AN INDIAN EPHEMERIS

A. D. 1800 TO A.D. 2000

L. D. SWAMIKANNU PILLAI

AN INDIAN EPHEMERIS
A. D. 1800 TO A.D. 2000

Showing, for every day in the year for two hundred years, A. D. 1800 to A. D. 2000

THE ENDING MOMENTS OF TITHIS AND NAKSHATRAS
with the English, Tamil, Malayalam and Muhammadan Equivalents;
and for every ten days, from A. D. 1910 to A. D. 2000,

THE GEOCENTRIC LONGITUDES OF PLANETS,
mainly according to the Surya Siddhanta;
Also
THE YEARS IN DIFFERENT ERAS, A.D., HIJRA, SAKA,
VIKRAMA, KALIYUGA, KOLLAM, Etc.
And
TABLES FOR ASCERTAINING LOCAL TIME,
with full instructions for casting Lagna & Horoscopes,
AND
TABLES OF HINDU FASTS, FEASTS AND FESTIVALS,
AND SOLAR AND LUNAR ECLIPSES.

BY
Dewan Bahadur L.D. Swamikannu Pillai,
Author of "PANCHANG AND HOROSCOPE"
AND "INDIAN CHRONOLOGY, SOLAR, LUNAR, PLANETARY

GYAN

Published by

Gyan Publishing House
5, Ansari Road
Daryaganj, New Delhi-110002
Phone: 011-47034999, 9811692060
E-mail: books@gyanbooks.com

Distribution Network
gyanbooks.com
India, USA, Canada, UK, Australia, France

ISBN : 978-81-212-4561-6 (HB)
First Published, Madras, 1915

2nd Impression 2020

Printed at: Gyan Press, Delhi.

AN INDIAN EPHEMERIS,

A.D. 1800—A.D. 2000.

CHAPTER I.

THE object of the present work, which is based on the author's previous work, *Indian Chronology* (1911, Grant & Co., Madras), and which will be found to agree in every respect* with the results arrived at in that work, is to show (1) for every day in the year, for two hundred years, from 1st January A.D. 1800 to 31st December A.D. 1999, the eras in use at present in different parts of India, Śaka, Vikrama, Kaliyuga, Kollam, Bengal San, Northern and Southern Cyclic years, Hijra and A.D.; the solar month and day of the Tamil and Malayâḷam Calendars; the solar months according to the râśis or signs of the zodiac; the tithi and the nakshatra, with the ending moments of each to two places of decimals, equivalent to half ghaṭikas; the lunar months and *pakshas* in use all over India and neighbouring countries; the Muhammadan months and days of the Muhammadan months; and (2) for every ten days in the year, from A.D. 1910† to A.D. 1999 inclusive, the *gochâras* or motions of the planets in geocentric longitude. For every one of these items the English month and day and week-day are given regularly throughout.

2. Every calendar, embracing a number of years, should, like the Roman god Janus, be two-faced: that is to say, it should cover a number of years past and a number of years to come, according to the size and scope of the work. All the Indian Calendars, published up to date, including the cheap Jantris, as well as the more ambitious Ephemerides of Mr. C. P. Brown (A.D. 1750 to A.D. 1850), Mr. Raghavachari of Nungambakam (A.D. 1850 to A.D. 1904), etc., are one-faced, in that they give the details for a certain number of years past and omit those of the future altogether. The reason of this procedure is that the computation of tithis and nakshatras is a tedious process, occupying two to three months, even where the compilation of a single year's details is in question. Naturally, therefore, Indian almanac-makers stop with the current year, or at most compile details for only one or two years in advance. An almanac which covers the space of one year only becomes so rapidly obsolete, that 'an old almanac' is an even more forcible expression in the Indian Vernaculars than it is in the European tongues for a thing that is utterly antiquated. Under such a system, the verification of the details of a year, even in the recent past, is a matter of some difficulty, and every person or office that has to make such references must keep a bundle of old panchângas, to be dived into as often as occasion may require.

3. The author, having hit upon a method of calculating by a mechanical process, but accurately to four places of decimals, all the elements required for the computation of a tithi (*i.e.*, mean ending moment of tithi and sun's and moon's equations of the centre) as well as all the elements required for nakshatras (*i.e.*, mean ending moment of nakshatra and moon's equation of the centre) successively for every day, for any number of years, past or future, offered to the Government of Madras to produce (1) an ephemeris in the present form for the whole of the period for which such information would ordinarily be required by epigraphists, from A.D. 700 to A.D. 1800, and (2) the present ephemeris from A.D. 1800 to A.D. 2000. Government accepted both the offers, undertaking to pay part of the cost of compiling the former ephemeris in manuscript and to purchase 1,500 copies of the latter, if published at the author's expense. The author takes the present opportunity of thanking the Government of Madras for their kind patronage of both parts of the work. Only one *manuscript* copy of the former work (A.D. 700 to A.D. 1800) has been produced for the present for the use of the Madras Epigraphist, but the author will be glad to furnish any other Administration or Epigraphist with manuscript copies of the same on terms to be settled by correspondence.

4. **Sûrya Siddhânta and Dṛig-gaṇita.**—Of the several calendrical systems based upon the Siddhântas, which, with their respective constants, are enumerated in

* Except as regards (1) leap years in the Muhammadan Calendar (*vide* paragraph 19 below): and (2) solar eclipses, as to which see paragraph 20. The author has also found, since the text was printed, that the adhika month in the year 1901 A.D. was *Ashâḍha* by the Sûrya Siddhânta, not Śrâvana (as shown in the text, p. 205 and on p. 126, Table X, *Indian Chronology*). By *Arya Siddhânta*, which is not usually followed in such cases, the *adhika* month was no doubt Śrâvana.

† The places of planets for the years A.D. 1840 to A.D. 1920 will be found in Table XVIII of *Indian Chronology*.

Varâhamihira's Pancha Siddhântika, the Sûrya Siddhânta is the one system which has found universal acceptance in India, and it has been adopted by almanac-makers through the length and breadth of the Indian Continent for at least a thousand years past; so that, in verifying any date in an Indian inscription, copper-plate, or literary work during this period, the principles of the Sûrya Siddhânta have to be applied in the first instance, and only if they fail, the applicability of any other Siddhânta may have to be considered. In Southern India alone, and even there, only in respect of Sankrântis, *i.e.*, the commencement of solar months, the *Ârya Siddhânta* has been in use for a long time past. Elsewhere, and for all other purposes, the Sûrya Siddhânta may be said to be in use and to have been in use, universally, throughout India.

5. Since panchângas, based on the Sûrya Siddhânta, are still the most popular ones in India, it may be affirmed that the Indian people, as a whole, are satisfied with their results to-day, just as they were satisfied a thousand years ago. New moons and full moons and the sun's tropical longitude, as well as eclipses, may still be calculated, with a very fair amount of precision, with the sole help of tables based on this venerable Indian system of Sûrya Siddhânta. As a system of pure chronology, it has probably not its equal anywhere in the world. Chronology is based on astronomy; but while astronomy is applied in the laboratories and observatories of a few mathematicians, chronology is meant to be applied and used by all. The chronological system of the Sûrya Siddhânta, though complicated, and inextricably interwoven with astrology, is yet sufficiently simple, as the author has endeavoured to show in his *Indian Chronology*, and its terms and methods have, by dint of use, been rendered familiar to the Indian people at large. If for no other reason, at least for the sake of its antiquity, of its use in the interpretation of ancient Indian dates and of its value in the reconstruction of Indian history as well as for the faithful representation of present day practice over a great part of India, such an ephemeris as the present one, based on the *Sûrya Siddhânta*, deserves to be on record.

6. During the last half century however, there has been a growing Indian sentiment in favour of something more accurate than the *Sûrya Siddhânta*. With the aid of the Nautical Almanacs published by observatories in Europe and America, or with the help of special works, such as Mr. Ketakar's *Jyotir-ganitam* (which unfortunately is not available in English, having been published only in Sanskrit), it is possible to construct an Indian panchânga, faithful in all its details to the results of the best modern astronomy; and certain of the more erudite almanac-makers in India have not been slow to avail themselves of this possibility and to produce almanacs of a refined type, called *Drig-ganita* in Southern India, and by other similar names in other parts of India. A yet further refinement is the adoption of the tropical year, giving rise to the *Sâyana panchângas* of Western India. Far be it from the author's intention to cavil at such reforms, but it must be confessed that they cannot make for better *chronology*. They do not aim at that simplicity of calculation which is essential in a chronology for all; they have not brought home to the Sûrya Siddhânta system any serious charge of inaccuracy for the purposes of the *Civil* Calendar, and the fact that along with them are used side by side the Sûrya Siddhânta panchângas, in the same households and for the purpose of the same rituals and festivals (though with occasional bickerings as to exact hour and date), shows that there is not much practical difference between the one and the other set of calendars. The advantage of practical simplicity and convenience, as well as of shastraic sanction, must remain with the Sûrya Siddhânta. For the first time, also, the author has shown that the Sûrya Siddhânta has another advantage over Drig-ganita, in that panchângas and trayângas under the former system can be compiled *for any length of time* backwards or forwards, so as to be permanently available for reference or research.

7. The main reason, indeed the sole reason, why Drig-ganita is preferred in certain quarters to Sûrya Siddhânta is that for *astrological* purposes the former yields more accurate positions for the planets. The benefits of astrology, and the 'maléfice' also, if one may still use the term, are dependent on the planets being in certain places at certain times. Shift the places by ever so small an arc, and you vary by, it may be, many times as much, the quantity or quality of planetary influence. *If* the influence is, in mathematical language, a rapidly variable function of the place of the planet, then the Sûrya Siddhânta must, for purposes of astrology, be rejected, or drop gradually out of use, to be replaced by Drig-ganita. This is the whole question at issue, and it is open to those who deny the '*if*', the premise, to deny also the conclusion and to argue that the whole question is begged by the upholders of Drig-ganita. Speaking more generally, astrology will have to make good its claims as a science before it can be allowed to impeach the Sûrya Siddhânta at the bar of its own tribunal.

8. **Method of Verification and Abbreviations.**—The only abbreviations used in the text are (1) the indication of ending moments of tithis and nakshatras as decimals of a day, instead of by *ghatikas* and *palas*, or hours and minutes; (2) the substitution of numbers for names of nakshatras. A key to the latter set of abbreviations will be found at the bottom of each page, while a key to the former has been inserted in each copy of the work as a detachable book-marker as well as on the inner side of the cover. For the rest, all the Indian and Muhammadan details corresponding to an English date are given *in its immediate neighbourhood*. Thus in the fortnight commencing with Sunday 10th April A.D. 1836 and

ending with Saturday 23rd April, there are several changes of Hindu and Muhammadan years and months, there is one day without its own tithi, one day without its own nakshatra, and one day with two tithis. All these changes and facts are visible at a glance without having to be gleaned with much trouble, from the top, bottom and sides of the page, as in an ordinary Indian panchânga. Thus, on Sunday 10th April A.D. 1836, it is clearly indicated that it was the 29th day of *Mina* or *Panguni* month of *Manmatha* year, and *Bahuḷa Navami* of Lunar *Chaitra*, ending at ·10 (=6 ghaṭikas, or 2 hours 24 minutes after mean sunrise), a day of Nakshatra 'Śravaṇa' (No. 22), ending at ·55 of day (=33 ghaṭikas, or 13 hours 12 minutes after mean sunrise), and lastly the 23rd day of *Zil Hijja* month of Hijra 1251. It is equally clear that the next day (Monday 11th April) was the first day of *Mesha* or *Chittirai*, month of a new year, *Durmukha*. The change from the last day of Hijra 1251 to the first day of Hijra 1252 on Monday 18th April A.D. 1836 is marked with equal clearness.

9. **Cyclic and other years.**—The headings at the top of each page comprise (1) the symbols for Solar and Lunar eclipse and the abbreviations for *Amâvâsya* and *Paurṇami*, (2) the numbers of years in the different eras, (3) the names of Samvatsaras or Cyclic years in Northern and Southern India, and (4) the commencement of the Indian year according to *Sûrya* and *Ârya* Siddhântas, according to the *Kollam* year, and according to *Hijra*. The Kollam year is a current one, like the A.D. year, while all the other Hindu years, Śaka, Vikrama and Kaliyuga, are expired years. It should be noted that the Kaliyuga years quoted in the ordinary South Indian panchângas are current and will be found to exceed in each case the Kaliyuga year marked in this book by one. The names of Solar Samvatsaras, *Prabhava*, *Vibhava*, etc., are quoted, not only at the top of each page, but above the name of each Tamil month. Thus it has been possible to give in this book, for each English date, the Tamil (or Malayâḷam), Telugu (or Canarese) and Muhammadan equivalents with as much fulness as in the ordinary pocket diaries. For example, against Tuesday 13th April A.D. 1915, one may read off, in this book, as in a pocket diary, '*Râkshasa* Samvat, *Chittirai* 1' *or* '*Medam* 1', 'Râkshasa Samvat Chaitra Bahuḷa Chaturdaśi', 'Nakshatra Uttara Bhadrapada', and 'Hijra 1333 Jumadalawwal 28'.

10. **Solar and Lunar Reckonings.**—The various calendar systems in use in India may be divided into two main groups as shown in this book, namely, the Solar reckoning comprising the English, Tamil, Malayâḷam, Orissa and Bengal reckonings; and the Lunar reckoning, used all over India, and including the Muhammadan and Jewish reckonings. The Indian Calendar is sometimes styled Luni-solar, because its lunar months and years cannot recede by more than 29 days from the corresponding solar months and years, whereas the Muhammadan or Hijra year recedes by 10 or 11 days every year and will therefore be found to commence in all months of the Indian and English years.

11. **Month and Day.**—Solar months in India are generally named in Sanskrit after the Râśis or signs of the zodiac, 'Mesha', 'Rishaba', etc., but in Tamil they are also known by another set of names, more or less modified from names of nakshatras or lunar months, namely, 'Chittirai', 'Vaikâśi', etc. Both sets of names, 'Mesha-Chittirai', 'Ṛishaba-Vaikâśi', 'Mithuna-Ani', etc., are quoted in this column. The days of the solar month are reckoned according to an ancient Tamil practice, from the Sankrânti of the *Ârya* Siddhânta. The rules for determining the commencement of the solar month, according to the Tamil, Malayâḷam, Orissa and Bengal systems, with examples, are given in sections 142 to 149 of *Indian Chronology*. The Malabar rule there stated entails an occasional difference between the Malayâḷam and Tamil modes of reckoning days of the solar month. In section 145 of *Indian Chronology*, the author presumed that there was no difference in practice between the two reckonings, but he has since learnt that there is an occasional difference justifying the rule. A difference of a whole day or of two days would ordinarily be found between Tamil days of the solar months and the corresponding Bengal days.

12. The days of the same Tamil month are not the same in number every year. Thus Chittirai has ordinarily 31 days, but may occasionally have 30. The fact stated by the ancient commentator of *Silapadhikâram* that Chittirai, in the year when the events described in that poem occurred, had only 30 days, and commenced on a Sunday, a day of 'Śvâti' nakshatra, enables us, without further mention of the year, to infer that the year in question was A.D. 756 and no other. Days of the solar month are now commonly quoted in the Tamil country, but we do not meet them before the beginning of the 8th century A.D. We learn from the ancient Tamil poem *Tolkâppiyam* that a day at that epoch was ordinarily called, as it still occasionally is, after its nakshatra. The practice of calling days by their tithi numbers apparently came into use at a subsequent date in the Tamil country, though elsewhere in India the calling of a day by its tithi number is an ancient, in fact, a Vedic, practice. Week-days do not seem to have been in use in the Tamil country much before the beginning of the 8th century A.D. Elsewhere in India, week-days have been traced to the 5th century A.D., but not much beyond. It is a curious circumstance, and deserving of careful study, that a date in India, one thousand and four hundred years ago was known by the same week-day as the corresponding day in Europe.

13. **Adhika and Kshaya Months.**—Occasionally, that is seven times in 19 years, a lunar month is repeated twice in the course of the same year. For instance, in the year 1915 there are two Vaiśâkhas, one reckoned from Thursday 15th April to Friday 14th May, and the other from Saturday 15th May to Saturday 12th June. The first month in such cases has the prefix *Adhika* (=additional), and the second the prefix *Nija* (=true). Both prefixes are duly and clearly marked in the Ephemeris. More rarely also, a lunar month is suppressed altogether, and in such cases is known as *Kshaya* (=suppressed). Thus in A.D. 1823, the month *Pausha*, which ought to have occurred in January-February, was suppressed. The next suppression of this kind will not occur till the year A.D. 1964. The omission of kshaya month is noted by N.B. at the foot of the page where required. The rules for determining the date of occurrence of additional and suppressed months are clearly given in sections 18 to 30 of *Indian Chronology*, where also, in Table II, the full names and day equivalents of tithis are given.

14. **Nakshatras and Ending Moments of Nakshatras.**—Below is a complete list of Indian nakshatras, with the fixed stars, as identified by different authorities. The practice of reckoning by nakshatras is peculiar to India and China, and has existed in each of these countries from very ancient times. In India, in Vedic times, a lunar month had no other name than that of the nakshatra in which the moon of that month became full. To this day, *Chaitra* is the month in which the moon becomes full when occupying 'Chitrâ' nakshatra, and so on for the other months. The concurrence of certain tithis with certain nakshatras is thus fixed within narrow limits for every month in the year, and the student of inscriptions should be familiar with the table of concurrence (see the author's *Eye Table* of Nakshatras and Tithis).

Order and names of Nakshatras.	Collective duration of Nakshatras (equal space). days.	Deities presiding over Nakshatras.	Nakshatras. Identified by BURGESS with	Identified by COLEBROOKE with	Identified by BENTLEY with
1 Aśvinî	1·01	Aśvin	*Beta* Arietis.	*Alpha* Arietis.	*Gamma* or *Beta* Arietis.
2 Bharani	2·02	Yama	*Alpha* Muscæ	Musca.	35 Arietis.
3 Krittikâ (**Tam.** Kiruttigai)	3·04	Agni	23 Tauri.	*Pi* Tauri.	Alcyone.
4 Rohini	4·05	Prajâpati	Al-Dabarân, *Alpha* Tauri.	*Alpha* Tauri	Aldebaran.
5 Mrigaśira (**Tam.** Mirugasîram)	5·06	Soma	*Lambda* Orionis.	*Lambda* Orionis.	113, 116, 117 Tauri
6 Ardrâ (**Tam.** Arudra or Tiruvâdirai)	6·07	Rudra	*Alpha* Orionis (?).	*Alpha* Orionis.	133 Tauri.
7 Punarvasu	7·08	Aditi	*Beta* Geminorum.	*Beta* Geminorum.	Pollux.
8 Pushya (**Tam.** Pûsam)	8·09	Brihaspati	*Delta* Cancri.	*Delta* Cancri.	*Delta* Cancri.
9 Aśleshâ (**Tam.** Âyilyam)	9·11	Sarpâh	*Epsilon* Hydræ.	*Alpha*, 1 and 2 Cancri.	49, 50 Cancri.
10 Maghâ (**Tam.** Magham)	10·12	Pitarah	Regulus.	*Alpha* Leonis.	Regulus.
11 Pûrva Phalgunî (**Tam.** Pûram)	11·13	Bhaga	*Delta* Leonis.	*Delta* Leonis.	70, 71 Leonis.
12 Uttara Phalgunî (**Tam.** Uttiram)	12·14	Âryaman	Al-Sarfa, *Beta* Leonis	*Beta* Leonis.	*Beta* Leonis.
13 Hasta (**Tam.** Hastam)	13·15	Savitri	*Gamma* or *Delta* Corvi.	*Gamma* or *Delta* Corvi.	7, 8 Corvi.
14 Chitrâ (**Tam.** Chittirai)	14·17	Tvashtri	Spica Virginis.	*Alpha* Virginis.	Spica.
15 Śvâti	15·18	Vâyu	Arcturus.	*Alpha* Bootes.	Arcturus.
16 Viśâkhâ (**Tam.** Visâkam)	16·19	Indrâgni	*Iota* Libræ.	*Alpha* or *Chi* Libræ.	24. Libræ.
17 Anurâdhâ (**Tam.** Anusham)	17·20	Mitra	*Delta* Scorpionis.	*Delta* Scorpionis.	*Beta* Scorpionis.
18 Jyeshthâ (**Tam.** Kettai)	18·21	Indra	Antares.	*Alpha* Scorpionis.	Antares.
19 Mûla (**Tam.** Mûlam)	19·23	Nirriti	*Lambda* Scorpionis.	*Lambda* Scorpionis.	34, 35 Scorpionis.
20 Pûrvâ Ashâdhâ (**Tam.** Pûrâdâm)	20·24	Âpah	*Delta* Sagittarii.	*Delta* Sagittarii	*Delta* Sagittarii.
21 Uttara Ashâdhâ (**Tam.** Uttirâdam)	21·25	Viśvadevâ	*Sigma* Sagittarii.	*Tau* Sagittarii.	*Phi* Sagittarii.
21 A. Âbhijit *	...	Brahma	Al-Nasr Al-waqi', Vega.	*Alpha* Lyræ	Vega.
22 Śravana (**Tam.** Tiruvônam)	22·26	Vishnu	Al-Nasr Al-târir, *Alpha* Aquilæ.	*Alpha* Aquilæ	*Alpha* Aquilæ.
23 Śravishtha or Dhanishthâ (**Tam.** Avittam)	23·27	Vasava	*Beta* Delphini.	*Alpha* Delphini	*Beta* Delphini.
24 Śatabhishaj or Satatârakâ (**Tam.** Sadayam)	24·29	Varuna	*Lambda* Aquarii.	*Lambda* Aquarii	*Lambda* Aquarii.
25 Pûrva Bhadrapadâ (**Tam.** Pûrattâdi)	25·30	Aja Ekapâd	*Alpha* Pegasi.	*Alpha* Pegasi	*Alpha* Pegasi.
26 Uttara Bhadrapadâ (**Tam.** Uttirattâdi)	26·31	Ahi Budhnya	*Gamma* Pegasi or *Alpha* Andromedæ.	*Alpha* Andromedæ	*Gamma* Pegasi
27 Revatî	27·32	Pûshan	*Zeta* Piscium.	*Zeta* Piscium.	*Zeta* Piscium.

* Abhijit is not usually reckoned when only 27 nakshatras are spoken of.

15. **Nakshatras and Tithis.**—Every Hindu feast, fast and festival (except Sankrântis) is connected with either a tithi or a nakshatra or both. Chapter II of this introduction,—for which the author is indebted partly to (1) Prof. KIELHORN's article in Vol. XXVI of *Indian Antiquary* and partly to (2) MR. VIDYÂRANYA PANCHÂNANA K. V. RÂMACHANDRA CHÂRYULU of Kalikivâyi, Singarâyakonda, Nellore District,—explains clearly the connection between a festival and its tithi or nakshatra in all ordinary cases.

16. A mean tithi extends over ·98 of a day, while a mean nakshatra extends over 1·01 days; but the solar and lunar anomalies may make a tithi longer or shorter by ·58 of a day as a maximum, while the lunar anomaly may similarly affect a nakshatra to the extent of ·41 of a day. Hence the irregular lengths, in time, of tithis and nakshatras, which make the Indian system so complicated in appearance, but which constitute a most valuable check in chronological studies. Hence also the curious fact that what ought to be a normal state of things, namely, each day having a single tithi and a single nakshatra, is very seldom noticed on the successive days of a *whole* month. Such a phenomenon occurred throughout the month of Pausha 4th January to 2nd February A.D. 1908, and will occur again throughout *Mârgaśira* month (7th December 1915 to 5th January 1916) in the current year. The curious reader may easily pursue the game with the help of this book. It follows from what has just been stated that in the course of a lunar month 2 tithis or 2 nakshatras may ordinarily be found either to occur on the same day or to cover parts of 3 days, the middle day in the latter case being without a tithi, or without a nakshatra of its own. Cases of the same day having 2 tithis *as well as* two nakshatras, as on *Kârttika, bahula 11 and 12* (Saturday 14th November A.D. 1914), and other cases (*e.g.*, Sunday 19th April 1914) in which a day had neither a tithi nor a nakshatra of its own can be easily traced with the aid of this book.

17. Such phenomena, which would mostly be astronomically true, may be multiplied *ad libitum*. To complete the scheme of astrology, we have to add the yet greater number of possible combinations, oppositions and 'aspects' of planets *inter se* (all of which may be studied by means of this and the companion book for five generations of human lives or 160 years, A.D. 1840 to A.D. 2000); and we have as the result an enormous number of possible phenomena, to each of which astrology may, and does, attach a meaning, so that on the one hand, one or other of the phenomena would be sure to occur every moment, (the public supposing all the while that some of them occur only once in a thousand or once in a hundred years, or only once in a lifetime), and on the other hand, when any event of importance does occur, whether in the natural, physical or political world, a phenomenon may be ready to be associated with it as its predestined partner. It is like placing something of value or of no value in each of a thousand chambers and letting loose a person blindfold among them. He no sooner finds something to rejoice or disappoint him than he begins to bless or curse his 'stars', not knowing that whatever his stars might be, he was sure to find or miss something in every one of the thousand chambers. In a country and under a system in which astronomy is only a stepping stone to astrology, it is impossible to write a work dealing with astronomic chronology without at the same time creating an apparatus for astrology: but a thoughtful study of astronomical facts will, it is believed, gradually dispel astrological errors.

18. These remarks seem relevant in connection with a phenomenon which, if not explained, is likely to be regarded as a triumph for astrology. Vyâsa says* to Dhritarâshtra in the *Mahâbhârata* (*Bhishma parva*, 3, 32) that he has known of lunar fortnights consisting of 14, 15 or 16 days, but never of one consisting of 13 days, but since such a one is in prospect or has occurred, there will be a great slaughter of human beings. Other Śâstras, quoted by Dr. Fleet in *Indian Antiquary*, Vol. XVI, for March 1887, reiterate this omen, and it is stated in one of the quotations (Commentary on the *Muhûrta Ganapati*) that the phenomenon occurs only once in 1,000 years. *If this was the case*, it would certainly be surprising that the great European War now raging should have broken out absolutely at the middle of a fortnight consisting of 13 days. The fortnight from *Sukla pratipada*, Friday 24th July, to *pûrnimâ*, Tuesday 4th August A.D. 1914, as will be seen from this Ephemeris, comprised only 13 days from *pratipada* to *panchadaśî*, owing to the occurrence twice, *i.e.*, on the 15th and on the last day of the paksha, of two tithis on a single day. *But it is not true that the phenomenon takes place only once in a thousand years.* In the absence of a compilation like this Ephemeris, it would have been difficult at any time to verify the statement, but any body can satisfy himself from this Ephemeris that the phenomenon occurred in 1805, 1813, 1830, 1847, 1849 (after 36 years as in the Mahâbhârata, *Mausala parva*, 11, 18, and with *grasthodayam* and *grâsthasthamanam* also as in the Mahâbhârata), 1861, 1864, 1872, 1878, 1880, 1892, 1900, 1903, 1914, and will occur in 1917, 1920, 1928, 1931, etcetera. Comment is needless after noting so many recurrences. The occurrence of such a fortnight in July 1914 was known in January 1914 when the new year's panchângas were published; nevertheless, no one then predicted that a great war was coming on in July: the 'prediction' came after the event.

19. **The Muhammadan Year.**—At page 197 of the tables appended to *Indian Chronology*, the author inserted the following note:—

The 2nd, 5th, 8th, 10th, 13th, 16th, 19th, 21st, 24th, 27th and 29th years in each cycle are leap years according to the present table, that is, they will be found to contain 355 days instead of 354. In certain

* Chaturdaśim panchadaśim bhûtapûrvâmcha shodaśim imâmtu nâbhijânâmi amâvâsyâm trayodaśim: chandrasûryâvubhau grasta vekâhnâ hitrayodaśîm.

countries, however, the 7th, 18th and 26th years of each cycle are reckoned as leap years instead of the 8th, 19th and 27th. Under the former reckoning, the 8th, 19th and 27th years, following as they do certain leap years, would begin one day later than they do according to the present table. For the convenience of reference, the 8th, 19th and 27th years of each cycle are marked by an asterisk. The reader will understand that the date of commencement of such Hijra years, as determined by the rules above laid down, is liable to be increased by one day in those countries where the 7th, 18th and 26th years of each cycle are regarded as leap years.

He has since found that the generality of authors have adopted the 7th, 18th and 26th years of each cycle as leap years, and he has decided in the present Ephemeris to follow their practice in this respect. To this extent there will be found an occasional difference between the Muhammadan dates entered in this Ephemeris and those shown at p. 196 of the tables appended to *Indian Chronology.*

20. Eclipses.—The solar eclipses, marked in Table X of the author's *Indian Chronology* for the years A.D. 1900 to A.D. 2000 include all solar eclipses visible *in any part of the world.* Attention was drawn to this fact in sec. 88, p. (34) of *Indian Chronology.* The author was at that time unable to refer to Oppolzer's *Canon der Finsternisse*, the standard work on the subject. He was since informed that a copy of this work was being used at the Kodaikānal Observatory, and, with the kind assistance of Mr. S. Sitaramaiyar, First Assistant at that Observatory, to whom he takes the present occasion to tender his thanks, he has been able to give, in this Ephemeris, the solar eclipses *visible in India* from A.D. 1800 to A.D. 2000.

The present opportunity is also taken to indicate a shorter method than that given in sec. 89, p. (34) of *Indian Chronology* for testing the possibility of eclipses, solar and lunar. The reader, being furnished in Table XVII of *Indian Chronology,* as illustrated in para. 23 below, with means of ascertaining directly the longitude of the sun and of the moon's nodes (called Rāhu and Ketu in Indian Astronomy), can find out readily whether the position of the sun with reference to either node falls within the limits given in the following table :—

Solar and Lunar Eclipses as determined by Sun's distance from node at New and Full Moon.

If Sun's distance from node at New Moon is		
Between 0° and 16·2 degrees or between 163·8° and 180 degrees	A SOLAR ECLIPSE IS	**Certain.**
Between 16·4° and 18·9 degrees or between 161·6° and 166·1 degrees		**Doubtful.**
Between 19·1° and 160·9 degrees ...		**Impossible.**
If Sun's distance from node at Full Moon is		
Between 0° and 10·4 degrees or between 169·6° and 180 degrees	A LUNAR ECLIPSE IS	**Certain.**
Between 10·6° and 13·9 degrees or between 169·4° and 166·1 degrees		**Doubtful.**
Between 14·0° and 166·0 degrees ...		**Impossible.**

21. Local Time.—Table XIII in *Indian Chronology,* showing local time, is reproduced as Appendix II to the present Ephemeris, but in a much simplified form, since only two decimal places are now required. (Three decimal places are actually given in Appendix II in view to accuracy when totalling. For the equivalents, in *ghaṭikas* and *palas* or *hours* and *minutes*, of three decimal places of a day, see table on inside of cover.) For the places actually given in that appendix, the local time for any particular day is found by simply adding (algebraically) the quantity noted in the last column under the place and against the day in question (in Appendix II), to the ending moment of the tithi or nakshatra for the day as given in the body of the Ephemeris. For places not noted in the appendix, the process described in Chapter IX of *Indian Chronology* should be followed. The method of determining the time of sunrise and sunset for any day in any year is given in Chapters IX and XI respectively of *Indian Chronology.*

22. Lagna.—The operation of determining the *lagna* of a particular moment (*e.g.*, the moment of a birth), or the moment when a particular degree of the zodiac will be *lagna* (say, to make an auspicious marriage) has often to be performed, not only by the astrologer, but also by the enquirer who wishes to verify a statement as to *lagna.* The rules on this subject, adapted from Prof. Jacobi's original article in the *Indian Antiquary* are given in Chapter X of *Indian Chronology.* For rapid working the following formula will be found useful. Let—

A = Sun's longitude at 6 a.m. (Lanka).

B = interval in decimals of a day between local sunrise and actual *local* time of birth or other moment. This interval may, for practical purposes, be taken also as the change of Sun's longitude corresponding to that interval; see N.B. to process (8) in First Example below.

a = seconds per degree of rise [table on page (31) of text of *Indian Chronology*].

T.L.S. = correction in seconds (Table XIII, *Indian Chronology*) for tropical longitude of Sun at actual local sunrise.

T.L.L. = correction in seconds (Table XIII, *Indian Chronology*) for tropical longitude of approximate degree of lagna.

Then approximate degree, which is lagna, $= (A - B) + (B \times 360^\circ)$ or $(A + 359\,B)$ degrees.

The formula $A + 359\,B$, process (12) below, is convenient for readily ascertaining the approximate lagna; and when the figure so obtained is well within a Rāśi, it will be unnecessary to proceed further. For exact calculation, and when lagna is on the borders of a Rāśi, we have,

$$\text{Actual lagna} = A^\circ + 359\,B^\circ - \frac{\text{T.L.S.} - \text{T.L.L.}}{a}$$

In order to render quite easy the performance of this important operation, we shall exhibit, in detail and by means of an example, the 17 processes of which operation consists. We propose to find the lagna child born at Madras at 12 noon (Standard or Ir. Railway time) on 1st April 1915.

Process.	Application.
(1) Interval from actual local sunrise to moment of birth.	(1) The time (12 noon, standard time) should be reduced by 9 minutes for all dates subsequent to 1st July 1906, the date of introduction of *Indian Standard,* or *Railway, time* which is in advance of *Madras mean astronomical time* by 9 minutes. The mean astronomical time of birth was 11 hours 51 minutes after midnight; or 5 hours 51 minutes or ·2437 of a day after mean Madras sunrise. To this should be added, by Table XIII (for lat. 13° and 1st April), *minus* 422 seconds for equation of time *plus* 351 seconds for tropical longitude = −71 seconds = −·0007 of a day. (*N.B.*—In order to find the tropical longitude for any day of the Solar year for the present time, from A.D. 1840 to A.D. 1920—we should add 20 days to the number of elapsed days in the Solar year and find under the given latitude in Table XIII the correction for tropical longitude appropriate to the resulting number of days.) The interval from actual Madras sunrise up to moment of birth was therefore 5 hours 51 minutes less 71 seconds = ·2430 of a day.
(2) Interval from Lanka sunrise to moment of birth.	This is obtained by subtracting from 5 hours 51 minutes (the given interval), the time difference due to Ujjain longitude of Madras, *i.e.*, 18 minutes; (2) will then be 5 hours 33 minutes = ·2312 of a day.
(3) Change of Sun's longitude corresponding to (1) "interval from actual sunrise to moment of birth"; use Table XVII *C, Indian Chronology.*	The change of Sun's longitude corresponding to ·2430 of a day is (by Table XVII, *Indian Chronology,* ·2365 + ·0030 = ·2395 of a degree.
(4) Change of Sun's longitude corresponding to (2) "interval from Lanka sunrise to moment of birth."—use Table XVII *C, Indian Chronology.*	The change of Sun's longitude corresponding to ·2312 of a day is (by Table XVII *C, Indian Chronology*) ·2267 + ·0012 = ·2279 of a degree. *N.B.*—Processes (3) and (4) may generally be dispensed with. See *N.B.* to (8) below.
(5) Days and fraction of a day (Lanka time) elapsed in Solar year up to moment of birth.	Take the given day of the English year (1st April) as reckoned from previous 1st April in Table VIII, *Indian Chronology,* and deduct the day and fraction of day in April when the Solar year 1914-15 commenced, according to Table. X, *Indian Chronology, i.e.,* April 12·2430. The given English day, April 1st A.D. 1915, is, by Table VIII, the 366th day reckoned from previous 1st April. Now, 366·2312 *minus* 13·2430 days = 352·9882 days.
(6) Longitude of Sun at Lanka mean sunrise on day of birth (Table XVIII).	According to Table XVIII, March 29, in the year 1915, which is not a leap year [see *Indian Chronology,* p. (112), sec. 295 (10)] is the 350th day of the Indian Solar year, when sun's mean longitude at Lanka 6 A.M. is 342·0° + ·6° and April 8th is the 360th day when sun's mean longitude at Lanka 6 A.M. is 351·8° + 6.°. April 1, the given day, is 3 days from March 29. Therefore the sun's mean longitude at Lanka mean sunrise on April 1, 1915, is 342·0° + ·6° (correction for the year—see *Indian Chronology,* sec. 295, foot-note) + $\frac{3}{10}$ of (difference between 342·6° and 352·4°) + 2·2° (the sun's equation of the centre) = 342·6° + ·3 × 9·8° + 2·2° = 342·6° + 2·94° + 2·2° = 347·7°.

(7) Longitude of sun at moment of birth.

N.B.—This is the *absolute* longitude of the sun for the moment of birth and does not depend on Lanka or any other time, though it is deduced by means of Lanka time. It is obtained by simply adding (6) *plus* (4).

Add (2) to (6). 347·7° + ·2° = 347·9°. To check this, the following direct method may be used (though it is not in general necessary for practical operations) by applying Table XVII A and Tab. XVII C, *Indian Chronology*, to (5).

By Table XVII A, the mean longitude of Sun for 352 days of the solar year is 344·7927°

Equation of centre for do. do. = +2·1717°

Longitude of Sun corresponding to ·98 of day = ·9659°

Do. do. ·0082 of day = ·0081°

Do. do. 352·9882 days = 347·9384°

(8) Longitude of sun at actual local sunrise.

To obtain this, we simply subtract (3) from (7); or we shall have equally correct results by subtracting (1) from (7).

N.B.—We see that we might equally well have taken (1) instead of (3), and in general a fraction of a day less than unity may be used equally well as the change of sun's longitude corresponding to that fraction of day, since the sun's motion per day is ready 1°

347·9° *minus* ·2° = 347·7°.

N.B.—This result is the same as (6), because the difference between the Sun's longitude at Lanka Sunrise and his longitude at Madras Sunrise is that due to 18 minutes of time, *i.e.*, ·0125 of a day or ·01 of a degree.

(9) Add to (8) as many minutes of an arc as there are years since 528 A.D. and deduct 360° if necessary.

1,915 − 528 = 1,387 minutes = 23 degrees 7 minutes = 23·1°:

347·7° + 23·1° = 370·8°
− 360°
10·8°

(10) Convert (9) into days by Table VII (*b*), *Indian Chronology*. Deduct 365·26 days *if necessary*.

10 degrees = 10·15 days.
·8 degree = ·8 day
10·8° = 10·95 days.

(11) Correction for tropical longitude of Sun (Table XIII) appropriate to latitude of given place (Madras, lat. 13°) and days arrived at in (10).

+428 seconds of time.

(12) Approximate lagna:—

Add the figure in (7) to 359 times the figure in (3) and deduct 360° *if necessary*.

347·9° + 359 × ·2395° = 433·9°
− 360°
73·9°

(13) Add to (12) same quantity as in (9) and convert result into days by Table VII (*b*), *Indian Chronology*. Deduct 365·26 days *if necessary*.

73·9° + 23·1° = 97·0° = 98·41 dads, (by Table VII (*b*), *Indian Chronology*. For,

90 degrees = 91·31 days.
7 degrees = 7·10 days.
97·0° = 98·41 days.

(14) Correction for tropical longitude of approximate lagna (Table XIII, *Indian Chronology*) appropriate to latitude of given place (Madras, lat. 13°) and days arrived at in (13).

+1,217 seconds.

(15) From (11) deduct (14) algebraically.

+428 − 1,217 = −789 seconds.

(16) Divide (15) by figure under latitude of given place in the table on page (31), *Indian Chronology*, and against sign of zodiac corresponding to degrees in (13).

Sign of zodiac corresponding to 97·0° of tropical longitude is IV.

The figure against sign IV and under lat. 13° in the table on page (31) of *Indian Chronology* is 266 seconds.

Now $\frac{-789}{266} = -3$ (approximately).

(17) Actual lagna is (12) *minus* (16) subtracted *algebraically*.

73·9° − (−3°) = 76·9° or **17° in Mithuna Rāśi.**

The above example is suited to a case in which the moment of birth is recorded in Indian Standard Time. But supposing the birth we are considering took place at 12 noon, Standard Time, on 1st April 1915 at *Vizagapatam*, where the same time is kept as at Madras, then in order to complete process (1) above, *i.e.*, to ascertain the interval between actual local sunrise and time of birth, we should increase or decrease the interval by the difference in time between the Ujjain longitude of Madras and that of Vizagapatam as given in Appendix I of this Ephemeris, or Table XIII, *Indian Chronology*. The interval will then be diminished by 1,804 − 1,072 = 732 seconds = 12 minutes 12 seconds = (by Table XX, *Indian Chronology*) ·0084 of a day.

If, on the other hand, strict Indian usage is followed (which is nowhere done at present, except by careful astrologers), and the moment of birth is recorded as so many ghaṭikas and palas after *actual local sunrise*, this is the very thing we want for process (1); and we need not trouble to calculate it.

We shall now indicate the processes for the converse problem of ascertaining the rising moment of a lagna, considered suitable for an act depending on the human will, say, the performance of a marriage, the undertaking of a journey, the taking charge of a house or an appointment, etc. The processes are only ten in number. Suppose we want to fix a suitable hour so as to have a marriage, etc., performed at Vellore (lat. 13°, time diff. + 808 seconds) on 15th May 1915, in the middle of Simha lagna (135° Sidereal longitude), then we proceed as follows :—

(1) Find longitude of Sun at Lanka mean sunrise on the given day. (Table XVIII). Proceed as in the first example.

26·6° + ·2 × 9·8° + 1·6° + ·4° = 26·6° + 1·96° + 1·6° + ·4° = 30·56°

(2) Find out by how much local sunrise precedes or follows Ujjain sunrise. (Table XIII, lat. 13°, 33rd day for equation of time; 33 + 20 or 53rd day for tropical longitude.)

May 15th is the 33rd day of the Indian Solar year at the present epoch. According to Table XIII the total correction for any moment at Vellore is − 348 + 1,592 + 808 seconds = 2,052 seconds = 34 minutes 12 seconds = + ·0240 of a day. That is (by section 70, *Indian Chronology*) local sunrise precedes Lanka mean sunrise by ·0240 of a day.

N.B.—In section 70, *Indian Chronology*, page (28) it is stated that "when we merely want to know by how many seconds local sunrise preceded or followed 6 a.m., we should simply add up the second and third corrections." By 6 a.m. in this passage is meant (according to strict Indian usage) local 6 a.m., *i.e.*, 6 a.m by a clock keeping mean astronomical time *for the locality in question*. (There is no such clock at present, except at astronomical observatories.) In the present case we want to know more, we want to know by how many seconds or minutes sunrise at Vellore on 15th May 1915 preceded or followed *Ujjain or Lanka* 6 a.m. We have in this case to take into account the first correction also, namely, that for terrestrial longitude, and we have done so in the above working. Again we took in the present case the correction for tropical longitude corresponding to the 53rd day of the year. The correct day, as shown in process (3) below, is the 52nd, but the difference will not lead to any appreciable error.

(3) Deduct (2) from (1) *algebraically* ... ...

30·56° − (+ ·024°) = 30·52°.

This is the longitude of the sun at actual local sunrise at Vellore on 15th May 1915.

(4) Deduct (3) from proposed lagna, increasing the latter, *if necessary*, by 360°.

135° *minus* 30·52° = 104·48°.

(5) Time of approximate lagna. Divide (4) by 360 ...

$\frac{104\cdot48}{360}$ = ·2902 of a day

= 17 ghaṭikas 25 palas, or 6 hours 58 minutes after local sunrise at Vellore.

(6) Increase (3) by 23·1° for tropical longitude as in process (9) in the first example, and convert into days by Table VII (*b*), *Indian Chronology*.

30·52° + 23·1° = 53·62 degrees.

50 degrees	=	50·73 days.
3 ,,	=	3·0 day.
·6 ,,	=	·61 ,,
53·6 degrees	=	54·34 days.

(7) Increase (4) by 23·1° for tropical longitude of proposed lagna and convert into days by Table VII (*b*), *Indian Chronology*.

104·48° + 23·1° = 127·6°.

100 degrees	=	101·5 days.
20 ,,	=	20·3 ,,
7 ,,	=	7·1 ,,
·6 ,,	=	·6 day.
127·6 degrees	=	129·5 days.

(8) Find from Table XIII, *Indian Chronology*, for given latitude (Vellore 13°) the correction for tropical longitude appropriate to (6).

+ 1,610 seconds.

(9) Find from Table XIII, *Indian Chronology*, for given latitude (Vellore 13°) the correction for tropical longitude of lagna, *i.e.*, (7).

+ 518 seconds.

(10) The actual moment of rising of the proposed lagna is {(9) *minus* (7)} added algebraically to (5).

(5) (9) − (7)
6 hrs. 58 min. + 518 sec. − 1,610 sec.
= 6 hrs. 58 min. less 1,092 sec.
= 6 hrs. 58 min. less 18 min. 12 sec.
= 6 hrs. 39 min. 48 sec.
= ·2776 of a day (Table XX, *Indian Chronology*.)

By Table XIX, *Indian Chronology*, this fraction = 1· ghaṭikas 39 palas after local sunrise at Vellore. This is the moment suitable, *cæteris paribus*, for a marriage to be celebrated under *Simha* lagna (135°) at Vellore on 15th May 1915.

---

22. Planetary Motions.—The example of the calculation of an actual horoscope given below will show the use to be made of the table of geocentric longitudes of the planets for every 10 days in the year given in *Indian Chronology* for the years A.D. 1840 to A.D. 1999 and in the present work for the years A.D. 1910 to A.D. 1999. For the accuracy of the places of planets entered in this table and an appreciation of the trouble which had to be taken in order to compile it, reference may be made to the following unsolicited opinion of MR. VENKATESH BAPU SHASTRI KETAKAR, the well-known author of *Jyotir-gaṇitam*, in his letter to the author, dated Poona, 8th December 1912:—

"The planetary places given in your Table XVIII for 1912, December 8 (page 224), tally fairly with those of my panchâng for the same date.

	My Panchâng. Longitude.		*Your Table XVIII.* Longitude.
Sun	...232°·9	...	232°·6
Mars	...222 ·9	...	223 ·1
Mercury	...235 ·1	...	233 ·6
Jupiter	...241 ·7	...	241 ·1
Saturn	... 36 ·8	...	37 ·6
Rahu	...346 ·4	...	
Venus	...271 ·5	...	271 ·4

"*But I wonder how you could bear the enormous trouble of preparing such a vast table as this!*"

It would have been impossible to attain even this measure of accuracy with a pure Sûrya Siddhânta constant without the use of Bîjas. The author (as explained in section 277 of *Indian Chronology*) used the mean places of planets as given by Leverrier and other modern authorities, and also the mean sidereal periods of revolution as given in modern astronomy, slightly corrected to suit the Indian ecliptic, and applied to these places the annual equations and corrections for anomaly, attributed to VÂVILÂLA KUCHINNA (by WARREN in his *Kâla Sankalita*), the value of which has been recognized by Professor JACOBI in his Planetary Tables (*Epigraphia Indica*, Vol. XII, April 1913, Part II).

It is hoped that these planetary tables, which we owe indirectly to the ingenuity of an obscure Telugu Astronomer, Vâviḷâla Kuchinna, will be used by others than astrologers.

Students of practical astronomy are exhorted to use them for the purpose of identifying the places of the planets in the nocturnal heavens and for studying those forward and retrograde motions of the planets, which, in every age and country, have afforded such rich material for the discoveries of astronomy and the inventions of astrology.

Example of an Actual Horoscope.—Provided the *lagna* and Sun's longitude at the moment of birth are determined as above, the rest of the horoscope can be cast in five minutes by means of the tables in *Indian Chronology* and *Indian Ephemeris*. Thus for a child born at Madras at 12 noon on 1st April 1915, which was a day of 'Chitrâ' Nakshatra (commenced ·65 of previous day and ended at ·59 of 1st April) the positions of the planets would be as follows:—

(1) Lagna (already determined) 77°.

(2) Sun (already determined) 347·9°.

(3) Moon: If we put (1) a = longitude at commencement of nakshatra, (2) b = total duration of nakshatra, and (3) c = fraction of day expired from commencement of nakshatra up to moment of birth, then the moon's longitude at moment of birth is given by $a + \left(\frac{c}{b} \times 13\frac{1}{3}°\right)$.

In this case b = ·94 of a day and c = ·58 of a day. (Both the quantities b and c are deduced from the entries in the Ephemeris against 31st March and 1st April 1915):

a, from footnote to App. II, is $173\frac{1}{3}°$.

∴ Longitude of moon at moment of birth $= 173\frac{1}{3}° + \frac{\cdot58}{\cdot94} \times 13\frac{1}{3}° = 181\cdot56°$

(4) Longitude of Mars $= 321\cdot9 + 3\cdot23 \times \cdot79 = 324\cdot45°$

(5) „ of Mercury $= 318\cdot6 + 3\cdot23 \times 1\cdot6 = 323\cdot77°$

(6) „ of Jupiter $= 319\cdot1 + 3\cdot23 \times \cdot23 = 319\cdot84°$

(7) „ of Venus $= 302\cdot8 + 3\cdot23 \times 1\cdot19 = 305\cdot84°$

(8) „ of Saturn $= 64\cdot9 + 3\cdot23 \times \cdot03 = 64\cdot93°$

The procedure for Mars, Mercury, Jupiter, Venus and Saturn is exactly the same. That is, being furnished in Table XVIII, *Indian Chronology*, or in Appendix II to this *Ephemeris*, with the places of the planets at Lanka sunrise for every ten days in the year, we take as an addition to the place of each planet at sunrise on March 29, A.D. 1914 (the 350th day of the Solar year 1914–15), the product of $3\cdot23 \times \frac{1}{10}$ of the change of longitude between the place of each planet on 29th March and its place on 8th April (the 360th day). The 3·23 days are the interval in days from sunrise on 29th March to the moment of birth on 1st April.

The position of *Rāhu* for 353·23 days, reckoned from 0 day of the Solar year, is found as follows :—

(Table XVII-B, *Indian Chronology*, or p. 432 of this book.) Mean place of Rāhu at sunrise on 0 day of Solar year A.D. 1914–15 = 323·85°.

Motion of Rāhu (backward) { for 350 days = − 18·54°; for 3 days = − ·166; for ·23 day = − ·01° }

Total: −18·71°

∴ The place of Rāhu at the moment of birth was $323\cdot85° - 18\cdot71° = 305\cdot14°$.

The place of Ketu was 180° less, *i.e.*, 125·14°.

The following are the Raśi and Navāmśa diagrams of this horoscope for a child born at Madras at noon on 1st April 1915 A.D. :—

<table>
<tr><td>Mina.
Pisces.
X
Sun (347·9°)</td><td>Mesha.
Aries.
XI</td><td>Rishabha.
Taurus.
XII</td><td>Mithuna.
Gemini.
I
Lagna (77°)
Saturn (64·9°)</td></tr>
<tr><td>Kumbha.
Aquarius
IX</td><td colspan="2" rowspan="2">Place and hour of birth, Madras, 12 noon, 1st April 1915.

Rasi.

N.B.—The degrees will enable the reader to construct other diagrams, *e.g.*, *Trimsamsa, Shashti, tamsa, etc.*

Roman numerals indicate Bhavas.</td><td>Karkataka.
Cancer.
II</td></tr>
<tr><td>Makara.
Capricornus.
VIII
Mars (324·4°)
Merc. (323·8°)
Jup. (319·8°)
Venus (305·8°)
Rāhu (305·1°)</td><td>Simha.
Leo.
III
Ketu (125·1°)</td></tr>
<tr><td>Dhanus.
Sagittarius.
VII</td><td>Vrischika.
Scorpio.
VI</td><td>Tula.
Libra.
V
Moon (181·6°)</td><td>Kanya.
Virgo.
IV</td></tr>
</table>

<table>
<tr><td>**XII**
Lagna.
Jupiter.</td><td>**I**</td><td>**II**
Ketu.
Mars.
Mercury.</td><td>**III**</td></tr>
<tr><td>**XI**</td><td colspan="2" rowspan="2">**Navamsa.**

This diagram is filled up by applying Table XXI to degrees of longitude.</td><td>**IV**</td></tr>
<tr><td>**X**</td><td>**V**</td></tr>
<tr><td>**IX**
Sun.</td><td>**VIII**
Saturn.
Venus.
Rāhu.</td><td>**VII**
Moon.</td><td>**VI**</td></tr>
</table>

CHAPTER II.

NOTES ON TITHIS IN RELATION TO FESTIVALS.

Day on which a festival is celebrated.—As a *tithi* generally covers a portion of two days, it sometimes happens that though for civil purposes the tithi of a day is that which is current at sunrise, yet, for religious purposes, the tithi may have to be celebrated on the previous day when it begins. When a tithi is appointed for the celebration of a feast or fast, to be kept at forenoon, midday, late afternoon, midnight, etc., it is obvious that the feast or fast must be observed on the day when the tithi covers the prescribed part of the day. The day for such purposes is divided, first of all, into five portions *between sunrise and sunset.*

(1) *Prâtahkâla*, or early forenoon, 6 ghaṭikas from sunrise.

(2) *Sangava*, or forenoon, 6 to 12 ghaṭikas from sunrise.

(3) *Madhyâhna*, or midday, 12 to 18 ghaṭikas from sunrise.

(4) *Aparâhna*, or afternoon, 18 to 24 ghaṭikas from sunrise.

(5) *Sâyâhna*, or late afternoon, 24 to 30 ghaṭikas from sunrise.

(*a*) The 4 ghaṭikas before sunrise are called *arunodaya* or rise of dawn.

(*b*) The 6 ghaṭikas after sunset are called *pradosha* or evening.

(*c*) The 2 ghaṭikas in the middle of the night are called *nisîtha*, midnight.

(*d*) A festival marked as *pûrvâviddha* is celebrated on the first day of the tithi, not on the second. A festival celebrated on the second day on which a tithi is current is said to be *paraviddha*.

N.B.—**Tithi dvayam**:—Two tithis meeting, *i.e.*, one commencing and the other ending, between 18 and 24 ghaṭikas after sunrise, when a similar meeting does not take place next day.

Festivals connected with Nakshatras as well as Tithis.—On the nakshatra Sravishṭha (No. 23) in lunar Śrâvana, the ceremony of Upâkarma (Âvani Aviṭṭam) is celebrated. The Eye-Table in *Indian Chronology* shows that this festival would ordinarily fall about full moon in Śrâvaṇa. In the same manner, all festivals associated with particular *nakshatras* may be equally well connected with particular *tithis*. In Southern India, however, it is usual to connect *nakshatra* festivals with certain *Solar* months in which they are celebrated; *e.g.*, *Panguni Uttaram* (*i.e.*, *Uttara Phâlguni* nakshatra in the solar month called *Pangunî*), *Chittirai Mûlam* (*i.e.*, *Mûla* nakshatra in the solar month called *Chittirai*); *Âvani Aviṭṭam* (*vide supra*), etc. *Tithi* festivals are also often connected in Southern India with solar months; and if a festival falls, for instance, on śukla panchami in a particular solar month, and there are two śukla panchamis in that month, the first is called *śûnya tithi* and the second only is celebrated.

Occasionally, something else is required for the celebration of a feast besides the concurrence of a *tithi* and a *nakshatra*; and there are also festivals and fasts which cannot conveniently be arranged under tithis. Such matters are arranged in the following alphabetical notes, which will be of interest to the general reader as well as to students of epigraphy :—

Amâvâsyâ should be in *aparâhna*. If it occurs in *aparâhna* on two days, and is less than 60 ghaṭikas in length, it is kept on the first day; otherwise (*i.e.*, if of normal length or longer) on second day. If not occurring in *aparâhna* of two days, it should be kept on the first day. The same rule is observed for Śrâddhas.

Śuklayajurveda.—Amâvâsyâ is kept on the third day before moonrise.

Time for yâgas (yāgnya kāla).—The last fourth part of a *parva* (*i.e.*, either amâvâsyâ or paurnamî) and first three parts of pratipada are suitable as *yâgakāla*. If there is yâgakāla on two days, then the day on which the kāla is current at noon is the proper day.

Ashṭami (8th tithi).—An *ashṭami* falling on Wednesday is special and receives the name of *Budhâshṭami*. The su. 8 of every month is sacred to Durgâ or Annapûrani, and, similarly, the ba. 8 of every month, called *kâlâshtami* (pûrvaviddha), is sacred to Krishna.

Chaturthi (4th tithi).—The Śukla Chaturthi in every month is called *Ganesa Chaturthi* or Vinâyaka Chaturthi, the chief being *Mâgha Chaturthi* (*Ganeśa Jayanti*). It is celebrated at midday. *Tila Chaturthi* is another name for *Mâgha Śukla Chaturthi*. It is performed in the evening and is *pûrvaviddha*. *Kuṇḍa Chaturthi* is another name for the same festival. Similarly, the bahula chaturthi in every month is Sankashṭa Chaturthi, and is a fast day for people who wish to emerge from difficulties: the fast is broken at moonrise. This chaturthi is called *Ângâraka Chaturthi* if it falls on Tuesday.

Chaturdaśî (14th tithi).—Bahula chaturdaśi in *every month* is *Śivârâtri*, but Mâgha ba. 14 is *Mahâ Śivarâtri.*

Châturmâsya dvitîyâs: Bhâdrapada ba. 2; Âshâḍha ba. 2; Phâlguṇa ba. 2; Kârttika ba. 2.

The *bahula dvitîyâ* in Âshâḍha, Śrâvana, Bhâdrapada and Âśvina is called Aśûnyasayana vrata and the fast is broken at moonrise.

Dvâdaśi (12th tithi).—The dvâdaśî is called *Mahâdvâdaśi* in the following circumstances:—

11th Tithi current at sunrise on two successive days: the next dvâdaśi is called *Unmîlanî.*

12th Tithi current at sunrise on two successive days: the dvâdaśi is called *Vanjulî.*

12th Tithi, to be followed by a full moon or a new-moon tithi, current at two sunrises—*Pakshavardhini.*

12th Tithi, joined with nakshatra 'Pushya', is *Jaya* [*i.e.*, by Eye-Table, bahuḷa 12 in Bhâd.; or sukḷa 12 in Phâlg. or Chait.].

12th Tithi, joined with nakshatra 'Śravaṇa', is *Vijaya* [*i.e.*, by Eye-Table sukḷa 12 in Bhâd.; Asv.; bahuḷa 12 in Phâlg.].

12th Tithi, joined with nakshatra 'Punarvasu', is *Jayanti* [*i.e.*, by Eye-Table, sukḷa 12 in Phâlg., bahuḷa 12 in Śrâvaṇa].

12th Tithi, joined with Nakshatra 'Rohiṇi', is Pâpanâsini [*i.e.*, by Eye-Table sukḷa 12 in Pausha, Mâgha; bahuḷa 12 in Âshâḍha.

N.B.—The *Eye-Table* referred to above is that appended to *Indian Chronology.*

Ekâdasî (11th Tithi).—Every Ekâdaśî is sacred, like every Amâvâsyâ, and receives a special name. It is called *Vijayâ* when joined with the nakshatra 'Punarvasu'. The following are the names of the 24 Ekâdaśis: 12 in bright halves and 12 in dark halves of the 12 lunar months):—

Month.	Śukḷa Paksha.	Bahuḷa Paksha.
Chaitra ...	Kâmadâ Ekâdaśî ...	Varûthinî Ekâdaśî.
Vaiśâkha ...	Mohinî do ...	Aparâ do.
Jyeshṭha ...	Nirjalâ do ...	Yogini do.
Âshâḍha ...	Vishnusayan o t s a v a; Sayani or Vishnu-sayani Ekâdaśî (*i. e.*, Vishnu going to sleep).	Kâmadâ do. or Kâmikâ do.
Śrâvaṇa ...	Putradâ Ekâdaśi ...	Ajâ do.
Bhâdrapada...	Vishnuparivartanotsava *or* Parivartini Ekâdaśi (Vishnu turning on his side, called Vishnu-srinkhala, when 11th and 12th tithis meet in nakshatra 'Śrâvaṇa'.)	Indirâ do.
Aśvina ...	Pâsânkusa Ekâdaśî ...	Ramâ do.
Kârttika ...	Prabodhinî E k â d a śi (waking of Vishnu), Bhishma panchaka-vrata commences.	Utpatti do.
Mârgaśira ...	Mokshada Ekâdaśi ...	Saphalâ do.
Pausha ...	Putradâ Ekâdaśi or Mukkotti or Vaikunṭha Ekâdaśi.	Shattilâ do.
Mâgha ...	Jayâ Ekâdaśi ...	Vijayâ Ekâdaśi.
Phâlguna ...	Amalakî Ekâdaśî ...	Pâpamochini do.

(Vaishṇavas).—If *dasami* ends after 56 ghaṭikas, the fast is on *dvâdaśî* day.

If on ekâdaśi day, there is any part of *navami* or *daśami* day, then also the fast should be kept on *dvâdaśi.*

If *dvâdaśi* touches three days, then the fast is on the day which is wholly *dvâdaśî* and paraṇam on the next day when dvâdaśî ends.

In any other case, *ekâdaśi* is the fast day and dvâdaśi the day of paranam.

Sanyâsins and widows of all creeds observe this rule for *ekâdaśi.*

(Smârthas)—Even if *daśami* ends after 56 ghaṭikas, the fast is kept on *ekâdaśi.*

If dvâdasi touches three days, Smârthas observe the first *dvâdaśî* day as *ekâdaśi.*

(Kâmyâ ekâdaśi).—Those who observe ekâdaśi for *kâmya* purposes (begetting children, etc.) observe the Smârtha rule: those who observe ekâdaśi for *môksha* (like Sanyâsins) observe the Vaishṇava rule.

If a death occurs on the day of ekâdaśî fast, whether it be ekâdaśî or dvâdaśî tithi, then the śrâddha is on the next day. Only Mâdhvas and Vaishṇavas observe this rule: Smârthas observe the śrâddha on ekâdaśi fast day also.

Grahaṇa.—For 9 hours before commencement of a lunar eclipse, and for 12 hours before commencement of a solar eclipse, neither śrâddha nor meals are allowed: they are allowed after *môksha, i.e.*, release of the eclipsed body. On the occasion of a *grasthôdaya*, eclipse of the moon (when moon rises in an eclipsed condition), neither śrâddha nor meals are allowed during day, and after *môksha*, performers of purṇimâ śrâddha must fast and perform śrâddha next day, but others may have food at night.

Grasthâsthamanam (Lunar eclipse).—If moon sets in an eclipsed condition, meals are allowed only after next moonrise, except to performer of śrâddha, who must fast in the night and perform śrâddha next day.

According to Manu, no śrâddha on account of a tithi can be performed at night, but śrâddhas on account of eclipse must be performed during time of eclipse, even if it be at night.

Jayanti—

1. *Matsya J.*—Chaitra **s. 5** (*aparâhna*).
2. *Kûrma J.*—Jyeshṭha **s. 12** (*pradôsha*).
3. *Varâha J.*—Chaitra **s. 9** (*aparâhna*).
4. *Nrisimha J.*—Vaiśâkha **s. 13** (*pradôsha*).
5. *Vâmana J.*—Bhâdrapada **s. 12** (*madhyâhna*).
6. *Paraśurâma J.*—Vaiśâkha **s. 3** (between 6 and 9 p.m.)
7. *Śri Râma J.*—Chaitra **s. 9** (*madyâhna*).
8. *Balarâma J.*—Bhâdrapada **s. 3** (*madyâhna*).
9. *Krishna J.*—Srâvaṇa **b. 8** (must be current at midnight).
10. *Bauddha J., Kalki J.*—Jyeshṭha **s. 3** (*pradôsha*).

Kalpâdi—

Kûrma kalpâdi—Chaitra su. 5.
or Chaitra Amâvâsyâ.
Pârthiva kalpâdi—Vaiśâkha ba. 3.
Sâvitri kalpâdi—Kârttika su. 7.
Praḷaya kalpâdi—Mârgaśîra su. 9.
Varâha kalpâdi—Mâgha su. 13.
Brahma kalpâdi—Phâlguna ba. 3.
} (*pûrvâhna.*)

Mâdhava tîrthams and Puṇyadinams.—South of Madras, Mâdhavas observe these commemorations as *aparâhna vyâpini* and North of Madras, they observe them as *udaya vyâpini*, because the days are days, not of birth, but of death.

These festivals are associated with lunar months and tithis, and are inserted in the general list accordingly.

Manvâdi—

List of *Manvâdis*—

1. Svârochisha—Âśvina su. 9.
2. Svâyambhuva—Kârttika su. 12.
3. Uttama—Chaitra su. 3.
4. Tâmasa—Bhâdrapada su. 3.
5. Agnisâvarṇi—Śrâvaṇa amâvâśyâ.
6. Raivata—Pushya su. 11.
7. Châkshusha—Ashâḍha su. 10.
8. Vaivasvata—Mâgha su. 7.
9. Sûryasâvarṇi—Bhâdrapada su. 7.
10. Rudrasâvarṇi—Âshâḍha ba. 8.
11. Indrasâvarṇi—Kârttika ba. 8.
12. Brahmasâvarṇi—Phālguṇa *pûrnimâ*.
13. Rauchyaka—Chaitra pūrṇimâ.
14. Bhauchya—Jyeshtha pūrṇimâ.

N.B.—*Manvadi* and *Yugadi*, occurring in *suklapaksha*, should be in *purvahna*, *i.e.*, before noon: if they occur in *krishnapaksha*, they should lie within *aparâhna*, *i.e.*, afternoon.

Mâsa Sivarâtri.—Every month, ba. 14 (*pradosha* or *pûrvaviddha*) is *Śivarâtri*. See *Chaturdasi*. *

Panchadaśî (15th Tithi).—A śukla 15 or Pûrṇimâ (full moon) is called *Somavati* when it falls on Monday and is special for donations.

It is called *chûḍâmaṇi* when it is *further* joined with a lunar eclipse.

Most pûrṇimâs receive special names, which are given in the general list.

Paraviddha, a tithi kept on the day on which it ends.

Pratipada (1st tithi).—The Chaitra śukla *pratipadâ*, *i.e.*, that which precedes the Mesha Sankrânti, is the beginning of the Hindu Lunar year, New Year's Day (Lunar) being that on which the pratipadâ is current at sunrise. (When there is an *Adhika Chaitra*, that begins the year.) The tithi is therefore called *Vatsarârambha* (commencement of the year). It is also *Navarâtrârambha*, there being another *Navarâtrârambha* on *Âśvina* śukḷa pratipadâ.

Pûrvaviddha.—A tithi kept on the day on which it begins, provided it begins more than 4 ghaṭikas before the sunset of one day and ends before sunset of following day.

Pushkara, or festival of a river, is celebrated when Jupiter enters certain signs of the Zodiac. The signs for the 12 chief rivers are—

Jupiter in Mesha–Gangâ	Jupiter in Tula–Kâveri.
„ in Vṛishabha–Revâ.	„ in Vrischika–Bhimarathî.
„ in Mithuna–Sarasvati.	„ in Dhanus–Pushkaram.
„ in Karkataka–Jumna.	„ in Makar–Gam.
„ in Simha–Godavari.	„ in Kumbha–Indus.
„ in Kanya–Krishna.	„ in Mina–Sapranitatasi.

The moment of Jupiter's entry into a Râśi is the Pushkaram, and the period for the feast is 12 days.

A Râśi into which Jupiter enters twice (*i.e.*, before retrogression and after) is counted only at second entry.

N.B.—For time of entry of Jupiter into the several Râśis, during the years A.D. 1840 to A.D. 1920 see *Ind. Chron.*, Tab XVIII, and for the time of his entry during the years A.D. 1910 to A.D. 1999 see Appendix II to this work.

Sankramaṇa.—When Sankrânti occurs during daylight, it should be observed as closely as possible: if after sunset, it is kept on the first day in the case of Sankrânti occurring before midnight: otherwise, next day. If at midnight, it may be kept on either day. Vṛishabha, Simha, Vṛischika, Kumbha Sankrântis (Sthira râśi Sankrântis) are called *Vishnupada*. Mithuna, Kanyâ, Dhanus, Mîna (Dvisvabhāva râśis) are called *Shadasiti puṇyakâla*.

Mésha and Tula Sakrântis are called Viśvat puṇyakâla. Karkaṭaka and Makara Sankrântis are called respectively Dakshinâyana and Uttarâyana punyakâla.

Saptami (7th Tithi).—A *Saptami* on Tuesday, combined with nakshatra 'Revati', (that is, by Eye-Table, bahuḷa 7 in Ashâdha or śukḷa 7 in Pausha or Mâgha) is very auspicious. *Śukla Saptami*, falling on Sunday, is called *Vijayâ*, and is special for donations. A śukla saptami, joined with the 1st quarter of nakshatra 'Hastâ', is called *Bhadrâ.* A śukla saptamî, coinciding with a Sankrânti is called Mahâjayâ, which, for making donations, is superior even to an eclipse.

Sopapadas.—Jyeshṭha. su. 2, Âśvina su. 10, Mâgha su. 4 and 12 (*purvāhna*).

Tisroshtakas.—7th, 8th and 9th tithis in bahuḷa paksha of Mârgaśîra, Pushya, Mâgha, Phâlguṇa (*aparâhna*).

Upâkarma.—Śrâvaṇa su. 15 (*samgavavyâpini* 6 ghaṭ. to 12). For Yâjurvedis, if Sankramaṇa, Mûḍham, heliacal setting of Jupiter or Venus or eclipse concur, then the upakarmam is on Bhâdrapada pûrṇimâ; if that also is objectionable, then the people observe it in Âshâḍha; but this is not according to the śâstras, which require it in this case to be performed in Śrâvaṇa month.

'Śravaṇa' nakshatra is the date for Ṛigvedis, whether the tithi be su. 14 or 15 or ba. 1.

For Vâjasaneyas, pûrnimâ must be *madhyâhṇa vyâpini.*

In Simha month, on 'Hasta' day is upakarma for Sâmavedis south of the Narbaḍha. For those north of the Narbaḍha, 'Hasta' nakshatra in Śrâvaṇa month is the appointed time.

Vaishnaya Tirunakshatras—

N.B.—*Tirunakshatra* among Vaishnavites means birth-star.

These nakshatras are observed according to Solar Months.

If a nakshatra occurs twice in a Solar Month, the second nakshatra is the one observed.

All nakshatras must have *Sangavakala vyapti.*

'*Aśvinî*'—

Mesha—Vaḍuganambi.
Kumbha—Śrîgovindaperumâl.

'*Bharaṇi*'—

Vṛischika—Îyuṇṇi Mâdhavaperumâl. Aruḷâḷaperumâḷ Emberumanâr.

'*Krittikâ*'—

Mesha—Uyyakonḍâr.
Vṛischika—Nambilai Tirumangaiâḷvâr.

'*Rohiṇî*'—

Vṛishabha—Tirukkottiyur Nambi.
Simha—Kaṇṇan. Periavâchâm Piḷḷai. Nâyanâr Achâm Piḷḷai.
Vṛischika—Tiruppâṇi Âḷwâr.
Mîna—Namberumâḷ.

'*Mrigaśîra*'—

Simha—Paravastu paṭṭarapirân Jîyar. Tirukkurugapîran Piḷḷân.
Makara—Emberumanâr Jiyar.
Kumbha—Tirukkachi Nambi.

'*Ardrâ*'—

Mesha—Emberumânâr.
Tula—Kûrakulôttama Dâśar.

'*Punarvasu*'—

Mésha—Chakravartti Tirumaganâr. Mudaliyâṇḍân.
Makara—Embâr.
Kumbham—Kulasekhara Āḷwâr Kandâḍayâṇḍân.

'*Pushyâ*'—

Karkaṭaka—Pratwâdi bhayankaram Aṇṇa.
Mina—Chelvapiḷḷâi.

'*Aśleshâ*'—

Mithuna—Mâraner Nambi.
Kumbha—Piḷḷai Urangavillidâśar.

'*Maghâ*'—

Makara—Tirumaḷisai Āḷwâr.
Kumbha—Maṇakkâl Nambi.

'*Pûrva Phalguṇî*'—

Karkaṭaka—Chûḍikkoḍutta Nâchiyâr. Kandaḍa Tôlappar. Edugiri Nâchiyâr.

'*Uttara Phâlguṇî*'—

Mîna—Śrîranga Nâchiyâr. Nanjîyār.

'*Hasta*'—

Mesha—Tevaperumâḷ.
Karkaṭaka—Badari Nârâyanapperumâḷ.
Makara—Kûrattâḷwâr.
Mîna—Tirunârâyaṇapperumâḷ. Tiruvarangattamudanâr.

'*Chitrâ*'—

Mesha—Madurakavi Āḷwâr. Ânanda Āḷwar.

'*Śvâti*'—

Vṛishabha—Aḷagya Singar. Tirumalai Nambi.
Mithuna—Periya Āḷwâr. Vaḍakku Tiruvidi Piḷḷai.

'*Viśâkha*'—

Vṛishaba—Nammâḷwâr. Piḷḷai Tirumalai Nambi. Tiruvâimoḷi Pillai.
Makara—Kurugâvala Appan.

'*Anurâdhâ*'—

Vṛishabha—Periya Paṭṭar. Srirâma Piḷḷai. Koil Kandâḍai Aṇṇan.
Mithuna—Śrîmannâtha Muṇigaḷ.

'*Jyeshṭha*'—

Dhanus—Tonḍaraḍipoḍi Āḷwâr. Periya Nambi. Nâlur Âcchân Piḷḷai. Aḷagiya Maṇavâla Perumâḷ Nâyanâr.

'*Mûla*'—

Tula—Maṇavâla Mahâmuni.

'*Pûrva Ashâḍha*'—

Tula—Senâmadurai Āḷwâr.

'*Uttara Ashâḍhâ*'—

Karkaṭaka—Āḷavandâr.
Puṇḍarîkâkshar.

'*Śravaṇâ*'—

Karkaṭaka—Terkâḷwâr.

Kanyâ—Tiruvengaḍam Uḍayān. Vedânta Deśikar.

Tula—Poigai Āḷwâr. Piḷḷai Lôkâchâryâr.

'*Dhanishṭha*'—

Tula—Pûdattāḷwâr. Tirumalayâṇḍân. Naḍuvil-tiruvidi paṭṭar.

'*Śatabhishaj*'—

Tula—Peyâlwâr. Pinpaḷagiya Perumâḷ Jiyar.

'*Pûrva Bhadrapada*'—

Makara—Choṭṭa Nambi. Nâlûrân.

'*Uttara Bhadrapadâ*'—

Tula—Viḷânjula pillai.

'*Revatî*'—

Mesha—Periya Perumâḷ.

Tula—Irumbilappar.

Vatsarârambha. lit: beginning of the year, is the name given to Chaitra, su. 1, which marks the commencement of the Hindu lunar year, and which is the su. 1 immediately preceding the Mesha Sankrânti. When there is an *adhikâ* Chaitra, su. 1 of that month begins the year. Pratipada is *paraviddhâ, i.e.,* it is kept on the day on which it ends. When Pratipadâ is *kshayâ,* it is kept on amâvâsyâ day: when it touches three days, it is kept on the third day.

Yogas—

Budhâshtamî.—su. 8 + Wednesday in any month.

Ekâdaśî Guruvâra vrata.—Ekâdaśi + Thursday in any month and either paksha.

Śanitrayôdaśi.—Shashṭhi + trayôdaśi in any month and either paksha.

Krishṇangâraka chaturdaśî vrata.—Krishna paksha 14 + Tuesday in any month (divavyâpini, *i.e.,* must be between sunrise and sunset).

Strînâm chandradarśanam.—The whole of the night from sunset to sunrise must be pûrṇimâ without occurrence of chaturdaśi.

Amâvâsyâ Sômâvâra vrata.—Monday + amâvâśya. *Bhânu Saptami.*—Sunday + saptami, any month and either paksha. *Angâraka Chaturthi.*—Tuesday + chaturthi. *Ashṭami Sômavâra vrata.*—Monday + ashṭami.	Tithi must be current at sunrise and noon (*divavyâpini*).

Mahâpaurṇamî vrata.—Moon and Jupiter should join in the Nakshatra whence the month takes its name.

Mahâmâgha.—*Saturn* in Mesha + *Moon* in 'Maghâ' + *Jupiter* in Simha + *Sun* in 'Śravaṇa' nakshatra.

Mahâvyatipâta.—*Jupiter* and *Mars* in Simha + *Venus* in Mesha + su. 12 + 'Hasta' nakshatra *in any month.*

Govindadvâdaśî.—*Sun* in Kumbha + *Jupiter* in Dhanus + śukha (*i.e., auspicious*) tithi, vâra, and nakshatra in Phâlguṇa sukla paksha;—

otherwise,

Sun in Kumbha + *Saturn* in Makara + su. 12 + 'Pushya' nakshatra.

Kûhayôga—Tyâjyam at meeting of amâvâsyâ and pratipadâ.

Yugâdi—

Kritâyugâdi—Kârttika su. 9.

Tretâyugâdi—Vaiśâkha su. 3.

Dvâparayugâdi—Mâgha amâvâsya.

Kaliyugâdi—Bhâdrapada ba. 13.

Manvâdi and Yugâdi occurring in *śukla paksha,* should be in *pûrvâhṇa, i.e.,* before-noon; if they occur in *krishṇa paksha,* they should be within *aparâhna, i.e.,* after-noon.

Yugântam—

Kretâyugântam—Simha Sankrânti. Tretâyugântam—Vrischika „ Dvâparayugântam—Vrishbha „ Kaliyugântam—Kumbha „	Same rule as for Sankrânti *q.v.* as regards time of day.

TABLE OF HINDU FASTS, FEASTS AND FESTIVALS.

NOTE.—The sign + means "combined with". The abbreviation "when +" means "when the tithi in question is combined with". *Asterisks* refer to the alphabetical list prefixed to this table.

Chaitra.

Su. 1. Chândra Vatsarârambha. Navarâtrârambha. Nimbakusuma pakshaṇa.

Su. 2. Védavyâsa Tîrtham (Mâdhavas).

Su. 3. Andôlana-tritiyâ (*paraviddha*). Gauri-tritiya. Matsajayanti (afternoon). Manvâdi.*

Su. 5. Lakshmi panchami or Srîpanchami (*pûrvaviddha*). Kalpâdi * (*pûrvâhna*).

Su. 8. Bhavâni-utpatti (*paraviddha*); bathing special, when + Wednesday + Nak. 'Punarvasu'. Aśokâshṭami.

Su. 9. Râma navami or **Srîrâma jayanti** (*madyâhna*). Varâha jayanti (aparâhna). Kavindira tîrtham (Mâdhavas).

Su. 10. Dharmarâja daśami.

Su. 11. Dôlotsava. Kâmadâ Ekâdaśi. See *Ekâdaśî.*

Su. 12. Vâmana dvâdaśi. Jayâ; when + nakshatra 'Pushya'. See *Dvâdaśi.**

Su. 13. Madana trayôdasi (*pûrvaviddha*) or Ananga pûjàna vrata; god of love worshipped. Satyavrata tirthânâm puṇyadinam (Mâdhavas).

Su. 15. Damanakôtsava (*pûrvaviddha*); (special for bathing when + Sunday, Thursday or Saturday. Manvâdi * (forenoon). Hanumat-jayanti. Virarâghava tirthânâm puṇya-dinam (Mâdhavas).

Ba. 3. Vagisa tirthânâm puṇyadinam (Mâdhavas).

Ba. 11. Varûthini Ekâdaśi. Satyavijaya tirthânâm puṇya-dinam (Mâdhavas).

Ba. 13. Varuṇi; when + Nak. 'Satabhishaj'. Mâhâ-varuṇi; when + Nak. 'Śatabhishaj' + Saturday. Mahâmahâvaruṇi; when + Nak. 'Satabhishaj' + Saturday + Yôga Śubha. Satyapriya tirthânâm puṇyadinam (Mâdhavas).

Ba. 15. Kalpâdi.*

Vaiśâkha.

Su. 3. Akshayatritiya (*pûrvaviddha*); special when + Wednesday + Nak. 'Rohiṇi'. Trétâ-yugâdi. See *Yugadi.** Parasurâma jayanti. Vidyadhiraja tirtham (Mâdhavas).

Su. 5. Râmachandra tirtham (Mâdhavas). Sankara's birthday.

Su. 7. Gangâ saptami or Gangôtpatti; birth of Gangâ; midday.

Su. 11. Paraśurâma Ekâdaśi. Môhini Ekâdaśi.

Su. 12. Vyatipâta (when Nak. 'Hasta' + *Jupiter* and *Mars* in Simha + *Sun* in Mésha).

Su. 13. Narasimha jayanti (*pradosha*).

Su. 14. Narasimha jayanti.

Su. 15. Vaiśâkhi pûrṇimâ. Sampat Gauri vrata (*paraviddha*). Kûrma jayanti (*pradôsha*). See *Jayanti.** Maha-Vaiśâkhi; when purṇimâ + *Sun* in Mésha + *Jupiter* in Dhanus + *Mars* in Makara + *Saturn* in Tula + *Nak.* 'Viśâkha' + Variya *yoga* + Sunday.

Ba. 3. Kalpâdi * (*pûrvâhna*).

Ba. 11. Aparâ Ekâdaśi.

Jyeshṭha.

Su. 2. Sopapada. Satyasandha tirtham (Mâdhavas).

Su. 3. Rambhâ-tritiyâ (*pûrvaviddha*); worship of Bhâvâni. Buddha jayanti. Kalki jayanti (*pradôsha*).

Su. 6. Araṇya Gauri vratam (*paraviddha*).

Su. 10. Daśaharâ (expiation of ten sins), *or* Gangâva-târa .Jyeshṭha Su. 10 + Wednesday (*or* Tuesday) + Nak. 'Hasta' + *Yoga* 'Vyati-pâta' is called DAŚAHARI.

Su. 11. Nirjalâ Ekâdaśi.

Su. 12. Râmalakshmaṇa Dvâdaśi. Kûrma jayanti* (*pradôsha*).

Su. 15. Vrishabha pûja. Mahâjyeshṭha (*Jupiter* in Aindra, *i.e.*, *Nak.* 'Jyeshṭhâ' + *Moon* in Aindra or Nak, 'Jyeshṭhâ' + *Sun* in Nak. 'Rohiṇi' + Jyeshṭha pûrṇimâ. Manvâdi* or Vaṭa Pûrṇimâ or Vaṭa Sâvitri (*purva-viddha*).

Ba. 2. Satya pûrṇa tirtham (Mâdhavas).

Ba. 3. Raghu variya tirtham (Mâdhavas).

Ba. 8. Trilôchana pûja.

Ba. 11. Yogini Ekâdaśi.

Ba. 15. Vaṭa Sâvitri vratam (*pûrvaviddha*).

Âshâḍha.

Su. 2. Ratha-yâtra dvitiyâ *or* Râmarathôtsava.

Su. 3. Satyâdhirâja tirtham (Mâdhavas).

Su. 5. Skanda-panchami (*paraviddha*).

Su. 6. Kumâra Shashṭhi (*paraviddha*).

Su. 7. Vivasvat saptami; (when + Nak. 'Pûrva Phalguṇi ").

Su. 10. Lakshmivratârambha. Sâka vratârambha. Manvâdi* (forenoon). Satyâbhinava tirtham (Mâdhavas).

Su. 11. Śayana Ekâdaśi (not to be observed in adhika month); *or* Vishnuśayana Ekâdaśi *or* Vishṇuśayanôtsava; (*i.e.* Vishnu going to sleep).

Su. 12. Gôpadma vratârambha. Châturmâsya* vrata commences.

Su. 14. Pavitrârôpanam (*paraviddha*). See *Upakarma**.

Su. 15. Vyâsapûrṇima (6 to 9 ghât. after sunrise). Hariśayanam. (*Sâyâhnavyâpini*). Manvâdi* Śivaśayanôtsava *or* Kokila vrata *or* Vyâsa-puja.

Ba. 2. Châturmâsya dvitiya.* Asûnyaśayana vrata; fast broken at moonrise.

Ba. 3. Śrivijaya tirtham (Mâdhavas).

Ba. 7. Special, when + Nak. 'Revati' + Tuesday.

Ba. 8. Manvâdi*.

Ba. 11. Kâmadâ or Kâmika Ekâdaśi. v. *Ekâdaśi* *.

Ba. 12. Pâpanâśini, when + Nak. 'Rôhini'. See *Dvâdasi* *.

Ba. 15. Satyâdiśa tirtham, (Mâdhavas).

Śrâvaṇa.

Su. 1. Râghavendraswâmi puṇyadinam (Mâdhavas).

Su. 3. Madhu-Śravâ (in Guzerat).

Su. 5. Nâgapanchami (*paraviddha*); worship of snakes.

Su. 6. Sûryashashṭhi (*paraviddha*). Hala-shasṭhi.

Su. 7. Satyavara tirthânâm puṇyadinam (Mâdhavas).

Su. 10. Dadhivratârambha.

Su. 11. Putradâ Ekâdaśi.

Su. 12. Dâmôdara dvâdaśi, Vishṇoh-pavitrâropanam.

Su. 14. Varalakshmi vrata, on Friday, nearest to purṇimâ in śuklapaksha.

Su. 15. Hayagrivôtpatti; Upâkarma *. Rig-yajuh-Srâvanî. Râkshabandhana (tying a string round the arm), or Rakipûrṇimâ; or Nârali-pûrṇimâ (when cocoanuts are thrown into the sea).

Hayagriva jayanti; or Hayagrivotpattî.

Ba. 2. Aśûnyaśayana vrata, See 'Châturmâsya dvitîyâ'.*

Ba. 3. Kajjalî-tritîyâ.

Ba. 4. Bahuḷa Chaturthi; when cows are worshipped.

Ba. 7. Sîtalā Saptamî or Sitalā-vrata (*pûrvaviddha*).

Ba. 8. Janmâshtami. Krishnâshtami or **Krishna-Jayanti.** Special when + Nak. 'Rohiṇi'; less so when joined only to Monday or Wednesday' Manvâdi. *

Ba. 11. Ajâ Ekâdaśî.

Ba. 12. Jayantî; (when + Nak. 'Punarvasu') See Dvâdasi. *

Ba. 13. Satyadharma tirthânâm puṇyadinam (Mâdhavas).

Ba. 15. Pithori or Kuśotpatinî (end of Śrāvaṇa) Manvâdi. *

Bhâdrapada.

Su. 1. Maunavratam (*pûrvaviddha*).

Su. 3. Shôḍaśomâvratam. Varâha jayanti (see *Jayanti* *). Haritâlika; worship of Pârvatî. Manvâdi *. Śivâ (a name for this tithi). Bâlarâma jayanti (*madhyâhna*).

Su. 4. **Vinâyaka Chaturthi** (*madhyâhnavyâpini*) Spl. when + Sunday or + Tuesday.

Su. 5. Ṛishipanchami (*aparâhanavyâpini*).

Su. 6. Champa Shashṭhi (when + Nak. 'Viśâkhâ' + Yoga Vaidhriti + Tuesday). Sûrya Shashṭhi (*paraviddha*) *or* Skanda Shashṭhi.

Su. 7. Amuktâbharaṇa Saptamî (*pûrvaviddha*). Jayasaptamî. Aparâjitâ. Manvâdi *.

Su. 8. Durvâshṭami (*pûrvaviddha*). Jyeshṭha pûja (when + Nak. 'Jyeshṭhâ'). Jyeshṭha-Gaurî-pûjâna-vrata, when + nakshatra 'Jyeshṭha'.

Su. 9. Nandanavamî. Aḍhukha-navamî.

Su. 10. Kshîravratârambha. Satyâshṭhakâma tirthânâm puṇyadinam (Mâdhavas).

Su. 11. Vishṇu parivartanôtsava *or* Parivarttana Ekâdaśi. Lakshminârâyaṇa Yôga.

Su. 12. Kalki-dvâdaśi. Sakrottâpanam. Vâmaṇa-jayanti (*madhyâhna*) (see *Jayanti* *). Srâvaṇa-dvâdaśi (when + Nak. Śravaṇa, + Wednesday). Vijaya, (when + Nak. 'Śravaṇa'). See *dvâdaśi.**

Su. 14. Anantavratam *or* Anantapadmanâbha Chaturdaśî (*pûrvaviddha*; must be current for 3 muhûrthas, *i.e.*, 6 ghaṭikas, after sunrise; and for those who perform this *vrata* for the first time, the tithi must be current at noon).

Su. 15. Praushṭhapadî pûrṇimâ *or* Śrâddha.

Ba. 1. Mahâlayapakshârambha. (Mahâbharaṇî, when + Nak. 'Bharaṇi' in *aparâhna*).

Ba. 2. Aśûnyaśayana-vrata. 'Châturmâsya dvitîya'*.

Ba. 3. Brihatyuma vratam (*paraviddha*).

Ba. 6. Chandrashasṭhivratam. Kapila Shasṭhi, (when + Nak. 'Rôhiṇi' + Yôga 'Vyatîpâta' + *Sun* in 'Hasta' + Tuesday).

Ba. 8. Rudrâshṭami (*pradôshakâla vyâpini*). Madhyâshṭami. Mahâlakshmî vrata (*pûrvaviddha*). Ashtaka Śrâddha.

Ba. 9. Durgâ navamî (in Maharâshtra). Gajagauri vratam (when + *Sun* entering nakshatra 'Hasta').

Ba. 10. Hariśankara Yôga (*pûrvaviddha*), when there is a concurrence (1) of ba. 9 and ba. 10. (2) of nak. 'Punarvasu' and nak. 'Pushya', (3) of 'Śivayôga' with 'Siddhayôga', and (4) of 'Garijakaraṇa' with 'Vanijakaraṇa'; for 8 ghaṭikas by day or night; may be kept in *adhika* months.

Ba. 11. Indirâ Ekâdaśi.

Ba. 12. Yatimahâlaya (*aparâhna vyâpini*). Jayâ (see Dvâdaśi *).

Ba. 13. Gajachchayâ (when + *Sun* in 'Hasta' + nak. 'Magha'). Kaliyugâdi. See *Yugâdi* *. Magha trayôdasi (nak. 'Magha').

Ba. 14. Vishaśastrahatânâm Mahâlaya. Mâdhava tîrthânâm puṇyadinam (Mâdhavas).

Ba. 15. Sarvapitṛi *or* **Mahâlaya Amâvâsya**; Special, when *Sun* and *Moon* are both in Nak. 'Hasta'.

Aśvina.

Su. 1. Chaṇḍîpûjârambha or commencement of **Navarâtri** (*paraviddha*). Stanavriddhî Gaurî vratam.

Su. 5. Upângalalita Gaurî vratam; esp. in Mahârâshṭra (*pûrvaviddha*). Sarasvatîpujârambha ('Mûla' Nak). Lalitâ panchami.

Su. 7. About this tithi, when it concurs with Nak. 'Mûla', Sarasvatî is worshipped. Satyaprâyana tîrthânâm puṇyadinam (Mâdhavas).

Su. 8. Mahâshṭami (Spl. when + Tuesday). Satyaparâkrama tirthânâm puṇyadinam (Mâdhavas).

Su. 9. Mahânavamî (*pûrvaviddha*) or Durgâ-navami Manvâdi *.

Su. 10. Vijayadaśami *or* **Daśara** (*pûrvaviddha*); (Spl. when + Nak. 'Śravaṇa)'.

Râjnyam paṭṭâbhishekha (*paraviddha*). Sarasvatîpûja (ends in 'Śravaṇa' nak.) Dvidaḷa vratârambha. Buddha-Jayanti. See *Jayanti* *. Sopapada.

Su. 11. Pâśânkuśa Ekâdaśi.

Su. 12. Padmanâbha dvâdaśi Godvâdaśi (*pradôsha vyâpini.*) Vijayâ (when + Nak. 'Śravaṇa'). See *Dvâdaśi* *.

Su. 15. Dhanapphalavratârambha, when + Sunday. Kaumudyutsava (*pûrvaviddha*). Kojâgari pûrṇimâ or Kojâgari vrata; worship of Lakshmi and Indra. Games of chance. Navânna pûrṇimâ (when new grain is cooked).

Ba. 2. Aśunyaśayana-vrata. See 'Châturmâsya dvitîya.' *

Ba. 3. Chandrôdaya Mâsa vratam (*paraviddha*).

Ba. 11. Ramâ Ekâdaśi.

Ba. 12. Gôvatsa Dvâdasi.

Ba. 13. Dhanatrayodaśi; when money lenders worship money.

Ba. 14. Narakachaturdaśi (*purvaviddha*). Yamadarpaṇam, Dîpadânam. Śvâtyabhyanga (at moonrise).

N.B.—Dîpâvali may fall on this tithi if joined to Nak. 'Śvâti.'

Ba. 15. **Dipâvali.** Kedâravratam (*paraviddha*).

Kârttika.

Su. 1. Balipratipada *or* Balipûja.

Su. 2. Yamadvitîya (*aparâhṇavyâpini*) *or* Bhrâtṛi dvitîya.

Su. 3. Âlochana Gaurî vratam (*paraviddha*).

Su. 4. Nâga Chaturthi (*paraviddha; madhyâhna vyâpini.*)

Su. 6. Mahâshasṭhi; special for feeding of Brahmans when it falls on Tuesday.

Su. 7. Kalpâdi * (*purvahna*).

Su. 8. Gô-ashṭâmi (*paraviddda*).

Su. 9. Kretâyugâdi. See *Yugâdi* *.

Su. 10. Satyavara tîrthânâm punyadinam (Mâdhavas).

Su. 11. Bôdhana Ekâdaśi *or* Prabodhini Ekâdaśi Bhîshmapanchaka vrata. Vedanidhi tîrthânâm puṇyadinam. (Mâdhavas).

Su. 12. Yôgeśvaradvâdaśi. Kshirâbdhi mahôtsava. Châturmâsya vrata * (begins). Prabôdhotsava *or* Utthâna dvâdaśi. (preparation for waking Vishnu). Tulasi vivâha. Manvâdi*

Su. 14. Vaikuṇṭha Chaturdaśi—midnight (*râtrivyâpini*). Tulasi vratodhyâpanam.

Su. 15. Special (when + Nak. 'Krittikâ'). Jvâlatoranam. (*pradôsha vyapini*). Dhatṛi yôga (when + Nak. 'Krittitkâ'). Manvâdi * Châturmâsya vrata (ends). Tripuri pûrṇimâ *or* tripurôtsava. Mahâkârttiki. (when + Nak. 'Rohiṇî'), or when *Moon* and *Jupiter* are both in Nak. 'Krittikâ' on Kârttika su. 15). Pâdmakayoga (when + *Sun* in Nak. 'Viśâkha' + *Moon* in Nak. 'Krittikâ'). **Krittika** Festival.

Ba. 2. Kârttika 'Châturmâsya dvitîya'*.

Ba. 3. Vidyânidhi tîrthânâm puṇyadinam (Mâdhavas.)

Ba. 8. Krishnâshtamî. v. *Ashtami* *. Kâla-Bhairâvâshtami *or* Kâla-Bhairava-jayanti. Manvâdi *.

Ba. 11. Utpatti Ekâdaśi.

Ba. 13. Yamadîpa (*pradosha vyâpini*).

Ba. 14. Padmanâbha tirthânâm punyadinam. (Mâdhavas).

Margaśîra.

Su. 5. Nâgapûja or Nâgapanchami.

Su. 6. Skanda Shashṭhî (*pûrvaviddha*), *or* Mahâ Shashṭhi. Champa Shashṭhî; Śiva worshipped as Khandoba. Spl. when + Sunday or Tuesday + Nak. 'Śatabhishaj' *or* + Yoga 'Vaidhriti'.

Su. 7. Mitra Saptamî (*pûrvaviddha*). Sûryavrata.

Su. 9. Kalpâdi (*purvâhna*).

Su. 11. Môkshadâ Ekâdasî. Satyanidhi tirthânâm puṇyadinam (Mâdhavas).

Su. 12. Matsya-dvâdaśi. Akaṇḍa dvâdaśi vratam-Sâtyanâtha tirthânâm puṇyadinam (Mâdhavas).

Su. 13. Hanumadvratam (*Abhijitvyâpini*).

Su. 14. Pâshâṇapakshana (*pradoshavyâpini*), *or* Pâshâṇa Chaturdaśi. Dattatreya jayanti (in some places; elsewhere it is su. 15).

Su. 15. Spl. for donations of salt, when + Nak. 'Mṛigaśirsha'. Chandra Pûja (*pradosha*). Śiva Pûja ('Ardrâ' Nak.). Dattatreya *or* Dattajayanti. Ardrâ festival.*

Ba. 7. Tisroshtaka * (*Aparâhna*).

Ba. 8. Kâlabhairava Ashṭami (*râtrivyâpini*). Ashṭaka-Srâddha. Tisroshtaka* (*aarâhna.*)

Ba. 9. Tisroshtaka (*aparâhna.*)

Ba. 11. Sapphala Ekâdasi.

Ba. 12. Raghunâtha tirthânâm puṇyadinam (Mâdhavas).

Ba. 15. Akshobhya tirthânâm puṇyadinam (Mâdhavas.)

Pausha.

Su. 2. Raghûttama tîrthanâm puṇyadinam (Mâdhavas).

Su. 8. Spl. when + Wednesday + Nak. 'Bharaṇî; † 'Rohiṇî' *or* 'Ardrâ', according to some).

Su. 11. Putradá Ekâdaśi *or* **Mukkotti Ekadaśi** *or* **Vaikunṭha Ekâdaśi.** Manvâdi.*

Su. 12. Kūrma dvâdaśi.

Ba. 6. Satyakâma tîrthânam puṇyadinam (Mâdhavas).

Ba. 7. Tisroshṭaka * (*aparâhna*). Naraharitîrthânâm puṇyadinam (Mádhavas).

Ba. 8. Tisroshtaka * (*aparâhna*). Ashṭaka Śrâddha.

Ba. 9. Tisroshtaka * (*aparâhna*).

Ba. 11. Shaṭṭilâ Ekâdaśi.

Ba. 14. Vidyádîśa tîrtham.

Ba. 15. Ardhodaya ; when + Sunday + Nak. 'Śravaṇa' + Yoga 'Vyatîpâta'. The tithi is called *Mahôdaya*, when any one of the above special features is wanting and the others are present. Purandaradáś a tîrtham (Mâdhavas).

Mâgha.

Su. 4. Tila chaturthi *or* Kuṇḍa Chaturthi (*pûrvaviddha*) Sopapada.

Su. 5. Madana panchami (*pûrvaviddha*). Vasanta panchami ; worship of Rathî and Kâma in forenoon; *or* Śripanchami.

Su. 7. Rathasaptamî (*paraviddha*). *or* Mahâsaptamî Chandrvrâkavartam. Manvâdi *

Su. 8. Bhîshmadarpaṇam (*purvaviddha*). Bhîshmâshṭami.

Su. 9. Mâdhva navamî *or* Ananta tîrthânâm puṇyadinam (Mâdhavas).

Su. 11. Bhîshmapanchakam. Jayâ Ekâdaśi.

Su. 12. Bhîshmadvâdâsi *or* Varâhadvâdaśi. Sopapada.*

Su. 13. Kalpàdi * (*purvâhna*).

Su. 15. Mahâ-Mâghi; when *Moon* and *Jupiter* are both in Nak. 'Maghā'.

Ba. 7. Tisroshṭaka.*

Ba. 8. Tisroshṭaka.* Ashtaka Srâddha.

Ba. 9. Râmadâsa Navamî. Tisroshtaka.*

Ba. 11. Vijayá Ekâdaśi.

Ba. 12. Tilâ dvâdasi *or* Vijaya when + Nak. 'Śravaṇa'.

Ba. 14. **Mahaśivarâtri**—midnight nearest ba. 14., when Nak. 'Śravaṇa' is current; spl. when + Yoga 'Śiva' + Sunday or Tuesday.

If Nak. 'Śravaṇa' is current at two successive midnights, the second is *Śivarâtri.*

Ba. 15. Dvâparayugâdi. See *Yugâdi.**

Phâlguṇa.

Su. 2. Satyabodha tîrthânam puṇyadinam (Mâdhavas.)

Su. 3. Vadiraja Svâmigaḷ puṇyadinam (Mâdhavas).

Su. 4. Śânta Chaturthi (*paravaddha*). Vyâsarâyaswâmigaḷ puṇyadinam (Mâdhavas).

Su. 6. Satyavratâtîrthânâm puṇyadinam (Mâdhavas).

Su. 11. Âmalakî Ekâdaśi.

Su. 12. Narasimhadvâdaśi.

Su. 13. Kâmadahanam (*paraviddha*) at midnight.

The concurrence of Sunday, Saturday, Tuesday or Friday is an objection to the feast: *chaturdaśî* (su. 14) is then the proper day. If that also is objectionable, then this festival is celebrated at that midnight at which Nak. 'Pûrva Phalguṇi' is current.

Su. 15. Helikotsava (*śâyâhana vyâpini*). Manvâdi.* Holikâ or Hutâsani pūrṇimâ. In South India, Kâman Paṇḍigai, commemorating the destruction of Cupid or Kâmadeva by Siva.

Ba. 1. Vasantotsava.

Ba. 2. Châturmâsya dvitiya. *

Ba. 3. Kalpâdi * (*purvâhna*).

Ba. 5. Rangapanchami; when colours are thrown about.

Ba. 7. Tisroshtaka.*

Ba. 8. Tisroshṭaka.* Ashtakaśrâddha.

Ba. 9. Tisroshṭaka.*

Ba. 11. Pápamôchini Ekâdaśi.

Ba. 13. Varuṇi, when + Nak. 'Śatabhishaj'.

Mahâvaruṇî, when + Nak Śatabhishaj + Saturday.

Mahâ-mahâ-Varuṇi, when + Nak. 'Śatabhishaj' + *Yoga* Śubha.'

Ba. 15. Manvâdi.*

THE EPHEMERIS

(A. D. 1800 to A. D. 2000)

A. D. 1800. **Mesha Sankranti.** (Commencement of Indian Sidereal Year). **Saka 1722: Kaliyuga 4901.**

Solar Eclipse. ● **(Surya Sid.) April 10·74.**

Lunar Eclipse. ○ **(Arya Sid.) April 10·64.** **(S. Cycle) Raudra.**

SOLAR reckoning: Cyclic Sidereal Year, Month and Day; Week-Day; English Month and Day. LUNAR reckoning: Tithi; Ending Moment; Nakshatra; Ending Moment; Muhammadan Year, Month and Day.

Jan.

Cyclic Sidereal Year, Month and Day	Week-Day	English Month and Day	Tithi	Ending Moment	Nakshatra	Ending Moment	Muhammadan Year, Month and Day
Siddharthi Dhanus—Margali 20	W	1	6	·42	25	·52	4
21	Th	2	7	·47	26	·59	5
22	Fr	3	8	·54	27	·69	6
23	Sa	4	9	·62	1	·79	7
24	Su	5	10	·70	2	·89	8
25	Mo	6	11	·80	...	...	9
26	Tu	7	12	·88	3	·00	10
27	We	8	13	·96	4	·10	11
28	Th	9	...	...	5	·19	12
—29	Fr	10	14	·02	6	·27	H. 1214 Shaban 13
Siddharthi Makara—Tai 1	Sa	11	Pausha P	·05	7	·32	14
2	Su	12	1	·07	8	·35	15
3	Mo	13	2	·06	9	·36	16
4	Tu	14	3 / 4	·04 / ·99	10	·35	17
5	We	15	5	·93	11	·33	18
6	Th	16	Bahula 6	·86	12	·29	19
7	Fr	17	7	·77	13	·24	20
8	Sa	18	8	·68	14	·18	21
9	Su	19	9	·57	15	·11	22
10	Mo	20	10	·48	16 / 17	·05 / ·98	23
11	Tu	21	11	·38	18	·91	24
12	We	22	12	·29	19	·85	25
13	Th	23	13	·22	20	·81	26
14	Fr	24	14	·14	21	·78	27
15	Sa	25	—A	·09	22	·77	28
16	Su	26	1	·06	23	·77	—29
17	Mo	27	2	·05	24	·79	1
18	Tu	28	3	·05	25	·83	2
19	We	29	4	·07	26	·91	3
20	Th	30	Sukla 5	·13	27	·99	4
21	Fr	31	6	·20	...	...	5

Feb.

Cyclic Sidereal Year, Month and Day	Week-Day	English Month and Day	Tithi	Ending Moment	Nakshatra	Ending Moment	Muhammadan Year, Month and Day
22	Sa	1	7	·27	1	·08	6
23	Su	2	8	·35	2	·19	7
24	Mo	3	9	·45	3	·30	8
25	Tu	4	10	·53	4	·40	9
26	We	5	11	·61	5	·50	10
27	Th	6	12	·66	6	·57	11
28	Fr	7	13	·70	7	·63	12
29	Sa	8	14	·71	8	·67	13
—30	Su	9	Magha P	·69	9	·68	14
Siddharthi Kumbha—Masi 1	Mo	10	1	·67	10	·69	H. 1214 Ramzan 15
2	Tu	11	2	·62	11	·66	16
3	We	12	3	·56	12	·63	17
4	Th	13	4	·48	13	·57	18
5	Fr	14	Bahula 5	·40	14	·51	19
6	Sa	15	6	·30	15	·46	20
7	Su	16	7	·19	16	·38	21
8	Mo	17	8	·11	17	·31	22
9	Tu	18	9 / 10	·00 / ·92	18	·25	23
10	We	19	11	·83	19	·19	24
11	Th	20	12	·76	20	·15	25
12	Fr	21	13	·71	21	·11	26
13	Sa	22	14	·69	22	·09	27
14	Su	23	—A	·67	23	·09	28
15	Mo	24	Phal. Suk. 1	·67	24	·11	29
·16	Tu	25	2	·70	25	·14	—30
17	We	26	3	·74	26	·21	1
18	Th	27	4	·81	27	·29	2
19	Fr	28	5	·90	1	·38	3

March

Cyclic Sidereal Year, Month and Day	Week-Day	English Month and Day	Tithi	Ending Moment	Nakshatra	Ending Moment	Muhammadan Year, Month and Day
Siddharthi Kumbha—Masi 20	Sa	1	6	·99	2	·49	4
21	Su	2	...	...	3	·59	5
22	Mo	3	7	·07	4	·71	6
23	Tu	4	Sukla 8	·14	5	·80	7
24	We	5	9	·22	6	·88	8
25	Th	6	10	·27	7	·94	9
26	Fr	7	11	·31	8	·98	10
27	Sa	8	12	·32	...	...	11
28	Su	9	13	·31	9	·01	12
—29	Mo	10	14	·27	10 / 11	·01 / ·99	13
Siddharthi Mina—Panguni 1	Tu	11	Phalguna P	·23	12	·96	H. 1214 Shawwal 14
2	We	12	1	·16	13	·91	15
3	Th	13	2	·08	14	·86	16
4	Fr	14	3 / 4	·00 / ·90	15	·79	17
5	Sa	15	5	·80	16	·72	18
6	Su	16	Bahula 6	·70	17	·65	19
7	Mo	17	7	·60	18	·58	20
8	Tu	18	8	·51	19	·53	21
9	We	19	9	·43	20	·48	22
10	Th	20	10	·36	21	·44	23
11	Fr	21	11	·31	22	·42	24
12	Sa	22	12	·28	23	·41	25
13	Su	23	13	·26	24	·42	26
14	Mo	24	14	·27	25	·47	27
15	Tu	25	—A	·30	26	·52	28
16	We	26	1	·33	27	·59	—29
17	Th	27	2	·40	1	·68	1
18	Fr	28	3	·48	2	·79	2
19	Sa	29	4	·57	3	·90	3
20	Su	30	5	·66	...	...	4
21	Mo	31	6	·74	4	·01	5

April

Cyclic Sidereal Year, Month and Day	Week-Day	English Month and Day	Tithi	Ending Moment	Nakshatra	Ending Moment	Muhammadan Year, Month and Day
22	Tu	1	Sukla 7	·80	5	·10	6
23	We	2	8	·86	6	·19	7
24	Th	3	9	·89	7	·25	8
25	Fr	4	10	·89	8	·31	9
26	Sa	5	11	·88	9	·33	10
27	Su	6	12	·84	10	·34	H. 1214 Zi-l-ka'da 11
28	Mo	7	13	·80	11	·32	12
29	Tu	8	14	·73	12	·29	13
30	We ○	9	Chaitra P	·65	13	·24	14
—31	Th	10	1	·56	14	·20	15
Raudra Mesha—Chittirai 1	Fr	11	2	·46	15	·13	16
2	Sa	12	3	·36	16 / 17	·06 / ·99	17
3	Su	13	4	·26	18	·92	18
4	Mo	14	5	·16	19	·87	19
5	Tu	15	6 / 7	·07 / ·99	20	·81	20
6	We	16	8	·91	21	·77	21
7	Th	17	Bahula 9	·86	22	·74	22
8	Fr	18	10	·83	23	·73	23
9	Sa	19	11	·81	24	·75	24
10	Su	20	12	·82	25	·78	25
11	Mo	21	13	·84	26	·83	26
12	Tu	22	14	·89	27	·90	27
13	We ●	23	—A	·94	1	·98	28
14	Th	24	Vaisak. Suk. ...	...	...	...	29
15	Fr	25	1	·03	2	·09	—30
16	Sa	26	2	·11	3	·20	Zi-l-hijja 1
17	Su	27	3	·20	4	·31	2
18	Mo	28	4	·27	5	·40	3
19	Tu	29	5	·34	6	·49	4
20	We	30	6	·40	7	·57	5

May

Cyclic Sidereal Year, Month and Day	Week-Day	English Month and Day	Tithi	Ending Moment	Nakshatra	Ending Moment	Muhammadan Year, Month and Day
Raudra Mesha—Chittirai 21	Th	1	7	·42	8	·62	6
22	Fr	2	8	·43	9	·65	7
23	Sa	3	Sukla 9	·41	10	·66	8
24	Su	4	10	·38	11	·65	9
25	Mo	5	11	·33	12	·62	10
26	Tu	6	12	·26	13	·59	11
27	We	7	13	·18	14	·53	12
28	Th	8	14	·09	15	·47	H. 1214 Zi-l-hijja 13
29	Fr	9	P / 1	·00 / ·89	16	·40	14
30	Sa	10	Vaisakha 2	·79	17	·33	15
—31	Su	11	3	·68	18	·27	16
Raudra Vrishabha—Vaikasi 1	Mo	12	4	·59	19	·20	17
2	Tu	13	5	·51	20	·15	18
3	We	14	6	·43	21	·10	19
4	Th	15	7	·39	22	·07	20
5	Fr	16	8	·34	23	·06	21
6	Sa	17	9	·33	24	·07	22
7	Su	18	Bahula 10	·33	25	·09	23
8	Mo	19	11	·36	26	·14	24
9	Tu	20	12	·41	27	·20	25
10	We	21	13	·45	1	·30	26
11	Th	22	14	·54	2	·39	27
12	Fr	23	—A	·62	3	·50	28
13	Sa	24	1	·71	4	·60	—29
14	Su	25	2	·77	5	·70	1
15	Mo	26	3	·84	6	·79	2
16	Tu	27	4	·90	7	·88	3
17	We	28	5	·92	8	·93	4
18	Th	29	Sukla 6	·93	9	·97	5
19	Fr	30	7	·91	10	·98	6
20	Sa	31	8	·89	11	·97	7

June

Cyclic Sidereal Year, Month and Day	Week-Day	English Month and Day	Tithi	Ending Moment	Nakshatra	Ending Moment	Muhammadan Year, Month and Day
21	Su	1	9	·83	12	·96	8
22	Mo	2	10	·77	13	·92	9
23	Tu	3	11	·68	14	·87	10
24	We	4	12	·59	15	·81	11
25	Th	5	13	·48	16	·74	12
26	Fr	6	14	·38	17	·68	H. 1215 Muharram 13
27	Sa	7	Jyeshtha P	·29	18	·61	14
28	Su	8	1	·18	19	·54	15
29	Mo	9	2	·10	20	·48	16
30	Tu	10	3 / 4	·01 / ·93	21	·43	17
—31	We	11	5	·87	22	·41	18
Raudra Mithuna—Ani 1	Th	12	6	·83	23	·39	19
2	Fr	13	Bahula 7	·82	24	·39	20
3	Sa	14	8	·81	25	·41	21
4	Su	15	9	·84	26	·45	22
5	Mo	16	10	·88	27	·52	23
6	Tu	17	11	·93	1	·60	24
7	We	18	...	...	2	·69	25
8	Th	19	12	·01	3	·79	26
9	Fr	20	13	·10	4	·90	27
10	Sa	21	14	·18	...	...	28
11	Su	22	—A	·24	5	·00	29
12	Mo	23	Ashadha Suk. 1	·32	6	·10	—30
13	Tu	24	2	·37	7	·19	H. 1215 Safar 1
14	We	25	3	·40	8	·25	2
15	Th	26	4	·41	9	·28	3
16	Fr	27	5	·39	10	·30	4
17	Sa	28	6	·37	11	·31	5
18	Su	29	7	·31	12	·29	6
19	Mo	30	8	·25	13	·25	7

Naksh :—1. Asvn. 2. Bhar. 3. Krit. 4. Rohi. 5. Mrig. 6. Ardh. 7. Punar. 8. Push. 9. Aslesh. 10. Magh. 11. P. Phal. 12. U. Phal. 13. Hasta. 14. Chit.

A. D. 1800. **Hijra 1215,** Commences, May 25. **Vikrama 1857.**

A.—Amavasya. **Kollam 976,** Commences { N. Malabar—Sept. / S. Malabar—Aug. **Bengal San 1206.**

P.—Pournami. (N. Cycle) **Prajapati.**

Columns: SOLAR reckoning (Cyclic Sidereal Year, Month and Day; Week-Day; English Month and Day) — LUNAR reckoning (Tithi, Ending Moment; Nakshatra, Ending Moment; Muhammadan Year, Month and Day).

July

Cyclic Sidereal Year, Month and Day	Week-Day	English Month and Day	Tithi	Ending Moment	Nakshatra	Ending Moment	Muhammadan Year, Month and Day
20	Tu	1	9	·17	14	·20	8
21	We	2	10 / 11	·08 / ·97	15	·14	9
22	Th	3	(Sukla) 12	·87	16	·09	10
(Raudra Mithuna—Ani) 23	Fr	4	13	·77	17 / 18	·01 / ·95	11
24	Sa	5	14	·66	19	·88	12
25	Su	6	(Ashadha) P	·58	20	·82	13
26	Mo	7	1	·49	21	·78	14
27	Tu	8	2	·41	22	·73	15
28	We	9	3	·35	23	·71	(H. 1215 Safar) 16
29	Th	10	4	·31	24	·71	17
30	Fr	11	5	·29	25	·72	18
31	Sa	12	6	·29	26	·76	19
32	Su	13	7	·32	27	·81	20
1	Mo	14	(Bahula) 8	·36	1	·90	21
2	Tu	15	9	·41	2	·99	22
3	We	16	10	·49	...	...	23
4	Th	17	11	·58	3	·10	24
5	Fr	18	12	·64	4	·20	25
6	Sa	19	13	·71	5	·31	26
7	Su	20	14	·80	6	·41	27
8	Mo	21	A	·85	7	·49	28
9	Tu	22	1	·88	8	·56	29
10	We	23	2	·89	9	·60	1
11	Th	24	3	·88	10	·62	2
12	Fr	25	4	·84	11	·63	3
13	Sa	26	5	·79	12	·62	4
(Raudra Karkata—Adi) 14	Su	27	(Sukla) 6	·73	13	·59	5
15	Mo	28	7	·66	14	·54	6
16	Tu	29	8	·56	15	·49	7
17	We	30	9	·46	16	·43	8
18	Th	31	10	·37	17	·35	9

Aug.

Cyclic Sidereal Year, Month and Day	Week-Day	English Month and Day	Tithi	Ending Moment	Nakshatra	Ending Moment	Muhammadan Year, Month and Day
19	Fr	1	11	·25	18	·28	10
20	Sa	2	12	·15	19	·22	11
21	Su	3	13 / 14	·06 / ·98	20	·15	12
22	Mo	4	(Sravana) P	·90	21	·11	13
23	Tu	5	1	·83	22	·07	14
24	We	6	2	·80	23	·04	15
25	Th	7	3	·78	24	·03	(H. 1215 Rabi-ul-awwal) 16
26	Fr	8	4	·78	25	·04	17
27	Sa	9	5	·79	26	·07	18
28	Su	10	6	·83	27	·13	19
29	Mo	11	7	·90	1	·20	20
30	Tu	12	8	·97	2	·29	21
31	We	13	...	...	3	·39	22
1	Th	14	(Bahula) 9	·05	4	·51	23
2	Fr	15	10	·13	5	·61	24
3	Sa	16	11	·22	6	·71	25
4	Su	17	12	·28	7	·80	26
5	Mo	18	13	·33	8	·86	27
6	Tu	19	14	·36	9	·92	28
7	We	20	A	·38	10	·95	29
8	Th	21	1	·37	11	·96	30
9	Fr	22	2	·34	12	·95	1
(Raudra Simha—Avani) 10	Sa	23	(Sukla) 3	·31	13	·92	(H. 1215 Rabi-ul-akhir) 2
11	Su	24	4	·23	14	·88	3
12	Mo	25	5	·16	15	·83	4
13	Tu	26	6 / 7	·06 / ·96	16	·76	5
14	We	27	8	·87	17	·69	6
15	Th	28	(Bhadra) 9	·76	18	·62	7
16	Fr	29	10	·67	19	·55	(H. 1215) 8
17	Sa	30	11	·56	20	·50	9
18	Su	31	12	·49	21	·44	10

Sep.

Cyclic Sidereal Year, Month and Day	Week-Day	English Month and Day	Tithi	Ending Moment	Nakshatra	Ending Moment	Muhammadan Year, Month and Day
19	Mo	1	(Suk.) 13	·41	22	·40	11
20	Tu	2	14	·35	23	·37	12
21	We	3	(Bhadrapada) P	·31	24	·35	13
22	Th	4	1	·29	25	·37	14
23	Fr	5	2	·30	26	·39	15
24	Sa	6	3	·31	27	·44	16
(Raudra Simha—Avani) 25	Su	7	4	·35	1	·54	17
26	Mo	8	5	·40	2	·59	(H. 1215 Rabi-ul-akhir) 18
27	Tu	9	6	·47	3	·70	19
28	We	10	7	·56	4	·81	20
29	Th	11	8	·64	5	·91	21
30	Fr	12	9	·73	...	...	22
31	Sa	13	10	·80	6	·01	23
1	Su	14	(Bahula) 11	·86	7	·10	24
2	Mo	15	12	·89	8	·18	25
3	Tu	16	13	·92	9	·24	26
4	We	17	14	·90	10	·27	27
5	Th	18	A	·87	11	·28	28
6	Fr	19	1	·84	12	·27	29
7	Sa	20	2	·76	13	·25	1
8	Su	21	3	·69	14	·22	2
9	Mo	22	4	·59	15	·16	3
10	Tu	23	5	·50	16	·10	4
(Raudra Kanya—Purattasi) 11	We	24	(Sukla) 6	·41	17 / 18	·03 / ·96	5
12	Th	25	7	·30	19	·90	(Jumadal-awwal) 6
13	Fr	26	8	·20	20	·84	7
14	Sa	27	9	·10	21	·78	8
15	Su	28	10 / 11	·03 / ·95	22	·73	9
16	Mo	29	12	·90	23	·69	10
17	Tu	30	13	·85	24	·69	11

Oct.

Cyclic Sidereal Year, Month and Day	Week-Day	English Month and Day	Tithi	Ending Moment	Nakshatra	Ending Moment	Muhammadan Year, Month and Day
18	We	1	14	·83	25	·69	(H. 1215) 12
19	Th	2	(Asvina) P	·83	26	·71	13
20	Fr	3	1	·85	27	·75	14
21	Sa	4	2	·90	1	·81	15
22	Su	5	3	·95	2	·90	16
23	Mo	6	...	...	...	...	17
24	Tu	7	4	·03	3	·00	18
25	We	8	5	·11	4	·10	19
26	Th	9	(Bahula) 6	·20	5	·21	20
27	Fr	10	7	·29	6	·31	21
28	Sa	11	8	·36	7	·41	22
29	Su	12	9	·42	8	·49	23
30	Mo	13	10	45	9	·55	24
31	Tu	14	11	·48	10	·59	25
1	We	15	12	·46	11	·60	26
2	Th	16	13	·44	12	·60	27
3	Fr	17	14	·40	13	·59	28
4	Sa	18	A	·33	14	·55	29
5	Su	19	1	·26	15	·50	30
6	Mo	20	2	·16	16	·44	1
7	Tu	21	3 / 4	·07 / ·98	17	·37	2
(Raudra Tula—Aippasi) 8	We	22	5	·88	18	·31	(H. 1215 Jumadal-akhir) 3
9	Th	23	(Sukla) 6	·78	19	·24	4
10	Fr	24	7	·68	20	·17	5
11	Sa	25	8	·61	21	·11	6
12	Su	26	9	·53	22	·06	7
13	Mo	27	10	·48	23	·03	8
14	Tu	28	(Kartika) 11	·43	24	·01	9
15	We	29	12	·42	25	·01	10
16	Th	30	13	·43	26	·02	11
17	Fr	31	14	·45	27	·06	12

Nov.

Cyclic Sidereal Year, Month and Day	Week-Day	English Month and Day	Tithi	Ending Moment	Nakshatra	Ending Moment	Muhammadan Year, Month and Day
18	Sa	1	(Kartika) P	·49	1	·13	(Jumadal-akhir) 13
19	Su	2	1	·55	2	·21	14
20	Mo	3	2	·63	3	·30	15
21	Tu	4	3	·70	4	·40	16
(Raudra Tula—Aippasi) 22	We	5	4	·81	5	·51	17
23	Th	6	5	·89	6	·61	18
24	Fr	7	6	·96	7	·72	19
25	Sa	8	...	...	8	·80	20
26	Su	9	(Bahula) 7	·01	9	·86	(H. 1215) 21
27	Mo	10	8	·04	10	·90	22
28	Tu	11	9	·08	11	·92	23
29	We	12	10	·06	12	·93	24
1	Th	13	11 / 12	·04 / ·99	13	·92	25
2	Fr	14	13	·94	14	·88	26
3	Sa	15	14	·86	15	·83	27
4	Su	16	A	·78	16	·77	28
5	Mo	17	1	·68	17	·71	29
6	Tu	18	2	·58	18	·65	1
7	We	19	3	·49	19	·58	2
8	Th	20	4	·39	20	·51	3
9	Fr	21	5	·30	21	·45	4
10	Sa	22	(Sukla) 6	·22	22	·40	5
11	Su	23	7	·15	23	·36	6
(Raudra Vrischika—Kartigai) 12	Mo	24	8	·09	24	·34	7
13	Tu	25	9	·05	25	·33	8
14	We	26	10	·04	26	·34	9
15	Th	27	11	·04	27	·38	10
16	Fr	28	12	·08	1	·44	11
17	Sa	29	13	·11	2	·51	12
18	Su	30	14	·18	3	·60	13

Dec.

Cyclic Sidereal Year, Month and Day	Week-Day	English Month and Day	Tithi	Ending Moment	Nakshatra	Ending Moment	Muhammadan Year, Month and Day
19	Mo	1	P	·26	4	·70	14
20	Tu	2	1	·34	5	·80	15
21	We	3	2	·43	6	·92	16
22	Th	4	(Margasira) 3	·51	...	...	(H. 1215 Rajab) 17
23	Fr	5	4	·59	7	·02	18
24	Sa	6	5	·65	8	·10	19
25	Su	7	6	·69	9	·17	20
26	Mo	8	7	·71	10	·22	21
27	Tu	9	8	·70	11	·25	22
28	We	10	9	·67	12	·26	23
29	Th	11	(Bahula) 10	·62	13	·24	24
30	Fr	12	11	·57	14	·21	25
1	Sa	13	12	·48	15	·17	26
2	Su	14	13	·40	16	·12	27
3	Mo	15	14	·31	17 / 18	·06 / ·99	28
4	Tu	16	A	·22	19	·92	29
5	We	17	1	·11	20	·85	30
6	Th	18	2 / 3	·02 / ·93	21	·79	1
7	Fr	19	4	·84	22	·74	2
8	Sa	20	5	·78	23	·69	3
9	Su	21	6	·72	24	·66	4
(Raudra Dhanus—Margali) 10	Mo	22	(Sukla) 7	·70	25	·65	5
11	Tu	23	8	·68	26	·66	6
12	We	24	9	·69	27	·70	7
13	Th	25	10	·72	1	·75	8
14	Fr	26	11	·76	2	·81	9
15	Sa	27	12	·84	3	·90	(H. 1215 Shaban) 10
16	Su	28	(Pausha) 13	·91	...	...	11
17	Mo	29	...	...	4	·00	12
18	Tu	30	14	00	5	·11	13
19	We	31	P	·09	6	·22	14

15. Svati. 16. Visak. 17. Anur. 18. Jyesh. 19. Mula. 20. P. Ash. 21. U. Ash. 22. Sravn. 23. Dani. 24. Satab. 25. P. Bhad. 26. U. Bhad. 27. Rev.

A. D. 1801.
Solar Eclipse. ●
Lunar Eclipse. ○

Mesha Sankranti. (Commencement of Indian Sidereal Year).
(Surya Sid.) April 11·00. **Saka 1723.** **Kaliyuga 4902.**
(Arya Sid.) April 10·90. **(S. Cycle) Durmati.**

Columns: SOLAR reckoning (Cyclic Sidereal Year, Month and Day; Week-Day, English Month and Day) — LUNAR reckoning (Tithi, Ending Moment; Nakshatra, Ending Moment) — Muhammadan Year, Month and Day.

Jan. — Solar: Raudra, Dhanus—Margali; Raudra, Makara—Tai. Lunar: Pausha (Bahula); Magha (Sukla). Muhammadan: H. 1215 Shaban; H. 1215 Ramzan.

Cyclic Sidereal Day	Week-Day	English Day	Tithi	Ending Moment	Nakshatra	Ending Moment	Muhammadan Day
20	Th	1	1	·18	7	·32	15
21	Fr	2	2	·24	8	·41	16
22	Sa	3	3	·29	9	·48	17
23	Su	4	4	·33	10	·54	18
24	Mo	5	5	·35	11	·57	19
25	Tu	6	6	·34	12	·58	20
26	We	7	7	·31	13	·57	21
27	Th	8	8	·28	14	·54	22
28	Fr	9	9	·21	15	·51	23
—29	Sa	10	10	·12	16	·46	24
1	Su	11	11 12	·05 ·95	17	·39	25
2	Mo	12	13	·85	18	·33	26
3	Tu	13	14	·76	19	·26	27
4	We	14	—A	·67	20	·19	28
5	Th	15	1	·57	21	·13	—29
6	Fr	16	2	·48	22	·07	1
7	Sa	17	3	·43	23 24	·02 ·99	2
8	Su	18	4	·37	25	·98	3
9	Mo	19	5	·34	26	·99	4
10	Tu	20	6	·33	...	...	5
11	We	21	7	·34	27	·01	6
12	Th	22	8	·36	1	·05	7
13	Fr	23	9	·41	2	·12	8
14	Sa	24	10	·49	3	·20	9
15	Su	25	11	·56	4	·31	10
16	Mo	26	12	·65	5	·41	11
17	Tu	27	13	·74	6	·52	12
18	We	28	14	·83	7	·62	13
19	Th	29	P	·89	8	·71	14
20	Fr	30	1	·95	9	·80	15
21	Sa	31	2	·98	10	·85	16

Feb. — Solar: Raudra, Kumbha—Mari. Lunar: Bahula; Phalguna (Sukla). Muhammadan: H. 1215 Shawwal.

Cyclic Sidereal Day	Week-Day	English Day	Tithi	Ending Moment	Nakshatra	Ending Moment	Muhammadan Day
22	Su	1	3	·99	11	·89	17
23	Mo	2	4	·98	12	·90	18
24	Tu	3	5	·95	13	·90	19
25	We	4	6	·92	14	·88	20
26	Th	5	7	·84	15	·84	21
27	Fr	6	8	·76	16	·79	22
28	Sa	7	9	·67	17	·73	23
29	Su	8	10	·59	18	·66	24
—30	Mo	9	11	·48	19	·59	25
1	Tu	10	12	·38	20	·53	26
2	We	11	13	·29	21	·47	27
3	Th	12	14	·19	22	·41	28
4	Fr	13	—A	·12	23	·36	29
5	Sa	14	1	·05	24	·32	—30
6	Su	15	2 3	·01 ·97	25	·31	1
7	Mo	16	4	·96	26	·31	2
8	Tu	17	5	·97	27	·33	3
9	We	18	...	...	1	·36	4
10	Th	19	6	·00	2	·42	5
11	Fr	20	7	·05	3	·51	6
12	Sa	21	8	·11	4	·61	7
13	Su	22	9	·19	5	·71	8
14	Mo	23	10	·29	6	·81	9
15	Tu	24	11	·36	7	·92	10
16	We	25	12	·45	...	...	11
17	Th	26	13	·51	8	·02	12
18	Fr	27	14	·57	9	·10	13
19	Sa	28	P	·60	10	·16	14

March — Solar: Raudra, Kumbha—Mari; Raudra, Mina—Panguni. Lunar: Phalguna (Bahula); Sukla; Chaitra. Muhammadan: H. 1215 Shawwal; H. 1215 Zi-l-ka'da.

Cyclic Sidereal Day	Week-Day	English Day	Tithi	Ending Moment	Nakshatra	Ending Moment	Muhammadan Day
20	Su	1	1	·62	11	·20	15
21	Mo	2	2	·60	12	·22	16
22	Tu	3	3	·58	13	·23	17
23	We	4	4	·52	14	·21	18
24	Th	5	5	·45	15	·18	19
25	Fr	6	6	·37	16	·13	20
26	Sa	7	7	·28	17	·07	21
27	Su	8	8	·19	18 19	·00 ·94	22
28	Mo	9	9	·08	20	·87	23
29	Tu	10	10 11	·00 ·90	21	·80	24
—30	We	11	12	·80	22	·74	25
1	Th	12	13	·72	23	·69	26
2	Fr	13	14	·65	24	·66	27
3	Sa	14	—A	·61	25	·64	28
4	Su	15	1	·57	26	·63	—29
5	Mo	16	2	·56	27	·64	1
6	Tu	17	3	·56	1	·68	2
7	We	18	4	·59	2	·74	3
8	Th	19	5	·64	3	·81	4
9	Fr	20	6	·72	4	·90	5
10	Sa	21	7	·80	...	...	6
11	Su	22	8	·88	5	·01	7
12	Mo	23	9	·98	6	·11	8
13	Tu	24	...	...	7	·23	9
14	We	25	10	·05	8	·32	10
15	Th	26	11	·11	9	·41	11
16	Fr	27	12	·16	10	·47	12
17	Sa	28	13	·19	11	·52	13
18	Su	29	14	·20	12	·54	14
19	Mo ○	30	P	·18	13	·56	15
20	Tu	31	1	·15	14	·54	16

April — Solar: Durmati, Mesha—Chittirai. Lunar: Bahula; Sukla; Vaisakha. Muhammadan: H. 1215 Zi-l-hijja.

Cyclic Sidereal Day	Week-Day	English Day	Tithi	Ending Moment	Nakshatra	Ending Moment	Muhammadan Day
21	We	1	2	·09	15	·51	17
22	Th	2	3 4	·04 ·95	16	·46	18
23	Fr	3	5	·86	17	·41	19
24	Sa	4	6	·77	18	·35	20
25	Su	5	7	·65	19	·28	21
26	Mo	6	8	·56	20	·21	22
27	Tu	7	9	·47	21	·14	23
28	We	8	10	·88	22	·08	24
29	Th	9	11	·29	23 24	·08 ·99	25
—30	Fr	10	12	·21	25	·96	26
1	Sa	11	13	·17	26	·95	27
2	Su	12	14	·13	27	·96	28
3	Mo ●	13	—A	·12	...	...	29
4	Tu	14	1	·12	1	·00	—30
5	We	15	2	·16	2	·05	1
6	Th	16	3	·20	3	·12	2
7	Fr	17	4	·27	4	·21	3
8	Sa	18	5	·35	5	·30	4
9	Su	19	6	·43	6	·41	5
10	Mo	20	7	·53	7	·53	6
11	Tu	21	8	·60	8	·63	7
12	We	22	9	·66	9	·71	8
13	Th	23	10	·70	10	·78	9
14	Fr	24	11	·72	11	·83	10
15	Sa	25	12	·74	12	·87	11
16	Su	26	13	·72	13	·88	12
17	Mo	27	14	·70	14	·87	13
18	Tu	28	P	·63	15	·84	14
19	We	29	1	·57	16	·80	15
20	Th	30	2	·48	17	·75	16

May — Solar: Durmati, Mesha—Chittirai; Durmati, Vrishabha—Vaikasi. Lunar: Vaisk. (Bahula); Jyeshtha (Sukla); Adhika. Muhammadan: H. 1215 Zi-l-hijja; H. 1216 Muharram.

Cyclic Sidereal Day	Week-Day	English Day	Tithi	Ending Moment	Nakshatra	Ending Moment	Muhammadan Day
21	Fr	1	3	·40	18	·69	17
22	Sa	2	4	·30	19	·62	18
23	Su	3	5	·19	20	·55	19
24	Mo	4	6	·10	21	·48	20
25	Tu	5	7 8	·00 ·91	22	·42	21
26	We	6	9	·81	23	·37	22
27	Th	7	10	·75	24	·32	23
28	Fr	8	11	·70	25	·29	24
29	Sa	9	12	·67	26	·27	25
30	Su	10	13	·65	27	·29	26
—31	Mo	11	14	·64	1	·31	27
1	Tu	12	—A	·68	2	·36	28
2	We	13	1	·72	3	·42	—29
3	Th	14	2	·79	4	·51	1
4	Fr	15	3	·86	5	·60	2
5	Sa	16	4	·95	6	·72	3
6	Su	17	...	...	7	·82	4
7	Mo	18	5	·03	8	·93	5
8	Tu	19	6	·10	...	...	6
9	We	20	7	·18	9	·02	7
10	Th	21	8	·22	10	·09	8
11	Fr	22	9	·24	11	·15	9
12	Sa	23	10	·25	12	·19	10
13	Su	24	11	·24	13	·20	11
14	Mo	25	12	·21	14	·19	12
15	Tu	26	13	·15	15	·17	13
16	We	27	14 P	·07 ·99	16	·14	14
17	Th	28	1	·91	17	·09	15
18	Fr	29	2	·81	18 19	·03 ·96	16
19	Sa	30	3	·70	20	·89	17
20	Su	31	4	·60	21	·83	18

June — Solar: Durmati, Mithuna—Ani. Lunar: Bahula; Sukla; Nija Jyeshtha; Bah. Muhammadan: H. 1216 Safar.

Cyclic Sidereal Day	Week-Day	English Day	Tithi	Ending Moment	Nakshatra	Ending Moment	Muhammadan Day
21	Mo	1	5	·49	22	·76	19
22	Tu	2	6	·40	23	·70	20
23	We	3	7	·32	24	·65	21
24	Th	4	8	·26	25	·62	22
25	Fr	5	9	·19	26	·60	23
26	Sa	6	10	·16	27	·61	24
27	Su	7	11	·14	1	·63	25
28	Mo	8	12	·14	2	·67	26
29	Tu	9	13	·15	3	·73	27
30	We	10	14	·19	4	·81	28
—31	Th	11	—A	·28	5	·90	29
1	Fr	12	1	·34	...	...	—30
2	Sa	13	2	·43	6	·02	1
3	Su	14	3	·51	7	·12	2
4	Mo	15	4	·58	8	·23	3
5	Tu	16	5	·65	9	·32	4
6	We	17	6	·70	10	·41	5
7	Th	18	7	·73	11	·47	6
8	Fr	19	8	·73	12	·50	7
9	Sa	20	9	·72	13	·52	8
10	Su	21	10	·69	14	·52	9
11	Mo	22	11	·63	15	·51	10
12	Tu	23	12	·56	16	·47	11
13	We	24	13	·49	17	·42	12
14	Th	25	14	·39	18	·36	13
15	Fr	26	P	·29	19	·30	14
16	Sa	27	1	·19	20	·24	15
17	Su	28	2 3	·08 ·98	21	·17	16
18	Mo	29	4	·89	22	·10	17
19	Tu	30	5	·81	23 24	·04 ·98	18

Naksh : 1. Asvn. 2. Bhar. 3. Krit. 4 Rohi. 5. Mrig. 6. Ardh. 7. Punar. 8. Push. 9. Aslesh. 10. Magh. 11. P. Phal. 12. U. Phal. 13. Hasta. 14. Chit.

A. D. 1801. **A.—Amavasya. P.—Pournami.** **Kollam 977,** Commences { **N. Malabar—Sept. S. Malabar—Aug.** **Hijra 1216,** Commences, **May 14.** **Vikrama 1858. Bengal San 1207. (N. Cycle) Angiras.**

July

Cyclic Sidereal Year, Month and Day	Week-Day	English Month and Day	Tithi	Ending Moment	Nakshatra	Ending Moment	Muhammadan Year, Month and Day
20	We	1	Nija. Jy. 6	·73	25	·95	Safar. 19
21	Th	2	7	·67	26	·93	20
22	Fr	3	8	·63	27	·93	21
23	Sa	4	9	·61	1	·94	22
24	Su	5	10	·62	2	·98	23
25	Mo	6	11	·64	...	...	24
26	Tu	7	12	·69	3	·04	25
27	We	8	13	·74	4	·12	26
28	Th	9	14	·83	5	·21	27
29	Fr	10	A	·91	6	·31	28
30	Sa	11	1	·98	7	·42	29
31	Su	12	...	...	8	·52	1
32	Mo	13	2	·06	9	·63	2
1	Tu	14	3	·13	10	·71	3
2	We	15	4	·18	11	·78	4
3	Th	16	5	·20	12	·82	5
4	Fr	17	6	·22	13	·84	6
5	Sa	18	7	·20	14	·85	7
6	Su	19	8	·16	15	·84	8
7	Mo	20	9	·11	16	·81	9
8	Tu	21	10 / 11	·04 / ·97	17	·76	10
9	We	22	12	·88	18	·70	11
10	Th	23	13	·79	19	·63	12
11	Fr	24	14	·68	20	·57	13
12	Sa	25	P	·57	21	·50	14
13	Su	26	1	·47	22	·43	15
14	Mo	27	2	·38	23	·37	16
15	Tu	28	3	·29	24	·32	17
16	We	29	4	·21	25	·29	18
17	Th	30	5	·16	26	·26	19
18	Fr	31	6	·12	27	·25	20

Solar: *Durmati Mithuna—Ani* (1–32); *Durmati Karkata—Adi* (from 1). Lunar: Nija. Jy. *Bahula*; *Sukla*; **Ashadha**. Muhammadan: H. 1216 *Safar*; H. 1216 *Rabi-ul-awwal* (from 10).

Aug.

Cyclic Sidereal Year, Month and Day	Week-Day	English Month and Day	Tithi	Ending Moment	Nakshatra	Ending Moment	Muhammadan Year, Month and Day
19	Sa	1	7	·10	1	·26	21
20	Su	2	8	·10	2	·29	22
21	Mo	3	9	·11	3	·35	23
22	Tu	4	10	·16	4	·42	24
23	We	5	11	·21	5	·51	25
24	Th	6	12	·30	6	·61	26
25	Fr	7	13	·38	7	·72	27
26	Sa	8	14	·47	8	·83	28
27	Su	9	A	·53	9	·93	29
28	Mo	10	1	·60	...	...	30
29	Tu	11	2	·65	10	·02	1
30	We	12	3	·69	11	·09	2
31	Th	13	4	·71	12	·13	3
1	Fr	14	5	·68	13	·17	4
2	Sa	15	6	·66	14	·18	5
3	Su	16	7	·61	15	·17	6
4	Mo	17	8	·55	16	·14	7
5	Tu	18	9	·47	17	·09	8
6	We	19	10	·37	18 / 19	·04 / ·98	9
7	Th	20	11	·27	20	·91	10
8	Fr	21	12	·17	21	·84	11
9	Sa	22	13 / 14	·08 / ·98	22	·77	12
10	Su	23	P	·88	23	·71	13
11	Mo	24	1	·79	24	·66	14
12	Tu	25	2	·72	25	·62	15
13	We	26	3	·66	26	·59	16
14	Th	27	4	·62	27	·57	17
15	Fr	28	5	·61	1	·58	18
16	Sa	29	6	·60	2	·61	19
17	Su	30	7	·62	3	·66	20
18	Mo	31	8	·66	4	·73	21

Solar: *Durmati Karkata—Adi*; *Durmati Simha—Avani* (from 1). Lunar: *Bahula*; *Sukla*; **Sravana**; *Bahula*. Muhammadan: H. 1216 *Rabi-ul-akhir* (from 1).

Sep.

Cyclic Sidereal Year, Month and Day	Week-Day	English Month and Day	Tithi	Ending Moment	Nakshatra	Ending Moment	Muhammadan Year, Month and Day
19	Tu	1	Srav. 9	·72	5	·81	Rabi-ul-akhir. 22
20	We	2	10	·80	6	·91	23
21	Th	3	11	·90	...	...	24
22	Fr	4	12	·97	7	·03	25
23	Sa	5	...	...	8	·13	26
24	Su	6	13	·06	9	·23	27
25	Mo	7	14	·12	10	·32	28
26	Tu	8	A	·16	11	·39	29
27	We	9	1	·20	12	·45	1
28	Th	10	2	·22	13	·49	2
29	Fr	11	3	·20	14	·50	3
30	Sa	12	4	·18	15	·49	4
31	Su	13	5	·13	16	·47	5
1	Mo	14	6 / 7	·07 / ·99	17	·43	6
2	Tu	15	8	·91	18	·38	7
3	We	16	9	·80	19	·32	8
4	Th	17	10	·70	20	·25	9
5	Fr	18	11	·60	21	·18	10
6	Sa	19	12	·49	22	·11	11
7	Su	20	13	·41	23	·05	12
8	Mo	21	14	·32	24 / 25	·00 / ·95	13
9	Tu	22 ○	P	·26	26	·91	14
10	We	23	1	·20	27	·90	15
11	Th	24	2	·15	1	·91	16
12	Fr	25	3	·14	2	·93	17
13	Sa	26	4	·13	3	·97	18
14	Su	27	5	·16	...	...	19
15	Mo	28	6	·21	4	·03	20
16	Tu	29	7	·27	5	·11	21
17	We	30	8	·34	6	·22	22

Solar: *Durmati Simha—Avani*; *Durmati Kanya—Purattasi* (from 1). Lunar: Srav. *Bahula*; *Sukla*; **Bhadrapada**. Muhammadan: *Rabi-ul-akhir*; H. 1216 *Jumadal-awwal* (from 1).

Oct.

Cyclic Sidereal Year, Month and Day	Week-Day	English Month and Day	Tithi	Ending Moment	Nakshatra	Ending Moment	Muhammadan Year, Month and Day
18	Th	1	9	·43	7	·32	23
19	Fr	2	10	·51	8	·43	24
20	Sa	3	11	·59	9	·53	25
21	Su	4	12	·67	10	·62	26
22	Mo	5	13	·72	11	·70	27
23	Tu	6	14	·75	12	·77	28
24	We	7	A	·77	13	·81	29
25	Th	8	1	·76	14	·82	30
26	Fr	9	2	·73	15	·82	1
27	Sa	10	3	·69	16	·80	2
28	Su	11	4	·63	17	·77	3
29	Mo	12	5	·55	18	·72	4
30	Tu	13	6	·46	19	·66	5
31	We	14	7	·36	20	·59	6
1	Th	15	8	·27	21	·52	7
2	Fr	16	9	·16	22	·46	8
3	Sa	17	10 / 11	·06 / ·98	23	·39	9
4	Su	18	12	·89	24	·33	10
5	Mo	19	13	·84	25	·28	11
6	Tu	20	14	·77	26	·24	12
7	We	21	P	·74	27	·23	13
8	Th	22	1	·72	1	·23	14
9	Fr	23	2	·73	2	·24	15
10	Sa	24	3	·74	3	·28	16
11	Su	25	4	·79	4	·34	17
12	Mo	26	5	·86	5	·42	18
13	Tu	27	6	·92	6	·52	19
14	We	28	...	...	7	·62	20
15	Th	29	7	·01	8	·73	21
16	Fr	30	8	·10	9	·83	22
17	Sa	31	9	·20	10	·93	23

Solar: *Durmati Kanya—Purattasi*; *Durmati Tula—Aippasi* (from 1). Lunar: *Bahula*; *Sukla*; **Asvina**; *Bahula*. Muhammadan: H. 1216 *Jumadal-akhir* (from 1).

Nov.

Cyclic Sidereal Year, Month and Day	Week-Day	English Month and Day	Tithi	Ending Moment	Nakshatra	Ending Moment	Muhammadan Year, Month and Day
18	Su	1	Asv. 10	·26	...	...	24
19	Mo	2	11	·31	11	·02	25
20	Tu	3	12	·34	12	·08	26
21	We	4	13	·36	13	·12	27
22	Th	5	14	·36	14	·14	28
23	Fr	6	A	·33	15	·14	29
24	Sa	7	1	·29	16	·14	1
25	Su	8	2	·22	17	·10	2
26	Mo	9	3	·15	18 / 19	·05 / ·99	3
27	Tu	10	4 / 5	·06 / ·96	20	·93	4
28	We	11	6	·87	21	·87	5
29	Th	12	7	·76	22	·80	6
30	Fr	13	8	·67	23	·73	7
1	Sa	14	9	·58	24	·67	8
2	Su	15	10	·51	25	·61	9
3	Mo	16	11	·44	26	·57	10
4	Tu	17	12	·37	27	·56	11
5	We	18	13	·34	1	·55	12
6	Th	19	14	·33	2	·56	13
7	Fr	20	P	·34	3	·59	14
8	Sa	21	1	·35	4	·65	15
9	Su	22	2	·41	5	·73	16
10	Mo	23	3	·48	6	·82	17
11	Tu	24	4	·55	7	·92	18
12	We	25	5	·64	...	...	19
13	Th	26	6	·72	8	·03	20
14	Fr	27	7	·82	9	·13	21
15	Sa	28	8	·88	10	·24	22
16	Su	29	9	·94	11	·32	23
17	Mo	30	10	·97	12	·39	24

Solar: *Durmati Tula—Aippasi*; *Durmati Vrischika—Kartigai* (from 1). Lunar: Asv. *Bahula*; *Sukla*; **Kartika**; *Bahula*. Muhammadan: *J. akhir*; H. 1216 *Rajab* (from 1).

Dec.

Cyclic Sidereal Year, Month and Day	Week-Day	English Month and Day	Tithi	Ending Moment	Nakshatra	Ending Moment	Muhammadan Year, Month and Day
18	Tu	1	...	...	13	·44	25
19	We	2	11 / 12	·00 / ·98	14	·46	26
20	Th	3	13	·95	15	·48	27
21	Fr	4	14	·90	16	·46	28
22	Sa	5	A	·84	17	·43	29
23	Su	6	1	·77	18	·39	30
24	Mo	7	2	·68	19	·33	1
25	Tu	8	3	·59	20	·28	2
26	We	9	4	·49	21	·21	3
27	Th	10	5	·38	22	·14	4
28	Fr	11	6	·29	23	·07	5
29	Sa	12	7	·20	24 / 25	·00 / ·95	6
1	Su	13	8	·13	26	·91	7
2	Mo	14	9	·06	27	·88	8
3	Tu	15	10 / 11	·02 / ·98	1	·87	9
4	We	16	12	·96	2	·88	10
5	Th	17	13	·98	3	·91	11
6	Fr	18	...	...	4	·97	12
7	Sa	19	14	·00	...	...	13
8	Su	20	P	·06	5	·03	14
9	Mo	21	1	·12	6	·12	15
10	Tu	22	2	·21	7	·23	16
11	We	23	3	·29	8	·32	17
12	Th	24	4	·38	9	·44	18
13	Fr	25	5	·47	10	·54	19
14	Sa	26	6	·53	11	·63	20
15	Su	27	7	·59	12	·70	21
16	Mo	28	8	·62	13	·75	22
17	Tu	29	9	·64	14	·79	23
18	We	30	10	·62	15	·80	24
19	Th	31	1	·61	16	·79	25

Solar: *Durmati Vrischika—Kartigai*; *Durmati Dhanus—Margali* (from 1). Lunar: *Sukla*; **Margasira**; *Bahula*. Muhammadan: H. 1216 *Shaban* (from 1).

15. Svati. 16. Visak. 17. Anur. 18. Jyesh. 19. Mula. 20. P. Ash. 21. U. Ash. 22. Sravn. 23. Dani. 24. Satab. 25. P. Bhad. 26. U. Bhad. 27. Rev.

A. D. 1802. **Mesha Sankranti** (Commencement of Indian Sidereal Year).
Solar Eclipse. ● **(Surya Sid.) April 11·26.** **Saka 1724.** **Kaliyuga 4903.**
Lunar Eclipse. ◯ **(Arya Sid.) April 11·16.** **(S. Cycle) Dundubhi.**

SOLAR reckoning	Cyclic Sidereal Year, Month and Day	Week-Day	English Month and Day	LUNAR reckoning	Tithi	Ending Moment	Nakshatra	Ending Moment	Muhammadan Year, Month and Day
		Jan.							
Durmati *Dhanus—Margali.*	20	Fr	1	Mr.	12	·55	17	·76	*Shaban.* 26
	21	Sa	2		13	·48	18	·72	27
	22	Su	3	*ha.*	14	·41	19	·67	28
	23	Mo	4		—A	·32	20	·61	—29
	24	Tu	5		1	·23	21	·55	1
	25	We	6		2	·13	22	·47	2
	26	Th	7		3 4	·04 ·94	23	·40	3
	27	Fr	8		5	·84	24	·34	4
	28	Sa	9		6	·78	25	·29	5
	29	Su	10	*Sukla*	7	·71	26	·24	6
	—30	Mo	11		8	·63	27	·21	7
	1	Tu	12		9	·62	1	·20	8
	2	We	13		10	·62	2	·20	9
	3	Th	14		11	·61	3	·23	10
	4	Fr	15		12	·65	4	·27	11
	5	Sa	16	Pausha	13	·70	5	·34	12
	6	Su	17		14	·78	6	·42	13
	7	Mo	18		P	·86	7	·52	14
	8	Tu	19		1	·94	8	·63	15
	9	We	20		...	...	9	·74	16
	10	Th	21		2	·04	10	·84	H. 1216 *Ramzan.* 17
	11	Fr	22		3	·12	11	·93	18
	12	Sa	23		4	·18	...	...	19
Durmati *Makara—Tai.*	13	Su	24		5	·23	12	·01	20
	14	Mo	25		6	·26	13	·07	21
	15	Tu	26	*Bahula*	7	·28	14	·11	22
	16	We	27		8	·26	15	·12	23
	17	Th	28		9	·25	16	·12	24
	18	Fr	29		10	·19	17	·09	25
	19	Sa	30		11	·12	18	·05	26
	20	Su	31		12 13	·04 ·96	19 20	·01 ·95	27
		Feb.							
	21	Mo	1		14	·86	21	·88	28
	22	Tu	2		—A	·76	22	·81	29
	23	We	3		1	·66	23	·74	—30
	24	Th	4		2	·57	24	·69	1
	25	Fr	5		3	·48	25	·63	2
	26	Sa	6		4	·40	26	·58	3
	27	Su	7		5	·35	27	·54	4
	28	Mo	8		6	·30	1	·52	5
	—29	Tu	9	*Sukla*	7	·26	2	·53	6
	1	We	10		8	·25	3	·55	7
	2	Th	11		9	·25	4	·58	8
	3	Fr	12		10	·29	5	·64	9
	4	Sa	13		11	·35	6	·72	10
	5	Su	14		12	·42	7	·83	11
	6	Mo	15		13	·49	8	·93	12
	7	Tu	16		14	·57	...	...	13
	8	We	17	Magha	P	·67	9	·04	14
	9	Th	18		1	·75	10	·14	15
Durmati *Kumbha—Masi.*	10	Fr	19		2	·82	11	·28	H. 1216 *Shawwal.* 16
	11	Sa	20		3	·87	12	·31	17
	12	Su	21		4	·89	13	·38	18
	13	Mo	22		5	·90	14	·42	19
	14	Tu	23		6	·90	15	·44	20
	15	We	24		7	·87	16	·44	21
	16	Th	25	*Bahula*	8	·80	17	·42	22
	17	Fr	26		9	·74	18	·40	23
	18	Sa	27		10	·66	19	·35	24
	19	Su	28		11	·57	20	·29	25

SOLAR reckoning	Cyclic Sidereal Year, Month and Day	Week-Day	English Month and Day	LUNAR reckoning	Tithi	Ending Moment	Nakshatra	Ending Moment	Muhammadan Year, Month and Day
		March							
Durmati *Kumbha—Masi.*	20	Mo	1	Mg.	12	·48	21	·22	*Shawal.* 26
	21	Tu	2		13	·39	22	·15	27
	22	We	3	*ha.*	14	·28	23	·09	28
	23	Th	4		—A	·18	24 25	·02 ·96	—29
	24	Fr	5		1	·09	26	·91	1
	25	Sa	6		2 3	·01 ·94	27	.87	2
	26	Su	7		4	·91	1	·86	3
	27	Mo	8		5	·88	2	·85	4
	28	Tu	9	*Sukla*	6	·86	3	·86	5
	29	We	10		7	·86	4	·90	6
	—30	Th	11		8	·91	5	·95	7
	1	Fr	12		9	·95	...	...	8
	2	Sa	13		...	...	6	·04	9
	3	Su	14		10	·03	7	·13	10
	4	Mo	15		11	·10	8	·23	11
	5	Tu	16	Phalguna	12	·19	9	·33	12
	6	We	17		13	·27	10	·44	13
	7	Th	18		14	·36	11	·54	14
	8	Fr ◯	19		P	·41	12	·63	15
	9	Sa	20		1	·46	13	·69	H. 1216 *Zi-ka'da.* 16
	10	Su	21		2	·50	14	·74	17
	11	Mo	22		3	·50	15	·76	18
	12	Tu	23		4	·49	16	·77	19
	13	We	24		5	·45	17	·76	20
Durmati *Mina—Panguni.*	14	Th	25	*Bahula*	6	·40	18	·73	21
	15	Fr	26		7	·33	19	·68	22
	16	Sa	27		8	·25	20	·63	23
	17	Su	28		9	·16	21	·56	24
	18	Mo	29		10 11	·05 ·95	22	·49	25
	19	Tu	30		12	·85	23	·43	26
	20	We	31		13	·77	24	·36	27
		April							
	21	Th	1		14	·67	25	·30	28
	22	Fr	2		—A	·59	26	·24	29
	23	Sa	3		1	·52	27	·21	—30
	24	Su	4		2	·48	1	·18	1
	25	Mo	5		3	·45	2	·17	2
	26	Tu	6		4	·43	3	·18	3
	27	We	7		5	·44	4	·21	4
	28	Th	8	*Sukla*	6	·48	5	·26	5
	29	Fr	9		7	·53	6	·34	6
	—30	Sa	10		8	·59	7	·43	7
	1	Su	11		9	·66	8	·53	8
	2	Mo	12		10	·75	9	·63	9
	3	Tu	13		11	·84	10	·74	10
	4	We	14		12	·92	11	·85	11
	5	Th	15	Chaitra	13	·97	12	·96	12
	6	Fr	16		...	...	...	...	13
	7	Sa	17		14	·03	13	·00	14
	8	Su	18		P	·03	14	·05	15
	9	Mo	19		1	·05	15	·08	16
Dundubhi *Mesha—Chittirai.*	10	Tu	20		2	·04	16	·10	H. 1216 *Zi-l-hijja.* 17
	11	We	21		3 4	·00 ·95	17	·09	18
	12	Th	22		5	·87	18	·06	19
	13	Fr	23		6	·79	19 20	·02 ·96	20
	14	Sa	24	*Bahula*	7	·70	21	·91	21
	15	Su	25		8	·61	22	·84	22
	16	Mo	26		9	·50	23	·77	23
	17	Tu	27		10	·40	24	·70	24
	18	We	28		11	·31	25	·63	25
	19	Th	29		12	·21	26	·59	26
	20	Fr	30		13	·13	27	·54	27

SOLAR reckoning	Cyclic Sidereal Year, Month and Day	Week-Day	English Month and Day	LUNAR reckoning	Tithi	Ending Moment	Nakshatra	Ending Moment	Muhammadan Year, Month and Day
		May							
Dundubhi *Mesha—Chittirai.*	21	Sa	1		14	·05	1	·51	28
	22	Su	2		A 1	·02 ·98	2	·49	29
	23	Mo	3		2	.96	3	·50	—30
	24	Tu	4		3	·97	4	·52	1
	25	We	5		...	...	5	·58	2
	26	Th	6		4	·00	6	·64	3
	27	Fr	7	*Sukla*	5	·05	7	·73	4
	28	Sa	8		6	·11	8	·82	5
	29	Su	9		7	·19	9	·93	6
	30	Mo	10		8	·28	...	...	7
	—31	Tu	11		9	·35	10	·05	8
	1	We	12		10	·43	11	·15	9
	2	Th	13		11	·49	12	·24	10
	3	Fr	14	Vaisakha	12	·55	13	·31	11
	4	Sa	15		13	·56	14	·36	12
	5	Su	16		14	·57	15	·41	13
	6	Mo	17		P	·55	16	·42	H. 1217 *Muharram.* 14
	7	Tu	18		1	·53	17	·41	15
	8	We	19		2	·46	18	·39	16
	9	Th	20		3	·39	19	·35	17
	10	Fr	21		4	·31	20	·31	18
	11	Sa	22		5	·21	21	·25	19
	12	Su	23		6	·12	22	·18	20
	13	Mo	24		7 8	·01 ·92	23	·11	21
Dundubhi *Vrishabha—Vaikasi.*	14	Tu	25	*Bahula*	9	·81	24 25	·04 ·97	22
	15	We	26		10	·71	26	·92	23
	16	Th	27		11	·64	27	·87	24
	17	Fr	28		12	·57	1	·84	25
	18	Sa	29		13	·52	2	·82	26
	19	Su	30		14	·48	3	·82	27
	20	Mo	31		—A	·47	4	·84	28
		June							
	21	Tu	1		1	·46	5	·89	29
	22	We	2		2	·49	6	·95	—30
	23	Th	3		3	·55	...	...	1
	24	Fr	4		4	·61	7	·03	2
	25	Sa	5	*Sukla*	5	·68	8	·12	3
	26	Su	6		6	·77	9	·24	4
	27	Mo	7		7	·86	10	·34	5
	28	Tu	8		8	·93	11	·45	6
	29	We	9		9	·98	12	·54	7
	30	Th	10	Jyeshtha	...	...	13	·62	8
	—31	Fr	11		10	·03	14	·69	9
	1	Sa	12		11	·05	15	·72	10
	2	Su	13		12	·06	16	·74	11
	3	Mo	14		13	·04	17	·74	12
	4	Tu	15		14 P	·01 ·95	18	·72	13
	5	We	16		1	·89	19	·68	14
	6	Th	17		2	·80	20	·64	15
	7	Fr	18		3	·71	21	·58	H. 1217 *Safar.* 16
	8	Sa	19		4	·61	22	·52	17
Dundubhi *Mithuna—Ani.*	9	Su	20		5	·50	23	·44	18
	10	Mo	21		6	·41	24	·37	19
	11	Tu	22	*Bahula*	7	·30	25	·32	20
	12	We	23		8	·21	26	·26	21
	13	Th	24		9	·13	27	·20	22
	14	Fr	25		10	·04	1	·17	23
	15	Sa	26		11 12	·00 ·96	2	·14	24
	16	Su	27		13	·94	3	·15	25
	17	Mo	28		14	·94	4	·16	26
	18	Tu	29		—A	·98	5	·20	27
	19	We	30		...	...	6	·26	28

Naksh :—1. Asvn. 2. Bhar. 3. Krit. 4. Rohi. 5. Mrig. 6. Ardh. 7. Punar. 8. Push. 9. Asleah. 10. Magh. 11. P. Phal. 12. U. Phal. 13. Hasta. 14. Chit.

A. D. 1802. **A.—Amavasya.** **P.—Pournami.**
Kollam 978, Commences { **N. Malabar—Sept.** **S. Malabar—Aug.**
Hijra 1217, Commences, **May 4.**
Vikrama 1859. **Bengal San 1208.** **(N. Cycle) Srimukha.**

Each table: SOLAR reckoning (Cyclic Sidereal Year, Month and Day; Week-Day; English Month and Day) and LUNAR reckoning (Tithi; Ending Moment; Nakshatra; Ending Moment; Muhammadan Year, Month and Day).

July — Solar: Dundubhi Mithuna—Ani. (20–32), Dundubhi Karkata—Adi. (1–18); Lunar: Sukla, Ashadha, Bahula; Muhammadan: H. 1217 Rabi-ul-awwal.

Cyclic Sidereal Year, Month and Day	Week-Day	English Month and Day	Tithi	Ending Moment	Nakshatra	Ending Moment	Muhammadan Year, Month and Day
20	Th	1	1	·02	7	·33	—29
21	Fr	2	2	·08	8	·43	1
22	Sa	3	3	·16	9	·53	2
23	Su	4	4	·24	10	·64	3
24	Mo	5	5	·32	11	·75	4
25	Tu	6	6	·39	12	·84	5
26	We	7	7	·46	13	·93	6
27	Th	8	8	·50	...	...	7
28	Fr	9	9	·53	14	·00	8
29	Sa	10	10	·54	15	·04	9
30	Su	11	11	·51	16	·06	10
31	Mo	12	12	·48	17	·06	11
—32	Tu	13	13	·43	18	·05	12
1	We	14	14	·37	19 / 20	·02 / ·98	13
2	Th	15	P	·27	21	·92	14
3	Fr	16	1	·19	22	·85	15
4	Sa	17	2 / 3	·09 / ·99	23	·78	16
5	Su	18	4	·88	24	·72	17
6	Mo	19	5	·78	25	·65	18
7	Tu	20	6	·69	26	·59	19
8	We	21	7	·61	27	·54	20
9	Th	22	8	·53	1	·50	21
10	Fr	23	9	·48	2	·48	22
11	Sa	24	10	·45	3	·47	23
12	Su	25	11	·42	4	·48	24
13	Mo	26	12	·43	5	·51	25
14	Tu	27	13	·46	6	·56	26
15	We	28	14	·49	7	·64	27
16	Th	29	—A	·56	8	·73	28
17	Fr	30	1	·63	9	·83	29
18	Sa	31	2	·72	10	·94	—30

Aug. — Solar: Dundubhi Simha—Avani.; Lunar: Sukla, Sravana, Bahula, Bh.; Muhammadan: H. 1217 Rabi-ul-akhir.

Cyclic Sidereal Year, Month and Day	Week-Day	English Month and Day	Tithi	Ending Moment	Nakshatra	Ending Moment	Muhammadan Year, Month and Day
19	Su	1	3	·79	...	...	1
20	Mo	2	4	·86	11	·04	2
21	Tu	3	5	·93	12	·14	3
22	We	4	6	·98	13	·24	4
23	Th	5	...	...	14	·31	5
24	Fr	6	7	·02	15	·35	6
25	Sa	7	8	·02	16	·38	7
26	Su	8	9 / 10	·01 / ·97	17	·39	8
27	Mo	9	11	·92	18	·39	9
28	Tu	10	12	·86	19	·36	10
29	We	11	13	·77	20	·31	11
30	Th	12	14	·69	21	·26	12
31	Fr	13	P	·59	22	·19	13
—32	Sa	14	1	·48	23	·13	14
1	Su	15	2	·38	24 / 25	·06 / ·99	15
2	Mo	16	3	·29	26	·93	16
3	Tu	17	4	·19	27	·87	17
4	We	18	5	·11	1	·84	18
5	Th	19	6 / 7	·03 / ·97	2	·81	19
6	Fr	20	8	·94	3	·79	20
7	Sa	21	9	·92	4	·80	21
8	Su	22	10	·93	5	·82	22
9	Mo	23	11	·94	6	·88	23
10	Tu	24	12	·98	7	·95	24
11	We	25	...	...	...	...	25
12	Th	26	13	·05	8	·04	26
13	Fr	27	14	·13	9	·13	27
14	Sa ●	28	—A	·21	10	·24	28
15	Su	29	1	·30	11	·34	—29
16	Mo	30	2	·37	12	·45	1
17	Tu	31	3	·44	13	·54	2

Sep. — Solar: Dundubhi Simha—Avani. (18–31), Dundubhi Kanya—Purattasi. (1–16); Lunar: Sukla, Bhadrapada, Bahula, Sukla; Muhammadan: H. 1217 Jumadal-awwal.

Cyclic Sidereal Year, Month and Day	Week-Day	English Month and Day	Tithi	Ending Moment	Nakshatra	Ending Moment	Muhammadan Year, Month and Day
18	We	1	4	·49	14	·61	3
19	Th	2	5	·52	15	·67	4
20	Fr	3	6	·53	16	·70	5
21	Sa	4	7	·52	17	·72	6
22	Su	5	8	·48	18	·71	7
23	Mo	6	9	·45	19	·69	8
24	Tu	7	10	·37	20	·65	9
25	We	8	11	·29	21	·59	10
26	Th	9	12	·20	22	·54	11
27	Fr	10	13	·10	23	·47	12
28	Sa ○	11	14 / P	·00 / ·90	24	·40	13
29	Su	12	1	·80	25	·33	14
30	Mo	13	2	·71	26	·26	15
—31	Tu	14	3	·63	27	·22	16
1	We	15	4	·56	1	·17	17
2	Th	16	5	·51	2	·13	18
3	Fr	17	6	·47	3	·12	19
4	Sa	18	7	·44	4	·12	20
5	Su	19	8	·44	5	·14	21
6	Mo	20	9	·47	6	·19	22
7	Tu	21	10	·52	7	·25	23
8	We	22	11	·57	8	·33	24
9	Th	23	12	·66	9	·43	25
10	Fr	24	13	·74	10	·53	26
11	Sa	25	14	·82	11	·65	27
12	Su	26	—A	·90	12	·75	28
13	Mo	27	1	·98	13	·85	29
14	Tu	28	...	...	14	·92	—30
15	We	29	2	·03	15	·98	1
16	Th	30	3	·06	...	...	2

Oct. — Solar: Dundubhi Tula—Aippasi.; Lunar: Asvina, Bahula, Kart. Suk.; Muhammadan: H. 1217 Jumadal-akhir., Rajab.

Cyclic Sidereal Year, Month and Day	Week-Day	English Month and Day	Tithi	Ending Moment	Nakshatra	Ending Moment	Muhammadan Year, Month and Day
17	Fr	1	4	·08	16	·03	3
18	Sa	2	5	·06	17	·04	4
19	Su	3	6 / 7	·03 / ·99	18	·04	5
20	Mo	4	8	·92	19 / 20	·02 / ·98	6
21	Tu	5	9	·84	21	·94	7
22	We	6	10	·75	22	·88	8
23	Th	7	11	·66	23	·81	9
24	Fr	8	12	·56	24	·74	10
25	Sa	9	13	·47	25	·67	11
26	Su	10	14	·36	26	·61	12
27	Mo	11	P	·27	27	·55	13
28	Tu	12	1	·19	1	·50	14
29	We	13	2	·12	2	·46	15
—30	Th	14	3	·08	3	·44	16
1	Fr	15	4	·03	4	·44	17
2	Sa	16	5	·02	5	·46	18
3	Su	17	6	·02	6	·50	19
4	Mo	18	7	·04	7	·56	20
5	Tu	19	8	·09	8	·64	21
6	We	20	9	·14	9	·73	22
7	Th	21	10	·23	10	·84	23
8	Fr	22	11	·32	11	·95	24
9	Sa	23	12	·41	...	...	25
10	Su	24	13	·49	12	·05	26
11	Mo	25	14	·56	13	·15	27
12	Tu	26	—A	·61	14	·23	28
13	We	27	1	·64	15	·30	—29
14	Th	28	2	·66	16	·34	1
15	Fr	29	3	·64	17	·36	2
16	Sa	30	4	·62	18	·36	3
17	Su	31	5	·58	19	·35	4

Nov. — Solar: Dundubhi Tula—Aippasi. (18–30), Dundubhi Vrischika—Kartigai. (1–17); Lunar: Sukla, Karttika, Bahula; Muhammadan: H. 1217 Rajab.

Cyclic Sidereal Year, Month and Day	Week-Day	English Month and Day	Tithi	Ending Moment	Nakshatra	Ending Moment	Muhammadan Year, Month and Day
18	Mo	1	6	·52	20	·32	5
19	Tu	2	7	·43	21	·27	6
20	We	3	8	·34	22	·21	7
21	Th	4	9	·25	23	·15	8
22	Fr	5	10	·15	24	·08	9
23	Sa	6	11 / 12	·06 / ·95	25 / 26	·01 / ·95	10
24	Su	7	13	·87	27	·89	11
25	Mo	8	14	·78	1	·83	12
26	Tu	9	P	·72	2	·79	13
27	We	10	1	·67	3	·77	14
28	Th	11	2	·63	4	·77	15
29	Fr	12	3	·62	5	·78	16
—30	Sa	13	4	·62	6	·81	17
1	Su	14	5	·66	7	·87	18
2	Mo	15	6	·70	8	·94	19
3	Tu	16	7	·77	...	...	20
4	We	17	8	·85	9	·04	21
5	Th	18	9	·94	10	·14	22
6	Fr	19	...	...	11	·25	23
7	Sa	20	10	·03	12	·35	24
8	Su	21	11	·11	13	·45	25
9	Mo	22	12	·18	14	·54	26
10	Tu	23	13	·23	15	·61	27
11	We	24	14	·28	16	·66	28
12	Th	25	—A	·28	17	·68	29
13	Fr	26	1	·26	18	·69	—30
14	Sa	27	2	·23	19	·68	1
15	Su	28	3	·19	20	·65	2
16	Mo	29	4	·13	21	·61	3
17	Tu	30	5 / 6	·05 / ·97	22	·55	4

Dec. — Solar: Dundubhi Vrischika—Kartigai. (18–29), Dundubhi Dhanus—Margali. (1–19); Lunar: Sukla, Margasira, Bahula, Pausha Sukla; Muhammadan: H. 1217 Shaban, H. 1217 Ramzan.

Cyclic Sidereal Year, Month and Day	Week-Day	English Month and Day	Tithi	Ending Moment	Nakshatra	Ending Moment	Muhammadan Year, Month and Day
18	We	1	7	·87	23	·49	5
19	Th	2	8	·77	24	·42	6
20	Fr	3	9	·67	25	·36	7
21	Sa	4	10	·57	26	·29	8
22	Su	5	11	·49	27	·22	9
23	Mo	6	12	·40	1	·17	10
24	Tu	7	13	·34	2	·12	11
25	We	8	14	·30	3	·10	12
26	Th	9	P	·26	4	·09	13
27	Fr	10	1	·25	5	·10	14
28	Sa	11	2	·25	6	·13	15
—29	Su	12	3	·30	7	·18	16
1	Mo	13	4	·34	8	·25	17
2	Tu	14	5	·42	9	·34	18
3	We	15	6	·50	10	·44	19
4	Th	16	7	·59	11	·54	20
5	Fr	17	8	·67	12	·65	21
6	Sa	18	9	·76	13	·76	22
7	Su	19	10	·83	14	·85	23
8	Mo	20	11	·87	15	·92	24
9	Tu	21	12	·91	16	·97	25
10	We	22	13	·92	...	...	26
11	Th	23	14	·91	17	·00	27
12	Fr	24	—A	·87	18	·01	28
13	Sa	25	1	·83	19 / 20	·01 / ·98	—29
14	Su	26	2	·77	21	·94	1
15	Mo	27	3	·68	22	·89	2
16	Tu	28	4	·61	23	·82	3
17	We	29	5	·50	24	·76	4
18	Th	30	6	·41	25	·69	5
19	Fr	31	7	·31	26	·62	6

15. Svati. 16. Visak. 17. Anur. 18. Jyesh. 19. Mula. 20. P. Ash. 21. U. Ash. 22. Sravn. 23. Dani. 24. Satab. 25. P. Bhad. 26. U. Bhad. 27. Rev.

A. D. 1803. **Mesha Sankranti** (Commencement of Indian Sidereal Year).

Solar Eclipse. ● **(Surya Sid.) April 11·52.** **Saka 1725.** **Kaliyuga 4904.**

Lunar Eclipse. ◯ **(Arya Sid.) April 11·42.** **(S. Cycle) Rudhirodgari.**

SOLAR reckoning.			LUNAR reckoning.				
Cyclic Sidereal Year, Month and Day.	Week-Day	English Month and Day.	Tithi	Ending Moment.	Nakshatra	Ending Moment.	Muhammadan Year, Month and Day.
	Jan.						
Dundubhi Dhanus—Margali. 20	Sa	1	*Suk.* 8	·22	27	·56	7
21	Su	2	9	·13	1	·50	8
22	Mo	3	10 11	·04 ·99	2	·46	9
23	Tu	4	12	·94	3	·43	10
24	We	5	**Pausha** 13	·91	4	·42	11
25	Th	6	14	·90	5	·42	12
26	Fr	7	P	·91	6	·44	13
27	Sa	8	1	·94	7	·49	14
28	Su	9	2	·99	8	·56	*H. 1217 Ramzan.* 15
29	Mo	10	...	...	9	·64	16
—30	Tu	11	3	·07	10	·74	17
1	We	12	4	·14	11	·84	18
2	Th	13	*Bahula* 5	·25	12	·95	19
3	Fr	14	6	·32	...	...	20
4	Sa	15	7	·41	13	·06	21
5	Su	16	8	·47	14	·15	22
6	Mo	17	9	·52	15	·23	23
7	Tu	18	10	·56	16	·28	24
8	We	19	11	·56	17	·32	25
9	Th	20	12	·56	18	·34	26
10	Fr	21	13	·52	19	·34	27
11	Sa	22	14	·48	20	·31	28
12	Su	23	—A	·40	21	·27	29
13	Mo	24	1	·33	22	·22	—30
Dundubhi Makara—Tai. 14	Tu	25	2	·23	23	·17	1
15	We	26	3	·13	24	·10	2
16	Th	27	4 5	·04 ·94	25 26	·03 ·96	3
17	Fr	28	6	·85	27	·89	4
18	Sa	29	*Sukla* 7	·76	1	·85	5
19	Su	30	8	·69	2	·80	6
20	Mo	31	9	·63	3	·76	7
	Feb.						
21	Tu	1	10	·58	4	·74	8
22	We	2	11	·55	5	·74	9
23	Th	3	12	·53	6	·77	10
24	Fr	4	**Magha** 13	·55	7	·81	11
25	Sa	5	14	·59	8	·86	12
26	Su	6	P	·64	9	·94	13
27	Mo	7	1	·71	...	...	14
28	Tu	8	2	·79	10	·04	*H. 1217 Shawwal.* 15
—29	We	9	3	·88	11	·14	16
1	Th	10	4	·96	12	·26	17
2	Fr	11	...	...	13	·36	18
3	Sa	12	5	·05	14	·45	19
4	Su	13	*Bahula* 6	·11	15	·53	20
5	Mo	14	7	·17	16	·59	21
6	Tu	15	8	·19	17	·64	22
Dundubhi Kumbha—Masi. 7	We	16	9	·20	18	·66	23
8	Th	17	10	·18	19	·66	24
9	Fr	18	11	·15	20	·64	25
10	Sa	19	12	·10	21	·61	26
11	Su	20	13 14	·02 ·95	22	·57	27
12	Mo	21	—A	·85	23	·51	28
13	Tu	22	1	·76	24	·44	—29
14	We	23	**Phalg.** *Suk.* 2	·67	25	·37	*Zi-l-ka'da.* 1
15	Th	24	3	·56	26	·30	2
16	Fr	25	4	·47	27	·24	3
17	Sa	26	5	·38	1	·18	4
18	Su	27	6	·30	2	·13	5
19	Mo	28	7	·23	3	·09	6

Cyclic Sidereal Year, Month and Day.	Week-Day	English Month and Day.	Tithi	Ending Moment.	Nakshatra	Ending Moment.	Muhammadan Year, Month and Day.
	March						
Dundubhi Kumbha—Masi. 20	Tu	1	*Sukla* 8	·21	4	·06	7
21	We	2	9	·17	5	·06	8
22	Th	3	10	·15	6	·08	9
23	Fr	4	11	·17	7	·12	10
24	Sa	5	12	·20	8	·17	11
25	Su	6	13	·26	9	·25	12
26	Mo	7	**Phalguna** 14	·32	10	·34	13
27	Tu	8	P	·42	11	·45	14
28	We	9	1	·50	12	·55	15
29	Th	10	2	·59	13	·66	*H. 1217 Zi-l-ka'da.* 16
—30	Fr	11	3	·67	14	·76	17
1	Sa	12	4	·72	15	·84	18
2	Su	13	5	·77	16	·91	19
3	Mo	14	*Bahula* 6	·79	17	·96	20
4	Tu	15	7	·80	18	·98	21
5	We	16	8	·78	19	·99	22
6	Th	17	9	·75	20	·97	23
7	Fr	18	10	·69	21	·95	24
8	Sa	19	11	·61	22	·90	25
9	Su	20	12	·55	23	·84	26
10	Mo	21	13	·45	24	·78	27
11	Tu	22	14	·35	25	.71	28
12	We	23	—A	·25	26	·65	29
13	Th	24	1	·15	27	·58	—30
Dundubhi Mina—Panguni. 14	Fr	25	2 3	·06 ·97	1	·52	1
15	Sa	26	4	·89	2	·46	2
16	Su	27	5	·82	3	·42	3
17	Mo	28	6	·79	4	·39	4
18	Tu	29	*Sukla* 7	·75	5	·39	5
19	We	30	8	·74	6	·40	6
20	Th	31	9	·76	7	·43	7
	April						
21	Fr	1	10	·79	8	·48	8
22	Sa	2	11	·84	9	·55	9
23	Su	3	12	·91	10	·65	10
24	Mo	4	13	·99	11	·75	*H. 1217 Zi-l-hijja.* 11
25	Tu	5	**Chaitra** ...	...	12	·85	12
26	We	6	14	·07	13	·96	13
27	Th	7	P	·17	...	...	14
28	Fr	8	1	·24	14	·06	15
29	Sa	9	2	·30	15	·15	16
—30	Su	10	3	·34	16	·22	17
1	Mo	11	4	·35	17	·27	18
2	Tu	12	5	·36	18	·30	19
3	We	13	*Bahula* 6	·34	19	·31	20
4	Th	14	7	·31	20	·31	21
5	Fr	15	8	·25	21	·28	22
6	Sa	16	9	·18	22	·24	23
Rudhirodgari Mesha—Chittirai. 7	Su	17	10	·10	23	·18	24
8	Mo	18	11 12	·01 ·91	24	·12	25
9	Tu	19	13	·81	25 26	·05 ·99	26
10	We	20	14	·71	27	·92	27
11	Th	21	—A	·61	1	·85	28
12	Fr	22	**Vaisakha** *Sukla* 1	·52	2	·80	—29
13	Sa	23	2	·43	3	·75	*H. 1218 Muharram.* 1
14	Su	24	3	·37	4	·73	2
15	Mo	25	4	·32	5	·71	3
16	Tu	26	5	·29	6	·72	4
17	We	27	6	·28	7	·74	5
18	Th	28	7	·29	8	·79	6
19	Fr	29	8	·33	9	·86	7
20	Sa	30	9	·37	10	·95	8

Cyclic Sidereal Year, Month and Day.	Week-Day	English Month and Day.	Tithi	Ending Moment.	Nakshatra	Ending Moment.	Muhammadan Year, Month and Day.
	May						
Rudhirodgari Mesha—Chittirai. 21	Su	1	*Sukla* 10	·44	...	...	9
22	Mo	2	11	·51	11	·04	10
23	Tu	3	12	·60	12	·15	11
24	We	4	13	·69	13	·26	12
25	Th	5	14	·76	14	·37	13
26	Fr	6	**Vaisakha** P	·82	15	·46	14
27	Sa	7	1	·86	16	·53	15
28	Su	8	2	·89	17	·58	16
29	Mo	9	3	·89	18	·62	17
30	Tu	10	4	·88	19	·64	*H. 1218 Muharram.* 18
—31	We	11	5	·83	20	·64	19
1	Th	12	6	·77	21	·61	20
2	Fr	13	*Bahula* 7	·70	22	·57	21
3	Sa	14	8	·62	23	·52	22
4	Su	15	9	·53	24	·46	23
5	Mo	16	10	·42	25	·40	24
6	Tu	17	11	·33	26	·33	25
7	We	18	12	·22	27	·26	26
8	Th	19	13	·12	1	·19	27
9	Fr	20	14 A	·03 ·94	2	·13	28
10	Sa	21	1	·89	3	·09	29
11	Su	22	2	·83	4	·06	—30
Rudhirodgari Vrishaba—Vaikasi. 12	Mo	23	3	·81	5	·04	1
13	Tu	24	4	·78	6	·04	2
14	We	25	5	·79	7	·06	3
15	Th	26	*Sukla* 6	·83	8	·11	4
16	Fr	27	7	·88	9	·17	5
17	Sa	28	8	·94	10	·25	6
18	Su	29	...	...	11	·34	7
19	Mo	30	9	·01	12	·45	8
20	Tu	31	10	·10	13	·56	9
	June						
21	We	1	11	.19	14	·67	*H. 1218 Safar.* 10
22	Th	2	**Jyeshtha** 12	·26	15	·76	11
23	Fr	3	13	·32	16	·84	12
24	Sa	4	14	·35	17	·90	13
25	Su	5	P	·39	18	·93	14
26	Mo	6	1	·38	19	·96	15
27	Tu	7	2	·37	20	·96	16
28	We	8	3	·33	21	·94	17
29	Th	9	4	·29	22	·90	18
30	Fr	10	5	·20	23	·85	19
31	Sa	11	6	·12	24	·80	20
—32	Su	12	7 8	·03 .92	25	·74	21
1	Mo	13	*Bahula* 9	·83	26	·66	22
2	Tu	14	10	·72	27	·59	23
3	We	15	11	·62	1	·53	24
4	Th	16	12	·52	2	·48	25
5	Fr	17	13	·44	3	·42	26
6	Sa	18	14	·38	4	·39	27
Rudhirodgari Mithuna—Ani. 7	Su	19	—A	·31	5	·36	28
8	Mo	20	1	·29	6	·36	—29
9	Tu	21	*Sukla* 2	·27	7	·38	1
10	We	22	3	·28	8	·42	2
11	Th	23	4	·30	9	·48	*H. 1218 Rabi-ul-awwal.* 3
12	Fr	24	5	·36	10	·55	4
13	Sa	25	**Ashadha** 6	·41	11	·64	5
14	Su	26	7	·48	12	·76	6
15	Mo	27	8	·56	13	·86	7
16	Tu	28	9	·65	14	·97	8
17	We	29	10	·73	...	...	9
18	Th	30	11	·79	15	·06	10

Naksh :—1. Asvn. 2. Bhar. 3. Krit. 4. Rohi. 5. Mrig. 6. Ardh. 7. Punar. 8. Push. 9. Aslesh. 10. Magh. 11. P. Phal. 12. U. Phal. 13. Hasta. 14. Chit.

A. D. 1803. **Kollam 979,** { **N. Malabar—Sept.** **S. Malabar—Aug.** **Hijra 1218,** Commences, April 23. **Vikrama 1860.** **Bengal San 1209.** **(N.Cycle) Bhava.**

A.—Amavasya. **P.—Paurnami.** Commences

Columns: SOLAR reckoning — Cyclic Sidereal Year, Month and Day; Week-Day; English Month and Day. LUNAR reckoning — Tithi, Ending Moment; Nakshatra, Ending Moment; Muhammadan Year, Month and Day.

July — Solar: Rudhirodgari *Mithuna—Ani.* (to 31), then Rudhirodgari *Karkata—Adi.* Lunar: Ashadha *Sukla*, *Bahula*; Sravana *Sukla*. Muhammadan: H. 1218 *Rabi-ul-awwal.*

Solar	Week-Day	Day	Tithi	Ending Moment	Nakshatra	Ending Moment	Muhammadan
19	Fr	1	12	·84	16	·14	11
20	Sa	2	13	·86	17	·21	12
21	Su	3	14	·86	18	·26	13
22	Mo	4	P	·85	19	·28	14
23	Tu	5	1	·80	20	·28	15
24	We	6	2	·76	21	·27	16
25	Th	7	3	·68	22	·23	17
26	Fr	8	4	·60	23	·20	18
27	Sa	9	5	·50	24	·14	19
28	Su	10	6	·41	25	·07	20
29	Mo	11	7	·29	26 / 27	·00 / ·93	21
30	Tu	12	8	·19	1	·87	22
31	We	13	9	·10	2	·81	23
1	Th	14	10 / 11	·00 / ·92	3	·76	24
2	Fr	15	12	·85	4	·72	25
3	Sa	16	13	·80	5	·69	26
4	Su	17	14	·76	6	·69	27
5	Mo	18	A	·74	7	·71	28
6	Tu	19	1	·76	8	·73	29
7	We	20	2	·78	9	·78	30
8	Th	21	3	·82	10	·85	1
9	Fr	22	4	·88	11	·94	2
10	Sa	23	5	·97	...	...	3
11	Su	24	...	...	12	·05	4
12	Mo	25	6	·04	13	·16	5
13	Tu	26	7	·12	14	·27	6
14	We	27	8	·20	15	·36	7
15	Th	28	9	·26	16	·45	8
16	Fr	29	10	·32	17	·53	9
17	Sa	30	11	·34	18	·57	10
18	Su	31	12	·35	19	·60	11

Aug. — Solar: Rudhirodgari *Karkata—Adi.* (to 32), then Rudhirodgari *Simha—Avani.* Lunar: Sravana *Bahula*; Bhadrapada *Sukla*. Muhammadan: H. 1218 *Rabi-ul-akhir.*, then H. 1218 *Jumadal-awwal.*

Solar	Week-Day	Day	Tithi	Ending Moment	Nakshatra	Ending Moment	Muhammadan
19	Mo	1	13	·82	20	·61	12
20	Tu	2	14	·29	21	·60	13
21	We	3	P	·28	22	·58	14
22	Th	4	1	·17	23	·53	15
23	Fr	5	2 / 3	·10 / ·99	24	·48	16
24	Sa	6	4	·90	25	·41	17
25	Su	7	5	·79	26	·34	18
26	Mo	8	6	·70	27	·28	19
27	Tu	9	7	·59	1	·21	20
28	We	10	8	·49	2	·15	21
29	Th	11	9	·42	3	·09	22
30	Fr	12	10	·35	4	·05	23
31	Sa	13	11	·29	5	·02	24
32	Su	14	12	·25	6	·01	25
1	Mo	15	13	·24	7	·02	26
2	Tu	16	14	·25	8	·04	27
3	We ●	17	A	·26	9	·09	28
4	Th	18	1	·32	10	·16	29
5	Fr	19	2	·37	11	·25	1
6	Sa	20	3	·46	12	·35	2
7	Su	21	4	·54	13	·46	3
8	Mo	22	5	·63	14	·56	4
9	Tu	23	6	·70	15	·66	5
10	We	24	7	·76	16	·76	6
11	Th	25	8	·81	17	·83	7
12	Fr	26	9	·83	18	·89	8
13	Sa	27	10	·85	19	·92	9
14	Su	28	11	·83	20	·93	10
15	Mo	29	12	·80	21	·93	11
16	Tu	30	13	·74	22	·91	12
17	We	31	14	·68	23	·86	13

Sep. — Solar: Rudhirodgari *Simha—Avani.* (to 31), then Rudhirodgari *Kanya—Purattasi.* Lunar: Bhadru. *Bahula*; Asvina *Sukla*. Muhammadan: H. 1218 *Jumadal-awwal.*, then *Jumadal-akhir.*

Solar	Week-Day	Day	Tithi	Ending Moment	Nakshatra	Ending Moment	Muhammadan
18	Th	1	P	·60	24	·81	14
19	Fr	2	1	·50	25	·75	15
20	Sa	3	2	·41	26	·69	16
21	Su	4	3	·30	27	·62	17
22	Mo	5	4	·21	1	·55	18
23	Tu	6	5	·11	2	·48	19
24	We	7	6 / 7	·01 / ·93	3	·42	20
25	Th	8	8	·86	4	·38	21
26	Fr	9	9	·80	5	·35	22
27	Sa	10	10	·77	6	·34	23
28	Su	11	11	·76	7	·34	24
29	Mo	12	12	·78	8	·36	25
30	Tu	13	13	·79	9	·40	26
31	We	14	14	·84	10	·47	27
1	Th	15	A	·90	11	·56	28
2	Fr	16	1	·98	12	·65	29
3	Sa	17	...	...	13	·76	30
4	Su	18	2	·06	14	·86	1
5	Mo	19	3	·14	15	·97	2
6	Tu	20	4	·21	...	...	3
7	We	21	5	·29	16	·07	4
8	Th	22	6	·34	17	·14	5
9	Fr	23	7	·37	18	·20	6
10	Sa	24	8	·38	19	·24	7
11	Su	25	9	·36	20	·26	8
12	Mo	26	10	·34	21	·26	9
13	Tu	27	11	·28	22	·24	10
14	We	28	12	·22	23	·20	11
15	Th	29	13	·14	24	·15	12
16	Fr	30	14 / P	·05 / ·95	25	·09	13

Oct. — Solar: Rudhirodgari *Kanya—Purattasi.* (to 30), then Rudhirodgari *Tula—Aippasi.* Lunar: Asvina *Bahula*; Karttika *Sukla*. Muhammadan: H. 1218 (Jumadal-akhir), then H. 1218 *Rajab.*

Solar	Week-Day	Day	Tithi	Ending Moment	Nakshatra	Ending Moment	Muhammadan
17	Sa	1	1	·86	26 / 27	·03 / ·96	14
18	Su	2	2	·76	1	·89	15
19	Mo	3	3	·65	2	·82	16
20	Tu	4	4	·56	3	·74	17
21	We	5	5	·48	4	·72	18
22	Th	6	6	·42	5	·68	19
23	Fr	7	7	·35	6	·66	20
24	Sa	8	8	·32	7	·66	21
25	Su	9	9	·31	8	·67	22
26	Mo	10	10	·34	9	·72	23
27	Tu	11	11	·35	10	·78	24
28	We	12	12	·40	11	·86	25
29	Th	13	13	·45	12	·95	26
30	Fr	14	14	·54	...	...	27
1	Sa	15	A	·63	13	·05	28
2	Su	16	1	·71	14	·17	29
3	Mo	17	2	·78	15	·27	1
4	Tu	18	3	·86	16	·37	2
5	We	19	4	·91	17	·45	3
6	Th	20	5	·94	18	·51	4
7	Fr	21	6	·95	19	·56	5
8	Sa	22	7	·95	20	·58	6
9	Su	23	8	·91	21	·58	7
10	Mo	24	9	·87	22	·56	8
11	Tu	25	10	·80	23	·53	9
12	We	26	11	·71	24	·48	10
13	Th	27	12	·63	25	·43	11
14	Fr	28	13	·53	26	·37	12
15	Sa	29	14	·43	27	·30	13
16	Su	30	P	·34	1	·23	14
17	Mo	31	1	·25	2	·16	15

Nov. — Solar: Rudhirodgari *Tula—Aippasi.* (to 30), then Rudhirodgari *Vrischika—Kartigai.* Lunar: Kartt. *Bahula*; *Sukla*. Muhammadan: H. 1218 *Rajab.*, then H. 1218 *Shaban.*

Solar	Week-Day	Day	Tithi	Ending Moment	Nakshatra	Ending Moment	Muhammadan
18	Tu	1	2	·15	3	·11	16
19	We	2	3	·07	4	·05	17
20	Th	3	4 / 5	·01 / ·94	5 / 6	·01 / ·99	18
21	Fr	4	6	·93	7	·98	19
22	Sa	5	7	·91	...	...	20
23	Su	6	8	·93	8	·00	21
24	Mo	7	9	·94	9	·03	22
25	Tu	8	10	·99	10	·09	23
26	We	9	...	...	11	·16	24
27	Th	10	11	·07	12	·25	25
28	Fr	11	12	·15	13	·36	26
29	Sa	12	13	·24	14	·47	27
30	Su	13	14	·32	15	·57	28
1	Mo	14	A	·40	16	·67	29
2	Tu	15	1	·47	17	·75	30
3	We	16	2	·53	18	·82	1
4	Th	17	3	·56	19	·88	2
5	Fr	18	4	·56	20	·90	3
6	Sa	19	5	·56	21	·91	4
7	Su	20	6	·52	22	·89	5
8	Mo	21	7	·48	23	·86	6
9	Tu	22	8	·41	24	·83	7
10	We	23	9	·34	25	·77	8
11	Th	24	10	·25	26	·71	9
12	Fr	25	11	·15	27	·64	10
13	Sa	26	12 / 13	·05 / ·96	1	·56	11
14	Su	27	14	·87	2	·51	12
15	Mo	28	P	·77	3	·44	13
16	Tu	29	1	·70	4	·39	14
17	We	30	2	·63	5	·34	15

Dec. — Solar: Rudhirodgari *Vrischika—Kartigai.* (to 30), then Rudhirodgari *Dhanus—Margali.* Lunar: Margasira *Bahula*, *Sukla*; Pausha *Bah.* Muhammadan: H. 1218 (Shaban), then H. 1218 *Ramzan.*

Solar	Week-Day	Day	Tithi	Ending Moment	Nakshatra	Ending Moment	Muhammadan
18	Th	1	3	·57	6	·31	16
19	Fr	2	4	·55	7	·31	17
20	Sa	3	5	·53	8	·32	18
21	Su	4	6	·56	9	·35	19
22	Mo	5	7	·58	10	·38	20
23	Tu	6	8	·63	11	·46	21
24	We	7	9	·69	12	·55	22
25	Th	8	10	·79	13	·66	23
26	Fr	9	11	·87	14	·77	24
27	Sa	10	12	·95	15	·87	25
28	Su	11	...	...	16	·97	26
29	Mo	13	13	·03	...	...	27
30	Tu	15	14	·11	17	·06	28
1	We	14	A	·17	18	·14	29
2	Th	15	1	·19	19	·19	1
3	Fr	16	2	·21	20	·22	2
4	Sa	17	3	·19	21	·23	3
5	Su	18	4	·15	22	·21	4
6	Mo	19	5	·11	23	·20	5
7	Tu	20	6 / 7	·04 / ·96	24	·16	6
8	We	21	8	·87	25	·11	7
9	Th	22	9	·79	26 / 27	·04 / ·97	8
10	Fr	23	10	·68	1	·91	9
11	Sa	24	11	·60	2	·84	10
12	Su	25	12	·49	3	·78	11
13	Mo	26	13	·40	4	·72	12
14	Tu	27	14	·33	5	·67	13
15	We	28	P	·27	6	·64	14
16	Th	29	1	·22	7	·63	15
17	Fr	30	2	·19	8	·64	16
18	Sa	31	3	·19	9	·66	17

15. Svati. 16. Visak. 17. Anur. 18. Jyesh. 19. Mula. 20. P. Ash. 21. U. Ash. 22. Sravn. 23. Dani. 24. Satab. 25. P. Bhad. 26. U. Bhad. 27. Rev.

A. D. 1804. **Mesha Sankranti.** (Commencement of Indian Sidereal Year).
Solar Eclipse. ● (Surya Sid.) April 10·78. **Saka 1726.** **Kaliyuga 4905.**
Lunar Eclipse. ○ (Arya Sid.) April 10·68. (S. Cycle) **Raktaksha.**

Cyclic Sidereal Year, Month and Day (SOLAR reckoning)	Week-Day	English Month and Day	Tithi (LUNAR reckoning)	Ending Moment	Nakshatra	Ending Moment	Muhammadan Year, Month and Day
		Jan.					
[Rudhirodgari Dhanus—Margali] 19	Su	1	[Pausha Bahula] 4	·20	10	·71	[H. 1218 Ramzan] 18
20	Mo	2	5	·22	11	·77	19
21	Tu	3	6	·28	12	·86	20
22	We	4	7	·35	13	·96	21
23	Th	5	8	·44	...	...	22
24	Fr	6	9	·52	14	·06	23
25	Sa	7	10	·61	15	·17	24
26	Su	8	11	·70	16	·27	25
27	Mo	9	12	·76	17	·37	26
28	Tu	10	13	·82	18	·45	27
29	We	11	14	·84	19	·50	28
[Rudhirodgari Makara—Tai] 1	Th	12	A	·85	20	·54	29
2	Fr	13	1	·84	21	·55	30
3	Sa	14	2	·81	22	·56	[H. 1218 Shawwal] 1
4	Su	15	3	·75	23	·53	2
5	Mo	16	4	·69	24	·49	3
6	Tu	17	5	·61	25	·44	4
7	We	18	6	·52	26	·38	5
8	Th	19	7	·42	27	·32	6
9	Fr	20	[Sukla] 8	·32	1	·25	7
10	Sa	21	9	·23	2	·18	8
11	Su	22	10	·12	3	·11	9
12	Mo	23	{11 / 12	·05 / ·98	4	·05	10
13	Tu	24	13	·91	5 / 6	·01 / ·98}	11
14	We	25	[Magha] 14	·86	7	·96	12
15	Th ○	26	P	·84	8	·96	13
16	Fr	27	1	·83	9	·98	14
17	Sa	28	2	·84	...	...	15
18	Su	29	3	·89	10	·02	16
19	Mo	30	4	·94	11	·09	17
20	Tu	31	...	...	12	·16	18
		Feb.					
21	We	1	[Bahula] 5	·01	13	·26	19
22	Th	2	6	·09	14	·36	20
23	Fr	3	7	·17	15	·47	21
24	Sa	4	8	·27	16	·58	22
25	Su	5	9	·35	17	·67	23
26	Mo	6	10	·42	18	·75	24
27	Tu	7	11	·46	19	·81	25
28	We	8	12	·48	20	·85	26
29	Th	9	13	·49	21	·88	27
30	Fr	10	14	·47	22	·88	28
[Rudhirodgari Kumbha—Masi] 1	Sa ●	11	A	·44	23	·86	29
2	Su	12	[Sukla] 1	·37	24	·83	[H. 1218 Zi-l-ka'da] 1
3	Mo	13	2	·31	25	·78	2
4	Tu	14	3	·23	26	·72	3
5	We	15	4	·15	27	·66	4
6	Th	16	{5 / 6	·04 / ·94	1	·59	5
7	Fr	17	7	·85	2	·52	6
8	Sa	18	8	·75	3	·45	7
9	Su	19	9	·67	4	·39	8
10	Mo	20	[Phalguna] 10	·59	5	·35	9
11	Tu	21	11	·53	6	·31	10
12	We	22	12	·48	7	·28	11
13	Th	23	13	·46	8	·28	12
14	Fr	24	14	·45	9	·29	13
15	Sa	25	P	·46	10	·34	14
16	Su	26	[Bah.] 1	·51	11	·39	15
17	Mo	27	2	·55	12	·47	16
18	Tu	28	3	·63	13	·56	17
19	We	29	4	·72	14	·66	18

Cyclic Sidereal Year, Month and Day (SOLAR reckoning)	Week-Day	English Month and Day	Tithi (LUNAR reckoning)	Ending Moment	Nakshatra	Ending Moment	Muhammadan Year, Month and Day
		March					
[Rudhirodgari Kumbha—Masi] 20	Th	1	[Phalg. Bahula] 5	·81	15	·77	[H. 1218 Zi-l-ka'da] 19
21	Fr	2	6	·89	16	·88	20
22	Sa	3	7	·96	17	·98	21
23	Su	4	...	...	...	...	22
24	Mo	5	8	·03	18	·06	23
25	Tu	6	9	·07	19	·12	24
26	We	7	10	·09	20	·18	25
27	Th	8	11	·10	21	·20*	26
28	Fr	9	12	·09	22	·21	27
29	Sa	10	{13 / 14	·05 / ·98	23	·19	28
30	Su	11	A	·92	24	·16	29
[Rudhirodgari Mina—Panguni] 1	Mo	12	1	·83	25	·11	30
2	Tu	13	2	·75	26	·06	[H. 1218 Zi-l-hijja] 1
3	We	14	3	·64	27 / 1	·00 / ·93}	2
4	Th	15	[Sukla] 4	·55	2	·86	3
5	Fr	16	5	·44	3	·79	4
6	Sa	17	6	·35	4	·74	5
7	Su	18	7	·26	5	·68	6
8	Mo	19	8	·19	6	·64	7
9	Tu	20	9	·13	7	·61	8
10	We	21	10	·08	8	·60	9
11	Th	22	[Adhika Chaitra] 11	·06	9	·62	10
12	Fr	23	12	·04	10	·65	11
13	Sa	24	13	·07	11	·70	12
14	Su	25	14	·10	12	·77	13
15	Mo	26	P	·14	13	·86	14
16	Tu	27	1	·23	14	·97	15
17	We	28	2	·30	...	...	16
18	Th	29	3	·39	15	·07	17
19	Fr	30	4	·47	16	·18	18
20	Sa	31	5	·56	17	·28	19
		April					
21	Su	1	[Bahula] 6	·61	18	·36	20
22	Mo	2	7	·65	19	·43	21
23	Tu	3	8	·68	20	·49	22
24	We	4	9	·67	21	·52	23
25	Th	5	10	·66	22	·53	24
26	Fr	6	11	·61	23	·52	25
27	Sa	7	12	·56	24	·49	26
28	Su	8	13	·49	25	·46	27
29	Mo	9	14	·41	26	·40	28
30	Tu	10	A	·32	27	·34	29
[Raktaksha Mesha—Chittirai] 1	We	11	1	·20	1	·27	30
2	Th	12	2	·11	2	·20	[H. 1219 Muharram] 1
3	Fr	13	{3 / 4	·00 / ·91	3	·14	2
4	Sa	14	5	·82	4	·07	3
5	Su	15	[Sukla] 6	·75	5 / 6	·01 / ·97}	4
6	Mo	16	7	·68	7	·94	5
7	Tu	17	8	·63	8	·93	6
8	We	18	9	·61	9	·94	7
9	Th	19	[Nija Chaitra] 10	·59	10	·96	8
10	Fr	20	11	·61	...	...	9
11	Sa	21	12	·65	11	·01	10
12	Su	22	13	·69	12	·07	11
13	Mo	23	14	·76	13	·17	12
14	Tu	24	P	·84	14	·26	13
15	We	25	1	·93	15	·37	14
16	Th	26	...	...	16	·48	15
17	Fr	27	[Bahula] 2	·02	17	·58	16
18	Sa	28	3	·09	18	·67	17
19	Su	29	4	·15	19	·75	18
20	Mo	30	5	·20	20	·81	19

Cyclic Sidereal Year, Month and Day (SOLAR reckoning)	Week-Day	English Month and Day	Tithi (LUNAR reckoning)	Ending Moment	Nakshatra	Ending Moment	Muhammadan Year, Month and Day
		May					
[Raktaksha Mesha—Chittirai] 21	Tu	1	[Nija Ch. Bah.] 6	·20	21	·84	[H. 1219 Muharram] 20
22	We	2	7	·21	22	·85	21
23	Th	3	8	·19	23	·84	22
24	Fr	4	9	·15	24	·83	23
25	Sa	5	10	·09	25	·79	24
26	Su	6	{11 / 12	·02 / ·93	26	·74	25
27	Mo	7	13	·83	27	·67	26
28	Tu	8	14	·74	1	·61	27
29	We	9	A	·64	2	·55	28
30	Th	10	1	·53	3	·47	29
31	Fr	11	2	·43	4	·41	30
[Raktaksha Vrishabha—Vaikasi] 1	Sa	12	3	·34	5	·35	[H. 1219 Safar] 1
2	Su	13	4	·27	6	·30	2
3	Mo	14	5	·20	7	·28	3
4	Tu	15	[Sukla] 6	·16	8	·26	4
5	We	16	7	·12	9	·26	5
6	Th	17	8	·10	10	·28	6
7	Fr	18	9	·12	11	·32	7
8	Sa	19	10	·16	12	·38	8
9	Su	20	11	·21	13	·47	9
10	Mo	21	[Vaisakha] 12	·27	14	·56	10
11	Tu	22	13	·35	15	·67	11
12	We	23	14	·44	16	·77	12
13	Th	24	P	·53	17	·88	13
14	Fr	25	1	·59	18	·98	14
15	Sa	26	2	·65	...	...	15
16	Su	27	3	·70	19	·06	16
17	Mo	28	4	·71	20	·12	17
18	Tu	29	5	·71	21	·15	18
19	We	30	6	·69	22	·17	19
20	Th	31	7	·66	23	·18	20
		June					
21	Fr	1	[Bahula] 8	·59	24	·16	21
22	Sa	2	9	·52	25	·12	22
23	Su	3	10	·43	26	·07	23
24	Mo	4	11	·33	27 / 1	·01 / ·95}	24
25	Tu	5	12	·23	2	·88	25
26	We	6	13	·13	3	·81	26
27	Th	7	{14 / A	·03 / ·93	4	·75	27
28	Fr	8	1	·85	5	·68	28
29	Sa	9	2	·76	6	·63	29
30	Su	10	3	·70	7	·61	[H. 1219 Rabi-ul-awwal] 1
31	Mo	11	4	·65	8	·58	2
[Raktaksha Mithuna—Ani] 1	Tu	12	[Sukla] 5	·61	9	·58	3
2	We	13	6	·60	10	·59	4
3	Th	14	7	·61	11	·63	5
4	Fr	15	8	·64	12	·70	6
5	Sa	16	9	·69	13	·77	7
6	Su	17	10	·75	14	·86	8
7	Mo	18	[Jyeshtha] 11	·83	15	·97	9
8	Tu	19	12	·91	...	...	10
9	We	20	...	...	16	·07	11
10	Th	21	13	·00	17	·19	12
11	Fr	22	14	·07	18	·28	13
12	Sa	23	P	·13	19	·36	14
13	Su	24	1	·17	20	·43	15
14	Mo	25	2	·19	21	·47	16
15	Tu	26	[Bahula] 3	·19	22	·50	17
16	We	27	4	·17	23	·50	18
17	Th	28	5	·14	24	·49	19
18	Fr	29	6	·07	25	·45	20
19	Sa	30	{7 / 8	·01 / ·92	26	·41	21

Naksh:—1. Asvn. 2. Bhar. 3. Krit. 4. Rohi. 5. Mrig. 6. Ardh. 7. Punar. 8. Push. 9. Aslesh. 10. Magh. 11. P. Phal. 12. U. Phal. 13. Hasta. 14. Chit.

A. D. 1804. **Koilam 980,** {N. Malabar—Sept. / S. Malabar—Aug.} **Hijra 1219,** **Vikrama 1861.**
A.—Amavasya. Commences Commences, April 12. **Bengal San 1210.**
P.—Paurnami. (N. Cycle) Yuvan.

SOLAR reckoning — LUNAR reckoning.

July

Cyclic Sidereal Year, Month and Day	Week-Day	English Month and Day	Tithi	Ending Moment	Nakshatra	Ending Moment	Muhammadan Year, Month and Day
Raktaksha *Mithuna—Ani.* 20	Su	1	*Jyesh. Bah.* 9	·83	27	·36	*Rabi-ul-awwal.* 22
21	Mo	2	10	·72	1	·29	23
22	Tu	3	11	·62	2	·22	24
23	We	4	12	·52	3	·15	25
24	Th	5	13	·41	4	·08	26
25	Fr	6	14	·33	5 / 6	·02 / ·98	27
26	Sa	7	A	·24	7	·94	28
27	Su	8	*Sukla* 1	·18	8	·91	29
28	Mo	9	2	·12	9	·90	30
29	Tu	10	3	·09	10	·91	*H. 1219 Rabi-ul-akhir.* 1
30	We	11	4	·07	11	·95	2
31	Th	12	5	·08	...	...	3
32	Fr	13	6	·12	12	·00	4
Raktaksha *Karkata—Adi.* 1	Sa	14	7	·17	13	·08	5
2	Su	15	8	·23	14	·16	6
3	Mo	16	9	·31	15	·26	7
4	Tu	17	10	·39	16	·38	8
5	We	18	**Ashadha** 11	·46	17	·49	9
6	Th	19	12	·53	18	·58	10
7	Fr	20	13	·61	19	·67	11
8	Sa	21	14	·65	20	·74	12
9	Su ○	22	P	·67	21	·79	13
10	Mo	23	*Bahula* 1	·67	22	·82	14
11	Tu	24	2	·66	23	·83	15
12	We	25	3	·61	24	·82	16
13	Th	26	4	·55	25	·79	17
14	Fr	27	5	·49	26	·74	18
15	Sa	28	6	·41	27	·70	19
16	Su	29	7	·31	1	·63	20
17	Mo	30	8	·21	2	·56	21
18	Tu	31	9	·12	3	·49	22

Aug.

Cyclic Sidereal Year, Month and Day	Week-Day	English Month and Day	Tithi	Ending Moment	Nakshatra	Ending Moment	Muhammadan Year, Month and Day
19	We	1	10 / 11	·00 / ·90	4	·42	23
20	Th	2	12	·82	5	·37	24
21	Fr	3	13	·73	6	·31	25
22	Sa	4	14	·65	7	·27	26
23	Su	5	A	·60	8	·24	27
24	Mo	6	*Sukla* 1	·58	9	·22	28
25	Tu	7	2	·56	10	·24	29
26	We	8	3	·56	11	·27	*H. 1219 Jumadal-awwal.* 1
27	Th	9	4	·59	12	·31	2
28	Fr	10	5	·64	13	·38	3
29	Sa	11	6	·71	14	.46	4
30	Su	12	7	·79	15	·57	5
31	Mo	13	8	·88	16	·68	6
Raktaksha *Simha—Avani.* 1	Tu	14	9	·95	17	·78	7
2	We	15	...	...	18	·88	8
3	Th	16	10	·03	19	·97	9
4	Fr	17	11	·09	...	...	10
5	Sa	18	**Sravana** 12	·13	20	·06	11
6	Su	19	13	·17	21	·11	12
7	Mo	20	14	·16	22	·14	13
8	Tu	21	P	·15	23	·15	14
9	We	22	*Bahula* 1	·11	24	·14	15
10	Th	23	2	·07	25	·12	16
11	Fr	24	3 / 4	·00 / ·90	26	·08	17
12	Sa	25	5	·81	27 / 1	·03 / ·97	18
13	Su	26	6	·71	2	·90	19
14	Mo	27	7	·62	3	·83	20
15	Tu	28	8	·51	4	·77	21
16	We	29	9	·42	5	·70	22
17	Th	30	10	·32	6	·64	23
18	Fr	31	11	24	7	·60	24

Sep.

Cyclic Sidereal Year, Month and Day	Week-Day	English Month and Day	Tithi	Ending Moment	Nakshatra	Ending Moment	Muhammadan Year, Month and Day
Raktaksha *Simha—Avani.* 19	Sa	1	*Bah.* 12	·17	8	·56	*Jl. awwal.* 25
20	Su	2	13	·11	9	·56	26
21	Mo	3	14	·09	10	·56	27
22	Tu	4	A	·07	11	·58	28
23	We	5	*Sukla* 1	·10	12	·62	29
24	Th	6	2	·11	13	·68	30
25	Fr	7	3	·16	14	·78	*H. 1219 Jumadal-akhir.* 1
26	Sa	8	4	·21	15	·87	2
27	Su	9	5	·29	16	·98	3
28	Mo	10	6	·38	...	...	4
29	Tu	11	7	·46	17	·08	5
30	We	12	8	·54	18	·18	6
31	Th	13	9	·61	19	·28	7
Raktaksha *Kanya—Purattasi.* 1	Fr	14	**Bhadrapada** 10	·66	20	·36	8
2	Sa	15	11	·68	21	·42	9
3	Su	16	12	·69	22	·46	10
4	Mo	17	13	·68	23	·47	11
5	Tu	18	14	·65	24	·47	12
6	We	19	P	·59	25	·46	13
7	Th	20	*Bahula* 1	·52	26	·42	14
8	Fr	21	2	·44	27	·37	15
9	Sa	22	3	·34	1	·31	16
10	Su	23	4	·25	2	·24	17
11	Mo	24	5	·15	3	·18	18
12	Tu	25	6 / 7	·05 / ·95	4	·11	19
13	We	26	8	·86	5 / 6	·04 / ·98	20
14	Th	27	9	·78	7	·93	21
15	Fr	28	10	·71	8	·90	22
16	Sa	29	11	·66	9	·88	23
17	Su	30	12	·63	10	·88	24

Oct.

Cyclic Sidereal Year, Month and Day	Week-Day	English Month and Day	Tithi	Ending Moment	Nakshatra	Ending Moment	Muhammadan Year, Month and Day
18	Mo	1	13	·61	11	·89	25
19	Tu	2	14	·64	12	·93	26
20	We	3	A	65	...	...	27
21	Th	4	*Sukla* 1	·71	13	·00	28
22	Fr	5	2	·76	14	·08	29
23	Sa	6	3	·85	15	·17	*H. 1219 Rajab.* 1
24	Su	7	4	·93	16	·27	2
25	Mo	8	...	...	17	·38	3
26	Tu	9	5	·01	18	·48	4
27	We	10	6	·10	19	·58	5
28	Th	11	7	·17	20	·67	6
29	Fr	12	8	·22	21	·73	7
30	Sa	13	9	·24	22	·77	8
31	Su	14	**Asvina** 10	·26	23	·79	9
Raktaksha *Tula—Aippasi.* 1	Mo	15	11	·24	24	·80	10
2	Tu	16	12	·22	25	·78	11
3	We	17	13	·16	26	·75	12
4	Th	18	14	·08	27	·70	13
5	Fr	19	P / 1	·01 / ·91	1	·64	14
6	Sa	20	*Bahula* 2	·82	2	·59	15
7	Su	21	3	·71	3	·52	16
8	Mo	22	4	·63	4	·45	17
9	Tu	23	5	·53	5	·38	18
10	We	24	6	·41	6	·31	19
11	Th	25	7	·36	7	·27	20
12	Fr	26	8	·29	8	·23	21
13	Sa	27	9	·24	9	·21	22
14	Su	28	10	·21	10	·20	23
15	Mo	29	11	·20	11	·21	24
16	Tu	30	12	·21	12	·24	25
17	We	31	13	·24	13	·31	26

Nov.

Cyclic Sidereal Year, Month and Day	Week-Day	English Month and Day	Tithi	Ending Moment	Nakshatra	Ending Moment	Muhammadan Year, Month and Day
Raktaksha *Tula—Aippasi.* 18	Th	1	14	·30	14	·38	*Rajab.* 27
19	Fr	2	A	·36	15	·47	28
20	Sa	3	*Sukla* 1	·45	16	·57	29
21	Su	4	2	·52	17	·67	30
22	Mo	5	3	·63	18	·79	*H. 1219 Shaban.* 1
23	Tu	6	4	·70	19	·89	2
24	We	7	5	·77	20	·97	3
25	Th	8	6	·81	...	...	4
26	Fr	9	7	·84	21	·04	5
27	Sa	10	8	·86	22	·09	6
28	Su	11	9	·84	23	·12	7
29	Mo	12	10	·81	24	·13	8
Raktaksha *Vrischika—Kartigai.* 1	Tu	13	11	.76	25	·11	9
2	We	14	12	·69	26	·08	10
3	Th	15	**Karttika** 13	·62	27 / 1	·04 / ·99	11
4	Fr	16	14	·52	2	·92	12
5	Sa	17	P	·43	3	·85	13
6	Su	18	*Bahula* 1	·32	4	·78	14
7	Mo	19	2	·24	5	·71	15
8	Tu	20	3	·14	6	·66	16
9	We	21	4 / 5	·05 / ·97	7	·61	17
10	Th	22	6	·91	8	·56	18
11	Fr	23	7	·86	9	·53	19
12	Sa	24	8	·83	10	·52	20
13	Su	25	9	·82	11	·53	21
14	Mo	26	10	·84	12	·57	22
15	Tu	27	11	·87	13	·62	23
16	We	28	12	.92	14	·69	24
17	Th	29	13	·99	15	·77	25
18	Fr	30	...	...	16	·87	26

Dec.

Cyclic Sidereal Year, Month and Day	Week-Day	English Month and Day	Tithi	Ending Moment	Nakshatra	Ending Moment	Muhammadan Year, Month and Day
19	Sa	1	14	·08	17	·99	27
20	Su	2	A	·16	...	...	28
21	Mo	3	*Sukla* 1	·25	18	·09	29
22	Tu	4	2	·32	19	·19	*H. 1219 Ramzan.* 1
23	We	5	3	·40	20	·28	2
24	Th	6	4	·45	21	·35	3
25	Fr	7	5	·48	22	·41	4
26	Sa	8	6	·49	23	·44	5
27	Su	9	7	·47	24	·45	6
28	Mo	10	8	·44	25	·44	7
29	Tu	11	9	·38	26	·41	8
30	We	12	10	·32	27	·38	9
Raktaksha *Dhanus—Margali.* 1	Th	13	11	·24	1	·33	10
2	Fr	14	12	·15	2	·26	11
3	Sa	15	13 / 14	·06 / ·96	3	·19	12
4	Su	16	**Margasira** P	·86	4	·12	13
5	Mo	17	*Bahula* 1	·76	5	·05	14
6	Tu	18	2	·68	6 / 7	·00 / ·94	15
7	We	19	3	·60	8	·89	16
8	Th	20	4	·54	9	·86	17
9	Fr	21	5	·49	10	·84	18
10	Sa	22	6	·48	11	·86	19
11	Su	23	7	·46	12	·88	20
12	Mo	24	8	·47	13	·93	21
13	Tu	25	9	·52	14	·99	22
14	We	26	10	·57	...	...	23
15	Th	27	11	·64	15	·07	24
16	Fr	28	12	·73	16	·18	25
17	Sa	29	13	·82	17	·28	26
18	Su	30	14	·90	18	·39	27
19	Mo	31	A	.98	19	·49	28

A. D. 1805. **Mesha Sankranti.** (Commencement of Indian Sidereal Year).

Solar Eclipse. ● **(Surya Sid.) April 11·04.** **Saka 1727.** **Kaliyuga 4906.**

Lunar Eclipse. ○ **(Arya Sid.) April 10·94.** **(S. Cycle) Krodhana.**

SOLAR reckoning: Cyclic Sidereal Year, Month and Day; Week-Day; English Month and Day. LUNAR reckoning: Tithi; Ending Moment; Nakshatra; Ending Moment; Muhammadan Year, Month and Day.

Jan.

Raktaksha, Dhanu—Margali. / Raktaksha, Makara—Tai. — Pausha (Sukla / Bahula) — H. 1219 Shawwal.

Cyclic Sidereal Year, Month and Day	Week-Day	English Month and Day	Tithi	Ending Moment	Nakshatra	Ending Moment	Muhammadan Year, Month and Day
20	Tu	1	...	...	20	·58	29
21	We	2	1	·05	21	·67	—30
22	Th	3	2	·09	22	·72	1
23	Fr	4	3	·12	23	·76	2
24	Sa	5	4	·13	24	·77	3
25	Su	6	5	·12	25	·77	4
26	Mo	7	6	·08	26	·74	5
27	Tu	8	7 8	·04 ·96	27	·71	6
28	We	9	9	·88	1	.66	7
—29	Th	10	10	·80	2	·60	8
1	Fr	11	11	·70	3	·53	9
2	Sa	12	12	·60	4	·46	10
3	Su	13	13	·51	5	·40	11
4	Mo	14	14	·42	6	·33	12
5	Tu ○	15	P	·32	7	·27	13
6	We	16	1	·24	8	·22	14
7	Th	17	2	·19	9	·19	15
8	Fr	18	3	·14	10	·18	16
9	Sa	19	4	·12	11	·18	17
10	Su	20	5	·11	12	·20	18
11	Mo	21	6	·13	13	·24	19
12	Tu	22	7	·16	14	·30	20
13	We	23	8	·22	15	·38	21
14	Th	24	9	·30	16	·48	22
15	Fr	25	10	·38	17	·58	23
16	Sa	26	11	·47	18	·69	24
17	Su	27	12	·56	19	·79	25
18	Mo	28	13	·64	20	·90	26
19	Tu	29	14	·70	21	·97	27
20	We	30	—A	·74	...	...	28
21	Th	31	1	·77	22	·03	—29

Feb.

Raktaksha, Kumbha—Masi. — Magha (Sukla / Bahula) — H. 1219 Zi-l-ka'da.

Cyclic Sidereal Year, Month and Day	Week-Day	English Month and Day	Tithi	Ending Moment	Nakshatra	Ending Moment	Muhammadan Year, Month and Day
22	Fr	1	2	·77	23	·07	1
23	Sa	2	3	·76	24	·09	2
24	Su	3	4	·72	25	·09	3
25	Mo	4	5	·67	26	·08	4
26	Tu	5	6	·59	27	·05	5
27	We	6	7	·52	1 2	·00 ·94	6
28	Th	7	8	·42	3	·87	7
29	Fr	8	9	·33	4	·81	8
—30	Sa	9	10	·23	5	·74	9
1	Su	10	11	·13	6	·67	10
2	Mo	11	12 13	·04 ·94	7	·61	11
3	Tu	12	14	·88	8	·56	12
4	We	13	P	·82	9	·53	13
5	Th	14	1	·77	10	·50	14
6	Fr	15	2	·75	11	·50	15
7	Sa	16	3	·74	12	·51	16
8	Su	17	4	·76	13	·55	17
9	Mo	18	5	·80	14	·61	18
10	Tu	19	6	·86	15	·69	19
11	We	20	7	·93	16	·78	20
12	Th	21	...	...	17	·88	21
13	Fr	22	8	·01	18	·99	22
14	Sa	23	9	·09	...	...	23
15	Su	24	10	·18	19	·09	24
16	Mo	25	11	·27	20	·20	25
17	Tu	26	12	·32	21	·28	26
18	We	27	13	·37	22	·34	27
19	Th	28	14	·38	23	·39	28

March

Raktaksha, Kumbha—Masi. / Raktaksha, Mina—Panguni. — Phalguna (Sukla / Bahula) — H. 1219 Zi-l-hijja.

Cyclic Sidereal Year, Month and Day	Week-Day	English Month and Day	Tithi	Ending Moment	Nakshatra	Ending Moment	Muhammadan Year, Month and Day
20	Fr	1	—A	·39	24	·42	29
21	Sa	2	1	·38	25	·43	—30
22	Su	3	2	·34	26	·41	1
23	Mo	4	3	·28	27	·38	2
24	Tu	5	4	·20	1	·33	3
25	We	6	5	·12	2	·27	4
26	Th	7	6 7	·03 ·94	3	·22	5
27	Fr	8	8	·84	4	·15	6
28	Sa	9	9	·75	5	·08	7
29	Su	10	10	·65	6 7	·01 ·94	8
—30	Mo	11	11	·55	8	·90	9
1	Tu	12	12	·48	9	·86	10
2	We	13	13	·41	10	·83	11
3	Th	14	14	·38	11	·82	12
4	Fr	15	P	·35	12	·83	13
5	Sa	16	1	·34	13	·87	14
6	Su	17	2	·35	14	·92	15
7	Mo	18	3	·39	15	·99	16
8	Tu	19	4	·45	...	...	17
9	We	20	5	·54	16	·08	18
10	Th	21	6	·62	17	·18	19
11	Fr	22	7	·70	18	·29	20
12	Sa	23	8	·79	19	·40	21
13	Su	24	9	·87	20	·50	22
14	Mo	25	10	·91	21	·58	23
15	Tu	26	11	·96	22	·65	24
16	We	27	12	·98	23	·71	25
17	Th	28	13	·98	24	·74	26
18	Fr	29	14	·96	25	·75	27
19	Sa	30	—A	·92	26	·74	28
20	Su	31	1	·86	27	·71	—29

April

Krodhana, Mesha—Chittirai. — Chaitra (Sukla / Bahula) — H. 1220 Muharram.

Cyclic Sidereal Year, Month and Day	Week-Day	English Month and Day	Tithi	Ending Moment	Nakshatra	Ending Moment	Muhammadan Year, Month and Day
21	Mo	1	2	·79	1	·67	1
22	Tu	2	3	·70	2	·62	2
23	We	3	4	·61	3	·56	3
24	Th	4	5	·50	4	·49	4
25	Fr	5	6	.40	5	·42	5
26	Sa	6	7	·31	6	·35	6
27	Su	7	8	·21	7	·29	7
28	Mo	8	9	·13	8	·23	8
29	Tu	9	10 11	·05 ·97	9	·19	9
—30	We	10	12	·94	10	·16	10
1	Th	11	13	·91	11	·14	11
2	Fr	12	14	·90	12	·16	12
3	Sa	13	P	·91	13	·18	13
4	Su	14	1	·96	14	·23	14
5	Mo	15	...	...	15	·30	15
6	Tu	16	2	·01	16	·38	16
7	We	17	3	·09	17	·49	17
8	Th	18	4	·17	18	·59	18
9	Fr	19	5	·25	19	·70	19
10	Sa	20	6	·34	20	·80	20
11	Su	21	7	·41	21	·89	21
12	Mo	22	8	·47	22	·96	22
13	Tu	23	9	·50	...	...	23
14	We	24	10	·52	23	·03	24
15	Th	25	11	·52	24	·06	25
16	Fr	26	12	·50	25	·07	26
17	Sa	27	13	·47	26	·06	27
18	Su	28	14	·40	27	·04	28
19	Mo	29	—A	·33	1 2	·01 ·96	29
20	Tu	30	1	·24	3	·89	—30

May

Krodhana, Mesha—Chittirai. / Krodhana, Vrishabha—Vaikasi. — Vaisakha (Sukla / Bahula) — H. 1220 Safar.

Cyclic Sidereal Year, Month and Day	Week-Day	English Month and Day	Tithi	Ending Moment	Nakshatra	Ending Moment	Muhammadan Year, Month and Day
21	We	1	2	·15	4	·83	1
22	Th	2	3 4	·04 ·94	5	·76	2
23	Fr	3	5	·84	6	·69	3
24	Sa	4	6	·74	7	·63	4
25	Su	5	7	·66	8	·57	5
26	Mo	6	8	·57	9	·52	6
27	Tu	7	9	·51	10	·49	7
28	We	8	10	·47	11	·48	8
29	Th	9	11	·44	12	·48	9
30	Fr	10	12	·43	13	·50	10
—31	Sa	11	13	·43	14	·54	11
1	Su	12	14	·48	15	·60	12
2	Mo	13	P	·53	16	·68	13
3	Tu	14	1	·61	17	·78	14
4	We	15	2	·68	18	·89	15
5	Th	16	3	·77	...	...	16
6	Fr	17	4	·85	19	·00	17
7	Sa	18	5	·92	20	·10	18
8	Su	19	6	·98	21	·19	19
9	Mo	20	...	...	22	·28	20
10	Tu	21	7	·02	23	·34	21
11	We	22	8	·03	24	·38	22
12	Th	23	9	·03	25	·39	23
13	Fr	24	10 11	·02 ·98	26	·39	24
14	Sa	25	12	·91	27	·38	25
15	Su	26	13	·83	1	·34	26
16	Mo	27	14	·74	2	·29	27
17	Tu	28	—A	·66	3	·23	28
18	We	29	1	·54	4	·16	—29
19	Th	30	2	·45	5	·10	1
20	Fr	31	3	·34	6 7	·03 ·96	2

June

Krodhana, Mithuna—Ani. — Jyeshtha (Sukla / Bahula); Ash. Su. — H. 1220 Rabi-ul-awwal.

Cyclic Sidereal Year, Month and Day	Week-Day	English Month and Day	Tithi	Ending Moment	Nakshatra	Ending Moment	Muhammadan Year, Month and Day
21	Sa	1	4	·24	8	·90	3
22	Su	2	5	·15	9	·85	4
23	Mo	3	6	·08	10	·82	5
24	Tu	4	7 8	·02 ·96	11	·80	6
25	We	5	9	·94	12	·80	7
26	Th	6	10	·92	13	·81	8
27	Fr	7	11	·94	14	·85	9
28	Sa	8	12	·96	15	·91	10
29	Su	9	...	...	16	·99	11
30	Mo	10	13	·01	...	...	12
—31	Tu	11	14	·10	17	·08	13
1	We	12	P	·15	18	·19	14
2	Th	13	1	·25	19	·29	15
3	Fr	14	2	·33	20	·40	16
4	Sa	15	3	·40	21	·50	17
5	Su	16	4	·46	22	·58	18
6	Mo	17	5	·49	23	·65	19
7	Tu	18	6	·52	24	·69	20
8	We	19	7	·51	25	·71	21
9	Th	20	8	.50	26	·72	22
10	F	21	9	·46	27	·71	23
11	Sa	22	10	·40	1	·67	24
12	Su	23	11	·32	2	·63	25
13	Mo	24	12	·24	3	·57	26
14	Tu	25	13	·15	4	·51	27
15	We ●	26	14 A	·03 ·94	5	·44	28
16	Th	27	1	·83	6	·37	29
17	Fr	28	2	·73	7	·30	—30
18	Sa	29	3	·64	8	·24	1
19	Su	30	4	·57	9	·19	2

Naksh:—1. Asvn. 2. Bhar. 3. Krit. 4. Rohi. 5. Mrig. 6. Ardh. 7. Punar. 8. Push. 9. Aslesh. 10. Magh. 11. P. Phal. 12. U. Phal. 13. Hasta. 14. Chit.

A. D. 1805.
A.—Amavasya. P.—Paurnami.

Kollam 981, Commences { N. Malabar—Sept. S. Malabar—Aug.

Hijra 1220, Commences, April 1.

Vikrama 1862. Bengal San 1211. (N. Cycle) Dhatri.

SOLAR reckoning. LUNAR reckoning.

July (Solar: Krodhana, Mithuna—Ani; from July 14 Krodhana, Karkata—Adi. Lunar: Sukla; Ashadha; Bahula. Muhammadan: H. 1220 Rabi-ul-akhir; from July 27 Jumadal-awwal.)

Cyclic Sidereal Year, Month and Day	Week-Day	English Month and Day	Tithi	Ending Moment	Nakshatra	Ending Moment	Muhammadan Year, Month and Day
20	Mo	1	5	·50	10	·15	3
21	Tu	2	6	·44	11	·13	4
22	We	3	7	·42	12	·12	5
23	Th	4	8	·40	13	·13	6
24	Fr	5	9	·41	14	·16	7
25	Sa	6	10	·44	15	·22	8
26	Su	7	11	·50	16	·30	9
27	Mo	8	12	·56	17	·38	10
28	Tu	9	13	·64	18	·48	11
29	We	10	14	·73	19	·59	12
30	Th ◯	11	P	·79	20	·71	13
31	Fr	12	1	·88	21	·80	14
32	Sa	13	2	·94	22	·89	15
1	Su	14	3	·99	23	·96	16
2	Mo	15	4	·99	...	...	17
3	Tu	16	...	...	24	·00	18
4	We	17	5 / 6	·00 / ·98	25	·04	19
5	Th	18	7	·93	26	·05	20
6	Fr	19	8	·88	27	·03	21
7	Sa	20	9	·80	1 / 2	·00 / ·96	22
8	Su	21	10	·72	3	·91	23
9	Mo	22	11	·63	4	·85	24
10	Tu	23	12	·53	5	·78	25
11	We	24	13	·43	6	·71	26
12	Th	25	14	·32	7	·64	27
13	Fr	26	A	·22	8	·58	28
14	Sa	27	1	·13	9	·53	29
15	Su	28	2	·05	10	·49	1
16	Mo	29	3 / 4	·03 / ·93	11	·46	2
17	Tu	30	5	·90	12	·44	3
18	We	31	6	·87	13	·45	4

Aug. (Solar: Krodhana, Karkata—Adi; from Aug. 14 Krodhana, Simha—Avani. Lunar: Sukla; Sravana; Bahula; Bhad. Sukla. Muhammadan: H. 1220 Jumadal-awwal; from Aug. 27 Jl. akhir.)

Cyclic Sidereal Year, Month and Day	Week-Day	English Month and Day	Tithi	Ending Moment	Nakshatra	Ending Moment	Muhammadan Year, Month and Day
19	Th	1	7	·89	14	·49	5
20	Fr	2	8	·91	15	·53	6
21	Sa	3	9	·97	16	·60	7
22	Su	4	...	...	17	·69	8
23	Mo	5	10	·03	18	·78	9
24	Tu	6	11	·12	19	·90	10
25	We	7	12	·20	...	...	11
26	Th	8	13	·29	20	·01	12
27	Fr	9	14	·35	21	·11	13
28	Sa	10	P	·41	22	·19	14
29	Su	11	1	·46	23	·27	15
30	Mo	12	2	·48	24	·33	16
31	Tu	13	3	·49	25	·36	17
1	We	14	4	·46	26	·37	18
2	Th	15	5	·43	27	·36	19
3	Fr	16	6	·38	1	·34	20
4	Sa	17	7	·30	2	·29	21
5	Su	18	8	·22	3	·25	22
6	Mo	19	9	·11	4	·19	23
7	Tu	20	10 / 11	·02 / ·92	5	·12	24
8	We	21	12	·83	6 / 7	·05 / ·98	25
9	Th	22	13	·72	8	·92	26
10	Fr	23	14	·63	9	·86	27
11	Sa	24	A	·55	10	·82	28
12	Su	25	1	·48	11	·78	29
13	Mo	26	2	·43	12	·77	30
14	Tu	27	3	·40	13	·78	1
15	We	28	4	·39	14	·80	2
16	Th	29	5	·39	15	·84	3
17	Fr	30	6	·42	16	·91	4
18	Sa	31	7	·47	17	·99	5

Sep. (Solar: Krodhana, Simha—Avani; from Sep. 14 Krodhana, Kanya—Purattasi. Lunar: Bhadrapa. Suk.; Bahula; Sukla. Muhammadan: H. 1220 Jumadal-akhir; from Sep. 25 Rajab.)

Cyclic Sidereal Year, Month and Day	Week-Day	English Month and Day	Tithi	Ending Moment	Nakshatra	Ending Moment	Muhammadan Year, Month and Day
19	Su	1	8	·53	...	...	6
20	Mo	2	9	·62	18	·09	7
21	Tu	3	10	·70	19	·20	8
22	We	4	11	·79	20	·30	9
23	Th	5	12	·87	21	·41	10
24	Fr	6	13	·94	22	·50	11
25	Sa	7	14	·97	23	·58	12
26	Su	8	P	·98	24	·64	13
27	Mo	9	...	...	25	·68	14
28	Tu	10	1 / 2	·00 / ·98	26	·69	15
29	We	11	3	·96	27	·69	16
30	Th	12	4	·90	1	·67	17
31	Fr	13	5	·83	2	·64	18
1	Sa	14	6	·74	3	·59	19
2	Su	15	7	·65	4	·53	20
3	Mo	16	8	·55	5	·46	21
4	Tu	17	9	·45	6	·39	22
5	We	18	10	·36	7	·53	23
6	Th	19	11	·24	8	·26	24
7	Fr	20	12	·16	9	·20	25
8	Sa	21	13	·08	10	·15	26
9	Su	22	14 / A	·02 / ·96	11	·11	27
10	Mo	23	1	·93	12	·10	28
11	Tu	24	2	·92	13	·10	29
12	We	25	3	·94	14	·11	1
13	Th	26	4	·97	15	·15	2
14	Fr	27	...	...	16	·21	3
15	Sa	28	5	·01	17	·30	4
16	Su	29	6	·08	18	·39	5
17	Mo	30	7	·16	19	·49	6

Oct. (Solar: Krodhana, Kanya—Purattasi; from Oct. 15 Krodhana, Tula—Aippasi. Lunar: Asvina; Bahula; Karttika Suk. Muhammadan: H. 1220 Rajab; from Oct. 25 Shaban.)

Cyclic Sidereal Year, Month and Day	Week-Day	English Month and Day	Tithi	Ending Moment	Nakshatra	Ending Moment	Muhammadan Year, Month and Day
18	Tu	1	8	·24	20	·60	7
19	We	2	9	·33	21	·69	8
20	Th	3	10	·40	22	·80	9
21	Fr	4	11	·48	23	·89	10
22	Sa	5	12	·52	24	·95	11
23	Su	6	13	·54	25	·99	12
24	Mo	7	14	·55	...	...	13
25	Tu	8	P	·54	26	·01	14
26	We	9	1	·51	27	·01	15
27	Th	10	2	·45	1 / 2	·00 / ·97	16
28	Fr	11	3	·39	3	·92	17
29	Sa	12	4	·30	4	·86	18
30	Su	13	5	·21	5	·80	19
31	Mo	14	6	·11	6	·74	20
1	Tu	15	7 / 8	·02 / ·92	7	·66	21
2	We	16	9	·81	8	·60	22
3	Th	17	10	·73	9	·53	23
4	Fr	18	11	·65	10	·48	24
5	Sa	19	12	·59	11	·45	25
6	Su	20	13	·53	12	·43	26
7	Mo	21	14	·52	13	·42	27
8	Tu	22	A	·51	14	·43	28
9	We	23	1	·52	15	·46	29
10	Th	24	2	·55	16	·53	30
11	Fr	25	3	·60	17	·60	1
12	Sa	26	4	·66	18	·69	2
13	Su	27	5	·74	19	·79	3
14	Mo	28	6	·83	20	·90	4
15	Tu	29	7	·91	...	...	5
16	We	30	...	...	21	·00	6
17	Th	31	8	·01	22	·11	7

Nov. (Solar: Krodhana, Tula—Aippasi; from Nov. 14 Krodhana, Vrischika—Kartigai. Lunar: Sukla; Karttika; Bahula; Sukla. Muhammadan: H. 1220 Shaban; from Nov. 23 Ramzan.)

Cyclic Sidereal Year, Month and Day	Week-Day	English Month and Day	Tithi	Ending Moment	Nakshatra	Ending Moment	Muhammadan Year, Month and Day
18	Fr	1	9	·07	23	·19	8
19	Sa	2	10	·11	24	·26	9
20	Su	3	11	·15	25	·31	10
21	Mo	4	12	·14	26	·33	11
22	Tu	5	13	·13	27	·35	12
23	We	6	14	·10	1	·33	13
24	Th	7	P / 1	·05 / ·98	2	·30	14
25	Fr	8	2	·89	3	·26	15
26	Sa	9	3	·80	4	·20	16
27	Su	10	4	·71	5	·14	17
28	Mo	11	5	·61	6	·07	18
29	Tu	12	6	·52	7 / 8	·00 / ·93	19
30	We	13	7	·42	9	·87	20
1	Th	14	8	·33	10	·82	21
2	Fr	15	9	·27	11	·78	22
3	Sa	16	10	·20	12	·75	23
4	Su	17	11	·14	13	·74	24
5	Mo	18	12	·12	14	·75	25
6	Tu	19	13	·12	15	·78	26
7	We	20	14	·13	16	·84	27
8	Th	21	A	·16	17	·91	28
9	Fr	22	1	·22	18	·99	29
10	Sa	23	2	·29	...	...	1
11	Su	24	3	·37	19	·09	2
12	Mo	25	4	·46	20	·20	3
13	Tu	26	5	·54	21	·31	4
14	We	27	6	·63	22	·41	5
15	Th	28	7	·69	23	·50	6
16	Fr	29	8	·75	24	·57	7
17	Sa	30	9	·77	25	·62	8

Dec. (Solar: Krodhana, Vrischika—Kartigai; from Dec. 13 Krodhana, Dhanus—Margali. Lunar: Margasira; Bahula; Pausha Sukla. Muhammadan: H. 1220 Ramzan; from Dec. 23 Shawwal.)

Cyclic Sidereal Year, Month and Day	Week-Day	English Month and Day	Tithi	Ending Moment	Nakshatra	Ending Moment	Muhammadan Year, Month and Day
18	Su	1	10	·77	26	·66	9
19	Mo	2	11	·76	27	·67	10
20	Tu	3	12	·71	1	·66	11
21	We	4	13	·66	2	·63	12
22	Th	5	14	·60	3	·59	13
23	Fr	6	P	·52	4	·55	14
24	Sa	7	1	·43	5	·48	15
25	Su	8	2	·34	6	·41	16
26	Mo	9	3	·24	7	·34	17
27	Tu	10	4	·14	8	27	18
28	We	11	5 / 6	·04 / ·96	9	·21	19
29	Th	12	7	·89	10	·16	20
1	Fr	13	8	·82	11	·11	21
2	Sa	14	9	·79	12	·08	22
3	Su	15	10	76	13	·06	23
4	Mo	16	11	·75	14	·07	24
5	Tu	17	12	·78	15	·10	25
6	We	18	13	·81	16	·15	26
7	Th	19	14	·87	17	·21	27
8	Fr	20	A	·93	18	·29	28
9	Sa	21	...	...	19	·39	29
10	Su	22	1	·03	20	·50	30
11	Mo	23	2	·11	21	·61	1
12	Tu	24	3	·19	22	·71	2
13	We	25	4	·28	23	·80	3
14	Th	26	5	·34	24	·88	4
15	Fr	27	6	·39	25	·94	5
16	Sa	28	7	·42	26	·98	6
17	Su	29	8	·42	27	·99	7
18	Mo	30	9	·40	1	·99	8
19	Tu	31	10	·36	2	·96	9

15. Svati. 16. Visak. 17. Anur. 18. Jyesh. 19. Mula. 20. P. Ash. 21. U. Ash. 22. Sravn. 23. Dani. 24. Satab. 25. P. Bhad. 26. U. Bhad. 27. Rev.

A. D. 1806. **Mesha Sankranti.** (Commencement of Indian Sidereal Year).

Solar Eclipse. ● **(Surya Sid.) April 11·30.** **Saka 1728.** **Kaliyuga 4907.**

Lunar Eclipse. ○ **(Arya Sid.) April 11·20.** **(S. Cycle) Kshaya** (Akshaya).

Cyclic Sidereal Year, Month and Day (SOLAR reckoning)	Week-Day	English Month and Day	Tithi (LUNAR reckoning)	Ending Moment	Nakshatra	Ending Moment	Muhammadan Year, Month and Day
		Jan.					
Krodhana *Dhanus—Margali.* 20	We	1	*Sukla* 11	·31	3	·93	*H. 1220 Shawwal.* 10
21	Th	2	12	·24	4	·88	11
22	Fr	3	13	·16	5	·82	12
23	Sa	○ 4	14 P	·06 ·98	6	·75	13
24	Su	5	Pausha 1	·87	7	·68	14
25	Mo	6	2	·78	8	·61	15
26	Tu	7	3	·69	9	·55	16
27	We	8	4	·60	10	·49	17
28	Th	9	5	·53	11	·44	18
29	Fr	10	6	·47	12	·41	19
—30	Sa	11	7	·43	13	·39	20
Krodhana *Makara—Tai.* 1	Su	12	8	·40	14	·40	21
2	Mo	13	*Bahula* 9	·41	15	·42	22
3	Tu	14	10	·42	16	·46	23
4	We	15	11	·45	17	·52	24
5	Th	16	12	·51	18	·59	25
6	Fr	17	13	·59	19	·70	26
7	Sa	18	14	·69	20	·80	27
8	Su	19	—A	·76	21	·91	28
9	Mo	20	1	.86	...	...	—29
10	Tu	21	2	·93	22	·01	1
11	We	22	3	·99	23	·11	2
12	Th	23	...	...	24	·19	3
13	Fr	24	4	·03	25	·25	4
14	Sa	25	*Sukla* 5	·06	26	·29	5
15	Su	26	6	·06	27	·31	6
16	Mo	27	7	·04	1	·31	7
17	Tu	28	8 9	·01 ·95	2	·29	8
18	We	29	10	·88	3	·27	9
19	Th	30	11	·79	4	·22	10
20	Fr	31	12	·70	5	·16	11
		Feb.					
21	Sa	1	13	·61	6	·09	*H. 1220 Zi-l-ka'da.* 12
22	Su	2	Magha 14	·50	7 8	·02 ·96	13
23	Mo	3	P	·41	9	·89	14
24	Tu	4	1	·32	10	·83	15
25	We	5	2	·24	11	·78	16
26	Th	6	3	·16	12	·74	17
27	Fr	7	4	·11	13	·72	18
28	Sa	8	5	·07	14	·72	19
—29	Su	9	6	·04	15	·73	20
Krodhana *Kumbha—Masi.* 1	Mo	10	*Bahula* 7	·04	16	·77	21
2	Tu	11	8	·05	17	·82	22
3	We	12	9	·10	18	·91	23
4	Th	13	10	·16	...	...	24
5	Fr	14	11	·23	19	·00	25
6	Sa	15	12	·32	20	·10	26
7	Su	16	13	·39	21	·21	27
8	Mo	17	14	·49	22	·31	28
9	Tu	18	—A	·56	23	·42	29
10	We	19	1	·63	24	·50	—30
11	Th	20	Phalg. *Sukla* 2	·67	25	.57	*H. 1220 Zi-l-hijja* 1
12	Fr	21	3	·69	26	·61	2
13	Sa	22	4	·68	27	·63	3
14	Su	23	5	·67	1	·64	4
15	Mo	24	6	·62	2	·63	5
16	Tu	25	7	·56	3	.60	6
17	We	26	8	·50	4	·55	7
18	Th	27	9	·41	5	·49	8
19	Fr	28	10	·32	6	·43	9

Cyclic Sidereal Year, Month and Day (SOLAR reckoning)	Week-Day	English Month and Day	Tithi (LUNAR reckoning)	Ending Moment	Nakshatra	Ending Moment	Muhammadan Year, Month and Day
		March					
Krodhana *Kumbha—Masi.* 20	Sa	1	*Suk.* 11	·23	7	·37	*H. 1220 Zi-l-hijja.* 10
21	Su	2	12	·13	8	·30	11
22	Mo	3	13 14	·03 ·93	9	·23	12
23	Tu	4	—P	·85	10	·16	13
24	We	5	Phalguna 1	·77	11	·11	14
25	Th	6	2	·71	12	·08	15
26	Fr	7	3	·67	13	·05	16
27	Sa	8	4	·66	14	·04	17
28	Su	9	5	·65	15	·05	18
29	Mo	10	6	·67	16	·08	19
—30	Tu	11	7	·71	17	·14	20
Krodhana *Mina—Panguni.* 1	We	12	8	·76	18	·21	21
2	Th	13	9	·84	19	·30	22
3	Fr	14	*Bahula* 10	·92	20	·40	23
4	Sa	15	...	...	21	·50	24
5	Su	16	11	·01	22	·61	25
6	Mo	17	12	·09	23	·72	26
7	Tu	18	13	·15	24	·80	27
8	We	19	14	·22	25	·87	28
9	Th	20	—A	·26	26	·92	—29
10	Fr	21	1	·29	27	·95	1
11	Sa	22	2	·28	1	·97	2
12	Su	23	3	·27	2	·96	3
13	Mo	24	*Sukla* 4	·21	3	·93	4
14	Tu	25	5	·16	4	·88	5
15	We	26	6	·09	5	·83	6
16	Th	27	7 8	·00 ·91	6	·77	7
17	Fr	28	9	·80	7	·71	8
18	Sa	29	10	·70	8	·63	9
19	Su	30	11	·61	9	·57	10
20	Mo	31	12	·52	10	·50	11
		April					
21	Tu	1	Chaitra 13	·43	11	·45	*H. 1221 Muharram.* 12
22	We	2	14	·34	12	·41	13
23	Th	3	P	·29	13	·38	14
24	Fr	4	1	·25	14	·36	15
25	Sa	5	2	·23	15	·37	16
26	Su	6	3	·22	16	·40	17
27	Mo	7	4	·25	17	·45	18
28	Tu	8	5	·28	18	·52	19
29	We	9	6	·33	19	·60	20
—30	Th	10	*Bahula* 7	·41	20	·70	21
Kshaya *Mesha—Chittirai.* 1	Fr	11	8	·48	21	·80	22
2	Sa	12	9	·57	22	·92	23
3	Su	13	10	·65	...	...	24
4	Mo	14	11	·72	23	·02	25
5	Tu	15	12	·78	24	·11	26
6	We	16	13	·83	25	·18	27
7	Th	17	14	·84	26	·24	28
8	Fr	18	—A	·83	27	·28	29
9	Sa	19	Vaisakha *Sukla* 1	·82	1	·29	—30
10	Su	20	2	·76	2	·28	*H. 1221 Safar.* 1
11	Mo	21	3	·71	3	·26	2
12	Tu	22	4	·63	4	·22	3
13	We	23	5	·55	5	·18	4
14	Th	24	6	·45	6	·11	5
15	Fr	25	7	·35	7 8	·04 ·97	6
16	Sa	26	8	·25	9	.90	7
17	Su	27	9	·15	10	·85	8
18	Mo	28	10 11	·06 ·97	11	·79	9
19	Tu	29	12	·88	12	·74	10
20	We	30	13	·82	13	·71	11

Cyclic Sidereal Year, Month and Day (SOLAR reckoning)	Week-Day	English Month and Day	Tithi (LUNAR reckoning)	Ending Moment	Nakshatra	Ending Moment	Muhammadan Year, Month and Day
		May					
Kshaya *Mesha—Chittirai.* 21	Th	1	Vaisakha 14	·79	14	·69	*H. 1221 Safar.* 12
22	Fr	2	P	·76	15	·69	13
23	Sa	3	1	·75	16	·72	14
24	Su	4	2	·78	17	·76	15
25	Mo	5	3	·81	18	·82	16
26	Tu	6	4	·86	19	·90	17
27	We	7	5	·93	...	...	18
28	Th	8	...	...	20	·00	19
29	Fr	9	6	·02	21	·11	20
30	Sa	10	7	·09	22	.22	21
—31	Su	11	8	·17	23	·32	22
Kshaya *Vrishabha—Vaikasi.* 1	Mo	12	*Bahula* 9	·25	24	·41	23
2	Tu	13	10	·30	25	·49	24
3	We	14	11	·35	26	·56	25
4	Th	15	12	·36	27	·60	26
5	Fr	16	13	·36	1	·61	27
6	Sa	17	14	·33	2	·61	28
7	Su	18	—A	·28	3	·59	—29
8	Mo	19	1	·22	4	·56	*Rabi-ul-awwal.* 1
9	Tu	20	2	·14	5	·51	2
10	We	21	3 4	·07 ·96	6	·45	3
11	Th	22	*Sukla* 5	·87	7	·38	4
12	Fr	23	6	·76	8	·31	5
13	Sa	24	7	·67	9	·25	6
14	Su	25	8	·56	10	·18	7
15	Mo	26	9	·46	11	·12	8
16	Tu	27	10	·39	12	·07	9
17	We	28	11	·34	13	·03	10
18	Th	29	12	·29	14	·01	11
19	Fr	30	13	·26	15	·02	12
20	Sa	31	14	·26	16	·03	13
		June					
21	Su	1	Jyeshtha P	·26	17	·07	H. 1221 14
22	Mo	2	1	·29	18	·13	15
23	Tu	3	2	·36	19	·20	16
24	We	4	3	·43	20	·30	17
25	Th	5	4	·51	21	·41	18
26	Fr	6	5	·59	22	·51	19
27	Sa	7	6	·68	23	·62	20
28	Su	8	7	·75	24	·71	21
29	Mo	9	8	·78	25	·80	22
30	Tu	10	*Bahula* 9	·83	26	·87	23
31	We	11	10	·85	27	·91	24
—32	Th	12	11	·84	1	·93	25
Kshaya *Mithuna—Ani.* 1	Fr	13	12	·82	2	·93	26
2	Sa	14	13	·78	3	·93	27
3	Su	15	14	·71	4	·89	28
4	Mo	16	—A	·64	5	·85	29
5	Tu	17	1	·56	6	·79	—30
6	We	18	2	·46	7	·72	*H. 1221 Rabi-ul-akhir.* 1
7	Th	19	*Sukla* 3	·35	8	·65	2
8	Fr	20	4	·25	9	·59	3
9	Sa	21	5	·16	10	·52	4
10	Su	22	6 7	·05 ·96	11	·46	5
11	Mo	23	8	·88	12	·41	6
12	Tu	24	9	·81	13	·36	7
13	We	25	Ashadha 10	·77	14	·35	8
14	Th	26	11	·74	15	·34	9
15	Fr	27	12	·73	16	·35	10
16	Sa	28	13	·74	17	·38	11
17	Su	29	14	·78	18	·43	12
18	Mo	30	P	·83	19	·52	13

Naksh:—1. Asvn. 2. Bhar. 3. Krit. 4. Rohi. 5. Mrig. 6. Ardh. 7. Punar. 8. Push. 9. Aslesh. 10. Magh. 11. P. Phal. 12. U. Phal. 13. Hasta. 14. Chit.

A. D. 1806. | Kollam 982, Commences { N. Malabar—Sept. S. Malabar—Aug. | Hijra 1221, Commences, Mar. 21. | Vikrama 1863. Bengal San 1212. (N. Cycle) Isvara.

A.—Amavasya.
P.—Paurnami.

July — Solar: Kshaya Mithuna—Ani (to 31), Kshaya Karkata—Adi. Lunar: Ashadha Bahula, Sukla; Sravana. Muhammadan: H. 1221 Rabi-ul-akhir; Jumadal-awwal.

Cyclic Sidereal Year, Month and Day.	Week-Day	English Month and Day.	Tithi	Ending Moment.	Nakshatra	Ending Moment.	Muhammadan Year, Month and Day.
19	Tu	1	1	·89	20	·60	14
20	We	2	2	·97	21	·71	15
21	Th	3	...	...	22	·81	16
22	Fr	4	3	·06	23	·92	17
23	Sa	5	4	·14	...	...	18
24	Su	6	5	·21	24	·03	19
25	Mo	7	6	·27	25	·11	20
26	Tu	8	7	·31	26	·18	21
27	We	9	8	·33	27	·22	22
28	Th	10	9	·32	1	·25	23
29	Fr	11	10	·30	2	·26	24
30	Sa	12	11	·25	3	·25	25
—31	Su	13	12	·19	4	·22	26
1	Mo	14	13	·12	5	·18	27
2	Tu	15	{14 / A	·04 / ·94	6	·12	28
3	We	16	1	·83	7	·06	—29
4	Th	17	2	·73	8 / 9	·00 / ·93}	1
5	Fr	18	3	·62	10	·86	2
6	Sa	19	4	·53	11	·80	3
7	Su	20	5	·44	12	·74	4
8	Mo	21	6	·36	13	·70	5
9	Tu	22	7	·30	14	·67	6
10	We	23	8	·25	15	·66	7
11	Th	24	9	·23	16	·67	8
12	Fr	25	10	·21	17	·70	9
13	Sa	26	11	·22	18	·75	10
14	Su	27	12	·25	19	·82	11
15	Mo	28	13	·30	20	·91	12
16	Tu	29	14	·37	...	...	13
17	We	30	P	·45	21	·00	14
18	Th	31	1	·54	22	·11	15

Aug. — Solar: Kshaya Karkata—Adi (to 32), Kshaya Simha—Avani. Lunar: Adhika Bahula, Sukla; Nija Sravana Bah. Muhammadan: H. 1221 Jumadal-awwal; H. 1221 Jumadal-akhir.

Cyclic Sidereal Year, Month and Day.	Week-Day	English Month and Day.	Tithi	Ending Moment.	Nakshatra	Ending Moment.	Muhammadan Year, Month and Day.
19	Fr	1	2	·61	23	·28	16
20	Sa	2	3	·68	24	·33	17
21	Su	3	4	·74	25	·41	18
22	Mo	4	5	·78	26	·49	19
23	Tu	5	6	·81	27	·54	20
24	We	6	7	·80	1	·57	21
25	Th	7	8	·79	2	·59	22
26	Fr	8	9	·74	3	·57	23
27	Sa	9	10	·68	4	·56	24
28	Su	10	11	·61	5	·51	25
29	Mo	11	12	·52	6	·46	26
30	Tu	12	13	·44	7	·41	27
31	We	13	14	·33	8	·34	28
—32	Th	14	—A	·23	9	·27	29
1	Fr	15	1	·12	10	·20	—30
2	Sa	16	{2 / 3	·03 / ·94	11	·13	1
3	Su	17	4	·86	12	·08	2
4	Mo	18	5	·80	13	·04	3
5	Tu	19	6	·74	14 / 15	·00 / ·99}	4
6	We	20	7	·72	16	·99	5
7	Th	21	8	·71	...	...	6
8	Fr	22	9	·72	17	02	7
9	Sa	23	10	·74	18	·06	8
10	Su	24	11	·79	19	·13	9
11	Mo	25	12	·87	20	·21	10
12	Tu	26	13	·95	21	·30	11
13	We	27	...	...	22	·41	12
14	Th	28	14	·03	23	·52	13
15	Fr	29	P	·12	24	·63	14
16	Sa	30	1	·19	25	·72	15
17	Su	31	2	·25	26	·79	16

Sep. — Solar: Kshaya Simha—Avani (to 31), Kshaya Kanya—Purattasi. Lunar: Nija Srav. Bahula, Sukla; Bhadrapada. Muhammadan: H. 1221 Jumadal-akhir; H. 1221 Rajab.

Cyclic Sidereal Year, Month and Day.	Week-Day	English Month and Day.	Tithi	Ending Moment.	Nakshatra	Ending Moment.	Muhammadan Year, Month and Day.
18	Mo	1	3	·28	27	·85	17
19	Tu	2	4	·32	1	·90	18
20	We	3	5	·31	2	·91	19
21	Th	4	6	·30	3	·91	20
22	Fr	5	7	·25	4	.88	21
23	Sa	6	8	·21	5	·85	22
24	Su	7	9	·12	6	·81	23
25	Mo	8	{10 / 11	·04 / ·95	7	·74	24
26	Tu	9	12	·84	8	·68	25
27	We	10	13	·75	9	·61	26
28	Th	11	14	·64	10	·54	27
29	Fr	12	A	·55	11	·48	28
30	Sa	13	1	·46	12	·42	—29
—31	Su	14	2	·39	13	·37	1
1	Mo	15	3	·31	14	·33	2
2	Tu	16	4	·27	15	·31	3
3	We	17	5	·25	16	·32	4
4	Th	18	6	·24	17	·34	5
5	Fr	19	7	·24	18	·37	6
6	Sa	20	8	·27	19	·43	7
7	Su	21	9	·33	20	·51	8
8	Mo	22	10	·39	21	·60	9
9	Tu	23	11	·47	22	·72	10
10	We	24	12	·56	23	·82	11
11	Th	25	13	·64	24	·93	12
12	Fr	26	14	·72	...	...	13
13	Sa	27	P	·78	25	·02	14
14	Su	28	1	·83	26	·10	15
15	Mo	29	2	·85	27	·17	16
16	Tu	30	3	·86	1	·24	17

Oct. — Solar: Kshaya Kanya—Purattasi (to 30), Kshaya Tula—Aippasi. Lunar: Bahula, Sukla; Asvina Bah. Muhammadan: H. 1221 Rajab; H 1221 Shaban.

Cyclic Sidereal Year, Month and Day.	Week-Day	English Month and Day.	Tithi	Ending Moment.	Nakshatra	Ending Moment.	Muhammadan Year, Month and Day.
17	We	1	4	·84	2	·23	18
18	Th	2	5	·80	3	·23	19
19	Fr	3	6	·75	4	·21	20
20	Sa	4	7	·67	5	·20	21
21	Su	5	8	·59	6	·14	22
22	Mo	6	9	·50	7	·08	23
23	Tu	7	10	·41	8 / 9	·02 / ·94}	24
24	We	8	11	·31	10	·88	25
25	Th	9	12	·19	11	·82	26
26	Fr	10	13	·11	12	·75	27
27	Sa	11	{14 / A	·02 / ·95	13	·70	28
28	Su	12	1	·89	14	·66	29
29	Mo	13	2	.84	15	·64	—30
—30	Tu	14	3	·81	16	·64	1
1	We	15	4	·81	17	·65	2
2	Th	16	5	·81	18	·68	3
3	Fr	17	6	·84	19	·74	4
4	Sa	18	7	·90	20	·81	5
5	Su	19	8	·96	21	·91	6
6	Mo	20	...	...	...	...	7
7	Tu	21	9	·05	22	·00	8
8	We	22	10	·14	23	·12	9
9	Th	23	11	·23	24	·22	10
10	Fr	24	12	·31	25	·32	11
11	Sa	25	13	·36	26	·42	12
12	Su	26	14	·41	27	·48	13
13	Mo	27	P	·44	1	·53	14
14	Tu	28	1	·44	2	·55	15
15	We	29	2	·42	3	·56	16
16	Th	30	3	·39	4	·55	17
17	Fr	31	4	·34	5	·52	18

Nov. — Solar: Kshaya Tula—Aippasi (to 30), Kshaya Vrischika—Kartigai. Lunar: Asv. Bahula, Sukla; Karttika. Muhammadan: H. 1221 Shaban; H. 1221 Ramzan.

Cyclic Sidereal Year, Month and Day.	Week-Day	English Month and Day.	Tithi	Ending Moment.	Nakshatra	Ending Moment.	Muhammadan Year, Month and Day.
18	Sa	1	5	·26	6	·48	19
19	Su	2	6	·18	7	·42	20
20	Mo	3	{7 / 8	·09 / ·99	8	·35	21
21	Tu	4	9	·90	9	·29	22
22	We	5	10	·80	10	·22	23
23	Th	6	11	·70	11	·15	24
24	Fr	7	12	.62	12	.09	25
25	Sa	8	13	·54	13 / 14	·08 / ·99}	26
26	Su	9	14	·48	15	·97	27
27	Mo	10	—A	·44	16	·96	28
28	Tu	11	1	·41	17	·97	—29
29	We	12	2	·41	...	...	1
—30	Th	13	3	.41	18	·00	2
1	Fr	14	4	·45	19	·05	3
2	Sa	15	5	·51	20	·13	4
3	Su	16	6	·58	21	·21	5
4	Mo	17	7	·67	22	·31	6
5	Tu	18	8	·75	23	·42	7
6	We	19	9	·85	24	·52	8
7	Th	20	10	·92	25	·63	9
8	Fr	21	11	·98	26	·72	10
9	Sa	22	...	...	27	·79	11
10	Su	23	12	·02	1	·84	12
11	Mo	24	13	·06	2	·87	13
12	Tu	25	14	·06	3	·89	14
13	We	26	P	·04	4	·88	15
14	Th	27	{1 / 2	·00 / ·95	5	85	16
15	Fr	28	3	·89	6	·81	17
16	Sa	29	4	·80	7	·75	18
17	Su	30	5	·71	8	·69	19

Dec. — Solar: Kshaya Vrischika—Kartigai (to 30), Kshaya Dhanus—Margali. Lunar: Bahula, Sukla; Margasira Bahula. Muhammadan: H. 1221 Ramzan; H. 1221 Shawwal.

Cyclic Sidereal Year, Month and Day.	Week-Day	English Month and Day.	Tithi	Ending Moment.	Nakshatra	Ending Moment.	Muhammadan Year, Month and Day.
18	Mo	1	6	·62	9	·63	20
19	Tu	2	7	·52	10	·56	21
20	We	3	8	·42	11	·49	22
21	Th	4	9	·32	12	·43	23
22	Fr	5	10	·24	13	·37	24
23	Sa	6	11	·16	14	·33	25
24	Su	7	12	·11	15	·30	26
25	Mo	8	13	·07	16	·28	27
26	Tu	9	14	·04	17	·29	28
27	We ●	10	—A	·04	18	·31	29
28	Th	11	1	·05	19	·37	—30
29	Fr	12	2	·10	20	·43	1
—30	Sa	13	3	·15	21	·51	2
1	Su	14	4	·28	22	·61	3
2	Mo	15	5	·32	23	·72	4
3	Tu	16	6	·40	24	·83	5
4	We	17	7	·49	25	·93	6
5	Th	18	8	·57	...	...	7
6	Fr	19	9	·64	26	·02	8
7	Sa	20	10	·67	27	·10	9
8	Su	21	11	·70	1	·15	10
9	Mo	22	12	·70	2	·20	11
10	Tu	23	13	·69	3	·21	12
11	We	24	14	·64	4	·21	13
12	Th	25	P	·59	5	·18	14
13	Fr	26	1	·52	6	·14	15
14	Sa	27	2	·43	7	·09	16
15	Su	28	3	·35	8 / 9	·04 / ·97}	17
16	Mo	29	4	·25	10	·90	18
17	Tu	30	5	·16	11	·83	19
18	We	31	{6 / 7	·06 / ·96	12	·76	20

15. Svati. 16. Visak. 17. Anur. 18. Jyesh. 19. Mula. 20. P. Ash. 21. U. Ash. 22. Sravn. 23. Dani. 24. Satab. 25. P. Bhad. 26. U. Bhad. 27. Rev.

A. D. 1807.
Solar Eclipse. ●
Lunar Eclipse. ○

Mesha Sankranti. (Commencement of Indian Sidereal Year).
(Surya Sid.) April 11·56.
(Arya Sid.) April 11·46.

Saka 1729. **Kaliyuga 4908.**
(S. Cycle) Prabhava.

SOLAR reckoning: Cyclic Sidereal Year, Month and Day	Week-Day	English Month and Day	LUNAR reckoning: Tithi	Ending Moment	Nakshatra	Ending Moment	Muhammadan Year, Month and Day
		Jan.					
Kshaya *Dhanus—Margali.* 19	Th	1	Marg. *Bah.* 8	·88	13	·71	H. 1221 *Shawwal.* 21
20	Fr	2	9	·80	14	·66	22
21	Sa	3	10	·76	15	·63	23
22	Su	4	11	·71	16	·61	24
23	Mo	5	12	·69	17	·61	25
24	Tu	6	13	·69	18	·64	26
25	We	7	14	·70	19	·68	27
26	Th	8	—A	·74	20	·74	28
27	Fr	9	1	·80	21	·82	—29
28	Sa	10	2	·88	22	·91	1
—29	Su	11	3	·96	...	...	2
1	Mo	12	...	...	23	·02	3
2	Tu	13	Pausha *Sukla* 4	·05	24	·13	4
3	We	14	5	·14	25	·23	5
4	Th	15	6	·22	26	·33	6
5	Fr	16	7	·28	27	·40	7
6	Sa	17	8	·32	1	·46	8
7	Su	18	9	·35	2	·51	9
8	Mo	19	10	·34	3	·53	10
9	Tu	20	11	·33	4	·53	11
10	We	21	12	·29	5	·51	12
11	Th	22	13	·24	6	·47	13
12	Fr	23	14	·16	7	·44	14
13	Sa	24	P 1	·06 ·98	8	·38	H. 1221 *Zi-l-ka'da.* 15
Kshaya *Makara—Tai.* 14	Su	25	*Bahula* 2	·88	9	·31	16
15	Mo	26	3	·78	10	·24	17
16	Tu	27	4	·69	11	·17	18
17	We	28	5	·60	12	·11	19
18	Th	29	6	·51	13	·05	20
19	Fr	30	7	·45	14 15	·00 ·96	21
20	Sa	31	8	·40	16	·93	22
		Feb.					
21	Su	1	9	·35	17	·94	23
22	Mo	2	10	·33	18	·95	24
23	Tu	3	11	·32	19	·99	25
24	We	4	12	·35	...	...	26
25	Th	5	13	·39	20	·04	27
26	Fr	6	14	·46	21	·12	28
27	Sa	7	—A	·52	22	·21	29
28	Su	8	1	·61	23	·32	—30
—29	Mo	9	2	·70	24	·43	1
Kshaya *Kumbha—Masi.* 1	Tu	10	Magha *Sukla* 3	·78	25	·53	H. 1221 *Zi-l-hijja.* 2
2	We	11	4	·86	26	·63	3
3	Th	12	5	·92	27	·71	4
4	Fr	13	6	·97	1	·78	5
5	Sa	14	7	·98	2	·83	6
6	Su	15	8	·97	3	·85	7
7	Mo	16	9	·96	4	·86	8
8	Tu	17	10	·91	5	·84	9
9	We	18	11	·86	6	·82	10
10	Th	19	12	·78	7	·77	11
11	Fr	20	13	·70	8	·71	12
12	Sa	21	14	·60	9	·65	13
13	Su	22	P	·51	10	·58	14
14	Mo	23	*Bahula* 1	·41	11	·52	15
15	Tu	24	2	·31	12	·45	16
16	We	25	3	·22	13	·38	17
17	Th	26	4	·13	14	·33	18
18	Fr	27	5	·06	15	·29	19
19	Sa	28	6 7	·00 ·98	16	·26	20

SOLAR reckoning: Cyclic Sidereal Year, Month and Day	Week-Day	English Month and Day	LUNAR reckoning: Tithi	Ending Moment	Nakshatra	Ending Moment	Muhammadan Year, Month and Day
		March					
Kshaya *Kumbha—Masi.* 20	Su	1	Magha. *Bah.* 8	·95	17	·26	H. 1221 *Zi-l-hijja.* 21
21	Mo	2	9	·94	18	·27	22
22	Tu	3	10	·97	19	·30	23
23	We	4	...	...	20	·35	24
24	Th	5	11	·00	21	·42	25
25	F	6	12	·07	22	·52	26
26	Sa	7	13	·14	23	·62	27
27	Su	8	14	24	24	·72	28
28	Mo	9	—A	·32	25	·83	29
29	Tu	10	1	·40	26	·93	—30
—30	We	11	2	·46	...	...	1
1	Th	12	Phalguna *Sukla* 3	·53	27	·03	H. 1222 *Muharram.* 2
2	Fr	13	4	·57	1	·09	3
3	Sa	14	5	·58	2	·14	4
4	Su	15	6	·58	3	·17	5
5	Mo	16	7	·56	4	·18	6
6	Tu	17	8	·51	5	·18	7
7	We	18	9	·45	6	·15	8
8	Th	19	10	·37	7	·10	9
9	Fr	20	11	·29	8 9	·05 ·98	10
10	Sa	21	12	·20	10	·92	11
11	Su	22	13 14	·10 ·99	11	·85	12
Kshaya *Mina—Panguni.* 12	Mo	23	P	·91	12	·79	13
13	Tu	24	1	·81	13	·72	14
14	We	25	2	·72	14	·66	15
15	Th	26	3	·65	15	·62	16
16	Fr	27	4	·58	16	·60	17
17	Sa	28	5	·56	17	·58	18
18	Su	29	6	·53	18	·59	19
19	Mo	30	7	·53	19	·61	20
20	Tu	31	8	·55	20	·66	21
		April					
21	We	1	*Bahula* 9	·58	21	·74	22
22	Th	2	10	·65	22	·82	23
23	Fr	3	11	·72	23	92	24
24	Sa	4	12	·81	...	...	25
25	Su	5	13	·89	24	·02	26
26	Mo	6	14	·98	25	·13	27
27	Tu	7	...	...	26	·24	28
28	We	8	—A	·04	27	·33	29
29	Th	9	1	·11	1	·40	—30
—30	Fr	10	2	·14	2	·46	1
Prabhava *Mesha—Chittirai.* 1	Sa	11	Chaitra *Sukla* 3	·14	3	·49	H. 1222 *Safar.* 2
2	Su	12	4	·14	4	·51	3
3	Mo	13	5	·12	5	·50	4
4	Tu	14	6	·07	6	·48	5
5	We	15	7 8	·01 ·94	7	·44	6
6	Th	16	9	·85	8	·39	7
7	Fr	17	10	·75	9	·33	8
8	Sa	18	11	·66	10	·26	9
9	Su	19	12	·55	11	·19	10
10	Mo	20	13	·46	12	·12	11
11	Tu	21	14	·36	13	·06	12
12	We	22	P	.27	14 15	·00 ·96	13
13	Th	23	*Bahula* 1	·19	16	·93	14
14	Fr	24	2	·13	17	·91	15
15	Sa	25	3	·10	18	·91	16
16	Su	26	4	·07	19	·93	17
17	Mo	27	5	·07	20	·98	18
18	Tu	28	6	·09	...	...	19
19	We	29	7	·13	21	·04	20
20	Th	30	8	·18	22	·12	21

SOLAR reckoning: Cyclic Sidereal Year, Month and Day	Week-Day	English Month and Day	LUNAR reckoning: Tithi	Ending Moment	Nakshatra	Ending Moment	Muhammadan Year, Month and Day
		May					
Prabhava *Mesha—Chittirai.* 21	Fr	1	Chait. *Bah.* 9	·25	23	·22	H. 1222 *Safar.* 22
22	Sa	2	10	·33	24	·32	23
23	Su	3	11	·42	25	·44	24
24	Mo	4	12	·50	26	·54	25
25	Tu	5	13	·57	27	·63	26
26	We	6	14	·63	1	·71	27
27	Th	7	—A	·66	2	·77	28
28	Fr	8	1	·68	3	·82	—29
29	Sa	9	2	·67	4	·83	1
30	Su	10	3	·65	5	·83	2
—31	Mo	11	4	·60	6	·81	3
Prabhava *Vrishabha—Vaikasi.* 1	Tu	12	Vaisakha *Sukla* 5	·53	7	·77	H. 1222 *Rabi-ul-awwal.* 4
2	We	13	6	·46	8	·72	5
3	Th	14	7	·37	9	·67	6
4	Fr	15	8	·28	10	·60	7
5	Sa	16	9	·17	11	·53	8
6	Su	17	10 11	·07 ·97	12	·46	9
7	Mo	18	12	·87	13	·39	10
8	Tu	19	13	·79	14	·34	11
9	We	20	14	·71	15	·29	12
10	Th ○	21	P	·65	16	·25	13
11	Fr	22	1	·61	17	·23	14
12	Sa	23	2	·59	18	·23	15
13	Su	24	3	·58	19	·25	16
14	Mo	25	4	·58	20	·29	17
15	Tu	26	5	·64	21	·35	18
16	We	27	6	·69	22	·42	19
17	Th	28	7	·77	23	·52	20
18	Fr	29	8	·83	24	·63	21
19	Sa	30	9	·93	25	·73	22
20	Su	31	...	...	26	·84	23
		June					
21	Mo	1	*Bahula.* 10	·00	27	·93	24
22	Tu	2	11	·06	...	...	25
23	We	3	12	·12	1	·02	26
24	Th	4	13	·15	2	·09	27
25	Fr	5	14	·18	3	·13	28
26	Sa ●	6	—A	·16	4	·15	29
27	Su	7	1	·15	5	·15	—30
28	Mo	8	2	·10	6	·14	1
29	Tu	9	3 4	·05 ·96	7	·10	2
30	We	10	Jyeshtha *Sukla* 5	·87	8	·07	3
31	Th	11	6	·78	9 10	·01 ·94	4
—32	Fr	12	7	·67	11	·87	5
Prabhava *Mithuna—Ani.* 1	Sa	13	8	·57	12	·80	H. 1222 *Rabi-ul-akhir.* 6
2	Su	14	9	·47	13	·74	7
3	Mo	15	10	·37	14	·68	8
4	Tu	16	11	·28	15	·63	9
5	We	17	12	·20	16	·58	10
6	Th	18	13	·14	17	·56	11
7	Fr	19	14	·09	18	·56	12
8	Sa	20	P	·07	19	·57	13
9	Su	21	*Bahula* 1	·06	20	·60	14
10	Mo	22	2	·07	21	·65	15
11	Tu	23	3	·11	22	·73	16
12	We	24	4	·16	23	·82	17
13	Th	25	5	·23	24	·93	18
14	Fr	26	6	·30	...	...	19
15	Sa	27	7	·40	25	·03	20
16	Su	28	8	·47	26	·14	21
17	Mo	29	9	·54	27	·24	22
18	Tu	30	10	·60	1	·32	23

Naksh:—1. Asvn. 2. Bhar. 3. Krit. 4. Rohi. 5, Mrig. 6. Ardh. 7. Punar. 8. Push. 9. Aslesh. 10. Magh. 11. P. Phal. 12. U. Phal. 13. Hasta. 14. Chit.

A. D. 1807.
A.—Amavasya.
P.—Paurnami.

Kollam 983, Commences {**N. Malabar—Sept.** / **S. Malabar—Aug.**}

Hijra 1222, Commences, **March 11.**

Vikrama 1864.
Bengal San 1213.
(N. Cycle) Bahudhanya.

SOLAR reckoning: Cyclic Sidereal Year, Month and Day	Week-Day	English Month and Day	LUNAR reckoning: Tithi	Ending Moment	Nakshatra	Ending Moment	Muhammadan Year, Month and Day
	July						
Prabhava, *Mithuna—Ani.* 19	We	1	Jy. *Bah.* 11	·64	2	·40	*R. akhir.* 24
20	Th	2	12	·65	3	·45	25
21	Fr	3	13	·64	4	·47	26
22	Sa	4	14	·63	5	·48	27
23	Su	5	—A	·57	6	·46	28
24	Mo	6	*Sukla* 1	·52	7	·44	—29
25	Tu	7	2	·44	8	·40	1
26	We	8	3	·35	9	·34	2
27	Th	9	4	·25	10	·28	3
28	Fr	10	5	·15	11	·21	4
29	Sa	11	{6 / 7}	.04 / ·94	12	·15	5
30	Su	12	8	·85	13	·08	6
—31	Mo	13	9	·76	{14 / 15}	·01 / ·96	7
Prabhava, *Karkata—Adi.* 1	Tu	14	**Ashadha** 10	·68	16	·91	8
2	We	15	11	·61	17	·89	9
3	Th	16	12	·58	18	·88	10
4	Fr	17	13	·54	19	·89	11
5	Sa	18	14	·53	20	·92	H. 1222 *Jumadal-awwal.* 12
6	Su	19	P	·55	21	·96	13
7	Mo	20	1	·59	...	...	14
8	Tu	21	2	·65	22	.03	15
9	We	22	3	·70	23	·13	16
10	Th	23	4	·79	24	·22	17
11	Fr	24	5	·87	25	·33	18
12	Sa	25	6	·94	26	·44	19
13	Su	26	...	...	27	·54	20
14	Mo	27	*Bahula* 7	·01	1	·63	21
15	Tu	28	8	·07	2	·71	22
16	We	29	9	·12	3	·76	23
17	Th	30	10	·18	4	·79	24
18	Fr	31	11	·13	5	·80	25
	Aug.						
19	Sa	1	12	·11	6	·80	26
20	Su	2	13	.05	7	·77	27
21	Mo	3	{14 / A}	·00 / ·93	8	·73	28
22	Tu	4	*Sukla* 1	·85	9	·68	29
23	We	5	2	·74	10	·62	—30
24	Th	6	3	·65	11	·56	1
25	Fr	7	4	·54	12	·49	2
26	Sa	8	5	·45	13	·42	3
27	Su	9	6	·34	14	·35	4
28	Mo	10	7	·25	15	·29	5
29	Tu	11	8	·18	16	·25	6
30	We	12	9	·10	17	·22	7
31	Th	13	10	·07	18	·21	8
—32	Fr	14	11	·03	19	·21	9
Prabhava, *Simha—Avani.* 1	Sa	15	**Sravana** 12	·03	20	·23	H. 1222 *Jumadal-akhir.* 10
2	Su	16	13	·03	21	·27	11
3	Mo	17	14	·07	22	·35	12
4	Tu	18	P	·13	23	·43	13
5	We	19	1	·19	24	·52	14
6	Th	20	2	·28	25	·63	15
7	Fr	21	3	·36	26	·73	16
8	Sa	22	4	·45	27	·85	17
9	Su	23	5	·51	1	·94	18
10	Mo	24	6	·56	...	...	19
11	Tu	25	7	·61	2	·01	20
12	We	26	8	·63	3	·07	21
13	Th	27	*Bahula* 9	·63	4	·11	22
14	Fr	28	10	·61	5	·13	23
15	Sa	29	11	·57	6	·13	24
16	Su	30	12	·51	7	·10	25
17	Mo	31	13	·44	8	·07	26

SOLAR reckoning: Cyclic Sidereal Year, Month and Day	Week-Day	English Month and Day	LUNAR reckoning: Tithi	Ending Moment	Nakshatra	Ending Moment	Muhammadan Year, Month and Day
	Sep.						
Prabhava, *Simha—Avani.* 18	Tu	1	14	·35	{9 / 10}	·02 / ·96	*J. akr.* 27
19	We	2	—A	·25	11	·90	28
20	Th	3	*Sukla* 1	·15	12	·83	—29
21	Fr	4	{2 / 3}	·05 / ·96	13	·75	1
22	Sa	5	4	·86	14	·69	2
23	Su	6	5	·77	15	·63	3
24	Mo	7	6	·69	16	·59	4
25	Tu	8	7	·62	17	·55	5
26	We	9	8	·58	18	·53	6
27	Th	10	9	·55	19	·53	7
28	Fr	11	10	·55	20	·55	8
29	Sa	12	11	·55	21	·59	9
30	Su	13	**Bhadrapada** 12	·60	22	·65	10
—31	Mo	14	13	·65	23	·73	11
Prabhava, *Kanya—Purattasi.* 1	Tu	15	14	·71	24	·82	H. 1222 *Rajab.* 12
2	We	16	P	·80	25	·93	13
3	Th	17	1	·88	...	...	14
4	Fr	18	2	·96	26	·04	15
5	Sa	19	...	...	27	·14	16
6	Su	20	3	·03	1	·24	17
7	Mo	21	4	·10	2	·32	18
8	Tu	22	*Bahula* 5	·14	3	·38	19
9	We	23	6	·16	4	·43	20
10	Th	24	7	·16	5	·45	21
11	Fr	25	8	·14	6	·45	22
12	Sa	26	9	·11	7	·43	23
13	Su	27	{10 / 11}	·04 / ·98	8	·40	24
14	Mo	28	12	·89	9	·35	25
15	Tu	29	13	·80	10	·30	26
16	We	30	14	·70	11	·23	27
	Oct.						
17	Th	1	—A	·60	12	·16	28
18	Fr	2	*Sukla* 1	·50	13	·09	29
19	Sa	3	2	·40	{14 / 15}	·03 / ·97	—30
20	Su	4	3	.32	16	·92	1
21	Mo	5	4	·24	17	·88	2
22	Tu	6	5	·18	18	·86	3
23	We	7	6	·12	19	·85	4
24	Th	8	7	·11	20	·87	5
25	Fr	9	8	·10	21	·91	6
26	Sa	10	9	·11	22	·96	7
27	Su	11	10	·16	...	...	8
28	Mo	12	11	·21	23	·03	9
29	Tu	13	12	·28	24	·13	10
—30	We	14	13	·38	25	.23	11
Prabhava, *Tula—Aippasi.* 1	Th	15	**Asvina** 14	·45	26	·34	H. 1222 *Shaban.* 12
2	Fr	16	P	·53	27	·45	13
3	Sa	17	1	·61	1	·54	14
4	Su	18	2	·67	2	·63	15
5	Mo	19	3	·71	3	·70	16
6	Tu	20	4	·74	4	·75	17
7	We	21	5	·73	5	·77	18
8	Th	22	6	·73	6	·78	19
9	Fr	23	7	·68	7	·76	20
10	Sa	24	8	·62	8	·73	21
11	Su	25	*Bahula* 9	·56	9	·69	22
12	Mo	26	10	·47	10	·64	23
13	Tu	27	11	·38	11	·57	24
14	We	28	12	·27	12	·50	25
15	Th	29	13	·18	13	·43	26
16	Fr	30	14	·08	14	·37	27
17	Sa	31	{A / 1}	·00 / ·91	15	·31	28

SOLAR reckoning: Cyclic Sidereal Year, Month and Day	Week-Day	English Month and Day	LUNAR reckoning: Tithi	Ending Moment	Nakshatra	Ending Moment	Muhammadan Year, Month and Day
	Nov.						
Prabhava, *Tula—Aippasi.* 18	Su	1	*Sukla* 2	·83	16	·25	—29
19	Mo	2	3	·77	17	·21	1
20	Tu	3	4	·71	18	·18	2
21	We	4	5	·71	19	·18	3
22	Th	5	6	·70	20	·19	4
23	Fr	6	7	·71	21	·22	5
24	Sa	7	8	·75	22	·27	6
25	Su	8	9	·80	23	·34	7
26	Mo	9	10	·89	24	·43	8
27	Tu	10	11	·97	25	·53	9
28	We	11	...	...	26	·64	10
29	Th	12	**Karttika** 12	·06	27	·74	H. 1222 *Ramzan.* 11
—30	Fr	13	13	·14	1	·84	12
Prabhava, *Vrischika—Kartigai.* 1	Sa	14	14	·22	2	·93	13
2	Su ○	15	P	·28	...	...	14
3	Mo	16	1	·32	3	·01	15
4	Tu	17	2	·35	4	·06	16
5	We	18	3	·34	5	·09	17
6	Th	19	4	·34	6	·10	18
7	Fr	20	*Bahula* 5	·29	7	·09	19
8	Sa	21	6	·24	8	·07	20
9	Su	22	7	·17	{9 / 10}	·03 / ·97	21
10	Mo	23	8	·09	11	·91	22
11	Tu	24	{9 / 10}	·00 / ·89	12	·84	23
12	We	25	11	·80	13	·78	24
13	Th	26	12	·69	14	·71	25
14	Fr	27	13	·62	15	·65	26
15	Sa	28	14	·52	16	·59	27
16	Su ●	29	—A	·45	17	·54	28
17	Mo	30	1	·38	18	·52	29
	Dec.						
18	Tu	1	*Sukla* 2	·34	19	·50	—30
19	We	2	3	·33	20	·51	1
20	Th	3	4	·32	21	·53	2
21	Fr	4	5	·34	22	·58	3
22	Sa	5	6	·39	23	·64	4
23	Su	6	7	·44	24	·73	5
24	Mo	7	8	·51	25	·83	6
25	Tu	8	9	·60	26	·94	7
26	We	9	10	·69	...	...	8
27	Th	10	11	·77	27	·04	9
28	Fr	11	**Margasira** 12	·86	1	·14	10
29	Sa	12	13	·92	2	·24	11
—30	Su	13	14	·97	3	·32	H. 1222 *Shawwal.* 12
Prabhava, *Dhanus—Margali.* 1	Mo	14	P	·98	4	·37	13
2	Tu	15	1	99	5	·41	14
3	We	16	2	·97	6	·42	15
4	Th	17	3	·92	7	·43	16
5	Fr	18	4	·87	8	·40	17
6	Sa	19	5	·80	9	·36	18
7	Su	20	6	·71	10	·31	19
8	Mo	21	7	·62	11	·25	20
9	Tu	22	*Bahula* 8	·53	12	·19	21
10	We	23	9	·43	13	·12	22
11	Th	24	10	·32	{14 / 15}	·05 / ·98	23
12	Fr	25	11	·24	16	·92	24
13	Sa	26	12	·15	17	·88	25
14	Su	27	13	·09	18	·85	26
15	Mo	28	{14 / A}	·03 / ·99	19	·83	27
16	Tu	29	*P. Suk.* 1	·97	20	·83	28
17	We	30	2	·98	21	·85	—29
18	Th	31	3	·99	22	·89	1

15. Svati. 16. Visak. 17. Anur. 18. Jyesh. 19. Mula. 20. P. Ash. 21. U. Ash. 22. Sravn. 23. Dani. 24. Satab. 25. P. Bhad. 26. U. Bhad. 27 Rev.

A. D. 1808. **Mesha Sankranti.** (Commencement of Indian Sidereal Year).

Solar Eclipse. ● **(Surya Sid.) April 10·81.** **Saka 1730.** **Kaliyuga 4909.**

Lunar Eclipse. ○ **(Arya Sid.) April 10·71.** **(S. Cycle) Vibhava.**

Columns: SOLAR reckoning — Cyclic Sidereal Year, Month and Day; Week-Day; English Month and Day. LUNAR reckoning — Tithi; Ending Moment; Nakshatra; Ending Moment; Muhammadan Year, Month and Day.

Jan.

Cyclic Sidereal Year, Month and Day	Week-Day	English Month and Day	Tithi	Ending Moment	Nakshatra	Ending Moment	Muhammadan Year, Month and Day
Prabhava *Dhanus–Margali.* 19	Fr	1	...	...	23	·96	2
20	Sa	2	4	·02	...	...	3
21	Su	3	5	·09	24	·04	4
22	Mo	4	6	·17	25	·13	5
23	Tu	5	7	·26	26	·23	6
24	We	6	*Sukla* 8	·34	27	·34	7
25	Th	7	9	·44	1	·45	8
26	Fr	8	10	·51	2	·55	9
27	Sa	9	11	·56	3	·63	10
28	Su	10	12	·62	4	·68	11
—29	Mo	11	13	·63	5	·72	12
1	Tu	12	14	·63	6	·75	13
2	We	13	P	·62	7	·75	14
3	Th	14	**Pausha** 1	·58	8	·73	15
4	Fr	15	2	·51	9	·69	16
5	Sa	16	3	·43	10	·65	H. 1222 *Zi-l-ka'da.* 17
6	Su	17	4	·36	11	·60	18
7	Mo	18	5	·27	12	.53	19
8	Tu	19	6	·17	13	·46	20
9	We	20	{ 7 8	.07 .97	14	·30	21
10	Th	21	9	.88	15	·32	22
11	Fr	22	10	80	16	·26	23
12	Sa	23	*Bahula* 11	·73	17	·22	24
13	Su	24	12	·67	18	·18	25
Prabhava *Makara–Tai.* 14	Mo	25	13	·63	19	·15	26
15	Tu	26	14	·61	20	·15	27
16	We	27	—A	·62	21	·16	28
17	Th	28	1	·63	22	·21	29
18	Fr	29	*Sukla* 2	·69	23	·26	—30
19	Sa	30	3	·74	24	·34	1
20	Su	31	4	·82	25	·43	2

Feb.

Cyclic Sidereal Year, Month and Day	Week-Day	English Month and Day	Tithi	Ending Moment	Nakshatra	Ending Moment	Muhammadan Year, Month and Day
21	Mo	1	5	·91	26	.53	3
22	Tu	2	6	·99	27	·65	4
23	We	3	...	...	1	·75	5
24	Th	4	7	·08	2	·85	6
25	Fr	5	8	·16	3	·93	7
26	Sa	6	9	·22	...	...	8
27	Su	7	10	·25	4	·00	9
28	Mo	8	11	·26	5	·05	10
29	Tu	9	12	·27	6	·07	11
—30	We	10	13	·25	7	·08	12
1	Th	11	14	·21	8	·06	13
2	Fr	12	**Magha** P	·13	9 10	·03 ·99 }	*Zi-l-hijja.* 14
3	Sa	13	{ 1 2	·06 ·98	11	·93	15
4	Su	14	3	·89	12	·87	H. 1222 16
5	Mo	15	4	·79	13	·80	17
6	Tu	16	5	·69	14	·73	18
7	We	17	6	·60	15	·66	19
8	Th	18	7	·50	16	·60	20
9	Fr	19	*Bahula* 8	·42	17	·55	21
10	Sa	20	9	·35	18	·51	22
11	Su	21	10	·30	19	·48	23
Prabhava *Kumbha–Masi.* 12	Mo	22	11	·25	20	·47	24
13	Tu	23	12	·24	21	·49	25
14	We	24	13	·24	22	·52	26
15	Th	25	14	·26	23	·57	27
16	Fr	26	—A	·31	24	·64	28
17	Sa	27	1	·36	25	·78	—29
18	Su	28	*P. Suk.* 2	·44	26	·84	1
19	Mo	29	3	·54	27	·95	2

March

Cyclic Sidereal Year, Month and Day	Week-Day	English Month and Day	Tithi	Ending Moment	Nakshatra	Ending Moment	Muhammadan Year, Month and Day
20	Tu	1	4	·62	...	...	3
21	We	2	5	·70	1	·05	4
22	Th	3	6	·77	2	·15	5
23	Fr	4	*Sukla* 7	·83	3	·24	6
Prabhava *Kumbha–Masi.* 24	Sa	5	8	·87	4	·31	7
25	Su	6	9	·88	5	·36	8
26	Mo	7	10	·88	6	·39	9
27	Tu	8	11	·85	7	·40	10
28	We	9	12	·81	8	·39	11
29	Th	10	13	·74	9	·36	12
—30	Fr	11	14	·67	10	·32	13
1	Sa	12	P	·58	11	·27	14
2	Su	13	**Phalguna** 1	·49	12	·20	15
3	Mo	14	2	·39	13	·14	16
4	Tu	15	3	·30	14	·06	17
5	We	16	4	·19	15 16	·00 ·94 }	H. 1223 *Muharram.* 18
6	Th	17	5	·09	17	·88	19
7	Fr ●	18	{ 6 7	·01 ·94	18	.84	20
8	Sa	29	8	·89	19	·81	21
9	Su	20	9	·85	20	·80	22
10	Mo	21	*Bahula* 10	·84	21	·81	23
11	Tu	22	11	·83	22	·83	24
12	We	23	12	·86	23	·88	25
Prabhava *Mina–Panguni.* 13	Th	24	13	·90	24	·95	26
14	Fr	25	14	·95	...	...	27
15	Sa	26	...	...	25	·04	28
16	Su	27	—A	·04	26	·14	29
17	Mo	28	1	·12	27	·24	—30
18	Tu	29	2	·21	1	·35	1
19	We	30	*Sukla* 3	·29	2	·45	2
20	Th	31	4	·36	3	·55	3

April

Cyclic Sidereal Year, Month and Day	Week-Day	English Month and Day	Tithi	Ending Moment	Nakshatra	Ending Moment	Muhammadan Year, Month and Day
21	Fr	1	5	·41	4	·62	4
22	Sa	2	6	·45	5	·68	5
23	Su	3	7	·45	6	·71	6
24	Mo	4	8	·45	7	·72	7
25	Tu	5	9	·42	8	·71	8
26	We	6	**Chaitra** 10	·38	9	·70	9
27	Th	7	11	·32	10	·66	10
28	Fr	8	12	·24	11	·60	11
29	Sa	9	13	·15	12	·54	12
—30	Su	10	{ 14 P	·06 ·95	13	·47	*Safar.* 13
1	Mo	11	1	·85	14	·41	14
2	Tu	12	2	·75	15	·34	H. 1223 15
3	We	13	3	·66	16	·28	16
4	Th	14	4	·57	17	·22	17
5	Fr	15	5	·50	18	·17	18
6	Sa	16	6	·44	19	·15	19
7	Su	17	7	.40	20	·13	20
8	Mo	18	*Bahula* 8	·39	21	·13	21
9	Tu	19	9	·38	22	·15	22
10	We	20	10	·42	23	·19	23
Vibhava *Mesha–Chittirai.* 11	Th	21	11	·45	24	·26	24
12	Fr	22	12	·50	25	·34	25
13	Sa	23	13	·57	26	·44	26
14	Su	24	14	·66	27	·54	27
15	Mo	25	—A	·75	1	·65	28
16	Tu	26	1	·82	2	·75	—29
17	We	27	*V. Suk.* 2	·90	3	·85	1
18	Th	28	3	·95	4	·93	*R-awwal.* 2
19	Fr	29	...	...	5	·99	3
20	Sa	30	{ 4 5	·00 ·99	...	...	4

May

Cyclic Sidereal Year, Month and Day	Week-Day	English Month and Day	Tithi	Ending Moment	Nakshatra	Ending Moment	Muhammadan Year, Month and Day
21	Su	1	6	·98	6	·03	5
22	Mo	2	*Sukla* 7	·96	7	·04	6
Vibhava *Mesha–Chittirai.* 23	Tu	3	8	·91	8	·05	7
24	We	4	9	·85	9 10	·03 ·99 }	8
25	Th	5	10	·77	11	·94	9
26	Fr	6	11	·68	12	·88	10
27	Sa	7	12	·58	13	·82	11
28	Su	8	13	·49	14	·75	12
29	Mo	9	14	·38	15	·68	13
30	Tu ○	10	**Vaisakha** P	·26	16	·61	14
—31	We	11	1	·18	17	·55	15
1	Th	12	2	·09	18	·51	16
2	Fr	13	{ 3 4	·02 ·97	19	·47	*Rabi-ul-awwal.* 17
3	Sa	14	5	·93	20	·45	H. 1223 18
4	Su	15	6	·90	21	·45	19
5	Mo	16	*Bahula* 7	·89	22	·46	20
6	Tu	17	8	·93	23	·51	21
7	We	18	9	·96	24	·57	22
8	Th	19	...	...	25	·64	23
9	Fr	20	10	·03	26	·74	24
10	Sa	21	11	·08	27	·84	25
11	Su	22	12	·17	1	·95	26
12	Mo	23	13	·26	...	...	27
13	Tu	24	14	·33	2	·06	28
Vibhava *Vrishabha–Vaikasi.* 14	We	25	—A	·40	3	·16	29
15	Th	26	1	·45	4	·24	—30
16	Fr	27	2	·49	5	·30	1
17	Sa	28	3	·50	6	·34	2
18	Su	29	*Sukla* 4	·50	.7	·37	3
19	Mo	30	5	·46	8	·37	4
20	Tu	31	6	·43	9	·36	5

June

Cyclic Sidereal Year, Month and Day	Week-Day	English Month and Day	Tithi	Ending Moment	Nakshatra	Ending Moment	Muhammadan Year, Month and Day
21	We	1	7	·36	10	·32	6
22	Th	2	8	·26	11	·27	7
23	Fr	3	9	·18	12	·23	8
24	Sa	4	{ 10 11	·08 ·99	13	·16	9
25	Su	5	12	·87	14	·09	10
26	Mo	6	13	·78	15 16	·02 ·95 }	11
27	Tu	7	14	·69	17	·90	12
28	We	8	P	·60	18	·84	13
29	Th	9	1	·52	19	·80	14
30	Fr	10	**Jyeshtha** 2	·46	20	·78	*Rabi-ul-akhir.* 15
—31	Sa	11	3	·42	21	·77	16
1	Su	12	4	·39	22	·78	H. 1223 17
2	Mo	13	5	·39	23	·82	18
3	Tu	14	6	·41	24	·88	19
4	We	15	7	·44	25	·95	20
5	Th	16	8	·50	...	...	21
6	Fr	17	*Bahula* 9	·57	26	·04	22
7	Sa	18	10	·65	27	·14	23
8	Su	19	11	·73	1	·25	24
9	Mo	20	12	·81	2	·36	25
Vibhava *Mithuna–Ani.* 10	Tu	21	13	·88	3	·46	26
11	We	22	14	·93	4	·54	27
12	Th	23	—A	·97	5	·61	28
13	Fr	24	1	·98	6	·67	—29
14	Sa	25	*Suk.* 2	·97	7	·69	1
15	Su	26	3	·94	8	·70	2
16	Mo	27	**Ashad.** 4	·91	9	·68	*J-awwal.* 3
17	Tu	28	5	·83	10	·65	4
18	We	29	6	·76	11	·62	5
19	Th	30	7	·67	12	·56	6

Naksh :—1. Asvn. 2. Bhar. 3. Krit. 4. Rohi. 5. Mrig. 6. Ardh. 7. Punar. 8. Push. 9. Aslesh. 10. Magh. 11. P. Phal. 12. U. Phal. 13. Hasta. 14. Chit.

A. D. 1808.		Hijra 1223,	Vikrama 1865.
A.—Amavasya.	Kollam 984, Commences { N. Malabar—Sept. S. Malabar—Aug.	Commences, Feb. 28.	Bengal San 1214.
P.—Paurnami.			(N. Cycle) Pramathin.

SOLAR reckoning. Cyclic Sidereal Year, Month and Day.	Week-Day	English Month and Day.	LUNAR reckoning. Tithi	Ending Moment.	Nakshatra	Ending Moment.	Muhammadan Year, Month and Day.
	July						
Vibhava Mithuna—Ani. 20	Fr	1	8	·57	13	·50	7
21	Sa	2	9	·46	14	·43	8
22	Su	3	Sukla 10	·36	15	·36	9
23	Mo	4	11	·27	16	·29	10
24	Tu	5	12	·16	17	·23	11
25	We	6	13	·08	18	·18	12
26	Th	7	{14 P	·00 ·94	19	·13	H. 1223 Jumadal-awval. 13
27	Fr	8	Ashadha 1	·89	20	·10	14
28	Sa	9	2	·87	21	·09	15
29	Su	10	3	·86	22	·10	16
30	Mo	11	4	·88	23	·14	17
31	Tu	12	5	·92	24	·18	18
—32	We	13	6	·98	25	·25	19
1	Th	14	...	...	26	·34	20
2	Fr	15	7	·05	27	·45	21
3	Sa	16	8	·13	1	·55	22
4	Su	17	Bahula 9	·19	2	·66	23
5	Mo	18	10	·27	3	76	24
6	Tu	19	11	·35	4	·85	25
7	We	20	12	·42	5	·93	26
8	Th	21	13	·45	6	·98	27
9	Fr	22	14	·46	...	...	28
10	Sa	23	—A	·45	7	·01	29
11	Su	24	1	·42	8	·02	—30
Vibhava Karkata—Adi. 12	Mo	25	2	·38	9 10	·01 ·99}	1
13	Tu	26	Sukla 3	·31	11	·95	2
14	We	27	4	·24	12	·90	3
15	Th	28	5	·16	13	·84	4
16	Fr	29	{6 7	·06 ·96	14	·77	5
17	Sa	30	8	·86	15	·70	6
18	Su	31	9	·76	16	·64	7
	Aug.						
19	Mo	1	10	·65	17	·57	8
20	Tu	2	11	·57	18	·51	H. 1223 Jumadal-akhir. 9
21	We	3	Sravana 12	·49	19	·47	10
22	Th	4	13	·43	20	·43	11
23	Fr	5	14	·37	21	·42	12
24	Sa	6	P	·36	22	·43	13
25	Su	7	1	·35	23	·45	14
26	Mo	8	2	·36	24	·49	15
27	Tu	9	3	·39	25	·56	16
28	We	10	4	·45	26	·65	17
29	Th	11	5	·53	27	·74	18
30	Fr	12	6	·61	1	·85	19
—31	Sa	13	Bahula 7	·70	2	·96	20
1	Su	14	8	·77	...	...	21
2	Mo	15	9	·83	3	·06	22
3	Tu	16	10	·90	4	·16	23
4	We	17	11	·93	5	·23	24
5	Th	18	12	96	6	·29	25
6	Fr	19	13	·94	7	·33	26
Vibhava Simha—Avani. 7	Sa	20	14	·92	8	·31	27
8	Su	21	—A	·88	9	·34	28
9	Mo	22	1	·83	10	·32	—29
10	Tu	23	Sukla. 2	·75	11	·29	1
11	We	24	3	·65	12	·23	H. 1223 Rajab. 2
12	Th	25	4	·56	13	·17	3
13	Fr	26	Bhad. 5	·46	14	·11	4
14	Sa	27	6	·36	15 16	·05 ·97}	5
15	Su	28	7	·26	17	·91	6
16	Mo	29	8	·17	18	·85	7
17	Tu	30	{9 10	·07 ·99	19	·80	8
18	We	31	11	·94	20	·77	9

SOLAR reckoning. Cyclic Sidereal Year, Month and Day.	Week-Day	English Month and Day.	LUNAR reckoning. Tithi	Ending Moment.	Nakshatra	Ending Moment.	Muhammadan Year, Month and Day.
	Sep.						
19	Th	1	Suk. 12	·88	21	·75	10
20	Fr	2	13	·87	22	·75	11
21	Sa	3	14	·86	23	·77	12
Vibhava Simha—Avani. 22	Su	4	Bhadrapada P	·88	24	·80	13
23	Mo	5	1	·91	25	·87	14
24	Tu	6	2	·97	26	·95	15
25	We	7	...	...	...	...	H. 1223 Rajab. 16
26	Th	8	3	·03	27	·04	17
27	Fr	9	4	·11	1	·15	18
28	Sa	10	5	·20	2	·25	19
29	Su	11	6	·28	3	·37	20
30	Mo	12	7	·36	4	·46	21
—31	Tu	13	8	·42	5	·54	22
1	We	14	Bahula 9	·48	6	·60	23
2	Th	15	10	·48	7	·64	24
3	Fr	16	11	·47	8	·66	25
4	Sa	17	12	·45	9	·67	26
5	Su	18	13	·41	10	+65	27
6	Mo	19	14	·35	11	·62	28
7	Tu	20	—A	·27	12	·57	29
Vibhava Kanya—Purattasi. 8	We	21	1	·19	13	·51	—30
9	Th	22	2	·09	14	·45	1
10	Fr	23	{3 4	·00 ·90	15	·38	2
11	Sa	24	5	·79	16	·31	3
12	Su	25	Sukla 6	·70	17	·24	4
13	Mo	26	7	·61	18	·18	5
14	Tu	27	8	·54	19	·14	6
15	We	28	9	·48	20	·09	7
16	Th	29	10	·43	21	·08	8
17	Fr	30	11	·41	22	·07	9
	Oct.						
18	Sa	1	12	·40	23	·08	10
19	Su	2	Asvina 13	·42	24	·13	H. 1223 Shaban. 11
20	Mo	3	14	·45	25	·18	12
21	Tu	4	P	·51	26	·25	13
22	We	5	1	·58	27	·34	14
23	Th	6	2	·67	1	·44	15
24	Fr	7	3	·75	2	·55	16
25	Sa	8	4	·83	3	·67	17
26	Su	9	5	·90	4	·76	18
27	Mo	10	6	·98	5	·85	19
28	Tu	11	...	...	6	·91	20
29	We	12	Bahula 7	·02	7	·96	21
30	Th	13	8	·04	8	·99	22
—31	Fr	14	9	·04	...	...	23
1	Sa	15	{10 11	·01 ·97	9 10	·00 ·98}	24
2	Su	16	12	·92	11	·95	25
3	Mo	17	13	·84	12	·90	26
4	Tu	18	14	·76	13	·86	27
Vibhava Tula—Aippasi 5	We	19	—A	·66	14	·79	28
6	Th	20	1	·57	15	·72	—29
7	Fr	21	2	·46	16	·65	1
8	Sa	22	3	·38	17	·58	2
9	Su	23	Sukla 4	·28	18	·53	H. 1223 Ramzan. 3
10	Mo	24	5	·19	19	·47	4
11	Tu	25	6	·12	20	·43	5
12	We	26	7	·06	21	·40	6
13	Th	27	{8 9	·01 ·99	22	·39	7
14	Fr	28	Kartt. 10	·99	23	·41	8
15	Sa	29	...	...	24	.44	9
16	Su	30	11	·01	25	·49	10
17	Mo	31	12	·04	26	·56	11

SOLAR reckoning. Cyclic Sidereal Year, Month and Day.	Week-Day	English Month and Day.	LUNAR reckoning. Tithi	Ending Moment.	Nakshatra	Ending Moment.	Muhammadan Year, Month and Day.
	Nov.						
18	Tu	1	Karttika 13	·11	27	·64	12
19	We	2	14	·18	1	·74	13
20	Th ○	3	P	·27	2	·86	14
Vibhava Tula—Aippasi. 21	Fr	4	1	·34	3	·96	15
22	Sa	5	2	·45	...	...	16
23	Su	6	3	·52	4	·06	H. 1223 Ramzan. 17
24	Mo	7	4	·57	5	·15	18
25	Tu	8	5	·61	6	·22	19
26	We	9	6	·63	7	·28	20
27	Th	10	7	·64	8	·31	21
28	Fr	11	Bahula 8	·61	9	·32	22
29	Sa	12	9	·57	10	·31	23
—30	Su	13	10	·52	11	·28	24
1	Mo	14	11	·45	12	·25	25
2	Tu	15	12	·37	13	·19	26
3	We	16	13	·27	14	·13	27
4	Th	17	14	·17	15 16	·06 ·99}	28
5	Fr ●	18	{A 1	·07 ·99	17	·93	29
6	Sa	19	2	·89	18	·86	—30
7	Su	20	3	·81	19	·81	1
8	Mo	21	4	·73	20	·76	2
9	Tu	22	5	·67	21	·73	3
Vibhava Vrischika—Kartigai. 10	We	23	6	·63	22	·71	4
11	Th	24	7	·61	23	·73	5
12	Fr	25	Sukla 8	.61	24	·75	6
13	Sa	26	9	·64	25	·80	7
14	Su	27	10	·67	26	·86	8
15	Mo	28	11	·73	27	·94	9
16	Tu	29	12	·80	...	...	10
17	We	30	13	·90	1	·05	11
	Dec.						
18	Th	1	Margasira 14	·98	2	·16	12
19	Fr	2	...	...	3	·26	13
20	Sa	3	P	·07	4	·36	14
21	Su	4	1	·14	5	·45	15
22	Mo	5	2	·21	6	·54	16
23	Tu	6	3	·25	7	·59	H. 1223 Shawval. 17
24	We	7	4	·27	8	·63	18
25	Th	8	5	·26	9	·64	19
26	Fr	9	6	·24	10	·64	20
27	Sa	10	7	·20	11	·62	21
28	Su	11	8	·14	12	·58	22
—29	Mo	12	{9 10	·07 ·99	13	·53	23
1	Tu	13	Bahula 11	·90	14	·47	24
2	We	14	12	·79	15	·40	25
3	Th	15	13	·70	16	·34	26
4	Fr	16	14	·61	17	·27	27
5	Sa	17	—A	·51	18	·20	28
6	Su	18	1	·44	19	·14	—29
7	Mo	19	2	·36	20	·09	1
8	Tu	20	3	·31	21	·06	2
9	We	21	Sukla 4	·26	22	·05	3
Vibhava Dhanus—Margali. 10	Th	22	5	·26	23	·05	4
11	Fr	23	6	·25	24	·07	5
12	Sa	24	7	·27	25	·11	6
13	Su	25	8	·33	26	·17	H. 1223 Zi-l-ka'da. 7
14	Mo	26	Pausha 9	·38	27	·26	8
15	Tu	27	10	·46	1	·35	9
16	We	28	11	·55	2	·45	10
17	Th	29	12	·64	3	·56	11
18	Fr	30	13	·72	4	·66	12
19	Sa	31	14	·80	5	·77	13

15. Svati. 16. Visak. 17. Anur. 18. Jyesh. 19. Mula. 20. P. Ash. 21. U. Ash. 22. Sravn. 23. Dani. 24. Satab. 25. P. Bhad. 26. U. Bhad. 27. Rev.

A. D. 1809. **Mesha Sankranti.** (Commencement of Indian Sidereal Year).
Solar Eclipse. ● (Surya Sid.) April 11·07. **Saka 1731.** **Kaliyuga 4910.**
Lunar Eclipse. ○ (Arya Sid.) April 10·97. (S. Cycle) **Sukla.**

SOLAR reckoning.			LUNAR reckoning.				
Cyclic Sidereal Year, Month and Day.	Week-Day	English Month and Day.	Tithi	Ending Moment.	Nakshatra	Ending Moment.	Muhammadan Year, Month and Day.
		Jan.					
Vibhava *Dhanus—Margali.* 20	Su	1	**Pausha** P	.86	6	·85	H. 1223 *Zi-l-ka'da.* 14
21	Mo	2	1	·89	7	·91	15
22	Tu	3	2	·91	8	·94	16
23	We	4	3	·91	9	·96	17
24	Th	5	4	·89	10	·97	18
25	Fr	6	5	·84	11	·94	19
26	Sa	7	6	·79	12	·91	20
27	Su	8	7	·72	13	·86	21
28	Mo	9	*Bahula* 8	·63	14	·80	22
—29	Tu	10	9	·55	15	·74	23
Vibhava *Makara—Tai.* 1	We	11	10	·44	16	·68	24
2	Th	12	11	·35	17	·61	25
3	Fr	13	12	·25	18	·54	26
4	Sa	14	13	·17	19	·48	27
5	Su	15	14	·08	20	·43	28
6	Mo	16	{ A 1	·00 ·96	21	·40	29
7	Tu	17	2	·91	22	·37	—30
8	We	18	3	·90	23	37	*Zi-l-hijja.* 1
9	Th	19	4	·90	24	·38	2
10	Fr	20	5	·93	25	·42	3
11	Sa	21	*Sukla* 6	·96	26	·48	4
12	Su	22	...	...	27	·56	5
13	Mo	23	7	·03	1	·65	6
14	Tu	24	8	·12	2	·75	7
15	We	25	9	·20	3	·86	8
16	Th	26	10	·29	4	·97	9
17	Fr	27	11	·38	...	...	10
18	Sa	28	**Magha** 12	·46	5	·07	11
19	Su	29	13	·51	6	·15	12
20	Mo	30	14	·53	7	·22	13
21	Tu	31	P	·56	8	·26	14
		Feb.					
22	We	1	*Bahula* 1	·55	9	·28	H. 1223 15
23	Th	2	2	·53	10	·29	16
24	Fr	3	3	·48	11	·28	17
25	Sa	4	4	·42	12	·25	18
26	Su	5	5	·35	13	·20	19
27	Mo	6	6	·27	14	·14	20
28	Tu	7	7	·17	15	·09	21
29	We	8	{ 8 9	·06 ·98	16 17	·02 ·95 }	22
—30	Th	9	10	·87	18	·88	23
Vibhava *Kumbha—Masi.* 1	Fr	10	11	·79	19	·81	24
2	Sa	11	12	·70	20	·77	25
3	Su	12	13	·63	21	·73	26
4	Mo	13	14	·59	22	·70	27
5	Tu	14	—A	·54	23	·69	28
6	We	15	1	·53	24	·70	—29
7	Th	16	2	·52	25	·74	H. 1224 *Muharram.* 1
8	Fr	17	3	·57	26	·79	2
9	Sa	18	4	·61	27	·86	3
10	Su	19	*Sukla* 5	·67	1	·95	4
11	Mo	20	6	·74	...	...	5
12	Tu	21	7	·82	2	·05	6
13	We	22	8	·91	3	·17	7
14	Th	23	...	...	4	·27	8
15	Fr	24	9	·00	5	·37	9
16	Sa	25	**Phalguna** 10	·08	6	·46	10
17	Su	26	11	·13	7	·52	11
18	Mo	27	12	·17	8	·57	12
19	Tu	28	13	·17	9	·61	13

SOLAR reckoning.			LUNAR reckoning.				
Cyclic Sidereal Year, Month and Day.	Week-Day	English Month and Day.	Tithi	Ending Moment.	Nakshatra	Ending Moment.	Muhammadan Year, Month and Day.
		March					
Vibhava *Kumbha—Masi.* 20	We	1	*Suk.* 14	·17	10	·62	H. 1224 *Muharram.* 14
21	Th	2	P	·15	11	·61	15
22	Fr	3	**Phalg.** 1	·09	12	·58	16
23	Sa	4	{ 2 3	·04 ·96	13	·53	17
24	Su	5	4	·88	14	·49	18
25	Mo	6	5	·78	15	·42	19
26	Tu	7	6	·68	16	·35	20
27	We	8	7	·59	17	·28	21
28	Th	9	8	·48	18	·21	22
29	Fr	10	9	·40	19	·16	23
—30	Sa	11	10	·31	20	·10	24
Vibhava *Mina—Panguni.* 1	Su	12	*Bahula* 11	·24	21	·06	25
2	Mo	13	12	·18	22	·03	26
3	Tu	14	13	·15	23	·01	27
4	We	15	14	·13	24	·03	28
5	Th	16	—A	·13	25	·05	29
6	Fr	17	1	·16	26	·10	—30
7	Sa	18	2	·20	27	·17	*Safar.* 1
8	Su	19	3	·26	1	·25	2
9	Mo	20	4	·35	2	·35	3
10	Tu	21	*Sukla* 5	·44	3	·46	4
11	We	22	6	·52	4	·57	5
12	Th	23	7	·61	5	·67	6
13	Fr	24	8	·67	6	·76	7
14	Sa	25	9	·72	7	·83	8
15	Su	26	10	·76	8	·90	9
16	Mo	27	**Chaitra** 11	·75	9	·93	10
17	Tu	28	12	·76	10	·94	11
18	We	29	13	·72	11	·93	12
19	Th	30	14	·68	12	·91	13
20	Fr	31	P	·62	13	·88	14
		April					
21	Sa	1	1	·54	14	·82	H. 1224 15
22	Su	2	2	·46	15	·76	16
23	Mo	3	3	·36	16	·69	17
24	Tu	4	4	·25	17	·62	18
25	We	5	5	·15	18	·56	19
26	Th	6	{ 6 7	·06 ·97	19	·50	20
27	Fr	7	8	·89	20	·44	21
28	Sa	8	9	·81	21	·39	22
29	Su	9	*Bahula* 10	·75	22	·35	23
—30	Mo	10	11	·71	23	·35	24
Sukla *Mesha—Chittirai.* 1	Tu	11	12	·69	24	·35	25
2	We	12	13	·69	25	·37	26
3	Th	13	14	·72	26	·41	27
4	Fr	14	—A	·77	27	·47	28
5	Sa	15	1	·82	1	·55	—29
6	Su	16	2	·90	2	·66	H. 1224 *Rabi-ul-awwal.* 1
7	Mo	17	3	·99	3	·76	2
8	Tu	18	...	...	4	·87	3
9	We	19	*Sukla* 4	·07	5	·97	4
10	Th	20	5	·16	...	...	5
11	Fr	21	6	·22	6	·06	6
12	Sa	22	7	·28	7	·15	7
13	Su	23	8	·30	8	·21	8
14	Mo	24	**Vaisakha** 9	·30	9	·25	9
15	Tu	25	10	·30	10	·26	10
16	We	26	11	·27	11	·26	11
17	Th	27	12	·22	12	·25	12
18	Fr	28	13	·16	13	·21	13
19	Sa ○	29	{ 14 P	·09 ·99	14	·16	14
20	Su	30	1	·90	15	·10	15

SOLAR reckoning.			LUNAR reckoning.				
Cyclic Sidereal Year, Month and Day.	Week-Day	English Month and Day.	Tithi	Ending Moment.	Nakshatra	Ending Moment.	Muhammadan Year, Month and Day.
		May					
Sukla *Mesha—Chittirai.* 21	Mo	1	**Vaisakha** 2	·79	16 17	·03 ·97 }	H. 1224 *Rabi-ul-awwal.* 16
22	Tu	2	3	·69	18	·90	17
23	We	3	4	·59	19	·83	18
24	Th	4	5	·49	20	·77	19
25	Fr	5	6	·42	21	·72	20
26	Sa	6	7	·33	22	·68	21
27	Su	7	8	·29	23	·67	22
28	Mo	8	9	·24	24	·67	23
29	Tu	9	10	·22	25	·68	24
30	We	10	*Bahula* 11	·22	26	·72	25
—31	Th	11	12	·24	27	·78	26
Sukla *Vrishabha—Vaikasi.* 1	Fr	12	13	·29	1	·86	27
2	Sa	13	14	·34	2	·96	28
3	Su	14	—A	·42	...	...	29
4	Mo	15	1	·50	3	·06	—30
5	Tu	16	2	·58	4	·17	H. 1224 *Rabi-ul-akhir.* 1
6	We	17	3	·66	5	·27	2
7	Th	18	4	·73	6	·38	3
8	Fr	19	*Sukla* 5	·79	7	·46	4
9	Sa	20	6	·81	8	·52	5
10	Su	21	7	·82	9	·56	6
11	Mo	22	8	·81	10	·58	7
12	Tu	23	9	·79	11	·59	8
13	We	24	10	·74	12	·58	9
14	Th	25	**Jyeshtha** 11	·66	13	·54	10
15	Fr	26	12	·59	14	·49	11
16	Sa	27	13	·49	15	·44	12
17	Su	28	14	·39	16	·38	13
18	Mo	29	P	·29	17	·31	14
19	Tu	30	1	·20	18	·24	15
20	We	31	{ 2 3	·09 ·98	19	·17	16
		June					
21	Th	1	4	·91	20	·11	17
22	Fr	2	5	·84	21	·05	18
23	Sa	3	6	·79	22	·02	19
24	Su	4	7	·73	23 24	·00 ·99 }	20
25	Mo	5	*Bahula* 8	·72	...	...	21
26	Tu	6	9	·71	25	·00	22
27	We	7	10	·74	26	·03	23
28	Th	8	11	·77	27	·10	24
29	Fr	9	12	·82	1	·17	25
30	Sa	10	13	·91	2	·26	26
—31	Su	11	14	·99	3	·36	27
Sukla *Mithuna—Ani.* 1	Mo	12	...	...	4	·46	28
2	Tu	13	—A	·08	5	·58	—29
3	We	14	*Sukla* 1	·14	6	·68	H. 1224 *Jumadal-awwal.* 1
4	Th	15	2	·22	7	·76	2
5	Fr	16	3	·26	8	·83	3
6	Sa	17	**Ashadha** 4	·29	9	·88	4
7	Su	18	5	·31	10	·91	5
8	Mo	19	6	·30	11	·92	6
9	Tu	20	7	·27	12	·90	7
10	We	21	8	·22	13	·87	8
11	Th	22	9	·17	14	·83	9
12	Fr	23	{ 10 11	.08 ·98	15	·78	10
13	Sa	24	**Adhika** 12	·89	16	·72	11
14	Su	25	13	·78	17	·65	12
15	Mo	26	14	·68	18	·58	13
16	Tu	27	P	·58	19	·51	14
17	We	28	*Bah.* 1	·48	20	·44	15
18	Th	29	2	·40	21	·40	16
19	Fr	30	3	·33	22	·38	17

Naksh :—1. Asvn. 2. Bhar. 3. Krit. 4. Rohi. 5. Mrig. 6. Ardh. 7. Punar. 8. Push. 9. Aslesh. 10. Magh. 11. P. Phal. 12. U. Phal. 13. Hasta. 14. Chit

A. D. 1809. | Vikrama 1866.
A.—Amavasya. Kollam 985, { N. Malabar—Sept. / S. Malabar—Aug. } Commences | Hijra 1224, Commences, Feb. 16. | Bengal San 1215.
P.—Paurnami. | (N. Cycle) Vikrama.

SOLAR reckoning: Cyclic Sidereal Year, Month and Day; Week-Day; English Month and Day. LUNAR reckoning: Tithi, Ending Moment; Nakshatra, Ending Moment; Muhammadan Year, Month and Day.

July — Solar: Sukla *Mithuna—Ani.* (to 32); Sukla *Karkata—Adi.* (from 1). Lunar: Adhika Ash. *Bahula*; Nija Ashadha *Sukla*. Muhammadan: H. 1224 *Jumadal-awwal.*; H. 1224 *Jumadal-akhir.*

Cyclic Sidereal	Week-Day	English Day	Tithi	Ending Moment	Nakshatra	Ending Moment	Muhammadan
20	Sa	1	4	·27	23	·32	18
21	Su	2	5	·21	24	·31	19
22	Mo	3	6	·20	25	·32	20
23	Tu	4	7	·19	26	·36	21
24	We	5	8	·21	27	·40	22
25	Th	6	9	·25	1	·47	23
26	Fr	7	10	·31	2	·56	24
27	Sa	8	11	·38	3	·66	25
28	Su	9	12	·46	4	·77	26
29	Mo	10	13	·55	5	·88	27
30	Tu	11	14	·61	6	·98	28
31	We	12	A	·69	...	...	29
32	Th	13	1	·74	7	·07	30
1	Fr	14	2	·78	8	·14	1
2	Sa	15	3	·78	9	·20	2
3	Su	16	4	·77	10	·23	3
4	Mo	17	5	·75	11	·24	4
5	Tu	18	6	·69	12	·23	5
6	We	19	7	·64	13	·20	6
7	Th	20	8	·55	14	·16	7
8	Fr	21	9	·47	15	·12	8
9	Sa	22	10	·37	16 / 17	·06 / ·99	9
10	Su	23	11	·28	18	·92	10
11	Mo	24	12	·17	19	·85	11
12	Tu	25	13 / 14	·06 / ·97	20	·79	12
13	We	26	P	·88	21	·73	13
14	Th	27	1	·81	22	·68	14
15	Fr	28	2	·74	23	·65	15
16	Sa	29	3	·70	24	·64	16
17	Su	30	4	·68	25	·65	17
18	Mo	31	5	·66	26	·67	18

Aug. — Solar: Sukla *Simha—Avani.* (from 1). Lunar: *Bahula*; Sravana *Sukla*; *Bahula*. Muhammadan: H. 1224 *Rajab.*

Cyclic Sidereal	Week-Day	English Day	Tithi	Ending Moment	Nakshatra	Ending Moment	Muhammadan
19	Tu	1	6	·69	27	·71	19
20	We	2	7	·72	1	·78	20
21	Th	3	8	·79	2	·86	21
22	Fr	4	9	·85	3	·96	22
23	Sa	5	10	·94	...	...	23
24	Su	6	...	...	4	·07	24
25	Mo	7	11	·02	5	·18	25
26	Tu	8	12	·09	6	·28	26
27	We	9	13	·16	7	·37	27
28	Th	10	14	·21	8	·44	28
29	Fr	11	A	·25	9	·51	29
30	Sa	12	1	·27	10	·55	1
31	Su	13	2	·27	11	·56	2
1	Mo	14	3	·24	12	·56	3
2	Tu	15	4	·19	13	·53	4
3	We	16	5	·14	14	·51	5
4	Th	17	6 / 7	·05 / ·97	15	·45	6
5	Fr	18	8	·87	16	·39	7
6	Sa	19	9	·77	17	·33	8
7	Su	20	10	·66	18	·25	9
8	Mo	21	11	·57	19	·19	10
9	Tu	22	12	·47	20	·13	11
10	We	23	13	·38	21	·07	12
11	Th	24	14	·31	22 / 23	·02 / ·98	13
12	Fr	25	P	·25	24	·97	14
13	Sa	26	1	·20	25	·97	15
14	Su	27	2	·18	26	·99	16
15	Mo	28	3	·18	...	...	17
16	Tu	29	4	·19	27	·02	18
17	We	30	5	·23	1	·08	19
18	Th	31	6	·29	2	·16	20

Sep. — Solar: Sukla *Simha—Avani.* (to 31); Sukla *Kanya—Purattasi.* (from 1). Lunar: Sravn. *Bahula*; Bhadrapada *Sukla*. Muhammadan: H. 1224 *Rajab.*; H. 1224 *Shaban.*

Cyclic Sidereal	Week-Day	English Day	Tithi	Ending Moment	Nakshatra	Ending Moment	Muhammadan
19	Fr	1	7	·35	3	·26	21
20	Sa	2	8	·44	4	·37	22
21	Su	3	9	·52	5	·47	23
22	Mo	4	10	·61	6	·58	24
23	Tu	5	11	·68	7	·67	25
24	We	6	12	·74	8	·76	26
25	Th	7	13	·76	9	·82	27
26	Fr	8	14	·78	10	·86	28
27	Sa	9	A	·78	11	·88	29
28	Su	10	1	·75	12	·88	30
29	Mo	11	2	·72	13	·87	1
30	Tu	12	3	·65	14	·84	2
31	We	13	4	·58	15	·79	3
1	Th	14	5	·49	16	·73	4
2	Fr	15	6	·39	17	·66	5
3	Sa	16	7	·30	18	·60	6
4	Su	17	8	·19	19	·53	7
5	Mo	18	9 / 10	·10 / ·99	20	·46	8
6	Tu	19	11	·91	21	·40	9
7	We	20	12	·84	22	·35	10
8	Th	21	13	·79	23	·32	11
9	Fr	22	14	·73	24	·30	12
10	Sa	23	P	·71	25	·29	13
11	Su	24	1	·71	26	·30	14
12	Mo	25	2	·72	27	·34	15
13	Tu	26	3	·77	1	·39	16
14	We	27	4	·82	2	·47	17
15	Th	28	5	·90	3	·56	18
16	Fr	29	6	·98	4	·67	19
17	Sa	30	...	...	5	·77	20

Oct. — Solar: Sukla *Tula—Aippasi.* (from 1). Lunar: *Bahula*; Asvina *Sukla*; *Bahula*. Muhammadan: H. 1224 *Ramzan.*

Cyclic Sidereal	Week-Day	English Day	Tithi	Ending Moment	Nakshatra	Ending Moment	Muhammadan
18	Su	1	7	·06	6	·87	21
19	Mo	2	8	·15	7	·98	22
20	Tu	3	9	·22	...	...	23
21	We	4	10	·28	8	·07	24
22	Th	5	11	·31	9	·13	25
23	Fr	6	12	·33	10	·18	26
24	Sa	7	13	·33	11	·20	27
25	Su	8	14	·30	12	·22	28
26	Mo	9	A	·28	13	·20	29
27	Tu	10	1	·21	14	·17	1
28	We	11	2	·14	15	·12	2
29	Th	12	3 / 4	·05 / ·96	16	·07	3
30	Fr	13	5	·86	17 / 18	·01 / ·94	4
31	Sa	14	6	·76	19	·87	5
1	Su	15	7	·66	20	·80	6
2	Mo	16	8	·56	21	·74	7
3	Tu	17	9	·48	22	·68	8
4	We	18	10	·41	23	·65	9
5	Th	19	11	·36	24	·62	10
6	Fr	20	12	·30	25	·61	11
7	Sa	21	13	·29	26	·62	12
8	Su	22	14	·29	27	·65	13
9	Mo ○	23	P	·30	1	·71	14
10	Tu	24	1	·35	2	·78	15
11	We	25	2	·41	3	·86	16
12	Th	26	3	·48	4	·96	17
13	Fr	27	4	·56	...	...	18
14	Sa	28	5	·65	5	·07	19
15	Su	29	6	·73	6	·19	20
16	Mo	30	7	·81	7	·28	21
17	Tu	31	8	·87	8	·37	22

Nov. — Solar: Sukla *Tula—Aippasi.* (to 30); Sukla *Vrischika—Kartigai.* (from 1). Lunar: Asvn. *Bah.*; Kartika *Sukla*. Muhammadan: H. 1224 *Ramzan.*; H. 1224 *Shawwal.*

Cyclic Sidereal	Week-Day	English Day	Tithi	Ending Moment	Nakshatra	Ending Moment	Muhammadan
18	We	1	9	·90	9	·44	23
19	Th	2	10	·93	10	·49	24
20	Fr	3	11	·92	11	·53	25
21	Sa	4	12	·90	12	·54	26
22	Su	5	13	·87	13	·53	27
23	Mo	6	14	·81	14	·50	28
24	Tu	7	A	·73	15	·46	29
25	We	8	1	·64	16	·41	30
26	Th	9	2	·55	17	·35	1
27	Fr	10	3	·46	18	·29	2
28	Sa	11	4	·36	19	·21	3
29	Su	12	5	·26	20	·14	4
30	Mo	13	6	·17	21	·07	5
1	Tu	14	7	·08	22 / 23	·03 / ·98	6
2	We	15	8 / 9	·02 / ·96	24	·95	7
3	Th	16	10	·91	25	·93	8
4	Fr	17	11	·90	26	·94	9
5	Sa	18	12	·90	27	·97	10
6	Su	19	13	·92	...	...	11
7	Mo	20	14	·96	1	·02	12
8	Tu	21	...	...	2	·08	13
9	We	22	P	·03	3	·17	14
10	Th	23	1	·11	4	·26	15
11	Fr	24	2	·19	5	·38	16
12	Sa	25	3	·28	6	·48	17
13	Su	26	4	·36	7	·59	18
14	Mo	27	5	·44	8	·68	19
15	Tu	28	6	·49	9	·75	20
16	We	29	7	·54	10	·81	21
17	Th	30	8	·55	11	·85	22

Dec. — Solar: Sukla *Dhanus—Margali.* (from 1). Lunar: *Bahula*; Margasira *Sukla*; *Bahula*. Muhammadan: H. 1224 *Zil-ka'da.*

Cyclic Sidereal	Week-Day	English Day	Tithi	Ending Moment	Nakshatra	Ending Moment	Muhammadan
18	Fr	1	9	·55	12	·86	23
19	Sa	2	10	·53	13	·85	24
20	Su	3	11	·48	14	·83	25
21	Mo	4	12	·42	15	·79	26
22	Tu	5	13	·35	16	·75	27
23	We	6	14	·28	17	·69	28
24	Th	7	A	·18	18	·62	29
25	Fr	8	1 / 2	·08 / ·99	19	·55	1
26	Sa	9	3	·88	20	·48	2
27	Su	10	4	·79	21	·42	3
28	Mo	11	5	·71	22	·36	4
29	Tu	12	6	·65	23	·31	5
1	We	13	7	·59	24	·28	6
2	Th	14	8	·56	25	·26	7
3	Fr	15	9	·54	26	·27	8
4	Sa	16	10	·53	27	·28	9
5	Su	17	11	·56	1	·33	10
6	Mo	18	12	·61	2	·39	11
7	Tu	19	13	·68	3	·47	12
8	We	20	14	·75	4	·57	13
9	Th	21	P	·84	5	·67	14
10	Fr	22	1	·93	6	·78	15
11	Sa	23	...	...	7	·88	16
12	Su	24	2	·01	8	·98	17
13	Mo	25	3	·08	...	...	18
14	Tu	26	4	·14	9	·07	19
15	We	27	5	·18	10	·13	20
16	Th	28	6	·19	11	·16	21
17	Fr	29	7	·20	12	·18	22
18	Sa	30	8	·17	13	·18	23
19	Su	31	9	·12	14	·16	24

15. Svati. 16. Visak. 17. Anur. 18. Jyesh. 19. Mula. 20. P. Ash. 21. U. Ash. 22. Sravn. 23. Dani. 24. Satab. 25. P. Bhad. 26. U. Bhad. 27. Rev.

A. D. 1810. **Mesha Sankranti** (Commencement of Indian Sidereal Year).

Solar Eclipse. ● **(Surya Sid.) April 11·33.** **Saka 1732.** **Kaliyuga 4911.**

Lunar Eclipse. ○ **(Arya Sid.) April 11·23.** **(S. Cycle) Pramodhuta.**

SOLAR reckoning: Cyclic Sidereal Year, Month and Day; Week-Day; English Month and Day. LUNAR reckoning: Tithi, Ending Moment; Nakshatra, Ending Moment; Muhammadan Year, Month and Day.

Jan.

Cyclic Sidereal Year, Month and Day	Week-Day	English Month and Day	Tithi	Ending Moment	Nakshatra	Ending Moment	Muhammadan Year, Month and Day
Sukla *Dhanus—Margali.* 20	Mo	1	Mr. *Bah.* 10 11	·07 ·99	15	·13	1224 *Zil-ka'da.* 25
21	Tu	2	12	·91	16	·08	26
22	We	3	13	·81	17 18	·02 ·96	27
23	Th	4	14	·72	19	·89	28
24	Fr	5	A	·62	20	·83	29
25	Sa	6	1	·53	21	·76	30
26	Su	7	2	·44	22	·70	1
27	Mo	8	3	·35	23	·65	2
28	Tu	9	4	·29	24	·61	3
29	We	10	5	·23	25	·59	4
30	Th	11	*Sukla* 6	·20	26	·59	5
1	Fr	12	7	·18	27	·60	6
2	Sa	13	8	·19	1	·64	7
3	Su	14	9	·21	2	·69	8
4	Mo	15	10	·25	3	·78	9
5	Tu	16	11	·32	4	·87	10
6	We	17	12	·41	5	·97	11
7	Th	18	Pausha 13	·50	...	...	12
8	Fr	19	14	·58	6	·08	13
9	Sa	20	P	·68	7	·18	H. 1224 *Zil-hijja.* 14
10	Su	21	1	·74	8	·28	15
Sukla *Makara—Tai.* 11	Mo	22	2	·78	9	·37	16
12	Tu	23	3	·83	10	·44	17
13	We	24	4	·84	11	·48	18
14	Th	25	5	·84	12	·50	19
15	Fr	26	6	·81	13	·50	20
16	Sa	27	7	·78	14	·50	21
17	Su	28	*Bahula* 8	·71	15	·47	22
18	Mo	29	9	·63	16	·42	23
19	Tu	30	10	·54	17	·36	24
20	We	31	11	·45	18	·30	25

Feb.

Cyclic Sidereal Year, Month and Day	Week-Day	English Month and Day	Tithi	Ending Moment	Nakshatra	Ending Moment	Muhammadan Year, Month and Day
21	Th	1	12	·35	19	·23	26
22	Fr	2	13	·25	20	·16	27
23	Sa	3	14	·16	21	·10	28
24	Su	4	A 1	·07 ·99	22 23	·03 ·98	29
25	Mo	5	2	·92	24	·95	30
26	Tu	6	3	·86	25	·92	1
27	We	7	4	·84	26	·91	2
28	Th	8	5	·82	27	·92	3
29	Fr	9	*Sukla* 6	·83	1	·95	4
1	Sa	10	7	·85	...	...	5
2	Su	11	8	·90	2	·01	6
3	Mo	12	9	·97	3	·08	7
4	Tu	13	...	...	4	·17	8
5	We	14	10	·05	5	·27	9
6	Th	15	11	·13	6	·38	10
7	Fr	16	12	·21	7	·48	H. 1225 *Muharram.* 11
8	Sa	17	Magha 13	·30	8	·59	12
9	Su	18	14	·38	9	·68	13
Sukla *Kumbha—Masi.* 10	Mo	19	P	·43	10	·74	14
11	Tu	20	1	·46	11	·79	15
12	We	21	2	·48	12	·82	16
13	Th	22	3	·46	13	·84	17
14	Fr	23	4	·43	14	·83	18
15	Sa	24	*Bahula* 5	·39	15	·80	19
16	Su	25	6	·32	16	·75	20
17	Mo	26	7	·25	17	·70	21
18	Tu	27	8	·16	18	·64	22
19	We	28	9 10	·07 ·96	19	·57	23

March

Cyclic Sidereal Year, Month and Day	Week-Day	English Month and Day	Tithi	Ending Moment	Nakshatra	Ending Moment	Muhammadan Year, Month and Day
Sukla *Kumbha—Masi.* 20	Th	1	Mg. *Bah.* 11	·87	20	·50	*Muharram.* 24
21	Fr	2	12	·78	21	·43	25
22	Sa	3	13	·68	22	·37	26
23	Su	4	14	·60	23	·32	27
24	Mo	5	A	·53	24	·28	28
25	Tu	6	1	·48	25	·25	29
26	We	7	2	·44	26	·23	30
27	Th	8	3	·44	27	·24	1
28	Fr	9	4	·44	1	·26	2
29	Sa	10	5	·48	2	·32	3
30	Su	11	*Sukla* 6	·51	3	·39	4
1	Mo	12	7	·57	4	·47	5
2	Tu	13	8	·66	5	·57	6
3	We	14	9	·74	6	·68	7
4	Th	15	10	·83	7	·79	8
5	Fr	16	11	·91	8	·89	9
6	Sa	17	Phalguna 12	·97	9	·98	10
7	Su	18	...	...	...	...	11
8	Mo	19	13	·03	10	·05	12
9	Tu	20	14	·06	11	·11	H. 1225 *Safar.* 13
10	We	21	P	·08	12	·15	14
11	Th	22	1	·06	13	·16	15
12	Fr	23	2 3	·03 ·98	14	·15	16
Sukla *Mina—Panguni.* 13	Sa	24	4	·91	15	·13	17
14	Su	25	5	·84	16	·09	18
15	Mo	26	6	·75	17 18	·04 ·98	19
16	Tu	27	7	·66	19	·91	20
17	We	28	*Bahula* 8	·54	20	·84	21
18	Th	29	9	·45	21	·77	22
19	Fr	30	10	·36	22	·71	23
20	Sa	31	11	·27	23	·66	24

April

Cyclic Sidereal Year, Month and Day	Week-Day	English Month and Day	Tithi	Ending Moment	Nakshatra	Ending Moment	Muhammadan Year, Month and Day
21	Su	1	12	·18	24	·61	25
22	Mo	2	13	·10	25	·57	26
23	Tu	3	14	·06	26	·56	27
24	We ●	4	A	·02	27	·56	28
25	Th	5	1	·01	1	·59	29
26	Fr	6	2	·01	2	·63	1
27	Sa	7	3	·04	3	·69	2
28	Su	8	4	·08	4	·77	3
29	Mo	9	5	·14	5	·87	4
30	Tu	10	6	·22	6	·98	5
1	We	11	*Sukla* 7	·30	...	...	6
2	Th	12	8	·39	7	·09	7
3	Fr	13	9	·47	8	·19	8
4	Sa	14	10	·54	9	·28	9
5	Su	15	11	·59	10	·36	10
6	Mo	16	12	·62	11	·43	11
7	Tu	17	13	·63	12	·47	12
8	We	18	Chaitra 14	·61	13	·48	13
9	Th	19	P	·58	14	·48	14
Pramodhuta *Mesha—Chittirai.* 10	Fr	20	1	·53	15	·46	H. 1225 *Rabi-ul-awwal.* 15
11	Sa	21	2	·48	16	·43	16
12	Su	22	3	·39	17	·38	17
13	Mo	23	4	·30	18	·32	18
14	Tu	24	5	·20	19	·25	19
15	We	25	6	·09	20	·18	20
16	Th	26	7 8	·00 ·89	21	·11	21
17	Fr	27	*Bahula* 9	·81	22 23	·05 ·99	22
18	Sa	28	10	·72	24	·94	23
19	Su	29	11	·65	25	·90	24
20	Mo	30	12	·59	26	·88	25

May

Cyclic Sidereal Year, Month and Day	Week-Day	English Month and Day	Tithi	Ending Moment	Nakshatra	Ending Moment	Muhammadan Year, Month and Day
Pramodhuta *Mesha—Chittirai.* 21	Tu	1	*Bah.* 13	·55	27	·89	*R. awwal.* 26
22	We	2	14	·54	1	·90	27
23	Th	3	A	·54	2	·94	28
24	Fr	4	1	·57	...	...	29
25	Sa	5	2	·61	3	·00	30
26	Su	6	3	·67	4	·08	1
27	Mo	7	4	·74	5	·18	2
28	Tu	8	5	·83	6	·28	3
29	We	9	6	·91	7	·39	4
30	Th	10	7	·99	8	·49	5
31	Fr	11	*Sukla* ...	...	9	·59	6
1	Sa	12	8	·06	10	·68	7
2	Su	13	9	·11	11	·74	8
3	Mo	14	10	·14	12	·78	9
4	Tu	15	11	·15	13	·80	10
5	We	16	12	·14	14	·80	11
6	Th	17	13	·10	15	·79	H. 1225 *Rabi-ul-akhir.* 12
7	Fr	18	14 P	·05 ·98	16	·76	13
8	Sa	19	Vaisakha 1	·90	17	·71	14
9	Su	20	2	·82	18	·66	15
10	Mo	21	3	·71	19	·59	16
11	Tu	22	4	·61	20	·52	17
Pramodhuta *Vrishabha—Vaikasi.* 12	We	23	5	·51	21	·46	18
13	Th	24	6	·40	22	·39	19
14	Fr	25	7	·31	23	·33	20
15	Sa	26	8	·22	24	·27	21
16	Su	27	9	·16	25	·23	22
17	Mo	28	*Bahula* 10	·10	26	·22	23
18	Tu	29	11	·06	27	·21	24
19	We	30	12	·04	1	·22	25
20	Th	31	13	·05	2	·25	26

June

Cyclic Sidereal Year, Month and Day	Week-Day	English Month and Day	Tithi	Ending Moment	Nakshatra	Ending Moment	Muhammadan Year, Month and Day
21	Fr	1	14	·06	3	·31	27
22	Sa	2	A	·10	4	·39	28
23	Su	3	1	·17	5	·48	29
24	Mo	4	2	·24	6	·58	1
25	Tu	5	3	·32	7	·68	2
26	We	6	4	·41	8	·79	3
27	Th	7	5	·49	9	·90	4
28	Fr	8	*Sukla* 6	·56	10	·98	5
29	Sa	9	7	·59	...	...	6
30	Su	10	8	·63	11	·05	7
31	Mo	11	9	·64	12	·10	8
32	Tu	12	10	·62	13	·12	9
1	We	13	11	·59	14	·13	10
2	Th	14	12	·55	15	·12	H. 1225 *Jumadul-awwal.* 11
3	Fr	15	Jyeshtha 13	·47	16	·09	12
4	Sa	16	14	·39	17 18	·05 ·99	13
5	Su	17	P	·31	19	·93	14
6	Mo	18	1	·21	20	·87	15
7	Tu	19	2	·10	21	·80	16
Pramodhuta *Mithuna—Ani.* 8	We	20	3 4	·00 ·90	22	·73	17
9	Th	21	5	·80	23	·66	18
10	Fr	22	6	·72	24	·61	19
11	Sa	23	7	·64	25	·57	20
12	Su	24	8	·58	26	·54	21
13	Mo	25	9	·54	27	·53	22
14	Tu	26	*Bahula* 10	·52	1	·54	23
15	We	27	11	·53	2	·57	24
16	Th	28	12	·54	3	·62	25
17	Fr	29	13	·59	4	·69	26
18	Sa	30	14	·64	5	·78	27

Naksh :—1. Asvn. 2. Bhar. 3. Krit. 4. Rohi. 5. Mrig. 6. Ardh. 7. Punar. 8. Push. 9. Aslesh. 10. Magh. 11. P. Phal. 12. U. Phal. 13. Hasta. 14. Chit.

A. D. 1810. **Vikrama 1867.**

A.—Amavasya. **Kollam 986,** Commences { **N. Malabar—Sept.** / **S. Malabar—Aug.** } **Hijra 1225,** Commences, **Feb. 6.** **Bengal San 1216.**

P.—Paurnami. **(N. Cycle) Vrisha.**

Columns: SOLAR reckoning (Cyclic Sidereal Year, Month and Day; Week-Day; English Month and Day) — LUNAR reckoning (Tithi; Ending Moment; Nakshatra; Ending Moment; Muhammadan Year, Month and Day).

July

Pramodhuta Mithuna—Ani. (19–31); Pramodhuta Karkata—Adi. (1–18) — Ashadha; Sukla; Bahula — H. 1225 Jumada-l-akhir.

Cyclic Sidereal Year, Month and Day	Week-Day	English Month and Day	Tithi	Ending Moment	Nakshatra	Ending Moment	Muhammadan Year, Month and Day
19	Su	1	—A	·71	6	·88	28
20	Mo	2	1	·79	7	·98	29
21	Tu	3	2	·88	...	...	—30
22	We	4	3	·96	8	·09	1
23	Th	5	...	...	9	·20	2
24	Fr	6	4	·02	10	·29	3
25	Sa	7	5	·08	11	·36	4
26	Su	8	6	·11	12	·41	5
27	Mo	9	7	·11	13	·44	6
28	Tu	10	8	·10	14	·46	7
29	We	11	9	·07	15	·45	8
30	Th	12	10 / 11	·02 / ·95	16	·42	9
—31	Fr	13	12	·88	17	·38	10
1	Sa	14	13	·79	18	·33	11
2	Su	15	14	·69	19	·27	12
3	Mo	16	P	·58	20	·21	13
4	Tu	17	1	·48	21	·14	14
5	We	18	2	·37	22	·06	15
6	Th	19	3	·28	23 / 24	·00 / ·95	16
7	Fr	20	4	·20	25	·90	17
8	Sa	21	5	·12	26	·87	18
9	Su	22	6	·06	27	·86	19
10	Mo	23	7	·02	1	·86	20
11	Tu	24	8	·00	2	·89	21
12	We	25	9	·00	3	·93	22
13	Th	26	10	·02	...	...	23
14	Fr	27	11	·06	4	·00	24
15	Sa	28	12	·11	5	·08	25
16	Su	29	13	·19	6	·18	26
17	Mo	30	14	·27	7	·28	27
18	Tu	31	—A	·36	8	·40	28

Aug.

Pramodhuta Simha—Avani. — Sravana; Sukla; Bahula — H. 1225 Rajab.

Cyclic Sidereal Year, Month and Day	Week-Day	English Month and Day	Tithi	Ending Moment	Nakshatra	Ending Moment	Muhammadan Year, Month and Day
19	We	1	1	·42	9	·50	—29
20	Th	2	2	·49	10	·59	1
21	Fr	3	3	·55	11	·67	2
22	Sa	4	4	·59	12	·72	3
23	Su	5	5	·60	13	·77	4
24	Mo	6	6	·58	14	·78	5
25	Tu	7	7	·56	15	·78	6
26	We	8	8	·51	16	·75	7
27	Th	9	9	·44	17	·71	8
28	Fr	10	10	·37	18	·67	9
29	Sa	11	11	·28	19	·61	10
30	Su	12	12	·18	20	·54	11
31	Mo	13	13 / 14	·08 / ·98	21	·47	12
—32	Tu	14	P	·87	22	·40	13
1	We	15	1	·78	23	·35	14
2	Th	16	2	·70	24	·29	15
3	Fr	17	3	·62	25	·24	16
4	Sa	18	4	·55	26	·20	17
5	Su	19	5	·51	27	·18	18
6	Mo	20	6	·50	1	·18	19
7	Tu	21	7	·50	2	·21	20
8	We	22	8	·52	3	·24	21
9	Th	23	9	·55	4	·30	22
10	Fr	24	10	·60	5	·38	23
11	Sa	25	11	·69	6	·47	24
12	Su	26	12	·76	7	·59	25
13	Mo	27	13	·85	8	·69	26
14	Tu	28	14	·93	9	·80	27
15	We	29	...	...	10	·89	28
16	Th	30	—A	·01	11	·97	29
17	Fr	31	1	·05	...	...	—30

Sep.

Pramodhuta Simha—Avani. (18–31); Pramodhuta Kanya—Purattasi. (1–16) — Bhadrapada; Sukla; Bahula — H. 1225 Shaban.

Cyclic Sidereal Year, Month and Day	Week-Day	English Month and Day	Tithi	Ending Moment	Nakshatra	Ending Moment	Muhammadan Year, Month and Day
18	Sa	1	2	·08	12	·04	1
19	Su	2	3	·11	13	·08	2
20	Mo	3	4	·09	14	·10	3
21	Tu	4	5	·07	15	·10	4
22	We	5	6 / 7	·03 / ·97	16	·08	5
23	Th	6	8	·89	17	·06	6
24	Fr	7	9	·78	18 / 19	·01 / ·95	7
25	Sa	8	10	·69	20	·88	8
26	Su	9	11	·59	21	·81	9
27	Mo	10	12	·49	22	·75	10
28	Tu	11	13	·39	23	·68	11
29	We	12	14	·31	24	·62	12
30	Th	13	P	·22	25	·57	13
—31	Fr	14	1	·15	26	·53	14
1	Sa	15	2	·09	27	·51	15
2	Su	16	3	·04	1	·51	16
3	Mo	17	4	·03	2	·52	17
4	Tu	18	5	·03	3	·56	18
5	We	19	6	·04	4	·61	19
6	Th	20	7	·08	5	·68	20
7	Fr	21	8	·13	6	·78	21
8	Sa	22	9	·21	7	·89	22
9	Su	23	10	·29	8	·99	23
10	Mo	24	11	·38	...	...	24
11	Tu	25	12	·45	9	·10	25
12	We	26	13	·54	10	·19	26
13	Th	27	14	·59	11	·29	27
14	Fr	28	—A	·63	12	·35	28
15	Sa	29	1	·65	13	·40	—29
16	Su	30	2	·63	14	·42	1

Oct.

Pramodhuta Tula—Aippasi. — Asvina; Sukla; Bahula; K. Suk. — H. 1225 Ramzan.

Cyclic Sidereal Year, Month and Day	Week-Day	English Month and Day	Tithi	Ending Moment	Nakshatra	Ending Moment	Muhammadan Year, Month and Day
17	Mo	1	3	·61	15	·43	2
18	Tu	2	4	·58	16	·42	3
19	We	3	5	·51	17	·39	4
20	Th	4	6	·43	18	·34	5
21	Fr	5	7	·34	19	·29	6
22	Sa	6	8	·24	20	·22	7
23	Su	7	9	·16	21	·15	8
24	Mo	8	10 / 11	·05 / ·94	22	·09	9
25	Tu	9	12	·86	23 / 24	·02 / ·96	10
26	We	10	13	·78	25	·90	11
27	Th	11	14	·71	26	·86	12
28	Fr	12	P	·65	27	·84	13
29	Sa	13	1	·61	1	·83	14
—30	Su	14	2	·59	2	·84	15
1	Mo	15	3	·59	3	·87	16
2	Tu	16	4	·61	4	·92	17
3	We	17	5	·65	...	...	18
4	Th	18	6	·71	5	·00	19
5	Fr	19	7	·78	6	·09	20
6	Sa	20	8	·87	7	·18	21
7	Su	21	9	·96	8	·29	22
8	Mo	22	...	...	9	·40	23
9	Tu	23	10	·05	10	·51	24
10	We	24	11	·12	11	·59	25
11	Th	25	12	·17	12	·66	26
12	Fr	26	13	·21	13	·71	27
13	Sa	27	14	·23	14	·74	28
14	Su	28	—A	·22	15	·75	29
15	Mo	29	1	·19	16	·75	—30
16	Tu	30	2	·16	17	·72	1
17	We	31	3	·10	18	·68	2

Nov.

Pramodhuta Tula—Aippasi. (18–30); Pramodhuta Vrischika—Kartigai. (1–17) — Kartika; Sukla; Bahula — H. 1225 Shawwal.

Cyclic Sidereal Year, Month and Day	Week-Day	English Month and Day	Tithi	Ending Moment	Nakshatra	Ending Moment	Muhammadan Year, Month and Day
18	Th	1	4 / 5	·02 / ·93	19	·62	3
19	Fr	2	6	·83	20	·56	4
20	Sa	3	7	·74	21	·50	5
21	Su	4	8	·63	22	·43	6
22	Mo	5	9	·55	23	·36	7
23	Tu	6	10	·45	24	·29	8
24	We	7	11	·37	25	·24	9
25	Th	8	12	·30	26	·20	10
26	Fr	9	13	·23	27	·17	11
27	Sa	10	14	·21	1	·15	12
28	Su	11	P	·19	2	·16	13
29	Mo	12	1	·20	3	·18	14
—30	Tu	13	2	·21	4	·24	15
1	We	14	3	·26	5	·30	16
2	Th	15	4	·33	6	·39	17
3	Fr	16	5	·40	7	·48	18
4	Sa	17	6	·49	8	·59	19
5	Su	18	7	·57	9	·70	20
6	Mo	19	8	·67	10	·81	21
7	Tu	20	9	·73	11	·90	22
8	We	21	10	·79	12	·97	23
9	Th	22	11	·83	...	...	24
10	Fr	23	12	·85	13	·02	25
11	Sa	24	13	·84	14	·06	26
12	Su	25	14	·81	15	·08	27
13	Mo	26	—A	·77	16	·07	28
14	Tu	27	1	·71	17	·05	—29
15	We	28	2	·65	18 / 19	·01 / ·96	1
16	Th	29	3	·55	20	·91	2
17	Fr	30	4	·45	21	·84	3

Dec.

Pramodhuta Vrischika—Kartigai. (18–30); Pramodhuta Dhanus—Margali. (1–18) — Margasira; Sukla; Bahula; Suk.; Psh. — H. 1225 Zi-l-ka'da; Zi-l-hijja.

Cyclic Sidereal Year, Month and Day	Week-Day	English Month and Day	Tithi	Ending Moment	Nakshatra	Ending Moment	Muhammadan Year, Month and Day
18	Sa	1	5	·37	22	·77	4
19	Su	2	6	·26	23	·70	5
20	Mo	3	7	·17	24	·63	6
21	Tu	4	8	·07	25	58	7
22	We	5	9 / 10	·00 / ·92	26	·53	8
23	Th	6	11	·87	27	·50	9
24	Fr	7	12	·84	1	·48	10
25	Sa	8	13	·82	2	·48	11
26	Su	9	14	·83	3	·51	12
27	Mo	10	P	·85	4	·55	13
28	Tu	11	1	·91	5	·61	14
29	We	12	2	·97	6	·69	15
—30	Th	13	...	...	7	·78	16
1	Fr	14	3	·05	8	·89	17
2	Sa	15	4	·14	...	...	18
3	Su	16	5	·22	9	·00	19
4	Mo	17	6	·31	10	·11	20
5	Tu	18	7	·38	11	·20	21
6	We	19	8	·44	12	·28	22
7	Th	20	9	·47	13	·34	23
8	Fr	21	10	·49	14	·38	24
9	Sa	22	11	·48	15	·40	25
10	Su	23	12	·45	16	·40	26
11	Mo	24	13	·41	17	·38	27
12	Tu	25	14	·35	18	·34	28
13	We	26	—A	·28	19	·30	29
14	Th	27	1	·18	20	·24	—30
15	Fr	28	2	·09	21	·18	1
16	Sa	29	3 / 4	·00 / ·90	22	·11	2
17	Su	30	5	·80	23 / 24	·03 / ·98	3
18	Mo	31	6	·71	25	·92	4

15. Svati. 16. Visak. 17. Anur. 18. Jyesh. 19. Mula. 20. P. Ash. 21. U. Ash. 22. Sravn. 23. Dani. 24. Satab. 25. P. Bhad. 26. U. Bhad. 27. Rev.

A. D. 1811. **Mesha Sankranti** (Commencement of Indian Sidereal Year).

Solar Eclipse. ● (Surya Sid.) April 11·59. **Saka 1733.** **Kaliyuga 4912.**

Lunar Eclipse. ○ (Arya Sid.) April 11·49. (S. Cycle) Prajapati.

Jan.

Solar: Pramodhuta Dhanus—Margali; Pramodhuta Makara—Tai. Lunar: Sukla, Pausha, Bahula, Sukla. Muhammadan: H. 1225 Zil-hijja.

Cyclic Sidereal Year, Month and Day	Week-Day	English Month and Day	Tithi	Ending Moment	Nakshatra	Ending Moment	Muhammadan Year, Month and Day
19	Tu	1	7	·64	26	·86	5
20	We	2	8	·56	27	·83	6
21	Th	3	9	·51	1	·80	7
22	Fr	4	10	·48	2	·81	8
23	Sa	5	11	·47	3	·82	9
24	Su	6	12	·47	4	·86	10
25	Mo	7	13	·50	5	·92	11
26	Tu	8	14	·55	6	·99	12
27	We	9	P	·61	...	...	13
28	Th	10	1	·70	7	·08	14
—29	Fr	11	2	·78	8	·19	15
1	Sa	12	3	·87	9	·30	16
2	Su	13	4	·96	10	·41	17
3	Mo	14	...	...	11	·50	18
4	Tu	15	5	·02	12	·58	19
5	We	16	6	·08	13	·66	20
6	Th	17	7	·11	14	·70	21
7	Fr	18	8	·14	15	·72	22
8	Sa	19	9	·12	16	·72	23
9	Su	20	10	·10	17	·71	24
10	Mo	21	11	·06	18	·69	25
11	Tu	22	{12 13	·00 ·91	19	·64	26
12	We	23	14	·81	20	·58	27
13	Th	24	—A	·73	21	·51	28
14	Fr	25	1	·63	22	·44	—29
15	Sa	26	2	·53	23	·38	1
16	Su	27	3	·44	24	·31	2
17	Mo	28	4	·35	25	·25	3
18	Tu	29	5	·27	26	·20	4
19	We	30	6	·20	27	·16	5
20	Th	31	7	·16	1	·13	6

Feb.

Solar: Pramodhuta Kumbha—Masi. Lunar: Magha, Bahula, Pl. Suk. Muhammadan: H. 1226 Muharram, Safar.

Cyclic Sidereal Year, Month and Day	Week-Day	English Month and Day	Tithi	Ending Moment	Nakshatra	Ending Moment	Muhammadan Year, Month and Day
21	Fr	1	8	·12	2	·12	7
22	Sa	2	9	·11	3	·14	8
23	Su	3	10	·11	4	·17	9
24	Mo	4	11	·16	5	·22	10
25	Tu	5	12	·20	6	·29	11
26	We	6	13	·27	7	·39	12
27	Th	7	14	·34	8	·49	13
28	Fr	8	P	·43	9	·60	14
—29	Sa	9	1	·52	10	·70	15
1	Su	10	2	·60	11	·80	16
2	Mo	11	3	·67	12	·90	17
3	Tu	12	4	·72	13	·97	18
4	We	13	5	·76	...	...	19
5	Th	14	6	·77	14	·01	20
6	Fr	15	7	·75	15	·04	21
7	Sa	16	8	·73	16	·05	22
8	Su	17	9	·68	17	·05	23
9	Mo	18	10	·62	18 19}	·02 ·97}	24
10	Tu	19	11	·53	20	·92	25
11	We	20	12	·45	21	·85	26
12	Th	21	13	·35	22	·79	27
13	Fr	22	14	·25	23	·72	28
14	Sa	23	—A	·16	24	·65	29
15	Su	24	{1 2	·06 ·97	25	·59	—30
16	Mo	25	3	·88	26	·53	1
17	Tu	26	4	·82	27	·49	2
18	We	27	5	·77	1	·47	3
19	Th	28	6	·74	2	·45	4

March

Solar: Pramodhuta Kumbha—Masi; Pramodhuta Mina—Panguni. Lunar: Sukla, Phalguna, Bahula, Sukla. Muhammadan: H. 1226 Safar.

Cyclic Sidereal Year, Month and Day	Week-Day	English Month and Day	Tithi	Ending Moment	Nakshatra	Ending Moment	Muhammadan Year, Month and Day
20	Fr	1	7	·73	3	·46	5
21	Sa	2	8	·73	4	·48	6
22	Su	3	9	·77	5	·53	7
23	Mo	4	10	·81	6	·61	8
24	Tu	5	11	·88	7	·69	9
25	We	6	12	·96	8	·79	10
26	Th	7	...	...	9	·90	11
27	Fr	8	13	·05	...	...	12
28	Sa	9	14	·14	10	·00	13
29	Su ○	10	P	·22	11	·11	14
—30	Mo	11	1	·28	12	·20	15
1	Tu	12	2	·33	13	·27	16
2	We	13	3	·37	14	·33	17
3	Th	14	4	·37	15	·36	18
4	Fr	15	5	·36	16	·37	19
5	Sa	16	6	·32	17	·37	20
6	Su	17	7	·27	18	·35	21
7	Mo	18	8	·21	19	·31	22
8	Tu	19	9	·12	20	·25	23
9	We	20	{10 11	·04 ·95	21	·19	24
10	Th	21	12	·84	22	·13	25
11	Fr	22	13	·74	23 24}	·06 ·99}	26
12	Sa	23	14	·66	25	·92	27
13	Su	24	—A	·56	26	·87	28
14	Mo	25	1	·47	27	·83	—29
15	Tu	26	2	·41	1	·78	1
16	We	27	3	·36	2	·78	2
17	Th	28	4	·33	3	·78	3
18	Fr	29	5	·31	4	·80	4
19	Sa	30	6	·32	5	·85	5
20	Su	31	7	·35	6	·91	6

April

Solar: Prajapati Mesha—Chittirai. Lunar: Chaitra, Bahula, Sukla, Vaisak. Muhammadan: H. 1226 Rabi-ul-awwal, R. akhir.

Cyclic Sidereal Year, Month and Day	Week-Day	English Month and Day	Tithi	Ending Moment	Nakshatra	Ending Moment	Muhammadan Year, Month and Day
21	Mo	1	8	·39	7	·99	7
22	Tu	2	9	·47	...	...	8
23	We	3	10	·54	8	·09	9
24	Th	4	11	·63	9	·19	10
25	Fr	5	12	·71	10	·31	11
26	Sa	6	13	·80	11	·41	12
27	Su	7	14	·85	12	·50	13
28	Mo	8	P	·90	13	·58	14
29	Tu	9	1	·94	14	·64	15
—30	We	10	2	·93	15	·68	16
1	Th	11	3	·92	16	·70	17
2	Fr	12	4	·88	17	·70	18
3	Sa	13	5	·84	18	·68	19
4	Su	14	6	·77	19	·64	20
5	Mo	15	7	·69	20	·59	21
6	Tu	16	8	·60	21	·54	22
7	We	17	9	·50	22	·47	23
8	Th	18	10	·39	23	·40	24
9	Fr	19	11	·30	24	·33	25
10	Sa	20	12	·21	25	·26	26
11	Su	21	13	·11	26	·21	27
12	Mo	22	{14 A	·02 ·95	27	·16	28
13	Tu	23	1	·90	1	·12	29
14	We	24	2	·87	2	·10	—30
15	Th	25	3	·85	3	·10	1
16	Fr	26	4	·86	4	·12	2
17	Sa	27	5	·89	5	·16	3
18	Su	28	6	·94	6	·22	4
19	Mo	29	7	·99	7	·30	5
20	Tu	30	...	...	8	·39	6

May

Solar: Prajapati Mesha—Chittirai; Prajapati Vrishabha—Vaikasi. Lunar: Sukla, Vaisakha, Bahula, Sukla. Muhammadan: H. 1226 Rabi-ul-akhir.

Cyclic Sidereal Year, Month and Day	Week-Day	English Month and Day	Tithi	Ending Moment	Nakshatra	Ending Moment	Muhammadan Year, Month and Day
21	We	1	8	·07	9	·49	7
22	Th	2	9	·16	10	·61	8
23	Fr	3	10	·23	11	·71	9
24	Sa	4	11	·32	12	·81	10
25	Su	5	12	·38	13	·89	11
26	Mo	6	13	·44	14	·95	12
27	Tu	7	14	·45	...	...	13
28	We	8	P	·47	15	·00	14
29	Th	9	1	·45	16	·02	15
30	Fr	10	2	·42	17	·02	16
—31	Sa	11	3	·37	18 19}	·01 ·97}	17
1	Su	12	4	·29	20	·93	18
2	Mo	13	5	·21	21	·87	19
3	Tu	14	6	·12	22	·81	20
4	We	15	{7 8	·03 ·92	23	·74	21
5	Th	16	9	·81	24	·67	22
6	Fr	17	10	·72	25	·61	23
7	Sa	18	11	·62	26	·55	24
8	Su	19	12	·54	27	·49	25
9	Mo	20	13	·47	1	·45	26
10	Tu	21	14	·42	2	·43	27
11	We	22	—A	·38	3	·43	28
12	Th	23	1	·37	4	·44	—29
13	Fr	24	2	·37	5	·47	1
14	Sa	25	3	·38	6	·53	2
15	Su	26	4	·44	7	·60	3
16	Mo	27	5	·50	8	·69	4
17	Tu	28	6	·58	9	·80	5
18	We	29	7	·65	10	·90	6
19	Th	30	8	·75	...	...	7
20	Fr	31	9	·82	11	·01	8

June

Solar: Prajapati Mithuna—Ani. Lunar: Jyeshtha, Bahula, Sukla, Ashadha. Muhammadan: H. 1226 Jumadal-awwal, J. akhir.

Cyclic Sidereal Year, Month and Day	Week-Day	English Month and Day	Tithi	Ending Moment	Nakshatra	Ending Moment	Muhammadan Year, Month and Day
21	Sa	1	10	·87	12	·11	9
22	Su	2	11	·92	13	·19	10
23	Mo	3	12	·95	14	·27	11
24	Tu	4	13	·97	15	·32	12
25	We	5	14	·94	16	·34	13
26	Th	6	P	·92	17	·35	14
27	Fr	7	1	·86	18	·33	15
28	Sa	8	2	·80	19	·31	16
29	Su	9	3	·71	20	·27	17
30	Mo	10	4	·62	21	·21	18
31	Tu	11	5	·53	22	·15	19
—32	We	12	6	·41	23	·08	20
1	Th	13	7	·32	24 25}	·02 ·95}	21
2	Fr	14	8	·22	26	·88	22
3	Sa	15	9	·12	27	·83	23
4	Su	16	{10 11	·03 ·96	1	·78	24
5	Mo	17	12	·91	2	·75	25
6	Tu	18	13	·86	3	·75	26
7	We	19	14	·85	4	·76	27
8	Th	20	—A	·85	5	·79	28
9	Fr	21	1	·87	6	·83	29
10	Sa	22	2	·91	7	·91	—30
11	Su	23	3	·97	...	...	1
12	Mo	24	...	...	8	·00	2
13	Tu	25	4	·04	9	·10	3
14	We	26	5	·12	10	·20	4
15	Th	27	6	·22	11	·34	5
16	Fr	28	7	·28	12	·41	6
17	Sa	29	8	·36	13	·51	7
18	Su	30	9	·40	14	·58	8

Naksh :—1. Asvn. 2. Bhar. 3. Krit. 4. Rohi. 5. Mrig. 6. Ardh. 7. Punar. 8. Push. 9. Aslesh. 10. Magh. 11. P. Phal. 12. U. Phal. 13. Hasta. 14. Chit.

A. D. 1811. **Kollam 987,** Commences {N. Malabar—Sept. / S. Malabar—Aug.} **Hijra 1226,** Commences, Jan. 26. **Vikrama 1868.** **Bengal San 1217.** **(N. Cycle) Chitrabhanu.**

A.—Amavasya. P.—Paurnami.

Columns: SOLAR reckoning (Cyclic Sidereal Year, Month and Day; Week-Day; English Month and Day) — LUNAR reckoning (Tithi; Ending Moment; Nakshatra; Ending Moment; Muhammadan Year, Month and Day).

July — Prajapati Mithuna—Ani. (19–31); Prajapati Karkata—Adi (1–18); Ashadha Suk.; Bahula; Sukla; H. 1226 Jumadal-akhir.

Cyclic Sidereal Year, Month and Day	Week-Day	English Month and Day	Tithi	Ending Moment	Nakshatra	Ending Moment	Muhammadan Year, Month and Day
19	Mo	1	10	·43	15	·63	9
20	Tu	2	11	·44	16	·66	10
21	We	3	12	·42	17	·67	11
22	Th	4	13	·40	18	·67	12
23	Fr	5	14	·34	19	·64	13
24	Sa	6	P	·27	20	·60	14
25	Su	7	1	·19	21	·55	15
26	Mo	8	2	·11	22	·48	16
27	Tu	9	3 4	·00 ·89	23	·43	17
28	We	10	5	·80	24	·36	18
29	Th	11	6	·69	25	·28	19
30	Fr	12	7	·60	26	·22	20
31	Sa	13	8	·51	27	·16	21
1	Su	14	9	·45	1	·11	22
2	Mo	15	10	·38	2	·09	23
3	Tu	16	11	·34	3	·08	24
4	We	17	12	·33	4	·08	25
5	Th	18	13	·32	5	·10	26
6	Fr	19	14	·35	6	·14	27
7	Sa	20	A	·39	7	·22	28
8	Su	21	1	·45	8	·30	29
9	Mo	22	2	·51	9	·40	1
10	Tu	23	3	·61	10	·50	2
11	We	24	4	·69	11	·61	3
12	Th	25	5	·75	12	·72	4
13	Fr	26	6	·83	13	·81	5
14	Sa	27	7	·88	14	·89	6
15	Su	28	8	·92	15	·94	7
16	Mo	29	9	·92	16	·98	8
17	Tu	30	10	·91	...	...	9
18	We	31	11	·88	17	·00	10

Aug. — Prajapati Simha—Avani; Sravana; Bahula; Bhadrapada Sukla; H. 1226 Rajab; H. 1226 Shaban.

Cyclic Sidereal Year, Month and Day	Week-Day	English Month and Day	Tithi	Ending Moment	Nakshatra	Ending Moment	Muhammadan Year, Month and Day
19	Th	1	12	·82	18 19	·00 ·97	11
20	Fr	2	13	·76	20	·93	12
21	Sa	3	14	·68	21	·88	13
22	Su	4	P	·60	22	·82	14
23	Mo	5	1	·49	23	·76	15
24	Tu	6	2	·39	24	·69	16
25	We	7	3	·29	25	·62	17
26	Th	8	4	·18	26	·56	18
27	Fr	9	5	·09	27	·50	19
28	Sa	10	6 7	·00 ·94	1	·46	20
29	Su	11	8	·87	2	·42	21
30	Mo	12	9	·84	3	·40	22
31	Tu	13	10	·81	4	·40	23
32	We	14	11	·82	5	·42	24
1	Th	15	12	·83	6	·46	25
2	Fr	16	13	·87	7	·52	26
3	Sa	17	14	·94	8	·60	27
4	Su	18	...	...	9	·69	28
5	Mo	19	A	·01	10	·80	29
6	Tu	20	1	·10	11	·91	30
7	We	21	2	·18	...	...	1
8	Th	22	3	·26	12	·02	2
9	Fr	23	4	·33	13	·11	3
10	Sa	24	5	·36	14	·19	4
11	Su	25	6	·40	15	·25	5
12	Mo	26	7	·42	16	·29	6
13	Tu	27	8	·41	17	·32	7
14	We	28	9	·38	18	·32	8
15	Th	29	10	·34	19	·30	9
16	Fr	30	11	·26	20	·27	10
17	Sa	31	12	·18	21	·22	11

Sep. — Prajapati Simha—Avani; Prajapati Kanya—Purattasi; Bhadra.; Bahula; Sukla; H. 1226 Shaban; Ramzan.

Cyclic Sidereal Year, Month and Day	Week-Day	English Month and Day	Tithi	Ending Moment	Nakshatra	Ending Moment	Muhammadan Year, Month and Day
18	Su	1	13	·10	22	·17	12
19	Mo ○	2	14 P	·00 ·90	23	·10	13
20	Tu	3	1	·80	24 25	·03 ·96	14
21	We	4	2	·70	26	·89	15
22	Th	5	3	·61	27	·84	16
23	Fr	6	4	·53	1	·79	17
24	Sa	7	5	·45	2	·75	18
25	Su	8	6	·39	3	·73	19
26	Mo	9	7	·35	4	·72	20
27	Tu	10	8	·33	5	·74	21
28	We	11	9	·34	6	·78	22
29	Th	12	10	·35	7	·83	23
30	Fr	13	11	·40	8	·90	24
31	Sa	14	12	·45	9	·99	25
1	Su	15	13	·53	...	...	26
2	Mo	16	14	·63	10	·11	27
3	Tu	17	A	·70	11	·21	28
4	We	18	1	·78	12	·32	29
5	Th	19	2	·85	13	·41	1
6	Fr	20	3	·90	14	·50	2
7	Sa	21	4	·93	15	·56	3
8	Su	22	5	·95	16	·62	4
9	Mo	23	6	·94	17	·64	5
10	Tu	24	7	·91	18	·65	6
11	We	25	8	·87	19	·63	7
12	Th	26	9	·80	20	·60	8
13	Fr	27	10	·73	21	·56	9
14	Sa	28	11	·64	22	·51	10
15	Su	29	12	·55	23	·44	11
16	Mo	30	13	·45	24	·37	12

Oct. — Prajapati Tula—Aippasi; Asvina; Bahula; Sukla; Kart.; H. 1226 Ramzan; H. 1226 Shawwal.

Cyclic Sidereal Year, Month and Day	Week-Day	English Month and Day	Tithi	Ending Moment	Nakshatra	Ending Moment	Muhammadan Year, Month and Day
17	Tu	1	14	·35	25	·30	13
18	We	2	P	·24	26	·24	14
19	Th	3	1	·15	27	·18	15
20	Fr	4	2	·07	1	·12	16
21	Sa	5	3 4	·00 ·93	2	·08	17
22	Su	6	5	·90	3	·05	18
23	Mo	7	6	·88	4	·05	19
24	Tu	8	7	·88	5	·06	20
25	We	9	8	·91	6	·09	21
26	Th	10	9	·96	7	·14	22
27	Fr	11	...	...	8	·21	23
28	Sa	12	10	·01	9	·30	24
29	Su	13	11	·09	10	·40	25
30	Mo	14	12	·20	11	·51	26
1	Tu	15	13	·27	12	·62	27
2	We	16	14	·34	13	·72	28
3	Th	17	A	·42	14	·80	29
4	Fr	18	1	·47	15	·88	30
5	Sa	19	2	·50	16	·93	1
6	Su	20	3	·53	17	·96	2
7	Mo	21	4	·51	18	·97	3
8	Tu	22	5	·50	19	·96	4
9	We	23	6	·45	20	·94	5
10	Th	24	7	·38	21	·90	6
11	Fr	25	8	·31	22	·84	7
12	Sa	26	9	·22	23	·78	8
13	Su	27	10	·12	24	·71	9
14	Mo	28	11 12	·02 ·93	25	·65	10
15	Tu	29	13	·83	26	·58	11
16	We	30	14	·74	27	·51	12
17	Th	31	P	·66	1	·46	13

Nov. — Prajapati Tula—Aippasi; Prajapati Vrischika—Kartigai; Kartika; Bahula; Sukla; Margasira; H. 1226 Shawwal; Zi-l-ka'da.

Cyclic Sidereal Year, Month and Day	Week-Day	English Month and Day	Tithi	Ending Moment	Nakshatra	Ending Moment	Muhammadan Year, Month and Day
18	Fr	1	1	·59	2	·41	14
19	Sa	2	2	·53	3	·39	15
20	Su	3	3	·49	4	·37	16
21	Mo	4	4	·49	5	·38	17
22	Tu	5	5	·49	6	·40	18
23	We	6	6	·51	7	·45	19
24	Th	7	7	·55	8	·51	20
25	Fr	8	8	·61	9	·61	21
26	Sa	9	9	·70	10	·70	22
27	Su	10	10	·79	11	·81	23
28	Mo	11	11	·88	12	·91	24
29	Tu	12	12	·96	...	...	25
30	We	13	...	...	13	·02	26
1	Th	14	13	·08	14	·12	27
2	Fr	15	14	·07	15	·19	28
3	Sa	16	A	·12	16	·24	29
4	Su	17	1	·13	17	·28	1
5	Mo	18	2	·12	18	·29	2
6	Tu	19	3	·10	19	·29	3
7	We	20	4	·05	20	·27	4
8	Th	21	5 6	·00 ·92	21	·23	5
9	Fr	22	7	·83	22	·18	6
10	Sa	23	8	·74	23	·12	7
11	Su	24	9	·64	24 25	·06 ·99	8
12	Mo	25	10	·54	26	·92	9
13	Tu	26	11	·44	27	·85	10
14	We	27	12	·37	1	·79	11
15	Th	28	13	·28	2	·74	12
16	Fr	29	14	·21	3	·72	13
17	Sa	30	P	·15	4	·70	14

Dec. — Prajapati Dhanus—Margali; Bahula; Sukla; Psh.; Bah.; H. 1226; H. 1226 Zi-l-hijja.

Cyclic Sidereal Year, Month and Day	Week-Day	English Month and Day	Tithi	Ending Moment	Nakshatra	Ending Moment	Muhammadan Year, Month and Day
18	Su	1	1	·12	5	·70	15
19	Mo	2	2	·11	6	·72	16
20	Tu	3	3	·11	7	·76	17
21	We	4	4	·14	8	·83	18
22	Th	5	5	·19	9	·91	19
23	Fr	6	6	·26	...	...	20
24	Sa	7	7	·33	10	·00	21
25	Su	8	8	·42	11	·11	22
26	Mo	9	9	·51	12	·21	23
27	Tu	10	10	·59	13	·33	24
28	We	11	11	·67	14	·42	25
29	Th	12	12	·73	15	·50	26
30	Fr	13	13	·76	16	·56	27
1	Sa	14	14	·77	17	·59	28
2	Su	15	A	·76	18	·62	29
3	Mo	16	1	·74	19	·62	30
4	Tu	17	2	·68	20	·60	1
5	We	18	3	·63	21	·56	2
6	Th	19	4	·55	22	·51	3
7	Fr	20	5	·46	23	·46	4
8	Sa	21	6	·36	24	·40	5
9	Su	22	7	·28	25	·33	6
10	Mo	23	8	·17	26	·25	7
11	Tu	24	9	·07	27	·19	8
12	We	25	10 11	·00 ·92	1	·13	9
13	Th	26	12	·86	2	·08	10
14	Fr	27	13	·80	3	·05	11
15	Sa	28	14	·77	4	·02	12
16	Su	29	P	·75	5	·02	13
17	Mo	30	1	·76	6	·03	14
18	Tu	31	2	·79	7	·08	15

15. Svati. 16. Visak. 17. Anur. 18. Jyesh. 19. Mula. 20. P. Ash. 21. U. Ash. 22. Sravn. 23. Dani. 24. Satab. 25. P. Bhad. 26. U. Bhad. 27. Rev.

A. D. 1812. **Mesha Sankranti** (Commencement of Indian Sidereal Year).
Solar Eclipse. ● **(Surya Sid.) April 10·85.** **Saka 1734.** **Kaliyuga 4913.**
Lunar Eclipse. ○ **(Arya Sid.) April 10·75.** **(S. Cycle) Angirasa.**

SOLAR reckoning: Cyclic Sidereal Year, Month and Day; Week-Day; English Month and Day. LUNAR reckoning: Tithi, Ending Moment; Nakshatra, Ending Moment; Muhammadan Year, Month and Day.

Jan.

Cyclic Sidereal Year, Month and Day	Week-Day	English Month and Day	Tithi	Ending Moment	Nakshatra	Ending Moment	Muhammadan Year, Month and Day
Prajapati Dhanu—Margali 19	We	1	Pausha 3	·84	8	·14	H. 1226 Zi-l-hijja 16
20	Th	2	4	·91	9	·21	17
21	Fr	3	5	·99	10	·30	18
22	Sa	4	...	...	11	·40	19
23	Su	5	6	·08	12	·52	20
24	Mo	6	7	·16	13	·62	21
25	Tu	7	8	·26	14	·72	22
26	We	8	Bahula 9	·32	15	·80	23
27	Th	9	10	·37	16	·87	24
28	Fr	10	11	·40	17	·92	25
29	Sa	11	12	·42	18	·94	26
1	Su	12	13	·41	19	·94	27
2	Mo	13	14	·38	20	·93	28
3	Tu	14	A	·34	21	·90	29
4	We	15	1	·27	22	·85	30
5	Th	16	2	·19	23	·80	Muharram 1
6	Fr	17	3	·10	24	·73	2
7	Sa	18	4 / 5	·01 / ·91	25	·66	3
8	Su	19	Sukla 6	·80	26	·59	4
9	Mo	20	7	·72	27	·52	5
10	Tu	21	8	·64	1	·47	6
11	We	22	9	·55	2	·42	7
Prajapati Makara—Tai 12	Th	23	10	·49	3	·38	8
13	Fr	24	11	·44	4	·35	9
14	Sa	25	12	·41	5	·34	10
15	Su	26	Magha 13	·39	6	·36	11
16	Mo	27	14	·41	7	·39	12
17	Tu	28	P	·43	8	·44	13
18	We	29	1	·50	9	·51	14
19	Th	30	2	·56	10	·60	15
20	Fr	31	3	·64	11	·71	16

Feb.

Cyclic Sidereal Year, Month and Day	Week-Day	English Month and Day	Tithi	Ending Moment	Nakshatra	Ending Moment	Muhammadan Year, Month and Day
21	Sa	1	4	·73	12	·82	H. 1227 17
22	Su	2	5	·81	13	·92	18
23	Mo	3	6	·90	...	...	19
24	Tu	4	7	·97	14	·02	20
25	We	5	Bahula ...	...	15	·11	21
26	Th	6	8	·03	16	·19	22
27	Fr	7	9	·04	17	·23	23
28	Sa	8	10	·05	18	·26	24
29	Su	9	11	·05	19	·27	25
30	Mo	10	12 / 13	·02 / ·96	20	·26	26
1	Tu	11	14	·89	21	·23	27
2	We	12	A	·82	22	·19	28
3	Th	13	1	·73	23	·14	29
4	Fr	14	2	·63	24	·07	30
5	Sa	15	3	·54	25 / 26	·00 / ·93	H. 1227 Safar 1
6	Su	16	Sukla 4	·43	27	·87	2
Prajapati Kumbha—Masi 7	Mo	17	5	·35	1	·81	3
8	Tu	18	6	·26	2	·75	4
9	We	19	7	·18	3	·71	5
10	Th	20	8	·11	4	·68	6
11	Fr	21	9	·07	5	·67	7
12	Sa	22	Phalguna 10	·03	6	·68	8
13	Su	23	11	·02	7	·70	9
14	Mo	24	12	·03	8	·75	10
15	Tu	25	13	·06	9	·82	11
16	We	26	14	·12	10	·91	12
17	Th	27 ○	P	·18	...	...	13
18	Fr	28	Bah. 1	·26	11	·01	14
19	Sa	29	2	·36	12	·12	15

March

Cyclic Sidereal Year, Month and Day	Week-Day	English Month and Day	Tithi	Ending Moment	Nakshatra	Ending Moment	Muhammadan Year, Month and Day
Prajapati Kumbha—Masi 20	Su	1	Phalg. 3	·44	13	·22	H. 1227 Safar 16
21	Mo	2	4	·52	14	·32	17
22	Tu	3	5	·58	15	·41	18
23	We	4	6	·64	16	·49	19
24	Th	5	7	·66	17	·55	20
25	Fr	6	8	·67	18	·58	21
26	Sa	7	9	·66	19	·59	22
27	Su	8	Bahula 10	·62	20	·58	23
28	Mo	9	11	·57	21	·57	24
29	Tu	10	12	·50	22	·53	25
30	We	11	13	·43	23	·47	26
1	Th	12	14	·33	24	·41	27
2	Fr	13	A	·24	25	·34	28
3	Sa	14	1	·13	26	·28	29
4	Su	15	2 / 3	·04 / ·94	27	·21	Rabi-ul-awwal 1
5	Mo	16	4	·84	1	·14	2
6	Tu	17	5	·77	2	·09	3
7	We	18	6	·70	3	·04	4
8	Th	19	Sukla 7	·67	4	·01	5
9	Fr	20	8	·63	5	·00	6
10	Sa	21	9	·62	6	·00	7
11	Su	22	10	·62	7	·02	8
12	Mo	23	11	·65	8	·06	9
Prajapati Mina—Panguni 13	Tu	24	Chaitra 12	·71	9	·12	10
14	We	25	13	·77	10	·21	11
15	Th	26	14	·86	11	·31	12
16	Fr	27	P	·94	12	·41	13
17	Sa	28	...	...	13	·52	14
18	Su	29	1	·03	14	·62	15
19	Mo	30	2	·11	15	·72	16
20	Tu	31	3	·17	16	·80	17

April

Cyclic Sidereal Year, Month and Day	Week-Day	English Month and Day	Tithi	Ending Moment	Nakshatra	Ending Moment	Muhammadan Year, Month and Day
21	We	1	4	·22	17	·86	H. 1227 18
22	Th	2	5	·24	18	·90	19
23	Fr	3	Bahula 6	·25	19	·91	20
24	Sa	4	7	·23	20	·92	21
25	Su	5	8	·20	21	·90	22
26	Mo	6	9	·14	22	·86	23
27	Tu	7	10	·08	23	·81	24
28	We	8	11 / 12	·00 / ·90	24	·75	25
29	Th	9	13	·80	25	·69	26
30	Fr	10	14	·69	26	·62	27
1	Sa	11	A	·60	27	·55	28
2	Su	12	1	·50	1	·48	29
3	Mo	13	2	·41	2	·42	30
4	Tu	14	Sukla 3	·33	3	·38	H. 1227 Rabi-ul-akhir 1
5	We	15	4	·25	4	·34	2
6	Th	16	5	·22	5	·32	3
7	Fr	17	6	·18	6	·32	4
8	Sa	18	7	·17	7	·33	5
Angirasa Mesha—Chittirai 9	Su	19	8	·17	8	·37	6
10	Mo	20	9	·21	9	·44	7
11	Tu	21	Adhika Vaisakha 10	·26	10	·52	8
12	We	22	11	·32	11	·61	9
13	Th	23	12	·40	12	·71	10
14	Fr	24	13	·48	13	·82	11
15	Sa	25	14	·57	14	·93	12
16	Su	26	P	·64	...	...	13
17	Mo	27	Bah. 1	·71	15	·03	14
18	Tu	28	2	·76	16	·11	15
19	We	29	3	·79	17	·17	16
20	Th	30	4	·78	18	·21	17

May

Cyclic Sidereal Year, Month and Day	Week-Day	English Month and Day	Tithi	Ending Moment	Nakshatra	Ending Moment	Muhammadan Year, Month and Day
Angirasa Mesha—Chittirai 21	Fr	1	Adh. Vak. 5	·76	19	·24	H. 1227 Rabi-ul-akhir 18
22	Sa	2	6	·74	20	·24	19
23	Su	3	7	·67	21	·23	20
24	Mo	4	8	·61	22	·19	21
25	Tu	5	9	·53	23	·14	22
26	We	6	10	·43	24	·09	23
27	Th	7	Bahula 11	·33	25 / 26	·03 / ·96	24
28	Fr	8	12	·23	27	·89	25
29	Sa	9	13	·13	1	·82	26
30	Su	10	14 / A	·03 / ·93	2	·76	27
31	Mo	11	1	·85	3	·71	28
1	Tu	12	2	·78	4	·67	29
2	We	13	3	·74	5	·65	Jumadal-awwal 1
3	Th	14	4	·71	6	·64	2
4	Fr	15	5	·69	7	·66	3
5	Sa	16	6	·68	8	·69	4
6	Su	17	Sukla 7	·73	9	·74	5
7	Mo	18	8	·77	10	·82	6
8	Tu	19	9	·84	11	·91	7
9	We	20	10	·91	...	...	8
10	Th	21	11	·99	12	·01	9
11	Fr	22	...	...	13	·13	10
Angirasa Vrishabha—Vaikasi 12	Sa	23	Nija Vaisakha 12	·07	14	·23	11
13	Su	24	13	·15	15	·33	12
14	Mo	25	14	·22	16	·41	13
15	Tu	26	P	·26	17	·48	14
16	We	27	1	·28	18	·54	15
17	Th	28	2	·29	19	·56	16
18	Fr	29	3	·28	20	·57	17
19	Sa	30	4	·24	21	·55	18
20	Su	31	5	·18	22	·52	19

June

Cyclic Sidereal Year, Month and Day	Week-Day	English Month and Day	Tithi	Ending Moment	Nakshatra	Ending Moment	Muhammadan Year, Month and Day
21	Mo	1	6	·11	23	·49	H. 1227 20
22	Tu	2	7 / 8	·02 / ·93	24	·43	21
23	We	3	9	·83	25	·37	22
24	Th	4	Bahula 10	·73	26	·30	23
25	Fr	5	11	·62	27	·23	24
26	Sa	6	12	·53	1	·17	25
27	Su	7	13	·44	2	·10	26
28	Mo	8	14	·36	3	·05	27
29	Tu	9	A	·28	4 / 5	·00 / ·97	28
30	We	10	1	·23	6	·97	29
31	Th	11	2	·20	7	·98	30
1	Fr	12	3	·17	...	...	H. 1227 Jumadal-akhir 1
2	Sa	13	4	·18	8	·01	2
3	Su	14	5	·21	9	·06	3
4	Mo	15	Sukla 6	·24	10	·12	4
5	Tu	16	7	·31	11	·21	5
6	We	17	8	·38	12	·32	6
7	Th	18	9	·47	13	·42	7
8	Fr	19	10	·55	14	·53	8
Angirasa Mithuna—Ani 9	Sa	20	11	·63	15	·63	9
10	Su	21	Jyeshtha 12	·69	16	·72	10
11	Mo	22	13	·74	17	·80	11
12	Tu	23	14	·76	18	·85	12
13	We	24	P	·77	19	·88	13
14	Th	25	1	·75	20	·89	14
15	Fr	26	2	·72	21	·88	15
16	Sa	27	Bahula 3	·67	22	·86	16
17	Su	28	4	·59	23	·82	17
18	Mo	29	5	·51	24	·77	18
19	Tu	30	6	·42	25	·70	19

Naksh:—1. Asvn. 2. Bhar. 3. Krit. 4. Rohi. 5. Mrig. 6. Ardh. 7. Punar. 8. Push. 9. Aslesh. 10. Magh. 11. P. Phal. 12. U. Phal. 13. Hasta. 14. Chit.

A. D. 1812.
A.—Amavasya.
P.—Paurnami.

Kollam 988, Commences { N. Malabar—Sept. / S. Malabar—Aug.

Hijra 1227, Commences Jan. 16.

Vikrama 1869.
Bengal San 1218.
(N. Cycle) Subhanu.

SOLAR reckoning: Cyclic Sidereal Year, Month and Day. — Week-Day, English Month and Day. — LUNAR reckoning: Tithi, Ending Moment; Nakshatra, Ending Moment; Muhammadan Year, Month and Day.

July — Solar: Angirasa *Mithuna—Ani*; Angirasa *Karkata—Adi*. Lunar: Jy. *Bahula*; *Sukla*; Ashadha. Muhammadan: H. 1227 *Jl. akhir.*; H. 1227 *Rajab.*

Cyclic Sidereal Year, Month and Day	Week-Day	English Month and Day	Tithi	Ending Moment	Nakshatra	Ending Moment	Muhammadan Year, Month and Day
20	We	1	7	·32	26	·64	20
21	Th	2	8	·21	27	·57	21
22	Fr	3	9	·11	1	·50	22
23	Sa	4	10 / 11	·02 / ·91	2	·44	23
24	Su	5	12	·84	3	·38	24
25	Mo	6	13	·76	4	·33	25
26	Tu	7	14	·70	5	·30	26
27	We	8	A	·68	6	·30	27
28	Th	9	1	·66	7	·30	28
29	Fr	10	2	·65	8	·32	—29
30	Sa	11	3	·68	9	·36	1
31	Su	12	4	·73	10	·43	2
—32	Mo	13	5	·79	11	·52	3
1	Tu	14	6	·86	12	·62	4
2	We	15	7	·95	13	·72	5
3	Th	16	...	...	14	·83	6
4	Fr	17	8	·03	15	·93	7
5	Sa	18	9	·11	...	...	8
6	Su	19	10	·16	16	·03	9
7	Mo	20	11	·22	17	·11	10
8	Tu	21	12	·24	18	·16	11
9	We	22	13	·26	19	·20	12
10	Th	23	14	·23	20	·21	13
11	Fr	24	P	·20	21	·22	14
12	Sa	25	1	·15	22	·19	15
13	Su	26	2	·07	23	·15	16
14	Mo	27	3 / 4	·00 / ·91	24	·10	17
15	Tu	28	5	·82	25 / 26	·04 / ·98	18
16	We	29	6	·70	27	·92	19
17	Th	30	7	·60	1	·84	20
18	Fr	31	8	·51	2	·78	21

Aug. — Solar: Angirasa *Simha—Avani*. Lunar: *Bahula*; *Sukla*; Sravana; *Bahula*. Muhammadan: H. 1227 *Shaban.*

Cyclic Sidereal Year, Month and Day	Week-Day	English Month and Day	Tithi	Ending Moment	Nakshatra	Ending Moment	Muhammadan Year, Month and Day
19	Sa	1	9	·41	3	·72	22
20	Su	2	10	·33	4	·67	23
21	Mo	3	11	·25	5	·64	24
22	Tu	4	12	·20	6	·62	25
23	We	5	13	·15	7	·62	26
24	Th	6	14	·14	8	·64	27
25	Fr	7	—A	·14	9	·67	28
26	Sa	8	1	·16	10	·74	29
27	Su	9	2	·20	11	·82	—30
28	Mo	10	3	·26	12	·92	1
29	Tu	11	4	·34	...	...	2
30	We	12	5	·43	13	·02	3
—31	Th	13	6	·52	14	·13	4
1	Fr	14	7	·58	15	·24	5
2	Sa	15	8	·64	16	·33	6
3	Su	16	9	·70	17	·41	7
4	Mo	17	10	·74	18	·47	8
5	Tu	18	11	·75	19	·51	9
6	We	19	12	·72	20	·54	10
7	Th	20	13	·69	21	·54	11
8	Fr	21	14	·65	22	·52	12
9	Sa	○ 22	P	·58	23	·49	13
10	Su	23	1	·50	24	·44	14
11	Mo	24	2	·40	25	·38	15
12	Tu	25	3	·31	26	·32	16
13	We	26	4	·20	27	·25	17
14	Th	27	5	·11	1	·18	18
15	Fr	28	6 / 7	·01 / ·92	2	·11	19
16	Sa	29	8	·83	3	·05	20
17	Su	30	9	·75	4 / 5	·01 / ·97	21
18	Mo	31	10	·71	6	·94	22

Sep. — Solar: Angirasa *Simha—Avani*; Angirasa *Kanya—Purattasi*. Lunar: Sr. *Bah.*; *Sukla*; Bhadrapada. Muhammadan: *Shaban.*; H. 1227 *Ramzan.*

Cyclic Sidereal Year, Month and Day	Week-Day	English Month and Day	Tithi	Ending Moment	Nakshatra	Ending Moment	Muhammadan Year, Month and Day
19	Tu	1	11	·66	7	·94	23
20	We	2	12	·65	8	·95	24
21	Th	3	13	·65	...	...	25
22	Fr	4	14	·68	9	·00	26
23	Sa	5	A	·72	10	·05	27
24	Su	6	1	·76	11	·13	28
25	Mo	7	2	·85	12	·22	—29
26	Tu	8	3	·93	13	·32	1
27	We	9	...	...	14	·43	2
28	Th	10	4	·02	15	·54	3
29	Fr	11	5	·09	16	·64	4
30	Sa	12	6	·17	17	·71	5
—31	Su	13	7	·22	18	·78	6
1	Mo	14	8	·24	19	·83	7
2	Tu	15	9	·27	20	·86	8
3	We	16	10	·25	21	·87	9
4	Th	17	11	·23	22	·85	10
5	Fr	18	12	·18	23	·82	11
6	Sa	19	13	·12	24	·77	12
7	Su	20	14 / P	·03 / ·94	25	·73	13
8	Mo	21	1	·84	26	·66	14
9	Tu	22	2	·74	27	·59	15
10	We	23	3	·65	1	·52	16
11	Th	24	4	·54	2	·46	17
12	Fr	25	5	·45	3	·40	18
13	Sa	26	6	·37	4	·34	19
14	Su	27	7	·30	5	·30	20
15	Mo	28	8	·25	6	·27	21
16	Tu	29	9	·20	7	·26	22
17	We	30	10	·19	8	·28	23

Oct. — Solar: Angirasa *Tula—Aippasi.* Lunar: *Bahula*; *Sukla*; Asvina; *Bahula*. Muhammadan: H. 1227 *Shawwal.*

Cyclic Sidereal Year, Month and Day	Week-Day	English Month and Day	Tithi	Ending Moment	Nakshatra	Ending Moment	Muhammadan Year, Month and Day
18	Th	1	11	·18	9	·31	24
19	Fr	2	12	·22	10	·36	25
20	Sa	3	13	·26	11	·43	26
21	Su	4	14	·32	12	·52	27
22	Mo	5	—A	·40	13	·63	28
23	Tu	6	1	·49	14	·73	29
24	We	7	2	·57	15	·84	—30
25	Th	8	3	·64	16	·94	1
26	Fr	9	4	·72	...	...	2
27	Sa	10	5	·78	17	·02	3
28	Su	11	6	·82	18	·09	4
29	Mo	12	7	·83	19	·15	5
30	Tu	13	8	·82	20	·18	6
—31	We	14	9	·79	21	·19	7
1	Th	15	10	·74	22	·18	8
2	Fr	16	11	·68	23	·15	9
3	Sa	17	12	·59	24	·12	10
4	Su	18	13	·51	25	·06	11
5	Mo	19	14	·41	26 / 27	·00 / ·92	12
6	Tu	20	P	·31	1	·86	13
7	We	21	1	·21	2	·80	14
8	Th	22	2	·12	3	·73	15
9	Fr	23	3 / 4	·03 / ·95	4	·68	16
10	Sa	24	5	·88	5	·63	17
11	Su	25	6	·83	6	·60	18
12	Mo	26	7	·79	7	·59	19
13	Tu	27	8	·77	8	·60	20
14	We	28	9	·78	9	·62	21
15	Th	29	10	·81	10	·67	22
16	Fr	30	11	·85	11	·73	23
17	Sa	31	12	·92	12	·82	24

Nov. — Solar: Angirasa *Tula—Aippasi.*; Angirasa *Vrischika—Kartigai.* Lunar: *Bah.*; *Sukla*; Kartika; *Bahula*. Muhammadan: *Shawwal.*; H. 1227 *Zi-l-ka'da.*

Cyclic Sidereal Year, Month and Day	Week-Day	English Month and Day	Tithi	Ending Moment	Nakshatra	Ending Moment	Muhammadan Year, Month and Day
18	Su	1	...	...	13	·92	25
19	Mo	2	13	·00	...	...	26
20	Tu	3	14	·08	14	·03	27
21	We	4	—A	·17	15	·14	28
22	Th	5	1	·26	16	·24	—29
23	Fr	6	2	·32	17	·33	1
24	Sa	7	3	·37	18	·41	2
25	Su	8	4	·42	19	·46	3
26	Mo	9	5	·42	20	·50	4
27	Tu	10	6	·42	21	·51	5
28	We	11	7	·38	22	·50	6
29	Th	12	8	·35	23	·49	7
—30	Fr	13	9	·28	24	·45	8
1	Sa	14	10	·19	25	·40	9
2	Su	15	11	·11	26	·34	10
3	Mo	16	12 / 13	·02 / ·92	27	·27	11
4	Tu	17	14	·82	1	·21	12
5	We	18	P	·72	2	·14	13
6	Th	19	1	·64	3	·07	14
7	Fr	20	2	·56	4 / 5	·01 / ·96	15
8	Sa	21	3	·48	6	·94	16
9	Su	22	4	·45	7	·92	17
10	Mo	23	5	·41	8	·92	18
11	Tu	24	6	·39	9	·94	19
12	We	25	7	·40	10	·98	20
13	Th	26	8	·42	...	...	21
14	Fr	27	9	·48	11	·04	22
15	Sa	28	10	·54	12	·13	23
16	Su	29	11	·62	13	·22	24
17	Mo	30	12	.71	14	·33	25

Dec. — Solar: Angirasa *Dhanus—Margali.* Lunar: *Sukla*; Margasira; *Bahula*. Muhammadan: H. 1227 *Zi-l-hijja.*

Cyclic Sidereal Year, Month and Day	Week-Day	English Month and Day	Tithi	Ending Moment	Nakshatra	Ending Moment	Muhammadan Year, Month and Day
18	Tu	1	13	·80	15	·43	26
19	We	2	14	·88	16	·54	27
20	Th	3	—A	·95	17	·64	28
21	Fr	4	...	...	18	·72	29
22	Sa	5	1	·01	19	·78	—30
23	Su	6	2	·05	20	·81	1
24	Mo	7	3	·05	21	·83	2
25	Tu	8	4	·04	22	·84	3
26	We	9	5 / 6	·01 / ·97	23	·82	4
27	Th	10	7	·90	24	·78	5
28	Fr	11	8	·82	25	·73	6
—29	Sa	12	9	·74	26	·67	7
1	Su	13	10	·65	27	·62	8
2	Mo	14	11	·54	1	·54	9
3	Tu	15	12	·45	2	·47	10
4	We	16	13	·35	3	·41	11
5	Th	17	14	·26	4	·35	12
6	Fr	18	P	·19	5	·29	13
7	Sa	19	1	·12	6	·27	14
8	Su	20	2	·08	7	·24	15
9	Mo	21	3	·04	8	·24	16
10	Tu	22	4	·03	9	·25	17
11	We	23	5	·04	10	·29	18
12	Th	24	6	·07	11	·36	19
13	Fr	25	7	·15	12	·43	20
14	Sa	26	8	·19	13	·52	21
15	Su	27	9	·28	14	·62	22
16	Mo	28	10	·37	15	·73	23
17	Tu	29	11	·46	16	·85	24
18	We	30	12	·53	17	·94	25
19	Th	31	13	·61	...	...	26

15. Svati. 16. Visak. 17. Anur. 18. Jyesh. 19. Mula. 20. P. Ash. 21. U. Ash. 22. Sravn. 23. Dani. 24. Satab. 25. P. Bhad. 26. U. Bhad. 27. Rev.

A. D. 1813. **Mesha Sankranti** (Commencement of Indian Sidereal Year). **Saka 1735.** **Kaliyuga 4914.**

Solar Eclipse. ● **(Surya Sid.) April 11·11.** **(S. Cycle) Srimukha.**

Lunar Eclipse. ○ **(Arya Sid.) April 11·01.**

SOLAR reckoning: Cyclic Sidereal Year, Month and Day; Week-Day; English Month and Day. LUNAR reckoning: Tithi; Ending Moment; Nakshatra; Ending Moment; Muhammadan Year, Month and Day.

Cyclic Sidereal Year, Month and Day	Week-Day	English Month and Day	Tithi	Ending Moment	Nakshatra	Ending Moment	Muhammadan Year, Month and Day
		Jan.					
Angirasa, Dhanus—Margali			*Pausha, Sukla*				
20	Fr	1	14	·66	18	·02	27
21	Sa	2	—A	·69	19	·09	28
22	Su	3	1	·70	20	·13	—29
							H. 1228 Muharram
23	Mo	4	2	·69	21	·16	1
24	Tu	5	3	·66	22	·16	2
25	We	6	4	·61	23	·15	3
26	Th	7	5	·55	24	·11	4
27	Fr	8	6	·47	25	·07	5
28	Sa	9	7	·38	26 27	·02 ·95	6
—29	Su	10	8	·30	1	·88	7
Angirasa, Makara—Tai							
1	Mo	11	9	·19	2	·81	8
2	Tu	12	10	·10	3	·74	9
3	We	13	11 12	·00 ·91	4	·68	10
4	Th	14	13	·83	5	·64	11
5	Fr	15	14	·76	6	·60	12
6	Sa	16	P	·73	7	·57	13
			Pausha, Bahula				
7	Su	17	1	·69	8	·56	14
8	Mo	18	2	·68	9	·58	15
9	Tu	19	3	·69	10	·61	16
10	We	20	4	·73	11	·66	17
11	Th	21	5	·77	12	·73	18
12	Fr	22	6	·85	13	·82	19
13	Sa	23	7	·93	14	·92	20
14	Su	24	...	...	...	...	21
15	Mo	25	8	·02	15	·04	22
16	Tu	26	9	·11	16	·14	23
17	We	27	10	·19	17	·24	24
18	Th	28	11	·27	18	·33	25
19	Fr	29	12	·30	19	·40	26
20	Sa	30	13	·33	20	·45	27
21	Su	31	14	·34	21	·48	28
		Feb.					
			Magha, Sukla				
22	Mo ●	1	—A	·33	22	·49	29
23	Tu	2	1	·30	23	·48	—30
							H. 1228 Safar
24	We	3	2	·25	24	·45	1
25	Th	4	3	·18	25	·40	2
26	Fr	5	4	·10	26	·36	3
27	Sa	6	5 6	·01 ·91	27	·29	4
28	Su	7	7	·81	1	·22	5
29	Mo	8	8	·72	2	·15	6
—30	Tu	9	9	·62	3	·08	7
Angirasa, Kumbha—Masi							
1	We	10	10	·54	4 5	·03 ·97	8
2	Th	11	11	·45	6	·93	9
3	Fr	12	12	·39	7	·90	10
4	Sa	13	13	·30	8	·88	11
5	Su	14	14	·32	9	·90	12
6	Mo ○	15	P	·31	10	·92	13
			Magha, Bahula				
7	Tu	16	1	·31	11	·97	14
8	We	17	2	·37	...	...	15
9	Th	18	3	·41	12	·04	16
10	Fr	19	4	·49	13	·12	17
11	Sa	20	5	·56	14	·23	18
12	Su	21	6	·64	15	·34	19
13	Mo	22	7	·73	16	·44	20
14	Tu	23	8	·82	17	·54	21
15	We	24	9	·89	18	·63	22
16	Th	25	10	·93	19	·70	23
17	Fr	26	11	·96	20	·77	24
18	Sa	27	12	·96	21	·80	25
19	Su	28	13	·94	22	·81	26

Cyclic Sidereal Year, Month and Day	Week-Day	English Month and Day	Tithi	Ending Moment	Nakshatra	Ending Moment	Muhammadan Year, Month and Day
		March					
Angirasa, Kumbha—Masi			*Phalguna, Sukla*				
20	Mo	1	14	·92	23	·80	27
21	Tu	2	—A	·86	24	·78	28
22	We	3	1	·80	25	·75	29
							H. 1228 Rabi-ul-awwal
23	Th	4	2	·71	26	·69	1
24	Fr	5	3	·63	27	·63	2
25	Sa	6	4	·52	1	·56	3
26	Su	7	5	·43	2	·49	4
27	Mo	8	6	·33	3	·43	5
28	Tu	9	7	·23	4	·36	6
29	We	10	8	·15	5	·31	7
—30	Th	11	9	·06	6	·26	8
Angirasa, Mina—Panguni							
1	Fr	12	10 11	·00 ·96	7	·22	9
2	Sa	13	12	·93	8	·22	10
3	Su	14	13	·91	9	·22	11
4	Mo	15	14	·92	10	·24	12
5	Tu	16	P	·96	11	·28	13
			Phalguna, Bahula				
6	We	17	...	...	12	·34	14
7	Th	18	1	·00	13	·43	15
8	Fr	19	2	·09	14	·53	16
9	Sa	20	3	·17	15	·63	17
10	Su	21	4	·26	16	·74	18
11	Mo	22	5	·34	17	·84	19
12	Tu	23	6	·43	18	·94	20
13	We	24	7	·48	...	...	21
14	Th	25	8	·52	19	·02	22
15	Fr	26	9	·56	20	·08	23
16	Sa	27	10	·55	21	·12	24
17	Su	28	11	·54	22	·13	25
18	Mo	29	12	·49	23	·13	26
19	Tu	30	13	·45	24	·12	27
20	We	31	14	·37	25	·08	28
		April					
			Chaitra, Sukla				
21	Th	1	—A	·29	26 27	·03 ·97	29
22	Fr	2	1	·20	1	·90	—30
							H. 1228 Rabi-ul-akhir
23	Sa	3	2	·09	2	·84	1
24	Su	4	3 4	·00 ·89	3	·77	2
25	Mo	5	5	·81	4	·70	3
26	Tu	6	6	·72	5	·64	4
27	We	7	7	·63	6	·59	5
28	Th	8	8	·57	7	·56	6
29	Fr	9	9	·53	8	·54	7
—30	Sa	10	10	·49	9	·54	8
Srimukha, Mesha—Chittirai							
1	Su	11	11	·47	10	·55	9
2	Mo	12	12	·48	11	·59	10
3	Tu	13	13	·52	12	·65	11
4	We	14	14	·57	13	·74	12
5	Th	15	P	·65	14	·83	13
			Chaitra, Bahula				
6	Fr	16	1	·72	15	·93	14
7	Sa	17	2	·81	...	...	15
8	Su	18	3	·89	16	·04	16
9	Mo	19	4	·98	17	·14	17
10	Tu	20	...	...	18	·25	18
11	We	21	5	·03	19	·33	19
12	Th	22	6	·08	20	·39	20
13	Fr	23	7	·09	21	·43	21
14	Sa	24	8	·09	22	·45	22
15	Su	25	9	·08	23	·46	23
16	Mo	26	10 11	·04 ·99	24	·45	24
17	Tu	27	12	·91	25	·41	25
18	We	28	13	·84	26	·36	26
19	Th	29	14	·74	27	·30	27
20	Fr	30	—A	·63	1	·25	28

Cyclic Sidereal Year, Month and Day	Week-Day	English Month and Day	Tithi	Ending Moment	Nakshatra	Ending Moment	Muhammadan Year, Month and Day
		May					
Srimukha, Mesha—Chittirai			*Vaisakha, Sukla*				
21	Sa	1	1	·54	2	·18	—29
							H. 1228 Jumadal-awwal
22	Su	2	2	·43	3	·11	1
23	Mo	3	3	·34	4 5	·04 ·98	2
24	Tu	4	4	·25	6	·93	3
25	We	5	5	·17	7	·89	4
26	Th	6	6	·09	8	·88	5
27	Fr	7	7	·06	9	·86	6
28	Sa	8	8	·02	10	·87	7
29	Su	9	9	·00	11	·90	8
30	Mo	10	10	·02	12	·97	9
—31	Tu	11	11	·04	...	...	10
Srimukha, Vrishabha—Vaikasi							
1	We	12	12	·10	13	·04	11
2	Th	13	13	·16	14	·13	12
3	Fr	14	14	·24	15	·23	13
4	Sa	15	P	·32	16	·34	14
			Vaisakha, Bahula				
5	Su	16	1	·39	17	·45	15
6	Mo	17	2	·48	18	·55	16
7	Tu	18	3	·54	19	·63	17
8	We	19	4	·59	20	·70	18
9	Th	20	5	·61	21	·75	19
10	Fr	21	6	·61	22	·78	20
11	Sa	22	7	·59	23	·78	21
12	Su	23	8	·55	24	·77	22
13	Mo	24	9	·50	25	·74	23
14	Tu	25	10	·42	26	·70	24
15	We	26	11	·34	27	·65	25
16	Th	27	12	·24	1	·59	26
17	Fr	28	13	·15	2	·51	27
18	Sa	29	14 A	·05 ·94	3	·45	28
19	Su	30	1	·84	4	·38	29
20	Mo	31	2	·75	5	·31	—30
		June					
			Jyeshtha, Sukla				*H. 1228 Jumadal-akhir*
21	Tu	1	3	·67	6	·27	1
22	We	2	4	·60	7	·22	2
23	Th	3	5	·56	8	·19	3
24	Fr	4	6	·52	9	·18	4
25	Sa	5	7	·50	10	·19	5
26	Su	6	8	·51	11	·23	6
27	Mo	7	9	·58	12	·28	7
28	Tu	8	10	·60	13	·34	8
29	We	9	11	·65	14	·43	9
30	Th	10	12	·73	15	·52	10
—31	Fr	11	13	·81	16	·64	11
Srimukha, Mithuna—Ani							
1	Sa	12	14	·89	17	·75	12
2	Su	13	P	·96	18	·85	13
			Jyeshtha, Bahula				
3	Mo	14	...	...	19	·94	14
4	Tu	15	1	·08	...	...	15
5	We	16	2	·06	20	·01	16
6	Th	17	3	·09	21	·07	17
7	Fr	18	4	·10	22	·10	18
8	Sa	19	5	·08	23	·11	19
9	Su	20	6 7	·04 ·99	24	·10	20
10	Mo	21	8	·92	25	·07	21
11	Tu	22	9	·83	26 27	·04 ·99	22
12	We	23	10	·73	1	·92	23
13	Th	24	11	·64	2	·85	24
14	Fr	25	12	·53	3	·78	25
15	Sa	26	13	·43	4	·71	26
16	Su	27	14	·33	5	·66	27
17	Mo	28	—A	·24	6	·60	28
			A. Suk.				
18	Tu	29	1	·15	7	·55	—29
19	We	30	2	·08	8	·52	1

Naksh:—1. Asvn. 2. Bhar. 3. Krit. 4. Rohi. 5. Mrig. 6. Ardh. 7. Punar. 8. Push. 9. Aslesh. 10. Magh. 11. P. Phal. 12. U. Phal. 13. Hasta. 14. Chit.

A. D. 1813.
A.—Amavasya. P.—Paurnami.
Kollam 989, Commences {**N. Malabar—Sept.** / **S. Malabar—Aug.**}
Hijra 1228, Jan. 4. **Hijra 1229, Dec. 24.**
Vikrama 1870. **Bengal San 1219.** **(N. Cycle) Tarana.**

SOLAR reckoning: Cyclic Sidereal Year, Month and Day; Week-Day; English Month and Day. LUNAR reckoning: Tithi, Ending Moment; Nakshatra, Ending Moment; Muhammadan Year, Month and Day.

July

Solar month	Cyclic Sidereal Day	Week-Day	English Day	Lunar month	Tithi	Ending Moment	Nakshatra	Ending Moment	Muhammadan Day
Srimukha Mithuna—Ani	20	Th	1	Ashadha Sukla	3, 4	·03, ·99	9	·51	2 (H. 1228 Rajab)
	21	Fr	2		5	·98	10	·52	3
	22	Sa	3		6	·99	11	·54	4
	23	Su	4		...	...	12	·58	5
	24	Mo	5		7	·01	13	·65	6
	25	Tu	6		8	·06	14	·73	7
	26	We	7		9	·13	15	·84	8
	27	Th	8		10	·20	16	·94	9
	28	Fr	9		11	·27	...	...	10
	29	Sa	10		12	·37	17	·05	11
	30	Su	11		13	·43	18	·15	12
	31	Mo	12		14	·50	19	·24	13
	32	Tu	13		P	·54	20	·33	14
Srimukha Karkata—Adi	1	We	14	Bahula	1	·58	21	·38	15
	2	Th	15		2	·57	22	·42	16
	3	Fr	16		3	·55	23	·43	17
	4	Sa	17		4	·52	24	·43	18
	5	Su	18		5	·46	25	·40	19
	6	Mo	19		6	·39	26	·36	20
	7	Tu	20		7	·31	27	·32	21
	8	We	21		8	·22	1	·26	22
	9	Th	22		9	·12	2	·19	23
	10	Fr	23		10, 11	·02, ·92	3	·12	24
	11	Sa	24		12	·81	4, 5	·06, ·99	25
	12	Su	25		13	·72	6	·94	26
	13	Mo	26		14	·63	7	·89	27
	14	Tu	27		A	·57	8	·85	28
	15	We	28	Sravana Sukla	1	·51	9	·84	29
	16	Th	29		2	·48	10	·84	30
	17	Fr	30		3	·46	11	·86	1 (Shaban)
	18	Sa	31		4	·47	12	·90	2

Aug.

Solar month	Cyclic Sidereal Day	Week-Day	English Day	Lunar month	Tithi	Ending Moment	Nakshatra	Ending Moment	Muhammadan Day
	19	Su	1	Sravana Sukla	5	·48	13	·95	3 (H. 1228 Shaban)
	20	Mo	2		6	·53	...	...	4
	21	Tu	3		7	·60	14	·04	5
	22	We	4		8	·67	15	·14	6
	23	Th	5		9	·76	16	·24	7
	24	Fr	6		10	·84	17	·35	8
	25	Sa	7		11	·91	18	·45	9
	26	Su	8		12	·98	19	·55	10
	27	Mo	9		...	...	20	·63	11
	28	Tu	10		13	·03	21	·69	12
	29	We	11		14	·06	22	·73	13
	30	Th ○	12		P	·06	23	·75	14
	31	Fr	13	Bahula	1	·05	24	·75	15
Srimukha Simha—Avani	1	Sa	14		2, 3	·01, ·96	25	·74	16
	2	Su	15		4	·89	26	·71	17
	3	Mo	16		5	·81	27	·66	18
	4	Tu	17		6	·72	1	·60	19
	5	We	18		7	·62	2	·53	20
	6	Th	19		8	·52	3	·47	21
	7	Fr	20		9	·41	4	·40	22
	8	Sa	21		10	·32	5	·33	23
	9	Su	22		11	·22	6	·27	24
	10	Mo	23		12	·14	7	·22	25
	11	Tu	24		13	·07	8	·19	26
	12	We	25		14, A	·00, ·98	9	·16	27
	13	Th	26	Bhad. Suk.	1	·96	10	·16	28
	14	Fr	27		2	·97	11	·17	29
	15	Sa	28		3	·99	12	·21	1 (Ramzan)
	16	Su	29		...	...	13	·27	2
	17	Mo	30		4	·03	14	·35	3
	18	Tu	31		5	·10	15	·44	4

Sep.

Solar month	Cyclic Sidereal Day	Week-Day	English Day	Lunar month	Tithi	Ending Moment	Nakshatra	Ending Moment	Muhammadan Day
Srimukha Simha—Avani	19	We	1	Bhadrapada Sukla	6	·17	16	·54	5 (H. 1228 Ramzan)
	20	Th	2		7	·26	17	·64	6
	21	Fr	3		8	·34	18	·75	7
	22	Sa	4		9	·43	19	·86	8
	23	Su	5		10	·49	20	·94	9
	24	Mo	6		11	·54	...	...	10
	25	Tu	7		12	·56	21	·00	11
	26	We	8		13	·57	22	·05	12
	27	Th	9		14	·56	23	·07	13
	28	Fr	10		P	·53	24	·09	14
	29	Sa	11	Bahula	1	·49	25	·07	15
	30	Su	12		2	·41	26, 27	·04, ·99	16
	31	Mo	13		3	·34	1	·93	17
Srimukha Kanya—Purattasi	1	Tu	14		4	·24	2	·88	18
	2	We	15		5	·14	3	·81	19
	3	Th	16		6, 7	·05, ·94	4	·74	20
	4	Fr	17		8	·85	5	·67	21
	5	Sa	18		9	·74	6	·61	22
	6	Su	19		10	·67	7	·56	23
	7	Mo	20		11	·60	8	·52	24
	8	Tu	21		12	·53	9	·49	25
	9	We	22		13	·51	10	·48	26
	10	Th	23		14	·49	11	·49	27
	11	Fr	24		A	·51	12	·52	28
	12	Sa	25	Asvina Sukla	1	·52	13	·58	29
	13	Su	26		2	·58	14	·65	30
	14	Mo	27		3	·63	15	·74	1 (Shawwal)
	15	Tu	28		4	·72	16	·84	2
	16	We	29		5	·80	17	·94	3
	17	Th	30		6	·88	...	...	4

Oct.

Solar month	Cyclic Sidereal Day	Week-Day	English Day	Lunar month	Tithi	Ending Moment	Nakshatra	Ending Moment	Muhammadan Day
Srimukha Kanya—Purattasi	18	Fr	1	Asvina Sukla	7	·96	18	·06	5 (H. 1228 Shawwal)
	19	Sa	2		...	...	19	·16	6
	20	Su	3		8	·03	20	·24	7
	21	Mo	4		9	·08	21	·31	8
	22	Tu	5		10	·11	22	·36	9
	23	We	6		11	·13	23	·40	10
	24	Th	7		12	·11	24	·41	11
	25	Fr	8		13	·08	25	·40	12
	26	Sa	9		14, P	·03, ·96	26	·37	13
	27	Su	10	Bahula	1	·90	27	·33	14
	28	Mo	11		2	·80	1	·28	15
	29	Tu	12		3	·71	2	·22	16
	30	We	13		4	·61	3	·15	17
	31	Th	14		5	·50	4	·08	18
Srimukha Tula—Aippasi	1	Fr	15		6	·41	5, 6	·01, ·95	19
	2	Sa	16		7	·31	7	·90	20
	3	Su	17		8	·24	8	·85	21
	4	Mo	18		9	·17	9	·82	22
	5	Tu	19		10	·12	10	·80	23
	6	We	20		11	·08	11	·81	24
	7	Th	21		12	·07	12	·84	25
	8	Fr	22		13	·10	13	·89	26
	9	Sa	23		14	·10	14	·95	27
	10	Su	24		A	·16	...	...	28
	11	Mo	25	Kartt. Suk.	1	·22	15	·04	29
	12	Tu	26		2	·30	16	·13	1 (Zi-l-ka'da)
	13	We	27		3	·38	17	·25	2
	14	Th	28		4	·47	18	·36	3
	15	Fr	29		5	·55	19	·46	4
	16	Sa	30		6	·62	20	·55	5
	17	Su	31		7	·68	21	·62	6

Nov.

Solar month	Cyclic Sidereal Day	Week-Day	English Day	Lunar month	Tithi	Ending Moment	Nakshatra	Ending Moment	Muhammadan Day
Srimukha Tula—Aippasi	18	Mo	1	Kartika Sukla	8	·70	22	·68	7 (H. 1228 Zi-l-ka'da)
	19	Tu	2		9	·72	23	·72	8
	20	We	3		10	·70	24	·73	9
	21	Th	4		11	·67	25	·72	10
	22	Fr	5		12	·63	26	·70	11
	23	Sa	6		13	·56	27	·67	12
	24	Su	7		14	·49	1	·62	13
	25	Mo	8		P	·39	2	·56	14
	26	Tu	9	Bahula	1	·30	3	·49	15
	27	We	10		2	·20	4	·42	16
	28	Th	11		3	·11	5	·35	17
	29	Fr	12		4, 5	·01, ·92	6	·29	18
	30	Sa	13		6	·84	7	·23	19
Srimukha Vrischika—Kartigai	1	Su	14		7	·78	8	·18	20
	2	Mo	15		8	·72	9	·15	21
	3	Tu	16		9	·69	10	·13	22
	4	We	17		10	·68	11	·14	23
	5	Th	18		11	·70	12	·16	24
	6	Fr	19		12	·72	13	·20	25
	7	Sa	20		13	·77	14	·26	26
	8	Su	21		14	·83	15	·34	27
	9	Mo	22		A	·93	16	·44	28
	10	Tu	23	Margasira Sukla	...	...	17	·55	29
	11	We	24		1	·01	18	·65	30
	12	Th	25		2	·10	19	·76	1 (Zi-l-hijja)
	13	Fr	26		3	·17	20	·85	2
	14	Sa	27		4	·25	21	·94	3
	15	Su	28		5	·31	...	...	4
	16	Mo	29		6	·34	22	·00	5
	17	Tu	30		7	·34	23	·03	6

Dec.

Solar month	Cyclic Sidereal Day	Week-Day	English Day	Lunar month	Tithi	Ending Moment	Nakshatra	Ending Moment	Muhammadan Day
Srimukha Vrischika—Kartigai	18	We	1	Margasira Sukla	8	·83	24	·05	7 (H. 1228 Zi-l-hijja)
	19	Th	2		9	·80	25	·05	8
	20	Fr	3		10	·24	26	·04	9
	21	Sa	4		11	·18	27, 1	·00, ·95	10
	22	Su	5		12	·11	2	·89	11
	23	Mo	6		13, 14	·03, ·93	3	·82	12
	24	Tu	7		P	·82	4	·75	13
	25	We	8	Bahula	1	·73	5	·69	14
	26	Th	9		2	·63	6	·63	15
	27	Fr	10		3	·54	7	·57	16
	28	Sa	11		4	·46	8	·51	17
	29	Su	12		5	·41	9	·48	18
Srimukha Dhanus—Margali	1	Mo	13		6	·35	10	·46	19
	2	Tu	14		7	·32	11	·46	20
	3	We	15		8	·32	12	·47	21
	4	Th	16		9	·33	13	·51	22
	5	Fr	17		10	·36	14	·57	23
	6	Sa	18		11	·42	15	·65	24
	7	Su	19		12	·49	16	·74	25
	8	Mo	20		13	·57	17	·85	26
	9	Tu	21		14	·66	18	·95	27
	10	We	22		A	·75	...	...	28
	11	Th	23	Pausha Sukla	1	·82	19	·06	29
	12	Fr	24		2	·89	20	·16	1 (H. 1229 Muharram)
	13	Sa	25		3	·95	21	·24	2
	14	Su	26		4	·98	22	·31	3
	15	Mo	27		5	·98	23	·35	4
	16	Tu	28		6	·98	24	·37	5
	17	We	29		7	·94	25	·37	6
	18	Th	30		8	·88	26	·37	7
	19	Fr	31		9	·83	27	·33	8

15. Svati. 16. Visak. 17. Anur. 18. Jyesh. 19. Mula. 20. P. Ash. 21. U. Ash. 22. Sravn. 23. Dani. 24. Satab. 25. P. Bhad. 26. U. Bhad. 27. Rev.

A. D. 1814. **Mesha Sankranti** (Commencement of Indian Sidereal Year).
Solar Eclipse. ● **(Surya Sid.) April 11·37.** **Saka 1736.** **Kaliyuga 4915.**
Lunar Eclipse. ○ **(Arya Sid.) April 11·27.** **(S. Cycle) Bhava.**

SOLAR reckoning: Cyclic Sidereal Year, Month and Day; Week-Day; English Month and Day. LUNAR reckoning: Tithi; Ending Moment; Nakshatra; Ending Moment; Muhammadan Year, Month and Day.

Jan. — Solar: Srimukha *Dhanu—Margali* (to 30), Srimukha *Makara—Tai* (from 1). Lunar: Pausha (*Sukla*, then *Bahula* from 8, *Sukla* from 1 after A). Muhammadan: H. 1229 *Muharram*.

Cyclic Sidereal Year, Month and Day	Week-Day	English Month and Day	Tithi	Ending Moment	Nakshatra	Ending Moment	Muhammadan Year, Month and Day
20	Sa	1	10	·74	1	·29	9
21	Su	2	11	·66	2	·23	10
22	Mo	3	12	·56	3	·16	11
23	Tu	4	13	·47	4	·10	12
24	We	5	14	·37	5 6	·03 ·96	13
25	Th	6	P	·27	7	·90	14
26	Fr	7	1	·19	8	·85	15
27	Sa	8	2	·11	9	·82	16
28	Su	9	3	·05	10	·79	17
29	Mo	10	4 5	·00 ·98	11	·78	18
30	Tu	11	6	·96	12	·79	19
1	We	12	7	·99	13	·82	20
2	Th	13	...	...	14	·88	21
3	Fr	14	8	·01	15	·95	22
4	Sa	15	9	·06	...	...	23
5	Su	16	10	·13	16	·04	24
6	Mo	17	11	·23	17	·14	25
7	Tu	18	12	·32	18	·25	26
8	We	19	13	·40	19	·37	27
9	Th	20	14	·49	20	·46	28
10	Fr	21	A	·55	21	·55	29
11	Sa	22	1	·59	22	·62	30
12	Su	23	2	·62	23	·66	1
13	Mo	24	3	·63	24	·69	2
14	Tu	25	4	·62	25	·71	3
15	We	26	5	·58	26	·70	4
16	Th	27	6	·54	27	·67	5
17	Fr	28	7	·46	1	·62	6
18	Sa	29	8	·37	2	·57	7
19	Su	30	9	·29	3	·51	8
20	Mo	31	10	·20	4	·44	9

Feb. — Solar: Srimukha *Kumbha—Masi*. Lunar: Magha (*Bahula* from 7), Phal. *Suk.* Muhammadan: H. 1229 *Safar*; H. 1229 *Rabi-ul-awwal*.

Cyclic Sidereal Year, Month and Day	Week-Day	English Month and Day	Tithi	Ending Moment	Nakshatra	Ending Moment	Muhammadan Year, Month and Day
21	Tu	1	11	·10	5	·37	10
22	We	2	12 13	·00 ·91	6	·30	11
23	Th	3	14	·81	7	·24	12
24	Fr	4	P	·75	8	·19	13
25	Sa	5	1	·69	9	·15	14
26	Su	6	2	·63	10	·12	15
27	Mo	7	3	·61	11	·10	16
28	Tu	8	4	·60	12	·11	17
29	We	9	5	·62	13	·14	18
1	Th	10	6	·65	14	·19	19
2	Fr	11	7	·71	15	·26	20
3	Sa	12	8	·77	16	·34	21
4	Su	13	9	·86	17	·44	22
5	Mo	14	10	·95	18	·55	23
6	Tu	15	...	...	19	·66	24
7	We	16	11	·03	20	·76	25
8	Th	17	12	·11	21	·85	26
9	Fr	18	13	·18	22	·92	27
10	Sa	19	14	·24	23	·98	28
11	Su	20	A	·25	...	...	29
12	Mo	21	1	·26	24	·02	1
13	Tu	22	2	·24	25	·08	2
14	We	23	3	·20	26	·02	3
15	Th	24	4	·15	27 1	·00 ·95	4
16	Fr	25	5	·08	2	·91	5
17	Sa	26	6 7	·00 ·91	3	·85	6
18	Su	27	8	·82	4	·78	7
19	Mo	28	9	·71	5	·71	8

March — Solar: Srimukha *Kumbha—Masi* (to 30), Srimukha *Mina—Panguni* (from 1). Lunar: Phalguna (*Sukla*, *Bahula* from 8, *Sukla* after A). Muhammadan: H. 1229 *Rabi-ul-awwal*.

Cyclic Sidereal Year, Month and Day	Week-Day	English Month and Day	Tithi	Ending Moment	Nakshatra	Ending Moment	Muhammadan Year, Month and Day
20	Tu	1	10	·62	6	·64	9
21	We	2	11	·52	7	·58	10
22	Th	3	12	·43	8	·52	11
23	Fr	4	13	·36	9	·48	12
24	Sa	5	14	·29	10	·44	13
25	Su	6	P	·25	11	·43	14
26	Mo	7	1	·22	12	·43	15
27	Tu	8	2	·21	13	·46	16
28	We	9	3	·23	14	·50	17
29	Th	10	4	·26	15	·56	18
30	Fr	11	5	·32	16	·65	19
1	Sa	12	6	·39	17	·74	20
2	Su	13	7	·48	18	·86	21
3	Mo	14	8	·56	19	·96	22
4	Tu	15	9	·65	...	...	23
5	We	16	10	·73	20	·06	24
6	Th	17	11	·78	21	·16	25
7	Fr	18	12	·83	22	·23	26
8	Sa	19	13	·84	23	·30	27
9	Su	20	14	·86	24	·34	28
10	Mo	21	A	·84	25	·35	29
11	Tu	22	1	·80	26	·35	30
12	We	23	2	·74	27	·33	1
13	Th	24	3	·67	1	·30	2
14	Fr	25	4	·59	2	·25	3
15	Sa	26	5	·50	3	·19	4
16	Su	27	6	·39	4	·12	5
17	Mo	28	7	·29	5 6	·05 ·99	6
18	Tu	29	8	·20	7	·92	7
19	We	30	9	·10	8	·86	8
20	Th	31	10 11	·01 ·94	9	·81	9

April — Solar: Srimukha *Mina—Panguni* (to 30), Bhava *Mesha—Chittirai* (from 1). Lunar: Chaitra (*Bahula* from 5), Vaisakha *Suk.* Muhammadan: H. 1229 *Rabi-ul-akhir*; H. 1229 *Jumadal-awwal*.

Cyclic Sidereal Year, Month and Day	Week-Day	English Month and Day	Tithi	Ending Moment	Nakshatra	Ending Moment	Muhammadan Year, Month and Day
21	Fr	1	12	·87	10	·77	10
22	Sa	2	13	·83	11	·75	11
23	Su	3	14	·80	12	·76	12
24	Mo	4	P	·79	13	·77	13
25	Tu	5	1	·81	14	·81	14
26	We	6	2	·85	15	·87	15
27	Th	7	3	·89	16	·95	16
28	Fr	8	4	·97	...	...	17
29	Sa	9	...	...	17	·05	18
30	Su	10	5	·05	18	·15	19
1	Mo	11	6	·12	19	·26	20
2	Tu	12	7	·21	20	·36	21
3	We	13	8	·29	21	·46	22
4	Th	14	9	·35	22	·55	23
5	Fr	15	10	·39	23	·61	24
6	Sa	16	11	·40	24	·65	25
7	Su	17	12	·41	25	·67	26
8	Mo	18	13	·39	26	·67	27
9	Tu	19	14	·36	27	·66	28
10	We	20	A	·29	1	·63	29
11	Th	21	1	·23	2	·58	1
12	Fr	22	2	·14	3	·52	2
13	Sa	23	3 4	·04 ·94	4	·46	3
14	Su	24	5	·84	5	·39	4
15	Mo	25	6	·74	6	·33	5
16	Tu	26	7	·64	7	·26	6
17	We	27	8	·56	8	·20	7
18	Th	28	9	·48	9	·14	8
19	Fr	29	10	·42	10	·10	9
20	Sa	30	11	·36	11	·09	10

May — Solar: Bhava *Mesha—Chittirai* (to 31), Bhava *Vrishabha—Vaikasi* (from 1). Lunar: Vaisakha (*Sukla*, *Bahula* from 9, *Sukla* from 6 after A). Muhammadan: H. 1229 *Jumadal-awwal*; *Jumadal-akhir*.

Cyclic Sidereal Year, Month and Day	Week-Day	English Month and Day	Tithi	Ending Moment	Nakshatra	Ending Moment	Muhammadan Year, Month and Day
21	Su	1	12	·33	12	·08	11
22	Mo	2	13	·32	13	·09	12
23	Tu	3	14	·33	14	·12	13
24	We	4	P	·38	15	·18	14
25	Th	5	1	·42	16	·26	15
26	Fr	6	2	·49	17	·35	16
27	Sa	7	3	·56	18	·45	17
28	Su	8	4	·64	19	·56	18
29	Mo	9	5	·73	20	·66	19
30	Tu	10	6	·81	21	·77	20
31	We	11	7	·87	22	·85	21
1	Th	12	8	·91	23	·92	22
2	Fr	13	9	·93	24	·97	23
3	Sa	14	10	·93	25	·99	24
4	Su	15	11	·92	...	...	25
5	Mo	16	12	·87	26 27	·01 ·99	26
6	Tu	17	13	·80	1	·96	27
7	We	18	14	·74	2	·92	28
8	Th	19	A	·65	3	·86	29
9	Fr	20	1	·57	4	·80	30
10	Sa	21	2	·46	5	·74	1
11	Su	22	3	·36	6	·66	2
12	Mo	23	4	·25	7	·60	3
13	Tu	24	5	·15	8	·53	4
14	We	25	6 7	·06 ·98	9	·48	5
15	Th	26	8	·93	10	·44	6
16	Fr	27	9	·87	11	·41	7
17	Sa	28	10	·84	12	·40	8
18	Su	29	11	·82	13	·41	9
19	Mo	30	12	·83	14	·44	10
20	Tu	31	13	·86	15	·50	11

June — Solar: Bhava *Vrishabha—Vaikasi* (to 32), Bhava *Mithuna—Ani* (from 1). Lunar: Jyeshtha (*Bahula* from 7), Ashadha *Sukla*. Muhammadan: H. 1229; H. 1229 *Rajab*.

Cyclic Sidereal Year, Month and Day	Week-Day	English Month and Day	Tithi	Ending Moment	Nakshatra	Ending Moment	Muhammadan Year, Month and Day
21	We	1	14	·91	16	·56	12
22	Th	2	P	·99	17	·65	13
23	Fr	3	...	...	18	·75	14
24	Sa	4	1	·06	19	·86	15
25	Su	5	2	·14	20	·97	16
26	Mo	6	3	·22	...	...	17
27	Tu	7	4	·31	21	·07	18
28	We	8	5	·36	22	·16	19
29	Th	9	6	·40	23	·23	20
30	Fr	10	7	·42	24	·28	21
31	Sa	11	8	·42	25	·31	22
32	Su	12	9	·41	26	·33	23
1	Mo	13	10	·36	27	·32	24
2	Tu	14	11	·31	1	·29	25
3	We	15	12	·24	2	·25	26
4	Th	16	13	·14	3	·20	27
5	Fr	17	14 A	·05 ·95	4	·14	28
6	Sa	18	1	·85	5	·07	29
7	Su	19	2	·74	6 7	·00 ·93	1
8	Mo	20	3	·65	8	·87	2
9	Tu	21	4	·56	9	·82	3
10	We	22	5	·47	10	·77	4
11	Th	23	6	·41	11	·74	5
12	Fr	24	7	·35	12	·72	6
13	Sa	25	8	·32	13	·73	7
14	Su	26	9	·30	14	·76	8
15	Mo	27	10	·32	15	·81	9
16	Tu	28	11	·34	16	·87	10
17	We	29	12	·39	17	·95	11
18	Th	30	13	·46	...	...	12

Naksh:—1. Asvn. 2. Bhar. 3. Krit. 4. Rohi. 5. Mrig. 6. Ardh. 7. Punar. 8. Push. 9. Aslesh. 10. Magh. 11. P. Phal. 12. U. Phal. 13. Hasta. 14. Chit.

A. D. 1814.
A.—Amavasya. **P.—Paurnami.**

Kollam 990, Commences {N. Malabar—Sept. S. Malabar—Aug.

Hijra 1230, Commences, Dec. 14.

Vikrama 1871. **Bengal San 1220.** **(N. Cycle) Parthiva.**

Columns: SOLAR reckoning (Cyclic Sidereal Year, Month and Day; Week-Day; English Month and Day) — LUNAR reckoning (Tithi; Ending Moment; Nakshatra; Ending Moment; Muhammadan Year, Month and Day).

July — marginal labels: Bhava *Mithuna—Ani.*; Ashadha; *Bahula*; H. 1229 *Rajab.*; Bhava *Karkata—Adi.*; *Sukla*; Sravana; *Shaban.*

Cyclic Sidereal Year, Month and Day	Week-Day	English Month and Day	Tithi	Ending Moment	Nakshatra	Ending Moment	Muhammadan Year, Month and Day
19	Fr	1	14	·53	18	·05	13
20	Sa	2	P	·61	19	·16	14
21	Su	3	1	·70	20	·27	15
22	Mo	4	2	·78	21	·37	16
23	Tu	5	3	·83	22	·46	17
24	We	6	4	·88	23	·54	18
25	Th	7	5	·90	24	·59	19
26	Fr	8	6	·89	25	·64	20
27	Sa	9	7	·88	26	·65	21
28	Su	10	8	·84	27	·65	22
29	Mo	11	9	·78	1	·62	23
30	Tu	12	10	·71	2	·58	24
—31	We	13	11	·63	3	·54	25
1	Th	14	12	·53	4	·48	26
2	Fr	15	13	·42	5	·41	27
3	Sa	16	14	·33	6	·34	28
4	Su ●	17	—A	·22	7	·27	29
5	Mo	18	1	·12	8	·21	—30
6	Tu	19	2; 3	·03; ·96	9	·15	1
7	We	20	4	·89	10	·11	2
8	Th	21	5	·83	11	·07	3
9	Fr	22	6	·80	12	·05	4
10	Sa	23	7	·78	13	·06	5
11	Su	24	8	·79	14	·08	6
12	Mo	25	9	·82	15	·12	7
13	Tu	26	10	·86	16	·18	8
14	We	27	11	·93	17	·25	9
15	Th	28	...	...	18	·35	10
16	Fr	29	12	·00	19	·46	11
17	Sa	30	13	·07	20	·57	12
18	Su	31	14	·17	21	·67	13

Aug. — marginal labels: *Bahula*; Adhika Bhadrapada *Sukla*; Bhava *Simha—Avani*; H. 1229 *Ramzan.*

Cyclic Sidereal Year, Month and Day	Week-Day	English Month and Day	Tithi	Ending Moment	Nakshatra	Ending Moment	Muhammadan Year, Month and Day
19	Mo	1	P	·24	22	·76	14
20	Tu	2	1	·30	23	·84	15
21	We	3	2	·35	24	·91	16
22	Th	4	3	·38	25	·95	17
23	Fr	5	4	·38	26	·97	18
24	Sa	6	5	·36	27	·97	19
25	Su	7	6	·32	1	·95	20
26	Mo	8	7	·28	2	·93	21
27	Tu	9	8	·20	3	·88	22
28	We	10	9	·12	4	·82	23
29	Th	11	10; 11	·02; ·92	5	·75	24
30	Fr	12	12	·83	6	·68	25
31	Sa	13	13	·73	7	·62	26
—32	Su	14	14	·62	8	·55	27
1	Mo	15	—A	·53	9	·49	28
2	Tu	16	1	·45	10	·44	—29
3	We	17	2	·39	11	·40	1
4	Th	18	3	·33	12	·38	2
5	Fr	19	4	·29	13	·38	3
6	Sa	20	5	·28	14	·39	4
7	Su	21	6	·29	15	·43	5
8	Mo	22	7	·31	16	·48	6
9	Tu	23	8	·37	17	·56	7
10	We	24	9	·42	18	·66	8
11	Th	25	10	·50	19	·76	9
12	Fr	26	11	·58	20	·86	10
13	Sa	27	12	·68	21	·97	11
14	Su	28	13	·75	...	...	12
15	Mo	29	14	·82	22	·07	13
16	Tu	30	P	·85	23	·16	14
17	We	31	1	·87	24	·22	15

Sep. — marginal labels: Bhava *Simha—Avani.*; Adhika Bhad.; *Bahula*; H. 1229 *Ramzan.*; *Sukla*; Bhadrapada; Bhava *Kanya—Purattasi.*; H. 1229 *Shawwal.*

Cyclic Sidereal Year, Month and Day	Week-Day	English Month and Day	Tithi	Ending Moment	Nakshatra	Ending Moment	Muhammadan Year, Month and Day
18	Th	1	2	·89	25	·27	16
19	Fr	2	3	·87	26	·29	17
20	Sa	3	4	·84	27	·30	18
21	Su	4	5	·79	1	·29	19
22	Mo	5	6	·73	2	·26	20
23	Tu	6	7	·64	3	·21	21
24	We	7	8	·53	4	·15	22
25	Th	8	9	·44	5	·09	23
26	Fr	9	10	·35	6; 7	·02; ·96	24
27	Sa	10	11	·24	8	·89	25
28	Su	11	12	·14	9	·83	26
29	Mo	12	13; 14	·06; ·97	10	·77	27
30	Tu	13	—A	·91	11	·73	28
—31	We	14	1	·85	12	·71	29
1	Th	15	2	·82	13	·70	—30
2	Fr	16	3	·81	14	·71	1
3	Sa	17	4	·83	15	·74	2
4	Su	18	5	·84	16	·79	3
5	Mo	19	6	·89	17	·87	4
6	Tu	20	7	·95	18	·96	5
7	We	21	...	...	...	...	6
8	Th	22	8	·03	19	·06	7
9	Fr	23	9	·11	20	·16	8
10	Sa	24	10	·20	21	·27	9
11	Su	25	11	·27	22	·38	10
12	Mo	26	12	·35	23	·46	11
13	Tu	27	13	·39	24	·53	12
14	We	28	14	·42	25	·58	13
15	Th	29	P	·43	26	·61	14
16	Fr	30	1	·41	27	·63	15

Oct. — marginal labels: Nija; *Bahula*; *Sukla*; Asvina; *Bah.*; Bhava *Tula—Aippasi.*; H. 1229 *Zi-l-ka'da.*

Cyclic Sidereal Year, Month and Day	Week-Day	English Month and Day	Tithi	Ending Moment	Nakshatra	Ending Moment	Muhammadan Year, Month and Day
17	Sa	1	2	·39	1	·62	16
18	Su	2	3	·33	2	·59	17
19	Mo	3	4	·27	3	·55	18
20	Tu	4	5	·18	4	·49	19
21	We	5	6; 7	·09; ·99	5	·43	20
22	Th	6	8	·90	6	·37	21
23	Fr	7	9	·80	7	·30	22
24	Sa	8	10	·69	8	·23	23
25	Su	9	11	·61	9	·16	24
26	Mo	10	12	·53	10	·10	25
27	Tu	11	13	·47	11	·07	26
28	We	12	14	·41	12	·04	27
29	Th	13	—A	·39	13	·02	28
—30	Fr	14	1	·37	14	·03	—29
1	Sa	15	2	·39	15	·05	1
2	Su	16	3	·41	16	·11	2
3	Mo	17	4	·46	17	·17	3
4	Tu	18	5	·52	18	·26	4
5	We	19	6	·60	19	·36	5
6	Th	20	7	·69	20	·46	6
7	Fr	21	8	·77	21	·58	7
8	Sa	22	9	·86	22	·68	8
9	Su	23	10	·93	23	·77	9
10	Mo	24	11	·97	24	·84	10
11	Tu	25	...	...	25	·90	11
12	We	26	12	·00	26	·93	12
13	Th	27	13	·01	27	·95	13
14	Fr	28	14; P	·00; ·96	1	·94	14
15	Sa	29	1	·91	2	·92	15
16	Su	30	2	·86	3	·88	16
17	Mo	31	3	·77	4	·83	17

Nov. — marginal labels: Asv.; *Bahula*; Bhava *Tula—Aippasi.*; H. 1229 *Zi-l-ka'da.*; *Sukla*; Kartika; Bhava *Vrischika—Kartigai.*; H. 1229 *Zi-l-hijja.*

Cyclic Sidereal Year, Month and Day	Week-Day	English Month and Day	Tithi	Ending Moment	Nakshatra	Ending Moment	Muhammadan Year, Month and Day
18	Tu	1	4	·68	5	·77	18
19	We	2	5	·58	6	·71	19
20	Th	3	6	·49	7	·64	20
21	Fr	4	7	·39	8	·56	21
22	Sa	5	8	·30	9	·50	22
23	Su	6	9	·21	10	·45	23
24	Mo	7	10	·12	11	·40	24
25	Tu	8	11	·06	12	·37	25
26	We	9	12; 13	·00; ·99	13	·35	26
27	Th	10	14	·97	14	·35	27
28	Fr	11	—A	·99	15	·38	28
29	Sa	12	...	...	16	·42	29
—30	Su	13	1	·01	17	·48	—30
1	Mo	14	2	·06	18	·56	1
2	Tu	15	3	·14	19	·65	2
3	We	16	4	·22	20	·77	3
4	Th	17	5	·31	21	·87	4
5	Fr	18	6	·39	22	·98	5
6	Sa	19	7	·48	...	...	6
7	Su	20	8	·54	23	·07	7
8	Mo	21	9	·59	24	·15	8
9	Tu	22	10	·62	25	·21	9
10	We	23	11	·63	26	·25	10
11	Th	24	12	·62	27	·27	11
12	Fr	25	13	·58	1	·27	12
13	Sa	26	14	·53	2	·25	13
14	Su	27	P	·48	3	·21	14
15	Mo	28	1	·40	4	·17	15
16	Tu	29	2	·30	5	·11	16
17	We	30	3	·20	6; 7	·04; ·97	17

Dec. — marginal labels: *Bahula*; *Sukla*; Margasira; *Bahula*; Bhava *Dhanus—Margali.*; H. 1230 *Muharram.*

Cyclic Sidereal Year, Month and Day	Week-Day	English Month and Day	Tithi	Ending Moment	Nakshatra	Ending Moment	Muhammadan Year, Month and Day
18	Th	1	4	·11	8	·90	18
19	Fr	2	5; 6	·01; ·92	9	·85	19
20	Sa	3	7	·83	10	·78	20
21	Su	4	8	·75	11	·73	21
22	Mo	5	9	·68	12	·70	22
23	Tu	6	10	·63	13	·67	23
24	We	7	11	·62	14	·68	24
25	Th	8	12	·60	15	·69	25
26	Fr	9	13	·62	16	·73	26
27	Sa	10	14	·65	17	·79	27
28	Su	11	—A	·72	18	·86	28
29	Mo	12	1	·78	19	·95	29
—30	Tu	13	2	·87	...	...	—30
1	We	14	3	·95	20	·07	1
2	Th	15	...	...	21	·17	2
3	Fr	16	4	·04	22	·28	3
4	Sa	17	5	·12	23	·37	4
5	Su	18	6	·18	24	·45	5
6	Mo	19	7	·24	25	·53	6
7	Tu	20	8	·26	26	·57	7
8	We	21	9	·27	27	·59	8
9	Th	22	10	·25	1	·59	9
10	Fr	23	11	·22	2	·58	10
11	Sa	24	12	·17	3	·55	11
12	Su	25	13	·09	4	·51	12
13	Mo ○	26	14; P	·02; ·93	5	·45	13
14	Tu	27	1	·84	6	·38	14
15	We	28	2	·74	7	·31	15
16	Th	29	3	·64	8	·25	16
17	Fr	30	4	·55	9	·18	17
18	Sa	31	5	·47	10	·12	18

15. Svati. 16. Visak. 17. Anur. 18. Jyesh. 19. Mula. 20. P. Ash. 21. U. Ash. 22. Srava. 23. Dani. 24. Satab. 25. P. Bhad. 26. U. Bhad. 27. Rev.

A. D. 1815. **Mesha Sankranti** (Commencement of Indian Sidereal Year).

Solar Eclipse. ● (Surya Sid.) April 11·63. **Saka 1737.** **Kaliyuga 4916.**

Lunar Eclipse. ○ (Arya Sid.) April 11·53. (S. Cycle) **Yuva.**

Columns: SOLAR reckoning (Cyclic Sidereal Year, Month and Day; Week-Day; English Month and Day) — LUNAR reckoning (Tithi; Ending Moment; Nakshatra; Ending Moment) — Muhammadan Year, Month and Day.

Jan.

Cyclic Sidereal Year, Month and Day	Week-Day	English Month and Day	Tithi	Ending Moment	Nakshatra	Ending Moment	Muhammadan Year, Month and Day
Bhava Dhanus—Margali 19	Su	1	Marg. Bahula 6	·39	11	·07	H. 1230 Muharram. 19
20	Mo	2	7	·32	12	·03	20
21	Tu	3	8	·28	13	·01	21
22	We	4	9	·26	14	·00	22
23	Th	5	10	·25	15	·01	23
24	Fr	6	11	·26	16	·04	24
25	Sa	7	12	·30	17	·09	25
26	Su	8	13	·36	18	·17	26
27	Mo	9	14	·42	19	·25	27
28	Tu	10	A	·52	20	·36	28
29	We	11	1	·60	21	·47	29
Bhava Makara—Tai 1	Th	12	Pausha Sukla 2	·69	22	·58	30
2	Fr	13	3	·77	23	·67	H. 1230 Safar. 1
3	Sa	14	4	·83	24	·77	2
4	Su	15	5	·88	25	·84	3
5	Mo	16	6	·90	26	·88	4
6	Tu	17	7	·92	27	·91	5
7	We	18	8	·90	1	·92	6
8	Th	19	9	·87	2	·92	7
9	Fr	20	10	·82	3	·89	8
10	Sa	21	11	·74	4	·84	9
11	Su	22	12	·66	5	·79	10
12	Mo	23	13	·57	6	·72	11
13	Tu	24	14	·48	7	·66	12
14	We	25	P	·37	8	·59	13
15	Th	26	1	·28	9	·52	14
16	Fr	27	2	·19	10	·46	15
17	Sa	28	3	·10	11	·40	16
18	Su	29	4 / 5	·03 / ·96	12	·36	17
19	Mo	30	6	·93	13	·34	18
20	Tu	31	7	·90	14	·32	19

Feb.

Cyclic Sidereal Year, Month and Day	Week-Day	English Month and Day	Tithi	Ending Moment	Nakshatra	Ending Moment	Muhammadan Year, Month and Day
21	We	1	Bahula 8	·89	15	·33	20
22	Th	2	9	·90	16	·36	21
23	Fr	3	10	·96	17	·40	22
24	Sa	4	...	...	18	·48	23
25	Su	5	11	·01	19	·56	24
26	Mo	6	12	·07	20	·66	25
27	Tu	7	13	·16	21	·77	26
28	We	8	14	·25	22	·87	27
29	Th	9	A	·34	23	·98	28
Bhava Kumbha—Masi 1	Fr	10	Magha Sukla 1	·41	...	...	29
2	Sa	11	2	·48	24	·07	H. 1230 Rabi-ul-awwal. 1
3	Su	12	3	·52	25	·15	2
4	Mo	13	4	·55	26	·20	3
5	Tu	14	5	·55	27	·23	4
6	We	15	6	·53	1	·25	5
7	Th	16	7	·50	2	·24	6
8	Fr	17	8	·43	3	·22	7
9	Sa	18	9	·37	4	·17	8
10	Su	19	10	·29	5	·12	9
11	Mo	20	11	·20	6	·06	10
12	Tu	21	12 / 13	·10 / ·99	7 / 8	·00 / ·93	11
13	We	22	14	·90	9	·86	12
14	Th	23	P	·81	10	·79	13
15	Fr	24	Bah. 1	·72	11	·73	14
16	Sa	25	2	·64	12	·70	15
17	Su	26	3	·58	13	·66	16
18	Mo	27	4	·54	14	·65	17
19	Tu	28	5	·51	15	·65	18

March

Cyclic Sidereal Year, Month and Day	Week-Day	English Month and Day	Tithi	Ending Moment	Nakshatra	Ending Moment	Muhammadan Year, Month and Day
Bhava Kumbha—Masi 20	We	1	Magha Bahula 6	·51	16	·67	H. 1230 Rabi-ul-awwal. 19
21	Th	2	7	·52	17	·72	20
22	Fr	3	8	·57	18	·78	21
23	Sa	4	9	·62	19	·87	22
24	Su	5	10	·69	20	·96	23
25	Mo	6	11	·78	...	...	24
26	Tu	7	12	·87	21	·07	25
27	We	8	13	·96	22	·18	26
28	Th	9	...	...	23	·28	27
29	Fr	10	14	·03	24	·38	28
30	Sa	11	A	·09	25	·45	29
Bhava Mina—Panguni 1	Su	12	Phalguna Sukla 1	·13	26	·51	30
2	Mo	13	2	·15	27	·56	H. 1230 Rabi-ul-akhir. 1
3	Tu	14	3	·15	1	·57	2
4	We	15	4	·14	2	·57	3
5	Th	16	5	·10	3	·55	4
6	Fr	17	6 / 7	·03 / ·96	4	·51	5
7	Sa	18	8	·88	5	·46	6
8	Su	19	9	·79	6	·41	7
9	Mo	20	10	·69	7	·34	8
10	Tu	21	11	·59	8	·27	9
11	We	22	12	·49	9	·20	10
12	Th	23	13	·40	10	·13	11
13	Fr	24	14	·31	11	·08	12
14	Sa	25	P	·23	12 / 13	·03 / ·99	13
15	Su	26	1	·17	14	·97	14
16	Mo	27	2	·13	15	·97	15
17	Tu	28	3	·11	16	·99	16
18	We	29	4	·09	...	...	17
19	Th	30	5	·12	17	03·	18
20	Fr	31	6	·15	18	·09	19

April

Cyclic Sidereal Year, Month and Day	Week-Day	English Month and Day	Tithi	Ending Moment	Nakshatra	Ending Moment	Muhammadan Year, Month and Day
21	Sa	1	Bahula 7	·20	19	·17	20
22	Su	2	8	·28	20	·26	21
23	Mo	3	9	·36	21	·37	22
24	Tu	4	10	·45	22	·48	23
25	We	5	11	·53	23	·58	24
26	Th	6	12	·61	24	·68	25
27	Fr	7	13	·66	25	·76	26
28	Sa	8	14	·70	26	·82	27
29	Su	9	A	·73	27	·87	28
30	Mo	10	1	·71	1	·89	29
31	Tu	11	2	·70	2	·89	H. 1230 Jumadal-awwal. 1
Yuva Mesha—Chittirai 1	We	12	Chaitra Sukla 3	·66	3	·87	2
2	Th	13	4	·60	4	·84	3
3	Fr	14	5	·52	5	·80	4
4	Sa	15	6	·44	6	·74	5
5	Su	16	7	·35	7	·63	6
6	Mo	17	8	·25	8	·61	7
7	Tu	18	9	·15	9	·54	8
8	We	19	10 / 11	·05 / ·96	10	·48	9
9	Th	20	12	·86	11	·41	10
10	Fr	21	13	·79	12	·36	11
11	Sa	22	14	·71	13	·32	12
12	Su	23	P	·67	14	·30	13
13	Mo	24	Bahula 1	·65	15	·30	14
14	Tu	25	2	·63	16	·31	15
15	We	26	3	·65	17	·34	16
16	Th	27	4	·69	18	·40	17
17	Fr	28	5	·75	19	·47	18
18	Sa	29	6	·82	20	·57	19
19	Su	30	7	·88	21	·67	20

May

Cyclic Sidereal Year, Month and Day	Week-Day	English Month and Day	Tithi	Ending Moment	Nakshatra	Ending Moment	Muhammadan Year, Month and Day
Yuva Mesha—Chittirai 20	Mo	1	Chait. Bah. 8	·97	22	·78	H. 1230 Jl.-awwal. 21
21	Tu	2	...	...	23	·88	22
22	We	3	9	·05	24	·98	23
23	Th	4	10	·14	...	...	24
24	Fr	5	11	·19	25	·06	25
25	Sa	6	12	·24	26	·14	26
26	Su	7	13	·24	27	·19	27
27	Mo	8	14	·25	1	·21	28
28	Tu	9	A	·23	2	·22	29
29	We	10	1	·19	3	·20	30
30	Th	11	2	·13	4	·18	H. 1230 Jumadal-akhir. 1
Yuva Vrishabha—Vaikasi 1	Fr	12	Vaisakha Sukla 3 / 4	·04 / ·96	5	·14	2
2	Sa	13	5	·87	6	·08	3
3	Su	14	6	·78	7 / 8	·01 / ·94	4
4	Mo	15	7	·67	9	·88	5
5	Tu	16	8	·56	10	·81	6
6	We	17	9	·47	11	·75	7
7	Th	18	10	·37	12	·70	8
8	Fr	19	11	·30	13	·65	9
9	Sa	20	12	·24	14	·63	10
10	Su	21	13	·19	15	·62	11
11	Mo	22	14	·16	16	·63	12
12	Tu	23	P	·14	17	·66	13
13	We	24	1	·16	18	·71	14
14	Th	25	2	·19	19	·78	15
15	Fr	26	3	·25	20	·87	16
16	Sa	27	4	·32	21	·97	17
17	Su	28	5	·40	...	...	18
18	Mo	29	6	·47	22	·08	19
19	Tu	30	7	·56	23	·18	20
20	We	31	8	·64	24	·28	21

June

Cyclic Sidereal Year, Month and Day	Week-Day	English Month and Day	Tithi	Ending Moment	Nakshatra	Ending Moment	Muhammadan Year, Month and Day
21	Th	1	Bahula 9	·68	25	·38	22
22	Fr	2	10	·72	26	·45	23
23	Sa	3	11	·74	27	·50	24
24	Su	4	12	·75	1	·53	25
25	Mo	5	13	·72	2	·54	26
26	Tu	6	14	·69	3	·54	27
27	We	7	A	·63	4	·51	28
28	Th	8	Jyeshtha Sukla 1	·55	5	·47	29
29	Fr	9	2	·46	6	·42	H. 1230 Rajab. 1
30	Sa	10	3	·37	7	·35	2
31	Su	11	4	·28	8	·29	3
32	Mo	12	5	·17	9	·22	4
Yuva Mithuna—Ani 1	Tu	13	6 / 7	·07 / ·96	10	·15	5
2	We	14	8	·86	11	·09	6
3	Th	15	9	·79	12 / 13	·03 / ·99	7
4	Fr	16	10	·72	14	·96	8
5	Sa	17	11	·68	15	·94	9
6	Su	18	12	·64	16	·95	10
7	Mo	19	13	·63	17	·97	11
8	Tu	20	14	·64	...	...	12
9	We ○	21	P	·68	18	·02	13
10	Th	22	1	·72	19	·09	14
11	Fr	23	2	·79	20	·17	15
12	Sa	24	3	·87	21	·27	16
13	Su	25	4	·94	22	·37	17
14	Mo	26	...	...	23	·48	18
15	Tu	27	Bahula 5	·03	24	·59	19
16	We	28	6	·11	25	·68	20
17	Th	29	7	·16	26	·76	21
18	Fr	30	8	·20	27	·81	22

Naksh:—1. Asvn. 2. Bhar. 3. Krit. 4. Rohi. 5. Mrig. 6. Aidh. 7. Punar. 8. Push. 9. Aslesh. 10. Magh. 11. P. Phal. 12. U. Phal. 13. Hasta. 14. Chit.

A. D. 1815. **Kollam 991,** Commences {N. Malabar—Sept. S. Malabar—Aug. **Hijra 1231,** Commences, Dec. 3. **Vikrama 1872.** **Bengal San 1221.** **(N. Cycle) Vyaya.**

A.—Amavasya. P.—Paurnami.

SOLAR reckoning: Cyclic Sidereal Year, Month and Day; Week-Day; English Month and Day. LUNAR reckoning: Tithi; Ending Moment; Nakshatra; Ending Moment; Muhammadan Year, Month and Day.

July — Solar: *Yuva Mithuna—Ani.* (19–30), *Yuva Karkata—Adi.* (1–18); Lunar: Jy. *Bah.*, *Sukla*, **Ashadha**, *Bahula*; H. 1230 *Rajab.*, H. 1230 *Shaban.*

Cyclic Sidereal Year, Month and Day	Week-Day	English Month and Day	Tithi	Ending Moment	Nakshatra	Ending Moment	Muhammadan Year, Month and Day
19	Sa	1	9	·22	1	·85	23
20	Su	2	10	·23	2	·87	24
21	Mo	3	11	·20	3	·87	25
22	Tu	4	12	·17	4	·84	26
23	We	5	13	·11	5	·80	27
24	Th ●	6	{14 A	·08 ·94	6	·75	28
25	Fr	7	1	·85	7	·70	29
26	Sa	8	2	·74	8	·63	—30
27	Su	9	3	·64	9	·56	1
28	Mo	10	4	·54	10	·49	2
29	Tu	11	5	·43	11	·42	3
30	We	12	6	·35	12	·36	4
—31	Th	13	7	·37	13	·32	5
1	Fr	14	8	·21	14	·29	6
2	Sa	15	9	·15	15	·27	7
3	Su	16	10	·12	16	·27	8
4	Mo	17	11	·11	17	·29	9
5	Tu	18	12	·11	18	·34	10
6	We	19	13	·15	19	·40	11
7	Th	20	14	·20	20	·47	12
8	Fr	21	P	·27	21	·57	13
9	Sa	22	1	·33	22	·67	14
10	Su	23	2	·42	23	·79	15
11	Mo	24	3	·51	24	·89	16
12	Tu	25	4	·57	25	·98	17
13	We	26	5	·63	...	...	18
14	Th	27	6	·68	26	·06	19
15	Fr	28	7	·71	27	·12	20
16	Sa	29	8	·70	1	·17	21
17	Su	30	9	·69	2	·19	22
18	Mo	31	10	·65	3	·19	23

Aug. — Solar: *Yuva Simha—Avani.*; Lunar: *Sukla*, **Sravana**, *Bahula*; H. 1230 *Ramzan*

Cyclic Sidereal Year, Month and Day	Week-Day	English Month and Day	Tithi	Ending Moment	Nakshatra	Ending Moment	Muhammadan Year, Month and Day
19	Tu	1	11	·58	4	·17	24
20	We	2	12	·52	5	·14	25
21	Th	3	13	·48	6	·10	26
22	Fr	4	14	·34	7 8	·05 ·97}	27
23	Sa	5	—A	·23	9	·90	28
24	Su	6	1	·14	10	·83	—29
25	Mo	7	{2 3	·04 ·93	11	·76	1
26	Tu	8	4	·84	12	·71	2
27	We	9	5	·76	13	·66	3
28	Th	10	6	·70	14	·62	4
29	Fr	11	7	·64	15	·59	5
30	Sa	12	8	·62	16	·59	6
31	Su	13	9	·59	17	·61	7
—32	Mo	14	10	·60	18	·65	8
1	Tu	15	11	·63	19	·70	9
2	We	16	12	·68	20	·78	10
3	Th	17	13	·76	21	·87	11
4	Fr	18	14	·82	22	·98	12
5	Sa	19	P	·92	...	...	13
6	Su	20	...	...	23	·09	14
7	Mo	21	1	·00	24	·19	15
8	Tu	22	2	·08	25	·29	16
9	We	23	3	·14	26	·37	17
10	Th	24	4	·17	27	·44	18
11	Fr	25	5	·19	1	·49	19
12	Sa	26	6	·20	2	·51	20
13	Su	27	7	·19	3	·52	21
14	Mo	28	8	·15	4	·50	22
15	Tu	29	9	·11	5	·47	23
16	We	30	{10 11	·03 ·93	6	·43	24
17	Th	31	12	·84	7	·37	25

Sep. — Solar: *Yuva Simha—Avani.* (18–31), *Yuva Kanya—Purattasi.* (1–16); Lunar: *Bah.*, *Sukla*, **Bhadrapada**, *Bahula*; *Ramzan.*, H. 1230 *Shawwal.*

Cyclic Sidereal Year, Month and Day	Week-Day	English Month and Day	Tithi	Ending Moment	Nakshatra	Ending Moment	Muhammadan Year, Month and Day
18	Fr	1	13	·74	8	·31	26
19	Sa	2	14	·65	9	·24	27
20	Su	3	—A	·55	10	·17	28
21	Mo	4	1	·45	11	·11	29
22	Tu	5	2	·36	12 13	·04 ·99}	—30
23	We	6	3	·28	14	·95	1
24	Th	7	4	·21	15	·92	2
25	Fr	8	5	·15	16	·92	3
26	Sa	9	6	·13	17	·93	4
27	Su	10	7	·11	18	·96	5
28	Mo	11	8	·13	...	...	6
29	Tu	12	9	·15	19	·01	7
30	We	13	10	·21	20	·08	8
—31	Th	14	11	·27	21	·18	9
1	Fr	15	12	·35	22	·28	10
2	Sa	16	13	·44	23	·38	11
3	Su	17	14	·52	24	·49	12
4	Mo	18	P	·60	25	·59	13
5	Tu	19	1	·66	26	·67	14
6	We	20	2	·71	27	·75	15
7	Th	21	3	·72	1	·80	16
8	Fr	22	4	·73	2	·83	17
9	Sa	23	5	·72	3	·84	18
10	Su	24	6	·69	4	·83	19
11	Mo	25	7	·64	5	·81	20
12	Tu	26	8	·56	6	·77	21
13	We	27	9	·48	7	·71	22
14	Th	28	10	·39	8	·65	23
15	Fr	29	11	·29	9	·58	24
16	Sa	30	12	·20	10	·52	25

Oct. — Solar: *Yuva Tula—Aippasi.*; Lunar: *Sukla*, **Asvina**, *Bahula*; H. 1230 *Zi-l-ka'da.*

Cyclic Sidereal Year, Month and Day	Week-Day	English Month and Day	Tithi	Ending Moment	Nakshatra	Ending Moment	Muhammadan Year, Month and Day
17	Su	1	{13 14	·09 ·99	11	·45	26
18	Mo	2	—A	·90	12	·38	27
19	Tu	3	1	·83	13	·32	28
20	We	4	2	·76	14	·28	—29
21	Th	5	3	·71	15	·26	1
22	Fr	6	4	·68	16	·24	2
23	Sa	7	5	·66	17	·25	3
24	Su	8	6	·69	18	·27	4
25	Mo	9	7	·71	19	·32	5
26	Tu	10	8	·77	20	·40	6
27	We	11	9	·83	21	·48	7
28	Th	12	10	·92	22	·58	8
29	Fr	13	...	...	23	·68	9
—30	Sa	14	11	·00	24	·79	10
1	Su	15	12	·08	25	·89	11
2	Mo	16	13	·16	26	·99	12
3	Tu	17	14	·23	...	...	13
4	We	18	P	·28	27	·06	14
5	Th	19	1	·29	1	·12	15
6	Fr	20	2	·31	2	·15	16
7	Sa	21	3	·29	3	·16	17
8	Su	22	4	·27	4	·16	18
9	Mo	23	5	·22	5	·14	19
10	Tu	24	6	·14	6	·10	20
11	We	25	{7 8	·06 ·96	7 8	·05 ·98}	21
12	Th	26	9	·87	9	·93	22
13	Fr	27	10	·77	10	·80	23
14	Sa	28	11	·68	11	·79	24
15	Su	29	12	·57	12	·72	25
16	Mo	30	13	·49	13	·66	26
17	Tu	31	14	·42	14	·62	27

Nov. — Solar: *Yuva Tula—Aippasi.* (18–30), *Yuva Vrischika—Kartigai.* (1–17); Lunar: *Sukla*, **Karttika**, *Bahula*; H. 1230 *Zi-l-hijja.*

Cyclic Sidereal Year, Month and Day	Week-Day	English Month and Day	Tithi	Ending Moment	Nakshatra	Ending Moment	Muhammadan Year, Month and Day
18	We	1	—A	·35	15	·59	28
19	Th	2	1	·30	16	·57	29
20	Fr	3	2	·27	17	·57	—30
21	Sa	4	3	·26	18	·59	1
22	Su	5	4	·28	19	·63	2
23	Mo	6	5	·30	20	·70	3
24	Tu	7	6	·36	21	·78	4
25	We	8	7	·43	22	·87	5
26	Th	9	8	·52	23	·98	6
27	Fr	10	9	·61	...	...	7
28	Sa	11	10	·70	24	·09	8
29	Su	12	11	·77	25	·20	9
—30	Mo	13	12	·84	26	·29	10
1	Tu	14	13	·88	27	·37	11
2	We	15	14	·91	1	·43	12
3	Th	16	P	·92	2	·47	13
4	Fr	17	1	·90	3	·49	14
5	Sa	18	2	·87	4	·49	15
6	Su	19	3	·83	5	·47	16
7	Mo	20	4	·76	6	·43	17
8	Tu	21	5	·67	7	·38	18
9	We	22	6	·57	8	·33	19
10	Th	23	7	·49	9	·26	20
11	Fr	24	8	·39	10	·19	21
12	Sa	25	9	·30	11	·12	22
13	Su	26	10	·19	12	·05	23
14	Mo	27	11	·11	13 14	·00 ·95}	24
15	Tu	28	{12 13	·03 ·96	15	·91	25
16	We	29	14	·92	16	·89	26
17	Th	30	—A	·90	17	·89	27

Dec. — Solar: *Yuva Dhanus—Margali.*; Lunar: *Sukla*, **Margasira**, *Bahula*; H. 1231 *Muharram.*

Cyclic Sidereal Year, Month and Day	Week-Day	English Month and Day	Tithi	Ending Moment	Nakshatra	Ending Moment	Muhammadan Year, Month and Day
18	Fr	1	1	·90	18	·90	28
19	Sa	2	2	·90	19	·95	—29
20	Su	3	3	·94	...	...	1
21	Mo	4	4	·99	20	·01	2
22	Tu	5	...	...	21	·08	3
23	We	6	5	·07	22	·17	4
24	Th	7	6	·15	23	·28	5
25	Fr	8	7	·24	24	·39	6
26	Sa	9	8	·33	25	·50	7
27	Su	10	9	·40	26	·59	8
28	Mo	11	10	·48	27	·67	9
29	Tu	12	11	·53	1	·74	10
—30	We	13	12	·55	2	·79	11
1	Th	14	13	·55	3	·81	12
2	Fr	15	14	·54	4	·81	13
3	Sa ○	16	P	·51	5	·80	14
4	Su	17	1	·44	6	·76	15
5	Mo	18	2	·38	7	·73	16
6	Tu	19	3	·30	8	·67	17
7	We	20	4	·21	9	·60	18
8	Th	21	5	·11	10	·53	19
9	Fr	22	{6 7	·02 ·92	11	·46	20
10	Sa	23	8	·82	12	·39	21
11	Su	24	9	·75	13	·34	22
12	Mo	25	10	·67	14	·29	23
13	Tu	26	11	·61	15	·24	24
14	We	27	12	·56	16	·22	25
15	Th	28	13	·55	17	·21	26
16	Fr	29	14	·53	18	·23	27
17	Sa	30	—A	·54	19	·26	28
18	Su	31	1	·60	20	·31	29

15. Svati. 16. Visak. 17. Anur. 18. Jyesh. 19. Mula. 20. P. Ash. 21. U. Ash. 22. Sravn. 23. Dani. 24. Satab. 25. P. Bhad. 26. U. Bhad. 27 Rev.

A. D. 1816. **Mesha Sankranti** (Commencement of Indian Sidereal Year). (Surya Sid.) April 10·88. (Arya Sid.) April 10·78.

Solar Eclipse. ● **Lunar Eclipse.** ○

Saka 1738. **Kaliyuga 4917.** **(S. Cycle) Dhatri.**

Columns: SOLAR reckoning (Cyclic Sidereal Year, Month and Day; Week-Day; English Month and Day) — LUNAR reckoning (Tithi; Ending Moment; Nakshatra; Ending Moment) — Muhammadan Year, Month and Day.

Jan. — Yuva, *Dhanus—Margali* / Yuva, *Makara—Tai*; Sukla / Pausha / Bahula; H. 1231 *Safar*.

Cyclic Sidereal	Week-Day	English	Tithi	Ending Moment	Nakshatra	Ending Moment	Muhammadan
19	Mo	1	2	·65	21	·39	—30
20	Tu	2	3	·72	22	·47	1
21	We	3	4	·80	23	·58	2
22	Th	4	5	·90	24	·69	3
23	Fr	5	6	·98	25	·80	4
24	Sa	6	...	...	26	·89	5
25	Su	7	7	·05	27	·98	6
26	Mo	8	8	·13	...	...	7
27	Tu	9	9	·17	1	·06	8
28	We	10	10	·20	2	·10	9
—29	Th	11	11	·20	3	·13	10
1	Fr	12	12	·19	4	·14	11
2	Sa	13	13	·15	5	·12	12
3	Su	14	14	·10	6	·10	13
4	Mo	15	P / 1	·03 / ·94	7	·06	14
• 5	Tu	16	2	·85	8 / 9	·00 / ·94	15
6	We	17	3	·76	10	·87	16
7	Th	18	4	·66	11	·80	17
8	Fr	19	5	·56	12	·74	18
9	Sa	20	6	·47	13	·68	19
10	Su	21	7	·39	14	·62	20
11	Mo	22	8	·31	15	·58	21
12	Tu	23	9	·25	16	·55	22
13	We	24	10	·21	17	·54	23
14	Th	25	11	·19	18	·55	24
15	Fr	26	12	·18	19	·58	25
16	Sa	27	13	·21	20	·62	26
17	Su	28	14	·25	21	·70	27
18	Mo	29	—A	·30	22	·79	28
19	Tu	30	1	·37	23	·88	—29
20	We	31	2	·47	24	·99	1

Feb. — Yuva, *Kumbha—Masi*; Sukla / Magha / Bahula; H. 1231 *Rabi-ul-awwal*.

Cyclic Sidereal	Week-Day	English	Tithi	Ending Moment	Nakshatra	Ending Moment	Muhammadan
21	Th	1	3	·55	...	...	2
22	Fr	2	4	·63	25	·10	3
23	Sa	3	5	·71	26	·20	4
24	Su	4	6	·78	27	·29	5
25	Mo	5	7	·82	1	·37	6
26	Tu	6	8	·84	2	·42	7
27	We	7	9	·83	3	·45	8
28	Th	8	10	·83	4	·46	9
29	Fr	9	11	·78	5	·45	10
—30	Sa	10	12	·72	6	·44	11
1	Su	11	13	·65	7	·39	12
2	Mo	12	14	·57	8	·34	13
3	Tu	13	P	·48	9	·28	14
4	We	14	1	·38	10	·21	15
5	Th	15	2	·28	11	·15	16
6	Fr	16	3	·18	12	·08	17
• 7	Sa	17	4	·10	13 / 14	·01 / ·95	18
8	Su	18	5 / 6	·01 / ·94	15	·91	19
9	Mo	19	7	·87	16	·88	20
10	Tu	20	8	·83	17	·87	21
11	We	21	9	·81	18	·87	22
12	Th	22	10	·81	19	·89	23
13	Fr	23	11	·84	20	·93	24
14	Sa	24	12	·87	...	...	25
15	Su	25	13	·93	21	·01	26
16	Mo	26	14	·99	22	·09	27
17	Tu	27	...	...	23	·18	28
18	We	28	—A	·07	24	·29	29
19	Th	29	1	·16	25	·39	—30

March — Yuva, *Kumbha—Masi* / Yuva, *Mina—Panguni*; Sukla / Phalguna / Bahula; H. 1231 *Rabi-ul-akhir*.

Cyclic Sidereal	Week-Day	English	Tithi	Ending Moment	Nakshatra	Ending Moment	Muhammadan
20	Fr	1	2	·25	26	·51	1
21	Sa	2	3	·33	27	·60	2
22	Su	3	4	·39	1	·67	3
23	Mo	4	5	·44	2	·73	4
24	Tu	5	6	·45	3	·77	5
25	We	6	7	·45	4	·78	6
26	Th	7	8	·43	5	·79	7
27	Fr	8	9	·38	6	·77	8
28	Sa	9	10	·33	7	·73	9
29	Su	10	11	·26	8	·68	10
—30	Mo	11	12	·18	9	·62	11
1	Tu	12	13 / 14	·08 / ·99	10	·55	12
2	We	13	P	·88	11	·49	13
3	Th	14	1	·78	12	·42	14
4	Fr	15	2	·69	13	·35	15
5	Sa	16	3	·60	14	·29	16
6	Su	17	4	·53	15	·25	17
7	Mo	18	5	·46	16	·21	18
8	Tu	19	6	·44	17	·19	19
9	We	20	7	·41	18	·19	20
10	Th	21	8	·41	19	·20	21
11	Fr	22	9	·43	20	·25	22
12	Sa	23	10	·46	21	·31	23
13	Su	24	11	·52	22	·39	24
14	Mo	25	12	·59	23	·48	25
15	Tu	26	13	·68	24	·58	26
16	We	27	14	·76	25	·69	27
17	Th	28	—A	·85	26	·80	28
18	Fr	29	1	·92	27	·90	—29
19	Sa	30	2	·97	1	·98	1
20	Su	31	...	...	...	...	2

April — Yuva, *Mina—Panguni* / Dhatri, *Mesha—Chittirai*; Sukla / Chaitra / Bahula / V. Suk.; H. 1231 *Jumadal-awwal*.

Cyclic Sidereal	Week-Day	English	Tithi	Ending Moment	Nakshatra	Ending Moment	Muhammadan
21	Mo	1	3	·02	2	·04	3
22	Tu	2	4	·03	3	·08	4
23	We	3	5	·03	4	·11	5
24	Th	4	6 / 7	·01 / ·96	5	·11	6
25	Fr	5	8	·90	6	·09	7
26	Sa	6	9	·84	7	·06	8
27	Su	7	10	·75	8 / 9	·01 / ·96	9
28	Mo	8	11	·65	10	·90	10
29	Tu	9	12	·55	11	·83	11
—30	We	10	13	·44	12	·75	12
1	Th	11	14	·35	13	·69	13
2	Fr	12	P	·25	14	·63	14
3	Sa	13	1	·17	15	·58	15
4	Su	14	2	·09	16	·54	16
5	Mo	15	3 / 4	·02 / ·99	17	·52	17
6	Tu	16	5	·96	18	·51	18
7	We	17	6	·96	19	·52	19
8	Th	18	7	·98	20	·56	20
9	Fr	19	...	...	21	·62	21
10	Sa	20	8	·02	22	·69	22
11	Su	21	9	·07	23	·78	23
12	Mo	22	10	·12	24	·88	24
13	Tu	23	11	·22	...	...	25
14	We	24	12	·30	25	·00	26
15	Th	25	13	·39	26	·10	27
16	Fr	26	14	·45	27	·20	28
17	Sa	27	—A	·52	1	·28	29
18	Su	28	1	·56	2	·35	—30
19	Mo	29	2	·58	3	·41	1
20	Tu	30	3	·56	4	·43	2

May — Dhatri, *Mesha—Chittirai* / Dhatri, *Vrishabha—Vaikasi*; Sukla / Vaisakha / Bahula; H. 1231 *Jumadal-akhir*.

Cyclic Sidereal	Week-Day	English	Tithi	Ending Moment	Nakshatra	Ending Moment	Muhammadan
21	We	1	4	·54	5	·44	3
22	Th	2	5	·49	6	·42	4
23	Fr	3	6	·43	7	·39	5
24	Sa	4	7	·37	8	·36	6
25	Su	5	8	·28	9	·30	7
26	Mo	6	9	·19	10	·23	8
27	Tu	7	10 / 11	·08 / ·97	11	·16	9
28	We	8	12	·88	12	·09	10
29	Th	9	13	·78	13 / 14	·03 / ·97	11
30	Fr	10	14	·70	15	·92	12
—31	Sa	11	P	·61	16	·87	13
1	Su	12	1	·56	17	·84	14
2	Mo	13	2	·51	18	·83	15
3	Tu	14	3	·48	19	·85	16
4	We	15	4	·48	20	·88	17
5	Th	16	5	·48	21	·93	18
6	Fr	17	6	·53	...	...	19
7	Sa	18	7	·58	22	·00	20
8	Su	19	8	·65	23	·08	21
9	Mo	20	9	·74	24	·19	22
10	Tu	21	10	·81	25	·30	23
11	We	22	11	·89	26	·40	24
12	Th	23	12	·96	27	·50	25
13	Fr	24	...	...	1	·59	26
14	Sa	25	13	·03	2	·67	27
15	Su	26	14	·05	3	·72	28
16	Mo	27	—A	·08	4	·75	—29
17	Tu	28	1	·07	5	·76	1
18	We	29	2	·06	6	·75	2
19	Th	30	3 / 4	·00 / ·94	7	·73	3
20	Fr	31	5	·87	8	·69	4

June — Dhatri, *Vrishabha—Vaikasi* / Dhatri, *Mithuna—Ani*; Sukla / Jyeshtha / Bahula / Ashad. Suk.; H. 1231 *Rajab* / *Shaban*.

Cyclic Sidereal	Week-Day	English	Tithi	Ending Moment	Nakshatra	Ending Moment	Muhammadan
21	Sa	1	6	·77	9	·64	5
22	Su	2	7	·68	10	·57	6
23	Mo	3	8	·58	11	·50	7
24	Tu	4	9	·48	12	·43	8
25	We	5	10	·37	13	·37	9
26	Th	6	11	·27	14	·31	10
27	Fr	7	12	·20	15	·25	11
28	Sa	8	13	·12	16	·20	12
29	Su	9	14	·05	17	·17	13
30	Mo ○	10	P / 1	·00 / ·98	18	·16	14
—31	Tu	11	2	·96	19	·17	15
1	We	12	3	·98	20	·19	16
2	Th	13	...	...	21	·24	17
3	Fr	14	4	·01	22	·30	18
4	Sa	15	5	·05	23	·39	19
5	Su	16	6	·13	24	·49	20
6	Mo	17	7	·20	25	·59	21
7	Tu	18	8	·29	26	·70	22
8	We	19	9	·36	27	·80	23
9	Th	20	10	·44	1	·90	24
10	Fr	21	11	·50	2	·98	25
11	Sa	22	12	·53	...	...	26
12	Su	23	13	·56	3	·03	27
13	Mo	24	14	·55	4	·07	28
14	Tu	25	—A	·53	5	·08	29
15	We	26	1	·48	6	·09	—30
16	Th	27	2	·43	7	·06	1
17	Fr	28	3	·35	8 / 9	·02 / ·97	2
18	Sa	29	4	·26	10	·91	3
19	Su	30	5	·17	11	·84	4

Naksh :—1. Asvn. 2. Bhar. 3. Krit. 4. Rohi. 5. Mrig. 6. Ardh. 7. Punar. 8. Push. 9. Aslesh. 10. Magh. 11. P. Phal. 12. U. Phal. 13. Hasta. 14. Chit.

A. D. 1816. **A.—Amavasya.** **P.—Paurnami.**

Kollam 992, Commences {**N. Malabar—Sept.** **S. Malabar—Aug.**

Hijra 1232, Commences, **Nov. 21.**

Vikrama 1873. **Bengal San 1222.** **(N. Cycle) Sarvajit.**

July

SOLAR reckoning: Cyclic Sidereal Year, Month and Day	Week-Day	English Month and Day	LUNAR reckoning: Tithi	Ending Moment	Nakshatra	Ending Moment	Muhammadan Year, Month and Day
Dhatri *Mithuna—Ani.* 20	Mo	1	Ashadha *Sukla* 6 7	·07 ·97	12	·78	H. 1231 *Shaban* 5
21	Tu	2	8	·86	13	·71	6
22	We	3	9	·77	14	·64	7
23	Th	4	10	·68	15	·58	8
24	Fr	5	11	·59	16	·53	9
25	Sa	6	12	·53	17	·51	10
26	Su	7	13	·49	18	·49	11
27	Mo	8	14	·45	19	·49	12
28	Tu	9	P	·44	20	·51	13
29	We	10	*Bahula* 1	·46	21	·55	14
30	Th	11	2	·48	22	·62	15
31	Fr	12	3	·54	23	·69	16
—32	Sa	13	4	·61	24	·79	17
Dhatri *Karkata—Adi.* 1	Su	14	5	·69	25	·89	18
2	Mo	15	6	·75	...	...	19
3	Tu	16	7	·84	26	·00	20
4	We	17	8	·93	27	·11	21
5	Th	18	9	·97	1	·21	22
6	Fr	19	...	...	2	·28	23
7	Sa	20	10	·02	3	·34	24
8	Su	21	11	·03	4	·38	25
9	Mo	22	12	·03	5	·40	26
10	Tu	23	13 14	·01 ·97	6	·41	27
11	We	24	—A	·91	7	·39	28
12	Th	25	*Sukla* 1	·83	8	·36	—29
13	Fr	26	2	·76	9	·31	1
14	Sa	27	3	·66	10	·25	2
15	Su	28	4	·56	11	·19	3
16	Mo	29	5	·45	12	·12	4
17	Tu	30	6	·36	13 14	·05 ·98	5
18	We	31	7	·26	15	·92	6

Aug.

SOLAR reckoning: Cyclic Sidereal Year, Month and Day	Week-Day	English Month and Day	LUNAR reckoning: Tithi	Ending Moment	Nakshatra	Ending Moment	Muhammadan Year, Month and Day
19	Th	1	Sravana 8	·15	16	·88	H. 1231 *Ramzan.* 7
20	Fr	2	9	·08	17	·84	8
21	Sa	3	10 11	·01 ·97	18	·81	9
22	Su	4	12	·93	19	·81	10
23	Mo	5	13	·93	20	·82	11
24	Tu	6	14	·93	21	·87	12
25	We	7	P	·96	22	·92	13
26	Th	8	...	...	...	...	14
27	Fr	9	1	·01	23	·00	15
28	Sa	10	2	·08	24	·09	16
29	Su	11	3	·16	25	·19	17
30	Mo	12	4	·25	26	·31	18
—31	Tu	13	5	·34	27	·41	19
Dhatri *Simha—Avani.* 1	We	14	*Bahula* 6	·40	1	·51	20
2	Th	15	7	·46	2	·59	21
3	Fr	16	8	·50	3	·65	22
4	Sa	17	9	·53	4	·70	23
5	Su	18	10	·53	5	·73	24
6	Mo	19	11	·50	6	·74	25
7	Tu	20	12	·46	7	·72	26
8	We	21	13	·41	8	·69	27
9	Th	22	14	·34	9	·64	28
10	Fr	23	—A	·26	10	·59	29
11	Sa	24	Bhad. *Suk.* 1	·15	11	.53	—30
12	Su	25	2 3	·05 ·95	12	·46	*Shawwal.* 1
13	Mo	26	4	·87	13	·39	2
14	Tu	27	5	·76	14	·32	3
15	We	28	6	·67	15	·26	4
16	Th	29	7	·58	16	·21	5
17	Fr	30	8	·52	17	·17	6
18	Sa	31	9	·47	18	·14	7

Sep.

SOLAR reckoning: Cyclic Sidereal Year, Month and Day	Week-Day	English Month and Day	LUNAR reckoning: Tithi	Ending Moment	Nakshatra	Ending Moment	Muhammadan Year, Month and Day
Dhatri *Simha—Avani.* 19	Su	1	Bhadrapada *Sukla* 10	·44	19	·13	H. 1231 *Shawwal.* 8
20	Mo	2	11	·44	20	·15	9
21	Tu	3	12	·44	21	·18	10
22	We	4	13	·48	22	·23	11
23	Th	5	14	·53	23	·30	12
24	Fr	6	P	·61	24	·39	13
25	Sa	7	1	·66	25	·49	14
26	Su	8	2	·75	26	·60	15
27	Mo	9	3	·84	27	·71	16
28	Tu	10	4	·92	1	·81	17
29	We	11	5	·98	2	·89	18
30	Th	12	...	...	3	·96	19
—31	Fr	13	6	·02	...	...	20
Dhatri *Kanya—Purattasi.* 1	Sa	14	7	·06	4	·02	21
2	Su	15	8	·05	5	·05	22
3	Mo	16	*Bahula* 9 10	·03 ·99	6	·06	23
4	Tu	17	11	·94	7	·05	24
5	We	18	12	·87	8 9	·02 ·98	25
6	Th	19	13	·78	10	·93	26
7	Fr	20	14	·69	11	·87	27
8	Sa	21	—A	·59	12	·80	28
9	Su	22	*Sukla* 1	·50	13	·73	—29
10	Mo	23	2	·39	14	·67	1
11	Tu	24	3	·29	15	·60	2
12	We	25	4	·20	16	·54	3
13	Th	26	5	·12	17	·50	4
14	Fr	27	6	·07	18	·47	5
15	Sa	28	7 8	·01 ·99	19	·46	6
16	Su	29	9	·98	20	·47	7
17	Mo	30	10	·98	21	·49	8

Oct.

SOLAR reckoning: Cyclic Sidereal Year, Month and Day	Week-Day	English Month and Day	LUNAR reckoning: Tithi	Ending Moment	Nakshatra	Ending Moment	Muhammadan Year, Month and Day
18	Tu	1	Asvina ...	...	22	·54	H. 1231 *Zi-l-ka'da.* 9
19	We	2	11	·02	23	·61	10
20	Th	3	12	·07	24	·69	11
21	Fr	4	13	·14	25	·80	12
22	Sa	5	14	·22	26	·90	13
23	Su	6	P	·31	...	...	14
24	Mo	7	1	·39	27	·01	15
25	Tu	8	2	·46	1	·11	16
26	We	9	3	·53	2	·20	17
27	Th	10	4	·58	3	·28	18
28	Fr	11	5	·62	4	·34	19
29	Sa	12	6	·61	5	·37	20
30	Su	13	*Bahula* 7	·60	6	·38	21
—31	Mo	14	8	·55	7	·37	22
Dhatri *Tula—Aippasi.* 1	Tu	15	9	·51	8	·36	23
2	We	16	10	·43	9	·32	24
3	Th	17	11	·34	10	·27	25
4	Fr	18	12	·25	11	·20	26
5	Sa	19	13	·15	12	·13	27
6	Su	20	14 A	·06 ·95	13	·07	28
7	Mo	21	Karttika *Sukla* 1	·87	14 15	·00 ·94	29
8	Tu	22	2	·78	16	·88	—30
9	We	23	3	·70	17	·83	H. 1231 *Zi-l-hijja.* 1
10	Th	24	4	·65	18	·80	2
11	Fr	25	5	·59	19	·79	3
12	Sa	26	6	·57	20	·79	4
13	Su	27	7	·56	21	·81	5
14	Mo	28	8	·57	22	·85	6
15	Tu	29	9	·61	23	·91	7
16	We	30	10	·66	...	...	8
17	Th	31	11	·74	24	·00	9

Nov.

SOLAR reckoning: Cyclic Sidereal Year, Month and Day	Week-Day	English Month and Day	LUNAR reckoning: Tithi	Ending Moment	Nakshatra	Ending Moment	Muhammadan Year, Month and Day
Dhatri *Tula—Aippasi.* 18	Fr	1	Kartika *Suk.* 12	·82	25	·10	H. 1231 *Zi-l-hijja.* 10
19	Sa	2	13	·90	26	·20	11
20	Su	3	14	·99	27	·31	12
21	Mo	4	...	...	1	·41	13
22	Tu	5	P	·07	2	·51	14
23	We	6	1	·13	3	·59	15
24	Th	7	2	·18	4	·65	16
25	Fr	8	3	·21	5	·69	17
26	Sa	9	4	·20	6	·70	18
27	Su	10	5	·19	7	·71	19
28	Mo	11	6	·15	8	·69	20
29	Tu	12	7	·11	9	·65	21
—30	We	13	*Bahula* 8 9	·03 ·95	10	·60	22
Dhatri *Vrischika—Kartigai.* 1	Th	14	10	·86	11	·54	23
2	Fr	15	11	·76	12	·47	24
3	Sa	16	12	·67	13	·41	25
4	Su	17	13	·56	14	·34	26
5	Mo	18	14	·47	15	·27	27
6	Tu ●	19	—A	·39	16	·21	28
7	We	20	*Sukla* 1	·32	17	·16	—29
8	Th	21	2	·25	18	·13	1
9	Fr	22	3	·20	19	·11	2
10	Sa	23	4	·19	20	·11	3
11	Su	24	5	·18	21	·12	4
12	Mo	25	6	·20	22	·16	5
13	Tu	26	7	·22	23	·23	6
14	We	27	8	·29	24	·30	7
15	Th	28	9	·36	25	·39	8
16	Fr	29	10	·45	26	·50	9
17	Sa	30	11	·53	27	·60	10

Dec.

SOLAR reckoning: Cyclic Sidereal Year, Month and Day	Week-Day	English Month and Day	LUNAR reckoning: Tithi	Ending Moment	Nakshatra	Ending Moment	Muhammadan Year, Month and Day
18	Su	1	Margasira 12	·62	1	·72	H. 1232 *Muharram.* 11
19	Mo	2	13	·70	2	·81	12
20	Tu	3	14	·75	3	·89	13
21	We ○	4	P	·81	4	·96	14
22	Th	5	1	·84	...	...	15
23	Fr	6	2	·84	5	·00	16
24	Sa	7	3	·82	6	·03	17
25	Su	8	4	·78	7	·03	18
26	Mo	9	5	·73	8 9	·01 ·98	19
27	Tu	10	6	·65	10	·94	20
28	We	11	*Bahula* 7	·57	11	·88	21
—29	Th	12	8	·49	12	·82	22
Dhatri *Dhanus—Margali.* 1	Fr	13	9	·39	13	·75	23
2	Sa	14	10	·29	14	·68	24
3	Su	15	11	·20	15	·61	25
4	Mo	16	12	·10	16	·55	26
5	Tu	17	13 14	·01 ·95	17	·51	27
6	We	18	—A	·89	18	·46	28
7	Th	19	Pausha *Sukla* 1	·85	19	·44	29
8	Fr	20	2	·82	20	·43	—30
9	Sa	21	3	·83	21	·44	H. 1232 *Safar.* 1
10	Su	22	4	·84	22	·48	2
11	Mo	23	5	·87	23	·53	3
12	Tu	24	6	·94	24	·61	4
13	We	25	...	...	25	·69	5
14	Th	26	7	·01	26	·80	6
15	Fr	27	8	·10	27	·91	7
16	Sa	28	9	·19	...	...	8
17	Su	29	10	·28	1	·02	9
18	Mo	30	11	·35	2	·12	10
19	Tu	31	12	·41	3	·20	11

15. Svati. 16. Visak. 17. Anur. 18. Jyesh. 19. Mula. 20. P. Ash. 21. U. Ash. 22. Sravu. 23. Dani. 24. Satab. 25. P. Bhad. 26. U. Bhad. 27. Rev·

A. D. 1817. **Mesha Sankranti** (Commencement of Indian Sidereal Year).
Solar Eclipse. ● **(Surya Sid.) April 11·14.** **Saka 1739.** **Kaliyuga 4918.**
Lunar Eclipse. ○ **(Arya Sid.) April 11·04.** **(S. Cycle) Isvara.**

SOLAR reckoning: Cyclic Sidereal Year, Month and Day; Week-Day; English Month and Day. LUNAR reckoning: Tithi, Ending Moment; Nakshatra, Ending Moment; Muhammadan Year, Month and Day.

Jan.

Cyclic Sidereal Year, Month and Day	Week-Day	English Month and Day	Tithi	Ending Moment	Nakshatra	Ending Moment	Muhammadan Year, Month and Day
Dhatri Dhanus—Margali 20	We	1	Pansha Suk. 13	·46	4	·27	12
21	Th	2	14	·48	5	·31	13
22	Fr	3	P	·48	6	·35	14
23	Sa	4	1	·47	7	·36	15
24	Su	5	2	·43	8	·34	16
25	Mo	6	3	·37	9	·31	17
26	Tu	7	4	·30	10	·27	18
27	We	8	5	·22	11	·22	H. 1232 Safar 19
28	Th	9	6	·13	12	·16	20
29	Fr	10	{ 7 8	·03 ·94	13	·09	21
Dhatri Makara—Tai 1	Sa	11	Bahula 9	·84	14 15	·02 ·95 }	22
2	Su	12	10	·74	16	·90	23
3	Mo	13	11	·67	17	·84	24
4	Tu	14	12	·59	18	·79	25
5	We	15	13	·53	19	·76	26
6	Th	16	14	·49	20	·75	27
7	Fr	17	A	·47	21	·77	28
8	Sa	18	1	·47	22	·80	29
9	Su	19	2	·48	23	·84	1
10	Mo	20	3	·53	24	·91	2
11	Tu	21	4	·59	...	...	3
12	We	22	Sukla 5	·66	25	·00	4
13	Th	23	6	·75	26	·10	5
14	Fr	24	7	·84	27	·21	6
15	Sa	25	8	·93	1	·33	7
16	Su	26	...	...	2	·42	Rabi-ul-awwal 8
17	Mo	27	9	·00	3	·50	9
18	Tu	28	10	·07	4	·58	10
19	We	29	Magha 11	·10	5	·64	11
20	Th	30	12	·13	6	·67	12
21	Fr	31	13	·12	7	·68	13

Feb.

Cyclic Sidereal Year, Month and Day	Week-Day	English Month and Day	Tithi	Ending Moment	Nakshatra	Ending Moment	Muhammadan Year, Month and Day
22	Sa	1	14	·11	8	·67	H. 1232 14
23	Su	2	P	·07	9	·65	15
24	Mo	3	{ 1 2	·00 ·93	10	·61	16
25	Tu	4	3	·85	11	·56	17
26	We	5	Bahula 4	·76	12	·50	18
27	Th	6	5	·66	13	·43	19
28	Fr	7	6	·56	14	·36	20
29	Sa	8	7	·47	15	·30	21
30	Su	9	8	·37	16	·23	22
Dhatri Kumbha—Masi 1	Mo	10	9	·29	17	·17	23
2	Tu	11	10	·21	18	·13	24
3	We	12	11	·17	19	·09	25
4	Th	13	12	·13	20	·09	26
5	Fr	14	13	·10	21	·09	27
6	Sa	15	14	·10	22	·11	28
7	Su	16	A	·12	23	·15	29
8	Mo	17	1	·17	24	·22	30
9	Tu	18	Sukla 2	·22	25	·30	1
10	We	19	3	·30	26	·40	Rabi-ul-akhir 2
11	Th	20	4	·38	27	·51	3
12	Fr	21	5	·47	1	·61	4
13	Sa	22	Phalguna 6	·55	2	·72	5
14	Su	23	7	·63	3	·81	6
15	Mo	24	8	·70	4	·89	H. 1232 7
16	Tu	25	9	·73	5	·95	8
17	We	26	10	·75	6	·99	9
18	Th	27	11	·74	...	...	10
19	Fr	28	12	·73	7	·00	11

March

Cyclic Sidereal Year, Month and Day	Week-Day	English Month and Day	Tithi	Ending Moment	Nakshatra	Ending Moment	Muhammadan Year, Month and Day
20	Sa	1	Phalg. Suk. 13	·68	8 9	·00 ·98 }	12
21	Su	2	14	·62	10	·95	13
Dhatri Kumbha—Masi 22	Mo	3	P	·55	11	·90	14
23	Tu	4	1	·46	12	·83	15
24	We	5	2	·37	13	·77	16
25	Th	6	3	·27	14	·71	Rabi-ul-akhir 17
26	Fr	7	4	·18	15	·64	18
27	Sa	8	{ 5 6	·08 ·99	16	·57	19
28	Su	9	7	·90	17	·51	20
29	Mo	10	8	·82	18	·46	21
30	Tu	11	9	·77	19	·43	H. 1232 22
1	We	12	Bahula 10	·73	20	·41	23
2	Th	13	11	·71	21	·41	24
3	Fr	14	12	·70	22	·43	25
4	Sa	15	13	·73	23	·46	26
5	Su	16	14	·76	24	·52	27
6	Mo	17	A	·82	25	·61	28
7	Tu	18	1	·90	26	·70	29
8	We	19	2	·98	27	·80	1
9	Th	20	...	...	1	·91	2
10	Fr	21	3	·08	...	...	3
11	Sa	22	Sukla 4	·16	2	·02	4
12	Su	23	5	·23	3	·12	5
Dhatri Mina—Panguni 13	Mo	24	6	·29	4	·20	Jumadal-awwal 6
14	Tu	25	7	·32	5	·26	7
15	We	26	8	·34	6	·30	8
16	Th	27	9	·33	7	·32	9
17	Fr	28	10	·32	8	·33	10
18	Sa	29	11	·26	9	·31	11
19	Su	30	12	·21	10	·28	12
20	Mo	31	Chaitra 13	·13	11	·23	13

April

Cyclic Sidereal Year, Month and Day	Week-Day	English Month and Day	Tithi	Ending Moment	Nakshatra	Ending Moment	Muhammadan Year, Month and Day
21	Tu	1	{ 14 P	·05 ·95 }	12	·17	H. 1232 14
22	We	2	1	·84	13	·12	15
23	Th	3	2	·74	14 15	·04 ·97 }	16
24	Fr	4	3	·65	16	·91	17
25	Sa	5	4	·56	17	·84	18
26	Su	6	Bahula 5	·47	18	·79	19
27	Mo	7	6	·40	19	·76	20
28	Tu	8	7	·34	20	·74	21
29	We	9	8	·30	21	·73	22
30	Th	10	9	·27	22	·74	23
1	Fr	11	10	·26	23	·77	24
2	Sa	12	11	·20	24	·84	25
3	Su	13	12	·32	25	·91	26
4	Mo	14	13	·39	...	...	27
5	Tu	15	14	·46	26	·00	28
6	We	16	A	·54	27	·10	29
7	Th	17	1	·63	1	·21	30
8	Fr	18	2	·71	2	·32	1
9	Sa	19	3	·78	3	·42	2
Isvara Mesha—Chittirai 10	Su	20	Sukla 4	·84	4	·51	Jumadal-akhir 3
11	Mo	21	5	·88	5	·57	4
12	Tu	22	6	·88	6	·62	5
13	We	23	7	·88	7	·65	6
14	Th	24	8	·86	8	·66	7
15	Fr	25	9	·80	9	·64	8
16	Sa	26	Vaisakha 10	·75	10	·61	H. 1232 9
17	Su	27	11	·67	11	·57	10
18	Mo	28	12	·59	12	·52	11
19	Tu	29	13	·49	13	·45	12
20	We	30	14	·39	14	·38	13

May

Cyclic Sidereal Year, Month and Day	Week-Day	English Month and Day	Tithi	Ending Moment	Nakshatra	Ending Moment	Muhammadan Year, Month and Day
21	Th	1	P	·28	15	·31	14
22	Fr	2	1	·18	16	·24	15
Isvara Mesha—Chittirai 23	Sa	3	2	·09	17	·18	16
24	Su	4	{ 3 4	·00 ·93	18	·13	Jumadal-akhir 17
25	Mo	5	Vaisak 5	·87	19	·09	18
26	Tu	6	6	·83	20	·06	19
27	We	7	7	·80	21	·05	20
28	Th	8	8	·79	22	·06	21
29	Fr	9	9	·82	23	·10	22
30	Sa	10	10	·84	24	·15	23
31	Su	11	11	·91	25	·22	H. 1232 24
1	Mo	12	Bahula 12	·97	26	·30	25
2	Tu	13	...	...	27	·40	26
3	We	14	13	·06	1	·52	27
4	Th	15	14	·14	2	·62	28
5	Fr ●	16	A	·23	3	·72	29
6	Sa	17	1	·29	4	·81	1
7	Su	18	2	·35	5	·88	2
8	Mo	19	3	·39	6	·94	3
9	Tu	20	4	·40	7	·97	4
10	We	21	Sukla 5	·40	8	·98	5
11	Th	22	6	·37	9	·97	6
12	Fr	23	7	·33	10	·94	7
13	Sa	24	8	·26	11	·90	8
Isvara Vrishabha—Vaikasi 14	Su	25	9	·18	12	·85	9
15	Mo	26	{ 10 11	·09 ·99	13	·79	Rajab 10
16	Tu	27	12	·90	14	·72	11
17	We	28	13	·79	15	·65	12
18	Th	29	Jyeshtha 14	·69	16	·58	13
19	Fr	30	P	·59	17	·53	H. 1232 14
20	Sa	31	1	·51	18	·47	15

June

Cyclic Sidereal Year, Month and Day	Week-Day	English Month and Day	Tithi	Ending Moment	Nakshatra	Ending Moment	Muhammadan Year, Month and Day
21	Su	1	2	·43	19	·42	16
22	Mo	2	3	·37	20	·39	17
23	Tu	3	4	·33	21	·37	18
24	We	4	5	·30	22	·39	19
25	Th	5	Bahula 6	·29	23	·41	20
26	Fr	6	7	·30	24	·46	21
27	Sa	7	8	·34	25	·52	22
28	Su	8	9	·41	26	·60	23
29	Mo	9	10	·46	27	·71	24
30	Tu	10	11	·55	1	·82	25
31	We	11	12	·63	2	·92	26
1	Th	12	13	·70	...	...	27
2	Fr	13	14	·77	3	·02	28
3	Sa	14	A	·84	4	·11	29
4	Su	15	1	·86	5	·19	30
5	Mo	16	2	·88	6	·25	1
6	Tu	17	3	·88	7	·29	2
7	We	18	4	·86	8	·30	3
Isvara Mithuna—Ani 8	Th	19	Sukla 5	·81	9	·29	4
9	Fr	20	6	·75	10	·27	Shaban 5
10	Sa	21	7	·68	11	·24	6
11	Su	22	8	·58	12	·19	7
12	Mo	23	9	·49	13	·13	8
13	Tu	24	10	·39	14 15	·06 ·99 }	9
14	We	25	Ashadha 11	·27	16	·98	H. 1232 10
15	Th	26	12	·18	17	·86	11
16	Fr	27	{ 13 14	·08 ·99	18	·80	12
17	Sa	28	P	·91	19	·75	13
18	Su	29	Bah. 1	·85	20	·72	14
19	Mo	30	2	·81	21	·71	15

Naksh :—1. Asvn. 2. Bhar. 3. Krit. 4. Rohi. 5. Mrig. 6. Ardh. 7. Punar. 8. Push. 9. Aslesh. 10. Magh. 11. P. Phal. 12. U. Phal. 13. Hasta. 14. Chit.

A. D. 1817.
A.—Amavasya. **P.—Paurnami.**

Kollam 993, Commences { **N. Malabar—Sept.** **S. Malabar—Aug.**

Hijra 1233, Commences, **Nov. 11.**

Vikrama 1874.
Bengal San 1223.
(N. Cycle) Sarvadharin.

Columns: SOLAR reckoning — Cyclic Sidereal Year, Month and Day; Week-Day; English Month and Day. LUNAR reckoning — Tithi; Ending Moment; Nakshatra; Ending Moment; Muhammadan Year, Month and Day.

July (Solar: Isvara *Mithuna—Adi* to 32; then Isvara *Karkata—Adi*. Lunar: Ashadha *Bahula*; Adhika Sravana *Sukla*. Muhammadan: H. 1232 *Shaban*; H. 1232 *Ramzan*.)

Cyclic Sidereal Year, Month and Day	Week-Day	English Month and Day	Tithi	Ending Moment	Nakshatra	Ending Moment	Muhammadan Year, Month and Day
20	Tu	1	3	·77	22	·71	16
21	We	2	4	·77	23	·73	17
22	Th	3	5	·78	24	·77	18
23	Fr	4	6	·81	25	·83	19
24	Sa	5	7	·87	26	·92	20
25	Su	6	8	·94	...	...	21
26	Mo	7	...	...	27	·01	22
27	Tu	8	9	·01	1	·11	23
28	We	9	10	·09	2	·22	24
29	Th	10	11	·18	3	·32	25
30	Fr	11	12	·24	4	·42	26
31	Sa	12	13	·31	5	·50	27
—32	Su	13	14	·34	6	·56	28
1	Mo	14	—A	·37	7	·60	—29
2	Tu	15	1	·36	8	·62	1
3	We	16	2	·34	9	·62	2
4	Th	17	3	·29	10	·61	3
5	Fr	18	4	·23	11	·57	4
6	Sa	19	5	·15	12	·53	5
7	Su	20	6 / 7	·06 / ·97	13	·47	6
8	Mo	21	8	·87	14	·40	7
9	Tu	22	9	·77	15	·34	8
10	We	23	10	·67	16	·27	9
11	Th	24	11	·57	17	·20	10
12	Fr	25	12	·48	18	·14	11
13	Sa	26	13	·39	19	·09	12
14	Su	27	14	·33	20	·06	13
15	Mo	28	P	·29	21	·03	14
16	Tu	29	1	·26	22	·03	15
17	We	30	2	·25	23	·04	16
18	Th	31	3	·26	24	·08	17

Aug. (Solar: Isvara *Simha—Avani*. Lunar: Adhika Sravana *Bahula*; Nija Sravana *Sukla*; *Bah.* Muhammadan: H. 1232 *Shawwal*.)

Cyclic Sidereal Year, Month and Day	Week-Day	English Month and Day	Tithi	Ending Moment	Nakshatra	Ending Moment	Muhammadan Year, Month and Day
19	Fr	1	4	·29	25	·13	18
20	Sa	2	5	·34	26	·22	19
21	Su	3	6	·42	27	·31	20
22	Mo	4	7	·49	1	·41	21
23	Tu	5	8	·58	2	·52	22
24	We	6	9	·65	3	·62	23
25	Th	7	10	·73	4	·73	24
26	Fr	8	11	·79	5	·81	25
27	Sa	9	12	·81	6	·87	26
28	Su	10	13	·85	7	·92	27
29	Mo	11	14	·84	8	·94	28
30	Tu	12	—A	·88	9	·96	29
—31	We	13	1	·78	10	·94	—30
1	Th	14	2	·73	11	·91	1
2	Fr	15	3	·65	12	·86	2
3	Sa	16	4	·56	13	·80	3
4	Su	17	5	·47	14	·75	4
5	Mo	18	6	·37	15	·68	5
6	Tu	19	7	·26	16	·61	6
7	We	20	8	·16	17	·54	7
8	Th	21	9 / 10	·07 / ·98	18	·47	8
9	Fr	22	11	·91	19	·43	9
10	Sa	23	12	·83	20	·39	10
11	Su	24	13	·78	21	·36	11
12	Mo	25	14	·76	22	·35	12
13	Tu	26	P	·75	23	·36	13
14	We	27	1	·76	24	·39	14
15	Th	28	2	·80	25	·45	15
16	Fr	29	3	·85	26	·52	16
17	Sa	30	4	·91	27	·61	17
18	Su	31	5	·99	1	·71	18

Sep. (Solar: Isvara *Simha—Avani* to 31; then Isvara *Kanya—Purattasi*. Lunar: Nija Srv. *Bahula*; Bhadrapada *Sukla*. Muhammadan: H. 1232 *Shawwal*; H. 1232 *Zil-ka'da*.)

Cyclic Sidereal Year, Month and Day	Week-Day	English Month and Day	Tithi	Ending Moment	Nakshatra	Ending Moment	Muhammadan Year, Month and Day
19	Mo	1	...	...	2	·81	19
20	Tu	2	6	·08	3	·93	20
21	We	3	7	·16	...	...	21
22	Th	4	8	·24	4	·03	22
23	Fr	5	9	·30	5	·12	23
24	Sa	6	10	·34	6	·18	24
25	Su	7	11	·36	7	·23	25
26	Mo	8	12	·35	8	·27	26
27	Tu	9	13	·34	9	·28	27
28	We	10	14	·29	10	·27	28
29	Th	11	—A	·25	11	·24	—29
30	Fr	12	1	·17	12	·19	1
—31	Sa	13	2 / 3	·09 / ·09	13	·15	2
1	Su	14	4	·90	14	·08	3
2	Mo	15	5	·79	15 / 16	·02 / ·94	4
3	Tu	16	6	·69	17	·88	5
4	We	17	7	·60	18	·81	6
5	Th	18	8	·51	19	·76	7
6	Fr	19	9	·43	20	·72	8
7	Sa	20	10	·36	21	·69	9
8	Su	21	11	·32	22	·67	10
9	Mo	22	12	·29	23	·68	11
10	Tu	23	13	·28	24	·71	12
11	We	24	14	·29	25	·76	13
12	Th	25	P	·33	26	·83	14
13	Fr	26	1	·39	27	·91	15
14	Sa	27	2	·47	...	...	16
15	Su	28	3	·56	1	·01	17
16	Mo	29	4	·63	2	·12	18
17	Tu	30	5	·70	3	·23	19

Oct. (Solar: Isvara *Kanya—Purattasi* to 31; then Isvara *Tula—Aippasi*. Lunar: *Bahula*; *Sukla*; Asvina; *Bahula*. Muhammadan: H. 1232 *Zil-ka'da*; H. 1232 *Zil-hijja*.)

Cyclic Sidereal Year, Month and Day	Week-Day	English Month and Day	Tithi	Ending Moment	Nakshatra	Ending Moment	Muhammadan Year, Month and Day
18	We	1	6	·77	4	·33	20
19	Th	2	7	·84	5	·42	21
20	Fr	3	8	·88	6	·49	22
21	Sa	4	9	·90	7	·56	23
22	Su	5	10	·91	8	·59	24
23	Mo	6	11	·89	9	·60	25
24	Tu	7	12	·86	10	·59	26
25	We	8	13	·80	11	·57	27
26	Th	9	14	·72	12	·54	28
27	Fr	10	—A	·65	13	·49	29
28	Sa	11	1	·55	14	·42	—30
29	Su	12	2	·46	15	·35	1
30	Mo	13	3	·35	16	·28	2
—31	Tu	14	4	·26	17	·21	3
1	We	15	5	·16	18	·16	4
2	Th	16	6	·07	19	·10	5
3	Fr	17	7 / 8	·00 / ·93	20	·05	6
4	Sa	18	9	·89	21	·02	7
5	Su	19	10	·86	22	·00	8
6	Mo	20	11	·86	23	·01	9
7	Tu	21	12	·87	24	·03	10
8	We	22	13	·91	25	·07	11
9	Th	23	14	·97	26	·13	12
10	Fr	24	...	...	27	·21	13
11	Sa	25	P	·03	1	·32	14
12	Su	26	1	·12	2	·42	15
13	Mo	27	2	·20	3	·53	16
14	Tu	28	3	·28	4	·63	17
15	We	29	4	·37	5	·72	18
16	Th	30	5	·44	6	·81	19
17	Fr	31	6	·48	7	·87	20

Nov. (Solar: Isvara *Tula—Aippasi* to 30; then Isvara *Vrischika—Kartigai*. Lunar: Asvn. *Bah.*; Kartika *Sukla*. Muhammadan: H. 1232 *Zil-hijja*; H. 1233 *Muharram*.)

Cyclic Sidereal Year, Month and Day	Week-Day	English Month and Day	Tithi	Ending Moment	Nakshatra	Ending Moment	Muhammadan Year, Month and Day
18	Sa	1	7	·50	8	·91	21
19	Su	2	8	·50	9	·92	22
20	Mo	3	9	·48	10	·92	23
21	Tu	4	10	·44	11	·90	24
22	We	5	11	·40	12	·87	25
23	Th	6	12	·33	13	·82	26
24	Fr	7	13	·24	14	·76	27
25	Sa	8	14	·14	15	·69	28
26	Su ●	9	A / 1	·04 / ·95	16	·62	29
27	Mo	10	2	·86	17	·56	—30
28	Tu	11	3	·76	18	·49	1
29	We	12	4	·68	19	·43	2
—30	Th	13	5	·60	20	·38	3
1	Fr	14	6	·54	21	·34	4
2	Sa	15	7	·50	22	·33	5
3	Su	16	8	·47	23	·33	6
4	Mo	17	9	·47	24	·34	7
5	Tu	18	10	·47	25	·38	8
6	We	19	11	·53	26	·44	9
7	Th	20	12	·58	27	·52	10
8	Fr	21	13	·66	1	·62	11
9	Sa	22	14	·74	2	·72	12
10	Su	23	P	·83	3	·82	13
11	Mo	24	1	·92	4	·93	14
12	Tu	25	2	·99	...	...	15
13	We	26	...	...	5	·03	16
14	Th	27	3	·05	6	·12	17
15	Fr	28	4	·11	7	·18	18
16	Sa	29	5	·18	8	·22	19
17	Su	30	6	·12	9	·24	20

Dec. (Solar: Isvara *Vrischika—Kartigai* to 29; then Isvara *Dhanus—Margali*. Lunar: *Bahula*; Margasira *Sukla*; *Bahula*. Muhammadan: H. 1233 *Muharram*; H. 1233 *Safar*.)

Cyclic Sidereal Year, Month and Day	Week-Day	English Month and Day	Tithi	Ending Moment	Nakshatra	Ending Moment	Muhammadan Year, Month and Day
18	Mo	1	7	·10	10	·24	21
19	Tu	2	8	·07	11	·24	22
20	We	3	9 / 10	·00 / ·95	12	·20	23
21	Th	4	11	·86	13	·16	24
22	Fr	5	12	·78	14	·10	25
23	Sa	6	13	·67	15 / 16	·03 / ·97	26
24	Su	7	14	·58	17	·90	27
25	Mo	8	—A	·48	18	·83	28
26	Tu	9	1	·38	19	·77	29
27	We	10	2	·30	20	·72	—30
28	Th	11	3	·22	21	·68	1
—29	Fr	12	4	·17	22	·66	2
1	Sa	13	5	·12	23	·65	3
2	Su	14	6	·11	24	·66	4
3	Mo	15	7	·11	25	·69	5
4	Tu	16	8	·12	26	·76	6
5	We	17	9	·17	27	·83	7
6	Th	18	10	·23	1	·92	8
7	Fr	19	11	·31	...	...	9
8	Sa	20	12	·39	2	·02	10
9	Su	21	13	·48	3	·12	11
10	Mo	22	14	·57	4	·23	12
11	Tu	23	P	·64	5	·34	13
12	We	24	1	·70	6	·42	14
13	Th	25	2	·75	7	·49	15
14	Fr	26	3	·77	8	·54	16
15	Sa	27	4	·77	9	·56	17
16	Su	28	5	·76	10	·58	18
17	Mo	29	6	·71	11	·56	19
18	Tu	30	7	·65	12	·53	20
19	We	31	8	·59	13	·49	21

15. Svati. 16. Visak. 17. Anur. 18. Jyesh. 19. Mula. 20. P. Ash. 21. U. Ash. 22. Sravn. 23. Dani. 24. Satab. 25. P. Bhad. 26. U. Bhad. 27. Rev.

A. D. 1818.
Solar Eclipse. ●
Lunar Eclipse. ○

Mesha Sankranti (Commencement of Indian Sidereal Year).
(Surya Sid.) April 11·40. **Saka 1740.** **Kaliyuga 4919.**
(Arya Sid.) April 11·30. **(S. Cycle) Bahudhanya.**

SOLAR reckoning: Cyclic Sidereal Year, Month and Day	Week-Day	English Month and Day	LUNAR reckoning: Tithi	Ending Moment	Nakshatra	Ending Moment	Muhammadan Year, Month and Day
	Jan.						
Isvara, Dhanus—Margali.			*Mr. Bah.*				*H. 1233 Safar.*
20	Th	1	9	·50	14	·43	22
21	Fr	2	10	·41	15	·38	23
22	Sa	3	11	·31	16	·31	24
23	Su	4	12	·22	17	·24	25
24	Mo	5	13	·11	18	·17	26
25	Tu	6	14 / A	·03 / ·95	19	·10	27
26	We	7	1	·87	20	·05	28
27	Th	8	2	·81	21 / 22	·01 / ·98	—29
28	Fr	9	3	·77	23	·97	1
29	Sa	10	4	·76	24	·98	2
—30	Su	11	5	·75	...	...	3
Isvara, Makara—Tai.			*Sukla*				
1	Mo	12	6	·78	25	·01	4
2	Tu	13	7	·82	26	·06	5
3	We	14	8	·87	27	·13	6
4	Th	15	9	·95	1	·22	7
5	Fr	16	...	...	2	·31	8
6	Sa	17	10	·05	3	·42	9
			Pausha				*H. 1233 Rabi-ul-awwal.*
7	Su	18	11	·14	4	·54	10
8	Mo	19	12	·22	5	·64	11
9	Tu	20	13	·29	6	·72	12
10.	We	21	14	·35	7	·80	13
11	Th	22	P	·40	8	·85	14
			Bahula				
12	Fr	23	1	·41	9	·89	15
13	Sa	24	2	·40	10	·90	16
14	Su	25	3	·40	11	·89	17
15	Mo	26	4	·35	12	·86	18
16	Tu	27	5	·29	13	·82	19
17	We	28	6	·22	14	·78	20
18	Th	29	7	·14	15	·72	21
19	Fr	30	8 / 9	·04 / ·93	16	·64	22
20	Sa	31	10	·84	17	·58	23
	Feb.						
Isvara, Kumbha—Masi.							
21	Su	1	11	·74	18	·51	24
22	Mo	2	12	·66	19	·45	25
23	Tu	3	13	·57	20	·39	26
24	We	4	14	·51	21	·35	27
25	Th	5	—A	·45	22	·31	28
			Sukla				
26	Fr	6	1	·41	23	·30	29
27	Sa	7	2	·39	24	·30	—30
							H. 1233 Rabi-ul-akhir.
28	Su	8	3	·39	25	·33	1
—29	Mo	9	4	·41	26	·37	2
1	Tu	10	5	·46	27	·44	3
2	We	11	6	·52	1	·52	4
3	Th	12	7	·59	2	·61	5
4	Fr	13	8	·69	3	·73	6
5	Sa	14	9	·77	4	·83	7
6	Su	15	10	·85	5	·94	8
			Magha				
7	Mo	16	11	·93	...	...	9
8	Tu	17	12	·99	6	·03	10
9	We	18	...	...	7	·10	11
10	Th	19	13	·04	8	·17	12
11	Fr	20	14	·04	9	·21	13
12	Sa	21	P	·04	10	·22	14
			Bahula				
13	Su	22	1 / 2	·02 / ·96	11	·22	15
14	Mo	23	3	·91	12	·19	16
15	Tu	24	4	·84	13	·17	17
16	We	25	5	·75	14	·12	18
17	Th	26	6	·66	15 / 16	·05 / ·99	19
18	Fr	27	7	·56	17	·92	20
19	Sa	28	8	·46	18	·84	21

SOLAR reckoning: Cyclic Sidereal Year, Month and Day	Week-Day	English Month and Day	LUNAR reckoning: Tithi	Ending Moment	Nakshatra	Ending Moment	Muhammadan Year, Month and Day
	March						
Isvara, Kumbha—Masi.			*Mg. Bah.*				*Rabi-ul-akhir.*
20	Su	1	9	·37	19	·79	22
21	Mo	2	10	·27	20	·73	23
22	Tu	3	11	·18	21	·68	24
23	We	4	12	·12	22	·64	25
24	Th	5	13	·05	23	·62	26
25	Fr	6	14	·02	24	·63	27
26	Sa	7	—A	·00	25	·65	28
			Sukla				
27	Su	8	1	·01	26	·68	—29
28	Mo	9	2	·03	27	·74	1
29	Tu	10	3	·07	1	·82	2
—30	We	11	4	·13	2	·92	3
Isvara, Mina—Panguni.							
1	Th	12	5	·21	...	...	4
2	Fr	13	6	·30	3	·03	5
3	Sa	14	7	·38	4	·13	6
4	Su	15	8	·47	5	·24	7
5	Mo	16	9	·53	6	·33	8
6	Tu	17	10	·58	7	·42	9
			Phalguna				*H. 1233 Jumadal-awwal.*
7	We	18	11	·63	8	·48	10
8	Th	19	12	·63	9	·52	11
9	Fr	20	13	·64	10	·54	12
10	Sa	21	14	·62	11	·54	13
11	Su	22	P	·57	12	·53	14
			Bahula				
12	Mo	23	1	·50	13	·50	15
13	Tu	24	2	·43	14	·45	16
14	We	25	3	·34	15	·39	17
15	Th	26	4	·25	16	·32	18
16	Fr	27	5	·14	17	·25	19
17	Sa	28	6 / 7	·04 / ·95	18	·19	20
18	Su	29	8	·85	19	·13	21
19	Mo	30	9	·77	20	·06	22
20	Tu	31	10	·70	21 / 22	·01 / ·97	23
	April						
21	We	1	11	·63	23	·96	24
22	Th	2	12	·60	24	·95	25
23	Fr	3	13	·58	25	·96	26
24	Sa	4	14	·58	...	...	27
25	Su	5	—A	·60	26	·00	28
			Sukla				
26	Mo	6	1	·65	27	·05	29
27	Tu	7	2	·70	1	·13	—30
							H. 1233 Jumadal-akhir.
28	We	8	3	·78	2	·22	1
29	Th	9	4	·87	3	·32	2
—30	Fr	10	5	·94	4	·43	3
Bahudhanya, Mesha—Chittirai.							
1	Sa	11	...	...	5	·54	4
2	Su	12	6	·03	6	·64	5
3	Mo	13	7	·09	7	·73	6
4	Tu	14	8	·15	8	·79	7
5	We	15	9	·19	9	·84	8
			Chaitra				
6	Th	16	10	·20	10	·86	9
7	Fr	17	11	·19	11	·87	10
8	Sa	18	12	·17	12	·86	11
9	Su	19	13	·12	13	·83	12
10	Mo ○	20	14 / P	·05 / ·98	14	·78	13
			Bahula				
11	Tu	21	1	·89	15	·73	14
12	We	22	2	·79	16	·66	15
13	Th	23	3	·69	17	·60	16
14	Fr	24	4	·59	18	·53	17
15	Sa	25	5	·49	19	·46	18
16	Su	26	6	·39	20	·40	19
17	Mo	27	7	·31	21	·34	20
18	Tu	28	8	·24	22	·31	21
19	We	29	9	·18	23	·28	22
20	Th	30	10	·13	24	·27	23

SOLAR reckoning: Cyclic Sidereal Year, Month and Day	Week-Day	English Month and Day	LUNAR reckoning: Tithi	Ending Moment	Nakshatra	Ending Moment	Muhammadan Year, Month and Day
	May						
Bahudhanya, Mesha—Chittirai.			*Ch. Bah.*				*Jl. akhir.*
21	Fr	1	11	·12	25	·28	24
22	Sa	2	12	·11	26	·31	25
23	Su	3	13	·13	27	·37	26
24	Mo	4	14	·18	1	·44	27
25	Tu ●	5	A	·23	2	·52	28
			Sukla				
26	We	6	1	·30	3	·62	—29
							H. 1233 Rajab.
27	Th	7	2	·38	4	·73	1
28	Fr	8	3	·47	5	·84	2
29	Sa	9	4	·55	6	·94	3
30	Su	10	5	·62	...	...	4
—31	Mo	11	6	·67	7	·03	5
Bahudhanya, Vrishabha—Vaikasi.							
1	Tu	12	7	·71	8	·10	6
2	We	13	8	·72	9	·15	7
3	Th	14	9	·71	10	·18	8
4	Fr	15	10	·69	11	·20	9
5	Sa	16	11	·64	12	·19	10
			Vaisakha				
6	Su	17	12	·56	13	·16	11
7	Mo	18	13	·49	14	·12	12
8	Tu	19	14	·40	15	·06	13
9	We	20	P	·31	16 / 17	·01 / ·94	14
			Bahula				
10	Th	21	1	·21	18	·87	15
11	Fr	22	2	·11	19	·80	16
12	Sa	23	3 / 4	·00 / ·91	20	·74	17
13	Su	24	5	·81	21	·69	18
14	Mo	25	6	·74	22	·64	19
15	Tu	26	7	·69	23	·61	20
16	We	27	8	·64	24	·59	21
17	Th	28	9	·63	25	·60	22
18	Fr	29	10	·61	26	·62	23
19	Sa	30	11	·63	27	·68	24
20	Su	31	12	·68	1	·74	25
	June						
21	Mo	1	13	·73	2	·82	26
22	Tu	2	14	·80	3	·92	27
23	We	3	—A	·88	...	...	28
			Sukla				
24	Th	4	1	·97	4	·03	29
25	Fr	5	...	...	5	·14	—30
							H. 1233 Shaban.
26	Sa	6	2	·04	6	·24	1
27	Su	7	3	·12	7	·33	2
28	Mo	8	4	·16	8	·41	3
29	Tu	9	5	·20	9	·46	4
30	We	10	6	·21	10	·51	5
31	Th	11	7	·20	11	·52	6
—32	Fr	12	8	·18	12	·52	7
Bahudhanya, Mithuna—Ani.							
1	Sa	13	9	·13	13	·49	8
			Jyeshtha				
2	Su	14	10 / 11	·07 / ·99	14	·45	9
3	Mo	15	12	·90	15	·41	10
4	Tu	16	13	·80	16	·35	11
5	We	17	14	·70	17	·28	12
6	Th	18	P	·60	18	·21	13
			Bahula				
7	Fr	19	1	·49	19	·14	14
8	Sa	20	2	·40	20	·08	15
9	Su	21	3	·31	21 / 22	·02 / ·97	16
10	Mo	22	4	·23	23	·94	17
11	Tu	23	5	·17	24	·92	18
12	We	24	6	·12	25	·92	19
13	Th	25	7	·10	26	·95	20
14	Fr	26	8	·09	27	·99	21
15	Sa	27	9	·12	...	...	22
16	Su	28	10	·14	1	·05	23
17	Mo	29	11	·20	2	·13	24
18	Tu	30	12	·27	3	·22	25

Naksh :—1. Asvn. 2. Bhar. 3. Krit. 4. Rohi. 5. Mrig. 6. Ardh. 7. Punar. 8. Push. 9. Aslesh. 10. Magh. 11. P. Phal. 12. U. Phal. 13. Hasta. 14. Chit.

A. D. 1818.
A.—Amavasya.
P.—Paurnami.

Kollam 994, Commences { **N. Malabar—Sept.** / **S. Malabar—Aug.**

Hijra 1234, Commences, **Oct. 31.**

Vikrama 1875.
Bengal San 1224.
(N. Cycle) Virodhin.

Columns: SOLAR reckoning — Cyclic Sidereal Year, Month and Day; Week-Day; English Month and Day. LUNAR reckoning — Tithi; Ending Moment; Nakshatra; Ending Moment; Muhammadan Year, Month and Day.

July

Solar month	Cyclic Sidereal Day	Week-Day	English Day	Lunar month	Tithi	Ending Moment	Nakshatra	Ending Moment	Muhammadan month	Muhammadan Day
Bahudhanya *Mithuna—Ani.*	19	We	1	*Bah.*	13	·35	4	·33	*Shaban*	26
	20	Th	2		14	·43	5	·44		27
	21	Fr	3		—A	·51	6	·54		28
	22	Sa	4	Ashadha *Sukla*	1	·59	7	·64		—29
	23	Su	5		2	·63	8	·72	H. 1233 *Ramzan.*	1
	24	Mo	6		3	·68	9	·78		2
	25	Tu	7		4	·69	10	·82		3
	26	We	8		5	·68	11	·84		4
	27	Th	9		6	·65	12	·84		5
	28	Fr	10		7	·61	13	·82		6
	29	Sa	11		8	·54	14	·79		7
	30	Su	12		9	·46	15	·75		8
	—31	Mo	13		10	·38	16	·69		9
Bahudhanya *Karkata—Adi.*	1	Tu	14		11	·28	17	·62		10
	2	We	15		12	·18	18	·55		11
	3	Th	16		13 14	·07 ·97	19	·48		12
	4	Fr	17		P	·87	20	·42		13
	5	Sa	18	*Bahula*	1	·78	21	·36		14
	6	Su	19		2	·71	22	·31		15
	7	Mo	20		3	·65	23	·27		16
	8	Tu	21		4	·60	24	·24		17
	9	We	22		5	·58	25	·25		18
	10	Th	23		6	·57	26	·26		19
	11	Fr	24		7	·59	27	·30		20
	12	Sa	25		8	·62	1	·35		21
	13	Su	26		9	·68	2	·43		22
	14	Mo	27		10	·74	3	·51		23
	15	Tu	28		11	·83	4	·63		24
	16	We	29		12	·91	5	·74		25
	17	Th	30		13	·99	6	·84		26
	18	Fr	31		...	...	7	·94		27

Aug.

Solar month	Cyclic Sidereal Day	Week-Day	English Day	Lunar month	Tithi	Ending Moment	Nakshatra	Ending Moment	Muhammadan month	Muhammadan Day
	19	Sa	1		14	·06	...	...		28
	20	Su	2		—A	·10	8	·03		29
	21	Mo	3	Sravana *Sukla*	1	·16	9	·10		—30
	22	Tu	4		2	·17	10	·14	H. 1233 *Shawwal.*	1
	23	We	5		3	·17	11	·16		2
	24	Th	6		4	·13	12	·17		3
	25	Fr	7		5	·10	13	·16		4
	26	Sa	8		6 7	·04 ·96	14	·13		5
	27	Su	9		8	·87	15	·08		6
	28	Mo	10		9	·77	16 17	·02 ·96		7
	29	Tu	11		10	·68	18	·89		8
	30	We	12		11	·57	19	·83		9
	31	Th	13		12	·48	20	·76		10
	—32	Fr	14		13	·37	21	·69		11
Bahudhanya *Simha—Avani.*	1	Sa	15		14	·29	22	·64		12
	2	Su	16		P	·21	23	·60		13
	3	Mo	17	*Bahula*	1	·14	24	·58		14
	4	Tu	18		2	·10	25	·57		15
	5	We	19		3	·07	26	·58		16
	6	Th	20		4	·07	27	·61		17
	7	Fr	21		5	·08	1	·66		18
	8	Sa	22		6	·12	2	·74		19
	9	Su	23		7	·18	3	·83		20
	10	Mo	24		8	·24	4	·93		21
	11	Tu	25		9	·32	...	...		22
	12	We	26		10	·40	5	·04		23
	13	Th	27		11	·49	6	·14		24
	14	Fr	28		12	·56	7	·25		25
	15	Sa	29		13	·62	8	·34		26
	16	Su	30		14	·65	9	·40		27
	17	Mo	31		—A	·67	10	·45		28

Sep.

Solar month	Cyclic Sidereal Day	Week-Day	English Day	Lunar month	Tithi	Ending Moment	Nakshatra	Ending Moment	Muhammadan month	Muhammadan Day
Bahudhanya *Simha—Avani.*	18	Tu	1	Bhadrapada *Sukla*	1	·67	11	·48		—29
	19	We	2		2	·64	12	·49	H. 1233 *Zi-l-ka'da.*	1
	20	Th	3		3	·61	13	·49		2
	21	Fr	4		4	·55	14	·46		3
	22	Sa	5		5	·48	15	·41		4
	23	Su	6		6	·39	16	·36		5
	24	Mo	7		7	·29	17	·29		6
	25	Tu	8		8	·19	18	·23		7
	26	We	9		9 10	·08 ·99	19	·16		8
	27	Th	10		11	·89	20	·09		9
	28	Fr	11		12	·81	21 22	·03 ·97		10
	29	Sa	12		13	·73	23	·94		11
	30	Su	13		14	·68	24	·91		12
	—31	Mo	14		P	·62	25	·89		13
Bahudhanya *Kanya—Purattasi.*	1	Tu	15	*Bahula*	1	·60	26	·90		14
	2	We	16		2	·60	27	·92		15
	3	Th	17		3	·61	1	·98		16
	4	Fr	18		4	·64	...	...		17
	5	Sa	19		5	·69	2	·05		18
	6	Su	20		6	·77	3	·13		19
	7	Mo	21		7	·85	4	·23		20
	8	Tu	22		8	·93	5	·33		21
	9	We	23		...	...	6	·45		22
	10	Th	24		9	·01	7	·55		23
	11	Fr	25		10	·08	8	·64		24
	12	Sa	26		11	·16	9	·71		25
	13	Su	27		12	·19	10	·77		26
	14	Mo	28		13	·21	11	·80		27
	15	Tu	29		14	·21	12	·82		28
	16	We	30		—A	·19	13	·81		29

Oct.

Solar month	Cyclic Sidereal Day	Week-Day	English Day	Lunar month	Tithi	Ending Moment	Nakshatra	Ending Moment	Muhammadan month	Muhammadan Day
	17	Th	1	Asvina *Sukla*	1	·15	14	·79		—30
	18	Fr	2		2	·09	15	·75	H. 1233 *Zi-l-hijja.*	1
	19	Sa	3		3 4	·02 ·93	16	·69		2
	20	Su	4		5	·84	17	·64		3
	21	Mo	5		6	·75	18	·57		4
	22	Tu	6		7	·65	19	·50		5
	23	We	7		8	·54	20	·43		6
	24	Th	8		9	·44	21	·37		7
	25	Fr	9		10	·36	22	·32		8
	26	Sa	10		11	·29	23	·27		9
	27	Su	11		12	·24	24	·24		10
	28	Mo	12		13	·18	25	·22		11
	29	Tu	13		14	·17	26	·22		12
	—30	We ○	14		P	·16	27	·25		13
Bahudhanya *Tula—Aippasi.*	1	Th	15	*Bahula*	1	·17	1	·29		14
	2	Fr	16		2	·21	2	·35		15
	3	Sa	17		3	·27	3	·43		16
	4	Su	18		4	·34	4	·53		17
	5	Mo	19		5	·42	5	·63		18
	6	Tu	20		6	·51	6	·75		19
	7	We	21		7	·59	7	·85		20
	8	Th	22		8	·68	8	·94		21
	9	Fr	23		9	·74	...	...		22
	10	Sa	24		10	·77	9	·02		23
	11	Su	25		11	·80	10	·08		24
	12	Mo	26		12	·79	11	·13		25
	13	Tu	27		13	·77	12	·14		26
	14	We	28		14	·73	13	·14		27
	15	Th	29		—A	·68	14	·12		28
	16	Fr	30	*Suk.*	1	·61	15	·08		—29
	17	Sa	31		2	·52	16 17	·04 ·98		1

Nov.

Solar month	Cyclic Sidereal Day	Week-Day	English Day	Lunar month	Tithi	Ending Moment	Nakshatra	Ending Moment	Muhammadan month	Muhammadan Day
Bahudhanya *Tula—Aippasi.*	18	Su	1	Kartika *Sukla*	3	·43	18	·91	H. 1234 *Muharram.*	2
	19	Mo	2		4	·33	19	·84		3
	20	Tu	3		5	·23	20	·77		4
	21	We	4		6	·13	21	·71		5
	22	Th	5		7 8	·05 ·96	22	·65		6
	23	Fr	6		9	·89	23	·60		7
	24	Sa	7		10	·83	24	·56		8
	25	Su	8		11	·77	25	·54		9
	26	Mo	9		12	·77	26	·54		10
	27	Tu	10		13	·76	27	·56		11
	28	We	11		14	·78	1	·60		12
	29	Th	12		P	·81	2	·66		13
	—30	Fr	13	*Bahula*	1	·88	3	·73		14
Bahudhanya *Vrischika—Karttigai.*	1	Sa	14		2	·96	4	·83		15
	2	Su	15		...	...	5	·94		16
	3	Mo	16		3	·04	...	...		17
	4	Tu	17		4	·13	6	·04		18
	5	We	18		5	·21	7	·15		19
	6	Th	19		6	·29	8	·25		20
	7	Fr	20		7	·35	9	·33		21
	8	Sa	21		8	·40	10	·40		22
	9	Su	22		9	·41	11	·44		23
	10	Mo	23		10	·41	12	·46		24
	11	Tu	24		11	·39	13	·46		25
	12	We	25		12	·35	14	·45		26
	13	Th	26		13	·30	15	·42		27
	14	Fr	27		14	·23	16	·37		28
	15	Sa	28		—A	·15	17	·32		29
	16	Su	29	Margasira *Sukla*	1 2	·05 ·96	18	·25		—30
	17	Mo	30		3	·85	19	·18		1

Dec.

Solar month	Cyclic Sidereal Day	Week-Day	English Day	Lunar month	Tithi	Ending Moment	Nakshatra	Ending Moment	Muhammadan month	Muhammadan Day
	18	Tu	1		4	·76	20	·12	H. 1234 *Safar.*	2
	19	We	2		5	·67	21 22	·05 ·99		3
	20	Th	3		6	·58	23	·93		4
	21	Fr	4		7	·50	24	·89		5
	22	Sa	5		8	·45	25	·87		6
	23	Su	6		9	·41	26	·87		7
	24	Mo	7		10	·39	27	·88		8
	25	Tu	8		11	·39	1	·91		9
	26	We	9		12	·42	2	·97		10
	27	Th	10		13	·45	...	...		11
	28	Fr	11		14	·52	3	·04		12
	29	Sa	12		P	·60	4	·14		13
	—30	Su	13	*Bahula*	1	·69	5	·24		14
Bahudhanya *Dhanus—Margali.*	1	Mo	14		2	·77	6	·34		15
	2	Tu	15		3	·86	7	·45		16
	3	We	16		4	·93	8	·55		17
	4	Th	17		5	·99	9	·64		18
	5	Fr	18		...	...	10	·71		19
	6	Sa	19		6	·04	11	·76		20
	7	Su	20		7	·05	12	·78		21
	8	Mo	21		8	·05	13	·79		22
	9	Tu	22		9	·02	14	·78		23
	10	We	23		10 11	·00 ·93	15	·75		24
	11	Th	24		12	·85	16	·71		25
	12	Fr	25		13	·78	17	·65		23
	13	Sa	26		14	·68	18	·59		27
	14	Su	27		—A	·60	19	·52		28
	15	Mo	28	*P. Suk.*	1	·49	20	·46		—29
	16	Tu	29		2	·40	21	·39		1
	17	We	30		3	·30	22	·32		2
	18	Th	31		4	·22	23	·27		3

15. Svati. 16. Visak. 17. Anur. 18. Jyesh. 19. Mula. 20. P. Ash. 21. U. Ash. 22. Sravn. 23. Dani. 24. Satab. 25. P. Bhad. 26. U. Bhad. 27. Rev.

A. D. 1819. **Mesha Sankranti** (Commencement of Indian Sidereal Year).

Solar Eclipse. ● **(Surya Sid.) April 11·66.** **Saka 1741.** **Kaliyuga 4920.**

Lunar Eclipse. ○ **(Arya Sid.) April 11·56.** **(S. Cycle) Pramathi.**

SOLAR reckoning: Cyclic Sidereal Year, Month and Day.	Week-Day	English Month and Day.	LUNAR reckoning: Tithi	Ending Moment.	Nakshatra	Ending Moment.	Muhammadan Year, Month and Day.
	Jan.						
Bahudhanya *Dhanus—Margali.* 19	Fr	1	*Sukla* 5	·15	24	·22	H. 1234 *Rabi-ul-awwal.* 4
20	Sa	2	6	·09	25	·20	5
21	Su	3	7	·05	26	·19	6
22	Mo	4	8	·04	27	·20	7
23	Tu	5	9	·04	1	·23	8
24	We	6	10	·06	2	·27	9
25	Th	7	11	·13	3	·35	10
26	Fr	8	12	·19	4	·44	11
27	Sa	9	13	·26	5	·54	12
28	Su	10	14	·34	6	·64	13
—29	Mo	11	**Pausha** P	·42	7	·75	14
Bahudhanya *Makara—Tai.* 1	Tu	12	1	·51	8	·86	15
2	We	13	2	·59	9	·95	16
3	Th	14	3	·65	...	...	17
4	Fr	15	4	·68	10	·02	18
5	Sa	16	5	·69	11	·07	19
6	Su	17	*Bahula* 6	·70	12	·10	20
7	Mo	18	7	·67	13	·12	21
8	Tu	19	8	·63	14	·11	22
9	We	20	9	·58	15	·08	23
10	Th	21	10	·51	16 17	·04 ·99	24
11	Fr	22	11	·41	18	·93	25
12	Sa	23	12	·31	19	·87	26
13	Su	24	13	·22	20	·80	27
14	Mo	25	14	·12	21	·73	28
15	Tu	26	A 1	·03 ·93	22	·66	29
16	We	27	2	·86	23	·60	—30
17	Th	28	3	·79	24	·57	1
18	Fr	29	*Sukla* 4	·74	25	·53	2
19	Sa	30	5	·70	26	·52	3
20	Su	31	6	·68	27	·52	4
	Feb.						
21	Mo	1	7	·68	1	·54	H. 1234 *Rabi-ul-akhir.* 5
22	Tu	2	8	·70	2	·59	6
23	We	3	9	·75	3	·66	7
24	Th	4	10	·82	4	·74	8
25	Fr	5	11	·90	5	·83	9
26	Sa	6	12	·98	6	·94	10
27	Su	7	...	...	...	...	11
28	Mo	8	13	·06	7	·06	12
—29	Tu	9	14	·16	8	·16	13
Bahudhanya *Kumbha—Masi.* 1	We	10	**Magha** P	·23	9	·25	14
2	Th	11	1	·29	10	·32	15
3	Fr	12	2	·31	11	·38	16
4	Sa	13	3	·33	12	·42	17
5	Su	14	4	·33	13	·44	18
6	Mo	15	5	·30	14	·45	19
7	Tu	16	6	·25	15	·41	20
8	We	17	7	·19	16	·38	21
9	Th	18	8	·13	17	·32	22
10	Fr	19	*Bahula* 9 10	·04 ·95	18	·27	23
11	Sa	20	11	·84	19	·21	24
12	Su	21	12	·75	20	·14	25
13	Mo	22	13	·65	21	·06	26
14	Tu	23	14	·56	22 23	·00 ·95	27
15	We	24	—A	·48	24	·90	28
16	Th	25	*P. Suk.* 1	·40	25	·86	—29
17	Fr	26	2	·36	26	·84	1
18	Sa	27	3	·31	27	·84	2
19	Su	28	4	·30	1	·87	3

SOLAR reckoning: Cyclic Sidereal Year, Month and Day.	Week-Day	English Month and Day.	LUNAR reckoning: Tithi	Ending Moment.	Nakshatra	Ending Moment.	Muhammadan Year, Month and Day.
	March						
Bahudhanya *Kumbha—Masi.* 20	Mo	1	*Sukla* 5	·30	2	·90	H. 1234 *Jumadal-awwal.* 4
21	Tu	2	6	·33	3	·96	5
22	We	3	7	·58	...	...	6
23	Th	4	8	·43	4	·04	7
24	Fr	5	9	·52	5	·13	8
25	Sa	6	10	·60	6	·25	9
26	Su	7	11	·69	7	·35	10
27	Mo	8	12	·78	8	·46	11
28	Tu	9	13	·84	9	·55	12
29	We	10	14	·90	10	·63	13
—30	Th	11	**Phalguna** P	·93	11	·69	14
Bahudhanya *Mina—Panguni.* 1	Fr	12	1	·94	12	·74	15
2	Sa	13	2	·93	13	·76	16
3	Su	14	3	·90	14	·76	17
4	Mo	15	4	·85	15	·74	18
5	Tu	16	5	·80	16	·71	19
6	We	17	*Bahula* 6	·72	17	·67	20
7	Th	18	7	·63	18	·61	21
8	Fr	19	8	·54	19	·54	22
9	Sa	20	9	·43	20	·47	23
10	Su	21	10	·34	21	·40	24
11	Mo	22	11	·24	22	·34	25
12	Tu	23	12	·16	23	·28	26
13	We	24	13 14	·07 ·99	24	·23	27
14	Th	25	—A	·94	25	·19	28
15	Fr	26	1	·90	26	·17	29
16	Sa	27	2	·89	27	·17	—30
17	Su	28	3	·88	1	·18	1
18	Mo	29	*Sukla* 4	·92	2	·22	2
19	Tu	30	5	·96	3	·27	3
20	We	31	...	...	4	·34	4
	April						
21	Th	1	6	·01	5	·43	H. 1234 *Jumadal-akhir.* 5
22	Fr	2	7	·10	6	·54	6
23	Sa	3	8	·18	7	·65	7
24	Su	4	9	·27	8	·76	8
25	Mo	5	10	·35	9	·85	9
26	Tu	6	11	·42	10	·94	10
27	We	7	12	·47	...	...	11
28	Th	8	13	·51	11	·01	12
29	Fr	9	14	·51	12	·06	13
30	Sa ○	10	**Chaitra** P	·50	13	·08	14
—31	Su	11	1	·47	14	·09	15
Pramathi *Mesha—Chittirai.* 1	Mo	12	2	·41	15	·07	16
2	Tu	13	3	·36	16	·05	17
3	We	14	4	·28	17 18	·00 ·95	18
4	Th	15	5	·20	19	·88	19
5	Fr	16	*Bahula* 6 7	·10 ·99	20	·81	20
6	Sa	17	8	·90	21	·75	21
7	Su	18	9	·79	22	·68	22
8	Mo	19	10	·71	23	·62	23
9	Tu	20	11	·62	24	·56	24
10	We	21	12	·55	25	·52	25
11	Th	22	13	·48	26	·50	26
12	Fr	23	14	·45	27	·49	27
13	Sa	24	—A	·43	1	·50	28
14	Su	25	**Vaisk.** *Suk.* 1	·42	2	·53	—29
15	Mo	26	2	·46	3	·58	*Rajab.* 1
16	Tu	27	3	·50	4	·65	2
17	We	28	4	·56	5	·73	3
18	Th	29	5	·64	6	·84	4
19	Fr	30	6	·72	7	·95	5

SOLAR reckoning: Cyclic Sidereal Year, Month and Day.	Week-Day	English Month and Day.	LUNAR reckoning: Tithi	Ending Moment.	Nakshatra	Ending Moment.	Muhammadan Year, Month and Day.
	May						
Pramathi *Mesha—Chittirai.* 20	Sa	1	*Sukla* 7	·80	...	...	H. 1234 *Rajab.* 6
21	Su	2	8	·87	8	·05	7
22	Mo	3	9	·95	9	·15	8
23	Tu	4	...	...	10	·25	9
24	We	5	10	·00	11	·32	10
25	Th	6	11	·04	12	·37	11
26	Fr	7	12	·03	13	·40	12
27	Sa	8	13	·03	14	·41	13
28	Su	9	14 **Vaisakha** P	·00 ·94	15	·41	14
29	Mo	10	1	·88	16	·38	15
—30	Tu	11	2	·80	17	·34	16
Pramathi *Vrishabha—Vaikasi.* 1	We	12	3	·72	18	·28	17
2	Th	13	4	·62	19	·22	18
3	Fr	14	5	·52	20	·16	19
4	Sa	15	6	·42	21	·09	20
5	Su	16	7	·31	22 23	·02 ·95	21
6	Mo	17	*Bahula* 8	·22	24	·90	22
7	Tu	18	9	·13	25	·85	23
8	We	19	10	·06	26	·83	24
9	Th	20	11 12	·01 ·96	27	·81	25
10	Fr	21	13	·94	1	·82	26
11	Sa	22	14	·94	2	·84	27
12	Su	23	—A	·97	3	·89	28
13	Mo	24	...	...	4	·96	29
14	Tu	25	1	·00	...	...	—30
15	We	26	2	·06	5	·04	1
16	Th	27	3	·13	6	·14	2
17	Fr	28	4	·22	7	·25	3
18	Sa	29	*Sukla* 5	·29	8	·35	4
19	Su	30	6	·38	9	·46	5
20	Mo	31	7	·45	10	·55	6
	June						
21	Tu	1	8	·48	11	·63	H. 1234 *Shaban.* 7
22	We	2	9	·52	12	·68	8
23	Th	3	10	·53	13	·72	9
24	Fr	4	11	·53	14	·74	10
25	Sa	5	12	·49	15	·74	11
26	Su	6	13	·45	16	·71	12
27	Mo	7	14	·39	17	·67	13
28	Tu	8	**Jyeshtha** P	·32	18	·62	14
29	We	9	1	·22	19	·56	15
30	Th	10	2	·12	20	·50	16
31	Fr	11	3 4	·01 ·91	21	·43	17
—32	Sa	12	5	·81	22	·36	18
Pramathi *Mithuna—Ani.* 1	Su	13	6	·72	23	·29	19
2	Mo	14	*Bahula* 7	·64	24	·23	20
3	Tu	15	8	·55	25	·19	21
4	We	16	9	·49	26	·16	22
5	Th	17	10	·45	27	·14	23
6	Fr	18	11	·43	1	·14	24
7	Sa	19	12	·42	2	·16	25
8	Su	20	13	·44	3	·21	26
9	Mo	21	14	·49	4	·27	27
10	Tu	22	—A	·53	5	·35	28
11	We	23	**Ashadha** *Suk.* 1	·60	6	·44	—29
12	Th	24	2	·69	7	·54	1234 *Ramzan.* 1
13	Fr	25	3	·76	8	·66	2
14	Sa	26	4	·85	9	·76	3
15	Su	27	5	·92	10	·86	4
16	Mo	28	6	·97	11	·94	5
17	Tu	29	...	...	...	...	6
18	We	30	7	·00	12	·00	7

Naksh :—1. Asvn. 2. Bhar. 3. Krit. 4. Rohi. 5. Mrig. 6. Ardh. 7. Punar. 8. Push. 9. Aslesh. 10. Magh. 11. P. Phal. 12. U. Phal. 13. Hasta. 14. Chit.

A. D. 1819.
A.—Amavasya. **Kollam 995,** Commences { **N. Malabar—Sept.** / **S. Malabar—Aug.** } **Hijra 1235,** Commences, **Oct. 20.** **Vikrama 1876.**
P.—Paurnami. **Bengal San 1225.** **(N. Cycle) Vikrita.**

Columns: SOLAR reckoning — Cyclic Sidereal Year, Month and Day; Week-Day; English Month and Day. LUNAR reckoning — Tithi; Ending Moment; Nakshatra; Ending Moment; Muhammadan Year, Month and Day.

July

(Solar: Pramathi *Mithuna—Ani.*; Pramathi *Karkata—Adi.* — Lunar: *Suk.*, **Ashadha**, *Bahula*, *Sukla* — H. 1234 *Ramzan*)

Cyclic Sidereal Year, Month and Day	Week-Day	English Month and Day	Tithi	Ending Moment	Nakshatra	Ending Moment	Muhammadan Year, Month and Day
19	Th	1	8	·02	13	·04	8
20	Fr	2	9 / 10	·01 / ·97	14	·06	9
21	Sa	3	11	·93	15	·06	10
22	Su	4	12	·87	16	·04	11
23	Mo	5	13	·79	17 / 18	·00 / ·95	12
24	Tu	6	14	·69	19	·90	13
25	We	7	P	·60	20	·84	14
26	Th	8	1	·49	21	·77	15
27	Fr	9	2	·39	22	·70	16
28	Sa	10	3	·29	23	·63	17
29	Su	11	4	·18	24	·58	18
30	Mo	12	5	·11	25	·53	19
—31	Tu	13	6 / 7	·03 / ·97	26	·49	20
1	We	14	8	·92	27	·46	21
2	Th	15	9	·91	1	·46	22
3	Fr	16	10	·90	2	·48	23
4	Sa	17	11	·91	3	·52	24
5	Su	18	12	·96	4	·57	25
6	Mo	19	...	...	5	·65	26
7	Tu	20	13	·01	6	·74	27
8	We	21	14	·08	7	·85	28
9	Th	22	—A	·15	8	·96	29
10	Fr	23	1	·25	...	...	—30
11	Sa	24	2	·32	9	·06	1
12	Su	25	3	·38	10	·16	2
13	Mo	26	4	·45	11	·24	3
14	Tu	27	5	·48	12	·31	4
15	We	28	6	·50	13	.36	5
16	Th	29	7	·48	14	·38	6
17	Fr	30	8	·46	15	·38	7
18	Sa	31	9	·41	16	·37	8

Aug.

(Solar: Pramathi *Simha—Avani.* — Lunar: **Sravana**, *Bahula*, **Bhadrapada** *Sukla* — H. 1234 *Shawwal.*; H. 1234 *Zi-l-ka'da.*)

Cyclic Sidereal Year, Month and Day	Week-Day	English Month and Day	Tithi	Ending Moment	Nakshatra	Ending Moment	Muhammadan Year, Month and Day
19	Su	1	10	·35	17	·35	9
20	Mo	2	11	·28	18	·30	10
21	Tu	3	12	·18	19	·24	11
22	We	4	13 / 14	·09 / ·98	20	·18	12
23	Th	5	P	·89	21	·11	13
24	Fr	6	1	·78	22 / 23	·04 / ·98	14
25	Sa	7	2	·69	24	·91	15
26	Su	8	3	·61	25	·86	16
27	Mo	9	4	·52	26	·82	17
28	Tu	10	5	·46	27	·79	18
29	We	11	6	·41	1	·79	19
30	Th	12	7	·40	2	·80	20
31	Fr	13	8	·39	3	·83	21
—32	Sa	14	9	·40	4	·88	22
1	Su	15	10	·44	5	·95	23
2	Mo	16	11	·49	...	...	24
3	Tu	17	12	·57	6	·05	25
4	We	18	13	·65	7	·15	26
5	Th	19	14	·74	8	·26	27
6	Fr	20	—A	·81	9	·36	28
7	Sa	21	1	·89	10	·46	—29
8	Su	22	2	·94	11	·56	1
9	Mo	23	3	·97	12	·62	2
10	Tu	24	4	·99	13	·67	3
11	We	25	5	·98	14	·70	4
12	Th	26	6	·96	15	·71	5
13	Fr	27	7	·92	16	·71	6
14	Sa	28	8	·87	17	·68	7
15	Su	29	9	·79	18	·63	8
16	Mo	30	10	·69	19	·58	9
17	Tu	31	11	·59	20	·51	10

Sep.

(Solar: Pramathi *Simha—Avani.*; Pramathi *Kanya—Purattasi.* — Lunar: *Suk.*, **Bhadra.**, *Bahula*, *Sukla* — H. 1234 *Zi-l-ka'da.*)

Cyclic Sidereal Year, Month and Day	Week-Day	English Month and Day	Tithi	Ending Moment	Nakshatra	Ending Moment	Muhammadan Year, Month and Day
18	We	1	12	·49	21	·44	11
19	Th	2	13	·40	22	·38	12
20	Fr	3	14	·29	23	·31	13
21	Sa	4	P	·20	24	·25	14
22	Su	5	1	·12	25	·19	15
23	Mo	6	2 / 3	·05 / ·98	26	·15	16
24	Tu	7	4	·92	27	·13	17
25	We	8	5	·91	1	·11	18
26	Th	9	6	·91	2	·12	19
27	Fr	10	7	·92	3	·14	20
28	Sa	11	8	·96	4	·19	21
29	Su	12	...	...	5	·27	22
30	Mo	13	9	·02	6	·35	23
—31	Tu	14	10	·09	7	·45	24
1	We	15	11	·17	8	·55	25
2	Th	16	12	·26	9	·66	26
3	Fr	17	13	·35	10	·77	27
4	Sa	18	14	·42	11	·86	28
5	Su ●	19	—A	·46	12	·93	29
6	Mo	20	1	·50	13	·99	—30
7	Tu	21	2	·51	...	...	1
8	We	22	3	·52	14	·02	2
9	Th	23	4	·49	15	·03	3
10	Fr	24	5	·46	16	·03	4
11	Sa	25	6	·40	17 / 18	·01 / ·97	5
12	Su	26	7	·31	19	·91	6
13	Mo	27	8	·23	20	·85	7
14	Tu	28	9	·13	21	·79	8
15	We	29	10 / 11	·04 / ·94	22	·72	9
16	Th	30	12	·83	23	·65	10

Oct.

(Solar: Pramathi *Tula—Aippasi.* — Lunar: **Asvina**, *Bahula*, *Sukla*, **Karttika** — H. 1234 *Zi-l-hijja.*; H. 1235 *Muharram.*)

Cyclic Sidereal Year, Month and Day	Week-Day	English Month and Day	Tithi	Ending Moment	Nakshatra	Ending Moment	Muhammadan Year, Month and Day
17	Fr	1	13	·74	24	·59	11
18	Sa	2	14	·66	25	·53	12
19	Su ○	3	P	·59	26	·49	13
20	Mo	4	1	·53	27	·45	14
21	Tu	5	2	·48	1	·44	15
22	We	6	3	·46	2	·44	16
23	Th	7	4	·46	3	·46	17
24	Fr	8	5	·47	4	·51	18
25	Sa	9	6	·52	5	·57	19
26	Su	10	7	·58	6	·65	20
27	Mo	11	8	·65	7	·75	21
28	Tu	12	9	·74	8	·85	22
29	We	13	10	·82	9	·96	23
—30	Th	14	11	·90	...	...	24
1	Fr	15	12	·98	10	·07	25
2	Sa	16	...	...	11	·16	26
3	Su	17	13	·03	12	·24	27
4	Mo	18	14	·07	13	·30	28
5	Tu	19	—A	·09	14	·34	—29
6	We	20	1	·09	15	·36	1
7	Th	21	2	·06	16	·36	2
8	Fr	22	3 / 4	·03 / ·98	17	·34	3
9	Sa	23	5	·89	18	·30	4
10	Su	24	6	·81	19	·25	5
11	Mo	25	7	·71	20	·19	6
12	Tu	26	8	·62	21	·13	7
13	We	27	9	·51	22 / 23	·06 / ·99	8
14	Th	28	10	·42	24	·92	9
15	Fr	29	11	·32	25	·87	10
16	Sa	30	12	·25	26	·82	11
17	Su	31	13	·18	27	·78	12

Nov.

(Solar: Pramathi *Tula—Aippasi.*; Pramathi *Vrischika—Kartigai.* — Lunar: **Karttika**, *Bahula*, *Sukla* — H. 1235 *Muharram.*)

Cyclic Sidereal Year, Month and Day	Week-Day	English Month and Day	Tithi	Ending Moment	Nakshatra	Ending Moment	Muhammadan Year, Month and Day
18	Mo	1	14	·12	1	·76	13
19	Tu	2	P	·07	2	·76	14
20	We	3	1	·05	3	·78	15
21	Th	4	2	·05	4	·82	16
22	Fr	5	3	·07	5	·88	17
23	Sa	6	4	·12	6	·95	18
24	Su	7	5	·18	...	...	19
25	Mo	8	6	·25	7	·05	20
26	Tu	9	7	·34	8	·15	21
27	We	10	8	·43	9	·27	22
28	Th	11	9	·52	10	·37	23
29	Fr	12	10	·58	11	·47	24
—30	Sa	13	11	·64	12	·55	25
1	Su	14	12	·67	13	·61	26
2	Mo	15	13	·70	14	·66	27
3	Tu	16	14	·70	15	·68	28
4	We	17	—A	·67	16	·68	29
5	[illegible]	18	1	·63	17	·67	—30
6	Fr	19	2	·58	18	·63	1
7	Sa	20	3	·51	19	·59	2
8	Su	21	4	·42	20	·54	3
9	Mo	22	5	·33	21	·47	4
10	Tu	23	6	·24	22	·40	5
11	We	24	7	·13	23	·33	6
12	Th	25	8 / 9	·04 / ·94	24	·27	7
13	Fr	26	10	·87	25	·21	8
14	Sa	27	11	·79	26	·15	9
15	Su	28	12	·74	27	·11	10
16	Mo	29	13	·69	1	·09	11
17	Tu	30	14	·68	2	·08	12

Dec.

(Solar: Pramathi *Dhanus—Margali.* — Lunar: **Margasira**, *Bahula*, *Sukla*, **Pausha** — H. 1235 *Safar.*; H. 1235 *Rabi-ul-awwal.*)

Cyclic Sidereal Year, Month and Day	Week-Day	English Month and Day	Tithi	Ending Moment	Nakshatra	Ending Moment	Muhammadan Year, Month and Day
18	We	1	P	·68	3	·10	13
19	Th	2	1	·70	4	·13	14
20	Fr	3	2	·74	5	·19	15
21	Sa	4	3	·81	6	·26	16
22	Su	5	4	·89	7	·35	17
23	Mo	6	5	·97	8	·46	18
24	Tu	7	...	...	9	·56	19
25	We	8	6	·06	10	·67	20
26	Th	9	7	·15	11	·77	21
27	Fr	10	8	·22	12	·85	22
28	Sa	11	9	·28	13	·93	23
29	Su	12	10	·32	14	·97	24
—30	Mo	13	11	·34	...	...	25
1	Tu	14	12	·33	15	·00	26
2	We	15	13	·31	16 / 17	·01 / ·99	27
3	Th	16	14	·27	18	·97	28
4	Fr	17	—A	·20	19	·93	—29
5	Sa	18	1	·13	20	·87	1
6	Su	19	2 / 3	·05 / ·96	21	·81	2
7	Mo	20	4	·86	22	·74	3
8	Tu	21	5	·76	23	·68	4
9	We	22	6	·67	24	·61	5
10	Th	23	7	·57	25	·54	6
11	Fr	24	8	·49	26	·49	7
12	Sa	25	9	·43	27	·44	8
13	Su	26	10	·38	1	·41	9
14	Mo	27	11	·33	2	·41	10
15	Tu	28	12	·33	3	·42	11
16	We	29	13	·32	4	·45	12
17	Th	30	14	·35	5	·49	13
18	Fr	31	P	·40	6	·56	14

15. Svati. 16. Visak. 17. Anur. 18. Jyesh. 19. Mula. 20. P. Ash. 21. U. Ash. 22. Sravn. 23. Dani. 24. Satab. 25. P. Bhad. 26. U. Bhad. 27. Rev.

A. D. 1820.
Solar Eclipse. ●
Lunar Eclipse. ○

Mesha Sankranti (Commencement of Indian Sidereal Year).
(Surya Sid.) April 10·92.
(Arya Sid.) April 10·82.

Saka 1742. **Kaliyuga 4921.**
(S. Cycle) Vikrama.

SOLAR reckoning: Cyclic Sidereal Year, Month and Day; Week-Day; English Month and Day. LUNAR reckoning: Tithi; Ending Moment; Nakshatra; Ending Moment; Muhammadan Year, Month and Day.

Jan.

Cyclic Sidereal Year, Month and Day	Week-Day	English Month and Day	Tithi	Ending Moment	Nakshatra	Ending Moment	Muhammadan Year, Month and Day
Pramathi Dhanus—Margali 19	Sa	1	Pausha Bahula 1	·46	7	·63	H. 1235 Rabi-ul-awwal 15
20	Su	2	2	·54	8	·76	16
21	Mo	3	3	·62	9	·86	17
22	Tu	4	4	·72	10	·97	18
23	We	5	5	·80	...	...	19
24	Th	6	6	·87	11	·07	20
25	Fr	7	7	·93	12	·17	21
26	Sa	8	8	·96	13	·24	22
27	Su	9	9	·98	14	·29	23
28	Mo	10	10	·98	15	·32	24
29	Tu	11	11	·96	16	·33	25
Pramathi Makara—Tai 1	We	12	12	·91	17	·33	26
2	Th	13	13	·86	18	·30	27
3	Fr	14	14	·78	19	·26	28
4	Sa	15	A	·69	20	·21	29
5	Su	16	Magha Sukla 1	·60	21	·15	30
6	Mo	17	2	·50	22	·08	Rabi-ul-akhir 1
7	Tu	18	3	·41	23 / 24	·02 / ·95	2
8	We	19	4	·31	25	·88	3
9	Th	20	5	·22	26	·82	4
10	Fr	21	6	·14	27	·77	5
11	Sa	22	7	·08	1	·75	6
12	Su	23	8 / 9	·02 / ·98	2	·74	7
13	Mo	24	10	·97	3	·74	8
14	Tu	25	11	·96	4	·76	9
15	We	26	...	...	5	·80	10
16	Th	27	12	·00	6	·88	11
17	Fr	28	13	·05	7	·96	12
18	Sa	29	14	·12	...	...	13
19	Su	30	P	·19	8	·05	14
20	Mo	31	1	·28	9	·16	15

Feb.

Cyclic Sidereal Year, Month and Day	Week-Day	English Month and Day	Tithi	Ending Moment	Nakshatra	Ending Moment	Muhammadan Year, Month and Day
21	Tu	1	Bahula 2	·37	10	·27	H. 1235 16
22	We	2	3	·45	11	·38	17
23	Th	3	4	·52	12	·47	18
24	Fr	4	5	·58	13	·54	19
25	Sa	5	6	·61	14	·60	20
26	Su	6	7	·62	15	·64	21
27	Mo	7	8	·61	16	·66	22
28	Tu	8	9	·60	17	·66	23
29	We	9	10	·55	18	·63	24
30	Th	10	11	·49	19	·60	25
Pramathi Kumbha—Masi 1	Fr	11	12	·40	20	·54	26
2	Sa	12	13	·32	21	·48	27
3	Su	13	14	·23	22	·43	28
4	Mo	14	A	·14	23	·35	29
5	Tu	15	Phalguna Sukla 1 / 2	·03 / ·93	24	·28	H. 1235 Jumadal-awwal 1
6	We	16	3	·84	25	·22	2
7	Th	17	4	·76	26	·16	3
8	Fr	18	5	·70	27	·12	4
9	Sa	19	6	·65	1	·08	5
10	Su	20	7	·61	2	·06	6
11	Mo	21	8	·59	3	·06	7
12	Tu	22	9	·58	4	·08	8
13	We	23	10	·63	5	·12	9
14	Th	24	11	·67	6	·18	10
15	Fr	25	12	·74	7	·26	11
16	Sa	26	13	·81	8	·35	12
17	Su	27	14	·91	9	·46	13
18	Mo	28	P	·99	10	·57	14
19	Tu	29	...	...	11	·68	15

March

Cyclic Sidereal Year, Month and Day	Week-Day	English Month and Day	Tithi	Ending Moment	Nakshatra	Ending Moment	Muhammadan Year, Month and Day
Pramathi Kumbha—Masi 20	We	1	Phalg. Bahula 1	·07	12	·77	H. 1235 Jumadal-awwal 16
21	Th	2	2	·14	13	·85	17
22	Fr	3	3	·19	14	·91	18
23	Sa	4	4	·23	15	·95	19
24	Su	5	5	·23	16	·98	20
25	Mo	6	6	·23	17	·98	21
26	Tu	7	7	·20	18	·96	22
27	We	8	8	·16	19	·93	23
28	Th	9	9	·09	20	·88	24
29	Fr	10	10 / 11	·01 / ·93	21	·83	25
30	Sa	11	12	·83	22	·76	26
Pramathi Mina—Panguni 1	Su	12	13	·73	23	·69	27
2	Mo	13	14	·63	24	·62	28
3	Tu	14	A	·54	25	·55	29
4	We	15	Chaitra Sukla 1	·44	26	·50	30
5	Th	16	2	·35	27	·45	Jumadal-akhir 1
6	Fr	17	3	·29	1	·41	2
7	Sa	18	4	·23	2	·39	3
8	Su	19	5	·21	3	·38	4
9	Mo	20	6	·19	4	·40	5
10	Tu	21	7	·19	5	·44	6
11	We	22	8	·22	6	·49	7
12	Th	23	9	·27	7	·56	8
13	Fr	24	10	·33	8	·65	9
14	Sa	25	11	·41	9	·77	10
15	Su	26	12	·50	10	·87	11
16	Mo	27	13	·58	11	·98	12
17	Tu	28	14	·67	...	...	13
18	We ○	29	P	·72	12	·07	14
19	Th	30	1	·78	13	·16	15
20	Fr	31	2	·82	14	·22	16

April

Cyclic Sidereal Year, Month and Day	Week-Day	English Month and Day	Tithi	Ending Moment	Nakshatra	Ending Moment	Muhammadan Year, Month and Day
21	Sa	1	Bahula 3	·81	15	·28	H. 1235 17
22	Su	2	4	·81	16	·30	18
23	Mo	3	5	·77	17	·31	19
24	Tu	4	6	·73	18	·29	20
25	We	5	7	·66	19	·26	21
26	Th	6	8	·59	20	·22	22
27	Fr	7	9	·50	21	·17	23
28	Sa	8	10	·40	22	·10	24
29	Su	9	11	·29	23 / 24	·03 / ·96	25
30	Mo	10	12	·19	25	·90	26
Vikrama Mesha—Chittirai 1	Tu	11	13	·10	26	·84	27
2	We	12	14 / A	·00 / ·91	27	·78	28
3	Th	13	Vaisakha Sukla 1	85	1	·74	29
4	Fr	14	2	·80	2	·71	H. 1235 Rajab 1
5	Sa	15	3	·76	3	·71	2
6	Su	16	4	·74	4	·72	3
7	Mo	17	5	·75	5	·75	4
8	Tu	18	6	·77	6	·80	5
9	We	19	7	·82	7	·87	6
10	Th	20	8	·88	8	·95	7
11	Fr	21	9	·97	...	...	8
12	Sa	22	...	...	9	·06	9
13	Su	23	10	·04	10	·17	10
14	Mo	24	11	·12	11	·28	11
15	Tu	25	12	·20	12	·37	12
16	We	26	13	·27	13	·46	13
17	Th	27	14	·32	14	·54	14
18	Fr	28	P	·36	15	·59	15
19	Sa	29	Bah. 1	·37	16	·62	16
20	Su	30	2	·35	17	·63	17

May

Cyclic Sidereal Year, Month and Day	Week-Day	English Month and Day	Tithi	Ending Moment	Nakshatra	Ending Moment	Muhammadan Year, Month and Day
Vikrama Mesha—Chittirai 21	Mo	1	Vaisk. Bahula 3	·31	18	·62	H. 1235 Rajab 18
22	Tu	2	4	·26	19	·60	19
23	We	3	5	·19	20	·56	20
24	Th	4	6	·12	21	·50	21
25	Fr	5	7 / 8	·03 / ·93	22	·44	22
26	Sa	6	9	·82	23	·37	23
27	Su	7	10	·73	24	·31	24
28	Mo	8	11	·63	25	·24	25
29	Tu	9	12	·53	26	·17	26
30	We	10	13	·45	27	·12	27
31	Th	11	14	·37	1	·07	28
Vikrama Vrishabha—Vaikasi 1	Fr	12	A	·32	2	·04	29
2	Sa	13	Adhika Jyeshtha Sukla 1	·28	3	·02	30
3	Su	14	2	·27	4	·04	H. 1235 Shaban 1
4	Mo	15	3	·27	5	·06	2
5	Tu	16	4	·28	6	·11	3
6	We	17	5	·33	7	·17	4
7	Th	18	6	·39	8	·27	5
8	Fr	19	7	·47	9	·36	6
9	Sa	20	8	·55	10	·47	7
10	Su	21	9	·63	11	·57	8
11	Mo	22	10	·71	12	·68	9
12	Tu	23	11	·78	13	·78	10
13	We	24	12	·84	14	·85	11
14	Th	25	13	·85	15	·90	12
15	Fr	26	14	·87	16	·94	13
16	Sa	27	P	·85	17	·95	14
17	Su	28	1	·83	18	·95	15
18	Mo	29	2	·77	19	·93	16
19	Tu	30	3	·71	20	·89	17
20	We	31	4	·62	21	·84	18

June

Cyclic Sidereal Year, Month and Day	Week-Day	English Month and Day	Tithi	Ending Moment	Nakshatra	Ending Moment	Muhammadan Year, Month and Day
21	Th	1	Bahula 5	·52	22	·78	19
22	Fr	2	6	·43	23	·72	20
23	Sa	3	7	·32	24	·65	21
24	Su	4	8	·23	25	·58	22
25	Mo	5	9	·12	26	·51	23
26	Tu	6	10 / 11	·03 / ·95	27	·45	24
27	We	7	12	·87	1	·40	25
28	Th	8	13	·81	2	·38	26
29	Fr	9	14	·77	3	·36	27
30	Sa	10	A	·76	4	·36	28
31	Su	11	Nija Jyeshtha Sukla 1	·75	5	·38	29
Vikrama Mithuna—Ani 1	Mo	12	2	·77	6	·42	H. 1235 Ramzan 1
2	Tu	13	3	·81	7	·49	2
3	We	14	4	·86	8	·57	3
4	Th	15	5	·94	9	·66	4
5	Fr	16	...	...	10	·76	5
6	Sa	17	6	·02	11	·87	6
7	Su	18	7	·10	12	·98	7
8	Mo	19	8	·19	...	...	8
9	Tu	20	9	·26	13	·08	9
10	We	21	10	·31	14	·16	10
11	Th	22	11	·35	15	·22	11
12	Fr	23	12	·35	16	·25	12
13	Sa	24	13	·33	17	·28	13
14	Su	25	14	·31	18	·28	14
15	Mo	26	P	·25	19	·26	15
16	Tu	27	1	·19	20	·22	16
17	We	28	2	·11	21	·17	17
18	Th	29	Bah. 3 / 4	·02 / ·92	22	·11	18
19	Fr	30	5	·81	23 / 24	·06 / ·99	19

Naksh:—1. Asvn. 2. Bhar. 3. Krit. 4. Rohi. 5. Mrig. 6. Ardh. 7. Punar. 8. Push. 9. Aslesh. 10. Magh. 11. P. Phal. 12. U. Phal. 13. Hasta. 14. Chit.

A. D. 1820.
A.—Amavasya.
P.—Paurnami.

Kollam 996, Commences { **N. Malabar—Sept.** / **S. Malabar—Aug.**

Hijra 1236, Commences, Oct. 9.

Vikrama 1877.
Bengal San 1226.
(N. Cycle) Khara.

Columns: SOLAR reckoning (Cyclic Sidereal Year, Month and Day; Week-Day; English Month and Day) — LUNAR reckoning (Tithi; Ending Moment; Nakshatra; Ending Moment; Muhammadan Year, Month and Day).

July

Solar: Vikrama *Mithuna—Ani* (to 32), then Vikrama *Karkata—Adi*. Lunar: Ni. Jy. *Bahula*, then Ashadha *Sukla* / *Bahula*. Muhammadan: H. 1235 *Ramzan*, then H. 1235 *Shawwal*.

Cyclic Sidereal Year, Month and Day	Week-Day	English Month and Day	Tithi	Ending Moment	Nakshatra	Ending Moment	Muhammadan Year, Month and Day
20	Sa	1	6	·72	25	·92	20
21	Su	2	7	·61	26	·85	21
22	Mo	3	8	·52	27	·79	22
23	Tu	4	9	·43	1	·75	23
24	We	5	10	·35	2	·71	24
25	Th	6	11	·29	3	·68	25
26	Fr	7	12	·26	4	·68	26
27	Sa	8	13	·23	5	·69	27
28	Su	9	14	·23	6	·74	28
29	Mo	10	—A	·25	7	·79	29
30	Tu	11	1	·28	8	·87	—30
31	We	12	2	·35	9	·96	1
—32	Th	13	3	·42	...	...	2
1	Fr	14	4	·51	10	·06	3
2	Sa	15	5	·58	11	·18	4
3	Su	16	6	·66	12	·28	5
4	Mo	17	7	·74	13	·38	6
5	Tu	18	8	·78	14	·46	7
6	We	19	9	·82	15	·53	8
7	Th	20	10	·83	16	·58	9
8	Fr	21	11	·82	17	·60	10
9	Sa	22	12	·78	18	·61	11
10	Su	23	13	·73	19	·59	12
11	Mo	24	14	·67	20	·56	13
12	Tu	25	P	·59	21	·51	14
13	We	26	1	·51	22	·46	15
14	Th	27	2	·41	23	·40	16
15	Fr	28	3	·31	24	·33	17
16	Sa	29	4	·20	25	·25	18
17	Su	30	5	·10	26	·19	19
18	Mo	31	{ 6 7	·01 ·91	27	·13	20

Aug.

Solar: Vikrama *Simha—Avani*. Lunar: *Bahula*, then Sravana *Sukla* / *Bahula*. Muhammadan: H. 1235 *Zi-l-ka'da*.

Cyclic Sidereal Year, Month and Day	Week-Day	English Month and Day	Tithi	Ending Moment	Nakshatra	Ending Moment	Muhammadan Year, Month and Day
19	Tu	1	8	·83	1	·08	21
20	We	2	9	·77	2	·04	22
21	Th	3	10	·74	3	·01	23
22	Fr	4	11	·71	4	·00	24
23	Sa	5	12	·72	5	·01	25
24	Su	6	13	·73	6	·05	26
25	Mo	7	14	·76	7	·10	27
26	Tu	8	—A	·82	8	·17	28
27	We	9	1	·89	9	·26	—29
28	Th	10	2	·98	10	·37	1
29	Fr	11	...	...	11	·48	2
30	Sa	12	3	·07	12	·58	3
—31	Su	13	4	·15	13	·68	4
1	Mo	14	5	·21	14	·77	5
2	Tu	15	6	·26	15	·83	6
3	We	16	7	·30	16	·89	7
4	Th	17	8	·32	17	·92	8
5	Fr	18	9	·31	18	·93	9
6	Sa	19	10	·27	19	·92	10
7	Su	20	11	·24	20	·89	11
8	Mo	21	12	·17	21	·85	12
9	Tu	22	13	·10	22	·80	13
10	We	23	{ 14 P	·01 ·91	23	·73	14
11	Th	24	1	·80	24	·66	15
12	Fr	25	2	·70	25	·59	16
13	Sa	26	3	·60	26	·53	17
14	Su	27	4	·51	27	·47	18
15	Mo	28	5	·43	1	·41	19
16	Tu	29	6	·35	2	·37	20
17	We	30	7	·28	3	·34	21
18	Th	31	8	·24	4	·33	22

Sep.

Solar: Vikrama *Simha—Avani* (to 31), then Vikrama *Kanya—Purattasi*. Lunar: Srv. *Bah.*, then Bhadrapada *Sukla* / *Bahula*. Muhammadan: *Zi-l-ka'da*, then H. 1235 *Zi-l-hijja*.

Cyclic Sidereal Year, Month and Day	Week-Day	English Month and Day	Tithi	Ending Moment	Nakshatra	Ending Moment	Muhammadan Year, Month and Day
19	Fr	1	9	·22	5	·34	23
20	Sa	2	10	·23	6	·36	24
21	Su	3	11	·24	7	·41	25
22	Mo	4	12	·29	8	·48	26
23	Tu	5	13	·34	9	·57	27
24	We	6	14	·40	10	·67	28
25	Th	7	—A	·48	11	·78	29
26	Fr	8	1	·57	12	·88	—30
27	Sa	9	2	·65	13	·98	1
28	Su	10	3	·73	...	...	2
29	Mo	11	4	·79	14	·07	3
30	Tu	12	5	·82	15	·15	4
—31	We	13	6	·85	16	·21	5
1	Th	14	7	·83	17	·24	6
2	Fr	15	8	·80	18	·25	7
3	Sa	16	9	·77	19	·24	8
4	Su	17	10	·70	20	·23	9
5	Mo	18	11	·63	21	·19	10
6	Tu	19	12	·53	22	·13	11
7	We	20	13	·44	23	·07	12
8	Th	21	14	·34	24 25	·00 ·94 }	13
9	Fr ○	22	P	·24	26	·87	14
10	Sa	23	1	·13	27	·81	15
11	Su	24	{ 2 3	·04 ·96	1	·75	16
12	Mo	25	4	·88	2	·70	17
13	Tu	26	5	·83	3	·67	18
14	We	27	6	·78	4	·66	19
15	Th	28	7	·77	5	·66	20
16	Fr	29	8	·76	6	·68	21
17	Sa	30	9	·78	7	·72	22

Oct.

Solar: Vikrama *Tula—Aippasi*. Lunar: *Bahula*, then Asvina *Sukla* / *Bahula*. Muhammadan: H. 1236 *Muharram*.

Cyclic Sidereal Year, Month and Day	Week-Day	English Month and Day	Tithi	Ending Moment	Nakshatra	Ending Moment	Muhammadan Year, Month and Day
18	Su	1	10	·83	8	·78	23
19	Mo	2	11	·87	9	·87	24
20	Tu	3	12	·96	10	·97	25
21	We	4	...	...	...	...	26
22	Th	5	13	·04	11	·07	27
23	Fr	6	14	·13	12	·18	28
24	Sa	7	—A	·20	13	·28	29
25	Su	8	1	·28	14	·38	—30
26	Mo	9	2	·34	15	·46	1
27	Tu	10	3	·38	16	·52	2
28	We	11	4	·41	17	·56	3
29	Th	12	5	·39	18	·57	4
30	Fr	13	6	·37	19	·58	5
—31	Sa	14	7	·33	20	·56	6
1	Su	15	8	·26	21	·52	7
2	Mo	16	9	·19	22	·47	8
3	Tu	17	10	·10	23	·41	9
4	We	18	{ 11 12	·00 ·90	24	·35	10
5	Th	19	13	·81	25	·28	11
6	Fr	20	14	·70	26	·21	12
7	Sa	21	P	·62	27	·14	13
8	Su	22	1	·54	1	·08	14
9	Mo	23	2	·46	2	·04	15
10	Tu	24	3	·41	3 4	·00 ·98 }	16
11	We	25	4	·36	5	·98	17
12	Th	26	5	·35	6	·99	18
13	Fr	27	6	·35	...	...	19
14	Sa	28	7	·37	7	·02	20
15	Su	29	8	·41	8	·10	21
16	Mo	30	9	·47	9	·18	22
17	Tu	31	10	·56	10	·27	23

Nov.

Solar: Vikrama *Tula—Aippasi* (to 30), then Vikrama *Vrischika—Karttigai*. Lunar: As. *Bah.*, then Karttika *Sukla* / *Bahula*. Muhammadan: *Muharram*, then H. 1236 *Safar*.

Cyclic Sidereal Year, Month and Day	Week-Day	English Month and Day	Tithi	Ending Moment	Nakshatra	Ending Moment	Muhammadan Year, Month and Day
18	We	1	11	·63	11	·37	24
19	Th	2	12	·72	12	·48	25
20	Fr	3	13	·80	13	·59	26
21	Sa	4	14	·88	14	·69	27
22	Su	5	—A	·94	15	·77	28
23	Mo	6	1	·97	16	·83	29
24	Tu	7	...	...	17	·87	—30
25	We	8	{ 2 3	·00 ·98	18	·90	1
26	Th	9	4	·95	19	·90	2
27	Fr	10	5	·92	20	·89	3
28	Sa	11	6	·87	21	·85	4
29	Su	12	7	·79	22	·80	5
—30	Mo	13	8	·70	23	·75	6
1	Tu	14	9	·60	24	·69	7
2	We	15	10	·51	25	·62	8
3	Th	16	11	·41	26	·55	9
4	Fr	17	12	·31	27	·48	10
5	Sa	18	13	·23	1	·42	11
6	Su	19	14	·15	2	·37	12
7	Mo	20	P	·08	3	·33	13
8	Tu	21	{ 1 2	·01 ·97	4	·31	14
9	We	22	3	·97	5	·30	15
10	Th	23	4	·97	6	·31	16
11	Fr	24	5	·99	7	·35	17
12	Sa	25	...	...	8	·41	18
13	Su	26	6	·03	9	·48	19
14	Mo	27	7	·10	10	·57	20
15	Tu	28	8	·18	11	·67	21
16	We	29	9	·26	12	·78	22
17	Th	30	10	·35	13	·89	23

Dec.

Solar: Vikrama *Dhanus—Margali*. Lunar: *Sukla*, then Margasira *Bahula*. Muhammadan: H. 1236 *Rabi-ul-awwal*.

Cyclic Sidereal Year, Month and Day	Week-Day	English Month and Day	Tithi	Ending Moment	Nakshatra	Ending Moment	Muhammadan Year, Month and Day
18	Fr	1	11	·43	14	·99	24
19	Sa	2	12	·51	...	...	25
20	Su	3	13	·57	15	·07	26
21	Mo	4	14	·61	16	·14	27
22	Tu	5	—A	·63	17	·20	28
23	We	6	1	·62	18	·22	—29
24	Th	7	2	·59	19	·23	1
25	Fr	8	3	·55	20	·21	2
26	Sa	9	4	·49	21	·18	3
27	Su	10	5	·41	22	·14	4
28	Mo	11	6	·32	23	·09	5
—29	Tu	12	7	·23	24 25	·03 ·96 }	6
1	We	13	8	·14	26	·89	7
2	Th	14	{ 9 10	·03 ·94	27	·82	8
3	Fr	15	11	·85	1	·76	9
4	Sa	16	12	·77	2	·71	10
5	Su	17	13	·71	3	·66	11
6	Mo	18	14	·65	4	·63	12
7	Tu	19	P	·62	5	·62	13
8	We	20	1	·60	6	·64	14
9	Th	21	2	·62	7	·67	15
10	Fr	22	3	·64	8	·71	16
11	Sa	23	4	·68	9	·78	17
12	Su	24	5	·75	10	·87	18
13	Mo	25	6	·83	11	·98	19
14	Tu	26	7	·92	...	...	20
15	We	27	...	...	12	·08	21
16	Th	28	8	·01	13	·19	22
17	Fr	29	9	·10	14	·29	23
18	Sa	30	10	·16	15	·38	24
19	Su	31	11	·21	16	·46	25

15. Svati. 16. Visak. 17. Anur. 18. Jyesh. 19. Mula. 20. P. Ash. 21. U. Ash. 22. Sravn. 23. Dani. 24. Satab. 25. P. Bhad. 26. U. Bhad. 27. Rev.

A. D. 1821. **Mesha Sankranti** (Commencement of Indian Sidereal Year).

Solar Eclipse. ● **(Surya Sid.) April 11·18.** **Saka 1743.** **Kaliyuga 4922.**

Lunar Eclipse. ○ **(Arya Sid.) April 11·08.** **(S. Cycle) Vrisha.**

SOLAR reckoning: Cyclic Sidereal Year, Month and Day; Week-Day; English Month and Day. LUNAR reckoning: Tithi; Ending Moment; Nakshatra; Ending Moment; Muhammadan Year, Month and Day.

Jan. — Vikrama *Dhanus—Margali.* / Vikrama *Makara—Tai.* — *Bah.* / *Sukla* / **Pausha** / *Bahula* — *R. awwal.* / H. 1236 *Rabi-ul-akhir.*

Cyclic Sidereal Year, Month and Day	Week-Day	English Month and Day	Tithi	Ending Moment	Nakshatra	Ending Moment	Muhammadan Year, Month and Day
20	Mo	1	12	·26	17	·51	26
21	Tu	2	13	·27	18	·54	27
22	We	3	14	·26	19	·55	28
23	Th	4	—A	·23	20	·54	29
24	Fr	5	1	·20	21	·51	—30
25	Sa	6	2	·13	22	·48	1
26	Su	7	3 / 4	·05 / ·97	23	·43	2
27	Mo	8	5	·87	24	·36	3
28	Tu	9	6	·78	25	·30	4
—29	We	10	7	·68	26	·24	5
1	Th	11	8	·59	27	·16	6
2	Fr	12	9	·49	1	·10	7
3	Sa	13	10	·42	2 / 3	·04 / ·99	8
4	Su	14	11	·35	4	·96	9
5	Mo	15	12	·29	5	·96	10
6	Tu	16	13	·26	6	·96	11
7	We	17	14	·25	7	·98	12
8	Th	18	P	·26	...	...	13
9	Fr	19	1	·28	8	·02	14
10	Sa	20	2	·34	9	·09	15
11	Su	21	3	·41	10	·18	16
12	Mo	22	4	·48	11	·28	17
13	Tu	23	5	·57	12	·38	18
14	We	24	6	·66	13	·49	19
15	Th	25	7	·75	14	·59	20
16	Fr	26	8	·81	15	·68	21
17	Sa	27	9	·88	16	·77	22
18	Su	28	10	·90	17	·82	23
19	Mo	29	11	·91	18	·86	24
20	Tu	30	12	·90	19	·87	25
21	We	31	13	·88	20	·87	26

Feb. — Vikrama *Kumbha—Masi.* — *Sukla* / **Magha** / *Bahula* — H. 1236 *Jumadal-awwal.*

Cyclic Sidereal Year, Month and Day	Week-Day	English Month and Day	Tithi	Ending Moment	Nakshatra	Ending Moment	Muhammadan Year, Month and Day
22	Th	1	14	·84	21	·85	27
23	Fr	2	—A	·76	22	·81	28
24	Sa	3	1	·69	23	·76	—29
25	Su	4	2	·60	24	·70	1
26	Mo	5	3	·51	25	·63	2
27	Tu	6	4	·41	26	·57	3
28	We	7	5	·30	27	·50	4
29	Th	8	6	·22	1	·44	5
—30	Fr	9	7	·13	2	·38	6
1	Sa	10	8 / 9	·05 / ·97	3	·33	7
2	Su	11	10	·93	4	·30	8
3	Mo	12	11	·90	5	·28	9
4	Tu	13	12	·88	6	·28	10
5	We	14	13	·89	7	·30	11
6	Th	15	14	·92	8	·33	12
7	Fr	16	P	·98	9	·40	13
8	Sa	17	...	...	10	·48	14
9	Su	18	1	·04	11	·57	15
10	Mo	19	2	·12	12	·68	16
11	Tu	20	3	·20	13	·78	17
12	We	21	4	·28	14	·89	18
13	Th	22	5	·37	15	·99	19
14	Fr	23	6	·44	...	...	20
15	Sa	24	7	·50	16	·07	21
16	Su	25	8	·53	17	·13	22
17	Mo	26	9	·54	18	·17	23
18	Tu	27	10	·52	19	·19	24
19	We	28	11	·50	20	·20	25

March — Vikrama *Kumbha—Masi.* / Vikrama *Mina—Panguni.* — *Bah.* / *Sukla* / **Phalguna** / *Bahula* — *J. awwal.* / H. 1236 *Jumadal-akhir.*

Cyclic Sidereal Year, Month and Day	Week-Day	English Month and Day	Tithi	Ending Moment	Nakshatra	Ending Moment	Muhammadan Year, Month and Day
20	Th	1	12	·44	21	·18	26
21	Fr	2	13	·38	22	·15	27
22	Sa	3	14	·31	23	·10	28
23	Su ●	4	—A	·21	24 / 25	·04 / ·98	29
24	Mo	5	1	·12	26	·91	—30
25	Tu	6	2 / 3	·02 / ·92	27	·84	1
26	We	7	4	·82	1	·77	2
27	Th	8	5	·73	2	·71	3
28	Fr	9	6	·66	3	·67	4
29	Sa	10	7	·58	4	·63	5
—30	Su	11	8	·54	5	·61	6
1	Mo	12	9	·50	6	·60	7
2	Tu	13	10	·49	7	·61	8
3	We	14	11	·49	8	·65	9
4	Th	15	12	·53	9	·71	10
5	Fr	16	13	·57	10	·78	11
6	Sa	17	14	·63	11	·87	12
7	Su	18	P	·72	12	·98	13
8	Mo	19	1	·80	...	...	14
9	Tu	20	2	·90	13	·08	15
10	We	21	3	·98	14	·20	16
11	Th	22	...	...	15	·29	17
12	Fr	23	4	·04	16	·38	18
13	Sa	24	5	·09	17	·44	19
14	Su	25	6	·12	18	·49	20
15	Mo	26	7	·13	19	·52	21
16	Tu	27	8	·11	20	·53	22
17	We	28	9	·08	21	·51	23
18	Th	29	10 / 11	·03 / ·97	22	·48	24
19	Fr	30	12	·88	23	·43	25
20	Sa	31	13	·79	24	·39	26

April — Vrisha *Mesha—Chittirai.* — *Sukla* / **Chaitra** / *Bahula* — H. 1236 *Rajab.*

Cyclic Sidereal Year, Month and Day	Week-Day	English Month and Day	Tithi	Ending Moment	Nakshatra	Ending Moment	Muhammadan Year, Month and Day
21	Su	1	14	·70	25	·32	27
22	Mo	2	—A	·59	26	·25	28
23	Tu	3	1	·49	27	·18	—29
24	We	4	2	·40	1	·11	1
25	Th	5	3	·31	2	·06	2
26	Fr	6	4	·23	3 / 4	·00 / ·96	3
27	Sa	7	5	·16	5	·93	4
28	Su	8	6	·11	6	·92	5
29	Mo	9	7	·07	7	·93	6
—30	Tu	10	8	·05	8	·97	7
1	We	11	9	·05	...	...	8
2	Th	12	10	·09	9	·02	9
3	Fr	13	11	·13	10	·09	10
4	Sa	14	12	·20	11	·18	11
5	Su	15	13	·28	12	·27	12
6	Mo	16	14	·36	13	·39	13
7	Tu	17	P	·45	14	·50	14
8	We	18	1	·53	15	·60	15
9	Th	19	2	·59	16	·68	16
10	Fr	20	3	·64	17	·75	17
11	Sa	21	4	·68	18	·81	18
12	Su	22	5	·67	19	·84	19
13	Mo	23	6	·65	20	·85	20
14	Tu	24	7	·63	21	·84	21
15	We	25	8	·57	22	·81	22
16	Th	26	9	·51	23	·78	23
17	Fr	27	10	·42	24	·72	24
18	Sa	28	11	·34	25	·66	25
19	Su	29	12	·24	26	·59	26
20	Mo	30	13	·14	27	·52	27

May — Vrisha *Mesha—Chittirai.* / Vrisha *Vrishabha—Vaikasi.* — *Sukla* / **Vaisakha** / *Bahula* — H. 1236 *Shaban.*

Cyclic Sidereal Year, Month and Day	Week-Day	English Month and Day	Tithi	Ending Moment	Nakshatra	Ending Moment	Muhammadan Year, Month and Day
21	Tu	1	14 / A	·03 / ·93	1	·45	28
22	We	2	1	·84	2	·39	29
23	Th	3	2	·75	3	·34	—30
24	Fr	4	3	·69	4	·29	1
25	Sa	5	4	·64	5	·26	2
26	Su	6	5	·60	6	·24	3
27	Mo	7	6	·58	7	·26	4
28	Tu	8	7	·58	8	·28	5
29	We	9	8	·62	9	·33	6
30	Th	10	9	·66	10	·39	7
—31	Fr	11	10	·72	11	·48	8
1	Sa	12	11	·79	12	·58	9
2	Su	13	12	·88	13	·69	10
3	Mo	14	13	·96	14	·79	11
4	Tu	15	...	...	15	·90	12
5	We	16	14	·04	16	·99	13
6	Th	17	P	·10	...	...	14
7	Fr	18	1	·15	17	·07	15
8	Sa	19	2	·18	18	·12	16
9	Su	20	3	·19	19	·16	17
10	Mo	21	4	·18	20	·17	18
11	Tu	22	5	·14	21	·16	19
12	We	23	6	·10	22	·15	20
13	Th	24	7 / 8	·02 / ·93	23	·11	21
14	Fr	25	9	·84	24	·06	22
15	Sa	26	10	·74	25 / 26	·00 / ·93	23
16	Su	27	11	·64	27	·86	24
17	Mo	28	12	·54	1	·80	25
18	Tu	29	13	·44	2	·73	26
19	We	30	14	·34	3	·67	27
20	Th	31	—A	·25	4	·62	28

June — Vrisha *Mithuna—Ani.* — *Sukla* / **Jyeshtha** / *Bahula* — H. 1236 *Ramzan.*

Cyclic Sidereal Year, Month and Day	Week-Day	English Month and Day	Tithi	Ending Moment	Nakshatra	Ending Moment	Muhammadan Year, Month and Day
21	Fr	1	1	·19	5	·59	—29
22	Sa	2	2	·13	6	·58	1
23	Su	3	3	·10	7	·58	2
24	Mo	4	4	·08	8	·60	3
25	Tu	5	5	·08	9	·64	4
26	We	6	6	·10	10	·70	5
27	Th	7	7	·15	11	·79	6
28	Fr	8	8	·22	12	·88	7
29	Sa	9	9	·28	13	·99	8
30	Su	10	10	·37	...	...	9
—31	Mo	11	11	·45	14	·09	10
1	Tu	12	12	·52	15	·20	11
2	We	13	13	·58	16	·30	12
3	Th	14	14	·64	17	·38	13
4	Fr	15	P	·66	18	·44	14
5	Sa	16	1	·67	19	·47	15
6	Su	17	2	·66	20	·49	16
7	Mo	18	3	·63	21	·49	17
8	Tu	19	4	·58	22	·48	18
9	We	20	5	·51	23	·44	19
10	Th	21	6	·43	24	·39	20
11	Fr	22	7	·33	25	·33	21
12	Sa	23	8	·23	26	·27	22
13	Su	24	9	·13	27	·21	23
14	Mo	25	10 / 11	·02 / ·98	1	·18	24
15	Tu	26	12	·83	2	·07	25
16	We	27	13	·74	3 / 4	·01 / ·95	26
17	Th	28	14	·67	5	·93	27
18	Fr	29	—A	·62	6	·90	28
19	Sa	30	1	·58	7	·90	29

Naksh:—1. Asvn. 2. Bhar. 3. Krit. 4. Rohi. 5. Mrig. 6. Ardh. 7. Punar. 8. Push. 9. Aslesh. 10. Magh. 11. P. Phal. 12. U. Phal. 13. Hasta. 14. Chit.

A. D. 1821.	Kollam 997, Commences	N. Malabar—Sept. S. Malabar—Aug.	Hijra 1237, Commences, Sep. 28.	Vikrama 1878. Bengal San 1227. (N. Cycle) Nandana.

A.—Amavasya.
P.—Paurnami.

SOLAR reckoning. / LUNAR reckoning.

July

Solar: Vrisha, Mithuna—Ani (1–12 July); Vrisha, Karkata—Adi (13–31 July). Lunar: Sukla, Ashadha, Bahula. Muhammadan: H. 1236 Shawwal.

Cyclic Sidereal Year, Month and Day.	Week-Day	English Month and Day.	Tithi	Ending Moment.	Nakshatra	Ending Moment.	Muhammadan Year, Month and Day.
20	Su	1	2	·56	8	·91	—30
21	Mo	2	3	·56	9	·95	1
22	Tu	3	4	·58	...	...	2
23	We	4	5	·63	10	·02	3
24	Th	5	6	·68	11	·09	4
25	Fr	6	7	·76	12	·18	5
26	Sa	7	8	·84	13	·28	6
27	Su	8	9	·91	14	·39	7
28	Mo	9	...	...	15	·50	8
29	Tu	10	10	·00	16	·60	9
30	We	11	11	·06	17	·68	10
31	Th	12	12	·11	18	·75	11
—32	Fr	13	13	·14	19	·79	12
1	Sa	14	14	·16	20	·81	13
2	Su	15	P	·14	21	·82	14
3	Mo	16	1	·10	22	·81	15
4	Tu	17	{ 2 3	·06 ·99	23	·78	16
5	We	18	4	·90	24	·73	17
6	Th	19	5	·81	25	·67	18
7	Fr	20	6	·72	26	·61	19
8	Sa	21	7	·61	27	·54	20
9	Su	22	8	·52	1	·47	21
10	Mo	23	9	·42	2	·40	22
11	Tu	24	10	·32	3	·34	23
12	We	25	11	·22	4	·30	24
13	Th	26	12	·15	5	·26	25
14	Fr	27	13	·10	6	·23	26
15	Sa	28	14	·06	7	·22	27
16	Su	29	—A	·04	8	·23	28
17	Mo	30	1	·04	9	·27	—29
18	Tu	31	2	·06	10	·32	1

Aug.

Solar: Vrisha, Simha—Avani. Lunar: Sukla, Sravana, Bahula, B. Suk. Muhammadan: H. 1236 Zi-l-ka'da.

Cyclic Sidereal Year, Month and Day.	Week-Day	English Month and Day.	Tithi	Ending Moment.	Nakshatra	Ending Moment.	Muhammadan Year, Month and Day.
19	We	1	3	·09	11	·39	2
20	Th	2	4	·15	12	·48	3
21	Fr	3	5	·23	13	·58	4
22	Sa	4	6	·31	14	·69	5
23	Su	5	7	·40	15	·80	6
24	Mo	6	8	·47	16	·90	7
25	Tu	7	9	·53	...	...	8
26	We	8	10	·59	17	·00	9
27	Th	9	11	·62	18	·06	10
28	Fr	10	12	·64	19	·10	11
29	Sa	11	13	·62	20	·14	12
30	Su	12	14	·60	21	·15	13
—31	Mo	13	P	·54	22	·14	14
1	Tu	14	1	·49	23	·11	15
2	We	15	2	·40	24	·06	16
3	Th	16	3	·31	25 26	·02 ·95 }	17
4	Fr	17	4	·22	27	·88	18
5	Sa	18	5	·11	1	·81	19
6	Su	19	{ 6 7	·01 ·91	2	·74	20
7	Mo	20	8	·82	3	·69	21
8	Tu	21	9	·73	4	·63	22
9	We	22	10	·66	5	·59	23
10	Th	23	11	·59	6	·56	24
11	Fr	24	12	·55	7	·54	25
12	Sa	25	13	·54	8	·55	26
13	Su	26	14	·54	9	·58	27
14	Mo	27	—A	·56	10	·63	28
15	Tu	28	1	·60	11	·70	29
16	We	29	2	·66	12	·78	—30
17	Th	30	3	·72	13	·88	1
18	Fr	31	4	·80	...	...	2

Sep.

Solar: Vrisha, Simha—Avani (1–14 Sep.); Vrisha, Kanya—Purattasi (15–30 Sep.). Lunar: Sukla, Bhadrapada, Bahula. Muhammadan: H. 1236 Zi-l-hijja.

Cyclic Sidereal Year, Month and Day.	Week-Day	English Month and Day.	Tithi	Ending Moment.	Nakshatra	Ending Moment.	Muhammadan Year, Month and Day.
19	Sa	1	5	·90	14	·00	3
20	Su	2	6	·98	15	·10	4
21	Mo	3	...	...	16	·20	5
22	Tu	4	7	·06	17	·29	6
23	We	5	8	·10	18	·36	7
24	Th	6	9	·14	19	·43	8
25	Fr	7	10	·16	20	·46	9
26	Sa	8	11	·13	21	·47	10
27	Su	9	12	·11	22	·46	11
28	Mo	10	13	·06	23	·44	12
29	Tu	11	{ 14 P	·00 ·92	24	·41	13
30	We	12	1	·84	25	·35	14
31	Th	13	2	·74	26	·29	15
—32	Fr	14	3	·65	27	·22	16
1	Sa	15	4	·54	1	·15	17
2	Su	16	5	·44	2	·09	18
3	Mo	17	6	·35	3 4	·02 ·97 }	19
4	Tu	18	7	·26	5	·92	20
5	We	19	8	·19	6	·88	21
6	Th	20	9	·13	7	·87	22
7	Fr	21	10	·09	8	·88	23
8	Sa	22	11	·07	9	·90	24
9	Su	23	12	·06	10	·94	25
10	Mo	24	13	·09	...	...	26
11	Tu	25	14	·13	11	·00	27
12	We	26	—A	·19	12	·08	28
13	Th	27	1	·27	13	·19	—29
14	Fr	28	2	·36	14	·29	1
15	Sa	29	3	·44	15	·40	2
16	Su	30	4	·52	16	·50	3

Oct.

Solar: Vrisha, Tula—Aippasi. Lunar: Sukla, Asvina, Bahula, Kartt. Suk. Muhammadan: H. 1237 Muharram; Sfar.

Cyclic Sidereal Year, Month and Day.	Week-Day	English Month and Day.	Tithi	Ending Moment.	Nakshatra	Ending Moment.	Muhammadan Year, Month and Day.
17	Mo	1	5	·60	17	·59	4
18	Tu	2	6	·64	18	·68	5
19	We	3	7	·68	19	·74	6
20	Th	4	8	·70	20	·78	7
21	Fr	5	9	·69	21	·79	8
22	Sa	6	10	·66	22	·79	9
23	Su	7	11	·61	23	·78	10
24	Mo	8	12	·55	24	·74	11
25	Tu	9	13	·47	25	·69	12
26	We	10	14	·40	26	·63	13
27	Th	11	P	·30	27	·56	14
28	Fr	12	1	·20	1	·49	15
29	Sa	13	2	·10	2	·43	16
—30	Su	14	{ 3 4	·00 ·91	3	·36	17
1	Mo	15	5	·82	4	·30	18
2	Tu	16	6	·76	5	·25	19
3	We	17	7	·70	6	·21	20
4	Th	18	8	·66	7	·20	21
5	Fr	19	9	·64	8	·20	22
6	Sa	20	10	·65	9	·21	23
7	Su	21	11	·67	10	·25	24
8	Mo	22	12	·71	11	·31	25
9	Tu	23	13	·78	12	·40	26
10	We	24	14	·85	13	·49	27
11	Th	25	—A	·94	14	·59	28
12	Fr	26	...	...	15	·70	29
13	Sa	27	1	·02	16	·80	—30
14	Su	28	2	·11	17	·91	1
15	Mo	29	3	·18	18	·99	2
16	Tu	30	4	·23	...	...	3
17	We	31	5	·27	19	·05	4

Nov.

Solar: Vrisha, Tula—Aippasi (1–13 Nov.); Vrisha, Vrischika—Kartigai (14–30 Nov.). Lunar: Sukla, Karttika, Bahula, Sukla. Muhammadan: H. 1237 Safar.

Cyclic Sidereal Year, Month and Day.	Week-Day	English Month and Day.	Tithi	Ending Moment.	Nakshatra	Ending Moment.	Muhammadan Year, Month and Day.
18	Th	1	6	·29	20	·09	5
19	Fr	2	7	·28	21	·11	6
20	Sa	3	8	·25	22	·12	7
21	Su	4	9	·21	23	·11	8
22	Mo	5	10	·14	24	·07	9
23	Tu	6	{ 11 12	·08 ·99	25 26	·02 ·96 }	10
24	We	7	13	·89	27	·90	11
25	Th	8	14	·79	1	·84	12
26	Fr	9	P	·69	2	·77	13
27	Sa	10	1	·60	3	·70	14
28	Su	11	2	·51	4	·64	15
29	Mo	12	3	·43	5	·58	16
—30	Tu	13	4	·36	6	·55	17
1	We	14	5	·29	7	·53	18
2	Th	15	6	·27	8	·52	19
3	Fr	16	7	·25	9	·53	20
4	Sa	17	8	·26	10	·56	21
5	Su	18	9	·27	11	·63	22
6	Mo	19	10	·33	12	·70	23
7	Tu	20	11	·39	13	·79	24
8	We	21	12	·48	14	·89	25
9	Th	22	13	·56	...	...	26
10	Fr	23	14	·65	15	·00	27
11	Sa	24	—A	·73	16	·10	28
12	Su	25	1	·80	17	·21	—29
13	Mo	26	2	·85	18	·29	1
14	Tu	27	3	·90	19	·36	2
15	We	28	4	·92	20	·41	3
16	Th	29	5	·90	21	·43	4
17	Fr	30	6	·87	22	·45	5

Dec.

Solar: Vrisha, Dhanus—Margali. Lunar: Margasira, Bahula, Pausha Suk. Muhammadan: H. 1237 Rabi-ul-awwal; R. akhir.

Cyclic Sidereal Year, Month and Day.	Week-Day	English Month and Day.	Tithi	Ending Moment.	Nakshatra	Ending Moment.	Muhammadan Year, Month and Day.
18	Sa	1	7	·83	23	·43	6
19	Su	2	8	·76	24	·40	7
20	Mo	3	9	·70	25	·36	8
21	Tu	4	10	·61	26	·30	9
22	We	5	11	·53	27	·25	10
23	Th	6	12	·42	1	·18	11
24	Fr	7	13	·32	2	·11	12
25	Sa	8	14	·22	3 4	·04 ·97 }	13
26	Su	9	P	·13	5	·93	14
27	Mo	10	{ 1 2	·05 ·98	6	·88	15
28	Tu	11	3	·94	7	·85	16
—29	We	12	4	·90	8	·84	17
1	Th	13	5	·89	9	·85	18
2	Fr	14	6	·90	10	·89	19
3	Sa	15	7	·92	11	·94	20
4	Su	16	8	·97	...	...	21
5	Mo	17	...	...	12	·00	22
6	Tu	18	9	·04	13	·09	23
7	We	19	10	·13	14	·19	24
8	Th	20	11	·21	15	·29	25
9	Fr	21	12	·30	16	·41	26
10	Sa	22	13	·38	17	·51	27
11	Su	23	14	·45	18	·60	28
12	Mo	24	—A	·50	19	·67	29
13	Tu	25	1	·54	20	·72	—30
14	We	26	2	·56	21	·76	1
15	Th	27	3	·54	22	·77	2
16	Fr	28	4	·53	23	·76	3
17	Sa	29	5	·47	24	·73	4
18	Su	30	6	·41	25	·69	5
19	Mo	31	7	·34	26	·65	6

15. Svati. 16. Visak. 17. Anur. 18. Jyesh. 19. Mula. 20. P. Ash. 21. U. Ash. 22. Sravn. 23. Dani. 24. Satab. 25. P. Bhad. 26. U. Bhad. 27. Rev.

A. D. 1822. **Mesha Sankranti** (Commencement of Indian Sidereal Year). **Saka 1744.** **Kaliyuga 4923.**

Solar Eclipse. ● **(Surya Sid.) April 11·44.**

Lunar Eclipse. ○ **(Arya Sid.) April 11·34.** **(S. Cycle) Chitrabhanu.**

Jan.

Cyclic Sidereal Year, Month and Day (SOLAR reckoning)	Week-Day	English Month and Day	Tithi (LUNAR reckoning)	Ending Moment	Nakshatra	Ending Moment	Muhammadan Year, Month and Day
[Vrisha Dhanus—Margali.] 20	Tu	1	[Suk.] 8	·25	27	·58	[H. 1237 Rabi-us-akhir.] 7
21	We	2	9	·15	1	·52	8
22	Th	3	10; 11	·05; ·96	2	·44	9
23	Fr	4	12	·86	3	·37	10
24	Sa	5	13	·78	4	·32	11
25	Su	6	14	·69	5	·26	12
26	Mo	7	[Pausha] P	·63	6	·21	13
27	Tu	8	1	·58	7	·18	14
28	We	9	2	·54	8	·17	15
29	Th	10	3	·54	9	·17	16
30	Fr	11	4	·54	10	·20	17
[Vrisha Makara—Tai.] 1	Sa	12	5	·57	11	·24	18
2	Su	13	6	·62	12	·31	19
3	Mo	14	7	·68	13	·39	20
4	Tu	15	[Bahula] 8	·77	14	·49	21
5	We	16	9	·86	15	·60	22
6	Th	17	10	·96	16	·71	23
7	Fr	18	...	...	17	·81	24
8	Sa	19	11	·04	18	·90	25
9	Su	20	12	·10	19	·98	26
10	Mo	21	13	·15	...	...	27
11	Tu	22	14	·18	20	·04	28
12	We	23	A	·20	21	·08	29
13	Th	24	1	·18	22	·09	1
14	Fr	25	2	·17	23	·09	2
15	Sa	26	3	·11	24	·06	3
16	Su	27	4; 5	·05; ·97	25; 26	·08; ·98	4
17	Mo	28	[Sukla] 6	·89	27	·94	5
18	Tu	29	7	·78	1	·85	6
19	We	30	8	·68	2	·78	7
20	Th	31	9	·59	3	·72	8

Feb.

Cyclic Sidereal Year, Month and Day	Week-Day	English Month and Day	Tithi	Ending Moment	Nakshatra	Ending Moment	Muhammadan Year, Month and Day
21	Fr	1	10	·49	4	·66	9
22	Sa	2	11	·41	5	·60	10
23	Su	3	12	·32	6	·55	[H. 1237 Jumada-awwal.] 11
24	Mo	4	13	·27	7	·51	12
25	Tu	5	14	·22	8	·49	13
26	We ○	6	[Magha] P	·18	9	·50	14
27	Th	7	1	·17	10	·52	15
28	Fr	8	2	·18	11	·55	16
29	Sa	9	3	·22	12	·61	17
[Vrisha Kumbha—Masi.] 1	Su	10	4	·27	13	·69	18
2	Mo	11	5	·34	14	·80	19
3	Tu	12	[Bahula] 6	·41	15	·90	20
4	We	13	7	·51	...	...	21
5	Th	14	8	·59	16	·01	22
6	Fr	15	9	·67	17	·11	23
7	Sa	16	10	·74	18	·20	24
8	Su	17	11	·80	19	·29	25
9	Mo	18	12	·82	20	·35	26
10	Tu	19	13	·83	21	·39	27
11	We	20	14	·82	22	·41	28
12	Th	21	A	·79	23	·41	29
13	Fr	22	[Sukla] 1	·73	24	·40	30
14	Sa	23	2	·67	25	·37	[J. akhir.] 1
15	Su	24	3	·59	26	·32	2
16	Mo	25	[Phal.] 4	·50	27	·26	3
17	Tu	26	5	·40	1	·19	4
18	We	27	6	·31	2	·12	5
19	Th	28	7	·20	3; 4	·05; ·99	6

March

Cyclic Sidereal Year, Month and Day	Week-Day	English Month and Day	Tithi	Ending Moment	Nakshatra	Ending Moment	Muhammadan Year, Month and Day
20	Fr	1	8	·11	5	·93	7
21	Sa	2	[Suk.] 9; 10	·03; ·94	6	·88	8
22	Su	3	11	·89	7	·84	9
23	Mo	4	12	·83	8	·82	[H. 1237 Jumada-akhir.] 10
24	Tu	5	13	·80	9	·82	11
25	We	6	14	·78	10	·83	12
26	Th	7	[Phalguna] P	·80	11	·87	13
27	Fr	8	1	·83	12	·92	14
28	Sa	9	2	·88	...	...	15
29	Su	10	3	·95	13	·01	16
30	Mo	11	...	...	14	·10	17
[Vrisha Mina—Panguni.] 1	Tu	12	4	·03	15	·20	18
2	We	13	5	·12	16	·30	19
3	Th	14	6	·20	17	·41	20
4	Fr	15	[Bahula] 7	·29	18	·52	21
5	Sa	16	8	·34	19	·60	22
6	Su	17	9	·39	20	·66	23
7	Mo	18	10	·42	21	·71	24
8	Tu	19	11	·42	22	·73	25
9	We	20	12	·41	23	·75	26
10	Th	21	13	·38	24	·73	27
11	Fr	22	14	·33	25	·70	28
12	Sa	23	A	·26	26	·65	29
13	Su	24	1	·18	27	·60	1
14	Mo	25	2; 3	·09; ·98	1	·53	2
15	Tu	26	4	·89	2	·47	3
16	We	27	5	·78	3	·40	4
17	Th	28	6	·70	4	·33	5
18	Fr	29	7	·61	5	·27	6
19	Sa	30	[Sukla] 8	·53	6	·21	7
20	Su	31	9	·46	7	·18	8

April

Cyclic Sidereal Year, Month and Day	Week-Day	English Month and Day	Tithi	Ending Moment	Nakshatra	Ending Moment	Muhammadan Year, Month and Day
21	Mo	1	10	·41	8	·15	9
22	Tu	2	11	·38	9	·14	10
23	We	3	12	·36	10	·15	11
24	Th	4	13	·37	11	·18	12
25	Fr	5	14	·40	12	·24	13
26	Sa	6	[Chaitra] P	·46	13	·31	[H. 1237 Rajab.] 14
27	Su	7	1	·53	14	·40	15
28	Mo	8	2	·60	15	·50	16
29	Tu	9	3	·69	16	·60	17
30	We	10	4	·76	17	·72	18
[Chitrabhanu Mesha—Chittirai.] 1	Th	11	5	·84	18	·82	19
2	Fr	12	6	·90	19	·90	20
3	Sa	13	7	·96	20	·97	21
4	Su	14	[Bahula] 8	·98	...	...	22
5	Mo	15	9	·98	21	·02	23
6	Tu	16	10	·97	22	·05	24
7	We	17	11	·98	23	·07	25
8	Th	18	12	·85	24	·06	26
9	Fr	19	13	·81	25; 26	·03; ·99	27
10	Sa	20	14	·74	27	·93	28
11	Su	21	A	·64	1	·88	29
12	Mo	22	[Vaisk. Suk.] 1	·54	2	·81	30
13	Tu	23	2	·44	3	·74	[H. 1237 Shaban.] 1
14	We	24	3	·33	4	·67	2
15	Th	25	4	·24	5	·60	3
16	Fr	26	5	·14	6	·56	4
17	Sa	27	6	·07	7	·51	5
18	Su	28	7; 8	·00; ·96	8	·48	6
19	Mo	29	9	·91	9	·46	7
20	Tu	30	10	·89	10	·47	8

May

Cyclic Sidereal Year, Month and Day	Week-Day	English Month and Day	Tithi	Ending Moment	Nakshatra	Ending Moment	Muhammadan Year, Month and Day
21	We	1	[Sukla] 11	·90	11	·50	9
22	Th	2	12	·93	12	·55	10
23	Fr	3	13	·99	13	·61	11
24	Sa	4	...	...	14	·70	12
25	Su	5	14	·05	15	·79	13
26	Mo	6	[Vaisakha] P	·12	16	·90	14
27	Tu	7	1	·20	...	...	15
28	We	8	2	·28	17	·02	16
29	Th	9	3	·37	18	·12	17
30	Fr	10	4	·43	19	·21	18
31	Sa	11	5	·49	20	·28	[H. 1237 Shaban.] 19
[Chitrabhanu Vrishabha—Vaikasi.] 1	Su	12	6	·50	21	·33	20
2	Mo	13	[Bahula] 7	·51	22	·38	21
3	Tu	14	8	·49	23	·39	22
4	We	15	9	·47	24	·38	23
5	Th	16	10	·40	25	·36	24
6	Fr	17	11	·32	26	·32	25
7	Sa	18	12	·25	27	·28	26
8	Su	19	13	·15	1	·22	27
9	Mo	20	14; A	·06; ·96	2	·15	28
10	Tu	21	1	·85	3	·08	29
11	We	22	2	·75	4; 5	·01; ·95	1
12	Th	23	3	·65	6	·89	2
13	Fr	24	4	·58	7	·84	3
14	Sa	25	5	·51	8	·81	4
15	Su	26	[Sukla] 6	·46	9	·79	5
16	Mo	27	7	·42	10	·80	6
17	Tu	28	8	·41	11	·82	7
18	We	29	9	·40	12	·86	8
19	Th	30	10	·43	13	·92	9
20	Fr	31	11	·49	...	...	10

June

Cyclic Sidereal Year, Month and Day	Week-Day	English Month and Day	Tithi	Ending Moment	Nakshatra	Ending Moment	Muhammadan Year, Month and Day
21	Sa	1	12	·54	14	·00	11
22	Su	2	13	·62	15	·09	12
23	Mo	3	14	·70	16	·21	13
24	Tu	4	[Jyeshtha] P	·79	17	·31	[H. 1237 Ramzan.] 14
25	We	5	1	·86	18	·42	15
26	Th	6	2	·92	19	·51	16
27	Fr	7	3	·97	20	·59	17
28	Sa	8	4	·99	21	·66	18
29	Su	9	...	...	22	·69	19
30	Mo	10	5; 6	·01; ·99	23	·71	20
31	Tu	11	[Bahula] 7	·96	24	·71	21
32	We	12	8	·89	25	·69	22
[Chitrabhanu Mithuna—Ani.] 1	Th	13	9	·83	26	·66	23
2	Fr	14	10	·75	27	·61	24
3	Sa	15	11	·64	1	·55	25
4	Su	16	12	·55	2	·49	26
5	Mo	17	13	·45	3	·41	27
6	Tu	18	14	·35	4	·35	28
7	We	19	A	·24	5	·29	29
8	Th	20	1	·15	6	·23	30
9	Fr	21	2	·07	7	·17	[H. 1237 Shawwal.] 1
10	Sa	22	3; 4	·00; ·94	8	·14	2
11	Su	23	[Sukla] 5	·90	9	·11	3
12	Mo	24	6	·88	10	·12	4
13	Tu	25	7	·88	11	·13	5
14	We	26	8	·91	12	·17	6
15	Th	27	[Ashad.] 9	·95	13	·23	7
16	Fr	28	...	...	14	·30	8
17	Sa	29	10	·02	15	·40	9
18	Su	30	11	·09	16	·51	10

Nakah:—1. Asvn. 2. Bhar. 3. Krit. 4. Rohi. 5. Mrig. 6. Ardh. 7. Punar. 8. Push. 9. Aslesh. 10. Magh. 11. P. Phal. 12. U. Phal. 13. Hasta. 14. Chit.

A. D. 1822.
A.—Amavasya.
P.—Paurnami.

Kollam 998, Commences { **N. Malabar—Sept.** / **S. Malabar—Aug.**

Hijra 1238, Commences, **Sep. 18.**

Vikrama 1879.
Bengal San 1228.
(N. Cycle) Vijaya.

SOLAR reckoning: Cyclic Sidereal Year, Month and Day. Week-Day, English Month and Day. LUNAR reckoning: Tithi, Ending Moment; Nakshatra, Ending Moment; Muhammadan Year, Month and Day.

July — Solar: Chitrabhanu *Mithuna—Ani.* (to 31), then Chitrabhanu *Karkata—Adi.* — Lunar: Ashadha *Suk.*, *Bahula*, *Sukla* — Muhammadan: H. 1237 *Shawwal.*

Cyclic Sidereal Year, Month and Day	Week-Day	English Month and Day	Tithi	Ending Moment	Nakshatra	Ending Moment	Muhammadan Year, Month and Day
19	Mo	1	12	·17	17	·61	11
20	Tu	2	13	·25	18	·72	12
21	We	3	14	·33	19	·81	13
22	Th	4	P	·40	20	·90	14
23	Fr	5	1	·44	21	·97	15
24	Sa	6	2	·47	...	...	16
25	Su	7	3	·48	22	·01	17
26	Mo	8	4	·45	23	·03	18
27	Tu	9	5	·43	24	·08	19
28	We	10	6	·37	25 / 26	·03 / ·99	20
29	Th	11	7	·30	27	·95	21
30	Fr	12	8	·22	1	·89	22
—31	Sa	13	9	·13	2	·82	23
1	Su	14	10 / 11	·03 / ·94	3	·76	24
2	Mo	15	12	·82	4	·69	25
3	Tu	16	13	·72	5	·62	26
4	We	17	14	·63	6	·56	27
5	Th	18	—A	·54	7	·51	28
6	Fr	19	1	·47	8	·47	—29
7	Sa	20	2	·42	9	·45	1
8	Su	21	3	·39	10	·44	2
9	Mo	22	4	·36	11	·45	3
10	Tu	23	5	·36	12	·48	4
11	We	24	6	·40	13	·53	5
12	Th	25	7	·42	14	·61	6
13	Fr	26	8	·49	15	·70	7
14	Sa	27	9	·56	16	·80	8
15	Su	28	10	·65	17	·91	9
16	Mo	29	11	·72	...	...	10
17	Tu	30	12	·80	18	·01	11
18	We	31	13	·87	19	·12	12

Aug. — Solar: Chitrabhanu *Karkata—Adi.* (to 32), then Chitrabhanu *Simha—Avani.* — Lunar: Sravana, *Bahula*, Bhadrapada *Sukla* — Muhammadan: H. 1237 *Zi-l-ka'da.*, H. 1237 *Zi-l-hijja.*

Cyclic Sidereal Year, Month and Day	Week-Day	English Month and Day	Tithi	Ending Moment	Nakshatra	Ending Moment	Muhammadan Year, Month and Day
19	Th	1	14	·91	20	·21	13
20	Fr ○	2	P	·95	21	·27	14
21	Sa	3	1	·96	22	·32	15
22	Su	4	2	·95	23	·35	16
23	Mo	5	3	·91	24	·37	17
24	Tu	6	4	·86	25	·36	18
25	We	7	5	·80	26	·33	19
26	Th	8	6	·72	27	·28	20
27	Fr	9	7	·62	1	·23	21
28	Sa	10	8	·52	2	·16	22
29	Su	11	9	·42	3	·10	23
30	Mo	12	10	·32	4 / 5	·03 / ·96	24
31	Tu	13	11	·23	6	·90	25
—32	We	14	12	·12	7	·84	26
1	Th	15	13 / 14	·04 / ·97	8	·81	27
2	Fr	16	—A	·91	9	·78	28
3	Sa	17	1	·88	10	·76	29
4	Su	18	2	·85	11	·77	—30
5	Mo	19	3	·86	12	·79	1
6	Tu	20	4	·88	13	·85	2
7	We	21	5	·93	14	·92	3
8	Th	22	6	·99	...	...	4
9	Fr	23	...	...	15	·00	5
10	Sa	24	7	·05	16	·10	6
11	Su	25	8	·13	17	·21	7
12	Mo	26	9	·23	18	·32	8
13	Tu	27	10	·31	19	·42	9
14	We	28	11	·37	20	·51	10
15	Th	29	12	·43	21	·58	11
16	Fr	30	13	·44	22	·64	12
17	Sa	31	14	·46	23	·68	13

Sep. — Solar: Chitrabhanu *Simha—Avani.* (to 31), then Chitrabhanu *Kanya—Purattasi.* — Lunar: Bhadra., *Bahula*, Asvina *Sukla* — Muhammadan: H. 1237 *Zi-l-hijja.*, *Muharram.*

Cyclic Sidereal Year, Month and Day	Week-Day	English Month and Day	Tithi	Ending Moment	Nakshatra	Ending Moment	Muhammadan Year, Month and Day
18	Su	1	P	·45	24	·69	14
19	Mo	2	1	·42	25	·68	15
20	Tu	3	2	·38	26	·66	16
21	We	4	3	·31	27	·62	17
22	Th	5	4	·23	1	·57	18
23	Fr	6	5	·14	2	·51	19
24	Sa	7	6 / 7	·03 / ·93	3	·44	20
25	Su	8	8	·83	4	·37	21
26	Mo	9	9	·74	5	·30	22
27	Tu	10	10	·64	6	·23	23
28	We	11	11	·57	7	·19	24
29	Th	12	12	·49	8	·14	25
30	Fr	13	13	·45	9	·10	26
—31	Sa	14	14	·40	10	·09	27
1	Su	15	—A	·38	11	·09	28
2	Mo	16	1	·39	12	·12	29
3	Tu	17	2	·41	13	·16	—30
4	We	18	3	·46	14	·22	1
5	Th	19	4	·50	15	·30	2
6	Fr	20	5	·58	16	·40	3
7	Sa	21	6	·67	17	·51	4
8	Su	22	7	·75	18	·62	5
9	Mo	23	8	·83	19	·72	6
10	Tu	24	9	·90	20	·82	7
11	We	25	10	·96	21	·89	8
12	Th	26	11	·98	22	·95	9
13	Fr	27	...	...	...	...	10
14	Sa	28	12 / 13	·01 / ·99	23	·00	11
15	Su	29	14	·97	24	·01	12
16	Mo	30	P	·92	25 / 26	·01 / ·99	13

Oct. — Solar: Chitrabhanu *Kanya—Purattasi.* (to 30), then Chitrabhanu *Tula—Aippasi.* — Lunar: Adhika, *Bahula*, Nija Asvina *Sukla* — Muhammadan: H. 1238, H 1238 *Safar.*

Cyclic Sidereal Year, Month and Day	Week-Day	English Month and Day	Tithi	Ending Moment	Nakshatra	Ending Moment	Muhammadan Year, Month and Day
17	Tu	1	1	·85	27	·95	14
18	We	2	2	·77	1	·91	15
19	Th	3	3	·68	2	·85	16
20	Fr	4	4	·59	3	·78	17
21	Sa	5	5	·49	4	·71	18
22	Su	6	6	·40	5	·64	19
23	Mo	7	7	·29	6	·58	20
24	Tu	8	8	·19	7	·52	21
25	We	9	9	·12	8	·47	22
26	Th	10	10	·05	9	·43	23
27	Fr	11	11 / 12	·00 / ·96	10	·41	24
28	Sa	12	13	·95	11	·42	25
29	Su	13	14	·95	12	·43	26
—30	Mo	14	—A	·97	13	·47	27
1	Tu	15	...	...	14	·53	28
2	We	16	1	·02	15	·61	29
3	Th	17	2	·07	16	·71	—30
4	Fr	18	3	·15	17	·81	1
5	Sa	19	4	·24	18	·92	2
6	Su	20	5	·33	...	...	3
7	Mo	21	6	·40	19	·02	4
8	Tu	22	7	·48	20	·12	5
9	We	23	8	·54	21	·20	6
10	Th	24	9	·56	22	·27	7
11	Fr	25	10	·59	23	·31	8
12	Sa	26	11	·57	24	·33	9
13	Su	27	12	·54	25	·33	10
14	Mo	28	13	·50	26	·32	11
15	Tu	29	14	·44	27	·29	12
16	We	30	P	·36	1	·24	13
17	Th	31	1	·27	2	·18	14

Nov. — Solar: Chitrabhanu *Tula—Aippasi.* (to 30), then Chitrabhanu *Vrischika—Kartigai.* — Lunar: Ni. Asv., *Bahula*, *Sukla* — Muhammadan: H. 1238 *Safar.*, *Rabi-ul-awwal.*

Cyclic Sidereal Year, Month and Day	Week-Day	English Month and Day	Tithi	Ending Moment	Nakshatra	Ending Moment	Muhammadan Year, Month and Day
18	Fr	1	2	·18	3	·12	15
19	Sa	2	3 / 4	·07 / ·98	4 / 5	·05 / ·90	16
20	Su	3	5	·88	6	·92	17
21	Mo	4	6	·80	7	·86	18
22	Tu	5	7	·72	8	·80	19
23	We	6	8	·64	9	·76	20
24	Th	7	9	·59	10	·75	21
25	Fr	8	10	·55	11	·74	22
26	Sa	9	11	·55	12	·75	23
27	Su	10	12	·55	13	·78	24
28	Mo	11	13	·58	14	·84	25
29	Tu	12	14	·62	15	·91	26
—30	We	13	—A	·69	...	...	27
1	Th	14	1	·78	16	·01	28
2	Fr	15	2	·86	17	·11	—29
3	Sa	16	3	·95	18	·22	1
4	Su	17	...	...	19	·33	2
5	Mo	18	4	·02	20	·42	3
6	Tu	19	5	·09	21	·51	4
7	We	20	6	·15	22	·58	5
8	Th	21	7	·19	23	·63	6
9	Fr	22	8	·20	24	·65	7
10	Sa	23	9	·18	25	·66	8
11	Su	24	10	·16	26	·65	9
12	Mo	25	11	·11	27	·62	10
13	Tu	26	12 / 13	·06 / ·98	1	·58	11
14	We	27	14	·90	2	·52	12
15	Th	28	P	·80	3	·46	13
16	Fr	29	1	·69	4	·40	14
17	Sa	30	2	·60	5	·33	15

Dec. — Solar: Chitrabhanu *Vrischika—Kartigai.* (to 30), then Chitrabhanu *Dhanus—Margali.* — Lunar: Kartika, *Bahula*, Margasira *Sukla* — Muhammadan: H. 1238, H. 1238 *Rabi-ul-akhir.*

Cyclic Sidereal Year, Month and Day	Week-Day	English Month and Day	Tithi	Ending Moment	Nakshatra	Ending Moment	Muhammadan Year, Month and Day
18	Su	1	3	·51	6	·26	16
19	Mo	2	4	·42	7	·19	17
20	Tu	3	5	·33	8	·14	18
21	We	4	6	·26	9	·09	19
22	Th	5	7	·22	10	·07	20
23	Fr	6	8	·19	11	·06	21
24	Sa	7	9	·17	12	·07	22
25	Su	8	10	·18	13	·10	23
26	Mo	9	11	·22	14	·15	24
27	Tu	10	12	·26	15	·22	25
28	We	11	13	·32	16	·31	26
29	Th	12	14	·42	17	·41	27
—30	Fr	13	—A	·51	18	·51	28
1	Sa	14	1	·59	19	·62	29
2	Su	15	2	·67	20	·73	—30
3	Mo	16	3	·74	21	·82	1
4	Tu	17	4	·79	22	·89	2
5	We	18	5	·84	23	·94	3
6	Th	19	6	·84	24	·97	4
7	Fr	20	7	·83	25	·99	5
8	Sa	21	8	·79	26	·98	6
9	Su	22	9	·75	27	·95	7
10	Mo	23	10	·69	1	·91	8
11	Tu	24	11	·61	2	·86	9
12	We	25	12	·53	3	·80	10
13	Th	26	13	·43	4	·73	11
14	Fr	27	14	·33	5	·66	12
15	Sa	28	P	·24	6	·59	13
16	Su	29	1	·15	7	·53	14
17	Mo	30	2 / 3	·05 / ·98	8	·47	15
18	Tu	31	4	·91	9	·43	16

15. Svati. 16. Visak. 17. Anur. 18. Jyesh. 19. Mula. 20. P. Ash. 21. U. Ash. 22. Sravn. 23. Dani. 24. Satab. 25. P. Bhad. 26. U. Bhad. 27. Rev

A. D. 1823. Solar Eclipse. ● Lunar Eclipse. ○

Mesha Sankranti (Commencement of Indian Sidereal Year). (Surya Sid.) April 11·70. (Arya Sid.) April 11·60.

Saka 1745. Kaliyuga 4924. (S. Cycle) Subhanu.

SOLAR reckoning: Cyclic Sidereal Year, Month and Day; Week-Day; English Month and Day. LUNAR reckoning: Tithi; Ending Moment; Nakshatra; Ending Moment; Muhammadan Year, Month and Day.

Jan. — Solar: Chitrabhanu Dhanus—Margali; Chitrabhanu Makara—Tai. Lunar: Marg. Bahula; Sukla; Magha. Muhammadan: H. 1238 Rabi-ul-akhir; H. 1238 Jumadal-awwal.

Cyclic Sidereal	Week-Day	English	Tithi	Ending Moment	Nakshatra	Ending Moment	Muhammadan
19	We	1	5	·86	10	·40	17
20	Th	2	6	·82	11	·39	18
21	Fr	3	7	·82	12	·39	19
22	Sa	4	8	·83	13	·41	20
23	Su	5	9	·86	14	·46	21
24	Mo	6	10	·91	15	·53	22
25	Tu	7	11	·98	16	·61	23
26	We	8	...	...	17	·71	24
27	Th	9	12	·06	18	·81	25
28	Fr	10	13	·16	19	·93	26
29	Sa	11	14	·24	...	...	27
1	Su	12	A	·32	20	·08	28
2	Mo	13	1	·40	21	·12	29
3	Tu	14	2	·44	22	·20	1
4	We	15	3	·48	23	·25	2
5	Th	16	4	·48	24	·30	3
6	Fr	17	5	·48	25	·31	4
7	Sa	18	6	·44	26	·31	5
8	Su	19	7	·40	27	·28	6
9	Mo	20	8	·33	1	·24	7
10	Tu	21	9	·26	2	·19	8
11	We	22	10	·15	3	·14	9
12	Th	23	11 / 12	·06 / ·96	4	·07	10
13	Fr	24	13	·87	5 / 6	·00 / ·93	11
14	Sa	25	14	·77	7	·86	12
15	Su ○	26	P	·69	8	·82	13
16	Mo	27	1	·62	9	·77	14
17	Tu	28	2	·55	10	·73	15
18	We	29	3	·50	11	·71	16
19	Th	30	4	·47	12	·71	17
20	Fr	31	5	·46	13	·74	18

Feb. — Solar: Chitrabhanu Makara—Tai; Chitrabhanu Kumbha—Masi. Lunar: Bahula; Sukla; Phalguna; Bah. Muhammadan: H. 1238 Jumadal-akhir.

Cyclic Sidereal	Week-Day	English	Tithi	Ending Moment	Nakshatra	Ending Moment	Muhammadan
21	Sa	1	6	·47	14	·78	19
22	Su	2	7	·51	15	·83	20
23	Mo	3	8	·56	16	·91	21
24	Tu	4	9	·63	...	...	22
25	We	5	10	·72	17	·01	23
26	Th	6	11	·80	18	·12	24
27	Fr	7	12	·88	19	·23	25
28	Sa	8	13	·97	20	·33	26
29	Su	9	...	...	21	·42	27
1	Mo	10	14	·04	22	·50	28
2	Tu ●	11	A	·09	23	·57	29
3	We	12	1	·11	24	·61	30
4	Th	13	2	·12	25	·63	1
5	Fr	14	3	·11	26	·63	2
6	Sa	15	4	·07	27	·61	3
7	Su	16	5 / 6	·02 / ·95	1	·58	4
8	Mo	17	7	·88	2	·54	5
9	Tu	18	8	·79	3	·48	6
10	We	19	9	·70	4	·41	7
11	Th	20	10	·59	5	·34	8
12	Fr	21	11	·49	6	·27	9
13	Sa	22	12	·39	7	·21	10
14	Su	23	13	·31	8	·15	11
15	Mo	24	14	·23	9	·10	12
16	Tu	25	P	·16	10	·06	13
17	We	26	1	·13	11	·03	14
18	Th	27	2	·09	12	·04	15
19	Fr	28	3	·08	13	·05	16

March — Solar: Chitrabhanu Kumbha—Masi; Chitrabhanu Mina—Panguni. Lunar: Phalg. Bahula; Sukla; Adhika Chaitra. Muhammadan: H. 1238 Jumadal-akhir; H. 1238 Rajab.

Cyclic Sidereal	Week-Day	English	Tithi	Ending Moment	Nakshatra	Ending Moment	Muhammadan
20	Sa	1	4	·09	14	·09	17
21	Su	2	5	·13	15	·14	18
22	Mo	3	6	·18	16	·22	19
23	Tu	4	7	·24	17	·32	20
24	We	5	8	·34	18	·42	21
25	Th	6	9	·42	19	·52	22
26	Fr	7	10	·51	20	·63	23
27	Sa	8	11	·59	21	·73	24
28	Su	9	12	·65	22	·81	25
29	Mo	10	13	·70	23	·88	26
30	Tu	11	14	·72	24	·93	27
1	We	12	A	·73	25	·95	28
2	Th	13	1	·71	26	·96	29
3	Fr	14	2	·68	27	·94	1
4	Sa	15	3	·62	1	·92	2
5	Su	16	4	·55	2	·87	3
6	Mo	17	5	·47	3	·81	4
7	Tu	18	6	·38	4	·75	5
8	We	19	7	·29	5	·68	6
9	Th	20	8	·18	6	·62	7
10	Fr	21	9 / 10	·09 / ·99	7	·55	8
11	Sa	22	11	·91	8	·49	9
12	Su	23	12	·82	9	·43	10
13	Mo	24	13	·75	10	·39	11
14	Tu	25	14	·72	11	·37	12
15	We	26	P.	·68	12	·36	13
16	Th	27	1	·67	13	·37	14
17	Fr	28	2	·67	14	·40	15
18	Sa	29	3	·72	15	·45	16
19	Su	30	4	·76	16	·53	17
20	Mo	31	5	·84	17	·62	18

April — Solar: Chitrabhanu Mina—Panguni; Subhanu Mesha—Chittirai. Lunar: Bahula; Sukla; Nija Chaitra; Bah. Muhammadan: H. 1238 Rajab; H. 1238 Shaban.

Cyclic Sidereal	Week-Day	English	Tithi	Ending Moment	Nakshatra	Ending Moment	Muhammadan
21	Tu	1	6	·92	18	·72	19
22	We	2	...	...	19	·82	20
23	Th	3	7	·00	20	·93	21
24	Fr	4	8	·09	...	...	22
25	Sa	5	9	·17	21	·03	23
26	Su	6	10	·23	22	·12	24
27	Mo	7	11	·27	23	·19	25
28	Tu	8	12	·30	24	·24	26
29	We	9	13	·30	25	·27	27
30	Th	10	14	·28	26	·28	28
31	Fr	11	A	·24	27	·28	29
1	Sa	12	1	·18	1	·25	30
2	Su	13	2	·12	2	·21	1
3	Mo	14	3 / 4	·03 / ·95	3	·15	2
4	Tu	15	5	·84	4	·09	3
5	We	16	6	·74	5 / 6	·03 / ·96	4
6	Th	17	7	·64	7	·89	5
7	Fr	18	8	·54	8	·82	6
8	Sa	19	9	·46	9	·77	7
9	Su	20	10	·37	10	·73	8
10	Mo	21	11	·31	11	·70	9
11	Tu	22	12	·26	12	·68	10
12	We	23	13	·22	13	·69	11
13	Th	24	14	·21	14	·71	12
14	Fr	25	P	·21	15	·76	13
15	Sa	26	1	·26	16	·83	14
16	Su	27	2	·30	17	·92	15
17	Mo	28	3	·38	...	...	16
18	Tu	29	4	·46	18	·01	17
19	We	30	5	·54	19	·12	18

May — Solar: Subhanu Mesha—Chittirai; Subhanu Vrishabha—Vaikasi. Lunar: Ni. Ch. Bahula; Sukla; Vaisakha. Muhammadan: H. 1238 Shaban; H. 1238 Ramzan.

Cyclic Sidereal	Week-Day	English	Tithi	Ending Moment	Nakshatra	Ending Moment	Muhammadan
20	Th	1	6	·61	20	·23	19
21	Fr	2	7	·69	21	·34	20
22	Sa	3	8	·76	22	·43	21
23	Su	4	9	·80	23	·50	22
24	Mo	5	10	·83	24	·55	23
25	Tu	6	11	·82	25	·59	24
26	We	7	12	·81	26	·61	25
27	Th	8	13	·77	27	·60	26
28	Fr	9	14	·71	1	·58	27
29	Sa	10	A	·65	2	·54	28
30	Su	11	1	·56	3	·49	29
31	Mo	12	2	·47	4	·44	1
1	Tu	13	3	·36	5	·37	2
2	We	14	4	·27	6	·30	3
3	Th	15	5	·16	7	·23	4
4	Fr	16	6 / 7	·05 / ·97	8	·16	5
5	Sa	17	8	·88	9	·11	6
6	Su	18	9	·82	10	·06	7
7	Mo	19	10	·78	11	·03	8
8	Tu	20	11	·74	12	·01	9
9	We	21	12	·72	13	·01	10
10	Th	22	13	·73	14	·03	11
11	Fr	23	14	·77	15	·08	12
12	Sa	24	P	·81	16	·14	13
13	Su	25	1	·88	17	·22	14
14	Mo	26	2	·95	18	·31	15
15	Tu	27	...	...	19	·42	16
16	We	28	3	·04	20	·53	17
17	Th	29	4	·12	21	·64	18
18	Fr	30	5	·20	22	·73	19
19	Sa	31	6	·26	23	·81	20

June — Solar: Subhanu Vrishabha—Vaikasi; Subhanu Mithuna—Ani. Lunar: Bahula; Sukla; Jyeshtha; Bahula. Muhammadan: H. 1238 Ramzan; H. 1238 Shawwal.

Cyclic Sidereal	Week-Day	English	Tithi	Ending Moment	Nakshatra	Ending Moment	Muhammadan
20	Su	1	7	·29	24	·87	21
21	Mo	2	8	·32	25	·91	22
22	Tu	3	9	·32	26	·93	23
23	We	4	10	·31	27	·93	24
24	Th	5	11	·27	1	·91	25
25	Fr	6	12	·22	2	·87	26
26	Sa	7	13	·14	3	·83	27
27	Su	8	14 / A	·06 / ·96	4	·77	28
28	Mo	9	1	·85	5	·71	29
29	Tu	10	2	·76	6	·63	30
30	We	11	3	·66	7	·56	1
31	Th	12	4	·56	8	·50	2
1	Fr	13	5	·47	9	·45	3
2	Sa	14	6	·39	10	·39	4
3	Su	15	7	·31	11	·36	5
4	Mo	16	8	·26	12	·33	6
5	Tu	17	9	·23	13	·33	7
6	We	18	10	·21	14	·35	8
7	Th	19	11	·21	15	·39	9
8	Fr	20	12	·24	16	·45	10
9	Sa	21	13	·29	17	·52	11
10	Su	22	14	·35	18	·61	12
11	Mo	23	P	·42	19	·73	13
12	Tu	24	1	·51	20	·83	14
13	We	25	2	·59	21	·94	15
14	Th	26	3	·67	...	...	16
15	Fr	27	4	·73	22	·03	17
16	Sa	28	5	·77	23	·11	18
17	Su	29	6	·80	24	·19	19
18	Mo	30	7	·80	25	·23	20

Naksh:—1. Asvu. 2. Bhar. 3. Krit. 4. Rohi. 5. Mrig. 6. Ardh. 7. Punar. 8. Push. 9. Aslesh. 10. Magh. 11. P. Phal. 12. U. Phal. 13. Hasta. 14. Chit.

N. B.—In this year the Lunar month **Pausha** is **Kshaya** *i.e.*, suppressed.

A. D. 1823.
A.—Amavasya. **P.—Paurnami.**
Kollam 999, Commences { **N. Malabar—Sept.** **S. Malabar—Aug.**
Hijra 1239, Commences, **Sep. 7.**
Vikrama 1880. **Bengal San 1229.** **(N. Cycle) Jaya.**

SOLAR reckoning. Cyclic Sidereal Year, Month and Day.	Week-Day	English Month and Day.	LUNAR reckoning. Tithi	Ending Moment.	Nakshatra	Ending Moment.	Muhammadan Year, Month and Day.
	July						
Subhanu *Mithuna—Ani.* 19	Tu	1	Jyesh. *Bahula* 8	·79	26	·25	H. 1238 *Shawwal.* 21
20	We	2	9	·74	27	·25	22
21	Th	3	10	·70	1	·24	23
22	Fr	4	11	·62	2	·20	24
23	Sa	5	12	·54	3	·17	25
24	Su	6	13	·44	4	·11	26
25	Mo	7	14	·35	5 6	·04 ·97	27
26	Tu	8	A	·24	7	·90	28
27	We	9	Ashadha *Sukla* 1	·13	8	·84	29
28	Th	10	2 3	·04 ·94	9	·78	H. 1238 *Zi-l-ka'da.* 1
29	Fr	11	4	·86	10	·73	2
30	Sa	12	5	·79	11	·69	3
31	Su	13	6	·75	12	·60	4
32	Mo	14	7	·70	13	·66	5
Subhanu *Karkata—Adi.* 1	Tu	15	8	·68	14	·67	6
2	We	16	9	·70	15	·70	7
3	Th	17	10	·71	16	·75	8
4	Fr	18	11	·77	17	·82	9
5	Sa	19	12	·83	18	·92	10
6	Su	20	13	·90	...	...	11
7	Mo	21	14	·97	19	·02	12
8	Tu	22	...	...	20	·13	13
9	We ○	23	P	·06	21	·24	14
10	Th	24	*Bahula* 1	·14	22	·33	15
11	Fr	25	2	·19	23	·43	16
12	Sa	26	3	·25	24	·50	17
13	Su	27	4	·28	25	·54	18
14	Mo	28	5	·29	26	·57	19
15	Tu	29	6	·27	27	·58	20
16	We	30	7	·28	1	·57	21
17	Th	31	8	·18	2	·55	22
	Aug.						
18	Fr	1	9	·11	3	·50	23
19	Sa	2	10 11	·03 ·93	4	·45	24
20	Su	3	12	·84	5	·38	25
21	Mo	4	13	·74	6	·31	26
22	Tu	5	14	·63	7	·25	27
23	We	6	A	·53	8	·18	28
24	Th	7	Sravana *Sukla* 1	·44	9	·12	29
25	Fr	8	2	·36	10	·06	30
26	Sa	9	3	·28	11	·02	H. 1238 *Zi-l-hijja.* 1
27	Su	10	4	·23	12 13	·00 ·98	2
28	Mo	11	5	·19	14	·99	3
29	Tu	12	6	·18	...	...	4
30	We	13	7	·19	15	·01	5
31	Th	14	8	·20	16	·06	6
Subhanu *Simha—Avani.* 1	Fr	15	9	·25	17	·14	7
2	Sa	16	10	·32	18	·22	8
3	Su	17	11	·39	19	·32	9
4	Mo	18	12	·47	20	·42	10
5	Tu	19	13	·56	21	·53	11
6	We	20	14	·63	22	·63	12
7	Th	21	P	·70	23	·73	13
8	Fr	22	*Bahula* 1	·74	24	·80	14
9	Sa	23	2	·78	25	·86	15
10	Su	24	3	·78	26	·89	16
11	Mo	25	4	·76	27	·90	17
12	Tu	26	5	·73	1	·90	18
13	We	27	6	·69	2	·88	19
14	Th	28	7	·62	3	·83	20
15	Fr	29	8	·54	4	·78	21
16	Sa	30	9	·43	5	·72	22
17	Su	31	10	·34	6	·66	23

SOLAR reckoning. Cyclic Sidereal Year, Month and Day.	Week-Day	English Month and Day.	LUNAR reckoning. Tithi	Ending Moment.	Nakshatra	Ending Moment.	Muhammadan Year, Month and Day.
	Sep.						
Subhanu *Simha—Avani.* 18	Mo	1	*Bah.* 11	·24	7	·59	*Zi-l-hijja.* 24
19	Tu	2	12	·14	8	·52	25
20	We	3	13 14	·04 ·96	9	·45	26
21	Th	4	A	·87	10	·39	27
22	Fr	5	Bhadrapada *Sukla* 1	·81	11	·36	28
23	Sa	6	2	·73	12	·32	29
24	Su	7	3	·70	13	·31	H. 1239 *Muharram.* 1
25	Mo	8	4	·69	14	·31	2
26	Tu	9	5	·71	15	·33	3
27	We	10	6	·72	16	·38	4
28	Th	11	7	·77	17	·44	5
29	Fr	12	8	·83	18	·53	6
30	Sa	13	9	·90	19	·62	7
31	Su	14	10	·98	20	·73	8
Subhanu *Kanya—Purattasi.* 1	Mo	15	...	...	21	·83	9
2	Tu	16	11	·08	22	·94	10
3	We	17	12	·15	...	...	11
4	Th	18	13	·22	23	·04	12
5	Fr	19	14	·26	24	·11	13
6	Sa	20	P	·30	25	·17	14
7	Su	21	*Bahula* 1	·31	26	·21	15
8	Mo	22	2	·29	27	·23	16
9	Tu	23	3	·27	1	·23	17
10	We	24	4	·22	2	·21	18
11	Th	25	5	·15	3	·17	19
12	Fr	26	6 7	·07 ·98	4	·12	20
13	Sa	27	8	·89	5	·07	21
14	Su	28	9	·80	6 7	·00 ·93	22
15	Mo	29	10	·69	8	·86	23
16	Tu	30	11	·58	9	·79	24
	Oct.						
17	We	1	12	·49	10	·74	25
18	Th	2	13	·41	11	·69	26
19	Fr	3	14	·34	12	·65	27
20	Sa	4	A	·28	13	·63	28
21	Su	5	Asvina *Sukla* 1	·26	14	·63	29
22	Mo	6	2	·24	15	·64	30
23	Tu	7	3	·26	16	·69	H. 1239 *Safar.* 1
24	We	8	4	·27	17	·75	2
25	Th	9	5	·32	18	·83	3
26	Fr	10	6	·59	19	·92	4
27	Sa	11	7	·46	...	...	5
28	Su	12	8	·56	20	·02	6
29	Mo	13	9	·64	21	·14	7
30	Tu	14	10	·72	22	·24	8
Subhanu *Tula—Aippasi.* 1	We	15	11	·79	23	·34	9
2	Th	16	12	·83	24	·42	10
3	Fr	17	13	·87	25	·48	11
4	Sa	18	14	·88	26	·53	12
5	Su	19	P	·87	27	·55	13
6	Mo	20	*Bahula* 1	·84	1	·55	14
7	Tu	21	2	·80	2	·53	15
8	We	22	3	·73	3	·50	16
9	Th	23	4	·65	4	·46	17
10	Fr	24	5	·56	5	·40	18
11	Sa	25	6	·46	6	·34	19
12	Su	26	7	·37	7	·27	20
13	Mo	27	8	·26	8	·20	21
14	Tu	28	9	·17	9	·14	22
15	We	29	10	·07	10	·08	23
16	Th	30	11 12	·00 ·94	11 12	·02 ·98	24
17	Fr	31	13	·87	13	·96	25

SOLAR reckoning. Cyclic Sidereal Year, Month and Day.	Week-Day	English Month and Day.	LUNAR reckoning. Tithi	Ending Moment.	Nakshatra	Ending Moment.	Muhammadan Year, Month and Day.
	Nov.						
Subhanu *Tula—Aippasi.* 18	Sa	1	14	·85	14	·95	*Safar.* 26
19	Su	2	A	·83	15	·97	27
20	Mo	3	Karttika *Sukla* 1	·84	...	...	28
21	Tu	4	2	·87	16	·00	29
22	We	5	3	·93	17	·06	H. 1239 *Rabi-ul-awwal.* 1
23	Th	6	4	·99	18	·13	2
24	Fr	7	...	...	19	·22	3
25	Sa	8	5	·07	20	·33	4
26	Su	9	6	·16	21	·44	5
27	Mo	10	7	·25	22	·54	6
28	Tu	11	8	·33	23	·64	7
29	We	12	9	·39	24	·72	8
30	Th	13	10	·44	25	·80	9
Subhanu *Vrischika—Kartigai.* 1	Fr	14	11	·48	26	·85	10
2	Sa	15	12	·49	27	·87	11
3	Su	16	13	·48	1	·88	12
4	Mo	17	14	·44	2	·86	13
5	Tu	18	P	·40	3	·84	14
6	We	19	*Bahula* 1	·34	4	·80	15
7	Th	20	2	·27	5	·74	16
8	Fr	21	3	·18	6	·68	17
9	Sa	22	4 5	·07 ·98	7	·61	18
10	Su	23	6	·88	8	·53	19
11	Mo	24	7	·79	9	·47	20
12	Tu	25	8	·69	10	·41	21
13	We	26	9	·63	11	·36	22
14	Th	27	10	·56	12	·31	23
15	Fr	28	11	·50	13	·28	24
16	Sa	29	12	·47	14	·28	25
17	Su	30	13	·45	15	·29	26
	Dec.						
18	Mo	1	14	·48	16	·32	27
19	Tu	2	A	·50	17	·37	28
20	We	3	Margasira *Sukla* 1	·55	18	·43	29
21	Th	4	2	·61	19	·53	30
22	Fr	5	3	·71	20	·63	H. 1239 *Rabi-ul-akhir.* 1
23	Sa	6	4	·79	21	·74	2
24	Su	7	5	·87	22	·84	3
25	Mo	8	6	·96	23	·94	4
26	Tu	9	...	...	...	...	5
27	We	10	7	·03	24	·04	6
28	Th	11	8	·09	25	·11	7
29	Fr	12	9	·11	26	·16	8
30	Sa	13	10	·13	27	·19	9
Subhanu *Dhanus—Margali.* 1	Su	14	11	·11	1	·20	10
2	Mo	15	12	·07	2	·20	11
3	Tu	16	13 14	·03 ·96	3	·17	12
4	We	17	P	·89	4	·13	13
5	Th	18	*Bahula* 1	·80	5	·09	14
6	Fr	19	2	·71	6 7	·01 ·94	15
7	Sa	20	3	·60	8	·88	16
8	Su	21	4	·51	9	·81	17
9	Mo	22	5	·42	10	·75	18
10	Tu	23	6	·32	11	·69	19
11	We	24	7	·25	12	·64	20
12	Th	25	8	·19	13	·62	21
13	Fr	26	9	·14	14	·60	22
14	Sa	27	10	·11	15	·61	23
15	Su	28	11	·11	16	·63	24
16	Mo	29	12	·12	17	·68	25
17	Tu	30	13	·14	18	·75	26
18	We	31	14	·21	19	·83	27

15. Svati. 16. Visak. 17. Anur. 18. Jyesh. 19. Mula. 20. P. Ash. 21. U. Ash. 22. Sravn. 23. Dani. 24. Satab. 25. P. Bhad. 26. U. Bhad. 27 Rev.

A. D. 1824. **Mesha Sankranti** (Commencement of Indian Sidereal Year).

Solar Eclipse. ● **(Surya Sid.) April 10·95.** **Saka 1746.** **Kaliyuga 4925.**

Lunar Eclipse. ○ **(Arya Sid.) April 10·85.** **(S. Cycle) Tarana.**

Columns: SOLAR reckoning (Cyclic Sidereal Year, Month and Day; Week-Day; English Month and Day) — LUNAR reckoning (Tithi; Ending Moment; Nakshatra; Ending Moment; Muhammadan Year, Month and Day).

Jan. — Solar: Subhanu *Dhanus—Margali*; Subhanu *Makara—Tai*. Lunar: Pausha (*Sukla*, *Bahula*). Muhammadan: H. 1239 *Jumadal-awwal*.

Cyclic Sidereal Year, Month and Day	Week-Day	English Month and Day	Tithi	Ending Moment	Nakshatra	Ending Moment	Muhammadan Year, Month and Day
19	Th	1	—A	·27	20	·93	28
20	Fr	2	1	·36	...	...	—29
21	Sa	3	2	·44	21	·03	1
22	Su	4	3	·54	22	·14	2
23	Mo	5	4	·61	23	·25	3
24	Tu	6	5	·68	24	·34	4
25	We	7	6	·74	25	·42	5
26	Th	8	7	·76	26	·47	6
27	Fr	9	8	·77	27	·51	7
28	Sa	10	9	·76	1	·52	8
—29	Su	11	10	·73	2	·53	9
1	Mo	12	11	·67	3	·50	10
2	Tu	13	12	·62	4	·46	11
3	We	14	13	·54	5	·41	12
4	Th	15	14	·44	6	·35	13
5	Fr ○	16	P	·35	7	·29	14
6	Sa	17	1	·25	8	·22	15
7	Su	18	2	·16	9	·15	16
8	Mo	19	3 4	·06 ·98	10	·08	17
9	Tu	20	5	·90	11 12	·02 ·99	18
10	We	21	6	·83	13	·95	19
11	Th	22	7	·78	14	·93	20
12	Fr	23	8	·76	15	·93	21
13	Sa	24	9	·75	16	·95	22
14	Su	25	10	·76	...	...	23
15	Mo	26	11	·80	17	·00	24
16	Tu	27	12	·86	18	·06	25
17	We	28	13	·93	19	·13	26
18	Th	29	...	...	20	·23	27
19	Fr	0	14	·01	21	·33	28
20	Sa	1	—A	·09	22	·44	29

Feb. — Solar: Subhanu *Kumbha—Masi*. Lunar: Magha (*Sukla*, *Bahula*). Muhammadan: H. 1239 *Jumadal-akhir*.

Cyclic Sidereal Year, Month and Day	Week-Day	English Month and Day	Tithi	Ending Moment	Nakshatra	Ending Moment	Muhammadan Year, Month and Day
21	Su	1	1	·19	23	·55	—30
22	Mo	2	2	·26	24	·64	1
23	Tu	3	3	·33	25	·72	2
24	We	4	4	·38	26	·78	3
25	Th	5	5	·41	27	·82	4
26	Fr	6	6	·41	1	·85	5
27	Sa	7	7	·39	2	·85	6
28	Su	8	8	·35	3	·83	7
29	Mo	9	9	·30	4	·80	8
—30	Tu	10	10	·24	5	·75	9
1	We	11	11	·16	6	·70	10
2	Th	12	12 13	·07 ·97	7	·63	11
3	Fr	13	14	·87	8	·56	12
4	Sa	14	P	·78	9	·49	13
5	Su	15	1	·68	10	·42	14
6	Mo	16	2	·59	11	·37	15
7	Tu	17	3	·52	12	·32	16
8	We	18	4	·46	13	·28	17
9	Th	19	5	·41	14	·25	18
10	Fr	20	6	·39	15	·25	19
11	Sa	21	7	·37	16	·27	20
12	Su	22	8	·38	17	·31	21
13	Mo	23	9	·43	18	·36	22
14	Tu	24	10	·48	19	·44	23
15	We	25	11	·55	20	·53	24
16	Th	26	12	·63	21	·63	25
17	Fr	27	13	·73	22	·74	26
18	Sa	28	14	·80	23	·85	27
19	Su	29	—A	·88	24	·95	28

March — Solar: Subhanu *Kumbha—Masi*; Subhanu *Mina—Panguni*. Lunar: Phalguna (*Sukla*, *Bahula*). Muhammadan: H. 1239 *Rajab*.

Cyclic Sidereal Year, Month and Day	Week-Day	English Month and Day	Tithi	Ending Moment	Nakshatra	Ending Moment	Muhammadan Year, Month and Day
20	Mo	1	1	·95	...	...	—29
21	Tu	2	...	...	25	·03	1
22	We	3	2	·00	26	·09	2
23	Th	4	3	·02	27	·15	3
24	Fr	5	4	·02	1	·17	4
25	Sa	6	5 6	·01 ·97	2	·18	5
26	Su	7	7	·91	3	·16	6
27	Mo	8	8	·85	4	·13	7
28	Tu	9	9	·76	5	·09	8
29	We	10	10	·68	6 7	·03 ·97	9
30	Th	11	11	·58	8	·90	10
—31	Fr	12	12	·48	9	·83	11
1	Sa	13	13	·38	10	·77	12
2	Su	14	14	·29	11	·71	13
3	Mo	15	P	·19	12	·65	14
4	Tu	16	1	·11	13	·61	15
5	We	17	2	·05	14	·58	16
6	Th	18	3 4	·00 ·99	15	·57	17
7	Fr	19	5	·97	16	·59	18
8	Sa	20	...	...	17	·62	19
9	Su	21	6	·00	18	·67	20
10	Mo	22	7	·02	19	·74	21
11	Tu	23	8	·07	20	·83	22
12	We	24	9	·15	21	·94	23
13	Th	25	10	·23	...	...	24
14	Fr	26	11	·32	22	·04	25
15	Sa	27	12	·40	23	·15	26
16	Su	28	13	·48	24	·25	27
17	Mo	29	14	·53	25	·33	28
18	Tu	30	—A	·58	26	·41	29
19	We	31	1	·61	27	·46	—30

April — Solar: Subhanu *Mina—Panguni*; Tarana *Mesha—Chittirai*. Lunar: Chaitra (*Sukla*, *Bahula*). Muhammadan: H. 1239 *Shaban*.

Cyclic Sidereal Year, Month and Day	Week-Day	English Month and Day	Tithi	Ending Moment	Nakshatra	Ending Moment	Muhammadan Year, Month and Day
20	Th	1	2	·60	1	·49	1
21	Fr	2	3	·59	2	·50	2
22	Sa	3	4	·54	3	·49	3
23	Su	4	5	·49	4	·47	4
24	Mo	5	6	·42	5	·43	5
25	Tu	6	7	·34	6	·37	6
26	We	7	8	·25	7	·31	7
27	Th	8	9	·14	8	·24	8
28	Fr	9	10 11	·04 ·94	9	·18	9
—29	Sa	10	12	·85	10	·11	10
1	Su	11	13	·75	11 12	·05 ·98	11
2	Mo	12	14	·68	13	·94	12
3	Tu	13	P	·61	14	·91	13
4	We	14	1	·56	15	·90	14
5	Th	15	2	·54	16	·91	15
6	Fr	16	3	·52	17	·93	16
7	Sa	17	4	·54	18	·98	17
8	Su	18	5	·57	...	...	18
9	Mo	19	6	·63	19	·04	19
10	Tu	20	7	·70	20	·14	20
11	We	21	8	·79	21	·23	21
12	Th	22	9	·86	22	·34	22
13	Fr	23	10	·94	23	·45	23
14	Sa	24	...	...	24	·55	24
15	Su	25	11	·01	25	·65	25
16	Mo	26	12	·07	26	·72	26
17	Tu	27	13	·13	27	·78	27
18	We	28	14	·14	1	·81	28
19	Th	29	—A	·15	2	·82	—29
20	Fr	30	1	·13	3	·82	1

May — Solar: Tarana *Mesha—Chittirai*; Tarana *Vrishabha—Vaikasi*. Lunar: Vaisakha (*Sukla*, *Bahula*). Muhammadan: H. 1239 *Ramzan*.

Cyclic Sidereal Year, Month and Day	Week-Day	English Month and Day	Tithi	Ending Moment	Nakshatra	Ending Moment	Muhammadan Year, Month and Day
21	Sa	1	2	·08	4	·80	2
22	Su	2	3 4	·02 ·95	5	·76	3
23	Mo	3	5	·87	6	·71	4
24	Tu	4	6	·78	7	·64	5
25	We	5	7	·69	8	·58	6
26	Th	6	8	·57	9	·52	7
27	Fr	7	9	·47	10	·44	8
28	Sa	8	10	·37	11	·38	9
29	Su	9	11	·28	12	·32	10
30	Mo	10	12	·21	13	·27	11
—31	Tu	11	13	·13	14	·25	12
1	We	12	14	·09	15	·23	13
2	Th	13	P	·06	16	·23	14
3	Fr	14	1	·05	17	·25	15
4	Sa	15	2	·06	18	·29	16
5	Su	16	3	·08	19	·36	17
6	Mo	17	4	·14	20	·44	18
7	Tu	18	5	·21	21	·53	19
8	We	19	6	·29	22	·64	20
9	Th	20	7	·37	23	·74	21
10	Fr	21	8	·45	24	·86	22
11	Sa	22	9	·53	25	·95	23
12	Su	23	10	·59	...	...	24
13	Mo	24	11	·64	26	·03	25
14	Tu	25	12	·64	27	·09	26
15	We	26	13	·65	1	·12	27
16	Th	27	14	·63	2	·15	28
17	Fr	28	—A	·60	3	·15	29
18	Sa	29	1	·53	4	·12	—30
19	Su	30	2	·45	5	·09	1
20	Mo	31	3	·37	6 7	·04 ·98	2

June — Solar: Tarana *Mithuna—Ani*. Lunar: Jyeshtha (*Sukla*, *Bahula*); A. *Suk.* Muhammadan: H. 1239 *Shawwal*.

Cyclic Sidereal Year, Month and Day	Week-Day	English Month and Day	Tithi	Ending Moment	Nakshatra	Ending Moment	Muhammadan Year, Month and Day
21	Tu	1	4	·27	8	·92	3
22	We	2	5	·17	9	·85	4
23	Th	3	6 7	·07 ·98	10	·78	5
24	Fr	4	8	·87	11	·72	6
25	Sa	5	9	·79	12	·65	7
26	Su	6	10	·71	13	·61	8
27	Mo	7	11	·64	14	·58	9
28	Tu	8	12	·59	15	·55	10
29	We	9	13	·55	16	·55	11
30	Th	10	14	·54	17	·56	12
—31	Fr	11	P	·55	18	·61	13
1	Sa	12	1	·58	19	·67	14
2	Su	13	2	·62	20	·74	15
3	Mo	14	3	·69	21	·83	16
4	Tu	15	4	·76	22	·94	17
5	We	16	5	·84	...	...	18
6	Th	17	6	·93	23	·05	19
7	Fr	18	...	...	24	·16	20
8	Sa	19	7	·01	25	·25	21
9	Su	20	8	·07	26	·33	22
10	Mo	21	9	·11	27	·40	23
11	Tu	22	10	·13	1	·44	24
12	We	23	11	·13	2	·47	25
13	Th	24	12	·11	3	·47	26
14	Fr	25	13	·08	4	·46	27
15	Sa ●	26	14 A	·01 ·95	5	·42	28
16	Su	27	1	·86	6	·38	—29
17	Mo	28	2	·77	7	·33	1
18	Tu	29	3	·66	8	·26	2
19	We	30	4	·56	9	·19	3

Naksh :—1. Asvn. 2. Bhar. 3. Krit. 4. Rohi. 5. Mrig. 6. Ardh. 7. Punar. 8. Push. 9. Aslesh. 10. Magh. 11. P. Phal. 12. U. Phal. 13. Hasta. 14. Chit.

A. D. 1824. **Vikrama 1881.**

A.—Amavasya. Kollam 1000, Commences { **N. Malabar—Sept.** / **S. Malabar—Aug.** } **Hijra 1240,** Commences, **Aug. 26.** **Bengal San 1230.**

P.—Paurnami. **(N. Cycle) Manmatha.**

Cyclic Sidereal Year, Month and Day.	Week-Day	English Month and Day.	Tithi	Ending Moment.	Nakshatra	Ending Moment.	Muhammadan Year, Month and Day.
	July						
20	Th	1	5	·46	10	·12	4
21	Fr	2	6	·35	11	·05	5
22	Sa	3	7	·27	12 / 13	·00 / ·95	6
23	Su	4	8	·19	14	·91	7
24	Mo	5	9	·12	15	·88	8
25	Tu	6	10	·06	16	·87	9
26	We	7	11	·03	17	·89	10
27	Th	8	12	·01	18	·92	11
28	Fr	9	13	·02	19	·97	12
29	Sa	10	14	·06	...	...	13
30	Su ○	11	P	·09	20	·05	14
31	Mo	12	1	·17	21	·13	15
32	Tu	13	2	·24	22	·24	16
1	We	14	3	·32	23	·35	17
2	Th	15	4	·40	24	·46	18
3	Fr	16	5	·48	25	·55	19
4	Sa	17	6	·55	26	·64	20
5	Su	18	7	·58	27	·71	21
6	Mo	19	8	·61	1	·76	22
7	Tu	20	9	·61	2	·79	23
8	We	21	10	·60	3	·80	24
9	Th	22	11	·55	4	·79	25
10	Fr	23	12	·49	5	·76	26
11	Sa	24	13	·43	6	·72	27
12	Su	25	14	·34	7	·67	28
13	Mo	26	A	·26	8	·60	29
14	Tu	27	1	·16	9	·53	30
15	We	28	2 / 3	·06 / ·94	10	·46	1
16	Th	29	4	·84	11	·40	2
17	Fr	30	5	·76	12	·34	3
18	Sa	31	6	·67	13	·28	4
	Aug.						
19	Su	1	7	·60	14	·24	5
20	Mo	2	8	·54	15	·21	6
21	Tu	3	9	·52	16	·20	7
22	We	4	10	·49	17	·21	8
23	Th	5	11	·51	18	·24	9
24	Fr	6	12	·53	19	·28	10
25	Sa	7	13	·57	20	·35	11
26	Su	8	14	·64	21	·43	12
27	Mo	9	P	·71	22	·54	13
28	Tu	10	1	·80	23	·64	14
29	We	11	2	·88	24	·75	15
30	Th	12	3	·97	25	·85	16
31	Fr	13	...	...	26	·94	17
1	Sa	14	4	·03	...	...	18
2	Su	15	5	·06	27	·03	19
3	Mo	16	6	·10	1	·08	20
4	Tu	17	7	·10	2	·11	21
5	We	18	8	·09	3	·12	22
6	Th	19	9	·05	4	·11	23
7	Fr	20	10 / 11	·00 / ·93	5	·10	24
8	Sa	21	12	·84	6	·05	25
9	Su	22	13	·76	7 / 8	·00 / ·94	26
10	Mo	23	14	·65	9	·87	27
11	Tu	24	A	·55	10	·81	28
12	We	25	1	·44	11	·74	29
13	Th	26	2	·35	12	·67	1
14	Fr	27	3	·26	13	·61	2
15	Sa	28	4	·19	14	·57	3
16	Su	29	5	·12	15	·53	4
17	Mo	30	6	·05	16	·53	5
18	Tu	31	7	·02	17	·53	6

Side labels: Tarana *Mithuna—Ani.*; Tarana *Karkata—Adi.*; Tarana *Simha—Avani.*; *Sukla*; Ashadha; *Bahula*; *Sukla*; Sravana; *Bahula*; Bhad. *Suk.*; H. 1239 *Zi-l-ka'da.*; H. 1239 *Zi-l-hijja.*; H. 1240 *M.*

Cyclic Sidereal Year, Month and Day.	Week-Day	English Month and Day.	Tithi	Ending Moment.	Nakshatra	Ending Moment.	Muhammadan Year, Month and Day.
	Sep.						
19	We	1	8	·00	18	·55	7
20	Th	2	9	·02	19	·59	8
21	Fr	3	10	·04	20	·65	9
22	Sa	4	11	·09	21	·75	10
23	Su	5	12	·16	22	·84	11
24	Mo	6	13	·22	23	·95	12
25	Tu	7	14	·30	...	...	13
26	We	8	P	·39	24	·05	14
27	Th	9	1	·47	25	·15	15
28	Fr	10	2	·54	26	·26	16
29	Sa	11	3	·59	27	·33	17
30	Su	12	4	·61	1	·39	18
31	Mo	13	5	·62	2	·43	19
1	Tu	14	6	·61	3	·44	20
2	We	15	7	·58	4	·45	21
3	Th	16	8	·53	5	·43	22
4	Fr	17	9	·46	6	·39	23
5	Sa	18	10	·38	7	·34	24
6	Su	19	11	·27	8	·28	25
7	Mo	20	12	·18	9	·22	26
8	Tu	21	13 / 14	·09 / ·98	10	·15	27
9	We	22	A	·88	11	·08	28
10	Th	23	1	·79	12 / 13	·01 / ·95	29
11	Fr	24	2	·72	14	·90	30
12	Sa	25	3	·65	15	·87	1
13	Su	26	4	·59	16	·85	2
14	Mo	27	5	·56	17	·85	3
15	Tu	28	6	·54	18	·86	4
16	We	29	7	·56	19	·90	5
17	Th	30	8	·58	20	·97	6
	Oct.						
18	Fr	1	9	·63	...	...	7
19	Sa	2	10	·69	21	·05	8
20	Su	3	11	·77	22	·14	9
21	Mo	4	12	·86	23	·24	10
22	Tu	5	13	·95	24	·35	11
23	We	6	...	...	25	·46	12
24	Th	7	14	·02	26	·56	13
25	Fr	8	P	·09	27	·64	14
26	Sa	9	1	·14	1	·70	15
27	Su	10	2	·16	2	·74	16
28	Mo	11	3	·19	3	·77	17
29	Tu	12	4	·17	4	·77	18
30	We	13	5	·15	5	·75	19
31	Th	14	6	·09	6	·72	20
1	Fr	15	7 / 8	·02 / ·94	7	·67	21
2	Sa	16	9	·84	8	·61	22
3	Su	17	10	·75	9	·56	23
4	Mo	18	11	·66	10	·49	24
5	Tu	19	12	·55	11	·42	25
6	We	20	13	·45	12	·35	26
7	Th	21	14	·36	13	·28	27
8	Fr	22	A	·29	14	·24	28
9	Sa	23	1	·23	15	·20	29
10	Su	24	2	·17	16	·18	1
11	Mo	25	3	·14	17	·17	2
12	Tu	26	4	·13	18	·18	3
13	We	27	5	·15	19	·22	4
14	Th	28	6	·17	20	·28	5
15	Fr	29	7	·22	21	·35	6
16	Sa	30	8	·29	22	·44	7
17	Su	31	9	·37	23	·54	8

Side labels: Tarana *Simha—Avani.*; Tarana *Kanya—Purattasi.*; Tarana *Tula—Aippasi.*; *Sukla*; Bhadrapada; *Bahula*; *Sukla*; Asvina; *Bahula*; Kartika *Sukla*; H. 1240 *Muharram.*; H. 1240 *Safar.*; *Rabi-ul-awwal.*

Cyclic Sidereal Year, Month and Day.	Week-Day	English Month and Day.	Tithi	Ending Moment.	Nakshatra	Ending Moment.	Muhammadan Year, Month and Day.
	Nov.						
18	Mo	1	10	·45	24	·66	9
19	Tu	2	11	·55	25	·76	10
20	We	3	12	·62	26	·86	11
21	Th	4	13	·69	27	·94	12
22	Fr	5	14	·74	...	...	13
23	Sa	6	P	·77	1	·01	14
24	Su	7	1	·78	2	·07	15
25	Mo	8	2	·76	3	·09	16
26	Tu	9	3	·73	4	·10	17
27	We	10	4	·69	5	·08	18
28	Th	11	5	·63	6	·05	19
29	Fr	12	6	·54	7 / 8	·01 / ·96	20
30	Sa	13	7	·44	9	·89	21
1	Su	14	8	·35	10	·82	22
2	Mo	15	9	·26	11	·75	23
3	Tu	16	10	·16	12	·68	24
4	We	17	11 / 12	·06 / ·98	13	·63	25
5	Th	18	13	·90	14	·58	26
6	Fr	19	14	·84	15	·53	27
7	Sa	20	A	·78	16	·50	28
8	Su	21	1	·75	17	·49	29
9	Mo	22	2	·75	18	·51	30
10	Tu	23	3	·76	19	·54	1
11	We	24	4	·79	20	·59	2
12	Th	25	5	·84	21	·66	3
13	Fr	26	6	·92	22	·74	4
14	Sa	27	...	...	23	·85	5
15	Su	28	7	·00	24	·96	6
16	Mo	29	8	·08	...	...	7
17	Tu	30	9	·17	25	·06	8
	Dec.						
18	We	1	10	·25	26	·16	9
19	Th	2	11	·32	27	·25	10
20	Fr	3	12	·37	1	·32	11
21	Sa	4	13	·40	2	·38	12
22	Su	5	14	·41	3	·41	13
23	Mo	6	P	·39	4	·42	14
24	Tu	7	1	·36	5	·41	15
25	We	8	2	·31	6	·38	16
26	Th	9	3	·25	7	·35	17
27	Fr	10	4	·16	8	·30	18
28	Sa	11	5 / 6	·07 / ·98	9	·23	19
29	Su	12	7	·89	10	·16	20
1	Mo	13	8	·78	11	·09	21
2	Tu	14	9	·68	12 / 13	·03 / ·97	22
3	We	15	10	·60	14	·91	23
4	Th	16	11	·52	15	·86	24
5	Fr	17	12	·46	16	·83	25
6	Sa	18	13	·42	17	·82	26
7	Su	19	14	·40	18	·83	27
8	Mo ●	20	A	·38	19	·85	28
9	Tu	21	1	·39	20	·90	29
10	We	22	2	·44	21	·96	1
11	Th	23	3	·49	...	...	2
12	Fr	24	4	·56	22	·05	3
13	Sa	25	5	·65	23	·15	4
14	Su	26	6	·74	24	·25	5
15	Mo	27	7	·82	25	·36	6
16	Tu	28	8	·91	26	·46	7
17	We	29	9	·97	27	·55	8
18	Th	30	...	...	1	·64	9
19	Fr	31	10	·01	2	·69	10

Side labels: Tarana *Tula—Aippasi.*; Tarana *Vrischika—Kartigai.*; Tarana *Dhanus—Margali.*; *Suk.*; Kartika; *Bahula*; *Sukla*; Margasira; *Bahula*; *Sukla*; Pausha; H. 1240 *Rabi-ul-awwal.*; H. 1240 *Rabi-ul-akhir.*; *Jumada-l-awwal.*

15. Svati. 16. Visak. 17. Anur. 18. Jyesh. 19. Mula. 20. P. Ash. 21. U. Ash. 22. Sravn. 23. Dani. 24. Satab. 25. P. Bhad. 26. U. Bhad. 27. Rev

A. D. 1825. **Mesha Sankranti** (Commencement of Indian Sidereal Year).
Solar Eclipse. ● **(Surya Sid.) April 11·21.** **Saka 1747.** **Kaliyuga 4926.**
Lunar Eclipse. ○ **(Arya Sid.) April 11·11.** **(S. Cycle) Parthiva.**

Column headings (each group of three months): SOLAR reckoning — Cyclic Sidereal Year, Month and Day; Week-Day; English Month and Day. LUNAR reckoning — Tithi; Ending Moment; Nakshatra; Ending Moment; Muhammadan Year, Month and Day.

Jan.

Cyclic Sidereal Year, Month and Day	Week-Day	English Month and Day	Tithi	Ending Moment	Nakshatra	Ending Moment	Muhammadan Year, Month and Day
Tarana Dhanus—Margali 20	Sa	1	*Suk.* 11	·05	3	·73	11
21	Su	2	12	·05	4	·74	12
22	Mo	3	13	·04	5	·74	13
23	Tu	4	{ 14 P	·00 ·96	6	·72	14
24	We	5	*Pausha* 1	·89	7	·68	*H. 1240 Jumadal-awwal* 15
25	Th	6	2	·80	8	·63	16
26	Fr	7	3	·72	9	·57	17
27	Sa	8	4	·63	10	·50	18
28	Su	9	5	·53	11	·44	19
29	Mo	10	6	·43	12	·37	20
—30	Tu	11	7	·34	13	·30	21
1	We	12	8	·25	14	·24	22
2	Th	13	*Bahula* 9	·17	15	·19	23
3	Fr	14	10	·11	16	·15	24
4	Sa	15	11	·06	17	·15	25
5	Su	16	12	·04	18	·15	26
6	Mo	17	13	·03	19	·17	27
7	Tu	18	14	·05	20	·21	28
8	We	19	—A	·08	21	·27	29
9	Th	20	1	·15	22	·35	—30
10	Fr	21	2	·22	23	·45	1
Tarana Makara—Tai 11	Sa	22	3	·30	24	·55	2
12	Su	23	4	·39	25	·66	3
13	Mo	24	5	·48	26	·76	4
14	Tu	25	*Sukla* 6	·56	27	·87	5
15	We	26	7	·62	1	·94	6
16	Th	27	8	·67	...	...	7
17	Fr	28	9	·69	2	·00	8
18	Sa	29	10	·69	3	·04	9
19	Su	30	11	·68	4	·06	10
20	Mo	31	12	·65	5	·07	11

Feb.

Cyclic Sidereal Year, Month and Day	Week-Day	English Month and Day	Tithi	Ending Moment	Nakshatra	Ending Moment	Muhammadan Year, Month and Day
21	Tu	1	*Magha* 13	·60	6	·05	*H. 1240 Jumadal-akhir* 12
22	We	2	14	·52	7 8	·02 } ·97	13
23	Th	3	P	·44	9	·91	14
24	Fr	4	1	·35	10	·85	15
25	Sa	5	2	·25	11	·78	16
26	Su	6	3	·15	12	·71	17
27	Mo	7	{ 4 5	·05 ·97	13	·64	18
28	Tu	8	6	·88	14	·58	19
—29	We	9	*Bahula* 7	·80	15	·54	20
1	Th	10	8	·74	16	·50	21
2	Fr	11	9	·70	17	·47	22
3	Sa	12	10	·67	18	·47	23
4	Su	13	11	·66	19	·48	24
5	Mo	14	12	·68	20	·52	25
6	Tu	15	13	·72	21	·58	26
7	We	16	14	·78	22	·66	27
8	Th	17	—A	·85	23	·75	28
9	Fr	18	1	·94	24	·85	—29
Tarana Kumbha—Masi 10	Sa	19	...	...	25	·96	*H. 1240 Rajab* 1
11	Su	20	*Sukla* 2	·02	...	...	2
12	Mo	21	3	·10	26	·07	3
13	Tu	22	4	·18	27	·17	4
14	We	23	*Phalguna* 5	·24	1	·25	5
15	Th	24	6	·30	2	·31	6
16	Fr	25	7	·31	3	·36	7
17	Sa	26	8	·32	4	·39	8
18	Su	27	9	·30	5	·40	9
19	Mo	28	10	·26	6	·38	10

March

Cyclic Sidereal Year, Month and Day	Week-Day	English Month and Day	Tithi	Ending Moment	Nakshatra	Ending Moment	Muhammadan Year, Month and Day
Tarana Kumbha—Masi 20	Tu	1	*Suk.* 11	·20	7	·35	11
21	We	2	12	·13	8	·30	12
22	Th	3	{ 13 14	·06 ·96	9	·25	13
23	Fr	4	P	·87	10	·19	14
24	Sa	5	*Phalguna* 1	·76	11	·12	15
25	Su	6	2	·67	12 13	·05 } ·98	16
26	Mo	7	3	·57	14	·91	*H. 1240 Rajab* 17
27	Tu	8	4	·49	15	·87	18
28	We	9	5	·41	16	·83	19
29	Th	10	6	·34	17	·80	20
—30	Fr	11	7	·31	18	·79	21
1	Sa	12	8	·28	19	·80	22
2	Su	13	*Bahula* 9	·27	20	·84	23
3	Mo	14	10	·28	21	·89	24
4	Tu	15	11	·32	22	·96	25
5	We	16	12	·38	...	...	26
6	Th	17	13	·45	23	·05	27
7	Fr	18	14	·54	24	·15	28
8	Sa	19	—A	·62	25	·26	29
9	Su	20	1	·72	26	·37	—30
10	Mo	21	2	·79	27	·47	1
11	Tu	22	3	·85	1	·55	2
12	We	23	*Sukla* 4	·89	2	·62	3
Tarana Mina—Panguni 13	Th	24	5	·91	3	·68	4
14	Fr	25	6	·91	4	·71	5
15	Sa	26	7	·89	5	·72	6
16	Su	27	*Chaitra* 8	·85	6	·71	7
17	Mo	28	9	·79	7	·68	8
18	Tu	29	10	·72	8	·64	9
19	We	30	11	·64	9	·59	10
20	Th	31	12	·54	10	·53	11

April

Cyclic Sidereal Year, Month and Day	Week-Day	English Month and Day	Tithi	Ending Moment	Nakshatra	Ending Moment	Muhammadan Year, Month and Day
21	Fr	1	13	·44	11	·46	*H. 1240 Shaban* 12
22	Sa	2	14	·33	12	·39	13
23	Su	3	P	·24	13	·32	14
24	Mo	4	1	·15	14	·26	15
25	Tu	5	{ 2 3	·06 ·98	15	·20	16
26	We	6	4	·91	16	·16	17
27	Th	7	*Bahula* 5	·88	17	·13	18
28	Fr	8	6	·85	18	·11	19
29	Sa	9	7	·83	19	·13	20
—30	Su	10	8	·84	20	·15	21
1	Mo	11	9	·89	21	·20	22
2	Tu	12	10	·94	22	·27	23
3	We	13	...	...	23	·35	24
4	Th	14	11	·02	24	·46	25
5	Fr	15	12	·10	25	·56	26
6	Sa	16	13	·18	26	·67	27
7	Su	17	14	·27	27	·77	28
8	Mo	18	—A	·34	1	·86	—29
Parthiva Mesha—Chittirai 9	Tu	19	1	·40	2	·94	1
10	We	20	*Sukla* 2	·44	...	...	2
11	Th	21	3	·46	3	·00	3
12	Fr	22	4	·46	4	·03	4
13	Sa	23	*Vaisakha* 5	·43	5	·04	*H 1240 Ramzan* 5
14	Su	24	6	·40	6	·03	6
15	Mo	25	7	·33	7 8	·01 } ·98	7
16	Tu	26	8	·26	9	·93	8
17	We	27	9	·18	10	·86	9
18	Th	28	{ 10 11	·09 ·99	11	·80	10
19	Fr	29	12	·88	12	·73	11
20	Sa	30	13	·78	13	·66	12

May

Cyclic Sidereal Year, Month and Day	Week-Day	English Month and Day	Tithi	Ending Moment	Nakshatra	Ending Moment	Muhammadan Year, Month and Day
21	Su	1	*Vaisakha* 14	·66	14	·60	13
22	Mo	2	P	·59	15	·54	14
Parthiva Mesha—Chittirai 23	Tu	3	1	·51	16	·49	15
24	We	4	2	·45	17	·46	16
25	Th	5	3	·41	18	·45	17
26	Fr	6	4	·38	19	·45	*H. 1240 Ramzan* 18
27	Sa	7	5	·36	20	·47	19
28	Su	8	6	·37	21	·51	20
29	Mo	9	7	·42	22	·57	21
30	Tu	10	*Bahula* 8	·47	23	·66	22
—31	We	11	9	·53	24	·75	23
1	Th	12	10	·61	25	·86	24
2	Fr	13	11	·70	26	·97	25
3	Sa	14	12	·78	...	...	26
4	Su	15	13	·85	27	·07	27
5	Mo	16	14	·91	1	·16	28
6	Tu	17	—A	·95	2	·25	29
7	We	18	1	·97	3	·31	—30
8	Th	19	2	·97	4	·35	1
9	Fr	20	3	·96	5	·36	2
10	Sa	21	4	·91	6	·36	3
11	Su	22	5	·84	7	·35	4
12	Mo	23	6	·77	8	·31	5
13	Tu	24	*Sukla* 7	·69	9	·26	6
Parthiva Vrishabha—Vaikasi 14	We	25	8	·59	10	·20	7
15	Th	26	9	·49	11	·13	8
16	Fr	27	10	·39	12	·07	9
17	Sa	28	11	·29	13 14	·00 } ·93	10
18	Su	29	12	·20	15	·87	*Shawwal* 11
19	Mo	30	13	·09	16	·82	12
20	Tu ○	31	{ 14 P	·02 ·95	17	·79	13

June

Cyclic Sidereal Year, Month and Day	Week-Day	English Month and Day	Tithi	Ending Moment	Nakshatra	Ending Moment	Muhammadan Year, Month and Day
21	We	1	*Jyeshtha* 1	·90	18	·77	*H. 1240* 14
22	Th	2	2	·88	19	·77	15
23	Fr	3	3	·86	20	·78	16
24	Sa	4	4	·87	21	·82	17
25	Su	5	5	·90	22	·89	18
26	Mo	6	6	·96	23	·96	19
27	Tu	7	...	...	...	...	20
28	We	8	7	·03	24	·05	21
29	Th	9	8	·10	25	·16	22
30	Fr	10	9	·19	26	·26	23
—31	Sa	11	*Bahula* 10	·27	27	·37	24
1	Su	12	11	·33	1	·47	25
2	Mo	13	12	·39	2	·55	26
3	Tu	14	13	·44	3	·62	27
4	We	15	14	·45	4	·66	28
5	Th ●	16	—A	·45	5	·68	—29
6	Fr	17	1	·44	6	·69	1
Parthiva Mithuna—Ani 7	Sa	18	2	·40	7	·68	2
8	Su	19	3	·34	8	·64	3
9	Mo	20	*Sukla* 4	·26	9	·60	4
10	Tu	21	5	·19	10	·54	5
11	We	22	{ 6 7	·09 ·98	11	·48	6
12	Th	23	8	·88	12	·41	*H. 1240 Zil-ka'da* 7
13	Fr	24	9	·78	13	·34	8
14	Sa	25	10	·68	14	·27	9
15	Su	26	*Ashadha* 11	·58	15	·21	10
16	Mo	27	12	·51	16	·17	11
17	Tu	28	13	·45	17	·12	12
18	We	29	14	·38	18	·10	13
19	Th	30	P	·36	19	·09	14

Naksh :—1. Asvn. 2. Bhar. 3. Krit. 4. Rohi. 5. Mrig. 6. Ardh. 7. Punar. 8. Push. 9. Aslesh. 10. Magh. 11. P. Phal. 12. U. Phal. 13. Hasta. 14. Chit.

A. D. 1825. | **A.—Amavasya.** **P.—Paurnami.** | **Kollam 1001,** Commences { **N. Malabar—Sept.** **S. Malabar—Aug.** | **Hijra 1241,** Commences **Aug. 16.** | **Vikrama 1882.** **Bengal San 1231.** **(N. Cycle) Durmukha.**

SOLAR reckoning.			LUNAR reckoning.				
Cyclic Sidereal Year, Month and Day.	Week-Day	English Month and Day.	Tithi	Ending Moment.	Nakshatra	Ending Moment.	Muhammadan Year, Month and Day.
	July						
Parthiva Mithuna—Ani. 20	Fr	1	Ashadha 1	·34	20	·10	H. 1240 Zi-l-ka'da. 15
21	Sa	2	2	·35	21	·13	16
22	Su	3	3	·38	22	·19	17
23	Mo	4	4	·44	23	·27	18
24	Tu	5	5	·50	24	·35	19
25	We	6	6	·58	25	·45	20
26	Th	7	7	·66	26	·56	21
27	Fr	8	8	·74	27	·68	22
28	Sa	9	Bahula 9	·82	1	·77	23
29	Su	10	10	·87	2	·86	24
30	Mo	11	11	·91	3	·93	25
31	Tu	12	12	·93	4	·97	26
32	We	13	13	·94	...	...	27
Parthiva Karkata—Adi. 1	Th	14	14	·92	5	·01	28
2	Fr	15	A	·87	6	·02	29
3	Sa	16	Sravana Sukla 1	·82	7 8	·00 ·97	30
4	Su	17	2	·74	9	·93	Zi-l-hijja. 1
5	Mo	18	3	·65	10	·88	2
6	Tu	19	4	·56	11	·82	3
7	We	20	5	·47	12	·75	4
8	Th	21	6	·36	13	·68	5
9	Fr	22	7	·26	14	·61	6
10	Sa	23	8	·17	15	·56	7
11	Su	24	9 10	·06 ·98	16	·50	8
12	Mo	25	11	·91	17	·46	9
13	Tu	26	12	·87	18	·43	10
14	We	27	13	·84	19	·41	11
15	Th	28	14	·82	20	·42	12
16	Fr	29	P	·83	21	·46	13
17	Sa	30	1	·85	22	·50	14
18	Su	31	2	·90	23	·57	15
	Aug.						
19	Mo	1	Adhika 3	·97	24	·66	H. 1240 16
20	Tu	2	...	...	25	·75	17
21	We	3	4	·05	26	·87	18
22	Th	4	5	·13	27	·98	19
23	Fr	5	6	·21	...	...	20
24	Sa	6	7	·29	1	·08	21
25	Su	7	8	·34	2	·16	22
26	Mo	8	Bahula 9	·39	3	·24	23
27	Tu	9	10	·41	4	·30	24
28	We	10	11	·42	5	·33	25
29	Th	11	12	·40	6	·34	26
30	Fr	12	13	·37	7	·33	27
31	Sa	13	14	·32	8	·31	28
32	Su	14	A	·23	9	·26	29
Parthiva Simha—Avani. 1	Mo	15	Nija Sravana Sukla 1	·15	10	·22	30
2	Tu	16	2 3	·06 ·97	11	·16	H. 1241 Muharram. 1
3	We	17	4	·86	12	·09	2
4	Th	18	5	·76	13 14	·02 ·95	3
5	Fr	19	6	·65	15	·89	4
6	Sa	20	7	·57	16	·83	5
7	Su	21	8	·49	17	·79	6
8	Mo	22	9	·42	18	·75	7
9	Tu	23	10	·37	19	·74	8
10	We	24	11	·33	20	·75	9
11	Th	25	12	·32	21	·77	10
12	Fr	26	13	·32	22	·81	11
13	Sa	27	14	·36	23	·88	12
14	Su	28	P	·41	24	·96	13
15	Mo	29	Bah. 1	·48	...	...	14
16	Tu	30	2	·54	25	·06	15
17	We	31	3	·62	26	·17	16

SOLAR reckoning.			LUNAR reckoning.				
Cyclic Sidereal Year, Month and Day.	Week-Day	English Month and Day.	Tithi	Ending Moment.	Nakshatra	Ending Moment.	Muhammadan Year, Month and Day.
	Sep.						
Parthiva Simha—Avani. 18	Th	1	Nija Srv. 4	·71	27	·27	H. 1241 Muharram. 17
19	Fr	2	5	·80	1	·38	18
20	Sa	3	6	·86	2	·47	19
21	Su	4	7	·90	3	·55	20
22	Mo	5	8	·93	4	·61	21
23	Tu	6	9	·94	5	·65	22
24	We	7	10	·91	6	·66	23
25	Th	8	Bahula 11	·89	7	·66	24
26	Fr	9	12	·83	8	·64	25
27	Sa	10	13	·76	9	·61	26
28	Su	11	14	·67	10	·56	27
29	Mo	12	A	·59	11	·50	28
30	Tu	13	Bhadrapada Sukla 1	·48	12	·43	29
31	We	14	2	·38	13	·36	30
Parthiva Kanya—Purattasi. 1	Th	15	3	·28	14	·30	H. 1241 Safar. 1
2	Fr	16	4	·18	15	·23	2
3	Sa	17	5	·10	16	·17	3
4	Su	18	6 7	·02 ·95	17	·12	4
5	Mo	19	8	·89	18	·08	5
6	Tu	20	9	·86	19	·07	6
7	We	21	10	·85	20	·07	7
8	Th	22	11	·87	21	·08	8
9	Fr	23	12	·89	22	·12	9
10	Sa	24	13	·94	23	·18	10
11	Su	25	...	...	24	·27	11
12	Mo	26	14	·01	25	·36	12
13	Tu	27	P	·08	26	·46	13
14	We	28	1	·18	27	·57	14
15	Th	29	2	·26	1	·67	15
16	Fr	30	3	·33	2	·77	16
	Oct.						
17	Sa	1	4	·40	3	·86	17
18	Su	2	5	·44	4	·92	18
19	Mo	3	6	·47	5	·96	19
20	Tu	4	Bahula 7	·48	6	·98	20
21	We	5	8	·47	7	·98	21
22	Th	6	9	·44	8	·97	22
23	Fr	7	10	·38	9	·94	23
24	Sa	8	11	·31	10	·89	24
25	Su	9	12	·22	11	·83	25
26	Mo	10	13	·14	12	·77	26
27	Tu	11	14 A	·04 ·95	13	·71	27
28	We	12	Asvina Sukla 1	·85	14	·63	28
29	Th	13	2	·74	15	·57	29
30	Fr	14	3	·66	16	·50	H. 1241 Rabi-ul-avval. 1
Parthiva Tula—Aippasi. 1	Sa	15	4	·58	17	·45	2
2	Su	16	5	·52	18	·42	3
3	Mo	17	6	·46	19	·40	4
4	Tu	18	7	·44	20	·39	5
5	We	19	8	·42	21	·40	6
6	Th	20	9	·44	22	·43	7
7	Fr	21	10	·46	23	·50	8
8	Sa	22	11	·52	24	·57	9
9	Su	23	12	·59	25	·66	10
10	Mo	24	13	·66	26	·76	11
11	Tu	25	14	·76	27	·87	12
12	We	26	P	·84	1	·97	13
13	Th	27	1	·93	...	...	14
14	Fr	28	2	·99	2	·08	15
15	Sa	29	Bah. ...	...	3	·16	16
16	Su	30	3	·02	4	·23	17
17	Mo	31	4	·06	5	·28	18

SOLAR reckoning.			LUNAR reckoning.				
Cyclic Sidereal Year, Month and Day.	Week-Day	English Month and Day.	Tithi	Ending Moment.	Nakshatra	Ending Moment.	Muhammadan Year, Month and Day.
	Nov.						
Parthiva Tula—Aippasi. 18	Tu	1	5	·07	6	·30	H. 1241 Rabi-ul-awwal. 19
19	We	2	6	·06	7	·32	20
20	Th	3	7 8	·02 ·98	8	·30	21
21	Fr	4	Asv. 9	·90	9	·27	22
22	Sa	5	10	·82	10	·23	23
23	Su	6	11	·74	11	·17	24
24	Mo	7	12	·63	12	·11	25
25	Tu	8	Bahula 13	·54	13 14	·04 ·97	26
26	We	9	14	·44	15	·90	27
27	Th	10	A	·35	16	·84	28
28	Fr	11	Kartika Sukla 1	·26	17	·79	29
29	Sa	12	2	·19	18	·75	30
30	Su	13	3	·12	19	·72	H. 1241 Rabi-ul-akhir. 1
Parthiva Vrischika—Kartigai. 1	Mo	14	4	·06	20	·71	2
2	Tu	15	5	·05	21	·72	3
3	We	16	6	·03	22	·75	4
4	Th	17	7	·05	23	·81	5
5	Fr	18	8	·07	24	·88	6
6	Sa	19	9	·14	25	·96	7
7	Su	20	10	·21	...	...	8
8	Mo	21	11	·29	26	·06	9
9	Tu	22	12	·38	27	·17	10
10	We	23	13	·47	1	·28	11
11	Th	24	14	·55	2	·38	12
12	Fr ○	25	P	·61	3	·47	13
13	Sa	26	1	·66	4	·54	14
14	Su	27	2	·69	5	·59	15
15	Mo	28	3	·70	6	·63	16
16	Tu	29	4	·68	7	·64	17
17	We	30	5	·64	8	·63	18
	Dec.						
18	Th	1	Bahula 6	·60	9	·60	19
19	Fr	2	7	·52	10	·56	20
20	Sa	3	8	·45	11	·52	21
21	Su	4	9	·36	12	·45	22
22	Mo	5	10	·27	13	·38	23
23	Tu	6	11	·17	14	·31	24
24	We	7	12 13	·06 ·97	15	·24	25
25	Th	8	14	·88	16	·19	26
26	Fr	9	A	·81	17	·13	27
27	Sa	10	Margasira Sukla 1	·74	18	·08	28
28	Su	11	2	·71	19	·05	29
29	Mo	12	3	·68	20	·03	H. 1241 Jumadal-awwal. 1
Parthiva Dhanus—Margali. 1	Tu	13	4	·66	21	·04	2
2	We	14	5	·69	22	·07	3
3	Th	15	6	·72	23	·12	4
4	Fr	16	7	·78	24	·18	5
5	Sa	17	8	·86	25	·26	6
6	Su	18	9	·95	26	·36	7
7	Mo	19	...	...	27	·47	8
8	Tu	20	10	·05	1	·58	9
9	We	21	11	·12	2	·68	10
10	Th	22	12	·20	3	·77	11
11	Fr	23	13	·26	4	·85	12
12	Sa	24	14	·31	5	·91	13
13	Su	25	P	·32	6	·95	14
14	Mo	26	Bah. 1	·34	7	·96	15
15	Tu	27	2	·32	8	·96	16
16	We	28	3	·29	9	·93	17
17	Th	29	4	·24	10	·90	18
18	Fr	30	5	·16	11	·85	19
19	Sa	31	6 7	·08 ·99	12	·79	20

15. Svati. 16. Visak. 17. Anur. 18. Jyesh. 19. Mula. 20. P. Ash. 21. U. Ash. 22. Sravn. 23. Dani. 24. Satab. 25. P. Bhad. 26. U. Bhad. 27. Rev.

A. D. 1826. **Mesha Sankranti** (Commencement of Indian Sidereal Year).

Solar Eclipse. ● **(Surya Sid.) April 11·47.** **Saka 1748.** **Kaliyuga 4927.**

Lunar Eclipse. ○ **(Arya Sid.) April 11·37.** **(S. Cycle) Vyaya.**

SOLAR reckoning: Cyclic Sidereal Year, Month and Day; Week-Day; English Month and Day. LUNAR reckoning: Tithi; Ending Moment; Nakshatra; Ending Moment; Muhammadan Year, Month and Day.

Jan.

Parthiva Dhanus—Margali; Parthiva Makara—Tai; Mr. Bahula; Sukla; Pausha; Bahula; H. 1241 Jt.-awwal; H. 1241 Jumadal-akhir.

Cyclic Sidereal Year, Month and Day	Week-Day	English Month and Day	Tithi	Ending Moment	Nakshatra	Ending Moment	Muhammadan Year, Month and Day
20	Su	1	8	·90	13	·72	21
21	Mo	2	9	·80	14	·65	22
22	Tu	3	10	·70	15	·58	23
23	We	4	11	·61	16	·52	24
24	Th	5	12	·52	17	·46	25
25	Fr	6	13	·45	18	·41	26
26	Sa	7	14	·39	19	·38	27
27	Su	8	—A	·35	20	·36	28
28	Mo	9	1	·32	21	·37	29
29	Tu	10	2	·32	22	·30	—30
—30	We	11	3	·33	23	·43	1
1	Th	12	4	·37	24	·49	2
2	Fr	13	5	·42	25	·56	3
3	Sa	14	6	·50	26	·67	4
4	Su	15	7	·60	27	·77	5
5	Mo	16	8	·68	1	·88	6
6	Tu	17	9	·77	2	·98	7
7	We	18	10	·84	...	...	8
8	Th	19	11	·91	3	·08	9
9	Fr	20	12	·96	4	·16	10
10	Sa	21	13	·97	5	·22	11
11	Su	22	14	·98	6	·26	12
12	Mo	23	P	·96	7	·28	13
13	Tu	24	1	·94	8	·28	14
14	We	25	2	·88	9	·26	15
15	Th	26	3	·80	10	·24	16
16	Fr	27	4	·72	11	·19	17
17	Sa	28	5	·62	12	·13	18
18	Su	29	6	·53	13 } 14	·06 } ·99	19
19	Mo	30	7	·43	15	·93	20
20	Tu	31	8	·34	16	·86	21

Feb.

Parthiva Kumbha—Masi; Sukla; Magha; Bah.; H. 1241 Rajab.

Cyclic Sidereal Year, Month and Day	Week-Day	English Month and Day	Tithi	Ending Moment	Nakshatra	Ending Moment	Muhammadan Year, Month and Day
21	We	1	9	·24	17	·80	22
22	Th	2	10	·16	18	·75	23
23	Fr	3	11	·08	19	·71	24
24	Sa	4	{12 {13	·04 ·99	20	·69	25
25	Su	5	14	·96	21	·69	26
26	Mo	6	—A	·96	22	·70	27
27	Tu	7	1	·97	23	·74	28
28	We	8	...	...	24	·79	—29
—29	Th	9	2	·02	25	·88	1
1	Fr	10	3	·07	26	·97	2
2	Sa	11	4	·15	...	...	3
3	Su	12	5	·24	27	·07	4
4	Mo	13	6	·32	1	·18	5
5	Tu	14	7	·41	2	·28	6
6	We	15	8	·48	3	·39	7
7	Th	16	9	·55	4	·47	8
8	Fr	17	10	·60	5	·53	9
9	Sa	18	11	·61	6	·58	10
10	Su	19	12	·61	7	·60	11
11	Mo	20	13	·59	8	·61	12
12	Tu	21	14	·56	9	·60	13
13	We	22	P	·49	10	·57	14
14	Th	23	1	·42	11	·52	15
15	Fr	24	2	·34	12	·46	16
16	Sa	25	3	·25	13	·40	17
17	Su	26	4	·15	14	·34	18
18	Mo	27	{5 {6	·06 ·96	15	·27	19
19	Tu	28	7	·86	16	·20	20

March

Parthiva Kumbha—Masi; Parthiva Mina—Panguni; Mg. Bahula; Sukla; Phalguna; H. 1241 Rajab; H. 1241 Shaban.

Cyclic Sidereal Year, Month and Day	Week-Day	English Month and Day	Tithi	Ending Moment	Nakshatra	Ending Moment	Muhammadan Year, Month and Day
20	We	1	8	·78	17	·13	21
21	Th	2	9	·70	18	·08	22
22	Fr	3	10	·64	19	·05	23
23	Sa	4	11	·60	20	·02	24
24	Su	5	12	·58	21	·01	25
25	Mo	6	13	·57	22	·02	26
26	Tu	7	14	·57	23	·05	27
27	We	8	—A	·62	24	·11	28
28	Th	9	1	·69	25	·18	29
29	Fr	10	2	·77	26	·27	—30
—30	Sa	11	3	·85	27	·37	1
1	Su	12	4	·94	1	·47	2
2	Mo	13	...	...	2	·58	3
3	Tu	14	5	·02	3	·69	4
4	We	15	6	·09	4	·77	5
5	Th	16	7	·15	5	·84	6
6	Fr	17	8	·19	6	·89	7
7	Sa	18	9	·21	7	·92	8
8	Su	19	10	·20	8	·94	9
9	Mo	20	11	·19	9	·93	10
10	Tu	21	12	·15	10	·90	11
11	We	22	13	·09	11	·85	12
12	Th	23	{14 {P	·02 ·93	12	·80	13
13	Fr	24	1	·84	13	·75	14
14	Sa	25	2	·73	14	·68	15
15	Su	26	3	·63	15	·61	16
16	Mo	27	4	·54	16	·54	17
17	Tu	28	5	·45	17	·47	18
18	We	29	6	·36	18	·42	19
19	Th	30	7	·28	19	·38	20
20	Fr	31	8	·22	20	·35	21

April

Bahula; Sukla; Chaitra; Bahula; Vyaya Mesha—Chittirai; H. 1241 Ramzan.

Cyclic Sidereal Year, Month and Day	Week-Day	English Month and Day	Tithi	Ending Moment	Nakshatra	Ending Moment	Muhammadan Year, Month and Day
21	Sa	1	9	·18	21	·33	22
22	Su	2	10	·16	22	·34	23
23	Mo	3	11	·15	23	·37	24
24	Tu	4	12	·18	24	·42	25
25	We	5	13	·21	25	·49	26
26	Th	6	14	·27	26	·57	27
27	Fr	7	—A	·34	27	·67	28
28	Sa	8	1	·42	1	·77	—29
29	Su	9	2	·51	2	·89	1
—30	Mo	10	3	·58	3	·99	2
1	Tu	11	4	·65	...	...	3
2	We	12	5	·71	4	·08	4
3	Th	13	6	·76	5	·15	5
4	Fr	14	7	·77	6	·21	6
5	Sa	15	8	·76	7	·25	7
6	Su	16	9	·74	8	·26	8
7	Mo	17	10	·69	9	·25	9
8	Tu	18	11	·64	10	·23	10
9	We	19	12	·57	11	·19	11
10	Th	20	13	·49	12	·15	12
11	Fr	21	14	·39	13	·08	13
12	Sa	22	P	·29	14 } 15	·01 } ·04	14
13	Su	23	1	·18	16	·87	15
14	Mo	24	{2 {3	·08 ·99	17	·32	16
15	Tu	25	4	·90	18	·76	17
16	We	26	5	·83	19	·71	18
17	Th	27	6	·76	20	·68	19
18	Fr	28	7	·73	21	·66	20
19	Sa	29	8	·70	22	·66	21
20	Su	30	9	·68	23	·69	22

May

Vyaya Mesha—Chittirai; Vyaya Vrishabha—Vaikasi; Ch. Bah.; Sukla; Vaisakha; Bahula; Ramzan; H. 1241 Shawwal.

Cyclic Sidereal Year, Month and Day	Week-Day	English Month and Day	Tithi	Ending Moment	Nakshatra	Ending Moment	Muhammadan Year, Month and Day
21	Mo	1	10	·71	24	·73	23
22	Tu	2	11	·74	25	·79	24
23	We	3	12	·80	26	·87	25
24	Th	4	13	·87	27	·97	26
25	Fr	5	14	·95	...	...	27
26	Sa	6	...	...	1	·08	28
27	Su	7	—A	·02	2	·19	29
28	Mo	8	1	·10	3	·29	—30
29	Tu	9	2	·18	4	·38	1
30	We	10	3	·24	5	·46	2
—31	Th	11	4	·29	6	·53	3
1	Fr	12	5	·29	7	·56	4
2	Sa	13	6	·29	8	·58	5
3	Su	14	7	·27	9	·58	6
4	Mo	15	8	·22	10	·56	7
5	Tu	16	9	·16	11	·53	8
6	We	17	10	·08	12	·48	9
7	Th	18	{11 {12	·00 ·90	13	·42	10
8	Fr	19	13	·81	14	·35	11
9	Sa	20	14	·70	15	·28	12
10	Su ○	21	P	·60	16	·22	13
11	Mo	22	1	·50	17	·15	14
12	Tu	23	2	·41	18	·09	15
13	We	24	3	·34	19	·04	16
14	Th	25	4	·27	20 } 21	·00 } ·98	17
15	Fr	26	5	·23	22	·99	18
16	Sa	27	6	·20	...	...	19
17	Su	28	7	·20	23	·00	20
18	Mo	29	8	·20	24	·04	21
19	Tu	30	9	·24	25	·10	22
20	We	31	10	·30	26	·17	23

June

Vyaya Mithuna—Ani; Sukla; Jyeshtha; Bahula; H. 1241 Zi-l-ka'da.

Cyclic Sidereal Year, Month and Day	Week-Day	English Month and Day	Tithi	Ending Moment	Nakshatra	Ending Moment	Muhammadan Year, Month and Day
21	Th	1	11	·35	27	·27	24
22	Fr	2	12	·44	1	·38	25
23	Sa	3	13	·52	2	·48	26
24	Su	4	14	·61	3	·59	27
25	Mo	5	—A	·67	4	·68	28
26	Tu	6	1	·73	5	·77	—29
27	We	7	2	·77	6	·84	1
28	Th	8	3	·79	7	·88	2
29	Fr	9	4	·78	8	·90	3
30	Sa	10	5	·76	9	·90	4
31	Su	11	6	·72	10	·90	5
—32	Mo	12	7	·65	11	·86	6
1	Tu	13	8	·58	12	·82	7
2	We	14	9	·50	13	·76	8
3	Th	15	10	·39	14	·69	9
4	Fr	16	11	·30	15	·62	10
5	Sa	17	12	·19	16	·56	11
6	Su	18	{13 {14	·10 ·99	17	·49	12
7	Mo	19	P	·91	18	·43	13
8	Tu	20	1	·83	19	·38	14
9	We	21	2	·75	20	·33	15
10	Th	22	3	·71	21	·32	16
11	Fr	23	4	·68	22	·31	17
12	Sa	24	5	·67	23	·32	18
13	Su	25	6	·68	24	·35	19
14	Mo	26	7	·72	25	·41	20
15	Tu	27	8	·76	26	·49	21
16	We	28	9	·83	27	·58	22
17	Th	29	10	·91	1	·68	23
18	Fr	30	11	·99	2	·78	24

Naksh:—1. Asvn. 2. Bhar. 3. Krit. 4. Rohi. 5. Mrig. 6. Ardh. 7. Punar. 8. Push. 9. Aslesh. 10. Magh. 11. P. Phal. 12. U. Phal. 13. Hasta. 14. Chit.

A. D. 1826.
A.—Amavasya. **P.—Paurnami.**
Kollam 1002, Commences { **N. Malabar—Sept.** **S. Malabar—Aug.**
Hijra 1242, Commences, **Aug. 5.**
Vikrama 1883. **Bengal San 1232,** **(N. Cycle) Hemalamba.**

SOLAR reckoning: Cyclic Sidereal Year, Month and Day; Week-Day; English Month and Day. LUNAR reckoning: Tithi; Ending Moment; Nakshatra; Ending Moment; Muhammadan Year, Month and Day.

July

Cyclic Sidereal Year, Month and Day	Week-Day	English Month and Day	Tithi	Ending Moment	Nakshatra	Ending Moment	Muhammadan Year, Month and Day
Vyaya Mithuna—Asi. 19	Sa	1	Jy. Bah. ...	...	3	·89	Zi-l-ka'da. 25
20	Su	2	12	·08	...	...	26
21	Mo	3	13	·14	4	·00	27
22	Tu	4	14	·21	5	·08	28
23	We	5	—A	·25	6	·15	29
24	Th	6	1	·27	7	·19	—30
25	Fr	7	2	·26	8	·22	1
26	Sa	8	3	·24	9	·24	2
27	Su	9	4	·19	10	·22	3
28	Mo	10	5	·13	11	·19	4
29	Tu	11	Sukla 6 / 7	·07 / ·97	12	·15	5
30	We	12	8	·88	13	·09	6
—31	Th	13	9	·78	14 / 15	·03 / ·97	7
1	Fr	14	10	·67	16	·90	8
2	Sa	15	11	·57	17	·83	9
3	Su	16	12	·47	18	·77	10
4	Mo	17	Ashadha 13	·39	19	·71	H. 1241 Zi-l-hijja. 11
5	Tu	18	14	·30	20	·68	12
6	We	19	P	·24	21	·65	13
7	Th	20	1	·19	22	·33	14
8	Fr	21	2	·17	23	·64	15
9	Sa	22	3	·15	24	·67	16
10	Su	23	4	·16	25	·72	17
11	Mo	24	5	·20	26	·79	18
Vyaya Karkata—Adi. 12	Tu	25	6	·23	27	·88	19
13	We	26	7	·30	1	·97	20
14	Th	27	Bahula 8	·38	...	...	21
15	Fr	28	9	·47	2	·08	22
16	Sa	29	10	·54	3	·20	23
17	Su	30	11	·61	4	·30	24
18	Mo	31	12	·68	5	·38	25

Aug.

Cyclic Sidereal Year, Month and Day	Week-Day	English Month and Day	Tithi	Ending Moment	Nakshatra	Ending Moment	Muhammadan Year, Month and Day
19	Tu	1	13	·71	6	·46	26
20	We	2	14	·75	7	·51	27
21	Th	3	—A	·74	8	·54	28
22	Fr	4	1	·72	9	·56	—29
23	Sa	5	2	·67	10	·55	1
24	Su	6	3	·62	11	·53	2
25	Mo	7	4	·56	12	·48	3
26	Tu	8	5	·47	13	·43	4
27	We	9	6	·37	14	·38	5
28	Th	10	Sukla 7	·27	15	·31	6
29	Fr	11	8	·17	16	·24	7
30	Sa	12	9 / 10	·08 / ·98	17	·17	8
31	Su	13	11	·88	18	·10	9
—32	Mo	14	12	·79	19	·05	10
1	Tu	15	13	·74	20 / 21	·01 / ·97	11
2	We	16	Sravana 14	·68	22	·96	12
3	Th	17	P	·66	23	·96	13
4	Fr	18	1	·64	24	·99	H. 1242 Muharram. 14
5	Sa	19	2	·65	...	...	15
6	Su	20	3	·68	25	·03	16
Vyaya Simha—Avani. 7	Mo	21	4	·73	26	·10	17
8	Tu	22	5	·80	27	·18	18
9	We	23	6	·87	1	·27	19
10	Th	24	7	·95	2	·33	20
11	Fr	25	Bahula ...	...	3	·49	21
12	Sa	26	8	·04	4	·60	22
13	Su	27	9	·12	5	·69	23
14	Mo	28	10	·18	6	·76	24
15	Tu	29	11	·23	7	·82	25
16	We	30	12	·25	8	·87	26
17	Th	31	13	·24	9	·88	27

Sep.

Cyclic Sidereal Year, Month and Day	Week-Day	English Month and Day	Tithi	Ending Moment	Nakshatra	Ending Moment	Muhammadan Year, Month and Day
18	Fr	1	14	·23	10	·88	28
Vyaya Simha—Avani. 19	Sa	2	—A	·18	11	·85	29
20	Su	3	1	·14	12	·82	—30
21	Mo	4	2 / 3	·07 / ·99	13	·78	1
22	Tu	5	4	·89	14	·71	2
23	We	6	5	·79	15	·65	3
24	Th	7	Sukla 6	·68	16	·58	4
25	Fr	8	7	·59	17	·51	5
26	Sa	9	8	·49	18	·45	6
27	Su	10	9	·40	19	·39	7
28	Mo	11	10	·32	20	·34	8
29	Tu	12	11	·26	21	·30	9
30	We	13	12	·20	22	·28	10
—31	Th	14	Bhadrapada 13	·18	23	·29	11
1	Fr	15	14	·17	24	·31	12
2	Sa	16	P	·18	25	·34	H. 1242 Safar. 13
3	Su	17	1	·21	26	·40	14
4	Mo	18	2	·27	27	·48	15
5	Tu	19	3	·32	1	·57	16
6	We	20	4	·40	2	·69	17
7	Th	21	5	·48	3	·79	18
8	Fr	22	6	·56	4	·90	19
9	Sa	23	Bahula 7	·65	5	·99	20
10	Su	24	8	·71	...	...	21
11	Mo	25	9	·76	6	·07	22
Vyaya Kanya—Purattasi. 12	Tu	26	10	·78	7	·14	23
13	We	27	11	·79	8	·18	24
14	Th	28	12	·77	9	·20	25
15	Fr	29	13	·73	10	·20	26
16	Sa	30	14	·68	11	·18	27

Oct.

Cyclic Sidereal Year, Month and Day	Week-Day	English Month and Day	Tithi	Ending Moment	Nakshatra	Ending Moment	Muhammadan Year, Month and Day
17	Su	1	—A	·60	12	·16	28
18	Mo	2	1	·53	13	·11	—29
19	Tu	3	2	·43	14 / 15	·05 / ·99	1
20	We	4	3	·35	16	·91	2
21	Th	5	Sukla 4	·24	17	·85	3
22	Fr	6	5	·14	18	·79	4
23	Sa	7	6 / 7	·04 / ·94	19	·72	5
24	Su	8	8	·87	20	·67	6
25	Mo	9	9	·82	21	·63	7
26	Tu	10	10	·77	22	·61	8
27	We	11	11	·74	23	·61	9
28	Th	12	12	·74	24	·62	10
29	Fr	13	Asvina 13	·74	25	·65	11
—30	Sa	14	14	·77	26	·71	12
1	Su	15	P	·83	27	·79	13
2	Mo	16	1	·89	1	·88	14
3	Tu	17	2	·97	2	·98	15
4	We	18	...	...	...	...	H. 1242 Rabi-ul-awwal. 16
5	Th	19	3	·06	3	·09	17
6	Fr	20	4	·15	4	·19	18
7	Sa	21	5	·23	5	·29	19
8	Su	22	6	·29	6	·39	20
9	Mo	23	Bahula 7	·34	7	·45	21
10	Tu	24	8	·37	8	·50	22
Vyaya Tula—Aippasi. 11	We	25	9	·37	9	·52	23
12	Th	26	10	·35	10	·53	24
13	Fr	27	11	·31	11	·52	25
14	Sa	28	12	·26	12	·49	26
15	Su	29	13	·19	13	·45	27
16	Mo	30	14	·12	14	·39	28
17	Tu	31	A / 1	·02 / ·92	15	·32	29

Nov.

Cyclic Sidereal Year, Month and Day	Week-Day	English Month and Day	Tithi	Ending Moment	Nakshatra	Ending Moment	Muhammadan Year, Month and Day
18	We	1	2	·83	16	·26	—30
Vyaya Tula—Aippasi. 19	Th	2	3	·74	17	·19	1
20	Fr	3	4	·63	18	·12	2
21	Sa	4	5	·54	19	·06	3
22	Su	5	Sukla 6	·47	20 / 21	·00 / ·97	4
23	Mo	6	7	·41	22	·94	5
24	Tu	7	8	·36	23	·93	6
25	We	8	9	·33	24	·94	7
26	Th	9	10	·33	25	·97	8
27	Fr	10	11	·34	...	...	9
28	Sa	11	12	·38	26	·03	10
29	Su	12	13	·43	27	·10	11
—30	Mo	13	Kartika 14	·50	1	·18	12
1	Tu ○	14	P	·58	2	·28	13
2	We	15	1	·68	3	·39	14
3	Th	16	2	·77	4	·49	H. 1242 Rabi-ul-akhir. 15
4	Fr	17	3	·84	5	·60	16
5	Sa	18	4	·90	6	·69	17
6	Su	19	5	·95	7	·76	18
7	Mo	20	6	·99	8	·81	19
8	Tu	21	Bahula 7	·98	9	·84	20
9	We	22	8	·96	10	·86	21
Vyaya Vrischika—Kartigai. 10	Th	23	9	·93	11	·85	22
11	Fr	24	10	·87	12	·82	23
12	Sa	25	11	·81	13	·78	24
13	Su	26	12	·73	14	·72	25
14	Mo	27	13	·65	15	·67	26
15	Tu	28	14	·54	16	·60	27
16	We	29	—A	·44	17	·53	28
17	Th	30	1	·35	18	·46	—29

Dec.

Cyclic Sidereal Year, Month and Day	Week-Day	English Month and Day	Tithi	Ending Moment	Nakshatra	Ending Moment	Muhammadan Year, Month and Day
18	Fr	1	2	·26	19	·40	1
19	Sa	2	3	·17	20	·35	2
20	Su	3	4	·08	21	·30	3
21	Mo	4	5 / 6	·03 / ·99	22	·27	4
22	Tu	5	Sukla 7	·96	23	·25	5
23	We	6	8	·96	24	·26	6
24	Th	7	9	·98	25	·28	7
25	Fr	8	...	...	26	·34	8
26	Sa	9	10	·02	27	·40	9
27	Su	10	11	·07	1	·48	10
28	Mo	11	Margasira 12	·14	2	·58	11
29	Tu	12	13	·24	3	·69	12
—30	We	13	14	·33	4	·80	13
1	Th	14	P	·41	5	·90	14
2	Fr	15	1	·49	6	·99	15
3	Sa	16	2	·55	...	...	H. 1242 Jumadal-awwal. 16
4	Su	17	3	·59	7	·07	17
5	Mo	18	4	·63	8	·12	18
6	Tu	19	5	·62	9	·17	19
7	We	20	Bahula 6	·61	10	·18	20
8	Th	21	7	·56	11	·18	21
9	Fr	22	8	·51	12	15	22
Vyaya Dhanus—Margali. 10	Sa	23	9	·44	13	·11	23
11	Su	24	10	·35	14	·07	24
12	Mo	25	11	·27	15 / 16	·01 / ·94	25
13	Tu	26	12	·17	17	·87	26
14	We	27	13 / 14	·08 / ·93	18	·80	27
15	Th	28	—A	·88	19	·78	28
16	Fr	29	P. Suk. 1	·80	20	·68	29
17	Sa	30	2	·73	21	·63	—30
18	Su	31	3	·68	22	·60	1

15. Svati. 16. Visak. 17. Anur. 18. Jyesh. 19. Mula. 20. P. Ash. 21. U. Ash. 22. Sravn. 23. Dani. 24. Satab. 25. P. Bhad. 26. U. Bhad. 27. Rev.

A. D. 1827.
Solar Eclipse. ●
Lunar Eclipse. ○

Mesha Sankranti (Commencement of Indian Sidereal Year).
(Surya Sid.) April 11·73.
(Arya Sid.) April 11·63.

Saka 1749. **Kaliyuga 4928.**
(S. Cycle) Sarvajit.

Columns: SOLAR reckoning — Cyclic Sidereal Year, Month and Day; Week-Day; English Month and Day. LUNAR reckoning — Tithi; Ending Moment; Nakshatra; Ending Moment; Muhammadan Year, Month and Day.

Jan. — Solar: Vyaya *Dhanus—Margali.* / Vyaya *Makara—Tai.* — Lunar: *Sukla*, **Pausha**, *Bahula* — H. 1242 *Jumadal-akhir.*

Cyclic Sidereal Year, Month and Day	Week-Day	English Month and Day	Tithi	Ending Moment	Nakshatra	Ending Moment	Muhammadan Year, Month and Day
19	Mo	1	4	·63	23	·58	2
20	Tu	2	5	·61	24	·58	3
21	We	3	6	·60	25	·61	4
22	Th	4	7	·63	26	·65	5
23	Fr	5	8	·66	27	·71	6
24	Sa	6	9	·71	1	·79	7
25	Su	7	10	·80	2	·88	8
26	Mo	8	11	·86	3	·99	9
27	Tu	9	12	·97	...	...	10
28	We	10	...	...	4	·10	11
—29	Th	11	13	·06	5	·20	12
1	Fr	12	14	·14	6	·30	13
2	Sa	13	P	·19	7	·37	14
3	Su	14	1	·24	8	·44	15
4	Mo	15	2	·27	9	·48	16
5	Tu	16	3	·26	10	·50	17
6	We	17	4	·25	11	·50	18
7	Th	18	5	·21	12	·48	19
8	Fr	19	6	·16	13	·45	20
9	Sa	20	7 / 8	·08 / ·99	14	·41	21
10	Su	21	9	·90	15	·35	22
11	Mo	22	10	·80	16	·28	23
12	Tu	23	11	·71	17	·21	24
13	We	24	12	·61	18	·14	25
14	Th	25	13	·52	19	·08	26
15	Fr	26	14	·43	20 / 21	·02 / ·97	27
16	Sa	27	—A	·38	22	·93	28
17	Su	28	1	·32	23	·90	—29
18	Mo	29	2	·27	24	·91	1
19	Tu	30	3	·25	25	·92	2
20	We	31	4	·25	26	·96	3

Feb. — Solar: Vyaya *Kumbha—Masi.* — Lunar: *Sukla*, **Magha**, *Bahula*, *Suk.* — H. 1242 *Rajab.*

Cyclic Sidereal Year, Month and Day	Week-Day	English Month and Day	Tithi	Ending Moment	Nakshatra	Ending Moment	Muhammadan Year, Month and Day
21	Th	1	5	·27	...	...	4
22	Fr	2	6	·31	27	·01	5
23	Sa	3	7	·37	1	·09	6
24	Su	4	8	·45	2	·19	7
25	Mo	5	9	·53	3	·29	8
26	Tu	6	10	·62	4	·40	9
27	We	7	11	·70	5	·50	10
28	Th	8	12	·79	6	·60	11
—29	Fr	9	13	·84	7	·69	12
1	Sa	10	14	·89	8	·75	13
2	Su	11	P	·90	9	·80	14
3	Mo	12	1	·90	10	·82	15
4	Tu	13	2	·89	11	·83	16
5	We	14	3	·84	12	·81	17
6	Th	15	4	·78	13	·79	18
7	Fr	16	5	·70	14	·74	19
8	Sa	17	6	·63	15	·68	20
9	Su	18	7	·54	16	·62	21
10	Mo	19	8	·44	17	·55	22
11	Tu	20	9	·34	18	·49	23
12	We	21	10	·23	19	·42	24
13	Th	22	11	·14	20	·35	25
14	Fr	23	12 / 13	·06 / ·99	21	·30	26
15	Sa	24	14	·93	22	·26	27
16	Su	25	—A	·90	23	·24	28
17	Mo	26	1	·87	24	·23	29
18	Tu	27	2	·86	25	·24	—30
19	We	28	3	·90	26	·27	1

March — Solar: Vyaya *Kumbha—Masi.* / Vyaya *Mina—Panguni.* — Lunar: *Sukla*, **Phalguna**, *Bahula* — H. 1242 *Shaban.*

Cyclic Sidereal Year, Month and Day	Week-Day	English Month and Day	Tithi	Ending Moment	Nakshatra	Ending Moment	Muhammadan Year, Month and Day
20	Th	1	4	·93	27	·32	2
21	Fr	2	5	·99	1	·40	3
22	Sa	3	...	...	2	·49	4
23	Su	4	6	·07	3	·59	5
24	Mo	5	7	·16	4	·69	6
25	Tu	6	8	·24	5	·80	7
26	We	7	9	·33	6	·91	8
27	Th	8	10	·39	7	·99	9
28	Fr	9	11	·45	...	...	10
29	Sa	10	12	·50	8	·06	11
—30	Su	11	13	·51	9	·11	12
1	Mo	12	14	·51	10	·14	13
2	Tu	13	P	·49	11	·15	14
3	We	14	1	·44	12	·15	15
4	Th	15	2	·38	13	·12	16
5	Fr	16	3	·30	14	·07	17
6	Sa	17	4	·22	15 / 16	·02 / ·96	18
7	Su	18	5	·13	17	·90	19
8	Mo	19	6 / 7	·03 / ·93	18	·83	20
9	Tu	20	8	·84	19	·76	21
10	We	21	9	·74	20	·69	22
11	Th	22	10	·65	21	·63	23
12	Fr	23	11	·58	22	·60	24
13	Sa	24	12	·52	23	·57	25
14	Su	25	13	·49	24	·55	26
15	Mo	26	14	·46	25	·56	27
16	Tu	27	—A	·46	26	·58	28
17	We	28	1	·48	27	·64	—29
18	Th	29	2	·52	1	·71	1
19	Fr	30	3	·57	2	·79	2
20	Sa	31	4	·65	3	·89	3

April — Solar: Sarvajit *Mesha—Chittirai.* — Lunar: *Sukla*, **Chaitra**, *Bahula*, **V.** *Suk.* — H. 1242 *Ramzan.*

Cyclic Sidereal Year, Month and Day	Week-Day	English Month and Day	Tithi	Ending Moment	Nakshatra	Ending Moment	Muhammadan Year, Month and Day
21	Su	1	5	·74	4	·99	4
22	Mo	2	6	·82	...	...	5
23	Tu	3	7	·91	5	·10	6
24	We	4	8	·97	6	·21	7
25	Th	5	...	...	7	·30	8
26	Fr	6	9	·03	8	·37	9
27	Sa	7	10	·07	9	·43	10
28	Su	8	11	·08	10	·46	11
29	Mo	9	12	·08	11	·48	12
30	Tu	10	13	·06	12	·47	13
—31	We	11	14 / P	·00 / ·94	13	·45	14
1	Th	12	1	·87	14	·41	15
2	Fr	13	2	·78	15	·35	16
3	Sa	14	3	·68	16	·30	17
4	Su	15	4	·59	17	·23	18
5	Mo	16	5	·49	18	·16	19
6	Tu	17	6	·39	19	·09	20
7	We	18	7	·29	20 / 21	·03 / ·98	21
8	Th	19	8	·21	22	·93	22
9	Fr	20	9	·13	23	·90	23
10	Sa	21	10	·08	24	·88	24
11	Su	22	11	·03	25	·88	25
12	Mo	23	12	·00	26	·91	26
13	Tu	24	13	·00	27	·95	27
14	We	25	14	·02	...	...	28
15	Th ●	26	—A	·06	1	·01	29
16	Fr	27	1	·11	2	·09	—30
17	Sa	28	2	·20	3	·19	1
18	Su	29	3	·28	4	·29	2
19	Mo	30	4	·35	5	·41	3

May — Solar: Sarvajit *Mesha—Chittirai.* / Sarvajit *Vrishabha—Vaikasi.* — Lunar: *Sukla*, **Vaisakha**, *Bahula* — H. 1242 *Shawwal.*

Cyclic Sidereal Year, Month and Day	Week-Day	English Month and Day	Tithi	Ending Moment	Nakshatra	Ending Moment	Muhammadan Year, Month and Day
20	Tu	1	5	·43	6	·51	4
21	We	2	6	·50	7	·60	5
22	Th	3	7	·57	8	·68	6
23	Fr	4	8	·60	9	·74	7
24	Sa	5	9	·62	10	·79	8
25	Su	6	10	·60	11	·80	9
26	Mo	7	11	·59	12	·80	10
27	Tu	8	12	·53	13	·78	11
28	We	9	13	·47	14	·74	12
29	Th	10	14	·40	15	·70	13
30	Fr ○	11	P	·31	16	·64	14
—31	Sa	12	1	·21	17	·57	15
1	Su	13	2	·11	18	·50	16
2	Mo	14	3 / 4	·02 / ·91	19	·43	17
3	Tu	15	5	·81	20	·36	18
4	We	16	6	·72	21	·31	19
5	Th	17	7	·64	22	·26	20
6	Fr	18	8	·60	23	·22	21
7	Sa	19	9	·55	24	·20	22
8	Su	20	10	·53	25	·20	23
9	Mo	21	11	·51	26	·22	24
10	Tu	22	12	·52	27	·26	25
11	We	23	13	·57	1	·32	26
12	Th	24	14	·62	2	·39	27
13	Fr	25	—A	·69	3	·49	28
14	Sa	26	1	·77	4	·60	—29
15	Su	27	2	·86	5	·70	1
16	Mo	28	3	·94	6	·81	2
17	Tu	29	...	...	7	·90	3
18	We	30	4	·01	8	·99	4
19	Th	31	5	·07	...	...	5

June — Solar: Sarvajit *Mithuna—Ani.* — Lunar: *Sukla*, **Jyeshtha**, *Bahula*, **Ash.** *Suk.* — H. 1242 *Zi-l-ka'da.* / *Zi-l-hijja.*

Cyclic Sidereal Year, Month and Day	Week-Day	English Month and Day	Tithi	Ending Moment	Nakshatra	Ending Moment	Muhammadan Year, Month and Day
20	Fr	1	6	·09	9	·06	6
21	Sa	2	7	·11	10	·10	7
22	Su	3	8	·10	11	·12	8
23	Mo	4	9	·09	12	·12	9
24	Tu	5	10 / 11	·04 / ·98	13	·11	10
25	We	6	12	·90	14	·08	11
26	Th	7	13	·80	15 / 16	·03 / ·98	12
27	Fr	8	14	·71	17	·91	13
28	Sa	9	P	·60	18	·84	14
29	Su	10	1	·51	19	·78	15
30	Mo	11	2	·41	20	·71	16
—31	Tu	12	3	·31	21	·65	17
1	We	13	4	·22	22	·60	18
2	Th	14	5	·14	23	·55	19
3	Fr	15	6	·08	24	·53	20
4	Sa	16	7	·03	25	·53	21
5	Su	17	8	·01	26	·54	22
6	Mo	18	9	·00	27	·57	23
7	Tu	19	10	·01	1	·63	24
8	We	20	11	·05	2	·70	25
9	Th	21	12	·11	3	·80	26
10	Fr	22	13	·16	4	·90	27
11	Sa	23	14	·24	...	...	28
12	Su	24	A	·33	5	·00	29
13	Mo	25	1	·40	6	·11	—30
14	Tu	26	2	·48	7	·21	1
15	We	27	3	·54	8	·30	2
16	Th	28	4	·57	9	·37	3
17	Fr	29	5	·59	10	·41	4
18	Sa	30	6	·58	11	·44	5

Naskh :—1. Asvn. 2. Bhar. 3. Krit. 4. Rohi. 5. Mrig. 6. Ardh. 7. Punar. 8. Push. 9. Aslesh. 10. Magh. 11. P. Phal. 12. U. Phal. 13. Hasta. 14. Chit.

A. D. 1827.

A.—Amavasya. Kollam 1003, Commences { **N. Malabar—Sept. / S. Malabar—Aug.**

P.—Paurnami.

Hijra 1243, Commences, **July 25.**

Vikrama 1884. Bengal San 1233. (N. Cycle) Vilamba.

Columns: SOLAR reckoning — Cyclic Sidereal Year, Month and Day; Week-Day; English Month and Day. LUNAR reckoning — Tithi; Ending Moment; Nakshatra; Ending Moment; Muhammadan Year, Month and Day.

July

Cyclic Sidereal Year, Month and Day	Week-Day	English Month and Day	Tithi	Ending Moment	Nakshatra	Ending Moment	Muhammadan Year, Month and Day
19	Su	1	7	·57	12	·45	6
20	Mo	2	8	·51	13	·44	7
21	Tu	3	9	·46	14	·41	8
22	We	4	10	·38	15	·37	9
23	Th	5	11	·29	16	·31	10
24	Fr	6	12	·19	17	·25	11
25	Sa	7	{ 13 14	·09 ·98	18	·18	12
26	Su	8	P	·88	19	·12	13
27	Mo	9	1	·79	20 21	·05 ·98 }	14
28	Tu	10	2	·69	22	·93	15
29	We	11	3	·62	23	·88	16
30	Th	12	4	·55	24	·86	17
31	Fr	13	5	·52	25	·85	18
32	Sa	14	6	·49	26	·86	19
1	Su	15	7	·47	27	·89	20
2	Mo	16	8	·49	1	·93	21
3	Tu	17	9	·52	...	...	22
4	We	18	10	·58	2	·01	23
5	Th	19	11	·63	3	·10	24
6	Fr	20	12	·72	4	·19	25
7	Sa	21	13	·80	5	·30	26
8	Su	22	14	·87	6	·41	27
9	Mo	23	A	·95	7	·51	28
10	Tu	24	...	...	8	·60	29
11	We	25	1	·02	9	·68	1
12	Th	26	2	·05	10	·73	2
13	Fr	27	3	·07	11	·76	3
14	Sa	28	4	·07	12	·77	4
15	Su	29	5	·05	13	·76	5
16	Mo	30	{ 6 7	·00 ·94	14	·74	6
17	Tu	31	8	·87	15	·70	7

(Side labels: Sarvajit *Mithuna—Ani.*; Sarvajit *Karkata—Adi.*; *Sukla*, Ashadha, *Bahula*, *Sukla*; H. 1242 *Zil-hijja.*)

Aug.

Cyclic Sidereal Year, Month and Day	Week-Day	English Month and Day	Tithi	Ending Moment	Nakshatra	Ending Moment	Muhammadan Year, Month and Day
18	We	1	9	·78	16	·65	8
19	Th	2	10	·68	17	·59	9
20	Fr	3	11	·59	18	·52	10
21	Sa	4	12	·48	19	·46	11
22	Su	5	13	·38	20	·39	12
23	Mo	6	14	·28	21	·32	13
24	Tu	7	P	·19	22	·26	14
25	We	8	1	·12	23	·23	15
26	Th	9	2	·04	24	·19	16
27	Fr	10	{ 3 4	·00 ·97	25	·18	17
28	Sa	11	5	·97	26	·18	18
29	Su	12	6	·97	27	·20	19
30	Mo	13	7	·99	1	·25	20
31	Tu	14	...	...	2	·32	21
1	We	15	8	·05	3	·40	22
2	Th	16	9	·12	4	·49	23
3	Fr	17	10	·21	5	·60	24
4	Sa	18	11	·29	6	·71	25
5	Su	19	12	·37	7	·82	26
6	Mo	20	13	·44	8	·91	27
7	Tu	21	14	·51	9	·98	28
8	We	22	A	·54	...	...	29
9	Th	23	1	·57	10	·04	30
10	Fr	24	2	·56	11	·08	1
11	Sa	25	3	·54	12	·10	2
12	Su	26	4	·50	13	·10	3
13	Mo	27	5	·45	14	·07	4
14	Tu	28	6	·38	15 16	·04 ·98 }	5
15	We	29	7	·29	17	·93	6
16	Th	30	8	·18	18	·87	7
17	Fr	31	{ 9 10	·09 ·98	19	·80	8

(Side labels: Sarvajit *Simha—Avani.*; Sravana, *Bahula*, *Sukla*, Bhadra.; H. 1243 *Muharram.*; H. 1243 *Safar.*)

Sep.

Cyclic Sidereal Year, Month and Day	Week-Day	English Month and Day	Tithi	Ending Moment	Nakshatra	Ending Moment	Muhammadan Year, Month and Day
18	Sa	1	11	·89	20	·73	9
19	Su	2	12	·79	21	·66	10
20	Mo	3	13	·71	22	·61	11
21	Tu	4	14	·63	23	·56	12
22	We	5	P	·56	24	·52	13
23	Th	6	1	·51	25	·50	14
24	Fr	7	2	·48	26	·50	15
25	Sa	8	3	·48	27	·53	16
26	Su	9	4	·48	1	·56	17
27	Mo	10	5	·52	2	·62	18
28	Tu	11	6	·58	3	·70	19
29	We	12	7	·64	4	·79	20
30	Th	13	8	·72	5	·90	21
31	Fr	14	9	·80	...	...	22
1	Sa	15	10	·89	6	·01	23
2	Su	16	11	·97	7	·12	24
3	Mo	17	...	...	8	·21	25
4	Tu	18	12	·04	9	·29	26
5	We	19	13	·07	10	·35	27
6	Th	20	14	·09	11	·40	28
7	Fr	21	A	·09	12	·42	29
8	Sa	22	1	·07	13	·42	1
9	Su	23	{ 2 3	·04 ·98	14	·40	2
10	Mo	24	4	·91	15	·37	3
11	Tu	25	5	·82	16	·33	4
12	We	26	6	·73	17	·27	5
13	Th	27	7	·64	18	·20	6
14	Fr	28	8	·53	19	·13	7
15	Sa	29	9	·43	20	·07	8
16	Su	30	10	·33	21 22	·01 ·94 }	9

(Side labels: Sarvajit *Simha—Avani.*; Sarvajit *Kanya—Purattasi.*; *Suk.*, Bhadrapada, *Bahula*, *Sukla*; H. 1243 *Safar.*)

Oct.

Cyclic Sidereal Year, Month and Day	Week-Day	English Month and Day	Tithi	Ending Moment	Nakshatra	Ending Moment	Muhammadan Year, Month and Day
17	Mo	1	11	·25	23	·89	10
18	Tu	2	12	·17	24	·85	11
19	We	3	13	·11	25	·83	12
20	Th	4	14	·06	26	·83	13
21	Fr	5	P	·04	27	·84	14
22	Sa	6	1	·03	1	·89	15
23	Su	7	2	·03	2	·93	16
24	Mo	8	3	·08	...	...	17
25	Tu	9	4	·13	3	·00	18
26	We	10	5	·21	4	·09	19
27	Th	11	6	·28	5	·20	20
28	Fr	12	7	·38	6	·31	21
29	Sa	13	8	·45	7	·42	22
30	Su	14	9	·53	8	·51	23
31	Mo	15	10	·60	9	·60	24
1	Tu	16	11	·68	10	·67	25
2	We	17	12	·67	11	·72	26
3	Th	18	13	·66	12	·74	27
4	Fr	19	14	·65	13	·75	28
5	Sa	20	A	·61	14	·73	29
6	Su	21	1	·56	15	·71	30
7	Mo	22	2	·49	16	·66	1
8	Tu	23	3	·40	17	·61	2
9	We	24	4	·31	18	·54	3
10	Th	25	5	·21	19	·47	4
11	Fr	26	6	·11	20	·41	5
12	Sa	27	{ 7 8	·01 ·92	21	·34	6
13	Su	28	9	·83	22	·28	7
14	Mo	29	10	·76	23	·22	8
15	Tu	30	11	·70	24	·18	9
16	We	31	12	·65	25	·15	10

(Side labels: Sarvajit *Tula—Aippasi.*; Asvina, *Bahula*, *Sukla*, Kartt.; H. 1243 *Rabi-ul-awwal.*; H. 1243 *Rabi-ul-akhir.*)

Nov.

Cyclic Sidereal Year, Month and Day	Week-Day	English Month and Day	Tithi	Ending Moment	Nakshatra	Ending Moment	Muhammadan Year, Month and Day
17	Th	1	13	·63	26	·15	11
18	Fr	2	14	·62	27	·16	12
19	Sa ☾	3	P	·63	1	·19	13
20	Su	4	1	·68	2	·24	14
21	Mo	5	2	·73	3	·31	15
22	Tu	6	3	·81	4	·40	16
23	We	7	4	·88	5	·50	17
24	Th	8	5	·98	6	·61	18
25	Fr	9	...	...	7	·71	19
26	Sa	10	6	·07	8	·81	20
27	Su	11	7	·14	9	·91	21
28	Mo	12	8	·20	10	·98	22
29	Tu	13	9	·24	...	...	23
1	We	14	10	·27	11	·03	24
2	Th	15	11	·26	12	·06	25
3	Fr	16	12	·26	13	·07	26
4	Sa	17	13	·22	14	·06	27
5	Su	18	14	·17	15	·04	28
6	Mo	19	A	·09	16 17	·00 ·94 }	29
7	Tu	20	{ 1 2	·02 ·92	18	·88	1
8	We	21	3	·82	19	·82	2
9	Th	22	4	·72	20	·75	3
10	Fr	23	5	·63	21	·68	4
11	Sa	24	6	·54	22	·62	5
12	Su	25	7	·45	23	·56	6
13	Mo	26	8	·38	24	·51	7
14	Tu	27	9	·31	25	·49	8
15	We	28	10	·27	26	·47	9
16	Th	29	11	·25	27	·48	10
17	Fr	30	12	·24	1	·50	11

(Side labels: Sarvajit *Tula—Aippasi.*; Sarvajit *Vrischika—Kartigai.*; *Suk.*, Kartika, *Bahula*, *Sukla*; H. 1243 *Rabi-ul-akhir.*)

Dec.

Cyclic Sidereal Year, Month and Day	Week-Day	English Month and Day	Tithi	Ending Moment	Nakshatra	Ending Moment	Muhammadan Year, Month and Day
18	Sa	1	13	·27	2	·55	12
19	Su	2	14	·30	3	·62	13
20	Mo	3	P	·36	4	·70	14
21	Tu	4	1	·43	5	·80	15
22	We	5	2	·53	6	·91	16
23	Th	6	3	·61	...	...	17
24	Fr	7	4	·70	7	·01	18
25	Sa	8	5	·78	8	·12	19
26	Su	9	6	·84	9	·21	20
27	Mo	10	7	·88	10	·29	21
28	Tu	11	8	·90	11	·34	22
29	We	12	9	·91	12	·38	23
30	Th	13	10	·89	13	·40	24
1	Fr	14	11	·84	14	·40	25
2	Sa	15	12	·80	15	·37	26
3	Su	16	13	·72	16	·33	27
4	Mo	17	14	·64	17	·28	28
5	Tu	18	A	·55	18	·22	29
6	We	19	1	·46	19	·16	30
7	Th	20	2	·35	20	·09	1
8	Fr	21	3	·25	21 22	·02 ·95 }	2
9	Sa	22	4	·17	23	·89	3
10	Su	23	5	·08	24	·85	4
11	Mo	24	{ 6 7	·01 ·95	25	·82	5
12	Tu	25	8	·91	26	·80	6
13	We	26	9	·89	27	·80	7
14	Th	27	10	·90	1	·82	8
15	Fr	28	11	·91	2	·87	9
16	Sa	29	12	·95	3	·93	10
17	Su	30	...	...	...	...	11
18	Mo	31	13	·02	4	·01	12

(Side labels: Sarvajit *Dhanus—Margali.*; Margasira, *Bahula*, *Sukla*, Pausha; H. 1243 *Jumada-l-awwal.*; H. 1243 *Jumada-l-akhir.*)

15. Svati. 16. Visak. 17. Anur. 18. Jyesh. 19. Mula. 20. P. Ash. 21. U. Ash. 22. Sravn. 23. Dani. 24. Satab. 25. P. Bhad. 26. U. Bhad. 27. Rev.

A. D. 1828. **Mesha Sankranti** (Commencement of Indian Sidereal Year).
Solar Eclipse: ● **(Surya Sid.) April 10·99.** **Saka 1750.** **Kaliyuga 4929.**
Lunar Eclipse. ○ **(Arya Sid.) April 10·89.** **(S. Cycle) Sarvadhari.**

SOLAR reckoning: Cyclic Sidereal Year, Month and Day; Week-Day; English Month and Day. LUNAR reckoning: Tithi, Ending Moment; Nakshatra, Ending Moment; Muhammadan Year, Month and Day.

Jan.

Cyclic Sidereal Year, Month and Day	Week-Day	English Month and Day	Tithi	Ending Moment	Nakshatra	Ending Moment	Muhammadan Year, Month and Day
Sarvajit Dhanus—Margali. 19	Tu	1	Pausha 14	·09	5	·10	H. 1243 Jumadal-akhir. 13
20	We	2	P	·18	6	·20	14
21	Th	3	1	·26	7	·32	15
22	Fr	4	2	·36	8	·42	16
23	Sa	5	3	·43	9	·52	17
24	Su	6	4	·48	10	·59	18
25	Mo	7	5	·54	11	·65	19
26	Tu	8	Bahula 6	·55	12	·70	20
27	We	9	7	·55	13	·72	21
28	Th	10	8	·54	14	·72	22
—29	Fr	11	9	·50	15	·70	23
1	Sa	12	10	·44	16	·66	24
2	Su	13	11	·37	17	·62	25
3	Mo	14	12	·29	18	·57	26
4	Tu	15	13	·19	19	·50	27
5	We	16	{14 / A	·09 / ·99	20	·43	28
6	Th	17	1	·91	21	·36	—29
7	Fr	18	2	·81	22	·29	1
8	Sa	19	3	·73	23	·24	2
9	Su	20	4	·66	24	·19	3
10	Mo	21	Sukla 5	·59	25	·15	4
11	Tu	22	6	·56	26	·12	5
12	We	23	7	·53	27	·12	6
Sarvajit Makara—Tai. 13	Th	24	8	·54	1	·14	7
14	Fr	25	9	·55	2	·18	8
15	Sa	26	10	·61	3	·23	9
16	Su	27	Magha 11	·67	4	·31	Rajab. 10
17	Mo	28	12	·74	5	·40	11
18	Tu	29	13	·83	6	·51	12
19	We	30	14	·91	7	·62	13
20	Th	31	...	...	8	·72	14

Feb.

Cyclic Sidereal Year, Month and Day	Week-Day	English Month and Day	Tithi	Ending Moment	Nakshatra	Ending Moment	Muhammadan Year, Month and Day
21	Fr	1	P	·01	9	·82	H. 1243 15
22	Sa	2	1	·08	10	·90	16
23	Su	3	2	·14	11	·96	17
24	Mo	4	3	·17	...	...	18
25	Tu	5	4	·20	12	·02	19
26	We	6	Bahula 5	·10	13	·04	20
27	Th	7	6	·17	14	·05	21
28	Fr	8	7	·13	15	·03	22
29	Sa	9	8	·06	16 / 17	·00 / ·95}	23
—30	Su	10	{9 / 10	·00 / ·91	18	·90	24
1	Mo	11	11	·32	19	·84	25
2	Tu	12	12	·71	20	·77	26
3	We	13	13	·62	21	·70	27
4	Th	14	14	·58	22	·64	28
5	Fr	15	—A	·43	23	·57	29
6	Sa	16	1	·35	24	·52	—30
7	Su	17	2	·28	25	·48	1
8	Mo	18	3	·23	26	·45	2
9	Tu	19	Sukla 4	·18	27	·45	H. 1243 Shaban. 3
10	We	20	5	·16	1	·46	4
11	Th	21	6	·16	2	·49	5
12	Fr	22	7	·18	3	·54	6
Sarvajit Kumbha—Masi. 13	Sa	23	Phalguna 8	·24	4	·61	7
14	Su	24	9	·29	5	·70	8
15	Mo	25	10	·37	6	·81	9
16	Tu	26	11	·46	7	·92	10
17	We	27	12	·54	...	...	11
18	Th	28	13	·62	8	·02	12
19	Fr	29	14	·70	9	·12	13

March

Cyclic Sidereal Year, Month and Day	Week-Day	English Month and Day	Tithi	Ending Moment	Nakshatra	Ending Moment	Muhammadan Year, Month and Day
Sarvajit Kumbha—Masi. 20	Sa	1	Phalguna P	·76	10	·21	14
21	Su	2	1	·80	11	·28	15
22	Mo	3	2	·81	12	·33	16
23	Tu	4	3	·80	13	·36	17
24	We	5	4	·79	14	·37	18
25	Th	6	5	·73	15	·36	H. 1243 Shaban. 19
26	Fr	7	6	·67	16	·34	20
27	Sa	8	7	·61	17	·29	21
28	Su	9	Bahula 8	·52	18	·24	22
29	Mo	10	9	·43	19	·17	23
30	Tu	11	10	·32	20	·10	24
—31	We	12	11	·23	21 / 22	·04 / ·97}	25
1	Th	13	12	·12	23	·91	26
2	Fr	14	{13 / 14	·03 / ·95	24	·85	27
3	Sa	15	—A	·87	25	·81	28
4	Su	16	1	·81	26	·79	—29
5	Mo	17	2	·77	27	·77	1
6	Tu	18	3	·76	1	·78	2
7	We	19	4	·76	2	·80	3
8	Th	20	5	·79	3	·85	4
9	Fr	21	6	·83	4	·92	5
10	Sa	22	Sukla 7	·88	...	...	6
11	Su	23	8	·97	5	·01	7
Sarvajit Mina—Panguni. 12	Mo	24	...	...	6	·11	8
13	Tu	25	9	·05	7	·21	9
14	We	26	10	·14	8	·32	10
15	Th	27	Chaitra 11	·22	9	·42	Ramzan. 11
16	Fr	28	12	·29	10	·52	12
17	Sa	29	13	·34	11	·59	13
18	Su	30	14	·38	12	·65	14
19	Mo	31	P	·39	13	·68	15

April

Cyclic Sidereal Year, Month and Day	Week-Day	English Month and Day	Tithi	Ending Moment	Nakshatra	Ending Moment	Muhammadan Year, Month and Day
20	Tu	1	1	·38	14	·69	H. 1243 16
21	We	2	2	·37	15	·69	17
22	Th	3	3	·31	16	·67	18
23	Fr	4	Bahula 4	·25	17	·63	19
24	Sa	5	5	·18	18	·57	20
25	Su	6	6	·09	19	·51	21
26	Mo	7	{7 / 8	·00 / ·89	20	·45	22
27	Tu	8	9	·79	21	·38	23
28	We	9	10	·69	22	·31	24
—29	Th	10	11	·60	23	·26	25
1	Fr	11	12	·50	24	·19	26
2	Sa	12	13	·43	25	·14	27
3	Su	13	14	·37	26	·12	28
4	Mo	● 14	—A	·33	27	·10	29
5	Tu	15	1	·32	1	·10	—30
6	We	16	2	·31	2	·12	1
7	Th	17	3	·34	3	·16	2
8	Fr	18	4	·38	4	·23	3
9	Sa	19	5	·44	5	·31	H. 1243 Shawwal. 4
10	Su	20	Sukla 6	·52	6	·41	5
11	Mo	21	7	·60	7	·51	6
12	Tu	22	8	·68	8	·62	7
Sarvadhari Mesha—Chittirai. 13	We	23	9	·75	9	·73	8
14	Th	24	10	·83	10	·82	9
15	Fr	25	Vaisakha 11	·88	11	·90	10
16	Sa	26	12	·93	12	·96	11
17	Su	27	13	·93	...	...	12
18	Mo	28	14	·93	13	·00	13
19	Tu	29	P	·91	14	·02	14
20	We	30	1	·84	15	·02	15

May

Cyclic Sidereal Year, Month and Day	Week-Day	English Month and Day	Tithi	Ending Moment	Nakshatra	Ending Moment	Muhammadan Year, Month and Day
Sarvadhari Mesha—Chittirai. 21	Th	1	Vaisk. 2	·78	16 / 17	·00 / ·96}	16
22	Fr	2	3	·71	18	·91	17
23	Sa	3	4	·62	19	·86	18
24	Su	4	5	·53	20	·79	H. 1243 Shawwal. 19
25	Mo	5	Bahula 6	·43	21	·72	20
26	Tu	6	7	·32	22	·65	21
27	We	7	8	·21	23	·58	22
28	Th	8	9	·12	24	·52	23
29	Fr	9	{10 / 11	·03 / ·97	25	·48	24
30	Sa	10	12	·90	26	·44	25
—31	Su	11	13	·86	27	·42	26
1	Mo	12	14	·84	1	·42	27
2	Tu	13	—A	·83	2	·43	28
3	We	14	1	·86	3	·48	—29
4	Th	15	2	·89	4	·54	1
5	Fr	16	3	·95	5	·61	2
6	Sa	17	...	...	6	·71	3
7	Su	18	4	·02	7	·81	4
8	Mo	19	5	·09	8	·93	5
9	Tu	20	Sukla 6	·19	...	...	6
10	We	21	7	·28	9	·03	7
11	Th	22	8	·34	10	·13	8
Sarvadhari Vrishabha—Vaikasi. 12	Fr	23	9	·39	11	·21	9
13	Sa	24	10	·44	12	·27	H. 1243 Zi-l-ka'da. 10
14	Su	25	11	·44	13	·32	11
15	Mo	26	Jyeshtha 12	·43	14	·34	12
16	Tu	27	13	·41	15	·34	13
17	We	28	14	·37	16	·33	14
18	Th	29	P	·29	17	·29	15
19	Fr	30	1	·20	18	·24	16
20	Sa	31	2	·12	19	·20	17

June

Cyclic Sidereal Year, Month and Day	Week-Day	English Month and Day	Tithi	Ending Moment	Nakshatra	Ending Moment	Muhammadan Year, Month and Day
21	Su	1	{3 / 4	·03 / ·92	20	·13	18
22	Mo	2	5	·82	21 / 22	·06 / ·99}	19
23	Tu	3	6	·72	23	·92	20
24	We	4	Bahula 7	·62	24	·87	21
25	Th	5	8	·53	25	·81	22
26	Fr	6	9	·47	26	·77	23
27	Sa	7	10	·40	27	·75	24
28	Su	8	11	·36	1	·74	25
29	Mo	9	12	·33	2	·76	26
30	Tu	10	13	·33	3	·79	27
—31	We	11	14	·34	4	·85	28
1	Th	12	—A	·38	5	·92	29
2	Fr	13	1	·43	...	...	—30
3	Sa	14	2	·49	6	·01	1
4	Su	15	Sukla 3	·58	7	·12	2
5	Mo	16	4	·66	8	·22	3
6	Tu	17	5	·76	9	·33	4
7	We	18	6	·82	10	·43	5
8	Th	19	7	·87	11	·51	H. 1243 Zi-l-hijja. 6
9	Fr	20	8	·91	12	·59	7
10	Sa	21	9	·92	13	·64	8
11	Su	22	Adhika Ashadha 10	·91	14	·66	9
12	Mo	23	11	·89	15	·67	10
Sarvadhari Mithuna—Ani. 13	Tu	24	12	·85	16	·65	11
14	We	25	13	·77	17	·62	12
15	Th	26	14	·70	18	·59	13
16	Fr	27	P	·61	19	·53	14
17	Sa	28	Bah. 1	·50	20	·47	15
18	Su	29	2	·41	21	·40	16
19	Mo	30	3	·31	22	·33	17

Naksh:—1. Asvn. 2. Bhar. 3. Krit. 4. Rohi. 5. Mrig. 6. Ardh. 7. Punar. 8. Push. 9. Aslesh. 10. Magh. 11. P. Phal. 12. U. Phal. 13. Hasta. 14. Chit.

A. D. 1828. **A.—Amavasya. P.—Paurnami.** **Kollam 1004,** Commences { **N. Malabar—Sept.** / **S. Malabar—Aug.** } **Hijra 1244,** Commences **July 14.** **Vikrama 1885. Bengal San 1234. (N. Cycle) Vikarin.**

Columns: SOLAR reckoning (Cyclic Sidereal Year, Month and Day; Week-Day; English Month and Day) — LUNAR reckoning (Tithi, Ending Moment; Nakshatra, Ending Moment; Muhammadan Year, Month and Day).

July

Sarvadhari Mithuna—Ani; Sarvadhari Karkata—Adi. Ash. — Adh. Bahula — Sukla — Nija~Ashadha Bahula. H. 1243 Zil-hijja; H. 1244 Muharram.

Cyclic Sidereal Day	Week-Day	English Day	Tithi	Ending Moment	Nakshatra	Ending Moment	Muhammadan Day
20	Tu	1	4	·21	23	·27	18
21	We	2	5	·10	24	·20	19
22	Th	3	6 / 7	·02 / ·95	25	·15	20
23	Fr	4	8	·88	26	·10	21
24	Sa	5	9	·83	27	·07	22
25	Su	6	10	·81	1	·07	23
26	Mo	7	11	·80	2	·08	24
27	Tu	8	12	·81	3	·11	25
28	We	9	13	·86	4	·15	26
29	Th	10	14	·91	5	·22	27
30	Fr	11	A	·98	6	·32	28
31	Sa	12	...	...	7	·42	29
32	Su	13	1	·06	8	·52	30
1	Mo	14	2	·14	9	·63	1
2	Tu	15	3	·22	10	·73	2
3	We	16	4	·29	11	·81	3
4	Th	17	5	·35	12	·90	4
5	Fr	18	6	·38	13	·95	5
6	Sa	19	7	·40	14	·98	6
7	Su	20	8	·39	15	·99	7
8	Mo	21	9	·37	16	·98	8
9	Tu	22	10	·32	17	·96	9
10	We	23	11	·25	18	·92	10
11	Th	24	12	·18	19	·87	11
12	Fr	25	13	·10	20	·81	12
13	Sa	26	14 / P	·00 / ·90	21	·74	13
14	Su	27	1	·81	22	·68	14
15	Mo	28	2	·70	23	·61	15
16	Tu	29	3	·59	24	·54	16
17	We	30	4	·51	25	·48	17
18	Th	31	5	·42	26	·44	18

Aug.

Sarvadhari Simha—Avani. Bahula — Sukla — Sravana — Bahula. H. 1244 Safar.

Cyclic Sidereal Day	Week-Day	English Day	Tithi	Ending Moment	Nakshatra	Ending Moment	Muhammadan Day
19	Fr	1	6	·36	27	·41	19
20	Sa	2	7	·31	1	·40	20
21	Su	3	8	·30	2	·40	21
22	Mo	4	9	·29	3	·42	22
23	Tu	5	10	·28	4	·46	23
24	We	6	11	·33	5	·54	24
25	Th	7	12	·38	6	·62	25
26	Fr	8	13	·46	7	·71	26
27	Sa	9	14	·53	8	·82	27
28	Su	10	A	·62	9	·93	28
29	Mo	11	1	·70	...	...	29
30	Tu	12	2	·78	10	·03	30
31	We	13	3	·83	11	·13	1
1	Th	14	4	·86	12	·20	2
2	Fr	15	5	·89	13	·26	3
3	Sa	16	6	·88	14	·30	4
4	Su	17	7	·86	15	·31	5
5	Mo	18	8	·82	16	·32	6
6	Tu	19	9	·76	17	·29	7
7	We	20	10	·68	18	·26	8
8	Th	21	11	·59	19	·20	9
9	Fr	22	12	·50	20	·14	10
10	Sa	23	13	·40	21	·09	11
11	Su	24	14	·29	22 / 23	·02 / ·94	12
12	Mo	25	P	·19	24	·88	13
13	Tu	26	1	·10	25	·82	14
14	We	27	2 / 3	·01 / ·93	26	·77	15
15	Th	28	4	·87	27	·74	16
16	Fr	29	5	·81	1	·72	17
17	Sa	30	6	·80	2	·72	18
18	Su	31	7	·79	3	·74	19

Sep.

Sarvadhari Simha—Avani; Sarvadhari Kanya—Purattasi. Srvn. Bah. — Sukla — Bhadrapada. H. 1244 Safar; H. 1244 Rabi-ul-awwal.

Cyclic Sidereal Day	Week-Day	English Day	Tithi	Ending Moment	Nakshatra	Ending Moment	Muhammadan Day
19	Mo	1	8	·81	4	·77	20
20	Tu	2	9	·84	5	·84	21
21	We	3	10	·90	6	·92	22
22	Th	4	11	·96	...	...	23
23	Fr	5	...	...	7	·01	24
24	Sa	6	12	·04	8	·12	25
25	Su	7	13	·11	9	·22	26
26	Mo	8	14	·20	10	·34	27
27	Tu	9	A	·29	11	·43	28
28	We	10	1	·34	12	·51	29
29	Th	11	2	·39	13	·57	1
30	Fr	12	3	·41	14	·61	2
31	Sa	13	4	·40	15	·64	3
1	Su	14	5	·38	16	·64	4
2	Mo	15	6	·34	17	·62	5
3	Tu	16	7	·29	18	·59	6
4	We	17	8	·21	19	·54	7
5	Th	18	9	·13	20	·49	8
6	Fr	19	10 / 11	·02 / ·93	21	·42	9
7	Sa	20	12	·83	22	·35	10
8	Su	21	13	·72	23	·28	11
9	Mo	22	14	·63	24	·21	12
10	Tu	23	P	·54	25	·15	13
11	We	24	1	·47	26	·11	14
12	Th	25	2	·41	27	·07	15
13	Fr	26	3	·36	1	·05	16
14	Sa	27	4	·34	2	·04	17
15	Su	28	5	·33	3	·05	18
16	Mo	29	6	·35	4	·10	19
17	Tu	30	7	·38	5	·15	20

Oct.

Sarvadhari Tula—Aippasi. Bahula — Sukla — Asvina — Bahula. H. 1244 Rabi-ul-akhir.

Cyclic Sidereal Day	Week-Day	English Day	Tithi	Ending Moment	Nakshatra	Ending Moment	Muhammadan Day
18	We	1	8	·44	6	·22	21
19	Th	2	9	·51	7	·31	22
20	Fr	3	10	·61	8	·41	23
21	Sa	4	11	·68	9	·53	24
22	Su	5	12	·75	10	·64	25
23	Mo	6	13	·83	11	·73	26
24	Tu	7	14	·89	12	·82	27
25	We	● 8	A	·94	13	·88	28
26	Th	9	1	·95	14	·94	29
27	Fr	10	2	·97	15	·96	30
28	Sa	11	3	·94	16	·97	1
29	Su	12	4	·91	17	·95	2
30	Mo	13	5	·85	18	·92	3
31	Tu	14	6	·77	19	·88	4
1	We	15	7	·69	20	·83	5
2	Th	16	8	·59	21	·76	6
3	Fr	17	9	·50	22	·69	7
4	Sa	18	10	·39	23	·62	8
5	Su	19	11	·30	24	·55	9
6	Mo	20	12	·20	25	·50	10
7	Tu	21	13	·11	26	·44	11
8	We	22	14 / P	·05 / ·99	27	·40	12
9	Th	23	1	·94	1	·37	13
10	Fr	24	2	·92	2	·36	14
11	Sa	25	3	·92	3	·38	15
12	Su	26	4	·93	4	·41	16
13	Mo	27	5	·96	5	·46	17
14	Tu	28	...	...	6	·53	18
15	We	29	6	·03	7	·61	19
16	Th	30	7	·11	8	·72	20
17	Fr	31	8	·19	9	·83	21

Nov.

Sarvadhari Tula—Aippasi; Sarvadhari Vrischika—Karttigai. Asv. Bah. — Sukla — Kartika — Bahula. Rabi-ul-akhir; H. 1244 Jumada-l-awwal.

Cyclic Sidereal Day	Week-Day	English Day	Tithi	Ending Moment	Nakshatra	Ending Moment	Muhammadan Day
18	Sa	1	9	·27	10	·93	22
19	Su	2	10	·36	...	...	23
20	Mo	3	11	·43	11	·05	24
21	Tu	4	12	·49	12	·12	25
22	We	5	13	·54	13	·20	26
23	Th	6	14	·56	14	·25	27
24	Fr	7	A	·56	15	·28	28
25	Sa	8	1	·53	16	·29	29
26	Su	9	2	·50	17	·28	1
27	Mo	10	3	·45	18	·25	2
28	Tu	11	4	·38	19	·22	3
29	We	12	5	·29	20	·16	4
30	Th	13	6	·19	21	·10	5
1	Fr	14	7	·10	22 / 23	·03 / ·96	6
2	Sa	15	8 / 9	·00 / ·91	24	·90	7
3	Su	16	10	·81	25	·83	8
4	Mo	17	11	·73	26	·78	9
5	Tu	18	12	·66	27	·73	10
6	We	19	13	·59	1	·70	11
7	Th	20	14	·55	2	·69	12
8	Fr	21	P	·53	3	·70	13
9	Sa	22	1	·54	4	·72	14
10	Su	23	2	·56	5	·77	15
11	Mo	24	3	·59	6	·83	16
12	Tu	25	4	·65	7	·92	17
13	We	26	5	·73	...	...	18
14	Th	27	6	·82	8	·02	19
15	Fr	28	7	·90	9	·13	20
16	Sa	29	8	·98	10	·23	21
17	Su	30	...	...	11	·33	22

Dec.

Sarvadhari Dhanus—Margali. Sukla — Margasira — Bahula. H. 1244 Jumada-l-akhir.

Cyclic Sidereal Day	Week-Day	English Day	Tithi	Ending Moment	Nakshatra	Ending Moment	Muhammadan Day
18	Mo	1	9	·05	12	·43	23
19	Tu	2	10	·14	13	·51	24
20	We	3	11	·17	14	·56	25
21	Th	4	12	·19	15	·60	26
22	Fr	5	13	·18	16	·61	27
23	Sa	6	14	·16	17	·60	28
24	Su	7	A	·13	18	·59	29
25	Mo	8	1	·06	19	·55	30
26	Tu	9	2 / 3	·00 / ·91	20	·50	1
27	We	10	4	·82	21	·44	2
28	Th	11	5	·73	22	·37	3
29	Fr	12	6	·62	23	·31	4
1	Sa	13	7	·53	24	·24	5
2	Su	14	8	·43	25	·17	6
3	Mo	15	9	·36	26	·11	7
4	Tu	16	10	·28	27	·06	8
5	We	17	11	·23	1	·04	9
6	Th	18	12	·19	2	·02	10
7	Fr	19	13	·18	3	·02	11
8	Sa	20	14	·17	4	·04	12
9	Su	21	P	·19	5	·08	13
10	Mo	22	1	·24	6	·15	14
11	Tu	23	2	·30	7	·23	15
12	We	24	3	·38	8	·32	16
13	Th	25	4	·47	9	·42	17
14	Fr	26	5	·56	10	·53	18
15	Sa	27	6	·64	11	·63	19
16	Su	28	7	·71	12	·74	20
17	Mo	29	8	·78	13	·82	21
18	Tu	30	9	·81	14	·87	22
19	We	31	10	·84	15	·91	23

15. Svati. 16. Visak. 17. Anur. 18. Jyesh. 19. Mula. 20. P. Ash. 21. U. Ash. 22. Sravn. 23. Dani. 24. Satab. 25. P. Bhad. 26. U. Bhad. 27. Rev.

A. D. 1829. **Mesha Sankranti** (Commencement of Indian Sidereal Year).
Solar Eclipse. ● **(Surya Sid.) April 11·25.** **Saka 1751.** **Kaliyuga 4930.**
Lunar Eclipse. ○ **(Arya Sid.) April 11·15.** **(S. Cycle) Virodhi.**

SOLAR reckoning: Cyclic Sidereal Year, Month and Day; Week-Day; English Month and Day. LUNAR reckoning: Tithi, Ending Moment; Nakshatra, Ending Moment; Muhammadan Year, Month and Day.

Jan.

Cyclic Sidereal Year, Month and Day	Week-Day	English Month and Day	Tithi	Ending Moment	Nakshatra	Ending Moment	Muhammadan Year, Month and Day
Sarvadhari *Dhanus—Margali.* 20	Th	1	Mr. *Bah.* 11	·83	16	·93	*Jl.-akhir.* 24
21	Fr	2	12	·81	17	·94	25
22	Sa	3	13	·77	18	·92	26
23	Su	4	14	·72	19	·68	27
24	Mo	5	—A	·64	20	·83	28
25	Tu	6	1	·55	21	·77	—29
26	We	7	2	·47	22	·71	1
27	Th	8	3	·37	23	·65	2
28	Fr	9	4	·27	24	·58	3
29	Sa	10	*Sukla* 5	·18	25	·51	4
—30	Su	11	6	·09	26	·45	5
1	Mo	12	7 8	·00 ·93	27	·41	6
2	Tu	13	9	·88	1	·37	7
3	We	14	10	·83	2	·34	8
4	Th	15	11	·82	3	·34	9
5	Fr	16	12	·82	4	·35	10
6	Sa	17	**Pausha** 13	·85	5	·40	11
7	Su	18	14	·88	6	·45	12
8	Mo	19	P	·95	7	·53	H. 1244 *Rajab.* 13
9	Tu	20	...	...	8	·62	14
10	We	21	1	·03	9	·72	15
11	Th	22	2	·12	10	·83	16
12	Fr	23	3	·21	11	·94	17
Sarvadhari *Makara—Tai.* 13	Sa	24	4	·30	...	...	18
14	Su	25	5	·37	12	·04	19
15	Mo	26	6	·42	13	·12	20
16	Tu	27	*Bahula* 7	·47	14	·18	21
17	We	28	8	·48	15	·23	22
18	Th	29	9	·47	16	·26	23
19	Fr	30	10	·45	17	·26	24
20	Sa	31	11	·41	18	·25	25

Feb.

Cyclic Sidereal Year, Month and Day	Week-Day	English Month and Day	Tithi	Ending Moment	Nakshatra	Ending Moment	Muhammadan Year, Month and Day
21	Su	1	12	·35	19	·22	26
22	Mo	2	13	·27	20	·17	27
23	Tu	3	14	·19	21	·12	28
24	We	4	—A	·09	22 23	·06 ·99	29
25	Th	5	1 2	·00 ·90	24	·92	—30
26	Fr	6	3	·80	25	·85	1
27	Sa	7	4	·71	26	·78	2
28	Su	8	5	·63	27	·74	3
—29	Mo	9	*Sukla* 6	·56	1	·70	4
1	Tu	10	7	·51	2	·67	5
2	We	11	8	·46	3	·66	6
3	Th	12	9	·45	4	·67	7
4	Fr	13	10	·45	5	·71	H. 1244 *Shaban.* 8
5	Sa	14	11	·49	6	·76	9
6	Su	15	12	·52	7	·83	10
Sarvadhari *Kumbha—Masi.* 7	Mo	16	13	·59	8	·92	11
8	Tu	17	**Magha** 14	·67	...	...	12
9	We	18	P	·76	9	·02	13
10	Th	19	1	·84	10	·14	14
11	Fr	20	2	·92	11	·24	15
12	Sa	21	3	·99	12	·34	16
13	Su	22	...	...	13	·43	17
14	Mo	23	4	·05	14	·49	18
15	Tu	24	5	·10	15	·55	19
16	We	25	*Bahula* 6	·10	16	·58	20
17	Th	26	7	·10	17	·59	21
18	Fr	27	8	·07	18	·58	22
19	Sa	28	9 10	·02 ·96	19	·55	23

March

Cyclic Sidereal Year, Month and Day	Week-Day	English Month and Day	Tithi	Ending Moment	Nakshatra	Ending Moment	Muhammadan Year, Month and Day
20	Su	1	Mg. *Bah.* 11	·89	20	·51	*Shaban.* 24
Sarvadhari *Kumbha—Masi.* 21	Mo	2	12	·81	21	·46	25
22	Tu	3	13	·71	22	·39	26
23	We	4	14	·62	23	·32	27
24	Th	5	—A	·51	24	·25	28
25	Fr	6	1	·41	25	·18	—29
26	Sa	7	2	·32	26	·13	1
27	Su	8	3	·24	27	*·07	2
28	Mo	9	4	17	1	·03	3
29	Tu	10	5	·11	2 3	·00 ·98	4
—30	We	11	*Sukla* 6	·08	...	...	5
1	Th	12	7	·06	4	·00	6
2	Fr	13	8	·06	5	·02	7
3	Sa	14	9	·09	6	·07	8
4	Su	15	10	·12	7	·14	9
5	Mo	16	11	·19	8	·22	10
6	Tu	17	12	·27	9	·33	11
7	We	18	13	·36	10	·43	12
8	Th	19	14	·44	11	·54	H. 1244 *Ramzan.* 13
9	Fr ○	20	**Phalguna** P	·54	12	·64	14
10	Sa	21	1	·60	13	·73	15
11	Su	22	2	·65	14	·81	16
Sarvadhari *Mina—Panguni.* 12	Mo	23	3	·69	15	·87	17
13	Tu	24	4	·69	16	·90	18
14	We	25	5	·69	17	·91	19
15	Th	26	6	·65	18	·90	20
16	Fr	27	*Bahula* 7	·61	19	·88	21
17	Sa	28	8	·55	20	·85	22
18	Su	29	9	·48	21	·79	23
19	Mo	30	10	·39	22	·73	24
20	Tu	31	11	·29	23	·66	25

April

Cyclic Sidereal Year, Month and Day	Week-Day	English Month and Day	Tithi	Ending Moment	Nakshatra	Ending Moment	Muhammadan Year, Month and Day
21	We	1	12	·18	24	·59	26
22	Th	2	13	·08	25	·53	27
23	Fr	3	14 A	·00 ·90	26	·47	28
24	Sa	4	1	·82	27	·41	29
25	Su	5	2	·74	1	·36	—30
26	Mo	6	3	·68	2	·32	1
27	Tu	7	4	·65	3	·32	2
28	We	8	5	·65	4	·32	3
29	Th	9	*Sukla* 6	·63	5	·34	4
—30	Fr	10	7	·65	6	·38	5
1	Sa	11	8	·69	7	·44	6
2	Su	12	9	·75	8	·53	7
3	Mo	13	10	·83	9	·63	8
4	Tu	14	11	·92	10	·73	9
5	We	15	...	...	11	·84	10
6	Th	16	12	·00	12	·94	H. 1244 *Shawwal.* 11
Virodhi *Mesha—Chittirai.* 7	Fr	17	**Chaitra** 13	·09	...	...	12
8	Sa	18	14	·15	13	·04	13
9	Su	19	P	·21	14	·12	14
10	Mo	20	1	·24	15	·18	15
11	Tu	21	2	·25	16	·22	16
12	We	22	3	·24	17	·23	17
13	Th	23	4	·20	18	·23	18
14	Fr	24	5	·15	19	·22	19
15	Sa	25	6	·09	20	·18	20
16	Su	26	7 8	·02 ·93	21	·13	21
17	Mo	27	*Bahula* 9	·84	22	·07	22
18	Tu	28	10	·73	23 24	·00 ·94	23
19	We	29	11	·63	25	·87	24
20	Th	30	12	·53	26	·80	25

May

Cyclic Sidereal Year, Month and Day	Week-Day	English Month and Day	Tithi	Ending Moment	Nakshatra	Ending Moment	Muhammadan Year, Month and Day
21	Fr	1	*Bah.* 13	·43	27	·74	26
Virodhi *Mesha—Chittirai.* 22	Sa	2	14	·35	1	·69	27
23	Su	3	—A	·27	2	·66	28
24	Mo	4	1	·23	3	·64	—29
25	Tu	5	2	·18	4	·64	1
26	We	6	3	·15	5	·65	2
27	Th	7	4	·15	6	·69	3
28	Fr	8	5	·18	7	·76	4
29	Sa	9	*Sukla* 6	·23	8	·84	5
30	Su	10	7	·28	9	·93	6
—31	Mo	11	8	·35	...	...	7
1	Tu	12	9	·43	10	·03	8
2	We	13	10	·52	11	·14	9
3	Th	14	11	·60	12	·24	10
4	Fr	15	**Vaisakha** 12	·67	13	·35	11
5	Sa	16	13	·72	14	·43	H. 1244 *Zi-l-ka'da.* 12
6	Su	17	14	·75	15	·49	13
7	Mo	18	P	·76	16	·53	14
8	Tu	19	1	·75	17	·55	15
9	We	20	2	·73	18	·56	16
10	Th	21	3	·67	19	·55	17
11	Fr	22	4	·60	20	·51	18
12	Sa	23	5	·53	21	·46	19
13	Su	24	6	·44	22	·41	20
Virodhi *Vrishabha—Vaikasi.* 14	Mo	25	*Bahula* 7	·34	23	·35	21
15	Tu	26	8	·23	24	·28	22
16	We	27	9	·14	25	·21	23
17	Th	28	10 11	·03 ·93	26	·14	24
18	Fr	29	12	·85	27	·08	25
19	Sa	30	13	·78	1 2	·03 ·99	26
20	Su	31	14	·72	3	·97	27

June

Cyclic Sidereal Year, Month and Day	Week-Day	English Month and Day	Tithi	Ending Moment	Nakshatra	Ending Moment	Muhammadan Year, Month and Day
21	Mo	1	—A	·67	4	·96	28
22	Tu	2	1	·66	5	·97	29
23	We	3	2	·65	...	...	—30
24	Th	4	3	·68	6	·01	1
25	Fr	5	4	·71	7	·07	2
26	Sa	6	5	·77	8	·14	3
27	Su	7	6	·85	9	·23	4
28	Mo	8	*Sukla* 7	·93	10	·33	5
29	Tu	9	...	...	11	·43	6
30	We	10	8	·01	12	·55	7
—31	Th	11	9	·09	13	·65	8
1	Fr	12	10	·16	14	·73	9
2	Sa	13	11	·20	15	·80	10
3	Su	14	**Jyeshtha** 12	·23	16	·85	H. 1244 *Zi-l-hijja.* 11
4	Mo	15	13	·25	17	·88	12
5	Tu	16	14	·23	18	·89	13
6	We	17	P	·21	19	·87	14
7	Th	18	1	·16	20	·84	15
8	Fr	19	2	·11	21	·80	16
Virodhi *Mithuna—Ani.* 9	Sa	20	3 4	·02 ·94	22	·75	17
10	Su	21	5	·84	23	·69	18
11	Mo	22	6	·78	24	·62	19
12	Tu	23	*Bahula* 7	·63	25	·55	20
13	We	24	8	·52	26	·48	21
14	Th	25	9	·43	27	·42	22
15	Fr	26	10	·34	1	·37	23
16	Sa	27	11	·27	2	·32	24
17	Su	28	12	·20	3	·29	25
18	Mo	29	13	·15	4	·28	26
19	Tu	30	14	·14	5	·29	27

Naksh:—1. Asvn. 2. Bhar. 3. Krit. 4. Rohi. 5. Mrig. 6. Ardh. 7. Punar. 8. Push. 9. Aslesh. 10. Magh. 11. P. Phal. 12. U. Phal. 13. Hasta. 14. Chit.

A. D. 1829.
A.—Amavasya.
P.—Paurnami.

Kollam 1005, Commences { **N. Malabar—Sept. S. Malabar—Aug.**

Hijra 1245, Commences, **July 3.**

Vikrama 1886.
Bengal San 1236.
(N. Cycle) Sarvari.

SOLAR reckoning.			LUNAR reckoning.				
Cyclic Sidereal Year, Month and Day.	Week-Day	English Month and Day.	Tithi	Ending Moment.	Nakshatra	Ending Moment.	Muhammadan Year, Month and Day.
	July						
Virodhi Mithuna—Ani. 20	We	1	—A	·13	6	·33	28
21	Th	2	Sukla 1	·15	7	·37	—29
22	Fr	3	2	·19	8	·44	H. 1245 Muharram. 1
23	Sa	4	3	·25	9	·53	2
24	Su	5	4	·31	10	·63	3
25	Mo	6	5	·39	11	·74	4
26	Tu	7	6	·48	12	·85	5
27	We	8	7	·55	13	·95	6
28	Th	9	8	·63	...	...	7
29	Fr	10	9	·68	14	·04	8
30	Sa	11	10	·71	15	·11	9
31	Su	12	11	·72	16	·17	10
—32	Mo	13	Ashadha 12	·72	17	·20	11
Virodhi Karkata—Adi. 1	Tu	14	13	·69	18	·21	12
2	We	15	14	·63	19	·20	13
3	Th	16	P	·58	20	·17	14
4	Fr	17	1	·50	21	·14	15
5	Sa	18	2	·41	22	·09	16
6	Su	19	3	·31	23 24	·03 ·96	17
7	Mo	20	4	·21	25	·89	18
8	Tu	21	5	·11	26	·82	19
9	We	22	6 7	·01 ·92	27	·76	20
10	Th	23	Bahula 8	·82	1	·70	21
11	Fr	24	9	·74	2	·66	22
12	Sa	25	10	·68	3	·62	23
13	Su	26	11	·64	4	·61	24
14	Mo	27	12	·62	5	·62	25
15	Tu	28	13	·60	6	·64	26
16	We	29	14	·63	7	·68	27
17	Th	30	—A	·66	8	·75	28
18	Fr	31	1	·71	9	·83	29
	Aug.						
19	Sa	1	2	·78	10	·94	—30
20	Su	2	3	·87	...	...	1
21	Mo	3	4	·95	11	·04	2
22	Tu	4	...	...	12	·15	3
23	We	5	5	·04	13	·25	4
24	Th	6	6	·10	14	·34	5
25	Fr	7	Sukla 7	·15	15	·42	6
26	Sa	8	8	·20	16	·48	7
27	Su	9	9	·21	17	·52	8
28	Mo	10	10	·20	18	·53	9
29	Tu	11	11	·17	19	·53	10
30	We	12	12	·13	20	·51	11
31	Th	13	13	·08	21	·48	12
—32	Fr	14	14 P	·00 ·91	22	·42	H. 1245 Safar. 13
1	Sa	15	Sravana 1	·81	23	·36	14
2	Su	16	2	·71	24	·30	15
3	Mo	17	3	·61	25	·22	16
4	Tu	18	4	·51	26	·16	17
5	We	19	5	·41	27	·10	18
Virodhi Simha—Avani. 6	Th	20	6	·32	1 2	·04 ·99	19
7	Fr	21	7	·25	3	·95	20
8	Sa	22	8	·19	4	·94	21
9	Su	23	Bahula 9	·14	5	·94	22
10	Mo	24	10	·11	6	·96	23
11	Tu	25	11	·11	7	·99	24
12	We	26	12	·12	...	...	25
13	Th	27	13	·17	8	·05	26
14	Fr	28	14	·22	9	·14	27
15	Sa	29	—A	·29	10	·23	28
16	Su	30	Suk. 1	·36	11	·34	—29
17	Mo	31	2	·44	12	·44	1

SOLAR reckoning.			LUNAR reckoning.				
Cyclic Sidereal Year, Month and Day.	Week-Day	English Month and Day.	Tithi	Ending Moment.	Nakshatra	Ending Moment.	Muhammadan Year, Month and Day.
	Sep.						
Virodhi Simha—Avani. 18	Tu	1	Sukla 3	·54	13	·55	2
19	We	2	4	·61	14	·65	3
20	Th	3	5	·67	15	·73	4
21	Fr	4	6	·70	16	·79	5
22	Sa	5	7	·72	17	·83	6
23	Su	6	8	·72	18	·85	7
24	Mo	7	9	·68	19	·85	8
25	Tu	8	10	·65	20	·84	9
26	We	9	11	·59	21	·81	10
27	Th	10	12	·52	22	·76	11
28	Fr	11	13	·42	23	·70	12
29	Sa	12	14	·33	24	·63	13
30	Su ○	13	P	·23	25	·57	14
—31	Mo	14	Bhadrapada 1	·13	26	·50	15
1	Tu	15	2 3	·03 ·93	27	·43	16
2	We	16	4	·86	1	·37	H. 1245 Rabi-ul-awwal. 17
3	Th	17	5	·78	2	·32	18
4	Fr	18	6	·72	3	·29	19
5	Sa	19	Bahula 7	·66	4	·27	20
6	Su	20	8	·64	5	·26	21
7	Mo	21	9	·64	6	·27	22
8	Tu	22	10	·65	7	·31	23
9	We	23	11	·70	8	·37	24
Virodhi Kanya—Purattasi. 10	Th	24	12	·75	9	·44	25
11	Fr	25	13	·82	10	·53	26
12	Sa	26	14	·90	11	·64	27
13	Su ●	27	—A	·99	12	·74	28
14	Mo	28	...	...	13	·85	29
15	Tu	29	1	·07	14	·95	—30
16	We	30	2	·15	...	...	1
	Oct.						
17	Th	1	3	·21	15	·04	2
18	Fr	2	4	·24	16	·10	3
19	Sa	3	5	·26	17	·15	4
20	Su	4	6	·26	18	·17	5
21	Mo	5	Sukla 7	·24	19	·19	6
22	Tu	6	8	·21	20	·17	7
23	We	7	9	·14	21	·14	8
24	Th	8	10 11	·07 ·97	22	·09	9
25	Fr	9	12	·88	23 24	·04 ·98	10
26	Sa	10	13	·79	25	·91	11
27	Su	11	Asvina 14	·70	26	·84	12
28	Mo	12	P	·59	27	·77	13
29	Tu	13	1	·49	1	·71	H. 1245 Rabi-ul-akhir. 14
—30	We	14	2	·42	2	·66	15
1	Th	15	3	·34	3	·62	16
2	Fr	16	4	·29	4	·59	17
3	Sa	17	5	·23	5	·58	18
4	Su	18	6	·22	6	·59	19
5	Mo	19	Bahula 7	·21	7	·63	20
6	Tu	20	8	·22	8	·68	21
Virodhi Tula—Aippasi. 7	We	21	9	·27	9	·75	22
8	Th	22	10	·33	10	·83	23
9	Fr	23	11	·40	11	·93	24
10	Sa	24	12	·48	...	...	25
11	Su	25	13	·57	12	·04	26
12	Mo	26	14	·66	13	·15	27
13	Tu	27	—A	·74	14	·25	28
14	We	28	K. Suk. 1	·79	15	·34	—29
15	Th	29	2	·82	16	·41	1
16	Fr	30	3	·86	17	·46	2
17	Sa	31	4	·85	18	·50	3

SOLAR reckoning.			LUNAR reckoning.				
Cyclic Sidereal Year, Month and Day.	Week-Day	English Month and Day.	Tithi	Ending Moment.	Nakshatra	Ending Moment.	Muhammadan Year, Month and Day.
	Nov.						
18	Su	1	5	·83	19	·51	4
19	Mo	2	6	·79	20	·50	5
20	Tu	3	7	·74	21	·47	6
Virodhi Tula—Aippasi. 21	We	4	8	·66	22	·43	7
22	Th	5	9	·57	23	·38	8
23	Fr	6	Sukla 10	·48	24	·32	9
24	Sa	7	11	·38	25	·25	10
25	Su	8	12	·28	26	·18	11
26	Mo	9	13	·16	27	·11	12
27	Tu	10	14	·10	1	·05	13
28	We	11	P 1	·02 ·94	2 3	·00 ·95	H. 1245 Jumadal-awwal. 14
29	Th	12	Kartika 2	·88	4	·92	15
—30	Fr	13	3	·83	5	·90	16
1	Sa	14	4	·82	6	·92	17
2	Su	15	5	·83	7	·94	18
3	Mo	16	6	·84	8	·99	19
4	Tu	17	7	·88	...	...	20
5	We	18	8	·95	9	·05	21
6	Th	19	...	...	10	·14	22
7	Fr	20	Bahula 9	·03	11	·24	23
8	Sa	21	10	·11	12	·35	24
9	Su	22	11	·20	13	·45	25
Virodhi Vrischika—Kartigai. 10	Mo	23	12	·28	14	·55	26
11	Tu	24	13	·36	15	·64	27
12	We	25	14	·41	16	·72	28
13	Th	26	—A	·46	17	·78	29
14	Fr	27	1	·48	18	·82	—30
15	Sa	28	2	·47	19	·83	1
16	Su	29	3	·45	20	·82	2
17	Mo	30	4	·40	21	·80	3
	Dec.						
18	Tu	1	5	·35	22	·77	4
19	We	2	Sukla 6	·28	23	·72	5
20	Th	3	7	·20	24	·66	6
21	Fr	4	8	·10	25	·59	7
22	Sa	5	9 10	·01 ·91	26	·52	8
23	Su	6	11	·81	27	·46	9
24	Mo	7	12	·72	1	·39	H. 1245 Jumadal-akhir. 10
25	Tu	8	13	·64	2	·33	11
26	We	9	14	·57	3	·28	12
27	Th	10	P	·51	4	·25	13
28	Fr	11	Margasira 1	·47	5	·23	14
—29	Sa	12	2	·46	6	·24	15
1	Su	13	3	·45	7	·26	16
2	Mo	14	4	·48	8	·30	17
3	Tu	15	5	·53	9	·36	18
4	We	16	6	·60	10	·44	19
5	Th	17	7	·67	11	·54	20
6	Fr	18	Bahula 8	·77	12	·64	21
7	Sa	19	9	·85	13	·75	22
8	Su	20	10	·92	14	·85	23
Virodhi Dhanus—Margali. 9	Mo	21	...	...	15	·95	24
10	Tu	22	11	·00	...	...	25
11	We	23	12	·06	16	·04	26
12	Th	24	13	·10	17	·09	27
13	Fr	25	14	·11	18	·13	28
14	Sa	26	—A	·12	19	·15	—29
15	Su	27	Suk. 1	·09	20	·15	1
16	Mo	28	2	·05	21	·14	2
17	Tu	29	3 4	·00 ·91	22	·10	Rajab. 3
18	We	30	Push. 5	·83	23 24	·05 ·99	4
19	Th	31	6	·74	25	·93	5

15. Svati. 16. Visak. 17. Anur. 18. Jyesh. 19. Mula. 20. P. Ash. 21. U. Ash. 22. Sravn. 23. Dani. 24. Satab. 25. P. Bhad. 26. U. Bhad. 27. Rev.

A. D. 1830. **Mesha Sankranti** (Commencement of Indian Sidereal Year).
Solar Eclipse. ● **(Surya Sid.) April 11·51.** **Saka 1752.** **Kaliyuga 4931.**
Lunar Eclipse. ○ **(Arya Sid.) April 11·41.** **(S. Cycle) Vikrita.**

SOLAR reckoning: Cyclic Sidereal Year, Month and Day; Week-Day; English Month and Day. LUNAR reckoning: Tithi; Ending Moment; Nakshatra; Ending Moment; Muhammadan Year, Month and Day.

Jan.

Cyclic Sidereal Year, Month and Day	Week-Day	English Month and Day	Tithi	Ending Moment	Nakshatra	Ending Moment	Muhammadan Year, Month and Day
Virodhi, *Dhanus—Margali.* 30	Fr	1	*Sukla* 7	·65	26	·87	H. 1245 *Rajab.* 6
21	Sa	2	8	·54	27	·80	7
22	Su	3	9	·45	1	·73	8
23	Mo	4	10	·36	2	·67	9
24	Tu	5	11	·27	3	·62	10
25	We	6	12	·21	4	·58	11
26	Th	7	13	·16	5	·56	12
27	Fr	8	14	·12	6	·56	13
28	Sa	9	Pausha P	·10	7	·57	14
29	Su	10	1	·11	8	·61	15
30	Mo	11	2	·13	9	·66	16
1	Tu	12	3	·17	10	·75	17
2	We	13	4	·25	11	·84	18
3	Th	14	5	·32	12	·94	19
4	Fr	15	*Bahula* 6	·41	...	...	20
5	Sa	16	7	·50	13	·05	21
6	Su	17	8	·59	14	·15	22
7	Mo	18	9	·65	15	·26	23
8	Tu	19	10	·71	16	·34	24
9	We	20	11	·75	17	·41	25
10	Th	21	12	·76	18	·45	26
11	Fr	22	13	·76	19	·47	27
12	Sa	23	14	·73	20	·48	28
13	Su	24	A	·70	21	·47	29
14	Mo	25	1	·63	22	·44	30
Virodhi, *Makara—Tai.* 15	Tu	26	2	·55	23	·39	1
16	We	27	3	·47	24	·33	2
17	Th	28	*Sukla* 4	·37	25	·27	3
18	Fr	29	5	·28	26	·20	4
19	Sa	30	6	·18	27	·13	5
20	Su	31	7 8	·09 ·99	1	·07	6

Feb.

Cyclic Sidereal Year, Month and Day	Week-Day	English Month and Day	Tithi	Ending Moment	Nakshatra	Ending Moment	Muhammadan Year, Month and Day
21	Mo	1	9	·91	2 3	·00 ·95	H. 1245 *Shaban.* 7
22	Tu	2	10	·85	4	·92	8
23	We	3	11	·80	5	·89	9
24	Th	4	12	·76	6	·88	10
25	Fr	5	13	·74	7	·89	11
26	Sa	6	14	·74	8	·92	12
27	Su	7	Magha P	·78	9	·98	13
28	Mo	8	1	·83	...	...	14
29	Tu	9	2	·89	10	·05	15
Virodhi, *Kumbha—Masi.* 1	We	10	3	·97	11	·14	16
2	Th	11	...	...	12	·24	17
3	Fr	12	4	·05	13	·35	18
4	Sa	13	5	·13	14	·46	19
5	Su	14	6	·22	15	·56	20
6	Mo	15	*Bahula* 7	·29	16	·65	21
7	Tu	16	8	·35	17	·71	22
8	We	17	9	·38	18	·76	23
9	Th	18	10	·40	19	·79	24
10	Fr	19	11	·39	20	·81	25
11	Sa	20	12	·36	21	·80	26
12	Su	21	13	·31	22	·77	27
13	Mo	22	14	·24	23	·72	28
14	Tu ●	23	A	·17	24	·67	29
15	We	24	1	·09	25	·61	*Ramzan.* 1
16	Th	25	*P. Suk.* 2 3	·00 ·90	26	·54	2
17	Fr	26	4	·79	27	·47	3
18	Sa	27	5	·70	1	·40	4
19	Su	28	6	·60	2	·34	5

March

Cyclic Sidereal Year, Month and Day	Week-Day	English Month and Day	Tithi	Ending Moment	Nakshatra	Ending Moment	Muhammadan Year, Month and Day
Virodhi, *Kumbha—Masi.* 20	Mo	1	*Sukla* 7	·53	3	·29	H. 1245 *Ramzan.* 6
21	Tu	2	8	·46	4	·25	7
22	We	3	9	·41	5	·22	8
23	Th	4	10	·37	6	·20	9
24	Fr	5	11	·36	7	·21	10
25	Sa	6	12	·35	8	·24	11
26	Su	7	13	·38	9	·29	12
27	Mo	8	14	·44	10	·36	13
28	Tu ○	9	Phalguna P	·50	11	·44	14
29	We	10	1	·59	12	·54	15
30	Th	11	2	·67	13	·65	16
1	Fr	12	3	·76	14	·76	17
2	Sa	13	4	·84	15	·86	18
3	Su	14	5	·89	16	·95	19
4	Mo	15	6	·95	...	...	20
5	Tu	16	*Bahula* 7	·98	17	·02	21
6	We	17	8	·99	18	·08	22
7	Th	18	9	·98	19	·12	23
8	Fr	19	10	·95	20	·13	24
9	Sa	20	11	·91	21	·12	25
10	Su	21	12	·85	22	·10	26
11	Mo	22	13	·77	23	·06	27
12	Tu	23	14	·68	24 25	·01 ·95	28
Virodhi, *Mina—Panguni.* 13	We	24	A	·59	26	·88	29
14	Th	25	1	·48	27	·81	30
15	Fr	26	2	·38	1	·74	1
16	Sa	27	*Sukla* 3	·29	2	·69	2
17	Su	28	4	·20	3	·63	3
18	Mo	29	5	·11	4	·58	4
19	Tu	30	6 7	·04 ·99	5	·54	5
20	We	31	8	·95	6	·53	6

April

Cyclic Sidereal Year, Month and Day	Week-Day	English Month and Day	Tithi	Ending Moment	Nakshatra	Ending Moment	Muhammadan Year, Month and Day
21	Th	1	9	·94	7	·54	H. 1245 *Shawwal.* 7
22	Fr	2	10	·93	8	·56	8
23	Sa	3	11	·97	9	·60	9
24	Su	4	...	...	10	·66	10
25	Mo	5	12	·01	11	·74	11
26	Tu	6	13	·07	12	·84	12
27	We	7	14	·16	13	·95	13
28	Th	8	Chaitra P	·24	...	...	14
29	Fr	9	1	·33	14	·06	15
30	Sa	10	2	·40	15	·16	16
Vikrita, *Mesha—Chittirai.* 1	Su	11	3	·46	16	·25	17
2	Mo	12	4	·51	17	·33	18
3	Tu	13	5	·55	18	·40	19
4	We	14	6	·55	19	·44	20
5	Th	15	*Bahula* 7	·54	20	·45	21
6	Fr	16	8	·51	21	·45	22
7	Sa	17	9	·46	22	·43	23
8	Su	18	10	·40	23	·40	24
9	Mo	19	11	·32	24	·35	25
10	Tu	20	12	·24	25	·29	26
11	We	21	13	·14	26	·22	27
12	Th	22	14 A	·04 ·93	27	·15	28
13	Fr	23	1	·83	1	·09	29
14	Sa	24	Vaisakha *Suk.* 2	·74	2 3	·02 ·96	H. 1245 *Zi-l-ka'da.* 1
15	Su	25	3	·65	4	·91	2
16	Mo	26	4	·59	5	·87	3
17	Tu	27	5	·53	6	·86	4
18	We	28	6	·49	7	·86	5
19	Th	29	7	·48	8	·87	6
20	Fr	30	8	·46	9	·91	7

May

Cyclic Sidereal Year, Month and Day	Week-Day	English Month and Day	Tithi	Ending Moment	Nakshatra	Ending Moment	Muhammadan Year, Month and Day
Vikrita, *Mesha—Chittirai.* 21	Sa	1	*Sukla* 9	·50	10	·97	H. 1245 *Zi-l-ka'da.* 8
22	Su	2	10	·54	...	...	9
23	Mo	3	11	·61	11	·05	10
24	Tu	4	12	·68	12	·15	11
25	We	5	13	·77	13	·25	12
26	Th	6	14	·84	14	·36	13
27	Fr	7	Vaisakha P	·92	15	·46	14
28	Sa	8	1	·99	16	·56	15
29	Su	9	...	...	17	·65	16
30	Mo	10	3	·04	18	·71	17
31	Tu	11	3	·08	19	·75	18
Vikrita, *Vrishabha—Vaikasi.* 1	We	12	4	·08	20	·77	19
2	Th	13	5	·07	21	·77	20
3	Fr	14	6 7	·04 ·98	22	·77	21
4	Sa	15	*Bahula* 8	·92	23	·73	22
5	Su	16	9	·83	24	·68	23
6	Mo	17	10	·75	25	·63	24
7	Tu	18	11	·65	26	·56	25
8	We	19	12	·56	27	·50	26
9	Th	20	13	·45	1	·43	27
10	Fr	21	14	·34	2	·36	28
11	Sa	22	A	·25	3	·30	29
12	Su	23	1	·16	4	·24	30
13	Mo	24	2	·10	5	·20	1
14	Tu	25	3	·03	6	·19	2
15	We	26	4 5	·00 ·98	7	·18	3
16	Th	27	6	·98	8	·19	4
17	Fr	28	7	·99	9	·22	5
18	Sa	29	*Sukla* ...	...	10	·28	6
19	Su	30	8	·04	11	·36	7
20	Mo	31	9	·11	12	·45	8

June

Cyclic Sidereal Year, Month and Day	Week-Day	English Month and Day	Tithi	Ending Moment	Nakshatra	Ending Moment	Muhammadan Year, Month and Day
21	Tu	1	10	·17	13	·55	H. 1245 *Zi-l-hijja.* 9
22	We	2	11	·26	14	·65	10
23	Th	3	12	·34	15	·76	11
24	Fr	4	13	·43	16	·87	12
25	Sa	5	14	·48	17	·95	13
26	Su	6	Jyeshtha P	·52	...	...	14
27	Mo	7	1	·57	18	·02	15
28	Tu	8	2	·57	19	·07	16
29	We	9	3	·56	20	·09	17
30	Th	10	4	·53	21	·11	18
31	Fr	11	5	·49	22	·09	19
32	Sa	12	6	·41	23	·06	20
Vikrita, *Mithuna—Ani.* 1	Su	13	*Bahula* 7	·34	24 25	·02 ·96	21
2	Mo	14	8	·25	26	·91	22
3	Tu	15	9	·15	27	·84	23
4	We	16	10 11	·04 ·94	1	·77	24
5	Th	17	12	·85	2	·70	25
6	Fr	18	13	·75	3	·63	26
7	Sa	19	14	·66	4	·58	27
8	Su	20	A	·59	5	·54	28
9	Mo	21	1	·52	6	·51	29
10	Tu	22	Ashadha *Sukla* 2	·48	7	·50	H. 1246 *Muharram.* 1
11	We	23	3	·46	8	·51	2
12	Th	24	4	·47	9	·54	3
13	Fr	25	5	·47	10	·60	4
14	Sa	26	6	·52	11	·66	5
15	Su	27	7	·58	12	·75	6
16	Mo	28	8	·64	13	·85	7
17	Tu	29	9	·73	14	·95	8
18	We	30	10	·81	...	...	9

Naksh:—1. Asvn. 2. Bhar. 3. Krit. 4. Rohi. 5. Mrig. 6. Ardb. 7. Punar. 8. Push. 9. Aslesh. 10. Magh. 11. P. Phal. 12. U. Phal. 13. Hasta. 14. Chit.

A. D. 1830.
A.—Amavasya.
P.—Paurnami.

Kollam 1006, Commences { N. Malabar—Sept. / S. Malabar—Aug.

Hijra 1246, Commences June 22.

Vikrama 1887.
Bengal San 1236.
(N. Cycle) Plava.

SOLAR reckoning: Cyclic Sidereal Year, Month and Day.	Week-Day	English Month and Day.	LUNAR reckoning: Tithi	Ending Moment.	Nakshatra	Ending Moment.	Muhammadan Year, Month and Day.
		July					
Vikrita *Mithuna—Ani.* 19	Th	1	Ashadha Suk. 11	·90	15	·07	H. 1246 *Muharram.* 10
20	Fr	2	12	·96	16	·17	11
21	Sa	3	...	...	17	·26	12
22	Su	4	13	·01	18	·33	13
23	Mo	5	14	·05	19	·38	14
24	Tu	6	P	·05	20	·42	15
25	We	7	1	·04	21	·43	16
26	Th	8	2 / 3	·01 / ·96	22	·42	17
27	Fr	9	*Bahula* 4	·89	23	·39	18
28	Sa	10	5	·82	24	·35	19
29	Su	11	6	·72	25	·30	20
30	Mo	12	7	·63	26	·24	21
—31	Tu	13	8	·52	27	·18	22
Vikrita *Karkata—Adi.* 1	We	14	9	·41	1	·11	23
2	Th	15	10	·32	2 / 3	·03 / ·97	24
3	Fr	16	11	·22	4	·92	25
4	Sa	17	12	·14	5	·87	26
5	Su	18	13	·06	6	·84	27
6	Mo	19	14 / A	·00 / ·96	7	·83	28
7	Tu	20	*Sukla* 1	·94	8	·83	29
8	We	21	2	·94	9	·86	—30
9	Th	22	3	·95	10	·90	1
10	Fr	23	...	...	11	·97	2
11	Sa	24	4	·00	...	...	3
12	Su	25	5	·04	12	·05	4
13	Mo	26	6	·12	13	·15	5
14	Tu	27	7	·20	14	·26	6
15	We	28	8	·29	15	·37	7
16	Th	29	9	·36	16	·47	8
17	Fr	30	10	·43	17	·56	9
18	Sa	31	11	·49	18	·64	10
		Aug.					
19	Su	1	Sravana 12	·52	19	·70	H. 1246 *Safar.* 11
20	Mo	2	13	·54	20	·74	12
21	Tu	3	14	·52	21	·75	13
22	We	4	P	·50	22	·75	14
23	Th	5	1	·44	23	·72	15
24	Fr	6	2	·38	24	·68	16
25	Sa	7	3	·31	25	·64	17
26	Su	8	4	·22	26	·58	18
27	Mo	9	5	·12	27	·51	19
28	Tu	10	6 / 7	·01 / ·92	1	·44	20
29	We	11	*Bahula* 8	·82	2	·37	21
30	Th	12	9	·72	3	·32	22
31	Fr	13	10	·63	4	·26	23
—32	Sa	14	11	·55	5	·21	24
Vikrita *Simha—Avani.* 1	Su	15	12	·49	6	·17	25
2	Mo	16	13	·45	7	·15	26
3	Tu	17	14	·44	8	·16	27
4	We	18	—A	·44	9	·18	28
5	Th	19	Bhadrapada *Sukla* 1	·44	10	·21	—29
6	Fr	20	2	·48	11	·27	H. 1246 *Rabi-ul-awwal.* 1
7	Sa	21	3	·54	12	·35	2
8	Su	22	4	·62	13	·46	3
9	Mo	23	5	·70	14	·56	4
10	Tu	24	6	·77	15	·66	5
11	We	25	7	·86	16	·77	6
12	Th	26	8	·94	17	·86	7
13	Fr	27	9	·99	18	·94	8
14	Sa	28	...	...	...	...	9
15	Su	29	10	·02	19	·01	10
16	Mo	30	11	·05	20	·05	11
17	Tu	31	12	·02	21	·07	12

SOLAR reckoning: Cyclic Sidereal Year, Month and Day.	Week-Day	English Month and Day.	LUNAR reckoning: Tithi	Ending Moment.	Nakshatra	Ending Moment.	Muhammadan Year, Month and Day.
		Sep.					
Vikrita *Simha—Avani.* 18	We	1	Bhadra. 13 / 14	·00 / ·96	22	·07	H. 1246 *Rabi-ul-awwal.* 13
19	Th ○	2	P	·90	23	·05	14
20	Fr	3	1	·82	24 / 25	·03 / ·98	15
21	Sa	4	2	·74	26	·92	16
22	Su	5	3	·64	27	·85	17
23	Mo	6	4	·53	1	·78	18
24	Tu	7	5	·43	2	·72	19
25	We	8	*Bahula* 6	·32	3	·65	20
26	Th	9	7	·24	4	·59	21
27	Fr	10	8	·15	5	·54	22
28	Sa	11	9	·08	6	·50	23
29	Su	12	10 / 11	·02 / ·97	7	·49	24
30	Mo	13	12	·96	8	·48	25
—31	Tu	14	13	·96	9	·49	26
Vikrita *Kanya—Purattasi.* 1	We	15	14	·97	10	·53	27
2	Th	16	...	...	11	·58	28
3	Fr	17	—A	·01	12	·65	29
4	Sa	18	Asvina *Sukla* 1	·07	13	·75	—30
5	Su	19	2	·13	14	·86	H. 1246 *Rabi-ul-akhir.* 1
6	Mo	20	3	·21	15	·96	2
7	Tu	21	4	·30	...	...	3
8	We	22	5	·38	16	·07	4
9	Th	23	6	·47	17	·16	5
10	Fr	24	7	·52	18	·26	6
11	Sa	25	8	·56	19	·32	7
12	Su	26	9	58	20	·37	8
13	Mo	27	10	·57	21	·39	9
14	Tu	28	11	·54	22	·40	10
15	We	29	12	·51	23	·39	11
16	Th	30	13	·44	24	·36	12
		Oct.					
17	Fr	1	14	·86	25	·31	H. 1246 13
18	Sa	2	P	·28	26	·26	14
19	Su	3	1	·18	27	·19	15
20	Mo	4	2 / 3	·09 / ·99	1	·18	16
21	Tu	5	*Bahula* 4	·88	2 / 3	·06 / ·99	17
22	We	6	5	·79	4	·93	18
23	Th	7	6	·70	5	·87	19
24	Fr	8	7	·63	6	·84	20
25	Sa	9	8	·58	7	·81	21
26	Su	10	9	·54	8	·80	22
27	Mo	11	10	·52	9	·81	23
28	Tu	12	11	·52	10	·84	24
29	We	13	12	·54	11	·89	25
—30	Th	14	13	·57	12	·97	26
Vikrita *Tula—Aippasi.* 1	Fr	15	14	·63	...	...	27
2	Sa	16	—A	·70	13	·06	28
3	Su	17	1	·79	14	·15	—29
4	Mo	18	Karttika *Sukla* 2	·88	15	·26	H. 1246 *Jumadal-awwal.* 1
5	Tu	19	3	·96	16	·37	2
6	We	20	...	...	17	·48	3
7	Th	21	4	·04	18	·56	4
8	Fr	22	5	·09	19	·63	5
9	Sa	23	6	·14	20	·68	6
10	Su	24	7	·16	21	·71	7
11	Mo	25	8	·15	22	·73	8
12	Tu	26	9	·12	23	·72	9
13	We	27	10	·09	24	·69	10
14	Th	28	11 / 12	·02 / ·94	25	·65	11
15	Fr	29	13	·86	26	·59	12
16	Sa	30	14	·77	27	·54	13
17	Su	31	P	·67	1	·47	14

SOLAR reckoning: Cyclic Sidereal Year, Month and Day.	Week-Day	English Month and Day.	LUNAR reckoning: Tithi	Ending Moment.	Nakshatra	Ending Moment.	Muhammadan Year, Month and Day.
		Nov.					
Vikrita *Tula—Aippasi.* 18	Mo	1	Kartika 1	·57	2	·40	H. 1246 *Jumadal-awwal.* 15
19	Tu	2	2	·47	3	·33	16
20	We	3	3	·38	4	·26	17
21	Th	4	4	·29	5	·21	18
22	Fr	5	5	·23	6	·17	19
23	Sa	6	6	·16	7	·14	20
24	Su	7	7	·13	8	·12	21
25	Mo	8	*Bahula* 8	·11	9	·13	22
26	Tu	9	9	·12	10	·15	23
27	We	10	10	·14	11	·21	24
28	Th	11	11	·19	12	·27	25
29	Fr	12	12	·24	13	·30	26
—30	Sa	13	13	·31	14	·45	27
Vikrita *Vrischika—Kartigai.* 1	Su	14	14	·40	15	·56	28
2	Mo	15	—A	·50	16	·67	29
3	Tu	16	1	·58	17	·78	—30
4	We	17	2	·65	18	·87	H. 1246 *Jumadal-akhir.* 1
5	Th	18	3	·71	19	·94	2
6	Fr	19	4	·76	20	·99	3
7	Sa	20	*Sukla* 5	·77	...	...	4
8	Su	21	6	·76	21	·04	5
9	Mo	22	7	·73	22	·05	6
10	Tu	23	8	·70	23	·04	7
11	We	24	9	·64	24 / 25	·02 / ·98	8
12	Th	25	Margasira 10	·57	26	·94	9
13	Fr	26	11	·48	27	·88	10
14	Sa	27	12	·40	1	·81	11
15	Su	28	13	·29	2	·74	12
16	Mo	29	14	·19	3	·67	13
17	Tu	30	P	·09	4	·60	14
		Dec.					
18	We	1	1 / 2	·01 / ·92	5	·55	H. 1246 15
19	Th	2	3	·84	6	·50	16
20	Fr	3	4	·79	7	·47	17
21	Sa	4	5	·76	8	·45	18
22	Su	5	*Bahula* 6	·74	9	·45	19
23	Mo	6	7	·75	10	·48	20
24	Tu	7	8	·78	11	·52	21
25	We	8	9	·83	12	·58	22
26	Th	9	10	·88	13	·66	23
27	Fr	10	11	·96	14	·75	24
28	Sa	11	...	...	15	·87	25
29	Su	12	12	·06	16	·97	26
—30	Mo	13	13	·14	...	...	27
Vikrita *Dhanus—Marguli.* 1	Tu	14	14	·22	17	·08	28
2	We	15	—A	·30	18	·17	—29
3	Th	16	1	·36	19	·25	H. 1246 *Rajub.* 1
4	Fr	17	2	·39	20	·32	2
5	Sa	18	3	·42	21	·35	3
6	Su	19	4	·40	22	·37	4
7	Mo	20	5	·38	23	·37	5
8	Tu	21	6	·33	24	·35	6
9	We	22	*Sukla* 7	·27	25	·31	7
10	Th	23	8	·20	26	·27	8
11	Fr	24	9	·11	27	·21	9
12	Sa	25	10 / 11	·01 / ·92	1	·15	10
13	Su	26	Pausha 12	·83	2	·08	11
14	Mo	27	13	·72	3 / 4	·01 / ·95	12
15	Tu	28	14	·64	5	·89	13
16	We	29	P	·56	6	·83	14
17	Th	30	*Bah.* 1	·48	7	·80	15
18	Fr	31	2	·44	8	·77	16

15. Svati. 16. Visak. 17. Anur. 18. Jyesh. 19. Mula. 20. P. Ash. 21. U. Ash. 22. Sravn. 23. Dani. 24. Satab. 25. P. Bhad. 26. U. Bhad. 27. Rev.

A. D. 1831.
Solar Eclipse. ●
Lunar Eclipse. ○

Mesha Sankranti (Commencement of Indian Sidereal Year).
(Surya Sid.) April 11·77.
(Arya Sid.) April 11·67.

Saka 1753. **Kaliyuga 4932.**
(S. Cycle) Khara.

Jan.

SOLAR reckoning: Cyclic Sidereal Year, Month and Day	Week-Day	English Month and Day	LUNAR reckoning: Tithi	Ending Moment	Nakshatra	Ending Moment	Muhammadan Year, Month and Day
Vikrita *Dhanus—Margali.* 19	Sa	1	Pausha *Bahula* 3	·40	9	·77	H. 1246 *Rajab.* 17
20	Su	2	4	·39	10	·79	18
21	Mo	3	5	·39	11	·83	19
22	Tu	4	6	·42	12	·89	20
23	We	5	7	·47	13	·96	21
24	Th	6	8	·53	...	...	22
25	Fr	7	9	·62	14	·06	23
26	Sa	8	10	·70	15	·16	24
27	Su	9	11	·79	16	·27	25
28	Mo	10	12	·87	17	·37	26
29	Tu	11	13	·95	18	·47	27
Vikrita *Makara—Tai.* 1	We	12	...	...	19	·56	28
2	Th	13	14	·00	20	·63	29
3	Fr	14	A	·04	21	·67	30
4	Sa	15	Magha *Sukla* 1	·06	22	·69	H. 1246 *Shaban.* 1
5	Su	16	2	·04	23	·69	2
6	Mo	17	3 4	·02 ·98	24	·68	3
7	Tu	18	5	·92	25	·66	4
8	We	19	6	·84	26	·61	5
9	Th	20	7	·74	27	·55	6
10	Fr	21	8	·65	1	·48	7
11	Sa	22	9	·55	2	·41	8
12	Su	23	10	·45	3	·35	9
13	Mo	24	11	·36	4	·28	10
14	Tu	25	12	·28	5	·22	11
15	We	26	13	·20	6	·17	12
16	Th	27	14	·13	7	·13	13
17	Fr	28	P	·08	8	·11	14
18	Sa	29	1	·04	9	·10	15
19	Su	30	2	·03	10	·11	16
20	Mo	31	3	·04	11	·14	17

Feb.

SOLAR reckoning: Cyclic Sidereal Year, Month and Day	Week-Day	English Month and Day	LUNAR reckoning: Tithi	Ending Moment	Nakshatra	Ending Moment	Muhammadan Year, Month and Day
21	Tu	1	*Bahula* 4	·07	12	·19	18
22	We	2	5	·12	13	·27	19
23	Th	3	6	·18	14	·36	20
24	Fr	4	7	·27	15	·46	21
25	Sa	5	8	·35	16	·57	22
26	Su	6	9	·44	17	·67	23
27	Mo	7	10	·52	18	·77	24
28	Tu	8	11	·60	19	·87	25
29	We	9	12	·65	20	·94	26
30	Th	10	13	·68	21	·98	27
Vikrita *Kumbha—Masi.* 1	Fr	11	14	·69	...	...	28
2	Sa	12	A	·67	22	·01	29
3	Su	13	Phalguna *Sukla* 1	·66	23	·02	H. 1246 *Ramzan.* 1
4	Mo	14	2	·60	24 25	·02 ·99	2
5	Tu	15	3	·54	26	·94	3
6	We	16	4	·46	27	·89	4
7	Th	17	5	·38	1	·82	5
8	Fr	18	6	·28	2	·76	6
9	Sa	19	7	·19	3	·69	7
10	Su	20	8 9	·08 ·98	4	·62	8
11	Mo	21	10	·89	5	·56	9
12	Tu	22	11	·81	6	·50	10
13	We	23	12	·75	7	·47	11
14	Th	24	13	·70	8	·44	12
15	Fr	25	14	·67	9	·42	13
16	Sa ○	26	P	·65	10	·43	14
17	Su	27	*Bah.* 1	·65	11	·45	15
18	Mo	28	2	·69	12	·51	16

March

SOLAR reckoning: Cyclic Sidereal Year, Month and Day	Week-Day	English Month and Day	LUNAR reckoning: Tithi	Ending Moment	Nakshatra	Ending Moment	Muhammadan Year, Month and Day
Vikrita *Kumbha—Mas.* 19	Tu	1	Phalg. *Bahula* 3	·74	13	·58	H. 1246 *Ramzan.* 17
20	We	2	4	·81	14	·66	18
21	Th	3	5	·89	15	·76	19
22	Fr	4	6	·98	16	·87	20
23	Sa	5	...	...	17	·97	21
24	Su	6	7	·06	...	...	22
25	Mo	7	8	·13	18	·08	23
26	Tu	8	9	·20	19	·17	24
27	We	9	10	·26	20	·24	25
28	Th	10	11	·30	21	·30	26
29	Fr	11	12	·30	22	·33	27
Vikrita *Mina—Panguni.* 1	Sa	12	13	·29	23	·35	28
2	Su	13	14	·25	24	·34	29
3	Mo	14	A	·21	25	·32	30
4	Tu	15	Chaitra *Sukla* 1	·14	26	·28	H. 1246 *Shawwal.* 1
5	We	16	2 3	·06 ·97	27	·23	2
6	Th	17	4	·87	1	·17	3
7	Fr	18	5	·78	2	·10	4
8	Sa	19	6	·67	3 4	·03 ·96	5
9	Su	20	7	·59	5	·89	6
10	Mo	21	8	·49	6	·85	7
11	Tu	22	9	·41	7	·80	8
12	We	23	10	·34	8	·76	9
13	Th	24	11	·29	9	·75	10
14	Fr	25	12	·26	10	·75	11
15	Sa	26	13	·24	11	·77	12
16	Su	27	14	·25	12	·82	13
17	Mo	28	P	·28	13	·88	14
18	Tu	29	1	·32	14	·96	15
19	We	30	2	·40	...	...	16
20	Th	31	3	·47	15	·06	17

April

SOLAR reckoning: Cyclic Sidereal Year, Month and Day	Week-Day	English Month and Day	LUNAR reckoning: Tithi	Ending Moment	Nakshatra	Ending Moment	Muhammadan Year, Month and Day
21	Fr	1	*Bahula* 4	·56	16	·16	18
22	Sa	2	5	·64	17	·28	19
23	Su	3	6	·73	18	·38	20
24	Mo	4	7	·79	19	·47	21
25	Tu	5	8	·84	20	·55	22
26	We	6	9	·87	21	·61	23
27	Th	7	10	·87	22	·66	24
28	Fr	8	11	·86	23	·67	25
29	Sa	9	12	·82	24	·67	26
30	Su	10	13	·77	25	·66	27
31	Mo	11	14	·70	26	·61	28
Khara *Mesha—Chittirai.* 1	Tu	12	A	·63	27	·57	29
2	We	13	Adhika Vaisak. *Sukla* 1	·53	1	·51	H. 1246 *Zi-l-ka'da.* 1
3	Th	14	2	·43	2	·44	2
4	Fr	15	3	·34	3	·37	3
5	Sa	16	4	·23	4	·30	4
6	Su	17	5	·14	5	·23	5
7	Mo	18	6 7	·04 ·96	6	·18	6
8	Tu	19	8	·89	7	·13	7
9	We	20	9	·84	8	·09	8
10	Th	21	10	·80	9	·07	9
11	Fr	22	11	·78	10	·07	10
12	Sa	23	12	·79	11	·09	11
13	Su	24	13	·82	12	·13	12
14	Mo	25	14	·87	13	·19	13
15	Tu	26	P	·93	14	·27	14
16	We	27	...	...	15	·36	15
17	Th	28	*Bah.* 1	·02	16	·47	16
18	Fr	29	2	·10	17	·58	17
19	Sa	30	3	·18	18	·68	18

May

SOLAR reckoning: Cyclic Sidereal Year, Month and Day	Week-Day	English Month and Day	LUNAR reckoning: Tithi	Ending Moment	Nakshatra	Ending Moment	Muhammadan Year, Month and Day
Khara *Mesha—Chittirai.* 20	Su	1	Adh. Vsk. *Bahula* 4	·25	19	·78	H. 1246 *Zi-l-ka'da.* 19
21	Mo	2	5	·31	20	·86	20
22	Tu	3	6	·37	21	·93	21
23	We	4	7	·40	22	·97	22
24	Th	5	8	·41	23	·99	23
25	Fr	6	9	·39	24	·99	24
26	Sa	7	10	·35	25	·98	25
27	Su	8	11	·30	26	·95	26
28	Mo	9	12	·23	27	·90	27
29	Tu	10	13	·16	1	·84	28
30	We	11	14 A	·06 ·96	2	·78	29
31	Th	12	Nija Vaisakha *Sukla* 1	·86	3	·71	30
Khara *Vrishabha—Vaikasi.* 1	Fr	13	2	·76	4	·64	H. 1246 *Zi-l-hijja.* 1
2	Sa	14	3	·66	5	·58	2
3	Su	15	4	·56	6	·52	3
4	Mo	16	5	·48	7	·46	4
5	Tu	17	6	·40	8	·42	5
6	We	18	7	·36	9	·40	6
7	Th	19	8	·32	10	·39	7
8	Fr	20	9	·31	11	·41	8
9	Sa	21	10	·30	12	·44	9
10	Su	22	11	·33	13	·50	10
11	Mo	23	12	·38	14	·57	11
12	Tu	24	13	·44	15	·67	12
13	We	25	14	·51	16	·77	13
14	Th	26	P	·59	17	·87	14
15	Fr	27	1	·68	18	·98	15
16	Sa	28	2	·76	...	...	16
17	Su	29	3	·81	19	·08	17
18	Mo	30	4	·87	20	·17	18
19	Tu	31	5	·89	21	·24	19

June

SOLAR reckoning: Cyclic Sidereal Year, Month and Day	Week-Day	English Month and Day	LUNAR reckoning: Tithi	Ending Moment	Nakshatra	Ending Moment	Muhammadan Year, Month and Day
20	We	1	*Bahula* 6	·90	22	·29	20
21	Th	2	7	·88	23	·31	21
22	Fr	3	8	·86	24	·32	22
23	Sa	4	9	·81	25	·30	23
24	Su	5	10	·74	26	·28	24
25	Mo	6	11	·65	27	·24	25
26	Tu	7	12	·55	1	·18	26
27	We	8	13	·46	2	·12	27
28	Th	9	14	·36	3 4	·05 ·99	28
29	Fr	10	A	·26	5	·92	29
30	Sa	11	Jyeshtha *Sukla* 1	·16	6	·85	30
31	Su	12	2 3	·06 ·98	7	·80	H. 1247 *Muharram.* 1
Khara *Mithuna—Ani.* 1	Mo	13	4	·90	8	·75	2
2	Tu	14	5	·84	9	·73	3
3	We	15	6	·80	10	·72	4
4	Th	16	7	·79	11	·73	5
5	Fr	17	8	·79	12	·76	6
6	Sa	18	9	·81	13	·81	7
7	Su	19	10	·85	14	·88	8
8	Mo	20	11	·91	15	·97	9
9	Tu	21	12	·98	...	...	10
10	We	22	...	...	16	·07	11
11	Th	23	13	·06	17	·17	12
12	Fr	24	14	·15	18	·28	13
13	Sa	25	P	·22	19	·39	14
14	Su	26	*Bah.* 1	·29	20	·48	15
15	Mo	27	2	·34	21	·56	16
16	Tu	28	3	·38	22	·60	17
17	We	29	4	·38	23	·63	18
18	Th	30	5	·36	24	·64	19

Naksh:—1. Asvn. 2. Bhar. 3. Krit. 4. Rohi. 5. Mrig. 6. Ardh. 7. Punar. 8. Push. 9. Aslesh. 10. Magh. 11. P. Phal. 12. U. Phal. 13. Hasta. 14. Chit.

A. D. 1831.
A.—Amavasya. **P.—Paurnami.**
Kollam 1007, Commences { **N. Malabar—Sept.** / **S. Malabar—Aug.**
Hijra 1247, Commences, **June 12.**
Vikrama 1888. **Bengal San 1237.** **(N. Cycle) Subhakrit.**

July — Solar: Khara, Mithuna—Ani; Khara, Karkata—Adi. Lunar: Jyesh., Bahula, Sukla, Ashadha. Muhammadan: H. 1247 Muharram; H. 1247 Safar.

Cyclic Sidereal Year, Month and Day	Week-Day	English Month and Day	Tithi	Ending Moment	Nakshatra	Ending Moment	Muhammadan Year, Month and Day
19	Fr	1	6	·84	25	·64	20
20	Sa	2	7	·29	26	·61	21
21	Su	3	8	·22	27	·57	22
22	Mo	4	9	·13	1	·52	23
23	Tu	5	10 / 11	·05 / ·94	2	·46	24
24	We	6	12	·84	3	·40	25
25	Th	7	13	·74	4	·33	26
26	Fr	8	14	·63	5	·25	27
27	Sa	9	A	·54	6	·19	28
28	Su	10	1	·45	7	·13	29
29	Mo	11	2	·38	8	·09	—30
30	Tu	12	3	·32	9	·06	1
31	We	13	4	·28	10	·05	2
—32	Th	14	5	·27	11	·05	3
1	Fr	15	6	·26	12	·07	4
2	Sa	16	7	·29	13	·12	5
3	Su	17	8	·33	14	·19	6
4	Mo	18	9	·38	15	·27	7
5	Tu	19	10	·45	16	·37	8
6	We	20	11	·54	17	·47	9
7	Th	21	12	·62	18	·58	10
8	Fr	22	13	·69	19	·69	11
9	Sa	23	14	·76	20	·78	12
10	Su	24	P	·82	21	·86	13
11	Mo	25	1	·85	22	·91	14
12	Tu	26	2	·86	23	·95	15
13	We	27	3	·85	24	·97	16
14	Th	28	4	·82	25	·97	17
15	Fr	29	5	·76	26	·94	18
16	Sa	30	6	·70	27	·90	19
17	Su	31	7	·62	1	·85	20

Aug. — Solar: Khara, Simha—Avani. Lunar: Bahula, Sukla, Sravana, Bah. Muhammadan: H. 1247 Rabi-ul-awwal.

Cyclic Sidereal Year, Month and Day	Week-Day	English Month and Day	Tithi	Ending Moment	Nakshatra	Ending Moment	Muhammadan Year, Month and Day
18	Mo	1	8	·53	2	·80	21
19	Tu	2	9	·43	3	·73	22
20	We	3	10	·33	4	·66	23
21	Th	4	11	·23	5	·59	24
22	Fr	5	12	·13	6	·53	25
23	Sa	6	13	·03	7	·48	26
24	Su	7	14 / A	·94 / ·87	8	·43	27
25	Mo	8	1	·80	9	·39	28
26	Tu	9	2	·77	10	·37	—29
27	We	10	3	·75	11	·37	1
28	Th	11	4	·76	12	·40	2
29	Fr	12	5	·77	13	·43	3
30	Sa	13	6	·80	14	·49	4
—31	Su	14	7	·87	15	·57	5
1	Mo	15	8	·94	16	·67	6
2	Tu	16	...	...	17	·77	7
3	We	17	9	·03	18	·88	8
4	Th	18	10	·11	19	·99	9
5	Fr	19	11	·19	...	...	10
6	Sa	20	12	·25	20	·08	11
7	Su	21	13	·30	21	·16	12
8	Mo	22	14	·34	22	·22	13
9	Tu ○	23	P	·36	23	·27	14
10	We	24	1	·34	24	·29	15
11	Th	25	2	·31	25	·29	16
12	Fr	26	3	·28	26	·27	17
13	Sa	27	4	·21	27	·24	18
14	Su	28	5	·13	1	·20	19
15	Mo	29	6 / 7	·04 / ·94	2	·14	20
16	Tu	30	8	·83	3	·07	21
17	We	31	9	·73	4 / 5	·00 / ·93	22

Sep. — Solar: Khara, Simha—Avani; Khara, Kanya—Purattasi. Lunar: Sr. Bah., Sukla, Bhadrapada, Bahula. Muhammadan: Rabi-ul-awwal; H. 1247 Rabi-ul-akhir.

Cyclic Sidereal Year, Month and Day	Week-Day	English Month and Day	Tithi	Ending Moment	Nakshatra	Ending Moment	Muhammadan Year, Month and Day
18	Th	1	10	·64	6	·87	23
19	Fr	2	11	·54	7	·81	24
20	Sa	3	12	·46	8	·76	25
21	Su	4	13	·39	9	·72	26
22	Mo	5	14	·33	10	·70	27
23	Tu	6	A	·29	11	·69	28
24	We	7	1	·26	12	·71	29
25	Th	8	2	·27	13	·75	—30
26	Fr	9	3	·28	14	·80	1
27	Sa	10	4	·33	15	·87	2
28	Su	11	5	·38	16	·96	3
29	Mo	12	6	·45	...	...	4
30	Tu	13	7	·54	17	·08	5
—31	We	14	8	·62	18	·18	6
1	Th	15	9	·71	19	·29	7
2	Fr	16	10	·78	20	·38	8
3	Sa	17	11	·84	21	·47	9
4	Su	18	12	·87	22	·54	10
5	Mo	19	13	·89	23	·59	11
6	Tu	20	14	·87	24	·61	12
7	We	21	P	·84	25	·62	13
8	Th	22	1	·81	26	·60	14
9	Fr	23	2	·74	27	·58	15
10	Sa	24	3	·66	1	·53	16
11	Su	25	4	·57	2	·48	17
12	Mo	26	5	·48	3	·41	18
13	Tu	27	6	·38	4	·34	19
14	We	28	7	·28	5	·28	20
15	Th	29	8	·18	6	·21	21
16	Fr	30	9	·08	7	·15	22

Oct. — Solar: Khara, Tula—Aippasi. Lunar: Sukla, Asvina, Bahula. Muhammadan: H. 1247 Jumadal-awwal.

Cyclic Sidereal Year, Month and Day	Week-Day	English Month and Day	Tithi	Ending Moment	Nakshatra	Ending Moment	Muhammadan Year, Month and Day
17	Sa	1	10 / 11	·00 / ·93	8	·09	23
18	Su	2	12	·88	9	·05	24
19	Mo	3	13	·83	10	·02	25
20	Tu	4	14	·81	11	·02	26
21	We	5	A	·81	12	·03	27
22	Th	6	1	·83	13	·06	28
23	Fr	7	2	·88	14	·11	—29
24	Sa	8	3	·93	15	·18	1
25	Su	9	...	...	16	·28	2
26	Mo	10	4	·01	17	·37	3
27	Tu	11	5	·10	18	·48	4
28	We	12	6	·20	19	·59	5
29	Th	13	7	·27	20	·69	6
30	Fr	14	8	·34	21	·78	7
—31	Sa	15	9	·40	22	·85	8
1	Su	16	10	·43	23	·90	9
2	Mo	17	11	·46	24	·93	10
3	Tu	18	12	·44	25	·94	11
4	We	19	13	·42	26	·94	12
5	Th	20	14	·37	27	·91	13
6	Fr	21	P	·31	1	·87	14
7	Sa	22	1	·24	2	·81	15
8	Su	23	2	·15	3	·75	16
9	Mo	24	3 / 4	·06 / ·95	4	·68	17
10	Tu	25	5	·86	5	·62	18
11	We	26	6	·76	6	·55	19
12	Th	27	7	·66	7	·48	20
13	Fr	28	8	·58	8	·43	21
14	Sa	29	9	·52	9	·38	22
15	Su	30	10	·46	10	·36	23
16	Mo	31	11	·42	11	·34	24

Nov. — Solar: Khara, Tula—Aippasi; Khara, Vrischika—Kartigai. Lunar: Bah., Sukla, Kartika, Bahula. Muhammadan: J. awwal; H. 1247 Jumadal-akhir.

Cyclic Sidereal Year, Month and Day	Week-Day	English Month and Day	Tithi	Ending Moment	Nakshatra	Ending Moment	Muhammadan Year, Month and Day
17	Tu	1	12	·41	12	·35	25
18	We	2	13	·41	13	·37	26
19	Th	3	14	·43	14	·42	27
20	Fr	4	A	·47	15	·49	28
21	Sa	5	1	·54	16	·58	29
22	Su	6	2	·62	17	·67	—30
23	Mo	7	3	·70	18	·78	1
24	Tu	8	4	·80	19	·88	2
25	We	9	5	·88	...	...	3
26	Th	10	6	·96	20	·00	4
27	Fr	11	...	...	21	·09	5
28	Sa	12	7	·00	22	·16	6
—29	Su	13	8	·03	23	·21	7
1	Mo	14	9	·06	24	·25	8
2	Tu	15	10	·04	25	·26	9
3	We	16	11 / 12	·02 / ·97	26	·26	10
4	Th	17	13	·92	27	·24	11
5	Fr	18	14	·84	1	·20	12
6	Sa	19	P	·77	2	·15	13
7	Su	20	1	·67	3	·09	14
8	Mo	21	2	·56	4 / 5	·03 / ·96	15
9	Tu	22	3	·47	6	·89	16
10	We	23	4	·38	7	·82	17
11	Th	24	5	·29	8	·76	18
12	Fr	25	6	·20	9	·72	19
13	Sa	26	7	·13	10	·69	20
14	Su	27	8	·08	11	·67	21
15	Mo	28	9	·04	12	·67	22
16	Tu	29	10	·03	13	·69	23
17	We	30	11	·03	14	·74	24

Dec. — Solar: Khara, Dhanus—Margali. Lunar: Sukla, Margasira, Bahula. Muhammadan: H. 1247 Rajab.

Cyclic Sidereal Year, Month and Day	Week-Day	English Month and Day	Tithi	Ending Moment	Nakshatra	Ending Moment	Muhammadan Year, Month and Day
18	Th	1	12	·06	15	·80	25
19	Fr	2	13	·10	16	·88	26
20	Sa	3	14	·17	17	·97	27
21	Su	4	A	·24	...	...	28
22	Mo	5	1	·34	18	·08	—29
23	Tu	6	2	·42	19	·19	1
24	We	7	3	·50	20	·30	2
25	Th	8	4	·60	21	·39	3
26	Fr	9	5	·64	22	·47	4
27	Sa	10	6	·68	23	·53	5
28	Su	11	7	·69	24	·56	6
29	Mo	12	8	·69	25	·59	7
—30	Tu	13	9	·66	26	·59	8
1	We	14	10	·60	27	·57	9
2	Th	15	11	·55	1	·53	10
3	Fr	16	12	·47	2	·48	11
4	Sa	17	13	·39	3	·43	12
5	Su	18	14	·30	4	·37	13
6	Mo	19	P	·20	5	·29	14
7	Tu	20	1 / 2	·10 / ·99	6	·22	15
8	We	21	3	·91	7	·16	16
9	Th	22	4	·83	8	·11	17
10	Fr	23	5	·77	9	·05	18
11	Sa	24	6	·72	10 / 11	·02 / ·99	19
12	Su	25	7	·69	12	·99	20
13	Mo	26	8	·67	...	...	21
14	Tu	27	9	·68	13	·01	22
15	We	28	10	·71	14	·05	23
16	Th	29	11	·75	15	·11	24
17	Fr	30	12	·83	16	·18	25
18	Sa	31	13	·91	17	·27	26

15. Svati. 16. Visak. 17. Anur. 18. Jyesh. 19. Mula. 20. P. Ash. 21. U. Ash. 22. Sravn. 23. Dani. 24. Satab. 25. P. Bhad. 26. U. Bhad. 27. Rev.

A. D. 1832. **Mesha Sankranti** (Commencement of Indian Sidereal Year).
Solar Eclipse. ● **(Surya Sid.) April 11·02.** **Saka 1754.** **Kaliyuga 4933.**
Lunar Eclipse. ○ **(Arya Sid.) April 10·92.** **(S. Cycle) Nandana.**

SOLAR reckoning: Cyclic Sidereal Year, Month and Day; Week-Day; English Month and Day. LUNAR reckoning: Tithi; Ending Moment; Nakshatra; Ending Moment; Muhammadan Year, Month and Day.

Jan.

Cyclic Sidereal Year, Month and Day	Week-Day	English Month and Day	Tithi	Ending Moment	Nakshatra	Ending Moment	Muhammadan Year, Month and Day
19 (Khara, Dhanus—Margali)	Su	1	...	...	18	·37	27 (Rajab)
20	Mo	2	14	·00	19	·49	28
21	Tu	3	A	·08	20	·59	29
22	We	4	1 (Sukla)	·16	21	·69	30
23	Th	5	2	·24	22	·77	1
24	Fr	6	3	·28	23	·84	2
25	Sa	7	4	·32	24	·89	3
26	Su	8	5	·34	25	·91	4
27	Mo	9	6	·33	26	·91	5
28	Tu	10	7	·30	27	·90	6
29	We	11	8	·26	1	·87	7
1	Th	12	9	·19	2	·83	8
2	Fr	13	10	·12	3	·77	9
3	Sa	14	11 / 12	·04 / ·94	4	·70	10
4	Su	15	13 (Pausha)	·84	5	·63	11
5	Mo	16	14	·74	6	·56	12
6	Tu	17	P	·65	7	·50	13 (H. 1247 Shaban)
7	We	18	1	·56	8	·44	14
8	Th	19	2	·47	9	·39	15
9	Fr	20	3	·42	10	·35	16
10	Sa	21	4	·36	11	·32	17
11	Su	22	5	·33	12	·32	18
12	Mo	23	6	·31	13	·33	19
13 (Khara, Makara—Tai)	Tu	24	7 (Bahula)	·35	14	·36	20
14	We	25	8	·35	15	·41	21
15	Th	26	9	·41	16	·48	22
16	Fr	27	10	·48	17	·57	23
17	Sa	28	11	·56	18	·68	24
18	Su	29	12	·65	19	·79	25
19	Mo	30	13	·73	20	·89	26
20	Tu	31	14	·82	21	·99	27

Feb.

Cyclic Sidereal Year, Month and Day	Week-Day	English Month and Day	Tithi	Ending Moment	Nakshatra	Ending Moment	Muhammadan Year, Month and Day
21	We	1	A	·80	...	...	28
22	Th	2	1 (Sukla)	·94	22	·08	29
23	Fr	3	2	·96	23	·16	1
24	Sa	4	3	·98	24	·20	2
25	Su	5	4	·97	25	·23	3
26	Mo	6	5	·94	26	·24	4
27	Tu	7	6	·88	27	·23	5
28	We	8	7	·82	1	·21	6
29	Th	9	8	·75	2	·16	7
30	Fr	10	9	·66	3	·11	8
1 (Khara, Kumbha—Masi)	Sa	11	10	·57	4 / 5	·04 / ·97	9
2	Su	12	11 (Magha)	·46	6	·91	10 (H. 1247 Ramzan)
3	Mo	13	12	·37	7	·84	11
4	Tu	14	13	·27	8	·78	12
5	We	15	14	·18	9	·72	13
6	Th	16	P	·10	10	·68	14
7	Fr	17	1	·04	11	·65	15
8	Sa	18	2 / 3	·00 / ·96	12	·64	16
9	Su	19	4	·94	13	·65	17
10	Mo	20	5	·95	14	·67	18
11	Tu	21	6	·98	15	·72	19
12	We	22	... (Bahula)	...	16	·79	20
13	Th	23	7	·04	17	·88	21
14	Fr	24	8	·10	18	·98	22
15	Sa	25	9	·19	...	...	23
16	Su	26	10	·28	19	·09	24
17	Mo	27	11	·38	20	·19	25
18	Tu	28	12	·43	21	·29	26
19	We	29	13	·51	22	·39	27

March

Cyclic Sidereal Year, Month and Day	Week-Day	English Month and Day	Tithi	Ending	Nakshatra	Ending Moment	Muhammadan Year, Month and Day
20 (Khara, Kumbha—Masi)	Th	1	14	·56	23	·46	28
21	Fr	2	A	·59	24	·52	29
22	Sa	3	1 (Sukla)	·60	25	·55	30
23	Su	4	2	·58	26	·56	1 (H. 1247 Shawwal)
24	Mo	5	3	·56	27	·56	2
25	Tu	6	4	·49	1	·54	3
26	We	7	5	·42	2	·50	4
27	Th	8	6	·36	3	·44	5
28	Fr	9	7	·27	4	·38	6
29	Sa	10	8	·17	5	·32	7
30	Su	11	9 / 10	·07 / ·98	6	·25	8
31	Mo	12	11	·87	7	·18	9
1 (Khara, Mina—Panguni)	Tu	13	12	·78	8	·11	10
2	We	14	13	·70	9	·06	11
3	Th	15	14 (Phalguna)	·63	10 / 11	·01 / ·98	12
4	Fr	16	P	·59	12	·97	13
5	Sa	17	1	·55	13	·97	14
6	Su	18	2	·54	14	·99	15
7	Mo	19	3	·55	...	...	16
8	Tu	20	4	·58	15	·03	17
9	We	21	5	·63	16	·10	18
10	Th	22	6 (Bahula)	·70	17	·18	19
11	Fr	23	7	·79	18	·28	20
12	Sa	24	8	·87	19	·38	21
13	Su	25	9	·96	20	·49	22
14	Mo	26	...	...	21	·60	23
15	Tu	27	10	·04	22	·69	24
16	We	28	11	·10	23	·77	25
17	Th	29	12	·14	24	·83	26
18	Fr	30	13	·17	25	·87	27
19	Sa	31	14	·18	26	·89	28

April

Cyclic Sidereal Year, Month and Day	Week-Day	English Month and Day	Tithi	Ending Moment	Nakshatra	Ending Moment	Muhammadan Year, Month and Day
20	Su	1	A	·16	27	·89	29
21	Mo	2	1 (Sukla)	·13	1	·87	1 (H. 1247 Zi-l-ka'da)
22	Tu	3	2	·07	2	·83	2
23	We	4	3 / 4	·01 / ·93	3	·78	3
24	Th	5	5	·84	4	·72	4
25	Fr	6	6	·73	5	·66	5
26	Sa	7	7	·63	6	·59	6
27	Su	8	8	·53	7	·52	7
28	Mo	9	9	·44	8	·45	8
29	Tu	10	10	·35	9	·39	9
1 (Nandana, Mesha—Chittirai)	We	11	11	·26	10	·35	10
2	Th	12	12	·19	11	·31	11
3	Fr	13	13 (Chaitra)	·15	12	·29	12
4	Sa	14	14	·11	13	·29	13
5	Su	15	P	·10	14	·30	14
6	Mo	16	1	·10	15	·35	15
7	Tu	17	2	·14	16	·41	16
8	We	18	3	·19	17	·49	17
9	Th	19	4	·27	18	·58	18
10	Fr	20	5	·34	19	·68	19
11	Sa	21	6 (Bahula)	·42	20	·80	20
12	Su	22	7	·50	21	·90	21
13	Mo	23	8	·57	...	...	22
14	Tu	24	9	·64	22	·00	23
15	We	25	10	·69	23	·08	24
16	Th	26	11	·72	24	·14	25
17	Fr	27	12	·72	25	·19	26
18	Sa	28	13	·70	26	·21	27
19	Su	29	14	·68	27	·21	28
20	Mo	30	A	·61	1	·20	29

May

Cyclic Sidereal Year, Month and Day	Week-Day	English Month and Day	Tithi	Ending Moment	Nakshatra	Ending Moment	Muhammadan Year, Month and Day
21 (Nandana, Mesha—Chittirai)	Tu	1	1	·54	2	·16	30
22	We	2	2	·46	3	·11	1
23	Th	3	3	·37	4	·06	2
24	Fr	4	4 (Sukla)	·27	5 / 6	·00 / ·93	3
25	Sa	5	5	·18	7	·86	4
26	Su	6	6 / 7	·06 / ·96	8	·79	5
27	Mo	7	8	·88	9	·74	6
28	Tu	8	9	·79	10	·68	7
29	We	9	10	·73	11	·64	8
30	Th	10	11	·68	12	·62	9
31	Fr	11	12 (Vaisakha)	·64	13	·61	10 (H. 1247 Zi-l-hijja)
1	Sa	12	13	·62	14	·63	11
2	Su	13	14	·62	15	·66	12
3	Mo	14	P	·66	16	·72	13
4	Tu	15	1	·71	17	·79	14
5	We	16	2	·77	18	·88	15
6	Th	17	3	·84	19	·99	16
7	Fr	18	4	·93	...	...	17
8	Sa	19	...	...	20	·10	18
9	Su	20	5	·01	21	·20	19
10	Mo	21	6 (Bahula)	·09	22	·30	20
11 (Nandana, Vrishabha—Vaikasi)	Tu	22	7	·15	23	·38	21
12	We	23	8	·20	24	·45	22
13	Th	24	9	·22	25	·51	23
14	Fr	25	10	·23	26	·53	24
15	Sa	26	11	·21	27	·54	25
16	Su	27	12	·18	1	·52	26
17	Mo	28	13	·13	2	·49	27
18	Tu	29	14 / A	·05 / ·96	3	·46	28
19	We	30	1	·87	4	·40	29
20	Th	31	2	·77	5	·34	1

June

Cyclic Sidereal Year, Month and Day	Week-Day	English Month and Day	Tithi	Ending Moment	Nakshatra	Ending Moment	Muhammadan Year, Month and Day
21	Fr	1	3	·67	6	·27	2
22	Sa	2	4	·56	7	·20	3
23	Su	3	5	·47	8	·14	4
24	Mo	4	6	·38	9	·07	5
25	Tu	5	7 (Sukla)	·29	10 / 11	·02 / ·97	6
26	We	6	8	·23	12	·94	7
27	Th	7	9	·17	13	·94	8
28	Fr	8	10	·14	14	·95	9
29	Sa	9	11	·11	15	·98	10
30	Su	10	12	·12	...	...	11 (H. 1248 Muharram)
31	Mo	11	13 (Jyeshtha)	·14	16	·03	12
1 (Nandana, Mithuna—Ani)	Tu	12	14	·18	17	·09	13
2	We	13	P	·25	18	·18	14
3	Th	14	1	·32	19	·29	15
4	Fr	15	2	·40	20	·39	16
5	Sa	16	3	·48	21	·50	17
6	Su	17	4	·57	22	·60	18
7	Mo	18	5	·63	23	·69	19
8	Tu	19	6	·68	24	·77	20
9	We	20	7 (Bahula)	·70	25	·82	21
10	Th	21	8	·71	26	·85	22
11	Fr	22	9	·69	27	·86	23
12	Sa	23	10	·66	1	·85	24
13	Su	24	11	·61	2	·83	25
14	Mo	25	12	·54	3	·79	26
15	Tu	26	13	·46	4	·74	27
16	We	27	14	·36	5	·67	28
17	Th	28	A	·25	6	·61	29
18	Fr	29	1	·16	7	·54	30
19	Sa	30	2 / 3	·05 / ·96	8	·47	1

Naksh:—1. Asvn. 2. Bhar. 3. Krit. 4. Rohi. 5. Mrig. 6. Ardh. 7. Punar. 8. Push. 9. Aslesh. 10. Magh. 11. P. Phal. 12. U. Phal. 13. Hasta. 14. Chit.

A. D. 1832.
A.—Amavasya. P.—Paurnami. **Kollam 1008,** Commences { **N. Malabar—Sept. S. Malabar—Aug.** **Hijra 1248,** Commences, **May 31.** **Vikrama 1889. Bengal San 1238. (N. Cycle) Sobhana.**

Cyclic Sidereal Year, Month and Day. (SOLAR reckoning)	Week-Day	English Month and Day.	Tithi (LUNAR reckoning)	Ending Moment.	Nakshatra	Ending Moment.	Muhammadan Year, Month and Day.
		July					
[Nandana Mithuna—Ani.] 20	Su	1	[Ashadha, Sukla] 4	·86	9	·41	[H. 1248 Safar.] 2
21	Mo	2	5	·78	10	·35	3
22	Tu	3	6	·71	11	·30	4
23	We	4	7	·64	12	·28	5
24	Th	5	8	·61	13	·27	6
25	Fr	6	9	·59	14	·27	7
26	Sa	7	10	·59	15	·29	8
27	Su	8	11	·61	16	·33	9
28	Mo	9	12	·67	17	·40	10
29	Tu	10	13	·73	18	·49	11
30	We	11	14	·80	19	·59	12
31	Th	12	P	·88	20	·69	13
32	Fr	13	[Bahula] 1	·96	21	·80	14
[Nandana Karkata—Adi.] 1	Sa	14	...	...	22	·90	15
2	Su	15	2	·05	...	...	16
3	Mo	16	3	·10	23	·00	17
4	Tu	17	4	·16	24	·08	18
5	We	18	5	·18	25	·13	19
6	Th	19	6	·19	26	·17	20
7	Fr	20	7	·17	27	·18	21
8	Sa	21	8	·14	1	·19	22
9	Su	22	9	·09	2	·16	23
10	Mo	23	10, 11	·01, ·94	3	·12	24
11	Tu	24	12	·85	4	·07	25
12	We	25	13	·75	5, 6	·01, ·95	26
13	Th	26	14	·65	7	·88	27
14	Fr ●	27	A	·55	8	·81	28
15	Sa	28	[Sravana, Sukla] 1	·45	9	·75	29
16	Su	29	2	·34	10	·69	[H. 1248 Rabi-ul-awwal.] 1
17	Mo	30	3	·27	11	·64	2
18	Tu	31	4	·19	12	·61	3
		Aug.					
19	We	1	5	·13	13	·59	4
20	Th	2	6	·09	14	·59	5
21	Fr	3	7	·08	15	·61	6
22	Sa	4	8	·08	16	·64	7
23	Su	5	9	·08	17	·71	8
24	Mo	6	10	·14	18	·79	9
25	Tu	7	11	·20	19	·89	10
26	We	8	12	·28	20	·99	11
27	Th	9	13	·35	...	...	12
28	Fr	10	14	·44	21	·10	13
29	Sa	11	P	·52	22	·21	14
30	Su	12	[Bahula] 1	·58	23	·30	15
31	Mo	13	2	·64	24	·38	16
[Nandana Simha—Avani.] 1	Tu	14	3	·66	25	·44	17
2	We	15	4	·68	26	·48	18
3	Th	16	5	·66	27	·51	19
4	Fr	17	6	·64	1	·51	20
5	Sa	18	7	·59	2	·49	21
6	Su	19	8	·52	3	·46	22
7	Mo	20	9	·44	4	·41	23
8	Tu	21	10	·34	5	·36	24
9	We	22	11	·25	6	·29	25
10	Th	23	12	·15	7	·22	26
11	Fr	24	13, 14	·04, ·94	8	·15	27
12	Sa	25	A	·85	9	·08	28
13	Su	26	[Bhad. Suk.] 1	·77	10, 11	·02, ·98	29
14	Mo	27	2	·70	12	·94	30
15	Tu	28	3	·64	13	·92	[R. akhir.] 1
16	We	29	4	·59	14	·91	2
17	Th	30	5	·58	15	·92	3
18	Fr	31	6	·58	16	·97	4

Cyclic Sidereal Year, Month and Day. (SOLAR reckoning)	Week-Day	English Month and Day.	Tithi (LUNAR reckoning)	Ending Moment.	Nakshatra	Ending Moment.	Muhammadan Year, Month and Day.
		Sep.					
[Nandana Simha—Avani.] 19	Sa	1	[Bhadrapada, Sukla] 7	·60	...	...	[H. 1248 Rabi-ul-akhir.] 5
20	Su	2	8	·65	17	·02	6
21	Mo	3	9	·71	18	·10	7
22	Tu	4	10	·78	19	·19	8
23	We	5	11	·87	20	·29	9
24	Th	6	12	·94	21	·40	10
25	Fr	7	...	...	22	·51	11
26	Sa	8	13	·02	23	·61	12
27	Su	9	14	·10	24	·69	13
28	Mo	10	P	·15	25	·75	14
29	Tu	11	[Bahula] 1	·18	26	·81	15
30	We	12	2	·20	27	·83	16
31	Th	13	3	·18	1	·84	17
[Nandana Kanya—Purattasi.] 1	Fr	14	4	·16	2	·82	18
2	Sa	15	5	·11	3	·79	19
3	Su	16	6, 7	·05, ·97	4	·74	20
4	Mo	17	8	·88	5	·70	21
5	Tu	18	9	·78	6	·63	22
6	We	19	10	·68	7	·56	23
7	Th	20	11	·58	8	·49	24
8	Fr	21	12	·47	9	·42	25
9	Sa	22	13	·38	10	·36	26
10	Su	23	14	·30	11	·31	27
11	Mo	24	A	·23	12	·27	28
12	Tu	25	[Asvina, Sukla] 1	·18	13	·24	29
13	We	26	2	·13	14	·23	[H. 1248 Jumadal-awwal.] 1
14	Th	27	3	·12	15	·25	2
15	Fr	28	4	·11	16	·28	3
16	Sa	29	5	·15	17	·33	4
17	Su	30	6	·19	18	·40	5
		Oct.					
18	Mo	1	7	·25	19	·49	6
19	Tu	2	8	·33	20	·60	7
20	We	3	9	·42	21	·70	8
21	Th	4	10	·49	22	·81	9
22	Fr	5	11	·57	23	·91	10
23	Sa	6	12	·65	24	·99	11
24	Su	7	13	·70	...	...	12
25	Mo	8	14	·73	25	·07	13
26	Tu	9	P	·75	26	·12	14
27	We	10	[Bahula] 1	·75	27	·15	15
28	Th	11	2	·72	1	·16	16
29	Fr	12	3	·67	2	·15	17
30	Sa	13	4	·61	3	·12	18
31	Su	14	5	·53	4	·09	19
[Nandana Tula—Aippasi.] 1	Mo	15	6	·44	5, 6	·03, ·97	20
2	Tu	16	7	·34	7	·90	21
3	We	17	8	·24	8	·83	22
4	Th	18	9	·14	9	·77	23
5	Fr	19	10, 11	·05, ·95	10	·70	24
6	Sa	20	12	·87	11	·65	25
7	Su	21	13	·81	12	·60	26
8	Mo	22	14	·76	13	·57	27
9	Tu	23	A	·72	14	·56	28
10	We	24	[Karttika Suk.] 1	·70	15	·57	29
11	Th	25	2	·71	16	·59	30
12	Fr	26	3	·73	17	·64	[J. akhir.] 1
13	Sa	27	4	·77	18	·70	2
14	Su	28	5	·84	19	·79	3
15	Mo	29	6	·92	20	·89	4
16	Tu	30	...	...	...	...	5
17	We	31	7	·00	21	·00	6

Cyclic Sidereal Year, Month and Day. (SOLAR reckoning)	Week-Day	English Month and Day.	Tithi (LUNAR reckoning)	Ending Moment.	Nakshatra	Ending Moment.	Muhammadan Year, Month and Day.
		Nov.					
[Nandana Tula—Aippasi.] 18	Th	1	[Kartika, Sukla] 8	·10	22	·11	[H. 1248 Jumadal-akhir.] 7
19	Fr	2	9	·18	23	·21	8
20	Sa	3	10	·24	24	·30	9
21	Su	4	11	·29	25	·38	10
22	Mo	5	12	·33	26	·43	11
23	Tu	6	13	·35	27	·47	12
24	We	7	14	·34	1	·48	13
25	Th	8	P	·31	2	·47	14
26	Fr	9	[Bahula] 1	·27	3	·46	15
27	Sa	10	2	·21	4	·42	16
28	Su	11	3	·13	5	·37	17
29	Mo	12	4, 5	·04, ·94	6	·31	18
30	Tu	13	6	·84	7	·24	19
[Nandana Vrischika—Kartigai.] 1	We	14	7	·74	8	·18	20
2	Th	15	8	·66	9	·11	21
3	Fr	16	9	·56	10, 11	·04, ·98	22
4	Sa	17	10	·49	12	·93	23
5	Su	18	11	·41	13	·91	24
6	Mo	19	12	·36	14	·89	25
7	Tu	20	13	·33	15	·89	26
8	We	21	14	·31	16	·91	27
9	Th	22	A	·32	17	·95	28
10	Fr	23	[Margasira, Sukla] 1	·35	...	...	29
11	Sa	24	2	·40	18	·01	[H. 1248 Rajab.] 1
12	Su	25	3	·46	19	·10	2
13	Mo	26	4	·54	20	·19	3
14	Tu	27	5	·64	21	·30	4
15	We	28	6	·72	22	·40	5
16	Th	29	7	·80	23	·51	6
17	Fr	30	8	·87	24	·61	7
		Dec.					
18	Sa	1	9	·94	25	·69	8
19	Su	2	10	·96	26	·75	9
20	Mo	3	11	·98	27	·78	10
21	Tu	4	12	·96	1	·80	11
22	We	5	13	·94	2	·81	12
23	Th	6	14	·89	3	·79	13
24	Fr	7	P	·82	4	·75	14
25	Sa	8	[Bahula] 1	·75	5	·70	15
26	Su	9	2	·66	6	·64	16
27	Mo	10	3	·57	7	·59	17
28	Tu	11	4	·47	8	·51	18
29	We	12	5	·37	9	·44	19
[Nandana Dhanus—Margali.] 1	Th	13	6	·28	10	·38	20
2	Fr	14	7	·18	11	·32	21
3	Sa	15	8	·11	12	·26	22
4	Su	16	9	·04	13	·24	23
5	Mo	17	10, 11	·00, ·97	14	·21	24
6	Tu	18	12	·95	15	·21	25
7	We	19	13	·96	16	·22	26
8	Th	20	14	·99	17	·26	27
9	Fr	21	...	...	18	·33	28
10	Sa	22	A	·05	19	·40	29
11	Su	23	[Pausha, Sukla] 1	·11	20	·49	30
12	Mo	24	2	·19	21	·59	[H. 1248 Shaban.] 1
13	Tu	25	3	·29	22	·70	2
14	We	26	4	·38	23	·82	3
15	Th	27	5	·45	24	·91	4
16	Fr	28	6	·52	25	·99	5
17	Sa	29	7	·58	...	...	6
18	Su	30	8	·61	26	·06	7
19	Mo	31	9	·63	27	·10	8

15. Svati. 16. Visak. 17. Anur. 18. Jyesh. 19. Mula. 20. P. Ash. 21. U. Ash. 22. Sravn. 23. Dani. 24. Satab. 25. P. Bhad. 26. U. Bhad. 27. Rev.

A. D. 1833.
Solar Eclipse. ●
Lunar Eclipse. ○

Mesha Sankranti (Commencement of Indian Sidereal Year).
(Surya Sid.) April 11·28.
(Arya Sid.) April 11·18.

Saka 1755. **Kaliyuga 4934.**
(S. Cycle) Vijaya.

Solar: Nandana, Dhanus—Margali (20–30); Nandana, Makara—Tai (1–20). Lunar: Suk., Pausha, Bahula, Sukla. Muhammadan: H. 1248 Shaban.

Cyclic Sidereal Year, Month and Day	Week-Day	English Month and Day	Tithi	Ending Moment	Nakshatra	Ending Moment	Muhammadan Year, Month and Day
	Jan.						
20	Tu	1	10	·61	1	·13	9
21	We	2	11	·58	2	·13	10
22	Th	3	12	·53	3	·12	11
23	Fr	4	13	·47	4	·08	12
24	Sa	5	14	·39	5 / 6	·04 / ·90	13
25	Su ○	6	P	·30	7	·92	14
26	Mo	7	1	·21	8	·85	15
27	Tu	8	2	·11	9	·78	16
28	We	9	3 / 4	·02 / ·93	10	·71	17
29	Th	10	5	·84	11	·65	18
—30	Fr	11	6	·76	12	·61	19
1	Sa	12	7	·69	13	·57	20
2	Su	13	8	·65	14	·54	21
3	Mo	14	9	·61	15	·53	22
4	Tu	15	10	·60	16	·54	23
5	We	16	11	·60	17	·58	24
6	Th	17	12	·64	18	·63	25
7	Fr	18	13	·69	19	·70	26
8	Sa	19	14	·76	20	·79	27
9	Su	20	—A	·86	21	·89	28
10	Mo	21	1	·94	...	...	—29
11	Tu	22	...	...	22	·01	1
12	We	23	2	·03	23	·11	2
13	Th	24	3	·11	24	·21	3
14	Fr	25	4	·18	25	·30	4
15	Sa	26	5	·22	26	·37	5
16	Su	27	6	·24	27	·42	6
17	Mo	28	7	·27	1	·45	7
18	Tu	29	8	·25	2	·46	8
19	We	30	9	·22	3	·45	9
20	Th	31	10	·17	4	·42	10

Solar: Nandana, Kumbha—Mani. Lunar: Magha, Bahula, Phalguna Suk. Muhammadan: H. 1248 Ramzan; H. 1248 Shawwal.

Cyclic Sidereal Year, Month and Day	Week-Day	English Month and Day	Tithi	Ending Moment	Nakshatra	Ending Moment	Muhammadan Year, Month and Day
	Feb.						
21	Fr	1	11	·11	5	·37	11
22	Su	2	12 / 13	·02 / ·94	6	·33	12
23	Su	3	14	·84	7	·26	13
24	Mo	4	P	·74	8	·19	14
25	Tu	5	1	·65	9	·12	15
26	We	6	2	·55	10	·05	16
27	Th	7	3	·46	11 / 12	·00 / ·94	17
28	Fr	8	4	·39	13	·90	18
—29	Sa	9	5	·32	14	·87	19
1	Su	10	6	·28	15	·85	20
2	Mo	11	7	·24	16	·87	21
3	Tu	12	8	·23	17	·89	22
4	We	13	9	·24	18	·94	23
5	Th	14	10	·29	...	...	24
6	Fr	15	11	·33	19	·01	25
7	Sa	16	12	·40	20	·09	26
8	Su	17	13	·49	21	·20	27
9	Mo	18	14	·57	22	·31	28
10	Tu	19	—A	·66	23	·41	29
11	We	20	1	·73	24	·51	—30
12	Th	21	2	·80	25	·60	1
13	Fr	22	3	·85	26	·68	2
14	Sa	23	4	·89	27	·74	3
15	Su	24	5	·89	1	·77	4
16	Mo	25	6	·88	2	·78	5
17	Tu	26	7	·84	3	·77	6
18	We	27	8	·78	4	·75	7
19	Th	28	9	·72	5	·72	8

Solar: Nandana, Kumbha—Mani (20–30); Nandana, Mina—Panguni (1–20). Lunar: Sukla, Phalguna, Bahula, Sukla. Muhammadan: H. 1248 Shawwal.

Cyclic Sidereal Year, Month and Day	Week-Day	English Month and Day	Tithi	Ending Moment	Nakshatra	Ending Moment	Muhammadan Year, Month and Day
	March						
20	Fr	1	10	·64	6	·66	9
21	Sa	2	11	·56	7	·60	10
22	Su	3	12	·46	8	·53	11
23	Mo	4	13	·36	9	·46	12
24	Tu	5	14	·26	10	·40	13
25	We	6	P	·16	11	·33	14
26	Th	7	1	·07	12	·28	15
27	Fr	8	2 / 3	·00 / ·93	13	·23	16
28	Sa	9	4	·89	14	·19	17
29	Su	10	5	·86	15	·19	18
—30	Mo	11	6	·84	16	·19	19
1	Tu	12	7	·84	17	·21	20
2	We	13	8	·89	18	·25	21
3	Th	14	9	·93	19	·31	22
4	Fr	15	...	...	20	·40	23
5	Sa	16	10	·01	21	·50	24
6	Su	17	11	·09	22	·60	25
7	Mo	18	12	·18	23	·71	26
8	Tu	19	13	·26	24	·81	27
9	We	20	14	·34	25	·91	28
10	Th	21	—A	·39	26	·99	—29
11	Fr	22	1	·45	...	...	1
12	Sa	23	2	·49	27	·05	2
13	Su	24	3	·48	1	·09	3
14	Mo	25	4	·47	2	·10	4
15	Tu	26	5	·42	3	·10	5
16	We	27	6	·38	4	·09	6
17	Th	28	7	·31	5	·05	7
18	Fr	29	8	·22	6 / 7	·00 / ·94	8
19	Sa	30	9	·14	8	·87	9
20	Su	31	10 / 11	·03 / ·93	9	·81	10

Solar: Vijaya, Mesha—Chittirai. Lunar: Chaitra, Bahula, Vaisakha Sukla. Muhammadan: H. 1248 Zi-l-ka'da; H. 1248 Zi-l-hijja.

Cyclic Sidereal Year, Month and Day	Week-Day	English Month and Day	Tithi	Ending Moment	Nakshatra	Ending Moment	Muhammadan Year, Month and Day
	April						
21	Mo	1	12	·83	10	·74	11
22	Tu	2	13	·74	11	·67	12
23	We	3	14	·65	12	·61	13
24	Th	4	P	·57	13	·56	14
25	Fr	5	1	·50	14	·53	15
26	Sa	6	2	·46	15	·51	16
27	Su	7	3	·43	16	·51	17
28	Mo	8	4	·41	17	·52	18
29	Tu	9	5	·42	18	·56	19
—30	We	10	6	·45	19	·62	20
1	Th	11	7	·50	20	·71	21
2	Fr	12	8	·57	21	·80	22
3	Sa	13	9	·65	22	·90	23
4	Su	14	10	·74	...	...	24
5	Mo	15	11	·82	23	·01	25
6	Tu	16	12	·90	24	·11	26
7	We	17	13	·96	25	·22	27
8	Th	18	...	...	26	·30	28
9	Fr	19	14	·01	27	·36	29
10	Sa	20	—A	·03	1	·40	—30
11	Su	21	1	·03	2	·42	1
12	Mo	22	2 / 3	·02 / ·97	3	·43	2
13	Tu	23	4	·92	4	·41	3
14	We	24	5	·85	5	·38	4
15	Th	25	6	·77	6	·33	5
16	Fr	26	7	·68	7	·27	6
17	Sa	27	8	·59	8	·21	7
18	Su	28	9	·48	9	·15	8
19	Mo	29	10	·38	10	·08	9
20	Tu	30	11	·27	11 / 12	·01 / ·95	10

Solar: Vijaya, Mesha—Chittirai (21–31); Vijaya, Vrishabha—Vaikasi (1–20). Lunar: Suk., Vaisakha, Bahula, Sukla. Muhammadan: H. 1248 Zi-l-hijja.

Cyclic Sidereal Year, Month and Day	Week-Day	English Month and Day	Tithi	Ending Moment	Nakshatra	Ending Moment	Muhammadan Year, Month and Day
	May						
21	We	1	12	·18	13	·90	11
22	Th	2	13	·10	14	·86	12
23	Fr	3	14	·03	15	·84	13
24	Sa	4	P / 1	·00 / ·96	16	·83	14
25	Su	5	2	·93	17	·84	15
26	Mo	6	3	·94	18	·87	16
27	Tu	7	4	·98	19	·94	17
28	We	8	...	...	...	...	18
29	Th	9	5	·03	20	·01	19
30	Fr	10	6	·09	21	·10	20
—31	Sa	11	7	·17	22	·20	21
1	Su	12	8	·25	23	·31	22
2	Mo	13	9	·33	24	·42	23
3	Tu	14	10	·41	25	·52	24
4	We	15	11	·48	26	·60	25
5	Th	16	12	·52	27	·67	26
6	Fr	17	13	·54	1	·72	27
7	Sa	18	14	·55	2	·75	28
8	Su	19	—A	·53	3	·76	29
9	Mo	20	1	·50	4	·74	—30
10	Tu	21	2	·44	5	·71	1
11	We	22	3	·36	6	·67	2
12	Th	23	4	·28	7	·62	3
13	Fr	24	5	·19	8	·56	4
14	Sa	25	6 / 7	·10 / ·99	9	·49	5
15	Su	26	8	·89	10	·42	6
16	Mo	27	9	·78	11	·35	7
17	Tu	28	10	·69	12	·28	8
18	We	29	11	·61	13	·24	9
19	Th	30	12	·54	14	·19	10
20	Fr	31	13	·50	15	·16	11

Solar: Vijaya, Mithuna—Ani. Lunar: Jyeshtha, Bahula, Ashadha Sukla. Muhammadan: H. 1249 Muharram; H. 1249 Safar.

Cyclic Sidereal Year, Month and Day	Week-Day	English Month and Day	Tithi	Ending Moment	Nakshatra	Ending Moment	Muhammadan Year, Month and Day
	June						
21	Sa	1	14	·45	16	·15	12
22	Su	2	P	·44	17	·16	13
23	Mo	3	1	·44	18	·20	14
24	Tu	4	2	·47	19	·25	15
25	We	5	3	·51	20	·31	16
26	Th	6	4	·59	21	·40	17
27	Fr	7	5	·67	22	·50	18
28	Sa	8	6	·75	23	·61	19
29	Su	9	7	·83	24	·72	20
30	Mo	10	8	·91	25	·82	21
31	Tu	11	9	·97	26	·91	22
—32	We	12	...	...	27	·98	23
1	Th	13	10	·00	...	...	24
2	Fr	14	11	·03	1	·04	25
3	Sa	15	12	·04	2	·07	26
4	Su	16	13 / 14	·01 / ·98	3	·08	27
5	Mo	17	—A	·93	4	·07	28
6	Tu	18	1	·87	5	·04	29
7	We	19	2	·77	6 / 7	·01 / ·96	—30
8	Th	20	3	·68	8	·89	1
9	Fr	21	4	·58	9	·82	2
10	Sa	22	5	·47	10	·75	3
11	Su	23	6	·37	11	·68	4
12	Mo	24	7	·27	12	·63	5
13	Tu	25	8	·18	13	·57	6
14	We	26	9	·09	14	·52	7
15	Th	27	10 / 11	·03 / ·97	15	·49	8
16	Fr	28	12	·93	16	·48	9
17	Sa	29	13	·92	17	·49	10
18	Su	30	14	·92	18	·51	11

Naksh :—1. Asvn. 2. Bhar. 3. Krit. 4 Rohi. 5. Mrig. 6. Ardh. 7. Punar. 8. Push. 9. Aslesh. 10. Magh. 11. P. Phal. 12. U. Phal. 13. Hasta. 14. Chit.

A. D. 1833. **Kollam 1009,** { **N. Malabar—Sept.** / **S. Malabar—Aug.** } Commences. **Hijra 1249,** Commences, **May 21.** **Vikrama 1890.** **Bengal San 1239.** **(N. Cycle) Krodhin.**

A.—Amavasya. **P.—Paurnami.**

July — Solar: Vijaya, *Mithuna—Ani.* / Vijaya, *Karkata—Adi.* Lunar: Ashadha, *Bahula*; Sravana, *Sukla*. Muhammadan: H. 1249 *Safar*; *Rabi-ul-awwal.*

SOLAR reckoning: Cyclic Sidereal Year, Month and Day	Week-Day	English Month and Day	LUNAR reckoning: Tithi	Ending Moment	Nakshatra	Ending Moment	Muhammadan Year, Month and Day
19	Mo	○ 1	P (Ashadha)	·95	19	·55	12
20	Tu	2	1	·99	20	·62	13
21	We	3	...	...	21	·70	14
22	Th	4	2	·06	22	·81	15
23	Fr	5	3	·13	23	·91	16
24	Sa	6	4	·21	...	...	17
25	Su	7	5	·30	24	·02	18
26	Mo	8	6	·37	25	·12	19
27	Tu	9	7	·44	26	·21	20
28	We	10	8	·48	27	·30	21
29	Th	11	9	·51	1	·35	22
30	Fr	12	10	·51	2	·39	23
—31	Sa	13	11	·49	3	·40	24
1	Su	14	12	·46	4	·40	25
2	Mo	15	13	·40	5	·37	26
3	Tu	16	14	·34	6	·34	27
4	We	● 17	—A	·25	7	·29	28
5	Th	18	1	·16	8	·23	—29
6	Fr	19	2 3	·06 ·97	9	·16	1
7	Sa	20	4	·86	10	·09	2
8	Su	21	5	·75	11 12	·03 ·96	3
9	Mo	22	6	·66	13	·91	4
10	Tu	23	7	·57	14	·86	5
11	We	24	8	·51	15	·82	6
12	Th	25	9	·45	16	·81	7
13	Fr	26	10	·42	17	·81	8
14	Sa	27	11	·40	18	·83	9
15	Su	28	12	·40	19	·87	10
16	Mo	29	13	·42	20	·92	11
17	Tu	30	14	·46	...	...	12
18	We	31	P (Sravana)	·53	21	·01	13

Aug. — Solar: Vijaya, *Simha—Avani.* Lunar: *Bahula*; Adhika Bhad., *Sukla*. Muhammadan: H. 1249; H. 1249 *Rabi-ul-akhir.*

Cyclic Sidereal Year, Month and Day	Week-Day	English Month and Day	Tithi	Ending Moment	Nakshatra	Ending Moment	Muhammadan Year, Month and Day
19	Th	1	1	·60	22	·11	14
20	Fr	2	2	·69	23	·21	15
21	Sa	3	3	·77	24	·32	16
22	Su	4	4	·85	25	·42	17
23	Mo	5	5	·91	26	·52	18
24	Tu	6	6	·95	27	·60	19
25	We	7	...	...	1	·66	20
26	Th	8	7	·00	2	·70	21
27	Fr	9	8 9	·00 ·98	3	·72	22
28	Sa	10	10	·94	4	·72	23
29	Su	11	11	·90	5	·71	24
30	Mo	12	12	·83	6	·68	25
31	Tu	13	13	·75	7	·63	26
—32	We	14	14	·65	8	·57	27
1	Th	15	—A	·55	9	·50	28
2	Fr	16	1	·46	10	·44	29
3	Sa	17	2	·35	11	·37	—30
4	Su	18	3	·26	12	·30	1
5	Mo	19	4	·16	13	·24	2
6	Tu	20	5	·07	14	·19	3
7	We	21	6 7	·01 ·95	15	·16	4
8	Th	22	8	·92	16	·13	5
9	Fr	23	9	·89	17	·13	6
10	Sa	24	10	·90	18	·14	7
11	Su	25	11	·92	19	·18	8
12	Mo	26	12	·96	20	·24	9
13	Tu	27	...	...	21	·32	10
14	We	28	13	·04	22	·41	11
15	Th	29	14	·11	23	·51	12
16	Fr	30	P	·18	24	·61	13
17	Sa	31	1	·26	25	·72	14

Sep. — Solar: Vijaya, *Simha—Avani.* / Vijaya, *Kanya—Purattasi.* Lunar: Adh. Bhadra., *Bahula*; Bhadrapada, *Sukla*. Muhammadan: H. 1249 *Rabi-ul-akhir.*; *Jumadal-awwal.*

Cyclic Sidereal Year, Month and Day	Week-Day	English Month and Day	Tithi	Ending Moment	Nakshatra	Ending Moment	Muhammadan Year, Month and Day
18	Su	1	2	·36	26	·83	15
19	Mo	2	3	·42	27	·91	16
20	Tu	3	4	·47	1	·97	17
21	We	4	5	·50	...	...	18
22	Th	5	6	·51	2	·02	19
23	Fr	6	7	·50	3	·04	20
24	Sa	7	8	·46	4	·06	21
25	Sa	8	9	·42	5	·04	22
26	Mo	9	10	·34	6 7	·01 ·96	23
27	Tu	10	11	·27	8	·90	24
28	We	11	12	·17	9	·85	25
29	Th	12	13 14	·07 ·98	10	·78	26
30	Fr	13	—A	·87	11	·71	27
—31	Sa	14	1	·78	12	·64	28
1	Su	15	2	·69	13	·58	—29
2	Mo	16	3	·61	14	·53	1
3	Tu	17	4	·54	15	·49	2
4	We	18	5	·48	16	·46	3
5	Th	19	6	·44	17	·45	4
6	Fr	20	7	·42	18	·46	5
7	Sa	21	8	·44	19	·50	6
8	Su	22	9	·46	20	·55	7
9	Mo	23	10	·51	21	·62	8
10	Tu	24	11	·56	22	·71	9
11	We	25	12	·64	23	·81	10
12	Th	26	13	·72	24	·91	11
13	Fr	27	14	·80	...	...	12
14	Sa	28	P	·89	25	·03	13
15	Su	29	1	·96	26	·13	14
16	Mo	30	...	...	27	·21	15

Oct. — Solar: Vijaya, *Tula—Aippasi.* Lunar: Nija, *Bahula*; Asvina, *Sukla*; *Bah.* Muhammadan: H. 1249; H. 1249 *Jumadal-akhir.*

Cyclic Sidereal Year, Month and Day	Week-Day	English Month and Day	Tithi	Ending Moment	Nakshatra	Ending Moment	Muhammadan Year, Month and Day
17	Tu	1	2	·01	1	·28	16
18	We	2	3	·04	2	·33	17
19	Th	3	4	·06	3	·37	18
20	Fr	4	5	·04	4	·38	19
21	Sa	5	6 7	·01 ·97	5	·37	20
22	Su	6	8	·89	6	·34	21
23	Mo	7	9	·82	7	·30	22
24	Tu	8	10	·72	8	·25	23
25	We	9	11	·63	9	·19	24
26	Th	10	12	·54	10	·12	25
27	Fr	11	13	·44	11 12	·05 ·98	26
28	Sa	12	14	·34	13	·92	27
29	Su	13	—A	·25	14	·87	28
—30	Mo	14	1	·17	15	·82	29
1	Tu	15	2	·10	16	·79	—30
2	We	16	3	·06	17	·77	1
3	Th	17	4	·01	18	·78	2
4	Fr	18	5	·00	19	·81	3
5	Sa	19	6	·02	20	·86	4
6	Su	20	7	·03	21	·92	5
7	Mo	21	8	·08	...	...	6
8	Tu	22	9	·15	22	·01	7
9	We	23	10	·22	23	·10	8
10	Th	24	11	·30	24	·22	9
11	Fr	25	12	·40	25	·33	10
12	Sa	26	13	·48	26	·43	11
13	Su	27	14	·54	27	·52	12
14	Mo	28	P	·59	1	·59	13
15	Tu	29	1	·62	2	·65	14
16	We	30	2	·65	3	·69	15
17	Th	31	3	·63	4	·70	16

Nov. — Solar: Vijaya, *Tula—Aippasi.* / Vijaya, *Vrischika—Kartigai.* Lunar: Asv., *Bahula*; Kartika, *Sukla*. Muhammadan: H. 1249 *Jumadal-akhir.*; H. 1249 *Rajab.*

Cyclic Sidereal Year, Month and Day	Week-Day	English Month and Day	Tithi	Ending Moment	Nakshatra	Ending Moment	Muhammadan Year, Month and Day
18	Fr	1	4	·59	5	·69	17
19	Sa	2	5	·56	6	·67	18
20	Su	3	6	·49	7	·64	19
21	Mo	4	7	·41	8	·59	20
22	Tu	5	8	·32	9	·53	21
23	We	6	9	·23	10	·46	22
24	Th	7	10	·13	11	·39	23
25	Fr	8	11 12	·03 ·93	12	·32	24
26	Sa	9	13	·85	13	·26	25
27	Su	10	14	·77	14	·20	26
28	Mo	11	—A	·70	15	·15	27
29	Tu	12	1	·64	16	·12	28
—30	We	13	2	·61	17	·10	—29
1	Th	14	3	·61	18	·11	1
2	Fr	15	4	·62	19	·13	2
3	Sa	16	5	·64	20	·17	3
4	Su	17	6	·69	21	·23	4
5	Mo	18	7	·76	22	·31	5
6	Tu	19	8	·84	23	·41	6
7	We	20	9	·92	24	·52	7
8	Th	21	...	...	25	·62	8
9	Fr	22	10	·02	26	·73	9
10	Sa	23	11	·10	27	·82	10
11	Su	24	12	·17	1	·91	11
12	Mo	25	13	·22	2	·97	12
13	Tu	26	14	·26	...	...	13
14	We	27	P	·26	3	·00	14
15	Th	28	1	·25	4	·02	15
16	Fr	29	2	·22	5	·02	16
17	Sa	30	3	·17	6 7	·01 ·97	17

Dec. — Solar: Vijaya, *Dhanus—Margali.* Lunar: *Bahula*; Margasira, *Sukla*; *Bah.* Muhammadan: H. 1249 *Shaban.*

Cyclic Sidereal Year, Month and Day	Week-Day	English Month and Day	Tithi	Ending Moment	Nakshatra	Ending Moment	Muhammadan Year, Month and Day
18	Su	1	4	·11	8	·92	18
19	Mo	2	5 6	·04 ·95	9	·86	19
20	Tu	3	7	·85	10	·80	20
21	We	4	8	·75	11	·72	21
22	Th	5	9	·66	12	·66	22
23	Fr	6	10	·56	13	·60	23
24	Sa	7	11	·46	14	·54	24
25	Su	8	12	·39	15	·48	25
26	Mo	9	13	·33	16	·45	26
27	Tu	10	14	·27	17	·43	27
28	We	11	—A	·24	18	·43	28
—29	Th	12	1	·24	19	·44	29
1	Fr	13	2	·25	20	·48	—30
2	Sa	14	3	·28	21	·54	1
3	Su	15	4	·34	22	·62	2
4	Mo	16	5	·41	23	·71	3
5	Tu	17	6	·49	24	·82	4
6	We	18	7	·59	25	·92	5
7	Th	19	8	·67	...	...	6
8	Fr	20	9	·74	26	·03	7
9	Sa	21	10	·81	27	·13	8
10	Su	22	11	·86	1	·21	9
11	Mo	23	12	·90	2	·28	10
12	Tu	24	13	·90	3	·32	11
13	We	25	14	·90	4	·34	12
14	Th	○ 26	P	·86	5	·34	13
15	Fr	27	1	·81	6	·34	14
16	Sa	28	2	·75	7	·31	15
17	Su	29	3	·67	8	·26	16
18	Mo	30	4	·58	9	·20	17
19	Tu	31	5	·49	10	·13	18

15. Svati. 16. Visak. 17. Anur. 18. Jyesh. 19. Mula. 20. P. Ash. 21. U. Ash. 22. Sravn. 23. Dani. 24. Satab. 25. P. Bhad. 26. U. Bhad. 27. Rev.

A. D. 1834.
Solar Eclipse. ●
Lunar Eclipse. ○

Mesha Sankranti (Commencement of Indian Sidereal Year).
(Surya Sid.) April 11·54.
(Arya Sid.) April 11·44.

Saka 1756.
(S. Cycle) Jaya.

Kaliyuga 4935.

Columns: SOLAR reckoning (Cyclic Sidereal Year, Month and Day; Week-Day; English Month and Day); LUNAR reckoning (Tithi; Ending Moment; Nakshatra; Ending Moment; Muhammadan Year, Month and Day).

Jan. (Solar: Vijaya, Dhanus—Margali; Vijaya, Makara—Tai. Lunar: Marga., Bahula; Sukla; Pausha. Muhammadan: H. 1249 Shaban.; H. 1249 Ramzan.)

Cyclic Sidereal Year, Month and Day	Week-Day	English Month and Day	Tithi	Ending Moment	Nakshatra	Ending Moment	Muhammadan Year, Month and Day
20	We	1	6	·40	11	·07	19
21	Th	2	7	·29	12 13	·00 ·93	20
22	Fr	3	8	·20	14	·87	21
23	Sa	4	9	·11	15	·82	22
24	Su	5	10 11	·03 ·97	16	·79	23
25	Mo	6	12	·92	17	·76	24
26	Tu	7	13	·90	18	·75	25
27	We	8	14	·88	19	·76	26
28	Th	9	A	91	20	·79	27
29	Fr	10	1	·93	21	·85	28
30	Sa	11	2	·98	22	·93	29
1	Su	12	...	...	...	...	1
2	Mo	13	3	·06	23	·01	2
3	Tu	14	4	·14	24	·11	3
4	We	15	5	·23	25	·22	4
5	Th	16	6	·31	26	·34	5
6	Fr	17	7	·40	27	·43	6
7	Sa	18	8	·46	1	·52	7
8	Su	19	9	·50	2	·59	8
9	Mo	20	10	·55	3	·63	9
10	Tu	21	11	·55	4	·66	10
11	We	22	12	·54	5	·68	11
12	Th	23	13	·50	6	·67	12
13	Fr	24	14	·46	7	·64	13
14	Sa	25	P	·39	8	·59	14
15	Su	26	1	·31	9	·54	15
16	Mo	27	2	·21	10	·48	16
17	Tu	28	3	·12	11	·41	17
18	We	29	4 5	·02 ·92	12	·34	18
19	Th	30	6	·83	13	·27	19
20	Fr	31	7	·74	14	·21	20

Feb. (Solar: Vijaya, Kumbha—Masi. Lunar: Bahula; Sukla; Magha; Bahula. Muhammadan: H. 1249 Shawwal.)

Cyclic Sidereal Year, Month and Day	Week-Day	English Month and Day	Tithi	Ending Moment	Nakshatra	Ending Moment	Muhammadan Year, Month and Day
21	Sa	1	8	·67	15	·16	21
22	Su	2	9	·61	16	·12	22
23	Mo	3	10	·55	17	·09	23
24	Tu	4	11	·54	18	·07	24
25	We	5	12	·52	19	·08	25
26	Th	6	13	·54	20	·12	26
27	Fr	7	14	·57	21	·16	27
28	Sa	8	A	·64	22	·23	28
29	Su	9	1	·70	23	·31	29
1	Mo	10	2	·78	24	·41	30
2	Tu	11	3	·87	25	·52	1
3	We	12	4	·95	26	·63	2
4	Th	13	...	...	27	·73	3
5	Fr	14	5	·04	1	·82	4
6	Sa	15	6	·10	2	·89	5
7	Su	16	7	·16	3	·95	6
8	Mo	17	8	·18	4	·99	7
9	Tu	18	9	·19	...	...	8
10	We	19	10	·17	5 6	·00 ·99	9
11	Th	20	11	·13	7	·97	10
12	Fr	21	12	·07	8	·92	11
13	Sa	22	13 14	·00 ·93	9	·88	12
14	Su	23	P	·84	10	·82	13
15	Mo	24	1	·75	11	·75	14
16	Tu	25	2	·64	12	·68	15
17	We	26	3	·54	13	·61	16
18	Th	27	4	·45	14	·55	17
19	Fr	28	5	·35	15	·50	18

March (Solar: Vijaya, Kumbha—Masi; Vijaya, Mina—Panguni. Lunar: Magha, Bahula; Sukla; Phalguna. Muhammadan: H. 1249 Shawwal.; H. 1249 Zi-l-ka'da.)

Cyclic Sidereal Year, Month and Day	Week-Day	English Month and Day	Tithi	Ending Moment	Nakshatra	Ending Moment	Muhammadan Year, Month and Day
20	Sa	1	6	·29	16	·45	19
21	Su	2	7	·22	17	·41	20
22	Mo	3	8	·18	18	·40	21
23	Tu	4	9	·15	19	·41	22
24	We	5	10	·13	20	·43	23
25	Th	6	11	·15	21	·47	24
26	Fr	7	12	·18	22	·53	25
27	Sa	8	13	·25	23	·62	26
28	Su	9	14	·32	24	·71	27
29	Mo	10	A	·41	25	·83	28
30	Tu	11	1	·49	26	·93	29
1	We	12	2	·58	...	...	1
2	Th	13	3	·65	27	·03	2
3	Fr	14	4	·70	1	·13	3
4	Sa	15	5	·76	2	·20	4
5	Su	16	6	·77	3	·27	5
6	Mo	17	7	·75	4	·31	6
7	Tu	18	8	·75	5	·32	7
8	We	19	9	·73	6	·32	8
9	Th	20	10	·67	7	·30	9
10	Fr	21	11	·60	8	·27	10
11	Sa	22	12	·53	9	·22	11
12	Su	23	13	·43	10	·16	12
13	Mo	24	14	·33	11	·09	13
14	Tu	25	P	·22	12 13	·02 ·96	14
15	We	26	1	·13	14	·89	15
16	Th	27	2 3	·04 ·95	15	·83	16
17	Fr	28	4	·87	16	·78	17
18	Sa	29	5	·80	17	·74	18
19	Su	30	6	·76	18	·72	19
20	Mo	31	7	·73	19	·73	20

April (Solar: Jaya, Mesha—Chittirai. Lunar: Bahula; Sukla; Chaitra; Bahula. Muhammadan: H. 1249 Zi-l-hijja.)

Cyclic Sidereal Year, Month and Day	Week-Day	English Month and Day	Tithi	Ending Moment	Nakshatra	Ending Moment	Muhammadan Year, Month and Day
21	Tu	1	8	·72	20	·74	21
22	We	2	9	·74	21	·78	22
23	Th	3	10	·77	22	·84	23
24	Fr	4	11	·82	23	·92	24
25	Sa	5	12	·89	...	...	25
26	Su	6	13	·98	24	·02	26
27	Mo	7	...	...	25	·12	27
28	Tu	8	14	·06	26	·23	28
29	We	9	A	·15	27	·33	29
30	Th	10	1	·22	1	·43	30
1	Fr	11	2	·27	2	·52	1
2	Sa	12	3	·32	3	·58	2
3	Su	13	4	·33	4	·62	3
4	Mo	14	5	·34	5	·64	4
5	Tu	15	6	·32	6	·64	5
6	We	16	7	·29	7	·63	6
7	Th	17	8	·22	8	·60	7
8	Fr	18	9	·16	9	·55	8
9	Sa	19	10 11	·08 ·99	10	·49	9
10	Su	20	12	·89	11	·43	10
11	Mo	21	13	·78	12	·36	11
12	Tu	22	14	·68	13	·30	12
13	We	23	P	·58	14	·23	13
14	Th	24	1	·49	15	·17	14
15	Fr	25	2	·42	16	·11	15
16	Sa	26	3	·35	17	·07	16
17	Su	27	4	·30	18	·06	17
18	Mo	28	5	·27	19	·05	18
19	Tu	29	6	·26	20	·06	19
20	We	30	7	·26	21	·09	20

May (Solar: Jaya, Mesha—Chittirai; Jaya, Vrishabha—Vaikasi. Lunar: Chait., Bah.; Sukla; Vaisakha. Muhammadan: H. 1249 Zi-l-hijja.; H. 1250 Muharram.)

Cyclic Sidereal Year, Month and Day	Week-Day	English Month and Day	Tithi	Ending Moment	Nakshatra	Ending Moment	Muhammadan Year, Month and Day
21	Th	1	8	·30	22	·15	21
22	Fr	2	9	·35	23	·23	22
23	Sa	3	10	·42	24	·32	23
24	Su	4	11	·50	25	·42	24
25	Mo	5	12	·59	26	·53	25
26	Tu	6	13	·66	27	·63	26
27	We	7	14	·73	1	·74	27
28	Th	8	A	·80	2	·82	28
29	Fr	9	1	·85	3	·89	29
30	Sa	10	2	·87	4	·94	1
31	Su	11	3	·86	5	·96	2
1	Mo	12	4	·85	6	·98	3
2	Tu	13	5	·81	7	·96	4
3	We	14	6	·74	8	·93	5
4	Th	15	7	·67	9	·89	6
5	Fr	16	8	·58	10	·83	7
6	Sa	17	9	·50	11	·76	8
7	Su	18	10	·40	12	·70	9
8	Mo	19	11	·30	13	·63	10
9	Tu	20	12	·20	14	·57	11
10	We	21	13	·09	15	·50	12
11	Th	22	14 P	·00 ·92	16	·45	13
12	Fr	23	1	·86	17	·41	14
13	Sa	24	2	·80	18	·38	15
14	Su	25	3	·78	19	·37	16
15	Mo	26	4	·76	20	·38	17
16	Tu	27	5	·77	21	·41	18
17	We	28	6	·79	22	·47	19
18	Th	29	7	·85	23	·58	20
19	Fr	30	8	·92	24	·62	21
20	Sa	31	...	...	25	·72	22

June (Solar: Jaya, Mithuna—Ani. Lunar: Bahula; Sukla; Jyeshtha; Bahula. Muhammadan: H. 1250 Safar.)

Cyclic Sidereal Year, Month and Day	Week-Day	English Month and Day	Tithi	Ending Moment	Nakshatra	Ending Moment	Muhammadan Year, Month and Day
21	Su	1	9	·00	26	·83	23
22	Mo	2	10	·08	27	·94	24
23	Tu	3	11	·16	...	...	25
24	We	4	12	·24	1	·04	26
25	Th	5	13	·30	2	·13	27
26	Fr	6	14	·33	3	·20	28
27	Sa	7	A	·36	4	·25	29
28	Su	8	1	·36	5	·28	30
29	Mo	9	2	·35	6	·30	1
30	Tu	10	3	·30	7	·29	2
31	We	11	4	·25	8	·26	3
32	Th	12	5	·18	9	·22	4
1	Fr	13	6	·09	10	·17	5
2	Sa	14	7 8	·00 ·90	11	·11	6
3	Su	15	9	·79	12 13	·04 ·97	7
4	Mo	16	10	·69	14	·90	8
5	Tu	17	11	·60	15	·84	9
6	We	18	12	·50	16	·79	10
7	Th	19	13	·42	17	·74	11
8	Fr	20	14	·35	18	·71	12
9	Sa ○	21	P	·29	19	·69	13
10	Su	22	1	·26	20	·70	14
11	Mo	23	2	·24	21	·73	15
12	Tu	24	3	·26	22	·78	16
13	We	25	4	·27	23	·84	17
14	Th	26	5	·33	24	·92	18
15	Fr	27	6	·39	...	...	19
16	Sa	28	7	·46	25	·02	20
17	Su	29	8	·55	26	·13	21
18	Mo	30	9	·63	27	·24	22

Naksh:—1. Asvn. 2. Bhar. 3. Krit. 4. Rohi. 5. Mrig. 6. Ardh. 7. Punar. 8. Push. 9. Aslesh. 10. Magh. 11. P. Phal. 12. U. Phal. 13. Hasta. 14. Chit.

A. D. 1834. **Kollam 1010,** Commences { **N. Malabar—Sept.** / **S. Malabar—Aug.** **Hijra 1250,** Commences, **May 10.** **Vikrama 1891.**

A.—Amavasya. **P.—Paurnami.** **Bengal San 1240.** **(N. Cycle) Visvavasu.**

Columns: SOLAR reckoning (Cyclic Sidereal Year, Month and Day; Week-Day; English Month and Day) — LUNAR reckoning (Tithi; Ending Moment; Nakshatra; Ending Moment; Muhammadan Year, Month and Day).

July

Solar month	Cyclic Sidereal Day	Week-Day	English Day	Lunar month	Tithi	Ending Moment	Nakshatra	Ending Moment	Muhammadan month	Muhammadan Day
Jaya Mithuna—Ani	19	Tu	1	Jy. Bah.	10	·71	1	·34	Safar	23
	20	We	2		11	·76	2	·43		24
	21	Th	3		12	·82	3	·51		25
	22	Fr	4		13	·84	4	·56		26
	23	Sa	5		14	·83	5	·61		27
	24	Su	6		—A	·82	6	·62		28
	25	Mo	7	Sukla	1	·78	7	·62		—29
	26	Tu	8		2	·72	8	·59		1
	27	We	9		3	·65	9	·55		2
	28	Th	10		4	·57	10	·51		3
	29	Fr	11		5	·47	11	·45		4
	30	Sa	12		6	·38	12	·38		5
	—31	Su	13		7	·27	13	·31		6
Jaya Karkata—Adi	1	Mo	14		8	·17	14	·24		7
	2	Tu	15		{ 9 10	·06 ·97	15	·18		8
	3	We	16	Ashadha	11	·89	16	·12	H. 1250 Rabi-ul-awwal	9
	4	Th	17		12	·82	17	·08		10
	5	Fr	18		13	·77	18	·04		11
	6	Sa	19		14	·74	19	·02		12
	7	Su	20		P	·72	20	·03		13
	8	Mo	21	Bahula	1	·73	21	·05		14
	9	Tu	22		2	·75	22	·09		15
	10	We	23		3	·80	23	·15		16
	11	Th	24		4	·85	24	·22		17
	12	Fr	25		5	·94	25	·32		18
	13	Sa	26		...	...	26	·43		19
	14	Su	27		6	·02	27	·54		20
	15	Mo	28		7	·10	1	·64		21
	16	Tu	29		8	·18	2	·73		22
	17	We	30		9	·24	3	·81		23
	18	Th	31		10	·30	4	·88		24

Aug.

Solar month	Cyclic Sidereal Day	Week-Day	English Day	Lunar month	Tithi	Ending Moment	Nakshatra	Ending Moment	Muhammadan month	Muhammadan Day
Jaya Karkata—Adi	19	Fr	1		11	·31	5	·92		25
	20	Sa	2		12	·32	6	·94		26
	21	Su	3		13	·30	7	·94		27
	22	Mo	4		14	·27	8	·92		28
	23	Tu	5		—A	·21	9	·90		29
	24	We	6	Sukla	1	·14	10	·85		—30
	25	Th	7		{ 2 3	·06 ·97	11	·79		1
	26	Fr	8		4	·87	12	·72		2
	27	Sa	9		5	·76	13	·65		3
	28	Su	10		6	·66	14	·58		4
	29	Mo	11		7	·56	15	·52		5
	30	Tu	12		8	·47	16	·46		6
	31	We	13		9	·40	17	·41		7
	—32	Th	14		10	·32	18	·37	H. 1250 Rabi-ul-akhir	8
Jaya Simha—Avani	1	Fr	15		11	·26	19	·35		9
	2	Sa	16		12	·23	20	·35		10
	3	Su	17	Sravana	13	·22	21	·36		11
	4	Mo	18		14	·23	22	·40		12
	5	Tu	19		P	·24	23	·45		13
	6	We	20	Bahula	1	·29	24	·53		14
	7	Th	21		2	·36	25	·63		15
	8	Fr	22		3	·44	26	·73		16
	9	Sa	23		4	·52	27	·83		17
	10	Su	24		5	·60	1	·94		18
	11	Mo	25		6	·68	...	...		19
	12	Tu	26		7	·75	2	·04		20
	13	We	27		8	·79	3	·13		21
	14	Th	28		9	·81	4	·19		22
	15	Fr	29		10	·83	5	·24		23
	16	Sa	30		11	·80	6	·26		24
	17	Su	31		12	·77	7	·27		25

Sep.

Solar month	Cyclic Sidereal Day	Week-Day	English Day	Lunar month	Tithi	Ending Moment	Nakshatra	Ending Moment	Muhammadan month	Muhammadan Day
Jaya Simha—Avani	18	Mo	1	Bhad.	13	·72	8	·26	R. Akr.	26
	19	Tu	2		14	·66	9	·23		27
	20	We	3		—A	·57	10	·18		28
	21	Th	4	Sukla	1	·48	11	·12		—29
	22	Fr	5		2	·38	12	·06		1
	23	Sa	6		3	·28	13 14	·00 ·93 }		2
	24	Su	7		4	·17	15	·86		3
	25	Mo	8		{ 5 6	·07 ·99	16	·80		4
	26	Tu	9		7	·91	17	·74		5
	27	We	10		8	·85	18	·70		6
	28	Th	11		9	·79	19	·68		7
	29	Fr	12		10	·75	20	·67		8
	30	Sa	13		11	·74	21	·68	H. 1250 Jumadal-awwal	9
	—31	Su	14	Bhadrapada	12	·76	22	·71		10
Jaya Kanya—Purattasi	1	Mo	15		13	·78	23	·76		11
	2	Tu	16		14	·82	24	·84		12
	3	We	17		P	·88	25	·93		13
	4	Th	18	Bahula	1	·95	...	...		14
	5	Fr	19		...	...	26	·03		15
	6	Sa	20		2	·03	27	·13		16
	7	Su	21		3	·12	1	·24		17
	8	Mo	22		4	·20	2	·35		18
	9	Tu	23		5	·28	3	·43		19
	10	We	24		6	·32	4	·50		20
	11	Th	25		7	·35	5	·55		21
	12	Fr	26		8	·36	6	·58		22
	13	Sa	27		9	·34	7	·60		23
	14	Su	28		10	·32	8	·59		24
	15	Mo	29		11	·26	9	·56		25
	16	Tu	30		12	·20	10	·52		26

Oct.

Solar month	Cyclic Sidereal Day	Week-Day	English Day	Lunar month	Tithi	Ending Moment	Nakshatra	Ending Moment	Muhammadan month	Muhammadan Day
Jaya Kanya—Purattasi	17	We	1		13	·12	11	·47		27
	18	Th	2		{ 14 A	·03 ·93	12	·41		28
	19	Fr	3	Sukla	1	·84	13	·34		29
	20	Sa	4		2	·73	14	·27		—30
	21	Su	5		3	·63	15	·20		1
	22	Mo	6		4	·54	16	·13		2
	23	Tu	7		5	·46	17	·08		3
	24	We	8		6	·40	18	·04		4
	25	Th	9		7	·34	19 20	·01 ·99 }		5
	26	Fr	10		8	·32	...	...		6
	27	Sa	11		9	·30	21	·00		7
	28	Su	12		10	·32	22	·02		8
	29	Mo	13		11	·34	23	·08		9
	—30	Tu	14	Asvina	12	·38	24	·14	H. 1250 Jumadal-akhir	10
Jaya Tula—Aippasi	1	We	15		13	·45	25	·23		11
	2	Th	16		14	·52	26	·33		12
	3	Fr	17		P	·61	27	·43		13
	4	Sa	18	Bahula	1	·69	1	·55		14
	5	Su	19		2	·77	2	·65		15
	6	Mo	20		3	·85	3	·74		16
	7	Tu	21		4	·89	4	·81		17
	8	We	22		5	·93	5	·86		18
	9	Th	23		6	·94	6	·91		19
	10	Fr	24		7	·93	7	·92		20
	11	Sa	25		8	·89	8	·91		21
	12	Su	26		9	·85	9	·89		22
	13	Mo	27		10	·78	10	·85		23
	14	Tu	28		11	·69	11	·80		24
	15	We	29		12	·61	12	·74		25
	16	Th	30		13	·51	13	·68		26
	17	Fr	31		14	·42	14	·61		27

Nov.

Solar month	Cyclic Sidereal Day	Week-Day	English Day	Lunar month	Tithi	Ending Moment	Nakshatra	Ending Moment	Muhammadan month	Muhammadan Day
Jaya Tula—Aippasi	18	Sa	1		—A	·31	15	·53		28
	19	Su	2	Sukla	1	·22	16	·47		—29
	20	Mo	3		2	·13	17	·42		1
	21	Tu	4		3	·05	18	·37		2
	22	We	5		{ 4 5	·00 ·94	19	·34		3
	23	Th	6		6	·91	20	·32		4
	24	Fr	7		7	·89	21	·32		5
	25	Sa	8		8	·91	22	·35		6
	26	Su	9		9	·94	23	·39		7
	27	Mo	10		10	·98	24	·45		8
	28	Tu	11		...	...	25	·53		9
	29	We	12		11	·05	26	·62		10
	—30	Th	13		12	·13	27	·74		11
Jaya Vrischika—Kartigai	1	Fr	14	Karttika	13	·23	1	·84		12
	2	Sa	15		14	·32	2	·95	H. 1250 Rajab	13
	3	Su	16		P	·40	...	...		14
	4	Mo	17	Bahula	1	·46	3	·04		15
	5	Tu	18		2	·51	4	·12		16
	6	We	19		3	·55	5	·19		17
	7	Th	20		4	·55	6	·22		18
	8	Fr	21		5	·54	7	·24		19
	9	Sa	22		6	·50	8	·24		20
	10	Su	23		7	·46	9	·22		21
	11	Mo	24		8	·40	10	·18		22
	12	Tu	25		9	·32	11	·14		23
	13	We	26		10	·22	12	·08		24
	14	Th	27		11	·13	13 14	·01 ·94 }		25
	15	Fr	28		{ 12 13	·04 ·93	15	·87		26
	16	Sa	29		14	·84	16	·81		27
	17	Su	30		—A	·76	17	·75		28

Dec.

Solar month	Cyclic Sidereal Day	Week-Day	English Day	Lunar month	Tithi	Ending Moment	Nakshatra	Ending Moment	Muhammadan month	Muhammadan Day
Jaya Vrischika—Kartigai	18	Mo	1	Sukla	1	·68	18	·70		29
	19	Tu	2		2	·61	19	·67		—30
	20	We	3		3	·56	20	·64		1
	21	Th	4		4	·54	21	·65		2
	22	Fr	5		5	·52	22	·66		3
	23	Sa	6		6	·54	23	·70		4
	24	Su	7		7	·57	24	·76		5
	25	Mo	8		8	·63	25	·83		6
	26	Tu	9		9	·69	26	·93		7
	27	We	10		10	·77	...	...		8
	28	Th	11		11	·86	27	·04		9
	29	Fr	12		12	·96	1	·14		10
	—30	Sa	13	Margasira	...	...	2	·25		11
Jaya Dhanus—Margali	1	Su	14		13	·04	3	·34		12
	2	Mo	15		14	·10	4	·42	H. 1250 Shaban	13
	3	Tu ○	16		P	·16	5	·50		14
	4	We	17	Bahula	1	·18	6	·54		15
	5	Th	18		2	·19	7	·56		16
	6	Fr	19		3	·18	8	·56		17
	7	Sa	20		4	·14	9	·55		18
	8	Su	21		5	·09	10	·52		19
	9	Mo	22		{ 6 7	·02 ·95	11	·48		20
	10	Tu	23		8	·85	12	·42		21
	11	We	24		9	·76	13	·35		22
	12	Th	25		10	·67	14	·28		23
	13	Fr	26		11	·57	15	·22		24
	14	Sa	27		12	·47	16	·15		25
	15	Su	28		13	·39	17	·09		26
	16	Mo	29		14	·31	18	·04		27
	17	Tu	30		—A	·25	19 20	·00 ·98 }		28
	18	We	31		1	·21	21	·97		—29

A. D. 1835. **Mesha Sankranti** (Commencement of Indian Sidereal Year).
Solar Eclipse. ● **(Surya Sid.) April 11·80.** **Saka 1757.** **Kaliyuga 4936.**
Lunar Eclipse. ○ **(Arya Sid.) April 11·70.** **.(S. Cycle) Manmatha.**

Jan.

Labels: Jaya, Dhanus—Margali. / Jaya, Makara—Tai. — Sukla; Pausha; Bahula — H. 1250 Ramzan.

Cyclic Sidereal Year, Month and Day	Week-Day	English Month and Day	Tithi	Ending Moment	Nakshatra	Ending Moment	Muhammadan Year, Month and Day
19	Th	1	2	·18	22	·98	1
20	Fr	2	3	·17	...	...	2
21	Sa	3	4	·18	23	·01	3
22	Su	4	5	·22	24	·06	4
23	Mo	5	6	·28	25	·14	5
24	Tu	6	7	·34	26	·23	6
25	We	7	8	·43	27	·34	7
26	Th	8	9	·52	1	·44	8
27	Fr	9	10	·61	2	·55	9
28	Sa	10	11	·69	3	·64	10
—29	Su	11	12	·75	4	·74	11
1	Mo	12	13	·80	5	·81	12
2	Tu	13	14	·83	6	·85	13
3	We	14	P	·84	7	·88	14
4	Th	15	1	·82	8	·89	15
5	Fr	16	2	·79	9	·88	16
6	Sa	17	3	·74	10	·86	17
7	Su	18	4	·68	11	·81	18
8	Mo	19	5	·59	12	·76	19
9	Tu	20	6	·49	13	·69	20
10	We	21	7	·40	14	·63	21
11	Th	22	8	·30	15	·56	22
12	Fr	23	9	·20	16	·49	23
13	Sa	24	10	·11	17	·43	24
14	Su	25	11 12	·03 ·95	18	·37	25
15	Mo	26	13	·90	19	·84	26
16	Tu	27	14	·85	20	·81	27
17	We	28	—A	·82	21	·29	28
18	Th	29	1	·81	22	·30	29
19	Fr	30	2	·83	23	·33	—30
20	Sa	31	3	·88	24	·37	1

Feb.

Labels: Jaya, Kumbha—Masi. — Sukla; Magha; Bahula — H. 1250 Shawwal.

Cyclic Sidereal Year, Month and Day	Week-Day	English Month and Day	Tithi	Ending Moment	Nakshatra	Ending Moment	Muhammadan Year, Month and Day
21	Su	1	4	·93	25	·45	2
22	Mo	2	5	·99	26	·53	3
23	Tu	3	...	...	27	·63	4
24	We	4	6	·08	1	·74	5
25	Th	5	7	·17	2	·84	6
26	Fr	6	8	·26	3	·95	7
27	Sa	7	9	·33	...	...	8
28	Su	8	10	·40	4	·04	9
29	Mo	9	11	·45	5	·11	10
—30	Tu	10	12	·47	6	·17	11
1	We	11	13	·47	7	·20	12
2	Th	12	14	·45	8	·22	13
3	Fr	13	P	·42	9	·21	14
4	Sa	14	1	·36	10	·19	15
5	Su	15	2	·30	11	·14	16
6	Mo	16	3	·21	12	·09	17
7	Tu	17	4	·12	13 14	·04 ·97	18
8	We	18	5 6	·03 ·93	15	·90	19
9	Th	19	7	·88	16	·83	20
10	Fr	20	8	·78	17	·76	21
11	Sa	21	9	·65	18	·70	22
12	Su	22	10	·56	19	·66	23
13	Mo	23	11	·51	20	·63	24
14	Tu	24	12	·47	21	·62	25
15	We	25	13	·45	22	·62	26
16	Th	26	14	·43	23	·64	27
17	Fr	27	—A	·44	24	·69	28
18	Sa	28	1	·49	25	·76	—29

March

Labels: Jaya, Kumbha—Masi. / Jaya, Mina—Panguni. — Sukla; Phalguna; Bahula — H. 1250 Zi-l-ka'da.

Cyclic Sidereal Year, Month and Day	Week-Day	English Month and Day	Tithi	Ending Moment	Nakshatra	Ending Moment	Muhammadan Year, Month and Day
19	Su	1	2	·55	26	·84	1
20	Mo	2	3	·62	27	·93	2
21	Tu	3	4	·71	...	...	3
22	We	4	5	·80	1	·04	4
23	Th	5	6	·88	2	·15	5
24	Fr	6	7	·94	3	·25	6
25	Sa	7	...	...	4	·35	7
26	Su	8	8	·01	5	·42	8
27	Mo	9	9	·06	6	·48	9
28	Tu	10	10	·08	7	·53	10
—29	We	11	11	·08	8	·54	11
1	Th	12	12	·07	9	·54	12
2	Fr	13	13 14	·03 ·97	10	·52	13
3	Sa	14	P	·90	11	·48	14
4	Su	15	1	·81	12	·44	15
5	Mo	16	2	·72	13	·38	16
6	Tu	17	3	·62	14	·31	17
7	We	18	4	·53	15	·24	18
8	Th	19	5	·43	16	·17	19
9	Fr	20	6	·34	17	·10	20
10	Sa	21	7	·25	18	·05	21
11	Su	22	8	·16	19 20	·00 ·96	22
12	Mo	23	9	·10	21	·94	23
13	Tu	24	10	·06	22	·94	24
14	We	25	11	·04	23	·96	25
15	Th	26	12	·02	...	...	26
16	Fr	27	13	·05	24	·00	27
17	Sa	28	14	·08	25	·06	28
18	Su	29	—A	·13	26	·14	29
19	Mo	30	1	·21	27	·23	—30
20	Tu	31	2	·29	1	·34	1

April

Labels: Jaya, Mina—Panguni. / Manmatha, Mesha—Chittirai. — Sukla; Chaitra; Bahula; Suk. — H. 1250 Zi-l-hijja.

Cyclic Sidereal Year, Month and Day	Week-Day	English Month and Day	Tithi	Ending Moment	Nakshatra	Ending Moment	Muhammadan Year, Month and Day
21	We	1	3	·38	2	·45	2
22	Th	2	4	·46	3	·55	3
23	Fr	3	5	·54	4	·65	4
24	Sa	4	6	·59	5	·73	5
25	Su	5	7	·63	6	·80	6
26	Mo	6	8	·66	7	·84	7
27	Tu	7	9	·65	8	·86	8
28	We	8	10	·64	9	·86	9
29	Th	9	11	·59	10	·84	10
30	Fr	10	12	·53	11	·81	11
—31	Sa	11	13	·46	12	·77	12
1	Su	12	14	·38	13	·71	13
2	Mo	13	P	·28	14	·65	14
3	Tu	14	1	·18	15	·58	15
4	We	15	2 3	·08 ·98	16	·51	16
5	Th	16	4	·89	17	·44	17
6	Fr	17	5	·80	18	·38	18
7	Sa	18	6	·72	19	·33	19
8	Su	19	7	·65	20	·29	20
9	Mo	20	8	·61	21	·27	21
10	Tu	21	9	·59	22	·27	22
11	We	22	10	·56	23	·28	23
12	Th	23	11	·58	24	·31	24
13	Fr	24	12	·62	25	·37	25
14	Sa	25	13	·68	26	·44	26
15	Su	26	14	·74	27	·54	27
16	Mo	27	—A	·83	1	·64	28
17	Tu	28	1	·92	2	·75	—29
18	We	29	...	...	3	·85	1
19	Th	30	2	·00	4	·95	2

May

Labels: Manmatha, Mesha—Chittirai. / Manmatha, Vrishabha—Vaikasi. — Sukla; Vaisakha; Bahula — H. 1251 Muharram.

Cyclic Sidereal Year, Month and Day	Week-Day	English Month and Day	Tithi	Ending Moment	Nakshatra	Ending Moment	Muhammadan Year, Month and Day
20	Fr	1	3	·06	...	...	3
21	Sa	2	4	·12	5	·04	4
22	Su	3	5	·17	6	·11	5
23	Mo	4	6	·18	7	·16	6
24	Tu	5	7	·19	8	·18	7
25	We	6	8	·17	9	·19	8
26	Th	7	9	·12	10	·17	9
27	Fr	8	10 11	·06 ·98	11	·15	10
28	Sa	9	12	·90	12	·11	11
29	Su	10	13	·81	13 14	·05 ·98	12
30	Mo	11	14	·71	15	·91	13
—31	Tu	12	P	·60	16	·85	14
1	We	13	1	·50	17	·78	15
2	Th	14	2	·41	18	·72	16
3	Fr	15	3	·32	19	·67	17
4	Sa	16	4	·23	20	·62	18
5	Su	17	5	·17	21	·60	19
6	Mo	18	6	·13	22	·59	20
7	Tu	19	7	·10	23	·60	21
8	We	20	8	·09	24	·63	22
9	Th	21	9	·09	25	·68	23
10	Fr	22	10	·13	26	·76	24
11	Sa	23	11	·19	27	·84	25
12	Su	24	12	·25	1	·94	26
13	Mo	25	13	·33	...	...	27
14	Tu	26	14	·41	2	·05	28
15	We	27	—A	·50	3	·15	29
16	Th	28	1	·57	4	·25	—30
17	Fr	29	2	·62	5	·35	1
18	Sa	30	3	·66	6	·42	2
19	Su	31	4	·68	7	·47	3

June

Labels: Manmatha, Mithuna—Ani. — Sukla; Jyeshtha; Bahula; A. Suk. — H. 1251 Safar; R'awwal.

Cyclic Sidereal Year, Month and Day	Week-Day	English Month and Day	Tithi	Ending Moment	Nakshatra	Ending Moment	Muhammadan Year, Month and Day
20	Mo	1	5	·68	8	·50	4
21	Tu	2	6	·66	9	·51	5
22	We	3	7	·63	10	·51	6
23	Th	4	8	·57	11	·48	7
24	Fr	5	9	·49	12	·44	8
25	Sa	6	10	·41	13	·39	9
26	Su	7	11	·30	14	·33	10
27	Mo	8	12	·21	15	·26	11
28	Tu	9	13	·10	16	·19	12
29	We ○	10	14 P	·01 ·91	17	·12	13
30	Th	11	1	·81	18	·06	14
—31	Fr	12	2	·73	19 20	·00 ·96	15
1	Sa	13	3	·66	21	·93	16
2	Su	14	4	·62	22	·91	17
3	Mo	15	5	·58	23	·92	18
4	Tu	16	6	·57	24	·94	19
5	We	17	7	·58	...	...	20
6	Th	18	8	·62	25	·00	21
7	Fr	19	9	·66	26	·06	22
8	Sa	20	10	·72	27	·14	23
9	Su	21	11	·80	1	·24	24
10	Mo	22	12	·88	2	·34	25
11	Tu	23	13	·97	3	·45	26
12	We	24	...	...	4	·56	27
13	Th	25	14	·04	5	·65	28
14	Fr	26	A	·10	6	·73	—29
15	Sa	27	1	·14	7	·78	1
16	Su	28	2	·16	8	·82	2
17	Mo	29	3	·16	9	·84	3
18	Tu	30	4	·14	10	·84	4

Naksh :—1. Asvn. 2. Bhar. 3. Krit. 4. Rohi. 5. Mrig. 6. Ardh. 7. Punar. 8. Push. 9. Aslesh. 10. Magh. 11. P. Phal. 12. U. Phal. 13. Hasta. 14. Chit.

A. D. 1835. | **Vikrama 1892.**
A.—Amavasya. **Kollam 1011,** Commences { **N. Malabar—Sept.** / **S. Malabar—Aug.** } **Hijra 1251,** Commences, April 29. | **Bengal San 1241.**
P.—Paurnami. | **(N. Cycle) Parabhava.**

July

SOLAR reckoning: Solar month	Cyclic Sidereal Year, Month and Day	Week-Day	English Month and Day	LUNAR reckoning: Lunar month	Tithi	Ending Moment	Nakshatra	Ending Moment	Muhammadan Year, Month	Day
Manmatha *Mithuna—Ani.*	19	We	1	Ashadha *Sukla*	5	·11	11	·81	H. 1251 *Rabi-ul-awwal.*	5
	20	Th	2		6 7	·05 ·97	12	·77		6
	21	Fr	3		8	·89	13	·72		7
	22	Sa	4		9	·80	14	·67		8
	23	Su	5		10	·69	15	·60		9
	24	Mo	6		11	·59	16	·53		10
	25	Tu	7		12	·49	17	·46		11
	26	We	8		13	·39	18	·39		12
	27	Th	9		14	·29	19	·34		13
	28	Fr	10		P	·21	20	·29		14
	29	Sa	11	*Bahula*	1	·14	21	·26		15
	30	Su	12		2	·09	22	·24		16
	31	Mo	13		3	·06	23	·24		17
	—32	Tu	14		4	·05	24	·26		18
Manmatha *Karkata—Adi.*	1	We	15		5	·05	25	·31		19
	2	Th	16		6	·09	26	·37		20
	3	Fr	17		7	·14	27	·44		21
	4	Sa	18		8	·19	1	·54		22
	5	Su	19		9	·27	2	·64		23
	6	Mo	20		10	·35	3	·75		24
	7	Tu	21		11	·44	4	·86		25
	8	We	22		12	·51	5	·95		26
	9	Th	23		13	·57	...	...		27
	10	Fr	24		14	·62	6	·03		28
	11	Sa	25		—A	·64	7	·09		29
	12	Su	26		1	·64	8	·14		—30
	13	Mo	27		2	·63	9	·16		1
	14	Tu	28		3	·59	10	·16		2
	15	We	29		4	·53	11	·14		3
	16	Th	30		5	·46	12	·11		4
	17	Fr	31		6	·38	13	·07		5

Aug.

Solar month	Cyclic Sidereal Year, Month and Day	Week-Day	English Month and Day	Lunar month	Tithi	Ending Moment	Nakshatra	Ending Moment	Muhammadan Year, Month	Day
Manmatha *Simha—Avani.*	18	Sa	1	Sravana *Sukla*	7	·28	14 15	·01 ·94	H. 1251 *Rabi-ul-akhir.*	6
	19	Su	2		8	·18	16	·87		7
	20	Mo	3		9 10	·08 ·98	17	·80		8
	21	Tu	4		11	·88	18	·73		9
	22	We	5		12	·78	19	·68		10
	23	Th	6		13	·70	20	·63		11
	24	Fr	7		14	·63	21	·59		12
	25	Sa	8		P	·57	22	·56		13
	26	Su	9	*Bahula*	1	·55	23	·56		14
	27	Mo	10		2	·53	24	·58		15
	28	Tu	11		3	·54	25	·62		16
	29	We	12		4	·57	26	·67		17
	30	Th	13		5	·61	27	·75		18
	—31	Fr	14		6	·67	1	·84		19
	1	Sa	15		7	·76	2	·95		20
	2	Su	16		8	·85	...	...		21
	3	Mo	17		9	·93	3	·06		22
	4	Tu	18		...	...	4	·16		23
	5	We	19		10	·01	5	·26		24
	6	Th	20		11	·06	6	·34		25
	7	Fr	21		12	·10	7	·41		26
	8	Sa	22		13	·14	8	·46		27
	9	Su	23		14	·14	9	·48		28
	10	Mo	24		—A	·13	10	·49		—29
	11	Tu	25	Bhad. *Suk.*	1	·08	11	·47	*Jumadal-[illegible]*	1
	12	We	26		2 3	·04 ·96	12	·43		2
	13	Th	27		4	·88	13	·40		3
	14	Fr	28		5	·79	14	·34		4
	15	Sa	29		6	·69	15	·28		5
	16	Su	30		7	·58	16	·21		6
	17	Mo	31		8	·48	17	·14		7

Sep.

Solar month	Cyclic Sidereal Year, Month and Day	Week-Day	English Month and Day	Lunar month	Tithi	Ending Moment	Nakshatra	Ending Moment	Muhammadan Year, Month	Day
Manmatha *Simha—Avani.*	18	Tu	1	Bhadrapada *Sukla*	9	·38	18	·08	H. 1251 *Jumadal-awwal.*	8
	19	We	2		10	·29	19 20	·02 ·96		9
	20	Th	3		11	·22	21	·92		10
	21	Fr	4		12	·15	22	·89		11
	22	Sa	5		13	·09	23	·89		12
	23	Su	6		14	·07	24	·90		13
	24	Mo	7		P	·05	25	·93		14
	25	Tu	8	*Bahula*	1	·07	26	·98		15
	26	We	9		2	·09	...	...		16
	27	Th	10		3	·14	27	·05		17
	28	Fr	11		4	·20	1	·15		18
	29	Sa	12		5	·27	2	·25		19
	30	Su	13		6	·36	3	·35		20
	—31	Mo	14		7	·44	4	·46		21
Manmatha *Kanya—Purattasi.*	1	Tu	15		8	·52	5	·56		22
	2	We	16		9	·59	6	·65		23
	3	Th	17		10	·64	7	·72		24
	4	Fr	18		11	·66	8	·77		25
	5	Sa	19		12	·66	9	·80		26
	6	Su	20		13	·65	10	·81		27
	7	Mo	21		14	·62	11	·80		28
	8	Tu	22		—A	·57	12	·78		29
	9	We	23	*Sukla*	1	·49	13	·75		—30
	10	Th	24		2	·41	14	·68		1
	11	Fr	25		3	·32	15	·61		2
	12	Sa	26		4	·23	16	·55		3
	13	Su	27		5	·13	17	·49		4
	14	Mo	28		6 7	·03 ·93	18	·42		5
	15	Tu	29		8	·83	19	·35		6
	16	We	30		9	·76	20	·29		7

Oct.

Solar month	Cyclic Sidereal Year, Month and Day	Week-Day	English Month and Day	Lunar month	Tithi	Ending Moment	Nakshatra	Ending Moment	Muhammadan Year, Month	Day
Manmatha *Kanya—Purattasi.*	17	Th	1	Asvina	10	·69	21	·25	H. 1251 *Jumadal-akhir.*	8
	18	Fr	2		11	·64	22	·23		9
	19	Sa	3		12	·61	23	·21		10
	20	Su	4		13	·59	24	·22		11
	21	Mo	5		14	·61	25	·24		12
	22	Tu	6		P	·63	26	·29		13
	23	We	7	*Bahula*	1	·69	27	·37		14
	24	Th	8		2	·75	1	·45		15
	25	Fr	9		3	·84	2	·55		16
	26	Sa	10		4	·92	3	·65		17
	27	Su	11		...	...	4	·76		18
	28	Mo	12		5	·00	5	·87		19
	29	Tu	13		6	·09	6	·96		20
	30	We	14		7	·15	...	...		21
	—31	Th	15		8	·20	7	·03		22
Manmatha *Tula—Aippasi.*	1	Fr	16		9	·22	8	·09		23
	2	Sa	17		10	·24	9	·12		24
	3	Su	18		11	·22	10	·13		25
	4	Mo	19		12	·20	11	·13		26
	5	Tu	20		13	·14	12	·11		27
	6	We	21		14 A	·06 ·98	13	·07		28
	7	Th	22	Karttika *Sukla*	1	·90	14 15	·02 ·96		—29
	8	Fr	23		2	·80	16	·90	H. 1251 *Rajab.*	1
	9	Sa	24		3	·70	17	·83		2
	10	Su	25		4	·60	18	·76		3
	11	Mo	26		5	·50	19	·69		4
	12	Tu	27		6	·41	20	·63		5
	13	We	28		7	·34	21	·59		6
	14	Th	29		8	·27	22	·56		7
	15	Fr	30		9	·23	23	·54		8
	16	Sa	31		10	·20	24	·54		9

Nov.

Solar month	Cyclic Sidereal Year, Month and Day	Week-Day	English Month and Day	Lunar month	Tithi	Ending Moment	Nakshatra	Ending Moment	Muhammadan Year, Month	Day
Manmatha *Tula—Aippasi.*	17	Su	1	Karttika *Suk.*	11	·19	25	·56	H. 1251 *Rajab.*	10
	18	Mo	2		12	·19	26	·61		11
	19	Tu	3		13	·22	27	·67		12
	20	We	4		14	·28	1	·75		13
	21	Th	5		P	·36	2	·84		14
	22	Fr	6	*Bahula*	1	·44	3	·95		15
	23	Sa	7		2	·52	...	...		16
	24	Su	8		3	·61	4	·06		17
	25	Mo	9		4	·69	5	·17		18
	26	Tu	10		5	·76	6	·26		19
	27	We	11		6	·80	7	·34		20
	28	Th	12		7	·85	8	·40		21
	29	Fr	13		8	·84	9	·43		22
	—30	Sa	14		9	·82	10	·46		23
Manmatha *Vrischika—Kartigai.*	1	Su	15		10	·80	11	·46		24
	2	Mo	16		11	·75	12	·44		25
	3	Tu	17		12	·68	13	·40		26
	4	We	18		13	·59	14	·35		27
	5	Th	19		14	·51	15	·30		28
	6	Fr ●	20		—A	·41	16	·23		29
	7	Sa	21	*Sukla*	1	·31	17	·16		—30
	8	Su	22		2	·21	18	·09		1
	9	Mo	23		3	·12	19 20	·03 ·97		2
	10	Tu	24		4 5	·04 ·96	21	·92		3
	11	We	25		6	·89	22	·89		4
	12	Th	26		7	·85	23	·86		5
	13	Fr	27		8	·82	24	·86		6
	14	Sa	28		9	·81	25	·88		7
	15	Su	29		10	·82	26	·92		8
	16	Mo	30		11	·87	27	·98		9

Dec.

Solar month	Cyclic Sidereal Year, Month and Day	Week-Day	English Month and Day	Lunar month	Tithi	Ending Moment	Nakshatra	Ending Moment	Muhammadan Year, Month	Day
Manmatha *Vrischika—Kartigai.*	17	Tu	1	Margasira	12	·92	...	...	H. 1251 *Shaban.*	10
	18	We	2		13	·99	1	·05		11
	19	Th	3		...	...	2	·14		12
	20	Fr	4		14	·06	3	·25		13
	21	Sa	5		P	·16	4	·36		14
	22	Su	6	*Bahula*	1	·25	5	·47		15
	23	Mo	7		2	·32	6	·56		16
	24	Tu	8		3	·39	7	·64		17
	25	We	9		4	·44	8	·71		18
	26	Th	10		5	·47	9	·76		19
	27	Fr	11		6	·47	10	·78		20
	28	Sa	12		7	·46	11	·78		21
	—29	Su	13		8	·43	12	·77		22
Manmatha *Dhanus—Margali.*	1	Mo	14		9	·37	13	·74		23
	2	Tu	15		10	·31	14	·70		24
	3	We	16		11	·23	15	·64		25
	4	Th	17		12	·14	16	·57		26
	5	Fr	18		13 14	·04 ·94	17	·50		27
	6	Sa	19		—A	·84	18	·43		28
	7	Su	20	Pausha *Sukla*	1	·74	19	·37		—29
	8	Mo	21		2	·66	20	·31	H. 1251 *Ramzan.*	1
	9	Tu	22		3	·59	21	·26		2
	10	We	23		4	·55	22	·21		3
	11	Th	24		5	·48	23	·19		4
	12	Fr	25		6	·46	24	·18		5
	13	Sa	26		7	·45	25	·20		6
	14	Su	27		8	·46	26	·23		7
	15	Mo	28		9	·51	27	·28		8
	16	Tu	29		10	·56	1	·36		9
	17	We	30		11	·64	2	·44		10
	18	Th	31		12	·72	3	·55		11

15. Svati. 16. Visak. 17. Anur. 18. Jyesh. 19. Mula. 20. P. Ash. 21. U. Ash. 22. Sravn. 23. Dani. 24. Satno. 25. P. Bhad. 26. U. Bhad. 27. Rev.

A. D. 1836. **Mesha Sankranti** (Commencement of Indian Sidereal Year).
Solar Eclipse. ● **(Surya Sid.) April 11·06.** **Saka 1758.** **Kaliyuga 4937.**
Lunar Eclipse. ○ **(Arya Sid.) April 10·96.** **(S. Cycle) Durmukha.**

Columns: SOLAR reckoning — Cyclic Sidereal Year, Month and Day; Week-Day; English Month and Day. LUNAR reckoning — Tithi; Ending Moment; Nakshatra; Ending Moment; Muhammadan Year, Month and Day.

Jan. (Solar: Manmatha, Dhanus—Margali, to 29; then Manmatha, Makara—Tai. Lunar: Pausha, Su., then Bahula, then Sukla. Muhammadan: H. 1251 Ramzan, then Shawwal.)

Cyclic Sidereal Day	Week-Day	English Day	Tithi	Ending Moment	Nakshatra	Ending Moment	Muhammadan Day
19	Fr	1	13	·82	4	·66	12
20	Sa	2	14	·90	5	·77	13
21	Su	3	P	·97	6	·86	14
22	Mo	4	...	...	7	·95	15
23	Tu	5	1	·04	...	...	16
24	We	6	2	·08	8	·03	17
25	Th	7	3	·11	9	·07	18
26	Fr	8	4	·12	10	·10	19
27	Sa	9	5	·11	11	·11	20
28	Su	10	6	·07	12	·09	21
—29	Mo	11	7 / 8	·03 / ·95	13	·07	22
1	Tu	12	9	·87	14 / 15	·08 / ·97	23
2	We	13	10	·79	16	·91	24
3	Th	14	11	·69	17	·84	25
4	Fr	15	12	·59	18	·77	26
5	Sa	16	13	·49	19	·71	27
6	Su	17	14	·40	20	·65	28
7	Mo	18	—A	·31	21	·59	29
8	Tu	19	1	·23	22	·55	—30
9	We	20	2	·18	23	·52	1
10	Th	21	3	·13	24	·51	2
11	Fr	22	4	·11	25	·52	3
12	Sa	23	5	·09	26	·55	4
13	Su	24	6	·12	27	·59	5
14	Mo	25	7	·15	1	·66	6
15	Tu	26	8	·21	2	·75	7
16	We	27	9	·30	3	·85	8
17	Th	28	10	·39	4	·96	9
18	Fr	29	11	·47	...	...	10
19	Sa	30	12	·55	5	·06	11
20	Su	31	13	·64	6	·16	12

Feb. (Solar: Manmatha, Kumbha—Masi, from 1. Lunar: Magha, Bahula; then Phalguna, Sukla. Muhammadan: H. 1251 Shawwal, then H. 1251 Zi-l-ka'da.)

Cyclic Sidereal Day	Week-Day	English Day	Tithi	Ending Moment	Nakshatra	Ending Moment	Muhammadan Day
21	Mo	1	14	·70	7	·26	13
22	Tu	2	P	·74	8	·34	14
23	We	3	1	·75	9	·39	15
24	Th	4	2	·76	10	·42	16
25	Fr	5	3	·75	11	·43	17
26	Sa	6	4	·71	12	·43	18
27	Su	7	5	·65	13	·41	19
28	Mo	8	6	·58	14	·36	20
29	Tu	9	7	·50	15	·31	21
—30	We	10	8	·41	16	·25	22
1	Th	11	9	·31	17	·19	23
2	Fr	12	10	·21	18	·12	24
3	Sa	13	11	·11	19 / 20	·05 / ·08	25
4	Su	14	12 / 13	·02 / ·93	21	·92	26
5	Mo	15	14	·86	22	·88	27
6	Tu	16	—A	·80	23	·85	28
7	We	17	1	·77	24	·84	—29
8	Th	18	2	·74	25	·84	1
9	Fr	19	3	·72	26	·86	2
10	Sa	20	4	·74	27	·90	3
11	Su	21	5	·78	1	·98	4
12	Mo	22	6	·84	...	...	5
13	Tu	23	7	·92	2	·06	6
14	We	24	...	...	3	·15	7
15	Th	25	8	·02	4	·26	8
16	Fr	26	9	·10	5	·37	9
17	Sa	27	10	·18	6	·48	10
18	Su	28	11	·25	7	·57	11
19	Mo	29	12	·31	8	·64	12

March (Solar: Manmatha, Kumbha—Masi, to 31; then Manmatha, Mina—Panguni. Lunar: Phalguna, Bahula; then Sukla. Muhammadan: H. 1251 Zi-l-ka'da, then Zi-l-hijja.)

Cyclic Sidereal Day	Week-Day	English Day	Tithi	Ending Moment	Nakshatra	Ending Moment	Muhammadan Day
20	Tu	1	13	·36	9	·70	13
21	We	2	14	·37	10	·74	14
22	Th	3	P	·38	11	·75	15
23	Fr	4	1	·36	12	·76	16
24	Sa	5	2	·32	13	·74	17
25	Su	6	3	·26	14	·70	18
26	Mo	7	4	·19	15	·65	19
27	Tu	8	5	·11	16	·59	20
28	We	9	6 / 7	·02 / ·92	17	·53	21
29	Th	10	8	·82	18	·46	22
30	Fr	11	9	·72	19	·39	23
—31	Sa	12	10	·62	20	·32	24
1	Su	13	11	·53	21	·26	25
2	Mo	14	12	·46	22	·22	26
3	Tu	15	13	·39	23	·18	27
4	We	16	14	·36	24	·16	28
5	Th	17	—A	·33	25	·16	29
6	Fr	18	1	·32	26	·18	—30
7	Sa	19	2	·35	27	·22	1
8	Su	20	3	·38	1	·28	2
9	Mo	21	4	·44	2	·36	3
10	Tu	22	5	·52	3	·45	4
11	We	23	6	·61	4	·55	5
12	Th	24	7	·69	5	·66	6
13	Fr	25	8	·78	6	·77	7
14	Sa	26	9	·84	7	·87	8
15	Su	27	10	·90	8	·95	9
16	Mo	28	11	·95	...	...	10
17	Tu	29	12	·96	9	·01	11
18	We	30	13	·96	10	·05	12
19	Th	31	14	·94	11	·08	13

April (Solar: Manmatha, Mina—Panguni, to 29; then Durmukha, Mesha—Chittirai. Lunar: Chaitra, Bahula; then Vaisakha, Sukla. Muhammadan: H. 1251 Zi-l-hijja, then H. 1252 Muharram.)

Cyclic Sidereal Day	Week-Day	English Day	Tithi	Ending Moment	Nakshatra	Ending Moment	Muhammadan Day
20	Fr	1	P	·90	12	·08	14
21	Sa	2	1	·84	13	·06	15
22	Su	3	2	·77	14 / 15	·03 / ·98	16
23	Mo	4	3	·68	16	·93	17
24	Tu	5	4	·58	17	·87	18
25	We	6	5	·48	18	·80	19
26	Th	7	6	·38	19	·72	20
27	Fr	8	7	·28	20	·66	21
28	Sa	9	8	·19	21	·60	22
—29	Su	10	9	·10	22	·55	23
1	Mo	11	10 / 11	·02 / ·95	23	·51	24
2	Tu	12	12	·92	24	·49	25
3	We	13	13	·89	25	·48	26
4	Th	14	14	·89	26	·50	27
5	Fr	15	—A	·90	27	·53	28
6	Sa	16	1	·94	1	·59	29
7	Su	17	2	·99	2	·66	—30
8	Mo	18	...	...	3	·75	1
9	Tu	19	3	·07	4	·85	2
10	We	20	4	·16	5	·96	3
11	Th	21	5	·24	...	...	4
12	Fr	22	6	·32	6	·07	5
13	Sa	23	7	·39	7	·17	6
14	Su	24	8	·45	8	·25	7
15	Mo	25	9	·49	9	·32	8
16	Tu	26	10	·50	10	·38	9
17	We	27	11	·50	11	·40	10
18	Th	28	12	·48	12	·41	11
19	Fr	29	13	·45	13	·39	12
20	Sa	30	14	·38	14	·36	13

May (Solar: Durmukha, Mesha—Chittirai, to 31; then Durmukha, Vrishabha—Vaikasi. Lunar: Vaisak., Bahula; then Sukla; then Jyeshtha. Muhammadan: H. 1252 Muharram, then Safar.)

Cyclic Sidereal Day	Week-Day	English Day	Tithi	Ending Moment	Nakshatra	Ending Moment	Muhammadan Day
21	Su ○	1	—P	·30	15	·33	14
22	Mo	2	1	·21	16	·27	15
23	Tu	3	2	·12	17	·20	16
24	We	4	3 / 4	·02 / ·92	18	·13	17
25	Th	5	5	·82	19	·06	18
26	Fr	6	6	·72	20 / 21	·00 / ·94	19
27	Sa	7	7	·63	22	·89	20
28	Su	8	8	·55	23	·84	21
29	Mo	9	9	·49	24	·81	22
30	Tu	10	10	·45	25	·81	23
—31	We	11	11	·42	26	·82	24
1	Th	12	12	·41	27	·85	25
2	Fr	13	13	·42	1	·90	26
3	Sa	14	14	·47	2	·97	27
4	Su	15	—A	·52	...	...	28
5	Mo	16	1	·58	3	·05	29
6	Tu	17	2	·67	4	·16	—30
7	We	18	3	·75	5	·27	1
8	Th	19	4	·83	6	·37	2
9	Fr	20	5	·90	7	·47	3
10	Sa	21	6	·96	8	·56	4
11	Su	22	7	·99	9	·64	5
12	Mo	23	...	...	10	·69	6
13	Tu	24	8	·02	11	·72	7
14	We	25	9 / 10	·01 / ·99	12	·73	8
15	Th	26	11	·95	13	·72	9
16	Fr	27	12	·88	14	·70	10
17	Sa	28	13	·81	15	·66	11
18	Su	29	14	·72	16	·61	12
19	Mo	30	P	·62	17	·54	13
20	Tu	31	1	·52	18	·47	14

June (Solar: Durmukha, Vrishabha—Vaikasi, to 31; then Durmukha, Mithuna—Ani. Lunar: Jyeshtha, Bahula; then Adhika Ashadha, Sukla; then Bahula. Muhammadan: H. 1252 Safar, then H. 1252 Rabi-ul-awwal.)

Cyclic Sidereal Day	Week-Day	English Day	Tithi	Ending Moment	Nakshatra	Ending Moment	Muhammadan Day
21	We	1	2	·42	19	·40	15
22	Th	2	3	·32	20	·34	16
23	Fr	3	4	·22	21	·28	17
24	Sa	4	5	·13	22	·22	18
25	Su	5	6 / 7	·05 / ·99	23	·17	19
26	Mo	6	8	·94	24	·14	20
27	Tu	7	9	·92	25	·13	21
28	We	8	10	·90	26	·14	22
29	Th	9	11	·92	27	·16	23
30	Fr	10	12	·95	1	·21	24
—31	Sa	11	13	·99	2	·27	25
1	Su	12	...	...	3	·36	26
2	Mo	13	14	·06	4	·46	27
3	Tu	14	—A	·14	5	·56	28
4	We	15	1	·22	6	·67	—29
5	Th	16	2	·30	7	·77	1
6	Fr	17	3	·38	8	·87	2
7	Sa	18	4	·44	9	·95	3
8	Su	19	5	·47	...	...	4
9	Mo	20	6	·50	10	·00	5
10	Tu	21	7	·49	11	·04	6
11	We	22	8	·47	12	·05	7
12	Th	23	9	·42	13	·06	8
13	Fr	24	10	·37	14 / 15	·03 / ·99	9
14	Sa	25	11	·30	16	·94	10
15	Su	26	12	·21	17	·88	11
16	Mo	27	13	·11	18	·82	12
17	Tu	28	14 / P	·01 / ·91	19	·75	13
18	We	29	1	·81	20	·68	14
19	Th	30	2	·71	21	·61	15

Naksh:—1. Asvn. 2. Bhar. 3. Krit. 4. Rohi. 5. Mrig. 6. Ardh. 7. Punar. 8. Push. 9. Aslesh. 10. Magh. 11. P. Phal. 12. U. Phal. 13. Hasta. 14. Chit.

A. D. 1836.
A.—Amavasya.
P.—Paurnami.

Kollam 1012, Commences {N. Malabar—Sept. / S. Malabar—Aug.}

Hijra 1252, Commences, April 18.

Vikrama 1893.
Bengal San 1243.
(N. Cycle) Plavanga.

Columns: SOLAR reckoning (Cyclic Sidereal Year, Month and Day; Week-Day; English Month and Day) — LUNAR reckoning (Tithi; Ending Moment; Nakshatra; Ending Moment; Muhammadan Year, Month and Day).

July

Solar: Durmukha *Mithuna—Ani* (to 32); Durmukha *Karkata—Adi* (from 1). Lunar: Adh. Ash. *Bahula*; Nija Ashadha *Sukla*. Muhammadan: H. 1252 *Rabi-ul-awwal* (to 30); H. 1252 *Rabi-ul-akhir* (from 1).

Cyclic Sidereal Year, Month and Day	Week-Day	English Month and Day	Tithi	Ending Moment	Nakshatra	Ending Moment	Muhammadan Year, Month and Day
20	Fr	1	3	·62	22	·55	16
21	Sa	2	4	·54	23	·50	17
22	Su	3	5	·47	24	·48	18
23	Mo	4	6	·42	25	·46	19
24	Tu	5	7	·39	26	·46	20
25	We	6	8	·38	27	·48	21
26	Th	7	9	·40	1	·52	22
27	Fr	8	10	·42	2	·59	23
28	Sa	9	11	·48	3	·66	24
29	Su	10	12	·54	4	·76	25
30	Mo	11	13	·61	5	·86	26
31	Tu	12	14	·70	6	·97	27
32	We	13	A	·78	...	...	28
1	Th	14	1	·86	7	·08	29
2	Fr	15	2	·91	8	·18	30
3	Sa	16	3	·96	9	·25	1
4	Su	17	4	·98	10	·31	2
5	Mo	18	5	·97	11	·35	3
6	Tu	19	6	·95	12	·37	4
7	We	20	7	·90	13	·37	5
8	Th	21	8	·85	14	·36	6
9	Fr	22	9	·77	15	·33	7
10	Sa	23	10	·69	16	·28	8
11	Su	24	11	·60	17	·22	9
12	Mo	25	12	·50	18	·16	10
13	Tu	26	13	·40	19	·09	11
14	We	27	14	·30	20 21	·02 ·95	12
15	Th	28	P	·20	22	·89	13
16	Fr	29	1	·10	23	·85	14
17	Sa	30	2 3	·02 ·95	24	·81	15
18	Su	31	4	·90	25	·78	16

Aug.

Solar: Durmukha *Karkata—Adi* (to 31); Durmukha *Simha—Arani* (from 1). Lunar: *Bahula*; Sravana *Sukla*; *Bah.* Muhammadan: H. 1252 *Rabi-ul-akhir* (to 29); H. 1252 *Jumadal-awwal* (from 1).

Cyclic Sidereal Year, Month and Day	Week-Day	English Month and Day	Tithi	Ending Moment	Nakshatra	Ending Moment	Muhammadan Year, Month and Day
19	Mo	1	5	·87	26	·78	17
20	Tu	2	6	·87	27	·79	18
21	We	3	7	·88	1	·84	19
22	Th	4	8	·89	2	·89	20
23	Fr	5	9	·95	3	·97	21
24	Sa	6	...	...	...	...	22
25	Su	7	10	·02	4	·06	23
26	Mo	8	11	·10	5	·16	24
27	Tu	9	12	·18	6	·27	25
28	We	10	13	·26	7	·38	26
29	Th	11	14	·33	8	·48	27
30	Fr	12	A	·39	9	·56	28
31	Sa	13	1	·44	10	·62	29
1	Su	14	2	·46	11	·67	1
2	Mo	15	3	·46	12	·70	2
3	Tu	16	4	·44	13	·71	3
4	We	17	5	·40	14	·69	4
5	Th	18.	6	·35	15	·66	5
6	Fr	19.	7	·27	16	·61	6
7	Sa	20	8	·19	17	·56	7
8	Su	21	9	·10	18	·50	8
9	Mo	22	10 11	·00 ·90	19	·43	9
10	Tu	23	12	·80	20	·36	10
11	We	24	13	·70	21	·29	11
12	Th	25	14	·61	22	·23	12
13	Fr	26	P	·53	23	·18	13
14	Sa	27	1	·46	24	·14	14
15	Su	28	2	·41	25	·11	15
16	Mo	29	3	·38	26	·10	16
17	Tu	30	4	·37	27	·12	17
18	We	31	5	·37	1	·15	18

Sep.

Solar: Durmukha *Simha—Arani* (to 31); Durmukha *Kanya—Purattasi* (from 1). Lunar: Sravn. *Bahula*; Bhadrapada *Sukla*. Muhammadan: H. 1252 *Jumadal-awwal* (to 30); H. 1252 *Jumadal-akhir* (from 1).

Cyclic Sidereal Year, Month and Day	Week-Day	English Month and Day	Tithi	Ending Moment	Nakshatra	Ending Moment	Muhammadan Year, Month and Day
19	Th	1	6	·41	2	·20	19
20	Fr	2	7	·46	3	·27	20
21	Sa	3	8	·52	4	·36	21
22	Su	4	9	·60	5	·46	22
23	Mo	5	10	·68	6	·57	23
24	Tu	6	11	·77	7	·68	24
25	We	7	12	·84	8	·78	25
26	Th	8	13	·91	9	·86	26
27	Fr	9	14	·95	10	·93	27
28	Sa	10	A	·98	11	·99	28
29	Su	11	1	·98	...	...	29
30	Mo	12	2	·96	12	·02	30
31	Tu	13	3	·92	13	·03	1
1	We	14	4	·87	14 15	·02 ·99	2
2	Th	15	5	·81	16	·95	3
3	Fr	16	6	·72	17	·90	4
4	Sa	17	7	·63	18	·84	5
5	Su	18	8	·53	19	·77	6
6	Mo	19	9	·43	20	·70	7
7	Tu	20	10	·33	21	·63	8
8	We	21	11	·23	22	·57	9
9	Th	22	12	·14	23	·51	10
10	Fr	23	13	·06	24	·47	11
11	Sa	24	14 P	·00 ·94	25	·44	12
12	Su	25	1	·91	26	·43	13
13	Mo	26	2	·91	27	·44	14
14	Tu	27	3	·92	1	·46	15
15	We	28	4	·95	2	·51	16
16	Th	29	...	...	3	·58	17
17	Fr	30	5	·00	4	·66	18

Oct.

Solar: Durmukha *Kanya—Purattasi* (to 31); Durmukha *Tula—Aippasi* (from 1). Lunar: *Bahula*; Asvina *Sukla*; *Bahula*. Muhammadan: H. 1252 *Jumadal-akhir* (to 29); H. 1252 *Rajab* (from 1).

Cyclic Sidereal Year, Month and Day	Week-Day	English Month and Day	Tithi	Ending Moment	Nakshatra	Ending Moment	Muhammadan Year, Month and Day
18	Sa	1	6	·06	5	·77	19
19	Su	2	7	·14	6	·88	20
20	Mo	3	8	·22	7	·98	21
21	Tu	4	9	·31	...	...	22
22	We	5	10	·39	8	·08	23
23	Th	6	11	·46	9	·17	24
24	Fr	7	12	·50	10	·25	25
25	Sa	8	13	·53	11	·31	26
26	Su	9	14	·54	12	·34	27
27	Mo	10	A	·53	13	·35	28
28	Tu	11	1	·48	14	·34	29
29	We	12	2	·43	15	·33	1
30	Th	13	3	·36	16	·29	2
31	Fr	14	4	·28	17	·24	3
1	Sa	15	5	·19	18	·17	4
2	Su	16	6 7	·09 ·99	19	·10	5
3	Mo	17	8	·89	20 21	·03 ·97	6
4	Tu	18	9	·79	22	·91	7
5	We	19	10	·71	23	·85	8
6	Th	20	11	·63	24	·80	9
7	Fr	21	12	·57	25	·77	10
8	Sa	22	13	·52	26	·76	11
9	Su	23	14	·50	27	·76	12
10	Mo ○	24	P	·49	1	·78	13
11	Tu	25	1	·50	2	·82	14
12	We	26	2	·53	3	·88	15
13	Th	27	3	·58	4	·97	16
14	Fr	28	4	·65	...	...	17
15	Sa	29	5	·72	5	·07	18
16	Su	30	6	·82	6	·17	19
17	Mo	31	7	·91	7	·28	20

Nov.

Solar: Durmukha *Tula—Aippasi* (to 30); Durmukha *Vrischika—Kartigai* (from 1). Lunar: Asv. *Bahula*; Kartika *Sukla*. Muhammadan: H. 1252 *Rajab* (to 30); H. 1252 *Shaban* (from 1).

Cyclic Sidereal Year, Month and Day	Week-Day	English Month and Day	Tithi	Ending Moment	Nakshatra	Ending Moment	Muhammadan Year, Month and Day
18	Tu	1	8	·99	8	·38	21
19	We	2	...	...	9	·48	22
20	Th	3	9	·05	10	·56	23
21	Fr	4	10	·09	11	·62	24
22	Sa	5	11	·13	12	·66	25
23	Su	6	12	·13	13	·67	26
24	Mo	7	13	·12	14	·68	27
25	Tu	8	14	·07	15	·66	28
26	We ●	9	A 1	·02 ·96	16	·62	29
27	Th	10	2	·88	17	·57	30
28	Fr	11	3	·79	18	·51	1
29	Sa	12	4	·69	19	·45	2
30	Su	13	5	·59	20	·38	3
1	Mo	14	6	·50	21	·31	4
2	Tu	15	7	·41	22	·24	5
3	We	16	8	·32	23	·18	6
4	Th	17	9	·24	24	·13	7
5	Fr	18	10	·18	25	·10	8
6	Sa	19	11	·13	26	·08	9
7	Su	20	12	·11	27	·08	10
8	Mo	21	13	·10	1	·09	11
9	Tu	22	14	·11	2	·13	12
10	We	23	P	·15	3	·20	13
11	Th	24	1	·21	4	·27	14
12	Fr	25	2	·28	5	·37	15
13	Sa	26	3	·36	6	·47	16
14	Su	27	4	·45	7	·57	17
15	Mo	28	5	·53	8	·68	18
16	Tu	29	6	·61	9	·78	19
17	We	30	7	·68	10	·86	20

Dec.

Solar: Durmukha *Vrischika—Kartigai* (to 29); Durmukha *Dhanus—Margali* (from 1). Lunar: *Bahula*; Margasira *Sukla*; *Bahula*. Muhammadan: H. 1252 *Shaban* (to 29); H. 1252 *Ramzan* (from 1).

Cyclic Sidereal Year, Month and Day	Week-Day	English Month and Day	Tithi	Ending Moment	Nakshatra	Ending Moment	Muhammadan Year, Month and Day
18	Th	1	8	·74	11	·93	21
19	Fr	2	9	·76	12	·97	22
20	Sa	3	10	·75	...	...	23
21	Su	4	11	·74	13	·00	24
22	Mo	5	12	·70	14 15	·00 ·99	25
23	Tu	6	13	·65	16	·95	26
24	We	7	14	·58	17	·91	27
25	Th	8	A	·50	18	·85	28
26	Fr	9	1	·41	19	·79	29
27	Sa	10	2	·32	20	·72	1
28	Su	11	3	·22	21	·65	2
29	Mo	12	4	·12	22	·58	3
1	Tu	13	5 6	·03 ·94	23	·52	4
2	We	14	7	·87	24	·47	5
3	Th	15	8	·81	25	·43	6
4	Fr	16	9	·77	26	·41	7
5	Sa	17	10	·75	27	·40	8
6	Su	18	11	·74	1	·41	9
7	Mo	19	12	·76	2	·45	10
8	Tu	20	13	·79	3	·50	11
9	We	21	14	·86	4	·58	12
10	Th	22	P	·93	5	·67	13
11	Fr	23	...	...	6	·77	14
12	Sa	24	1	·01	7	·88	15
13	Su	25	2	·11	8	·99	16
14	Mo	26	3	·19	...	...	17
15	Tu	27	4	·27	9	·09	18
16	We	28	5	·33	10	·17	19
17	Th	29	6	·38	11	·24	20
18	Fr	30	7	·40	12	·28	21
19	Sa	31	8	·40	13	·32	22

15. Svati. 16. Visak. 17. Anur. 18. Jyesh. 19. Mula. 20. P. Ash. 21. U. Ash. 22. Sravn. 23. Dani. 24. Satab. 25. P. Bhad. 26. U. Bhad. 27. Rev.

A. D. 1837. | **Mesha Sankranti** (Commencement of Indian Sidereal Year).
Solar Eclipse. ● | **(Surya Sid.) April 11·32.** | **Saka 1759.** | **Kaliyuga 4938.**
Lunar Eclipse. ○ | **(Arya Sid.) April 11·22.** | **(S. Cycle) Hemalamba.**

SOLAR reckoning: Cyclic Sidereal Year, Month and Day	Week-Day	English Month and Day	LUNAR reckoning: Tithi	Ending Moment	Nakshatra	Ending Moment	Muhammadan Year, Month and Day
		Jan.					
Durmukha Dhanus—Margali 20	Su	1	Mr. 9	·39	14	·33	H. 1252 Ramzan 23
21	Mo	2	10	·35	15	·31	24
22	Tu	3	Bah. 11	·29	16	·28	25
23	We	4	12	·22	17	·24	26
24	Th	5	13	·15	18	·19	27
25	Fr	6	14 / A	·05 / ·95	19	·13	28
26	Sa	7	1	·86	20 / 21	·06 / ·99	29
27	Su	8	2	·77	22	·93	30
28	Mo	9	3	·67	23	·87	1
29	Tu	10	4	·58	24	·81	2
30	We	11	5	·51	25	·77	3
Durmukha Makara—Tai 1	Th	12	Pausha Sukla 6	·45	26	·74	4
2	Fr	13	7	·42	27	·72	5
3 ●	Sa	14	8	·39	1	·74	6
4	Su	15	9	·39	2	·77	7
5	Mo	16	10	·40	3	·81	8
6	Tu	17	11	·45	4	·88	9
7	We	18	12	·50	5	·97	10
8	Th	19	13	·58	...	...	11
9	Fr	20	14	·67	6	·07	H. 1252 Shawwal 12
10	Sa	21	P	·76	7	·18	13
11	Su	22	1	·85	8	·29	14
12	Mo	23	2	·92	9	·39	15
13	Tu	24	3	·99	10	·47	16
14	We	25	...	...	11	·55	17
15	Th	26	Bahula 4	·02	12	·61	18
16	Fr	27	5	·04	13	·64	19
17	Sa	28	6	·05	14	·65	20
18	Su	29	7 / 8	·03 / ·99	15	·64	21
19	Mo	30	9	·93	16	·62	22
20	Tu	31	10	·86	17	·58	23
		Feb.					
21	We	1	11	·78	18	·53	24
22	Th	2	12	·68	19	·47	25
23	Fr	3	13	·58	20	·40	26
24	Sa	4	14	·49	21	·33	27
25	Su	5	A	·39	22	·26	28
26	Mo	6	1	·30	23	·20	29
27	Tu	7	2	·21	24	·14	H. 1252 Zi-l-ka'da 1
28	We	8	3	·15	25	·10	2
29	Th	9	4	·10	26	·06	3
Durmukha Kumbha—Masi 1	Fr	10	5	·05	27	·06	4
2	Sa	11	6	·02	1	·06	5
3	Su	12	7	·02	2	·08	6
4	Mo	13	Magha Sukla 8	·05	3	·12	7
5	Tu	14	9	·09	4	·19	8
6	We	15	10	·14	5	·27	9
7	Th	16	11	·22	6	·37	10
8	Fr	17	12	·30	7	·48	11
9	Sa	18	13	·39	8	·58	12
10	Su	19	14	·48	9	·68	13
11	Mo	20	P	·55	10	·78	14
12	Tu	21	1	·61	11	·86	15
13	We	22	2	·65	12	·92	16
14	Th	23	3	·68	13	·96	17
15	Fr	24	4	·67	14	·97	18
16	Sa ●	25	Bahula 5	·65	15	·97	19
17	Su	26	6	·60	16	·95	20
18	Mo	27	7	·54	17	·92	21
19	Tu	28	8	·47	18	·86	22

SOLAR reckoning: Cyclic Sidereal Year, Month and Day	Week-Day	English Month and Day	LUNAR reckoning: Tithi	Ending Moment	Nakshatra	Ending Moment	Muhammadan Year, Month and Day
		March					
Durmukha Kumbha—Masi 20	We	1	Mg. 9	·39	19	·80	23
21	Th	2	10	·30	20	·74	24
22	Fr	3	Bah. 11	·20	21	·68	25
23	Sa	4	12	·10	22	·61	26
24	Su	5	13 / 14	·00 / ·90	23	·54	27
25	Mo	6	A	·82	24	·48	28
26	Tu	7	1	·75	25	·43	29
27	We	8	2	·70	26	·40	30
28	Th	9	3	·66	27	·38	1
29	Fr	10	4	·64	1	·38	2
30	Sa	11	5	·63	2	·40	3
Durmukha Mina—Panguni 1	Su	12	Sukla 6	·65	3	·43	4
2	Mo	13	7	·69	4	·49	5
3	Tu	14	8	·74	5	·58	6
4	We	15	9	·82	6	·67	7
5	Th	16	10	·91	7	·77	8
6	Fr	17	...	...	8	·88	9
7	Sa	18	Phalguna 11	·00	9	·99	10
8	Su	19	12	·08	...	...	11
9	Mo	20	13	·15	10	·09	H. 1252 Zi-l-hijja 12
10	Tu	21	14	·21	11	·17	13
11	We	22	P	·25	12	·23	14
12	Th	23	1	·27	13	·27	15
13	Fr	24	2	·26	14	·29	16
14	Sa	25	3	·24	15	·30	17
15	Su	26	4	·19	16	·28	18
16	Mo	27	5	·14	17	·25	19
17	Tu	28	Bahula 6 / 7	·06 / ·97	18	·20	20
18	We	29	8	·88	19	·14	21
19	Th	30	9	·78	20	·08	22
20	Fr	31	10	·68	21 / 22	·01 / ·94	23
		April					
21	Sa	1	11	·58	23	·87	24
22	Su	2	12	·49	24	·81	25
23	Mo	3	13	·40	25	·76	26
24	Tu	4	14	·32	26	·73	27
25	We	5	A	·27	27	·71	28
26	Th	6	1	·23	1	·70	29
27	Fr	7	2	·21	2	·71	H. 1253 Muharram 1
28	Sa	8	3	·20	3	·74	2
29	Su	9	4	·22	4	·81	3
30	Mo	10	5	·25	5	·88	4
Hemalamba Mesha—Chittirai 1	Tu	11	6	·31	6	·97	5
2	We	12	Sukla 7	·39	...	...	6
3	Th	13	8	·47	7	·07	7
4	Fr	14	9	·56	8	·18	8
5	Sa	15	10	·64	9	·29	9
6	Su	16	11	·71	10	·39	10
7	Mo	17	Chaitra 12	·76	11	·48	11
8	Tu	18	13	·81	12	·54	12
9	We ○	19	14	·82	13	·59	13
10	Th	20	P	·81	14	·62	14
11	Fr	21	1	·80	15	·63	15
12	Sa	22	2	·74	16	·61	16
13	Su	23	3	·68	17	·58	17
14	Mo	24	4	·60	18	·54	18
15	Tu	25	5	·52	19	·49	19
16	We	26	Bahula 6	·42	20	·42	20
17	Th	27	7	·32	21	·35	21
18	Fr	28	8	·22	22	·28	22
19	Sa	29	9	·12	23	·21	23
20	Su	30	10 / 11	·02 / ·93	24	·15	24

SOLAR reckoning: Cyclic Sidereal Year, Month and Day	Week-Day	English Month and Day	LUNAR reckoning: Tithi	Ending Moment	Nakshatra	Ending Moment	Muhammadan Year, Month and Day
		May					
Hemalamba Mesha—Chittirai 21	Mo	1	Bah. 12	·86	25	·10	Muharram 25
22	Tu	2	13	·80	26	·06	26
23	We	3	14	·77	27	·03	27
24	Th	4	A	·74	1	·02	28
25	Fr	5	1	·73	2	·03	29
26	Sa	6	2	·75	3	·07	30
27	Su	7	3	·78	4	·12	1
28	Mo	8	4	·84	5	·19	2
29	Tu	9	5	·91	6	·27	3
30	We	10	...	...	7	·37	4
31	Th	11	Sukla 6	·00	8	·48	5
Hemalamba Vrishabha—Vaikasi 1	Fr	12	7	·08	9	·59	6
2	Sa	13	8	·15	10	·69	7
3	Su	14	9	·22	11	·78	8
4	Mo	15	10	·28	12	·85	9
5	Tu	16	11	·33	13	·91	10
6	We	17	Vaisakha 12	·34	14	·94	11
7	Th	18	13	·33	15	·95	12
8	Fr	19	14	·31	16	·94	13
9	Sa	20	P	·26	17	·91	H. 1253 Safar 14
10	Su	21	1	·20	18	·87	15
11	Mo	22	2	·12	19	·82	16
12	Tu	23	3 / 4	·03 / ·93	20	·76	17
13	We	24	5	·83	21	·69	18
14	Th	25	Bahula 6	·73	22	·62	19
15	Fr	26	7	·63	23	·56	20
16	Sa	27	8	·53	24	·50	21
17	Su	28	9	·44	25	·44	22
18	Mo	29	10	·37	26	·39	23
19	Tu	30	11	·31	27	·36	24
20	We	31	12	·27	1	·34	25
		June					
21	Th	1	13	·23	2	·36	26
22	Fr	2	14	·23	3	·38	27
23	Sa	3	A	·24	4	·43	28
24	Su	4	1	·27	5	·49	29
25	Mo	5	2	·33	6	·57	1
26	Tu	6	3	·40	7	·68	2
27	We	7	4	·49	8	·79	3
28	Th	8	5	·57	9	·89	4
29	Fr	9	Sukla 6	·65	10	·99	5
30	Sa	10	7	·71	...	...	6
31	Su	11	8	·76	11	·08	7
32	Mo	12	9	·80	12	·17	8
Hemalamba Mithuna—Ani 1	Tu	13	10	·82	13	·22	9
2	We	14	11	·82	14	·26	H. 1253 Rabi-ul-awwal 10
3	Th	15	12	·79	15	·27	11
4	Fr	16	Jyeshtha 13	·75	16	·27	12
5	Sa	17	14	·69	17	·24	13
6	Su	18	P	·62	18	·21	14
7	Mo	19	1	·52	19	·16	15
8	Tu	20	2	·42	20	·10	16
9	We	21	3	·32	21 / 22	·03 / ·96	17
10	Th	22	4	·22	23	·89	18
11	Fr	23	5	·12	24	·83	19
12	Sa	24	6 / 7	·02 / ·93	25	·77	20
13	Su	25	Bahula 8	·85	26	·72	21
14	Mo	26	9	·79	27	·69	22
15	Tu	27	10	·74	1	·68	23
16	We	28	11	·71	2	·68	24
17	Th	29	12	·71	3	·70	25
18	Fr	30	13	·72	4	·74	26

Naksh:—1. Asvn. 2. Bhar. 3. Krit. 4. Rohi. 5. Mrig. 6. Ardh. 7. Puna. 8. Push. 9. Aslesh. 10. Magh. 11. P. Phal. 12. U. Phal. 13. Hasta. 14. Chit.

A. D. 1837.
A.—Amavasya.
P.—Paurnami.

Kollam 1013, Commences { N. Malabar—Sept. / S. Malabar—Aug.

Hijra 1253, Commences, April 7.

Vikrama 1894.
Bengal San 1243.
(N. Cycle) Kilaka.

July

Solar: Hemalamba Mithuna—Adi; Hemalamba Karkata—Adi. Lunar: Sukla; Ashadha; Bahula. Muhammadan: H. 1253 Rabi-ul-akhir.

Cyclic Sidereal Year, Month and Day	Week-Day	English Month and Day	Tithi	Ending Moment	Nakshatra	Ending Moment	Muhammadan Year, Month and Day
19	Sa	1	14	·75	5	·80	27
20	Su	2	—A	·80	6	·89	28
21	Mo	3	1	·87	7	·98	29
22	Tu	4	2	·95	...	...	—30
23	We	5	...	...	8	·08	1
24	Th	6	3	·03	9	·19	2
25	Fr	7	4	·12	10	·29	3
26	Sa	8	5	·19	11	·39	4
27	Su	9	6	·25	12	·47	5
28	Mo	10	7	·28	13	·53	6
29	Tu	11	8	·31	14	·57	7
30	We	12	9	·29	15	·59	8
—31	Th	13	10	·27	16	·59	9
1	Fr	14	11	·23	17	·58	10
2	Sa	15	12	·17	18	·54	11
3	Su	16	13	·09	19	·50	12
4	Mo	17	{ 14 P	·00 ·90	20	·44	13
5	Tu	18	1	·80	21	·38	14
6	We	19	2	·70	22	·31	15
7	Th	20	3	·60	23	·24	16
8	Fr	21	4	·50	24	·17	17
9	Sa	22	5	·41	25	·11	18
10	Su	23	6	·33	26	·06	19
11	Mo	24	7	·27	27	·03	20
12	Tu	25	8	·22	1	·00	21
13	We	26	9	·20	2	·00	22
14	Th	27	10	·19	3	·01	23
15	Fr	28	11	·20	4	·05	24
16	Sa	29	12	·22	5	·10	25
17	Su	30	13	·27	6	·19	26
18	Mo	31	14	·34	7	·28	27

Aug.

Solar: Hemalamba Simha—Avani. Lunar: Sukla; Sravana; Bahula. Muhammadan: H. 1253 Jumadal-awwal.

Cyclic Sidereal Year, Month and Day	Week-Day	English Month and Day	Tithi	Ending Moment	Nakshatra	Ending Moment	Muhammadan Year, Month and Day
19	Tu	1	—A	·42	8	·38	28
20	We	2	1	·51	9	·49	—29
21	Th	3	2	·59	10	·59	1
22	Fr	4	3	·66	11	·70	2
23	Sa	5	4	·72	12	·78	3
24	Su	6	5	·76	13	·84	4
25	Mo	7	6	·79	14	·89	5
26	Tu	8	7	·78	15	·91	6
27	We	9	8	·76	16	·93	7
28	Th	10	9	·71	17	·91	8
29	Fr	11	10	·66	18	·88	9
30	Sa	12	11	·59	19	·83	10
31	Su	13	12	·50	20	·78	11
—32	Mo	14	13	·40	21	·72	12
1	Tu	15	14	·30	22	·65	13
2	We	16	P	·20	23	·58	14
3	Th	17	1	·10	24	·51	15
4	Fr	18	{ 2 3	·00 ·91	25	·44	16
5	Sa	19	4	·83	26	·40	17
6	Su	20	5	·77	27	·36	18
7	Mo	21	6	·72	1	·33	19
8	Tu	22	7	·70	2	·32	20
9	We	23	8	·68	3	·33	21
10	Th	24	9	·69	4	·36	22
11	Fr	25	10	·72	5	·42	23
12	Sa	26	11	·78	6	·49	24
13	Su	27	12	·85	7	·58	25
14	Mo	28	13	·92	8	·68	26
15	Tu	29	...	...	9	·79	27
16	We	30	14	·00	10	·90	28
17	Th	31	—A	·09	...	...	29

Sep.

Solar: Hemalamba Simha—Avani; Hemalamba Kanya—Purattasi. Lunar: Sukla; Bhadrapada; Bahula. Muhammadan: H. 1253 Jumadal-akhir.

Cyclic Sidereal Year, Month and Day	Week-Day	English Month and Day	Tithi	Ending Moment	Nakshatra	Ending Moment	Muhammadan Year, Month and Day
18	Fr	1	1	·17	11	·00	—30
19	Sa	2	2	·23	12	·09	1
20	Su	3	3	·27	13	·15	2
21	Mo	4	4	·30	14	·20	3
22	Tu	5	5	·29	15	·24	4
23	We	6	6	·28	16	·25	5
24	Th	7	7	·23	17	·24	6
25	Fr	8	8	·18	18	·21	7
26	Sa	9	9	·10	19	·17	8
27	Su	10	{ 10 11	·02 ·92	20	·12	9
28	Mo	11	12	·82	21 22	·06 ·99 }	10
29	Tu	12	13	·72	23	·92	11
30	We	13	14	·62	24	·85	12
—31	Th	14	P	·53	25	·78	13
1	Fr	15	1	·44	26	·73	14
2	Sa	16	2	·37	27	·69	15
3	Su	17	3	·30	1	·66	16
4	Mo	18	4	·25	2	·64	17
5	Tu	19	5	·22	3	·66	18
6	We	20	6	·21	4	·68	19
7	Th	21	7	·22	5	·73	20
8	Fr	22	8	·25	6	·80	21
9	Sa	23	9	·31	7	·88	22
10	Su	24	10	·37	8	·98	23
11	Mo	25	11	·45	...	...	24
12	Tu	26	12	·54	9	·09	25
13	We	27	13	·62	10	·20	26
14	Th	28	14	·70	11	·30	27
15	Fr	29	—A	·77	12	·39	28
16	Sa	30	1	·81	13	·46	—29

Oct.

Solar: Hemalamba Tula—Aippasi. Lunar: Sukla; Asvina; Bahula; Suk. Muhammadan: H. 1253 Rajab.

Cyclic Sidereal Year, Month and Day	Week-Day	English Month and Day	Tithi	Ending Moment	Nakshatra	Ending Moment	Muhammadan Year, Month and Day
17	Su	1	2	·83	14	·53	1
18	Mo	2	3	·84	15	·56	2
19	Tu	3	4	·82	16	·57	3
20	We	4	5	·78	17	·56	4
21	Th	5	6	·73	18	·54	5
22	Fr	6	7	·66	19	·51	6
23	Sa	7	8	·57	20	·45	7
24	Su	8	9	·48	21	·39	8
25	Mo	9	10	·38	22	·32	9
26	Tu	10	11	·28	23	·25	10
27	We	11	12	·18	24	·19	11
28	Th	12	13	·09	25	·13	12
29	Fr ◯	13	{ 14 P	·00 ·93	26	·07	13
—30	Sa	14	1	·86	27 1	·02 ·99 }	14
1	Su	15	2	·82	2	·98	15
2	Mo	16	3	·79	3	·98	16
3	Tu	17	4	·79	...	...	17
4	We	18	5	·79	4	·00	18
5	Th	19	6	·82	5	·04	19
6	Fr	20	7	·89	6	·10	20
7	Sa	21	8	·96	7	·18	21
8	Su	22	...	...	8	·28	22
9	Mo	23	9	·04	9	·39	23
10	Tu	24	10	·12	10	·50	24
11	We	25	11	·21	11	·60	25
12	Th	26	12	·29	12	·69	26
13	Fr	27	13	·35	13	·78	27
14	Sa	28	14	·39	14	·84	28
15	Su	29	—A	·42	15	·88	29
16	Mo	30	1	·43	16	·89	—30
17	Tu	31	2	·41	17	·89	1

Nov.

Solar: Hemalamba Tula—Aippasi; Hemalamba Vrischika—Karttigai. Lunar: Sukla; Karttika; Bahula. Muhammadan: H. 1253 Shaban.

Cyclic Sidereal Year, Month and Day	Week-Day	English Month and Day	Tithi	Ending Moment	Nakshatra	Ending Moment	Muhammadan Year, Month and Day
18	We	1	3	·37	18	·88	2
19	Th	2	4	·32	19	·84	3
20	Fr	3	5	·24	20	·79	4
21	Sa	4	6	·16	21	·73	5
22	Su	5	{ 7 8	·07 ·98	22	·67	6
23	Mo	6	9	·88	23	·60	7
24	Tu	7	10	·78	24	·53	8
25	We	8	11	·68	25	·46	9
26	Th	9	12	·60	26	·40	10
27	Fr	10	13	·53	27	·35	11
28	Sa	11	14	·46	1	·31	12
29	Su	12	P	·42	2	·30	13
—30	Mo	13	1	·39	3	·30	14
1	Tu	14	2	·39	4	·31	15
2	We	15	3	·40	5	·35	16
3	Th	16	4	·44	6	·41	17
4	Fr	17	5	·50	7	·49	18
5	Sa	18	6	·56	8	·59	19
6	Su	19	7	·65	9	·69	20
7	Mo	20	8	·74	10	·79	21
8	Tu	21	9	·83	11	·90	22
9	We	22	10	·90	...	...	23
10	Th	23	11	·97	12	·00	24
11	Fr	24	...	...	13	·09	25
12	Sa	25	12	·01	14	·15	26
13	Su	26	13	·04	15	·19	27
14	Mo	27	14	·04	16	·21	28
15	Tu	28	{ A 1	·03 ·99	17	·22	—29
16	We	29	2	·93	18	·21	1
17	Th	30	3	·87	19	·17	2

Dec.

Solar: Hemalamba Dhanus—Margali. Lunar: Sukla; Margasira; Bahula; P. Suk. Muhammadan: H. 1253 Ramzan.

Cyclic Sidereal Year, Month and Day	Week-Day	English Month and Day	Tithi	Ending Moment	Nakshatra	Ending Moment	Muhammadan Year, Month and Day
18	Fr	1	4	·79	20	·13	3
19	Sa	2	5	·70	21	·07	4
20	Su	3	6	·60	22 23	·01 ·94 }	5
21	Mo	4	7	·50	24	·87	6
22	Tu	5	8	·40	25	·80	7
23	We	6	9	·31	26	·74	8
24	Th	7	10	·22	27	·69	9
25	Fr	8	11	·15	1	·65	10
26	Sa	9	12	·09	2	·63	11
27	Su	10	13	·05	3	·62	12
28	Mo	11	14	·02	4	·63	13
29	Tu	12	P	·03	5	·66	14
—30	We	13	1	·04	6	·73	15
1	Th	14	2	·09	7	·80	16
2	Fr	15	3	·15	8	·89	17
3	Sa	16	4	·22	9	·99	18
4	Su	17	5	·30	...	...	19
5	Mo	18	6	·40	10	·10	20
6	Tu	19	7	·48	11	·21	21
7	We	20	8	·55	12	·31	22
8	Th	21	9	·62	13	·39	23
9	Fr	22	10	·66	14	·46	24
10	Sa	23	11	·69	15	·50	25
11	Su	24	12	·69	16	·54	26
12	Mo	25	13	·68	17	·55	27
13	Tu	26	14	·65	18	·53	28
14	We	27	—A	·57	19	·50	29
15	Th	28	1	·51	20	·46	--30
16	Fr	29	2	·42	21	·40	1
17	Sa	30	3	·33	22	·34	2
18	Su	31	4	·24	23	·28	3

15. Svati. 16. Visak. 17. Anur. 18. Jyesh. 19. Mula. 20. P. Ash. 21. U. Ash. 22. Sravn. 23. Dani. 24. Satab. 25. P. Bhad. 26. U. Bhad. 27. Rev.

A. D. 1838. **Mesha Sankranti** (Commencement of Indian Sidereal Year).
Solar Eclipse. ● **(Surya Sid.) April 11·58.** **Saka 1760.** **Kaliyuga 4939.**
Lunar Eclipse. ○ **(Arya Sid.) April 11·48.** **(S. Cycle) Vilamba.**

SOLAR reckoning: Cyclic Sidereal Year, Month and Day	Week-Day	English Month and Day	LUNAR reckoning: Tithi	Ending Moment	Nakshatra	Ending Moment	Muhammadan Year, Month and Day
		Jan.					
Hemalamba Dhanus—Margali. 19	Mo	1	5	·14	24	·21	4
20	Tu	2	*Sukla* 6 / 7	·04 / ·94	25	·14	5
21	We	3	8	·86	26	·07	6
22	Th	4	9	·79	27 / 1	·02 / ·98	7
23	Fr	5	10	·73	2	·95	8
24	Sa	6	11	·70	3	·94	9
25	Su	7	12	·68	4	·95	*H. 1253 Shawwal.* 10
26	Mo	8	*Pausha* 13	·67	5	·99	11
27	Tu	9	14	·70	...	...	12
28	We	10	P	·74	6	·03	13
29	Th	11	1	·79	7	·10	14
Hemalamba Makara—Tai. 1	Fr	12	2	·87	8	·19	15
2	Sa	13	3	·95	9	·29	16
3	Su	14	...	...	10	·40	17
4	Mo	15	4	·05	11	·51	18
5	Tu	16	*Bahula* 5	·13	12	·61	19
6	We	17	6	·20	13	·69	20
7	Th	18	7	·27	14	·77	21
8	Fr	19	8	·30	15	·82	22
9	Sa	20	9	·33	16	·86	23
10	Su	21	10	·33	17	·87	24
11	Mo	22	11	·32	18	·86	25
12	Tu	23	12	·27	19	·83	26
13	We	24	13	·22	20	·79	27
14	Th	25	14	·14	21	·75	28
15	Fr	26	A / 1	·05 / ·96	22	·69	29
16	Sa	27	2	·87	23	·62	1
17	Su	28	3	·77	24	·55	2
18	Mo	29	4	·67	25	·48	3
19	Tu	30	5	·58	26	·42	4
20	We	31	6	·50	27	·36	5
		Feb.					
21	Th	1	*Sukla* 7	·43	1	·32	6
22	Fr	2	8	·37	2	·28	7
23	Sa	3	9	·33	3	·27	8
24	Su	4	10	·32	4	·28	9
25	Mo	5	11	·31	5	·30	10
26	Tu	6	12	·33	6	·34	11
27	We	7	*Magha* 13	·38	7	·41	*H. 1253 Zi-l-ka'da.* 12
28	Th	8	14	·45	8	·49	13
29	Fr	9	P	·52	9	·59	14
Hemalamba Kumbha—Masi. 1	Sa	10	1	·60	10	·70	15
2	Su	11	2	·69	11	·81	16
3	Mo	12	3	·77	12	·91	17
4	Tu	13	4	·85	...	...	18
5	We	14	5	·91	13	·00	19
6	Th	15	*Bahula* 6	·95	14	·07	20
7	Fr	16	7	·96	15	·14	21
8	Sa	17	8	·96	16	·18	22
9	Su	18	9	·95	17	·19	23
10	Mo	19	10	·89	18	·19	24
11	Tu	20	11	·83	19	·17	25
12	We	21	12	·76	20	·14	26
13	Th	22	13	·68	21	·08	27
14	Fr	23	14	·59	22 / 23	·02 / ·96	28
15	Sa	24	A	·49	24	·89	29
16	Su	25	*P. Suk.* 1	·39	25	·82	30
17	Mo	26	2	·29	26	·76	1
18	Tu	27	3	·20	27	·70	2
19	We	28	4	·12	1	·65	3

SOLAR reckoning: Cyclic Sidereal Year, Month and Day	Week-Day	English Month and Day	LUNAR reckoning: Tithi	Ending Moment	Nakshatra	Ending Moment	Muhammadan Year, Month and Day
		March					
Hemalamba Kumbha—Masi. 20	Th	1	*Sukla* 5 / 6	·05 / ·99	2	·61	4
21	Fr	2	7	·96	3	·60	5
22	Sa	3	8	·93	4	·60	6
23	Su	4	9	·92	5	·62	7
24	Mo	5	10	·95	6	·65	8
25	Tu	6	11	·99	7	·71	9
26	We	7	...	...	8	·79	10
27	Th	8	*Phalguna* 12	·06	9	·89	11
28	Fr	9	13	·14	...	...	12
29	Sa	10	14	·23	10	·00	*H. 1253 Zi-l-hijja.* 13
30	Su	11	P	·31	11	·11	14
Hemalamba Mina—Panguni. 1	Mo	12	1	·39	12	·21	15
2	Tu	13	2	·46	13	·30	16
3	We	14	3	·51	14	·39	17
4	Th	15	4	·56	15	·45	18
5	Fr	16	5	·57	16	·49	19
6	Sa	17	*Bahula* 6	·56	17	·51	20
7	Su	18	7	·54	18	·51	21
8	Mo	19	8	·49	19	·50	22
9	Tu	20	9	·43	20	·47	23
10	We	21	10	·36	21	·42	24
11	Th	22	11	·28	22	·36	25
12	Fr	23	12	·18	23	·29	26
13	Sa	24	13 / 14	·07 / ·97	24	·23	27
14	Su	25	A	·88	25	·17	28
15	Mo	26	1	·79	26	·10	29
16	Tu	27	2	·70	27 / 1	·03 / ·98	1
17	We	28	3	·63	2	·95	2
18	Th	29	4	·57	3	·93	3
19	Fr	30	5	·54	4	·92	4
20	Sa	31	6	·51	5	·93	5
		April					
21	Su	1	*Sukla* 7	·51	6	·97	6
22	Mo	2	8	·53	...	...	7
23	Tu	3	9	·58	7	·02	8
24	We	4	10	·63	8	·10	9
25	Th	5	11	·71	9	·19	10
26	Fr	6	12	·80	10	·29	11
27	Sa	7	*Chaitra* 13	·88	11	·40	*H. 1254 Muharram.* 12
28	Su	8	14	·96	12	·51	13
29	Mo	9	...	...	13	·61	14
30	Tu	○ 10	P	·03	14	·70	15
Villamba Mesha—Chittirai. 1	We	11	1	·08	15	·76	16
2	Th	12	2	·12	16	·81	17
3	Fr	13	3	·12	17	·83	18
4	Sa	14	4	·12	18	·85	19
5	Su	15	5	·10	19	·83	20
6	Mo	16	*Bahula* 6 / 7	·05 / ·99	20	·80	21
7	Tu	17	8	·92	21	·75	22
8	We	18	9	·83	22	·70	23
9	Th	19	10	·73	23	·64	24
10	Fr	20	11	·63	24	·57	25
11	Sa	21	12	·53	25	·50	26
12	Su	22	13	·43	26	·43	27
13	Mo	23	14	·33	27	·37	28
14	Tu	24	A	·25	1	·31	29
15	We	25	*Vaisk. Suk.* 1	·17	2	·28	30
16	Th	26	2	·11	3	·25	*Safar.* 1
17	Fr	27	3	·07	4	·24	2
18	Sa	28	4	·05	5	·25	3
19	Su	29	5	·05	6	·28	4
20	Mo	30	6	·06	7	·34	5

SOLAR reckoning: Cyclic Sidereal Year, Month and Day	Week-Day	English Month and Day	LUNAR reckoning: Tithi	Ending Moment	Nakshatra	Ending Moment	Muhammadan Year, Month and Day
		May					
Villamba Mesha—Chittirai. 21	Tu	1	*Sukla* 7	·11	8	·41	6
22	We	2	8	·16	9	·49	7
23	Th	3	9	·24	10	·59	8
24	Fr	4	10	·33	11	·70	9
25	Sa	5	11	·41	12	·81	10
26	Su	6	12	·48	13	·91	11
27	Mo	7	*Vaisakha* 13	·55	...	...	12
28	Tu	8	14	·61	14	·00	13
29	We	9	P	·65	15	·07	*H. 1254 Safar.* 14
30	Th	10	1	·66	16	·12	15
31	Fr	11	2	·64	17	·16	16
Villamba Vrishabha—Vaikasi. 1	Sa	12	3	·62	18	·17	17
2	Su	13	4	·58	19	·16	18
3	Mo	14	5	·51	20	·13	19
4	Tu	15	6	·44	21	·09	20
5	We	16	*Bahula* 7	,34	22 / 23	·04 / ·98	21
6	Th	17	8	·24	24	·91	22
7	Fr	18	9	·14	25	·84	23
8	Sa	19	10 / 11	·04 / ·94	26	·77	24
9	Su	20	12	·85	27	·71	25
10	Mo	21	13	·76	1	·66	26
11	Tu	22	14	·68	2	·61	27
12	We	23	A	·63	3	·58	28
13	Th	24	1	·58	4	·56	29
14	Fr	25	2	·56	5	·57	1
15	Sa	26	3	·55	6	·60	2
16	Su	27	4	·56	7	·65	3
17	Mo	28	5	·61	8	·71	4
18	Tu	29	6	·66	9	·79	5
19	We	30	*Sukla* 7	·74	10	89	6
20	Th	31	8	·82	...	...	7
		June					
21	Fr	1	9	·90	11	·00	8
22	Sa	2	10	·98	12	·11	9
23	Su	3	...	...	13	·21	10
24	Mo	4	11	·05	14	·30	11
25	Tu	5	*Jyeshtha* 12	·10	15	·38	12
26	We	6	13	·13	16	·44	13
27	Th	7	14	·15	17	·48	14
28	Fr	8	P	·14	18	·49	*H. 1254 Rabi-ul-awwal.* 15
29	Sa	9	1	·13	19	·49	16
30	Su	10	2	·07	20	·46	17
31	Mo	11	3 / 4	·01 / ·94	21	·42	18
32	Tu	12	5	·84	22	·38	19
Villamba Mithuna—Ani. 1	We	13	6	·74	23	·32	20
2	Th	14	*Bahula* 7	·64	24	·25	21
3	Fr	15	8	·54	25	·18	22
4	Sa	16	9	·44	26	·11	23
5	Su	17	10	·34	27 / 1	·05 / ·99	24
6	Mo	18	11	·25	2	·94	25
7	Tu	19	12	·17	3	·91	26
8	We	20	13	·11	4	·89	27
9	Th	21	14	·06	5	·90	28
10	Fr	22	A	·04	6	·92	29
11	Sa	23	*Ashadha Suk.* 1	·03	7	·96	30
12	Su	24	2	·05	...	...	*Rabi-ul-akhir.* 1
13	Mo	25	3	·08	8	·02	2
14	Tu	26	4	·14	9	·10	3
15	We	27	5	·21	10	·20	4
16	Th	28	6	·28	11	·30	5
17	Fr	29	7	·37	12	·41	6
18	Sa	30	8	·45	13	·51	7

Naksh:—1. Asvn. 2. Bhar. 3. Krit. 4. Rohi. 5. Mrig. 6. Ardh. 7. Punar. 8. Push. 9. Aslesh. 10. Magh. 11. P. Phal. 12. U. Phal. 13. Hasta. 14. Chit.

A. D. 1838.
A.—Amavasya.
P.—Paurnami.

Kollam 1014, Commences { N. Malabar—Sept. / S. Malabar—Aug. }

Hijra 1254, Commences, March 27.

Vikrama 1895.
Bengal San 1244.
(N. Cycle) Saumya.

SOLAR reckoning. LUNAR reckoning.

July

Cyclic Sidereal Year, Month and Day	Week-Day	English Month and Day	Tithi	Ending Moment	Nakshatra	Ending Moment	Muhammadan Year, Month and Day
Vilamba Mithuna—Ani 19	Su	1	Ashadha Sukla 9	·52	14	·61	H. 1254 Rabi-ul-akhir 8
20	Mo	2	10	·57	15	·68	9
21	Tu	3	11	·62	16	·75	10
22	We	4	12	·63	17	·79	11
23	Th	5	13	·61	18	·81	12
24	Fr	6	14	·60	19	·81	13
25	Sa	7	P	·55	20	·79	14
26	Su	8	Bahula 1	·48	21	·76	15
27	Mo	9	2	·41	22	·72	16
28	Tu	10	3	·32	23	·66	17
29	We	11	4	·22	24	·59	18
30	Th	12	5	·11	25	·52	19
—31	Fr	13	6 / 7	·01 / ·91	26	·45	20
Vilamba Karkata—Adi 1	Sa	14	8	·81	27	·39	21
2	Su	15	9	·72	1	·33	22
3	Mo	16	10	·66	2	·28	23
4	Tu	17	11	·58	3	·24	24
5	We	18	12	·54	4	·22	25
6	Th	19	13	·52	5	·22	26
7	Fr	20	14	·51	6	·23	27
8	Sa	21	—A	·53	7	·27	28
9	Su	22	Sukla 1	·56	8	·32	—29
10	Mo	23	2	·61	9	·41	1
11	Tu	24	3	·68	10	·50	2
12	We	25	4	·76	11	·60	3
13	Th	26	5	·84	12	·71	4
14	Fr	27	6	·92	13	·81	5
15	Sa	28	...	...	14	·91	6
16	Su	29	7	·00	...	...	7
17	Mo	30	8	·05	15	·00	8
18	Tu	31	9	·10	16	·06	9

Aug.

Cyclic Sidereal Year, Month and Day	Week-Day	English Month and Day	Tithi	Ending Moment	Nakshatra	Ending Moment	Muhammadan Year, Month and Day
19	We	1	Sravana 10	·11	17	·11	H. 1254 Jumadal-awwal 10
20	Tu	2	11	·10	18	·13	11
21	Fr	3	12	·08	19	·14	12
22	Sa	4	13 / 14	·03 / ·97	20	·13	13
23	Su	5	P	·89	21	·10	14
24	Mo	6	Bahula 1	·81	22 / 23	·05 / ·99	15
25	Tu	7	2	·72	24	·93	16
26	We	8	3	·62	25	·87	17
27	Th	9	4	·51	26	·80	18
28	Fr	10	5	·41	27	·73	19
29	Sa	11	6	·31	1	·66	20
30	Su	12	7	·22	2	·61	21
31	Mo	13	8	·15	3	·58	22
—32	Tu	14	9	·08	4	·55	23
Vilamba Simha—Avani 1	We	15	10	·03	5	·54	24
2	Th	16	11	·02	6	·55	25
3	Fr	17	12	·01	7	·58	26
4	Sa	18	13	·01	8	·63	27
5	Su	19	14	·04	9	·71	28
6	Mo	20	—A	·10	10	·80	29
7	Tu	21	Bhadrapada Sukla 1	·17	11	·90	—30
8	We	22	2	·26	...	...	Jumadal-akhir 1
9	Th	23	3	·34	12	·01	2
10	Fr	24	4	·42	13	·12	3
11	Sa	25	5	·49	14	·22	4
12	Su	26	6	·54	15	·31	5
13	Mo	27	7	·59	16	·37	6
14	Tu	28	8	·61	17	·42	7
15	We	29	9	·61	18	·45	8
16	Th	30	10	·58	19	·47	9
17	Fr	31	11	·54	20	·46	10

Sep.

Cyclic Sidereal Year, Month and Day	Week-Day	English Month and Day	Tithi	Ending Moment	Nakshatra	Ending Moment	Muhammadan Year, Month and Day
Vilamba Simha—Avani 18	Sa	1	Bhadrapada Suk. 12	·48	21	·43	H. 1254 Jumadal-akhir 11
19	Su	2	13	·41	22	·38	12
20	Mo	3	14	·32	23	·33	13
21	Tu	4	P	·22	24	·27	14
22	We	5	Bahula 1	·12	25	·20	15
23	Th	6	2 / 3	·02 / ·92	26	·13	16
24	Fr	7	4	·82	27	·06	17
25	Sa	8	5	·74	1 / 2	·00 / ·95	18
26	Su	9	6	·67	3	·91	19
27	Mo	10	7	·60	4	·88	20
28	Tu	11	8	·55	5	·86	21
29	We	12	9	·53	6	·87	22
30	Th	13	10	·53	7	·89	23
—31	Fr	14	11	·54	8	·95	24
Vilamba Kanya—Purattasi 1	Sa	15	12	·58	...	...	25
2	Su	16	13	·63	9	·02	26
3	Mo	17	14	·70	10	·10	27
4	Tu	18	—A	·78	11	·20	28
5	We	19	Sukla 1	·85	12	·31	—29
6	Th	20	2	·94	13	·42	1
7	Fr	21	...	...	14	·52	2
8	Sa	22	3	·01	15	·61	3
9	Su	23	4	·08	16	·68	4
10	Mo	24	5	·12	17	·74	5
11	Tu	25	6	·14	18	·78	6
12	We	26	7	·14	19	·79	7
13	Th	27	8	·12	20	·78	8
14	Fr	28	9	·09	21	·76	9
15	Sa	29	10 / 11	·02 / ·95	22	·72	10
16	Su	30	12	·86	23	·67	11

Oct.

Cyclic Sidereal Year, Month and Day	Week-Day	English Month and Day	Tithi	Ending Moment	Nakshatra	Ending Moment	Muhammadan Year, Month and Day
17	Mo	1	Asvina 13	·77	24	·61	H. 1254 Rajab 12
18	Tu	2	14	·68	25	·54	13
19	We ○	3	P	·58	26	·47	14
20	Th	4	Bahula 1	·47	27	·40	15
21	Fr	5	2	·37	1	·34	16
22	Sa	6	3	·29	2	·29	17
23	Su	7	4	·21	3	·24	18
24	Mo	8	5	·16	4	·21	19
25	Tu	9	6	·11	5	·19	20
26	We	10	7	·10	6	·19	21
27	Th	11	8	·09	7	·22	22
28	Fr	12	9	·09	8	·26	23
29	Sa	13	10	·14	9	·32	24
—30	Su	14	11	·19	10	·40	25
Vilamba Tula—Aippasi 1	Mo	15	12	·26	11	·50	26
2	Tu	16	13	·35	12	·61	27
3	We	17	14	·43	13	·72	28
4	Th	18	—A	·51	14	·82	29
5	Fr	19	Karttika Sukla 1	·59	15	·91	—30
6	Sa	20	2	·65	16	·99	H. 1254 Shaban 1
7	Su	21	3	·69	...	...	2
8	Mo	22	4	·73	17	·06	3
9	Tu	23	5	·72	18	·10	4
10	We	24	6	·70	19	·11	5
11	Th	25	7	·66	20	·11	6
12	Fr	26	8	·60	21	·09	7
13	Sa	27	9	·53	22	·06	8
14	Su	28	10	·44	23 / 24	·01 / ·95	9
15	Mo	29	11	·35	25	·88	10
16	Tu	30	12	·26	26	·81	11
17	We	31	13	·16	27	·74	12

Nov.

Cyclic Sidereal Year, Month and Day	Week-Day	English Month and Day	Tithi	Ending Moment	Nakshatra	Ending Moment	Muhammadan Year, Month and Day
Vilamba Tula—Aippasi 18	Th	1	Karttika 14 / P	·06 / ·97	1	·68	H. 1254 Shaban 13
19	Fr	2	Bahula 1	·88	2	·62	14
20	Sa	3	2	·80	3	·57	15
21	Su	4	3	·75	4	·53	16
22	Mo	5	4	·71	5	·51	17
23	Tu	6	5	·69	6	·52	18
24	We	7	6	·68	7	·53	19
25	Th	8	7	·70	8	·57	20
26	Fr	9	8	·74	9	·63	21
27	Sa	10	9	·80	10	·70	22
28	Su	11	10	·87	11	·80	23
29	Mo	12	11	·95	12	·91	24
—30	Tu	13	...	...	...	...	25
Vilamba Vrischika—Kartigai 1	We	14	12	·04	13	·02	26
2	Th	15	13	·13	14	·12	27
3	Fr	16	14	·21	15	·22	28
4	Sa	17	—A	·26	16	·31	—29
5	Su	18	1	·30	17	·37	Ramzan 1
6	Mo	19	2	·34	18	·41	2
7	Tu	20	3	·33	19	·43	3
8	We	21	4	·31	20	·43	4
9	Th	22	5	·27	21	·42	5
10	Fr	23	6	·22	22	·39	6
11	Sa	24	7	·15	23	·34	7
12	Su	25	Sukla 8 / 9	·07 / ·97	24	·29	8
13	Mo	26	10	·87	25	·22	9
14	Tu	27	11	·77	26	·15	10
15	We	28	12	·68	27	·08	11
16	Th	29	13	·59	1 / 2	·02 / ·96	12
17	Fr	30	14	·50	3	·90	13

Dec.

Cyclic Sidereal Year, Month and Day	Week-Day	English Month and Day	Tithi	Ending Moment	Nakshatra	Ending Moment	Muhammadan Year, Month and Day
18	Sa	1	Margasira P	·43	4	·86	H. 1254 Ramzan 14
19	Su	2	Bahula 1	·37	5	·85	15
20	Mo	3	2	·32	6	·84	16
21	Tu	4	3	·31	7	·85	17
22	We	5	4	·31	8	·88	18
23	Th	6	5	·34	9	·94	19
24	Fr	7	6	·37	...	...	19/20
25	Sa	8	7	·44	10	·02	21
26	Su	9	8	·51	11	·11	22
27	Mo	10	9	·59	12	·21	23
28	Tu	11	10	·68	13	·31	24
29	We	12	11	·77	14	·42	25
—30	Th	13	12	·85	15	·53	26
Vilamba Dhanus—Margali 1	Fr	14	13	·91	16	·61	27
2	Sa	15	14	·96	17	·68	28
3	Su	16	—A	·97	18	·73	29
4	Mo	17	Pausha Sukla 1	·97	19	·75	—30
5	Tu	18	2	·95	20	·76	H. 1254 Shawwal 1
6	We	19	3	·91	21	·75	2
7	Th	20	4	·85	22	·72	3
8	Fr	21	5	·77	23	·68	4
9	Sa	22	6	·69	24	·62	5
10	Su	23	7	·60	25	·56	6
11	Mo	24	8	·51	26	·50	7
12	Tu	25	9	·41	27	·43	8
13	We	26	10	·31	1	·36	9
14	Th	27	11	·22	2	·29	10
15	Fr	28	12	·14	3	·24	11
16	Sa	29	13	·07	4	·20	12
17	Su	30	14 / P	·01 / ·98	5	·17	13
18	Mo	31	1	·96	6	·16	14

15. Svati. 16. Visak. 17. Anur. 18. Jyesh. 19. Mula. 20. P. Ash. 21. U. Ash. 22. Sravn. 23. Dani. 24. Satab. 25. P. Bhad. 26. U. Bhad. 27. Rev.

A. D. 1839. **Mesha Sankranti** (Commencement of Indian Sidereal Year).
Solar Eclipse. ● **(Surya Sid.) April 11·84.** **Saka 1761.** **Kaliyuga 4940.**
Lunar Eclipse. ○ **(Arya Sid.) April 11·74.** **(S. Cycle) Vikari.**

SOLAR reckoning: Cyclic Sidereal Year, Month and Day; Week-Day; English Month and Day. LUNAR reckoning: Tithi; Ending Moment; Nakshatra; Ending Moment; Muhammadan Year, Month and Day.

Jan.

Cyclic Sidereal Year, Month and Day	Week-Day	English Month and Day	Tithi	Ending Moment	Nakshatra	Ending Moment	Muhammadan Year, Month and Day
Vilamba Dhanus—Margali 19	Tu	1	Pausha Bahula 2	·96	7	·17	H. 1254 Shawwal 15
20	We	2	3	·98	8	·20	16
21	Th	3	...	...	9	·25	17
22	Fr	4	4	·02	10	·32	18
23	Sa	5	5	·09	11	·41	19
24	Su	6	6	·16	12	·51	20
25	Mo	7	7	·25	13	·61	21
26	Tu	8	8	·34	14	·72	22
27	We	9	9	·42	15	·83	23
28	Th	10	10	·50	16	·92	24
29	Fr	11	11	·55	17	·99	25
Vilamba Makara—Tai 1	Sa	12	12	·60	...	...	26
2	Su	13	13	·62	18	·04	27
3	Mo	14	14	·62	19	·07	28
4	Tu	15	A	·59	20	·09	29
5	We	16	Magha Sukla 1	·56	21	·08	Zi-l-ka'da 1
6	Th	17	2	·50	22	·05	2
7	Fr	18	3	·42	23 24	·01 ·96	3
8	Sa	19	4	·34	25	·91	4
9	Su	20	5	·24	26	·84	5
10	Mo	21	6	·14	27	·77	6
11	Tu	22	7 8	·04 ·95	1	·70	7
12	We	23	9	·86	2	·63	8
13	Th	24	10	·78	3	·58	9
14	Fr	25	11	·71	4	·54	10
15	Sa	26	12	·65	5	·50	11
16	Su	27	13	·62	6	·49	12
17	Mo	28	14	·60	7	·49	13
18	Tu	29	P	·60	8	·51	14
19	We	30	1	·62	9	·56	15
20	Th	31	2	·68	10	·63	16

Feb.

Cyclic Sidereal Year, Month and Day	Week-Day	English Month and Day	Tithi	Ending Moment	Nakshatra	Ending Moment	Muhammadan Year, Month and Day
21	Fr	1	Bahula 3	·74	11	·71	H. 1254 17
22	Sa	2	4	·81	12	·80	18
23	Su	3	5	·90	13	·91	19
24	Mo	4	6	·99	...	...	20
25	Tu	5	...	...	14	·02	21
26	We	6	7	·07	15	·13	22
27	Th	7	8	·14	16	·22	23
28	Fr	8	9	·21	17	·29	24
29	Sa	9	10	·24	18	·35	25
30	Su	10	11	·25	19	·40	26
Vilamba Kumbha—Masi 1	Mo	11	12	·25	20	·41	27
2	Tu	12	13	·22	21	·41	28
3	We	13	14	·19	22	·38	29
4	Th	14	A	·12	23	·35	30
5	Fr	15	Phalguna Sukla 1 2	·05 ·96	24	·30	H. 1254 Zi-l-hijja 1
6	Sa	16	3	·87	25	·24	2
7	Su	17	4	·78	26	·18	3
8	Mo	18	5	·68	27	·11	4
9	Tu	19	6	·58	1 2	·04 ·98	5
10	We	20	7	·48	3	·92	6
11	Th	21	8	·40	4	·87	7
12	Fr	22	9	·32	5	·83	8
13	Sa	23	10	·28	6	·81	9
14	Su	24	11	·24	7	·81	10
15	Mo	25	12	·22	8	·84	11
16	Tu	26	13	·22	9	·87	12
17	We	27	14	·25	10	·93	13
18	Th	28	P	·29	...	...	14

March

Cyclic Sidereal Year, Month and Day	Week-Day	English Month and Day	Tithi	Ending Moment	Nakshatra	Ending Moment	Muhammadan Year, Month and Day
Vilamba Kumbha—Masi 19	Fr	1	Phalguna Bahula 1	·36	11	·01	H. 1254 Zi-l-hijja 15
20	Sa	2	2	·44	12	·11	16
21	Su	3	3	·53	13	·22	17
22	Mo	4	4	·62	14	·33	18
23	Tu	5	5	·70	15	·43	19
24	We	6	6	·76	16	·52	20
25	Th	7	7	·82	17	·60	21
26	Fr	8	8	·86	18	·67	22
27	Sa	9	9	·87	19	·71	23
28	Su	10	10	·86	20	·73	24
29	Mo	11	11	·83	21	·73	25
Vilamba Mina—Panguni 1	Tu	12	12	·79	22	·71	26
2	We	13	13	·72	23	·69	27
3	Th	14	14	·65	24	·64	28
4	Fr	15	A	·56	25	·58	29
5	Sa	16	Chaitra Sukla 1	·47	26	·51	30
6	Su	17	2	·37	27	·44	Muharram 1
7	Mo	18	3	·27	1	·37	2
8	Tu	19	4	·17	2	·31	3
9	We	20	5	·08	3	·25	4
10	Th	21	6 7	·00 ·92	4	·20	5
11	Fr	22	8	·87	5	·10	6
12	Sa	23	9	·83	6	·14	7
13	Su	24	10	·82	7	·14	8
14	Mo	25	11	·82	8	·15	9
15	Tu	26	12	·85	9	·19	10
16	We	27	13	·88	10	·24	11
17	Th	28	14	·94	11	·31	12
18	Fr	29	...	...	12	·41	13
19	Sa	30	P	·02	13	·51	14
20	Su	31	1	·11	14	·62	15

April

Cyclic Sidereal Year, Month and Day	Week-Day	English Month and Day	Tithi	Ending Moment	Nakshatra	Ending Moment	Muhammadan Year, Month and Day
21	Mo	1	Bahula 2	·20	15	·72	H. 1255 16
22	Tu	2	3	·28	16	·82	17
23	We	3	4	·34	17	·92	18
24	Th	4	5	·40	18	·98	19
25	Fr	5	6	·43	...	...	20
26	Sa	6	7	·44	19	·03	21
27	Su	7	8	·43	20	·05	22
28	Mo	8	9	·40	21	·06	23
29	Tu	9	10	·36	22	·05	24
30	We	10	11	·30	23 24	·02 ·97	25
31	Th	11	12	·21	25	·92	26
Vikari Mesha—Chittirai 1	Fr	12	13	·12	26	·85	27
2	Sa	13	14 A	·03 ·93	27	·78	28
3	Su	14	Vaisakha Sukla 1	·83	1	·71	29
4	Mo	15	2	·73	2	·65	30
5	Tu	16	3	·64	3	·59	H. 1255 Safar 1
6	We	17	4	·55	4	·53	2
7	Th	18	5	·48	5	·49	3
8	Fr	19	6	·42	6	·47	4
9	Sa	20	7	·38	7	·46	5
10	Su	21	8	·37	8	·47	6
11	Mo	22	9	·36	9	·50	7
12	Tu	23	10	·39	10	·55	8
13	We	24	11	·42	11	·63	9
14	Th	25	12	·49	12	·71	10
15	Fr	26	13	·57	13	·81	11
16	Sa	27	14	·65	14	·92	12
17	Su	28	P	·74	...	...	13
18	Mo	29	Bah. 1	·82	15	·03	14
19	Tu	30	2	·88	16	·13	15

May

Cyclic Sidereal Year, Month and Day	Week-Day	English Month and Day	Tithi	Ending Moment	Nakshatra	Ending Moment	Muhammadan Year, Month and Day
Vikari Mesha—Chittirai 20	We	1	Vaisakha Bahula 3	·93	17	·22	H. 1255 Safar 16
21	Th	2	4	·97	18	·29	17
22	Fr	3	5	·97	19	·34	18
23	Sa	4	6	·96	20	·37	19
24	Su	5	7	·94	21	·38	20
25	Mo	6	8	·88	22	·38	21
26	Tu	7	9	·82	23	·35	22
27	We	8	10	·74	24	·31	23
28	Th	9	11	·66	25	·25	24
29	Fr	10	12	56	26	·19	25
30	Sa	11	13	·46	27	·13	26
31	Su	12	14	·35	1 2	·06 ·99	27
Vikari Vrishabha—Vaikasi 1	Mo	13	A	·25	3	·93	28
2	Tu	14	Adhika Jyeshtha Sukla 1	·16	4	·87	29
3	We	15	2 3	·07 ·99	5	·83	Rabi-ul-awwal 1
4	Th	16	4	·04	6	·80	2
5	Fr	17	5	·90	7	·78	3
6	Sa	18	6	·88	8	·79	4
7	Su	19	7	·87	9	·81	5
8	Mo	20	8	·90	10	·87	6
9	Tu	21	9	·93	11	·93	7
10	We	22	...	...	...	...	8
11	Th	23	10	·00	12	·01	9
12	Fr	24	11	·07	13	·11	10
13	Sa	25	12	·15	14	·22	11
14	Su	26	13	·23	15	·33	12
15	Mo	27	14	·31	16	·43	13
16	Tu	28	P	·39	17	·52	14
17	We	29	1	·43	18	·60	15
18	Th	30	2	·46	19	·65	16
19	Fr	31	3	·47	20	·69	17

June

Cyclic Sidereal Year, Month and Day	Week-Day	English Month and Day	Tithi	Ending Moment	Nakshatra	Ending Moment	Muhammadan Year, Month and Day
20	Sa	1	Bahula 4	·47	21	·71	H. 1255 18
21	Su	2	5	·43	22	·70	19
22	Mo	3	6	·39	23	·68	20
23	Tu	4	7	·33	24	·64	21
24	We	5	8	·24	25	·59	22
25	Th	6	9	·15	26	·54	23
26	Fr	7	10 11	·05 ·95	27	·47	24
27	Sa	8	12	·85	1	·40	25
28	Su	9	13	·75	2	·33	26
29	Mo	10	14	·66	3	·26	27
30	Tu	11	A	·57	4	·21	28
31	We	12	Nija Jyeshtha Sukla 1	·49	5	·10	29
Vikari Mithuna—Ani 1	Th	13	2	·43	6	·13	30
2	Fr	14	3	·39	7	·11	H. 1255 Rabi-ul-akhir 1
3	Sa	15	4	·36	8	·11	2
4	Su	16	5	·36	9	·14	3
5	Mo	17	6	·38	10	·18	4
6	Tu	18	7	·42	11	·24	5
7	We	19	8	·47	12	·32	6
8	Th	20	9	·54	13	·41	7
9	Fr	21	10	·62	14	·51	8
10	Sa	22	11	·70	15	·62	9
11	Su	23	12	·79	16	·73	10
12	Mo	24	13	·86	17	·83	11
13	Tu	25	14	·91	18	·91	12
14	We	26	P	·94	19	·96	13
15	Th	27	Bah. 1	·95	...	...	14
16	Fr	28	2	·94	20	·01	15
17	Sa	29	3	·91	21	·08	16
18	Su	30	4	·87	22	·03	17

Naksh:—1. Asvn. 2. Bhar. 3. Krit. 4. Rohi. 5. Mrig. 6. Ardh. 7. Punar. 8. Push. 9. Aslesh. 10. Magh. 11. P. Phal. 12. U. Phal. 13. Hasta. 14. Chit.

A. D. 1839.
A.—Amavasya. **Kollam 1015,** Commences { **N. Malabar—Sept.** / **S. Malabar—Aug.** } **Hijra 1255,** Commences, **Mar. 17.**
P.—Paurnami.

Vikrama 1896.
Bengal San 1245.
(N. Cycle) Sadharana.

SOLAR reckoning: Cyclic Sidereal Year, Month and Day; Week-Day; English Month and Day. LUNAR reckoning: Tithi; Ending Moment; Nakshatra; Ending Moment; Muhammadan Year, Month and Day.

July

Vikari Mithuna—Ani. / Vikari Karkata—Adi. — Nija Jy. Bahula / Sukla / Ashadha — H. 1255 Rabi-ul-akhir. / H. 1255 Jumadal-awwal.

Cyclic Sidereal Year, Month and Day	Week-Day	English Month and Day	Tithi	Ending Moment	Nakshatra	Ending Moment	Muhammadan Year, Month and Day
19	Mo	1	5	·81	23 / 24	·01 / ·97	18
20	Tu	2	6	·73	25	·93	19
21	We	3	7	·64	26	·87	20
22	Th	4	8	·54	27	·81	21
23	Fr	5	9	·43	1	·74	22
24	Sa	6	10	·33	2	·67	23
25	Su	7	11	·23	3	·61	24
26	Mo	8	12	·13	4	·55	25
27	Tu	9	13 / 14	·05 / ·97	5	·50	26
28	We	10	A	·91	6	·46	27
29	Th	11	1	·86	7	·43	28
30	Fr	12	2	·84	8	·44	—29
31	Sa	13	3	·84	9	·45	1
—32	Su	14	4	·85	10	·49	2
1	Mo	15	5	·90	11	·54	3
2	Tu	16	6	·95	12	·62	4
3	We	17	...	...	13	·71	5
4	Th	18	7	·01	14	·82	6
5	Fr	19	8	·09	15	·93	7
6	Sa	20	9	·17	...	...	8
7	Su	21	10	·26	16	·03	9
8	Mo	22	11	·33	17	·13	10
9	Tu	23	12	·39	18	·21	11
10	We	24	13	·42	19	·29	12
11	Th	25	14	·43	20	·33	13
12	Fr	26	P	·42	21	·35	14
13	Sa	27	1	·39	22	·35	15
14	Su	28	2	·35	23	·34	16
15	Mo	29	3	·29	24	·31	17
16	Tu	30	4	·22	25	·27	18
17	We	31	5	·13	26	·21	19

Aug.

Vikari Simha—Avani. — Bahula / Sukla / Sravana / Bahula — H. 1255 Jumadal-akhir.

Cyclic Sidereal Year, Month and Day	Week-Day	English Month and Day	Tithi	Ending Moment	Nakshatra	Ending Moment	Muhammadan Year, Month and Day
18	Th	1	6 / 7	·03 / ·93	27	·15	20
19	Fr	2	8	·83	1	·09	21
20	Sa	3	9	·73	2 / 3	·02 / ·95	22
21	Su	4	10	·63	4	·88	23
22	Mo	5	11	·54	5	·83	24
23	Tu	6	12	·46	6	·79	25
24	We	7	13	·40	7	·76	26
25	Th	8	14	·35	8	·76	27
26	Fr	9	A	·33	9	·77	28
27	Sa	10	1	·32	10	·80	29
28	Su	11	2	·33	11	·85	—30
29	Mo	12	3	·38	12	·92	1
30	Tu	13	4	·43	...	...	2
—31	We	14	5	·50	13	·02	3
1	Th	15	6	·58	14	·12	4
2	Fr	16	7	·67	15	·23	5
3	Sa	17	8	·75	16	·33	6
4	Su	18	9	·82	17	·43	7
5	Mo	19	10	·87	18	·53	8
6	Tu	20	11	·90	19	·59	9
7	We	21	12	·93	20	·64	10
8	Th	22	13	·92	21	·67	11
9	Fr	23	14	·90	22	·68	12
10	Sa	24	P	·85	23	·68	13
11	Su	25	1	·80	24	·65	14
12	Mo	26	2	·72	25	·60	15
13	Tu	27	3	·63	26	·55	16
14	We	28	4	·53	27	·48	17
15	Th	29	5	·43	1	·41	18
16	Fr	30	6	·33	2	·34	19
17	Sa	31	7	·23	3	·28	20

Sep.

Vikari Simha—Avani. / Vikari Kanya—Purattasi. — Sr. Bah. / Sukla / Bhadrapada / Bahula — Jumadal-akhir. / H. 1255 Rajab.

Cyclic Sidereal Year, Month and Day	Week-Day	English Month and Day	Tithi	Ending Moment	Nakshatra	Ending Moment	Muhammadan Year, Month and Day
18	Su	1	8	·14	4	·22	21
19	Mo	2	9 / 10	·05 / ·97	5	·16	22
20	Tu	3	11	·92	6	·12	23
21	We	4	12	·87	7	·10	24
22	Th	5	13	·85	8	·08	25
23	Fr	6	14	·83	9	·09	26
24	Sa	7	A	·85	10	·11	27
25	Su	8	1	·89	11	·16	28
26	Mo	9	2	·95	12	·24	—29
27	Tu	10	...	...	13	·32	1
28	We	11	3	·02	14	·42	2
29	Th	12	4	·10	15	·52	3
30	Fr	13	5	·18	16	·63	4
—31	Sa	14	6	·27	17	·74	5
1	Su	15	7	·35	18	·83	6
2	Mo	16	8	·40	19	·90	7
3	Tu	17	9	·44	20	·96	8
4	We	18	10	·46	21	·99	9
5	Th	19	11	·44	...	...	10
6	Fr	20	12	·42	22	·01	11
7	Sa	21	13	·39	23 / 24	·00 / ·98	12
8	Su	22	14	·33	25	·94	13
9	Mo	23	P	·25	26	·88	14
10	Tu	24	1	·17	27	·82	15
11	We	25	2 / 3	·07 / ·97	1	·76	16
12	Th	26	4	·87	2	·69	17
13	Fr	27	5	·77	3	·62	18
14	Sa	28	6	·68	4	·56	19
15	Su	29	7	·59	5	·50	20
16	Mo	30	8	·52	6	·46	21

Oct.

Vikari Tula—Aippasi. — Sukla / Asvina / Bahula — H. 1255 Shaban.

Cyclic Sidereal Year, Month and Day	Week-Day	English Month and Day	Tithi	Ending Moment	Nakshatra	Ending Moment	Muhammadan Year, Month and Day
17	Tu	1	9	·46	7	·42	22
18	We	2	10	·41	8	·41	23
19	Th	3	11	·39	9	·41	24
20	Fr	4	12	·38	10	·43	25
21	Sa	5	13	·40	11	·48	26
22	Su	6	14	·44	12	·54	27
23	Mo	7	A	·49	13	·62	28
24	Tu	8	1	·56	14	·72	29
25	We	9	2	·65	15	·82	—30
26	Th	10	3	·74	16	·93	1
27	Fr	11	4	·82	...	...	2
28	Sa	12	5	·90	17	·04	3
29	Su	13	6	·96	18	·13	4
30	Mo	14	...	...	19	·21	5
—31	Tu	15	7	·00	20	·27	6
1	We	16	8	·02	21	·31	7
2	Th	17	9 / 10	·02 / ·99	22	·33	8
3	Fr	18	11	·95	23	·33	9
4	Sa	19	12	·90	24	·31	10
5	Su	20	13	·82	25	·27	11
6	Mo	21	14	·74	26	·22	12
7	Tu	22	P	·65	27	·16	13
8	We	23	1	·55	1	·10	14
9	Th	24	2	·45	2 / 3	·03 / ·96	15
10	Fr	25	3	·35	4	·89	16
11	Sa	26	4	·26	5	·84	17
12	Su	27	5	·17	6	·79	18
13	Mo	28	6	·10	7	·75	19
14	Tu	29	7	·04	8	·73	20
15	We	30	8 / 9	·00 / ·98	9	·73	21
16	Th	31	10	·98	10	·75	22

Nov.

Vikari Tula—Aippasi. / Vikari Vrischiku—Kartigai. — Asv. Bah. / Sukla / Kartika / Bahula — Shaban. / H 1255 Ramzan.

Cyclic Sidereal Year, Month and Day	Week-Day	English Month and Day	Tithi	Ending Moment	Nakshatra	Ending Moment	Muhammadan Year, Month and Day
17	Fr	1	11	·99	11	·79	23
18	Sa	2	...	...	12	·85	24
19	Su	3	12	·03	13	·93	25
20	Mo	4	13	·09	...	...	26
21	Tu	5	14	·17	14	·02	27
22	We	6	A	·26	15	·13	28
23	Th	7	1	·35	16	·24	—29
24	Fr	8	2	·43	17	·34	1
25	Sa	9	3	·50	18	·44	2
26	Su	10	4	·56	19	·52	3
27	Mo	11	5	·60	20	·58	4
28	Tu	12	6	·62	21	·63	5
29	We	13	7	·62	22	·65	6
—30	Th	14	8	·59	23	·65	7
1	Fr	15	9	·56	24	·64	8
2	Sa	16	10	·51	25	·60	9
3	Su	17	11	·44	26	·56	10
4	Mo	18	12	·35	27	·51	11
5	Tu	19	13	·26	1	·44	12
6	We	20	14	·16	2	·37	13
7	Th	21	P / 1	·06 / ·96	3	·30	14
8	Fr	22	2	·87	4	·24	15
9	Sa	23	3	·79	5	·18	16
10	Su	24	4	·72	6	·12	17
11	Mo	25	5	·65	7	·08	18
12	Tu	26	6	·62	8	·06	19
13	We	27	7	·60	9	·06	20
14	Th	28	8	·60	10	·07	21
15	Fr	29	9	·62	11	·10	22
16	Sa	30	10	·67	12	·16	23

Dec.

Vikari Dhanus—Margali. — Sukla / Margasira / Bahula — H. 1255 Shawwal.

Cyclic Sidereal Year, Month and Day	Week-Day	English Month and Day	Tithi	Ending Moment	Nakshatra	Ending Moment	Muhammadan Year, Month and Day
17	Su	1	11	·72	13	·23	24
18	Mo	2	12	·80	14	·32	25
19	Tu	3	13	·88	15	·43	26
20	We	4	14	·97	16	·53	27
21	Th	5	...	...	17	·64	28
22	Fr	6	A	·06	18	·74	29
23	Sa	7	1	·13	19	·82	—30
24	Su	8	2	·20	20	·90	1
25	Mo	9	3	·24	21	·95	2
26	Tu	10	4	·26	22	·97	3
27	We	11	5	·25	23	·98	4
28	Th	12	6	·22	24	·96	5
—29	Fr	13	7	·19	25	·94	6
1	Sa	14	8	·13	26	·90	7
2	Su	15	9 / 10	·06 / ·97	27	·84	8
3	Mo	16	11	·88	1	·78	9
4	Tu	17	12	·79	2	·72	10
5	We	18	13	·69	3	·65	11
6	Th	19	14	·59	4	·58	12
7	Fr	20	P	·49	5	·51	13
8	Sa	21	1	·42	6	·46	14
9	Su	22	2	·35	7	·41	15
10	Mo	23	3	·30	8	·39	16
11	Tu	24	4	·25	9	·38	17
12	We	25	5	·24	10	·39	18
13	Th	26	6	·24	11	·42	19
14	Fr	27	7	·26	12	·46	20
15	Sa	28	8	·31	13	·53	21
16	Su	29	9	·37	14	·63	22
17	Mo	30	10	·45	15	·73	23
18	Tu	31	11	·54	16	·83	24

15. Svati. 16. Visak. 17. Anur. 18. Jyesh. 19. Mula. 20. P. Ash. 21. U. Ash. 22. Sravn. 23. Dani. 24. Satab. 25. P. Bhad. 26. U. Bhad. 27. Rev.

A. D. 1840. **Mesha Sankranti** (Commencement of Indian Sidereal Year).

Solar Eclipse. ● **(Surya Sid.) April 11·09.** **Saka 1762.** **Kaliyuga 4941.**

Lunar Eclipse. ○ **(Arya Sid.) April 10·99.** **(S. Cycle) Sarvari.**

Columns: SOLAR reckoning (Cyclic Sidereal Year, Month and Day; Week-Day; English Month and Day) — LUNAR reckoning (Tithi; Ending Moment; Nakshatra; Ending Moment; Muhammadan Year, Month and Day).

Jan. — Vikari Dhanus—Margali; Vikari Makara—Tai. Bah.; Sukla; Pausha; Bahula. Shawwal; H. 1255 Zi-l-ka'da.

Cyclic Sidereal Year, Month and Day	Week-Day	English Month and Day	Tithi	Ending Moment	Nakshatra	Ending Moment	Muhammadan Year, Month and Day
19	We	1	12	·64	17	·94	25
20	Th	2	13	·71	...	...	26
21	Fr	3	14	·78	18	·04	27
22	Sa	4	A	·85	19	·14	28
23	Su	5	1	·88	20	·21	29
24	Mo	6	2	·90	21	·26	1
25	Tu	7	3	·90	22	·29	2
26	We	8	4	·88	23	·30	3
27	Th	9	5	·83	24	·30	4
28	Fr	10	6	·78	25	·27	5
29	Sa	11	7	·71	26	·23	6
1	Su	12	8	·62	27	·18	7
2	Mo	13	9	·53	1	·12	8
3	Tu	14	10	·43	2 / 3	·06 / ·99	9
4	We	15	11	·33	4	·92	10
5	Th	16	12	·23	5	·85	11
6	Fr	17	13	·15	6	·79	12
7	Sa	18	14 / P	·07 / ·99	7	·75	13
8	Su	19	1	·94	8	·72	14
9	Mo	20	2	·90	9	·71	15
10	Tu	21	3	·89	10	·71	16
11	We	22	4	·88	11	·73	17
12	Th	23	5	·92	12	·77	18
13	Fr	24	6	·97	13	·85	19
14	Sa	25	...	...	14	·93	20
15	Su	26	7	·02	...	...	21
16	Mo	27	8	·11	15	·02	22
17	Tu	28	9	·20	16	·13	23
18	We	29	10	·29	17	·24	24
19	Th	30	11	·37	18	·35	25
20	Fr	31	12	·45	19	·44	26

Feb. — Vikari Kumbha—Masi. Sukla; Magha; Bahula. H. 1255 Zi-l-hijja.

Cyclic Sidereal Year, Month and Day	Week-Day	English Month and Day	Tithi	Ending Moment	Nakshatra	Ending Moment	Muhammadan Year, Month and Day
21	Sa	1	13	·50	20	·51	27
22	Su	2	14	·52	21	·57	28
23	Mo	3	A	·54	22	·61	29
24	Tu	4	1	·54	23	·63	30
25	We	5	2	·52	24	·63	1
26	Th	6	3	·47	25	·60	2
27	Fr	7	4	·40	26	·57	3
28	Sa	8	5	·32	27	·51	4
29	Su	9	6	·24	1	·45	5
30	Mo	10	7	·15	2	·39	6
1	Tu	11	8 / 9	·05 / ·95	3	·32	7
2	We	12	10	·85	4	·25	8
3	Th	13	11	·77	5	·19	9
4	Fr	14	12	·69	6	·13	10
5	Sa	15	13	·62	7	·09	11
6	Su	16	14	·57	8	·05	12
7	Mo ○	17	P	·53	9	·03	13
8	Tu	18	1	·52	10	·03	14
9	We	19	2	·51	11	·05	15
10	Th	20	3	·55	12	·09	16
11	Fr	21	4	·59	13	·15	17
12	Sa	22	5	·66	14	·23	18
13	Su	23	6	·74	15	·32	19
14	Mo	24	7	·84	16	·43	20
15	Tu	25	8	·92	17	·54	21
16	We	26	9	·99	18	·65	22
17	Th	27	...	...	19	·74	23
18	Fr	28	10	·06	20	·82	24
19	Sa	29	11	·11	21	·88	25

March — Vikari Kumbha—Masi; Vikari Mina—Panguni. Bah.; Sukla; Phalguna; Bahula. H. 1256 Muharram.

Cyclic Sidereal Year, Month and Day	Week-Day	English Month and Day	Tithi	Ending Moment	Nakshatra	Ending Moment	Muhammadan Year, Month and Day
20	Su	1	12	·16	22	·92	26
21	Mo	2	13	·17	23	·95	27
22	Tu	3	14	·16	24	·95	28
23	We ●	4	A	·13	25	·93	29
24	Th	5	1	·08	26	·90	1
25	Fr	6	2 / 3	·02 / ·94	27	·85	2
26	Sa	7	4	·86	1	·80	3
27	Su	8	5	·76	2	·73	4
28	Mo	9	6	·66	3	·66	5
29	Tu	10	7	·56	4	·59	6
30	We	11	8	·46	5	·52	7
31	Th	12	9	·37	6	·47	8
1	Fr	13	10	·28	7	·42	9
2	Sa	14	11	·22	8	·38	10
3	Su	15	12	·16	9	·36	11
4	Mo	16	13	·13	10	·35	12
5	Tu	17	14	·11	11	·37	13
6	We	18	P	·11	12	·41	14
7	Th	19	1	·15	13	·46	15
8	Fr	20	2	·19	14	·53	16
9	Sa	21	3	·26	15	·62	17
10	Su	22	4	·34	16	·73	18
11	Mo	23	5	·43	17	·84	19
12	Tu	24	6	·52	18	·95	20
13	We	25	7	·60	...	...	21
14	Th	26	8	·65	19	·04	22
15	Fr	27	9	·70	20	·13	23
16	Sa	28	10	·74	21	·19	24
17	Su	29	11	·75	22	·25	25
18	Mo	30	12	·74	23	·27	26
19	Tu	31	13	·70	24	·28	27

April — Sarvari Mesha—Chittirai. Sukla; Chaitra; Bahula. H. 1256 Safar.

Cyclic Sidereal Year, Month and Day	Week-Day	English Month and Day	Tithi	Ending Moment	Nakshatra	Ending Moment	Muhammadan Year, Month and Day
20	We	1	14	·66	25	·26	28
21	Th	2	A	·59	26	·23	29
22	Fr	3	1	·51	27	·19	30
23	Sa	4	2	·43	1	·14	1
24	Su	5	3	·33	2	·07	2
25	Mo	6	4	·23	3 / 4	·00 / ·93	3
26	Tu	7	5	·13	5	·86	4
27	We	8	6 / 7	·03 / ·94	6	·80	5
28	Th	9	8	·86	7	·75	6
29	Fr	10	9	·78	8	·71	7
1	Sa	11	10	·72	9	·68	8
2	Su	12	11	·69	10	·68	9
3	Mo	13	12	·67	11	·69	10
4	Tu	14	13	·67	12	·72	11
5	We	15	14	·70	13	·77	12
6	Th	16	P	·75	14	·84	13
7	Fr	17	1	·81	15	·92	14
8	Sa	18	2	·89	...	...	15
9	Su	19	3	·98	16	·03	16
10	Mo	20	...	...	17	·14	17
11	Tu	21	4	·06	18	·25	18
12	We	22	5	·14	19	·34	19
13	Th	23	6	·20	20	·43	20
14	Fr	24	7	·25	21	·51	21
15	Sa	25	8	·28	22	·56	22
16	Su	26	9	·29	23	·59	23
17	Mo	27	10	·28	24	·60	24
18	Tu	28	11	·25	25	·59	25
19	We	29	12	·20	26	·57	26
20	Th	30	13	·13	27	·53	27

May — Sarvari Mesha—Chittirai; Sarvari Vrishabha—Vaikasi. Sukla; Vaisakha; Bahula. H. 1256 Rabi-ul-awwal.

Cyclic Sidereal Year, Month and Day	Week-Day	English Month and Day	Tithi	Ending Moment	Nakshatra	Ending Moment	Muhammadan Year, Month and Day
21	Fr	1	14 / A	·05 / ·96	1	·47	28
22	Sa	2	1	·87	2	·41	29
23	Su	3	2	·77	3	·34	1
24	Mo	4	3	·67	4	·28	2
25	Tu	5	4	·57	5	·21	3
26	We	6	5	·47	6	·14	4
27	Th	7	6	·38	7	·09	5
28	Fr	8	7	·31	8	·04	6
29	Sa	9	8	·26	9	·02	7
30	Su	10	9	·22	10	·00	8
31	Mo	11	10	·19	11	·01	9
1	Tu	12	11	·19	12	·03	10
2	We	13	12	·22	13	·08	11
3	Th	14	13	·27	14	·14	12
4	Fr	15	14	·33	15	·23	13
5	Sa	16	P	·40	16	·33	14
6	Su	17	1	·48	17	·44	15
7	Mo	18	2	·57	18	·54	16
8	Tu	19	3	·65	19	·64	17
9	We	20	4	·71	20	·74	18
10	Th	21	5	·76	21	·82	19
11	Fr	22	6	·78	22	·87	20
12	Sa	23	7	·80	23	·91	21
13	Su	24	8	·79	24	·92	22
14	Mo	25	9	·76	25	·92	23
15	Tu	26	10	·71	26	·90	24
16	We	27	11	·64	27	·86	25
17	Th	28	12	·56	1	·81	26
18	Fr	29	13	·46	2	·75	27
19	Sa	30	14	·36	3	·69	28
20	Su	31	A	·26	4	·62	29

June — Sarvari Mithuna—Ani. Sukla; Jyeshtha; Bahula. H. 1256 Rabi-ul-akhir.

Cyclic Sidereal Year, Month and Day	Week-Day	English Month and Day	Tithi	Ending Moment	Nakshatra	Ending Moment	Muhammadan Year, Month and Day
21	Mo	1	1	·16	5	·55	30
22	Tu	2	2 / 3	·06 / ·96	6	·48	1
23	We	3	4	·88	7	·42	2
24	Th	4	5	·81	8	·37	3
25	Fr	5	6	·76	9	·35	4
26	Sa	6	7	·71	10	·33	5
27	Su	7	8	·70	11	·33	6
28	Mo	8	9	·69	12	·35	7
29	Tu	9	10	·71	13	·39	8
30	We	10	11	·75	14	·46	9
31	Th	11	12	·81	15	·54	10
1	Fr	12	13	·88	16	·63	11
2	Sa	13	14	·96	17	·73	12
3	Su	14	...	...	18	·84	13
4	Mo	15	P	·05	19	·95	14
5	Tu	16	1	·12	...	...	15
6	We	17	2	·19	20	·05	16
7	Th	18	3	·24	21	·13	17
8	Fr	19	4	·27	22	·19	18
9	Sa	20	5	·28	23	·22	19
10	Su	21	6	·27	24	·25	20
11	Mo	22	7	·25	25	·25	21
12	Tu	23	8	·19	26	·23	22
13	We	24	9	·13	27	·19	23
14	Th	25	10 / 11	·05 / ·95	1	·14	24
15	Fr	26	12	·85	2	·09	25
16	Sa	27	13	·75	3 / 4	·03 / ·96	26
17	Su	28	14	·65	5	·89	27
18	Mo	29	A	·55	6	·82	28
19	Tu	30	1	·46	7	·76	29

Naksh:—1. Asvn. 2. Bhar. 3. Krit. 4. Rohi. 5. Mrig. 6. Ardh. 7. Punar. 8. Push. 9. Aslesh. 10. Magh. 11. P. Phal. 12. U. Phal. 13. Hasta. 14. Chit.

A. D. 1840.
A.—Amavasya. **Kollam 1016,** Commences { **N. Malabar—Sept.** / **S. Malabar—Aug.**
P.—Paurnami.

Hijra 1256, Commences, **Mar. 5.**

Vikrama 1897.
Bengal San 1246.
(N. Cycle) Virodhakrit.

Cyclic Sidereal Year, Month and Day (SOLAR reckoning)	Week-Day	English Month and Day	Tithi (LUNAR reckoning)	Ending Moment	Nakshatra	Ending Moment	Muhammadan Year, Month and Day
		July					
20 [Sarvari Mithuna—Ani.]	We	1	2	·37	8	·72	1
21	Th	2	3	·30	9	·68	2
22	Fr	3	4	·24	10	·65	3
23	Sa	4	5	·19	11	·65	4
24	Su	5	6 [Sukla]	·17	12	·66	5
25	Mo	6	7	·16	13	·71	6
26	Tu	7	8	·19	14	·76	7
27	We	8	9	·22	15	·84	8
28	Th	9	10	·29	16	·93	9
29	Fr	10	11 [Ashadha]	·36	...	...	10 [Jumadal-awwal.]
30	Sa	11	12	·43	17	·03	11
31	Su	12	13	·52	18	·14	12
—32	Mo	13	14	·60	19	·25	13
1 [Sarvari Karkata—Adi.]	Tu	14	P	·67	20	·35	14
2	We	15	1	·71	21	·43	15
3	Th	16	2	·75	22	·50	16
4	Fr	17	3	·76	23	·55	17 [H. 1256 Jumadal-akhir]
5	Sa	18	4	·74	24	·57	18
6	Su	19	5	·72	25	·57	19
7	Mo	20	6 [Bahula]	·67	26	·56	20
8	Tu	21	7	·61	27	·53	21
9	We	22	8	·53	1	·48	22
10	Th	23	9	·45	2	·43	23
11	Fr	24	10	·35	3	·36	24
12	Sa	25	11	·25	4	·29	25
13	Su	26	12	·15	5	·22	26
14	Mo	27	{ 13 14	·05 ·95	6	·16	27
15	Tu	28	—A	·85	7	·10	28
16	We	29	1	·77	8	·05	29
17	Th	30	2	·71	9 10	·01 ·98 }	—30
18	Fr	31	3	·65	11	·97	1
		Aug.					
19	Sa	1	4	·64	12	·99	2
20	Su	2	5	·64	...	...	3
21	Mo	3	6 [Sukla]	·66	13	·02	4
22	Tu	4	7	·69	14	·07	5
23	We	5	8	·76	15	·14	6
24	Th	6	9	·83	16	·23	7
25	Fr	7	10	·91	17	·34	8
26	Sa	8	11	·99	18	·45	9
27	Su	9	...	...	19	·55	10
28	Mo	10	12 [Sravana]	·07	20	·65	11
29	Tu	11	13	·14	21	·74	12
30	We	12	14	·19	22	·80	13
—31	Th ○	13	P	·24	23	·86	14
1 [Sarvari Simha—Avani.]	Fr	14	1	·25	24	·89	15
2	Sa	15	2	·24	25	·90	16
3	Su	16	3	·21	26	·89	17 [H. 1256 Jumadal-akhir.]
4	Mo	17	4	·17	27	·86	18
5	Tu	18	5	·11	1	·82	19
6	We	19	{ 6 7 [Bahula]	·03 ·94	2	·77	20
7	Th	20	8	·84	3	·70	21
8	Fr	21	9	·74	4	·63	22
9	Sa	22	10	·64	5	·56	23
10	Su	23	11	·54	6	·50	24
11	Mo	24	12	·44	7	·44	25
12	Tu	25	13	·35	8	·38	26
13	We	26	14	·28	9	·34	27
14	Th ●	27	—A	·21	10	·31	28
15	Fr	28	1 [B. Suk.]	·18	11	·30	—29
16	Sa	29	2	·16	12	·31	1 [Rajab.]
17	Su	30	3	·15	13	·33	2
18	Mo	31	4	·16	14	·38	3
		Sep.					
19	Tu	1	5 [Sukla]	·21	15	·45	4
20	We	2	6	·27	16	·54	5
21	Th	3	7	·34	17	·64	6
22	Fr	4	8	·42	18	·75	7
23	Sa	5	9	·50	19	·85	8
24	Su	6	10	·59	20	·95	9
25	Mo	7	11 [Bhadrapada]	·66	...	...	10
26	Tu	8	12	·71	21	·04	11
27	We	9	13	·75	22	·12	12
28	Th	10	14	·77	23	·18	13
29	Fr	11	P	·76	24	·21	14 [H. 1256 Rajab.]
30	Sa	12	1	·73	25	·22	15
—31	Su	13	2	·70	26	·21	16
1 [Sarvari Kanya—Purattasi.]	Mo	14	3	·63	27	·20	17
2	Tu	15	4	·56	1	·16	18
3	We	16	5	·47	2	·10	19
4	Th	17	6 [Bahula]	·37	3 4	·04 ·97 }	20
5	Fr	18	7	·27	5	·90	21
6	Sa	19	8	·17	6	·84	22
7	Su	20	{ 9 10	·07 ·97	7	·78	23
8	Mo	21	11	·89	8	·72	24
9	Tu	22	12	·82	9	·67	25
10	We	23	13	·76	10	·64	26
11	Th	24	14	·71	11	·63	27
12	Fr	25	—A	·69	12	·63	28
13	Sa	26	1	·69	13	·65	29
14	Su	27	2	·70	14	·69	—30
15	Mo	28	3	·75	15	·75	1
16	Tu	29	4	·80	16	·84	2
17	We	30	5	·88	17	·94	3
		Oct.					
18	Th	1	6 [Sukla]	·96	...	...	4
19	Fr	2	...	...	18	·04	5
20	Sa	3	7	·04	19	·15	6
21	Su	4	8	·13	20	·25	7
22	Mo	5	9	·21	21	·35	8
23	Tu	6	10	·27	22	·43	9
24	We	7	11	·30	23	·49	10
25	Th	8	12	·33	24	·53	11
26	Fr	9	13 [Asvina]	·31	25	·54	12
27	Sa	10	14	·29	26	·55	13 [H. 1256 Shaban.]
28	Su	11	P	·26	27	·53	14
29	Mo	12	1	·19	1	·49	15
30	Tu	13	2	·12	2	·44	16
—31	We	14	{ 3 4	·03 ·94	3	·38	17
1 [Sarvari Tula—Aippasi.]	Th	15	5	·84	4	·32	18
2	Fr	16	6	·74	5	·25	19
3	Sa	17	7	·64	6	·18	20
4	Su	18	8 [Bahula]	·54	7	·11	21
5	Mo	19	9	·46	8	·05	22
6	Tu	20	10	·38	9 10	·01 ·97 }	23
7	We	21	11	·33	11	·95	24
8	Th	22	12	·29	12	·95	25
9	Fr	23	13	·28	13	·96	26
10	Sa	24	14	·28	...	...	27
11	Su	25	—A	·29	14	·00	28
12	Mo	26	1 [Kartt. Suk.]	·33	15	·07	—29
13	Tu	27	2	·39	16	·15	1 [Ramzan.]
14	We	28	3	·46	17	·24	2
15	Th	29	4	·54	18	·34	3
16	Fr	30	5	·64	19	·45	4
17	Sa	31	6	·73	20	·55	5
		Nov.					
18	Su	1	7 [Sukla]	·81	21	·66	6
19	Mo	2	8	·86	22	·74	7
20	Tu	3	9	·89	23	·80	8
21	We	4	10	·92	24	·84	9
22	Th	5	11	·91	25	·87	10
23	Fr	6	12	·89	26	·87	11
24	Sa	7	13 [Kartika]	·85	27	·86	12
25	Su	8	14	·79	1	·82	13
26	Mo	9	P	·71	2	·77	14
27	Tu	10	1	·63	3	·72	15
28	We	11	2	·54	4	·66	16
29	Th	12	3	·44	5	·59	17 [H. 1256 Ramzan.]
—30	Fr	13	4	·34	6	·52	18
1 [Sarvari Vrischika—Kartigai.]	Sa	14	5	·24	7	·45	19
2	Su	15	6	·15	8	·39	20
3	Mo	16	{ 7 8	·07 ·99	9	·34	21
4	Tu	17	9 [Bahula]	·93	10	·30	22
5	We	18	10	·90	11	·28	23
6	Th	19	11	·89	12	·27	24
7	Fr	20	12	·89	13	·28	25
8	Sa	21	13	·90	14	·32	26
9	Su	22	14	·95	15	·38	27
10	Mo	23	...	...	16	·45	28
11	Tu	24	—A	·02	17	·54	29
12	We	25	1	·09	18	·64	—30
13	Th	26	2	·17	19	·75	1
14	Fr	27	3	·27	20	·86	2
15	Sa	28	4	·35	21	·96	3
16	Su	29	5 [Sukla]	·43	...	...	4
17	Mo	30	6	·49	22	·04	5
		Dec.					
18	Tu	1	7	·54	23	·11	6
19	We	2	8	·55	24	·17	7
20	Th	3	9	·53	25	·19	8
21	Fr	4	10 [Margasira]	·51	26	·20	9
22	Sa	5	11	·47	27	·18	10
23	Su	6	12	·41	1	·15	11
24	Mo	7	13	·34	2	·12	12 [H. 1256 Shawwal.]
25	Tu	8	14	·26	3	·06	13
26	We	9	P	·16	4 5	·00 ·93 }	14
27	Th	10	{ 1 2	·06 ·96	6	·86	15
28	Fr	11	3	·86	7	·79	16
—29	Sa	12	4	·77	8	·73	17
1	Su	13	5	·69	9	·68	18
2	Mo	14	6	·63	10	·63	19
3	Tu	15	7 [Bahula]	·57	11	·60	20
4	We	16	8	·54	12	·59	21
5 [Sarvari Dhanus—Margali.]	Th	17	9	·52	13	·61	22
6	Fr	18	10	·53	14	·64	23
7	Sa	19	11	·56	15	·69	24
8	Su	20	12	·59	16	·75	25
9	Mo	21	13	·66	17	·84	26
10	Tu	22	14	·74	18	·95	27
11	We	23	—A	·83	...	...	28
12	Th	24	1	·92	19	·05	—29
13	Fr	25	... [Pausha Sukla]	...	20	·16	1 [Zi-l-ka'da.]
14	Sa	26	2	·00	21	·26	2
15	Su	27	3	·08	22	·35	3
16	Mo	28	4	·13	23	·43	4
17	Tu	29	5	·18	24	·48	5
18	We	30	6	·19	25	·51	6
19	Th	31	7	·18	26	·52	7

15. Svati. **16.** Visak. **17.** Anur. **18.** Jyesh. **19.** Mula. **20.** P. Ash. **21.** U. Ash. **22.** Sravn. **23.** Dani. **24.** Satab. **25.** P. Bhad. **26.** U. Bhad. **27.** Rev.

A. D. 1841.
Solar Eclipse. ●
Lunar Eclipse. ○

Mesha Sankranti (Commencement of Indian Sidereal Year).
(Surya Sid.) April 11·35.
(Arya Sid.) April 11·25.

Saka 1763. **Kaliyuga 4942.**
(S. Cycle) Plava.

Cyclic Sidereal Year, Month and Day.	Week-Day	English Month and Day.	Tithi	Ending Moment.	Nakshatra	Ending Moment.	Muhammadan Year, Month and Day.
SOLAR reckoning.			**LUNAR** reckoning.				
	Jan.						
Sarvari *Dhanus—Margali.* 20	Fr	1	*Suk.* 8	·16	27	·51	H. 1256 *Zi-l-ka'da.* 8
21	Sa	2	9	·11	1	·48	9
22	Su	3	10 11	·05 ·98	2	·45	10
23	Mo	4	**Pausha** 12	·90	3	·39	11
24	Tu	5	13	·81	4	·33	12
25	We	6	14	·71	5	·27	13
26	Th	7	P	·61	6	·20	14
27	Fr	8	1	·51	7	·13	15
28	Sa	9	2	·42	8	·07	16
29	Su	10	3	·34	9 10	·01 ·96	17
—30	Mo	11	4	·27	11	·93	18
Sarvari *Makara—Tai.* 1	Tu	12	*Bahula* 5	·21	12	·93	19
2	We	13	6	·19	13	·93	20
3	Th	14	7	·17	14	·95	21
4	Fr	15	8	·18	15	·99	22
5	Sa	16	9	·20	...	...	23
6	Su	17	10	·25	16	·06	24
7	Mo	18	11	·31	17	·15	25
8	Tu	19	12	·40	18	·25	26
9	We	20	13	·49	19	·35	27
10	Th	21	14	·58	20	·46	28
11	Fr	22	—A	·66	21	·56	29
12	Sa	23	*Sukla* 1	·73	22	·65	—30
13	Su	24	2	·79	23	·74	1
14	Mo	25	3	·82	24	·79	2
15	Tu	26	4	·83	25	·83	3
16	We	27	5	·83	26	·84	4
17	Th	28	6	·80	27	·84	5
18	Fr	29	7	·76	1	·82	6
19	Sa	30	8	·69	2	·78	7
20	Su	31	9	·62	3	·73	8
	Feb.						
21	Mo	1	**Magha** 10	·53	4	·67	H. 1256 *Zi-l-hijja.* 9
22	Tu	2	11	·43	5	·61	10
23	We	3	12	·33	6	·54	11
24	Th	4	13	·23	7	·47	12
25	Fr	5	14	·14	8	·41	13
26	Sa ○	6	P 1	·05 ·97	9	·35	14
27	Su	7	2	·90	10	·30	15
28	Mo	8	3	·85	11	·27	16
—29	Tu	9	4	·82	12	·25	17
Sarvari *Kumbha—Masi.* 1	We	10	*Bahula* 5	·80	13	·25	18
2	Th	11	6	·81	14	·27	19
3	Fr	12	7	·85	15	·30	20
4	Sa	13	8	·90	16	·37	21
5	Su	14	9	·95	17	·45	22
6	Mo	15	...	...	18	·55	23
7	Tu	16	10	·04	19	·65	24
8	We	17	11	·13	20	·75	25
9	Th	18	12	·21	21	·86	26
10	Fr	19	13	·29	22	·96	27
11	Sa	20	14	·36	...	...	28
12	Su	21	—A	·42	23	·04	29
13	Mo	22	**Phalg.** *Sukla* 1	·44	24	·10	—30
14	Tu	23	2	·46	25	·14	H. 1257 *Muharram.* 1
15	We	24	3	·45	26	·16	2
16	Th	25	4	·42	27	·17	3
17	Fr	26	5	·37	1	·15	4
18	Sa	27	6	·30	2	·12	5
19	Su	28	7	·23	3	·07	6

Cyclic Sidereal Year, Month and Day.	Week-Day	English Month and Day.	Tithi	Ending Moment.	Nakshatra	Ending Moment.	Muhammadan Year, Month and Day.
SOLAR reckoning.			**LUNAR** reckoning.				
	March						
Sarvari *Kumbha—Masi.* 20	Mo	1	*Suk.* 8	·14	4 5	·01 ·95	H. 1257 *Muharram.* 7
21	Tu	2	9 10	·05 ·95	6	·88	8
22	We	3	11	·85	7	·81	9
23	Th	4	**Phalguna** 12	·75	8	·74	10
24	Fr	5	13	·66	9	·68	11
25	Sa	6	14	·58	10	·64	12
26	Su	7	P	·50	11	·60	13
27	Mo	8	1	·46	12	·58	14
28	Tu	9	2	·43	13	·57	15
29	We	10	3	·42	14	·58	16
—30	Th	11	4	·42	15	·62	17
Sarvari *Mina—Panguni.* 1	Fr	12	5	·45	16	·68	18
2	Sa	13	*Bahula* 6	·50	17	·75	19
3	Su	14	7	·56	18	·84	20
4	Mo	15	8	·64	19	·95	21
5	Tu	16	9	·78	...	...	22
6	We	17	10	·82	20	·05	23
7	Th	18	11	·89	21	·16	24
8	Fr	19	12	·95	22	·26	25
9	Sa	20	...	...	23	·35	26
10	Su	21	13	·01	24	·41	27
11	Mo	22	14	·05	25	·46	28
12	Tu	23	—A	·06	26	·49	29
13	We	24	1	·04	27	·50	—30
14	Th	25	2 3	·01 ·96	1	·48	1
15	Fr	26	*Sukla* 4	·89	2	·45	2
16	Sa	27	5	·82	3	·40	3
17	Su	28	6	·72	4	·35	4
18	Mo	29	7	·62	5	·29	5
19	Tu	30	8	·52	6	·22	6
20	We	31	9	·42	7	·15	7
	April						
21	Th	1	10	·33	8	·08	H. 1257 *Safar.* 8
22	Fr	2	**Chaitra** 11	·24	9 10	·02 ·97	9
23	Sa	3	12	·16	11	·93	10
24	Su	4	13	·08	12	·90	11
25	Mo	5	14	·04	13	·89	12
26	Tu	6	P 1	·00 ·99	14	·90	13
27	We	7	2	·99	15	·94	14
28	Th	8	...	...	16	·99	15
29	Fr	9	3	·02	...	...	16
—30	Sa	10	4	·06	17	·06	17
Plava *Mesha—Chittirai.* 1	Su	11	5	·11	18	·15	18
2	Mo	12	*Bahula* 6	·20	19	·24	19
3	Tu	13	7	·29	20	·35	20
4	We	14	8	·38	21	·46	21
5	Th	15	9	·45	22	·57	22
6	Fr	16	10	·52	23	·65	23
7	Sa	17	11	·57	24	·72	24
8	Su	18	12	·60	25	·78	25
9	Mo	19	13	·61	26	·81	26
10	Tu	20	14	·59	27	·82	27
11	We	21	—A	·56	1	·81	28
12	Th	22	1	·51	2	·78	—29
13	Fr	23	2	·44	3	·75	*Rabi-ul-awwal.* 1
14	Sa	24	*Sukla* 3	·36	4	·69	2
15	Su	25	4	·27	5	·63	3
16	Mo	26	5	·17	6	·56	4
17	Tu	27	6 7	·07 ·97	7	·49	5
18	We	28	8	·87	8	·42	6
19	Th	29	9	·78	9	·36	7
20	Fr	30	**Vak.** 10	·69	10	·31	8

Cyclic Sidereal Year, Month and Day.	Week-Day	English Month and Day.	Tithi	Ending Moment.	Nakshatra	Ending Moment.	Muhammadan Year, Month and Day.
SOLAR reckoning.			**LUNAR** reckoning.				
	May						
Plava *Mesha—Chittirai.* 21	Sa	1	*Suk.* 11	·62	11	·26	H. 1257 *Rabi-ul-awwal.* 9
22	Su	2	12	·57	12	·23	10
23	Mo	3	13	·54	13	·21	11
24	Tu	4	**Vaisakha** 14	·52	14	·23	12
25	We	5	P	·52	15	·25	13
26	Th	6	1	·55	16	·30	14
27	Fr	7	2	·59	17	·36	15
28	Sa	8	3	·66	18	·45	16
29	Su	9	4	·73	19	·55	17
30	Mo	10	5	·81	20	·66	18
—31	Tu	11	6	·89	21	·77	19
Plava *Vrishabha—Vaikasi.* 1	We	12	*Bahula* 7	·98	22	·87	20
2	Th	13	...	...	23	·96	21
3	Fr	14	8	·04	...	...	22
4	Su	15	9	·09	24	·04	23
5	Su	16	10	·12	25	·09	24
6	Mo	17	11	·12	26	·13	25
7	Tu	18	12	·11	27	·14	26
8	We	19	13	·08	1	·13	27
9	Th	20	14 A	·04 ·96	2	·12	28
10	Fr	21	1	·87	3	·08	29
11	Sa	22	2	·78	4 5	·03 ·97	—30
12	Su	23	3	·68	6	·90	1
13	Mo	24	4	·58	7	·83	2
14	Tu	35	5	·48	8	·76	3
15	We	26	6	·38	9	·70	4
16	Th	27	*Sukla* 7	·28	10	·64	5
17	Fr	28	8	·20	11	·59	6
18	Sa	29	9	·13	12	·56	7
19	Su	30	10	·07	13	·55	8
20	Mo	31	11	·04	14	·55	9
	June						
21	Tu	1	**Jyeshtha** 12	·01	15	·57	H. 1257 *Rabi-ul-akhir.* 10
22	We	2	13	·02	16	·61	11
23	Th	3	14	·04	17	·67	12
24	Fr	4	P	·10	18	·76	13
25	Sa	5	1	·16	19	·85	14
26	Su	6	2	·23	20	·96	15
27	Mo	7	3	·31	...	...	16
28	Tu	8	4	·39	21	·06	17
29	We	9	5	·47	22	·17	18
30	Th	10	6	·53	23	·27	19
31	Fr	11	*Bahula* 7	·58	24	·35	20
—32	Sa	12	8	·60	25	·41	21
Plava *Mithuna—Ani.* 1	Su	13	9	·61	26	·44	22
2	Mo	14	10	·60	27	·46	23
3	Tu	15	11	·56	1	·46	24
4	We	16	12	·52	2	·45	25
5	Th	17	13	·45	3	·41	26
6	Fr	18	14	·37	4	·36	27
7	Sa	19	—A	·27	5	·30	28
8	Su	20	1	·17	6	·24	—29
9	Mo	21	2 3	·07 ·97	7	·18	H. 1257 *Jumadal-awwal.* 1
10	Tu	22	4	·87	8	·11	2
11	We	23	*Sukla* 5	·78	9 10	·04 ·98	3
12	Th	24	6	·70	11	·93	4
13	Fr	25	7	·62	12	·90	5
14	Sa	26	**Ashadha** 8	·56	13	·87	6
15	Su	27	9	·52	14	·87	7
16	Mo	28	10	·49	15	·88	8
17	Tu	29	11	·50	16	·92	9
18	We	30	12	·52	17	·99	10

Naksh :—1. Asvn. 2. Bhar. 3. Krit. 4 Rohi. 5. Mrig. 6. Ardh. 7. Punar 8. Push. 9. Aslesh. 10. Magh. 11. P. Phal. 12. U. Phal. 13. Hasta. 14. Chit.

A. D. 1841. | **Kollam 1017,** Commences { **N. Malabar—Sept.** / **S. Malabar—Aug.** | **Hijra 1257,** Commences, **Feb. 23.** | **Vikrama 1898.** **Bengal San 1247.** **(N. Cycle) Paridhavin.**

A.—Amavasya. P.—Paurnami.

Columns: SOLAR reckoning (Cyclic Sidereal Year, Month and Day; Week-Day; English Month and Day) — LUNAR reckoning (Tithi; Ending Moment; Nakshatra; Ending Moment; Muhammadan Year, Month and Day).

July

Solar: Plava *Mithuna—Ani*; Plava *Karkata—Adi*. Lunar: Ashadha *Suk.*; *Bahula*; *Sukla*. Muhammadan: H. 1257 *Jumadal-awval*.

Cyclic Sidereal	Week-Day	English	Tithi	Ending Moment	Nakshatra	Ending Moment	Muhammadan
19	Th	1	13	·57	...	...	11
20	Fr	2	14	·62	18	·06	12
21	Sa	3	P	·70	19	·15	13
22	Su	4	1	·78	20	·25	14
23	Mo	5	2	·86	21	·36	15
24	Tu	6	3	·94	22	·47	16
25	We	7	...	...	23	·57	17
26	Th	8	4	·00	24	·65	18
27	Fr	9	5	·05	25	·72	19
28	Sa	10	6	·08	26	·76	20
29	Su	11	7	·10	27	·78	21
30	Mo	12	8	·08	1	·79	22
31	Tu	13	9	·05	2	·78	23
1	We	14	10 / 11	·00 / ·93	3	·75	24
2	Th	15	12	·85	4	·70	25
3	Fr	16	13	·76	5	·64	26
4	Sa	17	14	·66	6	·58	27
5	Su	18	A	·56	7	·51	28
6	Mo	19	1	·46	8	·44	29
7	Tu	20	2	·35	9	·37	30
8	We	21	3	·25	10	·31	1
9	Th	22	4	·17	11	·27	2
10	Fr	23	5	·09	12	·23	3
11	Sa	24	6 / 7	·04 / ·99	13	·20	4
12	Su	25	8	·98	14	·19	5
13	Mo	26	9	·98	15	·20	6
14	Tu	27	...	...	16	·24	7
15	We	28	10	·00	17	·29	8
16	Th	29	11	·03	18	·36	9
17	Fr	30	12	·09	19	·45	10
18	Sa	31	13	·16	20	·55	11

Aug.

Solar: Plava *Simha—Avani*. Lunar: Sravana; *Bahula*; *Sukla*; Bhadrapada. Muhammadan: H. 1257 *Jumadal-akhir*; H. 1257 *Rajab*.

Cyclic Sidereal	Week-Day	English	Tithi	Ending Moment	Nakshatra	Ending Moment	Muhammadan
19	Su	1	14	·24	21	·66	12
20	Mo ○	2	P	·33	22	·77	13
21	Tu	3	1	·41	23	·87	14
22	We	4	2	·48	24	·96	15
23	Th	5	3	·52	...	...	16
24	Fr	6	4	·56	25	·03	17
25	Sa	7	5	·58	26	·07	18
26	Su	8	6	·56	27	·11	19
27	Mo	9	7	·53	1	·12	20
28	Tu	10	8	·48	2	·11	21
29	We	11	9	·43	3	·08	22
30	Th	12	10	·34	4 / 5	·04 / ·99	23
31	Fr	13	11	·25	6	·92	24
32	Sa	14	12	·15	7	·85	25
1	Su	15	13 / 14	·05 / ·95	8	·78	26
2	Mo	16	A	·85	9	·71	27
3	Tu	17	1	·76	10	·65	28
4	We	18	2	·67	11	·60	29
5	Th	19	3	·59	12	·56	1
6	Fr	20	4	·53	13	·53	2
7	Sa	21	5	·49	14	·51	3
8	Su	22	6	·46	15	·52	4
9	Mo	23	7	·47	16	·55	5
10	Tu	24	8	·49	17	·60	6
11	We	25	9	·53	18	·67	7
12	Th	26	10	·60	19	·75	8
13	Fr	27	11	·67	20	·85	9
14	Sa	28	12	·74	21	·96	10
15	Su	29	13	·83	...	...	11
16	Mo	30	14	·91	22	·07	12
17	Tu	31	P	·98	23	·17	13

Sep.

Solar: Plava *Simha—Avani*; Plava *Kanya—Purattasi*. Lunar: Bhadra.; *Bahula*; *Sukla*; Asvina. Muhammadan: H. 1257 *Rajab*; *Shaban*.

Cyclic Sidereal	Week-Day	English	Tithi	Ending Moment	Nakshatra	Ending Moment	Muhammadan
18	We	1	...	...	24	·26	14
19	Th	2	1	·03	25	·33	15
20	Fr	3	2	·07	26	·40	16
21	Sa	4	3	·09	27	·43	17
22	Su	5	4	·07	1	·44	18
23	Mo	6	5	·05	2	·43	19
24	Tu	7	6 / 7	·01 / ·94	3	·41	20
25	We	8	8	·86	4	·38	21
26	Th	9	9	·77	5	·32	22
27	Fr	10	10	·67	6	·26	23
28	Sa	11	11	·57	7	·19	24
29	Su	12	12	·47	8	·12	25
30	Mo	13	13	·37	9 / 10	·05 / ·99	26
31	Tu	14	14	·28	11	·94	27
1	We	15	A	·19	12	·89	28
2	Th	16	1	·13	13	·85	29
3	Fr	17	2	·07	14	·84	30
4	Sa	18	3	·03	15	·85	1
5	Su	19	4 / 5	·00 / ·99	16	·87	2
6	Mo	20	...	...	17	·91	3
7	Tu	21	6	·02	18	·97	4
8	We	22	7	·06	...	...	5
9	Th	23	8	·12	19	·05	6
10	Fr	24	9	·19	20	·15	7
11	Sa	25	10	·28	21	·26	8
12	Su	26	11	·36	22	·37	9
13	Mo	27	12	·44	23	·47	10
14	Tu	28	13	·52	24	·56	11
15	We	29	14	·57	25	·65	12
16	Th	30	P	·61	26	·71	13

Oct.

Solar: Plava *Tula—Aippasi*. Lunar: Adhika; *Bahula*; *Sukla*; Nija Asvina. Muhammadan: H. 1257; H. 1257 *Ramzan*.

Cyclic Sidereal	Week-Day	English	Tithi	Ending Moment	Nakshatra	Ending Moment	Muhammadan
17	Fr	1	1	·63	27	·75	14
18	Sa	2	2	·62	1	·76	15
19	Su	3	3	·60	2	·76	16
20	Mo	4	4	·57	3	·75	17
21	Tu	5	5	·49	4	·71	18
22	We	6	6	·40	5	·66	19
23	Th	7	7	·31	6	·60	20
24	Fr	8	8	·22	7	·53	21
25	Sa	9	9	·13	8	·46	22
26	Su	10	10 / 11	·03 / ·93	9	·39	23
27	Mo	11	12	·84	10	·33	24
28	Tu	12	13	·75	11	·27	25
29	We	13	14	·69	12	·22	26
30	Th	14	A	·63	13	·18	27
1	Fr	15	1	·59	14	·17	28
2	Sa	16	2	·57	15	·17	29
3	Su	17	3	·58	16	·18	1
4	Mo	18	4	·59	17	·22	2
5	Tu	19	5	·63	18	·28	3
6	We	20	6	·69	19	·37	4
7	Th	21	7	·77	20	·46	5
8	Fr	22	8	·85	21	·56	6
9	Sa	23	9	·94	22	·67	7
10	Su	24	...	...	23	·78	8
11	Mo	25	10	·03	24	·88	9
12	Tu	26	11	·10	25	·96	10
13	We	27	12	·16	...	...	11
14	Th	28	13	·19	26	·02	12
15	Fr	29	14	·21	27	·06	13
16	Sa	30	P	·20	1	·08	14
17	Su	31	1	·18	2	·09	15

Nov.

Solar: Plava *Tula—Aippasi*; Plava *Vrischika—Kartigai*. Lunar: Nija Asv.; *Bahula*; *Sukla*; Karttika. Muhammadan: H. 1257 *Ramzan*; *Shawwal*.

Cyclic Sidereal	Week-Day	English	Tithi	Ending Moment	Nakshatra	Ending Moment	Muhammadan
18	Mo	1	2	·15	3	·08	16
19	Tu	2	3	·08	4 / 5	·04 / ·99	17
20	We	3	4 / 5	·00 / ·91	6	·93	18
21	Th	4	6	·82	7	·87	19
22	Fr	5	7	·72	8	·81	20
23	Sa	6	8	·62	9	·74	21
24	Su	7	9	·52	10	·67	22
25	Mo	8	10	·43	11	·61	23
26	Tu	9	11	·35	12	·55	24
27	We	10	12	·28	13	·52	25
28	Th	11	13	·22	14	·50	26
29	Fr	12	14	·19	15	·49	27
30	Sa	13	A	·17	16	·50	28
1	Su	14	1	·18	17	·53	29
2	Mo	15	2	·20	18	·60	30
3	Tu	16	3	·25	19	·67	1
4	We	17	4	·31	20	·76	2
5	Th	18	5	·39	21	·86	3
6	Fr	19	6	·48	22	·97	4
7	Sa	20	7	·56	...	...	5
8	Su	21	8	·64	23	·08	6
9	Mo	22	9	·71	24	·18	7
10	Tu	23	10	·78	25	·26	8
11	We	24	11	·82	26	·33	9
12	Th	25	12	·84	27	·38	10
13	Fr	26	13	·82	1	·40	11
14	Sa	27	14	·80	2	·42	12
15	Su	28	P	·76	3	·40	13
16	Mo	29	1	·69	4	·37	14
17	Tu	30	2	·62	5	·33	15

Dec.

Solar: Plava *Dhanus—Margali*. Lunar: *Bahula*; *Sukla*; Margasira; *Bahula*. Muhammadan: H. 1257; H. 1257 *Zi-l-ka'da*.

Cyclic Sidereal	Week-Day	English	Tithi	Ending Moment	Nakshatra	Ending Moment	Muhammadan
18	We	1	3	·54	6	·28	16
19	Th	2	4	·44	7	·22	17
20	Fr	3	5	·34	8	·15	18
21	Sa	4	6	·24	9	·08	19
22	Su	5	7	·15	10 / 11	·01 / ·95	20
23	Mo	6	8 / 9	·06 / ·97	12	·90	21
24	Tu	7	10	·91	13	·85	22
25	We	8	11	·86	14	·82	23
26	Th	9	12	·82	15	·81	24
27	Fr	10	13	·81	16	·82	25
28	Sa	11	14	·82	17	·86	26
29	Su	12	A	·84	18	·91	27
30	Mo	13	1	·89	19	·97	28
1	Tu	14	2	·96	...	...	29
2	We	15	...	...	20	·06	1
3	Th	16	3	·04	21	·16	2
4	Fr	17	4	·13	22	·27	3
5	Sa	18	5	·23	23	·38	4
6	Su	19	6	·30	24	·48	5
7	Mo	20	7	·36	25	·57	6
8	Tu	21	8	·42	26	·64	7
9	We	22	9	·46	27	·69	8
10	Th	23	10	·48	1	·73	9
11	Fr	24	11	·47	2	·74	10
12	Sa	25	12	·45	3	·73	11
13	Su	26	13	·40	4	·70	12
14	Mo	27	14	·34	5	·66	13
15	Tu	28	P	·26	6	·62	14
16	We	29	1	·17	7	·55	15
17	Th	30	2 / 3	·08 / ·98	8	·48	16
18	Fr	31	4	·88	9	·41	17

15. Svati. 16. Visak. 17. Anur. 18. Jyesh. 19. Mula. 20. P. Ash. 21. U. Ash. 22. Sravn. 23 Dani. 24. Satab. 25. P. Bhad. 26. U. Bhad. 27. Rev.

A. D. 1842. **Mesha Sankranti** (Commencement of Indian Sidereal Year). **(Surya Sid.) April 11·61.** **(Arya Sid.) April 11·51.** **Saka 1764.** **Kaliyuga 4943.** **(S. Cycle) Subhakrit.**

Solar Eclipse. ●
Lunar Eclipse. ○

Jan.

Solar: Cyclic Sidereal Year, Month and Day	Week-Day	English Month and Day	Lunar month / Paksha	Tithi	Ending Moment	Nakshatra	Ending Moment	Muhammadan Year, Month and Day
Plava Dhanus—Margali 19	Sa	1	Marg. Bahula	5	·79	10	·34	H. 1257 Zi-l-ka'da 18
20	Su	2		6	·70	11	·28	19
21	Mo	3		7	·61	12	·23	20
22	Tu	4		8	·55	13	·18	21
23	We	5		9	·50	14	·15	22
24	Th	6		10	·46	15	·14	23
25	Fr	7		11	·45	16	·15	24
26	Sa	8		12	·46	17	·17	25
27	Su	9		13	·49	18	·21	26
28	Mo	10		14	·54	19	·28	27
29	Tu	11		A	·60	20	·36	28
Plava Makara—Tai 1	We	12	Sukla	1	·68	21	·46	29
2	Th	13		2	·78	22	·57	30
3	Fr	14		3	·87	23	·68	H. 1257 Zi-l-hijja 1
4	Sa	15		4	·95	24	·78	2
5	Su	16		...	...	25	·87	3
6	Mo	17		5	·02	26	·95	4
7	Tu	18		6	·07	...	...	5
8	We	19		7	·11	27	·01	6
9	Th	20		8	·12	1	·05	7
10	Fr	21		9	·11	2	·06	8
11	Sa	22		10	·09	3	·06	9
12	Su	23		11 12	·03 ·97	4	·03	10
13	Mo	24		13	·89	5 6	·00 ·95	11
14	Tu	25	Pausha	14	·81	7	·89	12
15	We ○	26		P	·71	8	·82	13
16	Th	27		1	·61	9	·75	14
17	Fr	28		2	·51	10	·69	15
18	Sa	29		3	·42	11	·63	16
19	Su	30		4	·33	12	·57	17
20	Mo	31		5	·25	13	·52	18

Feb.

Solar: Cyclic Sidereal Year, Month and Day	Week-Day	English Month and Day	Lunar month / Paksha	Tithi	Ending Moment	Nakshatra	Ending Moment	Muhammadan Year, Month and Day
Plava Kumbha—Masi 21	Tu	1	Bahula	6	·19	14	·48	19
22	We	2		7	·14	15	·47	20
23	Th	3		8	·10	16	·47	21
24	Fr	4		9	·10	17	·49	22
25	Sa	5		10	·11	18	·52	23
26	Su	6		11	·14	19	·58	24
27	Mo	7		12	·18	20	·66	25
28	Tu	8		13	·25	21	·77	26
29	We	9		14	·33	22	·87	27
1	Th	10		A	·43	23	·98	28
2	Fr	11	Sukla	1	·51	...	...	29
3	Sa	12		2	·59	24	·08	H. 1258 Muharram 1
4	Su	13		3	·66	25	·17	2
5	Mo	14		4	·71	26	·26	3
6	Tu	15		5	·74	27	·32	4
7	We	16		6	·75	1	·36	5
8	Th	17		7	·75	2	·38	6
9	Fr	18		8	·72	3	·38	7
10	Sa	19		9	·66	4	·37	8
11	Su	20		10	·59	5	·34	9
12	Mo	21	Magha	11	·51	6	·29	10
13	Tu	22		12	·43	7	·23	11
14	We	23		13	·34	8	·17	12
15	Th	24		14	·24	9	·10	13
16	Fr	25		P	·14	10 11	·03 ·96	14
17	Sa	26	Bah.	1 2	·04 ·95	12	·90	15
18	Su	27		3	·87	13	·85	16
19	Mo	28		4	·81	14	·81	17

March

Solar: Cyclic Sidereal Year, Month and Day	Week-Day	English Month and Day	Lunar month / Paksha	Tithi	Ending Moment	Nakshatra	Ending Moment	Muhammadan Year, Month and Day
Plava Kumbha—Masi 20	Tu	1	Magha Bahula	5	·76	15	·80	H. 1258 Muharram 18
21	We	2		6	·73	16	·79	19
22	Th	3		7	·71	17	·80	20
23	Fr	4		8	·72	18	·84	21
24	Sa	5		9	·75	19	·89	22
25	Su	6		10	·79	20	·98	23
26	Mo	7		11	·86	...	...	24
27	Tu	8		12	·96	21	·07	25
28	We	9		...	...	22	·17	26
29	Th	10		13	·05	23	·27	27
30	Fr	11		14	·13	24	·38	28
Plava Mina—Panguni 1	Sa	12		A	·21	25	·48	29
2	Su	13	Sukla	1	·27	26	·57	30
3	Mo	14		2	·31	27	·63	H. 1258 Safar 1
4	Tu	15		3	·35	1	·68	2
5	We	16		4	·35	2	·70	3
6	Th	17		5	·34	3	·72	4
7	Fr	18		6	·30	4	·70	5
8	Sa	19		7	·25	5	·67	6
9	Su	20		8	·19	6	·62	7
10	Mo	21		9	·12	7	·56	8
11	Tu	22		10 11	·03 ·93	8	·50	9
12	We	23	Phalguna	12	·82	9	·44	10
13	Th	24		13	·72	10	·37	11
14	Fr	25		14	·63	11	·30	12
15	Sa	26		P	·54	12	·24	13
16	Su	27		1	·46	13	·18	14
17	Mo	28		2	·39	14	·15	15
18	Tu	29		3	·34	15	·12	16
19	We	30		4	·31	16	·11	17
20	Th	31		5	·29	17	·12	18

April

Solar: Cyclic Sidereal Year, Month and Day	Week-Day	English Month and Day	Lunar month / Paksha	Tithi	Ending Moment	Nakshatra	Ending Moment	Muhammadan Year, Month and Day
Plava Mina—Panguni 21	Fr	1	Bahula	6	·30	18	·15	H. 1258 Safar 19
22	Sa	2		7	·33	19	·21	20
23	Su	3		8	·38	20	·28	21
24	Mo	4		9	·45	21	·37	22
25	Tu	5		10	·53	22	·47	23
26	We	6		11	·62	23	·57	24
27	Th	7		12	·70	24	·68	25
28	Fr	8		13	·78	25	·78	26
29	Sa	9		14	·84	26	·87	27
30	Su	10		A	·88	27	·94	28
31	Mo	11	Sukla	1	·91	1	·99	29
Subhakrit Mesha—Chittirai 1	Tu	12		2	·92	...	...	H. 1258 Rabi-ul-awwal 1
2	We	13		3	·90	2	·03	2
3	Th	14		4	·86	3	·04	3
4	Fr	15		5	·81	4	·03	4
5	Sa	16		6	·74	5 6	·00 ·96	5
6	Su	17	Chaitra	7	·67	7	·90	6
7	Mo	18		8	·58	8	·84	7
8	Tu	19		9	·48	9	·78	8
9	We	20		10	·38	10	·71	9
10	Th	21		11	·28	11	·64	10
11	Fr	22		12	·18	12	·58	11
12	Sa	23		13	·08	13	·53	12
13	Su	24		14 P	·00 ·94	14	·48	13
14	Mo	25	Bahula	1	·89	15	·45	14
15	Tu	26		2	·85	16	·43	15
16	We	27		3	·83	17	·44	16
17	Th	28		4	·84	18	·47	17
18	Fr	29		5	·86	19	·52	18
19	Sa	30		6	·91	20	·58	19

May

Solar: Cyclic Sidereal Year, Month and Day	Week-Day	English Month and Day	Lunar month / Paksha	Tithi	Ending Moment	Nakshatra	Ending Moment	Muhammadan Year, Month and Day
Subhakrit Mesha—Chittirai 20	Su	1	Chait. Bahula	7	·97	21	·67	H. 1258 Rabi-ul-awwal 20
21	Mo	2		...	...	22	·77	21
22	Tu	3		8	·06	23	·88	22
23	We	4		9	·15	24	·99	23
24	Th	5		10	·23	...	...	24
25	Fr	6		11	·30	25	·09	25
26	Sa	7		12	·36	26	·18	26
27	Su	8		13	·41	27	·25	27
28	Mo	9		14	·43	1	·30	28
29	Tu	10		A	·45	2	·35	29
30	We	11	Sukla	1	·43	3	·36	30
Subhakrit Vrishabha—Vaikasi 1	Th	12		2	·40	4	·35	H. 1258 Rabi-ul-akhir 1
2	Fr	13		3	·33	5	·33	2
3	Sa	14		4	·26	6	·29	3
4	Su	15		5	·19	7	·25	4
5	Mo	16		6 7	·09 ·99	8	·19	5
6	Tu	17		8	·89	9	·12	6
7	We	18		9	·79	10 11	·05 ·98	7
8	Th	19		10	·69	12	·92	8
9	Fr	20		11	·60	13	·86	9
10	Sa	21	Vaisakha	12	·51	14	·81	10
11	Su	22		13	·45	15	·78	11
12	Mo	23		14	·40	16	·76	12
13	Tu	24		P	·36	17	·77	13
14	We	25		1	·34	18	·79	14
15	Th	26		2	·34	19	·83	15
16	Fr	27		3	·37	20	·89	16
17	Sa	28		4	·42	21	·97	17
18	Su	29		5	·48	...	...	18
19	Mo	30		6	·56	22	·07	19
20	Tu	31		7	·64	23	·18	20

June

Solar: Cyclic Sidereal Year, Month and Day	Week-Day	English Month and Day	Lunar month / Paksha	Tithi	Ending Moment	Nakshatra	Ending Moment	Muhammadan Year, Month and Day
Subhakrit Vrishabha—Vaikasi 21	We	1	Bahula	8	·72	24	·29	H. 1258 Rabi-ul-akhir 21
22	Th	2		9	·80	25	·39	22
23	Fr	3		10	·87	26	·48	23
24	Sa	4		11	·90	27	·56	24
25	Su	5		12	·92	1	·63	25
26	Mo	6		13	·94	2	·66	26
27	Tu	7		14	·92	3	·68	27
28	We	8		A	·90	4	·68	28
29	Th	9		1	·84	5	·66	29
30	Fr	10		2	·77	6	·63	H. 1258 Jumadal-awwal 1
31	Sa	11		3	·69	7	·58	2
32	Su	12		4	·59	8	·52	3
Subhakrit Mithuna—Ani 1	Mo	13	Sukla	5	·49	9	·46	4
2	Tu	14		6	·39	10	·39	5
3	We	15		7	·29	11	·32	6
4	Th	16		8	·19	12	·26	7
5	Fr	17		9	·10	13	·20	8
6	Sa	18		10 11	·01 ·94	14	·14	9
7	Su	19	Jyeshtha	12	·88	15	·11	10
8	Mo	20		13	·84	16	·09	11
9	Tu	21		14	·82	17	·09	12
10	We	22		P	·82	18	·10	13
11	Th	23		1	·85	19	·14	14
12	Fr	24		2	·89	20	·20	15
13	Sa	25		3	·96	21	·27	16
14	Su	26		...	...	22	·37	17
15	Mo	27	Bahula	4	·03	23	·47	18
16	Tu	28		5	·10	24	·58	19
17	We	29		6	·19	25	·69	20
18	Th	30		7	·27	26	·78	21

Naksh :—1. Asvn, 2. Bhar. 3. Krit. 4. Rohi. 5. Mrig. 6. Ardh. 7. Punar. 8. Push. 9. Aslesh. 10. Magh. 11. P. Phal. 12. U. Phal. 13. Hasta. 14. Chit.

A. D. 1842.
A.—Amavasya. P.—Paurnami. **Kollam 1018,** Commences { **N. Malabar—Sept. S. Malabar—Aug.** **Hijra 1258,** Commences, **Feb. 12.** **Vikrama 1899. Bengal San 1248. (N. Cycle) Pramadin.**

Solar month	Cyclic Sidereal Year, Month and Day.	Week-Day	English Month and Day.	Lunar month	Tithi	Ending Moment.	Nakshatra	Ending Moment.	Muhammadan Year, Month and Day.	Muhammadan month
		July								
Subhakrit *Mithuna—Ani.*	19	Fr	1	Jyesh. Bah.	8	·34	27	·87	22	*Jumadal-awwal.*
	20	Sa	2		9	·38	1	·94	23	
	21	Su	3		10	·41	2	·98	24	
	22	Mo	4		11	·42	...	...	25	
	23	Tu	5		12	·40	3	·00	26	
	24	We	6		13	·37	4	·01	27	
	25	Th	7		14	·31	5 6	·00 ·96	28	
	26	Fr ●	8		—A	·24	7	·92	29	
	27	Sa	9	Sukla	1	·16	8	·86	—30	
	28	Su	10		2 3	·07 ·97	9	·80	1	
	29	Mo	11		4	·87	10	·73	2	
	30	Tu	12		5	·77	11	·66	3	
	—31	We	13		6	·67	12	·59	4	
Subhakrit *Karkata—Adi.*	1	Th	14	Ashadha	7	·58	13	·53	5	H. 1258 *Jumadal-akhir.*
	2	Fr	15		8	·49	14	·48	6	
	3	Sa	16		9	·42	15	·45	7	
	4	Su	17		10	·36	16	·42	8	
	5	Mo	18		11	·32	17	·41	9	
	6	Tu	19		12	·30	18	·42	10	
	7	We	20		13	·30	19	·45	11	
	8	Th	21		14	·33	20	·50	12	
	9	Fr ○	22		P	·36	21	·58	13	
	10	Sa	23	Bahula	1	·43	22	·67	14	
	11	Su	24		2	·50	23	·77	15	
	12	Mo	25		3	·58	24	·88	16	
	13	Tu	26		4	·66	25	·99	17	
	14	We	27		5	·75	...	...	18	
	15	Th	28		6	·81	26	·09	19	
	16	Fr	29		7	·85	27	·18	20	
	17	Sa	30		8	·89	1	·25	21	
	18	Su	31		9	·90	2	·29	22	
		Aug.								
	19	Mo	1		10	·88	3	·32	23	
	20	Tu	2		11	·85	4	·34	24	
	21	We	3		12	·80	5	·32	25	
	22	Th	4		13	·74	6	·30	26	
	23	Fr	5		14	·65	7	·25	27	
	24	Sa	6		—A	·56	8	·20	28	
	25	Su	7	Sukla	1	·46	9	·14	—29	
	26	Mo	8		2	·36	10	·07	1	
	27	Tu	9		3	·26	11 12	·00 ·93	2	
	28	We	10		4	·16	13	·87	3	
	29	Th	11		5 6	·07 ·98	14	·81	4	
	30	Fr	12		7	·91	15	·78	5	
	31	Sa	13		8	·84	16	·75	6	
	—32	Su	14		9	·81	17	·73	7	
Subhakrit *Simha—Avani.*	1	Mo	15	Sravana	10	·79	18	·74	8	H. 1258 *Rajab.*
	2	Tu	16		11	·80	19	·77	9	
	3	We	17		12	·81	20	·82	10	
	4	Th	18		13	·86	21	·89	11	
	5	Fr	19		14	·92	22	·97	12	
	6	Sa	20		P	·99	...	...	13	
	7	Su	21	Bahula	...	...	23	·07	14	
	8	Mo	22		1	·08	24	·18	15	
	9	Tu	23		2	·16	25	·29	16	
	10	We	24		3	·24	26	·39	17	
	11	Th	25		4	·30	27	·48	18	
	12	Fr	26		5	·36	1	·55	19	
	13	Sa	27		6	·38	2	·61	20	
	14	Su	28		7	·40	3	·65	21	
	15	Mo	29		8	·39	4	·66	22	
	16	Tu	30		9	·35	5	·65	23	
	17	We	31		10	·31	6	·63	24	

Solar month	Cyclic Sidereal Year, Month and Day.	Week-Day	English Month and Day.	Lunar month	Tithi	Ending Moment.	Nakshatra	Ending Moment.	Muhammadan Year, Month and Day.	Muhammadan month
		Sep.								
Subhakrit *Simha—Avani.*	18	Th	1		11	·24	7	·59	25	*Rajab.*
	19	Fr	2		12	·17	8	·54	26	
	20	Sa	3		13 14	·08 ·98	9	·46	27	
	21	Su	4		—A	·88	10	·41	28	
	22	Mo	5	Sukla	1	·78	11	·34	29	
	23	Tu	6		2	·68	12	·27	—30	
	24	We	7		3	·58	13	·21	1	
	25	Th	8		4	·50	14	·16	2	
	26	Fr	9		5	·43	15	·11	3	
	27	Sa	10		6	·38	16	·07	4	
	28	Su	11		7	·33	17	06	5	
	29	Mo	12		8	·31	18	·05	6	
	30	Tu	13		9	·32	19	·09	7	
	—31	We	14		10	·33	20	·13	8	
Subhakrit *Kanya—Purattasi.*	1	Th	15	Bhadrapada	11	·33	21	·19	9	H. 1258 *Shaban.*
	2	Fr	16		12	·44	22	·27	10	
	3	Sa	17		13	·52	23	·37	11	
	4	Su	18		14	·62	24	·48	12	
	5	Mo	19		P	·69	25	·59	13	
	6	Tu	20	Bahula	1	·76	26	·69	14	
	7	We	21		2	·83	27	·78	15	
	8	Th	22		3	·89	1	·86	16	
	9	Fr	23		4	·93	2	·93	17	
	10	Sa	24		5	·93	3	·97	18	
	11	Su	25		6	·92	4	·98	19	
	12	Mo	26		7	·90	5	·98	20	
	13	Tu	27		8	·85	6	·96	21	
	14	We	28		9	·78	7	·92	22	
	15	Th	29		10	·71	8	·88	23	
	16	Fr	30		11	·62	9	·82	24	
		Oct.								
	17	Sa	1		12	·52	10	·75	25	
	18	Su	2		13	·42	11	·68	26	
	19	Mo	3		14	·32	12	·61	27	
	20	Tu	4		—A	·22	13	·55	28	
	21	We	5	Sukla	1	·12	14	·49	—29	
	22	Th	6		2 3	·05 ·98	15	·44	1	
	23	Fr	7		4	·93	16	·40	2	
	24	Sa	8		5	·88	17	·38	3	
	25	Su	9		6	·87	18	·39	4	
	26	Mo	10		7	·88	19	·40	5	
	27	Tu	11		8	·90	20	·44	6	
	28	We	12		9	·95	21	·50	7	
	29	Th	13		...	...	22	·58	8	
	—30	Fr	14		10	·00	23	·68	9	
Subhakrit *Tula—Aippasi.*	1	Sa	15	Asvina	11	·08	24	·78	10	H. 1258 *Ramzan.*
	2	Su	16		12	·18	25	·89	11	
	3	Mo	17		13	·26	26	·99	12	
	4	Tu	18		14	·33	...	...	13	
	5	We	19		P	·40	27	·09	14	
	6	Th	20	Bahula	1	·46	1	·17	15	
	7	Fr	21		2	·49	2	·24	16	
	8	Sa	22		3	·52	3	·28	17	
	9	Su	23		4	·50	4	·30	18	
	10	Mo	24		5	·48	5	·30	19	
	11	Tu	25		6	·43	6	·28	20	
	12	We	26		7	·37	7	·26	21	
	13	Th	27		8	·29	8	·21	22	
	14	Fr	28		9	·20	9	·15	23	
	15	Sa	29		10	·11	10	·09	24	
	16	Su	30		11 12	·01 ·91	11 12	·03 ·96	25	
	17	Mo	31		13	·81	13	·89	26	

Solar month	Cyclic Sidereal Year, Month and Day.	Week-Day	English Month and Day.	Lunar month	Tithi	Ending Moment.	Nakshatra	Ending Moment.	Muhammadan Year, Month and Day.	Muhammadan month
		Nov.								
Subhakrit *Tula—Aippasi.*	18	Tu	1		14	·72	14	·83	27	
	19	We	2		—A	·64	15	·77	28	
	20	Th	3	Sukla	1	·57	16	·73	29	
	21	Fr	4		2	·52	17	·72	—30	
	22	Sa	5		3	·48	18	·71	1	
	23	Su	6		4	·47	19	·72	2	
	24	Mo	7		5	·47	20	·75	3	
	25	Tu	8		6	·49	21	·81	4	
	26	We	9		7	·54	22	·89	5	
	27	Th	10		8	·61	23	·98	6	
	28	Fr	11		9	·69	...	...	7	
	29	Sa	12		10	·77	24	·08	8	
	—30	Su	13		11	·86	25	·19	9	
Subhakrit *Vrischika—Kartigai.*	1	Mo	14	Karttika	12	·94	26	·29	10	H. 1258 *Shawwal.*
	2	Tu	15		...	...	27	·39	11	
	3	We	16		13	·02	1	·48	12	
	4	Th	17		14	·07	2	·55	13	
	5	Fr	18		P	·11	3	·60	14	
	6	Sa	19	Bahula	1	·12	4	·62	15	
	7	Su	20		2	·11	5	·63	16	
	8	Mo	21		3	·09	6	·62	17	
	9	Tu	22		4 5	·04 ·98	7	·59	18	
	10	We	23		6	·91	8	·55	19	
	11	Th	24		7	·82	9	·49	20	
	12	Fr	25		8	·73	10	·43	21	
	13	Sa	26		9	·63	11	·37	22	
	14	Su	27		10	·53	12	·30	23	
	15	Mo	28		11	·43	13	·23	24	
	16	Tu	29		12	·34	14	·16	25	
	17	We	30		13	·26	15	·11	26	
		Dec.								
	18	Th	1		14	·19	16	·07	27	
	19	Fr	2		—A	·14	17	·04	28	
	20	Sa	3	Sukla	1	·11	18	·03	—29	
	21	Su	4		2	·09	19	·04	1	
	22	Mo	5		3	·10	20	·07	2	
	23	Tu	6		4	·14	21	·12	3	
	24	We	7		5	·18	22	·19	4	
	25	Th	8		6	·25	23	·28	5	
	26	Fr	9		7	·32	24	·38	6	
	27	Sa	10		8	·40	25	·48	7	
	28	Su	11		9	·49	26	·59	8	
	29	Mo	12		10	·59	27	·70	9	
	—30	Tu	13		11	·66	1	·79	10	
Subhakrit *Dhanus—Margali.*	1	We	14	Margasira	12	·71	2	·86	11	H. 1258 *Zi-l-ka'da.*
	2	Th	15		13	·75	3	·91	12	
	3	Fr	16		14	·76	4	·94	13	
	4	Sa	17		P	·75	5	·96	14	
	5	Su	18	Bahula	1	·73	6	·95	15	
	6	Mo	19		2	·68	7	·92	16	
	7	Tu	20		3	·61	8	·88	17	
	8	We	21		4	·53	9	·83	18	
	9	Th	22		5	·45	10	·77	19	
	10	Fr	23		6	·35	11	·70	20	
	11	Sa	24		7	·25	12	·63	21	
	12	Su	25		8	·16	13	·56	22	
	13	Mo	26		9 10	·07 ·98	14	·50	23	
	14	Tu	27		11	·90	15	·45	24	
	15	We	28		12	·83	16	·40	25	
	16	Th	29		13	·78	17	·37	26	
	17	Fr	30		14	·76	18	·36	27	
	18	Sa	31		—A	·74	19	·36	28	

15. Svati. 16. Visak. 17. Anur. 18. Jyesh. 19. Mula. 20. P. Ash. 21. U. Ash. 22. Sravn. 23. Dani. 24. Satab. 25. P. Bhad. 26. U. Bhad. 27. Rev.

A. D. 1843.
Solar Eclipse. ●
Lunar Eclipse. ○

Mesha Sankranti (Commencement of Indian Sidereal Year).
(Surya Sid.) April 11·87.
(Arya Sid.) April 11·77.

Saka 1765. **Kaliyuga 4944.**
(S. Cycle) Sobhana (Sobhakrit.)

SOLAR reckoning: Year, Month	Cyclic Sidereal Day	Week-Day	English Month and Day	LUNAR reckoning: Month / Paksha	Tithi	Ending Moment	Nakshatra	Ending Moment	Muhammadan Year, Month	Muhammadan Day
			Jan.							
Subhakrit Dhanu—Margali.	19	Su	1		1	·75	20	·38		29
	20	Mo	2		2	·78	21	·43		—30
	21	Tu	3		3	·83	22	·50		1
	22	We	4		4	·90	23	·58		2
	23	Th	5		5	·97	24	·68		3
	24	Fr	6		...	...	25	·79		4
	25	Sa	7	Sukla	6	·07	26	·90		5
	26	Su	8		7	·16	...	...		6
	27	Mo	9		8	·24	27	·00		7
	28	Tu	10		9	·31	1	·09		8
	—29	We	11		10	·37	2	·17		9
	1	Th	12		11	·39	3	·22		10
	2	Fr	13		12	·40	4	·27		11
	3	Sa	14		13	·40	5	·28	H. 1258 Zi-l-hijja.	12
	4	Su	15		14	·37	6	·28		13
	5	Mo	16	Pausha	P	·32	7	·25		14
	6	Tu	17		1	·25	8	·21		15
	7	We	18		2	·18	9	·17		16
	8	Th	19		3 4	·09 ·99	10	·11		17
	9	Fr	20		5	·89	11 12	·04 ·97		18
	10	Sa	21	Bahula	6	·79	13	·90		19
	11	Su	22		7	·70	14	·84		20
	12	Mo	23		8	·61	15	·79		21
	13	Tu	24		9	·54	16	·74		22
Subhakrit Makara—Tai.	14	We	25		10	·47	17	·70		23
	15	Th	26		11	·42	18	·68		24
	16	Fr	27		12	·40	19	·68		25
	17	Sa	28		13	·38	20	·71		26
	18	Su	29		14	·39	21	·75		27
	19	Mo	30		—A	·42	22	·80		28
	20	Tu	31		1	·48	23	·88		—29
			Feb.							
	21	We	1		2	·55	24	·98		1
	22	Th	2		3	·63	...	...		2
	23	Fr	3		4	·72	25	·09		3
	24	Sa	4		5	·81	26	·20		4
	25	Su	5		6	·89	27	·30		5
	26	Mo	6		7	·95	1	·39		6
	27	Tu	7	Sukla	...	...	2	·47		7
	28	We	8		8	·01	3	·54		8
	29	Th	9		9	·03	4	·58		9
	—30	Fr	10		10	·05	5	·60		10
	1	Sa	11		11	·03	6	·60		11
	2	Su	12		12 13	·00 ·94	7	·58		12
	3	Mo	13		14	·88	8	·56	H. 1259 Muharram.	13
	4	Tu	14	Magha	P	·80	9	·51		14
	5	We	15		1	·71	10	·45		15
Subhakrit Kumbha—Mari.	6	Th	16		2	·62	11	·38		16
	7	Fr	17		3	·53	12	·31		17
	8	Sa	18		4	·43	13	·24		18
	9	Su	19		5	·33	14	·18		19
	10	Mo	20	Bahula	6	·23	15	·12		20
	11	Tu	21		7	·15	16	·07		21
	12	We	22		8	·08	17	·03		22
	13	Th	23		9	·05	18	·01		23
	14	Fr	24		10	·02	19	·01		24
	15	Sa	25		11	·01	20	·02		25
	16	Su	26		12	·01	21	·06		26
	17	Mo	27		13	·05	22	·11		27
	18	Tu	28		14	·10	23	·19		28
			March							
Subhakrit Kumbha—Mari.	19	We	1		—A	·17	24	·29		29
	20	Th	2		1	·26	25	·39		—30
	21	Fr	3		2	·35	26	·49		1
	22	Sa	4		3	·44	27	·60		2
	23	Su	5		4	·50	1	·70		3
	24	Mo	6	Sukla	5	·56	2	·79		4
	25	Tu	7		6	·62	3	·85		5
	26	We	8		7	·65	4	·90		6
	27	Th	9		8	·66	5	·92		7
	28	Fr	10		9	·64	6	·93		8
	—29	Sa	11		10	·61	7	·91		9
	1	Su	12		11	·55	8	·89		10
	2	Mo	13		12	·49	9	·84		11
	3	Tu	14		13	·40	10	·78	H. 1259 Safar.	12
	4	We	15		14	·31	11	·72		13
	5	Th	16	Phalguna	P	·22	12	·66		14
	6	Fr	17		1	·12	13	·59		15
	7	Sa	18		2 3	·02 ·92	14	·52		16
	8	Su	19		4	·83	15	·46		17
	9	Mo	20		5	·76	16	·40		18
	10	Tu	21	Bahula	6	·69	17	·36		19
	11	We	22		7	·65	18	·34		20
	12	Th	23		8	·61	19	·33		21
	13	Fr	24		9	·60	20	·34		22
Subhakrit Mina—Panguni.	14	Sa	25		10	·60	21	·37		23
	15	Su	26		11	·64	22	·42		24
	16	Mo	27		12	·69	23	·50		25
	17	Tu	28		13	·76	24	·59		26
	18	We	29		14	·84	25	·69		27
	19	Th	30		—A	·93	26	·79		28
	20	Fr	31		...	...	27	·90		—29
			April							
	21	Sa	1		1	·02	...	...		1
	22	Su	2		2	·09	1	·00		2
	23	Mo	3		3	·15	2	·09		3
	24	Tu	4		4	·20	3	·16		4
	25	We	5		5	·23	4	·21		5
	26	Th	6		6	·23	5	·24		6
	27	Fr	7	Sukla	7	·21	6	·25		7
	28	Sa	8		8	·17	7	·25		8
	29	Su	9		9	·12	8	·22		9
	30	Mo	10		10 11	·05 ·97	9	·18		10
	—31	Tu	11		12	·88	10	·12		11
	1	We	12		13	·78	11	·06		12
	2	Th	13	Chaitra	14	·68	12 13	·00 ·93		13
	3	Fr	14		P	·58	14	·86	H. 1259 Rabi-ul-awwal.	14
	4	Sa	15		1	·48	15	·79		15
	5	Su	16		2	·39	16	·74		16
	6	Mo	17		3	·31	17	·70		17
	7	Tu	18		4	·24	18	·67		18
Sobhana Mesha—Chittirai.	8	We	19		5	·20	19	·65		19
	9	Th	20	Bahula	6	·16	20	·66		20
	10	Fr	21		7	·15	21	·68		21
	11	Sa	22		8	·15	22	·74		22
	12	Su	23		9	·19	23	·81		23
	13	Mo	24		10	·23	24	·89		24
	14	Tu	25		11	·30	25	·98		25
	15	We	26		12	·39	...	...		26
	16	Th	27		13	·48	26	·09		27
	17	Fr	28		14	·56	27	·20		28
	18	Sa	29		—A	·62	1	·30		29
	19	Su	30		1	·68	2	·40		—30
			May							
Sobhana Mesha—Chittirai.	20	Mo	1		2	·73	3	·47		1
	21	Tu	2		3	·76	4	·52		2
	22	We	3		4	·76	5	·56		3
	23	Th	4		5	·75	6	·58		4
	24	Fr	5	Sukla	6	·71	7	·57		5
	25	Sa	6		7	·65	8	·55		6
	26	Su	7		8	·58	9	·51		7
	27	Mo	8		9	·49	10	·46		8
	28	Tu	9		10	·40	11	·40		9
	29	We	10		11	·30	12	·34		10
	30	Th	11		12	·20	13	·27		11
	—31	Fr	12		13	·10	14	·20	H. 1259 Rabi-ul-akhir.	12
	1	Sa	13		14 P	·00 ·91	15	·13		13
	2	Su	14	Vaisakha	1	·83	16	·08		14
	3	Mo	15		2	·76	17	·03		15
	4	Tu	16		3	·71	18 19	·00 ·98		16
	5	We	17		4	·68	20	·98		17
	6	Th	18		5	·66	...	...		18
	7	Fr	19		6	·67	21	·00		19
	8	Sa	20		7	·70	22	·05		20
	9	Su	21	Bahula	8	·74	23	·11		21
	10	Mo	22		9	·81	24	·19		22
	11	Tu	23		10	·89	25	·28		23
	12	We	24		11	·98	26	·39		24
Sobhana Vrishabha—Vaikasi.	13	Th	25		...	...	27	·50		25
	14	Fr	26		12	·06	1	·61		26
	15	Sa	27		13	·13	2	·70		27
	16	Su	28		14	·20	3	·78		28
	17	Mo	29		—A	·24	4	·84		—29
	18	Tu	30		1	·26	5	·88		1
	19	We	31		2	·26	6	·90		2
			June							
	20	Th	1		3	·25	7	·90		3
	21	Fr	2	Sukla	4	·21	8	·88		4
	22	Sa	3		5	·16	9	·84		5
	23	Su	4		6	·09	10	·80		6
	24	Mo	5		7 8	·00 ·90	11	·74		7
	25	Tu	6		9	·80	12	·67		8
	26	We	7		10	·70	13	·60		9
	27	Th	8		11	·60	14	·54	H. 1259 Jumadal-awwal.	10
	28	Fr	9	Jyeshtha	12	·50	15	·48		11
	29	Sa	10		13	·41	16	·42		12
	30	Su	11		14	·33	17	·36		13
	—31	Mo	12		P	·25	18	·33		14
	1	Tu	13		1	·20	19	·30		15
	2	We	14		2	·17	20	·30		16
	3	Th	15		3	·15	21	·32		17
	4	Fr	16		4	·15	22	·36		18
	5	Sa	17		5	·18	23	·42		19
	6	Su	18		6	·23	24	·49		20
Sobhana Mithuna—Ani.	7	Mo	19	Bahula	7	·28	25	·58		21
	8	Tu	20		8	·36	26	·69		22
	9	We	21		9	·45	27	·80		23
	10	Th	22		10	·53	1	·91		24
	11	Fr	23		11	·60	...	...		25
	12	Sa	24		12	·67	2	·00		26
	13	Su	25		13	·71	3	·08		27
	14	Mo	26		14	·74	4	·15		28
	15	Tu	27		—A	·75	5	·20		29
	16	We	28	A. Sud.	1	·72	6	·22		—30
	17	Th	29		2	·68	7	·22		1
	18	Fr	30		3	·68	8	·21		2

Naksh :—1. Asvn. 2. Bhar. 3. Krit. 4. Rohi. 5. Mrig. 6. Ardh. 7. Punar. 8. Push. 9. Aslesh. 10. Magh. 11. P. Phal. 12. U. Phal. 13. Hasta. 14. Chit.

A. D. 1843.
A.—Amavasya.
P.—Paurnami.

Kollam 1019, Commences { N. Malabar—Sept. S. Malabar—Aug.

Hijra 1259, Commences, Feb. 1.

Vikrama 1900.
Bengal San 1249.
(N. Cycle) Ananda.

SOLAR reckoning: Cyclic Sidereal Year, Month and Day; Week-Day; English Month and Day. LUNAR reckoning: Tithi, Ending Moment; Nakshatra, Ending Moment; Muhammadan Year, Month and Day.

Solar month	Cyclic Sidereal Day	Week-Day	English Month and Day	Lunar month	Tithi	Ending Moment	Nakshatra	Ending Moment	Muhammadan Year, Month and Day
			July						
	19	Sa	1		4	·57	9	·18	3
	20	Su	2		5	·48	10	·14	4
	21	Mo	3		6	·39	11	·08	5
	22	Tu	4	Sukla	7	·30	12 / 13	·01 / ·04	6
Sobhana Mithuna—Ani.	23	We	5		8	·19	14	·87	7
	24	Th	6		9 / 10	·08 / ·98	15	·81	8
	25	Fr	7		11	·88	16	·75	9
	26	Sa	8		12	·80	17	·70	10
	27	Su	9	Ashadha	13	·73	18	·66	11
	28	Mo	10		14	·68	19	·63	12
	29	Tu	11		P	·64	20	·63	13
	30	We	12		1	·62	21	·64	14
	31	Th	13		2	·63	22	·67	15
	32	Fr	14		3	·65	23	·72	16
	1	Sa	15		4	·70	24	·80	17
	2	Su	16		5	·76	25	·89	18
	3	Mo	17		6	·84	26	·99	H. 1259 Jumadal-akhir. 19
	4	Tu	18	Bahula	7	·92	...	...	20
	5	We	19		...	...	27	·09	21
	6	Th	20		8	·00	1	·20	22
	7	Fr	21		9	·07	2	·30	23
	8	Sa	22		10	·14	3	·40	24
	9	Su	23		11	·19	4	·47	25
	10	Mo	24		12	·22	5	·51	26
	11	Tu	25		13	·23	6	·54	27
	12	We	26		14	·20	7	·55	28
	13	Th	27		A	·17	8	·55	29
Sobhana Karkata—Adi.	14	Fr	28		1	·12	9	·52	1
	15	Sa	29		2 / 3	·05 / ·97	10	·47	2
	16	Su	30		4	·88	11	·42	3
	17	Mo	31		5	·78	12	·35	4
			Aug.						
	18	Tu	1		6	·68	13	·28	5
	19	We	2	Sukla	7	·58	14	·21	6
	20	Th	3		8	·48	15	·15	7
	21	Fr	4		9	·38	16	·09	8
	22	Sa	5		10	·29	17 / 18	·03 / ·99	9
	23	Su	6		11	·22	19	·97	10
	24	Mo	7		12	·17	20	·95	11
	25	Tu	8	Sravana	13	·13	21	·96	12
	26	We	9		14	·11	22	·99	13
	27	Th	10		P	·11	...	...	H. 1259 Rajab. 14
	28	Fr	11		1	·14	23	·03	15
	29	Sa	12		2	·18	24	·11	16
	30	Su	13		3	·25	25	·19	17
	31	Mo	14		4	·32	26	·29	18
	1	Tu	15		5	·40	27	·40	19
	2	We	16		6	·49	1	·51	20
	3	Th	17	Bahula	7	·57	2	·61	21
	4	Fr	18		8	·64	3	·70	22
	5	Sa	19		9	·68	4	·77	23
	6	Su	20		10	·71	5	·83	24
	7	Mo	21		11	·72	6	·86	25
Sobhana Simha—Avani.	8	Tu	22		12	·70	7	·87	26
	9	We	23		13	·67	8	·86	27
	10	Th	24		14	·62	9	·85	28
	11	Fr	25		A	·56	10	·80	29
	12	Sa	26		1	·47	11	·75	30
	13	Su	27	B. Suk.	2	·38	12	·69	1
	14	Mo	28		3	·28	13	·63	Shaban. 2
	15	Tu	29		4	·18	14	·56	3
	16	We	30		5 / 6	·08 / ·98	15	·49	4
	17	Th	31		7	·89	16	·42	5

Solar month	Cyclic Sidereal Day	Week-Day	English Month and Day	Lunar month	Tithi	Ending Moment	Nakshatra	Ending Moment	Muhammadan Year, Month and Day
			Sep.						
	18	Fr	1	Sukla	8	·81	17	·37	6
	19	Sa	2		9	·74	18	·33	7
	20	Su	3		10	·69	19	·29	8
	21	Mo	4		11	·64	20	·28	9
	22	Tu	5		12	·63	21	·28	10
Sobhana Simha—Avani.	23	We	6		13	·63	22	·30	11
	24	Th	7		14	·65	23	·35	12
	25	Fr	8	Bhadrapada	P	·69	24	·41	13
	26	Sa	9		1	·76	25	·50	14
	27	Su	10		2	·83	26	·59	15
	28	Mo	11		3	·91	27	·70	16
	29	Tu	12		...	...	1	·81	17
	30	We	13		4	·00	2	·91	18
	31	Th	14		5	·08	...	...	19
	1	Fr	15		6	·15	3	·01	H. 1259 Shaban. 20
	2	Sa	16	Bahula	7	·20	4	·08	21
	3	Su	17		8	·24	5	·14	22
	4	Mo	18		9	·25	6	·18	23
	5	Tu	19		10	·24	7	·20	24
	6	We	20		11	·20	8	·20	25
	7	Th	21		12	·15	9	·18	26
	8	Fr	22		13	·09	10	·14	27
	9	Sa	23		14 / A	·01 / ·92	11	·09	28
	10	Su	24		1	·82	12 / 13	·04 / ·97	29
	11	Mo	25		2	·72	14	·90	1
Sobhana Kanya—Purattasi.	12	Tu	26		3	·62	15	·83	2
	13	We	27		4	·52	16	·76	3
	14	Th	28	Sukla	5	·42	17	·71	4
	15	Fr	29		6	·34	18	·66	5
	16	Sa	30		7	·28	19	·62	6
			Oct.						
	17	Su	1		8	·23	20	·60	7
	18	Mo	2		9	·19	21	·60	8
	19	Tu	3		10	·17	22	·61	9
	20	We	4		11	·17	23	·66	10
	21	Th	5		12	·20	24	·72	11
	22	Fr	6		13	·24	25	·80	12
	23	Sa	7	Asvina	14	·31	26	·89	13
	24	Su	8		P	·38	27	·99	14
	25	Mo	9		1	·47	...	...	15
	26	Tu	10		2	·56	1	·10	H. 1259 Ramzan. 16
	27	We	11		3	·65	2	·21	17
	28	Th	12		4	·72	3	·31	18
	29	Fr	13		5	·77	4	·39	19
	30	Sa	14		6	·80	5	·45	20
	31	Su	15	Bahula	7	·81	6	·50	21
	1	Mo	16		8	·80	7	·52	22
	2	Tu	17		9	·77	8	·52	23
	3	We	18		10	·73	9	·50	24
	4	Th	19		11	·66	10	·47	25
	5	Fr	20		12	·58	11	·43	26
	6	Sa	21		13	·49	12	·37	27
	7	Su	22		14	·39	13	·31	28
	8	Mo	23		A	·29	14	·24	29
	9	Tu	24		1	·19	15	·17	30
Sobhana Tula—Aippasi.	10	We	25	Kartt. Suk.	2	·10	16	·11	1
	11	Th	26		3 / 4	·01 / ·93	17 / 18	·05 / ·99	Shawwal. 2
	12	Fr	27		5	·86	19	·95	3
	13	Sa	28		6	·81	20	·93	4
	14	Su	29		7	·78	21	·92	5
	15	Mo	30		8	·76	22	·94	6
	16	Tu	31		9	·77	23	·97	7

Solar month	Cyclic Sidereal Day	Week-Day	English Month and Day	Lunar month	Tithi	Ending Moment	Nakshatra	Ending Moment	Muhammadan Year, Month and Day
			Nov.						
	17	We	1	Sukla	10	·79	...	...	8
	18	Th	2		11	·84	24	·03	9
	19	Fr	3		12	·91	25	·10	10
	20	Sa	4		13	·99	26	·19	11
	21	Su	5		...	...	27	·30	12
Sobhana Tula—Aippasi.	22	Mo	6		14	·08	1	·41	13
	23	Tu	7	Karttika	P	·17	2	·51	14
	24	We	8		1	·25	3	·61	15
	25	Th	9		2	·31	4	·69	16
	26	Fr	10		3	·37	5	·77	17
	27	Sa	11		4	·41	6	·82	18
	28	Su	12		5	·41	7	·84	19
	29	Mo	13		6	·40	8	·85	20
	30	Tu	14	Bahula	7	·37	9	·83	H. 1259 Shawwal. 21
	1	We	15		8	·33	10	·81	22
	2	Th	16		9	·26	11	·77	23
	3	Fr	17		10	·18	12	·71	24
	4	Sa	18		11	·09	13	·65	25
	5	Su	19		12 / 13	·00 / ·90	14	·58	26
	6	Mo	20		14	·80	15	·51	27
	7	Tu	21		A	·71	16	·45	28
	8	We	22		1	·62	17	·39	29
	9	Th	23		2	·55	18	·33	1
	10	Fr	24		3	·48	19	·28	2
Sobhana Vrischika—Kartigai.	11	Sa	25		4	·43	20	·25	3
	12	Su	26		5	·39	21	·25	4
	13	Mo	27		6	·38	22	·26	5
	14	Tu	28	Sukla	7	·39	23	·29	6
	15	We	29		8	·41	24	·34	7
	16	Th	30		9	·46	25	·40	8
			Dec.						
	17	Fr	1		10	·54	26	·50	9
	18	Sa	2		11	·62	27	·60	10
	19	Su	3		12	·70	1	·71	11
	20	Mo	4		13	·78	2	·81	12
	21	Tu	5		14	·87	3	·91	13
	22	We	○ 6	Margasira	P	·95	...	...	14
	23	Th	7		...	...	4	·01	15
	24	Fr	8		1	·00	5	·08	16
	25	Sa	9		2	·04	6	·13	H. 1259 Zi-l-ka'da. 17
	26	Su	10		3	·05	7	·16	18
	27	Mo	11		4	·08	8	·17	19
	28	Tu	12		5 / 6	·00 / ·96	9	·17	20
	29	We	13	Bahula	7	·89	10	·14	21
	1	Th	14		8	·81	11	·10	22
	2	Fr	15		9	·72	12 / 13	·05 / ·98	23
	3	Sa	16		10	·63	14	·91	24
	4	Su	17		11	·53	15	·84	25
	5	Mo	18		12	·43	16	·78	26
	6	Tu	19		13	·34	17	·72	27
	7	We	20		14	·25	18	·66	28
	8	Th	● 21		A	·17	19	·61	29
	9	Fr	22		1	·11	20	·59	30
Sobhana Dhanus—Margali.	10	Sa	23		2	·07	21	·58	1
	11	Su	24	Sukla	3	·04	22	·58	2
	12	Mo	25		4	·03	23	·60	3
	13	Tu	26		5	·04	24	·65	4
	14	We	27	Pausha	6	·06	25	·72	H. 1259 Zi-l-hijja. 5
	15	Th	28		7	·12	26	·80	6
	16	Fr	29		8	·19	27	·90	7
	17	Sa	30		9	·27	...	...	8
	18	Su	31		10	·36	1	·00	9

15. Svati. 16. Visak. 17. Anur. 18. Jyesh. 19. Mula. 20. P. Ash. 21. U. Ash. 22. Sravn. 23. Dani. 24. Satab. 25. P. Bhad. 26. U. Bhad. 27. Rev.

A. D. 1844. **Mesha Sankranti** (Commencement of Indian Sidereal Year).

Solar Eclipse. ● **(Surya Sid.) April 11·13.** **Saka 1766.** **Kaliyuga 4945.**

Lunar Eclipse. ○ **(Arya Sid.) April 11·03.** **(S. Cycle) Krodhi.**

SOLAR reckoning: Cyclic Sidereal Year, Month and Day; Week-Day; English Month and Day. LUNAR reckoning: Tithi, Ending Moment; Nakshatra, Ending Moment; Muhammadan Year, Month and Day.

Jan.

Cyclic Sidereal Year, Month and Day	Week-Day	English Month and Day	Tithi	Ending Moment	Nakshatra	Ending Moment	Muhammadan Year, Month and Day
Sobhana *Dhanus—Margali.* 19	Mo	1	Pausha *Suk.* 11	·45	2	·11	H. 1259 *Zi-l-hijja.* 10
20	Tu	2	12	·53	3	·22	11
21	We	3	13	·60	4	·31	12
22	Th	4	14	·65	5	·39	13
23	Fr	5	P	·68	6	·44	14
24	Sa	6	*Bahula* 1	·69	7	·48	15
25	Su	7	2	·68	8	·50	16
26	Mo	8	3	·65	9	·50	17
27	Tu	9	4	·60	10	·47	18
28	We	10	5	·54	11	·43	19
—29	Th	11	6	·46	12	·38	20
Sobhana *Makara—Tai.* 1	Fr	12	7	·37	13	·32	21
2	Sa	13	8	·28	14	·26	22
3	Su	14	9	·18	15	·19	23
4	Mo	15	10 11	·08 ·99	16	·12	24
5	Tu	16	12	·90	17 18	·05 ·99	25
6	We	17	13	·82	19	·95	26
7	Th	18	14	·75	20	·92	27
8	Fr	19	—A	·71	21	·90	28
9	Sa	20	*Sukla* 1	·68	22	·90	29
10	Su	21	2	·67	23	·92	—30
11	Mo	22	3	·68	24	·97	1
12	Tu	23	4	·71	...	...	2
13	We	24	5	·78	25	·03	3
14	Th	25	6	·85	26	·10	4
15	Fr	26	7	·92	27	·20	5
16	Sa	27	...	...	1	·30	6
17	Su	28	8	·01	2	·41	7
18	Mo	29	9	·11	3	·52	8
19	Tu	30	10	·18	4	·61	9
20	We	31	11	·25	5	·69	10

Feb.

Cyclic Sidereal Year, Month and Day	Week-Day	English Month and Day	Tithi	Ending Moment	Nakshatra	Ending Moment	Muhammadan Year, Month and Day
21	Th	1	Magha 12	·30	6	·75	H. 1260 *Muharram.* 11
22	Fr	2	13	·33	7	·79	12
23	Sa	3	14	·33	8	·82	13
24	Su	4	P	·31	9	·82	14
25	Mo	5	*Bahula* 1	29	10	·80	15
26	Tu	6	2	·23	11	·77	16
27	We	7	3	·16	12	·72	17
28	Th	8	4	·08	13	·67	18
29	Fr	9	5 6	·00 ·90	14	·60	19
—30	Sa	10	7	·80	15	·53	20
Sobhana *Kumbha—Masi.* 1	Su	11	8	·70	16	·46	21
2	Mo	12	9	·60	17	·39	22
3	Tu	13	10	·52	18	·34	23
4	We	14	11	·44	19	·29	24
5	Th	15	12	·38	20	·25	25
6	Fr	16	13	·33	21	·22	26
7	Sa	17	14	·31	22	·22	27
8	Su	18	—A	·30	23	·24	28
9	Mo	19	Phalguna *Sukla* 1	·31	24	·28	29
10	Tu	20	2	·35	25	·33	—30
11	We	21	3	·40	26	·41	H. 1260 *Safar.* 1
12	Th	22	4	·47	27	·50	2
13	Fr	23	5	·55	1	·60	3
14	Sa	24	6	·65	2	·71	4
15	Su	25	7	·73	3	·82	5
16	Mo	26	8	·80	4	·92	6
17	Tu	27	9	·87	...	...	7
18	We	28	10	·91	5	·00	8
19	Th	29	11	·95	6	·06	9

March

Cyclic Sidereal Year, Month and Day	Week-Day	English Month and Day	Tithi	Ending Moment	Nakshatra	Ending Moment	Muhammadan Year, Month and Day
Sobhana *Kumbha—Masi.* 20	Fr	1	Phalguna *Suk.* 12	·95	7	·12	H. 1260 *Safar.* 10
21	Sa	2	13	·94	8	·14	11
22	Su	3	14	·90	9	·15	12
23	Mo	4	P	·85	10	·13	13
24	Tu	5	*Bahula* 1	·77	11	·10	14
25	We	6	2	·69	12	·06	15
26	Th	7	3	·61	13 14	·00 ·94	16
27	Fr	8	4	·52	15	·87	17
28	Sa	9	5	·42	16	·80	18
29	Su	10	6	·32	17	·74	19
30	Mo	11	7	·22	18	·68	20
—31	Tu	12	8	·12	19	·62	21
Sobhana *Mina—Panguni.* 1	We	13	9 10	·04 ·98	20	·58	22
2	Th	14	11	·93	21	·55	23
3	Fr	15	12	·91	22	·54	24
4	Sa	16	13	·89	23	·56	25
5	Su	17	14	·91	24	·59	26
6	Mo	18	—A	·95	25	·64	27
7	Tu	19	...	...	26	·71	28
8	We	20	Chaitra *Sukla* 1	·00	27	·80	—29
9	Th	21	2	·08	1	·90	1
10	Fr	22	3	·16	...	...	2
11	Sa	23	4	·25	2	·01	3
12	Su	24	5	·33	3	·12	4
13	Mo	25	6	·41	4	·22	5
14	Tu	26	7	·46	5	·30	6
15	We	27	8	·51	6	·38	7
16	Th	28	9	·54	7	·43	8
17	Fr	29	10	·53	8	·46	9
18	Sa	30	11	·51	9	·47	10
19	Su	31	12	·47	10	·46	11

April

Cyclic Sidereal Year, Month and Day	Week-Day	English Month and Day	Tithi	Ending Moment	Nakshatra	Ending Moment	Muhammadan Year, Month and Day
20	Mo	1	13	·42	11	·44	H. 1260 *Rabi-ul-awwal.* 12
21	Tu	2	14	·35	12	·40	13
22	We	3	P	·27	13	·34	14
23	Th	4	*Bahula* 1	·18	14	·28	15
24	Fr	5	2 3	·07 ·97	15	·22	16
25	Sa	6	4	·87	16	·15	17
26	Su	7	5	·78	17	·08	18
27	Mo	8	6	·69	18 19	·01 ·96	19
28	Tu	9	7	·61	20	·91	20
—29	We	10	8	·54	21	·88	21
Krodhi *Mesha—Chittirai.* 1	Th	11	9	·49	22	·87	22
2	Fr	12	10	·47	23	·88	23
3	Sa	13	11	·46	24	·90	24
4	Su	14	12	·47	25	·95	25
5	Mo	15	13	·50	...	...	26
6	Tu	16	14	·56	26	·01	27
7	We	17	—A	·63	27	·11	28
8	Th	18	Vaisakha *Sukla* 1	·72	1	·21	29
9	Fr	19	2	·80	2	·31	—30
10	Sa	20	3	·88	3	·42	H. 1260 *Rabi-ul-akhir.* 1
11	Su	21	4	·94	4	·52	2
12	Mo	22	...	...	5	·62	3
13	Tu	23	5	·00	6	·69	4
14	We	24	6	·05	7	·74	5
15	Th	25	7	·07	8	·78	6
16	Fr	26	8	·08	9	·79	7
17	Sa	27	9	·06	10	·79	8
18	Su	28	10 11	·02 ·97	11	·77	9
19	Mo	29	12	·89	12	·73	10
20	Tu	30	13	·80	13	·67	11

May

Cyclic Sidereal Year, Month and Day	Week-Day	English Month and Day	Tithi	Ending Moment	Nakshatra	Ending Moment	Muhammadan Year, Month and Day
Krodhi *Mesha—Chittirai.* 21	We	1	Vaisakha 14	·71	14	·61	H. 1260 *Rabi-ul-akhir.* 12
22	Th	2	P	·61	15	·55	13
23	Fr	3	*Bahula* 1	·51	16	·49	14
24	Sa	4	2	·41	17	·42	15
25	Su	5	3	·31	18	·35	16
26	Mo	6	4	·22	19	·29	17
27	Tu	7	5	·14	20	·24	18
28	We	8	6	·07	21	·22	19
29	Th	9	7 8	·03 ·99	22	·20	20
30	Fr	10	9	·98	23	·20	21
—31	Sa	11	10	·99	24	·22	22
Krodhi *Vrishabha—Vaikasi.* 1	Su	12	...	...	25	·26	23
2	Mo	13	11	·02	26	·33	24
3	Tu	14	12	·07	27	·41	25
4	We	15	13	·14	1	·50	26
5	Th	16	14	·22	2	·61	27
6	Fr	17	—A	·30	3	·72	28
7	Sa	18	Jyeshtha *Sukla* 1	·39	4	·83	—29
8	Su	19	2	·46	5	·92	*Jumadal-awwal.* 1
9	Mo	20	3	·51	...	...	2
10	Tu	21	4	·56	6	·00	3
11	We	22	5	·58	7	·06	4
12	Th	23	6	·58	8	·09	5
13	Fr	24	7	·56	9	·12	6
14	Sa	25	8	·53	10	·12	7
15	Su	26	9	·47	11	·10	8
16	Mo	27	10	·40	12	·06	9
17	Tu	28	11	·31	13 14	·01 ·95	10
18	We	29	12	·21	15	·89	11
19	Th	30	13	·11	16	·82	12
20	Fr ○	31	14 P	·01 ·91	17	·75	13

June

Cyclic Sidereal Year, Month and Day	Week-Day	English Month and Day	Tithi	Ending Moment	Nakshatra	Ending Moment	Muhammadan Year, Month and Day
21	Sa	1	*Bahula* 1	·81	18	·69	H. 1260 14
22	Su	2	2	·72	19	·63	15
23	Mo	3	3	·64	20	·58	16
24	Tu	4	4	·57	21	·55	17
25	We	5	5	·52	22	·52	18
26	Th	6	6	·49	23	·52	19
27	Fr	7	7	·48	24	·53	20
28	Sa	8	8	·48	25	·58	21
29	Su	9	9	·51	26	·64	22
30	Mo	10	10	·56	27	·71	23
—31	Tu	11	11	·61	1	·80	24
Krodhi *Mithuna—Ani.* 1	We	12	12	·70	2	·91	25
2	Th	13	13	·78	...	...	26
3	Fr	14	14	·86	3	·02	27
4	Sa	15	—A	·93	4	·13	28
5	Su	16	...	...	5	·22	29
6	Mo	17	Ashadha *Sukla* 1	·00	6	·30	—30
7	Tu	18	2	·05	7	·37	H. 1260 *Jumadal-akhir.* 1
8	We	19	3	·07	8	·41	2
9	Th	20	4	·07	9	·44	3
10	Fr	21	5	·05	10	·44	4
11	Sa	22	6 7	·01 ·95	11	·43	5
12	Su	23	8	·88	12	·39	6
13	Mo	24	9	·80	13	·35	7
14	Tu	25	10	·71	14	·30	8
15	We	26	11	·61	15	·23	9
16	Th	27	12	·50	16	·16	10
17	Fr	28	13	·40	17	·09	11
18	Sa	29	14	·30	18 19	·02 ·97	12
19	Su	30	P	·21	20	·92	13

Naksh:—1. Asvn. 2. Bhar. 3. Krit. 4. Rohi. 5. Mrig. 6. Ardh. 7. Punar. 8. Push. 9. Aslesh. 10. Magh. 11. P. Phal. 12. U. Phal. 13. Hasta. 14. Chit.

A. D. 1844.
A.—Amavasya.
P.—Paurnami.

Kollam 1020, Commences { **N. Malabar—Sept.** / **S. Malabar—Aug.**

Hijra 1260, Commences, **Jan. 22.**

Vikrama 1901.
Bengal San 1250.
(N. Cycle) Rakshasa.

SOLAR reckoning: Cyclic Sidereal Year, Month and Day; Week-Day, English Month and Day. LUNAR reckoning: Tithi, Ending Moment; Nakshatra, Ending Moment; Muhammadan Year, Month and Day.

July

Cyclic Sidereal Year, Month and Day	Week-Day	English Month and Day	Tithi	Ending Moment	Nakshatra	Ending Moment	Muhammadan Year, Month and Day
Krodhi *Mithuna—Ani.* 20	Mo	1	Ashadha *Bahula* 1	·13	21	·88	H. 1260 *Jumadal-akhir.* 14
21	Tu	2	2	·06	22	·85	15
22	We	3	3, 4	·00, ·96	23	·84	16
23	Th	4	5	·95	24	·86	17
24	Fr	5	6	·96	25	·89	18
25	Sa	6	7	·98	26	·94	19
26	Su	7	...	...	...	...	20
27	Mo	8	8	·03	27	·02	21
28	Tu	9	9	·10	1	·10	22
29	We	10	10	·17	2	·21	23
30	Th	11	11	·26	3	·32	24
31	Fr	12	12	·34	4	·43	25
32	Sa	13	13	·41	5	·52	26
Krodhi *Karkata—Adi.* 1	Su	14	14	·47	6	·61	27
2	Mo	15	A	·52	7	·68	28
3	Tu	16	Sravana *Sukla* 1	·55	8	·73	29
4	We	17	2	·55	9	·76	*Rajab.* 1
5	Th	18	3	·53	10	·77	2
6	Fr	19	4	·49	11	·75	3
7	Sa	20	5	·43	12	·73	4
8	Su	21	6	·36	13	·69	5
9	Mo	22	7	·28	14	·64	6
10	Tu	23	8	·19	15	·57	7
11	We	24	9, 10	·09, ·99	16	·50	8
12	Th	25	11	·89	17	·43	9
13	Fr	26	12	·79	18	·37	10
14	Sa	27	13	·70	19	·31	11
15	Su	28	14	·61	20	·25	12
16	Mo	29	P	·54	21	·21	13
17	Tu	30	1	·48	22	·18	14
18	We	31	2	·45	23	·17	15

Aug.

Cyclic Sidereal Year, Month and Day	Week-Day	English Month and Day	Tithi	Ending Moment	Nakshatra	Ending Moment	Muhammadan Year, Month and Day
19	Th	1	Adhika Sravana *Bahula* 3	·43	24	·18	H. 1260 16
20	Fr	2	4	·44	25	·21	17
21	Sa	3	5	·46	26	·25	18
22	Su	4	6	·50	27	·32	19
23	Mo	5	7	·57	1	·40	20
24	Tu	6	8	·65	2	·51	21
25	We	7	9	·74	3	·62	22
26	Th	8	10	·82	4	·72	23
27	Fr	9	11	·89	5	·82	24
28	Sa	10	12	·95	6	·91	25
29	Su	11	...	...	7	·99	26
30	Mo	12	13	·00	...	...	27
31	Tu	13	14	·03	8	·05	28
Krodhi *Simha—Avani.* 1	We	14	A	·03	9	·08	29
2	Th	15	Nija Sravana *Sukla* 1, 2	·02, ·98	10	·09	30
3	Fr	16	3	·94	11	·08	H. 1260 *Shaban.* 1
4	Sa	17	4	·87	12	·06	2
5	Su	18	5	·78	13, 14	·02, ·97	3
6	Mo	19	6	·69	15	·91	4
7	Tu	20	7	·59	16	·84	5
8	We	21	8	·49	17	·78	6
9	Th	22	9	·39	18	·71	7
10	Fr	23	10	·29	19	·64	8
11	Sa	24	11	·20	20	·58	9
12	Su	25	12	·12	21	·54	10
13	Mo	26	13, 14	·05, ·99	22	·51	11
14	Tu	27	P	·95	23	·50	12
15	We	28	Nija *Bah.* 1	·93	24	·50	13
16	Th	29	2	·95	25	·52	14
17	Fr	30	3	·97	26	·56	15
18	Sa	31	...	...	27	·63	16

Sep.

Cyclic Sidereal Year, Month and Day	Week-Day	English Month and Day	Tithi	Ending Moment	Nakshatra	Ending Moment	Muhammadan Year, Month and Day
Krodhi *Simha—Avani.* 19	Su	1	Nija Sravn. *Bahula* 4	·02	1	·72	H. 1260 *Shaban.* 17
20	Mo	2	5	·08	2	·81	18
21	Tu	3	6	·15	3	·92	19
22	We	4	7	·24	...	...	20
23	Th	5	8	·32	4	·02	21
24	Fr	6	9	·39	5	·12	22
25	Sa	7	10	·46	6	·22	23
26	Su	8	11	·52	7	·30	24
27	Mo	9	12	·54	8	·36	25
28	Tu	10	13	·56	9	·40	26
29	We	11	14	·54	10	·41	27
30	Th	12	A	·51	11	·42	28
31	Fr	13	Bhadrapada *Sukla* 1	·46	12	·40	29
Krodhi *Kanya—Purattasi.* 1	Sa	14	2	·39	13	·36	*Ramzan.* 1
2	Su	15	3	·31	14	·31	2
3	Mo	16	4	·22	15	·25	3
4	Tu	17	5	·12	16	·19	4
5	We	18	6, 7	·02, ·92	17	·12	5
6	Th	19	8	·82	18, 19	·05, ·98	6
7	Fr	20	9	·73	20	·92	7
8	Sa	21	10	·65	21	·87	8
9	Su	22	11	·58	22	·84	9
10	Mo	23	12	·52	23	·82	10
11	Tu	24	13	·49	24	·82	11
12	We	25	14	·47	25	·83	12
13	Th	26	P	·49	26	·87	13
14	Fr	27	1	·51	27	·94	14
15	Sa	28	2	·56	...	...	15
16	Su	29	3	·62	1	·02	16
17	Mo	30	4	·70	2	·11	17

Oct.

Cyclic Sidereal Year, Month and Day	Week-Day	English Month and Day	Tithi	Ending Moment	Nakshatra	Ending Moment	Muhammadan Year, Month and Day
18	Tu	1	*Bahula* 5	·78	3	·21	H. 1260 18
19	We	2	6	·87	4	·32	19
20	Th	3	7	·94	5	·48	20
21	Fr	4	...	...	6	·53	21
22	Sa	5	8	·01	7	·61	22
23	Su	6	9	·07	8	·67	23
24	Mo	7	10	·09	9	·71	24
25	Tu	8	11	·11	10	·74	25
26	We	9	12	·09	11	·74	26
27	Th	10	13	·07	12	·72	27
28	Fr	11	14, A	·02, ·95	13	·69	28
29	Sa	12	Asvina *Sukla* 1	·87	14	·64	29
30	Su	13	2	·73	15	·59	30
31	Mo	14	3	·69	16	·53	H. 1260 *Shawwal.* 1
Krodhi *Tula—Aippasi.* 1	Tu	15	4	·59	17	·46	2
2	We	16	5	·49	18	·39	3
3	Th	17	6	·39	19	·32	4
4	Fr	18	7	·30	20	·26	5
5	Sa	19	8	·22	21	·21	6
6	Su	20	9	·15	22	·17	7
7	Mo	21	10	·10	23	·15	8
8	Tu	22	11	·07	24	·14	9
9	We	23	12	·06	25	·15	10
10	Th	24	13	·07	26	·19	11
11	Fr	25	14	·09	27	·25	12
12	Sa	26	P	·14	1	·32	13
13	Su	27	Asvina *Bah.* 1	·20	2	·41	14
14	Mo	28	2	·28	3	·51	15
15	Tu	29	3	·37	4	·62	16
16	We	30	4	·47	5	·73	17
17	Th	31	5	·55	6	·83	18

Nov.

Cyclic Sidereal Year, Month and Day	Week-Day	English Month and Day	Tithi	Ending Moment	Nakshatra	Ending Moment	Muhammadan Year, Month and Day
Krodhi *Tula—Aippasi.* 18	Fr	1	Asvina *Bahula* 6	·62	7	·91	H. 1260 *Shawwal.* 19
19	Sa	2	7	·66	8	·98	20
20	Su	3	8	·69	...	...	21
21	Mo	4	9	·71	9	·04	22
22	Tu	5	10	·69	10	·06	23
23	We	6	11	·66	11	·07	24
24	Th	7	12	·61	12	·05	25
25	Fr	8	13	·55	13, 14	·02, ·98	26
26	Sa	9	14	·47	15	·93	27
27	Su	10	A	·38	16	·86	28
28	Mo	11	Kartika *Sukla* 1	·28	17	·79	29
29	Tu	12	2	·18	18	·72	H. 1260 *Zi-l-ka'da.* 1
30	We	13	3, 4	·08, ·99	19	·65	2
Krodhi *Vrischika—Kartigai.* 1	Th	14	5	·91	20	·60	3
2	Fr	15	6	·83	21	·55	4
3	Sa	16	7	·77	22	·50	5
4	Su	17	8	·71	23	·47	6
5	Mo	18	9	·68	24	·46	7
6	Tu	19	10	·67	25	·48	8
7	We	20	11	·68	26	·51	9
8	Th	21	12	·72	27	·56	10
9	Fr	22	13	·77	1	·63	11
10	Sa	23	14	·84	2	·71	12
11	Su ○	24	P	·91	3	·82	13
12	Mo	25	...	...	4	·93	14
13	Tu	26	1	·00	...	...	15
14	We	27	2	·09	5	·03	16
15	Th	28	3	·17	6	·13	17
16	Fr	29	4	·24	7	·22	18
17	Sa	30	5	·30	8	·29	19

Dec.

Cyclic Sidereal Year, Month and Day	Week-Day	English Month and Day	Tithi	Ending Moment	Nakshatra	Ending Moment	Muhammadan Year, Month and Day
18	Su	1	*Bahula* 6	·33	9	·35	20
19	Mo	2	7	·38	10	·38	21
20	Tu	3	8	·32	11	·39	22
21	We	4	9	·29	12	·38	23
22	Th	5	10	·23	13	·36	24
23	Fr	6	11	·17	14	·32	25
24	Sa	7	12	·09	15	·27	26
25	Su	8	13, 14	·00, ·91	16	·20	27
26	Mo	9	A	·81	17	·13	28
27	Tu	10	Margasira *Sukla* 1	·71	18	·06	29
28	We	11	2	·61	19, 20	·00, ·94	30
29	Th	12	3	·52	21	·88	H. 1260 *Zi-l-hijja.* 1
Krodhi *Dhanus—Margali.* 1	Fr	13	4	·45	22	·83	2
2	Sa	14	5	·39	23	·80	3
3	Su	15	6	·34	24	·79	4
4	Mo	16	7	·32	25	·80	5
5	Tu	17	8	·31	26	·82	6
6	We	18	9	·32	27	·87	7
7	Th	19	10	·36	1	·93	8
8	Fr	20	11	·41	...	...	9
9	Sa	21	12	·48	2	·02	10
10	Su	22	13	·56	3	·12	11
11	Mo	23	14	·65	4	·22	12
12	Tu	24	P	·74	5	·33	13
13	We	25	Margasira *Bahula* 1	·83	6	·43	14
14	Th	26	2	·89	7	·53	15
15	Fr	27	3	·94	8	·61	16
16	Sa	28	4	·97	9	·66	17
17	Su	29	5	·98	10	·70	18
18	Mo	30	6	·97	11	·71	19
19	Tu	31	7	·93	12	·71	20

15. Svati. 16. Visak. 17. Anur. 18. Jyesh. 19. Mula. 20. P. Ash. 21. U. Ash. 22. Sravn. 23. Dani. 24. Satab. 25. P. Bhad. 26. U. Bhad. 27. Rev.

A. D. 1845. **Mesha Sankranti** (Commencement of Indian Sidereal Year).

Solar Eclipse. ● **(Surya Sid.) April 11·39.** **Saka 1767.** **Kaliyuga 4946.**

Lunar Eclipse. ○ **(Arya Sid.) April 11·29.** **(S. Cycle) Visvavasu.**

SOLAR reckoning: Cyclic Sidereal Year, Month and Day; Week-Day; English Month and Day. LUNAR reckoning: Tithi; Ending Moment; Nakshatra; Ending Moment; Muhammadan Year, Month and Day.

Jan.

Solar Year, Month	Cyclic Sidereal Day	Week-Day	English Day	Lunar Month	Tithi	Ending Moment	Nakshatra	Ending Moment	Muhammadan Year, Month	Muhammadan Day
Krodhi Dhanus—Margali.	20	We	1	Marg. Bah.	8	·88	13	·69	H. 1260 Zi-l-hijja.	21
	21	Th	2		9	·81	14	·65		22
	22	Fr	3		10	·73	15	·60		23
	23	Sa	4		11	·65	16	·54		24
	24	Su	5		12	·55	17	·48		25
	25	Mo	6		13	·45	18	·41		26
	26	Tu	7		14	·35	19	·34		27
	27	We	8		A	·26	20	·27		28
	28	Th	9		1	·18	21	·21		29
	29	Fr	10		2	·11	22	·16	H. 1261 Muharram.	1
	30	Sa	11		3 / 4	·04 / ·99	23	·14		2
Krodhi Makara—Tai.	1	Su	12	Pausha Sukla	5	·97	24	·12		3
	2	Mo	13		6	·95	25	·12		4
	3	Tu	14		7	·97	26	·14		5
	4	We	15		...	...	27	·18		6
	5	Th	16		8	·01	1	·28		7
	6	Fr	17		9	·06	2	·32		8
	7	Sa	18		10	·13	3	·42		9
	8	Su	19		11	·22	4	·52		10
	9	Mo	20		12	·31	5	·63		11
	10	Tu	21		13	·40	6	·74		12
	11	We	22		14	·48	7	·83		13
	12	Th	23		P	·55	8	·91		14
	13	Fr	24	Bahula	1	·59	9	·97		15
	14	Sa	25		2	·61	...	...		16
	15	Su	26		3	·62	10	·01		17
	16	Mo	27		4	·61	11	·03		18
	17	Tu	28		5	·57	12	·04		19
	18	We	29		6	·52	13 / 14	·02 / ·99		20
	19	Th	30		7	·45	15	·94		21
	20	Fr	31		8	·37	16	·88		22

Feb.

Solar Year, Month	Cyclic Sidereal Day	Week-Day	English Day	Lunar Month	Tithi	Ending Moment	Nakshatra	Ending Moment	Muhammadan Year, Month	Muhammadan Day
Krodhi Makara—Tai.	21	Sa	1		9	·28	17	·82	H. 1261 Muharram.	23
	22	Su	2		10	·18	18	·75		24
	23	Mo	3		11 / 12	·08 / ·98	19	·68		25
	24	Tu	4		13	·89	20	·61		26
	25	We	5		14	·80	21	·55		27
	26	Th	6		A	·73	22	·51		28
	27	Fr	7	Magha Sukla	1	·67	23	·47		29
	28	Sa	8		2	·63	24	·44		30
	29	Su	9		3	·60	25	·44	H. 1261 Safar.	1
Krodhi Kumbha—Masi.	1	Mo	10		4	·58	26	·45		2
	2	Tu	11		5	·60	27	·50		3
	3	We	12		6	·64	1	·55		4
	4	Th	13		7	·70	2	·63		5
	5	Fr	14		8	·77	3	·72		6
	6	Sa	15		9	·85	4	·82		7
	7	Su	16		10	·94	5	·93		8
	8	Mo	17		...	...	...	...		9
	9	Tu	18		11	·03	6	·04		10
	10	We	19		12	·11	7	·14		11
	11	Th	20		13	·17	8	·22		12
	12	Fr	21		14	·22	9	·28		13
	13	Sa	22		P	·24	10	·33		14
	14	Su	23	Bah.	1	·25	11	·30		15
	15	Mo	24		2	·23	12	·37		16
	16	Tu	25		3	·19	13	·35		17
	17	We	26		4	·13	14	·32		18
	18	Th	27		5 / 6	·06 / ·98	15	·27		19
	19	Fr	28		7	·89	16	·22		20

March

Solar Year, Month	Cyclic Sidereal Day	Week-Day	English Day	Lunar Month	Tithi	Ending Moment	Nakshatra	Ending Moment	Muhammadan Year, Month	Muhammadan Day
Krodhi Kumbha—Masi.	20	Sa	1	Magha Bahula	8	·80	17	·16	H. 1261 Safar.	21
	21	Su	2		9	·70	18	·09		22
	22	Mo	3		10	·60	19 / 20	·02 / ·96		23
	23	Tu	4		11	·50	21	·90		24
	24	We	5		12	·41	22	·84		25
	25	Th	6		13	·34	23	·80		26
	26	Fr	7		14	·28	24	·77		27
	27	Sa	8		A	·24	25	·76		28
	28	Su	9	Phalguna Sukla	1	·21	26	·78		29
	29	Mo	10		2	·20	27	·81	H. 1261 Rabi-ul-awwal.	1
	30	Tu	11		3	·21	1	·86		2
Krodhi Mina—Panguni.	1	We	12		4	·25	2	·93		3
	2	Th	13		5	·31	...	...		4
	3	Fr	14		6	·38	3	·02		5
	4	Sa	15		7	·46	4	·12		6
	5	Su	16		8	·55	5	·23		7
	6	Mo	17		9	·64	6	·34		8
	7	Tu	18		10	·71	7	·44		9
	8	We	19		11	·77	8	·52		10
	9	Th	20		12	·82	9	·59		11
	10	Fr	21		13	·84	10	·65		12
	11	Sa	22		14	·84	11	·68		13
	12	Su	23		P	·82	12	·69		14
	13	Mo	24	Bahula	1	·78	13	·68		15
	14	Tu	25		2	·73	14	·65		16
	15	We	26		3	·66	15	·61		17
	16	Th	27		4	·57	16	·56		18
	17	Fr	28		5	·47	17	·50		19
	18	Sa	29		6	·37	18	·43		20
	19	Su	30		7	·27	19	·36		21
	20	Mo	31		8	·17	20	·29		22

April

Solar Year, Month	Cyclic Sidereal Day	Week-Day	English Day	Lunar Month	Tithi	Ending Moment	Nakshatra	Ending Moment	Muhammadan Year, Month	Muhammadan Day
Krodhi Mina—Panguni.	21	Tu	1		9	·08	21	·23	H. 1261 Rabi-ul-awwal.	23
	22	We	2		10 / 11	·00 / ·92	22	·17		24
	23	Th	3		12	·86	23	·13		25
	24	Fr	4		13	·81	24	·10		26
	25	Sa	5		14	·78	25	·08		27
	26	Su	6		A	·77	26	·10		28
	27	Mo	7	Chaitra Sukla	1	·79	27	·12		29
	28	Tu	8		2	·83	1	·17		30
	29	We	9		3	·88	2	·24	H. 1261 Rabi-ul-akhir.	1
	30	Th	10		4	·95	3	·32		2
Visvavasu Mesha—Chittirai.	1	Fr	11		...	...	4	·42		3
	2	Sa	12		5	·02	5	·53		4
	3	Su	13		6	·11	6	·64		5
	4	Mo	14		7	·20	7	·74		6
	5	Tu	15		8	·27	8	·83		7
	6	We	16		9	·33	9	·91		8
	7	Th	17		10	·37	10	·96		9
	8	Fr	18		11	·39	...	...		10
	9	Sa	19		12	·39	11	·00		11
	10	Su	20		13	·37	12	·01		12
	11	Mo	21		14	·33	13 / 14	·00 / ·98		13
	12	Tu	22		P	·27	15	·95		14
	13	We	23	Bahula	1	·20	16	·89		15
	14	Th	24		2	·11	17	·83		16
	15	Fr	25		3 / 4	·02 / ·92	18	·77		17
	16	Sa	26		5	·82	19	·71		18
	17	Su	27		6	·72	20	·64		19
	18	Mo	28		7	·62	21	·57		20
	19	Tu	29		8	·53	22	·51		21
	20	We	30		9	·45	23	·46		22

May

Solar Year, Month	Cyclic Sidereal Day	Week-Day	English Day	Lunar Month	Tithi	Ending Moment	Nakshatra	Ending Moment	Muhammadan Year, Month	Muhammadan Day
Visvavasu Mesha—Chittirai.	21	Th	1	Ch. Bah.	10	·39	24	·43	Rabi-ul-akhir.	23
	22	Fr	2		11	·34	25	·42		24
	23	Sa	3		12	·31	26	·42		25
	24	Su	4		13	·30	27	·44		26
	25	Mo	5		14	·31	1	·48		27
	26	Tu ●	6		A	·34	2	·54		28
	27	We	7	Vaisakha Sukla	1	·40	3	·63		29
	28	Th	8		2	·47	4	·72	H. 1261 Jumada-l-awwal.	1
	29	Fr	9		3	·55	5	·83		2
	30	Sa	10		4	·63	6	·94		3
	31	Su	11		5	·71	...	...		4
Visvavasu Vrishabha—Vaikasi.	1	Mo	12		6	·78	7	·04		5
	2	Tu	13		7	·85	8	·14		6
	3	We	14		8	·89	9	·22		7
	4	Th	15		9	·90	10	·28		8
	5	Fr	16		10	·90	11	·31		9
	6	Sa	17		11	·89	12	·33		10
	7	Su	18		12	·85	13	·34		11
	8	Mo	19		13	·79	14	·32		12
	9	Tu	20		14	·71	15	·28		13
	10	We ○	21		P	·62	16	·23		14
	11	Th	22	Bahula	1	·53	17	·17		15
	12	Fr	23		2	·43	18	·11		16
	13	Sa	24		3	·33	19 / 20	·04 / ·97		17
	14	Su	25		4	·23	21	·91		18
	15	Mo	26		5	·13	22	·85		19
	16	Tu	27		6 / 7	·04 / ·96	23	·79		20
	17	We	28		8	·89	24	·76		21
	18	Th	29		9	·84	25	·74		22
	19	Fr	30		10	·81	26	·74		23
	20	Sa	31		11	·79	27	·75		24

June

Solar Year, Month	Cyclic Sidereal Day	Week-Day	English Day	Lunar Month	Tithi	Ending Moment	Nakshatra	Ending Moment	Muhammadan Year, Month	Muhammadan Day
Visvavasu Vrishabha—Vaikasi.	21	Su	1		12	·81	1	·79	H. 1261 Jumada-l-awwal.	25
	22	Mo	2		13	·84	2	·86		26
	23	Tu	3		14	·89	3	·93		27
	24	We	4		A	·96	...	...		28
	25	Th	5	Jyeshtha Sukla	...	...	4	·02		29
	26	Fr	6		1	·04	5	·13		30
	27	Sa	7		2	·13	6	·23	H. 1261 Jumada-l-akhir.	1
	28	Su	8		3	·21	7	·34		2
	29	Mo	9		4	·28	8	·44		3
	30	Tu	10		5	·35	9	·52		4
	31	We	11		6	·37	10	·59		5
	32	Th	12		7	·39	11	·63		6
Visvavasu Mithuna—Ani.	1	Fr	13		8	·39	12	·66		7
	2	Sa	14		9	·38	13	·66		8
	3	Su	15		10	·34	14	·65		9
	4	Mo	16		11	·28	15	·61		10
	5	Tu	17		12	·21	16	·57		11
	6	We	18		13	·12	17	·51		12
	7	Th	19		14 / P	·02 / ·92	18	·45		13
	8	Fr	20	Bahula	1	·82	19	·38		14
	9	Sa	21		2	·72	20	·31		15
	10	Su	22		3	·62	21	·24		16
	11	Mo	23		4	·53	22	·18		17
	12	Tu	24		5	·44	23	·13		18
	13	We	25		6	·37	24	·09		19
	14	Th	26		7	·32	25	·07		20
	15	Fr	27		8	·29	26	·06		21
	16	Sa	28		9	·27	27	·07		22
	17	Su	29		10	·29	1	·11		23
	18	Mo	30		11	·32	2	·16		24

Naksh:—1. Asvn. 2. Bhar. 3. Krit. 4. Rohi. 5. Mrig. 6. Ardh. 7. Punar. 8. Push. 9. Aslesh. 10. Magh. 11. P. Phal. 12. U. Phal. 13. Hasta. 14. Chit.

A. D. 1845.
A.—Amavasya.
P.—Paurnami.

Kollam 1021, Commences { **N. Malabar—Sept.** / **S. Malabar—Aug.**

Hijra 1261, Jan. 10.
Hijra 1262, Dec. 30.

Vikrama 1902.
Bengal San 1251.
(N. Cycle) Anala.

Columns: SOLAR reckoning — Cyclic Sidereal Year, Month and Day; Week-Day; English Month and Day. LUNAR reckoning — Tithi; Ending Moment; Nakshatra; Ending Moment; Muhammadan Year, Month and Day.

July (Solar: Visvavasu Mithuna—Ani to 31; Visvavasu Karkata—Adi from 1. Lunar: J. Bah. to A; Ashadha Sukla, P, Bahula. Muhammadan: J.-akhir to 29; H. 1261 Rajab from 1)

Solar	Week-Day	Eng. Day	Tithi	Ending Moment	Nakshatra	Ending Moment	Muhammadan
19	Tu	1	12	·37	3	·24	25
20	We	2	13	·43	4	·33	26
21	Th	3	14	·51	5	·43	27
22	Fr	4	A	·59	6	·54	28
23	Sa	5	1	·68	7	·65	—29
24	Su	6	2	·75	8	·74	1
25	Mo	7	3	·80	9	·83	2
26	Tu	8	4	·84	10	·90	3
27	We	9	5	·87	11	·94	4
28	Th	10	6	·87	12	·97	5
29	Fr	11	7	·85	13	·99	6
30	Sa	12	8	·81	14	·97	7
—31	Su	13	9	·76	15	·94	8
1	Mo	14	10	·69	16	·90	9
2	Tu	15	11	·60	17	·85	10
3	We	16	12	·50	18	·79	11
4	Th	17	13	·40	19	·72	12
5	Fr	18	14	·30	20	·65	13
6	Sa	19	P	·20	21	·59	14
7	Su	20	1	·10	22	·53	15
8	Mo	21	2 / 3	·00 / ·92	23	·47	16
9	Tu	22	4	·85	24	·43	17
10	We	23	5	·80	25	·40	18
11	Th	24	6	·77	26	·38	19
12	Fr	25	7	·76	27	·40	20
13	Sa	26	8	·77	1	·43	21
14	Su	27	9	·79	2	·47	22
15	Mo	28	10	·84	3	·54	23
16	Tu	29	11	·90	4	·63	24
17	We	30	12	·98	5	·73	25
18	Th	31	...	...	6	·84	26

Aug. (Solar: Visvavasu Karkata to 32; Visvavasu Simha—Avani from 1. Lunar: Sravana Sukla, P, Bahula. Muhammadan: H. 1261 Shaban from 1)

Solar	Week-Day	Eng. Day	Tithi	Ending Moment	Nakshatra	Ending Moment	Muhammadan
19	Fr	1	13	·07	7	·94	27
20	Sa	2	14	·15	...	...	28
21	Su	3	—A	·22	8	·04	29
22	Mo	4	1	·28	9	·13	—30
23	Tu	5	2	·32	10	·21	1
24	We	6	3	·35	11	·27	2
25	Th	7	4	·36	12	·30	3
26	Fr	8	5	·34	13	·31	4
27	Sa	9	6	·30	14	·30	5
28	Su	10	7	·25	15	·28	6
29	Mo	11	8	·18	16	·24	7
30	Tu	12	9	·10	17	·19	8
31	We	13	10 / 11	·00 / ·90	18	·13	9
—32	Th	14	12	·80	19 / 20	·06 / ·99	10
1	Fr	15	13	·70	21	·93	11
2	Sa	16	14	·60	22	·86	12
3	Su	17	P	·51	23	·80	13
4	Mo	18	1	·42	24	·76	14
5	Tu	19	2	·35	25	·73	15
6	We	20	3	·30	26	·72	16
7	Th	21	4	·27	27	·72	17
8	Fr	22	5	·26	1	·74	18
9	Sa	23	6	·25	2	·78	19
10	Su	24	7	·29	3	·85	20
11	Mo	25	8	·34	4	·93	21
12	Tu	26	9	·40	...	...	22
13	We	27	10	·48	5	·03	23
14	Th	28	11	·56	6	·14	24
15	Fr	29	12	·65	7	·25	25
16	Sa	30	13	·72	8	·35	26
17	Su	31	14	·78	9	·44	27

Sep. (Solar: Visvavasu Simha—Avani to 31; Visvavasu Kanya—Purattasi from 1. Lunar: Bhadrapada Sukla, P, Bahula. Muhammadan: H. 1261 Ramzan from 1)

Solar	Week-Day	Eng. Day	Tithi	Ending Moment	Nakshatra	Ending Moment	Muhammadan
18	Mo	1	—A	·83	10	·52	28
19	Tu	2	1	·86	11	·58	—29
20	We	3	2	·87	12	·62	1
21	Th	4	3	·85	13	·63	2
22	Fr	5	4	·82	14	·63	3
23	Sa	6	5	·76	15	·62	4
24	Su	7	6	·69	16	·58	5
25	Mo	8	7	·61	17	·53	6
26	Tu	9	8	·52	18	·47	7
27	We	10	9	·42	19	·41	8
28	Th	11	10	·32	20	·34	9
29	Fr	12	11	·22	21	·27	10
30	Sa	13	12	·12	22	·20	11
—31	Su	14	13 / 14	·03 / ·95	23	·14	12
1	Mo	15	P	·88	24	·09	13
2	Tu	16	1	·83	25	·05	14
3	We	17	2	·79	26	·04	15
4	Th	18	3	·78	27	·04	16
5	Fr	19	4	·80	1	·06	17
6	Sa	20	5	·83	2	·09	18
7	Su	21	6	·87	3	·15	19
8	Mo	22	7	·93	4	·24	20
9	Tu	23	...	...	5	·33	21
10	We	24	8	·01	6	·43	22
11	Th	25	9	·10	7	·54	23
12	Fr	26	10	·18	8	·65	24
13	Sa	27	11	·26	9	·75	25
14	Su	28	12	·32	10	·83	26
15	Mo	29	13	·37	11	·89	27
16	Tu	30	14	·40	12	·93	28

Oct. (Solar: Visvavasu Kanya to 30; Visvavasu Tula—Aippasi from 1. Lunar: Asvina Sukla, P, Bahula. Muhammadan: H. 1261 Shawwal from 1)

Solar	Week-Day	Eng. Day	Tithi	Ending Moment	Nakshatra	Ending Moment	Muhammadan
17	We	1	—A	·41	13	·95	29
18	Th	2	1	·40	14	·96	—30
19	Fr	3	2	·37	15	·94	1
20	Sa	4	3	·31	16	·91	2
21	Su	5	4	·24	17	·86	3
22	Mo	6	5	·16	18	·80	4
23	Tu	7	6 / 7	07 / ·97	19	·74	5
24	We	8	8	·87	20	·68	6
25	Th	9	9	·77	21	·61	7
26	Fr	10	10	·68	22	·54	8
27	Sa	11	11	·59	23	·47	9
28	Su	12	12	·51	24	·42	10
29	Mo	13	13	·45	25	·39	11
—30	Tu	14	14	·40	26	·37	12
1	We	15	P	·37	27	·36	13
2	Th	16	1	·36	1	·37	14
3	Fr	17	2	·37	2	·40	15
4	Sa	18	3	·39	3	·47	16
5	Su	19	4	·44	4	·54	17
6	Mo	20	5	·51	5	·63	18
7	Tu	21	6	·59	6	·73	19
8	We	22	7	·68	7	·84	20
9	Th	23	8	·77	8	·95	21
10	Fr	24	9	·85	...	...	22
11	Sa	25	10	·91	9	·05	23
12	Su	26	11	·95	10	·13	24
13	Mo	27	12	·98	11	·20	25
14	Tu	28	13	·99	12	·25	26
15	We	29	14	·99	13	·28	27
16	Th	30	—A	·96	14	·29	28
17	Fr	31	1	·91	15	·27	—29

Nov. (Solar: Visvavasu Tula—Aippasi to 30; Visvavasu Vrischika—Kartigai from 1. Lunar: Karttika Sukla, P, Bahula. Muhammadan: H. 1261 Zi-l-ka'da from 1)

Solar	Week-Day	Eng. Day	Tithi	Ending Moment	Nakshatra	Ending Moment	Muhammadan
18	Sa	1	2	·84	16	·24	1
19	Su	2	3	·76	17	·20	2
20	Mo	3	4	·67	18	·14	3
21	Tu	4	5	·57	19	·08	4
22	We	5	6	·47	20 / 21	·01 / ·94	5
23	Th	6	7	·37	22	·87	6
24	Fr	7	8	·28	23	·81	7
25	Sa	8	9	·19	24	·76	8
26	Su	9	10	·12	25	·72	9
27	Mo	10	11 / 12	·05 / ·99	26	·69	10
28	Tu	11	13	·96	27	·68	11
29	We	12	14	·95	1	·69	12
—30	Th ○	13	P	·97	2	·73	13
1	Fr	14	...	...	3	·78	14
2	Sa	15	1	·00	4	·85	15
3	Su	16	2	·05	5	·93	16
4	Mo	17	3	·12	...	...	17
5	Tu	18	4	·21	6	·03	18
6	We	19	5	·30	7	·14	19
7	Th	20	6	·38	8	·25	20
8	Fr	21	7	·46	9	·35	21
9	Sa	22	8	·53	10	·44	22
10	Su	23	9	·58	11	·51	23
11	Mo	24	10	·61	12	·57	24
12	Tu	25	11	·62	13	·60	25
13	We	26	12	·61	14	·62	26
14	Th	27	13	·57	15	·60	27
15	Fr	28	14	·52	16	·57	28
16	Sa	29	—A	·46	17	·53	29
17	Su	30	1	·38	18	·49	—30

Dec. (Solar: Visvavasu Vrischika to 30; Visvavasu Dhanus—Margali from 1. Lunar: Margasira Sukla, P, Bahula; P. Suk. from A. Muhammadan: H. 1261 Zi-l-hijja from 1)

Solar	Week-Day	Eng. Day	Tithi	Ending Moment	Nakshatra	Ending Moment	Muhammadan
18	Mo	1	2	·29	19	·42	1
19	Tu	2	3	·20	20	·35	2
20	We	3	4	·10	21	·28	3
21	Th	4	5 / 6	·00 / ·90	22	·22	4
22	Fr	5	7	·81	23	·16	5
23	Sa	6	8	·73	24	·10	6
24	Su	7	9	·67	25	·05	7
25	Mo	8	10	·63	26	·02	8
26	Tu	9	11	·60	27	·00	9
27	We	10	12	·59	1	·02	10
28	Th	11	13	·61	2	·04	11
29	Fr	12	14	·65	3	·09	12
—30	Sa	13	P	·71	4	·15	13
1	Su	14	1	·78	5	·23	14
2	Mo	15	2	·86	6	·33	15
3	Tu	16	3	·95	7	·44	16
4	We	17	...	...	8	·55	17
5	Th	18	4	·04	9	·65	18
6	Fr	19	5	·12	10	·74	19
7	Sa	20	6	·18	11	·82	20
8	Su	21	7	·22	12	·88	21
9	Mo	22	8	·25	13	·92	22
10	Tu	23	9	·26	14	·93	23
11	We	24	10	·25	15	·93	24
12	Th	25	11	·22	16	·90	25
13	Fr	26	12	·16	17	·87	26
14	Sa	27	13	·09	18	·82	27
15	Su	28	14 / A	·01 / ·92	19	·76	28
16	Mo	29	1	·83	20	·69	—29
17	Tu	30	2	·73	21	·62	1
18	We	31	3	·63	22	·55	2

15. Svati. 16. Visak. 17. Anur. 18. Jyesh. 19. Mula. 20. P. Ash. 21. U. Ash. 22. Sravn. 23. Dani. 24. Satab. 25. P. Bhad. 26. U. Bhad. 27. Rev.

A. D. 1846. **Mesha Sankranti** (Commencement of Indian Sidereal Year).
Solar Eclipse. ● **(Surya Sid.) April 11·65.** **Saka 1768.** **Kaliyuga 4947.**
Lunar Eclipse. ○ **(Arya Sid.) April 11·65.** **(S. Cycle) Parabhava.**

SOLAR reckoning. — LUNAR reckoning.

Jan.

Visvavasu *Dhanus—Margali.* / Visvavasu *Makara—Tai.* — *Sukla*, **Pausha**, *Bahula* — H. 1262 *Muharram.*

Cyclic Sidereal Year, Month and Day	Week-Day	English Month and Day	Tithi	Ending Moment	Nakshatra	Ending Moment	Muhammadan Year, Month and Day
19	Th	1	4	·54	23	·49	3
20	Fr	2	5	·45	24	·43	4
21	Sa	3	6	·37	25	·38	5
22	Su	4	7	·31	26	·35	6
23	Mo	5	8	·27	27	·34	7
24	Tu	6	9	·25	1	·34	8
25	We	7	10	·24	2	·36	9
26	Th	8	11	·25	3	·40	10
27	Fr	9	12	·29	4	·46	11
28	Sa	10	13	·35	5	·54	12
—29	Su	11	14	·42	6	·64	13
1	Mo	12	P	·51	7	·74	14
2	Tu	13	1	·60	8	·85	15
3	We	14	2	·68	9	·95	16
4	Th	15	3	·76	...	...	17
5	Fr	16	4	·83	10	·05	18
6	Sa	17	5	·87	11	·13	19
7	Su	18	6	·89	12	·19	20
8	Mo	19	7	·90	13	·23	21
9	Tu	20	8	·89	14	·25	22
10	We	21	9	·86	15	·25	23
11	Th	22	10	·80	16	·24	24
12	Fr	23	11	·73	17	·21	25
13	Sa	24	12	·65	18	·16	26
14	Su	25	13	·56	19	·10	27
15	Mo	26	14	·46	20 21	·04 ·97	28
16	Tu	27	—A	·36	22	·90	29
17	We	28	1	·26	23	·83	—30
18	Th	29	2	·17	24	·77	1
19	Fr	30	3	·09	25	·72	2
20	Sa	31	4 5	·02 ·96	26	·69	3

Feb.

Visvavasu *Kumbha—Masi.* — *Sukla*, **Magha**, *Bahula*, **P.** *Suk.* — H. 1262 *Safar.*

Cyclic Sidereal Year, Month and Day	Week-Day	English Month and Day	Tithi	Ending Moment	Nakshatra	Ending Moment	Muhammadan Year, Month and Day
21	Su	1	6	·91	27	·67	4
22	Mo	2	7	·89	1	·66	5
23	Tu	3	8	·88	2	·67	6
24	We	4	9	·89	3	·71	7
25	Th	5	10	·94	4	·76	8
26	Fr	6	...	...	5	·85	9
27	Sa	7	11	·00	6	·94	10
28	Su	8	12	·07	...	...	11
—29	Mo	9	13	·15	7	·04	12
1	Tu	10	14	·23	8	·15	13
2	We	11	P	·32	9	·26	14
3	Th	12	1	·41	10	·36	15
4	Fr	13	2	·47	11	·44	16
5	Sa	14	3	·51	12	·50	17
6	Su	15	4	·53	13	·55	18
7	Mo	16	5	·54	14	·58	19
8	Tu	17	6	·53	15	·59	20
9	We	18	7	·49	16	·57	21
10	Th	19	8	·42	17	·54	22
11	Fr	20	9	·35	18	·49	23
12	Sa	21	10	·27	19	·43	24
13	Su	22	11	·18	20	·37	25
14	Mo	23	12 13	·08 ·98	21	·37	26
15	Tu	24	14	·88	22	·24	27
16	We	25	—A	·78	23	·17	28
17	Th	26	1	·69	24	·11	—29
18	Fr	27	2	·62	25	·06	1
19	Sa	28	3	·57	26 27	·02 ·99	2

March

Visvavasu *Kumbha—Masi.* / Visvavasu *Mina—Panguni.* — *Sukla*, **Phalguna**, *Bahula* — H. 1262 *Rabi-ul-awwal.*

Cyclic Sidereal Year, Month and Day	Week-Day	English Month and Day	Tithi	Ending Moment	Nakshatra	Ending Moment	Muhammadan Year, Month and Day
20	Su	1	4	·53	1	·98	3
21	Mo	2	5	·50	2	·99	4
22	Tu	3	6	·49	...	...	5
23	We	4	7	·51	3	·02	6
24	Th	5	8	·55	4	·08	7
25	Fr	6	9	·61	5	·15	8
26	Sa	7	10	·69	6	·24	9
27	Su	8	11	·78	7	·34	10
28	Mo	9	12	·87	8	·44	11
29	Tu	10	13	·95	9	·55	12
—30	We	11	...	...	10	·65	13
1	Th	12	14	·02	11	·74	14
2	Fr	13	P	·07	12	·81	15
3	Sa	14	1	·11	13	·86	16
4	Su	15	2	·13	14	·90	17
5	Mo	16	3	·13	15	·91	18
6	Tu	17	4	·12	16	·90	19
7	We	18	5	·08	17	·87	20
8	Th	19	6 7	·02 ·95	18	·83	21
9	Fr	20	8	·86	19	·78	22
10	Sa	21	9	·77	20	·72	23
11	Su	22	10	·67	21	·65	24
12	Mo	23	11	·57	22	·58	25
13	Tu	24	12	·47	23	·51	26
14	We	25	13	·38	24	·45	27
15	Th	26	14	·29	25	·39	28
16	Fr	27	—A	·21	26	·35	29
17	Sa	28	1	·15	27	·32	—30
18	Su	29	2	·11	1	·30	1
19	Mo	30	3	·09	2	·31	2
20	Tu	31	4	·08	3	·34	3

April

Parabhava *Mesha—Chittirai.* — *Sukla*, **Chaitra**, *Bahula*, **V.** *Suk.* — H. 1262 *Rabi-ul-akhir.* / *J. awwal.*

Cyclic Sidereal Year, Month and Day	Week-Day	English Month and Day	Tithi	Ending Moment	Nakshatra	Ending Moment	Muhammadan Year, Month and Day
21	We	1	5	·10	4	·39	4
22	Th	2	6	·13	5	·46	5
23	Fr	3	7	·19	6	·54	6
24	Sa	4	8	·27	7	·64	7
25	Su	5	9	·35	8	·75	8
26	Mo	6	10	·44	9	·86	9
27	Tu	7	11	·52	10	·96	10
28	We	8	12	·59	...	...	11
29	Th	9	13	·64	11	·05	12
30	Fr	10	14	·68	12	·12	13
—31	Sa	11	P	·69	13	·18	14
1	Su	12	1	·69	14	·22	15
2	Mo	13	2	·68	15	·23	16
3	Tu	14	3	·64	16	·22	17
4	We	15	4	·58	17	·20	18
5	Th	16	5	·51	18	·16	19
6	Fr	17	6	·42	19	·11	20
7	Sa	18	7	·33	20 21	·05 ·98	21
8	Su	19	8	·23	22	·91	22
9	Mo	20	9	·13	23	·85	23
10	Tu	21	10 11	·03 ·93	24	·79	24
11	We	22	12	·84	25	·73	25
12	Th	23	13	·76	26	·68	26
13	Fr	24	14	·70	27	·65	27
14	Sa	25	—A	·66	1	·63	28
15	Su	26	1	·63	2	·64	—29
16	Mo	27	2	·61	3	·66	1
17	Tu	28	3	·63	4	·70	2
18	We	29	4	·66	5	·76	3
19	Th	30	5	·72	6	·84	4

May

Parabhava *Mesha—Chittirai.* / Parabhava *Vrishabha—Vaikasi.* — *Sukla*, **Vaisakha**, *Bahula* — H. 1262 *Jumadul-awwal.*

Cyclic Sidereal Year, Month and Day	Week-Day	English Month and Day	Tithi	Ending Moment	Nakshatra	Ending Moment	Muhammadan Year, Month and Day
20	Fr	1	6	·80	7	·94	5
21	Sa	2	7	·89	...	...	6
22	Su	3	8	·97	8	·05	7
23	Mo	4	...	...	9	·16	8
24	Tu	5	9	·04	10	·26	9
25	We	6	10	·11	11	·35	10
26	Th	7	11	·17	12	·43	11
27	Fr	8	12	·22	13	·50	12
28	Sa	9	13	·25	14	·54	13
29	Su	10	14	·23	15	·55	14
—30	Mo	11	P	·20	16	·55	15
1	Tu	12	1	·16	17	·53	16
2	We	13	2	·10	18	·50	17
3	Th	14	3 4	·03 ·94	19	·45	18
4	Fr	15	5	·84	20	·39	19
5	Sa	16	6	·74	21	·32	20
6	Su	17	7	·64	22	·25	21
7	Mo	18	8	·54	23	·18	22
8	Tu	19	9	·44	24	·12	23
9	We	20	10	·34	25	·06	24
10	Th	21	11	·26	26 27	·01 ·97	25
11	Fr	22	12	·21	1	·96	26
12	Sa	23	13	·17	2	·96	27
13	Su	24	14	·14	3	·97	28
14	Mo	25	—A	·12	...	...	29
15	Tu	26	1	·13	4	·01	—30
16	We	27	2	·17	5	·07	1
17	Th	28	3	·22	6	·15	2
18	Fr	29	4	·29	7	·25	3
19	Sa	30	5	·38	8	·35	4
20	Su	31	6	·46	9	·45	5

June

Parabhava *Mithuna—Ani.* — *Sukla*, **Jyeshtha**, *Bahula*, **Ashad.** *Suk.* — H. 1262 *Jumadul-akhir.* / *Rajab.*

Cyclic Sidereal Year, Month and Day	Week-Day	English Month and Day	Tithi	Ending Moment	Nakshatra	Ending Moment	Muhammadan Year, Month and Day
21	Mo	1	7	·54	10	·56	6
22	Tu	2	8	·61	11	·65	7
23	We	3	9	·67	12	·74	8
24	Th	4	10	·70	13	·81	9
25	Fr	5	11	·72	14	·85	10
26	Sa	6	12	·72	15	·87	11
27	Su	7	13	·70	16	·87	12
28	Mo	8	14	·66	17	·86	13
29	Tu	9	P	·60	18	·83	14
30	We	10	1	·52	19	·79	15
31	Th	11	2	·43	20	·73	16
—32	Fr	12	3	·33	21	·67	17
1	Sa	13	4	·23	22	·60	18
2	Su	14	5	·13	23	·53	19
3	Mo	15	6 7	·03 ·93	24	·46	20
4	Tu	16	8	·84	25	·40	21
5	We	17	9	·76	26	·35	22
6	Th	18	10	·70	27	·31	23
7	Fr	19	11	·65	1	·29	24
8	Sa	20	12	·61	2	·28	25
9	Su	21	13	·60	3	·29	26
10	Mo	22	14	·61	4	·32	27
11	Tu	23	—A	·65	5	·38	28
12	We	24	1	·70	6	·46	—29
13	Th	25	2	·76	7	·55	1
14	Fr	26	3	·84	8	·65	2
15	Sa	27	4	·93	9	·75	3
16	Su	28	...	...	10	·86	4
17	Mo	29	5	·01	11	·96	5
18	Tu	30	6	·08	...	...	6

Naksh:—1. Asvn. 2. Bhar. 3. Krit. 4. Rohi. 5. Mrig. 6. Ardh. 7. Punar. 8. Push. 9. Aslesh. 10. Magh. 11. P. Phal. 12. U. Phal. 13. Hasta. 14. Chit.

A. D. 1846.
A.—Amavasya.
P.—Paurnami.

Kollam 1022, Commences { N. Malabar—Sept. / S. Malabar—Aug.

Hijra 1263, Commences, Dec. 20.

Vikrama 1903.
Bengal San 1252.
(N. Cycle) Pingala.

July

SOLAR reckoning: Cyclic Sidereal Year, Month and Day	Week-Day	English Month and Day	LUNAR reckoning: Tithi	Ending Moment	Nakshatra	Ending Moment	Muhammadan Year, Month and Day
Parabhava Mithuna—Ani. 19	We	1	Sukla 7	·14	12	·05	7
20	Th	2	8	·18	13	·12	8
21	Fr	3	9	·20	14	·16	9
22	Sa	4	10	·19	15	·19	10
23	Su	5	11	·17	16	·21	11
24	Mo	6	12	·14	17	·19	12
25	Tu	7	13	·08	18	·16	13
26	We	8	{ 14 / P	·00 / ·91	19	·12	14
27	Th	9	Ashadha 1	·81	20	·07	15
28	Fr	10	2	·71	{ 21 / 22	·01 / ·94	H. 1262 Rajab. 16
29	Sa	11	3	·61	23	·87	17
30	Su	12	4	·51	24	·80	18
—31	Mo	13	5	·41	25	·74	19
1	Tu	14	6	·32	26	·69	20
2	We	15	7	·24	27	·65	21
3	Th	16	Bahula 8	·17	1	·62	22
4	Fr	17	9	·12	2	·60	23
5	Sa	18	10	·10	3	·61	24
6	Su	19	11	·09	4	·64	25
7	Mo	20	12	·09	5	·69	26
8	Tu	21	13	·12	6	·76	27
9	We	22	14	·16	7	·85	28
10	Th	23	—A	·23	8	·94	29
11	Fr	24	1	·31	...	...	—30
Parabhava Karkata—Adi. 12	Sa	25	2	·40	9	·05	1
13	Su	26	3	·48	10	·16	2
14	Mo	27	4	·55	11	·27	3
15	Tu	28	5	·61	12	·36	4
16	We	29	Sukla 6	·66	13	·43	5
17	Th	30	7	·68	14	·48	6
18	Fr	31	8	·68	15	·52	7

Aug.

SOLAR reckoning: Cyclic Sidereal Year, Month and Day	Week-Day	English Month and Day	LUNAR reckoning: Tithi	Ending Moment	Nakshatra	Ending Moment	Muhammadan Year, Month and Day
19	Sa	1	9	·66	16	·53	8
20	Su	2	10	·62	17	·52	9
21	Mo	3	Sravana 11	·56	18	·50	10
22	Tu	4	12	·48	19	·46	11
23	We	5	13	·40	20	·41	12
24	Th	6	14	·31	21	·35	13
25	Fr	7	P	·21	22	·28	H. 1262 Shaban. 14
26	Sa	8	1	·11	23	·21	15
27	Su	9	{ 2 / 3	·01 / ·91	24	·14	16
28	Mo	10	4	·82	25	·08	17
29	Tu	11	5	·74	{ 26 / 27	·02 / ·98	18
30	We	12	6	·67	1	·95	19
31	Th	13	Bahula 7	·61	2	·93	20
—32	Fr	14	8	·59	3	·93	21
1	Sa	15	9	·58	4	·96	22
2	Su	16	10	·59	...	...	23
3	Mo	17	11	·61	5	·00	24
4	Tu	18	12	·66	6	·07	25
5	We	19	13	·73	7	·15	26
6	Th	20	14	·81	8	·24	27
7	Fr	21	—A	·90	9	·35	28
Parabhava Simha—Avani. 8	Sa	22	1	·98	10	·46	—29
9	Su	23	...	...	11	·57	1
10	Mo	24	Sukla 2	·05	12	·66	2
11	Tu	25	3	·11	13	·73	3
12	We	26	4	·16	14	·80	4
13	Th	27	Bhadra. 5	·19	15	·84	H. 1262 Ramzan. 5
14	Fr	28	6	·18	16	·85	6
15	Sa	29	7	·16	17	·85	7
16	Su	30	8	·12	18	·83	8
17	Mo	31	9	·07	19	·80	9

Sep.

SOLAR reckoning: Cyclic Sidereal Year, Month and Day	Week-Day	English Month and Day	LUNAR reckoning: Tithi	Ending Moment	Nakshatra	Ending Moment	Muhammadan Year, Month and Day
18	Tu	1	{ 10 / 11	·00 / ·92	20	·74	10
19	We	2	Suk. 12	·82	21	·68	11
Parabhava Simha—Avani. 20	Th	3	13	·72	22	·62	12
21	Fr	4	14	·62	23	·55	13
22	Sa	5	P	·52	24	·48	14
23	Su	6	Bhadrapada 1	·42	25	·42	15
24	Mo	7	2	·33	26	·36	16
25	Tu	8	3	·26	27	·31	17
26	We	9	4	·19	1	·27	18
27	Th	10	5	·14	2	·25	19
28	Fr	11	6	·11	3	·26	H. 1262 Ramzan. 20
29	Sa	12	7	·10	4	·28	21
30	Su	13	8	·11	5	·31	22
—31	Mo	14	Bahula 9	·14	6	·37	23
1	Tu	15	10	·19	7	·45	24
2	We	16	11	·25	8	·55	25
3	Th	17	12	·33	9	·66	26
4	Fr	18	13	·41	10	·77	27
5	Sa	19	14	·49	11	·87	28
6	Su	20	—A	·57	12	·96	29
7	Mo	21	1	·64	...	...	—30
8	Tu	22	2	·69	13	·04	1
9	We	23	3	·71	14	·11	2
Parabhava Kanya—Purattasi. 10	Th	24	4	·72	15	·15	3
11	Fr	25	5	·70	16	·17	4
12	Sa	26	6	·66	17	·17	5
13	Su	27	7	·61	18	·16	6
14	Mo	28	Sukla 8	·54	19	·13	7
15	Tu	29	9	·46	20	·08	8
16	We	30	10	·37	{ 21 / 22	·02 / ·96	9

Oct.

SOLAR reckoning: Cyclic Sidereal Year, Month and Day	Week-Day	English Month and Day	LUNAR reckoning: Tithi	Ending Moment	Nakshatra	Ending Moment	Muhammadan Year, Month and Day
17	Th	1	11	·27	23	·89	10
18	Fr	2	12	·17	24	·82	11
19	Sa	3	{ 13 / 14	·07 / ·97	25	·75	12
20	Su	4	Asvina P	·88	26	·69	H. 1262 Shawwal. 13
21	Mo	5	1	·80	27	·64	14
22	Tu	6	2	·74	1	·60	15
23	We	7	3	·69	2	·59	16
24	Th	8	4	·67	3	·59	17
25	Fr	9	5	·67	4	·69	18
26	Sa	10	6	·68	5	·62	19
27	Su	11	7	·70	6	·68	20
28	Mo	12	Bahula 8	·75	7	·76	21
29	Tu	13	9	·81	8	·85	22
—30	We	14	10	·89	9	·95	23
1	Th	15	11	·98	...	...	24
2	Fr	16	...	...	10	·06	25
3	Sa	17	12	·07	11	·17	26
4	Su	18	13	·15	12	·27	27
5	Mo	19	14	·21	13	·36	28
6	Tu	● 20	—A	·26	14	·42	—29
Parabhava Tula—Aippasi. 7	We	21	1	·30	15	·47	1
8	Th	22	2	·30	16	·49	2
9	Fr	23	3	·28	17	·50	3
10	Sa	24	Sukla 4	·24	18	·49	H. 1262 Zi-l-ka'da. 4
11	Su	25	5	·19	19	·46	5
12	Mo	26	6	·12	20	·42	6
13	Tu	27	{ 7 / 8	·04 / ·95	21	·36	7
14	We	28	Kartt. 9	·85	22	·30	8
15	Th	29	10	·75	23	·23	9
16	Fr	30	11	·66	24	·16	10
17	Sa	31	12	·57	25	·09	11

Nov.

SOLAR reckoning: Cyclic Sidereal Year, Month and Day	Week-Day	English Month and Day	LUNAR reckoning: Tithi	Ending Moment	Nakshatra	Ending Moment	Muhammadan Year, Month and Day
18	Su	1	Suk. 13	·48	{ 26 / 27	·03 / ·97	12
19	Mo	2	14	·40	1	·94	13
Parabhava Tula—Aippasi. 20	Tu	3	P	·33	2	·91	14
21	We	4	Kartika 1	·29	3	·90	15
22	Th	5	2	·27	4	·91	16
23	Fr	6	3	·26	5	·94	17
24	Sa	7	4	·26	...	...	18
25	Su	8	5	·30	6	·00	19
26	Mo	9	6	·36	7	·07	20
27	Tu	10	7	·43	8	·15	H. 1262 Zi-l-ka'da. 21
28	We	11	8	·51	9	·25	22
29	Th	12	Bahula 9	·59	10	·36	23
—30	Fr	13	10	·68	11	·47	24
1	Sa	14	11	·76	12	·57	25
2	Su	15	12	·83	13	·66	26
3	Mo	16	13	·88	14	·73	27
4	Tu	17	14	·91	15	·78	28
5	We	18	—A	·91	16	·81	29
6	Th	19	1	·89	17	·83	—30
7	Fr	20	2	·85	18	·82	1
8	Sa	21	3	·80	19	·79	2
9	Su	22	4	·74	20	·75	3
Parabhava Vrischika—Kartigai. 10	Mo	23	5	·66	21	·69	4
11	Tu	24	6	·57	22	·63	5
12	We	25	Sukla 7	·47	23	·57	6
13	Th	26	8	·37	24	·50	7
14	Fr	27	9	·28	25	·43	8
15	Sa	28	10	·19	26	·37	9
16	Su	29	11	·10	27	·32	10
17	Mo	30	{ 12 / 13	·02 / ·96	1	·27	11

Dec.

SOLAR reckoning: Cyclic Sidereal Year, Month and Day	Week-Day	English Month and Day	LUNAR reckoning: Tithi	Ending Moment	Nakshatra	Ending Moment	Muhammadan Year, Month and Day
18	Tu	1	Margasira 14	·91	2	·24	H. 1262 Zi-l-hijja. 12
19	We	2	P	·89	3	·22	13
20	Th	3	1	·89	4	·23	14
21	Fr	4	2	·90	5	·26	15
22	Sa	5	3	·94	6	·31	16
23	Su	6	4	·99	7	·37	17
24	Mo	7	...	...	8	·45	18
25	Tu	8	5	·06	9	·55	19
26	We	9	6	·14	10	·66	20
27	Th	10	Bahula 7	·23	11	·77	21
28	Fr	11	8	·32	12	·87	22
29	Sa	12	9	·40	13	·96	23
—30	Su	13	10	·47	...	...	24
1	Mo	14	11	·52	14	·04	25
2	Tu	15	12	·55	15	·09	26
3	We	16	13	·55	16	·13	27
4	Th	17	14	·53	17	·15	28
5	Fr	18	—A	·49	18	·15	29
6	Sa	19	1	·44	19	·12	—30
7	Su	20	2	·37	20	·08	1
Parabhava Dhanus—Marguli. 8	Mo	21	3	·29	{ 21 / 22	·04 / ·98	2
9	Tu	22	Sukla 4	·20	23	·91	H. 1263 Muharram. 3
10	We	23	5	·10	24	·84	4
11	Th	24	{ 6 / 7	·00 / ·91	25	·77	5
12	Fr	25	8	·82	26	·71	6
13	Sa	26	9	·74	27	·65	7
14	Su	27	Pausha 10	·66	1	·60	8
15	Mo	28	11	·60	2	·57	9
16	Tu	29	12	·55	3	·55	10
17	We	30	13	·53	4	·55	11
18	Th	31	14	·53	5	·58	12

15. Svati. 16. Visak. 17. Anur. 18. Jyesh. 19. Mula. 20. P. Ash. 21. U. Ash. 22. Sravu. 23. Dani. 24. Satab. 25. P. Bhad. 26. U. Bhad. 27. Rev.

A. D. 1847. **Mesha Sankranti** (Commencement of Indian Sidereal Year).
Solar Eclipse. ● **(Surya Sid.) April 11·91.** **Saka 1769.** **Kaliyuga 4948.**
Lunar Eclipse. ○ **(Arya Sid.) April 11·81.** **(S. Cycle) Plavanga.**

SOLAR reckoning: Cyclic Sidereal Year, Month and Day; Week-Day; English Month and Day. LUNAR reckoning: Tithi; Ending Moment; Nakshatra; Ending Moment; Muhammadan Year, Month and Day.

Jan.

Cyclic Sidereal Year, Month and Day	Week-Day	English Month and Day	Tithi	Ending Moment	Nakshatra	Ending Moment	Muhammadan Year, Month and Day
Parabhava *Dhanus—Margali.* 19	Fr	1	**Pausha** P	·55	6	·62	13
20	Sa	2	1	·59	7	·68	14
21	Su	3	2	·64	8	·76	15
22	Mo	4	3	·71	9	·85	16
23	Tu	5	4	·79	10	·96	17
24	We	6	5	·88	...	...	18
25	Th	7	6	·97	11	·07	19
26	Fr	8	...	...	12	·17	20
27	Sa	9	*Bahula* 7	·05	13	·27	H. 1263 *Muharram.* 21
28	Su	10	8	·12	14	·34	22
—29	Mo	11	9	·16	15	·40	23
1	Tu	12	10	·19	16	·45	24
2	We	13	11	·19	17	·47	25
3	Th	14	12	·17	18	·47	26
4	Fr	15	13	·13	19	·45	27
5	Sa	16	14	·08	20	·42	28
6	Su	17	A 1	·02 ·94	21	·38	29
7	Mo	18	2	·84	22	·32	—30
8	Tu	19	3	·74	23	·25	1
9	We	20	4	·64	24	·18	2
10	Th	21	5	·54	25	·11	3
11	Fr	22	6	·45	26 27	·05 ·99	4
Parabhava *Makara—Tai.* 12	Sa	23	*Sukla* 7	·37	1	·94	5
13	Su	24	8	·30	2	·90	6
14	Mo	25	9	·24	3	·87	7
15	Tu	26	10	·20	4	·87	8
16	We	27	11	·18	5	·89	9
17	Th	28	**Magha** 12	·17	6	·93	10
18	Fr	29	13	·19	7	·98	*Safar.* 11
19	Sa	30	14	·24	...	...	12
20	Su	31	P	·30	8	·06	13

Feb.

Cyclic Sidereal Year, Month and Day	Week-Day	English Month and Day	Tithi	Ending Moment	Nakshatra	Ending Moment	Muhammadan Year, Month and Day
21	Mo	1	1	·37	9	·16	H. 1263 14
22	Tu	2	2	·45	10	·26	15
23	We	3	3	·54	11	·37	16
24	Th	4	4	·62	12	·47	17
25	Fr	5	5	·70	13	·57	18
26	Sa	6	*Bahula* 6	·76	14	·66	19
27	Su	7	7	·81	15	·72	20
28	Mo	8	8	·83	16	·77	21
29	Tu	9	9	·83	17	·79	22
—30	We	10	10	·80	18	·80	23
1	Th	11	11	·76	19	·79	24
2	Fr	12	12	·71	20	·76	25
3	Sa	13	13	·64	21	·71	26
4	Su	14	14	·56	22	·65	27
5	Mo	15	—A	·47	23	·59	28
6	Tu	16	*Sukla* 1	·37	24	·53	—29
Parabhava *Kumbha—Masi.* 7	We	17	2	·27	25	·46	1
8	Th	18	3	·17	26	·39	*Rabi-ul-awwal.* 2
9	Fr	19	4 5	·08 ·99	27	·32	3
10	Sa	20	6	·91	1	·27	4
11	Su	21	7	·86	2	·23	5
12	Mo	22	8	·82	3	·21	6
13	Tu	23	9	·80	4	·20	7
14	We	24	**Phalguna** 10	·79	5	·21	H. 1263 8
15	Th	25	11	·81	6	·24	9
16	Fr	26	12	·85	7	·29	10
17	Sa	27	13	·92	8	·37	11
18	Su	28	...	...	9	·46	12

March

Cyclic Sidereal Year, Month and Day	Week-Day	English Month and Day	Tithi	Ending Moment	Nakshatra	Ending Moment	Muhammadan Year, Month and Day
19	Mo	1	**Phalguna** 14	·00	10	·56	13
Parabhava *Kumbha—Masi.* 20	Tu	2	P	·08	11	·66	14
21	We	3	1	·17	12	·77	15
22	Th	4	2	·25	13	·88	16
23	Fr	5	3	·32	14	·97	17
24	Sa	6	4	·37	...	...	18
25	Su	7	5	·41	15	·03	*Rabi-ul-awwal.* 19
26	Mo	8	6	·44	16	·08	20
27	Tu	9	*Bahula* 7	·44	17	·11	21
28	We	10	8	·42	18	·13	22
—29	Th	11	9	·37	19	·12	23
1	Fr	12	10	·31	20	·09	H. 1263 24
2	Sa	13	11	·24	21 22	·04 ·99	25
3	Su	14	12	·16	23	·93	26
4	Mo	15	13 14	·06 ·96	24	·87	27
5	Tu	16	—A	·86	25	·80	28
6	We	17	1	·76	26	·73	29
7	Th	18	2	·67	27	·66	—30
8	Fr	19	3	·59	1	·60	1
9	Sa	20	4	·51	2	·57	2
10	Su	21	5	·45	3	·54	3
11	Mo	22	6	·41	4	·52	4
Parabhava *Mina—Panguni.* 12	Tu	23	*Sukla* 7	·39	5	·53	5
13	We	24	8	·39	6	·55	6
14	Th	25	9	·41	7	·61	7
15	Fr	26	10	·45	8	·68	*Rabi-ul-akhir.* 8
16	Sa	27	**Chaitra** 11	·51	9	·76	9
17	Su	28	12	·58	10	·86	10
18	Mo	29	13	·66	11	·96	11
19	Tu	30	14	·75	...	...	12
20	We ○	31	P	·83	12	·07	13

April

Cyclic Sidereal Year, Month and Day	Week-Day	English Month and Day	Tithi	Ending Moment	Nakshatra	Ending Moment	Muhammadan Year, Month and Day
21	Th	1	1	·90	13	·17	H. 1263 14
22	Fr	2	2	·96	14	·27	15
23	Sa	3	...	...	15	·34	16
24	Su	4	3	·00	16	·40	17
25	Mo	5	4	·01	17	·43	18
26	Tu	6	5 6	·01 ·99	18	·45	19*
27	We	7	*Bahula* 7	·94	19	·44	20
28	Th	8	8	·88	20	·42	21
29	Fr	9	9	·80	21	·38	22
30	Sa	10	10	·72	22	·33	23
—31	Su	11	11	·63	23	·27	24
1	Mo	12	12	·53	24	·20	25
2	Tu	13	13	·48	25	·13	26
3	We	14	14	·33	26	·06	27
4	Th ●	15	—A	·23	27 1	·00 ·95	28
Plavanga *Mesha—Chittirai.* 5	Fr	16	1	·14	2	·90	—29
6	Sa	17	2	·06	3	·87	1
7	Su	18	3 4	·01 ·97	4	·85	*Jumadal-awwal.* 2
8	Mo	19	5	·94	5	·85	3
9	Tu	20	6	·93	6	·88	4
10	We	21	*Sukla* 7	·95	7	·92	5
11	Th	22	8	·99	8	·98	6
12	Fr	23	...	...	...	...	7
13	Sa	24	9	·05	9	·06	H. 1263 8
14	Su	25	**Vaisakha** 10	·12	10	·16	9
15	Mo	26	11	·20	11	·26	10
16	Tu	27	12	·29	12	·37	11
17	We	28	13	·37	13	·48	12
18	Th	29	14	·44	14	·57	13
19	Fr	30	P	·44	15	·65	14

May

Cyclic Sidereal Year, Month and Day	Week-Day	English Month and Day	Tithi	Ending Moment	Nakshatra	Ending Moment	Muhammadan Year, Month and Day
20	Sa	1	**Vaisakha** 1	·53	16	·71	15
21	Su	2	2	·55	17	·76	16
22	Mo	3	3	·55	18	·77	17
Plavanga *Mesha—Chittirai.* 23	Tu	4	4	·53	19	·77	18
24	We	5	5	·47	20	·75	19
25	Th	6	6	·40	21	·71	20
26	Fr	7	7	·33	22	·67	*Jumadal-awwal.* 21
27	Sa	8	8	·25	23	·61	22
28	Su	9	9	·15	24	·54	23
29	Mo	10	10 11	·05 ·95	25	·47	H. 1263 24
30	Tu	11	*Bahula* 12	·85	26	·40	25
—31	We	12	13	·75	27	·34	26
1	Th	13	14	·66	1	·28	27
2	Fr	14	—A	·59	2	·23	28
3	Sa	15	1	·53	3	·19	29
4	Su	16	2	·48	4	·17	—30
5	Mo	17	3	·46	5	·17	1
6	Tu	18	4	·45	6	·19	2
7	We	19	5	·46	7	·23	3
8	Th	20	6	·50	8	·29	4
9	Fr	21	*Sukla* 7	·56	9	·36	5
10	Sa	22	8	·63	10	·46	6
Plavanga *Vrishabha—Vaikasi.* 11	Su	23	9	·71	11	·57	7
12	Mo	24	10	·79	12	·68	8
13	Tu	25	11	·87	13	·78	9
14	We	26	12	·94	14	·87	*Jumadal-akhir.* 10
15	Th	27	**Jyeshtha** ...	...	15	·96	11
16	Fr	28	13	·00	...	...	12
17	Sa	29	14	·03	16	·03	13
18	Su	30	P	·05	17	·07	14
19	Mo	31	1	·04	18	·09	15

June

Cyclic Sidereal Year, Month and Day	Week-Day	English Month and Day	Tithi	Ending Moment	Nakshatra	Ending Moment	Muhammadan Year, Month and Day
20	Tu	1	**Adhika** 2 3	·02 ·98	19	·09	H. 1263 16
21	We	2	4	·92	20	·08	17
22	Th	3	5	·84	21	·05	18
23	Fr	4	6	·74	22 23	·01 ·95	19
24	Sa	5	7	·64	24	·88	20
25	Su	6	8	·54	25	·81	21
26	Mo	7	*Bahula* 9	·44	26	·74	22
27	Tu	8	10	·34	27	·68	23
28	We	9	11	·25	1	·62	24
29	Th	10	12	·16	2	·57	25
30	Fr	11	13	·08	3	·52	26
—31	Sa	12	14 A	·02 ·97	4	·50	27
1	Su	13	1	·94	5	·50	28
2	Mo	14	2	·93	6	·51	—29
3	Tu	15	3	·95	7	·54	1
4	We	16	*Sukla* 4	·98	8	·60	2
5	Th	17	...	...	9	·67	3
Plavanga *Mithuna—Ani.* 6	Fr	18	5	·03	10	·77	4
7	Sa	19	6	·10	11	·87	5
8	Su	20	7	·18	12	·97	*Rajab.* 6
9	Mo	21	8	·26	...	...	7
10	Tu	22	9	·34	13	·08	8
11	We	23	**Nija Jyeshtha** 10	·41	14	·18	9
12	Th	24	11	·47	15	·27	H. 1263 10
13	Fr	25	12	·51	16	·34	11
14	Sa	26	13	·53	17	·38	12
15	Su	27	14	·52	18	·41	13
16	Mo	28	P	·50	19	·42	14
17	Tu	29	*Bah.* 1	·46	20	·41	15
18	We	30	2	·40	21	·38	16

Naksh:—1. Asvn. 2. Bhar. 3. Krit. 4. Rohi. 5. Mrig. 6. Ardh. 7. Punar. 8. Push. 9. Aslesh. 10. Magh. 11. P. Phal. 12. U. Phal. 13. Hasta. 14. Chit.

A. D. 1847.
A.—Amavasya. **P.—Paurnami.**
Kollam 1023, Commences { **N. Malabar—Sept.** **S. Malabar—Aug.**
Hijra 1264, Commences, **Dec. 9.**
Vikrama 1904. **Bengal San 1253.** **(N. Cycle) Kalayukta.**

July (Solar: Plavanga *Mithuna—Ani* to 32, then Plavanga *Karkata—Adi*; Lunar: Nija Jyesh. Bahula, then Ashadha Sukla; Muhammadan: H. 1263 *Rajab.*, then H. 1263 *Shaban.*)

Cyclic Sidereal Year, Month and Day.	Week-Day	English Month and Day.	Tithi	Ending Moment.	Nakshatra	Ending Moment.	Muhammadan Year, Month and Day.
19	Th	1	3	·31	22	·34	17
20	Fr	2	4	·23	23	·28	18
21	Sa	3	5	·14	24	·22	19
22	Su	4	6 7	·04 ·93	25	·16	20
23	Mo	5	8	·82	26	·09	21
24	Tu	6	9	·72	27 1	·02 ·95	22
25	We	7	10	·63	2	·90	23
26	Th	8	11	·56	3	·85	24
27	Fr	9	12	·50	4	·83	25
28	Sa	10	13	·45	5	·82	26
29	Su	11	14	·42	6	·83	27
30	Mo	12	A	·41	7	·86	28
31	Tu	13	1	·43	8	·90	29
32	We	14	2	·46	9	·98	30
1	Th	15	3	·51	...	...	1
2	Fr	16	4	·58	10	·07	2
3	Sa	17	5	·65	11	·16	3
4	Su	18	6	·73	12	·27	4
5	Mo	19	7	·81	13	·38	5
6	Tu	20	8	·89	14	·48	6
7	We	21	9	·95	15	·57	7
8	Th	22	10	·99	16	·64	8
9	Fr	23	...	...	17	·70	9
10	Sa	24	11	·01	18	·73	10
11	Su	25	12 13	·00 ·98	19	·75	11
12	Mo	26	14	·94	20	·74	12
13	Tu	27	P	·88	21	·71	13
14	We	28	1	·80	22	·67	14
15	Th	29	2	·72	23	·62	15
16	Fr	30	3	·62	24	·56	16
17	Sa	31	4	·52	25	·50	17

Aug. (Solar: Plavanga *Karkata—Adi* to 31, then Plavanga *Simha—Avani*; Lunar: Ashadha Bahula, then Sravana Sukla, Bah.; Muhammadan: H. 1263 *Shaban.*, then H. 1263 *Ramzan.*)

Cyclic Sidereal Year, Month and Day.	Week-Day	English Month and Day.	Tithi	Ending Moment.	Nakshatra	Ending Moment.	Muhammadan Year, Month and Day.
18	Su	1	5	·42	26	·43	18
19	Mo	2	6	·32	27	·36	19
20	Tu	3	7	·22	1	·29	20
21	We	4	8	·12	2	·23	21
22	Th	5	9 10	·04 ·98	3	·19	22
23	Fr	6	11	·94	4	·16	23
24	Sa	7	12	·91	5	·15	24
25	Su	8	13	·90	6	·15	25
26	Mo	9	14	·90	7	·17	26
27	Tu	10	A	·93	8	·22	27
28	We	11	1	·98	9	·29	28
29	Th	12	...	...	10	·37	29
30	Fr	13	2	·05	11	·46	1
31	Sa	14	3	·14	12	·57	2
1	Su	15	4	·23	13	·68	3
2	Mo	16	5	·31	14	·78	4
3	Tu	17	6	·38	15	·87	5
4	We	18	7	·43	16	·95	6
5	Th	19	8	·47	...	...	7
6	Fr	20	9	·50	17	·01	8
7	Sa	21	10	·50	18	·05	9
8	Su	22	11	·47	19	·07	10
9	Mo	23	12	·43	20	·07	11
10	Tu	24	13	·38	21	·04	12
11	We	25	14	·31	22 23	·00 ·95	13
12	Th	26	P	·22	24	·90	14
13	Fr	27	1	·12	25	·84	15
14	Sa	28	2 3	·02 ·92	26	·77	16
15	Su	29	4	·82	27	·70	17
16	Mo.	30	5	·72	1	·63	18
17	Tu	31	6	·63	2	·58	19

Sep. (Solar: Plavanga *Simha—Avani* to 31, then Plavanga *Kanya—Purattasi*; Lunar: Sravn. Bahula, then Bhadrapada Sukla; Muhammadan: H. 1263 *Ramzan.*, then H. 1263 *Shawwal.*)

Cyclic Sidereal Year, Month and Day.	Week-Day	English Month and Day.	Tithi	Ending Moment.	Nakshatra	Ending Moment.	Muhammadan Year, Month and Day.
18	We	1	7	·56	3	·53	20
19	Th	2	8	·50	4	·49	21
20	Fr	3	9	·45	5	·47	22
21	Sa	4	10	·42	6	·47	23
22	Su	5	11	·41	7	·50	24
23	Mo	6	12	·42	8	·53	25
24	Tu	7	13	·45	9	·59	26
25	We	8	14	·50	10	·67	27
26	Th	9	A	·57	11	·76	28
27	Fr	10	1	·65	12	·87	29
28	Sa	11	2	·73	13	·98	30
29	Su	12	3	·82	...	...	1
30	Mo	13	4	·90	14	·09	2
31	Tu	14	5	·96	15	·18	3
1	We	15	...	...	16	·26	4
2	Th	16	6	·00	17	·32	5
3	Fr	17	7	·03	18	·37	6
4	Sa	18	8	·03	19	·39	7
5	Su	19	9 10	·01 ·97	20	·39	8
6	Mo	20	11	·91	21	·37	9
7	Tu	21	12	·84	22	·34	10
8	We	22	13	·76	23	·30	11
9	Th	23	14	·67	24	·24	12
10	Fr ○	24	P	·57	25	·17	13
11	Sa	25	1	·47	26	·10	14
12	Su	26	2	·37	27 1	·04 ·98	15
13	Mo	27	3	·27	2	·92	16
14	Tu	28	4	·18	3	·86	17
15	We	29	5	·10	4	·82	18
16	Th	30	6 7	·04 ·99	5	·80	19

Oct. (Solar: Plavanga *Kanya—Purattasi* to 31, then Plavanga *Tula—Aippasi*; Lunar: Bhadrapada Bahula, then Asvina Sukla, Bahula; Muhammadan: H. 1263 *Shawwal.*, then H. 1263 *Zi-l-ka'da.*)

Cyclic Sidereal Year, Month and Day.	Week-Day	English Month and Day.	Tithi	Ending Moment.	Nakshatra	Ending Moment.	Muhammadan Year, Month and Day.
17	Fr	1	8	·97	6	·80	20
18	Sa	2	9	·96	7	·81	21
19	Su	3	10	·97	8	·85	22
20	Mo	4	...	...	9	·90	23
21	Tu	5	11	·00	10	·97	24
22	We	6	12	·05	...	...	25
23	Th	7	13	·12	11	·06	26
24	Fr	8	14	·20	12	·17	27
25	Sa ●	9	A	·29	13	·28	28
26	Su	10	1	·38	14	·39	29
27	Mo	11	2	·46	15	·48	1
28	Tu	12	3	·53	16	·57	2
29	We	13	4	·57	17	·64	3
30	Th	14	5	·59	18	·69	4
31	Fr	15	6	·60	19	·71	5
1	Sa	16	7	·58	20	·72	6
2	Su	17	8	·54	21	·70	7
3	Mo	18	9	·48	22	·68	8
4	Tu	19	10	·41	23	·63	9
5	We	20	11	·33	24	·58	10
6	Th	21	12	·24	25	·51	11
7	Fr	22	13	·14	26	·44	12
8	Sa	23	14 P	·04 ·94	27	·37	13
9	Su	24	1	·85	1	·31	14
10	Mo	25	2	·76	2	·25	15
11	Tu	26	3	·69	3	·19	16
12	We	27	4	·63	4	·15	17
13	Th	28	5	·58	5	·12	18
14	Fr	29	6	·56	6	·12	19
15	Sa	30	7	·55	7	·13	20
16	Su	31	8	·56	8	·16	21

Nov. (Solar: Plavanga *Tula—Aippasi* to 30, then Plavanga *Vrischika—Karttigai*; Lunar: Asv. Bahula, then Kartika Sukla, Bahula; Muhammadan: *Zi-l-ka'da*, then H. 1263 *Zi-l-hijja.*)

Cyclic Sidereal Year, Month and Day.	Week-Day	English Month and Day.	Tithi	Ending Moment.	Nakshatra	Ending Moment.	Muhammadan Year, Month and Day.
17	Mo	1	9	·59	9	·21	22
18	Tu	2	10	·64	10	·28	23
19	We	3	11	·72	11	·37	24
20	Th	4	12	·81	12	·47	25
21	Fr	5	13	·90	13	·58	26
22	Sa	6	14	·98	14	·68	27
23	Su	7	...	...	15	·78	28
24	Mo	8	A	·06	16	·87	29
25	Tu	9	1	·12	17	·95	30
26	We	10	2	·17	...	...	1
27	Th	11	3	·20	18	·00	2
28	Fr	12	4	·19	19	·08	3
29	Sa	13	5	·17	20	·04	4
30	Sa	14	6	·14	21	·04	5
1	Mo	15	7	·09	22 23	·01 ·97	6
2	Tu	16	8 9	·02 ·94	24	·91	7
3	We	17	10	·85	25	·85	8
4	Th	18	11	·75	26	·79	9
5	Fr	19	12	·65	27	·72	10
6	Sa	20	13	·55	1	·65	11
7	Su	21	14	·46	2	·59	12
8	Mo	22	P	·38	3	·53	13
9	Tu	23	1	·31	4	·48	14
10	We	24	2	·25	5	·46	15
11	Th	25	3	·20	6	·44	16
12	Fr	26	4	·18	7	·45	17
13	Sa	27	5	·17	8	·47	18
14	Su	28	6	·19	9	·52	19
15	Mo	29	7	·22	10	·59	20
16	Tu	30	8	·28	11	·67	21

Dec. (Solar: Plavanga *Vrischika—Karttigai* to 29, then Plavanga *Dhanus—Margali*; Lunar: Kartika Bahula, then Margasira Sukla, Bahula; Muhammadan: H. 1263 *Zi-l-hijja.*, then H. 1264 *Muharram.*)

Cyclic Sidereal Year, Month and Day.	Week-Day	English Month and Day.	Tithi	Ending Moment.	Nakshatra	Ending Moment.	Muhammadan Year, Month and Day.
17	We	1	9	·35	12	·77	22
18	Th	2	10	·43	13	·88	23
19	Fr	3	11	·52	14	·99	24
20	Sa	4	12	·61	...	...	25
21	Su	5	13	·69	15	·09	26
22	Mo	6	14	·76	16	·18	27
23	Tu	7	A	·81	17	·26	28
24	We	8	1	·83	18	·31	29
25	Th	9	2	·83	19	·35	1
26	Fr	10	3	·81	20	·37	2
27	Sa	11	4	·77	21	·37	3
28	Su	12	5	·71	22	·34	4
29	Mo	13	6	·64	23	·30	5
1	Tu	14	7	·56	24	·25	6
2	We	15	8	·47	25	·19	7
3	Th	16	9	·38	26	·13	8
4	Fr	17	10	·28	27 1	·06 ·99	9
5	Sa	18	11	·18	2	·92	10
6	Su	19	12	·09	3	·86	11
7	Mo	20	13 14	·00 ·93	4	·82	12
8	Tu	21	P	·87	5	·79	13
9	We	22	1	·84	6	·77	14
10	Th	23	2	·82	7	·77	15
11	Fr	24	3	·82	8	·79	16
12	Sa	25	4	·83	9	·84	17
13	Su	26	5	·87	10	·90	18
14	Mo	27	6	·93	11	·98	19
15	Tu	28	...	...	...	...	20
16	We	29	7	·00	12	·07	21
17	Th	30	8	·09	13	·17	22
18	Fr	31	9	·18	14	·28	23

15. Svati. 16. Visak. 17. Anur. 18. Jyesh. 19. Mula. 20. P. Ash. 21. U. Ash. 22. Sravn. 23. Dani. 24. Satab. 25. P. Bhad. 26. U. Bhad. 27. Rev.

A. D. 1848. **Mesha Sankranti** (Commencement of Indian Sidereal Year).
Solar Eclipse. ● **(Surya Sid.) April 11·16.** **Saka 1770.** **Kaliyuga 4949.**
Lunar Eclipse. ○ **(Arya Sid.) April 11·06.** **(S. Cycle) Kilaka.**

SOLAR reckoning: Cyclic Sidereal Year, Month and Day; Week-Day; English Month and Day. LUNAR reckoning: Tithi; Ending Moment; Nakshatra; Ending Moment; Muhammadan Year, Month and Day.

Jan.

Cyclic Sidereal Year, Month and Day	Week-Day	English Month and Day	Tithi	Ending Moment	Nakshatra	Ending Moment	Muhammadan Year, Month and Day
Plavanga *Dhanus—Margali.* 19	Sa	1	Mr. *Bah.* 10	·27	15	·39	*Muharram.* 24
20	Su	2	11	·35	16	·48	25
21	Mo	3	12	·41	17	·56	26
22	Tu	4	13	·45	18	·62	27
23	We	5	14	·47	19	·67	28
24	Th	6	A	·48	20	·69	29
25	Fr	7	Pausha *Sukla* 1	·46	21	·69	30
26	Sa	8	2	·42	22	·67	H. 1264 *Safar.* 1
27	Su	9	3	·36	23	·63	2
28	Mo	10	4	·29	24	·59	3
29	Tu	11	5	·21	25	·53	4
Plavanga *Makara—Tai.* 1	We	12	6	·12	26	·47	5
2	Th	13	7 / 8	·02 / ·92	27	·40	6
3	Fr	14	9	·82	1	·33	7
4	Sa	15	10	·73	2	·26	8
5	Su	16	11	·65	3	·21	9
6	Mo	17	12	·58	4	·16	10
7	Tu	18	13	·52	5	·12	11
8	We	19	14	·48	6	·09	12
9	Th	20	P	·46	7	·09	13
10	Fr	21	*Bahula* 1	·46	8	·11	14
11	Sa	22	2	·48	9	·15	15
12	Su	23	3	·52	10	·20	16
13	Mo	24	4	·58	11	·28	17
14	Tu	25	5	·65	12	·37	18
15	We	26	6	·74	13	·48	19
16	Th	27	7	·83	14	·59	20
17	Fr	28	8	·92	15	·69	21
18	Sa	29	...	...	16	·78	22
19	Su	30	9	·00	17	·86	23
20	Mo	31	10	·06	18	·93	24

Feb.

Cyclic Sidereal Year, Month and Day	Week-Day	English Month and Day	Tithi	Ending Moment	Nakshatra	Ending Moment	Muhammadan Year, Month and Day
21	Tu	1	11	·10	19	·98	25
22	We	2	12	·12	...	...	26
23	Th	3	13	·12	20	·01	27
24	Fr	4	14	·10	21	·02	28
25	Sa	5	A / 1	·05 / ·99	22 / 23	·00 / ·97	29
26	Su	6	Magha *Sukla* 2	·92	24	·93	H. 1264 *Rabi-ul-awwal.* 1
27	Mo	7	3	·84	25	·87	2
28	Tu	8	4	·75	26	·81	3
29	We	9	5	·65	27	·74	4
30	Th	10	6	·53	1	·67	5
Plavanga *Kumbha—Masi.* 1	Fr	11	7	·45	2	·61	6
2	Sa	12	8	·36	3	·55	7
3	Su	13	9	·28	4	·49	8
4	Mo	14	10	·21	5	·45	9
5	Tu	15	11	·15	6	·42	10
6	We	16	12	·12	7	·42	11
7	Th	17	13	·10	8	·43	12
8	Fr	18	14	·09	9	·46	13
9	Sa	19	P	·11	10	·51	14
10	Su	20	*Bahula* 1	·15	11	·58	15
11	Mo	21	2	·21	12	·68	16
12	Tu	22	3	·29	13	·78	17
13	We	23	4	·37	14	·89	18
14	Th	24	5	·46	15	·99	19
15	Fr	25	6	·54	...	...	20
16	Sa	26	7	·61	16	·09	21
17	Su	27	8	·67	17	·18	22
18	Mo	28	9	·72	18	·25	23
19	Tu	29	10	·74	19	·30	24

March

Cyclic Sidereal Year, Month and Day	Week-Day	English Month and Day	Tithi	Ending Moment	Nakshatra	Ending Moment	Muhammadan Year, Month and Day
Plavanga *Kumbha—Masi.* 20	We	1	*Bah.* 11	·73	20	·83	*R.-awwal.* 25
21	Th	2	12	·71	21	·84	26
22	Fr	3	13	·66	22	·33	27
23	Sa	4	14	·60	23	·31	28
24	Su	5	A	·53	24	·26	29
25	Mo	6	Phalguna *Sukla* 1	·45	25	·21	30
26	Tu	7	2	·36	26	·14	H. 1264 *Rabi-ul-akhir.* 1
27	We	8	3	·26	27	·07	2
28	Th	9	4	·16	1 / 2	·00 / ·94	3
29	Fr	10	5 / 6	·06 / ·97	3	·88	4
30	Sa	11	7	·88	4	·82	5
31	Su	12	8	·80	5	·78	6
Plavanga *Mina—Panguni.* 1	Mo	13	9	·74	6	·76	7
2	Tu	14	10	·71	7	·74	8
3	We	15	11	·69	8	·75	9
4	Th	16	12	·68	9	·77	10
5	Fr	17	13	·71	10	·82	11
6	Sa	18	14	·76	11	·89	12
7	Su ○	19	P	·82	12	·98	13
8	Mo	20	*Bahula* 1	·89	...	...	14
9	Tu	21	2	·97	13	·08	15
10	We	22	...	...	14	·18	16
11	Th	23	3	·06	15	·29	17
12	Fr	24	4	·14	16	·39	18
13	Sa	25	5	·21	17	·48	19
14	Su	26	6	·27	18	·56	20
15	Mo	27	7	·30	19	·62	21
16	Tu	28	8	·32	20	·65	22
17	We	29	9	·31	21	·66	23
18	Th	30	10	·29	22	·66	24
19	Fr	31	11	·24	23	·64	25

April

Cyclic Sidereal Year, Month and Day	Week-Day	English Month and Day	Tithi	Ending Moment	Nakshatra	Ending Moment	Muhammadan Year, Month and Day
20	Sa	1	12	·18	24	·60	26
21	Su	2	13	·11	25	·54	27
22	Mo	3	14 / A	·03 / ·93	26	·48	28
23	Tu	4	Chaitra *Sukla* 1	·83	27	·42	29
24	We	5	2	·73	1	·35	H. 1264 *Jumadal-awwal.* 1
25	Th	6	3	·63	2	·28	2
26	Fr	7	4	·54	3	·22	3
27	Sa	8	5	·45	4	·16	4
28	Su	9	6	·37	5	·11	5
29	Mo	10	7	·31	6	·09	6
Kilaka *Mesha—Chittirai.* 1	Tu	11	8	·27	7	·07	7
2	We	12	9	·25	8	·07	8
3	Th	13	10	·25	9	·09	9
4	Fr	14	11	·28	10	·13	10
5	Sa	15	12	·32	11	·20	11
6	Su	16	13	·37	12	·28	12
7	Mo	17	14	·44	13	·38	13
8	Tu	18	P	·52	14	·48	14
9	We	19	*Bahula* 1	·61	15	·59	15
10	Th	20	2	·69	16	·70	16
11	Fr	21	3	·76	17	·79	17
12	Sa	22	4	·81	18	·87	18
13	Su	23	5	·84	19	·93	19
14	Mo	24	6	·86	20	·97	20
15	Tu	25	7	·86	21	·99	21
16	We	26	8	·84	22	·99	22
17	Th	27	9	·79	23	·97	23
18	Fr	28	10	·73	24	·93	24
19	Sa	29	11	·65	25	·88	25
20	Su	30	12	·56	26	·83	26

May

Cyclic Sidereal Year, Month and Day	Week-Day	English Month and Day	Tithi	Ending Moment	Nakshatra	Ending Moment	Muhammadan Year, Month and Day
Kilaka *Mesha—Chittirai.* 21	Mo	1	*Bah.* 13	·46	27	·76	27
22	Tu	2	14	·36	1	·69	28
23	We	3	A	·26	2	·62	29
24	Th	4	Vaisakha *Sukla* 1	·16	3	·55	30
25	Fr	5	2 / 3	·06 / ·97	4	·49	H. 1264 *Jumadal-akhir.* 1
26	Sa	6	4	·90	5	·44	2
27	Su	7	5	·84	6	·41	3
28	Mo	8	6	·80	7	·39	4
29	Tu	9	7	·77	8	·39	5
30	We	10	8	·77	9	·40	6
31	Th	11	9	·79	10	·45	7
Kilaka *Vrishabha—Vaikasi.* 1	Fr	12	10	·83	11	·51	8
2	Sa	13	11	·89	12	·58	9
3	Su	14	12	·96	13	·68	10
4	Mo	15	...	...	14	·78	11
5	Tu	16	13	·04	15	·89	12
6	We	17	14	·12	...	...	13
7	Th	18	P	·21	16	·00	14
8	Fr	19	*Bahula* 1	·27	17	·10	15
9	Sa	20	2	·32	18	·18	16
10	Su	21	3	·35	19	·24	17
11	Mo	22	4	·37	20	·29	18
12	Tu	23	5	·37	21	·31	19
13	We	24	6	·35	22	·31	20
14	Th	25	7	·30	23	·30	21
15	Fr	26	8	·23	24	·26	22
16	Sa	27	9	·15	25	·21	23
17	Su	28	10 / 11	·06 / ·96	26	·16	24
18	Mo	29	12	·86	27	·10	25
19	Tu	30	13	·76	1 / 2	·03 / ·96	26
20	We	31	14	·66	3	·90	27

June

Cyclic Sidereal Year, Month and Day	Week-Day	English Month and Day	Tithi	Ending Moment	Nakshatra	Ending Moment	Muhammadan Year, Month and Day
21	Th	1	A	·56	4	·84	28
22	Fr	2	Jyeshtha *Sukla* 1	·48	5	·78	29
23	Sa	3	2	·41	6	·74	H. 1264 *Rajab.* 1
24	Su	4	3	·34	7	·72	2
25	Mo	5	4	·30	8	·71	3
26	Tu	6	5	·27	9	·73	4
27	We	7	6	·27	10	·76	5
28	Th	8	7	·28	11	·82	6
29	Fr	9	8	·32	12	·89	7
30	Sa	10	9	·37	13	·98	8
31	Su	11	10	·43	...	...	9
Kilaka *Mithuna—Ani.* 1	Mo	12	11	·51	14	·09	10
2	Tu	13	12	·60	15	·19	11
3	We	14	13	·68	16	·30	12
4	Th	15	14	·75	17	·40	13
5	Fr	16	P	·81	18	·49	14
6	Sa	17	*Bahula* 1	·85	19	·56	15
7	Su	18	2	·86	20	·61	16
8	Mo	19	3	·85	21	·63	17
9	Tu	20	4	·83	22	·64	18
10	We	21	5	·78	23	·62	19
11	Th	22	6	·72	24	·59	20
12	Fr	23	7	·64	25	·56	21
13	Sa	24	8	·55	26	·50	22
14	Su	25	9	·45	27	·44	23
15	Mo	26	10	·35	1	·37	24
16	Tu	27	11	·25	2	·30	25
17	We	28	12	·15	3	·23	26
18	Th	29	13 / 14	·05 / ·96	4	·17	27
19	Fr	30	A	·88	5	·12	28

Naksh :—1. Asvn. 2. Bhar. 3. Krit. 4. Rohi. 5. Mrig. 6. Ardh. 7. Punar. 8. Push. 9. Aslesh. 10. Magh. 11. P. Phal. 12. U. Phal. 13. Hasta. 14. Chit.

A. D. 1848.
A.—Amavasya. **Kollam 1024,** { **N. Malabar—Sept.** **Hijra 1265,** **Vikrama 1905.**
P.—Paurnami. Commences { **S. Malabar—Aug.** Commences, **Nov. 27.** **Bengal San 1254.**
(N. Cycle) Siddharthin.

SOLAR reckoning: Cyclic Sidereal Year, Month and Day; Week-Day; English Month and Day. LUNAR reckoning: Tithi, Ending Moment; Nakshatra, Ending Moment; Muhammadan Year, Month and Day.

July

Kilaka, *Mithuna—Ani.* / Kilaka, *Karkata—Adi.* — Ashadha (*Sukla*, *Bahula*) — H. 1264 *Shaban.*

Cyclic Sidereal Year, Month and Day	Week-Day	English Month and Day	Tithi	Ending Moment	Nakshatra	Ending Moment	Muhammadan Year, Month and Day
20	Sa	1	1	·82	6	·07	29
21	Su	2	2	·77	7	·04	—30
22	Mo	3	3	·74	8	·04	1
23	Tu	4	4	·74	9	·05	2
24	We	5	5	·75	10	·08	3
25	Th	6	6	·79	11	·12	4
26	Fr	7	7	·84	12	·19	5
27	Sa	8	8	·91	13	·29	6
28	Su	9	9	·99	14	·39	7
29	Mo	10	...	...	15	·49	8
30	Tu	11	10	·08	16	·60	9
31	We	12	11	·16	17	·70	10
—32	Th	13	12	·23	18	·79	11
1	Fr	14	13	·28	19	·87	12
2	Sa	15	14	·32	20	·92	13
3	Su	16	P	·34	21	·95	14
4	Mo	17	1	·33	22	·96	15
5	Tu	18	2	·31	23	·95	16
6	We	19	3	·26	24	·93	17
7	Th	20	4	·20	25	·89	18
8	Fr	21	5	·13	26	·84	19
9	Sa	22	6 7	·04 ·94	27	·78	20
10	Su	23	8	·84	1	·72	21
11	Mo	24	9	·74	2	·65	22
12	Tu	25	10	·64	3	·58	23
13	We	26	11	·54	4	·51	24
14	Th	27	12	·45	5	·45	25
15	Fr	28	13	·36	6	·41	26
16	Sa	29	14	·30	7	·38	27
17	Su	30	—A	·25	8	·37	28
18	Mo	31	1	·23	9	·37	—29

Aug.

Kilaka, *Simha—Avani.* — Sravana (*Sukla*, *Bahula*, *Suk.*) — H. 1264 *Ramzan.*

Cyclic Sidereal Year, Month and Day	Week-Day	English Month and Day	Tithi	Ending Moment	Nakshatra	Ending Moment	Muhammadan Year, Month and Day
19	Tu	1	2	·22	10	·39	1
20	We	2	3	·24	11	·44	2
21	Th	3	4	·27	12	·51	3
22	Fr	4	5	·32	13	·59	4
23	Sa	5	6	·39	14	·68	5
24	Su	6	7	·47	15	·79	6
25	Mo	7	8	·56	16	·90	7
26	Tu	8	9	·64	...	...	8
27	We	9	10	·71	17	·00	9
28	Th	10	11	·76	18	·09	10
29	Fr	11	12	·80	19	·17	11
30	Sa	12	13	·83	20	·23	12
—31	Su	13	14	·82	21	·27	13
1	Mo	14	P	·80	22	·28	14
2	Tu	15	1	·76	23	·28	15
3	We	16	2	·70	24	·26	16
4	Th	17	3	·62	25	·23	17
5	Fr	18	4	·53	26	·17	18
6	Sa	19	5	·44	27	·11	19
7	Su	20	6	·34	1 2	·05 ·99	20
8	Mo	21	7	·24	3	·92	21
9	Tu	22	8	·14	4	·85	22
10	We	23	9 10	·05 ·96	5	·79	23
11	Th	24	11	·88	6	·74	24
12	Fr	25	12	·81	7	·71	25
13	Sa	26	13	·76	8	·69	26
14	Su	27	14	·73	9	·68	27
15	Mo	28	—A	·72	10	·71	28
16	Tu	29	1	·73	11	·75	29
17	We	30	2	·77	12	·81	—30
18	Th	31	3	·82	13	·89	1

Sep.

Kilaka, *Simha—Avani.* / Kilaka, *Kanya—Purattasi.* — Bhadrapada (*Sukla*, *Bahula*) — H. 1264 *Shawwal.*

Cyclic Sidereal Year, Month and Day	Week-Day	English Month and Day	Tithi	Ending Moment	Nakshatra	Ending Moment	Muhammadan Year, Month and Day
19	Fr	1	4	·89	14	·98	2
20	Sa	2	5	·97	...	...	3
21	Su	3	...	...	15	·09	4
22	Mo	4	6	·06	16	·20	5
23	Tu	5	7	·14	17	·30	6
24	We	6	8	·21	18	·40	7
25	Th	7	9	·27	19	·48	8
26	Fr	8	10	·32	20	·54	9
27	Sa	9	11	·34	21	·58	10
28	Su	10	12	·33	22	·61	11
29	Mo	11	13	·31	23	·61	12
30	Tu	12	14	·27	24	·59	13
31	We ○	13	P	·22	25	·56	14
—32	Th	14	1	·15	26	·51	15
1	Fr	15	2 3	·07 ·97	27	·46	16
2	Sa	16	4	·87	1	·39	17
3	Su	17	5	·77	2	·32	18
4	Mo	18	6	·67	3	·25	19
5	Tu	19	7	·57	4	·18	20
6	We	20	8	·48	5	·13	21
7	Th	21	9	·40	6	·08	22
8	Fr	22	10	·34	7	·04	23
9	Sa	23	11	·29	8	·02	24
10	Su	24	12	·27	9	·01	25
11	Mo	25	13	·26	10	·03	26
12	Tu	26	14	·27	11	·07	27
13	We	27	—A	·31	12	·12	28
14	Th	28	1	·37	13	·19	—29
15	Fr	29	2	·44	14	·28	1
16	Sa	30	3	·53	15	·38	2

Oct.

Kilaka, *Tula—Aippasi.* — Asvina (*Sukla*, *Bahula*), K. *Suk.* — H. 1264 *Zi-l-ka'da.*

Cyclic Sidereal Year, Month and Day	Week-Day	English Month and Day	Tithi	Ending Moment	Nakshatra	Ending Moment	Muhammadan Year, Month and Day
17	Su	1	4	·61	16	·49	3
18	Mo	2	5	·69	17	·60	4
19	Tu	3	6	·76	18	·70	5
20	We	4	7	·82	19	·79	6
21	Th	5	8	·87	20	·85	7
22	Fr	6	9	·89	21	·90	8
23	Sa	7	10	·89	22	·93	9
24	Su	8	11	·87	23	·94	10
25	Mo	9	12	·84	24	·92	11
26	Tu	10	13	·78	25	·89	12
27	We	11	14	·71	26	·85	13
28	Th	12	P	·62	27	·80	14
29	Fr	13	1	·53	1	·73	15
—30	Sa	14	2	·43	2	·66	16
1	Su	15	3	·33	3	·59	17
2	Mo	16	4	·23	4	·53	18
3	Tu	17	5	·13	5	·47	19
4	We	18	6 7	·04 ·97	6	·41	20
5	Th	19	8	·91	7	·37	21
6	Fr	20	9	·87	8	·34	22
7	Sa	21	10	·85	9	·33	23
8	Su	22	11	·85	10	·35	24
9	Mo	23	12	·86	11	·38	25
10	Tu	24	13	·90	12	·43	26
11	We	25	14	·95	13	·50	27
12	Th	26	...	...	14	·58	28
13	Fr	27	—A	·02	15	·69	29
14	Sa	28	1	·10	16	·80	—30
15	Su	29	2	·19	17	·90	1
16	Mo	30	3	·28	...	...	2
17	Tu	31	4	·36	18	·00	3

Nov.

Kilaka, *Tula—Aippasi.* / Kilaka, *Vrischika—Kartigai.* — Kartika (*Sukla*, *Bahula*) — H. 1264 *Zi-l-hijja.*

Cyclic Sidereal Year, Month and Day	Week-Day	English Month and Day	Tithi	Ending Moment	Nakshatra	Ending Moment	Muhammadan Year, Month and Day
18	We	1	5	·42	19	·09	4
19	Th	2	6	·46	20	·17	5
20	Fr	3	7	·48	21	·22	6
21	Sa	4	8	·49	22	·25	7
22	Su	5	9	·47	23	·26	8
23	Mo	6	10	·43	24	·25	9
24	Tu	7	11	·37	25	·22	10
25	We	8	12	·30	26	·19	11
26	Th	9	13	·22	27	·13	12
27	Fr	10	14	·13	1	·07	13
28	Sa	11	P 1	·03 ·93	2 3	·00 ·93	14
29	Su	12	2	·83	4	·87	15
—30	Mo	13	3	·74	5	·81	16
1	Tu	14	4	·66	6	·75	17
2	We	15	5	·59	7	·70	18
3	Th	16	6	·53	8	·67	19
4	Fr	17	7	·48	9	·66	20
5	Sa	18	8	·46	10	·67	21
6	Su	19	9	·46	11	·69	22
7	Mo	20	10	·47	12	·73	23
8	Tu	21	11	·51	13	·80	24
9	We	22	12	·57	14	·89	25
10	Th	23	13	·65	15	·99	26
11	Fr	24	14	·73	...	...	27
12	Sa	25	—A	·82	16	·10	28
13	Su	26	1	·91	17	·20	—29
14	Mo	27	2	·98	18	·30	1
15	Tu	28	...	...	19	·40	2
16	We	29	3	·04	20	·48	3
17	Th	30	4	·09	21	·53	4

Dec.

Kilaka, *Dhanus—Margali.* — Margasira (*Sukla*, *Bahula*), Psh. *Suk.* — H. 1265 *Muharram.*, *Safar.*

Cyclic Sidereal Year, Month and Day	Week-Day	English Month and Day	Tithi	Ending Moment	Nakshatra	Ending Moment	Muhammadan Year, Month and Day
18	Fr	1	5	·12	22	·56	5
19	Sa	2	6	·11	23	·58	6
20	Su	3	7	·09	24	·57	7
21	Mo	4	8 9	·05 ·99	25	·55	8
22	Tu	5	10	·92	26	·52	9
23	We	6	11	·84	27	·47	10
24	Th	7	12	·75	1	·41	11
25	Fr	8	13	·66	2	·35	12
26	Sa	9	14	·56	3	·28	13
27	Su	10	P	·46	4	·21	14
28	Mo	11	1	·36	5	·14	15
—29	Tu	12	2	·28	6	·08	16
1	We	13	3	·21	7	·04	17
2	Th	14	4	·16	8 9	·01 ·99	18
3	Fr	15	5	·12	10	·99	19
4	Sa	16	6	·10	...	...	20
5	Su	17	7	·10	11	·01	21
6	Mo	18	8	·11	12	·05	22
7	Tu	19	9	·16	13	·12	23
8	We	20	10	·22	14	·20	24
9	Th	21	11	·30	15	·29	25
10	Fr	22	12	·38	16	·39	26
11	Sa	23	13	·47	17	·50	27
12	Su	24	14	·56	18	·61	28
13	Mo	25	—A	·63	19	·71	29
14	Tu	26	1	·69	20	·79	—30
15	We	27	2	·74	21	·84	1
16	Th	28	3	·76	22	·88	2
17	Fr	29	4	·75	23	·90	3
18	Sa	30	5	·73	24	·91	4
19	Su	31	6	·70	25	·89	5

15. Svati. 16. Visak. 17. Anur. 18. Jyesh. 19. Mula. 20. P. Ash. 21. U. Ash. 22. Sravn. 23. Dani. 24. Satab. 25. P. Bhad. 26. U. Bhad. 27. Rev.

A. D. 1849. **Mesha Sankranti** (Commencement of Indian Sidereal Year). **(Surya Sid.) April 11·42.** **(Arya Sid.) April 11·32.**

Saka 1771. **Kaliyuga 4950.** **(S. Cycle) Saumya.**

Solar Eclipse. ●
Lunar Eclipse. ○

Columns: SOLAR reckoning — Cyclic Sidereal Year, Month and Day; Week-Day; English Month and Day. LUNAR reckoning — Tithi; Ending Moment; Nakshatra; Ending Moment; Muhammadan Year, Month and Day.

Jan.

Kilaka, Dhanus—Marguli (20–30); Kilaka, Makara—Tai (1–20). Pausha: Sukla, Bahula, Sukla. H. 1265 Sufar.

Cyclic Sidereal Year, Month and Day	Week-Day	English Month and Day	Tithi	Ending Moment	Nakshatra	Ending Moment	Muhammadan Year, Month and Day
20	Mo	1	7	·64	26	·85	6
21	Tu	2	8	·57	27	·80	7
22	We	3	9	·48	1	·75	8
23	Th	4	10	·39	2	·69	9
24	Fr	5	11	·30	3	·62	10
25	Sa	6	12	20	4	·55	11
26	Su	7	13	·10	5	·48	12
27	Mo	8	14 P	·01 ·92	6	·42	13
28	Tu	9	1	·85	7	·38	14
29	We	10	2	·80	8	·34	15
30	Th	11	3	·77	9	·31	16
1	Fr	12	4	·75	10	·31	17
2	Sa	13	5	·74	11	·32	18
3	Su	14	6	·76	12	·37	19
4	Mo	15	7	·80	13	·43	20
5	Tu	16	8	·86	14	·50	21
6	We	17	9	·94	15	·59	22
7	Th	18	...	...	16	·69	23
8	Fr	19	10	·04	17	·80	24
9	Sa	20	11	·13	18	·91	25
10	Su	21	12	·21	...	...	26
11	Mo	22	13	·29	19	·01	27
12	Tu	23	14	·34	20	·09	28
13	We	24	A	·38	21	·15	29
14	Th	25	1	·40	22	·20	1
15	Fr	26	2	·39	23	·23	2
16	Sa	27	3	·37	24	·23	3
17	Su	28	4	·34	25	·22	4
18	Mo	29	5	·28	26	·19	5
19	Tu	30	6	·20	27	·14	6
20	We	31	7	·12	1	·09	7

Feb.

Kilaka, Kumbha—Masi. Magha: Bahula; P. Sukla. H. 1265 Rabi-ul-awwal; R.-akhir.

Cyclic Sidereal Year, Month and Day	Week-Day	English Month and Day	Tithi	Ending Moment	Nakshatra	Ending Moment	Muhammadan Year, Month and Day
21	Th	1	8 9	·02 ·92	2 3	·03 ·96	8
22	Fr	2	10	·82	4	·89	9
23	Sa	3	11	·73	5	·82	10
24	Su	4	12	·64	6	·76	11
25	Mo	5	13	·55	7	·71	12
26	Tu	6	14	·48	8	·67	13
27	We	7	P	·43	9	·64	14
28	Th	8	1	·40	10	·63	15
29	Fr	9	2	·38	11	·64	16
1	Sa	10	3	·38	12	·68	17
2	Su	11	4	·41	13	·73	18
3	Mo	12	5	·45	14	·80	19
4	Tu	13	6	·51	15	·89	20
5	We	14	7	·58	16	·99	21
6	Th	15	8	·67	...	...	22
7	Fr	16	9	·76	17	·10	23
8	Sa	17	10	·84	18	·21	24
9	Su	18	11	·91	19	·31	25
10	Mo	19	12	·97	20	·40	26
11	Tu	20	...	...	21	·47	27
12	We	21	13	·01	22	·52	28
13	Th	22	14	·03	23	·55	29
14	Fr ●	23	A	·03	24	·56	30
15	Sa	24	1 2	·00 ·95	25	·55	1
16	Su	25	3	·89	26	·52	2
17	Mo	26	4	·81	27	·48	3
18	Tu	27	5	·73	1	·43	4
19	We	28	6	·64	2	·36	5

March

Kilaka, Kumbha—Masi (20–30); Kilaka, Mina—Panguni (1–20). Phalguna: Sukla, Bahula, Sukla. H. 1265 Rabi-ul-akhir.

Cyclic Sidereal Year, Month and Day	Week-Day	English Month and Day	Tithi	Ending Moment	Nakshatra	Ending Moment	Muhammadan Year, Month and Day
20	Th	1	7	·55	3	·29	6
21	Fr	2	8	·45	4	·22	7
22	Sa	3	9	·35	5	·16	8
23	Su	4	10	·25	6	·10	9
24	Mo	5	11	·16	7	·04	10
25	Tu	6	12	·09	8 9	·00 ·97	11
26	We	7	13	·04	10	·95	12
27	Th ○	8	14 P	·01 ·99	11	·96	13
28	Fr	9	1	·99	12	·09	14
29	Sa	10	...	...	...	...	15
30	Su	11	2	·02	13	·04	16
1	Mo	12	3	·06	14	·11	17
2	Tu	13	4	·12	15	·19	18
3	We	14	5	·19	16	·30	19
4	Th	15	6	·28	17	·41	20
5	Fr	16	7	·37	18	·51	21
6	Sa	17	8	·45	19	·61	22
7	Su	18	9	·52	20	·70	23
8	Mo	19	10	·57	21	·78	24
9	Tu	20	11	·61	22	·84	25
10	We	21	12	·62	23	·87	26
11	Th	22	13	·62	24	·88	27
12	Fr	23	14	·59	25	·87	28
13	Sa	24	A	·55	26	·85	29
14	Su	25	1	·49	27	·82	1
15	Mo	26	2	·41	1	·76	2
16	Tu	27	3	·32	2	·70	3
17	We	28	4	·22	3	·63	4
18	Th	29	5	·12	4	·56	5
19	Fr³	30	6 7	·02 ·92	5	·50	6
20	Sa	31	8	·83	6	·44	7

April

Saumya, Mesha—Chittirai. Chaitra: Bahula; Vaisakha: Suk. H. 1265 Jumadal-awwal; Jumadal-akhir.

Cyclic Sidereal Year, Month and Day	Week-Day	English Month and Day	Tithi	Ending Moment	Nakshatra	Ending Moment	Muhammadan Year, Month and Day
21	Su	1	9	·75	7	·38	8
22	Mo	2	10	·67	8	·33	9
23	Tu	3	11	·61	9	·29	10
24	We	4	12	·58	10	·28	11
25	Th	5	13	·56	11	·29	12
26	Fr	6	14	·56	12	·31	13
27	Sa	7	P	·59	13	·35	14
28	Su	8	1	·63	14	·41	15
29	Mo	9	2	·69	15	·50	16
30	Tu	10	3	·76	16	·60	17
1	We	11	4	·84	17	·70	18
2	Th	12	5	·93	18	·81	19
3	Fr	13	...	...	19	·91	20
4	Sa	14	6	·01	...	...	21
5	Su	15	7	·08	20	·01	22
6	Mo	16	8	·13	21	·09	23
7	Tu	17	9	·17	22	·15	24
8	We	18	10	·18	23	·19	25
9	Th	19	11	·17	24	·21	26
10	Fr	20	12	·14	25	·21	27
11	Sa	21	13	·10	26	·19	28
12	Su	22	14 A	·03 ·95	27	·15	29
13	Mo	23	1	·86	1	·10	30
14	Tu	24	2	·77	2 3	·04 ·97	1
15	We	25	3	·67	4	·91	2
16	Th	26	4	·57	5	·84	3
17	Fr	27	5	·47	6	·77	4
18	Sa	28	6	·37	7	·71	5
19	Su	29	7	·28	8	·66	6
20	Mo	30	8	·21	9	·63	7

May

Saumya, Mesha—Chittirai (21–31); Saumya, Vrishabha—Vaikasi (1–20). Vaisakha: Sukla, Bahula, Sukla. H. 1265 Jumadal-akhir.

Cyclic Sidereal Year, Month and Day	Week-Day	English Month and Day	Tithi	Ending Moment	Nakshatra	Ending Moment	Muhammadan Year, Month and Day
21	Tu	1	9	·15	10	·61	8
22	We	2	10	·11	11	·61	9
23	Th	3	11	·09	12	·63	10
24	Fr	4	12	·09	13	·66	11
25	Sa	5	13	·11	14	·73	12
26	Su	6	14	·15	15	·81	13
27	Mo	7	P	·21	16	·90	14
28	Tu	8	1	·28	...	...	15
29	We	9	2	·37	17	·00	16
30	Th	10	3	·45	18	·11	17
31	Fr	11	4	·52	19	·22	18
1	Sa	12	5	·59	20	·32	19
2	Su	13	6	·65	21	·40	20
3	Mo	14	7	·68	22	·46	21
4	Tu	15	8	·69	23	·50	22
5	We	16	9	·68	24	·52	23
6	Th	17	10	·66	25	·53	24
7	Fr	18	11	·61	26	·52	25
8	Sa	19	12	·54	27	·48	26
9	Su	20	13	·46	1	·43	27
10	Mo	21	14	·37	2	·38	28
11	Tu	22	A	·27	3	·32	29
12	We	23	1	·17	4	·25	1
13	Th	24	2 3	·07 ·97	5	·18	2
14	Fr	25	4	·88	6	·11	3
15	Sa	26	5	·79	7	·05	4
16	Su	27	6	·72	8 9	·00 ·96	5
17	Mo	28	7	·66	10	·94	6
18	Tu	29	8	·62	11	·93	7
19	We	30	9	·60	12	·94	8
20	Th	31	10	·59	13	·98	9

June

Saumya, Mithuna—Ani. Jyeshtha: Bahula; Ashadha: Sukla. H. 1265 Rajab; H. 1265 Shaban.

Cyclic Sidereal Year, Month and Day	Week-Day	English Month and Day	Tithi	Ending Moment	Nakshatra	Ending Moment	Muhammadan Year, Month and Day
21	Fr	1	11	·61	...	...	10
22	Sa	2	12	·65	14	·04	11
23	Su	3	13	·71	15	·11	12
24	Mo	4	14	·78	16	·20	13
25	Tu	5	P	·86	17	·30	14
26	We	6	1	·95	18	·41	15
27	Th	7	...	...	19	·52	16
28	Fr	8	2	·03	20	·62	17
29	Sa	9	3	·09	21	·70	18
30	Su	10	4	·14	22	·76	19
31	Mo	11	5	·17	23	·81	20
32	Tu	12	6	·18	24	·85	21
1	We	13	7	·17	25	·86	22
2	Th	14	8	·15	26	·84	23
3	Fr	15	9	·10	27	·81	24
4	Sa	16	10 11	·04 ·96	1	·77	25
5	Su	17	12	·87	2	·72	26
6	Mo	18	13	·77	3	·66	27
7	Tu	19	14	·67	4	·59	28
8	We	20	A	·57	5	·52	29
9	Th	21	1	·47	6	·45	30
10	Fr	22	2	·37	7	·39	1
11	Sa	23	3	·28	8	·34	2
12	Su	24	4	·20	9	·29	3
13	Mo	25	5	·14	10	·26	4
14	Tu	26	6	·09	11	·26	5
15	We	27	7	·07	12	·27	6
16	Th	28	8	·06	13	·30	7
17	Fr	29	9	·08	14	·35	8
18	Sa	30	10	·12	15	·41	9

Naksh :—1. Asvn. 2. Bhar. 3. Krit. 4 Rohi. 5. Mrig. 6. Ardh. 7. Punar. 8. Push. 9. Aslesh. 10. Magh. 11. P. Phal. 12. U. Phal. 13. Hasta. 14. Chit·

A. D. 1849. **A.—Amavasya.** **P.—Paurnami.** **Kollam 1025,** Commences { **N. Malabar—Sept.** **S. Malabar—Aug.** **Hijra 1266,** Commences, **Nov. 17.** **Vikrama 1906.** **Bengal San 1255.** **(N. Cycle) Raudra.**

SOLAR reckoning: Cyclic Sidereal Year, Month and Day; Week-Day; English Month and Day. LUNAR reckoning: Tithi; Ending Moment; Nakshatra; Ending Moment; Muhammadan Year, Month and Day.

July

Solar month	Cyclic Sidereal Day	Week-Day	English Day	Lunar month	Tithi	Ending Moment	Nakshatra	Ending Moment	Muhammadan Month	Day
Saumya Mithuna—Ani	19	Su	1	Suk.	11	·18	16	·50		10
	20	Mo	2		12	·25	17	·60		11
	21	Tu	3	Ashadha	13	·33	18	·71		12
	22	We	4		14	·41	19	·82		13
	23	Th	5		P	·49	20	·92		14
	24	Fr	6		1	·56	...	...		15
	25	Sa	7		2	·61	21	·01		16
	26	Su	8		3	·65	22	·08		17
	27	Mo	9		4	·66	23	·14	H. 1265 Shaban	18
	28	Tu	10		5	·66	24	·17		19
	29	We	11	Bahula	6	·62	25	·18		20
	30	Th	12		7	·58	26	·17		21
	31	Fr	13		8	·52	27	·14		22
Saumya Karkatu—Adi	1	Sa	14		9	·44	1	·11		23
	2	Su	15		10	·35	2	·06		24
	3	Mo	16		11	·25	3 4	·00 ·93		25
	4	Tu	17		12	·15	5	·86		26
	5	We	18		13 14	·05 ·95	6	·79		27
	6	Th	19		A	·85	7	·73		28
	7	Fr	20		1	·76	8	·67		29
	8	Sa	21		2	·68	9	·63		1
	9	Su	22		3	·62	10	·59		2
	10	Mo	23		4	·57	11	·58		3
	11	Tu	24		5	·55	12	·59		4
	12	We	25	Sukla	6	·55	13	·61		5
	13	Th	26		7	·57	14	·65		6
	14	Fr	27		8	·60	15	·72		7
	15	Sa	28		9	·65	16	·80		8
	16	Su	29		10	·72	17	·90		9
	17	Mo	30		11	·80	...	...		10
	18	Tu	31		12	·89	18	·01		11

Aug.

Solar month	Cyclic Sidereal Day	Week-Day	English Day	Lunar month	Tithi	Ending Moment	Nakshatra	Ending Moment	Muhammadan Month	Day
	19	We	1	Sravana	13	·97	19	·12	H. 1265 Ramzan	12
	20	Th	2		...	...	20	·22		13
	21	Fr	3		14	·04	21	·31		14
	22	Sa	4		P	·09	22	·39		15
	23	Su	5		1	·13	23	·45		16
	24	Mo	6		2	·14	24	·49		17
	25	Tu	7		3	·14	25	·50		18
	26	We	8		4	·11	26	·50		19
	27	Th	9		5	·07	27	·48		20
	28	Fr	10	Bahula	6 7	·01 ·93	1	·45		21
	29	Sa	11		8	·85	2	·39		22
	30	Su	12		9	·75	3	·33		23
	31	Mo	13		10	·65	4	·27		24
	32	Tu	14		11	·55	5	·20		25
Saumya Simha—Avani	1	We	15		12	·45	6	·13		26
	2	Th	16		13	·35	7	·07		27
	3	Fr	17		14	·26	8 9	·01 ·96		28
	4	Sa ●	18		A	·18	10	·92		29
	5	Su	19		1	·12	11	·91		30
	6	Mo	20	Sukla	2	·07	12	·91	H. 1265 Shawwal	1
	7	Tu	21		3	·05	13	·93		2
	8	We	22		4	·05	14	·96		3
	9	Th	23		5	·06	...	...		4
	10	Fr	24	Bhadrapada	6	·09	15	·04		5
	11	Sa	25		7	·15	16	·11		6
	12	Su	26		8	·22	17	·20		7
	13	Mo	27		9	·30	18	·31		8
	14	Tu	28		10	·39	19	·41		9
	15	We	29		11	·47	20	·52		10
	16	Th	30		12	·54	21	·62		11
	17	Fr	31		13	·60	22	·70		12

Sep.

Solar month	Cyclic Sidereal Day	Week-Day	English Day	Lunar month	Tithi	Ending Moment	Nakshatra	Ending Moment	Muhammadan Month	Day
Saumya Simha—Avani	18	Sa	1	Bhadrapada	14	·63	23	·76		13
	19	Su ○	2		P	·65	24	·80		14
	20	Mo	3		1	65	25	·82		15
	21	Tu	4		2	·62	26	·83		16
	22	We	5		3	·58	27	·81		17
	23	Th	6		4	·52	1	·78	H. 1265 Shawwal	18
	24	Fr	7		5	·45	2	·73		19
	25	Sa	8		6	·36	3	·67		20
	26	Su	9		7	·26	4	·61		21
	27	Mo	10		8	·16	5	·54		22
	28	Tu	11	Bahula	9 10	·06 ·96	6	·47		23
	29	We	12		11	·87	7	·40		24
	30	Th	13		12	·79	8	·34		25
	31	Fr	14		13	·71	9	·29		26
Saumya Kanya—Purattasi	1	Sa	15		14	·65	10	·26		27
	2	Su	16		A	·60	11	·24		28
	3	Mo	17		1	·57	12	·23		29
	4	Tu	18		2	·57	13	·24		1
	5	We	19		3	·58	14	·28		2
	6	Th	20		4	·62	15	·34		3
	7	Fr	21		5	·68	16	·41		4
	8	Sa	22	Sukla	6	·75	17	·50		5
	9	Su	23		7	·83	18	·61		6
	10	Mo	24		8	·91	19	·72		7
	11	Tu	25		...	...	20	·83	Zi-l-ka'da	8
	12	We	26	Asvina	9	·00	21	·92		9
	13	Th	27		10	·08	...	...		10
	14	Fr	28		11	·14	22	·00		11
	15	Sa	29		12	·17	23	·07		12
	16	Su	30		13	·19	24	·12		13

Oct.

Solar month	Cyclic Sidereal Day	Week-Day	English Day	Lunar month	Tithi	Ending Moment	Nakshatra	Ending Moment	Muhammadan Month	Day
	17	Mo	1		14	·19	25	·15	H. 1265	14
	18	Tu	2		P	·17	26	·16		15
	19	We	3		1	·13	27	·14		16
	20	Th	4		2	·07	1	·11		17
	21	Fr	5		3 4	·00 ·91	2	·06		18
	22	Sa	6		5	·82	3 4	·01 ·95		19
	23	Su	7	Bahula	6	·73	5	·88		20
	24	Mo	8		7	·63	6	·81		21
	25	Tu	9		8	·53	7	·74		22
	26	We	10		9	·43	8	·68		23
	27	Th	11		10	·35	9	·63		24
	28	Fr	12		11	·27	10	·59		25
	29	Sa	13		12	·21	11	·56		26
	30	Su	14		13	·17	12	·55		27
Saumya Tula—Aippasi	1	Mo	15		14	·15	13	·56		28
	2	Tu	16		A	·14	14	·60		29
	3	We	17		1	·16	15	·65		30
	4	Th	18		2	·20	16	·72		1
	5	Fr	19		3	·25	17	·80	H. 1265 Zi-l-hijja	2
	6	Sa	20		4	·32	18	·90		3
	7	Su	21	Sukla	5	·41	...	...		4
	8	Mo	22		6	·50	19	·01		5
	9	Tu	23		7	·59	20	·13		6
	10	We	24		8	·67	21	·22		7
	11	Th	25	Karttika	9	·72	22	·31		8
	12	Fr	26		10	·75	23	·38		9
	13	Sa	27		11	·77	24	·43		10
	14	Su	28		12	·77	25	·47		11
	15	Mo	29		13	·76	26	·48		12
	16	Tu	30		14	·72	27	·47		13
	17	We	31		P	·67	1	·44		14

Nov.

Solar month	Cyclic Sidereal Day	Week-Day	English Day	Lunar month	Tithi	Ending Moment	Nakshatra	Ending Moment	Muhammadan Month	Day
Saumya Tula—Aippasi	18	Th	1	Kartika	1	·59	2	·40		15
	19	Fr	2		2	·50	3	·35		16
	20	Sa	3		3	·41	4	·29		17
	21	Su	4		4	·31	5	·22		18
	22	Mo	5		5	·21	6	·15		19
	23	Tu	6		6	·11	7	·08	H. 1265 Zi-l-hijja	20
	24	We	7		7 8	·02 ·94	8 9	·02 ·97		21
	25	Th	8	Bahula	9	·87	10	·92		22
	26	Fr	9		10	·81	11	·89		23
	27	Sa	10		11	·77	12	·87		24
	28	Su	11		12	·75	13	·89		25
	29	Mo	12		13	·75	14	·91		26
	30	Tu	13		14	·77	15	·96		27
Saumya Vrischika—Karttigai	1	We	14		A	·81	...	...		28
	2	Th	15		1	·87	16	·02		29
	3	Fr	16		2	·94	17	·11		30
	4	Sa	17		...	...	18	·21		1
	5	Su	18		3	·03	19	·32		2
	6	Mo	19	Sukla	4	·12	20	·42		3
	7	Tu	20		5	·20	21	52		4
	8	We	21		6	·28	22	·61		5
	9	Th	22		7	·34	23	·69		6
	10	Fr	23		8	·39	24	·75		7
	11	Sa	24	Margasira	9	·40	25	·79		8
	12	Su	25		10	·39	26	·80		9
	13	Mo	26		11	·37	27	·79	Muharram	10
	14	Tu	27		12	·33	1	·77		11
	15	We	28		13	·28	2	·74		12
	16	Th	29		14	·21	3	·69		13
	17	Fr	30		P	·13	4	·63		14

Dec.

Solar month	Cyclic Sidereal Day	Week-Day	English Day	Lunar month	Tithi	Ending Moment	Nakshatra	Ending Moment	Muhammadan Month	Day
	18	Sa	1		1 2	·04 ·94	5	·56	H. 1266	15
	19	Su	2		3	·84	6	·49		16
	20	Mo	3		4	·74	7	·42		17
	21	Tu	4		5	·65	8	·36		18
	22	We	5	Bahula	6	·56	9	·30		19
	23	Th	6		7	·49	10	·25		20
	24	Fr	7		8	·44	11	·22		21
	25	Sa	8		9	·40	12	·21		22
	26	Su	9		10	·38	13	·21		23
	27	Mo	10		11	·38	14	·23		24
	28	Tu	11		12	·41	15	·27		25
	29	We	12		13	·45	16	·33		26
	30	Th	13		14	·51	17	·41		27
Saumya Dhanus—Margali	1	Fr	14		A	·59	18	·51		28
	2	Sa	15		1	·68	19	·61		29
	3	Su	16		2	·77	20	·72		30
	4	Mo	17		3	·85	21	·82		1
	5	Tu	18		4	·92	22	·92		2
	6	We	19		5	·98	...	...		3
	7	Th	20	Sukla	...	...	23	·01		4
	8	Fr	21		6	·02	24	·07		5
	9	Sa	22		7	·04	25	·10	H. 1266 Safar	6
	10	Su	23		8	·04	26	·12		7
	11	Mo	24		9 10	·01 ·97	27	·12		8
	12	Tu	25	Pausha	11	·92	1	·11		9
	13	We	26		12	·85	2	·07		10
	14	Th	27		13	·77	3 4	·02 ·96		11
	15	Fr	28		14	·67	5	·90		12
	16	Sa	29		P	·57	6	·84		13
	17	Su	30	Bah.	1	·47	7	·77		14
	18	Mo	31		2	·38	8	·70		15

15. Svati. 16. Visak. 17. Anur. 18. Jyesh. 19. Mula. 20. P. Ash. 21. U. Ash. 22. Sravn. 23. Dani. 24. Satab. 25. P. Bhad. 26. U. Bhad. 27. Rev.

A. D. 1850. **Mesha Sankranti** (Commencement of Indian Sidereal Year).
Solar Eclipse. ● **(Surya Sid.) April 11·68.** **Saka 1772.** **Kaliyuga 4951.**
Lunar Eclipse. ○ **(Arya Sid.) April 11·58.** **(S. Cycle) Sadharana.**

SOLAR reckoning: Cyclic Sidereal Year, Month and Day	Week-Day	English Month and Day	LUNAR reckoning: Tithi	Ending Moment	Nakshatra	Ending Moment	Muhammadan Year, Month and Day
	Jan.						
Saumya *Dhanus—Margali.* 19	Tu	1	**Pausha** 3	·29	9	·64	16
20	We	2	4	·21	10	·59	17
21	Th	3	5	·14	11	·55	18
22	Fr	4	6	·08	12	·53	H. 1266 *Safar.* 19
23	Sa	5	7	·04	13	·53	20
24	Su	6	8	·03	14	·54	21
25	Mo	7	*Bahula* 9	·03	15	·58	22
26	Tu	8	10	·05	16	·63	23
27	We	9	11	·10	17	·72	24
28	Th	10	12	·16	18	·81	25
—29	Fr	11	13	·24	19	·91	26
1	Sa	12	14	·33	...	...	27
2	Su	13	—A	·42	20	·02	28
3	Mo	14	1	·50	21	·13	—29
4	Tu	15	2	·57	22	·23	1
5	We	16	3	·63	23	·31	2
6	Th	17	4	·67	24	·38	3
7	Fr	18	*Sukla* 5	·68	25	·42	4
8	Sa	19	6	·68	26	·44	5
9	Su	20	7	·66	27	·45	6
10	Mo	21	8	·62	1	·44	7
11	Tu	22	9	·56	2	·41	8
12	We	23	10	·49	3	·36	9
13	Th	24	**Magha** 11	·40	4	·30	10
Saumya *Makara—Tai.* 14	Fr	25	12	·31	5	·24	11
15	Sa	26	13	·21	6	·17	12
16	Su	27	14	·11	7	·10	*Rabi-ul-awwal.* 13
17	Mo	28	P / 1	·01 / ·92	8 / 9	·03 / ·97	14
18	Tu	29	2	·84	10	·92	15
19	We	30	3	·78	11	·89	16
20	Th	31	4	·73	12	·86	17
	Feb.						
21	Fr	1	*Bahula* 5	·69	13	·85	H. 1266 18
22	Sa	2	6	·66	14	·86	19
23	Su	3	7	·67	15	·89	20
24	Mo	4	8	·70	16	·95	21
25	Tu	5	9	·75	...	...	22
26	We	6	10	·81	17	·02	23
27	Th	7	11	·89	18	·11	24
28	Fr	8	12	·97	19	·21	25
—29	Sa	9	...	...	20	·32	26
1	Su	10	13	·06	21	·43	27
2	Mo	11	14	·14	22	·53	28
3	Tu ●	12	—A	·22	23	·62	29
4	We	13	1	·28	24	·68	—30
5	Th	14	2	·31	25	·73	1
6	Fr	15	3	·32	26	·77	2
7	Sa	16	4	·31	27	·78	3
Saumya *Kumbha—Masi.* 8	Su	17	5	·29	1	·77	*Rabi-ul-akhir.* 4
9	Mo	18	*Sukla* 6	·24	2	·74	5
10	Tu	19	7	·18	3	·69	6
11	We	20	8	·11	4	·64	7
12	Th	21	9 / 10	·02 / ·93	5	·58	8
13	Fr	22	**Phalguna** 11	·83	6	·51	9
14	Sa	23	12	·73	7	·44	10
15	Su	24	13	·63	8	·37	11
16	Mo	25	14	·54	9	·31	12
17	Tu	26	P	·45	10	·26	13
18	We	27	1	·38	11	·22	14
19	Th	28	2	·34	12	·19	15

SOLAR reckoning: Cyclic Sidereal Year, Month and Day	Week-Day	English Month and Day	LUNAR reckoning: Tithi	Ending Moment	Nakshatra	Ending Moment	Muhammadan Year, Month and Day
	March						
Saumya *Kumbha—Masi.* 20	Fr	1	**Phalguna** 3	·31	13	·17	16
21	Sa	2	4	·29	14	·18	17
22	Su	3	5	·28	15	·21	*Rabi-ul-akhir.* 18
23	Mo	4	6	·31	16	·26	19
24	Tu	5	7	·36	17	·33	20
25	We	6	8	·42	18	·41	21
26	Th	7	9	·50	19	·51	22
27	Fr	8	*Bahula* 10	·59	20	·62	H. 1266 23
28	Sa	9	11	·68	21	·73	24
29	Su	10	12	·76	22	·83	25
—30	Mo	11	13	·82	23	·92	26
1	Tu	12	14	·87	24	·99	27
2	We	13	—A	·91	...	...	28
3	Th	14	1	·92	25	·05	—29
4	Fr	15	2	·91	26	·09	1
5	Sa	16	3	·88	27	·10	2
6	Su	17	4	·84	1	·09	3
7	Mo	18	5	·78	2	·07	4
8	Tu	19	6	·71	3 / 4	·03 / ·98	5
9	We	20	*Sukla* 7	·62	5	·92	6
10	Th	21	8	·52	6	·85	7
11	Fr	22	9	·42	7	·78	*Jumadal-awwal.* 8
12	Sa	23	10	·32	8	·71	9
13	Su	24	11	·22	9	·65	10
Saumya *Mina—Panguni.* 14	Mo	25	12	·13	10	·60	11
15	Tu	26	13 / 14	·05 / ·98	11	·55	12
16	We	27	**Chaitra** P	·92	12	·51	13
17	Th	28	1	·88	13	·50	H. 1266 14
18	Fr	29	2	·87	14	·51	15
19	Sa	30	3	·87	15	·53	16
20	Su	31	4	·90	16	·57	17
	April						
21	Mo	1	5	·94	17	·63	18
22	Tu	2	...	...	18	·71	19
23	We	3	6	·00	19	·82	20
24	Th	4	*Bahula* 7	·08	20	·93	21
25	Fr	5	8	·16	...	...	22
26	Sa	6	9	·26	21	·03	23
27	Su	7	10	·34	22	·13	24
28	Mo	8	11	·40	23	·22	25
29	Tu	9	12	·45	24	·30	26
30	We	10	13	·48	25	·37	27
—31	Th	11	14	·48	26	·41	28
1	Fr	12	—A	·47	27	·42	29
2	Sa	13	1	·44	1	·42	—30
3	Su	14	2	·39	2	·40	1
4	Mo	15	3	·33	3	·37	2
5	Tu	16	*Sukla* 4	·26	4	·32	3
6	We	17	5	·17	5	·26	*Jumadal-akhir.* 4
Sadharana *Mesha—Chittirai.* 7	Th	18	6 / 7	·07 / ·97	6	·19	5
8	Fr	19	8	·87	7	·12	6
9	Sa	20	**Adhika Vaisakha** 9	·77	8 / 9	·05 / ·99	7
10	Su	21	10	·67	10	·93	8
11	Mo	22	11	·59	11	·88	9
12	Tu	23	12	·52	12	·84	H. 1266 10
13	We	24	13	·46	13	·83	11
14	Th	25	14	·43	14	·83	12
15	Fr	26	P	·41	15	·84	13
16	Sa	27	*Bah.* 1	·40	16	·88	14
17	Su	28	2	·43	17	·94	15
18	Mo	29	3	·47	...	...	16
19	Tu	30	4	·53	18	·03	17

SOLAR reckoning: Cyclic Sidereal Year, Month and Day	Week-Day	English Month and Day	LUNAR reckoning: Tithi	Ending Moment	Nakshatra	Ending Moment	Muhammadan Year, Month and Day
	May						
Sadharana *Mesha—Chittirai.* 20	We	1	**Adh. Vsk** 5	·61	19	·12	18
21	Th	2	6	·71	20	·22	*Jumadal-akhir.* 19
22	Fr	3	7	·79	21	·33	20
23	Sa	4	8	·86	22	·43	21
24	Su	5	9	·92	23	·53	22
25	Mo	6	10	·97	24	·62	23
26	Tu	7	*Bah.* ...	...	25	·68	24
27	We	8	11	·00	26	·72	H. 1266 25
28	Th	9	12	·01	27	·74	26
29	Fr	10	13 / 14	·00 / ·97	1	·74	27
30	Sa	11	—A	·92	2	·73	28
—31	Su	12	1	·86	3	·70	—29
1	Mo	13	2	·78	4	·65	1
2	Tu	14	3	·69	5	·59	2
3	We	15	4	·59	6	·53	3
4	Th	16	5	·49	7	·47	4
5	Fr	17	*Sukla* 6	·39	8	·40	5
6	Sa	18	7	·29	9	·33	6
7	Su	19	8	·19	10	·27	7
8	Mo	20	9	·11	11	·21	8
9	Tu	21	10 / 11	·04 / ·98	12	·18	9
10	We	22	**Nija Vaisakha** 12	·94	13	·16	10
Sadharana *Vrishabha—Vaikasi.* 11	Th	23	13	·91	14	·15	11
12	Fr	24	14	·91	15	·16	12
13	Sa	25	P	·93	16	·19	*Rajab.* 13
14	Su	26	1	·98	17	·25	14
15	Mo	27	...	...	18	·33	15
16	Tu	28	2	·04	19	·42	H. 1266 16
17	We	29	3	·11	20	·52	17
18	Th	30	4	·19	21	·62	18
19	Fr	31	5	·27	22	·73	19
	June						
20	Sa	1	*Bahula* 6	·35	23	·84	20
21	Su	2	7	·41	24	·92	21
22	Mo	3	8	·46	25	·99	22
23	Tu	4	9	·49	...	...	23
24	We	5	10	·50	26	·04	24
25	Th	6	11	·50	27	·06	25
26	Fr	7	12	·47	1	·07	26
27	Sa	8	13	·42	2	·06	27
28	Su	9	14	·35	3 / 4	·03 / ·99	28
29	Mo	10	—A	·27	5	·93	29
30	Tu	11	1	·18	6	·87	—30
—31	We	12	2 / 3	·08 / ·98	7	·81	1
1	Th	13	4	·88	8	·74	2
2	Fr	14	5	·78	9	·67	3
3	Sa	15	6	·69	10	·61	4
4	Su	16	*Sukla* 7	·60	11	·56	5
5	Mo	17	8	·52	12	·51	6
Sadharana *Mithuna—Ani.* 6	Tu	18	9	·46	13	·48	*Shaban.* 7
7	We	19	10	·42	14	·47	8
8	Th	20	11	·40	15	·48	9
9	Fr	21	**Jyeshtha** 12	·39	16	·51	H. 1266 10
10	Sa	22	13	·41	17	·56	11
11	Su	23	14	·46	18	·63	12
12	Mo	24	P	·52	19	·72	13
13	Tu	25	1	·59	20	·82	14
14	We	26	2	·67	21	·92	15
15	Th	27	3	·75	...	...	16
16	Fr	28	4	·83	22	·03	17
17	Sa	29	*Bah.* 5	·89	23	·14	18
18	Su	30	6	·94	24	·23	19

Naksh :—1. Asvn. 2. Bhar. 3. Krit. 4. Rohi. 5. Mrig. 6. Ardh. 7. Punar. 8. Push. 9. Aslesh. 10. Magh. 11. P. Phal. 12. U. Phal. 13. Hasta. 14. Chit.

A. D. 1850.   **Vikrama 1907.**
A.—Âmavasya.   **Kollam 1026,** { **N. Malabar—Sept.** / **S. Malabar—Aug.** } Commences   **Hijra 1267,** Commences, **Nov. 6.**   **Bengal San 1256.**
P.—Paurnami.   **(N. Cycle) Durmati.**

SOLAR reckoning: Cyclic Sidereal Year, Month and Day; Week-Day; English Month and Day. LUNAR reckoning: Tithi, Ending Moment; Nakshatra, Ending Moment; Muhammadan Year, Month and Day.

July

Cyclic Sidereal Year, Month and Day	Week-Day	English Month and Day	Tithi	Ending Moment	Nakshatra	Ending Moment	Muhammadan Year, Month and Day	Notes
19	Mo	1	7	·97	25	·30	20	Sadharana, Mithuna—Âni; Jyesh. Bahula
20	Tu	2	8	·99	26	·36	21	H. 1266 Shaban
21	We	3	9	·98	27	·39	22	
22	Th	4	10	·95	1	·40	23	
23	Fr	5	11	·90	2	·39	24	
24	Sa	6	12	·83	3	·36	25	
25	Su	7	13	·75	4	·32	26	
26	Mo	8	14	·66	5	·27	27	
27	Tu	9	A	·56	6	·21	28	
28	We	10	1	·46	7	·15	29	Sukla
29	Th	11	2	·36	8	·08	1	H. 1266 Ramzan
30	Fr	12	3	·26	9 / 10	·01 / ·94	2	
31	Sa	13	4	·17	11	·89	3	
32	Su	14	5	·09	12	·84	4	
1	Mo	15	6 / 7	·02 / ·95	13	·81	5	Sadharana, Karkata—Adi
2	Tu	16	8	·90	14	·80	6	
3	We	17	9	·88	15	·80	7	
4	Th	18	10	·87	16	·83	8	
5	Fr	19	11	·89	17	·87	9	
6	Sa	20	12	·93	18	·94	10	
7	Su	21	13	·98	...	...	11	
8	Mo	22	...	...	19	·02	12	Ashadha
9	Tu	23	14	·05	20	·12	13	
10	We	24	P	·13	21	·23	14	
11	Th	25	1	·22	22	·34	15	
12	Fr	26	2	·30	23	·44	16	
13	Sa	27	3	·36	24	·53	17	
14	Su	28	4	·41	25	·61	18	
15	Mo	29	5	·45	26	·67	19	
16	Tu	30	6	·47	27	·71	20	
17	We	31	7	·45	1	·72	21	

Aug.

Cyclic Sidereal Year, Month and Day	Week-Day	English Month and Day	Tithi	Ending Moment	Nakshatra	Ending Moment	Muhammadan Year, Month and Day	Notes
18	Th	1	8	·42	2	·72	22	Bahula
19	Fr	2	9	·38	3	·69	23	
20	Sa	3	10	·32	4	·65	24	
21	Su	4	11	·24	5	·61	25	
22	Mo	5	12	·15	6	·55	26	
23	Tu	6	13 / 14	·06 / ·96	7	·48	27	
24	We	7	A	·86	8	·41	28	
25	Th	8	1	·76	9	·35	29	Sukla
26	Fr	9	2	·66	10	·29	30	
27	Sa	10	3	·57	11	·23	1	H. 1266 Shawwal
28	Su	11	4	·50	12	·18	2	
29	Mo	12	5	·44	13	·14	3	
30	Tu	13	6	·39	14	·12	4	
31	We	14	7	·37	15	·13	5	
1	Th	15	8	·36	16	·15	6	Sadharana, Simha—Avani
2	Fr	16	9	·38	17	·18	7	
3	Sa	17	10	·42	18	·24	8	
4	Su	18	11	·48	19	·32	9	
5	Mo	19	12	·55	20	·42	10	Sravana
6	Tu	20	13	·63	21	·53	11	
7	We	21	14	·72	22	·64	12	
8	Th	22	P	·80	23	·74	13	
9	Fr	23	1	·86	24	·83	14	Bahula
10	Sa	24	2	·91	25	·92	15	
11	Su	25	3	·94	26	·98	16	
12	Mo	26	4	·96	...	...	17	
13	Tu	27	5	·96	27	·02	18	
14	We	28	6	·94	1	·04	19	
15	Th	29	7	·89	2	·04	20	
16	Fr	30	8	·83	3	·02	21	
17	Sa	31	9	·76	4 / 5	·00 / ·95	22	

Sep.

Cyclic Sidereal Year, Month and Day	Week-Day	English Month and Day	Tithi	Ending Moment	Nakshatra	Ending Moment	Muhammadan Year, Month and Day	Notes
18	Su	1	10	·67	6	·89	23	Sr. Bah.; Shawwal
19	Mo	2	11	·57	7	·82	24	
20	Tu	3	12	·47	8	·75	25	
21	We	4	13	·37	9	·68	26	
22	Th	5	14	·27	10	·62	27	
23	Fr	6	A	·17	11	·56	28	
24	Sa	7	1	·09	12	·51	29	Sukla
25	Su	8	2 / 3	·02 / ·96	13	·47	1	H. 1266 Zi-l-ka'da
26	Mo	9	4	·91	14	·46	2	
27	Tu	10	5	·89	15	·45	3	
28	We	11	6	·88	16	·46	4	
29	Th	12	7	·90	17	·50	5	
30	Fr	13	8	·94	18	·55	6	
31	Sa	14	...	...	19	·63	7	
1	Su	15	9	·09	20	·72	8	Sadharana, Kanya—Purattasi
2	Mo	16	10	·07	21	·83	9	
3	Tu	17	11	·15	22	·94	10	Bhadrapada
4	We	18	12	·23	...	...	11	
5	Th	19	13	·31	23	·04	12	
6	Fr	20	14	·33	24	·13	13	
7	Sa	21	P	·44	25	·22	14	
8	Su	22	1	·48	26	·29	15	Bahula
9	Mo	23	2	·49	27	·34	16	
10	Tu	24	3	·49	1	·36	17	
11	We	25	4	·47	2	·37	18	
12	Th	26	5	·43	3	·36	19	
13	Fr	27	6	·37	4	·33	20	
14	Sa	28	7	·29	5	·28	21	
15	Su	29	8	·21	6	·22	22	
16	Mo	30	9	·12	7	·16	23	

Oct.

Cyclic Sidereal Year, Month and Day	Week-Day	English Month and Day	Tithi	Ending Moment	Nakshatra	Ending Moment	Muhammadan Year, Month and Day	Notes
17	Tu	1	10 / 11	·02 / ·92	8	·10	24	
18	We	2	12	·82	9 / 10	·03 / ·96	25	
19	Th	3	13	·72	11	·90	26	
20	Fr	4	14	·64	12	·84	27	
21	Sa	5	A	·57	13	·81	28	
22	Su	6	1	·51	14	·78	29	Sukla
23	Mo	7	2	·47	15	·77	30	
24	Tu	8	3	·45	16	·78	1	H. 1266 Zi-l-hijja
25	We	9	4	·45	17	·81	2	
26	Th	10	5	·46	18	·87	3	
27	Fr	11	6	·50	19	·94	4	
28	Sa	12	7	·56	...	...	5	
29	Su	13	8	·63	20	·03	6	
30	Mo	14	9	·71	21	·12	7	
1	Tu	15	10	·80	22	·23	8	Sadharana, Tula—Aippasi
2	We	16	11	·89	23	·34	9	
3	Th	17	12	·96	24	·45	10	
4	Fr	18	...	...	25	·53	11	Asvina
5	Sa	19	13	·01	26	·60	12	
6	Su	20	14	·05	27	·65	13	
7	Mo	21	P	·07	1	·68	14	
8	Tu	22	1	·08	2	·70	15	Bahula
9	We	23	2	·05	3	·69	16	
10	Th	24	3 / 4	·01 / ·95	4	·66	17	
11	Fr	25	5	·87	5	·62	18	
12	Sa	26	6	·79	6	·56	19	
13	Su	27	7	·70	7	·50	20	
14	Mo	28	8	·60	8	·44	21	
15	Tu	29	9	·50	9	·37	22	
16	We	30	10	·41	10	·30	23	
17	Th	31	11	·32	11	·24	24	

Nov.

Cyclic Sidereal Year, Month and Day	Week-Day	English Month and Day	Tithi	Ending Moment	Nakshatra	Ending Moment	Muhammadan Year, Month and Day	Notes
18	Fr	1	12	·23	12	·19	25	Bah.; Zi-l-hijja
19	Sa	2	13	·15	13	·14	26	
20	Su	3	14	·09	14	·11	27	Sadharana, Tula—Aippasi
21	Mo	4	A	·06	15	·09	28	
22	Tu	5	1	·04	16	·10	29	
23	We	6	2	·04	17	·12	1	H. 1267 Muharram
24	Th	7	3	·06	18	·18	2	
25	Fr	8	4	·10	19	·24	3	
26	Sa	9	5	·16	20	·33	4	
27	Su	10	6	·24	21	·42	5	Sukla
28	Mo	11	7	·33	22	·53	6	
29	Tu	12	8	·42	23	·64	7	
30	We	13	9	·50	24	·75	8	
1	Th	14	10	·57	25	·84	9	Sadharana, Vrischika—Kartigai
2	Fr	15	11	·63	26	·91	10	
3	Sa	16	12	·67	27	·96	11	
4	Su	17	13	·69	...	...	12	Kartika
5	Mo	18	14	·69	1	·01	13	
6	Tu	19	P	·66	2	·02	14	
7	We	20	1	·62	3 / 4	·01 / ·99	15	
8	Th	21	2	·56	5	·95	16	
9	Fr	22	3	·49	6	·91	17	
10	Sa	23	4	·41	7	·85	18	Bahula
11	Su	24	5	·32	8	·78	19	
12	Mo	25	6	·22	9	·71	20	
13	Tu	26	7	·12	10	·64	21	
14	We	27	8 / 9	·02 / ·93	11	·58	22	
15	Th	28	10	·85	12	·52	23	
16	Fr	29	11	·78	13	·47	24	
17	Sa	30	12	·72	14	·44	25	

Dec.

Cyclic Sidereal Year, Month and Day	Week-Day	English Month and Day	Tithi	Ending Moment	Nakshatra	Ending Moment	Muhammadan Year, Month and Day	Notes
18	Su	1	13	·68	15	·42	26	
19	Mo	2	14	·66	16	·42	27	
20	Tu	3	A	·67	17	·45	28	
21	We	4	1	·69	18	·49	29	Sukla
22	Th	5	2	·74	19	·55	30	
23	Fr	6	3	·80	20	·63	1	H. 1267 Safar
24	Sa	7	4	·88	21	·72	2	
25	Su	8	5	·96	22	·83	3	
26	Mo	9	...	...	23	·94	4	
27	Tu	10	6	·05	...	...	5	
28	We	11	7	·14	24	·05	6	
29	Th	12	8	·21	25	·14	7	
30	Fr	13	9	·27	26	·23	8	
1	Sa	14	10	·31	27	·29	9	Sadharana, Dhanus—Margali; Margasira
2	Su	15	11	·34	1	·32	10	
3	Mo	16	12	·33	2	·34	11	
4	Tu	17	13	·30	3	·34	12	
5	We	18	14	·25	4	·32	13	
6	Th	19	P	·19	5	·28	14	
7	Fr	20	1	·12	6	·24	15	Bahula
8	Sa	21	2 / 3	·04 / ·95	7	·18	16	
9	Su	22	4	·85	8	·12	17	
10	Mo	23	5	·75	9 / 10	·05 / ·98	18	
11	Tu	24	6	·65	11	·92	19	
12	We	25	7	·56	12	·86	20	
13	Th	26	8	·48	13	·81	21	
14	Fr	27	9	·41	14	·77	22	
15	Sa	28	10	·36	15	·74	23	
16	Su	29	11	·33	16	·74	24	
17	Mo	30	12	·32	17	·76	25	
18	Tu	31	13	·32	18	·80	26	

15. Svati. 16. Visak. 17. Anur. 18. Jyesh. 19. Mula. 20. P. Ash. 21. U. Ash. 22. Sravn. 23. Dani. 24. Satab. 25. P. Bhad. 26. U. Bhad. 27. Rev.

A. D. 1851. **Mesha Sankranti** (Commencement of Indian Sidereal Year).
Solar Eclipse. ● **(Surya Sid.) April 11·94.** **Saka 1773.** **Kaliyuga 4952.**
Lunar Eclipse. ○ **(Arya Sid.) April 11·84.** **(S. Cycle) Virodhakrit.**

Jan. (Solar: Sadharana, Dhanus—Margali; Sadharana, Makara—Tai. Lunar: Sukla; Pausha; Bahula. Muhammadan: H. 1267 Rabi-ul-awwal.)

SOLAR reckoning: Cyclic Sidereal Year, Month and Day.	Week-Day	English Month and Day.	LUNAR reckoning: Tithi	Ending Moment.	Nakshatra	Ending Moment.	Muhammadan Year, Month and Day.
19	We	1	14	·34	19	·86	27
20	Th	2	—A	·38	20	·93	28
21	Fr	3	1	·45	...	...	—29
22	Sa	4	2	·53	21	·03	1
23	Su	5	3	·62	22	·13	2
24	Mo	6	4	·71	23	·24	3
25	Tu	7	5	·79	24	·35	4
26	We	8	6	·87	25	·44	5
27	Th	9	7	·93	26	·53	6
28	Fr	10	8	·96	27	·60	7
—29	Sa	11	9	·98	1	·64	8
1	Su	12	10	·97	2	·66	9
2	Mo	13	11	·95	3	·66	10
3	Tu	14	12	·90	4	·65	11
4	We	15	13	·84	5	·63	12
5	Th	16	14	·77	6	·58	13
6	Fr ○	17	P	·68	7	·52	14
7	Sa	18	1	·59	8	·45	15
8	Su	19	2	·49	9	·38	16
9	Mo	20	3	·39	10	·31	17
10	Tu	21	4	·29	11	·25	18
11	We	22	5	·20	12	·19	19
12	Th	23	6	·12	13	·14	20
13	Fr	24	7	·05	14	·10	21
14	Sa	25	{8 / 9}	·00 / ·97	15	·08	22
15	Su	26	10	·96	16	·07	23
16	Mo	27	11	·96	17	·08	24
17	Tu	28	12	·99	18	·11	25
18	We	29	...	...	19	·16	26
19	Th	30	13	·04	20	·24	27
20	Fr	31	14	·11	21	·33	28

Feb. (Solar: Sadharana, Kumbha—Masi. Lunar: Sukla; Magha; Bahula. Muhammadan: H. 1267 Rabi-ul-akhir.)

SOLAR reckoning: Cyclic Sidereal Year, Month and Day.	Week-Day	English Month and Day.	LUNAR reckoning: Tithi	Ending Moment.	Nakshatra	Ending Moment.	Muhammadan Year, Month and Day.
21	Sa	1	—A	·18	22	·43	29
22	Su	2	1	·26	23	·54	—30
23	Mo	3	2	·36	24	·64	1
24	Tu	4	3	·44	25	·74	2
25	We	5	4	·51	26	·84	3
26	Th	6	5	·57	27	·91	4
27	Fr	7	6	·61	1	·95	5
28	Sa	8	7	·62	2	·98	6
29	Su	9	8	·61	3	·99	7
—30	Mo	10	9	·58	4	·99	8
1	Tu	11	10	·53	5	·96	9
2	We	12	11	·47	6	·91	10
3	Th	13	12	·39	7	·85	11
4	Fr	14	13	·31	8	·79	12
5	Sa	15	14	·21	9	·73	13
6	Su	16	P	·11	10	·66	14
7	Mo	17	{1 / 2}	·01 / ·91	11	·59	15
8	Tu	18	3	·82	12	·53	16
9	We	19	4	·74	13	·47	17
10	Th	20	5	·66	14	·44	18
11	Fr	21	6	·63	15	·41	19
12	Sa	22	7	·60	16	·39	20
13	Su	23	8	·58	17	·40	21
14	Mo	24	9	·58	18	·42	22
15	Tu	25	10	·61	19	·48	23
16	We	26	11	·65	20	·55	24
17	Th	27	12	·72	21	·63	25
18	Fr	28	13	·81	22	·73	26

March (Solar: Sadharana, Kumbha—Masi; Sadharana, Mina—Panguni. Lunar: Sukla; Phalguna; Bahula. Muhammadan: H. 1267 Jumadal-awwal.)

SOLAR reckoning: Cyclic Sidereal Year, Month and Day.	Week-Day	English Month and Day.	LUNAR reckoning: Tithi	Ending Moment.	Nakshatra	Ending Moment.	Muhammadan Year, Month and Day.
19	Sa	1	14	·90	23	·84	27
20	Su	2	—A	·98	24	·94	28
21	Mo	3	...	...	...	...	—29
22	Tu	4	1	·06	25	·05	1
23	We	5	2	·13	26	·14	2
24	Th	6	3	·18	27	·21	3
25	Fr	7	4	·22	1	·27	4
26	Sa	8	5	·23	2	·30	5
27	Su	9	6	·22	3	·32	6
28	Mo	10	7	·19	4	·31	7
—29	Tu	11	8	·14	5	·29	8
1	We	12	{9 / 10}	·07 / ·99	6	·25	9
2	Th	13	11	·90	7	·19	10
3	Fr	14	12	·81	8	·13	11
4	Sa	15	13	·71	9	·07	12
5	Su	16	14	·61	{10 / 11}	·00 / ·93	13
6	Mo	17	P	·51	12	·87	14
7	Tu	18	1	·42	13	·82	15
8	We	19	2	·34	14	·77	16
9	Th	20	3	·27	15	·73	17
10	Fr	21	4	·22	16	·72	18
11	Sa	22	5	·19	17	·72	19
12	Su	23	6	·17	18	·74	20
13	Mo	24	7	·18	19	·79	21
14	Tu	25	8	·21	20	·85	22
15	We	26	9	·25	21	·93	23
16	Th	27	10	·31	...	...	24
17	Fr	28	11	·39	22	·03	25
18	Sa	29	12	·48	23	·14	26
19	Su	30	13	·57	24	·25	27
20	Mo	31	14	·65	25	·35	28

April (Solar: Virodhakrit, Mesha—Chittirai. Lunar: Sukla; Chaitra; Bahula. Muhammadan: H. 1267 Jumadal-akhir.)

SOLAR reckoning: Cyclic Sidereal Year, Month and Day.	Week-Day	English Month and Day.	LUNAR reckoning: Tithi	Ending Moment.	Nakshatra	Ending Moment.	Muhammadan Year, Month and Day.
21	Tu	1	—A	·72	26	·44	29
22	We	2	1	·77	27	·52	—30
23	Th	3	2	·80	1	·58	1
24	Fr	4	3	·80	2	·63	2
25	Sa	5	4	·79	3	·64	3
26	Su	6	5	·75	4	·64	4
27	Mo	7	6	·70	5	·62	5
28	Tu	8	7	·64	6	·58	6
29	We	9	8	·56	7	·54	7
30	Th	10	9	·47	8	·48	8
—31	Fr	11	10	·37	9	·41	9
1	Sa	12	11	·27	10	·34	10
2	Su	13	12	·17	11	·27	11
3	Mo	14	{13 / 14}	·07 / ·98	12	·21	12
4	Tu	15	P	·90	13	·15	13
5	We	16	1	·83	14	·10	14
6	Th	17	2	·78	15	·06	15
7	Fr	18	3	·74	16	·04	16
8	Sa	19	4	·72	17	·04	17
9	Su	20	5	·73	18	·06	18
10	Mo	21	6	·75	19	·10	19
11	Tu	22	7	·80	20	·16	20
12	We	23	8	·86	21	·24	21
13	Th	24	9	·93	22	·33	22
14	Fr	25	...	...	23	·44	23
15	Sa	26	10	·02	24	·55	24
16	Su	27	11	·11	25	·65	25
17	Mo	28	12	·19	26	·75	26
18	Tu	29	13	·25	27	·83	27
19	We	30	14	·30	1	·90	28

May (Solar: Virodhakrit, Mesha—Chittirai; Virodhakrit, Vrishabha—Vaikasi. Lunar: Sukla; Vaisakha; Bahula. Muhammadan: H. 1267 Rajab.)

SOLAR reckoning: Cyclic Sidereal Year, Month and Day.	Week-Day	English Month and Day.	LUNAR reckoning: Tithi	Ending Moment.	Nakshatra	Ending Moment.	Muhammadan Year, Month and Day.
20	Th	1	—A	·33	2	·94	—29
21	Fr	2	1	·34	3	·96	1
22	Sa	3	2	·32	4	·96	2
23	Su	4	3	·29	5	·95	3
24	Mo	5	4	·24	6	·92	4
25	Tu	6	5	·17	7	·87	5
26	We	7	6	·09	8	·81	6
27	Th	8	{7 / 8}	·00 / ·90	9	·75	7
28	Fr	9	9	·80	10	·68	8
29	Sa	10	10	·70	11	·61	9
30	Su	11	11	·60	12	·55	10
—31	Mo	12	12	·50	13	·49	11
1	Tu	13	13	·41	14	·43	12
2	We	14	14	·34	15	·39	13
3	Th	15	P	·29	16	·37	14
4	Fr	16	1	·25	17	·37	15
5	Sa	17	2	·24	18	·38	16
6	Su	18	3	·24	19	·41	17
7	Mo	19	4	·27	20	·47	18
8	Tu	20	5	·31	21	·54	19
9	We	21	6	·36	22	·64	20
10	Th	22	7	·44	23	·74	21
11	Fr	23	8	·53	24	·85	22
12	Sa	24	9	·61	25	·95	23
13	Su	25	10	·68	...	...	24
14	Mo	26	11	·75	26	·05	25
15	Tu	27	12	·80	27	·14	26
16	We	28	13	·83	1	·21	27
17	Th	29	14	·84	2	·26	28
18	Fr	30	—A	·82	3	·28	29
19	Sa	31	1	·79	4	·29	—30

June (Solar: Virodhakrit, Mithuna—Ani. Lunar: Sukla; Jyeshtha; Bahula. Muhammadan: H. 1267 Shaban.)

SOLAR reckoning: Cyclic Sidereal Year, Month and Day.	Week-Day	English Month and Day.	LUNAR reckoning: Tithi	Ending Moment.	Nakshatra	Ending Moment.	Muhammadan Year, Month and Day.
20	Su	1	2	·75	5	·27	1
21	Mo	2	3	·68	6	·25	2
22	Tu	3	4	·59	7	·21	3
23	We	4	5	·49	8	·15	4
24	Th	5	6	·39	9	·09	5
25	Fr	6	7	·29	{10 / 11}	·03 / ·96	6
26	Sa	7	8	·19	12	·89	7
2.	Su	8	9	·10	13	·83	8
28	Mo	9	{10 / 11}	·01 / ·92	14	·77	9
29	Tu	10	12	·84	15	·72	10
30	We	11	13	·78	16	·70	11
—31	Th	12	14	·74	17	·69	12
1	Fr	13	P	·72	18	·70	13
2	Sa	14	1	·72	19	·73	14
3	Su	15	2	·75	20	·78	15
4	Mo	16	3	·79	21	·85	16
5	Tu	17	4	·85	22	·94	17
6	We	18	5	·92	...	...	18
7	Th	19	...	...	23	·04	19
8	Fr	20	6	·00	24	·14	20
9	Sa	21	7	·09	25	·25	21
10	Su	22	8	·16	26	·36	22
11	Mo	23	9	·23	27	·45	23
12	Tu	24	10	·28	1	·52	24
13	We	25	11	·31	2	·57	25
14	Th	26	12	·32	3	·60	26
15	Fr	27	13	·30	4	·61	27
16	Sa	28	14	·27	5	·61	28
17	Su	29	—A	·22	6	·58	—29
18	Mo	30	1	·16	7	·54	1

Naksh :—1. Asvn. 2. Bhar. 3. Krit. 4. Rohi. 5. Mrig. 6. Ardh. 7. Punar. 8. Push. 9. Aslesh. 10. Magh. 11. P. Phal. 12. U. Phal. 13. Hasta. 14. Chit.

A. D. 1851.
A.—Amavasya.
P.—Paurnami.

Kollam 1027, Commences { N. Malabar—Sept. S. Malabar—Aug.

Hijra 1268, Commences, Oct. 27.

Vikrama 1908.
Bengal San 1257.
(N. Cycle) Dundubhi.

Column headings. SOLAR reckoning: Cyclic Sidereal Year, Month and Day; Week-Day; English Month and Day. LUNAR reckoning: Tithi; Ending Moment; Nakshatra; Ending Moment; Muhammadan Year, Month and Day.

July — Solar: Virodhakrit *Mithuna—Ani.* (to 32), Virodhakrit *Karkata—Adi.* (from 1). Lunar: Ashadha *Sukla*, P, *Bahula*, A. Muhammadan: H. 1267 *Ramzan.*

Cyclic Sidereal Year, Month and Day	Week-Day	English Month and Day	Tithi	Ending Moment	Nakshatra	Ending Moment	Muhammadan Year, Month and Day
19	Tu	1	{ 2 / 3	·08 / ·98	8	·49	2
20	We	2	4	·88	9	·43	3
21	Th	3	5	·78	10	·36	4
22	Fr	4	6	·68	11	·29	5
23	Sa	5	7	·58	12	·22	6
24	Su	6	8	·48	13	·16	7
25	Mo	7	9	·39	14	·10	8
26	Tu	8	10	·32	15	·06	9
27	We	9	11	·26	16	·03	10
28	Th	10	12	·22	17	·02	11
29	Fr	11	13	·20	18	·02	12
30	Sa	12	14	·20	19	·04	13
31	Su	13 ☾	P	·22	20	·09	14
—32	Mo	14	1	·26	21	·16	15
1	Tu	15	2	·32	22	·24	16
2	We	16	3	·39	23	·34	17
3	Th	17	4	·47	24	·45	18
4	Fr	18	5	·55	25	·56	19
5	Sa	19	6	·63	26	·66	20
6	Su	20	7	·70	27	·75	21
7	Mo	21	8	·75	1	·83	22
8	Tu	22	9	·78	2	·88	23
9	We	23	10	·80	3	·92	24
10	Th	24	11	·78	4	·94	25
11	Fr	25	12	·75	5	·94	26
12	Sa	26	13	·70	6	·91	27
13	Su	27	14	·64	7	·87	28
14	Mo	28	—A	·56	8	·82	29
15	Tu	29	1	·47	9	·76	—30
16	We	30	2	·37	10	·70	1
17	Th	31	3	·27	11	·63	2

Aug. — Solar: Virodhakrit *Simha—Avani.* (from 1). Lunar: Sravana *Sukla*, P, *Bahula*, A; Bhad. *Suk.* Muhammadan: H. 1267 *Shawwal.*; *Zi-l-ka'da.*

Cyclic Sidereal Year, Month and Day	Week-Day	English Month and Day	Tithi	Ending Moment	Nakshatra	Ending Moment	Muhammadan Year, Month and Day
18	Fr	1	4	·17	12	·56	3
19	Sa	2	{ 5 / 6	·07 / ·97	13	·50	4
20	Su	3	7	·88	14	·45	5
21	Mo	4	8	·81	15	·40	6
22	Tu	5	9	·75	16	·36	7
23	We	6	10	·71	17	·34	8
24	Th	7	11	·69	18	·34	9
25	Fr	8	12	·68	19	·37	10
26	Sa	9	13	·70	20	·41	11
27	Su	10	14	·74	21	·46	12
28	Mo	11	P	·80	22	·54	13
29	Tu	12	1	·87	23	·64	14
30	We	13	2	·96	24	·75	15
—31	Th	14	...	...	25	·86	16
1	Fr	15	3	·05	26	·96	17
2	Sa	16	4	·13	...	...	18
3	Su	17	5	·19	27	·05	19
4	Mo	18	6	·24	1	·13	20
5	Tu	19	7	·27	2	·19	21
6	We	20	8	·29	3	·24	22
7	Th	21	9	·28	4	·26	23
8	Fr	22	10	·25	5	·26	24
9	Sa	23	11	·21	6	·24	25
10	Su	24	12	·14	7	·21	26
11	Mo	25	{ 13 / 14	·06 / ·97	8	·17	27
12	Tu	26	—A	·87	9	·11	28
13	We	27	1	·77	10 / 11 }	·04 / ·97	—29
14	Th	28	2	·67	12	·90	1
15	Fr	29	3	·57	13	·84	2
16	Sa	30	4	·47	14	·78	3
17	Su	31	5	·39	15	·73	4

Sep. — Solar: Virodhakrit *Simha—Avani.* (to 31), Virodhakrit *Kanya—Purattasi.* (from 1). Lunar: Bhadrapada *Sukla*, P, *Bahula*, A. Muhammadan: H. 1267 *Zi-l-ka'da.*

Cyclic Sidereal Year, Month and Day	Week-Day	English Month and Day	Tithi	Ending Moment	Nakshatra	Ending Moment	Muhammadan Year, Month and Day
18	Mo	1	6	·32	16	·69	5
19	Tu	2	7	·26	17	·67	6
20	We	3	8	·22	18	·66	7
21	Th	4	9	·20	19	·68	8
22	Fr	5	10	·20	20	·72	9
23	Sa	6	11	·22	21	·77	10
24	Su	7	12	·26	22	·85	11
25	Mo	8	13	·31	23	·94	12
26	Tu	9	14	·39	...	...	13
27	We	10	P	·47	24	·05	14
28	Th	11	1	·56	25	·16	15
29	Fr	12	2	·64	26	·26	16
30	Sa	13	3	·71	27	·36	17
—31	Su	14	4	·77	1	·44	18
1	Mo	15	5	·81	2	·51	19
2	Tu	16	6	·83	3	·56	20
3	We	17	7	·81	4	·58	21
4	Th	18	8	·78	5	·59	22
5	Fr	19	9	·74	6	·57	23
6	Sa	20	10	·67	7	·54	24
7	Su	21	11	·59	8	·50	25
8	Mo	22	12	·50	9	·45	26
9	Tu	23	13	·41	10	·38	27
10	We	24	14	·31	11	·31	28
11	Th	25	—A	·21	12	·24	29
12	Fr	26	1	·11	13	·18	—30
13	Sa	27	{ 2 / 3	·01 / ·93	14	·12	1
14	Su	28	4	·86	15	·06	2
15	Mo	29	5	·81	16 / 17 }	·02 / ·99	3
16	Tu	30	6	·77	18	·99	4

Oct. — Solar: Virodhakrit *Kanya—Purattasi.* (to 31), Virodhakrit *Tula—Aippasi.* (from 1). Lunar: Asvina *Sukla*, P, *Bahula*, A; Kartt. *Suk.* Muhammadan: H. 1267 *Zi-l-hijja.*; H. 1268 *Muharram.*

Cyclic Sidereal Year, Month and Day	Week-Day	English Month and Day	Tithi	Ending Moment	Nakshatra	Ending Moment	Muhammadan Year, Month and Day
17	We	1	7	·75	...	...	5
18	Th	2	8	·74	19	·00	6
19	Fr	3	9	·76	20	·03	7
20	Sa	4	10	·81	21	·08	8
21	Su	5	11	·87	22	·16	9
22	Mo	6	12	·94	23	·25	10
23	Tu	7	...	...	24	·35	11
24	We	8	13	·02	25	·45	12
25	Th	9	14	·12	26	·56	13
26	Fr	10	P	·20	27	·66	14
27	Sa	11	1	·27	1	·75	15
28	Su	12	2	·33	2	·82	16
29	Mo	13	3	·36	3	·87	17
30	Tu	14	4	·38	4	·90	18
—31	We	15	5	·37	5	·91	19
1	Th	16	6	·35	6	·91	20
2	Fr	17	7	·31	7	·88	21
3	Sa	18	8	·25	8	·84	22
4	Su	19	9	·17	9	·78	23
5	Mo	20	{ 10 / 11	·08 / ·99	10	·72	24
6	Tu	21	12	·89	11	·65	25
7	We	22	13	·79	12	·58	26
8	Th	23	14	·69	13	·51	27
9	Fr	24	—A	·60	14	·45	28
10	Sa	25	1	·52	15	·40	29
11	Su	26	2	·45	16	·35	—30
12	Mo	27	3	·39	17	·33	1
13	Tu	28	4	·35	18	·31	2
14	We	29	5	·34	19	·32	3
15	Th	30	6	·34	20	·34	4
16	Fr	31	7	·36	21	·39	5

Nov. — Solar: Virodhakrit *Tula—Aippasi.* (to 30), Virodhakrit *Vrischika—Kartigai.* (from 1). Lunar: Karttika *Sukla*, P, *Bahula*, A; *Sukla*. Muhammadan: H. 1268 *Muharram.*

Cyclic Sidereal Year, Month and Day	Week-Day	English Month and Day	Tithi	Ending Moment	Nakshatra	Ending Moment	Muhammadan Year, Month and Day
17	Sa	1	8	·40	22	·46	6
18	Su	2	9	·46	23	·55	7
19	Mo	3	10	·54	24	·65	8
20	Tu	4	11	·63	25	·75	9
21	We	5	12	·72	26	·86	10
22	Th	6	13	·80	27	·97	11
23	Fr	7	14	·87	...	...	12
24	Sa	8	P	·92	1	·06	13
25	Su	9	1	·96	2	·13	14
26	Mo	10	2	·99	3	·18	15
27	Tu	11	3	·98	4	·22	16
28	We	12	4	·95	5	·24	17
29	Th	13	5	·91	6	·23	18
—30	Fr	14	6	·85	7	·21	19
1	Sa	15	7	·77	8	·17	20
2	Su	16	8	·69	9	·12	21
3	Mo	17	9	·60	10	·06	22
4	Tu	18	10	·50	11 / 12 }	·00 / ·93	23
5	We	19	11	·40	13	·86	24
6	Th	20	12	·30	14	·79	25
7	Fr	21	13	·21	15	·73	26
8	Sa	22	14	·13	16	·69	27
9	Su	23	—A	·06	17	·66	28
10	Mo	24	{ 1 / 2	·00 / ·96	18	·64	29
11	Tu	25	3	·95	19	·64	—30
12	We	26	4	·96	20	·66	1
13	Th	27	5	·99	21	·71	2
14	Fr	28	...	...	22	·77	3
15	Sa	29	6	·03	23	·85	4
16	Su	30	7	·09	24	·94	5

Dec. — Solar: Virodhakrit *Vrischika—Kartigai.* (to 29), Virodhakrit *Dhanus—Margali.* (from 1). Lunar: Margasira P, *Bahula*, A; Pausha *Sukla*. Muhammadan: H. 1268 *Safar.*; *Rabi-ul-awwal.*

Cyclic Sidereal Year, Month and Day	Week-Day	English Month and Day	Tithi	Ending Moment	Nakshatra	Ending Moment	Muhammadan Year, Month and Day
17	Mo	1	8	·17	...	...	6
18	Tu	2	9	·26	25	·05	7
19	We	3	10	·35	26	·16	8
20	Th	4	11	·43	27	·27	9
21	Fr	5	12	·50	1	·36	10
22	Sa	6	13	·56	2	·44	11
23	Su	7	14	·60	3	·50	12
24	Mo	8	P	·62	4	·53	13
25	Tu	9	1	·61	5	·56	14
26	We	10	2	·58	6	·56	15
27	Th	11	3	·53	7	·54	16
28	Fr	12	4	·47	8	·50	17
—29	Sa	13	5	·40	9	·45	18
1	Su	14	6	·32	10	·40	19
2	Mo	15	7	·23	11	·33	20
3	Tu	16	8	·13	12	·26	21
4	We	17	{ 9 / 10	·03 / ·93	13	·19	22
5	Th	18	11	·84	14	·13	23
6	Fr	19	12	·76	15	·07	24
7	Sa	20	13	·69	16 / 17 }	·02 / ·99	25
8	Su	21	14	·64	18	·97	26
9	Mo	22	—A	·61	19	·96	27
10	Tu	23	1	·60	20	·98	28
11	We	24	2	·61	...	...	—29
12	Th	25	3	·63	21	·02	1
13	Fr	26	4	·67	22	·08	2
14	Sa	27	5	·74	23	·15	3
15	Su	28	6	·82	24	·24	4
16	Mo	29	7	·91	25	·35	5
17	Tu	30	...	...	26	·46	6
18	We	31	8	·00	27	·57	7

15. Svati. 16. Visak. 17. Anur. 18. Jyesh. 19. Mula. 20. P. Ash. 21. U. Ash. 22. Sravn. 23. Dani. 24. Satab. 25. P. Bhad. 26. U. Bhad. 27. Rev.

A. D. 1852. **Mesha Sankranti** (Commencement of Indian Sidereal Year). **Saka 1774.** **Kaliyuga 4953.**

Solar Eclipse. ● (Surya Sid.) April 11·20.

Lunar Eclipse. ○ (Arya Sid.) April 11·10. (S. Cycle) Paridhavi.

SOLAR reckoning. Cyclic Sidereal Year, Month and Day.	Week-Day	English Month and Day.	LUNAR reckoning. Tithi	Ending Moment.	Nakshatra	Ending Moment.	Muhammadan Year, Month and Day.
		Jan.					
Virodhakrit Dhanus—Margali. 19	Th	1	Suk. 9	·08	1	·66	8
20	Fr	2	10	·15	2	·74	9
21	Sa	3	11	·21	3	·81	10
22	Su	4	12	·25	4	·86	11
23	Mo	5	Pausha 13	·26	5	·88	12
24	Tu	6	14	·25	6	·88	13
25	We	○ 7	P	·23	7	·87	14
26	Th	8	1	·18	8	·84	H. 1268 Rabi-ul-awwal. 15
27	Fr	9	2	·12	9	·80	16
28	Sa	10	3 / 4	·04 / ·96	10	·74	17
—29	Su	11	5	·87	11	·67	18
1	Mo	12	Bahula 6	·77	12	·60	19
2	Tu	13	7	·67	13	·53	20
3	We	14	8	·57	14	·47	21
4	Th	15	9	·48	15	·41	22
5	Fr	16	10	·40	16	·36	23
6	Sa	17	11	·34	17	·32	24
7	Su	18	12	·29	18	·29	25
8	Mo	19	13	·26	19	·29	26
9	Tu	20	14	·24	20	·30	27
10	We	21	—A	·25	21	·33	28
11	Th	22	1	·28	22	·38	29
12	Fr	23	2	·33	23	·45	—30
Virodhakrit Makara—Tai. 13	Sa	24	3	·40	24	·54	1
14	Su	25	4	·48	25	·65	2
15	Mo	26	5	·57	26	·76	3
16	Tu	27	6	·65	27	·86	4
17	We	28	7	·73	1	·96	5
18	Th	29	Sukla 8	·80	...	...	6
19	Fr	30	9	·86	2	·05	7
20	Sa	31	10	·89	3	·13	8
		Feb.					
21	Su	1	11	·90	4	·17	9
22	Mo	2	12	·89	5	·20	H. 1268 Rabi-ul-akhir. 10
23	Tu	3	Magha 13	·87	6	·21	11
24	We	4	14	·83	7	·20	12
25	Th	5	P	·76	8	·18	13
26	Fr	6	1	·68	9	·13	14
27	Sa	7	2	·59	10	·08	15
28	Su	8	3	·49	11 / 12	·01 / ·94	16
29	Mo	9	4	·39	13	·87	17
—30	Tu	10	Bahula 5	·29	14	·81	18
1	We	11	6	·20	15	·75	19
2	Th	12	7	·11	16	·69	20
3	Fr	13	8 / 9	·03 / ·97	17	·65	21
4	Sa	14	10	·92	18	·62	22
5	Su	15	11	·89	19	·61	23
Virodhakrit Kumbha—Masi. 6	Mo	16	12	·87	20	·62	24
7	Tu	17	13	·88	21	·64	25
8	We	18	14	·91	22	·69	26
9	Th	19	—A	·96	23	·76	27
10	Fr	20	...	...	24	·85	28
11	Sa	21	Sukla 1	·08	25	·95	—29
12	Su	22	2	·11	...	...	Jumadal-awwal. 1
13	Mo	23	3	·20	26	·05	2
14	Tu	24	Phalguna 4	·28	27	·16	3
15	We	25	5	·36	1	·26	4
16	Th	26	6	·43	2	·35	5
17	Fr	27	7	·48	3	·43	6
18	Sa	28	8	·51	4	·49	7
19	Su	29	9	·53	5	·52	8

SOLAR reckoning. Cyclic Sidereal Year, Month and Day.	Week-Day	English Month and Day.	LUNAR reckoning. Tithi	Ending Moment.	Nakshatra	Ending Moment.	Muhammadan Year, Month and Day.
		March					
20	Mo	1	Suk. 10	·52	6	·53	9
21	Tu	2	11	·49	7	·53	10
Virodhakrit Kumbha—Masi. 22	We	3	12	·43	8	·51	11
23	Th	4	Phalg. 13	·36	9	·47	12
24	Fr	5	14	·28	10	·41	13
25	Sa	6	P	·19	11	·35	14
26	Su	7	1	·10	12	·29	15
27	Mo	8	2 / 3	·00 / ·90	13	·22	H. 1268 Jumadal-awwal. 16
28	Tu	9	4	·80	14	·15	17
29	We	10	5	·71	15	·08	18
30	Th	11	Bahula 6	·63	16 / 17	·03 / ·98	19
—31	Fr	12	7	·56	18	·95	20
1	Sa	13	8	·51	19	·94	21
2	Su	14	9	·48	20	·94	22
3	Mo	15	10	·47	21	·96	23
4	Tu	16	11	·48	...	...	24
5	We	17	12	·51	22	·00	25
6	Th	18	13	·56	23	·07	26
7	Fr	19	14	·63	24	·15	27
8	Sa	20	—A	·71	25	·25	28
9	Su	21	1	·80	26	·35	29
10	Mo	22	2	·89	27	·46	—30
11	Tu	23	3	·96	1	·57	1
Virodhakrit Mina—Panguni. 12	We	24	...	...	2	·66	2
13	Th	25	4	·02	3	·74	3
14	Fr	26	5	·07	4	·80	4
15	Sa	27	6	·10	5	·84	5
16	Su	28	Sukla 7	·11	6	·86	6
17	Mo	29	8	·09	7	·86	7
18	Tu	30	9	·06	8	·84	8
19	We	31	10 / 11	·01 / ·94	9	·80	9
		April					
20	Th	1	12	·86	10	·75	H. 1268 Jumadal-akhir. 10
21	Fr	2	Chaitra 13	·77	11	·69	11
22	Sa	3	14	·67	12	·63	12
23	Su	4	P	·57	13	·56	13
24	Mo	5	1	·47	14	·49	14
25	Tu	6	2	·37	15	·42	15
26	We	7	3	·28	16	·36	16
27	Th	8	4	·20	17	·32	17
28	Fr	9	5	·13	18	·28	18
—29	Sa	10	6	·08	19	·26	19
1	Su	11	Bahula 7	·05	20	·26	20
2	Mo	12	8	·03	21	·27	21
3	Tu	13	9	·04	22	·32	22
4	We	14	10	·07	23	·38	23
5	Th	15	11	·12	24	·46	24
6	Fr	16	12	·18	25	·55	25
7	Sa	17	13	·26	26	·65	26
Paridhavi Mesha—Chittirai. 8	Su	18	14	·35	27	·76	27
9	Mo	19	—A	·43	1	·87	28
10	Tu	20	1	·51	2	·97	—29
11	We	21	Sukla 2	·57	...	...	1
12	Th	22	3	·61	3	·05	2
13	Fr	23	4	·64	4	·11	3
14	Sa	24	5	·65	5	·16	H. 1268 Rajab. 4
15	Su	25	Vaisakha 6	·63	6	·18	5
16	Mo	26	7	·60	7	·18	6
17	Tu	27	8	·55	8	·17	7
18	We	28	9	·48	9	·13	8
19	Th	29	10	·40	10	·08	9
20	Fr	30	11	·30	11 / 12	·03 / ·97	10

SOLAR reckoning. Cyclic Sidereal Year, Month and Day.	Week-Day	English Month and Day.	LUNAR reckoning. Tithi	Ending Moment.	Nakshatra	Ending Moment.	Muhammadan Year, Month and Day.
		May					
21	Sa	1	Suk. 12	·21	13	·90	11
22	Su	2	13	·11	14	·83	12
Paridhavi Mesha—Chittirai. 23	Mo	3	14 / P	·01 / ·91	15	·77	13
24	Tu	4	Vaisakha 1	·81	16	·71	14
25	We	5	2	·73	17	·65	15
26	Th	6	3	·66	18	·61	16
27	Fr	7	4	·61	19	·59	H. 1268 Rajab. 17
28	Sa	8	5	·58	20	·58	18
29	Su	9	6	·56	21	·60	19
30	Mo	10	7	·56	22	·63	20
—31	Tu	11	8	·59	23	·69	21
1	We	12	Bahula 9	·63	24	·76	22
2	Th	13	10	·69	25	·85	23
3	Fr	14	11	·77	26	·96	24
4	Sa	15	12	·86	...	...	25
5	Su	16	13	·95	27	·07	26
6	Mo	17	...	...	1	·17	27
7	Tu	18	14	·02	2	·27	28
8	We	19	—A	·08	3	·35	29
9	Th	20	1	·13	4	·42	—30
10	Fr	21	2	·15	5	·48	1
11	Sa	22	3	·16	6	·50	2
12	Su	23	4	·15	7	·51	3
Paridhavi Vrishabha—Vaikasi. 13	Mo	24	5	·12	8	·49	4
14	Tu	25	Sukla 6 / 7	·06 / ·98	9	·46	5
15	We	26	8	·90	10	·42	6
16	Th	27	9	·81	11	·37	7
17	Fr	28	10	·71	12	·31	8
18	Sa	29	11	·61	13	·24	9
19	Su	30	12	·51	14	·17	10
20	Mo	31	13	·41	15	·11	11
		June					
21	Tu	1	Jyeshtha 14	·31	16 / 17	·05 / ·99	H. 1268 Shaban. 12
22	We	2	P	·23	18	·94	13
23	Th	3	1	·16	19	·91	14
24	Fr	4	2	·11	20	·91	15
25	Sa	5	3	·07	21	·92	16
26	Su	6	4	·05	22	·95	17
27	Mo	7	5	·06	...	...	18
28	Tu	8	6	·08	23	·00	19
29	We	9	Bahula 7	·12	24	·07	20
30	Th	10	8	·18	25	·16	21
—31	Fr	11	9	·25	26	·26	22
1	Sa	12	10	·34	27	·36	23
2	Su	13	11	·42	1	·47	24
3	Mo	14	12	·49	2	·57	25
4	Tu	15	13	·56	3	·66	26
5	We	16	14	·61	4	·74	27
6	Th	17	—A	·64	5	·79	28
7	Fr	18	1	·64	6	·82	—29
Paridhavi Mithuna—Ani. 8	Sa	19	2	·63	7	·83	1
9	Su	20	3	·60	8	·82	2
10	Mo	21	4	·54	9	·80	3
11	Tu	22	Sukla 5	·47	10	·76	H. 1268 Ramzan. 4
12	We	23	6	·39	11	·71	5
13	Th	24	7	·30	12	·64	6
14	Fr	25	8	·20	13	·57	7
15	Sa	26	9	·10	14	·50	8
16	Su	27	10 / 11	·00 / ·90	15	·44	9
17	Mo	28	Ash. 12	·80	16	·38	10
18	Tu	29	13	·71	17	·32	11
19	We	30	14	·64	18	·27	12

Naksh:—1. Asvn. 2. Bhar. 3. Krit. 4. Rohi. 5. Mrig. 6. Ardb. 7. Punar. 8. Push. 9. Aslesh. 10. Magh. 11. P. Phal. 12. U. Phal. 13. Hasta. 14. Chit.

A. D. 1852. Kollam 1028, { N. Malabar—Sept. / S. Malabar—Aug. } Commences. Hijra 1269, Commences Oct. 15. Vikrama 1909. Bengal San 1258. (N. Cycle) Rudhirodgarin

A.—Amavasya. P.—Paurnami.

SOLAR reckoning: Cyclic Sidereal Year, Month and Day.	Week-Day	English Month and Day.	LUNAR reckoning: Tithi	Ending Moment.	Nakshatra	Ending Moment.	Muhammadan Year, Month and Day.
	July						
Paridhavi Mithuna—Ani.			*Ashadha — Bahula*				*H. 1268 Ramzan.*
20	Th ○	1	P	·59	19	·25	13
21	Fr	2	1	·55	20	·24	14
22	Sa	3	2	·53	21	·24	15
23	Su	4	3	·53	22	·26	16
24	Mo	5	4	·55	23	·30	17
25	Tu	6	5	·60	24	·37	18
26	We	7	6	·66	25	·46	19
27	Th	8	7	·73	26	·56	20
28	Fr	9	8	·82	27	·66	21
29	Sa	10	9	·90	1	·77	22
30	Su	11	10	·97	2	·87	23
31	Mo	12	...	...	3	·97	24
—32	Tu	13	11	·03	...	...	25
Paridhavi Karkata—Adi.							
1	We	14	12	·08	4	·05	26
2	Th	15	13	·11	5	·10	27
3	Fr	16	14	·13	6	·14	28
4	Sa	17	—A	·11	7	·16	29
5	Su	18	1	·07	8	·16	—30
			Sukla				*Shawwal.*
6	Mo	19	2 / 3	·02 / ·96	9	·13	1
7	Tu	20	4	·88	10	·09	2
8	We	21	5	·79	11 / 12	·04 / ·98	3
9	Th	22	6	·69	13	·92	4
10	Fr	23	7	·59	14	·85	5
11	Sa	24	8	·49	15	·78	6
12	Su	25	9	·39	16	·71	7
			Sravana				
13	Mo	26	10	·29	17	·66	8
14	Tu	27	11	·20	18	·61	9
15	We	28	12	·13	19	·58	10
16	Th	29	13	·07	20	·56	11
17	Fr	30	14	·03	21	·56	12
18	Sa	31	P	·01	22	·58	13
	Aug.						
			Adhika Bhadrapada — Bahula				*H. 1268*
19	Su	1	1	·01	23	·62	14
20	Mo	2	2	·02	24	·68	15
21	Tu	3	3	·07	25	·76	16
22	We	4	4	·13	26	·86	17
23	Th	5	5	·20	27	·96	18
24	Fr	6	6	·29	...	...	19
25	Sa	7	7	·38	1	·07	20
26	Su	8	8	·45	2	·18	21
27	Mo	9	9	·51	3	·27	22
28	Tu	10	10	·56	4	·35	23
29	We	11	11	·60	5	·41	24
30	Th	12	12	·62	6	·45	25
—31	Fr	13	13	·60	7	·48	26
Paridhavi Simha—Avani.							
1	Sa	14	14	·57	8	·48	27
2	Su	15	—A	·52	9	·48	28
3	Mo	16	1	·46	10	·43	—29
			Sukla				*H. 1268 Zi-l-ka'da.*
4	Tu	17	2	·38	11	·38	1
5	We	18	3	·28	12	·33	2
6	Th	19	4	·18	13	·26	3
7	Fr	20	5 / 6	·08 / ·98	14	·19	4
8	Sa	21	7	·88	15	·12	5
9	Su	22	8	·79	16 / 17	·05 / ·99	6
10	Mo	23	9	·70	18	·94	7
11	Tu	24	10	·63	19	·90	8
12	We	25	11	·57	20	·88	9
13	Th	26	12	·54	21	·88	10
14	Fr	27	13	·52	22	·89	11
15	Sa	28	14	·51	23	·94	12
16	Su	29	P	·53	24	·99	13
17	Mo	30	1	·57	...	...	14
18	Tu	31	2	·63	25	·07	15

SOLAR reckoning: Cyclic Sidereal Year, Month and Day.	Week-Day	English Month and Day.	LUNAR reckoning: Tithi	Ending Moment.	Nakshatra	Ending Moment.	Muhammadan Year, Month and Day.
	Sep.						
Paridhavi Simha—Avani.			*Adh. Bhad. — Bahula*				*H. 1268 Zi-l-ka'da.*
19	We	1	3	·71	26	·16	16
20	Th	2	4	·80	27	·26	17
21	Fr	3	5	·89	1	·37	18
22	Sa	4	6	·97	2	·48	19
23	Su	5	...	...	3	·58	20
24	Mo	6	7	·04	4	·66	21
25	Tu	7	8	·08	5	·72	22
26	We	8	9	·11	6	·77	23
27	Th	9	10	·13	7	·80	24
28	Fr	10	11	·11	8	·81	25
29	Sa	11	12	·08	9	·79	26
30	Su	12	13 / 14	·04 / ·98	10	·76	27
31	Mo	13	—A	·90	11	·71	28
—32	Tu	14	1	·81	12	·66	29
Paridhavi Kanya—Purattasi.							
1	We	15	2	·71	13	·60	—30
			Sukla				*Zi-l-hijja.*
2	Th	16	3	·61	14	·53	1
3	Fr	17	4	·51	15	·46	2
4	Sa	18	5	·41	16	·40	3
5	Su	19	6	·32	17	·34	4
6	Mo	20	7	·24	18	·28	5
7	Tu	21	8	·17	19	·24	6
8	We	22	9	·11	20	·21	7
			Bhadrapada				
9	Th	23	10	·07	21	·20	8
10	Fr	24	11	·05	22	·22	9
11	Sa	25	12	·04	23	·25	10
12	Su	26	13	·07	24	·30	11
13	Mo	27	14	·12	25	·37	12
14	Tu	28	P	·18	26	·46	13
15	We	29	1	·26	27	·57	14
16	Th	30	2	·35	1	·68	15
	Oct.						
			Nija — Bahula				*H. 1268*
17	Fr	1	3	·43	2	·78	16
18	Sa	2	4	·51	3	·88	17
19	Su	3	5	·58	4	·96	18
20	Mo	4	6	·63	...	...	19
21	Tu	5	7	·66	5	·03	20
22	We	6	8	·68	6	·09	21
23	Th	7	9	·67	7	·12	22
24	Fr	8	10	·64	8	·13	23
25	Sa	9	11	·60	9	·12	24
26	Su	10	12	·54	10	·09	25
27	Mo	11	13	·46	11	·06	26
28	Tu	12	14	·37	12 / 13	·00 / ·94	27
29	We	13	—A	·27	14	·87	28
—30	Th	14	1	·17	15	·80	—29
Paridhavi Tula—Aippasi.							*H. 1269 Muharram.*
1	Fr	15	2 / 3	·07 / ·98	16	·74	1
2	Sa	16	4	·89	17	·68	2
3	Su	17	5	·81	18	·62	3
			Sukla				
4	Mo	18	6	·74	19	·57	4
5	Tu	19	7	·68	20	·54	5
6	We	20	8	·65	21	·53	6
7	Th	21	9	·63	22	·54	7
8	Fr	22	10	·64	23	·56	8
			Asvina				
9	Sa	23	11	·66	24	·61	9
10	Su	24	12	·70	25	·67	10
11	Mo	25	13	·76	26	·76	11
12	Tu	26	14	·84	27	·86	12
13	We	27	P	·93	1	·97	13
14	Th	28	...	...	...	...	14
			Bah.				
15	Fr	29	1	·02	2	·08	15
16	Sa	30	2	·10	3	·18	16
17	Su	31	3	·17	4	·27	17

SOLAR reckoning: Cyclic Sidereal Year, Month and Day.	Week-Day	English Month and Day.	LUNAR reckoning: Tithi	Ending Moment.	Nakshatra	Ending Moment.	Muhammadan Year, Month and Day.
	Nov.						
Paridhavi Tula—Aippasi.			*Asv. — Bahula*				*H. 1269 Muharram.*
18	Mo	1	4	·22	5	·35	18
19	Tu	2	5	·25	6	·40	19
20	We	3	6	·27	7	·44	20
21	Th	4	7	·26	8	·45	21
22	Fr	5	8	·24	9	·44	22
23	Sa	6	9	·20	10	·43	23
24	Su	7	10	·14	11	·39	24
25	Mo	8	11 / 12	·06 / ·97	12	·33	25
26	Tu	9	13	·88	13	·27	26
27	We	10	14	·78	14	·21	27
28	Th	11	—A	·68	15	·15	28
29	Fr	12	1	·58	16	·08	29
—30	Sa	13	2	·49	17 / 18	·01 / ·95	—30
Paridhavi Vrischika—Kartigai.			*Sukla*				*H. 1269 Safar.*
1	Su	14	3	·41	19	·91	1
2	Mo	15	4	·34	20	·88	2
3	Tu	16	5	·28	21	·86	3
4	We	17	6	·25	22	·86	4
5	Th	18	7	·24	23	·88	5
6	Fr	19	8	·25	24	·92	6
7	Sa	20	9	·27	25	·99	7
8	Su	21	10	·32	...	...	8
9	Mo	22	11	·39	26	·07	9
10	Tu	23	12	·47	27	·16	10
			Karttika				
11	We	24	13	·55	1	·27	11
12	Th	25	14	·64	2	·38	12
13	Fr	26	P	·72	3	·48	13
14	Sa	27	1	·79	4	·58	14
15	Su	28	2	·85	5	·66	15
16	Mo	29	3	·88	6	·72	16
17	Tu	30	4	·90	7	·75	17
	Dec.						
			Bahula				
18	We	1	5	·89	8	·77	18
19	Th	2	6	·86	9	·78	19
20	Fr	3	7	·81	10	·76	20
21	Sa	4	8	·75	11	·72	21
22	Su	5	9	·68	12	·67	22
23	Mo	6	10	·59	13	·61	23
24	Tu	7	11	·50	14	·55	24
25	We	8	12	·40	15	·48	25
26	Th	9	13	·30	16	·41	26
27	Fr	10	14	·20	17	·35	27
28	Sa ●	11	—A	·11	18	·29	28
—29	Su	12	1 / 2	·03 / ·97	19	·24	—29
Paridhavi Dhanus—Marguli.			*Sukla*				*H. 1269 Rabi-ul-awwal.*
1	Mo	13	3	·92	20	·21	1
2	Tu	14	4	·89	21	·18	2
3	We	15	5	·88	22	·18	3
4	Th	16	6	·89	23	·19	4
5	Fr	17	7	·91	24	·23	5
6	Sa	18	8	·96	25	·29	6
7	Su	19	...	...	26	·37	7
8	Mo	20	9	·03	27	·46	8
			Margasira				
9	Tu	21	10	·11	1	·57	9
10	We	22	11	·20	2	·68	10
11	Th	23	12	·29	3	·79	11
12	Fr	24	13	·37	4	·88	12
13	Sa	25	14	·44	5	·96	13
14	Su ○	26	P	·50	...	...	14
15	Mo	27	1	·53	6	·03	15
16	Tu	28	2	·55	7	·07	16
17	We	29	3	·54	8	·10	17
			Bah.				
18	Th	30	4	·51	9	·10	18
19	Fr	31	5	·46	10	·09	19

A. D. 1853. **Mesha Sankranti** (Commencement of Indian Sidereal Year).

Solar Eclipse. ● **(Surya Sid.) April 11·46.** **Saka 1775.** **Kaliyuga 4954.**

Lunar Eclipse. ○ **(Arya Sid.) April 11·36.** **(S. Cycle) Pramadicha.**

Columns: SOLAR reckoning — Cyclic Sidereal Year, Month and Day; Week-Day; English Month and Day. LUNAR reckoning — Tithi; Ending Moment; Nakshatra; Ending Moment; Muhammadan Year, Month and Day.

Jan.

Solar: Paridhavi *Dhanus—Marguli* (to 30); Paridhavi *Makara—Tai* (from 1). Lunar: Marg. *Bahula*; A; *Sukla*; Pausha P; *Bahula*. Muhammadan: H. 1269 *Rabi-ul-awwal* (to 30); H. 1269 *Rabi-ul-akhir* (from 1).

Cyclic Sidereal Year, Month and Day	Week-Day	English Month and Day	Tithi	Ending Moment	Nakshatra	Ending Moment	Muhammadan Year, Month and Day
20	Sa	1	6	·40	11	·05	20
21	Su	2	7	·32	12 13	·01 ·96	21
22	Mo	3	8	·23	14	·89	22
23	Tu	4	9	·14	15	·82	23
24	We	5	10 11	·04 ·94	16	·75	24
25	Th	6	12	·85	17	·68	25
26	Fr	7	13	·76	18	·63	26
27	Sa	8	14	·68	19	·58	27
28	Su	9	A	·62	20	·54	28
29	Mo	10	1	·57	21	·51	29
30	Tu	11	2	·54	22	·50	30
1	We	12	3	·53	23	·51	1
2	Th	13	4	·54	24	·55	2
3	Fr	14	5	·56	25	·60	3
4	Sa	15	6	·61	26	·67	4
5	Su	16	7	·69	27	·76	5
6	Mo	17	8	·77	1	·86	6
7	Tu	18	9	·86	2	·97	7
8	We	19	10	·95	...	...	8
9	Th	20	...	...	3	·08	9
10	Fr	21	11	·03	4	·18	10
11	Sa	22	12	·09	5	·27	11
12	Su	23	13	·14	6	·34	12
13	Mo	24	14	·17	7	·39	13
14	Tu	25	P	·19	8	·42	14
15	We	26	1	·18	9	·43	15
16	Th	27	2	·15	10	·42	16
17	Fr	28	3	·10	11	·39	17
18	Sa	29	4 5	·03 ·95	12	·35	18
19	Su	30	6	·87	13	·30	19
20	Mo	31	7	·77	14	·23	20

Feb.

Solar: Paridhavi *Makara—Tai* (to 29); Paridhavi *Kumbha—Masi* (from 1). Lunar: *Bahula*; A; *Sukla*; Magha P; *Bah.* Muhammadan: H. 1269 *Rabi-ul-akhir* (to 29); H. 1269 *Jumadal-awwal* (from 1).

Cyclic Sidereal Year, Month and Day	Week-Day	English Month and Day	Tithi	Ending Moment	Nakshatra	Ending Moment	Muhammadan Year, Month and Day
21	Tu	1	8	·67	15	·16	21
22	We	2	9	·57	16	·09	22
23	Th	3	10	·48	17 18	·03 ·97	23
24	Fr	4	11	·39	19	·91	24
25	Sa	5	12	·32	20	·87	25
26	Su	6	13	·26	21	·84	26
27	Mo	7	14	·21	22	·82	27
28	Tu	8	A	·17	23	·84	28
29	We	9	1	·16	24	·87	29
1	Th	10	2	·16	25	·91	1
2	Fr	11	3	·20	26	·98	2
3	Sa	12	4	·26	...	...	3
4	Su	13	5	·33	27	·07	4
5	Mo	14	6	·41	1	·17	5
6	Tu	15	7	·49	2	·28	6
7	We	16	8	·58	3	·38	7
8	Th	17	9	·66	4	·48	8
9	Fr	18	10	·72	5	·57	9
10	Sa	19	11	·77	6	·65	10
11	Su	20	12	·80	7	·71	11
12	Mo	21	13	·81	8	·74	12
13	Tu	22	14	·81	9	·75	13
14	We	23	P	·78	10	·74	14
15	Th	24	1	·72	11	·72	15
16	Fr	25	2	·65	12	·68	16
17	Sa	26	3	·57	13	·63	17
18	Su	27	4	·48	14	·57	18
19	Mo	28	5	·39	15	·50	19

March

Solar: Paridhavi *Kumbha—Masi* (to 30); Paridhavi *Mina—Panguni* (from 1). Lunar: Mg. *Bahula*; A; *Sukla*; Phalguna P; *Bahula*. Muhammadan: H. 1269 *Jumadal-awwal* (to 30); H. 1269 *Jumadal-akhir* (from 1).

Cyclic Sidereal Year, Month and Day	Week-Day	English Month and Day	Tithi	Ending Moment	Nakshatra	Ending Moment	Muhammadan Year, Month and Day
20	Tu	1	6	·29	16	·43	20
21	We	2	7	·19	17	·36	21
22	Th	3	8	·09	18	·30	22
23	Fr	4	9 10	·00 ·92	19	·24	23
24	Sa	5	11	·86	20	·20	24
25	Su	6	12	·82	21	·17	25
26	Mo	7	13	·79	22	·16	26
27	Tu	8	14	·77	23	·16	27
28	We	9	A	·78	24	·18	28
29	Th	10	1	·82	25	·22	29
30	Fr	11	2	·87	26	·28	30
1	Sa	12	3	·94	27	·37	1
2	Su	13	...	...	1	·47	2
3	Mo	14	4	·02	2	·58	3
4	Tu	15	5	·10	3	·68	4
5	We	16	6	·19	4	·78	5
6	Th	17	7	·26	5	·88	6
7	Fr	18	8	·32	6	·96	7
8	Sa	19	9	·37	...	...	8
9	Su	20	10	·41	7	·02	9
10	Mo	21	11	·41	8	·06	10
11	Tu	22	12	·40	9	·07	11
12	We	23	13	·36	10	·07	12
13	Th	24	14	·31	11	·06	13
14	Fr	25	P	·24	12 13	·02 ·97	14
15	Sa	26	1	·16	14	·91	15
16	Su	27	2 3	·06 ·96	15	·85	16
17	Mo	28	4	·86	16	·78	17
18	Tu	29	5	·76	17	·71	18
19	We	30	6	·67	18	·64	19
20	Th	31	7	·58	19	·58	20

April

Solar: Paridhavi *Mina—Panguni* (to 30); Pramadicha *Mesha—Chittirai* (from 1). Lunar: *Bahula*; A; *Sukla*; Chaitra P; *Bahula*. Muhammadan: H. 1269 *Jumadal-akhir* (to 29); H. 1269 *Rajab* (from 1).

Cyclic Sidereal Year, Month and Day	Week-Day	English Month and Day	Tithi	Ending Moment	Nakshatra	Ending Moment	Muhammadan Year, Month and Day
21	Fr	1	8	·50	20	·53	21
22	Sa	2	9	·44	21	·50	22
23	Su	3	10	·39	22	·48	23
24	Mo	4	11	·36	23	·48	24
25	Tu	5	12	·34	24	·49	25
26	We	6	13	·35	25	·53	26
27	Th	7	14	·39	26	·60	27
28	Fr	8	A	·44	27	·68	28
29	Sa	9	1	·50	1	·77	29
30	Su	10	2	·57	2	·87	1
1	Mo	11	3	·66	3	·98	2
2	Tu	12	4	·75	...	...	3
3	We	13	5	·83	4	·09	4
4	Th	14	6	·89	5	·19	5
5	Fr	15	7	·94	6	·27	6
6	Sa	16	8	·96	7	·33	7
7	Su	17	9	·96	8	·37	8
8	Mo	18	10	·95	9	·39	9
9	Tu	19	11	·91	10	·40	10
10	We	20	12	·85	11	·38	11
11	Th	21	13	·78	12	·35	12
12	Fr	22	14	·70	13	·30	13
13	Sa	23	P	·61	14	·24	14
14	Su	24	1	·51	15	·18	15
15	Mo	25	2	·41	16	·12	16
16	Tu	26	3	·31	17 18	·05 ·98	17
17	We	27	4	·21	19	·92	18
18	Th	28	5	·12	20	·87	19
19	Fr	29	6 7	·04 ·97	21	·83	20
20	Sa	30	8	·92	22	·81	21

May

Solar: Pramadicha *Mesha—Chittirai* (to 31); Pramadicha *Vrishabha—Vaikasi* (from 1). Lunar: Chait. *Bah.*; A; *Sukla*; Vaisakha P; *Bahula*. Muhammadan: H. 1269 *Rajab* (to 30); H. 1269 *Shaban* (from 1).

Cyclic Sidereal Year, Month and Day	Week-Day	English Month and Day	Tithi	Ending Moment	Nakshatra	Ending Moment	Muhammadan Year, Month and Day
21	Su	1	9	·89	23	·80	22
22	Mo	2	10	·87	24	·81	23
23	Tu	3	11	·88	25	·85	24
24	We	4	12	·91	26	·91	25
25	Th	5	13	·96	27	·99	26
26	Fr	6	...	...	...	...	27
27	Sa	7	14	·02	1	·07	28
28	Su	8	A	·10	2	·17	29
29	Mo	9	1	·19	3	·28	30
30	Tu	10	2	·27	4	·39	1
31	We	11	3	·34	5	·49	2
1	Th	12	4	·40	6	·57	3
2	Fr	13	5	·45	7	·64	4
3	Sa	14	6	·48	8	·69	5
4	Su	15	7	·49	9	·72	6
5	Mo	16	8	·47	10	·73	7
6	Tu	17	9	·43	11	·71	8
7	We	18	10	·37	12	·68	9
8	Th	19	11	·30	13	·64	10
9	Fr	20	12	·22	14	·59	11
10	Sa	21	13	·12	15	·53	12
11	Su	22	14 P	·02 ·92	16	·46	13
12	Mo	23	1	·82	17	·39	14
13	Tu	24	2	·72	18	·32	15
14	We	25	3	·63	19	·26	16
15	Th	26	4	·55	20	·21	17
16	Fr	27	5	·48	21	·16	18
17	Sa	28	6	·43	22	·13	19
18	Su	29	7	·39	23	·12	20
19	Mo	30	8	·38	24	·13	21
20	Tu	31	9	·38	25	·17	22

June

Solar: Pramadicha *Vrishabha—Vaikasi* (to 32); Pramadicha *Mithuna—Ani* (from 1). Lunar: A; *Sukla*; Jyeshtha P; *Bahula*. Muhammadan: H. 1269 *Shaban* (to 29); H. 1269 *Ramzan* (from 1).

Cyclic Sidereal Year, Month and Day	Week-Day	English Month and Day	Tithi	Ending Moment	Nakshatra	Ending Moment	Muhammadan Year, Month and Day
21	We	1	10	·41	26	·22	23
22	Th	2	11	·46	27	·28	24
23	Fr	3	12	·52	1	·37	25
24	Sa	4	13	·59	2	·47	26
25	Su	5	14	·68	3	·58	27
26	Mo	6	A	·77	4	·69	28
27	Tu	7	1	·84	5	·79	29
28	We	8	2	·90	6	·88	1
29	Th	9	3	·94	7	·95	2
30	Fr	10	4	·96	...	...	3
31	Sa	11	5	·97	8	·01	4
32	Su	12	6	·95	9	·04	5
1	Mo	13	7	·92	10	·05	6
2	Tu	14	8	·87	11	·04	7
3	We	15	9	·80	12 13	·01 ·98	8
4	Th	16	10	·71	14	·93	9
5	Fr	17	11	·61	15	·86	10
6	Sa	18	12	·51	16	·79	11
7	Su	19	13	·41	17	·72	12
8	Mo	20	14	·31	18	·66	13
9	Tu	○ 21	P	·21	19	·60	14
10	We	22	1	·12	20	·54	15
11	Th	23	2 3	·04 ·97	21	·49	16
12	Fr	24	4	·91	22	·46	17
13	Sa	25	5	·87	23	·44	18
14	Su	26	6	·85	24	·46	19
15	Mo	27	7	·86	25	·49	20
16	Tu	28	8	·89	26	·53	21
17	We	29	9	·93	27	·59	22
18	Th	30	10	·99	1	·67	23

Naksh:—1. Asvn. 2. Bhar. 3. Krit. 4. Rohi. 5. Mrig. 6. Ardh. 7. Punar. 8. Push. 9. Aslesh. 10. Mngh. 11. P. Phal. 12. U. Phal. 13. Hasta. 14. Chit.

A. D. 1853. | **Vikrama 1910.**

A.—Amavasya. **Kollam 1029,** Commences {N. Malabar—Sept. / S. Malabar—Aug.} **Hijra 1270,** Commences, Oct. 4. **Bengal San 1259.**

P.—Paurnami. **(N. Cycle) Raktaksha.**

Column headings: SOLAR reckoning (Cyclic Sidereal Year, Month and Day; Week-Day; English Month and Day) — LUNAR reckoning (Tithi; Ending Moment; Nakshatra; Ending Moment; Muhammadan Year, Month and Day).

July

Solar month	Cyclic Sidereal Day	Week-Day	English Day	Lunar month	Tithi	Ending Moment	Nakshatra	Ending Moment	Muhammadan month	Muhammadan Day
Pramadicha Mithuna—Ani	19	Fr	1	Jy. Bah.	...	...	2	·78	Ramzan	24
	20	Sa	2		11	·07	3	·88		25
	21	Su	3		12	·15	4	·99		26
	22	Mo	4		13	·23	...	...		27
	23	Tu	5		14	·30	5	·09		28
	24	We	6		—A	·37	6	·18		29
	25	Th	7	Ashadha Sukla	1	·41	7	·26		—30
	26	Fr	8		2	·44	8	·32	H. 1269 Shawwal	1
	27	Sa	9		3	·45	9	·36		2
	28	Su	10		4	·43	10	·37		3
	29	Mo	11		5	·39	11	·37		4
	30	Tu	12		6	·34	12	·35		5
	—31	We	13		7	·27	13	·31		6
Pramadicha Karkata—Adi	1	Th	14		8	·19	14	·26		7
	2	Fr	15		9	·10	15	·20		8
	3	Sa	16		10 11	·00 ·90	16	·13		9
	4	Su	17		12	·80	17	·06		10
	5	Mo	18		13	·70	18 19	·00 ·94		11
	6	Tu	19		14	·60	20	·88		12
	7	We	20		P	·51	21	·83		13
	8	Th	21	Bahula	1	·44	22	·79		14
	9	Fr	22		2	·39	23	·78		15
	10	Sa	23		3	·36	24	·78		16
	11	Su	24		4	·33	25	·80		17
	12	Mo	25		5	·33	26	·84		18
	13	Tu	26		6	·36	27	·90		19
	14	We	27		7	·40	1	·98		20
	15	Th	28		8	·46	...	...		21
	16	Fr	29		9	·54	2	·08		22
	17	Sa	30		10	·68	3	·18		23
	18	Su	31		11	·71	4	·29		24

Aug.

Solar month	Cyclic Sidereal Day	Week-Day	English Day	Lunar month	Tithi	Ending Moment	Nakshatra	Ending Moment	Muhammadan month	Muhammadan Day
	19	Mo	1		12	·78	5	·39		25
	20	Tu	2		13	·84	6	·49		26
	21	We	3		14	·89	7	·57		27
	22	Th	4		—A	·93	8	·63		28
	23	Fr	5	Sravana Sukla	1	·94	9	·67		—29
	24	Sa	6		2	·92	10	·69	H. 1269 Zi-l-ka'da	1
	25	Su	7		3	·88	11	·70		2
	26	Mo	8		4	·83	12	·68		3
	27	Tu	9		5	·77	13	·65		4
	28	We	10		6	·69	14	·60		5
	29	Th	11		7	·60	15	·54		6
	30	Fr	12		8	·50	16	·48		7
	31	Sa	13		9	·40	17	·41		8
	—32	Su	14		10	·30	18	·34		9
Pramadicha Simha—Avani	1	Mo	15		11	·20	19	·27		10
	2	Tu	16		12	·11	20	·21		11
	3	We	17		13 14	·02 ·94	21	·16		12
	4	Th	18		P	·88	22	·13		13
	5	Fr	19	Bahula	1	·85	23	·10		14
	6	Sa	20		2	·83	24	·10		15
	7	Su	21		3	·84	25	·11		16
	8	Mo	22		4	·86	26	·15		17
	9	Tu	23		5	·90	27	·21		18
	10	We	24		6	·96	1	·29		19
	11	Th	25		...	...	2	·38		20
	12	Fr	26		7	·04	3	·48		21
	13	Sa	27		8	·12	4	·59		22
	14	Su	28		9	·21	5	·70		23
	15	Mo	29		10	·28	6	·80		24
	16	Tu	30		11	·35	7	·88		25
	17	We	31		12	·40	8	·94		26

Sep.

Solar month	Cyclic Sidereal Day	Week-Day	English Day	Lunar month	Tithi	Ending Moment	Nakshatra	Ending Moment	Muhammadan month	Muhammadan Day
Pramadicha Simha—Avani	18	Th	1	Bah.	13	·43	9	·99		27
	19	Fr	2		14	·44	...	...		28
	20	Sa	3		—A	·43	10	·02		29
	21	Su	4	Bhadrupada Sukla	1	·40	11	·03		—30
	22	Mo	5		2	·35	12 13	·01 ·98	H. 1269 Zi-l-hijja	1
	23	Tu	6		3	·28	14	·93		2
	24	We	7		4	·20	15	·87		3
	25	Th	8		5	·11	16	·81		4
	26	Fr	9		6 7	·01 ·91	17	·75		5
	27	Sa	10		8	·81	18	·68		6
	28	Su	11		9	·71	19	·61		7
	29	Mo	12		10	·62	20	·55		8
	30	Tu	13		11	·54	21	·50		9
	—31	We	14		12	·47	22	·46		10
Pramadicha Kanya—Purattasi	1	Th	15		13	·42	23	·43		11
	2	Fr	16		14	·38	24	·42		12
	3	Sa	17		P	·36	25	·43		13
	4	Su	18	Bahula	1	·35	26	·47		14
	5	Mo	19		2	·38	27	·52		15
	6	Tu	20		3	·43	1	·59		16
	7	We	21		4	·49	2	·68		17
	8	Th	22		5	·57	3	·78		18
	9	Fr	23		6	·65	4	·89		19
	10	Sa	24		7	·73	...	...		20
	11	Su	25		8	·81	5	·00		21
	12	Mo	26		9	·88	6	·10		22
	13	Tu	27		10	·94	7	·18		23
	14	We	28		11	·97	8	·25		24
	15	Th	29		12	·99	9	·30		25
	16	Fr	30		13	·97	10	·34		26

Oct.

Solar month	Cyclic Sidereal Day	Week-Day	English Day	Lunar month	Tithi	Ending Moment	Nakshatra	Ending Moment	Muhammadan month	Muhammadan Day
	17	Sa	1		14	·94	11	·35		27
	18	Su	2		—A	·90	12	·34		28
	19	Mo	3	Asvina Sukla	1	·88	13	·31		—29
	20	Tu	4		2	·75	14	·27	H. 1270 Muharram	1
	21	We	5		3	·66	15	·22		2
	22	Th	6		4	·57	16	·16		3
	23	Fr	7		5	·47	17	·09		4
	24	Sa	8		6	·37	18 19	·02 ·95		5
	25	Su	9		7	·27	20	·89		6
	26	Mo	10		8	·18	21	·84		7
	27	Tu	11		9	·10	22	·79		8
	28	We	12		10 11	·03 ·98	23	·76		9
	29	Th	13		12	·94	24	·74		10
	—30	Fr	14		13	·93	25	·76		11
Pramadicha Tula—Aippasi	1	Sa	15		14	·93	26	·79		12
	2	Su	16		P	·95	27	·83		13
	3	Mo	17	Bahula	...	...	1	·89		14
	4	Tu	18		1	·00	2	·98		15
	5	We	19		2	·06	...	...		16
	6	Th	20		3	·14	3	·08		17
	7	Fr	21		4	·23	4	·19		18
	8	Sa	22		5	·32	5	·30		19
	9	Su	23		6	·40	6	·40		20
	10	Mo	24		7	·47	7	·49		21
	11	Tu	25		8	·52	8	·56		22
	12	We	26		9	·55	9	·62		23
	13	Th	27		10	·57	10	·66		24
	14	Fr	28		11	·55	11	·67		25
	15	Sa	29		12	·53	12	·66		26
	16	Su	30		13	·49	13	·64		27
	17	Mo	31		14	·42	14	·61		28

Nov.

Solar month	Cyclic Sidereal Day	Week-Day	English Day	Lunar month	Tithi	Ending Moment	Nakshatra	Ending Moment	Muhammadan month	Muhammadan Day
Pramadicha Tula—Aippasi	18	Tu	1		—A	·34	15	·56		29
	19	We	2	Kartika Sukla	1	·25	16	·50		—30
	20	Th	3		2	·16	17	·43	H. 1270 Safar	1
	21	Fr	4		3 4	·06 ·96	18	·36		2
	22	Sa	5		5	·86	19	·29		3
	23	Su	6		6	·77	20	·23		4
	24	Mo	7		7	·69	21	·17		5
	25	Tu	8		8	·63	22	·12		6
	26	We	9		9	·58	23	·09		7
	27	Th	10		10	·54	24	·07		8
	28	Fr	11		11	·53	25	·08		9
	29	Sa	12		12	·53	26	·10		10
	—30	Su	13		13	·57	27	·14		11
Pramadicha Vrischika—Kartigai	1	Mo	14		14	·62	1	·20		12
	2	Tu	15		P	·69	2	·28		13
	3	We	16	Bahula	1	·76	3	·38		14
	4	Th	17		2	·84	4	·48		15
	5	Fr	18		3	·94	5	·59		16
	6	Sa	19		...	...	6	·70		17
	7	Su	20		4	·02	7	·80		18
	8	Mo	21		5	·08	8	·88		19
	9	Tu	22		6	·13	9	·94		20
	10	We	23		7	·18	10	·97		21
	11	Th	24		8	·19	11	·99		22
	12	Fr	25		9	·17	12	·99		23
	13	Sa	26		10	·14	13	·98		24
	14	Su	27		11	·10	14	·94		25
	15	Mo	28		12 13	·04 ·96	15	·89		26
	16	Tu	29		14	·88	16	·83		27
	17	We	30		—A	·78	17	·77		28

Dec.

Solar month	Cyclic Sidereal Day	Week-Day	English Day	Lunar month	Tithi	Ending Moment	Nakshatra	Ending Moment	Muhammadan month	Muhammadan Day
	18	Th	1	Margasira Sukla	1	·68	18	·70		—29
	19	Fr	2		2	·58	19	·63	H. 1270 Rabi-ul-awwal	1
	20	Sa	3		3	·48	20	·56		2
	21	Su	4		4	·39	21	·50		3
	22	Mo	5		5	·31	22	·45		4
	23	Tu	6		6	·25	23	·42		5
	24	We	7		7	·21	24	·40		6
	25	Th	8		8	·18	25	·40		7
	26	Fr	9		9	·16	26	·41		8
	27	Sa	10		10	·17	27	·45		9
	28	Su	11		11	·21	1	·51		10
	29	Mo	12		12	·26	2	·59		11
	—30	Tu	13		13	·33	3	·68		12
Pramadicha Dhanus—Margali	1	We	14		14	·41	4	·78		13
	2	Th	15		P	·50	5	·89		14
	3	Fr	16	Bahula	1	·59	...	...		15
	4	Sa	17		2	·67	6	·00		16
	5	Su	18		3	·74	7	·10		17
	6	Mo	19		4	·79	8	·18		18
	7	Tu	20		5	·82	9	·25		19
	8	We	21		6	·83	10	·29		20
	9	Th	22		7	·82	11	·31		21
	10	Fr	23		8	·79	12	·32		22
	11	Sa	24		9	·74	13	·31		23
	12	Su	25		10	·68	14	·27		24
	13	Mo	26		11	·61	15	·23		25
	14	Tu	27		12	·52	16	·17		26
	15	We	28		13	·42	17	·11		27
	16	Th	29		14	·32	18 19	·04 ·97		28
	17	Fr	30		—A	·22	20	·90		29
	18	Sa	31		1	·13	21	·84		—30

15. Svati. 16. Visak. 17. Anur. 18. Jyesh. 19. Mula. 20. P. Ash. 21. U. Ash. 22. Sravn. 23. Dani. 24. Satab. 25. P. Bhad. 26. U. Bhad. 27. Rev.

A. D. 1854.
Solar Eclipse. ●
Lunar Eclipse. ○

Mesha Sankranti (Commencement of Indian Sidereal Year).
(Surya Sid.) April 11·72.
(Ârya Sid.) April 11·62.

Saka 1776. **Kaliyuga 4955.**
(S. Cycle) Ananda.

SOLAR reckoning: Cyclic Sidereal Year, Month and Day; Week-Day; English Month and Day. LUNAR reckoning: Tithi, Ending Moment; Nakshatra, Ending Moment; Muhammadan Year, Month and Day.

Jan.

Solar Year and Month	Cyclic Sidereal Day	Week-Day	English Day	Lunar Month	Tithi	Ending Moment	Nakshatra	Ending Moment	Muhammadan Month	Muhammadan Day
Pramadicha Dhanus—Margali.	19	Su	1	Sukla	2 / 3	·04 / ·96	22	·79	H. 1270 Rabi-ul-akhir.	1
	20	Mo	2		4	·90	23	·76		2
	21	Tu	3		5	·85	24	·73		3
	22	We	4		6	·82	25	·72		4
	23	Th	5		7	·81	26	·73		5
	24	Fr	6		8	·82	27	·76		6
	25	Sa	7		9	·85	1	·82		7
	26	Su	8		10	·90	2	·90		8
	27	Mo	9		11	·97	3	·98		9
	28	Tu	10		...	...	...	...		10
	—29	We	11	Pausha	12	·05	4	·08		11
Pramadicha Makara—Tai.	1	Th	12		13	·15	5	·19		12
	2	Fr	13		14	·24	6	·30		13
	3	Sa	14		P	·32	7	·40		14
	4	Su	15	Bahula	1	·39	8	·49		15
	5	Mo	16		2	·44	9	·56		16
	6	Tu	17		3	·47	10	·60		17
	7	We	18		4	·47	11	·63		18
	8	Th	19		5	·46	12	·65		19
	9	Fr	20		6	·43	13	·63		20
	10	Sa	21		7	·38	14	·60		21
	11	Su	22		8	·32	15	·56		22
	12	Mo	23		9	·24	16	·51		23
	13	Tu	24		10	·15	17	·45		24
	14	We	25		11 / 12	·05 / ·95	18	·38		25
	15	Th	26		13	·85	19	·31		26
	16	Fr	27		14	·76	20	·24		27
	17	Sa	28		—A	·67	21	·18		28
	18	Su	29		1	·60	22	·13		—29
	19	Mo	30		2	·54	23	·09		1
	20	Tu	31		3	·49	24	·06		2

Feb.

Solar Year and Month	Cyclic Sidereal Day	Week-Day	English Day	Lunar Month	Tithi	Ending Moment	Nakshatra	Ending Moment	Muhammadan Month	Muhammadan Day
Pramadicha Makara—Tai.	21	We	1	Sukla	4	·46	25	·04	H. 1270 Jumadal-awwal.	3
	22	Th	2		5	·44	26	·05		4
	23	Fr	3		6	·46	27	·09		5
	24	Sa	4		7	·50	1	·13		6
	25	Su	5		8	·55	2	·20		7
	26	Mo	6		9	·62	3	·28		8
	27	Tu	7		10	·70	4	·38		9
	28	We	8		11	·79	5	·49		10
	—29	Th	9		12	·88	6	·60		11
Pramadicha Kumbha—Masi.	1	Fr	10		13	·96	7	·70		12
	2	Sa	11	Magha	...	...	8	·79		13
	3	Su	12		14	·03	9	·86		14
	4	Mo	13		P	·08	10	·92		15
	5	Tu	14	Bahula	1	·10	11	·96		16
	6	We	15		2	·11	12	·97		17
	7	Th	16		3	·09	13	·96		18
	8	Fr	17		4	·06	14	·94		19
	9	Sa	18		5 / 6	·01 / ·94	15	·90		20
	10	Su	19		7	·86	16	·85		21
	11	Mo	20		8	·77	17	·79		22
	12	Tu	21		9	·67	18	·72		23
	13	We	22		10	·57	19	·65		24
	14	Th	23		11	·47	20	·58		25
	15	Fr	24		12	·38	21	·52		26
	16	Sa	25		13	·29	22	·46		27
	17	Su	26		14	·21	23	·42		28
	18	Mo	27		—A	·15	24	·39		29
	19	Tu	28		1	·11	25	·37		—30

March

Solar Year and Month	Cyclic Sidereal Day	Week-Day	English Day	Lunar Month	Tithi	Ending Moment	Nakshatra	Ending Moment	Muhammadan Month	Muhammadan Day
Pramadicha Kumbha—Masi.	20	We	1	Sukla	2	·08	26	·38	H. 1270 Jumadal-akhir.	1
	21	Th	2		3	·07	27	·40		2
	22	Fr	3		4	·08	1	·44		3
	23	Sa	4		5	·11	2	·51		4
	24	Su	5		6	·16	3	·59		5
	25	Mo	6		7	·23	4	·69		6
	26	Tu	7		8	·32	5	·80		7
	27	We	8		9	·41	6	·90		8
	28	Th	9		10	·50	...	...		9
	29	Fr	10		11	·58	7	·00		10
	—30	Sa	11		12	·64	8	·09		11
Pramadicha Mina—Panguni.	1	Su	12	Phalguna	13	·68	9	·17		12
	2	Mo	13		14	·70	10	·24		13
	3	Tu	14		P	·71	11	·28		14
	4	We	15	Bahula	1	·69	12	·29		15
	5	Th	16		2	·66	13	·29		16
	6	Fr	17		3	·60	14	·27		17
	7	Sa	18		4	·53	15	·24		18
	8	Su	19		5	·45	16	·19		19
	9	Mo	20		6	·36	17	·13		20
	10	Tu	21		7	·26	18 / 19	·06 / ·99		21
	11	We	22		8	·16	20	·92		22
	12	Th	23		9 / 10	·06 / ·97	21	·86		23
	13	Fr	24		11	·89	22	·80		24
	14	Sa	25		12	·81	23	·75		25
	15	Su	26		13	·74	24	·71		26
	16	Mo	27		14	·69	25	·70		27
	17	Tu	28		—A	·66	26	·70		28
	18	We	29		1	·65	27	·71		—29
	19	Th	30		2	·67	1	·75		1
	20	Fr	31		3	·70	2	·81		2

April

Solar Year and Month	Cyclic Sidereal Day	Week-Day	English Day	Lunar Month	Tithi	Ending Moment	Nakshatra	Ending Moment	Muhammadan Month	Muhammadan Day
Pramadicha Mina—Panguni.	21	Sa	1	Sukla	4	·75	3	·89	H. 1270 Rajab.	3
	22	Su	2		5	·82	4	·99		4
	23	Mo	3		6	·90	...	...		5
	24	Tu	4		7	·99	5	·09		6
	25	We	5		...	...	6	·20		7
	26	Th	6		8	·08	7	·30		8
	27	Fr	7		9	·15	8	·40		9
	28	Sa	8		10	·21	9	·49		10
	29	Su	9		11	·25	10	·55		11
	30	Mo	10		12	·27	11	·59		12
	—31	Tu	11		13	·27	12	·61		13
Ananda Mesha—Chittirai.	1	We	12	Chaitra	14	·25	13	·61		14
	2	Th	13		P	·22	14	·60		15
	3	Fr	14	Bahula	1	·16	15	·57		16
	4	Sa	15		2	·09	16	·52		17
	5	Su	16		3 / 4	·01 / ·92	17	·46		18
	6	Mo	17		5	·82	18	·40		19
	7	Tu	18		6	·72	19	·34		20
	8	We	19		7	·62	20	·27		21
	9	Th	20		8	·52	21	·20		22
	10	Fr	21		9	·43	22	·13		23
	11	Sa	22		10	·35	23	·08		24
	12	Su	23		11	·28	24	·04		25
	13	Mo	24		12	·23	25	·03		26
	14	Tu	25		13	·20	26	·02		27
	15	We	26		14	·19	27	·04		28
	16	Th	27		—A	·20	1	·07		29
	17	Fr	28	Suk.	1	·24	2	·12		—30
	18	Sa	29		2	·29	3	·20		1
	19	Su	30		3	·35	4	·29		2

May

Solar Year and Month	Cyclic Sidereal Day	Week-Day	English Day	Lunar Month	Tithi	Ending Moment	Nakshatra	Ending Moment	Muhammadan Month	Muhammadan Day
Ananda Mesha—Chittirai.	20	Mo	1	Sukla	4	·42	5	·39	H. 1270 Shaban.	3
	21	Tu	2		5	·51	6	·50		4
	22	We	3		6	·60	7	·61		5
	23	Th	4		7	·67	8	·71		6
	24	Fr	5		8	·73	9	·79		7
	25	Sa	6		9	·77	10	·86		8
	26	Su	7		10	·80	11	·91		9
	27	Mo	8		11	·80	12	·94		10
	28	Tu	9		12	·79	13	·95		11
	29	We	10	Vaisakha	13	·74	14	·93		12
	30	Th	11		14	·68	15	·90		13
	—31	Fr ○	12		P	·61	16	·86		14
Ananda Vrishabha—Vaikasi.	1	Sa	13	Bahula	1	·53	17	·80		15
	2	Su	14		2	·43	18	·74		16
	3	Mo	15		3	·33	19	·67		17
	4	Tu	16		4	·23	20	·60		18
	5	We	17		5	·13	21	·53		19
	6	Th	18		6 / 7	·03 / ·94	22	·47		20
	7	Fr	19		8	·86	23	·42		21
	8	Sa	20		9	·79	24	·38		22
	9	Su	21		10	·74	25	·35		23
	10	Mo	22		11	·72	26	·34		24
	11	Tu	23		12	·71	27	·35		25
	12	We	24		13	·71	1	·38		26
	13	Th	25		14	·74	2	·44		27
	14	Fr	26		—A	·79	3	·51		28
	15	Sa	27		1	·85	4	·59		—29
	16	Su	28		2	·93	5	·69		1
	17	Mo	29		...	...	6	·80		2
	18	Tu	30		3	·02	7	·91		3
	19	We	31		4	·10	...	...		4

June

Solar Year and Month	Cyclic Sidereal Day	Week-Day	English Day	Lunar Month	Tithi	Ending Moment	Nakshatra	Ending Moment	Muhammadan Month	Muhammadan Day
Ananda Vrishabha—Vaikasi.	20	Th	1	Sukla	5	·17	8	·01	H. 1270 Ramzan.	5
	21	Fr	2		6	·23	9	·10		6
	22	Sa	3		7	·27	10	·17		7
	23	Su	4		8	·29	11	·22		8
	24	Mo	5		9	·29	12	·26		9
	25	Tu	6		10	·28	13	·27		10
	26	We	7		11	·24	14	·26		11
	27	Th	8		12	·19	15	·23		12
	28	Fr	9		13	·12	16	·19		13
	29	Sa	10	Jyeshtha	14 / P	·03 / ·93	17	·14		14
	30	Su	11	Bahula	1	·83	18	·08		15
	—31	Mo	12		2	·73	19 / 20	·01 / ·94		16
Ananda Mithuna—Ani.	1	Tu	13		3	·63	21	·87		17
	2	We	14		4	·53	22	·81		18
	3	Th	15		5	·44	23	·76		19
	4	Fr	16		6	·36	24	·71		20
	5	Sa	17		7	·29	25	·68		21
	6	Su	18		8	·23	26	·66		22
	7	Mo	19		9	·20	27	·67		23
	8	Tu	20		10	·18	1	·70		24
	9	We	21		11	·19	2	·75		25
	10	Th	22		12	·21	3	·81		26
	11	Fr	23		13	·26	4	·89		27
	12	Sa	24		14	·32	5	·99		28
	13	Su	25		—A	·40	...	...		29
	14	Mo	26	Ash. Suk.	1	·49	6	·10		—30
	15	Tu	27		2	·57	7	·21	Shawwal.	1
	16	We	28		3	·64	8	·31		2
	17	Th	29		4	·70	9	·40		3
	18	Fr	30		5	·75	10	·48		4

Naksh:—1. Asvn. 2. Bhar. 3. Krit. 4. Rohi. 5. Mrig. 6. Ardh. 7. Punar. 8. Push. 9. Aslesh. 10. Magh. 11. P. Phal. 12. U. Phal. 13. Hasta. 14. Chit.

A. D. 1854. | Kollam 1030, Commences { N. Malabar—Sept. / S. Malabar—Aug. | Hijra 1271, Commences, Sep. 24. | Vikrama 1911.
A.—Amavasya. | | | Bengal San 1260.
P.—Paurnami. | | | (N. Cycle) Krodhana.

Each table has two parts: Solar reckoning (the first three columns) and Lunar reckoning (the remaining five).

July

Cyclic Sidereal Year, Month and Day.	Week-Day	English Month and Day.	Tithi	Ending Moment.	Nakshatra	Ending Moment.	Muhammadan Year, Month and Day.
Ananda Mithuna—Ani. 19	Sa	1	Ashadha Sukla 6	·77	11	·54	H. 1270 Shawwal. 5
20	Su	2	7	·78	12	·58	6
21	Mo	3	8	·76	13	·59	7
22	Tu	4	9	·72	14	·59	8
23	We	5	10	·66	15	·56	9
24	Th	6	11	·59	16	·52	10
25	Fr	7	12	·51	17	·48	11
26	Sa	8	13	·41	18	·42	12
27	Su	9	14	·31	19	·35	13
28	Mo	10	P	·21	20	·28	14
29	Tu	11	1	·11	21	·21	15
30	We	12	2 3	·01 ·91	22	·15	16
31	Th	13	4	·83	23	·09	17
32	Fr	14	5	·76	24	·04	18
Ananda Karkata—Adi. 1	Sa	15	6	·71	25 26	·01 ·99	19
2	Su	16	Bahula 7	·67	...	...	20
3	Mo	17	8	·65	27	·00	21
4	Tu	18	9	·66	1	·02	22
5	We	19	10	·69	2	·06	23
6	Th	20	11	·73	3	·12	24
7	Fr	21	12	·79	4	·20	25
8	Sa	22	13	·87	5	·30	26
9	Su	23	14	·96	6	·40	27
10	Mo	24	...	...	7	·51	28
11	Tu	25	A	·04	8	·61	29
12	We	26	1	·11	9	·70	1
13	Th	27	2	·17	10	·78	2
14	Fr	28	3	·23	11	·85	3
15	Sa	29	4	·25	12	·89	4
16	Su	30	5	·26	13	·91	5
17	Mo	31	6	·24	14	·91	6

Aug.

Cyclic Sidereal Year, Month and Day.	Week-Day	English Month and Day.	Tithi	Ending Moment.	Nakshatra	Ending Moment.	Muhammadan Year, Month and Day.
18	Tu	1	Sravana Sukla 7	·20	15	·89	H. 1270 Zi-l-ka'da. 7
19	We	2	8	·15	16	·86	8
20	Th	3	9	·08	17	·82	9
21	Fr	4	10 11	·00 ·90	18	·76	10
22	Sa	5	12	·80	19	·69	11
23	Su	6	13	·70	20	·62	12
24	Mo	7	14	·60	21	·55	13
25	Tu	8	P	·50	22	·49	14
26	We	9	1	·41	23	·43	15
27	Th	10	2	·33	24	·38	16
28	Fr	11	3	·26	25	·34	17
29	Sa	12	4	·20	26	·32	18
30	Su	13	5	·16	27	·32	19
31	Mo	14	Bahula 6	·15	1	·33	20
Ananda Simha—Avani. 1	Tu	15	7	·16	2	·37	21
2	We	16	8	·18	3	·43	22
3	Th	17	9	·23	4	·51	23
4	Fr	18	10	·29	5	·60	24
5	Sa	19	11	·36	6	·70	25
6	Su	20	12	·45	7	·81	26
7	Mo	21	13	·54	8	·91	27
8	Tu	22	14	·61	...	...	28
9	We	23	A	·67	9	·01	29
10	Th	24	Bhadra. Suk. 1	·72	10	·10	30
11	Fr	25	2	·75	11	·17	Zi-l-hijja. 1
12	Sa	26	3	·76	12	·21	2
13	Su	27	4	·74	13	·23	3
14	Mo	28	5	·71	14	·24	4
15	Tu	29	6	·66	15	·23	5
16	We	30	7	·59	16	·20	6
17	Th	31	8	·51	17	·15	7

Sep.

Cyclic Sidereal Year, Month and Day.	Week-Day	English Month and Day.	Tithi	Ending Moment.	Nakshatra	Ending Moment.	Muhammadan Year, Month and Day.
Ananda Simha—Avani. 18	Fr	1	Bhadrapada Sukla 9	·42	18	·09	H. 1270 Zi-l-hijja. 8
19	Sa	2	10	·32	19 20	·03 ·97	9
20	Su	3	11	·22	21	·90	10
21	Mo	4	12	·12	22	·83	11
22	Tu	5	13 14	·02 ·92	23	·76	12
23	We	6	P	·84	24	·71	13
24	Th	7	1	·77	25	·67	14
25	Fr	8	2	·71	26	·64	15
26	Sa	9	3	·68	27	·64	16
27	Su	10	4	·67	1	·65	17
28	Mo	11	5	·68	2	·68	18
29	Tu	12	6	·71	3	·73	19
30	We	13	7	·75	4	·81	20
31	Th	14	8	·81	5	·90	21
Ananda Kanya—Purattasi. 1	Fr	15	9	·89	...	...	22
2	Sa	16	Bahula 10	·97	6	·00	23
3	Su	17	...	...	7	·10	24
4	Mo	18	11	·05	8	·21	25
5	Tu	19	12	·13	9	·31	26
6	We	20	13	·20	10	·40	27
7	Th	21	14	·25	11	·47	28
8	Fr	22	A	·28	12	·52	29
9	Sa	23	Sukla 1	·29	13	·55	30
10	Su	24	2	·27	14	·57	1
11	Mo	25	3	·24	15	·56	2
12	Tu	26	4	·19	16	·53	3
13	We	27	5	·13	17	·49	4
14	Th	28	6 7	·05 ·96	18	·43	5
15	Fr	29	8	·86	19	·37	6
16	Sa	30	9	·76	20	·31	7

Oct.

Cyclic Sidereal Year, Month and Day.	Week-Day	English Month and Day.	Tithi	Ending Moment.	Nakshatra	Ending Moment.	Muhammadan Year, Month and Day.
17	Su	1	Asvina 10	·66	21	·24	8
18	Mo	2	11	·56	22	·17	H. 1271 Muharram. 9
19	Tu	3	12	·47	23	·10	10
20	We	4	13	·39	24	·05	11
21	Th	5	14	·32	25 26	·01 ·98	12
22	Fr	6	P	·27	27	·96	13
23	Sa	7	1	·24	1	·97	14
24	Su	8	2	·22	...	...	15
25	Mo	9	3	·24	2	·00	16
26	Tu	10	Bahula 4	·27	3	·05	17
27	We	11	5	·31	4	·12	18
28	Th	12	6	·37	5	·20	19
29	Fr	13	7	·45	6	·30	20
30	Sa	14	8	·54	7	·40	21
31	Su	15	9	·62	8	·51	22
Ananda Tula—Aippasi. 1	Mo	16	10	·70	9	·62	23
2	Tu	17	11	·77	10	·71	24
3	We	18	12	·82	11	·78	25
4	Th	19	13	·85	12	·84	26
5	Fr	20	14	·86	13	·88	27
6	Sa	21	A	·85	14	·89	28
7	Su	22	Kartt. Sukla 1	·82	15	·88	29
8	Mo	23	2	·78	16	·86	30
9	Tu	24	3	·71	17	·82	H. 1271 Safar. 1
10	We	25	4	·63	18	·77	2
11	Th	26	5	·54	19	·71	3
12	Fr	27	6	·44	20	·65	4
13	Sa	28	7	·34	21	·58	5
14	Su	29	8	·24	22	·51	6
15	Mo	30	9	·15	23	·44	7
16	Tu	31	10 11	·06 ·98	24	·39	8

Nov.

Cyclic Sidereal Year, Month and Day.	Week-Day	English Month and Day.	Tithi	Ending Moment.	Nakshatra	Ending Moment.	Muhammadan Year, Month and Day.
Ananda Tula—Aippasi. 17	We	1	Kartika Suk. 12	·91	25	·34	9
18	Th	2	13	·86	26	·31	10
19	Fr	3	14	·84	27	·29	11
20	Sa ○	4	P	·83	1	·29	12
21	Su	5	1	·84	2	·32	13
22	Mo	6	2	·86	3	·36	14
23	Tu	7	3	·91	4	·42	15
24	We	8	4	·98	5	·50	16
25	Th	9	...	...	6	·60	H. 1271 Safar. 17
26	Fr	10	Bahula 5	·06	7	·71	18
27	Sa	11	6	·15	8	·82	19
28	Su	12	7	·23	9	·92	20
29	Mo	13	8	·31	...	...	21
Ananda Vrischika—Kartigai. 1	Tu	14	9	·38	10	·01	22
2	We	15	10	·44	11	·09	23
3	Th	16	11	·47	12	·16	24
4	Fr	17	12	·48	13	·20	25
5	Sa	18	13	·47	14	·21	26
6	Su	19	14	·43	15	·21	27
7	Mo	20	A	·38	16	·19	28
8	Tu	21	1	·32	17	·15	29
9	We	22	2	·25	18	·11	1
10	Th	23	3	·16	19 20	·05 ·98	2
11	Fr	24	4 5	·06 ·96	21	·91	3
12	Sa	25	6	·87	22	·84	4
13	Su	26	Sukla 7	·78	23	·78	5
14	Mo	27	8	·69	24	·72	6
15	Tu	28	9	·61	25	·67	7
16	We	29	10	·54	26	·63	8
17	Th	30	11	·49	27	·61	9

Dec.

Cyclic Sidereal Year, Month and Day.	Week-Day	English Month and Day.	Tithi	Ending Moment.	Nakshatra	Ending Moment.	Muhammadan Year, Month and Day.
18	Fr	1	Margasira 12	·46	1	·62	H. 1271 Rabi-ul-awwal. 10
19	Sa	2	13	·44	2	·64	11
20	Su	3	14	·46	3	·67	12
21	Mo	4	P	·49	4	·73	13
22	Tu	5	1	·54	5	·80	14
23	We	6	2	·61	6	·90	15
24	Th	7	3	·69	...	...	16
25	Fr	8	4	·78	7	·01	17
26	Sa	9	5	·86	8	·12	18
27	Su	10	6	·94	9	·22	19
28	Mo	11	Bahula ...	...	10	·31	20
29	Tu	12	7	·02	11	·39	21
30	We	13	8	·08	12	·46	22
Ananda Dhanus—Margali. 1	Th	14	9	·11	13	·51	23
2	Fr	15	10	·12	14	·53	24
3	Sa	16	11	·10	15	·53	25
4	Su	17	12	·07	16	·52	26
5	Mo	18	13 14	·02 ·95	17	·49	27
6	Tu	19	A	·87	18	·45	28
7	We	20	1	·79	19	·39	29
8	Th	21	2	·70	20	·32	30
9	Fr	22	3	·60	21	·25	H. 1271 Rabi-ul-akhir. 1
10	Sa	23	Sukla 4	·50	22	·15	2
11	Su	24	5	·40	23	·12	3
12	Mo	25	6	·31	24	·06	4
13	Tu	26	7	·24	25 26	·01 ·97	5
14	We	27	Pausha 8	·18	27	·95	6
15	Th	28	9	·13	1	·94	7
16	Fr	29	10	·10	2	·95	8
17	Sa	30	11	·10	3	·98	9
18	Su	31	12	·11	...	...	10

15. Svati. 16. Visak. 17. Anur. 18. Jyesh. 19. Mula. 20. P. Ash. 21. U. Ash. 22. Sravn. 23. Dani. 24. Satab. 25. P. Bhad. 26. U. Bhad. 27. Rev.

A. D. 1855. **Mesha Sankranti** (Commencement of Indian Sidereal Year).

Solar Eclipse. ● **(Surya Sid.) April 11·98.** **Saka 1777.** **Kaliyuga 4956.**

Lunar Eclipse. ○ **(Arya Sid.) April 11·88.** **(S. Cycle) Rakshasa.**

SOLAR reckoning: Cyclic Sidereal Year, Month and Day; Week-Day; English Month and Day. LUNAR reckoning: Tithi, Ending Moment; Nakshatra, Ending Moment; Muhammadan Year, Month and Day.

Jan. (Ananda Dhanus—Margali; Ananda Makara—Tai. Pausha Suk. / Bahula / Sukla. H. 1271 Rabi-ul-akhir.)

Cyclic Sidereal Year, Month and Day	Week-Day	English Month and Day	Tithi	Ending Moment	Nakshatra	Ending Moment	Muhammadan Year, Month and Day
19	Mo	1	13	·13	4	·03	11
20	Tu	2	14	·19	5	·11	12
21	We	3	P	·26	6	·20	13
22	Th	4	1	·34	7	·30	14
23	Fr	5	2	·43	8	·41	15
24	Sa	6	3	·53	9	·52	16
25	Su	7	4	·61	10	·62	17
26	Mo	8	5	·68	11	·71	18
27	Tu	9	6	·73	12	·78	19
28	We	10	7	·75	13	·82	20
—29	Th	11	8	·76	14	·85	21
1	Fr	12	9	·75	15	·86	22
2	Sa	13	10	·72	16	·85	23
3	Su	14	11	·67	17	·82	24
4	Mo	15	12	·60	18	·78	25
5	Tu	16	13	·52	19	·72	26
6	We	17	14	·43	20	·66	27
7	Th	18	—A	·33	21	·60	28
8	Fr	19	1	·23	22	·53	—29
9	Sa	20	2	·13	23	·46	1
10	Su	21	{3 4	·04 ·96	24	·40	2
11	Mo	22	5	·89	25	·35	3
12	Tu	23	6	·82	26	·31	4
13	We	24	7	·77	27	·28	5
14	Th	25	8	·75	1	·26	6
15	Fr	26	9	·74	2	·27	7
16	Sa	27	10	·76	3	·30	8
17	Su	28	11	·80	4	·35	9
18	Mo	29	12	·85	5	·42	10
19	Tu	30	13	·92	6	·51	11
20	We	31	...	...	7	·61	12

Feb. (Ananda Kumbha—Masi. Magha / Bahula / Sukla / Phalguna. H. 1271 Jumadal-awwal; Jumadal-akhir.)

Cyclic Sidereal Year, Month and Day	Week-Day	English Month and Day	Tithi	Ending Moment	Nakshatra	Ending Moment	Muhammadan Year, Month and Day
21	Th	1	14	·00	8	·71	13
22	Fr	2	P	·08	9	·82	14
23	Sa	3	1	·17	10	·92	15
24	Su	4	2	·26	...	...	16
25	Mo	5	3	·33	11	·01	17
26	Tu	6	4	·37	12	·09	18
27	We	7	5	·39	13	·14	19
28	Th	8	6	·40	14	·17	20
29	Fr	9	7	·38	15	·19	21
—30	Sa	10	8	·35	16	·18	22
1	Su	11	9	·29	17	·16	23
2	Mo	12	10	·22	18	·11	24
3	Tu	13	11	·14	19	·06	25
4	We	14	{12 13	·05 ·95	20 21	·00 ·94}	26
5	Th	15	14	·85	22	·87	27
6	Fr	16	—A	·75	23	·80	28
7	Sa	17	1	·66	24	·73	29
8	Su	18	2	·58	25	·67	—30
9	Mo	19	3	·50	26	·63	1
10	Tu	20	4	·44	27	·60	2
11	We	21	5	·39	1	·59	3
12	Th	22	6	·37	2	·59	4
13	Fr	23	7	·36	3	·61	5
14	Sa	24	8	·37	4	·66	6
15	Su	25	9	·41	5	·73	7
16	Mo	26	10	·46	6	·81	8
17	Tu	27	11	·54	7	·90	9
18	We	28	12	·64	...	...	10

March (Ananda Kumbha—Masi; Ananda Mina—Panguni. Phalguna / Bahula / Sukla. H. 1271 Jumadal-akhir.)

Cyclic Sidereal Year, Month and Day	Week-Day	English Month and Day	Tithi	Ending Moment	Nakshatra	Ending Moment	Muhammadan Year, Month and Day
19	Th	1	13	·72	8	·01	11
20	Fr	2	14	·80	9	·12	12
21	Sa	3	P	·87	10	·23	13
22	Su	4	1	·93	11	·32	14
23	Mo	5	2	·98	12	·39	15
24	Tu	6	...	...	13	·45	16
25	We	7	3	·00	14	·50	17
26	Th	8	4	·01	15	·51	18
27	Fr	9	{5 6	·00 ·95	16	·51	19
28	Sa	10	7	·89	17	·49	20
29	Su	11	8	·82	18	·45	21
—30	Mo	12	9	·74	19	·41	22
1	Tu	13	10	·65	20	·35	23
2	We	14	11	·55	21	·28	24
3	Th	15	12	·45	22	·21	25
4	Fr	16	13	·35	23	·14	26
5	Sa	17	14	·26	24	·07	27
6	Su	18	—A	·17	25 26	·02 ·97}	28
7	Mo	19	1	·10	27	·98	—29
8	Tu	20	{2 3	·04 ·99	1	·91	1
9	We	21	4	·96	2	·91	2
10	Th	22	5	·95	3	·93	3
11	Fr	23	6	·97	4	·97	4
12	Sa	24	...	...	...	...	5
13	Su	25	7	·01	5	·03	6
14	Mo	26	8	·06	6	·11	7
15	Tu	27	9	·13	7	·20	8
16	We	28	10	·21	8	·31	9
17	Th	29	11	·30	9	·42	10
18	Fr	30	12	·38	10	·52	11
19	Sa	31	13	·46	11	·62	12

April (Ananda Mina—Panguni; Rakshasa Mesha—Chittirai. Chaitra / Bahula / Sukla / Vaisakha. H. 1271 Rajab; H. 1271 Shaban.)

Cyclic Sidereal Year, Month and Day	Week-Day	English Month and Day	Tithi	Ending Moment	Nakshatra	Ending Moment	Muhammadan Year, Month and Day
20	Su	1	14	·52	12	·70	13
21	Mo	2	P	·57	13	·77	14
22	Tu	3	1	·59	14	·81	15
23	We	4	2	·58	15	·83	16
24	Th	5	3	·56	16	·83	17
25	Fr	6	4	·52	17	·81	18
26	Sa	7	5	·47	18	·78	19
27	Su	8	6	·40	19	·74	20
28	Mo	9	7	·32	20	·68	21
29	Tu	10	8	·22	21	·62	22
—30	We	11	9	·12	22	·55	23
1	Th	12	{10 11	·02 ·92	23	·48	24
2	Fr	13	12	·82	24	·41	25
3	Sa	14	13	·73	25	·35	26
4	Su	15	14	·65	26	·30	27
5	Mo	16	—A	·59	27	·26	28
6	Tu	17	1	·55	1	·24	29
7	We	18	2	·52	2	·24	—30
8	Th	19	3	·50	3	·25	1
9	Fr	20	4	·52	4	·28	2
10	Sa	21	5	·55	5	·34	3
11	Su	22	6	·60	6	·41	4
12	Mo	23	7	·67	7	·51	5
13	Tu	24	8	·75	8	·61	6
14	We	25	9	·84	9	·72	7
15	Th	26	10	·93	10	·82	8
16	Fr	27	...	...	11	·92	9
17	Sa	28	11	·00	...	...	10
18	Su	29	12	·06	12	·01	11
19	Mo	30	13	·10	13	·08	12

May (Rakshasa Mesha—Chittirai; Rakshasa Vrishabha—Vaikasi. Vaisk. / Bahula / Sukla / Jyeshtha. H. 1271 Shaban; Ramzan.)

Cyclic Sidereal Year, Month and Day	Week-Day	English Month and Day	Tithi	Ending Moment	Nakshatra	Ending Moment	Muhammadan Year, Month and Day
20	Tu	1	14	·12	14	·13	13
21	We ○	2	P	·12	15	·15	14
22	Th	3	1	·10	16	·16	15
23	Fr	4	2	·06	17	·15	16
24	Sa	5	{3 4	·00 ·93	18	·12	17
25	Su	6	5	·84	19	·08	18
26	Mo	7	6	·74	20 21	·02 ·95}	19
27	Tu	8	7	·64	22	·88	20
28	We	9	8	·54	23	·81	21
29	Th	10	9	·44	24	·75	22
30	Fr	11	10	·34	25	·69	23
—31	Sa	12	11	·25	26	·64	24
1	Su	13	12	·18	27	·59	25
2	Mo	14	13	·11	1	·57	26
3	Tu	15	14	·06	2	·56	27
4	We ●	16	—A	·03	3	·57	28
5	Th	17	1	·02	4	·60	—29
6	Fr	18	2	·03	5	·65	1
7	Sa	19	3	·07	6	·72	2
8	Su	20	4	·12	7	·81	3
9	Mo	21	5	·18	8	·91	4
10	Tu	22	6	·26	...	...	5
11	We	23	7	·35	9	·02	6
12	Th	24	8	·43	10	·12	7
13	Fr	25	9	·50	11	·22	8
14	Sa	26	10	·56	12	·31	9
15	Su	27	11	·60	13	·39	10
16	Mo	28	12	·62	14	·44	11
17	Tu	29	13	·62	15	·47	12
18	We	30	14	·60	16	·48	13
19	Th	31	P	·56	17	·48	14

June (Rakshasa Mithuna—Ani. Bahula / Adh. Ashadha Sukla. H. 1271; H. 1271 Shawwal.)

Cyclic Sidereal Year, Month and Day	Week-Day	English Month and Day	Tithi	Ending Moment	Nakshatra	Ending Moment	Muhammadan Year, Month and Day
20	Fr	1	1	·50	18	·45	15
21	Sa	2	2	·48	19	·41	16
22	Su	3	3	·34	20	·35	17
23	Mo	4	4	·24	21	·29	18
24	Tu	5	5	·14	22	·23	19
25	We	6	{6 7	·04 ·94	23	·16	20
26	Th	7	8	·84	24	·09	21
27	Fr	8	9	·75	25 26	·03 ·97}	22
28	Sa	9	10	·67	27	·93	23
29	Su	10	11	·61	1	·90	24
30	Mo	11	12	·56	2	·88	25
—31	Tu	12	13	·52	3	·89	26
1	We	13	14	·51	4	·91	27
2	Th	14	—A	·52	5	·96	28
3	Fr	15	1	·55	...	...	29
4	Sa	16	2	·60	6	·08	—30
5	Su	17	3	·66	7	·11	1
6	Mo	18	4	·73	8	·21	2
7	Tu	19	5	·82	9	·31	3
8	We	20	6	·91	10	·42	4
9	Th	21	7	·98	11	·52	5
10	Fr	22	...	...	12	·62	6
11	Sa	23	8	·04	13	·70	7
12	Su	24	9	·08	14	·75	8
13	Mo	25	10	·10	15	·79	9
14	Tu	26	11	·10	16	·81	10
15	We	27	12	·08	17	·81	11
16	Th	28	{13 14	·04 ·98	18	·78	12
17	Fr	29	P	·91	19	·74	13
18	Sa	30	1	·83	20	·69	14

Naksh:—1. Asvn. 2. Bhar. 3. Krit. 4. Rohi. 5. Mrig. 6. Ardh. 7. Punar. 8. Push. 9. Asiesh. 10. Magh. 11. P. Phal. 12. U. Phal. 13. Hasta. 14. Chit.

A. D. 1855.   **Kollam 1031,** Commences { **N. Malabar—Sept.** / **S. Malabar—Aug.**   **Hijra 1272,** Commences, **Sep. 13.**   **Vikrama 1912.**

A.—Amavasya.   **P.—Paurnami.**   **Bengal San 1261.**   **(N. Cycle) Kshaya.**

SOLAR reckoning: Cyclic Sidereal Year, Month and Day; Week-Day, English Month and Day. LUNAR reckoning: Tithi, Ending Moment; Nakshatra, Ending Moment; Muhammadan Year, Month and Day.

July

Cyclic Sidereal Year, Month and Day	Week-Day	English Month and Day	Tithi	Ending Moment	Nakshatra	Ending Moment	Muhammadan Year, Month and Day
(Rakshasa, Mithuna—Ani.) 19	Su	1	(Adh. Ashad. Bahula) 2	·73	21	·64	(H. 1271 Shawwal.) 15
20	Mo	2	3	·63	22	·57	16
21	Tu	3	4	·53	23	·50	17
22	We	4	5	·43	24	·43	18
23	Th	5	6	·33	25	·36	19
24	Fr	6	7	·24	26	·31	20
25	Sa	7	8	·15	27	·26	21
26	Su	8	9	·08	1	·23	22
27	Mo	9	10 11	·03 ·99	2	·21	23
28	Tu	10	12	·98	3	·21	24
29	We	11	13	·99	4	·23	25
30	Th	12	...	...	5	·28	26
31	Fr	13	14	·03	6	·34	27
—32	Sa	14	—A	·08	7	·41	28
(Rakshasa, Karkata—Adi.) 1	Su	15	(Nija Ashadha, Sukla) 1	·14	8	·51	—29
2	Mo	16	2	·21	9	·62	(Zi-l-ka'da.) 1
3	Tu	17	3	·29	10	·73	2
4	We	18	4	·37	11	·83	3
5	Th	19	5	·44	12	·92	4
6	Fr	20	6	·51	...	...	5
7	Sa	21	7	·55	13	·00	6
8	Su	22	8	·58	14	·06	7
9	Mo	23	9	·58	15	·11	8
10	Tu	24	10	·56	16	·13	9
11	We	25	11	·52	17	·13	10
12	Th	26	12	·46	18	·11	11
13	Fr	27	13	·39	19	·08	12
14	Sa	28	14	·31	20 21	·04 ·98	13
15	Su	29	P	·22	22	·91	14
16	Mo	30	1	·12	23	·84	15
17	Tu	31	2 3	·02 ·92	24	·77	16

Aug.

Cyclic Sidereal Year, Month and Day	Week-Day	English Month and Day	Tithi	Ending Moment	Nakshatra	Ending Moment	Muhammadan Year, Month and Day
18	We	1	(Bahula) 4	·82	25	·71	(H. 1271) 17
19	Th	2	5	·72	26	·65	18
20	Fr	3	6	·63	27	·60	19
21	Sa	4	7	·56	1	·56	20
22	Su	5	8	·51	2	·53	21
23	Mo	6	9	·48	3	·53	22
24	Tu	7	10	·47	4	·55	23
25	We	8	11	·48	5	·59	24
26	Th	9	12	·50	6	·64	25
27	Fr	10	13	·55	7	·72	26
28	Sa	11	14	·62	8	·81	27
29	Su	12	—A	·70	9	·92	28
30	Mo	13	(Sravana, Sukla) 1	·79	...	...	29
—31	Tu	14	2	·87	10	·03	—30
(Rakshasa, Simha—Avani.) 1	We	15	3	·94	11	·13	(H. 1271 Zi-l-hijja.) 1
2	Th	16	...	...	12	·23	2
3	Fr	17	4	·00	13	·31	3
4	Sa	18	5	·04	14	·38	4
5	Su	19	6	·07	15	·43	5
6	Mo	20	7	·07	16	·45	6
7	Tu	21	8	·06	17	·46	7
8	We	22	9 10	·02 ·97	18	·45	8
9	Th	23	11	·90	19	·42	9
10	Fr	24	12	·81	20	·37	10
11	Sa	25	13	·72	21	·31	11
12	Su	26	14	·62	22	·25	12
13	Mo	27	P	·52	23	·18	13
14	Tu	28	(Bah.) 1	·42	24	·11	14
15	We	29	2	·32	25 26	·05 ·99	15
16	Th	30	3	·23	27	·93	16
17	Fr	31	4	·15	1	·89	17

Sep.

Cyclic Sidereal Year, Month and Day	Week-Day	English Month and Day	Tithi	Ending Moment	Nakshatra	Ending Moment	Muhammadan Year, Month and Day
(Rakshasa, Simha—Avani.) 18	Sa	1	(Sr.) 5	·08	2	·86	(H. 1271 Zi-l-hijja.) 18
19	Su	2	6	·03	3	·86	19
20	Mo	3	7 8	·00 ·99	4	·87	20
21	Tu	4	...	...	5	·90	21
22	We	5	9	·00	6	·95	22
23	Th	6	(Bahula) 10	·02	...	...	23
24	Fr	7	11	·07	7	·02	24
25	Sa	8	12	·13	8	·12	25
26	Su	9	13	·20	9	·23	26
27	Mo	10	14	·28	10	·33	27
28	Tu	11	—A	·37	11	·43	28
29	We	12	(Bhadrapada, Sukla) 1	·45	12	·53	—29
30	Th	13	2	·52	13	·62	(H. 1272 Muharram.) 1
—31	Fr	14	3	·57	14	·69	2
(Rakshasa, Kanya—Purattasi.) 1	Sa	15	4	·60	15	·74	3
2	Su	16	5	·61	16	·77	4
3	Mo	17	6	·59	17	·78	5
4	Tu	18	7	·55	18	·77	6
5	We	19	8	·50	19	·75	7
6	Th	20	9	·43	20	·70	8
7	Fr	21	10	·35	21	·65	9
8	Sa	22	11	·26	22	·59	10
9	Su	23	12	·16	23	·53	11
10	Mo	24	13 14	·06 ·96	24	·46	12
11	Tu	25	P	·86	25	·39	13
12	We	26	1	·77	26	·32	14
13	Th	27	2	·69	27	·26	15
14	Fr	28	3	·62	1	·22	16
15	Sa	29	4	·57	2	·19	17
16	Su	30	5	·54	3	·18	18

Oct.

Cyclic Sidereal Year, Month and Day	Week-Day	English Month and Day	Tithi	Ending Moment	Nakshatra	Ending Moment	Muhammadan Year, Month and Day
17	Mo	1	(Bahula) 6	·52	4	·19	19
18	Tu	2	7	·54	5	·21	20
19	We	3	8	·57	6	·26	21
20	Th	4	9	·61	7	·33	22
21	Fr	5	10	·67	8	·42	23
22	Sa	6	11	·75	9	·52	24
23	Su	7	12	·84	10	·62	25
24	Mo	8	13	·93	11	·73	26
25	Tu	9	...	...	12	·84	27
26	We	10	14	·01	13	·93	28
27	Th	11	—A	·08	...	...	29
28	Fr	12	(Asvina, Sukla) 1	·13	14	·00	—30
29	Sa	13	2	·15	15	·05	(H. 1272 Safar.) 1
30	Su	14	3	·16	16	·09	2
—31	Mo	15	4	·15	17	·10	3
(Rakshasa, Tula—Aippasi.) 1	Tu	16	5	·12	18	·10	4
2	We	17	6 7	·06 ·99	19	·08	5
3	Th	18	8	·91	20 21	·04 ·99	6
4	Fr	19	9	·82	22	·93	7
5	Sa	20	10	·73	23	·86	8
6	Su	21	11	·63	24	·79	9
7	Mo	22	12	·53	25	·72	10
8	Tu	23	13	·44	26	·63	11
9	We	24	14	·35	27	·60	12
10	Th ○	25	P	·27	1	·56	13
11	Fr	26	(Bah.) 1	·20	2	·53	14
12	Sa	27	2	·15	3	·51	15
13	Su	28	3	·12	4	·51	16
14	Mo	29	4	·12	5	·53	17
15	Tu	30	5	·13	6	·58	18
16	We	31	6	·16	7	·64	19

Nov.

Cyclic Sidereal Year, Month and Day	Week-Day	English Month and Day	Tithi	Ending Moment	Nakshatra	Ending Moment	Muhammadan Year, Month and Day
(Rakshasa, Tula—Aippasi.) 17	Th	1	(Asv. Bahula) 7	·21	8	·72	(H. 1272 Safar.) 20
18	Fr	2	8	·28	9	·82	21
19	Sa	3	9	·36	10	·92	22
20	Su	4	10	·45	...	...	23
21	Mo	5	11	·54	11	·03	24
22	Tu	6	12	·62	12	·14	25
23	We	7	13	·68	13	·23	26
24	Th	8	14	·72	14	·31	27
25	Fr	9	—A	·75	15	·37	28
26	Sa	10	(Kartika, Sukla) 1	·77	16	·41	—29
27	Su	11	2	·75	17	·43	(H. 1272 Rabi-ul-awwal.) 1
28	Mo	12	3	·72	18	·43	2
29	Tu	13	4	·67	19	·41	3
—30	We	14	5	·61	20	·37	4
(Rakshasa, Vrischika—Kartigai.) 1	Th	15	6	·53	21	·32	5
2	Fr	16	7	·44	22	·26	6
3	Sa	17	8	·34	23	·20	7
4	Su	18	9	·24	24	·13	8
5	Mo	19	10	·14	25 26	·06 ·99	9
6	Tu	20	11 12	·05 ·97	27	·94	10
7	We	21	13	·89	1	·89	11
8	Th	22	14	·82	2	·85	12
9	Fr	23	P	·77	3	·83	13
10	Sa	24	1	·74	4	·83	14
11	Su	25	2	·74	5	·85	15
12	Mo	26	3	·75	6	·89	16
13	Tu	27	4	·78	7	·95	17
14	We	28	5	·83	...	...	18
15	Th	29	6	·90	8	·02	19
16	Fr	30	7	·98	9	·12	20

Dec.

Cyclic Sidereal Year, Month and Day	Week-Day	English Month and Day	Tithi	Ending Moment	Nakshatra	Ending Moment	Muhammadan Year, Month and Day
17	Sa	1	(Bahula) ...	...	10	·23	21
18	Su	2	8	·07	11	·34	22
19	Mo	3	9	·16	12	·44	23
20	Tu	4	10	·24	13	·53	24
21	We	5	11	·31	14	·61	25
22	Th	6	12	·36	15	·68	26
23	Fr	7	13	·40	16	·73	27
24	Sa	8	14	·41	17	·75	28
25	Su	9	—A	·39	18	·75	29
26	Mo	10	(Margasira, Sukla) 1	·35	19	·74	—30
27	Tu	11	2	·30	20	·71	(H. 1272 Rabi-ul-akhir.) 1
28	We	12	3	·23	21	·67	2
—29	Th	13	4	·15	22	·61	3
(Rakshasa, Dhanus—Margali.) 1	Fr	14	5 6	·06 ·97	23	·54	4
2	Sa	15	7	·87	24	·47	5
3	Su	16	8	·77	25	·40	6
4	Mo	17	9	·67	26	·34	7
5	Tu	18	10	·58	27	·28	8
6	We	19	11	·51	1	·23	9
7	Th	20	12	·45	2	·18	10
8	Fr	21	13	·41	3	·16	11
9	Sa	22	14	·38	4	·15	12
10	Su	23	P	·37	5	·17	13
11	Mo	24	(Bahula) 1	·39	6	·20	14
12	Tu	25	2	·43	7	·25	15
13	We	26	3	·48	8	·33	16
14	Th	27	4	·56	9	·43	17
15	Fr	28	5	·64	10	·53	18
16	Sa	29	6	·73	11	·63	19
17	Su	30	7	·82	12	·74	20
18	Mo	31	8	·90	13	·84	21

15. Svati. 16. Visak. 17. Anur. 18. Jyesh. 19. Mula. 20. P. Ash. 21. U. Ash. 22. Sravn. 23. Dhni. 24. Satab. 25. P. Bhad. 26. U. Bhad. 27. Rev.

A. D. 1856. **Solar Eclipse.** ● **Lunar Eclipse.** ○

Mesha Sankranti (Commencement of Indian Sidereal Year). **(Surya Sid.) April 11·23.** **(Arya Sid.) April 11·13.**

Saka 1778. **Kaliyuga 4957.** **(S. Cycle) Anala** (Nala).

Columns: SOLAR reckoning (Cyclic Sidereal Year, Month and Day; Week-Day; English Month and Day) — LUNAR reckoning (Tithi, Ending Moment; Nakshatra, Ending Moment; Muhammadan Year, Month and Day).

Jan.

Solar: Rakshasa, *Dhanus—Margali* (to 30); Rakshasa, *Makara—Tai* (from 1). Lunar: Mr. Bah.; Sukla; Pausha; Bahula. Muhammadan: *Rabi-ul-akhir*; H. 1272 *Jumadal-awwal*.

Cyclic Sidereal Year, Month and Day	Week-Day	English Month and Day	Tithi	Ending Moment	Nakshatra	Ending Moment	Muhammadan Year, Month and Day
19	Tu	1	9	·96	14	·93	22
20	We	2	...	...	...	...	23
21	Th	3	10	·00	15	·00	24
22	Fr	4	11	·03	16	·04	25
23	Sa	5	12	·04	17	·07	26
24	Su	6	13	·03	18	·08	27
25	Mo	7	14 A	·00 ·95	19	·07	28
26	Tu	8	1	·88	20	·04	29
27	We	9	2	·80	21 22	·00 ·94	1
28	Th	10	3	·71	23	·88	2
29	Fr	11	4	·62	24	·82	3
30	Sa	12	5	·52	25	·75	4
1	Su	13	6	·42	26	·68	5
2	Mo	14	7	·32	27	·62	6
3	Tu	15	8	·23	1	·56	7
4	We	16	9	·16	2	·52	8
5	Th	17	10	·10	3	·49	9
6	Fr	18	11	·06	4	·48	10
7	Sa	19	12	·03	5	·49	11
8	Su	20	13	·02	6	·52	12
9	Mo	21	14	·04	7	·56	13
10	Tu	22	P	·08	8	·63	14
11	We	23	1	·14	9	·72	15
12	Th	24	2	·21	10	·82	16
13	Fr	25	3	·29	11	·93	17
14	Sa	26	4	·38	...	...	18
15	Su	27	5	·47	12	·04	19
16	Mo	28	6	·55	13	·14	20
17	Tu	29	7	·61	14	·23	21
18	We	30	8	·66	15	·31	22
19	Th	31	9	·68	16	·36	23

Feb.

Solar: Rakshasa, *Kumbha—Masi* (from 1). Lunar: Sukla; Magha; Bahula. Muhammadan: H. 1272 *Jumadal-akhir*.

Cyclic Sidereal Year, Month and Day	Week-Day	English Month and Day	Tithi	Ending Moment	Nakshatra	Ending Moment	Muhammadan Year, Month and Day
20	Fr	1	10	·68	17	·39	24
21	Sa	2	11	·67	18	·40	25
22	Su	3	12	·64	19	·40	26
23	Mo	4	13	·58	20	·38	27
24	Tu	5	14	·51	21	·33	28
25	We	6	A	·43	22	·28	29
26	Th	7	1	·34	23	·22	30
27	Fr	8	2	·24	24	·16	1
28	Sa	9	3	·14	25	·09	2
29	Su	10	4 5	·04 ·95	26 27	·02 ·95	3
1	Mo	11	6	·86	1	·89	4
2	Tu	12	7	·79	2	·85	5
3	We	13	8	·73	3	·82	6
4	Th	14	9	·69	4	·81	7
5	Fr	15	10	·66	5	·81	8
6	Sa	16	11	·65	6	·85	9
7	Su	17	12	·67	7	·88	10
8	Mo	18	13	·71	8	·95	11
9	Tu	19	14	·77	...	...	12
10	We	20	P	·84	9	·03	13
11	Th	21	1	·92	10	·12	14
12	Fr	22	...	...	11	·23	15
13	Sa	23	2	·01	12	·34	16
14	Su	24	3	·10	13	·45	17
15	Mo	25	4	·17	14	·54	18
16	Tu	26	5	·23	15	·61	19
17	We	27	6	·28	16	·67	20
18	Th	28	7	·30	17	·71	21
19	Fr	29	8	·31	18	·73	22

March

Solar: Rakshasa, *Kumbha—Masi* (to 31); Rakshasa, *Mina—Panguni* (from 1). Lunar: Bah.; Sukla; Phalguna; Bahula. Muhammadan: *Jumadal-akhir*; H. 1272 *Rajab*.

Cyclic Sidereal Year, Month and Day	Week-Day	English Month and Day	Tithi	Ending Moment	Nakshatra	Ending Moment	Muhammadan Year, Month and Day
20	Sa	1	9	·29	19	·72	23
21	Su	2	10	·25	20	·70	24
22	Mo	3	11	·19	21	·67	25
23	Tu	4	12	·12	22	·62	26
24	We	5	13 14	·04 ·95	23	·56	27
25	Th	6	A	·85	24	·50	28
26	Fr	7	1	·75	25	·43	29
27	Sa	8	2	·65	26	·36	1
28	Su	9	3	·55	27	·29	2
29	Mo	10	4	·46	1	·23	3
30	Tu	11	5	·39	2	·18	4
31	We	12	6	·33	3	·15	5
1	Th	13	7	·29	4	·13	6
2	Fr	14	8	·26	5	·13	7
3	Sa	15	9	·25	6	·15	8
4	Su	16	10	·26	7	·19	9
5	Mo	17	11	·30	8	·25	10
6	Tu	18	12	·37	9	·33	11
7	We	19	13	·45	10	·42	12
8	Th	20	14	·53	11	·53	13
9	Fr	21	P	·62	12	·64	14
10	Sa	22	1	·70	13	·75	15
11	Su	23	2	·77	14	·84	16
12	Mo	24	3	·83	15	·92	17
13	Tu	25	4	·87	16	·98	18
14	We	26	5	·89	...	...	19
15	Th	27	6	·89	17	·03	20
16	Fr	28	7	·87	18	·05	21
17	Sa	29	8	·83	19	·05	22
18	Su	30	9	·77	20	·03	23
19	Mo	31	10	·70	21 22	·00 ·96	24

April

Solar: *Mina—Panguni* (to 29); Anala, *Mesha—Chittirai* (from 1). Lunar: Sukla; Chaitra; Bahula. Muhammadan: H. 1272 *Shaban*.

Cyclic Sidereal Year, Month and Day	Week-Day	English Month and Day	Tithi	Ending Moment	Nakshatra	Ending Moment	Muhammadan Year, Month and Day
20	Tu	1	11	·61	23	·90	25
21	We	2	12	·51	24	·83	26
22	Th	3	13	·41	25	·76	27
23	Fr	4	14	·31	26	·69	28
24	Sa	5 ●	A	·21	27	·63	29
25	Su	6	1	·12	1	·57	30
26	Mo	7	2 3	·04 ·96	2	·52	1
27	Tu	8	4	·89	3	·48	2
28	We	9	5	·85	4	·46	3
29	Th	10	6	·82	5	·45	4
1	Fr	11	7	·81	6	·47	5
2	Sa	12	8	·82	7	·50	6
3	Su	13	9	·86	8	·56	7
4	Mo	14	10	·92	9	·63	8
5	Tu	15	...	...	10	·72	9
6	We	16	11	·00	11	·83	10
7	Th	17	12	·08	12	·94	11
8	Fr	18	13	·17	...	...	12
9	Sa	19	14	·25	13	·04	13
10	Su	20 ○	P	·32	14	·14	14
11	Mo	21	1	·38	15	·23	15
12	Tu	22	2	·41	16	·30	16
13	We	23	3	·43	17	·35	17
14	Th	24	4	·43	18	·37	18
15	Fr	25	5	·41	19	·38	19
16	Sa	26	6	·37	20	·36	20
17	Su	27	7	·31	21	·33	21
18	Mo	28	8	·24	22	·29	22
19	Tu	29	9	·15	23	·24	23
20	We	30	10 11	·05 ·95	24	·17	24

May

Solar: Anala, *Mesha—Chittirai* (to 31); Anala, *Vrishabha—Vaikasi* (from 1). Lunar: Ch. Bah.; Sukla; Vaisakha; Bahula. Muhammadan: *Shaban*; H. 1272 *Ramzan*.

Cyclic Sidereal Year, Month and Day	Week-Day	English Month and Day	Tithi	Ending Moment	Nakshatra	Ending Moment	Muhammadan Year, Month and Day
21	Th	1	12	·85	25	·10	25
22	Fr	2	13	·75	26 27	·03 ·97	26
23	Sa	3	14	·65	1	·91	27
24	Su	4	A	·56	2	·85	28
25	Mo	5	1	·48	3	·81	29
26	Tu	6	2	·42	4	·78	1
27	We	7	3	·38	5	·78	2
28	Th	8	4	·35	6	·79	3
29	Fr	9	5	·34	7	·82	4
30	Sa	10	6	·35	8	·87	5
31	Su	11	7	·39	9	·94	6
1	Mo	12	8	·44	...	...	7
2	Tu	13	9	·51	10	·03	8
3	We	14	10	·59	11	·13	9
4	Th	15	11	·68	12	·24	10
5	Fr	16	12	·76	13	·34	11
6	Sa	17	13	·83	14	·44	12
7	Su	18	14	·89	15	·53	13
8	Mo	19	P	·93	16	·61	14
9	Tu	20	1	·94	17	·66	15
10	We	21	2	·94	18	·69	16
11	Th	22	3	·93	19	·71	17
12	Fr	23	4	·89	20	·70	18
13	Sa	24	5	·82	21	·67	19
14	Su	25	6	·74	22	·63	20
15	Mo	26	7	·65	23	·57	21
16	Tu	27	8	·55	24	·51	22
17	We	28	9	·45	25	·45	23
18	Th	29	10	·35	26	·38	24
19	Fr	30	11	·25	27	·31	25
20	Sa	31	12	·15	1	·25	26

June

Solar: *Vrishabha—Vaikasi* (to 31); Anala, *Mithuna—Ani* (from 1). Lunar: Sukla; Jyeshtha; Bahula. Muhammadan: H. 1272 *Shawwal*.

Cyclic Sidereal Year, Month and Day	Week-Day	English Month and Day	Tithi	Ending Moment	Nakshatra	Ending Moment	Muhammadan Year, Month and Day
21	Su	1	13 14	·06 ·99	2	·19	27
22	Mo	2	A	·93	3	·15	28
23	Tu	3	1	·88	4	·12	29
24	We	4	2	·85	5	·10	30
25	Th	5	3	·83	6	·11	1
26	Fr	6	4	·84	7	·13	2
27	Sa	7	5	·87	8	·18	3
28	Su	8	6	·92	9	·25	4
29	Mo	9	7	·99	10	·33	5
30	Tu	10	...	...	11	·43	6
31	We	11	8	·07	12	·54	7
1	Th	12	9	·16	13	·64	8
2	Fr	13	10	·24	14	·74	9
3	Sa	14	11	·31	15	·84	10
4	Su	15	12	·37	16	·92	11
5	Mo	16	13	·41	17	·97	12
6	Tu	17	14	·43	...	...	13
7	We	18	P	·43	18	·01	14
8	Th	19	1	·41	19	·02	15
9	Fr	20	2	·37	20	·02	16
10	Sa	21	3	·31	21 22	·00 ·96	17
11	Su	22	4	·24	23	·91	18
12	Mo	23	5	·15	24	·85	19
13	Tu	24	6 7	·05 ·95	25	·79	20
14	We	25	8	·85	26	·72	21
15	Th	26	9	·75	27	·65	22
16	Fr	27	10	·65	1	·58	23
17	Sa	28	11	·56	2	·52	24
18	Su	29	12	·48	3	·48	25
19	Mo	30	13	·41	4	·45	26

Naksh:—1. Asvn. 2. Bhar. 3. Krit. 4. Rohi. 5. Mrig. 6. Ardh. 7. Punar. 8. Push. 9. Aslesh. 10. Magh. 11. P. Phal. 12. U. Phal. 13. Hasta. 14. Chit.

A. D. 1856. | Kollam 1032, Commences { N. Malabar—Sept. / S. Malabar—Aug. | Hijra 1273, Commences, Sep. 1. | Vikrama 1913.
A.—Amavasya. | | | Bengal San 1262.
P.—Paurnami. | | | (N. Cycle) Prabhava.

SOLAR reckoning: Cyclic Sidereal Year, Month and Day; Week-Day; English Month and Day. LUNAR reckoning: Tithi, Ending Moment; Nakshatra, Ending Moment; Muhammadan Year, Month and Day.

July

Solar: Anala, Mithuna—Ani. (to 32); Anala, Karkata—Adi. (from 1). Lunar: Sukla; Ashadha; Bahula. Muhammadan: H. 1272 Zi-l-ka'da.

Cyclic Sidereal Year, Month and Day	Week-Day	English Month and Day	Tithi	Ending Moment	Nakshatra	Ending Moment	Muhammadan Year, Month and Day
20	Tu	1	14	·36	5	·43	27
21	We	2	—A	·33	6	·43	28
22	Th	3	1	·32	7	·45	—29
23	Fr	4	2	·32	8	·50	1
24	Sa	5	3	·35	9	·56	2
25	Su	6	4	·40	10	·64	3
26	Mo	7	5	·47	11	·73	4
27	Tu	8	6	·55	12	·83	5
28	We	9	7	·64	13	·94	6
29	Th	10	8	·72	...	...	7
30	Fr	11	9	·79	14	·05	8
31	Sa	12	10	·85	15	·14	9
—32	Su	13	11	·89	16	·22	10
1	Mo	14	12	·91	17	·28	11
2	Tu	15	13	·91	18	·32	12
3	We	16	14	·89	19	·35	13
4	Th	17	P	·84	20	·35	14
5	Fr	18	1	·78	21	·34	15
6	Sa	19	2	·71	22	·30	16
7	Su	20	3	·63	23	·25	17
8	Mo	21	4	·54	24	·19	18
9	Tu	22	5	·44	25	·13	19
10	We	23	6	·34	26 27	·06 ·99	20
11	Th	24	7	·24	1	·92	21
12	Fr	25	8	·14	2	·87	22
13	Sa	26	9 10	·05 ·96	3	·82	23
14	Su	27	11	·89	4	·78	24
15	Mo	28	12	·84	5	·75	25
16	Tu	29	13	·81	6	·75	26
17	We	30	14	·79	7	·76	27
18	Th	31	—A	·80	8	·80	28

Aug.

Solar: Anala, Simha—Avani. (from 1). Lunar: Sukla; Sravana; Bahula. Muhammadan: H. 1272 Zi-l-hijja.

Cyclic Sidereal Year, Month and Day	Week-Day	English Month and Day	Tithi	Ending Moment	Nakshatra	Ending Moment	Muhammadan Year, Month and Day
19	Fr	1	1	·83	9	·86	29
20	Sa	2	2	·88	10	·94	—30
21	Su	3	3	·94	...	...	1
22	Mo	4	...	...	11	·03	2
23	Tu	5	4	·02	12	·13	3
24	We	6	5	·11	13	·24	4
25	Th	7	6	·19	14	·35	5
26	Fr	8	7	·26	15	·45	6
27	Sa	9	8	·32	16	·53	7
28	Su	10	9	·37	17	·59	8
29	Mo	11	10	·39	18	·64	9
30	Tu	12	11	·40	19	·67	10
31	We	13	12	·38	20	·68	11
—32	Th	14	13	·34	21	·66	12
1	Fr	15	14	·29	22	·63	13
2	Sa	16	P	·22	23	·59	14
3	Su	17	1	·13	24	·53	15
4	Mo	18	2 3	·03 ·93	25	·47	16
5	Tu	19	4	·83	26	·40	17
6	We	20	5	·73	27	·33	18
7	Th	21	6	·63	1	·27	19
8	Fr	22	7	·54	2	·21	20
9	Sa	23	8	·46	3	·15	21
10	Su	24	9	·39	4	·11	22
11	Mo	25	10	·34	5	·08	23
12	Tu	26	11	·31	6	·07	24
13	We	27	12	·30	7	·09	25
14	Th	28	13	·30	8	·12	26
15	Fr	29	14	·33	9	·17	27
16	Sa	30	—A	·38	10	·24	28
17	Su	31	1	·44	11	·33	—29

Sep.

Solar: Anala, Simha—Avani. (to 31); Anala, Kanya—Purattasi. (from 1). Lunar: Sukla; Bhadrapada; Bahula. Muhammadan: H. 1273 Muharram.

Cyclic Sidereal Year, Month and Day	Week-Day	English Month and Day	Tithi	Ending Moment	Nakshatra	Ending Moment	Muhammadan Year, Month and Day
18	Mo	1	2	·62	12	·43	1
19	Tu	2	3	·61	13	·54	2
20	We	3	4	·70	14	·65	3
21	Th	4	5	·78	15	·75	4
22	Fr	5	6	·84	16	·84	5
23	Sa	6	7	·88	17	·91	6
24	Su	7	8	·90	18	·96	7
25	Mo	8	9	·91	19	·99	8
26	Tu	9	10	·89	...	...	9
27	We	10	11	·86	20 21	·00 ·99	10
28	Th	11	12	·81	22	·96	11
29	Fr	12	13	·74	23	·92	12
30	Sa	13	14	·65	24	·87	13
—31	Su	14	P	·56	25	·81	14
1	Mo	15	1	·46	26	·74	15
2	Tu	16	2	·36	27	·67	16
3	We	17	3	·26	1	·60	17
4	Th	18	4	·16	2	·54	18
5	Fr	19	5 6	·07 ·99	3	·48	19
6	Sa	20	7	·92	4	·44	20
7	Su	21	8	·87	5	·41	21
8	Mo	22	9	·84	6	·40	22
9	Tu	23	10	·84	7	·41	23
10	We	24	11	·85	8	·43	24
11	Th	25	12	·87	9	·48	25
12	Fr	26	13	·92	10	·55	26
13	Sa	27	14	·99	11	·64	27
14	Su	28	...	...	12	·74	28
15	Mo ●	29	—A	·07	13	·84	29
16	Tu	30	1	.16	14	·95	—30

Oct.

Solar: Anala, Kanya—Purattasi. (to 30); Anala, Tula—Aippasi. (from 1). Lunar: Sukla; Asvina; Bahula; Suk. Muhammadan: H. 1273 Safar.

Cyclic Sidereal Year, Month and Day	Week-Day	English Month and Day	Tithi	Ending Moment	Nakshatra	Ending Moment	Muhammadan Year, Month and Day
17	We	1	2	·24	...	...	1
18	Th	2	3	·32	15	·05	2
19	Fr	3	4	·39	16	·14	3
20	Sa	4	5	·43	17	·22	4
21	Su	5	6	·45	18	·28	5
22	Mo	6	7	·46	19	·31	6
23	Tu	7	8	·45	20	·32	7
24	We	8	9	·42	21	·32	8
25	Th	9	10	·36	22	·30	9
26	Fr	10	11	·29	23	·26	10
27	Sa	11	12	·21	24	·21	11
28	Su	12	13	·12	25	·14	12
29	Mo ○	13	14 P	·03 ·93	26	·07	13
—30	Tu	14	1	·83	27 1	·00 ·94	14
1	We	15	2	·73	2	·88	15
2	Th	16	3	·64	3	·82	16
3	Fr	17	4	·56	4	·77	17
4	Sa	18	5	·49	5	·74	18
5	Su	19	6	·44	6	·73	19
6	Mo	20	7	·42	7	·73	20
7	Tu	21	8	·42	8	·75	21
8	We	22	9	·44	9	·79	22
9	Th	23	10	·47	10	·86	23
10	Fr	24	11	·51	11	·94	24
11	Sa	25	12	·57	...	...	25
12	Su	26	13	·65	12	·04	26
13	Mo	27	14	·74	13	·14	27
14	Tu	28	—A	·83	14	·25	28
15	We	29	1	·91	15	·36	—29
16	Th	30	2	·98	16	·45	1
17	Fr	31	...	...	17	·53	2

Nov.

Solar: Anala, Tula—Aippasi. (to 30); Anala, Vrischika—Kartigai. (from 1). Lunar: Sukla; Kartika; Bahula. Muhammadan: H. 1273 Rabi-ul-awwal.

Cyclic Sidereal Year, Month and Day	Week-Day	English Month and Day	Tithi	Ending Moment	Nakshatra	Ending Moment	Muhammadan Year, Month and Day
18	Sa	1	3	·03	18	·59	3
19	Su	2	4	·05	19	·63	4
20	Mo	3	5	·05	20	·64	5
21	Tu	4	6	·04	21	·64	6
22	We	5	7 8	·01 ·96	22	·63	7
23	Th	6	9	·89	23	·59	8
24	Fr	7	10	·81	24	·54	9
25	Sa	8	11	·72	25	·48	10
26	Su	9	12	·62	26	·42	11
27	Mo	10	13	·52	27	·35	12
28	Tu	11	14	·42	1	·28	13
29	We	12	P	·33	2	·21	14
—30	Th	13	1	·24	3	·15	15
1	Fr	14	2	·17	4	·11	16
2	Sa	15	3	·11	5	·07	17
3	Su	16	4	·06	6	·05	18
4	Mo	17	5	·05	7	·05	19
5	Tu	18	6	·03	8	·06	20
6	We	19	7	·04	9	·11	21
7	Th	20	8	·07	10	·17	22
8	Fr	21	9	·13	11	·24	23
9	Sa	22	10	·20	12	·34	24
10	Su	23	11	·28	13	·44	25
11	Mo	24	12	·37	14	·54	26
12	Tu	25	13	·46	15	·65	27
13	We	26	14	·54	16	·75	28
14	Th	27	—A	·60	17	·84	29
15	Fr	28	1	·65	18	·90	—30
16	Sa	29	2	·68	19	·94	1
17	Su	30	3	·69	20	·97	2

Dec.

Solar: Anala, Vrischika—Kartigai. (to 29); Anala, Dhanus—Margali. (from 1). Lunar: Sukla; Margasira; Bahula; P. Suk. Muhammadan: H. 1273 Rabi-ul-akhir; J. awwal.

Cyclic Sidereal Year, Month and Day	Week-Day	English Month and Day	Tithi	Ending Moment	Nakshatra	Ending Moment	Muhammadan Year, Month and Day
18	Mo	1	4	·66	21	·97	3
19	Tu	2	5	·62	22	·95	4
20	We	3	6	·57	23	·92	5
21	Th	4	7	·51	24	·88	6
22	Fr	5	8	·44	25	·83	7
23	Sa	6	9	·35	26	·76	8
24	Su	7	10	·25	27	·69	9
25	Mo	8	11	·15	1	·62	10
26	Tu	9	12 13	·05 ·95	2	·56	11
27	We	10	14	·87	3	·50	12
28	Th	11	P	·80	4	·44	13
—29	Fr	12	1	·74	5	·40	14
1	Sa	13	2	·70	6	·38	15
2	Su	14	3	·67	7	·37	16
3	Mo	15	4	·66	8	·39	17
4	Tu	16	5	·69	9	·42	18
5	We	17	6	·73	10	·48	19
6	Th	18	7	·78	11	·55	20
7	Fr	19	8	·85	12	·64	21
8	Sa	20	9	·93	13	·74	22
9	Su	21	...	...	14	·85	23
10	Mo	22	10	·02	15	·96	24
11	Tu	23	11	·10	...	...	25
12	We	24	12	·18	16	·06	26
13	Th	25	13	·25	17	·14	27
14	Fr	26	14	·30	18	·21	28
15	Sa	27	—A	·32	19	·27	—29
16	Su	28	1	·33	20	·29	1
17	Mo	29	2	·31	21	·30	2
18	Tu	30	3	·27	22	·28	3
19	We	31	4	·22	23	·25	4

15. Svati. 16. Visak. 17. Anur. 18. Jyesh. 19. Mula. 20. P. Ash. 21. U. Ash. 22. Sravn. 23. Dani. 24. Satab. 25. P. Bhad. 26. U. Bhad. 27. Rev.

A. D. 1857. **Mesha Sankranti** (Commencement of Indian Sidereal Year).

Solar Eclipse. ● **(Surya Sid.) April 11·49.** **Saka 1779.** **Kaliyuga 4958.**

Lunar Eclipse. ○ **(Arya Sid.) April 11·39.** **(S. Cycle) Pingala.**

Columns: SOLAR reckoning — Cyclic Sidereal Year, Month and Day; Week-Day; English Month and Day. LUNAR reckoning — Tithi; Ending Moment; Nakshatra; Ending Moment; Muhammadan Year, Month and Day.

Jan. (Solar: *Anala Dhanus—Margali* to 30; *Anala Makara—Tai* from 1. Lunar: *Sukla*, **Pausha** P, *Bahula*. Muhammadan: *H. 1273 Jumadal-awwal* to 30.)

Cyclic Sidereal Year, Month and Day	Week-Day	English Month and Day	Tithi	Ending Moment	Nakshatra	Ending Moment	Muhammadan Year, Month and Day
20	Th	1	5	·15	24	·21	5
21	Fr	2	6 / 7	·07 / ·98	25	·16	6
22	Sa	3	8	·88	26	·19	7
23	Su	4	9	·78	27 / 1	·03 / ·96	8
24	Mo	5	10	·69	2	·90	9
25	Tu	6	11	·60	3	·84	10
26	We	7	12	·51	4	·78	11
27	Th	8	13	·44	5	·73	12
28	Fr	9	14	·33	6	·70	13
29	Sa	10	P	·34	7	·69	14
30	Su	11	1	·32	8	·71	15
1	Mo	12	2	·32	9	·74	16
2	Tu	13	3	·33	10	·78	17
3	We	14	4	·37	11	·85	18
4	Th	15	5	·42	12	·94	19
5	Fr	16	6	·50	...	...	20
6	Sa	17	7	·59	13	·04	21
7	Su	18	8	·68	14	·15	22
8	Mo	19	9	·77	15	·26	23
9	Tu	20	10	·84	16	·36	24
10	We	21	11	·90	17	·45	25
11	Th	22	12	·94	18	·52	26
12	Fr	23	13	·97	19	·58	27
13	Sa	24	14	·97	20	·61	28
14	Su	25	A	·95	21	·62	29
15	Mo	26	1	·92	22	·61	30
16	Tu	27	2	·86	23	·59	1
17	We	28	3	·79	24	·55	2
18	Th	29	4	·70	25	·50	3
19	Fr	30	5	·61	26	·44	4
20	Sa	31	6	·51	27	·38	5

Feb. (Solar: *Anala Kumbha—Masi* from 1. Lunar: *Sukla*, **Magha** P, *Bahula*, *P. Suk.* Muhammadan: *H. 1273 Jumadal-akhir*; *Rajab* from 1.)

Cyclic Sidereal Year, Month and Day	Week-Day	English Month and Day	Tithi	Ending Moment	Nakshatra	Ending Moment	Muhammadan Year, Month and Day
21	Su	1	7	·41	1	·31	6
22	Mo	2	8	·32	2	·24	7
23	Tu	3	9	·23	3	·17	8
24	We	4	10	·15	4	·11	9
25	Th	5	11	·08	5	·07	10
26	Fr	6	12 / 13	·02 / ·98	6	·04	11
27	Sa	7	14	·95	7	·03	12
28	Su	8	P	·95	8	·08	13
29	Mo	9	1	·97	9	·05	14
1	Tu	10	...	...	10	·09	15
2	We	11	2	·01	11	·16	16
3	Th	12	3	·07	12	·25	17
4	Fr	13	4	·14	13	·35	18
5	Sa	14	5	·22	14	·45	19
6	Su	15	6	·31	15	·55	20
7	Mo	16	7	·40	16	·66	21
8	Tu	17	8	·47	17	·75	22
9	We	18	9	·53	18	·83	23
10	Th	19	10	·58	19	·89	24
11	Fr	20	11	·60	20	·93	25
12	Sa	21	12	·60	21	·94	26
13	Su	22	13	·58	22	·94	27
14	Mo	23	14	·53	23	·92	28
15	Tu	24	A	·47	24	·89	29
16	We	25	1	·40	25	·84	1
17	Th	26	2	·32	26	·78	2
18	Fr	27	3	·23	27	·71	3
19	Sa	28	4	·13	1	·64	4

March (Solar: *Anala Kumbha—Masi* to 30; *Anala Mina—Panguni* from 1. Lunar: *Sukla*, **Phalguna** P, *Bahula*. Muhammadan: *H. 1273 Rajab* to 30.)

Cyclic Sidereal Year, Month and Day	Week-Day	English Month and Day	Tithi	Ending Moment	Nakshatra	Ending Moment	Muhammadan Year, Month and Day
20	Su	1	5 / 6	·03 / ·93	2	·57	5
21	Mo	2	7	·84	3	·51	6
22	Tu	3	8	·76	4	·45	7
23	We	4	9	·68	5	·40	8
24	Th	5	10	·62	6	·37	9
25	Fr	6	11	·58	7	·35	10
26	Sa	7	12	·57	8	·35	11
27	Su	8	13	·57	9	·37	12
28	Mo	9	14	·58	10	·41	13
29	Tu	10	P	·62	11	·47	14
30	We	11	1	·68	12	·55	15
1	Th	12	2	·75	13	·64	16
2	Fr	13	3	·83	14	·75	17
3	Sa	14	4	·92	15	·86	18
4	Su	15	...	...	16	·97	19
5	Mo	16	5	·00	...	...	20
6	Tu	17	6	·07	17	·08	21
7	We	18	7	·13	18	·14	22
8	Th	19	8	·17	19	·20	23
9	Fr	20	9	·20	20	·24	24
10	Sa	21	10	·19	21	·26	25
11	Su	22	11	·17	22	·27	26
12	Mo	23	12	·13	23	·25	27
13	Tu	24	13	·07	24	·22	28
14	We	25	14 / A	·00 / ·91	25	·17	29
15	Th	26	1	·81	26	·11	30
16	Fr	27	2	·71	27 / 1	·05 / ·98	1
17	Sa	28	3	·61	2	·91	2
18	Su	29	4	·52	3	·85	3
19	Mo	30	5	·43	4	·79	4
20	Tu	31	6	·34	5	·74	5

April (Solar: *Pingala Mesha—Chittirai* from 1. Lunar: *Sukla*, **Chaitra** P, *Bahula*, *Vsk. Suk.* Muhammadan: *H. 1273 Shaban* to 29; *H. 1273 Ramzan* from 1.)

Cyclic Sidereal Year, Month and Day	Week-Day	English Month and Day	Tithi	Ending Moment	Nakshatra	Ending Moment	Muhammadan Year, Month and Day
21	We	1	7	·26	6	·70	6
22	Th	2	8	·20	7	·68	7
23	Fr	3	9	·16	8	·67	8
24	Sa	4	10	·14	9	·68	9
25	Su	5	11	·13	10	·72	10
26	Mo	6	12	·15	11	·78	11
27	Tu	7	13	·19	12	·85	12
28	We	8	14	·25	13	·94	13
29	Th	9	P	·32	...	...	14
30	Fr	10	1	·39	14	·05	15
1	Sa	11	2	·48	15	·16	16
2	Su	12	3	·56	16	·27	17
3	Mo	13	4	·63	17	·36	18
4	Tu	14	5	·69	18	·44	19
5	We	15	6	·74	19	·51	20
6	Th	16	7	·75	20	·56	21
7	Fr	17	8	·74	21	·59	22
8	Sa	18	9	·72	22	·60	23
9	Su	19	10	·67	23	·58	24
10	Mo	20	11	·61	24	·55	25
11	Tu	21	12	·54	25	·51	26
12	We	22	13	·46	26	·45	27
13	Th	23	14	·36	27	·39	28
14	Fr	24	A	·26	1	·32	29
15	Sa	25	1	·16	2	·25	1
16	Su	26	2 / 3	·06 / ·97	3	·19	2
17	Mo	27	4	·88	4	·13	3
18	Tu	28	5	·80	5	·07	4
19	We	29	6	·74	6	·03	5
20	Th	30	7	·70	7 / 8	·00 / ·99	6

May (Solar: *Pingala Mesha—Chittirai* to 31; *Pingala Vrishabha—Vaikasi* from 1. Lunar: *Sukla*, **Vaisakha** P, *Bahula*, *Sukla*. Muhammadan: *H. 1273 Ramzan* to 30.)

Cyclic Sidereal Year, Month and Day	Week-Day	English Month and Day	Tithi	Ending Moment	Nakshatra	Ending Moment	Muhammadan Year, Month and Day
21	Fr	1	8	·67	...	...	7
22	Sa	2	9	·66	9	·04	8
23	Su	3	10	·68	10	·04	9
24	Mo	4	11	·72	11	·09	10
25	Tu	5	12	·77	12	·16	11
26	We	6	13	·84	13	·24	12
27	Th	7	14	·92	14	·34	13
28	Fr	8	...	...	15	·45	14
29	Sa	9	P	·00	16	·56	15
30	Su	10	1	·08	17	·66	16
31	Mo	11	2	·15	18	·75	17
1	Tu	12	3	·21	19	·82	18
2	We	13	4	·26	20	·88	19
3	Th	14	5	·28	21	·91	20
4	Fr	15	6	·27	22	·92	21
5	Sa	16	7	·24	23	·91	22
6	Su	17	8	·20	24	·88	23
7	Mo	18	9	·13	25	·84	24
8	Tu	19	10 / 11	·05 / ·97	26	·79	25
9	We	20	12	·87	27	·73	26
10	Th	21	13	·77	1	·66	27
11	Fr	22	14	·67	2	·59	28
12	Sa	23	A	·57	3	·53	29
13	Su	24	1	·47	4	·47	30
14	Mo	25	2	·38	5	·41	1
15	Tu	26	3	·30	6	·36	2
16	We	27	4	·24	7	·33	3
17	Th	28	5	·20	8	·32	4
18	Fr	29	6	·17	9	·33	5
19	Sa	30	7	·16	10	·35	6
20	Su	31	8	·17	11	·40	7

June (Solar: *Pingala Vrishabha—Vaikasi* to 32; *Pingala Mithuna—Ani* from 1. Lunar: **Jyeshtha** P, *Bahula*, **Ashadha** *Sukla*. Muhammadan: *H. 1273 Shawwal* to 29; *Zu-l-ka'da* from 1.)

Cyclic Sidereal Year, Month and Day	Week-Day	English Month and Day	Tithi	Ending Moment	Nakshatra	Ending Moment	Muhammadan Year, Month and Day
21	Mo	1	9	·21	12	·46	8
22	Tu	2	10	·27	13	·54	9
23	We	3	11	·34	14	·65	10
24	Th	4	12	·42	15	·76	11
25	Fr	5	13	·51	16	·86	12
26	Sa	6	14	·59	17	·96	13
27	Su	7	P	·66	...	...	14
28	Mo	8	1	·71	18	·05	15
29	Tu	9	2	·74	19	·13	16
30	We	10	3	·76	20	·19	17
31	Th	11	4	·75	21	·23	18
32	Fr	12	5	·73	22	·24	19
1	Sa	13	6	·68	23	·24	20
2	Su	14	7	·62	24	·22	21
3	Mo	15	8	·55	25	·18	22
4	Tu	16	9	·46	26	·13	23
5	We	17	10	·36	27	·07	24
6	Th	18	11	·26	1 / 2	·01 / ·94	25
7	Fr	19	12	·16	3	·87	26
8	Sa	20	13 / 14	·06 / ·96	4	·80	27
9	Su	21	A	·87	5	·74	28
10	Mo	22	1	·79	6	·69	29
11	Tu	23	2	·73	7	·66	1
12	We	24	3	·68	8	·65	2
13	Th	25	4	·65	9	·63	3
14	Fr	26	5	·64	10	·67	4
15	Sa	27	6	·65	11	·71	5
16	Su	28	7	·68	12	·77	6
17	Mo	29	8	·74	13	·85	7
18	Tu	30	9	·82	14	·95	8

Naksh :—1. Asvn. 2. Bhar. 3 Krit. 4. Rohi. 5. Mrig. 6. Ardh. 7. Puna. 8. Push. 9. Aslesh. 10. Magh. 11. P. Phal. 12. U. Phal. 13. Hasta. 14. Chit

A. D. 1857.
A.—Amavasya.
P.—Paurnami.

Kollam 1033, Commences { **N. Malabar—Sept.** / **S. Malabar—Aug.**

Hijra 1274, Commences, **Aug. 22.**

Vikrama 1914.
Bengal San 1263.
(N. Cycle) Sukla.

SOLAR reckoning: Cyclic Sidereal Year, Month and Day; Week-Day; English Month and Day. LUNAR reckoning: Tithi; Ending Moment; Nakshatra; Ending Moment; Muhammadan Year, Month and Day.

July

Cyclic Sidereal Year, Month and Day	Week-Day	English Month and Day	Tithi	Ending Moment	Nakshatra	Ending Moment	Muhammadan Year, Month and Day
19	We	1	*Sukla* 10	·88	…	…	9
20	Th	2	11	·97	15	·05	10
21	Fr	3	…	…	16	·15	11
Pingala *Mithuna—Ani.* 22	Sa	4	12	·05	17	·26	12
23	Su	5	**Ashadha** 13	·12	18	·36	13
24	Mo	6	14	·18	19	·44	14
25	Tu	7	P	·22	20	·50	15
26	We	8	1	·24	21	·54	16
27	Th	9	2	·23	22	·56	H. 1273 *Zi-l-ka'da.* 17
28	Fr	10	3	·21	23	·57	18
29	Sa	11	4	·16	24	·55	19
30	Su	12	5	·10	25	·51	20
—31	Mo	13	6 / 7	·03 / ·94	26	·47	21
1	Tu	14	*Bahula* 8	·84	27	·41	22
2	We	15	9	·74	1	·35	23
3	Th	16	10	·64	2	·28	24
4	Fr	17	11	·54	3	·21	25
5	Sa	18	12	·44	4	·14	26
6	Su	19	13	·35	5	·08	27
7	Mo	20	14	·27	6	·03	28
8	Tu	21	—A	·21	7 / 8	·00 / ·98	29
9	We	22	1	·17	9	·97	—30
10	Th	23	2	·14	10	·98	1
11	Fr	24	3	·12	…	…	2
12	Sa	25	4	·13	11	·02	3
13	Su	26	5	·16	12	·08	4
Pingala *Karkata—Adi.* 14	Mo	27	6	·21	13	·16	5
15	Tu	28	7	·28	14	·25	6
16	We	29	*Sukla* 8	·36	15	·35	7
17	Th	30	9	·45	16	·46	8
18	Fr	31	10	·52	17	·57	9

Aug.

Cyclic Sidereal Year, Month and Day	Week-Day	English Month and Day	Tithi	Ending Moment	Nakshatra	Ending Moment	Muhammadan Year, Month and Day
19	Sa	1	11	·59	18	·67	10
20	Su	2	12	·65	19	·75	11
21	Mo	3	**Sravana** 13	·69	20	·82	12
22	Tu	4	14	·72	21	·86	13
23	We	5	P	·71	22	·89	H. 1273 *Zi-l-hijja.* 14
24	Th	6	1	·70	23	·90	15
25	Fr	7	2	·65	24	·88	16
26	Sa	8	3	·59	25	·85	17
27	Su	9	4	·52	26	·80	18
28	Mo	10	5	·43	27	·74	19
29	Tu	11	*Bahula* 6	·34	1	·68	20
30	We	12	7	·24	2	·62	21
31	Th	13	8	·14	3	·55	22
—32	Fr	14	9 / 10	·04 / ·94	4	·48	23
1	Sa	15	11	·85	5	·42	24
2	Su	16	12	·77	6	·37	25
3	Mo	17	13	·70	7	·33	26
4	Tu	18	14	·65	8	·30	27
5	We	19	—A	·63	9	·29	28
6	Th	20	1	·62	10	·30	29
7	Fr	21	*Sukla* 2	·63	11	·34	—30
8	Sa	22	3	·65	12	·39	1
Pingala *Simha—Avani.* 9	Su	23	4	·70	13	·46	2
10	Mo	24	**Bhadrapada** 5	·77	14	·55	H. 1274 *Muharram.* 3
11	Tu	25	6	·86	15	·65	4
12	We	26	7	·95	16	·76	5
13	Th	27	…	…	17	·87	6
14	Fr	28	8	·03	18	·97	7
15	Sa	29	9	·10	…	…	8
16	Su	30	10	·16	19	·06	9
17	Mo	31	11	·20	20	·13	10

Sep.

Cyclic Sidereal Year, Month and Day	Week-Day	English Month and Day	Tithi	Ending Moment	Nakshatra	Ending Moment	Muhammadan Year, Month and Day
18	Tu	1	12	·23	21	·18	11
19	We	2	*Suk.* 13	·23	22	·21	12
20	Th	3	14	·21	23	·22	13
21	Fr	4	P	·17	24	·21	14
22	Sa	5	1	·12	25	·18	15
Pingala *Simha—Avani.* 23	Su	6	2 / 3	·04 / ·95	26	·13	16
24	Mo	7	4	·85	27	·08	17
25	Tu	8	**Bhadra.** 5	·75	1 / 2	·02 / ·95	18
26	We	9	6	·65	3	·88	H. 1274 *Muharram.* 19
27	Th	10	7	·55	4	·82	20
28	Fr	11	8	·45	5	·76	21
29	Sa	12	9	·37	6	·70	22
30	Su	13	*Bahula* 10	·30	7	·66	23
—31	Mo	14	11	·24	8	·63	24
1	Tu	15	12	·19	9	·61	25
2	We	16	13	·16	10	·63	26
3	Th	17	14	·15	11	·66	27
4	Fr	18	—A	·15	12	·70	28
5	Sa	19	1	·18	13	·77	29
6	Su	20	2	·24	14	·85	—30
7	Mo	21	3	·31	15	·96	1
8	Tu	22	4	·39	…	…	2
9	We	23	5	·47	16	·07	3
Pingala *Kanya—Purattasi.* 10	Th	24	6	·55	17	·17	4
11	Fr	25	7	·63	18	·27	5
12	Sa	26	*Sukla* 8	·69	19	·36	6
13	Su	27	9	·74	20	·43	7
14	Mo	28	10	·76	21	·49	8
15	Tu	29	11	·77	22	·53	9
16	We	30	12	·75	23	·54	10

Oct.

Cyclic Sidereal Year, Month and Day	Week-Day	English Month and Day	Tithi	Ending Moment	Nakshatra	Ending Moment	Muhammadan Year, Month and Day
17	Th	1	**Asvina** 13	·71	24	·53	11
18	Fr	2	14	·66	25	·51	12
19	Sa	3	P	·59	26	·48	13
20	Su	4	1	·51	27	·42	H. 1274 *Safar.* 14
21	Mo	5	2	·42	1	·36	15
22	Tu	6	3	·32	2	·29	16
23	We	7	4	·22	3	·22	17
24	Th	8	5	·12	4	·16	18
25	Fr	9	6 / 7	·02 / ·93	5	·10	19
26	Sa	10	*Bahula* 8	·86	6 / 7	·04 / ·99	20
27	Su	11	9	·80	8	·96	21
28	Mo	12	10	·75	9	·95	22
29	Tu	13	11	·72	10	·95	23
—30	We	14	12	·71	11	·97	24
1	Th	15	13	·72	…	…	25
2	Fr	16	14	·75	12	·01	26
3	Sa	17	—A	·81	13	·07	27
4	Su	18	1	·88	14	·15	28
5	Mo	19	2	·96	15	·25	—29
6	Tu	20	…	…	16	·36	1
7	We	21	*Sukla* 3	·05	17	·47	2
8	Th	22	4	·14	18	·57	3
Pingala *Tula—Aippasi.* 9	Fr	23	5	·22	19	·66	H. 1274 *Rabi-ul-awwal.* 4
10	Sa	24	6	·28	20	·74	5
11	Su	25	7	·32	21	·81	6
12	Mo	26	**Kartika** 8	·35	22	·85	7
13	Tu	27	9	·35	23	·86	8
14	We	28	10	·33	24	·86	9
15	Th	29	11	·30	25	·85	10
16	Fr	30	12	·25	26	·81	11
17	Sa	31	13	·18	27	·76	12

Nov.

Cyclic Sidereal Year, Month and Day	Week-Day	English Month and Day	Tithi	Ending Moment	Nakshatra	Ending Moment	Muhammadan Year, Month and Day
18	Su	1	14	·09	1	·70	13
19	Mo	2	P / 1	·00 / ·90	2	·64	14
20	Tu	3	**Karttika** 2	·80	3	·57	15
Pingala *Tula—Aippasi.* 21	We	4	3	·70	4	·50	16
22	Th	5	4	·61	5	·43	17
23	Fr	6	5	·53	6	·37	18
24	Sa	7	6	·45	7	·32	19
25	Su	8	7	·39	8	·29	20
26	Mo	9	8	·35	9	·27	H. 1274 *Rabi-ul-awwal.* 21
27	Tu	10	*Bahula* 9	·33	10	·27	22
28	We	11	10	·32	11	·28	23
29	Th	12	11	·32	12	·32	24
—30	Fr	13	12	·36	13	·38	25
1	Sa	14	13	·42	14	·46	26
2	Su	15	14	·49	15	·56	27
3	Mo	16	—A	·57	16	·66	28
4	Tu	17	1	·66	17	·77	29
5	We	18	2	·75	18	·88	—30
6	Th	19	3	·83	19	·98	1
7	Fr	20	4	·89	…	…	2
8	Sa	21	*Sukla* 5	·94	20	·06	3
9	Su	22	6	·97	21	·12	4
Pingala *Vrischika—Karttigai.* 10	Mo	23	7	·97	22	·16	5
11	Tu	24	8	·95	23	·18	6
12	We	25	**Margasira** 9	·91	24	·19	7
13	Th	26	10	·86	25	·18	*Rabi-ul-akhir.* 8
14	Fr	27	11	·80	26	·14	9
15	Sa	28	12	·72	27	·09	10
16	Su	29	13	·63	1 / 2	·04 / ·98	11
17	Mo	30	14	·53	3	·91	12

Dec.

Cyclic Sidereal Year, Month and Day	Week-Day	English Month and Day	Tithi	Ending Moment	Nakshatra	Ending Moment	Muhammadan Year, Month and Day
18	Tu	1	P	·43	4	·84	H. 1274 13
19	We	2	1	·33	5	·77	14
20	Th	3	2	·23	6	·71	15
21	Fr	4	3	·14	7	·65	16
22	Sa	5	4	·07	8	·62	17
23	Su	6	5 / 6	·02 / ·98	9	·60	18
24	Mo	7	*Bahula* 7	·95	10	·59	19
25	Tu	8	8	·95	11	·60	20
26	We	9	9	·96	12	·63	21
27	Th	10	…	…	13	·69	22
28	Fr	11	10	·00	14	·77	23
29	Sa	12	11	·06	15	·86	24
—30	Su	13	12	·14	16	·96	25
1	Mo	14	13	·23	…	…	26
2	Tu	15	14	·32	17	·07	27
3	We	16	—A	·40	18	·18	28
4	Th	17	1	·48	19	·28	—29
5	Fr	18	2	·54	20	·36	1
6	Sa	19	*Sukla* 3	·58	21	·43	2
7	Su	20	4	·61	22	·48	3
Pingala *Dhanus—Margali.* 8	Mo	21	5	·61	23	·51	4
9	Tu	22	6	·60	24	·52	5
10	We	23	7	·56	25	·50	H. 1274 *Jumadi-awwal.* 6
11	Th	24	**Pausha** 8	·50	26	·47	7
12	Fr	25	9	·43	27	·43	8
13	Sa	26	10	·35	1	·38	9
14	Su	27	11	·26	2	·32	10
15	Mo	28	12	·17	3	·25	11
16	Tu	29	13 / 14	·07 / ·97	4	·18	12
17	We	30	P	·87	5	·11	13
18	Th	31	1	·79	6	·05	14

15. Svati. 16. Visak. 17. Anur. 18. Jyesh. 19. Mula. 20. P. Ash. 21. U. Ash. 22. Sravn. 23. Dani. 24. Satab. 25. P. Bhad. 26. U. Bhad. 27. Rev.

A. D. 1858. **Mesha Sankranti** (Commencement of Indian Sidereal Year).

Solar Eclipse. ● **(Surya Sid.) April 11·75.** **Saka 1780.** **Kaliyuga 4959.**

Lunar Eclipse. ○ **(Arya Sid.) April 11·65.** **(S. Cycle) Kalayukta.**

SOLAR reckoning: Cyclic Sidereal Year, Month and Day; Week-Day; English Month and Day. LUNAR reckoning: Tithi; Ending Moment; Nakshatra; Ending Moment; Muhammadan Year, Month and Day.

Jan.

Cyclic Sidereal Year, Month and Day	Week-Day	English Month and Day	Tithi	Ending Moment	Nakshatra	Ending Moment	Muhammadan Year, Month and Day
Pingala Dhanus—Margali 19	Fr	1	Pausha 2	·72	7 8	·00 ·95	H. 1274 Jumadal-awwal 15
20	Sa	2	3	·66	9	·92	16
21	Su	3	4	·62	10	·91	17
22	Mo	4	5	·60	11	·92	18
23	Tu	5	6	·59	12	·96	19
24	We	6	7	·61	...	...	20
25	Th	7	8	·65	13	·01	21
26	Fr	8	Bahula 9	·70	14	·07	22
27	Sa	9	10	·78	15	·16	23
28	Su	10	11	·87	16	·26	24
—29	Mo	11	12	·96	17	·37	25
1	Tu	12	...	...	18	·48	26
2	We	13	13	·05	19	·58	27
3	Th	14	14	·13	20	·67	28
4	Fr	15	—A	·19	21	·74	29
5	Sa	16	1	·23	22	·80	—30
6	Su	17	2	·26	23	·83	1
7	Mo	18	3	·26	24	·84	2
8	Tu	19	4	·24	25	·83	3
9	We	20	Sukla 5	·20	26	·80	4
10	Th	21	6	·14	27	·76	5
11	Fr	22	7 8	·07 ·98	1	·72	6
Pingala Makara—Tai. 12	Sa	23	9	·89	2	·66	7
13	Su	24	10	·79	3	·59	8
14	Mo	25	11	·69	4	·52	Jumadal-akhir. 9
15	Tu	26	12	·60	5	·45	10
16	We	27	13	·51	6	·39	11
17	Th	28	Magha 14	·43	7	·33	12
18	Fr	29	P	·36	8	·29	13
19	Sa	30	1	·30	9	·26	14
20	Su	31	2	·26	10	·24	15

Feb.

Cyclic Sidereal Year, Month and Day	Week-Day	English Month and Day	Tithi	Ending Moment	Nakshatra	Ending Moment	Muhammadan Year, Month and Day
21	Mo	1	3	·24	11	25	H. 1274 16
22	Tu	2	4	·23	12	·27	17
23	We	3	5	·26	13	·31	18
24	Th	4	6	·30	14	·38	19
25	Fr	5	Bahula 7	36	15	·40	20
26	Sa	6	8	·43	16	·56	21
27	Su	7	9	·52	17	·67	22
28	Mo	8	10	·61	18	·78	23
29	Tu	9	11	·69	19	·88	24
—30	We	10	12	·77	20	·97	25
1	Th	11	13	·83	...	...	26
2	Fr	12	14	·88	21	·05	27
3	Sa	13	—A	·89	22	·11	28
4	Su	14	1	·89	23	·15	—29
5	Mo	15	2	·86	24	·10	1
6	Tu	16	Sukla 3	·82	25	·16	2
7	We	17	4	·76	26	·14	3
Pingala Kumbha—Masi. 8	Th	18	5	·69	27	·11	4
9	Fr	19	Phalguna 6	·61	1 2	·05 ·99	5
10	Sa	20	7	·52	3	·93	H. 1274 Rajab. 6
11	Su	21	8	·42	4	·86	7
12	Mo	22	9	·32	5	·79	8
13	Tu	23	10	·22	6	·73	9
14	We	24	11	·13	7	·67	10
15	Th	25	12 13	·04 ·97	8	·62	11
16	Fr	26	14	·92	9	·58	12
17	Sa ○	27	P	·88	10	·57	13
18	Su	28	1	·86	11	·57	14

March

Cyclic Sidereal Year, Month and Day	Week-Day	English Month and Day	Tithi	Ending Moment	Nakshatra	Ending Moment	Muhammadan Year, Month and Day
Pingala Kumbha—Masi. 19	Mo	1	Phalguna 2	·85	12	·59	15
20	Tu	2	3	·88	13	·62	16
21	We	3	4	·92	14	·68	17
22	Th	4	5	·98	15	·76	18
23	Fr	5	...	...	16	·86	H. 1274 Rajab. 19
24	Sa	6	6	·05	17	·97	20
25	Su	7	7	·14	...	...	21
26	Mo	8	8	·23	18	·08	22
27	Tu	9	9	·31	19	·18	23
28	We	10	Bahula 10	·38	20	·27	24
—29	Th	11	11	·44	21	·35	25
1	Fr	12	12	·48	22	·42	26
2	Sa	13	13	·49	23	·46	27
3	Su	14	14	·49	24	·48	28
4	Mo ●	15	—A	·47	25	·48	29
5	Tu	16	1	·42	26	·47	—30
6	We	17	2	·36	27	·44	1
7	Th	18	3	·28	1	·39	2
8	Fr	19	4	·20	2	·33	3
9	Sa	20	5	·11	3	·27	4
10	Su	21	6 7	·01 ·91	4	·20	5
11	Mo	22	Sukla 8	·81	5	·13	6
12	Tu	23	9	·72	6	·06	7
Pingala Mina—Panguni. 13	We	24	10	·63	7 8	·00 ·95	8
14	Th	25	11	·56	9	·92	H. 1274 Shaban. 9
15	Fr	26	12	·50	10	·90	10
16	Sa	27	Chaitra 13	·46	11	·89	11
17	Su	28	14	·44	12	·00	12
18	Mo	29	P	·44	13	·94	13
19	Tu	30	1	·46	14	·99	14
20	We	31	2	·50	...	...	15

April

Cyclic Sidereal Year, Month and Day	Week-Day	English Month and Day	Tithi	Ending Moment	Nakshatra	Ending Moment	Muhammadan Year, Month and Day
21	Th	1	3	·56	15	·07	16
22	Fr	2	4	·63	16	·16	17
23	Sa	3	5	·71	17	·26	18
24	Su	4	Bahula 6	·80	18	·37	19
25	Mo	5	7	·88	19	·48	20
26	Tu	6	8	·95	20	·58	21
27	We	7	...	...	21	·67	22
28	Th	8	9	·01	22	·73	23
29	Fr	9	10	·05	23	·78	24
30	Sa	10	11	·06	24	·80	25
—31	Su	11	12	·05	25	·81	26
1	Mo	12	13 14	·03 ·98	26	·80	27
2	Tu	13	—A	·92	27	·77	28
3	We	14	1	·85	1	·73	—29
4	Th	15	2	·76	2	·67	1
5	Fr	16	3	·67	3	·61	2
6	Sa	17	4	·57	4	·54	3
Kalayukta Mesha—Chittirai. 7	Su	18	5	·47	5	·47	4
8	Mo	19	Sukla 6	·37	6	·40	H. 1274 Ramzan. 5
9	Tu	20	7	·27	7	·34	6
10	We	21	8	·18	8	·28	7
11	Th	22	9	·10	9	·25	8
12	Fr	23	10	·05	10	·22	9
13	Sa	24	11 12	·01 ·98	11	·21	10
14	Su	25	Vaisakha 13	·98	12	·22	11
15	Mo	26	...	...	13	·25	12
16	Tu	27	14	·00	14	·31	13
17	We	28	P	·04	15	·38	14
18	Th	29	1	·09	16	·46	15
19	Fr	30	2	·16	17	·56	16

May

Cyclic Sidereal Year, Month and Day	Week-Day	English Month and Day	Tithi	Ending Moment	Nakshatra	Ending Moment	Muhammadan Year, Month and Day
Kalayukta Mesha—Chittirai. 20	Sa	1	Vaisakha 3	·24	18	·67	17
21	Su	2	4	·33	19	·78	18
22	Mo	3	5	·41	20	·88	19
23	Tu	4	6	·48	21	·97	H. 1274 Ramzan. 20
24	We	5	7	·54	...	...	21
25	Th	6	8	·57	22	·04	22
26	Fr	7	9	·59	23	·09	23
27	Sa	8	10	·58	24	·13	24
28	Su	9	Bahula 11	·56	25	·14	25
29	Mo	10	12	·51	26	·12	26
30	Tu	11	13	·45	27	·10	27
—31	We	12	14	·37	1	·06	28
1	Th	13	—A	·28	2 3	·01 ·95	29
2	Fr	14	1	·18	4	·88	—30
3	Sa	15	2 3	·08 ·98	5	·81	1
4	Su	16	4	·88	6	·74	2
5	Mo	17	Sukla 5	·78	7	·68	3
6	Tu	18	6	·70	8	·63	4
7	We	19	7	·62	9	·58	5
8	Th	20	8	·56	10	·55	6
9	Fr	21	9	·52	11	·53	7
10	Sa	22	10	·50	12	·54	8
Kalayukta Vrishabha—Vaikasi. 11	Su	23	11	·49	13	·57	9
12	Mo	24	12	·50	14	·62	H. 1274 Shawwal. 10
13	Tu	25	Adhika Jyeshtha 13	·54	15	·68	11
14	We	26	14	·60	16	·76	12
15	Th	27	P	·67	17	·86	13
16	Fr	28	1	·75	18	·97	14
17	Sa	29	2	·84	...	...	15
18	Su	30	3	·92	19	·08	16
19	Mo	31	4	·98	20	·18	17

June

Cyclic Sidereal Year, Month and Day	Week-Day	English Month and Day	Tithi	Ending Moment	Nakshatra	Ending Moment	Muhammadan Year, Month and Day
20	Tu	1	...	...	21	·27	18
21	We	2	5	·03	22	·35	19
22	Th	3	6	·06	23	·41	20
23	Fr	4	Bahula 7	·08	24	·45	21
24	Sa	5	8	·07	25	·46	22
25	Su	6	9	·05	26	·46	23
26	Mo	7	10 11	·01 ·95	27	·43	24
27	Tu	8	12	·87	1	·39	25
28	We	9	13	·78	2	·35	26
29	Th	10	14	·68	3	·29	27
30	Fr	11	—A	·58	4	·22	28
—31	Sa	12	1	·48	5	·15	—29
1	Su	13	2	·38	6	·08	1
2	Mo	14	3	·28	7 8	·02 ·96	2
3	Tu	15	4	·19	9	·91	3
4	We	16	Sukla 5	·11	10	·88	4
5	Th	17	6	·05	11	·86	5
Kalayukta Mithuna—Ani. 6	Fr	18	7 8	·00 ·98	12	·87	H. 1274 Zilka'da. 6
7	Sa	19	9	·97	13	·89	7
8	Su	20	10	·98	14	·93	8
9	Mo	21	...	...	15	·99	9
10	Tu	22	Nija Jyeshtha 11	·02	...	...	10
11	We	23	12	·07	16	·07	11
12	Th	24	13	·14	17	·17	12
13	Fr	25	14	·22	18	·27	13
14	Sa	26	P	·31	19	·38	14
15	Su	27	1	·38	20	·48	15
16	Mo	28	Bah. 2	·45	21	·58	16
17	Tu	29	3	·51	22	·67	17
18	We	30	4	·55	23	·73	18

Naksh :—1. Asvn. 2. Bhar. 3. Krit. 4. Rohi. 5. Mrig. 6. Ardh. 7. Punar. 8. Push. 9. Aslesh. 10. Magh. 11. P. Phal. 12. U. Phal. 13. Hasta. 14. Chit.

A. D. 1858.
A.—Amavasya. **P.—Paurnami.**

Kollam 1034, Commences { **N. Malabar—Sept.** **S. Malabar—Aug.**

Hijra 1275, Commences, **Aug. 11.**

Vikrama 1915.
Bengal San 1264.
(N. Cycle) Pramoda.

SOLAR reckoning. | LUNAR reckoning.

July

Kalayukta Mithuna—Ani. / Kalayukta Karkata—Adi.
Ni. Jy. Bahula / Ashadha Sukla
H. 1274 Zi-l-ka'dag. / H. 1274 Zi-l-hijja.

Cyclic Sidereal Year, Month and Day	Week-Day	English Month and Day	Tithi	Ending Moment	Nakshatra	Ending Moment	Muhammadan Year, Month and Day
19	Th	1	5	·57	24	·76	19
20	Fr	2	6	·56	25	·78	20
21	Sa	3	7	·54	26	·78	21
22	Su	4	8	·50	27	·76	22
23	Mo	5	9	·44	1	·73	23
24	Tu	6	10	·36	2	·68	24
25	We	7	11	·26	3	·62	25
26	Th	8	12	·16	4	·56	26
27	Fr	9	13 / 14	·06 / ·96	5	·50	27
28	Sa	10	—A	·86	6	·43	28
29	Su	11	1	·76	7	·36	29
30	Mo	12	2	·66	8	·30	—30
31	Tu	13	3	·58	9	·25	1
—32	We	14	4	·53	10	·21	2
1	Th	15	5	·49	11	·19	3
2	Fr	16	6	·46	12	·19	4
3	Sa	17	7	·44	13	·20	5
4	Su	18	8	·46	14	·24	6
5	Mo	19	9	·30	15	·30	7.
6	Tu	20	10	·55	16	·38	8
7	We	21	11	·62	17	·47	9
8	Th	22	12	·70	18	·57	10
9	Fr	23	13	·78	19	·68	11
10	Sa	24	14	·85	20	·78	12
11	Su	25	P	·92	21	·88	13
12	Mo	26	1	·98	22	·97	14
13	Tu	27	...	...	...	...	15
14	We	28	2	·02	23	·03	16
15	Th	29	3	·04	24	·08	17
16	Fr	30	4	·04	25	·10	18
17	Sa	31	5 / 6	·02 / ·97	26	·11	19

Aug.

Kalayukta Simha—Avani.
Bahula / Sravana Sukla / Bahula
H. 1275 Muharram.

Cyclic Sidereal Year, Month and Day	Week-Day	English Month and Day	Tithi	Ending Moment	Nakshatra	Ending Moment	Muhammadan Year, Month and Day
18	Su	1	7	·91	27	·10	20
19	Mo	2	8	·84	1	·07	21
20	Tu	3	9	·75	2 / 3	·02 / ·96	22
21	We	4	10	·65	4	·90	23
22	Th	5	11	·55	5	·84	24
23	Fr	6	12	·45	6	·77	25
24	Sa	7	13	·35	7	·70	26
25	Su	8	14	·25	8	·63	27
26	Mo	9	—A	·16	9	·58	28
27	Tu	10	1	·09	10	·55	—29
28	We	11	2 / 3	·02 / ·97	11	·52	1
29	Th	12	4	·94	12	·51	2
30	Fr	13	5	·94	13	·52	3
—31	Sa	14	6	·95	14	·55	4
1	Su	15	7	·98	15	·60	5
2	Mo	16	...	...	16	·68	6
3	Tu	17	8	·04	17	·77	7
4	We	18	9	·11	18	·87	8
5	Th	19	10	·19	19	·98	9
6	Fr	20	11	·28	...	...	10
7	Sa	21	12	·36	20	·08	11
8	Su	22	13	·43	21	·18	12
9	Mo	23	14	·48	22	·27	13
10	Tu	○ 24	P	·52	23	·34	14
11	We	25	1	·54	24	·39	15
12	Th	26	2	·54	25	·42	16
13	Fr	27	3	·52	26	·44	17
14	Sa	28	4	·48	27	·43	18
15	Su	29	5	·42	1	·40	19
16	Mo	30	6	·35	2	·35	20
17	Tu	31	7	·26	3	·30	21

Sep.

Kalayukta Simha—Avani. / Kalayukta Kanya—Purattasi.
Sr. Bahula / Bhadrapada Sukla / Bahula
H. 1275 Muharram. / H. 1275 Safar.

Cyclic Sidereal Year, Month and Day	Week-Day	English Month and Day	Tithi	Ending Moment	Nakshatra	Ending Moment	Muhammadan Year, Month and Day
18	We	1	8	·16	4	·24	22
19	Th	2	9 / 10	·06 / ·96	5	·17	23
20	Fr	3	11	·86	6	·10	24
21	Sa	4	12	·77	7 / 8	·03 / ·97	25
22	Su	5	13	·68	9	·92	26
23	Mo	6	14	·60	10	·88	27
24	Tu	7	—A	·58	11	·85	28
25	We	8	1	·49	12	·83	29
26	Th	9	2	·46	13	·84	—30
27	Fr	10	3	·46	14	·86	1
28	Sa	11	4	·47	15	·92	2
29	Su	12	5	·51	16	·99	3
30	Mo	13	6	·56	...	...	4
—31	Tu	14	7	·63	17	·07	5
1	We	15	8	·72	18	·17	6
2	Th	16	9	·80	19	·28	7
3	Fr	17	10	·88	20	·39	8
4	Sa	18	11	·95	21	·49	9
5	Su	19	...	...	22	·58	10
6	Mo	20	12	·01	23	·65	11
7	Tu	21	13	·05	24	·71	12
8	We	22	14	·07	25	·75	13
9	Th	23	P	·07	26	·76	14
10	Fr	24	1	·05	27	·75	15
11	Sa	25	2 / 3	·01 / ·95	1	·72	16
12	Su	26	4	·88	2	·69	17
13	Mo	27	5	·80	3	·64	18
14	Tu	28	6	·71	4	·58	19
15	We	29	7	·61	5	·51	20
16	Th	30	8	·51	6	·44	21

Oct.

Kalayukta Tula—Aippasi.
Asvina Sukla / Bahula
H. 1275 Rabi-ul-awwal.

Cyclic Sidereal Year, Month and Day	Week-Day	English Month and Day	Tithi	Ending Moment	Nakshatra	Ending Moment	Muhammadan Year, Month and Day
17	Fr	1	9	·41	7	·37	22
18	Sa	2	10	·32	8	·31	23
19	Su	3	11	·23	9	·26	24
20	Mo	4	12	·15	10	·21	25
21	Tu	5	13	·09	11	·17	26
22	We	6	14	·04	12	·16	27
23	Th	7	—A	·02	13	·16	28
24	Fr	8	1	·01	14	·19	—29
25	Sa	9	2	·02	15	·23	1
26	Su	10	3	·06	16	·29	2
27	Mo	11	4	·12	17	·37	3
28	Tu	12	5	·20	18	·47	4
29	We	13	6	·28	19	·58	5
30	Th	14	7	·37	20	·69	6
—31	Fr	15	8	·45	21	·79	7
1	Sa	16	9	·52	22	·88	8
2	Su	17	10	·58	23	·96	9
3	Mo	18	11	·62	...	...	10
4	Tu	19	12	·65	24	·03	11
5	We	20	13	·65	25	·07	12
6	Th	21	14	·63	26	·08	13
7	Fr	22	P	·59	27	·08	14
8	Sa	23	1	·54	1	·06	15
9	Su	24	2	·47	2 / 3	·03 / ·98	16
10	Mo	25	3	·39	4	·92	17
11	Tu	26	4	·29	5	·85	18
12	We	27	5	·19	6	·78	19
13	Th	28	6 / 7	·09 / ·99	7	·71	20
14	Fr	29	8	·90	8	·65	21
15	Sa	30	9	·82	9	·59	22
16	Su	31	10	·74	10	·54	23

Nov.

Kalayukta Tula—Aippasi. / Kalayukta Vrischika—Kartigai.
Bahula / Karttika Sukla / Bahula
R.-awwal. / H. 1275 Rabi-ul-akhir.

Cyclic Sidereal Year, Month and Day	Week-Day	English Month and Day	Tithi	Ending Moment	Nakshatra	Ending Moment	Muhammadan Year, Month and Day
17	Mo	1	11	·68	11	·50	24
18	Tu	2	12	·64	12	·48	25
19	We	3	13	·62	13	·49	26
20	Th	4	14	·61	14	·51	27
21	Fr	5	—A	·62	15	·54	28
22	Sa	6	1	·66	16	·60	29
23	Su	7	2	·71	17	·68	—30
24	Mo	8	3	·79	18	·78	1
25	Tu	9	4	·88	19	·88	2
26	We	10	5	·97	20	·99	3
27	Th	11	...	...	...	...	4
28	Fr	12	6	·05	21	·09	5
—29	Sa	13	7	·13	22	·19	6
1	Su	14	8	·19	23	·28	7
2	Mo	15	9	·24	24	·34	8
3	Tu	16	10	·26	25	·38	9
4	We	17	11	·25	26	·40	10
5	Th	18	12	·23	27	·40	11
6	Fr	19	13	·20	1	·39	12
7	Sa	20	14	·15	2	·36	13
8	Su	21	P	·08	3	·31	14
9	Mo	22	1 / 2	·00 / ·91	4	·25	15
10	Tu	23	3	·81	5	·19	16
11	We	24	4	·71	6	·13	17
12	Th	25	5	·61	7 / 8	·06 / ·99	18
13	Fr	26	6	·52	9	·93	19
14	Sa	27	7	·43	10	·87	20
15	Su	28	8	·36	11	·84	21
16	Mo	29	9	·30	12	·82	22
17	Tu	30	10	·26	13	·81	23

Dec.

Kalayukta Dhanus—Margali.
Sukla / Margasira / Bahula
H. 1275 Jumadal-awwal.

Cyclic Sidereal Year, Month and Day	Week-Day	English Month and Day	Tithi	Ending Moment	Nakshatra	Ending Moment	Muhammadan Year, Month and Day
18	We	1	11	·24	14	.82	24
19	Th	2	12	·23	15	·85	25
20	Fr	3	13	·25	16	·91	26
21	Sa	4	14	·29	17	·99	27
22	Su	5	—A	·35	...	...	28
23	Mo	6	1	·42	18	·08	—29
24	Tu	7	2	·51	19	·18	1
25	We	8	3	·60	20	·28	2
26	Th	9	4	·68	21	·39	3
27	Fr	10	5	·76	22	·49	4
28	Sa	11	6	·83	23	·58	5
29	Su	12	7	·88	24	·65	6
—30	Mo	13	8	·90	25	·70	7
1	Tu	14	9	·90	26	·72	8
2	We	15	10	·88	27	·73	9
3	Th	16	11	·84	1	·72	10
4	Fr	17	12	·78	2	·69	11
5	Sa	18	13	·71	3	·65	12
6	Su	19	14	·63	4	·59	13
7	Mo	20	P	·54	5	·53	14
8	Tu	21	1	·44	6	·47	15
9	We	22	2	·34	7	·40	16
10	Th	23	3	·24	8	·33	17
11	Fr	24	4	·15	9	·26	18
12	Sa	25	5	·07	10	·21	19
13	Su	26	6 / 7	·00 / ·94	11	·17	20
14	Mo	27	8	·90	12	·14	21
15	Tu	28	9	·88	13	·13	22
16	We	29	10	·89	14	·14	23
17	Th	30	11	·91	15	·17	24
18	Fr	31	12	·94	16	·22	25

A. D. 1859. **Mesha Sankranti** (Commencement of Indian Sidereal Year).
Solar Eclipse. ● **(Surya Sid.) April 12·01.** **Saka 1781.** **Kaliyuga 4960.**
Lunar Eclipse. ○ **(Arya Sid.) April 11·91.** **(S. Cycle) Siddharthi.**

SOLAR reckoning: Cyclic Sidereal Year, Month and Day	Week-Day	English Month and Day	LUNAR reckoning: Tithi	Ending Moment	Nakshatra	Ending Moment	Muhammadan Year, Month and Day
		Jan.					
Kalayukta, Dhanus—Margali. 19	Sa	1	Bah. ...	...	17	·29	J. uowal. 26
20	Su	2	13	·00	18	·38	27
21	Mo	3	14	·08	19	·48	28
22	Tu	4	—A	·17	20	·58	29
23	We	5	1	·26	21	·69	—30
24	Th	6	2	·35	22	·80	1
25	Fr	7	3	·42	23	·89	2
26	Sa	8	4	·48	24	·96	3
27	Su	9	5	·52	...	...	4
28	Mo	10	6	·54	25	·01	5
—29	Tu	11	Sukla 7	·54	26	·04	6
1	We	12	8	·53	27	·06	7
2	Th	13	9	·48	1	·05	8
3	Fr	14	10	·42	2 3	·02 ·98	9
4	Sa	15	11	·35	4	·93	H. 1275 Jumadal-akhir. 10
5	Su	16	12	·27	5	·88	11
6	Mo	17	13	·18	6	·81	12
7	Tu	18	Pausha 14 P	·08 ·98	7	·74	13
8	We	19	1	·88	8	·67	14
9	Th	20	2	·79	9	·60	15
10	Fr	21	3	·71	10	·55	16
Kalayukta, Makara—Tai. 11	Sa	22	4	·64	11	·50	17
12	Su	23	5	·58	12	·47	18
13	Mo	24	6	·54	13	·46	19
14	Tu	25	Bahula 7	·52	14	·46	20
15	We	26	8	·53	15	·49	21
16	Th	27	9	·55	16	·53	22
17	Fr	28	10	·60	17	·60	23
18	Sa	29	11	·66	18	·68	24
19	Su	30	12	·73	19	·78	25
20	Mo	31	13	·81	20	·89	26
		Feb.					
21	Tu	1	14	·90	...	...	27
22	We	2	—A	·99	21	·00	28
23	Th	3	...	...	22	·10	—29
24	Fr	4	1	·07	23	·19	1
25	Sa	5	2	·13	24	·26	2
26	Su	6	3	·16	25	·32	3
27	Mo	7	4	·18	26	·37	4
28	Tu	8	5	·18	27	·38	5
29	We	9	Sukla 6	·16	1	·38	6
—30	Th	10	7	·11	2	·35	7
1	Fr	11	8 9	·04 ·97	3	·32	8
2	Sa	12	10	·89	4	·27	9
3	Sa	13	11	·80	5	·21	H. 1275 Rajab. 10
4	Mo	14	12	·70	6	·14	11
5	Tu	15	13	·60	7	·07	12
Kalayukta, Kumbha—Masi. 6	We	16	Magha 14	·30	8 9	·01 ·95	13
7	Th ○	17	P	·41	10	·89	14
8	Fr	18	1	·33	11	·84	15
9	Sa	19	2	·26	12	·80	16
10	Su	20	3	·20	13	·78	17
11	Mo	21	4	·16	14	·78	18
12	Tu	22	5	·15	15	·81	19
13	We	23	Bahula 6	·15	16	·84	20
14	Th	24	7	·17	17	·90	21
15	Fr	25	8	·22	18	·98	22
16	Sa	26	9	·28	...	...	23
17	Su	27	10	·35	19	·07	24
18	Mo	28	11	·44	20	·18	25

SOLAR reckoning: Cyclic Sidereal Year, Month and Day	Week-Day	English Month and Day	LUNAR reckoning: Tithi	Ending Moment	Nakshatra	Ending Moment	Muhammadan Year, Month and Day
		March					
Kalayukta, Kumbha—Masi. 19	Tu	1	Bah. 12	·53	21	·29	Rajab. 26
20	We	2	13	·61	22	·40	27
21	Th	3	14	·68	23	·49	28
22	Fr	4	—A	·74	24	·57	29
23	Sa	5	1	·78	25	·64	—30
24	Su	6	2	·79	26	·68	1
25	Mo	7	3	·79	27	·70	2
26	Tu	8	4	·76	1	·70	3
27	We	9	5	·71	2	·68	4
28	Th	10	6	·65	3	·66	5
29	Fr	11	Sukla 7	·58	4	·61	6
—30	Sa	12	8	·49	5	·55	7
1	Su	13	9	·40	6	·48	8
2	Mo	14	10	·30	7	·41	9
3	Tu	15	11	·20	8	·34	10
4	We	16	12	·10	9	·28	11
5	Th	17	13 14	·01 ·92	10	·22	H. 1275 Shaban. 12
6	Fr	18	Phalguna P	·85	11	·17	13
7	Sa	19	1	·80	12	·13	14
8	Su	20	2	·77	13	·11	15
9	Mo	21	3	·75	14	·11	16
10	Tu	22	4	·74	15	·12	17
11	We	23	5	·77	16	·16	18
Kalayukta, Mina—Panguni. 12	Th	24	6	·81	17	·21	19
13	Fr	25	7	·87	18	·28	20
14	Sa	26	8	·95	19	·37	21
15	Su	27	Bahula ...	...	20	·48	22
16	Mo	28	9	·03	21	·59	23
17	Tu	29	10	·12	22	·70	24
18	We	30	11	·20	23	·79	25
19	Th	31	12	·27	24	·88	26
		April					
20	Fr	1	13	·32	25	·95	27
21	Sa	2	14	·36	...	...	28
22	Su	3	—A	·37	26	·00	—29
23	Mo	4	1	·36	27	·02	1
24	Tu	5	2	·33	1	·03	2
25	We	6	3	·29	2 3	·02 ·99	3
26	Th	7	4	·23	4	·94	4
27	Fr	8	5	·15	5	·89	5
28	Sa	9	6 7	·06 ·96	6	·82	6
29	Su	10	Sukla 8	·86	7	·75	7
—30	Mo	11	9	·76	8	·68	8
1	Tu	12	10	·66	9	·62	9
2	We	13	11	·57	10	·56	10
3	Th	14	12	·48	11	·50	11
4	Fr	15	13	·41	12	·46	H. 1275 Ramzan. 12
5	Sa	16	Chaitra 14	·35	13	·44	13
6	Su	17	P	·31	14	·43	14
7	Mo	18	1	·30	15	·44	15
Siddharthi, Mesha—Chittirai. 8	Tu	19	2	·30	16	·47	16
9	We	20	3	·32	17	·53	17
10	Th	21	4	·35	18	·60	18
11	Fr	22	5	·41	19	·68	19
12	Sa	23	6	·48	20	·78	20
13	Su	24	Bahula 7	·57	21	·89	21
14	Mo	25	8	·66	...	...	22
15	Tu	26	9	·74	22	·00	23
16	We	27	10	·81	23	·10	24
17	Th	28	11	·86	24	·19	25
18	Fr	29	12	·89	25	·26	26
19	Sa	30	13	·90	26	·31	27

SOLAR reckoning: Cyclic Sidereal Year, Month and Day	Week-Day	English Month and Day	LUNAR reckoning: Tithi	Ending Moment	Nakshatra	Ending Moment	Muhammadan Year, Month and Day
		May					
Siddharthi, Mesha—Chittirai. 20	Su	1	14	·90	27	·34	28
21	Mo	2	—A	·87	1	·35	29
22	Tu	3	1	·82	2	·35	—30
23	We	4	2	·76	3	·32	1
24	Th	5	3	·68	4	·28	2
25	Fr	6	4	·59	5	·22	3
26	Sa	7	5	·49	6	·16	4
27	Su	8	6	·39	7	·10	5
28	Mo	9	Sukla 7	·29	8 9	·03 ·96	6
29	Tu	10	8	·19	10	·89	7
30	We	11	9	·09	11	·84	8
—31	Th	12	10 11	·00 ·93	12	·80	9
1	Fr	13	12	·87	13	·77	H. 1275 Shawwal. 10
2	Sa	14	Vaisakha 13	·83	14	·75	11
3	Su	15	14	·81	15	·76	12
4	Mo	16	P	·81	16	·78	13
5	Tu	17	1	·84	17	·84	14
6	We	18	2	·86	18	·91	15
7	Th	19	3	·93	19	·99	16
8	Fr	20	...	...	...	...	17
9	Sa	21	4	·00	20	·08	18
10	Su	22	5	·08	21	·19	19
Siddharthi, Vrishabha—Vaikasi. 11	Mo	23	6	·17	22	·30	20
12	Tu	24	Bahula 7	·25	23	·41	21
13	We	25	8	·31	24	·50	22
14	Th	26	9	·36	25	·57	23
15	Fr	27	10	·40	26	·62	24
16	Sa	28	11	·41	27	·66	25
17	Su	29	12	·40	1	·68	26
18	Mo	30	13	·37	2	·67	27
19	Tu	31	14	·33	3	·65	28
		June					
20	We	1	—A	·26	4	·61	—29
21	Th	2	1	·18	5	·56	1
22	Fr	3	2 3	·09 ·99	6	·51	2
23	Sa	4	4	·89	7	·44	3
24	Su	5	5	·79	8	·37	4
25	Mo	6	6	·69	9	·30	5
26	Tu	7	Sukla 7	·59	10	·23	6
27	We	8	8	·50	11	·18	7
28	Th	9	9	·43	12	·13	8
29	Fr	10	10	·37	13	·10	9
30	Sa	11	11	·32	14	·08	10
—31	Su	12	12	·30	15	·08	11
1	Mo	13	13	·30	16	·11	H. 1275 Zilka'da. 12
2	Tu	14	Jyeshtha 14	·31	17	·15	13
3	We	15	P	·35	18	·21	14
4	Th	16	1	·41	19	·29	15
5	Fr	17	2	·48	20	·38	16
6	Sa	18	3	·56	21	·48	17
Siddharthi, Mithuna—Ani. 7	Su	19	4	·64	22	·59	18
8	Mo	20	5	·72	23	·70	19
9	Tu	21	Bahula 6	·79	24	·80	20
10	We	22	7	·84	25	·88	21
11	Th	23	8	·88	26	·94	22
12	Fr	24	9	·89	27	·98	23
13	Sa	25	10	·88	...	...	24
14	Su	26	11	·85	1	·00	25
15	Mo	27	12	·81	2 3	·00 ·98	26
16	Tu	28	13	·75	4	·94	27
17	We	29	14	·67	5	·90	28
18	Th	30	—A	·58	6	·84	29

Naksh :—1. Asvn. 2. Bhar. 3. Krit. 4. Rohi. 5. Mrig. 6. Ardh. 7. Punar. 8. Push. 9. Aslesh. 10. Magh. 11. P. Phal. 12. U. Phal. 13. Hasta. 14. Chit.

A. D. 1859.			Vikrama 1916.
A.—Amavasya.	Kollam 1035, { N. Malabar—Sept.	Hijra 1276,	Bengal San 1265.
P.—Paurnami.	Commences { S. Malabar—Aug.	Commences, July 31.	(N. Cycle) Prajapati.

SOLAR reckoning: Cyclic Sidereal Year, Month and Day	Week-Day	English Month and Day	LUNAR reckoning: Tithi	Ending Moment	Nakshatra	Ending Moment	Muhammadan Year, Month and Day
		July					
19	Fr	1	1	·48	7	·78	—30
20	Sa	2	2	·38	8	·71	1
21	Su	3	3	·27	9	·64	2
22	Mo	4	4	·17	10	·58	3
Siddharthi *Mithuna—Ani.*			**Ashadha** *Sukla*				*H. 1275 Zi-l-hijja.*
23	Tu	5	5 6	·07 ·98	11	·52	4
24	We	6	7	·90	12	·47	5
25	Th	7	8	·85	13	·43	6
26	Fr	8	9	·80	14	·40	7
27	Sa	9	10	·77	15	·41	8
28	Su	10	11	·77	16	·43	9
29	Mo	11	12	·79	17	·46	10
30	Tu	12	13	·83	18	·51	11
31	We	13	14	·88	19	·59	12
—32	Th	14	P	·96	20	·68	13
1	Fr	15	...	...	21	·79	14
2	Sa	16	1	·04	22	·90	15
3	Su	17	2	·11	...	...	16
4	Mo	18	3	·18	23	·00	17
5	Tu	19	4	·25	24	·10	18
6	We	20	5	·32	25	·18	19
			Bahula				
7	Th	21	6	·35	26	·25	20
8	Fr	22	7	·37	27	·30	21
9	Sa	23	8	·36	1	·32	22
10	Su	24	9	·33	2	·32	23
Siddharthi *Karkata—Adi.*							
11	Mo	25	10	·28	3	·31	24
12	Tu	26	11	·22	4	·29	25
13	We	27	12	·15	5	·24	26
14	Th	28	13 14	·07 ·97	6	·18	27
15	Fr	29	—A	·87	7	·12	28
16	Sa	30	1	·77	8 9	·05 ·98	—29
17	Su	31	2	·67	10	·92	1
		Aug.					
18	Mo	1	3	·57	11	·85	2
19	Tu	2	4	·48	12	·80	3
20	We	3	5	·40	13	·76	4
			Sukla				
21	Th	4	6	·33	14	·73	5
22	Fr	5	7	·29	15	·73	6
23	Sa	6	8	·27	16	·74	7
24	Su	7	9	·26	17	·77	8
25	Mo	8	10	·26	18	·82	9
26	Tu	9	11	·30	19	·89	10
			Sravana				*H. 1276 Muharram.*
27	We	10	12	·36	20	·99	11
28	Th	11	13	·44	...	...	12
29	Fr	12	14	·52	21	·09	13
30	Sa ○	13	P	·60	22	·20	14
—31	Su	14	1	·68	23	·30	15
1	Mo	15	2	·75	24	·40	16
2	Tu	16	3	·81	25	·49	17
3	We	17	4	·84	26	·56	18
4	Th	18	5	·86	27	·61	19
5	Fr	19	6	·85	1	·64	20
			Bahula				
6	Sa	20	7	·83	2	·65	21
Siddharthi *Simha—Avani.*							
7	Su	21	8	·79	3	·65	22
8	Mo	22	9	·73	4	·62	23
9	Tu	23	10	·65	5	·57	24
10	We	24	11	·56	6	·52	25
11	Th	25	12	·47	7	·46	26
12	Fr	26	13	·37	8	·39	27
13	Sa	27	14	·27	9	·32	28
14	Su	28	—A	·17	10	·25	29
15	Mo	29	1 2	·07 ·98	11	·19	—30
16	Tu	30	3	·90	12	·13	1
17	We	31	4	·84	13	·09	2

SOLAR reckoning: Cyclic Sidereal Year, Month and Day	Week-Day	English Month and Day	LUNAR reckoning: Tithi	Ending Moment	Nakshatra	Ending Moment	Muhammadan Year, Month and Day
		Sep.					
18	Th	1	5	·80	14	·07	3
19	Fr	2	6	·78	15	·05	4
			Sukla				
20	Sa	3	7	·77	16	·06	5
Siddharthi *Simha—Avani.*							
21	Su	4	8	·79	17	·08	6
22	Mo	5	9	·82	18	·13	7
23	Tu	6	10	·87	19	·21	8
24	We	7	11	·94	20	·29	9
			Bhadrapada				
25	Th	8	...	...	21	·39	10
26	Fr	9	12	·02	22	·50	11
27	Sa	10	13	·11	23	·60	12
28	Su	11	14	·19	24	·70	13
							H. 1276 Safar.
29	Mo	12	P	·27	25	·79	14
30	Tu	13	1	·33	26	·87	15
—31	We	14	2	·37	27	·93	16
1	Th	15	3	·39	1	·96	17
2	Fr	16	4	·38	2	·98	18
3	Sa	17	5	·36	3	·97	19
4	Su	18	6	·32	4	·95	20
			Bahula				
5	Mo	19	7	·26	5	·91	21
6	Tu	20	8	·18	6	·85	22
7	We	21	9	·10	7	·79	23
8	Th	22	10 11	·01 ·91	8	·73	24
Siddharthi *Kanya—Purattasi.*							
9	Fr	23	12	·81	9	·66	25
10	Sa	24	13	·71	10	·59	26
11	Su	25	14	·61	11	·53	27
12	Mo	26	—A	·52	12	·47	28
13	Tu	27	1	·45	13	·43	—29
14	We	28	2	·39	14	·39	1
15	Th	29	3	·34	15	·38	2
16	Fr	30	4	·32	16	·38	3
		Oct.					
			Sukla				
17	Sa	1	5	·31	17	·40	4
18	Su	2	6	·33	18	·45	5
19	Mo	3	7	·36	19	·51	6
20	Tu	4	8	·42	20	·59	7
21	We	5	9	·49	21	·69	8
22	Th	6	10	·57	22	·80	9
23	Fr	7	11	·66	23	·91	10
			Asvina				*H. 1276 Rabi-ul-awwal.*
24	Sa	8	12	·75	...	...	11
25	Su	9	13	·83	24	·01	12
26	Mo	10	14	·89	25	·10	13
27	Tu	11	P	·93	26	·18	14
28	We	12	1	·95	27	·24	15
29	Th	13	2	·95	1	·28	16
30	Fr	14	3	·92	2	·30	17
—31	Sa	15	4	·88	3	·30	18
1	Su	16	5	·82	4	·28	19
			Bahula				
2	Mo	17	6	·75	5	·24	20
3	Tu	18	7	·67	6	·19	21
4	We	19	8	·58	7	·14	22
5	Th	20	9	·48	8	·07	23
Siddharthi *Tula—Aippasi.*							
6	Fr	21	10	·38	9 10	·00 ·93	24
7	Sa	22	11	·28	11	·86	25
8	Su	23	12	·19	12	·81	26
9	Mo	24	13	·10	13	·76	27
10	Tu	25	14 A	·03 ·97	14	·73	28
			Kartt. *Suk.*				*R.-akhir.*
11	We	26	1	·92	15	·70	29
12	Th	27	2	·90	16	·70	—30
13	Fr	28	3	·90	17	·72	1
14	Sa	29	4	·92	18	·76	2
15	Su	30	5	·96	19	·82	3
16	Mo	31	...	...	20	·90	4

SOLAR reckoning: Cyclic Sidereal Year, Month and Day	Week-Day	English Month and Day	LUNAR reckoning: Tithi	Ending Moment	Nakshatra	Ending Moment	Muhammadan Year, Month and Day
		Nov.					
			Sukla				
17	Tu	1	6	·02	21	·99	5
18	We	2	7	·09	...	...	6
19	Th	3	8	·18	22	·10	7
Siddharthi *Tula—Aippasi.*							
20	Fr	4	9	·27	23	·21	8
21	Sa	5	10	·36	24	·31	9
22	Su	6	11	·43	25	·41	10
23	Mo	7	12	·49	26	·49	11
			Karttika				*H. 1276 Rabi-ul-akhir.*
24	Tu	8	13	·52	27	·55	12
25	We	9	14	·54	1	·60	13
26	Th	10	P	·55	2	·62	14
27	Fr	11	1	·52	3	·62	15
28	Sa	12	2	·48	4	·61	16
29	Su	13	3	·43	5	·57	17
—30	Mo	14	4	·37	6	·53	18
1	Tu	15	5	·28	7	·48	19
2	We	16	6	·18	8	·41	20
3	Th	17	7 8	·08 ·98	9	·34	21
			Bahula				
4	Fr	18	9	·89	10	·27	22
5	Sa	19	10	·80	11	·21	23
6	Su	20	11	·72	12	·15	24
7	Mo	21	12	·65	13	·09	25
Siddharthi *Vrischika—Kartigai.*							
8	Tu	22	13	·58	14	·05	26
9	We	23	14	·54	15	·03	27
10	Th	24	—A	·52	16	·02	28
11	Fr	25	1	·53	17	·04	—29
12	Sa	26	2	·55	18	·07	1
13	Su	27	3	·58	19	·13	2
			Sukla				
14	Mo	28	4	·64	20	·20	3
15	Tu	29	5	·72	21	·29	4
16	We	30	6	·81	22	·39	5
		Dec.					
17	Th	1	7	·90	23	·50	6
18	Fr	2	8	·98	24	·61	7
19	Sa	3	...	...	25	·71	8
			Margasira				*H. 1276 Jumada-l-awwal.*
20	Su	4	9	·06	26	·79	9
21	Mo	5	10	·12	27	·87	10
22	Tu	6	11	·16	1	·92	11
23	We	7	12	·18	2	·94	12
24	Th	8	13	·18	3	·95	13
25	Fr	9	14	·15	4	·93	14
26	Sa	10	P	·11	5	·91	15
27	Su	11	1 2	·05 ·98	6	·87	16
28	Mo	12	3	·90	7	·81	17
—29	Tu	13	4	·81	8	·75	18
1	We	14	5	·71	9	·69	19
			Bahula				
2	Th	15	6	·61	10	·62	20
3	Fr	16	7	·52	11	·55	21
4	Sa	17	8	·43	12	·48	22
5	Su	18	9	·35	13	·42	23
Siddharthi *Dhanus—Margali.*							
6	Mo	19	10	·27	14	·38	24
7	Tu	20	11	·22	15	·36	25
8	We	21	12	·18	16	·35	26
9	Th	22	13	·17	17	·30	27
10	Fr	23	14	·17	18	·39	28
11	Sa	24	—A	·19	19	·48	29
			Pausha *Suk.*				*J.-akhir.*
12	Su	25	1	·24	20	·50	—30
13	Mo	26	2	·30	21	·60	1
14	Tu	27	3	·38	22	·70	2
15	We	28	4	·46	23	·80	3
16	Th	29	5	55	24	·91	4
17	Fr	30	6	·64	...	...	5
18	Sa	31	7	·71	25	·01	6

15. Svati. 16. Visak. 17. Anur. 18. Jyesh. 19. Mula. 20. P. Ash. 21. U. Ash. 22. Sravn. 23. Dani. 24. Satab. 25. P. Bhad. 26. U. Bhad. 27. Rev.

A. D. 1860. **Mesha Sankranti** (Commencement of Indian Sidereal Year).

Solar Eclipse. ● (Surya Sid.) April 11·27. Saka 1782. Kaliyuga 4961.

Lunar Eclipse. ○ (Arya Sid.) April 11·17. (S. Cycle) Randra.

SOLAR reckoning: Cyclic Sidereal Year, Month and Day; Week-Day; English Month and Day. LUNAR reckoning: Tithi; Ending Moment; Nakshatra; Ending Moment; Muhammadan Year, Month and Day.

Jan.

Cyclic Sidereal Year, Month and Day	Week-Day	English Month and Day	Tithi	Ending Moment	Nakshatra	Ending Moment	Muhammadan Year, Month and Day
19 *Siddharthi, Dhanus—Marguli*	Su	1	8 *Pausha, Sukla*	·77	26	·11	7 *H. 1276 Jumadal-akhir*
20	Mo	2	9	·81	27	·18	8
21	Tu	3	10	·83	1	·23	9
22	We	4	11	·82	2	·26	10
23	Th	5	12	·80	3	·27	11
24	Fr	6	13	·76	4	·27	12
25	Sa	7	14	·70	5	·24	13
26	Su	8	P	·63	6	·20	14
27	Mo	9	1 *Bahula*	·55	7	·15	15
28	Tu	10	2	·46	8	·09	16
29	We	11	3	·36	9 / 10	·03 / ·96	17
—30	Th	12	4	·26	11	·89	18
1 *Siddharthi, Makara—Tai*	Fr	13	5	·16	12	·82	19
2	Sa	14	6 / 7	·07 / ·99	13	·76	20
3	Su	15	8	·92	14	·71	21
4	Mo	16	9	·86	15	·69	22
5	Tu	17	10	·82	16	·68	23
6	We	18	11	·81	17	·68	24
7	Th	19	12	·82	18	·70	25
8	Fr	20	13	·84	19	·74	26
9	Sa	21	14	·88	20	·81	27
10	Su	22	—A	·95	21	·90	28
11	Mo	23	... *Sukla*	...	...	...	—29
12	Tu	24	1	·03	22	·00	1
13	We	25	2	·12	23	·10	2
14	Th	26	3	·21	24	·21	3
15	Fr	27	4	·29	25	·32	4
16	Sa	28	5	·36	26	·41	5
17	Su	29	6	·42	27	·49	6
18	Mo	30	7	·45	1	·54	7
19	Tu	31	8	·47	2	·58	8

Feb.

Cyclic Sidereal Year, Month and Day	Week-Day	English Month and Day	Tithi	Ending Moment	Nakshatra	Ending Moment	Muhammadan Year, Month and Day
20	We	1	9 *Magha*	46	3	·60	9 *H. 1276 Rajab*
21	Th	2	10	·44	4	·60	10
22	Fr	3	11	·39	5	·57	11
23	Sa	4	12	·33	6	·53	12
24	Su	5	13	·26	7	·48	13
25	Mo	6	14	·18	8	·43	14
26	Tu	○ 7	P / 1	·08 / ·98	9	·36	15
27	We	8	2 *Bahula*	·88	10	·29	16
28	Th	9	3	·78	11	·22	17
—29	Fr	10	4	69	12	·16	18
1 *Siddharthi, Kumbha—Masi*	Sa	11	5	·61	13	·10	19
2	Su	12	6	·55	14	·06	20
3	Mo	13	7	·50	15	·02	21
4	Tu	14	8	·46	16	·00	22
5	We	15	9	·44	17	·00	23
6	Th	16	10	·45	18	·02	24
7	Fr	17	11	·48	19	·06	25
8	Sa	18	12	·52	20	·12	26
9	Su	19	13	·58	21	·20	27
10	Mo	20	14	·65	22	·29	28
11	Tu	21	—A	·74	23	·40	29
12	We	22	1 *Phalg., Sukla*	·83	24	·51	—30
13	Th	23	2	·91	25	·62	1 *H. 1276 Shaban*
14	Fr	24	3	·98	26	·71	2
15	Sa	25	...	...	27	·79	3
16	Su	26	4	·04	1	·85	4
17	Mo	27	5	·03	2	·90	5
18	Tu	28	6	·09	3	·92	6
19	We	29	7	·08	4	·92	7

March

Cyclic Sidereal Year, Month and Day	Week-Day	English Month and Day	Tithi	Ending Moment	Nakshatra	Ending Moment	Muhammadan Year, Month and Day
20	Th	1	8	05	5	.90	8
21	Fr	2	9 / 10	·00 / ·94	6	·87	9
22	Sa	3	11 *Phalguna, Suk.*	·87	7	·82	10
23	Su	4	12	·79	8	·76	11
24	Mo	5	13	·70	9	·70	12
25	Tu	6	14	·60	10	·63	13
26	We	7	P	·50	11	·56	14
27	Th	8	1	·40	12	·49	15
28	Fr	9	2	·31	13	·44	16
29	Sa	10	3	·22	14	·39	17
30	Su	11	4	·15	15	·35	18
—31	Mo	12	5	·09	16	·33	19
1 *Siddharthi, Mina—Panguni*	Tu	13	6 *Bahula*	·06	17	·32	20
2	We	14	7	·04	18	·34	21
3	Th	15	8	·04	19	·38	22
4	Fr	16	9	·07	20	·43	23
5	Sa	17	10	·11	21	·50	24
6	Su	18	11	·18	22	·59	25
7	Mo	19	12	·26	23	·70	26
8	Tu	20	13	·35	24	·81	27
9	We	21	14	·44	25	·92	28
10	Th	22	—A	·52	...	...	—29
11	Fr	23	1	·58	26	·01	1
12	Sa	24	2	·63	27	·10	2
13	Su	25	3	·66	1	·17	3
14	Mo	26	4	·67	2	·22	4
15	Tu	27	5	·66	3	·24	5
16	We	28	6	·63	4	·25	6
17	Th	29	7 *Sukla*	·59	5	·23	7
18	Fr	30	8	·53	6	·20	8
19	Sa	31	9	·46	7	·16	9

April

Cyclic Sidereal Year, Month and Day	Week-Day	English Month and Day	Tithi	Ending Moment	Nakshatra	Ending Moment	Muhammadan Year, Month and Day
20	Su	1	10	·37	8	·11	10 *H. 1276 Ramzan*
21	Mo	2	11	·27	9 / 10	·04 / ·97	11
22	Tu	3	12	·17	11	·90	12
23	We	4	13 / 14 *Chaitra*	·07 / ·97	12	·84	13
24	Th	5	P	·88	13	·78	14
25	Fr	6	1	·80	14	·72	15
26	Sa	7	2	·72	15	·68	16
27	Su	8	3	·66	16	·65	17
28	Mo	9	4	·62	17	·65	18
—29	Tu	10	5	·60	18	·66	19
1 *Raudra, Mesha—Chittirai*	We	11	6	·60	19	·69	20
2	Th	12	7	·63	20	·74	21
3	Fr	13	8	·68	21	·81	22
4	Sa	14	9 *Bahula*	·74	22	·90	23
5	Su	15	10	·81	...	...	24
6	Mo	16	11	·90	23	·00	25
7	Tu	17	12	·98	24	·11	26
8	We	18	...	...	25	·22	27
9	Th	19	13	·06	26	·32	28
10	Fr	20	14	·13	27	·40	29
11	Sa	21	—A	·18	1	·47	—30
12	Su	22	1 *Vsk., Sukla*	·21	2	·53	1 *H. 1276 Shawwal*
13	Mo	23	2	·22	3	·56	2
14	Tu	24	3	·21	4	·57	3
15	We	25	4	·18	5	·56	4
16	Th	26	5	·13	6	·54	5
17	Fr	27	6 / 7	·07 / ·99	7	·50	6
18	Sa	28	8	·90	8	·44	7
19	Su	29	9	·80	9	·38	8
20	Mo	30	10	·70	10	·32	9

May

Cyclic Sidereal Year, Month and Day	Week-Day	English Month and Day	Tithi	Ending Moment	Nakshatra	Ending Moment	Muhammadan Year, Month and Day
21	Tu	1	11 *Vaisakha, Suk.*	·60	11	·25	10
22	We	2	12	·50	12	·18	11
23	Th	3	13	·40	13	·11	12
24	Fr	4	14	·32	14	·06	13
25	Sa	5	P	·25	15 / 16	·01 / ·99	14
26	Su	6	1	·19	17	·97	15
27	Mo	7	2	·15	18	·98	16
28	Tu	8	3	·13	...	...	17
29	We	9	4	·13	19	·00	18
30	Th	10	5	·15	20	·05	19
—31	Fr	11	6 *Bahula*	·20	21	·11	20
1 *Raudra, Vrishabha—Vaikasi*	Sa	12	7	·26	22	·20	21
2	Su	13	8	·33	23	·30	22
3	Mo	14	9	·41	24	·41	23
4	Tu	15	10	·50	25	·52	24
5	We	16	11	·57	26	·62	25
6	Th	17	12	·64	27	·72	26
7	Fr	18	13	·69	1	·79	27
8	Sa	19	14	·72	2	·84	28
9	Su	20	—A	·73	3	·88	—29
10	Mo	21	1	·72	4	·89	1
11	Tu	22	2	·70	5	·89	2
12	We	23	3	·65	6	·87	3
13	Th	24	4	·58	7	·83	4
14	Fr	25	5	·50	8	·78	5
15	Sa	26	6	·40	9	·72	6
16	Su	27	7 *Sukla*	·30	10	·66	7
17	Mo	28	8	·20	11	·59	8
18	Tu	29	9	·10	12	·52	9
19	We	30	10 / 11	·00 / ·90	13	·45	10
20	Th	31	12	·83	14	·39	11

June

Cyclic Sidereal Year, Month and Day	Week-Day	English Month and Day	Tithi	Ending Moment	Nakshatra	Ending Moment	Muhammadan Year, Month and Day
21	Fr	1	13 *Jyeshtha*	.76	15	·35	12 *H. 1276 Zi-l-ka'da*
22	Sa	2	14	·70	16	·32	13
23	Su	3	P	·65	17	·30	14
24	Mo	4	1	·63	18	·30	15
25	Tu	5	2	·62	19	·32	16
26	We	6	3	·65	20	·36	17
27	Th	7	4	·69	21	·43	18
28	Fr	8	5	·74	22	·51	19
29	Sa	9	6 *Bahula*	·82	23	·60	20
30	Su	10	7	·90	24	·70	21
—31	Mo	11	8	·98	25	·81	22
1 *Raudra, Mithuna—Ani*	Tu	12	...	...	26	·92	23
2	We	13	9	·06	...	...	24
3	Th	14	10	·13	27	·02	25
4	Fr	15	11	·17	1	·10	26
5	Sa	16	12	·20	2	·16	27
6	Su	17	13	·22	3	·19	28
7	Mo	18	14	·21	4	·22	29
8	Tu	19	—A	·18	5	·22	—30
9	We	20	1	·14	6	·20	1 *H. 1276 Zi-l-hijja*
10	Th	21	2 / 3 *Sukla*	·08 / ·99	7	·16	2
11	Fr	22	4	·89	8	·11	3
12	Sa	23	5	·79	9	·06	4
13	Su	24	6	·69	10 / 11	·00 / ·93	5
14	Mo	25	7 *Ashadha*	·59	12	·86	6
15	Tu	26	8	·49	13	·79	7
16	We	27	9	·39	14	·73	8
17	Th	28	10	·31	15	·68	9
18	Fr	29	11	·24	16	·65	10
19	Sa	30	12	·18	17	·62	11

Naksh:—1. Asvn. 2. Bhar. 3. Krit. 4. Rohi. 5. Mrig. 6. Ardh. 7. Punar. 8. Push. 9. Aslesh. 10. Magh. 11. P. Phal. 12. U. Phal. 13. Hasta. 14. Chit.

A. D. 1860. **Kollam 1036,** { N. Malabar—Sept. / S. Malabar—Aug. } Commences **Hijra 1277,** Commences, **July 20.** **Vikrama 1917.**

A.—Amavasya. **Bengal San 1266.**

P.—Paurnami. **(N. Cycle) Angiras.**

Solar columns: Cyclic Sidereal Year, Month and Day. Lunar columns: Week-Day; English Month and Day; Tithi and its Ending Moment; Nakshatra and its Ending Moment; Muhammadan Year, Month and Day.

Vertical labels printed beside the table rows:

- Solar: *Raudra Mithuna—Ani*.
- Lunar: *Ashadha Suk.*, *Bahula*, *Sukla*.
- Muhammadan: *H. 1276 Zil-hijja*.

SOLAR reckoning: Cyclic Sidereal Year, Month and Day	LUNAR reckoning: Week-Day	English Month and Day	Tithi	Ending Moment	Nakshatra	Ending Moment	Muhammadan Year, Month and Day
	July						
20	Su	1	13	·13	18	·62	12
21	Mo	2	14	·11	19	·63	13
22	Tu	3	P	·10	20	·68	14
23	We	4	1	·12	21	·74	15
24	Th	5	2	·16	22	·81	16
25	Fr	6	3	·22	23	·90	17
26	Sa	7	4	·29	...	...	18
27	Su	8	5	·37	24	·01	19
28	Mo	9	6	·45	25	·12	20
29	Tu	10	7	·53	26	·23	21
30	We	11	8	·60	27	·32	22
31	Th	12	9	·65	1	·40	23
—32	Fr	13	10	·68	2	·47	24
1	Sa	14	11	·69	3	·52	25
2	Su	15	12	·69	4	·54	26
3	Mo	16	13	·66	5	·54	27
4	Tu	17	14	·61	6	·53	28
5	We	18	—A	·55	7	·50	29
6	Th	19	1	·47	8	·46	—30
7	Fr	20	2	·38	9	·40	1
8	Sa	21	3	·28	10	·33	2
9	Su	22	4	·18	11	·26	3
10	Mo	23	5 / 6	·08 / ·98	12	·19	4
11	Tu	24	7	·88	13	·12	5
12	We	25	8	·79	14	·07	6
13	Th	26	9	·71	15 / 16	·02 / ·98	7
14	Fr	27	10	·65	17	·95	8
15	Sa	28	11	·61	18	·94	9
16	Su	29	12	·59	19	·96	10
17	Mo	30	13	·58	20	·99	11
18	Tu	31	14	·60	...	...	12

Vertical labels printed beside the table rows:

- Solar: *Raudra Karkata—Adi* (July 12–31), then *Raudra Simha—Avani*.
- Lunar: *Sravana*, *Bahula*, *Sukla*, *Bhadrapada*.
- Muhammadan: *Muharram*, *H. 1277*, *H. 1277 Safar*.

SOLAR reckoning: Cyclic Sidereal Year, Month and Day	LUNAR reckoning: Week-Day	English Month and Day	Tithi	Ending Moment	Nakshatra	Ending Moment	Muhammadan Year, Month and Day
	Aug.						
19	We ○	1	P	·64	21	·04	13
20	Th	2	1	·70	22	·11	14
21	Fr	3	2	·77	23	·20	15
22	Sa	4	3	·85	24	·31	16
23	Su	5	4	·93	25	·42	17
24	Mo	6	...	...	26	·52	18
25	Tu	7	5	·01	27	·62	19
26	We	8	6	·07	1	·71	20
27	Th	9	7	·12	2	·79	21
28	Fr	10	8	·16	3	·83	22
29	Sa	11	9	·18	4	·86	23
30	Su	12	10	·18	5	·87	24
31	Mo	13	11	·15	6	·86	25
—32	Tu	14	12	·11	7	·83	26
1	We	15	13 / 14	·05 / ·97	8	·79	27
2	Th	16	—A	·88	9	·74	28
3	Fr	17	1	·78	10	·67	29
4	Sa	18	2	·68	11	·60	—30
5	Su	19	3	·58	12	·53	1
6	Mo	20	4	·48	13	·47	2
7	Tu	21	5	·38	14	·41	3
8	We	22	6	·29	15	·35	4
9	Th	23	7	·22	16	·31	5
10	Fr	24	8	·16	17	·28	6
11	Sa	25	9	·11	18	·27	7
12	Su	26	10	·09	19	·28	8
13	Mo	27	11	·09	20	·30	9
14	Tu	28	12	·11	21	·35	10
15	We	29	13	·14	22	·42	11
16	Th	30	14	·20	23	·51	12
17	Fr	31	P	·27	24	·61	13

Vertical labels printed beside the table rows:

- Solar: *Raudra Simha—Avani*, *Raudra Kanya—Purattasi*, *Raudra Tula—Aippasi*.
- Lunar: *Bhadrapada*, *Bahula*, *Sukla*, *Asvina*, *Adhika*, *Nija Asvina*.
- Muhammadan: *H. 1277 Safar*, *Rabi-ul-awwal*, *H. 1277*, *Rabi-ul-akhir*.

SOLAR reckoning: Cyclic Sidereal Year, Month and Day	LUNAR reckoning: Week-Day	English Month and Day	Tithi	Ending Moment	Nakshatra	Ending Moment	Muhammadan Year, Month and Day
	Sep.						
18	Sa	1	1	·36	25	·72	14
19	Su	2	2	·43	26	·82	15
20	Mo	3	3	·52	27	·92	16
21	Tu	4	4	·59	...	...	17
22	We	5	5	·64	1	·02	18
23	Th	6	6	·67	2	·09	19
24	Fr	7	7	·69	3	·15	20
25	Sa	8	8	·69	4	·18	21
26	Su	9	9	·66	5	·19	22
27	Mo	10	10	·62	6	·19	23
28	Tu	11	11	·56	7	·17	24
29	We	12	12	·49	8	·13	25
30	Th	13	13	·40	9	·07	26
—31	Fr	14	14	·31	10 / 11	·01 / ·95	27
1	Sa	15	—A	·21	12	·88	28
2	Su	16	1	·11	13	·81	—29
3	Mo	17	2 / 3	·01 / ·91	14	·74	1
4	Tu	18	4	·82	15	·69	2
5	We	19	5	·75	16	·64	3
6	Th	20	6	·69	17	·61	4
7	Fr	21	7	·64	18	·60	5
8	Sa	22	8	·62	19	·60	6
9	Su	23	9	·62	20	·62	7
10	Mo	24	10	·63	21	·66	8
11	Tu	25	11	·68	22	·73	9
12	We	26	12	·74	23	·81	10
13	Th	27	13	·81	24	·91	11
14	Fr	28	14	·89	...	...	12
15	Sa	29	P	·98	25	·01	13
16	Su	30	...	...	26	·12	14
	Oct.						
17	Mo	1	1	·06	27	·22	15
18	Tu	2	2	·13	1	·32	16
19	We	3	3	·19	2	·40	17
20	Th	4	4	·22	3	·46	18
21	Fr	5	5	·24	4	·50	19
22	Sa	6	6	·24	5	·52	20
23	Su	7	7	·22	6	·52	21
24	Mo	8	8	·18	7	·50	22
25	Tu	9	9	·12	8	·46	23
26	We	10	10 / 11	·05 / ·96	9	·41	24
27	Th	11	12	·87	10	·35	25
28	Fr	12	13	·77	11	·29	26
29	Sa	13	14	·67	12	·22	27
—30	Su	14	—A	·57	13	·15	28
1	Mo	15	1	·47	14	·08	29
2	Tu	16	2	·39	15 / 16	·02 / ·98	—30
3	We	17	3	·32	17	·94	1
4	Th	18	4	·26	18	·92	2
5	Fr	19	5	·22	19	·92	3
6	Sa	20	6	·20	20	·93	4
7	Su	21	7	·20	21	·98	5
8	Mo	22	8	·22	...	...	6
9	Tu	23	9	·26	22	·04	7
10	We	24	10	·32	23	·12	8
11	Th	25	11	·39	24	·21	9
12	Fr	26	12	·47	25	·31	10
13	Sa	27	13	·56	26	·42	11
14	Su	28	14	·65	27	·53	12
15	Mo	29	P	·73	1	·63	13
16	Tu	30	1	·78	2	·71	14
17	We	31	2	·81	3	·77	15

Vertical labels printed beside the table rows:

- Solar: *Raudra Tula—Aippasi*, *Raudra Vrischika—Kartigai*, *Raudra Dhanus—Margali*.
- Lunar: *Nija Asv.*, *Bahula*, *Sukla*, *Kartika*, *Margasira*.
- Muhammadan: *H. 1277 Rabi-ul-akhir*, *Jumadal-awwal*, *H. 1277*, *H. 1277 Jumadal-akhir*.

SOLAR reckoning: Cyclic Sidereal Year, Month and Day	LUNAR reckoning: Week-Day	English Month and Day	Tithi	Ending Moment	Nakshatra	Ending Moment	Muhammadan Year, Month and Day
	Nov.						
18	Th	1	3	·83	4	·81	16
19	Fr	2	4	·83	5	·84	17
20	Sa	3	5	·81	6	·84	18
21	Su	4	6	·78	7	·83	19
22	Mo	5	7	·72	8	·79	20
23	Tu	6	8	·64	9	·74	21
24	We	7	9	·55	10	·69	22
25	Th	8	10	·46	11	·63	23
26	Fr	9	11	·37	12	·56	24
27	Sa	10	12	·27	13	·49	25
28	Su	11	13	·17	14	·43	26
29	Mo	12	14 / A	·08 / ·99	15	·37	27
—30	Tu	13	1	·92	16	·31	28
1	We	14	2	·87	17	·27	—29
2	Th	15	3	·83	18	·25	1
3	Fr	16	4	·81	19	·24	2
4	Sa	17	5	·81	20	·25	3
5	Su	18	6	·83	21	·29	4
6	Mo	19	7	·87	22	·35	5
7	Tu	20	8	·94	23	·42	6
8	We	21	...	...	24	·51	7
9	Th	22	9	·02	25	·61	8
10	Fr	23	10	·10	26	·72	9
11	Sa	24	11	·19	27	·83	10
12	Su	25	12	·27	1	·93	11
13	Mo	26	13	·35	...	...	12
14	Tu	27	14	·40	2	·01	13
15	We	28	P	·44	3	·08	14
16	Th	29	1	·46	4	·14	15
17	Fr	30	2	·46	5	·16	16
	Dec.						
18	Sa	1	3	·44	6	·17	17
19	Su	2	4	·39	7	·15	18
20	Mo	3	5	·33	8	·12	19
21	Tu	4	6	·26	9	·09	20
22	We	5	7	·19	10 / 11	·03 / ·97	21
23	Th	6	8	·10	12	·90	22
24	Fr	7	9 / 10	·00 / ·90	13	·83	23
25	Sa	8	11	·80	14	·76	24
26	Su	9	12	·70	15	·70	25
27	Mo	10	13	·62	16	·65	26
28	Tu	11	14	·55	17	·60	27
—29	We	12	—A	·50	18	·57	28
1	Th	13	1	·46	19	·56	29
2	Fr	14	2	·45	20	·58	—30
3	Sa	15	3	·45	21	·61	1
4	Su	16	4	·47	22	·65	2
5	Mo	17	5	·52	23	·72	3
6	Tu	18	6	·59	24	·81	4
7	We	19	7	·66	25	·91	5
8	Th	20	8	·75	...	...	6
9	Fr	21	9	·84	26	·02	7
10	Sa	22	10	·92	27	·13	8
11	Su	23	11	·99	1	·23	9
12	Mo	24	...	...	2	·32	10
13	Tu	25	12	·05	3	·40	11
14	We	26	13	·09	4	·45	12
15	Th	27	14	·10	5	·48	13
16	Fr	28	P	·10	6	·49	14
17	Sa	29	1	·08	7	·48	15
18	Su	30	2 / 3	·04 / ·98	8	·46	16
19	Mo	31	4	·90	9	·42	17

15. Svati. 16. Visak. 17. Anur. 18. Jyesh. 19. Mula. 20. P. Ash. 21. U. Ash. 22. Sravn. 23. Dani. 24. Satab. 25. P. Bhad. 26. U. Bhad. 27. Rev.

A. D. 1861.
Solar Eclipse. ●
Lunar Eclipse. ○

Mesha Sankranti (Commencement of Indian Sidereal Year).
(Surya Sid.) April 11·53. **(Arya Sid.) April 11·43.**

Saka 1783. **(S. Cycle) Durmati.** **Kaliyuga 4962.**

Columns: SOLAR reckoning (Cyclic Sidereal Year, Month and Day; Week-Day; English Month and Day) — LUNAR reckoning (Tithi; Ending Moment; Nakshatra; Ending Moment) — Muhammadan Year, Month and Day.

Jan. — Solar: Raudra *Dhanus—Margali*, then Raudra *Makara—Tai*. Lunar: Margasira Bahula, Sukla, Pausha. Muhammadan: H. 1277 *Jumadal-akhir*, *Rajab*.

Cyclic Sidereal Day	Week-Day	English Day	Tithi	Ending Moment	Nakshatra	Ending Moment	Muhammadan Day
20	Tu	1	5	·82	10	·37	18
21	We	2	6	·73	11	·31	19
22	Th	3	7	·64	12	·24	20
23	Fr	4	8	·54	13	·17	21
24	Sa	5	9	·44	14	·10	22
25	Su	6	10	·35	15 / 16	·04 / ·98	23
26	Mo	7	11	·27	17	·93	24
27	Tu	8	12	·20	18	·91	25
28	We	9	13	·14	19	·90	26
29	Th	10	14	·11	20	·90	27
30	Fr	● 11	A	·09	21	·92	28
1	Sa	12	1	·10	22	·96	29
2	Su	13	2	·12	...	...	1
3	Mo	14	3	·16	23	·03	2
4	Tu	15	4	·23	24	·12	3
5	We	16	5	·32	25	·22	4
6	Th	17	6	·41	26	·32	5
7	Fr	18	7	·50	27	·43	6
8	Sa	19	8	·58	1	·53	7
9	Su	20	9	·65	2	·63	8
10	Mo	21	10	·70	3	·71	9
11	Tu	22	11	·74	4	·76	10
12	We	23	12	·75	5	·80	11
13	Th	24	13	·75	6	·81	12
14	Fr	25	14	·73	7	·81	13
15	Sa	26	P	·69	8	·79	14
16	Su	27	1	·62	9	·75	15
17	Mo	28	2	·54	10	·70	16
18	Tu	29	3	·45	11	·64	17
19	We	30	4	·36	12	·58	18
20	Th	31	5	·26	13	·51	19

Feb. — Solar: Raudra *Kumbha—Masi*. Lunar: Bahula, Sukla, Magha, Bah. Muhammadan: H. 1277 *Shaban*.

Cyclic Sidereal Day	Week-Day	English Day	Tithi	Ending Moment	Nakshatra	Ending Moment	Muhammadan Day
21	Fr	1	6	·16	14	·44	20
22	Sa	2	7 / 8	·07 / ·98	15	·38	21
23	Su	3	9	·90	16	·32	22
24	Mo	4	10	·83	17	·27	23
25	Tu	5	11	·78	18	·24	24
26	We	6	12	·75	19	·22	25
27	Th	7	13	·73	20	·22	26
28	Fr	8	14	·74	21	·24	27
29	Sa	9	A	·76	22	·28	28
1	Su	10	1	·81	23	·34	29
2	Mo	11	2	·87	24	·42	30
3	Tu	12	3	·95	25	·51	1
4	We	13	...	...	26	·62	2
5	Th	14	4	·04	27	·73	3
6	Fr	15	5	·13	1	·84	4
7	Sa	16	6	·21	2	·93	5
8	Su	17	7	·28	...	...	6
9	Mo	18	8	·34	3	·01	7
10	Tu	19	9	·37	4	·07	8
11	We	20	10	·39	5	·11	9
12	Th	21	11	·37	6	·13	10
13	Fr	22	12	·34	7	·14	11
14	Sa	23	13	·30	8	·12	12
15	Su	24	14	·24	9	·09	13
16	Mo	25	P	·16	10 / 11	·04 / ·98	14
17	Tu	26	1 / 2	·07 / ·98	12	·92	15
18	We	27	3	·88	13	·85	16
19	Th	28	4	·78	14	·78	17

March — Solar: Raudra *Kumbha—Masi*, then Raudra *Mina—Panguni*. Lunar: Magha Bahula, Sukla, Phalguna. Muhammadan: H. 1277 *Shaban*, *Ramzan*.

Cyclic Sidereal Day	Week-Day	English Day	Tithi	Ending Moment	Nakshatra	Ending Moment	Muhammadan Day
20	Fr	1	5	·68	15	·71	18
21	Sa	2	6	·59	16	·65	19
22	Su	3	7	·51	17	·61	20
23	Mo	4	8	·44	18	·57	21
24	Tu	5	9	·39	19	·55	22
25	We	6	10	·36	20	·54	23
26	Th	7	11	·35	21	·55	24
27	Fr	8	12	·35	22	·60	25
28	Sa	9	13	·37	23	·65	26
29	Su	10	14	·42	24	·72	27
30	Mo	11	A	·48	25	·81	28
1	Tu	12	1	·56	26	·92	29
2	We	13	2	·65	...	...	1
3	Th	14	3	·74	27	·03	2
4	Fr	15	4	·82	1	·14	3
5	Sa	16	5	·88	2	·23	4
6	Su	17	6	·93	3	·31	5
7	Mo	18	7	·97	4	·38	6
8	Tu	19	8	·99	5	·43	7
9	We	20	9	·97	6	·46	8
10	Th	21	10	·94	7	·47	9
11	Fr	22	11	·89	8	·45	10
12	Sa	23	12	·83	9	·42	11
13	Su	24	13	·75	10	·37	12
14	Mo	25	14	·66	11	·32	13
15	Tu	26	P	·56	12	·26	14
16	We	27	1	·46	13	·19	15
17	Th	28	2	·36	14	·12	16
18	Fr	29	3	·27	15	·06	17
19	Sa	30	4	·18	16 / 17	·00 / ·94	18
20	Su	31	5	·09	18	·89	19

April — Solar: Raudra *Mina—Panguni*, then Durmati *Mesha—Chittirai*. Lunar: Bahula, Sukla, Chaitra, Bahula. Muhammadan: H. 1277 *Shawwal*.

Cyclic Sidereal Day	Week-Day	English Day	Tithi	Ending Moment	Nakshatra	Ending Moment	Muhammadan Day
21	Mo	1	6 / 7	·02 / ·97	19	·85	20
22	Tu	2	8	·93	20	·86	21
23	We	3	9	·92	21	·88	22
24	Th	4	10	·92	22	·91	23
25	Fr	5	11	·95	23	·96	24
26	Sa	6	12	·99	...	...	25
27	Su	7	...	...	24	·03	26
28	Mo	8	13	·05	25	·12	27
29	Tu	9	14	·13	26	·22	28
30	We	10	A	·21	27	·33	29
1	Th	11	1	·30	1	·44	30
2	Fr	12	2	·38	2	·54	1
3	Sa	13	3	·45	3	·62	2
4	Su	14	4	·50	4	·69	3
5	Mo	15	5	·53	5	·75	4
6	Tu	16	6	·54	6	·78	5
7	We	17	7	·52	7	·79	6
8	Th	18	8	·49	8	·78	7
9	Fr	19	9	·44	9	·75	8
10	Sa	20	10	·38	10	·71	9
11	Su	21	11	·30	11	·66	10
12	Mo	22	12	·21	12	·60	11
13	Tu	23	13	·11	13	·53	12
14	We	24	14 / P	·01 / ·91	14	·46	13
15	Th	25	1	·81	15	·40	14
16	Fr	26	2	·72	16	·34	15
17	Sa	27	3	·63	17	·28	16
18	Su	28	4	·56	18	·23	17
19	Mo	29	5	·50	19	·20	18
20	Tu	30	6	·46	20	·18	19

May — Solar: Durmati *Mesha—Chittirai*, then Durmati *Vrishabha—Vaikasi*. Lunar: Chait. Bahula, Sukla, Vaisakha, Bahula. Muhammadan: H. 1277 *Shawwal*, *Zu'l-ka'da*.

Cyclic Sidereal Day	Week-Day	English Day	Tithi	Ending Moment	Nakshatra	Ending Moment	Muhammadan Day
21	We	1	7	·45	21	·20	20
22	Th	2	8	·45	22	·23	21
23	Fr	3	9	·48	23	·27	22
24	Sa	4	10	·52	24	·33	23
25	Su	5	11	·58	25	·42	24
26	Mo	6	12	·65	26	·52	25
27	Tu	7	13	·73	27	·63	26
28	We	8	14	·82	1	·74	27
29	Th	9	A	·90	2	·84	28
30	Fr	10	1	·97	3	·93	29
31	Sa	11	...	...	...	...	1
1	Su	12	2	·02	4	·01	2
2	Mo	13	3	·05	5	·06	3
3	Tu	14	4	·06	6	·10	4
4	We	15	5	·04	7	·11	5
5	Th	16	6 / 7	·01 / ·96	8	·11	6
6	Fr	17	8	·89	9	·09	7
7	Sa	18	9	·81	10	·05	8
8	Su	19	10	·72	11 / 12	·00 / ·94	9
9	Mo	20	11	·62	13	·88	10
10	Tu	21	12	·52	14	·81	11
11	We	22	13	·42	15	·74	12
12	Th	23	14	·32	16	·67	13
13	Fr	24	P	·22	17	·61	14
14	Sa	25	1	·14	18	·56	15
15	Su	26	2	·07	19	·53	16
16	Mo	27	3 / 4	·01 / ·97	20	·52	17
17	Tu	28	5	·95	21	·52	18
18	We	29	6	·96	22	·54	19
19	Th	30	7	·98	23	·58	20
20	Fr	31	...	...	24	·64	21

June — Solar: Durmati *Vrishabha—Vaikasi*, then Durmati *Mithuna—Ani*. Lunar: Bahula, Sukla, Jyeshtha, Bahula. Muhammadan: H. 1277 *Zu'l-hijja*.

Cyclic Sidereal Day	Week-Day	English Day	Tithi	Ending Moment	Nakshatra	Ending Moment	Muhammadan Day
21	Sa	1	8	·02	25	·72	22
22	Su	2	9	·08	26	·82	23
23	Mo	3	10	·15	27	·93	24
24	Tu	4	11	·23	...	...	25
25	We	5	12	·32	1	·04	26
26	Th	6	13	·40	2	·14	27
27	Fr	7	14	·47	3	·23	28
28	Sa	8	A	·51	4	·32	29
29	Su	9	1	·54	5	·38	30
30	Mo	10	2	·55	6	·41	1
31	Tu	11	3	·53	7	·43	2
32	We	12	4	·50	8	·44	3
1	Th	13	5	·46	9	·42	4
2	Fr	14	6	·39	10	·38	5
3	Sa	15	7	·31	11	·33	6
4	Su	16	8	·22	12	·27	7
5	Mo	17	9	·12	13	·21	8
6	Tu	18	10 / 11	·02 / ·92	14	·15	9
7	We	19	12	·82	15	·08	10
8	Th	20	13	·72	16 / 17	·01 / ·95	11
9	Fr	21	14	·63	18	·89	12
10	Sa	22	P	·55	19	·86	13
11	Su	23	1	·49	20	·84	14
12	Mo	24	2	·45	21	·84	15
13	Tu	25	3	·43	22	·85	16
14	We	26	4	·44	23	·89	17
15	Th	27	5	·46	24	·96	18
16	Fr	28	6	·50	...	...	19
17	Sa	29	7	·55	25	·03	20
18	Su	30	8	·62	26	·12	21

Naksh:—1. Asvn. 2. Bhar. 3. Krit. 4. Rohi. 5. Mrig. 6. Ardh. 7. Punar. 8. Push. 9. Aslesh. 10. Magh. 11. P. Phal. 12. U. Phal. 13. Hasta. 14. Chit.

A. D. 1861.
A.—Amavasya.
P.—Paurnami.

Kollam 1037, Commences { **N. Malabar—Sept.** / **S. Malabar—Aug.**

Hijra 1278, Commences, **July 9.**

Vikrama 1918.
Bengal San 1267.
(N. Cycle) Srimukha.

SOLAR reckoning. Cyclic Sidereal Year, Month and Day.	Week-Day	English Month and Day.	LUNAR reckoning. Tithi	Ending Moment.	Nakshatra	Ending Moment.	Muhammadan Year, Month and Day.
	July						
Durmati Mithuna—Ani.			*Jyesh. Bah.*				*Zil-hijja.*
19	Mo	1	9	·70	27	·22	22
20	Tu	2	10	·79	1	·33	23
21	We	3	11	·87	2	·44	24
22	Th	4	12	·93	3	·54	25
23	Fr	5	13	·99	4	·62	26
24	Sa	6	...	...	5	·69	27
25	Su	7	14	·02	6	·73	28
26	Mo ●	8	A	·03	7	·75	29
27	Tu	9	1 2	·01 ·98	8	·76	1
28	We	10	3	·93	9	·75	2
29	Th	11	4	·86	10	·72	3
30	Fr	12	5	·78	11	·67	4
31	Sa	13	6	·69	12	·61	5
Durmati Karkata—Adi.			*Ashadha Sukla*				*H. 1278 Muharam.*
1	Su	14	7	·59	13	·55	6
2	Mo	15	8	·49	14	·48	7
3	Tu	16	9	·39	15	·41	8
4	We	17	10	·29	16	·34	9
5	Th	18	11	·19	17	·28	10
6	Fr	19	12	·11	18	·24	11
7	Sa	20	13 14	·03 ·97	19	·20	12
8	Su	21	P	·93	20	·17	13
			Bahula				
9	Mo	22	1	·91	21	·16	14
10	Tu	23	2	·91	22	·17	15
11	We	24	3	·93	23	·21	16
12	Th	25	4	·97	24	·26	17
13	Fr	26	...	...	25	·33	18
14	Sa	27	5	·03	26	·42	19
15	Su	28	6	·10	27	·52	20
16	Mo	29	7	·18	1	·63	21
17	Tu	30	8	·27	2	·74	22
18	We	31	9	·34	3	·84	23
	Aug.						
19	Th	1	10	·41	4	·93	24
20	Fr	2	11	·46	...	...	25
21	Sa	3	12	·50	5	·00	26
22	Su	4	13	·51	6	·04	27
23	Mo	5	14	·49	7	·08	28
24	Tu	6	A	·47	8	·09	29
25	We	7	1	·42	9	·08	30
			Sravana Sukla				*H. 1278 Safar*
26	Th	8	2	·35	10	·05	1
27	Fr	9	3	·28	11 12	·01 ·96	2
28	Sa	10	4	·19	13	·89	3
29	Su	11	5 6	·09 ·99	14	·82	4
30	Mo	12	7	·89	15	·75	5
31	Tu	13	8	·79	16	·69	6
32	We	14	9	·70	17	·63	7
Durmati Simha—Avani.							
1	Th	15	10	·61	18	·57	8
2	Fr	16	11	·53	19	·53	9
3	Sa	17	12	·47	20	·50	10
4	Su	18	13	·42	21	·48	11
5	Mo	19	14	·41	22	·50	12
6	Tu	20	P	·41	23	·53	13
			Bahula				
7	We	21	1	·43	24	·57	14
8	Th	22	2	·47	25	·64	15
9	Fr	23	3	·52	26	·72	16
10	Sa	24	4	·59	27	·82	17
11	Su	25	5	·67	1	·93	18
12	Mo	26	6	·76	...	...	19
13	Tu	27	7	·84	2	·04	20
14	We	28	8	·91	3	·14	21
15	Th	29	9	·96	4	·23	22
16	Fr	30	10	·99	5	·30	23
17	Sa	31	...	...	6	·37	24
	Sep.						
18	Su	1	11	·01	7	·40	25
19	Mo	2	12 13	·00 ·98	8	·41	26
20	Tu	3	14	·94	9	·40	27
21	We	4	A	·88	10	·38	28
22	Th	5	1	·80	11	·35	29
			Bhadrapada Sukla				*H. 1278 Rabi-ul-awwal.*
23	Fr	6	2	·70	12	·29	1
24	Sa	7	3	·60	13	·23	2
25	Su	8	4	·50	14	·16	3
26	Mo	9	5	·40	15	·09	4
27	Tu	10	6	·30	16 17	·03 ·97	5
28	We	11	7	·21	18	·91	6
29	Th	12	8	·13	19	·86	7
30	Fr	13	9	·06	20	·83	8
31	Sa	14	10 11	·00 ·95	21	·82	9
Durmati Kanya—Purattasi.							
1	Su	15	12	·94	22	·82	10
2	Mo	16	13	·94	23	·84	11
3	Tu	17	14	·95	24	·88	12
4	We	18	P	·99	25	·94	13
			Bahula				
5	Th	19	...	...	...	...	14
6	Fr	20	1	·05	26	·02	15
7	Sa	21	2	·12	27	·12	16
8	Su	22	3	·20	1	·23	17
9	Mo	23	4	·29	2	·34	18
10	Tu	24	5	·37	3	·44	19
11	We	25	6	·44	4	·53	20
12	Th	26	7	·50	5	·61	21
13	Fr	27	8	·54	6	·68	22
14	Sa	28	9	·56	7	·72	23
15	Su	29	10	·55	8	·73	24
16	Mo	30	11	·52	9	·73	25
	Oct.						
17	Tu	1	12	·48	10	·72	26
18	We	2	13	·42	11	·68	27
19	Th	3	14	·34	12	·63	28
20	Fr	4	A	·25	13	·57	29
21	Sa	5	1	·16	14	·51	30
			Asvina Sukla				*H. 1278 Rabi-ul-akhir.*
22	Su	6	2 3	·06 ·96	15	·44	1
23	Mo	7	4	·86	16	·37	2
24	Tu	8	5	·77	17	·30	3
25	We	9	6	·69	18	·24	4
26	Th	10	7	·62	19	·19	5
27	Fr	11	8	·56	20	·15	6
28	Sa	12	9	·52	21	·14	7
29	Su	13	10	·50	22	·14	8
30	Mo	14	11	·50	23	·15	9
Durmati Tula—Aippasi.							
1	Tu	15	12	·52	24	·19	10
2	We	16	13	·56	25	·25	11
3	Th	17	14	·62	26	·34	12
4	Fr	18	P	·69	27	·43	13
			Bahula				
5	Sa	19	1	·78	1	·53	14
6	Su	20	2	·87	2	·64	15
7	Mo	21	3	·96	3	·75	16
8	Tu	22	...	...	4	·85	17
9	We	23	4	·03	5	·93	18
10	Th	24	5	·08	6	·99	19
11	Fr	25	6	·12	...	...	20
12	Sa	26	7	·14	7	·03	21
13	Su	27	8	·13	8	·05	22
14	Mo	28	9	·11	9	·06	23
15	Tu	29	10	·07	10	·04	24
16	We	30	11 12	·01 ·93	11 12	·01 ·96	25
17	Th	31	13	·84	13	·90	26
	Nov.						
18	Fr	1	14	·75	14	·84	27
19	Sa	2	A	·65	15	·78	28
20	Su	3	1	·55	16	·71	29
			Karttika Sukla				*H. 1278 Jumadal-awwal.*
21	Mo	4	2	·45	17	·64	1
22	Tu	5	3	·36	18	·58	2
23	We	6	4	·28	19	·52	3
24	Th	7	5	·21	20	·49	4
25	Fr	8	6	·15	21	·47	5
26	Sa	9	7	·12	22	·46	6
27	Su	10	8	·10	23	·47	7
28	Mo	11	9	·11	24	·50	8
29	Tu	12	10	·13	25	·57	9
30	We	13	11	·17	26	·64	10
Durmati Vrischika—Kartigai.							
1	Th	14	12	·23	27	·73	11
2	Fr	15	13	·31	1	·83	12
3	Sa	16	14	·40	2	·94	13
4	Su	17	P	·49	...	...	14
			Bahula				
5	Mo	18	1	·57	3	·05	15
6	Tu	19	2	·64	4	·15	16
7	We	20	3	·70	5	·23	17
8	Th	21	4	·74	6	·30	18
9	Fr	22	5	·76	7	·35	19
10	Sa	23	6	·75	8	·37	20
11	Su	24	7	·72	9	·39	21
12	Mo	25	8	·68	10	·37	22
13	Tu	26	9	·62	11	·34	23
14	We	27	10	·55	12	·30	24
15	Th	28	11	·46	13	·24	25
16	Fr	29	12	·37	14	·18	26
17	Sa	30	13	·28	15	·12	27
	Dec.						
18	Su	1	14	·18	16 17	·05 ·98	28
19	Mo	2	A 1	·08 ·98	18	·92	29
20	Tu	3	2	·90	19	·86	30
			Margasira Sukla				*H. 1278 Jumadal-akhir.*
21	We	4	3	·83	20	·82	1
22	Th	5	4	·78	21	·79	2
23	Fr	6	5	·75	22	·78	3
24	Sa	7	6	·73	23	·79	4
25	Su	8	7	·74	24	·83	5
26	Mo	9	8	·76	25	·88	6
27	Tu	10	9	·81	26	·94	7
28	We	11	10	·88	...	...	8
29	Th	12	11	·96	27	·03	9
30	Fr	13	...	...	1	·13	10
Durmati Dhanus—Margali.							
1	Sa	14	12	·05	2	·24	11
2	Su	15	13	·14	3	·35	12
3	Mo	16	14	·22	4	·45	13
4	Tu ○	17	P	·29	5	·54	14
			Bahula				
5	We	18	1	·35	6	·61	15
6	Th	19	2	·38	7	·66	16
7	Fr	20	3	·40	8	·70	17
8	Sa	21	4	·39	9	·71	18
9	Su	22	5	·37	10	·70	19
10	Mo	23	6	·32	11	·67	20
11	Tu	24	7	·25	12	·63	21
12	We	25	8	·18	13	·59	22
13	Th	26	9	·09	14	·52	23
14	Fr	27	10 11	·00 ·91	15	·45	24
15	Sa	28	12	·81	16	·38	25
16	Su	29	13	·71	17	·32	26
17	Mo	30	14	·62	18	·26	27
18	Tu	31	A	·54	19	·20	28

15. Svati. 16. Visak. 17. Anur. 18. Jyesh. 19. Mula. 20. P. Ash. 21. U. Ash. 22. Sravn. 23. Dani. 24. Satab. 25. P. Bhad. 26. U. Bhad. 27. Rev.

A. D. 1862. **Mesha Sankranti** (Commencement of Indian Sidereal Year). **Saka 1784.** **Kaliyuga 4963.**

Solar Eclipse. ● (**Surya Sid.**) **April 11·79.**

Lunar Eclipse. ○ (**Arya Sid.**) **April 11·69.** (**S. Cycle**) **Dundubhi.**

Columns: SOLAR reckoning (Cyclic Sidereal Year, Month and Day; Week-Day; English Month and Day) — LUNAR reckoning (Tithi; Ending Moment; Nakshatra; Ending Moment; Muhammadan Year, Month and Day).

Jan.

Durmati *Dhanus—Margali.* / Durmati *Makara—Tai.* — *Sukla* / Pausha / *Bahula* — H. 1278 *Rajab.*

Cyclic Sidereal Year, Month and Day	Week-Day	English Month and Day	Tithi	Ending Moment	Nakshatra	Ending Moment	Muhammadan Year, Month and Day
19	We	1	1	·47	20	·15	—29
20	Th	2	2	·42	21	·12	1
21	Fr	3	3	·39	22	·11	2
22	Sa	4	4	·38	23	·12	3
23	Su	5	5	·38	24	·14	4
24	Mo	6	6	·41	25	·18	5
25	Tu	7	7	·46	26	·25	6
26	We	8	8	·52	27	·33	7
27	Th	9	9	·60	1	·43	8
28	Fr	10	10	·69	2	·54	9
—29	Sa	11	11	·78	3	·65	10
1	Su	12	12	·87	4	·75	11
2	Mo	13	13	·94	5	·84	12
3	Tu	14	14	·99	6	·92	13
4	We	15	...	...	7	·98	14
5	Th	16	P	·02	...	...	15
6	Fr	17	1	·04	8	·02	16
7	Sa	18	2	·03	9	·03	17
8	Su	19	3 4	·01 ·97	10	·03	18
9	Mo	20	5	·90	11 12	·00 ·97	19
10	Tu	21	6	·82	13	·92	20
11	We	22	7	·73	14	·86	21
12	Th	23	8	·64	15	·79	22
13	Fr	24	9	·54	16	·72	23
14	Sa	25	10	·44	17	·66	24
15	Su	26	11	·35	18	·60	25
16	Mo	27	12	·26	19	·54	26
17	Tu	28	13	·18	20	·49	27
18	We	29	14	·12	21	·45	28
19	Th	30	—A	·07	22	·44	29
20	Fr	31	1	·03	23	·44	—30

Feb.

Durmati *Kumbha—Masi.* — *Sukla* / Magha / *Bahula* — H. 1278 *Shaban.*

Cyclic Sidereal Year, Month and Day	Week-Day	English Month and Day	Tithi	Ending Moment	Nakshatra	Ending Moment	Muhammadan Year, Month and Day
21	Sa	1	2	·02	24	·46	1
22	Su	2	3	·02	25	·49	2
23	Mo	3	4	·06	26	·55	3
24	Tu	4	5	·11	27	·63	4
25	We	5	6	·18	1	·73	5
26	Th	6	7	·25	2	·84	6
27	Fr	7	8	·34	3	·95	7
28	Sa	8	9	·43	...	...	8
29	Su	9	10	·51	4	·05	9
—30	Mo	10	11	·58	5	·14	10
1	Tu	11	12	·63	6	·23	11
2	We	12	13	·67	7	·29	12
3	Th	13	14	·68	8	·33	13
4	Fr	14	P	·66	9	·35	14
5	Sa	15	1	·63	10	·35	15
6	Su	16	2	·59	11	·34	16
7	Mo	17	3	·53	12	·31	17
8	Tu	18	4	·45	13	·26	18
9	We	19	5	·36	14	·20	19
10	Th	20	6	·27	15	·14	20
11	Fr	21	7	·17	16	·07	21
12	Sa	22	8 9	·07 ·97	17 18	·00 ·93	22
13	Su	23	10	·88	19	·87	23
14	Mo	24	11	·79	20	·82	24
15	Tu	25	12	·73	21	·78	25
16	We	26	13	·68	22	·77	26
17	Th	27	14	·65	23	·76	27
18	Fr	28	—A	·64	24	·77	28

March

Durmati *Kumbha—Masi.* / Durmati *Mina—Panguni.* — *Sukla* / Phalguna / *Bahula* — H. 1278 *Ramzan.*

Cyclic Sidereal Year, Month and Day	Week-Day	English Month and Day	Tithi	Ending Moment	Nakshatra	Ending Moment	Muhammadan Year, Month and Day
19	Sa	1	1	·64	25	·81	—29
20	Su	2	2	·67	26	·86	1
21	Mo	3	3	·72	27	·94	2
22	Tu	4	4	·79	...	...	3
23	We	5	5	·87	1	·04	4
24	Th	6	6	·96	2	·14	5
25	Fr	7	...	...	3	·25	6
26	Sa	8	7	·05	4	·36	7
27	Su	9	8	·13	5	·46	8
28	Mo	10	9	·19	6	·54	9
—29	Tu	11	10	·24	7	·60	10
1	We	12	11	·28	8	·65	11
2	Th	13	12	·29	9	·67	12
3	Fr	14	13	·27	10	·69	13
4	Sa	15	14	·23	11	·67	14
5	Su	16	P	·18	12	·64	15
6	Mo	17	1	·12	13	·59	16
7	Tu	18	2 3	·04 ·95	14	·54	17
8	We	19	4	·85	15	·48	18
9	Th	20	5	·75	16	·41	19
10	Fr	21	6	·65	17	·34	20
11	Sa	22	7	·56	18	·27	21
12	Su	23	8	·47	19	·21	22
13	Mo	24	9	·38	20	·15	23
14	Tu	25	10	·32	21	·12	24
15	We	26	11	·27	22	·09	25
16	Th	27	12	·24	23	·08	26
17	Fr	28	13	·22	24	·09	27
18	Sa	29	14	·23	25	·12	28
19	Su	30	—A	·26	26	·18	29
20	Mo	31	1	·30	27	·25	—30

April

Dundubhi *Mesha—Chittirai.* — *Sukla* / Chaitra / *Bahula* — H. 1278 *Shawwal.*

Cyclic Sidereal Year, Month and Day	Week-Day	English Month and Day	Tithi	Ending Moment	Nakshatra	Ending Moment	Muhammadan Year, Month and Day
21	Tu	1	2	·37	1	·34	1
22	We	2	3	·45	2	·44	2
23	Th	3	4	·54	3	·55	3
24	Fr	4	5	·63	4	·66	4
25	Sa	5	6	·71	5	·76	5
26	Su	6	7	·77	6	·84	6
27	Mo	7	8	·82	7	·91	7
28	Tu	8	9	85	8	·96	8
29	We	9	10	·84	...	...	9
30	Th	10	11	·82	9	·00	10
—31	Fr	11	12	·79	10	·01	11
1	Sa	12	13	·75	11 12	·00 ·97	12 13
2	Su	13	14	·68	13	·93	14
3	Mo	14	P	·60	14	·88	15
4	Tu	15	1	·51	15	·82	16
5	We	16	2	·41	16	·75	17
6	Th	17	3	·31	17	·68	18
7	Fr	18	4	·21	18	·61	19
8	Sa	19	5	·11	19	·55	20
9	Su	20	6 7	·02 ·93	20	·50	21
10	Mo	21	8	·86	21	·45	22
11	Tu	22	9	·81	22	·42	23
12	We	23	10	·78	23	·40	24
13	Th	24	11	·76	24	·41	25
14	Fr	25	12	·77	25	·44	26
15	Sa	26	13	·80	26	·49	27
16	Su	27	14	·85	27	·56	28
17	Mo	28	—A	·91	1	·64	—29
18	Tu	29	1	·98	2	·74	1
19	We	30	...	...	3	·85	

May

Dundubhi *Mesha—Chittirai.* / Dundubhi *Vrishabha—Vaikasi.* — *Sukla* / Vaisakha / *Bahula* — H. 1278 *Zi-l-ka'da.*

Cyclic Sidereal Year, Month and Day	Week-Day	English Month and Day	Tithi	Ending Moment	Nakshatra	Ending Moment	Muhammadan Year, Month and Day
20	Th	1	2	·07	4	·96	2
21	Fr	2	3	·15	...	...	3
22	Sa	3	4	·23	5	·06	4
23	Su	4	5	·29	6	·15	5
24	Mo	5	6	·34	7	·22	6
25	Tu	6	7	·37	8	·27	7
26	We	7	8	·38	9	·31	8
27	Th	8	9	·36	10	·33	9
28	Fr	9	10	·32	11	·32	10
29	Sa	10	11	·27	12	·30	11
30	Su	11	12	·20	13	·26	12
—31	Mo	12	13	·12	14	·22	13
1	Tu	13	14 P	·03 ·93	15	·16	14
2	We	14	1	·83	16	·09	15
3	Th	15	2	·73	17 18	·02 ·95	16
4	Fr	16	3	·63	19	·89	17
5	Sa	17	4	·53	20	·83	18
6	Su	18	5	·45	21	·78	19
7	Mo	19	6	·38	22	·75	20
8	Tu	20	7	·33	23	·73	21
9	We	21	8	·29	24	·74	22
10	Th	22	9	·28	25	·76	23
11	Fr	23	10	·28	26	·80	24
12	Sa	24	11	·30	27	·86	25
13	Su	25	12	·35	1	·94	26
14	Mo	26	13	·41	...	...	27
15	Tu	27	14	·49	2	·04	28
16	We	28	—A	·57	3	·15	29
17	Th	29	1	·66	4	·25	—30
18	Fr	30	2	·73	5	·36	1
19	Sa	31	3	·79	6	·45	2

June

Dundubhi *Mithuna—Ani.* — *Sukla* / Jyeshtha / *Bahula* / A. *Suk.* — H. 1278 *Zi-l-hijja.*

Cyclic Sidereal Year, Month and Day	Week-Day	English Month and Day	Tithi	Ending Moment	Nakshatra	Ending Moment	Muhammadan Year, Month and Day
20	Su	1	4	·83	7	·53	3
21	Mo	2	5	·86	8	·60	4
22	Tu	3	6	·88	9	·63	5
23	We	4	7	·85	10	·65	6
24	Th	5	8	·82	11	·65	7
25	Fr	6	9	·77	12	·63	8
26	Sa	7	10	·71	13	·60	9
27	Su	8	11	·62	14	·55	10
28	Mo	9	12	·53	15	·49	11
29	Tu	10	13	·43	16	·42	12
30	We	11	14	·33	17	·35	13
—31	Th ○	12	P	·23	18	·29	14
1	Fr	13	1	·13	19	·23	15
2	Sa	14	2 3	·03 ·94	20	·17	16
3	Su	15	4	·87	21	·11	17
4	Mo	16	5	·81	22	·08	18
5	Tu	17	6	·77	23	·06	19
6	We	18	7	·76	24	·06	20
7	Th	19	8	·76	25	·07	21
8	Fr	20	9	·78	26	·11	22
9	Sa	21	10	·82	27	·17	23
10	Su	22	11	·88	1	·24	24
11	Mo	23	12	·95	2	·34	25
12	Tu	24	...	...	3	·44	26
13	We	25	13	·03	4	·55	27
14	Th	26	14	·12	5	·66	28
15	Fr	27	—A	·20	6	·75	29
16	Sa	28	1	·27	7	·84	—30
17	Su	29	2	·32	8	·91	1
18	Mo	30	3	·35	9	·95	2

Naksh:—1. Asvn. 2. Bhar. 3. Krit. 4. Rohi. 5. Mrig. 6. Ardh. 7. Punar. 8. Push. 9. Aslesh. 10. Magh. 11. P. Phal. 12. U. Phal. 13. Hasta. 14. Chit.

A. D. 1862. Kollam 1038, Commences { N. Malabar—Sept. S. Malabar—Aug. Hijra 1279, Commences June 29. Vikrama 1919. Bengal San 1268. (N. Cycle) Bhava.

A.—Amavasya. P.—Paurnami.

SOLAR reckoning: Cyclic Sidereal Year, Month and Day; Week-Day; English Month and Day. LUNAR reckoning: Tithi, Ending Moment; Nakshatra, Ending Moment; Muhammadan Year, Month and Day.

July (Solar: Dundubhi Mithuna—Ani to 32, then Dundubhi Karkata—Adi; Lunar: Ashadha Sukla, Bahula; Muhammadan: H. 1279 Muharram, Safar)

Cyclic Sidereal Year, Month and Day	Week-Day	English Month and Day	Tithi	Ending Moment	Nakshatra	Ending Moment	Muhammadan Year, Month and Day
19	Tu	1	4	·36	10	·97	3
20	We	2	5	·34	11	·97	4
21	Th	3	6	·31	12	·96	5
22	Fr	4	7	·25	13	·93	6
23	Sa	5	8	·18	14	·89	7
24	Su	6	9	·10	15	·83	8
25	Mo	7	{10 11	·01 ·91	16	·77	9
26	Tu	8	12	·81	17	·70	10
27	We	9	13	·71	18	·63	11
28	Th	10	14	·61	19	·56	12
29	Fr	11	P	·51	20	·50	13
30	Sa	12	1	·42	21	·45	14
31	Su	13	2	·35	22	·42	15
32	Mo	14	3	·29	23	·39	16
1	Tu	15	4	·25	24	·38	17
2	We	16	5	·24	25	·39	18
3	Th	17	6	·24	26	·42	19
4	Fr	18	7	·26	27	·47	20
5	Sa	19	8	·30	1	·55	21
6	Su	20	9	·36	2	·64	22
7	Mo	21	10	·43	3	·74	23
8	Tu	22	11	·52	4	·85	24
9	We	23	12	·60	5	·96	25
10	Th	24	13	·67	...	...	26
11	Fr	25	14	·74	6	·06	27
12	Sa	26	A	·79	7	·15	28
13	Su	27	1	·82	8	·22	29
14	Mo	28	2	·83	9	·26	30
15	Tu	29	3	·82	10	·29	1
16	We	30	4	·78	11	·31	2
17	Th	31	5	·73	12	·30	3

Aug. (Solar: Dundubhi Karkata—Adi to 31, then Dundubhi Simha—Avani; Lunar: Sukla, Sravana, Bahula, B. Suk.; Muhammadan: H. 1279 Safar, R.-awwal)

Cyclic Sidereal Year, Month and Day	Week-Day	English Month and Day	Tithi	Ending Moment	Nakshatra	Ending Moment	Muhammadan Year, Month and Day
18	Fr	1	6	·67	13	·27	4
19	Sa	2	7	·59	14	·22	5
20	Su	3	8	·50	15	·17	6
21	Mo	4	9	·40	16	·11	7
22	Tu	5	10	·30	17 18	·04 ·97}	8
23	We	6	11	·20	19	·90	9
24	Th	7	12	·10	20	·84	10
25	Fr	8	{13 14	·00 ·91	21	·78	11
26	Sa	9	P	·84	22	·75	12
27	Su	10	1	·78	23	·72	13
28	Mo	11	2	·75	24	·70	14
29	Tu	12	3	·73	25	·71	15
30	We	13	4	·73	26	·73	16
31	Th	14	5	·74	27	·79	17
1	Fr	15	6	·78	1	·86	18
2	Sa	16	7	·84	2	·94	19
3	Su	17	8	·92	...	...	20
4	Mo	18	...	...	3	·04	21
5	Tu	19	9	·01	4	·15	22
6	We	20	10	·09	5	·26	23
7	Th	21	11	·17	6	·36	24
8	Fr	22	12	·24	7	·45	25
9	Sa	23	13	·28	8	·52	26
10	Su	24	14	·31	9	·58	27
11	Mo	25	A	·33	10	·62	28
12	Tu	26	1	·32	11	·63	29
13	We	27	2	·29	12	·62	1
14	Th	28	3	·25	13	·60	2
15	Fr	29	4	·18	14	·56	3
16	Sa	30	5	·10	15	·51	4
17	Su	31	{6 7	·01 ·91	16	·45	5

Sep. (Solar: Dundubhi Simha—Avani to 31, then Dundubhi Kanya—Purattasi; Lunar: Sukla, Bhadrapada, Bahula, Sukla; Muhammadan: H. 1279 Rabi-ul-awwal)

Cyclic Sidereal Year, Month and Day	Week-Day	English Month and Day	Tithi	Ending Moment	Nakshatra	Ending Moment	Muhammadan Year, Month and Day
18	Mo	1	8	·81	17	·38	6
19	Tu	2	9	·71	18	·31	7
20	We	3	10	·61	19	·24	8
21	Th	4	11	·52	20	·18	9
22	Fr	5	12	·44	21	·13	10
23	Sa	6	13	·36	22	·08	11
24	Su	7	14	·30	23	·04	12
25	Mo	8	P	·26	24	·03	13
26	Tu	9	1	·24	25	·03	14
27	We	10	2	·25	26	·06	15
28	Th	11	3	·27	27	·10	16
29	Fr	12	4	·31	1	·16	17
30	Sa	13	5	·36	2	·24	18
31	Su	14	6	·44	3	·34	19
1	Mo	15	7	·53	4	·45	20
2	Tu	16	8	·61	5	·56	21
3	We	17	9	·69	6	·66	22
4	Th	18	10	·76	7	·76	23
5	Fr	19	11	·81	8	·83	24
6	Sa	20	12	·84	9	·90	25
7	Su	21	13	·86	10	·94	26
8	Mo	22	14	·85	11	·95	27
9	Tu	23	A	·82	12	·95	28
10	We	24	1	·78	13	·93	29
11	Th	25	2	·72	14	·89	30
12	Fr	26	3	·64	15	·85	1
13	Sa	27	4	·55	16	·79	2
14	Su	28	5	·46	17	·72	3
15	Mo	29	6	·36	18	·65	4
16	Tu	30	7	·26	19	·58	5

Oct. (Solar: Dundubhi Kanya—Purattasi to 31, then Dundubhi Tula—Aippasi; Lunar: Asvina, Bahula, Sus., Kartt.; Muhammadan: H. 1279 Rabi-ul-akhir, Jumadal-awwal)

Cyclic Sidereal Year, Month and Day	Week-Day	English Month and Day	Tithi	Ending Moment	Nakshatra	Ending Moment	Muhammadan Year, Month and Day
17	We	1	8	·16	20	·52	6
18	Th	2	{9 10	·06 ·98	21	·46	7
19	Fr	3	11	·91	22	·41	8
20	Sa	4	12	·85	23	·37	9
21	Su	5	13	·81	24	·35	10
22	Mo	6	14	·79	25	·36	11
23	Tu	7	P	·79	26	·37	12
24	We	8	1	·82	27	·41	13
25	Th	9	2	·87	1	·47	14
26	Fr	10	3	·93	2	·55	15
27	Sa	11	...	...	3	·65	16
28	Su	12	4	·01	4	·75	17
29	Mo	13	5	·10	5	·86	18
30	Tu	14	6	·18	6	·96	19
31	We	15	7	·26	...	...	20
1	Th	16	8	·33	7	·06	21
2	Fr	17	9	·38	8	·15	22
3	Sa	18	10	·41	9	·21	23
4	Su	19	11	·43	10	·25	24
5	Mo	20	12	·43	11	·27	25
6	Tu	21	13	·41	12	·27	26
7	We	22	14	·36	13	·26	27
8	Th	23	A	·29	14	·23	28
9	Fr	24	1	·22	15	·18	29
10	Sa	25	2	·13	16	·12	1
11	Su	26	{3 4	·04 ·94	17 18	·06 ·99}	2
12	Mo	27	5	·84	19	·92	3
13	Tu	28	6	·74	20	·86	4
14	We	29	7	·65	21	·80	5
15	Th	30	8	·57	22	·74	6
16	Fr	31	9	·50	23	·70	7

Nov. (Solar: Dundubhi Tula—Aippasi to 29, then Dundubhi Vrischika—Kartigai; Lunar: Sukla, Karttika, Bahula, Sukla; Muhammadan: H. 1279 Jumadal-awwal, Jumadal-akhir)

Cyclic Sidereal Year, Month and Day	Week-Day	English Month and Day	Tithi	Ending Moment	Nakshatra	Ending Moment	Muhammadan Year, Month and Day
17	Sa	1	10	·44	24	·69	8
18	Su	2	11	·41	25	·68	9
19	Mo	3	12	·39	26	·69	10
20	Tu	4	13	·40	27	·72	11
21	We	5	14	·42	1	·78	12
22	Th	6	P	·46	2	·86	13
23	Fr	7	1	·52	3	·95	14
24	Sa	8	2	·61	...	...	15
25	Su	9	3	·70	4	·05	16
26	Mo	10	4	·79	5	·16	17
27	Tu	11	5	·88	6	·26	18
28	We	12	6	·94	7	·36	19
29	Th	13	7	·99	8	·45	20
1	Fr	14	...	...	9	·52	21
2	Sa	15	8	·03	10	·57	22
3	Su	16	9	·05	11	·59	23
4	Mo	17	10	·03	12	·60	24
5	Tu	18	{11 12	·00 ·96	13	·59	25
6	We	19	13	·91	14	·56	26
7	Th	20	14	·84	15	·52	27
8	Fr	21	A	·75	16	·46	28
9	Sa	22	1	·65	17	·40	29
10	Su	23	2	·55	18	·34	30
11	Mo	24	3	·45	19	·27	1
12	Tu	25	4	·36	20	·20	2
13	We	26	5	·27	21	·13	3
14	Th	27	6	·19	22	·08	4
15	Fr	28	7	·12	23	·04	5
16	Sa	29	8	·06	24	·01	6
17	Su	30	9	·03	25	·00	7

Dec. (Solar: Dundubhi Vrischika—Kartigai to 30, then Dundubhi Dhanus—Margali; Lunar: Margasira, Bahula, Sukla, Pausha; Muhammadan: H. 1279 Jumadal-akhir, Rajab)

Cyclic Sidereal Year, Month and Day	Week-Day	English Month and Day	Tithi	Ending Moment	Nakshatra	Ending Moment	Muhammadan Year, Month and Day
18	Mo	1	10	·02	26	·01	8
19	Tu	2	11	·02	27	·04	9
20	We	3	12	·05	1	·09	10
21	Th	4	13	·10	2	·16	11
22	Fr	5	14	·17	3	·25	12
23	Sa ○	6	P	·24	4	·35	13
24	Su	7	1	·33	5	·45	14
25	Mo	8	2	·42	6	·56	15
26	Tu	9	3	·50	7	·67	16
27	We	10	4	·58	8	·76	17
28	Th	11	5	·64	9	·82	18
29	Fr	12	6	·67	10	·88	19
30	Sa	13	7	·68	11	·91	20
1	Su	14	8	·68	12	·93	21
2	Mo	15	9	·65	13	·92	22
3	Tu	16	10	·60	14	·89	23
4	We	17	11	·54	15	·85	24
5	Th	18	12	·46	16	·80	25
6	Fr	19	13	·37	17	·74	26
7	Sa	20	14	·28	18	·67	27
8	Su ●	21	A	·18	19	·60	28
9	Mo	22	{1 2	·08 ·98	20	·53	29
10	Tu	23	3	·90	21	·47	1
11	We	24	4	·83	22	·42	2
12	Th	25	5	·77	23	·37	3
13	Fr	26	6	·72	24	·34	4
14	Sa	27	7	·68	25	·33	5
15	Su	28	8	·66	26	·33	6
16	Mo	29	9	·67	27	·35	7
17	Tu	30	10	·70	1	·40	8
18	We	31	11	·75	2	·47	9

15. Svati. 16. Visak. 17. Anur. 18. Jyesh. 19. Mula. 20. P. Ash. 21. U. Ash. 22. Sravn. 23. Dani. 24. Satab. 25. P. Bhad. 26. U. Bhad. 27. Rev.

A. D. 1863.
Solar Eclipse. ●
Lunar Eclipse. ○

Mesha Sankranti (Commencement of Indian Sidereal Year).
(Surya Sid.) April 12·05.
(Arya Sid.) April 11·95.

Saka 1785.
Kaliyuga 4964.
(S. Cycle) Rudhirodgari.

SOLAR reckoning: Cyclic Sidereal Year, Month and Day; Week-Day; English Month and Day. LUNAR reckoning: Tithi; Ending Moment; Nakshatra; Ending Moment; Muhammadan Year, Month and Day.

Jan.

Cyclic Sidereal Year, Month and Day	Week-Day	English Month and Day	Tithi	Ending Moment	Nakshatra	Ending Moment	Muhammadan Year, Month and Day
Dundubhi Dhanus—Margali 19	Th	1	Pausha Suk. 12	·82	3	·55	H. 1279 Rajab 10
20	Fr	2	13	·90	4	·65	11
21	Sa	3	14	·99	5	·76	12
22	Su	4	...	...	6	·87	13
23	Mo	5	P	·08	7	·97	14
24	Tu	6	Bahula 1	·16	...	...	15
25	We	7	2	·23	8	·06	16
26	Th	8	3	·28	9	·14	17
27	Fr	9	4	·31	10	·19	18
28	Sa	10	5	·33	11	·23	19
29	Su	11	6	·32	12	·25	20
Dundubhi Makara—Tai 1	Mo	12	7	·29	13	·25	21
2	Tu	13	8	·25	14	·22	22
3	We	14	9	·18	15	·18	23
4	Th	15	10	·10	16	·14	24
5	Fr	16	11 / 12	·01 / ·92	17	·08	25
6	Sa	17	13	·82	18 / 19	·01 / ·94	26
7	Su	18	14	·72	20	·87	27
8	Mo	19	A	·63	21	·81	28
9	Tu	20	Sukla 1	·55	22	·76	29
10	We	21	2	·47	23	·71	30
11	Th	22	3	·40	24	·67	H. 1279 Shaban 1
12	Fr	23	4	·35	25	·65	2
13	Sa	24	5	·32	26	·66	3
14	Su	25	6	·30	27	·68	4
15	Mo	26	7	·32	1	·72	5
16	Tu	27	8	·35	2	·77	6
17	We	28	9	·40	3	·85	7
18	Th	29	10	·47	4	·95	8
19	Fr	30	11	·55	...	...	9
20	Sa	31	12	·64	5	·06	10

Feb.

Cyclic Sidereal Year, Month and Day	Week-Day	English Month and Day	Tithi	Ending Moment	Nakshatra	Ending Moment	Muhammadan Year, Month and Day
21	Su	1	Magha 13	·73	6	·17	H. 1279 Shaban 11
22	Mo	2	14	·81	7	·27	12
23	Tu	3	P	·88	8	·36	13
24	We	4	Bahula 1	·93	9	·44	14
25	Th	5	2	·95	10	·51	15
26	Fr	6	3	·96	11	·55	16
27	Sa	7	4	·96	12	·57	17
28	Su	8	5	·93	13	·57	18
29	Mo	9	6	·87	14	·55	19
30	Tu	10	7	·80	15	·53	20
Dundubhi Kumbha—Masi 1	We	11	8	·73	16	·48	21
2	Th	12	9	·64	17	·42	22
3	Fr	13	10	·55	18	·35	23
4	Sa	14	11	·45	19	·28	24
5	Su	15	12	·35	20	·21	25
6	Mo	16	13	·25	21	·15	26
7	Tu	17	14	·16	22	·09	27
8	We	18	A	·09	23	·04	28
9	Th	19	Phalguna Sukla 1 / 2	·03 / ·98	24 / 25	·00 / ·98	29
10	Fr	20	3	·94	26	·98	H. 1279 Ramzan 1
11	Sa	21	4	·93	27	·99	2
12	Su	22	5	·94	...	...	3
13	Mo	23	6	·97	1	·03	4
14	Tu	24	...	...	2	·08	5
15	We	25	7	·02	3	·16	6
16	Th	26	8	·09	4	·26	7
17	Fr	27	9	·17	5	·36	8
18	Sa	28	10	·26	6	·46	9

March

Cyclic Sidereal Year, Month and Day	Week-Day	English Month and Day	Tithi	Ending Moment	Nakshatra	Ending Moment	Muhammadan Year, Month and Day
Dundubhi Kumbha—Masi 19	Su	1	Phalguna Suk. 11	·35	7	·57	H. 1279 Ramzan 10
20	Mo	2	12	·43	8	·67	11
21	Tu	3	13	·49	9	·76	12
22	We	4	14	·54	10	·82	13
23	Th	5	P	·57	11	·87	14
24	Fr	6	Bahula 1	·58	12	·89	15
25	Sa	7	2	·56	13	·90	16
26	Su	8	3	·53	14	·89	17
27	Mo	9	4	·48	15	·86	18
28	Tu	10	5	·41	16	·81	19
29	We	11	6	·34	17	·75	20
30	Th	12	7	·25	18	·69	21
Dundubhi Mina—Panguni 1	Fr	13	8	·15	19	·63	22
2	Sa	14	9 / 10	·05 / ·95	20	·56	23
3	Su	15	11	·85	21	·49	24
4	Mo	16	12	·76	22	·43	25
5	Tu	17	13	·68	23	·37	26
6	We	18	14	·61	24	·33	27
7	Th	19	A	·57	25	·31	28
8	Fr	20	Sukla 1	·54	26	·30	29
9	Sa	21	2	·53	27	·31	30
10	Su	22	3	·53	1	·34	H. 1279 Shawwal 1
11	Mo	23	4	·56	2	·39	2
12	Tu	24	5	·62	3	·47	3
13	We	25	6	·69	4	·56	4
14	Th	26	7	·77	5	·66	5
15	Fr	27	8	·85	6	·76	6
16	Sa	28	9	·94	7	·87	7
17	Su	29	...	...	8	·97	8
18	Mo	30	10	·02	...	...	9
19	Tu	31	11	·08	9	·06	10

April

Cyclic Sidereal Year, Month and Day	Week-Day	English Month and Day	Tithi	Ending Moment	Nakshatra	Ending Moment	Muhammadan Year, Month and Day
20	We	1	Chaitra 12	·13	10	·13	H. 1279 Shawwal 11
21	Th	2	13	·15	11	·18	12
22	Fr	3	14	·16	12	·21	13
23	Sa	4	P	·14	13	·23	14
24	Su	5	Bahula 1	·10	14	·22	15
25	Mo	6	2 / 3	·05 / ·99	15	·19	16
26	Tu	7	4	·91	16	·15	17
27	We	8	5	·81	17	·09	18
28	Th	9	6	·71	18 / 19	·03 / ·97	19
29	Fr	10	7	·61	20	·90	20
30	Sa	11	8	·51	21	·83	21
Rudhirodgari Mesha—Chittirai 1	Su	12	9	·41	22	·76	22
2	Mo	13	10	·32	23	·71	23
3	Tu	14	11	·24	24	·67	24
4	We	15	12	·18	25	·64	25
5	Th	16	13	·13	26	·62	26
6	Fr	17	14	·09	27	·63	27
7	Sa	18	A	·08	1	·65	28
8	Su	19	Vaisakha Sukla 1	·09	2	·70	29
9	Mo	20	2	·12	3	·77	H. 1279 Zi-l-ka'da 1
10	Tu	21	3	·16	4	·86	2
11	We	22	4	·23	5	·96	3
12	Th	23	5	·31	...	...	4
13	Fr	24	6	·39	6	·07	5
14	Sa	25	7	·48	7	·18	6
15	Su	26	8	·56	8	·28	7
16	Mo	27	9	·62	9	·37	8
17	Tu	28	10	·66	10	·44	9
18	We	29	11	·69	11	·49	10
19	Th	30	12	·69	12	·53	11

May

Cyclic Sidereal Year, Month and Day	Week-Day	English Month and Day	Tithi	Ending Moment	Nakshatra	Ending Moment	Muhammadan Year, Month and Day
Rudhirodgari Mesha—Chittirai 20	Fr	1	Vaisakha 13	·67	13	·55	H. 1279 Zi-l-ka'da 12
21	Sa	2	14	·64	14	·54	13
22	Su	3	P	·58	15	·52	14
23	Mo	4	Bahula 1	·51	16	·48	15
24	Tu	5	2	·43	17	·43	16
25	We	6	3	·34	18	·33	17
26	Th	7	4	·24	19	·31	18
27	Fr	8	5	·14	20	·24	19
28	Sa	9	6 / 7	·04 / ·94	21	·17	20
29	Su	10	8	·84	22	·10	21
30	Mo	11	9	·76	23	·05	22
31	Tu	12	10	·69	24 / 25	·00 / ·97	23
Rudhirodgari Vrishabha—Vaikasi 1	We	13	11	·65	26	·95	24
2	Th	14	12	·62	27	·95	25
3	Fr	15	13	·60	1	·98	26
4	Sa	16	14	·59	...	...	27
5	Su	17	A	·63	2	·02	28
6	Mo	18	Sukla 1	·68	3	·08	29
7	Tu	19	2	·75	4	·16	30
8	We	20	3	·82	5	·25	Zi-l-hijja 1
9	Th	21	4	·90	6	·36	2
10	Fr	22	5	·98	7	·47	3
11	Sa	23	...	...	8	·58	4
12	Su	24	6	·06	9	·67	5
13	Mo	25	7	·12	10	·75	6
14	Tu	26	8	·17	11	·81	7
15	We	27	9	·19	12	·85	8
16	Th	28	10	·20	13	·87	9
17	Fr	29	11	·18	14	·87	10
18	Sa	30	12	·15	15	·85	11
19	Su	31	13	·10	16	·81	12

June

Cyclic Sidereal Year, Month and Day	Week-Day	English Month and Day	Tithi	Ending Moment	Nakshatra	Ending Moment	Muhammadan Year, Month and Day
20	Mo ○	1	Jyeshtha 14 / P	·02 / ·93	17	·77	H. 1279 13
21	Tu	2	Bahula 1	·83	18	·71	14
22	We	3	2	·73	19	·64	15
23	Th	4	3	·63	20	·57	16
24	Fr	5	4	·53	21	·51	17
25	Sa	6	5	·44	22	·45	18
26	Su	7	6	·35	23	·39	19
27	Mo	8	7	·26	24	·33	20
28	Tu	9	8	·19	25	·30	21
29	We	10	9	·14	26	·28	22
30	Th	11	10	·10	27	·28	23
31	Fr	12	11	·08	1	·29	24
Rudhirodgari Mithuna—Ani 1	Sa	13	12	·09	2	·33	25
2	Su	14	13	·11	3	·39	26
3	Mo	15	14	·15	4	·46	27
4	Tu	16	A	·22	5	·56	28
5	We	17	Ashadha Sukla 1	·29	6	·67	29
6	Th	18	2	·37	7	·78	H. 1280 Muharram 1
7	Fr	19	3	·46	8	·88	2
8	Sa	20	4	·54	9	·97	3
9	Su	21	5	·60	...	...	4
10	Mo	22	6	·65	10	·05	5
11	Tu	23	7	·67	11	·12	6
12	We	24	8	·67	12	·17	7
13	Th	25	9	·66	13	·19	8
14	Fr	26	10	·63	14	·19	9
15	Sa	27	11	·57	15	·18	10
16	Su	28	12	·50	16	·15	11
17	Mo	29	13	·42	17	·11	12
18	Tu	30	14	·32	18 / 19	·05 / ·98	13

Naksh:—1. Asvn. 2. Bhar. 3. Krit. 4. Rohi. 5. Mrig. 6. Ardh. 7. Punar. 8. Push. 9. Aslesh. 10. Magh. 11. P. Phal. 12. U. Phal. 13. Hasta. 14. Chit.

A. D. 1863. — Vikrama 1920.
A.—Amavasya. P.—Paurnami. Kollam 1039, Commences { N. Malabar—Sept. S. Malabar—Aug. Hijra 1280, Commences, June 18. Bengal San 1269. (N. Cycle) Yuvan.

Columns: SOLAR reckoning (Cyclic Sidereal Year, Month and Day; Week-Day; English Month and Day) · LUNAR reckoning (Tithi; Ending Moment; Nakshatra; Ending Moment) · Muhammadan Year, Month and Day.

July — Solar: Rudhirodgari, Mithuna—Ani, to 32; Rudhirodgari, Karkata—Adi, from 1. Lunar: Ashadha (Bahula from tithi 1 after P, to A); Sravana (Sukla), from 1 after A. Muhammadan: H. 1280 Muharram, to 30; Safar, from 1.

Cyclic Sidereal Year, Month and Day	Week-Day	English Month and Day	Tithi	Ending Moment	Nakshatra	Ending Moment	Muhammadan Year, Month and Day
19	We	1	P	·22	20	·91	14
20	Th	2	1	·12	21	·84	15
21	Fr	3	2 3	·02 ·92	22	·78	16
22	Sa	4	4	·82	23	·72	17
23	Su	5	5	·74	24	·67	18
24	Mo	6	6	·67	25	·63	19
25	Tu	7	7	·62	26	·61	20
26	We	8	8	·58	27	·60	21
27	Th	9	9	·55	1	·61	22
28	Fr	10	10	·56	2	·64	23
29	Sa	11	11	·59	3	·68	24
30	Su	12	12	·64	4	·76	25
31	Mo	13	13	·70	5	·86	26
32	Tu	14	14	·77	6	·96	27
1	We	15	A	·86	...	...	28
2	Th	16	1	·94	7	·07	29
3	Fr	17	...	...	8	·18	30
4	Sa	18	2	·00	9	·28	1
5	Su	19	3	·07	10	·37	2
6	Mo	20	4	·13	11	·44	3
7	Tu	21	5	·15	12	·48	4
8	We	22	6	·16	13	·51	5
9	Th	23	7	·14	14	·52	6
10	Fr	24	8	·11	15	·52	7
11	Sa	25	9 10	·05 ·98	16	·49	8
12	Su	26	11	·90	17	·44	9
13	Mo	27	12	·81	18	·38	10
14	Tu	28	13	·71	19	·32	11
15	We	29	14	·61	20	·26	12
16	Th	30	P	·51	21	·19	13
17	Fr	31	1	·41	22	·12	14

Aug. — Solar: Rudhirodgari, Karkata—Adi, to 31; Rudhirodgari, Simha—Avani, from 1. Lunar: Adhika Sravana (Bahula, to A); Nija Sravana (Sukla), from 1 after A. Muhammadan: H. 1280 Safar, to 29; H. 1280 Rabi-ul-awwal, from 1.

Cyclic Sidereal Year, Month and Day	Week-Day	English Month and Day	Tithi	Ending Moment	Nakshatra	Ending Moment	Muhammadan Year, Month and Day
18	Sa	1	2	·31	23	·06	15
19	Su	2	3	·23	24 25	·00 ·97	16
20	Mo	3	4	·16	26	·94	17
21	Tu	4	5	·10	27	·92	18
22	We	5	6	·06	1	·93	19
23	Th	6	7	·05	2	·95	20
24	Fr	7	8	·05	...	...	21
25	Sa	8	9	·07	3	·00	22
26	Su	9	10	·11	4	·08	23
27	Mo	10	11	·17	5	·16	24
28	Tu	11	12	·25	6	·26	25
29	We	12	13	·34	7	·37	26
30	Th	13	14	·42	8	·48	27
31	Fr	14	A	·49	9	·58	28
1	Sa	15	1	·55	10	·67	29
2	Su	16	2	·60	11	·74	1
3	Mo	17	3	·63	12	·80	2
4	Tu	18	4	·65	13	·83	3
5	We	19	5	·65	14	·85	4
6	Th	20	6	·60	15	·84	5
7	Fr	21	7	·56	16	·82	6
8	Sa	22	8	·49	17	·77	7
9	Su	23	9	·41	18	·72	8
10	Mo	24	10	·32	19	·66	9
11	Tu	25	11	·22	20	·60	10
12	We	26	12	·12	21	·53	11
13	Th	27	13 14	·02 ·92	22	·46	12
14	Fr	28	P	·82	23	·39	13
15	Sa	29	1	·73	24	·33	14
16	Su	30	2	·66	25	·29	15
17	Mo	31	3	·61	26	·26	16

Sep. — Solar: Rudhirodgari, Simha—Avani, to 31; Rudhirodgari, Kanya—Purattasi, from 1. Lunar: Nija Srav. (Bahula, to A); Bhadrapada (Sukla), from 1 after A. Muhammadan: H. 1280 Rabi-ul-awwal, to 30; H. 1280 Rabi-ul-akhir, from 1.

Cyclic Sidereal Year, Month and Day	Week-Day	English Month and Day	Tithi	Ending Moment	Nakshatra	Ending Moment	Muhammadan Year, Month and Day
18	Tu	1	4	·57	27	·25	17
19	We	2	5	·56	1	·25	18
20	Th	3	6	·56	2	·27	19
21	Fr	4	7	·59	3	·32	20
22	Sa	5	8	·62	4	·39	21
23	Su	6	9	·67	5	·47	22
24	Mo	7	10	·75	6	·56	23
25	Tu	8	11	·84	7	·67	24
26	We	9	12	·93	8	·78	25
27	Th	10	...	...	9	·88	26
28	Fr	11	13	·01	10	·97	27
29	Sa	12	14	·08	...	...	28
30	Su	13	A	·13	11	·05	29
31	Mo	14	1	·16	12	·11	30
1	Tu	15	2	·18	13	·16	1
2	We	16	3	·16	14	·17	2
3	Th	17	4	·14	15	·17	3
4	Fr	18	5	·09	16	·14	4
5	Sa	19	6 7	·02 ·94	17	·11	5
6	Su	20	8	·85	18	·07	6
7	Mo	21	9	·75	19 20	·01 ·94	7
8	Tu	22	10	·65	21	·87	8
9	We	23	11	·55	22	·80	9
10	Th	24	12	·45	23	·73	10
11	Fr	25	13	·36	24	·68	11
12	Sa	26	14	·28	25	·63	12
13	Su	27	P	·21	26	·59	13
14	Mo	28	1	·16	27	·57	14
15	Tu	29	2	·12	1	·57	15
16	We	30	3	·10	2	·59	16

Oct. — Solar: Rudhirodgari, Kanya—Purattasi, to 31; Rudhirodgari, Tula—Aippasi, from 1. Lunar: Bhadrapada (Bahula, to A); Asvina (Sukla), from 1 after A; Asvina (Bah.), from 1 after P. Muhammadan: H. 1280 Rabi-ul-akhir, to 29; H. 1280 Jumadal-awwal, from 1.

Cyclic Sidereal Year, Month and Day	Week-Day	English Month and Day	Tithi	Ending Moment	Nakshatra	Ending Moment	Muhammadan Year, Month and Day
17	Th	1	4	·09	3	·63	17
18	Fr	2	5	·12	4	·69	18
19	Sa	3	6	·17	5	·77	19
20	Su	4	7	·23	6	·86	20
21	Mo	5	8	·31	7	·97	21
22	Tu	6	9	·40	...	...	22
23	We	7	10	·48	8	·08	23
24	Th	8	11	·56	9	·18	24
25	Fr	9	12	·64	10	·28	25
26	Sa	10	13	·69	11	·36	26
27	Su	11	14	·73	12	·43	27
28	Mo	12	A	·74	13	·47	28
29	Tu	13	1	·73	14	·49	29
30	We	14	2	·70	15	·49	1
31	Th	15	3	·65	16	·47	2
1	Fr	16	4	·59	17	·44	3
2	Sa	17	5	·51	18	·40	4
3	Su	18	6	·42	19	·34	5
4	Mo	19	7	·32	20	·28	6
5	Tu	20	8	·22	21	·21	7
6	We	21	9	·12	22	·14	8
7	Th	22	10 11	·03 ·94	23	·08	9
8	Fr	23	12	·86	24 25	·02 ·96	10
9	Sa	24	13	·79	26	·92	11
10	Su	25	14	·74	27	·90	12
11	Mo	26	P	·70	1	·90	13
12	Tu	27	1	·68	2	·91	14
13	We	28	2	·70	3	·94	15
14	Th	29	3	·72	...	...	16
15	Fr	30	4	·76	4	·00	17
16	Sa	31	5	·83	5	·07	18

Nov. — Solar: Rudhirodgari, Tula—Aippasi, to 30; Rudhirodgari, Vrischika—Kartigai, from 1. Lunar: Asv. (Bahula, to A); Karttika (Sukla), from 1 after A. Muhammadan: H. 1280 Jumadal-awwal, to 30; H. 1280 Jumadal-akhir, from 1.

Cyclic Sidereal Year, Month and Day	Week-Day	English Month and Day	Tithi	Ending Moment	Nakshatra	Ending Moment	Muhammadan Year, Month and Day
17	Su	1	6	·91	6	·17	19
18	Mo	2	7	·99	7	·27	20
19	Tu	3	...	...	8	·38	21
20	We	4	8	·09	9	·48	22
21	Th	5	9	·17	10	·58	23
22	Fr	6	10	·24	11	·66	24
23	Sa	7	11	·29	12	·74	25
24	Su	8	12	·33	13	·79	26
25	Mo	9	13	·34	14	·81	27
26	Tu	10	14	·32	15	·82	28
27	We	11	A	·29	16	·80	29
28	Th	12	1	·25	17	·78	30
29	Fr	13	2	·19	18	·74	1
30	Sa	14	3	·12	19	·68	2
1	Su	15	4 5	·03 ·93	20	·61	3
2	Mo	16	6	,83	21	·54	4
3	Tu	17	7	·73	22	·48	5
4	We	18	8	·64	23	·42	6
5	Th	19	9	·55	24	·36	7
6	Fr	20	10	·47	25	·30	8
7	Sa	21	11	·40	26	·25	9
8	Su	22	12	·35	27	·23	10
9	Mo	23	13	·32	1	·22	11
10	Tu	24	14	·30	2	·23	12
11	We ○	25	P	·31	3	·26	13
12	Th	26	1	·34	4	·31	14
13	Fr	27	2	·39	5	·38	15
14	Sa	28	3	·45	6	·47	16
15	Su	29	4	·55	7	·57	17
16	Mo	30	5	·63	8	·68	18

Dec. — Solar: Rudhirodgari, Vrischika—Kartigai, to 29; Rudhirodgari, Dhanus—Marguli, from 1. Lunar: Karttika (Bahula, to A); Margasira (Sukla), from 1 after A; Margasira (Bahula), from 1 after P. Muhammadan: H. 1280 Jumadal-akhir, to 29; H. 1280 Rajab, from 1.

Cyclic Sidereal Year, Month and Day	Week-Day	English Month and Day	Tithi	Ending Moment	Nakshatra	Ending Moment	Muhammadan Year, Month and Day
17	Tu	1	6	·71	9	·78	19
18	We	2	7	·79	10	·88	20
19	Th	3	8	·86	11	·98	21
20	Fr	4	9	·92	...	...	22
21	Sa	5	10	·96	12	·05	23
22	Su	6	11	·97	13	·10	24
23	Mo	7	12	·95	14	·13	25
24	Tu	8	13	·92	15	·14	26
25	We	9	14	·88	16	·14	27
26	Th	10	A	·82	17	·11	28
27	Fr	11	1	·74	18	·07	29
28	Sa	12	2	·65	19 20	·02 ·96	1
29	Su	13	3	·56	21	·89	2
1	Mo	14	4	·46	22	·82	3
2	Tu	15	5	·36	23	·75	4
3	We	16	6	·26	24	·69	5
4	Th	17	7	·18	25	·63	6
5	Fr	18	8	·10	26	·59	7
6	Sa	19	9 10	·03 ·99	27	·56	8
7	Su	20	11	·96	1	·54	9
8	Mo	21	12	·95	2	·55	10
9	Tu	22	13	·96	3	·57	11
10	We	23	14	·99	4	·62	12
11	Th	24	...	...	5	·69	13
12	Fr	25	P	·04	6	·77	14
13	Sa	26	1	·10	7	·87	15
14	Su	27	2	·19	8	·97	16
15	Mo	28	3	·28	...	...	17
16	Tu	29	4	·37	9	·08	18
17	We	30	5	·45	10	·19	19
18	Th	31	6	·52	11	·28	20

15. Svati. 16. Visak. 17. Anur. 18. Jyesh. 19. Mula. 20. P. Ash. 21. U. Ash. 22. Sravu. 23. Dani. 24. Satab. 25. P. Bhad. 26. U. Bhad. 27. Rev.

A. D. 1864. **Mesha Sankranti** (Commencement of Indian Sidereal Year).
Solar Eclipse. ● **(Surya Sid.) April 11·30.** **Saka 1786.** **Kaliyuga 4965.**
Lunar Eclipse. ○ **(Arya Sid.) April 11·20.** **(S. Cycle) Raktaksha.**

SOLAR reckoning: Cyclic Sidereal Year, Month and Day; Week-Day; English Month and Day. LUNAR reckoning: Tithi, Ending Moment; Nakshatra, Ending Moment; Muhammadan Year, Month and Day.

Jan.

Solar: **Rudhirodgari** *Dhanus—Margali* (to 30); **Rudhirodgari** *Makara—Tai* (from 1). Lunar: **Marg.** *Bah.*; *Sukla*, **Pausha**. Muhammadan: H 1280 *Rajab*; H. 1280 *Shaban*.

Cyclic Sidereal Year, Month and Day	Week-Day	English Month and Day	Tithi	Ending Moment	Nakshatra	Ending Moment	Muhammadan Year, Month and Day
19	Fr	1	7	·57	12	·36	21
20	Sa	2	8	·60	13	·41	22
21	Su	3	9	·62	14	·45	23
22	Mo	4	10	·60	15	·47	24
23	Tu	5	11	·57	16	·47	25
24	We	6	12	·52	17	·44	26
25	Th	7	13	·46	18	·40	27
26	Fr	8	14	·39	19	·35	28
27	Sa	9	—A	·31	20	·30	29
28	Su	10	1	·21	21	·23	—30
29	Mo	11	2	·11	22	·16	1
—30	Tu	12	3 4	·01 ·91	23	·09	2
1	We	13	5	·82	24 25	·02 ·97	3
2	Th	14	6	·74	26	·93	4
3	Fr	15	7	·67	27	·90	5
4	Sa	16	8	·63	1	·87	6
5	Su	17	9	·60	2	·87	7
6	Mo	18	10	·59	3	·89	8
7	Tu	19	11	·60	4	·94	9
8	We	20	12	·64	...	...	10
9	Th	21	13	·69	5	·00	11
10	Fr	22	14	·76	6	·07	12
11	Sa	23	P	·84	7	·17	13
12	Su	24	1	·93	8	·27	14
13	Mo	25	...	...	9	·38	15
14	Tu	26	2	·02	10	·49	16
15	We	27	3	·11	11	·58	17
16	Th	28	4	·18	12	·66	18
17	Fr	29	5	·21	13	·72	19
18	Sa	30	6	·24	14	·77	20
19	Su	31	7	·26	15	·79	21

Feb.

Solar: **Rudhirodgari** *Kumbha—Masi* (from 1). Lunar: *Bahula*; *Sukla*, **Magha**; *Bahula*. Muhammadan: H. 1280 *Ramzan*.

Cyclic Sidereal Year, Month and Day	Week-Day	English Month and Day	Tithi	Ending Moment	Nakshatra	Ending Moment	Muhammadan Year, Month and Day
20	Mo	1	8	·24	16	·79	22
21	Tu	2	9	·21	17	·77	23
22	We	3	10	·16	18	·74	24
23	Th	4	11	·10	19	·70	25
24	Fr	5	12 13	·02 ·93	20	·64	26
25	Sa	6	14	·83	21	·57	27
26	Su	7	—A	·73	22	·50	28
27	Mo	8	1	·63	23	·43	—29
28	Tu	9	2	·53	24	·36	1
—29	We	10	3	·45	25	·31	2
1	Th	11	4	·37	26	·26	3
2	Fr	12	5	·31	27	·22	4
3	Sa	13	6	·27	1	·19	5
4	Su	14	7	·23	2	·10	6
5	Mo	15	8	·22	3	·21	7
6	Tu	16	9	·23	4	·25	8
7	We	17	10	·27	5	·30	9
8	Th	18	11	·32	6	·38	10
9	Fr	19	12	·40	7	·47	11
10	Sa	20	13	·48	8	·57	12
11	Su	21	14	·56	9	·68	13
12	Mo	22	P	·65	10	·79	14
13	Tu	23	1	·73	11	·89	15
14	We	24	2	·80	12	·97	16
15	Th	25	3	·84	...	...	17
16	Fr	26	4	·87	13	·04	18
17	Sa	27	5	·88	14	·08	19
18	Su	28	6	·87	15	·11	20
19	Mo	29	7	·83	16	·12	21

March

Solar: **Rudhirodgari** *Kumbha—Masi* (to 31); **Rudhirodgari** *Mina—Panguni* (from 1). Lunar: **Magha** *Bah.*; *Sukla*, **Phalguna**; *Bahula*. Muhammadan: H. 1280 *Ramzan*; H. 1280 *Shawwal*.

Cyclic Sidereal Year, Month and Day	Week-Day	English Month and Day	Tithi	Ending Moment	Nakshatra	Ending Moment	Muhammadan Year, Month and Day
20	Tu	1	8	·77	17	·10	22
21	We	2	9	·71	18	·08	23
22	Th	3	10	·63	19 20	·03 ·97	24
23	Fr	4	11	·54	21	·91	25
24	Sa	5	12	·44	22	·84	26
25	Su	6	13	·34	23	·77	27
26	Mo	7	14	·24	24	·71	28
27	Tu	8	—A	·14	25	·65	29
28	We	9	1 2	·05 ·97	26	·59	—30
29	Th	10	3	·91	27	·55	1
30	Fr	11	4	·87	1	·52	2
—31	Sa	12	5	·84	2	·52	3
1	Su	13	6	·82	3	·53	4
2	Mo	14	7	·82	4	·56	5
3	Tu	15	8	·86	5	·61	6
4	We	16	9	·91	6	·68	7
5	Th	17	10	·99	7	·78	8
6	Fr	18	...	...	8	·88	9
7	Sa	19	11	·08	9	·98	10
8	Su	20	12	·17	...	...	11
9	Mo	21	13	·25	10	·09	12
10	Tu	22	14	·33	11	·19	13
11	We	23	P	·39	12	·28	14
12	Th	24	1	·43	13	·35	15
13	Fr	25	2	·46	14	·40	16
14	Sa	26	3	·46	15	·43	17
15	Su	27	4	·44	16	·44	18
16	Mo	28	5	·40	17	·43	19
17	Tu	29	6	·35	18	·41	20
18	We	30	7	·28	19	·37	21
19	Th	31	8	·20	20	·31	22

April

Solar: **Raktaksha** *Mesha—Chittirai* (from 1). Lunar: *Sukla*, **Chaitra**; *Bahula*. Muhammadan: H. 1280 *Zi-l-ka'da*.

Cyclic Sidereal Year, Month and Day	Week-Day	English Month and Day	Tithi	Ending Moment	Nakshatra	Ending Moment	Muhammadan Year, Month and Day
20	Fr	1	9	·11	21	·25	23
21	Sa	2	10 11	·01 ·91	22	·19	24
22	Su	3	12	·81	23	·12	25
23	Mo	4	13	·72	24 25	·05 ·98	26
24	Tu	5	14	·63	26	·92	27
25	We	6	—A	·55	27	·88	28
26	Th	7	1	·49	1	·86	—29
27	Fr	8	2	·44	2	·84	1
28	Sa	9	3	·40	3	·85	2
—29	Su	10	4	·38	4	·87	3
1	Mo	11	5	·39	5	·92	4
2	Tu	12	6	·43	6	·99	5
3	We	13	7	·48	...	...	6
4	Th	14	8	·55	7	·08	7
5	Fr	15	9	·63	8	·18	8
6	Sa	16	10	·72	9	·28	9
7	Su	17	11	·81	10	·39	10
8	Mo	18	12	·89	11	·50	11
9	Tu	19	13	·94	12	·59	12
10	We	20	14	·98	13	·66	13
11	Th	21	...	...	14	·72	14
12	Fr	22	P	·00	15	·75	15
13	Sa	23	1 2	·00 ·99	16	·76	16
14	Su	24	3	·95	17	·76	17
15	Mo	25	4	·90	18	·74	18
16	Tu	26	5	·83	19	·70	19
17	We	27	6	·75	20	·65	20
18	Th	28	7	·65	21	·59	21
19	Fr	29	8	·55	22	·53	22
20	Sa	30	9	·45	23	·46	23

May

Solar: **Raktaksha** *Mesha—Chittirai* (to 31); **Raktaksha** *Vrishabha—Vaikasi* (from 1). Lunar: **Ch.** *Bah.*; *Sukla*, **Vaisakha**; *Bahula*. Muhammadan: *Zi-l-ka'da*; H. 1280 *Zi-l-hijja*.

Cyclic Sidereal Year, Month and Day	Week-Day	English Month and Day	Tithi	Ending Moment	Nakshatra	Ending Moment	Muhammadan Year, Month and Day
21	Su	1	10	·35	24	·39	24
22	Mo	2	11	·25	25	·32	25
23	Tu	3	12	·16	26	·26	26
24	We	4	13	·08	27	·22	27
25	Th ●	5	14 A	·01 ·96	1	·19	28
26	Fr	6	1	·93	2	·17	29
27	Sa	7	2	·91	3	·17	—30
28	Su	8	3	·93	4	·19	1
29	Mo	9	4	·96	5	·24	2
30	Tu	10	...	...	6	·30	3
—31	We	11	5	·01	7	·38	4
1	Th	12	6	·07	8	·47	5
2	Fr	13	7	·15	9	·58	6
3	Sa	14	8	·23	10	·69	7
4	Su	15	9	·31	11	·80	8
5	Mo	16	10	·39	12	·89	9
6	Tu	17	11	·45	13	·97	10
7	We	18	12	·50	...	...	11
8	Th	19	13	·52	14	·03	12
9	Fr	20	14	·53	15	·06	13
10	Sa	21	P	·50	16	·09	14
11	Su	22	1	·46	17	·09	15
12	Mo	23	2	·41	18	·07	16
13	Tu	24	3	·34	19 20	·03 ·98	17
14	We	25	4	·25	21	·92	18
15	Th	26	5	·15	22	·86	19
16	Fr	27	6 7	·05 ·95	23	·79	20
17	Sa	28	8	·85	24	·72	21
18	Su	29	9	·75	25	·66	22
19	Mo	30	10	·66	26	·60	23
20	Tu	31	11	·58	27	·55	24

June

Solar: **Raktaksha** *Mithuna—Ani* (from 1). Lunar: *Sukla*, **Jyeshtha**; *Bahula*. Muhammadan: H. 1281 *Muharram*.

Cyclic Sidereal Year, Month and Day	Week-Day	English Month and Day	Tithi	Ending Moment	Nakshatra	Ending Moment	Muhammadan Year, Month and Day
21	We	1	12	·52	1	·52	25
22	Th	2	13	·47	2	·49	26
23	Fr	3	14	·43	3	·49	27
24	Sa	4	—A	·41	4	·50	28
25	Su	5	1	·42	5	·55	—29
26	Mo	6	2	·45	6	·61	1
27	Tu	7	3	·50	7	·68	2
28	We	8	4	·56	8	·77	3
29	Th	9	5	·64	9	·88	4
30	Fr	10	6	·72	10	·99	5
31	Sa	11	7	·80	...	...	6
—32	Su	12	8	·87	11	·10	7
1	Mo	13	9	·93	12	·19	8
2	Tu	14	10	·97	13	·27	9
3	We	15	...	...	14	·34	10
4	Th	16	11	·00	15	·39	11
5	Fr	17	12 13	·01 ·99	16	·41	12
6	Sa	18	14	·95	17	·41	13
7	Su	19	P	·90	18	·40	14
8	Mo	20	1	·83	19	·37	15
9	Tu	21	2	·74	20	·33	16
10	We	22	3	·64	21	·27	17
11	Th	23	4	·54	22	·20	18
12	Fr	24	5	·44	23	·13	19
13	Sa	25	6	·34	24	·06	20
14	Su	26	7	·24	25 26	·00 ·94	21
15	Mo	27	8	·15	27	·89	22
16	Tu	28	9	·07	1	·85	23
17	We	29	10 11	·00 ·94	2	·82	24
18	Th	30	12	·90	3	·81	25

Naksh:—1. Asvn. 2. Bhar. 3. Krit. 4. Rohi. 5. Mrig. 6. Ardh. 7. Punar. 8. Push. 9. Aslesh. 10. Magh. 11. P. Phal. 12. U. Phal. 13. Hasta. 14. Chit.

A. D. 1864. **Kollam 1040,** { **N. Malabar—Sept.** **Hijra 1281,** **Vikrama 1921.**
A.—Amavasya. Commences { **S. Malabar—Aug.** Commences, **June 6.** **Bengal San 1270.**
P.—Paurnami. **(N. Cycle) Dhatri.**

SOLAR reckoning: Cyclic Sidereal Year, Month and Day; Week-Day; English Month and Day. LUNAR reckoning: Tithi, Ending Moment; Nakshatra, Ending Moment; Muhammadan Year, Month and Day.

Solar month	Cyclic Sidereal Day	Week-Day	July	Lunar month	Tithi	Ending Moment	Nakshatra	Ending Moment	Muhammadan month	Muhammadan Day
Raktaksha Mithuna—Ani	19	Fr	1	Bah.	13	·89	4	·83	Muharram	26
	20	Sa	2		14	·90	5	·86		27
	21	Su	3		A	·92	6	·91		28
	22	Mo	4	Sukla Ashadha	1	·97	7	·99		29
	23	Tu	5		...	...	...	...		30
	24	We	6		2	·03	8	·08	H. 1281 Safar	1
	25	Th	7		3	·10	9	·18		2
	26	Fr	8		4	·18	10	·29		3
	27	Sa	9		5	·27	11	·40		4
	28	Su	10		6	·34	12	·49		5
	29	Mo	11		7	·41	13	·58		6
	30	Tu	12		8	·46	14	·65		7
	31	We	13		9	·49	15	·70		8
Raktaksha Karkata—Adi	1	Th	14		10	·48	16	·73		9
	2	Fr	15		11	·46	17	·74		10
	3	Sa	16		12	·43	18	·73		11
	4	Su	17		13	·37	19	·71		12
	5	Mo	18		14	·30	20	·66		13
	6	Tu	19		P	·22	21	·61		14
	7	We	20	Bahula	1	·13	22	·54		15
	8	Th	21		2 / 3	·03 / ·93	23	·47		16
	9	Fr	22		4	·83	24	·40		17
	10	Sa	23		5	·73	25	·34		18
	11	Su	24		6	·63	26	·28		19
	12	Mo	25		7	·55	27	·22		20
	13	Tu	26		8	·48	1	·18		21
	14	We	27		9	·42	2	·15		22
	15	Th	28		10	·39	3	·14		23
	16	Fr	29		11	·37	4	·15		24
	17	Sa	30		12	·38	5	·18		25
	18	Su	31		13	·39	6	·22		26

Solar month	Cyclic Sidereal Day	Week-Day	Aug.	Lunar month	Tithi	Ending Moment	Nakshatra	Ending Moment	Muhammadan month	Muhammadan Day
Raktaksha Karkata—Adi	19	Mo	1	Bahula	14	·44	7	·29		27
	20	Tu	2		A	·51	8	·38		28
	21	We	3	Sukla Sravana	1	·58	9	·48		29
	22	Th	4		2	·67	10	·59	H. 1281 Rabi-ul-awwal	1
	23	Fr	5		3	·75	11	·69		2
	24	Sa	6		4	·82	12	·79		3
	25	Su	7		5	·88	13	·89		4
	26	Mo	8		6	·93	14	·97		5
	27	Tu	9		7	·97	...	...		6
	28	We	10		8	·98	15	·02		7
	29	Th	11		9	·96	16	·05		8
	30	Fr	12		10	·92	17	·06		9
	31	Sa	13		11	·87	18	·06		10
	32	Su	14		12	·80	19 / 20	·04 / ·99		11
Raktaksha Simha—Avani	1	Mo	15		13	·72	21	·94		12
	2	Tu	16		14	·63	22	·88		13
	3	We	17		P	·53	23	·82		14
	4	Th	18	Bahula	1	·43	24	·75		15
	5	Fr	19		2	·33	25	·68		16
	6	Sa	20		3	·23	26	·61		17
	7	Su	21		4	·13	27	·55		18
	8	Mo	22		5 / 6	·05 / ·98	1	·51		19
	9	Tu	23		7	·92	2	·48		20
	10	We	24		8	·89	3	·47		21
	11	Th	25		9	·87	4	·47		22
	12	Fr	26		10	·88	5	·49		23
	13	Sa	27		11	·90	6	·53		24
	14	Su	28		12	·94	7	·60		25
	15	Mo	29		...	...	8	·69		26
	16	Tu	30		13	·01	9	·78		27
	17	We	31		14	·08	10	·88		28

Solar month	Cyclic Sidereal Day	Week-Day	Sep.	Lunar month	Tithi	Ending Moment	Nakshatra	Ending Moment	Muhammadan month	Muhammadan Day
Raktaksha Simha—Avani	18	Th	1		A	·17	11	·99		29
	19	Fr	2	Sukla Bhadrapada	1	·25	...	...		30
	20	Sa	3		2	·33	12	·10	H. 1281 Rabi-ul-akhir	1
	21	Su	4		3	·40	13	·20		2
	22	Mo	5		4	·45	14	·27		3
	23	Tu	6		5	·47	15	·33		4
	24	We	7		6	·48	16	·37		5
	25	Th	8		7	·47	17	·38		6
	26	Fr	9		8	·44	18	·39		7
	27	Sa	10		9	·40	19	·37		8
	28	Su	11		10	·33	20	·33		9
	29	Mo	12		11	·25	21	·28		10
	30	Tu	13		12	·15	22	·22		11
	31	We	14		13 / 14	·05 / ·95	23	·16		12
Raktaksha Kanya—Purattasi	1	Th	15		P	·85	24	·09		13
	2	Fr	16	Bahula	1	·75	25 / 26	·02 / ·95		14
	3	Sa	17		2	·66	27	·89		15
	4	Su	18		3	·58	1	·84		16
	5	Mo	19		4	·51	2	·81		17
	6	Tu	20		5	·45	3	·79		18
	7	We	21		6	·42	4	·79		19
	8	Th	22		7	·40	5	·80		20
	9	Fr	23		8	·42	6	·85		21
	10	Sa	24		9	·44	7	·91		22
	11	Su	25		10	·49	8	·99		23
	12	Mo	26		11	·55	...	...		24
	13	Tu	27		12	·63	9	·08		25
	14	We	28		13	·71	10	·18		26
	15	Th	29		14	·79	11	·29		27
	16	Fr	30		A	·87	12	·40		28

Solar month	Cyclic Sidereal Day	Week-Day	Oct.	Lunar month	Tithi	Ending Moment	Nakshatra	Ending Moment	Muhammadan month	Muhammadan Day
Raktaksha Kanya—Purattasi	17	Sa	1	Sukla Asvina	1	·94	13	·50		29
	18	Su	2		...	...	14	·58	H. 1281 Jumadal-awwal	1
	19	Mo	3		2	·00	15	·64		2
	20	Tu	4		3	·02	16	·68		3
	21	We	5		4	·04	17	·71		4
	22	Th	6		5 / 6	·02 / ·99	18	·71		5
	23	Fr	7		7	·94	19	·69		6
	24	Sa	8		8	·88	20	·66		7
	25	Su	9		9	·81	21	·61		8
	26	Mo	10		10	·72	22	·56		9
	27	Tu	11		11	·62	23	·50		10
	28	We	12		12	·52	24	·43		11
	29	Th	13		13	·42	25	·36		12
	30	Fr	14		14	·32	26	·29		13
Raktaksha Tula—Aippasi	1	Sa	15		P	·23	27	·23		14
	2	Su	16	Bahula	1	·15	1	·18		15
	3	Mo	17		2	·08	2	·14		16
	4	Tu	18		3 / 4	·02 / ·99	3	·12		17
	5	We	19		5	·98	4	·11		18
	6	Th	20		...	...	5	·13		19
	7	Fr	21		6	·00	6	·16		20
	8	Sa	22		7	·02	7	·22		21
	9	Su	23		8	·07	8	·29		22
	10	Mo	24		9	·13	9	·38		23
	11	Tu	25		10	·21	10	·48		24
	12	We	26		11	·29	11	·59		25
	13	Th	27		12	·38	12	·70		26
	14	Fr	28		13	·46	13	·80		27
	15	Sa	29		14	·53	14	·88		28
	16	Su	30		A	·58	15	·95		29
	17	Mo	31		1	·61	...	...		30

Solar month	Cyclic Sidereal Day	Week-Day	Nov.	Lunar month	Tithi	Ending Moment	Nakshatra	Ending Moment	Muhammadan month	Muhammadan Day
Raktaksha Tula—Aippasi	18	Tu	1	Sukla Karttika	2	·63	16	·01	H. 1281 Jumadal-akhir	1
	19	We	2		3	·61	17	·03		2
	20	Th	3		4	·58	18	·04		3
	21	Fr	4		5	·54	19 / 20	·02 / ·99		4
	22	Sa	5		6	·48	21	·96		5
	23	Su	6		7	·40	22	·90		6
	24	Mo	7		8	·31	23	·83		7
	25	Tu	8		9	·21	24	·76		8
	26	We	9		10	·11	25	·69		9
	27	Th	10		11 / 12	·01 / ·92	26	·63		10
	28	Fr	11		13	·83	27	·57		11
	29	Sa	12		14	·75	1	·52		12
	30	Su	13		P	·66	2	·47		13
Raktaksha Vrischika—Kartigai	1	Mo	14	Bahula	1	·63	3	·44		14
	2	Tu	15		2	·60	4	·44		15
	3	We	16		3	·59	5	·45		16
	4	Th	17		4	·61	6	·48		17
	5	Fr	18		5	·64	7	·53		18
	6	Sa	19		6	·68	8	·60		19
	7	Su	20		7	·74	9	·69		20
	8	Mo	21		8	·83	10	·79		21
	9	Tu	22		9	·92	11	·90		22
	10	We	23		...	...	...	...		23
	11	Th	24		10	·01	12	·00		24
	12	Fr	25		11	·08	13	·10		25
	13	Sa	26		12	·15	14	·19		26
	14	Su	27		13	·21	15	·27		27
	15	Mo	28		14	·24	16	·32		28
	16	Tu	29		A	·25	17	·35		29
	17	We	30		1	·23	18	·36		1

Solar month	Cyclic Sidereal Day	Week-Day	Dec.	Lunar month	Tithi	Ending Moment	Nakshatra	Ending Moment	Muhammadan month	Muhammadan Day
Raktaksha Vrischika—Kartigai	18	Th	1	Sukla Margasira	2	·20	19	·35	H. 1281 Rajab	2
	19	Fr	2		3	·15	20	·33		3
	20	Sa	3		4	·09	21	·29		4
	21	Su	4		5 / 6	·02 / ·94	22	·24		5
	22	Mo	5		7	·84	23	·17		6
	23	Tu	6		8	·74	24	·11		7
	24	We	7		9	·64	25 / 26	·04 / ·97		8
	25	Th	8		10	·54	27	·91		9
	26	Fr	9		11	·45	1	·85		10
	27	Sa	10		12	·37	2	·80		11
	28	Su	11		13	·31	3	·77		12
	29	Mo	12		14	·26	4	·76		13
	30	Tu	13		P	·24	5	·77		14
Raktaksha Dhanus—Margali	1	We	14	Bahula	1	·23	6	·79		15
	2	Th	15		2	·24	7	·84		16
	3	Fr	16		3	·28	8	·91		17
	4	Sa	17		4	·33	9	·99		18
	5	Su	18		5	·40	...	...		19
	6	Mo	19		6	·48	10	·09		20
	7	Tu	20		7	·57	11	·19		21
	8	We	21		8	·66	12	·30		22
	9	Th	22		9	·73	13	·40		23
	10	Fr	23		10	·80	14	·50		24
	11	Sa	24		11	·86	15	·58		25
	12	Su	25		12	·89	16	·63		26
	13	Mo	26		13	·90	17	·67		27
	14	Tu	27		14	·89	18	·68		28
	15	We	28		A	·85	19	·68		29
	16	Th	29	Suk.	1	·80	20	·66		30
	17	Fr	30		2	·74	21	·62		1
	18	Sa	31		3	·66	22	·57		2

15. Svati. 16. Visak. 17. Anur. 18. Jyesh. 19. Mula. 20. P. Ash. 21. U. Ash. 22. Sravn. 23. Dani. 24. Satab. 25. P. Bhad. 26. U. Bhad. 27. Rev.

A. D. 1865. **Mesha Sankranti** (Commencement of Indian Sidereal Year).

Solar Eclipse. ● (Surya Sid.) April 11·56. **Saka 1787.** **Kaliyuga 4966.**

Lunar Eclipse. ○ (Arya Sid.) April 11·46. (S. Cycle) **Krodhana.**

Columns: SOLAR reckoning — Cyclic Sidereal Year, Month and Day; Week-Day; English Month and Day. LUNAR reckoning — Tithi, Ending Moment; Nakshatra, Ending Moment; Muhammadan Year, Month and Day.

Jan. — Cyclic: Raktaksha *Dhanus—Margali* (to 29); Raktaksha *Makara—Tai* (from 1). Lunar: *Sukla*, Pausha, *Bahula*. Muhammadan: H. 1281 *Shaban*.

Cyclic Sidereal Day	Week-Day	English Day	Tithi	Ending Moment	Nakshatra	Ending Moment	Muhammadan Day
19	Su	1	4	·57	23	·51	3
20	Mo	2	5	·47	24	·45	4
21	Tu	3	6	·37	25	·38	5
22	We	4	7	·28	26	·31	6
23	Th	5	8	·19	27	·24	7
24	Fr	6	9	·10	1	·18	8
25	Sa	7	10 / 11	·02 / ·96	2	·13	9
26	Su	8	12	·92	3	·11	10
27	Mo	9	13	·89	4	·09	11
28	Tu	10	14	·87	5	·09	12
29	We	11	P	·89	6	·11	13
1	Th	12	1	·92	7	·15	14
2	Fr	13	2	·97	8	·22	15
3	Sa	14	...	...	9	·29	16
4	Su	15	3	·04	10	·39	17
5	Mo	16	4	·13	11	·50	18
6	Tu	17	5	·23	12	·61	19
7	We	18	6	·32	13	·71	20
8	Th	19	7	·40	14	·80	21
9	Fr	20	8	·46	15	·88	22
10	Sa	21	9	·50	16	·94	23
11	Su	22	10	·53	17	·98	24
12	Mo	23	11	·54	...	...	25
13	Tu	24	12	·53	18	·01	26
14	We	25	13	·49	19 / 20	·01 / ·99	27
15	Th	26	14	·44	21	·96	28
16	Fr	27	A	·37	22	·91	29
17	Sa	28	1	·29	23	·85	1
18	Su	29	2	·20	24	·79	2
19	Mo	30	3	·11	25	·72	3
20	Tu	31	4 / 5	·01 / ·91	26	·65	4

Feb. — Cyclic: Raktaksha *Kumbha—Masi*. Lunar: *Sukla*, Magha, *Bahula*, P. *Suk.* Muhammadan: H. 1281 *Ramzan*.

Cyclic Sidereal Day	Week-Day	English Day	Tithi	Ending Moment	Nakshatra	Ending Moment	Muhammadan Day
21	We	1	6	·82	27	·58	5
22	Th	2	7	·73	1	·52	6
23	Fr	3	8	·66	2	·48	7
24	Sa	4	9	·60	3	·44	8
25	Su	5	10	·55	4	·41	9
26	Mo	6	11	·52	5	·41	10
27	Tu	7	12	·51	6	·42	11
28	We	8	13	·53	7	·47	12
29	Th	9	14	·56	8	·52	13
1	Fr	10	P	·62	9	·60	14
2	Sa	11	1	·69	10	·69	15
3	Su	12	2	·77	11	·79	16
4	Mo	13	3	·86	12	·90	17
5	Tu	14	4	·94	...	...	18
6	We	15	...	...	13	·01	19
7	Th	16	5	·02	14	·11	20
8	Fr	17	6	·09	15	·19	21
9	Sa	18	7	·14	16	·25	22
10	Su	19	8	·16	17	·30	23
11	Mo	20	9	·17	18	·33	24
12	Tu	21	10	·15	19	·34	25
13	We	22	11	·11	20	·32	26
14	Th	23	12 / 13	·06 / ·99	21	·29	27
15	Fr	24	14	·91	22	·24	28
16	Sa	25	A	·82	23	·19	29
17	Su	26	1	·73	24	·13	30
18	Mo	27	2	·63	25 / 26	·06 / ·99	1
19	Tu	28	3	·53	27	·92	2

March — Cyclic: Raktaksha *Kumbha—Masi* (to 30); Raktaksha *Mina—Panguni* (from 1). Lunar: *Sukla*, Phalguna, *Bahula*. Muhammadan: H. 1281 *Shawwal*.

Cyclic Sidereal Day	Week-Day	English Day	Tithi	Ending Moment	Nakshatra	Ending Moment	Muhammadan Day
20	We	1	4	·43	1	·86	3
21	Th	2	5	·34	2	·81	4
22	Fr	3	6	·27	3	·77	5
23	Sa	4	7	·20	4	·74	6
24	Su	5	8	·16	5	·73	7
25	Mo	6	9	·14	6	·75	8
26	Tu	7	10	·13	7	·78	9
27	We	8	11	·14	8	·83	10
28	Th	9	12	·17	9	·90	11
29	Fr	10	13	·23	10	·99	12
30	Sa	11	14	·30	...	...	13
1	Su	12	P	·38	11	·10	14
2	Mo	13	1	·47	12	·21	15
3	Tu	14	2	·56	13	·31	16
4	We	15	3	·64	14	·41	17
5	Th	16	4	·70	15	·49	18
6	Fr	17	5	·74	16	·56	19
7	Sa	18	6	·76	17	·62	20
8	Su	19	7	·77	18	·65	21
9	Mo	20	8	·75	19	·66	22
10	Tu	21	9	·71	20	·65	23
11	We	22	10	·65	21	·62	24
12	Th	23	11	·58	22	·59	25
13	Fr	24	12	·50	23	·53	26
14	Sa	25	13	·40	24	·47	27
15	Su	26	14	·30	25	·40	28
16	Mo	27	A	·20	26	·33	29
17	Tu	28	1	·10	27	·27	1
18	We	29	2 / 3	·01 / ·93	1	·20	2
19	Th	30	4	·85	2	·14	3
20	Fr	31	5	·78	3	·10	4

April — Cyclic: Krodhana *Mesha—Chittirai*. Lunar: *Sukla*, Chaitra, *Bahula*, V. *Suk.* Muhammadan: H. 1281 *Zi-l-ka'da*; *Zi-l-hijja*.

Cyclic Sidereal Day	Week-Day	English Day	Tithi	Ending Moment	Nakshatra	Ending Moment	Muhammadan Day
21	Sa	1	6	·74	4	·07	5
22	Su	2	7	·71	5	·06	6
23	Mo	3	8	·70	6	·07	7
24	Tu	4	9	·72	7	·09	8
25	We	5	10	·76	8	·14	9
26	Th	6	11	·81	9	·21	10
27	Fr	7	12	·88	10	·29	11
28	Sa	8	13	·96	11	·40	12
29	Su	9	...	...	12	·50	13
30	Mo	10	14	·04	13	·61	14
1	Tu ○	11	P	·12	14	·71	15
2	We	12	1	·20	15	·80	16
3	Th	13	2	·26	16	·88	17
4	Fr	14	3	·30	17	·93	18
5	Sa	15	4	·31	18	·97	19
6	Su	16	5	·32	19	·98	20
7	Mo	17	6	·30	20	·97	21
8	Tu	18	7	·27	21	·96	22
9	We	19	8	·21	22	·92	23
10	Th	20	9	·14	23	·87	24
11	Fr	21	10 / 11	·05 / ·95	24	·80	25
12	Sa	22	12	·85	25	·74	26
13	Su	23	13	·75	26	·68	27
14	Mo	24	14	·65	27	·60	28
15	Tu	25	A	·55	1	·54	29
16	We	26	1	·47	2	·48	30
17	Th	27	2	·39	3	·43	1
18	Fr	28	3	·32	4	·41	2
19	Sa	29	4	·27	5	·39	3
20	Su	30	5	·24	6	·39	4

May — Cyclic: Krodhana *Mesha—Chittirai* (to 31); Krodhana *Vrishabha—Vaikasi* (from 1). Lunar: *Sukla*, Vaisakha, *Bahula*. Muhammadan: H. 1281 *Zi-l-hijja*.

Cyclic Sidereal Day	Week-Day	English Day	Tithi	Ending Moment	Nakshatra	Ending Moment	Muhammadan Day
21	Mo	1	6	·23	7	·41	5
22	Tu	2	7	·24	8	·45	6
23	We	3	8	·28	9	·51	7
24	Th	4	9	·33	10	·60	8
25	Fr	5	10	·40	11	·69	9
26	Sa	6	11	·47	12	·80	10
27	Su	7	12	·55	13	·91	11
28	Mo	8	13	·64	...	...	12
29	Tu	9	14	·72	14	·01	13
30	We	10	P	·78	15	·11	14
31	Th	11	1	·82	16	·19	15
1	Fr	12	2	·84	17	·25	16
2	Sa	13	3	·84	18	·29	17
3	Su	14	4	·82	19	·30	18
4	Mo	15	5	·78	20	·31	19
5	Tu	16	6	·72	21	·29	20
6	We	17	7	·65	22	·25	21
7	Th	18	8	·56	23	·20	22
8	Fr	19	9	·46	24	·14	23
9	Sa	20	10	·36	25	·08	24
10	Su	21	11	·26	26 / 27	·01 / ·94	25
11	Mo	22	12	·16	1	·87	26
12	Tu	23	13 / 14	·06 / ·97	2	·81	27
13	We	24	A	·89	3	·76	28
14	Th	25	1	·83	4	·73	29
15	Fr	26	2	·78	5	·71	30
16	Sa	27	3	·75	6	·71	1
17	Su	28	4	·73	7	·72	2
18	Mo	29	5	·75	8	·76	3
19	Tu	30	6	·78	9	·83	4
20	We	31	7	·82	10	·90	5

June — Cyclic: Krodhana *Vrishabha—Vaikasi* (to 32); Krodhana *Mithuna—Ani* (from 1). Lunar: *Sukla*, Jyeshtha, *Bahula*, Ashad. *Suk.* Muhammadan: H. 1282 *Muharram*; *Safar*.

Cyclic Sidereal Day	Week-Day	English Day	Tithi	Ending Moment	Nakshatra	Ending Moment	Muhammadan Day
21	Th	1	8	·89	11	·99	6
22	Fr	2	9	·97	...	...	7
23	Sa	3	...	...	12	·10	8
24	Su	4	10	·06	13	·21	9
25	Mo	5	11	·14	14	·32	10
26	Tu	6	12	·21	15	·41	11
27	We	7	13	·27	16	·49	12
28	Th	8	14	·31	17	·56	13
29	Fr	9	P	·33	18	·60	14
30	Sa	10	1	·33	19	·63	15
31	Su	11	2	·31	20	·63	16
32	Mo	12	3	·27	21	·62	17
1	Tu	13	4	·22	22	·58	18
2	We	14	5	·15	23	·54	19
3	Th	15	6 / 7	·06 / ·96	24	·48	20
4	Fr	16	8	·86	25	·42	21
5	Sa	17	9	·76	26	·35	22
6	Su	18	10	·66	27	·28	23
7	Mo	19	11	·56	1	·21	24
8	Tu	20	12	·47	2	·15	25
9	We	21	13	·39	3	·10	26
10	Th	22	14	·32	4	·06	27
11	Fr	23	A	·26	5	·04	28
12	Sa	24	1	·23	6	·03	29
13	Su	25	2	·21	7	·04	30
14	Mo	26	3	·23	8	·08	1
15	Tu	27	4	·26	9	·13	2
16	We	28	5	·30	10	·21	3
17	Th	29	6	·36	11	·29	4
18	Fr	30	7	·44	12	·39	5

Naksh :—1 Asvn. 2. Bhar. 3. Krit. 4. Rohi. 5. Mrig. 6. Ardh. 7. Punar. 8. Push. 9. Aslesh. 10. Magh. 11. P. Phal. 12. U. Phal. 13. Hasta. 14. Chit.

A. D. 1865.
A.—Amavasya.
P.—Paurnami.

Kollam 1041, Commences { **N. Malabar—Sept.** / **S. Malabar—Aug.**

Hijra 1282, Commences **May 27.**

Vikrama 1922.
Bengal San 1271.
(N. Cycle) Isvara.

Cyclic Sidereal Year, Month and Day. (SOLAR reckoning)	Week-Day	English Month and Day.	Tithi (LUNAR reckoning)	Ending Moment.	Nakshatra	Ending Moment.	Muhammadan Year, Month and Day.
		July					
Krodhana Mithuna—Ani. 19	Sa	1	Sukla 8	·52	13	·50	6
20	Su	2	9	·61	14	·61	7
21	Mo	3	10	·69	15	·71	8
22	Tu	4	11	·75	16	·80	9
23	We	5	12	·79	17	·87	10
24	Th	6	13	·81	18	·91	11
25	Fr	7	14	·80	19	·95	12
26	Sa	8	Ashadha P	·79	20	·96	13
27	Su	9	1	·75	21	·94	14
28	Mo	10	2	·69	22	·91	15
29	Tu	11	3	·62	23	·87	16
30	We	12	4	·54	24	·82	17
—31	Th	13	5	·44	25	·76	H. 1282 Safar, 18
1	Fr	14	Bahula 6	·34	26	·69	19
2	Sa	15	7	·24	27	·62	20
3	Su	16	8	·14	1	·56	21
4	Mo	17	9 / 10	·04 / ·95	2	50	22
5	Tu	18	11	·87	3	·44	23
6	We	19	12	·80	4	·40	24
7	Th	20	13	·74	5	·37	25
8	Fr	21	14	·71	6	·35	26
9	Sa	22	—A	·69	7	·37	27
10	Su	23	1	·70	8	·40	28
11	Mo	24	2	·73	9	·44	—29
Krodhana Karkata—Adi. 12	Tu	25	3	·77	10	·51	1
13	We	26	4	·84	11	·60	2
14	Th	27	5	·91	12	·70	3
15	Fr	28	...	...	13	·81	4
16	Sa	29	Sukla 6	·00	14	·92	5
17	Su	30	7	·08	...	...	6
18	Mo	31	8	·15	15	·02	7
		Aug.					
19	Tu	1	9	·21	16	·10	8
20	We	2	10	·26	17	·18	9
21	Th	3	11	·29	18	·24	10
22	Fr	4	12	·30	19	·27	11
23	Sa	5	13	·28	20	·28	12
24	Su.	6	14	·24	21	·27	13
25	Mo	7	Sravana P	·19	22	·25	14
26	Tu	8	1	·12	23	·21	15
27	We	9	2 / 3	·03 / ·94	24	·16	H. 1282 Rabi-ul-awwal, 16
28	Th	10	4	·84	25	·10	17
29	Fr	11	5	·74	26 / 27	·03 / ·96	18
30	Sa	12	Bahula 6	·64	1	·89	19
31	Su	13	7	·54	2	·83	20
—32	Mo	14	8	·44	3	·77	21
1	Tu	15	9	·36	4	·73	22
2	We	16	10	·30	5	·70	23
3	Th	17	11	·24	6	·69	24
4	Fr	18	12	·20	7	·69	25
5	Sa	19	13	·19	8	·71	26
6	Su	20	14	·20	9	·75	27
Krodhana Simha—Avani. 7	Mo	21	—A	·23	10	·82	28
8	Tu	22	Suk. 1	·28	11	·90	29
9	We	23	2	·34	...	...	—30
10	Th	24	3	·41	12	·00	Rabi-ul-akhir. 1
11	Fr	25	4	·49	13	·11	2
12	Sa	26	5	·58	14	·22	3
13	Su	27	6	·66	15	·32	4
14	Mo	28	7	·72	16	·41	5
15	Tu	29	8	·76	17	·49	6
16	We	30	9	·78	18	·55	7
17	Th	31	Bhadrapada 10	·80	19	·59	8

Cyclic Sidereal Year, Month and Day. (SOLAR reckoning)	Week-Day	English Month and Day.	Tithi (LUNAR reckoning)	Ending Moment.	Nakshatra	Ending Moment.	Muhammadan Year, Month and Day.
		Sep.					
18	Fr	1	Sukla 11	·78	20	·60	9
19	Sa	2	12	·75	21	·60	10
20	Su	3	13	·70	22	·59	11
21	Mo	4	14	·64	23	·55	12
Krodhana Simha—Avani. 22	Tu	5	Bhadra. P	·55	24	·50	13
23	We	6	1	·45	25	·44	14
24	Th	7	2	·35	26	·38	15
25	Fr	8	3	·25	27	·31	16
26	Sa	9	4	·15	1	·24	17
27	Su	10	Bahula 5 / 6	·05 / ·97	2	·17	18
28	Mo	11	7	·89	3	·11	H. 1282 Rabi-ul-akhir. 19
29	Tu	12	8	·82	4	·06	20
30	We	13	9	·76	5	·03	21
—31	Th	14	10	·73	6	·01	22
1	Fr	15	11	·72	7	·01	23
2	Sa	16	12	·73	8	·02	24
3	Su	17	13	·75	9	·06	25
4	Mo	18	14	·80	10	·12	26
5	Tu	19	—A	·86	11	·21	27
6	We	20	1	·94	12	·30	28
7	Th	21	...	...	13	·40	—29
8	Fr	22	2	·02	14	·51	1
Krodhana Kanya—Purattasi. 9	Sa	23	3	·11	15	·62	2
10	Su	24	4	·19	16	·72	3
11	Mo	25	5	·26	17	·80	4
12	Tu	26	6	·30	18	·86	5
13	We	27	7	·33	19	·90	6
14	Th	28	Sukla 8	·34	20	·92	7
15	Fr	29	9	·32	21	·93	8
16	Sa	30	10	·29	22	·91	9
		Oct.					
17	Su	1	11	·24	23	·88	H. 1282 Jumadal-awwal, 10
18	Mo	2	12	·17	24	·83	11
19	Tu	3	13	·09	25	·78	12
20	We	○ 4	Asvina 14 / P	·00 / ·91	26	·72	13
21	Th	5	1	·81	27	·65	14
22	Fr	6	2	·71	1	·58	15
23	Sa	7	3	·61	2	·51	16
24	Su	8	4	·52	3	·44	17
25	Mo	9	5	·44	4	·39	18
26	Tu	10	6	·38	5	·36	19
27	We	11	Bahula 7	·33	6	·34	20
28	Th	12	8	·30	7	·33	21
29	Fr	13	9	·28	8	·34	22
—30	Sa	14	10	·30	9	·37	23
1	Su	15	11	·33	10	·44	24
2	Mo	16	12	·37	11	·51	25
3	Tu	17	13	·43	12	·60	26
4	We	18	14	·51	13	·70	27
5	Th	19	—A	·60	14	·81	28
Krodhana Tula—Aippasi. 6	Fr	20	1	·69	15	·92	29
7	Sa	21	2	·77	...	...	—30
8	Su	22	Sukla 3	·84	16	·02	H. 1282 Jumadal-akhir. 1
9	Mo	23	4	·88	17	·10	2
10	Tu	24	5	·91	18	·17	3
11	We	25	6	·92	19	·22	4
12	Th	26	7	·91	20	·25	5
13	Fr	27	8	·88	21	·26	6
14	Sa	28	9	·83	22	·24	7
15	Su	29	10	·76	23	·21	8
16	Mo	30	11	·68	24	·17	9
17	Tu	31	Karttika 12	·59	25	·11	10

Cyclic Sidereal Year, Month and Day. (SOLAR reckoning)	Week-Day	English Month and Day.	Tithi (LUNAR reckoning)	Ending Moment.	Nakshatra	Ending Moment.	Muhammadan Year, Month and Day.
		Nov.					
18	We	1	Karttika 13	·50	26 / 27	·05 / ·98	11
19	Th	2	14	·40	1	·91	12
20	Fr	3	P	·30	2	·84	13
Krodhana Tula—Aippasi. 21	Sa	4	1	·21	3	·78	14
22	Su	5	2	·12	4	·73	15
23	Mo	6	3 / 4	·04 / ·97	5	·69	16
24	Tu	7	5	·92	6	·66	17
25	We	8	6	·89	7	·65	18
26	Th	9	Bahula 7	·88	8	·66	H. 1282 Jumadal-akhir, 19
27	Fr	10	8	·90	9	·70	20
28	Sa	11	9	·93	10	·75	21
29	Su	12	10	·98	11	·82	22
—30	Mo	13	...	...	12	·90	23
1	Tu	14	11	·05	...	...	24
2	We	15	12	·13	13	·00	25
3	Th	16	13	·22	14	·11	26
4	Fr	17	14	·31	15	·22	27
5	Sa	18	—A	·39	16	·32	28
6	Su	19	1	·45	17	·41	—29
7	Mo	20	2	·50	18	·48	1
8	Tu	21	3	·53	19	·54	2
Krodhana Vrischika—Kartigai. 9	We	22	4	·54	20	·57	3
10	Th	23	5	·52	21	·58	4
11	Fr	24	6	·49	22	·57	5
12	Sa	25	Sukla 7	·45	23	·54	6
13	Su	26	8	·39	24	·50	7
14	Mo	27	9	·31	25	·46	8
15	Tu	28	10	·21	26	·39	9
16	We	29	11	·11	27	·32	10
17	Th	30	12 / 13	·01 / ·91	1	·25	11
		Dec.					
18	Fr	1	Margasira 14	·82	2	·19	H. 1282 Rajab. 12
19	Sa	2	P	·74	3	·13	13
20	Su	3	1	·66	4	·07	14
21	Mo	4	2	·59	5 / 6	·02 / ·99	15
22	Tu	5	3	·55	7	·97	16
23	We	6	4	·52	8	·99	17
24	Th	7	5	·51	...	...	18
25	Fr	8	6	·53	9	·01	19
26	Sa	9	7	·56	10	·06	20
27	Su	10	Bahula 8	·62	11	·12	21
28	Mo	11	9	·69	12	·20	22
29	Tu	12	10	·77	13	·30	23
—30	We	13	11	·86	14	·41	24
1	Th	14	12	·95	15	·52	25
2	Fr	15	...	...	16	·62	26
3	Sa	16	13	·05	17	·71	27
4	Su	17	14	·09	18	·78	28
5	Mo	18	—A	·14	19	·84	29
6	Tu	19	1	·17	20	·89	—30
7	We	20	2	·18	21	·90	1
8	Th	21	3	·16	22	·90	2
9	Fr	22	4	·13	23	·87	3
10	Sa	23	Sukla 5	·08	24	·84	4
Krodhana Dhanus—Margali. 11	Su	24	6 / 7	·01 / ·94	25	·79	5
12	Mo	25	8	·85	26	·73	H. 1282 Shaban. 6
13	Tu	26	9	·75	27	·66	7
14	We	27	10	·65	1	·59	8
15	Th	28	11	·55	2	·52	9
16	Fr	29	12	·46	3	·46	10
17	Sa	30	13	·38	4	·40	11
18	Su	31	Pausha 14	·30	5	·35	12.

15. Svati. 16. Visak. 17. Anur. 18. Jyesh. 19. Mula. 20. P. Ash. 21. U. Ash. 22. Sravn. 23. Dani. 24. Satab. 25. P. Bhad 26. U. Bhad. 27. Rev

A. D. 1866.
Solar Eclipse. ●
Lunar Eclipse. ○

Mesha Sankranti (Commencement of Indian Sidereal Year).
(Surya Sid.) April 11·82. **Saka 1788.** **Kaliyuga 4967.**
(Arya Sid.) April 11·72. **(S. Cycle) Kshaya** (Akshaya).

SOLAR reckoning: Cyclic Sidereal Year, Month and Day; Week-Day; English Month and Day. LUNAR reckoning: Tithi, Ending Moment; Nakshatra, Ending Moment; Muhammadan Year, Month and Day.

Jan.

Cyclic Sidereal Year, Month	Cyclic Sidereal Day	Week-Day	English Day	Lunar Month	Tithi	Ending Moment	Nakshatra	Ending Moment	Muhammadan Year, Month	Muhammadan Day
Krodhana Dhanus—Margali.	19	Mo	1	Pausha Bahula	P	·24	6	·32	H. 1282 Shaban.	13
	20	Tu	2		1	·19	7	·31		14
	21	We	3		2	·17	8	·31		15
	22	Th	4		3	·16	9	·33		16
	23	Fr	5		4	·17	10	·37		17
	24	Sa	6		5	·21	11	·43		18
	25	Su	7		6	·27	12	·52		19
	26	Mo	8		7	·34	13	·61		20
	27	Tu	9		8	·42	14	·71		21
	28	We	10		9	·51	15	·82		22
	29	Th	11		10	·60	16	·92		23
Krodhana Makaru—Tai.	1	Fr	12		11	·68	...	...		24
	2	Sa	13		12	·74	17	·02		25
	3	Su	14		13	·79	18	·10		26
	4	Mo	15		14	·81	19	·16		27
	5	Tu	16		A	·83	20	·20		28
	6	We	17	Maghu Sukla	1	·81	21	·22		29
	7	Th	18		2	·78	22	·22	Ramzan.	1
	8	Fr	19		3	·73	23	·21		2
	9	Sa	20		4	·66	24	·18		3
	10	Su	21		5	·58	25	·13		4
	11	Mo	22		6	·48	26	·07		5
	12	Tu	23		7	·38	27, 1	·01, ·94		6
	13	We	24		8	·28	2	·87		7
	14	Th	25		9	·19	3	·80		8
	15	Fr	26		10	·10	4	·74		9
	16	Sa	27		11, 12	·01, ·94	5	·69		10
	17	Su	28		13	·88	6	·66		11
	18	Mo	29		14	·84	7	·63		12
	19	Tu	30		P	·81	8	·63		13
	20	We	31		1	·80	9	·64		14

Feb.

Cyclic Sidereal Year, Month	Cyclic Sidereal Day	Week-Day	English Day	Lunar Month	Tithi	Ending Moment	Nakshatra	Ending Moment	Muhammadan Year, Month	Muhammadan Day
	21	Th	1	Bahula	2	·82	10	·68	H. 1282	15
	22	Fr	2		3	·86	11	·73		16
	23	Sa	3		4	·92	12	·82		17
	24	Su	4		5	·99	13	·91		18
	25	Mo	5		...	...	...	...		19
	26	Tu	6		6	·07	14	·01		20
	27	We	7		7	·16	15	·12		21
	28	Th	8		8	·25	16	·22		22
	29	Fr	9		9	·32	17	·32		23
	30	Sa	10		10	·38	18	·41		24
Krodhana Kumbha—Masi.	1	Su	11		11	·43	19	·47		25
	2	Mo	12		12	·45	20	·52		26
	3	Tu	13		13	·46	21	·54		27
	4	We	14		14	·45	22	·56		28
	5	Th	15		A	·41	23	·54		29
	6	Fr	16	Phalguna Sukla	1	·35	24	·51		30
	7	Sa	17		2	·28	25	·46	H. 1282 Shawwal.	1
	8	Su	18		3	·20	26	·40		2
	9	Mo	19		4	·11	27	·34		3
	10	Tu	20		5, 6	·01, ·91	1	·28		4
	11	We	21		7	·81	2	·21		5
	12	Th	22		8	·72	3	·14		6
	13	Fr	23		9	·63	4	·07		7
	14	Sa	24		10	·55	5, 6	·03, ·99		8
	15	Su	25		11	·49	7	·96		9
	16	Mo	26		12	·45	8	·95		10
	17	Tu	27		13	·43	9	·96		11
	18	We	28		14	·42	10	·99		12

March

Cyclic Sidereal Year, Month	Cyclic Sidereal Day	Week-Day	English Day	Lunar Month	Tithi	Ending Moment	Nakshatra	Ending Moment	Muhammadan Year, Month	Muhammadan Day
Krodhana Kumbha—Masi.	19	Th	1	Phalguna Bahula	P	·44	...	...	H. 1282 Shawwal.	13
	20	Fr	2		1	·48	11	·05		14
	21	Sa	3		2	·53	12	·12		15
	22	Su	4		3	·60	13	·21		16
	23	Mo	5		4	·69	14	·31		17
	24	Tu	6		5	·78	15	·42		18
	25	We	7		6	·87	16	·53		19
	26	Th	8		7	·95	17	·63		20
	27	Fr	9		...	...	18	·71		21
	28	Sa	10		8	·00	19	·78		22
	29	Su	11		9	·04	20	·83		23
Krodhana Mina—Panguni.	1	Mo	12		10	·06	21	·87		24
	2	Tu	13		11	·06	22	·88		25
	3	We	14		12	·05	23	·87		26
	4	Th	15		13, 14	·01, ·95	24	·84		27
	5	Fr	16		A	·87	25	·80		28
	6	Sa	17	Chaitra Sukla	1	·79	26	·75		29
	7	Su	18		2	·70	27	·69	Zi-l-ka'da.	1
	8	Mo	19		3	·60	1	·62		2
	9	Tu	20		4	·50	2	·55		3
	10	We	21		5	·40	3	·48		4
	11	Th	22		6	·31	4	·41		5
	12	Fr	23		7	·22	5	·36		6
	13	Sa	24		8	·15	6	·32		7
	14	Su	25		9	·08	7	·29		8
	15	Mo	26		10	·04	8	·27		9
	16	Tu	27		11	·02	9	·28		10
	17	We	28		12	·00	10	·31		11
	18	Th	29		13	·03	11	·36		12
	19	Fr	30		14	·07	12	·43		13
	20	Sa ○	31		P	·12	13	·51		14

April

Cyclic Sidereal Year, Month	Cyclic Sidereal Day	Week-Day	English Day	Lunar Month	Tithi	Ending Moment	Nakshatra	Ending Moment	Muhammadan Year, Month	Muhammadan Day
	21	Su	1	Bahula	1	·19	14	·61	H. 1282	15
	22	Mo	2		2	·27	15	·72		16
	23	Tu	3		3	·36	16	·83		17
	24	We	4		4	·44	17	·93		18
	25	Th	5		5	·52	...	...		19
	26	Fr	6		6	·57	18	·02		20
	27	Sa	7		7	·61	19	·09		21
	28	Su	8		8	·64	20	·15		22
	29	Mo	9		9	·62	21	·19		23
	30	Tu	10		10	·61	22	·20		24
	31	We	11		11	·57	23	·19		25
Kshaya Mesha—Chittirai.	1	Th	12		12	·51	24	·17		26
	2	Fr	13		13	·44	25	·14		27
	3	Sa	14		14	·36	26	·09		28
	4	Su	15		A	·26	27, 1	·02, ·95		29
	5	Mo	16	Vaisakha Sukla	1	·16	2	·88		30
	6	Tu	17		2, 3	·06, ·96	3	·82	H. 1282 Zi-l-hijja.	1
	7	We	18		4	·87	4	·76		2
	8	Th	19		5	·78	5	·70		3
	9	Fr	20		6	·70	6	·65		4
	10	Sa	21		7	·63	7	·62		5
	11	Su	22		8	·59	8	·60		6
	12	Mo	23		9	·56	9	·61		7
	13	Tu	24		10	·54	10	·63		8
	14	We	25		11	·56	11	·67		9
	15	Th	26		12	·60	12	·73		10
	16	Fr	27		13	·66	13	·81		11
	17	Sa	28		14	·73	14	·91		12
	18	Su	29		P	·80	...	...		13
	19	Mo	30		1	·89	15	·02		14

May

Cyclic Sidereal Year, Month	Cyclic Sidereal Day	Week-Day	English Day	Lunar Month	Tithi	Ending Moment	Nakshatra	Ending Moment	Muhammadan Year, Month	Muhammadan Day
Kshaya Mesha—Chittirai.	20	Tu	1	Vaisak. Bahula	2	·97	16	·13	H. 1282 Zi-l-hijja.	15
	21	We	2		...	...	17	·23		16
	22	Th	3		3	·04	18	·32		17
	23	Fr	4		4	·10	19	·40		18
	24	Sa	5		5	·14	20	·47		19
	25	Su	6		6	·15	21	·51		20
	26	Mo	7		7	·16	22	·52		21
	27	Tu	8		8	·14	23	·52		22
	28	We	9		9	·11	24	·50		23
	29	Th	10		10, 11	·04, ·96	25	·47		24
	30	Fr	11		12	·87	26	·42		25
	31	Sa	12		13	·78	27	·36		26
Kshaya Vrishabha—Vaikasi.	1	Su	13		14	·68	1	·29		27
	2	Mo	14		A	·58	2	·22		28
	3	Tu	15	Adhika Jyeshtha Sukla	1	·48	3	·15		29
	4	We	16		2	·38	4	·09	H. 1283 Muharram.	1
	5	Th	17		3	·29	5, 6	·03, ·98		2
	6	Fr	18		4	·21	7	·94		3
	7	Sa	19		5	·15	8	·93		4
	8	Su	20		6	·10	9	·93		5
	9	Mo	21		7	·07	10	·94		6
	10	Tu	22		8	·06	11	·98		7
	11	We	23		9	·07	...	...		8
	12	Th	24		10	·11	12	·04		9
	13	Fr	25		11	·16	13	·12		10
	14	Sa	26		12	·23	14	·21		11
	15	Su	27		13	·31	15	·31		12
	16	Mo	28		14	·39	16	·42		13
	17	Tu	29		P	·47	17	·53		14
	18	We	30		1	·54	18	·62		15
	19	Th	31		2	·60	19	·70		16

June

Cyclic Sidereal Year, Month	Cyclic Sidereal Day	Week-Day	English Day	Lunar Month	Tithi	Ending Moment	Nakshatra	Ending Moment	Muhammadan Year, Month	Muhammadan Day
	20	Fr	1	Bahula	3	·63	20	·77		17
	21	Sa	2		4	·65	21	·82		18
	22	Su	3		5	·66	22	·84		19
	23	Mo	4		6	·63	23	·84		20
	24	Tu	5		7	·60	24	·83		21
	25	We	6		8	·54	25	·80		22
	26	Th	7		9	·47	26	·76		23
	27	Fr	8		10	·38	27	·70		24
	28	Sa	9		11	·28	1	·63		25
	29	Su	10		12	·18	2	·57		26
	30	Mo	11		13, 14	·08, ·98	3	·50		27
	31	Tu	12		A	·85	4	·43		28
Kshaya Mithuna—Ani.	1	We	13	Nija Jyeshtha Sukla	1	·79	5	·37		29
	2	Th	14		2	·71	6	·32		30
	3	Fr	15		3	·64	7	·28	H. 1283 Safar.	1
	4	Sa	16		4	·59	8	·26		2
	5	Su	17		5	·56	9	·25		3
	6	Mo	18		6	·54	10	·26		4
	7	Tu	19		7	·56	11	·29		5
	8	We	20		8	·59	12	·35		6
	9	Th	21		9	·63	13	·43		7
	10	Fr	22		10	·70	14	·52		8
	11	Sa	23		11	·78	15	·62		9
	12	Su	24		12	·86	16	·72		10
	13	Mo	25		13	·94	17	·83		11
	14	Tu	26		...	...	18	·93		12
	15	We	27		14	·02	...	...		13
	16	Th	28		P	·07	19	·02		14
	17	Fr	29		1	·11	20	·09		15
	18	Sa	30		2	·14	21	·13		16

Naksh :—1. Asvn. 2. Bhar. 3. Krit. 4. Rohi. 5. Mrig. 6. Ardh. 7. Punar. 8. Push. 9. Aslesh. 10. Magh. 11. P. Phal. 12. U. Phal. 13. Hasta. 14. Chit.

A. D. 1866. | Kollam 1042, Commences { N. Malabar—Sept. S. Malabar—Aug. | Hijra 1283, Commences, May 16. | Vikrama 1923. Bengal San 1272. (N. Cycle) Bahudhanya.

A.—Amavasya. P.—Paurnami.

Columns: SOLAR reckoning (Cyclic Sidereal Year, Month and Day; Week-Day; English Month and Day) — LUNAR reckoning (Tithi; Ending Moment; Nakshatra; Ending Moment; Muhammadan Year, Month and Day).

July

Side labels: Solar — Kshaya Mithuna—Ani.; Kshaya Karkata—Adi. Lunar — Jy.; Nija.; Bahula; Sukla; Ashadha. Muhammadan — H. 1283 Sofur.; Rabi-ul-awwal.

Cyclic Sidereal Year, Month and Day	Week-Day	English Month and Day	Tithi	Ending Moment	Nakshatra	Ending Moment	Muhammadan Year, Month and Day
19	Su	1	3	·14	22	·16	17
20	Mo	2	4	·12	23	·18	18
21	Tu	3	5	·08	24	·16	19
22	We	4	6 7	·02 ·94	25	·13	20
23	Th	5	8	·85	26	·09	21
24	Fr	6	9	·75	27 1	·03 ·97	22
25	Sa	7	10	·65	2	·91	23
26	Su	8	11	·55	3	·84	24
27	Mo	9	12	·45	4	·77	25
28	Tu	10	13	·35	5	·71	26
29	We	11	14	·26	6	·66	27
30	Th	12	A	·19	7	·61	28
31	Fr	13	1	·12	8	·58	29
32	Sa	14	2	·07	9	·57	1
1	Su	15	3	·04	10	·58	2
2	Mo	16	4	·02	11	·61	3
3	Tu	17	5	·03	12	·66	4
4	We	18	6	·06	13	·73	5
5	Th	19	7	·11	14	·82	6
6	Fr	20	8	·18	15	·92	7
7	Sa	21	9	·25	...	...	8
8	Su	22	10	·34	16	·02	9
9	Mo	23	11	·42	17	·13	10
10	Tu	24	12	·49	18	·23	11
11	We	25	13	·55	19	·32	12
12	Th	26	14	·59	20	·40	13
13	Fr	27	P	·62	21	·45	14
14	Sa	28	1	·61	22	·49	15
15	Su	29	2	·60	23	·50	16
16	Mo	30	3	·56	24	·49	17
17	Tu	31	4	·50	25	·47	18

Aug.

Side labels: Solar — Kshaya Simha—Avani. Lunar — Bahula; Sukla; Sravana; Bah. Muhammadan — H. 1283; H. 1283 Rabi-ul-akhir.

Cyclic Sidereal Year, Month and Day	Week-Day	English Month and Day	Tithi	Ending Moment	Nakshatra	Ending Moment	Muhammadan Year, Month and Day
18	We	1	5	·43	26	·43	19
19	Th	2	6	·34	27	·38	20
20	Fr	3	7	·25	1	·32	21
21	Sa	4	8	·15	2	·25	22
22	Su	5	9 10	·05 ·95	3	·18	23
23	Mo	6	11	·85	4	·11	24
24	Tu	7	12	·75	5 6	·05 ·99	25
25	We	8	13	·67	7	·95	26
26	Th	9	14	·61	8	·91	27
27	Fr	10	A	·56	9	·90	28
28	Sa	11	1	·52	10	·90	29
29	Su	12	2	·50	11	·93	30
30	Mo	13	3	·52	12	·97	1
31	Tu	14	4	·55	...	...	2
1	We	15	5	·60	13	·04	3
2	Th	16	6	·67	14	·12	4
3	Fr	17	7	·75	15	·21	5
4	Sa	18	8	·83	16	·32	6
5	Su	19	9	·91	17	·43	7
6	Mo	20	10	·99	18	·54	8
7	Tu	21	...	...	19	·63	9
8	We	22	11	·05	20	·70	10
9	Th	23	12	·08	21	·77	11
10	Fr	24	13	·10	22	·81	12
11	Sa	25	14	·11	23	·82	13
12	Su	26	P	·09	24	·82	14
13	Mo	27	1	·06	25	·80	15
14	Tu	28	2 3	·01 ·94	26	·77	16
15	We	29	4	·85	27	·71	17
16	Th	30	5	·76	1	·65	18
17	Fr	31	6	·66	2	·59	19

Sep.

Side labels: Solar — Kshaya Simha—Avani.; Kshaya Kanya—Purattasi. Lunar — Srav.; Bahula; Sukla; Bhadrapada. Muhammadan — Rabi-ul-akhir.; H. 1283 Jumadal-awwal.

Cyclic Sidereal Year, Month and Day	Week-Day	English Month and Day	Tithi	Ending Moment	Nakshatra	Ending Moment	Muhammadan Year, Month and Day
18	Sa	1	7	·56	3	·52	20
19	Su	2	8	·46	4	·45	21
20	Mo	3	9	·36	5	·39	22
21	Tu	4	10	·27	6	·33	23
22	We	5	11	·19	7	·28	24
23	Th	6	12	·12	8	·24	25
24	Fr	7	13	·07	9	·22	26
25	Sa	8	14	·04	10	·23	27
26	Su	9	A	·02	11	·25	28
27	Mo	10	1	·04	12	·28	29
28	Tu	11	2	·07	13	·34	1
29	We	12	3	·12	14	·42	2
30	Th	13	4	·18	15	·52	3
31	Fr	14	5	·26	16	·62	4
1	Sa	15	6	·35	17	·73	5
2	Su	16	7	·43	18	·83	6
3	Mo	17	8	·51	19	·93	7
4	Tu	18	9	·57	...	...	8
5	We	19	10	·61	20	·02	9
6	Th	20	11	·64	21	·08	10
7	Fr	21	12	·65	22	·12	11
8	Sa	22	13	·63	23	·14	12
9	Su	23	14	·60	24	·14	13
10	Mo ○	24	P	·54	25	·13	14
11	Tu	25	1	·47	26	·16	15
12	We	26	2	·39	27 1	·05 ·99	16
13	Th	27	3	·30	2	·92	17
14	Fr	28	4	·21	3	·85	18
15	Sa	29	5	·11	4	·79	19
16	Su	30	6 7	·01 ·91	5	·73	20

Oct.

Side labels: Solar — Kshaya Tula—Aippasi. Lunar — Bahula; Sukla; Asvina; Bahula. Muhammadan — H. 1283 Jumadal-akhir.

Cyclic Sidereal Year, Month and Day	Week-Day	English Month and Day	Tithi	Ending Moment	Nakshatra	Ending Moment	Muhammadan Year, Month and Day
17	Mo	1	8	·82	6	·67	21
18	Tu	2	9	·74	7	·61	22
19	We	3	10	·67	8	·57	23
20	Th	4	11	·62	9	·56	24
21	Fr	5	12	·59	10	·55	25
22	Sa	6	13	·58	11	·56	26
23	Su	7	14	·60	12	·59	27
24	Mo	8	A	·63	13	·65	28
25	Tu	9	1	·68	14	·73	29
26	We	10	2	·74	15	·82	30
27	Th	11	3	·82	16	·92	1
28	Fr	12	4	·91	...	...	2
29	Sa	13	...	...	17	·03	3
30	Su	14	5	·00	18	·14	4
31	Mo	15	6	·08	19	·24	5
1	Tu	16	7	·15	20	·33	6
2	We	17	8	·19	21	·39	7
3	Th	18	9	·21	22	·44	8
4	Fr	19	10	·22	23	·46	9
5	Sa	20	11	·20	24	·47	10
6	Su	21	12	·17	25	·46	11
7	Mo	22	13	·13	26	·43	12
8	Tu	23	14 P	·06 ·97	27	·39	13
9	We	24	1	·88	1	·33	14
10	Th	25	2	·78	2	·27	15
11	Fr	26	3	·68	3	·20	16
12	Sa	27	4	·58	4	·13	17
13	Su	28	5	·49	5	·06	18
14	Mo	29	6	·41	6 7	·00 ·94	19
15	Tu	30	7	·33	8	·91	20
16	We	31	8	·26	9	·88	21

Nov.

Side labels: Solar — Kshaya Tula—Aippasi.; Kshaya Vrischika—Kartigai. Lunar — Asv.; Bah.; Sukla; Karttika; Bahula. Muhammadan — Jumadal-akhir.; H. 1283 Rajub.

Cyclic Sidereal Year, Month and Day	Week-Day	English Month and Day	Tithi	Ending Moment	Nakshatra	Ending Moment	Muhammadan Year, Month and Day
17	Th	1	9	·21	10	·87	22
18	Fr	2	10	·18	11	·88	23
19	Sa	3	11	·17	12	·91	24
20	Su	4	12	·19	13	·97	25
21	Mo	5	13	·22	...	...	26
22	Tu	6	14	·27	14	·04	27
23	We	7	A	·34	15	·12	28
24	Th	8	1	·43	16	·22	29
25	Fr	9	2	·52	17	·33	1
26	Sa	10	3	·61	18	·44	2
27	Su	11	4	·68	19	·54	3
28	Mo	12	5	·75	20	·63	4
29	Tu	13	6	·79	21	·70	5
30	We	14	7	·82	22	·75	6
1	Th	15	8	·83	23	·78	7
2	Fr	16	9	·81	24	·80	8
3	Sa	17	10	·78	25	·79	9
4	Su	18	11	·74	26	·76	10
5	Mo	19	12	·67	27	·72	11
6	Tu	20	13	·58	1	·66	12
7	We	21	14	·49	2	·60	13
8	Th	22	P	·40	3	·54	14
9	Fr	23	1	·30	4	·47	15
10	Sa	24	2	·20	5	·40	16
11	Su	25	3	·10	6	·34	17
12	Mo	26	4 5	·02 ·94	7	·29	18
13	Tu	27	6	·88	8	·24	19
14	We	28	7	·84	9	·21	20
15	Th	29	8	·82	10	·19	21
16	Fr	30	9	·81	11	·20	22

Dec.

Side labels: Solar — Kshaya Dhanus—Margali. Lunar — Sukla; Margasira; Bahula. Muhammadan — H. 1283 Shaban.

Cyclic Sidereal Year, Month and Day	Week-Day	English Month and Day	Tithi	Ending Moment	Nakshatra	Ending Moment	Muhammadan Year, Month and Day
17	Sa	1	10	·81	12	·23	23
18	Su	2	11	·84	13	·28	24
19	Mo	3	12	·90	14	·34	25
20	Tu	4	13	·98	15	·43	26
21	We	5	...	...	16	·52	27
22	Th	6	14	·07	17	·63	28
23	Fr	7	A	·16	18	·74	29
24	Sa	8	1	·24	19	·84	30
25	Su	9	2	·32	20	·93	1
26	Mo	10	3	·39	...	...	2
27	Tu	11	4	·44	21	·01	3
28	We	12	5	·46	22	·06	4
29	Th	13	6	·47	23	·10	5
1	Fr	14	7	·46	24	·12	6
2	Sa	15	8	·42	25	·12	7
3	Su	16	9	·36	26	·09	8
4	Mo	17	10	·29	27	·05	9
5	Tu	18	11	·21	1 2	·01 ·95	10
6	We	19	12	·12	3	·88	11
7	Th	20	13 14	·03 ·93	4	·81	12
8	Fr	21	P	·83	5	·74	13
9	Sa	22	1	·74	6	·68	14
10	Su	23	2	·65	7	·62	15
11	Mo	24	3	·58	8	·57	16
12	Tu.	25	4	·52	9	·54	17
13	We	26	5	·48	10	·52	18
14	Th	27	6	·46	11	·52	19
15	Fr	28	7	·45	12	·55	20
16	Sa	29	8	·47	13	·59	21
17	Su	30	9	·51	14	·65	22
18	Mo	31	10	·56	15	·73	23

A. D. 1867. **Mesha Sankranti** (Commencement of Indian Sidereal Year).

Solar Eclipse. ● **(Surya Sid.) April 12·08.** **Saka 1789.** **Kaliyuga 4968.**

Lunar Eclipse. ○ **(Arya Sid.) April 11·98.** **(S. Cycle) Prabhava.**

Columns: SOLAR reckoning (Cyclic Sidereal Year, Month and Day; Week-Day; English Month and Day) — LUNAR reckoning (Tithi; Ending Moment; Nakshatra; Ending Moment; Muhammadan Year, Month and Day).

Jan.

Solar: *Kshaya, Dhanus—Margali* (to 29); *Kshaya, Makara—Tai*. Lunar: Bah.; Sukla; Pausha; Bahula. Muhammadan: Shaban; H. 1283 Ramzan.

Cyclic Sidereal Year, Month and Day	Week-Day	English Month and Day	Tithi	Ending Moment	Nakshatra	Ending Moment	Muhammadan Year, Month and Day
19	Tu	1	11	·63	16	·82	24
20	We	2	12	·71	17	·93	25
21	Th	3	13	·80	...	...	26
22	Fr	4	14	·89	18	·04	27
23	Sa	5	—A	·97	19	·14	28
24	Su	6	...	...	20	·23	—29
25	Mo	7	1	·04	21	·31	1
26	Tu	8	2	·09	22	·28	2
27	We	9	3	·11	23	·42	3
28	Th	10	4	·11	24	·44	4
—29	Fr	11	5	·09	25	·44	5
1	Sa	12	6	·06	26	·42	6
2	Su	13	7 / 8	·01 / ·94	27	·39	7
3	Mo	14	9	·86	1	·35	8
4	Tu	15	10	·77	2	·29	9
5	We	16	11	·67	3	·23	10
6	Th	17	12	·57	4	·16	11
7	Fr	18	13	·47	5	·09	12
8	Sa	19	14	·38	6 / 7	·02 / ·96	13
9	Su	20	P	·30	8	·91	14
10	Mo	21	1	·22	9	·87	15
11	Tu	22	2	·16	10	·84	16
12	We	23	3	·12	11	·85	17
13	Th	24	4	·10	12	·87	18
14	Fr	25	5	·09	13	·90	19
15	Sa	26	6	·12	14	·95	20
16	Su	27	7	·16	...	...	21
17	Mo	28	8	·23	15	·03	22
18	Tu	29	9	·31	16	·18	23
19	We	30	10	·39	17	·23	24
20	Th	31	11	·47	18	·34	25

Feb.

Solar: *Kshaya, Kumbha—Masi*. Lunar: Sukla; Magha; Bahula. Muhammadan: H. 1283 Shawwal.

Cyclic Sidereal Year, Month and Day	Week-Day	English Month and Day	Tithi	Ending Moment	Nakshatra	Ending Moment	Muhammadan Year, Month and Day
21	Fr	1	12	·55	19	·44	26
22	Sa	2	13	·62	20	·54	27
23	Su	3	14	·68	21	·63	28
24	Mo	4	—A	·73	22	·69	29
25	Tu	5	1	·75	23	·74	—30
26	We	6	2	·76	24	·76	1
27	Th	7	3	·74	25	·77	2
28	Fr	8	4	·69	26	·76	3
29	Sa	9	5	·63	27	·72	4
—30	Su	10	6	·56	1	·68	5
1	Mo	11	7	·48	2	·62	6
2	Tu	12	8	·39	3	·56	7
3	We	13	9	·29	4	·50	8
4	Th	14	10	·19	5	·43	9
5	Fr	15	11	·09	6	·36	10
6	Sa	16	12 / 13	·00 / ·92	7	·20	11
7	Su	17	14	·85	8	·24	12
8	Mo	18	P	·79	9	·20	13
9	Tu	19	1	·75	10	·18	14
10	We	20	2	·72	11	·17	15
11	Th	21	3	·72	12	·18	16
12	Fr	22	4	·74	13	·21	17
13	Sa	23	5	·78	14	·26	18
14	Su	24	6	·84	15	·34	19
15	Mo	25	7	·91	16	·43	20
16	Tu	26	...	...	17	·53	21
17	We	27	8	·00	18	·63	22
18	Th	28	9	·09	19	·74	23

March

Solar: *Kshaya, Kumbha—Masi* (to 30); *Kshaya, Mina—Panguni*. Lunar: Mg. Bah.; Sukla; Phalguna; Bahula. Muhammadan: Shawwal; H. 1283 Zi-l-ka'da.

Cyclic Sidereal Year, Month and Day	Week-Day	English Month and Day	Tithi	Ending Moment	Nakshatra	Ending Moment	Muhammadan Year, Month and Day
19	Fr	1	10	·17	20	·85	24
20	Sa	2	11	·24	21	·94	25
21	Su	3	12	·30	...	...	26
22	Mo	4	13	·34	22	00	27
23	Tu	5	14	·36	23	·05	28
24	We ●	6	—A	·36	24	·08	—29
25	Th	7	1	·34	25	·10	1
26	Fr	8	2	·30	26	·09	2
27	Sa	9	3	·24	27	·06	3
28	Su	10	4	·17	1 / 2	·01 / ·96	4
29	Mo	11	5	·09	3	·90	5
—30	Tu	12	6 / 7	·00 / ·90	4	·84	6
1	We	13	8	·80	5	·77	7
2	Th	14	9	·70	6	·70	8
3	Fr	15	10	·60	7	·63	9
4	Sa	16	11	·52	8	·58	10
5	Su	17	12	·44	9	·54	11
6	Mo	18	13	·38	10	·51	12
7	Tu	19	14	·34	11	·49	13
8	We ○	20	P	·32	12	·50	14
9	Th	21	1	·32	13	·52	15
10	Fr	22	2	·34	14	·58	16
11	Sa	23	3	·38	15	·65	17
12	Su	24	4	·43	16	·73	18
13	Mo	25	5	·50	17	·83	19
14	Tu	26	6	·58	18	·94	20
15	We	27	7	·67	...	...	21
16	Th	28	8	·76	19	·05	22
17	Fr	29	9	·83	20	·15	23
18	Sa	30	10	·89	21	·24	24
19	Su	31	11	·93	22	·31	25

April

Solar: *Prabhava, Mesha—Chittirai*. Lunar: Sukla; Chaitra; Bahula. Muhammadan: H. 1283 Zi-l-hijja.

Cyclic Sidereal Year, Month and Day	Week-Day	English Month and Day	Tithi	Ending Moment	Nakshatra	Ending Moment	Muhammadan Year, Month and Day
20	Mo	1	12	·95	23	·37	26
21	Tu	2	13	·94	24	·40	27
22	We	3	14	·92	25	·42	28
23	Th	4	—A	·87	26	·41	29
24	Fr	5	1	·81	27	·39	—30
25	Sa	6	2	·74	1	·35	1
26	Su	7	3	·66	2	·30	2
27	Mo	8	4	·56	3	·24	3
28	Tu	9	5	·46	4	·17	4
29	We	10	6	·36	5	·10	5
—30	Th	11	7	·26	6 / 7	·03 / ·97	6
1	Fr	12	8	·16	8	·92	7
2	Sa	13	9	·08	9	·87	8
3	Su	14	10 / 11	·00 / ·94	10	·84	9
4	Mo	15	12	·90	11	·82	10
5	Tu	16	13	·87	12	·82	11
6	We	17	14	·87	13	·85	12
7	Th	18	P	·89	14	·89	13
8	Fr	19	1	·93	15	·95	14
9	Sa	20	2	·98	...	...	15
10	Su	21	...	...	16	·03	16
11	Mo	22	3	·04	17	·13	17
12	Tu	23	4	·13	18	·24	18
13	We	24	5	·22	19	·35	19
14	Th	25	6	·30	20	·45	20
15	Fr	26	7	·37	21	·54	21
16	Sa	27	8	·43	22	·62	22
17	Su	28	9	·47	23	·68	23
18	Mo	29	10	·49	24	·73	24
19	Tu	30	11	·47	25	·74	25

May

Solar: *Prabhava, Mesha—Chittirai* (to 31); *Prabhava, Vrishabha—Vaikasi*. Lunar: Bah.; Sukla; Vaisakha; Bahula. Muhammadan: H. 1284 Muharram.

Cyclic Sidereal Year, Month and Day	Week-Day	English Month and Day	Tithi	Ending Moment	Nakshatra	Ending Moment	Muhammadan Year, Month and Day
20	We	1	12	·45	26	·74	26
21	Th	2	13	·41	27	·72	27
22	Fr	3	14	·35	1	·68	28
23	Sa	4	—A	·28	2	·64	—29
24	Su	5	1	·19	3	·58	1
25	Mo	6	2 / 3	·09 / ·99	4	·51	2
26	Tu	7	4	·89	5	·44	3
27	We	8	5	·79	6	·37	4
28	Th	9	6	·69	7	·31	5
29	Fr	10	7	·60	8	·25	6
30	Sa	11	8	·52	9	·20	7
—31	Su	12	9	·47	10	·16	8
1	Mo	13	10	·43	11	·14	9
2	Tu	14	11	·40	12	·15	10
3	We	15	12	·38	13	·16	11
4	Th	16	13	·40	14	·20	12
5	Fr	17	14	·44	15	·26	13
6	Sa	18	P	·49	16	·33	14
7	Su	19	1	·56	17	·43	15
8	Mo	20	2	·64	18	·54	16
9	Tu	21	3	·72	19	·65	17
10	We	22	4	·80	20	·75	18
11	Th	23	5	·87	21	·84	19
12	Fr	24	6	·93	22	·93	20
13	Sa	25	7	·97	...	...	21
14	Su	26	8	·99	23	·00	22
15	Mo	27	9	·98	24	·04	23
16	Tu	28	10	·96	25	·06	24
17	We	29	11	·91	26	·06	25
18	Th	30	12	·85	27	·05	26
19	Fr	31	13	·77	1 / 2	·02 / ·98	27

June

Solar: *Prabhava, Mithuna—Ani*. Lunar: Sukla; Jyeshtha; Bahula. Muhammadan: H. 1284 Safar.

Cyclic Sidereal Year, Month and Day	Week-Day	English Month and Day	Tithi	Ending Moment	Nakshatra	Ending Moment	Muhammadan Year, Month and Day
20	Sa	1	14	·68	3	·92	28
21	Su	2	—A	·58	4	·85	29
22	Mo	3	1	·48	5	·78	—30
23	Tu	4	2	·38	6	·71	1
24	We	5	3	·28	7	·65	2
25	Th	6	4	·19	8	·59	3
26	Fr	7	5	·10	9	·54	4
27	Sa	8	6 / 7	·02 / ·96	10	·50	5
28	Su	9	8	·91	11	·48	6
29	Mo	10	9	·88	12	·47	7
30	Tu	11	10	·87	13	·48	8
—31	We	12	11	·89	14	·51	9
1	Th	13	12	·92	15	·57	10
2	Fr	14	13	·97	16	·64	11
3	Sa	15	...	...	17	·74	12
4	Su	16	14	·04	18	·84	13
5	Mo	17	P	·11	19	·94	14
6	Tu	18	1	·19	...	...	15
7	We	19	2	·27	20	·05	16
8	Th	20	3	·34	21	·15	17
9	Fr	21	4	·40	22	·24	18
10	Sa	22	5	·45	23	·31	19
11	Su	23	6	·47	24	·36	20
12	Mo	24	7	·46	25	·38	21
13	Tu	25	8	·43	26	·39	22
14	We	26	9	·39	27	·38	23
15	Th	27	10	·33	1	·35	24
16	Fr	28	11	·26	2	·31	25
17	Sa	29	12	·18	3	·25	26
18	Su	30	13 / 14	·09 / ·99	4	·19	27

Naksh :—1. Asvn. 2. Bhar. 3. Krit. 4. Rohi. 5. Mrig. 6. Ardh. 7. Punar. 8. Push. 9. Aslesh. 10. Magh. 11. P. Phal. 12. U. Phal. 13. Hasta. 14. Chit.

A. D. 1867.
A.—Amavasya.
P.—Paurnami.

Kollam 1043, Commences { **N. Malabar—Sept.** / **S. Malabar—Aug.**

Hijra 1284, Commences, **May 5.**

Vikrama 1924.
Bengal San 1273.
(N. Cycle) Pramathin.

SOLAR reckoning: Cyclic Sidereal Year, Month and Day; Week-Day; English Month and Day. LUNAR reckoning: Tithi; Ending Moment; Nakshatra; Ending Moment; Muhammadan Year, Month and Day.

July

Solar: Prabhava *Mithuna—Ani.* (to 32); Prabhava *Karkata—Adi.* (from 1). Lunar: Ashadha (Sukla, Bahula). Muhammadan: H. 1284 *Rabi-ul-awwal.*

Cyclic Sidereal Year, Month and Day	Week-Day	English Month and Day	Tithi	Ending Moment	Nakshatra	Ending Moment	Muhammadan Year, Month and Day
19	Mo	1	—A	·87	5	·13	28
20	Tu	2	1	·77	6 / 7	·06 / ·99	—29
21	We	3	2	·67	8	·92	1
22	Th	4	3	·58	9	·87	2
23	Fr	5	4	·50	10	·82	3
24	Sa	6	5	·44	11	·80	4
25	Su	7	6	·39	12	·79	5
26	Mo	8	7	·36	13	·80	6
27	Tu	9	8	·35	14	·83	7
28	We	10	9	·36	15	·88	8
29	Th	11	10	·39	16	·95	9
30	Fr	12	11	·45	...	...	10
31	Sa	13	12	·52	17	·04	11
—32	Su	14	13	·59	18	·13	12
1	Mo	15	14	·67	19	·24	13
2	Tu	16	P	·75	20	·35	14
3	We	17	1	·82	21	·45	15
4	Th	18	2	·88	22	·54	16
5	Fr	19	3	·93	23	·62	17
6	Sa	20	4	·95	24	·67	18
7	Su	21	5	·94	25	·70	19
8	Mo	22	6	·92	26	·72	20
9	Tu	23	7	·88	27	·71	21
10	We	24	8	·81	1	·68	22
11	Th	25	9	·74	2	·64	23
12	Fr	26	10	·66	3	·59	24
13	Sa	27	11	·57	4	·53	25
14	Su	28	12	·47	5	·47	26
15	Mo	29	13	·37	6	·40	27
16	Tu	30	14	·27	7	·33	28
17	We	31	—A	·17	8	·26	29

Aug.

Solar: Prabhava *Simha—Avani.* (from 1). Lunar: Sravana (Sukla, Bahula); Suk. Muhammadan: H. 1284 *Rabi-ul-akhir.*

Cyclic Sidereal Year, Month and Day	Week-Day	English Month and Day	Tithi	Ending Moment	Nakshatra	Ending Moment	Muhammadan Year, Month and Day
18	Th	1	1 / 2	·07 / ·99	9	·20	—30
19	Fr	2	3	·92	10	·16	1
20	Sa	3	4	·87	11	·13	2
21	Su	4	5	·85	12	·12	3
22	Mo	5	6	·84	13	·12	4
23	Tu	6	7	·84	14	·14	5
24	We	7	8	·87	15	·19	6
25	Th	8	9	·92	16	·26	7
26	Fr	9	10	·99	17	·34	8
27	Sa	10	...	...	18	·43	9
28	Su	11	11	·07	19	·54	10
29	Mo	12	12	·16	20	·65	11
30	Tu	13	13	·24	21	·76	12
—31	We	14	14	·31	22	·85	13
1	Th	15	P	·37	23	·92	14
2	Fr	16	1	·41	24	·98	15
3	Sa	17	2	·44	...	...	16
4	Su	18	3	·43	25	·03	17
5	Mo	19	4	·41	26	·04	18
6	Tu	20	5	·38	27	·04	19
7	We	21	6	·33	1 / 2	·01 / ·97	20
8	Th	22	7	·25	3	·92	21
9	Fr	23	8	·16	4	·87	22
10	Sa	24	9 / 10	·06 / ·96	5	·81	23
11	Su	25	11	·86	6	·74	24
12	Mo	26	12	·76	7	·67	25
13	Tu	27	13	·67	8	·60	26
14	We	28	14	·58	9	·55	27
15	Th	29	—A	·49	10	·50	28
16	Fr	30	1	·43	11	·46	—29
17	Sa	31	2	·38	12	·44	1

Sep.

Solar: Prabhava *Simha—Arani.* (to 31); Prabhava *Kanya—Purattasi.* (from 1). Lunar: Bhadrapada (Sukla, Bahula). Muhammadan: H. 1284 *Jumadal-awwal.*

Cyclic Sidereal Year, Month and Day	Week-Day	English Month and Day	Tithi	Ending Moment	Nakshatra	Ending Moment	Muhammadan Year, Month and Day
18	Su	1	3	·35	13	·44	2
19	Mo	2	4	·35	14	·47	3
20	Tu	3	5	·36	15	·50	4
21	We	4	6	·39	16	·56	5
22	Th	5	7	·44	17	·64	6
23	Fr	6	8	·50	18	·73	7
24	Sa	7	9	·57	19	·84	8
25	Su	8	10	·66	20	·95	9
26	Mo	9	11	·75	...	...	10
27	Tu	10	12	·83	21	·06	11
28	We	11	13	·89	22	·15	12
29	Th	12	14	·93	23	·23	13
30	Fr ○	13	P	·96	24	·29	14
—31	Sa	14	1	·97	25	·34	15
1	Su	15	2	·95	26	·36	16
2	Mo	16	3	·90	27	·36	17
3	Tu	17	4	·84	1	·34	18
4	We	18	5	·77	2	·31	19
5	Th	19	6	·69	3	·27	20
6	Fr	20	7	·60	4	·21	21
7	Sa	21	8	·50	5	·14	22
8	Su	22	9	·40	6	·07	23
9	Mo	23	10	·30	7 / 8	·00 / ·94	24
10	Tu	24	11	·20	9	·88	25
11	We	25	12	·11	10	·83	26
12	Th	26	13 / 14	·03 / ·97	11	·79	27
13	Fr	27	—A	·92	12	·77	28
14	Sa	28	1	·90	13	·77	29
15	Su	29	2	·89	14	·78	—30
16	Mo	30	3	·89	15	·82	1

Oct.

Solar: Prabhava *Tula—Aippasi.* (from 1). Lunar: Asvina (Sukla, Bahula); K. Suk. Muhammadan: H. 1284 *Jumadal-akhir.*; *Rajab.*

Cyclic Sidereal Year, Month and Day	Week-Day	English Month and Day	Tithi	Ending Moment	Nakshatra	Ending Moment	Muhammadan Year, Month and Day
17	Tu	1	4	·93	16	·87	2
18	We	2	5	·98	17	·94	3
19	Th	3	...	...	...	...	4
20	Fr	4	6	·05	18	·04	5
21	Sa	5	7	·13	19	·15	6
22	Su	6	8	·22	20	·26	7
23	Mo	7	9	·30	21	·36	8
24	Tu	8	10	·38	22	·45	9
25	We	9	11	·45	23	·54	10
26	Th	10	12	·49	24	·61	11
27	Fr	11	13	·52	25	·66	12
28	Sa	12	14	·52	26	·68	13
29	Su	13	P	·51	27	·69	14
30	Mo	14	1	·47	1	·67	15
—31	Tu	15	2	·41	2	·64	16
1	We	16	3	·34	3	·60	17
2	Th	17	4	·26	4	·55	18
3	Fr	18	5	·17	5	·48	19
4	Sa	19	6 / 7	·07 / ·97	6	·41	20
5	Su	20	8	·87	7	·34	21
6	Mo	21	9	·77	8	·28	22
7	Tu	22	10	·68	9	·22	23
8	We	23	11	·61	10	·16	24
9	Th	24	12	·55	11	·12	25
10	Fr	25	13	·50	12	·10	26
11	Sa	26	14	·48	13	·09	27
12	Su	27	—A	·47	14	·10	28
13	Mo	28	1	·49	15	·13	—29
14	Tu	29	2	·52	16	·18	1
15	We	30	3	·58	17	·25	2
16	Th	31	4	·65	18	·34	3

Nov.

Solar: Prabhava *Tula—Aippasi.* (to 30); Prabhava *Vrischika—Kartigai.* (from 1). Lunar: Sukla; Karttika; Bahula. Muhammadan: H. 1284 *Rajab.*

Cyclic Sidereal Year, Month and Day	Week-Day	English Month and Day	Tithi	Ending Moment	Nakshatra	Ending Moment	Muhammadan Year, Month and Day
17	Fr	1	5	·73	19	·44	4
18	Sa	2	6	·81	20	·55	5
19	Su	3	7	·90	21	·65	6
20	Mo	4	8	·98	22	·75	7
21	Tu	5	...	...	23	·85	8
22	We	6	9	·04	24	·92	9
23	Th	7	10	·09	25	·97	10
24	Fr	8	11	·12	...	...	11
25	Sa	9	12	·12	26	·00	12
26	Su	10	13	·10	27	·01	13
27	Mo	11	14	·06	1 / 2	·01 / ·98	14
28	Tu	12	P / 1	·01 / ·94	3	·94	15
29	We	13	2	·86	4	·88	16
—30	Th	14	3	·77	5	·82	17
1	Fr	15	4	·67	6	·76	18
2	Sa	16	5	·57	7	·69	19
3	Su	17	6	·47	8	·62	20
4	Mo	18	7	·38	9	·56	21
5	Tu	19	8	·30	10	·50	22
6	We	20	9	·23	11	·46	23
7	Th	21	10	·17	12	·43	24
8	Fr	22	11	·13	13	·41	25
9	Sa	23	12	·10	14	·42	26
10	Su	24	13	·09	15	·44	27
11	Mo	25	14	·11	16	·49	28
12	Tu	26	—A	·14	17	·56	29
13	We	27	1	·20	18	·64	—30
14	Th	28	2	·27	19	·74	1
15	Fr	29	3	·36	20	·85	2
16	Sa	30	4	·45	21	·96	3

Dec.

Solar: Prabhava *Dhanus—Margali.* (from 1). Lunar: Margasira (Sukla, Bahula); Paush. Suk. Muhammadan: H. 1284 *Shaban.*; *Ramzan.*

Cyclic Sidereal Year, Month and Day	Week-Day	English Month and Day	Tithi	Ending Moment	Nakshatra	Ending Moment	Muhammadan Year, Month and Day
17	Su	1	5	·53	...	...	4
18	Mo	2	6	·61	22	·06	5
19	Tu	3	7	·68	23	·15	6
20	We	4	8	·73	24	·23	7
21	Th	5	9	·75	25	·28	8
22	Fr	6	10	·76	26	·32	9
23	Sa	7	11	·74	27	·34	10
24	Su	8	12	·70	1	·34	11
25	Mo	9	13	·64	2	·31	12
26	Tu	10	14	·57	3	·27	13
27	We	11	P	·49	4	·22	14
28	Th	12	1	·40	5	·17	15
—29	Fr	13	2	·31	6	·10	16
1	Sa	14	3	·21	7 / 8	·03 / ·96	17
2	Su	15	4	·11	9	·89	18
3	Mo	16	5 / 6	·01 / ·93	10	·83	19
4	Tu	17	7	·86	11	·79	20
5	We	18	8	·80	12	·76	21
6	Th	19	9	·76	13	·74	22
7	Fr	20	10	·74	14	·74	23
8	Sa	21	11	·74	15	·76	24
9	Su	22	12	·75	16	·81	25
10	Mo	23	13	·79	17	·87	26
11	Tu	24	14	·85	18	·95	27
12	We	25	—A	·93	...	...	28
13	Th	26	...	...	19	·04	—29
14	Fr	27	1	·02	20	·14	1
15	Sa	28	2	·10	21	·25	2
16	Su	29	3	·19	22	·36	3
17	Mo	30	4	·27	23	·46	4
18	Tu	31	5	·33	24	·54	5

15. Svati. 16. Visak. 17. Anur. 18. Jyesh. 19. Mula. 20. P. Ash. 21. U. Ash. 22. Sravn. 23. Dani. 24. Satab. 25. P. Bhad. 26. U. Bhad. 27. Rev.

A. D. 1868. **Mesha Sankranti** (Commencement of Indian Sidereal Year).
Solar Eclipse. ● **(Surya Sid.) April 11·34.** **Saka 1790.** **Kaliyuga 4969.**
Lunar Eclipse. ○ **(Arya Sid.) April 11·24.** **(S. Cycle) Vibhava.**

Column headings: SOLAR reckoning — Cyclic Sidereal Year, Month and Day; Week-Day; English Month and Day. LUNAR reckoning — Tithi; Ending Moment; Nakshatra; Ending Moment; Muhammadan Year, Month and Day.

Jan.

Cyclic Sidereal Year, Month and Day	Week-Day	English Month and Day	Tithi	Ending Moment	Nakshatra	Ending Moment	Muhammadan Year, Month and Day
Prabhava Dhanus—Marguli, 19	We	1	Sukla 6	·37	25	·59	6
20	Th	2	7	·39	26	·64	7
21	Fr	3	8	·39	27	·66	8
22	Sa	4	9	·38	1	·66	9
23	Su	5	10	·34	2	·64	10
24	Mo	6	11	·28	3	·61	11
25	Tu	7	12	·21	4	·57	12
26	We	8	13	·13	5	·51	13
27	Th	9	{14 / P	·04 / ·95	6	·44	H. 1284 Ramzan. 14
28	Fr	10	Pausha Bahula 1	·85	7	·37	15
29	Sa	11	2	·75	8	·30	16
30	Su	12	3	·66	9	·23	17
Prabhava Makara—Tai. 1	Mo	13	4	·58	10	·18	18
2	Tu	14	5	·50	11	·13	19
3	We	15	6	·44	12	·09	20
4	Tu	16	7	·41	13	·06	21
5	Fr	17	8	·39	14	·06	22
6	Sa	18	9	·38	15	·08	23
7	Su	19	10	·40	16	·12	24
8	Mo	20	11	·44	17	·18	25
9	Tu	21	12	·50	18	·25	26
10	We	22	13	·58	19	·34	27
11	Th	23	14	·66	20	·45	28
12	Fr	24	A	·75	21	·56	29
13	Sa	25	Sukla 1	·84	22	·66	30
14	Su	26	2	·92	23	·76	1
15	Mo	27	3	·98	24	·84	2
16	Tu	28	...	...	25	·91	3
17	We	29	4	·01	26	·96	4
18	Th	30	5	·03	27	·98	5
19	Fr	31	6	·04	1	·99	6

Feb.

Cyclic Sidereal Year, Month and Day	Week-Day	English Month and Day	Tithi	Ending Moment	Nakshatra	Ending Moment	Muhammadan Year, Month and Day
20	Sa	1	{7 / 8	·02 / ·97	2	·97	H. 1284 Shawwal. 7
21	Su	2	9	·91	3	·94	8
22	Mo	3	10	·84	4	·90	9
23	Tu	4	11	·76	5	·84	10
24	We	5	12	·67	6	·78	11
25	Th	6	13	·58	7	·71	12
26	Fr	7	14	·48	8	·64	13
27	Sa	8	P	·38	9	·57	14
28	Su	9	Magha Bahula 1	·28	10	·51	15
29	Mo	10	2	·20	11	·46	16
Prabhava Kumbha—Masi. 1	Tu	11	3	·13	12	·42	17
2	We	12	4	·08	13	·39	18
3	Th	13	5	·04	14	·39	19
4	Fr	14	6	·02	15	·40	20
5	Sa	15	7	·01	16	·43	21
6	Su	16	8	·04	17	·48	22
7	Mo	17	9	·08	18	·55	23
8	Tu	18	10	·13	19	·65	24
9	We	19	11	·21	20	·75	25
10	Th	20	12	·29	21	·86	26
11	Fr	21	13	·38	22	·96	27
12	Sa	22	14	·47	...	...	28
13	Su	23	A	·54	23	·06	29
14	Mo	24	Phalg. Suk. 1	·60	24	·15	Zi-l-ka'da. 1
15	Tu	25	2	·64	25	·22	2
16	We	26	3	·66	26	·27	3
17	Th	27	4	·65	27	·30	4
18	Fr	28	5	·63	1	·31	5
19	Sa	29	6	·59	2	·30	6

March

Cyclic Sidereal Year, Month and Day	Week-Day	English Month and Day	Tithi	Ending Moment	Nakshatra	Ending Moment	Muhammadan Year, Month and Day
Prabhava Kumbha—Masi. 20	Su	1	Sukla 7	·53	3	·28	H. 1284 Zi-l-ka'da. 7
21	Mo	2	8	·46	4	·23	8
22	Tu	3	9	·37	5	·18	9
23	We	4	10	·28	6	·12	10
24	Th	5	11	·19	7 / 8}	·05 / ·98	11
25	Fr	6	{12 / 13	·00 / ·99	9	·91	12
26	Sa	7	14	·90	10	·85	13
27	Su	8	P	·81	11	·79	14
28	Mo	9	Phalguna Bahula 1	·74	12	·75	15
29	Tu	10	2	·68	13	·73	16
30	We	11	3	·64	14	·71	17
31	Th	12	4	·62	15	·72	18
Prabhava Mina—Panguni. 1	Fr	13	5	·61	16	·74	19
2	Sa	14	6	·64	17	·79	20
3	Su	15	7	·68	18	·87	21
4	Mo	16	8	·73	19	·95	22
5	Tu	17	9	·81	...	...	23
6	We	18	10	·90	20	·05	24
7	Th	19	11	·99	21	·15	25
8	Fr	20	...	...	22	·26	26
9	Sa	21	12	·07	23	·36	27
10	Su	22	13	·14	24	·46	28
11	Mo	23	14	·20	25	·53	29
12	Tu	24	A	·24	26	·59	30
13	We	25	Sukla 1	·25	27	·62	1
14	Th	26	2	·24	1	·63	2
15	Fr	27	3	·23	2	·63	3
16	Sa	28	4	·17	3	·61	4
17	Su	29	5	·12	4	·57	5
18	Mo	30	{6 / 7	·04 / ·95	5	·51	6
19	Tu	31	8	·85	6	·45	7

April

Cyclic Sidereal Year, Month and Day	Week-Day	English Month and Day	Tithi	Ending Moment	Nakshatra	Ending Moment	Muhammadan Year, Month and Day
20	We	1	9	·75	7	·39	H. 1284 Zi-l-hijja. 8
21	Th	2	10	·65	8	·32	9
22	Fr	3	11	·56	9	·25	10
23	Sa	4	12	·47	10	·19	11
24	Su	5	13	·38	11	·13	12
25	Mo	6	14	·31	12	·09	13
26	Tu	7	P	·25	13	·06	14
27	We	8	Chaitra Bahula 1	·21	14	·04	15
28	Th	9	2	·18	15	·04	16
29	Fr	10	3	·17	16	·06	17
Vibhava Mesha—Chittirai. 1	Sa	11	4	·19	17	·10	18
2	Su	12	5	·23	18	·17	19
3	Mo	13	6	·30	19	·25	20
4	Tu	14	7	·38	20	·35	21
5	We	15	8	·46	21	·45	22
6	Th	16	9	·54	22	·56	23
7	Fr	17	10	·62	23	·67	24
8	Sa	18	11	·69	24	·76	25
9	Su	19	12	·75	25	·84	26
10	Mo	20	13	·79	26	·90	27
11	Tu	21	14	·80	27	·94	28
12	We	22	A	·79	1	·96	29
13	Th	23	Vaisak. Sukla 1	·76	2	·95	30
14	Fr	24	2	·72	3	·93	1285 Muharram. 1
15	Sa	25	3	·66	4	·90	2
16	Su	26	4	·59	5	·85	3
17	Mo	27	5	·50	6	·80	4
18	Tu	28	6	·40	7	·73	5
19	We	29	7	·30	8	·66	6
20	Th	30	8	·20	9	·59	7

May

Cyclic Sidereal Year, Month and Day	Week-Day	English Month and Day	Tithi	Ending Moment	Nakshatra	Ending Moment	Muhammadan Year, Month and Day
Vibhava Mesha—Chittirai. 21	Fr	1	9	·10	10	·53	H. 1285 Muharram. 8
22	Sa	2	{10 / 11	·00 / ·91	11	·47	9
23	Su	3	Vaisakha Suk. 12	·84	12	·42	10
24	Mo	4	13	·78	13	·38	11
25	Tu	5	14	·74	14	·36	12
26	We	6	P	·71	15	·36	13 ●
27	Th	7	1	·71	16	·37	14
28	Fr	8	2	·73	17	·42	15
29	Sa	9	3	·76	18	·48	16
30	Su	10	4	·82	19	·55	17
31	Mo	11	5	·89	20	·65	18
Vibhava Vrishabha—Vaikasi. 1	Tu	12	6	·97	21	·75	19
2	We	13	...	...	22	·86	20
3	Th	14	Bahula 7	·05	23	·97	21
4	Fr	15	8	·13	...	...	22
5	Sa	16	9	·20	24	·07	23
6	Su	17	10	·26	25	·15	24
7	Mo	18	11	·30	26	·21	25
8	Tu	19	12	·31	27	·26	26
9	We	20	13	·31	1	·28	27
10	Th	21	14	·28	2	·28	28
11	Fr	22	A	·24	3	·26	29
12	Sa	23	Sukla 1	·17	4	·23	30
13	Su	24	2	·09	5	·19	1
14	Mo	25	{3 / 4	·00 / ·90	6	·14	2
15	Tu	26	5	·80	7	·07	3
16	We	27	6	·70	8 / 9}	·00 / ·93	4
17	Th	28	7	·60	10	·87	5
18	Fr	29	8	·50	11	·81	6
19	Sa	30	9	·41	12	·75	7
20	Su	31	10	·34	13	·71	8

June

Cyclic Sidereal Year, Month and Day	Week-Day	English Month and Day	Tithi	Ending Moment	Nakshatra	Ending Moment	Muhammadan Year, Month and Day
21	Mo	1	Jyeshtha 11	·28	14	·69	H. 1285 Safar. 9
22	Tu	2	12	·24	15	·68	10
23	We	3	13	·21	16	·70	11
24	Th	4	14	·20	17	·73	12
25	Fr	5	P	·21	18	·79	13
26	Sa	6	Bahula 1	·25	19	·86	14
27	Su	7	2	·31	20	·95	15
28	Mo	8	3	·38	...	...	16
29	Tu	9	4	·46	21	·05	17
30	We	10	5	·54	22	·16	18
31	Th	11	6	·61	23	·27	19
32	Fr	12	7	·68	24	·37	20
Vibhava Mithuna—Ani. 1	Sa	13	8	·74	25	·46	21
2	Su	14	9	·78	26	·53	22
3	Mo	15	10	·80	27	·58	23
4	Tu	16	11	·79	1	·60	24
5	We	17	12	·77	2	·61	25
6	Th	18	13	·72	3	·59	26
7	Fr	19	14	·66	4	·57	27
8	Sa	20	A	·58	5	·53	28
9	Su	21	Ashada. Sukla 1	·49	6	·47	29
10	Mo	22	2	·39	7	·41	1285 Rabi-ul-awwal. 1
11	Tu	23	3	·29	8	·34	2
12	We	24	4	·19	9	·27	3
13	Th	25	{5 / 6	·09 / ·99	10	·21	4
14	Fr	26	7	·90	11	·15	5
15	Sa	27	8	·82	12	·09	6
16	Su	28	9	·76	13	·04	7
17	Mo	29	10	·72	14	·01	8
18	Tu	30	11	·69	15	·01	9

Naksh:—1. Asvn. 2. Bhar. 3. Krit. 4. Rohi. 5. Mrig. 6. Ardh. 7. Punar. 8. Push. 9. Aslesh. 10. Magh. 11. P. Phal. 12. U. Phal. 13. Hasta. 14. Chit.

A. D. 1868.
A.—Amavasya.
P.—Paurnami.

Kollam 1044, Commences { **N. Malabar—Sept.** / **S. Malabar—Aug.**

Hijra 1285, Commences, **Apr. 24.**

Vikrama 1925.
Bengal San 1274.
(N. Cycle) Vikrama.

SOLAR reckoning: Month	Cyclic Sidereal Year, Month and Day	Week-Day	English Month and Day	LUNAR reckoning: Month	Tithi	Ending Moment	Nakshatra	Ending Moment	Muhammadan Month	Muhammadan Year, Month and Day
		July								
Vibhava *Mithuna—Ani.*	19	We	1	Ashadha *Suk.*	12	·68	16	·02	H. 1285 *Rabi-ul-awwal.*	10
	20	Th	2		13	·69	17	·05		11
	21	Fr	3		14	·72	18	·10		12
	22	Sa	4		P	·78	19	·17		13
	23	Su	5	*Bahula*	1	·85	20	·26		14
	24	Mo	6		2	·93	21	·36		15
	25	Tu	7		...	...	22	·46		16
	26	We	8		3	·01	23	·57		17
	27	Th	9		4	·09	24	·67		18
	28	Fr	10		5	·16	25	·77		19
	29	Sa	11		6	·22	26	·84		20
	30	Su	12		7	·26	27	·89		21
	—31	Mo	13		8	·28	1	·92		22
Vibhava *Karkata—Adi.*	1	Tu	14		9	·27	2	·93		23
	2	We	15		10	·25	3	·92		24
	3	Th	16		11	·20	4	·90		25
	4	Fr	17		12	·14	5	·86		26
	5	Sa	18		13 14	·06 ·97	6	·81		27
	6	Su	19	*Sukla*	A	·88	7	·75		28
	7	Mo	20		1	·78	8	·69		29
	8	Tu	21		2	·68	9	·62		—30
	9	We	22		3	·58	10	·55		1
	10	Th	23		4	·48	11	·48		2
	11	Fr	24		5	·38	12	·42		3
	12	Sa	25		6	·30	13	·38		4
	13	Su	26		7	·24	14	·35		5
	14	Mo	27		8	·20	15	·34		6
	15	Tu	28		9	·17	16	·34		7
	16	We	29		10	·16	17	·36		8
	17	Th	30		11	·18	18	·40		9
	18	Fr	31		12	·21	19	·47		10
		Aug.								
	19	Sa	1	Sravana	13	·25	20	·56	H. 1285 *Rabi-ul-akhir.*	11
	20	Su	2		14	·32	21	·65		12
	21	Mo	3		P	·40	22	·76		13
	22	Tu	4	*Bahula*	1	·49	23	·87		14
	23	We	5		2	·57	24	·98		15
	24	Th	6		3	·64	...	...		16
	25	Fr	7		4	·70	25	·07		17
	26	Sa	8		5	·73	26	·14		18
	27	Su	9		6	·75	27	·20		19
	28	Mo	10		7	·75	1	·24		20
	29	Tu	11		8	·73	2	·25		21
	30	We	12		9	·69	3	·26		22
	31	Th	13		10	·64	4	·24		23
	—32	Fr	14		11	·56	5	·20		24
Vibhava *Simha—Avani.*	1	Sa	15		12	·47	6	·14		25
	2	Su	16		13	·38	7	·08		26
	3	Mo	17		14	·28	8 9	·02 ·96		27
	4	Tu ●	18		A	·18	10	·89		28
	5	We	19	Bhadrapada *Sukla*	1 2	·08 ·98	11	·82		—29
	6	Th	20		3	·89	12	·76	H. 1285 *Jumadal-awwal.*	1
	7	Fr	21		4	·81	13	·72		2
	8	Sa	22		5	·74	14	·68		3
	9	Su	23		6	·69	15	·66		4
	10	Mo	24		7	·67	16	·66		5
	11	Tu	25		8	·66	17	·68		6
	12	We	26		9	·67	18	·72		7
	13	Th	27		10	·71	19	·78		8
	14	Fr	28		11	·76	20	·86		9
	15	Sa	29		12	·82	21	·95		10
	16	Su	30		13	·90	...	...		11
	17	Mo	31		14	·99	22	·06		12

SOLAR reckoning: Month	Cyclic Sidereal Year, Month and Day	Week-Day	English Month and Day	LUNAR reckoning: Month	Tithi	Ending Moment	Nakshatra	Ending Moment	Muhammadan Month	Muhammadan Year, Month and Day
		Sep.								
Vibhava *Simha—Avani.*	18	Tu	1	Bhadra.	...	...	23	·17	H. 1285 *Jumadal-awwal.*	13
	19	We	2		P	·07	24	·28		14
	20	Th	3	*Bahula*	1	·15	25	·37		15
	21	Fr	4		2	·21	26	·45		16
	22	Sa	5		3	·25	27	·51		17
	23	Su	6		4	·27	1	·55		18
	24	Mo	7		5	·27	2	·58		19
	25	Tu	8		6	·25	3	·58		20
	26	We	9		7	·21	4	·56		21
	27	Th	10		8	·16	5	·53		22
	28	Fr	11		9	·09	6	·48		23
	29	Sa	12		10 11	·00 ·90	7	·42		24
	30	Su	13		12	·80	8	·36		25
	—31	Mo	14		13	·70	9	·29		26
Vibhava *Kanya—Purattasi.*	1	Tu	15		14	·60	10	·22		27
	2	We	16	*Sukla*	A	·51	11	·15		28
	3	Th	17		1	·42	12	·10		29
	4	Fr	18		2	·34	13	·05		—30
	5	Sa	19		3	·27	14 15	·01 ·99	*Jumadal-akhir.*	1
	6	Su	20		4	·23	16	·98		2
	7	Mo	21		5	·20	17	·99		3
	8	Tu	22		6	·19	...	...		4
	9	We	23		7	·20	18	·03		5
	10	Th	24		8	·24	19	·09		6
	11	Fr	25		9	·30	20	·16		7
	12	Sa	26		10	·37	21	·25		8
	13	Su	27		11	·45	22	·36		9
	14	Mo	28		12	·53	23	·47		10
	15	Tu	29		13	·62	24	·58		11
	16	We	30		14	·69	25	·67		12
		Oct.								
	17	Th	1	Asvina	P	·75	26	·75	H. 1285	13
	18	Fr	2	*Bahula*	1	·79	27	·82		14
	19	Sa	3		2	·81	1	·87		15
	20	Su	4		3	·82	2	·90		16
	21	Mo	5		4	·80	3	·91		17
	22	Tu	6		5	·77	4	·89		18
	23	We	7		6	·71	5	·86		19
	24	Th	8		7	·64	6	·82		20
	25	Fr	9		8	·56	7	·77		21
	26	Sa	10		9	·47	8	·70		22
	27	Su	11		10	·37	9	·63		23
	28	Mo	12		11	·27	10	·56		24
	29	Tu	13		12	·17	11	·50		25
	—30	We	14		13 14	·07 ·98	12	·44		26
Vibhava *Tula—Aippasi.*	1	Th	15	*Sukla*	A	·91	13	·38		27
	2	Fr	16		1	·85	14	·34		28
	3	Sa	17		2	·80	15	·31		—29
	4	Su	18		3	·77	16	·30	H. 1285 *Rajab.*	1
	5	Mo	19		4	·77	17	·32		2
	6	Tu	20		5	·79	18	·35		3
	7	We	21		6	·83	19	·40		4
	8	Th	22		7	·88	20	·47		5
	9	Fr	23		8	·94	21	·56		6
	10	Sa	24		...	...	22	·66		7
	11	Su	25		9	·02	23	·77		8
	12	Mo	26	Karttika	10	·11	24	·87		9
	13	Tu	27		11	·20	25	·97		10
	14	We	28		12	·28	...	...		11
	15	Th	29		13	·35	26	·06		12
	16	Fr	30		14	·39	27	·14		13
	17	Sa	31		P	·41	1	·19		14

SOLAR reckoning: Month	Cyclic Sidereal Year, Month and Day	Week-Day	English Month and Day	LUNAR reckoning: Month	Tithi	Ending Moment	Nakshatra	Ending Moment	Muhammadan Month	Muhammadan Year, Month and Day
		Nov.								
Vibhava *Tula—Aippasi.*	18	Su	1	Karttika *Bahula*	1	·41	2	·22	H. 1285 *Rajab.*	15
	19	Mo	2		2	·39	3	·23		16
	20	Tu	3		3	·36	4	·22		17
	21	We	4		4	·31	5	·20		18
	22	Th	5		5	·24	6	·16		19
	23	Fr	6		6	·15	7	·10		20
	24	Sa	7		7 8	·05 ·95	8 9	·04 ·97		21
	25	Su	8		9	·86	10	·90		22
	26	Mo	9		10	·77	11	·84		23
	27	Tu	10		11	·68	12	·78		24
	28	We	11		12	·59	13	·72		25
	29	Th	12		13	·51	14	·67		26
	—30	Fr	13		14	·45	15	·64		27
Vibhava *Vrischika—Kartigai.*	1	Sa	14	*Sukla*	A	·41	16	·63		28
	2	Su	15		1	·38	17	·64		29
	3	Mo	16		2	·38	18	·66		—30
	4	Tu	17		3	·39	19	·71	*Shaban.*	1
	5	We	18		4	·43	20	·77		2
	6	Th	19		5	·49	21	·86		3
	7	Fr	20		6	·57	22	·96		4
	8	Sa	21		7	·65	...	...		5
	9	Su	22		8	·74	23	·07		6
	10	Mo	23	Margasira	9	·83	24	·17		7
	11	Tu	24		10	·90	25	·27		8
	12	We	25		11	·96	26	·37		9
	13	Th	26		...	...	27	·45		10
	14	Fr	27		12	·01	1	·50		11
	15	Sa	28		13	·04	2	·53		12
	16	Su	29		14	·03	3	·55		13
	17	Mo	30		P 1	·02 ·98	4	·55		14
		Dec.								
	18	Tu	1	*Bahula*	2	·92	5	·53	H. 1285	15
	19	We	2		3	·85	6	·49		16
	20	Th	3		4	·77	7	·44		17
	21	Fr	4		5	·69	8	·38		18
	22	Sa	5		6	·59	9	·32		19
	23	Su	6		7	·49	10	·25		20
	24	Mo	7		8	·39	11	·18		21
	25	Tu	8		9	·29	12	·11		22
	26	We	9		10	·21	13	·05		23
	27	Th	10		11	·14	14 15	·00 ·98		24
	28	Fr	11		12	·08	16	·96		25
	29	Sa	12		13	·04	17	·96		26
	—30	Su	13		14	·02	18	·98		27
Vibhava *Dhanus—Margali.*	1	Mo	14	*Sukla*	A	·01	...	...		28
	2	Tu	15		1	·03	19	·02		—29
	3	We	16		2	·08	20	·09	H. 1285 *Ramzan.*	1
	4	Th	17		3	·14	21	·17		2
	5	Fr	18		4	·22	22	·26		3
	6	Sa	19		5	·30	23	·36		4
	7	Su	20		6	·39	24	·47		5
	8	Mo	21		7	·48	25	·58		6
	9	Tu	22		8	·56	26	·68		7
	10	We	23		9	·61	27	·76		8
	11	Th	24		10	·65	1	·81		9
	12	Fr	25		11	·68	2	·85		10
	13	Sa	26		12	·68	3	·87		11
	14	Su	27	Pausha	13	·66	4	·88		12
	15	Mo	28		14	·62	5	·86		13
	16	Tu	29		P	·56	6	·82		14
	17	We	30		1	·49	7	·77		15
	18	Th	31		2	·41	8	·71		16

15. Svati. 16. Visak. 17. Anur. 18. Jyesh. 19. Mula. 20. P. Ash. 21. U. Ash. 22. Sravn. 23. Dani. 24. Satab. 25. P. Bhad. 26. U. Bhad. 27. Rev.

A. D. 1869. **Mesha Sankranti** (Commencement of Indian Sidereal Year).

Solar Eclipse. ● **(Surya Sid.) April 11·60.** **Saka 1791.** **Kaliyuga 4970.**

Lunar Eclipse. ○ **(Arya Sid.) April 11·50.** **(S. Cycle) Sukla.**

Columns: SOLAR reckoning (Cyclic Sidereal Year, Month and Day; Week-Day; English Month and Day) — LUNAR reckoning (Tithi; Ending Moment; Nakshatra; Ending Moment; Muhammadan Year, Month and Day).

Jan. — Solar: Vibhava, *Dhanus—Margali* (19–29); Vibhava, *Makara—Tai* (1–20). Lunar: Psh. *Bahula*; *Sukla*; Magha. Muhammadan: H. 1285 *Ramzan*; H. 1285 *Shawwal*.

Cyclic Sidereal Year, Month and Day	Week-Day	English Month and Day	Tithi	Ending Moment	Nakshatra	Ending Moment	Muhammadan Year, Month and Day
19	Fr	1	3	·32	9	·65	17
20	Sa	2	4	·22	10	·59	18
21	Su	3	5	·12	11	·52	19
22	Mo	4	6 7	·02 ·94	12	·45	20
23	Tu	5	8	·86	13	·39	21
24	We	6	9	·78	14	·35	22
25	Th	7	10	·72	15	·31	23
26	Fr	8	11	·68	16	·28	24
27	Sa	9	12	·67	17	·28	25
28	Su	10	13	·67	18	·29	26
29	Mo	11	14	·69	19	·33	27
1	Tu	12	A	·73	20	·39	28
2	We	13	1	·79	21	·47	29
3	Th	14	2	·86	22	·56	30
4	Fr	15	3	·95	23	·66	1
5	Sa	16	...	...	24	·77	2
6	Su	17	4	·05	25	·88	3
7	Mo	18	5	·13	26	·98	4
8	Tu	19	6	·20	...	...	5
9	We	20	7	·26	27	·06	6
10	Th	21	8	·30	1	·13	7
11	Fr	22	9	·32	2	·17	8
12	Sa	23	10	·32	3	·20	9
13	Su	24	11	·30	4	·20	10
14	Mo	25	12	·26	5	·19	11
15	Tu	26	13	·20	6	·16	12
16	We	27	14	·13	7	·11	13
17	Th ○	28	P 1	·05 ·95	8	·06	14
18	Fr	29	2	·85	9 10	·00 ·93	15
19	Sa	30	3	·75	11	·86	16
20	Su	31	4	·65	12	·79	17

Feb. — Solar: Vibhava, *Kumbha—Masi*. Lunar: *Bahula*; *Sukla*; Phalguna. Muhammadan: H. 1285 *Zi-l-ka'da*.

Cyclic Sidereal Year, Month and Day	Week-Day	English Month and Day	Tithi	Ending Moment	Nakshatra	Ending Moment	Muhammadan Year, Month and Day
21	Mo	1	5	·56	13	·73	18
22	Tu	2	6	·48	14	·68	19
23	We	3	7	·41	15	·64	20
24	Th	4	8	·36	16	·61	21
25	Fr	5	9	·32	17	·60	22
26	Sa	6	10	·30	18	·61	23
27	Su	7	11	·30	19	·65	24
28	Mo	8	12	·32	20	·70	25
29	Tu	9	13	·37	21	·77	26
1	We	10	14	·43	22	·86	27
2	Th	11	A	·51	23	96	28
3	Fr	12	1	·60	...	...	29
4	Sa	13	2	·68	24	·07	1
5	Su	14	3	·76	25	·18	2
6	Mo	15	4	·84	26	·28	3
7	Tu	16	5	·90	27	·37	4
8	We	17	6	·94	1	·43	5
9	Th	18	7	·96	2	·48	6
10	Fr	19	8	·95	3	·51	7
11	Sa	20	9	·93	4	·53	8
12	Su	21	10	·88	5	·52	9
13	Mo	22	11	·82	6	·49	10
14	Tu	23	12	·75	7	·45	11
15	We	24	13	·67	8	·40	12
16	Th	25	14	·57	9	·33	13
17	Fr	26	P	·47	10	·26	14
18	Sa	27	1	·37	11	·19	15
19	Su	28	2	·27	12	·13	16

March — Solar: Vibhava, *Kumbha—Masi* (20–30); Vibhava, *Mina—Panguni* (1–20). Lunar: Pal. *Bahula*; *Sukla*; Chaitra. Muhammadan: H. 1285 *Zi-l-ka'da*; H. 1285 *Zi-l-hijja*.

Cyclic Sidereal Year, Month and Day	Week-Day	English Month and Day	Tithi	Ending Moment	Nakshatra	Ending Moment	Muhammadan Year, Month and Day
20	Mo	1	3	·18	13	·07	17
21	Tu	2	4	·09	14 15	·01 ·97	18
22	We	3	5 6	·02 ·96	16	·94	19
23	Th	4	7	·93	17	·92	20
24	Fr	5	8	·91	18	·94	21
25	Sa	6	9	·92	19	·96	22
26	Su	7	10	·94	...	...	23
27	Mo	8	11	·98	20	·01	24
28	Tu	9	...	...	21	·08	25
29	We	10	12	·04	22	·16	26
30	Th	11	13	·12	23	·26	27
1	Fr	12	14	·21	24	·37	28
2	Sa	13	A	·29	25	·48	29
3	Su	14	1	·37	26	·58	30
4	Mo	15	2	·44	27	·67	1
5	Tu	16	3	·50	1	·75	2
6	We	17	4	·54	2	·81	3
7	Th	18	5	·55	3	·84	4
8	Fr	19	6	·54	4	·85	5
9	Sa	20	7	·52	5	·84	6
10	Su	21	8	·48	6	·83	7
11	Mo	22	9	·42	7	·79	8
12	Tu	23	10	·34	8	·73	9
13	We	24	11	·25	9	·67	10
14	Th	25	12	·15	10	·60	11
15	Fr	26	13 14	·05 ·95	11	·53	12
16	Sa	27	P	·85	12	·47	13
17	Su	28	1	·76	13	·41	14
18	Mo	29	2	·68	14	·35	15
19	Tu	30	3	·61	15	·30	16
20	We	31	4	·55	16	·27	17

April — Solar: Sukla, *Mesha—Chittirai*. Lunar: *Sukla*; Adhika Vaisakha *Sukla*; *Bah.* Muhammadan: H. 1286 *Muharram*.

Cyclic Sidereal Year, Month and Day	Week-Day	English Month and Day	Tithi	Ending Moment	Nakshatra	Ending Moment	Muhammadan Year, Month and Day
21	Th	1	5	·51	17	·26	18
22	Fr	2	6	·49	18	·26	19
23	Sa	3	7	·49	19	·28	20
24	Su	4	8	·51	20	·32	21
25	Mo	5	9	·56	21	·38	22
26	Tu	6	10	·62	22	·47	23
27	We	7	11	·70	23	·57	24
28	Th	8	12	·78	24	·67	25
29	Fr	9	13	·86	25	·78	26
30	Sa	10	14	·94	26	·88	27
1	Su	11	...	...	27	·98	28
2	Mo	12	A	·01	...	...	29
3	Tu	13	1	·06	1	·06	1
4	We	14	2	·09	2	·12	2
5	Th	15	3	·11	3	·16	3
6	Fr	16	4	·10	4	·17	4
7	Sa	17	5	·08	5	·18	5
8	Su	18	6 7	·03 ·97	6	·16	6
9	Mo	19	8	·89	7	·12	7
10	Tu	20	9	·80	8	·07	8
11	We	21	10	·70	9 10	·01 ·95	9
12	Th	22	11	·60	11	·88	10
13	Fr	23	12	·50	12	·81	11
14	Sa	24	13	·40	13	·74	12
15	Su	25	14	·30	14	·68	13
16	Mo	26	P	·22	15	·63	14
17	Tu	27	1	·15	16	·60	15
18	We	28	2	·09	17	·58	16
19	Th	29	3	·05	18	·58	17
20	Fr	30	4	·03	19	·59	18

May — Solar: Sukla, *Mesha—Chittirai* (21–31); Sukla, *Vrishabha—Vaikasi* (1–20). Lunar: Adh. Vsk. *Bahula*; *Sukla*; Nija Vaisakha. Muhammadan: H. 1286 *Muharram*; H. 1286 *Safar*.

Cyclic Sidereal Year, Month and Day	Week-Day	English Month and Day	Tithi	Ending Moment	Nakshatra	Ending Moment	Muhammadan Year, Month and Day
21	Sa	1	5	·02	20	·63	19
22	Su	2	6	·04	21	·70	20
23	Mo	3	7	·08	22	·78	21
24	Tu	4	8	·14	23	·87	22
25	We	5	9	·21	24	·97	23
26	Th	6	10	·29	...	...	24
27	Fr	7	11	·38	25	·08	25
28	Sa	8	12	·46	26	·19	26
29	Su	9	13	·53	27	·29	27
30	Mo	10	14	·58	1	·37	28
31	Tu	11	A	·62	2	·43	29
1	We	12	1	·63	3	·47	30
2	Th	13	2	·62	4	·50	1
3	Fr	14	3	·60	5	·50	2
4	Sa	15	4	·55	6	·49	3
5	Su	16	5	·48	7	·45	4
6	Mo	17	6	·40	8	·40	5
7	Tu	18	7	·31	9	·35	6
8	We	19	8	·22	10	·29	7
9	Th	20	9	·12	11	·22	8
10	Fr	21	10 11	·02 ·92	12	·15	9
11	Sa	22	12	·82	13	·08	10
12	Su	23	13	·73	14 15	·02 ·97	11
13	Mo	24	14	·66	16	·93	12
14	Tu	25	P	·60	17	·91	13
15	We	26	1	·56	18	·90	14
16	Th	27	2	·53	19	·91	15
17	Fr	28	3	·52	20	·95	16
18	Sa	29	4	·54	...	...	17
19	Su	30	5	·58	21	·01	18
20	Mo	31	6	·64	22	·08	19

June — Solar: Sukla, *Vrishabha—Vaikasi* (21–32); Sukla, *Mithuna—Ani* (1–18). Lunar: *Bahula*; *Sukla*; Jyeshtha; *Bahula*. Muhammadan: H. 1286 *Rabi-ul-awwal*.

Cyclic Sidereal Year, Month and Day	Week-Day	English Month and Day	Tithi	Ending Moment	Nakshatra	Ending Moment	Muhammadan Year, Month and Day
21	Tu	1	7	·71	23	·17	20
22	We	2	8	·79	24	·27	21
23	Th	3	9	·87	25	·38	22
24	Fr	4	10	·95	26	·49	23
25	Sa	5	...	...	27	·59	24
26	Su	6	11	·02	1	·67	25
27	Mo	7	12	·07	2	·74	26
28	Tu	8	13	·11	3	·79	27
29	We	9	14	·12	4	·82	28
30	Th	10	A	·11	5	·83	29
31	Fr	11	1	·09	6	·81	1
32	Sa	12	2 3	·04 ·98	7	·78	2
1	Su	13	4	·90	8	·74	3
2	Mo	14	5	·81	9	·69	4
3	Tu	15	6	·71	10	·63	5
4	We	16	7	·61	11	·56	6
5	Th	17	8	·51	12	·49	7
6	Fr	18	9	·41	13	·42	8
7	Sa	19	10	·31	14	·36	9
8	Su	20	11	·22	15	·31	10
9	Mo	21	12	·14	16	·26	11
10	Tu	22	13	·08	17	·23	12
11	We	23	14	·03	18	·22	13
12	Th	24	P	·01	19	·24	14
13	Fr	25	1	·00	20	·27	15
14	Sa	26	2	·02	21	·31	16
15	Su	27	3	·06	22	·38	17
16	Mo	28	4	·11	23	·47	18
17	Tu	29	5	·18	24	·57	19
18	We	30	6	·27	25	·68	20

Naksh:—1. Asvn. 2. Bhar. 3. Krit. 4. Rohi. 5. Mrig. 6. Ardh. 7. Punar. 8. Push. 9. Aslesh. 10. Magh. 11. P. Phal. 12. U. Phal. 13. Hasta. 14. Chit.

A. D. 1869.
A.—Amavasya.
P.—Paurnami.

Kollam 1045, Commences {**N. Malabar—Sept.** / **S. Malabar—Aug.**}

Hijra 1286, Commences, **April 13.**

Vikrama 1926.
Bengal San 1275.
(N. Cycle) Vrisha.

SOLAR reckoning: Cyclic Sidereal Year, Month and Day.	Week-Day	English Month and Day.	LUNAR reckoning: Tithi	Ending Moment.	Nakshatra	Ending Moment.	Muhammadan Year, Month and Day.
		July					
19	Th	1	Jyesh. 7	·34	26	·79	21
20	Fr	2	8	·42	27	·89	22
21	Sa	3	9	49	1	·98	23
Sukla Mithuna—Ani. 22	Su	4	10	·54	...	...	Rabi-ul-awwal. 24
23	Mo	5	Bahula 11	·58	2	·06	25
24	Tu	6	12	·60	3	·11	26
25	We	7	13	·59	4	·14	27
26	Th	8	14	·56	5	·15	28
27	Fr	9	—A	·52	6	·14	29
28	Sa	10	1	·45	7	·12	—30
29	Su	11	2	·37	8	·08	1
30	Mo	12	3	·28	9 / 10	·03 / ·97	2
—31	Tu	13	4	·18	11	·90	3
1	We	14	5 / 6	·08 / ·98	12	·83	4
2	Th	15	Sukla 7	·88	13	·76	5
3	Fr	16	8	·78	14	·70	6
4	Sa	17	9	·69	15	·64	7
5	Su	18	10	·62	16	·60	8
6	Mo	19	11	·56	17	·57	9
7	Tu	20	12	·52	18	·55	10
8	We	21	Ashadha 13	·49	19	·56	11
9	Th	22	14	·49	20	·58	12
10	Fr ○	23	P	·51	21	·62	13
11	Sa	24	1	·53	22	·69	H. 1286 Rabi-ul-akhir. 14
12	Su	25	2	·58	23	·77	15
Sukla Karkata—Adi. 13	Mo	26	3	·65	24	·87	16
14	Tu	27	4	·73	25	·98	17
15	We	28	5	·82	...	...	18
16	Th	29	6	·90	26	·09	19
17	Fr	30	7	·97	27	·19	20
18	Sa	31	...	...	1	·28	21
		Aug.					
19	Su	1	Bahula 8	·02	2	·36	22
20	Mo	2	9	·06	3	·42	23
21	Tu	3	10	·08	4	·46	24
22	We	4	11	·08	5	·47	25
23	Th	5	12	·05	6	·47	26
24	Fr	6	13 / 14	·01 / ·95	7	·45	27
25	Sa	7	—A	·87	8	·42	28
26	Su	8	1	·78	9	·36	—29
27	Mo	9	2	·68	10	·30	1
28	Tu	10	3	·58	11	·24	2
29	We	11	4	·48	12	·17	3
30	Th	12	5	·38	13	·10	4
31	Fr	13	6	·28	14 / 15	·04 / ·98	5
—32	Sa	14	Sukla 7	·20	16	·93	6
1	Su	15	8	·12	17	·89	7
2	Mo	16	9	·05	18	·88	8
3	Tu	17	10 / 11	·01 / ·98	19	·88	9
4	We	18	12	·98	20	·90	H. 1286 Jumadal-awwal. 10
5	Th	19	Sravana 13	·99	21	·93	11
6	Fr	20	...	...	22	·99	12
Sukla Simha—Avani. 7	Sa	21	14	·03	...	...	13
8	Su	22	P	·09	23	·08	14
9	Mo	23	1	·15	24	·18	15
10	Tu	24	2	·23	25	·28	16
11	We	25	3	·31	26	·38	17
12	Th	26	4	·40	27	·49	18
13	Fr	27	Bahula 5	·47	1	·59	19
14	Sa	28	6	·53	2	·67	20
15	Su	29	7	·57	3	·73	21
16	Mo	30	8	·59	4	·77	22
17	Tu	31	9	·58	5	·79	23

SOLAR reckoning: Cyclic Sidereal Year, Month and Day.	Week-Day	English Month and Day.	LUNAR reckoning: Tithi	Ending Moment.	Nakshatra	Ending Moment.	Muhammadan Year, Month and Day.
		Sep.					
18	We	1	Sr. 10	·56	6	·80	Jl-awwal. 24
19	Th	2	11	·52	7	·78	25
20	Fr	3	Bah. 12	·46	8	·75	26
21	Sa	4	13	·39	9	·70	27
22	Su	5	14	·30	10	·64	28
Sukla Simha—Avani. 23	Mo	6	—A	·20	11	·58	29
24	Tu	7	1	·10	12	·51	—30
25	We	8	2 / 3	·00 / ·90	13	·44	1
26	Th	9	4	·80	14	·37	2
27	Fr	10	5	·72	15	·31	3
28	Sa	11	Sukla 6	·64	16	·26	4
29	Su	12	7	·58	17	·23	5
30	Mo	13	8	·53	18	·21	6
—31	Tu	14	9	·51	19	·20	7
1	We	15	10	·51	20	·21	8
2	Th	16	11	·52	21	·25	9
3	Fr	17	Bhadrapada 12	·55	22	·31	10
4	Sa	18	13	·60	23	·38	H. 1286 Jumadal-akhir. 11
5	Su	19	14	·68	24	·47	12
6	Mo	20	P	·76	25	·58	13
7	Tu	21	1	·84	26	·69	14
8	We	22	2	·92	27	·80	15
Sukla Kanya—Purattasi. 9	Th	23	3	·99	1	·89	16
10	Fr	24	...	...	2	·97	17
11	Sa	25	4	·06	...	...	18
12	Su	26	5	·10	3	·04	19
13	Mo	27	6	·12	4	·09	20
14	Tu	28	Bahula 7	·12	5	·12	21
15	We	29	8	·10	6	·13	22
16	Th	30	9	·06	7	·11	23
		Oct.					
17	Fr	1	10 / 11	·00 / ·93	8	·08	24
18	Sa	2	12	·84	9 / 10	·03 / ·98	25
19	Su	3	13	·75	11	·92	26
20	Mo	4	14	·65	12	·85	27
21	Tu	5	—A	·55	13	·78	28
22	We	6	1	·45	14	·71	—29
23	Th	7	2	·35	15	·65	1
24	Fr	8	3	·27	16	·60	2
25	Sa	9	4	·20	17	·56	3
26	Su	10	5	·14	18	·53	4
27	Mo	11	6	·10	19	·52	5
28	Tu	12	Sukla 7	·08	20	·53	6
29	We	13	8	·07	21	·57	7
—30	Th	14	9	·09	22	.62	8
1	Fr	15	10	·12	23	·69	9
2	Sa	16	11	·18	24	·77	H. 1286 Rajab. 10
3	Su	17	12	·25	25	·88	11
4	Mo	18	Asvina 13	·33	26	·99	12
5	Tu	19	14	·42	...	...	13
6	We	20	P	·51	27	·10	14
7	Th	21	1	·59	1	·19	15
Sukla Tula—Aippasi. 8	Fr	22	2	·65	2	·28	16
9	Sa	23	3	·69	3	·35	17
10	Su	24	4	·71	4	·40	18
11	Mo	25	5	·70	5	·44	19
12	Tu	26	Bahula 6	·68	6	·45	20
13	We	27	7	·64	7	·44	21
14	Th	28	8	·59	8	·41	22
15	Fr	29	9	·52	9	·37	23
16	Sa	30	10	·44	10	·32	24
17	Su	31	11	·34	11	·26	25

SOLAR reckoning: Cyclic Sidereal Year, Month and Day.	Week-Day	English Month and Day.	LUNAR reckoning: Tithi	Ending Moment.	Nakshatra	Ending Moment.	Muhammadan Year, Month and Day.
		Nov.					
18	Mo	1	Bah. 12	·24	12	·19	Rajab. 26
19	Tu	2	13	·14	13	·12	27
20	We	3	14 / A	·04 / ·95	14 / 15	·05 / ·99	28
21	Th	4	1	·87	16	·94	29
Sukla Tula—Aippasi. 22	Fr	5	2	·80	17	·89	—30
23	Sa	6	3	·74	18	·86	1
24	Su	7	4	·69	19	·84	2
25	Mo	8	5	·67	20	·86	3
26	Tu	9	6	·67	21	·89	4
27	We	10	Sukla 7	·69	22	·93	5
28	Th	11	8	·73	23	·99	6
29	Fr	12	9	·79	...	...	7
—30	Sa	13	10	·87	24	·08	8
1	Su	14	11	·95	25	·18	9
2	Mo	15	...	...	26	·29	10
3	Tu	16	Karttika 12	·04	27	·39	11
4	We	17	13	·12	1	·49	H. 1286 Shaban. 12
5	Th	18	14	·20	2	·58	13
6	Fr	19	P	·26	3	·66	14
7	Sa	20	1	·30	4	·72	15
8	Su	21	2	·32	5	·76	16
9	Mo	22	3	·33	6	77	17
Sukla Vrischika—Kartigai. 10	Tu	23	Bahula 4	·30	7	·76	18
11	We	24	5	·26	8	·74	19
12	Th	25	6	·21	9	·71	20
13	Fr	26.	7	·14	10	·66	21
14	Sa	27	8 / 9	·06 / ·96	11	·60	22
15	Su	28	10	·86	12	·53	23
16	Mo	29	11	·76	13	·46	24
17	Tu	30	12	·67	14	·39	25
		Dec.					
18	We	1	13	·58	15	·33	26
19	Th	2	14	·49	16	·27	27
20	Fr	3	—A	·41	17	·22	28
21	Sa	4	1	·36	18	·19	—29
22	Su	5	2	·32	19	·18	1
23	Mo	6	3	·30	20	·18	2
24	Tu	7	4	·30	21	·20	3
25	We	8	5	·33	22	·24	4
26	Th	9	Sukla 6	·37	23	·30	5
27	Fr	10	7	·43	24	·38	6
28	Sa	11	8	·51	25	·48	7
29	Su	12	9	·60	26	·59	8
—30	Mo	13	10	·69	27	·69	9
1	Tu	14	11	·77	1	·79	10
2	We	15	12	·84	2	·89	11
3	Th	16	Margasira 13	·90	3	·98	H. 1286 Ramzan. 12
4	Fr	17	14	·94	...	...	13
5	Sa	18	P	·96	4	·04	14
6	Su	19	1	·96	5	·07	15
7	Mo	20	2	·94	6	·09	16
Sukla Dhanus—Margali. 8	Tu	21	3	·90	7	·09	17
9	We	22	4	·84	8	·08	18
10	Th	23	5	·77	9 / 10	·04 / ·99	19
11	Fr	24	6	·69	11	·93	20
12	Sa	25	Bahula 7	·60	12	·87	21
13	Su	26	8	·50	13	·81	22
14	Mo	27	9	·40	14	·74	23
15	Tu	28	10	·30	15	·67	24
16	We	29	11	·21	16	·61	25
17	Th	30	12	·13	17	·56	26
18	Fr	31	13	·06	18	·53	27

15. Svati. 16. Visak. 17. Anur. 18. Jyesh. 19. Mula. 20. P. Ash. 21. U. Ash. 22. Sravn. 23. Dani. 24. Satab. 25. P. Bhad. 26. U. Bhad. 27. Rev.

A. D. 1870. **Mesha Sankranti** (Commencement of Indian Sidereal Year).

Solar Eclipse. ● **(Surya Sid.) April 11·86.** **Saka 1792.** **Kaliyuga 4971.**

Lunar Eclipse. ○ **(Arya Sid.) April 11·76.** **(S. Cycle) Pramodhuta.**

Solar month	Cyclic Sidereal Year, Month and Day	Week-Day	English Month and Day	Lunar month	Tithi	Ending Moment	Nakshatra	Ending Moment	Muhammadan month	Muhammadan Year, Month and Day
			Jan.							
Sukla Dhanus—Margali	19	Sa	1		14 A	·00 ·96	19	·51		28
	20	Su	2		1	·95	20	·50		29
	21	Mo	3		2	·95	21	·52		—30
	22	Tu	4		3	·97	22	·55		1
	23	We	5		...	...	23	·60		2
	24	Th	6	Sukla	4	·02	24	·69		3
	25	Fr	7		5	·08	25	·78		4
	26	Sa	8		6	·15	26	·88		5
	27	Su	9		7	·24	27	·99		6
	28	Mo	10		8	·33	...	...		7
	—29	Tu	11		9	·42	1	·09		8
Sukla Makara—Tai	1	We	12		10	·50	2	·19	H. 1286 Shawwal	9
	2	Th	13		11	·56	3	·28		10
	3	Fr	14		12	·59	4	·35		11
	4	Sa	15	Pausha	13	·60	5	·39		12
	5	Su	16		14	·61	6	·41		13
	6	Mo ○	17		P	·58	7	·42		14
	7	Tu	18		1	·54	8	·41		15
	8	We	19		2	·49	9	·38		16
	9	Th	20		3	·42	10	·33		17
	10	Fr	21		4	·32	11	·27		18
	11	Sa	22		5	·22	12	·21		19
	12	Su	23		6	·12	13	·14		20
	13	Mo	24	Bahula	7 8	·03 ·94	14	·07		21
	14	Tu	25		9	·85	15 16	·00 ·94		22
	15	We	26		10	·77	17	·89		23
	16	Th	27		11	·70	18	·86		24
	17	Fr	28		12	·65	19	·83		25
	18	Sa	29		13	·61	20	·82		26
	19	Su	30		14	·59	21	·83		27
	20	Mo	31		—A	·59	22	·86		28
			Feb.							
	21	Tu	1		1	·61	23	·92		—29
	22	We	2		2	·66	24	·99		1
	23	Th	3		3	·73	...	...		2
	24	Fr	4		4	·81	25	·08		3
	25	Sa	5		5	·89	26	·18		4
	26	Su	6		6	·97	27	·29		5
	27	Mo	7	Sukla	...	...	1	·40		6
	28	Tu	8		7	·06	2	·50		7
	29	We	9		8	·14	3	·59		8
	—30	Th	10		9	·20	4	·65		9
Sukla Kumbha—Masi	1	Fr	11		10	·23	5	·70	H. 1286 Zi-l-ka'da	10
	2	Sa	12		11	·24	6	·74		11
	3	Su	13	Magha	12	·24	7	·75		12
	4	Mo	14		13	·21	8	·74		13
	5	Tu	15		14	·16	9	·71		14
	6	We	16		P	·10	10	·66		15
	7	Th	17		1 2	·03 ·95	11	·61		16
	8	Fr	18		3	·86	12	·55		17
	9	Sa	19		4	·76	13	·48		18
	10	Su	20		5	·66	14	·41		19
	11	Mo	21	Bahula	6	·56	15	·34		20
	12	Tu	22		7	·47	16	·28		21
	13	We	23		8	·39	17	·23		22
	14	Th	24		9	·31	18	·19		23
	15	Fr	25		10	·26	19	·16		24
	16	Sa	26		11	·22	20	·14		25
	17	Su	27		12	·21	21	·15		26
	18	Mo	28		13	·21	22	·18		27

Solar month	Cyclic Sidereal Year, Month and Day	Week-Day	English Month and Day	Lunar month	Tithi	Ending Moment	Nakshatra	Ending Moment	Muhammadan month	Muhammadan Year, Month and Day
			March							
Sukla Kumbha—Masi	19	Tu	1		14	·24	23	·23		28
	20	We	2		—A	·29	24	·30		29
	21	Th	3		1	·35	25	·38		—30
	22	Fr	4		2	·43	26	·48		1
	23	Sa	5		3	·51	27	·59		2
	24	Su	6		4	·60	1	·70		3
	25	Mo	7		5	·69	2	·80		4
	26	Tu	8	Sukla	6	·76	3	·89		5
	27	We	9		7	·81	4	·96		6
	28	Th	10		8	·84	...	...		7
	—29	Fr	11		9	·85	5	·02		8
Sukla Mina—Panguni	1	Sa	12		10	·84	6	·06		9
	2	Su	13		11	·81	7	·07		10
	3	Mo	14		12	·76	8	·06		11
	4	Tu	15	Phalguna	13	·70	9	·04	H. 1286 Zi-l-hijja	12
	5	We	16		14	·63	10 11	·00 ·95		13
	6	Th	17		P	·54	12	·89		14
	7	Fr	18		1	·45	13	·82		15
	8	Sa	19		2	·35	14	·75		16
	9	Su	20		3	·25	15	·69		17
	10	Mo	21		4	·15	16	·63		18
	11	Tu	22	Bahula	5 6	·06 ·98	17	·57		19
	12	We	23		7	·90	18	·52		20
	13	Th	24		8	·85	19	·48		21
	14	Fr	25		9	·81	20	·47		22
	15	Sa	26		10	·80	21	·48		23
	16	Su	27		11	·80	22	·50		24
	17	Mo	28		12	·83	23	·54		25
	18	Tu	29		13	·87	24	·60		26
	19	We	30		14	·93	25	·68		27
	20	Th	31		...	...	26	·78		28
			April							
	21	Fr	1		—A	·01	27	·89		29
	22	Sa	2		1	·09	...	...		—30
	23	Su	3		2	·16	1	·00		1
	24	Mo	4		3	·26	2	·10		2
	25	Tu	5		4	·33	3	·19		3
	26	We	6		5	·38	4	·27		4
	27	Th	7		6	·41	5	·34		5
	28	Fr	8	Sukla	7	·42	6	·38		6
	29	Sa	9		8	·41	7	·39		7
	30	Su	10		9	·38	8	·39		8
	—31	Mo	11		10	·33	9	·37		9
Pramodhuta Mesha—Chittirai	1	Tu	12		11	·27	10	·34	H. 1287 Muharram	10
	2	We	13		12	·19	11	·29		11
	3	Th	14		13	·11	12	·23		12
	4	Fr	15		14 P	·01 ·91	13	·16		13
	5	Sa	16	Chaitra	1	·81	14	·09		14
	6	Su	17		2	·71	15 16	·02 ·96		15
	7	Mo	18		3	·62	17	·90		16
	8	Tu	19		4	·53	18	·85		17
	9	We	20		5	·45	19	·81		18
	10	Th	21		6	·39	20	·80		19
	11	Fr	22	Bahula	7	·36	21	·80		20
	12	Sa	23		8	·34	22	·81		21
	13	Su	24		9	·33	23	·85		22
	14	Mo	25		10	·36	24	·91		23
	15	Tu	26		11	·41	...	...		24
	16	We	27		12	·47	25	·00		25
	17	Th	28		13	·55	26	·09		26
	18	Fr	29		14	·63	27	·19		27
	19	Sa	30		—A	·71	1	·30		28

Solar month	Cyclic Sidereal Year, Month and Day	Week-Day	English Month and Day	Lunar month	Tithi	Ending Moment	Nakshatra	Ending Moment	Muhammadan month	Muhammadan Year, Month and Day
			May							
Pramodhuta Mesha—Chittirai	20	Su	1		1	·79	2	·40		29
	21	Mo	2		2	·86	3	·50		—30
	22	Tu	3		3	·91	4	·59		1
	23	We	4		4	·94	5	·65		2
	24	Th	5		5	·95	6	·69		3
	25	Fr	6	Sukla	6	·94	7	·71		4
	26	Sa	7		7	·91	8	·71		5
	27	Su	8		8	·86	9	·70		6
	28	Mo	9		9	·80	10	·67		7
	29	Tu	10		10	·72	11	·62		8
	30	We	11		11	·63	12	·56		9
	—31	Th	12		12	·53	13	·50		10
Pramodhuta Vrishabha—Vaikasi	1	Fr	13	Vaisakha	13	·43	14	·44	H. 1287 Safar	11
	2	Sa	14		14	·33	15	·37		12
	3	Su	15		P	·23	16	·30		13
	4	Mo	16		1	·13	17	·24		14
	5	Tu	17		2 3	·04 ·97	18	·18		15
	6	We	18		4	·91	19	·15		16
	7	Th	19		5	·87	20	·13		17
	8	Fr	20	Bahula	6	·85	21	·12		18
	9	Sa	21		7	·85	22	·13		19
	10	Su	22		8	·87	23	·16		20
	11	Mo	23		9	·91	24	·22		21
	12	Tu	24		10	·97	25	·30		22
	13	We	25		...	...	26	·39		23
	14	Th	26		11	·04	27	·49		24
	15	Fr	27		12	·12	1	·59		25
	16	Sa	28		13	·21	2	·70		26
	17	Su	29		14	·29	3	·80		27
	18	Mo	30		—A	·36	4	·89		28
	19	Tu	31		1	·41	5	·96		—29
			June							
	20	We	1		2	·43	...	...		1
	21	Th	2		3	·44	6	·00		2
	22	Fr	3		4	·44	7	·03		3
	23	Sa	4		5	·41	8	·05		4
	24	Su	5	Sukla	6	·36	9	·03		5
	25	Mo	6		7	·30	10 11	·00 ·96		6
	26	Tu	7		8	·22	12	·90		7
	27	We	8		9	·12	13	·84		8
	28	Th	9		10 11	·02 ·92	14	·78		9
	29	Fr	10		12	·82	15	·71		10
	30	Sa	11	Jyeshtha	13	·72	16	·64	H. 1287 Rabi-ul-awwal	11
	—31	Su	12		14	·63	17	·57		12
Pramodhuta Mithuna—Ani	1	Mo	13		P	·54	18	·52		13
	2	Tu	14		1	·46	19	·48		14
	3	We	15		2	·40	20	·45		15
	4	Th	16		3	·36	21	·44		16
	5	Fr	17		4	·34	22	·45		17
	6	Sa	18		5	·33	23	·48		18
	7	Su	19	Bahula	6	·35	24	·53		19
	8	Mo	20		7	·39	25	·60		20
	9	Tu	21		8	·45	26	·69		21
	10	We	22		9	·52	27	·79		22
	11	Th	23		10	·60	1	·90		23
	12	Fr	24		11	·68	...	...		24
	13	Sa	25		12	·76	2	·01		25
	14	Su	26		13	·83	3	·11		26
	15	Mo	27		14	·88	4	·20		27
	16	Tu	28		—A	·91	5	·27		28
	17	We	29	Suk.	1	·93	6	·32		29
	18	Th	30		2	·91	7	·36		—30

Naksh:—1. Asvn. 2. Bhar. 3. Krit. 4. Rohi. 5. Mrig. 6. Ardh. 7. Punar. 8. Push. 9. Aslesh. 10. Magh. 11. P. Phal. 12. U. Phal. 13. Hasta. 14. Chit.

A. D. 1870. **A.—Amavasya. P.—Paurnami.** **Kollam 1046, Commences { N. Malabar—Sept. S. Malabar—Aug.** **Hijra 1287, Commences, April 3.** **Vikrama 1927. Bengal San 1276. (N. Cycle) Chitrabhanu.**

SOLAR reckoning: Cyclic Sidereal Year, Month and Day; Week-Day; English Month and Day. LUNAR reckoning: Tithi, Ending Moment; Nakshatra, Ending Moment; Muhammadan Year, Month and Day.

July

Solar Year, Month	Cyclic Sidereal Day	Week-Day	English Day	Lunar Month	Tithi	Ending Moment	Nakshatra	Ending Moment	Muhammadan Month	Muhammadan Day
Pramodhuta *Mithuna—Ani.*	19	Fr	1		3	·88	8	·37		1
	20	Sa	2		4	·84	9	·36		2
	21	Su	3		5	·78	10	·33		3
	22	Mo	4		6	·70	11	·29		4
	23	Tu	5		7	·60	12	·24		5
	24	We	6	*Sukla*	8	·50	13	·18		6
	25	Th	7		9	·40	14	·12		7
	26	Fr	8		10	·30	15 / 16	·05 / ·98		8
	27	Sa	9		11	·20	17	·91		9
	28	Su	10		12	·10	18	·86		10
	29	Mo	11		13 / 14	·02 / ·94	19	·81		11
	30	Tu ○	12	Ashadha	P	·88	20	·78	H. 1287 *Rabi-ul-akhir.*	12
	31	We	13		1	·84	21	·77		13
	32	Th	14		2	·82	22	·77		14
Pramodhuta *Karkata—Adi.*	1	Fr	15		3	·81	23	·80		15
	2	Sa	16		4	·82	24	·84		16
	3	Su	17		5	·86	25	·91		17
	4	Mo	18		6	·92	26	·99		18
	5	Tu	19		7	·99	...	...		19
	6	We	20		...	...	27	·09		20
	7	Th	21	*Bahula*	8	·07	1	·20		21
	8	Fr	22		9	·16	2	·31		22
	9	Sa	23		10	·23	3	·41		23
	10	Su	24		11	·29	4	·50		24
	11	Mo	25		12	·34	5	·57		25
	12	Tu	26		13	·38	6	·63		26
	13	We	27		14	·40	7	·67		27
	14	Th	28		A	·39	8	·69		28
	15	Fr	29		1	·37	9	·69		29
	16	Sa	30		2	·33	10	·66		1
	17	Su	31		3	·27	11	·63		2

Aug.

Solar Year, Month	Cyclic Sidereal Day	Week-Day	English Day	Lunar Month	Tithi	Ending Moment	Nakshatra	Ending Moment	Muhammadan Month	Muhammadan Day
	18	Mo	1		4	·19	12	·58		3
	19	Tu	2		5	·10	13	·52		4
	20	We	3		6 / 7	·00 / ·90	14	·45		5
	21	Th	4	*Sukla*	8	·80	15	·38		6
	22	Fr	5		9	·70	16	·32		7
	23	Sa	6		10	·60	17	·26		8
	24	Su	7		11	·51	18	·20		9
	25	Mo	8		12	·43	19	·15		10
	26	Tu	9		13	·37	20	·11		11
	27	We	10	Sravana	14	·33	21	·09		12
	28	Th	11		P	·31	22	·10		13
	29	Fr	12		1	·30	23	·12	H. 1287 *Jumadal-awwal.*	14
	30	Sa	13		2	·31	24	·15		15
	31	Su	14		3	·35	25	·21		16
Pramodhuta *Simha—Avani.*	1	Mo	15		4	·40	26	·29		17
	2	Tu	16		5	·48	27	·39		18
	3	We	17	*Bahula*	6	·56	1	·50		19
	4	Th	18		7	·65	2	·60		20
	5	Fr	19		8	·73	3	·70		21
	6	Sa	20		9	·80	4	·80		22
	7	Su	21		10	·85	5	·89		23
	8	Mo	22		11	·89	6	·95		24
	9	Tu	23		12	·90	7	·99		25
	10	We	24		13	·89	...	...		26
	11	Th	25		14	·87	8	·01		27
	12	Fr	26		A	·83	9 / 10	·01 / ·99		28
	13	Sa	27	Bhad. *Suk.*	1	·78	11	·97		29
	14	Su	28		2	·70	12	·92		30
	15	Mo	29		3	·60	13	·86		1
	16	Tu	30		4	·50	14	·79		2
	17	We	31		5	·40	15	·72		3

Sep.

Solar Year, Month	Cyclic Sidereal Day	Week-Day	English Day	Lunar Month	Tithi	Ending Moment	Nakshatra	Ending Moment	Muhammadan Month	Muhammadan Day
Pramodhuta *Simha—Avani.*	18	Th	1	*Sukla*	6	·30	16	·65		4
	19	Fr	2		7	·20	17	·59		5
	20	Sa	3		8	·11	18	·53		6
	21	Su	4		9 / 10	·03 / ·96	19	·48		7
	22	Mo	5	Bhadrapada	11	·89	20	·45		8
	23	Tu	6		12	·84	21	·43		9
	24	We	7		13	·82	22	·42		10
	25	Th	8		14	·81	23	·43		11
	26	Fr	9		P	·83	24	·47		12
	27	Sa	10		1	·87	25	·52		13
	28	Su	11		2	·93	26	·60		14
	29	Mo	12		...	...	27	·69		15
	30	Tu	13		3	·00	1	·79		16
	31	We	14		4	·09	2	·90	H. 1287 *Jumadal-akhir.*	17
Pramodhuta *Kanya—Purattasi.*	1	Th	15		5	·17	...	...		18
	2	Fr	16		6	·25	3	·01		19
	3	Sa	17	*Bahula*	7	·32	4	·11		20
	4	Su	18		8	·37	5	·20		21
	5	Mo	19		9	·41	6	·26		22
	6	Tu	20		10	·42	7	·31		23
	7	We	21		11	·42	8	·33		24
	8	Th	22		12	·40	9	·34		25
	9	Fr	23		13	·37	10	·33		26
	10	Sa	24		14	·31	11	·30		27
	11	Su	25		A	·23	12	·25		28
	12	Mo	26		1	·14	13	·19		29
	13	Tu	27		2 / 3	·05 / ·95	14	·13		1
	14	We	28		4	·85	15	·07		2
	15	Th	29		5	·75	16 / 17	·00 / ·93		3
	16	Fr	30		6	·65	18	·87		4

Oct.

Solar Year, Month	Cyclic Sidereal Day	Week-Day	English Day	Lunar Month	Tithi	Ending Moment	Nakshatra	Ending Moment	Muhammadan Month	Muhammadan Day
	17	Sa	1	*Sukla*	7	·57	19	·82		5
	18	Su	2		8	·50	20	·78		6
	19	Mo	3		9	·44	21	·75		7
	20	Tu	4		10	·39	22	·74		8
	21	We	5		11	·37	23	·75		9
	22	Th	6		12	·37	24	·78		10
	23	Fr	7	Asvina	13	·38	25	·84		11
	24	Sa	8		14	·42	26	·91		12
	25	Su	9		P	·48	...	...		13
	26	Mo	10		1	·56	27	·00		14
	27	Tu	11		2	·65	1	·10	H. 1287 *Rajab.*	15
	28	We	12		3	·73	2	·20		16
	29	Th	13		4	·81	3	·31		17
	30	Fr	14		5	·88	4	·41		18
	31	Sa	15		6	·94	5	·50		19
Pramodhuta *Tula—Aippasi.*	1	Su	16	*Bahula*	7	·98	6	·57		20
	2	Mo	17		...	...	7	·62		21
	3	Tu	18		8	·00	8	·65		22
	4	We	19		9 / 10	·00 / ·97	9	·67		23
	5	Th	20		11	·94	10	·66		24
	6	Fr	21		12	·88	11	·63		25
	7	Sa	22		13	·81	12	·59		26
	8	Su	23		14	·72	13	·53		27
	9	Mo	24		A	·63	14	·47		28
	10	Tu	25	Kartt. *Suk.*	1	·53	15	·41		29
	11	We	26		2	·43	16	·34		30
	12	Th	27		3	·33	17	·27	*Shaban.*	1
	13	Fr	28		4	·24	18	·21		2
	14	Sa	29		5	·16	19	·16		3
	15	Su	30		6	·09	20	·11		4
	16	Mo	31		7 / 8	·03 / ·98	21	·08		5

Nov.

Solar Year, Month	Cyclic Sidereal Day	Week-Day	English Day	Lunar Month	Tithi	Ending Moment	Nakshatra	Ending Moment	Muhammadan Month	Muhammadan Day
Pramodhuta *Tula—Aippasi.*	17	Tu	1	*Sukla*	9	·96	22	·06		6
	18	We	2		10	·96	23	·07		7
	19	Th	3		11	·98	24	·09		8
	20	Fr	4		...	...	25	·14		9
	21	Sa	5		12	·03	26	·21		10
	22	Su	6	Kartika	13	·09	27	·30		11
	23	Mo	7		14	·16	1	·39		12
	24	Tu	8		P	·25	2	·50		13
	25	We	9		1	·34	3	·61		14
	26	Th	10		2	·42	4	·72		15
	27	Fr	11		3	·49	5	·81	H. 1287 *Shaban.*	16
	28	Sa	12		4	·55	6	·88		17
	29	Su	13		5	·59	7	·93		18
	30	Mo	14	*Bahula*	6	·62	8	·97		19
Pramodhuta *Vrischika—Kartigai.*	1	Tu	15		7	·61	9	·99		20
	2	We	16		8	·58	10	·98		21
	3	Th	17		9	·54	11	·96		22
	4	Fr	18		10	·49	12	·92		23
	5	Sa	19		11	·42	13	·88		24
	6	Su	20		12	·34	14	·82		25
	7	Mo	21		13	·25	15	·75		26
	8	Tu	22		14	·15	16	·68		27
	9	We	23		A / 1	·05 / ·95	17	·61		28
	10	Th	24		2	·86	18	·55		29
	11	Fr	25		3	·78	19	·49		1
	12	Sa	26		4	·70	20	·44		2
	13	Su	27		5	·64	21	·41		3
	14	Mo	28	*Sukla*	6	·60	22	·39		4
	15	Tu	29		7	·59	23	·39		5
	16	We	30		8	·59	24	·42		6

Dec.

Solar Year, Month	Cyclic Sidereal Day	Week-Day	English Day	Lunar Month	Tithi	Ending Moment	Nakshatra	Ending Moment	Muhammadan Month	Muhammadan Day
	17	Th	1		9	·61	25	·46		7
	18	Fr	2		10	·65	26	·52		8
	19	Sa	3		11	·72	27	·60		9
	20	Su	4		12	·80	1	·69		10
	21	Mo	5		13	·88	2	·80		11
	22	Tu	6		14	·97	3	·91		12
	23	We	7	Margasira	...	...	...	...		13
	24	Th	8		P	·06	4	·02		14
	25	Fr	9		1	·13	5	·11		15
	26	Sa	10		2	·19	6	·19	H. 1287 *Ramzan.*	16
	27	Su	11		3	·23	7	·25		17
	28	Mo	12		4	·25	8	·29		18
	29	Tu	13		5	·24	9	·31		19
Pramodhuta *Dhanus—Margali.*	1	We	14	*Bahula*	6	·22	10	·31		20
	2	Th	15		7	·17	11	·29		21
	3	Fr	16		8	·11	12	·26		22
	4	Sa	17		9 / 10	·04 / ·96	13	·21		23
	5	Su	18		11	·87	14	·15		24
	6	Mo	19		12	·77	15	·09		25
	7	Tu	20		13	·67	16 / 17	·02 / ·95		26
	8	We	21		14	·57	18	·89		27
	9	Th	22		A	·48	19	·83		28
	10	Fr	23		1	·40	20	·77		29
	11	Sa	24	*Sukla*	2	·34	21	·73		30
	12	Su	25		3	·29	22	·71		1
	13	Mo	26		4	·25	23	·72	*Shawal.*	2
	14	Tu	27	Pausha	5	·24	24	·74		3
	15	We	28		6	·24	25	·77		4
	16	Th	29		7	·26	26	·83		5
	17	Fr	30		8	·31	27	·90		6
	18	Sa	31		9	·37	...	...		7

15. Svati. 16. Visak. 17. Anur. 18. Jyesh. 19. Mula. 20. P. Ash. 21. U. Ash. 22. Sravn. 23. Dani. 24. Satab. 25. P. Bhad. 26. U. Bhad. 27 Rev.

A. D. 1871. **Mesha Sankranti** (Commencement of Indian Sidereal Year).

Solar Eclipse. ● **(Surya Sid.) April 12·12.** **Saka 1793.** **Kaliyuga 4972.**

Lunar Eclipse. ○ **(Arya Sid.) April 12·02.** **(S. Cycle) Prajapati.**

SOLAR reckoning: Cyclic Sidereal Year, Month and Day; Week-Day; English Month and Day. LUNAR reckoning: Tithi; Ending Moment; Nakshatra; Ending Moment; Muhammadan Year, Month and Day.

Jan.

Cyclic Sidereal Year, Month and Day	Week-Day	English Month and Day	Tithi	Ending Moment	Nakshatra	Ending Moment	Muhammadan Year, Month and Day
Pramodhuta *Dhanu—Margali.* 19	Su	1	Pausha *Suk.* 10	·45	1	·00	H. 1287 *Shawwal.* 8
20	Mo	2	11	·54	2	·10	9
21	Tu	3	12	·63	3	·21	10
22	We	4	13	·71	4	·31	11
23	Th	5	14	·78	5	·41	12
24	Fr ○	6	P	·84	6	·59	13
25	Sa	7	1	·87	7	·57	14
26	Su	8	2	·89	8	·61	15
27	Mo	9	3	·89	9	·63	16
28	Tu	10	4	·87	10	·64	17
—29	We	11	5	·82	11	·63	18
1	Th	12	*Bahula* 6	·76	12	·60	19
2	Fr	13	7	·69	13	·55	20
3	Sa	14	8	·61	14	·49	21
4	Su	15	9	·51	15	·42	22
5	Mo	16	10	·41	16	·35	23
6	Tu	17	11	·31	17	·28	24
7	We	18	12	·22	18	·22	25
8	Th	19	13	·13	19	·16	26
9	Fr	20	{14 A	·05 ·99	20	·11	27
10	Sa	21	1	·93	21	·07	28
11	Su	22	2	·89	22	·05	—29
Pramodhuta *Makara—Tai.* 12	Mo	23	3	·88	23	·04	1
13	Tu	24	4	·88	24	·05	2
14	We	25	5	·91	25	·08	3
15	Th	26	6	·96	26	·13	4
16	Fr	27	...	...	27	·21	5
17	Sa	28	*Sukla* 7	·03	1	·30	6
18	Su	29	8	·11	2	·40	7
19	Mo	30	9	·19	3	·51	8
20	Tu	31	10	·28	4	·62	9

Feb.

Cyclic Sidereal Year, Month and Day	Week-Day	English Month and Day	Tithi	Ending Moment	Nakshatra	Ending Moment	Muhammadan Year, Month and Day
21	We	1	11	·36	5	·72	H 1287 *Zi-l-ka'da.* 10
22	Th	2	Magha 12	·43	6	·81	11
23	Fr	3	13	·49	7	·88	12
24	Sa	4	14	·52	8	·92	13
25	Su	5	P	·53	9	·95	14
26	Mo	6	1	·53	10	·96	15
27	Tu	7	2	·50	11	·96	16
28	We	8	3	·46	12	·93	17
29	Th	9	4	·39	13	·88	18
—30	Fr	10	*Bahula* 5	·31	14	·82	19
Pramodhuta *Kumbha—Masi.* 1	Sa	11	6	·23	15	·76	20
2	Su	12	7	·14	16	·70	21
3	Mo	13	{8 9	·04 ·94	17	·63	22
4	Tu	14	10	·84	18	·56	23
5	We	15	11	·75	19	·50	24
6	Th	16	12	·67	20	·44	25
7	Fr	17	13	·61	21	·41	26
8	Sa	18	14	·56	22	·38	27
9	Su	19	—A	·52	23	·36	28
10	Mo	20	Phalguna *Sukla* 1	·50	24	·37	29
11	Tu	21	2	·50	25	·39	—30
12	We	22	3	·53	26	·45	*Zi-l-hijja.* 1
13	Th	23	4	·58	27	·52	2
14	Fr	24	5	·65	1	·60	3
15	Sa	25	6	·73	2	·70	4
16	Su	26	7	·82	3	·81	5
17	Mo	27	8	·90	4	·92	6
18	Tu	28	9	·98	...	...	7

March

Cyclic Sidereal Year, Month and Day	Week-Day	English Month and Day	Tithi	Ending Moment	Nakshatra	Ending Moment	Muhammadan Year, Month and Day
Pramodhuta *Kumbha—Masi.* 19	We	1	Phalg. *Suk.* ...	...	5	·02	H. 1287 *Zi-l-hijja.* 8
20	Th	2	10	·05	6	·11	9
21	Fr	3	11	·10	7	·18	10
22	Sa	4	12	·14	8	·24	11
23	Su	5	13	·15	9	·27	12
24	Mo	6	14	·14	10	·29	13
25	Tu	7	P	·11	11	·28	14
26	We	8	1	·07	12	·26	15
27	Th	9	{2 3	·00 ·92	13	·22	16
28	Fr	10	4	·84	14	·16	17
29	Sa	11	5	·74	15	·10	18
—30	Su	12	*Bahula* 6	·64	16 17}	·04 ·97	19
1	Mo	13	7	·54	18	·90	20
2	Tu	14	8	·44	19	·83	21
3	We	15	9	·35	20	·78	22
4	Th	16	10	·26	21	·74	23
5	Fr	17	11	·20	22	·71	24
6	Sa	18	12	·15	23	·69	25
7	Su	19	13	·12	24	·69	26
8	Mo	20	14	·10	25	·72	27
9	Tu	21	—A	·10	26	·76	28
10	We	22	1	·13	27	·82	—29
11	Th	23	2	·18	1	·90	1
Pramodhuta *Mina—Panguni.* 12	Fr	24	3	·24	...	...	2
13	Sa	25	4	·32	2	·00	3
14	Su	26	5	·41	3	·10	4
15	Mo	27	6	·49	4	·21	5
16	Tu	28	*Sukla* 7	·57	5	·32	6
17	We	29	8	·63	6	·41	7
18	Th	30	9	·68	7	·49	8
19	Fr	31	10	·72	8	·55	9

April

Cyclic Sidereal Year, Month and Day	Week-Day	English Month and Day	Tithi	Ending Moment	Nakshatra	Ending Moment	Muhammadan Year, Month and Day
20	Sa	1	11	·78	9	·59	H. 1288 *Muharram.* 10
21	Su	2	12	·72	10	·61	11
22	Mo	3	Chaitra 13	·68	11	·61	12
23	Tu	4	14	·63	12	·59	13
24	We	5	P	·57	13	·55	14
25	Th	6	1	·50	14	·51	15
26	Fr	7	2	·41	15	·45	16
27	Sa	8	3	·31	16	·38	17
28	Su	9	4	·21	17	·31	18
29	Mo	10	5	·11	18	·24	19
—30	Tu	11	{6 7	·01 ·91	19	·18	20
1	We	12	*Bahula* 8	·83	20	·12	21
2	Th	13	9	·76	21	·07	22
3.	Fr	14	10	·71	22	·03	23
4	Sa	15	11	·67	23	·01	24
5	Su	16	12	·65	24	·01	25
6	Mo	17	13	·66	25	·03	26
Prajapati *Mesha—Chittirai.* 7	Tu	18	14	·68	26	·07	27
8	We	19	—A	·73	27	·13	28
9	Th	20	1	·79	1	·21	29
10	Fr	21	2	·87	2	·30	—30
11	Sa	22	*Sukla* 3	·95	3	·41	H. 1288 *Safar.* 1
12	Su	23	...	...	4	·52	2
13	Mo	24	Vaisakha 4	·03	5	·62	3
14	Tu	25	5	·11	6	·72	4
15	We	26	6	·18	7	·80	5
16	Th	27	7	·23	8	·87	6
17	Fr	28	8	·27	9	·91	7
18	Sa	29	9	·28	10	·93	8
19	Su	30	10	·26	11	·93	9

May

Cyclic Sidereal Year, Month and Day	Week-Day	English Month and Day	Tithi	Ending Moment	Nakshatra	Ending Moment	Muhammadan Year, Month and Day
Prajapati *Mesha—Chittirai.* 20	Mo	1	Vaisakha *Suk.* 11	·23	12	·92	H. 1288 *Safar.* 10
21	Tu	2	12	·17	13	·89	11
22	We	3	13	·10	14	·84	12
23	Th	4	{14 P	·03 ·94	15	·78	13
24	Fr	5	1	·84	16	·72	14
25	Sa	6	2	·74	17	·66	15
26	Su	7	3	·64	18	·59	16
27	Mo	8	4	·54	19	·52	17
28	Tu	9	5	·44	20	·46	18
29	We	10	6	·35	21	·40	19
30	Th	11	7	·28	22	·36	20
—31	Fr	12	*Bahula* 8	·23	23	·34	21
1	Sa	13	9	·20	24	·34	22
2	Su	14	10	·18	25	·35	23
3	Mo	15	11	·17	26	·38	24
4	Tu	16	12	·19	27	·44	25
5	We	17	13	·24	1	·51	26
6	Th	18	14	·30	2	·61	27
7	Fr	19	—A	·38	3	·71	28
8	Sa	20	1	·46	4	·81	—29
9	Su	21	2	·54	5	·92	1
10	Mo	22	3	·62	...	...	2
Prajapati *Vrishabha—Vaikasi.* 11	Tu	23	4	·69	6	·02	3
12	We	24	5	·74	7	·11	4
13	Th	25	6	·76	8	·18	5
14	Fr	26	*Sukla* 7	·78	9	·23	6
15	Sa	27	8	·76	10	·25	7
16	Su	28	9	·73	11	·26	8
17	Mo	29	10	·68	12	·25	9
18	Tu	30	11	·62	13	·22	10
19	We	31	12	·53	14	·18	11

June

Cyclic Sidereal Year, Month and Day	Week-Day	English Month and Day	Tithi	Ending Moment	Nakshatra	Ending Moment	Muhammadan Year, Month and Day
20	Th	1	Jyeshta 13	·43	15	·12	H. 1288 *Rabi-ul-awwal.* 12
21	Fr	2	14	·33	16 17}	·06 ·99	13
22	Sa	3	P	·23	18	·92	14
23	Su	4	1	·13	19	·86	15
24	Mo	5	{2 3	·03 ·94	20	·80	16
25	Tu	6	4	·86	21	·74	17
26	We	7	5	·78	22	·69	18
27	Th	8	*Bahula* 6	·72	23	·67	19
28	Fr	9	7	·68	24	·66	20
29	Sa	10	8	·66	25	·67	21
30	Su	11	9	·66	26	·70	22
—31	Mo	12	10	·68	27	·75	23
1	Tu	13	11	·72	1	·82	24
2	We	14	12	·78	2	·91	25
3	Th	15	13	·85	...	...	26
4	Fr	16	14	·93	3	·01	27
5	Sa	17	...	...	4	·11	28
6	Su ●	18	—A	·02	5	·22	29
Prajapati *Mithuna—Ani.* 7	Mo	19	Ashadha *Sukla* 1	·10	6	·33	—30
8	Tu	20	2	·17	7	·42	H. 1288 *Rabi-ul-akhir.* 1
9	We	21	3	·22	8	·49	2
10	Th	22	4	·25	9	·54	3
11	Fr	23	5	·26	10	·57	4
12	Sa	24	6	·24	11	·59	5
13	Su	25	7	·21	12	·58	6
14	Mo	26	8	·16	13	·55	7
15	Tu	27	9	·10	14	·51	8
16	We	28	{10 11	·02 ·93	15	·46	9
17	Th	29	12	·83	16	·40	10
18	Fr	30	13	·73	17	·34	11

Naksh:- 1. Asvn. 2. Bhar. 3. Krit. 4. Rohi. 5. Mrig. 6. Ardh. 7. Punar. 8. Push. 9. Aslesh. 10. Magh. 11. P. Phal. 12. U. Phal. 13. Hasta. 14. Chit.

A. D. 1871. **A.—Amavasya.** **P.—Paurnami.** **Kollam 1047,** Commences { **N. Malabar—Sept.** **S. Malabar—Aug.** **Hijra 1288,** Commences, **Mar. 23.** **Vikrama 1928.** **Bengal San 1277.** **(N. Cycle) Subhanu.**

Columns: SOLAR reckoning — Cyclic Sidereal Year, Month and Day; Week-Day; English Month and Day. LUNAR reckoning — Tithi; Ending Moment; Nakshatra; Ending Moment; Muhammadan Year, Month and Day.

July

Prajapati Mithuna—Ani. (solar 19–32); *Prajapati Karkata—Adi.* (solar 1–17); Lunar: **Ashadha**, *Bahula*, *Sukla*; *H. 1288 Rabi-ul-akhir.*

Cyclic Sidereal Year, Month and Day	Week-Day	English Month and Day	Tithi	Ending Moment	Nakshatra	Ending Moment	Muhammadan Year, Month and Day
19	Sa	1	14	·62	18	·26	12
20	Su	2	P	·52	19	·19	13
21	Mo	3	1	·42	20	·13	14
22	Tu	4	2	·33	21	·07	15
23	We	5	3	·26	22	·03	16
24	Th	6	4	·20	23 / 24	·00 / ·99	17
25	Fr	7	5	·16	25	·99	18
26	Sa	8	6	·14	...	...	19
27	Su	9	7	·14	26	·01	20
28	Mo	10	8	·15	27	·06	21
29	Tu	11	9	·19	1	·13	22
30	We	12	10	·26	2	·21	23
31	Th	13	11	·33	3	·31	24
32	Fr	14	12	·41	4	·42	25
1	Sa	15	13	·49	5	·53	26
2	Su	16	14	·57	6	·63	27
3	Mo	17	A	·64	7	·72	28
4	Tu	18	1	·69	8	·80	29
5	We	19	2	·73	9	·85	1
6	Th	20	3	·74	10	·89	2
7	Fr	21	4	·72	11	·91	3
8	Sa	22	5	·69	12	·91	4
9	Su	23	6	·65	13	·88	5
10	Mo	24	7	·58	14	·84	6
11	Tu	25	8	·50	15	·79	7
12	We	26	9	·41	16	·73	8
13	Th	27	10	·31	17	·67	9
14	Fr	28	11	·21	18	·60	10
15	Sa	29	12	·11	19	·53	11
16	Su	30	13 / 14	·01 / ·91	20	·47	12
17	Mo	31	P	·82	21	·42	13

Aug.

Prajapati Karkata—Adi. (solar 18–31); *Prajapati Simha—Avani.* (solar 1–17); Lunar: **Sravana**, *Bahula*, *Sukla*, **Adhika Bhadra.**; *H. 1288 Jumadal-awwal.*, *H. 1288 Jumadal-akhir.*

Cyclic Sidereal Year, Month and Day	Week-Day	English Month and Day	Tithi	Ending Moment	Nakshatra	Ending Moment	Muhammadan Year, Month and Day
18	Tu	1	1	·74	22	·37	14
19	We	2	2	·68	23	·33	15
20	Th	3	3	·64	24	·31	16
21	Fr	4	4	·62	25	·31	17
22	Sa	5	5	·62	26	·34	18
23	Su	6	6	·64	27	·38	19
24	Mo	7	7	·67	1	·43	20
25	Tu	8	8	·73	2	·51	21
26	We	9	9	·80	3	·61	22
27	Th	10	10	·89	4	·72	23
28	Fr	11	11	·98	5	·83	24
29	Sa	12	...	...	6	·93	25
30	Su	13	12	·05	...	...	26
31	Mo	14	13	·12	7	·02	27
1	Tu	15	14	·18	8	·10	28
2	We	16	A	·21	9	·16	29
3	Th	17	1	·23	10	·21	30
4	Fr	18	2	·22	11	·23	1
5	Sa	19	3	·19	12	·23	2
6	Su	20	4	·15	13	·21	3
7	Mo	21	5	·08	14	·18	4
8	Tu	22	6 / 7	·00 / ·91	15	·14	5
9	We	23	8	·81	16	·08	6
10	Th	24	9	·71	17 / 18	·01 / ·94	7
11	Fr	25	10	·61	19	·87	8
12	Sa	26	11	·51	20	·81	9
13	Su	27	12	·42	21	·75	10
14	Mo	28	13	·33	22	·70	11
15	Tu	29	14	·25	23	·66	12
16	We	30	P	·19	24	·64	13
17	Th	31	1	·15	25	·64	14

Sep.

Prajapati Simha—Avani. (solar 18–31); *Prajapati Kanya—Purattasi.* (solar 1–16); Lunar: **Adh. Bhadra.**, *Bahula*, *Sukla*, **Bhadrapada**; *H. 1288 Jumadal-akhir.*, *Rajab.*

Cyclic Sidereal Year, Month and Day	Week-Day	English Month and Day	Tithi	Ending Moment	Nakshatra	Ending Moment	Muhammadan Year, Month and Day
18	Fr	1	2	·13	26	·65	15
19	Sa	2	3	·14	27	·69	16
20	Su	3	4	·16	1	·74	17
21	Mo	4	5	·20	2	·82	18
22	Tu	5	6	·25	3	·91	19
23	We	6	7	·31	...	...	20
24	Th	7	8	·39	4	·01	21
25	Fr	8	9	·46	5	·12	22
26	Sa	9	10	·56	6	·23	23
27	Su	10	11	·64	7	·33	24
28	Mo	11	12	·70	8	·41	25
29	Tu	12	13	·74	9	·48	26
30	We	13	14	·76	10	·53	27
31	Th	14	A	·74	11	·55	28
1	Fr	15	1	·71	12	·56	29
2	Sa	16	2	·67	13	·54	1
3	Su	17	3	·61	14	·51	2
4	Mo	18	4	·53	15	·47	3
5	Tu	19	5	·45	16	·42	4
6	We	20	6	·35	17	·35	5
7	Th	21	7	·25	18	·28	6
8	Fr	22	8	·15	19	·21	7
9	Sa	23	9 / 10	·05 / ·95	20	·15	8
10	Su	24	11	·87	21	·09	9
11	Mo	25	12	·79	22 / 23	·03 / ·99	10
12	Tu	26	13	·74	24	·97	11
13	We	27	14	·70	25	·96	12
14	Th	28	P	·68	26	·97	13
15	Fr	29	1	·67	...	...	14
16	Sa	30	2	·69	27	·00	15

Oct.

Prajapati Kanya—Purattasi. (solar 17–31); *Prajapati Tula—Aippasi.* (solar 1–16); Lunar: **Nija** (Bhadrapada), *Bahula*, *Sukla*, **Asvina**, *Bah.*; *H. 1288* (Rajab), *H. 1288 Shaban.*

Cyclic Sidereal Year, Month and Day	Week-Day	English Month and Day	Tithi	Ending Moment	Nakshatra	Ending Moment	Muhammadan Year, Month and Day
17	Su	1	3	·73	1	·05	16
18	Mo	2	4	·78	2	·12	17
19	Tu	3	5	·86	3	·22	18
20	We	4	6	·95	4	·32	19
21	Th	5	...	...	5	·42	20
22	Fr	6	7	·04	6	·53	21
23	Sa	7	8	·12	7	·63	22
24	Su	8	9	·19	8	·72	23
25	Mo	9	10	·25	9	·79	24
26	Tu	10	11	·29	10	·84	25
27	We	11	12	·32	11	·87	26
28	Th	12	13	·30	12	·88	27
29	Fr	13	14	·28	13	·88	28
30	Sa	14	A	·24	14	·85	29
31	Su	15	1	·18	15	·81	30
1	Mo	16	2	·10	16	·75	1
2	Tu	17	3 / 4	·01 / ·91	17	·69	2
3	We	18	5	·81	18	·63	3
4	Th	19	6	·71	19	·56	4
5	Fr	20	7	·62	20	·49	5
6	Sa	21	8	·53	21	·42	6
7	Su	22	9	·45	22	·37	7
8	Mo	23	10	·37	23	·33	8
9	Tu	24	11	·31	24	·30	9
10	We	25	12	·27	25	·28	10
11	Th	26	13	·26	26	·29	11
12	Fr	27	14	·26	27	·31	12
13	Sa	28	P	·28	1	·36	13
14	Su	29	1	·32	2	·43	14
15	Mo	30	2	·38	3	·52	15
16	Tu	31	3	·46	4	·61	16

Nov.

Prajapati Tula—Aippasi. (solar 17–30); *Prajapati Vrischika—Kartigai.* (solar 1–16); Lunar: **Asvina**, *Bahula*, *Sukla*, **Karttika**; *H. 1288 Shaban.*, *H. 1288 Ramzan.*

Cyclic Sidereal Year, Month and Day	Week-Day	English Month and Day	Tithi	Ending Moment	Nakshatra	Ending Moment	Muhammadan Year, Month and Day
17	We	1	4	·54	5	·72	17
18	Th	2	5	·63	6	·83	18
19	Fr	3	6	·71	7	·94	19
20	Sa	4	7	·79	...	...	20
21	Su	5	8	·85	8	·03	21
22	Mo	6	9	·89	9	·10	22
23	Tu	7	10	·91	10	·15	23
24	We	8	11	·90	11	·19	24
25	Th	9	12	·88	12	·21	25
26	Fr	10	13	·84	13	·20	26
27	Sa	11	14	·78	14	·18	27
28	Su	12	A	·70	15	·14	28
29	Mo	13	1	·61	16	·09	29
30	Tu	14	2	·52	17 / 18	·03 / ·97	1
1	We	15	3	·42	19	·90	2
2	Th	16	4	·32	20	·83	3
3	Fr	17	5	·22	21	·76	4
4	Sa	18	6	·14	22	·70	5
5	Su	19	7 / 8	·06 / ·99	23	·66	6
6	Mo	20	9	·93	24	·63	7
7	Tu	21	10	·89	25	·61	8
8	We	22	11	·88	26	·61	9
9	Th	23	12	·88	27	·63	10
10	Fr	24	13	·90	1	·68	11
11	Sa	25	14	·95	2	·74	12
12	Su	26	...	...	3	·82	13
13	Mo	27	P	·01	4	·91	14
14	Tu	28	1	·09	...	...	15
15	We	29	2	·18	5	·02	16
16	Th	30	3	·27	6	·13	17

Dec.

Prajapati Vrischika—Kartigai. (solar 17–29); *Prajapati Dhanus—Margali.* (solar 1–18); Lunar: *Bahula*, *Sukla*, **Margasira**, *Bah.*; *H. 1288 Shawwal.*

Cyclic Sidereal Year, Month and Day	Week-Day	English Month and Day	Tithi	Ending Moment	Nakshatra	Ending Moment	Muhammadan Year, Month and Day
17	Fr	1	4	·35	7	·24	18
18	Sa	2	5	·42	8	·33	19
19	Su	3	6	·48	9	·41	20
20	Mo	4	7	·52	10	·47	21
21	Tu	5	8	·54	11	·51	22
22	We	6	9	·53	12	·53	23
23	Th	7	10	·51	13	·53	24
24	Fr	8	11	·46	14	·51	25
25	Sa	9	12	·40	15	·47	26
26	Su	10	13	·32	16	·42	27
27	Mo	11	14	·24	17	·37	28
28	Tu	12	A	·15	18	·30	29
29	We	13	1 / 2	·05 / ·95	19	·28	30
1	Th	14	3	·85	20	·16	1
2	Fr	15	4	·76	21	·10	2
3	Sa	16	5	·68	22 / 23	·04 / ·99	3
4	Su	17	6	·61	24	·96	4
5	Mo	18	7	·56	25	·93	5
6	Tu	19	8	·53	26	·93	6
7	We	20	9	·51	27	·95	7
8	Th	21	10	·53	1	·99	8
9	Fr	22	11	·55	...	...	9
10	Sa	23	12	·59	2	·05	10
11	Su	24	13	·66	3	·12	11
12	Mo	25	14	·74	4	·21	12
13	Tu	26	P	·83	5	·32	13
14	We	27	1	·92	6	·43	14
15	Th	28	...	...	7	·54	15
16	Fr	29	2	·00	8	·63	16
17	Sa	30	3	·07	9	·71	17
18	Su	31	4	·13	10	·78	18

15. Svati. 16. Visak. 17. Anur. 18. Jyesh. 19. Mula. 20. P. Ash. 21. U. Ash. 22. Sravn. 23. Dani. 24. Satab. 25. P. Bhad. 26. U. Bhad. 27. Rev.

A. D. 1872. **Mesha Sankranti** (Commencement of Indian Sidereal Year).

Solar Eclipse. ● **(Surya Sid.) April 11·37.** **Saka 1794.** **Kaliyuga 4973.**

Lunar Eclipse. ○ **(Arya Sid.) April 11·27.** **(S. Cycle) Angirasa.**

SOLAR reckoning: Cyclic Sidereal Year, Month and Day; Week-Day; English Month and Day. LUNAR reckoning: Tithi; Ending Moment; Nakshatra; Ending Moment; Muhammadan Year, Month and Day.

Jan.

Cyclic Sidereal Year, Month and Day	Week-Day	English Month and Day	Tithi	Ending Moment	Nakshatra	Ending Moment	Muhammadan Year, Month and Day
Prajapati Dhanus—Margali. 19	Mo	1	Marga. 5	·17	11	·83	H. 1288 Shawwal. 19
20	Tu	2	6	·18	12	·85	20
21	We	3	7	·17	13	·85	21
22	Th	4	8	·15	14	·84	22
23	Fr	5	9	·11	15	·81	23
24	Sa	6	Bahula {10 / 11	·05 / ·98	16	·77	24
25	Su	7	12	·89	17	·71	25
26	Mo	8	13	·79	18	·64	26
27	Tu	9	14	·69	19	·57	27
28	We	10	A	·59	20	·50	28
29	Th	11	1	·50	21	·44	—29
—30	Fr	12	2	·41	22	·38	1
1	Sa	13	3	·33	23	·33	2
2	Su	14	4	·26	24	·29	3
3	Mo	15	5	·21	25	·26	4
4	Tu	16	Sukla 6	·18	26	·26	5.
5	We	17	7	·16	27	·27	6
6	Th	18	8	·17	1	·30	7
7	Fr	19	9	·20	2	·35	8
8	Sa	20	10	·25	3	·42	9
9	Su	21	11	·32	4	·52	10
10	Mo	22	12	·40	5	·62	11
11	Tu	23	Pausha 13	·49	6	·73	H. 1288 Zi-l-ka'da. 12
12	We	24	14	·58	7	·83	13
Prajapati Makara—Tai. 13	Th	25	P	·66	8	·93	14
14	Fr	26	1	·73	...	...	15
15	Sa	27	2	·78	9	·02	16
16	Su	28	3	·81	10	·10	17
17	Mo	29	4	·83	11	·14	18
18	Tu	30	5	·82	12	·17	19
19	We	31	6	·79	13	·18	20

Feb.

Cyclic Sidereal Year, Month and Day	Week-Day	English Month and Day	Tithi	Ending Moment	Nakshatra	Ending Moment	Muhammadan Year, Month and Day
20	Th	1	Bahula 7	·74	14	·17	21
21	Fr	2	8	·67	15	·15	22
22	Sa	3	9	·60	16	·10	23
23	Su	4	10	·52	17 / 18}	·05 / ·98	24
24	Mo	5	11	·42	19	·91	25
25	Tu	6	12	·32	20	·84	26
26	We	7	13	·22	21	·78	27
27	Th	8	14	·12	22	·72	28
28	Fr	9	{A / 1	·03 / ·95	23	·66	29
—29	Sa	10	2	·38	24	·62	—30
1	Su	11	3	·84	25	·60	1
2	Mo	12	4	·81	26	·59	2
3	Tu	13	5	·79	27	·59	3
4	We	14	6	·80	1	·61	4
5	Th	15	Sukla 7	·84	2	·66	5
6	Fr	16	8	·89	3	·73	6
Prajapati Kumbha—Masi. 7	Sa	17	9	·95	4	·82	H. 1288 Zi-l-hijja. 7
8	Su	18	...	...	5	·92	8
9	Mo	19	10	·03	...	...	9
10	Tu	20	11	·11	6	·08	10
11	We	21	Maghu 12	·20	7	·13	11
12	Th	22	13	·28	8	·23	12
13	Fr	23	14	·35	9	·32	13
14	Sa	24	P	·41	10	·40	14
15	Su	25	1	·44	11	·46	15
16	Mo	26	2	·45	12	·49	16
17	Tu	27	3	·43	13	·50	17
18	We	28	Bah. 4	·41	14	·50	·18
19	Th	29	5	·36	15	·48	19

March

Cyclic Sidereal Year, Month and Day	Week-Day	English Month and Day	Tithi	Ending Moment	Nakshatra	Ending Moment	Muhammadan Year, Month and Day
20	Fr	1	Mag. 6	·29	16	·44	20
21	Sa	2	7	·22	17	·38	21
22	Su	3	8	·13	18	·32	H 1288 Zi-l-hijja. 22
Prajapati Kumbha—Masi. 23	Mo	4	9 / 10	·03 / ·93	19	·26	23
24	Tu	5	Bahula 11	·83	20	·19	24
25	We	6	12	·74	21	·12	25
26	Th	7	13	·65	22	·05	26
27	Fr	8	14	·57	23 / 24}	·00 / ·96	27
28	Sa	9	—A	·50	25	·93	28
29	Su	10	1	·45	26	·91	—29
30	Mo	11	2	·41	27	·91	1
—31	Tu	12	3	·40	1	·93	2
1	We	13	4	·41	2	·97	3
2	Th	14	5	·44	...	...	4
3	Fr	15	Sukla 6	·48	3	·04	5
4	Sa	16	7	·55	4	·12	6
5	Su	17	8	·63	5	·22	7
6	Mo	18	9	·72	6	·32	8
7	Tu	19	10	·81	7	·43	9
8	We	20	Phalguna 11	·89	8	·54	10
9	Th	21	12	·95	9	·64	11
10	Fr	22	...	...	10	·71	12
11	Sa	23	13	·00	11	·77	13
12	Su	24	14	·03	12	·81	H. 1289 Muharram. 14
13	Mo	25	P	·04	13	·83	15
Prajapati Mina—Pangunı. 14	Tu	26	1 / 2	·02 / ·99	14	·83	16
15	We	27	3	·94	15	·81	17
16	Th	28	4	·88	16	·77	18
17	Fr	29	5	·80	17	·72	19
18	Sa	30	6	·71	18	·66	20
19	Su	31	7	·61	19	·60	21

April

Cyclic Sidereal Year, Month and Day	Week-Day	English Month and Day	Tithi	Ending Moment	Nakshatra	Ending Moment	Muhammadan Year, Month and Day
20	Mo	1	Bahula 8	·51	20	·53	22
21	Tu	2	9	·41	21	·46	23
22	We	3	10	·31	22	·39	24
23	Th	4	11	·22	23	·33	25
24	Fr	5	12	·14	24	·29	26
25	Sa	6	13	·07	25	·25	27
26	Su	7	{14 / A	·02 / ·98	26	·23	28
27	Mo	8	1	·96	27	·23	29
28	Tu	9	2	·97	1	·24	—30
—29	We	10	...	...	2	·29	1
1	Th	11	3	·00	3	·35	2
2	Fr	12	4	·04	4	·43	3
3	Sa	13	5	·11	5	·52	4
4	Su	14	6	·19	6	·62	5
5	Mo	15	Sukla 7	·27	7	·73	6
6	Tu	16	8	·36	8	·84	7
7	We	17	9	·44	9	·94	8
8	Th	18	10	·50	...	...	9
9	Fr	19	11	·55	10	·02	H. 1289 Safar. 10
Angirasa Mesha—Chittirai. 10	Sa	20	12	·58	11	·08	11
11	Su	21	Chaitra 13	·58	12	·13	12
12	Mo	22	14	·56	13	·15	13
13	Tu	23	P	·53	14	·15	14
14	We	24	1	·48	15	·13	15
15	Th	25	2	·42	16	·10	16
16	Fr	26	3	·34	17	·06	17
17	Sa	27	Bahula 4	·25	18 / 19}	·00 / ·94	18
18	Su	28	5	·15	20	·87	19
19	Mo	29	6 / 7	·05 / ·95	21	·80	20
20	Tu	30	8	·85	22	·74	21

May

Cyclic Sidereal Year, Month and Day	Week-Day	English Month and Day	Tithi	Ending Moment	Nakshatra	Ending Moment	Muhammadan Year, Month and Day
21	We	1	Ch. 9	·75	23	·68	H. 1289 Safar. 22
22	Th	2	10	·67	24	·62	23
23	Fr	3	11	·60	25	·58	24
Angirasa Mesha—Chittirai. 24	Sa	4	Bah. 12	·55	26	·56	25
25	Su	5	13	·51	27	·55	26
26	Mo	6	14	·49	1	·57	27
27	Tu	7	—A	·49	2	·60	28
28	We	8	1	·52	3	·66	—29
29	Th	9	2	·57	4	·73	1
30	Fr	10	3	·63	5	·82	2
—31	Sa	11	4	·70	6	·93	3
1	Su	12	Sukla 5	·79	...	...	4
2	Mo	13	6	·87	7	·04	5
3	Tu	14	7	·95	8	·14	6
4	We	15	...	...	9	·24	7
5	Th	16	Vaisakha 8	·01	10	·33	8
6	Fr	17	9	·06	11	·40	9
7	Sa	18	10	·09	12	·45	10
8	Su	19	11	·10	13	·47	11
9	Mo	20	12	·09	14	·48	12
10	Tu	21	13	·05	15	·46	H. 1289 Rabi-ul-awwal. 13
11	We ○	22	{14 / P	·00 / ·93	16	·43	14
12	Th	23	1	·84	17	·40	15
13	Fr	24	2	·75	18	·34	16
Angirasa Vrishabha—Vaikasi. 14	Sa	25	3	·65	19	·28	17
15	Su	26	4	·55	20	·21	18
16	Mo	27	5	·45	21	·14	19
17	Tu	28	6	·35	22	·08	20
18	We	29	Bahula 7	·25	23 / 24}	·02 / ·96	21
19	Th	30	8	·17	25	·91	22
20	Fr	31	9	·10	26	·88	23

June

Cyclic Sidereal Year, Month and Day	Week-Day	English Month and Day	Tithi	Ending Moment	Nakshatra	Ending Moment	Muhammadan Year, Month and Day
21	Sa	1	10	·04	27	·88	24
22	Su	2	{11 / 12	·01 / ·99	1	·89	25
23	Mo	3	13	·99	2	·02	26
24	Tu	4	...	...	3	·97	27
25	We	5	14	·01	...	...	28
26	Th ●	6	—A	·06	4	·03	29
27	Fr	7	1	·12	5	·13	—30
28	Sa	8	2	·19	6	·23	1
29	Su	9	3	·28	7	·33	2
30	Mo	10	4	·36	8	·44	3
31	Tu	11	5	·43	9	·54	4
—32	We	12	Sukla 6	·49	10	·63	5
1	Th	13	7	·54	11	·71	6
2	Fr	14	8	·57	12	·76	7
3	Sa	15	9	·58	13	·79	8
4	Su	16	10	·57	14	·80	H. 1289 Rabi-ul-akhir. 9
5	Mo	17	11	·54	15	·79	10
6	Tu	18	Jyeshtha 12	·49	16	·77	11
7	We	19	13	·42	17	·73	12
Angirasa Mithuna—Ani. 8	Th	20	14	·34	18	·68	13
9	Fr	21	P	·24	19	·61	14
10	Sa	22	1	·14	20	·54	15
11	Su	23	2 / 3	·04 / ·94	21	·47	16
12	Mo	24	4	·84	22	·41	17
13	Tu	25	5	·74	23	·35	18
14	We	26	Bahula 6	·65	24	·29	19
15	Th	27	7	·58	25	·24	20
16	Fr	28	8	·53	26	·22	21
17	Sa	29	9	·49	27	·21	22
18	Su	30	10	·47	1	·21	23

Naksh :—1. Asvn. 2. Bhar. 3. Krit. 4. Rohi. 5. Mrig. 6. Ardh. 7. Punar. 8. Push. 9. Aslesh. 10. Magh. 11. P. Phal. 12. U. Phal. 13. Hasta. 14. Chit.

A. D. 1872.
A.—Amavasya. **P.—Paurnami.**
Kollam 1048, Commences { **N. Malabar—Sept.** / **S. Malabar—Aug.**
Hijra 1289, Commences, **Mar. 11.**
Vikrama 1929.
Bengal San 1278.
(N. Cycle) Tarana.

Columns: SOLAR reckoning — Cyclic Sidereal Year, Month and Day; Week-Day; English Month and Day. LUNAR reckoning — Tithi; Ending Moment; Nakshatra; Ending Moment; Muhammadan Year, Month and Day.

July

Side labels: *Angirasa Mithuna—Ani.*; *Angirasa Karkata—Adi.*; *Jy. Bah.*; *Sukla*; **Ashadha**; *Bahula*; *R.-akhir.*; *H. 1289 Jumadal-awwal.*

Cyclic Sidereal Year, Month and Day	Week-Day	English Month and Day	Tithi	Ending Moment	Nakshatra	Ending Moment	Muhammadan Year, Month and Day
19	Mo	1	11	·47	2	·23	24
20	Tu	2	12	·49	3	·27	25
21	We	3	13	·53	4	·34	26
22	Th	4	14	·59	5	·43	27
23	Fr	5	—A	·67	6	·53	28
24	Sa	6	1	·75	7	·63	—29
25	Su	7	2	·83	8	·74	1
26	Mo	8	3	·91	9	·84	2
27	Tu	9	4	·97	10	·94	3
28	We	10	...	...	...	...	4
29	Th	11	5	·02	11	·02	5
30	Fr	12	6	·05	12	·07	6
—31	Sa	13	7	·07	13	·11	7
1	Su	14	8	·05	14	·12	8
2	Mo	15	9 10	·02 ·97	15	·12	9
3	Tu	16	11	·90	16	·10	10
4	We	17	12	·82	17	·06	11
5	Th	18	13	·73	18 19	·01 ·95	12
6	Fr	19	14	·63	20	·80	13
7	Sa	20	P	·53	21	·82	14
8	Su	21	1	·43	22	·75	15
9	Mo	22	2	·33	23	·68	16
10	Tu	23	3	·23	24	·63	17
11	We	24	4	·14	25	·59	18
12	Th	25	5	·06	26	·55	19
13	Fr	26	6 7	·01 ·97	27	·53	20
14	Sa	27	8	·95	1	·53	21
15	Su	28	9	·95	2	·55	22
16	Mo	29	10	·97	3	·59	23
17	Tu	30	...	...	4	·65	24
18	We	31	11	·01	5	·73	25

Aug.

Side labels: *Angirasa Simha—Avani.*; *Sukla*; **Sravana**; *Bahula*; *H. 1289 Jumadal-akhir.*

Cyclic Sidereal Year, Month and Day	Week-Day	English Month and Day	Tithi	Ending Moment	Nakshatra	Ending Moment	Muhammadan Year, Month and Day
19	Th	1	12	·06	6	·83	26
20	Fr	2	13	·14	7	·93	27
21	Sa	3	14	·22	...	...	28
22	Su	4	—A	·30	8	·04	29
23	Mo	5	1	·38	9	·15	—30
24	Tu	6	2	·45	10	·24	1
25	We	7	3	·50	11	·32	2
26	Th	8	4	·53	12	·38	3
27	Fr	9	5	·55	13	·42	4
28	Sa	10	6	·53	14	·45	5
29	Su	11	7	·50	15	·45	6
30	Mo	12	8	·45	16	·43	7
31	Tu	13	9	·39	17	·40	8
—32	We	14	10	·31	18	·36	9
1	Th	15	11	·22	19	·30	10
2	Fr	16	12	·12	20	·23	11
3	Sa	17	13 14	·02 ·92	21	·16	12
4	Su	18	P	·82	22	·09	13
5	Mo	19	1	·73	23 24	·03 ·97	14
6	Tu	20	2	·64	25	·92	15
7	We	21	3	·56	26	·88	16
8	Th	22	4	·49	27	·85	17
9	Fr	23	5	·46	1	·85	18
10	Sa	24	6	·45	2	·86	19
11	Su	25	7	·45	3	·90	20
12	Mo	26	8	·47	4	·96	21
13	Tu	27	9	·51	...	...	22
14	We	28	10	·57	5	·04	23
15	Th	29	11	·63	6	·13	24
16	Fr	30	12	·71	7	·23	25
17	Sa	31	13	·81	8	·34	26

Sep.

Side labels: *Angirasa Simha—Avani.*; *Angirasa Kanya—Purattasi.*; *Sukla*; **Bhadrapada**; *Bahula*; *H. 1289 Rajab.*

Cyclic Sidereal Year, Month and Day	Week-Day	English Month and Day	Tithi	Ending Moment	Nakshatra	Ending Moment	Muhammadan Year, Month and Day
18	Su	1	14	·89	9	·46	27
19	Mo	2	—A	·96	10	·55	28
20	Tu	3	...	...	11	·63	—29
21	We	4	1	·01	12	·69	1
22	Th	5	2	·05	13	·74	2
23	Fr	6	3	·07	14	·77	3
24	Sa	7	4	·05	15	·78	4
25	Su	8	5 6	·02 ·97	16	·76	5
26	Mo	9	7	·91	17	·73	6
27	Tu	10	8	·84	18	·69	7
28	We	11	9	·75	19	·63	8
29	Th	12	10	·65	20	·57	9
30	Fr	13	11	·55	21	·50	10
—31	Sa	14	12	·45	22	·43	11
1	Su	15	13	·35	23	·37	12
2	Mo	16	14	·26	24	·31	13
3	Tu	17	P	·17	25	·25	14
4	We	18	1	·10	26	·21	15
5	Th	19	2	·04	27	·18	16
6	Fr	20	3 4	·00 ·98	1	·17	17
7	Sa	21	5	·97	2	·19	18
8	Su	22	...	...	3	·22	19
9	Mo	23	6	·00	4	·27	20
10	Tu	24	7	·04	5	·34	21
11	We	25	8	·10	6	·43	22
12	Th	26	9	·17	7	·53	23
13	Fr	27	10	·26	8	·64	24
14	Sa	28	11	·35	9	·75	25
15	Su	29	12	·43	10	·85	26
16	Mo	30	13	·50	11	·93	27

Oct.

Side labels: *Angirasa Tula—Aippasi.*; *Sukla*; **Asvina**; *Bahula*; *H. 1289 Shaban.*

Cyclic Sidereal Year, Month and Day	Week-Day	English Month and Day	Tithi	Ending Moment	Nakshatra	Ending Moment	Muhammadan Year, Month and Day
17	Tu	1	14	·55	...	...	28
18	We	2	—A	·59	12	·00	29
19	Th	3	1	·61	13	·06	—30
20	Fr	4	2	·60	14	·09	1
21	Sa	5	3	·57	15	·10	2
22	Su	6	4	·52	16	·00	3
23	Mo	7	5	·46	17	·07	4
24	Tu	8	6	·39	18 19	·03 ·97	5
25	We	9	7	·31	20	·91	6
26	Th	10	8	·21	21	·84	7
27	Fr	11	9	·11	22	·77	8
28	Sa	12	10 11	·01 ·91	23	·71	9
29	Su	13	12	·82	24	·65	10
—30	Mo	14	13	·74	25	·59	11
1	Tu	15	14	·67	26	·54	12
2	We	16	P	·61	27	·51	13
3	Th	17	1	·57	1	·50	14
4	Fr	18	2	·55	2	·51	15
5	Sa	19	3	·56	3	·53	16
6	Su	20	4	·58	4	·58	17
7	Mo	21	5	·62	5	·64	18
8	Tu	22	6	·69	6	·73	19
9	We	23	7	·77	7	·83	20
10	Th	24	8	·86	8	·94	21
11	Fr	25	9	·94	...	...	22
12	Sa	26	...	...	9	·05	23
13	Su	27	10	·02	10	·15	24
14	Mo	28	11	·09	11	·24	25
15	Tu	29	12	·14	12	·32	26
16	We	30	13	·18	13	·37	27
17	Th	31	14	·20	14	·41	28

Nov.

Side labels: *Angirasa Tula—Aippasi.*; *Angirasa Vrischika—Kartigai.*; *Sukla*; **Karttika**; *Bahula*; *H. 1289 Ramzan.*

Cyclic Sidereal Year, Month and Day	Week-Day	English Month and Day	Tithi	Ending Moment	Nakshatra	Ending Moment	Muhammadan Year, Month and Day
18	Fr	1	—A	·19	15	·42	—29
19	Sa	2	1	·16	16	·41	1
20	Su	3	2	·12	17	·39	2
21	Mo	4	3 4	·06 ·99	18	·36	3
22	Tu	5	5	·90	19	·30	4
23	We	6	6	·80	20	·24	5
24	Th	7	7	·70	21	·18	6
25	Fr	8	8	·60	22	·12	7
26	Sa	9	9	·51	23 24	·05 ·98	8
27	Su	10	10	·42	25	·92	9
28	Mo	11	11	·34	26	·88	10
29	Tu	12	12	·27	27	·85	11
—30	We	13	13	·21	1	·83	12
1	Th	14	14	·18	2	·83	13
2	Fr ○	15	P	·16	3	·85	14
3	Sa	16	1	·17	4	·89	15
4	Su	17	2	·19	5	·96	16
5	Mo	18	3	·24	...	...	17
6	Tu	19	4	·30	6	·04	18
7	We	20	5	·38	7	·13	19
8	Th	21	6	·47	8	·23	20
9	Fr	22	7	·56	9	·34	21
10	Sa	23	8	·64	10	·45	22
11	Su	24	9	·71	11	·55	23
12	Mo	25	10	·77	12	·63	24
13	Tu	26	11	·81	13	·69	25
14	We	27	12	·83	14	·72	26
15	Th	28	13	·81	15	·74	27
16	Fr	29	14	·78	16	·75	28
17	Sa	30	—A	·73	17	·73	29

Dec.

Side labels: *Angirasa Dhanus—Margali.*; *Sukla*; **Margasira**; *Bahula*; *H. 1289 Shawwal.*

Cyclic Sidereal Year, Month and Day	Week-Day	English Month and Day	Tithi	Ending Moment	Nakshatra	Ending Moment	Muhammadan Year, Month and Day
18	Su	1	1	·67	18	·69	—30
19	Mo	2	2	·60	19	·64	1
20	Tu	3	3	52	20	·58	2
21	We	4	4	·43	21	·52	3
22	Th	5	5	·33	22	·45	4
23	Fr	6	6	·23	23	·38	5
24	Sa	7	7	·13	24	·32	6
25	Su	8	8 9	·04 ·96	25	·26	7
26	Mo	9	10	·90	26	·21	8
27	Tu	10	11	·85	27	·18	9
28	We	11	12	·81	1	·16	10
29	Th	12	13	·80	2	·15	11
—30	Fr	13	14	·81	3	·16	12
1	Sa	14	P	·83	4	·20	13
2	Su	15	1	·88	5	·26	14
3	Mo	16	2	·95	6	·34	15
4	Tu	17	...	...	7	·43	16
5	We	18	3	·03	8	·53	17
6	Th	19	4	·12	9	·64	18
7	Fr	20	5	·21	10	·75	19
8	Sa	21	6	·29	11	·85	20
9	Su	22	7	·36	12	·93	21
10	Mo	23	8	·41	...	...	22
11	Tu	24	9	·45	13	·00	23
12	We	25	10	·47	14	·04	24
13	Th	26	11	·46	15	·07	25
14	Fr	27	12	·44	16	·07	26
15	Sa	28	13	·39	17	·05	27
16	Su	29	14	·32	18 19	·02 ·98	28
17	Mo	30	—A	·24	20	·93	—29
18	Tu	31	1	·16	21	·86	1

15. Svati. 16. Visak. 17. Anur. 18. Jyesh. 19. Mula. 20. P. Ash. 21. U. Ash. 22. Sravn. 23. Dani. 24. Satab. 25. P. Bhad. 26. U. Bhad. 27. Rev.

A. D. 1873. **Mesha Sankranti** (Commencement of Indian Sidereal Year). (Surya Sid.) April 11·63. (Arya Sid.) April 11·53. **Saka 1795.** **Kaliyuga 4974.** (S. Cycle) **Srimukha.**

Solar Eclipse. ● **Lunar Eclipse.** ○

Jan.

Cyclic Sidereal Year, Month and Day (SOLAR reckoning)	Week-Day	English Month and Day	Tithi (LUNAR reckoning)	Ending Moment	Nakshatra	Ending Moment	Muhammadan Year, Month and Day
19	We	1	2 / 3	·07 / ·97	22	·79	2
20	Th	2	4	·87	23	·72	3
21	Fr	3	5	·77	24	·66	4
22	Sa	4	6	·68	25	·60	5
23	Su	5	7	·60	26	·55	6
24	Mo	6	8	·54	27	·51	7
25	Tu	7	9	·49	1	·48	8
26	We	8	10	·46	2	·47	9
27	Th	9	11	·45	3	·48	10
28	Fr	10	12	·45	4	·52	11
—29	Sa	11	13	·48	5	·57	12
1	Su	12	14	·53	6	·65	13
2	Mo	13	P	·59	7	·73	14
3	Tu	14	1	·67	8	·83	15
4	We	15	2	·76	9	·94	16
5	Th	16	3	·86	...	...	17
6	Fr	17	4	·94	10	·05	18
7	Sa	18	...	...	11	·15	19
8	Su	19	5	·01	12	·24	20
9	Mo	20	6	·06	13	·31	21
10	Tu	21	7	·10	14	·36	22
11	We	22	8	·11	15	·39	23
12	Th	23	9	·09	16	·40	24
13	Fr	24	10	·07	17	·39	25
14	Sa	25	11 / 12	·02 / ·96	18	·36	26
15	Su	26	13	·89	19	·32	27
16	Mo	27		·80	20	·26	28
17	Tu	28	—A	·70	21	·20	29
18	We	29	1	·60	22	·13	—30
19	Th	30	2	·50	23 / 24	·06 / ·99	1
20	Fr	31	3	·40	25	·93	2

Margin labels: *Angirasa Dhanus—Margali* (19–29); *Angirasa Makara—Tai* (1–20); *Pausha*, *Sukla* (to P), *Bahula* (after P); *H. 1289 Zi-l-ka'da.*

Feb.

Cyclic Sidereal Year, Month and Day	Week-Day	English Month and Day	Tithi	Ending Moment	Nakshatra	Ending Moment	Muhammadan Year, Month and Day
21	Sa	1	4	·32	26	·88	3
22	Su	2	5	·24	27	·84	4
23	Mo	3	6	·18	1	·81	5
24	Tu	4	7	·13	2	·79	6
25	We	5	8	·09	3	·81	7
26	Th	6	9	·08	4	·84	8
27	Fr	7	10	·09	5	·88	9
28	Sa	8	11	·13	6	·95	10
—29	Su	9	12	·18	...	...	11
1	Mo	10	13	·25	7	·04	12
2	Tu	11	14	·33	8	·14	13
3	We	12	P	·42	9	·25	14
4	Th	13	1	·50	10	·35	15
5	Fr	14	2	·58	11	·45	16
6	Sa	15	3	·65	12	·54	17
7	Su	16	4	·70	13	·62	18
8	Mo	17	5	·73	14	·68	19
9	Tu	18	6	·74	15	·71	20
10	We	19	7	·73	16	·72	21
11	Th	20	8	·69	17	·71	22
12	Fr	21	9	·64	18	·69	23
13	Sa	22	10	·58	19	·65	24
14	Su	23	11	·50	20	·60	25
15	Mo	24	12	·41	21	·54	26
16	Tu	25	13	·31	22	·47	27
17	We	26	14	·21	23	·40	28
18	Th	27	—A	·11	24	·34	29
19	Fr	28	1 / 2	·02 / ·94	25	·28	—30

Margin labels: *Angirasa Kumbha—Masi*; *Magha*, *Sukla*, *Bahula*; *H. 1289 Zi-l-hijja.*

March

Cyclic Sidereal Year, Month and Day	Week-Day	English Month and Day	Tithi	Ending Moment	Nakshatra	Ending Moment	Muhammadan Year, Month and Day
20	Sa	1	3	·86	26	·22	1
21	Su	2	4	·79	27	·17	2
22	Mo	3	5	·74	1	·14	3
23	Tu	4	6	·71	2	·13	4
24	We	5	7	·69	3	·13	5
25	Th	6	8	·70	4	·15	6
26	Fr	7	9	·74	5	·19	7
27	Sa	8	10	·79	6	·25	8
28	Su	9	11	·86	7	·34	9
29	Mo	10	12	·94	8	·44	10
—30	Tu	11	...	...	9	·55	11
1	We	12	13	·03	10	·65	12
2	Th	13	14	·11	11	·75	13
3	Fr	14	P	·19	12	·85	14
4	Sa	15	1	·25	13	·93	15
5	Su	16	2	·30	14	·99	16
6	Mo	17	3	·33	...	...	17
7	Tu	18	4	·33	15	·03	18
8	We	19	5	·31	16	·04	19
9	Th	20	6	·28	17	·04	20
10	Fr	21	7	·24	18 / 19	·03 / ·99	21
11	Sa	22	8	·18	20	·94	22
12	Su	23	9	·10	21	·88	23
13	Mo	24	10 / 11	·00 / ·90	22	·82	24
14	Tu	25	12	·80	23	·75	25
15	We	26	13	·70	24	·68	26
16	Th	27	14	·61	25	·61	27
17	Fr	28	—A	·52	26	·55	28
18	Sa	29	1	·44	27	·50	29
19	Su	30	2	·37	1	·47	—30
20	Mo	31	3	·32	2	·45	1

Margin labels: *Angirasa Kumbha—Masi*; *Angirasa Mina—Panguni*; *Phalguna*, *Sukla*, *Bahula*; *H. 1290 Muharram.*

April

Cyclic Sidereal Year, Month and Day	Week-Day	English Month and Day	Tithi	Ending Moment	Nakshatra	Ending Moment	Muhammadan Year, Month and Day
21	Tu	1	4	·29	3	·45	2
22	We	2	5	·27	4	·46	3
23	Th	3	6	·28	5	·50	4
24	Fr	4	7	·31	6	·57	5
25	Sa	5	8	·37	7	·65	6
26	Su	6	9	·44	8	·74	7
27	Mo	7	10	·52	9	·84	8
28	Tu	8	11	·60	10	·95	9
29	We	9	12	·68	...	...	10
30	Th	10	13	·75	11	·06	11
—31	Fr	11	14	·81	12	·16	12
1	Sa	12	P	·86	13	·24	13
2	Su	13	1	·89	14	·30	14
3	Mo	14	2	·90	15	·34	15
4	Tu	15	3	·88	16	·36	16
5	We	16	4	·84	17	·37	17
6	Th	17	5	·79	18	·35	18
7	Fr	18	6	·72	19	·32	19
8	Sa	19	7	·64	20	·27	20
9	Su	20	8	·55	21	·21	21
10	Mo	21	9	·45	22	·15	22
11	Tu	22	10	·35	23	·09	23
12	We	23	11	·25	24 / 25	·02 / ·95	24
13	Th	24	12	·15	26	·89	25
14	Fr	25	13 / 14	·06 / ·98	27	·84	26
15	Sa	26	—A	·91	1	·80	27
16	Su	27	1	·86	2	·78	28
17	Mo	28	2	·82	3	·77	—29
18	Tu	29	3	·80	4	·78	1
19	We	30	4	·81	5	·82	2

Margin labels: *Srimukha Mesha—Chittirai*; *Chaitra*, *Sukla*, *Bahula*; *V. Suk.*; *H. 1290 Safar.*

May

Cyclic Sidereal Year, Month and Day	Week-Day	English Month and Day	Tithi	Ending Moment	Nakshatra	Ending Moment	Muhammadan Year, Month and Day
20	Th	1	5	·84	6	·88	3
21	Fr	2	6	·89	7	·95	4
22	Sa	3	7	·96	...	...	5
23	Su	4	...	...	8	·04	6
24	Mo	5	8	·04	9	·14	7
25	Tu	6	9	·12	10	·25	8
26	We	7	10	·20	11	·36	9
27	Th	8	11	·28	12	·46	10
28	Fr	9	12	·34	13	·54	11
29	Sa	10	13	·38	14	·61	12
—30	Su	11	14	·40	15	·66	13
1	Mo ○	12	P	·42	16	·69	14
2	Tu	13	1	·40	17	·70	15
3	We	14	2	·37	18	·68	16
4	Th	15	3	·31	19	·65	17
5	Fr	16	4	·24	20	·61	18
6	Sa	17	5	·16	21	·56	19
7	Su	18	6 / 7	·06 / ·96	22	·50	20
8	Mo	19	8	·86	23	·43	21
9	Tu	20	9	·76	24	·36	22
10	We	21	10	·66	25	·29	23
11	Th	22	11	·57	26	·23	24
12	Fr	23	12	·49	27	·18	25
13	Sa	24	13	·42	1	·13	26
14	Su	25	14	·37	2	·10	27
15	Mo	26	—A	·34	3	·09	28
16	Tu	27	1	·32	4	·10	29
17	We	28	2	·31	5	·14	—30
18	Th	29	3	·34	6	·19	1
19	Fr	30	4	·39	7	·25	2
20	Sa.	31	5	·45	8	·34	3

Margin labels: *Srimukha Mesha—Chittirai*; *Srimukha Vrishabha—Vaikasi*; *Vaisakha*, *Sukla*, *Bahula*; *H. 1290 Rabi-ul-awwal.*

June

Cyclic Sidereal Year, Month and Day	Week-Day	English Month and Day	Tithi	Ending Moment	Nakshatra	Ending Moment	Muhammadan Year, Month and Day
21	Su	1	6	·53	9	·44	4
22	Mo	2	7	·61	10	·55	5
23	Tu	3	8	·70	11	·66	6
24	We	4	9	·77	12	·76	7
25	Th	5	10	·83	13	·85	8
26	Fr	6	11	·88	14	·92	9
27	Sa	7	12	·90	15	·98	10
28	Su	8	13	·91	...	...	11
29	Mo	9	14	·89	16	·01	12
30	Tu	10	P	·86	17	·02	13
31	We	11	1	·81●	18 / 19	·01 / ·99	14
—32	Th	12	2	·74	20	·95	15
1	Fr	13	3	·66	21	·90	16
2	Sa	14	4	·56	22	·83	17
3	Su	15	5	·46	23	·76	18
4	Mo	16	6	·36	24	·69	19
5	Tu	17	7	·26	25	·63	20
6	We	18	8	·16	26	·57	21
7	Th	19	9 / 10	·06 / ·98	27	·51	22
8	Fr	20	11	·91	1	·46	23
9	Sa	21	12	·85	2	·43	24
10	Su	22	13	·81	3	·41	25
11	Mo	23	14	·79	4	·43	26
12	Tu	24	—A	·79	5	·46	27
13	We	25	1	·82	6	·50	28
14	Th	26	2	·87	7	·56	—29
15	Fr	27	3	·93	8	·64	1
16	Sa	28	...	...	9	·74	2
17	Su	29	4	·00	10	·85	3
18	Mo	30	5	·08	11	·96	4

Margin labels: *Srimukha Mithuna—Ani*; *Jyeshtha*, *Sukla*, *Bahula*; *Ashad. Suk.*; *H. 1290 Rabi-ul-akhir.*; *J. awwal.*

Naksh :—1. Asvn. 2. Bhar. 3. Krit. 4. Rohi. 5. Mrig. 6. Ardh. 7. Punar. 8. Push. 9. Aslesh. 10. Magh. 11. P. Phal. 12. U. Phal. 13. Hasta. 14. Chit.

A. D. 1873. | **Kollam 1049,** { N. Malabar—Sept. / S. Malabar—Aug. } Commences | **Hijra 1290,** Commences, Mar. 1. | **Vikrama 1930.**

A.—Amavasya. P.—Paurnami. | **Bengal San 1279.** | **(N. Cycle) Parthiva.**

Solar months: Srimukha *Mithuna—Ani.*; Srimukha *Karkata—Adi.*; Srimukha *Simha—Avani.* Lunar months: *Sukla*; Ashadha; *Bahula*; *Sukla*; Sravana; *Bahula*; Bhadra. *Suk.* Muhammadan months: H. 1290 *Jumadal-awwal.*; H. 1290 *Jumadal-akhir.*; H. 1290 *Rajab.*

Cyclic Sidereal Year, Month and Day	Week-Day	English Month and Day	Tithi	Ending Moment	Nakshatra	Ending Moment	Muhammadan Year, Month and Day
	July						
19	Tu	1	6	·16	...	...	5
20	We	2	7	·24	12	·06	6
21	Th	3	8	·31	13	·15	7
22	Fr	4	9	·35	14	·23	8
23	Sa	5	10	·38	15	·29	9
24	Su	6	11	·39	16	·33	10
25	Mo	7	12	·38	17	·34	11
26	Tu	8	13	·34	18	·34	12
27	We	9	14	·28	19	·32	13
28	Th	10	P	·21	20	·28	14
29	Fr	11	1	·13	21	·23	15
30	Sa	12	2 3	·04 ·94	22	·17	16
—31	Su	13	4	·84	23	·10	17
1	Mo	14	5	·74	24 25	·03 ·96	18
2	Tu	15	6	·64	26	·90	19
3	We	16	7	·54	27	·84	20
4	Th	17	8	·45	1	·80	21
5	Fr	18	9	·38	2	·77	22
6	Sa	19	10	·33	3	·75	23
7	Su	20	11	·29	4	·75	24
8	Mo	21	12	·27	5	·77	25
9	Tu	22	13	·27	6	·81	26
10	We	23	14	·30	7	·87	27
11	Th	24	—A	·34	8	·95	28
12	Fr	25	1	·40	...	...	29
13	Sa	26	2	·47	9	·05	—30
14	Su	27	3	·55	10	·15	1
15	Mo	28	4	·63	11	·26	2
16	Tu	29	5	·71	12	·36	3
17	We	30	6	·78	13	·46	4
18	Th	31	7	·83	14	·54	5
	Aug.						
19	Fr	1	8	·86	15	·60	6
20	Sa	2	9	·87	16	·64	7
21	Su	3	10	·85	17	·66	8
22	Mo	4	11	·82	18	·67	9
23	Tu	5	12	·77	19	·65	10
24	We	6	13	·71	20	·62	11
25	Th	7	14	·63	21	·57	12
26	Fr	8	P	·53	22	·51	13
27	Sa	9	1	·43	23	·45	14
28	Su	10	2	·33	24	·38	15
29	Mo	11	3	·23	25	·31	16
30	Tu	12	4	·13	26	·24	17
31	We	13	5 6	·03 ·95	27	·18	18
—32	Th	14	7	·88	1	·13	19
1	Fr	15	8	·82	2	·10	20
2	Sa	16	9	·78	3	·08	21
3	Su	17	10	·76	4	·07	22
4	Mo	18	11	·77	5	·08	23
5	Tu	19	12	·79	6	·12	24
6	We	20	13	·84	7	·18	25
7	Th	21	14	·90	8	·26	26
8	Fr	22	—A	·96	9	·35	27
9	Sa	23	...	...	10	·45	28
10	Su	24	1	·04	11	·56	—29
11	Mo	25	2	·14	12	·67	1
12	Tu	26	3	·22	13	·77	2
13	We	27	4	·28	14	·85	3
14	Th	28	5	·33	15	·91	4
15	Fr	29	6	·35	16	·96	5
16	Sa	30	7	·37	17	·98	6
17	Su	31	8	·36	...	...	7

Solar months: Srimukha *Simha—Avani.*; Srimukha *Kanya—Purattasi.*; Srimukha *Tula—Aippasi.* Lunar months: *Sukla*; Bhadrapada; *Bahula*; *Sukla*; Asvina; *Bahula*; Kartika *Suk.* Muhammadan months: H. 1290 *Rajab.*; H. 1290 *Shaban.*; H. 1290 *Ramzan.*

Cyclic Sidereal Year, Month and Day	Week-Day	English Month and Day	Tithi	Ending Moment	Nakshatra	Ending Moment	Muhammadan Year, Month and Day
	Sep.						
18	Mo	1	9	·33	18 19	·00 ·98	8
19	Tu	2	10	·28	20	·95	9
20	We	3	11	·22	21	·90	10
21	Th	4	12	·14	22	·84	11
22	Fr	5	13 14	·05 ·95	23	·78	12
23	Sa	6	P	·85	24	·72	13
24	Su	7	1	·75	25	·65	14
25	Mo	8	2	·65	26	·58	15
26	Tu	9	3	·56	27	·52	16
27	We	10	4	·48	1	·47	17
28	Th	11	5	·41	2	·43	18
29	Fr	12	6	·35	3	·40	19
30	Sa	13	7	·31	4	·39	20
—31	Su	14	8	·28	5	·40	21
1	Mo	15	9	·30	6	·44	22
2	Tu	16	10	·33	7	·49	23
3	We	17	11	·37	8	·56	24
4	Th	18	12	·42	9	·65	25
5	Fr	19	13	·49	10	·75	26
6	Sa	20	14	·57	11	·86	27
7	Su	21	—A	·66	12	·97	28
8	Mo	22	1	·74	...	...	29
9	Tu	23	2	·81	13	·07	—30
10	We	24	3	·87	14	·15	1
11	Th	25	4	·90	15	·22	2
12	Fr	26	5	·92	16	·27	3
13	Sa	27	6	·91	17	·31	4
14	Su	28	7	·88	18	·32	5
15	Mo	29	8	·83	19	·31	6
16	Tu	30	9	·76	20	·28	7
	Oct.						
17	We	1	10	·68	21	·24	8
18	Th	2	11	·59	22	·19	9
19	Fr	3	12	·50	23	·13	10
20	Sa	4	13	·40	24 25	·06 ·99	11
21	Su	5	14	·30	26	·92	12
22	Mo	6	P	·20	27	·86	13
23	Tu	7	1	·11	1	·81	14
24	We	8	2 3	·08 ·96	2	·76	15
25	Th	9	4	·91	3	·73	16
26	Fr	10	5	·87	4	·71	17
27	Sa	11	6	·86	5	·73	18
28	Su	12	7	·86	6	·76	19
29	Mo	13	8	·88	7	·80	20
—30	Tu	14	9	·93	8	·86	21
1	We	15	10	·99	9	·95	22
2	Th	16	...	...	...	...	23
3	Fr	17	11	·06	10	·05	24
4	Sa	18	12	·15	11	·16	25
5	Su	19	13	·24	12	·27	26
6	Mo	20	14	·32	13	·37	27
7	Tu	21	—A	·40	14	·46	28
8	We	22	1	·45	15	·53	—29
9	Th	23	2	·48	16	·59	1
10	Fr	24	3	·50	17	·63	2
11	Sa	25	4	·48	18	·64	3
12	Su	26	5	·45	19	·63	4
13	Mo	27	6	·41	20	·61	5
14	Tu	28	7	·35	21	·58	6
15	We	29	8	·27	22	·53	7
16	Th	30	9	·18	23	·47	8
17	Fr	31	10 11	·09 ·99	24	·40	9

Solar months: Srimukha *Tula—Aippasi.*; Srimukha *Vrischika—Kartigai.*; Srimukha *Dhanus—Margali.* Lunar months: Kartika *Suk.*; *Bahula*; *Sukla*; Margasira; *Bahula*; Pausha *Sukla*. Muhammadan months: H. 1290 *Ramzan.*; H. 1290 *Shawwal.*; H. 1290 *Zi-l-ka'da.*

Cyclic Sidereal Year, Month and Day	Week-Day	English Month and Day	Tithi	Ending Moment	Nakshatra	Ending Moment	Muhammadan Year, Month and Day
	Nov.						
18	Sa	1	12	·89	25	·33	10
19	Su	2	13	·79	26	·26	11
20	Mo	3	14	·70	27	·20	12
21	Tu ○	4	P	·62	1	·14	13
22	We	5	1	·55	2	·09	14
23	Th	6	2	·50	3	·06	15
24	Fr	7	3	·46	4	·04	16
25	Sa	8	4	·45	5	·05	17
26	Su	9	5	·46	6	·07	18
27	Mo	10	6	·49	7	·11	19
28	Tu	11	7	·53	8	·17	20
29	We	12	8	·60	9	·25	21
—30	Th	13	9	·68	10	·35	22
1	Fr	14	10	·77	11	·46	23
2	Sa	15	11	·86	12	·57	24
3	Su	16	12	·93	13	·67	25
4	Mo	17	...	...	14	·76	26
5	Tu	18	13	·00	15	·84	27
6	We	19	14	·06	16	·91	28
7	Th	20	—A	·10	17	·94	29
8	Fr	21	1	·11	18	·96	—30
9	Sa	22	2	·10	19	·96	1
10	Su	23	3	·07	20	·95	2
11	Mo	24	4 5	·02 ·96	21	·91	3
12	Tu	25	6	·89	22	·86	4
13	We	26	7	·81	23	·80	5
14	Th	27	8	·71	24	·74	6
15	Fr.	28	9	·61	25	·67	7
16	Sa	29	10	·51	26	·60	8
17	Su	30	11	·41	27	·54	9
	Dec.						
18	Mo	1	12	·32	1	.48	10
19	Tu	2	13	·24	2	·42	11
20	We	3	14	·18	3	·39	12
21	Th	4	P	·13	4	·37	13
22	Fr	5	1	·10	5	·37	14
23	Sa	6	2	·08	6	·38	15
24	Su	7	3	·09	7	·42	16
25	Mo	8	4	·12	8	·48	17
26	Tu	9	5	·17	9	·56	18
27	We	10	6	·24	10	·65	19
28	Th	11	7	·33	11	·75	20
29	Fr	12	8	·42	12	·86	21
—30	Sa	13	9	·50	13	·97	22
1	Su	14	10	·58	...	...	23
2	Mo	15	11	·65	14	·07	24
3	Tu	16	12	·70	15	·15	25
4	We	17	13	·74	16	·22	26
5	Th	18	14	·75	17	·26	27
6	Fr	19	—A	·74	18	·28	28
7	Sa	20	1	·71	19	·29	—29
8	Su	21	2	·67	20	·27	1
9	Mo	22	3	·60	21	·24	2
10	Tu	23	4	·52	22	·20	3
11	We	24	5	·44	23	·14	4
12	Th	25	6	·34	24	·08	5
13	Fr	26	7	·24	25 26	·01 ·94	6
14	Sa	27	8	·15	27	·87	7
15	Su	28	9 10	·06 ·97	1	·81	8
16	Mo	29	11	·89	2	·77	9
17	Tu	30	12	·82	3	·73	10
18	We	31	13	·77	4	·70	11

15. Svati. 16. Visak. 17. Anur. 18. Jyesh. 19. Mula. 20. P. Ash. 21. U. Ash. 22. Sravn. 23. Dani. 24. Satab. 25. P. Bhad. 26. U. Bhad. 27. Rev.

A. D. 1874.
Solar Eclipse. ●
Lunar Eclipse. ○

Mesha Sankranti (Commencement of Indian Sidereal Year).
(Surya Sid.) April 11·89.
(Arya Sid.) April 11·79.

Saka 1796. **Kaliyuga 4975.**
(S. Cycle) Bhava.

Columns: SOLAR reckoning (Cyclic Sidereal Year, Month and Day; Week-Day; English Month and Day) — LUNAR reckoning (Tithi, Ending Moment; Nakshatra, Ending Moment; Muhammadan Year, Month and Day).

Jan.

Srimukha, Dhanus—Margali; Srimukha, Makara—Tai. Pausha; Bahula; Sukla. H. 1290 Zi-l-ka'da.

Cyclic Sidereal Year, Month and Day	Week-Day	English Month and Day	Tithi	Ending Moment	Nakshatra	Ending Moment	Muhammadan Year, Month and Day
19	Th	1	14	·74	5	·69	12
20	Fr	2	P	·73	6	·70	13
21	Sa	3	1	·74	7	·73	14
22	Su	4	2	·77	8	·79	15
23	Mo	5	3	·82	9	·87	16
24	Tu	6	4	·89	10	·95	17
25	We	7	5	·97	...	...	18
26	Th	8	...	...	11	·05	19
27	Fr	9	6	·07	12	·16	20
28	Sa	10	7	·15	13	·27	21
29	Su	11	8	·23	14	·37	22
1	Mo	12	9	·30	15	·46	23
2	Tu	13	10	·36	16	·53	24
3	We	14	11	·39	17	·58	25
4	Th	15	12	·39	18	·61	26
5	Fr	16	13	·38	19	·62	27
6	Sa	17	14	·35	20	·60	28
7	Su	18	A	·31	21	·57	29
8	Mo	19	1	·25	22	·53	30
9	Tu	20	2	·17	23	·48	1
10	We	21	3 4	·07 ·97	24	·42	2
11	Th	22	5	·87	25	·35	3
12	Fr	23	6	·77	26	·28	4
13	Sa	24	7	·68	27	·22	5
14	Su	25	8	·59	1	·16	6
15	Mo	26	9	·52	2	·10	7
16	Tu	27	10	·46	3	·06	8
17	We	28	11	·41	4	·03	9
18	Th	29	12	·38	5	·01	10
19	Fr	30	13	·37	6	·02	11
20	Sa	31	14	·38	7	·05	12

Feb.

Srimukha, Kumbha—Masi. Magha; Bahula; Phalg. Sukla. H. 1290 Zi-l-hijja; H. 1291 Muharram.

Cyclic Sidereal Year, Month and Day	Week-Day	English Month and Day	Tithi	Ending Moment	Nakshatra	Ending Moment	Muhammadan Year, Month and Day
21	Su	1	P	·42	8	·10	13
22	Mo	2	1	·47	9	·17	14
23	Tu	3	2	·54	10	·25	15
24	We	4	3	·62	11	·35	16
25	Th	5	4	·71	12	·46	17
26	Fr	6	5	·80	13	·57	18
27	Sa	7	6	·88	14	·67	19
28	Su	8	7	·95	15	·76	20
29	Mo	9	...	...	16	·84	21
30	Tu	10	8	·00	17	·90	22
1	We	11	9	·02	18	·93	23
2	Th	12	10	·03	19	·94	24
3	Fr	13	11 12	·02 ·93	20	·93	25
4	Sa	14	13	·93	21	·91	26
5	Su	15	14	·87	22	·87	27
6	Mo	16	A	·79	23	·82	28
7	Tu	17	1	·70	24	·76	29
8	We	18	2	·61	25	·69	1
9	Th	19	3	·51	26	·62	2
10	Fr	20	4	·41	27	·55	3
11	Sa	21	5	·31	1	·49	4
12	Su	22	6	·22	2	·43	5
13	Mo	23	7	·14	3	·39	6
14	Tu	24	8	·08	4	·36	7
15	We	25	9	·04	5	·34	8
16	Th	26	10 11	·01 ·99	6	·35	9
17	Fr	27	...	...	7	·37	10
18	Sa	28	12	·01	8	·41	11

March

Srimukha, Kumbha—Masi; Srimukha, Mina—Panguni. Phalguna; Bahula; Sukla. H. 1291 Muharram.

Cyclic Sidereal Year, Month and Day	Week-Day	English Month and Day	Tithi	Ending Moment	Nakshatra	Ending Moment	Muhammadan Year, Month and Day
19	Su	1	13	·04	9	·48	12
20	Mo	2	14	·09	10	·56	13
21	Tu	3	P	·16	11	·66	14
22	We	4	1	·24	12	·77	15
23	Th	5	2	·33	13	·87	16
24	Fr	6	3	·42	14	·97	17
25	Sa	7	4	·50	...	...	18
26	Su	8	5	·56	15	·07	19
27	Mo	9	6	·61	16	·15	20
28	Tu	10	7	·63	17	·21	21
29	We	11	8	·64	18	·25	22
1	Th	12	9	·62	19	·26	23
2	Fr	13	10	·59	20	·26	24
3	Sa	14	11	·55	21	·24	25
4	Su	15	12	·46	22	·21	26
5	Mo	16	13	·38	23	·16	27
6	Tu	17	14	·29	24	·10	28
7	We	18	A	·20	25 26	·03 ·96	29
8	Th	19	1	·10	27	·89	30
9	Fr	20	2 3	·00 ·90	1	·83	1
10	Sa	21	4	·80	2	·77	2
11	Su	22	5	·72	3	·72	3
12	Mo	23	6	·66	4	·68	4
13	Tu	24	7	·62	5	·67	5
14	We	25	8	·59	6	·67	6
15	Th	26	9	·58	7	·68	7
16	Fr	27	10	·59	8	·72	8
17	Sa	28	11	·62	9	·78	9
18	Su	29	12	·67	10	·87	10
19	Mo	30	13	·75	11	·96	11
20	Tu	31	14	·83	...	...	12

April

Bhava, Mesha—Chittirai. Chaitra; Bahula; Sukla; Vaisakha. H. 1291 Safar; H. 1291 Rabi-ul-awwal.

Cyclic Sidereal Year, Month and Day	Week-Day	English Month and Day	Tithi	Ending Moment	Nakshatra	Ending Moment	Muhammadan Year, Month and Day
21	We	1	P	·91	12	·06	13
22	Th	2	...	...	13	·17	14
23	Fr	3	1	·00	14	·28	15
24	Sa	4	2	·08	15	·38	16
25	Su	5	3	·14	16	·46	17
26	Mo	6	4	·18	17	·52	18
27	Tu	7	5	·21	18	·56	19
28	We	8	6	·21	19	·58	20
29	Th	9	7	·19	20	·58	21
30	Fr	10	8	·15	21	·57	22
31	Sa	11	9	·09	22	·54	23
1	Su	12	10 11	·02 ·94	23	·49	24
2	Mo	13	12	·85	24	·43	25
3	Tu	14	13	·75	25	·37	26
4	We	15	14	·65	26	·31	27
5	Th	16	A	·55	27	·24	28
6	Fr	17	1	·45	1	·17	29
7	Sa	18	2	·36	2	·10	1
8	Su	19	3	·28	3	·05	2
9	Mo	20	4	·22	4	·02	3
10	Tu	21	5	·17	5 6	·00 ·99	4
11	We	22	6	·13	...	...	5
12	Th	23	7	·12	7	·00	6
13	Fr	24	8	·13	8	·03	7
14	Sa	25	9	·16	9	·09	8
15	Su	26	10	·21	10	·17	9
16	Mo	27	11	·29	11	·26	10
17	Tu	28	12	·37	12	·36	11
18	We	29	13	·45	13	·47	12
19	Th	30	14	·53	14	·57	13

May

Bhava, Mesha—Chittirai; Bhava, Vrishabha—Vaikasi. Vaisakha; Bahula; Sukla; Jyeshtha. H. 1291 Rabi-ul-awwal; Rabi-ul-akhir.

Cyclic Sidereal Year, Month and Day	Week-Day	English Month and Day	Tithi	Ending Moment	Nakshatra	Ending Moment	Muhammadan Year, Month and Day
20	Fr ○	1	P	·60	15	·67	14
21	Sa	2	1	·66	16	·76	15
22	Su	3	2	·71	17	·83	16
23	Mo	4	3	·74	18	·88	17
24	Tu	5	4	·74	19	·91	18
25	We	6	5	·72	20	·92	19
26	Th	7	6	·68	21	·90	20
27	Fr	8	7	·62	22	·87	21
28	Sa	9	8	·55	23	·83	22
29	Su	10	9	·46	24	·77	23
30	Mo	11	10	·37	25	·71	24
31	Tu	12	11	·27	26	·64	25
1	We	13	12	·17	27	·57	26
2	Th	14	13 14	·07 ·97	1	·50	27
3	Fr	15	A	·88	2	·44	28
4	Sa	16	1	·80	3	·39	29
5	Su	17	2	·74	4	·35	30
6	Mo	18	3	·69	5	·32	1
7	Tu	19	4	·65	6	·31	2
8	We	20	5	·63	7	·32	3
9	Th	21	6	·64	8	·36	4
10	Fr	22	7	·68	9	·41	5
11	Sa	23	8	·73	10	·48	6
12	Su	24	9	·79	11	·56	7
13	Mo	25	10	·86	12	·66	8
14	Tu	26	11	·94	13	·77	9
15	We	27	...	...	14	·88	10
16	Th	28	12	·03	15	·98	11
17	Fr	29	13	·11	...	...	12
18	Sa	30	14	·17	16	·07	13
19	Su	31	P	·21	17	·14	14

June

Bhava, Mithuna—Ani. Bahula; Sukla; Adhika Ashadha. H. 1291; H. 1291 Jumada-l-awwal.

Cyclic Sidereal Year, Month and Day	Week-Day	English Month and Day	Tithi	Ending Moment	Nakshatra	Ending Moment	Muhammadan Year, Month and Day
20	Mo	1	1	·23	18	·19	15
21	Tu	2	2	·23	19	·23	16
22	We	3	3	·22	20	·24	17
23	Th	4	4	·18	21	·23	18
24	Fr	5	5	·12	22	·20	19
25	Sa	6	6 7	·05 ·97	23	·16	20
26	Su	7	8	·87	24	·11	21
27	Mo	8	9	·77	25 26	·05 ·98	22
28	Tu	9	10	·67	27	·91	23
29	We	10	11	·57	1	·85	24
30	Th	11	12	·47	2	·79	25
31	Fr	12	13	·38	3	·73	26
1	Sa	13	14	·30	4	·68	27
2	Su	14	A	·23	5	·65	28
3	Mo	15	1	·17	6	·63	29
4	Tu	16	2	·14	7	·64	1
5	We	17	3	·12	8	·67	2
6	Th	18	4	·12	9	·72	3
7	Fr	19	5	·15	10	·78	4
8	Sa	20	6	·20	11	·86	5
9	Su	21	7	·26	12	·96	6
10	Mo	22	8	·33	...	...	7
11	Tu	23	9	·41	13	·07	8
12	We	24	10	·49	14	·18	9
13	Th	25	11	·57	15	·28	10
14	Fr	26	12	·64	16	·37	11
15	Sa	27	13	·68	17	·45	12
16	Su	28	14	·71	18	·51	13
17	Mo	29	P	·72	19	·55	14
18	Tu	30	1	·70	20	·56	15

Naksh:—1. Asvn. 2. Bhar. 3. Krit. 4. Rohi. 5. Mrig. 6. Ardh. 7. Punar. 8. Push. 9. Aslesh. 10. Magh. 11. P. Phal. 12. U. Phal. 13. Hasta. 14. Chit.

A. D. 1874.
A.—Amavasya.
P.—Paurnami.

Kollam 1050, Commences { **N. Malabar—Sept.** / **S. Malabar—Aug.**

Hijra 1291, Commences, **Feb. 18.**

Vikrama 1931.
Bengal San 1280.
(N. Cycle) Vyaya.

SOLAR reckoning: Cyclic Sidereal Year, Month and Day; Week-Day; English Month and Day. LUNAR reckoning: Tithi, Ending Moment; Nakshatra, Ending Moment; Muhammadan Year, Month and Day.

July — Solar: Bhava Mithuna—Ani (to 32), Bhava Karkata—Adi (from 1). Lunar: Adh. Ash. (Bahula), Nija Ashadha (Sukla; Bahula from 2). Muhammadan: H. 1291 Jumadal-awwal; Jumadal-akhir (from 1).

Cyclic Sidereal Year, Month and Day	Week-Day	English Month and Day	Tithi	Ending Moment	Nakshatra	Ending Moment	Muhammadan Year, Month and Day
19	We	1	2	·66	21	·56	16
20	Th	2	3	·61	22	·54	17
21	Fr	3	4	·54	23	·50	18
22	Sa	4	5	·45	24	·44	19
23	Su	5	6	·35	25	·38	20
24	Mo	6	7	·25	26	·32	21
25	Tu	7	8	·15	27	·25	22
26	We	8	9 / 10	·05 / ·95	1	·18	23
27	Th	9	11	·85	2	·12	24
28	Fr	10	12	·77	3	·06	25
29	Sa	11	13	·70	4 / 5	·01 / ·98	26
30	Su	12	14	·65	6	·96	27
31	Mo	13	A	·61	7	·97	28
32	Tu	14	1	·59	8	·99	29
1	We	15	2	·60	...	...	30
2	Th	16	3	·63	9	·03	1
3	Fr	17	4	·68	10	·09	2
4	Sa	18	5	·74	11	·17	3
5	Su	19	6	·81	12	·27	4
6	Mo	20	7	·89	13	·37	5
7	Tu	21	8	·97	14	·48	6
8	We	22	...	...	15	·58	7
9	Th	23	9	·05	16	·67	8
10	Fr	24	10	·12	17	·75	9
11	Sa	25	11	·16	18	·82	10
12	Su	26	12	·19	19	·86	11
13	Mo	27	13	·20	20	·88	12
14	Tu	28	14	·18	21	·88	13
15	We	29	P	·14	22	·87	14
16	Th	30	1	·09	23	·84	15
17	Fr	31	2 / 3	·02 / ·94	24	·79	16

Aug. — Solar: Bhava Simha—Avani. Lunar: Bahula; Sravana (Sukla); Bah. Muhammadan: H. 1291 (Jumadal-akhir); H. 1291 Rajab (from 1).

Cyclic Sidereal Year, Month and Day	Week-Day	English Month and Day	Tithi	Ending Moment	Nakshatra	Ending Moment	Muhammadan Year, Month and Day
18	Sa	1	4	·84	25	·73	17
19	Su	2	5	·74	26	·66	18
20	Mo	3	6	·64	27	·59	19
21	Tu	4	7	·54	1	·52	20
22	We	5	8	·44	2	·46	21
23	Th	6	9	·35	3	·40	22
24	Fr	7	10	·27	4	·35	23
25	Sa	8	11	·20	5	·31	24
26	Su	9	12	·14	6	·29	25
27	Mo	10	13	·11	7	·29	26
28	Tu	11	14	·09	8	·30	27
29	We	12	A	·10	9	·34	28
30	Th	13	1	·12	10	·40	29
31	Fr	14	2	·16	11	·48	1
1	Sa	15	3	·22	12	·57	2
2	Su	16	4	·30	13	·67	3
3	Mo	17	5	·38	14	·78	4
4	Tu	18	6	·46	15	·88	5
5	We	19	7	·54	16	·93	6
6	Th	20	8	·61	...	...	7
7	Fr	21	9	·66	17	·07	8
8	Sa	22	10	·69	18	·13	9
9	Su	23	11	·69	19	·17	10
10	Mo	24	12	·67	20	·20	11
11	Tu	25	13	·64	21	·22	12
12	We	26	14	·60	22	·20	13
13	Th	27	P	·53	23	·17	14
14	Fr	28	1	·45	24	·12	15
15	Sa	29	2	·35	25	·06	16
16	Su	30	3	·25	26 / 27	·00 / ·94	17
17	Mo	31	4	·15	1	·87	18

Sep. — Solar: Bhava Simha—Avani (to 31), Bhava Kanya—Purattasi (from 1). Lunar: Srav. (Bahula); Bhadrapada (Sukla). Muhammadan: H. 1291 Rajab; H. 1291 Shaban (from 1).

Cyclic Sidereal Year, Month and Day	Week-Day	English Month and Day	Tithi	Ending Moment	Nakshatra	Ending Moment	Muhammadan Year, Month and Day
18	Tu	1	5 / 6	·05 / ·95	2	·80	19
19	We	2	7	·86	3	·74	20
20	Th	3	8	·78	4	·68	21
21	Fr	4	9	·71	5	·64	22
22	Sa	5	10	·65	6	·62	23
23	Su	6	11	·61	7	·61	24
24	Mo	7	12	·60	8	·62	25
25	Tu	8	13	·61	9	·65	26
26	We	9	14	·64	10	·71	27
27	Th	10	A	·68	11	·78	28
28	Fr	11	1	·74	12	·87	29
29	Sa	12	2	·81	13	·97	30
30	Su	13	3	·89	...	...	1
31	Mo	14	4	·98	14	·08	2
1	Tu	15	...	...	15	·19	3
2	We	16	5	·06	16	·29	4
3	Th	17	6	·13	17	·37	5
4	Fr	18	7	·17	18	·44	6
5	Sa	19	8	·20	19	·49	7
6	Su	20	9	·22	20	·52	8
7	Mo	21	10	·21	21	·54	9
8	Tu	22	11	·18	22	·53	10
9	We	23	12	·13	23	·50	11
10	Th	24	13 / 14	·06 / ·98	24	·46	12
11	Fr	25	P	·89	25	·40	13
12	Sa	26	1	·79	26	·34	14
13	Su	27	2	·69	27	·28	15
14	Mo	28	3	·59	1	·21	16
15	Tu	29	4	·49	2	·14	17
16	We	30	5	·40	3	·07	18

Oct. — Solar: Bhava Tula—Aippasi (from 1). Lunar: Bahula; Asvina (Sukla); Bahula. Muhammadan: H. 1291 Ramzan (from 1).

Cyclic Sidereal Year, Month and Day	Week-Day	English Month and Day	Tithi	Ending Moment	Nakshatra	Ending Moment	Muhammadan Year, Month and Day
17	Th	1	6	·32	4 / 5	·02 / ·98	19
18	Fr	2	7	·25	6	·95	20
19	Sa	3	8	·20	7	·93	21
20	Su	4	9	·17	8	·94	22
21	Mo	5	10	·15	9	·97	23
22	Tu	6	11	·16	...	...	24
23	We	7	12	·19	10	·02	25
24	Th	8	13	·23	11	·09	26
25	Fr	9	14	·30	12	·17	27
26	Sa ●	10	A	·38	13	·27	28
27	Su	11	1	·47	14	·38	29
28	Mo	12	2	·55	15	·49	1
29	Tu	13	3	·63	16	·59	2
30	We	14	4	·70	17	·68	3
31	Th	15	5	·74	18	·75	4
1	Fr	16	6	·77	19	·80	5
2	Sa	17	7	·79	20	·84	6
3	Su	18	8	·78	21	·86	7
4	Mo	19	9	·75	22	·85	8
5	Tu	20	10	·71	23	·83	9
6	We	21	11	·64	24	·79	10
7	Th	22	12	·56	25	·74	11
8	Fr	23	13	·47	26	·68	12
9	Sa	24	14	·37	27	·62	13
10	Su ○	25	P	·27	1	·55	14
11	Mo	26	1	·17	2	·48	15
12	Tu	27	2 / 3	·08 / ·99	3	·42	16
13	We	28	4	·92	4	·36	17
14	Th	29	5	·85	5	·31	18
15	Fr	30	6	·79	6	·28	19
16	Sa	31	7	·76	7	·26	20

Nov. — Solar: Bhava Tula—Aippasi (to 30), Bhava Vrischika—Kartigai (from 1). Lunar: Asv. (Bahula); Kartika (Sukla). Muhammadan: H. 1291 Ramzan; H. 1291 Shawwal (from 1).

Cyclic Sidereal Year, Month and Day	Week-Day	English Month and Day	Tithi	Ending Moment	Nakshatra	Ending Moment	Muhammadan Year, Month and Day
17	Su	1	8	·74	8	·27	21
18	Mo	2	9	·75	9	·29	22
19	Tu	3	10	·78	10	·33	23
20	We	4	11	·84	11	·39	24
21	Th	5	12	·91	12	·47	25
22	Fr	6	13	·98	13	·57	26
23	Sa	7	...	...	14	·68	27
24	Su	8	14	·07	15	·79	28
25	Mo	9	A	·16	16	·89	29
26	Tu	10	1	·24	17	·98	30
27	We	11	2	·30	...	...	1
28	Th	12	3	·35	18	·06	2
29	Fr	13	4	·39	19	·12	3
30	Sa	14	5	·40	20	·16	4
1	Su	15	6	·38	21	·18	5
2	Mo	16	7	·35	22	·18	6
3	Tu	17	8	·31	23	·16	7
4	We	18	9	·25	24	·13	8
5	Th	19	10	·18	25	·08	9
6	Fr	20	11 / 12	·09 / ·99	26 / 27	·02 / ·95	10
7	Sa	21	13	·89	1	·88	11
8	Su	22	14	·79	2	·82	12
9	Mo	23	P	·70	3	·76	13
10	Tu	24	1	·61	4	·70	14
11	We	25	2	·53	5	·64	15
12	Th	26	3	·46	6	·60	16
13	Fr	27	4	·41	7	·58	17
14	Sa	28	5	·38	8	·59	18
15	Su	29	6	·36	9	·61	19
16	Mo	30	7	·38	10	·64	20

Dec. — Solar: Bhava Dhanus—Margali (from 1). Lunar: Bahula; Margasira (Sukla); Bahula. Muhammadan: H. 1291 Zi-l-ka'da (from 1).

Cyclic Sidereal Year, Month and Day	Week-Day	English Month and Day	Tithi	Ending Moment	Nakshatra	Ending Moment	Muhammadan Year, Month and Day
17	Tu	1	8	·41	11	·69	21
18	We	2	9	·46	12	·77	22
19	Th	3	10	·53	13	·87	23
20	Fr	4	11	·61	14	·98	24
21	Sa	5	12	·70	...	...	25
22	Su	6	13	·79	15	·09	26
23	Mo	7	14	·87	16	·19	27
24	Tu	8	A	·94	17	·28	28
25	We	9	1	·99	18	·37	29
26	Th	10	...	...	19	·44	1
27	Fr	11	2	·02	20	·48	2
28	Sa	12	3	·04	21	·50	3
29	Su	13	4 / 5	·02 / ·99	22	·50	4
1	Mo	14	6	·94	23	·49	5
2	Tu	15	7	·87	24	·46	6
3	We	16	8	·80	25	·42	7
4	Th	17	9	·72	26	·36	8
5	Fr	18	10	·62	27	·30	9
6	Sa	19	11	·53	1	·23	10
7	Su	20	12	·42	2	·16	11
8	Mo	21	13	·32	3	·10	12
9	Tu	22	14	·23	4 / 5	·04 / ·98	13
10	We	23	P	·16	6	·94	14
11	Th	24	1	·10	7	·92	15
12	Fr	25	2	·05	8	·91	16
13	Sa	26	3	·03	9	·92	17
14	Su	27	4	·02	10	·95	18
15	Mo	28	5	·03	...	...	19
16	Tu	29	6	·06	11	·00	20
17	We	30	7	·11	12	·08	21
18	Th	31	8	·18	13	·17	22

15. Svati. 16. Visak. 17. Anur. 18. Jyesh. 19. Mula. 20. P. Ash. 21. U. Ash. 22. Sravn. 23. Dani. 24. Satab. 25. P. Bhad. 26. U. Bhad. 27. Rev.

A. D. 1875. **Mesha Sankranti** (Commencement of Indian Sidereal Year).

Solar Eclipse. ● **(Surya Sid.) April 12·15.** **Saka 1797.** **Kaliyuga 4976.**

Lunar Eclipse. ○ **(Arya Sid.) April 12·05.** **(S. Cycle) Yuva.**

SOLAR reckoning: Cyclic Sidereal Year, Month and Day.	Week-Day	English Month and Day.	LUNAR reckoning: Tithi	Ending Moment.	Nakshatra	Ending Moment.	Muhammadan Year, Month and Day.
	Jan.						
Bhava *Dhanus—Marguli.* 19	Fr	1	Mar. *Bah.* 9	·26	14	·27	*Zi-l-ka'da.* 23
20	Sa	2	10	·35	15	·38	24
21	Su	3	11	·44	16	·49	25
22	Mo	4	12	·52	17	·59	26
23	Tu	5	13	·59	18	·68	27
24	We	6	14	·64	19	·75	28
25	Th	7	—A	·67	20	·79	29
26	Fr	8	1	·68	21	·82	—30
27	Sa	9	2	·67	22	·84	1
28	Su	10	3	·64	23	·82	2
—29	Mo	11	4	·59	24	·79	3
1	Tu	12	5	·53	25	·75	4
2	We	13	6	·45	26	·69	5
3	Th	14	*Sukla* 7	·36	27	·63	6
4	Fr	15	8	·26	1	·57	7
5	Sa	16	9	·16	2	·50	8
6	Su	17	{10 / 11	·06 / ·97	3	·43	9
7	Mo	18	12	·89	4	·37	10
8	Tu	19	Pausha 13	·81	5	·32	11
9	We	20	14	·75	6	·28	12
10	Th	21	P	·70	7	·25	13
11	Fr	22	1	·67	8	·23	14
12	Sa	23	2	·66	9	·24	15
13	Su	24	3	·67	10	·27	H. 1291 *Zi-l-hijja.* 16
Bhava *Makara—Tai.* 14	Mo	25	4	·70	11	·32	17
15	Tu	26	5	·76	12	·39	18
16	We	27	6	·84	13	·47	19
17	Th	28	*Bahula* 7	·92	14	·57	20
18	Fr	29	...	...	15	·68	21
19	Sa	30	8	·00	16	·79	22
20	Su	31	9	·09	17	·89	23
	Feb.						
21	Mo	1	10	·17	18	·98	24
22	Tu	2	11	·24	...	...	25
23	We	3	12	·29	19	·06	26
24	Th	4	13	·32	20	·11	27
25	Fr	5	14	·32	21	·15	28
26	Sa	6	—A	·30	22	·16	—29
27	Su	7	1	·27	23	·15	1
28	Mo	8	2	·22	24	·12	2
29	Tu	9	3	·15	25	·08	3
—30	We	10	{4 / 5	·07 / ·98	26 / 27	·03 / ·97}	4
1	Th	11	*Sukla* 6	·89	1	·91	5
2	Fr	12	7	·79	2	·84	6
3	Sa	13	8	·69	3	·77	7
4	Su	14	9	·59	4	·71	8
5	Mo	15	10	·50	5	·65	9
6	Tu	16	11	·43	6	·60	10
Bhava *Kumbha—Mani.* 7	We	17	12	·37	7	·57	11
8	Th	18	Magha 13	·33	8	·56	12
9	Fr	19	14	·30	9	·56	13
10	Sa	20	P	·28	10	·59	14
11	Su	21	1	·30	11	·63	H. 1292 *Muharram.* 15
12	Mo	22	2	·34	12	·70	16
13	Tu	23	3	·39	13	·78	17
14	We	24	4	·46	14	·87	18
15	Th	25	*Bahula* 5	·54	15	·98	19
16	Fr	26	6	·63	...	...	20
17	Sa	27	7	·71	16	·09	21
18	Su	28	8	·79	17	·20	22

SOLAR reckoning: Cyclic Sidereal Year, Month and Day.	Week-Day	English Month and Day.	LUNAR reckoning: Tithi	Ending Moment.	Nakshatra	Ending Moment.	Muhammadan Year, Month and Day.
	March						
Bhava *Kumbha—Mani.* 19	Mo	1	Mag. *Bah.* 9	·86	18	·29	*Muharram.* 23
20	Tu	2	10	·91	19	·36	24
21	We	3	11	·93	20	·42	25
22	Th	4	12	·93	21	·46	26
23	Fr	5	13	·92	22	·48	27
24	Sa	6	14	·88	23	·48	28
25	Su	7	—A	·83	24	·46	29
26	Mo	8	1	·76	25	·43	—30
27	Tu	9	2	·68	26	·38	1
28	We	10	3	·59	27	·32	2
29	Th	11	4	·49	1	·25	3
—30	Fr	12	*Sukla* 5	·39	2	·18	4
1	Sa	13	6	·29	3	·11	5
2	Su	14	7	·19	4 / 5	·05 / ·99}	6
3	Mo	15	8	·10	6	·94	7
4	Tu	16	{9 / 10	·02 / ·96	7	·90	8
5	We	17	11	·92	8	·88	9
6	Th	18	12	·90	9	·89	10
7	Fr	19	Phalguna 13	·89	10	·91	11
8	Sa	20	14	·91	11	·94	12
9	Su	21	P	·94	...	...	13
10	Mo	22	1	·98	12	·00	H. 1292 *Safar.* 14
11	Tu	23	...	...	13	·08	15
Bhava *Mina—Panguni.* 12	We	24	2	·05	14	·18	16
13	Th	25	3	·14	15	·28	17
14	Fr	26	4	·23	16	·39	18
15	Sa	27	5	·31	17	·49	19
16	Su	28	6	·38	18	·59	20
17	Mo	29	*Bahula* 7	·44	19	·67	21
18	Tu	30	8	·49	20	·74	22
19	We	31	9	·52	21	·78	23
	April						
20	Th	1	10	·51	22	·80	24
21	Fr	2	11	·49	23	·80	25
22	Sa	3	12	·45	24	·78	26
23	Su	4	13	·40	25	·75	27
24	Mo	5	14	·33	26	·71	28
25	Tu ●	6	—A	·25	27	·65	—29
26	We	7	1	·15	1	·59	1
27	Th	8	{2 / 3	·05 / ·95	2	·52	2
28	Fr	9	4	·85	3	·45	3
29	Sa	10	5	·75	4	·38	4
—30	Su	11	6	·66	5	·32	5
1	Mo	12	*Sukla* 7	·58	6	·27	6
2	Tu	13	8	·52	7	·24	7
3	We	14	9	·48	8	·22	8
4	Th	15	10	·45	9	·21	9
5	Fr	16	11	·43	10	·22	10
6	Sa	17	12	·45	11	·25	11
7	Su	18	Chaitra 13	·48	12	·31	12
8	Mo	19	14	·54	13	·38	13
9	Tu	20	P	·61	14	·48	H. 1292 *Rabi-ul-awwal.* 14
Yuva *Mesha—Chittirai.* 10	We	21	1	·69	15	·58	15
11	Th	22	2	·77	16	·69	16
12	Fr	23	3	·85	17	·79	17
13	Sa	24	4	·92	18	·89	18
14	Su	25	5	·98	19	·98	19
15	Mo	26	*Bahula* ...	...	...	...	20
16	Tu	27	6	·03	20	·05	21
17	We	28	7	·05	21	·10	22
18	Th	29	8	·06	22	·12	23
19	Fr	30	{9 / 10	·03 / ·99	23	·13	24

SOLAR reckoning: Cyclic Sidereal Year, Month and Day.	Week-Day	English Month and Day.	LUNAR reckoning: Tithi	Ending Moment.	Nakshatra	Ending Moment.	Muhammadan Year, Month and Day.
	May						
20	Sa	1	Ch. 11	·93	24	·12	*R.-awwal.* 25
21	Su	2	12	·86	25	·09	26
Yuva *Mesha—Chittirai.* 22	Mo	3	*Bah.* 13	·78	26 / 27	·05 / ·99}	27
23	Tu	4	14	·69	1	·93	28
24	We	5	—A	·59	2	·86	29
25	Th	6	1	·49	3	·79	—30
26	Fr	7	2	·39	4	·72	1
27	Sa	8	3	·29	5	·66	2
28	Su	9	*Sukla* 4	·19	6	·61	3
29	Mo	10	5	·11	7	·57	4
30	Tu	11	6	·05	8	·54	5
—31	We	12	{7 / 8	·00 / ·97	9	·53	6
1	Th	13	9	·96	10	·54	7
2	Fr	14	10	·96	11	·57	8
3	Sa	15	11	·99	12	·62	9
4	Su	16	...	...	13	·69	10
5	Mo	17	Vaisakha 12	·04	14	·78	11
6	Tu	18	13	·11	15	·88	12
7	We	19	14	·19	16	·99	13
8	Th	20	P	·27	...	...	14
9	Fr	21	1	·36	17	·10	15
10	Sa	22	2	·44	18	·20	H. 1292 *Rabi-ul-akhir.* 16
11	Su	23	3	·50	19	·29	17
12	Mo	24	4	·54	20	·36	18
13	Tu	25	5	·56	21	·41	19
Yuva *Vrishabha—Vaikasi.* 14	We	26	6	·56	22	·44	20
15	Th	27	*Bahula* 7	·54	23	·46	21
16	Fr	28	8	·50	24	·45	22
17	Sa	29	9	·44	25	·42	23
18	Su	30	10	·37	26	·38	24
19	Mo	31	11	·28	27	·33	25
	June						
20	Tu	1	12	·18	1	·27	26
21	We	2	{13 / 14	·08 / ·98	2	·20	27
22	Th	3	—A	·88	3	·13	28
23	Fr	4	1	·78	4	·06	—29
24	Sa	5	2	·70	5 / 6	·00 / ·94}	1
25	Su	6	3	·62	7	·90	2
26	Mo	7	4	·55	8	·87	3
27	Tu	8	5	·49	9	·85	4
28	We	9	6	·46	10	·86	5
29	Th	10	*Sukla* 7	·45	11	·89	6
30	Fr	11	8	·46	12	·94	7
—31	Sa	12	9	·49	...	...	8
1	Su	13	10	·53	13	·00	9
2	Mo	14	11	·59	14	·08	10
3	Tu	15	12	·67	15	·18	11
4	We	16	Jyeshtha 13	·75	16	·29	12
5	Th	17	14	·83	17	·40	13
6	Fr	18	P	·91	18	·50	14
7	Sa	19	1	·98	19	·59	H. 1292 *Jumada-l-awwal.* 15
8	Su	20	...	...	20	·67	16
Yuva *Mithuna—Ani.* 9	Mo	21	2	·02	21	·72	17
10	Tu	22	3	·04	22	·76	18
11	We	23	4	·04	23	·78	19
12	Th	24	{5 / 6	·02 / ·98	24	·78	20
13	Fr	25	*Bahula* 7	·92	25	·75	21
14	Sa	26	8	·85	26	·71	22
15	Su	27	9	·76	27	·66	23
16	Mo	28	10	·67	1	·60	24
17	Tu	29	11	·57	2	·54	25
18	We	30	12	·47	3	·47	26

Naksh:—1 Asvn. 2, Bhar. 3, Krit. 4, Rohi. 5, Mrig. 6, Ardh. 7, Punar. 8, Push. 9, Aslesh. 10, Magh. 11. P. Pha'.. [illegible] J. Phal. 13, Hasta. 14, Chit·

A. D. 1875. **Vikrama 1932.**

A.—Amavasya. **Kollam 1051,** Commences {N. Malabar—Sept. / S. Malabar—Aug.} **Hijra 1292,** Commences, **Feb. 7.** **Bengal San 1281.**

P.—Paurnami. **(N. Cycle) Sarvajit.**

July – August (Solar months: Yuva Mithuna—Ani.; Yuva Karkata—Adi.; Yuva Simha—Avani. Lunar months: Bah.; Sukla Ashadha; Bahula; Sukla Sravana; Bahula. Muhammadan months: H. 1292 Jumadal-akhir.; H. 1292 Rajab.)

SOLAR reckoning: Cyclic Sidereal Year, Month and Day	Week-Day	English Month and Day	LUNAR reckoning: Tithi	Ending Moment	Nakshatra	Ending Moment	Muhammadan Year, Month and Day
	July						
19	Th	1	13	·36	4	·40	27
20	Fr	2	14	·26	5	·33	28
21	Sa	3	—A	·17	6	·28	29
22	Su	4	1	·09	7	·23	—30
23	Mo	5	2 3	·02 ·97	8	·20	1
24	Tu	6	4	·94	9	·18	2
25	We	7	5	·92	10	·18	3
26	Th	8	6	·93	11	·21	4
27	Fr	9	7	·96	12	·25	5
28	Sa	10	...	...	13	·31	6
29	Su	11	8	·01	14	·38	7
30	Mo	12	9	·08	15	·48	8
31	Tu	13	10	·15	16	·59	9
—32	We	14	11	·23	17	·70	10
1	Th	15	12	·31	18	·80	11
2	Fr	16	13	·39	19	·90	12
3	Sa	17	14	·45	20	·98	13
4	Su	18	P	·49	...	...	14
5	Mo	19	1	·52	21	·04	15
6	Tu	20	2	·52	22	·08	16
7	We	21	3	·50	23	·10	17
8	Th	22	4	·46	24	·10	18
9	Fr	23	5	·40	25	·08	19
10	Sa	24	6	·33	26	·05	20
11	Su	25	7	·25	27 1	·01 ·95	21
12	Mo	26	8	·16	2	·88	22
13	Tu	27	9 10	·06 ·96	3	·81	23
14	We	28	11	·86	4	·74	24
15	Th	29	12	·76	5	·68	25
16	Fr	30	13	·66	6	·62	26
17	Sa	31	14	·58	7	·57	27
	Aug.						
18	Su	1	—A	·51	8	·53	28
19	Mo	2	1	·45	9	·50	—29
20	Tu	3	2	·42	10	·51	1
21	We	4	3	·40	11	·53	2
22	Th	5	4	·41	12	·56	3
23	Fr	6	5	·44	13	·61	4
24	Sa	7	6	·49	14	·69	5
25	Su	8	7	·55	15	·79	6
26	Mo	9	8	·62	16	·89	7
27	Tu	10	9	·70	...	...	8
28	We	11	10	·79	17	·00	9
29	Th	12	11	·87	18	·10	10
30	Fr	13	12	·93	19	·20	11
—31	Sa	14	13	·97	20	·28	12
1	Su	15	...	...	21	·35	13
2	Mo	16	14	·00	22	·40	14
3	Tu	17	P 1	·01 ·99	23	·42	15
4	We	18	2	·96	24	·43	16
5	Th	19	3	·91	25	·42	17
6	Fr	20	4	·84	26	·39	18
7	Sa	21	5	·76	27	·34	19
8	Su	22	6	·66	1	·28	20
9	Mo	23	7	·56	2	·22	21
10	Tu	24	8	·46	3	·16	22
11	We	25	9	·36	4	·09	23
12	Th	26	10	·26	5 6	·02 ·95	24
13	Fr	27	11	·17	7	·90	25
14	Sa	28	12	·09	8	·86	26
15	Su	29	13 14	·02 ·96	9	·84	27
16	Mo	30	—A	·93	10	·83	28
17	Tu	31	1	·91	11	·84	29

September – October (Solar months: Yuva Simha—Avani.; Yuva Kanya—Purattasi.; Yuva Tula—Aippasi. Lunar months: Sukla Bhadrapada; Bahula; Sukla Asvina; Bahula; Suk. Muhammadan months: H. 1292 Shaban.; H. 1292 Ramzan.)

SOLAR reckoning: Cyclic Sidereal Year, Month and Day	Week-Day	English Month and Day	LUNAR reckoning: Tithi	Ending Moment	Nakshatra	Ending Moment	Muhammadan Year, Month and Day
	Sep.						
18	We	1	2	·93	12	·87	—30
19	Th	2	3	·96	13	·92	1
20	Fr	3	...	...	...	...	2
21	Sa	4	4	·00	14	·00	3
22	Su	5	5	·06	15	·09	4
23	Mo	6	6	·13	16	·19	5
24	Tu	7	7	·21	17	·29	6
25	We	8	8	·30	18	·40	7
26	Th	9	9	·38	19	·50	8
27	Fr	10	10	·45	20	·59	9
28	Sa	11	11	·50	21	·66	10
29	Su	12	12	·53	22	·71	11
30	Mo	13	13	·54	23	·74	12
—31	Tu	14	14	·52	24	·75	13
1	We	15	P	·49	25	·75	14
2	Th	16	1	·44	26	·72	15
3	Fr	17	2	·37	27	·68	16
4	Sa	18	3	·28	1	·62	17
5	Su	19	4	·19	2	·56	18
6	Mo	20	5 6	·09 ·99	3	·50	19
7	Tu	21	7	·89	4	·43	20
8	We	22	8	·79	5	·36	21
9	Th	23	9	·70	6	·29	22
10	Fr	24	10	·62	7	·24	23
11	Sa	25	11	·55	8	·20	24
12	Su	26	12	·50	9	·17	25
13	Mo	27	13	·47	10	·15	26
14	Tu	28	14	·45	11	·16	27
15	We ●	29	—A	·47	12	·18	28
16	Th	30	1	·50	13	·23	—29
	Oct.						
17	Fr	1	2	·54	14	·30	1
18	Sa	2	3	·60	15	·39	2
19	Su	3	4	·68	16	·49	3
20	Mo	4	5	·77	17	·59	4
21	Tu	5	6	·86	18	·70	5
22	We	6	7	·93	19	·81	6
23	Th	7	...	...	20	·90	7
24	Fr	8	8	·00	21	·97	8
25	Sa	9	9	·05	...	...	9
26	Su	10	10	·08	22	·03	10
27	Mo	11	11	·10	23	·06	11
28	Tu	12	12	·08	24	·08	12
29	We	13	13	·05	25	·07	13
30	Th	14	14 P	·00 ·93	26	·05	14
—31	Fr	15	1	·85	27 1	·01 ·96	15
1	Sa	16	2	·76	2	·90	16
2	Su	17	3	·66	3	·83	17
3	Mo	18	4	·56	4	·76	18
4	Tu	19	5	·46	5	·69	19
5	We	20	6	·36	6	·63	20
6	Th	21	7	·28	7	·58	21
7	Fr	22	8	·20	8	·53	22
8	Sa	23	9	·13	9	·50	23
9	Su	24	10	·08	10	·48	24
10	Mo	25	11	·05	11	·48	25
11	Tu	26	12	·04	12	·50	26
12	We	27	13	·06	13	·55	27
13	Th	28	14	·09	14	·61	28
14	Fr	29	—A	·14	15	·69	29
15	Sa	30	1	·20	16	·79	—30
16	Su	31	2	·28	17	·90	1

November – December (Solar months: Yuva Tula—Aippasi.; Yuva Vrischika—Kartigai.; Yuva Dhanus—Margali. Lunar months: Sukla Karttika; Bahula; Sukla Margasira; Bahula; P. Suk. Muhammadan months: H. 1292 Shawwal.; H. 1292 Zi-l-ka'da.)

SOLAR reckoning: Cyclic Sidereal Year, Month and Day	Week-Day	English Month and Day	LUNAR reckoning: Tithi	Ending Moment	Nakshatra	Ending Moment	Muhammadan Year, Month and Day
	Nov.						
17	Mo	1	3	·36	...	...	2
18	Tu	2	4	·45	18	·01	3
19	We	3	5	·53	19	·11	4
20	Th	4	6	·60	20	·20	5
21	Fr	5	7	·65	21	·28	6
22	Sa	6	8	·68	22	·34	7
23	Su	7	9	·69	23	·38	8
24	Mo	8	10	·68	24	·40	9
25	Tu	9	11	·65	25	·40	10
26	We	10	12	·60	26	·38	11
27	Th	11	13	·53	27	·35	12
28	Fr	12	14	·45	1	·30	13
29	Sa	13	P	·36	2	·24	14
—30	Su	14	1	·27	3	·17	15
1	Mo	15	2	·17	4	·10	16
2	Tu	16	3 4	·07 ·97	5 6	·03 ·97	17
3	We	17	5	·89	7	·91	18
4	Th	18	6	·81	8	·86	19
5	Fr	19	7	·74	9	·82	20
6	Sa	20	8	·69	10	·80	21
7	Su	21	9	·67	11	·80	22
8	Mo	22	10	·66	12	·82	23
9	Tu	23	11	·67	13	·86	24
10	We	24	12	·70	14	·92	25
11	Th	25	13	·76	15	·99	26
12	Fr	26	14	·83	...	...	27
13	Sa	27	—A	·91	16	·09	28
14	Su	28	1	·99	17	·20	—29
15	Mo	29	...	...	18	·31	1
16	Tu	30	2	·08	19	·41	2
	Dec.						
17	We	1	3	·16	20	·50	3
18	Th	2	4	·23	21	·58	4
19	Fr	3	5	·28	22	·65	5
20	Sa	4	6	·31	23	·70	6
21	Su	5	7	·32	24	·72	7
22	Mo	6	8	·30	25	·72	8
23	Tu	7	9	·27	26	·71	9
24	We	8	10	·22	27	·68	10
25	Th	9	11	·16	1	·64	11
26	Fr	10	12 13	·08 ·99	2	·58	12
27	Sa	11	14	·89	3	·51	13
28	Su	12	P	·79	4	·44	14
—29	Mo	13	1	·69	5	·37	15
1	Tu	14	2	·60	6	·31	16
2	We	15	3	·52	7	·25	17
3	Th	16	4	·45	8	·19	18
4	Fr	17	5	·39	9	·15	19
5	Sa	18	6	·34	10	·13	20
6	Su	19	7	·31	11	·13	21
7	Mo	20	8	·29	12	·14	22
8	Tu	21	9	·31	13	·17	23
9	We	22	10	·35	14	·22	24
10	Th	23	11	·41	15	·30	25
11	Fr	24	12	·48	16	·40	26
12	Sa	25	13	·56	17	·50	27
13	Su	26	14	·65	18	·60	28
14	Mo	27	—A	·74	19	·71	29
15	Tu	28	1	·32	20	·81	—30
16	We	29	2	·88	21	·90	1
17	Th	30	3	·93	22	·97	2
18	Fr	31	4	·96	...	...	3

15. Svati. 16. Visak. 17. Anur. 18. Jyesh. 19. Mula. 20. P. Ash. 21. U. Ash. 22. Sravn. 23. Dani. 24. Satab. 25. P. Bhad. 26. U. Bhad. 27. Rev.

A. D. 1876. **Mesha Sankranti** (Commencement of Indian Sidereal Year).

Solar Eclipse. ● (**Surya Sid.**) **April 11·41.** **Saka 1798.** **Kaliyuga 4977.**

Lunar Eclipse. ○ (**Arya Sid.**) **April 11·31.** **(S. Cycle) Dhatri.**

SOLAR reckoning: Cyclic Sidereal Year, Month and Day; Week-Day; English Month and Day. LUNAR reckoning: Tithi; Ending Moment; Nakshatra; Ending Moment; Muhammadan Year, Month and Day.

Jan.

Cyclic Sidereal Year, Month and Day	Week-Day	English Month and Day	Tithi	Ending Moment	Nakshatra	Ending Moment	Muhammadan Year, Month and Day
Yuva Dhanus—Margali 19	Sa	1	5	·96	23	·01	H. 1292 Zil-hijja 4
20	Su	2	6	·95	24	·04	5
21	Mo	3	7	·92	25	·95	6
22	Tu	4	Sukla 8	·87	26	·03	7
23	We	5	9	·80	27 1	·01 ·97	8
24	Th	6	10	·72	2	·91	9
25	Fr	7	11	·63	3	·85	10
26	Sa	8	12	·54	4	·76	11
27	Su	9	Pausha 13	·44	5	·71	12
28	Mo	10	14	·34	6	·65	13
29	Tu	11	P	·25	7	·59	14
—30	We	12	1	·17	8	·53	15
1	Th	13	2	·09	9	·49	16
2	Fr	14	3 4	·02 ·97	10	·47	17
3	Sa	15	5	·95	11	·45	18
4	Su	16	6	·34	12	·46	19
5	Mo	17	Bahula 7	·96	13	·49	20
6	Tu	18	...	...	14	·54	21
7	We	19	8	·00	15	·61	22
8	Th	20	9	·06	16	·70	23
9	Fr	21	10	·13	17	·79	24
10	Sa	22	11	·21	18	·90	25
11	Su	23	12	·30	...	...	26
12	Mo	24	13	·39	19	·01	27
13	Tu	25	14	·47	20	·11	28
Yuva Makara—Tai 14	We	26	—A	·54	21	·20	29
15	Th	27	1	·58	22	·28	—30
16	Fr	28	2	·60	23	·33	1
17	Sa	29	3	·60	24	·36	2
18	Su	30	4	·59	25	·37	3
19	Mo	31	5	·56	26	·37	4

Feb.

Cyclic Sidereal Year, Month and Day	Week-Day	English Month and Day	Tithi	Ending Moment	Nakshatra	Ending Moment	Muhammadan Year, Month and Day
20	Tu	1	Sukla 6	·51	27	·34	5
21	We	2	7	·44	1	·30	6
22	Th	3	8	·36	2	·25	7
23	Fr	4	9	·26	3	·19	8
24	Sa	5	10	·16	4	·13	9
25	Su	6	Magha 11 12	·06 ·96	5 6	·06 ·99	H. 1293 Muharram 10
26	Mo	7	13	·87	7	·92	11
27	Tu	8	14	·79	8	·86	12
28	We	9	P	·71	9	·82	13
—29	Th	10	1	·65	10	·79	14
1	Fr	11	2	·61	11	·78	15
2	Sa	12	3	·58	12	·78	16
3	Su	13	4	·57	13	·80	17
4	Mo	14	5	·59	14	·85	18
5	Tu	15	6	·63	15	·92	19
6	We	16	Bahula 7	·69	...	...	20
Yuva Kumbha—Masi 7	Th	17	8	·76	16	·00	21
8	Fr	18	9	·84	17	·09	22
9	Sa	19	10	·93	18	·20	23
10	Su	20	...	...	19	·31	24
11	Mo	21	11	·01	20	·42	25
12	Tu	22	12	·09	21	·51	26
13	We	23	13	·16	22	·58	27
14	Th	24	14	·20	23	·64	28
15	Fr	25	—A	·22	24	·68	29
16	Sa	26	P. Suk. 1	·23	25	·70	—30
17	Su	27	2	·21	26	·70	Safar. 1
.18	Mo	28	3	·18	27	·68	2
19	Tu	29	4	·12	1	·64	3

March

Cyclic Sidereal Year, Month and Day	Week-Day	English Month and Day	Tithi	Ending Moment	Nakshatra	Ending Moment	Muhammadan Year, Month and Day
20	We	1	5 6	·05 ·97	2	·59	H. 1293 Safar. 4
Yuva Kumbha—Masi 21	Th	2	7	·88	3	·53	5
22	Fr	3	Sukla 8	·78	4	·47	6
23	Sa	4	9	·68	5	·40	7
24	Su	5	10	·58	6	·33	8
25	Mo	6	11	·49	7	·27	9
26	Tu	7	12	·40	8	·21	10
27	We	8	Phalguna 13	·32	9	·16	11
28	Th	9	14	·26	10	·12	12
29	Fr ○	10	P	·22	11	·10	13
30	Sa	11	1	·19	12	·10	14
—31	Su	12	2	·18	13	·12	15
1	Mo	13	3	·19	14	·16	16
2	Tu	14	4	·23	15	·22	17
3	We	15	5	·29	16	·30	18
4	Th	16	Bahula 6	·36	17	·39	19
5	Fr	17	7	·45	18	·50	20
6	Sa	18	8	·54	19	·61	21
7	Su	19	9	·63	20	·72	22
8	Mo	20	10	·70	21	·81	23
9	Tu	21	11	·76	22	·89	24
10	We	22	12	·80	23	·95	25
11	Th	23	13	·82	...	...	26
12	Fr	24	14	·82	24	·00	27
13	Sa	25	—A	·80	25	·02	28
14	Su	26	1	·76	26	·02	—29
Yuva Mina—Panguni 15	Mo	27	2	·70	27 1	·00 ·97	1
16	Tu	28	3	·63	2	·93	2
17	We	29	Sukla 4	·55	3	·87	3
18	Th	30	5	·45	4	·80	4
19	Fr	31	6	·35	5	·73	5

April

Cyclic Sidereal Year, Month and Day	Week-Day	English Month and Day	Tithi	Ending Moment	Nakshatra	Ending Moment	Muhammadan Year, Month and Day
20	Sa	1	7	·25	6	·66	6
21	Su	2	8	·15	7	·60	7
22	Mo	3	9 10	·06 ·97	8	·54	8
23	Tu	4	11	·89	9	·49	H. 1293 Rabi-ul-awwal. 9
24	We	5	Chaitra 12	·83	10	·45	10
25	Th	6	13	·79	11	·43	11
26	Fr	7	14	·76	12	·42	12
27	Sa	8	P	·75	13	·44	13
28	Su	9	1	·76	14	·47	14
—29	Mo	10	2	·79	15	·53	15
1	Tu	11	3	·85	16	·60	16
2	We	12	4	·93	17	·69	17
3	Th	13	...	...	18	·80	18
4	Fr	14	5	·01	19	·91	19
5	Sa	15	Bahula 6	·10	...	...	20
6	Su	16	7	·18	20	·01	21
Dhatri Mesha—Chittirai 7	Mo	17	8	·25	21	·11	22
8	Tu	18	9	·31	22	·20	23
9	We	19	10	·35	23	·27	24
10	Th	20	11	·37	24	·32	25
11	Fr	21	12	·36	25	·34	26
12	Sa	22	13	·34	26	·35	27
13	Su	23	14	·30	27	·33	28
14	Mo	24	—A	·24	1	·30	29
15	Tu	25	1	·17	2	·26	—30
16	We	26	2	·09	3	·21	Rabi-ul-akhir. 1
17	Th	27	V. Suk. 3 4	·00 ·90	4	·14	2
18	Fr	28	5	·80	5	·07	3
19	Sa	29	6	·70	6 7	·00 ·94	4
20	Su	30	7	·60	8	·88	5

May

Cyclic Sidereal Year, Month and Day	Week-Day	English Month and Day	Tithi	Ending Moment	Nakshatra	Ending Moment	Muhammadan Year, Month and Day
21	Mo	1	Sukla 8	·50	9	·82	6
22	Tu	2	9	·42	10	·78	7
Dhatri Mesha—Chittirai 23	We	3	10	·36	11	·75	8
24	Th	4	11	·32	12	·75	9
25	Fr	5	12	·29	13	·76	10
26	Sa	6	Vaisakha 13	·27	14	·79	11
27	Su	7	14	·29	15	·84	H. 1293 Rabi-ul-akhir. 12
28	Mo	8	P	·33	16	·91	13
29	Tu	9	1	·38	...	...	14
30	We	10	2	·44	17	·00	15
—31	Th	11	3	·52	18	·10	16
1	Fr	12	4	·61	19	·21	17
2	Sa	13	5	·69	20	·31	18
3	Su	14	Bahula 6	·76	21	·41	19
4	Mo	15	7	·82	22	·51	20
5	Tu	16	8	·86	23	·58	21
6	We	17	9	·88	24	·63	22
7	Th	18	10	·88	25	·66	23
8	Fr	19	11	·86	26	·67	24
9	Sa	20	12	·82	27	·66	25
10	Su	21	13	·76	1	·64	26
11	Mo	22	14	·69	2	·60	27
12	Tu	23	—A	·60	3	·54	28
Dhatri Vrishabha—Vaikasi 13	We	24	1	·50	4	·48	—29
14	Th	25	2	·40	5	·42	1
15	Fr	26	3	·30	6	·35	2
16	Sa	27	4	·20	7	·28	3
17	Su	28	Sukla 5	·10	8	·22	4
18	Mo	29	6 7	·00 ·92	9	·16	5
19	Tu	30	8	·86	10	·12	6
20	We	31	9	·82	11	·09	7

June

Cyclic Sidereal Year, Month and Day	Week-Day	English Month and Day	Tithi	Ending Moment	Nakshatra	Ending Moment	Muhammadan Year, Month and Day
21	Th	1	10	·79	12	·07	8
22	Fr	2	11	·77	13	·08	9
23	Sa	3	Jyeshtha 12	·78	14	·10	H. 1293 Jumadal-awwal. 10
24	Su	4	13	·81	15	·15	11
25	Mo	5	14	·87	16	·22	12
26	Tu	6	P	·94	17	·30	13
27	We	7	...	...	18	·40	14
28	Th	8	1	·02	19	·51	15
29	Fr	9	2	·10	20	·61	16
30	Sa	10	3	·18	21	·71	17
31	Su	11	4	·25	22	·81	18
—32	Mo	12	5	·30	23	·89	19
1	Tu	13	6	·34	24	·94	20
2	We	14	Bahula 7	·37	25	·97	21
3	Th	15	8	·37	26	·99	22
4	Fr	16	9	·35	...	...	23
5	Sa	17	10	·32	27 1	·00 ·97	24
6	Su	18	11	·26	2	·93	25
Dhatri Mithuna—Ani 7	Mo	19	12	·18	3	·88	26
8	Tu	20	13 14	·09 ·99	4	·82	27
9	We	21	—A	·89	5	·76	28
10	Th	22	1	·79	6	·69	29
11	Fr	23	Ashadha Sukla 2	·69	7	·62	—30
12	Sa	24	3	·59	8	·55	Jumadal-akhir. 1
13	Su	25	4	·49	9	·49	2
14	Mo	26	5	·41	10	·45	3
15	Tu	27	6	·35	11	·42	4
16	We	28	7	·30	12	·40	5
17	Th	29	8	·27	13	·40	6
18	Fr	30	9	·25	14	·42	7

Naksh:—1. Asvn. 2. Bhar. 3. Krit. 4. Rohi. 5. Mrig. 6. Ardh. 7. Punar. 8. Push. 9. Aslesh. 10. Magh. 11. P. Phal. 12. U. Phal. 13. Hasta. 14. Chit.

A. D. 1876.
A.—Amavasya.
P.—Paurnami.

Kollam 1052, Commences { **N. Malabar—Sept.** / **S. Malabar—Aug.**

Hijra 1293, Commences, **Jan. 28.**

Vikrama 1933.
Bengal San 1282.
(N. Cycle) Sarvadharin.

SOLAR reckoning: Cyclic Sidereal Year, Month and Day; Week-Day; English Month and Day. LUNAR reckoning: Tithi; Ending Moment; Nakshatra; Ending Moment; Muhammadan Year, Month and Day.

July

Solar: Dhatri *Mithuna—Ani.* (to 31); Dhatri *Karkata—Adi.* Lunar: Ashadha *Suk.*, *Bahula*, *Sukla*. Muhammadan: H. 1293 *Jumadal-akhir.*

Cyclic Sidereal Year, Month and Day	Week-Day	English Month and Day	Tithi	Ending Moment	Nakshatra	Ending Moment	Muhammadan Year, Month and Day
19	Sa	1	10	·26	15	·47	8
20	Su	2	11	·29	16	·53	9
21	Mo	3	12	·34	17	·61	10
22	Tu	4	13	·41	18	·70	11
23	We	5	14	·49	19	·80	12
24	Th	6	P	·57	20	·91	13
25	Fr	7	1	·65	...	...	14
26	Sa	8	2	·72	21	·02	15
27	Su	9	3	·78	22	·12	16
28	Mo	10	4	·82	23	·19	17
29	Tu	11	5	·84	24	·25	18
30	We	12	6	·85	25	·29	19
—31	Th	13	7	·83	26	·32	20
1	Fr	14	8	·78	27	·32	21
2	Sa	15	9	·72	1	·30	22
3	Su	16	10	·65	2	·27	23
4	Mo	17	11	·57	3	·22	24
5	Tu	18	12	·48	4	·16	25
6	We	19	13	·38	5	·10	26
7	Th	20	14	·28	6 / 7	·03 / ·96	27
8	Fr	21	—A	·13	8	·90	28
9	Sa	22	1 / 2	·08 / ·98	9	·84	—29
10	Su	23	3	·88	10	·79	1
11	Mo	24	4	·82	11	·75	2
12	Tu	25	5	·78	12	·72	3
13	We	26	6	·75	13	·72	4
14	Th	27	7	·73	14	·74	5
15	Fr	28	8	·74	15	·78	6
16	Sa	29	9	·76	16	·83	7
17	Su	30	10	·81	17	·91	8
18	Mo	31	11	·88	...	...	9

Aug.

Solar: Dhatri *Simha—Avani.* Lunar: Sravana, *Bahula*, Bhadrapada *Sukla*. Muhammadan: H. 1293 *Rajab.*; H. 1293 *Shaban.*

Cyclic Sidereal Year, Month and Day	Week-Day	English Month and Day	Tithi	Ending Moment	Nakshatra	Ending Moment	Muhammadan Year, Month and Day
19	Tu	1	12	·96	18	·00	10
20	We	2	...	...	19	·10	11
21	Th	3	13	·04	20	·21	12
22	Fr	4	14	·12	21	·32	13
23	Sa	5	P	·19	22	·42	14
24	Su	6	1	·25	23	·50	15
25	Mo	7	2	·30	24	·56	16
26	Tu	8	3	·32	25	·61	17
27	We	9	4	·33	26	·64	18
28	Th	10	5	·31	27	·65	19
29	Fr	11	6	·28	1	·63	20
30	Sa	12	7	·23	2	·60	21
31	Su	13	8	·16	3	·56	22
—32	Mo	14	9 / 10	·07 / ·97	4	·50	23
1	Tu	15	11	·87	5	·44	24
2	We	16	12	·77	6	·37	25
3	Th	17	13	·67	7	·30	26
4	Fr	18	14	·57	8	·24	27
5	Sa	19	—A	·48	9	·18	28
6	Su	20	1	·40	10	·12	29
7	Mo	21	2	·33	11	·08	—30
8	Tu	22	3	·28	12	·05	1
9	We	23	4	·24	13	·04	2
10	Th	24	5	·23	14	·06	3
11	Fr	25	6	·24	15	·09	4
12	Sa	26	7	·27	16	·14	5
13	Su	27	8	·32	17	·21	6
14	Mo	28	9	·38	18	·30	7
15	Tu	29	10	·45	19	·40	8
16	We	30	11	·53	20	·51	9
17	Th	31	12	·62	21	·62	10

Sep.

Solar: Dhatri *Simha—Avani.* (to 31); Dhatri *Kanya—Purattasi.* Lunar: Bhadrapada, *Bahula*, *Sukla*. Muhammadan: H. 1293 *Shaban.*

Cyclic Sidereal Year, Month and Day	Week-Day	English Month and Day	Tithi	Ending Moment	Nakshatra	Ending Moment	Muhammadan Year, Month and Day
18	Fr	1	13	·70	22	·72	11
19	Sa	2	14	·77	23	·81	12
20	Su	○ 3	P	·82	24	·88	13
21	Mo	4	1	·84	25	·93	14
22	Tu	5	2	·85	26	·96	15
23	We	6	3	·83	27	·97	16
24	Th	7	4	·80	1	·96	17
25	Fr	8	5	·74	2	·94	18
26	Sa	9	6	·67	3	·90	19
27	Su	10	7	·58	4	·84	20
28	Mo	11	8	·49	5	·78	21
29	Tu	12	9	·39	6	·71	22
30	We	13	10	·29	7	·64	23
—31	Th	14	11	·19	8	·57	24
1	Fr	15	12	·09	9	·51	25
2	Sa	16	13 / 14	·01 / ·93	10	·45	26
3	Su	17	—A	·86	11	·41	27
4	Mo	18	1	·81	12	·38	28
5	Tu	19	2	·78	13	·37	—29
6	We	20	3	·76	14	·38	1
7	Th	21	4	·78	15	·40	2
8	Fr	22	5	·81	16	·45	3
9	Sa	23	6	·85	17	·52	4
10	Su	24	7	·91	18	·61	5
11	Mo	25	8	·99	19	·71	6
12	Tu	26	...	...	20	·81	7
13	We	27	9	·09	21	·92	8
14	Th	28	10	·17	...	...	9
15	Fr	29	11	·24	22	·02	10
16	Sa	30	12	·30	23	·11	11

Oct.

Solar: Dhatri *Tulu—Aippasi.* Lunar: Asvina, *Bahula*, Kartika *Sukla*. Muhammadan: H. 1293 *Ramzan.*; H. 1293 *Shawwal.*

Cyclic Sidereal Year, Month and Day	Week-Day	English Month and Day	Tithi	Ending Moment	Nakshatra	Ending Moment	Muhammadan Year, Month and Day
17	Su	1	13	·35	24	·19	12
18	Mo	2	14	·38	25	·25	13
19	Tu	3	P	·39	26	·28	14
20	We	4	1	·38	27	·29	15
21	Th	5	2	·35	1	·28	16
22	Fr	6	3	·29	2	·26	17
23	Sa	7	4	·22	3	·23	18
24	Su	8	5	·14	4	·17	19
25	Mo	9	6 / 7	·06 / ·96	5	·11	20
26	Tu	10	8	·86	6 / 7	·05 / ·98	21
27	We	11	9	·76	8	·91	22
28	Th	12	10	·66	9	·85	23
29	Fr	13	11	·57	10	·79	24
—30	Sa	14	12	·49	11	·75	25
1	Su	15	13	·43	12	·72	26
2	Mo	16	14	·38	13	·70	27
3	Tu	17	—A	·35	14	·70	28
4	We	18	1	·33	15	·72	29
5	Th	19	2	·35	16	·76	—30
6	Fr	20	3	·38	17	·83	1
7	Sa	21	4	·43	18	·91	2
8	Su	22	5	·50	...	...	3
9	Mo	23	6	·58	19	·01	4
10	Tu	24	7	·67	20	·11	5
11	We	25	8	·76	21	·22	6
12	Th	26	9	·84	22	·32	7
13	Fr	27	10	·90	23	·42	8
14	Sa	28	11	·94	24	·50	9
15	Su	29	12	·97	25	·56	10
16	Mo	30	13	·98	26	·60	11
17	Tu	31	14	·97	27	·62	12

Nov.

Solar: Dhatri *Tula—Aippasi.* (to 30); Dhatri *Vrischika—Kartigai.* Lunar: Karttika, *Bahula*, Margasira *Sukla*. Muhammadan: H. 1293 *Shawwal.*; *Zu-l-ka'da.*

Cyclic Sidereal Year, Month and Day	Week-Day	English Month and Day	Tithi	Ending Moment	Nakshatra	Ending Moment	Muhammadan Year, Month and Day
18	We	1	P	·94	1	·62	13
19	Th	2	1	·89	2	·60	14
20	Fr	3	2	·82	3	·56	15
21	Sa	4	3	·74	4	·51	16
22	Su	5	4	·65	5	·45	17
23	Mo	6	5	·55	6	·39	18
24	Tu	7	6	·45	7	·32	19
25	We	8	7	·35	8	·25	20
26	Th	9	8	·26	9	·18	21
27	Fr	10	9	·18	10	·12	22
28	Sa	11	10	·10	11	·07	23
29	Su	12	11 / 12	·03 / ·98	12	·04	24
—30	Mo	13	13	·95	13	·02	25
1	Tu	14	14	·94	14	·02	26
2	We	15	—A	·96	15	·04	27
3	Th	16	1	·99	16	·08	28
4	Fr	17	...	...	17	·14	—29
5	Sa	18	2	·05	18	·22	1
6	Su	19	3	·12	19	·31	2
7	Mo	20	4	·20	20	·41	3
8	Tu	21	5	·29	21	·51	4
9	We	22	6	·38	22	·62	5
10	Th	23	7	·46	23	·72	6
11	Fr	24	8	·52	24	·81	7
12	Sa	25	9	·57	25	·87	8
13	Su	26	10	·60	26	·91	9
14	Mo	27	11	·61	27	·94	10
15	Tu	28	12	·59	1	·94	11
16	We	29	13	·55	2	·92	12
17	Th	30	14	·50	3	·89	13

Dec.

Solar: Dhatri *Dhanus—Margali.* Lunar: *Bahula*, Pausha *Sukla*. Muhammadan: H. 1293; H. 1293 *Zu-l-hijja.*

Cyclic Sidereal Year, Month and Day	Week-Day	English Month and Day	Tithi	Ending Moment	Nakshatra	Ending Moment	Muhammadan Year, Month and Day
18	Fr	1	P	·43	4	·85	14
19	Sa	2	1	·35	5	·80	15
20	Su	3	2	·27	6	·73	16
21	Mo	4	3	·18	7	·66	17
22	Tu	5	4 / 5	·08 / ·98	8	·59	18
23	We	6	6	·88	9	·53	19
24	Th	7	7	·79	10	·47	20
25	Fr	8	8	·72	11	·42	21
26	Sa	9	9	·66	12	·38	22
27	Su	10	10	·62	13	·35	23
28	Mo	11	11	·59	14	·34	24
29	Tu	12	12	·58	15	·36	25
—30	We	13	13	·60	16	·39	26
1	Th	14	14	·63	17	·45	27
2	Fr	15	—A	·69	18	·52	28
3	Sa	16	1	·76	19	·61	29
4	Su	17	2	·85	20	·71	—30
5	Mo	18	3	·94	21	·82	1
6	Tu	19	...	...	22	·93	2
7	We	20	4	·03	...	...	3
8	Th	21	5	·10	23	·03	4
9	Fr	22	6	·16	24	·11	5
10	Sa	23	7	·21	25	·18	6
11	Su	24	8	·24	26	·23	7
12	Mo	25	9	·25	27	·26	8
13	Tu	26	10	·23	1	·27	9
14	We	27	11	·20	2	·25	10
15	Th	28	12	·14	3	·22	11
16	Fr	29	13 / 14	·07 / ·99	4	·18	12
17	Sa	30	P	·91	5	·13	13
18	Su	31	1	·81	6	·07	14

15. Svati. 16. Visak. 17. Anur. 18. Jyesh. 19. Mula. 20. P. Ash. 21. U. Ash. 22. Sravn. 23. Dani. 24. Satab. 25. P. Bhad. 26. U. Bhad. 27. Rev.

A. D. 1877. **Mesha Sankranti** (Commencement of Indian Sidereal Year).

Solar Eclipse. ● **(Surya Sid.) April 11·67.** **Saka 1799.** **Kaliyuga 4978.**

Lunar Eclipse. ○ **(Arya Sid.) April 11·57.** **(S. Cycle) Isvara.**

SOLAR reckoning. Cyclic Sidereal Year, Month and Day.	Week-Day	English Month and Day.	LUNAR reckoning. Tithi	Ending Moment.	Nakshatra	Ending Moment.	Muhammadan Year, Month and Day.
		Jan.					
Dhatri *Dhanus—Margali.* 19	Mo	1	Pausha *Bahula* 2	·71	7 8	·00 ·93	H. 1293 *Zi-l-hijja.* 15
20	Tu	2	3	·61	9	·87	16
21	We	3	4	·52	10	·81	17
22	Th	4	5	·44	11	·75	18
23	Fr	5	6	·36	12	·70	19
24	Sa	6	7	·30	13	·67	20
25	Su	7	8	·26	14	·66	21
26	Mo	8	9	·23	15	·68	22
27	Tu	9	10	·23	16	·71	23
28	We	10	11	·24	17	·76	24
—29	Th	11	12	·28	18	·82	25
Dhatri *Makara—Tai.* 1	Fr	12	13	·34	19	·91	26
2	Sa	13	14	·42	...	...	27
3	Su	14	—A	·51	20	·01	28
4	Mo	15	Magha *Sukla* 1	·59	21	·12	—29
5	Tu	16	2	·68	22	·23	*Muharram.* 1
6	We	17	3	·75	23	·33	2
7	Th	18	4	·82	24	·42	3
8	Fr	19	5	·86	25	·50	4
9	Sa	20	6	·88	26	·55	5
10	Su	21	7	·89	27	·58	6
11	Mo	22	8	·87	1	·59	7
12	Tu	23	9	·84	2	·58	8
13	We	24	10	·78	3	·56	9
14	Th	25	11	·71	4	·52	10
15	Fr	26	12	·63	5	·47	11
16	Sa	27	13	·54	6	·41	12
17	Su	28	14	·44	7	·35	13
18	Mo	29	P	·34	8	·28	14
19	Tu	30	1	·25	9	·21	15
20	We	31	2	·16	10	·14	16
		Feb.					
21	Th	1	*Bahula* 3 4	·07 ·99	11	·08	H. 1294 17
22	Fr	2	5	·94	12	·04	18
23	Sa	3	6	·90	13	·01	19
24	Su	4	7	·88	14	·00	20
25	Mo	5	8	·87	15	·00	21
26	Tu	6	9	·89	16	·02	22
27	We	7	10	·93	17	·06	23
28	Th	8	11	·98	18	·13	24
—29	Fr	9	...	...	19	·22	25
Dhatri *Kumbha—Masi.* 1	Sa	10	12	·06	20	·32	26
2	Su	11	13	·15	21	·42	27
3	Mo	12	14	·24	22	·53	28
4	Tu	13	—A	·32	23	·63	29
5	We	14	Phalguna *Sukla* 1	·39	24	·72	—30
6	Th	15	2	·45	25	·80	H. 1294 *Safar.* 1
7	Fr	16	3	·50	26	·86	2
8	Sa	17	4	·52	27	·90	3
9	Su	18	5	·52	1	·92	4
10	Mo	19	6	·50	2	·92	5
11	Tu	20	7	·46	3	·89	6
12	We	21	8	·40	4	·85	7
13	Th	22	9	·33	5	·80	8
14	Fr	23	10	·25	6	·74	9
15	Sa	24	11	·16	7	·68	10
16	Su	25	12 13	·06 ·96	8	·62	11
17	Mo	26	14	·86	9	·55	12
18	Tu ○	27	P	·76	10	·48	13
19	We	28	1	·68	11	·42	14

SOLAR reckoning. Cyclic Sidereal Year, Month and Day.	Week-Day	English Month and Day.	LUNAR reckoning. Tithi	Ending Moment.	Nakshatra	Ending Moment.	Muhammadan Year, Month and Day.
		March					
Dhatri *Kumbha—Masi.* 20	Th	1	Phalguna *Bahula* 2	·61	12	·37	H. 1294 *Safar.* 15
21	Fr	2	3	·55	13	·34	16
22	Sa	3	4	·51	14	·32	17
23	Su	4	5	·49	15	·32	18
24	Mo	5	6	·48	16	·34	19
25	Tu	6	7	·50	17	·38	20
26	We	7	8	·54	18	·44	21
27	Th	8	9	·60	19	·52	22
28	Fr	9	10	·68	20	·62	23
29	Sa	10	11	·76	21	·72	24
—30	Su	11	12	·85	22	·82	25
Dhatri *Mina—Panguni.* 1	Mo	12	13	·93	23	·93	26
2	Tu	13	...	...	...	...	27
3	We	14	14	·00	24	·03	28
4	Th ●	15	—A	·06	25	·11	—29
5	Fr	16	Chaitra *Sukla* 1	·10	26	·17	*Rabi-ul-awwal.* 1
6	Sa	17	2	·12	27	·21	2
7	Su	18	3	·11	1	·24	3
8	Mo	19	4	·10	2	·24	4
9	Tu	20	5	·06	3	·22	5
10	We	21	6 7	·00 ·93	4	·19	6
11	Th	22	8	·84	5	·14	7
12	Fr	23	9	·74	6	·08	8
13	Sa	24	10	·64	7 8	·02 ·95	9
14	Su	25	11	·54	9	·88	10
15	Mo	26	12	·45	10	·82	11
16	Tu	27	13	·36	11	·76	12
17	We	28	14	·27	12	·71	13
18	Th	29	P	·19	13	·67	14
19	Fr	30	1	·13	14	·65	15
20	Sa	31	2	·09	15	·64	16
		April					
21	Su	1	*Bahula* 3	·07	16	·65	H. 1294 17
22	Mo	2	4	·06	17	·69	18
23	Tu	3	5	·08	18	·75	19
24	We	4	6	·12	19	·82	20
25	Th	5	7	·18	20	·91	21
26	Fr	6	8	·25	...	...	22
27	Sa	7	9	·33	21	·02	23
28	Su	8	10	·41	22	·13	24
29	Mo	9	11	·49	23	·24	25
30	Tu	10	12	·56	24	·34	26
—31	We	11	13	·62	25	·42	27
Isvara *Mesha—Chittirai.* 1	Th	12	14	·66	26	·48	28
2	Fr	13	—A	·68	27	·53	29
3	Sa	14	Vaisakha *Sukla* 1	·67	1	·56	—30
4	Su	15	2	·65	2	·57	H. 1294 *Rabi-ul-akhir.* 1
5	Mo	16	3	·61	3	·55	2
6	Tu	17	4	·55	4	·52	3
7	We	18	5	·48	5	·48	4
8	Th	19	6	·40	6	·42	5
9	Fr	20	7	·30	7	·36	6
10	Sa	21	8	·20	8	·29	7
11	Su	22	9	·10	9	·22	8
12	Mo	23	10 11	·00 ·90	10	·16	9
13	Tu	24	12	·81	11	·10	10
14	We	25	13	·74	12	·04	11
15	Th	26	14	·68	13 14	·00 ·97	12
16	Fr	27	P	·64	15	·96	13
17	Sa	28	1	·61	16	·98	14
18	Su	29	2	·59	...	...	15
19	Mo	30	3	·61	17	·01	16

SOLAR reckoning. Cyclic Sidereal Year, Month and Day.	Week-Day	English Month and Day.	LUNAR reckoning. Tithi	Ending Moment.	Nakshatra	Ending Moment.	Muhammadan Year, Month and Day.
		May					
Isvara *Mesha—Chittirai.* 20	Tu	1	Vaisakha *Bahula* 4	·65	18	·06	H. 1294 *Rabi-ul-akhir.* 17
21	We	2	5	·71	19	·13	18
22	Th	3	6	·78	20	·21	19
23	Fr	4	7	·86	21	·31	20
24	Sa	5	8	·94	22	·42	21
25	Su	6	...	...	23	·53	22
26	Mo	7	9	·02	24	·63	23
27	Tu	8	10	·09	25	·72	24
28	We	9	11	·15	26	·79	25
29	Th	10	12	·19	27	·85	26
—30	Fr	11	13	·20	1	·88	27
Isvara *Vrishabha—Vaikasi.* 1	Sa	12	14	·20	2	·89	28
2	Su	13	—A	·18	3	·88	—29
3	Mo	14	Adhika Jyeshtha *Sukla* 1	·13	4	·85	*Jumadal-awwal.* 1
4	Tu	15	2 3	·07 ·99	5	·81	2
5	We	16	4	·91	6	·76	3
6	Th	17	5	·81	7	·70	4
7	Fr	18	6	·71	8	·63	5
8	Sa	19	7	·61	9	·56	6
9	Su	20	8	·51	10	·50	7
10	Mo	21	9	·41	11	·44	8
11	Tu	22	10	·32	12	·38	9
12	We	23	11	·24	13	·33	10
13	Th	24	12	·18	14	·30	11
14	Fr	25	13	·14	15	·29	12
15	Sa	26	14	·12	16	·30	13
16	Su	27	P	·11	17	·32	14
17	Mo	28	1	·12	18	·37	15
18	Tu	29	2	·16	19	·43	16
19	We	30	3	·21	20	·51	17
20	Th	31	4	·27	21	·61	18
		June					
21	Fr	1	*Bahula* 5	·35	22	·72	H. 1294 19
22	Sa	2	6	·43	23	·83	20
23	Su	3	7	·51	24	·93	21
24	Mo	4	8	·58	...	...	22
25	Tu	5	9	·64	25	·02	23
26	We	6	10	·68	26	·10	24
27	Th	7	11	·70	27	·16	25
28	Fr	8	12	·69	1	·20	26
29	Sa	9	13	·67	2	·21	27
30	Su	10	14	·63	3	·21	28
31	Mo	11	—A	·57	4	·19	29
—32	Tu	12	Nija Jyeshtha *Sukla* 1	·50	5	·15	—30
Isvara *Mithuna—Ani.* 1	We	13	2	·41	6	·10	H. 1294 *Jumadal-akhir.* 1
2	Th	14	3	·31	7 8	·04 ·98	2
3	Fr	15	4	·21	9	·91	3
4	Sa	16	5	·11	10	·84	4
5	Su	17	6 7	·01 ·91	11	·77	5
6	Mo	18	8	·82	12	·71	6
7	Tu	19	9	·74	13	·66	7
8	We	20	10	·67	14	·63	8
9	Th	21	11	·62	15	·62	9
10	Fr	22	12	·59	16	·62	10
11	Sa	23	13	·59	17	·64	11
12	Su	24	14	·60	18	·68	12
13	Mo	25	P	·63	19	·74	13
14	Tu	26	*Bah.* 1	·68	20	·82	14
15	We	27	2	·74	21	·92	15
16	Th	28	3	·82	...	...	16
17	Fr	29	4	·90	22	·02	17
18	Sa	30	5	·99	23	·13	18

Naksh:—1. Asvn. 2. Bhar. 3. Krit. 4. Rohi. 5. Mrig. 6. Ardh. 7. Punar. 8. Push. 9. Aslesh. 10. Magh. 11. P. Phal. 12. U. Phal. 13. Hasta. 14. Chit.

A. D. 1877. **A.—Amavasya. P.—Paurnami.** **Kollam 1053, Commences {N. Malabar—Sept. S. Malabar—Aug.** **Hijra 1294, Commences, Jan. 16.** **Vikrama 1934. Bengal San 1283. (N. Cycle) Virodhin.**

SOLAR reckoning. / LUNAR reckoning.

July

Labels: Isvara *Mithuna—Ani.* (to 31); Isvara *Karkata—Adi.* (from 1); Tithi: Ni. Jy., *Bahula* (to 14), *Sukla*, Ashadha; Muhammadan: H. 1294 *Jumada-l-akhir.* (to 29), H. 1294 *Rajab.* (from 1)

Cyclic Sidereal Year, Month and Day.	Week-Day	English Month and Day.	Tithi	Ending Moment.	Nakshatra	Ending Moment.	Muhammadan Year, Month and Day.
19	Su	1	...	...	24	·23	19
20	Mo	2	6	·05	25	·33	20
21	Tu	3	7	·12	26	·41	21
22	We	4	8	·16	27	·47	22
23	Th	5	9	·18	1	·51	23
24	Fr	6	10	·17	2	·53	24
25	Sa	7	11	·15	3	·54	25
26	Su	8	12	·10	4	·52	26
27	Mo	9	13 14	·04 ·97	5	·49	27
28	Tu	10	—A	·89	6	·44	28
29	We	11	1	·79	7	·38	—29
30	Th	12	2	·69	8	·32	1
—31	Fr	13	3	·59	9	·25	2
1	Sa	14	4	·49	10	·18	3
2	Su	15	5	·39	11	·11	4
3	Mo	16	6	·29	12	·05	5
4	Tu	17	7	·21	13 14	·00 ·97	6
5	We	18	8	·15	15	·95	7
6	Th	19	9	·11	16	·94	8
7	Fr	20	10	·08	17	·95	9
8	Sa	21	11	·06	18	·99	10
9	Su	22	12	·07	...	...	11
10	Mo	23	13	·10	19	·05	12
11	Tu	24	14	·14	20	·13	13
12	We	25	P	·21	21	·22	14
13	Th	26	1	·29	22	·32	15
14	Fr	27	2	·37	23	·43	16
15	Sa	28	3	·45	24	·54	17
16	Su	29	4	·52	25	·64	18
17	Mo	30	5	·59	26	·72	19
18	Tu	31	6	·64	27	·78	20

Aug.

Labels: Isvara *Simha—Avani.*; Tithi: *Bahula*, *Sukla*, Sravana, *Bahula*; Muhammadan: H. 1294 *Shaban.*

Cyclic Sidereal Year, Month and Day.	Week-Day	English Month and Day.	Tithi	Ending Moment.	Nakshatra	Ending Moment.	Muhammadan Year, Month and Day.
19	We	1	7	·66	1	·83	21
20	Th	2	8	·65	2	·86	22
21	Fr	3	9	·63	3	·87	23
22	Sa	4	10	·59	4	·85	24
23	Su	5	11	·54	5	·82	25
24	Mo	6	12	·47	6	·77	26
25	Tu	7	13	·38	7	·71	27
26	We	8	14	·28	8	·65	28
27	Th	9	—A	·18	9	·59	29
28	Fr	10	1 2	·08 ·98	10	·52	—30
29	Sa	11	3	·88	11	·45	1
30	Su	12	4	·79	12	·39	2
31	Mo	13	5	·71	13	·34	3
—32	Tu	14	6	·65	14	·30	4
1	We	15	7	·60	15	·27	5
2	Th	16	8	·57	16	·26	6
3	Fr	17	9	·55	17	·27	7
4	Sa	18	10	·56	18	·31	8
5	Su	19	11	·59	19	·36	9
6	Mo	20	12	·64	20	·43	10
7	Tu	21	13	·71	21	·52	11
8	We	22	14	·78	22	·62	12
9	Th ○	23	P	·86	23	·73	13
10	Fr	24	1	·95	24	·84	14
11	Sa	25	...	...	25	·94	15
12	Su	26	2	·03	...	...	16
13	Mo	27	3	·09	26	·03	17
14	Tu	28	4	·14	27	·10	18
15	We	29	5	·17	1	·15	19
16	Th	30	6	·16	2	·18	20
17	Fr	31	7	·14	3	·19	21

Sep.

Labels: Isvara *Simha—Avani.* (to 31); Isvara *Kanya—Purattasi.* (from 1); Tithi: Sr. *Bah.*, *Sukla*, Bhadrupada, *Bahula*; Muhammadan: H. 1294 *Shaban.* (to 29), H. 1294 *Ramzan.* (from 1)

Cyclic Sidereal Year, Month and Day.	Week-Day	English Month and Day.	Tithi	Ending Moment.	Nakshatra	Ending Moment.	Muhammadan Year, Month and Day.
18	Sa	1	8	·10	4	·18	22
19	Su	2	9 10	·05 ·98	5	·15	23
20	Mo	3	11	·90	6	·11	24
21	Tu	4	12	·80	7 8	·05 ·99	25
22	We	5	13	·70	9	·92	26
23	Th	6	14	·60	10	·85	27
24	Fr	7	—A	·50	11	·79	28
25	Sa	8	1	·40	12	·73	—29
26	Su	9	2	·31	13	·67	1
27	Mo	10	3	·23	14	·63	2
28	Tu	11	4	·17	15	·60	3
29	We	12	5	·12	16	·58	4
30	Th	13	6	·09	17	·60	5
—31	Fr	14	7	·08	18	·63	6
1	Sa	15	8	·09	19	·67	7
2	Su	16	9	·12	20	·74	8
3	Mo	17	10	·17	21	·82	9
4	Tu	18	11	·23	22	·92	10
5	We	19	12	·31	...	...	11
6	Th	20	13	·39	23	·03	12
7	Fr	21	14	·47	24	·14	13
8	Sa	22	P	·55	25	·24	14
9	Su	23	1	·62	26	·33	15
10	Mo	24	2	·67	27	·40	16
11	Tu	25	3	·69	1	·46	17
12	We	26	4	·70	2	·50	18
13	Th	27	5	·68	3	·51	19
14	Fr	28	6	·64	4	·50	20
15	Sa	29	7	·59	5	·48	21
16	Su	30	8	·52	6	·45	22

Oct.

Labels: Isvara *Tula—Aippasi.*; Tithi: *Sukla*, Asvina, *Bahula*; Muhammadan: H. 1294 *Shawwal.*

Cyclic Sidereal Year, Month and Day.	Week-Day	English Month and Day.	Tithi	Ending Moment.	Nakshatra	Ending Moment.	Muhammadan Year, Month and Day.
17	Mo	1	9	·44	7	·39	23
18	Tu	2	10	·35	8	·33	24
19	We	3	11	·25	9	·26	25
20	Th	4	12	·15	10	·19	26
21	Fr	5	13 14	·05 ·95	11	·13	27
22	Sa	6	—A	·85	12	·07	28
23	Su	7	1	·77	13 14	·01 ·96	29
24	Mo	8	2	·72	15	·93	—30
25	Tu	9	3	·68	16	·92	1
26	We	10	4	·66	17	·92	2
27	Th	11	5	·65	18	·94	3
28	Fr	12	6	·66	19	·98	4
29	Sa	13	7	·69	...	...	5
—30	Su	14	8	·74	20	·04	6
1	Mo	15	9	·80	21	·13	7
2	Tu	16	10	·88	22	·23	8
3	We	17	11	·97	23	·33	9
4	Th	18	...	...	24	·44	10
5	Fr	19	12	·06	25	·54	11
6	Sa	20	13	·14	26	·63	12
7	Su	21	14	·20	27	·71	13
8	Mo	22	P	·25	1	·78	14
9	Tu	23	1	·28	2	·82	15
10	We	24	2	·23	3	·83	16
11	Th	25	3	·26	4	·83	17
12	Fr	26	4	·22	5	·82	18
13	Sa	27	5	·17	6	·78	19
14	Su	28	6	·10	7	·73	20
15	Mo	29	7 8	·02 ·93	8	·67	21
16	Tu	30	9	·84	9	·61	22
17	We	31	10	·74	10	·54	23

Nov.

Labels: Isvara *Tula—Aippasi.* (to 30); Isvara *Vrischika—Kartigai.* (from 1); Tithi: *Bah.*, *Sukla*, Karttika, *Bahula*; Muhammadan: *Shawwal.* (to 29), H. 1294 *Zi-l-ka'da.* (from 1)

Cyclic Sidereal Year, Month and Day.	Week-Day	English Month and Day.	Tithi	Ending Moment.	Nakshatra	Ending Moment.	Muhammadan Year, Month and Day.
18	Th	1	11	·64	11	·47	24
19	Fr	2	12	·54	12	·40	25
20	Sa	3	13	·45	13	·34	26
21	Su	4	14	·38	14	·29	27
22	Mo	5	—A	·32	15	·26	28
23	Tu	6	1	·27	16	·24	—29
24	We	7	2	·24	17	·24	1
25	Th	8	3	·24	18	·25	2
26	Fr	9	4	·26	19	·29	3
27	Sa	10	5	·29	20	·35	4
28	Su	11	6	·34	21	·43	5
29	Mo	12	7	·41	22	·53	6
—30	Tu	13	8	·49	23	·63	7
1	We	14	9	·58	24	·74	8
2	Th	15	10	·67	25	·85	9
3	Fr	16	11	·75	26	·95	10
4	Sa	17	12	·81	...	...	11
5	Su	18	13	·86	27	·03	12
6	Mo	19	14	·89	1	·09	13
7	Tu	20	P	·89	2	·13	14
8	We	21	1	·87	3	·15	15
9	Th	22	2	·83	4	·16	16
10	Fr	23	3	·78	5	·14	17
11	Sa	24	4	·72	6	·11	18
12	Su	25	5	·64	7	·07	19
13	Mo	26	6	·55	8 9	·01 ·95	20
14	Tu	27	7	·45	10	·88	21
15	We	28	8	·35	11	·81	22
16	Th	29	9	·25	12	·74	23
17	Fr	30	10	·16	13	·68	24

Dec.

Labels: Isvara *Dhanus—Margali.*; Tithi: *Sukla*, Margasira, *Bahula*; Muhammadan: H. 1294 *Zi-l-hijja.*

Cyclic Sidereal Year, Month and Day.	Week-Day	English Month and Day.	Tithi	Ending Moment.	Nakshatra	Ending Moment.	Muhammadan Year, Month and Day.
18	Sa	1	11 12	·07 ·99	14	·62	25
19	Su	2	13	·94	15	·59	26
20	Mo	3	14	·90	16	·57	27
21	Tu	4	—A	·88	17	·56	28
22	We	5	1	·87	18	·57	29
23	Th	6	2	·89	19	·60	—30
24	Fr	7	3	·93	20	·66	1
25	Sa	8	4	·98	21	·74	2
26	Su	9	...	...	22	·83	3
27	Mo	10	5	·05	23	·93	4
28	Tu	11	6	·14	...	...	5
29	We	12	7	·24	24	·04	6
—30	Th	13	8	·32	25	·15	7
1	Fr	14	9	·40	26	·25	8
2	Sa	15	10	·46	27	·33	9
3	Su	16	11	·50	1	·40	10
4	Mo	17	12	·53	2	·45	11
5	Tu	18	13	·53	3	·48	12
6	We	19	14	·51	4	·49	13
7	Th	20	P	·47	5	·47	14
8	Fr	21	1	·42	6	·44	15
9	Sa	22	2	·35	7	·40	16
10	Su	23	3	·27	8	·35	17
11	Mo	24	4	·19	9	·29	18
12	Tu	25	5 6	·09 ·99	10	·22	19
13	We	26	7	·89	11	·15	20
14	Th	27	8	·80	12	·08	21
15	Fr	28	9	·71	13 14	·02 ·96	22
16	Sa	29	10	·63	15	·92	23
17	Su	30	11	·58	16	·89	24
18	Mo	31	12	·54	17	·83	25

15. Svati. 16. Visak. 17. Anur. 18. Jyesh. 19. Mula. 20. P. Ash. 21. U. Ash. 22. Sravn. 23. Dani. 24. Satab. 25. P. Bhad. 26. U. Bhad. 27. Rev.

A. D. 1878. **Mesha Sankranti** (Commencement of Indian Sidereal Year).

Solar Eclipse. ● **(Surya Sid.) April 11·93.** **Saka 1800.** **Kaliyuga 4979.**

Lunar Eclipse. ○ **(Arya Sid.) April 11·83.** **(S. Cycle) Bahudhanya.**

Cyclic Sidereal Year, Month and Day (SOLAR reckoning)	Week-Day	English Month and Day	Tithi (LUNAR reckoning)	Ending Moment	Nakshatra	Ending Moment	Muhammadan Year, Month and Day
		Jan.					
19 (Isvara, Dhanu—Margali)	Tu	1	13 (Bah.)	·52	18	·89	26
20	We	2	14	·51	19	·93	27
21	Th	3	—A	·53	20	·98	28
22	Fr	4	1 (Pausha, Sukla)	·57	...	...	—29
23	Sa	5	2	·63	21	·04	1 (H. 1295 Muharram)
24	Su	6	3	·71	22	·13	2
25	Mo	7	4	·79	23	·23	3
26	Tu	8	5	·88	24	·34	4
27	We	9	6	·97	25	·45	5
28	Th	10	...	...	26	·55	6
—29	Fr	11	7	·04	27	·63	7
1 (Isvara, Makara—Tai)	Sa	12	8	·10	1	·71	8
2	Su	13	9	·15	2	·77	9
3	Mo	14	10	·18	3	·80	10
4	Tu	15	11	·18	4	·81	11
5	We	16	12	·16	5	·80	12
6	Th	17	13	·12	6	·77	13
7	Fr	18	14 P	·06 ·99	7	·73	14
8	Sa	19	1 (Bahula)	·91	8	·69	15
9	Su	20	2	·82	9	·63	16
10	Mo	21	3	·72	10	·56	17
11	Tu	22	4	·62	11	·49	18
12	We	23	5	·52	12	·42	19
13	Th	24	6	·43	13	·36	20
14	Fr	25	7	·35	14	·30	21
15	Sa	26	8	·28	15	·25	22
16	Su	27	9	·22	16	·22	23
17	Mo	28	10	·18	17	·21	24
18	Tu	29	11	·16	18	·22	25
19	We	30	12	·16	19	·24	26
20	Th	31	13	·18	20	·28	27
		Feb.					
21	Fr	1	14	·22	21	·35	28
22	Sa	2	—A	·28	22	·43	29
23	Su	3	1 (Magha, Sukla)	·36	23	·53	—30
24	Mo	4	2	·44	24	·64	1 (H. 1295 Safar)
25	Tu	5	3	·53	25	·75	2
26	We	6	4	·61	26	·85	3
27	Th	7	5	·69	27	·94	4
28	Fr	8	6	·75	...	...	5
29	Sa	9	7	·79	1	·02	6
—30	Su	10	8	·81	2	·08	7
1 (Isvara, Kumbha—Masi)	Mo	11	9	·81	3	·12	8
2	Tu	12	10	·79	4	·13	9
3	We	13	11	·75	5	·13	10
4	Th	14	12	·69	6	·11	11
5	Fr	15	13	·62	7	·08	12
6	Sa	16	14	·54	8 9	·02 ·96	13
7	Su ○	17	P	·45	10	·90	14
8	Mo	18	1 (Bahula)	·35	11	·88	15
9	Tu	19	2	·25	12	·76	16
10	We	20	3	·15	13	·70	17
11	Th	21	4 5	·05 ·97	14	·64	18
12	Fr	22	6	·90	15	·59	19
13	Sa	23	7	·84	16	·55	20
14	Su	24	8	·80	17	·54	21
15	Mo	25	9	·78	18	·54	22
16	Tu	26	10	·78	19	·56	23
17	We	27	11	·60	20	·59	24
18	Th	28	12	·84	21	·65	25

Cyclic Sidereal Year, Month and Day (SOLAR reckoning)	Week-Day	English Month and Day	Tithi (LUNAR reckoning)	Ending Moment	Nakshatra	Ending Moment	Muhammadan Year, Month and Day
		March					
19 (Isvara, Kumbha—Masi)	Fr	1	13 (Bah.)	·90	22	·74	26 (Safar)
20	Sa	2	14	·98	23	·83	27
21	Su	3	...	...	24	·93	28
22	Mo	4	—A	·07	...	...	—29
23	Tu	5	1 (Phalguna, Sukla)	·15	25	·04	1 (H. 1295 Rabi-ul-awwal)
24	We	6	2	·23	26	·15	2
25	Th	7	3	·30	27	·24	3
26	Fr	8	4	·36	1	·32	4
27	Sa	9	5	·40	2	·39	5
28	Su	10	6	·42	3	·43	6
—29	Mo	11	7	·42	4	·45	7
1 (Isvara, Mina—Panguni)	Tu	12	8	·40	5	·45	8
2	We	13	9	·35	6	·44	9
3	Th	14	10	·29	7	·41	10
4	Fr	15	11	·22	8	·36	11
5	Sa	16	12	·14	9	·30	12
6	Su	17	13 14	·04 ·94	10	·24	13
7	Mo	18	P	·84	11	·17	14
8	Tu	19	1 (Bahula)	·74	12	·10	15
9	We	20	2	·65	13 14	·03 ·97	16
10	Th	21	3	·57	15	·92	17
11	Fr	22	4	·49	16	·89	18
12	Sa	23	5	·43	17	·87	19
13	Su	24	6	·39	18	·86	20
14	Mo	25	7	·37	19	·87	21
15	Tu	26	8	·37	20	·91	22
16	We	27	9	·39	21	·97	23
17	Th	28	10	·43	...	...	24
18	Fr	29	11	·48	22	·04	25
19	Sa	30	12	·56	23	·13	26
20	Su	31	13	·65	24	·23	27
		April					
21	Mo	1	14	·74	25	·34	28
22	Tu	2	—A	·82	26	·45	29
23	We	3	1 (Chaitra, Sukla)	·89	27	·55	—30
24	Th	4	2	·94	1	·64	1 (H. 1295 Rabi-ul-akhir)
25	Fr	5	3	·97	2	·70	2
26	Sa	6	4	·99	3	·75	3
27	Su	7	5	·99	4	·78	4
28	Mo	8	6	·96	5	·79	5
29	Tu	9	7	·91	6	·77	6
30	We	10	8	·85	7	·74	7
—31	Th	11	9	·78	8	·69	8
1 (Bahudhanya, Mesha—Chittirai)	Fr	12	10	·69	9	·63	9
2	Sa	13	11	·60	10	·57	10
3	Su	14	12	·50	11	·51	11
4	Mo	15	13	·40	12	·44	12
5	Tu	16	14	·30	13	·37	13
6	We	17	P	·20	14	·31	14
7	Th	18	1 (Bahula)	·12	15	·26	15
8	Fr	19	2 3	·05 ·99	16	·22	16
9	Sa	20	4	·94	17	·19	17
10	Su	21	5	·91	18	·18	18
11	Mo	22	6	·91	19	·19	19
12	Tu	23	7	·93	20	·22	20
13	We	24	8	·97	21	·28	21
14	Th	25	...	...	22	·35	22
15	Fr	26	9	·03	23	·43	23
16	Sa	27	10	·11	24	·53	24
17	Su	28	11	·19	25	·64	25
18	Mo	29	12	·27	26	·75	26
19	Tu	30	13	·34	27	·85	27

Cyclic Sidereal Year, Month and Day (SOLAR reckoning)	Week-Day	English Month and Day	Tithi (LUNAR reckoning)	Ending Moment	Nakshatra	Ending Moment	Muhammadan Year, Month and Day
		May					
20 (Bahudhanya, Mesha—Chittirai)	We	1	14	·41	1	·94	28
21	Th	2	—A	·47	...	...	—29
22	Fr	3	1 (Vaisakha, Sukla)	·51	2	·01	1 (H. 1295 Jumadal-awwal)
23	Sa	4	2	·53	3	·06	2
24	Su	5	3	·52	4	·10	3
25	Mo	6	4	·49	5	·11	4
26	Tu	7	5	·44	6	·10	5
27	We	8	6	·38	7	·07	6
28	Th	9	7	·31	8 9	·03 ·98	7
29	Fr	10	8	·22	10	·92	8
30	Sa	11	9	·12	11	·85	9
—31	Su	12	10 11	·02 ·92	12	·78	10
1 (Bahudhanya, Vrishabha—Vaikasi)	Mo	13	12	·82	13	·71	11
2	Tu	14	13	·72	14	·65	12
3	We	15	14	·63	15	·59	13
4	Th	16	P	·56	16	·55	14
5	Fr	17	1 (Bahula)	·51	17	·52	15
6	Sa	18	2	·47	18	·50	16
7	Su	19	3	·44	19	·51	17
8	Mo	20	4	·42	20	·54	18
9	Tu	21	5	·44	21	·59	19
10	We	22	6	·48	22	·65	20
11	Th	23	7	·53	23	·73	21
12	Fr	24	8	·60	24	·83	22
13	Sa	25	9	·68	25	·94	23
14	Su	26	10	·77	...	...	24
15	Mo	27	11	·85	26	·05	25
16	Tu	28	12	·92	27	·15	26
17	We	29	13	·97	1	·24	27
18	Th	30	...	...	2	·32	28
19	Fr	31	14	·00	3	·38	29
		June					
20	Sa	1	—A	·02	4	·42	—30
21	Su	2	1 (Jyeshtha, Sukla) 2	·01 ·99	5	·43	1 (H. 1295 Jumadal-akhir)
22	Mo	3	3	·95	6	·42	2
23	Tu	4	4	·89	7	·40	3
24	We	5	5	·81	8	·37	4
25	Th	6	6	·72	9	·32	5
26	Fr	7	7	·62	10	·26	6
27	Sa	8	8	·52	11	·19	7
28	Su	9	9	·42	12	·12	8
29	Mo	10	10	·32	13 14	·05 ·99	9
30	Tu	11	11	·23	15	·93	10
—31	We	12	12	·14	16	·88	11
1 (Bahudhanya, Mithuna—Ani)	Th	13	13 14	·06 ·99	17	·85	12
2	Fr	14	P	·94	18	·83	13
3	Sa	15	1 (Bahula)	·92	19	·84	14
4	Su	16	2	·91	20	·86	15
5	Mo	17	3	·92	21	·90	16
6	Tu	18	4	·95	22	·96	17
7	We	19	...	...	...	...	18
8	Th	20	5	·00	23	·04	19
9	Fr	21	6	·07	24	·14	20
10	Sa	22	7	·15	25	·24	21
11	Su	23	8	·24	26	·35	22
12	Mo	24	9	·32	27	·45	23
13	Tu	25	10	·39	1	·55	24
14	We	26	11	·45	2	·63	25
15	Th	27	12	·48	3	·69	26
16	Fr	28	13	·50	4	·73	27
17	Sa	29	14	·49	5	·75	28
18	Su	30	—A	·47	6	·75	—29

Naksh:—1. Asvn. 2. Bhar. 3. krit. 4. Rohi. 5. Mrig. 6. Ardh. 7. Punar. 8. Push. 9. Aslesh. 10. Magh. 11. P. Phal. 12. U. Phal. 13. Hasta. 14. Chit.

A. D. 1878. **A.—Amavasya.** **P.—Paurnami.** **Kollam 1054,** Commences { **N. Malabar—Sept.** **S. Malabar—Aug.** **Hijra** Commences { **1295, Jan. 5.** **1296, Dec. 26.** **Vikrama 1935.** **Bengal San 1284.** **(N. Cycle) Vikrita.**

SOLAR reckoning: Bahudhanya *Mithuna—Ani.* / Bahudhanya *Karkata—Adi.* LUNAR reckoning: Sukla Ashadha P Bahula A. H. 1295 *Rajab.*

Cyclic Sidereal Year, Month and Day.	Week-Day	English Month and Day.	Tithi	Ending Moment.	Nakshatra	Ending Moment.	Muhammadan Year, Month and Day.
	July						
19	Mo	1	1	·43	7	·73	1
20	Tu	2	2	·37	8	·70	2
21	We	3	3	·29	9	·65	3
22	Th	4	4	·20	10	·59	4
23	Fr	5	5	·10	11	·53	5
24	Sa	6	6 7	·00 ·90	12	·47	6
25	Su	7	8	·80	13	·40	7
26	Mo	8	9	·70	14	·33	8
27	Tu	9	10	·61	15	·27	9
28	We	10	11	·53	16	·22	10
29	Th	11	12	·47	17	·18	11
30	Fr	12	13	·43	18	·16	12
31	Sa	13	14	·40	19	·16	13
—32	Su	14	P	·38	20	·17	14
1	Mo	15	1	·40	21	·21	15
2	Tu	16	2	·43	22	·27	16
3	We	17	3	·48	23	·35	17
4	Th	18	4	·54	24	·44	18
5	Fr	19	5	·62	25	·54	19
6	Sa	20	6	·71	26	·65	20
7	Su	21	7	·79	27	·76	21
8	Mo	22	8	·86	1	·86	22
9	Tu	23	9	·92	2	·94	23
10	We	24	10	·96	...	...	24
11	Th	25	11	·98	3	·01	25
12	Fr	26	12	·98	4	·05	26
13	Sa	27	13	·95	5	·07	27
14	Su	28	14	·91	6	·08	28
15	Mo	29	—A	·85	7	·07	29
16	Tu	30	1	·78	8 9	·04 ·99	—30
17	We	31	2	·69	10	·93	1

SOLAR: Bahudhanya *Simha—Avani.* LUNAR: Sukla Sravana P Bahula A. H. 1295 *Shaban.* / *Ramzan.*

Cyclic Sidereal Year, Month and Day.	Week-Day	English Month and Day.	Tithi	Ending Moment.	Nakshatra	Ending Moment.	Muhammadan Year, Month and Day.
	Aug.						
18	Th	1	3	·59	11	·87	2
19	Fr	2	4	·49	12	·81	3
20	Sa	3	5	·39	13	·74	4
21	Su	4	6	·29	14	·67	5
22	Mo	5	7	·19	15	·61	6
23	Tu	6	8	·10	16	·55	7
24	We	7	9 10	·02 ·95	17	·51	8
25	Th	8	11	·91	18	·49	9
26	Fr	9	12	·89	19	·48	10
27	Sa	10	13	·88	20	·49	11
28	Su	11	14	·88	21	·52	12
29	Mo ○	12	P	·91	22	·58	13
30	Tu	13	1	·96	23	·65	14
—31	We	14	...	...	24	·74	15
1	Th	15	2	·03	25	·84	16
2	Fr	16	3	·11	26	·95	17
3	Sa	17	4	·20	...	...	18
4	Su	18	5	·28	27	·06	19
5	Mo	19	6	·35	1	·16	20
6	Tu	20	7	·41	2	·24	21
7	We	21	8	·45	3	·31	22
8	Th	22	9	·47	4	·36	23
9	Fr	23	10	·47	5	·39	24
10	Sa	24	11	·45	6	·41	25
11	Su	25	12	·41	7	·40	26
12	Mo	26	13	·36	8	·37	27
13	Tu	27	14	·29	9	·33	28
14	We	28	—A	·20	10	·27	—29
15	Th	29	1	·10	11	·21	1
16	Fr	30	2 3	·00 ·90	12	·14	2
17	Sa	31	4	·80	13	·07	3

SOLAR: Bahudhanya *Simha—Avani.* / Bahudhanya *Kanya—Purattasi.* LUNAR: Sukla Bhadrapada P Bahula A. H. 1295 *Ramzan.*

Cyclic Sidereal Year, Month and Day.	Week-Day	English Month and Day.	Tithi	Ending Moment.	Nakshatra	Ending Moment.	Muhammadan Year, Month and Day.
	Sep.						
18	Su	1	5	·70	14 15	·00 ·94	4
19	Mo	2	6	·62	16	·89	5
20	Tu	3	7	·54	17	·85	6
21	We	4	8	·48	18	·82	7
22	Th	5	9	·43	19	·80	8
23	Fr	6	10	·40	20	·81	9
24	Sa	7	11	·39	21	·84	10
25	Su	8	12	·39	22	·89	11
26	Mo	9	13	·42	23	·96	12
27	Tu	10	14	·48	...	...	13
28	We	11	P	·55	24	·04	14
29	Th	12	1	·63	25	·14	15
30	Fr	13	2	·71	26	·24	16
—31	Sa	14	3	·80	27	·35	17
1	Su	15	4	·88	1	·46	18
2	Mo	16	5	·95	2	·55	19
3	Tu	17	6	·98	3	·62	20
4	We	18	...	...	4	·68	21
5	Th	19	7	·00	5	·72	22
6	Fr	20	8 9	·00 ·98	6	·73	23
7	Sa	21	10	·95	7	·72	24
8	Su	22	11	·89	8	·70	25
9	Mo	23	12	·82	9	·66	26
10	Tu	24	13	·74	10	·61	27
11	We	25	14	·65	11	·55	28
12	Th	26	—A	·55	12	·48	29
13	Fr	27	1	·45	13	·41	—30
14	Sa	28	2	·35	14	·35	1
15	Su	29	3	·25	15	·29	2
16	Mo	30	4	·16	16	·23	3

SOLAR: Bahudhanya *Tula—Aippasi.* LUNAR: Sukla Asvina P Bahula; Kartt. Suk. A. H. 1295 *Shawal.* / *Zi-l-ka'da.*

Cyclic Sidereal Year, Month and Day.	Week-Day	English Month and Day.	Tithi	Ending Moment.	Nakshatra	Ending Moment.	Muhammadan Year, Month and Day.
	Oct.						
17	Tu	1	5	·08	17	·18	4
18	We	2	6 7	·02 ·97	18	·14	5
19	Th	3	8	·95	19	·13	6
20	Fr	4	9	·94	20	·13	7
21	Sa	5	10	·95	21	·16	8
22	Su	6	11	·98	22	·20	9
23	Mo	7	...	...	23	·26	10
24	Tu	8	12	·04	24	·34	11
25	We	9	13	·12	25	·44	12
26	Th	10	14	·20	26	·55	13
27	Fr	11	P	·29	27	·66	14
28	Sa	12	1	·37	1	·76	15
29	Su	13	2	·44	2	·85	16
30	Mo	14	3	·50	3	·93	17
—31	Tu	15	4	·54	...	...	18
1	We	16	5	·57	4	·00	19
2	Th	17	6	·57	5	·04	20
3	Fr	18	7	·55	6	·05	21
4	Sa	19	8	·52	7	·05	22
5	Su	20	9	·47	8	·03	23
6	Mo	21	10	·40	9 10	·00 ·95	24
7	Tu	22	11	·32	11	·89	25
8	We	23	12	·22	12	·82	26
9	Th	24	13	·12	13	·75	27
10	Fr	25	14 A	·02 ·92	14	·68	28
11	Sa	26	1	·82	15	·62	—29
12	Su	27	2	·74	16	·56	1
13	Mo	28	3	·67	17	·51	2
14	Tu	29	4	·61	18	·47	3
15	We	30	5	·56	19	·45	4
16	Th	31	6	·54	20	·46	5

SOLAR: Bahudhanya *Tula—Aippasi.* / Bahudhanya *Vrischika—Kartigai.* LUNAR: Sukla Kartika P Bahula A. H. 1295 *Zi-l-ka'da.*

Cyclic Sidereal Year, Month and Day.	Week-Day	English Month and Day.	Tithi	Ending Moment.	Nakshatra	Ending Moment.	Muhammadan Year, Month and Day.
	Nov.						
17	Fr	1	7	·53	21	·48	6
18	Sa	2	8	·55	22	·51	7
19	Su	3	9	·59	23	·57	8
20	Mo	4	10	·65	24	·65	9
21	Tu	5	11	·72	25	·75	10
22	We	6	12	·80	26	·85	11
23	Th	7	13	·89	27	·96	12
24	Fr	8	14	·97	...	...	13
25	Sa	9	...	...	1	·06	14
26	Su	10	P	·05	2	·16	15
27	Mo	11	1	·11	3	·25	16
28	Tu	12	2	·15	4	·31	17
29	We	13	3	·17	5	·35	18
—30	Th	14	4	·17	6	·37	19
1	Fr	15	5	·16	7	·37	20
2	Sa	16	6	·13	8	·36	21
3	Su	17	7	·08	9	·33	22
4	Mo	18	8 9	·01 ·93	10	·28	23
5	Tu	19	10	·83	11	·22	24
6	We	20	11	·73	12	·16	25
7	Th	21	12	·63	13	·09	26
8	Fr	22	13	·53	14 15	·02 ·96	27
9	Sa	23	14	·44	16	·90	28
10	Su	24	—A	·36	17	·84	29
11	Mo	25	1	·29	18	·81	—30
12	Tu	26	2	·23	19	·79	1
13	We	27	3	·19	20	·78	2
14	Th	28	4	·16	21	·79	3
15	Fr	29	5	·15	22	·82	4
16	Sa	30	6	·17	23	·88	5

SOLAR: Bahudhanya *Dhanus—Margali.* LUNAR: Sukla Margasira P Bahula A; Pausha Sukla. H. 1295 *Zi-l-hijja.* / H. 1296 *Muharram.*

Cyclic Sidereal Year, Month and Day.	Week-Day	English Month and Day.	Tithi	Ending Moment.	Nakshatra	Ending Moment.	Muhammadan Year, Month and Day.
	Dec.						
17	Su	1	7	·21	24	·96	6
18	Mo	2	8	·27	...	...	7
19	Tu	3	9	·35	25	·05	8
20	We	4	10	·43	26	·15	9
21	Th	5	11	·52	27	·25	10
22	Fr	6	12	·60	1	·36	11
23	Sa	7	13	·68	2	·46	12
24	Su	8	14	·75	3	·55	13
25	Mo	9	P	·79	4	·62	14
26	Tu	10	1	·81	5	·67	15
27	We	11	2	·82	6	·70	16
28	Th	12	3	·80	7	·71	17
—29	Fr	13	4	·76	8	·69	18
1	Sa	14	5	·70	9	·66	19
2	Su	15	6	·65	10	·62	20
3	Mo	16	7	·55	11	·56	21
4	Tu	17	8	·46	12	·50	22
5	We	18	9	·36	13	·44	23
6	Th	19	10	·26	14	·37	24
7	Fr	20	11	·16	15	·30	25
8	Sa	21	12 13	·07 ·99	16	·24	26
9	Su	22	14	·92	17	·18	27
10	Mo	23	—A	·86	18	·14	28
11	Tu	24	1	·82	19	·11	29
12	We	25	2	·80	20	·10	—30
13	Th	26	3	·81	21	·11	1
14	Fr	27	4	·85	22	·14	2
15	Sa	28	5	·87	23	·19	3
16	Su	29	6	·95	24	·26	4
17	Mo	30	...	...	25	·35	5
18	Tu	31	7	·00	26	·45	6

15. Svati. 16. Visak. 17. Anur. 18. Jyesh. 19. Mula. 20. P. Ash. 21. U. Asa. 22. Sravn. 23. Dani. 24. Satab. 25. P. Bhad. 26. U. Bhad 27. Rev'

A. D. 1879. **Mesha Sankranti** (Commencement of Indian Sidereal Year).

Solar Eclipse. ● **(Surya Sid.) April 12·19.** **Saka 1801.** ***Kaliyuga* 4980.**

Lunar Eclipse. ○ **(Arya Sid.) April 12·09.** **(S. Cycle) Pramathi.**

Jan. — Bahudhanya, *Dhanus—Margali* / Bahudhanya, *Makara—Tai*; Pausha Sukla / Bahula / Sukla; H. 1296 *Muharram*.

Cyclic Sidereal Year, Month and Day.	Week-Day	English Month and Day.	Tithi	Ending Moment.	Nakshatra	Ending Moment.	Muhammadan Year, Month and Day.
19	We	1	8	·08	27	·56	7
20	Th	2	9	·17	1	·67	8
21	Fr	3	10	·26	2	·77	9
22	Sa	4	11	·34	3	·86	10
23	Su	5	12	·40	4	·93	11
24	Mo	6	13	·44	5	·98	12
25	Tu	7	14	·46	...	...	13
26	We	8	P	·47	6	·01	14
27	Th	9	1	·45	7	·03	15
28	Fr	10	2	·41	8 9	·02 ·99	16
—29	Sa	11	3	·35	10	·95	17
1	Su	12	4	·28	11	·90	18
2	Mo	13	5	·20	12	·84	19
3	Tu	14	6	·10	13	·78	20
4	We	15	7 8	·00 ·90	14	·71	21
5	Th	16	9	·81	15	·64	22
6	Fr	17	10	·72	16	·58	23
7	Sa	18	11	·64	17	·52	24
8	Su	19	12	·56	18	·48	25
9	Mo	20	13	·50	19	·45	26
10	Tu	21	14	·46	20	·43	27
11	We ●	22	—A	·44	21	·43	28
12	Th	23	1	·45	22	·46	29
13	Fr	24	2	·47	23	·51	—30
14	Sa	25	3	·52	24	·57	1
15	Su	26	4	·58	25	·65	2
16	Mo	27	5	·66	26	·75	3
17	Tu	28	6	·74	27	·86	4
18	We	29	7	·83	1	·97	5
19	Th	30	8	·92	...	...	6
20	Fr	31	9	·99	2	·07	7

Feb. — Bahudhanya, *Kumbha—Masi*; Magha / Bahula / Phalg. Suk.; H. 1296 *Safar* / *R.-awwal*.

Cyclic Sidereal Year, Month and Day.	Week-Day	English Month and Day.	Tithi	Ending Moment.	Nakshatra	Ending Moment.	Muhammadan Year, Month and Day.
21	Sa	1	...	...	3	·16	8
22	Su	2	10	·05	4	·23	9
23	Mo	3	11	·08	5	·29	10
24	Tu	4	12	·10	6	·33	11
25	We	5	13	·10	7	·35	12
26	Th	6	14	·08	8	·35	13
27	Fr	7	P 1	·03 ·97	9	·33	14
28	Sa	8	2	·90	10	·29	15
29	Su	9	3	·32	11	·24	16
—30	Mo	10	4	·73	12	·18	17
1	Tu	11	5	·63	13	·12	18
2	We	12	6	·53	14 15	·05 ·98	19
3	Th	13	7	·43	16	·92	20
4	Fr	14	8	·34	17	·86	21
5	Sa	15	9	·26	18	·81	22
6	Su	16	10	·19	19	·77	23
7	Mo	17	11	·14	20	·75	24
8	Tu	18	12	·10	21	·76	25
9	We	19	13	·08	22	·78	26
10	Th	20	14	·07	23	·81	27
11	Fr	21	—A	·09	24	·87	28
12	Sa	22	1	·14	25	·95	—29
13	Su	23	2	·20	...	...	1
14	Mo	24	3	·28	26	·04	2
15	Tu	25	4	·37	27	·15	3
16	We	26	5	·45	1	·26	4
17	Th	27	6	·53	2	·36	5
18	Fr	28	7	·61	3	·46	6

March — Bahudhanya, *Kumbha—Masi* / Bahudhanya, *Mina—Panguni*; Sukla / Phalguna / Bahula / Sukla; H. 1296 *Rabi-ul-awwal*.

Cyclic Sidereal Year, Month and Day.	Week-Day	English Month and Day.	Tithi	Ending Moment.	Nakshatra	Ending Moment.	Muhammadan Year, Month and Day.
19	Sa	1	8	·67	4	·54	7
20	Su	2	9	·71	5	·61	8
21	Mo	3	10	·72	6	·65	9
22	Tu	4	11	·71	7	·67	10
23	We	5	12	·69	8	·67	11
24	Th	6	13	·64	9	·65	12
25	Fr	7	14	·58	10	·62	13
26	Sa	8	P	·51	11	·58	14
27	Su	9	1	·43	12	·52	15
28	Mo	10	2	·33	13	·45	16
29	Tu	11	3	·23	14	·38	17
—30	We	12	4	·13	15	·31	18
1	Th	13	5 6	·03 ·94	16	·25	19
2	Fr	14	7	·86	17	·19	20
3	Sa	15	8	·78	18	·14	21
4	Su	16	9	·72	19	·10	22
5	Mo	17	10	·68	20	·08	23
6	Tu	18	11	·67	21	·08	24
7	We	19	12	·68	22	·09	25
8	Th	20	13	·70	23	·13	26
9	Fr	21	14	·74	24	·18	27
10	Sa	22	—A	·79	25	·25	28
11	Su	23	1	·87	26	·34	29
12	Mo	24	2	·96	27	·45	—30
13	Tu	25	...	...	1	·56	1
14	We	26	3	·05	2	·67	2
15	Th	27	4	·13	3	·77	3
16	Fr	28	5	·20	4	·86	4
17	Sa	29	6	·25	5	·93	5
18	Su	30	7	·29	6	·97	6
19	Mo	31	8	·30	7	·99	7

April — Pramathi, *Mesha—Chittirai*; Chaitra / Bahula / Vaisakha Sukla; H. 1296 *Rabi-ul-akhir* / *Jumadul-awwal*.

Cyclic Sidereal Year, Month and Day.	Week-Day	English Month and Day.	Tithi	Ending Moment.	Nakshatra	Ending Moment.	Muhammadan Year, Month and Day.
20	Tu	1	9	·29	...	...	8
21	We	2	10	·27	8 9	·00 ·99	9
22	Th	3	11	·22	10	·96	10
23	Fr	4	12	·16	11	·91	11
24	Sa	5	13	·09	12	·85	12
25	Su	6	14 P	·00 ·90	13	·79	13
26	Mo	7	1	·80	14	·73	14
27	Tu	8	2	·70	15	·66	15
28	We	9	3	·60	16	·59	16
29	Th	10	4	·50	17	·53	17
—30	Fr	11	5	·41	18	·47	18
1	Sa	12	6	·34	19	·43	19
2	Su	13	7	·28	20	·41	20
3	Mo	14	8	·25	21	·40	21
4	Tu	15	9	·23	22	·41	22
5	We	16	10	·23	23	·44	23
6	Th	17	11	·25	24	·49	24
7	Fr	18	12	·29	25	·56	25
8	Sa	19	13	·35	26	·65	26
9	Su	20	14	·43	27	·75	27
10	Mo	21	—A	·51	1	·86	28
11	Tu	22	1	·59	2	·97	—29
12	We	23	2	·67	...	...	1
13	Th	24	3	·74	3	·07	2
14	Fr	25	4	·79	4	·16	3
15	Sa	26	5	·83	5	·23	4
16	Su	27	6	·84	6	·28	5
17	Mo	28	7	·83	7	·31	6
18	Tu	29	8	·80	8	·33	7
19	We	30	9	·75	9	·32	8

May — Pramathi, *Mesha—Chittirai* / Pramathi, *Vrishabha—Vaikasi*; Vaisakha Suk. / Bahula / Sukla; H. 1296 *Jumadal-awwal*.

Cyclic Sidereal Year, Month and Day.	Week-Day	English Month and Day.	Tithi	Ending Moment.	Nakshatra	Ending Moment.	Muhammadan Year, Month and Day.
20	Th	1	10	·69	10	·29	9
21	Fr	2	11	·62	11	·25	10
22	Sa	3	12	·53	12	·19	11
23	Su	4	13	·43	13	·13	12
24	Mo	5	14	·33	14	·07	13
25	Tu	6	P	·23	15 16	·00 ·93	14
26	We	7	1	·13	17	·87	15
27	Th	8	2 3	·03 ·94	18	·81	16
28	Fr	9	4	·87	19	·77	17
29	Sa	10	5	·81	20	·74	18
30	Su	11	6	·77	21	·72	19
—31	Mo	12	7	·75	22	·73	20
1	Tu	13	8	·75	23	·76	21
2	We	14	9	·76	24	·81	22
3	Th	15	10	·80	25	·88	23
4	Fr	16	11	·86	26	·96	24
5	Sa	17	12	·93	...	...	25
6	Su	18	...	...	27	·05	26
7	Mo	19	13	·01	1	·16	27
8	Tu	20	14	·10	2	·27	28
9	We	21	—A	·18	3	·37	29
10	Th	22	1	·25	4	·46	—30
11	Fr	23	2	·30	5	·54	1
12	Sa	24	3	·34	6	·59	2
13	Su	25	4	·35	7	·63	3
14	Mo	26	5	·34	8	·65	4
15	Tu	27	6	·32	9	·64	5
16	We	28	7	·27	10	·62	6
17	Th	29	8	·20	11	·58	7
18	Fr	30	9	·12	12	·53	8
19	Sa	31	10 11	·03 ·93	13	·47	9

June — Pramathi, *Mithuna—Ani*; Jyeshtha / Bahula / Sukla / Ashadha; H. 1296 *Jumadal-akhir* / H. 1296 *Rajab*.

Cyclic Sidereal Year, Month and Day.	Week-Day	English Month and Day.	Tithi	Ending Moment.	Nakshatra	Ending Moment.	Muhammadan Year, Month and Day.
20	Su	1	12	·83	14	·41	10
21	Mo	2	13	·73	15	·34	11
22	Tu	3	14	·63	16	·27	12
23	We	4	P	·53	17	·21	13
24	Th	5	1	·45	18	·15	14
25	Fr	6	2	·37	19	·10	15
26	Sa	7	3	·31	20	·07	16
27	Su	8	4	·26	21	·05	17
28	Mo	9	5	·24	22	·05	18
29	Tu	10	6	·24	23	·08	19
30	We	11	7	·25	24	·12	20
—31	Th	12	8	·29	25	·18	21
1	Fr	13	9	·34	26	·26	22
2	Sa	14	10	·40	27	·35	23
3	Su	15	11	·48	1	·46	24
4	Mo	16	12	·57	2	·57	25
5	Tu	17	13	·65	3	·67	26
6	We	18	14	·72	4	·77	27
7	Th	19	—A	·78	5	·85	28
8	Fr	20	1	·82	6	·91	—29
9	Sa	21	2	·83	7	·95	1
10	Su	22	3	·82	8	·97	2
11	Mo	23	4	·80	9	·97	3
12	Tu	24	5	·75	10	·93	4
13	We	25	6	·69	11	·92	5
14	Th	26	7	·61	12	·87	6
15	Fr	27	8	·52	13	·81	7
16	Sa	28	9	·42	14	·75	8
17	Su	29	10	·32	15	·68	9
18	Mo	30	11	·22	16	·61	10

Naksh:—1. Asvn. 2. Bhar. 3. Krit. 4. Rohi. 5. Mrig. 6. Ardh. 7. Punar. 8. Push. 9. Aslesh. 10. Magh. 11. P. Phal. 12. U. Phal. 13. Hasta. 14. Chit.

A. D. 1879. **Vikrama 1936.**

A.—Amavasya. **Kollam 1055,** Commences { **N. Malabar—Sept.** / **S. Malabar—Aug.** **Hijra 1297,** Commences, **Dec. 15.** **Bengal San 1285.**

P.—Paurnami. **(N. Cycle) Khara.**

SOLAR reckoning: Solar month	Cyclic Sidereal Year, Month and Day.	Week-Day	English Month and Day.	LUNAR reckoning: Lunar month	Tithi	Ending Moment.	Nakshatra	Ending Moment.	Muhammadan Year, Month and Day.
			July						
Pramathi Mithuna—Ani.	19	Tu	1	Ashadha	12	·11	17	·55	11
	20	We	2		13 / 14	·01 / ·93	18	·49	12
	21	Th	3		P	·85	19	·44	13
	22	Fr	4		1	·79	20	·40	14
	23	Sa	5		2	·74	21	·37	15
	24	Su	6		3	·71	22	·38	16
	25	Mo	7		4	·71	23	·39	H. 1296 Rajab. 17
	26	Tu	8		5	·72	24	·43	18
	27	We	9		6	·76	25	·48	19
	28	Th	10	Bahula	7	·81	26	·56	20
	29	Fr	11		8	·89	27	·66	21
	30	Sa	12		9	·97	1	·76	22
	31	Su	13		...	...	2	·87	23
	—32	Mo	14		10	·05	3	·97	24
Pramathi Karkata—Adi.	1	Tu	15		11	·13	...	...	25
	2	We	16		12	·20	4	·07	26
	3	Th	17		13	·26	5	·15	27
	4	Fr	18		14	·29	6	·23	28
	5	Sa ●	19		—A	·31	7	·27	29
	6	Su	20		1	·30	8	·29	—30
	7	Mo	21		2	·28	9	·29	1
	8	Tu	22		3	·23	10	·28	2
	9	We	23		4	·17	11	·26	3
	10	Th	24		5	·09	12	·21	4
	11	Fr	25	Sukla	6 / 7	·00 / ·91	13	·15	5
	12	Sa	26		8	·81	14	·09	6
	13	Su	27		9	·71	15 / 16	·02 / ·95	7
	14	Mo	28		10	·61	17	·89	8
	15	Tu	29		11	·51	18	·83	9
	16	We	30		12	·42	19	·77	10
	17	Th	31		13	·34	20	·73	11
			Aug.						
	18	Fr	1	Sravana	14	·27	21	·71	H. 1296 Shaban. 12
	19	Sa	2		P	·22	22	·70	13
	20	Su	3		1	·20	23	·71	14
	21	Mo	4		2	·19	24	·74	15
	22	Tu	5		3	·20	25	·79	16
	23	We	6		4	·24	26	·86	17
	24	Th	7		5	·29	27	·96	18
	25	Fr	8		6	·30	...	...	19
	26	Sa	9	Bahula	7	·44	1	·06	20
	27	Su	10		8	·53	2	·17	21
	28	Mo	11		9	·61	3	·27	22
	29	Tu	12		10	·68	4	·37	23
	30	We	13		11	·75	5	·47	24
	—31	Th	14		12	·77	6	·53	25
Pramathi Simha—Avani.	1	Fr	15		13	·80	7	·58	26
	2	Sa	16		14	·79	8	·61	27
	3	Su	17		—A	·77	9	·62	28
	4	Mo	18		1	·73	10	·62	—29
	5	Tu	19		2	·67	11	·59	1
	6	We	20	Sukla	3	·61	12	·54	2
	7	Th	21		4	·50	13	·48	3
	8	Fr	22	Bhadrapada	5	·40	14	·42	4
	9	Sa	23		6	·30	15	·36	5
	10	Su	24		7	·20	16	·29	6
	11	Mo	25		8	·10	17	·22	7
	12	Tu	26		9 / 10	·01 / ·92	18	·16	H. 1296 Ramzan. 8
	13	We	27		11	·85	19	·10	9
	14	Th	28		12	·78	20	·06	10
	15	Fr	29		13	·73	21	·04	11
	16	Sa	30		14	·71	22	·02	12
	17	Su	31		P	·70	23	·03	13

SOLAR reckoning: Solar month	Cyclic Sidereal Year, Month and Day.	Week-Day	English Month and Day.	LUNAR reckoning: Lunar month	Tithi	Ending Moment.	Nakshatra	Ending Moment.	Muhammadan Year, Month and Day.
			Sep.						
Pramathi Simha—Avani.	18	Mo	1	Bhadrapada	1	·72	24	·05	14
	19	Tu	2		2	·76	25	·10	15
	20	We	3		3	·81	26	·18	16
	21	Th	4		4	·87	27	·26	17
	22	Fr	5		5	·94	1	·36	18
	23	Sa	6		...	...	2	·47	19
	24	Su	7		6	·03	3	·58	20
	25	Mo	8		7	·12	4	·68	H. 1296 Ramzan. 21
	26	Tu	9		8	·20	5	·77	22
	27	We	10	Bahula	9	·26	6	·84	23
	28	Th	11		10	·30	7	·90	24
	29	Fr	12		11	·32	8	·93	25
	30	Sa	13		12	·31	9	·95	26
	31	Su	14		13	·29	10	·94	27
	—32	Mo	15		14	·25	11	·92	28
Pramathi Kanya—Purattasi.	1	Tu	16		—A	·20	12	·88	29
	2	We	17		1	·12	13	·82	—30
	3	Th	18		2 / 3	·04 / ·94	14	·76	1
	4	Fr	19		4	·84	15	·70	2
	5	Sa	20		5	·74	16	·63	3
	6	Su	21		6	·64	17	·56	4
	7	Mo	22	Sukla	7	·54	18	·50	5
	8	Tu	23		8	·45	19	·44	6
	9	We	24		9	38	20	·40	7
	10	Th	25		10	·32	21	·36	8
	11	Fr	26	Asvina	11	·27	22	·35	Shawwal. 9
	12	Sa	27		12	·25	23	·35	10
	13	Su	28		13	·24	24	·37	11
	14	Mo	29		14	·26	25	·42	12
	15	Tu	30		P	·30	26	·48	13
			Oct.						
	16	We	1	Adhika	1	·35	27	·56	H. 1296 14
	17	Th	2		2	·42	1	·66	15
	18	Fr	3		3	·50	2	·76	16
	19	Sa	4		4	·58	3	·87	17
	20	Su	5		5	·66	4	·98	18
	21	Mo	6		6	·74	...	...	19
	22	Tu	7	Bahula	7	·80	5	·07	20
	23	We	8		8	·85	6	·15	21
	24	Th	9		9	·88	7	·21	22
	25	Fr	10		10	·88	8	·26	23
	26	Sa	11		11	·86	9	·27	24
	27	Su	12		12	·82	10	·27	25
	28	Mo	13		13	·76	11	·25	26
	29	Tu	14		14	·68	12	·21	27
	—31	We	15		—A	·60	13	·16	28
Pramathi Tula—Aippasi.	1	Th	16		1	·51	14	·11	—29
	2	Fr	17		2	·41	15 / 16	·04 / ·97	1
	3	Sa	18	Sukla	3	·31	17	·90	2
	4	Su	19		4	·21	18	·83	3
	5	Mo	20		5	·11	19	·78	4
	6	Tu	21		6 / 7	·03 / ·96	20	·73	H. 1296 Zi-l-ka'da. 5
	7	We	22		8	·90	21	·69	6
	8	Th	23		9	·85	22	·67	7
	9	Fr	24	Nija Asvina	10	·81	23	·67	8
	10	Sa	25		11	·83	24	·69	9
	11	Su	26		12	·84	25	·73	10
	12	Mo	27		13	·88	26	·79	11
	13	Tu	28		14	·95	27	·87	12
	14	We	29		...	...	1	·96	13
	15	Th	30		P	·02	...	...	14
	16	Fr	31		1	·10	2	·07	15

SOLAR reckoning: Solar month	Cyclic Sidereal Year, Month and Day.	Week-Day	English Month and Day.	LUNAR reckoning: Lunar month	Tithi	Ending Moment.	Nakshatra	Ending Moment.	Muhammadan Year, Month and Day.
			Nov.						
Pramathi Tula—Aippasi.	17	Sa	1	Nija Asvina	2	·18	3	·18	16
	18	Su	2		3	·27	4	·28	17
	19	Mo	3		4	·35	5	·38	18
	20	Tu	4		5	·41	6	·46	19
	21	We	5		6	·45	7	·53	20
	22	Th	6		7	·47	8	·57	21
	23	Fr	7		8	·47	9	·59	22
	24	Sa	8		9	·45	10	·59	H. 1296 Zi-l-ka'da. 23
	25	Su	9		10	·42	11	·58	24
	26	Mo	10	Bahula	11	·36	12	·54	25
	27	Tu	11		12	·29	13	·50	26
	28	We	12		13	·20	14	·44	27
	29	Th	13		14	·11	15	·38	28
	—30	Fr	14		A / 1	·02 / ·92	16	·31	29
Pramathi Vrischika—Kartigai.	1	Sa	15		2	·82	17	·24	—30
	2	Su	16		3	·73	18	·18	1
	3	Mo	17		4	·65	19	·12	2
	4	Tu	18		5	·57	20	·06	3
	5	We	19		6	·51	21	·02	4
	6	Th	20	Sukla	7	·46	22	·00	5
	7	Fr	21		8	·44	23	·00	6
	8	Sa	22		9	·45	24	·01	7
	9	Su	23		10	·47	25	·04	8
	10	Mo	24		11	·51	26	·10	9
	11	Tu	25	Kartika	12	·57	27	·17	10
	12	We	26		13	·65	1	27	Zi-l-hijja. 11
	13	Th	27		14	·73	2	·37	12
	14	Fr	28		P	·81	3	·47	13
	15	Sa	29		1	·89	4	·58	14
	16	Su	30		2	·97	5	·68	15
			Dec.						
	17	Mo	1		...	...	6	·76	H. 1296 16
	18	Tu	2		3	·04	7	·84	17
	19	We	3		4	·08	8	·89	18
	20	Th	4	Bahula	5	·10	9	·91	19
	21	Fr	5		6	·10	10	·92	20
	22	Sa	6		7	·08	11	·90	21
	23	Su	7		8 / 9	·04 / ·98	12	·88	22
	24	Mo	8		10	·91	13	·84	23
	25	Tu	9		11	·82	14	·78	24
	26	We	10		12	·73	15	·72	25
	27	Th	11		13	·64	16	·66	26
	28	Fr	12		14	·54	17	·59	27
	—29	Sa	13		—A	·44	18	·52	28
Pramathi Dhanus—Margali.	1	Su	14		1	·35	19	·45	—29
	2	Mo	15		2	·27	20	·40	1
	3	Tu	16		3	·20	21	35	2
	4	We	17		4	·15	22	·33	3
	5	Th	18	Sukla	5	·11	23	·32	4
	6	Fr	19		6	·09	24	·33	5
	7	Sa	20		7	·08	25	·36	6
	8	Su	21		8	·11	26	·41	7
	9	Mo	22		9	·15	27	·48	8
	10	Tu	23	Margasira	10	·21	1	·57	H. 1297 Muharram. 9
	11	We	24		11	·29	2	·67	10
	12	Th	25		12	·38	3	·77	11
	13	Fr	26		13	·47	4	·88	12
	14	Sa	27		14	·56	5	·98	13
	15	Su ◯	28		P	·63	...	...	14
	16	Mo	29	Bah.	1	·69	6	·08	15
	17	Tu	30		2	·73	7	·15	16
	18	We	31		3	·75	8	·20	17

15. Svati. 16. Visak. 17. Anur. 18. Jyesh. 19. Mula. 20. P. Ash. 21. U. Asu. 22. Sravn. 23. Dani. 24. Satab. 25. P. Bund. 26 U. Bund 27. Rev.

A. D. 1880. **Mesha Sankranti** (Commencement of Indian Sidereal Year).

Solar Eclipse. ● **(Surya Sid.) April 11·44.** **Saka 1802.** **Kaliyuga 4981.**

Lunar Eclipse. ○ **(Arya Sid.) April 11·34.** **(S. Cycle) Vikrama.**

Columns: SOLAR reckoning (Cyclic Sidereal Year, Month and Day; Week-Day; English Month and Day) — LUNAR reckoning (Tithi, Ending Moment; Nakshatra, Ending Moment) — Muhammadan Year, Month and Day.

Jan. (Solar: Pramathi Dhanus—Marguli; Pramathi Makara—Tai. Lunar: Margasira Bahula; Sukla; Paushu. Muhammadan: H. 1297 Muharram; H. 1297 Safar.)

Cyclic Sidereal Year, Month and Day	Week-Day	English Month and Day	Tithi	Ending Moment	Nakshatra	Ending Moment	Muhammadan Year, Month and Day
19	Th	1	4	·74	9	·23	18
20	Fr	2	5	·72	10	·24	19
21	Sa	3	6	·69	11	·24	20
22	Su	4	7	·63	12	·21	21
23	Mo	5	8	·55	13	·17	22
24	Tu	6	9	·47	14	·12	23
25	We	7	10	·39	15	·06	24
26	Th	8	11	·29	16 17	·00 ·93	25
27	Fr	9	12	·19	18	·86	26
28	Sa	10	13	·09	19	·79	27
29	Su	11	14 A	·00 ·92	20	·73	28
—30	Mo	12	1	·85	21	·68	29
1	Tu	13	2	·79	22	·66	—30
2	We	14	3	·75	23	·65	1
3	Th	15	4	·74	24	·65	2
4	Fr	16	5	·75	25	·67	3
5	Sa	17	6	·77	26	·71	4
6	Su	18	7	·81	27	·79	5
7	Mo	19	8	·88	1	·87	6
8	Tu	20	9	·95	2	·97	7
9	We	21	...	...	...	...	8
10	Th	22	10	·03	3	·07	9
11	Fr	23	11	·12	4	·18	10
12	Sa	24	12	·21	5	·29	11
13	Su	25	13	·28	6	·38	12
14	Mo	26	14	·33	7	·46	13
15	Tu	27	P	·37	8	·51	14
16	We	28	1	·39	9	·55	15
17	Th	29	2	·38	10	·57	16
18	Fr	30	3	·36	11	·57	17
19	Sa	31	4	·33	12	·54	18

Feb. (Solar: Pramathi Kumbha—Masi. Lunar: Bahula; Sukla; Maghu; Bah. Muhammadan: H. 1297 Rabi-ul-awwal.)

Cyclic Sidereal Year, Month and Day	Week-Day	English Month and Day	Tithi	Ending Moment	Nakshatra	Ending Moment	Muhammadan Year, Month and Day
20	Su	1	5	·26	13	·50	19
21	Mo	2	6	·18	14	·45	20
22	Tu	3	7	·10	15	·40	21
23	We	4	8 9	·01 ·91	16	·33	22
24	Th	5	10	·31	17	·26	23
25	Fr	6	11	·72	18	·19	24
26	Sa	7	12	·63	19	·13	25
27	Su	8	13	·54	20	·07	26
28	Mo	9	14	·47	21 22	·03 ·99	27
—29	Tu	10	—A	·42	23	·97	28
1	We	11	1	·39	24	·97	—29
2	Th	12	2	·37	25	·99	1
3	Fr	13	3	·37	...	...	2
4	Sa	14	4	·40	26	·03	3
5	Su	15	5	·44	27	·09	4
6	Mo	16	6	·50	1	·17	5
7	Tu	17	7	·58	2	·27	6
8	We	18	8	·67	3	·37	7
9	Th	19	9	·75	4	·48	8
10	Fr	20	10	·83	5	·59	9
11	Sa	21	11	·91	6	·68	10
12	Su	22	12	·97	7	·76	11
13	Mo	23	...	...	8	·82	12
14	Tu	24	13	·01	9	·87	13
15	We	25	14	·02	10	·89	14
16	Th	26	P 1	·01 ·98	11	·89	15
17	Fr	27	2	·94	12	·87	16
18	Sa	28	3	·88	13	·84	17
19	Su	29	4	·80	14	·79	18

March (Solar: Pramathi Kumbha—Masi; Pramathi Mina—Panguni. Lunar: Mag. Bahula; Sukla; Phalguna. Muhammadan: H. 1297 Rabi-ul-awwal; H. 1297 Rabi-ul-akhir.)

Cyclic Sidereal Year, Month and Day	Week-Day	English Month and Day	Tithi	Ending Moment	Nakshatra	Ending Moment	Muhammadan Year, Month and Day
20	Mo	1	5	·72	15	·74	19
21	Tu	2	6	·63	16	·67	20
22	We	3	7	·53	17	·60	21
23	Th	4	8	·43	18	·53	22
24	Fr	5	9	·33	19	·46	23
25	Sa	6	10	·24	20	·41	24
26	Su	7	11	·15	21	·36	25
27	Mo	8	12	·08	22	·32	26
28	Tu	9	13 14	·02 ·99	23	·30	27
29	We	10	—A	·97	24	·29	28
30	Th	11	1	·97	25	·31	29
—31	Fr	12	...	...	26	·35	—30
1	Sa	13	2	·00	27	·40	1
2	Su	14	3	·04	1	·47	2
3	Mo	15	4	·10	2	·56	3
4	Tu	16	5	·18	3	·67	4
5	We	17	6	·27	4	·78	5
6	Th	18	7	·36	5	·89	6
7	Fr	19	8	·44	6	·98	7
8	Sa	20	9	·51	...	...	8
9	Su	21	10	·56	7	·07	9
10	Mo	22	11	·60	8	·14	10
11	Tu	23	12	·61	9	·19	11
12	We	24	13	·60	10	·21	12
13	Th	25	14	·57	11	·22	13
14	Fr	26	P	·52	12	·20	14
15	Sa	27	1	·46	13	·17	15
16	Su	28	2	·39	14	·13	16
17	Mo	29	3	·30	15	·08	17
18	Tu	30	4	·20	16 17	·01 ·94	18
19	We	31	5	·10	18	·87	19

April (Solar: Vikrama Meshu—Chittirai. Lunar: Bahula; Sukla; Chaitra; Bahula. Muhammadan: H. 1297 Jumadal-awwal.)

Cyclic Sidereal Year, Month and Day	Week-Day	English Month and Day	Tithi	Ending Moment	Nakshatra	Ending Moment	Muhammadan Year, Month and Day
20	Th	1	6 7	·00 ·90	19	·81	20
21	Fr	2	8	·81	20	·75	21
22	Sa	3	9	·73	21	·69	22
23	Su	4	10	·66	22	·65	23
24	Mo	5	11	·60	23	·62	24
25	Tu	6	12	·56	24	·62	25
26	We	7	13	·54	25	·63	26
27	Th	8	14	·54	26	·66	27
28	Fr	9	—A	·56	27	·71	28
—29	Sa	10	1	·60	1	·78	—29
1	Su	11	2	·67	2	·88	1
2	Mo	12	3	·75	3	·98	2
3	Tu	13	4	·83	...	...	3
4	We	14	5	·91	4	·08	4
5	Th	15	...	...	5	·19	5
6	Fr	16	6	·00	6	·29	6
7	Sa	17	7	·07	7	·37	7
8	Su	18	8	·12	8	·45	8
9	Mo	19	9	·15	9	·50	9
10	Tu	20	10	·16	10	·53	10
11	We	21	11	·15	11	·54	11
12	Th	22	12	·11	12	·53	12
13	Fr	23	13	·06	13	·51	13
14	Sa	24	14 P	·00 ·93	14	·47	14
15	Su	25	1	·84	15	·41	15
16	Mo	26	2	·74	16	·35	16
17	Tu	27	3	·64	17	·29	17
18	We	28	4	·54	18	·22	18
19	Th	29	5	·44	19	·15	19
20	Fr	30	6	·34	20	·08	20

May (Solar: Vikrama Meshu—Chittirai; Vikrama Vrishabha—Vaikasi. Lunar: Bah. Chaitra; Sukla; Vaisakha; Bahula. Muhammadan: H. 1297 Jumadal-awwal; H. 1297 Jumadal-akhir.)

Cyclic Sidereal Year, Month and Day	Week-Day	English Month and Day	Tithi	Ending Moment	Nakshatra	Ending Moment	Muhammadan Year, Month and Day
21	Sa	1	7	·26	21 22	·03 ·98	21
22	Su	2	8	·19	23	·96	22
23	Mo	3	9	·14	24	·94	23
24	Tu	4	10	·10	25	·95	24
25	We	5	11	·07	26	·97	25
26	Th	6	12	·06	...	...	26
27	Fr	7	13	·09	27	·02	27
28	Sa	8	14	·14	1	·09	28
29	Su	9	—A	·19	2	·18	29
30	Mo	10	1	·26	3	·27	—30
—31	Tu	11	2	·34	4	·38	1
1	We	12	3	·43	5	·49	2
2	Th	13	4	·51	6	·59	3
3	Fr	14	5	·58	7	·69	4
4	Sa	15	6	·63	8	·76	5
5	Su	16	7	·66	9	·81	6
6	Mo	17	8	·68	10	·85	7
7	Tu	18	9	·66	11	·86	8
8	We	19	10	·63	12	·86	9
9	Th	20	11	·58	13	·84	10
10	Fr	21	12	·52	14	·89	11
11	Sa	22	13	·44	15	·75	12
12	Su	23	14	·35	16	·69	13
13	Mo	24	P	·25	17	·63	14
14	Tu	25	1	·15	18	·56	15
15	We	26	2 3	·05 ·95	19	·49	16
16	Th	27	4	·86	20	·42	17
17	Fr	28	5	·77	21	·36	18
18	Sa	29	6	·70	22	·32	19
19	Su	30	7	·64	23	·29	20
20	Mo	31	8	·59	24	·27	21

June (Solar: Vikrama Mithuna—Ani. Lunar: Sukla; Jyeshtha; Bahula. Muhammadan: H. 1297 Rajab.)

Cyclic Sidereal Year, Month and Day	Week-Day	English Month and Day	Tithi	Ending Moment	Nakshatra	Ending Moment	Muhammadan Year, Month and Day
21	Tu	1	9	·57	25	·27	22
22	We	2	10	·56	26	·29	23
23	Th	3	11	·59	27	·33	24
24	Fr	4	12	·63	1	·40	25
25	Sa	5	13	·68	2	·48	26
26	Su	6	14	·76	3	·57	27
27	Mo	7	—A	·84	4	·68	28
28	Tu	8	1	·92	5	·79	—29
29	We	9	...	...	6	·90	1
30	Th	10	2	·00	7	·99	2
31	Fr	11	3	·07	...	...	3
—32	Sa	12	4	·11	8	·07	4
1	Su	13	5	·14	9	·13	5
2	Mo	14	6	·16	10	·16	6
3	Tu	15	7	·15	11	·19	7
4	We	16	8	·12	12	·19	8
5	Th	17	9	·08	13	·17	9
6	Fr	18	10 11	·02 ·94	14	·13	10
7	Sa	19	12	·85	15	·08	11
8	Su	20	13	·75	16 17	·03 ·97	12
9	Mo	21	14	·65	18	·90	13
10	Tu ○	22	P	·54	19	·83	14
11	We	23	1	·44	20	·76	15
12	Th	24	2	·34	21	·70	16
13	Fr	25	3	·25	22	·65	17
14	Sa	26	4	·18	23	·62	18
15	Su	27	5	·12	24	·59	19
16	Mo	28	6	·07	25	·59	20
17	Tu	29	7	·05	26	·60	21
18	We	30	8	·04	27	·65	22

Naksh :—1. Asvn. 2. Bhar. 3. Krit. 4. Rohi. 5. Mrig. 6. Ardh. 7. Punar. 8. Push. 9. Aslesh. 10. Magh. 11. P. Phal. 12. U. Phal. 13. Hasta. 14. Chit.

A. D. 1880.
A.—Amavasya. **P.—Paurnami.**
Kollam 1056, Commences { **N. Malabar—Sept.** **S. Malabar—Aug.**
Hijra 1298, Commences, **Dec. 4.**
Vikrama 1937. **Bengal San 1286.** **(N. Cycle) Nandana.**

Solar: Vikrama Mithuna—Ani; Vikrama Karkata—Adi; Vikrama Simha—Avani. Lunar: Jy. Bahula; Sukla; Ashadha; Bahula; Sukla; Sravana; Bahula. Muhammadan: H. 1297 Rajab; H. 1297 Shaban; H. 1297 Ramzan.

SOLAR reckoning: Cyclic Sidereal Year, Month and Day.	Week-Day	English Month and Day.	LUNAR reckoning: Tithi	Ending Moment.	Nakshatra	Ending Moment.	Muhammadan Year, Month and Day.
		July					
19	Th	1	9	·06	1	·71	23
20	Fr	2	10	·10	2	·78	24
21	Sa	3	11	·16	3	·87	25
22	Su	4	12	·23	4	·97	26
23	Mo	5	13	·31	...	...	27
24	Tu	6	14	·39	5	·03	28
25	We	7	—A	·47	6	·19	29
26	Th	8	1	·54	7	·29	30
27	Fr	9	2	·59	8	·37	1
28	Sa	10	3	·62	9	·44	2
29	Su	11	4	·63	10	·49	3
30	Mo	12	5	·63	11	·51	4
—31	Tu	13	6	·6)	12	·51	5
1	We	14	7	·55	13	·50	6
2	Th	15	8	·49	14	·47	7
3	Fr	16	9	·41	15	·43	8
4	Sa	17	10	·33	16	·37	9
5	Su	18	11	·22	17	·30	10
6	Mo	19	12	·12	18	·23	11
7	Tu	20	13; 14	·02; ·92	19	·16	12
8	We	21	P	·82	20	·09	13
9	Th	22	1	·73	21; 22	·04; ·99	14
10	Fr	23	2	·65	23	·95	15
11	Sa	24	3	·59	24	·92	16
12	Su	25	4	·55	25	·91	17
13	Mo	26	5	·53	26	·93	18
14	Tu	27	6	·52	27	·96	19
15	We	28	7	·54	...	...	20
16	Th	29	8	·58	1	·01	21
17	Fr	30	9	·63	2	·08	22
18	Sa	31	10	·69	3	·17	23
		Aug.					
19	Su	1	11	·77	4	·28	24
20	Mo	2	12	·86	5	·39	25
21	Tu	3	13	·95	6	·49	26
22	We	4	...	...	7	·59	27
23	Th	5	14	·02	8	·68	28
24	Fr	6	—A	·07	9	·76	—29
25	Sa	7	1	·11	10	·80	1
26	Su	8	2	·12	11	·83	2
27	Mo	9	3	·11	12	·84	3
28	Tu	10	4	·08	13	·83	4
29	We	11	5; 6	·04; ·99	14	·80	5
30	Th	12	7	·91	15	·76	6
31	Fr	13	8	·82	16	·71	7
—32	Sa	14	9	·72	17	·64	8
1	Su	15	10	·62	18	·57	9
2	Mo	16	11	·52	19	·50	10
3	Tu	17	12	·42	20	·44	11
4	We	18	13	·32	21	·38	12
5	Th	19	14	·24	22	·32	13
6	Fr	20	P	·16	23	·28	14
7	Sa	21	1	·10	24	·25	15
8	Su	22	2	·05	25	·24	16
9	Mo	23	3	·02	26	·25	17
10	Tu	24	4	·02	27	·27	18
11	We	25	5	·04	1	·32	19
12	Th	26	6	·08	2	·39	20
13	Fr	27	7	·13	3	·48	21
14	Sa	28	8	·20	4	·58	22
15	Su	29	9	·28	5	·69	23
16	Mo	30	10	·36	6	·79	24
17	Tu	31	11	·45	7	·89	25

Solar: Vikrama Simha—Avani; Vikrama Kanya—Purattasi; Vikrama Tula—Aippasi. Lunar: Bah.; Sukla; Bhadrapada; Bahula; Sukla; Asvina; Bahula. Muhammadan: Ramzan; H. 1297 Shawwal; H. 1297 Zi-l-ka'da.

SOLAR reckoning: Cyclic Sidereal Year, Month and Day.	Week-Day	English Month and Day.	LUNAR reckoning: Tithi	Ending Moment.	Nakshatra	Ending Moment.	Muhammadan Year, Month and Day.
		Sep.					
18	We	1	12	·52	8	·99	26
19	Th	2	13	·58	...	...	27
20	Fr	3	14	·61	9	·06	28
21	Sa	4	—A	·63	10	·12	29
22	Su	5	1	·63	11	·15	—30
23	Mo	6	2	·60	12	·16	1
24	Tu	7	3	·56	13	·15	2
25	We	8	4	·50	14	·14	3
26	Th	9	5	·43	15	·10	4
27	Fr	10	6	·34	16; 17	·04; ·98	5
28	Sa	11	7	·24	18	·92	6
29	Su	12	8	·14	19	·85	7
30	Mo	13	9; 10	·04; ·94	20	·78	8
—31	Tu	14	11	·85	21	·71	9
1	We	15	12	·77	22	·66	10
2	Th	16	13	·69	23	·61	11
3	Fr	17	14	·63	24	·58	12
4	Sa	18	P	·58	25	·57	13
5	Su	19	1	·55	26	·57	14
6	Mo	20	2	·55	27	·59	15
7	Tu	21	3	·57	1	·63	16
8	We	22	4	·61	2	·70	17
9	Th	23	5	·66	3	·78	18
10	Fr	24	6	·73	4	·88	19
11	Sa	25	7	·82	5	·98	20
12	Su	26	8	·91	...	...	21
13	Mo	27	9	·99	6	·09	22
14	Tu	28	...	...	7	·19	23
15	We	29	10	·06	8	·29	24
16	Th	30	11	·12	9	·37	25
		Oct.					
17	Fr	1	12	·15	10	·43	26
18	Sa	2	13	·17	11	·47	27
19	Su	3	14	·17	12	·48	28
20	Mo	4	—A	·15	13	·49	—29
21	Tu	5	1	·12	14	·47	1
22	We	6	2; 3	·06; ·98	15	·43	2
23	Th	7	4	·89	16	·38	3
24	Fr	8	5	·80	17	·32	4
25	Sa	9	6	·71	18	·26	5
26	Su	10	7	·61	19	·19	6
27	Mo	11	8	·51	20	·12	7
28	Tu	12	9	·41	21; 22	·05; ·99	8
29	We	13	10	·33	23	·95	9
—30	Th	14	11	·26	24	·91	10
1	Fr	15	12	·20	25	·89	11
2	Sa	16	13	·15	26	·89	12
3	Su	17	14	·13	27	·90	—13
4	Mo	18	P	·12	1	·95	14
5	Tu	19	1	·14	...	...	15
6	We	20	2	·15	2	·01	16
7	Th	21	3	·24	3	·09	17
8	Fr	22	4	·31	4	·18	18
9	Sa	23	5	·39	5	·28	19
10	Su	24	6	·49	6	·39	20
11	Mo	25	7	·57	7	·50	21
12	Tu	26	8	·65	8	·60	22
13	We	27	9	·70	9	·63	23
14	Th	28	10	·74	10	·74	24
15	Fr	29	11	·77	11	·78	25
16	Sa	30	12	·76	12	·81	26
17	Su	31	13	·74	13	·81	27

Solar: Vikrama Tula—Aippasi; Vikrama Vrischika—Karttigai; Vikrama Dhanus—Margali. Lunar: Sukla; Karttika; Bahula; Sukla; Margasira; Bahula. Muhammadan: H. 1297 Zi-l-hijja; H. 1298 Muharram.

SOLAR reckoning: Cyclic Sidereal Year, Month and Day.	Week-Day	English Month and Day.	LUNAR reckoning: Tithi	Ending Moment.	Nakshatra	Ending Moment.	Muhammadan Year, Month and Day.
		Nov.					
18	Mo	1	14	·70	14	·80	28
19	Tu	2	—A	·65	15	·76	29
20	We	3	1	·57	16	·71	—30
21	Th	4	2	·48	17	·66	1
22	Fr	5	3	·39	18	·60	2
23	Sa	6	4	·29	19	·53	3
24	Su	7	5	·19	20	·46	4
25	Mo	8	6	·09	21	·40	5
26	Tu	9	7; 8	·01; ·93	22	·34	6
27	We	10	9	·86	23	·28	7
28	Th	11	10	·79	24	·24	8
29	Fr	12	11	·75	25	·22	9
—30	Sa	13	12	·74	26	·21	10
1	Su	14	13	·74	27	·22	11
2	Mo	15	14	·75	1	·26	12
3	Tu	16	P	·79	2	·32	13
4	We	17	1	·86	3	·39	14
5	Th	18	2	·94	4	·48	15
6	Fr	19	...	...	5	·58	16
7	Sa	20	3	·02	6	·69	17
8	Su	21	4	·11	7	·80	18
9	Mo	22	5	·19	8	·90	19
10	Tu	23	6	·27	9	·98	20
11	We	24	7	·33	...	...	21
12	Th	25	8	·37	10	·05	22
13	Fr	26	9	·39	11	·11	23
14	Sa	27	10	·38	12	·13	24
15	Su	28	11	·36	13	·14	25
16	Mo	29	12	·32	14	·12	26
17	Tu	30	13	·27	15	·09	27
		Dec.					
18	We	1	14	·19	16	·06	28
19	Th	2	—A	·11	17; 18	·00; ·94	29
20	Fr	3	1; 2	·02; ·92	19	·87	—30
21	Sa	4	3	·82	20	·80	1
22	Su	5	4	·72	21	·74	2
23	Mo	6	5	·63	22	·68	3
24	Tu	7	6	·55	23	·62	4
25	We	8	7	·48	24	·57	5
26	Th	9	8	·42	25	·54	6
27	Fr	10	9	·38	26	·53	7
28	Sa	11	10	·37	27	·55	8
29	Su	12	11	·37	1	·58	9
—30	Mo	13	12	·39	2	·63	10
1	Tu	14	13	·44	3	·69	11
2	We	15	14	·51	4	·78	12
3	Th ○	16	P	·59	5	·88	13
4	Fr	17	1	·68	6	·99	14
5	Sa	18	2	·76	...	...	15
6	Su	19	3	·84	7	·10	16
7	Mo	20	4	·91	8	·20	17
8	Tu	21	5	·97	9	·29	18
9	We	22	...	...	10	·37	19
10	Th	23	6	·01	11	·42	20
11	Fr	24	7	·02	12	·45	21
12	Sa	25	8	·03	13	·46	22
13	Su	26	9; 10	·00; ·96	14	·45	23
14	Mo	27	11	·91	15	·43	24
15	Tu	28	12	·83	16	·39	25
16	We	29	13	·75	17	·33	26
17	Th	30	14	·66	18	·27	27
18	Fr	31	—A	·56	19	·21	28

15. Svati. 16. Visak. 17. Anur. 18. Jyesh. 19. Mula. 20. P. Ash. 21. U. Ash. 22. Sravn. 23. Dani. 24. Satab. 25. P. Bhad. 26. U. Bhad. 27. Rev.

A. D. 1881. **Mesha Sankranti** (Commencement of Indian Sidereal Year).

Solar Eclipse. ● **(Surya Sid.) April 11·70.** **Saka 1803.** **Kaliyuga 4982.**

Lunar Eclipse. ○ **(Arya Sid.) April 11·60.** **(S. Cycle) Vrisha.**

SOLAR reckoning: Cyclic Sidereal Year, Month and Day.	Week-Day	English Month and Day.	LUNAR reckoning: Tithi	Ending Moment.	Nakshatra	Ending Moment.	Muhammadan Year, Month and Day.
	Jan.						
Vikrama Dhanus—Margali. 19	Sa	1	Pausha Sukla 1	·46	20	·14	29
20	Su	2	2	·36	21	·07	—30
21	Mo	3	3	·28	22 / 23	·01 / ·95	H. 1298 Safar. 1
22	Tu	4	4	·20	24	·90	2
23	We	5	5	·13	25	·87	3
24	Th	6	6	·07	26	·87	4
25	Fr	7	7	·03	27	·87	5
26	Sa	8	8	·01	1	·89	6
27	Su	9	9	·02	2	·93	7
28	Mo	10	10	·04	...	...	8
—29	Tu	11	11	·09	3	·00	9
1	We	12	12	·16	4	·09	10
2	Th	13	13	·24	5	·19	11
3	Fr	14	14	·32	6	·29	12
4	Sa	15	P	·41	7	·40	13
5	Su	16	Bahula 1	·50	8	·50	14
6	Mo	17	2	·57	9	·60	15
7	Tu	18	3	·62	10	·68	16
8	We	19	4	·66	11	·73	17
9	Th	20	5	·67	12	·77	18
10	Fr	21	6	·67	13	·78	19
11	Sa	22	7	·65	14	·78	20
12	Su	23	8	·61	15	·76	21
13	Mo	24	9	·54	16	·72	22
14	Tu	25	10	·46	17	·67	23
15	We	26	11	·38	18	·61	24
Vikrama Makara—Tai. 16	Th	27	12	·29	19	·55	25
17	Fr	28	13	·19	20	·48	26
18	Sa	29	14	·09	21	·41	27
19	Su	30	A / 1	·00 / 91	22	·35	28
20	Mo	31	2	·83	23	·29	—29
	Feb.						
21	Tu	1	Magha Sukla 3	·70	24	·24	1
22	We	2	4	·71	25	·21	2
23	Th	3	5	·67	26	·19	3
24	Fr	4	6	·65	27	·19	4
25	Sa	5	7	·65	1	·21	5
26	Su	6	8	·68	2	·24	6
27	Mo	7	9	·74	3	·31	7
28	Tu	8	10	·80	4	·39	8
—29	We	9	11	·88	5	·49	9
1	Th	10	12	·96	6	·59	H. 1298 Rabi-ul-awwal. 10
2	Fr	11	...	...	7	·69	11
3	Sa	12	13	·05	8	·80	12
4	Su	13	14	·14	9	·90	13
5	Mo	14	P	·21	10	·98	14
6	Tu	15	Bahula 1	·26	...	...	15
7	We	16	2	·29	11	·04	16
8	Th	17	3	·31	12	·08	17
9	Fr	18	4	·30	13	·10	18
10	Sa	19	5	·27	14	·11	19
Vikrama Kumbha—Masi. 11	Su	20	6	·22	15	·09	20
12	Mo	21	7	·15	16	·06	21
13	Tu	22	8	·08	17 / 18	·01 / ·95	22
14	We	23	9 / 10	·00 / ·91	19	·89	23
15	Th	24	11	·81	20	·82	24
16	Fr	25	12	·71	21	·75	25
17	Sa	26	13	·61	22	·68	26
18	Su	27	14	·52	23	·62	27
19	Mo	28	—A	·44	24	·58	28

SOLAR reckoning: Cyclic Sidereal Year, Month and Day.	Week-Day	English Month and Day.	LUNAR reckoning: Tithi	Ending Moment.	Nakshatra	Ending Moment.	Muhammadan Year, Month and Day.
	March						
20	Tu	1	Phalguna Sukla 1	·34	25	·54	29
21	We	2	2	·32	26	·52	—30
Vikrama Kumbha—Masi. 22	Th	3	3	·29	27	·51	H. 1298 Rabi-ul-akhir. 1
23	Fr	4	4	·27	1	·52	2
24	Sa	5	5	·26	2	·57	3
25	Su	6	6	·29	3	·62	4
26	Mo	7	7	·35	4	·69	5
27	Tu	8	8	·42	5	·78	6
28	We	9	9	·50	6	·88	7
29	Th	10	10	·58	7	·99	8
—30	Fr	11	11	·67	...	...	9
1	Sa	12	12	·75	8	·10	10
2	Su	13	13	·81	9	·20	11
3	Mo	14	14	·86	10	·29	12
4	Tu	15	P	·89	11	·35	13
5	We	16	Bahula 1	·90	12	·41	14
6	Th	17	2	·89	13	·43	15
7	Fr	18	3	·86	14	·44	16
8	Sa	19	4	·82	15	·42	17
9	Su	20	5	·76	16	·39	18
10	Mo	21	6	·68	17	·35	19
11	Tu	22	7	·59	18	·30	20
12	We	23	8	·50	19	·23	21
13	Th	24	9	·40	20	·16	22
14	Fr	25	10	·30	21	·09	23
15	Sa	26	11	·20	22 / 23	·03 / ·97	24
Vikrama Mina—Panguni. 16	Su	27	12	·11	24	·91	25
17	Mo	28	13 / 14	·02 / ·95	25	·87	26
18	Tu	29	—A	·90	26	·84	27
19	We	30	1	·86	27	·83	28
20	Th	31	2	·85	1	·85	—29
	April						
21	Fr	1	Chaitra Sukla 3	·65	2	·88	1
22	Sa	2	4	·88	3	·93	2
23	Su	3	5	·92	...	...	3
24	Mo	4	6	·99	4	·00	4
25	Tu	5	...	...	5	·09	5
26	We	6	7	·07	6	·19	6
27	Th	7	8	·15	7	·30	7
28	Fr	8	9	·24	8	·41	8
29	Sa	9	10	·32	9	·51	9
30	Su	10	11	·38	10	·59	H. 1298 Jumadal-awwal. 10
—31	Mo	11	12	·43	11	·67	11
1	Tu	12	13	·46	12	·72	12
2	We	13	14	·46	13	·75	13
3	Th	14	P	·45	14	·76	14
4	Fr	15	Bahula 1	·42	15	·75	15
5	Sa	16	2	·37	16	·72	16
6	Su	17	3	·31	17	·69	17
7	Mo	18	4	·24	18	·63	18
8	Tu	19	5	·15	19	·57	19
Vrisha Mesha—Chittirai. 9	We	20	6 / 7	·05 / ·95	20	·50	20
10	Th	21	8	·85	21	·43	21
11	Fr	22	9	·75	22	·37	22
12	Sa	23	10	·65	23	·31	23
13	Su	24	11	·57	24	·25	24
14	Mo	25	12	·50	25	·20	25
15	Tu	26	13	·44	26	·17	26
16	We	27	14	·41	27	·16	27
17	Th	28	—A	·39	1	·17	28
18	Fr	29	Suk. 1	·38	2	·19	29
19	Sa	30	2	·41	3	·24	—30

SOLAR reckoning: Cyclic Sidereal Year, Month and Day.	Week-Day	English Month and Day.	LUNAR reckoning: Tithi	Ending Moment.	Nakshatra	Ending Moment.	Muhammadan Year, Month and Day.
	May						
20	Su	1	Vaisakha Sukla 3	·45	4	·30	1
21	Mo	2	4	·52	5	·29	2
22	Tu	3	5	·60	6	·49	3
23	We	4	6	·69	7	·60	4
Vrisha Mesha—Chittirai. 24	Th	5	7	·76	8	·71	5
25	Fr	6	8	·83	9	·81	6
26	Sa	7	9	·90	10	·90	7
27	Su	8	10	·95	11	·98	8
28	Mo	9	11	·98	...	...	9
29	Tu	10	12	·99	12	·03	H. 1298 Jumadal-akhir. 10
30	We	11	13	·98	13	·07	11
—31	Th	12	14	·95	14	·08	12
1	Fr	13	P	·90	15	·07	13
2	Sa	14	Bahula 1	·83	16	·06	14
3	Su	15	2	·75	17 / 18	·02 / ·97	15
4	Mo	16	3	·66	19	·91	16
5	Tu	17	4	·56	20	·85	17
6	We	18	5	·46	21	·78	18
7	Th	19	6	·36	22	·71	19
8	Fr	20	7	·26	23	·64	20
9	Sa	21	8	·16	24	·58	21
10	Su	22	9	·08	25	·53	22
11	Mo	23	10 / 11	·01 / ·95	26	·50	23
12	Tu	24	12	·91	27	·49	24
13	We	25	13	·89	1	·49	25
Vrisha Vrishabha—Vaikasi. 14	Th	26	14	·89	2	·51	26
15	Fr ●	27	—A	·90	3	·55	27
16	Sa	28	1	·95	4	·61	28
17	Su	29	...	...	5	·70	—29
18	Mo	30	2	·02	6	·79	1
19	Tu	31	3	·09	7	·89	2
	June						
20	We	1	Jyeshtha Sukla 4	·17	...	...	3
21	Th	2	5	·26	8	·00	4
22	Fr	3	6	·34	9	·11	5
23	Sa	4	7	·40	10	·21	6
24	Su	5	8	·44	11	·29	7
25	Mo	6	9	·47	12	·35	8
26	Tu	7	10	·48	13	·38	9
27	We	8	11	·48	14	·40	10
28	Th	9	12	·45	15	·41	11
29	Fr	10	13	·40	16	·39	12
30	Sa	11	14	·33	17	·35	13
—31	Su ○	12	P	·25	18	·30	H. 1298 Rajab. 14
1	Mo	13	Bahula 1	·16	19	·24	15
2	Tu	14	2 / 3	·06 / ·96	20	·18	16
3	We	15	4	·86	21	·12	17
4	Th	16	5	·76	22 / 23	·05 / ·98	18
5	Fr	17	6	·66	24	·92	19
6	Sa	18	7	·57	25	·87	20
7	Su	19	8	·50	26	·84	21
8	Mo	20	9	·43	27	·81	22
9	Tu	21	10	·39	1	·81	23
Vrisha Mithuna—Ani. 10	We	22	11	·37	2	·82	24
11	Th	23	12	·38	3	·86	25
12	Fr	24	13	·39	4	·93	26
13	Sa	25	14	·43	...	...	27
14	Su	26	—A	·49	5	·00	28
15	Mo	27	A. Suk. 1	·56	6	·09	29
16	Tu	28	2	·64	7	·19	—30
17	We	29	3	·72	8	·30	1
18	Th	30	4	·81	9	·41	2

Naksh :—1. Asvn. 2. Bhar. 3. Krit. 4. Rohi. 5. Mrig. 6. Ardh. 7. Punar. 8. Push. 9. Aslesh. 10. Magh. 11. P. Phal. 12. U. Phal. 13. Hasta. 14. Chit.

A. D. 1881. | A.—Amavasya. | P.—Paurnami. | Kollam 1057, Commences {N. Malabar—Sept. / S. Malabar—Aug. | Hijra 1299, Commences, Nov. 23. | Vikrama 1938. | Bengal San 1287. | (N. Cycle) Vijaya.

Columns: SOLAR reckoning — Cyclic Sidereal Year, Month and Day; Week-Day; English Month and Day. LUNAR reckoning — Tithi, Ending Moment; Nakshatra, Ending Moment; Muhammadan Year, Month and Day.*

July

Solar month	Cyclic Sidereal Day	Week-Day	English Day	Lunar month / Paksha	Tithi	Ending Moment	Nakshatra	Ending Moment	Muhammadan Month	Muhammadan Day
Vrisha Mithuna—Ani.	19	Fr	1	Ashadha Sukla	5	·87	10	·51		3
	20	Sa	2		6	·92	11	·69		4
	21	Su	3		7	·96	12	·66		5
	22	Mo	4		8	·97	13	·70		6
	23	Tu	5		9	·95	14	·73		7
	24	We	6		10	·92	15	·73		8
	25	Th	7		11	·87	16	·72		9
	26	Fr	8		12	·80	17	·69		10
	27	Sa	9		13	·73	18	·64		11
	28	Su	10		14	·64	19	·59		12
	29	Mo	11		P	·54	20	·52		13
	30	Tu	12	Bahula	1	·43	21	·45	H. 1298 Shaban.	14
	31	We	13		2	·33	22	·38		15
	32	Th	14		3	·23	23	·31		16
Vrisha Karkata—Adi.	1	Fr	15		4	·13	24	·25		17
	2	Sa	16		5 6	·05 ·97	25	·21		18
	3	Su	17		7	·91	26	·17		19
	4	Mo	18		8	·87	27	·14		20
	5	Tu	19		9	·86	1	·13		21
	6	We	20		10	·85	2	·14		22
	7	Th	21		11	·87	3	·18		23
	8	Fr	22		12	·91	4	·23		24
	9	Sa	23		13	·96	5	·30		25
	10	Su	24		...	...	6	·39		26
	11	Mo	25		14	·08	7	·49		27
	12	Tu	26		A	·11	8	·60		28
	13	We	27	Sravana Sukla	1	·20	9	·71		29
	14	Th	28		2	·27	10	·81	Ramzan	1
	15	Fr	29		3	·34	11	·90		2
	16	Sa	30		4	·40	12	·97		3
	17	Su	31		5	·43	...	...		4

Aug.

Solar month	Cyclic Sidereal Day	Week-Day	English Day	Lunar month / Paksha	Tithi	Ending Moment	Nakshatra	Ending Moment	Muhammadan Month	Muhammadan Day
	18	Mo	1	Sravana Sukla	6	·45	13	·02	H. 1298 Ramzan.	5
	19	Tu	2		7	·43	14	·05		6
	20	We	3		8	·40	15	·06		7
	21	Th	4		9	·35	16	·05		8
	22	Fr	5		10	·29	17 18	·02 ·98		9
	23	Sa	6		11	·22	19	·93		10
	24	Su	7		12	·13	20	·86		11
	25	Mo	8		13 14	·03 ·93	21	·79		12
	26	Tu	9		P	·83	22	·72		13
	27	We	10	Bahula	1	·73	23	·66		14
	28	Th	11		2	·64	24	·60		15
	29	Fr	12		3	·55	25	·54		16
	30	Sa	13		4	·46	26	·50		17
	31	Su	14		5	·40	27	·47		18
Vrisha Simha—Avani.	1	Mo	15		6	·37	1	·45		19
	2	Tu	16		7	·35	2	·47		20
	3	We	17		8	·33	3	·49		21
	4	Th	18		9	·35	4	·54		22
	5	Fr	19		10	·39	5	·61		23
	6	Sa	20		11	·45	6	·70		24
	7	Su	21		12	·53	7	·80		25
	8	Mo	22		13	·61	8	·91		26
	9	Tu	23		14	·69	...	...		27
	10	We	24		A	·77	9	·01		28
	11	Th	25	Bhadra. Suk.	1	·85	10	·11		29
	12	Fr	26		2	·90	11	·20		30
	13	Sa	27		3	·93	12	·28	Shawwal.	1
	14	Su	28		4	·96	13	·34		2
	15	Mo	29		5	·93	14	·37		3
	16	Tu	30		6	·91	15	·38		4
	17	We	31		7	·87	16	·37		5

Sep.

Solar month	Cyclic Sidereal Day	Week-Day	English Day	Lunar month / Paksha	Tithi	Ending Moment	Nakshatra	Ending Moment	Muhammadan Month	Muhammadan Day
Vrisha Simha—Avani.	18	Th	1	Bhadrapada Sukla	8	·81	17	·35	H. 1298 Shawwal.	6*
	19	Fr	2		9	·73	18	·32		7
	20	Sa	3		10	·64	19	·26		8
	21	Su	4		11	·54	20	·20		9
	22	Mo	5		12	·44	21	·13		10
	23	Tu	6		13	·34	22	·06		11
	24	We	7		14	·24	23 24	·00 ·94		12
	25	Th	8		P	·16	25	·88		13
	26	Fr	9	Bahula	1 2	·06 ·99	26	·83		14
	27	Sa	10		3	·93	27	·80		15
	28	Su	11		4	·88	1	·79		16
	29	Mo	12		5	·87	2	·79		17
	30	Tu	13		6	·87	3	·81		18
	31	We	14		7	·88	4	·85		19
Vrisha Kanya—Purattasi.	1	Th	15		8	·92	5	·91		20
	2	Fr	16		9	·98	...	...		21
	3	Sa	17		...	...	6	·00		22
	4	Su	18		10	·05	7	·10		23
	5	Mo	19		11	·13	8	·20		24
	6	Tu	20		12	·21	9	·31		25
	7	We	21		13	·29	10	·41		26
	8	Th	22		14	·37	11	·51		27
	9	Fr	23		A	·43	12	·59		28
	10	Sa	24	Sukla	1	·47	13	·65		29
	11	Su	25		2	·49	14	·69	Zi-l-ka'da	1
	12	Mo	26		3	·48	15	·70		2
	13	Tu	27		4	·46	16	·70		3
	14	We	28		5	·42	17	·69		4
	15	Th	29		6	·35	18	·65		5
	16	Fr	30		7	·27	19	·60		6

Oct.

Solar month	Cyclic Sidereal Day	Week-Day	English Day	Lunar month / Paksha	Tithi	Ending Moment	Nakshatra	Ending Moment	Muhammadan Month	Muhammadan Day
	17	Sa	1	Asvina	8	·19	20	·54	H. 1298 Zi-l-ka'da.	7
	18	Su	2		9	·10	21	·48		8
	19	Mo	3		10 11	·00 ·90	22	·41		9
	20	Tu	4		12	·79	23	·34		10
	21	We	5		13	·70	24	·27		11
	22	Th	6		14	·61	25	·21		12
	23	Fr	7		P	·54	26	·16		13
	24	Sa	8	Bahula	1	·49	27	·13		14
	25	Su	9		2	·45	1	·11		15
	26	Mo	10		3	·43	2	·11		16
	27	Tu	11		4	·44	3	·12		17
	28	We	12		5	·45	4	·16		18
	29	Th	13		6	·48	5	·23		19
	30	Fr	14		7	·54	6	·31		20
Vrisha Tula—Aippasi.	1	Sa	15		8	·61	7	·40		21
	2	Su	16		9	·70	8	·50		22
	3	Mo	17		10	·79	9	·61		23
	4	Tu	18		11	·87	10	·72		24
	5	We	19		12	·95	11	·82		25
	6	Th	20		...	...	12	·90		26
	7	Fr	21		13	·00	13	·96		27
	8	Sa	22		14	·05	...	...		28
	9	Su	23		A	·07	14	·00		29
	10	Mo	24	Kartika Suk.	1	·06	15	·02		30
	11	Tu	25		2	·03	16	·03	H. 1298 Zi-l-hijja.	1
	12	We	26		3 4	·00 ·93	17 18	·02 ·98		2
	13	Th	27		5	·85	19	·93		3
	14	Fr	28		6	·77	20	·88		4
	15	Sa	29		7	·68	21	·82		5
	16	Su	30		8	·58	22	·75		6
	17	Mo	31		9	·48	23	·68		7

Nov.

Solar month	Cyclic Sidereal Day	Week-Day	English Day	Lunar month / Paksha	Tithi	Ending Moment	Nakshatra	Ending Moment	Muhammadan Month	Muhammadan Day
Vrisha Tula—Aippasi.	18	Tu	1	Karttika Sukla	10	·38	24	·61	H. 1298 Zi-l-hijja.	8
	19	We	2		11	·29	25	·55		9
	20	Th	3		12	·21	26	·50		10
	21	Fr	4		13	·14	27	·46		11
	22	Sa	5		14	·08	1	·44		12
	23	Su	6		P	·04	2	·43		13
	24	Mo	7	Bahula	1	·02	3	·44		14
	25	Tu	8		2	·03	4	·48		15
	26	We	9		3	·05	5	·54		16
	27	Th	10		4	·10	6	·61		17
	28	Fr	11		5	·15	7	·70		18
	29	Sa	12		6	·22	8	·80		19
	30	Su	13		7	·31	9	·91		20
Vrisha Vrischika—Kartigai.	1	Mo	14		8	·41	...	...		21
	2	Tu	15		9	·49	10	·02		22
	3	We	16		10	·56	11	·12		23
	4	Th	17		11	·62	12	·20		24
	5	Fr	18		12	·67	13	·27		25
	6	Sa	19		13	·68	14	·32		26
	7	Su	20		14	·67	15	·35		27
	8	Mo	21		A	·64	16	·36		28
	9	Tu	22	Sukla	1	·61	17	·34		29
	10	We	23		2	·55	18	·31	Muharram	1
	11	Th	24		3	·48	19	·27		2
	12	Fr	25		4	·39	20	·22		3
	13	Sa	26		5	·39	21	·16		4
	14	Su	27		6	·20	22	·09		5
	15	Mo	28		7	·10	23 24	·02 ·95		6
	16	Tu	29		8 9	·00 ·92	25	·89		7
	17	We	30		10	·83	26	·84		8

Dec.

Solar month	Cyclic Sidereal Day	Week-Day	English Day	Lunar month / Paksha	Tithi	Ending Moment	Nakshatra	Ending Moment	Muhammadan Month	Muhammadan Day
	18	Th	1	Margasira	11	·75	27	·79	H. 1299 Muharram.	9
	19	Fr	2		12	·70	1	·76		10
	20	Sa	3		13	·67	2	·75		11
	21	Su	4		14	·65	3	·76		12
	22	Mo ○	5		P	·66	4	·80		13
	23	Tu	6		1	·69	5	·85		14
	24	We	7		2	·74	6	·91		15
	25	Th	8		3	·79	...	...		16
	26	Fr	9		4	·87	7	·00		17
	27	Sa	10		5	·97	8	·10		18
	28	Su	11		...	...	9	·21		19
	29	Mo	12	Bahula	6	·05	10	·32		20
	30	Tu	13		7	·13	11	·42		21
Vrisha Dhanus—Margali.	1	We	14		8	·20	12	·51		22
	2	Th	15		9	·27	13	·58		23
	3	Fr	16		10	·30	14	·64		24
	4	Sa	17		11	·32	15	·67		25
	5	Su	18		12	·31	16	·68		26
	6	Mo	19		13	·29	17	·67		27
	7	Tu	20		14	·24	18	·64		28
	8	We	21		A	·18	19	·61		29
	9	Th	22	Pausha Sukla	1	·11	20	·56		30
	10	Fr	23		2 3	·02 ·93	21	·49	H. 1299 Safar.	1
	11	Sa	24		4	·84	22	·42		2
	12	Su	25		5	·74	23	·35		3
	13	Mo	26		6	·64	24	·29		4
	14	Tu	27		7	·55	25	·23		5
	15	We	28		8	·47	26	·17		6
	16	Th	29		9	·40	27	·12		7
	17	Fr	30		10	·35	1	·09		8
	18	Sa	31		11	·31	2	·08		9

15. Svati. 16. Visak. 17. Anur 18. Jyesh. 19. Mula. 20. P. Ash. 21. U. Ash. 22. Sravn. 23. Dani. 24. Satab. 25. P. Bhad. 26. U. Bhad. 27. Rev.

A. D. 1882.
Solar Eclipse. ●
Lunar Eclipse. ○

Mesha Sankranti (Commencement of Indian Sidereal Year).
(Surya Sid.) April 11·96.
(Arya Sid.) April 11·86.

Saka 1804. **Kaliyuga 4983.**
(S. Cycle) Chitrabhanu.

January–February

Solar months: Vrisha, *Dhanus—Margali* (Jan. 1–11); Vrisha, *Makara—Tai* (Jan. 12 – Feb. 10); Vrisha, *Kumbha—Masi* (from Feb. 11). Lunar: Pausha Suk., Bahula, Sukla; Magha Suk., Bahula; Phalguna Sukla. Muhammadan: H. 1299 Safar; H. 1299 Rabi-ul-awwal; Rabi-ul-akhir.

Cyclic Sidereal Year, Month and Day.	Week-Day	English Month and Day.	Tithi	Ending Moment.	Nakshatra	Ending Moment.	Muhammadan Year, Month and Day.
		Jan.					
19	Su	1	12	·30	3	·09	10
20	Mo	2	13	·30	4	·11	11
21	Tu	3	14	·34	5	·15	12
22	We	4	P	·38	6	·22	13
23	Th	5	1	·44	7	·31	14
24	Fr	6	2	·53	8	·41	15
25	Sa	7	3	·62	9	·51	16
26	Su	8	4	·70	10	·62	17
27	Mo	9	5	·78	11	·72	18
28	Tu	10	6	·86	12	·81	19
29	We	11	7	·91	13	·89	20
1	Th	12	8	·95	14	·95	21
2	Fr	13	9	·97	15	·99	22
3	Sa	14	10	·95	...	...	23
4	Su	15	11	·93	16	·00	24
5	Mo	16	12	·89	17 / 18	·00 / ·98	25
6	Tu	17	13	·83	19	·94	26
7	We	18	14	·75	20	·89	27
8	Th	19	A	·66	21	·83	28
9	Fr	20	1	·56	22	·76	29
10	Sa	21	2	·46	23	·69	1
11	Su	22	3	·36	24	·63	2
12	Mo	23	4	·27	25	·57	3
13	Tu	24	5	·19	26	·51	4
14	We	25	6	·11	27	·46	5
15	Th	26	7 / 8	·05 / ·99	1	·42	6
16	Fr	27	9	·95	2	·41	7
17	Sa	28	10	·94	3	·41	8
18	Su	29	11	·95	4	·43	9
19	Mo	30	12	·98	5	·46	10
20	Tu	31	...	...	6	·52	11
		Feb.					
21	We	1	13	·03	7	·61	12
22	Th	2	14	·10	8	·71	13
23	Fr	3	P	·18	9	·81	14
24	Sa	4	1	·26	10	·92	15
25	Su	5	2	·35	...	...	16
26	Mo	6	3	·43	11	·02	17
27	Tu	7	4	·51	12	·12	18
28	We	8	5	·56	13	·20	19
29	Th	9	6	·59	14	·26	20
30	Fr	10	7	·60	15	·30	21
1	Sa	11	8	·59	16	·32	22
2	Su	12	9	·57	17	·32	23
3	Mo	13	10	·52	18	·31	24
4	Tu	14	11	·45	19	·28	25
5	We	15	12	·37	20	·23	26
6	Th	16	13	·28	21	·17	27
7	Fr	17	14	·19	22	·11	28
8	Sa	18	A / 1	·10 / ·99	23 / 24	·04 / ·97	29
9	Su	19	2	·89	25	·90	30
10	Mo	20	3	·80	26	·84	1
11	Tu	21	4	·72	27	·79	2
12	We	22	5	·66	1	·76	3
13	Th	23	6	·61	2	·73	4
14	Fr	24	7	·58	3	·73	5
15	Sa	25	8	·56	4	·74	6
16	Su	26	9	·56	5	·78	7
17	Mo	27	10	·60	6	·84	8
18	Tu	28	11	·65	7	·92	9

March–April

Solar months: Vrisha, *Kumbha—Masi* (Mar. 1–12); Vrisha, *Mina—Panguni* (Mar. 13 – Apr. 11); Chitrabhanu, *Mesha—Chittirai* (from Apr. 12). Lunar: Phalguna Suk., Bahula, Sukla; Chaitra Suk., Bahula; Vaisakha Sukla. Muhammadan: H. 1299 Rabi-ul-akhir; H. 1299 Jumadal-awwal.

Cyclic Sidereal Year, Month and Day.	Week-Day	English Month and Day.	Tithi	Ending Moment.	Nakshatra	Ending Moment.	Muhammadan Year, Month and Day.
		March					
19	We	1	12	·72	...	...	10
20	Th	2	13	·80	8	·01	11
21	Fr	3	14	·89	9	·11	12
22	Sa	4	P	·97	10	·22	13
23	Su	5	...	...	11	·33	14
24	Mo	6	1	·05	12	·43	15
25	Tu	7	2	·12	13	·52	16
26	We	8	3	·17	14	·58	17
27	Th	9	4	·21	15	·62	18
28	Fr	10	5	·21	16	·64	19
29	Sa	11	6	·20	17	·66	20
30	Su	12	7	·17	18	·64	21
1	Mo	13	8	·12	19	·61	22
2	Tu	14	9 / 10	·05 / ·97	20	·56	23
3	We	15	11	·89	21	·51	24
4	Th	16	12	·79	22	·45	25
5	Fr	17	13	·69	23	·38	26
6	Sa	18	14	·59	24	·31	27
7	Su	19	A	·50	25	·24	28
8	Mo	20	1	·40	26	·18	29
9	Tu	21	2	·32	27	·13	1
10	We	22	3	·25	1	·09	2
11	Th	23	4	·20	2	·06	3
12	Fr	24	5	·17	3	·05	4
13	Sa	25	6	·15	4	·06	5
14	Su	26	7	·16	5	·10	6
15	Mo	27	8	·19	6	·15	7
16	Tu	28	9	·24	7	·22	8
17	We	29	10	·31	8	·31	9
18	Th	30	11	·38	9	·41	10
19	Fr	31	12	·47	10	·52	11
		April					
20	Sa	1	13	·56	11	·63	12
21	Su	2	14	·64	12	·73	13
22	Mo	3	P	·70	13	·81	14
23	Tu	4	1	·75	14	·88	15
24	We	5	2	·78	15	·93	16
25	Th	6	3	·78	16	·97	17
26	Fr	7	4	·77	17	·98	18
27	Sa	8	5	·73	18	·97	19
28	Su	9	6	·68	19	·94	20
29	Mo	10	7	·61	20	·90	21
30	Tu	11	8	·54	21	·85	22
1	We	12	9	·45	22	·79	23
2	Th	13	10	·35	23	·72	24
3	Fr	14	11	·25	24	·65	25
4	Sa	15	12	·15	25	·58	26
5	Su	16	13 / 14	·05 / ·96	26	·52	27
6	Mo	17	A	·88	27	·47	28
7	Tu	18	1	·81	1	·42	29
8	We	19	2	·76	2	·39	30
9	Th	20	3	·72	3	·37	1
10	Fr	21	4	·69	4	·39	2
11	Sa	22	5	·70	5	·41	3
12	Su	23	6	·73	6	·46	4
13	Mo	24	7	·78	7	·52	5
14	Tu	25	8	·84	8	·61	6
15	We	26	9	·93	9	·71	7
16	Th	27	...	...	10	·82	8
17	Fr	28	10	·01	11	·93	9
18	Sa	29	11	·09	...	...	10
19	Su	30	12	·16	12	·03	11

May–June

Solar months: Chitrabhanu, *Mesha—Chittirai* (May 1–12); Chitrabhanu, *Vrishabha—Vaikasi* (May 13 – June 12); Chitrabhanu, *Mithuna—Ani* (from June 13). Lunar: Vaisakha Suk., Bahula, Sukla; Jyeshtha Suk., Bahula; Ashadha Sukla. Muhammadan: H. 1299 Jumadal-akhir; H. 1299 Rajab; H. 1299 Shaban.

Cyclic Sidereal Year, Month and Day.	Week-Day	English Month and Day.	Tithi	Ending Moment.	Nakshatra	Ending Moment.	Muhammadan Year, Month and Day.
		May					
20	Mo	1	13	·22	13	·12	12
21	Tu	2	14	·28	14	·19	13
22	We	3	P	·31	15	·25	14
23	Th	4	1	·32	16	·29	15
24	Fr	5	2	·30	17	·30	16
25	Sa	6	3	·26	18	·29	17
26	Su	7	4	·21	19	·27	18
27	Mo	8	5	·15	20	·24	19
28	Tu	9	6 / 7	·07 / ·97	21	·19	20
29	We	10	8	·87	22	·13	21
30	Th	11	9	·77	23 / 24	·06 / ·99	22
31	Fr	12	10	·67	25	·92	23
1	Sa	13	11	·57	26	·86	24
2	Su	14	12	·47	27	·80	25
3	Mo	15	13	·39	1	·75	26
4	Tu	16	14	·32	2	·72	27
5	We ●	17	A	·27	3	·70	28
6	Th	18	1	·24	4	·71	29
7	Fr	19	2	·22	5	·73	1
8	Sa	20	3	·21	6	·77	2
9	Su	21	4	·24	7	·83	3
10	Mo	22	5	·29	8	·91	4
11	Tu	23	6	·35	...	...	5
12	We	24	7	·42	9	·01	6
13	Th	25	8	·50	10	·12	7
14	Fr	26	9	·59	11	·23	8
15	Sa	27	10	·67	12	·33	9
16	Su	28	11	·73	13	·43	10
17	Mo	29	12	·78	14	·51	11
18	Tu	30	13	·80	15	·57	12
19	We	31	14	·82	16	·60	13
		June					
20	Th	1	P	·80	17	·62	14
21	Fr	2	1	·77	18	·62	15
22	Sa	3	2	·72	19	·61	16
23	Su	4	3	·65	20	·57	17
24	Mo	5	4	·56	21	·52	18
25	Tu	6	5	·47	22	·46	19
26	We	7	6	·37	23	·40	20
27	Th	8	7	·27	24	·34	21
28	Fr	9	8	·17	25	·27	22
29	Sa	10	9 / 10	·07 / ·98	26	·20	23
30	Su	11	11	·89	27	·14	24
31	Mo	12	12	·81	1	·08	25
1	Tu	13	13	·75	2	·05	26
2	We	14	14	·71	3	·03	27
3	Th	15	A	·70	4	·03	28
4	Fr	16	1	·70	5	·04	29
5	Sa	17	2	·72	6	·08	30
6	Su	18	3	·76	7	·14	1
7	Mo	19	4	·83	8	·22	2
8	Tu	20	5	·90	9	·31	3
9	We	21	6	·97	10	·41	4
10	Th	22	...	...	11	·52	5
11	Fr	23	7	·06	12	·63	6
12	Sa	24	8	·14	13	·73	7
13	Su	25	9	·20	14	·81	8
14	Mo	26	10	·25	15	·88	9
15	Tu	27	11	·29	16	·92	10
16	We	28	12	·29	17	·94	11
17	Th	29	13	·27	18	·95	12
18	Fr	30	14	·25	19	·94	13

Naksh.:—1. Asvn. 2. Bhar. 3. Krit. 4. Rohi. 5. Mrig. 6. Ardh. 7. Punar. 8. Push. 9. Asleah. 10. Magh. 11. P. Phal. 12. U. Phal. 13. Hasta. 14. Chit.

A. D. 1882. **Vikrama 1939.**

A.—Amavasya. **Kollam 1058,** { **N. Malabar—Sept.** **S. Malabar—Aug.** } Commences **Hijra 1300,** Commences, **Nov. 12.** **Bengal San 1288.**

P.—Paurnami. **(N. Cycle) Jaya.**

SOLAR reckoning: Cyclic Sidereal Year, Month and Day; Week-Day; English Month and Day. LUNAR reckoning: Tithi; Ending Moment; Nakshatra; Ending Moment; Muhammadan Year, Month and Day.

July

Cyclic Sidereal Year, Month and Day	Week-Day	English Month and Day	Tithi	Ending Moment	Nakshatra	Ending Moment	Muhammadan Year, Month and Day
Chitrabhanu, Mithuna—Ani. 19	Sa	1	P	·20	20	·90	14
20	Su	2	1	·13	21	·86	15
21	Mo	3	Ashadha, Bahula: 2 3	·04 ·95	22	·80	16
22	Tu	4	4	·85	23	·74	17
23	We	5	5	·75	24	·67	H. 1299 Shaban. 18
24	Th	6	6	·65	25	·60	19
25	Fr	7	7	·55	26	·53	20
26	Sa	8	8	·45	27	·47	21
27	Su	9	9	·36	1	·42	22
28	Mo	10	10	·29	2	·39	23
29	Tu	11	11	·23	3	·36	24
30	We	12	12	·20	4	·35	25
31	Th	13	13	·18	5	·36	26
—32	Fr	14	14	·17	6	·39	27
Chitrabhanu, Karkata—Adi. 1	Sa	15	—A	·20	7	·45	28
2	Su	16	Sravana, Sukla: 1	·24	8	·52	—29
3	Mo	17	2	·29	9	·61	Ramzan. 1
4	Tu	18	3	·36	10	·70	2
5	We	19	4	·45	11	·81	3
6	Th	20	5	·53	12	·92	4
7	Fr	21	6	·60	...	...	5
8	Sa	22	7	·67	13	·03	6
9	Su	23	8	·73	14	·12	7
10	Mo	24	9	·76	15	·19	8
11	Tu	25	10	·77	16	·33	9
12	We	26	11	·76	17	·26	10
13	Th	27	12	·73	18	·28	11
14	Fr	28	13	·67	19	·27	12
15	Sa	29	14	·61	20	·24	13
16	Su	30	P	·53	21	·19	14
17	Mo	31	1	·44	22	·14	15

Aug.

Cyclic Sidereal Year, Month and Day	Week-Day	English Month and Day	Tithi	Ending Moment	Nakshatra	Ending Moment	Muhammadan Year, Month and Day
18	Tu	1	Adh. Sravana, Bahula: 2	·34	23	·08	H. 1299 16
19	We	2	3	·24	24 25	·01 ·94	17
20	Th	3	4	·14	26	·87	18
21	Fr	4	5 6	·04 ·94	27	·81	19
22	Sa	5	7	·85	1	·76	20
23	Su	6	8	·78	2	·72	21
24	Mo	7	9	·72	3	·69	22
25	Tu	8	10	·68	4	·67	23
26	We	9	11	·66	5	·68	24
27	Th	10	12	·67	6	·71	25
28	Fr	11	13	·68	7	·76	26
29	Sa	12	14	·71	8	·83	27
30	Su	13	—A	·78	9	·91	28
—31	Mo	14	Nija Sravana, Sukla: 1	·86	...	...	29
Chitrabhanu, Simha—Avani. 1	Tu	15	2	·94	10	·01	—30
2	We	16	...	...	11	·12	H. 1299 Shawwal. 1
3	Th	17	3	·02	12	·23	2
4	Fr	18	4	·10	13	·33	3
5	Sa	19	5	·16	14	·42	4
6	Su	20	6	·22	15	·49	5
7	Mo	21	7	·25	16	·55	6
8	Tu	22	8	·27	17	·59	7
9	We	23	9	·26	18	·60	8
10	Th	24	10	·23	19	·59	9
11	Fr	25	11	·19	20	·57	10
12	Sa	26	12	·12	21	·53	11
13	Su	27	13 14	·04 ·95	22	·48	12
14	Mo	28	P	·85	23	·42	13
15	Tu	29	1	·75	24	·35	14
16	We	30	2	·65	25	·28	15
17	Th	31	3	·55	26	·21	16

Sep.

Cyclic Sidereal Year, Month and Day	Week-Day	English Month and Day	Tithi	Ending Moment	Nakshatra	Ending Moment	Muhammadan Year, Month and Day
Chitrabhanu, Simha—Avani. 18	Fr	1	Nija Srvn., Bahula: 4	·45	27	·15	17
19	Sa	2	5	·37	1	·10	18
20	Su	3	6	·30	2	·05	19
21	Mo	4	7	·24	3	·01	20
22	Tu	5	8	·20	4	·00	21
23	We	6	9	·17	5	·01	22
24	Th	7	10	·18	6	·03	23
25	Fr	8	11	·20	7	·07	24
26	Sa	9	12	·24	8	·13	25
27	Su	10	13	·29	9	·21	26
28	Mo	11	14	·37	10	·31	27
29	Tu	12	—A	·45	11	·42	28
30	We	13	Bhadrapada, Sukla: 1	·53	12	·53	—29
—31	Th	14	2	·62	13	·63	H. 1299 Zi-l-ka'da. 1
Chitrabhanu, Kanya—Purattasi. 1	Fr	15	3	·69	14	·73	2
2	Sa	16	4	·75	15	·80	3
3	Su	17	5	·78	16	·87	4
4	Mo	18	6	·80	17	·91	5
5	Tu	19	7	·78	18	·92	6
6	We	20	8	·78	19	·92	7
7	Th	21	9	·72	20	·90	8
8	Fr	22	10	·65	21	·87	9
9	Sa	23	11	·57	22	·82	10
10	Su	24	12	·48	23	·76	11
11	Mo	25	13	·39	24	·69	12
12	Tu	26	14	·29	25	·62	13
13	We	27	P	·19	26	·55	14
14	Th	28	1 2	·09 ·99	27	·49	15
15	Fr	29	3	·91	1	·43	16
16	Sa	30	4	·84	2	·38	17

Oct.

Cyclic Sidereal Year, Month and Day	Week-Day	English Month and Day	Tithi	Ending Moment	Nakshatra	Ending Moment	Muhammadan Year, Month and Day
17	Su	1	5	·79	3	·34	18
18	Mo	2	Bahula: 6	·75	4	·33	19
19	Tu	3	7	·73	5	·33	20
20	We	4	8	·72	6	·34	21
21	Th	5	9	·74	7	·38	22
22	Fr	6	10	·79	8	·44	23
23	Sa	7	11	·85	9	·52	24
24	Su	8	12	·93	10	·62	25
25	Mo	9	...	...	11	·72	26
26	Tu	10	13	·02	12	·83	27
27	We	11	14	·11	13	·93	28
28	Th	12	—A	·18	...	...	29
29	Fr	13	Asvina, Sukla: 1	·25	14	·03	—30
30	Sa	14	2	·31	15	·12	H. 1299 Zi-l-hijja. 1
—31	Su	15	3	·34	16	·18	2
Chitrabhanu, Tula—Aippasi. 1	Mo	16	4	·37	17	·22	3
2	Tu	17	5	·35	18	·24	4
3	We	18	6	·33	19	·24	5
4	Th	19	7	·28	20	·23	6
5	Fr	20	8	·22	21	·20	7
6	Sa	21	9	·15	22	·15	8
7	Su	22	10 11	·06 ·97	23	·09	9
8	Mo	23	12	·87	24 25	·03 ·97	10
9	Tu	24	13	·77	26	·90	11
10	We	25	14	·67	27	·83	12
11	Th	26	P	·58	1	·77	13
12	Fr	27	1	·49	2	·71	14
13	Sa	28	2	·42	3	·67	15
14	Su	29	3	·37	4	·66	16
15	Mo	30	Bah.: 4	·33	5	·65	17
16	Tu	31	5	·32	6	·66	18

Nov.

Cyclic Sidereal Year, Month and Day	Week-Day	English Month and Day	Tithi	Ending Moment	Nakshatra	Ending Moment	Muhammadan Year, Month and Day
Chitrabhanu, Tula—Aippasi. 17	We	1	Asvina, Bahula: 6	·32	7	·69	19
18	Th	2	7	·34	8	·75	20
19	Fr	3	8	·38	9	·83	21
20	Sa	4	9	·45	10	·92	22
21	Su	5	10	·53	...	...	23
22	Mo	6	11	·61	11	·02	H. 1299 Zi-l-hijja. 24
23	Tu	7	12	·71	12	·13	25
24	We	8	13	·79	13	·24	26
25	Th	9	14	·87	14	·34	27
26	Fr	10	—A	·92	15	·42	28
27	Sa	11	Kartika, Sukla: 1	·95	16	·49	—29
28	Su	12	2	·97	17	·54	H. 1300 Muharram. 1
29	Mo	13	3	·96	18	·56	2
—30	Tu	14	4	·94	19	·58	3
Chitrabhanu, Vrischika—Kartigai. 1	We	15	5	·89	20	·56	4
2	Th	16	6	·83	21	·53	5
3	Fr	17	7	·76	22	·49	6
4	Sa	18	8	·68	23	·43	7
5	Su	19	9	·58	24	·37	8
6	Mo	20	10	·48	25	·31	9
7	Tu	21	11	·38	26	·24	10
8	We	22	12	·29	27	·17	11
9	Th	23	13	·20	1	·10	12
10	Fr	24	14	·11	2	·05	13
11	Sa	25	P 1	·04 ·99	3 4	·01 ·98	14
12	Su	26	2	·95	5	·97	15
13	Mo	27	3	·94	6	·98	16
14	Tu	28	4	·95	...	...	17
15	We	29	5	·98	7	·01	18
16	Th	30	...	...	8	·07	19

Dec.

Cyclic Sidereal Year, Month and Day	Week-Day	English Month and Day	Tithi	Ending Moment	Nakshatra	Ending Moment	Muhammadan Year, Month and Day
17	Fr	1	Bahula: 6	·02	9	·14	20
18	Sa	2	7	·08	10	·22	21
19	Su	3	8	·16	11	·32	22
20	Mo	4	9	·26	12	·42	23
21	Tu	5	10	·34	13	·52	24
22	We	6	11	·42	14	·63	25
23	Th	7	12	·50	15	·73	26
24	Fr	8	13	·55	16	·80	27
25	Sa	9	14	·59	17	·85	28
26	Su	10	—A	·60	18	·89	29
27	Mo	11	Margasira, Sukla: 1	·60	19	·90	—30
28	Tu	12	2	·57	20	·89	H. 1300 Safar. 1
—29	We	13	3	·52	21	·86	2
Chitrabhanu, Dhanus—Margali. 1	Th	14	4	·46	22	·82	3
2	Fr	15	5	·38	23	·77	4
3	Sa	16	6	·30	24	·71	5
4	Su	17	7	·21	25	·61	6
5	Mo	18	8	·11	26	·57	7
6	Tu	19	9 10	·01 ·91	27	·50	8
7	We	20	11	·83	1	·44	9
8	Th	21	12	·75	2	·39	10
9	Fr	22	13	·68	3	·34	11
10	Sa	23	14	·63	4	·31	12
11	Su	24	P	·60	5	·30	13
12	Mo	25	Bahula: 1	·58	6	·30	14
13	Tu	26	2	·59	7	·33	15
14	We	27	3	·62	8	·37	16
15	Th	28	4	·66	9	·44	17
16	Fr	29	5	·73	10	·52	18
17	Sa	30	6	·82	11	·62	19
18	Su	31	7	·91	12	·73	20

15. Svati. 16. Visak. 17. Anur. 18. Jyesh. 19. Mula. 20. P. Ash. 21. U. Ash. 22. Sravn. 23. Dani. 24. Satab. 25. P. Bhad. 26. U. Bhad. 27. Rev.

A. D. 1883. **Mesha Sankranti** (Commencement of Indian Sidereal Year).

Solar Eclipse. ● **(Surya Sid.) April 12·22.** **Saka 1805.** **Kaliyuga 4984.**

Lunar Eclipse. ○ **(Arya Sid.) April 12·12.** **(S. Cycle) Subhanu.**

SOLAR reckoning. / LUNAR reckoning.

Jan.

Solar: Chitrabhanu *Dhanus—Margali.* (to 30); Chitrabhanu *Makara—Tai.* (from 1). Lunar: Marg. *Bahula*; Pausha *Sukla* / *Bahula*. Muhammadan: H. 1300 *Safar.*; H. 1300 *Rabi-ul-awwal.*

Cyclic Sidereal Year, Month and Day.	Week-Day	English Month and Day.	Tithi	Ending Moment.	Nakshatra	Ending Moment.	Muhammadan Year, Month and Day.
19	Mo	1	8	·99	13	·84	21
20	Tu	2	...	...	14	·94	22
21	We	3	9	·07	...	...	23
22	Th	4	10	·15	15	·03	24
23	Fr	5	11	·20	16	·11	25
24	Sa	6	12	·23	17	·17	26
25	Su	7	13	·25	18	·21	27
26	Mo	8	14	·24	19	·22	28
27	Tu	9	—A	·21	20	·22	—29
28	We	10	1	·17	21	·19	1
29	Th	11	2	·10	22	·15	2
—30	Fr	12	3 4	·03 ·95	23	·11	3
1	Sa	13	5	·85	24 25	·05 ·98	4
2	Su	14	6	·75	26	·91	5
3	Mo	15	7	·65	27	·84	6
4	Tu	16	8	·56	1	·78	7
5	We	17	9	·47	2	·73	8
6	Th	18	10	·39	3	·68	9
7	Fr	19	11	·33	4	·64	10
8	Sa	20	12	·27	5	·62	11
9	Su	21	13	·24	6	·63	12
10	Mo	22	14	·22	7	·65	13
11	Tu	23	P	·24	8	·69	14
12	We	24	1	·27	9	·74	15
13	Th	25	2	·32	10	·82	16
14	Fr	26	3	·39	11	·92	17
15	Sa	27	4	·47	...	...	18
16	Su	28	5	·56	12	·03	19
17	Mo	29	6	·65	13	·14	20
18	Tu	30	7	·73	14	·24	21
19	We	31	8	·80	15	·33	22

Feb.

Solar: Chitrabhanu *Kumbha—Masi.* Lunar: Magha *Sukla* / *Bahula*. Muhammadan: H. 1300 *Rabi-ul-akhir.*

Cyclic Sidereal Year, Month and Day.	Week-Day	English Month and Day.	Tithi	Ending Moment.	Nakshatra	Ending Moment.	Muhammadan Year, Month and Day.
20	Th	1	9	·85	16	·41	23
21	Fr	2	10	·88	17	·48	24
22	Sa	3	11	·90	18	·52	25
23	Su	4	12	·88	19	·54	26
24	Mo	5	13	·85	20	·54	27
25	Tu	6	14	·79	21	·52	28
26	We	7	—A	·73	22	·50	29
27	Th	8	1	·66	23	·45	—30
28	Fr	9	2	·57	24	·39	1
—29	Sa	10	3	·48	25	·32	2
1	Su	11	4	·38	26	·25	3
2	Mo	12	5	·28	27	·18	4
3	Tu	13	6	·18	1	·12	5
4	We	14	7	·09	2	·06	6
5	Th	15	8 9	·01 ·95	3 4	·01 ·97	7
6	Fr	16	10	·91	5	·96	8
7	Sa	17	11	·87	6	·95	9
8	Su	18	12	·85	7	·96	10
9	Mo	19	13	·86	...	...	11
10	Tu	20	14	·89	8	·00	12
11	We	21	P	·95	9	·06	13
12	Th	22	...	...	10	·13	14
13	Fr	23	1	·02	11	·23	15
14	Sa	24	2	·10	12	·33	16
15	Su	25	3	·19	13	·43	17
16	Mo	26	4	·27	14	·54	18
17	Tu	27	5	·34	15	·64	19
18	We	28	6	·41	16	·73	20

March

Solar: Chitrabhanu *Kumbha—Masi.* (to 30); Chitrabhanu *Mina—Panguni.* (from 1). Lunar: Magha *Bahula*; Phalguna *Sukla* / *Bahula*. Muhammadan: *Rabi-ul-akhir.*; H. 1300 *Jumadal-awwal.*

Cyclic Sidereal Year, Month and Day.	Week-Day	English Month and Day.	Tithi	Ending Moment.	Nakshatra	Ending Moment.	Muhammadan Year, Month and Day.
19	Th	1	7	·47	17	·79	21
20	Fr	2	8	·50	18	·84	22
21	Sa	3	9	·51	19	·86	23
22	Su	4	10	·49	20	·87	24
23	Mo	5	11	·46	21	·86	25
24	Tu	6	12	·40	22	·83	26
25	We	7	13	·34	23	·78	27
26	Th	8	14	·27	24	·72	28
27	Fr	9	—A	·18	25	·66	—29
28	Sa	10	1 2	·08 ·98	26	·60	1
29	Su	11	3	·88	27	·53	2
—30	Mo	12	4	·78	1	·46	3
1	Tu	13	5	·69	2	·40	4
2	We	14	6	·61	3	·34	5
3	Th	15	7	·55	4	·31	6
4	Fr	16	8	·50	5	·28	7
5	Sa	17	9	·46	6	·27	8
6	Su	18	10	·45	7	·28	9
7	Mo	19	11	·46	8	·31	10
8	Tu	20	12	·50	9	·36	11
9	We	21	13	·55	10	·44	12
10	Th	22	14	·62	11	·53	13
11	Fr	23	P	·70	12	·63	14
12	Sa	24	1	·78	13	·73	15
13	Su	25	2	·87	14	·84	16
14	Mo	26	3	·95	15	·94	17
15	Tu	27	...	...	...	...	18
16	We	28	4	·01	16	·03	19
17	Th	29	5	·05	17	·10	20
18	Fr	30	6	·08	18	·15	21
19	Sa	31	7	·09	19	·18	22

April

Solar: Subhanu *Mesha—Chittirai.* Lunar: Phalguna *Bahula*; Chaitra *Sukla* / *Bahula*. Muhammadan: H. 1300 *Jumadal-akhir.*

Cyclic Sidereal Year, Month and Day.	Week-Day	English Month and Day.	Tithi	Ending Moment.	Nakshatra	Ending Moment.	Muhammadan Year, Month and Day.
20	Su	1	8	·07	20	·20	23
21	Mo	2	9 10	·04 ·98	21	·19	24
22	Tu	3	11	·92	22	·16	25
23	We	4	12	·84	23	·12	26
24	Th	5	13	·74	24	·06	27
25	Fr	6	14	·64	25 26	·01 ·94	28
26	Sa	7	—A	·54	27	·87	29
27	Su	8	1	·44	1	·80	—30
28	Mo	9	2	·34	2	·73	1
29	Tu	10	3	·26	3	·68	2
—30	We	11	4	·18	4	·64	3
1	Th	12	5	·11	5	·61	4
2	Fr	13	6	·06	6	·59	5
3	Sa	14	7	·02	7	·60	6
4	Su	15	8	·01	8	·62	7
5	Mo	16	9	·01	9	·68	8
6	Tu	17	10	·05	10	·74	9
7	We	18	11	·11	11	·83	10
8	Th	19	12	·18	12	·93	11
9	Fr	20	13	·25	...	...	12
10	Sa	21	14	·33	13	·03	13
11	Su	○ 22	P	·41	14	·14	14
12	Mo	23	1	·48	15	·25	15
13	Tu	24	2	·55	16	·34	16
14	We	25	3	·60	17	·41	17
15	Th	26	4	·63	18	·46	18
16	Fr	27	5	·63	19	·50	19
17	Sa	28	6	·61	20	·52	20
18	Su	29	7	·58	21	·51	21
19	Mo	30	8	·52	22	·49	22

May

Solar: Subhanu *Mesha—Chittirai.* (to 31); Subhanu *Vrishabha—Vaikasi.* (from 1). Lunar: Ch. *Bah.*; Vaisakha *Sukla* / *Bahula*. Muhammadan: *Jumadal-akhir.*; H. 1300 *Rajab.*

Cyclic Sidereal Year, Month and Day.	Week-Day	English Month and Day.	Tithi	Ending Moment.	Nakshatra	Ending Moment.	Muhammadan Year, Month and Day.
20	Tu	1	9	·45	23	·45	23
21	We	2	10	·37	24	·41	24
22	Th	3	11	·28	25	·35	25
23	Fr	4	12	·18	26	·28	26
24	Sa	5	13 14	·08 ·98	27	·21	27
25	Su	6	—A	·88	1	·14	28
26	Mo	7	1	·79	2	·07	—29
27	Tu	8	2	·71	3 4	·02 ·97	1
28	We	9	3	·64	5	·94	2
29	Th	10	4	·58	6	·92	3
30	Fr	11	5	·55	7	·92	4
—31	Sa	12	6	·53	8	·95	5
1	Su	13	7	·53	9	·99	6
2	Mo	14	8	·57	...	...	7
3	Tu	15	9	·62	10	·05	8
4	We	16	10	·68	11	·13	9
5	Th	17	11	·75	12	·22	10
6	Fr	18	12	·84	13	·33	11
7	Sa	19	13	·92	14	·44	12
8	Su	20	...	...	15	·55	13
9	Mo	21	14	·00	16	·64	14
10	Tu	22	P	·06	17	·72	15
11	We	23	1	·11	18	·79	16
12	Th	24	2	·13	19	·82	17
13	Fr	25	3	·13	20	·84	18
14	Sa	26	4	·12	21	·84	19
15	Su	27	5	·09	22	·82	20
16	Mo	28	6 7	·04 ·96	23	·78	21
17	Tu	29	8	·87	24	·74	22
18	We	30	9	·78	25	·68	23
19	Th	31	10	·68	26	·61	24

June

Solar: Subhanu *Vrishabha—Vaikasi.* (to 31); Subhanu *Mithuna—Ani.* (from 1). Lunar: Jyeshtha *Sukla* / *Bahula*. Muhammadan: H. 1300 *Shaban.*

Cyclic Sidereal Year, Month and Day.	Week-Day	English Month and Day.	Tithi	Ending Moment.	Nakshatra	Ending Moment.	Muhammadan Year, Month and Day.
20	Fr	1	11	·58	27	·54	25
21	Sa	2	12	·48	1	·48	26
22	Su	3	13	·38	2	·42	27
23	Mo	4	14	·29	3	·36	28
24	Tu	5	—A	·21	4	·30	29
25	We	6	1	·14	5	·27	—30
26	Th	7	2	·08	6	·25	1
27	Fr	8	3	·04	7	·25	2
28	Sa	9	4	·02	8	·26	3
29	Su	10	5	·03	9	·30	4
30	Mo	11	6	·05	10	·36	5
—31	Tu	12	7	·10	11	·43	6
1	We	13	8	·16	12	·53	7
2	Th	14	9	·23	13	·64	8
3	Fr	15	10	·31	14	·75	9
4	Sa	16	11	·39	15	·85	10
5	Su	17	12	·48	16	·94	11
6	Mo	18	13	·54	...	...	12
7	Tu	19	14	·59	17	·03	13
8	We	20	P	·61	18	·10	14
9	Th	21	1	·61	19	·14	15
10	Fr	22	2	·60	20	·16	16
11	Sa	23	3	·57	21	·16	17
12	Su	24	4	·51	22	·15	18
13	Mo	25	5	·44	23	·12	19
14	Tu	26	6	·36	24	·08	20
15	We	27	7	·26	25 26	·02 ·95	21
16	Th	28	8	·16	27	·88	22
17	Fr	29	9 10	·06 ·96	1	·81	23
18	Sa	30	11	·86	2	·75	24

Naksh:—1 Asvn. 2. Bhar. 3. Krit. 4. Rohi. 5. Mrig. 6. Ardh. 7. Punar. 8. Push. 9. Aslesh. 10. Maghi. 11. P. Phal. 12. U. Phal. 13. Hasta. 14. Chit.

A. D. 1883. **A.—Amavasya.** **P.—Paurnami.**

Kollam 1059, Commences { **N. Malabar—Sept.** **S. Malabar—Aug.**

Hijra 1301, Commences, **Nov. 2.**

Vikrama 1940. **Bengal San 1289.** **(N. Cycle) Manmatha.**

SOLAR reckoning.			LUNAR reckoning.				
Cyclic Sidereal Year, Month and Day.	Week-Day	English Month and Day.	Tithi	Ending Moment.	Nakshatra	Ending Moment.	Muhammadan Year, Month and Day.
	July						
Subhanu *Mithuna—Ani.* 19	Su	1	*Bah.* 12	·77	3	·69	*Shaban.* 25
20	Mo	2	13	·69	4	·64	26
21	Tu	3	14	·62	5	·60	27
22	We	4	—A	·56	6	·58	28
23	Th	5	*Sukla* 1	·52	7	·57	—29
24	Fr	6	2	·50	8	·58	1
25	Sa	7	3	·50	9	·61	2
26	Su	8	4	·53	10	·66	3
27	Mo	9	5	·57	11	·73	4
28	Tu	10	6	·63	12	·83	5
29	We	11	7	·71	13	·93	6
30	Th	12	8	·79	...	...	7
31	Fr	13	9	·87	14	·04	8
—32	Sa	14	10	·95	15	·15	9
Subhanu *Karkata—Adi.* 1	Su	15	...	...	16	·25	10
2	Mo	16	11	·01	17	·34	11
3	Tu	17	12	·06	18	·41	12
4	We	18	13	·08	19	·45	13
5	Th	19	14	·10	20	·48	14
6	Fr	20	**Ashadha** P	·08	21	·49	15
7	Sa	21	1 2	·05 ·99	22	·48	H. 1300 *Ramzan.* 16
8	Su	22	*Bahula* 3	·92	23	·46	17
9	Mo	23	4	·85	24	·41	18
10	Tu	24	5	·76	25	·35	19
11	We	25	6	·66	26	·29	20
12	Th	26	7	·56	27	·23	21
13	Fr	27	8	·46	1	·16	22
14	Sa	28	9	·36	2	·09	23
15	Su	29	10	·26	3 4	·03 ·97	24
16	Mo	30	11	·17	5	·94	25
17	Tu	31	12	·09	6	·91	26
	Aug.						
18	We	1	13	·04	7	·89	27
19	Th	2	14 A	·01 ·99	8	·90	28
20	Fr	3	*Sukla* 1	·98	9	·92	29
21	Sa	4	...	...	10	·97	—30
22	Su	5	2	·00	...	...	H. 1300 *Shawwal.* 1
23	Mo	6	3	·05	11	·05	2
24	Tu	7	4	·11	12	·13	3
25	We	8	5	·18	13	·23	4
26	Th	9	6	·26	14	·34	5
27	Fr	10	7	·35	15	·45	6
28	Sa	11	8	·43	16	·55	7
29	Su	12	9	·50	17	·64	8
30	Mo	13	10	·54	18	·71	9
31	Tu	14	11	·57	19	·77	10
—32	We	15	12	·59	20	·80	11
Subhanu *Simha—Avani.* 1	Th	16	13	·57	21	·82	12
2	Fr	17	14	·54	22	·81	13
3	Sa	18	**Sravana** P	·49	23	·79	14
4	Su	19	1	·43	24	·74	15
5	Mo	20	2	·35	25	·69	16
6	Tu	21	3	·25	26	·63	17
7	We	22	4	·15	27	·57	18
8	Th	23	5 6	·05 ·95	1	·50	19
9	Fr	24	*Bahula* 7	·85	2	·43	20
10	Sa	25	8	·76	3	·36	21
11	Su	26	9	·68	4	·30	22
12	Mo	27	10	·61	5	·26	23
13	Tu	28	11	·55	6	·23	24
14	We	29	12	·51	7	·22	25
15	Th	30	13	·49	8	·22	26
16	Fr	31	14	·49	9	·24	27

SOLAR reckoning.			LUNAR reckoning.				
Cyclic Sidereal Year, Month and Day.	Week-Day	English Month and Day.	Tithi	Ending Moment.	Nakshatra	Ending Moment.	Muhammadan Year, Month and Day.
	Sep.						
Subhanu *Simha—Avani.* 17	Sa	1	—A	·51	10	·29	28
18	Su	2	*Sukla* 1	·56	11	·35	—29
19	Mo	3	2	·63	12	·43	H. 1300 *Zi-l-ka'da.* 1
20	Tu	4	3	·70	13	·53	2
21	We	5	4	·78	14	·64	3
22	Th	6	5	·86	15	·75	4
23	Fr	7	6	·94	16	·85	5
24	Sa	8	...	...	17	·94	6
25	Su	9	7	·01	...	...	7
26	Mo	10	8	·06	18	·02	8
27	Tu	11	9	·09	19	·08	9
28	We	12	10	·11	20	·12	10
29	Th	13	11	·09	21	·14	11
30	Fr	14	12	·07	22	·14	12
—31	Sa	15	13 14	·02 ·96	23	·12	13
Subhanu *Kanya—Purattasi.* 1	Su	16	**Bhadrapada** P	·88	24	·09	14
2	Mo	17	1	·79	25 26	·04 ·98	15
3	Tu	18	2	·69	27	·91	16
4	We	19	3	·59	1	·84	17
5	Th	20	4	·49	2	·77	18
6	Fr	21	5	·39	3	·70	19
7	Sa	22	6	·29	4	·65	20
8	Su	23	7	·21	5	·60	21
9	Mo	24	8	·14	6	·56	22
10	Tu	25	*Bahula* 9	·09	7	·54	23
11	We	26	10	·05	8	·54	24
12	Th	27	11	·03	9	·56	25
13	Fr	28	12	·02	10	·60	26
14	Sa	29	13	·06	11	·66	27
15	Su	30	14	·10	12	·74	28
	Oct.						
16	Mo	1	—A	·16	13	·83	29
17	Tu	2	*Sukla* 1	·24	14	·94	—30
18	We	3	2	·33	...	...	H. 1300 *Zi-l-hijja.* 1
19	Th	4	3	·41	15	·05	2
20	Fr	5	4	·49	16	·15	3
21	Sa	6	5	·56	17	·25	4
22	Su	7	6	·61	18	·33	5
23	Mo	8	7	·64	19	·40	6
24	Tu	9	8	·67	20	·44	7
25	We	10	9	·66	21	·46	8
26	Th	11	10	·63	22	·46	9
27	Fr	12	11	·58	23	·44	10
28	Sa	13	12	·52	24	·41	11
29	Su	14	13	·44	25	·36	12
—30	Mo	15	14	·35	26	·31	13
Subhanu *Tula—Aippasi.* 1	Tu ○	16	**Asvina** P	·26	27	·25	14
2	We	17	1	·16	1	·18	15
3	Th	18	2 3	·06 ·96	2	·11	16
4	Fr	19	4	·87	3 4	·05 ·99	17
5	Sa	20	5	·79	5	·93	18
6	Su	21	*Bahula* 6	·72	6	·89	19
7	Mo	22	7	·67	7	·87	20
8	Tu	23	8	·63	8	·87	21
9	We	24	9	·61	9	·88	22
10	Th	25	10	·62	10	·91	23
11	Fr	26	11	·64	11	·97	24
12	Sa	27	12	·68	...	...	25
13	Su	28	13	·75	12	·04	26
14	Mo	29	14	·83	13	·14	27
15	Tu	30	—A	·91	14	·24	28
16	We	31	...	...	15	·35	29

SOLAR reckoning.			LUNAR reckoning.				
Cyclic Sidereal Year, Month and Day.	Week-Day	English Month and Day.	Tithi	Ending Moment.	Nakshatra	Ending Moment.	Muhammadan Year, Month and Day.
	Nov.						
Subhanu *Tula—Aippasi.* 17	Th	1	1	·01	16	·45	—30
18	Fr	2	2	·09	17	·55	H. 1301 *Muharram.* 1
19	Sa	3	3	·15	18	·64	2
20	Su	4	4	·19	19	·71	3
21	Mo	5	5	·23	20	·76	4
22	Tu	6	*Sukla* 6	·26	21	·78	5
23	We	7	7	·25	22	·79	6
24	Th	8	8	·22	23	·77	7
25	Fr	9	9	·18	24	·75	8
26	Sa	10	10	·12	25	·71	9
27	Su	11	11 12	·04 ·95	26	·65	10
28	Mo	12	13	·86	27	·59	11
29	Tu	13	14	·76	1	·52	12
—30	We	14	**Kartika** P	·66	2	·45	13
Subhanu *Vrischika—Kartigai.* 1	Th	15	1	·56	3	·39	14
2	Fr	16	2	·47	4	·33	15
3	Sa	17	3	·39	5	·27	16
4	Su	18	4	·32	6	·22	17
5	Mo	19	5	·24	7	·20	18
6	Tu	20	*Bahula* 6	·27	8	·19	19
7	We	21	7	·22	9	·20	20
8	Th	22	8	·24	10	·23	21
9	Fr	23	9	·27	11	·28	22
10	Sa	24	10	·31	12	·35	23
11	Su	25	11	·37	13	·44	24
12	Mo	26	12	·46	14	·54	25
13	Tu	27	13	·55	15	·65	26
14	We	28	14	·63	16	·75	27
15	Th	29	—A	·71	17	·85	28
16	Fr	30	1	·78	18	·95	29
	Dec.						
17	Sa	1	2	·84	...	...	—30
18	Su	2	3	·87	19	·02	H. 1301 *Safar.* 1
19	Mo	3	*Sukla* 4	·88	20	·07	2
20	Tu	4	5	·88	21	·10	3
21	We	5	6	·85	22	·11	4
22	Th	6	7	·80	23	·11	5
23	Fr	7	8	·74	24	·08	6
24	Sa	8	9	·66	25 26	·04 ·99	7
25	Su	9	10	·58	27	·93	8
26	Mo	10	11	·48	1	·86	9
27	Tu	11	12	·38	2	·79	10
28	We	12	13	·28	3	·72	11
—29	Th	13	14	·19	4	·66	12
Subhanu *Dhanus—Margali.* 1	Fr	14	**Margasira** P	·10	5	·60	13
2	Sa	15	1 2	·02 ·96	6	·56	14
3	Su	16	3	·92	7	·53	15
4	Mo	17	4	·88	8	·51	16
5	Tu	18	5	·87	9	·52	17
6	We	19	6	·88	10	·54	18
7	Th	20	*Bahula* 7	·91	11	·59	19
8	Fr	21	8	·96	12	·66	20
9	Sa	22	...	...	13	·74	21
10	Su	23	9	·03	14	·84	22
11	Mo	24	10	·11	15	·94	23
12	Tu	25	11	·20	...	...	24
13	We	26	12	·29	16	·05	25
14	Th	27	13	·37	17	·16	26
15	Fr	28	14	·43	18	·25	27
16	Sa	29	—A	·48	19	·33	28
17	Su	30	*Suk.* 1	·52	20	·38	—29
18	Mo	31	2	·54	21	·42	1

15. Svati. 16. Visak. 17. Anur. 18. Jyesh. 19. Mula. 20. P. Ash. 21. U. Ash. 22. Sravn. 23. Dani. 24. Satab. 25. P. Bhad. 26. U. Bhad. 27. Rev.

A. D. 1884. **Mesha Sankranti** (Commencement of Indian Sidereal Year).

Solar Eclipse. ● **(Surya Sid.) April 11·48.** **Saka 1806.** **Kaliyuga 4985.**

Lunar Eclipse. ○ **(Arya Sid.) April 11·38.** **(S. Cycle) Tarana.**

Columns: SOLAR reckoning (Cyclic Sidereal Year, Month and Day; Week-Day; English Month and Day) — LUNAR reckoning (Tithi; Ending Moment; Nakshatra; Ending Moment; Muhammadan Year, Month and Day).

Jan.

Cyclic Sidereal Year, Month and Day	Week-Day	English Month and Day	Tithi	Ending Moment	Nakshatra	Ending Moment	Muhammadan Year, Month and Day
Subhanu, *Dhanus—Margali.* 19	Tu	1	Sukla 3	·52	22	·44	2
20	We	2	4	·49	23	·44	3
21	Th	3	5	·45	24	·41	4
22	Fr	4	6	·38	25	·37	5
23	Sa	5	7	·30	26	·32	6
24	Su	6	8	·22	27	·27	7
25	Mo	7	9	·13	1	·20	8
26	Tu	8	10 11	·03 ·93	2	·13	9
27	We	9	12	·84	3 4	·06 ·99	H. 1301 *Rabi-ul-awwal.* 10
28	Th	10	Pausha 13	·75	5	·94	11
29	Fr	11	14	·67	6	·90	12
—30	Sa	12	P	·61	7	·86	13
Subhanu, *Makara—Tai.* 1	Su	13	1	·56	8	·84	14
2	Mo	14	2	·52	9	·84	15
3	Tu	15	3	·51	10	·86	16
4	We	16	4	·52	11	·91	17
5	Th	17	5	·56	12	·97	18
6	Fr	18	Bahula 6	·61	...	...	19
7	Sa	19	7	·68	13	·04	20
8	Su	20	8	·77	14	·14	21
9	Mo	21	9	·86	15	·25	22
10	Tu	22	10	·94	16	·36	23
11	We	23	...	...	17	·46	24
12	Th	24	11	·02	18	·55	25
13	Fr	25	12	·09	19	·63	26
14	Sa	26	13	·14	20	·69	27
15	Su	27	14	·17	21	·74	28
16	Mo	28	—A	·18	22	·76	29
17	Tu	29	1	·16	23	·76	—30
18	We	30	2	·13	24	·74	1
19	Th	31	3	·09	25	·71	2

Feb.

Cyclic Sidereal Year, Month and Day	Week-Day	English Month and Day	Tithi	Ending Moment	Nakshatra	Ending Moment	Muhammadan Year, Month and Day
20	Fr	1	Sukla 4 5	·02 ·94	26	·67	3
21	Sa	2	6	·85	27	·61	4
22	Su	3	7	·76	1	·54	5
23	Mo	4	8	·66	2	·47	6
24	Tu	5	9	·56	3	·40	7
25	We	6	10	·46	4	·34	8
26	Th	7	11	·38	5	·28	H. 1301 *Rabi-ul-akhir.* 9
27	Fr	8	12	·30	6	·23	10
28	Sa	9	Magha 13	·24	7	·19	11
—29	Su	10	14	·19	8	·16	12
Subhanu, *Kumbha—Masi.* 1	Mo	11	P	·16	9	·16	13
2	Tu	12	1	·15	10	·18	14
3	We	13	2	·16	11	·22	15
4	Th	14	3	·20	12	·27	16
5	Fr	15	4	·25	13	·35	17
6	Sa	16	5	·32	14	·44	18
7	Su	17	6	·40	15	·54	19
8	Mo	18	Bahula 7	·49	16	·65	20
9	Tu	19	8	·57	17	·76	21
10	We	20	9	·64	18	·86	22
11	Th	21	10	·71	19	·94	23
12	Fr	22	11	·76	...	...	24
13	Sa	23	12	·80	20	·01	25
14	Su	24	13	·80	21	·06	26
15	Mo	25	14	·79	22	·08	27
16	Tu	26	—A	·75	23	·09	28
17	We	27	P. Suk. 1	·70	24	·07	—29
18	Th	28	2	·64	25	·05	1
19	Fr	29	3	·56	26 27	·00 ·94	2

March

Cyclic Sidereal Year, Month and Day	Week-Day	English Month and Day	Tithi	Ending Moment	Nakshatra	Ending Moment	Muhammadan Year, Month and Day
Subhanu, *Kumbha—Masi.* 20	Sa	1	Sukla 4	·47	1	·88	3
21	Su	2	5	·57	2	·81	4
22	Mo	3	6	·27	3	·74	5
23	Tu	4	7	·17	4	·68	6
24	We	5	8 9	·07 ·98	5	·62	7
25	Th	6	10	·91	6	·56	8
26	Fr	7	11	·85	7	·52	9
27	Sa	8	Phalguna 12	·80	8	·49	H. 1301 *Jumadal-awwal.* 10
28	Su	9	13	·77	9	·49	11
29	Mo	10	14	·75	10	·50	12
30	Tu	11	P	·76	11	·53	13
—31	We	12	1	·80	12	·58	14
Subhanu, *Mina—Panguni.* 1	Th	13	2	·85	13	·65	15
2	Fr	14	3	·92	14	·75	16
3	Sa	15	...	...	15	·85	17
4	Su	16	4	·00	16	·95	18
5	Mo	17	5	·09	...	...	19
6	Tu	18	Bahula 6	·18	17	·06	20
7	We	19	7	·26	18	·16	21
8	Th	20	8	·32	19	·25	22
9	Fr	21	9	·36	20	·32	23
10	Sa	22	10	·39	21	·37	24
11	Su	23	11	·59	22	·40	25
12	Mo	24	12	·38	23	·41	26
13	Tu	25	13	·34	24	·40	27
14	We	26	14	·29	25	·38	28
15	Th	27	—A	·22	26	·34	29
16	Fr	28	1	·14	27	·28	—30
17	Sa	29	2 3	·05 ·95	1	·22	1
18	Su	30	4	·85	2	·16	2
19	Mo	31	5	·75	3	·09	3

April

Cyclic Sidereal Year, Month and Day	Week-Day	English Month and Day	Tithi	Ending Moment	Nakshatra	Ending Moment	Muhammadan Year, Month and Day
20	Tu	1	Sukla 6	·65	4 5	·02 ·95	4
21	We	2	7	·56	6	·89	5
22	Th	3	8	·48	7	·85	6
23	Fr	4	9	·41	8	·83	7
24	Sa	5	10	·37	9	·81	8
25	Su	6	11	·34	10	·82	H. 1301 *Jumadal-akhir.* 9
26	Mo	7	12	·32	11	·84	10
27	Tu	8	Chaitra 13	·33	12	·89	11
28	We	9	14	·36	13	·96	12
—29	Th	○ 10	P	·41	...	...	13
Tarana, *Mesha—Chittirai.* 1	Fr	11	1	·46	14	·05	14
2	Sa	12	2	·56	15	·15	15
3	Su	13	3	·65	16	·25	16
4	Mo	14	4	·75	17	·36	17
5	Tu	15	5	·81	18	·47	18
6	We	16	6	·87	19	·56	19
7	Th	17	Bahula 7	·92	20	·63	20
8	Fr	18	8	·94	21	·68	21
9	Sa	19	9	·95	22	·72	22
10	Su	20	10	·93	23	·73	23
11	Mo	21	11	·89	24	·73	24
12	Tu	22	12	·85	25	·71	25
13	We	23	13	·76	26	·67	26
14	Th	24	14	·68	27	·62	27
15	Fr	25	—A	·59	1	·56	28
16	Sa	26	1	·49	2	·50	—29
17	Su	27	V. Suk. 2	·39	3	·43	*Rajab.* 1
18	Mo	28	3	·29	4	·36	2
19	Tu	29	4	·19	5	·29	3
20	We	30	5	·09	6	·23	4

May

Cyclic Sidereal Year, Month and Day	Week-Day	English Month and Day	Tithi	Ending Moment	Nakshatra	Ending Moment	Muhammadan Year, Month and Day
Tarana, *Mesha—Chittirai.* 21	Th	1	Sukla 6 7	·01 ·95	7	·19	5
22	Fr	2	8	·91	8	·16	6
23	Sa	3	9	·87	9	·14	7
24	Su	4	10	·84	10	·14	8
25	Mo	5	11	·85	11	·16	9
26	Tu	6	12	·89	12	·21	10
27	We	7	Vaisakha 13	·24	13	·27	11
28	Th	8	...	...	14	·35	12
29	Fr	9	14	·00	15	·45	13
30	Sa	10	P	·08	16	·55	H. 1301 *Rajab.* 14
—31	Su	11	1	·16	17	·65	15
1	Mo	12	2	·24	18	·76	16
2	Tu	13	3	·32	19	·86	17
3	We	14	4	·39	20	·94	18
4	Th	15	5	·44	...	...	19
5	Fr	16	Bahula 6	·45	21	·00	20
6	Sa	17	7	·46	22	·03	21
7	Su	18	8	·44	23	·06	22
8	Mo	19	9	·41	24	·06	23
9	Tu	20	10	·35	25	·04	24
10	We	21	11	·27	26 27	·00 ·95	25
11	Th	22	12	·19	1	·89	26
12	Fr	23	13	·10	2	·83	27
Tarana, *Vrishabha—Vaikasi.* 13	Sa	24	14 A	·00 ·90	3	·76	28
14	Su	25	1	·80	4	·69	29
15	Mo	26	2	·70	5	·63	—30
16	Tu	27	3	·60	6	·57	1
17	We	28	4	·52	7	·52	2
18	Th	29	5	·45	8	·49	3
19	Fr	30	Sukla 6	·40	9	·46	4
20	Sa	31	7	·36	10	·46	5

June

Cyclic Sidereal Year, Month and Day	Week-Day	English Month and Day	Tithi	Ending Moment	Nakshatra	Ending Moment	Muhammadan Year, Month and Day
21	Su	1	8	·35	11	·48	6
22	Mo	2	9	·35	12	·52	7
23	Tu	3	10	·38	13	·58	8
24	We	4	11	·43	14	·65	9
25	Th	5	Jyeshtha 12	·50	15	·74	10
26	Fr	6	13	·58	16	·85	11
27	Sa	7	14	·66	17	·96	H. 1301 *Shaban.* 12
28	Su	8	P	·74	...	...	13
29	Mo	9	1	·82	18	·07	14
30	Tu	10	2	·88	19	·16	15
31	We	11	3	·91	20	·24	16
—32	Th	12	4	·94	21	·31	17
Tarana, *Mithuna—Ani.* 1	Fr	13	5	·95	22	·36	18
2	Sa	14	6	·93	23	·38	19
3	Su	15	Bahula 7	·89	24	·38	20
4	Mo	16	8	·84	25	·37	21
5	Tu	17	9	·77	26	·34	22
6	We	18	10	·68	27	·30	23
7	Th	19	11	·58	1	·24	24
8	Fr	20	12	·48	2	·17	25
9	Sa	21	13	·38	3	·10	26
10	Su	22	14	·28	4 5	·03 ·97	27
11	Mo	23	—A	·18	6	·91	28
12	Tu	24	1	·09	7	·86	—29
13	We	25	2 3	·01 ·94	8	·82	1
14	Th	26	Ash. Suk. 4	·88	9	·79	*Ramzan.* 2
15	Fr	27	5	·84	10	·78	3
16	Sa	28	6	·83	11	·80	4
17	Su	29	7	·83	12	·83	5
18	Mo	30	8	·86	13	·88	6

Naksh:—1. Asvn. 2. Bhar. 3. Krit. 4. Rohi. 5. Mrig. 6. Ardh. 7. Punar. 8. Push. 9. Aslesh. 10. Magh. 11. P. Phal. 12. U. Phal. 13. Hasta. 14. Chit.

A. D. 1884.
A.—Amavasya.
P.—Paurnami.

Kollam 1060, Commences { **N. Malabar—Sept.** / **S. Malabar—Aug.**

Hijra 1302, Commences, Oct. 21.

Vikrama 1941.
Bengal San 1290.
(N. Cycle) Durmukha.

SOLAR reckoning: Cyclic Sidereal Year, Month and Day.	Week-Day	English Month and Day.	LUNAR reckoning: Tithi	Ending Moment.	Nakshatra	Ending Moment.	Muhammadan Year, Month and Day.
	July						
(Tarana Mithuna—Ani.) 19	Tu	1	(Sukla) 9	·91	14	·95	7
20	We	2	10	·97	...	...	8
21	Th	3	...	...	15	·04	9
22	Fr	4	11	·04	16	·15	10
23	Sa	5	(Ashadha) 12	·12	17	·26	11
24	Su	6	13	·21	18	·37	12
25	Mo	7	14	·29	19	·46	13
26	Tu	8	P	·35	20	·55	14
27	We	9	1	·39	21	·63	15
28	Th	10	2	·42	22	·67	(H. 1301 Ramzan.) 16
29	Fr	11	3	:42	23	·70	17
30	Sa	12	4	·41	24	·71	18
—31	Su	13	(Bahula) 5	·37	25	·70	19
(Tarana Karkata—Adi.) 1	Mo	14	6	·31	26	·68	20
2	Tu	15	7	·24	27	·63	21
3	We	16	8	·16	1	·58	22
4	Th	17	9, 10	·07, ·97	2	·51	23
5	Fr	18	11	·87	3	·44	24
6	Sa	19	12	·77	4	·37	25
7	Su	20	13	·67	5	·31	26
8	Mo	21	14	·57	6	·25	27
9	Tu	22	—A	·49	7	·19	28
10	We	23	1	·42	8	·15	29
11	Th	24	2	·37	9	·12	—30
12	Fr	25	3	·33	10	·11	1
13	Sa	26	4	·31	11	·12	2
14	Su	27	5	·31	12	·15	3
15	Mo	28	6	·33	13	·19	4
16	Tu	29	(Sukla) 7	·37	14	·26	5
17	We	30	8	·44	15	·35	6
18	Th	31	9	·52	16	·45	7
	Aug.						
19	Fr	1	10	·60	17	·56	8
20	Sa	2	11	·68	18	·66	9
21	Su	3	12	·76	19	·76	10
22	Mo	4	(Sravana) 13	·82	20	·86	11
23	Tu	5	14	·87	21	·94	(H. 1301 Shawwal.) 12
24	We	6	P	·90	22	·99	13
25	Th	7	1	·91	...	...	14
26	Fr	8	2	·89	23	·02	15
27	Sa	9	3	·86	24	·03	16
28	Su	10	4	·81	25	·03	17
29	Mo	11	5	·74	26, 27	·01, ·96	18
30	Tu	12	(Bahula) 6	·66	1	·91	19
31	We	13	7	·57	2	·85	20
—32	Th	14	8	·47	3	·79	21
(Tarana Sinha—Avani.) 1	Fr	15	9	·37	4	·72	22
2	Sa	16	10	·27	5	·65	23
3	Su	17	11	·17	6	·58	24
4	Mo	18	12, 13	·07, ·99	7	·52	25
5	Tu	19	14	·92	8	·48	26
6	We	20	—A	·87	9	·45	27
7	Th	21	(Sukla) 1	·83	10	·44	28
8	Fr	22	2	·80	11	·44	—29
9	Sa	23	3	·81	12	·46	(H. 1301 Zi-l-ka'da.) 1
10	Su	24	(Bhadrapada) 4	·83	13	·50	2
11	Mo	25	5	·88	14	·57	3
12	Tu	26	6	·95	15	·66	4
13	We	27	...	...	16	·76	5
14	Th	28	7	·02	17	·86	6
15	Fr	29	8	·09	18	·97	7
16	Sa	30	9	·17	...	...	8
17	Su	31	10	·26	19	·07	9

SOLAR reckoning: Cyclic Sidereal Year, Month and Day.	Week-Day	English Month and Day.	LUNAR reckoning: Tithi	Ending Moment.	Nakshatra	Ending Moment.	Muhammadan Year, Month and Day.
	Sep.						
(Tarana Sinha—Avani.) 18	Mo	1	(Bhadrapada) 11	·33	20	·16	10
19	Tu	2	12	·38	21	·24	11
20	We	3	13	·41	22	·30	12
21	Th	4	14	·42	23	·34	13
22	Fr	5	P	·41	24	·35	14
23	Sa	6	1	·38	25	·36	15
24	Su	7	2	·33	26	·34	16
25	Mo	8	3	·26	27	·30	17
26	Tu	9	4	·18	1	·25	(H. 1301 Zi-l-ka'da.) 18
27	We	10	(Bahula) 5, 6	·09, ·99	2	·19	19
28	Th	11	7	·89	3	·13	20
29	Fr	12	8	·79	4, 5	·06, ·99	21
30	Sa	13	9	·69	6	·92	22
—31	Su	14	10	·60	7	·86	23
(Tarana Kanya—Purattasi.) 1	Mo	15	11	·52	8	·82	24
2	Tu	16	12	·45	9	·78	25
3	We	17	13	·40	10	·76	26
4	Th	18	14	·35	11	·76	27
5	Fr	19	—A	·33	12	·78	28
6	Sa	20	1	·35	13	·82	29
7	Su	21	2	·37	14	·88	—30
8	Mo	22	3	·42	15	·96	1
9	Tu	23	4	·48	...	...	2
10	We	24	5	·55	16	·05	3
11	Th	25	6	·63	17	·15	4
12	Fr	26	7	·72	18	·26	5
13	Sa	27	(Sukla) 8	·80	19	·37	6
14	Su	28	9	·87	20	·47	7
15	Mo	29	10	·92	21	·55	8
16	Tu	30	11	·95	22	·61	9
	Oct.						
17	We	1	(Asvina) 12	·97	23	·65	10
18	Th	2	13	·95	24	·68	11
19	Fr	3	14	·93	25	·68	(H. 1301 Zi-l-hijja.) 12
20	Sa ○	4	P	·88	26	·66	13
21	Su	5	1	·81	27	·63	14
22	Mo	6	2	·73	1	·58	15
23	Tu	7	3	·64	2	·53	16
24	We	8	4	·55	3	·47	17
25	Th	9	5	·45	4	·40	18
26	Fr	10	(Bahula) 6	·35	5	·33	19
27	Sa	11	7	·25	6	·26	20
28	Su	12	8	·16	7	·20	21
29	Mo	13	9	·08	8	·15	22
—30	Tu	14	10, 11	·01, ·96	9	·11	23
(Tarana Tula—Aippasi.) 1	We	15	12	·92	10	·09	24
2	Th	16	13	·91	11	·08	25
3	Fr	17	14	·92	12	·10	26
4	Sa	18	—A	·94	13	·13	27
5	Su	19	1	·99	14	·19	28
6	Mo	20	...	...	15	·26	—29
7	Tu	21	2	·06	16	·35	(H. 1302 Muharram.) 1
8	We	22	(Sukla) 3	·14	17	·45	2
9	Th	23	4	·22	18	·56	3
10	Fr	24	5	·31	19	·67	4
11	Sa	25	6	·39	20	·77	5
12	Su	26	(Karttika) 7	·46	21	·85	6
13	Mo	27	8	·50	22	·92	7
14	Tu	28	9	·53	23	·97	8
15	We	29	10	·56	...	...	9
16	Th	30	11	·54	24	·00	10
17	Fr	31	12	·51	25, 26	·01, ·99	11

SOLAR reckoning: Cyclic Sidereal Year, Month and Day.	Week-Day	English Month and Day.	LUNAR reckoning: Tithi	Ending Moment.	Nakshatra	Ending Moment.	Muhammadan Year, Month and Day.
	Nov.						
(Tarana Tula—Aippasi.) 18	Sa	1	(Kartt.) 13	·47	27	·96	12
19	Su	2	14	·40	1	·93	13
20	Mo	3	P	·32	2	·87	14
21	Tu	4	1	·23	3	·80	15
22	We	5	2	·14	4	·73	16
23	Th	6	3, 4	·04, ·94	5	·66	(H. 1302 Muharram.) 17
24	Fr	7	5	·84	6	·60	18
25	Sa	8	(Bahula) 6	·76	7	·54	19
26	Su	9	7	·68	8	·49	20
27	Mo	10	8	·61	9	·44	21
28	Tu	11	9	·55	10	·41	22
29	We	12	10	·52	11	·41	23
—30	Th	13	11	·52	12	·42	24
1	Fr	14	12	·53	13	·45	25
2	Sa	15	13	·55	14	·50	26
3	Su	16	14	·60	15	·57	27
4	Mo	17	—A	·67	16	·66	28
5	Tu	18	1	·75	17	·76	29
6	We	19	2	·83	18	·87	—30
7	Th	20	3	·92	19	·97	1
8	Fr	21	...	...	...	...	2
(Tarana Vrischika—Kartigai.) 9	Sa	22	4	·00	20	·07	3
10	Su	23	5	·08	21	·16	4
11	Mo	24	6	·13	22	·24	5
12	Tu	25	(Sukla) 7	·17	23	·29	6
13	We	26	8	·17	24	·32	7
14	Th	27	9	·16	25	·33	8
15	Fr	28	10	·13	26	·32	9
16	Sa	29	11	·08	27	·30	10
17	Su	30	12, 13	·02, ·95	1	·26	11
	Dec.						
18	Mo	1	(Margasira) 14	·86	2	·21	(H. 1302 Safar.) 12
19	Tu	2	P	·77	3	·14	13
20	We	3	1	·67	4	·07	14
21	Th	4	2	·57	5, 6	·00, ·94	15
22	Fr	5	3	·47	7	·88	16
23	Sa	6	4	·38	8	·82	17
24	Su	7	5	·50	9	·77	18
25	Mo	8	6	·24	10	·74	19
26	Tu	9	(Bahula) 7	·19	11	·73	20
27	We	10	8	·16	12	·74	21
28	Th	11	9	·15	13	·76	22
29	Fr	12	10	·16	14	·80	23
—30	Sa	13	11	·19	15	·87	24
(Tarana Dhanus—Margali.) 1	Su	14	12	·25	16	·96	25
2	Mo	15	13	·32	...	...	26
3	Tu	16	14	·40	17	·06	27
4	We	17	—A	·50	18	·16	28
5	Th	18	1	·58	19	·27	—29
6	Fr	19	2	·65	20	·37	1
7	Sa	20	3	·72	21	·47	(H. 1302 Rabi-ul-awwal.) 2
8	Su	21	4	·77	22	·55	3
9	Mo	22	5	·81	23	·60	4
10	Tu	23	(Sukla) 6	·82	24	·64	5
11	We	24	7	·81	25	·65	6
12	Th	25	8	·78	26	·66	7
13	Fr	26	9	·73	27	·63	8
14	Sa	27	(Pausha) 10	·66	1	·59	9
15	Su	28	11	·58	2	·54	10
16	Mo	29	12	·49	3	·48	11
17	Tu	30	13	·40	4	·42	12
18	We	31	14	·30	5	·35	13

15. Svati. 16. Visak. 17. Anur. 18. Jyesh. 19. Mula. 20. P. Ash. 21. U. Ash. 22. Sravn. 23. Dani. 24. Satab. 25. P. Bhad. 26. U. Bhad. 27. Reve.

A. D. 1885. **Mesha Sankranti** (Commencement of Indian Sidereal Year).

Solar Eclipse. ● **(Surya Sid.) April 11·74.** **Saka 1807.** **Kaliyuga 4986.**

Lunar Eclipse. ○ **(Arya Sid.) April 11·64.** **(S. Cycle) Parthiva.**

Columns: SOLAR reckoning (Cyclic Sidereal Year, Month and Day; Week-Day; English Month and Day) — LUNAR reckoning (Tithi; Ending Moment; Nakshatra; Ending Moment; Muhammadan Year, Month and Day).

Jan.

Cyclic Sidereal Year, Month and Day	Week-Day	English Month and Day	Tithi	Ending Moment	Nakshatra	Ending Moment	Muhammadan Year, Month and Day
Tarana, Dhanus—Margali. 19	Th	1	P	·20	6	·28	H. 1302 Rabi-ul-awwal. 14
20	Fr	2	Pausha, Bah. 1	·11	7	·21	15
21	Sa	3	2 / 3	·02 / ·94	8	·15	16
22	Su	4	4	·88	9	·10	17
23	Mo	5	5	·84	10	·08	18
24	Tu	6	6	·81	11	·06	19
25	We	7	7	·79	12	·06	20
26	Th	8	8	·81	13	·08	21
27	Fr	9	9	·84	14	·12	22
28	Sa	10	10	·89	15	·18	23
29	Su	11	11	·97	16	·26	24
Tarana, Makara—Tai. 1	Mo	12	...	...	17	·36	25
2	Tu	13	12	·05	18	·46	26
3	We	14	13	·14	19	·57	27
4	Th	15	14	·23	20	·68	28
5	Fr	16	A	·31	21	·78	29
6	Sa	17	Magha, Sukla. 1	·37	22	·85	30
7	Su	18	2	·42	23	·91	Rabi-ul-akhir. 1
8	Mo	19	3	·45	24	·95	2
9	Tu	20	4	·46	25	·98	3
10	We	21	5	·45	26	·98	4
11	Th	22	6	·42	27	·96	5
12	Fr	23	7	·37	1	·93	6
13	Sa	24	8	·30	2	·88	7
14	Su	25	9	·22	3	·82	8
15	Mo	26	10	·13	4	·76	9
16	Tu	27	11 / 12	·03 / ·93	5	·39	10
17	We	28	13	·83	6	·62	11
18	Th	29	14	·74	7	·55	12
19	Fr	30	P	·65	8	·49	13
20	Sa	31	1	·58	9	·45	14

Feb.

Cyclic Sidereal Year, Month and Day	Week-Day	English Month and Day	Tithi	Ending Moment	Nakshatra	Ending Moment	Muhammadan Year, Month and Day
21	Su	1	Bahula. 2	·52	10	·41	H. 1302. 15
22	Mo	2	3	·47	11	·38	16
23	Tu	3	4	·45	12	·38	17
24	We	4	5	·43	13	·39	18
25	Th	5	6	·45	14	·43	19
26	Fr	6	7	·49	15	·49	20
27	Sa	7	8	·55	16	·57	21
28	Su	8	9	·62	17	·66	22
29	Mo	9	10	·70	18	·76	23
Tarana, Kumbha—Masi. 1	Tu	10	11	·78	19	·87	24
2	We	11	12	·86	20	·98	25
3	Th	12	13	·94	...	...	26
4	Fr	13	...	...	21	·08	27
5	Sa	14	14	·01	22	·16	28
6	Su	15	A	·06	23	·22	29
7	Mo	16	Phalguna, Sukla. 1	·08	24	·27	H. 1302 Jumadal-awwal. 1
8	Tu	17	2	·10	25	·30	2
9	We	18	3	·08	26	·31	3
10	Th	19	4 / 5	·04 / ·98	27	·20	4
11	Fr	20	6	·91	1	·26	5
12	Sa	21	7	·84	2	·21	6
13	Su	22	8	·75	3	·16	7
14	Mo	23	9	·65	4	·10	8
15	Tu	24	10	·55	5 / 6	·03 / ·96	9
16	We	25	11	·45	7	·80	10
17	Th	26	12	·35	8	·83	11
18	Fr	27	13	·26	9	·78	12
19	Sa	28	14	·19	10	·74	13

March

Cyclic Sidereal Year, Month and Day	Week-Day	English Month and Day	Tithi	Ending Moment	Nakshatra	Ending Moment	Muhammadan Year, Month and Day
Tarana, Kumbha—Masi. 20	Su	1	Phalguna. P	·13	11	·71	H. 1302 Jumadal-awwal. 14
21	Mo	2	Bahula. 1	·09	12	·70	15
22	Tu	3	2	·06	13	·72	16
23	We	4	3	·05	14	·75	17
24	Th	5	4	·06	15	·80	18
25	Fr	6	5	·09	16	·87	19
26	Sa	7	6	·15	17	·96	20
27	Su	8	7	·23	...	...	21
28	Mo	9	8	·32	18	·06	22
29	Tu	10	9	·41	19	·17	23
30	We	11	10	·49	20	·28	24
Tarana, Mina—Panguni. 1	Th	12	11	·56	21	·38	25
2	Fr	13	12	·61	22	·46	26
3	Sa	14	13	·66	23	·53	27
4	Su	15	14	·68	24	·59	28
5	Mo	16	A	·69	25	·62	29
6	Tu	17	1	·67	26	·63	30
7	We	18	Chaitra, Sukla. 2	·64	27	·63	Jumadal-akhir. 1
8	Th	19	3	·59	1	·60	2
9	Fr	20	4	·52	2	·56	3
10	Sa	21	5	·44	3	·50	4
11	Su	22	6	·34	4	·44	5
12	Mo	23	7	·24	5	·37	6
13	Tu	24	8	·14	6	·30	7
14	We	25	9 / 10	·04 / ·95	7	·23	8
15	Th	26	11	·86	8	·17	9
16	Fr	27	12	·78	9	·11	10
17	Sa	28	13	·72	10	·07	11
18	Su	29	14	·67	11	·04	12
19	Mo ○	30	P	·64	12	·03	13
20	Tu	31	1	·63	13	·04	14

April

Cyclic Sidereal Year, Month and Day	Week-Day	English Month and Day	Tithi	Ending Moment	Nakshatra	Ending Moment	Muhammadan Year, Month and Day
21	We	1	Bahula. 2	·65	14	·06	H. 1302. 15
22	Th	2	3	·68	15	·11	16
23	Fr	3	4	·73	16	·18	17
24	Sa	4	5	·80	17	·27	18
25	Su	5	6	·88	18	·37	19
26	Mo	6	7	·97	19	·47	20
27	Tu	7	...	...	20	·58	21
28	We	8	8	·06	21	·68	22
29	Th	9	9	·13	22	·77	23
30	Fr	10	10	·18	23	·85	24
31	Sa	11	11	·22	24	·90	25
Parthiva, Mesha—Chittirai. 1	Su	12	12	·25	25	·94	26
2	Mo	13	13	·25	26	·95	27
3	Tu	14	14	·23	27	·94	28
4	We	15	A	·20	1	·93	29
5	Th	16	Vaisakha, Sukla. 1	·14	2	·89	H. 1302 Rajab. 1
6	Fr	17	2 / 3	·07 / ·99	3	·84	2
7	Sa	18	4	·90	4	·78	3
8	Su	19	5	·80	5	·71	4
9	Mo	20	6	·69	6	·64	5
10	Tu	21	7	·59	7	·57	6
11	We	22	8	·49	8	·51	7
12	Th	23	9	·40	9	·45	8
13	Fr	24	10	·32	10	·40	9
14	Sa	25	11	·26	11	·38	10
15	Su	26	12	·21	12	·36	11
16	Mo	27	13	·18	13	·36	12
17	Tu	28	14	·17	14	·38	13
18	We	29	P	·18	15	·42	14
19	Th	30	1	·21	16	·48	15

May

Cyclic Sidereal Year, Month and Day	Week-Day	English Month and Day	Tithi	Ending Moment	Nakshatra	Ending Moment	Muhammadan Year, Month and Day
Parthiva, Mesha—Chittirai. 20	Fr	1	Vaisakha, Bahula. 2	·26	17	·56	H. 1302 Rajab. 16
21	Sa	2	3	·33	18	·66	17
22	Su	3	4	·41	19	·77	18
23	Mo	4	5	·50	20	·88	19
24	Tu	5	6	·57	21	·98	20
25	We	6	7	·64	...	...	21
26	Th	7	8	·71	22	·08	22
27	Fr	8	9	·76	23	·16	23
28	Sa	9	10	·78	24	·22	24
29	Su	10	11	·77	25	·26	25
30	Mo	11	12	·76	26	27	26
31	Tu	12	13	·72	27	·28	27
Parthiva, Vrishabha—Vaikasi. 1	We	13	14	·66	1	·26	28
2	Th	14	A	·59	2	·22	29
3	Fr	15	Adhika Jyeshtha, Sukla. 1	·50	3	·17	30
4	Sa	16	2	·41	4	·11	Shaban. 1
5	Su	17	3	·31	5 / 6	·05 / ·98	2
6	Mo	18	4	·21	7	·91	3
7	Tu	19	5	·11	8	·84	4
8	We	20	6 / 7	·01 / ·91	9	·78	5
9	Th	21	8	·83	10	·73	6
10	Fr	22	9	·77	11	·70	7
11	Sa	23	10	·72	12	·68	8
12	Su	24	11	·69	13	·68	9
13	Mo	25	12	·67	14	·69	10
14	Tu	26	13	·69	15	·73	11
15	We	27	14	·72	16	·79	12
16	Th	28	P	·76	17	·87	13
17	Fr	29	1	·82	18	·96	14
18	Sa	30	2	·89	...	...	15
19	Su	31	3	·98	19	·07	16

June

Cyclic Sidereal Year, Month and Day	Week-Day	English Month and Day	Tithi	Ending Moment	Nakshatra	Ending Moment	Muhammadan Year, Month and Day
20	Mo	1	Bahula. ...	...	20	·18	H. 1302. 17
21	Tu	2	4	·07	21	·29	18
22	We	3	5	·15	22	·38	19
23	Th	4	6	·21	23	·46	20
24	Fr	5	7	·24	24	·53	21
25	Sa	6	8	·27	25	·57	22
26	Su	7	9	·27	26	·60	23
27	Mo	8	10	·26	27	·60	24
28	Tu	9	11	·22	1	·59	25
29	We	10	12	·16	2	·55	26
30	Th	11	13 / 14	·08 / ·99	3	·51	27
31	Fr	12	A	·90	4	·46	28
Parthiva, Mithuna—Ani. 1	Sa	13	Nija Jyeshtha, Sukla. 1	·80	5	·39	29
2	Su	14	2	·70	6	·32	H. 1302 Ramzan. 1
3	Mo	15	3	·60	7	·25	2
4	Tu	16	4	·50	8	·18	3
5	We	17	5	·41	9	·12	4
6	Th	18	6	·33	10	·07	5
7	Fr	19	7	·26	11	·03	6
8	Sa	20	8	·21	12	·01	7
9	Su	21	9	·17	13	·00	8
10	Mo	22	10	·15	14	·01	9
11	Tu	23	11	·17	15	·05	10
12	We	24	12	·19	16	·10	11
13	Th	25	13	·24	17	·17	12
14	Fr	26	14	·30	18	·26	13
15	Sa	27	P	·37	19	·37	14
16	Su	28	Bah. 1	·45	20	·48	15
17	Mo	29	2	·54	21	·59	16
18	Tu	30	3	·62	22	·68	17

Naksh:—1. Asvn. 2. Bhar. 3. Krit. 4. Rohi. 5. Mrig. 6. Ardh. 7. Punar. 8. Push. 9. Aslesh. 10. Magh. 11. P. Phal. 12. U. Phal. 13. Hasta. 14. Chit.

A. D. 1885.
A.—Amavasya. P.—Paurnami.
Kollam 1061, Commences { N. Malabar—Sept. S. Malabar—Aug.
Hijra 1303, Commences, Oct. 10.
Vikrama 1942. Bengal San 1291. (N. Cycle) Hemalamba.

July – August

Solar: Parthiva Mithuna—Ani (to July 14); Parthiva Karkata—Adi (July 15 – Aug. 15); Parthiva Simha—Avani (from Aug. 16).
Lunar: Nija Jyesh. Bahula; Ashadha Sukla; Ashadha Bahula; Sravana Sukla; Sravana Bahula.
Muhammadan: H. 1302 Ramzan; H. 1302 Shawwal; H. 1302 Zi-l-ka'da.

Cyclic Sidereal Year, Month and Day	Week-Day	English Month and Day	Tithi	Ending Moment	Nakshatra	Ending Moment	Muhammadan Year, Month and Day
		July					
19	We	1	4	·67	23	·77	18
20	Th	2	5	·72	24	·84	19
21	Fr	3	6	·75	25	·89	20
22	Sa	4	7	·75	26	·92	21
23	Su	5	8	·73	27	·93	22
24	Mo	6	9	·69	1	·91	23
25	Tu	7	10	·63	2	·88	24
26	We	8	11	·56	3	·84	25
27	Th	9	12	·48	4	·79	26
28	Fr	10	13	·38	5	·73	27
29	Sa	11	14	·28	6	·66	28
30	Su	12	—A	·18	7	·59	29
31	Mo	13	1 / 2	·08 / ·98	8	·52	—30
—32	Tu	14	3	·88	9	·46	1
1	We	15	4	·80	10	·41	2
2	Th	16	5	·73	11	·37	3
3	Fr	17	6	·68	12	·34	4
4	Sa	18	7	·65	13	·32	5
5	Su	19	8	·63	14	·34	6
6	Mo	20	9	·64	15	·37	7
7	Tu	21	10	·66	16	·41	8
8	We	22	11	·71	17	·48	9
9	Th	23	12	·77	18	·57	10
10	Fr	24	13	·85	19	·67	11
11	Sa	25	14	·93	20	·78	12
12	Su	26	...	...	21	·89	13
13	Mo	27	P	·02	22	·99	14
14	Tu	28	1	·10	...	...	15
15	We	29	2	·16	23	·08	16
16	Th	30	3	·21	24	·16	17
17	Fr	31	4	·23	25	·21	18
		Aug.					
18	Sa	1	5	·23	26	·24	19
19	Su	2	6	·21	27	·25	20
20	Mo	3	7	·18	1	·24	21
21	Tu	4	8	·12	2	·22	22
22	We	5	9 / 10	·05 / ·97	3	·18	23
23	Th	6	11	·88	4	·13	24
24	Fr	7	12	·78	5	·07	25
25	Sa	8	13	·68	6 / 7	·00 / ·93	26
26	Su	9	14	·58	8	·86	27
27	Mo	10	—A	·48	9	·80	28
28	Tu	11	1	·38	10	·74	—29
29	We	12	2	·30	11	·70	1
30	Th	13	3	·23	12	·67	2
—31	Fr	14	4	·17	13	·66	3
1	Sa	15	5	·14	14	·66	4
2	Su	16	6	·13	15	·68	5
3	Mo	17	7	·13	16	·72	6
4	Tu	18	8	·16	17	·79	7
5	We	19	9	·20	18	·88	8
6	Th	20	10	·27	19	·98	9
7	Fr	21	11	·35	...	...	10
8	Sa	22	12	·43	20	·08	11
9	Su	23	13	·51	21	·19	12
10	Mo	24	14	·59	22	·29	13
11	Tu	25	P	·66	23	·38	14
12	We	26	1	·70	24	·46	15
13	Th	27	2	·72	25	·52	16
14	Fr	28	3	·74	26	·56	17
15	Sa	29	4	·71	27	·57	18
16	Su	30	5	·68	1	·57	19
17	Mo	31	6	·63	2	·56	20

September – October

Solar: Parthiva Simha—Avani (to Sep. 14); Parthiva Kanya—Purattasi (Sep. 15 – Oct. 15); Parthiva Tula—Aippasi (from Oct. 16).
Lunar: Sr. Bah.; Bhadrupada Sukla; Bhadrupada Bahula; Asvina Sukla; Asvina Bahula.
Muhammadan: H. 1302 Zi-l-ka'da; H. 1302 Zi-l-hijja; H. 1303 Muharram.

Cyclic Sidereal Year, Month and Day	Week-Day	English Month and Day	Tithi	Ending Moment	Nakshatra	Ending Moment	Muhammadan Year, Month and Day
		Sep.					
18	Tu	1	7	·56	3	·52	21
19	We	2	8	·48	4	·47	22
20	Th	3	9	·39	5	·41	23
21	Fr	4	10	·29	6	·35	24
22	Sa	5	11	·19	7	·28	25
23	Su	6	12 / 13	·09 / ·99	8	·21	26
24	Mo	7	14	·90	9	·14	27
25	Tu	8	—A	·82	10	·08	28
26	We	9	1	·75	11	·03	29
27	Th	10	2	·69	12 / 13	·00 / ·98	—30
28	Fr	11	3	·66	14	·98	1
29	Sa	12	4	·65	15	·99	2
30	Su	13	5	·67	...	...	3
—31	Mo	14	6	·69	16	·03	4
1	Tu	15	7	·73	17	·09	5
2	We	16	8	·79	18	·17	6
3	Th	17	9	·86	19	·27	7
4	Fr	18	10	·94	20	·37	8
5	Sa	19	...	...	21	·48	9
6	Su	20	11	·03	22	·59	10
7	Mo	21	12	·11	23	·69	11
8	Tu	22	13	·18	24	·77	12
9	We	23	14	·23	25	·83	13
10	Th ○	24	P	·26	26	·87	14
11	Fr	25	1	·27	27	·89	15
12	Sa	26	2	·26	1	·90	16
13	Su	27	3	·23	2	·88	17
14	Mo	28	4	·18	3	·85	18
15	Tu	29	5	·11	4	·80	19
16	We	30	6 / 7	·03 / ·94	5	·75	20
		Oct.					
17	Th	1	8	·84	6	·69	21
18	Fr	2	9	·74	7	·62	22
19	Sa	3	10	·64	8	·55	23
20	Su	4	11	·54	9	·48	24
21	Mo	5	12	·45	10	·42	25
22	Tu	6	13	·37	11	·37	26
23	We	7	14	·30	12	·33	27
24	Th	8	—A	·25	13	·31	28
25	Fr	9	1	·23	14	·30	—29
26	Sa	10	2	·21	15	·31	1
27	Su	11	3	·23	16	·34	2
28	Mo	12	4	·25	17	·41	3
29	Tu	13	5	·29	18	·48	4
30	We	14	6	·36	19	·57	5
—31	Th	15	7	·44	20	·67	6
1	Fr	16	8	·52	21	·78	7
2	Sa	17	9	·61	22	·89	8
3	Su	18	10	·69	23	·99	9
4	Mo	19	11	·76	...	...	10
5	Tu	20	12	·80	24	·07	11
6	We	21	13	·81	25	·14	12
7	Th	22	14	·85	26	·19	13
8	Fr	23	P	·84	27	·22	14
9	Sa	24	1	·81	1	·23	15
10	Su	25	2	·76	2	·21	16
11	Mo	26	3	·69	3	·18	17
12	Tu	27	4	·61	4	·14	18
13	We	28	5	·52	5	·09	19
14	Th	29	6	·43	6 / 7	·02 / ·95	20
15	Fr	30	7	·33	8	·88	21
16	Sa	31	8	·23	9	·81	22

November – December

Solar: Parthiva Tula—Aippasi (to Nov. 13); Parthiva Vrischika—Kartigai (Nov. 14 – Dec. 13); Parthiva Dhanus—Margali (from Dec. 14).
Lunar: Bah.; Kartika Sukla; Kartika Bahula; Margasira Sukla; Margasira Bahula.
Muhammadan: Muharram; H. 1303 Safar; H. 1303 Rabi-ul-awwal.

Cyclic Sidereal Year, Month and Day	Week-Day	English Month and Day	Tithi	Ending Moment	Nakshatra	Ending Moment	Muhammadan Year, Month and Day
		Nov.					
17	Su	1	9	·13	10	·75	23
18	Mo	2	10 / 11	·04 / ·97	11	·70	24
19	Tu	3	12	·91	12	·66	25
20	We	4	13	·85	13	·63	26
21	Th	5	14	·82	14	·62	27
22	Fr	6	—A	·80	15	·63	28
23	Sa	7	1	·82	16	·67	29
24	Su	8	2	·85	17	·72	—30
25	Mo	9	3	·90	18	·79	1
26	Tu	10	4	·97	19	·87	2
27	We	11	...	...	20	·97	3
28	Th	12	5	·04	...	...	4
—29	Fr	13	6	·13	21	·08	5
1	Sa	14	7	·23	22	·19	6
2	Su	15	8	·31	23	·29	7
3	Mo	16	9	·37	24	·38	8
4	Tu	17	10	·42	25	·45	9
5	We	18	11	·46	26	·51	10
6	Th	19	12	·46	27	·54	11
7	Fr	20	13	·44	1	·55	12
8	Sa	21	14	·41	2	·54	13
9	Su	22	P	·37	3	·51	14
10	Mo	23	1	·31	4	·48	15
11	Tu	24	2	·23	5	·43	16
12	We	25	3	·14	6	·36	17
13	Th	26	4 / 5	·04 / ·94	7	·29	18
14	Fr	27	6	·84	8	·22	19
15	Sa	28	7	·75	9	·16	20
16	Su	29	8	·67	10	·10	21
17	Mo	30	9	·59	11 / 12	·04 / ·99	22
		Dec.					
18	Tu	1	10	·52	13	·96	23
19	We	2	11	·47	14	·94	24
20	Th	3	12	·44	15	·96	25
21	Fr	4	13	·43	16	·99	26
22	Sa	5	14	·45	...	...	27
23	Su	6	—A	·48	17	·03	28
24	Mo	7	1	·54	18	·09	—29
25	Tu	8	2	·60	19	·17	1
26	We	9	3	·68	20	·27	2
27	Th	10	4	·77	21	·39	3
28	Fr	11	5	·87	22	·49	4
29	Sa	12	6	·95	23	·58	5
—30	Su	13	...	...	24	·67	6
1	Mo	14	7	·02	25	·76	7
2	Tu	15	8	·07	26	·82	8
3	We	16	9	·09	27	·85	9
4	Th	17	10	·10	1	·87	10
5	Fr	18	11	·09	2	·87	11
6	Sa	19	12	·06	3	·84	12
7	Su	20	13 / 14	·00 / ·93	4	·81	13
8	Mo	21	P	·86	5	·76	14
9	Tu	22	1	·77	6	·70	15
10	We	23	2	·68	7	·63	16
11	Th	24	3	·58	8	·56	17
12	Fr	25	4	·48	9	·49	18
13	Sa	26	5	·38	10	·43	19
14	Su	27	6	·30	11	·37	20
15	Mo	28	7	·22	12	·32	21
16	Tu	29	8	·16	13	·29	22
17	We	30	9	·12	14	·28	23
18	Th	31	10	·09	15	·28	24

15. Svati. 16. Visak. 17. Anur. 18. Jyesh. 19. Mula. 20. P. Ash. 21. U. Ash. 22. Sravn. 23. Dani. 24. Satab. 25. P. Bhad. 26. U. Bhad. 27. Rev.

A. D. 1886. **Mesha Sankranti** (Commencement of Indian Sidereal Year).

Solar Eclipse. ● **(Surya Sid.) April 12·00.** **Saka 1808.** **Kaliyuga 4987.**

Lunar Eclipse. ○ **(Arya Sid.) April 11·90.** **(S. Cycle) Vyaya.**

SOLAR reckoning.			LUNAR reckoning.				
Cyclic Sidereal Year, Month and Day.	Week-Day	English Month and Day.	Tithi	Ending Moment.	Nakshatra	Ending Moment.	Muhammadan Year, Month and Day.
	Jan.						
Parthiva *Dhanus—Margali.* 19	Fr	1	**Mr.** *Bah.* 11	·08	16	·30	*R.-awwal.* 25
20	Sa	2	12	·09	17	·34	26
21	Su	3	13	·13	18	·40	27
22	Mo	4	14	·19	19	·48	28
23	Tu	5	A	·26	20	·58	29
24	We	6	1	·34	21	·68	30
25	Th	7	2	·43	22	·79	H. 1303 *Rabi-ul-akhir.* 1
26	Fr	8	3	·52	23	·90	2
27	Sa	9	4	·60	...	...	3
28	Su	10	5	·67	24	·00	4
29	Mo	11	6	·71	25	·07	5
Parthiva *Makara—Tai.* 1	Tu	12	**Pausha** *Sukla* 7	·74	26	·13	6
2	We	13	8	·75	27	·17	7
3	Th	14	9	·73	1	·19	8
4	Fr	15	10	·70	2	·19	9
5	Sa	16	11	·65	3	·18	10
6	Su	17	12	·59	4	·15	11
7	Mo	18	13	·51	5	·10	12
8	Tu	19	14	·41	6 7	·04 ·98	13
9	We	20	P	·31	8	·91	14
10	Th	21	*Bahula* 1	·21	9	·84	15
11	Fr	22	2	·11	10	·77	16
12	Sa	23	3 4	·02 ·94	11	·71	17
13	Su	24	5	·87	12	·66	18
14	Mo	25	6	·81	13	·63	19
15	Tu	26	7	·76	14	·60	20
16	We	27	8	·73	15	·60	21
17	Th	28	9	·72	16	·61	22
18	Fr	29	10	·74	17	·65	23
19	Sa	30	11	·78	18	·71	24
20	Su	31	12	·84	19	·79	25
	Feb.						
21	Mo	1	13	·91	20	·88	26
22	Tu	2	14	·99	21	·98	27
23	We	3	...	...	...	...	28
24	Th	4	A	·08	22	·09	29
25	Fr	5	**Magha** *Sukla* 1	·17	23	·20	H. 1303 *Jumadal-awwal.* 1
26	Sa	6	2	·25	24	·50	2
27	Su	7	3	·31	25	·38	3
28	Mo	8	4	·36	26	·44	4
29	Tu	9	5	·38	27	·49	5
30	We	10	6	·38	1	·51	6
Parthiva *Kumbha—Masi.* 1	Th	11	7	·36	2	·53	7
2	Fr	12	8	·33	3	·51	8
3	Sa	13	9	·28	4	·48	9
4	Su	14	10	·21	5	·43	10
5	Mo	15	11	·13	6	·38	11
6	Tu	16	12 13	·04 ·94	7	·32	12
7	We	17	14	·84	8	·25	13
8	Th	18	P	·74	9	·18	14
9	Fr	19	*Bahula* 1	·64	10	·11	15
10	Sa	20	2	·56	11	·05	16
11	Su	21	3	·48	12 13	·00 ·96	17
12	Mo	22	4	·42	14	·93	18
13	Tu	23	5	·38	15	·92	19
14	We	24	6	·36	16	·93	20
15	Th	25	7	·34	17	·97	21
16	Fr	26	8	·35	...	...	22
17	Sa	27	9	·40	18	·02	23
18	Su	28	10	·46	19	·09	24

SOLAR reckoning.			LUNAR reckoning.				
Cyclic Sidereal Year, Month and Day.	Week-Day	English Month and Day.	Tithi	Ending Moment.	Nakshatra	Ending Moment.	Muhammadan Year, Month and Day.
	March						
Parthiva *Kumbha—Masi.* 19	Mo	1	**Mg.** *Bah.* 11	·53	20	·18	*J.-awwal.* 25
20	Tu	2	12	·62	21	·28	26
21	We	3	13	·71	22	·39	27
22	Th	4	14	·79	23	·50	28
23	Fr	5	A	·86	24	·60	29
24	Sa	6	**Phalguna** *Sukla* 1	·92	25	·68	30
25	Su	7	2	·97	26	·75	H. 1303 *Jumadal-akhir.* 1
26	Mo	8	3	·99	27	·80	2
27	Tu	9	4	·99	1	·84	3
28	We	10	5	·98	2	·85	4
29	Th	11	6	·94	3	·84	5
30	Fr	12	7	·88	4	·81	6
Parthiva *Mina—Panguni.* 1	Sa	13	8	·81	5	·77	7
2	Su	14	9	·73	6	·72	8
3	Mo	15	10	·64	7	·66	9
4	Tu	16	11	·54	8	·59	10
5	We	17	12	·44	9	·52	11
6	Th	18	13	·34	10	·45	12
7	Fr	19	14	·24	11	·39	13
8	Sa	20	P	·15	12	·33	14
9	Su	21	*Bahula* 1	·07	13	·29	15
10	Mo	22	2 3	·01 ·97	14	·26	16
11	Tu	23	4	·95	15	·24	17
12	We	24	5	·93	16	·25	18
13	Th	25	6	·95	17	·28	19
14	Fr	26	7	·99	18	·33	20
15	Sa	27	...	...	19	·40	21
16	Su	28	8	·05	20	·48	22
17	Mo	29	9	·12	21	·58	23
18	Tu	30	10	·20	22	·69	24
19	We	31	11	·29	23	·80	25
	April						
20	Th	1	12	·37	24	·90	26
21	Fr	2	13	·45	...	...	27
22	Sa	3	14	·51	25	·00	28
23	Su	4	A	·55	26	·07	29
24	Mo	5	**Chaitra** *Sukla* 1	·57	27	·13	H. 1303 *Rajab.* 1
25	Tu	6	2	·56	1	·16	2
26	We	7	3	·54	2	·17	3
27	Th	8	4	·50	3	·16	4
28	Fr	9	5	·44	4	·14	5
29	Sa	10	6	·37	5	·11	6
30	Su	11	7	·29	6 7	·06 ·99	7
Vyaya *Mesha—Chittirai.* 1	Mo	12	8	·19	8	·92	8
2	Tu	13	9 10	·09 ·99	9	·85	9
3	We	14	11	·89	10	·79	10
4	Th	15	12	·80	11	·73	11
5	Fr	16	13	·71	12	·67	12
6	Sa	17	14	·63	13	·62	13
7	Su	18	P	·56	14	·59	14
8	Mo	19	*Bahula* 1	·52	15	·57	15
9	Tu	20	2	·50	16	·58	16
10	We	21	3	·48	17	·60	17
11	Th	22	4	·49	18	·64	18
12	Fr	23	5	·53	19	·70	19
13	Sa	24	6	·59	20	·78	20
14	Su	25	7	·66	21	·88	21
15	Mo	26	8	·75	22	·99	22
16	Tu	27	9	·83	...	...	23
17	We	28	10	·91	23	·10	24
18	Th	29	11	·97	24	·20	25
19	Fr	30	...	...	25	·29	26

SOLAR reckoning.			LUNAR reckoning.				
Cyclic Sidereal Year, Month and Day.	Week-Day	English Month and Day.	Tithi	Ending Moment.	Nakshatra	Ending Moment.	Muhammadan Year, Month and Day.
	May						
Vyaya *Mesha—Chittirai.* 20	Sa	1	*Bah.* 12	·03	26	·38	*Rajab.* 27
21	Su	2	13	·07	27	·44	28
22	Mo	3	14	·09	1	·48	29
23	Tu	4	A	·10	2	·49	30
24	We	5	**Vaisakha** *Sukla* 1	·08	3	·49	H. 1303 *Shaban.* 1
25	Th	6	2 3	·03 ·97	4	·48	2
26	Fr	7	4	·90	5	·44	3
27	Sa	8	5	·82	6	·39	4
28	Su	9	6	·72	7	·33	5
29	Mo	10	7	·62	8	·26	6
30	Tu	11	8	·52	9	·19	7
31	We	12	9	·42	10	·12	8
Vyaya *Vrishabha—Vaikasi.* 1	Th	13	10	·32	11	·06	9
2	Fr	14	11	·22	12 13	·00 ·95	10
3	Sa	15	12	·14	14	·91	11
4	Su	16	13	·08	15	·90	12
5	Mo	17	14	·04	16	·90	13
6	Tu	18	P	·01	17	·91	14
7	We	19	*Bahula* 1	·00	18	·95	15
8	Th	20	2	·00	...	...	16
9	Fr	21	3	·04	19	·01	17
10	Sa	22	4	·10	20	·09	18
11	Su	23	5	·16	21	·18	19
12	Mo	24	6	·24	22	·28	20
13	Tu	25	7	·32	23	·39	21
14	We	26	8	·41	24	·50	22
15	Th	27	9	·48	25	·60	23
16	Fr	28	10	·53	26	·68	24
17	Sa	29	11	·57	27	·75	25
18	Su	30	12	·59	1	·79	26
19	Mo	31	13	·59	2	·81	27
	June						
20	Tu	1	14	·57	3	·81	28
21	We	2	A	·54	4	·80	29
22	Th	3	**Jyeshtha** *Sukla* 1	·48	5	·77	H. 1303 *Ramzan.* 1
23	Fr	4	2	·40	6	·73	2
24	Sa	5	3	·32	7	·67	3
25	Su	6	4	·22	8	·61	4
26	Mo	7	5	·12	9	·54	5
27	Tu	8	6 7	·02 ·92	10	·47	6
28	We	9	8	·82	11	·40	7
29	Th	10	9	·73	12	·34	8
30	Fr	11	10	·64	13	·29	9
31	Sa	12	11	·57	14	·25	10
Vyaya *Mithuna—Ani.* 1	Su	13	12	·52	15	·23	11
2	Mo	14	13	·49	16	·22	12
3	Tu	15	14	·48	17	·23	13
4	We	16	P	·49	18	·26	14
5	Th	17	*Bahula* 1	·53	19	·32	15
6	Fr	18	2	·57	20	·40	16
7	Sa	19	3	·63	21	·49	17
8	Su	20	4	·71	22	·59	18
9	Mo	21	5	·79	23	·70	19
10	Tu	22	6	·88	24	·81	20
11	We	23	7	·95	25	·91	21
12	Th	24	...	...	26	·99	22
13	Fr	25	8	·01	...	...	23
14	Sa	26	9	·05	27	·06	24
15	Su	27	10	·08	1	·10	25
16	Mo	28	11	·07	2	·13	26
17	Tu	29	12	·05	3	·15	27
18	We	30	13 14	·02 ·96	4	·13	28

Naksh:—1. Asvn. 2. Bhar. 3. Krit. 4. Rohi. 5. Mrig. 6. Ardh. 7. Punar. 8. Push. 9. Aslesh. 10. Magh. 11. P. Phal. 12. U. Phal. 13. Hasta. 14. Chit.

A. D. 1886. **A.—Amavasya.** **P.—Paurnami.** | **Kollam 1062,** Commences {**N. Malabar—Sept.** **S. Malabar—Aug.** | **Hijra 1304,** Commences, **Sep. 30.** | **Vikrama 1943.** **Bengal San 1292.** **(N. Cycle) Vilamba.**

SOLAR reckoning: Cyclic Sidereal Year, Month and Day.	Week-Day	English Month and Day.	LUNAR reckoning: Tithi	Ending Moment.	Nakshatra	Ending Moment.	Muhammadan Year, Month and Day.
	July						
19	Th	1	—A	·88	5	·10	29
20	Fr	2	1	·80	6	·06	—30
21	Sa	3	2	·70	7 / 8	·01 / ·95	1
22	Su	4	3	·60	9	·88	2
23 *Vyaya Mithuna—Ani.*	Mo	5	4	·49	10	·81	3
24	Tu	6	5	·39	11	·74	4
25	We	7	6	·29	12	·68	5
26	Th	8	7 *Sukla*	·20	13	·63	6
27	Fr	9	8	·12	14	·58	7
28	Sa	10	9	·05	15	·55	8
29	Su	11	10 / 11	·00 / ·97	16	·54	9
30	Mo	12	12	·96	17	·55	10
31	Tu	13	13	·96	18	·58	11
—32	We	14	...	...	19	·63	12
1	Th	15	14 **Ashadha**	·00	20	·70	13
2	Fr	16	P	·05	21	·79	14
3	Sa	17	1	·11	22	·89	15
4	Su	18	2	·18	23	·99	16 *H. 1303 Shawwal.*
5	Mo	19	3	·27	...	...	17
6	Tu	20	4	·35	24	·10	18
7	We	21	5	·42	25	·20	19
8	Th	22	6	·48	26	·29	20
9	Fr	23	7 *Bahula*	·53	27	·37	21
10	Sa	24	8	·55	1	·42	22
11	Su	25	9	·55	2	·46	23
12	Mo	26	10	·54	3	·47	24
13 *Vyaya Karkata—Adi.*	Tu	27	11	·50	4	·46	25
14	We	28	12	·44	5	·44	26
15	Th	29	13	·37	6	·40	27
16	Fr	30	14	·29	7	·35	28
17	Sa	31	—A	·19	8	·29	—29
	Aug.						
18	Su	1	1 / 2	·09 / ·99	9	·22	1
19	Mo	2	3	·89	10	·15	2
20	Tu	3	4	·79	11	·08	3
21	We	4	5	·69	12 / 13	·02 / ·96	4
22	Th	5	6	·61	14	·92	5
23	Fr	6	7 *Sukla*	·54	15	·88	6
24	Sa	7	8	·49	16	·87	7
25	Su	8	9	·46	17	·88	8
26	Mo	9	10	·44	18	·90	9
27	Tu	10	11	·46	19	·94	10
28	We	11	12	·48	...	...	11
29	Th	12	13	·53	20	·01	12
30	Fr	13	14 **Sravana**	·59	21	·09	13
—31	Sa	14	P	·67	22	·19	14
1	Su	15	1	·76	23	·30	15 *H. 1303 Zi-l-ka'da.*
2	Mo	16	2	·84	24	·41	16
3	Tu	17	3	·92	25	·51	17
4	We	18	4	·97	26	·60	18
5	Th	19	...	...	27	·68	19
6	Fr	20	5	·01	1	·74	20
7	Sa	21	6 *Bahula*	·04	2	·78	21
8	Su	22	7	·05	3	·79	22
9 *Vyaya Simha—Avani.*	Mo	23	8	·04	4	·79	23
10	Tu	24	9 / 10	·00 / ·95	5	·77	24
11	We	25	11	·88	6	·74	25
12	Th	26	12	·80	7	·69	26
13	Fr	27	13	·70	8	·63	27
14	Sa	28	14	·60	9	·56	28
15	Su	29	—A	·50	10	·49	29
16	Mo	30	1 *Suk.*	·40	11	·42	—30
17	Tu	31	2	·30	12	·36	1

SOLAR reckoning: Cyclic Sidereal Year, Month and Day.	Week-Day	English Month and Day.	LUNAR reckoning: Tithi	Ending Moment.	Nakshatra	Ending Moment.	Muhammadan Year, Month and Day.
	Sep.						
18	We	1	3	·21	13	·30	2
19	Th	2	4	·13	14	·25	3
20	Fr	3	5	·06	15	·21	4
21	Sa	4	6 / 7	·00 / ·97	16	·19	5
22	Su	5	8 *Sukla*	·95	17	·19	6
23 *Vyaya Simha—Avani.*	Mo	6	9	·97	18	·22	7
24	Tu	7	...	...	19	·25	8
25	We	8	10	·00	20	·31	9
26	Th	9	11	·05	21	·39	10
27	Fr	10	12	·11	22	·49	11
28	Sa	11	13	·18	23	·59	12
29	Su	12	14 **Bhadrapada**	·26	24	·70	13
30	Mo	13	P	·35	25	·81	14
—31	Tu	14	1	·43	26	·91	15
1	We	15	2	·50	27	·99	16
2	Th	16	3	·55	...	...	17 *H. 1303 Zi-l-hijja.*
3	Fr	17	4	·57	1	·05	18
4	Sa	18	5	·58	2	·09	19
5	Su	19	6	·56	3	·11	20
6	Mo	20	7 *Bahula*	·53	4	·11	21
7	Tu	21	8	·48	5	·10	22
8	We	22	9	·40	6	·07	23
9	Th	23	10	·32	7 / 8	·02 / ·96	24
10	Fr	24	11	·23	9	·90	25
11	Sa	25	12	·14	10	·83	26
12 *Vyaya Kanya—Purattasi.*	Su	26	13 / 14	·04 / ·94	11	·76	27
13	Mo	27	—A	·84	12	·70	28
14	Tu	28	1	·75	13	·64	29
15	We	29	2	·67	14	·58	—30
16	Th	30	3	·60	15	·54	1
	Oct.						
17	Fr	1	4	·55	16	·53	2
18	Sa	2	5	·52	17	·52	3
19	Su	3	6	·50	18	·53	4
20	Mo	4	7 *Sukla*	·52	19	·56	5
21	Tu	5	8	·55	20	·62	6
22	We	6	9	·60	21	·70	7
23	Th	7	10	·66	22	·79	8
24	Fr	8	11	·74	23	·89	9
25	Sa	9	12	·83	...	...	10
26	Su	10	13	·92	24	·00	11
27	Mo	11	...	...	25	·11	12
28	Tu	12	14 **Asvina**	·00	26	·21	13
29	We	13	P	·06	27	·30	14
30	Th	14	1	·10	1	·36	15
—31	Fr	15	2	·13	2	·41	16 *H. 1304 Muharram.*
1	Sa	16	3	·15	3	·43	17
2	Su	17	4	·13	4	·45	18
3	Mo	18	5	·10	5	·43	19
4	Tu	19	6 / 7	·05 / ·98	6	·40	20
5	We	20	8 *Bahula*	·90	7	·36	21
6	Th	21	9	·81	8	·30	22
7	Fr	22	10	·71	9	·24	23
8	Sa	23	11	·61	10	·17	24
9 *Vyaya Tula—Aippasi.*	Su	24	12	·51	11	·10	25
10	Mo	25	13	·41	12 / 13	·03 / ·97	26
11	Tu	26	14	·32	14	·91	27
12	We	27	—A	·25	15	·88	28
13	Th	28	1 **K.** *Suk.*	·19	16	·85	29
14	Fr	29	2	·14	17	·84	—30
15	Sa	30	3	·11	18	·85	1
16	Su	31	4	·10	19	·88	2

SOLAR reckoning: Cyclic Sidereal Year, Month and Day.	Week-Day	English Month and Day.	LUNAR reckoning: Tithi	Ending Moment.	Nakshatra	Ending Moment.	Muhammadan Year, Month and Day.
	Nov.						
17	Mo	1	5	·10	20	·94	3
18	Tu	2	6	·14	...	...	4
19	We	3	7 *Sukla*	·20	21	·01	5
20	Th	4	8	·27	22	·09	6
21 *Vyaya Tula—Aippasi.*	Fr	5	9	·35	23	·19	7
22	Sa	6	10	·43	24	·30	8
23	Su	7	11	·52	25	·41	9
24	Mo	8	12	·60	26	·51	10
25	Tu	9	13	·67	27	·60	11
26	We	10	14 **Kartika**	·71	1	·67	12
27	Th	11	P	·74	2	·72	13
28	Fr	12	1	·75	3	·75	14
29	Sa	13	2	·73	4	·77	15
—30	Su	14	3	·71	5	·76	16 *H. 1304 Safar.*
1	Mo	15	4	·66	6	·73	17
2	Tu	16	5	·59	7	·69	18
3	We	17	6 *Bahula*	·51	8	·64	19
4	Th	18	7	·42	9	·58	20
5	Fr	19	8	·32	10	·51	21
6	Sa	20	9	·22	11	·44	22
7	Su	21	10	·12	12	·37	23
8	Mo	22	11 / 12	·03 / ·95	13	·31	24
9	Tu	23	13	·87	14	·25	25
10	We	24	14	·80	15	·21	26
11	Th	25	—A	·76	16	·18	27
12 *Vyaya Vrischika—Kartigai.*	Fr	26	1	·73	17	·16	28
13	Sa	27	2	·72	18	·17	—29
14	Su	28	3	·73	19	·20	1
15	Mo	29	4	·77	20	·25	2
16	Tu	30	5	·83	21	·31	3
	Dec.						
17	We	1	6 *Sukla*	·90	22	·39	4
18	Th	2	7	·98	23	·49	5
19	Fr	3	...	...	24	·60	6
20	Sa	4	8	·07	25	·71	7
21	Su	5	9	·16	26	·81	8
22	Mo	6	10	·24	27	·90	9
23	Tu	7	11	·31	1	·97	10
24	We	8	12	·35	...	...	11
25	Th	9	13 **Margasira**	·38	2	·03	12
26	Fr	10	14	·39	3	·07	13
27	Sa	11	P	·38	4	·09	14
28	Su	12	1	·34	5	·09	15
—29	Mo	13	2	·28	6	·06	16 *H. 1304 Rabi-ul-awwal.*
1	Tu	14	3	·21	7 / 8	·02 / ·98	17
2	We	15	4	·13	9	·92	18
3	Th	16	5 / 6	·05 / ·95	10	·85	19
4	Fr	17	7 *Bahula*	·85	11	·78	20
5	Sa	18	8	·75	12	·71	21
6	Su	19	9	·65	13	·65	22
7	Mo	20	10	·57	14	·59	23
8	Tu	21	11	·50	15	·54	24
9 *Vyaya Dhanus—Margali.*	We	22	12	·44	16	·51	25
10	Th	23	13	·40	17	·49	26
11	Fr	24	14	·38	18	·50	27
12	Sa	25	—A	·36	19	·52	28
13	Su	26	1 **Psh.** *Sukla*	·37	20	·56	29
14	Mo	27	2	·42	21	·62	—30
15	Tu	28	3	·48	22	·70	1 *R.-akhir.*
16	We	29	4	·55	23	·79	2
17	Th	30	5	·63	24	·90	3
18	Fr	31	6	·73	...	...	4

15. Svati. 16. Visak. 17. Anur. 18. Jyesh. 19. Mula. 20. P. Ash. 21. U. Ash. 22. Sravn. 23. Dani. 24. Satab. 25. P. Bhad. 26. U. Bhad. 27. Rev.

A. D. 1887.
Solar Eclipse. ●
Lunar Eclipse. ○

Mesha Sankranti (Commencement of Indian Sidereal Year).
(Surya Sid.) April 12·26.
(Arya Sid.) April 12·15.

Saka 1809.
(S. Cycle) Sarvajit.

Kaliyuga 4988.

Jan. (Solar: Vyaya, Dhanus—Margali; Vyaya, Makara—Tai. Lunar: Sukla; Pausha; Bahula; Sukla. Muhammadan: H. 1304 Rabi-ul-akhir.)

SOLAR reckoning: Cyclic Sidereal Year, Month and Day.	Week-Day	English Month and Day.	LUNAR reckoning: Tithi	Ending Moment.	Nakshatra	Ending Moment.	Muhammadan Year, Month and Day.
19	Sa	1	7	·81	25	·01	5
20	Su	2	8	·89	26	·11	6
21	Mo	3	9	·95	27	·21	7
22	Tu	4	10	·99	1	·23	8
23	We	5	...	...	2	·35	9
24	Th	6	11	·02	3	·39	10
25	Fr	7	12	·03	4	·41	11
26	Sa	8	13 14	·02 ·98	5	·41	12
27	Su	9	P	·93	6	·39	13
28	Mo	10	1	·86	7	·36	14
29	Tu	11	2	·78	8	·32	15
30	We	12	3	·70	9	·26	16
1	Th	13	4	·60	10	·19	17
2	Fr	14	5	·50	11	·12	18
3	Sa	15	6	·40	12 13	·05 ·99	19
4	Su	16	7	·31	14	·93	20
5	Mo	17	8	·22	15	·88	21
6	Tu	18	9	·15	16	·84	22
7	We	19	10	·09	17	·82	23
8	Th	20	11	·05	18	·82	24
9	Fr	21	12	·02	19	·83	25
10	Sa	22	13	·00	20	·87	26
11	Su	23	14	·03	21	·92	27
12	Mo	24	A	·07	...	...	28
13	Tu	25	1	·13	22	·00	29
14	We	26	2	·21	23	·10	1
15	Th	27	3	·29	24	·20	2
16	Fr	28	4	·38	25	·31	3
17	Sa	29	5	·47	26	·41	4
18	Su	30	6	·55	27	·51	5
19	Mo	31	7	·61	1	·60	6

Feb. (Solar: Vyaya, Kumbha—Masi. Lunar: Magha; Bahula; Phalg. Suk. Muhammadan: H. 1304 Jumadal-awwal; J.-akhir.)

SOLAR reckoning: Cyclic Sidereal Year, Month and Day.	Week-Day	English Month and Day.	LUNAR reckoning: Tithi	Ending Moment.	Nakshatra	Ending Moment.	Muhammadan Year, Month and Day.
20	Tu	1	8	·65	2	·66	7
21	We	2	9	·66	3	·71	8
22	Th	3	10	·67	4	·73	9
23	Fr	4	11	·66	5	·74	10
24	Sa	5	12	·62	6	·73	11
25	Su	6	13	·56	7	·70	12
26	Mo	7	14	·49	8	·65	13
27	Tu ○	8	P	·41	9	·59	14
28	We	9	1	·32	10	·53	15
29	Th	10	2	·22	11	·47	16
1	Fr	11	3	·12	12	·40	17
2	Sa	12	4 5	·02 ·93	13	·33	18
3	Su	13	6	·84	14	·26	19
4	Mo	14	7	·77	15	·21	20
5	Tu	15	8	·72	16	·17	21
6	We	16	9	·68	17	·15	22
7	Th	17	10	·65	18	·14	23
8	Fr	18	11	·63	19	·15	24
9	Sa	19	12	·65	20	·18	25
10	Su	20	13	·69	21	·23	26
11	Mo	21	14	·75	22	·31	27
12	Tu	22	A	·83	23	·40	28
13	We	23	1	·92	24	·50	29
14	Th	24	...	...	25	·60	30
15	Fr	25	2	·01	26	·71	1
16	Sa	26	3	·09	27	·82	2
17	Su	27	4	·16	1	·91	3
18	Mo	28	5	·22	2	·97	4

March (Solar: Vyaya, Kumbha—Masi; Vyaya, Mina—Panguni. Lunar: Sukla; Phalguna; Bahula; Sukla. Muhammadan: H. 1304 Jumadal-akhir.)

SOLAR reckoning: Cyclic Sidereal Year, Month and Day.	Week-Day	English Month and Day.	LUNAR reckoning: Tithi	Ending Moment.	Nakshatra	Ending Moment.	Muhammadan Year, Month and Day.
19	Tu	1	6	·27	...	...	5
20	We	2	7	·28	3	·02	6
21	Th	3	8	·27	4	·05	7
22	Fr	4	9	·25	5	·07	8
23	Sa	5	10	·23	6	·06	9
24	Su	6	11	·17	7 8	·03 ·98	10
25	Mo	7	12	·10	9	·93	11
26	Tu	8	13 14	·02 ·93	10	·88	12
27	We	9	P	·83	11	·81	13
28	Th	10	1	·73	12	·74	14
29	Fr	11	2	·63	13	·67	15
30	Sa	12	3	·53	14	·60	16
1	Su	13	4	·44	15	·54	17
2	Mo	14	5	·37	16	·51	18
3	Tu	15	6	·31	17	·48	19
4	We	16	7	·27	18	·46	20
5	Th	17	8	·24	19	·47	21
6	Fr	18	9	·23	20	·49	22
7	Sa	19	10	·25	21	·55	23
8	Su	20	11	·29	22	·62	24
9	Mo	21	12	·35	23	·70	25
10	Tu	22	13	·43	24	·80	26
11	We	23	14	·52	25	·91	27
12	Th	24	A	·60	...	...	28
13	Fr	25	1	·68	26	·02	29
14	Sa	26	2	·75	27	·12	1
15	Su	27	3	·82	1	·21	2
16	Mo	28	4	·86	2	·28	3
17	Tu	29	5	·87	3	·34	4
18	We	30	6	·87	4	·37	5
19	Th	31	7	·85	5	·39	6

April (Solar: Sarvajit, Mesha—Chittirai. Lunar: Chaitra; Bahula; Vaisak. Sukla. Muhammadan: H. 1304 Rajab; Shaban.)

SOLAR reckoning: Cyclic Sidereal Year, Month and Day.	Week-Day	English Month and Day.	LUNAR reckoning: Tithi	Ending Moment.	Nakshatra	Ending Moment.	Muhammadan Year, Month and Day.
20	Fr	1	8	·81	6	·38	7
21	Sa	2	9	·75	7	·36	8
22	Su	3	10	·68	8	·32	9
23	Mo	4	11	·59	9	·27	10
24	Tu	5	12	·49	10	·21	11
25	We	6	13	·39	11	·14	12
26	Th	7	14	·29	12	·07	13
27	Fr	8	P	·19	13 14	·00 ·94	14
28	Sa	9	1	·09	15	·89	15
29	Su	10	2 3	·01 ·93	16	·84	16
30	Mo	11	4	·87	17	·81	17
1	Tu	12	5	·83	18	·79	18
2	We	13	6	·80	19	·79	19
3	Th	14	7	·80	20	·82	20
4	Fr	15	8	·81	21	·86	21
5	Sa	16	9	·85	22	·92	22
6	Su	17	10	·91	...	...	23
7	Mo	18	11	·99	23	·00	24
8	Tu	19	...	...	24	·10	25
9	We	20	12	·07	25	·21	26
10	Th	21	13	·15	26	·32	27
11	Fr	22	14	·23	27	·42	28
12	Sa	23	A	·30	1	·51	29
13	Su	24	1	·36	2	·59	30
14	Mo	25	2	·40	3	·65	1
15	Tu	26	3	·41	4	·68	2
16	We	27	4	·41	5	·71	3
17	Th	28	5	·39	6	·71	4
18	Fr	29	6	·35	7	·69	5
19	Sa	30	7	·28	8	·65	6

May (Solar: Sarvajit, Mesha—Chittirai; Sarvajit, Vrishabha—Vaikasi. Lunar: Suk.; Vaisakha; Bahula; Sukla. Muhammadan: H. 1304 Shaban.)

SOLAR reckoning: Cyclic Sidereal Year, Month and Day.	Week-Day	English Month and Day.	LUNAR reckoning: Tithi	Ending Moment.	Nakshatra	Ending Moment.	Muhammadan Year, Month and Day.
20	Su	1	8	·20	9	·61	7
21	Mo	2	9	·12	10	·55	8
22	Tu	3	10 11	·03 ·93	11	·48	9
23	We	4	12	·83	12	·41	10
24	Th	5	13	·73	13	·34	11
25	Fr	6	14	·63	14	·28	12
26	Sa	7	P	·54	15	·22	13
27	Su	8	1	·46	16	·17	14
28	Mo	9	2	·40	17	·13	15
29	Tu	10	3	·35	18	·11	16
30	We	11	4	·33	19	·12	17
31	Th	12	5	·32	20	·13	18
1	Fr	13	6	·33	21	·17	19
2	Sa	14	7	·37	22	·23	20
3	Su	15	8	·42	23	·30	21
4	Mo	16	9	·49	24	·40	22
5	Tu	17	10	·57	25	·51	23
6	We	18	11	·66	26	·62	24
7	Th	19	12	·74	27	·72	25
8	Fr	20	13	·81	1	·81	26
9	Sa	21	14	·87	2	·90	27
10	Su	22	A	·91	3	·97	28
11	Mo	23	1	·93	...	...	29
12	Tu	24	2	·92	4	·01	1
13	We	25	3	·90	5	·03	2
14	Th	26	4	·86	6	·03	3
15	Fr	27	5	·79	7 8	·02 ·99	4
16	Sa	28	6	·71	9	·95	5
17	Su	29	7	·62	10	·89	6
18	Mo	30	8	·52	11	·82	7
19	Tu	31	9	·42	12	·75	8

June (Solar: Sarvajit, Mithuna—Ani. Lunar: Jyeshtha; Bahula; Ashad. Sukla. Muhammadan: H. 1304 Ramzan; H. 1304 Shawwal.)

SOLAR reckoning: Cyclic Sidereal Year, Month and Day.	Week-Day	English Month and Day.	LUNAR reckoning: Tithi	Ending Moment.	Nakshatra	Ending Moment.	Muhammadan Year, Month and Day.
20	We	1	10	·32	13	·68	9
21	Th	2	11	·22	14	·62	10
22	Fr	3	12	·13	15	·56	11
23	Sa	4	13 14	·04 ·96	16	·51	12
24	Su	5	P	·90	17	·47	13
25	Mo	6	1	·85	18	·45	14
26	Tu	7	2	·82	19	·44	15
27	We	8	3	·81	20	·45	16
28	Th	9	4	·83	21	·48	17
29	Fr	10	5	·85	22	·54	18
30	Sa	11	6	·90	23	·62	19
31	Su	12	7	·97	24	·71	20
1	Mo	13	...	...	25	·81	21
2	Tu	14	8	·05	26	·91	22
3	We	15	9	·13	...	...	23
4	Th	16	10	·21	27	·02	24
5	Fr	17	11	·29	1	·12	25
6	Sa	18	12	·35	2	·21	26
7	Su	19	13	·39	3	·28	27
8	Mo	20	14	·41	4	·33	28
9	Tu	21	A	·40	5	·35	29
10	We	22	1	·38	6	·36	30
11	Th	23	2	·33	7	·35	1
12	Fr	24	3	·27	8	·32	2
13	Sa	25	4	·20	9	·28	3
14	Su	26	5	·12	10	·22	4
15	Mo	27	6 7	·02 ·92	11	·16	5
16	Tu	28	8	·82	12	·10	6
17	We	29	9	·72	13 14	·03 ·96	7
18	Th	30	10	·62	15	·89	8

Naksh:—1. Asvn. 2. Bhar. 3. Krit. 4. Rohi. 5. Mrig. 6. Ardra. 7. Punar. 8. Push. 9. Aslesh. 10. Magh. 11. P. Phal. 12. U. Phal. 13. Hasta. 14. Chit.

A. D. 1887.
A.—Amavasya.
P.—Paurnami.

Kollam 1063, Commences { **N. Malabar—Sept.** / **S. Malabar—Aug.**

Hijra 1305, Commences, **Sep. 19.**

Vikrama 1944.
Bengal San 1293.
(N. Cycle) Vikarin.

SOLAR reckoning.			LUNAR reckoning.				
Cyclic Sidereal Year, Month and Day.	Week-Day.	English Month and Day.	Tithi	Ending Moment.	Nakshatra	Ending Moment.	Muhammadan Year, Month and Day.
		July					
Sarvajit *Mithuna—Ani.* 19	Fr	1	Ashadha *Suk.* 11	·52	16	·84	H. 1304 *Shawwal.* 9
20	Sa	2	12	·45	17	·79	10
21	Su	3	13	·38	18	·77	11
22	Mo	4	14	·32	19	·76	12
23	Tu	5	P	·30	20	·77	13
24	We	6	*Bahula* 1	·29	21	·80	14
25	Th	7	2	·30	22	·85	15
26	Fr	8	3	·33	23	·92	16
27	Sa	9	4	·38	...	...	17
28	Su	10	5	·44	24	·01	18
29	Mo	11	6	·52	25	·10	19
30	Tu	12	7	·61	26	·21	20
31	We	13	8	·69	27	·32	21
—32	Th	14	9	·76	1	·42	22
Sarvajit *Karkata—Adi.* 1	Fr	15	10	·82	2	·51	23
2	Sa	16	11	·86	3	·59	24
3	Su	17	12	·88	4	·64	25
4	Mo	18	13	·88	5	·67	26
5	Tu	19	14	·86	6	·69	27
6	We	20	—A	·81	7	·68	28
7	Th	21	*Sukla* 1	·75	8	·65	—29
8	Fr	22	2	·68	9	·61	1
9	Sa	23	3	·60	10	·56	2
10	Su	24	4	·51	11	·51	3
11	Mo	25	5	·41	12	·44	4
12	Tu	26	6	·31	13	·37	5
13	We	27	7	·21	14	·30	6
14	Th	28	8	·11	15	·23	7
15	Fr	29	{ 9 10	·01 ·93	16	·17	8
16	Sa	30	11	·86	17	·13	9
17	Su	31	12	·81	18	·10	10
		Aug.					
18	Mo	1	Sravana 13	·78	19	·09	H. 1304 *Zi-l-ka'da.* 11
19	Tu	2	14	77	20	·09	12
20	We ○	3	P	·77	21	·11	13
21	Th	4	*Bahula* 1	·80	22	·16	14
22	Fr	5	2	·85	23	·23	15
23	Sa	6	3	·92	24	·31	16
24	Su	7	...	...	25	·40	17
25	Mo	8	4	·00	26	·51	18
26	Tu	9	5	·09	27	·62	19
27	We	10	6	·17	1	·73	20
28	Th	11	7	·24	2	·82	21
29	Fr	12	8	·30	3	·89	22
30	Sa	13	9	·34	4	·95	23
31	Su	14	10	·37	...	...	24
—32	Mo	15	11	·37	5	·00	25
Sarvajit *Simha—Avani.* 1	Tu	16	12	·35	6	·01	26
2	We	17	13	·31	7 8	·01 } ·98 }	27
3	Th	18	14	·25	9	·95	28
4	Fr ●	19	—A	·18	10	·90	29
5	Sa	20	*Sukla* 1	·10	11	·84	—30
6	Su	21	{ 2 3	01 ·91	12	·78	H. 1304 *Zi-l-hijja.* 1
7	Mo	22	4	·81	13	·71	2
8	Tu	23	5	·71	14	·64	3
9	We	24	6	·61	15	·58	4
10	Th	25	7	·52	16	·53	5
11	Fr	26	8	·44	17	·47	6
12	Sa	27	9	·37	18	·43	7
13	Su	28	Bhadra. 10	·32	19	·41	8
14	Mo	29	11	·29	20	·41	9
15	Tu	30	12	·28	21	·44	10
16	We	31	13	·28	22	·47	11

SOLAR reckoning.			LUNAR reckoning.				
Cyclic Sidereal Year, Month and Day.	Week-Day.	English Month and Day.	Tithi	Ending Moment.	Nakshatra	Ending Moment.	Muhammadan Year, Month and Day.
		Sep.					
Sarvajit *Simha—Avani.* 17	Th	1	Bhadrapada 14	·32	23	·53	H. 1304 *Zi-l-hijja.* 12
18	Fr	2	P	·37	24	·61	13
19	Sa	3	*Bahula* 1	·43	25	·70	14
20	Su	4	2	·51	26	·81	15
21	Mo	5	3	·59	27	·92	16
22	Tu	6	4	·67	...	...	17
23	We	7	5	·74	1	·03	18
24	Th	8	6	·81	2	·12	19
25	Fr	9	7	·86	3	·20	20
26	Sa	10	8	·90	4	·26	21
27	Su	11	9	·89	5	·31	22
28	Mo	12	10	·87	6	·33	23
29	Tu	13	11	·83	7	·33	24
30	We	14	12	·78	8	·31	25
—31	Th	15	13	·71	9	·28	26
Sarvajit *Kanya—Purattasi.* 1	Fr	16	14	·63	10	·24	27
2	Sa	17	—A	·54	11	·18	28
3	Su	18	*Sukla* 1	·44	12	·11	—29
4	Mo	19	2	·34	13 14	·04 } ·97 }	*Muharrum.* 1
5	Tu	20	3	·24	15	·91	2
6	We	21	4	·14	16	·85	3
7	Th	22	{ 5 6	·05 ·97	17	·80	4
8	Fr	23	7	·90	18	·76	5
9	Sa	24	8	·85	19	·74	6
10	Su	25	9	·82	20	·74	7
11	Mo	26	10	·82	21	·75	8
12	Tu	27	11	·83	22	·79	9
13	We	28	12	·86	23	·84	10
14	Th	29	13	·91	24	·91	11
15	Fr	30	14	·97	...	...	12
		Oct.					
16	Sa	1	Asvina ...	...	25	·01	H. 1305 13
17	Su	2	P	·05	26	·11	14
18	Mo	3	*Bahula* 1	·14	27	·22	15
19	Tu	4	2	·22	1	·32	16
20	We	5	3	·29	2	·42	17
21	Th	6	4	·37	3	·51	18
22	Fr	7	5	·41	4	·58	19
23	Sa	8	6	·44	5	·63	20
24	Su	9	7	·45	6	·65	21
25	Mo	10	8	·43	7	·66	22
26	Tu	11	9	·39	8	·64	23
27	We	12	10	·34	9	·61	24
28	Th	13	11	·28	10	·57	25
29	Fr	14	12	·20	11	·52	26
—30	Sa	15	13	·11	12	·46	27
Sarvajit *Tula—Aippasi.* 1	Su	16	{ 14 A	·01 ·91	13	·39	28
2	Mo	17	*Sukla* 1	·81	14	·32	29
3	Tu	18	2	·71	15	·25	—30
4	We	19	3	·62	16	·19	H. 1305 *Safar.* 1
5	Th	20	4	·55	17	·13	2
6	Fr	21	5	·49	18	·09	3
7	Sa	22	6	·44	19	·07	4
8	Su	23	7	·41	20	·06	5
9	Mo	24	8	·40	21	·07	6
10	Tu	25	9	·41	22	·10	7
11	We	26	10	·44	23	·15	8
12	Th	27	11	·48	24	·22	9
13	Fr	28	Kartika 12	·56	25	·31	10
14	Sa	29	13	·65	26	·41	11
15	Su	30	14	·74	27	·52	12
16	Mo	31	P	·82	1	·62	13

SOLAR reckoning.			LUNAR reckoning.				
Cyclic Sidereal Year, Month and Day.	Week-Day.	English Month and Day.	Tithi	Ending Moment.	Nakshatra	Ending Moment.	Muhammadan Year, Month and Day.
		Nov.					
Sarvajit *Tula—Aippasi.* 17	Tu	1	Kartika 1	·90	2	·72	H. 1305 *Safar.* 14
18	We	2	2	·96	3	·82	15
19	Th	3	...	...	4	·89	16
20	Fr	4	3	·01	5	·94	17
21	Sa	5	4	·04	6	·97	18
22	Su	6	5	·04	7	·98	19
23	Mo	7	{ 6 7	·03 ·99	8	·98	20
24	Tu	8	*Bahula* 8	·94	9	·95	21
25	We	9	9	·88	10	·91	22
26	Th	10	10	·80	11	·85	23
27	Fr	11	11	·71	12	·79	24
28	Sa	12	12	·61	13	·73	25
29	Su	13	13	·51	14	·66	26
—30	Mo	14	14	·41	15	·59	27
Sarvajit *Vrischika—Kartiyai.* 1	Tu	15	—A	·32	16	·53	28
2	We	16	*Sukla* 1	·23	17	·47	—29
3	Th	17	2	·15	18	·43	*Rabi-ul-awwal.* 1
4	Fr	18	3	·09	19	·40	2
5	Sa	19	4	·04	20	·38	3
6	Su	20	5	·02	21	·39	4
7	Mo	21	6	·01	22	·41	5
8	Tu	22	7	·03	23	·46	6
9	We	23	8	·06	24	·53	7
10	Th	24	9	·12	25	·61	8
11	Fr	25	10	·19	26	·71	9
12	Sa	26	11	·27	27	·82	10
13	Su	27	12	·36	1	·93	11
14	Mo	28	13	·44	...	...	12
15	Tu	29	14	·52	2	·03	13
16	We	30	Margasira P	·59	3	·12	14
		Dec.					
17	Th	1	1	·64	4	·20	H. 1305 15
18	Fr	2	2	·67	5	·25	16
19	Sa	3	3	·67	6	·29	17
20	Su	4	4	·66	7	·31	18
21	Mo	5	5	·62	8	·31	19
22	Tu	6	6	·56	9	·28	20
23	We	7	*Bahula* 7	·49	10	·24	21
24	Th	8	8	·42	11	·19	22
25	Fr	9	9	·33	12	·14	23
26	Sa	10	10	·23	13	·07	24
27	Su	11	11	·13	14 15	·00 } ·93 }	25
28	Mo	12	{ 12 13	·03 ·94	16	·86	26
—29	Tu	13	14	·86	17	·80	27
Sarvajit *Dhanus—Margali.* 1	We	14	—A	·79	18	·76	28
2	Th	15	*Sukla* 1	·73	19	·73	29
3	Fr	16	2	·69	20	·71	—30
4	Sa	17	3	·66	21	·71	H. 1305 *Rabi-ul-akhir.* 1
5	Su	18	4	·65	22	·73	2
6	Mo	19	5	·67	23	·78	3
7	Tu	20	6	·71	24	·84	4
8	We	21	7	·77	25	·92	5
9	Th	22	8	·84	...	...	6
10	Fr	23	9	·93	26	·01	7
11	Sa	24	...	...	27	·11	8
12	Su	25	10	·02	1	·22	9
13	Mo	26	11	·11	2	·33	10
14	Tu	27	Pausha 12	·18	3	·43	11
15	We	28	13	·24	4	·51	12
16	Th	29	14	·29	5	·57	13
17	Fr	30	P	·31	6	·61	14
18	Sa	31	1	·32	7	·63	15

15. Svati. 16. Visak. 17. Anur. 18. Jyesh. 19. Mula. 20. P. Ash. 21. U. Ash. 22. Sravn. 23. Dani. 24. Satab. 25. P. Bhad. 26. U. Bhad. 27. Rev.

A. D. 1888. **Mesha Sankranti** (Commencement of Indian Sidereal Year).

Solar Eclipse. ● **(Surya Sid.) April 11·51.** **Saka 1810.** **Kaliyuga 4989.**

Lunar Eclipse. ○ **(Arya Sid.) April 11·40.** **(S. Cycle) Sarvadhari.**

SOLAR reckoning: Cyclic Sidereal Year, Month and Day; Week-Day; English Month and Day. LUNAR reckoning: Tithi; Ending Moment; Nakshatra; Ending Moment; Muhammadan Year, Month and Day.

Jan.

Sarvajit Dhanus—Margali. Sarvajit Makara—Tai. Pausha ~ Bahula. Sukla. Magha. H. 1305 Rub-ul-akhir. H. 1305 Jumadal-awal.

Cyclic Sidereal Year, Month and Day	Week-Day	English Month and Day	Tithi	Ending Moment	Nakshatra	Ending Moment	Muhammadan Year, Month and Day
19	Su	1	2	·30	8	·63	16
20	Mo	2	3	·26	9	·61	17
21	Tu	3	4	·20	10	·58	18
22	We	4	5	·13	11	·54	19
23	Th	5	6 7	·06 ·97	12	·48	20
24	Fr	6	8	·88	13	·41	21
25	Sa	7	9	·78	14	·34	22
26	Su	8	10	·68	15	·27	23
27	Mo	9	11	·58	16	·21	24
28	Tu	10	12	·49	17	·15	25
29	We	11	13	·42	18	·10	26
—30	Th	12	14	·37	19	·06	27
1	Fr	13	—A	·33	20	·03	28
2	Sa	14	1	·30	21	·03	—29
3	Su	15	2	·30	22	·05	1
4	Mo	16	3	·32	23	·09	2
5	Tu	17	4	·36	24	·14	3
6	We	18	5	·42	25	·22	4
7	Th	19	6	·50	26	·31	5
8	Fr	20	7	·59	27	·42	6
9	Sa	21	8	·68	1	·58	7
10	Su	22	9	·76	2	·63	8
11	Mo	23	10	·84	3	·73	9
12	Tu	24	11	·90	4	·81	10
13	We	25	12	·94	5	·88	11
14	Th	26	13	·96	6	·93	12
15	Fr	27	14	·96	7	·95	13
16	Sa ○	28	P	94	8	·96	14
17	Su	29	1	·90	9	·94	15
18	Mo	30	2	·84	10	·91	16
19	Tu	31	3	·77	11	·67	17

Feb.

Sarvajit Kumbha—Masi. Bahula. Sukla. Phalguna. H. 1305 Jumadal-akhir.

Cyclic Sidereal Year, Month and Day	Week-Day	English Month and Day	Tithi	Ending Moment	Nakshatra	Ending Moment	Muhammadan Year, Month and Day
20	We	1	4	·69	12	·81	18
21	Th	2	5	·60	13	·75	19
22	Fr	3	6	·50	14	·68	20
23	Sa	4	7	·40	15	·61	21
24	Su	5	8	·30	16	·54	22
25	Mo	6	9	·21	17	·48	23
26	Tu	7	10	·13	18	·43	24
27	We	8	11	·06	19	·39	25
28	Th	9	12 13	·01 ·96	20	·36	26
—29	Fr	10	14	·93	21	·30	27
1	Sa	11	—A	·94	22	·37	28
2	Su	12	1	·96	23	·40	29
3	Mo	13	...	...	24	·45	—30
4	Tu	14	2	·00	25	·52	1
5	We	15	3	·06	26	·62	2
6	Th	16	4	·14	27	·72	3
7	Fr	17	5	·22	1	·83	4
8	Sa	18	6	·31	2	·93	5
9	Su	19	7	·39	...	...	6
10	Mo	20	8	·46	3	·03	7
11	Tu	21	9	·52	4	·12	8
12	We	22	10	·57	5	·19	9
13	Th	23	11	·59	6	·24	10
14	Fr	24	12	·58	7	·27	11
15	Sa	25	13	·56	8	·28	12
16	Su	26	14	·51	9	·27	13
17	Mo	27	P	·45	10	·25	14
18	Tu	28	1	·38	11	·20	15
19	We	29	2	·30	12	·14	16

March

Sarvajit Kumbha—Masi. Sarvajit Mina—Panguni. Phalg. ~ Bahula. Sukla. Adhika ~ Chaitra. H. 1305 Jumadal-akhir. H. 1305 Rajab.

Cyclic Sidereal Year, Month and Day	Week-Day	English Month and Day	Tithi	Ending Moment	Nakshatra	Ending Moment	Muhammadan Year, Month and Day
20	Th	1	3	·22	13	·08	17
21	Fr	2	4	·12	14 15	·02 ·95	18
22	Sa	3	5 6	·02 ·92	16	·88	19
23	Su	4	7	·82	17	·82	20
24	Mo	5	8	·73	18	·76	21
25	Tu	6	9	·66	19	·72	22
26	We	7	10	·61	20	·70	23
27	Th	8	11	·57	21	·68	24
28	Fr	9	12	·55	22	·69	25
29	Sa	10	13	·54	23	·71	26
30	Su	11	14	·56	24	·76	27
—31	Mo	12	—A	·60	25	·83	28
1	Tu	13	1	·66	26	·92	—29
2	We	14	2	·74	...	...	1
3	Th	15	3	·82	27	·02	2
4	Fr	16	4	·91	1	·12	3
5	Sa	17	5	·99	2	·23	4
6	Su	18	...	...	3	·33	5
7	Mo	19	6	·06	4	·42	6
8	Tu	20	7	·12	5	·50	7
9	We	21	8	·16	6	·56	8
10	Th	22	9	·18	7	·59	9
11	Fr	23	10	·17	8	·60	10
12	Sa	24	11	·15	9	·60	11
13	Su	25	12	·10	10	·58	12
14	Mo	26	13 14	·04 ·97	11	·54	13
15	Tu	27	P	·89	12	·48	14
16	We	28	1	·79	13	·42	15
17	Th	29	2	·69	14	·36	16
18	Fr	30	3	·59	15	·29	17
19	Sa	31	4	·49	16	·22	18

April

Sarvadhari Mesha—Chittirai. Bahula. Sukla. Nija Chaitra ~ Bah. H. 1305 Shaban.

Cyclic Sidereal Year, Month and Day	Week-Day	English Month and Day	Tithi	Ending Moment	Nakshatra	Ending Moment	Muhammadan Year, Month and Day
20	Su	1	5	·40	17	·16	19
21	Mo	2	6	·31	18	·10	20
22	Tu	3	7	·24	19	·06	21
23	We	4	8	·18	20	·03	22
24	Th	5	9	·14	21	·01	23
25	Fr	6	10	·12	22	·01	24
26	Sa	7	11	·11	23	·03	25
27	Su	8	12	·13	24	·07	26
28	Mo	9	13	·16	25	·14	27
—29	Tu	10	14	·22	26	·22	28
1	We	11	—A	·30	27	·32	29
2	Th	12	1	·38	1	·42	—30
3	Fr	13	2	·47	2	·53	1
4	Sa	14	3	·55	3	·64	2
5	Su	15	4	·62	4	·73	3
6	Mo	16	5	·67	5	·81	4
7	Tu	17	6	·71	6	·87	5
8	We	18	7	·73	7	·91	6
9	Th	19	8	·72	8	·93	7
10	Fr	20	9	·70	9	·98	8
11	Sa	21	10	·65	10	·91	9
12	Su	22	11	·59	11	·87	10
13	Mo	23	12	·51	12	·82	11
14	Tu	24	13	·43	13	·76	12
15	We	25	14	·34	14	·70	13
16	Th	26	P	·24	15	·63	14
17	Fr	27	1	·14	16	·56	15
18	Sa	28	2 3	·04 ·94	17	·49	16
19	Su	29	4	·85	18	·44	17
20	Mo	30	5	·77	19	·39	18

May

Sarvadhari Mesha—Chittirai. Sarvadhari Vrishabha—Vaikasi. Nija Ch. Bahula. Sukla. Vaisakha. H. 1305 Shaban. H. 1305 Ramzan.

Cyclic Sidereal Year, Month and Day	Week-Day	English Month and Day	Tithi	Ending Moment	Nakshatra	Ending Moment	Muhammadan Year, Month and Day
21	Tu	1	6	·72	20	·35	19
22	We	2	7	·68	21	·33	20
23	Th	3	8	·65	22	·33	21
24	Fr	4	9	·64	23	·35	22
25	Sa	5	10	·66	24	·39	23
26	Su	6	11	·69	25	·45	24
27	Mo	7	12	·75	26	·53	25
28	Tu	8	13	·82	27	·62	26
29	We	9	14	·90	1	·72	27
30	Th	10	—A	·98	2	·83	28
—31	Fr	11	...	...	3	·94	—29
1	Sa	12	1	·06	...	...	1
2	Su	13	2	·18	4	·04	2
3	Mo	14	3	·19	5	·12	3
4	Tu	15	4	·23	6	·18	4
5	We	16	5	·24	7	·28	5
6	Th	17	6	·24	8	·25	6
7	Fr	18	7	·22	9	·25	7
8	Sa	19	8	·18	10	·23	8
9	Su	20	9	·11	11	·20	9
10	Mo	21	10 11	·03 ·94	12	·16	10
11	Tu	22	12	·85	13	·11	11
12	We	23	13	·75	14 15	·04 ·97	12
13	Th	24	14	·64	16	·90	13
14	Fr	25	P	·54	17	·84	14
15	Sa	26	1	·44	18	·78	15
16	Su	27	2	·35	19	·72	16
17	Mo	28	3	·28	20	·68	17
18	Tu	29	4	·22	21	·66	18
19	We	30	5	·17	22	·66	19
20	Th	31	6	·14	23	·67	20

June

Sarvadhari Mithuna—Ani. Bahula. Sukla. Jyeshtha ~ Bah. H. 1305 Shawwal.

Cyclic Sidereal Year, Month and Day	Week-Day	English Month and Day	Tithi	Ending Moment	Nakshatra	Ending Moment	Muhammadan Year, Month and Day
21	Fr	1	7	·14	24	·70	21
22	Sa	2	8	·15	25	·76	22
23	Su	3	9	·18	26	·83	23
24	Mo	4	10	·24	27	·92	24
25	Tu	5	11	·31	...	...	25
26	We	6	12	·39	1	·02	26
27	Th	7	13	·48	2	·13	27
28	Fr	8	14	·56	3	·24	28
29	Sa	9	—A	·62	4	·34	29
30	Su	10	1	·67	5	·42	—30
31	Mo	11	2	·71	6	·49	1
—32	Tu	12	3	·73	7	·54	2
1	We	13	4	·73	8	·57	3
2	Th	14	5	·70	9	·58	4
3	Fr	15	6	·66	10	·56	5
4	Sa	16	7	·60	11	·54	6
5	Su	17	8	·53	12	·50	7
6	Mo	18	9	·44	13	·44	8
7	Tu	19	10	·34	14	·38	9
8	We	20	11	·24	15	·32	10
9	Th	21	12	·14	16	·25	11
10	Fr	22	13 14	·04 ·94	17	·18	12
11	Sa	23	P	·84	18	·11	13
12	Su	24	1	·76	19	·05	14
13	Mo	25	2	·70	20 21	·01 ·99	15
14	Tu	26	3	·65	22	·98	16
15	We	27	4	·62	23	·99	17
16	Th	28	5	·62	...	...	18
17	Fr	29	6	·63	24	·02	19
18	Sa	30	7	·67	25	·06	20

Naksh:—1. Asvn. 2. Bhar. 3. Krit. 4. Rohi. 5. Mrig. 6. Ardh. 7. Punar. 8. Push. 9. Aslesh. 10. Magh. 11. P. Phal. 12. U. Phal. 13. Hasta. 14. Chit.

A. D. 1888.
A.—Amavasya. **P.—Paurnami.**
Kollam 1064, Commences { **N. Malabar—Sept.** **S. Malabar—Aug.**
Hijra 1306, Commences, **Sep. 7.**
Vikrama 1945. **Bengal San 1294.** **(N. Cycle) Sarvari.**

SOLAR reckoning: Cyclic Sidereal Year, Month and Day; Week-Day; English Month and Day. LUNAR reckoning: Tithi; Ending Moment; Nakshatra; Ending Moment; Muhammadan Year, Month and Day.

July

Solar: Sarvadhari, Mithuna—Ani (19–31); Sarvadhari, Karkata—Adi (1–18). Lunar: Jyesh. Bahula (to A); Ashadha Sukla (1–P); Bahula. Muhammadan: H. 1305 Shawwal (21–29); H. 1305 Zi-l-ka'da (1–22).

Cyclic Sidereal Year, Month and Day	Week-Day	English Month and Day	Tithi	Ending Moment	Nakshatra	Ending Moment	Muhammadan Year, Month and Day
19	Su	1	8	·72	26	·13	21
20	Mo	2	9	·79	27	·22	22
21	Tu	3	10	·87	1	·33	23
22	We	4	11	·95	2	·44	24
23	Th	5	...	...	3	·54	25
24	Fr	6	12	·03	4	·64	26
25	Sa	7	13	·10	5	·73	27
26	Su	8	14	·16	6	·81	28
27	Mo	9	A	·20	7	·86	29
28	Tu	10	1	·22	8	·89	1
29	We	11	2	·20	9	·90	2
30	Th	12	3	·18	10	·90	3
31	Fr	13	4	·14	11	·87	4
1	Sa	14	5	·08	12	·83	5
2	Su	15	6 7	·01 ·92	13	·78	6
3	Mo	16	8	·82	14	·72	7
4	Tu	17	9	·72	15	·66	8
5	We	18	10	·62	16	·59	9
6	Th	19	11	·51	17	·52	10
7	Fr	20	12	·41	18	·45	11
8	Sa	21	13	·32	19	·39	12
9	Su	22	14	·25	20	·35	13
10	Mo ○	23	P	·19	21	·32	14
11	Tu	24	1	·14	22	·31	15
12	We	25	2	·12	23	·31	16
13	Th	26	3	·11	24	·33	17
14	Fr	27	4	·11	25	·37	18
15	Sa	28	5	·13	26	·44	19
16	Su	29	6	·18	27	·53	20
17	Mo	30	7	·25	1	·63	21
18	Tu	31	8	·33	2	·73	22

Aug.

Solar: Sarvadhari, Karkata—Adi (19–32); Sarvadhari, Simha—Avani (1–17). Lunar: Bahula (to A); Sravana Sukla (1–P); Bahula. Muhammadan: (to 30); H. 1305 Zi-l-hijja (1–23).

Cyclic Sidereal Year, Month and Day	Week-Day	English Month and Day	Tithi	Ending Moment	Nakshatra	Ending Moment	Muhammadan Year, Month and Day
19	We	1	9	·42	3	·84	23
20	Th	2	10	·50	4	·95	24
21	Fr	3	11	·57	...	...	25
22	Sa	4	12	·63	5	·04	26
23	Su	5	13	·67	6	·11	27
24	Mo	6	14	·70	7	·17	28
25	Tu	7	A	·70	8	·21	29
26	We	8	1	·67	9	·23	30
27	Th	9	2	·63	10	·23	1
28	Fr	10	3	·58	11	·20	2
29	Sa	11	4	·50	12	·17	3
30	Su	12	5	·41	13	·12	4
31	Mo	13	6	·31	14	·06	5
32	Tu	14	7	·21	15 16	·00 ·93	6
1	We	15	8	·11	17	·86	7
2	Th	16	9 10	·01 ·92	18	·79	8
3	Fr	17	11	·83	19	·73	9
4	Sa	18	12	·75	20	·69	10
5	Su	19	13	·69	21	·65	11
6	Mo	20	14	·64	22	·63	12
7	Tu	21	P	·61	23	·63	13
8	We	22	1	·59	24	·65	14
9	Th	23	2	·60	25	·69	15
10	Fr	24	3	·63	26	·75	16
11	Sa	25	4	·69	27	·83	17
12	Su	26	5	·76	1	·92	18
13	Mo	27	6	·84	...	...	19
14	Tu	28	7	·92	2	·03	20
15	We	29	...	...	3	·14	21
16	Th	30	8	·00	4	·25	22
17	Fr	31	9	·08	5	·34	23

Sep.

Solar: Sarvadhari, Simha—Avani (18–31); Sarvadhari, Kanya—Purattasi (1–16). Lunar: Sr. Bah. (to A); Bhadrapada Sukla (1–P); Bahula. Muhammadan: Zi-l-hijja (24–29); H. 1306 Muharram (1–24).

Cyclic Sidereal Year, Month and Day	Week-Day	English Month and Day	Tithi	Ending Moment	Nakshatra	Ending Moment	Muhammadan Year, Month and Day
18	Sa	1	10	·14	6	·42	24
19	Su	2	11	·18	7	·48	25
20	Mo	3	12	·21	8	·53	26
21	Tu	4	13	·20	9	·55	27
22	We	5	14	·18	10	·55	28
23	Th	6	A	·14	11	·53	29
24	Fr	7	1	·09	12	·50	1
25	Sa	8	2 3	·02 ·93	13	·45	2
26	Su	9	4	·85	14	·40	3
27	Mo	10	5	·78	15	·33	4
28	Tu	11	6	·63	16	·26	5
29	We	12	7	·53	17	·19	6
30	Th	13	8	·44	18	·12	7
31	Fr	14	9	·36	19	·07	8
1	Sa	15	10	·28	20 21	·02 ·98	9
2	Su	16	11	·21	22	·96	10
3	Mo	17	12	·16	23	·95	11
4	Tu	18	13	·13	24	·97	12
5	We	19	14	·12	...	...	13
6	Th	20	P	·13	25	·01	14
7	Fr	21	1	·16	26	·06	15
8	Sa	22	2	·22	27	·13	16
9	Su	23	3	·29	1	·22	17
10	Mo	24	4	·37	2	·33	18
11	Tu	25	5	·45	3	·44	19
12	We	26	6	·53	4	·55	20
13	Th	27	7	·61	5	·64	21
14	Fr	28	8	·68	6	·72	22
15	Sa	29	9	·72	7	·79	23
16	Su	30	10	·74	8	·84	24

Oct.

Solar: Sarvadhari, Kanya—Purattasi (17–30); Sarvadhari, Tula—Aippasi (1–17). Lunar: Bahula (to A); Asvina Sukla (1–P); Bahula. Muhammadan: (to 30); H. 1306 Safar (1–25).

Cyclic Sidereal Year, Month and Day	Week-Day	English Month and Day	Tithi	Ending Moment	Nakshatra	Ending Moment	Muhammadan Year, Month and Day
17	Mo	1	11	·75	9	·87	25
18	Tu	2	12	·73	10	·88	26
19	We	3	13	·69	11	·86	27
20	Th	4	14	·63	12	·83	28
21	Fr	5	A	·56	13	·79	29
22	Sa	6	1	·48	14	·74	30
23	Su	7	2	·39	15	·67	1
24	Mo	8	3	·30	16	·60	2
25	Tu	9	4	·20	17	·53	3
26	We	10	5	·10	18	·47	4
27	Th	11	6 7	·00 ·91	19	·41	5
28	Fr	12	8	·84	20	·35	6
29	Sa	13	9	·78	21	·31	7
30	Su	14	10	·73	22	·28	8
1	Mo	15	11	·70	23	·28	9
2	Tu	16	12	·70	24	·29	10
3	We	17	13	·71	25	·32	11
4	Th	18	14	·74	26	·37	12
5	Fr	19	P	·80	27	·44	13
6	Sa	20	1	·87	1	·53	14
7	Su	21	2	·95	2	·63	15
8	Mo	22	...	...	3	·74	16
9	Tu	23	3	·03	4	·84	17
10	We	24	4	·12	5	·94	18
11	Th	25	5	·20	...	...	19
12	Fr	26	6	·26	6	·03	20
13	Sa	27	7	·30	7	·11	21
14	Su	28	8	·33	8	·16	22
15	Mo	29	9	·34	9	·19	23
16	Tu	30	10	·32	10	·20	24
17	We	31	11	·28	11	·19	25

Nov.

Solar: Sarvadhari, Tula—Aippasi (18–30); Sarvadhari, Vrischika—Kartigai (1–17). Lunar: Bah. (to A); Kartika Sukla (1–P); Bahula. Muhammadan: Safar (26–29); H. 1306 Rabi-ul-awwal (1–26).

Cyclic Sidereal Year, Month and Day	Week-Day	English Month and Day	Tithi	Ending Moment	Nakshatra	Ending Moment	Muhammadan Year, Month and Day
18	Th	1	12	·23	12	·17	26
19	Fr	2	13	·16	13	·13	27
20	Sa	3	14 A	·07 ·98	14	·07	28
21	Su	4	1	·89	15 16	·01 ·95	29
22	Mo	5	2	·79	17	·88	1
23	Tu	6	3	·69	18	·81	2
24	We	7	4	·59	19	·74	3
25	Th	8	5	·51	20	·69	4
26	Fr	9	6	·43	21	·65	5
27	Sa	10	7	·37	22	·62	6
28	Su	11	8	·33	23	·60	7
29	Mo	12	9	·30	24	·61	8
30	Tu	13	10	·30	25	·63	9
1	We	14	11	·32	26	·68	10
2	Th	15	12	·36	27	·74	11
3	Fr	16	13	·41	1	·83	12
4	Sa	17	14	·48	2	·93	13
5	Su	18	P	·56	...	...	14
6	Mo	19	1	·65	3	·04	15
7	Tu	20	2	·74	4	·14	16
8	We	21	3	·82	5	·24	17
9	Th	22	4	·88	6	·34	18
10	Fr	23	5	·92	7	·42	19
11	Sa	24	6	·95	8	·47	20
12	Su	25	7	·95	9	·50	21
13	Mo	26	8	·94	10	·52	22
14	Tu	27	9	·90	11	·53	23
15	We	28	10	·85	12	·50	24
16	Th	29	11	·78	13	·46	25
17	Fr	30	12	·70	14	·41	26

Dec.

Solar: Sarvadhari, Vrischika—Kartigai (18–30); Sārvadhari, Dhanus—Margali (1–18). Lunar: Bahula (to A); Margasira Sukla (1–P); Bahula. Muhammadan: (to 30); H. 1306 Rabi-ul-akhir (1–27).

Cyclic Sidereal Year, Month and Day	Week-Day	English Month and Day	Tithi	Ending Moment	Nakshatra	Ending Moment	Muhammadan Year, Month and Day
18	Sa	1	13	·61	15	·35	27
19	Su	2	14	·51	16	·29	28
20	Mo	3	A	·41	17	·22	29
21	Tu	4	1	·31	18	·15	30
22	We	5	2	·22	19	·08	1
23	Th	6	3	·13	20 21	·02 ·98	2
24	Fr	7	4	·06	22	·95	3
25	Sa	8	5 6	·00 ·96	23	·93	4
26	Su	9	7	·93	24	·93	5
27	Mo	10	8	·94	25	·95	6
28	Tu.	11	9	·96	26	·99	7
29	We	12	...	...	...	...	8
30	Th	13	10	·00	27	·05	9
1	Fr	14	11	·06	1	·13	10
2	Sa	15	12	·14	2	·23	11
3	Su	16	13	·22	3	·33	12
4	Mo	17	14	·31	4	·44	13
5	Tu	18	P	·39	5	·55	14
6	We	19	1	·46	6	·65	15
7	Th	20	2	·52	7	·73	16
8	Fr	21	3	·57	8	·79	17
9	Sa	22	4	·60	9	·83	18
10	Su	23	5	·59	10	·85	19
11	Mo	24	6	·58	11	·85	20
12	Tu	25	7	·54	12	·83	21
13	We	26	8	·49	13	·79	22
14	Th	27	9	·42	14	·74	23
15	Fr	28	10	·34	15	·69	24
16	Sa	29	11	·25	16	·63	25
17	Su	30	12	·15	17	·56	26
18	Mo	31	13 14	·05 ·95	18	·49	27

15. Svati. 16. Visak. 17. Anur. 18. Jyesh. 19. Mula. 20. P. Ash. 21. U. Ash. 22. Sravn. 23. Dani. 24. Satab. 25. P. Bhad. 26. U. Bhad. 27. Rev.

A. D. 1889. **Mesha Sankranti** (Commencement of Indian Sidereal Year).

Solar Eclipse. ● **(Surya Sid.) April 11·77.** **Saka 1811.** **Kaliyuga 4990.**

Lunar Eclipse. ○ **(Arya Sid.) April 11·66.** **(S. Cycle) Virodhi.**

Jan.

Solar month (SOLAR reckoning)	Cyclic Sidereal Year, Month and Day	Week-Day	English Month and Day	Lunar month (LUNAR reckoning)	Tithi	Ending Moment	Nakshatra	Ending Moment	Muhammadan Year, Month	Muhammadan Day
Sarvadhari *Dhanus—Margali.*	19	Tu	1		—A	·85	19	·42		28
	20	We	2		1	·77	20	·36		—29
	21	Th	3		2	·70	21	·32	H. 1306 *Jumadal-awwal.*	1
	22	Fr	4		3	·64	22	·28		2
	23	Sa	5		4	·6?	23	·25		3
	24	Su	6		5	·59	24	·25		4
	25	Mo	7		6	·58	25	·26		5
	26	Tu	8	Pausha *Sukla*	7	·60	26	·30		6
	27	We	9		8	·64	27	·36		7
	28	Th	10		9	·70	1	·44		8
	—29	Fr	11		10	·78	2	·53		9
Sarvadhari *Makara—Tai.*	1	Sa	12		11	·86	3	·63		10
	2	Su	13		12	·96	4	·74		11
	3	Mo	14		...	...	5	·85		12
	4	Tu	15		13	·04	6	·95		13
	5	We	16		14	·11	...	...		14
	6	Th ○	17		P	·17	7	·03		15
	7	Fr	18	*Bahula*	1	·21	8	·10		16
	8	Sa	19		2	·24	9	·15		17
	9	Su	20		3	·24	10	·17		18
	10	Mo	21		4	·23	11	·17		19
	11	Tu	22		5	·19	12	·16		20
	12	We	23		6	·13	13	·13		21
	13	Th	24		7 8	·06 ·98	14	·09		22
	14	Fr	25		9	·88	15 16	·03 ·97		23
	15	Sa	26		10	·78	17	·90		24
	16	Su	27		11	·68	18	·83		25
	17	Mo	28		12	·58	19	·76		26
	18	Tu	29		13	·49	20	·70		27
	19	We	30		14	·41	21	·65		28
	20	Th	31		—A	·34	22	·61		29

Feb.

Solar month (SOLAR reckoning)	Cyclic Sidereal Year, Month and Day	Week-Day	English Month and Day	Lunar month (LUNAR reckoning)	Tithi	Ending Moment	Nakshatra	Ending Moment	Muhammadan Year, Month	Muhammadan Day
	21	Fr	1	Magha *Sukla*	1	·28	23	·58		—30
	22	Sa	2		2	·24	24	·57	H. 1306 *Jumadal-akhir.*	1
	23	Su	3		3	·23	25	·59		2
	24	Mo	4		4	·22	26	·62		3
	25	Tu	5		5	·24	27	·67		4
	26	We	6		6	·29	1	·74		5
	27	Th	7		7	·36	2	·83		6
	28	Fr	8		8	·43	3	·94		7
	29	Sa	9		9	·51	...	...		8
	—30	Su	10		10	·60	4	·05		9
Sarvadhari *Kumbha—Masi.*	1	Mo	11		11	·68	5	·15		10
	2	Tu	12		12	·76	6	·25		11
	3	We	13		13	·82	7	·34		12
	4	Th	14		14	·86	8	·41		13
	5	Fr	15		P	·87	9	·46		14
	6	Sa	16	*Bahula*	1	·88	10	·49		15
	7	Su	17		2	·85	11	·50		16
	8	Mo	18		3	·80	12	·49		17
	9	Tu	19		4	·74	13	·46		18
	10	We	20		5	·67	14	·42		19
	11	Th	21		6	·59	15	·37		20
	12	Fr	22		7	·50	16	·30		21
	13	Sa	23		8	·40	17	·23		22
	14	Su	24		9	·30	18	·16		23
	15	Mo	25		10	·20	19	·10		24
	16	Tu	26		11	·11	20 21	·04 ·98		25
	17	We	27		12 13	·03 ·96	22	·94		26
	18	Th	28		14	·90	23	·91		27

March

Solar month (SOLAR reckoning)	Cyclic Sidereal Year, Month and Day	Week-Day	English Month and Day	Lunar month (LUNAR reckoning)	Tithi	Ending Moment	Nakshatra	Ending Moment	Muhammadan Year, Month	Muhammadan Day
Sarvadhari *Kumbha—Masi.*	19	Fr	1		—A	·87	24	·90		28
	20	Sa	2	Phalguna *Sukla*	1	·84	25	·91		—29
	21	Su	3		2	·83	26	·93	H. 1306 *Rajab.*	1
	22	Mo	4		3	·86	27	·98		2
	23	Tu	5		4	·90	...	...		3
	24	We	6		5	·97	1	·05		4
	25	Th	7		...	...	2	·14		5
	26	Fr	8		6	·05	3	·24		6
	27	Sa	9		7	·14	4	·34		7
	28	Su	10		8	·23	5	·45		8
	—29	Mo	11		9	·31	6	·35		9
Sarvadhari *Mina—Panguni.*	1	Tu	12		10	·37	7	·64		10
	2	We	13		11	·42	8	·72		11
	3	Th	14		12	·46	9	·78		12
	4	Fr	15		13	·47	10	·81		13
	5	Sa	16		14	·47	11	·82		14
	6	Su	17		P	·45	12	·81		15
	7	Mo	18	*Bahula*	1	·40	13	·80		16
	8	Tu	19		2	·34	14	·76		17
	9	We	20		3	·27	15	·70		18
	10	Th	21		4	·18	16	·64		19
	11	Fr	22		5 6	·09 ·99	17	·58		20
	12	Sa	23		7	·89	18	·51		21
	13	Su	24		8	·79	19	·44		22
	14	Mo	25		9	·70	20	·38		23
	15	Tu	26		10	·61	21	·32		24
	16	We	27		11	·54	22	·27		25
	17	Th	28		12	·48	23	·24		26
	18	Fr	29		13	·45	24	·23		27
	19	Sa	30		14	·42	25	·23		28
	20	Su	31		—A	·42	26	·25		29

April

Solar month (SOLAR reckoning)	Cyclic Sidereal Year, Month and Day	Week-Day	English Month and Day	Lunar month (LUNAR reckoning)	Tithi	Ending Moment	Nakshatra	Ending Moment	Muhammadan Year, Month	Muhammadan Day
	21	Mo	1	Chaitra *Sukla*	1	·44	27	·29		—30
	22	Tu	2		2	·48	1	·36	H. 1306 *Shaban.*	1
	23	We	3		3	·54	2	·44		2
	24	Th	4		4	·62	3	·54		3
	25	Fr	5		5	·71	4	·64		4
	26	Sa	6		6	·79	5	·75		5
	27	Su	7		7	·87	6	·85		6
	28	Mo	8		8	·94	7	·95		7
	29	Tu	9		9	·99	...	...		8
	30	We	10		...	...	8	·03		9
	—31	Th	11		10	·02	9	·09		10
Virodhi *Mesha—Chittirai.*	1	Fr	12		11	·03	10	·13		11
	2	Sa	13		12	·03	11	·14		12
	3	Su	14		13 14	·01 ·96	12	·15		13
	4	Mo	15		P	·90	13	·13		14
	5	Tu	16	*Bahula*	1	·88	14	·09		15
	6	We	17		2	·74	15 16	·04 ·98		16
	7	Th	18		3	·64	17	·92		17
	8	Fr	19		4	·54	18	·85		18
	9	Sa	20		5	·44	19	·78		19
	10	Su	21		6	·34	20	·71		20
	11	Mo	22		7	·24	21	·65		21
	12	Tu	23		8	·16	22	·61		22
	13	We	24		9	·08	23	·57		23
	14	Th	25		10 11	·02 ·98	24	·55		24
	15	Fr	26		12	·96	25	·55		25
	16	Sa	27		13	·96	26	·56		26
	17	Su	28		14	·98	27	·60		27
	18	Mo	29		...	...	1	·66		28
	19	Tu	30		—A	·02	2	·74		—29

May

Solar month (SOLAR reckoning)	Cyclic Sidereal Year, Month and Day	Week-Day	English Month and Day	Lunar month (LUNAR reckoning)	Tithi	Ending Moment	Nakshatra	Ending Moment	Muhammadan Year, Month	Muhammadan Day
Virodhi *Mesha—Chittirai.*	20	We	1	Vaisakha *Sukla*	1	·07	3	·84	H. 1306 *Ramzan.*	1
	21	Th	2		2	·15	4	·94		2
	22	Fr	3		3	·24	...	...		3
	23	Sa	4		4	·32	5	·05		4
	24	Su	5		5	·39	6	·16		5
	25	Mo	6		6	·46	7	·26		6
	26	Tu	7		7	·52	8	·24		7
	27	We	8		8	·56	9	·40		8
	28	Th	9		9	·57	10	·44		9
	29	Fr	10		10	·56	11	·47		10
	30	Sa	11		11	·54	12	·47		11
	—31	Su	12		12	·49	13	·46		12
Virodhi *Vrishabha—Vaikasi.*	1	Mo	13		13	·42	14	·42		13
	2	Tu	14		14	·35	15	·37		14
	3	We	15		P	·26	16	·22		15
	4	Th	16	*Bahula*	1	·16	17	·26		16
	5	Fr	17		2 3	·06 ·96	18	·19		17
	6	Sa	18		4	·86	19	·12		18
	7	Su	19		5	·76	20	·06		19
	8	Mo	20		6	·67	21 22	·00 ·94		20
	9	Tu	21		7	·59	23	·91		21
	10	We	22		8	·53	24	·88		22
	11	Th	23		9	·49	25	·87		23
	12	Fr	24		10	·47	26	·88		24
	13	Sa	25		11	·46	27	·92		25
	14	Su	26		12	·47	1	·98		26
	15	Mo	27		13	·52	...	...		27
	16	Tu	28		14	·58	2	·05		28
	17	We	29		—A	·65	3	·14		29
	18	Th	30		1	·73	4	·24		—30
	19	Fr	31		2	·81	5	·35		1

June

Solar month (SOLAR reckoning)	Cyclic Sidereal Year, Month and Day	Week-Day	English Month and Day	Lunar month (LUNAR reckoning)	Tithi	Ending Moment	Nakshatra	Ending Moment	Muhammadan Year, Month	Muhammadan Day
	20	Sa	1	Jyeshtha *Sukla*	3	·89	6	·46	H. 1306 *Shawwal.*	2
	21	Su	2		4	·96	7	·56		3
	22	Mo	3		...	...	8	·64		4
	23	Tu	4		5	·01	9	·71		5
	24	We	5		6	·05	10	·76		6
	25	Th	6		7	·06	11	·79		7
	26	Fr	7		8	·05	12	·80		8
	27	Sa	8		9 10	·03 ·98	13	·78		9
	28	Su	9		11	·92	14	·75		10
	29	Mo	10		12	·85	15	·71		11
	30	Tu	11		13	·76	16	·66		12
	—31	We	12		14	·66	17	·60		13
Virodhi *Mithuna—Ani.*	1	Th	13		P	·55	18	·53		14
	2	Fr	14	*Bahula*	1	·45	19	·46		15
	3	Sa	15		2	·35	20	·39		16
	4	Su	16		3	·25	21	·33		17
	5	Mo	17		4	·16	22	·28		18
	6	Tu	18		5	·08	23	·23		19
	7	We	19		6 7	·02 ·97	24	·20		20
	8	Th	20		8	·95	25	·19		21
	9	Fr	21		9	·94	26	·21		22
	10	Sa	22		10	·96	27	·24		23
	11	Su	23		11	·99	1	·28		24
	12	Mo	24		...	...	2	·35		25
	13	Tu	25		12	·05	3	·44		26
	14	We	26		13	·12	4	·54		27
	15	Th	27		14	·20	5	·65		28
	16	Fr ●	28		—A	·28	6	·76		—29
	17	Sa	29	*Suk.*	1	·36	7	·86		1
	18	Su	30		2	·44	8	·95		2

Naksh :—1. Asvn. 2. Bhar. 3. Krit. 4. Rohi. 5. Mrig. 6. Ardh. 7. Punar. 8. Push. 9. Aslesh. 10. Magh. 11. P. Phal. 12. U. Phal. 13. Hasta 14. Chit.

A. D. 1889. | **Kollam 1065,** Commences { **N. Malabar—Sept.** / **S. Malabar—Aug.** | **Hijra 1307,** Commences, **Aug. 28.** | **Vikrama 1946.**

A.—Amavasya. **P.—Paurnami.** | **Bengal San 1295.** | **(N. Cycle) Plava.**

SOLAR reckoning.			LUNAR reckoning.				
Cyclic Sidereal Year, Month and Day.	Week-Day	English Month and Day.	Tithi	Ending Moment.	Nakshatra	Ending Moment.	Muhammadan Year, Month and Day.
	July						
Virodhi *Mithuna—Ani.* 19	Mo	1	Ashadha *Sukla* 3	·48	...	...	H. 1306 *Zi-l-ka'da.* 3
20	Tu	2	4	·52	9	·03	4
21	We	3	5	·54	10	·08	5
22	Th	4	6	·53	11	·11	6
23	Fr	5	7	·51	12	·12	7
24	Sa	6	8	·46	13	·11	8
25	Su	7	9	·39	14	·09	9
26	Mo	8	10	·32	15	·05	10
27	Tu	9	11	·23	16 17	·00 ·94	11
28	We	10	12	·13	18	·87	12
29	Th	11	13 14	·03 ·93	19	·80	13
30	Fr ○	12	P	·83	20	·73	14
31	Sa	13	*Bahula* 1	·73	21	·67	15
—32	Su	14	2	·64	22	·61	16
Virodhi *Karkata—Adi.* 1	Mo	15	3	·56	23	·56	17
2	Tu	16	4	·50	24	·53	18
3	We	17	5	·45	25	·52	19
4	Th	18	6	·43	26	·53	20
5	Fr	19	7	·42	27	·55	21
6	Sa	20	8	·44	1	·59	22
7	Su	21	9	·47	2	·66	23
8	Mo	22	10	·52	3	·74	24
9	Tu	23	11	·59	4	·84	25
10	We	24	12	·67	5	·95	26
11	Th	25	13	·75	...	...	27
12	Fr	26	14	·83	6	·06	28
13	Sa	27	—A	·90	7	·16	29
14	Su	28	Sravana *Sukla* 1	·96	8	·25	—30
15	Mo	29	...	...	9	·33	H. 1306 *Zi-l-hijja.* 1
16	Tu	30	2	·00	10	·39	2
17	We	31	3	·02	11	·43	3
	Aug.						
18	Th	1	4 5	·01 ·99	12	·44	4
19	Fr	2	6	·95	13	·44	5
20	Sa	3	7	·89	14	·42	6
21	Su	4	8	·81	15	·39	7
22	Mo	5	9	·72	16	·33	8
23	Tu	6	10	·63	17	·27	9
24	We	7	11	·53	18	·21	10
25	Th	8	12	·43	19	·14	11
26	Fr	9	13	·33	20	·07	12
27	Sa	10	14	·23	21 22	·01 ·95	13
28	Su	11	P	·14	23	·90	14
29	Mo	12	*Bahula* 1 2	·06 ·98	24	·87	15
30	Tu	13	3	·94	25	·85	16
—31	We	14	4	·92	26	·85	17
Virodhi *Simha—Avani.* 1	Th	15	5	·92	27	·87	18
2	Fr	16	6	·93	1	·90	19
3	Sa	17	7	·96	2	·97	20
4	Su	18	...	...	...	...	21
5	Mo	19	8	·01	3	·05	22
6	Tu	20	9	·08	4	·14	23
7	We	21	10	·16	5	·25	24
8	Th	22	11	·25	6	·36	25
9	Fr	23	12	·33	7	·47	26
10	Sa	24	13	·40	8	·56	27
11	Su	25	14	·46	9	·64	28
12	Mo	26	—A	·50	10	·70	29
13	Tu	27	B. *Sukla* 1	·52	11	·74	—30
14	We	28	2	·52	12	·76	H. 1307 *Muharam.* 1
15	Th	29	3	·49	13	·77	2
16	Fr	30	4	·45	14	·75	3
17	Sa	31	5	·39	15	·72	4

SOLAR reckoning.			LUNAR reckoning.				
Cyclic Sidereal Year, Month and Day.	Week-Day	English Month and Day.	Tithi	Ending Moment.	Nakshatra	Ending Moment.	Muhammadan Year, Month and Day.
	Sep.						
Virodhi *Simha—Avani.* 18	Su	1	Bhadrapada *Sukla* 6	·32	16	·67	H. 1307 *Muharram.* 5
19	Mo	2	7	·23	17	·61	6
20	Tu	3	8	·14	18	·55	7
21	We	4	9 10	·04 ·94	19	·48	8
22	Th	5	11	·84	20	·41	9
23	Fr	6	12	·74	21	·34	10
24	Sa	7	13	·66	22	·28	11
25	Su	8	14	·58	23	·24	12
26	Mo	9	P	·51	24	·20	13
27	Tu	10	*Bahula* 1	·46	25	·18	14
28	We	11	2	·44	26	·17	15
29	Th	12	3	·44	27	·18	16
30	Fr	13	4	·45	1	·22	17
—31	Sa	14	5	·49	2	·28	18
Virodhi *Kanya—Purattasi.* 1	Su	15	6	·54	3	·35	19
2	Mo	16	7	·61	4	·44	20
3	Tu	17	8	·69	5	·55	21
4	We	18	9	·77	6	·66	22
5	Th	19	10	·85	7	·77	23
6	Fr	20	11	·92	8	·86	24
7	Sa	21	12	·98	9	·94	25
8	Su	22	...	...	...	...	26
9	Mo	23	13	·03	10	·01	27
10	Tu	24	14	·05	11	·06	28
11	We	25	—A	·05	12	·09	29
12	Th	26	Asvina *Sukla* 1 2	·03 ·99	13	·10	—30
13	Fr	27	3	·93	14	·08	H. 1307 *Safar.* 1
14	Sa	28	4	·86	15	·05	2
15	Su	29	5	·78	16 17	·01 ·96	3
16	Mo	30	6	·69	18	·89	4
	Oct.						
17	Tu	1	7	·59	19	·82	5
18	We	2	8	·49	20	·75	6
19	Th	3	9	·38	21	·68	7
20	Fr	4	10	·28	22	·62	8
21	Sa	5	11	·20	23	·57	9
22	Su	6	12	·13	24	·53	10
23	Mo	7	13	·07	25	·50	11
24	Tu	8	14	·02	26	·49	12
25	We	9	P	·01	27	·50	13
26	Th	10	*Bahula* 1	·00	1	·54	14
27	Fr	11	2	·00	2	·59	15
28	Sa	12	3	·04	3	·66	16
29	Su	13	4	·10	4	·74	17
30	Mo	14	5	·17	5	·84	18
—31	Tu	15	6	·25	6	·95	19
Virodhi *Tula—Aippasi.* 1	We	16	7	·34	...	...	20
2	Th	17	8	·42	7	·06	21
3	Fr	18	9	·50	8	·16	22
4	Sa	19	10	·56	9	·25	23
5	Su	20	11	·61	10	·32	24
6	Mo	21	12	·64	11	·38	25
7	Tu	22	13	·63	12	·41	26
8	We	23	14	·61	13	·42	27
9	Th	24	—A	·57	14	·41	28
10	Fr	25	Kart. *Suk.* 1	·51	15	·38	—29
11	Sa	26	2	·44	16	·35	*Rabi-ul-awwal.* 1
12	Su	27	3	·36	17	·29	2
13	Mo	28	4	·27	18	·23	3
14	Tu	29	5	·18	19	·16	4
15	We	30	6 7	·08 ·98	20	·09	5
16	Th	31	8	·88	21 22	·02 ·96	6

SOLAR reckoning.			LUNAR reckoning.				
Cyclic Sidereal Year, Month and Day.	Week-Day	English Month and Day.	Tithi	Ending Moment.	Nakshatra	Ending Moment.	Muhammadan Year, Month and Day.
	Nov.						
Virodhi *Tula—Aippasi.* 17	Fr	1	Kartika *Sukla* 9	·79	23	·91	H. 1307 *Rabi-ul-awwal.* 7
18	Sa	2	10	·72	24	·86	8
19	Su	3	11	·66	25	·83	9
20	Mo	4	12	·62	26	·81	10
21	Tu	5	13	·60	27	·83	11
22	We	6	14	·59	1	·85	12
23	Th	7	P	·61	2	·90	13
24	Fr	8	*Bahula* 1	·65	3	·97	14
25	Sa	9	2	·71	...	...	15
26	Su	10	3	·78	4	·05	16
27	Mo	11	4	·86	5	·15	17
28	Tu	12	5	·95	6	·26	18
—29	We	13	...	...	7	·37	19
Virodhi *Vrischika—Kartigai.* 1	Th	14	6	·04	8	·47	20
2	Fr	15	7	·12	9	·56	21
3	Sa	16	8	·18	10	·64	22
4	Su	17	9	·22	11	·69	23
5	Mo	18	10	·24	12	·73	24
6	Tu	19	11	·24	13	·74	25
7	We	20	12	·22	14	·73	26
8	Th	21	13	·18	15	·71	27
9	Fr	22	14	·13	16	·68	28
10	Sa	23	A Margasira *Sukla* 1	·06 ·98	17	·63	29
11	Su	24	2	·89	18	·57	—30
12	Mo	25	3	·79	19	·50	H. 1307 *Rabi-ul-akhir.* 1
13	Tu	26	4	·69	20	·43	2
14	We	27	5	·59	21	·36	3
15	Th	28	6	·50	22	·30	4
16	Fr	29	7	·41	23	·24	5
17	Sa	30	8	·34	24	·19	6
	Dec.						
18	Su	1	9	·28	25	·16	7
19	Mo	2	10	·24	26	·15	8
20	Tu	3	11	·22	27	·15	9
21	We	4	12	·22	1	·17	10
22	Th	5	13	·25	2	·21	11
23	Fr	6	14	·29	3	·27	12
24	Sa	7	P	·35	4	·36	13
25	Su	8	*Bahula* 1	·42	5	·45	14
26	Mo	9	2	·50	6	·55	15
27	Tu	10	3	·59	7	·66	16
28	We	11	4	·68	8	·77	17
29	Th	12	5	·76	9	·87	18
—30	Fr	13	6	·82	10	·95	19
Virodhi *Dhanus—Margali.* 1	Sa	14	7	·87	...	...	20
2	Su	15	8	·88	11	·01	21
3	Mo	16	9	·38	12	·04	22
4	Tu	17	10	·86	13	·06	23
5	We	18	11	·82	14	·07	24
6	Th	19	12	·76	15	·05	25
7	Fr	20	13	·69	16 17	·01 ·96	26
8	Sa	21	14	·61	18	·90	27
9	Su	22	—A	·52	19	·84	28
10	Mo	23	Pausha *Sukla* 1	·42	20	·78	—29
11	Tu	24	2	·32	21	·71	*Jumadal-awwal.* 1
12	We	25	3	·22	22	·64	2
13	Th	26	4	·13	23	·58	3
14	Fr	27	5 6	·05 ·98	24	·53	4
15	Sa	28	7	·92	25	·50	5
16	Su	29	8	·89	26	·47	6
17	Mo	30	9	·87	27	·47	7
18	Tu	31	10	·87	1	·48	8

15. Svati. 16. Visak. 17. Anur. 18. Jyesh. 19. Mula. 20. P. Ash. 21. U. Ash. 22. Sravn. 23. Dani. 24. Satab. 25. P. Bhad. 26. U. Bhad. 27. Rev.

A. D. 1890. **Mesha Sankránti** (Commencement of Indian Sidereal Year).
Solar Eclipse. ● **(Surya Sid.) April 12·03.** **Saka 1812.** **Kaliyuga 4991.**
Lunar Eclipse. ○ **(Arya Sid.) April 11·92.** **(S. Cycle) Vikrita.**

Columns: SOLAR reckoning — Cyclic Sidereal Year, Month and Day; Week-Day; English Month and Day. LUNAR reckoning — Tithi; Ending Moment; Nakshatra; Ending Moment; Muhammadan Year, Month and Day.

Jan. — Solar: Virodhi, *Dhanus—Margali* (19–29); Virodhi, *Makara—Tai* (1–20). Lunar: Pausha, *Sukla* / *Bahula* / *Sukla*. Muhammadan: H. 1307 *Jumadal-awwal*.

Cyclic Sidereal Year, Month and Day	Week-Day	English Month and Day	Tithi	Ending Moment	Nakshatra	Ending Moment	Muhammadan Year, Month and Day
19	We	1	11	·89	2	·52	9
20	Th	2	12	·93	3	·58	10
21	Fr	3	13	·99	4	·66	11
22	Sa	4	...	...	5	·75	12
23	Su	5	14	·07	6	·85	13
24	Mo	6	P	·16	7	·96	14
25	Tu	7	1	·25	...	...	15
26	We	8	2	·33	8	·07	16
27	Th	9	3	·41	9	·17	17
28	Fr	10	4	·47	10	·25	18
29	Sa	11	5	·51	11	·32	19
1	Su	12	6	·53	12	·36	20
2	Mo	13	7	·53	13	·38	21
3	Tu	14	8	·50	14	·39	22
4	We	15	9	·47	15	·38	23
5	Th	16	10	·41	16	·35	24
6	Fr	17	11	·34	17	·30	25
7	Sa	18	12	·25	18	·24	26
8	Su	19	13	·16	19	·18	27
9	Mo	20	14 A	·06 ·96	20	·11	28
10	Tu	21	1	·86	21 22	·04 ·98	29
11	We	22	2	·77	23	·82	30
12	Th	23	3	·69	24	·87	1
13	Fr	24	4	·62	25	·83	2
14	Sa	25	5	·56	26	·80	3
15	Su	26	6	·53	27	·79	4
16	Mo	27	7	·51	1	·80	5
17	Tu	28	8	·51	2	·84	6
18	We	29	9	·54	3	·89	7
19	Th	30	10	·59	4	·96	8
20	Fr	31	11	·65	...	...	9

Feb. — Solar: Virodhi, *Kumbha—Masi* (from 1). Lunar: Magha, *Bahula*; Phalguna, *Sukla*. Muhammadan: H. 1307 *Jumadal-akhir*; H. 1307 *Rajab* (from 1).

Cyclic Sidereal Year, Month and Day	Week-Day	English Month and Day	Tithi	Ending Moment	Nakshatra	Ending Moment	Muhammadan Year, Month and Day
21	Sa	1	12	·72	5	·05	10
22	Su	2	13	·81	6	·16	11
23	Mo	3	14	·90	7	·27	12
24	Tu	4	P	·98	8	·38	13
25	We	5	...	...	9	·47	14
26	Th	6	1	·05	10	·55	15
27	Fr	7	2	·11	11	·62	16
28	Sa	8	3	·15	12	·67	17
29	Su	9	4	·17	13	·71	18
30	Mo	10	5	·16	14	·72	19
1	Tu	11	6	·13	15	·71	20
2	We	12	7	·09	16	·68	21
3	Th	13	8 9	·03 ·96	17	·64	22
4	Fr	14	10	·88	18	·59	23
5	Sa	15	11	·79	19	·52	24
6	Su	16	12	·69	20	·45	25
7	Mo	17	13	·59	21	·38	26
8	Tu	18	14	·49	22	·31	27
9	We	19	A	·39	23	·25	28
10	Th	20	1	·31	24	·20	29
11	Fr	21	2	·24	25	·16	1
12	Sa	22	3	·19	26	·13	2
13	Su	23	4	·15	27	·11	3
14	Mo	24	5	·13	1	·13	4
15	Tu	25	6	·13	2	·15	5
16	We	26	7	·16	3	·20	6
17	Th	27	8	·20	4	·27	7
18	Fr	28	9	·27	5	·35	8

March — Solar: Virodhi, *Kumbha—Masi* (19–30); Virodhi, *Mina—Panguni* (1–19). Lunar: Phalguna, *Suk.* / *Bahula*; *Sukla*. Muhammadan: H. 1307 *Rajab*.

Cyclic Sidereal Year, Month and Day	Week-Day	English Month and Day	Tithi	Ending Moment	Nakshatra	Ending Moment	Muhammadan Year, Month and Day
19	Sa	1	10	·35	6	·45	9
20	Su	2	11	·44	7	·56	10
21	Mo	3	12	·53	8	·67	11
22	Tu	4	13	·61	9	·77	12
23	We	5	14	·67	10	·86	13
24	Th	6	P	·73	11	·93	14
25	Fr	7	1	·77	12	·99	15
26	Sa	8	2	·78	...	...	16
27	Su	9	3	·77	13	·03	17
28	Mo	10	4	·74	14	·04	18
29	Tu	11	5	·70	15	·03	19
30	We	12	6	·64	16 17	·01 ·98	20
1	Th	13	7	·56	18	·92	21
2	Fr	14	8	·47	19	·86	22
3	Sa	15	9	·38	20	·79	23
4	Su	16	10	·28	21	·72	24
5	Mo	17	11	·18	22	·66	25
6	Tu	18	12	·09	23	·60	26
7	We	19	13 14	·00 ·91	24	·54	27
8	Th	20	A	·84	25	49	28
9	Fr	21	1	·78	26	·46	29
10	Sa	22	2	·74	27	·45	30
11	Su	23	3	·73	1	·45	1
12	Mo	24	4	·72	2	·47	2
13	Tu	25	5	·75	3	·51	3
14	We	26	6	·79	4	·57	4
15	Th	27	7	·85	5	·65	5
16	Fr	28	8	·93	6	·75	6
17	Sa	29	...	...	7	·86	7
18	Su	30	9	·02	8	·97	8
19	Mo	31	10	·11	...	...	9

April — Solar: Vikrita, *Mesha—Chittirai* (from 1). Lunar: Chaitra, *Bahula*; Vaisakha, *Sukla*. Muhammadan: H. 1307 *Shaban*; H. 1307 *Ramzan* (from 1).

Cyclic Sidereal Year, Month and Day	Week-Day	English Month and Day	Tithi	Ending Moment	Nakshatra	Ending Moment	Muhammadan Year, Month and Day
20	Tu	1	11	·19	9	·07	10
21	We	2	12	·26	10	·16	11
22	Th	3	13	·31	11	·24	12
23	Fr	4	14	·34	12	·31	13
24	Sa	5	P	·35	13	·35	14
25	Su	6	1	·34	14	·36	15
26	Mo	7	2	·31	15	·36	16
27	Tu	8	3	·27	16	·35	17
28	We	9	4	·21	17	·31	18
29	Th	10	5	·13	18	·26	19
30	Fr	11	6 7	·04 ·94	19	·20	20
1	Sa	12	8	·84	20	·14	21
2	Su	13	9	·74	21	·07	22
3	Mo	14	10	·64	22 23	·00 ·93	23
4	Tu	15	11	·55	24	·87	24
5	We	16	12	·46	25	·82	25
6	Th	17	13	·39	26	·78	26
7	Fr	18	14	·33	27	·77	27
8	Sa	19	A	·29	1	·77	28
9	Su	20	1	·28	2	·78	29
10	Mo	21	2	·27	3	·82	1
11	Tu	22	3	·30	4	·88	2
12	We	23	4	·34	5	·96	3
13	Th	24	5	·40	...	...	4
14	Fr	25	6	·48	6	·06	5
15	Sa	26	7	·56	7	·16	6
16	Su	27	8	·65	8	·27	7
17	Mo	28	9	·73	9	·38	8
18	Tu	29	10	·79	10	·48	9
19	We	30	11	·84	11	·56	10

May — Solar: Vikrita, *Mesha—Chittirai* (20–31); Vikrita, *Vrishabha—Vaikasi* (1–19). Lunar: Vaisakha, *Bahula*; *Sukla*. Muhammadan: H. 1307 *Ramzan*.

Cyclic Sidereal Year, Month and Day	Week-Day	English Month and Day	Tithi	Ending Moment	Nakshatra	Ending Moment	Muhammadan Year, Month and Day
20	Th	1	12	·88	12	·62	11
21	Fr	2	13	·89	13	·66	12
22	Sa	3	14	·88	14	·68	13
23	Su	4	P	·85	15	·69	14
24	Mo	5	1	·79	16	·68	15
25	Tu	6	2	·73	17	·64	16
26	We	7	3	·65	18	·59	17
27	Th	8	4	·57	19	·53	18
28	Fr	9	5	·47	20	·47	19
29	Sa	10	6	·37	21	·41	20
30	Su	11	7	·27	22	·34	21
31	Mo	12	8	·17	23	·27	22
1	Tu	13	9 10	·07 ·98	24	·21	23
2	We	14	11	·91	25	·15	24
3	Th	15	12	·85	26	·12	25
4	Fr	16	13	·81	27	·10	26
5	Sa	17	14	·79	1	·09	27
6	Su	18	A	·78	2	·10	28
7	Mo	19	1	·81	3	·14	29
8	Tu	20	2	·85	4	·20	30
9	We	21	3	·91	5	·27	1
10	Th	22	4	·98	6	·36	2
11	Fr	23	...	...	7	·46	3
12	Sa	24	5	·06	8	·57	4
13	Su	25	6	·15	9	·68	5
14	Mo	26	7	·23	10	·78	6
15	Tu	27	8	·30	11	·86	7
16	We	28	9	·35	12	·93	8
17	Th	29	10	·37	13	·98	9
18	Fr	30	11	·38	...	...	10
19	Sa	31	12	·38	14	·01	11

June — Solar: Vikrita, *Mithuna—Ani* (from 1). Lunar: Jyeshtha, *Bahula*; Ashadha, *Sukla*. Muhammadan: H. 1307 *Shawwal*; H. 1307 *Zi-l-ka'da* (from 1).

Cyclic Sidereal Year, Month and Day	Week-Day	English Month and Day	Tithi	Ending Moment	Nakshatra	Ending Moment	Muhammadan Year, Month and Day
20	Su	1	13	·35	15	·02	12
21	Mo	2	14	·30	16 17	·01 ·97	13
22	Tu ○	3	P	·23	18	·93	14
23	We	4	1	·15	19	·88	15
24	Th	5	2 3	·06 ·97	20	·82	16
25	Fr	6	4	·87	21	·75	17
26	Sa	7	5	·77	22	·68	18
27	Su	8	6	·67	23	·61	19
28	Mo	9	7	·57	24	·55	20
29	Tu	10	8	·48	25	·50	21
30	We	11	9	·40	26	·45	22
31	Th	12	10	·34	27	·42	23
1	Fr	13	11	·30	1	·41	24
2	Sa	14	12	·27	2	·42	25
3	Su	15	13	·27	3	·45	26
4	Mo	16	14	·29	4	·50	27
5	Tu ●	17	A	·33	5	·57	28
6	We	18	1	·38	6	·66	29
7	Th	19	2	·45	7	·76	1
8	Fr	20	3	·53	8	·87	2
9	Sa	21	4	·62	9	·98	3
10	Su	22	5	·70	...	...	4
11	Mo	23	6	·77	10	·08	5
12	Tu	24	7	·82	11	·17	6
13	We	25	8	·85	12	·24	7
14	Th	26	9	·86	13	·29	8
15	Fr	27	10	·85	14	·33	9
16	Sa	28	11	·82	15	·34	10
17	Su	29	12	·78	16	·34	11
18	Mo	30	13	·72	17	·30	12

Naksh:—1. Asvn. 2. Bhar. 3. Krit. 4. Rohi. 5. Mrig. 6. Ardh. 7. Punar. 8. Push. 9. Aslesh. 10. Magh. 11. P .Phal. 12. U. Phal. 13. Hasta. 14. Chit.

A. D. 1890. | **Kollam 1066,** { N. Malabar—Sept. / S. Malabar—Aug. } Commences | **Hijra 1308,** Commences, Aug. 17. | **Vikrama 1947.** **Bengal San 1296.** **(N. Cycle) Subhakrit.**

A.—Amavasya.
P.—Paurnami.

SOLAR reckoning: Cyclic Sidereal Year, Month and Day; Week-Day; English Month and Day. LUNAR reckoning: Tithi, Ending Moment; Nakshatra, Ending Moment; Muhammadan Year, Month and Day.

July

Cyclic Sidereal Year, Month and Day	Week-Day	English Month and Day	Tithi	Ending Moment	Nakshatra	Ending Moment	Muhammadan Year, Month and Day
(Vikrita Mithuna—Ani) 19	Tu	1	(Ashadha) 14	·64	18	·26	(H. 1307 Zi-l-ka'da) 13
20	We	2	P	·55	19	·21	14
21	Th	3	1	·45	20	·15	15
22	Fr	4	2	·35	21	·09	16
23	Sa	5	3	·25	22 / 23	·02 / ·95	17
24	Su	6	4	·15	24	·89	18
25	Mo	7	(Bahula) 5 / 6	·05 / ·96	25	·83	19
26	Tu	8	7	·88	26	·78	20
27	We	9	8	·82	27	·75	21
28	Th	10	9	·77	1	·74	22
29	Fr	11	10	·75	2	·75	23
30	Sa	12	11	·75	3	·77	24
31	Su	13	12	·77	4	·81	25
32	Mo	14	13	·81	5	·88	26
(Vikrita Karkata—Adi) 1	Tu	15	14	·86	6	·97	27
2	We	16	A	·92	...	...	28
3	Th	17	...	...	7	·07	29
4	Fr	18	(Sravana Sukla) 1	·00	8	·17	30
5	Sa	19	2	·08	9	·28	(Zi-l-hijja) 1
6	Su	20	3	·17	10	·38	2
7	Mo	21	4	·24	11	·47	3
8	Tu	22	5	·30	12	·55	4
9	We	23	6	·33	13	·61	5
10	Th	24	7	·34	14	·65	6
11	Fr	25	8	·33	15	·66	7
12	Sa	26	9	·31	16	·66	8
13	Su	27	10	·26	17	·63	9
14	Mo	28	11	·20	18	·60	10
15	Tu	29	12	·13	19	·55	11
16	We	30	13 / 14	·04 / ·94	20	·49	12
17	Th	31	P	·84	21	·42	13

Aug.

Cyclic Sidereal Year, Month and Day	Week-Day	English Month and Day	Tithi	Ending Moment	Nakshatra	Ending Moment	Muhammadan Year, Month and Day
(Vikrita Simha—Avani) 18	Fr	1	(Bahula) 1	·74	22	·35	(H. 1307) 14
19	Sa	2	2	·64	23	·29	15
20	Su	3	3	·54	24	·23	16
21	Mo	4	4	·45	25	·17	17
22	Tu	5	5	·37	26	·12	18
23	We	6	6	·31	27	·08	19
24	Th	7	7	·26	1	·07	20
25	Fr	8	8	·24	2	·07	21
26	Sa	9	9	·28	3	·09	22
27	Su	10	10	·24	4	·12	23
28	Mo	11	11	·28	5	·18	24
29	Tu	12	12	·34	6	·26	25
30	We	13	13	·41	7	·36	26
31	Th	14	14	·49	8	·47	27
1	Fr	15	A	·58	9	·58	28
2	Sa	16	(Adh. Bhadrapada Sukla) 1	·66	10	·68	29
3	Su	17	2	·73	11	·77	(H. 1308 Muharram) 1
4	Mo	18	3	·78	12	·85	2
5	Tu	19	4	·81	13	·92	3
6	We	20	5	·84	14	·96	4
7	Th	21	6	·83	15	·98	5
8	Fr	22	7	·81	16	·98	6
9	Sa	23	8	·77	17	·97	7
10	Su	24	9	·71	18	·94	8
11	Mo	25	10	·63	19	·89	9
12	Tu	26	11	·54	20	·83	10
13	We	27	12	·44	21	·77	11
14	Th	28	13	·34	22	·70	12
15	Fr	29	14	·24	23	·63	13
16	Sa	30	P	·14	24	·56	14
17	Su	31	1 / 2	·05 / ·96	25	·50	15

Sep.

Cyclic Sidereal Year, Month and Day	Week-Day	English Month and Day	Tithi	Ending Moment	Nakshatra	Ending Moment	Muhammadan Year, Month and Day
(Vikrita Simha—Avani) 18	Mo	1	(Adh. Bhadra.) 3	·89	26	·45	(H. 1308 Muharram) 16
19	Tu	2	4	·83	27	·42	17
20	We	3	5	·79	1	·40	18
21	Th	4	6	·76	2	·39	19
22	Fr	5	7	·74	3	·40	20
23	Sa	6	8	·76	4	·44	21
24	Su	7	9	·80	5	·49	22
25	Mo	8	10	·86	6	·57	23
26	Tu	9	11	·92	7	·66	24
27	We	10	...	...	8	·76	25
28	Th	11	(Bahula) 12	·00	9	·87	26
29	Fr	12	13	·09	10	·98	27
30	Sa	13	14	·17	...	...	28
31	Su	14	A	·25	11	·08	29
(Vikrita Kanya—Purattasi) 1	Mo	15	1	·31	12	·17	30
2	Tu	16	2	·35	13	·23	(H. 1308 Safar) 1
3	We	17	3	·37	14	·28	2
4	Th	18	4	·35	15	·30	3
5	Fr	19	5	·33	16	·32	4
6	Sa	20	6	·30	17	·30	5
7	Su	21	(Bhadrapada Sukla) 7	·24	18	·27	6
8	Mo	22	8	·16	19	·22	7
9	Tu	23	9 / 10	·08 / ·99	20	·16	8
10	We	24	11	·89	21	·10	9
11	Th	25	12	·79	22 / 23	·04 / ·97	10
12	Fr	26	13	·68	24	·90	11
13	Sa	27	14	·59	25	·84	12
14	Su	28	P	·50	26	·79	13
15	Mo	29	1	·43	27	·75	14
16	Tu	30	2	·37	1	·72	15

Oct.

Cyclic Sidereal Year, Month and Day	Week-Day	English Month and Day	Tithi	Ending Moment	Nakshatra	Ending Moment	Muhammadan Year, Month and Day
(Vikrita Kanya—Purattasi) 17	We	1	(Nija Bahula) 3	·33	2	·71	16
18	Th	2	4	·30	3	·72	17
19	Fr	3	5	·29	4	·75	18
20	Sa	4	6	·31	5	·81	19
21	Su	5	7	·35	6	·88	20
22	Mo	6	8	·40	7	·96	21
23	Tu	7	9	·47	...	...	22
24	We	8	10	·56	8	·06	23
25	Th	9	11	·65	9	·17	24
26	Fr	10	12	·73	10	·28	25
27	Sa	11	13	·81	11	·38	26
28	Su	12	14	·87	12	·47	27
29	Mo	13	A	·91	13	·54	28
30	Tu	14	1	·93	14	·59	29
31	We	15	2	·93	15	·63	(H. 1308 Rabi-ul-awwal) 1
(Vikrita Tula—Aippasi) 1	Th	16	3	·90	16	·64	2
2	Fr	17	4	·87	17	·63	3
3	Sa	18	5	·81	18	·60	4
4	Su	19	(Asvina Sukla) 6	·73	19	·56	5
5	Mo	20	7	·65	20	·51	6
6	Tu	21	8	·56	21	·45	7
7	We	22	9	·46	22	·38	8
8	Th	23	10	·36	23	·31	9
9	Fr	24	11	·26	24	·24	10
10	Sa	25	12	·17	25	·18	11
11	Su	26	13	·08	26	·13	12
12	Mo	27	14 / P	·01 / ·95	27	·08	13
13	Tu	28	(Bahula) 1	·91	1	·05	14
14	We	29	2	·89	2	·03	15
15	Th	30	3	·89	3	·04	16
16	Fr	31	4	·90	4	·07	17

Nov.

Cyclic Sidereal Year, Month and Day	Week-Day	English Month and Day	Tithi	Ending Moment	Nakshatra	Ending Moment	Muhammadan Year, Month and Day
(Vikrita Tula—Aippasi) 17	Sa	1	(Asvina Bahula) 5	·94	5	·12	(H. 1308 Rabi-ul-awwal) 18
18	Su	2	...	...	6	·18	19
19	Mo	3	6	·00	7	·26	20
20	Tu	4	7	·08	8	·36	21
21	We	5	8	·17	9	·47	22
22	Th	6	9	·25	10	·58	23
23	Fr	7	10	·33	11	·69	24
24	Sa	8	11	·41	12	·78	25
25	Su	9	12	·48	13	·85	26
26	Mo	10	13	·51	14	·91	27
27	Tu	11	14	·53	15	·95	28
28	We	12	A	·53	16	·96	29
29	Th	13	1	·50	17	·95	30
30	Fr	14	2	·47	18	·93	(H. 1308 Rabi-ul-akhir) 1
(Vikrita Vrischika—Kartigai) 1	Sa	15	3	·42	19	·89	2
2	Su	16	(Kartika Sukla) 4	·35	20	·85	3
3	Mo	17	5	·26	21	·79	4
4	Tu	18	6	·17	22	·72	5
5	We	19	7 / 8	·07 / ·97	23	·65	6
6	Th	20	9	·87	24	·58	7
7	Fr	21	10	·78	25	·52	8
8	Sa	22	11	·70	26	·46	9
9	Su	23	12	·63	27	·41	10
10	Mo	24	13	·57	1	·38	11
11	Tu	25	14	·53	2	·36	12
12	We ○	26	P	·50	3	·37	13
13	Th	27	1	·51	4	·39	14
14	Fr	28	2	·53	5	·43	15
15	Sa	29	3	·57	6	·49	16
16	Su	30	4	·63	7	·57	17

Dec.

Cyclic Sidereal Year, Month and Day	Week-Day	English Month and Day	Tithi	Ending Moment	Nakshatra	Ending Moment	Muhammadan Year, Month and Day
(Vikrita Vrischika—Kartigai) 17	Mo	1	(Kartika Bahula) 5	·71	8	·67	(H. 1308 Rabi-ul-akhir) 18
18	Tu	2	6	·79	9	·78	19
19	We	3	7	·88	10	·89	20
20	Th	4	8	·97	11	·99	21
21	Fr	5	...	...	...	...	22
22	Sa	6	9	·05	12	·08	23
23	Su	7	10	·11	13	·16	24
24	Mo	8	11	·15	14	·23	25
25	Tu	9	12	·17	15	·26	26
26	We	10	13	·16	16	·28	27
27	Th	11	14	·14	17	·28	28
28	Fr ●	12	A	·10	18	·26	29
29	Sa	13	1 / 2	·04 / ·97	19	·23	(H. 1308 Jumada-l-awwal) 1
(Vikrita Dhanus—Margali) 1	Su	14	3	·89	20	·18	2
2	Mo	15	4	·80	21	·12	3
3	Tu	16	5	·70	22 / 23	·06 / ·99	4
4	We	17	(Margasira Sukla) 6	·60	24	·92	5
5	Th	18	7	·50	25	·86	6
6	Fr	19	8	·41	26	·80	7
7	Sa	20	9	·33	27	·74	8
8	Su	21	10	·26	1	·71	9
9	Mo	22	11	·21	2	·69	10
10	Tu	23	12	·17	3	·69	11
11	We	24	13	·15	4	·70	12
12	Th	25	14	·15	5	·74	13
13	Fr	26	P	·18	6	·80	14
14	Sa	27	(Marg. Bah.) 1	·23	7	·88	15
15	Su	28	2	·29	8	·97	16
16	Mo	29	3	·36	...	...	17
17	Tu	30	4	·44	9	·07	18
18	We	31	5	·53	10	·18	19

15. Svati. 16. Visak. 17. Anur. 18. Jyesh. 19. Mula. 20. P. Ash. 21. U. Ash. 22. Sravn. 23. Dani. 24. Satab. 25. P. Bhad. 26. U. Bhad. 27. Rev.

A. D. 1891. **Mesha Sankranti** (Commencement of Indian Sidereal Year).
Solar Eclipse. ● **(Surya Sid.) April 12·29.** **Saka 1813.** **Kaliyuga 4992.**
Lunar Eclipse. ○ **(Arya Sid.) April 12·18.** **(S. Cycle) Khara.**

SOLAR reckoning: Cyclic Sidereal Year, Month and Day.	Week-Day	English Month and Day.	LUNAR reckoning: Tithi	Ending Moment.	Nakshatra	Ending Moment.	Muhammadan Year, Month and Day.
	Jan.						
Vikrita, *Dhanus—Margali.* 19	Th	1	Marga. *Bahula* 6	·62	11	·29	*Jumadal-awwal.* 20
20	Fr	2	7	·70	12	·39	21
21	Sa	3	8	·76	13	·47	22
22	Su	4	9	·79	14	·54	23
23	Mo	5	10	·81	15	·58	24
24	Tu	6	11	·81	16	·60	25
25	We	7	12	·79	17	·61	26
26	Th	8	13	·75	18	·60	27
27	Fr	9	14	·69	19	·57	28
28	Sa	10	—A	·62	20	·52	29
29	Su	11	Pausha *Sukla* 1	·54	21	·46	—30
—30	Mo	12	2	·44	22	·40	H. 1308 *Jumadal-akhir.* 1
Vikrita, *Makara—Tai.* 1	Tu	13	3	·34	23	·33	2
2	We	14	4	·24	24	·26	3
3	Th	15	5	·15	25	·19	4
4	Fr	16	6 / 7	·06 / ·98	26	·13	5
5	Sa	17	8	·91	27	·08	6
6	Su	18	9	·86	1	·05	7
7	Mo	19	10	·82	2	·02	8
8	Tu	20	11	·80	3	·01	9
9	We	21	12	·79	4	·02	10
10	Th	22	13	·83	5	·05	11
11	Fr	23	14	·88	6	·10	12
12	Sa	24	P	·94	7	·18	13
13	Su	25	*Bahula* ...	...	8	·27	14
14	Mo	26	1	·02	9	·37	15
15	Tu	27	2	·11	10	·48	16
16	We	28	3	·20	11	·59	17
17	Th	29	4	·28	12	·69	18
18	Fr	30	5	·35	13	·78	19
19	Sa	31	6	·41	14	·85	20
	Feb.						
20	Su	1	7	·44	15	·89	21
21	Mo	2	8	·45	16	·92	22
22	Tu	3	9	·45	17	·94	23
23	We	4	10	·43	18	·93	24
24	Th	5	11	·38	19	·90	25
25	Fr	6	12	·32	20	·85	26
26	Sa	7	13	·24	21	·80	27
27	Su	8	14	·16	22	·74	28
28	Mo	9	A / 1	·06 / ·96	23	·67	—29
—29	Tu	10	Magha *Sukla* 2	·86	24	·60	H. 1308 *Rajab.* 1
Vikrita, *Kumbha—Masi.* 1	We	11	3	·76	25	·53	2
2	Th	12	4	·67	26	·47	3
3	Fr	13	5	·59	27	·41	4
4	Sa	14	6	·53	1	·38	5
5	Su	15	7	·48	2	·35	6
6	Mo	16	8	·45	3	·33	7
7	Tu	17	9	·43	4	·34	8
8	We	18	10	·43	5	·37	9
9	Th	19	11	·46	6	·42	10
10	Fr	20	12	·50	7	·49	11
11	Sa	21	13	·57	8	·57	12
12	Su	22	14	·65	9	·67	13
13	Mo	23	P	·74	10	·78	14
14	Tu	24	*Bah.* 1	·83	11	·89	15
15	We	25	2	·90	12	·99	16
16	Th	26	3	·97	...	...	17
17	Fr	27	...	...	13	·08	18
18	Sa	28	4	·02	14	·15	19
	March						
Vikrita, *Kumbha—Masi.* 19	Su	1	Mag. *Bahula* 5	·06	15	·21	H. 1308 *Rajab.* 20
20	Mo	2	6	·07	16	·25	21
21	Tu	3	7	·07	17	·26	22
22	We	4	8 / 9	·04 / ·99	18	·25	23
23	Th	5	10	·93	19	·23	24
24	Fr	6	11	·85	20	·19	25
25	Sa	7	12	·77	21	·14	26
26	Su	8	13	·68	22	·08	27
27	Mo	9	14	·58	23 / 24	·01 / ·94	28
28	Tu	10	—A	·48	25	·87	29
29	We	11	Phalguna *Sukla* 1	·38	26	·81	—30
—30	Th	12	2	·28	27	·76	H. 1308 *Shaban.* 1
Vikrita, *Mina—Panguni.* 1	Fr	13	3	·20	1	·71	2
2	Sa	14	4	·13	2	·67	3
3	Su	15	5	·07	3	·66	4
4	Mo	16	6	·04	4	·66	5
5	Tu	17	7	·02	5	·69	6
6	We	18	8	·02	6	·73	7
7	Th	19	9	·06	7	·79	8
8	Fr	20	10	·11	8	·87	9
9	Sa	21	11	·17	9	·97	10
10	Su	22	12	·25	...	...	11
11	Mo	23	13	·34	10	·08	12
12	Tu	24	14	·42	11	·19	13
13	We	25	P	·50	12	·29	14
14	Th	26	1	·56	13	·38	15
15	Fr	27	2	·61	14	·46	16
16	Sa	28	3	·65	15	·53	17
17	Su	29	4	·66	16	·57	18
18	Mo	30	5	·65	17	·58	19
19	Tu	31	6	·61	18	·58	20
	April						
20	We	1	*Bahula* 7	·57	19	·56	21
21	Th	2	8	·51	20	·53	22
22	Fr	3	9	·43	21	·48	23
23	Sa	4	10	·34	22	·42	24
24	Su	5	11	·25	23	·35	25
25	Mo	6	12	·15	24	·28	26
26	Tu	7	13 / 14	·05 / ·95	25	·21	27
27	We	8	—A	·85	26	·15	28
28	Th	9	Chaitra *Sukla* 1	·76	27	·09	—29
29	Fr	10	2	·69	1	·04	H. 1308 *Ramzan.* 1
—30	Sa	11	3	·64	2 / 3	·00 / ·98	2
Khara, *Mesha—Chittirai.* 1	Su	12	4	·60	4	·99	3
2	Mo	13	5	·58	...	...	4
3	Tu	14	6	·58	5	·00	5
4	We	15	7	·61	6	·04	6
5	Th	16	8	·66	7	·10	7
6	Fr	17	9	·73	8	·18	8
7	Sa	18	10	·81	9	·28	9
8	Su	19	11	·89	10	·38	10
9	Mo	20	12	·97	11	·49	11
10	Tu	21	...	...	12	·59	12
11	We	22	13	·04	13	·69	13
12	Th	23	14	·10	14	·77	14
13	Fr	24	P	·15	15	·84	15
14	Sa	25	*Bah.* 1	·19	16	·88	16
15	Su	26	2	·20	17	·90	17
16	Mo	27	3	·19	18	·90	18
17	Tu	28	4	·16	19	·88	19
18	We	29	5	·11	20	·86	20
19	Th	30	6 / 7	·04 / ·96	21	·81	21
	May						
Khara, *Mesha—Chittirai.* 20	Fr	1	Chait. *Bahula* 8	·87	22	·75	H. 1308 *Ramzan.* 22
21	Sa	2	9	·78	23	·69	23
22	Su	3	10	·68	24	·63	24
23	Mo	4	11	·58	25	·56	25
24	Tu	5	12	·47	26	·49	26
25	We	6	13	·37	27	·43	27
26	Th	7	14	·29	1	·37	28
27	Fr	8	—A	·22	2	·33	29
28	Sa	9	Vaisakha *Sukla* 1	·17	3	·32	—30
29	Su	10	2	·13	4	·31	H. 1308 *Shawwal.* 1
30	Mo	11	3	·11	5	·32	2
—31	Tu	12	4	·10	6	·35	3
Khara, *Vrishabha—Vaikasi.* 1	We	13	5	·14	7	·41	4
2	Th	14	6	·18	8	·49	5
3	Fr	15	7	·23	9	·58	6
4	Sa	16	8	·30	10	·68	7
5	Su	17	9	·39	11	·79	8
6	Mo	18	10	·48	12	·89	9
7	Tu	19	11	·56	13	·99	10
8	We	20	12	·63	...	...	11
9	Th	21	13	·67	14	·08	12
10	Fr	22	14	·69	15	·15	13
11	Sa ○	23	P	·71	16	·20	14
12	Su	24	*Bahula* 1	·69	17	·22	15
13	Mo	25	2	·67	18	·23	16
14	Tu	26	3	·62	19	·22	17
15	We	27	4	·55	20	·19	18
16	Th	28	5	·47	21	·15	19
17	Fr	29	6	·38	22	·09	20
18	Sa	30	7	·28	23 / 24	·03 / ·97	21
19	Su	31	8	·17	25	·90	22
	June						
20	Mo	1	9 / 10	·07 / ·97	26	·83	23
21	Tu	2	11	·88	27	·76	24
22	We	3	12	·79	1	·71	25
23	Th	4	13	·72	2	·67	26
24	Fr	5	14	·66	3	·64	27
25	Sa	6	—A	·62	4	·63	28
26	Su	7	Jyeshtha *Sukla* 1	·60	5	·64	—29
27	Mo	8	2	·59	6	·67	H. 1308 *Zi-l-ka'da.* 1
28	Tu	9	3	·62	7	·72	2
29	We	10	4	·66	8	·79	3
30	Th	11	5	·72	9	·88	4
31	Fr	12	6	·79	10	·98	5
—32	Sa	13	7	·87	...	...	6
Khara, *Mithuna—Ani.* 1	Su	14	8	·95	11	·08	7
2	Mo	15	...	...	12	·19	8
3	Tu	16	9	·03	13	·30	9
4	We	17	10	·10	14	·39	10
5	Th	18	11	·15	15	·46	11
6	Fr	19	12	·18	16	·51	12
7	Sa	20	13	·19	17	·54	13
8	Su	21	14	·18	18	·56	14
9	Mo	22	P	·15	19	·55	15
10	Tu	23	*Bahula* 1	·10	20	·52	16
11	We	24	2 / 3	·04 / ·96	21	·48	17
12	Th	25	4	·87	22	·43	18
13	Fr	26	5	·77	23	·37	19
14	Sa	27	6	·67	24	·30	20
15	Su	28	7	·57	25	·23	21
16	Mo	29	8	·47	26	·16	22
17	Tu	30	9	·37	27	·10	23

Naksh:—1 Asvn. 2. Bhar. 3. Krit. 4. Rohi. 5. Mrig. 6. Ardh. 7. Punar. 8. Push. 9. Aslesh. 10. Magh. 11. P. Phal. 12. U. Phal. 13. Hasta. 14. Chit.

A. D. 1891.
A.—Amavasya.
P.—Paurnami.

Kollam 1067, Commences { **N. Malabar—Sept.** / **S. Malabar—Aug.**

Hijra 1309, Commences, **Aug. 7.**

Vikrama 1948.
Bengal San 1297.
(N. Cycle) Sobhana.

SOLAR reckoning. / LUNAR reckoning.

July

Solar month	Cyclic Sidereal Year, Month and Day	Week-Day	English Month and Day	Lunar month	Tithi	Ending Moment	Nakshatra	Ending Moment	Muhammadan month	Muhammadan Year, Month and Day
Khara Mithuna—Ani.	18	We	1	Jyesh Bah.	10	·27	1	05	Zi-l-ka'da.	24
	19	Th	2		11	·21	2 3	·00 ·97		25
	20	Fr	3		12	·15	4	·96		26
	21	Sa	4		13	·10	5	96		27
	22	Su	5		14	·08	6	98		28
	23	Mo	6		—A	·07	...	...		29
	24	Tu	7	Ashadha Sukla	1	·09	7	·03		—30
	25	We	8		2	·13	8	·10	H. 1308 Zi-l-hijja.	1
	26	Th	9		3	·19	9	·18		2
	27	Fr	10		4	·26	10	·28		3
	28	Sa	11		5	·35	11	·39		4
	29	Su	12		6	·43	12	·50		5
	30	Mo	13		7	·51	13	·60		6
	—31	Tu	14		8	·57	14	·69		7
Khara Karkata—Adi.	1	We	15		9	·62	15	·77		8
	2	Th	16		10	·66	16	·83		9
	3	Fr	17		11	·67	17	·87		10
	4	Sa	18		12	·66	18	·88		11
	5	Su	19		13	·63	19	·88		12
	6	Mo	20		14	·59	20	·85		13
	7	Tu	21		P	·52	21	·83		14
	8	We	22	Bahula	1	·44	22	·77		15
	9	Th	23		2	·36	23	·71		16
	10	Fr	24		3	·26	24	·64		17
	11	Sa	25		4	·16	25	·57		18
	12	Su	26		5 6	·06 ·96	26	·50		19
	13	Mo	27		7	·86	27	·44		20
	14	Tu	28		8	·77	1	·39		21
	15	We	29		9	·69	2	·34		22
	16	Th	30		10	·62	3	·30		23
	17	Fr	31		11	·58	4	·28		24

Aug.

Solar month	Cyclic Sidereal Year, Month and Day	Week-Day	English Month and Day	Lunar month	Tithi	Ending Moment	Nakshatra	Ending Moment	Muhammadan month	Muhammadan Year, Month and Day
Khara Karkata—Adi.	18	Sa	1		12	·56	5	·28		25
	19	Su	2		13	·56	6	·31		26
	20	Mo	3		14	·57	7	·35		27
	21	Tu	4		—A	·61	8	·40		28
	22	We	5	Sravana Sukla	1	·67	9	·48		29
	23	Th	6		2	·74	10	·58		—30
	24	Fr	7		3	·82	11	·69	H. 1309 Muharram.	1
	25	Sa	8		4	·90	12	·80		2
	26	Su	9		5	·98	13	·90		3
	27	Mo	10		...	...	14	·99		4
	28	Tu	11		6	·03	...	...		5
	29	We	12		7	·11	15	·07		6
	30	Th	13		8	·15	16	·14		7
	31	Fr	14		9	·16	17	·18		8
	—32	Sa	15		10	·15	18	·20		9
Khara Simha—Avani.	1	Su	16		11	·12	19	·20		10
	2	Mo	17		12	·08	20	·18		11
	3	Tu	18		13 14	·02 ·94	21	·15		12
	4	We	19		P	·85	22	·11		13
	5	Th	20	Bahula	1	·75	23 24	·03 ·98		14
	6	Fr	21		2	·65	25	·91		15
	7	Sa	22		3	·55	26	·84		16
	8	Su	23		4	·45	27	·78		17
	9	Mo	24		5	·35	1	·72		18
	10	Tu	25		6	·27	2	·67		19
	11	We	26		7	·20	3	·63		20
	12	Th	27		8	·13	4	·60		21
	13	Fr	28		9	·09	5	·61		22
	14	Sa	29		10	·06	6	·63		23
	15	Su	30		11	·06	7	·66		24
	16	Mo	31		12	·03	8	·71		25

Sep.

Solar month	Cyclic Sidereal Year, Month and Day	Week-Day	English Month and Day	Lunar month	Tithi	Ending Moment	Nakshatra	Ending Moment	Muhammadan month	Muhammadan Year, Month and Day
Khara Simha—Avani.	17	Tu	1	Bah.	13	·12	9	·79	Muharram	26
	18	We	2		14	·18	10	·83		27
	19	Th	3		—A	·25	11	·99		28
	20	Fr	4	Bhadrapada Sukla	1	·33	...	...		29
	21	Sa	5		2	·41	12	·09		—30
	22	Su	6		3	·49	13	·20	H. 1309 Safar.	1
	23	Mo	7		4	·56	14	·30		2
	24	Tu	8		5	·62	15	·38		3
	25	We	9		6	·66	16	·45		4
	26	Th	10		7	·69	17	·50		5
	27	Fr	11		8	·67	18	·52		6
	28	Sa	12		9	·64	19	·53		7
	29	Su	13		10	·60	20	·51		8
	30	Mo	14		11	·54	21	·48		9
	—31	Tu	15		12	·47	22	·44		10
Khara Kanya—Purattasi.	1	We	16		13	·38	23	·39		11
	2	Th	17		14	·29	24	·33		12
	3	Fr	18		P	·19	25	·26		13
	4	Sa	19	Bahula	1 2	·09 ·98	26	·19		14
	5	Su	20		3	·88	27	·12		15
	6	Mo	21		4	·80	1	·06		16
	7	Tu	22		5	·73	2 3	·00 ·96		17
	8	We	23		6	·67	4	·94		18
	9	Th	24		7	·63	5	·93		19
	10	Fr	25		8	·61	6	·94		20
	11	Sa	26		9	·60	7	·97		21
	12	Su	27		10	·62	...	...		22
	13	Mo	28		11	·66	8	·02		23
	14	Tu	29		12	·72	9	·10		24
	15	We	30		13	·79	10	·19		25

Oct.

Solar month	Cyclic Sidereal Year, Month and Day	Week-Day	English Month and Day	Lunar month	Tithi	Ending Moment	Nakshatra	Ending Moment	Muhammadan month	Muhammadan Year, Month and Day
Khara Kanya—Purattasi.	16	Th	1		14	·87	11	·29		26
	17	Fr	2		—A	·96	12	·39		27
	18	Sa	3	Asvina Sukla	...	...	13	·50		28
	19	Su	4		1	·04	14	·60		—29
	20	Mo	5		2	·12	15	·69	H. 1309 Rabi-ul-awwal.	1
	21	Tu	6		3	·18	16	·76		2
	22	We	7		4	·22	17	·81		3
	23	Th	8		5	·24	18	·84		4
	24	Fr	9		6	·23	19	·85		5
	25	Sa	10		7	·21	20	·85		6
	26	Su	11		8	·17	21	·82		7
	27	Mo	12		9	·11	22	·78		8
	28	Tu	13		10 11	·03 ·94	23	·72		9
	29	We	14		12	·85	24	·66		10
	—30	Th	15		13	·75	25	·60		11
Khara Tula—Aippasi.	1	Fr	16		14	·65	26	·53		12
	2	Sa	17		P	·53	27	·46		13
	3	Su	18	Bahula	1	·46	1	·39		14
	4	Mo	19		2	·37	2	·34		15
	5	Tu	20		3	·29	3	·30		16
	6	We	21		4	·24	4	·27		17
	7	Th	22		5	·20	5	·25		18
	8	Fr	23		6	·19	6	·26		19
	9	Sa	24		7	·19	7	·29		20
	10	Su	25		8	·21	8	·34		21
	11	Mo	26		9	·24	9	·40		22
	12	Tu	27		10	·30	10	·48		23
	13	We	28		11	·37	11	·58		24
	14	Th	29		12	·46	12	·69		25
	15	Fr	30		13	·55	13	·80		26
	16	Sa	31		14	·64	14	·91		27

Nov.

Solar month	Cyclic Sidereal Year, Month and Day	Week-Day	English Month and Day	Lunar month	Tithi	Ending Moment	Nakshatra	Ending Moment	Muhammadan month	Muhammadan Year, Month and Day
Khara Tula—Aippasi.	17	Su	1		—A	·72	...	...		28
	18	Mo	2	Kartika Sukla	1	·77	15	·00		29
	19	Tu	3		2	·81	16	·07		—30
	20	We	4		3	·84	17	·12	H. 1309 Rabi-ul-akhir.	1
	21	Th	5		4	·82	18	·16		2
	22	Fr	6		5	·80	19	·18		3
	23	Sa	7		6	·76	20	·17		4
	24	Su	8		7	·70	21	·15		5
	25	Mo	9		8	·63	22	·11		6
	26	Tu	10		9	·55	23	·06		7
	27	We	11		10	·45	24 25	·01 ·94		8
	28	Th	12		11	·35	26	·87		9
	29	Fr	13		12	·25	27	·80		10
	—30	Sa	14		13	·15	1	·73		11
Khara Vrischika—Kartigai.	1	Su ○	15		14 P	·06 ·98	2	·68		12
	2	Mo	16	Bahula	1	·91	3	·63		13
	3	Tu	17		2	·85	4	·60		14
	4	We	18		3	·82	5	·58		15
	5	Th	19		4	·80	6	·58		16
	6	Fr	20		5	·80	7	·60		17
	7	Sa	21		6	·83	8	·65		18
	8	Su	22		7	·86	9	·71		19
	9	Mo	23		8	·92	10	·79		20
	10	Tu	24		...	...	11	·88		21
	11	We	25		9	·00	12	·99		22
	12	Th	26		10	·10	...	...		23
	13	Fr	27		11	·18	13	·10		24
	14	Sa	28		12	·26	14	·21		25
	15	Su	29		13	·34	15	·30		26
	16	Mo	30		14	·41	16	·38		27

Dec.

Solar month	Cyclic Sidereal Year, Month and Day	Week-Day	English Month and Day	Lunar month	Tithi	Ending Moment	Nakshatra	Ending Moment	Muhammadan month	Muhammadan Year, Month and Day
Khara Vrischika—Kartigai.	17	Tu	1		—A	·45	17	·44		28
	18	We	2	Margasira Sukla	1	·46	18	·48		—29
	19	Th	3		2	·45	19	·50	H. 1309 Jumadal-awwal.	1
	20	Fr	4		3	·43	20	·50		2
	21	Sa	5		4	·38	21	·48		3
	22	Su	6		5	·32	22	·44		4
	23	Mo	7		6	·25	23	·40		5
	24	Tu	8		7	·17	24	·34		6
	25	We	9		8 9	·08 ·98	25	·27		7
	26	Th	10		10	·88	26	·20		8
	27	Fr	11		11	·78	27	·14		9
	28	Sa	12		12	·69	1	·08		10
	—29	Su	13		13	·61	2 3	·02 ·96		11
Khara Dhanus—Margali.	1	Mo	14		14	·54	4	·93		12
	2	Tu	15		P	·48	5	·90		13
	3	We	16	Bahula	1	·45	6	·90		14
	4	Th	17		2	·44	7	·92		15
	5	Fr	18		3	·45	8	·96		16
	6	Sa	19		4	·47	...	...		17
	7	Su	20		5	·51	9	·02		18
	8	Mo	21		6	·58	10	·09		19
	9	Tu	22		7	·66	11	·18		20
	10	We	23		8	·74	12	·29		21
	11	Th	24		9	·84	13	·40		22
	12	Fr	25		10	·92	14	·51		23
	13	Sa	26		11	·99	15	·60		24
	14	Su	27		...	...	16	·68		25
	15	Mo	28		12	·05	17	·75		26
	16	Tu	29		13	·09	18	·80		27
	17	We	30		* 14	·10	19	·82		28
	18	Th	31		—A	·10	20	·82		29

15. Svati. 16. Visak. 17. Anur. 18. Jyesh. 19. Mula. 20. P. Ash. 21. U. Ash. 22. Sravn. 23. Dani. 24. Satab. 25. P. Bhad. 26. U. Bhad. 27. Rev.

A. D. 1892. **Mesha Sankranti** (Commencement of Indian Sidereal Year).

Solar Eclipse. ● **(Surya Sid.) April 11·55.** **Saka 1814.** **Kaliyuga 4993.**

Lunar Eclipse. ○ **(Arya Sid.) April 11·44.** **(S. Cycle) Nandana.**

SOLAR reckoning: Solar month	Cyclic Sidereal Year, Month and Day	Week-Day	English Month and Day	LUNAR reckoning: Lunar month	Tithi	Ending Moment	Nakshatra	Ending Moment	Muhammadan Year, Month and Day
		Jan.							
Khara *Dhanus—Margali.*	19	Fr	1	**Pausha** *Sukla*	1	·07	21	·81	—30
	20	Sa	2		2 3	·02 ·96	22	·78	1 (H. 1309 *Jumadal-akhir.*)
	21	Su	3		4	·89	23	·74	2
	22	Mo	4		5	·81	24	·68	3
	23	Tu	5		6	·72	25	·61	4
	24	We	6		7	·62	26	·54	5
	25	Th	7		8	·52	27	·47	6
	26	Fr	8		9	·42	1	·41	7
	27	Sa	9		10	·34	2	·35	8
	28	Su	10		11	·26	3	·30	9
	29	Mo	11		12	·18	4	·26	10
	—30	Tu	12		13	·13	5	·23	11
Khara *Makara—Tai.*	1	We	13		14	·10	6	·23	12
	2	Th	14		P	·08	7	·24	13
	3	Fr	15	*Bahula*	1	·09	8	·27	14
	4	Sa	16		2	·12	9	·32	15
	5	Su	17		3	·17	10	·39	16
	6	Mo	18		4	·23	11	·49	17
	7	Tu	19		5	·31	12	·59	18
	8	We	20		6	·40	13	·70	19
	9	Th	21		7	·49	14	·80	20
	10	Fr	22		8	·57	15	·90	21
	11	Sa	23		9	·64	...	...	22
	12	Su	24		10	·70	16	·00	23
	13	Mo	25		11	·74	17	·07	24
	14	Tu	26		12	·76	18	·11	25
	15	We	27		13	·74	19	·14	26
	16	Th	28		14	·71	20	·15	27
	17	Fr	29		—A	·66	21	·15	28
	18	Sa	30	**Magha** *Sukla*	1	·60	22	·12	—29
	19	Su	31		2	·53	23	·08	1 (H. 1309 *Rajab.*)
		Feb.							
	20	Mo	1		3	·44	24 25	·02 ·95	2
	21	Tu	2		4	·35	26	·88	3
	22	We	3		5	·25	27	·81	4
	23	Th	4		6	·15	1	·75	5
	24	Fr	5		7 8	·05 ·96	2	·69	6
	25	Sa	6		9	·88	3	·63	7
	26	Su	7		10	·81	4	·59	8
	27	Mo	8		11	·76	5	·57	9
	28	Tu	9		12	·73	6	·55	10
	—29	We	10		13	·72	7	·56	11
Khara *Kumbha—Masi.*	1	Th	11		14	·72	8	·58	12
	2	Fr	12		P	·76	9	·63	13
	3	Sa	13	*Bahula*	1	·81	10	·71	14
	4	Su	14		2	·87	11	·79	15
	5	Mo	15		3	·95	12	·89	16
	6	Tu	16		...	...	...	...	17
	7	We	17		4	·04	13	·00	18
	8	Th	18		5	·13	14	·11	19
	9	Fr	19		6	·20	15	·21	20
	10	Sa	20		7	·27	16	·30	21
	11	Su	21		8	·33	17	·37	22
	12	Mo	22		9	·36	18	·43	23
	13	Tu	23		10	·38	19	·46	24
	14	We	24		11	·36	20	·47	25
	15	Th	25		12	·33	21	·47	26
	16	Fr	26		13	·28	22	·45	27
	17	Sa	27		14	·21	23	·41	28
	18.	Su	28		—A	·14	24	·35	29
	19	Mo	29	**Phalguna** *Sukla*	1 2	·06 ·97	25	·29	—30

SOLAR reckoning: Solar month	Cyclic Sidereal Year, Month and Day	Week-Day	English Month and Day	LUNAR reckoning: Lunar month	Tithi	Ending Moment	Nakshatra	Ending Moment	Muhammadan Year, Month and Day
		March							
Khara *Kumbha—Masi.*	20	Tu	1		3	·87	26	·23	1 (H. 1309 *Shaban.*)
	21	We	2		4	·77	27	·16	2
	22	Th	3		5	·67	1	·09	3
	23	Fr	4		6	·58	2 3	·02 ·97	4
	24	Sa	5		7	·49	4	·93	5
	25	Su	6		8	·42	5	·90	6
	26	Mo	7		9	·37	6	·88	7
	27	Tu	8		10	·34	7	·88	8
	28	We	9		11	·33	8	·90	9
	29	Th	10		12	·34	9	·95	10
	30	Fr	11		13	·37	...	...	11
	—31	Sa	12		14	·41	10	·01	12
Khara *Mina—Panguni.*	1	Su	13		P	·47	11	·09	13
	2	Mo	14	*Bahula*	1	·55	12	·19	14
	3	Tu	15		2	·64	13	·30	15
	4	We	16		3	·73	14	·41	16
	5	Th	17		4	·81	15	·51	17
	6	Fr	18		5	·88	16	·60	18
	7	Sa	19		6	·93	17	·68	19
	8	Su	20		7	·96	18	·74	20
	9	Mo	21		8	·97	19	·78	21
	10	Tu	22		9	·95	20	·80	22
	11	We	23		10	·93	21	·80	23
	12	Th	24		11	·88	22	·78	24
	13	Fr	25		12	·81	23	·74	25
	14	Sa	26		13	·73	24	·69	26
	15	Su	27		14	·64	25	·63	27
	16	Mo	28		—A	·54	26	·57	28
	17	Tu	29	**Chaitra** *Sukla*	1	·44	27	·50	—29
	18	We	30		2	·34	1	·43	1 (H. 1309 *Ramzan.*)
	19	Th	31		3	·24	2	·36	2
		April							
	20	Fr	1		4	·15	3	·31	3
	21	Sa	2		5	·07	4	·26	4
	22	Su	3		6 7	·00 ·95	5	·22	5
	23	Mo	4		8	·91	6	·20	6
	24	Tu	5		9	·90	7	·20	7
	25	We	6		10	·90	8	·22	8
	26	Th	7		11	·93	9	·26	9
	27	Fr	8		12	·97	10	·32	10
	28	Sa	9		...	...	11	·40	11
	—29	Su	10		13	·05	12	·49	12
Nandana *Mesha—Chittirai.*	1	Mo	11		14	·12	13	·59	13
	2	Tu	12		P	·21	14	·70	14
	3	We	13	*Bahula*	1	·29	15	·81	15
	4	Th	14		2	·36	16	·91	16
	5	Fr	15		3	·45	17	·99	17
	6	Sa	16		4	·48	...	...	18
	7	Su	17		5	·52	18	·05	19
	8	Mo	18		6	·52	19	·10	20
	9	Tu	19		7	·51	20	·12	21
	10	We	20		8	·47	21	·12	22
	11	Th	21		9	·42	22	·11	23
	12	Fr	22		10	·35	23	·07	24
	13	Sa	23		11	·27	24 25	·03 ·97	25
	14	Su	24		12	·18	26	·91	26
	15	Mo	25		13 14	·08 ·98	27	·84	27
	16	Tu	26		—A	·88	1	·77	28
	17	We	27	**V.** *Suk.*	1	·78	2	·71	29
	18	Th	28		2	·69	3	·65	—30
	19	Fr	29		3	·60	4	·59	1 (H. 1309 *Shawwal.*)
	20	Sa	30		4	·53	5	·55	2

SOLAR reckoning: Solar month	Cyclic Sidereal Year, Month and Day	Week-Day	English Month and Day	LUNAR reckoning: Lunar month	Tithi	Ending Moment	Nakshatra	Ending Moment	Muhammadan Year, Month and Day
		May							
Nandana *Mesha—Chittirai.*	21	Su	1	**Vaisakha** *Sukla*	5	·45	6	·53	3
	22	Mo	2		6	·45	7	·52	4
	23	Tu	3		7	·43	8	·54	5
	24	We	4		8	·44	9	·57	6
	25	Th	5		9	·46	10	·63	7
	26	Fr	6		10	·50	11	·70	8
	27	Sa	7		11	·57	12	·79	9
	28	Su	8		12	·64	13	·90	10
	29	Mo	9		13	·72	...	...	11
	30	Tu	10		14	·81	14	·01	12
	—31	We ○	11		P	·89	15	·11	13
Nandana *Vrishabha—Vaikasi.*	1	Th	12	*Bahula*	1	·95	16	·21	14
	2	Fr	13		...	...	17	·29	15
	3	Sa	14		2	·00	18	·36	16
	4	Su	15		3	·03	19	·42	17
	5	Mo	16		4	·03	20	·44	18
	6	Tu	17		5 6	·02 ·99	21	·45	19
	7	We	18		7	·94	22	·43	20
	8	Th	19		8	·87	23	·41	21
	9	Fr	20		9	·78	24	·37	22
	10	Sa	21		10	·69	25	·31	23
	11	Su	22		11	·59	26	·25	24
	12	Mo	23		12	·49	27	·19	25
	13	Tu	24		13	·39	1	·12	26
	14	We	25		14	·29	2 3	·05 ·98	27
	15	Th	26		—A	·19	4	·93	28
	16	Fr	27	**Jyeshtha** *Sukla*	1	·11	5	·88	—29
	17	Sa	28		2 3	·04 ·98	6	·85	1 (H. 1309 *Zul-ka'da.*)
	18	Su	29		4	·95	7	·85	2
	19	Mo	30		5	·92	8	·86	3
	20	Tu	31		6	·93	9	·89	4
		June							
	21	We	1		7	·95	10	·94	5
	22	Th	2		...	...	...	...	6
	23	Fr	3		8	·00	11	·01	7
	24	Sa	4		9	·06	12	·10	8
	25	Su	5		10	·13	13	·20	9
	26	Mo	6		11	·21	14	·30	10
	27	Tu	7		12	·30	15	·41	11
	28	We	8		13	·38	16	·51	12
	29	Th	9		14	·44	17	·61	13
	30	Fr	10		P	·49	18	·68	14
	31	Sa	11	*Bahula*	1	·51	19	·73	15
	—32	Su	12		2	·52	20	·76	16
Nandana *Mithuna—Ani.*	1	Mo	13		3	·51	21	·77	17
	2	Tu	14		4	·48	22	·77	18
	3	We	15		5	·43	23	·74	19
	4	Th	16		6	·37	24	·70	20
	5	Fr	17		7	·29	25	·65	21
	6	Sa	18		8	·19	26	·58	22
	7	Su	19		9 10	·09 ·99	27	·51	23
	8	Mo	20		11	·89	1	·44	24
	9	Tu	21		12	·79	2	·38	25
	10	We	22		13	·69	3	·32	26
	11	Th	23		14	·60	4	·26	27
	12	Fr	24		—A	·52	5	·21	28
	13	Sa	25	**Ash.** *Suk.*	1	·47	6	·19	29
	14	Su	26		2	·43	7	·18	—30
	15	Mo	27		3	·40	8	·18	1 (*Zil-hijja.*)
	16	Tu	28		4	·41	9	·20	2
	17	We	29		5	·43	10	·24	3
	18	Th	30		6	·48	11	·31	4

Naksh:—1. Asvn. 2. Bhar. 3. Krit. 4. Rohi. 5. Mrig. 6. Ardh. 7. Punar. 8. Push. 9. Aslesh. 10. Magh. 11. P. Phal. 12. U. Phal. 13. Hasta. 14. Chit.

A. D. 1892.
A.—Amavasya.
P.—Paurnami.

Kollam 1068, Commences { N. Malabar—Sept. / S. Malabar—Aug.

Hijra 1310, Commences, July 26.

Vikrama 1949.
Bengal San 1298.
(N. Cycle) Krodhin.

SOLAR reckoning: Cyclic Sidereal Year, Month and Day; Week-Day; English Month and Day. LUNAR reckoning: Tithi, Ending Moment; Nakshatra, Ending Moment; Muhammadan Year, Month and Day.

July — Solar: Nandana *Mithuna—Ani*; Nandana *Karkata—Adi*. Lunar: Ashadha Sukla, Bahula; Sukla. Muhammadan: H. 1309 *Zu-l-hijja*.

Cyclic Sidereal Year, Month and Day	Week-Day	English Month and Day	Tithi	Ending Moment	Nakshatra	Ending Moment	Muhammadan Year, Month and Day
19	Fr	1	7	·54	12	·40	5
20	Sa	2	8	·61	13	·50	6
21	Su	3	9	·69	14	·61	7
22	Mo	4	10	·77	15	·72	8
23	Tu	5	11	·85	16	·83	9
24	We	6	12	·91	17	·93	10
25	Th	7	13	·96	18	·99	11
26	Fr	8	14	·99	...	...	12
27	Sa	9	...	...	19	·04	13
28	Su	10	P 1	·01 ·99	20	·08	14
29	Mo	11	2	·96	21	·10	15
30	Tu	12	3	·91	22	·10	16
31	We	13	4	·84	23	·07	17
1	Th	14	5	·76	24 25	·03 ·98	18
2	Fr	15	6	·67	26	·92	19
3	Sa	16	7	·57	27	·86	20
4	Su	17	8	·47	1	·79	21
5	Mo	18	9	·37	2	·72	22
6	Tu	19	10	·26	3	·65	23
7	We	20	11	·16	4	·60	24
8	Th	21	12	·08	5	·56	25
9	Fr	22	13 14	·01 ·95	6	·52	26
10	Sa	23	A	·90	7	·50	27
11	Su	24	1	·89	8	·50	28
12	Mo	25	2	·89	9	·52	29
13	Tu	26	3	·91	10	·56	1
14	We	27	4	·94	11	·62	2
15	Th	28	...	...	12	·70	3
16	Fr	29	5	·00	13	·80	4
17	Sa	30	6	·08	14	·91	5
18	Su	31	7	·16	...	...	6

Aug. — Solar: Nandana *Simha—Avani*. Lunar: Sravana Sukla, Bahula; Bhadra Sukla. Muhammadan: H. 1310 *Muharram*; H. 1310 *Safar*.

Cyclic Sidereal Year, Month and Day	Week-Day	English Month and Day	Tithi	Ending Moment	Nakshatra	Ending Moment	Muhammadan Year, Month and Day
19	Mo	1	8	·24	15	·02	7
20	Tu	2	9	·32	16	·12	8
21	We	3	10	·39	17	·21	9
22	Th	4	11	·44	18	·29	10
23	Fr	5	12	·47	19	·35	11
24	Sa	6	13	·49	20	·39	12
25	Su	7	14	·47	21	·42	13
26	Mo	8	P	·44	22	·42	14
27	Tu	9	1	·39	23	·40	15
28	We	10	2	·33	24	·37	16
29	Th	11	3	·25	25	·32	17
30	Fr	12	4	·16	26	·26	18
31	Sa	13	5 6	·06 ·96	27	·20	19
32	Su	14	7	·86	1	·13	20
1	Mo	15	8	·76	2 3	·06 ·99	21
2	Tu	16	9	·67	4	·94	22
3	We	17	10	·59	5	·89	23
4	Th	18	11	·51	6	·85	24
5	Fr	19	12	·44	7	·82	25
6	Sa	20	13	·40	8	·82	26
7	Su	21	14	·39	9	·84	27
8	Mo	22	A	·39	10	·88	28
9	Tu	23	1	·40	11	·94	29
10	We	24	2	·44	...	...	30
11	Th	25	3	·50	12	·01	1
12	Fr	26	4	·58	13	·10	2
13	Sa	27	5	·66	14	·20	3
14	Su	28	6	·74	15	·31	4
15	Mo	29	7	·82	16	·42	5
16	Tu	30	8	·89	17	·52	6
17	We	31	9	·94	18	·60	7

Sep. — Solar: Nandana *Simha—Avani*; Nandana *Kanya—Purattasi*. Lunar: Bhadrapada Suk., Bahula; Sukla. Muhammadan: H. 1310 *Safar*.

Cyclic Sidereal Year, Month and Day	Week-Day	English Month and Day	Tithi	Ending Moment	Nakshatra	Ending Moment	Muhammadan Year, Month and Day
18	Th	1	10	·98	19	·66	8
19	Fr	2	...	...	20	·71	9
20	Sa	3	11 12	·00 ·98	21	·74	10
21	Su	4	13	·96	22	·75	11
22	Mo	5	14	·92	23	·73	12
23	Tu	6	P	·85	24	·70	13
24	We	7	1	·77	25	·66	14
25	Th	8	2	·68	26	·60	15
26	Fr	9	3	·58	27	·54	16
27	Sa	10	4	·48	1	·47	17
28	Su	11	5	·38	2	·40	18
29	Mo	12	6	·28	3	·34	19
30	Tu	13	7	·19	4	·28	20
31	We	14	8	·11	5	·22	21
1	Th	15	9 10	·04 ·98	6	·18	22
2	Fr	16	11	·94	7	·15	23
3	Sa	17	12	·91	8	·15	24
4	Su	18	13	·90	9	·16	25
5	Mo	19	14	·93	10	·19	26
6	Tu	20	A	·97	11	·24	27
7	We	21	...	...	12	·31	28
8	Th	22	1	·03	13	·40	29
9	Fr	23	2	·10	14	·50	1
10	Sa	24	3	·18	15	·61	2
11	Su	25	4	·27	16	·72	3
12	Mo	26	5	·36	17	·82	4
13	Tu	27	6	·43	18	·90	5
14	We	28	7	·48	19	·98	6
15	Th	29	8	·52	...	...	7
16	Fr	30	9	·54	20	·03	8

Oct. — Solar: Nandana *Tula—Aippasi*. Lunar: Asvina Sukla, Bahula; Karttika Sukla. Muhammadan: H. 1310 *Rabi-ul-awwal*; *Rabi-ul-akhir*.

Cyclic Sidereal Year, Month and Day	Week-Day	English Month and Day	Tithi	Ending Moment	Nakshatra	Ending Moment	Muhammadan Year, Month and Day
17	Sa	1	10	·53	21	·06	9
18	Su	2	11	·51	22	·07	10
19	Mo	3	12	·47	23	·06	11
20	Tu	4	13	·40	24	·04	12
21	We	5	14	·32	25 26	·00 ·94	13
22	Th	6	P	·23	27	·88	14
23	Fr	7	1	·14	1	·82	15
24	Sa	8	2 3	·04 ·94	2	·75	16
25	Su	9	4	·84	3	·68	17
26	Mo	10	5	·75	4	·61	18
27	Tu	11	6	·67	5	·56	19
28	We	12	7	·60	6	·52	20
29	Th	13	8	·54	7	·49	21
30	Fr	14	9	·50	8	·47	22
1	Sa	15	10	·48	9	·48	23
2	Su	16	11	·49	10	·50	24
3	Mo	17	12	·51	11	·55	25
4	Tu	18	13	·55	12	·62	26
5	We	19	14	·60	13	·71	27
6	Th	20	A	·67	14	·81	28
7	Fr	21	1	·76	15	·91	29
8	Sa	22	2	·85	...	...	30
9	Su	23	3	·94	16	·02	1
10	Mo	24	...	...	17	·12	2
11	Tu	25	4	·01	18	·22	3
12	We	26	5	·07	19	·29	4
13	Th	27	6	·10	20	·34	5
14	Fr	28	7	·12	21	·37	6
15	Sa	29	8	·11	22	·39	7
16	Su	30	9	·09	23	·39	8
17	Mo	31	10 11	·06 ·99	24	·37	9

Nov. — Solar: Nandana *Tula—Aippasi*; Nandana *Vrischika—Kartigai*. Lunar: Karttika Suk., Bahula; Sukla. Muhammadan: H. 1310 *Rabi-ul-akhir*.

Cyclic Sidereal Year, Month and Day	Week-Day	English Month and Day	Tithi	Ending Moment	Nakshatra	Ending Moment	Muhammadan Year, Month and Day
18	Tu	1	12	·91	25	·33	10
19	We	2	13	·82	26	·28	11
20	Th	3	14	·73	27	·22	12
21	Fr ○	4	P	·63	1	·16	13
22	Sa	5	1	·53	2	·09	14
23	Su	6	2	·44	3 4	·02 ·95	15
24	Mo	7	3	·35	5	·89	16
25	Tu	8	4	·27	6	·84	17
26	We	9	5	·20	7	·82	18
27	Th	10	6	·14	8	·80	19
28	Fr	11	7	·10	9	·80	20
29	Sa	12	8	·08	10	·82	21
30	Su	13	9	·09	11	·86	22
1	Mo	14	10	·11	12	·93	23
2	Tu	15	11	·16	...	...	24
3	We	16	12	·22	13	·01	25
4	Th	17	13	·30	14	·10	26
5	Fr	18	14	·39	15	·21	27
6	Sa	19	A	·48	16	·32	28
7	Su	20	1	·56	17	·43	29
8	Mo	21	2	·63	18	·52	1
9	Tu	22	3	·69	19	·60	2
10	We	23	4	·73	20	·66	3
11	Th	24	5	·75	21	·70	4
12	Fr	25	6	·73	22	·72	5
13	Sa	26	7	·71	23	·72	6
14	Su	27	8	·66	24	·70	7
15	Mo	28	9	·60	25	·66	8
16	Tu	29	10	·53	26	·61	9
17	We	30	11	·45	27	·55	10

Dec. — Solar: Nandana *Dhanus—Margali*. Lunar: Margasira Sukla, Bahula; Pausha Sukla. Muhammadan: H. 1310 *Jumada-l-awwal*; H. 1310 *Jumada-l-akhir*.

Cyclic Sidereal Year, Month and Day	Week-Day	English Month and Day	Tithi	Ending Moment	Nakshatra	Ending Moment	Muhammadan Year, Month and Day
18	Th	1	12	·36	1	·49	11
19	Fr	2	13	·26	2	·42	12
20	Sa	3	14	·16	3	·35	13
21	Su	4	P 1	·06 ·97	4	·29	14
22	Mo	5	2	·89	5	·23	15
23	Tu	6	3	·82	6	·18	16
24	We	7	4	·77	7	·15	17
25	Th	8	5	·73	8	·12	18
26	Fr	9	6	·72	9	·12	19
27	Sa	10	7	·73	10	·14	20
28	Su	11	8	·75	11	·18	21
29	Mo	12	9	·80	12	·24	22
30	Tu	13	10	·87	13	·32	23
1	We	14	11	·95	14	·41	24
2	Th	15	...	...	15	·51	25
3	Fr	16	12	·04	16	·62	26
4	Sa	17	13	·13	17	·73	27
5	Su	18	14	·21	18	·82	28
6	Mo	19	A	·28	19	·90	29
7	Tu	20	1	·33	20	·97	30
8	We	21	2	·37	...	...	1
9	Th	22	3	·39	21	·02	2
10	Fr	23	4	·37	22	·04	3
11	Sa	24	5	·34	23	·04	4
12	Su	25	6	·30	24 25	·03 ·99	5
13	Mo	26	7	·24	26	·95	6
14	Tu	27	8	·16	27	·90	7
15	We	28	9 10	·08 ·99	1	·83	8
16	Th	29	11	·90	2	·76	9
17	Fr	30	12	·81	3	·69	10
18	Sa	31	13	·71	4	·63	11

15. Svati. 16. Visak. 17. Anur. 18. Jyesh. 19. Mula. 20. P. Ash. 21. U. Ash. 22. Sravn. 23. Dani. 24. Satab. 25. P. Bhad. 26. U. Bhad. 27. Rev.

A. D. 1893. **Mesha Sankranti** (Commencement of Indian Sidereal Year).

Solar Eclipse. ● **(Surya Sid.) April 11·81.** **Saka 1815.** **Kaliyuga 4994.**

Lunar Eclipse. ○ **(Arya Sid.) April 11·70.** **(S. Cycle) Vijaya.**

Columns: SOLAR reckoning (Cyclic Sidereal Year, Month and Day; Week-Day; English Month and Day) — LUNAR reckoning (Tithi; Ending Moment; Nakshatra; Ending Moment; Muhammadan Year, Month and Day).

Jan.

Cyclic Sidereal Year, Month and Day	Week-Day	English Month and Day	Tithi	Ending Moment	Nakshatra	Ending Moment	Muhammadan Year, Month and Day
Nandana *Dhanus—Margali.* 19	Su	1	**Pausha** 14	·61	5	·57	H. 1310 *Jumadal-akhir.* 12
20	Mo	2	P	·52	6	·52	13
21	Tu	3	1	·46	7	·48	14
22	We	4	2	·41	8	·45	15
23	Th	5	3	·38	9	·44	16
24	Fr	6	4	·37	10	·46	17
25	Sa	7	5	·37	11	·49	18
26	Su	8	6	·40	12	·54	19
27	Mo	9	*Bahula* 7	·45	13	·62	20
28	Tu	10	8	·52	14	·71	21
—29	We	11	9	·59	15	·81	22
1	Th	12	10	·68	16	·92	23
2	Fr	13	11	·77	...	...	24
3	Sa	14	12	·85	17	·03	25
4	Su	15	13	·92	18	·13	26
5	Mo	16	14	·98	19	·21	27
6	Tu	17	...	...	20	·28	28
7	We	18	—A	·02	21	·33	—29
8	Th	19	1	·03	22	·30	*Rajab.* 1
9	Fr	20	2	·02	23	·37	2
10	Sa	21	{ 3 / 4	·00 / ·95	24	·36	3
11	Su	22	5	·88	25	·33	4
12	Mo	23	6	·80	26	·29	5
13	Tu	24	*Sukla* 7	·72	27	·24	6
14	We	25	8	·63	1	·17	7
Nandana *Makara—Tai.* 15	Th	26	9	·53	2	·10	8
16	Fr	27	10	·43	3 / 4	·03 / ·97 }	9
17	Sa	28	11	·33	5	·91	10
18	Su	29	12	·24	6	·86	11
19	Mo	30	13	·16	7	·81	12
20	Tu	31	14	·10	8	·78	13

Feb.

Cyclic Sidereal Year, Month and Day	Week-Day	English Month and Day	Tithi	Ending Moment	Nakshatra	Ending Moment	Muhammadan Year, Month and Day
21	We	1	**Magha** P	·05	9	·77	H. 1310 14
22	Th	2	1	·02	10	·78	15
23	Fr	3	2	·01	11	·80	16
24	Sa	4	3	·01	12	·85	17
25	Su	5	4	·04	13	·92	18
26	Mo	6	5	·09	...	...	19
27	Th	7	6	·16	14	·01	20
28	We	8	*Bahula* 7	·24	15	·11	21
29	Th	9	8	·33	16	·22	22
—30	Fr	10	9	·42	17	·32	23
1	Sa	11	10	·50	18	·42	24
2	Su	12	11	·57	19	·51	25
3	Mo	13	12	·62	20	·59	26
4	Tu	14	13	·65	21	·65	27
5	We	15	14	·68	22	·68	28
6	Th	16	—A	·66	23	·69	29
7	Fr	17	1	·61	24	·68	—30
8	Sa	18	2	·57	25	·66	H. 1310 *Shaban.* 1
9	Su	19	3	·50	26	·62	2
10	Mo	20	4	·42	27	·57	3
Nandana *Kumbha—Masi.* 11	Tu	21	*Sukla* 5	·34	1	·51	4
12	We	22	6	·25	2	·45	5
13	Th	23	7	·15	3	·38	6
14	Fr	24	{ 8 / 9	·05 / ·95	4	·31	7
15	Sa	25	**Phalg.** 10	·85	5	·24	8
16	Su	26	11	·77	6	·18	9
17	Mo	27	12	·71	7	·14	10
18	Tu	28	13	·67	8	·11	11

March

Cyclic Sidereal Year, Month and Day	Week-Day	English Month and Day	Tithi	Ending Moment	Nakshatra	Ending Moment	Muhammadan Year, Month and Day
Nandana *Kumbha—Masi.* 19	We	1	**Phalguna** 14	·64	9	·10	H. 1310 *Shaban.* 12
20	Th	2	P	·62	10	·10	13
21	Fr	3	1	·63	11	·12	14
22	Sa	4	2	·66	12	·16	15
23	Su	5	3	·70	13	·22	16
24	Mo	6	4	·77	14	·31	17
25	Tu	7	5	·86	15	·41	18
26	We	8	6	·96	16	·52	19
27	Th	9	*Bahula* ...	...	17	·62	20
28	Fr	10	7	·04	18	·72	21
—29	Sa	11	8	·12	19	·82	22
1	Su	12	9	·18	20	·90	23
2	Mo	13	10	·22	21	·96	24
3	Tu	14	11	·25	...	...	25
4	We	15	12	·26	22	·00	26
5	Th	16	13	·25	23	·01	27
6	Fr	17	14	·21	24	·02	28
7	Sa	18	—A	·16	25 / 26	·00 / ·96 }	—29
8	Su	19	1	·10	27	·91	*Ramzan.* 1
9	Mo	20	{ 2 / 3	·03 / ·94	1	·85	2
10	Tu	21	4	·84	2	·79	3
11	We	22	5	·74	3	·73	4
Nandana *Mina—Panguni.* 12	Th	23	*Sukla* 6	·64	4	·65	5
13	Fr	24	7	·54	5	·58	6
14	Sa	25	8	·45	6	·52	7
15	Su	26	9	·37	7	·48	8
16	Mo	27	**Chaitra** 10	·30	8	·44	9
17	Tu	28	11	·25	9	·42	10
18	We	29	12	·22	10	·42	11
19	Th	30	13	·20	11	·45	12
20	Fr	31	14	·21	12	·48	13

April

Cyclic Sidereal Year, Month and Day	Week-Day	English Month and Day	Tithi	Ending Moment	Nakshatra	Ending Moment	Muhammadan Year, Month and Day
21	Sa	1	P	·24	13	·54	H. 1310 14
22	Su	2	1	·29	14	·62	15
23	Mo	3	2	·36	15	·71	16
24	Tu	4	3	·44	16	·81	17
25	We	5	4	·53	17	·92	18
26	Th	6	5	·61	...	...	19
27	Fr	7	*Bahula* 6	·69	18	·03	20
28	Sa	8	7	·75	19	·13	21
29	Su	9	8	·79	20	·21	22
30	Mo	10	9	·82	21	·27	23
—31	Tu	11	10	·83	22	·31	24
1	We	12	11	·81	23	·34	25
2	Th	13	12	·77	24	·34	26
3	Fr	14	13	·72	25	·32	27
4	Sa	15	14	·66	26	·29	28
5	Su	16	—A	·58	27	·24	29
6	Mo	17	1	·49	1	·19	—30
7	Tu	18	2	·39	2	·13	H. 1310 *Shawwal.* 1
Vijaya *Mesha—Chittirai.* 8	We	19	*Sukla* 3	·29	3 / 4	·05 / ·99 }	2
9	Th	20	4	·19	5	·92	3
10	Fr	21	{ 5 / 6	·09 / ·99	6	·86	4
11	Sa	22	7	·91	7	·81	5
12	Su	23	8	·85	8	·77	6
13	Mo	24	9	·80	9	·75	7
14	Tu	25	**Vaisakha** 10	·76	10	·74	8
15	We	26	11	·75	11	·75	9
16	Th	27	12	·75	12	·79	10
17	Fr	28	13	·78	13	·85	11
18	Sa	29	14	·82	14	·92	12
19	Su	30	P	·88	...	...	13

May

Cyclic Sidereal Year, Month and Day	Week-Day	English Month and Day	Tithi	Ending Moment	Nakshatra	Ending Moment	Muhammadan Year, Month and Day
Vijaya *Mesha—Chittirai.* 20	Mo	1	**Vaisakha** 1	·96	15	·01	H. 1310 *Shawwal.* 14
21	Tu	2	...	...	16	·11	15
22	We	3	2	·06	17	·22	16
23	Th	4	3	·14	18	·33	17
24	Fr	5	4	·21	19	·43	18
25	Sa	6	5	·27	20	·51	19
26	Su	7	6	·31	21	·58	20
27	Mo	8	7	·34	22	·64	21
28	Tu	9	*Bahula* 8	·36	23	·66	22
29	We	10	9	·34	24	·67	23
30	Th	11	10	·31	25	·65	24
—31	Fr	12	11	·25	26	·62	25
1	Sa	13	12	·18	27	·59	26
2	Su	14	13	·10	1	·53	27
3	Mo	15	{ 14 / A	·01 / ·91	2	·46	28
4	Tu	16	1	·81	3	·39	—29
5	We	17	2	·71	4	·32	*Zil-ka'da.* 1
6	Th	18	3	·61	5	·26	2
7	Fr	19	4	·52	6	·20	3
8	Sa	20	5	·43	7	·15	4
9	Su	21	6	·36	8	·10	5
10	Mo	22	*Sukla* 7	·31	9	·07	6
Vijaya *Vrishabha—Vaikasi.* 11	Tu	23	8	·27	10	·06	7
12	We	24	9	·25	11	·08	8
13	Th	25	10	·25	12	·11	9
14	Fr	26	**Jyeshtha** 11	·28	13	·16	10
15	Sa	27	12	·33	14	·22	11
16	Su	28	13	·39	15	·31	12
17	Mo	29	14	·47	16	·42	13
18	Tu	30	P	·55	17	·53	14
19	We	31	1	·63	18	·63	15

June

Cyclic Sidereal Year, Month and Day	Week-Day	English Month and Day	Tithi	Ending Moment	Nakshatra	Ending Moment	Muhammadan Year, Month and Day
20	Th	1	2	·71	19	·73	H. 1310 16
21	Fr	2	3	·77	20	·82	17
22	Sa	3	4	·81	21	·90	18
23	Su	4	5	·83	22	·95	19
24	Mo	5	6	·85	23	·98	20
25	Tu	6	*Bahula* 7	·83	24	·99	21
26	We	7	8	·80	25	·98	22
27	Th	8	9	·75	26	·95	23
28	Fr	9	10	·68	27	·92	24
29	Sa	10	11	·60	1	·87	25
30	Su	11	12	·50	2	·80	26
—31	Mo	12	13	·40	3	·73	27
1	Tu	13	14	·30	4	·66	28
2	We	14	—A	·20	5	·60	29
3	Th	15	1	·10	6	·54	—30
4	Fr	16	{ 2 / 3	·01 / ·92	7	·48	H. 1310 *Zil-hijja.* 1
5	Sa	17	4	·85	8	·43	2
6	Su	18	*Sukla* 5	·79	9	·40	3
Vijaya *Mithuna—Ani.* 7	Mo	19	6	·75	10	·39	4
8	Tu	20	7	·73	11	·40	5
9	We	21	**Adhika Ashadha** 8	·73	12	·42	6
10	Th	22	9	·76	13	·47	7
11	Fr	23	10	·81	14	·54	8
12	Sa	24	11	·87	15	·62	9
13	Su	25	12	·94	16	·72	10
14	Mo	26	...	...	17	·82	11
15	Tu	27	13	·02	18	·93	12
16	We	28	14	·10	...	...	13
17	Th	29	P	·18	19	·03	14
18	Fr	30	1	·25	20	·12	15

Naksh:—1. Asvn. 2. Bhar. 3. Krit. 4. Rohi. 5. Mrig. 6. Ardh. 7. Punar. 8. Push. 9. Aslesh. 10. Magh. 11. P. Phal. 12. U. Phal. 13. Hasta. 14. Chit.

A. D. 1893. **A.—Amavasya.** **P.—Paurnami.**

Kollam 1069, Commences { **N. Malabar—Sept.** **S. Malabar—Aug.**

Hijra 1311, Commences, **July 15.**

Vikrama 1950. **Bengal San 1299.** **(N. Cycle) Visvavasu.**

SOLAR reckoning. Cyclic Sidereal Year, Month and Day.	Week-Day	English Month and Day.	LUNAR reckoning. Tithi	Ending Moment.	Nakshatra	Ending Moment.	Muhammadan Year, Month and Day.
		July					
[Vijaya Mithuna—Ani.] 19	Sa	1	[Adh. Ashad.] 2	·30	21	·21	[H. 1310 Zi-l-hijja.] 16
20	Su	2	3	·32	22	·26	17
21	Mo	3	4	·33	23	·30	18
22	Tu	4	5	·32	24	·31	19
23	We	5	6	·28	25	·31	20
24	Th	6	7	·22	26	·29	21
25	Fr	7	8	·15	27	·25	22
26	Sa	8	9 / 10	·07 / ·98	1	·20	23
27	Su	9	[Bahula] 11	·88	2	·14	24
28	Mo	10	12	·78	3	·08	25
29	Tu	11	13	·68	4 / 5	·01 / ·94	26
30	We	12	14	58	6	·87	27
31	Th	13	A	·49	7	·81	28
32	Fr	14	[Nija Ashadha] 1	·40	8	·77	29
[Vijaya Karkata—Adi.] 1	Sa	15	2	·33	9	·74	[H. 1311 Muharram.] 1
2	Su	16	3	·27	10	·72	2
3	Mo	17	4	·23	11	·72	3
4	Tu	18	5	·21	12	·74	4
5	We	19	[Sukla] 6	·22	13	·78	5
6	Th	20	7	·24	14	·84	6
7	Fr	21	8	·28	15	·92	7
8	Sa	22	9	·34	...	...	8
9	Su	23	10	·41	16	·02	9
10	Mo	24	11	·49	17	·12	10
11	Tu	25	12	·58	18	·23	11
12	We	26	13	·66	19	·33	12
13	Th	27	14	·72	20	·43	13
14	Fr	28	P	·77	21	·51	14
15	Sa	29	1	·80	22	·57	15
16	Su	30	2	·81	23	·61	16
17	Mo	31	3	·79	24	·63	17
		Aug.					
18	Tu	1	4	·76	25	·64	18
19	We	2	5	·71	26	·62	19
20	Th	3	[Bahula] 6	·64	27	·59	20
21	Fr	4	7	·56	1	·54	21
22	Sa	5	8	·47	2	·48	22
23	Su	6	9	·37	3	·42	23
24	Mo	7	10	·27	4	·35	24
25	Tu	8	11	·17	5	·28	25
26	We	9	12 / 13	·07 / ·98	6	·21	26
27	Th	10	14	·90	7	·15	27
28	Fr	11	A	·82	8	·10	28
29	Sa	12	[Sravana] 1	·76	9	·07	29
30	Su	13	2	·72	10	·04	30
31	Mo	14	3	·70	11	·04	[H. 1311 Safar.] 1
[Vijaya Simha—Avani.] 1	Tu	15	4	·71	12	·05	2
2	We	16	5	·73	13	·09	3
3	Th	17	6	·77	14	·15	4
4	Fr	18	7	·83	15	·23	5
5	Sa	19	[Sukla] 8	·90	16	·32	6
6	Su	20	9	·98	17	·42	7
7	Mo	21	...	...	18	·53	8
8	Tu	22	10	·07	19	·64	9
9	We	23	11	·15	20	·74	10
10	Th	24	12	·21	21	·82	11
11	Fr	25	13	·26	22	·88	12
12	Sa	26	14	·29	23	·93	13
13	Su	27	P	·31	24	·96	14
14	Mo	28	[Bah.] 1	·30	25	·97	15
15	Tu	29	2	·27	26	·95	16
16	We	30	3	·22	27	·92	17
17	Th	31	4	·16	1	·87	18

SOLAR reckoning. Cyclic Sidereal Year, Month and Day.	Week-Day	English Month and Day.	LUNAR reckoning. Tithi	Ending Moment.	Nakshatra	Ending Moment.	Muhammadan Year, Month and Day.
		Sep.					
[Vijaya Simha—Avani.] 18	Fr	1	[Sravn. Bahula] 5 / 6	·08 / ·99	2	·82	[H. 1311 Safar.] 19
19	Sa	2	7	·89	3	·76	20
20	Su	3	8	·79	4	·69	21
21	Mo	4	9	·69	5	·62	22
22	Tu	5	10	·59	6	·55	23
23	We	6	11	·49	7	·49	24
24	Th	7	12	·41	8	·44	25
25	Fr	8	13	·34	9	·40	26
26	Sa	9	14	·28	10	·37	27
27	Su	10	A	·24	11	·36	28
28	Mo	11	[Bhadrupada] 1	·22	12	·37	29
29	Tu	12	2	·23	13	·41	[H. 1311 Rabi-ul-awwal.] 1
30	We	13	3	·25	14	·46	2
31	Th	14	4	·30	15	·53	3
[Vijaya Kanya—Purattasi.] 1	Fr	15	5	·36	16	·62	4
2	Sa	16	[Sukla] 6	·43	17	·72	5
3	Su	17	7	·51	18	·83	6
4	Mo	18	8	·59	19	·94	7
5	Tu	19	9	·67	...	...	8
6	We	20	10	·74	20	·03	9
7	Th	21	11	·80	21	·12	10
8	Fr	22	12	·83	22	·19	11
9	Sa	23	13	·85	23	·25	12
10	Su	24	14	·83	24	·28	13
11	Mo	25	P	·80	25	·29	14
12	Tu	26	1	·76	26	·28	15
13	We	27	2	·70	27	·25	16
14	Th	28	3	·62	1	·21	17
15	Fr	29	4	·53	2	·16	18
16	Sa	30	5	·44	3	·10	19
		Oct.					
17	Su	1	[Bahula] 6	·34	4 / 5	·03 / ·96	20
18	Mo	2	7	·24	6	·89	21
19	Tu	3	8	·14	7	·83	22
20	We	4	9 / 10	·04 / ·96	8	·77	23
21	Th	5	11	·89	9	·73	24
22	Fr	6	12	·84	10	·70	25
23	Sa	7	13	·80	11	·68	26
24	Su	8	14	·79	12	·70	27
25	Mo	9	A	·79	13	·72	28
26	Tu	10	[Asvina] 1	·81	14	·77	29
27	We	11	2	·85	15	·83	30
28	Th	12	3	·91	16	·92	[H. 1311 Rabi-ul-akhir.] 1
29	Fr	13	4	·99	...	...	2
30	Sa	14	...	...	17	·02	3
31	Su	15	5	·08	18	·13	4
[Vijaya Tula—Aippasi.] 1	Mo	16	6	·16	19	·24	5
2	Tu	17	[Sukla] 7	·24	20	·34	6
3	We	18	8	·31	21	·43	7
4	Th	19	9	·37	22	·51	8
5	Fr	20	10	·41	23	·57	9
6	Sa	21	11	·43	24	·60	10
7	Su	22	12	·41	25	·61	11
8	Mo	23	13	·38	26	·60	12
9	Tu	24	14	·34	27	·59	13
10	We	25	P	·28	1	·55	14
11	Th	26	1	·20	2	·50	15
12	Fr	27	2	·11	3	·44	16
13	Sa	28	[Bahula] 3 / 4	·02 / ·92	4	·37	17
14	Su	29	5	·82	5	·30	18
15	Mo	30	6	·72	6	·23	19
16	Tu	31	7	·63	7	·17	20

SOLAR reckoning. Cyclic Sidereal Year, Month and Day.	Week-Day	English Month and Day.	LUNAR reckoning. Tithi	Ending Moment.	Nakshatra	Ending Moment.	Muhammadan Year, Month and Day.
		Nov.					
[Vijaya Tula—Aippasi.] 17	We	1	[Asvn. Bah.] 8	·55	8	·11	[Rabi-ul-akhir.] 21
18	Th	2	9	·48	9	·06	22
19	Fr	3	10	·42	10	·03	23
20	Sa	4	11	·39	11	·02	24
21	Su	5	12	·38	12	·02	25
22	Mo	6	13	·38	13	·04	26
23	Tu	7	14	·40	14	·08	27
24	We	8	A	·45	15	·14	28
25	Th	9	[Kartika] 1	·52	16	·22	29
26	Fr	10	2	·60	17	·32	[H. 1311 Jumadal-awwal.] 1
27	Sa	11	3	·68	18	·43	2
28	Su	12	4	·77	19	·54	3
29	Mo	13	5	·85	20	·64	4
30	Tu	14	6	·92	21	·74	5
[Vijaya Vrischika—Kartigai.] 1	We	15	7	·98	22	·82	6
2	Th	16	[Sukla] ...	...	23	·88	7
3	Fr	17	8	·02	24	·91	8
4	Sa	18	9	·03	25	·93	9
5	Su	19	10	·02	26	·93	10
6	Mo	20	11 / 12	·00 / ·95	27	·92	11
7	Tu	21	13	·89	1	·88	12
8	We	22	14	·82	2	·83	13
9	Th	23	P	·74	3	·77	14
10	Fr	24	1	·64	4	·71	15
11	Sa	25	2	·54	5	·64	16
12	Su	26	3	·44	6	·57	17
13	Mo	27	4	·34	7	·50	18
14	Tu	28	5	·25	8	·44	19
15	We	29	6	·17	9	·39	20
16	Th	30	7	·10	10	·36	21
		Dec.					
17	Fr	1	[Bahula] 8	·05	11	·34	22
18	Sa	2	9	·02	12	·34	23
19	Su	3	10	·00	13	·35	24
20	Mo	4	11	·01	14	·39	25
21	Tu	5	12	·04	15	·45	26
22	We	6	13	·08	16	·53	27
23	Th	7	14	·15	17	·62	28
24	Fr	8	A	·23	18	·72	29
25	Sa	9	[Margasira] 1	·32	19	·83	30
26	Su	10	2	·41	20	·94	[H. 1311 Jumadal-akhir.] 1
27	Mo	11	3	·50	...	...	2
28	Tu	12	4	·57	21	·04	3
29	We	13	5	·62	22	·12	4
[Vijaya Dhanus—Margali.] 1	Th	14	6	·66	23	·19	5
2	Fr	15	[Sukla] 7	·67	24	·23	6
3	Sa	16	8	·66	25	·25	7
4	Su	17	9	·64	26	·26	8
5	Mo	18	10	·59	27	·25	9
6	Tu	19	11	·52	1	·21	10
7	We	20	12	·44	2	·17	11
8	Th	21	13	·36	3	·11	12
9	Fr	22	14	·27	4 / 5	·05 / ·98	13
10	Sa	23	P	·17	6	·91	14
11	Su	24	1 / 2	·07 / ·97	7	·84	15
12	Mo	25	[Bahula] 3	·88	8	·78	16
13	Tu	26	4	·80	9	·74	17
14	We	27	5	·74	10	·70	18
15	Th	28	6	·70	11	·67	19
16	Fr	29	7	·67	12	·66	20
17	Sa	30	8	·65	13	·67	21
18	Su	31	9	·66	14	·71	22

A. D. 1894. **Mesha Sankranti** (Commencement of Indian Sidereal Year).
Solar Eclipse. ● **(Surya Sid.) April 12·07.** **Saka 1816.** **Kaliyuga 4995.**
Lunar Eclipse. ○ **(Arya Sid.) April 11·96.** **(S. Cycle) Jaya.**

SOLAR reckoning: Cyclic Sidereal Year, Month and Day	Week-Day	English Month and Day	LUNAR reckoning: Tithi	Ending Moment	Nakshatra	Ending Moment	Muhammadan Year, Month and Day
		Jan.					
Vijaya Dhanus—Margali 19	Mo	1	*Mr. Bah.* 10	·69	15	·76	*J.-akhir.* 23
20	Tu	2	11	·74	16	·83	24
21	We	3	12	·81	17	·92	25
22	Th	4	13	·89	...	...	26
23	Fr	5	14	·98	18	·02	27
24	Sa	6	...	...	19	·13	28
25	Su	7	—A	·07	20	·24	—29
26	Mo	8	*Pausha Sukla* 1	·15	21	·34	*H. 1311 Rajab.* 1
27	Tu	9	2	·22	22	·43	2
28	We	10	3	·27	23	·50	3
—29	Th	11	4	·30	24	·55	4
Vijaya Makara—Tai 1	Fr	12	5	·31	25	·58	5
2	Sa	13	6	·31	26	·59	6
3	Su	14	7	·28	27	·58	7
4	Mo	15	8	·23	1	·55	8
5	Tu	16	9	·17	2	·51	9
6	We	17	10	·09	3	·46	10
7	Th	18	11 / 12	·00 / ·90	4	·39	11
8	Fr	19	13	·80	5	·32	12
9	Sa	20	14	·70	6	·25	13
10	Su	21	P	·61	7	·18	14
11	Mo	22	*Bahula* 1	·52	8	·12	15
12	Tu	23	2	·45	9	·07	16
13	We	24	3	·39	10	·03	17
14	Th	25	4	·34	11 / 12	·00 / ·98	18
15	Fr	26	5	·31	13	·99	19
16	Sa	27	6	·29	...	...	20
17	Su	28	7	·30	14	·03	21
18	Mo	29	8	·33	15	·08	22
19	Tu	30	9	·39	16	·14	23
20	We	31	10	·46	17	·22	24
		Feb.					
21	Th	1	11	·54	18	·32	25
22	Fr	2	12	·63	19	·43	26
23	Sa	3	13	·72	20	·54	27
24	Su	4	14	·80	21	·64	28
25	Mo	5	—A	·86	22	·73	29
26	Tu	6	*Magha Sukla* 1	·91	23	·81	—30
27	We	7	2	·94	24	·87	*H. 1311 Shaban.* 1
28	Th	8	3	·96	25	·90	2
29	Fr	9	4	·94	26	·91	3
—30	Sa	10	5	·91	27	·90	4
Vijaya Kumbha—Mani 1	Su	11	6	·86	1	·88	5
2	Mo	12	7	·79	2	·84	6
3	Tu	13	8	·71	3	·79	7
4	We	14	9	·62	4	·73	8
5	Th	15	10	·53	5	·66	9
6	Fr	16	11	·44	6	·59	10
7	Sa	17	12	·34	7	·52	11
8	Su	18	13	·24	8	·46	12
9	Me	19	14	·15	9	·40	13
10	Tu	20	P	·07	10	·35	14
11	We	21	*Bahula* 1 / 2	·00 / ·96	11	·32	15
12	Th	22	3	·93	12	·31	16
13	Fr	23	4	·92	13	·32	17
14	Sa	24	5	·92	14	·34	18
15	Su	25	6	·96	15	·38	19
16	Mo	26	...	...	16	·44	20
17	Tu	27	7	·01	17	·53	21
18	We	28	8	·08	18	·63	22

SOLAR reckoning: Cyclic Sidereal Year, Month and Day	Week-Day	English Month and Day	LUNAR reckoning: Tithi	Ending Moment	Nakshatra	Ending Moment	Muhammadan Year, Month and Day
		March					
Vijaya Kumbha—Mani 19	Th	1	*Mg. Bah.* 9	·17	19	·74	*Shaban.* 23
20	Fr	2	10	·26	20	·84	24
21	Sa	3	11	·35	21	·94	25
22	Su	4	12	·42	...	...	26
23	Mo	5	13	·48	22	·04	27
24	Tu	6	14	·53	23	·12	28
25	We	7	—A	·56	24	·18	—29
26	Th	8	*Phalguna Sukla* 1	·57	25	·22	*H. 1311 Ramzan.* 1
27	Fr	9	2	·55	26	·23	2
28	Sa	10	3	·52	27	·23	3
29	Su	11	4	·46	1	·22	4
—30	Mo	12	5	·39	2	·18	5
Vijaya Mina—Panguni 1	Tu	13	6	·31	3	·13	6
2	We	14	7	·22	4	·07	7
3	Th	15	8	·13	5 / 6	·00 / ·93	8
4	Fr	16	9 / 10	·03 / ·93	7	·86	9
5	Sa	17	11	·83	8	·80	10
6	Su	18	12	·74	9	·74	11
7	Mo	19	13	·66	10	·69	12
8	Tu	20	14	·59	11	·65	13
9	We ○	21	P	·55	12	·64	14
10	Th	22	*Bahula* 1	·52	13	·64	15
11	Fr	23	2	·51	14	·65	16
12	Sa	24	3	·51	15	·69	17
13	Su	25	4	·55	16	·75	18
14	Mo	26	5	·61	17	·83	19
15	Tu	27	6	·68	18	·93	20
16	We	28	7	·76	...	...	21
17	Th	29	8	·85	19	·03	22
18	Fr	30	9	·93	20	·14	23
19	Sa	31	...	...	21	·25	24
		April					
20	Su	1	10	·00	22	·35	25
21	Mo	2	11	·06	23	·43	26
22	Tu	3	12	·11	24	·49	27
23	We	4	13	·14	25	·53	28
24	Th	5	14	·14	26	·55	29
25	Fr ●	6	—A	·12	27	·56	—30
26	Sa	7	*Chaitra Sukla* 1	·08	1	·54	*H. 1311 Shawwal.* 1
27	Su	8	2 / 3	·03 / ·96	2	·51	2
28	Mo	9	4	·88	3	·46	3
29	Tu	10	5	·79	4	·40	4
—30	We	11	6	·69	5	·34	5
Jaya Mesha—Chittirai 1	Th	12	7	·59	6	·28	6
2	Fr	13	8	·49	7	·21	7
3	Sa	14	9	·39	8	·14	8
4	Su	15	10	·30	9	·07	9
5	Mo	16	11	·22	10 / 11	·02 / ·99	10
6	Tu	17	12	·16	12	·97	11
7	We	18	13	·11	13	·96	12
8	Th	19	14	·08	14	·97	13
9	Fr	20	P	·06	...	...	14
10	Sa	21	*Bahula* 1	·06	15	·00	15
11	Su	22	2	·09	16	·06	16
12	Mo	23	3	·14	17	·14	17
13	Tu	24	4	·21	18	·23	18
14	We	25	5	·30	19	·33	19
15	Th	26	6	·39	20	·44	20
16	Fr	27	7	·47	21	·55	21
17	Sa	28	8	·53	22	·65	22
18	Su	29	9	·59	23	·73	23
19	Mo	30	10	·64	24	·80	24

SOLAR reckoning: Cyclic Sidereal Year, Month and Day	Week-Day	English Month and Day	LUNAR reckoning: Tithi	Ending Moment	Nakshatra	Ending Moment	Muhammadan Year, Month and Day
		May					
Jaya Mesha—Chittirai 20	Tu	1	*Bah.* 11	·67	25	·85	*Shawwal.* 25
21	We	2	12	·67	26	·87	26
22	Th	3	13	·66	27	·89	27
23	Fr	4	14	·62	1	·87	28
24	Sa	5	—A	·56	2	·84	29
25	Su	6	*Vaisakha Sukla* 1	·49	3	·80	*H. 1311 Zi-l-ka'da.* 1
26	Mo	7	2	·41	4	·74	2
27	Tu	8	3	·32	5	·68	3
28	We	9	4	·22	6	·61	4
29	Th	10	5	·12	7	·54	5
30	Fr	11	6 / 7	·02 / ·92	8	·47	6
—31	Sa	12	8	·82	9	·41	7
Jaya Vrishabha—Vaikasi 1	Su	13	9	·74	10	·36	8
2	Mo	14	10	·67	11	·32	9
3	Tu	15	11	·62	12	·29	10
4	We	16	12	·59	13	·28	11
5	Th	17	13	·57	14	·29	12
6	Fr	18	14	·58	15	·33	13
7	Sa	19	P	·61	16	·38	14
8	Su	20	*Bahula* 1	·65	17	·45	15
9	Mo	21	2	·72	18	·53	16
10	Tu	22	3	·80	19	·63	17
11	We	23	4	·89	20	·74	18
12	Th	24	5	·97	21	·85	19
13	Fr	25	...	...	22	·95	20
14	Sa	26	6	·04	...	...	21
15	Su	27	7	·10	23	·04	22
16	Mo	28	8	·15	24	·11	23
17	Tu	29	9	·17	25	·16	24
18	We	30	10	·17	26	·20	25
19	Th	31	11	·16	27	·21	26
		June					
20	Fr	1	12	·12	1	·20	27
21	Sa	2	13	·07	2	·17	28
22	Su	3	14 / A	·00 / ·91	3	·13	29
23	Mo	4	*Jyeshtha Sukla* 1	·81	4	·08	—30
24	Tu	5	2	·71	5 / 6	·02 / ·95	*H. 1311 Zi-l-hijja.* 1
25	We	6	3	·61	7	·88	2
26	Th	7	4	·51	8	·82	3
27	Fr	8	5	·41	9	·76	4
28	Sa	9	6	·32	10	·70	5
29	Su	10	7	·24	11	·65	6
30	Mo	11	8	·17	12	·62	7
—31	Tu	12	9	·12	13	·60	8
Jaya Mithuna—Ani 1	We	13	10	·08	14	·61	9
2	Th	14	11	·05	15	·64	10
3	Fr	15	12	·06	16	·69	11
4	Sa	16	13	·09	17	·75	12
5	Su	17	14	·14	18	·83	13
6	Mo	18	P	·20	19	·93	14
7	Tu	19	*Bahula* 1	·28	...	...	15
8	We	20	2	·36	20	·04	16
9	Th	21	3	·44	21	·15	17
10	Fr	22	4	·51	22	·25	18
11	Sa	23	5	·57	23	·34	19
12	Su	24	6	·62	24	·42	20
13	Mo	25	7	·65	25	·48	21
14	Tu	26	8	·66	26	·52	22
15	We	27	9	·63	27	·53	23
16	Th	28	10	·59	1	·53	24
17	Fr	29	11	·54	2	·50	25
18	Sa	30	12	·48	3	·47	26

Nakah:—1. Asvn. 2. Bhar. 3. Krit. 4. Rohi. 5. Mrig. 6. Ardh. 7. Punar. 8. Push. 9. Aslesh. 10. Magh. 11. P. Phal. 12. U. Phal. 13. Hasta. 14. Chit.

A. D. 1894. **A.—Amavasya. P.—Paurnami.** **Kollam 1070,** Commences {N. Malabar—Sept. S. Malabar—Aug. **Hijra 1312,** Commences, **July 5.** **Vikrama 1951. Bengal San 1300. (N. Cycle) Parabhava.**

Solar month	Cyclic Sidereal Year, Month and Day	Week-Day	English Month and Day	Lunar	Tithi	Ending Moment	Nakshatra	Ending Moment	Muhammadan Year, Month and Day
			July						
Jaya Mithuna—Ani	19	Su	1	Bah.	13	·39	4	·42	Zi-l-hijja 27
	20	Mo	2		14	·30	5	·36	28
	21	Tu	3		A	·20	6	·29	29
	22	We	4		1 / 2	·09 / ·99	7	·22	30
	23	Th	5	Sukla	3	·89	8	·15	1
	24	Fr	6		4	·79	9	·09	2
	25	Sa	7		5	·71	10 / 11	·03 / ·98	3
	26	Su	8		6	·64	12	·95	4
	27	Mo	9		7	·59	13	·93	5
	28	Tu	10		8	·55	14	·94	6
	29	We	11		9	·54	15	·96	7
	30	Th	12		10	·54	...	...	8
	31	Fr	13	Ashadha	11	·57	16	·00	9
	—32	Sa	14		12	·61	17	·06	H. 1312 Muharram 10
Jaya Karkatu—Adi	1	Su	15		13	·67	18	·14	11
	2	Mo	16		14	·75	19	·24	12
	3	Tu	17		P	·83	20	·34	13
	4	We	18		1	·91	21	·45	14
	5	Th	19		2	·99	22	·55	15
	6	Fr	20		...	...	23	·64	16
	7	Sa	21	Bahula	3	·06	24	·72	17
	8	Su	22		4	·10	25	·79	18
	9	Mo	23		5	·13	26	·83	19
	10	Tu	24		6	·14	27	·85	20
	11	We	25		7	·11	1	·85	21
	12	Th	26		8	·08	2	·84	22
	13	Fr	27		9 / 10	·03 / ·96	3	·81	23
	14	Sa	28		11	·88	4	·76	24
	15	Su	29		12	·79	5	·70	25
	16	Mo	30		13	·69	6	·63	26
	17	Tu	31		14	·58	7	·56	27

Solar month	Cyclic Sidereal Year, Month and Day	Week-Day	English Month and Day	Lunar	Tithi	Ending Moment	Nakshatra	Ending Moment	Muhammadan Year, Month and Day
			Aug.						
Jaya Karkatu—Adi	18	We	1		—A	·48	8	·49	28
	19	Th	2	Sukla	1	·38	9	·43	29
	20	Fr	3		2	·29	10	·37	—30
	21	Sa	4		3	·20	11	·32	H. 1312 Safar 1
	22	Su	5		4	·13	12	·28	2
	23	Mo	6		5	·08	13	·26	3
	24	Tu	7		6	·04	14	·26	4
	25	We	8		7	·02	15	·27	5
	26	Th	9		8	·02	16	·31	6
	27	Fr	10		9	·05	17	·37	7
	28	Sa	11		10	·10	18	·45	8
	29	Su	12	Sravana	11	·16	19	·54	9
	30	Mo	13		12	·23	20	·64	10
	—31	Tu	14		13	·31	21	·75	11
Jaya Simha—Avani	1	We	15		14	·40	22	·86	12
	2	Th	16		P	·48	23	·96	13
	3	Fr	17		1	·55	...	...	14
	4	Sa	18		2	·59	24	·04	15
	5	Su	19		3	·63	25	·10	16
	6	Mo	20		4	·63	26	·15	17
	7	Tu	21	Bahula	5	·61	27	·17	18
	8	We	22		6	·58	1	·19	19
	9	Th	23		7	·53	2	·17	20
	10	Fr	24		8	·46	3	·14	21
	11	Sa	25		9	·38	4	·09	22
	12	Su	26		10	·29	5 / 6	·03 / ·97	23
	13	Mo	27		11	·19	7	·91	24
	14	Tu	28		12 / 13	·09 / ·99	8	·84	25
	15	We	29		14	·89	9	·77	26
	16	Th	30		—A	·79	10	·70	27
	17	Fr	31		1	·71	11	·65	28

Solar month	Cyclic Sidereal Year, Month and Day	Week-Day	English Month and Day	Lunar	Tithi	Ending Moment	Nakshatra	Ending Moment	Muhammadan Year, Month and Day
			Sep.						
Jaya Simha—Avani	18	Sa	1		2	·65	12	·62	—29
	19	Su	2		3	·60	13	·59	H. 1312 Rabi-ul-awal 1
	20	Mo	3		4	·56	14	·58	2
	21	Tu	4		5	·54	15	·59	3
	22	We	5	Sukla	6	·53	16	·62	4
	23	Th	6		7	·56	17	·68	5
	24	Fr	7		8	·60	18	·75	6
	25	Sa	8		9	·66	19	·84	7
	26	Su	9		10	·74	20	·94	8
	27	Mo	10		11	·83	...	...	9
	28	Tu	11		12	·91	21	·05	10
	29	We	12	Bhadrapada	13	·99	22	·16	11
	30	Th	13		...	...	23	·26	12
	—31	Fr	14		14	·06	24	·34	13
Jaya Kanya—Purattasi	1	Sa	○ 15		P	·11	25	·41	14
	2	Su	16		1	·15	26	·46	15
	3	Mo	17		2	·16	27	·49	16
	4	Tu	18		3	·15	1	·51	17
	5	We	19		4	·11	2	·50	18
	6	Th	20		5	·06	3	·47	19
	7	Fr	21	Bahula	6 / 7	·00 / ·92	4	·43	20
	8	Sa	22		8	·83	5	·38	21
	9	Su	23		9	·73	6	·32	22
	10	Mo	24		10	·63	7	·25	23
	11	Tu	25		11	·53	8	·18	24
	12	We	26		12	·43	9	·11	25
	13	Th	27		13	·34	10 / 11	·04 / ·99	26
	14	Fr	28		14	·26	12	·95	27
	15	Sa	● 29		—A	·19	13	·92	28
	16	Su	30		1	·14	14	·90	29

Solar month	Cyclic Sidereal Year, Month and Day	Week-Day	English Month and Day	Lunar	Tithi	Ending Moment	Nakshatra	Ending Moment	Muhammadan Year, Month and Day
			Oct.						
Jaya Kanya—Purattasi	17	Mo	1		2	·10	15	·91	—30
	18	Tu	2		3	·08	16	·94	H. 1312 Rabi-ul-akhir 1
	19	We	3		4	·08	17	·99	2
	20	Th	4		5	·11	...	...	3
	21	Fr	5	Sukla	6	·15	18	·06	4
	22	Sa	6		7	·21	19	·14	5
	23	Su	7		8	·29	20	·24	6
	24	Mo	8		9	·38	21	·35	7
	25	Tu	9		10	·47	22	·46	8
	26	We	10		11	·56	23	·56	9
	27	Th	11		12	·63	24	·65	10
	28	Fr	12	Asvina	13	·68	25	·72	11
	29	Sa	13		14	·71	26	·78	12
	30	Su	14		P	·72	27	·82	13
	—31	Mo	15		1	·71	1	·83	14
Jaya Tula—Aippasi	1	Tu	16		2	·68	2	·82	15
	2	We	17		3	·64	3	·80	16
	3	Th	18		4	·57	4	·76	17
	4	Fr	19		5	·49	5	·71	18
	5	Sa	20	Bahula	6	·40	6	·65	19
	6	Su	21		7	·31	7	·59	20
	7	Mo	22		8	·21	8	·52	21
	8	Tu	23		9	·11	9	·45	22
	9	We	24		10 / 11	·01 / ·92	10	·39	23
	10	Th	25		12	·84	11	·33	24
	11	Fr	26		13	·77	12	·28	25
	12	Sa	27		14	·72	13	·25	26
	13	Su	28		—A	·69	14	·23	27
	14	Mo	29	K. Suk.	1	·67	15	·24	28
	15	Tu	30		2	·68	16	·26	—29
	16	We	31		3	·70	17	·30	1

Solar month	Cyclic Sidereal Year, Month and Day	Week-Day	English Month and Day	Lunar	Tithi	Ending Moment	Nakshatra	Ending Moment	Muhammadan Year, Month and Day
			Nov.						
Jaya Tula—Aippasi	17	Th	1		4	·75	18	·36	2
	18	Fr	2		5	·82	19	·44	3
	19	Sa	3		6	·90	20	·54	4
	20	Su	4		7	·99	21	·65	5
	21	Mo	5	Sukla	...	...	22	·76	6
	22	Tu	6		8	·07	23	·86	7
	23	We	7		9	·15	24	·95	8
	24	Th	8		10	·22	...	...	9
	25	Fr	9		11	·28	25	·03	10
	26	Sa	10		12	·32	26	·10	11
	27	Su	11	Karttika	13	·32	27	·14	H. 1312 Jumadal-awal 12
	28	Mo	12		14	·31	1	·15	13
	29	Tu	13		P	·28	2	·15	14
	—30	We	14		1	·24	3	·13	15
Jaya Vrischika—Kartigai	1	Th	15		2	·18	4	·11	16
	2	Fr	16		3	·10	5 / 6	·05 / ·99	17
	3	Sa	17		4 / 5	·01 / ·92	7	·93	18
	4	Su	18	Bahula	6	·82	8	·85	19
	5	Mo	19		7	·72	9	·78	20
	6	Tu	20		8	·63	10	·72	21
	7	We	21		9	·54	11	·66	22
	8	Th	22		10	·46	12	·61	23
	9	Fr	23		11	·39	13	·57	24
	10	Sa	24		12	·34	14	·55	25
	11	Su	25		13	·30	15	·56	26
	12	Mo	26		14	·29	16	·57	27
	13	Tu	27		—A	·30	17	·61	28
	14	We	28		1	·32	18	·67	29
	15	Th	29		2	·37	19	·74	—30
	16	Fr	30		3	·45	20	·84	1

Solar month	Cyclic Sidereal Year, Month and Day	Week-Day	English Month and Day	Lunar	Tithi	Ending Moment	Nakshatra	Ending Moment	Muhammadan Year, Month and Day
			Dec.						
Jaya Vrischika—Kartigai	17	Sa	1		4	·53	21	·95	2
	18	Su	2		5	·61	...	...	3
	19	Mo	3	Sukla	6	·70	22	·06	4
	20	Tu	4		7	·79	23	·16	5
	21	We	5		8	·86	24	·25	6
	22	Th	6		9	·91	25	·34	7
	23	Fr	7		10	·95	26	·41	8
	24	Sa	8		11	·96	27	·45	9
	25	Su	9		12	·94	1	·47	10
	26	Mo	10	Margasira	13	·91	2	·47	11
	27	Tu	11		14	·87	3	·46	12
	28	We	12		P	·80	4	·43	13
	—29	Th	13		1	·72	5	·39	14
Jaya Dhanus—Margali	1	Fr	14		2	·63	6	·33	H. 1312 Jumadal-akhir 15
	2	Sa	15		3	[illegible]	7	·27	16
	3	Su	16		4	[illegible]	8	·20	17
	4	Mo	17		5	·35	9	·13	18
	5	Tu	18		6	·26	10	·06	19
	6	We	19	Bahula	7	·16	11 / 12	·00 / ·95	20
	7	Th	20		8	·08	13	·91	21
	8	Fr	21		9 / 10	·02 / ·97	14	·89	22
	9	Sa	22		11	·94	15	·88	23
	10	Su	23		12	·94	16	·89	24
	11	Mo	24		13	·95	17	·92	25
	12	Tu	25		14	·98	18	·97	26
	13	We	26		...	...	...	...	27
	14	Th	27		—A	·03	19	·05	28
	15	Fr	28	P. Suk.	1	·10	20	·14	—29
	16	Sa	29		2	·18	21	·24	Rajab 1
	17	Su	30		3	·27	22	·35	2
	—18	Mo	31		4	·36	23	·46	3

15. Savati. 16. Visak. 17. Anur. 18. Jyesh. 19. Mula. 20. P. Ash. 21. U. Ash. 22. Sravn. 23. Dani. 24. Satab. 25. P. Bhad. 26. U. Bhad. 27. Rev

A. D. 1895. **Mesha Sankranti** (Commencement of Indian Sidereal Year).

Solar Eclipse. ● **(Surya Sid.) April 12·33.** **Saka 1817.** **Kaliyuga 4996.**

Lunar Eclipse. ○ **(Arya Sid.) April 12·22.** **(S. Cycle) Manmatha.**

Columns: SOLAR reckoning — Cyclic Sidereal Year, Month and Day; Week-Day; English Month and Day. LUNAR reckoning — Tithi; Ending Moment; Nakshatra; Ending Moment; Muhammadan Year, Month and Day.

Jan.

Solar: Jaya Dhanus—Margali (19–30); Jaya Makara—Tai (1–19). Lunar: Pausha Sukla; Bahula. Muhammadan: H. 1312 Rajab.

Cyclic Sidereal Year, Month and Day	Week-Day	English Month and Day	Tithi	Ending Moment	Nakshatra	Ending Moment	Muhammadan Year, Month and Day
19	Tu	1	5	·44	24	·56	4
20	We	2	6	·51	25	·65	5
21	Th	3	7	·56	26	·72	6
22	Fr	4	8	·59	27	·76	7
23	Sa	5	9	·60	1	·79	8
24	Su	6	10	·59	2	·81	9
25	Mo	7	11	·56	3	·79	10
26	Tu	8	12	·51	4	·76	11
27	We	9	13	·45	5	·72	12
28	Th	10	14	·37	6	·66	13
29	Fr	11	P	·28	7	·60	14
30	Sa	12	1	·19	8	·54	15
1	Su	13	2 / 3	·09 / ·99	9	·47	16
2	Mo	14	4	·89	10	·40	17
3	Tu	15	5	·81	11	·34	18
4	We	16	6	·73	12	·29	19
5	Th	17	7	·67	13	·25	20
6	Fr	18	8	·62	14	·22	21
7	Sa	19	9	·59	15	·20	22
8	Su	20	10	·58	16	·21	23
9	Mo	21	11	·59	17	·24	24
10	Tu	22	12	·62	18	·29	25
11	We	23	13	·68	19	·36	26
12	Th	24	14	·76	20	·45	27
13	Fr	25	A	·84	21	·55	28
14	Sa	26	1	·92	22	·66	29
15	Su	27	...	...	23	·77	30
16	Mo	28	2	·01	24	·87	1
17	Tu	29	3	·09	25	·95	2
18	We	30	4	·16	...	...	3
19	Th	31	5	·21	26	·02	4

Feb.

Solar: Jaya Kumbha—Masi. Lunar: Sukla; Magha; Bahula; P. Suk. Muhammadan: H. 1312 Shaban.

Cyclic Sidereal Year, Month and Day	Week-Day	English Month and Day	Tithi	Ending Moment	Nakshatra	Ending Moment	Muhammadan Year, Month and Day
20	Fr	1	6	·24	27	·08	5
21	Sa	2	7	·24	1	·12	6
22	Su	3	8	·22	2	·13	7
23	Mo	4	9	·19	3	·12	8
24	Tu	5	10	·14	4	·10	9
25	We	6	11 / 12	·07 / ·99	5	·06	10
26	Th	7	13	·91	6 / 7	·01 / ·95	11
27	Fr	8	14	·82	8	·88	12
28	Sa	9	P	·72	9	·81	13
29	Su	10	1	·62	10	·74	14
1	Mo	11	2	·52	11	·67	15
2	Tu	12	3	·43	12	·62	16
3	We	13	4	·35	13	·58	17
4	Th	14	5	·29	14	·55	18
5	Fr	15	6	·25	15	·53	19
6	Sa	16	7	·23	16	·53	20
7	Su	17	8	·21	17	·56	21
8	Mo	18	9	·22	18	·60	22
9	Tu	19	10	·26	19	·67	23
10	We	20	11	·31	20	·75	24
11	Th	21	12	·38	21	·85	25
12	Fr	22	13	·46	22	·96	26
13	Sa	23	14	·55	...	...	27
14	Su	24	A	·64	23	·07	28
15	Mo	25	1	·72	24	·17	29
16	Tu	26	2	·78	25	·26	1
17	We	27	3	·82	26	·33	2
18	Th	28	4	·86	27	·39	3

March

Solar: Jaya Kumbha—Masi (19–30); Jaya Mina—Panguni (1–19). Lunar: Sukla; Phalguna; Bahula. Muhammadan: H. 1312 Ramzan.

Cyclic Sidereal Year, Month and Day	Week-Day	English Month and Day	Tithi	Ending Moment	Nakshatra	Ending Moment	Muhammadan Year, Month and Day
19	Fr	1	5	·86	1	·43	4
20	Sa	2	6	·85	2	·45	5
21	Su	3	7	·81	3	·45	6
22	Mo	4	8	·75	4	·43	7
23	Tu	5	9	·68	5	·39	8
24	We	6	10	·60	6	·35	9
25	Th	7	11	·52	7	·29	10
26	Fr	8	12	·43	8	·22	11
27	Sa	9	13	·33	9	·15	12
28	Su	10	14	·23	10	·08	13
29	Mo ○	11	P	·13	11 / 12	·02 / ·96	14
30	Tu	12	1 / 2	·08 / ·96	13	·91	15
1	We	13	3	·89	14	·87	16
2	Th	14	4	·84	15	·85	17
3	Fr	15	5	·82	16	·86	18
4	Sa	16	6	·80	17	·87	19
5	Su	17	7	·82	18	·91	20
6	Mo	18	8	·86	19	·97	21
7	Tu	19	9	·92	...	...	22
8	We	20	10	·99	20	·05	23
9	Th	21	...	...	21	·15	24
10	Fr	22	11	·07	22	·25	25
11	Sa	23	12	·16	23	·36	26
12	Su	24	13	·24	24	·46	27
13	Mo	25	14	·32	25	·56	28
14	Tu	26	A	·38	26	·64	29
15	We	27	1	·42	27	·71	30
16	Th	28	2	·45	1	·75	1
17	Fr	29	3	·44	2	·77	2
18	Sa	30	4	·43	3	·77	3
19	Su	31	5	·39	4	·75	4

April

Solar: Jaya Mina—Panguni (20–30); Manmatha Mesha—Chittirai (1–19). Lunar: Sukla; Chaitra; Bahula; Vaisak. Suk. Muhammadan: H. 1312 Shawwal; Zi-l-ka'da.

Cyclic Sidereal Year, Month and Day	Week-Day	English Month and Day	Tithi	Ending Moment	Nakshatra	Ending Moment	Muhammadan Year, Month and Day
20	Mo	1	6	·34	5	·72	5
21	Tu	2	7	·27	6	·68	6
22	We	3	8	·19	7	·62	7
23	Th	4	9 / 10	·09 / ·99	8	·56	8
24	Fr	5	11	·89	9	·49	9
25	Sa	6	12	·79	10	·42	10
26	Su	7	13	·69	11	·35	11
27	Mo	8	14	·60	12	·29	12
28	Tu	9	P	·52	13	·24	13
29	We	10	1	·45	14	·20	14
30	Th	11	2	·41	15	·19	15
1	Fr	12	3	·38	16	·18	16
2	Sa	13	4	·36	17	·19	17
3	Su	14	5	·38	18	·22	18
4	Mo	15	6	·41	19	·28	19
5	Tu	16	7	·47	20	·36	20
6	We	17	8	·54	21	·45	21
7	Th	18	9	·62	22	·55	22
8	Fr	19	10	·71	23	·66	23
9	Sa	20	11	·79	24	·76	24
10	Su	21	12	·86	25	·86	25
11	Mo	22	13	·92	26	·95	26
12	Tu	23	14	·96	...	...	27
13	We	24	A	·98	27	·02	28
14	Th	25	1	·99	1	·07	29
15	Fr	26	2	·97	2	·09	1
16	Sa	27	3	·93	3	·10	2
17	Su	28	4	·87	4	·09	3
18	Mo	29	5	·80	5	·06	4
19	Tu	30	6	·72	6 / 7	·02 / ·96	5

May

Solar: Manmatha Mesha—Chittirai (20–31); Manmatha Vrishabha—Vaikasi (1–19). Lunar: Sukla; Vaisakha; Bahula. Muhammadan: H. 1312 Zi-l-ka'da.

Cyclic Sidereal Year, Month and Day	Week-Day	English Month and Day	Tithi	Ending Moment	Nakshatra	Ending Moment	Muhammadan Year, Month and Day
20	We	1	7	·63	8	·90	6
21	Th	2	8	·53	9	·83	7
22	Fr	3	9	·43	10	·76	8
23	Sa	4	10	·33	11	·69	9
24	Su	5	11	·23	12	·63	10
25	Mo	6	12	·13	13	·57	11
26	Tu	7	13 / 14	·05 / ·99	14	·54	12
27	We	8	P	·94	15	·51	13
28	Th	9	1	·90	16	·50	14
29	Fr	10	2	·89	17	·51	15
30	Sa	11	3	·90	18	·54	16
31	Su	12	4	·93	19	·59	17
1	Mo	13	5	·98	20	·66	18
2	Tu	14	...	...	21	·75	19
3	We	15	6	·04	22	·85	20
4	Th	16	7	·12	23	·96	21
5	Fr	17	8	·21	...	...	22
6	Sa	18	9	·30	24	·07	23
7	Su	19	10	·37	25	·17	24
8	Mo	20	11	·43	26	·26	25
9	Tu	21	12	·47	27	·33	26
10	We	22	13	·49	1	·38	27
11	Th	23	14	·50	2	·41	28
12	Fr	24	A	·48	3	·43	29
13	Sa	25	1	·44	4	·42	30
14	Su	26	2	·38	5	·39	1
15	Mo	27	3	·31	6	·35	2
16	Tu	28	4	·23	7	·30	3
17	We	29	5	·13	8	·24	4
18	Th	30	6 / 7	·03 / ·92	9	·17	5
19	Fr	31	8	·82	10	·10	6

June

Solar: Manmatha Vrishabha—Vaikasi (20–32); Manmatha Mithuna—Ani (1–17). Lunar: Sukla; Jyeshtha; Bahula; Ashad. Sukla. Muhammadan: H. 1312 Zi-l-hijja; H. 1313 Muharram.

Cyclic Sidereal Year, Month and Day	Week-Day	English Month and Day	Tithi	Ending Moment	Nakshatra	Ending Moment	Muhammadan Year, Month and Day
20	Sa	1	9	·72	11 / 12	·03 / ·97	7
21	Su	2	10	·63	13	·91	8
22	Mo	3	11	·55	14	·87	9
23	Tu	4	12	·48	15	·84	10
24	We	5	13	·43	16	·82	11
2-	Th	6	14	·40	17	·83	12
26	Fr	7	P	·39	18	·85	13
27	Sa	8	1	·39	19	·90	14
28	Su	9	2	·42	20	·97	15
29	Mo	10	3	·47	...	...	16
30	Tu	11	4	·53	21	·05	17
31	We	12	5	·61	22	·15	18
32	Th	13	6	·69	23	·26	19
1	Fr	14	7	·77	24	·37	20
2	Sa	15	8	·84	25	·47	21
3	Su	16	9	·91	26	·56	22
4	Mo	17	10	·96	27	·64	23
5	Tu	18	11	·98	1	·69	24
6	We	19	12	·98	2	·73	25
7	Th	20	13	·96	3	·75	26
8	Fr	21	14	·92	4	·75	27
9	Sa	22	A	·86	5	·72	28
10	Su	23	1	·79	6	·68	29
11	Mo	24	2	·71	7	·63	1
12	Tu	25	3	·62	8	·57	2
13	We	26	4	·52	9	·51	3
14	Th	27	5	·41	10	·44	4
15	Fr	28	6	·31	11	·37	5
16	Sa	29	7	·21	12	·30	6
17	Su	30	8	·12	13	·24	7

Nakah:—1. Asvn. 2. Bhar. 3. Krit. 4. Rohi. 5. Mrig. 6. Ardh. 7. Punar. 8. Push. 9. Aslesh. 10. Magh. 11. P. Phal. 12. U. Phal. 13. Hasta. 14. Chit.

A. D. 1895. **Kollam 1071,** { **N. Malabar—Sept.** **S. Malabar—Aug.** Commences **Hijra 1313,** Commences, **June 24.** **Vikrama 1952.**

A.—Amavasya. **Bengal San 1301.**

P.—Paurnami. **(N. Cycle) Plavanga.**

SOLAR reckoning. Cyclic Sidereal Year, Month and Day.	Week-Day.	English Month and Day.	LUNAR reckoning. Tithi	Ending Moment.	Nakshatra	Ending Moment.	Muhammadan Year, Month and Day.
		July					
18	Mo	1	9 / 10	·03 / ·96	14	·20	8
19	Tu	2	Suk. 11	·91	15	·17	9
Manmatha Mithuna—Ani. 20	We	3	12	·88	16	·15	10
21	Th	4	13	·86	17	·15	11
22	Fr	5	Ashadha 14	·87	18	·18	12
23	Sa	6	P	·89	19	·22	13
24	Su	7	1	·94	20	·28	14
25	Mo	8	...	...	21	·36	15
26	Tu	9	2	·01	22	·45	16
27	We	10	3	·09	23	·56	17
28	Th	11	4	·17	24	·67	18
29	Fr	12	5	·25	25	·77	*H. 1313 Muharram.* 19
30	Sa	13	6	·32	26	·87	20
—31	Su	14	*Bahula* 7	·38	27	·95	21
1	Mo	15	8	·43	...	...	22
2	Tu	16	9	·46	1	·01	23
3	We	17	10	·45	2	·05	24
4	Th	18	11	·44	3	·07	25
5	Fr	19	12	·40	4	·07	26
6	Sa	20	13	·34	5	·05	27
7	Su	21	14	·27	6 / 7	·02 / ·98	28
8	Mo	22	—A	·19	8	·92	29
9	Tu	23	1	·11	9	·85	—30
10	We	24	2 / 3	·01 / ·91	10	·78	1
11	Th	25	4	·81	11	·71	2
Manmatha Karkata—Adi. 12	Fr	26	5	·71	12	·65	3
13	Sa	27	6	·61	13	·59	4
14	Su	28	7	·52	14	·54	5
15	Mo	29	8	·45	15	·50	6
16	Tu	30	*Sukla* 9	·39	16	·47	7
17	We	31	10	·36	17	·48	8
		Aug.					
18	Th	1	11	·34	18	·50	9
19	Fr	2	12	·35	19	·53	10
20	Sa	3	Sravana 13	·37	20	·58	11
21	Su	4	14	·41	21	·66	*H. 1313 Safar.* 12
22	Mo	5	P	·48	22	·76	13
23	Tu	6	1	·56	23	·86	14
24	We	7	2	·65	24	·97	15
25	Th	8	3	·73	...	...	16
26	Fr	9	4	·80	25	·07	17
27	Sa	10	5	·86	26	·17	18
28	Su	11	6	·92	27	·25	19
29	Mo	12	*Bahula* 7	·95	1	·32	20
30	Tu	13	8	·94	2	·37	21
31	We	14	9	·93	3	·39	22
—32	Th	15	10	·90	4	·40	23
1	Fr	16	11	·85	5	·39	24
2	Sa	17	12	·78	6	·36	25
3	Su	18	13	·69	7	·31	26
4	Mo	19	14	·60	8	·25	27
5	Tu ●	20	—A	·50	9	·19	28
6	We	21	1	·40	10	·12	—29
7	Th	22	2	·30	11 / 12	·05 / ·99	1
8	Fr	23	3	·20	13	·93	2
9	Sa	24	*Sukla* 4	·11	14	·87	3
Manmatha Simha—Avani. 10	Su	25	5 / 6	·03 / ·96	15	·83	4
11	Mo	26	7	·90	16	·81	*H. 1313 Rabi-ul-awwal.* 5
12	Tu	27	Bhadra. 8	·86	17	·80	6
13	We	28	9	·84	18	·81	7
14	Th	29	10	·86	19	·84	8
15	Fr	30	11	·88	20	·89	9
16	Sa	31	12	·93	21	·97	10

SOLAR reckoning. Cyclic Sidereal Year, Month and Day.	Week-Day.	English Month and Day.	LUNAR reckoning. Tithi	Ending Moment.	Nakshatra	Ending Moment.	Muhammadan Year, Month and Day.
		Sep.					
17	Su	1	Suk. 13	·99	...	...	11
18	Mo	2	...	...	22	·06	12
19	Tu	3	14	·07	23	·16	13
20	We ○	4	P	·15	24	·26	14
21	Th	5	1	·24	25	·37	15
Manmatha Simha—Avani. 22	Fr	6	Bhadrapada 2	·32	26	·47	16
23	Sa	7	3	·38	27	·56	17
24	Su	8	4	·43	1	·63	18
25	Mo	9	5	·46	2	·68	19
26	Tu	10	6	·47	3	·71	20
27	We	11	7	·45	4	·73	*H. 1313 Rabi-ul-awwal.* 21
28	Th	12	8	·42	5	·72	22
29	Fr	13	*Bahula* 9	·37	6	·69	23
30	Sa	14	10	·30	7	·64	24
—31	Su	15	11	·22	8	·59	25
1	Mo	16	12	·13	9	·53	26
2	Tu	17	13 / 14	·03 / ·93	10	·47	27
3	We	18	—A	·83	11	·40	28
4	Th	19	1	·73	12	·33	29
5	Fr	20	2	·64	13	·26	—30
6	Sa	21	3	·56	14	·21	1
7	Su	22	4	·49	15	·17	2
8	Mo	23	5	·43	16	·14	3
9	Tu	24	6	·40	17	·12	4
10	We	25	7	·39	18	·13	5
Manmatha Kanya—Purattasi. 11	Th	26	8	·40	19	·16	6
12	Fr	27	*Sukla* 9	·42	20	·21	7
13	Sa	28	10	·46	21	·28	8
14	Su	29	11	·52	22	·36	9
15	Mo	30	12	·60	23	·46	10
		Oct.					
16	Tu	1	Asvina 13	·69	24	·57	11
17	We	2	14	·78	25	·68	12
18	Th	3	P	·86	26	·78	13
19	Fr	4	1	·92	27	·87	14
20	Sa	5	2	·97	1	·94	15
21	Su	6	...	...	...	...	16
22	Mo	7	3	·00	2	·00	*H. 1313 Rabi-ul-akhir.* 17
23	Tu	8	4	·03	3	·03	18
24	We	9	5 / 6	·01 / ·98	4	·05	19
25	Th	10	7	·93	5	·04	20
26	Fr	11	*Bahula* 8	·86	6 / 7	·02 / ·98	21
27	Sa	12	9	·78	8	·93	22
28	Su	13	10	·69	9	·87	23
29	Mo	14	11	·60	10	·80	24
—30	Tu	15	12	·50	11	·73	25
1	We	16	13	·40	12	·66	26
2	Th	17	14	·30	13	·60	27
3	Fr	18	—A	·21	14	·55	28
4	Sa	19	1	·13	15	·50	—29
5	Su	20	2	·06	16	·47	1
6	Mo	21	3 / 4	·01 / ·98	17	·45	2
7	Tu	22	*Sukla* 5	·97	18	·45	3
8	We	23	6	·99	19	·48	4
Manmatha Tula—Aippasi. 9	Th.	24	...	...	20	·52	5
10	Fr	25	7	·01	21	·58	*H. 1313 Jumadal-awwal.* 6
11	Sa	26	8	·05	22	·66	7
12	Su	27	Karttika 9	·11	23	·76	8
13	Mo	28	10	·19	24	·87	9
14	Tu	29	11	·28	25	·98	10
15	We	30	12	·38	...	...	11
16	Th	31	13	·48	26	·08	12

SOLAR reckoning. Cyclic Sidereal Year, Month and Day.	Week-Day.	English Month and Day.	LUNAR reckoning. Tithi	Ending Moment.	Nakshatra	Ending Moment.	Muhammadan Year, Month and Day.
		Nov.					
17	Fr	1	Karttika 14	·53	27	·17	13
18	Sa	2	P	·57	1	·25	14
19	Su	3	1	·60	2	·31	15
20	Mo	4	2	·62	3	·35	16
21	Tu	5	3	·60	4	·37	17
Manmatha Tula—Aippasi. 22	We	6	4	·57	5	·37	18
23	Th	7	5	·52	6	·35	19
24	Fr	8	6	·46	7	·31	*H. 1313 Jumadal-awwal.* 20
25	Sa	9	*Bahula* 7	·38	8	·27	21
26	Su	10	8	·30	9	·21	22
27	Mo	11	9	·20	10	·14	23
28	Tu	12	10	·10	11	·07	24
29	We	13	11 / 12	·00 / ·91	12 / 13	·00 / ·94	25
—30	Th	14	13	·82	14	·88	26
1	Fr	15	14	·74	15	·83	27
2	Sa	16	—A	·67	16	·79	28
3	Su	17	1	·62	17	·77	29
4	Mo	18	2	·59	18	·78	—30
5	Tu	19	3	·58	19	·79	1
6	We	20	4	·59	20	·83	2
7	Th	21	*Sukla* 5	·63	21	·89	3
8	Fr	22	6	·68	22	·96	4
9	Sa	23	7	·75	...	...	5
10	Su	24	8	·83	23	·05	6
Manmatha Vrischika—Kartigai. 11	Mo	25	Margasira 9	·92	24	·16	*Jumadal-akhir.* 7
12	Tu	26	...	...	25	·27	8
13	We	27	10	·00	26	·38	9
14	Th	28	11	·08	27	·47	10
15	Fr	29	12	·15	1	·55	11
16	Sa	30	13	·20	2	·62	12
		Dec.					
17	Su	1	14	·23	3	·67	13
18	Mo	2	P	·24	4	·69	14
19	Tu	3	1	·22	5	·69	*H. 1313* 15
20	We	4	2	·19	6	·68	16
21	Th	5	3	·14	7	·65	17
22	Fr	6	4 / 5	·07 / ·99	8	·61	18
23	Sa	7	6	·91	9	·55	19
24	Su	8	7	·82	10	·48	20
25	Mo	9	*Bahula* 8	·72	11	·41	21
26	Tu	10	9	·62	12	·34	22
27	We	11	10	·52	13	·28	23
28	Th	12	11	·44	14	·22	24
29	Fr	13	12	·37	15	·17	25
—30	Sa	14	13	·31	16	·13	26
1	Su	15	14	·26	17	·10	27
2	Mo	16	—A	·23	18	·10	28
3	Tu	17	1	·22	19	·11	—29
4	We	18	2	·24	20	·14	1
5	Th	19	3	·27	21	·19	2
6	Fr	20	4	·32	22	·27	3
7	Sa	21	5	·39	23	·36	4
8	Su	22	6	·47	24	·46	5
9	Mo	23	*Sukla* 7	·56	25	·57	6
Manmatha Dhanus—Margali. 10	Tu	24	8	·65	26	·68	*H. 1313 Rajab.* 7
11	We	25	9	·73	27	·78	8
12	Th	26	10	·80	1	·87	9
13	Fr	27	11	·85	2	·94	10
14	Sa	28	Pausha 12	·88	3	·98	11
15	Su	29	13	·88	...	...	12
16	Mo	30	14	·87	4	·01	13
17	Tu	31	P	·84	5	·02	14

15. Svati. 16. Visak. 17. Anur. 18. Jyesh. 19. Mula. 20. P. Ash. 21. U. Ash. 22. Sravu. 23. Dhani. 24. Satab. 25. P. Bhad. 26. U. Bhad. 27. Rev.

A. D. 1896. **Mesha Sankranti** (Commencement of Indian Sidereal Year).

Solar Eclipse. ● (Surya Sid.) April 11·58. **Saka 1818.** **Kaliyuga 4997.**

Lunar Eclipse. ○ (Arya Sid.) April 11·47. (S. Cycle) Durmukha.

Column headings: SOLAR reckoning: Cyclic Sidereal Year, Month and Day; Week-Day; English Month and Day. LUNAR reckoning: Tithi; Ending Moment; Nakshatra; Ending Moment; Muhammadan Year, Month and Day.

Jan.

Manmatha *Dhanus—Margali*; Pausha *Bahula*; H. 1313 *Rajab*

Cyclic Sidereal Day	Week-Day	English Day	Tithi	Ending Moment	Nakshatra	Ending Moment	Muhammadan Day
18	We	1	1	·79	6 / 7	·01 / ·98	15
19	Th	2	2	·72	8	·94	16
20	Fr	3	3	·64	9	·88	17
21	Sa	4	4	·56	10	·82	18
22	Su	5	5	·46	11	·76	19
23	Mo	6	6	·36	12	·69	20
24	Tu	7	7	·26	13	·62	21
25	We	8	8	·17	14	·56	22
26	Th	9	9	·09	15	·50	23
27	Fr	10	10 / 11	·02 / ·95	16	·46	24
28	Sa	11	12	·90	17	·44	25
29	Su	12	13	·88	18	·42	26
1	Mo	13	14	·86	19	·43	27
2	Tu	14	A	·88	20	·46	28
3	We	15	1	·92	21	·51	29
4	Th	16	2	·97	22	·58	30
5	Fr	17	...	...	23	·67	1
6	Sa	18	3	·04	24	·77	2
7	Su	19	4	·13	25	·87	3
8	Mo	20	5	·22	26	·98	4
9	Tu	21	6	·31	...	...	5
10	We	22	7	·39	27	·08	6
11	Th	23	8	·46	1	·17	7
12	Fr	24	9	·50	2	·25	8
13	Sa	25	10	·52	3	·30	9
14	Su	26	11	·54	4	·33	10
15	Mo	27	12	·52	5	·35	11
16	Tu	28	13	·48	6	·34	12
17	We	29	14	·43	7	·31	13
18	Th	30	P	·36	8	·27	14
19	Fr	31	1	·28	9	·22	15

From Jan. 1 (cyclic): Manmatha *Makara—Tai*; from Jan. 5: *Sukla*, Magha; H. 1313 *Shaban*

Feb.

Bahula; H. 1313

Cyclic Sidereal Day	Week-Day	English Day	Tithi	Ending Moment	Nakshatra	Ending Moment	Muhammadan Day
20	Sa	1	2	·19	10	·16	16
21	Su	2	3 / 4	·09 / ·99	11	·10	17
22	Mo	3	5	·89	12 / 13	·03 / ·96	18
23	Tu	4	6	·80	14	·89	19
24	We	5	7	·71	15	·83	20
25	Th	6	8	·64	16	·79	21
26	Fr	7	9	·58	17	·76	22
27	Sa	8	10	·54	18	·75	23
28	Su	9	11	·51	19	·75	24
29	Mo	10	12	·49	20	·77	25
1	Tu	11	13	·51	21	·82	26
2	We	12	14	·55	22	·89	27
3	Th	13	A	·61	23	·97	28
4	Fr	14	1	·68	...	...	29
5	Sa	15	2	·76	24	·06	1
6	Su	16	3	·85	25	·17	2
7	Mo	17	4	·94	26	·28	3
8	Tu	18	...	...	27	·39	4
9	We	19	5	·02	1	·48	5
10	Th	20	6	·08	2	·55	6
11	Fr	21	7	·13	3	·61	7
12	Sa	22	8	·15	4	·65	8
13	Su	23	9	·16	5	·67	9
14	Mo	24	10	·14	6	·67	10
15	Tu	25	11	·10	7	·64	11
16	We	26	12 / 13	·04 / ·97	8	·61	12
17	Th	27	14	·89	9	·56	13
18	Fr ○	28	P	·80	10	·50	14
19	Sa	29	1	·71	11	·44	15

From Feb. 5 (cyclic 1): Manmatha *Kumbha—Masi*; Phalguna *Sukla*; H. 1313 *Ramzan*

March

Manmatha *Kumbha—Masi*; Phalguna *Bahula*; H. 1313 *Ramzan*

Cyclic Sidereal Day	Week-Day	English Day	Tithi	Ending Moment	Nakshatra	Ending Moment	Muhammadan Day
20	Su	1	2	·61	12	·37	16
21	Mo	2	3	·51	13	·30	17
22	Tu	3	4	·41	14	·24	18
23	We	4	5	·32	15	·18	19
24	Th	5	6	·25	16	·13	20
25	Fr	6	7	·19	17	·09	21
26	Sa	7	8	·15	18	·07	22
27	Su	8	9	·12	19	·07	23
28	Mo	9	10	·11	20	·09	24
29	Tu	10	11	·12	21	·13	25
30	We	11	12	·16	22	·19	26
31	Th	12	13	·22	23	·27	27
1	Fr	13	14	·29	24	·36	28
2	Sa	14	A	·37	25	·47	29
3	Su	15	1	·46	26	·58	30
4	Mo	16	2	·55	27	·69	1
5	Tu	17	3	·63	1	·78	2
6	We	18	4	·69	2	·86	3
7	Th	19	5	·73	3	·92	4
8	Fr	20	6	·75	4	·97	5
9	Sa	21	7	·75	5	·99	6
10	Su	22	8	·73	6	·99	7
11	Mo	23	9	·69	7	·97	8
12	Tu	24	10	·64	8	·94	9
13	We	25	11	·57	9	·90	10
14	Th	26	12	·48	10	·84	11
15	Fr	27	13	·38	11	·78	12
16	Sa	28	14	·28	12	·71	13
17	Su	29	P	·18	13	·64	14
18	Mo	30	1 / 2	·08 / ·99	14	·57	15
19	Tu	31	3	·91	15	·51	16

From March 14 (cyclic 2): Chaitra *Sukla*; from March 25 (cyclic 13): Manmatha *Mina—Panguni*; H. 1313 *Shawwal*

April

Chaitra *Bahula*; H. 1313 *Shawwal*

Cyclic Sidereal Day	Week-Day	English Day	Tithi	Ending Moment	Nakshatra	Ending Moment	Muhammadan Day
20	We	1	4	·83	16	·46	17
21	Th	2	5	·77	17	·42	18
22	Fr	3	6	·72	18	·40	19
23	Sa	4	7	·69	19	·40	20
24	Su	5	8	·68	20	·41	21
25	Mo	6	9	·70	21	·44	22
26	Tu	7	10	·74	22	·50	23
27	We	8	11	·79	23	·58	24
28	Th	9	12	·86	24	·67	25
29	Fr	10	13	·94	25	·77	26
1	Sa	11	...	...	26	·88	27
2	Su	12	14	·03	27	·98	28
3	Mo	13	A	·11	...	...	29
4	Tu	14	1	·18	1	·08	1
5	We	15	2	·24	2	·17	2
6	Th	16	3	·28	3	·24	3
7	Fr	17	4	·30	4	·29	4
8	Sa	18	5	·30	5	·31	5
9	Su	19	6	·28	6	·32	6
10	Mo	20	7	·24	7	·30	7
11	Tu	21	8	·18	8	·28	8
12	We	22	9	·11	9	·24	9
13	Th	23	10 / 11	·03 / ·94	10	·18	10
14	Fr	24	12	·84	11	·11	11
15	Sa	25	13	·74	12 / 13	·04 / ·97	12
16	Su	26	14	·63	14	·91	13
17	Mo	27	P	·53	15	·85	14
18	Tu	28	1	·44	16	·79	15
19	We	29	2	·36	17	·75	16
20	Th	30	3	·30	18	·73	17

From April 11 (cyclic 1): Durmukha *Mesha—Chittirai*; from April 14: Vaisakha *Sukla*; H. 1313 *Zi-l-ka'da*; from April 28: *Bah.*

May

Durmukha *Mesha—Chittirai*; Vaisakha *Bahula*; H. 1313 *Zi-l-ka'da*

Cyclic Sidereal Day	Week-Day	English Day	Tithi	Ending Moment	Nakshatra	Ending Moment	Muhammadan Day
21	Fr	1	4	·26	19	·72	18
22	Sa	2	5	·23	20	·73	19
23	Su	3	6	·21	21	·76	20
24	Mo	4	7	·22	22	·81	21
25	Tu	5	8	·26	23	·88	22
26	We	6	9	·31	24	·97	23
27	Th	7	10	·38	...	...	24
28	Fr	8	11	·46	25	·07	25
29	Sa	9	12	·55	26	·18	26
30	Su	10	13	·63	27	·28	27
31	Mo	11	14	·70	1	·38	28
1	Tu	12	A	·76	2	·48	29
2	We	13	1	·80	3	·55	30
3	Th	14	2	·82	4	·60	1
4	Fr	15	3	·81	5	·63	2
5	Sa	16	4	·80	6	·64	3
6	Su	17	5	·76	7	·64	4
7	Mo	18	6	·70	8	·61	5
8	Tu	19	7	·63	9	·57	6
9	We	20	8	·54	10	·51	7
10	Th	21	9	·44	11	·45	8
11	Fr	22	10	·34	12	·39	9
12	Sa	23	11	·24	13	·32	10
13	Su	24	12	·14	14	·25	11
14	Mo	25	13 / 14	·04 / ·94	15	·19	12
15	Tu	26	P	·86	16	·13	13
16	We	27	1	·80	17	·08	14
17	Th	28	2	·75	18	·06	15
18	Fr	29	3	·72	19	·04	16
19	Sa	30	4	·70	20	·05	17
20	Su	31	5	·72	21	·07	18

From May 13: *Sukla*; H. 1313 *Zi-l-hijja*; from May 24 (cyclic 13): Durmukha *Vrishabha—Vaikasi*; Jyeshtha

June

Adhika Jyeshtha *Bahula*

Cyclic Sidereal Day	Week-Day	English Day	Tithi	Ending Moment	Nakshatra	Ending Moment	Muhammadan Day
21	Mo	1	6	·75	22	·12	19
22	Tu	2	7	·81	23	·19	20
23	We	3	8	·88	24	·27	21
24	Th	4	9	·96	25	·37	22
25	Fr	5	...	...	26	·48	23
26	Sa	6	10	·04	27	·59	24
27	Su	7	11	·12	1	·69	25
28	Mo	8	12	·19	2	·78	26
29	Tu	9	13	·25	3	·86	27
30	We	10	14	·29	4	·91	28
31	Th	11	A	·31	5	·95	29
32	Fr	12	1	·30	6	·97	1
1	Sa	13	2	·29	7	·97	2
2	Su	14	3	·25	8	·94	3
3	Mo	15	4	·19	9	·90	4
4	Tu	16	5	·12	10	·85	5
5	We	17	6 / 7	·04 / ·94	11	·79	6
6	Th	18	8	·84	12	·73	7
7	Fr	19	9	·74	13	·66	8
8	Sa	20	10	·63	14	·59	9
9	Su	21	11	·53	15	·52	10
10	Mo	22	12	·44	16	·46	11
11	Tu	23	13	·36	17	·42	12
12	We	24	14	·29	18	·39	13
13	Th	25	P	·24	19	·37	14
14	Fr	26	1	·20	20	·37	15
15	Sa	27	2	·18	21	·39	16
16	Su	28	3	·20	22	·44	17
17	Mo	29	4	·24	23	·50	18
18	Tu	30	5	·29	24	·58	19

From June 12: Nija Jyeshtha *Sukla*; H. 1314 *Muharram*; from June 13 (cyclic 1): Durmukha *Mithuna—Ani*; from June 26: *Bah.*

Naksh :—1. Asvn. 2. Bhar. 3. Krit. 4. Rohi. 5. Mrig. 6. Ardh. 7. Punar. 8. Push. 9. Aslesh. 10. Magh. 11. P. Phal. 12. U. Phal. 13. Hasta. 14. Chit.

A. D. 1896.
A.—Amavasya. P.—Paurnami.
Kollam 1072, Commences { **N. Malabar—Sept. S. Malabar—Aug.**
Hijra 1314, Commences, **June 12.**
Vikrama 1953. Bengal San 1302. (N. Cycle) Kilaka.

Columns: SOLAR reckoning (Cyclic Sidereal Year, Month and Day; Week-Day; English Month and Day); LUNAR reckoning (Tithi; Ending Moment; Nakshatra; Ending Moment; Muhammadan Year, Month and Day).

July — Solar: Durmukha, *Mithuna—Ani.* (to 31); Durmukha, *Karkata—Adi.* Lunar: Nija Jy. *Bahula*; Ashadha *Sukla*. Muhammadan: H. 1314 *Muharram.*; H. 1314 *Safar.*

Cyclic Sidereal Year, Month and Day	Week-Day	English Month and Day	Tithi	Ending Moment	Nakshatra	Ending Moment	Muhammadan Year, Month and Day
19	We	1	6	·35	25	·67	20
20	Th	2	7	·43	26	·77	21
21	Fr	3	8	·51	27	·88	22
22	Sa	4	9	·59	1	·95	23
23	Su	5	10	·66	...	...	24
24	Mo	6	11	·72	2	·09	25
25	Tu	7	12	·76	3	·16	26
26	We	8	13	·78	4	·22	27
27	Th	9	14	·79	5	·27	28
28	Fr	10	—A	·77	6	·29	29
29	Sa	11	1	·73	7	·29	—30
30	Su	12	2	·67	8	·27	1
—31	Mo	13	3	·60	9	·23	2
1	Tu	14	4	·51	10	·19	3
2	We	15	5	·41	11	·14	4
3	Th	16	6	·31	12	·07	5
4	Fr	17	7	·21	13 / 14	·00 / ·93	6
5	Sa	18	8	·11	15	·87	7
6	Su	19	9 / 10	·01 / ·92	16	·81	8
7	Mo	20	11	·84	17	·76	9
8	Tu	21	12	·77	18	·72	10
9	We	22	13	·72	19	·69	11
10	Th	23	14	·68	20	·69	12
11	Fr	24	P	·67	21	·71	13
12	Sa	25	1	·68	22	·75	14
13	Su	26	2	·71	23	·81	15
14	Mo	27	3	·75	24	·88	16
15	Tu	28	4	·81	25	·97	17
16	We	29	5	·89	...	...	18
17	Th	30	6	·97	26	·08	19
18	Fr	31	...	...	27	·19	20

Aug. — Solar: Durmukha, *Simha—Avani.* Lunar: *Bahula*; Sravana *Sukla*; *Bahula*. Muhammadan: H. 1314 *Rabi-ul-awwal.*

Cyclic Sidereal Year, Month and Day	Week-Day	English Month and Day	Tithi	Ending Moment	Nakshatra	Ending Moment	Muhammadan Year, Month and Day
19	Sa	1	7	·06	1	·29	21
20	Su	2	8	·13	2	·39	22
21	Mo	3	9	·19	3	[illegible]	23
22	Tu	4	10	·23	4	·54	24
23	We	5	11	·26	5	·59	25
24	Th	6	12	·27	6	·62	26
25	Fr	7	13	·25	7	·62	27
26	Sa	8	14	·22	8	·60	28
27	Su ●	9	—A	·16	9	·57	—29
28	Mo	10	1	·09	10	·53	1
29	Tu	11	2 / 3	·01 / ·92	11	·47	2
30	We	12	4	·82	12	·41	3
31	Th	13	5	·71	13	·34	4
—32	Fr	14	6	·61	14	·27	5
1	Sa	15	7	·52	15	·20	6
2	Su	16	8	·43	16	·14	7
3	Mo	17	9	·34	17	·09	8
4	Tu	18	10	·26	18	·05	9
5	We	19	11	·21	19	·02	10
6	Th	20	12	·18	20	·02	11
7	Fr	21	13	·17	21	·03	12
8	Sa	22	14	·18	22	·06	13
9	Su ○	23	P	·20	23	·12	14
10	Mo	24	1	·25	24	·19	15
11	Tu	25	2	·32	25	·28	16
12	We	26	3	·40	26	·38	17
13	Th	27	4	·48	27	·48	18
14	Fr	28	5	·56	1	·59	19
15	Sa	29	6	·63	2	·69	20
16	Su	30	7	·69	3	·78	21
17	Mo	31	8	·74	4	·85	22

Sep. — Solar: Durmukha, *Simha—Avani.* (to 31); Durmukha, *Kanya—Purattasi.* Lunar: Sr. *Bah.*; Bhadrapada *Sukla*; *Bahula*. Muhammadan: *R.-awwal.*; H. 1314 *Rabi-ul-akhir.*

Cyclic Sidereal Year, Month and Day	Week-Day	English Month and Day	Tithi	Ending Moment	Nakshatra	Ending Moment	Muhammadan Year, Month and Day
18	Tu	1	9	·77	5	·90	23
19	We	2	10	·78	6	·93	24
20	Th	3	11	·76	7	·94	25
21	Fr	4	12	·73	8	·93	26
22	Sa	5	13	·67	9	·90	27
23	Su	6	14	·60	10	·86	28
24	Mo	7	—A	·52	11	·81	29
25	Tu	8	1	·43	12	·75	—30
26	We	9	2	·33	13	·68	1
27	Th	10	3	·23	14	·61	2
28	Fr	11	4	·13	15	·54	3
29	Sa	12	5 / 6	·03 / ·94	16	·48	4
30	Su	13	7	·86	17	·42	5
—31	Mo	14	8	·79	18	·38	6
1	Tu	15	9	·74	19	·36	7
2	We	16	10	·71	20	·34	8
3	Th	17	11	·69	21	·35	9
4	Fr	18	12	·70	22	·37	10
5	Sa	19	13	·73	23	·42	11
6	Su	20	14	·78	24	·49	12
7	Mo	21	P	·84	25	·58	13
8	Tu	22	1	·92	26	·68	14
9	We	23	...	...	27	·78	15
10	Th	24	2	·01	1	·89	16
11	Fr	25	3	·09	2	·99	17
12	Sa	26	4	·17	...	...	18
13	Su	27	5	·24	3	·08	19
14	Mo	28	6	·29	4	·16	20
15	Tu	29	7	·31	5	·22	21
16	We	30	8	·32	6	·25	22

Oct. — Solar: Durmukha, *Kanya—Purattasi.* (to 30); Durmukha, *Tula—Aippasi.* Lunar: Asvina *Sukla*; *Bahula*. Muhammadan: H. 1314 *Jumadal-awwal.*

Cyclic Sidereal Year, Month and Day	Week-Day	English Month and Day	Tithi	Ending Moment	Nakshatra	Ending Moment	Muhammadan Year, Month and Day
17	Th	1	9	·31	7	·26	23
18	Fr	2	10	·28	8	·26	24
19	Sa	3	11	·22	9	·24	25
20	Su	4	12	·15	10	·20	26
21	Mo	5	13 / 14	·07 / ·98	11	·15	27
22	Tu	6	—A	·89	12	·09	28
23	We	7	1	·79	13 / 14	·02 / ·95	—29
24	Th	8	2	·69	15	·88	1
25	Fr	9	3	·59	16	·82	2
26	Sa	10	4	·50	17	·76	3
27	Su	11	5	·42	18	·72	4
28	Mo	12	6	·36	19	·69	5
29	Tu	13	7	·31	20	·67	6
—30	We	14	8	·28	21	·67	7
1	Th	15	9	·26	22	·69	8
2	Fr	16	10	·28	23	·73	9
3	Sa	17	11	·31	24	·80	10
4	Su	18	12	·35	25	·88	11
5	Mo	19	13	·41	26	·98	12
6	Tu	20	14	·49	...	...	13
7	We	21	P	·58	27	·08	14
8	Th	22	1	·67	1	·19	15
9	Fr	23	2	·75	2	·30	16
10	Sa	24	3	·82	3	·39	17
11	Su	25	4	·87	4	·47	18
12	Mo	26	5	·89	5	·53	19
13	Tu	27	6	·90	6	·57	20
14	We	28	7	·89	7	·59	21
15	Th	29	8	·86	8	·59	22
16	Fr	30	9	·82	9	·57	23
17	Sa	31	10	·75	10	·53	24

Nov. — Solar: Durmukha, *Tula—Aippasi.* (to 30); Durmukha, *Vrischika—Kartigai.* Lunar: *Bah.*; Kartika *Sukla*; *Bahula*. Muhammadan: *J.-awwal.*; H. 1314 *Jumadal-akhir.*

Cyclic Sidereal Year, Month and Day	Week-Day	English Month and Day	Tithi	Ending Moment	Nakshatra	Ending Moment	Muhammadan Year, Month and Day
18	Su	1	11	·67	11	·48	25
19	Mo	2	12	·58	12	·42	26
20	Tu	3	13	·48	13	·36	27
21	We	4	14	·38	14	·29	28
22	Th	5	—A	·28	15	·22	29
23	Fr	6	1	·19	16	·16	—30
24	Sa	7	2	·10	17	·10	1
25	Su	8	3 / 4	·02 / ·96	18	·05	2
26	Mo	9	5	·91	19 / 20	·01 / ·99	3
27	Tu	10	6	·88	21	·99	4
28	We	11	7	·86	...	...	5
29	Th	12	8	·88	22	·01	6
—30	Fr	13	9	·91	23	·05	7
1	Sa	14	10	·96	24	·11	8
2	Su	15	...	...	25	·19	9
3	Mo	16	11	·03	26	·28	10
4	Tu	17	12	·12	27	·38	11
5	We	18	13	·21	1	·49	12
6	Th	19	14	·29	2	·60	13
7	Fr	20	P	·37	3	·70	14
8	Sa	21	1	·43	4	·78	15
9	Su	22	2	·48	5	·84	16
10	Mo	23	3	·52	6	·89	17
11	Tu	24	4	·53	7	·91	18
12	We	25	5	·51	8	·91	19
13	Th	26	6	·48	9	·90	20
14	Fr	27	7	·43	10	·87	21
15	Sa	28	8	·37	11	·83	22
16	Su	29	9	·29	12	·77	23
17	Mo	30	10	·20	13	·70	24

Dec. — Solar: Durmukha, *Vrischika—Kartigai.* (to 30); Durmukha, *Dhanus—Margali.* Lunar: Margasira *Sukla*; *Bahula*. Muhammadan: H. 1314 *Rajab.*

Cyclic Sidereal Year, Month and Day	Week-Day	English Month and Day	Tithi	Ending Moment	Nakshatra	Ending Moment	Muhammadan Year, Month and Day
18	Tu	1	11	·11	14	·63	25
19	We	2	12 / 13	·01 / ·91	15	·56	26
20	Th	3	14	·81	16	·50	27
21	Fr	4	—A	·72	17	·44	28
22	Sa	5	1	·64	18	·39	—29
23	Su	6	2	·58	19	·35	1
24	Mo	7	3	·54	20	·32	2
25	Tu	8	4	·51	21	·31	3
26	We	9	5	·50	22	·33	4
27	Th	10	6	·51	23	·37	5
28	Fr	11	7	·55	24	·42	6
29	Sa	12	8	·61	25	·49	7
—30	Su	13	9	·68	26	·58	8
1	Mo	14	10	·76	27	·68	9
2	Tu	15	11	·85	1	·79	10
3	We	16	12	·94	2	·90	11
4	Th	17	...	...	...	...	12
5	Fr	18	13	·02	3	·00	13
6	Sa	19	14	·08	4	·09	14
7	Su	20	P	·13	5	·16	15
8	Mo	21	1	·16	6	·21	16
9	Tu	22	2	·17	7	·23	17
10	We	23	3	·15	8	·24	18
11	Th	24	4	·12	9	·22	19
12	Fr	25	5 / 6	·06 / ·99	10	·19	20
13	Sa	26	7	·91	11	·15	21
14	Su	27	8	·83	12	·10	22
15	Mo	28	9	·74	13 / 14	·04 / ·97	23
16	Tu	29	10	·64	15	·90	24
17	We	30	11	·55	16	·83	25
18	Th	31	12	·45	17	·77	26

15. Svati. 16. Visak. 17. Anur. 18. Jyesh. 19. Mula. 20. P. Ash. 21. U. Ash. 22. Sravn. 23. Dani. 24. Satab. 25. P. Bhad. 26. U. Bhad. 27. Rev.

A. D. 1897. **Mesha Sankranti** (Commencement of Indian Sidereal Year). (Surya Sid.) April 11·84. (Arya Sid.) April 11·73. **Saka 1819.** **Kaliyuga 4998.** (S. Cycle) **Hemalamba.**

Solar Eclipse. ●
Lunar Eclipse. ○

SOLAR reckoning: Cyclic Sidereal Year, Month and Day; Week-Day; English Month and Day. LUNAR reckoning: Tithi; Ending Moment; Nakshatra; Ending Moment; Muhammadan Year, Month and Day.

Jan.

Solar: Durmukha, Dhanus—Marguli (to 29); Durmukha, Makara—Tai (from 1). Lunar: Bah. (1–3); Sukla (4–17); Pausha; Bahula (from 18). Muhammadan: Rajab (to 30); H. 1314 Shaban (from 1).

Cyclic Sidereal Year, Month and Day	Week-Day	English Month and Day	Tithi	Ending Moment	Nakshatra	Ending Moment	Muhammadan Year, Month and Day
19	Fr	1	13	·36	18	·72	27
20	Sa	2	14	·23	19	·67	28
21	Su	3	—A	·22	20	·64	29
22	Mo	4	1	·18	21	·64	—30
23	Tu	5	2	·15	22	·65	1
24	We	6	3	·15	23	·68	2
25	Th	7	4	·16	24	·72	3
26	Fr	8	5	·20	25	·79	4
27	Sa	9	6	·26	26	·88	5
28	Su	10	7	·33	27	·98	6
—29	Mo	11	8	·41	...	...	7
1	Tu	12	9	·50	1	·09	8
2	We	13	10	·59	2	·20	9
3	Th	14	11	·67	3	·30	10
4	Fr	15	12	·73	4	·39	11
5	Sa	16	13	·78	5	·47	12
6	Su	17	14	·81	6	·52	13
7	Mo	18	P	·81	7	·55	14
8	Tu	19	1	·80	8	·56	15
9	We	20	2	·77	9	·55	16
10	Th	21	3	·71	10	·53	17
11	Fr	22	4	·64	11	·49	18
12	Sa	23	5	·56	12	·44	19
13	Su	24	6	·47	13	·38	20
14	Mo	25	7	·37	14	·32	21
15	Tu	26	8	·27	15	·25	○ 22
16	We	27	9	·17	16	·18	23
17	Th	28	10 11	·07 ·99	17	·11	24
18	Fr	29	12	·92	18	·05	25
19	Sa	30	13	·86	19 20	·01 ·98	26
20		31	14	·82	21	·97	27

Feb.

Solar: Durmukha, Kumbha—Masi. Lunar: Sukla (to 14); Magha; Bahula (from 21). Muhammadan: H. 1314 Ramzan (from 1).

Cyclic Sidereal Year, Month and Day	Week-Day	English Month and Day	Tithi	Ending Moment	Nakshatra	Ending Moment	Muhammadan Year, Month and Day
21	Mo	1	—A	·79	22	·97	28
22	Tu	2	1	·79	23	·99	—29
23	We	3	2	·80	...	...	1
24	Th	4	3	·84	24	·04	2
25	Fr	5	4	·90	25	·11	3
26	Sa	6	5	·98	26	·19	4
27	Su	7	...	...	27	·28	5
28	Mo	8	6	·06	1	·38	6
29	Tu	9	7	·15	2	·49	7
—30	We	10	8	·23	3	·60	8
1	Th	11	9	·31	4	·70	9
2	Fr	12	10	·37	5	·78	10
3	Sa	13	11	·42	6	·83	11
4	Su	14	12	·44	7	·86	12
5	Mo	15	13	·44	8	·88	13
6	Tu	16	14	·43	9	·89	14
7	We	17	P	·39	10	·87	15
8	Th	18	1	·32	11	·83	16
9	Fr	19	2	·26	12	·78	17
10	Sa	20	3	·18	13	·72	18
11	Su	21	4 5	·09 ·99	14	·66	19
12	Mo	22	6	·89	15	·59	20
13	Tu	23	7	·79	16	·52	21
14	We	24	8	·69	17	·45	22
15	Th	25	9	·61	18	·39	23
16	Fr	26	10	·53	19	·35	24
17	Sa	27	11	·47	20	·31	25
18	Su	28	12	·44	21	·29	26

March

Solar: Durmukha, Kumbha—Masi (to 29); Durmukha, Mina—Panguni (from 1). Lunar: Bah. (1–3); Sukla (4–15); Phalguna; Bahula (from 20). Muhammadan: Ramzan (to 30); H. 1314 Shawwal (from 1).

Cyclic Sidereal Year, Month and Day	Week-Day	English Month and Day	Tithi	Ending Moment	Nakshatra	Ending Moment	Muhammadan Year, Month and Day
19	Mo	1	13	·42	22	·29	27
20	Tu	2	14	·40	23	·31	28
21	We	3	—A	[illegible]	24	·35	29
22	Th	4	1	·46	25	·41	—30
23	Fr	5	2	·51	26	·49	1
24	Sa	6	3	·59	27	·58	2
25	Su	7	4	·68	1	·69	3
26	Mo	8	5	·78	2	·80	4
27	Tu	9	6	·86	3	·91	5
28	●We	10	7	·93	...	...	6
—29	Th	11	8	·98	4	·09	7
1	Fr	12	...	...	5	·08	8
2	Sa	13	9	·02	6	·14	9
3	Su	14	10	·04	7	·18	10
4	Mo	15	11	·04	8	·21	11
5	Tu	16	12 13	·03 ·99	9	·21	12
6	We	17	14	·93	10	·19	13
7	Th	18	P	·85	11	·16	14
8	Fr	19	1	·77	12	·11	15
9	Sa	20	2	·68	13 14	·06 ·99	16
10	Su	21	3	·58	15	·92	17
11	Mo	22	4	·48	16	·85	18
12	Tu	23	5	·38	17	·79	19
13	We	24	6	·29	18	·73	20
14	Th	25	7	·20	19	·68	21
15	Fr	26	8	·12	20	·64	22
16	Sa	27	9	·06	21	·62	23
17	Su	28	10	·02	22	·61	24
18	Mo	29	11 12	·00 ·99	23	·63	25
19	Tu	30	...	...	24	·67	26
20	We	31	13	·01	25	·72	27

April

Solar: Durmukha, Mina—Panguni (to 31); Hemalamba, Mesha—Chittirai (from 1). Lunar: Sukla (3–17); Chaitra; Bahula (from 19). Muhammadan: H. 1314 Zi-l-ka'da (from 1).

Cyclic Sidereal Year, Month and Day	Week-Day	English Month and Day	Tithi	Ending Moment	Nakshatra	Ending Moment	Muhammadan Year, Month and Day
21	Th	1	14	·04	26	·79	28
22	Fr	2	—A	·10	27	·88	—29
23	Sa	3	1	·18	1	·99	1
24	Su	4	2	·26	...	...	2
25	Mo	5	3	·35	2	·10	3
26	Tu	6	4	·43	3	·21	4
27	We	7	5	·50	4	·30	5
28	Th	8	6	·56	5	·38	6
29	Fr	9	7	·59	6	·45	7
30	Sa	10	8	·60	7	·50	8
—31	Su	11	9	·61	8	·53	9
1	Mo	12	10	·59	9	·54	10
2	Tu	13	11	·55	10	·52	11
3	We	14	12	·49	11	·49	12
4	Th	15	13	·41	12	·45	13
5	Fr	16	14	·33	13	·40	14
6	Sa	17	P	·24	14	·33	15
7	Su	18	1	·14	15	·26	16
8	Mo	19	2 3	·04 ·94	16	·19	17
9	Tu	20	4	·84	17	·13	18
10	We	21	5	·75	18	·07	19
11	Th	22	6	·67	19 20	·01 ·97	20
12	Fr	23	7	·61	21	·94	21
13	Sa	24	8	·57	22	·93	22
14	Su	25	9	·54	23	·95	23
15	Mo	26	10	·52	24	·98	24
16	Tu	27	11	·54	...	...	25
17	We	28	12	·58	25	·03	26
18	Th	29	13	·63	26	·10	27
19	Fr	30	14	·70	27	·19	28

May

Solar: Hemalamba, Mesha—Chittirai (to 31); Hemalamba, Vrushabha—Vaikasi (from 1). Lunar: Sukla (to 14); Vaisakha; Bahula (from 21). Muhammadan: H. 1314 Zi-l-hijja (from 1).

Cyclic Sidereal Year, Month and Day	Week-Day	English Month and Day	Tithi	Ending Moment	Nakshatra	Ending Moment	Muhammadan Year, Month and Day
20	Sa	1	—A	·79	1	·29	29
21	Su	2	1	·88	2	·40	—30
22	Mo	3	2	·96	3	·50	1
23	Tu	4	...	...	4	·60	2
24	We	5	3	·03	5	·69	3
25	Th	6	4	·08	6	·77	4
26	Fr	7	5	·12	7	·82	5
27	Sa	8	6	·13	8	·85	6
28	Su	9	7	·14	9	·86	7
29	Mo	10	8	·12	10	·85	8
30	Tu	11	9	·08	11	·83	9
—31	We	12	10 11	·02 ·94	12	·79	10
1	Th	13	12	·85	13	·73	11
2	Fr	14	13	·75	14	·67	12
3	Sa	15	14	·65	15	·60	13
4	Su	16	P	·55	16	·53	14
5	Mo	17	1	·45	17	·47	15
6	Tu	18	2	·35	18	·41	16
7	We	19	3	·26	19	·35	17
8	Th	20	4	·18	20	·30	18
9	Fr	21	5	·12	21	·27	19
10	Sa	22	6	·08	22	·26	20
11	Su	23	7	·05	23	·27	21
12	Mo	24	8	·03	24	·29	22
13	Tu	25	9	·05	25	·33	23
14	We	26	10	·09	26	·40	24
15	Th	27	11	·14	27	·49	25
16	Fr	28	12	·21	1	·59	26
17	Sa	29	13	·29	2	·70	27
18	Su	30	14	·37	3	·80	28
19	Mo	31	A	·45	4	·90	29

June

Solar: Hemalamba, Vrushabha—Vaikasi (to 31); Hemalamba, Mithuna—Ani (from 1). Lunar: Sukla (to 14); Jyeshtha; Bahula (from 21). Muhammadan: H. 1315 Muharram (from 1).

Cyclic Sidereal Year, Month and Day	Week-Day	English Month and Day	Tithi	Ending Moment	Nakshatra	Ending Moment	Muhammadan Year, Month and Day
20	Tu	1	1	·52	...	...	—30
21	We	2	2	·58	5	·00	1
22	Th	3	3	·62	6	·08	2
23	Fr	4	4	·63	7	·14	3
24	Sa	5	5	·63	8	·17	4
25	Su	6	6	·62	9	·18	5
26	Mo	7	7	·58	10	·18	6
27	Tu	8	8	·52	11	·16	7
28	We	9	9	·44	12	·12	8
29	Th	10	10	·35	13	·07	9
30	Fr	11	11	·25	14 15	·01 ·95	10
—31	Sa	12	12	·15	16	·88	11
1	Su	13	13 14	·05 ·95	17	·81	12
2	Mo	14	P	·85	18	·74	13
3	Tu	15	1	·76	19	·68	14
4	We	16	2	·68	20	·64	15
5	Th	17	3	·61	21	·61	16
6	Fr	18	4	·56	22	·59	17
7	Sa	19	5	·53	23	·59	18
8	Su	20	6	·52	24	·61	19
9	Mo	21	7	·53	25	·65	20
10	Tu	22	8	·56	26	·72	21
11	We	23	9	·61	27	·80	22
12	Th	24	10	·68	1	·89	23
13	Fr	25	11	·76	2	·99	24
14	Sa	26	12	·84	...	...	25
15	Su	27	13	·92	3	·10	26
16	Mo	28	14	·99	4	·21	27
17	Tu	29	...	...	5	·31	28
18	We	30	—A	·06	6	·39	29

Naksh :—1. Asvn. 2. Bhar. 3. Krit. 4. Rohi. 5. Mrig. 6 Ardh. 7. Punar. 8. Push. 9. Aslesh. 10. Magh. 11. P. Phal. 12. U. Phal. 13. Hasta 14. Chit.

A. D. 1897. A.—Amavasya. P.—Paurnami. Kollam 1073, Commences { N. Malabar—Sept. S. Malabar—Aug. Hijra 1315, Commences, June 2. Vikrama 1954. Bengal San 1303. (N. Cycle) Ulauam.

SOLAR reckoning. LUNAR reckoning.

July

Solar month	Cyclic Sidereal Year, Month and Day	Week-Day	English Month and Day	Lunar month	Tithi	Ending Moment	Nakshatra	Ending Moment	Muhammadan Year, Month and Day
Hemalamba Mithuna—Ani	19	Th	1		1	·10	7	·44	—30
	20	Fr	2		2	·11	8	·48	1
	21	Sa	3		3	·11	9	·50	2
	22	Su	4		4	·00	10	·51	3
	23	Mo	5	Sukla	5 / 6	·05 / ·90	11	·49	4
	24	Tu	6		7	·92	12	·46	5
	25	We	7		8	·83	13	·41	6
	26	Th	8		9	·73	14	·35	7
	27	Fr	9		10	·63	15	·29	8
	28	Sa	10		11	·53	16	·22	9
	29	Su	11		12	·43	17	·15	10
	30	Mo	12	Ashadha	13	·33	18	·08	11
	31	Tu	13		14	·24	19 / 20	·02 / ·93	12
	—32	We	14		P	·16	21	·04	13
Hemalamba Karkata—Adi	1	Th	15		1	·09	22	·91	H. 1315 Safar. 14
	2	Fr	16		2	·04	23	·91	15
	3	Sa	17		3	·01	24	·93	16
	4	Su	18		4	·00	25	·97	17
	5	Mo	19		5	·01	...	...	18
	6	Tu	20	Bahula	6	·04	26	·03	19
	7	We	21		7	·08	27	·10	20
	8	Th	22		8	·15	1	·19	21
	9	Fr	23		9	·23	2	·29	22
	10	Sa	24		10	·31	3	·40	23
	11	Su	25		11	·39	4	·51	24
	12	Mo	26		12	·47	5	·61	25
	13	Tu	27		13	·53	6	·69	26
	14	We	28		14	·57	7	·76	27
	15	Th	29		—A	·59	8	·80	28
	16	Fr	30		1	·59	9	·83	—29
	17	Sa	31		2	·57	10	·84	1

Aug.

Solar month	Cyclic Sidereal Year, Month and Day	Week-Day	English Month and Day	Lunar month	Tithi	Ending Moment	Nakshatra	Ending Moment	Muhammadan Year, Month and Day
	18	Su	1		3	·53	11	·62	2
	19	Mo	2		4	·48	12	·79	3
	20	Tu	3		5	·41	13	·75	4
	21	We	4	Sukla	6	·32	14	·69	5
	22	Th	5		7	·22	15	·63	6
	23	Fr	6		8	·12	16	·56	7
	24	Sa	7		9 / 10	·02 / ·92	17	·49	8
	25	Su	8		11	·82	18	·42	H. 1315 Rabi-ul-awwal. 9
	26	Mo	9	Sravana	12	·73	19	·36	10
	27	Tu	10		13	·65	20	·31	11
	28	We	11		14	·58	21	·27	12
	29	Th	12		P	·53	22	·24	13
	30	Fr	13		1	·50	23	·23	14
	—31	Sa	14		2	·49	24	·25	15
Hemalamba Simha—Avani	1	Su	15		3	·50	25	·28	16
	2	Mo	16		4	·53	26	·33	17
	3	Tu	17		5	·58	27	·40	18
	4	We	18		6	·64	1	·49	19
	5	Th	19	Bahula	7	·72	2	·59	20
	6	Fr	20		8	·81	3	·70	21
	7	Sa	21		9	·89	4	·81	22
	8	Su	22		10	·96	5	·91	23
	9	Mo	23		...	...	...	...	24
	10	Tu	24		11	·02	6	·00	25
	11	We	25		12	·07	7	·07	26
	12	Th	26		13	·10	8	·12	27
	13	Fr	27		14	·10	9	·15	28
	14	Sa	28		—A	·08	10	·16	29
	15	Su	29		1 / 2	·04 / ·97	11	·15	—30
	16	Mo	30	Suk.	3	·91	12	·12	1
	17	Tu	31		4	·83	13	·08	2

Sep.

Solar month	Cyclic Sidereal Year, Month and Day	Week-Day	English Month and Day	Lunar month	Tithi	Ending Moment	Nakshatra	Ending Moment	Muhammadan Year, Month and Day
	18	We	1		5	·74	14 / 15	·03 / ·97	3
	19	Th	2		6	·64	16	·90	4
	20	Fr	3	Sukla	7	·54	17	·83	5
Hemalamba Simha—Avani	21	Sa	4		8	·44	18	·76	6
	22	Su	5		9	·34	19	·70	7
	23	Mo	6		10	·25	20	·64	8
	24	Tu	7		11	·17	21	·60	9
	25	We	8		12	·10	22	·57	10
	26	Th	9	Bhadrapada	13	·05	23	·55	11
	27	Fr	10		14	·02	24	·56	12
	28	Sa	11		P	·01	25	·59	13
	29	Su	12		1	·02	26	·64	14
	30	Mo	13		2	·05	27	·71	15
	—31	Tu	14		3	·10	1	·80	16
Hemalamba Kanya—Purattasi	1	We	15		4	·17	2	·90	H. 1315 Rabi-ul-akhir. 17
	2	Th	16		5	·25	...	...	18
	3	Fr	17		6	·33	3	·00	19
	4	Sa	18	Bahula	7	·41	4	·11	20
	5	Su	19		8	·48	5	·21	21
	6	Mo	20		9	·55	6	·30	22
	7	Tu	21		10	·60	7	·38	23
	8	We	22		11	·62	8	·44	24
	9	Th	23		12	·63	9	·47	25
	10	Fr	24		13	·61	10	·43	26
	11	Sa	25		14	·57	11	·47	27
	12	Su	26		—A	·52	12	·45	28
	13	Mo	27		1	·45	13	·41	—29
	14	Tu	28		2	·37	14	·36	1
	15	We	29		3	·28	15	·30	2
	16	Th	30		4	·19	16	·24	3

Oct.

Solar month	Cyclic Sidereal Year, Month and Day	Week-Day	English Month and Day	Lunar month	Tithi	Ending Moment	Nakshatra	Ending Moment	Muhammadan Year, Month and Day
	17	Fr	1		5 / 6	·09 / ·99	17	·17	4
	18	Sa	2	Sukla	7	·89	18	·10	5
	19	Su	3		8	·79	19 / 20	·04 / ·98	6
	20	Mo	4		9	·71	21	·93	7
	21	Tu	5		10	·65	22	·90	8
	22	We	6		11	·60	23	·89	9
	23	Th	7		12	·57	24	·89	10
	24	Fr	8	Asvina	13	·57	25	·91	H. 1315 Jumadal-awwal. 11
	25	Sa	9		14	·58	26	·95	12
	26	Su	10		P	·61	...	...	13
	27	Mo	11		1	·66	27	·01	14
	28	Tu	12		2	·72	1	·10	15
	29	We	13		3	·80	2	·20	16
	30	Th	14		4	·89	3	·30	17
	—31	Fr	15		5	·98	4	·41	18
Hemalamba Tula—Aippasi	1	Sa	16		...	...	5	·51	19
	2	Su	17		6	·06	6	·61	20
	3	Mo	18	Bahula	7	·12	7	·69	21
	4	Tu	19		8	·17	8	·75	22
	5	We	20		9	·20	9	·79	23
	6	Th	21		10	·20	10	·80	24
	7	Fr	22		11	·18	11	·81	25
	8	Sa	23		12	·15	12	·79	26
	9	Su	24		13	·10	13	·75	27
	10	Mo	25		14 / A	·03 / ·95	14	·70	28
	11	Tu	26	Suk.	1	·86	15	·64	29
	12	We	27	Kart.	2	·76	16	·58	—30
	13	Th	28		3	·65	17	·51	J. akhir. 1
	14	Fr	29		4	·57	18	·44	2
	15	Sa	30		5	·48	19	·37	3
	16	Su	31		6	·39	20	·31	4

Nov.

Solar month	Cyclic Sidereal Year, Month and Day	Week-Day	English Month and Day	Lunar month	Tithi	Ending Moment	Nakshatra	Ending Moment	Muhammadan Year, Month and Day
	17	Mo	1		7	·31	21	·26	5
	18	Tu	2	Sukla	8	·24	22	·23	6
Hemalamba Tula—Aippasi	19	We	3		9	·19	23	·21	7
	20	Th	4		10	·17	24	·21	8
	21	Fr	5		11	·17	25	·22	9
	22	Sa	6		12	·18	26	·26	10
	23	Su	7	Kartika	13	·21	27	·32	11
	24	Mo	8		14	·26	1	·40	12
	25	Tu	9		P	·33	2	·50	13
	26	We	10		1	·41	3	·60	14
	27	Th	11		2	·50	4	·71	15
	28	Fr	12		3	·59	5	·82	16
	29	Sa	13		4	·67	6	·92	17
	—30	Su	14		5	·74	...	...	H. 1315 Jumadal-akhir. 18
Hemalamba Vruchika—Kartigai	1	Mo	15	Bahula	6	·79	7	·03	19
	2	Tu	16		7	·82	8	·03	20
	3	We	17		8	·82	9	·10	21
	4	Th	18		9	·80	10	·13	22
	5	Fr	19		10	·76	11	·13	23
	6	Sa	20		11	·71	12	·11	24
	7	Su	21		12	·65	13	·03	25
	8	Mo	22		13	·57	14 / 15	·03 / ·93	26
	9	Tu	23		14	·48	16	·92	27
	10	We	24		—A	·39	17	·85	28
	11	Th	25		1	·29	18	·78	—29
	12	Fr	26		2	·19	19	·71	1
	13	Sa	27		3	·09	20	·65	2
	14	Su	28		4 / 5	·00 / ·92	21	·60	3
	15	Mo	29		6	·86	22	·56	4
	16	Tu	30		7	·82	23	·54	5

Dec.

Solar month	Cyclic Sidereal Year, Month and Day	Week-Day	English Month and Day	Lunar month	Tithi	Ending Moment	Nakshatra	Ending Moment	Muhammadan Year, Month and Day
	17	We	1	Sukla	8	·80	24	·53	6
	18	Th	2		9	·79	25	·54	7
	19	Fr	3		10	·81	26	·58	8
	20	Sa	4		11	·85	27	·64	9
	21	Su	5		12	·90	1	·71	10
	22	Mo	6		13	·97	2	·80	11
	23	Tu	7		...	...	3	·90	H. 1315 Rajab. 12
	24	We	8	Margasira	14	·05	...	...	13
	25	Th	9		P	·14	4	·01	14
	26	Fr	10		1	·23	5	·12	15
	27	Sa	11		2	·31	6	·22	16
	28	Su	12		3	·38	7	·30	17
	—29	Mo	13		4	·43	8	·37	18
Hemalamba Dhanus—Margali	1	Tu	14		5	·46	9	·42	19
	2	We	15		6	·45	10	·45	20
	3	Th	16	Bahula	7	·43	11	·46	21
	4	Fr	17		8	·40	12	·44	22
	5	Sa	18		9	·35	13	·41	23
	6	Su	19		10	·28	14	·37	24
	7	Mo	20		11	·20	15	·32	25
	8	Tu	21		12	·11	16	·26	26
	9	We	22		13 / 14	·02 / ·92	17	·10	27
	10	Th	23		—A	·82	18	·12	28
	11	Fr	24		1	·73	19 / 20	·05 / ·92	29
	12	Sa	25	Sukla	2	·61	21	·94	—30
	13	Su	26		3	·56	22	·90	1
	14	Mo	27	Pausha	4	·50	23	·86	Shaban. 2
	15	Tu	28		5	·46	24	·85	3
	16	We	29		6	·44	25	·87	4
	17	Th	30		7	·44	26	·90	5
	18	Fr	31		8	·46	27	·94	6

15. Svati. 16. Visak. 17. Anur. 18. Jyesh. 19. Mula. 20. P. Asn. 21. U. Asn. 22. Sravn. 23. Dani. 24. Satab. 25. P. Bhad. 26. U. Bhad. 27. Rev.

A. D. 1898.
Solar Eclipse. ●
Lunar Eclipse. ○

Mesha Sankranti (Commencement of Indian Sidereal Year).
(Surya Sid.) April 12·10.
(Arya Sid.) April 11·99.

Saka 1820. **Kaliyuga 4999.**
(S. Cycle) Vilamba.

SOLAR reckoning: Cyclic Sidereal Year, Month and Day; Week-Day; English Month and Day. LUNAR reckoning: Tithi, Ending Moment; Nakshatra, Ending Moment; Muhammadan Year, Month and Day.

Jan.

Solar: Hemalamba *Dhanus—Margali.* (to 29); Hemalamba *Makara—Tai.* Lunar: *Sukla*; **Pausha**; *Bahula*; *Sukla*. Muhammadan: H. 1315 *Shaban.*

Cyclic Sidereal Year, Month and Day	Week-Day	English Month and Day	Tithi	Ending Moment	Nakshatra	Ending Moment	Muhammadan Year, Month and Day
19	Sa	1	9	·49	...	...	7
20	Su	2	10	·54	1	·01	8
21	Mo	3	11	·62	2	·10	9
22	Tu	4	12	·70	3	·20	10
23	We	5	13	·79	4	·31	11
24	Th	6	14	·88	5	·42	12
25	Fr ○	7	P	·96	6	·52	13
26	Sa	8	...	...	7	·61	14
27	Su	9	1	·02	8	·68	15
28	Mo	10	2	·07	9	·74	16
—29	Tu	11	3	·10	10	·77	17
1	We	12	4	·09	11	·78	18
2	Th	13	5	·08	12	·77	19
3	Fr	14	6 7	·04 ·99	13	·74	20
4	Sa	15	8	·93	14	·71	21
5	Su	16	9	·85	15	·66	22
6	Mo	17	10	·75	16	·60	23
7	Tu	18	11	·65	17	·53	24
8	We	19	12	·55	18	·46	25
9	Th	20	13	·45	19	·39	26
10	Fr	21	14	·36	20	·33	27
11	Sa ●	22	—A	·28	21	·27	28
12	Su	23	1	·21	22	·23	—29
13	Mo	24	2	·15	23	·20	1
14	Tu	25	3	·11	24	·18	2
15	We	26	4	·09	25	·19	3
16	Th	27	5	·08	26	·21	4
17	Fr	28	6	·10	27	·25	5
18	Sa	29	7	·14	1	·32	6
19	Su	30	8	·20	2	·40	7
20	Mo	31	9	·28	3	·50	8

Feb.

Solar: Hemalamba *Kumbha—Masi.* Lunar: **Magha**; *Bahula*; *Sukla*; **Phalg.** Muhammadan: H. 1315 *Ramzan.*; *Shawwal.*

Cyclic Sidereal Year, Month and Day	Week-Day	English Month and Day	Tithi	Ending Moment	Nakshatra	Ending Moment	Muhammadan Year, Month and Day
21	Tu	1	10	·37	4	·61	9
22	We	2	11	·45	5	·72	10
23	Th	3	12	·53	6	·82	11
24	Fr	4	13	·61	7	·91	12
25	Sa	5	14	·67	8	·99	13
26	Su	6	P	·71	...	...	14
27	Mo	7	1	·74	9	·05	15
28	Tu	8	2	·74	10	·09	16
29	We	9	3	·72	11	·10	17
—30	Th	10	4	·68	12	·10	18
1	Fr	11	5	·62	13	·08	19
2	Sa	12	6	·55	14 15	·04 ·99	20
3	Su	13	7	·47	16	·93	21
4	Mo	14	8	·38	17	·87	22
5	Tu	15	9	·29	18	·80	23
6	We	16	10	·19	19	·73	24
7	Th	17	11 12	·09 ·99	20	·67	25
8	Fr	18	13	·90	21	·61	26
9	Sa	19	14	·82	22	·56	27
10	Su	20	—A	·76	23	·52	28
11	Mo	21	1	·73	24	·51	29
12	Tu	22	2	·71	25	·51	—30
13	We	23	3	·71	26	·53	1
14	Th	24	4	·73	27	·56	2
15	Fr	25	5	·77	1	·62	3
16	Sa	26	6	·82	2	·70	4
17	Su	27	7	·90	3	·80	5
18	Mo	28	8	·99	4	·91	6

March

Solar: Hemalamba *Kumbha—Masi.* (to 30); Hemalamba *Mina—Panguni.* Lunar: *Sukla*; **Phalguna**; *Bahula*; *Sukla*. Muhammadan: H. 1315 *Shawwal.*

Cyclic Sidereal Year, Month and Day	Week-Day	English Month and Day	Tithi	Ending Moment	Nakshatra	Ending Moment	Muhammadan Year, Month and Day
19	Tu	1	...	...	...	...	7
20	We	2	9	·08	5	·02	8
21	Th	3	10	·16	6	·12	9
22	Fr	4	11	·23	7	·22	10
23	Sa	5	12	·28	8	·30	11
24	Su	6	13	·32	9	·36	12
25	Mo	7	14	·34	10	·40	13
26	Tu	8	P	·35	11	·42	14
27	We	9	1	·33	12	·43	15
28	Th	10	2	·28	13	·41	16
29	Fr	11	3	·22	14	·38	17
—30	Sa	12	4	·15	15	·33	18
1	Su	13	5 6	·07 ·98	16	·27	19
2	Mo	14	7	·88	17	·21	20
3	Tu	15	8	·78	18	·14	21
4	We	16	9	·68	19	·07	22
5	Th	17	10	·58	20 21	·00 ·94	23
6	Fr	18	11	·49	22	·89	24
7	Sa	19	12	·42	23	·86	25
8	Su	20	13	·36	24	·84	26
9	Mo	21	14	·32	25	·83	27
10	Tu	22	—A	·30	26	·84	28
11	We	23	1	·30	27	·88	—29
12	Th	24	2	·32	1	·94	1
13	Fr	25	3	·36	...	...	2
14	Sa	26	4	·42	2	·01	3
15	Su	27	5	·49	3	·10	4
16	Mo	28	6	·57	4	·20	5
17	Tu	29	7	·66	5	·31	6
18	We	30	8	·74	6	·42	7
19	Th	31	9	·81	7	·52	8

April

Solar: Villamba *Mesha—Chittirai.* Lunar: **Chaitra**; *Bahula*; *Sukla*; **Vaisakha**. Muhammadan: H. 1315 *Zi-l-ka'da.*; H. 1315 *Zi-l-hijja.*

Cyclic Sidereal Year, Month and Day	Week-Day	English Month and Day	Tithi	Ending Moment	Nakshatra	Ending Moment	Muhammadan Year, Month and Day
20	Fr	1	10	·87	8	·60	9
21	Sa	2	11	·91	9	·67	10
22	Su	3	12	·93	10	·72	11
23	Mo	4	13	·92	11	·75	12
24	Tu	5	14	·89	12	·76	13
25	We	6	P	·85	13	·74	14
26	Th	7	1	·79	14	·71	15
27	Fr	8	2	·72	15	·66	16
28	Sa	9	3	·63	16	·61	17
29	Su	10	4	·54	17	·55	18
—30	Mo	11	5	·44	18	·48	19
1	Tu	12	6	·34	19	·41	20
2	We	13	7	·24	20	·34	21
3	Th	14	8	·14	21	·28	22
4	Fr	15	9 10	·05 ·98	22	·23	23
5	Sa	16	11	·92	23	·19	24
6	Su	17	12	·88	24	·16	25
7	Mo	18	13	·85	25	·15	26
8	Tu	19	14	·85	26	·16	27
9	We	20	—A	·86	27	·20	28
10	Th	21	1	·90	1	·25	29
11	Fr	22	2	·96	2	·32	—30
12	Sa	23	...	...	3	·40	1
13	Su	24	3	·04	4	·50	2
14	Mo	25	4	·12	5	·61	3
15	Tu	26	5	·21	6	·72	4
16	We	27	6	·29	7	·82	5
17	Th	28	7	·35	8	·91	6
18	Fr	29	8	·40	9	·98	7
19	Sa	30	9	·44	...	...	8

May

Solar: Vilamba *Mesha—Chittirai.* (to 31); Vilamba *Vrishabha—Vaikasi.* Lunar: **Vaisakha** *Suk.*; *Bahula*; *Sukla*. Muhammadan: H. 1315 *Zi-l-hijja.*

Cyclic Sidereal Year, Month and Day	Week-Day	English Month and Day	Tithi	Ending Moment	Nakshatra	Ending Moment	Muhammadan Year, Month and Day
20	Su	1	10	·46	10	·03	9
21	Mo	2	11	·45	11	·06	10
22	Tu	3	12	·43	12	·08	11
23	We	4	13	·38	13	·07	12
24	Th	5	14	·32	14	·04	13
25	Fr	6	P	·24	15 16	·00 ·95	14
26	Sa	7	1	·16	17	·89	15
27	Su	8	2 3	·07 ·97	18	·82	16
28	Mo	9	4	·87	19	·75	17
29	Tu	10	5	·76	20	·68	18
30	We	11	6	·66	21	·62	19
—31	Th	12	7	·57	22	·57	20
1	Fr	13	8	·50	23	·52	21
2	Sa	14	9	·44	24	·49	22
3	Su	15	10	·39	25	·47	23
4	Mo	16	11	·37	26	·49	24
5	Tu	17	12	·36	27	·52	25
6	We	18	13	·38	1	·56	26
7	Th	19	14	·42	2	·62	27
8	Fr	20	—A	·47	3	·70	28
9	Sa	21	1	·54	4	·80	—29
10	Su	22	2	·62	5	·91	1
11	Mo	23	3	·71	...	...	2
12	Tu	24	4	·79	6	·02	3
13	We	25	5	·86	7	·12	4
14	Th	26	6	·91	8	·21	5
15	Fr	27	7	·94	9	·29	6
16	Sa	28	8	·96	10	·35	7
17	Su	29	9	·95	11	·39	8
18	Mo	30	10	·93	12	·40	9
19	Tu	31	11	·89	13	·40	10

June

Solar: Vilamba *Mithuna—Ani.* Lunar: **Jyeshtha**; *Bahula*; *Sukla*; **Ashadha**. Muhammadan: H. 1316 *Muharram.*; H. 1316 *Safar.*

Cyclic Sidereal Year, Month and Day	Week-Day	English Month and Day	Tithi	Ending Moment	Nakshatra	Ending Moment	Muhammadan Year, Month and Day
20	We	1	12	·83	14	·38	11
21	Th	2	13	·75	15	·34	12
22	Fr	3	14	·66	16	·29	13
23	Sa	4	P	·56	17	·23	14
24	Su	5	1	·46	18	·16	15
25	Mo	6	2	·36	19	·09	16
26	Tu	7	3	·26	20 21	·02 ·96	17
27	We	8	4	·16	22	·90	18
28	Th	9	5	·07	23	·85	19
29	Fr	10	6 7	·00 ·94	24	·82	20
30	Sa	11	8	·89	25	·81	21
—31	Su	12	9	·86	26	·81	22
1	Mo	13	10	·84	27	·83	23
2	Tu	14	11	·86	1	·87	24
3	We	15	12	·89	2	·93	25
4	Th	16	13	·94	...	...	26
5	Fr	17	...	...	3	·01	27
6	Sa	18	14	·01	4	·11	28
7	Su	19	—A	·09	5	·21	29
8	Mo	20	1	·18	6	·32	—30
9	Tu	21	2	·26	7	·42	1
10	We	22	3	·33	8	·52	2
11	Th	23	4	·38	9	·61	3
12	Fr	24	5	·42	10	·67	4
13	Sa	25	6	·44	11	·70	5
14	Su	26	7	·44	12	·72	6
15	Mo	27	8	·41	13	·72	7
16	Tu	28	9	·37	14	·70	8
17	We	29	10	·31	15	·67	9
18	Th	30	11	·24	16	·62	10

Naksh :—1. Asvn. 2. Bhar. 3. Krit. 4. Rohi. 5. Mrig. 6. Ardh. 7. Punar. 8. Push. 9. Aslesh. 10. Magh. 11. P. Phal. 12. U. Phal. 13. Hasta. 14. Chit.

A. D. 1898.
A.—Amavasya.
P.—Paurnami.

Kollam 1074, Commences { **N. Malabar—Sept.** / **S. Malabar—Aug.**

Hijra 1316, Commences, **May 22.**

Vikrama 1955.
Bengal San 1304.
(N. Cycle) Sadharana.

Solar month	Cyclic Sidereal Year, Month and Day.	Week-Day	English Month and Day.	Lunar month	Tithi	Ending Moment.	Nakshatra	Ending Moment.	Muhammadan Year, Month and Day.
		July							
Vilamba Mithuna—Ani.	19	Fr	1	Ashadha Bahula	12	·15	17	·56	H. 1316 Safar 11
	20	Sa	2		13 14	·05 ·95	18	·50	12
	21	Su ○	3		P	·85	19	·44	13
	22	Mo	4		1	·74	20	·37	14
	23	Tu	5		2	·64	21	·30	15
	24	We	6		3	·55	22	·24	16
	25	Th	7		4	·47	23	·19	17
	26	Fr	8		5	·41	24	·15	18
	27	Sa	9		6	·36	25	·13	19
	28	Su	10		7	·33	26	·13	20
	29	Mo	11		8	·32	27	·14	21
	30	Tu	12		9	·34	1	·18	22
	31	We	13		10	·38	2	·24	23
	—32	Th	14		11	·43	3	·32	24
Vilamba Karkata—Adi.	1	Fr	15		12	·50	4	·41	25
	2	Sa	16		13	·57	5	·51	26
	3	Su	17		14	·65	6	·62	27
	4	Mo	18		—A	·73	7	·73	28
	5	Tu	19	Sravana Sukla	1	·80	8	·83	—29
	6	We	20		2	·86	9	·91	Rabi-ul-awwal. 1
	7	Th	21		3	·90	10	·98	2
	8	Fr	22		4	·92	...	...	3
	9	Sa	23		5	·92	11	·02	4
	10	Su	24		6	·89	12	·04	5
	11	Mo	25		7	·85	13	·05	6
	12	Tu	26		8	·79	14	·04	7
	13	We	27		9	·72	15 16	·01 ·96	8
	14	Th	28		10	·63	17	·90	9
	15	Fr	29		11	·54	18	·84	10
	16	Sa	30		12	.44	19	·78	11
	17	Su	31		13	.33	20	·71	12
		Aug.							
	18	Mo	1		14	·23	21	·64	H. 1316 13
	19	Tu	2		P	·13	22	·57	14
	20	We	3	Bahula	1 2	·04 ·96	23	·52	15
	21	Th	4		3	·89	24	·49	16
	22	Fr	5		4	·85	25	·46	17
	23	Sa	6		5	·82	26	·45	18
	24	Su	7		6	·81	27	·46	19
	25	Mo	8		7	·82	1	·49	20
	26	Tu	9		8	·85	2	·55	21
	27	We	10		9	·90	3	·62	22
	28	Th	11		10	·97	4	·71	23
	29	Fr	12		...	...	5	·81	24
	30	Sa	13		11	·05	6	·92	25
	—31	Su	14		12	·14	...	...	26
Vilamba Simha—Avani.	1	Mo	15		13	·22	7	·03	27
	2	Tu	16		14	·29	8	·13	28
	3	We	17		—A	·35	9	·22	29
	4	Th	18	Bhadra. Sukla	1	·38	10	·28	—30
	5	Fr	19		2	·41	11	·33	H. 1316 Rabi-ul-akhir. 1
	6	Sa	20		3	·41	12	·37	2
	7	Su	21		4	·39	13	·38	3
	8	Mo	22		5	·35	14	·37	4
	9	Tu	23		6	·29	15	·34	5
	10	We	24		7	·22	16	·29	6
	11	Th	25		8	·14	17	·24	7
	12	Fr	26		9 10	·04 ·94	18	·18	8
	13	Sa	27		11	·84	19	·11	9
	14	Su	28		12	·74	20 21	·04 ·97	10
	15	Mo	29		13	·64	22	·91	11
	16	Tu	30		14	·55	23	·86	12
	17	We	31		P	·47	24	·82	13

Solar month	Cyclic Sidereal Year, Month and Day.	Week-Day	English Month and Day.	Lunar month	Tithi	Ending Moment.	Nakshatra	Ending Moment.	Muhammadan Year, Month and Day.
		Sep.							
Vilamba Simha—Avani.	18	Th	1	Bhadrapada Bahula	1	·41	25	·79	H. 1316 Rabi-ul-akhir. 14
	19	Fr	2		2	·36	26	·77	15
	20	Sa	3		3	·33	27	·78	16
	21	Su	4		4	·32	1	·81	17
	22	Mo	5		5	·33	2	·86	18
	23	Tu	6		6	·36	3	·93	19
	24	We	7		7	·41	...	...	20
	25	Th	8		8	·48	4	·01	21
	26	Fr	9		9	·56	5	·11	22
	27	Sa	10		10	·64	6	·22	23
	28	Su	11		11	·73	7	·33	24
	29	Mo	12		12	·81	8	·43	25
	30	Tu	13		13	·87	9	·52	26
	—31	We	14		14	·91	10	·59	27
Vilamba Kanya—Purattasi.	1	Th	15		—A	·94	11	·65	28
	2	Fr	16	Asvina Sukla	1	·94	12	·69	—29
	3	Sa	17		2	·92	13	·70	Jumadal-awwal. 1
	4	Su	18		3	·88	14	·69	2
	5	Mo	19		4	·82	15	·67	3
	6	Tu	20		5	·75	16	·63	4
	7	We	21		6	·66	17	·58	5
	8	Th	22		7	·56	18	·52	6
	9	Fr	23		8	·46	19	·45	7
	10	Sa	24		9	·36	20	·38	8
	11	Su	25		10	·26	21	·32	9
	12	Mo	26		11	·17	22	·26	10
	13	Tu	27		12	·09	23	·20	11
	14	We	28		13 14	·02 ·96	24	·15	12
	15	Th	29		P	·91	25	·12	13
	16	Fr	30		1	·88	26	·10	14
		Oct.							
	17	Sa	1	Adhika Bahula	2	·87	27	·11	H. 1316 15
	18	Su	2		3	·88	1	·13	16
	19	Mo	3		4	·91	2	·17	17
	20	Tu	4		5	·96	3	·23	18
	21	We	5		...	...	4	·31	19
	22	Th	6		6	·03	5	·41	20
	23	Fr	7		7	·11	6	·52	21
	24	Sa	8		8	·20	7	·63	22
	25	Su	9		9	·29	8	·73	23
	26	Mo	10		10	·37	9	·82	24
	27	Tu	11		11	·44	10	·90	25
	28	We	12		12	·48	11	·96	26
	29	Th	13		13	·51	...	...	27
	30	Fr	14		14	·50	12	·00	28
	—31	Sa	15		—A	·48	13	·02	29
Vilamba Tula—Aippasi.	1	Su	16	Nija Asvina Sukla	1	·44	14	·02	—30
	2	Mo	17		2	·39	15 16	·00 ·97	H. 1316 Jumadal-akhir. 1
	3	Tu	18		3	·32	17	·92	2
	4	We	19		4	·24	18	·86	3
	5	Th	20		5	·15	19	·79	4
	6	Fr	21		6 7	·06 ·96	20	·72	5
	7	Sa	22		8	·86	21	·65	6
	8	Su	23		9	·76	22	·59	7
	9	Mo	24		10	·67	23	·53	8
	10	Tu	25		11	·59	24	·48	9
	11	We	26		12	·53	25	·45	10
	12	Th	27		13	·49	26	·43	11
	13	Fr	28		14	·47	27	·43	12
	14	Sa	29		P	·46	1	·44	13
	15	Su	30	Bah.	1	·47	2	·48	14
	16	Mo	31		2	·50	3	·54	15

Solar month	Cyclic Sidereal Year, Month and Day.	Week-Day	English Month and Day.	Lunar month	Tithi	Ending Moment.	Nakshatra	Ending Moment.	Muhammadan Year, Month and Day.
		Nov.							
Vilamba Tula—Aippasi.	17	Tu	1	Nija Asvina Bahula	3	·56	4	·62	H. 1316 Jumadal-akhir. 16
	18	We	2		4	·63	5	·72	17
	19	Th	3		5	·71	6	·82	18
	20	Fr	4		6	·80	7	·93	19
	21	Sa	5		7	·89	...	...	20
	22	Su	6		8	·97	8	·03	21
	23	Mo	7		...	...	9	·13	22
	24	Tu	8		9	·03	10	·22	23
	25	We	9		10	·08	11	·28	24
	26	Th	10		11	·11	12	·32	25
	27	Fr	11		12	·11	13	·34	26
	28	Sa	12		13	·09	14	·34	27
	29	Su	13		14	·05	15	·33	28
	—30	Mo	14		A 1	·00 ·93	16	·30	—29
Vilamba Vrischika—Kartigai.	1	Tu	15	Karttika Sukla	2	·85	17	·26	H. 1316 Rajab. 1
	2	We	16		3	·76	18	·20	2
	3	Th	17		4	·66	19	·14	3
	4	Fr	18		5	·56	20	·07	4
	5	Sa	19		6	·46	21 22	·00 ·93	5
	6	Su	20		7	·37	23	·87	6
	7	Mo	21		8	·28	24	·82	7
	8	Tu	22		9	·21	25	·78	8
	9	We	23		10	·15	26	·76	9
	10	Th	24		11	·11	27	·75	10
	11	Fr	25		12	·08	1	·76	11
	12	Sa	26		13	·08	2	·79	12
	13	Su	27		14	·10	3	·85	13
	14	Mo	28		P	·13	4	·93	14
	15	Tu	29		1	·19	...	...	15
	16	We	30		2	·26	5	·02	16
		Dec.							
	17	Th	1	Bahula	3	·34	6	·12	17
	18	Fr	2		4	·43	7	·23	18
	19	Sa	3		5	·52	8	·34	19
	20	Su	4		6	·60	9	·44	20
	21	Mo	5		7	·66	10	·52	21
	22	Tu	6		8	·71	11	·59	22
	23	We	7		9	·74	12	·64	23
	24	Th	8		10	·74	13	·67	24
	25	Fr	9		11	·72	14	·68	25
	26	Sa	10		12	·68	15	·66	26
	27	Su	11		13	·63	16	·63	27
	28	Mo	12		14	·56	17	·59	28
	—29	Tu	13		—A	·48	18	·53	29
Vilamba Dhanus—Margali.	1	We	14	Margasira Sukla	1	·39	19	·47	—30
	2	Th	15		2	·29	20	·41	H. 1316 Shaban. 1
	3	Fr	16		3	·19	21	·34	2
	4	Sa	17		4	·09	22	·27	3
	5	Su	18		5 6	·00 ·92	23	·20	4
	6	Mo	19		7	·84	24	·15	5
	7	Tu	20		8	·78	25	·11	6
	8	We	21		9	·74	26	·08	7
	9	Th	22		10	·72	27	·07	8
	10	Fr	23		11	·73	1	·08	9
	11	Sa	24		12	·75	2	·11	10
	12	Su	25		13	·78	3	·16	11
	13	Mo	26		14	·84	4	·23	12
	14	Tu ○	27		P	·92	5	·32	13
	15	We	28		...	...	6	·42	14
	16	Th	29		1	·00	7	·53	15
	17	Fr	30	Bah.	2	09	8	·64	16
	18	Sa	31		3	·18	9	·74	17

5. Svati. 16. Visak. 17. Anur. 18. Jyesh. 19. Mula. 20. P. Ash. 21. U. Ash. 22. Sravn. 23. Dani. 24. Satab. 25. P. Bhad. 26. U. Bhad. 27. Reve

A. D. 1899. **Mesha Sankranti** (Commencement of Indian Sidereal Year). **Saka 1821.** **Kaliyuga 5000.**
Solar Eclipse. ● **(Surya Sid.) April 12·36.** **(S. Cycle) Vikari.**
Lunar Eclipse. ○ **(Arya Sid.) April 12·25.**

SOLAR reckoning: Cyclic Sidereal Year, Month and Day; Week-Day; English Month and Day. LUNAR reckoning: Tithi; Ending Moment; Nakshatra; Ending Moment; Muhammadan Year, Month and Day.

Jan. — Solar: Vilamba Dhanus—Margali (to 30); Vilamba Makara—Tai. Lunar: Marga. Bahula; Sukla Pausha. H. 1316 Shaban; H. 1316 Ramzan.

Cyclic Sidereal Year, Month and Day	Week-Day	English Month and Day	Tithi	Ending Moment	Nakshatra	Ending Moment	Muhammadan Year, Month and Day
19	Su	1	4	·26	10	·83	18
20	Mo	2	5	·32	11	·90	19
21	Tu	3	6	·36	12	·95	20
22	We	4	7	·38	13	·99	31
23	Th	5	8	·38	...	...	23
24	Fr	6	9	·36	14 15	·00 ·99	23
25	Sa	7	10	·33	16	·96	24
26	Su	8	11	·27	17	·92	25
27	Mo	9	12	·20	18	·88	26
28	Tu	10	13	·12	19	·82	27
29	We	11	14 A	·03 ·93	20	·75	28
30	Th	12	1	·83	21	·68	29
1	Fr	13	2	·73	22	·61	1
2	Sa	14	3	·64	23	·54	2
3	Su	15	4	·56	24	·48	3
4	Mo	16	5	·49	25	·44	4
5	Tu	17	6	·43	26	·41	5
6	We	18	7	·39	27	·40	6
7	Th	19	8	·37	1	·40	7
8	Fr	20	9	·37	2	·43	8
9	Sa	21	10	·38	3	·48	9
10	Su	22	11	·42	4	·54	10
11	Mo	23	12	·49	5	·62	11
12	Tu	24	13	·57	6	·72	12
13	We	25	14	·65	7	·83	13
14	Th	26	P	·74	8	·94	14
15	Fr	27	1	·82	...	...	15
16	Sa	28	2	·90	9	·04	16
17	Su	29	3	·97	10	·13	17
18	Mo	30	...	...	11	·20	18
19	Tu	31	4	·01	12	·26	19

Feb. — Solar: Vilamba Kumbha—Masi (from 1). Lunar: Bahula; Sukla Magha; Bah. H. 1316 Shawwal (from 1).

Cyclic Sidereal Year, Month and Day	Week-Day	English Month and Day	Tithi	Ending Moment	Nakshatra	Ending Moment	Muhammadan Year, Month and Day
20	We	1	5	·03	13	·30	20
21	Th	2	6	·02	14	·32	21
22	Fr	3	7 8	·00 ·96	15	·32	22
23	Sa	4	9	·90	16	·30	23
24	Su	5	10	·83	17	·26	24
25	Mo	6	11	·75	18	·21	25
26	Tu	7	12	·66	19	·15	26
27	We	8	13	·56	20	·08	27
28	Th	9	14	·46	21 22	·01 ·95	28
29	Fr	10	A	·36	23	·89	29
1	Sa	11	1	·27	24	·83	30
2	Su	12	2	·19	25	·78	1
3	Mo	13	3	·12	26	·74	2
4	Tu	14	4	·06	27	·72	3
5	We	15	5	·02	1	·73	4
6	Th	16	6	·01	2	·75	5
7	Fr	17	7	·00	3	·78	6
8	Sa	18	8	·02	4	·84	7
9	Su	19	9	·06	5	·92	8
10	Mo	20	10	·12	...	...	9
11	Tu	21	11	·19	6	·02	10
12	We	22	12	·28	7	·13	11
13	Th	23	13	·37	8	·24	12
14	Fr	24	14	·45	9	·34	13
15	Sa	25	P	·52	10	·44	14
16	Su	26	1	·58	11	·52	15
17	Mo	27	2	·62	12	·53	16
18	Tu	28	3	·65	13	·62	17

March — Solar: Vilamba Kumbha—Masi (to 30); Vilamba Mina—Panguni. Lunar: Magha Bahula; Sukla Phalguna. H. 1316 Shawwal; H. 1316 Zi-l-ka'da.

Cyclic Sidereal Year, Month and Day	Week-Day	English Month and Day	Tithi	Ending Moment	Nakshatra	Ending Moment	Muhammadan Year, Month and Day
19	We	1	4	·64	14	·64	18
20	Th	2	5	·62	15	·64	19
21	Fr	3	6	·57	16	·62	20
22	Sa	4	7	·51	17	·59	21
23	Su	5	8	·44	18	·55	23
24	Mo	6	9	·36	19	·49	23
25	Tu	7	10	·27	20	·42	24
26	We	8	11	·18	21	·35	25
27	Th	9	12 13	·03 ·98	22	·28	26
28	Fr	10	14	·88	23	·22	27
29	Sa	11	A	·79	24	·16	28
30	Su	12	1	·71	25	·11	29
1	Mo	13	2	·65	26	·08	1
2	Tu	14	3	·62	27	·06	2
3	We	15	4	·60	1	·05	3
4	Th	16	5	·59	2	·07	4
5	Fr	17	6	·62	3	·10	5
6	Sa	18	7	·66	4	·15	6
7	Su	19	8	·72	5	·23	7
8	Mo	20	9	·80	6	·32	8
9	Tu	21	10	·89	7	·42	9
10	We	22	11	·97	8	·53	10
11	Th	23	...	...	9	·64	11
12	Fr	24	12	·05	10	·74	12
13	Sa	25	13	·12	11	·83	13
14	Su	26	14	·18	12	·89	14
15	Mo	27	P	·22	13	·93	15
16	Tu	28	1	·23	14	·96	16
17	We	29	2	·22	15	·97	17
18	Th	30	3	·20	16	·96	18
19	Fr	31	4	·16	17	·93	19

April — Solar: Vikari Mesha—Chittirai (from 1). Lunar: Bahula; Sukla Chaitra; Bah. H. 1316 Zi-l-hijja (from 1).

Cyclic Sidereal Year, Month and Day	Week-Day	English Month and Day	Tithi	Ending Moment	Nakshatra	Ending Moment	Muhammadan Year, Month and Day
20	Sa	1	5	·10	18	·88	20
21	Su	2	6 7	·03 ·94	19	·88	21
22	Mo	3	8	·84	20	·77	22
23	Tu	4	9	·74	21	·70	23
24	We	5	10	·64	22	·63	24
25	Th	6	11	·54	23	·56	25
26	Fr	7	12	·45	24	·50	26
27	Sa	8	13	·36	25	·45	27
28	Su	9	14	·28	26	·41	28
29	Mo	10	A	·22	27	·38	29
30	Tu	11	1	·18	1	·37	30
1	We	12	2	·16	2 ●	·38	1
2	Th	13	3	·15	3	·41	2
3	Fr	14	4	·18	4	·47	3
4	Sa	15	5	·22	5	·54	4
5	Su	16	6	·28	6	·62	5
6	Mo	17	7	·36	7	·72	6
7	Tu	18	8	·44	8	·83	7
8	We	19	9	·53	9	·94	8
9	Th	20	10	·61	...	...	9
10	Fr	21	11	·67	10	·04	10
11	Sa	22	12	·72	11	·13	11
12	Su	23	13	·76	12	·20	12
13	Mo	24	14	·77	13	·25	13
14	Tu	25	P	·77	14	·28	14
15	We	26	1	·74	15	·30	15
16	Th	27	2	·69	16	·29	16
17	Fr	28	3	·63	17	·26	17
18	Sa	29	4	·55	18	·22	18
19	Su	30	5	·47	19	·17	19

May — Solar: Vikari Mesha—Chittirai (to 31); Vikari Vrishabha—Vaikasi. Lunar: Chait. Bahula; Sukla Vaisakha; Bahula. H. 1316 Zi-l-hijja; H. 1317 Muharram.

Cyclic Sidereal Year, Month and Day	Week-Day	English Month and Day	Tithi	Ending Moment	Nakshatra	Ending Moment	Muhammadan Year, Month and Day
20	Mo	1	6	·38	20	·11	20
21	Tu	2	7	·28	21 22	·04 ·97	21
22	We	3	8	·17	23	·90	22
23	Th	4	9 10	·07 ·97	24	·84	23
24	Fr	5	11	·88	25	·78	24
25	Sa	6	12	·81	26	·74	25
26	Su	7	13	·76	27	·71	26
27	Mo	8	14	·72	1	·69	27
28	Tu	9	A	·69	2	·70	28
29	We	10	1	·68	3	·73	29
30	Th	11	2	·70	4	·78	30
31	Fr	12	3	·74	5	·85	1
1	Sa	13	4	·83	6	·93	2
2	Su	14	5	·87	...	...	3
3	Mo	15	6	·95	7	·03	4
4	Tu	16	...	...	8	·14	5
5	We	17	7	·04	9	·25	6
6	Th	18	8	·12	10	·35	7
7	Fr	19	9	·18	11	·44	8
8	Sa	20	10	·23	12	·51	9
9	Su	21	11	·26	13	·56	10
10	Mo	22	12	·28	14	·60	11
11	Tu	23	13	·28	15	·62	12
12	We	24	14	·26	16	·61	13
13	Th	25	P	·22	17	·59	14
14	Fr	26	1	·15	18	·56	15
15	Sa	27	2 3	·07 ·98	19	·51	16
16	Su	28	4	·88	20	·45	17
17	Mo	29	5	·78	21	·38	18
18	Tu	30	6	·68	22	·31	19
19	We	31	7	·58	23	·24	20

June — Solar: Vikari Mithuna—Ani (from 1). Lunar: Sukla Jyeshtha; Bah. H. 1317 Safar (from 1).

Cyclic Sidereal Year, Month and Day	Week-Day	English Month and Day	Tithi	Ending Moment	Nakshatra	Ending Moment	Muhammadan Year, Month and Day
20	Th	1	8	·48	24	·18	21
21	Fr	2	9	·39	25	·12	22
22	Sa	3	10	·31	26	·07	23
23	Su	4	11	·25	27	·04	24
24	Mo	5	12	·21	1	·02	25
25	Tu	6	13	·18	2	·02	26
26	We	7	14	·18	3	·05	27
27	Th	8	A	·19	4	·09	28
28	Fr	9	1	·23	5	·15	29
29	Sa	10	2	·28	6	·23	30
30	Su	11	3	·34	7	·32	1
31	Mo	12	4	·42	8	·43	2
32	Tu	13	5	·51	9	·54	3
1	We	14	6	·59	10	·64	4
2	Th	15	7	·66	11	·74	5
3	Fr	16	8	·72	12	·82	6
4	Sa	17	9	·76	13	·88	7
5	Su	18	10	·77	14	·92	8
6	Mo	19	11	·76	15	·94	9
7	Tu	20	12	·74	16	·94	10
8	We	21	13	·69	17	·92	11
9	Th	22	14	·63	18	·89	12
10	Fr ○	23	P	·56	19	·84	13
11	Sa	24	1	·47	20	·78	14
12	Su	25	2	·37	21	·72	15
13	Mo	26	3	·26	22	·65	16
14	Tu	27	4	·16	23	·58	17
15	We	28	5 6	·06 ·96	24	·52	18
16	Th	29	7	·87	25	·46	19
17	Fr	30	8	·79	26	·41	20

Naksh:—1. Asvu. 2. Bhar. 3. Krit. 4. Rohi. 5. Mrig. 6. Ardh. 7. Punar. 8. Push. 9. Aslesh. 10. Magh. 11. P. Phal. 12. U. Phal. 13. Hasta. 14. Chit.

A. D. 1899. | Kollam 1075, N. Malabar—Sept., S. Malabar—Aug. Commences | Hijra 1317, Commences, May 12. | Vikrama 1956. Bengal San 1305. (N. Cycle) Virodhakrit.

A.—Amavasya. P.—Paurnami.

July (SOLAR reckoning / LUNAR reckoning)

Cyclic Sidereal Year, Month and Day	Week-Day English Month and Day	Tithi Ending Moment	Nakshatra Ending Moment	Muhammadan Year, Month and Day
Vikari Mithuna—Ani. 18	Sa 1	Jy. Bahula 9 ·73	27 ·37	H. 1317 Safar. 21
19	Su 2	10 ·69	1 ·34	22
20	Mo 3	11 ·65	2 ·35	23
21	Tu 4	12 ·65	3 ·36	24
22	We 5	13 ·66	4 ·40	25
23	Th 6	14 ·70	5 ·45	26
24	Fr 7	A ·75	6 ·53	27
25	Sa 8	Ashadha Sukla 1 ·83	7 ·63	28
26	Su 9	2 ·91	8 ·73	29
27	Mo 10	3 ·99	9 ·84	H. 1317 Rabi-ul-awwal. 1
28	Tu 11	... ...	10 ·94	2
29	We 12	4 ·07	... ...	3
30	Th 13	5 ·14	11 ·04	4
31	Fr 14	6 ·20	12 ·13	5
Vikari Karkata—Adi. 1	Sa 15	7 ·23	13 ·20	6
2	Su 16	8 ·25	14 ·24	7
3	Mo 17	9 ·24	15 ·26	8
4	Tu 18	10 ·22	16 ·26	9
5	We 19	11 ·17	17 ·25	10
6	Th 20	12 ·10	18 ·23	11
7	Fr 21	13 ·04 14 ·95	19 ·18	12
8	Sa 22	P ·86	20 ·12	13
9	Su 23	Bahula 1 ·75	21 ·06 22 ·99	14
10	Mo 24	2 ·65	23 ·92	15
11	Tu 25	3 ·55	24 ·86	16
12	We 26	4 ·45	25 ·79	17
13	Th 27	5 ·37	26 ·74	18
14	Fr 28	6 ·27	27 ·70	19
15	Sa 29	7 ·21	1 ·68	20
16	Su 30	8 ·16	2 ·67	21
17	Mo 31	9 ·14	3 ·68	22

Aug.

Cyclic Sidereal Year, Month and Day	Week-Day English Month and Day	Tithi Ending Moment	Nakshatra Ending Moment	Muhammadan Year, Month and Day
18	Tu 1	10 ·13	4 ·71	23
19	We 2	11 ·15	5 ·76	24
20	Th 3	12 ·18	6 ·84	25
21	Fr 4	13 ·22	7 ·93	26
22	Sa 5	14 ·30	... ...	27
23	Su 6	A ·38	8 ·03	28
24	Mo 7	Sravana Sukla 1 ·47	9 ·14	29
25	Tu 8	2 ·54	10 ·24	30
26	We 9	3 ·62	11 ·35	H. 1317 Rabi-ul-akhir. 1
27	Th 10	4 ·67	12 ·44	2
28	Fr 11	5 ·71	13 ·50	3
29	Sa 12	6 ·74	14 ·55	4
30	Su 13	7 ·72	15 ·58	5
31	Mo 14	8 ·71	16 ·59	6
32	Tu 15	9 ·66	17 ·59	7
Vikari Simha—Avani. 1	We 16	10 ·61	18 ·56	8
2	Th 17	11 ·54	19 ·51	9
3	Fr 18	12 ·45	20 ·46	10
4	Sa 19	13 ·35	21 ·39	11
5	Su 20	14 ·24	22 ·33	12
6	Mo 21	P ·15	23 ·26	13
7	Tu 22	Bahula 1 ·04 2 ·95	24 ·19	14
8	We 23	3 ·86	25 ·13	15
9	Th 24	4 ·79	26 ·07	16
10	Fr 25	5 ·72	27 ·04	17
11	Sa 26	6 ·66	1 ·01 2 ·99	18
12	Su 27	7 ·65	... ...	19
13	Mo 28	8 ·63	3 ·00	20
14	Tu 29	9 ·64	4 ·02	21
15	We 30	10 ·68	5 ·08	22
16	Th 31	11 ·74	6 ·15	23

Sep.

Cyclic Sidereal Year, Month and Day	Week-Day English Month and Day	Tithi Ending Moment	Nakshatra Ending Moment	Muhammadan Year, Month and Day
Vikari Simha—Avani. 17	Fr 1	Sr. Bah. 12 ·80	7 ·23	24
18	Sa 2	13 ·88	8 ·33	25
19	Su 3	14 ·97	9 ·44	26
20	Mo 4	... ...	10 ·54	27
21	Tu 5	A ·05	11 ·65	28
22	We 6	Bhadrapada Sukla 1 ·13	12 ·74	29
23	Th 7	2 ·18	13 ·81	H. 1317 Jumadal-awwal. 1
24	Fr 8	3 ·23	14 ·87	2
25	Sa 9	4 ·25	15 ·90	3
26	Su 10	5 ·25	16 ·92	4
27	Mo 11	6 ·23	17 ·91	5
28	Tu 12	7 ·18	18 ·89	6
29	We 13	8 ·13	19 ·85	7
30	Th 14	9 ·06 10 ·98	20 ·79	8
31	Fr 15	11 ·88	21 ·74	9
Vikari Kanya—Purattasi. 1	Sa 16	12 ·78	22 ·67	10
2	Su 17	13 ·68	23 ·60	11
3	Mo 18	14 ·56	24 ·53	12
4	Tu 19	P ·48	25 ·47	13
5	We 20	Bahula 1 ·38	26 ·42	14
6	Th 21	2 ·32	27 ·37	15
7	Fr 22	3 ·25	1 ·33	16
8	Sa 23	4 ·20	2 ·32	17
9	Su 24	5 ·18	3 ·32	18
10	Mo 25	6 ·17	4 ·35	19
11	Tu 26	7 ·18	5 ·39	20
12	We 27	8 ·22	6 ·45	21
13	Th 28	9 ·28	7 ·53	22
14	Fr 29	10 ·34	8 ·63	23
15	Sa 30	11 ·43	9 ·73	24

Oct.

Cyclic Sidereal Year, Month and Day	Week-Day English Month and Day	Tithi Ending Moment	Nakshatra Ending Moment	Muhammadan Year, Month and Day
16	Su 1	12 ·51	10 ·85	25
17	Mo 2	13 ·60	11 ·95	26
18	Tu 3	14 ·67	... ...	27
19	We 4	A ·73	12 ·04	28
20	Th 5	Asvina Sukla 1 ·78	13 ·12	29
21	Fr 6	2 ·79	14 ·18	30
22	Sa 7	3 ·80	15 ·23	H. 1317 Jumadal-akhir. 1
23	Su 8	4 ·78	16 ·24	2
24	Mo 9	5 ·75	17 ·24	3
25	Tu 10	6 ·69	18 ·22	4
26	We 11	7 ·62	19 ·18	5
27	Th 12	8 ·53	20 ·14	6
28	Fr 13	9 ·44	21 ·08	7
29	Sa 14	10 ·34	22 ·01 23 ·94	8
30	Su 15	11 ·24	24 ·87	9
Vikari Tula—Aippasi. 1	Mo 16	12 ·14	25 ·81	10
2	Tu 17	13 ·04 14 ·95	26 ·75	11
3	We 18	P ·89	27 ·70	12
4	Th 19	Bahula 1 ·82	1 ·66	13
5	Fr 20	2 ·78	2 ·64	14
6	Sa 21	3 ·76	3 ·64	15
7	Su 22	4 ·76	4 ·66	16
8	Mo 23	5 ·76	5 ·70	17
9	Tu 24	6 ·81	6 ·76	18
10	We 25	7 ·86	7 ·84	19
11	Th 26	8 ·92	8 ·93	20
12	Fr 27	... ...	... ...	21
13	Sa 28	9 ·01	9 ·04	22
14	Su 29	10 ·10	10 ·15	23
15	Mo 30	11 ·20	11 ·25	24
16	Tu 31	12 ·27	12 ·35	25

Nov.

Cyclic Sidereal Year, Month and Day	Week-Day English Month and Day	Tithi Ending Moment	Nakshatra Ending Moment	Muhammadan Year, Month and Day
Vikari Tula—Aippasi. 17	We 1	Bah. 13 ·33	13 ·43	J. akhir. 26
18	Th 2	14 ·37	14 ·50	27
19	Fr 3	A ·39	15 ·54	28
20	Sa 4	Karttika Sukla 1 ·40	16 ·56	29
21	Su 5	2 ·38	17 ·56	H. 1317 Rajab. 1
22	Mo 6	3 ·34	18 ·55	2
23	Tu 7	4 ·28	19 ·52	3
24	We 8	5 ·21	20 ·47	4
25	Th 9	6 ·13	21 ·42	5
26	Fr 10	7 ·05 8 ·94	22 ·35	6
27	Sa 11	9 ·84	23 ·28	7
28	Su 12	10 ·74	24 ·22	8
29	Mo 13	11 ·64	25 ·15	9
30	Tu 14	12 ·57	26 ·09	10
Vikari Vrischika—Kartigai. 1	We 15	13 ·50	27 ·03 1 ·99	11
2	Th 16	14 ·43	2 ·97	12
3	Fr 17	P ·38	3 ·97	13
4	Sa 18	Bahula 1 ·37	4 ·98	14
5	Su 19	2 ·37	... ...	15
6	Mo 20	3 ·37	5 ·01	16
7	Tu 21	4 ·42	6 ·07	17
8	We 22	5 ·48	7 ·14	18
9	Th 23	6 ·56	8 ·24	19
10	Fr 24	7 ·64	9 ·34	20
11	Sa 25	8 ·72	10 ·44	21
12	Su 26	9 ·82	11 ·55	22
13	Mo 27	10 ·89	12 ·65	23
14	Tu 28	11 ·95	13 ·74	24
15	We 29	... ...	14 ·81	25
16	Th 30	12 ·00	15 ·86	26

Dec.

Cyclic Sidereal Year, Month and Day	Week-Day English Month and Day	Tithi Ending Moment	Nakshatra Ending Moment	Muhammadan Year, Month and Day
17	Fr 1	13 ·03	16 ·88	27
18	Sa 2	14 ·02	17 ·89	28
19	Su 3	A ·01 1 ·96	18 ·88	29
20	Mo 4	Margasira Sukla 2 ·90	19 ·85	30
21	Tu 5	3 ·83	20 ·81	H. 1317 Shaban. 1
22	We 6	4 ·75	21 ·75	2
23	Th 7	5 ·66	22 ·69	3
24	Fr 8	6 ·57	23 ·62	4
25	Sa 9	7 ·47	24 ·56	5
26	Su 10	8 ·36	25 ·49	6
27	Mo 11	9 ·27	26 ·42	7
28	Tu 12	10 ·19	27 ·37	8
29	We 13	11 ·12	1 ·32	9
30	Th 14	12 ·07	2 ·30	10
Vikari Dhanus—Margali. 1	Fr 15	13 ·02	3 ·29	11
2	Sa 16	14 ·01	4 ·30	12
3	Su ○ 17	P ·01	5 ·33	13
4	Mo 18	Bahula 1 ·02	6 ·37	14
5	Tu 19	2 ·07	7 ·45	15
6	We 20	3 ·12	8 ·54	16
7	Th 21	4 ·21	9 ·64	17
8	Fr 22	5 ·29	10 ·74	18
9	Sa 23	6 ·38	11 ·85	19
10	Su 24	7 ·47	12 ·96	20
11	Mo 25	8 ·55	... ...	21
12	Tu 26	9 ·60	13 ·05	22
13	We 27	10 ·65	14 ·12	23
14	Th 28	11 ·67	15 ·17	24
15	Fr 29	12 ·66	16 ·20	25
16	Sa 30	13 ·65	17 ·22	26
17	Su 31	14 ·61	18 ·21	27

15. Svati. 16. Visak. 17. Anur. 18. Jyesh. 19. Mula. 20. P. Ash. 21. U. Ash. 22. Sravn. 23. Dani. 24 Satab. 25. P. Bhad. 26. U. Bhad. 27. Rev.

A. D. 1900. **Mesha Sankranti** (Commencement of Indian Sidereal Year).
Solar Eclipse. ● (Surya Sid.) April 12·62. Saka 1822. Kaliyuga 5001.
Lunar Eclipse. ○ (Arya Sid.) April 12·51. (S. Cycle) Sarvari.

Cyclic Sidereal Year, Month and Day (SOLAR reckoning)	Week-Day English Month and Day (SOLAR reckoning)	Tithi Ending Moment (LUNAR reckoning)	Nakshatra Ending Moment (LUNAR reckoning)	Muhammadan Year, Month and Day
	Jan.			
[Vikari Dhanus—Margali] 18	Mo 1	—A ·55	19 ·18	28
19	Tu 2	[Sukla] 1 ·47	20 ·14	—29
20	We 3	2 ·39	21 ·09	[H. 1317 Ramzan] 1
21	Th 4	3 ·30	22 ·02 / 23 ·97	2
22	Fr 5	4 ·20	24 ·90	3
25	Sa 6	5 ·12	25 ·82	4
24	Su 7	6 ·01 / 7 ·92	26 ·76	5
25	Mo 8	8 ·84	27 ·70	6
26	Tu 9	9 ·76	1 ·66	7
27	We 10	10 ·71	2 ·63	8
28	Th 11	11 ·67	3 ·62	9
—29	Fr 12	12 ·66	4 ·62	10
[Vikari Makara—Tai] 1	Sa 13	[Pausha] 13 ·65	5 ·64	11
2	Su 14	14 ·67	6 ·69	12
3	Mo 15	P ·71	7 ·76	13
4	Tu 16	[Bahula] 1 ·78	8 ·84	14
5	We 17	2 ·86	9 ·94	15
6	Th 18	3 ·94	... ...	16
7	Fr 19	... ...	10 ·04	17
8	Sa 20	4 ·04	11 ·16	18
9	Su 21	5 ·12	12 ·26	19
10	Mo 22	6 ·20	13 ·35	20
11	Tu 23	7 ·24	14 ·43	21
12	We 24	8 ·30	15 ·48	22
13	Th 25	9 ·31	16 ·52	23
14	Fr 26	10 ·30	17 ·54	24
15	Sa 27	11 ·29	18 ·54	25
16	Su 28	12 ·25	19 ·51	26
17	Mo 29	13 ·19	20 ·47	27
18	Tu 30	14 ·10	21 ·42	28
19	We 31	A ·03 / 1 ·93	22 ·37	29
	Feb.			
20	Th 1	[Sukla] 2 ·84	23 ·30	—30
21	Fr 2	3 ·73	24 ·23	[H. 1317 Shawwal] 1
22	Sa 3	4 ·64	25 ·16	2
23	Su 4	5 ·55	26 ·10	3
24	Mo 5	6 ·46	27 ·05	4
25	Tu 6	7 ·39	1 ·00 / 2 ·96	5
26	We 7	8 ·35	3 ·94	6
27	Th 8	9 ·31	4 ·94	7
28	Fr 9	10 ·29	5 ·97	8
—29	Sa 10	11 ·28	... ...	9
[Vikari Kumbha—Masi] 1	Su 11	[Magha] 12 ·32	6 ·00	10
2	Mo 12	13 ·36	7 ·06	11
3	Tu 13	14 ·42	8 ·14	12
4	We 14	P ·49	9 ·23	13
5	Th 15	[Bahula] 1 ·58	10 ·34	14
6	Fr 16	2 ·67	11 ·45	15
7	Sa 17	3 ·75	12 ·56	16
8	Su 18	4 ·83	13 ·65	17
9	Mo 19	5 ·88	14 ·73	18
10	Tu 20	6 ·93	15 ·79	19
11	We 21	7 ·93	16 ·84	20
12	Th 22	8 ·94	17 ·86	21
13	Fr 23	9 ·91	18 ·86	22
14	Sa 24	10 ·87	19 ·84	23
15	Su 25	11 ·80	20 ·81	24
16	Mo 26	12 ·72	21 ·77	25
17	Tu 27	13 ·64	22 ·71	26
18	We 28	14 ·55	23 ·64	27

Cyclic Sidereal Year, Month and Day (SOLAR reckoning)	Week-Day English Month and Day (SOLAR reckoning)	Tithi Ending Moment (LUNAR reckoning)	Nakshatra Ending Moment (LUNAR reckoning)	Muhammadan Year, Month and Day
	March			
[Vikari Kumbha—Masi] 19	Th 1	—A ·46	24 ·57	28
20	Fr 2	[Sukla] 1 ·35	25 ·50	—29
21	Sa 3	2 ·26	26 ·44	[H. 1317 Zi-l-ka'da] 1
22	Su 4	3 ·16	27 ·38	2
23	Mo 5	4 ·07	1 ·33	3
24	Tu 6	5 ·00 / 6 ·95	2 ·29	4
25	We 7	7 ·92	3 ·27	5
26	Th 8	8 ·90	4 ·27	6
27	Fr 9	9 ·90	5 ·28	7
28	Sa 10	10 ·93	6 ·32	8
29	Su 11	11 ·96	7 ·37	9
—30	Mo 12	... ...	8 ·44	10
[Vikari Mina—Panguni] 1	Tu 13	[Phalguna] 12 ·03	9 ·53	11
2	We 14	13 ·10	10 ·65	12
3	Th 15	14 ·19	11 ·75	13
4	Fr 16	P ·28	12 ·86	14
5	Sa 17	[Bahula] 1 ·36	13 ·95	15
6	Su 18	2 ·42	... ...	16
7	Mo 19	3 ·48	14 ·04	17
8	Tu 20	4 ·53	15 ·11	18
9	We 21	5 ·53	16 ·16	19
10	Th 22	6 ·53	17 ·18	20
11	Fr 23	7 ·49	18 ·19	21
12	Sa 24	8 ·46	19 ·17	22
13	Su 25	9 ·39	20 ·15	23
14	Mo 26	10 ·32	21 ·10	24
15	Tu 27	11 ·23	22 ·05 / 23 ·98	25
16	We 28	12 ·13	24 ·91	26
17	Th 29	13 ·03 / 14 ·92	25 ·85	27
18	Fr 30	—A ·84	26 ·78	28
19	Sa 31	1 ·74	27 ·72	29
	April			
20	Su 1	[Sukla] 2 ·66	1 ·66	—30
21	Mo 2	3 ·58	2 ·62	[H. 1317 Zi-l-hijja] 1
22	Tu 3	4 ·52	3 ·59	2
23	We 4	5 ·49	4 ·59	3
24	Th 5	6 ·47	5 ·60	4
25	Fr 6	7 ·47	6 ·63	5
26	Sa 7	8 ·50	7 ·68	6
27	Su 8	9 ·54	8 ·75	7
28	Mo 9	10 ·59	9 ·85	8
29	Tu 10	11 ·68	10 ·96	9
30	We 11	12 ·75	... ...	10
—31	Th 12	13 ·84	11 ·05	11
[Sarvari Mesha—Chittirai] 1	Fr 13	[Chaitra] 14 ·92	12 ·16	12
2	Sa 14	P ·98	13 ·26	13
3	Su 15	[Bahula]	14 ·35	14
4	Mo 16	1 ·04	15 ·42	45
5	Tu 17	2 ·08	16 ·47	16
6	We 18	3 ·09	17 ·50	17
7	Th 19	4 ·08	18 ·51	18
8	Fr 20	5 ·04	19 ·51	19
9	Sa 21	6 ·01 / 7 ·93	20 ·48	20
10	Su 22	8 ·86	21 ·44	21
11	Mo 23	9 ·77	22 ·38	22
12	Tu 24	10 ·68	23 ·32	23
13	We 25	11 ·58	24 ·26	24
14	Th 26	12 ·48	25 ·19	25
15	Fr 27	13 ·38	26 ·13	26
16	Sa 28	14 ·28	27 ·05	27
17	Su 29	—A ·19	1 ·00 / 2 ·95	28
18	Mo 30	1 ·11	3 ·93	—29

Cyclic Sidereal Year, Month and Day (SOLAR reckoning)	Week-Day English Month and Day (SOLAR reckoning)	Tithi Ending Moment (LUNAR reckoning)	Nakshatra Ending Moment (LUNAR reckoning)	Muhammadan Year, Month and Day
	May			
[Sarvari Mesha—Chittirai] 19	Tu 1	[Sukla] 2 ·07	4 ·91	[H. 1318 Muharram] 1
20	We 2	3 ·92	5 ·92	2
21	Th 3	4 ·01	6 ·94	3
22	Fr 4	5 ·00	7 ·99	4
23	Sa 5	6 ·02	... ...	5
24	Su 6	7 ·06	8 ·06	6
25	Mo 7	8 ·12	9 ·15	7
26	Tu 8	9 ·20	10 ·24	8
27	We 9	10 ·28	11 ·35	9
28	Th 10	11 ·36	12 ·45	10
29	Fr 11	[Vaisakha] 12 ·43	13 ·57	11
—30	Sa 12	13 ·50	14 ·66	12
[Sarvari Vrishabha—Vaikasi] 1	Su 13	14 ·57	15 ·73	13
2	Mo 14	P ·60	16 ·78	14
3	Tu 15	[Bahula] 1 ·60	17 ·82	15
4	We 16	2 ·59	18 ·84	16
5	Th 17	3 ·57	19 ·83	17
6	Fr 18	4 ·53	20 ·81	18
7	Sa 19	5 ·46	21 ·77	19
8	Su 20	6 ·37	22 ·72	20
9	Mo 21	7 ·28	23 ·66	21
10	Tu 22	8 ·19	24 ·60	22
11	We 23	9 ·09 / 10 ·99	25 ·53	23
12	Th 24	11 ·88	26 ·46	24
13	Fr 25	12 ·79	27 ·39	25
14	Sa 26	13 ·70	1 ·33	26
15	Su 27	14 ·63	2 ·29	27
16	Mo 28	—A ·57	3 ·26	28
17	Tu 29	1 ·52	4 ·24	29
18	We 30	2 ·51	5 ·24	—30
19	Th 31	3 ·49	6 ·26	[H. 1318 Safar] 1
	June			
20	Fr 1	[Sukla] 4 ·52	7 ·31	2
21	Sa 2	5 ·56	8 ·37	3
22	Su 3	6 ·62	9 ·45	4
23	Mo 4	7 ·69	10 ·54	5
24	Tu 5	8 ·77	11 ·65	6
25	We 6	9 ·86	12 ·76	7
26	Th 7	10 ·94	13 ·87	8
27	Fr 8	11 ·99	14 ·96	9
28	Sa 9	[Jyeshtha]	... ...	10
29	Su 10	12 ·05	15 ·04	11
30	Mo 11	13 ·09	16 ·10	12
31	Tu 12	14 ·09	17 ·14	13
—32	We ○ 13	P ·08	18 ·16	14
[Sarvari Mithuna—Ani] 1	Th 14	[Bahula] 1 ·06	19 ·16	15
2	Fr 15	2 ·01 / 3 ·95	20 ·14	16
3	Sa 16	4 ·87	21 ·10	17
4	Su 17	5 ·79	22 ·05	18
5	Mo 18	6 ·68	23 ·00 / 24 ·94	19
6	Tu 19	7 ·58	25 ·87	20
7	We 20	8 ·48	26 ·79	21
8	Th 21	9 ·37	27 ·73	22
9	Fr 22	10 ·28	1 ·68	23
10	Sa 23	11 ·19	2 ·62	24
11	Su 24	12 ·11	3 ·59	25
12	Mo 25	13 ·05	4 ·56	26
13	Tu 26	14 ·00 / A ·98	5 ·56	27
14	We 27	[A. Suk.] 1 ·97	6 ·58	28
15	Th 28	... ...	7 ·62	—29
16	Fr 29	2 ·00	8 ·68	1
17	Sa 30	3 ·03	9 ·75	2

Naksh :—1. Asvn. 2. Bhar. 3. Krit. 4. Rohi. 5. Mrig. 6. Ardh. 7. Punar. 8. Push. 9. Aslesh. 10. Magh. 11. P. Phal. 12. U. Phal. 13. Hasta. 14. Chit.

A. D. 1900. **A.—Amavasya.** **P.—Paurnami.**

Kollam 1076, Commences { **N. Malabar—Sept.** / **S. Malabar—Aug.**

Hijra 1318, Commences, **May 1.**

Vikrama 1957. **Bengal San 1306.** **(N. Cycle) Paridhavin.**

Cyclic Sidereal Year, Month and Day. (SOLAR reckoning)	Week-Day English Month and Day.	Tithi Ending Moment. (LUNAR reckoning)	Nakshatra Ending Moment.	Muhammadan Year, Month and Day.
	July			
Sarvari Mithuna—Adi. 18	Su 1	4 ·09	10 ·84	3
19	Mo 2	5 ·16	11 ·95	4
20	Tu 3	Sukla 6 ·25	... ...	5
21	We 4	7 ·32	12 ·06	6
22	Th 5	8 ·40	13 ·17	7
23	Fr 6	9 ·47	14 ·26	8
24	Sa 7	10 ·52	15 ·34	9
25	Su 8	11 ·56	16 ·41	10
26	Mo 9	12 ·57	17 ·46	11
27	Tu 10	Ashadha 13 ·56	18 ·48	12
28	We 11	14 ·53	19 ·48	H. 1318 Rabi-ul-awwal. 13
29	Th 12	P ·49	20 ·47	14
30	Fr 13	1 ·43	21 ·44	15
31	Sa 14	2 ·34	22 ·40	16
1	Su 15	3 ·26	23 ·34	17
2	Mo 16	4 ·16	24 ·27	18
3	Tu 17	{ 5 ·07 / 6 ·95	25 ·20	19
4	We 18	7 ·85	26 ·13	20
5	Th 19	Bahula 8 ·76	27 ·07	21
6	Fr 20	9 ·66	1 ·01 / 2 ·96 }	22
7	Sa 21	10 ·59	3 ·92	23
8	Su 22	11 ·53	4 ·89	24
9	Mo 23	12 ·49	5 ·89	25
10	Tu 24	13 ·46	6 ·90	26
Sarvari Karkata—Adi. 11	We 25	14 ·46	7 ·93	27
12	Th 26	—A ·48	8 ·98	28
13	Fr 27	1 ·50	... ...	29
14	Sa 28	2 ·56	9 ·05	—30
15	Su 29	3 ·63	10 ·15	1
16	Mo 30	4 ·72	11 ·25	2
17	Tu 31	5 ·79	12 ·36	3
	Aug.			
18	We 1	6 ·88	13 ·46	4
19	Th 2	Sukla 7 ·94	14 ·56	5
20	Fr 3	... ...	15 ·65	6
21	Sa 4	8 ·00	16 ·73	7
22	Su 5	9 ·04	17 ·77	8
23	Mo 6	10 ·05	18 ·80	9
24	Tu 7	11 ·05	19 ·81	10
25	We 8	{ 12 ·02 / 13 ·98	20 ·80	11
26	Th 9	14 ·92	21 ·78	12
27	Fr 10	P ·85	22 ·73	13
28	Sa 11	Sravana 1 ·76	23 ·68	14
29	Su 12	2 ·66	24 ·61	15
30	Mo 13	3 ·56	25 ·54	16
31	Tu 14	4 ·45	26 ·48	H. 1318 Rabi-ul-akhir. 17
—32	We 15	5 ·36	27 ·41	18
1	Th 16	6 ·26	1 ·35	19
2	Fr 17	7 ·18	2 ·29	20
3	Sa 18	8 ·09	3 ·25	21
4	Su 19	{ 9 ·03 / 10 ·98	4 ·23	22
5	Mo 20	11 ·96	5 ·21	23
6	Tu 21	Bahula 12 ·96	6 ·22	24
7	We 22	13 ·96	7 ·24	25
Sarvari Simha—Avani. 8	Th 23	... ...	8 ·29	26
9	Fr 24	14 ·00	9 ·36	27
10	Sa 25	—A ·06	10 ·45	28
11	Su 26	Bhad. Suk. 1 ·13	11 ·55	—29
12	Mo 27	2 ·22	12 ·66	J. awwal. 1
13	Tu 28	3 ·29	13 ·76	2
14	We 29	4 ·38	14 ·86	3
15	Th 30	5 ·45	15 ·96	4
16	Fr 31	6 ·51	... ...	5

Cyclic Sidereal Year, Month and Day. (SOLAR reckoning)	Week-Day English Month and Day.	Tithi Ending Moment. (LUNAR reckoning)	Nakshatra Ending Moment.	Muhammadan Year, Month and Day.
	Sep.			
17	Sa 1	7 ·54	16 ·03	6
18	Su 2	8 ·57	17 ·09	7
19	Mo 3	9 ·56	18 ·12	8
20	Tu 4	Sukla 10 ·53	19 ·13	9
21	We 5	11 ·50	20 ·13	10
Sarvari Simha—Avani. 22	Th 6	12 ·43	21 ·11	11
23	Fr 7	13 ·36	22 ·07	12
24	Sa 8	14 ·27	23 ·01 / 24 ·95 }	13
25	Su 9	P ·18	25 ·89	14
26	Mo 10	{ 1 ·07 / 2 ·97	26 ·82	15
27	Tu 11	3 ·88	27 ·75	16
28	We 12	4 ·78	1 ·68	17
29	Th 13	5 ·70	2 ·63	H. 1318 Jumadal-awwal. 18
30	Fr 14	Bhadrapada 6 ·62	3 ·58	19
—31	Sa 15	7 ·57	4 ·55	20
1	Su 16	8 ·51	5 ·54	21
2	Mo 17	9 ·48	6 ·54	22
3	Tu 18	10 ·48	7 ·56	23
4	We 19	11 ·49	8 ·60	24
5	Th 20	Bahula 12 ·53	9 ·67	25
6	Fr 21	13 ·58	10 ·75	26
7	Sa 22	14 ·66	11 ·85	27
8	Su 23	—A ·74	12 ·95	28
9	Mo 24	1 ·83	... ...	29
Sarvari Kanya—Purattasi. 10	Tu 25	2 ·91	13 ·06	—30
11	We 26	3 ·99	14 ·17	1
12	Th 27	... ...	15 ·26	2
13	Fr 28	4 ·05	16 ·33	3
14	Sa 29	Sukla 5 ·08	17 ·40	4
15	Su 30	6 ·10	18 ·44	5
	Oct.			
16	Mo 1	7 ·10	19 ·46	6
17	Tu 2	8 ·08	20 ·46	7
18	We 3	{ 9 ·05 / 10 ·98	21 ·44	8
19	Th 4	11 ·91	22 ·40	9
20	Fr 5	12 ·82	23 ·35	10
21	Sa 6	13 ·73	24 ·30	11
22	Su 7	14 ·63	25 ·23	12
23	Mo 8	P ·54	26 ·16	13
24	Tu 9	Asvina 1 ·44	27 ·09	14
25	We 10	2 ·34	1 ·02 / 2 ·96 }	15
26	Th 11	3 ·26	3 ·92	16
27	Fr 12	4 ·18	4 ·88	H. 1318 Jumadal-akhir. 17
28	Sa 13	5 ·13	5 ·86	18
29	Su 14	6 ·07	6 ·86	19
—30	Mo 15	7 ·06	7 ·87	20
1	Tu 16	8 ·05	8 ·92	21
2	We 17	Bahula 9 ·07	9 ·98	22
3	Th 18	10 ·11	... ...	23
4	Fr 19	11 ·16	10 ·06	24
5	Sa 20	12 ·23	11 ·15	25
6	Su 21	13 ·32	12 ·26	26
Sarvari Tula—Aippasi. 7	Mo 22	14 ·41	13 ·37	27
8	Tu 23	—A ·50	14 ·47	28
9	We 24	1 ·58	15 ·57	—29
10	Th 25	Kartika Sukla 2 ·63	16 ·65	1
11	Fr 26	3 ·66	17 ·71	H. 1318 Rajab. 2
12	Sa 27	4 ·69	18 ·76	3
13	Su 28	5 ·68	19 ·78	4
14	Mo 29	6 ·67	20 ·78	5
15	Tu 30	7 ·63	21 ·77	6
16	We 31	8 ·58	22 ·73	7

Cyclic Sidereal Year, Month and Day. (SOLAR reckoning)	Week-Day English Month and Day.	Tithi Ending Moment. (LUNAR reckoning)	Nakshatra Ending Moment.	Muhammadan Year, Month and Day.
	Nov.			
17	Th 1	9 ·50	23 ·68	8
18	Fr 2	Sukla 10 ·42	24 ·63	9
19	Sa 3	11 ·32	25 ·57	10
20	Su 4	12 ·22	26 ·50	11
21	Mo 5	13 ·13	27 ·43	12
22	Tu 6	{ 14 ·02 / P ·94	1 ·36	13
23	We 7	1 ·85	2 ·31	14
Sarvari Tula—Aippasi. 24	Th 8	Kartika 2 ·79	3 ·25	15
25	Fr 9	3 ·73	4 ·21	H. 1318 Rajab. 16
26	Sa 10	4 ·67	5 ·19	17
27	Su 11	5 ·66	6 ·18	18
28	Mo 12	6 ·65	7 ·20	19
29	Tu 13	7 ·68	8 ·23	20
—30	We 14	8 ·72	9 ·29	21
1	Th 15	Bahula 9 ·78	10 ·36	22
2	Fr 16	10 ·85	11 ·45	23
3	Sa 17	11 ·94	12 ·56	24
4	Su 18	... ...	13 ·67	25
5	Mo 19	12 ·03	14 ·77	26
6	Tu 20	13 ·11	15 ·87	27
7	We 21	14 ·19	16 ·95	28
8	Th 22	—A ·25	... ...	29
9	Fr 23	1 ·30	17 ·03	—30
10	Sa 24	2 ·31	18 ·08	1
Sarvari Vrischika—Kartigai. 11	Su 25	3 ·31	19 ·10	2
12	Mo 26	4 ·28	20 ·11	3
13	Tu 27	5 ·24	21 ·09	4
14	We 28	6 ·19	22 ·06	5
15	Th 29	Sukla 7 ·12	23 ·03 / 24 ·97 }	6
16	Fr 30	{ 8 ·04 / 9 ·95	25 ·91	7
	Dec.			
17	Sa 1	10 ·85	26 ·84	8
18	Su 2	11 ·75	27 ·77	H. 1318 Shaban. 9
19	Mo 3	12 ·64	1 ·71	10
20	Tu 4	13 ·57	2 ·64	11
21	We 5	14 ·47	3 ·59	12
22	Th 6	Margasira P ·40	4 ·54	13
23	Fr 7	1 ·35	5 ·51	14
24	Sa 8	2 ·31	6 ·51	15
25	Su 9	3 ·29	7 ·52	16
26	Mo 10	4 ·28	8 ·55	17
27	Tu 11	5 ·32	9 ·60	18
28	We 12	6 ·36	10 ·66	19
29	Th 13	7 ·42	11 ·76	20
—30	Fr 14	Bahula 8 ·50	12 ·86	21
1	Sa 15	9 ·59	13 ·96	22
2	Su 16	10 ·67	... ...	23
3	Mo 17	11 ·77	14 ·07	24
4	Tu 18	12 ·84	15 ·17	25
5	We 19	13 ·89	16 ·26	26
6	Th 20	14 ·93	17 ·34	27
7	Fr 21	—A ·95	18 ·39	28
8	Sa 22	1 ·95	19 ·42	—29
Sarvari Dhanus—Margali. 9	Su 23	2 ·92	20 ·43	1
10	Mo 24	Sukla 3 ·89	21 ·42	2
11	Tu 25	4 ·83	22 ·40	H. 1318 Ramzan. 3
12	We 26	5 ·75	23 ·36	4
13	Th 27	6 ·68	24 ·31	5
14	Fr 28	7 ·58	25 ·24	6
15	Sa 29	Pausha 8 ·48	26 ·18	7
16	Su 30	9 ·39	27 ·11	8
17	Mo 31	10 ·29	1 ·04 / 2 ·98 }	9

15. Svati. 16. Visak. 17. Anur. 18. Jyesh. 19. Mula. 20. P. Ash. 21. U. Ash. 22. Sravn. 23. Dani. 24. Satab. 25. P. Bhad. 26. U. Bhad. 27. Rev.

A. D. 1901. **Mesha Sankranti** (Commencement of Indian Sidereal Year).

Solar Eclipse. ● (Surya Sid.) April 12·88. Saka 1823. Kaliyuga 5002.

Lunar Eclipse. ○ (Arya Sid.) April 12·77. (S. Cycle) Plava.

Columns: SOLAR reckoning — Cyclic Sidereal Year, Month and Day; Week-Day, English Month and Day. LUNAR reckoning — Tithi Ending Moment; Nakshatra Ending Moment; Muhammadan Year, Month and Day.

Jan.

Cyclic Sidereal Year, Month and Day	Week-Day, English Month and Day	Tithi Ending Moment	Nakshatra Ending Moment	Muhammadan Year, Month and Day
Sarvari Dhanus—Margali 18	Tu 1	Suk. 11 ·20	3 ·92	H. 1318 Ramzan 10
19	We 2	12 ·11	4 ·87	11
20	Th 3	13 ·05 / 14 ·99	5 ·85	12
21	Fr 4	Pausha P ·95	6 ·84	13
22	Sa 5	1 ·94	7 ·84	14
23	Su 6	2 ·94	8 ·86	15
24	Mo 7	3 ·96	9 ·90	16
25	Tu 8	... ...	10 ·98	17
26	We 9	4 ·02	... ...	18
27	Th 10	5 ·07	11 ·06	19
28	Fr 11	6 ·14	12 ·16	20
29	Sa 12	Bahula 7 ·25	13 ·26	21
Sarvari Makara—Tai 1	Su 13	8 ·32	14 ·37	22
2	Mo 14	9 ·41	15 ·47	23
3	Tu 15	10 ·48	16 ·57	24
4	We 16	11 ·55	17 ·65	25
5	Th 17	12 ·58	18 ·70	26
6	Fr 18	13 ·59	19 ·74	27
7	Sa 19	14 ·60	20 ·75	28
8	Su 20	A ·57	21 ·76	29
9	Mo 21	1 ·53	22 ·73	30
10	Tu 22	2 ·47	23 ·69	1
11	We 23	3 ·40	24 ·64	2
12	Th 24	4 ·31	25 ·58	3
13	Fr 25	5 ·22	26 ·52	4
14	Sa 26	6 ·12	27 ·45	5
15	Su 27	7 ·02 / 8 ·92	1 ·38	6
16	Mo 28	9 ·83	2 ·32	7
17	Tu 29	Sukla 10 ·75	3 ·26	8
18	We 30	11 ·69	4 ·22	9
19	Th 31	12 ·64	5 ·18	10

Feb.

Cyclic Sidereal Year, Month and Day	Week-Day, English Month and Day	Tithi Ending Moment	Nakshatra Ending Moment	Muhammadan Year, Month and Day
20	Fr 1	Magha 13 ·59	6 ·16	H. 1318 Shawwal 11
21	Sa 2	14 ·57	7 ·16	12
22	Su 3	P ·58	8 ·18	13
23	Mo 4	1 ·61	9 ·21	14
24	Tu 5	2 ·66	10 ·28	15
25	We 6	3 ·71	11 ·36	16
26	Th 7	4 ·80	12 ·46	17
27	Fr 8	5 ·88	13 ·56	18
28	Sa 9	6 ·96	14 ·67	19
29	Su 10	... ...	15 ·78	20
30	Mo 11	Bahula 7 ·05	16 ·87	21
Sarvari Kumbha—Masi 1	Tu 12	8 ·12	17 ·95	22
2	We 13	9 ·19	... ...	23
3	Th 14	10 ·22	18 ·01	24
4	Fr 15	11 ·23	19 ·05	25
5	Sa 16	12 ·22	20 ·08	26
6	Su 17	13 ·21	21 ·08	27
7	Mo 18	14 ·15	22 ·06	28
8	Tu 19	A ·09	23 ·03 / 24 ·98	29
9	We 20	1 ·02 / 2 ·92	25 ·93	H. 1318 Zi-l-Ka'da 1
10	Th 21	3 ·84	26 ·86	2
11	Fr 22	Sukla 4 ·74	27 ·79	3
12	Sa 23	5 ·65	1 ·72	4
13	Su 24	6 ·54	2 ·65	5
14	Mo 25	7 ·44	3 ·60	6
15	Tu 26	8 ·37	4 ·55	7
16	We 27	9 ·29	5 ·51	8
17	Th 28	Phalg. 10 ·25	6 ·48	9

March

Cyclic Sidereal Year, Month and Day	Week-Day, English Month and Day	Tithi Ending Moment	Nakshatra Ending Moment	Muhammadan Year, Month and Day
Sarvari Kumbha—Masi 18	Fr 1	Sukla 11 ·21	7 ·48	H. 1318 Zi-l-Ka'da 10
19	Sa 2	12 ·20	8 ·49	11
20	Su 3	13 ·19	9 ·54	12
21	Mo 4	14 ·22	10 ·59	13
22	Tu 5	Phalguna P ·27	11 ·67	14
23	We 6	1 ·32	12 ·76	15
24	Th 7	2 ·42	13 ·86	16
25	Fr 8	3 ·50	14 ·97	17
26	Sa 9	4 ·60	... ...	18
27	Su 10	5 ·67	15 ·08	19
28	Mo 11	6 ·74	16 ·18	20
29	Tu 12	7 ·79	17 ·26	21
Sarvari Mina—Panguni 1	We 13	Bahula 8 ·82	18 ·32	22
2	Th 14	9 ·83	19 ·38	23
3	Fr 15	10 ·82	20 ·40	24
4	Sa 16	11 ·79	21 ·41	25
5	Su 17	12 ·74	22 ·39	26
6	Mo 18	13 ·69	23 ·36	27
7	Tu 19	14 ·63	24 ·32	28
8	We 20	A ·52	25 ·27	29
9	Th 21	1 ·43	26 ·20	30
10	Fr 22	2 ·32	27 ·13	1
11	Sa 23	3 ·23	1 ·06 / 2 ·99	2
12	Su 24	4 ·13	3 ·94	3
13	Mo 25	5 ·04 / 6 ·96	4 ·88	4
14	Tu 26	7 ·88	5 ·84	5
15	We 27	Sukla 8 ·83	6 ·81	6
16	Th 28	9 ·79	7 ·80	7
17	Fr 29	10 ·78	8 ·82	8
18	Sa 30	11 ·77	9 ·85	9
19	Su 31	12 ·81	10 ·90	10

April

Cyclic Sidereal Year, Month and Day	Week-Day, English Month and Day	Tithi Ending Moment	Nakshatra Ending Moment	Muhammadan Year, Month and Day
20	Mo 1	Chaitra 13 ·85	11 ·97	H. 1318 Zi-l-hijja 11
21	Tu 2	14 ·91	... ...	12
22	We 3	P ·99	12 ·06	13
23	Th 4	... ...	13 ·17	14
24	Fr 5	1 ·07	14 ·27	15
25	Sa 6	2 ·17	15 ·38	16
26	Su 7	3 ·24	16 ·48	17
27	Mo 8	4 ·31	17 ·56	18
28	Tu 9	5 ·36	18 ·64	19
29	We 10	6 ·39	19 ·69	20
30	Th 11	Bahula 7 ·39	20 ·72	21
31	Fr 12	8 ·38	21 ·73	22
Plava Mesha—Chittirai 1	Sa 13	9 ·35	22 ·72	23
2	Su 14	10 ·30	23 ·69	24
3	Mo 15	11 ·25	24 ·66	25
4	Tu 16	12 ·17	25 ·60	26
5	We 17	13 ·08 / 14 ·98	26 ·54	27
6	Th 18	A ·89	27 ·47	28
7	Fr 19	1 ·78	1 ·40	29
8	Sa 20	2 ·68	2 ·34	H. 1319 Muharram 1
9	Su 21	Sukla 3 ·58	3 ·27	2
10	Mo 22	4 ·50	4 ·22	3
11	Tu 23	5 ·43	5 ·17	4
12	We 24	6 ·37	6 ·14	5
13	Th 25	7 ·34	7 ·13	6
14	Fr 26	8 ·32	8 ·14	7
15	Sa 27	9 ·31	9 ·16	8
16	Su 28	Vaisakha 10 ·35	10 ·21	9
17	Mo 29	11 ·38	11 ·27	10
18	Tu 30	12 ·44	12 ·37	11

May

Cyclic Sidereal Year, Month and Day	Week-Day, English Month and Day	Tithi Ending Moment	Nakshatra Ending Moment	Muhammadan Year, Month and Day
19	We 1	Suk. 13 ·52	13 ·46	12
20	Th 2	14 ·62	14 ·57	13
21	Fr 3	Vaisakha P ·70	15 ·68	14
22	Sa 4	1 ·76	16 ·78	15
23	Su 5	2 ·83	17 ·88	16
24	Mo 6	3 ·88	18 ·95	17
25	Tu 7	4 ·92	... ...	18
26	We 8	5 ·92	19 ·00	H. 1319 Muharram 19
27	Th 9	6 ·92	20 ·04	20
28	Fr 10	7 ·88	21 ·05	21
29	Sa 11	8 ·83	22 ·04	22
30	Su 12	Bahula 9 ·77	23 ·03 / 24 ·99	23
31	Mo 13	10 ·68	25 ·94	H. 1319 24
Plava Vrishabha—Vaikasi 1	Tu 14	11 ·60	26 ·88	25
2	We 15	12 ·49	27 ·81	26
3	Th 16	13 ·40	1 ·75	27
4	Fr 17	14 ·29	2 ·68	28
5	Sa ● 18	A ·20	3 ·61	29
6	Su 19	1 ·10	4 ·55	30
7	Mo 20	2 ·00 / 3 ·94	5 ·50	1
8	Tu 21	4 ·89	6 ·48	2
9	We 22	5 ·85	7 ·46	3
10	Th 23	6 ·82	8 ·46	4
11	Fr 24	Sukla 7 ·82	9 ·48	5
12	Sa 25	8 ·84	10 ·52	6
13	Su 26	9 ·89	11 ·59	7
14	Mo 27	10 ·95	12 ·67	8
15	Tu 28	... ...	13 ·76	9
16	We 29	11 ·02	14 ·87	10
17	Th 30	12 ·10	15 ·97	11
18	Fr 31	13 ·17	... ...	12

June

Cyclic Sidereal Year, Month and Day	Week-Day, English Month and Day	Tithi Ending Moment	Nakshatra Ending Moment	Muhammadan Year, Month and Day
19	Sa 1	Jyeshtha 14 ·26	16 ·08	H. 1319 Safar 13
20	Su 2	P ·33	17 ·18	14
21	Mo 3	1 ·38	18 ·26	15
22	Tu 4	2 ·41	19 ·32	16
23	We 5	3 ·41	20 ·35	17
24	Th 6	4 ·41	21 ·37	18
25	Fr 7	5 ·38	22 ·38	19
26	Sa 8	6 ·34	23 ·36	20
27	Su 9	7 ·26	24 ·32	21
28	Mo 10	8 ·19	25 ·27	22
29	Tu 11	9 ·10 / 10 ·99	26 ·21	23
30	We 12	Bahula 11 ·90	27 ·16	24
31	Th 13	12 ·79	1 ·08	25
Plava Mithuna—Ani 1	Fr 14	13 ·69	2 ·01 / 3 ·95	26
2	Sa 15	14 ·59	4 ·89	27
3	Su 16	A ·51	5 ·84	28
4	Mo 17	1 ·44	6 ·81	29
5	Tu 18	2 ·37	7 ·78	H. 1319 Rabi-ul-awwal 1
6	We 19	3 ·33	8 ·78	2
7	Th 20	Sukla 4 ·31	9 ·79	3
8	Fr 21	5 ·30	10 ·84	4
9	Sa 22	6 ·32	11 ·90	5
10	Su 23	7 ·37	12 ·97	6
11	Mo 24	8 ·42	... ...	7
12	Tu 25	Ashadha 9 ·50	13 ·06	8
13	We 26	10 ·58	14 ·16	9
14	Th 27	11 ·65	15 ·27	10
15	Fr 28	12 ·74	16 ·39	11
16	Sa 29	13 ·80	17 ·48	12
17	Su 30	14 ·86	18 ·56	13

Naksh:—1. Asvn. 2. Bhar. 3. Krit. 4. Rohi. 5. Mrig. 6. Ardh. 7. Punar. 8. Push. 9. Aslesh. 10. Magh. 11. P. Phal. 12. U. Phal. 13. Hasta. 14. Chit.

A. D. 1901.	Kollam 1077, Commences { N. Malabar—Sept. / S. Malabar—Aug.	Hijra 1319, Commences, April 20.	Vikrama 1958.
A.—Amavasya.			Bengal San 1307.
P.—Paurnami.			(N. Cycle) Pramadin.

July

Solar month	SOLAR reckoning: Cyclic Sidereal Year, Month and Day	Week-Day	English Month and Day	Lunar month	LUNAR reckoning: Tithi Ending Moment	Nakshatra Ending Moment	Muhammadan month	Muhammadan Year, Month and Day
Plava Mithuna—Ani.	18	Mo	1	Ashadha	P ·88	19 ·63	H, 1319 Rabi-ul-awwal.	14
	19	Tu	2		1 ·90	20 ·67		15
	20	We	3		2 ·89	21 ·70		16
	21	Th	4		3 ·85	22 ·70		17
	22	Fr	5		4 ·81	23 ·69		18
	23	Sa	6		5 ·74	24 ·65		19
	24	Su	7		6 ·66	25 ·61		20
	25	Mo	8		7 ·57	26 ·56		21
	26	Tu	9	Bahula	8 ·48	27 ·49		22
	27	We	10		9 ·37	1 ·42		23
	28	Th	11		10 ·27	2 ·35		24
	29	Fr	12		11 ·17	3 ·28		25
	30	Sa	13		12 ·07	4 ·28		26
	31	Su	14		{13 ·00 / 14 ·94	5 ·18		27
	—32	Mo	15		—A ·86	6 ·14		28
Plava Karkata—Adi.	1	Tu	16		1 ·80	7 ·11		29
	2	We	17		2 ·79	8 ·10		—30
	3	Th	18		3 ·78	9 ·11		1
	4	Fr	19		4 ·80	10 ·15		2
	5	Sa	20		5 ·84	11 ·20		3
	6	Su	21	Sukla	6 ·89	12 ·27		4
	7	Mo	22		7 ·97	13 ·36		5
	8	Tu	23		... ...	14 ·46		6
	9	We	24		8 ·04	15 ·58		7
	10	Th	25		9 ·13	16 ·68		8
	11	Fr	26	Sravana.	10 ·21	17 ·78		9
	12	Sa	27		11 ·27	18 ·87		10
	13	Su	28		12 ·32	19 ·94		11
	14	Mo	29		13 ·36	20 ·99		12
	15	Tu	30		14 ·38	... ...		13
	16	We	31		P ·36	21 ·02		14

Aug.

Solar month	SOLAR reckoning: Cyclic Sidereal Year, Month and Day	Week-Day	English Month and Day	Lunar month	LUNAR reckoning: Tithi Ending Moment	Nakshatra Ending Moment	Muhammadan month	Muhammadan Year, Month and Day
	17	Th	1	Adhika	1 ·34	22 ·03	H, 1319 Rabi-ul-akhir.	15
	18	Fr	2		2 ·29	23 ·02 / 24 ·99}		16
	19	Sa	3		3 ·24	25 ·95		17
	20	Su	4		4 ·16	26 ·90		18
	21	Mo	5		{5 ·06 / 6 ·97	27 ·83		19
	22	Tu	6		7 ·87	1 ·76		20
	23	We	7	Bahula	8 ·77	2 ·69		21
	24	Th	8		9 ·68	3 ·63		22
	25	Fr	9		10 ·57	4 ·57		23
	26	Sa	10		11 ·48	5 ·51		24
	27	Su	11		12 ·41	6 ·47		25
	28	Mo	12		13 ·35	7 ·44		26
	29	Tu	13		14 ·29	8 ·42		27
	30	We	14		—A ·28	9 ·44		28
	—31	Th	15		1 ·27	10 ·46		—29
Plava Simha—Avani.	1	Fr	16		2 ·29	11 ·51	H, 1319 Jumadal-awwal.	1
	2	Sa	17		3 ·33	12 ·58		2
	3	Su	18		4 ·38	13 ·66		3
	4	Mo	19	Sukla	5 ·46	14 ·77		4
	5	Tu	20		6 ·54	15 ·88		5
	6	We	21		7 ·63	16 ·98		6
	7	Th	22		8 ·71	... ...		7
	8	Fr	23	Nija Sravana.	9 ·77	17 ·08		8
	9	Sa	24		10 ·82	18 ·17		9
	10	Su	25		11 ·86	19 ·25		10
	11	Mo	26		12 ·88	20 ·31		11
	12	Tu	27		13 ·87	21 ·34		12
	13	We	28		14 ·85	22 ·35		13
	14	Th	29		P ·80	23 ·34		14
	15	Fr	30		1 ·74	24 ·32		15
	16	Sa	31		2 ·66	25 ·29		16

Sep.

Solar month	SOLAR reckoning: Cyclic Sidereal Year, Month and Day	Week-Day	English Month and Day	Lunar month	LUNAR reckoning: Tithi Ending Moment	Nakshatra Ending Moment	Muhammadan month	Muhammadan Year, Month and Day
Plava Simha—Avani.	17	Su	1	Nija Srvn.	3 ·58	26 ·23	H. 1319 Jumadal-awwal.	17
	18	Mo	2		4 ·48	27 ·17		18
	19	Tu	3		5 ·38	1 ·10		19
	20	We	4		6 ·28	2 ·03 / 3 ·97}		20
	21	Th	5		7 ·18	4 ·90		21
	22	Fr	6		{8 ·08 / 9 ·99	5 ·85		22
	23	Sa	7		10 ·93	6 ·90		23
	24	Su	8	Bahula	11 ·87	7 ·76		24
	25	Mo	9		12 ·81	8 ·76		25
	26	Tu	10		13 ·80	9 ·76		26
	27	We	11		14 ·79	10 ·78		27
	28	Th	12		—A ·81	11 ·82		28
	29	Fr	13		1 ·85	12 ·88		29
	30	Sa	14		2 ·91	13 ·97		—30
	—31	Su	15		3 ·98	... ...	H. 1319 Jumadal-akhir.	1
Plava Kanya—Purattasi.	1	Mo	16		... ...	14 ·07		2
	2	Tu	17	Sukla	4 ·07	15 ·17		3
	3	We	18		5 ·14	16 ·28		4
	4	Th	19		6 ·22	17 ·38		5
	5	Fr	20		7 ·30	18 ·49		6
	6	Sa	21		8 ·35	19 ·56		7
	7	Su	22	Bhadrapada	9 ·39	20 ·62		8
	8	Mo	23		10 ·40	21 ·66		9
	9	Tu	24		11 ·41	22 ·67		10
	10	We	25		12 ·38	23 ·67		11
	11	Th	26		13 ·35	24 ·66		12
	12	Fr	27		14 ·28	25 ·62		13
	13	Sa	28		P ·20	26 ·57		14
	14	Su	29		1 ·12	27 ·51		15
	15	Mo	30		{2 ·02 / 3 ·94	1 ·44		16

Oct.

Solar month	SOLAR reckoning: Cyclic Sidereal Year, Month and Day	Week-Day	English Month and Day	Lunar month	LUNAR reckoning: Tithi Ending Moment	Nakshatra Ending Moment	Muhammadan month	Muhammadan Year, Month and Day
	16	Tu	1		4 ·83	2 ·38		17
	17	We	2		5 ·73	3 ·31		18
	18	Th	3		6 ·63	4 ·24		19
	19	Fr	4	Bahula	7 ·54	5 ·18		20
	20	Sa	5		8 ·48	6 ·13		21
	21	Su	6		9 ·42	7 ·10		22
	22	Mo	7		10 ·37	8 ·08		23
	23	Tu	8		11 ·35	9 ·08		24
	24	We	9		12 ·36	10 ·09		25
	25	Th	10		13 ·37	11 ·13		26
	26	Fr	11		14 ·41	12 ·20		27
	27	Sa	12		—A ·47	13 ·28		28
	28	Su	13		1 ·54	14 ·37		—29
	29	Mo	14		2 ·63	15 ·47	H. 1319 Rajab.	1
	30	Tu	15		3 ·71	16 ·58		2
	—31	We	16		4 ·80	17 ·68		3
Plava Tula—Aippasi.	1	Th	17		5 ·87	18 ·79		4
	2	Fr	18	Sukla	6 ·92	19 ·88		5
	3	Sa	19		7 ·96	20 ·93		6
	4	Su	20		8 ·98	21 ·97		7
	5	Mo	21		9 ·99	22 ·99		8
	6	Tu	22		10 ·96	... ...		9
	7	We	23		11 ·93	23 ·00 / 24 ·99}		10
	8	Th	24	Asvina	12 ·89	25 ·95		11
	9	Fr	25		13 ·79	26 ·90		12
	10	Sa	26		14 ·70	27 ·84		13
	11	Su ○	27		P ·60	1 ·79		14
	12	Mo	28		1 ·51	2 ·72		15
	13	Tu	29		2 ·41	3 ·65		16
	14	We	30	Bah.	3 ·32	4 ·58		17
	15	Th	31		4 ·22	5 ·52		18

Nov.

Solar month	SOLAR reckoning: Cyclic Sidereal Year, Month and Day	Week-Day	English Month and Day	Lunar month	LUNAR reckoning: Tithi Ending Moment	Nakshatra Ending Moment	Muhammadan month	Muhammadan Year, Month and Day
Plava Tula—Aippasi.	16	Fr	1		5 ·14	6 ·47	H. 1319 Rajab.	19
	17	Sa	2		{6 ·07 / 7 ·99	7 ·43		20
	18	Su	3	Asv.	8 ·97	8 ·41		21
	19	Mo	4		9 ·95	9 ·40		22
	20	Tu	5		10 ·95	10 ·41		23
	21	We	6		11 ·96	11 ·45		24
	22	Th	7	Bahula	... ...	12 ·51		25
	23	Fr	8		12 ·01	13 ·58		26
	24	Sa	9		13 ·08	14 ·67		27
	25	Su	10		14 ·15	15 ·77		28
	26	Mo ●	11		—A ·24	16 ·88		29
	27	Tu	12		1 ·32	17 ·99		—30
	28	We	13		2 ·41	... ...	H. 1319 Shaban.	1
	29	Th	14		3 ·48	18 ·09		2
	—30	Fr	15		4 ·54	19 ·17		3
Plava Vrischika—Kartigai.	1	Sa	16		5 ·59	20 ·24		4
	2	Su	17	Sukla	6 ·60	21 ·29		5
	3	Mo	18		7 ·60	22 ·32		6
	4	Tu	19		8 ·57	23 ·33		7
	5	We	20		9 ·53	24 ·31		8
	6	Th	21	Karttika	10 ·47	25 ·28		9
	7	Fr	22		11 ·41	26 ·24		10
	8	Sa	23		12 ·32	27 ·19		11
	9	Su	24		13 ·23	1 ·13		12
	10	Mo	25		14 ·12	2 ·06 / 3 ·99}		13
	11	Tu	26		{P ·03 / 1 ·94	4 ·92		14
	12	We	27		2 ·84	5 ·86		15
	13	Th	28		3 ·76	6 ·81		16
	14	Fr	29		4 ·69	7 ·76		17
	15	Sa	30		5 ·63	8 ·73		18

Dec.

Solar month	SOLAR reckoning: Cyclic Sidereal Year, Month and Day	Week-Day	English Month and Day	Lunar month	LUNAR reckoning: Tithi Ending Moment	Nakshatra Ending Moment	Muhammadan month	Muhammadan Year, Month and Day
	16	Su	1		6 ·59	9 ·72		19
	17	Mo	2	Bahula	7 ·57	10 ·73		20
	18	Tu	3		8 ·59	11 ·77		21
	19	We	4		9 ·60	12 ·82		22
	20	Th	5		10 ·65	13 ·88		23
	21	Fr	6		11 ·71	14 ·97		24
	22	Sa	7		12 ·79	... ...		25
	23	Su	8		13 ·87	15 ·07		26
	24	Mo	9		14 ·96	16 ·18		27
	25	Tu	10		... ...	17 ·29		28
	26	We	11		—A ·05	18 ·39		—29
	27	Th	12		1 ·13	19 ·48	H. 1319 Ramzan.	1
	28	Fr	13		2 ·18	20 ·55		2
	—29	Sa	14		3 ·22	21 ·61		3
Plava Dhanus—Margali.	1	Su	15		4 ·25	22 ·64		4
	2	Mo	16		5 ·23	23 ·65		5
	3	Tu	17	Sukla	6 ·21	24 ·64		6
	4	We	18		7 ·17	25 ·61		7
	5	Th	19		8 ·10	26 ·58		8
	6	Fr	20		{9 ·03 / 10 ·94	27 ·53		9
	7	Sa	21	Margasira	11 ·86	1 ·46		10
	8	Su	22		12 ·75	2 ·39		11
	9	Mo	23		13 ·66	3 ·32		12
	10	Tu	24		14 ·57	4 ·26		13
	11	We	25		P ·48	5 ·19		14
	12	Th	26		1 ·39	6 ·14		15
	13	Fr	27		2 ·33	7 ·09		16
	14	Sa	28		3 ·27	8 ·06		17
	15	Su	29		4 ·23	9 ·05		18
	16	Mo	30	Bah.	5 ·23	10 ·06		19
	17	Tu	31		6 ·23	11 ·08		20

15. Svati. 16. Visak. 17. Anur. 18. Jyesh. 19. Mula. 20. P. Ash. 21. U. Ash. 22. Sravn. 23. Dani. 24. Satab. 25. P. Bhad. 26. U. Bhad. 27. Rev.

A. D. 1902.   **Mesha Sankranti** (Commencement of Indian Sidereal Year).
Solar Eclipse. ●   **(Surya Sid.) April 13·14.**   **Saka 1824.**   **Kaliyuga 5003.**
Lunar Eclipse. ○   **(Arya Sid.) April 13·03.**   **(S. Cycle) Subhakrit.**

Jan.

SOLAR reckoning: Cyclic Sidereal Year, Month and Day	Week-Day English Month and Day	LUNAR reckoning: Tithi Ending Moment	Nakshatra Ending Moment	Muhammadan Year, Month and Day
Plava, Dhanus—Margali 18	We 1	*Marg. Bahula* 7 ·25	12 ·12	*H. 1319 Ramzan.* 21
19	Th 2	8 ·29	13 ·19	22
20	Fr 3	9 ·36	14 ·27	23
21	Sa 4	10 ·44	15 ·38	24
22	Su 5	11 ·52	16 ·48	25
23	Mo 6	12 ·62	17 ·59	26
24	Tu 7	13 ·70	18 ·69	27
25	We 8	14 ·78	19 ·78	28
26	Th 9	—A ·84	20 ·87	29
27	Fr 10	*Pausha Sukla* 1 ·87	21 ·92	—30
28	Sa 11	2 ·89	22 ·96	*H. 1319 Shawwal.* 1
—29	Su 12	3 ·88	23 ·97	2
Plava, Makara—Tai. 1	Mo 13	4 ·86	24 ·97	3
2	Tu 14	5 ·81	25 ·95	4
3	We 15	6 ·75	26 ·91	5
4	Th 16	7 ·68	27 ·86	6
5	Fr 17	8 ·60	1 ·80	7
6	Sa 18	9 ·50	2 ·73	8
7	Su 19	10 ·39	3 ·66	9
8	Mo 20	11 ·30	4 ·60	10
9	Tu 21	12 ·20	5 ·53	11
10	We 22	13 ·11	6 ·48	12
11	Th 23	{14 ·04 P ·97	7 ·43	13
12	Fr 24	1 ·91	8 ·39	14
13	Sa 25	2 ·88	9 ·38	15
14	Su 26	3 ·87	10 ·38	16
15	Mo 27	4 ·87	11 ·40	17
16	Tu 28	5 ·89	12 ·44	18
17	We 29	6 ·95	13 ·49	19
18	Th 30	... ...	14 ·58	20
19	Fr 31	7 ·02	15 ·68	21

Feb.

Cyclic Sidereal Year, Month and Day	Week-Day English Month and Day	Tithi Ending Moment	Nakshatra Ending Moment	Muhammadan Year, Month and Day
20	Sa 1	*Bahula* 8 ·09	16 ·78	22
21	Su 2	9 ·17	17 ·89	23
22	Mo 3	10 ·27	18 ·09	24
23	Tu 4	11 ·35	... ...	25
24	We 5	12 ·43	19 ·09	26
25	Th 6	13 ·48	20 ·17	27
26	Fr 7	14 ·52	21 ·23	28
27	Sa 8	—A ·53	22 ·27	—29
28	Su 9	*Magha Sukla* 1 ·52	23 ·29	*H. 1319 Zi-l-ka'da.* 1
29	Mo 10	2 ·49	24 ·29	2
—30	Tu 11	3 ·44	25 ·26	3
Plava, Kumbha—Masi. 1	We 12	4 ·37	26 ·25	4
2	Th 13	5 ·30	27 ·20	5
3	Fr 14	6 ·22	1 ·14	6
4	Sa 15	7 ·12	2 ·07	7
5	Su 16	{8 ·02 9 ·93	3 ·01 4 ·94}	8
6	Mo 17	10 ·82	5 ·87	9
7	Tu 18	11 ·74	6 ·81	10
8	We 19	12 ·65	7 ·76	11
9	Th 20	13 ·58	8 ·73	12
10	Fr 21	14 ·53	9 ·70	13
11	Sa 22	P ·51	10 ·70	14
12	Su 23	*Bahula* 1 ·49	11 ·71	15
13	Mo 24	2 ·49	12 ·75	16
14	Tu 25	3 ·52	13 ·81	17
15	We 26	4 ·56	14 ·89	18
16	Th 27	5 ·63	15 ·98	19
17	Fr 28	6 ·72	... ...	20

March

Cyclic Sidereal Year, Month and Day	Week-Day English Month and Day	Tithi Ending Moment	Nakshatra Ending Moment	Muhammadan Year, Month and Day
18	Sa 1	*Magha Bahula* 7 ·81	16 ·08	*H. 1319 Zi-l-ka'da.* 21
19	Su 2	8 ·89	17 ·18	22
20	Mo 3	9 ·97	18 ·30	23
21	Tu 4	... ...	19 ·40	24
22	We 5	10 ·04	20 ·48	25
23	Th 6	11 ·09	21 ·54	26
24	Fr 7	12 ·13	22 ·59	27
25	Sa 8	13 ·14	23 ·61	28
26	Su 9	14 ·13	24 ·63	29
27	Mo 10	—A ·09	25 ·61	—30
28	Tu 11	*Phalguna Sukla* {1 ·05 2 ·98	26 ·58	*H. 1319 Zi-l-hijja.* 1
29	We 12	3 ·90	27 ·53	2
—30	Th 13	4 ·82	1 ·47	3
Plava, Mina—Panguni. 1	Fr 14	5 ·72	2 ·42	4
2	Sa 15	6 ·62	3 ·35	5
3	Su 16	7 ·52	4 ·28	6
4	Mo 17	8 ·42	5 ·21	7
5	Tu 18	9 ·33	6 ·15	8
6	We 19	10 ·26	7 ·10	9
7	Th 20	11 ·18	8 ·06	10
8	Fr 21	12 ·13	9 ·03	11
9	Sa 22	13 ·10	10 ·02	12
10	Su 23	14 ·08	11 ·03	13
11	Mo 24	P ·09	12 ·07	14
12	Tu 25	1 ·12	13 ·11	15
13	We 26	2 ·16	14 ·19	16
14	Th 27	3 ·22	15 ·28	17
15	Fr 28	4 ·30	16 ·38	18
16	Sa 29	5 ·39	17 ·48	19
17	Su 30	6 ·48	18 ·60	20
18	Mo 31	7 ·56	19 ·70	21

April

Cyclic Sidereal Year, Month and Day	Week-Day English Month and Day	Tithi Ending Moment	Nakshatra Ending Moment	Muhammadan Year, Month and Day
19	Tu 1	*Bahula* 8 ·62	20 ·78	22
20	We 2	9 ·68	21 ·85	23
21	Th 3	10 ·71	22 ·90	24
22	Fr 4	11 ·71	23 ·94	25
23	Sa 5	12 ·70	24 ·95	26
24	Su 6	13 ·66	25 ·94	27
25	Mo 7	14 ·62	26 ·91	28
26	Tu 8	—A ·55	27 ·87	29
27	We 9	*Chaitra Sukla* 1 ·47	1 ·82	—30
28	Th 10	2 ·38	2 ·76	*H. 1320 Muharram.* 1
29	Fr 11	3 ·29	3 ·69	2
—30	Sa 12	4 ·18	4 ·62	3
Subhakrit, Mesha—Chittirai. 1	Su 13	{5 ·08 6 ·98	5 ·55	4
2	Mo 14	7 ·89	6 ·49	5
3	Tu 15	8 ·81	7 ·44	6
4	We 16	9 ·73	8 ·39	7
5	Th 17	10 ·69	9 ·36	8
6	Fr 18	11 ·65	10 ·34	9
7	Sa 19	12 ·63	11 ·36	10
8	Su 20	13 ·64	12 ·38	11
9	Mo 21	14 ·66	13 ·43	12
10	Tu ○ 22	P ·71	14 ·49	13
11	We 23	1 ·76	15 ·58	14
12	Th 24	2 ·85	16 ·67	15
13	Fr 25	3 ·93	17 ·79	16
14	Sa 26	... ...	18 ·90	17
15	Su 27	*Bahula* 4 ·00	... ...	18
16	Mo 28	5 ·09	19 ·00	19
17	Tu 29	6 ·16	20 ·09	20
18	We 30	7 ·21	21 ·16	21

May

Cyclic Sidereal Year, Month and Day	Week-Day English Month and Day	Tithi Ending Moment	Nakshatra Ending Moment	Muhammadan Year, Month and Day
Subhakrit, Mesha—Chittirai. 19	Th 1	*Ch. Bah.* 8 ·24	22 ·22	*H. 1320 Muharram.* 22
20	Fr 2	9 ·25	23 ·26	23
21	Sa 3	10 ·23	24 ·27	24
22	Su 4	11 ·21	25 ·26	25
23	Mo 5	12 ·15	26 ·24	26
24	Tu 6	13 ·07	27 ·21	27
25	We 7	{14 ·00 A ·91	1 ·16	28
26	Th 8	*Vaisakha Sukla* 1 ·82	2 ·09	29
27	Fr 9	2 ·71	3 ·03 4 ·96}	—30
28	Sa 10	3 ·61	5 ·90	*H. 1320 Safar.* 1
29	Su 11	4 ·50	6 ·83	2
30	Mo 12	5 ·41	7 ·77	3
—31	Tu 13	6 ·33	8 ·72	4
Subhakrit, Vrishabha—Vaikasi. 1	We 14	7 ·25	9 ·69	5
2	Th 15	8 ·20	10 ·67	6
3	Fr 16	9 ·16	11 ·68	7
4	Sa 17	10 ·15	12 ·70	8
5	Su 18	11 ·15	13 ·74	9
6	Mo 19	12 ·18	14 ·80	10
7	Tu 20	13 ·22	15 ·88	11
8	We 21	14 ·27	16 ·98	12
9	Th 22	P ·36	... ...	13
10	Fr 23	*Bahula* 1 ·44	17 ·09	14
11	Sa 24	2 ·52	18 ·19	15
12	Su 25	3 ·59	19 ·30	16
13	Mo 26	4 ·67	20 ·39	17
14	Tu 27	5 ·72	21 ·48	18
15	We 28	6 ·73	22 ·54	19
16	Th 29	7 ·75	23 ·57	20
17	Fr 30	8 ·73	24 ·59	21
18	Sa 31	9 ·70	25 ·59	22

June

Cyclic Sidereal Year, Month and Day	Week-Day English Month and Day	Tithi Ending Moment	Nakshatra Ending Moment	Muhammadan Year, Month and Day
19	Su 1	10 ·65	26 ·58	23
20	Mo 2	11 ·59	27 ·54	24
21	Tu 3	12 ·50	1 ·49	25
22	We 4	13 ·40	2 ·43	26
23	Th 5	14 ·30	3 ·37	27
24	Fr 6	—A ·20	4 ·30	28
25	Sa 7	*Jyeshtha Sukla* 1 ·11	5 ·23	—29
26	Su 8	{2 ·00 3 ·92	6 ·17	*H. 1320 Rabi-ul-awwal.* 1
27	Mo 9	4 ·83	7 ·11	2
28	Tu 10	5 ·74	8 ·05	3
29	We 11	6 ·69	9 ·02	4
30	Th 12	7 ·65	10 ·00	5
—31	Fr 13	8 ·64	11 ·00	6
Subhakrit, Mithuna—Ani. 1	Sa 14	9 ·63	12 ·01	7
2	Su 15	10 ·66	13 ·05	8
3	Mo 16	11 ·70	14 ·11	9
4	Tu 17	12 ·76	15 ·19	10
5	We 18	13 ·83	16 ·28	11
6	Th 19	14 ·91	17 ·39	12
7	Fr 20	... ...	18 ·49	13
8	Sa 21	P ·00	19 ·60	14
9	Su 22	*Bahula* 1 ·06	20 ·70	15
10	Mo 23	2 ·14	21 ·78	16
11	Tu 24	3 ·19	22 ·85	17
12	We 25	4 ·22	23 ·89	18
13	Th 26	5 ·23	24 ·91	19
14	Fr 27	6 ·21	25 ·92	20
15	Sa 28	7 ·18	26 ·91	21
16	Su 29	8 ·13	27 ·87	22
17	Mo 30	{9 ·07 10 ·99	1 ·83	23

Naksh :—1. Asvn. 2. Bhar. 3. Krit. 4. Rohi. 5. Mrig. 6. Ardh. 7. Punar. 8. Push. 9. Aslesh. 10. Magh. 11. P. Phal. 12 U. Phal. 13. Hasta. 14. Chit.

A. D. 1902. **Kollam 1078,** Commences { **N. Malabar—Sept.** **S. Malabar—Aug.** **Hijra 1320,** Commences, April 10. **Vikrama 1959.**

A.—Amavasya. **Bengal San 1308.**

P.—Paurnami. **(N. Cycle) Ananda.**

July

SOLAR reckoning: Cyclic Sidereal Year, Month and Day.	Week-Day English Month and Day.	LUNAR reckoning: Tithi Ending Moment.	Nakshatra Ending Moment.	Muhammadan Year, Month and Day.
Subhakrit Mithuna—Ani. 18	Tu 1	Jy. Bah. 11 ·89	2 ·77	R.-awwal. 24
19	We 2	12 ·79	3 ·70	25
20	Th 3	13 ·70	4 ·64	26
21	Fr 4	14 ·58	5 ·57	27
22	Sa 5	—A ·48	6 ·50	28
23	Su 6	Ashadha Sukla 1 ·40	7 ·44	29
24	Mo 7	2 ·30	8 ·39	—30
25	Tu 8	3 ·23	9 ·36	H. 1320 Rabi-ul-akhir. 1
26	We 9	4 ·17	10 ·33	2
27	Th 10	5 ·13	11 ·32	3
28	Fr 11	6 ·11	12 ·33	4
29	Sa 12	7 ·11	13 ·36	5
30	Su 13	8 ·14	14 ·42	6
31	Mo 14	9 ·17	15 ·50	7
—32	Tu 15	10 ·23	16 ·58	8
Subhakrit Karkata—Adi. 1	We 16	11 ·81	17 ·68	9
2	Th 17	12 ·38	18 ·79	10
3	Fr 18	13 ·46	19 ·91	11
4	Sa 19	14 ·53	... ...	12
5	Su 20	P ·62	20 ·00	13
6	Mo 21	Bahula 1 ·66	21 ·09	14
7	Tu 22	2 ·70	22 ·16	15
8	We 23	3 ·71	23 ·20	16
9	Th 24	4 ·69	24 ·24	17
10	Fr 25	5 ·66	25 ·25	18
11	Sa 26	6 ·62	26 ·23	19
12	Su 27	7 ·55	27 ·21	20
13	Mo 28	8 ·47	1 ·16	21
14	Tu 29	9 ·38	2 ·11	22
15	We 30	10 ·28	{3 ·05; 4 ·98}	23
16	Th 31	11 ·18	5 ·91	24

Aug.

Cyclic Sidereal Year, Month and Day.	Week-Day English Month and Day.	Tithi Ending Moment.	Nakshatra Ending Moment.	Muhammadan Year, Month and Day.
17	Fr 1	{12 ·07; 13 98}	6 ·84	25
18	Sa 2	14 ·88	7 ·78	26
19	Su 3	—A ·79	8 ·73	27
20	Mo 4	Sravana Sukla 1 ·72	9 ·69	28
21	Tu 5	2 ·65	10 ·66	—29
22	We 6	3 ·62	11 ·64	H. 1320 Jumadal-awwal. 1
23	Th 7	4 ·59	12 ·65	2
24	Fr 8	5 ·60	13 ·69	3
25	Sa 9	6 ·61	14 ·73	4
26	Su 10	7 ·65	15 ·80	5
27	Mo 11	8 ·72	16 ·88	6
28	Tu 12	9 ·78	17 ·98	7
29	We 13	10 ·87	... ...	8
30	Th 14	11 ·95	18 ·10	9
—31	Fr 15	... ...	19 ·20	10
Subhakrit Simha—Avani. 1	Sa 16	12 ·04	20 ·30	11
2	Su 17	13 ·10	21 ·39	12
3	Mo 18	14 ·16	22 ·46	13
4	Tu 19	P ·18	23 ·52	14
5	We 20	Bahula 1 ·20	24 ·56	15
6	Th 21	2 ·19	25 ·57	16
7	Fr 22	3 ·16	26 ·56	17
8	Sa 23	4 ·12	27 ·54	18
9	Su 24	{5 ·05; 6 ·98}	1 ·49	19
10	Mo 25	7 ·88	2 ·45	20
11	Tu 26	8 ·78	3 ·39	21
12	We 27	9 ·69	4 ·32	22
13	Th 28	10 ·58	5 ·25	23
14	Fr 29	11 ·48	6 ·18	24
15	Sa 30	12 ·38	7 ·12	25
16	Su 31	13 ·31	8 ·07	26

Sep.

Cyclic Sidereal Year, Month and Day.	Week-Day English Month and Day.	Tithi Ending Moment.	Nakshatra Ending Moment.	Muhammadan Year, Month and Day.
17	Mo 1	14 ·23	{9 ·02; 10 ·98}	J.-awwal. 27
18	Tu 2	—A ·17	11 ·97	28
19	We 3	Bhadrapada Sukla 1 ·13	12 ·98	29
Subhakrit Simha—Avani. 20	Th 4	2 ·11	... ...	30
21	Fr 5	3 ·12	13 ·00	H. 1320 Jumadal-akhir. 1
22	Sa 6	4 ·12	14 ·04	2
23	Su 7	5 ·17	15 ·10	3
24	Mo 8	6 ·22	16 ·19	4
25	Tu 9	7 ·30	17 ·28	5
26	We 10	8 ·38	18 ·40	6
27	Th 11	9 ·46	19 ·50	7
28	Fr 12	10 ·55	20 ·60	8
29	Sa 13	11 ·62	21 ·70	9
30	Su 14	12 ·68	22 ·77	10
—31	Mo 15	13 ·71	23 ·84	11
Subhakrit Kanya—Purattasi. 1	Tu 16	14 ·74	24 ·88	12
2	We 17	P ·72	25 ·89	13
3	Th 18	Bahula 1 ·68	26 ·89	14
4	Fr 19	2 ·65	27 ·87	15
5	Sa 20	3 ·58	1 ·84	16
6	Su 21	4 ·51	2 ·79	17
7	Mo 22	5 ·41	3 ·73	18
8	Tu 23	6 ·32	4 ·66	19
9	We 24	7 ·23	5 ·59	20
10	Th 25	8 ·13	6 ·53	21
11	Fr 26	{9 ·02; 10 ·92}	7 ·46	22
12	Sa 27	11 ·85	8 ·40	23
13	Su 28	12 ·77	9 ·35	24
14	Mo 29	13 ·72	10 ·31	25
15	Tu 30	14 ·67	11 ·30	26

Oct.

Cyclic Sidereal Year, Month and Day.	Week-Day English Month and Day.	Tithi Ending Moment.	Nakshatra Ending Moment.	Muhammadan Year, Month and Day.
16	We 1	—A ·66	12 ·30	27
17	Th 2	Asvina Sukla 1 ·65	13 ·31	28
18	Fr 3	2 ·67	14 ·35	—29
19	Sa 4	3 ·72	15 ·41	H. 1320 Rajab. 1
20	Su 5	4 ·77	16 ·49	2
21	Mo 6	5 ·85	17 ·59	3
22	Tu 7	6 ·93	18 ·69	4
23	We 8	... ...	19 ·80	5
24	Th 9	7 ·03	20 ·90	6
25	Fr 10	8 ·11	... ...	7
26	Sa 11	9 ·18	21 ·00	8
27	Su 12	10 ·24	22 ·09	9
28	Mo 13	11 ·27	23 ·15	10
29	Tu 14	12 ·30	24 ·19	11
30	We 15	13 ·28	25 ·21	12
—31	Th 16	14 ·26	26 ·21	13
Subhakrit Tula—Aippasi. 1	Fr ○ 17	P ·22	27 ·20	14
2	Sa 18	Bahula 1 ·16	1 ·17	15
3	Su 19	{2 ·08; 3 ·98}	2 ·12	16
4	Mo 20	4 ·90	3 ·07	17
5	Tu 21	5 ·80	{4 ·00; 5 ·94}	18
6	We 22	6 ·70	6 ·87	19
7	Th 23	7 ·60	7 ·80	20
8	Fr 24	8 ·51	8 ·74	21
9	Sa 25	9 ·43	9 ·68	22
10	Su 26	10 ·35	10 ·64	23
11	Mo 27	11 ·30	11 ·63	24
12	Tu 28	12 ·25	12 ·62	25
13	We 29	13 ·25	13 ·63	26
14	Th 30	14 ·25	14 ·66	27
15	Fr ● 31	—A ·27	15 ·72	28

Nov.

Cyclic Sidereal Year, Month and Day.	Week-Day English Month and Day.	Tithi Ending Moment.	Nakshatra Ending Moment.	Muhammadan Year, Month and Day.
16	Sa 1	Karttika Sukla 1 ·31	16 ·80	29
17	Su 2	2 ·37	17 ·89	—30
18	Mo 3	3 ·45	18 ·99	H. 1320 Shaban. 1
19	Tu 4	4 ·54	... ...	2
Subhakrit Tula—Aippasi. 20	We 5	5 ·63	19 ·10	3
21	Th 6	6 ·71	20 ·20	4
22	Fr 7	7 ·78	21 ·31	5
23	Sa 8	8 ·83	22 ·39	6
24	Su 9	9 ·88	23 ·46	7
25	Mo 10	10 ·90	24 ·51	8
26	Tu 11	11 ·88	25 ·53	9
27	We 12	12 ·86	26 ·55	10
28	Th 13	13 ·81	27 ·53	11
29	Fr 14	14 ·77	1 ·50	12
—30	Sa 15	P ·68	2 ·46	13
Subhakrit Vrischika—Kartigai. 1	Su 16	Bahula 1 ·60	3 ·40	14
2	Mo 17	2 ·50	4 ·35	15
3	Tu 18	3 ·41	5 ·28	16
4	We 19	4 ·31	6 ·20	17
5	Th 20	5 ·21	7 ·14	18
6	Fr 21	6 ·12	8 ·07	19
7	Sa 22	{7 ·05; 8 ·97}	{9 ·02; 10 ·98}	20
8	Su 23	9 ·91	11 ·95	21
9	Mo 24	10 ·87	12 ·94	22
10	Tu 25	11 ·87	13 ·95	23
11	We 26	12 ·87	14 ·98	24
12	Th 27	13 ·90	... ...	25
13	Fr 28	14 ·93	15 ·04	26
14	Sa 29	... ...	16 ·10	27
15	Su 30	—A ·01	17 ·19	28

Dec.

Cyclic Sidereal Year, Month and Day.	Week-Day English Month and Day.	Tithi Ending Moment.	Nakshatra Ending Moment.	Muhammadan Year, Month and Day.
16	Mo 1	Margasira Sukla 1 ·08	18 ·29	—29
17	Tu 2	2 ·17	19 ·40	H. 1320 Ramzan. 1
18	We 3	3 ·25	20 ·51	2
19	Th 4	4 ·34	21 ·61	3
20	Fr 5	5 ·41	22 ·70	4
21	Sa 6	6 ·47	23 ·77	5
22	Su 7	7 ·52	24 ·82	6
23	Mo 8	8 ·53	25 ·86	7
24	Tu 9	9 ·52	26 ·87	8
25	We 10	10 ·49	27 ·86	9
26	Th 11	11 ·45	1 ·83	10
27	Fr 12	12 ·39	2 ·79	11
28	Sa 13	13 ·30	3 ·74	12
—29	Su 14	14 ·23	4 ·68	13
Subhakrit Dhanus—Margali. 1	Mo 15	P ·13	5 ·61	14
2	Tu 16	Bahula {1 ·04; 2 ·94}	6 ·54	15
3	We 17	3 ·85	7 ·47	16
4	Th 18	4 ·75	8 ·41	17
5	Fr 19	5 ·66	9 ·36	18
6	Sa 20	6 ·60	10 ·31	19
7	Su 21	7 ·55	11 ·28	20
8	Mo 22	8 ·52	12 ·26	21
9	Tu 23	9 ·51	13 ·27	22
10	We 24	10 ·52	14 ·30	23
11	Th 25	11 ·54	15 ·35	24
12	Fr 26	12 ·58	16 ·41	25
13	Sa 27	13 ·66	17 ·49	26
14	Su 28	14 ·73	18 ·59	27
15	Mo 29	—A ·82	19 ·70	28
16	Tu 30	1 ·91	20 ·81	29
17	We 31	... ...	21 ·91	—30

15. Svati. 16. Visak. 17. Anur. 18. Jyesh. 19 Mula. 20. P. Ash. 21. U. Ash. 22. Sravn. 23. Dani. 24. Satab. 25. P. Bhad. 26. U. Bhad. 27. Rev.

A. D. 1903. **Mesha Sankranti** (Commencement of Indian Sidereal Year).
Solar Eclipse. ● **(Surya Sid.) April 13·40.** **Saka 1825.** **Kaliyuga 5004.**
Lunar Eclipse. ○ **(Arya Sid.) April 13·29.** **(S. Cycle) Sobhana** (Sobhakrit).

SOLAR reckoning: Cyclic Sidereal Year, Month and Day; Week-Day English Month and Day. LUNAR reckoning: Tithi Ending Moment; Nakshatra Ending Moment. Muhammadan Year, Month and Day.

Jan.

Solar month	Cyclic Sidereal Day	Week-Day	English Day	Lunar month	Tithi	Tithi Ending Moment	Nakshatra	Nakshatra Ending Moment	Muhammadan Day	Muhammadan month
Subhakrit *Dhanus—Margali.*	18	Th	1		2	·00	...	...	1	
	19	Fr	2		3	·06	22	·00	2	
	20	Sa	3		4	·11	23	·08	3	
	21	Su	4		5	·16	24	·14	4	
	22	Mo	5	*Sukla*	6	·17	25	·18	5	
	23	Tu	6		7	·16	26	·19	6	
	24	We	7		8	·14	27	·19	7	
	25	Th	8		9	·10	1	·16	8	
	26	Fr	9		10 11	·03 ·96	2	·12	9	
	27	Sa	10		12	·87	3	·08	10	
	28	Su	11		13	·77	4 5	·02 ·95	11	
	29	Mo	12	**Pausha**	14	·68	6	·88	12	H. 1320 *Shawwal.*
	30	Tu	13		P	·58	7	·81	13	
Subhakrit *Makara—Tai.*	1	We	14		1	·49	8	·75	14	
	2	Th	15		2	·39	9	·69	15	
	3	Fr	16		3	·32	10	·65	16	
	4	Sa	17		4	·25	11	·61	17	
	5	Su	18		5	·19	12	·59	18	
	6	Mo	19		6	·17	13	·60	19	
	7	Tu	20	*Bahula*	7	·15	14	·62	20	
	8	We	21		8	·16	15	·66	21	
	9	Th	22		9	·18	16	·72	22	
	10	Fr	23		10	·25	17	·79	23	
	11	Sa	24		11	·31	18	·90	24	
	12	Su	25		12	·38	...	...	25	
	13	Mo	26		13	·48	19	·00	26	
	14	Tu	27		14	·56	20	·11	27	
	15	We	28		A	·65	21	·21	28	
	16	Th	29		1	·71	22	·30	29	
	17	Fr	30		2	·78	23	·38	1	
	18	Sa	31		3	·80	24	·45	2	

Feb.

Solar month	Cyclic Sidereal Day	Week-Day	English Day	Lunar month	Tithi	Tithi Ending Moment	Nakshatra	Nakshatra Ending Moment	Muhammadan Day	Muhammadan month
	19	Su	1		4	·82	25	·49	3	
	20	Mo	2		5	·80	26	·51	4	
	21	Tu	3		6	·78	27	·51	5	
	22	We	4		7	·74	1	·49	6	
	23	Th	5		8	·66	2	·47	7	
	24	Fr	6	*Sukla*	9	·58	3	·42	8	
	25	Sa	7		10	·50	4	·36	9	
	26	Su	8		11	·41	5	·29	10	
	27	Mo	9		12	·30	6	·22	11	
	28	Tu	10		13	·20	7	·16	12	
	29	We	11		14	·11	8	·09	13	
Subhakrit *Kumbha—Masi.*	1	Th	12		P 1	·02 ·94	9 10	·03 ·98	14	
	2	Fr	13		2	·87	11	·94	15	
	3	Sa	14		3	·83	12	·92	16	
	4	Su	15	**Magha**	4	·80	13	·92	17	H. 1320 *Zi-l-ka'da.*
	5	Mo	16		5	·78	14	·93	18	
	6	Tu	17		6	·79	15	·97	19	
	7	We	18		7	·82	...	...	20	
	8	Th	19		8	·87	16	·02	21	
	9	Fr	20		9	·93	17	·11	22	
	10	Sa	21	*Bahula*	...	...	18	·20	23	
	11	Su	22		10	·02	19	·30	24	
	12	Mo	23		11	·11	20	·40	25	
	13	Tu	24		12	·19	21	·51	26	
	14	We	25		13	·27	22	·61	27	
	15	Th	26		14	·33	23	·70	28	
	16	Fr	27		A	·39	24	·76	29	
	17	Sa	28		1	·42	25	·81	30	

March

Solar month	Cyclic Sidereal Day	Week-Day	English Day	Lunar month	Tithi	Tithi Ending Moment	Nakshatra	Nakshatra Ending Moment	Muhammadan Day	Muhammadan month
	18	Su	1		2	·44	26	·83	1	
	19	Mo	2		3	·42	27	·84	2	
	20	Tu	3		4	·40	1	·88	3	
Subhakrit *Kumbha—Masi.*	21	We	4		5	·34	2	·80	4	
	22	Th	5	*Sukla*	6	·27	3	·75	5	
	23	Fr	6		7	·19	4	·69	6	
	24	Sa	7		8	·10	5	·63	7	
	25	Su	8		9 10	·02 ·92	6	·57	8	
	26	Mo	9		11	·82	7	·50	9	
	27	Tu	10		12	·72	8	·43	10	
	28	We	11		13	·63	9	·37	11	
	29	Th	12		14	·54	10	·31	12	
	30	Fr	13	**Phalguna**	P	·47	11	·28	13	
	1	Sa	14		1	·43	12	·25	14	
	2	Su	15		2	·39	13	·24	15	
	3	Mo	16		3	·38	14	·25	16	H. 1320 *Zi-l-hijja.*
	4	Tu	17		4	·38	15	·28	17	
	5	We	18		5	·42	16	·33	18	
	6	Th	19		6	·47	17	·41	19	
	7	Fr	20	*Bahula*	7	·54	18	·50	20	
	8	Sa	21		8	·62	19	·60	21	
	9	Su	22		9	·70	20	·70	22	
	10	Mo	23		10	·80	21	·81	23	
	11	Tu	24		11	·87	22	·92	24	
Subhakrit *Mina—Panguni.*	12	We	25		12	·93	...	...	25	
	13	Th	26		13	·98	23	·00	26	
	14	Fr	27		...	...	24	·07	27	
	15	Sa	28		14	·01	25	·12	28	
	16	Su ●	29		A	·02	26	·15	29	
	17	Mo	30		1 2	·00 ·97	27	·17	1	
	18	Tu	31		3	·91	1	·16	2	

April

Solar month	Cyclic Sidereal Day	Week-Day	English Day	Lunar month	Tithi	Tithi Ending Moment	Nakshatra	Nakshatra Ending Moment	Muhammadan Day	Muhammadan month
	19	We	1		4	·86	2	·13	3	
	20	Th	2		5	·77	3	·09	4	
	21	Fr	3		6	·69	4 5	·03 ·98	5	
	22	Sa	4		7	·59	6	·91	6	
	23	Su	5	*Sukla*	8	·47	7	·84	7	
	24	Mo	6		9	·38	8	·77	8	
	25	Tu	7		10	·29	9	·70	9	
	26	We	8		11	·20	10	·65	10	
	27	Th	9		12	·10	11	·61	11	
	28	Fr	10		13 14	·04 ·99	12	·58	12	
	29	Sa ○	11		P	·95	13	·56	13	
	30	Su	12	**Chaitra**	1	·94	14	·57	14	
	1	Mo	13		2	·94	15	·59	15	H. 1321 *Muharram.*
	2	Tu	14		3	·98	16	·65	16	
	3	We	15		...	...	17	·71	17	
	4	Th	16		4	·02	18	·80	18	
	5	Fr	17		5	·09	19	·89	19	
	6	Sa	18		6	·17	...	...	20	
Sobhana *Mesha—Chittirai.*	7	Su	19	*Bahula*	7	·25	20	·00	21	
	8	Mo	20		8	·35	21	·12	22	
	9	Tu	21		9	·42	22	·22	23	
	10	We	22		10	·48	23	·31	24	
	11	Th	23		11	·52	24	·38	25	
	12	Fr	24		12	·56	25	·44	26	
	13	Sa	25		13	·56	26	·48	27	
	14	Su	26		14	·55	27	·49	28	
	15	Mo	27		A	·52	1	·48	29	
	16	Tu	28	*Suk.*	1	·45	2	·46	30	
	17	We	29		2	·39	3	·42	1	
	18	Th	30		3	·30	4	·38	2	

May

Solar month	Cyclic Sidereal Day	Week-Day	English Day	Lunar month	Tithi	Tithi Ending Moment	Nakshatra	Nakshatra Ending Moment	Muhammadan Day	Muhammadan month
	19	Fr	1		4	·22	5	·31	3	
	20	Sa	2		5	·12	6	·25	4	
	21	Su	3		6 7	·02 ·92	7	·18	5	
Sobhana *Mesha—Chittirai.*	22	Mo	4	*Sukla*	8	·82	8	·10	6	
	23	Tu	5		9	·73	9 10	·04 ·99	7	
	24	We	6		10	·63	11	·94	8	
	25	Th	7		11	·57	12	·91	9	
	26	Fr	8		12	·52	13	·89	10	
	27	Sa	9		13	·49	14	·89	11	
	28	Su	10	**Vaisakha**	14	·47	15	·92	12	
	29	Mo	11		P	·46	16	·96	13	
	30	Tu	12		1	·50	...	...	14	
	31	We	13		2	·54	17	·02	15	H. 1321 *Safar.*
	1	Th	14		3	·61	18	·10	16	
	2	Fr	15		4	·68	19	·19	17	
	3	Sa	16		5	·77	20	·31	18	
	4	Su	17		6	·85	21	·41	19	
	5	Mo	18		7	·93	22	·52	20	
	6	Tu	19	*Bahula*	...	...	23	·61	21	
	7	We	20		8	·00	24	·69	22	
	8	Th	21		9	·04	25	·76	23	
	9	Fr	22		10	·06	26	·79	24	
	10	Sa	23		11	·07	27	·81	25	
	11	Su	24		12	·06	1	·81	26	
Sobhana *Vrishabha—Vaikasi.*	12	Mo	25		13 14	·03 ·97	2	·79	27	
	13	Tu	26		A	·89	3	·75	28	
	14	We	27		1	·81	4	·71	29	
	15	Th	28		2	·73	5	·65	1	
	16	Fr	29		3	·62	6	·58	2	
	17	Sa	30		4	·52	7	·51	3	
	18	Su	31		5	·42	8	·44	4	

June

Solar month	Cyclic Sidereal Day	Week-Day	English Day	Lunar month	Tithi	Tithi Ending Moment	Nakshatra	Nakshatra Ending Moment	Muhammadan Day	Muhammadan month
	19	Mo	1		6	·31	9	·39	5	
	20	Tu	2	*Sukla*	7	·22	10	·32	6	
	21	We	3		8	·15	11	·27	7	
	22	Th	4		9	·08	12	·24	8	
	23	Fr	5		10 11	·01 ·98	13	·21	9	
	24	Sa	6		12	·96	14	·22	10	
	25	Su	7		13	·97	15	·23	11	
	26	Mo	8		14	·98	16	·27	12	
	27	Tu	9	**Jyeshtha**	...	...	17	·33	13	
	28	We	10		P	·03	18	·40	14	H. 1321 *Rabi-ul-awwal.*
	29	Th	11		1	·10	19	·50	15	
	30	Fr	12		2	·16	20	·61	16	
	31	Sa	13		3	·25	21	·71	17	
	32	Su	14		4	·33	22	·82	18	
	1	Mo	15		5	·40	23	·91	19	
	2	Tu	16		6	·47	...	...	20	
	3	We	17		7	·52	24	·00	21	
	4	Th	18	*Bahula*	8	·55	25	·07	22	
	5	Fr	19		9	·55	26	·11	23	
	6	Sa	20		10	·54	27	·13	24	
Sobhana *Mithuna—Ani.*	7	Su	21		11	·51	1	·13	25	
	8	Mo	22		12	·45	2	·12	26	
	9	Tu	23		13	·38	3	·09	27	
	10	We	24		14	·31	4 5	·05 ·99	28	
	11	Th	25		A	·21	6	·92	29	
	12	Fr	26		1	·12	7	·85	30	
	13	Sa	27		2 3	·01 ·90	8	·79	1	*R. akhir.*
	14	Su	28	*Suk.*	4	·80	9	·72	2	
	15	Mo	29		5	·71	10	·66	3	
	16	Tu	30		6	·63	11	·61	4	

Naksh :—1. Asvn. 2. Bhar. 3. Krit. 4. Rohi. 5. Mrig. 6. Ardh. 7. Punar. 8. Push. 9. Aslesh. 10. Magh. 11. P. Phal. 12. U. Phal. 13. Hasta. 14. Chit.

A. D. 1903.
A.—Amavasya.
P.—Paurnami.

Kollam 1079, Commences { **N. Malabar—Sept.** / **S. Malabar—Aug.**

Hijra 1321, Commences, **March 30.**

Vikrama 1960.
Bengal San 1309.
(N. Cycle), Rakshasa.

SOLAR reckoning: Sobhana *Mithuna—Ani.*; Sobhana *Kurkata—Adi.*; Sobhana *Simha—Avani.* — LUNAR reckoning: *Sukla*, **Ashadha**, *Bahula*; *Sukla*, **Sravana**, *Bahula*; *Sukla*, **Bhadra.** — Muhammadan: H. 1321 *Rabi-ul-akhir.*; H. 1321 *Jumadal-awwal.*; *Jl.-akhir.*

Cyclic Sidereal Year, Month and Day.	Week-Day English Month and Day.	Tithi Ending Moment.	Nakshatra Ending Moment.	Muhammadan Year, Month and Day.
	July			
17	We 1	7 ·55	12 ·57	5
18	Th 2	8 ·50	13 ·55	6
19	Fr 3	9 ·46	14 ·54	7
20	Sa 4	10 ·44	15 ·55	8
21	Su 5	11 ·44	16 ·58	9
22	Mo 6	12 ·46	17 ·63	10
23	Tu 7	13 ·51	18 ·72	11
24	We 8	14 ·56	19 ·80	12
25	Th 9	P ·65	20 ·90	13
26	Fr 10	1 ·73	... ...	14
27	Sa 11	2 ·80	21 ·01	15
28	Su 12	3 ·88	22 ·12	16
29	Mo 13	4 ·95	23 ·21	17
30	Tu 14	... ...	24 ·31	18
—31	We 15	5 ·00	25 ·38	19
1	Th 16	6 ·02	26 ·42	20
2	Fr 17	7 ·04	27 ·45	21
3	Sa 18	8 ·02 9 ·99	1 ·46	22
4	Su 19	10 ·93	2 ·45	23
5	Mo 20	11 ·86	3 ·43	24
6	Tu 21	12 ·79	4 ·38	25
7	We 22	13 ·70	5 83	26
8	Th 23	14 ·61	6 ·26	27
9	Fr 24	—A ·50	7 ·20	28
10	Sa 25	1 ·40	8 ·13	—29
11	Su 26	2 ·29	9 ·06	1
12	Mo 27	3 ·20	10 ·00 11 ·94	2
13	Tu 28	4 ·11	12 ·91	3
14	We 29	5 ·03 6 ·98	13 ·88	4
15	Th 30	7 ·93	14 ·86	5
16	Fr 31	8 ·92	15 ·87	6
	Aug.			
17	Sa 1	9 ·92	16 ·90	7
18	Su 2	10 ·93	17 ·95	8
19	Mo 3	11 ·98	... ...	9
20	Tu 4	... ...	18 ·02	10
21	We 5	12 ·03	19 ·10	11
22	Th 6	13 ·12	20 ·20	12
23	Fr 7	14 ·20	21 ·31	13
24	Sa 8	P ·29	22 ·41	14
25	Su 9	1 ·36	23 ·52	15
26	Mo 10	2 ·43	24 ·61	16
27	Tu 11	3 ·47	25 ·69	17
28	We 12	4 ·51	26 ·74	18
29	Th 13	5 ·53	27 ·77	19
30	Fr 14	6 ·50	1 ·79	20
31	Sa 15	7 ·48	2 ·78	21
—32	Su 16	8 ·43	3 ·76	22
1	Mo 17	9 ·37	4 ·71	23
2	Tu 18	10 ·29	5 ·66	24
3	We 19	11 ·19	6 ·61	25
4	Th 20	12 ·09 13 ·99	7 ·54	26
5	Fr 21	14 ·90	8 ·47	27
6	Sa 22	—A ·79	9 ·40	28
7	Su 23	1 ·70	10 ·33	29
8	Mo 24	2 ·61	11 ·28	—30
9	Tu 25	3 ·55	12 ·24	1
10	We 26	4 ·48	13 ·20	2
11	Th 27	5 ·44	14 ·19	3
12	Fr 28	6 ·43	15 ·19	4
13	Sa 29	7 ·42	16 ·21	5
14	Su 30	8 ·44	17 ·26	6
15	Mo 31	9 ·48	18 ·32	7

SOLAR reckoning: Sobhana *Simha—Avani.*; Sobhana *Kanya—Purattasi.*; Sobhana *Tula—Aippasi.* — LUNAR reckoning: *Suk.*, **Bhadrapada**, *Bahula*, *Sukla*; **Asvina**, *Bahula*, *Sukla*, **Karttika** — Muhammadan: H. 1321 *Jumadal-akhir.*; H. 1321 *Rajab.*; H. 1821 *Shaban.*

Cyclic Sidereal Year, Month and Day.	Week-Day English Month and Day.	Tithi Ending Moment.	Nakshatra Ending Moment.	Muhammadan Year, Month and Day.
	Sep.			
16	Tu 1	10 ·55	19 ·41	8
17	We 2	11 ·62	20 ·50	9
18	Th 3	12 ·72	21 ·61	10
19	Fr 4	13 ·81	22 ·72	11
20	Sa 5	14 ·88	23 ·82	12
21	Su 6	P ·95	24 ·92	13
22	Mo 7	1 ·98	25 ·99	14
23	Tu 8	... ...	... ...	15
24	We 9	2 ·02	26 ·05	16
25	Th 10	3 ·04	27 ·10	17
26	Fr 11	4 ·02	1 ·11	18
27	Sa 12	5 ·00 6 ·95	2 ·11	19
28	Su 13	7 ·89	3 ·09	20
29	Mo 14	8 ·81	4 ·05	21
30	Tu 15	9 ·73	5 ·01 6 ·95	22
—31	We 16	10 ·62	7 ·88	23
1	Th 17	11 ·53	8 ·81	24
2	Fr 18	12 ·42	9 ·74	25
3	Sa 19	13 ·31	10 ·68	26
4	Su 20	14 ·23	11 ·62	27
5	Mo 21	—A ·14	12 ·57	28
6	Tu 22	1 ·08	13 ·53	—29
7	We 23	2 ·02 3 ·98	14 ·51	1
8	Th 24	4 ·96	15 ·51	2
9	Fr 25	5 ·95	16 ·53	3
10	Sa 26	6 ·98	17 ·57	4
11	Su 27	... ...	18 ·63	5
12	Mo 28	7 ·03	19 ·71	6
13	Tu 29	8 ·09	20 ·80	7
14	We 30	9 ·18	21 ·91	8
	Oct.			
15	Th 1	10 ·27	... ...	9
16	Fr 2	11 ·33	22 ·02	10
17	Sa 3	12 ·41	23 ·12	11
18	Su 4	13 ·49	24 ·22	12
19	Mo 5	14 ·54	25 ·30	13
20	Tu ○ 6	P ·57	26 ·37	14
21	We 7	1 ·59	27 ·41	15
22	Th 8	2 ·58	1 ·43	16
23	Fr 9	3 ·55	2 ·43	17
24	Sa 10	4 ·52	3 ·41	18
25	Su 11	5 ·45	4 ·39	19
26	Mo 12	6 ·37	5 ·34	20
27	Tu 13	7 ·28	6 ·28	21
28	We 14	8 ·18	7 ·22	22
29	Th 15	9 ·09 10 ·98	8 ·15	23
—30	Fr 16	11 ·89	9 ·08	24
1	Sa 17	12 ·80	10 ·02 11 ·95	25
2	Su 18	13 ·71	12 ·90	26
3	Mo 19	14 ·66	13 ·86	27
4	Tu 20	—A ·59	14 ·84	28
5	We 21	1 ·56	15 ·84	29
6	Th 22	2 ·54	16 ·85	—30
7	Fr 23	3 ·55	17 ·88	1
8	Sa 24	4 ·56	18 ·94	2
9	Su 25	5 ·61	... ...	3
10	Mo 26	6 ·68	19 ·01	4
11	Tu 27	7 ·76	20 ·11	5
12	We 28	8 ·85	21 ·21	6
13	Th 29	9 ·92	22 ·32	7
14	Fr 30	... ...	23 ·42	8
15	Sa 31	10 ·02	24 ·52	9

SOLAR reckoning: Sobhana *Tula—Aippasi.*; Sobhana *Vrischika—Kartigai.*; Sobhana *Dhanus—Margali.* — LUNAR reckoning: *Suk.*, **Kartt.**, *Bahula*, *Sukla*; **Margasira**, *Bahula*, *Sukla*, **Pausha** — Muhammadan: H. 1321 *Shaban.*; H. 1321 *Ramzan.*; H. 1321 *Shawwal.*

Cyclic Sidereal Year, Month and Day.	Week-Day English Month and Day.	Tithi Ending Moment.	Nakshatra Ending Moment.	Muhammadan Year, Month and Day.
	Nov.			
16	Su 1	11 ·08	25 ·61	10
17	Mo 2	12 ·14	26 ·68	11
18	Tu 3	13 ·16	27 ·73	12
19	We 4	14 ·18	1 ·75	13
20	Th 5	P ·18	2 ·76	14
21	Fr 6	1 ·15	3 ·74	15
22	Sa 7	2 ·11	4 ·72	16
23	Su 8	3 ·04 4 ·97	5 ·68	17
24	Mo 9	5 87	6 ·62	18
25	Tu 10	6 ·78	7 ·55	19
26	We 11	7 ·69	8 ·48	20
27	Th 12	8 ·58	9 ·42	21
28	Fr 13	9 ·49	10 ·35	22
29	Sa 14	10 ·40	11 ·29	23
—30	Su 15	11 ·33	12 ·24	24
1	Mo 16	12 ·26	13 ·19	25
2	Tu 17	13 ·20	14 ·17	26
3	We 18	14 ·16	15 ·16	27
4	Th 19	—A ·15	16 ·17	28
5	Fr 20	1 ·16	17 ·20	—29
6	Sa 21	2 ·17	18 ·25	1
7	Su 22	3 ·23	19 ·33	2
8	Mo 23	4 ·30	20 ·41	3
9	Tu 24	5 ·38	21 ·51	4
10	We 25	6 ·46	22 ·62	5
11	Th 26	7 ·54	23 ·72	6
12	Fr 27	8 ·64	24 ·83	7
13	Sa 28	9 ·70	25 ·92	8
14	Su 29	10 ·76	26 ·99	9
15	Mo 30	11 ·79	... ...	10
	Dec.			
16	Tu 1	12 ·82	27 ·04	11
17	We 2	13 ·80	1 ·07	12
18	Th 3	14 ·77	2 ·08	13
19	Fr 4	P ·72	3 ·08	14
20	Sa 5	1 ·66	4 ·05	15
21	Su 6	2 ·59	5 ·01 6 ·96	16
22	Mo 7	3 ·50	7 ·89	17
23	Tu 8	4 ·41	8 ·83	18
24	We 9	5 ·31	9 ·76	19
25	Th 10	6 ·21	10 ·69	20
26	Fr 11	7 ·11	11 ·63	21
27	Sa 12	8 ·02 9 ·95	12 ·57	22
28	Su 13	10 ·88	13 ·53	23
29	Mo 14	11 ·84	14 ·50	24
—30	Tu 15	12 ·80	15 ·48	25
1	We 16	13 ·79	16 ·49	26
2	Th 17	14 ·80	17 ·51	27
3	Fr 18	—A ·82	18 ·57	28
4	Sa 19	1 ·88	19 ·63	29
5	Su 20	2 ·94	20 ·71	—30
6	Mo 21	... ...	21 .81	1
7	Tu 22	3 ·03	22 ·91	2
8	We 23	4 ·11	... ...	3
9	Th 24	5 ·20	23 ·02	4
10	Fr 25	6 ·29	24 ·13	5
11	Sa 26	7 ·35	25 ·22	6
12	Su 27	8 ·41	26 ·30	7
13	Mo 28	9 ·44	27 ·35	8
14	Tu 29	10 ·46	1 ·39	9
15	We 30	11 ·44	2 ·41	10
16	Th 31	12 ·43	3 ·41	11

15. Svati. 16. Visak. 17. Anur. 18. Jyesh. 19. Mula. 20. P. Ash. 21. U. Ash. 22. Sravn. 23. Dani. 24. Satab. 25. P. Bhad. 26. U. Bhad. 27. Rev,

A. D. 1904. **Mesha Sankranti** (Commencement of Indian Sidereal Year).
Solar Eclipse. ● **(Surya Sid.) April 12·65.** **Saka 1826.** **Kaliyuga 5005.**
Lunar Eclipse. ○ **(Arya Sid.) April 12·54.** **(S. Cycle) Krodhi.**

SOLAR reckoning: Cyclic Sidereal Year, Month and Day; Week-Day English Month and Day. LUNAR reckoning: Tithi Ending Moment; Nakshatra Ending Moment; Muhammadan Year, Month and Day.

Jan.

Solar month	Cyclic Sidereal Day	Week-Day	English Day	Lunar month	Tithi Ending Moment	Nakshatra Ending Moment	Muhammadan month	Muhammadan Day
Sobhana Dhanus—Margali	17	Fr	1	Suk.	13 ·37	4 ·38	H. 1321 Shawwal	12
	18	Sa	2		14 ·31	5 ·34		13
	19	Su	3		P ·23	6 ·29		14
	20	Mo	4		1 ·14	7 ·24		15
	21	Tu	5	Pausha	2 ·05 3 ·95	8 ·17		16
	22	We	6		4 ·85	9 ·10		17
	23	Th	7		5 ·76	10 ·03 11 ·96		18
	24	Fr	8		6 ·67	12 ·91		19
	25	Sa	9		7 ·59	13 ·86		20
	26	Su	10		8 .53	14 ·83		21
	27	Mo	11		9 ·48	15 ·81		22
	28	Tu	12	Bahula	10 ·44	16 ·81		23
	—29	We	13		11 ·44	17 ·84		24
Sobhana Makara—Tai	1	Th	14		12 ·44	18 ·88		25
	2	Fr	15		13 ·47	19 ·95		26
	3	Sa	16		14 ·52	... ...		27
	4	Su	17		—A ·60	20 ·01		28
	5	Mo	18		1 ·68	21 ·11		—29
	6	Tu	19		2 .76	22 ·21		1
	7	We	20		3 ·86	23 ·32		2
	8	Th	21		4 ·94	24 ·43		3
	9	Fr	22		... ...	25 ·52		4
	10	Sa	23	Sukla	5 ·00	26 ·60		5
	11	Su	24		6 ·05	27 ·66		6
	12	Mo	25		7 ·09	1 ·71		7
	13	Tu	26		8 ·10	2 ·73		8
	14	We	27		9 ·08	3 ·73		9
	15	Th	28		10 ·07	4 ·71		10
	16	Fr	29		11 ·01 12 ·94	5 ·68		11
	17	Sa	30		13 ·86	6 ·64		12
	18	Su	31		14 ·78	7 ·58		13

Feb.

Solar month	Cyclic Sidereal Day	Week-Day	English Day	Lunar month	Tithi Ending Moment	Nakshatra Ending Moment	Muhammadan month	Muhammadan Day
	19	Mo	1	Magha	P ·68	8 ·51	H. 1321 Zi-l-ka'da	14
	20	Tu	2		1 ·58	9 ·44		15
	21	We	3		2 ·48	10 ·37		16
	22	Th	4		3 ·39	11 ·31		17
	23	Fr	5		4 ·30	12 ·25		18
	24	Sa	6		5 ·22	13 ·20		19
	25	Su	7		6 ·17	14 ·16		20
	26	Mo	8	Bahula	7 ·12	15 ·13		21
	27	Tu	9		8 ·09	16 ·13		22
	28	We	10		9 ·07	17 ·15		23
	—29	Th	11		10 ·07	18 ·19		24
Sobhana Kumbha—Masi	1	Fr	12		11 ·11	19 ·24		25
	2	Sa	13		12 ·17	20 ·32		26
	3	Su	14		13 ·24	21 ·41		27
	4	Mo	15		14 ·31	22 ·52		28
	5	Tu	16		—A ·40	23 ·62		29
	6	We	17		1 ·49	24 ·73		—30
	7	Th	18		2 ·57	25 ·83	H. 1321 Zi-l-hijja	1
	8	Fr	19		3 ·64	26 ·91		2
	9	Sa	20		4 ·69	27 ·98		3
	10	Su	21	Sukla	5 ·71	... ...		4
	11	Mo	22		6 ·72	1 ·03		5
	12	Tu	23		7 ·72	2 ·05		6
	13	We	24		8 ·69	3 ·06		7
	14	Th	25	Phalguna	9 ·62	4 ·04		8
	15	Fr	26		10 ·56	5 ·02 6 ·97		9
	16	Sa	27		11 ·48	7 ·91		10
	17	Su	28		12 ·39	8 ·85		11
	18	Mo	29		13 ·29	9 ·78		12

March

Solar month	Cyclic Sidereal Day	Week-Day	English Day	Lunar month	Tithi Ending Moment	Nakshatra Ending Moment	Muhammadan month	Muhammadan Day
Sobhana Kumbha—Masi	19	Tu	1	Suk.	14 .21	10 ·72		13
	20	We	2		P ·10	11 ·65		14
	21	Th	3	Phalg.	1 ·01 2 ·91	12 ·58		15
	22	Fr	4		3 ·83	13 ·53	H. 1321 Zi-l-hijja	16
	23	Sa	5		4 ·76	14 ·49		17
	24	Su	6		5 ·73	15 ·46		18
	25	Mo	7		6 ·70	16 ·46		19
	26	Tu	8		7 ·68	17 ·47		20
	27	We	9		8 ·69	18 ·50		21
	28	Th	10	Bahula	9 ·73	19 ·55		22
	29	Fr	11		10 ·77	20 ·62		23
	30	Sa	12		11 ·85	21 ·72		24
	—31	Su	13		12 ·92	22 ·82		25
Sobhana Mina—Panguni	1	Mo	14		... ...	23 ·92		26
	2	Tu	15		13 ·01	... ...		27
	3	We	16		14 ·09	24 ·03		28
	4	Th	● 17		—A ·18	25 ·13		—29
	5	Fr	18		1 ·23	26 ·22		1
	6	Sa	19		2 ·28	27 ·29		2
	7	Su	20		3 ·32	1 ·34		3
	8	Mo	21		4 ·32	2 ·37		4
	9	Tu	22	Sukla	5 ·31	3 ·38		5
	10	We	23		6 ·27	4 ·38		6
	11	Th	24		7 ·22	5 ·35		7
	12	Fr	25		8 ·15	6 ·31		8
	13	Sa	26		9 ·08 10 ·98	7 ·25		9
	14	Su	27		11 ·87	8 ·19		10
	15	Mo	28	Chaitra	12 ·77	9 ·12		11
	16	Tu	29		13 ·67	10 ·06 11 ·99		12
	17	We	30		14 ·59	12 ·92		13
	18	Th	31		P ·49	13 ·86		14

April

Solar month	Cyclic Sidereal Day	Week-Day	English Day	Lunar month	Tithi Ending Moment	Nakshatra Ending Moment	Muhammadan month	Muhammadan Day
	19	Fr	1		1 ·42	14 ·82	H. 1322 Muharram	15
	20	Sa	2		2 ·34	15 ·80		16
	21	Su	3		3 ·30	16 ·78		17
	22	Mo	4		4 ·27	17 ·79		18
	23	Tu	5		5 ·25	18 ·81		19
	24	We	6		6 ·26	19 ·86		20
	25	Th	7	Bahula	7 ·30	20 ·94		21
	26	Fr	8		8 ·35	... ...		22
	27	Sa	9		9 ·41	21 ·02		23
	28	Su	10		10 ·48	22 ·12		24
	29	Mo	11		11 ·57	23 ·22		25
	—30	Tu	12		12 ·66	24 ·33		26
Krodhi Mesha—Chittirai	1	We	13		13 ·74	25 ·44		27
	2	Th	14		14 ·79	26 ·53		28
	3	Fr	15		—A ·85	27 ·60		29
	4	Sa	16		1 ·87	1 ·66		—30
	5	Su	17		2 ·88	2 ·69	H. 1322 Safar	1
	6	Mo	18	Sukla	3 ·86	3 ·71		2
	7	Tu	19		4 ·82	4 ·70		3
	8	We	20		5 ·77	5 ·68		4
	9	Th	21		6 ·69	6 ·64		5
	10	Fr	22	Vaisakha	7 ·61	7 ·59		6
	11	Sa	23		8 ·52	8 ·52		7
	12	Su	24		9 ·43	9 ·47		8
	13	Mo	25		10 ·32	10 ·40		9
	14	Tu	26		11 ·22	11 ·32		10
	15	We	27		12 ·13	12 ·26		11
	16	Th	28		13 ·03 14 ·95	13 ·20		12
	17	Fr	29		P ·87	14 ·16		13
	18	Sa	30		1 ·84	15 ·13		14

May

Solar month	Cyclic Sidereal Day	Week-Day	English Day	Lunar month	Tithi Ending Moment	Nakshatra Ending Moment	Muhammadan month	Muhammadan Day
Krodhi Mesha—Chittirai	19	Su	1	Vaisakha	2 ·80	16 ·11	H. 1322 Safar	15
	20	Mo	2		3 ·78	17 ·11		16
	21	Tu	3		4 ·79	18 ·13		17
	22	We	4		5 ·82	19 ·18		18
	23	Th	5		6 ·87	20 ·24		19
	24	Fr	6		7 ·93	21 ·32		20
	25	Sa	7		... ...	22 ·41		21
	26	Su	8		8 ·01	23 ·52		22
	27	Mo	9	Bahula	9 ·10	24 ·64		23
	28	Tu	10		10 ·19	25 ·74		24
	29	We	11		11 ·25	26 ·83		25
	—30	Th	12		12 ·31	27 ·91		26
Krodhi Vrishabha—Vaikasi	1	Fr	13		13 ·37	1 ·97		27
	2	Sa	14		14 ·38	... ...		28
	3	Su	15		—A ·40	2 ·00		—29
	4	Mo	16		1 ·37	3 ·03	H. 1322 Rabi-ul-awwal	1
	5	Tu	17		2 ·35	4 ·03		2
	6	We	18	Sukla	3 ·28	5 ·01 6 ·97		3
	7	Th	19		4 ·21	7 ·92		4
	8	Fr	20		5 ·13	8 ·87		5
	9	Sa	21		6 ·03 7 ·94	9 ·80		6
	10	Su	22		8 ·83	10 ·73		7
	11	Mo	23		9 ·74	11 ·66		8
	12	Tu	24		10 ·63	12 ·60		9
	13	We	25		11 ·54	13 ·54		10
	14	Th	26	Jyeshtha	12 ·46	14 ·49		11
	15	Fr	27		13 ·39	15 ·46		12
	16	Sa	28		14 ·34	16 ·48		13
	17	Su	29		P ·30	17 ·43		14
	18	Mo	30		1 ·29	18 ·45		15
	19	Tu	31		2 ·28	19 ·49		16

June

Solar month	Cyclic Sidereal Day	Week-Day	English Day	Lunar month	Tithi Ending Moment	Nakshatra Ending Moment	Muhammadan month	Muhammadan Day
	20	We	1	Adhika	3 ·32	20 ·55		17
	21	Th	2		4 ·37	21 ·62		18
	22	Fr	3		5 ·43	22 ·71		19
	23	Sa	4		6 ·50	23 ·82		20
	24	Su	5		7 ·59	24 .93		21
	25	Mo	6		8 ·68	... ...		22
	26	Tu	7	Bahula	9 ·75	25 ·04		23
	27	We	8		10 ·80	26 ·13		24
	28	Th	9		11 ·85	27 ·21		25
	29	Fr	10		12 ·87	1 ·28		26
	30	Sa	11		13 ·88	2 ·33		27
	31	Su	12		14 ·86	3 ·35		28
	—32	Mo	13		—A ·83	4 ·35		29
Krodhi Mithuna—Ani	1	Tu	14		1 ·77	5 ·34		—30
	2	We	15		2 ·71	6 ·30	H. 1322 Rabi-ul-akhir	1
	3	Th	16		3 ·62	7 ·27		2
	4	Fr	17		4 ·54	8 ·21		3
	5	Sa	18		5 ·43	9 ·14		4
	6	Su	19		6 ·32	10 ·07		5
	7	Mo	20	Sukla	7 ·23	11 ·00 12 ·94		6
	8	Tu	21		8 ·12	13 ·88		7
	9	We	22	Nija Jyeshtha	9 ·03 10 ·95	14 ·83		8
	10	Th	23		11 ·87	15 ·78		9
	11	Fr	24		12 ·82	16 ·76		10
	12	Sa	25		13 ·78	17 ·76		11
	13	Su	26		14 ·76	18 ·77		12
	14	Mo	27		P ·76	19 ·80		13
	15	Tu	28		1 ·80	20 ·85		14
	16	We	29		2 ·84	21 ·93		15
	17	Th	30		3 ·90	... ...		16

Naksh :—1. Asvn. 2. Bhar. 3. Krit. 4. Rohi. 5. Mrig. 6. Ardh. 7. Punar. 8. Push. 9. Aslesh. 10. Magh. 11. P. Phal. 12. U. Phal. 13. Hasta. 14. Chit.

A. D. 1904. A.—Amavasya. P.—Paurnami.	Kollam 1080, Commences { N. Malabar—Sept. S. Malabar—Aug.	Hijra 1322, Commences, March 18.	Vikrama 1961. Bengal San 1310. (N. Cycle) Anala.

SOLAR reckoning: Cyclic Sidereal Year, Month and Day; Week-Day English Month and Day. LUNAR reckoning: Tithi Ending Moment; Nakshatra Ending Moment; Muhammadan Year, Month and Day.

July

Solar: Krodhi Mithuna—Ani (18–31); Krodhi Karkata—Adi (1–17). Lunar: Nija Jyesh. Bahula; Ashadha Sukla. Muhammadan: H. 1322 Rabi-ul-akhir (17–29); H. 1322 Jumadal-awwal (1–18).

Cyclic Sidereal Year, Month and Day	Week-Day English Month and Day	Tithi Ending Moment	Nakshatra Ending Moment	Muhammadan Year, Month and Day
18	Fr 1	4 ·98	22 ·01	17
19	Sa 2	... ...	23 ·12	18
20	Su 3	5 ·06	24 ·23	19
21	Mo 4	6 ·14	25 ·34	20
22	Tu 5	7 ·21	26 ·43	21
23	We 6	8 ·28	27 ·52	22
24	Th 7	9 ·32	1 ·60	23
25	Fr 8	10 ·35	2 ·64	24
26	Sa 9	11 ·36	3 ·67	25
27	Su 10	12 ·34	4 ·68	26
28	Mo 11	13 ·30	5 ·66	27
29	Tu 12	14 ·25	6 ·64	28
30	We 13	A ·19	7 ·60	29
31	Th 14	1 ·10	8 ·54	1
1	Fr 15	2 ·01; 3 ·91	9 ·48	2
2	Sa 16	4 ·81	10 ·41	3
3	Su 17	5 ·70	11 ·35	4
4	Mo 18	6 ·60	12 ·28	5
5	Tu 19	7 ·51	13 ·22	6
6	We 20	8 ·43	14 ·16	7
7	Th 21	9 ·35	15 ·12	8
8	Fr 22	10 ·30	16 ·09	9
9	Sa 23	11 ·27	17 ·08	10
10	Su 24	12 ·24	18 ·09	11
11	Mo 25	13 ·24	19 ·12	12
12	Tu 26	14 ·28	20 ·16	13
13	We 27	P ·31	21 ·23	14
14	Th 28	1 ·37	22 ·33	15
15	Fr 29	2 ·45	23 ·42	16
16	Sa 30	3 ·54	24 ·53	17
17	Su 31	4 ·61	25 ·63	18

Aug.

Solar: Krodhi Karkata—Adi (18–32); Krodhi Simha—Avani (1–16). Lunar: Ashadha Bahula; Sravana Sukla; Bahula. Muhammadan: H. 1322 Jumadal-awwal (19–30); H. 1322 Jumadal-akhir (1–19).

Cyclic Sidereal Year, Month and Day	Week-Day English Month and Day	Tithi Ending Moment	Nakshatra Ending Moment	Muhammadan Year, Month and Day
18	Mo 1	5 ·69	26 ·74	19
19	Tu 2	6 ·75	27 ·83	20
20	We 3	7 ·80	1 ·91	21
21	Th 4	8 ·84	2 ·96	22
22	Fr 5	9 ·84	3 ·99	23
23	Sa 6	10 ·83	... ...	24
24	Su 7	11 ·79	4 ·00	25
25	Mo 8	12 ·74	5 ·00; 6 ·98	26
26	Tu 9	13 ·68	7 ·93	27
27	We 10	14 ·59	8 ·88	28
28	Th 11	A ·51	9 ·82	29
29	Fr 12	1 ·41	10 ·76	30
30	Sa 13	2 ·30	11 ·69	1
31	Su 14	3 ·20	12 ·62	2
32	Mo 15	4 ·11	13 ·55	3
1	Tu 16	5 ·01; 6 ·94	14 ·49	4
2	We 17	7 ·85	15 ·45	5
3	Th 18	8 ·79	16 ·42	6
4	Fr 19	9 ·76	17 ·41	7
5	Sa 20	10 ·74	18 ·41	8
6	Su 21	11 ·75	19 ·43	9
7	Mo 22	12 ·76	20 ·47	10
8	Tu 23	13 ·81	21 ·55	11
9	We 24	14 ·87	22 ·63	12
10	Th 25	P ·95	23 ·72	13
11	Fr 26	... ...	24 ·83	14
12	Sa 27	1 ·03	25 93	15
13	Su 28	2 ·12	... ...	16
14	Mo 29	3 ·19	26 ·05	17
15	Tu 30	4 ·26	27 ·15	18
16	We 31	5 ·31	1 ·22	19

Sep.

Solar: Krodhi Simha—Avani (17–31); Krodhi Kanya—Purattasi (1–15). Lunar: Srv. Bahula; Bhadrapada Sukla. Muhammadan: H. 1322 Jumadal-akhir (20–29); H. 1322 Rajab (1–20).

Cyclic Sidereal Year, Month and Day	Week-Day English Month and Day	Tithi Ending Moment	Nakshatra Ending Moment	Muhammadan Year, Month and Day
17	Th 1	6 ·34	2 ·27	20
18	Fr 2	7 ·35	3 ·31	21
19	Sa 3	8 ·34	4 ·33	22
20	Su 4	9 ·30	5 ·33	23
21	Mo 5	10 ·27	6 ·31	24
22	Tu 6	11 ·19	7 ·27	25
23	We 7	12 ·11	8 ·22	26
24	Th 8	13 ·02; 14 ·93	9 ·16	27
25	Fr 9	A ·82	10 ·10	28
26	Sa 10	1 ·72	11 ·03; 12 ·96	29
27	Su 11	2 ·62	13 ·89	1
28	Mo 12	3 ·53	14 ·83	2
29	Tu 13	4 ·45	15 ·79	3
30	We 14	5 ·38	16 ·75	4
31	Th 15	6 ·34	17 ·73	5
1	Fr 16	7 ·29	18 ·73	6
2	Sa 17	8 ·27	19 .75	7
3	Su 18	9 ·26	20 ·79	8
4	Mo 19	10 ·29	21 ·85	9
5	Tu 20	11 ·34	22 ·93	10
6	We 21	12 ·39	... ...	11
7	Th 22	13 ·48	23 ·02	12
8	Fr 23	14 ·56	24 ·12	13
9	Sa 24	P ·64	25 ·24	14
10	Su 25	1 ·72	26 ·34	15
11	Mo 26	2 ·80	27 ·44	16
12	Tu 27	3 ·85	1 ·52	17
13	We 28	4 ·88	2 ·58	18
14	Th 29	5 ·90	3 ·63	19
15	Fr 30	6 ·88	4 ·65	20

Oct.

Solar: Krodhi Kanya—Purattasi (16–30); Krodhi Tula—Aippasi (1–16). Lunar: Bahula; Asvina Sukla; Bahula. Muhammadan: H. 1322 Rajab (21–30); H. 1322 Shaban (1–21).

Cyclic Sidereal Year, Month and Day	Week-Day English Month and Day	Tithi Ending Moment	Nakshatra Ending Moment	Muhammadan Year, Month and Day
16	Sa 1	7 ·86	5 ·65	21
17	Su 2	8 ·81	6 ·63	22
18	Mo 3	9 ·74	7 ·60	23
19	Tu 4	10 ·66	8 ·55	24
20	We 5	11 ·57	9 ·50	25
21	Th 6	12 ·48	10 ·44	26
22	Fr 7	13 ·38	11 ·37	27
23	Sa 8	14 ·29	12 ·29	28
24	Su 9	A ·18	13 ·23	29
25	Mo 10	1 ·09	14 ·17	30
26	Tu 11	2 ·01; 3 ·94	15 ·12	1
27	We 12	4 ·90	16 ·08	2
28	Th 13	5 ·85	17 ·06	3
29	Fr 14	6 ·84	18 ·05	4
30	Sa 15	7 ·84	19 ·07	5
1	Su 16	8 ·86	20 ·10	6
2	Mo 17	9 ·91	21 ·16	7
3	Tu 18	10 ·96	22 ·23	8
4	We 19	... ...	23 ·32	9
5	Th 20	11 ·05	24 ·43	10
6	Fr 21	12 ·14	25 ·54	11
7	Sa 22	13 ·23	26 ·64	12
8	Su 23	14 ·31	27 ·74	13
9	Mo 24	P ·39	1 ·82	14
10	Tu 25	1 ·43	2 ·89	15
11	We 26	2 ·46	3 ·95	16
12	Th 27	3 ·48	4 ·97	17
13	Fr 28	4 ·46	5 ·98	18
14	Sa 29	5 ·44	6 ·96	19
15	Su 30	6 ·40	7 ·93	20
16	Mo 31	7 ·34	8 ·90	21

Nov.

Solar: Krodhi Tula—Aippasi (17–30); Krodhi Vrischika—Kartigai (1–16). Lunar: Asv. Bahula; Kartika Sukla. Muhammadan: H. 1322 Shaban (22–29); H. 1322 Ramzan (1–22).

Cyclic Sidereal Year, Month and Day	Week-Day English Month and Day	Tithi Ending Moment	Nakshatra Ending Moment	Muhammadan Year, Month and Day
17	Tu 1	8 ·25	9 ·84	22
18	We 2	9 ·16	10 ·77	23
19	Th 3	10 ·07; 11 ·97	11 ·70	24
20	Fr 4	12 ·88	12 ·63	25
21	Sa 5	13 ·77	13 ·57	26
22	Su 6	14 ·69	14 ·51	27
23	Mo 7	A ·60	15 ·46	28
24	Tu 8	1 ·55	16 ·41	29
25	We 9	2 ·49	17 ·38	1
26	Th 10	3 ·45	18 ·38	2
27	Fr 11	4 ·44	19 ·39	3
28	Sa 12	5 ·44	20 ·42	4
29	Su 13	6 ·47	21 ·47	5
30	Mo 14	7 ·52	22 ·54	6
1	Tu 15	8 ·60	23 ·63	7
2	We 16	9 ·67	24 ·73	8
3	Th 17	10 ·75	25 ·84	9
4	Fr 18	11 ·85	26 ·94	10
5	Sa 19	12 ·93	... ...	11
6	Su 20	13 ·99	27 ·04	12
7	Mo 21	... ...	1 ·13	13
8	Tu 22	14 ·04	2 ·21	14
9	We 23	P ·10	3 ·26	15
10	Th 24	1 ·10	4 ·29	16
11	Fr 25	2 ·08	5 ·30	17
12	Sa 26	3 ·05	6 ·29	18
13	Su 27	4 ·01; 5 ·96	7 ·27	19
14	Mo 28	6 ·87	8 ·23	20
15	Tu 29	7 ·79	9 ·18	21
16	We 30	8 ·69	10 ·11	22

Dec.

Solar: Krodhi Vrischika—Kartigai (17–30); Krodhi Dhanus—Margali (1–17). Lunar: Bahula; Margasira Sukla; Bahula. Muhammadan: H. 1322 Ramzan (23–30); H. 1322 Shawwal (1–23).

Cyclic Sidereal Year, Month and Day	Week-Day English Month and Day	Tithi Ending Moment	Nakshatra Ending Moment	Muhammadan Year, Month and Day
17	Th 1	9 ·60	11 ·04; 12 ·98	23
18	Fr 2	10 ·49	13 ·91	24
19	Sa 3	11 ·39	14 ·85	25
20	Su 4	12 ·31	15 ·79	26
21	Mo 5	13 ·22	16 ·74	27
22	Tu 6	14 ·16	17 ·72	28
23	We 7	A ·12	18 ·70	29
24	Th 8	1 ·09	19 .71	30
25	Fr 9	2 ·07	20 .73	1
26	Sa 10	3 ·07	21 .78	2
27	Su 11	4 ·12	22 .84	3
28	Mo 12	5 ·16	23 .93	4
29	Tu 13	6 ·24	... ...	5
30	We 14	7 ·32	24 ·03	6
1	Th 15	8 ·41	25 ·13	7
2	Fr 16	9 ·49	26 ·24	8
3	Sa 17	10 ·58	27 ·34	9
4	Su 18	11 ·65	1 ·44	10
5	Mo 19	12 ·69	2 ·52	11
6	Tu 20	13 ·73	3 ·57	12
7	We 21	14 ·74	4 ·61	13
8	Th 22	P ·73	5 ·62	14
9	Fr 23	1 ·69	6 ·63	15
10	Sa 24	2 ·66	7 ·60	16
11	Su 25	3 ·59	8 ·56	17
12	Mo 26	4 ·50	9 ·51	18
13	Tu 27	5 ·43	10 ·45	19
14	We 28	6 ·32	11 ·39	20
15	Th 29	7 ·23	12 ·32	21
16	Fr 30	8 ·13	13 ·25	22
17	Sa 31	9 ·04; 10 ·95	14 ·18	23

15. Svati. 16. Visak. 17. Anur. 18. Jyesh. 19. Mula. 20 P. Ash. 21. U. Ash. 22. Sravn. 23. Dani. 24. Satab. 25. P. Bhad. 26. U. Bhad. 27. Rev.

A. D. 1905.
Solar Eclipse. ●
Lunar Eclipse. ○

Mesha Sankranti (Commencement of Indian Sidereal Year)
(Surya Sid.) April 12·91. **Saka 1827.** **Kaliyuga 5006.**
(Arya Sid.) April 12·80. **(S. Cycle) Visvavasu.**

Jan.

SOLAR reckoning: Cyclic Sidereal Year, Month and Day.	SOLAR reckoning: Week-Day English Month and Day.	LUNAR reckoning: Tithi Ending Moment.	LUNAR reckoning: Nakshatra Ending Moment.	LUNAR reckoning: Muhammadan Year, Month and Day.
Krodhi Dhanus—Margali. 18	Su 1	Mr. Bah. 11 ·86	15 ·12	Shawwal. 24
19	Mo 2	12 ·81	16 ·07	25
20	Tu 3	13 ·76	17 ·05	26
21	We 4	14 ·73	18 ·03	27
22	Th 5	—A ·72	19 ·03	28
23	Fr 6	1 ·73	20 ·05	—29
24	Sa 7	2 ·76	21 ·09	1
25	Su 8	3 ·81	22 ·16	2
26	Mo 9	4 ·89	23 ·24	3
27	Tu 10	5 ·96	24 ·33	4
28	We 11	... ...	25 ·43	5
—29	Th 12	Sukla 6 ·06	26 ·54	6
1	Fr 13	7 ·14	27 ·65	7
2	Sa 14	8 ·23	1 ·75	8
3	Su 15	9 ·29	2 ·82	9
4	Mo 16	10 ·35	3 ·88	H. 1322 Zi-l-ka'da. 10
5	Tu 17	11 ·38	4 ·92	11
6	We 18	12 ·38	5 ·95	12
7	Th 19	Pausha 13 ·37	6 ·95	13
8	Fr 20	14 ·34	7 ·93	14
9	Sa 21	P. ·30	8 ·90	15
10	Su 22	1 ·22	9 ·85	16
11	Mo 23	2 ·15	10 ·80	17
12	Tu 24	{ 3 ·05 / 4 ·95	11 ·73	18
13	We 25	5 ·86	12 ·66	19
Krodhi Makara—Tai. 14	Th 26	Bahula 6 ·76	13 ·59	20
15	Fr 27	7 ·67	14 ·52	21
16	Sa 28	8 ·58	15 ·46	22
17	Su 29	9 ·51	16 ·42	23
18	Mo 30	10 ·45	17 ·38	24
19	Tu 31	11 ·41	18 ·35	25

Feb.

Cyclic Sidereal Year, Month and Day.	Week-Day English Month and Day.	Tithi Ending Moment.	Nakshatra Ending Moment.	Muhammadan Year, Month and Day.
20	We 1	12 ·37	19 ·35	26
21	Th 2	13 ·35	20 ·36	27
22	Fr 3	14 ·37	21 ·41	28
23	Sa 4	—A ·41	22 ·46	29
24	Su 5	1 ·46	23 ·54	—30
25	Mo 6	2 ·53	24 ·63	1
26	Tu 7	3 ·62	25 ·73	2
27	We 8	4 ·70	26 ·85	3
28	Th 9	5 ·78	27 ·95	4
29	Fr 10	6 ·87	... ...	5
—30	Sa 11	7 ·93	1 ·05	6
1	Su 12	Sukla 8 ·99	2 ·13	7
2	Mo 13	... ...	3 ·19	8
3	Tu 14	9 ·01	4 ·25	9
4	We 15	10 ·02	5 ·27	H. 1322 Zi-l-hijja. 10
5	Th 16	{ 11 ·00 / 12 ·97	6 ·28	11
6	Fr 17	13 ·92	7 ·26	12
7	Sa 18	Magha 14 ·84	8 ·23	13
8	Su ○ 19	P ·77	9 ·18	14
9	Mo 20	1 ·67	10 ·13	15
Krodhi Kumbha—Masi. 10	Tu 21	2 ·58	11 ·07	16
11	We 22	3 ·49	12 ·00 / 13 ·93 }	17
12	Th 23	4 ·39	14 ·86	18
13	Fr 24	Bahula 5 ·29	15 ·80	19
14	Sa 25	6 ·20	16 ·75	20
15	Su 26	7 ·12	17 ·71	21
16	Mo 27	8 ·05	18 ·68	22
17	Tu 28	{ 9 ·08 / 10 ·99	19 ·67	23

March

Cyclic Sidereal Year, Month and Day.	Week-Day English Month and Day.	Tithi Ending Moment.	Nakshatra Ending Moment.	Muhammadan Year, Month and Day.
18	We 1	Mg. 11 ·98	20 ·69	Zi-l-hijja. 24
19	Th 2	12 ·99	21 ·72	25
20	Fr 3	... ...	22 ·77	26
21	Sa 4	Bah. 13 ·02	23 ·84	27
Krodhi Kumbha—Masi. 22	Su 5	14 ·08	24 ·93	28
23	Mo 6	—A ·14	... ...	29
24	Tu 7	1 ·24	25 ·04	—30
25	We 8	2 ·32	26 ·14	1
26	Th 9	3 ·41	27 ·25	2
27	Fr 10	4 ·49	1 ·35	3
28	Sa 11	Sukla 5 ·54	2 ·43	4
—29	Su 12	6 ·59	3 ·51	5
1	Mo 13	7 ·61	4 ·56	6
2	Tu 14	8 ·62	5 ·59	7
3	We 15	9 ·60	6 ·60	8
4	Th 16	10 ·57	7 ·59	9
5	Fr 17	11 ·51	8 ·56	10
6	Sa 18	Phalguna 12 ·44	9 ·52	11
7	Su 19	13 ·36	10 ·47	12
8	Mo 20	14 ·27	11 ·41	13
9	Tu 21	P ·17	12 ·34	H. 1323 Muharram. 14
10	We 22	{ 1 ·07 / 2 ·97	13 ·27	15
11	Th 23	3 ·88	14 ·21	16
12	Fr 24	4 ·80	15 ·14	17
Krodhi Mina—Panguni. 13	Sa 25	5 ·71	16 ·08	18
14	Su 26	6 ·64	17 ·04	19
15	Mo 27	Bahula 7 ·61	18 ·01	20
16	Tu 28	8 ·57	19 ·00	21
17	We 29	9 ·56	20 ·01	22
18	Th 30	10 ·58	21 ·03	23
19	Fr 31	11 ·61	22 ·08	24

April

Cyclic Sidereal Year, Month and Day.	Week-Day English Month and Day.	Tithi Ending Moment.	Nakshatra Ending Moment.	Muhammadan Year, Month and Day.
20	Sa 1	12 ·66	23 ·15	25
21	Su 2	13 ·73	24 ·24	26
22	Mo 3	14 ·81	25 ·34	27
23	Tu 4	—A ·89	26 ·44	28
24	We 5	1 ·99	27 ·55	29
25	Th 6	... ...	1 ·65	—30
26	Fr 7	2 ·06	2 ·74	1
27	Sa 8	3 ·12	3 ·82	2
28	Su 9	4 ·16	4 ·83	3
29	Mo 10	5 ·18	5 ·91	4
30	Tu 11	6 ·18	6 ·92	5
—31	We 12	Sukla 7 ·16	7 ·91	6
1	Th 13	8 ·13	8 ·90	7
2	Fr 14	9 ·07	9 ·86	8
3	Sa 15	{ 10 ·00 / 11 ·92	10 ·81	9
4	Su 16	12 ·83	11 ·74	H. 1323 Safar. 10
5	Mo 17	13 ·73	12 ·67	11
6	Tu 18	Chaitra 14 ·63	13 ·61	12
7	We 19	P ·53	14 ·54	13
Visvavasu Mesha—Chittirai. 8	Th 20	1 ·43	15 ·48	14
9	Fr 21	2 ·34	16 ·42	15
10	Sa 22	3 ·25	17 ·37	16
11	Su 23	4 ·19	18 ·35	17
12	Mo 24	5 ·14	19 ·33	18
13	Tu 25	6 ·12	20 ·33	19
14	We 26	Bahula 7 ·10	21 ·35	20
15	Th 27	8 ·11	22 ·39	21
16	Fr 28	9 ·15	23 ·46	22
17	Sa 29	10 ·19	24 ·54	23
18	Su 30	11 ·26	25 ·64	24

May

Cyclic Sidereal Year, Month and Day.	Week-Day English Month and Day.	Tithi Ending Moment.	Nakshatra Ending Moment.	Muhammadan Year, Month and Day.
19	Mo 1	Bah. 12 ·33	26 ·74	Safar. 25
20	Tu 2	13 ·43	27 ·85	26
21	We 3	14 ·51	1 ·95	27
Visvavasu Mesha—Chittirai. 22	Th 4	—A ·58	... ...	28
23	Fr 5	1 ·64	2 ·05	—29
24	Sa 6	2 ·68	3 ·13	1
25	Su 7	3 ·71	4 ·18	2
26	Mo 8	4 ·71	5 ·23	3
27	Tu 9	5 ·70	6 ·24	4
28	We 10	6 ·65	7 ·25	5
29	Th 11	Sukla 7 ·59	8 ·23	6
30	Fr 12	8 ·52	9 ·19	7
—31	Sa 13	9 ·44	10 ·14	8
1	Su 14	10 ·35	11 ·08	9
2	Mo 15	11 ·24	12 ·02 / 13 ·95 }	10
3	Tu 16	12 ·15	14 ·88	11
4	We 17	{ 13 ·04 / 14 ·95	15 ·81	12
5	Th 18	Vaisakha P ·85	16 ·75	13
6	Fr 19	1 ·76	17 ·70	14
7	Sa 20	2 ·71	18 ·67	15
8	Su 21	3 ·65	19 ·65	16
9	Mo 22	4 ·63	20 ·65	17
10	Tu 23	5 ·60	21 ·66	H. 1323 Rabi-ul-awwal. 18
11	We 24	6 ·62	22 ·70	19
12	Th 25	7 ·65	23 ·77	20
13	Fr 26	8 ·70	24 ·84	21
Visvavasu Vrishabha—Vaikasi. 14	Sa 27	9 ·77	25 ·93	22
15	Su 28	10 ·83	... ...	23
16	Mo 29	Bahula 11 ·93	26 ·04	24
17	Tu 30	... ...	27 ·14	25
18	We 31	12 ·01	1 ·26	26

June

Cyclic Sidereal Year, Month and Day.	Week-Day English Month and Day.	Tithi Ending Moment.	Nakshatra Ending Moment.	Muhammadan Year, Month and Day.
19	Th 1	13 ·08	2 ·35	27
20	Fr 2	14 ·14	3 ·43	28
21	Sa 3	—A ·17	4 ·50	29
22	Su 4	1 ·21	5 ·54	—30
23	Mo 5	2 ·20	6 ·57	1
24	Tu 6	3 ·19	7 ·57	2
25	We 7	Sukla 4 ·15	8 ·56	3
26	Th 8	5 ·11	9 ·52	4
27	Fr 9	6 ·02 / 7 ·95	10 ·48	5
28	Sa 10	8 ·86	11 ·43	6
29	Su 11	9 ·74	12 ·36	7
30	Mo 12	10 ·65	13 ·29	8
—31	Tu 13	11 ·54	14 ·22	9
1	We 14	12 ·44	15 ·15	H. 1323 Rabi-ul-akhir. 10
2	Th 15	Jyeshtha 13 ·34	16 ·09	11
3	Fr 16	14 ·27	17 ·05	12
4	Sa 17	P ·20	18 ·00 / 19 ·98 }	13
5	Su 18	1 ·13	20 ·97	14
6	Mo 19	2 ·11	21 ·98	15
7	Tu 20	3 ·09	... ...	16
8	We 21	4 ·10	22 ·02	17
Visvavasu Mithuna—Ani. 9	Th 22	5 ·12	23 ·07	18
10	Fr 23	6 ·18	24 ·15	19
11	Sa 24	Bahula 7 ·23	25 ·23	20
12	Su 25	8 ·31	26 ·34	21
13	Mo 26	9 ·40	27 ·45	22
14	Tu 27	10 ·47	1 ·56	23
15	We 28	11 ·55	2 ·66	24
16	Th 29	12 ·61	3 ·74	25
17	Fr 80	13 ·66	4 ·81	26

Naksh :—1. Asvn. 2. Bhar. 3. Krit. 4. Rohi. 5. Mrig. 6. Ardh. 7. Punar. 8. Push. 9. Aslesh. 10. Magh. 11. P. Phal. 12. U. Phal. 13. Hasta. 14. Chit.

A. D. 1905. | Kollam 1081, Commences { N. Malabar—Sept. S. Malabar—Aug. | Hijra 1323, Commences, March 8. | Vikrama 1962.
A.—Amavasya. | | | Bengal San 1311.
P.—Paurnami. | | | (N. Cycle) Pingala.

Columns: SOLAR reckoning (Cyclic Sidereal Year, Month and Day; Week-Day English Month and Day) — LUNAR reckoning (Tithi Ending Moment; Nakshatra Ending Moment; Muhammadan Year, Month and Day).

July — Visvavasu *Mithuna—Ani.*; *Sukla*; **Ashadha**; *Bahula*; *R.akr.*; H. 1323 *Jumadal-awwal.*

Cyclic Sidereal Year, Month and Day	Week-Day English Month and Day	Tithi Ending Moment	Nakshatra Ending Moment	Muhammadan Year, Month and Day
18	Sa 1	14 ·68	5 ·86	27
19	Su 2	—A ·69	6 ·89	28
20	Mo 3	1 ·67	7 ·90	—29
21	Tu 4	2 ·62	8 ·88	1
22	We 5	3 ·68	9 ·85	2
23	Th 6	4 ·50	10 ·81	3
24	Fr 7	5 ·42	11 ·76	4
25	Sa 8	6 ·32	12 ·70	5
26	Su 9	7 ·23	13 ·63	6
27	Mo 10	8 ·11	14 ·56	7
28	Tu 11	9 ·01 10 ·92	15 ·49	8
29	We 12	11 ·82	16 ·44	9
30	Th 13	12 ·74	17 ·38	10
31	Fr 14	13 ·67	18 ·33	11
—32	Sa 15	14 ·62	19 ·30	12
1	Su 16	P ·58	20 ·29	13
2	Mo 17	1 ·57	21 ·31	14
3	Tu 18	2 ·58	22 ·34	15
4	We 19	3 ·60	23 ·38	16
5	Th 20	4 ·64	24 ·45	17
6	Fr 21	5 ·70	25 ·54	18
7	Sa 22	6 ·79	26 ·64	19
8	Su 23	7 ·86	27 ·75	20
9	Mo 24	8 ·95	1 ·86	21
10	Tu 25	... ...	2 ·96	22
11	We 26	9 ·02	... ...	23
12	Th 27	10 ·09	3 ·04	24
13	Fr 28	11 ·15	4 ·13	25
14	Sa 29	12 ·16	5 ·18	26
15	Su 30	13 ·17	6 ·21	27
16	Mo 31	14 ·15	7 ·22	28

Aug. — Visvavasu *Karkata—Adi.*; Visvavasu *Simha—Avani.*; *Sukla*; **Sravana**; *Bahula*; H. 1323 *Jumadal-akhir.*

Cyclic Sidereal Year, Month and Day	Week-Day English Month and Day	Tithi Ending Moment	Nakshatra Ending Moment	Muhammadan Year, Month and Day
17	Tu 1	—A ·11	8 ·21	29
18	We 2	1 ·05 2 ·99	9 ·19	—30
19	Th 3	3 ·92	10 ·15	1
20	Fr 4	4 ·81	11 ·10	2
21	Sa 5	5 ·72	12 ·04 13 ·97	3
22	Su 6	6 ·61	14 ·90	4
23	Mo 7	7 ·52	15 ·84	5
24	Tu 8	8 ·41	16 ·77	6
25	We 9	9 ·32	17 ·71	7
26	Th 10	10 ·24	18 ·67	8
27	Fr 11	11 ·17	19 ·63	9
28	Sa 12	12 ·11	20 ·68	10
29	Su 13	13 ·07	21 ·68	11
30	Mo 14	14 ·06	22 ·65	12
—31	Tu ○ 15	P ·07	23 ·69	13
1	We 16	1 ·09	24 ·76	14
2	Th 17	2 ·14	25 ·85	15
3	Fr 18	3 ·19	26 ·94	16
4	Sa 19	4 ·28	... ...	17
5	Su 20	5 ·36	27 ·05	18
6	Mo 21	6 ·45	1 ·15	19
7	Tu 22	7 ·52	2 ·26	20
8	We 23	8 ·58	3 ·35	21
9	Th 24	9 ·63	4 ·43	22
10	Fr 25	10 ·65	5 ·49	23
11	Sa 26	11 ·67	6 ·53	24
12	Su 27	12 ·65	7 ·54	25
13	Mo 28	13 ·62	8 ·54	26
14	Tu 29	14 ·56	9 ·52	27
15	We ● 30	—A ·50	10 ·49	28
16	Th 31	1 ·42	11 ·44	—29

Sep. — Visvavasu *Simha—Avani.*; *Sukla*; **Bhadrapada**; *Bahula*; H. 1323 *Rajab.*

Cyclic Sidereal Year, Month and Day	Week-Day English Month and Day	Tithi Ending Moment	Nakshatra Ending Moment	Muhammadan Year, Month and Day
17	Fr 1	2 ·33	12 ·37	1
18	Sa 2	3 ·23	13 ·31	2
19	Su 3	4 ·12	14 ·25	3
20	Mo 4	5 ·03 6 ·93	15 ·18	4
21	Tu 5	7 ·83	16 ·11	5
22	We 6	8 ·75	17 ·05	6
23	Th 7	9 ·69	18 ·00 19 ·97	7
24	Fr 8	10 ·62	20 ·95	8
25	Sa 9	11 ·59	21 ·95	9
26	Su 10	12 ·58	22 ·97	10
27	Mo 11	13 ·60	... ...	11
28	Tu 12	14 ·61	23 ·00	12
29	We 13	P ·66	24 ·07	13
30	Th 14	1 ·72	25 ·15	14
—31	Fr 15	2 ·80	26 ·24	15
1	Sa 16	3 ·88	27 ·35	16
2	Su 17	4 ·96	1 ·45	17
3	Mo 18	... ...	2 ·56	18
4	Tu 19	5 ·03	3 ·66	19
5	We 20	6 ·11	4 ·74	20
6	Th 21	7 ·16	5 ·80	21
7	Fr 22	8 ·19	6 ·84	22
8	Sa 23	9 ·20	7 ·86	23
9	Su 24	10 ·19	8 ·87	24
10	Mo 25	11 ·16	9 ·85	25
11	Tu 26	12 ·10	10 ·82	26
12	We 27	13 ·04 14 ·96	11 ·77	27
13	Th 28	—A ·87	12 ·71	28
14	Fr 29	1 ·77	13 ·66	29
15	Sa 30	2 ·68	14 ·58	—30

Oct. — Visvavasu *Kanya—Purattasi.*; Visvavasu *Tula—Aippasi.*; *Sukla*; **Asvina**; *Bahula*; H. 1323 *Shaban.*

Cyclic Sidereal Year, Month and Day	Week-Day English Month and Day	Tithi Ending Moment	Nakshatra Ending Moment	Muhammadan Year, Month and Day
16	Su 1	3 ·58	15 ·51	1
17	Mo 2	4 ·47	16 ·45	2
18	Tu 3	5 ·38	17 ·38	3
19	We 4	6 ·30	18 ·34	4
20	Th 5	7 ·24	19 ·30	5
21	Fr 6	8 ·17	20 ·28	6
22	Sa 7	9 ·15	21 ·27	7
23	Su 8	10 ·13	22 ·28	8
24	Mo 9	11 ·17	23 ·31	9
25	Tu 10	12 ·17	24 ·38	10
26	We 11	13 ·22	25 ·45	11
27	Th 12	14 ·28	26 ·54	12
28	Fr 13	P ·36	27 ·64	13
29	Sa 14	1 ·45	1 ·75	14
30	Su 15	2 ·53	2 ·86	15
—31	Mo 16	3 ·61	3 ·96	16
1	Tu 17	4 ·68	... ...	17
2	We 18	5 ·73	4 ·05	18
3	Th 19	6 ·76	5 ·11	19
4	Fr 20	7 ·77	6 ·16	20
5	Sa 21	8 ·77	7 ·19	21
6	Su 22	9 ·73	8 ·20	22
7	Mo 23	10 ·69	9 ·18	23
8	Tu 24	11 ·62	10 ·15	24
9	We 25	12 ·53	11 ·11	25
10	Th 26	13 ·45	12 ·06 13 ·99	26
11	Fr 27	14 ·85	14 ·92	27
12	Sa 28	—A ·25	15 ·85	28
13	Su 29	1 ·16	16 ·78	—29
14	Mo 30	2 ·07 3 ·97	17 ·72	1
15	Tu 31	4 ·90	18 ·67	2

Nov. — Visvavasu *Tula—Aippasi.*; Visvavasu *Vrischika—Kartigai.*; *Sukla*; **Karttika**; *Bahula*; H. 1323 *Ramzan.*

Cyclic Sidereal Year, Month and Day	Week-Day English Month and Day	Tithi Ending Moment	Nakshatra Ending Moment	Muhammadan Year, Month and Day
16	We 1	5 ·83	19 ·63	3
17	Th 2	6 ·76	20 ·60	4
18	Fr 3	7 ·75	21 ·59	5
19	Sa 4	8 ·73	22 ·60	6
20	Su 5	9 ·75	23 ·64	7
21	Mo 6	10 ·76	24 ·69	8
22	Tu 7	11 ·82	25 ·76	9
23	We 8	12 ·89	26 ·84	10
24	Th 9	13 ·97	27 ·96	11
25	Fr 10	... ...	... ...	12
26	Sa 11	14 ·06	1 ·06	13
27	Su 12	P ·14	2 ·16	14
28	Mo 13	1 ·22	3 ·26	15
29	Tu 14	2 ·29	4 ·35	16
—30	We 15	3 ·35	5 ·42	17
1	Th 16	4 ·38	6 ·48	18
2	Fr 17	5 ·38	7 ·51	19
3	Sa 18	6 ·38	8 ·52	20
4	Su 19	7 ·84	9 ·51	21
5	Mo 20	8 ·30	10 ·48	22
6	Tu 21	9 ·23	11 ·45	23
7	We 22	10 ·16	12 ·39	24
8	Th 23	11 ·07 12 ·98	13 ·33	25
9	Fr 24	13 ·87	14 ·26	26
10	Sa 25	14 ·77	15 ·19	27
11	Su 26	—A ·69	16 ·12	28
12	Mo 27	1 ·59	17 ·07	29
13	Tu 28	2 ·52	18 ·01 19 ·96	—30
14	We 29	3 ·44	20 ·93	1
15	Th 30	4 ·40	21 ·91	2

Dec. — Visvavasu *Dhanus—Margali.*; *Sukla*; **Margasira**; *Bahula*; **Pah.** *Suk.*; H. 1323 *Shawwal.*; *Zi-l-ka'da.*

Cyclic Sidereal Year, Month and Day	Week-Day English Month and Day	Tithi Ending Moment	Nakshatra Ending Moment	Muhammadan Year, Month and Day
16	Fr 1	5 ·37	22 ·93	3
17	Sa 2	6 ·35	23 ·95	4
18	Su 3	7 ·37	... ...	5
19	Mo 4	8 ·40	24 ·00	6
20	Tu 5	9 ·45	25 ·06	7
21	We 6	10 ·51	26 ·14	8
22	Th 7	11 ·61	27 ·25	9
23	Fr 8	12 ·69	1 ·36	10
24	Sa 9	13 ·77	2 ·46	11
25	Su 10	14 ·85	3 ·56	12
26	Mo 11	P ·93	4 ·65	13
27	Tu 12	1 ·99	5 ·74	14
28	We 13	... ...	6 ·79	15
—29	Th 14	2 ·01	7 ·83	16
1	Fr 15	3 ·03	8 ·84	17
2	Sa 16	4 ·01 5 ·98	9 ·84	18
3	Su 17	6 ·93	10 ·81	19
4	Mo 18	7 ·86	11 ·78	20
5	Tu 19	8 ·78	12 ·73	21
6	We 20	9 ·69	13 ·67	22
7	Th 21	10 ·61	14 ·60	23
8	Fr 22	11 ·50	15 ·53	24
9	Sa 23	12 ·41	16 ·47	25
10	Su 24	13 ·31	17 ·40	26
11	Mo 25	14 ·22	18 ·34	27
12	Tu 26	—A ·15	19 ·29	28
13	We 27	1 ·09	20 ·26	—29
14	Th 28	2 ·04	21 ·25	1
15	Fr 29	3 ·01	22 ·25	2
16	Sa 30	4 ·01	23 ·27	3
17	Su 31	5 ·02	24 ·31	4

15. Svati. 16. Visak. 17. Anur. 18. Jyesh. 19 Mula. 20. P. Ash. 21. U. Ash. 22 Sravn. 23. Dani. 24. Satab. 25. P. Bhad. 26. U. Bhad. 27. Rev.

A. D. 1906. **Mesha Sankranti** (Commencement of Indian Sidereal Year).

Solar Eclipse. ● **(Surya Sid.) April 13·17.** **Saka 1828.** **Kaliyuga 5007.**

Lunar Eclipse. ○ **(Arya Sid.) April 13·06.** **(S. Cycle) Parabhava.**

SOLAR reckoning: Cyclic Sidereal Year, Month and Day.	Week-Day English Month and Day.	LUNAR reckoning: Tithi Ending Moment.	Nakshatra Ending Moment.	Muhammadan Year, Month and Day.
	Jan.			
18	Mo 1	6 ·05	25 ·37	5
19	Tu 2	7 ·10	26 ·46	6
Visvavasu Dhanus—Margali. 20	We 3	*Sukla* 8 ·17	27 ·55	7
21	Th 4	9 ·26	1 ·65	8
22	Fr 5	10 ·34	2 ·76	9
23	Sa 6	11 ·44	3 ·86	10
24	Su 7	12 ·52	4 ·97	11
25	Mo 8	13 ·59	... ...	12
26	Tu 9	14 ·64	5 ·04	13
27	We 10	**Pausha** P ·66	6 ·10	14
28	Th 11	1 ·67	7 ·14	15
—29	Fr 12	2 ·66	8 ·16	16
1	Sa 13	3 ·63	9 ·16	17
2	Su 14	4 ·57	10 ·15	*H. 1323 Zi-l-ka'da.* 18
3	Mo 15	5 ·51	11 ·11	19
4	Tu 16	6 ·48	12 ·07	20
5	We 17	*Bahula* 7 ·34	13 ·01 14 ·94	21
6	Th 18	8 ·24	15 ·88	22
7	Fr 19	9 ·14	16 ·81	23
8	Sa 20	10 ·05 11 ·94	17 ·74	24
9	Su 21	12 ·87	18 ·68	25
10	Mo 22	13 ·80	19 ·63	26
11	Tu 23	14 ·74	20 ·60	27
12	We 24	—A ·68	21 ·57	28
13	Th 25	1 ·65	22 ·57	29
14	Fr 26	2 ·65	23 ·58	—30
Visvavasu Makara—Tai. 15	Sa 27	3 ·66	24 ·62	1
16	Su 28	4 ·71	25 ·68	2
17	Mo 29	*Sukla* 5 ·76	26 ·76	3
18	Tu 30	6 ·84	27 ·85	4
19	We 31	7 ·91	1 ·95	5
	Feb.			
20	Th 1	8 ·99	... ...	6
21	Fr 2	... ...	2 ·06	7
22	Sa 3	9 ·08	3 ·16	8
23	Su 4	10 ·17	4 ·27	9
24	Mo 5	11 ·24	5 ·35	10
25	Tu 6	12 ·28	6 ·41	11
26	We 7	13 ·30	7 ·46	12
27	Th 8	**Magha** 14 ·31	8 ·48	*H. 1323 Zi-l-hijja.* 13
28	Fr ○ 9	P ·29	9 ·50	14
29	Sa 10	1 ·26	10 ·48	15
—30	Su 11	2 ·19	11 45.	16
1	Mo 12	3 ·13	12 ·40	17
2	Tu 13	4 ·05 5 ·97	13 ·34	18
3	We 14	6 ·86	14 ·29	19
4	Th 15	7 ·77	15 ·22	20
5	Fr 16	8 ·67	16 ·15	21
6	Sa 17	*Bahula* 9 ·57	17 ·08	22
7	Su 18	10 ·49	18 ·01 19 ·97	23
8	Mo 19	11 ·41	20 ·93	24
Visvavasu Kumbha—Masi. 9	Tu 20	12 ·35	21 ·90	25
10	We 21	13 ·30	22 ·89	26
11	Th 22	14 ·29	23 ·90	27
12	Fr 23	—A ·27	24 ·94	28
13	Sa 24	1 ·28	25 ·99	—29
14	Su 25	**Phal.** *Suk.* 2 ·33	... ...	*H. 1324 Muharram* 1
15	Mo 26	3 ·37	26 ·06	2
16	Tu 27	4 ·45	27 ·15	3
17	We 28	5 ·56	1 ·25	4

SOLAR reckoning: Cyclic Sidereal Year, Month and Day.	Week-Day English Month and Day.	LUNAR reckoning: Tithi Ending Moment.	Nakshatra Ending Moment.	Muhammadan Year, Month and Day.
	March			
18	Th 1	6 ·63	2 ·35	5
19	Fr 2	7 ·71	3 ·47	6
20	Sa 3	*Sukla* 8 ·78	4 ·57	7
Visvavasu Kumbha—Masi. 21	Su 4	9 ·85	5 ·66	8
22	Mo 5	10 ·89	6 ·72	9
23	Tu 6	11 ·91	7 ·77	10
24	We 7	12 ·92	8 ·81	11
25	Th 8	13 ·91	9 ·82	12
26	Fr 9	**Phalguna** 14 ·87	10 ·81	13
27	Sa 10	P ·81	11 ·78	14
28	Su 11	1 ·74	12 ·73	15
29	Mo 12	2 ·65	13 ·69	16
—30	Tu 13	3 ·57	14 ·63	*H. 1324 Muharram.* 17
1	We 14	4 ·46	15 ·56	18
2	Th 15	5 ·37	16 ·48	19
3	Fr 16	*Bahula* 6 ·26	17 ·42	20
4	Sa 17	7 ·17	18 ·36	21
5	Su 18	8 ·08	19 ·30	22
6	Mo 19	9 ·01 10 ·95	20 ·26	23
7	Tu 20	11 ·90	21 ·23	24
8	We 21	12 ·88	22 ·21	25
9	Th 22	13 ·86	23 ·22	26
10	Fr 23	14 ·89	24 ·25	27
11	Sa 24	—A ·92	25 ·30	28
12	Su 25	1 ·96	26 ·37	29
13	Mo 26	... ...	27 ·45	—30
Visvavasu Mina—Panguni. 14	Tu 27	2 ·05	1 ·55	1
15	We 28	3 ·12	2 ·66	2
16	Th 29	*Sukla* 4 ·21	3 ·77	3
17	Fr 30	5 ·29	4 ·87	4
18	Sa 31	6 ·38	5 ·96	5
	April			
19	Su 1	7 ·43	... ...	6
20	Mo 2	8 ·48	6 ·03	7
21	Tu 3	9 ·50	7 ·10	8
22	We 4	10 ·49	8 ·13	9
23	Th 5	11 ·48	9 ·14	10
24	Fr 6	12 ·43	10 ·13	11
25	Sa 7	**Chaitra** 13 ·38	11 ·11	*H. 1324 Safur.* 12
26	Su 8	14 ·31	12 ·08	13
27	Mo 9	P ·23	13 ·03 14 ·96	14
28	Tu 10	1 ·13	15 ·89	15
29	We 11	2 ·02 3 ·93	16 ·82	16
—30	Th 12	4 ·82	17 ·76	17
1	Fr 13	5 ·73	18 ·70	18
2	Sa 14	6 ·64	19 ·64	19
3	Su 15	*Bahula* 7 ·57	20 ·59	20
4	Mo 16	8 ·50	21 ·56	21
5	Tu 17	9 ·46	22 ·54	22
6	We 18	10 ·43	23 ·55	23
7	Th 19	11 ·41	24 ·57	24
Parabhava Mesha—Chittirai. 8	Fr 20	12 ·43	25 ·61	25
9	Sa 21	13 ·46	26 ·67	26
10	Su 22	14 ·51	27 ·75	27
11	Mo 23	—A ·58	1 ·86	28
12	Tu 24	1 ·67	2 ·96	—29
13	We 25	2 ·75	... ...	1
14	Th 26	**Vaisk.** *Sukla* 3 ·84	3 ·07	*R. awwal.* 2
15	Fr 27	4 ·91.	4 ·17	3
16	Sa 28	5 ·97	5 ·26	4
17	Su 29	... ...	6 ·35	5
18	Mo 30	6 ·01	7 ·41	6

SOLAR reckoning: Cyclic Sidereal Year, Month and Day.	Week-Day English Month and Day.	LUNAR reckoning: Tithi Ending Moment.	Nakshatra Ending Moment.	Muhammadan Year, Month and Day.
	May			
19	Tu 1	*Suk.* 7 ·02	8 ·45	7
20	We 2	8 ·03	9 ·46	8
21	Th 3	9 ·01 10 ·97	10 ·46	9
Parabhava Mesha—Chittirai. 22	Fr 4	11 ·91	11 ·45	10
23	Sa 5	12 ·83	12 ·41	11
24	Su 6	**Vaisakha** 13 ·75	13 ·36	12
25	Mo 7	14 ·65	14 ·30	13
26	Tu 8	P ·56	15 ·23	14
27	We 9	1 ·46	16 ·16	15
28	Th 10	2 ·35	17 ·10	16
29	Fr 11	3 ·25	18 ·08 19 ·97	*H. 1324 Rabi-ul-awwal.* 17
30	Sa 12	4 ·16	20 ·92	18
—31	Su 13	5 ·09	21 ·88	19
1	Mo 14	6 ·02 7 ·97	22 ·87	20
2	Tu 15	8 ·94	23 ·87	21
3	We 16	*Bahula* 9 ·93	24 ·88	22
4	Th 17	10 ·94	25 ·92	23
5	Fr 18	11 ·98	26 ·98	24
6	Sa 19	... ...	... ...	25
7	Su 20	12 ·02	27 ·06	26
8	Mo 21	13 ·09	1 ·16	27
9	Tu 22	14 ·17	2 ·26	28
10	We 23	—A ·26	3 ·36	29
11	Th 24	1 ·34	4 ·47	—30
12	Fr 25	2 ·41	5 ·57	1
Parabhava Vrishabha—Vaikasi. 13	Sa 26	3 ·47	6 ·66	2
14	Su 27	4 ·52	7 ·72	3
15	Mo 28	5 ·52	8 ·76	4
16	Tu 29	6 ·58	9 ·78	5
17	We 30	*Sukla* 7 ·51	10 ·78	6
18	Th 31	8 ·46	11 ·78	7
	June			
19	Fr 1	9 ·41	12 ·74	8
20	Sa 2	10 ·35	13 ·70	9
21	Su 3	11 ·26	14 ·64	10
22	Mo 4	12 ·14	15 ·57	11
23	Tu 5	13 ·05 14 ·95	16 ·51	12
24	We 6	P ·85	17 ·44	13
25	Th 7	1 ·75	18 ·87	14
26	Fr 8	**Jyeshtha** 2 ·67	19 ·31	*H. 1324 Rabi-ul-akhir.* 15
27	Sa 9	3 ·58	20 ·26	16
28	Su 10	4 ·52	21 ·22	17
29	Mo 11	5 ·46	22 ·20	18
30	Tu 12	6 ·43	23 ·19	19
—31	We 13	7 ·42	24 ·20	20
1	Th 14	8 ·42	25 ·23	21
2	Fr 15	*Bahula* 9 ·46	26 ·30	22
3	Sa 16	10 ·51	27 ·37	23
4	Su 17	11 ·57	1 ·46	24
5	Mo 18	12 ·64	2 ·56	25
6	Tu 19	13 ·78	3 ·66	26
7	We 20	14 ·82	4 ·78	27
Parabhava Mithuna—Ani. 8	Th 21	—A ·88	5 ·88	28
9	Fr 22	1 ·95	6 ·96	—29
10	Sa 23	*Sukla* 2 ·99	... ...	1
11	Su 24	... ...	7 ·03	2
12	Mo 25	3 ·01	8 ·08	*Jumadal-awwal.* 3
13	Tu 26	4 ·01 5 ·99	9 ·10	4
14	We 27	**Ashad.** 6 ·95	10 ·12	5
15	Th 28	7 ·89	11 ·10	6
16	Fr 29	8 ·83	12 ·07	7
17	Sa 30	9 ·74	13 ·03 14 ·97	8

Naksh :—1. Asvn. 2. Bhar. 3. Krit. 4. Rohi. 5. Mrig. 6. Ardh. 7. Punar. 8. Push. 9. Aslesh. 10. Magh. 11 P. Phal. 12. U. Phal. 13. Hasta. 14. Chit.

A. D. 1906.	Kollam 1082, Commences	N. Malabar—Sept. S. Malabar—Aug.	Hijra 1324, Commences, Feb. 25.	Vikrama 1963.
A.—Amavasya.				Bengal San 1313.
P.—Paurnami.				(N. Cycle) Kalayukta.

Columns: SOLAR reckoning — Cyclic Sidereal Year, Month and Day; Week-Day English Month and Day. LUNAR reckoning — Tithi Ending Moment; Nakshatra Ending Moment; Muhammadan Year, Month and Day.

July

Solar: Parabhava *Mithuna—Ani.* (to 32); Parabhava *Karkata—Adi.* (from 1). Lunar: Ashadha Sud.; *Bahula*; *Sukla*. Muhammadan: H. 1324 *Jumadal-awwal.*

Cyclic Sidereal Year, Month and Day	Week-Day	English Day	Tithi Ending Moment	Nakshatra Ending Moment	Muhammadan Year, Month and Day
18	Su	1	10 ·64	15 ·92	9
19	Mo	2	11 ·54	16 ·85	10
20	Tu	3	12 ·44	17 ·78	11
21	We	4	13 33	18 ·71	12
22	Th	5	14 ·23	19 ·64	13
23	Fr	6	P ·15	20 ·60	14
24	Sa	7	1 ·05	21 ·55	15
25	Su	8	2 ·00 3 ·94	22 ·52	16
26	Mo	9	4 ·91	23 ·51	17
27	Tu	10	5 ·89	24 ·52	18
28	We	11	6 ·90	25 ·56	19
29	Th	12	7 ·94	26 ·60	20
30	Fr	13	8 ·98	27 ·67	21
31	Sa	14	... ...	1 ·76	22
32	Su	15	9 ·05	2 ·85	23
1	Mo	16	10 ·13	3 ·96	24
2	Tu	17	11 ·20	... ...	25
3	We	18	12 ·28	4 ·08	26
4	Th	19	13 ·35	5 ·18	27
5	Fr	20	14 ·43	6 ·26	28
6	Sa	21	A ·46	7 ·34	29
7	Su	22	1 ·49	8 ·40	30
8	Mo	23	2 ·49	9 ·43	1
9	Tu	24	3 ·47	10 ·44	2
10	We	25	4 ·43	11 ·43	3
11	Th	26	5 ·37	12 ·40	4
12	Fr	27	6 ·31	13 ·36	5
13	Sa	28	7 ·22	14 ·32	6
14	Su	29	8 ·13	15 ·26	7
15	Mo	30	9 ·03 10 ·93	16 ·19	8
16	Tu	31	11 ·82	17 ·12	9

Aug.

Solar: Parabhava *Simha—Avani.* (from 1). Lunar: Sravana; *Bahula*; *Sukla*; Bhadra. Muhammadan: H. 1324 *Jumadal-akhir.*; H. 1324 *Rajab.*

Cyclic Sidereal Year, Month and Day	Week-Day	English Day	Tithi Ending Moment	Nakshatra Ending Moment	Muhammadan Year, Month and Day
17	We	1	12 ·78	18 ·05 19 ·99	10
18	Th	2	13 ·64	20 ·93	11
19	Fr	3	14 ·55	21 ·89	12
20	Sa ☉	4	P ·47	22 ·85	13
21	Su	5	1 ·42	23 ·84	14
22	Mo	6	2 ·40	24 ·85	15
23	Tu	7	3 ·38	25 ·87	16
24	We	8	4 ·39	26 ·91	17
25	Th	9	5 ·41	27 ·98	18
26	Fr	10	6 ·46	... ...	19
27	Sa	11	7 ·53	1 ·06	20
28	Su	12	8 ·61	2 ·16	21
29	Mo	13	9 ·69	3 ·27	22
30	Tu	14	10 ·77	4 ·37	23
31	We	15	11 ·85	5 ·48	24
1	Th	16	12 ·91	6 ·57	25
2	Fr	17	13 ·95	7 ·65	26
3	Sa	18	14 ·98	8 ·71	27
4	Su	19	A ·98	9 ·75	28
5	Mo	20	1 ·97	10 ·76	29
6	Tu	21	2 ·93	11 ·76	1
7	We	22	3 ·89	12 ·73	2
8	Th	23	4 ·81	13 ·71	3
9	Fr	24	5 ·73	14 ·66	4
10	Sa	25	6 ·63	15 ·59	5
11	Su	26	7 ·53	16 ·53	6
12	Mo	27	8 ·44	17 ·46	7
13	Tu	28	9 ·33	18 ·40	8
14	We	29	10 ·23	19 ·33	9
15	Th	30	11 ·14	20 ·27	10
16	Fr	31	12 ·06 13 ·99	21 ·22	11

Sep.

Solar: Parabhava *Simha—Avani.* (to 32); Parabhava *Kanya—Purattasi.* (from 1). Lunar: Bhadrapada; *Bahula*; *Sukla*. Muhammadan: H. 1324 *Rajab.*

Cyclic Sidereal Year, Month and Day	Week-Day	English Day	Tithi Ending Moment	Nakshatra Ending Moment	Muhammadan Year, Month and Day
17	Sa	1	14 ·93	22 ·18	12
18	Su	2	P ·91	23 ·17	13
19	Mo	3	1 ·89	24 ·17	14
20	Tu	4	2 ·92	25 ·19	15
21	We	5	3 ·93	26 ·22	16
22	Th	6	4 ·98	27 ·23	17
23	Fr	7	... ...	1 ·37	18
24	Sa	8	5 ·03	2 ·46	19
25	Su	9	6 ·11	3 ·57	20
26	Mo	10	7 ·20	4 ·67	21
27	Tu	11	8 ·28	5 ·78	22
28	We	12	9 ·36	6 ·87	23
29	Th	13	10 ·43	7 ·96	24
30	Fr	14	11 ·48	... ...	25
31	Sa	15	12 ·50	8 ·02	26
32	Su	16	13 ·52	9 ·06	27
1	Mo	17	14 ·50	10 ·08	28
2	Tu	18	A ·46	11 ·08	29
3	We	19	1 ·41	12 ·07	30
4	Th	20	2 ·84	13 ·04 14 ·99	1
5	Fr	21	3 ·26	15 ·93	2
6	Sa	22	4 16	16 ·86	3
7	Su	23	5 ·07 6 ·97	17 ·80	4
8	Mo	24	7 ·87	18 ·73	5
9	Tu	25	8 ·77	19 ·67	6
10	We	26	9 ·68	20 ·60	7
11	Th	27	10 ·60	21 ·55	8
12	Fr	28	11 ·53	22 ·52	9
13	Sa	29	12 ·48	23 ·50	10
14	Su	30	13 ·45	24 ·49	11

Oct.

Solar: Parabhava *Tula—Aippasi.* (from 1). Lunar: Asvina; *Bahula*; *Sukla*; Karttika. Muhammadan: H. 1324 *Shaban.*; H. 1324 *Ramzan.*

Cyclic Sidereal Year, Month and Day	Week-Day	English Day	Tithi Ending Moment	Nakshatra Ending Moment	Muhammadan Year, Month and Day
15	Mo	1	14 ·44	25 ·50	12
16	Tu	2	P ·46	26 ·54	13
17	We	3	1 ·47	27 ·59	14
18	Th	4	2 ·53	1 ·67	15
19	Fr	5	3 ·58	2 ·76	16
20	Sa	6	4 ·67	3 ·86	17
21	Su	7	5 ·75	4 ·97	18
22	Mo	8	6 ·84	... ...	19
23	Tu	9	7 ·92	5 ·08	20
24	We	10	8 ·99	6 ·18	21
25	Th	11	... ...	7 ·27	22
26	Fr	12	9 ·04	8 ·33	23
27	Sa	13	10 ·06	9 ·38	24
28	Su	14	11 ·08	10 ·40	25
29	Mo	15	12 ·06	11 ·42	26
30	Tu	16	13 ·04 14 ·98	12 ·40	27
1	We	17	A ·90	13 ·37	28
2	Th	18	1 ·83	14 ·32	29
3	Fr	19	2 ·73	15 ·27	1
4	Sa	20	3 ·64	16 ·21	2
5	Su	21	4 ·54	17 ·14	3
6	Mo	22	5 ·45	18 ·07	4
7	Tu	23	6 ·35	19 ·00 20 ·94	5
8	We	24	7 ·27	21 ·89	6
9	Th	25	8 ·18	22 ·85	7
10	Fr	26	9 ·11	23 ·82	8
11	Sa	27	10 ·06	24 ·81	9
12	Su	28	11 ·03	25 ·82	10
13	Mo	29	12 ·03	26 ·85	11
14	Tu	30	13 ·03	27 ·91	12
15	We	31	14 ·07	1 ·98	13

Nov.

Solar: Parabhava *Tula—Aippasi.* (to 30); Parabhava *Vrischika—Kartigai.* (from 1). Lunar: Karttika; *Bahula*; *Sukla*; Margasira. Muhammadan: H. 1324 *Ramzan.*

Cyclic Sidereal Year, Month and Day	Week-Day	English Day	Tithi Ending Moment	Nakshatra Ending Moment	Muhammadan Year, Month and Day
16	Th	1	P ·12	... ..	14
17	Fr	2	1 ·18	2 ·06	15
18	Sa	3	2 ·27	3 ·16	16
19	Su	4	3 ·30	4 ·27	17
20	Mo	5	4 ·45	5 ·38	18
21	Tu	6	5 ·52	6 ·48	19
22	We	7	6 ·59	7 ·57	20
23	Th	8	7 ·63	8 ·64	21
24	Fr	9	8 ·67	9 ·69	22
25	Sa	10	9 ·68	10 ·73	23
26	Su	11	10 ·66	11 ·74	24
27	Mo	12	11 ·63	12 ·73	25
28	Tu	13	12 ·58	13 ·70	26
29	We	14	13 ·52	14 ·66	27
30	Th	15	14 ·44	15 ·61	28
1	Fr	16	A ·35	16 ·55	29
2	Sa	17	1 ·25	17 ·48	30
3	Su	18	2 ·15	18 ·41	1
4	Mo	19	3 ·06 4 ·96	19 ·34	2
5	Tu	20	5 ·87	20 ·28	3
6	We	21	6 ·80	21 ·23	4
7	Th	22	7 ·73	22 ·18	5
8	Fr	23	8 ·68	23 ·15	6
9	Sa	24	9 ·65	24 ·13	7
10	Su	25	10 ·65	25 ·14	8
11	Mo	26	11 ·66	26 ·17	9
12	Tu	27	12 ·69	27 ·22	10
13	We	28	13 ·74	1 ·28	11
14	Th	29	14 ·82	2 ·36	12
15	Fr	30	P ·90	3 ·46	13

Dec.

Solar: Parabhava *Dhanus—Marguli.* (from 1). Lunar: *Bahula*; *Sukla*; Pausha. Muhammadan: H. 1324 *Shawwal.*; H. 1324 *Zi-l-ka'da.*

Cyclic Sidereal Year, Month and Day	Week-Day	English Day	Tithi Ending Moment	Nakshatra Ending Moment	Muhammadan Year, Month and Day
16	Sa	1	1 ·98	4 ·58	14
17	Su	2	... ...	5 ·68	15
18	Mo	3	2 ·07	6 ·78	16
19	Tu	4	3 ·15	7 ·87	17
20	We	5	4 ·22	8 ·95	18
21	Th	6	5 ·27	... ...	19
22	Fr	7	6 ·30	9 ·01	20
23	Sa	8	7 ·31	10 ·05	21
24	Su	9	8 ·30	11 ·06	22
25	Mo	10	9 ·26	12 ·06	23
26	Tu	11	10 ·21	13 ·03	24
27	We	12	11 ·14	14 ·00 15 ·95	25
28	Th	13	12 ·06 13 ·97	16 ·89	26
29	Fr	14	14 ·88	17 ·82	27
1	Sa	15	A ·78	18 ·75	28
2	Su	16	1 ·68	19 ·68	29
3	Mo	17	2 ·59	20 ·62	1
4	Tu	18	3 ·50	21 ·56	2
5	We	19	4 ·42	22 ·51	3
6	Th	20	5 ·36	23 ·48	4
7	Fr	21	6 ·32	24 ·46	5
8	Sa	22	7 ·30	25 ·47	6
9	Su	23	8 ·28	26 ·49	7
10	Mo	24	9 31	27 ·53	8
11	Tu	25	10 ·34	1 ·59	9
12	We	26	11 ·39	2 ·67	10
13	Th	27	12 ·47	3 ·77	11
14	Fr	28	13 ·55	4 ·87	12
15	Sa	29	14 ·64	5 ·98	13
16	Su	30	P ·78	... ...	14
17	Mo	31	1 ·81	6 ·08	15

15. Svati. 16. Visak. 17. Anur. 18. Jyesh. 19. Mula. 20. P. Ash. 21. U. Ash. 22. Sravn. 23. Dani. 24. Satab. 25. P. Bhad. 26. U. Bhad. 27. Rev.

A. D. 1907.
Solar Eclipse. ●
Lunar Eclipse. ○

Mesha Sankranti (Commencement of Indian Sidereal Year).
(Surya Sid.) April 13·43.
(Arya Sid.) April 13·32.

Saka 1829. **Kaliyuga 5008.**
(S. Cycle) Plavanga.

Columns: SOLAR reckoning — Cyclic Sidereal Year, Month and Day; Week-Day English Month and Day. LUNAR reckoning — Tithi Ending Moment; Nakshatra Ending Moment; Muhammadan Year, Month and Day.

Jan.

Solar: Parabhava Dhanus—Margali (to 30); Parabhava Makara—Tai (from 1). Lunar: Pausha, Bahula, Sukla, Magha. Muhammadan: H. 1324 Zi-l-ka'da; H. 1324 Zi-l-hijja.

Cyclic Sidereal	Week-Day	Day	Tithi	Nakshatra	Muhammadan
18	Tu	1	Pausha 2 ·87	7 ·18	16
19	We	2	3 ·91	8 ·27	17
20	Th	3	4 ·95	9 ·32	18
21	Fr	4	5 ·95	10 ·36	19
22	Sa	5	6 ·94	11 ·38	20
23	Su	6	7 ·91	12 ·38	21
24	Mo	7	8 ·86	13 ·36	22
25	Tu	8	Bahula 9 ·78	14 ·33	23
26	We	9	10 ·71	15 ·29	24
27	Th	10	11 ·62	16 ·23	25
28	Fr	11	12 ·52	17 ·16	26
29	Sa	12	13 ·43	18 ·09	27
30	Su	13	14 ·33	19 ·03 20 ·96	28
1	Mo ●	14	A ·24	21 ·90	29
2	Tu	15	1 ·14	22 ·85	30
3	We	16	2 ·08	23 ·81	1
4	Th	17	3 ·01 4 ·96	24 ·79	2
5	Fr	18	5 ·95	25 ·79	3
6	Sa	19	6 ·93	26 ·80	4
7	Su	20	7 ·95	27 ·84	5
8	Mo	21	Sukla 8 ·98	1 ·89	6
9	Tu	22	... ...	2 ·98	7
10	We	23	9 ·06	... ...	8
11	Th	24	10 ·12	3 ·07	9
12	Fr	25	11 ·20	4 ·17	10
13	Sa	26	12 ·30	5 ·28	11
14	Su	27	Magha 13 ·38	6 ·38	12
15	Mo	28	14 ·46	7 ·49	13
16	Tu ○	29	P ·52	8 ·57	14
17	We	30	1 ·58	9 ·64	15
18	Th	31	2 ·59	10 ·68	16

Feb.

Solar: Parabhava Kumbha—Masi. Lunar: Bahula, Sukla, Phalguna. Muhammadan: H. 1325 Muharram.

Cyclic Sidereal	Week-Day	Day	Tithi	Nakshatra	Muhammadan
19	Fr	1	3 ·59	11 ·70	17
20	Sa	2	4 ·58	12 ·71	18
21	Su	3	5 ·55	13 ·70	19
22	Mo	4	6 ·49	14 ·67	20
23	Tu	5	Bahula 7 ·41	15 ·62	21
24	We	6	8 ·34	16 ·56	22
25	Th	7	9 ·25	17 ·50	23
26	Fr	8	10 ·16	18 ·44	24
27	Sa	9	11 ·05 12 ·95	19 ·37	25
28	Su	10	13 ·86	20 ·30	26
29	Mo	11	14 ·76	21 ·23	27
1	Tu	12	A ·70	22 ·18	28
2	We	13	1 ·64	23 ·15	29
3	Th	14	2 ·60	24 ·12	1
4	Fr	15	3 ·57	25 ·11	2
5	Sa	16	4 ·56	26 ·12	3
6	Su	17	5 ·58	27 ·15	4
7	Mo	18	6 ·62	1 ·21	5
8	Tu	19	Sukla 7 ·68	2 ·28	6
9	We	20	8 ·75	3 ·37	7
10	Th	21	9 ·83	4 ·47	8
11	Fr	22	10 ·93	5 ·58	9
12	Sa	23	... ...	6 ·68	10
13	Su	24	Phalguna 11 ·01	7 ·79	11
14	Mo	25	12 ·09	8 ·88	12
15	Tu	26	13 ·14	9 ·94	13
16	We	27	14 ·19	10 ·99	14
17	Th	28	P ·20	... ...	15

March

Solar: Parabhava Kumbha—Masi (to 30); Parabhava Mina—Panguni (from 1). Lunar: Phalg., Bahula, Sukla, Chaitra. Muhammadan: H. 1325 Muharram; H. 1325 Safar.

Cyclic Sidereal	Week-Day	Day	Tithi	Nakshatra	Muhammadan
18	Fr	1	Phalg. 1 ·22	11 ·02	16
19	Sa	2	2 ·20	12 ·04	17
20	Su	3	3 ·17	13 ·03	18
21	Mo	4	4 ·10	14 ·00 15 ·95	19
22	Tu	5	5 ·02 6 ·94	16 ·90	20
23	We	6	Bahula 7 ·85	17 ·84	21
24	Th	7	8 ·77	18 ·77	22
25	Fr	8	9 ·66	19 ·70	23
26	Sa	9	10 ·57	20 ·63	24
27	Su	10	11 ·47	21 ·57	25
28	Mo	11	12 ·37	22 ·52	26
29	Tu	12	13 ·30	23 ·48	27
30	We	13	14 ·23	24 ·45	28
1	Th	14	A ·20	25 ·43	29
2	Fr	15	1 ·17	26 ·44	30
3	Sa	16	2 ·16	27 ·47	1
4	Su	17	3 ·17	1 ·52	2
5	Mo	18	4 ·22	2 ·59	3
6	Tu	19	5 ·28	3 ·67	4
7	We	20	6 ·36	4 ·77	5
8	Th	21	Sukla 7 ·44	5 ·87	6
9	Fr	22	8 ·52	6 ·99	7
10	Sa	23	9 ·61	... ...	8
11	Su	24	10 ·68	7 ·09	9
12	Mo	25	11 ·74	8 ·18	10
13	Tu	26	12 ·78	9 ·25	11
14	We	27	13 ·80	10 ·31	12
15	Th	28	Chaitra 14 ·80	11 ·35	13
16	Fr	29	P ·78	12 ·36	14
17	Sa	30	1 ·74	13 ·35	15
18	Su	31	2 ·68	14 ·33	16

April

Solar: Plavanga Mesha—Chittirai. Lunar: Adhika, Bahula, Sukla, Nija Chaitra. Muhammadan: H. 1325 Rabi-ul-awwal.

Cyclic Sidereal	Week-Day	Day	Tithi	Nakshatra	Muhammadan
19	Mo	1	Adhika 3 ·61	15 ·29	17
20	Tu	2	4 ·52	16 ·24	18
21	We	3	5 ·42	17 ·18	19
22	Th	4	6 ·32	18 ·11	20
23	Fr	5	7 ·22	19 ·04 20 ·97	21
24	Sa	6	8 ·13	21 ·92	22
25	Su	7	9 ·03 10 ·95	22 ·86	23
26	Mo	8	Bahula 11 ·86	23 ·81	24
27	Tu	9	12 ·80	24 ·78	25
28	We	10	13 ·76	25 ·76	26
29	Th	11	14 ·73	26 ·76	27
30	Fr	12	A ·72	27 ·79	28
1	Sa	13	1 ·73	1 ·83	29
2	Su	14	2 ·78	2 ·89	1
3	Mo	15	3 ·83	3 ·97	2
4	Tu	16	4 ·92	... ...	3
5	We	17	5 ·99	4 ·07	4
6	Th	18	Sukla	5 ·18	5
7	Fr	19	6 ·07	6 ·29	6
8	Sa	20	7 ·16	7 ·39	7
9	Su	21	8 ·23	8 ·48	8
10	Mo	22	9 ·29	9 ·56	9
11	Tu	23	Nija Chaitra 10 ·32	10 ·63	10
12	We	24	11 ·34	11 ·67	11
13	Th	25	12 ·34	12 ·68	12
14	Fr	26	13 ·32	13 ·68	13
15	Sa	27	14 ·29	14 ·66	14
16	Su	28	P ·22	15 ·63	15
17	Mo	29	1 ·15	16 ·58	16
18	Tu	30	2 ·06 3 ·97	17 ·52	17

May

Solar: Plavanga Mesha—Chittirai (to 31); Plavanga Vrishabha—Vaikasi (from 1). Lunar: Nija Chait., Bahula, Sukla, Vaisakha. Muhammadan: H. 1325 Rabi-ul-awwal; H. 1325 Rabi-ul-akhir.

Cyclic Sidereal	Week-Day	Day	Tithi	Nakshatra	Muhammadan
19	We	1	Nija Chait. 4 ·86	18 ·45	18
20	Th	2	5 ·77	19 ·38	19
21	Fr	3	6 ·66	20 ·31	20
22	Sa	4	7 ·56	21 ·25	21
23	Su	5	8 ·48	22 ·19	22
24	Mo	6	9 ·39	23 ·14	23
25	Tu	7	10 ·33	24 ·10	24
26	We	8	Bahula 11 ·29	25 ·08	25
27	Th	9	12 ·27	26 ·09	26
28	Fr	10	13 ·24	27 ·10	27
29	Sa	11	14 ·25	1 ·14	28
30	Su	12	A ·30	2 ·20	29
31	Mo	13	1 ·35	3 ·27	30
1	Tu	14	2 ·43	4 ·38	1
2	We	15	3 ·50	5 ·48	2
3	Th	16	4 ·59	6 ·59	3
4	Fr	17	5 ·67	7 ·69	4
5	Sa	18	6 ·74	8 ·79	5
6	Su	19	Sukla 7 ·80	9 ·88	6
7	Mo	20	8 ·84	10 ·94	7
8	Tu	21	9 ·85	11 ·98	8
9	We	22	10 ·85	... ...	9
10	Th	23	11 ·84	12 ·00	10
11	Fr	24	12 ·80	13 ·00	11
12	Sa	25	Vaisakha 13 ·74	14 ·00 15 ·96	12
13	Su	26	14 ·65	16 ·91	13
14	Mo	27	P ·56	17 ·86	14
15	Tu	28	1 ·48	18 ·79	15
16	We	29	2 ·36	19 ·72	16
17	Th	30	3 ·27	20 ·66	17
18	Fr	31	4 ·16	21 ·59	18

June

Solar: Plavanga Mithuna—Ani. Lunar: Bahula, Sukla, Jyeshtha, Bahula. Muhammadan: H. 1325 Rabi-ul-akhir; H. 1325 Jumadal-awwal.

Cyclic Sidereal	Week-Day	Day	Tithi	Nakshatra	Muhammadan
19	Sa	1	5 ·06 6 ·97	22 ·53	19
20	Su	2	Bahula 7 ·90	23 ·47	20
21	Mo	3	8 ·84	24 ·43	21
22	Tu	4	9 ·78	25 ·42	22
23	We	5	10 ·76	26 ·41	23
24	Th	6	11 ·74	27 ·42	24
25	Fr	7	12 ·76	1 ·45	25
26	Sa	8	13 ·78	2 ·51	26
27	Su	9	14 ·84	3 ·59	27
28	Mo	10	A ·92	4 ·68	28
29	Tu	11	1 ·98	5 ·78	29
30	We	12	... ...	6 ·88	1
31	Th	13	2 ·07	7 ·99	2
32	Fr	14	Sukla 3 ·15	... ...	3
1	Sa	15	4 ·23	8 ·10	4
2	Su	16	5 ·28	9 ·18	5
3	Mo	17	6 ·32	10 ·25	6
4	Tu	18	Jyeshtha 7 ·34	11 ·30	7
5	We	19	8 ·34	12 ·32	8
6	Th	20	9 ·32	13 ·33	9
7	Fr	21	10 ·28	14 ·32	10
8	Sa	22	11 ·23	15 ·29	11
9	Su	23	12 ·14	16 ·25	12
10	Mo	24	13 ·06 14 ·97	17 ·19	13
11	Tu	25	P ·85	18 ·13	14
12	We	26	1 ·76	19 ·07	15
13	Th	27	Bahula 2 ·65	20 ·00 21 ·93	16
14	Fr	28	3 ·55	22 ·86	17
15	Sa	29	4 ·46	23 ·81	18
16	Su	30	5 ·39	24 ·77	19

Naksh:—1. Asvn. 2. Bhar. 3. Krit. 4. Rohi. 5. Mrig. 6. Ardh. 7. Punar. 8. Push. 9. Aslesh. 10. Magh. 11. P. Phal. 12. U. Phal. 13. Hasta. 14. Chit.

A. D. 1907. A.—Amavasya. P.—Paurnami.	Kollam 1083, Commences { N. Malabar—Sept. S. Malabar—Aug.	Hijra 1325, Commences, Feb. 14.	Vikrama 1964. Bengal San 1313. (N. Cycle) Siddharthin.

Solar month	SOLAR reckoning: Cyclic Sidereal Year, Month and Day	Week-Day	English Month and Day	Lunar month	LUNAR reckoning: Tithi	Tithi Ending Moment	Nakshatra	Nakshatra Ending Moment	Muhammadan Year, Month and Day
			July						
Playanga Mithuna—Ani	17	Mo	1	Jyesh.	6	·32	25	·74	H. 1325 Jumadal-awwal 20
	18	Tu	2		7	·27	26	·73	21
	19	We	3		8	·24	27	·74	22
	20	Th	4		9	·21	1	·77	23
	21	Fr	5		10	·23	2	·82	24
	22	Sa	6	Bahula	11	·26	3	·89	25
	23	Su	7		12	·32	4	·98	26
	24	Mo	8		13	·38	...	...	27
	25	Tu	9		14	·47	5	·08	28
	26	We	10		—A	·55	6	·18	29
	27	Th	11		1	·62	7	·30	30
	28	Fr	12		2	·70	8	·40	H. 1325 Jumadal-akhir 1
	29	Sa	13		3	·76	9	·49	2
	30	Su	14		4	·81	10	·56	3
	—31	Mo	15		5	·81	11	·61	4
	1	Tu	16	Sukla	6	·82	12	·64	5
	2	We	17		7	·79	13	·66	6
	3	Th	18		8	·75	14	·65	7
	4	Fr	19		9	·70	15	·62	8
	5	Sa	20	Ashadha	10	·62	16	·58	9
	6	Su	21		11	·54	17	·53	10
	7	Mo	22		12	·45	18	·48	11
	8	Tu	23		13	·35	19	·41	12
	9	We	24		14	·25	20	·34	13
	10	Th○	25		P	·15	21	·27	14
	11	Fr	26		{ 1 / 2	·04 / ·95	22	·20	15
	12	Sa	27		3	·87	23	·15	16
	13	Su	28		4	·79	24	·11	17
	14	Mo	29		5	·75	25	·07	18
	15	Tu	30		6	·72	26	·06	19
	16	We	31		7	·70	27	·06	20
			Aug.						
Playanga Karkata—Adi	17	Th	1	Bahula	8	·71	1	·09	21
	18	Fr	2		9	·73	2	·13	22
	19	Sa	3		10	·79	3	·20	23
	20	Su	4		11	·85	4	·28	24
	21	Mo	5		12	·94	5	·37	25
	22	Tu	6		...	...	6	·48	26
	23	We	7		13	·02	7	·60	27
	24	Th	8		14	·11	8	·70	28
	25	Fr	9		—A	·17	9	·79	—29
	26	Sa	10		1	·23	10	·86	H. 1325 Rajab 1
	27	Su	11		2	·28	11	·92	2
	28	Mo	12		3	·30	12	·97	3
	29	Tu	13		4	·31	13	·98	4
	30	We	14		5	·28	14	.98	5
	31	Th	15	Sukla	6	·25	15	·95	6
	—32	Fr	16		7	·20	16	·92	7
Playanga Simha—Avani	1	Sa	17		8	·13	17	·87	8
	2	Su	18		{ 9 / 10	·04 / ·93	18	·81	9
	3	Mo	19		11	·84	19	·75	10
	4	Tu	20		12	·74	20	·68	11
	5	We	21	Sravana	13	·65	21	·60	12
	6	Th	22		14	·54	22	·55	13
	7	Fr	23		P	·46	23	·49	14
	8	Sa	24		1	·37	24	·44	15
	9	Su	25		2	·30	25	·40	16
	10	Mo	26		3	·25	26	·38	17
	11	Tu	27		4	·22	27	·39	18
	12	We	28		5	·21	1	·41	19
	13	Th	29	Bahula	6	·21	2	·44	20
	14	Fr	30		7	·24	3	·50	21
	15	Sa	31		8	·29	4	·58	22

Solar month	SOLAR reckoning: Cyclic Sidereal Year, Month and Day	Week-Day	English Month and Day	Lunar month	LUNAR reckoning: Tithi	Tithi Ending Moment	Nakshatra	Nakshatra Ending Moment	Muhammadan Year, Month and Day
			Sep.						
Playanga Simha—Avani	16	Su	1	Sravn.	9	·36	5	·67	H. 1325 Rajab 23
	17	Mo	2		10	·44	6	·79	24
	18	Tu	3		11	·52	7	·89	25
	19	We	4		12	·61	...	...	26
	20	Th	5	Bah.	13	·69	8	·00	27
	21	Fr	6		14	·76	9	·09	28
	22	Sa	7		—A.	·79	10	·17	29
	23	Su	8		1	·81	11	·24	—30
	24	Mo	9		2	·82	12	·28	H. 1325 Shaban 1
	25	Tu	10		3	·80	13	·30	2
	26	We	11		4	·78	14	·30	3
	27	Th	12		5	·72	15	·28	4
	28	Fr	13		6	·65	16	·26	5
	29	Sa	14	Sukla	7	·56	17	·21	6
	30	Su	15		8	·47	18	·15	7
	—31	Mo	16		9	·37	19	·08	8
	1	Tu	17		10	·27	{ 20 / 21	·01 / ·95 }	9
	2	We	18		11	·18	22	·88	10
	3	Th	19		{ 12 / 13	·06 / ·98	23	·82	11
	4	Fr	20	Bhadrapada	14	·90	24	·77	12
	5	Sa	21		P	·84	25	·73	13
	6	Su	22		1	·78	26	·71	14
	7	Mo	23		2	·76	27	·71	15
	8	Tu	24		3	·75	1	·72	16
	9	We	25		4	·76	2	·76	17
	10	Th	26		5	·78	3	·81	18
	11	Fr	27		6	·83	4	·88	19
	12	Sa	28		7	·90	5	·98	20
	13	Su	29		8	·98	...	...	21
	14	Mo	30		...	...	6	·08	22
			Oct.						
Playanga Kanya—Purattasi	15	Tu	1	Bahula	9	·07	7	·19	23
	16	We	2		10	·15	8	·30	24
	17	Th	3		11	·22	9	·39	25
	18	Fr	4		12	·30	10	·49	26
	19	Sa	5		13	·34	11	·55	27
	20	Su	6		14	·36	12	·60	28
	21	Mo	7		—A	·37	13	·62	—29
	22	Tu	8		1	·36	14	·63	H. 1325 Ramzan 1
	23	We	9		2	·33	15	·62	2
	24	Th	10		3	·27	16	·59	3
	25	Fr	11		4	·21	17	·54	4
	26	Sa	12		5	·12	18	·49	5
	27	Su	13		{ 6 / 7	·03 / ·93	19	·42	6
	28	Mo	14	Sukla	8	·84	20	·36	7
	29	Tu	15		9	·74	21	·29	8
	—30	We	16		10	·64	22	·22	9
Playanga Tula—Aippasi	1	Th	17		11	·55	23	·16	10
	2	Fr	18		12	·47	24	·10	11
	3	Sa	19	Asvina	13	·41	25	·06	12
	4	Su	20		14	·35	26	·04	13
	5	Mo	21		P	·33	27	·03	14
	6	Tu	22		1	·33	1	·04	15
	7	We	23		2	·35	2	·07	16
	8	Th	24		3	·37	3	·12	17
	9	Fr	25		4	·42	4	·20	18
	10	Sa	26		5	·48	5	·28	19
	11	Su	27		6	·56	6	·38	20
	12	Mo	28	Bahula	7	·65	7	·49	21
	13	Tu	29		8	·73	8	·59	22
	14	We	30		9	·83	9	·70	23
	15	Th	31		10	·89	10	·79	24

Solar month	SOLAR reckoning: Cyclic Sidereal Year, Month and Day	Week-Day	English Month and Day	Lunar month	LUNAR reckoning: Tithi	Tithi Ending Moment	Nakshatra	Nakshatra Ending Moment	Muhammadan Year, Month and Day
			Nov.						
Playanga Tula—Aippasi	16	Fr	1	Asv.	11	·93	11	·86	Ramzan 25
	17	Sa	2		12	·97	12	·91	26
	18	Su	3	Bah.	13	·96	13	·94	27
	19	Mo	4		14	·95	14	·96	28
	20	Tu	5		—A	·92	15	·95	29
	21	We	6		1	·87	16	·92	—30
	22	Th	7		2	·80	17	·88	H. 1325 Shawwal 1
	23	Fr	8		3	·72	18	·82	2
	24	Sa	9		4	·62	19	·76	3
	25	Su	10		5	·53	20	·70	4
	26	Mo	11		6	·43	21	·63	5
	27	Tu	12	Sukla	7	·34	22	·56	6
	28	We	13		8	·24	23	·49	7
	29	Th	14		9	·15	24	·44	8
	—30	Fr	15		10	·09	25	·40	9
	1	Sa	16		{ 11 / 12	·02 / ·96	26	·37	10
	2	Su	17		13	·95	27	·35	11
	3	Mo	18	Karttika	14	·94	1	·36	12
	4	Tu	19		P	·95	2	·38	13
	5	We	20		1	·98	3	·44	14
	6	Th	21		...	...	4	·50	15
	7	Fr	22		2	·04	5	·58	16
	8	Sa	23		3	·11	6	·68	17
	9	Su	24		4	·20	7	·79	18
	10	Mo	25		5	·28	8	·90	19
	11	Tu	26		6	·36	...	...	20
	12	We	27	Bahula	7	·45	9	·00	21
	13	Th	28		8	·51	10	·09	22
	14	Fr	29		9	·57	11	·17	23
	15	Sa	30		10	·59	12	·22	24
			Dec.						
Playanga Vrischika—Kartigai	16	Su	1		11	·60	13	·26	25
	17	Mo	2		12	·58	14	·28	26
	18	Tu	3		13	·53	15	·27	27
	19	We	4		14	·48	16	·25	28
	20	Th	5		—A	·42	17	·21	—29
	21	Fr	6		1	·84	18	·16	H. 1325 Zi-l-ka'da 1
	22	Sa	7		2	·25	19	·11	2
	23	Su	8		3	·16	{ 20 / 21	·04 / ·97 }	3
	24	Mo	9		{ 4 / 5	·06 / ·96	22	·90	4
	25	Tu	10		6	·86	23	·83	5
	26	We	11	Sukla	7	·78	24	·78	6
	27	Th	12		8	·71	25	·73	7
	28	Fr	13		9	·64	26	·70	8
	29	Sa	14		10	·61	27	·68	9
	—30	Su	15		11	·58	1	·68	10
Playanga Dhanus—Margali	1	Mo	16		12	·58	2	·71	11
	2	Tu	17	Margasira	13	·60	3	·75	12
	3	We	18		14	·63	4	·81	13
	4	Th	19		P	·69	5	·89	14
	5	Fr	20		1	·75	6	·98	15
	6	Sa	21		2	·85	...	...	16
	7	Su	22		3	·93	7	·09	17
	8	Mo	23		...	...	8	·20	18
	9	Tu	24		4	·02	9	·30	19
	10	We	25		5	·09	10	·40	20
	11	Th	26		6	·16	11	·48	21
	12	Fr	27	Bahula	7	·21	12	·53	22
	13	Sa	28		8	·23	13	·58	23
	14	Su	29		9	·24	14	·60	24
	15	Mo	30		10	·22	15	·60	25
	16	Tu	31		11	·18	16	·58	26

15. Svati. 16. Visak. 17. Anur. 18. Jyesh. 19. Mula. 20. P. Ash. 21. U. Ash. 22. Sravn. 23. Dani. 24. Satab. 25. P. Bhad. 26. U. Bhad. 27. Rev.

A. D. 1908.
Solar Eclipse. ●
Lunar Eclipse. ○

Mesha Sankranti (Commencement of Indian Sidereal Year).
(Surya Sid.) April 12·69.
(Arya Sid.) April 12·58.

Saka 1830. **Kaliyuga 5009.**
(S. Cycle) Kilaka.

SOLAR reckoning: Cyclic Sidereal Year, Month and Day; Week-Day, English Month and Day. LUNAR reckoning: Tithi Ending Moment; Nakshatra Ending Moment; Muhammadan Year, Month and Day.

Jan. — Solar: Playanga, Dhanus—Margali (to 29); Playanga, Makara—Tai (from 1). Lunar: Sukla; Pausha (from P); Bahula. Muhammadan: Zilkada (to 30); H. 1325 Zi-l-hijja (from 1).

Cyclic Sidereal Day	Week-Day	English Day	Tithi	Ending Moment	Nakshatra	Ending Moment	Muhammadan Day
17	We	1	12	·13	17	·54	27
18	Th	2	13 14	·06 ·98	18	·50	28
19	Fr	3	—A	·88	19	·44	29
20	Sa	4	1	·80	20	·38	—30
21	Su	5	2	·69	21	·31	1
22	Mo	6	3	·60	22	·24	2
23	Tu	7	4	·51	23	·18	3
24	We	8	5	·43	24	·12	4
25	Th	9	6	·35	25	·07	5
26	Fr	10	7	·29	26	·03	6
27	Sa	11	8	·25	27	·00	7
28	Su	12	9	·22	1	·01	8
—29	Mo	13	10	·23	2	·02	9
1	Tu	14	11	·24	3	·06	10
2	We	15	12	·28	4	·11	11
3	Th	16	13	·33	5	·19	12
4	Fr	17	14	·41	6	·28	13
5	Sa	18	P	·51	7	·39	14
6	Su	19	1	·58	8	·50	15
7	Mo	20	2	·68	9	·60	16
8	Tu	21	3	·75	10	·70	17
9	We	22	4	·81	11	·78	18
10	Th	23	5	·85	12	·86	19
11	Fr	24	6	·88	13	·90	20
12	Sa	25	7	·88	14	·92	21
13	Su	26	8	·86	15	·92	22
14	Mo	27	9	·83	16	·91	23
15	Tu	28	10	·77	17	·89	24
16	We	29	11	·70	18	·84	25
17	Th	30	12	·61	19	·78	26
18	Fr	31	13	·53	20	·72	27

Feb. — Solar: Playanga, Kumbha—Masi (from 1). Lunar: Sukla; Magha (from P); Bahula. Muhammadan: H. 1326 Muharram (from 1).

Cyclic Sidereal Day	Week-Day	English Day	Tithi	Ending Moment	Nakshatra	Ending Moment	Muhammadan Day
19	Sa	1	14	·43	21	·65	28
20	Su	2	—A	·32	22	·59	29
21	Mo	3	1	·23	23	·52	—30
22	Tu	4	2	·14	24	·45	1
23	We	5	3 4	·06 ·98	25	40	2
24	Th	6	5	·93	26	·36	3
25	Fr	7	6	·89	27	·34	4
26	Sa	8	7	·86	1	·33	5
27	Su	9	8	·86	2	·34	6
28	Mo	10	9	·87	3	·37	7
—29	Tu	11	10	·92	4	·42	8
1	We	12	11	·98	5	·49	9
2	Th	13	...	...	6	·59	10
3	Fr	14	12	·05	7	·69	11
4	Sa	15	13	·14	8	·80	12
5	Su	16	14	·21	9	·90	13
6	Mo	17	P	·31	...	...	14
7	Tu	18	1	·38	10	·00	15
8	We	19	2	·45	11	·10	16
9	Th	20	3	·49	12	·16	17
10	Fr	21	4	·51	13	·21	18
11	Sa	22	5	·50	14	·24	19
12	Su	23	6	·50	15	·25	20
13	Mo	24	7	·44	16	·25	21
14	Tu	25	8	·38	17	·22	22
15	We	26	9	·32	18	·17	23
16	Th	27	10	·23	19	·12	24
17	Fr	28	11	·14	20 21	·05 ·99	25
18	Sa	29	12 13	·04 ·95	22	·92	26

March — Solar: Playanga, Kumbha—Masi (to 31); Playanga, Mina—Panguni (from 1). Lunar: Sukla; Phalguna (from P); Bahula. Muhammadan: H. 1326 Safar (from 1).

Cyclic Sidereal Day	Week-Day	English Day	Tithi	Ending Moment	Nakshatra	Ending Moment	Muhammadan Day
19	Su	1	14	·84	23	·85	27
20	Mo	2	—A	·75	24	·79	28
21	Tu	3	1	·67	25	·73	29
22	We	4	2	·59	26	·69	—30
23	Th	5	3	·53	27	·67	1
24	Fr	6	4	·49	1	65	2
25	Sa	7	5	·48	2	·66	3
26	Su	8	6	·47	3	·68	4
27	Mo	9	7	·50	4	·73	5
28	Tu	10	8	·53	5	·81	6
29	We	11	9	·58	6	·89	7
30	Th	12	10	·66	7	·99	8
—31	Fr	13	11	·74	...	...	9
1	Sa	14	12	·83	8	·09	10
2	Su	15	13	·91	9	·20	11
3	Mo	16	14	·98	10	·31	12
4	Tu	17	...	...	11	·40	13
5	We	18	P	·04	12	.47	14
6	Th	19	1	·08	13	·53	15
7	Fr	20	2	·11	●14	·56	16
8	Sa	21	3	·10	15	·58	17
9	Su	22	4	·09	16	·57	18
10	Mo	23	5 6	·03 ·98	17	·55	19
11	Tu	24	7	·91	18	·51	20
12	We	25	8	·82	19	·45	21
13	Th	26	9	·73	20	·40	22
14	Fr	27	10	·62	21	·33	23
15	Sa	28	11	·52	22	·26	24
16	Su	29	12	·43	23	·19	25
17	Mo	30	13	·34	24	·18	26
18	Tu	31	14	·25	25	07	27

April — Solar: Kilaka, Mesha—Chittirai (from 1). Lunar: Sukla; Chaitra (from P); Bahula. Muhammadan: H. 1326 Rabi-ul-awwal (from 1).

Cyclic Sidereal Day	Week-Day	English Day	Tithi	Ending Moment	Nakshatra	Ending Moment	Muhammadan Day
19	We	1	—A	·17	26 27	·03 ·99	28
20	Th	2	1	·11	1	·98	—29
21	Fr	3	2	·07	2	·98	1
22	Sa	4	3	·05	...	...	2
23	Su	5	4	·04	3	·00	3
24	Mo	6	5	·07	4	·05	4
25	Tu	7	6	·10	5	·11	5
26	We	8	7	·16	6	·19	6
27	Th	9	8	·28	7	·29	7
28	Fr	10	9	·30	8	·39	8
29	Sa	11	10	·39	9	·51	9
—30	Su	12	11	·47	10	·61	10
1	Mo	13	12	·54	11	·70	11
2	Tu	14	13	·60	12	·78	12
3	We	15	14	·65	13	·84	13
4	Th	16	P	·66	14	·89	14
5	Fr	17	1	·65	15	·90	15
6	Sa	18	2	·64	16	·90	16
7	Su	19	3	·58	17	·88	17
8	Mo	20	4	·53	18	·84	18
9	Tu	21	5	·45	19	·79	19
10	We	22	6	·37	20	·74	20
11	Th	23	7	·27	21	·67	21
12	Fr	24	8	·18	22	·60	22
13	Sa	25	9 10	·07 ·97	23	·53	23
14	Su	26	11	·88	24	·46	24
15	Mo	27	12	·79	25	·41	25
16	Tu	28	13	·71	26	·36	26
17	We	29	14	·64	27	·32	27
18	Th	30	—A	·61	1	·80	28

May — Solar: Kilaka, Mesha—Chittirai (to 31); Kilaka, Vrishabha—Vaikasi (from 1). Lunar: Sukla; Vaisakha (from P); Bahula. Muhammadan: H. 1326 Rabi-ul-akhir (from 1).

Cyclic Sidereal Day	Week-Day	English Day	Tithi	Ending Moment	Nakshatra	Ending Moment	Muhammadan Day
19	Fr	1	1	·58	2	·80	29
20	Sa	2	2	·57	3	·32	—30
21	Su	3	3	·60	4	·36	1
22	Mo	4	4	·63	5	·42	2
23	Tu	5	5	·68	6	·50	3
24	We	6	6	·75	7	·59	4
25	Th	7	7	·84	8	·70	5
26	Fr	8	8	·91	9	·81	6
27	Sa	9.	9	·99	10	·91	7
28	Su	10	...	...	...	...	8
29	Mo	11	10	·07	11	·01	9
30	Tu	12	11	·12	12	·09	10
—31	We	13	12	·17	13	·16	11
1	Th	14	13	·18	14	·20	12
2	Fr	15	14	·18	15	·22	13
3	Sa	16	P	·15	16	.22	14
4	Su	17	1	·11	17	·21	15
5	Mo	18	2 3	·04 ·96	18	·17	16
6	Tu	19	4	·89	19	·13	17
7	We	20	5	·78	20	·08	18
8	Th	21	6	·69	21 22	·01 ·94	19
9	Fr	22	7	·58	23	·87	20
10	Sa	23	8	·49	24	·81	21
11	Su	24	9	·38	25	·75	22
12	Mo	25	10	·28	26	·69	23
13	Tu	26	11	·21	27	·65	24
14	We	27	12	·16	1	·63	25
15	Th	28	13	·11	2	·63	26
16	Fr	29	14	·08	3	·64	27
17	Sa	30	—A	·08	4	·67	28
18	Su	31	1	·08	5	·73	—29

June — Solar: Kilaka, Mithuna—Ani (from 1). Lunar: Sukla; Jyeshtha (from P); Bahula; A. Suk. Muhammadan: H. 1326 Jumadal-awwal.

Cyclic Sidereal Day	Week-Day	English Day	Tithi	Ending Moment	Nakshatra	Ending Moment	Muhammadan Day
19	Mo	1	2	·12	6	·80	1
20	Tu	2	3	·18	7	·90	2
21	We	3	4	·25	...	...	3
22	Th	4	5	·33	8	·00	4
23	Fr	5	6	·41	9	·10	5
24	Sa	6	7	·50	10	·21	6
25	Su	7	8	·57	11	·31	7
26	Mo	8	9	·61	12	·39	8
27	Tu	9	10	·65	13	·47	9
28	We	10	11	·67	14	·52	10
29	Th	11	12	·66	15	·54	11
30	Fr	12	13	·64	16	·55	12
—31	Sa	13	14	·60	17	·53	13
1	Su	14	P	·53	18	·51	14
2	Mo	15	1	·46	19	·47	15
3	Tu	16	2	·38	20	·41	16
4	We	17	3	·28	21	·35	17
5	Th	18	4	·17	22	·28	18
6	Fr	19	5 6	·07 ·98	23	·22	19
7	Sa	20	7	·87	24	·15	20
8	Su	21	8	·78	25	·08	21
9	Mo	22	9	·70	26 27	·03 ·98	22
10	Tu	23	10	·65	1	·96	23
11	We	24	11	·59	2	·95	24
12	Th	25	12	·56	3	·96	25
13	Fr	26	13	·55	4	·99	26
14	Sa	27	14	·56	...	...	27
15	Su	28	—A	·60	5	·03	28
16	Mo	29	1	·65	6	·10	29
17	Tu	30	2	·73	7	·20	—30

Naksh :—1. Asvn. 2. Bhar. 3. Krit. 4. Rohi. 5. Mrig. 6. Ardh. 7. Punar. 8. Push. 9. Aslesh. 10. Magh. 11. P. Phal. 12. U. Phal. 13. Hasta. 14. Chit.

A. D. 1908.
A.—Amavasya.
P.—Paurnami.

Kollam 1084, Commences { N. Malabar—Sept. S. Malabar—Aug.

Hijra 1326, Commences, Feb. 4.

Vikrama 1965.
Bengal San 1314.
(N. Cycle) Raudra.

Columns: SOLAR reckoning (Cyclic Sidereal Year, Month and Day; Week-Day English Month and Day) — LUNAR reckoning (Tithi Ending Moment; Nakshatra Ending Moment; Muhammadan Year, Month and Day).

July — Solar: Kilaka Mithuna—Ani.; Kilaka Karkata—Adi. Lunar: Sukla, Ashadha, Bahula. Muhammadan: H. 1326 Jumadal-akhir.

Cyclic Sidereal Year, Month and Day	Week-Day	English Day	Tithi Ending Moment	Nakshatra Ending Moment	Muhammadan Year, Month and Day
18	We	1	3 ·79	8 ·80	1
19	Th	2	4 ·88	9 ·40	2
20	Fr	3	5 ·97	10 ·51	3
21	Sa	4	... ...	11 ·61	4
22	Su	5	6 ·03	12 ·71	5
23	Mo	6	7 ·09	13 ·78	6
24	Tu	7	8 ·13	14 ·83	7
25	We	8	9 ·15	15 ·86	8
26	Th	9	10 ·14	16 ·87	9
27	Fr	10	11 ·12	17 ·87	10
28	Sa	11	12 ·07	18 ·84	11
29	Su	12	13 ·01 / 14 ·94	19 ·80	12
30	Mo	13	P ·86	20 ·75	13
31	Tu	14	1 ·76	21 ·69	14
32	We	15	2 ·65	22 ·63	15
1	Th	16	3 ·56	23 ·56	16
2	Fr	17	4 ·44	24 ·49	17
3	Sa	18	5 ·35	25 ·42	18
4	Su	19	6 ·26	26 ·36	19
5	Mo	20	7 ·18	27 ·33	20
6	Tu	21	8 ·12	1 ·29	21
7	We	22	9 ·07	2 ·28	22
8	Th	23	10 ·05	3 ·28	23
9	Fr	24	11 ·03	4 ·30	24
10	Sa	25	12 ·04	5 ·34	25
11	Su	26	13 ·07	6 ·42	26
12	Mo	27	14 ·12	7 ·50	27
13	Tu	28	A ·19	8 ·59	28
14	We	29	1 ·27	9 ·70	29
15	Th	30	2 ·36	10 ·81	1
16	Fr	31	3 ·43	11 ·92	2

Aug. — Solar: Kilaka Simha—Avani. Lunar: Sukla, Sravana, Bahula, Bhad. Suk. Muhammadan: H. 1326 Rajab; Shaban.

Cyclic Sidereal Year, Month and Day	Week-Day	English Day	Tithi Ending Moment	Nakshatra Ending Moment	Muhammadan Year, Month and Day
17	Sa	1	4 ·50	... ...	3
18	Su	2	5 ·56	12 ·01	4
19	Mo	3	6 ·60	13 ·08	5
20	Tu	4	7 ·63	14 ·14	6
21	We	5	8 ·62	15 ·18	7
22	Th	6	9 ·61	16 ·20	8
23	Fr	7	10 ·56	17 ·20	9
24	Sa	8	11 ·51	18 ·17	10
25	Su	9	12 ·43	19 ·14	11
26	Mo	10	13 ·34	20 ·08	12
27	Tu	11	14 ·26	21 ·03 / 22 ·97	13
28	We	12	P ·15	23 ·89	14
29	Th	13	1 ·05 / 2 ·94	24 ·82	15
30	Fr	14	3 ·85	25 ·76	16
31	Sa	15	4 ·76	26 ·70	17
1	Su	16	5 ·68	27 ·66	18
2	Mo	17	6 ·62	1 ·62	19
3	Tu	18	7 ·56	2 ·60	20
4	We	19	8 ·54	3 ·60	21
5	Th	20	9 ·53	4 ·62	22
6	Fr	21	10 ·54	5 ·66	23
7	Sa	22	11 ·56	6 ·72	24
8	Su	23	12 ·62	7 ·80	25
9	Mo	24	13 ·69	8 ·89	26
10	Tu	25	14 ·77	... ...	27
11	We	26	A ·85	9 ·00	28
12	Th	27	1 ·94	10 ·11	29
13	Fr	28	... ...	11 ·22	30
14	Sa	29	2 ·02	12 ·31	1
15	Su	30	3 ·06	13 ·39	2
16	Mo	31	4 ·11	14 ·45	3

Sep. — Solar: Kilaka Simha—Avani.; Kilaka Kanya—Purattasi. Lunar: Sukla, Bhadrapada, Bahula. Muhammadan: H. 1326 Shaban.

Cyclic Sidereal Year, Month and Day	Week-Day	English Day	Tithi Ending Moment	Nakshatra Ending Moment	Muhammadan Year, Month and Day
17	Tu	1	5 ·14	15 ·50	4
18	We	2	6 ·13	16 ·52	5
19	Th	3	7 ·12	17 ·52	6
20	Fr	4	8 ·07	18 ·50	7
21	Sa	5	9 ·03 / 10 ·95	19 ·47	8
22	Su	6	11 ·86	20 ·43	9
23	Mo	7	12 ·77	21 ·37	10
24	Tu	8	13 ·66	22 ·30	11
25	We	9	14 ·57	23 ·23	12
26	Th	10	P ·46	24 ·16	13
27	Fr	11	1 ·37	25 ·09	14
28	Sa	12	2 ·28	26 ·04 / 27 ·99	15
29	Su	13	3 ·21	1 ·95	16
30	Mo	14	4 ·15	2 ·93	17
31	Tu	15	5 ·10	3 ·92	18
1	We	16	6 ·07	4 ·94	19
2	Th	17	7 ·06	5 ·98	20
3	Fr	18	8 ·06	... ...	21
4	Sa	19	9 ·09	6 ·03	22
5	Su	20	10 ·15	7 ·10	23
6	Mo	21	11 ·21	8 ·19	24
7	Tu	22	12 ·30	9 ·31	25
8	We	23	13 ·38	10 ·41	26
9	Th	24	14 ·46	11 ·52	27
10	Fr	25	A ·54	12 ·61	28
11	Sa	26	1 ·60	13 ·70	29
12	Su	27	2 ·65	14 ·77	1
13	Mo	28	3 ·67	15 ·82	2
14	Tu	29	4 ·68	16 ·84	3
15	We	30	5 ·66	17 ·85	4

Oct. — Solar: Kilaka Tula—Aippasi. Lunar: Sukla, Asvina, Bahula, Kartt. Suk. Muhammadan: H. 1326 Ramzan; Shawwal.

Cyclic Sidereal Year, Month and Day	Week-Day	English Day	Tithi Ending Moment	Nakshatra Ending Moment	Muhammadan Year, Month and Day
16	Th	1	6 ·62	18 ·83	5
17	Fr	2	7 ·57	19 ·80	6
18	Sa	3	8 ·49	20 ·76	7
19	Su	4	9 ·41	21 ·71	8
20	Mo	5	10 ·32	22 ·64	9
21	Tu	6	11 ·23	23 ·57	10
22	We	7	12 ·13	24 ·50	11
23	Th	8	13 ·02 / 14 ·93	25 ·44	12
24	Fr	9	P ·84	26 ·38	13
25	Sa	10	1 ·77	27 ·32	14
26	Su	11	2 ·71	1 ·28	15
27	Mo	12	3 ·66	2 ·25	16
28	Tu	13	4 ·63	3 ·25	17
29	We	14	5 ·63	4 ·26	18
30	Th	15	6 ·63	5 ·29	19
1	Fr	16	7 ·66	6 ·34	20
2	Sa	17	8 ·72	7 ·41	21
3	Su	18	9 ·78	8 ·50	22
4	Mo	19	10 ·87	9 ·60	23
5	Tu	20	11 ·96	10 ·71	24
6	We	21	... ...	11 ·82	25
7	Th	22	12 ·05	12 ·91	26
8	Fr	23	13 ·13	... ...	27
9	Sa	24	14 ·18	13 ·01	28
10	Su	25	A ·23	14 ·08	29
11	Mo	26	1 ·26	15 ·13	30
12	Tu	27	2 ·26	16 ·16	1
13	We	28	3 ·24	17 ·17	2
14	Th	29	4 ·21	18 ·16	3
15	Fr	30	5 ·16	19 ·14	4
16	Sa	31	6 ·09	20 ·10	5

Nov. — Solar: Kilaka Tula—Aippasi.; Kilaka Vrischika—Karttigai. Lunar: Sukla, Karttika, Bahula. Muhammadan: H. 1326 Shawwal.

Cyclic Sidereal Year, Month and Day	Week-Day	English Day	Tithi Ending Moment	Nakshatra Ending Moment	Muhammadan Year, Month and Day
17	Su	1	7 ·00 / 8 ·91	21 ·04 / 22 ·98	6
18	Mo	2	9 ·81	23 ·91	7
19	Tu	3	10 ·71	24 ·85	8
20	We	4	11 ·62	25 ·78	9
21	Th	5	12 ·52	26 ·71	10
22	Fr	6	13 ·44	27 ·66	11
23	Sa	7	14 ·36	1 ·61	12
24	Su	8	P ·30	2 ·59	13
25	Mo	9	1 ·26	3 ·57	14
26	Tu	10	2 ·23	4 ·58	15
27	We	11	3 ·23	5 ·60	16
28	Th	12	4 ·23	6 ·65	17
29	Fr	13	5 ·27	7 ·71	18
30	Sa	14	6 ·33	8 ·81	19
1	Su	15	7 ·41	9 ·90	20
2	Mo	16	8 ·49	... ...	21
3	Tu	17	9 ·57	10 ·01	22
4	We	18	10 ·67	11 ·11	23
5	Th	19	11 ·74	12 ·21	24
6	Fr	20	12 ·80	13 ·31	25
7	Sa	21	13 ·84	14 ·39	26
8	Su	22	14 ·89	15 ·44	27
9	Mo	23	A ·88	16 ·48	28
10	Tu	24	1 ·86	17 ·49	29
11	We	25	2 ·82	18 ·49	1
12	Th	26	3 ·77	19 ·47	2
13	Fr	27	4 ·71	20 ·43	3
14	Sa	28	5 ·62	21 ·38	4
15	Su	29	6 ·53	22 ·32	5
16	Mo	30	7 ·44	23 ·26	6

Dec. — Solar: Kilaka Vrischika—Karttigai.; Kilaka Dhanus—Margali. Lunar: Sukla, Margasira, Bahula, Pahs. Sukla. Muhammadan: H. 1326 Zi-l-ka'da; H. 1326 Zi-l-hijja.

Cyclic Sidereal Year, Month and Day	Week-Day	English Day	Tithi Ending Moment	Nakshatra Ending Moment	Muhammadan Year, Month and Day
17	Tu	1	8 ·34	24 ·19	7
18	We	2	9 ·24	25 ·12	8
19	Th	3	10 ·14	26 ·05 / 27 ·99	9
20	Fr	4	11 ·06 / 12 ·98	1 ·95	10
21	Sa	5	13 ·93	2 ·92	11
22	Su	6	14 ·89	3 ·90	12
23	Mo	7	P ·87	4 ·90	13
24	Tu	8	1 ·86	5 ·92	14
25	We	9	2 ·87	6 ·96	15
26	Th	10	3 ·92	... ...	16
27	Fr	11	4 ·97	7 ·03	17
28	Sa	12	... ...	8 ·11	18
29	Su	13	5 ·05	9 ·20	19
30	Mo	14	6 ·14	10 ·30	20
1	Tu	15	7 ·23	11 ·41	21
2	We	16	8 ·31	12 ·52	22
3	Th	17	9 ·39	13 ·62	23
4	Fr	18	10 ·46	14 ·70	24
5	Sa	19	11 ·49	15 ·76	25
6	Su	20	12 ·52	16 ·79	26
7	Mo	21	13 ·52	17 ·82	27
8	Tu	22	14 ·51	18 ·82	28
9	We	23	A ·46	19 ·80	29
10	Th	24	1 ·41	20 ·76	30
11	Fr	25	2 ·34	21 ·71	1
12	Sa	26	3 ·25	22 ·66	2
13	Su	27	4 ·17	23 ·60	3
14	Mo	28	5 ·07 / 6 ·98	24 ·53	4
15	Tu	29	7 ·88	25 ·46	5
16	We	30	8 ·79	26 ·39	6
17	Th	31	9 ·70	27 ·33	7

15. Svati. 16. Visak. 17. Anur. 18. Jyesh. 19. Mula. 20. P. Ash. 21. U. Ash. 22. Sravn. 23. Dani. 24. Satab. 25. P. Bhad. 26. U. Bhad. 27. Rev.

A. D. 1909.
Solar Eclipse. ●
Lunar Eclipse. ☉

Mesha Sankranti (Commencement of Indian Sidereal Year).
(Surya Sid.) April 12·95.
(Arya Sid.) April 12·84.

Saka 1831. Kaliyuga 5010.
(S. Cycle) Saumya.

Column groups: SOLAR reckoning (Cyclic Sidereal Year, Month and Day; Week-Day, English Month and Day); LUNAR reckoning (Tithi Ending Moment; Nakshatra Ending Moment; Muhammadan Year, Month and Day).

Jan.

Cyclic Sidereal Year, Month	Day	Week-Day	English Day	Lunar month / Paksha	Tithi	Ending Moment	Nakshatra	Ending Moment	Muhammadan Year, Month	Day
Kilaka Dhanus—Margali.	18	Fr	1	Sukla	10	·62	1	·29	H. 1326 Zi-l-hijja.	8
	19	Sa	2		11	·58	2	·25		9
	20	Su	3		12	·53	3	·23		10
	21	Mo	4		13	·51	4	·22		11
	22	Tu	5		14	·50	5	·23		12
	23	We	6	Pausha	P	·58	6	·28		13
	24	Th	7		1	·56	7	·33		14
	25	Fr	8		2	·61	8	·41		15
	26	Sa	9		3	·70	9	·50		16
	27	Su	10		4	·78	10	·60		17
	28	Mo	11		5	·87	11	·72		18
	—29	Tu	12		6	·96	12	·82		19
Kilaka Makara—Tai.	1	We	13		...	...	13	·92		20
	2	Th	14		7	·04	...	...		21
	3	Fr	15	Bahula	8	·10	14	·00		22
	4	Sa	16		9	·13	15	·07		23
	5	Su	17		10	·17	16	·12		24
	6	Mo	18		11	·16	17	·14		25
	7	Tu	19		12	·15	18	·14		26
	8	We	20		13	·11	19	·13		27
	9	Th	21		14 A	·06 ·98	20	·10		28
	10	Fr	22		1	·89	21	·06		—29
	11	Sa	23		2	·80	22 23	·00 ·94		1
	12	Su	24		3	·70	24	·86		2
	13	Mo	25		4	·60	25	·79		3
	14	Tu	26		5	·51	26	·73		4
	15	We	27		6	·42	27	·67		5
	16	Th	28	Sukla	7	33	1	·62		6
	17	Fr	29		8	·27	2	·58		7
	18	Sa	30		9	·22	3	·55		8
	19	Su	31		10	·17	4	·54		9

Feb.

Cyclic Sidereal Year, Month	Day	Week-Day	English Day	Lunar month / Paksha	Tithi	Ending Moment	Nakshatra	Ending Moment	Muhammadan Year, Month	Day
	20	Mo	1		11	·15	5	·56	H. 1327 Muharram.	10
	21	Tu	2		12	·14	6	·59		11
	22	We	3		13	·17	7	·64		12
	23	Th	4	Magha	14	·21	8	·71		13
	24	Fr	5		P	·28	9	·80		14
	25	Sa	6		1	·34	10	·91		15
	26	Su	7		2	·44	...	...		16
	27	Mo	8		3	·52	11	·02		17
	28	Tu	9		4	·60	12	·12		18
	29	We	10		5	·68	13	·22		19
	—30	Th	11		6	·74	14	·31		20
Kilaka Kumbha—Masi.	1	Fr	12	Bahula	7	·79	15	·38		21
	2	Sa	13		8	·80	16	·43		22
	3	Su	14		9	·80	17	·46		23
	4	Mo	15		10	·78	18	·47		24
	5	Tu	16		11	·73	19	·46		25
	6	We	17		12	·68	20	·43		26
	7	Th	18		13	·60	21	·39		27
	8	Fr	19		14	·52	22	·34		28
	9	Sa	20		—A	·42	23	·27		29
	10	Su	21	Sukla	1	·33	24	20		—30
	11	Mo	22		2	·23	25	·13	H. 1327 Safar.	1
	12	Tu	23		3	·13	26	·07		2
	13	We	24		4 5	·04 ·95	27 1	·01 ·95		3
	14	Th	25	Phalg.	6	·88	2	·91		4
	15	Fr	26		7	·82	3	·88		5
	16	Sa	27		8	·80	4	·87		6
	17	Su	28		9	·77	5	·88		7

March

Cyclic Sidereal Year, Month	Day	Week-Day	English Day	Lunar month / Paksha	Tithi	Ending Moment	Nakshatra	Ending Moment	Muhammadan Year, Month	Day
Kilaka Kumbha—Masi.	18	Mo	1	Sukla	10	·77	6	·90	H. 1327 Safar.	·8
	19	Tu	2		11	·79	7	·95		9
	20	We	3		12	·82	...	...		10
	21	Th	4		13	·89	8	·02		11
	22	Fr	5		14	·96	9	·11		12
	23	Sa	6	Phalguna	...	...	10	·21		13
	24	Su	7		P	·06	11	·32		14
	25	Mo	8		1	·14	12	·42		15
	26	Tu	9		2	·23	13	·52		16
	27	We	10		3	·29	14	·62		17
	28	Th	11		4	·35	15	·69		18
	29	Fr	12		5	·39	16	·75		19
	—30	Sa	13		6	·40	17	·78		20
Kilaka Mina—Panguni.	1	Su	14	Bahula	7	·40	18	.79		21
	2	Mo	15		8	·38	19	.78		22
	3	Tu	16		9	·33	20	·77		23
	4	We	17		10	·27	21	·73		24
	5	Th	18		11	·19	22	·67		25
	6	Fr	19		12	·11	23	·61		26
	7	Sa	20		13 14	·02 ·92	24	·54		27
	8	Su	21		—A	·81	25	·48		28
	9	Mo	22		1	·73	26	·41		—29
	10	Tu	23		2	·63	27	·35		1
	11	We	24		3	·55	1	·29		2
	12	Th	25		4	·47	2	·24		3
	13	Fr	26		5	·40	3	·21		4
	14	Sa	27		6	·38	4	·20		5
	15	Su	28	Sukla	7	·35	5	·20		6
	16	Mo	29		8	·35	6	·22		7
	17	Tu	30		9	·37	7	·26		8
	18	We	31		10	·41	8	·33		9

April

Cyclic Sidereal Year, Month	Day	Week-Day	English Day	Lunar month / Paksha	Tithi	Ending Moment	Nakshatra	Ending Moment	Muhammadan Year, Month	Day
	19	Th	1		11	·47	9	·41	H. 1327 Rabi-ul-awwal.	10
	20	Fr	2		12	·54	10	·51		11
	21	Sa	3	Chaitra	13	·63	11	·61		12
	22	Su	4		14	·71	12	·72		13
	23	Mo	5		P	·80	13	·82		14
	24	Tu	6		1	·86	14	·92		15
	25	We	7		2	·93	...	...		16
	26	Th	8		3	·96	15	·00		17
	27	Fr	9		4	·96	16	·06		18
	28	Sa	10		5	·96	17	·10		19
	29	Su	11		6	·94	18	·11		20
	—30	Mo	12	Bahula	7	·89	19	·12		21
Saumya Mesha—Chittirai.	1	Tu	13		8	·83	20	·10		22
	2	We	14		9	·76	21	·06		23
	3	Th	15		10	·67	22 23	·01 ·95		24
	4	Fr	16		11	·58	24	·89		25
	5	Sa	·17		12	·48	25	·82		26
	6	Su	18		13	·37	26	·75		27
	7	Mo	19		14	·28	27	·68		28
	8	Tu	20		—A	·18	1	·62		29
	9	We	21		1	·09	2	·58		—30
	10	Th	22	Sukla	2 3	·01 ·95	3	·54	H. 1327 Rabi-ul-akhir.	1
	11	Fr	23		4	·92	4	·52		2
	12	Sa	24		5	·89	5	·52		3
	13	Su	25		6	·89	6	·53		4
	14	Mo	26	Vaisak.	7	·91	7	·57		5
	15	Tu	27		8	·95	8	·64		6
	16	We	28		...	...	9	·72		7
	17	Th	29		9	·00	10	·81		8
	18	Fr	30		10	·07	11	·91		9

May

Cyclic Sidereal Year, Month	Day	Week-Day	English Day	Lunar month / Paksha	Tithi	Ending Moment	Nakshatra	Ending Moment	Muhammadan Year, Month	Day
Saumya Mesha—Chittirai.	19	Sa	1	Sukla	11	·15	...	...	H. 1327 Rabi-ul-akhir.	10
	20	Su	2		12	·25	12	·02		11
	21	Mo	3		13	·32	13	·13		12
	22	Tu	4	Vaisakha	14	·39	14	·23		13
	23	We	5		P	·45	15	·31		14
	24	Th	6		1	·48	16	·37		15
	25	Fr	7		2	·50	17	·41		16
	26	Sa	8		3	·49	18	·44		17
	27	Su	9		4	·48	19	·44		18
	28	Mo	10		5	·42	20	·43		19
	29	Tu	11	Bahula	6	·35	21	·39		20
	30	We	12		7	·28	22	·34		21
	—31	Th	13		8	·19	23	·29		22
Saumya Vrishabha—Vaikasi.	1	Fr	14		9	·10	24	·23		23
	2	Sa	15		10 11	·00 ·89	25	·16		24
	3	Su	16		12	·79	26	·09		25
	4	Mo	17		13	·69	27 1	·02 ·97		26
	5	Tu	18		14	·61	2	·91		27
	6	We	19		—A	·53	3	·87		28
	7	Th	20		1	·47	4	·85		—29
	8	Fr	21		2	·43	5	·84		1
	9	Sa	22	Sukla	3	·41	6	·85		2
	10	Su	23		4	·40	7	·89		3
	11	Mo	24		5	·41	8	·95		4
	12	Tu	25		6	·46	...	...		5
	13	We	26		7	·51	9	·02		6
	14	Th	27	Jyeshtha	8	·59	10	·11		7
	15	Fr	28		9	·65	11	·21		8
	16	Sa	29		10	·75	12	·32		9
	17	Su	30		11	·82	13	·43		10
	18	Mo	31		12	·89	14	·53		11

June

Cyclic Sidereal Year, Month	Day	Week-Day	English Day	Lunar month / Paksha	Tithi	Ending Moment	Nakshatra	Ending Moment	Muhammadan Year, Month	Day
	19	Tu	1		13	·94	15	·61	H. 1327 Jumadal-awwal.	12
	20	We	2		14	·97	16	·68		13
	21	Th	3		...	...	17	·74		14
	22	Fr ☉	4		P 1	·00 ·98	18	·76		15
	23	Sa	5		2	·97	19	·77		16
	24	Su	6		3	·92	20	·75		17
	25	Mo	7		4	·87	21	·72		18
	26	Tu	8		5	·78	22	·69		19
	27	We	9	Bahula	6	·69	23	·63		20
	28	Th	10		7	·60	24	·57		21
	29	Fr	11		8	·49	25	·50		22
	30	Sa	12		9	·39	26	·43		23
	—31	Su	13		10	·29	27	·36		24
Saumya Mithuna—Ani.	1	Mo	14		11	·19	1	·30		25
	2	Tu	15		12	·10	2	·25		26
	3	We	16		13 14	·03 ·96	3	·20		27
	4	Th	17		—A	91	4	·17		28
	5	Fr	18		1	·89	5	·16		29
	6	Sa	19		2	·88	6	·18		—30
	7	Su	20		3	·89	7	·21	H. 1327 Jumadal-akhir.	1
	8	Mo	21		4	·93	8	·26		2
	9	Tu	22	Sukla	5	·99	9	·32		3
	10	We	23		...	...	10	·41		4
	11	Th	24		6	·05	11	·52		5
	12	Fr	25		7	·12	12	·62		6
	13	Sa	26	Ashadha	8	·22	13	·73		7
	14	Su	27		9	·29	14	·83		8
	15	Mo	28		10	·36	15	·92		9
	16	Tu	29		11	·42	...	...		10
	17	We	30		12	·46	16	·00		11

Naksh:—1. Asvn. 2. Bhar. 3. Krit. 4. Rohi. 5. Mrig. 6. Ardh. 7. Punar. 8. Push. 9. Aslesh. 10. Magh. 11. P. Phal. 12. U. Phal. 13. Hasta. 14. Chit.

A. D. 1909.
A.—Amavasya.
P.—Paurnami.

Kollam 1085, Commences { N. Malabar—Sept. / S. Malabar—Aug.

Hijra 1327, Commences, Jan. 23.

Vikrama 1966.
Bengal San 1315.
(N. Cycle) Durmati.

SOLAR reckoning: Cyclic Sidereal Year, Month and Day.	Week-Day English Month and Day.	LUNAR reckoning: Tithi Ending Moment.	Nakshatra Ending Moment.	Muhammadan Year, Month and Day.
	July			
18 [Saumya Mithuna—Ani]	Th 1	13 ·47 [Ashadha]	17 ·05	12 [H. 1327 Jumadal-akhir]
19	Fr 2	14 ·47	18 ·08	13
20	Sa 3	P ·46	19 ·09	14
21	Su 4	1 ·40	20 ·08	15
22	Mo 5	2 ·35	21 ·06	16
23	Tu 6	3 ·27	22 ·02 / 23 ·97	17
24	We 7	4 ·18	24 ·90	18
25	Th 8	5 ·08 / 6 ·98	25 ·84	19
26	Fr 9	7 ·86 [Bahula]	26 ·77	20
27	Sa 10	8 ·76	27 ·70	21
28	Su 11	9 ·67	1 ·64	22
29	Mo 12	10 ·56	2 ·58	23
30	Tu 13	11 ·49	3 ·53	24
31	We 14	12 ·43	4 ·50	25
—32	Th 15	13 ·40	5 ·50	26
1 [Saumya Karkata—Adi]	Fr 16	14 ·37	6 ·50	27
2	Sa 17	—A ·35	7 ·52	28
3	Su 18	1 ·37 [Sukla]	8 ·56	—29
4	Mo 19	2 ·41	9 ·63	1
5	Tu 20	3 ·47	10 ·72	2
6	We 21	4 ·52	11 ·82	3
7	Th 22	5 ·61	12 ·92	4
8	Fr 23	6 ·69	... ...	5
9	Sa 24	7 ·77	13 ·03	6
10	Su 25	8 ·83	14 ·13	7
11	Mo 26	9 ·89	15 ·23	8
12	Tu 27	10 ·94 [Sravana]	16 ·31	9
13	We 28	11 ·95	17 ·36	10
14	Th 29	12 ·95	18 ·40	11
15	Fr 30	13 ·93	19 ·41	12
16	Sa 31	14 ·88	20 ·41	13
	Aug.			
17 [Saumya Simha—Avani]	Su 1	P ·82 [Adhika]	21 ·39	14 [H. 1327 Rajab]
18	Mo 2	1 ·75	22 ·35	15
19	Tu 3	2 ·67	23 ·30	16
20	We 4	3 ·56	24 ·24	17
21	Th 5	4 ·47	25 ·17	18
22	Fr 6	5 ·36	26 ·11	19
23	Sa 7	6 ·27 [Bahula]	27 ·04 / 1 ·98	20
24	Su 8	7 ·16	2 ·92	21
25	Mo 9	8 ·07	3 ·87	22
26	Tu 10	9 ·00 / 10 ·92	4 ·84	23
27	We 11	11 ·89	5 ·82	24
28	Th 12	12 ·85	6 ·82	25
29	Fr 13	13 ·85	7 ·84	26
30	Sa 14	14 ·85	8 ·87	27
—31	Su 15	—A ·90	9 ·94	28
1	Mo 16	1 ·95 [Sukla]	... ...	29
2	Tu 17	... ...	10 ·02	—30
3	We 18	2 ·01	11 ·12	1 [H. 1327 Shaban]
4	Th 19	3 ·10	12 ·22	2
5	Fr 20	4 ·18	13 ·32	3
6	Sa 21	5 ·27	14 ·44	4
7	Su 22	6 ·34	15 ·53	5
8	Mo 23	7 ·39 [Nija Sravana]	16 ·61	6
9	Tu 24	8 ·43	17 ·67	7
10	We 25	9 ·45	18 ·71	8
11	Th 26	10 ·45	19 ·73	9
12	Fr 27	11 ·43	20 ·74	10
13	Sa 28	12 ·39	21 ·72	11
14	Su 29	13 ·33	22 ·69	12
15	Mo 30	14 ·26	23 ·64	13
16	Tu 31	P ·17	24 ·58	14

SOLAR reckoning: Cyclic Sidereal Year, Month and Day.	Week-Day English Month and Day.	LUNAR reckoning: Tithi Ending Moment.	Nakshatra Ending Moment.	Muhammadan Year, Month and Day.
	Sep.			
17 [Saumya Simha—Avani]	We 1	1 ·07 / 2 ·97 [Nija Srvn.]	25 ·52	15 [H. 1327 Shaban]
18	Th 2	3 ·87	26 ·45	16
19	Fr 3	4 ·78	27 ·88	17
20	Sa 4	5 ·68	1 ·31	18
21	Su 5	6 ·59	2 ·25	19
22	Mo 6	7 ·51	3 ·21	20
23	Tu 7	8 ·45	4 ·17	21
24	We 8	9 ·40	5 ·15	22
25	Th 9	10 ·37	6 ·14	23
26	Fr 10	11 ·37 [Bahula]	7 ·14	24
27	Sa 11	12 ·37	8 ·20	25
28	Su 12	13 ·42	9 ·25	26
29	Mo 13	14 ·47	10 ·32	27
30	Tu 14	—A ·54	11 ·41	28
—31	We 15	1 ·61 [Sukla]	12 ·52	—29
1 [Saumya Kanya—Purattasi]	Th 16	2 ·70	13 ·62	1 [H. 1327 Ramzan]
2	Fr 17	3 ·79	14 ·74	2
3	Sa 18	4 ·85	15 ·83	3
4	Su 19	5 ·92	16 ·92	4
5	Mo 20	6 ·96	17 ·98	5
6	Tu 21	7 ·98	... ...	6
7	We 22	8 ·98	18 ·03	7
8	Th 23	9 ·96	19 ·06	8
9	Fr 24	10 ·93 [Bhadrapada]	20 ·07	9
10	Sa 25	11 ·86	21 ·05	10
11	Su 26	12 ·80	22 ·02 / 23 ·97	11
12	Mo 27	13 ·71	24 ·93	12
13	Tu 28	14 ·62	25 ·86	13
14	We 29	P ·52	26 ·79	14
15	Th 30	1 ·43	27 ·72	15
	Oct.			
16	Fr 1	2 ·32	1 ·65	16
17	Sa 2	3 ·22	2 ·60	17
18	Su 3	4 ·14	3 ·54	18
19	Mo 4	5 ·06	4 ·50	19
20	Tu 5	6 ·00 / 7 ·94 [Bahula]	5 ·47	20
21	We 6	8 ·93	6 ·46	21
22	Th 7	9 ·92	7 ·48	22
23	Fr 8	10 ·95	8 ·51	23
24	Sa 9	11 ·98	9 ·56	24
25	Su 10	... ...	10 ·63	25
26	Mo 11	12 ·03	11 ·72	26
27	Tu 12	13 ·10	12 ·81	27
28	We 13	14 ·20	13 ·93	28
29	Th 14	—A ·27	... ...	29
30	Fr 15	1 ·35 [Sukla]	14 ·04	—30
—31	Sa 16	2 ·44	15 ·14	1 [H. 1327 Shawwal]
1 [Saumya Tula—Aippasi]	Su 17	3 ·49	16 ·22	2
2	Mo 18	4 ·53	17 ·29	3
3	Tu 19	5 ·56	18 ·35	4
4	We 20	6 ·55	19 ·38	5
5	Th 21	7 ·55	20 ·39	6
6	Fr 22	8 ·50	21 ·38	7
7	Sa 23	9 ·45	22 ·35	8
8	Su 24	10 ·38	23 ·32	9
9	Mo 25	11 ·29	24 ·26	10
10	Tu 26	12 ·20	25 ·20	11
11	We 27	13 ·09	26 ·13	12
12	Th 28	14 ·00 / P ·90	27 ·06	13
13	Fr 29	1 ·82 [Asvina]	1 ·00 / 2 ·93	14
14	Sa 30	2 ·73	3 ·88	15
15	Su 31	3 ·65	4 ·83	16

SOLAR reckoning: Cyclic Sidereal Year, Month and Day.	Week-Day English Month and Day.	LUNAR reckoning: Tithi Ending Moment.	Nakshatra Ending Moment.	Muhammadan Year, Month and Day.
	Nov.			
16 [Saumya Tula—Aippasi]	Mo 1	4 ·59 [Asvina]	5 ·80	17 [H. 1327 Shawwal]
17	Tu 2	5 ·53	6 ·78	18
18	We 3	6 ·53	7 ·80	19
19	Th 4	7 ·52	8 ·82	20
20	Fr 5	8 ·53	9 ·87	21
21	Sa 6	9 ·57	10 ·93	22
22	Su 7	10 ·63 [Bahula]	... ...	23
23	Mo 8	11 ·71	11 ·02	24
24	Tu 9	12 ·79	12 ·12	25
25	We 10	13 ·88	13 ·23	26
26	Th 11	14 ·96	14 ·33	27
27	Fr 12	... ...	15 ·44	28
28	Sa 13	—A ·04	16 ·53	—29
29	Su 14	1 ·09	17 ·61	1 [H. 1327 Zi-l-ka'da]
—30	Mo 15	2 ·15	18 ·66	2
1 [Saumya Vrischika—Kartigai]	Tu 16	3 ·17 [Sukla]	19 ·70	3
2	We 17	4 ·16	20 ·71	4
3	Th 18	5 ·15	21 ·70	5
4	Fr 19	6 ·11	22 ·69	6
5	Sa 20	7 ·06 / 8 ·99	23 ·65	7
6	Su 21	9 ·91	24 ·60	8
7	Mo 22	10 ·82	25 ·54	9
8	Tu 23	11 ·71	26 ·47	10
9	We 24	12 ·62	27 ·40	11
10	Th 25	13 ·51 [Karttika]	1 ·34	12
11	Fr 26	14 ·42	2 ·27	13
12	Sa ○ 27	P ·34	3 ·21	14
13	Su 28	1 ·27	4 ·16	15
14	Mo 29	2 ·20	5 ·13	16
15	Tu 30	3 ·17	6 ·12	17
	Dec.			
16	We 1	4 ·15 [Bahula]	7 ·12	18
17	Th 2	5 ·14	8 ·14	19
18	Fr 3	6 ·16	9 ·18	20
19	Sa 4	7 ·21	10 ·24	21
20	Su 5	8 ·26	11 ·33	22
21	Mo 6	9 ·33	12 ·42	23
22	Tu 7	10 ·43	13 ·53	24
23	We 8	11 ·51	14 ·63	25
24	Th 9	12 ·59	15 ·74	26
25	Fr 10	13 ·68	16 ·84	27
26	Sa 11	14 ·74	17 ·92	28
27	Su 12	—A ·79	18 ·98	29
28	Mo 13	1 ·80	... ...	—30
—29	Tu 14	2 ·81 [Sukla]	19 ·01	1 [H. 1327 Zi-l-hijja]
1 [Saumya Dhanu—Margali]	We 15	3 ·79	20 ·08	2
2	Th 16	4 ·74	21 ·04	3
3	Fr 17	5 ·69	22 ·02 / 23 ·98	4
4	Sa 18	6 ·62	24 ·93	5
5	Su 19	7 ·53	25 ·87	6
6	Mo 20	8 ·44	26 ·81	7
7	Tu 21	9 ·35	27 ·75	8
8	We 22	10 ·25	1 ·68	9
9	Th 23	11 ·15	2 ·61	10
10	Fr 24	12 ·06 / 13 ·97	3 ·55	11
11	Sa 25	14 ·91 [Margasira]	4 ·49	12
12	Su 26	P ·85	5 ·47	13
13	Mo 27	1 ·81	6 ·44	14
14	Tu 28	2 ·79	7 ·44	15
15	We 29	3 ·80	8 ·45	16
16	Th 30	4 ·81	9 ·49	17
17	Fr 31	5 ·85	10 ·56	18

15. Svati. 16. Visak. 17. Anur. 18. Jyesh. 19. Mula. 20. P. Ash. 21. U. Ash. 22. Sravn. 23. Dani. 24. Satab. 25. P. Bhad. 26. U. Bhad. 27. Rev.

A. D. 1910.
Solar Eclipse. ●
Lunar Eclipse. ○

Mesha Sankranti (Commencement of Indian Sidereal Year).
(Surya Sid.) April 13·21. (Arya Sid.) April 13·10.

Saka 1832. (S. Cycle) Sadharana.

Kaliyuga 5011.

SOLAR reckoning: Cyclic Sidereal Year, Month and Day; Week-Day, English Month and Day. LUNAR reckoning: Tithi Ending Moment; Nakshatra Ending Moment; Muhammadan Year, Month and Day.

Jan.

Cyclic Sidereal Year, Month and Day	Week-Day, English Month and Day	Tithi Ending Moment	Nakshatra Ending Moment	Muhammadan Year, Month and Day
18 (Saumya, Dhanus—Margali.)	Sa 1	6 ·91 (Marg., Bahula)	11 ·63	19 (H. 1327 Zil-hijja.)
19	Su 2	7 ·99	12 ·72	20
20	Mo 3	... ...	13 ·82	21
21	Tu 4	8 ·08	14 ·93	22
22	We 5	9 ·16	... ...	23
23	Th 6	10 ·26	15 ·04	24
24	Fr 7	11 ·33	16 ·14	25
25	Sa 8	12 ·38	17 ·22	26
26	Su 9	13 ·44	18 ·29	27
27	Mo. 10	14 ·45	19 ·33	28
28	Tu 11	—A ·45	20 ·35	29
—29	We 12	1 ·43 (Pausha, Sukla)	21 ·36	—30
1 (Saumya, Makara—Tai.)	Th 13	2 ·40	22 ·85	1 (H. 1328 Muharram.)
2	Fr 14	3 ·33	23 ·32	2
3	Sa 15	4 ·26	24 ·27	3
4	Su 16	5 ·18	25 ·21	4
5	Mo 17	6 ·09 / 7 ·99	26 ·15	5
6	Tu 18	8 ·89	27 ·08	6
7	We 19	9 ·79	1 ·01 / 2 ·94	7
8	Th 20	10 ·70	3 ·88	8
9	Fr 21	11 ·62	4 ·84	9
10	Sa 22	12 ·55	5 ·80	10
11	Su 23	13 ·49	6 ·77	11
12	Mo 24	14 ·45	7 ·76	12
13	Tu 25	P ·43	8 ·77	13
14	We 26	1 ·44	9 ·81	14
15	Th 27	2 ·45	10 ·86	15
16	Fr 28	3 ·51	11 ·93	16
17	Sa 29	4 ·56	... ...	17
18	Su 30	5 ·65	12 ·02	18
19	Mo 31	6 ·78	13 ·12	19

Feb.

Cyclic Sidereal Year, Month and Day	Week-Day, English Month and Day	Tithi Ending Moment	Nakshatra Ending Moment	Muhammadan Year, Month and Day
20	Tu 1	7 ·81 (Bahula)	14 ·24	20
21	We 2	8 ·90	15 ·34	21
22	Th 3	9 ·98	16 ·44	22
23	Fr 4	... ...	17 ·53	23
24	Sa 5	10 ·04	18 ·60	24
25	Su 6	11 ·07	19 ·64	25
26	Mo 7	12 ·09	20 ·68	26
27	Tu 8	13 ·09	21 ·69	27
28	We 9	14 ·07	22 ·68	28
29	Th 10	A ·03 / 1 ·95 (Magha, Sukla)	23 ·65	29
—30	Fr 11	2 ·88	24 ·60	—30
1 (Saumya, Kumbha—Masi.)	Sa 12	3 ·80	25 ·56	1 (H. 1328 Safar.)
2	Su 13	4 ·71	26 ·49	2
3	Mo 14	5 ·61	27 ·42	3
4	Tu 15	6 ·51	1 ·35	4
5	We 16	7 ·42	2 ·28	5
6	Th 17	8 ·32	3 ·28	6
7	Fr 18	9 ·24	4 ·17	7
8	Sa 19	10 ·17	5 ·13	8
9	Su 20	11 ·12	6 ·10	9
10	Mo 21	12 ·07	7 ·08	10
11	Tu 22	13 ·07	8 ·10	11
12	We 23	14 ·06	9 ·12	12
13	Th 24	P ·08	10 ·17	13
14	Fr 25	1 ·13 (Bahula)	11 ·24	14
15	Sa 26	2 ·18	12 ·32	15
16	Su 27	3 ·26	13 ·42	16
17	Mo 28	4 ·36	14 ·54	17

March

Cyclic Sidereal Year, Month and Day	Week-Day, English Month and Day	Tithi Ending Moment	Nakshatra Ending Moment	Muhammadan Year, Month and Day
18 (Saumya, Kumbha—Masi.)	Tu 1	5 ·45 (Magha, Bahula)	15 ·64	18 (H. 1328 Safar.)
19	We 2	6 ·52	16 ·74	19
20	Th 3	7 ·59	17 ·83	20
21	Fr 4	8 ·65	18 ·90	21
22	Sa 5	9 ·69	19 ·97	22
23	Su 6	10 ·70	... ...	23
24	Mo 7	11 ·70	20 ·00	24
25	Tu 8	12 ·67	21 ·01	25
26	We 9	13 ·63	22 ·00 / 23 ·98	26
27	Th 10	14 ·56	24 ·95	27
28	Fr 11	—A ·49	25 ·89	25
29	Sa 12	1 ·40 (Phalguna, Sukla)	26 ·83	—29
—30	Su 13	2 ·31	27 ·76	1 (H. 1328 Rabi-ul-awwal.)
1 (Saumya, Mina—Panguni.)	Mo 14	3 ·21	1 ·69	2
2	Tu 15	4 ·12	2 ·63	3
3	We 16	5 ·01 / 6 ·92	3 ·56	4
4	Th 17	7 ·83	4 ·51	5
5	Fr 18	8 ·75	5 ·46	6
6	Sa 19	9 ·71	6 42	7
7	Su 20	10 ·67	7 ·42	8
8	Mo 21	11 ·66	8 ·42	9
9	Tu 22	12 ·65	9 ·44	10
10	We 23	13 ·68	10 ·48	11
11	Th 24	14 ·72	11 ·54	12
12	Fr 25	P ·77	12 ·62	13
13	Sa 26	1 ·86	13 ·73	14
14	Su 27	2 ·94	14 ·83	15
15	Mo 28	... ...	15 ·94	16
16	Tu 29	3 ·03	... ...	17
17	We 30	4 ·11	16 ·04	18
18	Th 31	5 ·18	17 ·13	19

April

Cyclic Sidereal Year, Month and Day	Week-Day, English Month and Day	Tithi Ending Moment	Nakshatra Ending Moment	Muhammadan Year, Month and Day
19	Fr 1	6 ·23 (Bahula)	18 ·22	20
20	Sa 2	7 ·27	19 ·28	21
21	Su 3	8 ·28	20 ·31	22
22	Mo 4	9 ·27	21 ·33	23
23	Tu 5	10 ·24	22 ·33	24
24	We 6	11 ·20	23 ·32	25
25	Th 7	12 ·14	24 ·28	26
26	Fr 8	13 ·06 / 14 ·98	25 ·28	27
27	Sa 9	—A ·87	26 ·17	28
28	Su 10	1 ·77 (Chaitra, Sukla)	27 ·10	29
29	Mo 11	2 ·67	1 ·04 / 2 ·97	—30
—30	Tu 12	3 ·57	3 ·90	1 (H. 1328 Rabi-ul-akhir.)
1 (Sadharana, Msha—Chittirai.)	We 13	4 ·48	4 ·84	2
2	Th 14	5 ·39	5 ·79	3
3	Fr 15	6 ·32	6 ·75	4
4	Sa 16	7 ·26	7 ·74	5
5	Su 17	8 ·22	8 ·74	6
6	Mo 18	9 ·21	9 ·75	7
7	Tu 19	10 ·20	10 ·79	8
8	We 20	11 ·24	11 ·85	9
9	Th 21	12 ·26	12 ·94	10
10	Fr 22	13 ·32	... ...	11
11	Sa 23	14 ·39	13 ·03	12
12	Su 24	P ·49	14 ·13	13
13	Mo 25	1 ·57 (Bahula)	15 ·24	14
14	Tu 26	2 ·64	16 ·34	15
15	We 27	3 ·72	17 ·45	16
16	Th 28	4 ·77	18 .53	17
17	Fr 29	5 ·81	19 ·59	18
18	Sa 30	6 ·81	20 ·63	19

May

Cyclic Sidereal Year, Month and Day	Week-Day, English Month and Day	Tithi Ending Moment	Nakshatra Ending Moment	Muhammadan Year, Month and Day
19 (Sadharana, Msha—Chittirai.)	Su 1	7 ·81 (Chaitra, Bahula)	21 ·65	20 (Rabi-ul-akhir.)
20	Mo 2	8 ·78	22 ·66	21
21	Tu 3	9 ·73	23 ·65	22
22	We 4	10 ·67	24 ·61	23
23	Th 5	11 ·58	25 ·56	24
24	Fr 6	12 ·50	26 ·50	25
25	Sa 7	13 ·40	27 ·45	26
26	Su 8	14 ·31	1 ·38	27
27	Mo 9	—A ·20	2 ·31	28
28	Tu 10	1 ·09 (Vaisakha, Sukla)	3 ·24	—29
29	We 11	2 ·00 / 3 ·91	4 ·18	1 (H. 1328 Jumadal-awwal.)
30	Th 12	4 ·84	5 ·12	2
—31	Fr 13	5 ·79	6 ·09	3
1 (Sadharana, Vrishabha—Vaikasi.)	Sa 14	6 ·74	7 ·07	4
2	Su 15	7 ·72	8 ·06	5
3	Mo 16	8 .72	9 ·07	6
4	Tu 17	9 ·75	10 ·10	7
5	We 18	10 ·78	11 ·17	8
6	Th 19	11 ·85	12 ·24	9
7	Fr 20	12 ·90	13 ·33	10
8	Sa 21	13 ·99	14 ·43	11
9	Su 22	... ...	15 ·53	12
10	Mo 23	14 ·08	16 ·65	13
11	Tu ○ 24	P ·16	17 ·75	14
12	We 25	1 ·22 (Bahula)	18 ·83	15
13	Th 26	2 ·27	19 ·90	16
14	Fr 27	3 ·31	20 ·95	17
15	Sa 28	4 ·32	21 ·98	18
16	Su 29	5 ·31	22 ·99	19
17	Mo 30	6 ·28	23 ·97	20
18	Tu 31	7 ·25	24 ·94	21

June

Cyclic Sidereal Year, Month and Day	Week-Day, English Month and Day	Tithi Ending Moment	Nakshatra Ending Moment	Muhammadan Year, Month and Day
19	We 1	8 ·17	25 ·90	22
20	Th 2	9 ·08	26 ·84	23
21	Fr 3	10 ·00 / 11 ·90	27 ·79	24
22	Sa 4	12 ·80	1 ·72	25
23	Su 5	13 ·69	2 ·65	26
24	Mo 6	14 ·60	3 ·58	27
25	Tu 7	—A ·51	4 ·51	28
26	We 8	1 ·42 (Jyeshtha, Sukla)	5 ·47	29
27	Th 9	2 ·33	6 ·42	—30
28	Fr 10	3 ·28	7 ·39	1 (H. 1328 Jumadal-akhir.)
29	Sa 11	4 ·23	8 ·38	2
30	Su 12	5 ·21	9 ·39	3
—31	Mo 13	6 ·21	10 ·43	4
1 (Sadharana, Mithuna—Ani.)	Tu 14	7 ·22	11 ·48	5
2	We 15	8 ·26	12 ·54	6
3	Th 16	9 ·32	13 ·63	7
4	Fr 17	10 ·39	14 ·73	8
5	Sa 18	11 ·46	15 ·84	9
6	Su 19	12 ·55	16 ·95	10
7	Mo 20	13 ·63	... ...	11
8	Tu 21	14 ·69	17 ·05	12
9	We 22	P ·75	18 ·14	13
10	Th 23	1 ·79 (Bahula)	19 ·21	14
11	Fr 24	2 ·79	20 ·26	15
12	Sa 25	3 ·79	21 ·30	16
13	Su 26	4 ·76	22 ·31	17
14	Mo 27	5 ·72	23 ·30	18
15	Tu 28	6 ·65	24 ·27	19
16	We 29	7 ·58	25 ·23	20
17	Th 30	8 ·49	26 ·19	21

Naksh :—1. Asvn. 2. Bhar. 3. Krit. 4. Rohi. 5. Mrig. 6. Ardh. 7. Punar. 8. Push. 9. Aslesh. 10. Magh. 11. P. Phal. 12. U. Phal. 13. Hasta. 14. Chit.

A. D. 1910.
A.—Amavasya.
P.—Paurnami.

Kollam 1086, Commences { **N. Malabar—Sept.** / **S. Malabar—Aug.**

Hijra 1328, Commences, **Jan. 13.**

Vikrama 1967.
Bengal San 1316.
(N. Cycle) Dundubhi.

Columns: SOLAR reckoning — Cyclic Sidereal Year, Month and Day | Week-Day, English Month and Day | LUNAR reckoning — Tithi Ending Moment | Nakshatra Ending Moment | Muhammadan Year, Month and Day.

July

Cyclic Sidereal Year, Month and Day	Week-Day	Day	Tithi	Ending Moment	Nakshatra	Ending Moment	Muhammadan Year, Month and Day	Notes
18	Fr	1	Jy. Bah. 9	·39	27	·12	22	H. 1328 J-akhir.
19	Sa	2	10	·29	1 2	·06 ·99	23	
20	Su	3	11	·18	3	·91	24	
21	Mo	4	12 13	·08 ·98	4	·86	25	
22	Tu	5	14	·90	5	·80	26	Sadharana Mithuna—Ani.
23	We	6	—A	·81	6	·75	27	
24	Th	7	1	·76	7	·72	28	Ashadha, Sukla
25	Fr	8	2	·71	8	·71	—29	
26	Sa	9	3	68	9	·72	1	
27	Su	10	4	·68	10	·74	2	
28	Mo	11	5	·70	11	·78	3	
29	Tu	12	6	·74	12	·85	4	
30	We	13	7	·79	13	·93	5	
31	Th	14	8	·87	...	...	6	
—32	Fr	15	9	·95	14	·04	7	
1	Sa	16	..	...	15	·14	8	
2	Su	17	10	·02	16	·25	9	
3	Mo	18	11	·09	17	·35	10	
4	Tu	19	12	·17	18	·44	11	
5	We	20	13	·25	19	·52	12	
6	Th	21	14	·27	20	·58	13	
7	Fr	22	P	·28	21	·62	14	
8	Sa	23	1	·27	22	·63	15	
9	Su	24	2	·25	23	·63	16	
10	Mo	25	3	·20	24	·60	17	
11	Tu	26	4	·13	25	·57	18	
12	We	27	5 6	·06 ·98	26	·52	19	Sadharana Karkata—Adi.; H. 1328 Rajab.
13	Th	28	7	·88	27	·46	20	Bahula
14	Fr	29	8	·78	1	·39	21	
15	Sa	30	9	·68	2	·32	22	
16	Su	31	10	·57	3	·26	23	

Aug.

Cyclic Sidereal Year, Month and Day	Week-Day	Day	Tithi	Ending Moment	Nakshatra	Ending Moment	Muhammadan Year, Month and Day	Notes
17	Mo	1	11	·47	4	·20	24	
18	Tu	2	12	·39	5	·14	25	
19	We	3	13	·31	6	·09	26	
20	Th	4	14	·24	7	·05	27	
21	Fr	5	—A	·19	8	·04	28	
22	Sa	6	1	·18	9	·04	29	Sravana, Sukla
23	Su	7	2	·17	10	·06	—30	
24	Mo	8	3	·18	11	·09	1	
25	Tu	9	4	·21	12	·15	2	
26	We	10	5	·27	13	·23	3	
27	Th	11	6	·35	14	·34	4	
28	Fr	12	7	·43	15	·44	5	
29	Sa	13	8	·51	16	·54	6	
30	Su	14	9	·59	17	·65	7	
31	Mo	15	10	·66	18	·74	8	
—32	Tu	16	11	·72	19	·83	9	
1	We	17	12	·75	20	·89	10	Sadharana Simha—Avani.; H. 1328 Shaban.
2	Th	18	13	·77	21	·93	11	
3	Fr	19	14	·76	22	·95	12	
4	Sa	20	P	·74	23	·95	13	
5	Su	21	1	·70	24	·94	14	Bahula
6	Mo	22	2	·65	25	·91	15	
7	Tu	23	3	·56	26	·86	16	
8	We	24	4	·47	27	·80	17	
9	Th	25	5	·38	1	·73	18	
10	Fr	26	6	·28	2	·67	19	
11	Sa	27	7	·18	3	·60	20	
12	Su	28	8 9	·08 ·98	4	·53	21	
13	Mo	29	10	·89	5	·47	22	
14	Tu	30	11	·82	6	·42	23	
15	We	31	12	·76	7	·39	24	

Sep.

Cyclic Sidereal Year, Month and Day	Week-Day	Day	Tithi	Ending Moment	Nakshatra	Ending Moment	Muhammadan Year, Month and Day	Notes
16	Th	1	Bah. 13	·70	8	·37	25	Shaban.
17	Fr	2	14	·69	9	·36	26	
18	Sa	3	—A	·68	10	·37	27	
19	Su	4	1	·70	11	·41	28	Bhadrapada, Sukla
20	Mo	5	2	·72	12	·46	—29	Sadharana Simha—Avani.
21	Tu	6	3	·79	13	·55	1	
22	We	7	4	·85	14	·63	2	
23	Th	8	5	·93	15	·74	3	
24	Fr	9	...	...	16	·84	4	
25	Sa	10	6	·02	17	·95	5	
26	Su	11	7	·10	...	...	6	
27	Mo	12	8	·18	18	·05	7	
28	Tu	13	9	·24	19	·14	8	
29	We	14	10	·28	20	·20	9	
30	Th	15	11	·30	21	·25	10	
—31	Fr	16	12	·29	22	·27	11	
1	Sa	17	13	·27	23	·29	12	
2	Su	18	14	·23	24	·27	13	
3	Mo	19	P	·17	25	·24	14	
4	Tu	20	1	·09	26	·19	15	Bahula
5	We	21	2 3	·01 ·91	27	·14	16	
6	Th	22	4	·83	1	·08	17	H. 1328 Ramzan.
7	Fr	23	5	·72	2 3	·01 ·94	18	
8	Sa	24	6	·61	4	·87	19	Sadharana Kanya—Purattasi.
9	Su	25	7	·52	5	·81	20	
10	Mo	26	8	·43	6	·75	21	
11	Tu	27	9	·36	7	·70	22	
12	We	28	10	·30	8	·69	23	
13	Th	29	11	·25	9	·68	24	
14	Fr	30	12	·23	10	·69	25	

Oct.

Cyclic Sidereal Year, Month and Day	Week-Day	Day	Tithi	Ending Moment	Nakshatra	Ending Moment	Muhammadan Year, Month and Day	Notes
15	Sa	1	13	·22	11	·72	26	
16	Su	2	14	·24	12	·78	27	
17	Mo	3	—A	·27	13	·85	28	
18	Tu	4	1	·33	14	·94	29	Asvina, Sukla
19	We	5	2	·40	...	...	—30	
20	Th	6	3	·49	15	·03	1	
21	Fr	7	4	·57	16	·14	2	
22	Sa	8	5	·66	17	·26	3	
23	Su	9	6	·74	18	·36	4	
24	Mo	10	7	·80	19	·44	5	
25	Tu	11	8	·84	20	·51	6	
26	We	12	9	·86	21	·56	7	
27	Th	13	10	·86	22	·60	8	
28	Fr	14	11	·83	23	·61	9	
29	Sa	15	12	·80	24	·60	10	
—30	Su	16	13	·74	25	·57	11	H. 1328 Shawwal.
1	Mo	17	14	·66	26	·53	12	
2	Tu	18	P	·58	27	·48	13	
3	We	19	1	·48	1	·42	14	Bahula
4	Th	20	2	·39	2	·35	15	
5	Fr	21	3	·30	3	·28	16	
6	Sa	22	4	·20	4	·21	17	Sadharana Tula—Aippasi.
7	Su	23	5	·10	5	·14	18	
8	Mo	24	6 7	·01 ·94	6	·10	19	
9	Tu	25	8	·88	7	·05	20	
10	We	26	9	·83	8	·02	21	
11	Th	27	10	·81	9	·00	22	
12	Fr	28	11	·82	10	·01	23	
13	Sa	29	12	·83	11	·04	24	
14	Su	30	13	·87	12	·09	25	
15	Mo	31	14	·93	13	·15	26	

Nov.

Cyclic Sidereal Year, Month and Day	Week-Day	Day	Tithi	Ending Moment	Nakshatra	Ending Moment	Muhammadan Year, Month and Day	Notes
16	Tu	1	...	...	14	·24	27	
17	We	2	—A	·00	15	·33	28	
18	Th	3	1	·09	16	·45	—29	Kartika, Sukla
19	Fr	4	2	·18	17	·55	1	
20	Sa	5	3	·27	18	·65	2	Sadharana Tula—Aippasi.
21	Su	6	4	·34	19	·75	3	
22	Mo	7	5	·40	20	·82	4	
23	Tu	8	6	·43	21	·88	5	
24	We	9	7	·46	22	·92	6	
25	Th	10	8	·46	23	·93	7	
26	Fr	11	9	·43	24	·92	8	
27	Sa	12	10	·39	25	·90	9	
28	Su	13	11	·34	26	·86	10	
29	Mo	14	12	·28	27	·82	11	
—30	Tu	15	13	·19	1	·76	12	
1	We ○	16	14 P	·09 ·99	2	·69	13	
2	Th	17	1	·90	3	·62	14	Bahula; H. 1328 Zi-l-ka'da.
3	Fr	18	2	·81	4	·55	15	
4	Sa	19	3	·71	5	·49	16	
5	Su	20	4	·63	6	·43	17	
6	Mo	21	5	·55	7	·38	18	
7	Tu	22	6	·50	8	·35	19	Sadharana Vrischika—Kartigai.
8	We	23	7	·45	9	·33	20	
9	Th	24	8	·43	10	·34	21	
10	Fr	25	9	·43	11	·36	22	
11	Sa	26	10	·46	12	·40	23	
12	Su	27	11	·49	13	·46	24	
13	Mo	28	12	·55	14	·54	25	
14	Tu	29	13	·63	15	·64	26	
15	We	30	14	·72	16	·75	27	

Dec.

Cyclic Sidereal Year, Month and Day	Week-Day	Day	Tithi	Ending Moment	Nakshatra	Ending Moment	Muhammadan Year, Month and Day	Notes
16	Th	1	—A	·80	17	·85	28	
17	Fr	2	1	·89	18	·96	29	Margasira, Sukla
18	Sa	3	2	·96	..	...	—30	
19	Su	4	...	...	19	·05	1	
20	Mo	5	3	·04	20	·14	2	
21	Tu	6	4	·07	21	·20	3	
22	We	7	5	·09	22	·28	4	
23	Th	8	6	·09	23	·25	5	
24	Fr	9	7	·06	24	·25	6	
25	Sa	10	8 9	·02 ·96	25	·28	7	
26	Su	11	10	·90	26	·20	8	
27	Mo	12	11	·81	27	·15	9	
28	Tu	13	12	·72	1	·09	10	
—29	We	14	13	·62	2 3	·03 ·96	11	H. 1328 Zi-l-hijja.
1	Th	15	14	·53	4	·90	12	
2	Fr	16	P	·43	5	·83	13	
3	Sa	17	1	·34	6	·77	14	Bahula
4	Su	18	2	·26	7	·71	15	
5	Mo	19	3	·18	8	·68	16	
6	Tu	20	4	·18	9	·66	17	
7	We	21	5	·09	10	·66	18	Sadharana Dhanus—Margali.
8	Th	22	6	·08	11	·67	19	
9	Fr	23	7	·07	12	·71	20	
10	Sa	24	8	·10	13	·77	21	
11	Su	25	9	·15	14	·83	22	
12	Mo	26	10	·20	15	·94	23	
13	Tu	27	11	·29	...	...	24	
14	We	28	12	·37	16	·04	25	
15	Th	29	13	·46	17	·15	26	
16	Fr	30	14	·55	18	·25	27	
17	Sa	31	—A	·63	19	·35	28	

15. Svati. 16. Visak. 17. Anur. 18. Jyesh. 19. Mula. 20. P. Ash. 21. U. Ash. 22. Sravn. 23. Dani. 24. Satab. 25. P. Bhad. 26. U. Bhad. 27. Rev.

A. D. 1911.
Solar Eclipse. ●
Lunar Eclipse. ○

Mesha Sankranti (Commencement of Indian Sidereal Year).
(Surya Sid.) April 13·47. **Saka 1833.** **Kaliyuga 5012.**
(Arya Sid.) April 13·36. **(S. Cycle) Virodhakrit.**

Columns: SOLAR reckoning — Cyclic Sidereal Year, Month and Day; Week-Day, English Month and Day. LUNAR reckoning — Tithi Ending Moment; Nakshatra Ending Moment; Muhammadan Year, Month and Day.

Jan.

Sadharana *Dhanus—Margali*; Sadharana *Makara—Tai*. Sukla; Pausha; Bahula. H. 1329 *Muharram.*

Cyclic Sidereal Year, Month and Day	Week-Day	English Day	Tithi Ending Moment	Nakshatra Ending Moment	Muhammadan Year, Month and Day
18	Su	1	1 ·68	20 ·44	—29
19	Mo	2	2 ·71	21 ·51	1
20	Tu	3	3 ·74	22 ·55	2
21	We	4	4 ·73	23 ·57	3
22	Th	5	5 ·71	24 ·57	4
23	Fr	6	6 ·67	25 ·57	5
24	Sa	7	7 ·62	26 ·54	6
25	Su	8	8 ·54	27 ·49	7
26	Mo	9	9 ·46	1 ·43	8
27	Tu	10	10 ·37	2 ·36	9
28	We	11	11 ·26	3 ·30	10
29	Th	12	12 ·18	4 ·23	11
—30	Fr	13	{13 ·07, 14 ·99	5 ·16	12
1	Sa	14	P ·90	6 ·10	13
2	Su	15	1 ·83	7 ·05	14
3	Mo	16	2 ·78	8 ·02, 9 ·99}	15
4	Tu	17	3 ·73	10 ·98	16
5	We	18	4 ·73	11 ·99	17
6	Th	19	5 ·72	... ...	18
7	Fr	20	6 ·75	12 ·02	19
8	Sa	21	7 ·79	13 ·07	20
9	Su	22	8 ·87	14 ·15	21
10	Mo	23	9 ·94	15 ·24	22
11	Tu	24	... ...	16 ·34	23
12	We	25	10 ·02	17 ·45	24
13	Th	26	11 ·12	18 ·55	25
14	Fr	27	12 ·20	19 ·66	26
15	Sa	28	13 ·28	20 ·75	27
16	Su	29	14 ·83	21 ·82	28
17	Mo	30	—A ·36	22 ·86	29
18	Tu	31	1 83	23 ·89	—30

Feb.

Sadharana *Kumbha—Masi.* Sukla; Magha; Bahula. H. 1329 *Safar.*

Cyclic Sidereal Year, Month and Day	Week-Day	English Day	Tithi Ending Moment	Nakshatra Ending Moment	Muhammadan Year, Month and Day
19	We	1	2 ·37	24 ·91	1
20	Th	2	3 ·35	25 ·90	2
21	Fr	3	4 ·30	26 ·87	3
22	Sa	4	5 ·25	27 ·82	4
23	Su	5	6 ·17	1 ·77	5
24	Mo	6	{7 ·09, 8 ·99	2 ·71	6
25	Tu	7	9 ·89	3 ·64	7
26	We	8	10 ·80	4 ·57	8
27	Th	9	11 ·69	5 ·50	9
28	Fr	10	12 ·61	6 ·44	10
—29	Sa	11	13 ·52	7 ·39	11
1	Su	12	14 ·46	8 ·35	12
2	Mo	13	P ·41	9 ·32	13
3	Tu	14	1 ·37	10 ·30	14
4	We	15	2 ·35	11 ·31	15
5	Th	16	3 ·34	12 ·33	16*
6	Fr	17	4 ·39	13 ·39	17
7	Sa	18	5 ·43	14 ·46	18
8	Su	19	6 ·49	15 ·54	19
9	Mo	20	7 ·56	16 ·64	20
10	Tu	21	8 ·65	17 ·75	21
11	We	22	9 ·75	18 ·86	22
12	Th	23	10 ·82	19 ·96	23
13	Fr	24	11 ·90	... ...	24
14	Sa	25	12 ·95	20 ·05	25
15	Su	26	13 ·99	21 ·12	26
16	Mo	27	14 ·99	22 ·18	27
17	Tu	28	... ...	23 ·22	28

March

Sadharana *Kumbha—Masi*; Sadharana *Mina—Panguni.* Sukla; Phalguna; Bahula. H. 1329 *Rabi-ul-awwal.*

Cyclic Sidereal Year, Month and Day	Week-Day	English Day	Tithi Ending Moment	Nakshatra Ending Moment	Muhammadan Year, Month and Day
18	We	1	{A ·00, 1 ·97	24 ·23	--29
19	Th	2	2 ·91	25 ·22	1
20	Fr	3	3 ·86	26 ·20	2
21	Sa	4	4 ·78	27 ·16	3
22	Su	5	5 ·70	1 ·11	4
23	Mo	6	6 ·60	2 ·05, 3 ·98}	5
24	Tu	7	7 ·51	4 ·91	6
25	We	8	8 ·41	5 ·84	7
26	Th	9	9 ·31	6 ·77	8
27	Fr	10	10 ·22	7 ·73	9
28	Sa	11	11 ·13	8 68	10
29	Su	12	12 ·06	9 ·64	11
—30	Mo	13	{13 ·00, 14 ·97	10 ·63	12
1	Tu	14	P ·95	11 ·63	13
2	We	15	1 ·95	12 ·66	14
3	Th	16	2 ·98	13 ·70	15
4	Fr	17	... ...	14 ·76	16
5	Sa	18	3 ·02	15 ·84	17
6	Su	19	4 ·09	16 ·94	18
7	Mo	20	5 ·17	... ...	19
8	Tu	21	6 ·26	17 ·05	20
9	We	22	7 ·34	18 ·16	21
10	Th	23	8 ·43	19 ·26	22
11	Fr	24	9 ·49	20 ·35	23
12	Sa	25	10 ·55	21 ·43	24
13	Su	26	11 ·58	22 ·50	25
14	Mo	27	12 ·58	23 ·54	26
15	Tu	28	13 ·58	24 ·55	27
16	We	29	14 ·54	25 ·55	28
17	Th	30	—A ·50	26 ·53	29
18	Fr	31	1 ·44	27 ·50	—30

April

Virodhakrit *Mesha—Chittirai.* Sukla; Chaitra; Bahula; Suk. H. 1329 *Rabi-ul-akhir.*

Cyclic Sidereal Year, Month and Day	Week-Day	English Day	Tithi Ending Moment	Nakshatra Ending Moment	Muhammadan Year, Month and Day
19	Sa	1	2 ·37	1 ·45	1
20	Su	2	3 ·28	2 ·40	2
21	Mo	3	4 ·18	3 ·32	3
22	Tu	4	{5 ·07, 6 ·97	4 ·25	4
23	We	5	7 ·88	5 ·18	5
24	Th	6	8 ·79	6 ·12	6
25	Fr	7	9 ·71	7 ·06	7
26	Sa	8	10 ·63	8 ·01, 9 ·97}	8
27	Su	9	11 ·56	10 ·95	9
•28	Mo	10	12 ·53	11 ·96	10
29	Tu	11	13 ·51	12 ·97	11
—30	We	12	14 ·51	... ...	12
1	Th	13	P ·54	13 ·01	13
2	Fr	14	1 ·59	14 ·07	14
3	Sa	15	2 ·64	15 ·15	15
4	Su	16	3 73	16 ·25	16
5	Mo	17	4 ·81	17 ·35	17
6	Tu	18	5 ·89	18 ·46	18
7	We	19	6 ·98	19 ·56	19
8	Th	20	... ...	20 ·66	20
9	Fr	21	7 ·04	21 ·75	21
10	Sa	22	8 ·09	22 ·81	22
11	Su	23	9 ·12	23 ·85	23
12	Mo	24	10 ·13	24 ·87	24
13	Tu	25	11 ·12	25 ·87	25
14	We	26	12 ·09	26 ·86	26
15	Th	27	{13 ·04, 14 ·98	27 ·83	27
16	Fr	28	—A ·91	1 ·78	28
17	Sa	29	1 ·81	2 ·72	—29
18	Su	30	2 ·72	3 ·66	1

May

Virodhakrit *Mesha—Chittirai*; Virodhakrit *Vrishabha—Vaikasi.* Sukla; Vaisakha; Bahula. H. 1329 *Jumadal-awwal.*

Cyclic Sidereal Year, Month and Day	Week-Day	English Day	Tithi Ending Moment	Nakshatra Ending Moment	Muhammadan Year, Month and Day
19	Mo	1	3 ·61	4 ·59	2
20	Tu	2	4 ·51	5 ·53	3
21	We	3	5 ·41	6 ·46	4
22	Th	4	6 ·31	7 ·40	5
23	Fr	5	7 ·21	8 ·34	6
24	Sa	6	8 ·15	9 ·30	7
25	Su	7	9 ·11	10 ·29	8
26	Mo	8	10 ·06	11 ·28	9
27	Tu	9	11 ·05	12 ·29	10
28	We	10	12 ·04	13 ·32	11
29	Th	11	13 ·06	14 ·38	12
30	Fr	12	14 ·11	15 ·46	13
—31	Sa	13	P ·16	16 ·55	14
1	Su	14	1 ·24	17 ·65	15
2	Mo	15	2 ·32	18 ·76	16
3	Tu	16	3 ·41	19 ·86	17
4	We	17	4 ·48	20 ·97	18
5	Th	18	5 ·55	... ...	19
6	Fr	19	6 ·61	21 ·05	20
7	Sa	20	7 ·62	22 ·12	21
8	Su	21	8 ·64	23 ·17	22
9	Mo	22	9 ·63	24 ·19	23
10	Tu	23	10 ·61	25 ·20	24
11	We	24	11 ·56	26 ·19	25
12	Th	25	12 ·48	27 ·16	26
13	Fr	26	13 ·41	1 ·12	27
14	Sa	27	14 ·31	2 ·06	28
15	Su	28	—A ·22	3 ·00, 4 ·94}	29
16	Mo	29	1 ·11	5 ·87	—30
17	Tu	30	{2 ·02, 3 ·91	6 ·80	1
18	We	31	4 ·81	7 ·73	2

June

Virodhakrit *Mithuna—Ani.* Sukla; Jyeshtha; Bahula; Ash. Suk. H. 1329 *Jumadal-akhir*; *Rajab.*

Cyclic Sidereal Year, Month and Day	Week-Day	English Day	Tithi Ending Moment	Nakshatra Ending Moment	Muhammadan Year, Month and Day
19	Th	1	5 ·74	8 ·68	3
20	Fr	2	6 ·66	9 ·64	4
21	Sa	3	7 ·61	10 ·61	5
22	Su	4	8 ·56	11 ·60	6
23	Mo	5	9 ·54	12 ·61	7
24	Tu	6	10 ·53	13 ·64	8
25	We	7	11 ·56	14 ·70	9
26	Th	8	12 ·60	15 ·76	10
27	Fr	9	13 ·64	16 ·85	11
28	Sa	10	14 ·73	17 ·95	12
29	Su	11	P ·81	... ...	13
30	Mo	12	1 ·90	18 ·06	14
31	Tu	13	2 ·97	19 ·16	15
—32	We	14	... ...	20 ·27	16
1	Th	15	3 ·04	21 ·36	17
2	Fr	16	4 ·08	22 ·43	18
3	Sa	17	5 ·12	23 ·48	19
4	Su	18	6 ·13	24 ·51	20
5	Mo	19	7 ·12	25 ·53	21
6	Tu	20	8 ·09	26 ·52	22
7	We	21	{9 ·04, 10 ·99	27 ·49	23
8	Th	22	11 ·90	1 ·45	24
9	Fr	23	12 ·81	2 ·40	25
10	Sa	24	13 ·71	3 ·34	26
11	Su	25	14 ·60	4 ·28	27
12	Mo	26	—A ·50	5 ·20	28
13	Tu	27	1 ·40	6 ·13	—29
14	We	28	2 ·30	7 ·07	1
15	Th	29	3 ·22	8 ·02, 9 ·97}	2
16	Fr	30	4 ·15	10 ·94	3

Nakah:—1. Asvn, 2. Bhar, 3. Krit, 4. Rohi, 5. Mrig, 6. Ardh, 7. Punar, 8. Push, 9. Aslesh, 10. Magh, 11. P. Phal, 12. U. Phal, 13. Hasta, 14. Chit.

A. D. 1911.			Vikrama 1968.
A.—Amavasya.	Kollam 1087, Commences { N. Malabar—Sept. / S. Malabar—Aug.	Hijra 1329, Jan. 2.	Bengal San 1317.
P.—Paurnami.		Hijra 1330, Dec. 22.	(N. Cycle) Rudhirodgarin.

Column headings: SOLAR reckoning — Cyclic Sidereal Year, Month and Day; Week-Day English Month and Day. LUNAR reckoning — Tithi Ending Moment; Nakshatra Ending Moment; Muhammadan Year, Month and Day.

July — Solar: Virodhakrit, Mithuna—Ani. (to 31); Virodhakrit, Karkata—Adi. (from 1). Lunar: Ashadha, Sukla; Bahula. Muhammadan: H. 1329 Rajab.

Cyclic Sidereal	Week-Day	Day	Tithi	Moment	Nakshatra	Moment	Muhammadan
17	Sa	1	5	·09	11	·93	4
18	Su	2	6	·03	12	·98	5
19	Mo	3	7	·02	13	·96	6
20	Tu	4	8	·01	...	...	7
21	We	5	9	·08	14	·00	8
22	Th	6	10	·07	15	·07	9
23	Fr	7	11	·13	16	·15	10
24	Sa	8	12	·20	17	·25	11
25	Su	9	13	·29	18	·35	12
26	Mo	10	14	·37	19	·47	13
27	Tu	11	P	·44	20	·57	14
28	We	12	1	·51	21	·66	15
29	Th	13	2	·56	22	·74	16
30	Fr	14	3	·60	23	·79	17
—31	Sa	15	4	·60	24	·84	18
1	Su	16	5	·60	25	·85	19
2	Mo	17	6	·57	26	·85	20
3	Tu	18	7	·51	27	·82	21
4	We	19	8	·45	1	·78	22
5	Th	20	9	·37	2	·74	23
6	Fr	21	10	·29	3	·68	24
7	Sa	22	11	·19	4	·61	25
8	Su	23	{ 12 / 13	·10 / ·99	5	·54	26
9	Mo	24	14	·88	6	·47	27
10	Tu	25	—A	·79	7	·42	28
11	We	26	1	·69	8	·36	29
12	Th	27	2	·63	9	·31	—30
13	Fr	28	3	·56	10	·27	1
14	Sa	29	4	·52	11	·25	2
15	Su	30	5	·50	12	·25	3
16	Mo	31	6	·49	13	·28	4

Aug. — Solar: Virodhakrit, Karkata—Adi. (to 32); Virodhakrit, Simha—Avani. (from 1). Lunar: Sravana, Sukla; Bahula; Bhadra. Suk. Muhammadan: H. 1329 Shaban.; Ramzan.

Cyclic Sidereal	Week-Day	Day	Tithi	Moment	Nakshatra	Moment	Muhammadan
17	Tu	1	7	·51	14	·31	5
18	We	2	8	·54	15	·37	6
19	Th	3	9	·61	16	·45	7
20	Fr	4	10	·68	17	·55	8
21	Sa	5	11	·76	18	·66	9
22	Su	6	12	·84	19	·77	10
23	Mo	7	13	·92	20	·87	11
24	Tu	8	14	·99	21	·96	12
25	We	9	...	...	...	...	13
26	Th	10	P	·03	22	·04	14
27	Fr	11	1	·07	23	·11	15
28	Sa	12	2	·09	24	·15	16
29	Su	13	3	·09	25	·17	17
30	Mo	14	4	·06	26	·17	18
31	Tu	15	{ 5 / 6	·01 / ·96	27	·15	19
—32	We	16	7	·87	1	·13	20
1	Th	17	8	·79	2	·08	21
2	Fr	18	9	·69	3 / 4	·02 / ·95 }	22
3	Sa	19	10	·59	5	·88	23
4	Su	20	11	·48	6	·81	24
5	Mo	21	12	·39	7	·75	25
6	Tu	22	13	·29	8	·69	26
7	We	23	14	·21	9	·64	27
8	Th	24	—A	·13	10	·60	28
9	Fr	25	1	·07	11	·58	—29
10	Sa	26	2	·03	12	·58	1
11	Su	27	3	·00	13	·59	2
12	Mo	28	4	·00	14	·63	3
13	Tu	29	5	·01	15	·68	4
14	We	30	6	·05	16	·76	5
15	Th	31	7	·11	17	·86	6

Sep. — Solar: Virodhakrit, Simha—Avani. (to 31); Virodhakrit, Kanya—Purattasi. (from 1). Lunar: Bhadrapada, Sukla; Bahula; Sukla. Muhammadan: H. 1329 Ramzan.

Cyclic Sidereal	Week-Day	Day	Tithi	Moment	Nakshatra	Moment	Muhammadan
16	Fr	1	8	·17	18	·96	7
17	Sa	2	9	·26	...	...	8
18	Su	3	10	·34	19	·06	9
19	Mo	4	11	·43	20	·17	10
20	Tu	5	12	·50	21	·27	11
21	We	6	13	·56	22	·36	12
22	Th	7	14	·58	23	·42	13
23	Fr	8	P	·61	24	·47	14
24	Sa	9	1	·60	25	·49	15
25	Su	10	2	·57	26	·50	16
26	Mo	11	3	·54	27	·49	17
27	Tu	12	4	·47	1	·46	18
28	We	13	5	·40	2	·41	19
29	Th	14	6	·31	3	·36	20
30	Fr	15	7	·22	4	·29	21
—31	Sa	16	8	·12	5	·22	22
1	Su	17	{ 9 / 10	·01 / ·92	6	·16	23
2	Mo	18	11	·81	7	·09	24
3	Tu	19	12	·73	8 / 9	·03 / ·97 }	25
4	We	20	13	·67	10	·93	26
5	Th	21	14	·61	11	·91	27
6	Fr	22	—A	·55	12	·90	28
7	Sa	23	1	·53	13	·91	29
8	Su	24	2	·53	14	·94	—30
9	Mo	25	3	·54	15	·99	1
10	Tu	26	4	·59	...	...	2
11	We	27	5	·64	16	·07	3
12	Th	28	6	·72	17	·16	4
13	Fr	29	7	·80	18	·26	5
14	Sa	30	8	·89	19	·36	6

Oct. — Solar: Virodhakrit, Kanya—Purattasi. (to 30); Virodhakrit, Tula—Aippasi. (from 1). Lunar: Asvina, Bahula; Karttika, Sukla. Muhammadan: H. 1329 Shawwal.; H. 1329 Zi-l-ka'da.

Cyclic Sidereal	Week-Day	Day	Tithi	Moment	Nakshatra	Moment	Muhammadan
15	Su	1	9	·97	20	·47	7
16	Mo	2	...	...	21	·58	8
17	Tu	3	10	·04	22	·66	9
18	We	4	11	·10	23	·73	10
19	Th	5	12	·13	24	·78	11
20	Fr	6	13	·15	25	·81	12
21	Sa	7	14	·15	26	·82	13
22	Su	8	P	·13	27	·82	14
23	Mo	9	1	·10	1	·79	15
24	Tu	10	{ 2 / 3	·03 / ·96	2	·75	16
25	We	11	4	·87	3	·69	17
26	Th	12	5	·78	4	·63	18
27	Fr	13	6	·68	5	·57	19
28	Sa	14	7	·58	6	·50	20
29	Su	15	8	·48	7	·43	21
—30	Mo	16	9	·38	8	·36	22
1	Tu	17	10	·30	9	·31	23
2	We	18	11	·23	10	·27	24
3	Th	19	12	·18	11	·24	25
4	Fr	20	13	·12	12	·22	26
5	Sa	21	14	·11	13	·23	27
6	Su ●	22	—A	·11	14	·25	28
7	Mo	23	1	·13	15	·31	—29
8	Tu	24	2	·17	16	·37	1
9	We	25	3	·23	17	·46	2
10	Th	26	4	·30	18	·55	3
11	Fr	27	5	·38	19	·66	4
12	Sa	28	6	·47	20	·78	5
13	Su	29	7	·55	21	·88	6
14	Mo	30	8	·64	22	·97	7
15	Tu	31	9	·69	...	...	8

Nov. — Solar: Virodhakrit, Tula—Aippasi. (to 30); Virodhakrit, Vrischika—Kartigai. (from 1). Lunar: Karttika, Sukla; Bahula; Sukla. Muhammadan: H. 1329 Zi-l-ka'da.

Cyclic Sidereal	Week-Day	Day	Tithi	Moment	Nakshatra	Moment	Muhammadan
16	We	1	10	·72	23	·04	9
17	Th	2	11	·75	24	·09	10
18	Fr	3	12	·74	25	·13	11
19	Sa	4	13	·72	26	·15	12
20	Su	5	14	·69	27	·14	13
21	Mo	6	P	·63	1	·12	14
22	Tu	7	1	·55	2	·08	15
23	We	8	2	·46	3 / 4	·03 / ·98 }	16
24	Th	9	3	·37	5	·91	17
25	Fr	10	4	·28	6	·84	18
26	Sa	11	5	·18	7	·77	19
27	Su	12	{ 6 / 7	·08 / ·99	8	·70	20
28	Mo	13	8	·90	9	·65	21
29	Tu	14	9	·84	10	·60	22
—30	We	15	10	·78	11	·57	23
1	Th	16	11	·73	12	·55	24
2	Fr	17	12	·72	13	·55	25
3	Sa	18	13	·72	14	·58	26
4	Su	19	14	·74	15	·62	27
5	Mo	20	—A	·78	16	·68	28
6	Tu	21	1	·85	17	·76	29
7	We	22	2	·93	18	·85	—30
8	Th	23	...	...	19	·96	1
9	Fr	24	3	·01	...	...	2
10	Sa	25	4	·10	20	·07	3
11	Su	26	5	·18	21	·18	4
12	Mo	27	6	·26	22	·27	5
13	Tu	28	7	·31	23	·35	6
14	We	29	8	·36	24	·41	7
15	Th	30	9	·37	25	·45	8

Dec. — Solar: Virodhakrit, Vrischika—Kartigai. (to 30); Virodhakrit, Dhanus—Margali. (from 1). Lunar: Margasira; Bahula; Pausha, Sukla. Muhammadan: H. 1329 Zi-l-hijja.; H. 1330 Muharram.

Cyclic Sidereal	Week-Day	Day	Tithi	Moment	Nakshatra	Moment	Muhammadan
16	Fr	1	10	·37	26	·47	9
17	Sa	2	11	·35	27	·47	10
18	Su	3	12	·30	1	·45	11
19	Mo	4	13	·24	2	·41	12
20	Tu	5	14	·17	3	·37	13
21	We	6	P	·10	4	·31	14
22	Th	7	{ 1 / 2	·00 / ·91	5	·25	15
23	Fr	8	3	·81	6	·17	16
24	Sa	9	4	·70	7	·10	17
25	Su	10	5	·61	8 / 9	·05 / ·99 }	18
26	Mo	11	6	·52	10	·93	19
27	Tu	12	7	·47	11	·90	20
28	We	13	8	·41	12	·87	21
29	Th	14	9	·37	13	·88	22
—30	Fr	15	10	·36	14	·89	23
1	Sa	16	11	·35	15	·93	24
2	Su	17	12	·38	16	·99	25
3	Mo	18	13	·43	...	...	26
4	Tu	19	14	·50	17	·06	27
5	We	20	—A	·57	18	·15	28
6	Th	21	1	·66	19	·26	—29
7	Fr	22	2	·75	20	·37	1
8	Sa	23	3	·84	21	·48	2
9	Su	24	4	·90	22	·57	3
10	Mo	25	5	·96	23	·65	4
11	Tu	26	...	...	24	·73	5
12	We	27	6	·00	25	·77	6
13	Th	28	7	·01	26	·79	7
14	Fr	29	{ 8 / 9	·02 / ·99	27	·79	8
15	Sa	30	10	·95	1	·78	9
16	Su	31	11	·89	2	·75	10

15. Svati. 16. Visak. 17. Anur. 18. Jyesh. 19. Mula. 20. P. Ash. 21. U. Ash. 22. Sravn. 23. Dani. 24 Satab. 25. P. Bhad. 26. U. Bhad. 27. Rev.

A. D. 1912. **Mesha Sankranti** (Commencement of Indian Sidereal Year).

Solar Eclipse. ● (Surya Sid.) April 12·72. **Saka 1834.** **Kaliyuga 5013.**

Lunar Eclipse. ○ (Arya Sid.) April 12·61. (S. Cycle) Paridhavi.

Jan.

SOLAR reckoning: Cyclic Sidereal Year, Month and Day	Week-Day English Month and Day		LUNAR reckoning: Tithi Ending Moment	Nakshatra Ending Moment	Muhammadan Year, Month and Day
Virodhakrit Dhanus—Margali. 17	Mo	1	*Suk.* Pausha 12 ·81	3 ·71	H. 1330 *Muharram.* 11
18	Tu	2	13 ·73	4 ·65	12
19	We	3	14 ·63	5 ·58	13
20	Th	4	P ·55	6 ·51	14
21	Fr	5	1 ·44	7 ·45	15
22	Sa	6	2 ·35	8 ·38	16
23	Su	7	3 ·26	9 ·32	17
24	Mo	8	4 ·17	10 ·27	18
25	Tu	9	5 ·11	11 ·23	19
26	We	10	6 ·05	12 ·20	20
27	Th	11	*Bahula* 7 ·02	13 ·20	21
28	Fr	12	8 ·00	14 ·21	22
—29	Sa	13	9 ·01	15 ·24	23
1	Su	14	10 ·03	16 ·29	24
2	Mo	15	11 ·08	17 ·36	25
3	Tu	16	12 ·14	18 ·46	26
4	We	17	13 ·23	19 ·56	27
5	Th	18	14 ·32	20 ·67	28
6	Fr	19	—A ·40	21 ·77	29
7	Sa	20	1 ·50	22 ·87	—30
8	Su	21	2 ·56	23 ·97	1
9	Mo	22	3 ·61	... ...	2
10	Tu	23	4 ·65	24 ·04	3
11	We	24	5 ·66	25 ·08	4
12	Th	25	6 ·66	26 ·11	5
Virodhakrit Makara—Tai. 13	Fr	26	7 ·63	27 ·12	6
14	Sa	27	*Sukla* 8 ·60	1 ·12	7
15	Su	28	9 ·53	2 ·09	8
16	Mo	29	10 ·45	3 ·04 4 ·99	9
17	Tu	30	11 ·36	5 ·92	10
18	We	31	12 ·27	6 ·86	11

Feb.

Cyclic Sidereal Year, Month and Day	Week-Day English Month and Day		Tithi Ending Moment	Nakshatra Ending Moment	Muhammadan Year, Month and Day
19	Th	1	13 ·17	7 ·79	H. 1330 *Safar.* 12
20	Fr	2	Magha 14 ·07 P ·98	8 ·72	13
21	Sa	3	1 ·89	9 ·66	14
22	Su	4	2 ·81	10 ·60	15
23	Mo	5	3 ·74	11 ·56	16
24	Tu	6	4 ·69	12 ·54	17
25	We	7	5 ·66	13 ·52	18
26	Th	8	6 ·64	14 ·53	19
27	Fr	9	7 ·65	15 ·55	20
28	Sa	10	*Bahula* 8 ·67	16 ·60	21
—29	Su	11	9 ·72	17 ·68	22
1	Mo	12	10 ·78	18 ·76	23
2	Tu	13	11 ·87	19 ·86	24
3	We	14	12 ·95	20 ·97	25
4	Th	15	... ...	... ...	26
5	Fr	16	13 ·03	21 ·07	27
6	Sa	17	14 ·12	22 ·18	28
Virodhakrit Kumbha—Masi. 7	Su	18	—A ·20	23 ·27	—29
8	Mo	19	1 ·25	24 ·34	H. 1330 *Rabi-ul-awwal.* 1
9	Tu	20	2 ·28	25 ·40	2
10	We	21	3 ·30	26 ·43	3
11	Th	22	4 ·28	27 ·45	4
12	Fr	23	*Sukla* 5 ·25	1 ·44	5
13	Sa	24	6 ·21	2 ·42	6
14	Su	25	7 ·14	3 ·38	7
15	Mo	26	8 ·07 9 ·98	4 ·32	8
16	Tu	27	Phal. 10 ·89	5 ·26	9
17	We	28	11 ·79	6 ·20	10
18	Th	29	12 ·70	7 ·13	11

March

Cyclic Sidereal Year, Month and Day	Week-Day English Month and Day		Tithi Ending Moment	Nakshatra Ending Moment	Muhammadan Year, Month and Day
19	Fr	1	*Suk.* 13 ·60	8 ·06 9 ·99	12
20	Sa	2	14 ·50	10 ·94	13
Virodhakrit Kumbha—Masi. 21	Su	3	Phalguna P ·42	11 ·90	14
22	Mo	4	1 ·35	12 ·86	H. 1330 *Rabi-ul-awwal.* 15
23	Tu	5	2 ·30	13 ·85	16
24	We	6	3 ·26	14 ·85	17
25	Th	7	4 ·26	15 ·87	18
26	Fr	8	5 ·26	16 ·92	19
27	Sa	9	6 ·28	17 ·98	20
28	Su	10	7 ·33	... ...	21
29	Mo	11	*Bahula* 8 ·39	18 ·06	22
30	Tu	12	9 ·48	19 ·16	23
—31	We	13	10 ·56	20 ·26	24
1	Th	14	11 ·65	21 ·38	25
2	Fr	15	12 ·73	22 ·48	26
3	Sa	16	13 ·80	23 ·58	27
4	Su	17	14 ·85	24 ·65	28
5	Mo	18	—A ·88	25 ·71	29
6	Tu	19	1 ·90	26 ·75	—30
7	We	20	2 ·88	27 ·77	1
8	Th	21	3 ·85	1 ·77	2
9	Fr	22	4 ·80	2 ·75	3
10	Sa	23	5 ·74	3 ·71	4
11	Su	24	6 ·66	4 ·66	5
Virodhakrit Mina—Panguni. 12	Mo	25	*Sukla* 7 ·57	5 ·61	6
13	Tu	26	8 ·48	6 ·54	7
14	We	27	9 ·36	7 ·47	8
15	Th	28	10 ·27	8 ·40	9
16	Fr	29	11 ·18	9 ·33	10
17	Sa	30	12 ·09	10 ·28	11
18	Su	31	13 ·00 14 ·92	11 ·23	12

April

Cyclic Sidereal Year, Month and Day	Week-Day English Month and Day		Tithi Ending Moment	Nakshatra Ending Moment	Muhammadan Year, Month and Day
19	Mo ○	1	Chaitra P ·88	12 ·19	H. 1330 *Rabi-ul-akhir.* 13
20	Tu	2	1 ·84	13 ·17	14
21	We	3	2 ·83	14 ·17	15
22	Th	4	3 ·83	15 ·19	16
23	Fr	5	4 ·86	16 ·23	17
24	Sa	6	5 ·90	17 ·29	18
25	Su	7	6 ·97	18 ·37	19
26	Mo	8	... ...	19 ·46	20
27	Tu	9	*Bahula* 7 ·04	20 ·57	21
28	We	10	8 ·12	21 ·68	22
29	Th	11	9 ·21	22 ·78	23
—30	Fr	12	10 ·29	23 ·88	24
1	Sa	13	11 ·36	24 ·96	25
2	Su	14	12 ·41	... ...	26
3	Mo	15	13 ·45	25 ·02	27
4	Tu	16	14 ·45	26 ·07	28
5	We ●	17	—A ·43	27 ·09	—29
6	Th	18	1 ·40	1 ·09	1
Paridhavi Mesha—Chittirai. 7	Fr	19	2 ·35	2 ·07	2
8	Sa	20	3 ·29	3 ·04	H. 1330 *Jumadal-awwal.* 3
9	Su	21	*Sukla* 4 ·21	4 ·00 5 ·94	4
10	Mo	22	5 ·12	6 ·88	5
11	Tu	23	6 ·02 7 ·91	7 ·81	6
12	We	24	8 ·82	8 ·74	7
13	Th	25	Vaisakha 9 ·71	9 ·68	8
14	Fr	26	10 ·63	10 ·62	9
15	Sa	27	11 ·54	11 ·56	10
16	Su	28	12 ·47	12 ·52	11
17	Mo	29	13 ·41	13 ·50	12
18	Tu	30	14 ·38	14 ·50	13

May

Cyclic Sidereal Year, Month and Day	Week-Day English Month and Day		Tithi Ending Moment	Nakshatra Ending Moment	Muhammadan Year, Month and Day
19	We	1	Vaisakha P ·36	15 ·51	14
20	Th	2	1 ·36	16 ·54	15
21	Fr	3	2 ·39	17 ·60	16
Paridhavi Mesha—Chittirai. 22	Sa	4	3 ·48	18 ·67	H. 1330 *Jumadal-awwal.* 17
23	Su	5	4 ·49	19 ·76	18
24	Mo	6	5 ·56	20 ·87	19
25	Tu	7	6 ·65	21 ·98	20
26	We	8	*Bahula* 7 ·73	... ...	21
27	Th	9	8 ·81	22 ·08	22
28	Fr	10	9 ·88	23 ·18	23
29	Sa	11	10 ·93	24 ·26	24
30	Su	12	11 ·96	25 ·34	25
—31	Mo	13	12 ·97	26 ·39	26
1	Tu	14	13 ·96	27 ·41	27
2	We	15	14 ·92	1 ·42	28
3	Th	16	—A ·87	2 ·40	29
4	Fr	17	1 ·80	3 ·38	—30
5	Sa	18	2 ·72	4 ·34	1
6	Su	19	3 ·64	5 ·28	2
7	Mo	20	4 ·53	6 ·22	3
8	Tu	21	5 ·43	7 ·15	4
9	We	22	6 ·38	8 ·09	5
10	Th	23	*Sukla* 7 ·28	9 ·02 10 ·95	6
Paridhavi Vrishabha—Vaikasi. 11	Fr	24	8 ·13	11 ·90	7
12	Sa	25	9 ·04 10 ·98	12 ·85	8
13	Su	26	Jyeshtha 11 ·92	13 ·83	*Jumadal-akhir.* 9
14	Mo	27	12 ·88	14 ·82	10
15	Tu	28	13 ·86	15 ·88	11
16	We	29	14 ·87	16 ·86	12
17	Th	30	P ·88	17 ·91	13
18	Fr	31	1 ·92	18 ·97	14

June

Cyclic Sidereal Year, Month and Day	Week-Day English Month and Day		Tithi Ending Moment	Nakshatra Ending Moment	Muhammadan Year, Month and Day
19	Sa	1	2 ·99	... ...	H. 1330 15
20	Su	2	... ...	19 ·07	16
21	Mo	3	3 ·06	20 ·17	17
22	Tu	4	4 ·14	21 ·27	18
23	We	5	5 ·23	22 ·38	19
24	Th	6	*Bahula* 6 ·31	23 ·48	20
25	Fr	7	7 ·38	24 ·58	21
26	Sa	8	8 ·42	25 ·65	22
27	Su	9	9 ·45	26 ·70	23
28	Mo	10	10 ·46	27 ·73	24
29	Tu	11	11 ·44	1 ·74	25
30	We	12	12 ·41	2 ·74	26
—31	Th	13	13 ·37	3 ·71	27
1	Fr	14	14 ·29	4 ·67	28
2	Sa	15	—A ·22	5 ·62	—29
3	Su	16	1 ·13	6 ·55	1
4	Mo	17	2 ·03 3 ·93	7 ·49	2
5	Tu	18	*Sukla* 4 ·82	8 ·42	3
6	We	19	5 ·72	9 ·35	4
Paridhavi Mithuna—Ani. 7	Th	20	6 ·63	10 ·29	H. 1330 *Rajab.* 5
8	Fr	21	7 ·54	11 ·23	6
9	Sa	22	Adhika Ashadha 8 ·46	12 ·18	7
10	Su	23	9 ·40	13 ·16	8
11	Mo	24	10 ·36	14 ·15	9
12	Tu	25	11 ·34	15 ·15	10
13	We	26	12 ·35	16 ·17	11
14	Th	27	13 ·36	17 ·21	12
15	Fr	28	14 ·41	18 ·29	13
16	Sa	29	P ·46	19 ·37	14
17	Su	30	1 ·54	20 ·47	15

Naksh :—1. Asvn. 2. Bhar. 3. Krit. 4. Rohi. 5. Mrig. 6. Ardh. 7. Punar. 8. Push. 9. Aslesh. 10. Magh. 11. P. Phal. 12. U. Phal. 13. Hasta. 14. Chit.

A. D. 1912.
A.—Amavasya.
P.—Paurnami.

Kollam 1088, Commences { N. Malabar—Sept. S. Malabar—Aug.

Hijra 1331, Commences, Dec. 11.

Vikrama 1969.
Bengal San 1318.
(N. Cycle) Raktaksha.

SOLAR reckoning: Cyclic Sidereal Year, Month and Day	Week-Day English Month and Day		LUNAR reckoning: Tithi Ending Moment	Nakshatra Ending Moment	Muhammadan Year, Month and Day
	July				
Paridhavi Mithuna—Ani. 18	Mo	1	Adhika Ashadha. Bahula 2 ·61	21 ·57	H. 1330 Rajab. 16
19	Tu	2	3 ·70	22 ·68	17
20	We	3	4 ·78	23 ·79	18
21	Th	4	5 ·84	24 ·88	19
22	Fr	5	6 ·90	25 ·96	20
23	Sa	6	7 ·93	... ...	21
24	Su	7	8 ·94	26 ·01	22
25	Mo	8	9 ·92	27 ·05	23
26	Tu	9	10 ·89	1 ·07	24
27	We	10	11. ·84	2 ·07	25
28	Th	11	12 ·77	3 ·04	26
29	Fr	12	13 ·70	4 ·00 5 ·95	27
30	Sa	13	14 ·61	6 ·90	28
31	Su	14	—A ·51	7 ·88	29
—32	Mo	15	1 ·40	8 ·76	—30
1	Tu	16	2 ·30	9 ·69	1
2	We	17	3 ·19	10 ·62	2
3	Th	18	4 ·10	11 ·57	3
4	Fr	19	5 ·02 6 ·94	12 ·53	4
5	Sa	20	Sukla 7 ·88	13 ·49	5
6	Su	21	8 ·84	14 ·47	6
7	Mo	22	9 ·83	15 ·47	7
8	Tu	23	10 ·82	16 ·49	8
9	We	24	11 ·84	17 ·54	9
Paridhavi Karkata—Adi. 10	Th	25	12 ·88	18 ·59	H. 1330 Shaban. 10
11	Fr	26	13 ·93	19 ·67	11
12	Sa	27	... ...	20 ·77	12
13	Su	28	Ashadha 14 ·01	21 ·87	13
14	Mo	29	P ·09	22 ·99	14
15	Tu	30	1 ·18	... ...	15
16	We	31	2 ·24	23 ·09	16
	Aug.				
17	Th	1	Nija 3 ·31	24 ·18	17
18	Fr	2	4 ·37	25 ·26	18
19	Sa	3	5 ·41	26 ·32	19
20	Su	4	6 ·42	27 ·36	20
21	Mo	5	Bahula 7 ·40	1 ·39	21
22	Tu	6	8 ·38	2 ·39	22
23	We	7	9 ·33	3 ·37	23
24	Th	8	10 ·26	4 ·34	24
25	Fr	9	11 ·19	5 ·29	25
26	Sa	10	12 ·10	6 ·24	26
27	Su	11	13 ·00 14 ·90	7 ·17	27
28	Mo	12	—A ·80	8 ·10	28
29	Tu	13	1 ·69	9 ·03 10 ·96	—29
30	We	14	2 ·61	11 ·91	1
—31	Th	15	3 ·52	12 ·86	2
1	Fr	16	4 ·44	13 ·82	3
2	Sa	17	5 ·38	14 ·79	4
3	Su	18	6 ·33	15 ·79	5
4	Mo	19	Sukla 7 ·32	16 ·81	6
Paridhavi Simha—Avani. 5	Tu	20	8 ·32	17 ·85	H. 1330 Ramzan. 7
6	We	21	9 ·34	18 ·90	8
7	Th	22	10 ·38	19 ·98	9
8	Fr	23	11 ·43	... ...	10
9	Sa	24	Sravana 12 ·51	20 ·07	11
10	Su	25	13 ·58	21 ·18	12
11	Mo	26	14 ·67	22 ·28	13
12	Tu	27	P ·75	23 ·39	14
13	We	28	1 ·83	24 ·49	15
14	Th	29	2 ·87	25 ·57	16
15	Fr	30	Bah. 3 ·91	26 ·63	17
16	Sa	31	4 ·93	27 ·69	18

SOLAR reckoning: Cyclic Sidereal Year, Month and Day	Week-Day English Month and Day		LUNAR reckoning: Tithi Ending Moment	Nakshatra Ending Moment	Muhammadan Year, Month and Day
	Sep.				
Paridhavi Simha—Avani. 17	Su	1	Sravana 5 ·91	1 ·71	H. 1330 Ramzan. 19
18	Mo	2	6 ·89	2 ·72	20
19	Tu	3	7 ·85	3 ·70	21
20	We	4	8 ·79	4 ·67	22
21	Th	5	9 ·71	5 ·63	23
22	Fr	6	10 ·62	6 ·57	24
23	Sa	7	Bahula 11 ·51	7 ·51	25
24	Su	8	12 ·41	8 ·44	26
25	Mo	9	13 ·31	9 ·37	27
26	Tu	10	14 ·21	10 ·31	28
27	We	11	—A ·13	11 ·25	29
28	Th	12	1 ·04 2 ·97	12 ·19	—30
29	Fr	13	3 ·91	13 ·15	1
30	Sa	14	4 ·86	14 ·12	2
—31	Su	15	5 ·85	15 ·12	3
1	Mo	16	6 ·85	16 ·13	4
2	Tu	17	Sukla 7 ·86	17 ·16	5
3	We	18	8 ·90	18 ·21	6
4	Th	19	9 ·95	19 ·28	7
5	Fr	20	... ...	20 ·37	8
6	Sa	21	10 ·03	21 ·48	9
7	Su	22	11 ·12	22 ·58	10
Paridhavi Kanya—Purattasi. 8	Mo	23	Bhadrapada 12 ·20	23 ·69	H. 1330 Shawwal. 11
9	Tu	24	13 ·27	24 ·79	12
10	We	25	14 ·36	25 ·87	13
11	Th ○	26	P ·41	26 ·95	14
12	Fr	27	1 ·45	... ...	15
13	Sa	28	2 ·47	27 ·00	16
14	Su	29	3 ·46	1 ·03	17
15	Mo	30	4 ·43	2 ·04	18
	Oct.				
16	Tu	1	5 ·40	3 ·03	19
17	We	2	Bahula 6 ·33	4 ·01 5 ·97	20
18	Th	3	7 ·25	6 ·91	21
19	Fr	4	8 ·16	7 ·85	22
20	Sa	5	9 ·06 10 ·97	8 ·78	23
21	Su	6	11 ·87	9 ·72	24
22	Mo	7	12 ·76	10 ·65	25
23	Tu	8	13* ·68	11 ·58	26
24	We	9	14 ·60	12 ·53	27
25	Th	10	—A ·53	13 ·48	28
26	Fr	11	1 ·47	14 ·46	—29
27	Sa	12	2 ·43	15 ·44	1
28	Su	13	3 ·41	16 ·45	2
29	Mo	14	4 ·42	17 ·47	3
30	Tu	15	5 ·43	18 ·52	4
—31	We	16	6 ·47	19 ·58	5
1	Th	17	Sukla 7 ·53	20 ·68	6
2	Fr	18	8 ·60	21 ·77	7
3	Sa	19	9 ·69	22 ·88	8
4	Su	20	10 ·77	23 ·99	9
5	Mo	21	11 ·87	... ...	H. 1330 Zi-l-ka'da. 10
Paridhavi Tula—Aippasi. 6	Tu	22	12 ·94	24 ·09	11
7	We	23	13 ·99	25 ·19	12
8	Th	24	Asvina	26 ·26	13
9	Fr	25	14 ·03	27 ·31	14
10	Sa	26	P ·05	1 ·35	15
11	Su	27	1 ·04	2 ·36	16
12	Mo	28	2 ·01 3 ·98	3 ·36	17
13	Tu	29	Bahula 4 ·92	4 ·34	18
14	We	30	5 ·84	5 ·30	19
15	Th	31	6 ·75	6 ·25	20

SOLAR reckoning: Cyclic Sidereal Year, Month and Day	Week-Day English Month and Day		LUNAR reckoning: Tithi Ending Moment	Nakshatra Ending Moment	Muhammadan Year, Month and Day
	Nov.				
16	Fr	1	Asvn. 7 ·65	7 ·19	H. 1330 Zi-l-ka'da. 21
17	Sa	2	8 ·56	8 ·13	22
18	Su	3	9 ·46	9 ·06 10 ·99	23
Paridhavi Tula—Aippasi. 19	Mo	4	Bahula 10 ·37	11 ·92	24
20	Tu	5	11 ·27	12 ·86	25
21	We	6	12 ·20	13 ·81	26
22	Th	7	13 ·12	14 ·79	27
23	Fr	8	14 ·05	15 ·77	28
24	Sa	9	—A ·03	16 ·77	29
25	Su	10	1 ·01	17 ·79	—30
26	Mo	11	2 ·02	18 ·83	1
27	Tu	12	3 ·03	19 ·90	2
28	We	13	4 ·08	20 ·93	3
—29	Th	14	5 ·15	... ...	4
1	Fr	15	6 ·22	21 ·07	5
2	Sa	16	Sukla 7 ·31	22 ·18	6
3	Su	17	8 ·39	23 ·28	7
4	Mo	18	9 ·49	24 ·40	8
5	Tu	19	10 ·55	25 ·49	9
6	We	20	11 ·61	26 ·57	10
7	Th	21	12 ·65	27 ·63	11
8	Fr	22	Karttika 13 ·68	1 ·66	12
9	Sa	23	14 ·66	2 ·69	H. 1330 Zi-l-hijja. 13
Paridhavi Vrischika—Kartigai. 10	Su	24	P ·63	3 ·69	14
11	Mo	25	1 ·59	4 ·67	15
12	Tu	26	2 ·53	5 ·63	16
13	We	27	3 ·47	6 ·58	17
14	Th	28	4 ·37	7 ·53	18
15	Fr	29	5 ·28	8 ·47	19
16	Sa	30	6 ·19	9 ·39	20
	Dec.				
17	Su	1	Bahula 7 ·08 8 ·99	10 ·32	21
18	Mo	2	9 ·89	11 ·26	22
19	Tu	3	10 ·81	12 ·20	23
20	We	4	11 ·74	13 ·15	24
21	Th	5	12 ·69	14 ·12	25
22	Fr	6	13 ·66	15 ·09	26
23	Sa	7	14 ·64	16 ·09	27
24	Su	8	—A ·65	17 ·10	28
25	Mo	9	1 ·67	18 ·15	29
26	Tu	10	2 ·73	19 ·21	—30
27	We	11	3 ·79	20 ·28	1
28	Th	12	4 ·87	21 ·37	2
29	Fr	13	5 ·96	22 ·48	3
—30	Sa	14	... ...	23 ·59	4
1	Su	15	Sukla 6 ·05	24 ·70	5
2	Mo	16	7 ·13	25 ·79	6
3	Tu	17	8 ·20	26 ·88	7
4	We	18	9 ·26	27 ·94	8
5	Th	19	10 ·29	1 ·99	9
6	Fr	20	11 ·31	... ...	H. 1331 Muharram. 10
Paridhavi Dhanus—Margali. 7	Sa	21	Margasira 12 ·30	2 ·01	11
8	Su	22	13 ·28	3 ·01	12
9	Mo	23	14 ·23	4 ·00 5 ·96	13
10	Tu	24	P ·17	6 ·92	14
11	We	25	1 ·10	7 ·87	15
12	Th	26	2 ·00 3 ·91	8 ·80	16
13	Fr	27	Bahula 4 ·82	9 ·73	17
14	Sa	28	5 ·72	10 ·66	18
15	Su	29	6 ·62	11 ·59	19
16	Mo	30	7 ·53	12 ·54	20
17	Tu	31	8 ·46	13 ·49	21

15. Svati. 16. Visak. 17. Anur. 18. Jyesh. 19. Mula. 20. P. Ash. 21. U. Ash. 22. Sravn. 23. Dani. 24. Satab. 25. P. Bhad. 26. U. Bhad. 27. Rev.

A. D. 1913.
Solar Eclipse. ●
Lunar Eclipse. ○

Mesha Sankranti (Commencement of Indian Sidereal Year).
(Surya Sid.) April 12·98. Saka 1835. Kaliyuga 5014.
(Arya Sid.) April 12·87. (S. Cycle) Pramadicha.

Columns: SOLAR reckoning — Cyclic Sidereal Year, Month and Day; Week-Day English Month and Day. LUNAR reckoning — Tithi Ending Moment; Nakshatra Ending Moment; Muhammadan Year, Month and Day.

Jan. (Solar: Paridhavi *Dhanus—Margali* to 29, then Paridhavi *Makara—Tai*. Lunar: *Bah.* Marg., then *Sukla* Pausha, then *Bahula*. Muhammadan: H. 1331 *Muharram*, then H. 1331 *Safar*.)

Cyclic Sidereal Year, Month and Day	Week-Day	English Day	Tithi Ending Moment	Nakshatra Ending Moment	Muhammadan Year, Month and Day
18	We	1	9 ·88	14 ·45	22
19	Th	2	10 ·33	15 ·42	23
20	Fr	3	11 ·30	16 ·41	24
21	Sa	4	12 ·29	17 ·43	25
22	Su	5	13 ·29	18 ·46	26
23	Mo	6	14 ·33	19 ·51	27
24	Tu	7	A ·37	20 ·59	28
25	We	8	1 ·43	21 ·67	29
26	Th	9	2 ·52	22 ·78	30
27	Fr	10	3 ·60	23 ·89	1
28	Sa	11	4 ·69	... ...	2
29	Su	12	5 ·78	24 ·00	3
1	Mo	13	6 ·85	25 ·09	4
2	Tu	14	7 ·90	26 ·18	5
3	We	15	8 ·93	27 ·25	6
4	Th	16	9 ·96	1 ·30	7
5	Fr	17	10 ·94	2 ·38	8
6	Sa	18	11 ·92	3 ·34	9
7	Su	19	12 ·88	4 ·33	10
8	Mo	20	13 ·82	5 ·30	11
9	Tu	21	14 ·73	6 ·26	12
10	We	22	P ·63	7 ·21	13
11	Th	23	1 ·55	8 ·14	14
12	Fr	24	2 ·45	9 ·07	15
13	Sa	25	3 ·35	10 ·00; 11 ·94	16
14	Su	26	4 ·26	12 ·88	17
15	Mo	27	5 ·17	13 ·82	18
16	Tu	28	6 ·09	14 ·78	19
17	We	29	7 ·03; 8 ·98	15 ·75	20
18	Th	30	9 ·94	16 ·74	21
19	Fr	31	10 ·93	17 ·75	22

Feb. (Solar: Paridhavi *Kumbha—Masi* from 1. Lunar: *Sukla* Magha, then *Bahula*. Muhammadan: H. 1331 *Rabi-ul-awwal*.)

Cyclic Sidereal Year, Month and Day	Week-Day	English Day	Tithi Ending Moment	Nakshatra Ending Moment	Muhammadan Year, Month and Day
20	Sa	1	11 ·98	18 ·78	23
21	Su	2	12 ·98	19 ·82	24
22	Mo	3	... ...	20 ·89	25
23	Tu	4	13 ·02	21 ·98	26
24	We	5	14 ·09	... ...	27
25	Th	6	A ·16	22 ·08	28
26	Fr	7	1 ·25	23 ·19	29
27	Sa	8	2 ·34	24 ·29	1
28	Su	9	3 ·42	25 ·39	2
29	Mo	10	4 ·49	26 ·48	3
30	Tu	11	5 ·54	27 ·56	4
1	We	12	6 ·58	1 ·62	5
2	Th	13	7 ·59	2 ·65	6
3	Fr	14	8 ·58	3 ·66	7
4	Sa	15	9 ·55	4 ·65	8
5	Su	16	10 ·50	5 ·64	9
6	Mo	17	11 ·44	6 ·59	10
7	Tu	18	12 ·35	7 ·54	11
8	We	19	13 ·27	8 ·48	12
9	Th	20	14 ·17	9 ·41	13
10	Fr	21	P ·08; 1 ·98	10 ·35	14
11	Sa	22	2 ·88	11 ·28	15
12	Su	23	3 ·79	12 ·21	16
13	Mo	24	4 ·70	13 ·16	17
14	Tu	25	5 ·64	14 ·11	18
15	We	26	6 ·59	15 ·08	19
16	Th	27	7 ·56	16 ·07	20
17	Fr	28	8 ·55	17 ·07	21

March (Solar: Paridhavi *Kumbha—Masi* to 30, then Paridhavi *Mina—Panguni*. Lunar: *Bah.* Mag., then *Sukla* Phalguna, then *Bahula*. Muhammadan: *Rabi-ul-awwal*, then H. 1331 *Rabi-ul-akhir*.)

Cyclic Sidereal Year, Month and Day	Week-Day	English Day	Tithi Ending Moment	Nakshatra Ending Moment	Muhammadan Year, Month and Day
18	Sa	1	9 ·55	18 ·09	22
19	Su	2	10 ·59	19 ·13	23
20	Mo	3	11 ·63	20 ·19	24
21	Tu	4	12 ·70	21 ·29	25
22	We	5	13 ·78	22 ·38	26
23	Th	6	14 ·87	23 ·49	27
24	Fr	7	A ·96	24 ·59	28
25	Sa	8	... ...	25 ·69	29
26	Su	9	1 ·05	26 ·80	30
27	Mo	10	2 ·10	27 ·87	1
28	Tu	11	3 ·15	1 ·93	2
29	We	12	4 ·19	2 ·97	3
30	Th	13	5 ·19	3 ·98	4
1	Fr	14	6 ·18	4 ·99	5
2	Sa	15	7 ·14	5 ·97	6
3	Su	16	8 ·10	6 ·98	7
4	Mo	17	9 ·03; 10 ·94	7 ·88	8
5	Tu	18	11 ·86	8 ·82	9
6	We	19	12 ·77	9 ·76	10
7	Th	20	13 ·66	10 ·69	11
8	Fr	21	14 ·56	11 ·62	12
9	Sa ○	22	P ·48	12 ·55	13
10	Su	23	1 ·38	13 ·49	14
11	Mo	24	2 ·29	14 ·45	15
12	Tu	25	3 ·23	15 ·41	16
13	We	26	4 ·18	16 ·39	17
14	Th	27	5 ·15	17 ·39	18
15	Fr	28	6 ·13	18 ·40	19
16	Sa	29	7 ·14	19 ·44	20
17	Su	30	8 ·17	20 ·51	21
18	Mo	31	9 ·22	21 ·59	22

April (Solar: Paridhavi *Mina—Panguni* to 30, then Pramadicha *Mesha—Chittirai*. Lunar: *Sukla* Chaitra, then *Bahula*. Muhammadan: H. 1331 *Rabi-ul-akhir*, then H. 1331 *Jumadal-awwal*.)

Cyclic Sidereal Year, Month and Day	Week-Day	English Day	Tithi Ending Moment	Nakshatra Ending Moment	Muhammadan Year, Month and Day
19	Tu	1	10 ·29	22 ·68	23
20	We	2	11 ·36	23 ·78	24
21	Th	3	12 ·45	24 ·89	25
22	Fr	4	13 ·53	... ...	26
23	Sa	5	14 ·62	25 ·00	27
24	Su	6	A ·67	26 ·10	28
25	Mo	7	1 ·73	27 ·18	29
26	Tu	8	2 ·76	1 ·24	1
27	We	9	3 ·75	2 ·28	2
28	Th	10	4 ·74	3 ·31	3
29	Fr	11	5 ·70	4 ·31	4
30	Sa	12	6 ·66	5 ·29	5
1	Su	13	7 ·59	6 ·26	6
2	Mo	14	8 ·51	7 ·21	7
3	Tu	15	9 ·42	8 ·16	8
4	We	16	10 ·32	9 ·10	9
5	Th	17	11 ·21	10 ·08; 11 ·96	10
6	Fr	18	12 ·12	12 ·89	11
7	Sa	19	13 ·03; 14 ·93	13 ·83	12
8	Su	20	P ·84	14 ·78	13
9	Mo	21	1 ·77	15 ·74	14
10	Tu	22	2 ·73	16 ·72	15
11	We	23	3 ·69	17 ·71	16
12	Th	24	4 ·67	18 ·72	17
13	Fr	25	5 ·68	19 ·76	18
14	Sa	26	6 ·71	20 ·82	19
15	Su	27	7 ·76	21 ·89	20
16	Mo	28	8 ·82	22 ·98	21
17	Tu	29	9 ·89	... ...	22
18	We	30	10 ·98	23 ·08	23

May (Solar: Pramadicha *Mesha—Chittirai* to 31, then Pramadicha *Vrishabha—Vaikasi*. Lunar: *Bah.* Ch., then *Sukla* Vaisakha, then *Bahula*. Muhammadan: *Jl-awwal*, then H. 1331 *Jumadal-akhir*.)

Cyclic Sidereal Year, Month and Day	Week-Day	English Day	Tithi Ending Moment	Nakshatra Ending Moment	Muhammadan Year, Month and Day
19	Th	1	... ...	24 ·20	24
20	Fr	2	11 ·06	25 ·30	25
21	Sa	3	12 ·14	26 ·40	26
22	Su	4	13 ·20	27 ·48	27
23	Mo	5	14 ·26	1 ·55	28
24	Tu	6	A ·27	2 ·61	29
25	We	7	1 ·29	3 ·63	30
26	Th	8	2 ·27	4 ·64	1
27	Fr	9	3 ·25	5 ·62	2
28	Sa	10	4 ·19	6 ·59	3
29	Su	11	5 ·11	7 ·56	4
30	Mo	12	6 ·03; 7 ·94	8 ·50	5
31	Tu	13	8 ·85	9 ·44	6
1	We	14	9 ·74	10 ·37	7
2	Th	15	10 ·64	11 ·29	8
3	Fr	16	11 ·54	12 ·23	9
4	Sa	17	12 ·44	13 ·17	10
5	Su	18	13 ·36	14 ·12	11
6	Mo	19	14 ·29	15 ·07	12
7	Tu	20	P ·24	16 ·04	13
8	We	21	1 ·20	17 ·03	14
9	Th	22	2 ·19	18 ·05	15
10	Fr	23	3 ·19	19 ·08	16
11	Sa	24	4 ·20	20 ·13	17
12	Su	25	5 ·26	21 ·19	18
13	Mo	26	6 ·32	22 ·28	19
14	Tu	27	7 ·40	23 ·39	20
15	We	28	8 ·47	24 ·50	21
16	Th	29	9 ·57	25 ·60	22
17	Fr	30	10 ·64	26 ·70	23
18	Sa	31	11 ·70	27 ·79	24

June (Solar: Pramadicha *Vrishabha—Vaikasi* to 31, then Pramadicha *Mithuna—Ani*. Lunar: *Sukla* Jyeshtha, then *Bahula*. Muhammadan: H. 1331 *Jumadal-akhir*, then H. 1331 *Rajab*.)

Cyclic Sidereal Year, Month and Day	Week-Day	English Day	Tithi Ending Moment	Nakshatra Ending Moment	Muhammadan Year, Month and Day
19	Su	1	12 ·74	1 ·87	25
20	Mo	2	13 ·77	2 ·92	26
21	Tu	3	14 ·79	3 ·95	27
22	We	4	A ·76	4 ·96	28
23	Th	5	1 ·74	5 ·95	29
24	Fr	6	2 ·69	6 ·92	1
25	Sa	7	3 ·63	7 ·89	2
26	Su	8	4 ·53	8 ·84	3
27	Mo	9	5 ·44	9 ·77	4
28	Tu	10	6 ·35	10 ·70	5
29	We	11	7 ·24	11 ·68	6
30	Th	12	8 ·14	12 ·57	7
31	Fr	13	9 ·04; 10 ·94	13 ·51	8
1	Sa	14	11 ·85	14 ·45	9
2	Su	15	12 ·78	15 ·40	10
3	Mo	16	13 ·73	16 ·37	11
4	Tu	17	14 ·68	17 ·36	12
5	We	18	P ·67	18 ·37	13
6	Th	19	1 ·67	19 ·39	14
7	Fr	20	2 ·69	20 ·44	15
8	Sa	21	3 ·73	21 ·50	16
9	Su	22	4 ·80	22 ·59	17
10	Mo	23	5 ·86	23 ·69	18
11	Tu	24	6 ·94	24 ·79	19
12	We	25	... ...	25 ·90	20
13	Th	26	7 ·03	... ...	21
14	Fr	27	8 ·10	26 ·00	22
15	Sa	28	9 ·18	27 ·10	23
16	Su	29	10 ·22	1 ·18	24
17	Mo	30	11 ·26	2 ·23	25

Naksh:—1. Asvn. 2. Bhar. 3. Krit. 4. Rohi. 5. Mrig. 6. Ardh. 7. Punar. 8. Push. 9. Aslesh. 10. Magh. 11. P. Phal. 12. U. Phal. 13. Hasta. 14. Chit.

A. D. 1913.
A.—Amavasya.
P.—Paurnami.

Kollam 1089, Commences { N. Malabar—Sept. S. Malabar—Aug.

Hijra 1332, Commences, Nov. 30.

Vikrama 1970.
Bengal San 1319.
(N. Cycle) Krodhana.

SOLAR reckoning.		LUNAR reckoning.		
Cyclic Sidereal Year, Month and Day.	Week-Day English Month and Day.	Tithi Ending Moment.	Nakshatra Ending Moment.	Muhammadan Year, Month and Day.
	July			
Pramadicha Mithuna—Ani. 18	Tu 1	J. Bah. 12 ·27	3 ·27	*Rajab.* 26
19	We 2	13 ·24	4 ·28	27
20	Th 3	14 ·22	5 ·28	28
21	Fr 4	—A ·16	6 ·26	29
22	Sa 5	1 ·09	7 ·22	—30
23	Su 6	2 ·01 3 ·93	8 ·17	1
24	Mo 7	4 ·82	9 ·11	2
25	Tu 8	5 ·71	10 ·04 11 ·98	3
26	We 9	6 ·62	12 ·91	4
27	Th 10	*Sukla* 7 ·51	13 ·84	5
28	Fr 11	8 ·42	14 ·78	6
29	Sa 12	9 ·33	15 ·74	7
30	Su 13	10 ·27	16 ·71	8
31	Mo 14	11 ·20	17 ·69	9
—32	Tu 15	12 ·17	18 ·69	10
1	We 16	**Ashadha** 13 ·15	19 ·71	11
2	Th 17	14 ·14	20 ·75	12
3	Fr 18	P ·17	21 ·82	*H. 1331 Shaban.* 13
4	Sa 19	1 ·21	22 ·89	14
5	Su 20	2 ·27	23 ·99	15
6	Mo 21	3 ·33	... ...	16
7	Tu 22	4 ·48	24 ·09	17
8	We 23	5 ·51	25 ·20	18
9	Th 24	6 ·58	26 ·30	19
Pramadicha Karkata—Adi. 10	Fr 25	*Bahula* 7 ·65	27 ·40	20
11	Sa 26	8 ·70	1 ·48	21
12	Su 27	9 ·74	2 ·54	22
13	Mo 28	10 ·74	3 ·58	23
14	Tu 29	11 ·73	4 ·60	24
15	We 30	12 ·70	5 ·61	25
16	Th 31	13 ·64	6 ·59	26
	Aug.			
17	Fr 1	14 ·58	7 ·56	27
18	Sa 2	—A ·50	8 ·51	28
19	Su 3	1 ·42	9 ·45	—29
20	Mo 4	2 ·31	10 ·39	1
21	Tu 5	3 21	11 ·32	2
22	We 6	4 ·11	12 ·25	3
23	Th 7	5 ·01 6 ·91	13 ·18	4
24	Fr 8	*Sukla* 7 ·82	14 ·12	5
25	Sa 9	8 ·76	15 ·08	6
26	Su 10	9 ·69	16 ·04	7
27	Mo 11	10 ·66	17 ·01	8
28	Tu 12	11 ·63	18 ·01	9
29	We 13	12 ·64	19 ·02	10
30	Th 14	**Sravana** 13 ·65	20 ·06	11
—31	Fr 15	14 ·69	21 ·12	12
1	Sa 16	P ·76	22 ·20	13
2	Su 17	1 ·83.	23 ·29	14
3	Mo 18	2 ·92	24 ·39	15
4	Tu 19	... ...	25 ·49	16
5	We 20	3 ·00	26 ·61	17
6	Th 21	4 ·08	27 ·71	*H. 1331 Ramzan.* 18
7	Fr 22	5 .15	1 ·79	19
8	Sa 23	6 ·19	2 ·85	20
9	Su 24	*Bahula* 7 ·22	3 ·90	21
Pramadicha Simha—Avani. 10	Mo 25	8 ·24	4 ·93	22
11	Tu 26	9 ·23	5 ·94	23
12	We 27	10 ·20	6 ·92	24
13	Th 28	11 ·16	7 ·89	25
14	Fr 29	12 ·08	8 ·84	26
15	Sa 30	13 ·01 14 ·92	9 ·79	27
16	Su 31	—A ·82	10 ·73	28

SOLAR reckoning.		LUNAR reckoning.		
Cyclic Sidereal Year, Month and Day.	Week-Day English Month and Day.	Tithi Ending Moment.	Nakshatra Ending Moment.	Muhammadan Year, Month and Day.
	Sep.			
17	Mo 1	1 ·72	11 ·66	29
18	Tu 2	2 ·62	12 ·59	—30
19	We 3	3 ·52	13 ·52	1
Pramadicha Simha—Avani. 20	Th 4	4 ·43	14 ·47	2
21	Fr 5	5 ·35	15 ·41	3
22	Sa 6	6 ·27	16 ·37	4
23	Su 7	*Sukla* 7 ·21	17 ·34	5
24	Mo 8	8 ·17	18 ·33	6
25	Tu 9	9 ·15	19 ·34	7
26	We 10	10 ·16	20 ·38	8
27	Th 11	11 ·17	21 ·43	9
28	Fr 12	**Bhadrapada** 12 ·22	22 ·50	10
29	Sa 13	13 ·27	23 ·59	11
30	Su 14	14 ·36	24 ·69	12
—31	Mo ○ 15	P ·46	25 ·80	13
1	Tu 16	1 ·58	26 ·91	14
2	We 17	2 ·60	... ...	15
3	Th 18	3 ·67	27 ·01	*H. 1831 Shawwal.* 16
4	Fr 19	4 ·72	1 ·09	17
5	Sa 20	5 ·75	2 ·16	18
6	Su 21	6 ·78	3 ·22	19
7	Mo 22	*Bahula* 7 ·76	4 ·25	20
8	Tu 23	8 ·73	5 ·26	21
9	We 24	9 ·69	6 ·25	22
Pramadicha Kanya—Purattasi. 10	Th 25	10 ·62	7 ·22	23
11	Fr 26	11 ·55	8 ·19	24
12	Sa 27	12 ·46	9 ·18	25
13	Su 28	13 ·37	10 ·07	26
14	Mo 29	14 ·27	11 ·00 12 ·93	27
15	Tu 30	—A ·17	13 ·86	28
	Oct.			
16	We 1	1 ·06 2 ·97	14 ·80	—29
17	Th 2	3 ·89	15 ·74	1
18	Fr 3	4 ·82	16 ·70	2
19	Sa 4	5 ·76	17 ·67	3
20	Su 5	6 ·72	18 ·66	4
21	Mo 6	*Sukla* 7 ·71	19 ·67	5
22	Tu 7	8 ·70	20 ·69	6
23	We 8	9 ·73	21 ·74	7
24	Th 9	10 ·78	22 ·80	8
25	Fr 10	11 ·83	28 ·89	9
26	Sa 11	12 ·92	24 ·99	10
27	Su 12	... ...	... ...	11
28	Mo 13	13 ·02	25 ·10	12
29	Tu 14	**Asvina** 14 ·09	26 ·21	13
30	We 15	P ·16	27 ·31	14
—31	Th 16	1 ·24	1 ·40	15
1	Fr 17	2 ·29	2 ·48	16
2	Sa 18	3 ·32	3 ·53	17
3	Su 19	4 ·35	4 ·57	*H. 1331 Zi-l-ka'da.* 18
4	Mo 20	5 ·33	5 ·58	19
5	Tu 21	6 ·32	6 ·57	20
6	We 22	*Bahula* 7 ·27	7 ·56	21
7	Th 23	8 ·20	8 ·52	22
8	Fr 24	9 ·13	9 ·47	23
9	Sa 25	10 ·04 11 ·94	10 ·40	24
Pramadicha Tula—Aippasi. 10	Su 26	12 ·84	11 ·34	25
11	Mo 27	13 ·75	12 ·28	26
12	Tu 28	14 ·65	13 ·20	27
13	We 29	—A ·57	14 ·14	28
14	Th 30	*Suk.* 1 ·48	15 ·08	29
15	Fr 31	2 ·41	16 ·03	—30

SOLAR reckoning.		LUNAR reckoning.		
Cyclic Sidereal Year, Month and Day.	Week-Day English Month and Day.	Tithi Ending Moment.	Nakshatra Ending Moment.	Muhammadan Year, Month and Day.
	Nov.			
16	Sa 1	3 ·35	17 ·01 18 ·99	1
17	Su 2	4 ·31	19 ·99	2
18	Mo 3	5 ·30	... ...	3
Pramadicha Tula—Aippasi. 19	Tu 4	6 ·31	20 ·01	4
20	We 5	*Sukla* 7 ·33	21 ·05	5
21	Th 6	8 37	22 ·11	6
22	Fr 7	9 ·43	23 ·20	7
23	Sa 8	10 ·52	24 ·29	8
24	Su 9	11 ·61	25 ·40	9
25	Mo 10	**Kartika** 12 ·70	26 ·50	10
26	Tu 11	13 ·78	27 ·61	11
27	We 12	14 ·85	1 ·71	12
28	Th 13	P ·89	2 ·79	13
29	Fr 14	1 ·94	3 ·85	14
—30	Sa 15	2 ·96	4 ·88	15
1	Su 16	3 ·94	5 ·90	16
2	Mo 17	4 ·92	6 ·91	*H. 1331 Zi-l-hijja.* 17
3	Tu 18	5 ·87	7 ·89	18
4	We 19	6 ·82	8 ·85	19
5	Th 20	*Bahula* 7 ·74	9 ·80	20
6	Fr 21	8 ·66	10 ·74	21
7	Sa 22	9 ·56	11 ·68	22
8	Su 23	10 ·46	12 ·61	23
Pramadicha Vrischika—Kartigai. 9	Mo 24	11 ·36	13 ·54	24
10	Tu 25	12 ·27	14 ·48	25
11	We 26	13 ·19	15 ·41	26
12	Th 27	14 ·10	16 ·36	27
13	Fr 28	A ·03 1 ·97	17 ·34	28
14	Sa 29	2 ·94	18 ·31	—29
15	Su 30	3 ·93	19 ·31	1
	Dec.			
16	Mo 1	4 ·93	20 ·32	2
17	Tu 2	5 ·96	21 ·36	3
18	We 3	... ...	22 ·43	4
19	Th 4	6 ·01	23 ·50	5
20	Fr 5	*Sukla* 7 ·08	24 ·59	6
21	Sa 6	8 ·15	25 ·70	7
22	Su 7	9 ·25	26 ·80	8
23	Mo 8	10 ·33	27 ·92	9
24	Tu 9	11 ·41	... ...	10
25	We 10	12 ·49	1 ·01	11
26	Th 11	**Margasira** 13 ·55	2 ·09	12
27	Fr 12	14 ·58	3 ·16	13
28	Sa 13	P ·59	4 ·20	14
—29	Su 14	1 ·59	5 ·23	15
1	Mo 15	2 ·56	6 ·23	16
2	Tu 16	3 ·50	7 ·22	*H. 1332 Muharram.* 17
3	We 17	4 ·45	8 ·18	18
4	Th 18	5 ·37	9 ·14	19
5	Fr 19	*Bahula* 6 ·28	10 ·08	20
Pramadicha Dhanus—Margali. 6	Sa 20	7 ·18	11 ·02 12 ·94	21
7	Su 21	8 ·10 9 ·99	13 ·88	22
8	Mo 22	10 ·89	14 ·81	23
9	Tu 23	11 ·81	15 ·75	24
10	We 24	12 ·73	16 ·71	25
11	Th 25	13 ·68	17 ·67	26
12	Fr 26	14 ·62	18 ·64	27
13	Sa 27	—A ·59	19 ·63	28
14	Su 28	*P. Suk.* 1 ·57	20 ·64	29
15	Mo 29	2 ·59	21 ·68	—30
16	Tu 30	3 ·61	22 ·73	1
17	We 31	4 ·66	23 ·81	2

15. Svati. 16. Visak. 17. Anur. 18. Jyesh. 19. Mula, 20. P. Ash. 21. U. Ash. 22, Sravn. 23. Dani. 24. Satab. 25. P. Bhad. 26. U. Bhad. 27. Rev,

A. D. 1914. **Mesha Sankranti** (Commencement of Indian Sidereal Year).
Solar Eclipse. ● **(Surya Sid.) April 13·24.** **Saka 1836.** **Kaliyuga 5015.**
Lunar Eclipse. ○ **(Arya Sid.) April 13·13.** **(S. Cycle) Ananda.**

SOLAR reckoning: Cyclic Sidereal Year, Month and Day; Week-Day, English Month and Day. LUNAR reckoning: Tithi Ending Moment; Nakshatra Ending Moment; Muhammadan Year, Month and Day.

Jan.

Solar month	Cyclic Sidereal Day	Week-Day	Day	Lunar month / fortnight	Tithi Ending Moment	Nakshatra Ending Moment	Muh. month	Muhammadan Day
Pramadicha Dhanus—Margali.	18	Th	1	Sukla	5 ·73	24 ·90	H. 1332 Safar.	3
	19	Fr	2		6 ·80	25 ·99		4
	20	Sa	3		7 ·90	... ...		5
	21	Su	4		8 ·98	26 ·11		6
	22	Mo	5		... ...	27 ·22		7
	23	Tu	6		9 ·07	1 ·31		8
	24	We	7		10 ·14	2 ·40		9
	25	Th	8		11 ·19	3 ·47		10
	26	Fr	9		12 ·22	4 ·52		11
	27	Sa	10		13 ·24	5 ·55		12
	28	Su	11	Pausha	14 ·28	6 ·56		13
	29	Mo	12		P ·20	7 ·54		14
	—30	Tu	13		1 ·16	8 ·52		15
Pramadicha Makara—Tai.	1	We	14		2 ·09	9 ·47		16
	2	Th	15		3 ·01 4 ·92	10 ·43		17
	3	Fr	16		5 ·83	11 ·36		18
	4	Sa	17		6 ·73	12 ·29		19
	5	Su	18	Bahula	7 ·62	13 ·22		20
	6	Mo	19		8 ·54	14 ·15		21
	7	Tu	20		9 ·46	15 ·10		22
	8	We	21		10 ·38	16 ·04		23
	9	Th	22		11 ·31	17 ·00 18 ·97		24
	10	Fr	23		12 ·26	19 ·95		25
	11	Sa	24		13 ·23	20 ·97		26
	12	Su	25		14 ·21	... ...		27
	13	Mo	26		—A ·23	21 ·00		28
	14	Tu	27		1 ·26	22 ·04		—29
	15	We	28		2 ·32	23 ·11		1
	16	Th	29		3 ·38	24 ·19		2
	17	Fr	30		4 ·46	25 ·30		3
	18	Sa	31		5 ·55	26 ·41		4

Feb.

Solar month	Cyclic Sidereal Day	Week-Day	Day	Lunar month / fortnight	Tithi Ending Moment	Nakshatra Ending Moment	Muh. month	Muhammadan Day
	19	Su	1	Sukla	6 ·63	27 ·51	H. 1332 Rabi-ul-awwal.	5
	20	Mo	2		7 ·72	1 ·61		6
	21	Tu	3		8 ·79	2 ·70		7
	22	We	4		9 ·85	3 ·78		8
	23	Th	5		10 ·86	4 ·84		9
	24	Fr	6		11 ·88	5 ·87		10
	25	Sa	7		12 ·87	6 ·88		11
	26	Su	8	Magha	13 ·84	7 ·87		12
	27	Mo	9		14 ·78	8 ·85		13
	28	Tu	10		P ·71	9 ·81		14
	—29	We	11		1 ·64	10 ·76		15
Pramadicha Kumbha—Masi.	1	Th	12		2 ·55	11 ·70		16
	2	Fr	13		3 ·46	12 ·63		17
	3	Sa	14		4 ·36	13 ·56		18
	4	Su	15	Bahula	5 ·25	14 ·50		19
	5	Mo	16		6 ·16	15 ·43		20
	6	Tu	17		7 ·07	16 ·37		21
	7	We	18		8 ·00 9 ·93	17 ·33		22
	8	Th	19		10 ·80	18 ·20		23
	9	Fr	20		11 ·85	19 ·29		24
	10	Sa	21		12 ·84	20 ·29		25
	11	Su	22		13 ·86	21 ·31		26
	12	Mo	23		14 ·88	22 ·35		27
	13	Tu	24		—A ·94	23 ·41		28
	14	We	25	P. Suk.	... ...	24 ·51		29
	15	Th	26		1 ·00	25 ·60		—30
	16	Fr	27		2 ·08	26 ·71		1
	17	Sa	28		3 ·18	27 ·81		2

March

Solar month	Cyclic Sidereal Day	Week-Day	Day	Lunar month / fortnight	Tithi Ending Moment	Nakshatra Ending Moment	Muh. month	Muhammadan Day
Pramadicha Kumbha—Masi.	18	Su	1	Sukla	4 ·27	1 ·91	H. 1332 Rabi-ul-akhir.	3
	19	Mo	2		5 ·34	... ...		4
	20	Tu	3		6 ·40	2 ·01		5
	21	We	4		7 ·46	3 ·09		6
	22	Th	5		8 ·48	4 ·15		7
	23	Fr	6		9 ·49	5 ·19		8
	24	Sa	7		10 ·47	6 ·20		9
	25	Su	8	Phalguna	11 ·45	7 ·20		10
	26	Mo	9		12 ·39	8 ·19		11
	27	Tu	10		13 ·32	9 ·15		12
	28	We	11		14 ·25	10 ·10		13
	29	Th ○	12		P ·15	11 ·04 12 ·97		14
	—30	Fr	13		1 ·06 2 ·95	13 ·91		15
Pramadicha Mina—Panguni.	1	Sa	14		3 ·86	14 ·84		16
	2	Su	15		4 ·76	15 ·77		17
	3	Mo	16		5 ·66	16 ·71		18
	4	Tu	17	Bahula	6 ·59	17 ·66		19
	5	We	18		7 ·52	18 ·63		20
	6	Th	19		8 ·49	19 ·61		21
	7	Fr	20		9 ·45	20 ·61		22
	8	Sa	21		10 ·44	21 ·62		23
	9	Su	22		11 ·44	22 ·66		24
	10	Mo	23		12 ·48	23 ·72		25
	11	Tu	24		13 ·53	24 ·81		26
	12	We	25		14 ·60	25 ·90		27
	13	Th	26		—A ·68	... ...		28
	14	Fr	27		1 ·76	26 ·00		—29
	15	Sa	28		2 ·85	27 ·11		1
	16	Su	29		3 ·93	1 ·21		2
	17	Mo	30		4 ·99	2 ·32		3
	18	Tu	31		... ...	3 ·40		4

April

Solar month	Cyclic Sidereal Day	Week-Day	Day	Lunar month / fortnight	Tithi Ending Moment	Nakshatra Ending Moment	Muh. month	Muhammadan Day
	19	We	1	Sukla	5 ·04	4 ·46	H. 1332 Jumadal-awwal.	5
	20	Th	2		6 ·06	5 ·50		6
	21	Fr	3		7 ·07	6 ·52		7
	22	Sa	4		8 ·05	7 ·53		8
	23	Su	5		9 ·02 10 ·96	8 ·51		9
	24	Mo	6		11 ·90	9 ·48		10
	25	Tu	7		12 ·82	10 ·43		11
	26	We	8	Chaitra	13 ·72	11 ·37		12
	27	Th	9		14 ·62	12 ·32		13
	28	Fr	10		P ·51	13 ·25		14
	29	Sa	11		1 ·42	14 ·18		15
	—30	Su	12		2 ·32	15 ·11		16
Ananda Mesha—Chittirai.	1	Mo	13		3 ·23	16 ·04		17
	2	Tu	14		4 ·15	17 ·00 18 ·96		18
	3	We	15		5 ·09	19 ·94		19
	4	Th	16		6 ·04	20 ·93		20
	5	Fr	17	Bahula	7 ·00 8 ·99	21 ·94		21
	6	Sa	18		9 ·99	22 ·98		22
	7	Su	19		... ...	... ...		23
	8	Mo	20		10 ·03	23 ·04		24
	9	Tu	21		11 ·07	24 ·11		25
	10	We	22		12 ·14	25 ·20		26
	11	Th	23		13 ·22	26 ·30		27
	12	Fr	24		14 ·30	27 ·41		28
	13	Sa	25		—A ·39	1 ·52		29
	14	Su	26	V. Suk.	1 ·46	2 ·62	J.-akhir.	—30
	15	Mo	27		2 ·53	3 ·70		1
	16	Tu	28		3 ·58	4 ·77		2
	17	We	29		4 ·60	5 ·82		3
	18	Th	30		5 ·60	6 ·85		4

May

Solar month	Cyclic Sidereal Day	Week-Day	Day	Lunar month / fortnight	Tithi Ending Moment	Nakshatra Ending Moment	Muh. month	Muhammadan Day
Ananda Mesha—Chittirai.	19	Fr	1	Sukla	6 ·59	7 ·86	H. 1332 Jumadal-akhir.	5
	20	Sa	2		7 ·56	8 ·84		6
	21	Su	3		8 ·49	9 ·81		7
	22	Mo	4		9 ·43	10 ·77		8
	23	Tu	5		10 ·35	11 ·72		9
	24	We	6		11 ·25	12 ·65		10
	25	Th	7		12 ·15	13 ·58		11
	26	Fr	8		13 ·06 14 ·95	14 ·51		12
	27	Sa	9	Vaisakha	P ·85	15 ·44		13
	28	Su	10		1 ·75	16 ·38		14
	29	Mo	11		2 ·67	17 ·34		15
	30	Tu	12		3 ·60	18 ·29		16
	—31	We	13		4 ·56	19 ·26		17
Ananda Vrishabha—Vaikasi.	1	Th	14		5 ·53	20 ·25		18
	2	Fr	15		6 ·50	21 ·26		19
	3	Sa	16		7 ·50	22 ·30		20
	4	Su	17	Bahula	8 ·55	23 ·35		21
	5	Mo	18		9 ·59	24 ·42		22
	6	Tu	19		10 ·66	25 ·50		23
	7	We	20		11 ·72	26 ·60		24
	8	Th	21		12 ·81	27 ·72		25
	9	Fr	22		13 ·89	1 ·82		26
	10	Sa	23		14 ·98	2 ·92		27
	11	Su	24		... ...	... ...		28
	12	Mo	25		—A ·03	3 ·01		—29
	13	Tu	26		1 ·08	4 ·08		1
	14	We	27		2 ·10	5 ·14		2
	15	Th	28		3 ·11	6 ·17		3
	16	Fr	29		4 ·09	7 ·18		4
	17	Sa	30		5 ·06	8 ·17		5
	18	Su	31		6 ·01 7 ·93	9 ·14		6

June

Solar month	Cyclic Sidereal Day	Week-Day	Day	Lunar month / fortnight	Tithi Ending Moment	Nakshatra Ending Moment	Muh. month	Muhammadan Day
	19	Mo	1	Sukla	8 ·84	10 ·11	H. 1332 Rajab.	7
	20	Tu	2		9 ·75	11 ·06 12 ·99		8
	21	We	3		10 ·65	13 ·92		9
	22	Th	4		11 ·54	14 ·83		10
	23	Fr	5	Jyeshtha	12 ·44	15 ·78		11
	24	Sa	6		13 ·35	16 ·78		12
	25	Su	7		14 ·26	17 ·67		13
	26	Mo	8		P ·17	18 ·62		14
	27	Tu	9		1 ·10	19 ·59		15
	28	We	10		2 ·05	20 ·57		16
	29	Th	11		3 ·01 4 ·99	21 ·59		17
	30	Fr	12		... ...	22 ·61		18
	—31	Sa	13		5 ·00	23 ·66		19
Ananda Mithuna—Ani.	1	Su	14	Bahula	6 ·02	24 ·72		20
	2	Mo	15		7 ·07	25 ·80		21
	3	Tu	16		8 ·13	26 ·91		22
	4	We	17		9 ·20	... ...		23
	5	Th	18		10 ·28	27 ·01		24
	6	Fr	19		11 ·37	1 ·12		25
	7	Sa	20		12 ·45	2 ·22		26
	8	Su	21		13 ·50	3 ·31		27
	9	Mo	22		14 ·56	4 ·40		28
	10	Tu	23		—A ·58	5 ·45		29
	11	We	24	Ashad. Suk.	1 ·58	6 ·49	Shaban.	—30
	12	Th	25		2 ·57	7 ·50		1
	13	Fr	26		3 ·54	8 ·50		2
	14	Sa	27		4 ·48	9 ·47		3
	15	Su	28		5 ·41	10 ·44		4
	16	Mo	29		6 ·33	11 ·39		5
	17	Tu	30		7 ·24	12 ·33		6

Naksh :—1. Asvn. 2. Bhar. 3. Krit. 4. Rohi. 5. Mrig. 6. Ardh. 7. Punar. 8. Push. 9. Aslesh. 10. Magh. 11. P. Phal. 12 U. Phal. 13. Hasta. 14. Chit.

A. D. 1914.
A.—Amavasya.
P.—Paurnami.

Kollam 1090, Commences { **N. Malabar—Sept.** / **S. Malabar—Aug.**

Hijra 1333, Commences, **Nov. 19.**

Vikrama 1971.
Bengal San 1321.
(N. Cycle) Kshaya.

SOLAR reckoning: Cyclic Sidereal Year, Month and Day	Week-Day English Month and Day	LUNAR reckoning: Tithi Ending Moment	Nakshatra Ending Moment	Muhammadan Year, Month and Day
	July			
18	We 1	8 ·13	13 ·26	7
19	Th 2	9 ·03 / 10 ·93	14 ·19	8
20	Fr 3	11 ·83	15 ·13	9
21	Sa 4	*Sukla* 12 ·73	16 ·06	10
Ananda *Mithuna—Ani.* 22	Su 5	13 ·66	17 ·00 / 18 ·95	11
23	Mo 6	14 ·58	19 ·92	12
24	Tu 7	**Ashadha** P ·53	20 ·91	13
25	We 8	1 ·49	21 ·91	14
26	Th 9	2 ·47	22 ·93	15
27	Fr 10	3 ·47	23 ·97	16
28	Sa 11	4 ·50	...	17
29	Su 12	5 ·55	24 ·03	18
30	Mo 13	6 ·61	25 ·11	19
31	Tu 14	*Bahula* 7 ·68	26 ·21	H. 1332 *Shaban.* 20
—32	We 15	8 ·77	27 ·31	21
1	Th 16	9 ·85	1 ·42	22
2	Fr 17	10 ·91	2 ·52	23
3	Sa 18	11 ·98	3 ·62	24
4	Su 19	...	4 ·70	25
5	Mo 20	12 ·04	5 ·76	26
6	Tu 21	13 ·06	6 ·80	27
7	We 22	14 ·07	7 ·82	28
8	Th 23	—A ·05	8 ·82	—29
9	Fr 24	1 ·03 / 2 ·96	9 ·81	1
10	Sa 25	3 ·89	10 ·78	2
11	Su 26	4 ·82	11 ·73	3
Ananda *Karkata—Adi.* 12	Mo 27	5 ·73	12 ·67	4
13	Tu 28	6 ·63	13 ·60	5
14	We 29	7 ·52	14 ·54	6
15	Th 30	8 ·43	15 ·47	7
16	Fr 31	*Sukla* 9 ·32	16 ·40	8
	Aug.			
17	Sa 1	10 ·22	17 ·34	9
18	Su 2	11 ·15	18 ·29	10
19	Mo 3	12 ·07	19 ·26	11
20	Tu 4	13 ·01 / 14 ·97	20 ·23	12
21	We 5	P ·96	21 ·23	13
22	Th 6	**Sravana** 1 ·96	22 ·24	H. 1332 *Ramzan.* 14
23	Fr 7	2 ·97	23 ·28	15
24	Sa 8	...	24 ·34	16
25	Su 9	3 ·02	25 ·42	17
26	Mo 10	4 ·08	26 ·51	18
27	Tu 11	5 ·16	27 ·61	19
28	We 12	6 ·25	1 ·71	20
29	Th 13	7 ·33	2 ·82	21
30	Fr 14	*Bahula* 8 ·40	3 ·93	22
31	Sa 15	9 ·47	...	23
—32	Su 16	10 ·52	4 ·01	24
1	Mo 17	11 ·54	5 ·07	25
2	Tu 18	12 ·56	6 ·12	26
3	We 19	13 ·54	7 ·14	27
4	Th 20	14 ·51	8 ·16	28
5	Fr ● 21	—A ·47	9 ·14	29
6	Sa 22	1 ·41	10 ·11	—30
7	Su 23	2 ·31	11 ·06	1
8	Mo 24	3 ·22	12 ·00 / 13 ·95	2
Ananda *Simha—Avani.* 9	Tu 25	*Sukla* 4 ·13	14 ·88	H. 1332 *Shawwal.* 3
10	We 26	5 ·02 / 6 ·93	15 81	4
11	Th 27	7 ·83	16 ·74	5
12	Fr 28	8 ·73	17 ·67	6
13	Sa 29	9 ·65	18 ·63	7
14	Su 30	10 ·57	19 ·59	8
15	Mo 31	**Bhadra.** 11 ·53	20 ·56	9

SOLAR reckoning: Cyclic Sidereal Year, Month and Day	Week-Day English Month and Day	LUNAR reckoning: Tithi Ending Moment	Nakshatra Ending Moment	Muhammadan Year, Month and Day
	Sep.			
16	Tu 1	*Suk.* 12 ·48	21 ·55	10
17	We 2	13 ·47	22 ·56	11
18	Th 3	14 ·47	23 ·59	12
19	Fr ○ 4	P ·50	24 ·65	13
20	Sa 5	1 ·54	25 ·72	14
Ananda *Simha—Avani.* 21	Su 6	2 ·59	26 ·81	15
22	Mo 7	3 ·67	27 ·91	16
23	Tu 8	**Bhadrapada** 4 ·75	...	17
24	We 9	5 ·84	1 ·01	18
25	Th 10	6 ·91	2 ·13	19
26	Fr 11	7 ·99	3 ·23	20
27	Sa 12	...	4 ·31	H. 1332 *Shawwal.* 21
28	Su 13	*Bahula* 8 ·04	5 ·38	22
29	Mo 14	9 ·07	6 ·43	23
30	Tu 15	10 ·09	7 ·47	24
—31	We 16	11 ·07	8 ·48	25
1	Th 17	12 ·05	9 ·47	26
2	Fr 18	13 ·00 / 14 ·93	10 ·44	27
3	Sa 19	—A ·84	11 ·40	28
4	Su 20	1 ·76	12 ·35	—29
5	Mo 21	2 ·66	13 ·29	1
6	Tu 22	3 ·56	14 ·22	2
7	We 23	4 ·47	15 ·15	3
8	Th 24	5 ·36	16 ·08	4
9	Fr 25	6 ·27	17 ·02 / 18 ·96	5
Ananda *Kanya—Purattasi.* 10	Sa 26	7 ·19	19 ·93	6
11	Su 27	*Sukla* 8 ·12	20 ·89	7
12	Mo 28	9 ·07	21 ·87	8
13	Tu 29	10 ·03	22 ·88	9
14	We 30	11 ·01	23 ·91	10
	Oct.			
15	Th 1	12 ·00	24 ·96	11
16	Fr 2	13 ·04	...	12
17	Sa 3	14 ·08	25 ·03	13
18	Su 4	**Asvina** P ·14	26 ·11	14
19	Mo 5	1 ·22	27 ·21	15
20	Tu 6	2 ·31	1 ·32	H. 1332 *Zi-l-ka'da.* 16
21	We 7	3 ·39	2 ·43	17
22	Th 8	4 ·46	3 ·53	18
23	Fr 9	5 ·54	4 ·62	19
24	Sa 10	6 ·60	5 ·69	20
25	Su 11	7 ·64	6 ·76	21
26	Mo 12	*Bahula* 8 ·65	7 ·79	22
27	Tu 13	9 ·64	8 ·80	23
28	We 14	10 ·61	9 ·79	24
29	Th 15	11 ·57	10 ·77	25
—30	Fr 16	12 ·50	11 ·74	26
1	Sa 17	13 ·41	12 ·69	27
2	Su 18	14 ·33	13 ·62	28
3	Mo 19	—A ·23	14 ·56	29
4	Tu 20	1 ·13	15 ·49	—30
5	We 21	2 ·04 / 3 ·95	16 ·42	1
6	Th 22	4 ·85	17 ·36	2
Ananda *Tula—Aippasi.* 7	Fr 23	5 ·77	18 ·30	3
8	Sa 24	*Sukla* 6 ·70	19 ·25	4
9	Su 25	7 ·65	20 ·22	5
10	Mo 26	8 ·61	21 ·20	H. 1332 *Zi-l-hijja.* 6
11	Tu 27	9 ·59	22 ·21	7
12	We 28	10 ·61	23 ·23	8
13	Th 29	11 ·63	24 ·27	9
14	Fr 30	12 ·67	25 ·33	10
15	Sa 31	**Karttika** 13 ·74	26 ·41	11

SOLAR reckoning: Cyclic Sidereal Year, Month and Day	Week-Day English Month and Day	LUNAR reckoning: Tithi Ending Moment	Nakshatra Ending Moment	Muhammadan Year, Month and Day
	Nov.			
16	Su 1	**Kartt.ka** 14 ·82	27 ·51	12
17	Mo 2	P ·90	1 ·62	13
18	Tu 3	...	2 ·73	14
19	We 4	1 ·00	3 ·83	15
20	Th 5	2 ·08	4 ·92	16
Ananda *Tula—Aippasi.* 21	Fr 6	3 ·15	...	17
22	Sa 7	4 ·20	5 ·01	H. 1332 *Zi-l-hijja.* 18
23	Su 8	5 ·24	6 ·07	19
24	Mo 9	*Bahula* 6 ·24	7 ·11	20
25	Tu 10	7 ·24	8 ·12	21
26	We 11	8 ·20	9 ·12	22
27	Th 12	9 ·17	10 ·11	23
28	Fr 13	10 ·10	11 ·07	24
29	Sa 14	11 ·02 / 12 ·94	12 ·02 / 13 ·96	25
—30	Su 15	13 ·84	14 ·89	26
1	Mo 16	14 ·74	15 ·82	27
2	Tu 17	—A ·64	16 ·76	28
3	We 18	1 ·55	17 ·70	—29
4	Th 19	2 ·46	18 ·63	1
5	Fr 20	3 ·38	19 ·58	2
6	Sa 21	4 ·30	20 ·54	3
7	Su 22	5 ·26	21 ·53	4
8	Mo 23	6 ·23	22 ·53	5
9	Tu 24	7 ·21	23 ·54	6
Ananda *Vrischika—Kartigai.* 10	We 25	*Sukla* 8 ·22	24 ·58	7
11	Th 26	9 ·25	25 ·64	8
12	Fr 27	10 ·30	26 ·72	9
13	Sa 28	11 ·36	27 ·81	10
14	Su 29	12 ·45	1 ·92	11
15	Mo 30	13 ·54	...	12
	Dec.			
16	Tu 1	**Margas.ra** 14 ·62	2 ·02	13
17	We 2	P ·70	3 ·13	14
18	Th 3	1 ·77	4 ·23	15
19	Fr 4	2 ·84	5 ·31	16
20	Sa 5	3 ·87	6 ·38	17
21	Su 6	4 ·88	7 ·42	H. 1333 *Muharram.* 18
22	Mo 7	5 ·87	8 ·44	19
23	Tu 8	6 ·83	9 ·44	20
24	We 9	7 ·79	10 ·43	21
25	Th 10	*Bahula* 8 ·72	11 ·40	22
26	Fr 11	9 ·65	12 ·36	23
27	Sa 12	10 ·56	13 ·30	24
28	Su 13	11 ·47	14 ·23	25
—29	Mo 14	12 ·37	15 ·17	26
1	Tu 15	13 ·27	16 ·10	27
2	We 16	14 ·17	17 ·03 / 18 ·97	28
3	Th 17	—A ·09	19 ·92	29
4	Fr 18	1 ·01 / 2 ·94	20 ·88	—30
5	Sa 19	3 ·90	21 ·86	1
6	Su 20	4 ·87	22 ·85	2
7	Mo 21	5 ·86	23 ·86	3
8	Tu 22	6 ·86	24 ·89	4
Ananda *Dhanus—Margali.* 9	We 23	*Sukla* 7 ·90	25 ·95	H. 1333 *Safar.* 5
10	Th 24	8 ·95	...	6
11	Fr 25	...	26 ·03	7
12	Sa 26	9 ·01	27 ·11	8
13	Su 27	10 ·11	1 ·21	9
14	Mo 28	11 ·19	2 ·32	10
15	Tu 29	12 ·29	3 ·43	11
16	We 30	13 ·36	4 ·53	12
17	Th 31	**Pausha** 14 ·43	5 ·62	13

*15. Svati. 16. Visak. 17. Anur. 18. Jyesh. 19. Mula. 20. P. Ash. 21. U. Ash. 22. Sravn. 23. Dani. 24. Satab. 25. P. Bhad. 26. U. Bhad. 27. Rev.

A. D. 1915. **Mesha Sankranti** (Commencement of Indian Sidereal Year).

Solar Eclipse. ● **(Surya Sid.) April 13·50.** **Saka 1837.** **Kaliyuga 5016.**

Lunar Eclipse. ◯ **(Arya Sid.) April 13·39.** **(S. Cycle) Rakshasa.**

Jan. — Solar: *Ananda Dhanus—Margali*, then *Ananda Makara—Tai*. Lunar: *Pausha Bahula*, *Sukla*, *Magha*. Muhammadan: *H. 1333 Safar*, *Rabi-ul-awwal*.

SOLAR reckoning: Cyclic Sidereal Year, Month and Day	Week-Day English Month and Day	LUNAR reckoning: Tithi Ending Moment	Nakshatra Ending Moment	Muhammadan Year, Month and Day
18	Fr 1	P ·48	6 ·69	14
19	Sa 2	1 ·51	7 ·73	15
20	Su 3	2 ·53	8 ·76	16
21	Mo 4	3 ·51	9 ·78	17
22	Tu 5	4 ·48	10 ·76	18
23	We 6	5 ·44	11 ·73	19
24	Th 7	6 ·38	12 ·69	20
25	Fr 8	7 ·29	13 ·63	21
26	Sa 9	8 ·21	14 ·58	22
27	Su 10	9 ·12	15 ·51	23
28	Mo 11	10 ·01 11 ·92	16 ·44	24
29	Tu 12	12 ·82	17 ·37	25
—30	We 13	13 ·74	18 ·31	26
1	Th 14	14 ·65	19 ·26	27
2	Fr 15	—A ·58	20 ·22	28
3	Sa 16	1 ·55	21 ·19	—29
4	Su 17	2 ·51	22 ·17	1
5	Mo 18	3 ·50	23 ·18	2
6	Tu 19	4 ·51	24 ·22	3
7	We 20	5 ·55	25 ·26	4
8	Th 21	6 ·59	26 ·33	5
9	Fr 22	7 ·67	27 ·42	6
10	Sa 23	8 ·76	1 ·51	7
11	Su 24	9 ·84	2 ·62	8
12	Mo 25	10 ·98	3 ·74	9
13	Tu 26	... ...	4 ·84	10
14	We 27	11 ·02	5 ·92	11
15	Th 28	12 ·09	6 ·99	12
16	Fr 29	13 ·12	... ...	13
17	Sa 30	14 ·16	7 ·05	14
18	Su 31	P ·17	8 ·09	15

Feb. — Solar: *Ananda Kumbha—Masi*. Lunar: *Bahula*, *Sukla*, *Phalguna*. Muhammadan: *H. 1333*, *H. 1333 Rabi-ul-akhir*.

Cyclic Sidereal Year, Month and Day	Week-Day English Month and Day	Tithi Ending Moment	Nakshatra Ending Moment	Muhammadan Year, Month and Day
19	Mo 1	1 ·15	9 ·10	16
20	Tu 2	2 ·12	10 ·09	17
21	We 3	3 ·07	11 ·07	18
22	Th 4	4 ·01 5 ·92	12 ·02 13 ·98	19
23	Fr 5	6 ·83	14 ·92	20
24	Sa 6	7 ·73	15 ·85	21
25	Su 7	8 ·64	16 ·78	22
26	Mo 8	9 ·54	17 ·71	23
27	Tu 9	10 ·44	18 ·65	24
28	We 10	11 ·36	19 ·59	25
—29	Th 11	12 ·27	20 ·55	26
1	Fr 12	13 ·22	21 ·51	27
2	Sa 13	14 ·18	22 ·50	28
3	Su 14	—A ·14	23 ·50	29
4	Mo 15	1 ·13	24 ·53	—30
5	Tu 16	2 ·14	25 ·57	1
6	We 17	3 ·19	26 ·64	2
7	Th 18	4 ·23	27 ·72	3
8	Fr 19	5 ·31	1 ·81	4
9	Sa 20	6 ·38	2 ·93	5
10	Su 21	7 ·47	... ...	6
11	Mo 22	8 ·56	3 ·08	7
12	Tu 23	9 ·64	4 ·14	8
13	We 24	10 ·71	5 ·23	9
14	Th 25	11 ·75	6 ·80	10
15	Fr 26	12 ·78	7 ·37	11
16	Sa 27	13 ·78	8 ·41	12
17	Su 28	14 ·78	9 ·42	13

March — Solar: *Ananda Kumbha—Masi*, then *Ananda Mina—Panguni*. Lunar: *Phalguna*, *Bahula*, *Sukla*, *Chaitra*. Muhammadan: *H. 1333 Rabi-ul-akhir*, *Jumadal-awwal*.

Cyclic Sidereal Year, Month and Day	Week-Day English Month and Day	Tithi Ending Moment	Nakshatra Ending Moment	Muhammadan Year, Month and Day
18	Mo 1	P 74	10 ·42	14
19	Tu 2	1 ·68	11 ·40	15
20	We 3	2 ·62	12 ·37	16
21	Th 4	3 ·53	13 ·32	17
22	Fr 5	4 ·45	14 ·26	18
23	Sa 6	5 ·35	15 ·19	19
24	Su 7	6 ·26	16 ·12	20
25	Mo 8	7 ·15	17 ·06 18 ·99	21
26	Tu 9	8 ·05 9 ·97	19 ·93	22
27	We 10	10 ·88	20 ·88	23
28	Th 11	11 ·82	21 ·84	24
29	Fr 12	12 ·78	22 ·82	25
—30	Sa 13	13 ·75	23 ·83	26
1	Su 14	14 ·73	24 ·84	27
2	Mo 15	—A ·74	25 ·88	28
3	Tu 16	1 ·78	26 ·95	—29
4	We 17	2 ·82	... ...	1
5	Th 18	3 ·91	27 02	2
6	Fr 19	4 ·99	1 ·12	3
7	Sa 20	... ...	2 ·22	4
8	Su 21	5 ·08	3 ·33	5
9	Mo 22	6 ·16	4 ·43	6
10	Tu 23	7 ·25	5 ·53	7
11	We 24	8 ·30	6 ·62	8
12	Th 25	9 ·34	7 ·68	9
13	Fr 26	10 ·38	8 ·72	10
14	Sa 27	11 ·37	9 ·74	11
15	Su 28	12 ·36	10 ·74	12
16	Mo 29	13 ·31	11 ·73	13
17	Tu 30	14 ·26	12 ·70	14
18	We 31	P ·19	13 ·65	15

April — Solar: *Rakshasa Mesha—Chittirai*. Lunar: *Bahula*, *Sukla*, *Adhika Vaisakha*. Muhammadan: *H. 1333*, *H. 1333 Jumadal-akhir*.

Cyclic Sidereal Year, Month and Day	Week-Day English Month and Day	Tithi Ending Moment	Nakshatra Ending Moment	Muhammadan Year, Month and Day
19	Th 1	1 ·12	14 ·59	16
20	Fr 2	2 ·02 3 ·91	15 ·53	17
21	Sa 3	4 ·82	16 ·46	18
22	Su 4	5 ·71	17 ·39	19
23	Mo 5	6 ·63	18 ·33	20
24	Tu 6	7 ·54	19 ·26	21
25	We 7	8 ·46	20 ·21	22
26	Th 8	9 ·39	21 ·17	23
27	Fr 9	10 ·34	22 ·16	24
28	Sa 10	11 ·31	23 ·15	25
29	Su 11	12 ·29	24 ·16	26
—30	Mo 12	13 ·30	25 ·19	27
1	Tu 13	14 ·34	26 ·25	28
2	We 14	—A ·39	27 ·33	29
3	Th 15	1 ·47	1 ·42	—30
4	Fr 16	2 ·54	2 ·52	1
5	Sa 17	3 ·63	3 ·63	2
6	Su 18	4 ·71	4 ·73	3
7	Mo 19	5 ·80	5 ·84	4
8	Tu 20	6 ·85	6 ·93	5
9	We 21	7 ·89	7 ·99	6
10	Th 22	8 ·91	... ...	7
11	Fr 23	9 ·92	8 04	8
12	Sa 24	10 ·90	9 ·06	9
13	Su 25	11 ·86	10 ·08	10
14	Mo 26	12 ·81	11 ·06	11
15	Tu 27	13 ·74	12 ·08 13 ·99	12
16	We 28	14 ·66	14 ·93	13
17	Th 29	P ·55	15 ·86	14
18	Fr 30	1 ·46	16 ·80	15

May — Solar: *Rakshasa Mesha—Chittirai*, then *Rakshasa Vrishabha—Vaikasi*. Lunar: *Adh. Vsk.*, *Bahula*, *Sukla*, *Nija Vaisakha*. Muhammadan: *H. 1333 Jumadal-akhir*, *H. 1333 Rajab*.

Cyclic Sidereal Year, Month and Day	Week-Day English Month and Day	Tithi Ending Moment	Nakshatra Ending Moment	Muhammadan Year, Month and Day
19	Sa 1	2 ·36	17 ·73	16
20	Su 2	3 ·25	18 ·66	17
21	Mo 3	4 ·16	19 ·60	18
22	Tu 4	5 ·07 6 ·98	20 ·55	19
23	We 5	7 ·91	21 ·51	20
24	Th 6	8 ·87	22 ·48	21
25	Fr 7	9 ·84	23 ·47	22
26	Sa 8	10 ·82	24 ·48	23
27	Su 9	11 ·83	25 ·51	24
28	Mo 10	12 ·86	26 ·57	25
29	Tu 11	13 ·92	27 ·64	26
30	We 12	14 ·98	1 ·72	27
—31	Th 13	... ...	2 ·82	28
1	Fr 14	—A ·06	3 ·93	—29
2	Sa 15	1 ·13	... ...	1
3	Su 16	2 ·22	4 ·04	2
4	Mo 17	3 ·30	5 ·14	3
5	Tu 18	4 ·36	6 ·23	4
6	We 19	5 ·41	7 ·30	5
7	Th 20	6 ·43	8 ·35	6
8	Fr 21	7 ·43	9 ·88	7
9	Sa 22	8 ·41	10 ·40	8
10	Su 23	9 ·38	11 ·39	9
11	Mo 24	10 32	12 ·36	10
12	Tu 25	11 ·24	13 ·32	11
13	We 26	12 ·16	14 ·27	12
14	Th 27	13 ·06 14 ·97	15 ·21	13
15	Fr 28	P ·86	16 ·14	14
16	Sa 29	1 ·76	17 ·07	15
17	Su 30	2 ·66	18 ·00 19 ·94	16
18	Mo 31	3 ·56	20 ·89	17

June — Solar: *Rakshasa Mit'una—Ani*. Lunar: *Bahula*, *Sukla*, *Jyeshtha*, *Bah.* Muhammadan: *H. 1333 Shaban*.

Cyclic Sidereal Year, Month and Day	Week-Day English Month and Day	Tithi Ending Moment	Nakshatra Ending Moment	Muhammadan Year, Month and Day
19	Tu 1	4 ·49	21 ·84	18
20	We 2	5 ·42	22 ·81	19
21	Th 3	6 ·38	23 ·79	20
22	Fr 4	7 ·33	24 ·80	21
23	Sa 5	8 ·32	25 ·83	22
24	Su 6	9 ·33	26 ·88	23
25	Mo 7	10 ·36	27 ·94	24
26	Tu 8	11 ·41	... ...	25
27	We 9	12 ·47	1 ·02	26
28	Th 10	13 ·55	2 ·12	27
29	Fr 11	14 ·62	3 ·23	28
30	Sa 12	—A ·71	4 ·34	29
31	Su 13	1 ·78	5 ·44	—30
—32	Mo 14	2 ·84	6 ·53	1
1	Tu 15	3 ·88	7 ·61	2
2	We 16	4 ·91	8 ·66	3
3	Th 17	5 ·92	9 ·71	4
4	Fr 18	6 ·89	10 ·72	5
5	Sa 19	7 ·86	11 ·72	6
6	Su 20	8 ·81	12 ·69	7
7	Mo 21	9 ·73	13 ·65	8
8	Tu 22	10 ·65	14 ·61	9
9	We 23	11 ·56	15 ·55	10
10	Th 24	12 ·45	16 ·46	11
11	Fr 25	13 ·35	17 ·41	12
12	Sa 26	14 ·25	18 ·34	13
13	Su 27	P ·14	19 ·28	14
14	Mo 28	1 ·06 2 ·98	20 ·22	15
15	Tu 29	3 ·91	21 ·17	16
16	We 30	4 ·84	22 ·14	17

Naksh :—1. Asvn. 2. Bhar. 3. Krit. 4. Rohi. 5. Mrig. 6. Ardh. 7. Punar. 8. Push. 9. Aslesh. 10. Magh. 11. P. Phal. 12. U. Phal. 13. Hasta. 14. Chit.

A. D. 1915.
A.—Amavasya.
P.—Paurnami.

Kollam 1091, Commences { N. Malabar—Sept. / S. Malabar—Aug.

Hijra 1334, Commences, Nov. 9.

Vikrama 1972.
Bengal San 1321.
(N. Cycle) Prabhava.

SOLAR reckoning: Cyclic Sidereal Year, Month and Day.	Week-Day English Month and Day.	LUNAR reckoning: Tithi Ending Moment.	Nakshatra Ending Moment.	Muhammadan Year, Month and Day.
	July			
Rakshasa Mithuna—Ani. 17	Th 1	Jyesh. Bahula 5 ·81	23 ·12	H. 1333 Shaban. 18
18	Fr 2	6 ·80	24 ·13	19
19	Sa 3	7 ·80	25 ·15	20
20	Su 4	8 ·83	26 ·19	21
21	Mo 5	9 ·88	27 ·25	22
22	Tu 6	10 ·94	1 ·32	23
23	We 7	... ...	2 ·42	24
24	Th 8	11 ·01	3 ·53	25
25	Fr 9	12 ·09	4 ·64	26
26	Sa 10	13 ·18	5 ·74	27
27	Su 11	14 ·25	6 ·84	28
28	Mo 12	—A ·32	7 ·91	—29
29	Tu 13	Ashadha Sukla 1 ·36	8 ·98	H. 1333 Ramzan. 1
30	We 14	2 ·89	... ...	2
—31	Th 15	3 ·29	9 ·02	3
Rakshasa Karkata—Adi. 1	Fr 16	4 ·38	10 ·04	4
2	Sa 17	5 ·33	11 ·04	5
3	Su 18	6 ·28	12 ·02	6
4	Mo 19	7 ·21	{ 13 ·00 / 14 ·95 }	7
5	Tu 20	8 ·13	15 ·89	8
6	We 21	{ 9 ·04 / 10 ·94 }	16 ·82	9
7	Th 22	11 ·85	17 ·75	10
8	Fr 23	12 ·74	18 ·69	11
9	Sa 24	13 ·63	19 ·62	12
10	Su 25	14 ·54	20 ·56	13
11	Mo 26	P ·45	21 ·51	14
12	Tu 27	1 ·39	22 ·47	15
13	We 28	2 ·33	23 ·45	16
14	Th 29	3 ·30	24 ·45	17
15	Fr 30	4 ·28	25 ·46	18
16	Sa 31	5 ·28	26 ·50	19

SOLAR: Cyclic Sidereal Year, Month and Day.	Week-Day English Month and Day.	Tithi Ending Moment.	Nakshatra Ending Moment.	Muhammadan Year, Month and Day.
	Aug.			
17	Su 1	Bahula 6 ·30	27 ·55	H. 1333 Ramzan. 20
18	Mo 2	7 ·35	1 ·63	21
19	Tu 3	8 ·42	2 ·73	22
20	We 4	9 ·49	3 ·83	23
21	Th 5	10 ·58	4 ·94	24
22	Fr 6	11 ·66	... ...	25
23	Sa 7	12 ·74	5 ·04	26
24	Su 8	13 ·79	6 ·14	27
25	Mo 9	14 ·83	7 ·23	28
26	Tu 10	—A ·88	8 ·29	29
27	We 11	Sravana Sukla 1 ·88	9 ·34	—30
28	Th 12	2 ·87	10 ·36	H. 1333 Shawwal. 1
29	Fr 13	3 ·83	11 ·37	2
30	Sa 14	4 ·79	12 ·36	3
31	Su 15	5 ·71	13 ·33	4
—32	Mo 16	6 ·63	14 ·28	5
Rakshasa Simha—Avani. 1	Tu 17	7 ·54	15 ·22	6
2	We 18	8 ·43	16 ·16	7
3	Th 19	9 ·34	17 ·10	8
4	Fr 20	10 ·23	{ 18 ·03 / 19 ·96 }	9
5	Sa 21	11 ·14	20 ·89	10
6	Su 22	{ 12 ·04 / 13 ·96 }	21 ·34	11
7	Mo 23	14 ·89	22 ·80	12
8	Tu 24	P ·82	23 ·78	13
9	We 25	Bah. 1 ·80	24 ·77	14
10	Th 26	2 ·78	25 ·78	15
11	Fr 27	3 ·79	26 ·81	16
12	Sa 28	4 ·80	27 ·86	17
13	Su 29	5 ·86	1 ·94	18
14	Mo 30	6 ·92	... ...	19
15	Tu 31	7 ·99	2 ·03	20

SOLAR: Cyclic Sidereal Year, Month and Day.	Week-Day English Month and Day.	Tithi Ending Moment.	Nakshatra Ending Moment.	Muhammadan Year, Month and Day.
	Sep.			
Rakshasa Simha—Avani. 16	We 1	Sravn. Bahula	3 ·18	H. 1333 Shawwal. 21
17	Th 2	8 ·08	4 ·23	22
18	Fr 3	9 ·16	5 ·34	23
19	Sa 4	10 ·25	6 ·45	24
20	Su 5	11 ·31	7 ·53	25
21	Mo 6	12 ·35	8 ·60	26
22	Tu 7	13 ·38	9 ·65	27
23	We 8	14 ·39	10 ·68	28
24	Th 9	—A ·38	11 ·70	—29
25	Fr 10	Bhadrapada Sukla 1 ·35	12 ·69	H. 1333 Zi-l-ka'da. 1
26	Sa 11	2 ·31	13 ·66	2
27	Su 12	3 ·23	14 ·61	3
28	Mo 13	4 ·16	15 ·56	4
29	Tu 14	{ 5 ·06 / 6 ·96 }	16 ·50	5
30	We 15	7 ·87	17 ·44	6
—31	Th 16	8 ·76	18 ·37	7
Rakshasa Kanya—Purattasi. 1	Fr 17	9 ·67	19 ·30	8
2	Sa 18	10 ·56	20 ·23	9
3	Su 19	11 ·49	21 ·17	10
4	Mo 20	12 ·42	22 ·14	11
5	Tu 21	13 ·36	23 ·11	12
6	We 22	14 ·33	24 ·09	13
7	Th 23	P ·32	25 ·10	14
8	Fr 24	1 ·34	26 ·12	15
9	Sa 25	2 ·35	27 ·18	16
10	Su 26	3 ·40	1 ·25	17
11	Mo 27	4 ·45	2 ·33	18
12	Tu 28	5 ·54	3 ·43	19
13	We 29	6 ·62	4 ·53	20
14	Th 30	7 ·71	5 ·65	21

SOLAR: Cyclic Sidereal Year, Month and Day.	Week-Day English Month and Day.	Tithi Ending Moment.	Nakshatra Ending Moment.	Muhammadan Year, Month and Day.
	Oct.			
Rakshasa Kanya—Purattasi. 15	Fr 1	Bahula 8 ·78	6 ·75	H. 1333 Zi-l-ka'da. 22
16	Sa 2	9 ·85	7 ·84	23
17	Su 3	10 ·91	8 ·91	24
18	Mo 4	11 ·93	9 ·97	25
19	Tu 5	12 ·95	... ...	26
20	We 6	13 ·93	10 ·01	27
21	Th 7	14 ·91	11 ·02	28
22	Fr 8	—A ·85	{ 12 ·01 / 13 ·99 }	29
23	Sa 9	Asvina Sukla 1 ·80	14 ·95	—30
24	Su 10	2 ·72	15 ·90	H. 1333 Zi-l-hijja. 1
25	Mo 11	3 ·62	16 ·84	2
26	Tu 12	4 ·52	17 ·77	3
27	We 13	5 ·43	18 ·70	4
28	Th 14	6 ·33	19 ·63	5
29	Fr 15	7 ·23	20 ·57	6
—30	Sa 16	8 ·14	21 ·52	7
Rakshasa Tula—Aippasi. 1	Su 17	{ 9 ·06 / 10 ·99 }	22 ·47	8
2	Mo 18	11 ·93	23 ·44	9
3	Tu 19	12 ·90	24 ·42	10
4	We 20	13 ·90	25 ·42	11
5	Th 21	14 ·92	26 ·45	12
6	Fr 22	P ·93	27 ·49	13
7	Sa 23	1 ·98	1 ·55	14
8	Su 24	... ...	2 ·63	15
9	Mo 25	Bahula 2 ·04	3 ·73	16
10	Tu 26	3 ·12	4 ·84	17
11	We 27	4 ·20	5 ·95	18
12	Th 28	5 ·29	... ...	19
13	Fr 29	6 ·38	6 ·05	20
14	Sa 30	7 ·45	7 ·14	21
15	Su 31	8 ·50	8 ·22	22

SOLAR: Cyclic Sidereal Year, Month and Day.	Week-Day English Month and Day.	Tithi Ending Moment.	Nakshatra Ending Moment.	Muhammadan Year, Month and Day.
	Nov.			
Rakshasa Tula—Aippasi. 16	Mo 1	Asv. Bah. 9 ·53	9 ·28	Zi-l-hijja. 23
17	Tu 2	10 ·54	10 ·33	24
18	We 3	11 ·52	11 ·34	25
19	Th 4	12 ·50	12 ·34	26
20	Fr 5	13 ·45	13 ·32	27
21	Sa 6	14 ·39	14 ·28	28
22	Su 7	—A ·31	15 ·24	29
23	Mo 8	Kartika Sukla 1 ·22	16 ·18	—30
24	Tu 9	2 ·13	17 ·11	H. 1334 Muharram. 1
25	We 10	{ 3 ·02 / 4 ·93 }	{ 18 ·04 / 19 ·97 }	2
26	Th 11	5 ·83	20 ·91	3
27	Fr 12	6 ·74	21 ·85	4
28	Sa 13	7 ·67	22 ·80	5
29	Su 14	8 ·61	23 ·76	6
—30	Mo 15	9 ·54	24 ·74	7
Rakshasa Vrischika—Kartigai. 1	Tu 16	10 ·51	25 ·75	8
2	We 17	11 ·51	26 ·76	9
3	Th 18	12 ·52	27 ·80	10
4	Fr 19	13 ·54	1 ·86	11
5	Sa 20	14 ·59	2 ·93	12
6	Su 21	P ·67	... ...	13
7	Mo 22	1 ·75	3 ·04	14
8	Tu 23	2 ·84	4 ·14	15
9	We 24	3 ·92	5 ·24	16
10	Th 25	4 ·99	6 ·35	17
11	Fr 26	... ...	7 ·44	18
12	Sa 27	Bahula 5 ·07	8 ·52	19
13	Su 28	6 ·13	9 ·60	20
14	Mo 29	7 ·16	10 ·64	21
15	Tu 30	8 ·16	11 ·66	22

SOLAR: Cyclic Sidereal Year, Month and Day.	Week-Day English Month and Day.	Tithi Ending Moment.	Nakshatra Ending Moment.	Muhammadan Year, Month and Day.
	Dec.			
Rakshasa Vrischika—Kartigai. 16	We 1	9 ·16	12 ·66	H. 1334 Muharram. 23
17	Th 2	10 ·12	13 ·65	24
18	Fr 3	11 ·06	14 ·62	25
19	Sa 4	{ 12 ·00 / 13 ·94 }	15 ·58	26
20	Su 5	14 ·85	16 ·52	27
21	Mo 6	—A ·75	17 ·45	28
22	Tu 7	Margasira Sukla 1 ·66	18 ·38	29
23	We 8	2 ·56	19 ·32	—30
24	Th 9	3 ·46	20 ·25	H. 1334 Safar. 1
25	Fr 10	4 ·36	21 ·19	2
26	Sa 11	5 ·29	22 ·14	3
27	Su 12	6 ·23	23 ·09	4
28	Mo 13	7 ·17	24 ·08	5
29	Tu 14	8 ·16	25 ·07	6
—30	We 15	9 ·14	26 ·08	7
Rakshasa Dhanus—Margali. 1	Th 16	10 ·16	27 ·11	8
2	Fr 17	11 ·19	1 ·16	9
3	Sa 18	12 ·24	2 ·24	10
4	Su 19	13 ·31	3 ·34	11
5	Mo 20	14 ·39	4 ·44	12
6	Tu 21	P ·49	5 ·54	13
7	We 22	1 ·57	6 ·65	14
8	Th 23	2 ·65	7 ·75	15
9	Fr 24	3 ·72	8 ·84	16
10	Sa 25	4 ·77	9 ·91	17
11	Su 26	5 ·80	10 ·95	18
12	Mo 27	6 ·81	11 ·98	19
13	Tu 28	Bahula 7 ·80	12 ·99	20
14	We 29	8 ·76	13 ·98	21
15	Th 30	9 ·72	14 ·95	22
16	Fr 31	10 ·65	15 ·91	23

15. Svati. 16. Visak. 17. Anur. 18. Jyesh. 19. Mula. 20. P. Ash. 21. U. Ash. 22. Sravn. 23. Dani. 24. Satab. 25. P. Bhad. 26. U. Bhad. 27. Rev.

A. D. 1916.
Solar Eclipse. ●
Lunar Eclipse. ○

Mesha Sankranti (Commencement of Indian Sidereal Year).
(Surya Sid.) April 12·76. **Saka 1838.** **Kaliyuga 5017.**
(Arya Sid.) April 12·65. **(S. Cycle) Anala** (Nala).

SOLAR reckoning: Cyclic Sidereal Year, Month and Day; Week-Day, English Month and Day. LUNAR reckoning: Tithi Ending Moment; Nakshatra Ending Moment; Muhammadan Year, Month, and Day.

Jan.

Solar month	Cyclic Sidereal Day	Week-Day	Jan.	Lunar month	Tithi	Ending Moment	Nakshatra	Ending Moment	Muhammadan month	Day
Rakshasa Dhanus—Margali.	17	Sa	1	Mr. Bah.	11	·57	16	·85	Safar.	24
	18	Su	2		12	·48	17	·79		25
	19	Mo	3		13	·39	18	·73		26
	20	Tu	4		14	·29	19	·66		27
	21	We	5		—A	·19	20	·59		28
	22	Th	6		1	·11	21	·53		—29
	23	Fr	7		2 / 3	·01 / ·94	22	·47	H. 1334 Rabi-ul-awwal.	1
	24	Sa	8	Sukla	4	·88	23	·44		2
	25	Su	9		5	·82	24	·41		3
	26	Mo	10		6	·80	25	·39		4
	27	Tu	11		7	·79	26	·40		5
	28	We	12		8	·81	27	·43		6
	—29	Th	13		9	·83	1	·47		7
Rakshasa Makara—Tai.	1	Fr	14		10	·89	2	·55		8
	2	Sa	15		11	·96	3	·64		9
	3	Su	16		...	...	4	·73		10
	4	Mo	17	Pausha	12	·05	5	·84		11
	5	Tu	18		13	·14	6	·95		12
	6	We	19		14	·23	...	...		13
	7	Th	○20		P	·31	7	·06		14
	8	Fr	21	Bahula	1	·87	8	·14		15
	9	Sa	22		2	·42	9	·22		16
	10	Su	23		3	·45	10	·27		17
	11	Mo	24		4	·46	11	·30		18
	12	Tu	25		5	·44	12	·32		19
	13	We	26		6	·41	13	·31		20
	14	Th	27		7	·36	14	·29		21
	15	Fr	28		8	·28	15	·24		22
	16	Sa	29		9	:20	16	·19		23
	17	Su	30		10	·11	17	·13		24
	18	Mo	31		11 / 12	·03 / ·92	18	·07		25

Feb.

Solar month	Cyclic Sidereal Day	Week-Day	Feb.	Lunar month	Tithi	Ending Moment	Nakshatra	Ending Moment	Muhammadan month	Day
	19	Tu	1		13	·82	19 / 20	·00 / ·93		26
	20	We	2		14	·73	21	·86		27
	21	Th	3		—A	·64	22	·80		28
	22	Fr	4	Sukla	1	·57	23	·77		29
	23	Sa	5		2	·51	24	·73		—30
	24	Su	6		3	·46	25	·72	H. 1334 Rabi-ul-akhir.	1
	25	Mo	7		4	·44	26	·72		2
	26	Tu	8		5	·42	27	·74		3
	27	We	9		6	·44	1	·79		4
	28	Th	10		7	·47	2	·86		5
	29	Fr	11		8	·53	3	·94		6
	—30	Sa	12		9	·60	...	...		7
Rakshasa Kumbha—Masi.	1	Su	13		10	·69	4	·03		8
	2	Mo	14		11	·77	5	·14		9
	3	Tu	15		12	·86	6	·25		10
	4	We	16		13	·94	7	·36		11
	5	Th	17	Magha	...	...	8	·45		12
	6	Fr	18		14	·00	9	·52		13
	7	Sa	19		P	·06	10	·58		14
	8	Su	20		1	·07	11	·63		15
	9	Mo	21		2	·08	12	·64		16
	10	Tu	22		3	·06	13	·64		17
	11	We	23		4 / 5	·04 / ·97	14	·61		18
	12	Th	24	Bahula	6	·90	15	·58		19
	13	Fr	25		7	·82	16	·53		20
	14	Sa	26		8	·73	17	·47		21
	15	Su	27		9	·64	18	·41		22
	16	Mo	28		10	·54	19	·34		23
	17	Tu	29		11	·45	20	·27		24

March

Solar month	Cyclic Sidereal Day	Week-Day	March	Lunar month	Tithi	Ending Moment	Nakshatra	Ending Moment	Muhammadan month	Day
Rakshasa Kumbha—Masi.	18	We	1	Bah.	12	·84	21	·20	R.-akhir.	25
	19	Th	2		13	·26	22	·15		26
	20	Fr	3		14	·18	23	·10		27
	21	Sa	4		—A	·11	24	·06		28
	22	Su	5	Sukla	1	·07	25	·04		—29
	23	Mo	6		2	·05	26	·04	H. 1334 Jumadal-awwal.	1
	24	Tu	7		3	·04	27	·07		2
	25	We	8		4	·05	1	·10		3
	26	Th	9		5	·09	2	·16		4
	27	Fr	10		6	·14	3	·24		5
	28	Sa	11		7	·21	4	·33		6
	29	Su	12		8	·30	5	·45		7
	—30	Mo	13		9	·38	6	·55		8
Rakshasa Mina—Panguni.	1	Tu	14		10	·47	7	·66		9
	2	We	15		11	·55	8	·75		10
	3	Th	16	Phalguna	12	·61	9	·83		11
	4	Fr	17		13	·65	10	·89		12
	5	Sa	18		14	·67	11	·94		13
	6	Su	19		P	·68	12	·96		14
	7	Mo	20	Bahula	1	·66	13	·96		15
	8	Tu	21		2	·62	14	·94		16
	9	We	22		3	·56	15	·91		17
	10	Th	23		4	·49	16	·87		18
	11	Fr	24		5	·41	17	·81		19
	12	Sa	25		6	·32	18	·75		20
	13	Su	26		7	·21	19	·67		21
	14	Mo	27		8	·11	20	·60		22
	15	Tu	28		9 / 10	·02 / ·92	21	·54		23
	16	We	29		11	·84	22	·48		24
	17	Th	30		12	·76	23	·43		25
	18	Fr	31		13	·70	24	·39		26

April

Solar month	Cyclic Sidereal Day	Week-Day	April	Lunar month	Tithi	Ending Moment	Nakshatra	Ending Moment	Muhammadan month	Day
	19	Sa	1		14	·65	25	·37		27
	20	Su	2		—A	·62	26	·37		28
	21	Mo	3	Sukla	1	·61	27	·38		29
	22	Tu	4		2	·63	1	·41		—30
	23	We	5		3	·67	2	·47	H. 1334 Jumadal-akhir.	1
	24	Th	6		4	·72	3	·54		2
	25	Fr	7		5	·80	4	·64		3
	26	Sa	8		6	·87	5	·74		4
	27	Su	9		7	·94	6	·85		5
	28	Mo	10		...	...	7	·95		6
	29	Tu	11		8	·03	...	...		7
	—30	We	12		9	·11	8	·05		8
Anala Mesha—Chittirai.	1	Th	13		10	·17	9	·14		9
	2	Fr	14		11	·21	10	·21		10
	3	Sa	15	Chaitra	12	·23	11	·26		11
	4	Su	16		13	·23	12	·28		12
	5	Mo	17		14	·22	13	·29		13
	6	Tu	18		P	·18	14	·27		14
	7	We	19		1	·12	15	·25		15
	8	Th	20		2 / 3	·05 / ·96	16	·21		16
	9	Fr	21		4	·87	17	·15		17
	10	Sa	22		5	·76	18	·08		18
	11	Su	23		6	·67	19 / 20	·01 / ·95		19
	12	Mo	24	Bahula	7	·56	21	·88		20
	13	Tu	25		8	·46	22	·82		21
	14	We	26		9	·38	23	·76		22
	15	Th	27		10	·30	24	·72		23
	16	Fr	28		11	·24	25	·70		24
	17	Sa	29		12	·18	26	·69		25
	18	Su	30		13	·16	27	·70		26

May

Solar month	Cyclic Sidereal Day	Week-Day	May	Lunar month	Tithi	Ending Moment	Nakshatra	Ending Moment	Muhammadan month	Day
Anala Mesha—Chittirai.	19	Mo	1		14	·14	1	·73		27
	20	Tu	2		—A	·15	2	·78		28
	21	We	3	Sukla	1	·20	3	·85		—29
	22	Th	4		2	·24	4	·94	H. 1334 Rajab.	1
	23	Fr	5		3	·31	...	...		2
	24	Sa	6		4	·38	5	·04		3
	25	Su	7		5	·47	6	·15		4
	26	Mo	8		6	·55	7	·25		5
	27	Tu	9		7	·64	8	·35		6
	28	We	10		8	·69	9	·45		7
	29	Th	11		9	·73	10	·52		8
	30	Fr	12		10	·75	11	·57		9
	—31	Sa	13		11	·75	12	·60		10
Anala Vrishabha—Vaikasi.	1	Su	14	Vaisakha	12	·74	13	·61		11
	2	Mo	15		13	·69	14	·61		12
	3	Tu	16		14	·63	15	·58		13
	4	We	17		P	·56	16	·54		14
	5	Th	18	Bahula	1	·47	17	·48		15
	6	Fr	19		2	·38	18	·42		16
	7	Sa	20		3	·27	19	·36		17
	8	Su	21		4	·18	20	·29		18
	9	Mo	22		5 / 6	·07 / ·93	21	·22		19
	10	Tu	23		7	·88	22	·16		20
	11	We	24		8	·81	23	·10		21
	12	Th	25		9	·75	24	.06		22
	13	Fr	26		10	·69	25	·03		23
	14	Sa	27		11	·67	26	·01		24
	15	Su	28		12	·64	27	·02		25
	16	Mo	29		13	·66	1	·04		26
	17	Tu	30		14	·70	2	·09		27
	18	We	31		—A	·74	3	·16		28

June

Solar month	Cyclic Sidereal Day	Week-Day	June	Lunar month	Tithi	Ending Moment	Nakshatra	Ending Moment	Muhammadan month	Day
	19	Th	1	Sukla	1	·81	4	·24		29
	20	Fr	2		2	·88	5	·34		—30
	21	Sa	3		3	·97	6	·45	H. 1334 Shaban.	1
	22	Su	4		...	...	7	·55		2
	23	Mo	5		4	·04	8	·66		3
	24	Tu	6		5	·13	9	·75		4
	25	We	7		6	·18	10	·83		5
	26	Th	8		7	·23	11	·88		6
	27	Fr	9		8	·24	12	·92		7
	28	Sa	10		9	·24	13	·94		8
	29	Su	11		10	·23	14	·94		9
	30	Mo	12		11	·18	15	·91		10
	—31	Tu	13		12	·13	16	·87		11
Anala Mithuna—Ani.	1	We	14	Jyeshtha	13 / 14	·06 / ·97	17	·82		12
	2	Th	15		P	·88	18	·77		13
	3	Fr	16	Bahula	1	·78	19	·70		14
	4	Sa	17		2	·68	20	·63		15
	5	Su	18		3	·56	21	·56		16
	6	Mo	19		4	·47	22	·49		17
	7	Tu	20		5	·38	23	·43		18
	8	We	21		6	·30	24	·39		19
	9	Th	22		7	·23	25	·36		20
	10	Fr	23		8	·18	26	·34		21
	11	Sa	24		9	·14	27	·34		22
	12	Su	25		10	·12	1	·36		23
	13	Mo	26		11	·14	2	·41		24
	14	Tu	27		12	·16	3	·47		25
	15	We	28		13	·21	4	·55		26
	16	Th	29		14	·28	5	·64		27
	17	Fr	30		—A	·36	6	·74		28

Naksh :—1. Asvn. 2. Bhar. 3. Krit. 4. Rohi. 5. Mrig. 6. Ardh. 7. Punar. 8. Push. 9. Aslesh. 10. Magh. 11. P. Phal. 12. U. Phal. 13. Hasta. 14 Chit.

A. D. 1916.
A.—Amavasya.
P.—Paurnami.

Kollam 1092, Commences { N. Malabar—Sept. S. Malabar—Aug.

Hijra 1335, Commences, Oct. 28.

Vikrama 1973.
Bengal San 1323.
(N. Cycle) Vibhava.

SOLAR reckoning: Cyclic Sidereal Year, Month and Day; Week-Day English Month and Day. LUNAR reckoning: Tithi Ending Moment; Nakshatra Ending Moment; Muhammadan Year, Month and Day.

July — Anala Mithuna—Ani. / Anala Karkata—Adi. — Sukla / Ashadha / Bahula — H. 1334 Ramzan.

Cyclic Sidereal Year, Month and Day	Week-Day English Month and Day	Tithi Ending Moment	Nakshatra Ending Moment	Muhammadan Year, Month and Day
18	Sa 1	1 ·43	7 ·86	—29
19	Su 2	2 ·52	8 ·96	1
20	Mo 3	3 ·60	... ...	2
21	Tu 4	4 ·65	9 ·06	3
22	We 5	5 ·70	10 ·13	4
23	Th 6	6 ·72	11 ·19	5
24	Fr 7	7 ·72	12 ·24	6
25	Sa 8	8 ·70	13 ·26	7
26	Su 9	9 ·67	14 ·26	8
27	Mo 10	10 ·60	15 ·24	9
28	Tu 11	11 ·53	16 ·20	10
29	We 12	12 ·45	17 ·16	11
30	Th 13	13 ·35	18 ·11	12
31	Fr 14	14 ·25	19 ·04 20 ·97	13
—32	Sa ○ 15	P ·15	21 ·90	14
1	Su 16	1 ·05 2 ·94	22 ·83	15
2	Mo 17	3 ·85	23 ·78	16
3	Tu 18	4 ·78	24 ·73	17
4	We 19	5 ·71	25 ·69	18
5	Th 20	6 ·65	26 ·66	19
6	Fr 21	7 ·62	27 ·66	20
7	Sa 22	8 ·61	1 ·68	21
8	Su 23	9 ·61	2 ·72	22
9	Mo 24	10 ·64	3 ·77	23
10	Tu 25	11 ·68	4 ·85	24
11	We 26	12 ·75	5 ·94	25
12	Th 27	13 ·82	... ...	26
13	Fr 28	14 ·91	6 ·05	27
14	Sa 29	... ...	7 ·16	28
15	Su ● 30	—A ·00	8 ·26	29
16	Mo 31	1 ·07	9 ·36	—30

Aug. — Anala Simha—Avani. — Sukla / Sravana / Bahula / Suk. — H. 1334 Shawwal.

Cyclic Sidereal Year, Month and Day	Week-Day English Month and Day	Tithi Ending Moment	Nakshatra Ending Moment	Muhammadan Year, Month and Day
17	Tu 1	2 ·13	10 ·44	1
18	We 2	3 ·17	11 ·51	2
19	Th 3	4 ·20	12 ·56	3
20	Fr 4	5 ·21	13 ·58	4
21	Sa 5	6 ·18	14 ·50	5
22	Su 6	7 ·15	15 ·57	6
23	Mo 7	8 ·10	16 ·54	7
24	Tu 8	9 ·04 10 ·94	17 ·50	8
25	We 9	11 ·84	18 ·44	9
26	Th 10	12 ·75	19 ·38	10
27	Fr 11	13 ·65	20 ·31	11
28	Sa 12	14 ·55	21 ·24	12
29	Su 13	P ·44	22 ·18	13
30	Mo 14	1 ·36	23 ·11	14
—31	Tu 15	2 ·27	24 ·06	15
1	We 16	3 ·22	25 ·02 26 ·99	16
2	Th 17	4 ·15	27 ·99	17
3	Fr 18	5 ·11	... ...	18
4	Sa 19	6 ·10	1 ·00	19
5	Su 20	7 ·11	2 ·08	20
6	Mo 21	8 ·14	3 ·08	21
7	Tu 22	9 ·19	4 ·15	22
8	We 23	10 ·25	5 ·25	23
9	Th 24	11 ·32	6 ·35	24
10	Fr 25	12 ·40	7 ·45	25
11	Sa 26	13 ·50	8 ·56	26
12	Su 27	14 ·57	9 ·66	27
13	Mo 28	—A ·64	10 ·75	28
14	Tu 29	1 ·67	11 ·82	—29
15	We 30	2 ·70	12 ·87	1
16	Th 31	3 ·71	13 ·90	2

Sep. — Anala Simha—Avani. / Anala Kanya—Purattasi. — Sukla / Bhadrapada / Bahula — H. 1334 Zi-l-ka'da.

Cyclic Sidereal Year, Month and Day	Week-Day English Month and Day	Tithi Ending Moment	Nakshatra Ending Moment	Muhammadan Year, Month and Day
17	Fr 1	4 ·69	14 ·91	3
18	Sa 2	5 ·66	15 ·90	4
19	Su 3	6 ·61	16 ·88	5
20	Mo 4	7 ·55	17 ·83	6
21	Tu 5	8 ·46	18 ·78	7
22	We 6	9 ·36	19 ·72	8
23	Th 7	10 ·26	20 ·65	9
24	Fr 8	11 ·17	21 ·59	10
25	Sa 9	12 ·06 13 ·96	22 ·52	11
26	Su 10	14 ·88	23 ·45	12
27	Mo 11	P ·79	24 ·39	13
28	Tu 12	1 ·73	25 ·35	14
29	We 13	2 ·67	26 ·33	15
30	Th 14	3 ·65	27 ·31	16
—31	Fr 15	4 ·63	1 ·32	17
1	Sa 16	5 ·65	2 ·34	18
2	Su 17	6 ·66	3 ·39	19
3	Mo 18	7 ·71	4 ·47	20
4	Tu 19	8 ·77	5 ·55	21
5	We 20	9 ·85	6 ·65	22
6	Th 21	10 ·94	7 ·75	23
7	Fr 22	... ...	8 ·86	24
8	Sa 23	11 ·02	9 ·96	25
9	Su 24	12 ·09	... ...	26
10	Mo 25	13 ·17	10 ·06	27
11	Tu 26	14 ·21	11 ·13	28
12	We 27	—A ·24	12 ·19	29
13	Th 28	1 ·25	13 ·22	—30
14	Fr 29	2 ·24	14 ·23	1
15	Sa 30	3 ·21	15 ·23	2

Oct. — Anala Tula—Aippasi. — Sukla / Asvina / Bahula / K. Suk. — H. 1334 Zi-l-hijja. / H. 1335 Muharm.

Cyclic Sidereal Year, Month and Day	Week-Day English Month and Day	Tithi Ending Moment	Nakshatra Ending Moment	Muhammadan Year, Month and Day
16	Su 1	4 ·16	16 ·21	3
17	Mo 2	5 ·09	17 ·17	4
18	Tu 3	6 ·00 7 ·91	18 ·11	5
19	We 4	8 ·82	19 ·05 20 ·99	6
20	Th 5	9 ·73	21 ·92	7
21	Fr 6	10 ·62	22 ·85	8
22	Sa 7	11 ·52	23 ·79	9
23	Su 8	12 ·43	24 ·73	10
24	Mo 9	13 ·35	25 ·69	11
25	Tu 10	14 ·29	26 ·66	12
26	We 11	P ·23	27 ·64	13
27	Th 12	1 ·21	1 ·64	14
28	Fr 13	2 ·19	2 ·66	15
29	Sa 14	3 ·21	3 ·70	16
30	Su 15	4 ·23	4 ·77	17
—31	Mo 16	5 ·28	5 ·85	18
1	Tu 17	6 ·34	6 ·95	19
2	We 18	7 ·42	... ...	20
3	Th 19	8 ·51	7 ·05	21
4	Fr 20	9 ·59	8 ·16	22
5	Sa 21	10 ·69	9 ·27	23
6	Su 22	11 ·75	10 ·36	24
7	Mo 23	12 ·80	11 ·44	25
8	Tu 24	13 ·82	12 ·50	26
9	We 25	14 ·83	13 ·54	27
10	Th 26	—A ·82	14 ·56	28
11	Fr 27	1 ·78	15 ·56	—29
12	Sa 28	2 ·74	16 ·54	1
13	Su 29	3 ·68	17 ·50	2
14	Mo 30	4 ·60	18 ·45	3
15	Tu 31	5 ·50	19 ·40	4

Nov. — Anala Tula—Aippasi. / Anala Vrischika—Kartigai. — Sukla / Karttika / Bahula — H. 1335 Muharram.

Cyclic Sidereal Year, Month and Day	Week-Day English Month and Day	Tithi Ending Moment	Nakshatra Ending Moment	Muhammadan Year, Month and Day
16	We 1	6 ·40	20 ·33	5
17	Th 2	7 ·31	21 ·26	6
18	Fr 3	8 ·20	22 ·19	7
19	Sa 4	9 ·12	23 ·12	8
20	Su 5	10 ·03 11 ·95	24 ·07	9
21	Mo 6	12 ·88	25 ·02 26 ·98	10
22	Tu 7	13 ·83	27 ·96	11
23	We 8	14 ·81	1 ·96	12
24	Th 9	P ·79	2 ·97	13
25	Fr 10	1 ·81	... ...	14
26	Sa 11	2 ·83	3 ·02	15
27	Su 12	3 ·89	4 ·08	16
28	Mo 13	4 ·96	5 ·15	17
—29	Tu 14	... ...	6 ·25	18
1	We 15	5 ·05	7 ·35	19
2	Th 16	6 ·13	8 ·46	20
3	Fr 17	7 ·21	9 ·57	21
4	Sa 18	8 ·30	10 ·66	22
5	Su 19	9 ·36	11 ·75	23
6	Mo 20	10 ·41	12 ·81	24
7	Tu 21	11 ·44	13 ·86	25
8	We 22	12 ·46	14 ·88	26
9	Th 23	13 ·44	15 ·88	27
10	Fr 24	14 ·40	16 ·87	28
11	Sa 25	—A ·35	17 ·83	29
12	Su 26	1 ·30	18 ·80	—30
13	Mo 27	2 ·22	19 ·74	1
14	Tu 28	3 ·12	20 ·67	2
15	We 29	4 ·03 5 ·93	21 ·60	3
16	Th 30	6 ·84	22 ·53	4

Dec. — Anala Dhanus—Margali. — Sukla / Margasira / Bahula / Suk. / Pausha — H. 1335 Safar. / R.-awwal.

Cyclic Sidereal Year, Month and Day	Week-Day English Month and Day	Tithi Ending Moment	Nakshatra Ending Moment	Muhammadan Year, Month and Day
17	Fr 1	7 ·74	23 ·46	5
18	Sa 2	8 ·65	24 ·41	6
19	Su 3	9 ·56	25 ·36	7
20	Mo 4	10 ·50	26 ·31	8
21	Tu 5	11 ·46	27 ·29	9
22	We 6	12 ·43	1 ·28	10
23	Th 7	13 ·43	2 ·30	11
24	Fr 8	14 ·44	3 ·33	12
25	Sa 9	P ·47	4 ·39	13
26	Su 10	1 ·53	5 ·46	14
27	Mo 11	2 ·60	6 ·55	15
28	Tu 12	3 ·69	7 ·66	16
29	We 13	4 ·77	8 ·76	17
—30	Th 14	5 ·87	9 ·87	18
1	Fr 15	6 ·94	10 ·97	19
2	Sa 16	... ...	... ...	20
3	Su 17	7 ·00	11 ·05	21
4	Mo 18	8 ·06	12 ·13	22
5	Tu 19	9 ·08	13 ·17	23
6	We 20	10 ·09	14 ·20	24
7	Th 21	11 ·07	15 ·21	25
8	Fr 22	12 ·05 13 ·99	16 ·19	26
9	Sa 23	14 ·92	17 ·17	27
10	Su 24	—A ·85	18 ·13	28
11	Mo 25	1 ·75	19 ·07	—29
12	Tu 26	2 ·66	20 ·01 21 ·94	1
13	We 27	3 ·56	22 ·87	2
14	Th 28	4 ·47	23 ·81	3
15	Fr 29	5 ·38	24 ·74	4
16	Sa 30	6 ·30	25 ·69	5
17	Su 31	7 ·21	26 ·64	6

15. Svati. 16. Visak. 17. Anur. 18. Jyesh. 19. Mula. 20 P. Ash. 21. U. Ash. 22. Sravn. 23. Dani. 24. Satab. 25. P. Bhad. 26. U. Bhad. 27. Rev.

A. D. 1917. **Mesha Sankranti** (Commencement of Indian Sidereal Year).
Solar Eclipse. ● **(Surya Sid.) April 13·02.** **Saka 1839.** **Kaliyuga 5018.**
Lunar Eclipse. ○ **(Arya Sid.) April 12·91.** **(S. Cycle) Pingala.**

SOLAR reckoning: Cyclic Sidereal Year, Month and Day; Week-Day, English Month and Day. LUNAR reckoning: Tithi Ending Moment; Nakshatra Ending Moment; Muhammadan Year, Month and Day.

Jan.

Solar Year—Month	Cyclic Sidereal Day	Week-Day	English Day	Lunar Month / Paksha	Tithi	Tithi Ending Moment	Nakshatra	Nakshatra Ending Moment	Muhammadan Year, Month	Muhammadan Day
Anala Dhanus—Margali.	18	Mo	1	Sukla	8	·14	27	·61	H. 1335 Rabi-ul-awwal.	7
	19	Tu	2		9	·10	1	·61		8
	20	We	3		10	·08	2	·62		9
	21	Th	4		11	·07	3	·65		10
	22	Fr	5		12	·08	4	·69		11
	23	Sa	6		13	·13	5	·76		12
	24	Su	7	Pausha	14	·18	6	·86		13
	25	Mo	○ 8		P	·25	7	·95		14
	26	Tu	9		1	·34	...	...		15
	27	We	10		2	·42	8	·06		16
	28	Th	11		3	·51	9	·17		17
	—29	Fr	12		4	·59	10	·27		18
	1	Sa	13		5	·66	11	·36		19
	2	Su	14	Bahula	6	·70	12	·44		20
	3	Mo	15		7	·73	13	·49		21
	4	Tu	16		8	·74	14	·52		22
	5	We	17		9	·72	15	·53		23
	6	Th	18		10	·69	16	·52		24
	7	Fr	19		11	·64	17	·50		25
	8	Sa	20		12	·57	18	·46		26
	9	Su	21		13	·49	19	·41		27
	10	Mo	22		14	·39	20	·35		28
	11	Tu	● 23		—A	·30	21	·28		29
	12	We	24		1	·19	22	·22		—30
	13	Th	25		2	·10	23	·15		1
	14	Fr	26		3 4	·01 ·92	24	·08		2
Anala Makara—Tai.	15	Sa	27		5	·85	25 26	·02 ·98		3
	16	Su	28		6	·79	27	·95		4
	17	Mo	29	Sukla	7	·75	1	·94		5
	18	Tu	30		8	·73	2	·94		6
	19	We	31		9	·71	3	·96		7

Feb.

Solar Year—Month	Cyclic Sidereal Day	Week-Day	English Day	Lunar Month / Paksha	Tithi	Tithi Ending Moment	Nakshatra	Nakshatra Ending Moment	Muhammadan Year, Month	Muhammadan Day
	20	Th	1		10	·72	...	...	H. 1335 Rabi-ul-akhir.	8
	21	Fr	2		11	·77	4	·00		9
	22	Sa	3		12	·83	5	·08		10
	23	Su	4		13	·90	6	·16		11
	24	Mo	5	Magha	14	·98	7	·25		12
	25	Tu	6		...	...	8	·36		13
	26	We	7		P	·07	9	·46		14
	27	Th	8		1	·16	10	·57		15
	28	Fr	9		2	·23	11	·67		16
	29	Sa	10		3	·30	12	·74		17
	—30	Su	11		4	·34	13	·80		18
	1	Mo	12		5	·36	14	·84		19
	2	Tu	13		6	·37	15	·85		20
	3	We	14	Bahula	7	·36	16	·86		21
	4	Th	15		8	·32	17	·83		22
	5	Fr	16		9	·25	18	·80		23
	6	Sa	17		10	·19	19	·74		24
	7	Su	18		11	·11	20	·68		25
Anala Kumbha—Masi.	8	Mo	19		12 13	·02 ·92	21	·63		26
	9	Tu	20		14	·82	22	·56		27
	10	We	21		—A	·72	23	·49		28
	11	Th	22	Suk.	1	·64	24	·42		—29
	12	Fr	23		2	·54	25	·36	J.-awwal.	1
	13	Sa	24		3	·46	26	·32		2
	14	Su	25	Phalg.	4	·40	27	·28		3
	15	Mo	26		5	·36	1	·20		4
	16	Tu	27		6	·34	2	·26		5
	17	We	28		7	·33	3	·28		6

March

Solar Year—Month	Cyclic Sidereal Day	Week-Day	English Day	Lunar Month / Paksha	Tithi	Tithi Ending Moment	Nakshatra	Nakshatra Ending Moment	Muhammadan Year, Month	Muhammadan Day
Anala Kumbha—Masi.	18	Th	1	Sukla	8	·35	4	·32	H. 1335 Jumadal-awwal.	7
	19	Fr	2		9	·39	5	·38		8
	20	Sa	3		10	·44	6	·46		9
	21	Su	4		11	·51	7	·55		10
	22	Mo	5	Phalguna	12	·60	8	·66		11
	23	Tu	6		13	·69	9	·76		12
	24	We	7		14	·78	10	·88		13
	25	Th	8		P	·86	11	·97		14
	26	Fr	9		1	·91	...	...		15
	27	Sa	10		2	·95	12	·05		16
	28	Su	11		3	·97	13	·11		17
	29	Mo	12		4	·97	14	·15		18
	—30	Tu	13		5	·96	15	·18		19
	1	We	14		6	·92	16	·18		20
	2	Th	15	Bahula	7	·86	17	·16		21
	3	Fr	16		8	·78	18	·13		22
	4	Sa	17		9	·71	19	·08		23
	5	Su	18		10	·61	20 21	·03 ·96		24
	6	Mo	19		11	·51	22	·89		25
	7	Tu	20		12	·41	23	·82		26
	8	We	21		13	·31	24	·76		27
	9	Th	22		14	·23	25	·70		28
	10	Fr	23		—A	·13	26	·65		29
	11	Sa	24		1 2	·06 ·99	27	·61		—30
Anala Mina—Panguni.	12	Su	25		3	·95	1	·59		1
	13	Mo	26		4	·93	2	·58		2
	14	Tu	27		5	·91	3	·59		3
	15	We	28		6	·94	4	·64		4
	16	Th	29	Sukla	7	·97	5	·69		5
	17	Fr	30		...	...	6	·76		6
	18	Sa	31		8	·03	7	·85		7

April

Solar Year—Month	Cyclic Sidereal Day	Week-Day	English Day	Lunar Month / Paksha	Tithi	Tithi Ending Moment	Nakshatra	Nakshatra Ending Moment	Muhammadan Year, Month	Muhammadan Day
	19	Su	1		9	·10	8	·95	H. 1335 Jumadal-akhir.	8
	20	Mo	2		10	·18	...	...		9
	21	Tu	3		11	·27	9	·07		10
	22	We	4		12	·35	10	·18		11
	23	Th	5	Chaitra	13	·48	11	·27		12
	24	Fr	6		14	·48	12	·36		13
	25	Sa	7		P	·53	13	·42		14
	26	Su	8		1	·55	14	·48		15
	27	Mo	9		2	·55	15	·50		16
	28	Tu	10		3	·52	16	·51		17
	29	We	11		4	·48	17	·49		18
	—30	Th	12		5	·42	18	·46		19
	1	Fr	13	Bahula	6	·34	19	·42		20
	2	Sa	14		7	·27	20	·37		21
	3	Su	15		8	·17	21	·30		22
	4	Mo	16		9 10	·08 ·97	22	·28		23
	5	Tu	17		11	·87	23	·16		24
	6	We	18		12	·78	24	·10		25
Pingala Mesha—Chittirai.	7	Th	19		13	·68	25 26	·04 ·98		26
	8	Fr	20		14	·60	27	·94		27
	9	Sa	21		—A	·53	1	·91		28
	10	Su	22	Sukla	1	·50	2	·90		—29
	11	Mo	23		2	·47	3	·92	H. 1335 Rajab.	1
	12	Tu	24		3	·46	4	·95		2
	13	We	25	Vaisakha	4	·47	...	...		3
	14	Th	26		5	·51	5	·00		4
	15	Fr	27		6	·57	6	·07		5
	16	Sa	28		7	·64	7	·15		6
	17	Su	29		8	·71	8	·26		7
	18	Mo	30		9	·80	9	·37		8

May

Solar Year—Month	Cyclic Sidereal Day	Week-Day	English Day	Lunar Month / Paksha	Tithi	Tithi Ending Moment	Nakshatra	Nakshatra Ending Moment	Muhammadan Year, Month	Muhammadan Day
Pingala Mesha—Chittirai.	19	Tu	1	Suk.	10	·88	10	·47	H. 1335 Rajab.	9
	20	We	2		11	·96	11	·57		10
	21	Th	3	Vaisakha	...	...	12	·66		11
	22	Fr	4		12	·01	13	·74		12
	23	Sa	5		13	·06	14	·79		13
	24	Su	6		14	·06	15	·82		14
	25	Mo	7		P	·07	16	·83		15
	26	Tu	8		1	·05	17	·82		16
	27	We	9		2 3	·02 ·95	18	·80		17
	28	Th	10		4	·86	19	·76		18
	29	Fr	11		5	·78	20	·70		19
	30	Sa	12		6	·69	21	·64		20
	—31	Su	13	Bahula	7	·60	22	·57		21
	1	Mo	14		8	·49	23	·50		22
	2	Tu	15		9	·39	24	·44		23
	3	We	16		10	·29	25	·38		24
	4	Th	17		11	·20	26	·32		25
	5	Fr	18		12	·12	27	·27		26
	6	Sa	19		13	·06	1	·24		27
	7	Su	20		14 A	·01 ·98	2	·23		28
	8	Mo	21		1	·97	3	·24		29
	9	Tu	22		2	·98	4	·26		—30
Pingala Vrishabha—Vaikasi.	10	We	23		...	...	5	·31		1
	11	Th	24		3	·02	6	·37		2
	12	Fr	25		4	·07	7	·46		3
	13	Sa	26		5	·14	8	·56		4
	14	Su	27		6	·22	9	·67		5
	15	Mo	28	Sukla	7	·29	10	·77		6
	16	Tu	29		8	·38	11	·87		7
	17	We	30		9	·46	12	·97		8
	18	Th	31		10	·51	...	...		9

June

Solar Year—Month	Cyclic Sidereal Day	Week-Day	English Day	Lunar Month / Paksha	Tithi	Tithi Ending Moment	Nakshatra	Nakshatra Ending Moment	Muhammadan Year, Month	Muhammadan Day
	19	Fr	1		11	·54	13	·05	H. 1335 Shaban.	10
	20	Sa	2		12	·56	14	·10		11
	21	Su	3	Jyeshtha	13	·57	15	·14		12
	22	Mo	4		14	·54	16	·15		13
	23	Tu	5		P	·51	17	·16		14
	24	We	6		1	·45	18	·13		15
	25	Th	7		2	·38	19	·09		16
	26	Fr	8		3	·29	20 21	·04 ·98		17
	27	Sa	9		4	·20	22	·91		18
	28	Su	10	Bahula	5 6	·09 ·99	23	·85		19
	29	Mo	11		7	·89	24	·78		20
	30	Tu	12		8	·78	25	·71		21
	—31	We	13		9	·70	26	·65		22
	1	Th	14		10	·61	27	·60		23
	2	Fr	15		11	·55	1	·58		24
	3	Sa	16		12	·50	2	·56		25
	4	Su	17		13	·47	3	·56		26
	5	Mo	18		14	·45	4	·58		27
	6	Tu	● 19		—A	·46	5	·62		28
Pingala Mithuna—Ani.	7	We	20		1	·50	6	·69		—29
	8	Th	21		2	·54	7	·77	H. 1335 Ramzan.	1
	9	Fr	22	Sukla	3	·62	8	·86		2
	10	Sa	23		4	·69	9	·96		3
	11	Su	24		5	·76	...	...		4
	12	Mo	25		6	·85	10	·07		5
	13	Tu	26	Ashadha	7	·93	11	·18		6
	14	We	27		8	·98	12	·28		7
	15	Th	28		...	...	13	·35		8
	16	Fr	29		9	·02	14	·41		9
	17	Sa	30		10	·05	15	·45		10

Nakah :—1. Asvn. 2. Bhar. 3. Krit. 4. Rohi. 5. Mrig. 6. Ardh. 7. Punar. 8. Push. 9. Aslesh. 10. Magh. 11. P. Phal. 12. U. Phal. 13. Hasta. 14. Chit.

A. D. 1917.
A.—Amavasya.
P.—Paurnami.

Kollam 1093, Commences { N. Malabar—Sept. / S. Malabar—Aug.

Hijra 1336, Commences, Oct. 17.

Vikrama 1974.
Bengal San 1323.
(N. Cycle) Sukla.

SOLAR reckoning: Cyclic Sidereal Year, Month and Day	Week-Day English Month and Day	LUNAR reckoning: Tithi Ending Moment	Nakshatra Ending Moment	Muhammadan Year, Month and Day
	July			
18	Su 1	11 ·05	16 ·47	11
19	Mo 2	{ 12 ·03 / 13 ·99 (Ashadha)	17 ·48	12
20	Tu 3	14 ·93	18 ·46	13
21	We ○ 4	P ·85	19 ·42	14
Pingala Mithuna—Ani. 22	Th 5	1 ·76	20 ·38	15
23	Fr 6	2 ·68	21 ·32	16
24	Sa 7	3 ·57	22 ·26	17
25	Su 8	4 ·47	23 ·19	18
26	Mo 9	5 ·36	24 ·12	19
27	Tu 10	Bahula 6 ·25	{ 25 ·05 / 26 ·99	H. 1335 Ramzan. 20
28	We 11	7 ·17	27 ·95	21
29	Th 12	8 ·10	1 ·91	22
30	Fr 13	{ 9 ·03 / 10 ·97	2 ·88	23
31	Sa 14	11 ·95	3 ·88	24
—32	Su 15	12 ·93	4 ·89	25
1	Mo 16	13 ·94	5 ·94	26
2	Tu 17	14 ·97	6 ·99	27
3	We 18	... ...	... ...	28
4	Th 19	—A ·02	7 ·07	29
5	Fr 20	1 ·09	8 ·16	—30
6	Sa 21	2 ·16	9 ·26	1
7	Su 22	3 ·25	10 ·38	2
8	Mo 23	4 ·33	11 ·48	3
9	Tu 24	5 ·40	12 ·58	4
10	We 25	6 ·45	13 ·66	5
11	Th 26	Sukla 7 ·50	14 ·72	6
12	Fr 27	8 ·58	15 ·77	7
13	Sa 28	9 ·52	16 ·80	8
14	Su 29	10 ·51	17 ·81	9
15	Mo 30	11 ·47	18 ·79	10
16	Tu 31	12 ·41	19 ·76	11
	Aug.			
17	We 1	13 ·34	20 ·71	12
18	Th 2	14 ·25	21 ·66	13
19	Fr 3	P ·17	22 ·60	14
Pingala Karkata—Adi. 20	Sa 4	{ 1 ·05 / 2 ·96 (Sravana)	23 ·53	15
21	Su 5	3 ·86	24 ·46	16
22	Mo 6	4 ·76	25 ·39	17
23	Tu 7	5 ·66	26 ·33	18
24	We 8	6 ·59	27 ·28	H. 1335 Shawwal. 19
25	Th 9	7 ·52	1 ·24	20
26	Fr 10	8 ·46	2 ·21	21
27	Sa 11	9 ·44	3 ·20	22
28	Su 12	Bahula 10 ·41	4 ·22	23
29	Mo 13	11 ·43	5 ·25	24
30	Tu 14	12 ·45	6 ·30	25
—31	We 15	13 ·51	7 ·37	26
1	Th 16	14 ·58	8 ·46	27
2	Fr 17	—A ·65	9 ·56	28
3	Sa 18	1 ·74	10 ·68	—29
4	Su 19	2 ·82	11 ·78	1
5	Mo 20	3 ·90	12 ·88	2
6	Tu 21	4 ·96	13 ·97	3
7	We 22	... ...	... ...	4
8	Th 23	Sukla 5 ·00	14 ·03	5
Pingala Simha—Avani. 9	Fr 24	6 ·01	15 ·09	6
10	Sa 25	7 ·02	16 ·12	7
11	Su 26	{ 8 ·01 / 9 ·97	17 ·13	H. 1335 Zi-l-ka'da. 8
12	Mo 27	Adh. Bhad. 10 ·93	18 ·12	9
13	Tu 28	11 ·85	19 ·09	10
14	We 29	12 ·76	20 ·05	11
15	Th 30	13 ·67	{ 21 ·00 / 22 ·93	12
16	Fr 31	14 ·57	23 ·86	13

SOLAR reckoning: Cyclic Sidereal Year, Month and Day	Week-Day English Month and Day	LUNAR reckoning: Tithi Ending Moment	Nakshatra Ending Moment	Muhammadan Year, Month and Day
	Sep.			
17	Sa 1	P ·47	24 ·79	14
18	Su 2	1 ·37 (Adhika—Bhadra.)	25 ·73	15
19	Mo 3	2 ·27	26 ·67	16
20	Tu 4	3 ·18	27 ·61	17
Pingala Simha—Avani. 21	We 5	4 ·11	1 ·57	18
22	Th 6	{ 5 ·03 / 6 ·98	2 ·54	19
23	Fr 7	7 ·95	3 ·52	20
24	Sa 8	8 ·93	4 ·54	21
25	Su 9	9 ·95	5 ·56	H. 1335 Zi-l-ka'da. 22
26	Mo 10	10 ·97	6 ·61	23
27	Tu 11	... ...	7 ·68	24
28	We 12	Bahula 11 ·03	8 ·76	25
29	Th 13	12 ·09	9 ·87	26
30	Fr 14	13 ·18	10 ·97	27
—31	Sa 15	14 ·26	... ...	28
1	Su 16	—A ·34	11 ·08	29
2	Mo 17	1 ·42	12 ·18	—30
3	Tu 18	2 ·48	13 ·27	1
4	We 19	3 ·53	14 ·35	2
5	Th 20	4 ·54	15 ·41	3
6	Fr 21	5 ·56	16 ·44	4
7	Sa 22	6 ·54	17 ·45	5
8	Su 23	Sukla 7 ·52	18 ·44	6
9	Mo 24	8 ·46	19 ·43	7
10	Tu 25	9 ·38	20 ·39	8
11	We 26	10 ·30	21 ·33	9
12	Th 27	11 ·21	22 ·27	10
13	Fr 28	12 ·12	23 ·20	11
14	Sa 29	{ 13 ·02 / 14 ·92	24 ·14	12
15	Su 30	P ·81	25 ·07	13
	Oct.			
16	Mo 1	1 ·72 (Nija Bhadrapada)	{ 26 ·01 / 27 ·95	14
Pingala Kanya—Purattasi. 17	Tu 2	2 ·65	1 ·90	15
18	We 3	3 ·58	2 ·87	16
19	Th 4	4 ·53	3 ·86	17
20	Fr 5	5 ·50	4 ·86	H. 1335 Zi-l-hijja. 18
21	Sa 6	6 ·49	5 ·88	19
22	Su 7	7 ·51	6 ·92	20
23	Mo 8	8 ·53	7 ·98	21
24	Tu 9	9 ·59	... ...	22
25	We 10	10 ·65	8 ·07	23
26	Th 11	11 ·74	9 ·17	24
27	Fr 12	Bahula 12 ·82	10 ·27	25
28	Sa 13	13 ·91	11 ·38	26
29	Su 14	14 ·98	12 ·48	27
30	Mo 15	... ...	13 ·58	28
—31	Tu 16	—A ·06	14 ·66	—29
1	We 17	1 ·10	15 ·72	1
2	Th 18	2 ·11	16 ·76	2
3	Fr 19	3 ·13	17 ·77	3
4	Sa 20	4 ·11	18 ·78	4
5	Su 21	5 ·09	19 ·76	5
6	Mo 22	{ 6 ·04 / 7 ·97	20 ·72	6
Pingala Tula—Aippasi. 7	Tu 23	Sukla 8 ·88	21 ·67	H. 1336 Muharram. 7
8	We 24	9 ·78	22 ·61	8
9	Th 25	10 ·69	23 ·54	9
10	Fr 26	11 ·59	24 ·48	10
11	Sa 27	12 ·50	25 ·41	11
12	Su 28	13 ·39	26 ·34	12
13	Mo 29	Asvina 14 ·32	27 ·28	13
14	Tu 30	P ·24	1 ·23	14
15	We 31	1 ·18	2 ·20	15

SOLAR reckoning: Cyclic Sidereal Year, Month and Day	Week-Day English Month and Day	LUNAR reckoning: Tithi Ending Moment	Nakshatra Ending Moment	Muhammadan Year, Month and Day
	Nov.			
16	Th 1	Asvina 2 ·12	3 ·18	16
17	Fr 2	3 ·09	4 ·18	17
18	Sa 3	4 ·08	5 ·19	18
19	Su 4	5 ·10	6 ·23	19
20	Mo 5	6 ·13	7 ·30	20
21	Tu 6	7 ·18	8 ·37	21
22	We 7	8 ·26	9 ·47	22
Pingala Tula—Aippasi. 23	Th 8	Bahula 9 ·34	10 ·57	H. 1336 Muharram. 23
24	Fr 9	10 ·43	11 ·68	24
25	Sa 10	11 ·52	12 ·79	25
26	Su 11	12 ·59	13 ·89	26
27	Mo 12	13 ·66	14 ·97	27
28	Tu 13	14 ·70	... ...	28
29	We 14	—A ·74	15 ·03	29
—30	Th 15	1 ·74	16 ·07	—30
1	Fr 16	2 ·72	17 ·10	1
2	Sa 17	3 ·69	18 ·10	2
3	Su 18	4 ·65	19 ·09	3
4	Mo 19	5 ·58	20 ·05	4
5	Tu 20	6 ·49	{ 21 ·00 / 22 ·95	5
6	We 21	Sukla 7 ·40	23 ·89	6
7	Th 22	8 ·31	24 ·82	7
8	Fr 23	9 ·22	25 ·75	8
9	Sa 24	10 ·12	26 ·68	9
Pingala Vrischika—Kartigai. 10	Su 25	{ 11 ·02 / 12 ·94 (Karttika)	27 ·62	10
11	Mo 26	13 ·85	1 ·57	11
12	Tu 27	14 ·79	2 ·53	12
13	We 28	P ·74	3 ·51	Safar. 13
14	Th 29	1 ·73	4 ·50	14
15	Fr 30	2 ·72	5 ·51	15
	Dec.			
16	Sa 1	3 ·72	6 ·55	H. 1336 16
17	Su 2	4 ·76	7 ·61	17
18	Mo 3	5 ·81	8 ·68	18
19	Tu 4	6 ·89	9 ·77	19
20	We 5	7 ·97	10 ·87	20
21	Th 6	Bahula	11 ·98	21
22	Fr 7	8 ·07	... ...	22
23	Sa 8	9 ·15	12 ·09	23
24	Su 9	10 ·22	13 ·19	24
25	Mo 10	11 ·30	14 ·27	25
26	Tu 11	12 ·35	15 ·34	26
27	We 12	13 ·37	16 ·39	27
28	Th 13	14 ·37	17 ·42	28
—29	Fr 14	—A ·36	18 ·43	—29
1	Sa 15	1 ·33	19 ·41	1
2	Su 16	2 ·27	20 ·38	2
3	Mo 17	3 ·20	21 ·34	3
4	Tu 18	4 ·12	22 ·29	4
5	We 19	{ 5 ·03 / 6 ·93 (Sukla)	23 ·23	5
6	Th 20	7 ·84	24 ·16	6
Pingala Dhanus—Margali. 7	Fr 21	8 ·74	25 ·09	7
8	Sa 22	9 ·65	{ 26 ·02 / 27 ·96	8
9	Su 23	10 ·56	1 ·91	H. 1336 Rabi-ul-awwal. 9
10	Mo 24	Margasira 11 ·49	2 ·86	10
11	Tu 25	12 ·43	3 ·83	11
12	We 26	13 ·38	4 ·82	12
13	Th 27	14 ·37	5 ·84	13
14	Fr ○ 28	P ·36	6 ·87	14
15	Sa 29	1 ·37	7 ·91	15
16	Su 30	Bah. 2 ·42	8 ·98	16
17	Mo 31	3 ·47	... ...	17

15. Svati. 16. Visak. 17. Anur. 18. Jyesh. 19 Mula. 20. P. Ash. 21. U. Ash. 22 Sravn. 23. Dani. 24. Satab. 25. P. Bhad. 26. U. Bhad. 27. Rev.

A. D. 1918.
Solar Eclipse. ●
Lunar Eclipse. ○

Mesha Sankranti (Commencement of Indian Sidereal Year).
(Surya Sid.) April 13·28. **Saka 1840.** **Kaliyuga 5019.**
(Arya Sid.) April 13·17. **(S. Cycle) Kalayukta.**

SOLAR reckoning: Cyclic Sidereal Year, Month and Day	Week-Day	English Month and Day	LUNAR reckoning: Tithi Ending Moment	Nakshatra Ending Moment	Muhammadan Year, Month and Day
		Jan.			
Pingala, *Dhanus—Margali.* 18	Tu	1	**Marg.** 4 ·54	9 ·07	H. 1336 *Rabi-ul-awwal.* 18
19	We	2	5 ·62	10 ·18	19
20	Th	3	6 ·72	11 ·28	20
21	Fr	4	7 ·80	12 ·39	21
22	Sa	5	8 ·88	13 ·49	22
23	Su	6	*Bahula* 9 ·95	14 ·58	23
24	Mo	7	... ...	15 ·65	24
25	Tu	8	10 ·00	16 ·71	25
26	We	9	11 ·02	17 ·74	26
27	Th	10	12 ·02	18 ·75	27
28	Fr	11	13 ·01 / 14 ·97	19 ·74	28
29	Sa	12	—A ·92	20 ·71	29
—30	Su	13	1 ·85	21 ·68	—30
1	Mo	14	2 ·77	22 ·63	1
2	Tu	15	3 ·67	23 ·57	2
3	We	16	4 ·58	24 ·50	3
4	Th	17	5 ·48	25 ·43	4
5	Fr	18	6 ·38	26 ·37	5
6	Sa	19	7 ·29	27 ·30	6
7	Su	20	*Sukla* 8 ·21	1 ·24	7
8	Mo	21	9 ·14	2 ·20	8
9	Tu	22	10 ·07	3 ·16	9
10	We	23	11 ·04	4 ·16	H. 1336 *Rabi-ul-akhir.* 10
11	Th	24	12 ·01	5 ·16	11
12	Fr	25	13 ·00	6 ·18	12
Pingala, *Makara—Tai.* 13	Sa	26	**Pausha** 14 ·03	7 ·22	13
14	Su	27	P ·07	8 ·29	14
15	Mo	28	1 ·13	9 ·37	15
16	Tu	29	2 ·19	10 ·47	16
17	We	30	3 ·29	11 ·58	17
18	Th	31	4 ·37	12 ·69	18
		Feb.			
19	Fr	1	*Bahula* 5 ·45	13 ·79	19
20	Sa	2	6 ·53	14 ·88	20
21	Su	3	7 ·60	15 ·96	21
22	Mo	4	8 ·64	... ...	22
23	Tu	5	9 ·66	16 ·02	23
24	We	6	10 ·66	17 ·06	24
25	Th	7	11 ·65	18 ·07	25
26	Fr	8	12 ·60	19 ·07	26
27	Sa	9	13 ·54	20 ·05	27
28	Su	10	14 ·47	21 ·02 / 22 ·96	28
—29	Mo	11	—A ·39	23 ·90	—29
1	Tu	12	1 ·30	24 ·84	1
2	We	13	2 ·21	25 ·78	2
3	Th	14	3 ·10	26 ·70	3
4	Fr	15	4 ·01 / 5 ·92	27 ·64	H. 1336 *Jumadal-awwal.* 4
5	Sa	16	6 ·83	1 ·58	5
6	Su	17	*Sukla* 7 ·76	2 ·53	6
7	Mo	18	8 ·69	3 ·50	7
8	Tu	19	9 ·66	4 ·48	8
9	We	20	10 ·63	5 ·48	9
Pingala, *Kumbha—Masi.* 10	Th	21	11 ·63	6 ·50	10
11	Fr	22	**Magha** 12 ·66	7 ·53	11
12	Sa	23	13 ·69	8 ·59	12
13	Su	24	14 ·75	9 ·68	13
14	Mo	25	P ·81	10 ·77	14
15	Tu	26	*Bah.* 1 ·91	11 ·88	15
16	We	27	2 ·99	12 ·98	16
17	Th	28	... ...	... ...	17

SOLAR reckoning: Cyclic Sidereal Year, Month and Day	Week-Day	English Month and Day	LUNAR reckoning: Tithi Ending Moment	Nakshatra Ending Moment	Muhammadan Year, Month and Day
		March			
Pingala, *Kumbha—Masi.* 18	Fr	1	**Magha** 3 ·08	13 ·09	H. 1336 *Jumadal-awwal.* 18
19	Sa	2	4 ·15	14 ·19	19
20	Su	3	5 ·21	15 ·27	20
21	Mo	4	6 ·26	16 ·33	21
22	Tu	5	7 ·27	17 ·37	22
23	We	6	8 ·27	18 ·39	23
24	Th	7	*Bahula* 9 ·25	19 ·40	24
25	Fr	8	10 ·21	20 ·38	25
26	Sa	9	11 ·15	21 ·35	26
27	Su	10	12 ·09	22 ·30	27
28	Mo	11	13 ·00 / 14 ·90	23 ·24	28
29	Tu	12	—A ·81	24 ·18	29
—30	We	13	1 ·70	25 ·11	—30
1	Th	14	2 ·61	26 ·04 / 27 ·97	1
2	Fr	15	3 ·51	1 ·92	2
3	Sa	16	4 ·43	2 ·86	3
4	Su	17	5 ·35	3 ·83	4
5	Mo	18	6 ·28	4 ·81	5
6	Tu	19	*Sukla* 7 ·26	5 ·80	6
7	We	20	8 ·23	6 ·81	7
8	Th	21	9 ·23	7 ·85	8
9	Fr	22	10 ·25	8 ·91	H. 1336 *Jumadal-akhir.* 9
10	Sa	23	11 ·29	9 ·98	10
11	Su	24	12 ·34	... ...	11
12	Mo	25	**Phalguna** 13 ·41	10 ·07	12
Pingala, *Mina—Panguni.* 13	Tu	26	14 ·50	11 ·17	13
14	We	27	P ·58	12 ·28	14
15	Th	28	1 ·67	13 ·40	15
16	Fr	29	2 ·73	14 ·49	16
17	Sa	30	3 ·80	15 ·58	17
18	Su	31	4 ·84	16 ·64	18
		April			
19	Mo	1	5 ·86	17 ·69	19
20	Tu	2	6 ·85	18 ·72	20
21	We	3	*Bahula* 7 ·83	19 ·73	21
22	Th	4	8 ·78	20 ·71	22
23	Fr	5	9 ·72	21 ·68	23
24	Sa	6	10 ·66	22 ·63	24
25	Su	7	11 ·57	23 ·58	25
26	Mo	8	12 ·48	24 ·52	26
27	Tu	9	13 ·37	25 ·45	27
28	We	10	14 ·26	26 ·38	28
29	Th	11	—A ·17	27 ·31	—29
—30	Fr	12	1 ·07 / 2 ·99	1 ·25	1
1	Sa	13	3 ·91	2 ·20	2
2	Su	14	4 ·85	3 ·16	3
3	Mo	15	5 ·81	4 ·13	4
4	Tu	16	6 ·79	5 ·12	5
5	We	17	*Sukla* 7 ·78	6 ·13	6
6	Th	18	8 ·80	7 ·17	7
7	Fr	19	9 ·84	8 ·22	H. 1336 *Rajab.* 8
8	Sa	20	10 ·89	9 ·29	9
9	Su	21	11 ·95	10 ·37	10
Kalayukta, *Mesha—Chittirai.* 10	Mo	22	... ...	11 ·47	11
11	Tu	23	**Chaitra** 12 ·04	12 ·59	12
12	We	24	13 ·13	13 ·69	13
13	Th	25	14 ·21	14 ·79	14
14	Fr	26	P ·27	15 ·88	15
15	Sa	27	1 ·34	16 ·95	16
16	Su	28	2 ·38	... ...	17
17	Mo	29	*Bah.* 3 ·40	17 ·01	18
18	Tu	30	4 ·38	18 ·04	19

SOLAR reckoning: Cyclic Sidereal Year, Month and Day	Week-Day	English Month and Day	LUNAR reckoning: Tithi Ending Moment	Nakshatra Ending Moment	Muhammadan Year, Month and Day
		May			
Kalayukta, *Mesha—Chittirai.* 19	We	1	**Ch.** 5 ·37	19 ·05	H. 1336 *Rajab.* 20
20	Th	2	6 ·31	20 ·04	21
21	Fr	3	7 ·25	21 ·01 / 22 ·97	22
22	Sa	4	*Bahula* 8 ·19	23 ·92	23
23	Su	5	9 ·10	24 ·86	24
24	Mo	6	10 ·00 / 11 ·90	25 ·79	25
25	Tu	7	12 ·80	26 ·72	26
26	We	8	13 ·70	27 ·65	27
27	Th	9	14 ·61	1 ·59	28
28	Fr	10	—A ·51	2 ·54	29
29	Sa	11	1 ·43	3 ·49	—30
30	Su	12	2 ·38	4 ·46	1
—31	Mo	13	3 ·33	5 ·44	2
1	Tu	14	4 ·31	6 ·46	3
2	We	15	5 ·29	7 ·48	4
3	Th	16	6 ·31	8 ·53	5
4	Fr	17	7 ·35	9 ·59	6
5	Sa	18	*Sukla* 8 ·40	10 ·67	7
6	Su	19	9 ·47	11 ·78	8
7	Mo	20	10 ·55	12 ·89	9
8	Tu	21	11 ·63	13 ·99	10
9	We	22	12 ·71	... ...	11
10	Th	23	**Vaisakha** 13 ·79	14 ·09	12
11	Fr	24	14 ·84	15 ·18	13
Kalayukta, *Vrishabha—Vaikasi.* 12	Sa	25	P ·87	16 ·26	H. 1336 *Shaban.* 14
13	Su	26	1 ·90	17 ·32	15
14	Mo	27	2 ·89	18 ·36	16
15	Tu	28	3 ·87	19 ·37	17
16	We	29	4 ·82	20 ·36	18
17	Th	30	5 ·77	21 ·34	19
18	Fr	31	6 ·68	22 ·31	20
		June			
19	Sa	1	*Bahula* 7 ·60	23 ·26	21
20	Su	2	8 ·50	24 ·20	22
21	Mo	3	9 ·40	25 ·13	23
22	Tu	4	10 ·29	26 ·06	24
23	We	5	11 ·19	27 ·00 / 1 ·93	25
24	Th	6	12 ·10	2 ·87	26
25	Fr	7	13 ·02 / 14 ·93	3 ·82	27
26	Sa ●	8	—A ·87	4 ·79	28
27	Su	9	1 ·82	5 ·78	—29
28	Mo	10	2 ·79	6 ·78	1
29	Tu	11	3 ·78	7 ·80	2
30	We	12	4 ·80	8 ·84	3
—31	Th	13	5 ·82	9 ·90	4
1	Fr	14	6 ·88	10 ·99	5
2	Sa	15	*Sukla* 7 ·95	... ...	6
3	Su	16	... ...	11 ·08	7
4	Mo	17	8 ·02	12 ·19	8
5	Tu	18	9 ·10	13 ·29	9
6	We	19	10 ·18	14 ·39	H. 1336 *Ramzan.* 10
7	Th	20	11 ·26	15 ·49	11
8	Fr	21	**Jyeshtha** 12 ·32	16 ·58	12
9	Sa	22	13 ·36	17 ·63	13
Kalayukta, *Mithuna—Ani.* 10	Su	23	14 ·38	18 ·67	14
11	Mo ○	24	P ·38	19 ·69	15
12	Tu	25	1 ·35	20 ·69	16
13	We	26	2 ·30	21 ·68	17
14	Th	27	*Bah.* 3 ·25	22 ·64	18
15	Fr	28	4 ·17	23 ·59	19
16	Sa	29	5 ·09 / 6 ·99	24 ·53	20
17	Su	30	7 ·90	25 ·47	21

Naksh :—1. Asvn. 2. Bhar. 3. Krit. 4. Rohi. 5. Mrig. 6. Ardh 7. Punar. 8. Push. 9. Aslesh. 10. Magh. 11 P. Phal. 12. U. Phal. 13. Hasta. 14. Chit.

A. D. 1918.
A.—Amavasya.
P.—Paurnami.

Kollam 1094, Commences { N. Malabar—Sept. / S. Malabar—Aug.

Hijra 1337, Commences, Oct. 7.

Vikrama 1975.
Bengal San 1324.
(N. Cycle) Pramoda.

July

Cyclic Sidereal Year, Month and Day	Week-Day	English Month Day	Tithi	Ending Moment	Nakshatra	Ending Moment	Muhammadan Year, Month and Day	Notes
18	Mo	1	8	·78	26	·41	22	Kalayukta *Mithuna—Ani*; Jyesh. *Bahula*; H. 1336 *Ramzan*
19	Tu	2	9	·68	27	·34	23	
20	We	3	10	·59	1	·27	24	
21	Th	4	11	·49	2	·21	25	
22	Fr	5	12	·41	3	·16	26	
23	Sa	6	13	·35	4	·13	27	
24	Su	7	14	·30	5	·10	28	
25	Mo	8	—A	·27	6	·10	29	
26	Tu	9	1	·27	7	·11	—30	*Sukla*
27	We	10	2	·27	8	·15	1	H. 1336 *Shavval*
28	Th	11	3	·30	9	·20	2	
29	Fr	12	4	·36	10	·29	3	
30	Sa	13	5	·43	11	·38	4	
31	Su	14	6	·50	12	·48	5	
—32	Mo	15	7	·57	13	·59	6	
1	Tu	16	8	·66	14	·69	7	Kalayukta *Karkata—Adi*
2	We	17	9	·73	15	·80	8	
3	Th	18	10	·79	16	·88	9	
4	Fr	19	11	·84	17	·95	10	
5	Sa	20	12	·86	18	·99	11	
6	Su	21	13	·85	...	...	12	Ashadha
7	Mo	22	14	·83	19	·01	13	
8	Tu	23	P	·79	20	·02	14	
9	We	24	1	·72	21 / 22	·01 / ·98	15	*Bahula*
10	Th	25	2	·65	23	·93	16	
11	Fr	26	3	·58	24	·87	17	
12	Sa	27	4	·48	25	·82	18	
13	Su	28	5	·38	26	·75	19	
14	Mo	29	6	·27	27	·68	20	
15	Tu	30	7	·18	1	·61	21	
16	We	31	8 / 9	·07 / ·98	2	·54	22	

Aug.

Cyclic Sidereal Year, Month and Day	Week-Day	English Month Day	Tithi	Ending Moment	Nakshatra	Ending Moment	Muhammadan Year, Month and Day	Notes
17	Th	1	10	·90	3	·50	23	
18	Fr	2	11	·83	4	·46	24	
19	Sa	3	12	·78	5	·43	25	
20	Su	4	13	·75	6	·42	26	
21	Mo	5	14	·75	7	·43	27	
22	Tu	6	—A	·75	8	·46	28	
23	We	7	1	·78	9	·52	—29	*Sukla*
24	Th	8	2	·83	10	·59	1	H. 1336 *Zi-l-ka'ida*
25	Fr	9	3	·90	11	·68	2	
26	Sa	10	4	·98	12	·78	3	
27	Su	11	...	...	13	·89	4	
28	Mo	12	5	·07	...	...	5	
29	Tu	13	6	·15	14	·00	6	
30	We	14	7	·22	15	·10	7	
31	Th	15	8	·28	16	·19	8	
—32	Fr	16	9	·32	17	·25	9	
1	Sa	17	10	·35	18	·30	10	Kalayukta *Simha—Avani*; Sravana
2	Su	18	11	·34	19	·34	11	
3	Mo	19	12	·32	20	·35	12	
4	Tu	20	13	·28	21	·34	13	
5	We	21	14	23	22	·31	14	
6	Th	22	P	·16	23	·26	15	
7	Fr	23	1 / 2	·08 / ·98	24	·22	16	*Bahula*
8	Sa	24	3	·87	25	·15	17	
9	Su	25	4	·77	26	·08	18	
10	Mo	26	5	·68	27 / 1	·01 / ·94	19	
11	Tu	27	6	·58	2	·88	20	
12	We	28	7	·49	3	·83	21	
13	Th	29	8	·40	4	·79	22	
14	Fr	30	9	·34	5	·76	23	
15	Sa	31	10	·29	6	·74	24	

Sep.

Cyclic Sidereal Year, Month and Day	Week-Day	English Month Day	Tithi	Ending Moment	Nakshatra	Ending Moment	Muhammadan Year, Month and Day	Notes
16	Su	1	11	·26	7	·75	25	Sr. *Bah.*; *Zi-l-ka'ida*
17	Mo	2	12	·26	8	·78	26	
18	Tu	3	13	·26	9	·83	27	
19	We	4	14	·30	10	·90	28	
20	Th	5	—A	·35	11	·98	29	
21	Fr	6	1	·41	...	...	—30	*Sukla*
22	Sa	7	2	·48	12	·08	1	H. 1336 *Zi-l-hijja*
23	Su	8	3	·57	13	·19	2	
24	Mo	9	4	·66	14	·30	3	
25	Tu	10	5	·74	15	·40	4	
26	We	11	6	·80	16	·49	5	
27	Th	12	7	·84	17	·56	6	
28	Fr	13	8	·88	18	·63	7	
29	Sa	14	9	·87	19	·66	8	
30	Su	15	10	·86	20	·67	9	
—31	Mo	16	11	·81	21	·66	10	
1	Tu	17	12	·76	22	·64	11	Kalayukta *Kanya—Purattasi*; Bhadrapada
2	We	18	13	·68	23	·61	12	
3	Th	19	14	·60	24	·55	13	
4	Fr	20	P	·51	25	·49	14	
5	Sa	21	1	·41	26	·42	15	*Bahula*
6	Su	22	2	·32	27	·35	16	
7	Mo	23	3	·20	1	·28	17	
8	Tu	24	4	·11	2	·23	18	
9	We	25	5 / 6	·02 / ·94	3	·17	19	
10	Th	26	7	·89	4	·12	20	
11	Fr	27	8	·83	5	·08	21	
12	Sa	28	9	·81	6	·07	22	
13	Su	29	10	·80	7	·08	23	
14	Mo	30	11	·81	8	·10	24	

Oct.

Cyclic Sidereal Year, Month and Day	Week-Day	English Month Day	Tithi	Ending Moment	Nakshatra	Ending Moment	Muhammadan Year, Month and Day	Notes
15	Tu	1	12	·84	9	·14	25	
16	We	2	13	·89	10	·20	26	
17	Th	3	14	·96	11	·28	27	
18	Fr	4	...	...	12	·39	28	
19	Sa	5	—A	·04	13	·49	29	
20	Su	6	1	·13	14	·60	—30	*Sukla*
21	Mo	7	2	·21	15	·70	1	H. 1337 *Muharram*
22	Tu	8	3	·29	16	·79	2	
23	We	9	4	·36	17	·88	3	
24	Th	10	5	·40	18	·94	4	
25	Fr	11	6	·44	19	·98	5	
26	Sa	12	7	·43	20	·99	6	
27	Su	13	8	·42	21	·99	7	
28	Mo	14	9	·37	22	·97	8	
29	Tu	15	10	·33	23	·94	9	
—30	We	16	11	·25	24	·89	10	
1	Th	17	12	·16	25	·83	11	Kalayukta *Tula—Aippasi*; Asvina
2	Fr	18	13 / 14	·07 / ·97	26	·76	12	
3	Sa	19	P	·88	27	·69	13	
4	Su	20	1	·78	1	·63	14	*Bahula*
5	Mo	21	2	·69	2	·56	15	
6	Tu	22	3	·59	3	·50	16	
7	We	23	4	·52	4	·45	17	
8	Th	24	5	·46	5	·41	18	
9	Fr	25	6	·41	6	·40	19	
10	Sa	26	7	·39	7	·40	20	
11	Su	27	8	·38	8	·41	21	
12	Mo	28	9	·39	9	·45	22	
13	Tu	29	10	·43	10	·51	23	
14	We	30	11	·49	11	·60	24	
15	Th	31	12	·56	12	·69	25	

Nov.

Cyclic Sidereal Year, Month and Day	Week-Day	English Month Day	Tithi	Ending Moment	Nakshatra	Ending Moment	Muhammadan Year, Month and Day	Notes
16	Fr	1	13	·64	13	·79	26	*Bah.*; *Muharram*
17	Sa	2	14	·72	14	·90	27	
18	Su	3	—A	·81	...	..	28	
19	Mo	4	1	·90	15	·00	29	*Sukla*
20	Tu	5	2	·95	16	·10	—30	
21	We	6	...	...	17	·19	1	H. 1337 *Safar*
22	Th	7	3	·00	18	·25	2	
23	Fr	8	4	·03	19	·29	3	
24	Sa	9	5	·02	20	·31	4	
25	Su	10	6 / 7	·02 / ·97	21	·31	5	
26	Mo	11	8	·93	22	·31	6	
27	Tu	12	9	·85	23	·27	7	
28	We	13	10	·77	24	·22	8	
29	Th	14	11	·69	25	·17	9	
—30	Fr	15	12	·59	26	·10	10	
1	Sa	16	13	·49	27 / 1	·04 / ·97	11	Kalayukta *Vrischika—Kartigai*; Karttika
2	Su	17	14	·38	2	·90	12	
3	Mo	18	P	·30	3	·84	13	
4	Tu	19	1	·21	4	·78	14	*Bahula*
5	We	20	2	·14	5	·75	15	
6	Th	21	3	·07	6	·78	16	
7	Fr	22	4	·04	7	·72	17	
8	Sa	23	5	·01	8	·73	18	
9	Su	24	6	·00	9	·76	19	
10	Mo	25	7	·02	10	·83	20	
11	Tu	26	8	·05	11	·90	21	
12	We	27	9	·11	12	·99	22	
13	Th	28	10	·18	...	...	23	
14	Fr	29	11	·27	13	·09	24	
15	Sa	30	12	·36	14	·19	25	

Dec.

Cyclic Sidereal Year, Month and Day	Week-Day	English Month Day	Tithi	Ending Moment	Nakshatra	Ending Moment	Muhammadan Year, Month and Day	Notes
16	Su	1	13	·44	15	·30	26	
17	Mo	2	14	·52	16	·41	27	
18	Tu	3	—A	·57	17	·49	28	
19	We	4	1	·64	18	·56	—29	*Sukla*
20	Th	5	2	·66	19	·61	1	H. 1337 *Rabi-ul-awwal*
21	Fr	6	3	·66	20	·63	2	
22	Sa	7	4	·65	21	·65	3	
23	Su	8	5	·61	22	·63	4	
24	Mo	9	6	·55	23	·60	5	
25	Tu	10	7	·47	24	·56	6	
26	We	11	8	·40	25	·50	7	
27	Th	12	9	·31	26	·45	8	
28	Fr	13	10	·21	27	·38	9	
—29	Sa	14	11	·12	1	·31	10	
1	Su	15	12 / 13	·02 / ·92	2	·24	11	Kalayukta *Dhanus—Margali*; Margasira
2	Mo	16	14	·84	3	·17	12	
3	Tu	17	P	·77	4	·13	13	
4	We	18	1	·71	5	·08	14	*Bahula*
5	Th	19	2	·67	6	·05	15	
6	Fr	20	3	·65	7	·04	16	
7	Sa	21	4	·65	8	·05	17	
8	Su	22	5	·66	9	·08	18	
9	Mo	23	6	·71	10	·13	19	
10	Tu	24	7	·76	11	·20	20	
11	We	25	8	·83	12	·29	21	
12	Th	26	9	·92	13	·39	22	
13	Fr	27	...	...	14	·49	23	
14	Sa	28	10	·01	15	·61	24	
15	Su	29	11	·10	16	·71	25	
16	Mo	30	12	·18	17	·80	26	
17	Tu	31	13	·24	18	·87	27	

15. Svati. 16. Visak. 17. Anur. 18. Jyesh. 19. Mula. 20. P. Ash. 21. U. Ash. 22. Sravn. 23. Dani. 24. Satab. 25. P. Bhad. 26. U. Bhad. 27. Rev.

A. D. 1919. **Mesha Sankranti** (Commencement of Indian Sidereal Year).

Solar Eclipse. ● (Surya Sid.) April 13·54. **Saka 1841.** **Kaliyuga 5020.**

Lunar Eclipse. ○ (Arya Sid.) April 13·43. (S. Cycle) Siddharthi.

Jan.

Solar reckoning: Kalayukta, *Dhanus—Margali* (18–30); Kalayukta, *Makara—Tai* (1–18). Lunar reckoning: *Sukla*, Pausha, *Bahula*; H. 1337 *Rabi-ul-akhir*.

Cyclic Sidereal Year, Month and Day	Week-Day English Month and Day	Tithi Ending Moment	Nakshatra Ending Moment	Muhammadan Year, Month and Day
18	We 1	14 ·28	19 ·92	28
19	Th 2	—A ·30	20 ·96	29
20	Fr 3	1 ·30	21 ·97	—30
21	Sa 4	2 ·29	22 ·96	1
22	Su 5	3 ·25	23 ·93	2
23	Mo 6	4 ·19	24 ·89	3
24	Tu 7	5 ·13	25 ·85	4
25	We 8	6 ·04 7 ·95	26 ·79	5
26	Th 9	8 ·86	27 ·72	6
27	Fr 10	9 ·76	1 ·65	7
28	Sa 11	10 ·66	2 ·58	8
29	Su 12	11 ·57	3 ·52	9
—30	Mo 13	12 ·49	4 ·46	10
1	Tu 14	13 ·41	5 ·42	11
2	We 15	14 ·36	6 ·33	12
3	Th 16	P ·32	7 ·37	13
4	Fr 17	1 ·29	8 ·37	14
5	Sa 18	2 ·29	9 ·40	15
6	Su 19	3 ·31	10 ·44	16
7	Mo 20	4 ·35	11 ·51	17
8	Tu 21	5 ·41	12 ·59	18
9	We 22	6 ·49	13 ·68	19
10	Th 23	7 ·58	14 ·80	20
11	Fr 24	8 ·66	15 ·91	21
12	Sa 25	9 ·75	... ...	22
13	Su 26	10 ·83	16 ·01	23
14	Mo 27	11 ·89	17 ·10	24
15	Tu 28	12 ·92	18 ·17	25
16	We 29	13 ·95	19 ·24	26
17	Th 30	14 ·96	20 ·28	27
18	Fr 31	—A ·93	21 ·29	28

Feb.

Solar reckoning: Kalayukta, *Kumbha—Masi*. Lunar reckoning: *Sukla*, Magha, *Bahula*; H. 1337 *Jumadal-awwal*.

Cyclic Sidereal Year, Month and Day	Week-Day English Month and Day	Tithi Ending Moment	Nakshatra Ending Moment	Muhammadan Year, Month and Day
19	Sa 1	1 ·89	22 ·29	—29
20	Su 2	2 ·82	23 ·26	1
21	Mo 3	3 ·76	24 ·24	2
22	Tu 4	4 ·67	25 ·18	3
23	We 5	5 ·58	26 ·12	4
24	Th 6	6 ·48	27 ·06 1 ·98	5
25	Fr 7	7 ·40	2 ·91	6
26	Sa 8	8 ·29	3 ·86	7
27	Su 9	9 ·19	4 ·80	8
28	Mo 10	10 ·11	5 ·75	9
—29	Tu 11	11 ·05	6 ·71	10
1	We 12	12 ·00 13 ·95	7 ·69	11
2	Th 13	14 ·93	8 ·70	12
3	Fr 14	P ·92	9 ·72	13
4	Sa 15	1 ·95	10 ·75	14
5	Su 16	2 ·99	11 ·81	15
6	Mo 17	... ...	12 ·89	16
7	Tu 18	3 04	18 ·99	17
8	We 19	4 ·12	... ...	18
9	Th 20	5 ·20	14 ·10	19
10	Fr 21	6 ·29	15 ·20	20
11	Sa 22	7 ·38	16 ·31	21
12	Su 23	8 ·45	17 ·40	22
13	Mo 24	9 ·52	18 ·49	23
14	Tu 25	10 ·55	19 ·55	24
15	We 26	11 ·57	20 ·59	25
16	Th 27	12 ·56	21 ·61	26
17	Fr 28	13 ·55	22 ·61	27

March

Solar reckoning: Kalayukta, *Kumbha—Masi* (18–30); Kalayukta, *Mina—Panguni* (1–18). Lunar reckoning: *Sukla*, Phalguna, *Bahula*; H. 1337 *Jumadal-akhir*.

Cyclic Sidereal Year, Month and Day	Week-Day English Month and Day	Tithi Ending Moment	Nakshatra Ending Moment	Muhammadan Year, Month and Day
18	Sa 1	14 ·50	23 ·60	28
19	Su 2	—A ·45	24 ·57	29
20	Mo 3	1 ·37	25 ·52	—30
21	Tu 4	2 ·28	26 ·46	1
22	We 5	3 ·19	27 ·39	2
23	Th 6	4 ·09	1 ·82	3
24	Fr 7	5 ·00 6 ·90	2 ·26	4
25	Sa 8	7 ·81	3 ·19	5
26	Su 9	8 ·72	4 ·13	6
27	Mo 10	9 ·64	5 ·08	7
28	Tu 11	10 ·59	6 ·04	8
29	We 12	11 ·55	7 ·03	9
—30	Th 13	12 ·53	8 ·02	10
1	Fr 14	13 ·52	9 ·03	11
2	Sa 15	14 ·55	10 ·07	12
3	Su 16	P ·58	11 ·12	13
4	Mo 17	1 ·64	12 ·20	14
5	Tu 18	2 ·72	13 ·29	15
6	We 19	3 ·81	14 ·40	16
7	Th 20	4 ·90	15 ·50	17
8	Fr 21	5 ·98	16 ·61	18
9	Sa 22	... ...	17 ·71	19
10	Su 23	6 ·05	18 ·80	20
11	Mo 24	7 ·11	19 ·86	21
12	Tu 25	8 ·15	20 ·91	22
13	We 26	9 ·16	21 ·93	23
14	Th 27	10 ·15	22 ·94	24
15	Fr 28	11 ·14	23 ·93	25
16	Sa 29	12 ·08	24 ·90	26
17	Su 30	13 ·03 14 ·95	25 ·85	27
18	Mo 31	—A ·87	26 ·80	28

April

Solar reckoning: Siddharthi, *Mesha—Chittirai*. Lunar reckoning: *Sukla*, Chaitra, *Bahula*; H. 1337 *Rajab*.

Cyclic Sidereal Year, Month and Day	Week-Day English Month and Day	Tithi Ending Moment	Nakshatra Ending Moment	Muhammadan Year, Month and Day
19	Tu 1	1 ·77	27 ·73	—29
20	We 2	2 ·66	1 ·67	1
21	Th 3	3 ·56	2 ·60	2
22	Fr 4	4 ·47	3 ·53	3
23	Sa 5	5 ·38	4 ·47	4
24	Su 6	6 ·29	5 ·41	5
25	Mo 7	7 ·22	6 ·38	6
26	Tu 8	8 ·16	7 ·35	7
27	We 9	9 ·12	8 ·34	8
28	Th 10	10 ·09	9 ·35	9
29	Fr 11	11 ·08	10 ·38	10
—30	Sa 12	12 ·11	11 ·44	11
1	Su 13	13 ·14	12 ·51	12
2	Mo 14	14 ·21	13 ·59	13
3	Tu 15	P ·28	14 ·69	14
4	We 16	1 ·37	15 ·80	15
5	Th 17	2 ·45	16 ·92	16
6	Fr 18	3 ·53	... ...	17
7	Sa 19	4 ·60	17 ·01	18
8	Su 20	5 ·66	18 ·10	19
9	Mo 21	6 ·69	19 ·17	20
10	Tu 22	7 ·70	20 ·22	21
11	We 23	8 ·70	21 ·25	22
12	Th 24	9 ·68	22 ·27	23
13	Fr 25	10 ·62	23 ·26	24
14	Sa 26	11 ·57	24 ·23	25
15	Su 27	12 ·49	25 ·19	26
16	Mo 28	13 ·41	26 ·13	27
17	Tu 29	14 ·30	27 ·08	28
18	We 30	—A ·21	1 ·01 2 ·94	29

May

Solar reckoning: Siddharthi, *Mesha—Chittirai* (19–31); Siddharthi, *Vrishabha—Vaikasi* (1–18). Lunar reckoning: *Sukla*, Vaisakha, *Bahula*; H. 1337 *Shaban*.

Cyclic Sidereal Year, Month and Day	Week-Day English Month and Day	Tithi Ending Moment	Nakshatra Ending Moment	Muhammadan Year, Month and Day
19	Th 1	1 ·10	3 ·87	—30
20	Fr 2	2 ·01 3 ·91	4 ·80	1
21	Sa 3	4 ·82	5 ·76	2
22	Su 4	5 ·74	6 ·71	3
23	Mo 5	6 ·68	7 ·68	4
24	Tu 6	7 ·65	8 ·66	5
25	We 7	8 ·62	9 ·67	6
26	Th 8	9 ·62	10 ·70	7
27	Fr 9	10 ·64	11 ·75	8
28	Sa 10	11 ·66	12 ·81	9
29	Su 11	12 ·72	13 ·90	10
30	Mo 12	13 ·79	14 ·99	11
—31	Tu 13	14 ·88	... ...	12
1	We 14	P ·96	15 ·10	13
2	Th 15	... ...	16 ·21	14
3	Fr 16	1 ·04	17 ·31	15
4	Sa 17	2 ·11	18 ·40	16
5	Su 18	3 ·17	19 ·48	17
6	Mo 19	4 ·21	20 ·53	18
7	Tu 20	5 ·22	21 ·58	19
8	We 21	6 ·21	22 ·59	20
9	Th 22	7 ·19	23 ·58	21
10	Fr 23	8 ·15	24 ·56	22
11	Sa 24	9 ·08	25 ·52	23
12	Su 25	10 ·00 11 ·91	26 ·48	24
13	Mo 26	12 ·81	27 ·42	25
14	Tu 27	13 ·72	1 ·35	26
15	We 28	14 ·61	2 ·28	27
16	Th ● 29	—A ·51	3 ·21	28
17	Fr 30	1 ·41	4 ·15	—29
18	Sa 31	2 ·32	5 ·09	1

June

Solar reckoning: Siddharthi, *Mithuna—Ani*. Lunar reckoning: *Sukla*, Jyeshtha, *Bahula*, *Suk.* A.; H. 1337 *Ramzan*.

Cyclic Sidereal Year, Month and Day	Week-Day English Month and Day	Tithi Ending Moment	Nakshatra Ending Moment	Muhammadan Year, Month and Day
19	Su 1	3 ·25	6 ·04	2
20	Mo 2	4 ·18	7 ·01 8 ·99	3
21	Tu 3	5 ·15	9 ·99	4
22	We 4	6 ·11	... ...	5
23	Th 5	7 ·11	10 ·02	6
24	Fr 6	8 ·12	11 ·06	7
25	Sa 7	9 ·16	12 ·12	8
26	Su 8	10 ·22	13 ·20	9
27	Mo 9	11 ·29	14 ·29	10
28	Tu 10	12 ·37	15 ·40	11
29	We 11	13 ·44	16 ·51	12
30	Th 12	14 ·52	17 ·61	13
31	Fr 13	P ·59	18 ·71	14
—32	Sa 14	1 ·65	19 ·79	15
1	Su 15	2 ·68	20 ·86	16
2	Mo 16	3 ·71	21 ·89	17
3	Tu 17	4 ·70	22 ·91	18
4	We 18	5 ·67	23 ·91	19
5	Th 19	6 ·68	24 ·89	20
6	Fr 20	7 ·57	25 ·86	21
7	Sa 21	8 ·49	26 ·81	22
8	Su 22	9 ·40	27 ·75	23
9	Mo 23	10 ·31	1 ·69	24
10	Tu 24	11 ·20	2 ·62	25
11	We 25	12 ·09	3 ·56	26
12	Th 26	13 ·00 14 ·89	4 ·49	27
13	Fr 27	—A ·81	5 ·42	28
14	Sa 28	1 ·73	6 ·38	29
15	Su 29	2 ·67	7 ·34	—30
16	Mo 30	3 ·62	8 ·31	1

Naksh:—1. Asvn. 2. Bhar. 3. Krit. 4. Rohi. 5. Mrig. 6. Ardh. 7. Punar. 8. Push. 9. Aslesh. 10. Magh. 11. P. Phal. 12. U. Phal. 13. Hasta. 14. Chit.

A. D. 1919.
A.—Amavasya.
P.—Paurnami.

Kollam 1095, Commences { **N. Malabar—Sept.** / **S. Malabar—Aug.**

Hijra 1338, Commences, Sep. 26.

Vikrama 1976.
Bengal San 1325.
(N. Cycle) Prajapati.

SOLAR reckoning: Cyclic Sidereal Year, Month and Day; Week-Day English Month and Day. LUNAR reckoning: Tithi Ending Moment; Nakshatra Ending Moment; Muhammadan Year, Month and Day.

July — Siddharthi *Mithuna—Ani.* — Lunar: *Sukla*, Ashadha, *Bahula* — H. 1337 *Shawwal.*

Cyclic Sidereal	Week-Day	Day	Tithi	Nakshatra	Muhammadan
17	Tu	1	4 ·60	9 ·32	2
18	We	2	5 ·59	10 ·33	3
19	Th	3	6 ·60	11 ·37	4
20	Fr	4	7 ·63	12 ·42	5
21	Sa	5	8 ·69	13 ·50	6
22	Su	6	9 ·76	14 ·60	7
23	Mo	7	10 ·83	15 ·70	8
24	Tu	8	11 ·92	16 ·81	9
25	We	9	... ...	17 ·91	10
26	Th	10	12 ·00	... ...	11
27	Fr	11	13 ·06	18 ·01	12
28	Sa	12	14 ·12	19 ·10	13
29	Su	13	P ·16	20 ·17	14
30	Mo	14	1 ·19	21 ·21	15
—31	Tu	15	2 ·17	22 ·23	16
1	We	16	3 ·16	23 ·23	17
2	Th	17	4 ·11	24 ·23	18
3	Fr	18	5 ·04; 6 ·97	25 ·20	19
4	Sa	19	7 ·88	26 ·15	20
5	Su	20	8 ·79	27 ·09	21
6	Mo	21	9 ·68	1 ·03; 2 ·95	22
7	Tu	22	10 ·59	3 ·89	23
8	We	23	11 ·49	4 ·83	24
9	Th	24	12 ·39	5 ·76	25
10	Fr	25	13 ·30	6 ·71	26
11	Sa	26	14 ·21	7 ·67	27
12	Su	27	—A ·15	8 ·65	28
13	Mo	28	1 ·10	9 ·64	—29
14	Tu	29	2 ·08	10 ·65	1
15	We	30	3 ·07	11 ·68	2
16	Th	31	4 ·09	12 ·73	3

Aug. — Siddharthi *Karkata—Adi.*; Siddharthi *Simha—Avani.* — Lunar: *Sukla*, Sravana, *Bahula*, Bhad. *Suk.* — H. 1337 *Zi-l-ka'da.*; *Zi-l-hijja.*

Cyclic Sidereal	Week-Day	Day	Tithi	Nakshatra	Muhammadan
17	Fr	1	5 ·11	13 ·81	4
18	Sa	2	6 ·16	14 ·90	5
19	Su	3	7 ·23	... ...	6
20	Mo	4	8 ·30	15 ·00	7
21	Tu	5	9 ·40	16 ·11	8
22	We	6	10 ·48	17 ·21	9
23	Th	7	11 ·55	18 ·32	10
24	Fr	8	12 ·60	19 ·41	11
25	Sa	9	13 ·63	20 ·47	12
26	Su	10	14 ·67	21 ·52	13
27	Mo	11	P ·66	22 ·55	14
28	Tu	12	1 ·65	23 ·57	15
29	We	13	2 ·60	24 ·56	16
30	Th	14	3 ·55	25 ·53	17
31	Fr	15	4 ·47	26 ·48	18
—32	Sa	16	5 ·39	27 ·43	19
1	Su	17	6 ·29	1 ·36	20
2	Mo	18	7 ·18	2 ·30	21
3	Tu	19	8 ·08; 9 ·98	3 ·23	22
4	We	20	10 ·89	4 ·16	23
5	Th	21	11 ·80	5 ·10	24
6	Fr	22	12 ·72	6 ·04	25
7	Sa	23	13 ·65	7 ·01; 8 ·98	26
8	Su	24	14 ·60	9 ·96	27
9	Mo	25	—A ·58	10 ·97	28
10	Tu	26	1 ·57	11 ·99	29
11	We	27	2 ·58	... ...	—30
12	Th	28	3 ·61	12 ·05	1
13	Fr	29	4 ·67	13 ·12	2
14	Sa	30	5 ·73	14 ·20	3
15	Su	31	6 ·81	15 ·30	4

Sep. — Siddharthi *Simha—Avani.* — Lunar: *Sukla*, Bhadrapada, *Bahula* — H. 1337 *Zi-l-hijja.*

Cyclic Sidereal	Week-Day	Day	Tithi	Nakshatra	Muhammadan
16	Mo	1	7 ·90	16 ·41	5
17	Tu	2	8 ·98	17 ·52	6
18	We	3	... ...	18 ·62	7
19	Th	4	9 ·06	19 ·71	8
20	Fr	5	10 ·12	20 ·78	9
21	Sa	6	11 ·16	21 ·84	10
22	Su	7	12 ·18	22 ·87	11
23	Mo	8	13 ·18	23 ·89	12
24	Tu	9	14 ·16	24 ·88	13
25	We	10	P ·12	25 ·86	14
26	Th	11	1 ·07; 2 ·99	26 ·82	15
27	Fr	12	3 ·91	27 ·77	16
28	Sa	13	4 ·81	1 ·71	17
29	Su	14	5 ·72	2 ·64	18
30	Mo	15	6 ·61	3 ·57	19
—31	Tu	16	7 ·51	4 ·50	20
1	We	17	8 ·42	5 ·44	21
2	Th	18	9 ·32	6 ·39	22
3	Fr	19	10 ·25	7 ·34	23
4	Sa	20	11 ·18	8 ·30	24
5	Su	21	12 ·14	9 ·29	25
6	Mo	22	13 ·11	10 ·29	26
7	Tu	23	14 ·11	11 ·32	27
8	We	24	—A ·11	12 ·36	28
9	Th	25	1 ·15	13 ·42	—29
10	Fr	26	2 ·21	14 ·50	1
11	Sa	27	3 ·27	15 ·60	2
12	Su	28	4 ·36	16 ·71	3
13	Mo	29	5 ·44	17 ·82	4
14	Tu	30	6 ·53	18 ·92	5

Oct. — Siddharthi *Kanya—Purattasi.*; Siddharthi *Tula—Aippasi.* — Lunar: *Sukla*, Asvina, *Bahula*, Kartt. *Sukla* — H. 1338 *Muharram.*; H. 1338 *Safar.*

Cyclic Sidereal	Week-Day	Day	Tithi	Nakshatra	Muhammadan
15	We	1	7 ·59	... ...	6
16	Th	2	8 ·66	19 ·01	7
17	Fr	3	9 ·70	20 ·09	8
18	Sa	4	10 ·72	21 ·15	9
19	Su	5	11 ·73	22 ·20	10
20	Mo	6	12 ·71	23 ·21	11
21	Tu	7	13 ·68	24 ·21	12
22	We	8	14 ·62	25 ·19	13
23	Th	9	P ·55	26 ·15	14
24	Fr	10	1 ·47	27 ·11	15
25	Sa	11	2 ·37	1 ·05; 2 ·98	16
26	Su	12	3 ·28	3 ·91	17
27	Mo	13	4 ·17	4 ·84	18
28	Tu	14	5 ·08; 6 ·98	5 ·78	19
29	We	15	7 ·90	6 ·72	20
—30	Th	16	8 ·82	7 ·67	21
1	Fr	17	9 ·75	8 ·63	22
2	Sa	18	10 ·71	9 ·61	23
3	Su	19	11 ·68	10 ·61	24
4	Mo	20	12 ·69	11 ·63	25
5	Tu	21	13 ·69	12 ·67	26
6	We	22	14 ·74	13 ·73	27
7	Th	23	—A ·79	14 ·81	28
8	Fr	24	1 ·85	15 ·90	29
9	Sa	25	2 ·94	... ...	—30
10	Su	26	... ...	16 ·01	1
11	Mo	27	3 ·02	17 ·12	2
12	Tu	28	4 ·11	18 ·22	3
13	We	29	5 ·20	19 ·32	4
14	Th	30	6 ·26	20 ·40	5
15	Fr	31	7 ·30	21 ·47	6

Nov. — Siddharthi *Tula—Aippasi.* — Lunar: *Sukla*, Karttika, *Bahula*, *Sukla* — H. 1338 *Safar.*

Cyclic Sidereal	Week-Day	Day	Tithi	Nakshatra	Muhammadan
16	Sa	1	8 ·32	22 ·51	7
17	Su	2	9 ·32	23 ·53	8
18	Mo	3	10 ·30	24 ·53	9
19	Tu	4	11 ·27	25 ·52	10
20	We	5	12 ·22	26 ·49	11
21	Th	6	13 ·15	27 ·44	12
22	Fr ○	7	14 ·06; P ·97	1 ·38	13
23	Sa	8	1 ·86	2 ·32	14
24	Su	9	2 ·77	3 ·25	15
25	Mo	10	3 ·68	4 ·19	16
26	Tu	11	4 ·58	5 ·12	17
27	We	12	5 ·50	6 ·06	18
28	Th	13	6 ·42	7 ·00; 8 ·96	19
29	Fr	14	7 ·36	9 ·94	20
—30	Sa	15	8 ·32	10 ·94	21
1	Su	16	9 ·29	11 ·95	22
2	Mo	17	10 ·29	12 ·98	23
3	Tu	18	11 ·30	... ...	24
4	We	19	12 ·35	13 ·04	25
5	Th	20	13 ·40	14 ·11	26
6	Fr	21	14 ·48	15 ·21	27
7	Sa	22	—A ·56	16 ·31	28
8	Su	23	1 ·65	17 ·41	—29
9	Mo	24	2 ·74	18 ·52	1
10	Tu	25	3 ·81	19 ·62	2
11	We	26	4 ·88	20 ·71	3
12	Th	27	5 ·93	21 ·78	4
13	Fr	28	6 ·95	22 ·83	5
14	Sa	29	7 ·94	23 ·85	6
15	Su	30	8 ·94	24 ·86	7

Dec. — Siddharthi *Vrischika—Karttigai.*; Siddharthi *Dhanus—Margali.* — Lunar: Margasira, *Bahula*, Pausha *Sukla* — H. 1338 *Rabi-ul-awwal.*; *Rabi-ul-akhir.*

Cyclic Sidereal	Week-Day	Day	Tithi	Nakshatra	Muhammadan
16	Mo	1	9 ·89	25 ·85	8
17	Tu	2	10 ·83	26 ·82	9
18	We	3	11 ·77	27 ·78	10
19	Th	4	12 ·68	1 ·72	11
20	Fr	5	13 ·60	2 ·66	12
21	Sa	6	14 ·49	3 ·59	13
22	Su	7	P ·40	4 ·53	14
23	Mo	8	1 ·30	5 ·46	15
24	Tu	9	2 ·20	6 ·40	16
25	We	10	3 ·12	7 ·34	17
26	Th	11	4 ·05; 5 ·99	8 ·29	18
27	Fr	12	6 ·94	9 ·27	19
28	Sa	13	7 ·93	10 ·26	20
29	Su	14	8 ·93	11 ·27	21
—30	Mo	15	9 ·95	12 ·30	22
1	Tu	16	... ...	13 ·35	23
2	We	17	10 ·00	14 ·42	24
3	Th	18	11 ·05	15 ·51	25
4	Fr	19	12 ·13	16 ·61	26
5	Sa	20	13 ·21	17 ·71	27
6	Su	21	14 ·31	18 ·82	28
7	Mo	22	—A ·39	19 ·93	29
8	Tu	23	1 ·47	... ...	—30
9	We	24	2 ·53	20 ·02	1
10	Th	25	3 ·57	21 ·09	2
11	Fr	26	4 ·59	22 ·14	3
12	Sa	27	5 ·59	23 ·17	4
13	Su	28	6 ·58	24 ·19	5
14	Mo	29	7 ·53	25 ·18	6
15	Tu	30	8 ·48	26 ·15	7
16	We	31	9 ·41	27 ·11	8

15. Svati. 16. Visak. 17. Anur. 18. Jyesh. 19. Mula. 20. P. Ash. 21 U. Ash. 22. Sravn. 23. Dani. 24. Satab. 25. P. Bhad. 26. U. Bhad. 27. Rev.

A. D. 1920. **Mesha Sankranti** (Commencement of Indian Sidereal Year). **Kaliyuga 5021.**

Solar Eclipse. ● **(Surya Sid.) April 12·79.** **Saka 1842.**

Lunar Eclipse. ○ **(Arya Sid.) April 12·68.** **(S. Cycle) Raudra.**

SOLAR reckoning: Cyclic Sidereal Year, Month and Day; Week-Day, English Month and Day. LUNAR reckoning: Tithi Ending Moment; Nakshatra Ending Moment; Muhammadan Year, Month and Day.

Jan.

Cyclic Sidereal Year, Month and Day	Week-Day	Day	Tithi	Tithi Ending Moment	Nakshatra	Nakshatra Ending Moment	Muhammadan Year, Month and Day
Siddharthi Dhanus—Margali 17	Th	1	Sukla 10	·32	1	·06	H. 1338 Rabi-ul-akhir 9
18	Fr	2	11	·23	2 3	·00 ·94	10
19	Sa	3	12	·13	4	·87	11
20	Su	4	13 14	·04 ·94	5	·79	12
21	Mo	5	Pausha P	·86	6	·73	13
22	Tu	6	1	·77	7	·67	14
23	We	7	2	·70	8	·63	15
24	Th	8	3	·64	9	·60	16
25	Fr	9	4	·59	10	·59	17
26	Sa	10	5	·58	11	·59	18
27	Su	11	Bahula 6	·57	12	·61	19
28	Mo	12	7	·60	13	·66	20
29	Tu	13	8	·64	14	·73	21
Siddharthi Makara—Tai 1	We	14	9	·70	15	·81	22
2	Th	15	10	·77	16	·91	23
3	Fr	16	11	·86	...	...	24
4	Sa	17	12	·96	17	·01	25
5	Su	18	...	...	18	·13	26
6	Mo	19	13	·04	19	·23	27
7	Tu	20	14	·12	20	·32	28
8	We	21	A	·17	21	·40	29
9	Th	22	1	·22	22	·45	1
10	Fr	23	2	·23	23	·49	2
11	Sa	24	3	·23	24	·51	3
12	Su	25	4	·22	25	·51	4
13	Mo	26	Sukla 5	·17	26	·48	5
14	Tu	27	6	·12	27	·44	6
15	We	28	7 8	·04 ·96	1	·39	7
16	Th	29	9	·86	2	·34	8
17	Fr	30	10	·77	3	·27	9
18	Sa	31	11	·67	4	·20	10

Feb.

Cyclic Sidereal Year, Month and Day	Week-Day	Day	Tithi	Tithi Ending Moment	Nakshatra	Nakshatra Ending Moment	Muhammadan Year, Month and Day
19	Su	1	12	·57	5	·13	H. 1338 Jumadal-awwal 11
20	Mo	2	13	·48	6	·07	12
21	Tu	3	14	·39	7 8	·02 ·97	13
22	We	4	Magha P	·33	9	·93	14
23	Th	5	1	·27	10	·91	15
24	Fr	6	2	·23	11	·91	16
25	Sa	7	3	22	12	·94	17
26	Su	8	4	·21	13	·97	18
27	Mo	9	5	·23	...	...	19
28	Tu	10	6	·28	14	·03	20
29	We	11	Bahula 7	·34	15	·11	21
30	Th	12	8	·42	16	·21	22
Siddharthi Kumbha—Masi 1	Fr	13	9	·51	17	·32	23
2	Sa	14	10	·59	18	·42	24
3	Su	15	11	·67	19	·53	25
4	Mo	16	12	·76	20	·62	26
5	Tu	17	13	·81	21	·70	27
6	We	18	14	·86	22	·76	28
7	Th	19	A	·86	23	·81	29
8	Fr	20	1	·86	24	·83	30
9	Sa	21	2	·84	25	·83	Jumadal-akhir 1
10	Su	22	Sukla 3	·80	26	·81	2
11	Mo	23	4	·73	27	·78	3
12	Tu	24	5	·06	1	·74	4
13	We	25	6	·57	2	·68	5
14	Th	26	7	·48	3	·61	6
15	Fr	27	8	·38	4	·54	7
16	Sa	28	9	·29	5	·47	8
17	Su	29	Phalguna 10	·19	6	·41	9

March

Cyclic Sidereal Year, Month and Day	Week-Day	Day	Tithi	Tithi Ending Moment	Nakshatra	Nakshatra Ending Moment	Muhammadan Year, Month and Day
Siddharthi Kumbha—Masi 18	Mo	1	11	·09	7	·35	H. 1338 Jumadal-akhir 10
19	Tu	2	12 13	·00 ·93	8	·30	11
20	We	3	14	·87	9	·26	12
21	Th	4	Phalguna P	·84	10	·24	13
22	Fr	5	1	·83	11	·24	14
23	Sa	6	2	·83	12	·25	15
24	Su	7	3	·85	13	·29	16
25	Mo	8	4	·90	14	·34	17
26	Tu	9	5	·95	15	·41	18
27	We	10	...	...	16	·50	19
28	Th	11	6	·03	17	·62	20
29	Fr	12	Bahula 7	·12	18	·72	21
30	Sa	13	8	·20	19	·83	22
Siddharthi Mina—Panguni 1	Su	14	9	·29	20	·92	23
2	Mo	15	10	·35	...	...	24
3	Tu	16	11	·41	21	·01	25
4	We	17	12	·44	22	·08	26
5	Th	18	13	·45	23	·13	27
6	Fr	19	14	·46	24	·15	28
7	Sa	20	A	·44	25	·16	29
8	Su	21	1	·39	26	·14	1
9	Mo	22	2	·32	27	·12	2
10	Tu	23	3	·25	1	·07	3
11	We	24	4	16	2 3	·02 ·95	4
12	Th	25	5 6	·07 ·96	4	·88	5
13	Fr	26	7	·86	5	·82	6
14	Sa	27	8	·77	6	·75	7
15	Su	28	Sukla 9	·67	7	·69	8
16	Mo	29	10	·59	8	·63	9
17	Tu	30	11	·52	9	·59	10
18	We	31	12	·46	10	·56	11

April

Cyclic Sidereal Year, Month and Day	Week-Day	Day	Tithi	Tithi Ending Moment	Nakshatra	Nakshatra Ending Moment	Muhammadan Year, Month and Day
19	Th	1	Chaitra 13	·42	11	·56	H. 1338 Rajab 12
20	Fr	2	14	·40	12	·57	13
21	Sa	3	P	·40	13	·60	14
22	Su	4	1	·42	14	·65	15
23	Mo	5	2	·47	15	·72	16
24	Tu	6	3	·52	16	·82	17
25	We	7	4	·61	17	·91	18
26	Th	8	5	·69	...	...	19
27	Fr	9	6	·77	18	·02	20
28	Sa	10	Bahula 7	·85	19	·13	21
29	Su	11	8	·91	20	·23	22
30	Mo	12	9	·97	21	·32	23
Raudra Mesha—Chittirai 1	Tu	13	...	...	22	·30	24
2	We	14	10	·01	23	·44	25
3	Th	15	11	·02	24	·47	26
4	Fr	16	12 13	·01 ·99	25	·48	27
5	Sa	17	14	·94	26	·48	28
6	Su	18	A	·87	27	·45	29
7	Mo	19	1	·80	1	·41	30
8	Tu	20	2	·71	2	·35	H. 1338 Shaban 1
9	We	21	3	·61	3	·29	2
10	Th	22	Sukla 4	·51	4	·23	3
11	Fr	23	5	·42	5	·16	4
12	Sa	24	6	·31	6	·09	5
13	Su	25	7	·21	7 8	·02 ·97	6
14	Mo	26	Vaisakha 8	·13	9	·92	7
15	Tu	27	9	·06	10	·90	8
16	We	28	10 11	·00 ·95	11	·88	9
17	Th	29	12	·94	12	·89	10
18	Fr	30	13	·93	13	·91	11

May

Cyclic Sidereal Year, Month and Day	Week-Day	Day	Tithi	Tithi Ending Moment	Nakshatra	Nakshatra Ending Moment	Muhammadan Year, Month and Day
Raudra Mesha—Chittirai 19	Sa	1	Vaisakha 14	·95	14	·96	H. 1338 Shaban 12
20	Su	2	...	...	...	...	13
21	Mo ○	3	P	00	15	·03	14
22	Tu	4	1	·05	16	·12	15
23	We	5	2	·12	17	·21	16
24	Th	6	3	·20	18	·32	17
25	Fr	7	4	·29	19	·42	18
26	Sa	8	5	·37	20	·54	19
27	Su	9	6	·44	21	·63	20
28	● Mo	10	Bahula 7	·49	22	·70	21
29	Tu	11	8	·53	23	·75	22
30	We	12	9	·54	24	·79	23
31	Th	13	10	·53	25	·81	24
Raudra Vrishabha—Vaikasi 1	Fr	14	11	·51	26	·80	25
2	Sa	15	12	·47	27	·78	26
3	Su	16	13	·39	1	·74	27
4	Mo	17	14	·31	2	·69	28
5	Tu	18	A	·22	3	·63	29
6	We	19	1	·13	4	·57	1
7	Th	20	2 3	·03 ·93	5	·50	2
8	Fr	21	4	·82	6	·43	3
9	Sa	22	5	·73	7	·36	4
10	Su	23	6	·64	8	·30	5
11	Mo	24	Sukla 7	·56	9	·26	6
12	Tu	25	8	·51	10	·23	7
13	We	26	9	·46	11	·21	8
14	Th	27	10	·45	12	·21	9
15	Fr	28	11	·43	13	·23	10
16	Sa	29	12	·45	14	·28	11
17	Su	30	13	·50	15	·34	12
18	Mo	31	14	·55	16	·42	13

June

Cyclic Sidereal Year, Month and Day	Week-Day	Day	Tithi	Tithi Ending Moment	Nakshatra	Nakshatra Ending Moment	Muhammadan Year, Month and Day
19	Tu	1	Jyeshtha P	·62	17	·51	H. 1338 Ramzan 14
20	We	2	1	·70	18	·62	15
21	Th	3	2	·79	19	·73	16
22	Fr	4	3	·86	20	·84	17
23	Sa	5	4	·94	21	·93	18
24	Su	6	5	·99	...	...	19
25	Mo	7	...	...	22	·01	20
26	Tu	8	Bahula 6	·03	23	·07	21
27	We	9	7	·03	24	·11	22
28	Th	10	8	·02	25	·13	23
29	Fr	11	9 10	·00 ·95	26	·13	24
30	Sa	12	11	·80	27	·11	25
31	Su	13	12	·81	1	·07	26
Raudra Mithuna—Ani 1	Mo	14	13	·72	2 3	·02 ·97	27
2	Tu	15	14	·62	4	·91	28
3	We	16	A	·52	5	·84	29
4	Th	17	1	·42	6	·77	30
5	Fr	18	2	·31	7	·70	H. 1338 Shawwal 1
6	Sa	19	3	·22	8	·64	2
7	Su	20	4	·13	9	·59	3
8	Mo	21	5 6	·05 ·99	10	·56	4
9	Tu	22	Sukla 7	·95	11	·53	5
10	We	23	8	·92	12	·53	6
11	Th	24	9	·91	13	·55	7
12	Fr	25	10	·94	14	·59	8
13	Sa	26	11	·96	15	·65	9
14	Su	27	...	...	16	·72	10
15	Mo	28	Ashadha 12	·02	17	·81	11
16	Tu	29	13	·09	18	·92	12
17	We	30	14	·17	...	...	13

Naksh :—1. Asvn. 2. Bhar. 3. Krit. 4. Rohi. 5. Mrig. 6. Ardh. 7. Punar. 8. Push. 9. Aslesh. 10. Magh. 11. P. Phal. 12. U. Phal. 13. Hasta. 14. Chit.

A. D. 1920.
A.—Amavasya.
P.—Paurnami.

Kollam 1096, Commences { N. Malabar—Sept. S. Malabar—Aug.

Hijra 1339, Commences, Sep. 15.

Vikrama 1977.
Bengal San 1326.
(N. Cycle) Angiras.

July

SOLAR reckoning: Cyclic Sidereal Year, Month and Day	Week-Day	English Month and Day	LUNAR reckoning: Tithi Ending Moment	Nakshatra Ending Moment	Muhammadan Year, Month and Day
Raudra *Mithuna—Ani.* 18	Th	1	Ashadha P ·25	19 ·03	H. 1338 *Shawwal.* 14
19	Fr	2	1 ·33	20 ·13	15
20	Sa	3	2 ·41	21 ·23	16
21	Su	4	3 ·46	22 ·31	17
22	Mo	5	4 ·50	23 ·38	18
23	Tu	6	5 ·51	24 ·43	19
24	We	7	6 ·50	25 ·45	20
25	Th	8	*Bahula* 7 ·47	26 ·45	21
26	Fr	9	8 ·43	27 ·44	22
27	Sa	10	9 ·36	1 ·41	23
28	Su	11	10 ·28	2 ·37	24
29	Mo	12	11 ·20	3 ·31	25
30	Tu	13	12 ·10	4 ·24	26
31	We	14	13 ·00 14 ·89	5 ·17	27
—32	Th	15	—A ·80	6 ·10	28
Raudra *Karkata—Adi.* 1	Fr	16	Sravana *Sukla* 1 ·70	7 ·04 8 ·98	—29
2	Sa	17	2 ·60	9 ·93	H. 1338 *Zi-l-ka'da.* 1
3	Su	18	3 ·53	10 ·89	2
4	Mo	19	4 ·47	11 ·86	3
5	Tu	20	5 ·43	12 ·86	4
6	We	21	6 ·40	13 ·87	5
7	Th	22	7 ·40	14 ·90	6
8	Fr	23	8 ·42	15 ·95	7
9	Sa	24	9 ·44	... ...	8
10	Su	25	10 ·50	16 ·02	9
11	Mo	26	11 ·56	17 ·12	10
12	Tu	27	12 ·65	18 ·22	11
13	We	28	13 ·73	19 ·33	12
14	Th	29	14 ·81	20 ·43	13
15	Fr	30	P ·88	21 ·53	14
16	Sa	31	1 ·93	22 ·62	15

Aug.

SOLAR reckoning: Cyclic Sidereal Year, Month and Day	Week-Day	English Month and Day	LUNAR reckoning: Tithi Ending Moment	Nakshatra Ending Moment	Muhammadan Year, Month and Day
17	Su	1	Adhika 2 ·98	23 ·70	16
18	Mo	2	3 ·99	24 ·74	17
19	Tu	3	4 ·99	25 ·77	18
20	We	4	5 ·96	26 ·78	19
21	Th	5	6 ·92	27 ·77	20
22	Fr	6	7 ·86	1 ·75	21
23	Sa	7	*Bahula* 8 ·79	2 ·70	22
24	Su	8	9 ·69	3 ·65	23
25	Mo	9	10 ·59	4 ·58	24
26	Tu	10	11 ·50	5 ·51	25
27	We	11	12 ·39	6 ·44	26
28	Th	12	13 ·30	7 ·38	27
29	Fr	13	14 ·19	8 ·32	28
30	Sa	14	—A ·11	9 ·26	29
—31	Su	15	1 ·03 2 ·96	10 ·22	—30
Raudra *Simha—Avani.* 1	Mo	16	Nija Sravana *Sukla* 3 ·92	11 ·20	H. 1338 *Zi-l-hijja.* 1
2	Tu	17	4 ·89	12 ·18	2
3	We	18	5 ·89	13 ·19	3
4	Th	19	6 ·90	14 ·21	4
5	Fr	20	7 ·94	15 ·26	5
6	Sa	21	... ...	16 ·33	6
7	Su	22	8 ·00	17 ·42	7
8	Mo	23	9 ·07	18 ·52	8
9	Tu	24	10 ·14	19 ·63	9
10	We	25	11 ·22	20 ·73	10
11	Th	26	12 ·31	21 ·83	11
12	Fr	27	13 ·38	22 ·93	12
13	Sa	28	14 ·44	... ...	13
14	Su	29	P ·47	23 ·00	14
15	Mo	30	1 ·50	24 ·06	15
16	Tu	31	2 ·49	25 ·09	16

Sep.

SOLAR reckoning: Cyclic Sidereal Year, Month and Day	Week-Day	English Month and Day	LUNAR reckoning: Tithi Ending Moment	Nakshatra Ending Moment	Muhammadan Year, Month and Day
Raudra *Simha—Avani.* 17	We	1	Nija Sravn. 3 .46	26 ·10	H. 1338 *Zi-l-hijja.* 17
18	Th	2	4 ·43	27 ·10	18
19	Fr	3	5 ·37	1 ·08	19
20	Sa	4	6 ·30	2 ·04 3 ·98	20
21	Su	5	7 ·21	4 ·92	21
22	Mo	6	8 ·11	5 ·86	22
23	Tu	7	*Bahula* 9 ·01 10 ·90	6 ·79	23
24	We	8	11 ·81	7 ·72	24
25	Th	9	12 ·71	8 ·65	25
26	Fr	10	13 ·63	9 ·60	26
27	Sa	11	14 ·55	10 ·56	27
28	Su	12	—A ·50	11 ·52	28
29	Mo	13	1 ·45	12 ·51	29
30	Tu	14	2 ·43	13 ·51	—30
—31	We	15	3 ·42	14 ·53	H. 1339 *Muharram.* 1
Raudra *Kanya—Purattasi.* 1	Th	16	Bhadrapada *Sukla* 4 ·48	15 ·57	2
2	Fr	17	5 ·47	16 ·64	3
3	Sa	18	6 ·51	17 ·72	4
4	Su	19	7 ·59	18 ·82	5
5	Mo	20	8 ·67	19 ·92	6
6	Tu	21	9 ·76	... ...	7
7	We	22	10 ·83	20 ·03	8
8	Th	23	11 ·90	21 ·14	9
9	Fr	24	12 ·97	22 ·23	10
10	Sa	25	... ...	23 ·31	11
11	Su	26	13 ·01	24 ·37	12
12	Mo	27	14 ·03	25 ·41	13
13	Tu	28	P ·03	26 ·43	14
14	We	29	1 ·01 2 ·98	27 ·43	15
15	Th	30	3 ·91	1 ·41	16

Oct.

SOLAR reckoning: Cyclic Sidereal Year, Month and Day	Week-Day	English Month and Day	LUNAR reckoning: Tithi Ending Moment	Nakshatra Ending Moment	Muhammadan Year, Month and Day
16	Fr	1	4 ·84	2 ·37	17
17	Sa	2	5 ·75	3 ·32	18
18	Su	3	6 ·66	4 ·27	19
19	Mo	4	7 ·57	5 ·20	20
20	Tu	5	*Bahula* 8 ·47	6 ·13	21
21	We	6	9 ·36	7 ·06 8 ·99	22
22	Th	7	10 ·27	9 ·93	23
23	Fr	8	11 ·18	10 ·89	24
24	Sa	9	12 ·11	11 ·85	25
25	Su	10	13 ·06	12 ·83	26
26	Mo	11	14 ·00 A ·99	13 ·83	27
27	Tu	12	1 ·98	14 ·84	28
28	We	13	... ...	15 ·89	29
29	Th	14	2 ·00	16 ·95	—30
30	Fr	15	3 ·03	... ...	H. 1339 *Safar.* 1
—31	Sa	16	4 ·09	17 ·03	2
Raudra *Tula—Aippasi.* 1	Su	17	Asvina *Sukla* 5 ·16	18 ·12	3
2	Mo	18	6 ·24	19 ·22	4
3	Tu	19	7 ·33	20 ·34	5
4	We	20	8 ·41	21 ·44	6
5	Th	21	9 ·50	22 ·54	7
6	Fr	22	10 ·56	23 ·62	8
7	Sa	23	11 ·59	24 ·68	9
8	Su	24	12 ·62	25 ·73	10
9	Mo	25	13 ·61	26 ·75	11
10	Tu	26	14 ·59	27 ·75	12
11	We ○	27	P ·55	1 ·74	13
12	Th	28	1 ·50	2 ·70	14
13	Fr	29	*Bah.* 2 ·43	3 ·65	15
14	Sa	30	3 ·35	4 ·60	16
15	Su	31	4 ·25	5 .54	17

Nov.

SOLAR reckoning: Cyclic Sidereal Year, Month and Day	Week-Day	English Month and Day	LUNAR reckoning: Tithi Ending Moment	Nakshatra Ending Moment	Muhammadan Year, Month and Day
Raudra *Tula—Aippasi.* 16	Mo	1	5 ·15	6 ·47	H. 1339 *Safar.* 18
17	Tu	2	Asv. 6 ·05 7 ·95	7 ·40	19
18	We	3	8 ·87	8 ·33	20
19	Th	4	9 ·78	9 ·27	21
20	Fr	5	*Bahula* 10 ·71	10 ·22	22
21	Sa	6	11 ·65	11 ·18	23
22	Su	7	12 ·60	12 ·16	24
23	Mo	8	13 ·59	13 ·15	25
24	Tu	9	14 ·58	14 ·17	26
25	We	10	—A ·60	15 ·20	27
26	Th	11	1 ·63	16 ·26	28
27	Fr	12	2 ·70	17 ·33	—29
28	Sa	13	3 ·78	18 ·42	H. 1339 *Rabi-ul-awwal.* 1
—29	Su	14	4 ·87	19 ·53	2
Raudra *Vrischika—Kartigai.* 1	Mo	15	Kartika *Sukla* 5 ·95	20 ·64	3
2	Tu	16	... ...	21 ·74	4
3	We	17	6 ·03	22 ·84	5
4	Th	18	7 ·10	23 ·92	6
5	Fr	19	8 ·17	... ...	7
6	Sa	20	9 ·22	24 ·00	8
7	Su	21	10 ·23	25 ·05	9
8	Mo	22	11 ·23	26 ·07	10
9	Tu	23	12 ·21	27 ·08	11
10	We	24	13 ·17	1 ·06	12
11	Th	25	14 ·12	2 ·03	13
12	Fr	26	P ·05 1 ·97	3 ·00 4 ·94	14
13	Sa	27	2 ·87	5 ·88	15
14	Su	28	3 ·78	6 ·81	16
15	Mo	29	4 ·67	7 ·74	17
16	Tu	30	5 ·58	8 ·67	18

Dec.

SOLAR reckoning: Cyclic Sidereal Year, Month and Day	Week-Day	English Month and Day	LUNAR reckoning: Tithi Ending Moment	Nakshatra Ending Moment	Muhammadan Year, Month and Day
17	We	1	*Bahula* 6 ·49	9 ·61	19
18	Th	2	7 ·40	10 ·56	20
19	Fr	3	8 ·32	11 ·51	21
20	Sa	4	9 ·27	12 ·48	22
21	Su	5	10 ·23	13 ·48	23
22	Mo	6	11 ·21	14 ·49	24
23	Tu	7	12 ·22	15 ·52	25
24	We	8	13 ·24	16 ·57	26
25	Th	9	14 ·27	17 ·63	27
26	Fr	10	—A ·34	18 ·73	28
27	Sa	11	1 ·42	19 ·83	29
28	Su	12	2 ·51	20 ·93	—30
29	Mo	13	3 ·59	... ...	H. 1339 *Rabi-ul-akhir.* 1
—30	Tu	14	4 ·69	21 ·04	2
Raudra *Dhanus—Margali.* 1	We	15	Margasira *Sukla* 5 ·75	22 ·14	3
2	Th	16	6 ·81	23 ·23	4
3	Fr	17	7 ·86	24 ·31	5
4	Sa	18	8 ·87	25 ·36	6
5	Su	19	9 ·87	26 ·39	7
6	Mo	20	10 ·84	27 ·40	8
7	Tu	21	11 ·82	1 ·39	9
8	We	22	12 ·75	2 ·37	10
9	Th	23	13 ·68	3 ·33	11
10	Fr	24	14 ·60	4 ·28	12
11	Sa	25	P ·30	5 ·21	13
12	Su	26	1 ·41	6 ·15	14
13	Mo	27	2 ·31	7 ·08	15
14	Tu	28	*Bah.* 3 ·21	8 ·01 9 ·95	16
15	We	29	4 ·12	10 ·89	17
16	Th	30	5 ·05 6 ·97	11 ·84	18
17	Fr	31	7 ·91	12 ·81	19

15. Svati. 16. Visak. 17. Anur. 18. Jyesh. 19. Mula. 20. P. Ash. 21. U, Ash. 22. Sravn. 23. Dani. 24. Satab. 25. P. Bhad. 26. U. Bhad. 27. Rev.

A. D. 1921.
Solar Eclipse. ●
Lunar Eclipse. ○

Mesha Sankranti (Commencement of Indian Sidereal Year).
(Surya Sid.) April 13·05.
(Arya Sid.) April 12·94.

Saka 1843. **Kaliyuga 5022.**
(S. Cycle) Durmati.

SOLAR reckoning: Cyclic Sidereal Year, Month and Day; Week-Day, English Month and Day. LUNAR reckoning: Tithi Ending Moment; Nakshatra Ending Moment; Muhammadan Year, Month and Day.

Jan.

Solar label	Cyclic Sidereal Day	Week-Day	Jan.	Lunar label	Tithi	Ending Moment	Nakshatra	Ending Moment	Muhammadan label	Muhammadan Day
Raudra Dhanus—Margali.	18	Sa	1	Marg.	8	·87	13	·81		20
	19	Su	2		9	·86	14	·81	Rabi-ul-akhir.	21
	20	Mo	3		10	·86	15	·83		22
	21	Tu	4	Bahula	11	·88	16	·87		23
	22	We	5		12	·93	17	·95		24
	23	Th	6		13	·99	…	…		25
	24	Fr	7		…	…	18	·03		26
	25	Sa	8		14	·06	19	·13		27
	26	Su	9		—A	·16	20	·23		28
	27	Mo	10		1	·24	21	·34		—29
	28	Tu	11		2	·33	22	·44		1
	—29	We	12		3	·41	23	·54		2
	1	Th	13		4	·47	24	·62		3
Raudra Makara—Tai.	2	Fr	14		5	·50	25	·67		4
	3	Sa	15		6	·51	26	·71		5
	4	Su	16	Sukla	7	·52	27	·72		6
	5	Mo	17		8	·49	1	·73		7
	6	Tu	18		9	·45	2	·70		8
	7	We	19		10	·40	3	·66		9
	8	Th	20		11	·33	4	·61		10
	9	Fr	21		12	·23	5	·55		11
	10	Sa	22		13	·14	6	·49	H. 1339 Jumadal-awwal.	12
	11	Su	23		14 P	·03 ·94	7	·42		13
	12	Mo	24	Pausha	1	·85	8	·35		14
	13	Tu	25		2	·75	9	·29		15
	14	We	26		3	·68	10	·23		16
	15	Th	27		4	·61	11	·19		17
	16	Fr	28		5	·56	12	·15		18
	17	Sa	29		6	·51	13	·13		19
	18	Su	30		7	·50	14	·13		20
	19	Mo	31		8	·50	15	·15		21

Feb.

Solar label	Cyclic Sidereal Day	Week-Day	Feb.	Lunar label	Tithi	Ending Moment	Nakshatra	Ending Moment	Muhammadan label	Muhammadan Day
	20	Tu	1	Bahula	9	·52	16	·18		22
	21	We	2		10	·57	17	·25		23
	22	Th	3		11	·64	18	·33		24
	23	Fr	4		12	·72	19	·43		25
	24	Sa	5		13	·80	20	·53		26
	25	Su	6		14	·89	21	·64		27
	26	Mo	7		—A	·98	22	·75		28
	27	Tu	8		…	…	23	·84		29
	28	We	9		1	·05	24	92		—30
	29	Th	10		2	·11	25	·98		1
	—30	Fr	11		3	·13	…	…		2
	1	Sa	12		4	·15	26	·02		3
	2	Su	13		5	·15	27	·05		4
	3	Mo	14	Sukla	6	·13	1	·05	H. 1339 Jumadal-akhir.	5
	4	Tu	15		7	·07	2	·03		6
	5	We	16		8 9	·01 ·95	3 4	·00 ·95		7
Raudra Kumbha—Masi.	6	Th	17		10	·86	5	·90		8
	7	Fr	18		11	·77	6	·83		9
	8	Sa	19		12	·66	7	·76		10
	9	Su	20	Magha	13	·57	8	·69		11
	10	Mo	21		14	·47	9	·62		12
	11	Tu	22		P	·38	10	·57		13
	12	We	23		1	·30	11	·52		14
	13	Th	24		2	·22	12	·48		15
	14	Fr	25	Bahula	3	·17	13	·46		16
	15	Sa	26		4	·13	14	·45		17
	16	Su	27		5	·12	15	·46		18
	17	Mo	28		6	·12	16	·51		19

March

Solar label	Cyclic Sidereal Day	Week-Day	March	Lunar label	Tithi	Ending Moment	Nakshatra	Ending Moment	Muhammadan label	Muhammadan Day
	18	Tu	1	Magha	7	·16	17	·56		20
Raudra Kumbha—Masi.	19	We	2		8	·20	18	·64	Jumadal-akhir.	21
	20	Th	3		9	·25	19	.73		22
	21	Fr	4		10	·34	20	·83		23
	22	Sa	5		11	·42	21	·94		24
	23	Su	6	Bahula	12	·51	…	…		25
	24	Mo	7		13	·60	22	·05		26
	25	Tu	8		14	·67	23	·15		27
	26	We	9		—A	·72	24	·23		28
	27	Th	10		1	·75	25	·29		—29
	28	Fr	11		2	·76	26	·35		1
	29	Sa	12		3	·75	27	·37		2
	—30	Su	13		4	·72	1	·38		3
	1	Mo	14		5	·67	2	·36		4
	2	Tu	15		6	·62	3	·33		5
	3	We	16	Sukla	7	·54	4	·29		6
	4	Th	17		8	·45	5	·24		7
	5	Fr	18		9	·36	6	·17		8
	6	Sa	19		10	·25	7	·10		9
	7	Su	20		11	·16	8 9	·03 ·96		10
	8	Mo	21		12 13	·06 ·98	10	·90		11
Raudra Mina—Panguni.	9	Tu	22	Phalguna	14	·89	11	·85		12
	10	We	23		P	·82	12	·81		13
	11	Th	24		1	·76	13	·78	H. 1339 Rajab.	14
	12	Fr	25		2	·72	14	·77		15
	13	Sa	26		3	·71	15	·79		16
	14	Su	27		4	·70	16	·82		17
	15	Mo	28		5	·74	17	·87		18
	16	Tu	29		6	·78	18	·94		19
	17	We	30		7	·84	…	…		20
	18	Th	31		8	·92	19	·03		21

April

Solar label	Cyclic Sidereal Day	Week-Day	April	Lunar label	Tithi	Ending Moment	Nakshatra	Ending Moment	Muhammadan label	Muhammadan Day
	19	Fr	1	Bahula	…	…	20	·14		22
	20	Sa	2		9	·00	21	·24		23
	21	Su	3		10	·09	22	·35		24
	22	Mo	4		11	·17	23	·45		25
	23	Tu	5		12	·24	24	·53		26
	24	We	6		13	·29	25	·61		27
	25	Th	7		14	·33	26	·66		28
	26	Fr ●	8		—A	·33	27	·69		29
	27	Sa	9		1	·32	1	·70		—30
	28	Su	10		2	·29	2	·69		1
	29	Mo	11		3	·24	3	·67		2
	—30	Tu	12	Sukla	4	·18	4	·63		3
	1	We	13		5	·10	5	·57		4
	2	Th	14		6 7	·02 ·92	6	·51		5
	3	Fr	15		8	·82	7	·44		6
	4	Sa	16		9	·72	8	·37		7
	5	Su	17		10	·61	9	·30	H. 1339 Shaban.	8
	6	Mo	18		11	·53	10	·24		9
Durmati Mesha—Chittirai.	7	Tu	19		12	·44	11	·19		10
	8	We	20	Chaitra	13	·37	12	·14		11
	9	Th	21		14	·30	13	·11		12
	10	Fr ○	22		P	·27	14	·10		13
	11	Sa	23		1	·25	15	·11		14
	12	Su	24		2	·24	16	·13		15
	13	Mo	25		3	·28	17	·18		16
	14	Tu	26		4	·32	18	·24		17
	15	We	27	Bahula	5	·38	19	·34		18
	16	Th	28		6	·46	20	·44		19
	17	Fr	29		7	·54	21	·54		20
	18	Sa	30		8	·62	22	·65		21

May

Solar label	Cyclic Sidereal Day	Week-Day	May	Lunar label	Tithi	Ending Moment	Nakshatra	Ending Moment	Muhammadan label	Muhammadan Day
	19	Su	1	Ch.	9	·70	23	·75		22
	20	Mo	2		10	·77	24	·85		23
Durmati Mesha—Chittirai.	21	Tu	3	Bahula	11	·82	25	·92	Shaban.	24
	22	We	4		12	·86	26	·97		25
	23	Th	5		13	·85	…	…		26
	24	Fr	6		14	·85	27	·01		27
	25	Sa	7		—A	·82	1	·02		28
	26	Su	8		1	·77	2	·01		—29
	27	Mo	9		2	·71	3 4	·00 ·96		1
	28	Tu	10		3	·62	5	·91		2
	29	We	11		4	·54	6	·85		3
	30	Th	12	Sukla	5	·44	7	·79		4
	—31	Fr	13		6	·34	8	·72		5
	1	Sa	14		7	·24	9	·66		6
	2	Su	15		8	·13	10	·58		7
	3	Mo	16		9 10	·04 ·95	11	·52		8
	4	Tu	17		11	·88	12	·47		9
	5	We	18		12	·83	13	·45		10
	6	Th	19	Vaisakha	13	·78	14	·48		11
	7	Fr	20		14	·76	15	·43		12
	8	Sa	21		P	·76	16	·45	H. 1339 Ramzan.	13
	9	Su	22		1	·79	17	·49		14
Durmati Vrishabha—Vaikasi.	10	Mo	23		2	·89	18	·56		15
	11	Tu	24		3	·88	19	·64		16
	12	We	25		4	·95	20	·73		17
	13	Th	26		…	…	21	·84		18
	14	Fr	27		5	·04	22	·94		19
	15	Sa	28	Bahula	6	·12	…	…		20
	16	Su	29		7	·20	23	·05		21
	17	Mo	30		8	·27	24	·15		22
	18	Tu	31		9	·33	25	·23		23

June

Solar label	Cyclic Sidereal Day	Week-Day	June	Lunar label	Tithi	Ending Moment	Nakshatra	Ending Moment	Muhammadan label	Muhammadan Day
	19	We	1		10	·34	26	·29		24
	20	Th	2		11	·35	27	·32		25
	21	Fr	3		12	·35	1	·34		26
	22	Sa	4		13	·32	2	·35		27
	23	Su	5		14	·27	3	·33		28
	24	Mo	6		—A	·21	4	·29		29
	25	Tu	7		1	·14	5	·24		—30
	26	We	8		2 3	·04 ·94	6	·18		1
	27	Th	9		4	·83	7	·12		2
	28	Fr	10		5	·73	8 9	·05 ·98		3
	29	Sa	11		6	·63	10	·92		4
	30	Su	12	Sukla	7	·54	11	·86		5
	—31	Mo	13		8	·46	12	·81	H. 1339 Shawwal.	6
	1	Tu	14		9	·37	13	·78		7
	2	We	15		10	·32	14	·75		8
	3	Th	16		11	·27	15	·75		9
Durmati Mithuna—Ani.	4	Fr	17	Jyeshtha	12	·25	16	·76		10
	5	Sa	18		13	·24	17	·81		11
	6	Su	19		14	·26	18	·87		12
	7	Mo	20		P	·31	19	·94		13
	8	Tu	21		1	·36	…	…		14
	9	We	22		2	·43	20	·03		15
	10	Th	23		3	·51	21	·13		16
	11	Fr	24		4	·59	22	·24		17
	12	Sa	25		5	·67	23	·36		18
	13	Su	26	Bahula	6	·74	24	·45		19
	14	Mo	27		7	·79	25	·53		20
	15	Tu	28		8	·82	26	·60		21
	16	We	29		9	·84	27	·64		22
	17	Th	30		10	·83	1	·67		23

Nakṣh:—1. Asvn. 2. Bhar. 3. Krit. 4. Rohi. 5. Mrig. 6. Ardh. 7. Punar. 8. Push. 9. Aslesh. 10. Magh. 11. P. Phal. 12. U. Phal. 13. Hasta. 14. Chit.

A. D. 1921.	Kollam 1097, Commences { N. Malabar—Sept. / S. Malabar—Aug.	Hijra 1340, Commences, Sep. 4.	Vikrama 1978.
A.—Amavasya.			Bengal San 1327.
P.—Paurnami.			(N. Cycle) Srimukha.

SOLAR reckoning: Cyclic Sidereal Year, Month and Day; Week-Day English Month and Day. LUNAR reckoning: Tithi Ending Moment; Nakshatra Ending Moment; Muhammadan Year, Month and Day.

July

Solar: Durmati Mithuna—Ani. (to 32); Durmati Karkata—Adi. (from 1). Lunar: Jy. Bah.; Sukla; Ashadha; Bahula. Muhammadan: Shawwal.; H. 1339 Zi-l-ka'da.

Cyclic Sidereal	Week-Day	Day	Tithi	Moment	Nakshatra	Moment	Muhammadan
18	Fr	1	Jy. 11	·79	2	·67	24
19	Sa	2	12	·75	3	·66	25
20	Su	3	13	·69	4	·62	26
21	Mo	4	14	·61	5	·58	27
22	Tu	5	—A	·51	6	·53	28
23	We	6	1	·42	7	·46	-29
24	Th	7	2	·31	8	·39	1
25	Fr	8	3	·22	9	·32	2
26	Sa	9	4	·11	10	·25	3
27	Su	10	5 6	·01 ·93	11	·20	4
28	Mo	11	7	·85	12	·15	5
29	Tu	12	8	·80	13	·11	6
30	We	13	9	·75	14	·08	7
31	Th	14	10	·73	15	·07	8
—32	Fr	15	11	·72	16	·08	9
1	Sa	16	12	·73	17	·12	10
2	Su	17	13	·78	18	·17	11
3	Mo	18	14	·83	19	·24	12
4	Tu	19	P	·90	20	·33	13
5	We	20	1	·97	21	·43	14
6	Th	21	...	...	22	·55	15
7	Fr	22	2	·07	23	·65	16
8	Sa	23	3	·14	24	·75	17
9	Su	24	4	·20	25	·84	18
10	Mo	25	5	·25	26	·91	19
11	Tu	26	6	·30	27	·96	20
12	We	27	7	·32	1	·99	21
13	Th	28	8	·31	...	...	22
14	Fr	29	9	·28	2 3	·00 ·99	23
15	Sa	30	10	·23	4	·96	24
16	Su	31	11	·18	5	·92	25

Aug.

Solar: Durmati Simha—Avani. Lunar: Sukla; Sravana; Bahula. Muhammadan: H. 1339 Zi-l-hijja.

Cyclic Sidereal	Week-Day	Day	Tithi	Moment	Nakshatra	Moment	Muhammadan
17	Mo	1	12	·10	6	·87	26
18	Tu	2	13 14	·00 ·91	7	·80	27
19	We	3	—A	·81	8	·73	28
20	Th	4	1	·71	9	·66	29
21	Fr	5	2	·60	10	·60	—30
22	Sa	6	3	·51	11	·54	1
23	Su	7	4	·43	12	·48	2
24	Mo	8	5	·34	13	·44	3
25	Tu	9	6	·28	14	·41	4
26	We	10	7	·23	15	·39	5
27	Th	11	8	·22	16	·41	6
28	Fr	12	9	·21	17	·43	7
29	Sa	13	10	·22	18	·48	8
30	Su	14	11	·26	19	·55	9
—31	Mo	15	12	·32	20	·63	10
1	Tu	16	13	·39	21	·74	11
2	We	17	14	·47	22	·85	12
3	Th	18	P	·56	23	·95	13
4	Fr	19	1	·68	...	...	14
5	Sa	20	2	·70	24	·05	15
6	Su	21	3	·76	25	·14	16
7	Mo	22	4	·80	26	·22	17
8	Tu	23	5	·81	27	·28	18
9	We	24	6	·80	1	·31	19
10	Th	25	7	·78	2	·32	20
11	Fr	26	8	·74	3	·31	21
12	Sa	27	9	·69	4	·30	22
13	Su	28	10	·61	5	·26	23
14	Mo	29	11	·51	6	·20	24
15	Tu	30	12	·41	7	·14	25
16	We	31	13	·31	8	·07	26

Sep.

Solar: Durmati Simha—Avani. (to 31); Durmati Kanya—Purattasi. (from 1). Lunar: Sukla; Bhadrapada; Bahula. Muhammadan: H. 1340 Muharram.

Cyclic Sidereal	Week-Day	Day	Tithi	Moment	Nakshatra	Moment	Muhammadan
17	Th	1	14	·21	9 10	·00 ·93	27
18	Fr	2	—A	·11	11	·87	28
19	Sa	3	1 2	·02 ·94	12	·82	—29
20	Su	4	3	·87	13	·77	1
21	Mo	5	4	·80	14	·73	2
22	Tu	6	5	·75	15	·73	3
23	We	7	6	·73	16	·73	4
24	Th	8	7	·72	17	·75	5
25	Fr	9	8	·74	18	·79	6
26	Sa	10	9	·78	19	·85	7
27	Su	11	10	·84	20	·94	8
28	Mo	12	11	·91	...	...	9
29	Tu	13	...	...	21	·04	10
30	We	14	12	·00	22	·14	11
—31	Th	15	13	·08	23	·25	12
1	Fr	16	14	·15	24	·35	13
2	Sa	17	P	·28	25	·46	14
3	Su	18	1	·28	26	·53	15
4	Mo	19	2	·32	27	·59	16
5	Tu	20	3	·33	1	·63	17
6	We	21	4	·34	2	·64	18
7	Th	22	5	·31	3	·65	19
8	Fr	23	6	·28	4	·63	20
9	Sa	24	7	·22	5	·59	21
10	Su	25	8	·13	6	·54	22
11	Mo	26	9 10	·05 ·95	7	·48	23
12	Tu	27	11	·86	8	·41	24
13	We	28	12	·76	9	·33	25
14	Th	29	13	·66	10	·28	26
15	Fr	80	14	·56	11	·21	27

Oct.

Solar: Durmati Tula—Aippasi. Lunar: Sukla; Asvina; Bahula. Muhammadan: H. 1340 Safar.

Cyclic Sidereal	Week-Day	Day	Tithi	Moment	Nakshatra	Moment	Muhammadan
16	Sa	1	—A	·47	12	·15	28
17	Su	2	1	·41	13	·10	29
18	Mo	3	2	·35	14	·07	—30
19	Tu	4	3	·30	15	·05	1
20	We	5	4	·28	16	·05	2
21	Th	6	5	·28	17	·06	3
22	Fr	7	6	·29	18	·10	4
23	Sa	8	7	·33	19	·17	5
24	Su	9	8	·40	20	·25	6
25	Mo	10	9	·47	21	·34	7
26	Tu	11	10	·55	22	·44	8
27	We	12	11	·63	23	·55	9
28	Th	13	12	·72	24	·66	10
29	Fr	14	13	·80	25	·76	11
30	Sa	15	14	·85	26	·84	12
—31	Su ○	16	P	·89	27	·90	13
1	Mo	17	1	·91	1	·94	14
2	Tu	18	2	·91	2	·96	15
3	We	19	3	·88	3	·97	16
4	Th	20	4	·85	4	·95	17
5	Fr	21	5	·80	5	·92	18
6	Sa	22	6	·72	6	·87	19
7	Su	23	7	·63	7	·82	20
8	Mo	24	8	·53	8	·76	21
9	Tu	25	9	·44	9	·69	22
10	We	26	10	·33	10	·62	23
11	Th	27	11	·24	11	·55	24
12	Fr	28	12	·14	12	·49	25
13	Sa	29	13	·07	13	·44	26
14	Su	30	14 A	·00 ·94	14	·40	27
15	Mo	31	1	·89	15	·38	28

Nov.

Solar: Durmati Tula—Aippasi. (to 30); Durmati Vrischika—Kartigai. (from 1). Lunar: Sukla; Karttika; Bahula. Muhammadan: H. 1340 Rabi-ul-awwal.

Cyclic Sidereal	Week-Day	Day	Tithi	Moment	Nakshatra	Moment	Muhammadan
16	Tu	1	2	·87	16	·37	—29
17	We	2	3	·87	17	·38	1
18	Th	3	4	·89	18	·42	2
19	Fr	4	5	·94	19	·48	3
20	Sa	5	...	...	20	·55	4
21	Su	6	6	·00	21	·64	5
22	Mo	7	7	·08	22	·74	6
23	Tu	8	8	·16	23	·86	7
24	We	9	9	·25	24	·96	8
25	Th	10	10	·34	...	...	9
26	Fr	11	11	·40	25	·06	10
27	Sa	12	12	·46	26	·14	11
28	Su	13	13	·49	27	·21	12
29	Mo	14	14	·52	1	·26	13
—30	Tu	15	P	·52	2	·29	14
1	We	16	1	·49	3	·30	15
2	Th	17	2	·45	4	·28	16
3	Fr	18	3	·40	5	·25	17
4	Sa	19	4	·33	6	·21	18
5	Su	20	5	·24	7	·16	19
6	Mo	21	6	·15	8	·10	20
7	Tu	22	7 8	·06 ·95	9 10	·03 ·96	21
8	We	23	9	·86	11	·89	22
9	Th	24	10	·76	12	·83	23
10	Fr	25	11	·69	13	·78	24
11	Sa	26	12	·61	14	·73	25
12	Su	27	13	·56	15	·70	26
13	Mo	28	14	·51	16	·69	27
14	Tu	29	—A	·50	17	·71	28
15	We	30	1	·50	18	·74	29

Dec.

Solar: Durmati Dhanus—Margali. Lunar: Sukla; Margasira; Bahula; Suk. Muhammadan: H. 1340 Rabi-ul-akhir.

Cyclic Sidereal	Week-Day	Day	Tithi	Moment	Nakshatra	Moment	Muhammadan
16	Th	1	2	·52	19	·79	—30
17	Fr	2	3	·56	20	·85	1
18	Sa	3	4	·62	21	·94	2
19	Su	4	5	·71	...	...	3
20	Mo	5	6	·79	22	·04	4
21	Tu	6	7	·88	23	·15	5
22	We	7	8	·97	24	·26	6
23	Th	8	...	...	25	·36	7
24	Fr	9	9	·01	26	·45	8
25	Sa	10	10	·10	27	·52	9
26	Su	11	11	·13	1	·58	10
27	Mo	12	12	·16	2	·61	11
28	Tu	13	13	·15	3	·62	12
—29	We	14	14	·13	4	·61	13
1	Th	15	P	·09	5	·58	14
2	Fr	16	1 2	·02 ·95	6	·55	15
3	Sa	17	3	·87	7	·50	16
4	Su	18	4	·78	8	·43	17
5	Mo	19	5	·68	9	·36	18
6	Tu	20	6	·58	10	·29	19
7	We	21	7	·49	11	·23	20
8	Th	22	8	·40	12	·17	21
9	Fr	23	9	·31	13	·11	22
10	Sa	24	10	25	14	·06	23
11	Su	25	11	·20	15	·03	24
12	Mo	26	12	·15	16	·02	25
13	Tu	27	13	·15	17	·08	26
14	We	28	14	·14	18	·05	27
15	Th	29	—A	·17	19	·09	28
16	Fr	30	1	·22	20	·16	—29
17	Sa	31	2	·28	21	·24	1

15. Svati. 16. Visak. 17. Anur. 18. Jyesh. 19. Mula. 20. P. Ash. 21. U. Ash. 22. Sravn. 23. Dani. 24. Satab. 25. P. Bhad. 26. U. Bhad. 27. Rev.

A. D. 1922. **Mesha Sankranti** (Commencement of Indian Sidereal Year).
Solar Eclipse. ●
Lunar Eclipse. ○

(Surya Sid.) April 13·31 — (Arya Sid.) April 13·20.

Saka 1844. **Kaliyuga 5023.** **(S. Cycle) Dundubhi.**

Columns: SOLAR reckoning — Cyclic Sidereal Year, Month and Day; Week-Day English Month and Day. LUNAR reckoning — Tithi Ending Moment; Nakshatra Ending Moment; Muhammadan Year, Month and Day.

Jan. — Solar: Durmati, Dhanus—Margali (to 30), then Durmati, Makara—Tai. Lunar: Pausha (Sukla, Bahula). Muhammadan: H. 1340 Jumadal-awwal.

Cyclic Sidereal	Week-Day	Day	Tithi	Moment	Nakshatra	Moment	Muhammadan
18	Su	1	3	·36	22	·34	2
19	Mo	2	4	·44	23	·45	3
20	Tu	3	5	·54	24	·56	4
21	We	4	6	·62	25	·66	5
22	Th	5	7	·69	26	·75	6
23	Fr	6	8	·75	27	·84	7
24	Sa	7	9	·78	1	·89	8
25	Su	8	10	·80	2	·93	9
26	Mo	9	11	·80	3	·94	10
27	Tu	10	12	·78	4	·94	11
28	We	11	13	·73	5	·92	12
29	Th	12	14	·68	6	·88	13
—30	Fr	13	P	·60	7	·83	14
1	Sa	14	1	·52	8	·77	15
2	Su	15	2	·42	9	·70	16
3	Mo	16	3	·32	10	·64	17
4	Tu	17	4	·23	11	·57	18
5	We	18	5	·13	12	·50	19
6	Th	19	6	·04	13	·45	20
			7	·96			
7	Fr	20	8	·90	14	·40	21
8	Sa	21	9	·84	15	·36	22
9	Su	22	10	·80	16	·35	23
10	Mo	23	11	·79	17	·35	24
11	Tu	24	12	·78	18	·37	25
12	We	25	13	·82	19	·41	26
13	Th	26	14	·87	20	·46	27
14	Fr	27	—A	·94	21	·55	28
15	Sa	28	...	...	22	·65	29
16	Su	29	1	·01	23	·75	—30
17	Mo	30	2	·11	24	·86	1
18	Tu	31	3	·19	25	·96	2

Feb. — Solar: Durmati, Makara—Tai (to 29), then Durmati, Kumbha—Masi. Lunar: Magha (Sukla, Bahula), Suk. Muhammadan: H. 1340 Jumadal-akhir.

Cyclic Sidereal	Week-Day	Day	Tithi	Moment	Nakshatra	Moment	Muhammadan
19	We	1	4	·27	...	...	3
20	Th	2	5	·34	26	·06	4
21	Fr	3	6	·39	27	·14	5
22	Sa	4	7	·43	1	·20	6
23	Su	5	8	·44	2	·24	7
24	Mo	6	9	·44	3	·26	8
25	Tu	7	10	·41	4	·27	9
26	We	8	11	·37	5	·25	10
27	Th	9	12	·30	6	·22	11
28	Fr	10	13	·22	7	·17	12
—29	Sa	11	14	·14	8	·11	13
1	Su	12	P	·04	9	·04	14
			1	·95	10	98	
2	Mo	13	2	·85	11	·91	15
3	Tu	14	3	·75	12	·84	16
4	We	15	4	·66	13	·78	17
5	Th	16	5	·58	14	·73	18
6	Fr	17	6	·52	15	·70	19
7	Sa	18	7	·47	16	·67	20
8	Su	19	8	·43	17	·67	21
9	Mo	20	9	·41	18	·68	22
10	Tu	21	10	·41	19	·72	23
11	We	22	11	·45	20	·78	24
12	Th	23	12	·49	21	·86	25
13	Fr	24	13	·56	22	·93	26
14	Sa	25	14	·63	...	...	27
15	Su	26	—A	·73	23	·05	28
16	Mo	27	1	·82	24	·15	—29
17	Tu	28	2	·90	25	·27	1

March — Solar: Durmati, Kumbha—Masi (to 30), then Durmati, Mina—Panguni. Lunar: Phalguna (Sukla, Bahula). Muhammadan: H. 1340 Rajab.

Cyclic Sidereal	Week-Day	Day	Tithi	Moment	Nakshatra	Moment	Muhammadan
18	We	1	3	·96	26	·37	2
19	Th	2	...	...	27	·45	3
20	Fr	3	4	·01	1	·51	4
21	Sa	4	5	·05	2	·56	5
22	Su	5	6	·05	3	·59	6
23	Mo	6	7	·05	4	·60	7
24	Tu	7	8	·02	5	·59	8
			9	·98			
25	We	8	10	·91	6	55	9
26	Th	9	11	·83	7	·50	10
27	Fr	10	12	·75	8	·45	11
28	Sa	11	13	·65	9	·39	12
29	Su	12	14	·56	10	·32	13
—30	Mo	13	P	·45	11	·25	14
1	Tu	14	1	·36	12	·18	15
2	We	15	2	·26	13	·12	16
3	Th	16	3	·18	14	·07	17
4	Fr	17	4	·11	15	·03	18
5	Sa	18	5	·05	16	·00	19
					17	·99	
6	Su	19	6	·03	...	...	20
7	Mo	20	7	·01	18	·00	21
8	Tu	21	8	·01	19	·04	22
9	We	22	9	·04	20	·09	23
10	Th	23	10	·09	21	·16	24
11	Fr	24	11	·15	22	·25	25
12	Sa	25	12	·23	23	·35	26
13	Su	26	13	·32	24	·46	27
14	Mo	27	14	·40	25	·57	28
15	Tu	● 28	—A	48	26	·67	29
16	We	29	1	·54	27	·75	—30
17	Th	30	2	·60	1	·82	1
18	Fr	31	3	·64	2	·87	2

April — Solar: Durmati, Mina—Panguni (to 30), then Dundubhi, Mesha—Chittirai. Lunar: Chaitra (Sukla, Bahula), Y. Suk. Muhammadan: H. 1340 Shaban.

Cyclic Sidereal	Week-Day	Day	Tithi	Moment	Nakshatra	Moment	Muhammadan
19	Sa	1	4	·63	3	·91	3
20	Su	2	5	·62	4	·92	4
21	Mo	3	6	·59	5	·91	5
22	Tu	4	7	·55	6	·88	6
23	We	5	8	·48	7	·84	7
24	Th	6	9	·41	8	·79	8
25	Fr	7	10	·32	9	·73	9
26	Sa	8	11	·23	10	·66	10
27	Su	9	12	·12	11	·59	11
28	Mo	10	13	·01	12	·52	12
			14	·92			
29	Tu	11	P	·82	13	·46	13
—30	We	12	1	·74	14	·41	14
1	Th	13	2	·67	15	·36	15
2	Fr	14	3	·62	16	·33	16
3	Sa	15	4	·58	17	·31	17
4	Su	16	5	·56	18	·33	18
5	Mo	17	6	·57	19	·35	19
6	Tu	18	7	·59	20	·40	20
7	We	19	8	·64	21	·46	21
8	Th	20	9	·70	22	·55	22
9	Fr	21	10	·78	23	·65	23
10	Sa	22	11	·86	24	·76	24
11	Su	23	12	·95	25	·87	25
12	Mo	24	...	...	26	·97	26
13	Tu	25	13	·02	...	...	27
14	We	26	14	·09	27	·06	28
15	Th	27	—A	·14	1	·13	—29
16	Fr	28	1	·18	2	·19	1
17	Sa	29	2	·19	3	·28	2
18	Su	30	3	·16	4	·24	3

May — Solar: Dundubhi, Mesha—Chittirai (to 31), then Dundubhi, Vrishabha—Vaikasi. Lunar: Vaisakha (Sukla, Bahula). Muhammadan: H. 1340 Ramzan.

Cyclic Sidereal	Week-Day	Day	Tithi	Moment	Nakshatra	Moment	Muhammadan
19	Mo	1	4	·14	5	·23	4
20	Tu	2	5	·08	6	·21	5
21	We	3	6	·01	7	·18	6
			7	·94			
22	Th	4	8	·85	8	·13	7
23	Fr	5	9	·75	9	·07	8
24	Sa	6	10	·64	10	·00	9
					11	·93	
25	Su	7	11	·55	12	·86	10
26	Mo	8	12	·45	13	·80	11
27	Tu	9	13	·35	14	·74	12
28	We	10	14	·26	15	·69	13
29	Th	11	P	·19	16	·66	14
30	Fr	12	1	·14	17	·65	15
—31	Sa	13	2	·10	18	·65	16
1	Su	14	3	·09	19	·67	17
2	Mo	15	4	·08	20	·71	18
3	Tu	16	5	·11	21	·77	19
4	We	17	6	·15	22	·85	20
5	Th	18	7	·21	23	·95	21
6	Fr	19	8	·29	...	...	22
7	Sa	20	9	·36	24	·06	23
8	Su	21	10	·45	25	·16	24
9	Mo	22	11	·53	26	·27	25
10	Tu	23	12	·61	27	·36	26
11	We	24	13	·65	1	·45	27
12	Th	25	14	·67	2	·51	28
13	Fr	26	—A	·69	3	·54	29
14	Sa	27	1	·67	4	·56	—30
15	Su	28	2	·64	5	·56	1
16	Mo	29	3	·59	6	·55	2
17	Tu	30	4	·53	7	·51	3
18	We	31	5	·43	8	·46	4

June — Solar: Dundubhi, Vrishabha—Vaikasi (to 32), then Dundubhi, Mithuna—Ani. Lunar: Jyeshtha (Sukla, Bahula), A. Suk. Muhammadan: H. 1340 Shawwal, then Zi-l-ka'da.

Cyclic Sidereal	Week-Day	Day	Tithi	Moment	Nakshatra	Moment	Muhammadan
19	Th	1	6	·34	9	·40	5
20	Fr	2	7	·25	10	·34	6
21	Sa	3	8	·14	11	·27	7
22	Su	4	9	·04	12	·20	8
			10	·94			
23	Mo	5	11	·85	13	·14	9
24	Tu	6	12	·77	14	·08	10
25	We	7	13	·69	15	·03	11
26	Th	8	14	·63	16	·00	12
					17	·97	
27	Fr	9	P	·59	18	·97	13
28	Sa	10	1	·57	19	·98	14
29	Su	11	2	·57	...	...	15
30	Mo	12	3	·59	20	·02	16
31	Tu	13	4	·63	21	·08	17
—32	We	14	5	·69	22	·16	18
1	Th	15	6	·76	23	·25	19
2	Fr	16	7	·84	24	·36	20
3	Sa	17	8	·93	25	·46	21
4	Su	18	...	...	26	·57	22
5	Mo	19	9	·00	27	·67	23
6	Tu	20	10	·08	1	·75	24
7	We	21	11	·13	2	·82	25
8	Th	22	12	·16	3	·86	26
9	Fr	23	13	·17	4	·88	27
10	Sa	24	14	·15	5	·89	28
11	Su	25	—A	·12	6	·88	29
12	Mo	26	1	·07	7	·84	1
13	Tu	27	2	·01	8	·80	2
			3	·92			
14	We	28	4	·84	9	·74	3
15	Th	29	5	·74	10	·68	4
16	Fr	30	6	·64	11	·61	5

Naksh :—1. Asvn. 2. Bhar. 3. Krit. 4. Rohi. 5. Mrig. 6. Ardh. 7. Punar. 8. Push. 9. Aslesh. 10. Magh. 11. P. Phal. 12. U. Phal. 13. Hasta. 14. Chit.

A. D. 1922.
A.—Amavasya.
P.—Paurnami.

Kollam 1098, Commences { N. Malabar—Sept. / S. Malabar—Aug.

Hijra 1341, Commences, Aug. 24.

Vikrama 1979.
Bengal San 1328.
(N. Cycle) Bhava.

SOLAR reckoning: Cyclic Sidereal Year, Month and Day; Week-Day English Month and Day. LUNAR reckoning: Tithi Ending Moment; Nakshatra Ending Moment; Muhammadan Year, Month and Day.

July

Solar month	Cyclic Sidereal Day	Week-Day	Day	Lunar month / paksha	Tithi	Ending Moment	Nakshatra	Ending Moment	Muhammadan month	Day
Dundubhi Mithuna—Ani.	17	Sa	1	Sukla	7	·53	12	·54	H. 1340 Zi-l-ka'da.	6
	18	Su	2		8	·43	13	·47		7
	19	Mo	3		9	·34	14	·41		8
	20	Tu	4		10	·24	15	·36		9
	21	We	5		11	·17	16	·33		10
	22	Th	6		12	·11	17	·30		11
	23	Fr	7	Ashadha	13	·07	18	·29		12
	24	Sa	8		14	·05	19	·30		13
	25	Su	9		P	·05	20	·33		14
	26	Mo	10		1	·06	21	·39		15
	27	Tu	11		2	·10	22	·47		16
	28	We	12		3	·17	23	·55		17
	29	Th	13		4	·24	24	·65		18
	30	Fr	14		5	·32	25	·76		19
	31	Sa	15		6	·40	26	·88		20
Dundubhi Karkata—Adi.	1	Su	16	Bahula	7	·49	27	·97		21
	2	Mo	17		8	·55	...	...		22
	3	Tu	18		9	·60	1	·06		23
	4	We	19		10	·64	2	·13		24
	5	Th	20		11	·65	3	·17		25
	6	Fr	21		12	·63	4	·21		26
	7	Sa	22		13	·60	5	·22		27
	8	Su	23		14	·56	6	·20		28
	9	Mo	24		A	·48	7	·18		29
	10	Tu	25		1	·41	8	·13		30
	11	We	26		2	·33	9	·08		1
	12	Th	27		3	·23	10 / 11	·02 / ·95		2
	13	Fr	28		4	·12	12	·88		3
	14	Sa	29	Sukla	5 / 6	·02 / ·92	13	·81		4
	15	Su	30		7	·82	14	·75		5
	16	Mo	31		8	·73	15	·70		6

Aug.

Solar month	Cyclic Sidereal Day	Week-Day	Day	Lunar month / paksha	Tithi	Ending Moment	Nakshatra	Ending Moment	Muhammadan month	Day
	17	Tu	1		9	·65	16	·66		7
	18	We	2		10	·59	17	·63		8
	19	Th	3		11	·55	18	·61		9
	20	Fr	4		12	·53	19	·62	H. 1340 Zi-l-hijja.	10
	21	Sa	5	Sravana	13	·54	20	·66		11
	22	Su	6		14	·55	21	·70		12
	23	Mo	7		P	·58	22	·77		13
	24	Tu	8		1	·64	23	·85		14
	25	We	9		2	·71	24	·95		15
	26	Th	10		3	·80	...	...		16
	27	Fr	11		4	·89	25	·07		17
	28	Sa	12		5	·97	26	·17		18
	29	Su	13		...	...	27	·27		19
	30	Mo	14		6	·03	1	·36		20
	31	Tu	15	Bahula	7	·09	2	·43		21
	32	We	16		8	·12	3	·50		22
Dundubhi Simha—Avani.	1	Th	17		9	·14	4	·53		23
	2	Fr	18		10	·13	5	·54		24
	3	Sa	19		11	·09	6	·53		25
	4	Su	20		12 / 13	·06 / ·99	7	·51		26
	5	Mo	21		14	·92	8	·47		27
	6	Tu	22		A	·83	9	·42		28
	7	We	23		1	·72	10	·36		29
	8	Th	24		2	·62	11	·29	H. 1341 Muharram.	1
	9	Fr	25	Sukla	3	52	12	·22		2
	10	Sa	26		4	·42	13	·15		3
	11	Su	27		5	·33	14	·09		4
	12	Mo	28	Bhadra.	6	·25	15 / 16	·04 / ·99		5
	13	Tu	29		7	·16	17	·95		6
	14	We	30		8	·11	18	·94		7
	15	Th	31		9	·06	19	·95		8

Sep.

Solar month	Cyclic Sidereal Day	Week-Day	Day	Lunar month / paksha	Tithi	Ending Moment	Nakshatra	Ending Moment	Muhammadan month	Day
	16	Fr	1	Suk.	10	·04	20	·97		9
	17	Sa	2		11	·05	...	...		10
	18	Su	3		12	·06	21	·01		11
	19	Mo	4		13	·11	22	·07		12
Dundubhi Simha—Avani.	20	Tu	5	Bhadrapada	14	·16	23	·16		13
	21	We	6		P	·22	24	·26	H. 1341 Muharram.	14
	22	Th	7		1	·30	25	·37		15
	23	Fr	8		2	·39	26	·47		16
	24	Sa	9		3	·47	27	·57		17
	25	Su	10		4	·55	1	·67		18
	26	Mo	11		5	·61	2	·74		19
	27	Tu	12	Bahula	6	·64	3	·81		20
	28	We	13		7	·67	4	·85		21
	29	Th	14		8	·65	5	·86		22
	30	Fr	15		9	·62	6	·86		23
	31	Sa	16		10	·59	7	·84		24
	1	Su	17		11	·52	8	·81		25
	2	Mo	18		12	·44	9	·76		26
	3	Tu	19		13	·35	10	·70		27
	4	We	20		14	·26	11	·63		28
	5	Th	21		A	·16	12	·56		29
	6	Fr	22		1 / 2	·06 / ·95	13	·50		30
Dundubhi Kanya—Purattasi.	7	Sa	23		3	·86	14	·43		1
	8	Su	24		4	·78	15	·37		2
	9	Mo	25		5	·70	16	·32		3
	10	Tu	26	Sukla	6	·65	17	·28		4
	11	We	27		7	·60	18	·27		5
	12	Th	28		8	·59	19	·27		6
	13	Fr	29		9	·58	20	·28		7
	14	Sa	30		10	·60	21	·32		8

Oct.

Solar month	Cyclic Sidereal Day	Week-Day	Day	Lunar month / paksha	Tithi	Ending Moment	Nakshatra	Ending Moment	Muhammadan month	Day
	15	Su	1		11	·65	22	·38		9
	16	Mo	2		12	·70	23	·47	H. 1341 Safar.	10
	17	Tu	3	Asvina	13	·78	24	·56		11
	18	We	4		14	·86	25	·66		12
	19	Th	5		P	·95	26	·77		13
	20	Fr	6		...	...	27	·87		14
	21	Sa	7		1	·03	1	·97		15
	22	Su	8		2	·11	...	...		16
	23	Mo	9		3	·17	2	·06		17
	24	Tu	10		4	·20	3	·12		18
	25	We	11		5	·23	4	·16		19
	26	Th	12		6	·21	5	·18		20
	27	Fr	13	Bahula	7	·19	6	·18		21
	28	Sa	14		8	·15	7	·17		22
	29	Su	15		9	·09	8	·14		23
	30	Mo	16		10 / 11	·01 / ·92	9	·09		24
Dundubhi Tula—Aippasi.	1	Tu	17		12	·82	10 / 11	·03 / ·97		25
	2	We	18		13	·72	12	·91		26
	3	Th	19		14	·63	13	84		27
	4	Fr	20		A	·58	14	·77		28
	5	Sa	21		1	·45	15	·71		29
	6	Su	22		2	·36	16	·65	H. 1341 Rabi-ul-awwal.	1
	7	Mo	23	Sukla	3	·28	17	·62		2
	8	Tu	24		4	·23	18	·60		3
	9	We	25		5	·18	19	·59		4
	10	Th	26		6	·17	20	·60		5
	11	Fr	27	Karttika	7	·17	21	·63		6
	12	Sa	28		8	·19	22	·69		7
	13	Su	29		9	·24	23	·77		8
	14	Mo	30		10	·30	24	·86		9
	15	Tu	31		11	·38	25	·96		10

Nov.

Solar month	Cyclic Sidereal Day	Week-Day	Day	Lunar month / paksha	Tithi	Ending Moment	Nakshatra	Ending Moment	Muhammadan month	Day
	16	We	1	Suk.	12	·45	...	...		11
	17	Th	2		13	·54	26	·07		12
	18	Fr	3		14	·62	27	·17		13
	19	Sa	4	Karttika	P	·71	1	·28		14
Dundubhi Tula—Aippasi.	20	Su	5		1	·76	2	·36		15
	21	Mo	6		2	·80	3	·43	H. 1341 Rabi-ul-awwal.	16
	22	Tu	7		3	·82	4	·48		17
	23	We	8		4	·81	5	·50		18
	24	Th	9		5	·79	6	·52		19
	25	Fr	10	Bahula	6	·74	7	·50		20
	26	Sa	11		7	·69	8	·47		21
	27	Su	12		8	·61	9	·43		22
	28	Mo	13		9	·52	10	·38		23
	29	Tu	14		10	·43	11	·32		24
	30	We	15		11	·33	12	·25		25
	1	Th	16		12	·23	13	·18		26
	2	Fr	17		13	·13	14	·11		27
	3	Sa	18		14 / A	·05 / ·97	15	·05		28
	4	Su	19		1	·90	16 / 17	·00 / ·95		29
	5	Mo	20		2	·83	18	·92		30
	6	Tu	21		3	·81	19	·91		1
Dundubhi Vrischika—Kartigai.	7	We	32		4	·79	20	·92		2
	8	Th	23		5	·79	21	·95		3
	9	Fr	24		6	·81	...	...		4
	10	Sa	25	Sukla	7	·86	22	·01		5
	11	Su	26		8	·92	23	·07		6
	12	Mo	27		...	...	24	·16		7
	13	Tu	28		9	·00	25	·26		8
	14	We	29		10	·09	26	·37		9
	15	Th	30		11	·18	27	·48		10

Dec.

Solar month	Cyclic Sidereal Day	Week-Day	Day	Lunar month / paksha	Tithi	Ending Moment	Nakshatra	Ending Moment	Muhammadan month	Day
	16	Fr	1	Margasira	12	·26	1	·58	H. 1341 Rabi-ul-akhir.	11
	17	Sa	2		13	·33	2	·67		12
	18	Su	3		14	·39	3	·74		13
	19	Mo	4		P	·44	4	·79		14
	20	Tu	5		1	·45	5	·83		15
	21	We	6		2	·44	6	·84		16
	22	Th	7		3	·42	7	·83		17
	23	Fr	8		4	·37	8	·80		18
	24	Sa	9		5	·31	9	·76		19
	25	Su	10		6	·23	10	·72		20
	26	Mo	11		7	·15	11	·65		21
	27	Tu	12	Bahula	8 / 9	·06 / ·96	12	·58		22
	28	We	13		10	·86	13	·51		23
	29	Th	14		11	·77	14	·44		24
	30	Fr	15		12	·67	15	·38		25
Dundubhi Dhanus—Margali.	1	Sa	16		13	·59	16	·33		26
	2	Su	17		14	·53	17	·28		27
	3	Mo	18		A	·47	18	·25		28
	4	Tu	19		1	·44	19	·23		29
	5	We	20		2	·42	20	·24	H. 1341 Jumadal-awwal.	1
	6	Th	21		3	·44	21	·27		2
	7	Fr	22		4	·46	22	·32		3
	8	Sa	23	Sukla	5	·50	23	·38		4
	9	Su	24		6	·57	24	·46		5
	10	Mo	25		7	·65	25	·56		6
	11	Tu	26		8	·74	26	·67		7
	12	We	27		9	·83	27	·78		8
	13	Th	28	Pausha	10	·92	1	·88		9
	14	Fr	29		11	·98	2	·97		10
	15	Sa	30		...	...	...	...		11
	16	Su	31		12	·05	3	·05		12

15. Svati. 16. Visak. 17. Anur. 18. Jyesh. 19. Mula. 20. P. Ash. 21. U. Ash. 22. Sravn. 23. Dani. 24. Satab. 25. P. Bhad. 26. U. Bhad. 27. Rev.

A. D. 1923. **Mesha Sankranti** (Commencement of Indian Sidereal Year).

Solar Eclipse. ● **(Surya Sid.) April 13·57.** **Saka 1845.** **Kaliyuga 5024.**

Lunar Eclipse. ○ **(Arya Sid.) April 13·46.** **(S. Cycle) Rudhirodgari.**

Columns: SOLAR reckoning — Cyclic Sidereal Year, Month and Day; Week-Day, English Month and Day. LUNAR reckoning — Tithi Ending Moment; Nakshatra Ending Moment; Muhammadan Year, Month and Day.

Jan.

Solar month	Cyclic Sidereal Day	Week-Day	Eng. Day	Lunar month / Paksha	Tithi Ending Moment	Nakshatra Ending Moment	Muhammadan month	Muh. Day
Dundubhi Dhanus—Margali	17	Mo	1	Sukla	13 ·08	4 ·11	H. 1341 Jumadal-awwal	13
	18	Tu	2		14 ·09	5 ·15		14
	19	We	3		P ·08	6 ·16		15
	20	Th	4	Pausha	1 ·06	7 ·16		16
	21	Fr	5		2 ·02 / 3 ·96	8 ·13		17
	22	Sa	6		4 ·89	9 ·10		18
	23	Su	7		5 ·79	10 ·05 / 11 ·99		19
	24	Mo	8		6 ·69	12 ·92		20
	25	Tu	9		7 ·60	13 ·85		21
	26	We	10		8 ·50	14 ·78		22
	27	Th	11	Bahula	9 ·41	15 ·72		23
	28	Fr	12		10 ·32	16 ·66		24
	—29	Sa	13		11 ·25	17 ·62		25
Dundubhi Makara—Tai	1	Su	14		12 ·17	18 ·58		26
	2	Mo	15		13 ·11	19 ·56		27
	3	Tu	16		14 ·09	20 ·57		28
	4	We	17		—A ·07	21 ·59		29
	5	Th	18		1 ·08	22 ·63		—30
	6	Fr	19		2 ·11	23 ·69		1
	7	Sa	20		3 ·16	24 ·76		2
	8	Su	21		4 ·23	25 ·87		3
	9	Mo	22		5 ·31	26 ·97		4
	10	Tu	23		6 ·40	... ...		5
	11	We	24	Sukla	7 ·48	27 ·08		6
	12	Th	25		8 ·57	1 ·18		7
	13	Fr	26		9 ·64	2 ·27		8
	14	Sa	27		10 ·70	3 ·36		9
	15	Su	28		11 ·72	4 ·42		10
	16	Mo	29		12 ·74	5 ·46		11
	17	Tu	30		13 ·78	6 ·48		12
	18	We	31		14 ·70	7 ·48		13

Feb.

Solar month	Cyclic Sidereal Day	Week-Day	Eng. Day	Lunar month / Paksha	Tithi Ending Moment	Nakshatra Ending Moment	Muhammadan month	Muh. Day
	19	Th	1	Magha	P ·66	8 ·46	H. 1341 Jumadal-akhir	14
	20	Fr	2		1 ·59	9 ·44		15
	21	Sa	3		2 ·51	10 ·39		16
	22	Su	4		3 ·42	11 ·33		17
	23	Mo	5		4 ·33	12 ·26		18
	24	Tu	6		5 ·23	13 ·19		19
	25	We	7		6 ·13	14 ·13		20
	26	Th	8	Bahula	7 ·04 / 8 ·94	15 ·06		21
	27	Fr	9		9 ·86	16 ·00 / 17 ·95		22
	28	Sa	10		10 ·79	18 ·91		23
	—29	Su	11		11 ·75	19 ·89		24
Dundubhi Kumbha—Masi	1	Mo	12		12 ·72	20 ·89		25
	2	Tu	13		13 ·71	21 ·90		26
	3	We	14		14 ·71	22 ·94		27
	4	Th	15		—A ·74	23 ·99		28
	5	Fr	16		1 ·80	... ...		—29
	6	Sa	17		2 ·86	24 ·08	H. 1341 Rajab	1
	7	Su	18		3 ·94	25 ·17		2
	8	Mo	19	Sukla	... ...	26 ·27		3
	9	Tu	20		4 ·02	27 ·37		4
	10	We	21		5 ·11	1 ·48		5
	11	Th	22		6 ·19	2 ·58		6
	12	Fr	23	Phalguna	7 ·26	3 ·67		7
	13	Sa	24		8 ·32	4 ·73		8
	14	Su	25		9 ·35	5 ·78		9
	15	Mo	26		10 ·36	6 ·80		10
	16	Tu	27		11 ·34	7 ·81		11
	17	We	28		12 ·32	8 ·80		12

March

Solar month	Cyclic Sidereal Day	Week-Day	Eng. Day	Lunar month / Paksha	Tithi Ending Moment	Nakshatra Ending Moment	Muhammadan month	Muh. Day
Dundubhi Kumbha—Masi	18	Th	1	Suk.	13 ·27	9 ·77	H. 1341 Rajab	13
	19	Fr	2		14 ·20	10 ·72		14
	20	Sa ○	3		P ·13	11 ·66		15
	21	Su	4	Phalguna	1 ·03 / 2 ·94	12 ·60		16
	22	Mo	5		3 ·84	13 ·54		17
	23	Tu	6		4 ·74	14 ·47		18
	24	We	7		5 ·65	15 ·40		19
	25	Th	8		6 ·56	16 ·34		20
	26	Fr	9		7 ·48	17 ·28		21
	27	Sa	10		8 ·40	18 ·25		22
	28	Su	11		9 ·36	19 ·22		23
	29	Mo	12	Bahula	10 ·32	20 ·21		24
	—30	Tu	13		11 ·31	21 ·22		25
Dundubhi Mina—Panguni	1	We	14		12 ·31	22 ·25		26
	2	Th	15		13 ·35	23 ·31		27
	3	Fr	16		14 ·39	24 ·38		28
	4	Sa ●	17		—A ·45	25 ·47		29
	5	Su	18		1 ·54	26 ·57		—30
	6	Mo	19		2 ·63	27 ·67		1
	7	Tu	20		3 ·72	1 ·78		2
	8	We	21		4 ·80	2 ·89		3
	9	Th	22		5 ·86	3 ·97		4
	10	Fr	23		6 ·91	... ...		5
	11	Sa	24	Sukla	7 ·94	4 ·04		6
	12	Su	25		8 ·95	5 ·09		7
	13	Mo	26		9 ·93	6 ·12		8
	14	Tu	27		10 ·90	7 ·14		9
	15	We	28		11 ·85	8 ·13		10
	16	Th	29		12 ·78	9 ·10		11
	17	Fr	30		13 ·70	10 ·06		12
	18	Sa	31		14 ·62	11 ·01 / 12 ·95		13

April

Solar month	Cyclic Sidereal Day	Week-Day	Eng. Day	Lunar month / Paksha	Tithi Ending Moment	Nakshatra Ending Moment	Muhammadan month	Muh. Day
	19	Su	1	Chaitra	P ·52	13 ·88	H. 1341 Shaban	14
	20	Mo	2		1 ·41	14 ·81		15
	21	Tu	3		2 ·31	15 ·74		16
	22	We	4		3 ·22	16 ·68		17
	23	Th	5		4 ·13	17 ·63		18
	24	Fr	6		5 ·05 / 6 ·98	18 ·58		19
	25	Sa	7		7 ·93	19 ·55		20
	26	Su	8	Bahula	8 ·88	20 ·53		21
	27	Mo	9		9 ·87	21 ·54		22
	28	Tu	10		10 ·87	22 ·56		23
	29	We	11		11 ·91	23 ·62		24
	—30	Th	12		12 ·95	24 ·68		25
Rudhirodgari Mesha—Chittirai	1	Fr	13		... ...	25 ·77		26
	2	Sa	14		13 ·02	26 ·87		27
	3	Su	15		14 ·10	27 ·97		28
	4	Mo	16		—A ·19	... ...		—29
	5	Tu	17		1 ·27	1 ·09	H. 1341 Ramzan	1
	6	We	18		2 ·35	2 ·19		2
	7	Th	19	Sukla	3 ·41	3 ·28		3
	8	Fr	20		4 ·46	4 ·35		4
	9	Sa	21		5 ·50	5 ·40		5
	10	Su	22		6 ·49	6 ·45		6
	11	Mo	23		7 ·48	7 ·46		7
	12	Tu	24	Vaisakha	8 ·45	8 ·45		8
	13	We	25		9 ·39	9 ·43		9
	14	Th	26		10 ·32	10 ·39		10
	15	Fr	27		11 ·24	11 ·34		11
	16	Sa	28		12 ·16	12 ·28		12
	17	Su	29		13 ·06 / 14 ·96	13 ·22		13
	18	Mo	30		P ·85	14 ·15		14

May

Solar month	Cyclic Sidereal Day	Week-Day	Eng. Day	Lunar month / Paksha	Tithi Ending Moment	Nakshatra Ending Moment	Muhammadan month	Muh. Day
Rudhirodgari Mesha—Chittirai	19	Tu	1	Vaisakha	1 ·75	15 ·08	H. 1341 Ramzan	15
	20	We	2		2 ·66	16 ·02 / 17 ·96		16
	21	Th	3		3 ·37	18 ·91		17
	22	Fr	4		4 ·51	19 ·88		18
	23	Sa	5		5 ·45	20 ·86		19
	24	Su	6		6 ·42	21 ·86		20
	25	Mo	7	Bahula	7 ·40	22 ·89		21
	26	Tu	8		8 ·41	23 ·93		22
	27	We	9		9 ·44	24 ·99		23
	28	Th	10		10 ·47	... ...		24
	29	Fr	11		11 ·54	25 ·07		25
	30	Sa	12		12 ·61	26 ·16		26
	—31	Su	13		13 ·70	27 ·28		27
Rudhirodgari Vrishabha—Vaikasi	1	Mo	14		14 ·78	1 ·38		28
	2	Tu	15		—A ·86	2 ·49		29
	3	We	16		1 ·92	3 ·58		—30
	4	Th	17		2 ·97	4 ·66	H. 1341 Shawwal	1
	5	Fr	18	Sukla	... ...	5 ·73		2
	6	Sa	19		3 ·00	6 ·76		3
	7	Su	20		4 ·01 / 5 ·99	7 ·78		4
	8	Mo	21	Adhika Jyeshtha	6 ·96	8 ·78		5
	9	Tu	22		7 ·92	9 ·76		6
	10	We	23		8 ·84	10 ·73		7
	11	Th	24		9 ·75	11 ·68		8
	12	Fr	25		10 ·66	12 ·62		9
	13	Sa	26		11 ·56	13 ·55		10
	14	Su	27		12 ·46	14 ·48		11
	15	Mo	28		13 ·35	15 ·41		12
	16	Tu	29		14 ·26	16 ·35		13
	17	We	30		P ·16	17 ·29		14
	18	Th	31		1 ·08	18 ·24		15

June

Solar month	Cyclic Sidereal Day	Week-Day	Eng. Day	Lunar month / Paksha	Tithi Ending Moment	Nakshatra Ending Moment	Muhammadan month	Muh. Day
	19	Fr	1		2 ·01 / 3 ·95	19 ·21	H. 1341 Shawwal	16
	20	Sa	2		4 ·92	20 ·18		17
	21	Su	3		5 ·89	21 ·19		18
	22	Mo	4		6 ·90	22 ·20		19
	23	Tu	5	Bahula	7 ·92	23 ·24		20
	24	We	6		8 ·97	24 ·30		21
	25	Th	7		... ...	25 ·37		22
	26	Fr	8		9 ·03	26 ·47		23
	27	Sa	9		10 ·10	27 ·58		24
	28	Su	10		11 ·19	1 ·68		25
	29	Mo	11		12 ·27	2 ·79		26
	30	Tu	12		13 ·34	3 ·88		27
	31	We	13		14 ·40	4 ·97		28
	—32	Th	14		—A ·45	... ...		—29
Rudhirodgari Mithuna—Ani	1	Fr	15		1 ·48	5 ·04	H. 1341 Zi-l-ka'da	1
	2	Sa	16		2 ·49	6 ·08		2
	3	Su	17		3 ·48	7 ·10		3
	4	Mo	18		4 ·44	8 ·10		4
	5	Tu	19		5 ·40	9 ·10		5
	6	We	20		6 ·33	10 ·06		6
	7	Th	21	Sukla	7 ·24	11 ·02 / 12 ·96		7
	8	Fr	22		8 ·15	13 ·89		8
	9	Sa	23		9 ·06 / 10 ·95	14 ·82		9
	10	Su	24	Nija Jyeshtha	11 ·85	15 ·75		10
	11	Mo	25		12 ·75	16 ·69		11
	12	Tu	26		13 ·65	17 ·63		12
	13	We	27		14 ·56	18 ·58		13
	14	Th	28		P ·49	19 ·54		14
	15	Fr	29		1 ·44	20 ·52		15
	16	Sa	30		2 ·40	21 ·51		16

Naksh :—1. Asvn. 2. Bhar. 3. Krit. 4. Rohi. 5. Mrig. 6. Ardh. 7. Punar. 8. Push. 9. Aslesh. 10. Magh. 11. P. Phal. 12. U. Phal. 13. Hasta. 14. Chit.

A. D. 1923. **Vikrama 1980.**
A.—Amavasya. **Kollam 1099,** Commences { **N. Malabar—Sept.** / **S. Malabar—Aug.** **Hijra 1342,** Commences, **Aug. 14.** **Bengal San 1329.**
P.—Paurnami. **(N. Cycle) Yuvan.**

Columns: SOLAR reckoning — Cyclic Sidereal Year, Month and Day; Week-Day English Month and Day. LUNAR reckoning — Tithi Ending Moment; Nakshatra Ending Moment; Muhammadan Year, Month and Day.

July

Solar: Rudhirodgari Mithuna—Ani. / Rudhirodgari Karkata—Adi. Lunar: Nija Jyesh. Bahula / Sukla Ashadha. Muhammadan: H. 1341 Zil-ka'da. / H. 1341 Zil-hijja.

Cyclic Sidereal Year, Month and Day	Week-Day	English Month and Day	Tithi Ending Moment	Nakshatra Ending Moment	Muhammadan Year, Month and Day
17	Su	1	3 ·37	22 ·52	17
18	Mo	2	4 ·38	23 ·55	18
19	Tu	3	5 ·40	24 ·60	19
20	We	4	6 ·44	25 ·68	20
21	Th	5	7 ·50	26 ·77	21
22	Fr	6	8 ·58	27 ·87	22
23	Sa	7	9 ·65	1 ·98	23
24	Su	8	10 ·74	... ...	24
25	Mo	9	11 ·82	2 ·09	25
26	Tu	10	12 ·88	3 ·18	26
27	We	11	13 ·93	4 ·28	27
28	Th	12	14 ·96	5 ·35	28
29	Fr	13	—A ·98	6 ·39	29
30	Sa	14	1 ·95	7 ·42	—30
—31	Su	15	2 ·93	8 ·43	1
1	Mo	16	3 ·88	9 ·42	2
2	Tu	17	4 ·80	10 ·40	3
3	We	18	5 ·72	11 ·35	4
4	Th	19	6 ·63	12 ·30	5
5	Fr	20	7 ·53	13 ·24	6
6	Sa	21	8 ·43	14 ·17	7
7	Su	22	9 ·34	15 ·10	8
8	Mo	23	10 ·24	16 ·03 17 ·97	9
9	Tu	24	11 ·13	18 ·91	10
10	We	25	12 ·04 13 ·97	19 ·88	11
11	Th	26	14 ·92	20 ·85	12
12	Fr	27	P ·87	21 ·83	13
13	Sa	28	1 ·86	22 ·84	14
14	Su	29	2 ·86	23 ·87	15
15	Mo	30	3 ·88	24 ·92	16
16	Tu	31	4 ·91	25 ·99	17

Aug.

Solar: Rudhirodgari Simha—Avani. Lunar: Bahula / Sukla / Sravana / Bah. Muhammadan: H. 1342 Muharram.

Cyclic Sidereal Year, Month and Day	Week-Day	English Month and Day	Tithi Ending Moment	Nakshatra Ending Moment	Muhammadan Year, Month and Day
17	We	1	5 ·97	... ...	18
18	Th	2	... ...	26 ·07	19
19	Fr	3	6 ·04	27 ·17	20
20	Sa	4	7 ·12	1 ·28	21
21	Su	5	8 ·22	2 ·38	22
22	Mo	6	9 ·29	3 ·49	23
23	Tu	7	10 ·36	4 ·58	24
24	We	8	11 ·40	5 ·65	25
25	Th	9	12 ·44	6 ·71	26
26	Fr	10	13 ·46	7 ·74	27
27	Sa	11	14 ·44	8 ·76	28
28	Su	12	—A ·42	9 ·75	29
29	Mo	13	1 ·36	10 ·73	—30
30	Tu	14	2 ·30	11 ·68	1
31	We	15	3 ·22	12 ·63	2
—32	Th	16	4 ·13	13 ·58	3
1	Fr	17	5 ·08 6 ·93	14 ·51	4
2	Sa	18	7 ·83	15 ·44	5
3	Su	19	8 ·73	16 ·37	6
4	Mo	20	9 ·64	17 ·30	7
5	Tu	21	10 ·55	18 ·25	8
6	We	22	11 ·48	19 ·21	9
7	Th	23	12 ·41	20 ·17	10
8	Fr	24	13 ·37	21 ·16	11
9	Sa	25	14 ·36	22 ·16	12
10	Su ○	26	P ·36	23 ·18	13
11	Mo	27	1 ·38	24 ·23	14
12	Tu	28	2 ·42	25 ·30	15
13	We	29	3 ·48	26 ·38	16
14	Th	30	4 ·54	27 ·47	17
15	Fr	31	5 ·62	1 ·58	18

Sep.

Solar: Rudhirodgari Simha—Avani. / Rudhiroigari Kanya—Purattasi. Lunar: Sr. vn. Bahula / Sukla Bhadrapada. Muhammadan: H. 1342 Muharram. / H. 1342 Safar.

Cyclic Sidereal Year, Month and Day	Week-Day	English Month and Day	Tithi Ending Moment	Nakshatra Ending Moment	Muhammadan Year, Month and Day
16	Sa	1	6 ·72	2 ·69	19
17	Su	2	7 ·80	3 ·79	20
18	Mo	3	8 ·88	4 ·89	21
19	Tu	4	9 ·92	5 ·96	22
20	We	5	10 ·96	... ...	23
21	Th	6	11 ·97	6 ·02	24
22	Fr	7	12 ·95	7 ·07	25
23	Sa	8	13 ·93	8 ·08	26
24	Su	9	14 ·88	9 ·08	27
25	Mo	10	—A ·82	10 ·06	28
26	Tu	11	1 ·74	11 ·02 12 ·98	29
27	We	12	2 ·66	13 ·92	—30
28	Th	13	3 ·56	14 ·85	1
29	Fr	14	4 ·46	15 ·78	2
30	Sa	15	5 ·36	16 ·71	3
—31	Su	16	6 ·26	17 ·65	4
1	Mo	17	7 ·17	18 ·59	5
2	Tu	18	8 ·08	19 ·54	6
3	We	19	9 ·01 10 ·95	20 ·50	7
4	Th	20	11 ·91	21 ·48	8
5	Fr	21	12 ·89	22 ·48	9
6	Sa	22	13 ·88	23 ·50	10
7	Su	23	14 ·91	24 ·54	11
8	Mo	24	P ·95	25 ·60	12
9	Tu	25	... ...	26 ·68	13
10	We	26	1 ·01	27 ·77	14
11	Th	27	2 ·08	1 ·88	15
12	Fr	28	3 ·18	2 ·99	16
13	Sa	29	4 ·26	... ...	17
14	Su	30	5 ·34	3 ·09	18

Oct.

Solar: Rudhirodgari Tula—Aippasi. Lunar: Bahula / Sukla Asvina / Bah. Muhammadan: H. 1342 Rabi-ul-awwal.

Cyclic Sidereal Year, Month and Day	Week-Day	English Month and Day	Tithi Ending Moment	Nakshatra Ending Moment	Muhammadan Year, Month and Day
15	Mo	1	6 ·42	4 ·19	19
16	Tu	2	7 ·46	5 ·27	20
17	We	3	8 ·50	6 ·34	21
18	Th	4	9 ·52	7 ·38	22
19	Fr	5	10 ·51	8 ·40	23
20	Sa	6	11 ·48	9 ·40	24
21	Su	7	12 ·44	10 ·38	25
22	Mo	8	13 ·37	11 ·36	26
23	Tu	9	14 ·30	12 ·31	27
24	We	10	—A ·22	13 ·25	28
25	Th	11	1 ·12	14 ·19	—20
26	Fr	12	2 ·02 3 ·92	15 ·12	1
27	Sa	13	4 ·82	16 ·05 17 ·98	2
28	Su	14	5 ·73	18 ·92	3
29	Mo	15	6 ·64	19 ·87	4
—30	Tu	16	7 ·58	20 ·83	5
1	We	17	8 ·52	21 ·81	6
2	Th	18	9 ·48	22 ·81	7
3	Fr	19	10 ·46	23 ·82	8
4	Sa	20	11 ·48	24 ·85	9
5	Su	21	12 ·49	25 ·91	10
6	Mo	22	13 ·54	26 ·98	11
7	Tu	23	14 ·60	... ...	12
8	We	24	P ·68	27 ·08	13
9	Th	25	1 ·77	1 ·18	14
10	Fr	26	2 ·85	2 ·29	15
11	Sa	27	3 ·93	3 ·39	16
12	Su	28	... ...	4 ·49	17
13	Mo	29	4 ·00	5 ·58	18
14	Tu	30	5 ·06	6 ·65	19
15	We	31	6 ·09	7 ·70	20

Nov.

Solar: Rudhirodgari Tula—Aippasi. / Rudhiroigari Vrischika—Kartigai. Lunar: Asvn. Bahula / Sukla Karttika. Muhammadan: Rabi-ul-awwal. / H. 1342 Rabi-ul-akhir.

Cyclic Sidereal Year, Month and Day	Week-Day	English Month and Day	Tithi Ending Moment	Nakshatra Ending Moment	Muhammadan Year, Month and Day
16	Th	1	7 ·11	8 ·72	21
17	Fr	2	8 ·10	9 ·73	22
18	Sa	3	9 ·07	10 ·72	23
19	Su	4	10 ·03 11 ·97	11 ·69	24
20	Mo	5	12 ·90	12 ·65	25
21	Tu	6	13 ·81	13 ·59	26
22	We	7	14 ·71	14 ·52	27
23	Th	8	—A ·61	15 ·45	28
24	Fr	9	1 ·52	16 ·39	29
25	Sa	10	2 ·42	17 ·32	—30
26	Su	11	3 ·33	18 ·26	1
27	Mo	12	4 ·25	19 ·21	2
28	Tu	13	5 ·18	20 ·16	3
29	We	14	6 ·13	21 ·14	4
—30	Th	15	7 ·09	22 ·13	5
1	Fr	16	8 ·07	23 ·14	6
2	Sa	17	9 ·08	24 ·17	7
3	Su	18	10 ·09	25 ·22	8
4	Mo	19	11 ·15	26 ·30	9
5	Tu	20	12 ·21	27 ·38	10
6	We	21	13 ·30	1 ·48	11
7	Th	22	14 ·39	2 ·59	12
8	Fr	23	P ·47	3 ·69	13
9	Sa	24	1 ·55	4 ·80	14
10	Su	25	2 ·62	5 ·89	15
11	Mo	26	3 ·68	6 ·96	16
12	Tu	27	4 ·71	... ...	17
13	We	28	5 ·74	7 ·01	18
14	Th	29	6 ·72	8 ·04	19
15	Fr	30	7 ·69	9 ·05	20

Dec.

Solar: Rudhirodgari Dhanus—Margali. Lunar: Bahula / Sukla Margasira / Bahula. Muhammadan: H. 1342 Jumadal-awwal.

Cyclic Sidereal Year, Month and Day	Week-Day	English Month and Day	Tithi Ending Moment	Nakshatra Ending Moment	Muhammadan Year, Month and Day
16	Sa	1	8 ·65	10 ·05	21
17	Su	2	9 ·58	11 ·02 12 ·98	22
18	Mo	3	10 ·52	13 ·93	23
19	Tu	4	11 ·44	14 ·87	24
20	We	5	12 ·35	15 ·80	25
21	Th	6	13 ·25	16 ·73	26
22	Fr	7	14 ·15	17 ·66	27
23	Sa	8	A ·04 1 ·95	18 ·60	28
24	Su	9	2 ·87	19 ·54	—29
25	Mo	10	3 ·80	20 ·50	1
26	Tu	11	4 ·76	21 ·47	2
27	We	12	5 ·72	22 ·46	3
28	Th	13	6 ·72	23 ·46	4
29	Fr	14	7 ·72	24 ·48	5
—30	Sa	15	8 ·74	25 ·54	6
1	Su	16	9 ·80	26 ·60	7
2	Mo	17	10 ·86	27 ·68	8
3	Tu	18	11 ·95	1 ·78	9
4	We	19	... ...	2 ·88	10
5	Th	20	12 ·03	3 ·99	11
6	Fr	21	13 ·12	... ...	12
7	Sa	22	14 ·20	4 ·10	13
8	Su	23	P ·28	5 ·19	14
9	Mo	24	1 ·33	6 ·27	15
10	Tu	25	2 ·36	7 ·32	16
11	We	26	3 ·38	8 ·36	17
12	Th	27	4 ·37	9 ·38	18
13	Fr	28	5 ·35	10 ·38	19
14	Sa	29	6 ·29	11 ·35	20
15	Su	30	7 ·23	12 ·31	21
16	Mo	31	8 ·15	13 ·26	22

15. Svati. 16. Visak. 17. Anur. 18. Jyesh. 19. Mula. 20. P. Ash. 21. U. Ash. 22. Sravn. 23. Dani. 24 Satab. 25. P. Bhad. 26. U. Bhad. 27. Rev.

A. D. 1924. **Mesha Sankranti** (Commencement of Indian Sidereal Year).
Solar Eclipse. ● (Surya Sid.) April 12·83. **Saka 1846.** **Kaliyuga 5025.**
Lunar Eclipse. ○ (Arya Sid.) April 12·72. **(S. Cycle) Raktaksha.**

SOLAR reckoning: Cyclic Sidereal Year, Month and Day; Week-Day English Month and Day. LUNAR reckoning: Tithi Ending Moment; Nakshatra Ending Moment; Muhammadan Year, Month and Day.

Jan.

Cyclic Sidereal Year, Month and Day	Week-Day English Month and Day	Tithi Ending Moment	Nakshatra Ending Moment	Muhammadan Year, Month and Day
17	Tu 1	9 ·07 / 10 ·97	14 ·21	23
18	We 2	(Mr.) 11 ·87	15 ·14	24
(Rudhirodgari Dhanus—Margali) 19	Th 3	12 ·78	16 ·07	25
20	Fr 4	(Bah.) 13 ·68	17 ·00 / 18 ·93	26
21	Sa 5	14 ·60	19 ·88	(Jumadal-awwal) 27
22	Su 6	—A ·52	20 ·83	28
23	Mo 7	1 ·45	21 ·80	29
24	Tu 8	2 ·40	22 ·78	—30
25	We 9	3 ·37	23 ·78	1
26	Th 10	4 ·36	24 ·81	2
27	Fr 11	5 ·36	25 ·85	3
28	Sa 12	6 ·39	26 ·91	4
—29	Su 13	(Sukla) 7 ·44	27 ·98	5
1	Mo 14	8 ·51	... ...	6
2	Tu 15	9 ·59	1 ·08	7
3	We 16	10 ·68	2 ·18	8
4	Th 17	11 ·78	3 ·30	9
5	Fr 18	12 ·86	4 ·40	10
6	Sa 19	13 ·92	5 ·49	(H. 1342 Jumadal-akhir) 11
7	Su 20	(Pausha) 14 ·97	6 ·57	12
8	Mo 21	... ...	7 ·63	13
9	Tu 22	P ·01	8 ·68	14
10	We 23	1 ·02	9 ·70	15
11	Th 24	2 ·01 / 3 ·99	10 ·70	16
(Rudhirodgari Makara—Tai) 12	Fr 25	4 ·93	11 ·68	17
13	Sa 26	5 ·87	12 ·65	18
14	Su 27	6 ·79	13 ·61	19
15	Mo 28	(Bahula) 7 ·71	14 ·55	20
16	Tu 29	8 ·61	15 ·48	21
17	We 30	9 ·51	16 ·41	22
18	Th 31	10 ·41	17 ·34	23

Feb.

Cyclic Sidereal Year, Month and Day	Week-Day English Month and Day	Tithi Ending Moment	Nakshatra Ending Moment	Muhammadan Year, Month and Day
19	Fr 1	11 ·31	18 ·28	24
20	Sa 2	12 ·23	19 ·22	25
21	Su 3	13 ·16	20 ·17	26
22	Mo 4	14 ·10	21 ·13	27
23	Tu 5	—A ·04	22 ·10	28
24	We 6	1 ·01	23 ·10	—29
25	Th 7	2 ·00	24 ·12	1
26	Fr 8	3 ·00	25 ·16	2
27	Sa 9	4 ·04	26 ·21	3
28	Su 10	5 ·09	27 ·29	4
29	Mo 11	6 ·16	1 ·38	5
—30	Tu 12	(Sukla) 7 ·24	2 ·49	6
1	We 13	8 ·33	3 ·60	7
2	Th 14	9 ·41	4 ·70	8
3	Fr 15	10 ·49	5 ·80	9
4	Sa 16	11 ·57	6 ·88	(H. 1342 Rajab.) 10
5	Su 17	12 ·62	7 ·95	11
(Rudhirodgari Kumbha—Masi.) 6	Mo 18	13 ·64	... ...	12
7	Tu 19	14 ·65	8 ·00	13
8	We ○ 20	(Magha) P ·64	9 ·02	14
9	Th 21	1 ·61	10 ·03	15
10	Fr 22	2 ·55	11 ·01 / 12 ·99	16
11	Sa 23	3 ·49	13 ·94	17
12	Su 24	4 ·41	14 ·88	18
13	Mo 25	(Bahula) 5 ·32	15 ·82	19
14	Tu 26	6 ·22	16 ·76	20
15	We 27	7 ·13	17 ·69	21
16	Th 28	● 8 ·03 / 9 ·94	18 ·62	22
17	Fr 29	10 ·85	19 ·56	23

March

Cyclic Sidereal Year, Month and Day	Week-Day English Month and Day	Tithi Ending Moment	Nakshatra Ending Moment	Muhammadan Year, Month and Day
18	Sa 1	(Mg.) 11 ·77	20 ·50	24
19	Su 2	12 ·71	21 ·46	25
(Rudhirodgari Kumbha—Masi) 20	Mo 3	(Bah.) 13 ·65	22 ·43	(Rajab.) 26
21	Tu 4	14 ·62	23 ·43	27
22	We 5	—A ·60	24 ·44	28
23	Th 6	1 ·62	25 ·47	29
24	Fr 7	2 ·65	26 ·52	—30
25	Sa 8	3 ·70	27 ·59	1
26	Su 9	4 ·77	1 ·69	2
27	Mo 10	5 ·85	2 ·79	3
28	Tu 11	6 ·94	3 ·89	4
29	We 12	... ...	... ...	5
—30	Th 13	(Sukla) 7 ·02	4 ·00	6
1	Fr 14	8 ·10	5 ·10	7
2	Sa 15	9 ·16	6 ·19	8
3	Su 16	10 ·22	7 ·26	9
4	Mo 17	11 ·24	8 ·31	10
5	Tu 18	(Phalguna) 12 ·24	9 ·34	11
6	We 19	13 ·24	10 ·35	12
7	Th 20	14 ·20	11 ·35	13
8	Fr 21	P ·15	12 ·32	14
9	Sa 22	1 ·08	13 ·28	(H. 1342 Shaban.) 15
10	Su 23	2 ·01 / 3 ·91	14 ·22	16
11	Mo 24	4 ·81	15 ·16	17
(Rudhirodgari Mina—Panguni.) 12	Tu 25	5 ·71	16 ·09	18
13	We 26	6 ·61	17 ·03 / 18 ·96	19
14	Th 27	(Bahula) 7 ·52	19 ·89	20
15	Fr 28	8 ·43	20 ·83	21
16	Sa 29	9 ·35	21 ·79	22
17	Su 30	10 ·28	22 ·77	23
18	Mo 31	11 ·23	23 ·75	24

April

Cyclic Sidereal Year, Month and Day	Week-Day English Month and Day	Tithi Ending Moment	Nakshatra Ending Moment	Muhammadan Year, Month and Day
19	Tu 1	12 ·20	24 ·76	25
20	We 2	13 ·18	25 ·78	26
21	Th 3	14 ·19	26 ·83	27
22	Fr 4	—A ·22	27 ·91	28
23	Sa 5	1 ·28	1 ·99	—29
24	Su 6	2 ·35	... ...	1
25	Mo 7	3 ·43	2 ·09	2
26	Tu 8	4 ·51	3 ·19	3
27	We 9	5 ·58	4 ·30	4
28	Th 10	6 ·66	5 ·41	5
29	Fr 11	(Sukla) 7 ·72	6 ·50	6
—30	Sa 12	8 ·78	7 ·57	7
1	Su 13	9 ·80	8 ·63	8
2	Mo 14	10 ·81	9 ·66	9
3	Tu 15	11 ·79	10 ·68	(H. 1342 Ramzan.) 10
4	We 16	12 ·75	11 ·67	11
5	Th 17	(Chaitra) 13 ·70	12 ·65	12
6	Fr 18	14 ·63	13 ·61	13
7	Sa 19	P ·56	14 ·56	14
(Raktaksha Mesha—Chittirai.) 8	Su 20	1 ·46	15 ·50	15
9	Mo 21	2 ·36	16 ·44	16
10	Tu 22	3 ·26	17 ·37	17
11	We 23	4 ·15	18 ·29	18
12	Th 24	5 ·06 / 6 ·96	19 ·23	19
13	Fr 25	(Bahula) 7 ·89	20 ·17	20
14	Sa 26	8 ·82	21 ·13	21
15	Su 27	9 ·78	22 ·10	22
16	Mo 28	10 ·74	23 ·08	23
17	Tu 29	11 ·72	24 ·08	24
18	We 30	12 ·72	25 ·10	25

May

Cyclic Sidereal Year, Month and Day	Week-Day English Month and Day	Tithi Ending Moment	Nakshatra Ending Moment	Muhammadan Year, Month and Day
19	Th 1	13 ·75	26 ·15	26
20	Fr 2	(Bah.) 14 ·81	27 ·21	(Ramzan.) 27
(Raktaksha Mesha—Chittirai.) 21	Sa 3	—A ·87	1 ·29	28
22	Su 4	1 ·94	2 ·38	29
23	Mo 5	... ...	3 ·49	—30
24	Tu 6	2 ·02	4 ·61	1
25	We 7	3 ·11	5 ·71	2
26	Th 8	4 ·19	6 ·80	3
27	Fr 9	5 ·25	7 ·88	4
28	Sa 10	6 ·31	8 ·94	5
29	Su 11	7 ·32	9 ·97	6
30	Mo 12	(Sukla) 8 ·33	... ...	7
—31	Tu 13	9 ·31	10 ·00	8
1	We 14	10 ·29	11 ·00 / 12 ·98	9
2	Th 15	11 ·22	13 ·94	10
3	Fr 16	12 ·15	14 ·89	11
4	Sa 17	13 ·07 / 14 ·97	15 ·84	(H. 1342 Shavval.) 12
5	Su 18	(Vaisakha) P ·88	16 ·77	13
6	Mo 19	1 ·78	17 ·70	14
7	Tu 20	2 ·67	18 ·63	15
8	We 21	3 ·57	19 ·57	16
9	Th 22	4 ·48	20 ·51	17
10	Fr 23	5 ·40	21 ·46	18
11	Sa 24	6 ·33	22 ·43	19
(Raktaksha Vrishabha—Vaikasi.) 12	Su 25	7 ·28	23 ·40	20
13	Mo 26	(Bahula) 8 ·24	24 ·40	21
14	Tu 27	9 ·23	25 ·42	22
15	We 28	10 ·22	26 ·46	23
16	Th 29	11 ·25	27 ·52	24
17	Fr 30	12 ·31	1 ·59	25
18	Sa 31	13 ·37	2 ·68	26

June

Cyclic Sidereal Year, Month and Day	Week-Day English Month and Day	Tithi Ending Moment	Nakshatra Ending Moment	Muhammadan Year, Month and Day
19	Su 1	14 ·44	3 ·80	27
20	Mo 2	—A ·52	4 ·90	28
21	Tu 3	1 ·61	... ...	—29
22	We 4	2 ·68	5 ·01	1
23	Th 5	3 ·74	6 ·10	2
24	Fr 6	4 ·79	7 ·18	3
25	Sa 7	5 ·82	8 ·25	4
26	Su 8	6 ·82	9 ·30	5
27	Mo 9	(Sukla) 7 ·80	10 ·82	6
28	Tu 10	8 ·78	11 ·32	7
29	We 11	9 ·72	12 ·31	8
30	Th 12	10 ·65	13 ·28	9
—31	Fr 13	11 ·57	14 ·24	10
1	Sa 14	12 ·47	15 ·18	11
2	Su 15	(Jyeshtha) 13 ·37	16 ·11	12
3	Mo 16	14 ·27	17 ·04 / 18 ·97	13
4	Tu 17	P ·17	19 ·91	14
5	We 18	1 ·06 / 2 ·97	20 ·85	(H. 1342 Zi-l-ka'da.) 15
(Raktaksha Mithuna—Ani.) 6	Th 19	3 ·89	21 ·80	16
7	Fr 20	4 ·82	22 ·75	17
8	Sa 21	5 ·76	23 ·73	18
9	Su 22	6 ·72	24 ·73	19
10	Mo 23	(Bahula) 7 ·70	25 ·74	20
11	Tu 24	8 ·70	26 ·77	21
12	We 25	9 ·73	27 ·82	22
13	Th 26	10 ·77	1 ·90	23
14	Fr 27	11 ·84	2 ·98	24
15	Sa 28	12 ·91	... ...	25
16	Su 29	... ...	3 ·09	26
17	Mo 30	13 ·00	4 ·20	27

Naksh :—1. Asvn. 2. Bhar. 3. Krit. 4. Rohi. 5. Mrig. 6. Ardh. 7. Punar. 8. Push. 9. Aslesh. 10. Magh. 11. P. Phal. 12. U. Phal. 13. Hasta. 14. Chit.

A. D. 1924.
A.—Amavasya.
P.—Paurnami.

Kollam 1100, Commences { **N. Malabar—Sept.** / **S. Malabar—Aug.**

Hijra 1343, Commences, **Aug. 2.**

Vikrama 1981.
Bengal San 1330.
(N. Cycle) Dhatri.

Columns: SOLAR reckoning (Cyclic Sidereal Year, Month and Day; Week-Day English Month and Day) — LUNAR reckoning (Tithi Ending Moment; Nakshatra Ending Moment; Muhammadan Year, Month and Day).

July — Solar: Raktaksha *Mithuna—Ani* (18–—32); Raktaksha *Karkata—Adi* (1–16). Lunar: Ashadha (*Sukla*, *Bahula*). Muhammadan: H. 1342 *Zi-l-hijja*.

Cyclic Sidereal Year, Month and Day	Week-Day	English Day	Tithi Ending Moment	Nakshatra Ending Moment	Muhammadan Year, Month and Day
18	Tu	1	14 ·08	5 ·31	28
19	We	2	—A ·15	6 ·40	29
20	Th	3	1 ·22	7 ·49	—30
21	Fr	4	2 ·27	8 ·57	1
22	Sa	5	3 ·29	9 ·61	2
23	Su	6	4 ·30	10 ·64	3
24	Mo	7	5 ·29	11 ·65	4
25	Tu	8	6 ·25	12 ·63	5
26	We	9	7 ·19	13 ·61	6
27	Th	10	8 ·13	14 ·57	7
28	Fr	11	9 ·04 10 ·95	15 ·51	8
29	Sa	12	11 ·85	16 ·45	9
30	Su	13	12 ·75	17 ·39	10
31	Mo	14	13 ·64	18 ·32	11
—32	Tu	15	14 ·54	19 ·25	12
1	We	16	P ·45	20 ·19	13
2	Th	17	1 ·36	21 ·13	14
3	Fr	18	2 ·29	22 ·09	15
4	Sa	19	3 ·24	23 ·06	16
5	Su	20	4 ·21	24 ·05	17
6	Mo	21	5 ·18	25 ·06	18
7	Tu	22	6 ·19	26 ·09	19
8	We	23	7 ·22	27 ·13	20
9	Th	24	8 ·25	1 ·20	21
10	Fr	25	9 ·31	2 ·30	22
11	Sa	26	10 ·38	3 ·39	23
12	Su	27	11 ·47	4 ·50	24
13	Mo	28	12 ·55	5 ·60	25
14	Tu	29	13 ·63	6 ·71	26
15	We	30	14 ·69	7 ·80	27
16	Th	31	—A ·73	8 ·88	28

Aug. — Solar: Raktaksha *Simha—Avani*. Lunar: Sravana (*Sukla*, *Bahula*). Muhammadan: H. 1343 *Muharram*.

Cyclic Sidereal Year, Month and Day	Week-Day	English Day	Tithi Ending Moment	Nakshatra Ending Moment	Muhammadan Year, Month and Day
17	Fr	1	1 ·77	9 ·93	—29
18	Sa	2	2 ·78	10 ·96	1
19	Su	3	3 ·77	11 ·97	2
20	Mo	4	4 ·73	12 ·97	3
21	Tu	5	5 ·68	13 ·95	4
22	We	6	6 ·62	14 ·90	5
23	Th	7	7 ·54	15 ·85	6
24	Fr	8	8 ·44	16 ·79	7
25	Sa	9	9 ·34	17 ·73	8
26	Su	10	10 ·24	18 ·66	9
27	Mo	11	11 ·14	19 ·59	10
28	Tu	12	12 ·05 13 ·95	20 ·52	11
29	We	13	14 ·87	21 ·46	12
30	Th ○	14	P ·79	22 ·42	13
—31	Fr	15	1 ·73	23 ·39	14
1	Sa	16	2 ·70	24 ·38	15
2	Su	17	3 ·67	25 ·38	16
3	Mo	18	4 ·68	26 ·40	17
4	Tu	19	5 ·70	27 ·44	18
5	We	20	6 ·75	1 ·52	19
6	Th	21	7 ·81	2 ·60	20
7	Fr	22	8 ·87	3 ·69	21
8	Sa	23	9 ·95	4 ·80	22
9	Su	24	... ...	5 ·91	23
10	Mo	25	10 ·05	... ...	24
11	Tu	26	11 ·13	6 ·02	25
12	We	27	12 ·19	7 ·11	26
13	Th	28	13 ·25	8 ·18	27
14	Fr	29	14 ·27	9 ·24	28
15	Sa	30	—A ·29	10 ·28	29
16	Su	31	1 ·27	11 ·30	—30

Sep. — Solar: Raktaksha *Simha—Avani* (17–—31); Raktaksha *Kanya—Purattasi* (1–15). Lunar: Bhadrapada (*Sukla*, *Bahula*). Muhammadan: H. 1343 *Safar*.

Cyclic Sidereal Year, Month and Day	Week-Day	English Day	Tithi Ending Moment	Nakshatra Ending Moment	Muhammadan Year, Month and Day
17	Mo	1	2 ·24	12 ·30	1
18	Tu	2	3 ·20	13 ·28	2
19	We	3	4 ·13	14 ·24	3
20	Th	4	5 ·05 6 ·96	15 ·19	4
21	Fr	5	7 ·86	16 ·13	5
22	Sa	6	8 ·75	17 ·07	6
23	Su	7	9 ·65	18 ·00 19 ·93	7
24	Mo	8	10 ·56	20 ·86	8
25	Tu	9	11 ·47	21 ·81	9
26	We	10	12 ·39	22 ·76	10
27	Th	11	13 ·32	23 ·72	11
28	Fr	12	14 ·27	24 ·70	12
29	Sa	13	P ·22	25 ·70	13
30	Su	14	1 ·20	26 ·72	14
—31	Mo	15	2 ·21	27 ·76	15
1	Tu	16	3 ·23	1 ·82	16
2	We	17	4 ·28	2 ·90	17
3	Th	18	5 ·32	3 ·99	18
4	Fr	19	6 ·40	... ...	19
5	Sa	20	7 ·49	4 ·09	20
6	Su	21	8 ·58	5 ·20	21
7	Mo	22	9 ·65	6 ·31	22
8	Tu	23	10 ·72	7 ·41	23
9	We	24	11 ·78	8 ·49	24
10	Th	25	12 ·81	9 ·55	25
11	Fr	26	13 ·83	10 ·60	26
12	Sa	27	14 ·81	11 ·62	27
13	Su	28	—A ·79	12 ·62	28
14	Mo	29	1 ·74	13 ·60	—29
15	Tu	30	2 ·67	14 ·57	1

Oct. — Solar: Raktaksha *Kanya—Purattasi* (16–—31); Raktaksha *Tula—Aippasi* (1–15). Lunar: Asvina (*Sukla*, *Bahula*; *Suk.*). Muhammadan: H. 1343 *Rabi-ul-awwal*.

Cyclic Sidereal Year, Month and Day	Week-Day	English Day	Tithi Ending Moment	Nakshatra Ending Moment	Muhammadan Year, Month and Day
16	We	1	3 ·59	15 ·53	2
17	Th	2	4 ·50	16 ·47	3
18	Fr	3	5 ·41	17 ·41	4
19	Sa	4	6 ·31	18 ·34	5
20	Su	5	7 ·22	19 ·27	6
21	Mo	6	8 ·11	20 ·20	7
22	Tu	7	9 ·01 10 ·94	21 ·14	8
23	We	8	11 ·87	22 ·09	9
24	Th	9	12 ·83	23 ·05	10
25	Fr	10	13 ·79	24 ·03	11
26	Sa	11	14 ·77	25 ·02	12
27	Su	12	P ·77	26 ·04	13
28	Mo	13	1 ·80	27 ·07	14
29	Tu	14	2 ·84	1 ·13	15
30	We	15	3 ·89	2 ·20	16
—31	Th	16	4 ·97	3 ·29	17
1	Fr	17	... ...	4 ·40	18
2	Sa	18	5 ·06	5 ·51	19
3	Su	19	6 ·15	6 ·61	20
4	Mo	20	7 ·22	7 ·71	21
5	Tu	21	8 ·30	8 ·79	22
6	We	22	9 ·36	9 ·87	23
7	Th	23	10 ·39	10 ·92	24
8	Fr	24	11 ·41	11 ·94	25
9	Sa	25	12 ·39	12 ·95	26
10	Su	26	13 ·36	13 ·93	27
11	Mo	27	14 ·32	14 ·91	28
12	Tu	28	—A ·26	15 ·87	29
13	We	29	1 ·18	16 ·81	—30
14	Th	30	2 ·09	17 ·74	1
15	Fr	31	3 ·00 4 ·89	18 ·67	2

Nov. — Solar: Raktaksha *Tula—Aippasi* (16–—30); Raktaksha *Vrischika—Kartigai* (1–15). Lunar: Karttika (*Sukla*, *Bahula*). Muhammadan: H. 1343 *Rabi-ul-akhir*.

Cyclic Sidereal Year, Month and Day	Week-Day	English Day	Tithi Ending Moment	Nakshatra Ending Moment	Muhammadan Year, Month and Day
16	Sa	1	5 ·80	19 ·60	3
17	Su	2	6 ·70	20 ·54	4
18	Mo	3	7 ·62	21 ·48	5
19	Tu	4	8 ·54	22 ·43	6
20	We	5	9 ·47	23 ·38	7
21	Th	6	10 ·41	24 ·35	8
22	Fr	7	11 ·37	25 ·35	9
23	Sa	8	12 ·36	26 ·36	10
24	Su	9	13 ·37	27 ·39	11
25	Mo	10	14 ·40	1 ·44	12
26	Tu	11	P ·44	2 ·51	13
27	We	12	1 ·51	3 ·60	14
28	Th	13	2 ·59	4 ·70	15
29	Fr	14	3 ·68	5 ·81	16
—30	Sa	15	4 ·77	6 ·91	17
1	Su	16	5 ·84	... ...	18
2	Mo	17	6 ·91	7 ·01	19
3	Tu	18	7 ·97	8 ·11	20
4	We	19	... ...	9 ·18	21
5	Th	20	8 ·01	10 ·23	22
6	Fr	21	9 ·02	11 ·26	23
7	Sa	22	10 ·01 11 ·98	12 ·27	24
8	Su	23	12 ·93	13 ·26	25
9	Mo	24	13 ·87	14 ·24	26
10	Tu	25	14 ·79	15 ·20	27
11	We	26	—A ·72	16 ·15	28
12	Th	27	1 ·62	17 ·08	—29
13	Fr	28	2 ·52	18 ·01 19 ·94	1
14	Sa	29	3 ·42	20 ·88	2
15	Su	30	4 ·33	21 ·82	3

Dec. — Solar: Raktaksha *Vrischika—Kartigai* (16–—29); Raktaksha *Dhanus—Margali* (1–17). Lunar: Margasira (*Sukla*, *Bahula*); P. *Suk.* Muhammadan: H. 1343 *Jumadal-awwal*; *J.-akhir.*

Cyclic Sidereal Year, Month and Day	Week-Day	English Day	Tithi Ending Moment	Nakshatra Ending Moment	Muhammadan Year, Month and Day
16	Mo	1	5 ·24	22 ·76	4
17	Tu	2	6 ·15	23 ·71	5
18	We	3	7 ·08	24 ·69	6
19	Th	4	8 ·04	25 ·67	7
20	Fr	5	9 ·01 10 ·99	26 ·68	8
21	Sa	6	... ...	27 ·70	9
22	Su	7	11 ·00	1 ·75	10
23	Mo	8	12 ·04	2 ·82	11
24	Tu	9	13 ·08	3 ·90	12
25	We	10	14 ·14	... ...	13
26	Th	11	P ·24	4 ·00	14
27	Fr	12	1 ·33	5 ·10	15
28	Sa	13	2 ·41	6 ·21	16
—29	Su	14	3 ·50	7 ·32	17
1	Mo	15	4 ·56	8 ·41	18
2	Tu	16	5 ·61	9 ·49	19
3	We	17	6 ·66	10 ·54	20
4	Th	18	7 ·67	11 ·58	21
5	Fr	19	8 ·65	12 ·59	22
6	Sa	20	9 ·61	13 ·60	23
7	Su	21	10 ·58	14 ·57	24
8	Mo	22	11 ·51	15 ·53	25
9	Tu	23	12 ·43	16 ·48	26
10	We	24	13 ·35	17 ·42	27
11	Th	25	14 ·25	18 ·36	28
12	Fr	26	—A ·15	19 ·29	29
13	Sa	27	1 ·06 2 ·97	20 ·22	—30
14	Su	28	3 ·88	21 ·15	1
15	Mo	29	4 ·80	22 ·09	2
16	Tu	30	5 ·73	23 ·05	3
17	We	31	6 ·68	24 ·02	4

15. Svati. 16. Visak. 17. Anur. 18. Jyesh. 19. Mula. 20. P. Ash. 21. U. Ash. 22. Sravn. 23. Dani. 24. Satab. 25. P. Bhad. 26. U. Bhad. 27. Rev.

A. D. 1925.
Solar Eclipse. ●
Lunar Eclipse. ○

Mesha Sankranti (Commencement of Indian Sidereal Year).
(Surya Sid.) April 13·09. Saka 1847. Kaliyuga 5026.
(Arya Sid.) April 12·98. (S. Cycle) Krodhana.

SOLAR reckoning: Cyclic Sidereal Year, Month and Day; Week-Day, English Month and Day.
LUNAR reckoning: Tithi Ending Moment; Nakshatra Ending Moment; Muhammadan Year, Month and Day.

Jan.

Cyclic Sidereal Year, Month	Day	Week-Day	English Day	Lunar month / Paksha	Tithi	Ending Moment	Nakshatra	Ending Moment	Muhammadan Year, Month	Day
Raktaksha Dhanus—Margali	18	Th	1	Pausha, Sukla	7	65	25	·00	H. 1343 Jumadal-akhir	5
	19	Fr	2		8	·64	26	·00		6
	20	Sa	3		9	·65	27	·02		7
	21	Su	4		10	·68	1	·07		8
	22	Mo	5		11	·74	2	·13		9
	23	Tu	6		12	·80	3	·20		10
	24	We	7		13	·88	4	·30		11
	25	Th	8		14	·97	5	·40		12
	26	Fr	9		...	...	6	·51		13
	27	Sa	10		P	·06	7	·62		14
	28	Su	11	Bahula	1	·14	8	·72		15
	29	Mo	12		2	·21	9	·79		16
Raktaksha Makara—Tai	1	Tu	13		3	·27	10	·85		17
	2	We	14		4	·30	11	·89		18
	3	Th	15		5	·30	12	·92		19
	4	Fr	16		6	·29	13	·92		20
	5	Sa	17		7	·26	14	·90		21
	6	Su	18		8	·22	15	·87		22
	7	Mo	19		9	·15	16	·82		23
	8	Tu	20		10 / 11	08 / ·98	17	·77		24
	9	We	21		12	·88	18	·70		25
	10	Th	22		13	·78	19	·63		26
	11	Fr	23		14	·69	20	·56		27
	12	Sa	24		A	·59	21	·49		28
	13	Su	25	Sukla	1	·50	22	·44		29
	14	Mo	26		2	·43	23	·39		1
	15	Tu	27		3	·37	24	·35		2
	16	We	28		4	·83	25	·32		3
	17	Th	29		5	·29	26	·32		4
	18	Fr	30		6	·28	27	·34		5
	19	Sa	31		7	·29	1	·38		6

Feb.

Cyclic Sidereal Year, Month	Day	Week-Day	English Day	Lunar month / Paksha	Tithi	Ending Moment	Nakshatra	Ending Moment	Muhammadan Year, Month	Day
	20	Su	1	Magha	8	·33	2	·43	H. 1343 Rajab.	7
	21	Mo	2		9	·38	3	·51		8
	22	Tu	3		10	·45	4	·60		9
	23	We	4		11	·54	5	·70		10
	24	Th	5		12	·62	6	·81		11
	25	Fr	6		13	·70	7	·92		12
	26	Sa	7		14	·79	...	...		13
	27	Su ○	8		P	·86	8	·02		14
	28	Mo	9	Bahula	1	·91	9	·10		15
	29	Tu	10		2	·93	10	·16		16
	30	We	11		3	·94	11	·22		17
Raktaksha Kumbha—Masi	1	Th	12		4	·93	12	·24		18
	2	Fr	13		5	·90	13	·25		19
	3	Sa	14		6	·84	14	·23		20
	4	Su	15		7	·77	15	·20		21
	5	Mo	16		8	·70	16	·16		22
	6	Tu	17		9	·61	17	·10		23
	7	We	18		10	·52	18 / 19	·04 / ·97		24
	8	Th	19		11	·42	20	·90		25
	9	Fr	20		12	·32	21	·83		26
	10	Sa	21		13	·21	22	·77		27
	11	Su	22		14	·13	23	·72		28
	12	Mo	23	Pl. Suk.	A / 1	·05 / ·98	24	·68		29
	13	Tu	24		2	·94	25	·65		30
	14	We	25		3	·91	26	·64	Shaban.	1
	15	Th	26		4	·90	27	·66		2
	16	Fr	27		5	·91	1	·69		3
	17	Sa	28		6	·95	2	·74		4

March

Cyclic Sidereal Year, Month	Day	Week-Day	English Day	Lunar month / Paksha	Tithi	Ending Moment	Nakshatra	Ending Moment	Muhammadan Year, Month	Day
Raktaksha Kumbha—Masi	18	Su	1	Phalguna, Sukla	...	...	3	·81	H. 1343 Shaban.	5
	19	Mo	2		7	·00	4	·90		6
	20	Tu	3		8	·06	...	...		7
	21	We	4		9	·15	5	·00		8
	22	Th	5		10	·24	6	·11		9
	23	Fr	6		11	·33	7	·22		10
	24	Sa	7		12	·41	8	·32		11
	25	Su	8		13	·48	9	·40		12
	26	Mo	9		14	·52	10	·48		13
	27	Tu	10		P	·54	11	·53		14
	28	We	11	Bahula	1	·55	12	·56		15
	29	Th	12		2	·53	13	·57		16
	30	Fr	13		3	·50	14	·56		17
Raktaksha Mina—Panguni	1	Sa	14		4	·44	15	·54		18
	2	Su	15		5	·38	16	·49		19
	3	Mo	16		6	·29	17	·44		20
	4	Tu	17		7	·20	18	·38		21
	5	We	18		8	·11	19	·31		22
	6	Th	19		9 / 10	·00 / ·91	20	·25		23
	7	Fr	20		11	·81	21	·18		24
	8	Sa	21		12	·73	22	·11		25
	9	Su	22		13	·64	23	·05		26
	10	Mo	23		14	·57	24 / 25	·01 / ·98		27
	11	Tu	24		A	·54	26	·97		28
	12	We	25		1	·51	27	·98		29
	13	Th	26		2	·49	...	...		1
	14	Fr	27		3	·49	1	·00		2
	15	Sa	28		4	·54	2	·05		3
	15	Su	29		5	·59	3	·12		4
	17	Mo	30		6	·67	4	·21		5
	18	Tu	31		7	·74	5	·31		6

April

Cyclic Sidereal Year, Month	Day	Week-Day	English Day	Lunar month / Paksha	Tithi	Ending Moment	Nakshatra	Ending Moment	Muhammadan Year, Month	Day
	19	We	1	Chaitra, Sukla	8	·82	6	·41	H. 1343 Ramzan.	7
	20	Th	2		9	·91	7	·52		8
	21	Fr	3		10	·99	8	·62		9
	22	Sa	4		...	...	9	·72		10
	23	Su	5		11	·05	10	·79		11
	24	Mo	6		12	·09	11	·85		12
	25	Tu	7		13	·13	12	·88		13
	26	We	8		14	·12	13	·89		14
	27	Th	9		P	·10	14	·89		15
	28	Fr	10	Bahula	1	·06	15	·87		16
	29	Sa	11		2 / 3	·00 / ·94	16	·83		17
	30	Su	12		4	·85	17	·78		18
Krodhana Mesha—Chittirai	1	Mo	13		5	·76	18	·71		19
	2	Tu	14		6	·66	19	·64		20
	3	We	15		7	·56	20	·57		21
	4	Th	16		8	·46	21	·51		22
	5	Fr	17		9	·36	22	·45		23
	6	Sa	18		10	·28	23	·39		24
	7	Su	19		11	·19	24	·34		25
	8	Mo	20		12	·13	25	·32		26
	9	Tu	21		13	·08	26	·30		27
	10	We	22		14	·05	27	·30		28
	11	Th	23		A	·03	1	·32		29
	12	Fr	24	Vaisak. Suk.	1	·03	2	·36		30
	13	Sa	25		2	·07	3	·43	Shawwal.	1
	14	Su	26		3	·12	4	·51		2
	15	Mo	27		4	·20	5	·61		3
	16	Tu	28		5	·28	6	·71		4
	17	We	29		6	·36	7	·82		5
	18	Th	30		7	·43	8	·93		6

May

Cyclic Sidereal Year, Month	Day	Week-Day	English Day	Lunar month / Paksha	Tithi	Ending Moment	Nakshatra	Ending Moment	Muhammadan Year, Month	Day
Krodhana Mesha—Chittirai	19	Fr	1	Vaisakha, Sukla	8	·51	...	...	H. 1343 Shawwal.	7
	20	Sa	2		9	·58	9	·02		8
	21	Su	3		10	·62	10	·10		9
	22	Mo	4		11	·65	11	·16		10
	23	Tu	5		12	·64	12	·20		11
	24	We	6		13	·63	13	·22		12
	25	Th	7		14	·59	14	·22		13
	26	Fr	8		P	·53	15	20		14
	27	Sa	9	Bahula	1	·46	16	·16		15
	28	Su	10		2	·37	17	·11		16
	29	Mo	11		3	·28	18 / 19	·05 / ·99		17
	30	Tu	12		4	·18	20	·92		18
	31	We	13		5 / 6	·08 / ·98	21	·85		19
Krodhana Vrishabha—Vaikasi	1	Th	14		7	·88	22	·78		20
	2	Fr	15		8	·79	23	·72		21
	3	Sa	16		9	·70	24	·68		22
	4	Su	17		10	·64	25	·64		23
	5	Mo	18		11	·60	26	·62		24
	6	Tu	19		12	·57	27	·62		25
	7	We	20		13	·54	1	·63		26
	8	Th	21		14	·55	2	·68		27
	9	Fr	22		A	·59	3	·74		28
	10	Sa	23	Sukla	1	·63	4	·81		29
	11	Su	24		2	·70	5	·91		1
	12	Mo	25		3	·77	...	...		2
	13	Tu	26		4	·86	6	·01		3
	14	We	27		5	·94	7	·12		4
	15	Th	28		...	...	8	·23		5
	16	Fr	29		6	·02	9	·32		6
	17	Sa	30		7	·08	10	·40		7
	18	Su	31		8	·12	11	·47		8

June

Cyclic Sidereal Year, Month	Day	Week-Day	English Day	Lunar month / Paksha	Tithi	Ending Moment	Nakshatra	Ending Moment	Muhammadan Year, Month	Day
	19	Mo	1	Jyeshtha	9	·14	12	·51	H. 1343 Zi-l-ka'da.	9
	20	Tu	2		10	·14	13	·54		10
	21	We	3		11	·13	14	·54		11
	22	Th	4		12	·09	15	·53		12
	23	Fr	5		13 / 14	·04 / ·96	16	·49		13
	24	Sa	6		P	·88	17	·45		14
	25	Su	7	Bahula	1	·78	18	·40		15
	26	Mo	8		2	·68	19	·33		16
	27	Tu	9		3	·58	20	·26		17
	28	We	10		4	·48	21	·19		18
	29	Th	11		5	·38	22	·12		19
	30	Fr	12		6	·29	23	·07		20
	31	Sa	13		7	·21	24 / 25	·02 / ·97		21
Krodhana Mithuna—Ani	1	Su	14		8	·13	26	·95		22
	2	Mo	15		9	·08	27	·94		23
	3	Tu	16		10	·05	1	·96		24
	4	We	17		11	·03	2	·99		25
	5	Th	18		12	·03	...	...		26
	6	Fr	19		13	·06	3	·04		27
	7	Sa	20		14	·11	4	·12		28
	8	Su	21		A	·17	5	·21		29
	9	Mo	22	Ashadha, Sukla	1	·25	6	·31		30
	10	Tu	23		2	·33	7	·42	H. 1343 Zi-l-hijja.	1
	11	We	24		3	·41	8	·53		2
	12	Th	25		4	·49	9	·63		3
	13	Fr	26		5	·55	10	·71		4
	14	Sa	27		6	·59	11	·78		5
	15	Su	28		7	·62	12	·83		6
	16	Mo	29		8	·63	13	·86		7
	17	Tu	30		9	·61	14	·87		8

Naksh :—1. Asvn. 2. Bhar. 3. Krit. 4. Rohi. 5. Mrig. 6. Ardh. 7. Punar. 8. Push. 9. Aslesh. 10. Magh. 11. P. Phal. 12. U. Phal. 13. Hasta. 14. Chit.

A. D. 1925.
A.—Amavasya.
P.—Paurnami.

Kollam 1101, Commences { N. Malabar—Sept. S. Malabar—Aug.

Hijra 1344, Commences, July 22.

Vikrama 1982.
Bengal San 1331.
(N. Cycle) Isvara.

SOLAR reckoning: Cyclic Sidereal Year, Month and Day. LUNAR reckoning: Week-Day, English Month and Day; Tithi Ending Moment; Nakshatra Ending Moment; Muhammadan Year, Month and Day.

July

Cyclic Sidereal Year, Month and Day	Week-Day	English Day	Tithi	Ending Moment	Nakshatra	Ending Moment	Muhammadan Year, Month and Day
18	We	1	10	·57	15	·85	9
19	Th	2	Sukla 11	·52	16	·82	10
20	Fr	3	12	·44	17	·79	11
21	Sa	4	13	·36	18	·73	12
Krodhana Mithuna—Ani. 22	Su	5	14	·26	19	·67	13
23	Mo	6	P	·17	20	·60	14
24	Tu	7	1 2	·06 ·95	21	·53	15
25	We	8	Ashadha 3	·86	22	·47	16
26	Th	9	4	·76	23	·41	17
27	Fr	10	5	·68	24	·35	18
28	Sa	11	6	·61	25	·31	19
29	Su	12	7	·56	26	·28	H. 1343 Zil-hijja. 20
30	Mo	13	8	·52	27	·27	21
31	Tu	14	9	·51	1	·28	22
—32	We	15	Bahula 10	·52	2	·31	23
1	Th	16	11	·54	3	·35	24
2	Fr	17	12	·59	4	·42	25
3	Sa	18	13	·64	5	·51	26
4	Su	19	14	·72	6	·61	27
5	Mo	20	—A	·80	7	·72	28
6	Tu	21	1	·88	8	·83	—29
7	We	22	2	·96	9	·93	1
8	Th	23	...	...	...	...	2
9	Fr	24	3	03	10	·02	3
10	Sa	25	4	·07	11	·10	4
11	Su	26	5	·10	12	·15	5
12	Mo	27	6	·11	13	·18	6
Krodhana Karkata—Adi. 13	Tu	28	Sukla 7	·09	14	·19	7
14	We	29	8	·05	15	·18	8
15	Th	30	9 10	·00 ·93	16	·17	9
16	Fr	31	11	·85	17	·12	10

Aug.

Cyclic Sidereal Year, Month and Day	Week-Day	English Day	Tithi	Ending Moment	Nakshatra	Ending Moment	Muhammadan Year, Month and Day
17	Sa	1	12	·75	18	·07	11
18	Su	2	13	·66	19 20	·01 95	12
19	Mo	3	Sravana 14	·56	21	·88	13
20	Tu ○	4	P	·45	22	·81	14
21	We	5	1	·35	23	·74	15
22	Th	6	2	·27	24	·68	16
23	Fr	7	3	·18	25	·64	H. 1344 Muharram. 17
24	Sa	8	4	·10	26	·61	18
25	Su	9	5	·05	27	·60	19
26	Mo	10	6	·01	1	·60	20
27	Tu	11	Bahula 7	·00	2	·62	21
28	We	12	8	·01	3	·66	22
29	Th	13	9	·02	4	·73	23
30	Fr	14	10	·07	5	·82	24
—31	Sa	15	11	·13	6	·91	25
1	Su	16	12	·21	...	...	26
2	Mo	17	13	·29	7	·02	27
3	Tu	18	14	·38	8	·12	28
4	We	19	—A	·45	9	·28	29
5	Th	20	1	·52	10	·33	—30
6	Fr	21	2	·57	11	·40	1
7	Sa	22	3	·61	12	·46	2
8	Su	23	4	·60	13	·50	3
9	Mo	24	5	·58	14	·51	4
Krodhana Simha—Avani. 10	Tu	25	Sukla 6	·55	15	·52	5
11	We	26	7	·51	16	·49	6
12	Th	27	8	·44	17	·46	H. 1344 Safar. 7
13	Fr	28	Bhadra. 9	·36	18	·41	8
14	Sa	29	10	·26	19	·35	9
15	Su	30	11	·16	20	·29	10
16	Mo	31	12 13	·06 ·96	21	·22	11

Sep.

Cyclic Sidereal Year, Month and Day	Week-Day	English Day	Tithi	Ending Moment	Nakshatra	Ending Moment	Muhammadan Year, Month and Day
17	Tu	1	Bhadrapada 14	·86	22	·15	12
18	We	2	P	·77	23	·08	13
19	Th	3	1	·69	24 25	·02 ·97	14
20	Fr	4	2	·62	26	·94	15
21	Sa	5	3	·55	27	·92	16
Krodhana Simha—Avani. 22	Su	6	4	·52	1	·92	17
23	Mo	7	5	·51	2	·94	18
24	Tu	8	6	·52	3	·97	19
25	We	9	Bahula 7	·54	...	...	20
26	Th	10	8	·59	4	·04	H. 1344 Safar. 21
27	Fr	11	9	·65	5	·12	22
28	Sa	12	10	·72	6	·21	23
29	Su	13	11	·81	7	·32	24
30	Mo	14	12	·90	8	·43	25
—31	Tu	15	13	·97	9	·54	26
1	We	16	...	...	10	·63	27
2	Th	17	14	·04	11	·71	28
3	Fr	18	—A	·09	12	·77	—29
4	Sa	19	1	·12	13	·81	1
5	Su	20	2	·13	14	·84	2
6	Mo	21	3	12	15	·84	3
7	Tu	22	4	·09	16	·82	4
8	We	23	5 6	·04 ·97	17	·79	5
9	Th	24	Sukla 7	·89	18	·74	6
Krodhana Kanya—Purattasi. 10	Fr	25	8	·80	19	·68	7
11	Sa	26	9	·70	20	·62	8
12	Su	27	10	·61	21	·55	9
13	Mo	28	11	·51	22	·48	10
14	Tu	29	12	·40	23	·41	11
15	We	30	13	·31	24	·35	12

Oct.

Cyclic Sidereal Year, Month and Day	Week-Day	English Day	Tithi	Ending Moment	Nakshatra	Ending Moment	Muhammadan Year, Month and Day
16	Th	1	Asvina 14	·23	25	·31	13
17	Fr	2	P	·17	26	·27	14
18	Sa	3	1	·11	27	·25	15
19	Su	4	2	·08	1	·24	16
20	Mo	5	3	·06	2	·25	17
21	Tu	6	4	·06	3	·30	18
22	We	7	5	·09	4	·35	19
23	Th	8	6	·14	5	·42	20
24	Fr	9	Bahula 7	·21	6	·51	H. 1344 Rabi-ul-awwal. 21
25	Sa	10	8	·28	7	·61	22
26	Su	11	9	·38	8	·72	23
27	Mo	12	10	·46	9	·88	24
28	Tu	13	11	·54	10	·93	25
29	We	14	12	·61	...	...	26
30	Th	15	13	·65	11	·02	27
—31	Fr	16	14	·69	12	·08	28
1	Sa	17	—A	·70	13	·14	29
2	Su	18	1	·69	14	·16	—30
3	Mo	19	2	·66	15	·17	1
4	Tu	20	3	·62	16	·15	2
5	We	21	4	·55	17	·12	3
6	Th	22	5	·47	18	·08	4
7	Fr	23	Sukla 6	·38	19 20	·03 ·96	5
8	Sa	24	7	·28	21	·89	6
Krodhana Tula—Aippasi. 9	Su	25	8	·19	22	·82	7
10	Mo	26	9 10	·08 ·99	23	·76	H. 1344 Rabi-ul-akhir. 8
11	Tu	27	Karttika 11	·89	24	·70	9
12	We	28	12	82	25	·64	10
13	Th	29	13	·76	26	·60	11
14	Fr	30	14	·70	27	·57	12
15	Sa	31	P	·67	1	·56	13

Nov.

Cyclic Sidereal Year, Month and Day	Week-Day	English Day	Tithi	Ending Moment	Nakshatra	Ending Moment	Muhammadan Year, Month and Day
16	Su	1	Karttika 1	·65	2	·58	14
17	Mo	2	2	·66	3	·61	15
18	Tu	3	3	·69	4	·66	16
19	We	4	4	·75	5	·73	17
20	Th	5	5	·81	6	·81	18
Krodhana Tula—Aippasi. 21	Fr	6	6	·89	7	·92	19
22	Sa	7	7	·98	...	...	20
23	Su	8	...	...	8	·03	21
24	Mo	9	Bahula 8	·07	9	·13	22
25	Tu	10	9	·15	10	·23	23
26	We	11	10	·21	11	·32	H. 1344 Rabi-ul-akhir. 24
27	Th	12	11	·26	12	·39	25
28	Fr	13	12	·30	13	·45	26
29	Sa	14	13	·32	14	·48	27
—30	Su	15	14	·30	15	·49	28
1	Mo	16	—A	·26	16	·48	—29
2	Tu	17	1	·22	17	·45	1
3	We	18	2	·16	18	·42	2
4	Th	19	3 4	·09 ·99	19	·36	3
5	Fr	20	5	·90	20	·30	4
6	Sa	21	Sukla 6	·79	21	·23	5
7	Su	22	7	·70	22	·16	6
8	Mo	23	8	·60	28	·10	7
Krodhana Vrischika—Kartigai. 9	Tu	24	9	·51	24 25	·04 ·98	8
10	We	25	Margasira 10	·44	26	·93	Jumadal-awwal. 9
11	Th	26	11	·37	27	·90	10
12	Fr	27	12	·32	1	·89	11
13	Sa	28	13	·29	2	·90	12
14	Su	29	14	·27	3	·92	13
15	Mo	30	P	·30	4	·97	14

Dec.

Cyclic Sidereal Year, Month and Day	Week-Day	English Day	Tithi	Ending Moment	Nakshatra	Ending Moment	Muhammadan Year, Month and Day
16	Tu	1	1	·33	...	...	15
17	We	2	2	·37	5	·03	H. 1344 16
18	Th	3	3	·43	6	·12	17
19	Fr	4	4	·52	7	·22	18
20	Sa	5	5	·61	8	·33	19
21	Su	6	Bahula 6	·70	9	·43	20
22	Mo	7	7	·78	10	·53	21
23	Tu	8	8	·85	11	·62	22
24	We	9	9	·91	12	·71	23
25	Th	10	10	·93	13	·76	24
26	Fr	11	11	·95	14	·80	25
27	Sa	12	12	·93	15	·81	26
28	Su	13	13	·90	16	·81	27
—29	Mo	14	14	·85	17	·79	28
1	Tu	15	—A	·78	18	·75	29
2	We	16	1	·71	19	·70	—30
3	Th	17	2	·62	20	·64	1
4	Fr	18	3	·53	21	·58	2
5	Sa	19	4	·42	22	·51	3
6	Su	20	5	·33	23	·44	4
7	Mo	21	Sukla 6	·24	24	·37	5
8	Tu	22	7	·14	25	·31	6
Krodhana Dhanus—Margali. 9	We	23	8	07	26	·26	7
10	Th	24	9 10	·01 ·96	27	·24	8
11	Fr	25	11	·93	1	·22	H. 1344 Jumadal-akhir. 9
12	Sa	26	12	·93	2	·22	10
13	Su	27	Pausha 13	·94	3	·24	11
14	Mo	28	14	·97	4	·28	12
15	Tu	29	...	...	5	·34	13
16	We	30	P	·03	6	·43	14
17	Th	31	1	·09	7	·52	15

15 Svati. 16. Visak. 17. Anur. 18. Jyesh. 19. Mula. 20. P. Ash. 21. U. Ash. 22. Sravn. 23. Dani. 24. Satab. 25 P. Bhad. 26. U. Bhad. 27. Rev.

A. D. 1926.
Solar Eclipse. ●
Lunar Eclipse. ○

Mesha Sankranti (Commencement of Indian Sidereal Year).
(Surya Sid.) April 13·35. **Saka 1848.** **Kaliyuga 5027.**
(Arya Sid.) April 13·24. **(S. Cycle) Kshaya** (Akshaya).

Columns: SOLAR reckoning — Cyclic Sidereal Year, Month and Day; Week-Day English Month and Day. LUNAR reckoning — Tithi Ending Moment; Nakshatra Ending Moment; Muhammadan Year, Month and Day.

Jan.

Solar: Krodhana Dhanus—Margali; Krodhana Makara—Tai. Lunar: Pausha, Bahula; Sukla; Magha. Muhammadan: H. 1344 Jumadal-akhir; H. 1344 Rajab.

Cyclic Sidereal	Week-Day	Tithi	Nakshatra	Muhammadan
18	Fr 1	2 ·17	8 ·62	16
19	Sa 2	3 ·26	9 ·73	17
20	Su 3	4 ·36	10 ·83	18
21	Mo 4	5 ·43	11 ·94	19
22	Tu 5	6 ·50	... ...	20
23	We 6	7 ·56	12 ·01	21
24	Th 7	8 ·58	13 ·07	22
25	Fr 8	9 ·59	14 ·11	23
26	Sa 9	10 ·58	15 ·13	24
27	Su 10	11 ·55	16 ·14	25
28	Mo 11	12 ·49	17 ·12	26
29	Tu 12	13 ·44	18 ·08	27
—30	We 13	14 ·36	19 ·04 / 20 ·98	28
1	Th ● 14	—A ·26	21 ·92	—29
2	Fr 15	1 ·17	22 ·85	1
3	Sa 16	2 ·07 / 3 ·98	23 ·78	2
4	Su 17	4 ·88	24 ·71	3
5	Mo 18	5 ·79	25 ·65	4
6	Tu 19	6 ·72	26 ·60	5
7	We 20	7 ·66	27 ·57	6
8	Th 21	8 ·60	1 ·54	7
9	Fr 22	9 ·57	2 ·54	8
10	Sa 23	10 ·57	3 ·55	9
11	Su 24	11 ·58	4 ·59	10
12	Mo 25	12 ·61	5 ·65	11
13	Tu 26	13 ·68	6 ·73	12
14	We 27	14 ·75	7 ·82	13
15	Th 28	P ·83	8 ·92	14
16	Fr 29	1 ·91	... ...	15
17	Sa 30	... ...	9 ·03	16
18	Su 31	2 ·01	10 ·14	17

Feb.

Solar: Krodhana Kumbha—Masi. Lunar: Bahula; Sukla; Phalguna. Muhammadan: H. 1344 Shaban.

Cyclic Sidereal	Week-Day	Tithi	Nakshatra	Muhammadan
19	Mo 1	3 ·08	11 ·24	18
20	Tu 2	4 ·15	12 ·32	19
21	We 3	5 ·20	13 ·38	20
22	Th 4	6 ·23	14 ·43	21
23	Fr 5	7 ·23	15 ·46	22
24	Sa 6	8 ·22	16 ·47	23
25	Su 7	9 ·18	17 ·45	24
26	Mo 8	10 ·12	18 ·42	25
27	Tu 9	11 ·06 / 12 ·98	19 ·37	26
28	We 10	13 ·89	20 ·32	27
—29	Th 11	14 ·79	21 ·26	28
1	Fr 12	—A ·70	22 ·19	29
2	Sa 13	1 ·60	23 ·12	—30
3	Su 14	2 ·50	24 ·05 / 25 ·98	1
4	Mo 15	3 ·41	26 ·94	2
5	Tu 16	4 ·34	27 ·90	3
6	We 17	5 ·28	1 ·87	4
7	Th 18	6 ·23	2 ·86	5
8	Fr 19	7 ·21	3 ·87	6
9	Sa 20	8 ·19	4 ·91	7
10	Su 21	9 ·20	5 ·96	8
11	Mo 22	10 ·25	... ...	9
12	Tu 23	11 ·30	6 ·03	10
13	We 24	12 ·37	7 ·12	11
14	Th 25	13 ·45	8 ·22	12
15	Fr 26	14 ·55	9 ·33	13
16	Sa 27	P ·63	10 ·44	14
17	Su 28	1 ·71	11 ·54	15

March

Solar: Krodhana Kumbha—Masi; Krodhana Mina—Panguni. Lunar: Phalguna, Bahula; Sukla; Adhika Chaitra. Muhammadan: H. 1344 Shaban; H. 1344 Ramzan.

Cyclic Sidereal	Week-Day	Tithi	Nakshatra	Muhammadan
18	Mo 1	2 ·77	12 ·63	16
19	Tu 2	3 ·82	13 ·69	17
20	We 3	4 ·84	14 ·75	18
21	Th 4	5 ·84	15 ·78	19
22	Fr 5	6 ·83	16 ·79	20
23	Sa 6	7 ·79	17 ·78	21
24	Su 7	8 ·74	18 ·75	22
25	Mo 8	9 ·67	19 ·71	23
26	Tu 9	10 ·59	20 ·66	24
27	We 10	11 ·50	21 ·60	25
28	Th 11	12 ·40	22 ·53	26
29	Fr 12	13 ·30	23 ·46	27
—30	Sa 13	14 ·20	24 ·39	28
1	Su 14	—A ·11	25 ·33	—29
2	Mo 15	1 ·01 / 2 ·93	26 ·27	1
3	Tu 16	3 ·87	27 ·23	2
4	We 17	4 ·82	1 ·20	3
5	Th 18	5 ·80	2 ·18	4
6	Fr 19	6 ·79	3 ·20	5
7	Sa 20	7 ·81	4 ·22	6
8	Su 21	8 ·84	5 ·27	7
9	Mo 22	9 ·90	6 ·34	8
10	Tu 23	10 ·97	7 ·42	9
11	We 24	... ...	8 ·53	10
12	Th 25	11 ·05	9 ·63	11
13	Fr 26	12 ·14	10 ·74	12
14	Sa 27	13 ·22	11 ·84	13
15	Su 28	14 ·30	12 ·93	14
16	Mo 29	P ·36	... ...	15
17	Tu 30	1 ·41	13 ·01	16
18	We 31	2 ·43	14 ·07	17

April

Solar: Krodhana Mina—Panguni; Kshaya Mesha—Chittirai. Lunar: Bahula; Sukla; Nija Chaitra. Muhammadan: H. 1344 Ramzan; H. 1344 Shawwal.

Cyclic Sidereal	Week-Day	Tithi	Nakshatra	Muhammadan
19	Th 1	3 ·42	15 ·10	18
20	Fr 2	4 ·41	16 ·11	19
21	Sa 3	5 ·36	17 ·10	20
22	Su 4	6 ·31	18 ·08	21
23	Mo 5	7 ·24	19 ·05 / 20 ·99	22
24	Tu 6	8 ·16	21 ·93	23
25	We 7	9 ·07 / 10 ·96	22 ·86	24
26	Th 8	11 ·86	23 ·79	25
27	Fr 9	12 ·76	24 ·73	26
28	Sa 10	13 ·67	25 ·67	27
29	Su 11	14 ·58	26 ·61	28
—30	Mo 12	—A ·50	27 ·56	29
1	Tu 13	1 ·43	1 ·53	—30
2	We 14	2 ·39	2 ·52	1
3	Th 15	3 ·36	3 ·52	2
4	Fr 16	4 ·34	4 ·54	3
5	Sa 17	5 ·36	5 ·58	4
6	Su 18	6 ·39	6 ·64	5
7	Mo 19	7 ·45	7 ·73	6
8	Tu 20	8 ·52	8 ·83	7
9	We 21	9 ·60	9 ·98	8
10	Th 22	10 ·68	... ...	9
11	Fr 23	11 ·76	10 ·04	10
12	Sa 24	12 ·83	11 ·14	11
13	Su 25	13 ·89	12 ·23	12
14	Mo 26	14 ·95	13 ·32	13
15	Tu 27	P ·96	14 ·38	14
16	We 28	1 ·96	15 ·42	15
17	Th 29	2 ·94	16 ·43	16
18	Fr 30	3 ·91	17 ·43	17

May

Solar: Kshaya Mesha—Chittirai; Kshaya Vrishabha—Vaikasi. Lunar: Ni. Ch., Bahula; Sukla; Vaisakha. Muhammadan: H. 1344 Shawwal; H. 1344 Zi-l-ka'da.

Cyclic Sidereal	Week-Day	Tithi	Nakshatra	Muhammadan
19	Sa 1	4 ·84	18 ·42	18
20	Su 2	5 ·77	19 ·38	19
21	Mo 3	6 ·69	20 ·33	20
22	Tu 4	7 ·60	21 ·27	21
23	We 5	8 ·50	22 ·21	22
24	Th 6	9 ·39	23 ·14	23
25	Fr 7	10 ·30	24 ·07	24
26	Sa 8	11 ·19	25 ·00 / 26 ·94	25
27	Su 9	12 ·10	27 ·89	26
28	Mo 10	13 ·02 / 14 ·95	1 ·86	27
29	Tu 11	—A ·91	2 ·84	28
30	We 12	1 ·88	3 ·84	—29
—31	Th 13	2 ·87	4 ·85	1
1	Fr 14	3 ·87	5 ·89	2
2	Sa 15	4 ·90	6 ·96	3
3	Su 16	5 ·96	... ...	4
4	Mo 17	... ...	7 ·03	5
5	Tu 18	6 ·02	8 ·13	6
6	We 19	7 ·10	9 ·23	7
7	Th 20	8 ·18	10 ·33	8
8	Fr 21	9 ·27	11 ·44	9
9	Sa 22	10 ·35	12 ·54	10
10	Su 23	11 ·42	13 ·63	11
11	Mo 24	12 ·46	14 ·69	12
12	Tu 25	13 ·47	15 ·73	13
13	We 26	14 ·47	16 ·75	14
14	Th 27	P ·45	17 ·76	15
15	Fr 28	1 ·42	18 ·75	16
16	Sa 29	2 ·35	19 ·71	17
17	Su 30	3 ·28	20 ·67	18
18	Mo 31	4 ·19	21 ·61	19

June

Solar: Kshaya Mithuna—Ani. Lunar: Bahula; Sukla; Jyeshtha; Bah. Muhammadan: H. 1344 Zi-l-hijja.

Cyclic Sidereal	Week-Day	Tithi	Nakshatra	Muhammadan
19	Tu 1	5 ·09 / 6 ·99	22 ·55	20
20	We 2	7 ·89	23 ·48	21
21	Th 3	8 ·80	24 ·41	22
22	Fr 4	9 ·69	25 ·34	23
23	Sa 5	10 ·61	26 ·28	24
24	Su 6	11 ·53	27 ·23	25
25	Mo 7	12 ·46	1 ·19	26
26	Tu 8	13 ·40	2 ·17	27
27	We 9	14 ·37	3 ·16	28
28	Th 10	—A ·36	4 ·17	29
29	Fr 11	1 ·38	5 ·20	—30
30	Sa 12	2 ·40	6 ·27	1
31	Su 13	3 ·44	7 ·34	2
—32	Mo 14	4 ·51	8 ·43	3
1	Tu 15	5 ·58	9 ·53	4
2	We 16	6 ·66	10 ·63	5
3	Th 17	7 ·75	11 ·74	6
4	Fr 18	8 ·82	12 ·85	7
5	Sa 19	9 ·89	13 ·93	8
6	Su 20	10 ·93	... ...	9
7	Mo 21	11 ·95	14 ·00	10
8	Tu 22	12 ·95	15 ·04	11
9	We 23	13 ·93	16 ·08	12
10	Th 24	14 ·89	17 ·09	13
11	Fr 25	P ·88	18 ·07	14
12	Sa 26	1 ·77	19 ·04	15
13	Su 27	2 ·68	20 ·00 / 21 ·95	16
14	Mo 28	3 ·59	22 ·89	17
15	Tu 29	4 ·48	23 ·82	18
16	We 30	5 ·38	24 ·75	19

Naksh :—1. Asvn 2. Bhar. 3. Krit. 4. Rohi. 5. Mrig. 6. Ardh. 7. Punar. 8. Push. 9. Aslesh. 10. Magh. 11. P. Phal 12 U. Phal. 13. Hasta. 14. Chit.

A. D. 1926.
A.—Amavasya.
P.—Paurnami.

Kollam 1102, Commences { **N. Malabar—Sept.** / **S. Malabar—Aug.**

Hijra 1345, Commences, **July 12.**

Vikrama 1983.
Bengal San 1332.
(N. Cycle) Bahudhanya.

Solar month	Cyclic Sidereal Year, Month and Day	Week-Day	English Month and Day	Lunar month / fortnight	Tithi	Tithi Ending Moment	Nakshatra	Nakshatra Ending Moment	Muhammadan Year and Month	Muhammadan Day
		July								
Kshaya. Mithuna—Ani.	17	Th	1	Jy.	6	·27	25	·68	H. 1344 Zi-l-hijja.	20
	18	Fr	2		7	·17	26	·62		21
	19	Sa	3		8	·09	27	·57		22
	20	Su	4	Bahula	9 10	·01 ·94	1	·52		23
	21	Mo	5		11	·88	2	·49		24
	22	Tu	6		12	·85	3	·48		25
	23	We	7		13	·83	4	·49		26
	24	Th	8		14	·84	5	·53		27
	25	Fr ●	9		—A	·87	6	·57		28
	26	Sa	10		1	·91	7	·64		29
	27	Su	11		2	·98	8	·73		—30
	28	Mo	12		...	...	9	·83	H. 1345 Muharram.	1
	29	Tu	13		3	·06	10	·94		2
	30	We	14		4	·13	...	...		3
	—31	Th	15		5	·22	11	·05		4
Kshaya. Karkata—Adi.	1	Fr	16	Sukla	6	·30	12	·15		5
	2	Sa	17		7	·36	13	·23		6
	3	Su	18		8	·40	14	·31		7
	4	Mo	19		9	·43	15	·37		8
	5	Tu	20		10	·43	16	·40		9
	6	We	21	Ashadha	11	·41	17	·41		10
	7	Th	22		12	·37	18	·40		11
	8	Fr	23		13	·32	19	·37		12
	9	Sa	24		14	·24	20	·34		13
	10	Su	25		P	·16	21	·29		14
	11	Mo	26		1 2	·07 ·97	22	·23		15
	12	Tu	27		3	·87	23	·16		16
	13	We	28		4	·77	24	·09		17
	14	Th	29	Bahula	5	·67	25 26	·02 ·96		18
	15	Fr	30		6	·58	27	·90		19
	16	Sa	31		7	·49	1	·86		20
		Aug.								
	17	Su	1		8	·42	2	·82		21
	18	Mo	2		9	·36	3	·81		22
	19	Tu	3		10	·34	4	·82		23
	20	We	4		11	·31	5	·84		24
	21	Th	5		12	·33	6	·88		25
	22	Fr	6		13	·35	7	·95		26
	23	Sa	7		14	·39	...	...		27
	24	Su	8		—A	·46	8	·03		28
	25	Mo	9		1	·53	9	·13		29
	26	Tu	10		2	·61	10	·24		—30
	27	We	11		3	·70	11	·34	H. 1345 Safar.	1
	28	Th	12		4	·79	12	·45		2
	29	Fr	13		5	·85	13	·54		3
	30	Sa	14		6	·89	14	·62		4
	31	Su	15		7	·92	15	·68		5
	—32	Mo	16	Sukla	8	·92	16	·72		6
Kshaya. Simha—Avani.	1	Tu	17		9	·91	17	·73		7
	2	We	18		10	·87	18	·73		8
	3	Th	19		11	·82	19	·71		9
	4	Fr	20		12	·75	20	·68		10
	5	Sa	21	Sravana	13	·67	21	·62		11
	6	Su	22		14	·58	22	·56		12
	7	Mo	23		P	·47	23	·50		13
	8	Tu	24		1	·37	24	·44		14
	9	We	25		2	·26	25	·37		15
	10	Th	26		3	·17	26	·30		16
	11	Fr	27		4	·09	27	·24		17
	12	Sa	28	Bahula	5 6	·01 ·93	1	·19		18
	13	Su	29		7	·86	2	·15		19
	14	Mo	30		8	·84	3	·14		20
	15	Tu	31		9	·83	4	·14		21

Solar month	Cyclic Sidereal Year, Month and Day	Week-Day	English Month and Day	Lunar month / fortnight	Tithi	Tithi Ending Moment	Nakshatra	Nakshatra Ending Moment	Muhammadan Year and Month	Muhammadan Day
		Sep.								
Kshaya. Simha—Avani.	16	We	1	Srv.	10	·84	5	·16	H. 1345 Safar.	22
	17	Th	2		11	·86	6	·19		23
	18	Fr	3		12	·91	7	·25		24
	19	Sa	4	Bah.	13	·98	8	·34		25
	20	Su	5		...	...	9	·43		26
	21	Mo	6		14	·05	10	·54		27
	22	Tu	7		—A	·12	11	·64		28
	23	We	8		1	·21	12	·75		—29
	24	Th	9		2	·29	13	·85	H. 1345 Rabi-ul-awwal.	1
	25	Fr	10		3	·35	14	·93		2
	26	Sa	11		4	·41	15	·99		3
	27	Su	12		5	·48	...	...		4
	28	Mo	13		6	·45	16	·03		5
	29	Tu	14	Sukla	7	·43	17	·05		6
	30	We	15		8	·40	18	·05		7
	—31	Th	16		9	·35	19	·04		8
Kshaya. Kanya—Purattasi.	1	Fr	17		10	·28	20 21	·01 ·96		9
	2	Sa	18		11	·19	22	·90		10
	3	Su	19		12	·09	23	·84		11
	4	Mo	20	Bhadrapada	13 14	·00 ·91	24	·77		12
	5	Tu	21		P	·80	25	·70		13
	6	We	22		1	·70	26	·63		14
	7	Th	23		2	·61	27	·57		15
	8	Fr	24		3	·54	1	·52		16
	9	Sa	25		4	·47	2	·49		17
	10	Su	26		5	·41	3	·47		18
	11	Mo	27		6	·38	4	·46		19
	12	Tu	28		7	·37	5	·47		20
	13	We	29		8	·39	6	·51		21
	14	Th	30		9	·40	7	·57		22
		Oct.								
	15	Fr	1	Bahula	10	·45	8	·64		23
	16	Sa	2		11	·51	9	·73		24
	17	Su	3		12	·59	10	·83		25
	18	Mo	4		13	·68	11	·94		26
	19	Tu	5		14	·77	...	...		27
	20	We	6		—A	·84	12	·05		28
	21	Th	7		1	·91	13	·15		29
	22	Fr	8		2	·96	14	·24		—30
	23	Sa	9		3	·99	15	·30	H. 1345 Rabi-ul-akhir.	1
	24	Su	10		...	...	16	·35		2
	25	Mo	11		4 5	·01 ·99	17	·37		3
	26	Tu	12	Sukla	6	·96	18	·39		4
	27	We	13		7	·91	19	·37		5
	28	Th	14		8	·85	20	·34		6
	29	Fr	15		9	·76	21	·29		7
	—30	Sa	16		10	·66	22	·24		8
Kshaya. Tula—Aippasi.	1	Su	17		11	·57	23	·18		9
	2	Mo	18		12	·47	24	·11		10
	3	Tu	19	Asvina	13	·37	25 26	·04 ·97		11
	4	We	20		14	·28	27	·91		12
	5	Th	21		P	·20	1	·86		13
	6	Fr	22		1	·12	2	·82		14
	7	Sa	23		2 3	·05 ·99	3	·79		15
	8	Su	24		4	·96	4	·78		16
	9	Mo	25		5	·95	5	·79		17
	10	Tu	26		6	·97	6	·83		18
	11	We °	27	Bahula	7	·99	7	·88		19
	12	Th	28		...	...	8	·95		20
	13	Fr	29		8	·05	...	...		21
	14	Sa	30		9	·11	9	·03		22
	15	Su	31		10	·19	10	·13		23

Solar month	Cyclic Sidereal Year, Month and Day	Week-Day	English Month and Day	Lunar month / fortnight	Tithi	Tithi Ending Moment	Nakshatra	Nakshatra Ending Moment	Muhammadan Year and Month	Muhammadan Day
		Nov.								
Kshaya. Tula—Aippasi.	16	Mo	1	Bah.	11	·27	11	·24	R.-akhir.	24
	17	Tu	2		12	·37	12	·35		25
	18	We	3		13	·44	13	·45		26
	19	Th	4		14	·51	14	·54		27
	20	Fr	5		—A	·56	15	·61		28
	21	Sa	6		1	·60	16	·66		—29
	22	Su	7		2	·60	17	·70	H 1345 Jumadal-awwal.	1
	23	Mo	8		3	·58	18	·71		2
	24	Tu	9		4	·56	19	·70		3
	25	We	10		5	·51	20	·67		4
	26	Th	11		6	·45	21	·63		5
	27	Fr	12	Sukla	7	·36	22	·58		6
	28	Sa	13		8	·27	23	·52		7
	29	Su	14		9	·18	24	·45		8
	—30	Mo	15		10 11	·08 ·98	25	·38		9
Kshaya. Vrischika—Kartigai.	1	Tu	16		12	·89	26	·32		10
	2	We	17	Karttika	13	·81	27	·26		11
	3	Th	18		14	·73	1	·20		12
	4	Fr	19		P	·66	2	·15		13
	5	Sa	20		1	·60	3	·12		14
	6	Su	21		2	·58	4	·10		15
	7	Mo	22		3	·57	5	·11		16
	8	Tu	23		4	·58	6	·14		17
	9	We	24		5	·61	7	·19		18
	10	Th	25	Bahula	6	·67	8	·25		19
	11	Fr	26		7	·74	9	·33		20
	12	Sa	27		8	·82	10	·43		21
	13	Su	28		9	·91	11	·54		22
	14	Mo	29		10	·99	12	·65		23
	15	Tu	30		...	...	13	·75		24
		Dec.								
	16	We	1		11	·07	14	·84		25
	17	Th	2		12	·14	15	·92		26
	18	Fr	3		13	·19	16	·98		27
	19	Sa	4		14	·22	...	...		28
	20	Su	5		—A	·23	17	·02		29
	21	Mo	6		1	·22	18	·03		—30
	22	Tu	7		2	·18	19	·03	H. 1345 Jumadal-akhir.	1
	23	We	8		3	·13	20 21	·00 ·97		2
	24	Th	9		4 5	·07 ·98	22	·92		3
	25	Fr	10		6	·89	23	·86		4
	26	Sa	11	Sukla	7	·80	24	·79		5
	27	Su	12		8	·71	25	·72		6
	28	Mo	13		9	·60	26	·65		7
	29	Tu	14		10	·51	27	·59		8
	—30	We	15		11	·43	1	·53		9
Kshaya. Dhanus—Margali.	1	Th	16	Margasira	12	·35	2	·48		10
	2	Fr	17		13	·30	3	·45		11
	3	Sa	18		14	·25	4	·43		12
	4	Su ○	19		P	·22	5	·44		13
	5	Mo	20		1	·20	6	·46		14
	6	Tu	21		2	·23	7	·50		15
	7	We	22		3	·26	8	·56		16
	8	Th	23		4	·31	9	·64		17
	9	Fr	24		5	·39	10	·74		18
	10	Sa	25	Bahula	6	·47	11	·84		19
	11	Su	26		7	·56	12	·95		20
	12	Mo	27		8	·65	...	...		21
	13	Tu	28		9	·73	13	·05		22
	14	We	29		10	·79	14	·15		23
	15	Th	30		11	·84	15	·23		24
	16	Fr	31		12	·87	16	·29		25

15. Svati. 16. Visak. 17. Anur. 18. Jyesh. 19. Mula. 20. P. Ash. 21. U. Ash. 22. Sravn. 23. Dani. 24. Satab. 25. P. Bhad. 26. U. Bhad. 27. Rev.

A. D. 1927. | **Mesha Sankranti** (Commencement of Indian Sidereal Year).
Solar Eclipse. ● | **(Surya Sid.) April 13·61.** | **Saka 1849.** | **Kaliyuga 5028.**
Lunar Eclipse. ○ | **(Arya Sid.) April 13·50.** | **(S. Cycle) Prabhava.**

SOLAR reckoning: Cyclic Sidereal Year, Month and Day; Week-Day English Month and Day. LUNAR reckoning: Tithi Ending Moment; Nakshatra Ending Moment; Muhammadan Year, Month and Day.

Jan. (Solar: Kshaya, Dhanus—Margali; Kshaya, Makara—Tai. Lunar: Bah., Sukla, Pausha, Bahula. Muhammadan: J-akr.; H. 1345 Rajab.)

Cyclic Sidereal Year, Month and Day	Week-Day	Day	Tithi	Tithi Ending Moment	Nakshatra	Nakshatra Ending Moment	Muhammadan Year, Month and Day
17	Sa	1	13	·87	17	·33	26
18	Su	2	14	·86	18	·35	27
19	Mo	3	—A	·83	19	·35	28
20	Tu	4	1	·78	20	·33	—29
21	We	5	2	·71	21	·30	1
22	Th	6	3	·64	22	·26	2
23	Fr	7	4	·54	23	·20	3
24	Sa	8	5	·44	24	·13	4
25	Su	9	6	·35	25	·06	5
26	Mo	10	7	·25	26 27	·00 ·93	6
27	Tu	11	8	·16	1	·87	7
28	We	12	9	·08	2	·82	8
—29	Th	13	10 11	·00 ·93	3	·78	9
1	Fr	14	12	·88	4	·76	10
2	Sa	15	13	·86	5	·76	11
3	Su	16	14	·85	6	·77	12
4	Mo	17	P	·87	7	·81	13
5	Tu	18	1	·91	8	·86	14
6	We	19	2	·97	9	·95	15
7	Th	20	...	...	...	...	16
8	Fr	21	3	·04	10	·04	17
9	Sa	22	4	·12	11	·14	18
10	Su	23	5	·22	12	·25	19
11	Mo	24	6	·30	13	·35	20
12	Tu	25	7	·38	14	·46	21
13	We	26	8	·45	15	·54	22
14	Th	27	9	·49	16	·60	23
15	Fr	28	10	51	17	·65	24
16	Sa	29	11	·52	18	·67	25
17	Su	30	12	·51	19	·68	26
18	Mo	31	13	·47	20	·67	27

Feb. (Solar: Kshaya, Kumbha—Masi. Lunar: Sukla, Magha, Bahula. Muhammadan: H. 1345 Shaban.)

Cyclic Sidereal Year, Month and Day	Week-Day	Day	Tithi	Tithi Ending Moment	Nakshatra	Nakshatra Ending Moment	Muhammadan Year, Month and Day
19	Tu	1	14	·42	21	·64	28
20	We	2	—A	·34	22	·59	29
21	Th	3	1	·26	23	·53	—30
22	Fr	4	2	·17	24	·47	1
23	Sa	5	3 4	·08 ·97	25	·41	2
24	Su	6	5	·87	26	·34	3
25	Mo	7	6	·79	27	·27	4
26	Tu	8	7	·71	1	·20	5
27	We	9	8	·63	2	·15	6
28	Th	10	9	·56	3	·12	7
—29	Fr	11	10	·52	4	·09	8
1	Sa	12	11	·50	5	·08	9
2	Su	13	12	·48	6	·09	10
3	Mo	14	13	·50	7	·12	11
4	Tu	15	14	·54	8	·18	12
5	We	16	P	·61	9	·25	13
6	Th	17	1	68	10	·34	14
7	Fr	18	2	·76	11	·44	15
8	Sa	19	3	·84	12	·55	16
9	Su	20	4	·93	13	·65	17
10	Mo	21	...	...	14	·76	18
11	Tu	22	5	·00	15	·85	19
12	We	23	6	·07	16	·91	20
13	Th	24	7	·12	17	·96	21
14	Fr	25	8	·13	18	·99	22
15	Sa	26	9	·14	...	...	23
16	Su	27	10	·12	19	·01	24
17	Mo	28	11	·09	20 21	·00 ·97	25

March (Solar: Kshaya, Kumbha—Masi; Kshaya, Mina—Panguni. Lunar: Sukla, Phalguna, Bahula. Muhammadan: Shaban.; H. 1345 Ramzan.)

Cyclic Sidereal Year, Month and Day	Week-Day	Day	Tithi	Tithi Ending Moment	Nakshatra	Nakshatra Ending Moment	Muhammadan Year, Month and Day
18	Tu	1	12 13	·03 ·96	22	·92	26
19	We	2	14	·88	23	·87	27
20	Th	3	—A	·78	24	·81	28
21	Fr	4	1	·69	25	·74	—29
22	Sa	5	2	·58	26	·67	1
23	Su	6	3	·49	27	·60	2
24	Mo	7	4	·40	1	·54	3
25	Tu	8	5	·31	2	·49	4
26	We	9	6	·23	3	·45	5
27	Th	10	7	·16	4	·42	6
28	Fr	11	8	·13	5	·40	7
29	Sa	12	9	·10	6	·41	8
—30	Su	13	10	·09	7	·44	9
1	Mo	14	11	·10	8	·49	10
2	Tu	15	12	·15	9	·56	11
3	We	16	13	·20	10	·64	12
4	Th	17	14	·27	11	·74	13
5	Fr	18	P	·36	12	·84	14
6	Sa	19	1	·45	13	·95	15
7	Su	20	2	·54	...	...	16
8	Mo	21	3	·61	14	·06	17
9	Tu	22	4	·67	15	·15	18
10	We	23	5	·71	16	·22	19
11	Th	24	6	·73	17	·28	20
12	Fr	25	7	·73	18	·32	21
13	Sa	26	8	·71	19	·33	22
14	Su	27	9	·67	20	·32	23
15	Mo	28	10	·61	21	·30	24
16	Tu	29	11	·54	22	·26	25
17	We	30	12	·46	23	·21	26
18	Th	31	13	·36	24	·15	27

April (Solar: Prabhava, Mesha—Chittirai. Lunar: Sukla, Chaitra, Bahula. Muhammadan: H. 1345 Shawwal.)

Cyclic Sidereal Year, Month and Day	Week-Day	Day	Tithi	Tithi Ending Moment	Nakshatra	Nakshatra Ending Moment	Muhammadan Year, Month and Day
19	Fr	1	14	·26	25	·08	28
20	Sa	2	—A	·15	26 27	·01 ·94	·29
21	Su	3	1 2	·06 ·97	1	·88	—30
22	Mo	4	3	·88	2	·83	1
23	Tu	5	4	·80	3	·78	2
24	We	6	5	·74	4	·75	3
25	Th	7	6	·70	5	·73	4
26	Fr	8	7	·67	6	·73	5
27	Sa	9	8	·65	7	·76	6
28	Su	10	9	·66	8	·80	7
29	Mo	11	10	·71	9	·86	8
—30	Tu	12	11	·76	10	·94	9
1	We	13	12	·84	...	...	10
2	Th	14	13	·92	11	·04	11
3	Fr	15	...	...	12	·15	12
4	Sa	16	14	·00	13	·26	13
5	Su	17	P	·09	14	·36	14
6	Mo	18	1	·16	15	·45	15
7	Tu	19	2	·22	16	·53	16
8	We	20	3	·26	17	·60	17
9	Th	21	4	·28	18	·64	18
10	Fr	22	5	·27	19	·65	19
11	Sa	23	6	·26	20	·65	20
12	Su	24	7	·22	21	·63	21
13	Mo	25	8	·15	22	·60	22
14	Tu	26	9	·08	23	·55	23
15	We	27	10 11	·00 ·91	24	·49	24
16	Th	28	12	·81	25	·42	25
17	Fr	29	13	·70	26	·35	26
18	Sa	30	14	·60	27	·28	27

May (Solar: Prabhava, Mesha—Chittirai; Prabhava, Vrishabha—Vaikasi. Lunar: Sukla, Vaisakha, Bahula. Muhammadan: H. 1345 Zi-l-ka'da.)

Cyclic Sidereal Year, Month and Day	Week-Day	Day	Tithi	Tithi Ending Moment	Nakshatra	Nakshatra Ending Moment	Muhammadan Year, Month and Day
19	Su	1	—A	·50	1	·22	28
20	Mo	2	1	·41	2	·16	—29
21	Tu	3	2	·33	3	·11	1
22	We	4	3	·27	4	·07	2
23	Th	5	4	·22	5	·05	3
24	Fr	6	5	·20	6	·06	4
25	Sa	7	6	·18	7	·07	5
26	Su	8	7	·19	8	·11	6
27	Mo	9	8	·23	9	·17	7
28	Tu	10	9	·28	10	·25	8
29	We	11	10	·35	11	·35	9
30	Th	12	11	·43	12	·45	10
—31	Fr	13	12	·52	13	·56	11
1	Sa	14	13	·60	14	·66	12
2	Su	15	14	·67	15	·76	13
3	Mo	16	P	·73	16	·85	14
4	Tu	17	1	·77	17	·91	15
5	We	18	2	·79	18	95	16
6	Th	19	3	·79	19	·97	17
7	Fr	20	4	·77	20	·97	18
8	Sa	21	5	·73	21	·96	19
9	Su	22	6	·67	22	·93	20
10	Mo	23	7	·59	23	·88	21
11	Tu	24	8	·50	24	·83	22
12	We	25	9	·41	25	·76	23
13	Th	26	10	·31	26	·69	24
14	Fr	27	11	·21	27	·62	25
15	Sa	28	12	·11	1	·56	26
16	Su	29	13 14	·01 ·91	2	·50	27
17	Mo	30	—A	·83	3	·44	28
18	Tu	31	1	·77	4	·40	29

June (Solar: Prabhava, Mithuna—Ani. Lunar: Sukla, Jyeshtha, Bahula. Muhammadan: H. 1345 Zi-l-hijja.)

Cyclic Sidereal Year, Month and Day	Week-Day	Day	Tithi	Tithi Ending Moment	Nakshatra	Nakshatra Ending Moment	Muhammadan Year, Month and Day
19	We	1	2	·73	5	·39	—30
20	Th	2	3	·70	6	·38	1
21	Fr	3	4	·68	7	·39	2
22	Sa	4	5	·69	8	·42	3
23	Su	5	6	·72	9	·48	4
24	Mo	6	7	·78	10	·56	5
25	Tu	7	8	·84	11	·65	6
26	We	8	9	·92	12	·75	7
27	Th	9	...	...	13	·85	8
28	Fr	10	10	·01	14	·96	9
29	Sa	11	11	·09	...	...	10
30	Su	12	12	·16	15	·06	11
31	Mo	13	13	·21	16	·15	12
—32	Tu	14	14	·26	17	·22	13
1	We ○	15	P	·27	18	·27	14
2	Th	16	1	·27	19	·29	15
3	Fr	17	2	·26	20	·30	16
4	Sa	18	3	·22	21	·29	17
5	Su	19	4	·16	22	·26	18
6	Mo	20	5	·08	23	·22	19
7	Tu	21	6 7	·00 ·90	24	·16	20
8	We	22	8	·80	25	·10	21
9	Th	23	9	·70	26 27	·04 ·97	22
10	Fr	24	10	·59	1	·90	23
11	Sa	25	11	·50	2	·83	24
12	Su	26	12	·40	3	·78	25
13	Mo	27	13	·33	4	·74	26
14	Tu	28	14	·26	5	·71	27
15	We ●	29	—A	·21	6	·70	28
16	Th	30	1	·18	7	·71	—29

Naksh :—1. Asvn. 2. Bhar. 3. Krit. 4. Rohi. 5. Mrig. 6. Ardh. 7. Punar, 8. Push. 9. Aslesh. 10. Magh. 11. P. Phal. 12. U. Phal. 13. Hasta. 14. Chit

A. D. 1927.
A.—Amavasya.
P.—Paurnami.

Kollam 1103, Commences { N. Malabar—Sept. / S. Malabar—Aug.

Hijra 1346, Commences, July 1.

Vikrama 1984.
Bengal San 1333.
(N. Cycle) Pramathin.

Columns: SOLAR reckoning — Cyclic Sidereal Year, Month and Day; Week-Day English Month and Day. LUNAR reckoning — Tithi Ending Moment; Nakshatra Ending Moment; Muhammadan Year, Month and Day.

July — Solar: Prabhava Mithuna—Ani (to 31), Prabhava Karkata—Adi (from 1). Lunar: Ashadha (Sukla; Bahula). H. 1346 Muharram.

Cyclic Sidereal	Week-Day	Day	Tithi	Moment	Nakshatra	Moment	Muhammadan
17	Fr	1	2	·16	8	·74	1
18	Sa	2	3	·17	9	·79	2
19	Su	3	4	·20	10	·86	3
20	Mo	4	5	·25	11	·95	4
21	Tu	5	6	·32	...	...	5
22	We	6	7	·40	12	·05	6
23	Th	7	8	·47	13	·15	7
24	Fr	8	9	·55	14	·26	8
25	Sa	9	10	·64	15	·37	9
26	Su	10	11	·69	16	·46	10
27	Mo	11	12	·73	17	·53	11
28	Tu	12	13	·75	18	·58	12
29	We	13	14	·76	19	·61	13
30	Th	14	P	·73	20	·63	14
—31	Fr	15	1	·70	21	·62	15
1	Sa	16	2	·64	22	·59	16
2	Su	17	3	·56	23	·55	17
3	Mo	18	4	·47	24	·50	18
4	Tu	19	5	·38	25	·45	19
5	We	20	6	·29	26	·38	20
6	Th	21	7	·19	27	·31	21
7	Fr	22	8 / 9	·09 / ·99	1	·24	22
8	Sa	23	10	·88	2	·17	23
9	Su	24	11	·80	3	·12	24
10	Mo	25	12	·73	4	·08	25
11	Tu	26	13	·69	5	·04	26
12	We	27	14	·65	6	·03	27
13	Th	28	—A	·64	7	·03	28
14	Fr	29	1	·65	8	·06	29
15	Sa	30	2	·67	9	·10	—30
16	Su	31	3	·72	10	·17	1

Aug. — Solar: Prabhava Simha—Avani (from 1). Lunar: Sravana (Sukla; Bahula), B. Suk. H. 1346 Safar; R.-awl.

Cyclic Sidereal	Week-Day	Day	Tithi	Moment	Nakshatra	Moment	Muhammadan
17	Mo	1	4	·79	11	·25	2
18	Tu	2	5	·86	12	·34	3
19	We	3	6	·94	13	·45	4
20	Th	4	...	...	14	·56	5
21	Fr	5	7	·08	15	·67	6
22	Sa	6	8	·11	16	·76	7
23	Su	7	9	·17	17	·83	8
24	Mo	8	10	·20	18	·89	9
25	Tu	9	11	·23	19	·94	10
26	We	10	12	·24	20	·95	11
27	Th	11	13	·22	21	·95	12
28	Fr	12	14	·19	22	·92	13
29	Sa	13	P	·14	23	·89	14
30	Su	14	1 / 2	·06 / ·97	24	·84	15
31	Mo	15	3	·88	25	·78	16
—32	Tu	16	4	·78	26	·72	17
1	We	17	5	·68	27	·65	18
2	Th	18	6	·58	1	·58	19
3	Fr	19	7	·48	2	·52	20
4	Sa	20	8	·39	3	·46	21
5	Su	21	9	·31	4	·41	22
6	Mo	22	10	·24	5	·37	23
7	Tu	23	11	·18	6	·35	24
8	We	24	12	·15	7	·36	25
9	Th	25	13	·14	8	·38	26
10	Fr	26	14	·14	9	·41	27
11	Sa	27	—A	·18	10	·47	28
12	Su	28	1	·23	11	·55	—29
13	Mo	29	2	·29	12	·64	1
14	Tu	30	3	·36	13	·75	2
15	We	31	4	·44	14	·86	3

Sep. — Solar: Prabhava Simha—Avani (to 31), Prabhava Kanya—Purattasi (from 1). Lunar: Bhadrapada (Sukla; Bahula). H. 1346 Rabi-ul-awwal.

Cyclic Sidereal	Week-Day	Day	Tithi	Moment	Nakshatra	Moment	Muhammadan
16	Th	1	5	·53	15	·97	4
17	Fr	2	6	·62	...	...	5
18	Sa	3	7	·68	16	·06	6
19	Su	4	8	·72	17	·14	7
20	Mo	5	9	·75	18	·21	8
21	Tu	6	10	·75	19	·25	9
22	We	7	11	·73	20	·27	10
23	Th	8	12	·71	21	·27	11
24	Fr	9	13	·65	22	·25	12
25	Sa	10	14	·58	23	·23	13
26	Su	11	P	·49	24	·18	14
27	Mo	12	1	·40	25	·12	15
28	Tu	13	2	·30	26 / 27	·05 / ·98	16
29	We	14	3	·20	1	·92	17
30	Th	15	4	·11	2	·85	18
—31	Fr	16	5 / 6	·01 / ·92	3	·79	19
1	Sa	17	7	·83	4	·74	20
2	Su	18	8	·77	5	·70	21
3	Mo	19	9	·71	6	·68	22
4	Tu	20	10	·69	7	·68	23
5	We	21	11	·67	8	·69	24
6	Th	22	12	·69	9	·73	25
7	Fr	23	13	·71	10	·78	26
8	Sa	24	14	·76	11	·85	27
9	Su	25	—A	·83	12	·95	28
10	Mo	26	1	·91	...	...	29
11	Tu	27	...	...	13	·05	—30
12	We	28	2	·00	14	·16	1
13	Th	29	3	·08	15	·27	2
14	Fr	30	4	·15	16	·36	3

Oct. — Solar: Prabhava Tula—Aippasi (from 1). Lunar: Asvina (Sukla; Bahula), K. Suk. H. 1346 Rabi-ul-akhir; J.-awwal.

Cyclic Sidereal	Week-Day	Day	Tithi	Moment	Nakshatra	Moment	Muhammadan
15	Sa	1	5	·22	17	·45	4
16	Su	2	6	·26	18	·52	5
17	Mo	3	7	·29	19	·57	6
18	Tu	4	8	·30	20	·59	7
19	We	5	9	·29	21	·60	8
20	Th	6	10	·26	22	·59	9
21	Fr	7	11	·21	23	·56	10
22	Sa	8	12	·13	24	·51	11
23	Su	9	13 / 14	·04 / ·96	25	·46	12
24	Mo	10	P	·86	26	·39	13
25	Tu	11	1	·77	27	·33	14
26	We	12	2	·67	1	·26	15
27	Th	13	3	·57	2	·19	16
28	Fr	14	4	·48	3	·13	17
29	Sa	15	5	·40	4	·07	18
—30	Su	16	6	·34	5	·03	19
1	Mo	17	7	·28	6	·01	20
2	Tu	18	8	·26	7	·00	21
3	We	19	9	·25	8	·01	22
4	Th	20	10	·27	9	·04	23
5	Fr	21	11	·29	10	·09	24
6	Sa	22	12	·34	11	·17	25
7	Su	23	13	·41	12	·25	26
8	Mo	24	14	·48	13	·35	27
9	Tu	25	—A	·57	14	·46	28
10	We	26	1	·66	15	·56	—29
11	Th	27	2	·75	16	·67	1
12	Fr	28	3	·81	17	·76	2
13	Sa	29	4	·86	18	·83	3
14	Su	30	5	·88	19	·88	4
15	Mo	31	6	·89	20	·91	5

Nov. — Solar: Prabhava Tula—Aippasi (to 30), Prabhava Vrischika—Kartigai (from 1). Lunar: Karttika (Sukla; Bahula). H. 1346 Jumadal-awwal.

Cyclic Sidereal	Week-Day	Day	Tithi	Moment	Nakshatra	Moment	Muhammadan
16	Tu	1	7	·88	21	·93	6
17	We	2	8	·84	22	·92	7
18	Th	3	9	·80	23	·89	8
19	Fr	4	10	·73	24	·85	9
20	Sa	5	11	·65	25	·79	10
21	Su	6	12	·56	26	·73	11
22	Mo	7	13	·46	27	·67	12
23	Tu	8	14	·36	1	·60	13
24	We	9	P	·27	2	·53	14
25	Th	10	1	·17	3	·46	15
26	Fr	11	2	·08	4	·41	16
27	Sa	12	3 / 4	·01 / ·94	5	·37	17
28	Su	13	5	·89	6	·34	18
29	Mo	14	6	·87	7	·32	19
—30	Tu	15	7	·85	8	·33	20
1	We	16	8	·87	9	·35	21
2	Th	17	9	·90	10	·41	22
3	Fr	18	10	·96	11	·47	23
4	Sa	19	...	...	12	·55	24
5	Su	20	11	·03	13	·65	25
6	Mo	21	12	·11	14	·76	26
7	Tu	22	13	·20	15	·87	27
8	We	23	14	·29	16	·97	28
9	Th	24	—A	·37	...	...	29
10	Fr	25	1	·43	17	·06	—30
11	Sa	26	2	·49	18	·14	1
12	Su	27	3	·51	19	·19	2
13	Mo	28	4	·52	20	·24	3
14	Tu	29	5	·50	21	·25	4
15	We	30	6	·47	22	·24	5

Dec. — Solar: Prabhava Dhanus—Margali (from 1). Lunar: Margasira (Sukla; Bahula), P. Sukla. H. 1346 Jumadal-akhir; H. 1346 Rajab.

Cyclic Sidereal	Week-Day	Day	Tithi	Moment	Nakshatra	Moment	Muhammadan
16	Th	1	7	·42	23	·22	6
17	Fr	2	8	·35	24	·18	7
18	Sa	3	9	·27	25	·13	8
19	Su	4	10	·19	26	·08	9
20	Mo	5	11 / 12	·09 / ·99	27 / 1	·01 / ·94	10
21	Tu	6	13	·88	2	·87	11
22	We	7	14	·79	3	·80	12
23	Th ○	8	P	·70	4	·75	13
24	Fr	9	1	·63	5	·70	14
25	Sa	10	2	·56	6	·67	15
26	Su	11	3	·53	7	·65	16
27	Mo	12	4	·50	8	·65	17
28	Tu	13	5	·49	9	·68	18
29	We	14	6	·51	10	·72	19
—30	Th	15	7	·54	11	·78	20
1	Fr	16	8	·60	12	·86	21
2	Sa	17	9	·68	13	·95	22
3	Su	18	10	·77	...	...	23
4	Mo	19	11	·85	14	·06	24
5	Tu	20	12	·94	15	·17	25
6	We	21	...	...	16	·27	26
7	Th	22	13	·02	17	·37	27
8	Fr	23	14	·08	18	·45	28
9	Sa	24	—A	·13	19	·50	—29
10	Su	25	1	·15	20	·55	1
11	Mo	26	2	·16	21	·57	2
12	Tu	27	3	·14	22	·57	3
13	We	28	4	·11	23	·55	4
14	Th	29	5 / 6	·06 / ·99	24	·51	5
15	Fr	30	7	·90	25	·47	6
16	Sa	31	8	·81	26	·41	7

15. Svati. 16. Visak. 17. Anur. 18. Jyesh. 19. Mula. 20. P. Ash. 21. U. Ash. 22. Sravn. 23. Dani. 24. Satab. 25. P. Bhad. 26. U. Bhad. 27. Rev,

A. D. 1928. **Mesha Sankranti** (Commencement of Indian Sidereal Year).
Solar Eclipse. ● **(Surya Sid.) April 12·87.** **Saka 1850.** **Kaliyuga 5029.**
Lunar Eclipse. ○ **(Arya Sid.) April 12·76.** **(S. Cycle) Vibhava.**

Columns: SOLAR reckoning — Cyclic Sidereal Year, Month and Day; Week-Day English Month and Day. LUNAR reckoning — Tithi Ending Moment; Nakshatra Ending Moment; Muhammadan Year, Month and Day.

Jan.

Cyclic Sidereal Year, Month and Day	Week-Day English Month and Day	Tithi Ending Moment	Nakshatra Ending Moment	Muhammadan Year, Month and Day
(Prabhava, Dhanus—Margali) 17	Su 1	(Sukla) 9 ·72	27 ·35	(H. 1346 Rajab) 8
18	Mo 2	10 ·62	1 ·28	9
19	Tu 3	11 ·53	2 ·21	10
20	We 4	12 ·43	3 ·15	11
21	Th 5	13 ·35	4 ·09	12
22	Fr 6	(Pausha) 14 ·27	5 ·04 6 ·99	13
23	Sa 7	P ·21	7 ·97	14
24	Su 8	(Bahula) 1 ·17	8 ·98	15
25	Mo 9	2 ·14	9 ·99	16
26	Tu 10	3 ·14	... ...	17
27	We 11	4 ·15	10 ·03	18
28	Th 12	5 ·20	11 ·08	19
—29	Fr 13	6 ·25	12 ·16	20
(Prabhava, Makara—Tai) 1	Sa 14	7 ·32	13 ·25	21
2	Su 15	8 ·40	14 ·36	22
3	Mo 16	9 ·50	15 ·47	23
4	Tu 17	10 ·60	16 ·57	24
5	We 18	11 ·67	17 ·67	25
6	Th 19	12 ·73	18 ·75	26
7	Fr 20	13 ·78	19 ·83	27
8	Sa 21	14 ·80	20 ·87	28
9	Su 22	—A ·80	21 ·89	29
10	Mo 23	(Sukla) 1 ·79	22 ·89	—30
11	Tu 24	2 ·76	23 ·88	1
12	We 25	3 ·70	24 ·86	2
13	Th 26	4 ·63	25 ·81	3
14	Fr 27	5 ·54	26 ·75	4
15	Sa 28	6 ·45	27 ·69	5
16	Su 29	7 ·35	1 ·62	6
17	Mo 30	8 ·26	2 ·56	7
18	Tu 31	9 ·16	3 ·49	8

Feb.

Cyclic Sidereal Year, Month and Day	Week-Day English Month and Day	Tithi Ending Moment	Nakshatra Ending Moment	Muhammadan Year, Month and Day
19	We 1	(Magha) 10 ·06 11 ·98	4 ·42	(H. 1346 Shaban) 9
20	Th 2	12 ·91	5 ·37	10
21	Fr 3	13 ·86	6 ·33	11
22	Sa 4	14 ·81	7 ·31	12
23	Su 5	P ·78	8 ·30	13
24	Mo 6	(Bahula) 1 ·79	9 ·31	14
25	Tu 7	2 ·79	10 ·34	15
26	We 8	3 ·84	11 ·30	16
27	Th 9	4 ·89	12 ·46	17
28	Fr 10	5 ·97	13 ·56	18
29	Sa 11	... ...	14 ·66	19
—30	Su 12	6 ·06	15 ·77	20
(Prabhava, Kumbha—Masi) 1	Mo 13	7 ·15	16 ·87	21
2	Tu 14	8 ·23	17 ·97	22
3	We 15	9 ·30	... ...	23
4	Th 16	10 ·37	18 ·07	24
5	Fr 17	11 ·42	19 ·13	25
6	Sa 18	12 ·43	20 ·19	26
7	Su 19	13 ·43	21 ·21	27
8	Mo 20	14 ·42	22 ·22	28
9	Tu 21	—A ·38	23 ·22	—29
10	We 22	(Sukla) 1 ·32	24 ·19	(H. 1346 Ramzan) 1
11	Th 23	2 ·25	25 ·14	2
12	Fr 24	3 ·16	26 ·09	3
13	Sa 25	4 ·07 5 ·97	27 ·02 1 ·96	4
14	Su 26	(Phalg.) 6 ·87	2 ·89	5
15	Mo 27	7 ·77	3 ·82	6
16	Tu 28	8 ·68	4 ·76	7
17	We 29	9 ·60	5 ·70	8

March

Cyclic Sidereal Year, Month and Day	Week-Day English Month and Day	Tithi Ending Moment	Nakshatra Ending Moment	Muhammadan Year, Month and Day
(Prabhava, Kumbha—Masi) 18	Th 1	(Suk.) 10 ·52	6 ·66	(H. 1346 Ramzan) 9
19	Fr 2	11 ·46	7 ·64	10
20	Sa 3	12 ·42	8 ·62	11
21	Su 4	(Phalguna) 13 ·40	9 ·63	12
22	Mo 5	14 ·39	10 ·65	13
23	Tu 6	P ·41	11 ·70	14
24	We 7	(Bahula) 1 ·46	12 ·78	15
25	Th 8	2 ·51	13 ·86	16
26	Fr 9	3 ·59	14 ·96	17
27	Sa 10	4 ·67	... ...	18
28	Su 11	5 ·76	15 ·06	19
29	Mo 12	6 ·84	16 ·17	20
—30	Tu 13	7 ·91	17 ·28	21
(Prabhava, Mina—Panguni) 1	We 14	8 ·97	18 ·37	22
2	Th 15	... ...	19 ·44	23
3	Fr 16	9 ·01	20 ·50	24
4	Sa 17	10 ·03	21 ·53	25
5	Su 18	11 ·02	22 ·55	26
6	Mo 19	12 ·01 13 ·97	23 ·54	27
7	Tu 20	14 ·91	24 ·52	28
8	We 21	—A ·84	25 ·48	29
9	Th 22	(Sukla) 1 ·76	26 ·43	—30
10	Fr 23	2 ·66	27 ·37	1
11	Sa 24	3 ·55	1 ·30	2
12	Su 25	4 ·45	2 ·23	3
13	Mo 26	5 ·36	3 ·16	4
14	Tu 27	6 ·27	4 ·10	5
15	We 28	7 ·18	5 ·04	6
16	Th 29	8 ·11	6 ·00 7 ·96	7
17	Fr 30	9 ·04	8 ·95	8
18	Sa 31	10 ·00 11 ·98	9 ·95	9

April

Cyclic Sidereal Year, Month and Day	Week-Day English Month and Day	Tithi Ending Moment	Nakshatra Ending Moment	Muhammadan Year, Month and Day
19	Su 1	12 ·97	10 ·97	(H. 1346 Shawwal) 10
20	Mo 2	... ...	... ...	11
21	Tu 3	(Chaitra) 13 ·00	11 ·02	12
22	We 4	14 ·03	12 ·08	13
23	Th 5	P ·09	13 ·16	14
24	Fr 6	(Bahula) 1 ·16	14 ·26	15
25	Sa 7	2 ·24	15 ·36	16
26	Su 8	3 ·33	16 ·47	17
27	Mo 9	4 ·40	17 ·58	18
28	Tu 10	5 ·47	18 ·67	19
29	We 11	6 ·53	19 ·75	20
—30	Th 12	7 ·58	20 ·81	21
(Vibhava, Mesha—Chittirai) 1	Fr 13	8 ·59	21 ·86	22
2	Sa 14	9 ·59	22 ·87	23
3	Su 15	10 ·57	23 ·87	24
4	Mo 16	11 ·52	24 ·85	25
5	Tu 17	12 ·46	25 ·81	26
6	We 18	13 ·39	26 ·76	27
7	Th 19	14 ·31	27 ·71	28
8	Fr 20	—A ·21	1 ·64	—29
9	Sa 21	(Vaisak. Sukla) 1 ·11	2 ·57	(H. 1346 Zi-l-ka'da) 1
10	Su 22	2 ·00 3 ·90	3 ·50	2
11	Mo 23	4 ·81	4 ·43	3
12	Tu 24	5 ·72	5 ·38	4
13	We 25	6 ·65	6 ·33	5
14	Th 26	7 ·59	7 ·29	6
15	Fr 27	8 ·55	8 ·27	7
16	Sa 28	9 ·52	9 ·27	8
17	Su 29	10 ·50	10 ·29	9
18	Mo 30	11 ·53	11 ·33	10

May

Cyclic Sidereal Year, Month and Day	Week-Day English Month and Day	Tithi Ending Moment	Nakshatra Ending Moment	Muhammadan Year, Month and Day
(Vibhava, Mesha—Chittirai) 19	Tu 1	(Suk.) 12 ·56	12 ·39	(H. 1346 Zi-l-ka'da) 11
20	We 2	13 ·62	13 ·47	12
21	Th 3	14 ·68	14 ·56	13
22	Fr 4	(Vaisakha) P ·75	15 ·67	14
23	Sa 5	(Bahula) 1 ·84	16 ·78	15
24	Su 6	2 ·93	17 ·88	16
25	Mo 7	... ...	18 ·98	17
26	Tu 8	3 ·00	... ...	18
27	We 9	4 ·06	19 ·06	19
28	Th 10	5 ·11	20 ·13	20
29	Fr 11	6 ·12	21 ·17	21
30	Sa 12	7 ·11	22 ·19	22
—31	Su 13	8 ·09	23 ·19	23
(Vibhava, Vrishabha—Vaikasi) 1	Mo 14	9 ·05 10 ·98	24 ·18	24
2	Tu 15	11 ·90	25 ·14	25
3	We 16	12 ·82	26 ·10	26
4	Th 17	13 ·72	27 ·05 1 ·98	27
5	Fr 18	14 ·62	2 ·91	28
6	Sa 19	—A ·52	3 ·84	29
7	Su 20	(Sukla) 1 ·42	4 ·78	—30
8	Mo 21	2 ·32	5 ·72	1
9	Tu 22	3 ·23	6 ·66	2
10	We 23	4 ·16	7 ·62	3
11	Th 24	5 ·09	8 ·60	4
12	Fr 25	6 ·05	9 ·60	5
13	Sa 26	7 ·02	10 ·61	6
14	Su 27	8 ·02	11 ·64	7
15	Mo 28	9 ·03	12 ·70	8
16	Tu 29	10 ·07	13 ·77	9
17	We 30	11 ·12	14 ·87	10
18	Th 31	12 ·18	15 ·97	11

June

Cyclic Sidereal Year, Month and Day	Week-Day English Month and Day	Tithi Ending Moment	Nakshatra Ending Moment	Muhammadan Year, Month and Day
19	Fr 1	(Jyeshtha) 13 ·27	... ...	(H. 1346 Zi-l-hijja) 12
20	Sa 2	14 ·35	16 ·07	13
21	Su ○ 3	P ·43	17 ·18	14
22	Mo 4	(Bahula) 1 ·49	18 ·28	15
23	Tu 5	2 ·55	19 ·36	16
24	We 6	3 ·59	20 ·44	17
25	Th 7	4 ·61	21 ·49	18
26	Fr 8	5 ·60	22 ·51	19
27	Sa 9	6 ·58	23 ·52	20
28	Su 10	7 ·54	24 ·50	21
29	Mo 11	8 ·48	25 ·48	22
30	Tu 12	9 ·41	26 ·44	23
—31	We 13	10 ·32	27 ·38	24
(Vibhava, Mithuna—Ani) 1	Th 14	11 ·22	1 ·32	25
2	Fr 15	12 ·12	2 ·25	26
3	Sa 16	13 ·02 14 ·92	3 ·19	27
4	Su 17	—A ·82	4 ·12	28
5	Mo 18	(Sukla) 1 ·73	5 ·05	29
6	Tu 19	2 ·65	6 ·00 7 ·95	—30
7	We 20	3 ·58	8 ·93	(H. 1347 Muharram) 1
8	Th 21	4 ·53	9 ·92	2
9	Fr 22	5 ·50	10 ·93	3
10	Sa 23	6 ·50	11 ·96	4
11	Su 24	7 ·51	... ...	5
12	Mo 25	8 ·54	12 ·00	6
13	Tu 26	(Ashadha) 9 ·59	13 ·08	7
14	We 27	10 ·65	14 ·17	8
15	Th 28	11 ·73	15 ·27	9
16	Fr 29	12 ·81	16 ·37	10
17	Sa 30	13 ·90	17 ·48	11

Naksh :—1. Asvn. 2. Bhar. 3. Krit. 4. Rohi. 5. Mrig. 6. Ardh. 7. Punar. 8. Push. 9. Aslesh. 10. Magh. 11. P. Phal. 12. U. Phal. 13. Hasta. 14 Chit.

A. D. 1928.			Vikrama 1985.
A.—Amavasya.	Kollam 1104, Commences { N. Malabar—Sept.	Hijra 1347,	Bengal San 1334.
P.—Paurnami.	{ S. Malabar—Aug.	Commences, June 20.	(N. Cycle) Vikrama.

SOLAR reckoning: Cyclic Sidereal Year, Month and Day.	SOLAR reckoning: Week-Day English Month and Day.	LUNAR reckoning: Tithi Ending Moment.	LUNAR reckoning: Nakshatra Ending Moment.	LUNAR reckoning: Muhammadan Year, Month and Day.
	July			
(Vibhava Mithuna—Ani.) 18	Su 1	(Ashadha) 14 ·97	18 ·58	(H. 1347 Muharram.) 12
19	Mo 2	... ...	19 ·68	13
20	Tu 3	P ·03	20 ·75	14
21	We 4	1 ·07	21 ·80	15
22	Th 5	2 ·09	22 ·83	16
23	Fr 6	3 ·08	23 ·84	17
24	Sa 7	4 ·06	24 ·84	18
25	Su 8	(Bahula) 5 ·01; 6 ·95	25 ·81	19
26	Mo 9	7 ·88	26 ·77	20
27	Tu 10	8 ·79	27 ·72	21
28	We 11	9 ·70	1 ·66	22
29	Th 12	10 ·60	2 ·60	23
30	Fr 13	11 ·50	3 ·53	24
31	Sa 14	12 ·39	4 ·46	25
—32	Su 15	13 ·29	5 ·39	26
1	Mo 16	14 ·20	6 ·33	27
2	Tu 17	—A ·12	7 ·30	28
3	We 18	1 ·06	8 ·27	29
4	Th 19	2 ·01; 3 ·99	9 ·26	—30
5	Fr 20	4 ·97	10 ·25	1
6	Sa 21	5 ·98	11 ·27	2
7	Su 22	... ...	12 ·31	3
8	Mo 23	(Sukla) 6 ·01	13 ·39	4
9	Tu 24	7 ·05	14 ·47	5
(Vibhava Karkata—Adi.) 10	We 25	8 ·12	15 ·56	6
11	Th 26	9 ·20	16 ·67	7
12	Fr 27	(Sravana) 10 ·29	17 ·78	8
13	Sa 28	11 ·37	18 ·89	9
14	Su 29	12 ·44	19 ·98	10
15	Mo 30	13 ·50	... ...	11
16	Tu 31	14 ·54	20 ·05	12
	Aug.			
17	We 1	(Adhika) P ·57	21 ·11	(H. 1347 Safar.) 13
18	Th 2	1 ·56	22 ·15	14
19	Fr 3	2 ·54	23 ·17	15
20	Sa 4	3 ·49	24 ·17	16
21	Su 5	4 ·44	25 ·14	17
22	Mo 6	5 ·38	26 ·10	18
23	Tu 7	(Bahula) 6 ·29	27 ·05	19
24	We 8	7 ·19	1 ·00; 2 ·94	20
25	Th 9	8 ·09; 9 ·99	3 ·86	21
26	Fr 10	10 ·90	4 ·79	22
27	Sa 11	11 ·80	5 ·73	23
28	Su 12	12 ·70	6 ·67	24
29	Mo 13	13 ·62	7 ·63	25
30	Tu 14	14 ·56	8 ·59	26
—31	We 15	—A ·51	9 ·57	27
1	Th 16	1 ·48	10 ·57	28
2	Fr 17	2 ·46	11 ·59	—29
3	Sa 18	3 ·47	12 ·63	1
4	Su 19	4 ·50	13 ·69	2
5	Mo 20	(Sukla) 5 ·56	14 ·77	3
(Vibhava Simha—Avani.) 6	Tu 21	6 ·63	15 ·86	4
7	We 22	7 ·70	16 ·97	5
8	Th 23	8 ·77	... ...	6
9	Fr 24	9 ·86	17 ·08	7
10	Sa 25	(Nija Sravana) 10 ·94	18 ·19	(H. 1347 Rabi-ul-awwal.) 8
11	Su 26	... ...	19 ·28	9
12	Mo 27	11 ·00	20 ·36	10
13	Tu 28	12 ·05	21 ·42	11
14	We 29	13 ·08	22 ·47	12
15	Th 30	14 ·06	23 ·49	13
16	Fr 31	P ·04	24 ·49	14

SOLAR reckoning: Cyclic Sidereal Year, Month and Day.	SOLAR reckoning: Week-Day English Month and Day.	LUNAR reckoning: Tithi Ending Moment.	LUNAR reckoning: Nakshatra Ending Moment.	LUNAR reckoning: Muhammadan Year, Month and Day.
	Sep.			
(Vibhava Simha—Avani.) 17	Sa 1	(Nija Sravn.) 1 ·00; 2 ·96	25 ·48	(H. 1347 Rabi-ul-awwal.) 15
18	Su 2	3 ·89	26 ·44	16
19	Mo 3	4 ·81	27 ·40	17
20	Tu 4	5 ·71	1 ·34	18
21	We 5	6 ·61	2 ·27	19
22	Th 6	7 ·51	3 ·20	20
23	Fr 7	8 ·41	4 ·13	21
24	Sa 8	9 ·31	5 ·06	22
25	Su 9	(Bahula) 10 ·22	6 ·01; 7 ·96	23
26	Mo 10	11 ·14	8 ·92	24
27	Tu 11	12 ·08	9 ·90	25
28	We 12	13 ·03	10 ·89	26
29	Th 13	14 ·00; A ·99	11 ·91	27
30	Fr 14	... ...	12 ·95	28
—31	Sa 15	1 ·00	... ...	29
1	Su 16	2 ·03	13 ·00	—30
2	Mo 17	3 ·09	14 ·07	1
3	Tu 18	4 ·15	15 ·16	2
4	We 19	5 ·22	16 ·27	3
5	Th 20	(Sukla) 6 ·30	17 ·38	4
6	Fr 21	7 ·38	18 ·49	5
7	Sa 22	8 ·47	19 ·58	6
8	Su 23	9 ·53	20 ·67	7
(Vibhava Kanya—Purattasi.) 9	Mo 24	(Bhadrapada) 10 ·58	21 ·74	8
10	Tu 25	11 ·60	22 ·79	9
11	We 26	12 ·61	23 ·81	(Rabi-ul-akhir.) 10
12	Th 27	13 ·59	24 ·82	11
13	Fr 28	14 ·56	25 ·80	12
14	Sa 29	P ·50	26 ·77	13
15	Su 30	1 ·43	27 ·73	14
	Oct.			
16	Mo 1	2 ·35	1 ·68	(H. 1347) 15
17	Tu 2	3 ·25	2 ·61	16
18	We 3	4 ·16	3 ·54	17
19	Th 4	(Bahula) 5 ·06; 6 ·96	4 ·47	18
20	Fr 5	7 ·86	5 ·41	19
21	Sa 6	8 ·76	6 ·35	20
22	Su 7	9 ·69	7 ·29	21
23	Mo 8	10 ·64	8 ·25	22
24	Tu 9	11 ·59	9 ·22	23
25	We 10	12 ·56	10 ·22	24
26	Th 11	13 ·56	11 ·23	25
27	Fr 12	14 ·57	12 ·26	26
28	Sa 13	—A ·59	13 ·31	27
29	Su 14	1 ·65	14 ·38	28
30	Mo 15	2 ·71	15 ·47	—29
—31	Tu 16	3 ·79	16 ·57	1
1	We 17	4 ·88	17 ·68	2
2	Th 18	5 ·97	18 ·79	3
3	Fr 19	(Sukla)	19 ·89	4
4	Sa 20	6 ·05	20 ·98	5
5	Su 21	7 ·11	... ...	6
(Vibhava Tula—Aippasi.) 6	Mo 22	8 ·16	21 ·05	(H. 1347 Jumadal-awwal.) 7
7	Tu 23	9 ·19	22 ·10	8
8	We 24	(Asvina) 10 ·19	23 ·13	9
9	Th 25	11 ·17	24 ·14	10
10	Fr 26	12 ·13	25 ·13	11
11	Sa 27	13 ·08	26 ·11	12
12	Su 28	14 ·01; P ·93	27 ·07	13
13	Mo 29	1 ·84	1 ·01; 2 ·95	14
14	Tu 30	(Bah.) 2 ·74	3 ·88	15
15	We 31	3 ·64	4 ·82	16

SOLAR reckoning: Cyclic Sidereal Year, Month and Day.	SOLAR reckoning: Week-Day English Month and Day.	LUNAR reckoning: Tithi Ending Moment.	LUNAR reckoning: Nakshatra Ending Moment.	LUNAR reckoning: Muhammadan Year, Month and Day.
	Nov.			
(Vibhava Tula—Aippasi.) 16	Th 1	(Asvina) 4 ·55	5 ·75	(H. 1347 Jumadal-awwal.) 17
17	Fr 2	5 ·45	6 ·68	18
18	Sa 3	6 ·36	7 ·63	19
19	Su 4	7 ·29	8 ·58	20
20	Mo 5	8 ·23	9 ·56	21
21	Tu 6	(Bahula) 9 ·18	10 ·54	22
22	We 7	10 ·15	11 ·55	23
23	Th 8	11 ·15	12 ·57	24
24	Fr 9	12 ·16	13 ·62	25
25	Sa 10	13 ·20	14 ·69	26
26	Su 11	14 ·25	15 ·78	27
27	Mo ● 12	—A ·32	16 ·87	28
28	Tu 13	1 ·40	17 ·98	29
29	We 14	2 ·50	... ...	—30
—30	Th 15	3 ·59	18 ·08	1
1	Fr 16	4 ·66	19 ·18	2
2	Sa 17	5 ·72	20 ·28	3
3	Su 18	6 ·77	21 ·36	4
4	Mo 19	(Sukla) 7 ·81	22 ·41	5
5	Tu 20	8 ·80	23 ·45	6
6	We 21	9 ·78	24 ·46	7
7	Th 22	10 ·75	25 ·46	8
8	Fr 23	11 ·69	26 ·44	9
9	Sa 24	12 ·63	27 ·40	10
(Vibhava Vrischika—Kartigai.) 10	Su 25	(Karttika) 13 ·55	1 ·35	(Jumadal-akhir.) 11
11	Mo 26	14 ·47	2 ·29	12
12	Tu ○ 27	P ·37	3 ·23	13
13	We 28	1 ·27	4 ·16	14
14	Th 29	2 ·17	5 ·09	15
15	Fr 30	3 ·08; 4 ·99	6 ·02; 7 ·96	16
	Dec.			
16	Sa 1	5 ·91	8 ·92	(H. 1347) 17
17	Su 2	(Bahula) 6 ·85	9 ·89	18
18	Mo 3	7 ·81	10 ·87	19
19	Tu 4	8 ·79	11 ·87	20
20	We 5	9 ·78	12 ·89	21
21	Th 6	10 ·80	13 ·94	22
22	Fr 7	11 ·84	... ...	23
23	Sa 8	12 ·89	14 ·00	24
24	Su 9	13 ·96	15 ·08	25
25	Mo 10	... ...	16 ·17	26
26	Tu 11	14 ·05	17 ·27	27
27	We 12	—A ·15	18 ·38	28
28	Th 13	1 ·23	19 ·49	—29
—29	Fr 14	2 ·31	20 ·59	1
1	Sa 15	(Sukla) 3 ·37	21 ·67	2
2	Su 16	4 ·41	22 ·73	3
3	Mo 17	5 ·44	23 ·76	4
4	Tu 18	6 ·44	24 ·79	5
5	We 19	7 ·43	25 ·79	6
6	Th 20	(Margasira) 8 ·39	26 ·77	7
(Vibhava Dhanus—Margali.) 7	Fr 21	9 ·34	27 ·73	(H. 1347 Rajab.) 8
8	Sa 22	10 ·26	1 ·68	9
9	Su 23	11 ·17	2 ·63	10
10	Mo 24	12 ·09; 13 ·99	3 ·57	11
11	Tu 25	14 ·90	4 ·50	12
12	We 26	P ·80	5 ·43	13
13	Th 27	1 ·71	6 ·36	14
14	Fr 28	(Bahula) 2 ·62	7 ·31	15
15	Sa 29	3 ·55	8 ·26	16
16	Su 30	4 ·50	9 ·22	17
17	Mo 31	5 ·45	10 ·19	18

15. Svati. 16. Visak. 17. Anur. 18. Jyesh. 19. Mula. 20. P. Ash. 21. U. Ash. 22. Sravn. 23. Dani. 24. Satab. 25. P. Bhad. 26. U. Bhad 27. Rev.

A. D. 1929.
Solar Eclipse. ●
Lunar Eclipse. ○

Mesha Sankranti (Commencement of Indian Sidereal Year).
(Surya Sid.) April 13·12.
(Arya Sid.) April 13·01.

Saka 1851.
(S. Cycle) Sukla.

Kaliyuga 5030.

SOLAR reckoning. | **LUNAR reckoning.**

Jan.

Solar: Vibhava, Dhanus—Margali (to 29); Vibhava, Makara—Tai (from 1). Lunar: Marg. Bahula (to A); Sukla; Pausha (from P). Muhammadan: H. 1347 Rajab (to 30); H. 1347 Shaban (from 1).

Cyclic Sidereal Year, Month and Day	Week-Day English Month and Day	Tithi Ending Moment	Nakshatra Ending Moment	Muhammadan Year, Month and Day
18	Tu 1	6 ·43	11 ·19	19
19	We 2	7 ·42	12 ·20	20
20	Th 3	8 ·45	13 ·25	21
21	Fr 4	9 ·48	14 ·30	22
22	Sa 5	10 ·53	15 ·38	23
23	Su 6	11 ·61	16 ·47	24
24	Mo 7	12 ·70	17 ·57	25
25	Tu 8	13 ·79	18 ·68	26
26	We 9	14 ·88	19 ·79	27
27	Th 10	—A ·96	20 ·89	28
28	Fr 11	... ...	21 ·97	29
—29	Sa 12	1 ·02	... ...	—30
1	Su 13	2 ·07	22 ·04	1
2	Mo 14	3 ·09	23 ·09	2
3	Tu 15	4 ·08	24 ·11	3
4	We 16	5 ·07	25 ·11	4
5	Th 17	6 ·03 7 ·98	26 ·10	5
6	Fr 18	8 ·90	27 ·07	6
7	Sa 19	9 ·82	1 ·03 2 ·97	7
8	Su 20	10 ·73	3 ·91	8
9	Mo 21	11 ·63	4 ·83	9
10	Tu 22	12 ·53	5 ·76	10
11	We 23	13 ·48	6 ·70	11
12	Th 24	14 ·34	7 ·64	12
13	Fr 25	P ·26	8 ·59	13
14	Sa 26	1 ·20	9 ·55	14
15	Su 27	2 ·14	10 ·52	15
16	Mo 28	3 ·09	11 ·51	16
17	Tu 29	4 ·07	12 ·53	17
18	We 30	5 ·07	13 ·56	18
19	Th 31	6 ·09	14 ·61	19

Feb.

Solar: Vibhava, Kumbha—Masi. Lunar: Bahula; Sukla; Magha (from 11); Bah. Muhammadan: H. 1347 Ramzan (from 1).

Cyclic Sidereal Year, Month and Day	Week-Day English Month and Day	Tithi Ending Moment	Nakshatra Ending Moment	Muhammadan Year, Month and Day
20	Fr 1	7 ·13	15 ·68	20
21	Sa 2	8 ·19	16 ·77	21
22	Su 3	9 ·27	17 ·88	22
23	Mo 4	10 ·36	18 ·99	23
24	Tu 5	11 ·44	... ...	24•
25	We 6	12 ·52	19 ·09	25
26	Th 7	13 ·60	20 ·19	26
27	Fr 8	14 ·66	21 ·28	27
28	Sa 9	—A ·71	22 ·35	28
29	Su 10	1 ·72	23 ·40	—29
—30	Mo 11	2 ·72	24 ·43	1
1	Tu 12	3 ·71	25 ·44	2
2	We 13	4 ·66	26 ·43	3
3	Th 14	5 ·60	27 ·41	4
4	Fr 15	6 ·53	1 ·36	5
5	Sa 16	7 ·45	2 ·31	6
6	Su 17	8 ·36	3 ·24	7
7	Mo 18	9 ·26	4 ·17	8
8	Tu 19	10 ·16	5 ·10	9
9	We 20	11 ·06 12 ·96	6 ·04 7 ·98	10
10	Th 21	13 ·88	8 ·92	11
11	Fr 22	14 ·81	9 ·88	12
12	Sa 23	P ·75	10 ·85	13
13	Su 24	1 ·72	11 ·84	14
14	Mo 25	2 ·69	12 ·85	15
15	Tu 26	3 ·69	13 ·87	16
16	We 27	4 ·72	14 ·92	17
17	Th 28	5 ·75	15 ·99	18

March

Solar: Vibhava, Kumbha—Masi (to 30); Vibhava, Mina—Panguni (from 1). Lunar: Magha Bahula (to A); Sukla; Phalguna (from P). Muhammadan: H. 1347 Ramzan (to 30); H. 1347 Shawwal (from 1).

Cyclic Sidereal Year, Month and Day	Week-Day English Month and Day	Tithi Ending Moment	Nakshatra Ending Moment	Muhammadan Year, Month and Day
18	Fr 1	6 ·81	... ...	19
19	Sa 2	7 ·89	16 ·08	20
20	Su 3	8 ·98	17 ·18	21
21	Mo 4	... ...	18 ·29	22
22	Tu 5	9 ·06	19 ·39	23
23	We 6	10 ·14	20 ·49	24
24	Th 7	11 ·21	21 ·59	25
25	Fr 8	12 ·27	22 ·66	26
26	Sa 9	13 ·32	23 ·72	27
27	Su 10	14 ·33	24 ·75	28
28	Mo 11	—A ·33	25 ·76	29
29	Tu 12	1 ·31	26 ·75	—30
—30	We 13	2 ·26	27 ·74	1
1	Th 14	3 ·20	1 ·70	2
2	Fr 15	4 ·13	2 ·64	3
3	Sa 16	5 ·04 6 ·95	3 ·58	4
4	Su 17	7 ·85	4 ·51	5
5	Mo 18	8 ·75	5 ·45	6
6	Tu 19	9 ·66	6 ·38	7
7	We 20	10 ·56	7 ·32	8
8	Th 21	11 ·48	8 ·26	9
9	Fr 22	12 ·40	9 ·21	10
10	Sa 23	13 ·34	10 ·18	11
11	Su 24	14 ·31	11 ·17	12
12	Mo 25	P ·28	12 ·17	13
13	Tu 26	1 ·28	13 ·19	14
14	We 27	2 ·30	14 ·23	15
15	Th 28	3 ·34	15 ·30	16
16	Fr 29	4 ·39	16 ·38	17
17	Sa 30	5 ·47	17 ·48	18
18	Su 31	6 ·56	18 ·58	19

April

Solar: Sukla, Mesha—Chittirai (from 1). Lunar: Bahula; Sukla; Chaitra (from P); Bahula. Muhammadan: H. 1347 Zi-l-ka'da (from 1).

Cyclic Sidereal Year, Month and Day	Week-Day English Month and Day	Tithi Ending Moment	Nakshatra Ending Moment	Muhammadan Year, Month and Day
19	Mo 1	7 ·64	19 ·69	20
20	Tu 2	8 ·72	20 ·80	21
21	We 3	9 ·79	21 ·89	22
22	Th 4	10 ·85	22 ·97	23
23	Fr 5	11 ·89	... ...	24
24	Sa 6	12 ·91	23 ·03	25
25	Su 7	13 ·90	24 ·07	26
26	Mo 8	14 ·88	25 ·08	27
27	Tu 9	—A ·82	26 ·09	28
28	We 10	1 ·76	27 ·07	—29
29	Th 11	2 ·69	1 ·08 2 ·98	1
—30	Fr 12	3 ·60	3 ·92	2
1	Sa 13	4 ·51	4 ·86	3
2	Su 14	5 ·41	5 ·79	4
3	Mo 15	6 ·31	6 ·72	5
4	Tu 16	7 ·21	7 ·65	6
5	We 17	8 ·11	8 ·59	7
6	Th 18	9 ·03 10 ·95	9 ·55	8
7	Fr 19	11 ·90	10 ·51	9
8	Sa 20	12 ·85	11 ·49	10
9	Su 21	13 ·82	12 ·49	11
10	Mo 22	14 ·82	13 ·50	12
11	Tu 23	P ·84	14 ·55	13
12	We 24	1 ·88	15 ·61	14
13	Th 25	2 ·93	16 ·69	15
14	Fr 26	... ...	17 ·78	16
15	Sa 27	3 ·01	18 ·88	17
16	Su 28	4 ·10	19 ·99	18
17	Mo 29	5 ·19	... ...	19
18	Tu 30	6 ·26	20 ·10	20

May

Solar: Sukla, Mesha—Chittirai (to 31); Sukla, Vrishabha—Vaikasi (from 1). Lunar: Chait. Bahula (to A); Sukla; Vaisakha (from P); Bahula. Muhammadan: H. 1347 Zi-l-ka'da (to 30); H. 1347 Zi-l-hijja (from 1).

Cyclic Sidereal Year, Month and Day	Week-Day English Month and Day	Tithi Ending Moment	Nakshatra Ending Moment	Muhammadan Year, Month and Day
19	We 1	7 ·32	21 ·20	21
20	Th 2	8 ·38	22 ·28	22
21	Fr 3	9 ·42	23 ·34	23
22	Sa 4	10 ·44	24 ·38	24
23	Su 5	11 ·43	25 ·41	25
24	Mo 6	12 ·41	26 ·41	26
25	Tu 7	13 ·35	27 ·40	27
26	We 8	14 ·29	1 ·36	28
27	Th ● 9	—A ·22	2 ·31	29
28	Fr 10	1 ·13	3 ·26	—30
29	Sa 11	2 ·03 3 ·93	4 ·20	1
30	Su 12	4 ·83	5 ·13	2
—31	Mo 13	5 ·73	6 ·06 7 ·99	3
1	Tu 14	6 ·68	8 ·93	4
2	We 15	7 ·54	9 ·88	5
3	Th 16	8 ·46	10 ·84	6
4	Fr 17	9 ·41	11 ·82	7
5	Sa 18	10 ·37	12 ·81	8
6	Su 19	11 ·35	13 ·83	9
7	Mo 20	12 ·33	14 ·86	10
8	Tu 21	13 ·35	15 ·92	11
9	We 22	14 ·39	16 ·99	12
10	Th ○ 23	P ·44	... ...	13
11	Fr 24	1 ·51	17 ·08	14
12	Sa 25	2 ·59	18 ·18	15
13	Su 26	3 ·68	19 ·29	16
14	Mo 27	4 ·76	20 ·40	17
15	Tu 28	5 ·83	21 ·50	18
16	We 29	6 ·89	22 ·58	19
17	Th 30	7 ·91	23 ·65	20
18	Fr 31	8 ·98	24 ·71	21

June

Solar: Sukla, Mithuna—Ani (from 1). Lunar: Sukla; Jyeshtha (from P); Bahula. Muhammadan: H. 1348 Muharram (from 1).

Cyclic Sidereal Year, Month and Day	Week-Day English Month and Day	Tithi Ending Moment	Nakshatra Ending Moment	Muhammadan Year, Month and Day
19	Sa 1	9 ·92	25 ·73	22
20	Su 2	10 ·91	26 ·74	23
21	Mo 3	11 ·86	27 ·72	24
22	Tu 4	12 ·80	1 ·69	25
23	We 5	13 ·72	2 ·66	26
24	Th 6	14 ·63	3 ·60	27
25	Fr 7	—A ·53	4 ·54	28
26	Sa 8	1 ·43	5 ·47	—29
27	Su 9	2 ·33	6 ·40	1
28	Mo 10	3 ·23	7 ·34	2
29	Tu 11	4 ·13	8 ·27	3
30	We 12	5 ·04 6 ·97	9 ·22	4
—31	Th 13	7 ·90	10 ·17	5
1	Fr 14	8 ·85	11 ·14	6
2	Sa 15	9 ·83	12 ·13	7
3	Su 16	10 ·82	13 ·15	8
4	Mo 17	11 ·83	14 ·18	9
5	Tu 18	12 ·86	15 ·28	10
6	We 19	13 ·92	16 ·29	11
7	Th 20	14 ·98	17 ·38	12
8	Fr 21	... ...	18 ·48	13
9	Sa 22	P ·06	19 ·59	14
10	Su 23	1 ·15	20 ·70	15
11	Mo 24	2 ·23	21 ·80	16
12	Tu 25	3 ·30	22 ·89	17
13	We 26	4 ·36	23 ·97	18
14	Th 27	5 ·39	... ...	19
15	Fr 28	6 ·41	24 ·02	20
16	Sa 29	7 ·41	25 ·05	21
17	Su 30	8 ·39	26 ·06	22

Naksh :—1. Asvn. 2. Bhar. 3 Krit. 4. Rohi. 5. Mrig. 6. Ardh. 7. Punar. 8. Push. 9. Aslesh. 10. Magh. 11. P. Phal. 12. U. Phal. 13. Hasta. 14. Chit

A. D. 1929.
A.—Amavasya.
P.—Paurnami.

Kollam 1105, Commences { N. Malabar—Sept. / S. Malabar—Aug.

Hijra 1348, Commences, June 9.

Vikrama 1986.
Bengal San 1335.
(N. Cycle) Vrisha.

SOLAR reckoning: Cyclic Sidereal Year, Month and Day; Week-Day English Month and Day. LUNAR reckoning: Tithi Ending Moment; Nakshatra Ending Moment; Muhammadan Year, Month and Day.

July

Month labels	Cyclic Sidereal Day	Week-Day	Eng. Day	Tithi	Tithi Moment	Nakshatra	Nakshatra Moment	Muhammadan
Sukla Mithuna—Ani; Jy. Bahula; H. 1348 Muharram	18	Mo	1	Jy. 9	·34	27	·05	23
	19	Tu	2	10	·28	1 / 2	·03 / ·99	24
	20	We	3	11	·20	3	·91	25
	21	Th	4	12	·11	4	·87	26
	22	Fr	5	13 / 14	·01 / ·91	5	·81	27
	23	Sa	6	—A	·81	6	·74	28
Ashadha Sukla	24	Su	7	1	·71	7	·67	29
	25	Mo	8	2	·61	8	·61	—30
H. 1348 Safar	26	Tu	9	3	·52	9	·55	1
	27	We	10	4	·44	10	·50	2
	28	Th	11	5	·37	11	·47	3
	29	Fr	12	6	·34	12	·46	4
	30	Sa	13	7	·31	13	·47	5
	31	Su	14	8	·29	14	·49	6
	—32	Mo	15	9	·31	15	·53	7
Sukla Karkata—Adi	1	Tu	16	10	·34	16	·60	8
	2	We	17	11	·40	17	·69	9
	3	Th	18	12	·46	18	·79	10
	4	Fr	19	13	·54	19	·89	11
	5	Sa	20	14	·62	...	...	12
	6	Su	21	P	·70	20	·00	13
Bahula	7	Mo	22	1	·77	21	·10	14
	8	Tu	23	2	·84	22	·20	15
	9	We	24	3	·87	23	·28	16
	10	Th	25	4	·89	24	·33	17
	11	Fr	26	5	·89	25	·37	18
	12	Sa	27	6	·87	26	·38	19
	13	Su	28	7	·82	27	·39	20
	14	Mo	29	8	·76	1	·36	21
	15	Tu	30	9	·69	2	·32	22
	16	We	31	10	·60	3	·27	23

Aug.

Month labels	Cyclic Sidereal Day	Week-Day	Eng. Day	Tithi	Tithi Moment	Nakshatra	Nakshatra Moment	Muhammadan
	17	Th	1	11	·50	4	·21	24
	18	Fr	2	12	·40	5	·14	25
	19	Sa	3	13	·30	6	·08	26
	20	Su	4	14	·20	7 / 8	·01 / ·95	27
	21	Mo	5	—A	·10	9	·89	28
Sravana Sukla	22	Tu	6	1 / 2	·01 / ·91	10	·84	—29
H. 1948 Rabi-ul-awwal	23	We	7	3	·85	11	·81	1
	24	Th	8	4	·82	12	·79	2
	25	Fr	9	5	·80	13	·79	3
	26	Sa	10	6	·79	14	·81	4
	27	Su	11	7	·79	15	·84	5
	28	Mo	12	8	·82	16	·91	6
	29	Tu	13	9	·88	17	·99	7
	30	We	14	10	·95	...	...	8
	—31	Th	15	...	..	18	·09	9
Sukla Simha—Avani	1	Fr	16	11	·03	19	·19	10
	2	Sa	17	12	·11	20	·29	11
	3	Su	18	13	·19	21	·40	12
	4	Mo	19	14	·26	22	·50	13
	5	Tu	20	P	·33	23	·58	14
Bahula	6	We	21	1	·36	24	·64	15
	7	Th	22	2	·39	25	·68	16
	8	Fr	23	3	·38	26	·71	17
	9	Sa	24	4	·36	27	·71	18
	10	Su	25	5	·32	1	·69	19
	11	Mo	26	6	·27	2	·66	20
	12	Tu	27	7	·20	3	·61	21
	13	We	28	8	·11	4	·55	22
	14	Th	29	9 / 10	·01 / ·91	5	·49	23
	15	Fr	30	11	·81	6	·42	24
	16	Sa	31	12	·71	7	·35	25

Sep.

Month labels	Cyclic Sidereal Day	Week-Day	Eng. Day	Tithi	Tithi Moment	Nakshatra	Nakshatra Moment	Muhammadan
Bah.; R. awl.	17	Su	1	13	·61	8	·28	26
	18	Mo	2	14	·53	9	·22	27
	19	Tu	3	—A	·45	10	·18	28
Bhadrapada Sukla	20	We	4	1	·39	11	·14	29
	21	Th	5	2	·34	12	·12	—30
H. 1348 Rabi-ul-akhir	22	Fr	6	3	·30	13	·11	1
	23	Sa	7	4	·29	14	·12	2
	24	Su	8	5	·30	15	·17	3
	25	Mo	9	6	·34	16	·22	4
	26	Tu	10	7	·40	17	29	5
	27	We	11	8	·46	18	·38	6
	28	Th	12	9	·54	19	·49	7
	29	Fr	13	10	·62	20	·60	8
	30	Sa	14	11	·71	21	·71	9
	—31	Su	15	12	·79	22	·80	10
Sukla Kanya—Purattasi	1	Mo	16	13	·86	23	·89	11
	2	Tu	17	14	·89	24	·95	12
	3	We	18	P	·91	...	...	13
Bahula	4	Th	19	1	·91	25	·00	14
	5	Fr	20	2	·90	26	·03	15
	6	Sa	21	3	·86	27	·04	16
	7	Su	22	4	·80	1 / 2	·02 / ·99	17
	8	Mo	23	5	·73	3	·95	18
	9	Tu	24	6	·64	4	·90	19
	10	We	25	7	·55	5	·83	20
	11	Th	26	8	·46	6	·76	21
	12	Fr	27	9	·36	7	·69	22
	13	Sa	28	10	·25	8	·62	23
	14	Su	29	11	·15	9	·56	24
	15	Mo	30	12 / 13	·07 / ·99	10	·51	25

Oct.

Month labels	Cyclic Sidereal Day	Week-Day	Eng. Day	Tithi	Tithi Moment	Nakshatra	Nakshatra Moment	Muhammadan
	16	Tu	1	14	·93	11	·47	26
	17	We	2	—A	·88	12	·44	27
Asvina Sukla	18	Th	3	1	·86	13	·43	28
	19	Fr	4	2	·85	14	·45	—29
H. 1348 Jumadal-awwal	20	Sa	5	3	·85	15	·48	1
	21	Su	6	4	·90	16	·53	2
	22	Mo	7	5	·95	17	·60	3
	23	Tu	8	...	...	18	·69	4
	24	We	9	6	·02	19	·79	5
	25	Th	10	7	·10	20	·90	6
	26	Fr	11	8	·20	...	...	7
	27	Sa	12	9	·28	21	·01	8
	28	Su	13	10	·36	22	·11	9
	29	Mo	14	11	·42	23	·19	10
	30	Tu	15	12	·45	24	·26	11
	—31	We	16	13	·48	25	·32	12
Sukla Tula—Aippasi	1	Th	17	14	·48	26	·35	13
	2	Fr	18	P	·47	27	·36	14
Bahula	3	Sa	19	1	·43	1	·35	15
	4	Su	20	2	·38	2	·32	16
	5	Mo	21	3	·31	3	·29	17
	6	Tu	22	4	·22	4	·23	18
	7	We	23	5	·13	5	·17	19
	8	Th	24	6 / 7	·03 / ·93	6	·10	20
	9	Fr	25	8	·83	7 / 8	·08 / ·97	21
	10	Sa	26	9	·74	9	·91	22
	11	Su	27	10	·65	10	·85	23
	12	Mo	28	11	·58	11	·80	24
	13	Tu	29	12	·52	12	·77	25
	14	We	30	13	·47	13	·76	26
	15	Th	31	14	·45	14	·77	27

Nov.

Month labels	Cyclic Sidereal Day	Week-Day	Eng. Day	Tithi	Tithi Moment	Nakshatra	Nakshatra Moment	Muhammadan
	16	Fr ●	1	—A	·44	15	·79	28
Kartika Sukla	17	Sa	2	1	·45	16	·84	29
	18	Su	3	2	·49	17	·90	—30
H. 1348 Jumadal-akhir	19	Mo	4	3	·56	18	·99	1
	20	Tu	5	4	·63	...	...	2
	21	We	6	5	·71	19	·09	3
	22	Th	7	6	·80	20	·20	4
	23	Fr	8	7	·88	21	·30	5
	24	Sa	9	8	·96	22	·41	6
	25	Su	10	...	...	23	·50	7
	26	Mo	11	9	·02	24	·58	8
	27	Tu	12	10	·06	25	·63	9
	28	We	13	11	·09	26	·67	10
	29	Th	14	12	·08	27	·68	11
	—30	Fr	15	13	·08	1	·67	12
Sukla Vrischika—Kartigai	1	Sa	16	14 / P	·04 / ·99	2	·66	13
Bahula	2	Su	17	1	·92	3	·62	14
	3	Mo	18	2	·84	4	·57	15
	4	Tu	19	3	·74	5	·51	16
	5	We	20	4	·64	6	·45	17
	6	Th	21	5	·54	7	·38	18
	7	Fr	22	6	·45	8	·31	19
	8	Sa	23	7	·36	9	·24	20
	9	Su	24	8	·27	10	·18	21
	10	Mo	25	9	·20	11	·13	22
	11	Tu	26	10	·13	12	·10	23
	12	We	27	11	·10	13	·09	24
	13	Th	28	12	·07	14	·09	25
	14	Fr	29	13	·06	15	·11	26
	15	Sa	30	14	·09	16	·15	27

Dec.

Month labels	Cyclic Sidereal Day	Week-Day	Eng. Day	Tithi	Tithi Moment	Nakshatra	Nakshatra Moment	Muhammadan
	16	Su	1	—A	·12	17	·21	28
Margasira Sukla	17	Mo	2	1	·18	18	·30	—29
H. 1348 Rajab	18	Tu	3	2	·25	19	·39	1
	19	We	4	3	·34	20	·50	2
	20	Th	5	4	·43	21	·61	3
	21	Fr	6	5	·51	22	·71	4
	22	Sa	7	6	·59	23	·81	5
	23	Su	8	7	·66	24	·89	6
	24	Mo	9	8	·70	25	·95	7
	25	Tu	10	9	·72	26	·98	8
	26	We	11	10	·73	...	...	9
	27	Th	12	11	·71	27	·00	10
	28	Fr	13	12	·67	1 / 2	·01 / ·99	11
	—29	Sa	14	13	·62	3	·95	12
Sukla Dhanus—Margali	1	Su	15	14	·54	4	·90	13
	2	Mo	16	P	·46	5	·85	14
Bahula	3	Tu	17	1	·37	6	·79	15
	4	We	18	2	·27	7	·72	16
	5	Th	19	3	·17	8	·65	17
	6	Fr	20	4 / 5	·08 / ·99	9	·58	18
	7	Sa	21	6	·90	10	·52	19
	8	Su	22	7	·83	11	·47	20
	9	Mo	23	8	·77	12	·44	21
	10	Tu	24	9	·74	13	·41	22
	11	We	25	10	·71	14	·41	23
	12	Th	26	11	·72	15	·42	24
	13	Fr	27	12	·74	16	·46	25
	14	Sa	28	13	·77	17	·53	26
	15	Su	29	14	·83	18	·60	27
	16	Mo	30	—A	·91	19	·69	28
	17	Tu	31	...	...	20	·79	29

15. Svati. 16. Visak. 17. Anur. 18. Jyesh. 19 Mula. 20. P. Ash. 21. U. Ash. 22. Sravn. 23. Dani. 24. Satab. 25. P. Bhad. 26. U. Bhad. 27. Rev.

A. D. 1930.
Solar Eclipse. ●
Lunar Eclipse. ○

Mesha Sankranti (Commencement of Indian Side. eal Year).
(Surya Sid.) April 13·38.
(Arya Sid.) April 13·27.

Saka 1852. **Kaliyuga 5031.**
(S. Cycle) Pramodhuta.

SOLAR reckoning: Cyclic Sidereal Year, Month and Day; Week-Day English Month and Day. LUNAR reckoning: Tithi Ending Moment; Nakshatra Ending Moment; Muhammadan Year, Month and Day.

Jan.

Solar month	Cyclic Sidereal Day	Week-Day	Date	Lunar month	Tithi Ending Moment	Nakshatra Ending Moment	Muhammadan
Sukla Dhanus—Margali	18	We	1	Sukla	1 ·00	21 ·90	—30
	19	Th	2		2 ·09	... ...	1 (H. 1348 Shaban)
	20	Fr	3		3 ·18	22 ·01	2
	21	Sa	4		4 ·25	23 ·11	3
	22	Su	5		5 ·31	24 ·19	4
	23	Mo	6		6 ·36	25 ·26	5
	24	Tu	7		7 ·37	26 ·30	6
	25	We	8		8 ·37	27 ·33	7
	26	Th	9		9 ·35	1 ·33	8
	27	Fr	10		10 ·32	2 ·32	9
	28	Sa	11		11 ·26	3 ·29	10
	29	Su	12		12 ·19	4 ·24	11
	—30	Mo	13		13 ·11	5 ·18	12
Sukla Makara—Tai	1	Tu	14	Pausha	14 ·01; P ·91	6 ·12	13
	2	We	15		1 ·81	7 ·05; 8 ·98	14
	3	Th	16		2 ·72	9 ·91	15
	4	Fr	17		3 ·63	10 ·85	16
	5	Sa	18		4 ·55	11 ·81	17
	6	Su	19		5 ·48	12 ·77	18
	7	Mo	20	Bahula	6 ·41	13 ·74	19
	8	Tu	21		7 ·38	14 ·73	20
	9	We	22		8 ·35	15 ·74	21
	10	Th	23		9 ·36	16 ·78	22
	11	Fr	24		10 ·38	17 ·83	23
	12	Sa	25		11 ·43	18 ·90	24
	13	Su	26		12 ·49	19 ·99	25
	14	Mo	27		13 ·57	... ...	26
	15	Tu	28		14 ·65	20 ·09	27
	16	We	29		—A ·73	21 ·20	28
	17	Th	30		1 ·82	22 ·31	—29
	18	Fr	31		2 ·90	23 ·41	1

Feb.

Solar month	Cyclic Sidereal Day	Week-Day	Date	Lunar month	Tithi Ending Moment	Nakshatra Ending Moment	Muhammadan
	19	Sa	1		3 ·96	24 ·50	2
	20	Su	2		4 ·99	25 ·57	3
	21	Mo	3		... ...	26 ·62	4
	22	Tu	4		5 ·02	27 ·65	5
	23	We	5	Sukla	6 ·01; 7 ·99	1 ·66	6
	24	Th	6		8 ·95	2 ·65	7
	25	Fr	7		9 ·89	3 ·62	8
	26	Sa	8		10 ·82	4 ·57	9 (H. 1348 Ramzan)
	27	Su	9		11 ·73	5 ·53	10
	28	Mo	10		12 ·64	6 ·46	11
	—29	Tu	11	Magha	13 ·54	7 ·39	12
Sukla Kumbha—Masi	1	We	12		14 ·45	8 ·32	13
	2	Th	13		P ·35	9 ·26	14
	3	Fr	14		1 ·25	10 ·20	15
	4	Sa	15		2 ·17	11 ·14	16
	5	Su	16		3 ·10	12 ·10	17
	6	Mo	17		4 ·05	13 ·07	18
	7	Tu	18	Bahula	5 ·01; 6 ·99	14 ·05	19
	8	We	19		7 ·98	15 ·07	20
	9	Th	20		... ...	16 ·09	21
	10	Fr	21		8 ·00	17 ·14	22
	11	Sa	22		9 ·05	18 ·21	23
	12	Su	23		10 ·11	19 ·29	24
	13	Mo	24		11 ·19	20 ·40	25
	14	Tu	25		12 ·28	21 ·51	26
	15	We	26		13 ·36	22 ·61	27
	16	Th	27		14 ·44	23 ·71	28
	17	Fr	28		—A ·53	24 ·80	29

March

Solar month	Cyclic Sidereal Day	Week-Day	Date	Lunar month	Tithi Ending Moment	Nakshatra Ending Moment	Muhammadan
Sukla Kumbha—Masi	18	Sa	1		1 ·58	25 ·87	—30
	19	Su	2		2 ·62	26 ·94	1 (H. 1348 Shawwal)
	20	Mo	3		3 ·63	27 ·97	2
	21	Tu	4		4 ·62	1 ·98	3
	22	We	5		5 ·61	2 ·97	4
	23	Th	6		6 ·56	3 ·95	5
	24	Fr	7	Sukla	7 ·50	4 ·92	6
	25	Sa	8		8 ·43	5 ·86	7
	26	Su	9		9 ·34	6 ·80	8
	27	Mo	10		10 ·24	7 ·73	9
	28	Tu	11		11 ·14	8 ·66	10
	29	We	12		12 ·04; 13 ·94	9 ·60	11
	—30	Th	13	Phalguna	14 ·85	10 ·53	12
Sukla Mina—Panguni	1	Fr	14		P ·77	11 ·48	13
	2	Sa	15		1 ·69	12 ·43	14
	3	Su	16		2 ·63	13 ·39	15
	4	Mo	17		3 ·59	14 ·38	16
	5	Tu	18		4 ·58	15 ·39	17
	6	We	19		5 ·58	16 ·41	18
	7	Th	20		6 ·61	17 ·45	19
	8	Fr	21	Bahula	7 ·65	18 ·51	20
	9	Sa	22		8 ·70	19 ·60	21
	10	Su	23		9 ·78	20 ·70	22
	11	Mo	24		10 ·87	21 ·80	23
	12	Tu	25		11 ·96	22 ·91	24
	13	We	26		... ...	... ...	25
	14	Th	27		12 ·04	23 ·01	26
	15	Fr	28		13 ·11	24 ·10	27
	16	Sa	29		14 ·16	25 ·19	28
	17	Su	30		—A ·20	26 ·25	—29
	18	Mo	31		1 ·21	27 ·29	1

April

Solar month	Cyclic Sidereal Day	Week-Day	Date	Lunar month	Tithi Ending Moment	Nakshatra Ending Moment	Muhammadan
	19	Tu	1		2 ·20	1 ·30	2
	20	We	2		3 ·18	2 ·30	3
	21	Th	3		4 ·13	3 ·29	4
	22	Fr	4		5 ·07	4 ·25	5
	23	Sa	5	Sukla	6 ·00; 7 ·92	5 ·20	6
	24	Su	6		8 ·82	6 ·14	7
	25	Mo	7		9 ·71	7 ·07	8
	26	Tu	8		10 ·61	8 ·01; 9 ·94	9 (H. 1348 Zi-l-ka'da)
	27	We	9		11 ·51	10 ·87	10
	28	Th	10		12 ·42	11 ·81	11
	29	Fr	11		13 ·33	12 ·76	12
	—30	Sa	12	Chaitra	14 ·26	13 ·73	13
Pramodhuta Mesha—Chittirai	1	Su ○	13		P ·19	14 ·71	14
	2	Mo	14		1 ·15	15 ·71	15
	3	Tu	15		2 ·14	16 ·72	16
	4	We	16		3 ·14	17 ·76	17
	5	Th	17		4 ·16	18 ·82	18
	6	Fr	18		5 ·20	19 ·91	19
	7	Sa	19	Bahula	6 ·26	... ...	20
	8	Su	20		7 ·34	20 ·00	21
	9	Mo	21		8 ·42	21 ·10	22
	10	Tu	22		9 ·50	22 ·21	23
	11	We	23		10 ·57	23 ·31	24
	12	Th	24		11 ·64	24 ·42	25
	13	Fr	25		12 ·70	25 ·50	26
	14	Sa	26		13 ·75	26 ·56	27
	15	Su	27		14 ·76	27 ·60	28
	16	Mo	28		—A ·75	1 ·62	29
	17	Tu	29	Suk.	1 ·72	2 ·68	—30
	18	We	30		2 ·66	3 ·62	1

May

Solar month	Cyclic Sidereal Day	Week-Day	Date	Lunar month	Tithi Ending Moment	Nakshatra Ending Moment	Muhammadan
Pramodhuta Mesha—Chittirai	19	Th	1		3 ·60	4 ·58	2
	20	Fr	2		4 ·53	5 ·53	3
	21	Sa	3		5 ·44	6 ·47	4
	22	Su	4	Sukla	6 ·34	7 ·41	5
	23	Mo	5		7 ·24	8 ·35	6
	24	Tu	6		8 ·14	9 ·28	7
	25	We	7		9 ·04; 10 ·94	10 ·21	8
	26	Th	8		11 ·85	11 ·15	9
	27	Fr	9		12 ·78	12 ·09	10
	28	Sa	10		13 ·72	13 ·06	11 (H. 1348 Zi-l-hijja)
	29	Su	11	Vaisakha	14 ·68	14 ·04	12
	30	Mo	12		P ·66	15 ·03	13
	—31	Tu	13		1 ·66	16 ·04	14
Pramodhuta Vrishabha—Vaikasi	1	We	14		2 ·67	17 ·07	15
	2	Th	15		3 ·71	18 ·14	16
	3	Fr	16		4 ·77	19 ·21	17
	4	Sa	17		5 ·84	20 ·30	18
	5	Su	18		6 ·93	21 ·40	19
	6	Mo	19	Bahula	... ...	22 ·50	20
	7	Tu	20		7 ·01	23 ·61	21
	8	We	21		8 ·09	24 ·72	22
	9	Th	22		9 ·16	25 ·80	23
	10	Fr	23		10 ·21	26 ·87	24
	11	Sa	24		11 ·25	27 ·92	25
	12	Su	25		12 ·26	1 ·95	26
	13	Mo	26		13 ·25	2 ·96	27
	14	Tu	27		14 ·23	3 ·94	28
	15	We	28		—A ·19	4 ·91	—29
	16	Th	29		1 ·11	5 ·87	1
	17	Fr	30		2 ·03; 3 ·94	6 ·82	2
	18	Sa	31		4 ·84	7 ·76	3

June

Solar month	Cyclic Sidereal Day	Week-Day	Date	Lunar month	Tithi Ending Moment	Nakshatra Ending Moment	Muhammadan
	19	Su	1		5 ·74	8 ·69	4
	20	Mo	2		6 ·64	9 ·62	5
	21	Tu	3	Sukla	7 ·54	10 ·55	6
	22	We	4		8 ·44	11 ·48	7
	23	Th	5		9 ·36	12 ·43	8
	24	Fr	6		10 ·29	13 ·39	9 (H. 1349 Muharram)
	25	Sa	7		11 ·22	14 ·36	10
	26	Su	8		12 ·17	15 ·35	11
	27	Mo	9		13 ·15	16 ·36	12
	28	Tu	10	Jyeshtha	14 ·15	17 ·40	13
	29	We	11		P ·16	18 ·45	14
	30	Th	12		1 ·20	19 ·51	15
	31	Fr	13		2 ·25	20 ·60	16
	—32	Sa	14		3 ·32	21 ·70	17
Pramodhuta Mithuna—Ani	1	Su	15		4 ·40	22 ·81	18
	2	Mo	16		5 ·48	23 ·92	19
	3	Tu	17	Bahula	6 ·56	... ...	20
	4	We	18		7 ·63	24 ·02	21
	5	Th	19		8 ·69	25 ·11	22
	6	Fr	20		9 ·73	26 ·18	23
	7	Sa	21		10 ·74	27 ·24	24
	8	Su	22		11 ·73	1 ·27	25
	9	Mo	23		12 ·71	2 ·28	26
	10	Tu	24		13 ·66	3 ·27	27
	11	We	25		14 ·59	4 ·24	28
	12	Th	26		—A ·52	5 ·20	29
	13	Fr	27	Ash. Suk.	1 ·42	6 ·16	—30
	14	Sa	28		2 ·33	7 ·09	1 (Safar)
	15	Su	29		3 ·23	8 ·03; 9 ·96	2
	16	Mo	30		4 ·13	10 ·89	3

Naksh :—1. Asvn. 2. Bhar. 3. Krit. 4. Rohi. 5. Mrig. 6. Ardh. 7. Punar. 8. Push. 9. Aslesh. 10. Magh. 11. P. Phal. 12. U. Phal. 13. Hasta. 14. Chit.

A. D. 1930.
A.—Amavasya.
P.—Paurnami.

Kollam 1106, Commences { N. Malabar—Sept. / S. Malabar—Aug.

Hijra 1349, Commences, May 29.

Vikrama 1987.
Bengal San 1336.
(N. Cycle) Chitrabhanu.

July (SOLAR reckoning / LUNAR reckoning)

Cyclic Sidereal Year, Month and Day	Week-Day English Month and Day	Tithi Ending Moment	Nakshatra Ending Moment	Muhammadan Year, Month and Day
17	Tu 1	{ 5 ·02 / 6 ·92	11 ·83	4
18	We 2	Sukla 7 ·84	12 ·77	5
19	Th 3	8 ·76	13 ·72	6
Pramodhuta Mithuna—Ani. 20	Fr 4	9 ·70	14 ·69	7
21	Sa 5	10 ·65	15 ·68	8
22	Su 6	11 ·62	16 ·69	9
23	Mo 7	12 ·62	17 ·71	10
24	Tu 8	Ashadha 13 ·63	18 ·75	11
25	We 9	14 ·67	19 ·82	12
26	Th 10	P ·72	20 ·90	13
27	Fr 11	1 ·80	... ...	14
28	Sa 12	2 ·88	21 ·00	H. 1349 Safar. 15
29	Su 13	3 ·96	22 ·11	16
30	Mo 14	... ...	23 ·22	17
—31	Tu 15	4 ·04	24 ·32	18
1	We 16	5 ·11	25 ·41	19
2	Th 17	Bahula 6 ·17	26 ·50	20
3	Fr 18	7 ·20	27 ·55	21
4	Sa 19	8 ·22	1 ·59	22
5	Su 20	9 ·21	2 ·60	23
6	Mo 21	10 ·19	3 ·60	24
7	Tu 22	11 ·14	4 ·57	25
8	We 23	12 ·07	5 ·54	26
9	Th 24	{ 13 ·00 / 14 ·91	6 ·49	27
Pramodhuta Karkata—Adi. 10	Fr 25	—A ·82	7 ·43	28
11	Sa 26	1 ·72	8 ·36	—29
12	Su 27	2 ·62	9 ·29	1
13	Mo 28	3 ·52	10 ·23	2
14	Tu 29	4 ·42	11 ·17	3
15	We 30	5 ·33	12 ·11	4
16	Th 31	6 ·25	13 ·06	5

Aug.

Cyclic Sidereal Year, Month and Day	Week-Day English Month and Day	Tithi Ending Moment	Nakshatra Ending Moment	Muhammadan Year, Month and Day
17	Fr 1	Sukla 7 ·18	14 ·02	6
18	Sa 2	8 ·13	15 ·01	7
19	Su 3	9 ·11	16 ·01	8
20	Mo 4	10 ·10	17 ·03	9
21	Tu 5	11 ·11	18 ·06	10
22	We 6	12 ·15	19 ·12	11
23	Th 7	Sravana 13 ·20	20 ·21	12
24	Fr 8	14 ·27	21 ·31	13
25	Sa 9	P ·35	22 ·41	14
26	Su 10	1 ·44	23 ·51	H. 1349 Rabi-ul-awwal. 15
27	Mo 11	2 ·52	24 ·61	16
28	Tu 12	3 ·59	25 ·71	17
29	We 13	4 ·64	26 ·80	18
30	Th 14	5 ·68	27 ·86	19
31	Fr 15	6 ·71	1 ·90	20
—32	Sa 16	Bahula 7 ·70	2 ·92	21
1	Su 17	8 ·68	3 ·92	22
2	Mo 18	9 ·63	4 ·91	23
3	Tu 19	10 ·57	5 ·88	24
4	We 20	11 ·50	6 ·83	25
5	Th 21	12 ·42	7 ·77	26
Pramodhuta Simha—Avani. 6	Fr 22	13 ·32	8 ·71	27
7	Sa 23	14 ·21	9 ·64	28
8	Su 24	—A ·11	10 ·57	29
9	Mo 25	{ 1 ·01 / 2 ·92	11 ·50	—30
10	Tu 26	Bhad. Suk. 3 ·83	12 ·44	1
11	We 27	4 ·76	13 ·39	Rabi-ul-akhir. 2
12	Th 28	5 ·69	14 ·36	3
13	Fr 29	6 ·64	15 ·34	4
14	Sa 30	7 ·62	16 ·33	5
15	Su 31	8 ·61	17 ·34	6

Sep.

Cyclic Sidereal Year, Month and Day	Week-Day English Month and Day	Tithi Ending Moment	Nakshatra Ending Moment	Muhammadan Year, Month and Day
16	Mo 1	Sukla 9 ·63	18 ·38	7
17	Tu 2	10 ·66	19 ·44	8
18	We 3	11 ·72	20 ·51	9
19	Th 4	12 ·78	21 ·61	10
Pramodhuta Simha—Avani. 20	Fr 5	13 ·85	22 ·71	11
21	Sa 6	14 ·94	23 ·81	12
22	Su 7	Bhadrapada	24 ·92	13
23	Mo 8	P ·02	... ...	14
24	Tu 9	1 ·10	25 ·02	15
25	We 10	2 ·16	26 ·11	16
26	Th 11	3 ·21	27 ·17	17
27	Fr 12	4 ·23	1 ·22	18
28	Sa 13	5 ·23	2 ·24	H. 1349 Rabi-ul-akhir. 19
29	Su 14	Bahula 6 ·20	3 ·26	20
30	Mo 15	7 ·16	4 ·24	21
—31	Tu 16	8 ·11	5 ·21	22
1	We 17	{ 9 ·08 / 10 ·95	6 ·16	23
2	Th 18	11 ·85	7 ·11	24
3	Fr 19	12 ·75	{ 8 ·05 / 9 ·98	25
4	Sa 20	13 ·65	10 ·91	26
5	Su 21	14 ·55	11 ·84	27
6	Mo 22	—A ·45	12 ·78	28
Pramodhuta Kanya—Purattasi. 7	Tu 23	1 ·36	13 ·72	—29
8	We 24	2 ·29	14 ·68	1
9	Th 25	3 ·23	15 ·66	2
10	Fr 26	4 ·18	16 ·65	3
11	Sa 27	5 ·16	17 ·66	4
12	Su 28	Sukla 6 ·15	18 ·69	5
13	Mo 29	7 ·17	19 ·75	6
14	Tu 30	8 ·20	20 ·82	7

Oct.

Cyclic Sidereal Year, Month and Day	Week-Day English Month and Day	Tithi Ending Moment	Nakshatra Ending Moment	Muhammadan Year, Month and Day
15	We 1	9 ·26	21 ·91	8
16	Th 2	10 ·32	... ...	9
17	Fr 3	11 ·41	22 ·00	10
18	Sa 4	12 ·50	23 ·11	11
19	Su 5	Asvina 13 ·58	24 ·22	12
20	Mo 6	14 ·65	25 ·32	13
21	Tu 7	P ·71	26 ·41	14
22	We 8	1 ·76	27 ·48	15
23	Th 9	2 ·79	1 ·53	16
24	Fr 10	3 ·79	2 ·57	H. 1349 Jumadal-awwal. 17
25	Sa 11	4 ·76	3 ·58	18
26	Su 12	5 ·73	4 ·57	19
27	Mo 13	Bahula 6 ·67	5 ·54	20
28	Tu 14	7 ·59	6 ·50	21
29	We 15	8 ·51	7 ·45	22
—30	Th 16	9 ·41	8 ·39	23
1	Fr 17	10 ·31	9 ·32	24
2	Sa 18	11 ·21	10 ·25	25
3	Su 19	12 ·12	11 ·18	26
4	Mo 20	{ 13 ·03 / 14 ·95	12 ·11	27
Pramodhuta Tula—Aippasi. 5	Tu 21	—A ·87	13 ·06	28
6	We 22	1 ·81	{ 14 ·02 / 15 ·99	29
7	Th 23	Sukla 2 ·76	16 ·97	—30
8	Fr 24	3 ·74	17 ·98	1
9	Sa 25	4 ·74	... ...	Jumadal-akhir. 2
10	Su 26	5 ·75	18 ·01	3
11	Mo 27	Karttika 6 ·79	19 ·06	4
12	Tu 28	7 ·86	20 ·12	5
13	We 29	8 ·93	21 ·21	6
14	Th 30	... ...	22 ·30	7
15	Fr 31	9 ·01	23 ·41	8

Nov.

Cyclic Sidereal Year, Month and Day	Week-Day English Month and Day	Tithi Ending Moment	Nakshatra Ending Moment	Muhammadan Year, Month and Day
16	Sa 1	Suk. 10 ·09	24 ·52	9
17	Su 2	11 ·18	25 ·63	10
18	Mo 3	12 ·25	26 ·72	11
19	Tu 4	13 ·32	27 ·79	12
Pramodhuta Tula—Aippasi. 20	We 5	Karttika 14 ·36	1 ·85	13
21	Th 6	P ·38	2 ·89	14
22	Fr 7	1 ·38	3 ·90	15
23	Sa 8	2 ·36	4 ·89	16
24	Su 9	3 ·33	5 ·87	17
25	Mo 10	4 ·27	6 ·83	18
26	Tu 11	5 ·20	7 ·79	19
27	We 12	6 ·11	8 ·73	20
28	Th 13	{ 7 ·02 / 8 ·93	9 ·66	H. 1349 Jumadal-akhir. 21
29	Fr 14	Bahula 9 ·83	10 ·59	22
—30	Sa 15	10 ·73	11 ·52	23
1	Su 16	11 ·63	12 ·46	24
2	Mo 17	12 ·55	13 ·40	25
3	Tu 18	13 ·48	14 ·35	26
4	We 19	14 ·42	15 ·32	27
5	Th 20	—A ·37	16 ·30	28
6	Fr 21	1 ·35	17 ·31	—29
7	Sa 22	2 ·36	18 ·33	1
Pramodhuta Vrischika—Kartigai. 8	Su 23	3 ·38	19 ·37	2
9	Mo 24	4 ·41	20 ·43	3
10	Tu 25	5 ·47	21 ·51	4
11	We 26	6 ·56	22 ·61	5
12	Th 27	7 ·64	23 ·72	6
13	Fr 28	Sukla 8 ·72	24 ·83	7
14	Sa 29	9 ·80	25 ·93	8
15	Su 30	10 ·88	... ...	9

Dec.

Cyclic Sidereal Year, Month and Day	Week-Day English Month and Day	Tithi Ending Moment	Nakshatra Ending Moment	Muhammadan Year, Month and Day
16	Mo 1	11 ·95	26 ·02	10
17	Tu 2	12 ·99	27 ·11	11
18	We 3	... ...	1 ·17	12
19	Th 4	13 ·01	2 ·20	H. 1349 Rajab. 13
20	Fr 5	{ 14 ·01 / P ·99	3 ·22	14
21	Sa 6	Margasira 1 ·95	4 ·22	15
22	Su 7	2 ·89	5 ·20	16
23	Mo 8	3 ·82	6 ·17	17
24	Tu 9	4 ·73	7 ·12	18
25	We 10	5 ·64	8 ·06	19
26	Th 11	6 ·55	{ 9 ·00 / 10 ·93	20
27	Fr 12	7 ·45	11 ·87	21
28	Sa 13	Bahula 8 ·35	12 ·80	22
29	Su 14	9 ·26	13 ·74	23
—30	Mo 15	10 ·18	14 ·68	24
1	Tu 16	11 ·11	15 ·65	25
2	We 17	12 ·06	16 ·63	26
3	Th 18	13 ·02	17 ·63	27
4	Fr 19	{ 14 ·00 / A ·99	18 ·64	28
5	Sa 20	... ...	19 ·68	29
6	Su 21	1 ·02	20 ·74	—30
Pramodhuta Dhanus—Margali. 7	Mo 22	2 ·06	21 ·82	1
8	Tu 23	Sukla 3 ·12	22 ·91	2
9	We 24	4 ·20	... ...	3
10	Th 25	5 ·29	23 ·01	4
11	Fr 26	6 ·38	24 ·12	H. 1349 Shaban. 5
12	Sa 27	7 ·47	25 ·22	6
13	Su 28	Pausha 8 ·54	26 ·32	7
14	Mo 29	9 ·60	27 ·41	8
15	Tu 30	10 ·64	1 ·48	9
16	We 31	11 ·66	2 ·52	10

15. Svati. 16. Visak. 17. Anur. 18. Jyesh. 19. Mula. 20. P. Ash. 21. U. Ash. 22. Sravn. 23. Dani. 24. Satab. 25. P. Bhad. 26. U. Bhad. 27. Rev.

A. D. 1931. **Mesha Sankranti** (Commencement of Indian Sidereal Year).

Solar Eclipse. ● **(Surya Sid.) April 13·64.** **Saka 1853.** **Kaliyuga 5032.**

Lunar Eclipse. ○ **(Arya Sid.) April 13·53.** **(S. Cycle) Prajapati.**

SOLAR reckoning.		LUNAR reckoning.		
Cyclic Sidereal Year, Month and Day.	Week-Day English Month and Day.	Tithi Ending Moment.	Nakshatra Ending Moment.	Muhammadan Year, Month and Day.
	Jan.			
Pramodhuta *Dhanus—Margali.* 17	Th 1	Pausha *Suk.* 12 ·65	3 ·54	11
18	Fr 2	13 ·63	4 ·54	12
19	Sa 3	14 ·60	5 ·53	13
20	Su 4	P ·54	6 ·51	14
21	Mo 5	1 ·46	7 ·46	15
22	Tu 6	2 ·38	8 ·40	16
23	We 7	3 ·29	9 ·33	H. 1349 *Shaban.* 17
24	Th 8	4 ·19	10 ·27	18
25	Fr 9	5 ·10	11 ·20	19
26	Sa 10	*Bahula* 6 ·00 7 ·91	12 ·13	20
27	Su 11	8 ·83	13 ·07	21
28	Mo 12	9 ·75	14 ·02 15 ·99	22
—29	Tu 13	10 ·70	16 96	23
1	We 14	11 ·66	17 ·95	24
2	Th 15	12 ·65	18 ·96	25
3	Fr 16	13 ·65	19 ·99	26
4	Sa 17	14 ·67	... ...	27
5	Su 18	—A ·71	20 ·05	28
6	Mo 19	1 ·78	21 ·12	29
7	Tu 20	2 ·86	22 ·21	1
8	We 21	3 ·94	23 ·31	2
9	Th 22	... ...	24 ·42	3
10	Fr 23	4 ·03	25 ·52	4
Pramodhuta *Makara—Tai.* 11	Sa 24	5 ·12	26 ·63	5
12	Su 25	6 ·19	27 ·72	6
13	Mo 26	*Sukla* 7 ·24	1 ·79	7
14	Tu 27	8 ·29	2 ·83	8
15	We 28	9 ·30	3 ·86	9
16	Th 29	10 ·29	4 ·88	10
17	Fr 30	11 ·27	5 ·87	11
18	Sa 31	12 ·24	6 ·84	12
	Feb.			
19	Su 1	13 ·17	7 ·79	H. 1349 *Ramzan.* 13
20	Mo 2	14 ·09	8 ·74	14
21	Tu 3	Magha P ·01 1 ·92	9 ·68	15
22	We 4	2 ·83	10 ·61	16
23	Th 5	3 72	11 ·54	17
24	Fr 6	4 ·62	12 ·47	18
25	Sa 7	5 ·53	13 ·41	19
26	Su 8	6 ·45	14 ·36	20
27	Mo 9	*Bahula* 7 ·38	15 ·32	21
28	Tu 10	8 ·33	16 ·29	22
—29	We 11	9 ·29	17 ·27	23
1	Th 12	10 ·28	18 ·28	24
2	Fr 13	11 ·28	19 ·30	25
3	Sa 14	12 ·31	20 ·36	26
4	Su 15	13 ·35	21 ·43	27
Pramodhuta *Kumbha—Masi.* 5	Mo 16	14 ·42	22 ·51	28
6	Tu 17	—A ·49	23 ·61	29
7	We 18	1 ·58	24 ·72	—30
8	Th 19	2 ·66	25 ·83	1
9	Fr 20	Phalguna *Sukla* 3 ·74	26 ·93	H. 1349 *Shawwal.* 2
10	Sa 21	4 ·81	... ...	3
11	Su 22	5 ·88	27 ·02	4
12	Mo 23	6 ·92	1 ·09	5
13	Tu 24	7 ·93	2 ·15	6
14	We 25	8 ·92	3 ·19	7
15	Th 26	9 ·89	4 ·20	8
16	Fr 27	10 ·85	5 ·19	9
17	Sa 28	11 ·79	6 ·17	10

SOLAR reckoning.		LUNAR reckoning.		
Cyclic Sidereal Year, Month and Day.	Week-Day English Month and Day.	Tithi Ending Moment.	Nakshatra Ending Moment.	Muhammadan Year, Month and Day.
	March			
Pramodhuta *Kumbha—Masi.* 18	Su 1	*Suk.* 12 ·71	7 ·13	11
19	Mo 2	13 ·62	8 ·08	12
20	Tu 3	Phalguna 14 ·53	9 ·02 10 ·95	13
21	We 4	P ·44	11 ·88	14
22	Th 5	1 ·34	12 ·81	15
23	Fr 6	2 ·24	13 ·75	H. 1349 *Shawwal.* 16
24	Sa 7	3 ·15	14 ·70	17
25	Su 8	4 ·06 5 ·99	15 ·65	18
26	Mo 9	6 ·93	16 ·61	19
27	Tu 10	*Bahula* 7 ·90	17 ·60	20
28	We 11	8 ·88	18 ·60	21
29	Th 12	9 ·88	19 ·63	22
—30	Fr 13	10 ·91	20 ·67	23
1	Sa 14	11 ·94	21 ·73	24
2	Su 15	... ...	22 ·81	25
3	Mo 16	12 ·01	23 ·91	26
4	Tu 17	13 ·09	... ...	27
5	We 18	14 ·18	24 ·02	28
6	Th 19	—A ·27	25 ·13	—29
7	Fr 20	1 ·36	26 ·23	1
8	Sa 21	2 ·42	27 ·32	2
9	Su 22	3 ·48	1 ·40	3
10	Mo 23	4 ·51	2 ·47	4
Pramodhuta *Mina—Panguni.* 11	Tu 24	5 ·52	3 ·51	5
12	We 25	6 ·51	4 ·52	6
13	Th 26	*Sukla* 7 ·48	5 ·52	7
14	Fr 27	8 ·43	6 ·50	8
15	Sa 28	9 ·37	7 ·47	9
16	Su 29	10 ·30	8 ·42	10
17	Mo 30	11 ·21	9 ·36	11
18	Tu 31	12 ·11	10 ·29	12
	April			
19	We 1	Chaitra 13 ·00 14 ·90	11 ·22	H. 1349 *Zi-l-ka'da.* 13
20	Th ○ 2	P ·81	12 ·15	14
21	Fr 3	1 ·72	13 ·09	15
22	Sa 4	2 ·64	14 ·03 15 ·98	16
23	Su 5	3 ·56	16 ·94	17
24	Mo 6	4 ·50	17 ·92	18
25	Tu 7	5 ·47	18 ·93	19
26	We 8	6 ·45	19 ·94	20
27	Th 9	*Bahula* 7 ·44	20 ·98	21
28	Fr 10	8 ·47	... ...	22
29	Sa 11	9 ·51	21 ·04	23
30	Su 12	10 ·57	22 ·12	24
—31	Mo 13	11 ·65	23 ·22	25
1	Tu 14	12 ·74	24 ·32	26
2	We 15	13 ·82	25 ·43	27
3	Th 16	14 ·90	26 ·53	28
4	Fr 17	—A ·97	27 ·63	29
5	Sa 18	... ...	1 ·72	—30
6	Su 19	1 ·03	2 ·78	1
7	Mo 20	*Sukla* 2 ·06	3 ·82	2
Prajapati *Mesha—Chittirai.* 8	Tu 21	3 ·07	4 ·84	H 1349 *Zi-l-hijja.* 3
9	We 22	4 ·05	5 ·84	4
10	Th 23	5 ·02 6 ·97	6 ·83	5
11	Fr 24	7 ·91	7 ·80	6
12	Sa 25	Vaisakha 8 ·84	8 ·75	7
13	Su 26	9 ·75	9 ·69	8
14	Mo 27	10 ·65	10 ·63	9
15	Tu 28	11 ·55	11 ·57	10
16	We 29	12 ·45	12 ·50	11
17	Th 30	13 ·35	13 ·43	12

SOLAR reckoning.		LUNAR reckoning.		
Cyclic Sidereal Year, Month and Day.	Week-Day English Month and Day.	Tithi Ending Moment.	Nakshatra Ending Moment.	Muhammadan Year, Month and Day.
	May			
18	Fr 1	14 ·25	14 ·37	13
19	Sa 2	P ·17	15 ·31	14
20	Su 3	1 ·09	16 ·27	15
Prajapati *Mesha—Chittirai.* 21	Mo 4	Vaisakha 2 ·04 3 ·99	17 ·26	16
22	Tu 5	4 ·97	18 ·25	H. 1349 *Zi-l-hijja.* 17
23	We 6	5 ·97	19 ·26	18
24	Th 7	... ...	20 ·29	19
25	Fr 8	6 ·00	21 ·35	20
26	Sa 9	7 ·05	22 ·43	21
27	Su 10	8 ·10	23 ·52	22
28	Mo 11	9 ·17	24 ·62	23
29	Tu 12	*Bahula* 10 ·25	25 ·73	24
—30	We 13	11 ·34	26 ·83	25
1	Th 14	12 ·42	27 ·93	26
2	Fr 15	13 ·48	... ...	27
3	Sa 16	14 ·54	1 ·02	28
4	Su 17	—A ·57	2 09	29
5	Mo 18	1 ·59	3 ·14	—30
6	Tu 19	2 ·57	4 ·16	1
7	We 20	3 ·54	5 ·17	2
8	Th 21	4 ·49	6 ·16	3
9	Fr 22	5 ·43	7 ·13	4
10	Sa 23	6 ·35	8 ·09	5
11	Su 24	*Sukla* 7 ·25	9 ·03 10 ·97	6
Brajapati *Vrishabha—Vaikasi.* 12	Mo 25	8 ·15	11 ·91	7
13	Tu 26	9 ·05 10 ·95	12 84	8
14	We 27	11 ·85	13 ·77	*Muharram.* 9
15	Th 28	12 ·76	14 ·70	10
16	Fr 29	13 ·67	15 ·65	11
17	Sa 30	14 ·60	16 ·61	12
18	Su 31	P ·54	17 ·53	13
	June			
19	Mo 1	Jyeshtha 1 ·49	18 ·57	H. 1350 14
20	Tu 2	2 ·48	19 ·58	15
21	We 3	3 ·48	20 ·61	16
22	Th 4	4 ·50	21 ·67	17
23	Fr 5	5 ·53	22 ·74	18
24	Sa 6	6 ·59	23 ·82	19
25	Su 7	7 ·66	24 ·92	20
26	Mo 8	*Bahula* 8 ·74	... ...	21
27	Tu 9	9 ·83	25 ·02	22
28	We 10	10 ·91	26 ·13	23
29	Th 11	11 ·97	27 ·24	24
30	Fr 12	... ...	1 ·33	25
31	Sa 13	12 ·02	2 ·40	26
—32	Su 14	13 ·06	3 ·45	27
1	Mo 15	14 ·06	4 ·48	28
2	Tu 16	—A ·05	5 ·50	29
3	We 17	1 ·03 2 ·98	6 ·49	—30
4	Th 18	3 ·92	7 ·46	1
5	Fr 19	4 ·84	8 ·42	2
Prajapati *Mithuna—Ani.* 6	Sa 20	Adh. Ashadha *Sukla* 5 ·75	9 ·37	3
7	Su 21	6 ·65	10 ·31	4
8	Mo 22	7 ·55	11 ·24	H. 1350 *Safar.* 5
9	Tu 23	8 ·45	12 ·17	6
10	We 24	9 ·35	13 ·10	7
11	Th 25	10 ·25	14 ·04 15 ·99	8
12	Fr 26	11 ·16	16 ·94	9
13	Sa 27	12 ·08	17 ·91	10
14	Su 28	13 ·02 14 ·97	18 ·90	11
15	Mo 29	P ·95	19 ·90	12
16	Tu 30	1 ·94	20 ·93	13

Naksh :—1. Asvn. 2. Bhar. 3. Krit. 4. Rohi. 5. Mrig. 6. Ardh. 7. Punar. 8. Push. 9. Aslesh. 10. Magh. 11. P. Phal. 12. U. Phal. 13. Hasta. 14. Chit.

A. D. 1931.
A.—Amavasya.
P.—Paurnami.

Kollam 1107, Commences { N. Malabar—Sept. / S. Malabar—Aug.

Hijra 1350, Commences, May 19.

Vikrama 1988.
Bengal San. 1337.
(N. Cycle) Subhanu.

Columns: SOLAR reckoning — Cyclic Sidereal Year, Month and Day; Week-Day English Month and Day. LUNAR reckoning — Tithi Ending Moment; Nakshatra Ending Moment; Muhammadan Year, Month and Day.

July (Solar: Prajapati Mithuna—Ani; Lunar: Adhika Ashadha, Bahula / Sukla, Nija Ashadha; Muhammadan: H. 1350 Safar / Rabi-ul-awwal)

Cyclic Sidereal	Week-Day	Day	Tithi	Moment	Nakshatra	Moment	Muhammadan
17	We	1	2	·97	21	·97	14
18	Th	2	...	...	...	...	15
19	Fr	3	3	·01	22	·04	16
20	Sa	4	4	·06	23	·12	17
21	Su	5	5	·13	24	·22	18
22	Mo	6	6	·21	25	·33	19
23	Tu	7	7	·29	26	·44	20
24	We	8	8	·38	27	·54	21
25	Th	9	9	·45	1	·63	22
26	Fr	10	10	·49	2	·71	23
27	Sa	11	11	·53	3	·76	24
28	Su	12	12	·54	4	·81	25
29	Mo	13	13	·54	5	·82	26
30	Tu	14	14	·50	6	·82	27
—31	We	15	—A	·45	7	·79	28
1	Th	16	1	·40	8	·75	—29
2	Fr	17	2	·32	9	·71	1
3	Sa	18	3	·23	10	·65	2
4	Su	19	4	·13	11	·58	3
5	Mo	20	5 / 6	·03 / ·93	12	·51	4
6	Tu	21	7	·83	13	·44	5
7	We	22	8	·73	14	·38	6
8	Th	23	9	·64	15	·33	7
9	Fr	24	10	·56	16	·28	8
10	Sa	25	11	·50	17	·24	9
11	Su	26	12	·46	18	·22	10
12	Mo	27	13	·44	19	·22	11
13	Tu	28	14	·43	20	·25	12
14	We	29	P	·45	21	·28	13
15	Th	30	1	·48	22	·34	14
16	Fr	31	2	·53	23	·42	15.

Aug. (Solar: Prajapati Karkata—Adi / Prajapati Simha—Avani; Lunar: Bahula / Sukla, Sravana, Bah.; Muhammadan: H. 1350 / H. 1350 Rabi-ul-akhir)

Cyclic Sidereal	Week-Day	Day	Tithi	Moment	Nakshatra	Moment	Muhammadan
17	Sa	1	3	·60	24	·52	16
18	Su	2	4	·69	25	·63	17
19	Mo	3	5	·77	26	·74	18
20	Tu	4	6	·85	27	·84	19
21	We	5	7	·92	1	·93	20
22	Th	6	8	·97	...	...	21
23	Fr	7	...	...	2	·01	22
24	Sa	8	9	·02	3	·08	23
25	Su	9	10	·03	4	·12	24
26	Mo	10	11 / 12	·02 / ·99	5	·14	25
27	Tu	11	13	·95	6	·14	26
28	We	12	14	·90	7	·12	27
29	Th	13	—A	·82	8	·10	28
30	Fr	14	1	·73	9 / 10	·05 / ·99	29
31	Sa	15	2	·63	11	·92	—30
—32	Su	16	3	·53	12	·85	1
1	Mo	17	4	·43	13	·78	2
2	Tu	18	5	·33	14	·72	3
3	We	19	6	·23	15	·66	4
4	Th	20	7	·15	16	·61	5
5	Fr	21	8	·07	17	·57	6
6	Sa	22	9 / 10	·01 / ·95	18	·55	7
7	Su	23	11	·93	19	·55	8
8	Mo	24	12	·93	20	·56	9
9	Tu	25	13	·94	21	·60	10
10	We	26	14	·99	22	·65	11
11	Th	27	...	...	23	·73	12
12	Fr	28	P	·04	24	·83	13
13	Sa	29	1	·10	25	·93	14
14	Su	30	2	·18	...	...	15
15	Mo	31	3	·26	26	·03	16

Sep. (Solar: Prajapati Simha—Avani; Lunar: Sravana, Bahula / Sukla, Bhadrapada; Muhammadan: H. 1350 Rabi-ul-akhir / Jumadal-awwal)

Cyclic Sidereal	Week-Day	Day	Tithi	Moment	Nakshatra	Moment	Muhammadan
16	Tu	1	4	·36	27	·14	17
17	We	2	5	·43	1	·24	18
18	Th	3	6	·49	2	·33	19
19	Fr	4	7	·52	3	·39	20
20	Sa	5	8	·55	4	·44	21
21	Su	6	9	·53	5	·46	22
22	Mo	7	10	·50	6	·47	23
23	Tu	8	11	·47	7	·46	24
24	We	9	12	·41	8	·43	25
25	Th	10	13	·33	9	·38	26
26	Fr	11	14	·24	10	·33	27
27	Sa	12	—A	·15	11	·26	28
28	Su	13	1 / 2	·05 / ·95	12	·19	—29
29	Mo	14	3	·85	13	·12	1
30	Tu	15	4	·75	14	·06	2
—31	We	16	5	·67	15 / 16	·00 / ·94	3
1	Th	17	6	·59	17	·90	4
2	Fr	18	7	·53	18	·88	5
3	Sa	19	8	·48	19	·87	6
4	Su	20	9	·46	20	·88	7
5	Mo	21	10	·46	21	·91	8
6	Tu	22	11	·47	22	·96	9
7	We	23	12	·52	...	...	10
8	Th	24	13	·57	23	·04	11
9	Fr	25	14	·64	24	·13	12
10	Sa ○	26	P	·72	25	·23	13
11	Su	27	1	·81	26	·33	14
12	Mo	28	2	·89	27	·44	15
13	Tu	29	3	·97	1	·55	16
14	We	30	...	...	2	·63	17

Oct. (Solar: Prajapati Kanya—Purattasi / Prajapati Tula—Aippasi; Lunar: Bahula / Sukla, Asvina, Bah.; Muhammadan: H. 1350 / H. 1350 Jumadal-akhir)

Cyclic Sidereal	Week-Day	Day	Tithi	Moment	Nakshatra	Moment	Muhammadan
15	Th	1	4	·03	3	·70	18
16	Fr	2	5	·06	4	·75	19
17	Sa	3	6	·08	5	·78	20
18	Su	4	7	·08	6	·79	21
19	Mo	5	8	·06	7	·79	22
20	Tu	6	9 / 10	·03 / ·96	8	·76	23
21	We	7	11	·88	9	·72	24
22	Th	8	12	·79	10	·66	25
23	Fr	9	13	·70	11	·60	26
24	Sa	10	14	·61	12	·54	27
25	Su	11	—A	·51	13	·47	28
26	Mo	12	1	·41	14	·40	29
27	Tu	13	2	·32	15	·33	—30
28	We	14	3	·24	16	·28	1
29	Th	15	4	·16	17	·24	2
—30	Fr	16	5	·11	18	·21	3
1	Sa	17	6	·06	19	·19	4
2	Su	18	7	·04	20	·20	5
3	Mo	19	8	·03	21	·22	6
4	Tu	20	9	·05	22	·28	7
5	We	21	10	·10	23	·34	8
6	Th	22	11	·15	24	·43	9
7	Fr	23	12	·22	25	·52	10
8	Sa	24	13	·30	26	·63	11
9	Su	25	14	·40	27	·74	12
10	Mo	26	P	·48	1	·85	13
11	Tu	27	1	·56	2	·94	14
12	We	28	2	·61	...	...	15
13	Th	29	3	·65	3	·01	16
14	Fr	30	4	·68	4	·06	17
15	Sa	31	5	·67	5	·10	18

Nov. (Solar: Prajapati Tula—Aippasi; Lunar: Asvina, Bahula / Sukla, Karttika; Muhammadan: H. 1350 Jumadal-akhir / H. 1350 Rajab)

Cyclic Sidereal	Week-Day	Day	Tithi	Moment	Nakshatra	Moment	Muhammadan
16	Su	1	6	·65	6	·12	19
17	Mo	2	7	·61	7	·11	20
18	Tu	3	8	·56	8	·09	21
19	We	4	9	·49	9	·05	22
20	Th	5	10	·40	10 / 11	·00 / ·95	23
21	Fr	6	11	·30	12	·88	24
22	Sa	7	12	·20	13	·81	25
23	Su	8	13	·10	14	·74	26
24	Mo	9	14 / A	·01 / ·92	15	·67	27
25	Tu	10	1	·84	16	·62	28
26	We	11	2	·77	17	·57	—29
27	Th	12	3	·70	18	·54	1
28	Fr	13	4	·66	19	·52	2
29	Sa	14	5	·65	20	·52	3
—30	Su	15	6	·64	21	·55	4
1	Mo	16	7	·66	22	·59	5
2	Tu	17	8	·71	23	·65	6
3	We	18	9	·77	24	·73	7
4	Th	19	10	·85	25	·82	8
5	Fr	20	11	·93	26	·93	9
6	Sa	21	...	...	...	...	10
7	Su	22	12	·02	27	·04	11
8	Mo	23	13	·10	1	·15	12
9	Tu	24	14	·18	2	·24	13
10	We	25	P	·23	3	·32	14
11	Th	26	1	·28	4	·39	15
12	Fr	27	2	·30	5	·42	16
13	Sa	28	3	·30	6	·44	17
14	Su	29	4	·27	7	·44	18
15	Mo	30	5	·22	8	·42	19

Dec. (Solar: Prajapati Vrischika—Kartigai / Prajapati Dhanus—Margali; Lunar: Bahula / Sukla, Margasira, Bahula; Muhammadan: H. 1350 Shaban)

Cyclic Sidereal	Week-Day	Day	Tithi	Moment	Nakshatra	Moment	Muhammadan
16	Tu	1	6	·17	9	·38	20
17	We	2	7	·10	10	·34	21
18	Th	3	8 / 9	·02 / ·93	11	·28	22
19	Fr	4	10	·83	12	·21	23
20	Sa	5	11	·73	13	·14	24
21	Su	6	12	·63	14	·08	25
22	Mo	7	13	·54	15 / 16	·02 / ·96	26
23	Tu	8	14	·46	17	·90	27
24	We	9	—A	·39	18	·87	28
25	Th	10	1	·33	19	·85	29
26	Fr	11	2	·30	20	·85	—30
27	Sa	12	3	·28	21	·86	1
28	Su	13	4	·27	22	·90	2
29	Mo	14	5	·31	23	·96	3
—30	Tu	15	6	·35	...	...	4
1	We	16	7	·42	24	·03	5
2	Th	17	8	·50	25	·13	6
3	Fr	18	9	·59	26	·23	7
4	Sa	19	10	·67	27	·34	8
5	Su	20	11	·75	1	·45	9
6	Mo	21	12	·83	2	·54	10
7	Tu	22	13	·88	3	·63	11
8	We	23	14	·92	4	·70	12
9	Th	24	P	·94	5	·74	13
10	Fr	25	1	·94	6	·76	14
11	Sa	26	2	·91	7	·76	15
12	Su	27	3	·88	8	·75	16
13	Mo	28	4	·82	9	·72	17
14	Tu	29	5	·74	10	·68	18
15	We	30	6	·66	11	·62	19
16	Th	31	7	·56	12	·55	20

15. Svati. 16. Visak. 17. Anur. 18. Jyesh. 19. Mula. 20. P. Ash. 21. U. Ash. 22. Sravn. 23. Dani. 24. Satab. 25. P. Bhad. 26. U. Bhad. 27. Rev.

A. D. 1932. **Mesha Sankranti** (Commencement of Indian Sidereal Year).
Solar Eclipse. ● **(Surya Sid.) April 12·90.** **Saka 1854.** **Kaliyuga 5033.**
Lunar Eclipse. ○ **(Arya Sid.) April 12·79.** **(S. Cycle) Angirasa.**

SOLAR reckoning: Cyclic Sidereal Year, Month and Day; Week-Day English Month and Day. LUNAR reckoning: Tithi Ending Moment; Nakshatra Ending Moment; Muhammadan Year, Month and Day.

Jan.

Cyclic Sidereal Year, Month and Day	Week-Day English Month and Day	Tithi Ending Moment	Nakshatra Ending Moment	Muhammadan Year, Month and Day
Prajapati, Dhanus—Margali 17	Fr 1	Mar. Bah. 8 ·46	13 ·48	H. 1350 Shaban 21
18	Sa 2	9 ·36	14 ·41	22
19	Su 3	10 ·27	15 ·35	23
20	Mo 4	11 ·18	16 ·29	24
21	Tu 5	12 ·11	17 ·24	25
22	We 6	13 ·04 / 14 ·98	18 ·20	26
23	Th 7	—A ·94	19 ·18	27
24	Fr 8	1 ·93	20 ·17	28
25	Sa 9	2 ·93	21 ·18	—29
26	Su 10	3 ·95	22 ·21	H. 1350 Ramzan 1
27	Mo 11	... ...	23 ·26	2
28	Tu 12	4 ·01	24 ·34	3
—29	We 13	5 ·07	25 ·43	4
Prajapati, Makara—Tai 1	Th 14	Sukla 6 ·14	26 ·53	5
2	Fr 15	7 ·23	27 ·64	6
3	Sa 16	8 ·33	1 ·74	7
4	Su 17	9 ·42	2 ·84	8
5	Mo 18	10 ·48	3 ·94	9
6	Tu 19	11 ·53	... ...	10
7	We 20	12 ·57	4 ·01	11
8	Th 21	13 ·58	5 ·05	12
9	Fr 22	14 ·58	6 ·08	13
10	Sa 23	Pausha P ·56	7 ·09	14
11	Su 24	1 ·52	8 ·08	15
12	Mo 25	2 ·45	9 ·06	16
13	Tu 26	3 ·37	10 ·01 / 11 ·95	17
14	We 27	4 ·29	12 ·89	18
15	Th 28	5 ·20	13 ·83	19
16	Fr 29	6 ·10	14 ·76	20
17	Sa 30	7 ·00 / 8 ·90	15 ·69	21
18	Su 31	9 ·81	16 ·63	22

Feb.

Cyclic Sidereal Year, Month and Day	Week-Day English Month and Day	Tithi Ending Moment	Nakshatra Ending Moment	Muhammadan Year, Month and Day
19	Mo 1	Bahula 10 ·78	17 ·57	23
20	Tu 2	11 ·67	18 ·54	24
21	We 3	12 ·62	19 ·51	25
22	Th 4	13 ·58	20 ·49	26
23	Fr 5	14 ·56	21 ·50	27
24	Sa 6	—A ·56	22 ·52	28
25	Su 7	1 ·60	23 ·57	29
26	Mo 8	2 ·65	24 ·65	—30
27	Tu 9	3 ·71	25 ·73	H. 1350 Shawwal 1
28	We 10	4 ·79	26 ·83	2
29	Th 11	5 ·87	27 ·94	3
—30	Fr 12	6 ·96	... ...	4
Prajapati, Kumbha—Masi 1	Sa 13	Sukla	1 ·05	5
2	Su 14	7 ·06	2 ·15	6
3	Mo 15	8 ·12	3 ·24	7
4	Tu 16	9 ·17	4 ·31	8
5	We 17	10 ·21	5 ·37	9
6	Th 18	11 ·22	6 ·40	10
7	Fr 19	Magha 12 ·21	7 ·42	11
8	Sa 20	13 ·19	8 ·41	12
9	Su 21	14 ·13	9 ·39	13
10	Mo 22	P ·06 / 1 ·99	10 ·35	14
11	Tu 23	2 ·91	11 ·29	15
12	We 24	3 ·82	12 ·23	16
13	Th 25	4 ·72	13 ·17	17
14	Fr 26	5 ·62	14 ·10	18
15	Sa 27	Bahula 6 ·52	15 ·03 / 16 ·96	19
16	Su 28	7 ·43	17 ·91	20
17	Mo 29	8 ·35	18 ·87	21

March

Cyclic Sidereal Year, Month and Day	Week-Day English Month and Day	Tithi Ending Moment	Nakshatra Ending Moment	Muhammadan Year, Month and Day
Prajapati, Kumbha—Masi 18	Tu 1	Mag. Bah. 9 ·28	19 ·83	Shawwal 22
19	We 2	10 ·23	20 ·82	23
20	Th 3	11 ·19	21 ·82	24
21	Fr 4	12 ·18	22 ·84	25
22	Sa 5	13 ·18	23 ·89	26
23	Su 6	14 ·21	24 ·95	27
24	Mo 7	—A ·26	... ...	28
25	Tu 8	1 ·32	25 ·03	—29
26	We 9	2 ·40	26 ·13	H. 1350 Zi-l-ka'da 1
27	Th 10	3 ·49	27 ·23	2
28	Fr 11	4 ·58	1 ·34	3
29	Sa 12	5 ·66	2 ·45	4
—30	Su 13	6 ·72	3 ·55	5
Prajapati, Mina—Panguni 1	Mo 14	Sukla 7 ·77	4 ·62	6
2	Tu 15	8 ·80	5 ·68	7
3	We 16	9 ·81	6 ·73	8
4	Th 17	10 ·80	7 ·74	9
5	Fr 18	11 ·78	8 ·74	10
6	Sa 19	12 ·73	9 ·72	11
7	Su 20	Phalguna 13 ·67	10 ·68	12
8	Mo 21	14 ·59	11 ·64	13
9	Tu ○ 22	P ·50	12 ·58	14
10	We 23	1 ·40	13 ·51	15
11	Th 24	2 ·30	14 ·44	16
12	Fr 25	3 ·20	15 ·37	17
13	Sa 26	4 ·11	16 ·30	18
14	Su 27	Bahula 5 ·02 / 6 ·94	17 ·25	19
15	Mo 28	7 ·87	18 ·20	20
16	Tu 29	8 ·81	19 ·16	21
17	We 30	9 ·77	20 ·14	22
18	Th 31	10 ·76	21 ·14	23

April

Cyclic Sidereal Year, Month and Day	Week-Day English Month and Day	Tithi Ending Moment	Nakshatra Ending Moment	Muhammadan Year, Month and Day
19	Fr 1	11 ·76	22 ·16	24
20	Sa 2	12 ·79	23 ·20	25
21	Su 3	13 ·83	24 ·26	26
22	Mo 4	14 ·90	25 ·34	27
23	Tu 5	—A ·98	26 ·43	28
24	We 6	... ...	27 ·54	29
25	Th 7	1 ·06	1 ·65	—30
26	Fr 8	2 ·15	2 ·75	H. 1350 Zi-l-hijja 1
27	Sa 9	3 ·23	3 ·85	2
28	Su 10	4 ·28	4 ·93	3
29	Mo 11	5 ·33	... ...	4
—30	Tu 12	6 ·37	5 ·00	5
Angirasa, Mesha—Chittirai 1	We 13	Sukla 7 ·37	6 ·04	6
2	Th 14	8 ·36	7 ·06	7
3	Fr 15	9 ·33	8 ·06	8
4	Sa 16	10 ·28	9 ·04	9
5	Su 17	11 ·22	10 ·02 / 11 ·97	10
6	Mo 18	12 ·14	12 ·91	11
7	Tu 19	Chaitra 13 ·06 / 14 ·96	13 ·85	12
8	We 20	P ·86	14 ·78	13
9	Th 21	1 ·76	15 ·71	14
10	Fr 22	2 ·66	16 ·65	15
11	Sa 23	3 ·56	17 ·59	16
12	Su 24	4 ·47	18 ·53	17
13	Mo 25	5 ·41	19 ·49	18
14	Tu 26	6 ·35	20 ·47	19
15	We 27	Bahula 7 ·32	21 ·47	20
16	Th 28	8 ·30	22 ·48	21
17	Fr 29	9 ·29	23 ·51	22
18	Sa 30	10 ·32	24 ·57	23

May

Cyclic Sidereal Year, Month and Day	Week-Day English Month and Day	Tithi Ending Moment	Nakshatra Ending Moment	Muhammadan Year, Month and Day
Angirasa, Mesha—Chittirai 19	Su 1	Ch. Bah. 11 ·36	25 ·64	Zi-l-hijja 24
20	Mo 2	12 ·43	26 ·74	25
21	Tu 3	13 ·50	27 ·84	26
22	We 4	14 ·59	1 ·95	27
23	Th 5	—A ·67	... ...	28
24	Fr 6	1 ·74	2 ·05	—29
25	Sa 7	2 ·81	3 ·15	H. 1351 Muharram 1
26	Su 8	3 ·86	4 ·24	2
27	Mo 9	4 ·90	5 ·31	3
28	Tu 10	Sukla 5 ·90	6 ·36	4
29	We 11	6 ·89	7 ·38	5
30	Th 12	7 ·86	8 ·39	6
—31	Fr 13	8 ·81	9 ·37	7
Angirasa, Vrishabha—Vaikasi 1	Sa 14	9 ·74	10 ·35	8
2	Su 15	10 ·66	11 ·31	9
3	Mo 16	11 ·57	12 ·25	10
4	Tu 17	Vaisakha 12 ·47	13 ·19	11
5	We 18	13 ·37	14 ·13	12
6	Th 19	14 ·27	15 ·06 / 16 ·99	13
7	Fr 20	P ·17	17 ·92	14
8	Sa 21	1 ·07 / 2 ·98	18 ·87	15
9	Su 22	3 ·91	19 ·82	16
10	Mo 23	4 ·85	20 ·80	17
11	Tu 24	5 ·82	21 ·79	18
12	We 25	Bahula 6 ·80	22 ·80	19
13	Th 26	7 ·80	23 ·83	20
14	Fr 27	8 ·81	24 ·88	21
15	Sa 28	9 ·86	25 ·95	22
16	Su 29	10 ·92	... ...	23
17	Mo 30	11 ·99	26 ·04	24
18	Tu 31	... ...	27 ·14	25

June

Cyclic Sidereal Year, Month and Day	Week-Day English Month and Day	Tithi Ending Moment	Nakshatra Ending Moment	Muhammadan Year, Month and Day
19	We 1	12 ·08	1 ·24	26
20	Th 2	13 ·16	2 ·35	27
21	Fr 3	14 ·24	3 ·46	28
22	Sa 4	—A ·31	4 ·55	29
23	Su 5	1 ·35	5 ·62	—30
24	Mo 6	2 ·39	6 ·67	H. 1351 Safar 1
25	Tu 7	3 ·39	7 ·70	2
26	We 8	4 ·38	8 ·71	3
27	Th 9	5 ·35	9 ·71	4
28	Fr 10	Sukla 6 ·31	10 ·68	5
29	Sa 11	7 ·24	11 ·64	6
30	Su 12	8 ·16	12 ·59	7
—31	Mo 13	9 ·07 / 10 ·97	13 ·53	8
Angirasa, Mithuna—Ani 1	Tu 14	11 ·87	14 ·46	9
2	We 15	12 ·77	15 ·39	10
3	Th 16	Jyeshtha 13 ·67	16 ·32	11
4	Fr 17	14 ·57	17 ·26	12
5	Sa 18	P ·48	18 ·20	13
6	Su 19	1 ·41	19 ·16	14
7	Mo 20	2 ·35	20 ·13	15
8	Tu 21	3 ·30	21 ·12	16
9	We 22	4 ·28	22 ·12	17
10	Th 23	5 ·28	23 ·14	18
11	Fr 24	6 ·29	24 ·19	19
12	Sa 25	Bahula 7 ·34	25 ·26	20
13	Su 26	8 ·40	26 ·34	21
14	Mo 27	9 ·47	27 ·44	22
15	Tu 28	10 ·55	1 ·54	23
16	We 29	11 ·63	2 ·65	24
17	Th 30	12 ·72	3 ·76	25

Naksh :—1. Asvn. 2. Bhar. 3. Krit. 4. Rohi. 5. Mrig. 6. Ardh. 7. Punar. 8. Push. 9. Aslesh. 10. Magh. 11. P. Phal. 12. U. Phal. 13. Hasta. 14. Chit.

A. D. 1932.
A.—Amavasya.
P.—Paurnami.

Kollam 1108, Commences { N. Malabar—Sept. / S. Malabar—Aug.

Hijra 1351, Commences, May 7.

Vikrama 1989.
Bengal San 1338.
(N. Cycle) Tarana.

SOLAR reckoning: Cyclic Sidereal Year, Month and Day; Week-Day English Month and Day. LUNAR reckoning: Tithi Ending Moment; Nakshatra Ending Moment; Muhammadan Year, Month and Day.

July

Solar: Angirasa Mithuna—Ani. (18–32); Angirasa Karkata—Adi. (1–16)
Lunar: Bah. (13–A); Sukla; Ashadha; Bahula
Muhammadan: Safar. (26–29); H. 1351 Rabi-ul-awwal. (1–27)

Cyclic Sidereal Year, Month and Day	Week-Day	English Day	Tithi	Tithi Moment	Nakshatra	Nakshatra Moment	Muhammadan Year, Month and Day
18	Fr	1	13	·78	4	·85	26
19	Sa	2	14	·83	5	·93	27
20	Su	3	—A	·87	6	·98	28
21	Mo	4	1	·88	...	...	—29
22	Tu	5	2	·86	7	·02	1
23	We	6	3	·83	8	·04	2
24	Th	7	4	·78	9	·04	3
25	Fr	8	5	·71	10 / 11	·01 / ·97	4
26	Sa	9	6	·64	12	·92	5
27	Su	10	7	·54	13	·87	6
28	Mo	11	8	·44	14	·80	7
29	Tu	12	9	·34	15	·73	8
30	We	13	10	·24	16	·66	9
31	Th	14	11	·14	17	·60	10
—32	Fr	15	12 / 13	·04 / ·96	18	·55	11
1	Sa	16	14	·88	19	·50	12
2	Su	17	P	·82	20	·46	13
3	Mo	18	1	·78	21	·44	14
4	Tu	19	2	·77	22	·44	15
5	We	20	3	·76	23	·47	16
6	Th	21	4	·77	24	·51	17
7	Fr	22	5	·82	25	·56	18
8	Sa	23	6	·87	26	·64	19
9	Su	24	7	·94	27	·74	20
10	Mo	25	...	...	1	·85	21
11	Tu	26	8	·02	2	·96	22
12	We	27	9	·11	...	...	23
13	Th	28	10	·18	3	·06	24
14	Fr	29	11	·25	4	·15	25
15	Sa	30	12	·31	5	·23	26
16	Su	31	13	·34	6	·29	27

Aug.

Solar: Angirasa Simha—Avani. (1–16)
Lunar: Sukla; Sravana; Bahula
Muhammadan: H. 1351 Rabi-ul-akhir. (1–28)

Cyclic Sidereal Year, Month and Day	Week-Day	English Day	Tithi	Tithi Moment	Nakshatra	Nakshatra Moment	Muhammadan Year, Month and Day
17	Mo	1	14	·36	7	·34	28
18	Tu	2	—A	·34	8	·36	29
19	We	3	1	·32	9	·36	—30
20	Th	4	2	·27	10	·34	1
21	Fr	5	3	·21	11	·31	2
22	Sa	6	4	·13	12	·27	3
23	Su	7	5 / 6	·04 / ·94	13	·21	4
24	Mo	8	7	·84	14	·14	5
25	Tu	9	8	·74	15	·07	6
26	We	10	9	·64	16 / 17	·00 / ·94	7
27	Th	11	10	·55	18	·88	8
28	Fr	12	11	·46	19	·83	9
29	Sa	13	12	·37	20	·79	10
30	Su	14	13	·31	21	·76	11
—31	Mo	15	14	·27	22	·76	12
1	Tu	16	P	·26	23	·78	13
2	We	17	1	·26	24	·82	14
3	Th	18	2	·27	25	·87	15
4	Fr	19	3	·30	26	·95	16
5	Sa	20	4	·36	...	...	17
6	Su	21	5	·43	27	·04	18
7	Mo	22	6	·51	1	·15	19
8	Tu	23	7	·59	2	·25	20
9	We	24	8	·68	3	·36	21
10	Th	25	9	·76	4	·46	22
11	Fr	26	10	·81	5	·54	23
12	Sa	27	11	·85	6	·61	24
13	Su	28	12	·87	7	·66	25
14	Mo	29	13	·85	8	·68	26
15	Tu	30	14	·82	9	·69	27
16	We	31	—A	·78	10	·67	28

Sep.

Solar: Angirasa Simha—Avani. (17–31); Angirasa Kanya—Purattasi. (1–15)
Lunar: Sukla; Bhadrapada; Bahula
Muhammadan: H. 1351 Jumadal-awwal. (1–29)

Cyclic Sidereal Year, Month and Day	Week-Day	English Day	Tithi	Tithi Moment	Nakshatra	Nakshatra Moment	Muhammadan Year, Month and Day
17	Th	1	1	·72	11	·65	—29
18	Fr	2	2	·64	12	·60	1
19	Sa	3	3	·55	13	·54	2
20	Su	4	4	·45	14	·48	3
21	Mo	5	5	·35	15	·41	4
22	Tu	6	6	·25	16	·34	5
23	We	7	7	·15	17	·28	6
24	Th	8	8 / 9	·06 / ·97	18	·22	7
25	Fr	9	10	·90	19	·16	8
26	Sa	10	11	·84	20	·12	9
27	Su	11	12	·80	21	·09	10
28	Mo	12	13	·78	22	·09	11
29	Tu	13	14	·78	23	·10	12
30	We ○	14	P	·79	24	·13	13
—31	Th	15	1	·83	25	·18	14
1	Fr	16	2	·89	26	·25	15
2	Sa	17	3	·96	27	·35	16
3	Su	18	...	...	1	·45	17
4	Mo	19	4	·04	2	·55	18
5	Tu	20	5	·12	3	·66	19
6	We	21	6	·20	4	·76	20
7	Th	22	7	·29	5	·85	21
8	Fr	23	8	·34	6	·92	22
9	Sa	24	9	·38	7	·97	23
10	Su	25	10	·40	...	...	24
11	Mo	26	11	·39	8	·00	25
12	Tu	27	12	·36	9	·01	26
13	We	28	13	·33	10 / 11	·01 / ·98	27
14	Th	29	14	·26	12	·94	28
15	Fr	30	—A	·18	13	·88	29

Oct.

Solar: Angirasa Tula—Aippasi. (1–15)
Lunar: Sukla; Asvina; Bahula; K. Suk.
Muhammadan: H. 1351 Jumadal-akhir. (1–29)

Cyclic Sidereal Year, Month and Day	Week-Day	English Day	Tithi	Tithi Moment	Nakshatra	Nakshatra Moment	Muhammadan Year, Month and Day
16	Sa	1	1	·10	14	·82	—30
17	Su	2	2 / 3	·01 / ·91	15	·76	1
18	Mo	3	4	·81	16	·69	2
19	Tu	4	5	·71	17	·62	3
20	We	5	6	·61	18	·55	4
21	Th	6	7	·52	19	·50	5
22	Fr	7	8	·45	20	·45	6
23	Sa	8	9	·39	21	·43	7
24	Su	9	10	·36	22	·41	8
25	Mo	10	11	·34	23	·42	9
26	Tu	11	12	·35	24	·44	10
27	We	12	13	·36	25	·49	11
28	Th	13	14	·39	26	·56	12
29	Fr	14	P	·45	27	·65	13
30	Sa	15	1	·52	1	·74	14
—31	Su	16	2	·61	2	·85	15
1	Mo	17	3	·70	3	·96	16
2	Tu	18	4	·78	...	...	17
3	We	19	5	·86	4	·07	18
4	Th	20	6	·91	5	·16	19
5	Fr	21	7	·96	6	·23	20
6	Sa	22	8	·98	7	·28	21
7	Su	23	9	·97	8	·32	22
8	Mo	24	10	·94	9	·33	23
9	Tu	25	11	·91	10	·33	24
10	We	26	12	·84	11	·31	25
11	Th	27	13	·77	12	·27	26
12	Fr	28	14	·68	13	·22	27
13	Sa	29	—A	·59	14	·16	28
14	Su	30	1	·49	15	·10	—29
15	Mo	31	2	·39	16 / 17	·03 / ·96	1

Nov.

Solar: Angirasa Tula—Aippasi. (16–30); Angirasa Vrischika—Kartigai. (1–15)
Lunar: Sukla; Karttika; Bahula
Muhammadan: H. 1351 Rajab. (1–29)

Cyclic Sidereal Year, Month and Day	Week-Day	English Day	Tithi	Tithi Moment	Nakshatra	Nakshatra Moment	Muhammadan Year, Month and Day
16	Tu	1	3	·29	18	·89	2
17	We	2	4	·20	19	·83	3
18	Th	3	5	·12	20	·79	4
19	Fr	4	6 / 7	·05 / ·98	21	·76	5
20	Sa	5	8	·95	22	·74	6
21	Su	6	9	·93	23	·74	7
22	Mo	7	10	·94	24	·76	8
23	Tu	8	11	·96	25	·81	9
24	We	9	...	...	26	·87	10
25	Th	10	12	·01	27	·95	11
26	Fr	11	13	·06	...	...	12
27	Sa	12	14	·13	1	·04	13
28	Su	13	P	·22	2	·15	14
29	Mo	14	1	·32	3	·26	15
—30	Tu	15	2	·40	4	·37	16
1	We	16	3	·47	5	·47	17
2	Th	17	4	·53	6	·54	18
3	Fr	18	5	·58	7	·60	19
4	Sa	19	6	·60	8	·63	20
5	Su	20	7	·58	9	·66	21
6	Mo	21	8	·55	10	·66	22
7	Tu	22	9	·52	11	·64	23
8	We	23	10	·46	12	·60	24
9	Th	24	11	·39	13	·55	25
10	Fr	25	12	·30	14	·50	26
11	Sa	26	13	·21	15	·43	27
12	Su	27	14	·11	16	·36	28
13	Mo	28	A / 1	·01 / ·91	17	·29	29
14	Tu	29	2	·82	18	·23	—30
15	We	30	3	·74	19	·17	1

Dec.

Solar: Angirasa Dhanus—Margali. (1–17)
Lunar: Sukla; Margasira; Bahula; P. Suk.
Muhammadan: H. 1351 Shaban. (1–29)

Cyclic Sidereal Year, Month and Day	Week-Day	English Day	Tithi	Tithi Moment	Nakshatra	Nakshatra Moment	Muhammadan Year, Month and Day
16	Th	1	4	·66	20	·12	2
17	Fr	2	5	·61	21	·09	3
18	Sa	3	6	·58	22	·06	4
19	Su	4	7	·56	23	·06	5
20	Mo	5	8	·57	24	·08	6
21	Tu	6	9	·60	25	·12	7
22	We	7	10	·65	26	·18	8
23	Th	8	11	·70	27	·25	9
24	Fr	9	12	·78	1	·34	10
25	Sa	10	13	·88	2	·45	11
26	Su	11	14	·96	3	·56	12
27	Mo	12	...	...	4	·67	13
28	Tu	13	P	·04	5	·76	14
—29	We	14	1	·11	6	·84	15
1	Th	15	2	·18	7	·91	16
2	Fr	16	3	·21	8	·96	17
3	Sa	17	4	·23	9	·98	18
4	Su	18	5	·22	10	·98	19
5	Mo	19	6	·20	11	·97	20
6	Tu	20	7	·15	12	·94	21
7	We	21	8	·09	13	·90	22
8	Th	22	9 / 10	·02 / ·93	14	·84	23
9	Fr	23	11	·84	15	·77	24
10	Sa	24	12	·74	16	·70	25
11	Su	25	13	·64	17	·63	26
12	Mo	26	14	·54	18	·57	27
13	Tu	27	—A	·46	19	·51	28
14	We	28	1	·38	20	·46	—29
15	Th	29	2	·30	21	·42	1
16	Fr	30	3	·26	22	·39	2
17	Sa	31	4	·23	23	·39	3

15. Svati. 16. Visak. 17. Anur. 18. Jyesh. 19. Mula. 20. P. Ash. 21. U. Ash. 22. Sravn. 23. Dani. 24. Satab. 25 P. Bhad. 26. U. Bhad. 27. Rev.

A. D. 1933.
Solar Eclipse. ●
Lunar Eclipse. ○

Mesha Sankranti (Commencement of Indian Sidereal Year).
(Surya Sid.) April 13·16.
(Arya Sid.) April 13·05.

Saka 1855. **Kaliyuga 5034.**
(S. Cycle) Srimukha.

Columns: SOLAR reckoning — Cyclic Sidereal Year, Month and Day; Week-Day, English Month and Day. LUNAR reckoning — Tithi Ending Moment; Nakshatra Ending Moment; Muhammadan Year, Month and Day.

Jan. (Solar: Angirasa, Dhanus—Margali; Angirasa, Makara—Tai. Lunar: Sukla, Pausha, Bahula. H. 1351 Ramzan.)

Cyclic Sidereal	Week-Day	Tithi	Nakshatra	Muhammadan
18	Su 1	5 ·21	24 ·40	4
19	Mo 2	6 ·21	25 ·43	5
20	Tu 3	7 ·25	26 ·48	6
21	We 4	8 ·29	27 ·56	7
22	Th 5	9 ·35	1 ·64	8
23	Fr 6	10 ·43	2 ·75	9
24	Sa 7	11 ·52	3 ·86	10
25	Su 8	12 ·61	4 ·97	11
26	Mo 9	13 ·69	... ...	12
27	Tu 10	14 ·77	5 ·06	13
28	We 11	P ·82	6 ·15	14
29	Th 12	1 ·86	7 ·23	15
1	Fr 13	2 ·88	8 ·27	16
2	Sa 14	3 ·86	9 ·30	17
3	Su 15	4 ·84	10 ·31	18
4	Mo 16	5 ·80	11 ·30	19
5	Tu 17	6 ·74	12 ·28	20
6	We 18	7 ·66	13 ·23	21
7	Th 19	8 ·57	14 ·18	22
8	Fr 20	9 ·47	15 ·11	23
9	Sa 21	10 ·37	16 ·04 / 17 ·97	24
10	Su 22	11 ·27	18 ·91	25
11	Mo 23	12 ·18	19 ·85	26
12	Tu 24	13 ·10	20 ·79	27
13	We 25	14 ·02 / A ·96	21 ·75	28
14	Th 26	1 ·90	22 ·72	29
15	Fr 27	2 ·86	23 ·71	30
16	Sa 28	3 ·85	24 72	1
17	Su 29	4 ·86	25 ·75	2
18	Mo 30	5 ·89	26 ·79	3
19	Tu 31	6 ·94	27 ·86	4

March (Solar: Angirasa, Kumbha—Masi; Angirasa, Mina—Panguni. Lunar: Sukla, Phalguna, Bahula. H. 1351 Zi-l-ka'da.)

Cyclic Sidereal	Week-Day	Tithi	Nakshatra	Muhammadan
18	We 1	5 ·63	1 ·26	4
19	Th 2	6 ·71	2 ·35	5
20	Fr 3	7 ·80	3 ·46	6
21	Sa 4	8 ·88	4 ·56	7
22	Su 5	9 ·96	5 ·67	8
23	Mo 6	... ...	6 ·77	9
24	Tu 7	10 ·02	7 ·84	10
25	We 8	11 ·08	8 ·90	11
26	Th 9	12 ·12	9 ·94	12
27	Fr 10	13 ·12	10 ·96	13
28	Sa 11	14 ·11	11 ·96	14
29	Su 12	P ·07	12 ·94	15
30	Mo 13	1 ·03 / 2 ·96	13 ·90	16
1	Tu 14	3 ·88	14 ·85	17
2	We 15	4 ·79	15 ·79	18
3	Th 16	5 ·69	16 ·73	19
4	Fr 17	6 ·59	17 ·66	20
5	Sa 18	7 ·49	18 ·59	21
6	Su 19	8 ·40	19 ·52	22
7	Mo 20	9 ·31	20 ·46	23
8	Tu 21	• 10 ·23	21 ·42	24
9	We 22	11 ·16	22 ·38	25
10	Th 23	12 ·11	23 ·36	26
11	Fr 24	13 ·08	24 ·36	27
12	Sa 25	14 ·06	25 ·37	28
13	Su 26	A ·07	26 ·42	29
14	Mo 27	1 ·10	27 ·48	30
15	Tu 28	2 ·15	1 ·56	1
16	We 29	3 ·22	2 ·65	2
17	Th 30	4 ·29	3 ·75	3
18	Fr 31	5 ·38	4 ·86	4

May (Solar: Srimukha, Mesha—Chittirai; Srimukha, Vrishabha—Vaikasi. Lunar: Sukla, Vaisakha, Bahula, Sukla. H. 1352 Muharram.)

Cyclic Sidereal	Week-Day	Tithi	Nakshatra	Muhammadan
19	Mo 1	6 ·13	7 ·45	6
20	Tu 2	7 ·19	8 ·52	7
21	We 3	8 ·22	9 ·58	8
22	Th 4	9 ·23	10 ·60	9
23	Fr 5	10 ·21	11 ·61	10
24	Sa 6	11 ·18	12 ·59	11
25	Su 7	12 ·12	13 ·56	12
26	Mo 8	13 ·05 / 14 ·98	14 ·53	13
27	Tu 9	P ·88	15 ·47	14
28	We 10	1 ·78	16 ·41	15
29	Th 11	2 ·68	17 ·34	16
30	Fr 12	3 ·58	18 ·27	17
31	Sa 13	4 ·48	19 ·21	18
1	Su 14	5 ·38	20 ·15	19
2	Mo 15	6 ·30	21 ·09	20
3	Tu 16	7 ·22	22 ·04	21
4	We 17	8 ·18	23 ·01	22
5	Th 18	9 ·14	24 ·01	23
6	Fr 19	10 ·13	25 ·02	24
7	Sa 20	11 ·12	26 ·05	25
8	Su 21	12 ·15	27 ·10	26
9	Mo 22	13 ·20	1 ·16	27
10	Tu 23	14 ·26	2 ·25	28
11	We 24	A ·33	3 ·36	29
12	Th 25	1 ·41	4 ·47	30
13	Fr 26	2 ·50	5 ·57	1
14	Sa 27	3 ·58	6 ·67	2
15	Su 28	4 ·64	7 ·76	3
16	Mo 29	5 ·69	8 ·84	4
17	Tu 30	6 ·71	9 ·89	5
18	We 31	7 ·72	10 ·92	6

Feb. (Solar: Angirasa, Kumbha—Masi. Lunar: Sukla, Magha, Bahula, P. Suk. H. 1351 Shawwal.)

Cyclic Sidereal	Week-Day	Tithi	Nakshatra	Muhammadan
20	We 1	... ...	1 ·95	5
21	Th 2	7 ·00	... ...	6
22	Fr 3	8 ·08	2 ·05	7
23	Sa 4	9 ·17	3 ·16	8
24	Su 5	10 ·26	4 ·26	9
25	Mo 6	11 ·34	5 ·36	10
26	Tu 7	12 ·42	6 ·46	11
27	We 8	13 ·47	7 ·53	12
28	Th 9	14 ·50	8 ·59	13
29	Fr 10	P ·51	9 ·62	14
30	Sa 11	1 ·50	10 ·63	15
1	Su 12	2 ·48	11 ·63	16
2	Mo 13	3 ·42	12 ·61	17
3	Tu 14	4 ·36	13 ·56	18
4	We 15	5 ·28	14 ·51	19
5	Th 16	6 ·19	15 ·45	20
6	Fr 17	7 ·10	16 ·39	21
7	Sa 18	8 ·00 / 9 ·90	17 ·32	22
8	Su 19	10 ·80	18 ·25	23
9	Mo 20	11 ·71	19 ·18	24
10	Tu 21	12 ·63	20 ·13	25
11	We 22	13 ·57	21 ·08	26
12	Th 23	14 ·52	22 ·05	27
13	Fr ● 24	A ·49	23 ·04	28
14	Sa 25	1 ·47	24 ·04	29
15	Su 26	2 ·47	25 ·06	1
16	Mo 27	3 ·51	26 ·10	2
17	Tu 28	4 ·56	27 ·17	3

April (Solar: Srimukha, Mesha—Chittirai. Lunar: Sukla, Chaitra, Bahula, Vaisk. Suk. H. 1351 Zi-l-hijja; H. 1352 Muharram.)

Cyclic Sidereal	Week-Day	Tithi	Nakshatra	Muhammadan
19	Sa 1	6 ·46	5 ·97	5
20	Su 2	7 ·54	... ...	6
21	Mo 3	8 ·60	6 ·07	7
22	Tu 4	9 ·66	7 ·15	8
23	We 5	10 ·69	8 ·21	9
24	Th 6	11 ·69	9 ·25	10
25	Fr 7	12 ·68	10 ·28	11
26	Sa 8	13 ·64	11 ·28	12
27	Su 9	14 ·59	12 ·26	13
28	Mo 10	P ·52	13 ·23	14
29	Tu 11	1 ·45	14 ·18	15
30	We 12	2 ·36	15 ·13	16
1	Th 13	3 ·26	16 ·07	17
2	Fr 14	4 ·16	17 ·00 / 18 ·93	18
3	Sa 15	5 ·06 / 6 ·96	19 ·87	19
4	Su 16	7 ·86	20 ·81	20
5	Mo 17	8 ·78	21 ·75	21
6	Tu 18	9 ·71	22 ·71	22
7	We 19	10 ·67	23 ·69	23
8	Th 20	11 ·63	24 ·68	24
9	Fr 21	12 ·60	25 ·70	25
10	Sa 22	13 ·61	26 ·73	26
11	Su 23	14 ·64	27 ·79	27
12	Mo 24	A ·69	1 ·86	28
13	Tu 25	1 ·75	2 ·95	29
14	We 26	2 ·84	... ...	1
15	Th 27	3 ·92	3 ·06	2
16	Fr 28	... ...	4 ·17	3
17	Sa 29	4 ·00	5 ·27	4
18	Su 30	5 ·07	6 ·37	5

June (Solar: Srimukha, Mithuna—Ani. Lunar: Jyeshtha, Bahula, Ashadha Suk. H. 1352 Safar; Rabi-ul-awwal.)

Cyclic Sidereal	Week-Day	Tithi	Nakshatra	Muhammadan
19	Th 1	8 ·70	11 ·93	7
20	Fr 2	9 ·68	12 ·92	8
21	Sa 3	10 ·63	13 ·90	9
22	Su 4	11 ·56	14 ·86	10
23	Mo 5	12 ·47	15 ·81	11
24	Tu 6	13 ·38	16 ·74	12
25	We 7	14 ·28	17 ·67	13
26	Th 8	P ·18	18 ·60	14
27	Fr 9	1 ·08 / 2 ·98	19 ·54	15
28	Sa 10	3 ·88	20 ·48	16
29	Su 11	4 ·80	21 ·42	17
30	Mo 12	5 ·78	22 ·37	18
31	Tu 13	6 ·66	23 ·35	19
1	We 14	7 ·62	24 ·33	20
2	Th 15	8 ·61	25 ·34	21
3	Fr 16	9 ·61	26 ·36	22
4	Sa 17	10 ·68	27 ·41	23
5	Su 18	11 ·67	1 ·47	24
6	Mo 19	12 ·74	2 ·56	25
7	Tu 20	13 ·81	3 ·66	26
8	We 21	14 ·88	4 ·76	27
9	Th 22	A ·97	5 ·87	28
10	Fr 23	... ...	6 ·97	29
11	Sa 24	1 ·05	... ...	1
12	Su 25	2 ·11	7 ·07	2
13	Mo 26	3 ·16	8 ·15	3
14	Tu 27	4 ·20	9 ·20	4
15	We 28	5 ·20	10 ·24	5
16	Th 29	6 ·18	11 ·25	6
17	Fr 30	7 ·16	12 ·25	7

Naksh:—1. Asvn. 2. Bhar. 3. Krit. 4. Rohi. 5. Mrig. 6. Ardh. 7. Punar. 8. Push. 9. Asleah. 10. Magh. 11. P. Phal. 12. U. Phal. 13. Hasta. 14. Chit.

A. D. 1933.
A.—Amavasya.
P.—Paurnami.

Kollam 1109, Commences { N. Malabar—Sept. S. Malabar—Aug.

Hijra 1352, Commences, April 26.

Vikrama 1990.
Bengal San 1339.
(N. Cycle) Parthiva.

SOLAR reckoning: Cyclic Sidereal Year, Month and Day.	Week-Day English Month and Day.	LUNAR reckoning: Tithi Ending Moment.	Nakshatra Ending Moment.	Muhammadan Year, Month and Day.
	July			
Srimukha Mithuna—Ani 18	Sa 1	8 ·11	13 ·23	H. 1352 Rabi-ul-awwal 8
19	Su 2	Sukla { 9 ·04 / 10 ·95	14 ·19	9
20	Mo 3	11 ·86	15 ·14	10
21	Tu 4	12 ·76	16 ·08	11
22	We 5	13 ·66	17 ·02 / 18 ·95 }	12
23	Th 6	Ashadha 14 ·56	19 ·88	13
24	Fr 7	P ·46	20 ·81	14
25	Sa 8	1 ·36	21 ·75	15
26	Su 9	2 ·27	22 ·71	16
27	Mo 10	3 ·20	23 ·68	17
28	Tu 11	4 ·14	24 ·66	18
29	We 12	5 ·11	25 ·66	19
30	Th 13	Bahula 6 ·09	26 ·68	20
31	Fr 14	7 ·08	27 ·72	21
—32	Sa 15	8 ·11	1 ·79	22
Srimukha Karkata—Adi 1	Su 16	9 ·15	2 ·86	23
2	Mo 17	10 ·20	3 ·96	24
3	Tu 18	11 ·27	... ...	25
4	We 19	12 ·36	4 ·06	26
5	Th 20	13 ·44	5 ·17	27
6	Fr 21	14 ·51	6 ·28	28
7	Sa 22	—A ·58	7 ·37	29
8	Su 23	1 ·64	8 ·45	—30
9	Mo 24	2 ·67	9 ·51	1
10	Tu 25	3 ·68	10 ·55	2
11	We 26	4 ·67	11 ·58	3
12	Th 27	5 ·64	12 ·58	4
13	Fr 28	6 ·59	13 ·56	5
14	Sa 29	Sukla 7 ·52	14 ·53	6
15	Su 30	8 ·44	15 ·48	7
16	Mo 31	9 ·35	16 ·43	8

SOLAR reckoning: Cyclic Sidereal Year, Month and Day.	Week-Day English Month and Day.	LUNAR reckoning: Tithi Ending Moment.	Nakshatra Ending Moment.	Muhammadan Year, Month and Day.
	Aug.			
17	Tu 1	10 ·25	17 ·36	H. 1352 Rabi-ul-akhir 9
18	We 2	11 ·15	18 ·29	10
19	Th 3	{ 12 ·05 / 13 ·95	19 ·22	11
20	Fr 4	Sravana 14 ·85	20 ·15	12
21	Sa 5	P ·77	21 ·09	13
22	Su 6	1 ·69	22 ·05	14
23	Mo 7	2 ·62	23 ·01 / 24 ·99 }	15
24	Tu 8	3 ·59	25 ·98	16
25	We 9	4 ·58	26 ·99	17
26	Th 10	5 ·58	... ...	18
27	Fr 11	Bahula 6 ·59	27 ·04	19
28	Sa 12	7 ·62	1 ·09	20
29	Su 13	8 ·69	2 ·17	21
30	Mo 14	9 ·76	3 ·26	22
—31	Tu 15	10 ·85	4 ·36	23
Srimukha Simha—Avani 1	We 16	11 ·93	5 ·47	24
2	Th 17	... ...	6 ·58	25
3	Fr 18	12 ·01	7 ·68	26
4	Sa 19	13 ·07	8 ·76	27
5	Su 20	14 ·13	9 ·82	28
6	Mo 21	—A ·16	10 ·88	—29
7	Tu 22	1 ·18	11 ·90	H. 1352 Jumadal-awwal 1
8	We 23	2 ·17	12 ·91	2
9	Th 24	3 ·14	13 ·89	3
10	Fr 25	Sukla 4 ·10	14 ·86	4
11	Sa 26	{ 5 ·03 / 6 ·95	15 ·81	5
12	Su 27	7 ·86	16 ·76	6
13	Mo 28	8 ·76	17 ·70	7
14	Tu 29	9 ·66	18 ·63	8
15	We 30	Bhadra. 10 ·56	19 ·56	9
16	Th 31	11 ·46	20 ·50	10

SOLAR reckoning: Cyclic Sidereal Year, Month and Day.	Week-Day English Month and Day.	LUNAR reckoning: Tithi Ending Moment.	Nakshatra Ending Moment.	Muhammadan Year, Month and Day.
	Sep.			
17	Fr 1	Suk. 12 ·36	21 ·44	H. 1352 Jumadal-awwal 11
18	Sa 2	13 ·28	22 ·38	12
19	Su 3	14 ·21	23 ·34	13
20	Mo 4	Bhadrapada P ·16	24 ·31	14
Srimukha Simha—Avani 21	Tu 5	1 ·11	25 ·30	15
22	We 6	2 ·08	26 ·32	16
23	Th 7	3 ·09	27 ·35	17
24	Fr 8	4 ·10	1 ·40	18
25	Sa 9	5 ·15	2 ·47	19
26	Su 10	6 ·20	3 ·56	20
27	Mo 11	7 ·28	4 ·67	21
28	Tu 12	Bahula 8 ·36	5 ·77	22
29	We 13	9 ·44	6 ·88	23
30	Th 14	10 ·53	7 ·98	24
—31	Fr 15	11 ·60	... ...	25
Srimukha Kanya—Purattasi 1	Sa 16	12 ·66	8 ·06	26
2	Su 17	13 ·69	9 ·14	27
3	Mo 18	14 ·71	10 ·19	28
4	Tu 19	—A ·69	11 ·22	29
5	We 20	1 ·67	12 ·23	—30
6	Th 21	2 ·63	13 ·22	H. 1352 Jumadal-akhir 1
7	Fr 22	3 ·56	14 ·19	2
8	Sa 23	4 ·48	15 ·16	3
9	Su 24	5 ·39	16 ·10	4
10	Mo 25	6 ·30	17 ·04 / 18 ·97 }	5
11	Tu 26	Sukla 7 ·20	19 ·90	6
12	We 27	8 ·10	20 ·83	7
13	Th 28	9 ·00 / 10 ·90	21 ·77	8
14	Fr 29	11 ·82	22 ·72	9
15	Sa 30	12 ·75	23 ·67	10

SOLAR reckoning: Cyclic Sidereal Year, Month and Day.	Week-Day English Month and Day.	LUNAR reckoning: Tithi Ending Moment.	Nakshatra Ending Moment.	Muhammadan Year, Month and Day.
	Oct.			
16	Su 1	Asvina 13 ·70	24 ·64	11
17	Mo 2	14 ·65	25 ·63	12
18	Tu 3	P ·64	26 ·64	13
19	We 4	1 ·63	27 ·66	14
20	Th 5	2 ·65	1 ·71	15
21	Fr 6	3 ·70	2 ·78	16
22	Sa 7	4 ·75	3 ·87	17
23	Su 8	5 ·83	4 ·97	18
24	Mo 9	6 ·92	... ...	19
25	Tu 10	... ...	5 ·07	20
26	We 11	Bahula 7 ·02	6 ·18	21
27	Th 12	8 ·09	7 ·28	22
28	Fr 13	9 ·16	8 ·37	23
29	Sa 14	10 ·22	9 ·45	24
30	Su 15	11 ·25	10 ·50	25
—31	Mo 16	12 ·28	11 ·54	26
Srimukha Tula—Aippasi 1	Tu 17	13 ·26	12 ·55	27
2	We 18	14 ·23	13 ·54	28
3	Th 19	—A ·19	14 ·53	—29
4	Fr 20	1 ·14	15 ·49	H. 1352 Rajab. 1
5	Sa 21	{ 2 ·06 / 3 ·97	16 ·44	2
6	Su 22	4 ·88	17 ·38	3
7	Mo 23	5 ·78	18 ·31	4
8	Tu 24	Sukla 6 ·68	19 ·24	5
9	We 25	7 ·58	20 ·17	6
10	Th 26	8 ·49	21 ·11	7
11	Fr 27	9 ·40	22 ·05	8
12	Sa 28	Karttika 10 ·33	23 ·01 / 24 ·98 }	9
13	Su 29	11 ·28	25 ·96	10
14	Mo 30	12 ·24	26 ·96	11
15	Tu 31	13 ·23	27 ·98	12

SOLAR reckoning: Cyclic Sidereal Year, Month and Day.	Week-Day English Month and Day.	LUNAR reckoning: Tithi Ending Moment.	Nakshatra Ending Moment.	Muhammadan Year, Month and Day.
	Nov.			
16	We 1	Karttika 14 ·23	... ...	13
17	Th 2	P ·25	1 ·02	14
18	Fr 3	1 ·29	2 ·08	15
Srimukha Tula—Aippasi 19	Sa 4	2 ·36	3 ·17	16
20	Su 5	3 ·44	4 ·26	17
21	Mo 6	4 ·52	5 ·37	18
22	Tu 7	5 ·61	6 ·48	H. 1352 Rajab. 19
23	We 8	6 ·69	7 ·58	20
24	Th 9	Bahula 7 ·77	8 ·68	21
25	Fr 10	8 ·82	9 ·76	22
26	Sa 11	9 ·86	10 ·82	23
27	Su 12	10 ·88	11 ·85	24
28	Mo 13	11 ·86	12 ·87	25
29	Tu 14	12 ·84	13 ·88	26
—30	We 15	13 ·79	14 ·86	27
Srimukha Vrischika—Kartigai 1	Th 16	14 ·74	15 ·82	28
2	Fr 17	—A ·67	16 ·77	29
3	Sa 18	1 ·59	17 ·71	—30
4	Su 19	2 ·49	18 ·65	1
5	Mo 20	3 ·39	19 ·58	2
6	Tu 21	4 ·29	20 ·51	3
7	We 22	5 ·20	21 ·44	4
8	Th 23	6 ·11	22 ·38	5
9	Fr 24	{ 7 ·02 / 8 ·95	23 ·34	6
10	Sa 25	9 ·90	24 ·31	7
11	Su 26	Sukla 10 ·87	25 ·28	8
12	Mo 27	11 ·85	26 ·28	9
13	Tu 28	12 ·85	27 ·29	10
14	We 29	13 ·88	1 ·33	11
15	Th 30	14 ·92	2 ·40	12

SOLAR reckoning: Cyclic Sidereal Year, Month and Day.	Week-Day English Month and Day.	LUNAR reckoning: Tithi Ending Moment.	Nakshatra Ending Moment.	Muhammadan Year, Month and Day.
	Dec.			
16	Fr 1	Margasira P ·98	3 ·47	H. 1352 Shaban. 13
17	Sa 2	... ...	4 ·56	14
18	Su 3	1 ·06	5 ·67	15
19	Mo 4	2 ·16	6 ·78	16
20	Tu 5	3 ·25	7 ·89	17
21	We 6	4 ·33	8 ·98	18
22	Th 7	5 ·41	... ...	19
23	Fr 8	6 ·46	9 ·08	20
24	Sa 9	Bahula 7 ·50	10 ·13	21
25	Su 10	8 ·51	11 ·17	22
26	Mo 11	9 ·51	12 ·20	23
27	Tu 12	10 ·48	13 ·20	24
28	We 13	11 ·42	14 ·19	25
—29	Th 14	12 ·36	15 ·15	26
1	Fr 15	13 ·29	16 ·11	27
2	Sa 16	14 ·21	17 ·06 / 18 ·99 }	28
3	Su 17	—A ·12	19 ·92	—29
4	Mo 18	{ 1 ·02 / 2 ·92	20 ·85	1
5	Tu 19	3 ·82	21 ·78	2
Srimukha Dhanus—Margali 6	We 20	4 ·73	22 ·72	3
7	Th 21	5 ·65	23 ·68	4
8	Fr 22	6 ·59	24 ·64	H. 1352 Ramzan. 5
9	Sa 23	Sukla 7 ·54	25 ·61	6
10	Su 24	8 ·51	26 ·60	7
11	Mo 25	9 ·40	27 ·61	8
12	Tu 26	10 ·50	1 ·65	9
13	We 27	11 ·58	2 ·70	10
14	Th 28	Pausha 12 ·57	3 ·78	11
15	Fr 29	13 ·64	4 ·86	12
16	Sa 30	14 ·73	5 ·96	13
17	Su 31	P ·82	... ...	14

A. D. 1934.
Solar Eclipse. ●
Lunar Eclipse. ○

Mesha Sankranti (Commencement of Indian Sidereal Year).
(Surya Sid.) April 13·42.
(Arya Sid.) April 13·31.

Saka 1856. Kaliyuga 5035.
(S. Cycle) Bhava.

Columns: SOLAR reckoning — Cyclic Sidereal Year, Month and Day; Week-Day English Month and Day. LUNAR reckoning — Tithi Ending Moment; Nakshatra Ending Moment; Muhammadan Year, Month and Day.

Jan.

Cyclic Sidereal Year, Month	Day	Week-Day	Day	Lunar Month	Tithi	Ending Moment	Nakshatra	Ending Moment	Muhammadan Year, Month	Day
Srimukha *Dhanus—Margali.*	18	Mo	1	Pausha *Bahula*	1	·90	6	·07	H. 1352 *Ramzan.*	15
	19	Tu	2		2	·98	7	·18		16
	20	We	3		...	...	8	·28		17
	21	Th	4		3	·06	9	·37		18
	22	Fr	5		4	·10	10	·44		19
	23	Sa	6		5	·14	11	·49		20
	24	Su	7		6	·16	12	·52		21
	25	Mo	8		7	·15	13	·53		22
	26	Tu	9		8	·12	14	·51		23
	27	We	10		9	·08	15	·49		24
	28	Th	11		10 11	·01 ·94	16	·45		25
	29	Fr	12		12	·86	17	·40		26
	—30	Sa	13		13	·76	18	·33		27
Srimukha *Makara—Tai.*	1	Su	14		14	·66	19	·26		28
	2	Mo	15		—A	·56	20	·19		29
	3	Tu	16	Magha *Sukla*	1	·47	21	·12		—30
	4	We	17		2	·38	22	·06	*Shawwal.*	1
	5	Th	18		3	·30	23 24	·01 ·97		2
	6	Fr	19		4	·24	25	·94		3
	7	Sa	20		5	·18	26	·92		4
	8	Su	21		6	·15	27	·94		5
	9	Mo	22		7	·18	1	·97		6
	10	Tu	23		8	·15	...	...		7
	11	We	24		9	·17	2	·01		8
	12	Th	25		10	·23	3	·08		9
	13	Fr	26		11	·30	4	·16		10
	14	Sa	27		12	·38	5	·27		11
	15	Su	28		13	·46	6	·38		12
	16	Mo	29		14	·55	7	·48		13
	17	Tu ○	30		P	·64	8	·58		14
	18	We	31		1	·71	9	·67		15

Feb.

Cyclic Sidereal Year, Month	Day	Week-Day	Day	Lunar Month	Tithi	Ending Moment	Nakshatra	Ending Moment	Muhammadan Year, Month	Day
	19	Th	1	*Bahula*	2	·76	10	·75	H. 1352	16
	20	Fr	2		3	·79	11	·81		17
	21	Sa	3		4	·81	12	·84		18
	22	Su	4		5	·79	13	·85		19
	23	Mo	5		6	·76	14	·84		20
	24	Tu	6		7	·70	15	·82		21
	25	We	7		8	·64	16	·78		22
	26	Th	8		9	·57	17	·73		23
	27	Fr	9		10	·48	18	·67		24
	28	Sa	10		11	·39	19	·60		25
	—29	Su	11		12	·29	20	·53		26
Srimukha *Kumbha—Masi.*	1	Mo	12		13	·19	21	·46		27
	2	Tu	13		14	·09	22	·40		28
	3	We ●	14		A 1	·00 ·92	23	·34		—29
	4	Th	15	Phalguna *Sukla*	2	·86	24	·30	H. 1352 *Zi-l-ka'da.*	1
	5	Fr	16		3	·82	25	·27		2
	6	Sa	17		4	·78	26	·26		3
	7	Su	18		5	·77	27	·26		4
	8	Mo	19		6	·77	1	·28		5
	9	Tu	20		7	·80	2	·32		6
	10	We	21		8	·86	3	·39		7
	11	Th	22		9	·92	4	·48		8
	12	Fr	23		...	...	5	·58		9
	13	Sa	24		10	·01	6	·68		10
	14	Su	25		11	·10	7	·78		11
	15	Mo	26		12	·18	8	·88		12
	16	Tu	27		13	·25	9	·98		13
	17	We	28		14	·32	...	...		14

March

Cyclic Sidereal Year, Month	Day	Week-Day	Day	Lunar Month	Tithi	Ending Moment	Nakshatra	Ending Moment	Muhammadan Year, Month	Day
Srimukha *Kumbha—Masi.*	18	Th	1	Phalguna	P	·38	10	·06	H. 1352 *Zi-l-ka'da.*	15
	19	Fr	2	*Bahula*	1	·41	11	·12		16
	20	Sa	3		2	·42	12	·16		17
	21	Su	4		3	·40	13	·17		18
	22	Mo	5		4	·37	14	·17		19
	23	Tu	6		5	·31	15	·16		20
	24	We	7		6	·25	16	·12		21
	25	Th	8		7	·18	17	·07		22
	26	Fr	9		8 9	·09 ·99	18 19	·01 ·95		23
	27	Sa	10		10	·89	20	·83		24
	28	Su	11		11	·79	21	·81		25
	29	Mo	12		12	·69	22	·74		26
	—30	Tu	13		13	·60	23	·68		27
Srimukha *Mina—Panguni.*	1	We	14		14	·52	24	·63		28
	2	Th	15		—A	·45	25	·60		29
	3	Fr	16	Chaitra *Sukla*	1	·41	26	·58		—30
	4	Sa	17		2	·37	27	·58	*Zi-l-hijja.*	1
	5	Su	18		3	·36	1	·59		2
	6	Mo	19		4	·37	2	·63		3
	7	Tu	20		5	·41	3	·69		4
	8	We	21		6	·45	4	·78		5
	9	Th	22		7	·52	5	·87		6
	10	Fr	23		8	·60	6	·97		7
	11	Sa	24		9	·69	...	...		8
	12	Su	25		10	·78	7	·08		9
	13	Mo	26		11	·86	8	·18		10
	14	Tu	27		12	·92	9	·28		11
	15	We	28		13	·96	10	·37		12
	16	Th	29		14	·99	11	·43		13
	17	Fr	30		...	...	12	·47		14
	18	Sa	31		P 1	·00 ·98	13	·49		15

April

Cyclic Sidereal Year, Month	Day	Week-Day	Day	Lunar Month	Tithi	Ending Moment	Nakshatra	Ending Moment	Muhammadan Year, Month	Day
	19	Su	1	*Bahula*	2	·95	14	·50	H. 1352	16
	20	Mo	2		3	·89	15	·48		17
	21	Tu	3		4	·83	16	·45		18
	22	We	4		5	·75	17	·40		19
	23	Th	5		6	·66	18	·34		20
	24	Fr	6		7	·56	19	·28		21
	25	Sa	7		8	·45	20	·22		22
	26	Su	8		9	·35	21	·15		23
	27	Mo	9		10	·25	22	·08		24
	28	Tu	10		11	·16	23 24	·02 ·97		25
	29	We	11		12	·08	25	·93		26
	—30	Th	12		13 14	·02 ·97	26	·91		27
Bhava *Mesha—Chittirai.*	1	Fr	13		—A	·93	27	·90		28
	2	Sa	14	Adhika Vaisakha *Sukla*	1	·92	1	·91		29
	3	Su	15		2	·92	2	·94		—30
	4	Mo	16		3	·96	...	...	H. 1353 *Muharram.*	1
	5	Tu	17		...	...	3	·01		2
	6	We	18		4	·01	4	·08		3
	7	Th	19		5	·08	5	·17		4
	8	Fr	20		6	·16	6	27		5
	9	Sa	21		7	·24	7	·38		6
	10	Su	22		8	·32	8	·49		7
	11	Mo	23		9	·39	9	·59		8
	12	Tu	24		10	·46	10	·67		9
	13	We	25		11	·51	11	·74		10
	14	Th	26		12	·54	12	·79		11
	15	Fr	27		13	·54	13	·82		12
	16	Sa	28		14	·53	14	·83		13
	17	Su	29		P	·50	15	·81		14
	18	Mo	30		1	·43	16	·78		15

May

Cyclic Sidereal Year, Month	Day	Week-Day	Day	Lunar Month	Tithi	Ending Moment	Nakshatra	Ending Moment	Muhammadan Year, Month	Day
Bhava *Mesha—Chittirai.*	19	Tu	1	Adh. Vsk. *Bahula*	2	·36	17	·74	H. 1353 *Muharram.*	16
	20	We	2		3	·28	18	·69		17
	21	Th	3		4	·19	19	·62		18
	22	Fr	4		5 6	·09 ·99	20	·55		19
	23	Sa	5		7	·89	21	·48		20
	24	Su	6		8	·79	22	·41		21
	25	Mo	7		9	·70	23	·35		22
	26	Tu	8		10	·62	24	·30		23
	27	We	9		11	·55	25	·26		24
	28	Th	10		12	·49	26	·23		25
	29	Fr	11		13	·46	27	·22		26
	30	Sa	12		14	·44	1	·23		27
	—31	Su	13		—A	·45	2	·27		28
Bhava *Vrishabha—Vaikasi.*	1	Mo	14	Nija Vaisakha *Sukla*	1	·48	3	·32		29
	2	Tu	15		2	·52	4	·39		—30
	3	We	16		3	·59	5	·47	*Safar.*	1
	4	Th	17		4	·66	6	·57		2
	5	Fr	18		5	·75	7	·68		3
	6	Sa	19		6	·83	8	·79		4
	7	Su	20		7	·91	9	·89		5
	8	Mo	21		8	·97	10	·98		6
	9	Tu	22		...	...	...	...		7
	10	We	23		9	·02	11	·05		8
	11	Th	24		10	·04	12	·11		9
	12	Fr	25		11	·04	13	·14		10
	13	Sa	26		12	·03	14	·15		11
	14	Su	27		13 14	·00 ·95	15	·14		12
	15	Mo	28		P	·87	16	·11		13
	16	Tu	29		1	·78	17	·08		14
	17	We	30		2	·69	18 19	·03 ·96		15
	18	Th	31		3	·59	20	·89		16

June

Cyclic Sidereal Year, Month	Day	Week-Day	Day	Lunar Month	Tithi	Ending Moment	Nakshatra	Ending Moment	Muhammadan Year, Month	Day
	19	Fr	1	*Bahula*	4	·49	21	·82	H. 1353	17
	20	Sa	2		5	·39	22	·76		18
	21	Su	3		6	·29	23	·70		19
	22	Mo	4		7	·20	24	·64		20
	23	Tu	5		8	·12	25	·59		21
	24	We	6		9 10	·05 ·99	26	·56		22
	25	Th	7		11	·95	27	·54		23
	26	Fr	8		12	·93	1	·56		24
	27	Sa	9		13	·94	2	·58		25
	28	Su	10		14	·95	3	·63		26
	29	Mo	11		...	...	4	·69		27
	30	Tu	12		—A	·01	5	·77		28
	31	We	13	Jyeshtha *Sukla*	1	·07	6	·87		—29
	—32	Th	14		2	·14	7	·98	H. 1353 *Rabi-ul-awwal.*	1
Bhava *Mithuna—Ani.*	1	Fr	15		3	·22	...	...		2
	2	Sa	16		4	·30	8	·09		3
	3	Su	17		5	·39	9	·19		4
	4	Mo	18		6	·45	10	·28		5
	5	Tu	19		7	·50	11	·37		6
	6	We	20		8	·52	12	·42		7
	7	Th	21		9	·52	13	·46		8
	8	Fr	22		10	·51	14	·47		9
	9	Sa	23		11	·48	15	·47		10
	10	Su	24		12	·42	16	·45		11
	11	Mo	25		13	·35	17	·41		12
	12	Tu	26		14	·27	18	·36		13
	13	We	27		P	·18	19	·30		14
	14	Th	28	*Bah.*	1 2	·08 ·98	20	·23		15
	15	Fr	29		3	·88	21	·16		16
	16	Sa	30		4	·78	22	·10		17

Naksh :—1. Asvn. 2. Bhar. 3. Krit. 4. Rohi. 5. Mrig. 6. Ardh. 7. Punar. 8. Push. 9. Aslesh. 10. Magh. 11. P. Phal. 12. U. Phal. 13. Hasta. 14. Chit.

A. D, 1934.
A.—Amavasya.
P.—Paurnami.

Kollam 1110, Commences { **N. Malabar—Sept.** / **S. Malabar—Aug.**

Hijra 1353, Commences, April 16.

Vikrama 1991.
Bengal San 1340.
(N. Cycle) Vyaya.

Columns: SOLAR reckoning — Cyclic Sidereal Year, Month and Day; Week-Day English Month and Day. LUNAR reckoning — Tithi Ending Moment; Nakshatra Ending Moment; Muhammadan Year, Month and Day.

July

Solar: Bhava, Mithuna—Ani (to 31); Bhava, Karkata—Adi. Lunar: Jyeshtha (Bahula, Sukla); Ashadha. Muhammadan: H. 1353 Rabi-ul-awwal; H. 1353 Rabi-ul-akhir.

Cyclic Sidereal Day	Week-Day	Day	Tithi	Tithi Ending Moment	Nakshatra	Nakshatra Ending Moment	Muhammadan Day
17	Su	1	5	·68	23 / 24	·08 / ·97	18
18	Mo	2	6	·60	25	·92	19
19	Tu	3	7	·53	26	·89	20
20	We	4	8	·47	27	·88	21
21	Th	5	9	·43	1	·88	22
22	Fr	6	10	·41	2	·90	23
23	Sa	7	11	·41	3	·94	24
24	Su	8	12	·43	...	...	25
25	Mo	9	13	·48	4	·00	26
26	Tu	10	14	·54	5	·08	27
27	We	11	—A	·62	6	·18	28
28	Th	12	1	·70	7	·28	29
29	Fr	13	2	·78	8	·39	—30
30	Sa	14	3	·86	9	·49	1
—31	Su	15	4	·92	10	·59	2
1	Mo	16	5	·97	11	·67	3
2	Tu	17	6	·99	12	·73	4
3	We	18	...	...	13	·77	5
4	Th	19	7 / 8	·00 / ·99	14	·79	6
5	Fr	20	9	·97	15	·79	7
6	Sa	21	10	·90	16	·78	8
7	Su	22	11	·83	17	·75	9
8	Mo	23	12	·76	18	·70	10
9	Tu	24	13	·67	19	·64	11
10	We	25	14	·57	20	·58	12
11	Th ○	26	P	·47	21	·51	13
12	Fr	27	1	·37	22	·44	14
13	Sa	28	2	·27	23	·37	15
14	Su	29	3	·17	24	·31	16
15	Mo	30	4	·08	25	·26	17
16	Tu	31	5 / 6	·00 / ·95	26	·23	18

Aug.

Solar: Bhava, Simha—Avani (from 1). Lunar: Bahula; Sukla; Sravana (Bahula). Muhammadan: H. 1353 Jumadal-awwal.

Cyclic Sidereal Day	Week-Day	Day	Tithi	Tithi Ending Moment	Nakshatra	Nakshatra Ending Moment	Muhammadan Day
17	We	1	7	·91	27	·20	19
18	Th	2	8	·90	1	·20	20
19	Fr	3	9	·89	2	·21	21
20	Sa	4	10	·91	3	·25	22
21	Su	5	11	·96	4	·31	23
22	Mo	6	...	...	5	·39	24
23	Tu	7	12	·02	6	·48	25
24	We	8	13	·09	7	·58	26
25	Th	9	14	·17	8	·69	27
26	Fr ●	10	—A	·26	9	·79	28
27	Sa	11	1	·34	10	·90	—29
28	Su	12	2	·41	11	·98	1
29	Mo	13	3	·45	...	...	2
30	Tu	14	4	·48	12	·04	3
31	We	15	5	·50	13	·09	4
—32	Th	16	6	·48	14	·11	5
1	Fr	17	7	·45	15	·13	6
2	Sa	18	8	·40	16	·11	7
3	Su	19	9	·34	17	·08	8
4	Mo	20	10	·26	18 / 19	·03 / ·97	9
5	Tu	21	11	·16	20	·91	10
6	We	22	12 / 13	·06 / ·96	21	·85	11
7	Th	23	14	·86	22	·78	12
8	Fr	24	P	·76	23	·71	13
9	Sa	25	1	·67	24	·65	14
10	Su	26	2	·59	25	60	15
11	Mo	27	3	·52	26	·56	16
12	Tu	28	4	·46	27	·53	17
13	We	29	5	·41	1	·52	18
14	Th	30	6	·40	2	·53	19
15	Fr	31	7	·40	3	·56	20

Sep.

Solar: Bhava, Simha—Avani (to 31); Bhava, Kanya—Purattasi. Lunar: Sravn. (Bah.); Sukla; Bhadrapada (Bahula). Muhammadan: Jumadal-awwal; H. 1353 Jumadal-akhir.

Cyclic Sidereal Day	Week-Day	Day	Tithi	Tithi Ending Moment	Nakshatra	Nakshatra Ending Moment	Muhammadan Day
16	Sa	1	8	·42	4	·62	21
17	Su	2	9	·47	5	·69	22
18	Mo	3	10	·54	6	·78	23
19	Tu	4	11	·61	7	·88	24
20	We	5	12	·69	8	·99	25
21	Th	6	13	·77	...	...	26
22	Fr	7	14	·85	9	·10	27
23	Sa	8	—A	·92	10	·20	28
24	Su	9	1	·97	11	·28	29
25	Mo	10	...	...	12	·35	—30
26	Tu	11	2	·00	13	·40	1
27	We	12	3	·01	14	·44	2
28	Th	13	4 / 5	·00 / ·98	15	·45	3
29	Fr	14	6	·93	16	·44	4
30	Sa	15	7	·87	17	·41	5
—31	Su	16	8	·79	18	·37	6
1	Mo	17	9	·70	19	·32	7
2	Tu	18	10	·60	20	·26	8
3	We	19	11	·50	21	·19	9
4	Th	20	12	·40	22	·12	10
5	Fr	21	13	·30	23 / 24	·05 / ·99	11
6	Sa	22	14	·20	25	·93	12
7	Su	23	P	·12	26	·89	13
8	Mo	24	1	·05	27	·86	14
9	Tu	25	2 / 3	·00 / ·96	1	·84	15
10	We	26	4	·94	2	·85	16
11	Th	27	5	·93	3	·88	17
12	Fr	28	6	·97	4	·93	18
13	Sa	29	...	...	...	...	19
14	Su	30	7	·01	5	·00	20

Oct.

Solar: Bhava, Kanya—Purattasi (to 30); Bhava, Tula—Aippasi. Lunar: Sukla; Asvina (Bahula). Muhammadan: H. 1353 Rajab.

Cyclic Sidereal Day	Week-Day	Day	Tithi	Tithi Ending Moment	Nakshatra	Nakshatra Ending Moment	Muhammadan Day
15	Mo	1	8	·07	6	·08	21
16	Tu	2	9	·15	7	·18	22
17	We	3	10	·24	8	·29	23
18	Th	4	11	·32	9	·40	24
19	Fr	5	12	·39	10	·50	25
20	Sa	6	13	·46	11	·59	26
21	Su	7	14	·52	12	·66	27
22	Mo	8	—A	·55	13	·72	28
23	Tu	9	1	·58	14	·76	—29
24	We	10	2	·57	15	·77	1
25	Th	11	3	·54	16	·76	2
26	Fr	12	4	·50	17	·74	3
27	Sa	13	5	·43	18	·71	4
28	Su	14	6	·35	19	·65	5
29	Mo	15	7	·26	20	·59	6
—30	Tu	16	8	·16	21	·53	7
1	We	17	9 / 10	·06 / ·96	22	·46	8
2	Th	18	11	·87	23	·39	9
3	Fr	19	12	·78	24	·33	10
4	Sa	20	13	·70	25	·27	11
5	Su	21	14	·63	26	·22	12
6	Mo	22	P	·58	27	·19	13
7	Tu	23	1	·54	1	·17	14
8	We	24	2	·52	2	·18	15
9	Th	25	3	·53	3	·20	16
10	Fr	26	4	·55	4	·24	17
11	Sa	27	5	·59	5	·30	18
12	Su	28	6	·66	6	·38	19
13	Mo	29	7	·74	7	·48	20
14	Tu	30	8	·82	8	·59	21
15	We	31	9	·92	9	·70	22

Nov.

Solar: Bhava, Tula—Aippasi (to 30); Bhava, Vrischika—Kartigai. Lunar: Asv. (Bah.); Sukla; Karttika (Bahula). Muhammadan: H. 1353 Rajab; H. 1353 Shaban.

Cyclic Sidereal Day	Week-Day	Day	Tithi	Tithi Ending Moment	Nakshatra	Nakshatra Ending Moment	Muhammadan Day
16	Th	1	...	...	10	·80	23
17	Fr	2	10	·00	11	·89	24
18	Sa	3	11	·07	12	·98	25
19	Su	4	12	·13	...	...	26
20	Mo	5	13	·15	13	·04	27
21	Tu	6	14	·17	14	·07	28
22	We	7	—A	·16	15	·09	29
23	Th	8	1	·13	16	·09	—30
24	Fr	9	2	·09	17	·08	1
25	Sa	10	3 / 4	·03 / ·95	18 / 19	·04 / ·99	2
26	Su	11	5	·86	20	·93	3
27	Mo	12	6	·76	21	·86	4
28	Tu	13	7	·66	22	·79	5
29	We	14	8	·56	23	·73	6
—30	Th	15	9	·47	24	·67	7
1	Fr	16	10	·38	25	·61	8
2	Sa	17	11	·30	26	·55	9
3	Su	18	12	·23	27	·52	10
4	Mo	19	13	·19	1	·50	11
5	Tu	20	14	·15	2	·50	12
6	We	21	P	·13	3	·51	13
7	Th	22	1	·15	4	·55	14
8	Fr	23	2	·17	5	·61	15
9	Sa	24	3	·22	6	·69	16
10	Su	25	4	·28	7	·78	17
11	Mo	26	5	·37	8	·88	18
12	Tu	27	6	·46	9	·99	19
13	We	28	7	·54	...	...	20
14	Th	29	8	·62	10	·10	21
15	Fr	30	9	·69	11	·20	22

Dec.

Solar: Bhava, Vrischika—Kartigai (to 30); Bhava, Dhanus—Margali. Lunar: Sukla; Margasira (Bahula). Muhammadan: H. 1353 Ramzan.

Cyclic Sidereal Day	Week-Day	Day	Tithi	Tithi Ending Moment	Nakshatra	Nakshatra Ending Moment	Muhammadan Day
16	Sa	1	10	·76	12	·28	23
17	Su	2	11	·79	13	·35	24
18	Mo	3	12	·79	14	·39	25
19	Tu	4	13	·78	15	·41	26
20	We	5	14	·76	16	·41	27
21	Th	6	—A	·71	17	·40	28
22	Fr	7	1	·65	18	·37	—29
23	Sa	8	2	·57	19	·33	1
24	Su	9	3	·48	20	·27	2
25	Mo	10	4	·39	21	·21	3
26	Tu	11	5	·29	22	·14	4
27	We	12	6	·19	23	·07	5
28	Th	13	7	·10	24 / 25	·00 / ·94	6
29	Fr	14	8 / 9	·01 / ·94	26	·89	7
—30	Sa	15	10	·87	27	·85	8
1	Su	16	11	·88	1	·83	9
2	Mo	17	12	·79	2	·82	10
3	Tu	18	13	·78	3	·83	11
4	We	19	14	·78	4	·86	12
5	Th	20	P	·82	5	·92	13
6	Fr	21	1	·87	...	...	14
7	Sa	22	2	·93	6	·00	15
8	Su	23	...	...	7	·08	16
9	Mo	24	3	·02	8	·18	17
10	Tu	25	4	·11	9	·29	18
11	We	26	5	·20	10	·40	19
12	Th	27	6	·28	11	·50	20
13	Fr	28	7	·34	12	·59	21
14	Sa	29	8	·40	13	·66	22
15	Su	30	9	·43	14	·70	23
16	Mo	31	10	·45	15	·73	24

15. Svati. **16.** Visak. **17.** Anur. **18.** Jyesh. **19.** Mula. **20.** P. Ash. **21.** U. Ash. **22** Sravn. **23.** Dani. **24.** Satab. **25.** P. Bhad. **26.** U. Bhad. **27.** Rev.

A. D. 1935.
Solar Eclipse. ●
Lunar Eclipse. ○

Mesha Sankranti (Commencement of Indian Sidereal Year).
(Surya Sid.) April 13·68.
(Arya Sid.) April 13·57.

Saka 1857. **Kaliyuga 5036.**
(S. Cycle) Yuva.

SOLAR reckoning: Cyclic Sidereal Year, Month and Day; Week-Day English Month and Day. LUNAR reckoning: Tithi Ending Moment; Nakshatra Ending Moment; Muhammadan Year, Month and Day.

Jan.

Solar month	Cyclic Sidereal Day	Week-Day	Eng. Day	Lunar month	Tithi	Tithi Ending Moment	Nakshatra	Nakshatra Ending Moment	Muhammadan month	Muhammadan Day
Bhava Dhanus—Margali	17	Tu	1	Mr.	11	·43	16	·75	Ramzan	25
	18	We	2		12	·40	17	·73		26
	19	Th	3	Bah.	13	·36	18	·70		27
	20	Fr	4		14	·30	19	·66		28
	21	Sa	5		—A	·22	20	·60		29
	22	Su	6		1	·13	21	·54		—30
	23	Mo	7		2 3	·04 ·94	22	·48		1
	24	Tu	8		4	·84	23	·41		2
	25	We	9		5	·75	24	·34		3
	26	Th	10		6	·66	25	·28		4
	27	Fr	11	Sukla	7	·58	26	·23		5
	28	Sa	12		8	·51	27	·19		6
	—29	Su	13		9	·47	1	·16		7
Bhava Makara—Tai.	1	Mo	14		10	·43	2	·14		8
	2	Tu	15		11	·42	3	·15		9
	3	We	16		12	·43	4	·19		10
	4	Th	17		13	·47	5	·23		11
	5	Fr	18	Pausha	14	·51	6	·30		12
	6	Sa ○	19		P	·59	7	·39		13
	7	Su	20		1	·67	8	·48		14
	8	Mo	21		2	·76	9	·59	H. 1353 Shawwal.	15
	9	Tu	22		3	·85	10	·70		16
	10	We	23		4	·93	11	·80		17
	11	Th	24		5	·99	12	·89		18
	12	Fr	25		...	...	13	·97		19
	13	Sa	26	Bahula	6	·04	...	...		20
	14	Su	27		7	·08	14	·02		21
	15	Mo	28		8	·09	15	·06		22
	16	Tu	29		9	·07	16	·07		23
	17	We	30		10	·04	17	·06		24
	18	Th	31		11 12	·00 ·93	18 19	·04 ·99		25

Feb.

Solar month	Cyclic Sidereal Day	Week-Day	Eng. Day	Lunar month	Tithi	Tithi Ending Moment	Nakshatra	Nakshatra Ending Moment	Muhammadan month	Muhammadan Day
	19	Fr	1		13	·85	20	·94		26
	20	Sa	2		14	·76	21	·88		27
	21	Su	3		—A	·66	22	·82		28
	22	Mo	4		1	·56	23	·75		—29
	23	Tu	5		2	·46	24	·68		1
	24	We	6		3	·37	25	·62		2
	25	Th	7		4	·29	26	·56		3
	26	Fr	8		5	·21	27	·52		4
	27	Sa	9		6	·14	1	·48		5
	28	Su	10	Sukla	7	·10	2	·47		6
	—29	Mo	11		8	·07	3	·48		7
Bhava Kumbha—Masi.	1	Tu	12		9	·06	4	·50		8
	2	We	13		10	·07	5	·54		9
	3	Th	14		11	·11	6	·61	H. 1353 Zi-l-ka'da.	10
	4	Fr	15		12	·16	7	·69		11
	5	Sa	16		13	·23	8	·78		12
	6	Su	17	Magha	14	·31	9	·89		13
	7	Mo	18		P	·40	...	...		14
	8	Tu	19		1	·48	10	·00		15
	9	We	20		2	·55	11	·11		16
	10	Th	21		3	·62	12	·20		17
	11	Fr	22		4	·68	13	·27		18
	12	Sa	23		5	·71	14	·34		19
	13	Su	24	Bahula	6	·71	15	·38		20
	14	Mo	25		7	·70	16	·39		21
	15	Tu	26		8	·66	17	·39		22
	16	We	27		9	·60	18	·37		23
	17	Th	28		10	·54	19	·34		24

March

Solar month	Cyclic Sidereal Day	Week-Day	Eng. Day	Lunar month	Tithi	Tithi Ending Moment	Nakshatra	Nakshatra Ending Moment	Muhammadan month	Muhammadan Day
Bhava Kumbha—Masi.	18	Fr	1	Mg.	11	·46	20	·29	Zi-l-ka'da.	25
	19	Sa	2		12	·38	21	·23		26
	20	Su	3	Bah.	13	·28	22	·16		27
	21	Mo	4		14	·18	23	·09		28
	22	Tu	5		A 1	·08 ·99	24 25	·02 ·96		29
	23	We	6		2	·90	26	·90		—30
	24	Th	7		3	·82	27	·85		1
	25	Fr	8		4	·75	1	·81		2
	26	Sa	9		5	·71	2	·79		3
	27	Su	10		6	·68	3	·80		4
	28	Mo	11	Sukla	7	·66	4	·82		5
	29	Tu	12		8	·67	5	·85		6
	—30	We	13		9	·71	6	·91		7
Bhava Mina—Panguni.	1	Th	14		10	·75	7	·99		8
	2	Fr	15		11	·83	...	...		9
	3	Sa	16		12	·91	8	·09		10
	4	Su	17		...	...	9	·19		11
	5	Mo	18		13	·00	10	·30		12
	6	Tu	19	Phalguna	14	·09	11	·40		13
	7	We	20		P	·17	12	·50		14
	8	Th	21		1	·23	13	·59	H. 1353 Zi-l-hijja.	15
	9	Fr	22		2	·27	14	·65		16
	10	Sa	23		3	·30	15	·69		17
	11	Su	24		4	·30	16	·71		18
	12	Mo	25		5	·29	17	·71		19
	13	Tu	26	Bahula	6	·25	18	·70		20
	14	We	27		7	·20	19	·67		21
	15	Th	28		8	·13	20	·62		22
	16	Fr	29		9 10	·05 ·95	21	·56		23
	17	Sa	30		11	·85	22	·50		24
	18	Su	31		12	·75	23	·43		25

April

Solar month	Cyclic Sidereal Day	Week-Day	Eng. Day	Lunar month	Tithi	Tithi Ending Moment	Nakshatra	Nakshatra Ending Moment	Muhammadan month	Muhammadan Day
	19	Mo	1		13	·65	24	·36		26
	20	Tu	2		14	·56	25	·30		27
	21	We	3		—A	·47	26	·24		28
	22	Th	4		1	·39	27	·18		—29
	23	Fr	5		2	·32	1	·14		1
	24	Sa	6		3	·28	2	·13		2
	25	Su	7		4	·25	3	·12		3
	26	Mo	8		5	·23	4	·13		4
	27	Tu	9		6	·22	5	·17		5
	28	We	10	Sukla	7	·26	6	·22		6
	29	Th	11		8	·32	7	·30		7
	30	Fr	12		9	·39	8	·39		8
	—31	Sa	13		10	·47	9	·49		9
Yuva Mesha—Chittirai.	1	Su	14		11	·56	10	·60		10
	2	Mo	15		12	·64	11	·70		11
	3	Tu	16	Chaitra	13	·72	12	·80		12
	4	We	17		14	·78	13	·89		13
	5	Th	18		P	·83	14	·96		14
	6	Fr	19		1	·85	...	...		15
	7	Sa	20		2	·86	15	·01	H. 1354 Muharram.	16
	8	Su	21		3	·88	16	·03		17
	9	Mo	22		4	·79	17	·05		18
	10	Tu	23		5	·74	18	·03		19
	11	We	24		6	·67	19 20	·00 ·96		20
	12	Th	25	Bahula	7	·59	21	·90		21
	13	Fr	26		8	·50	22	·84		22
	14	Sa	27		9	·40	23	·77		23
	15	Su	28		10	·30	24	·70		24
	16	Mo	29		11	·20	25	·63		25
	17	Tu	30		12	·10	26	·57		26

May

Solar month	Cyclic Sidereal Day	Week-Day	Eng. Day	Lunar month	Tithi	Tithi Ending Moment	Nakshatra	Nakshatra Ending Moment	Muhammadan month	Muhammadan Day
Yuva Mesha—Chittirai.	18	We	1		13 14	·00 ·92	27	·52	Muharram.	27
	19	Th	2		—A	·85	1	·48		28
	20	Fr	3		1	·81	2	·45		29
	21	Sa	4		2	·78	3	·44		30
	22	Su	5		3	·76	4	·45		1
	23	Mo	6		4	·76	5	·48		2
	24	Tu	7		5	·80	6	·54		3
	25	We	8		6	·85	7	·61		4
	26	Th	9	Sukla	7	·92	8	·69		5
	27	Fr	10		8	·99	9	·79		6
	28	Sa	11		...	...	10	·90		7
	29	Su	12		9	·07	...	...		8
	—30	Mo	13		10	·16	11	·01		9
Yuva Vrishabha—Vaikasi.	1	Tu	14		11	·23	12	·11		10
	2	We	15		12	·30	13	·20		11
	3	Th	16	Vaisakha	13	·34	14	·27		12
	4	Fr	17		14	·36	15	·32		13
	5	Sa	18		P	·37	16	·35		14
	6	Su	19		1	·35	17	·37	H. 1354 Safar.	15
	7	Mo	20		2	·32	18	·36		16
	8	Tu	21		3	·25	19	·33		17
	9	We	22		4	·18	20	·29		18
	10	Th	23		5	·10	21	·24		19
	11	Fr	24	Bahula	6 7	·01 ·91	22	·18		20
	12	Sa	25		8	·81	23	·11		21
	13	Su	26		9	·71	24 25	·04 ·97		22
	14	Mo	27		10	·61	26	·91		23
	15	Tu	28		11	·51	27	·86		24
	16	We	29		12	·43	1	·81		25
	17	Th	30		13	·36	2	·78		26
	18	Fr	31		14	·31	3	·76		27

June

Solar month	Cyclic Sidereal Day	Week-Day	Eng. Day	Lunar month	Tithi	Tithi Ending Moment	Nakshatra	Nakshatra Ending Moment	Muhammadan month	Muhammadan Day
	19	Sa	1		—A	·27	4	·77		28
	20	Su	2		1	·26	5	·80		—29
	21	Mo	3		2	·26	6	·85		1
	22	Tu	4		3	·29	7	·91		2
	23	We	5		4	·33	8	·99		3
	24	Th	6		5	·41	...	...		4
	25	Fr	7		6	·49	9	·09		5
	26	Sa	8	Sukla	7	·57	10	·20		6
	27	Su	9		8	·65	11	·31		7
	28	Mo	10		9	·73	12	·41		8
	29	Tu	11		10	·78	13	·50		9
	30	We	12		11	·82	14	·58	H. 1354 Rabi-ul-awwal.	10
	31	Th	13		12	·85	15	·63		11
	—32	Fr	14	Jyeshtha	13	·85	16	·68		12
Yuva Mithuna—Ani.	1	Sa	15		14	·83	17	·69		13
	2	Su	16		P	·80	18	·69		14
	3	Mo	17		1	·75	19	·66		15
	4	Tu	18		2	·68	20	·62		16
	5	We	19		3	·59	21	·58		17
	6	Th	20		4	·49	22	·52		18
	7	Fr	21		5	·39	23	·45		19
	8	Sa	22	Bahula	6	·29	24	·38		20
	9	Su	23		7	·19	25	·31		21
	10	Mo	24		8	·09	26	·25		22
	11	Tu	25		9 10	·00 ·92	27	·19		23
	12	We	26		11	·85	1	·14		24
	13	Th	27		12	·79	2	·11		25
	14	Fr	28		13	·75	3	·09		26
	15	Sa	29		14	·74	4	·10		27
	16	Su	30		—A	·73	5	·12		28

Naksh :—1. Asvn. 2. Bhar. 3. Krit. 4. Rohi. 5. Mrig. 6. Ardh. 7. Punar. 8. Push. 9. Aslesh. 10. Magh. 11. P. Phal. 12. U. Phal. 13. Hasta. 14. Chit.

A. D. 1935. | **Kollam 1111,** Commences { **N. Malabar—Sept.** / **S. Malabar—Aug.** | **Hijra 1354,** Commences, **April 5.** | **Vikrama 1992.**

A.—Amavasya. | **Bengal San 1341.**

P.—Paurnami. | **(N. Cycle) Sarvajit.**

SOLAR reckoning: Cyclic Sidereal Year, Month and Day; Week-Day English Month and Day. LUNAR reckoning: Tithi Ending Moment; Nakshatra Ending Moment; Muhammadan Year, Month and Day.

July

Solar: Yuva Mithuna—Ani. / Yuva Karkata—Adi. — Lunar: Sukla, Ashadha, Bahula — H. 1354 Rabi-ul-akhir.

Cyclic Sidereal Year, Month and Day	Week-Day English Month and Day	Tithi Ending Moment	Nakshatra Ending Moment	Muhammadan Year, Month and Day
17	Mo 1	1 ·77	6 ·16	29
18	Tu 2	2 ·81	7 ·22	—30
19	We 3	3 ·88	8 ·29	1
20	Th 4	4 ·95	9 ·39	2
21	Fr 5	... ...	10 ·50	3
22	Sa 6	5 ·03	11 ·61	4
23	Su 7	6 ·11	12 ·71	5
24	Mo 8	7 ·19	13 ·81	6
25	Tu 9	8 ·26	14 ·88	7
26	We 10	9 ·30	15 ·95	8
27	Th 11	10 ·33	16 ·99	9
28	Fr 12	11 ·33	... ...	10
29	Sa 13	12 ·32	17 ·01	11
30	Su 14	13 ·28	18 ·01 19 ·99	12
31	Mo 15	14 ·22	20 ·97	13
—32	Tu ○16	P ·15	21 ·92	14
1	We 17	1 ·07 2 ·98	22 ·86	15
2	Th 18	3 ·88	23 ·79	16
3	Fr 19	4 ·78	24 ·72	17
4	Sa 20	5 ·68	25 ·65	18
5	Su 21	6 ·58	26 ·59	19
6	Mo 22	7 ·48	27 ·53	20
7	Tu 23	8 ·39	1 ·48	21
8	We 24	9 ·32	2 ·44	22
9	Th 25	10 ·27	3 ·42	23
10	Fr 26	11 ·24	4 ·42	24
11	Sa 27	12 ·22	5 ·43	25
12	Su 28	13 ·22	6 ·47	26
13	Mo 29	14 ·24	7 ·52	27
14	Tu 30	—A ·28	8 ·60	28
15	We 31	1 ·35	9 ·70	—29

Aug.

Solar: Yuva Simha—Avani. — Lunar: Sukla, Sravana, Bahula, B. Suk. — H. 1354 Jumadal-awwal.

Cyclic Sidereal Year, Month and Day	Week-Day English Month and Day	Tithi Ending Moment	Nakshatra Ending Moment	Muhammadan Year, Month and Day
16	Th 1	2 ·42	10 ·80	1
17	Fr 2	3 ·51	11 ·91	2
18	Sa 3	4 ·59	... ...	3
19	Su 4	5 ·67	12 ·01	4
20	Mo 5	6 ·73	13 ·11	5
21	Tu 6	7 ·78	14 ·20	6
22	We 7	8 ·81	15 ·26	7
23	Th 8	9 ·81	16 ·31	8
24	Fr 9	10 ·80	17 ·33	9
25	Sa 10	11 ·77	18 ·34	10
26	Su 11	12 ·72	19 ·33	11
27	Mo 12	13 ·65	20 ·30	12
28	Tu 13	14 ·56	21 ·25	13
29	We 14	P ·47	22 ·19	14
30	Th 15	1 ·37	23 ·13	15
—31	Fr 16	2 ·27	24 ·07	16
1	Sa 17	3 ·17	25 ·00 26 ·93	17
2	Su 18	4 ·07 5 ·98	27 ·86	18
3	Mo 19	6 ·90	1 ·81	19
4	Tu 20	7 ·83	2 ·77	20
5	We 21	8 ·77	3 ·75	21
6	Th 22	9 ·73	4 ·74	22
7	Fr 23	10 ·71	5 ·75	23
8	Sa 24	11 ·72	6 ·78	24
9	Su 25	12 ·74	7 ·83	25
10	Mo 26	13 ·79	8 ·91	26
11	Tu 27	14 ·85	... ...	27
12	We 28	—A ·92	9 ·00	28
13	Th 29	... ...	10 ·10	29
14	Fr 30	1 ·00	11 ·20	—30
15	Sa 31	2 ·08	12 ·31	1

Sep.

Solar: Yuva Simha—Avani. / Yuva Kanya—Purattasi. — Lunar: Sukla, Bhadrapada, Bahula — H. 1354 Jumadal-akhir.

Cyclic Sidereal Year, Month and Day	Week-Day English Month and Day	Tithi Ending Moment	Nakshatra Ending Moment	Muhammadan Year, Month and Day
16	Su 1	3 ·17	13 ·41	2
17	Mo 2	4 ·24	14 ·50	3
18	Tu 3	5 ·29	15 ·57	4
19	We 4	6 ·32	16 ·62	5
20	Th 5	7 ·33	17 ·65	6
21	Fr 6	8 ·31	18 ·67	7
22	Sa 7	9 ·28	19 ·66	8
23	Su 8	10 ·23	20 ·63	9
24	Mo 9	11 ·16	21 ·58	10
25	Tu 10	12 ·08 13 ·99	22 ·53	11
26	We 11	14 ·90	23 ·48	12
27	Th 12	P ·80	24 ·41	13
28	Fr 13	1 ·70	25 ·34	14
29	Sa 14	2 ·60	26 ·27	15
30	Su 15	3 ·51	27 ·20	16
—31	Mo 16	4 ·43	1 ·14	17
1	Tu 17	5 ·36	2 ·11	18
2	We 18	6 ·31	3 ·08	19
3	Th 19	7 ·26	4 ·06	20
4	Fr 20	8 ·24	5 ·07	21
5	Sa 21	9 ·26	6 ·09	22
6	Su 22	10 ·28	7 ·15	23
7	Mo 23	11 ·33	8 ·22	24
8	Tu 24	12 ·39	9 ·30	25
9	We 25	13 ·46	10 ·40	26
10	Th 26	14 ·54	11 ·51	27
11	Fr 27	—A ·62	12 ·62	28
12	Sa 28	1 ·71	13 ·72	—29
13	Su 29	2 ·78	14 ·81	1
14	Mo 30	3 ·83	15 ·88	2

Oct.

Solar: Yuva Tula—Aippasi. — Lunar: Sukla, Asvina, Bahula, K. Suk. — H. 1354 Rajab.

Cyclic Sidereal Year, Month and Day	Week-Day English Month and Day	Tithi Ending Moment	Nakshatra Ending Moment	Muhammadan Year, Month and Day
15	Tu 1	4 ·86	16 ·94	3
16	We 2	5 ·88	17 ·98	4
17	Th 3	6 ·86	18 ·99	5
18	Fr 4	7 ·84	19 ·98	6
19	Sa 5	8 ·79	20 ·96	7
20	Su 6	9 ·71	21 ·92	8
21	Mo 7	10 ·63	22 ·87	9
22	Tu 8	11 ·55	23 ·81	10
23	We 9	12 ·46	24 ·74	11
24	Th 10	13 ·36	25 ·67	12
25	Fr 11	14 ·26	26 ·60	13
26	Sa 12	P ·16	27 ·54	14
27	Su 13	1 ·07 2 ·99	1 ·49	15
28	Mo 14	3 ·92	2 ·44	16
29	Tu 15	4 ·87	3 ·41	17
—30	We 16	5 ·83	4 ·39	18
1	Th 17	6 ·82	5 ·39	19
2	Fr 18	7 ·83	6 ·42	20
3	Sa 19	8 ·86	7 ·46	21
4	Su 20	9 ·91	8 ·52	22
5	Mo 21	10 ·97	9 ·60	23
6	Tu 22	... ...	10 ·70	24
7	We 23	11 ·04	11 ·81	25
8	Th 24	12 ·12	12 ·92	26
9	Fr 25	13 ·21	... ...	27
10	Sa 26	14 ·30	13 ·02	28
11	Su 27	—A ·37	14 ·11	29
12	Mo 28	1 ·41	15 ·19	—30
13	Tu 29	2 ·45	16 ·25	1
14	We 30	3 ·47	17 ·30	2
15	Th 31	4 ·45	18 ·31	3

Nov.

Solar: Yuva Tula—Aippasi. / Yuva Vrischika—Karttigai. — Lunar: Sukla, Karttika, Bahula — H. 1354 Shaban.

Cyclic Sidereal Year, Month and Day	Week-Day English Month and Day	Tithi Ending Moment	Nakshatra Ending Moment	Muhammadan Year, Month and Day
16	Fr 1	5 ·42	19 ·31	4
17	Sa 2	6 ·38	20 ·29	5
18	Su 3	7 ·31	21 ·25	6
19	Mo 4	8 ·24	22 ·21	7
20	Tu 5	9 ·15	23 ·15	8
21	We 6	10 ·05 11 ·95	24 ·08	9
22	Th 7	12 ·85	25 ·01 26 ·94	10
23	Fr 8	13 ·76	27 ·88	11
24	Sa 9	14 ·67	1 ·82	12
25	Su 10	P ·59	2 ·77	13
26	Mo 11	1 ·53	3 ·73	14
27	Tu 12	2 ·47	4 ·71	15
28	We 13	3 ·44	5 ·71	16
29	Th 14	4 ·43	6 ·73	17
—30	Fr 15	5 ·44	7 ·77	18
1	Sa 16	6 ·46	8 ·83	19
2	Su 17	7 ·51	9 ·90	20
3	Mo 18	8 ·58	... ...	21
4	Tu 19	9 ·66	10 ·00	22
5	We 20	10 ·75	11 ·11	23
6	Th 21	11 ·84	12 ·22	24
7	Fr 22	12 ·92	13 ·32	25
8	Sa 23	13 ·99	14 ·41	26
9	Su 24	... ...	15 ·49	27
10	Mo 25	14 ·04	16 ·57	28
11	Tu 26	—A ·07	17 ·61	—29
12	We 27	1 ·07	18 ·63	1
13	Th 28	2 ·06	19 ·63	2
14	Fr 29	3 ·04 4 ·99	20 ·62	3
15	Sa 30	5 ·94	21 ·59	4

Dec.

Solar: Yuva Dhanus—Margali. — Lunar: Sukla, Margasira, Bahula, Pah. Suk. — H. 1354 Ramzan. / Shawwal.

Cyclic Sidereal Year, Month and Day	Week-Day English Month and Day	Tithi Ending Moment	Nakshatra Ending Moment	Muhammadan Year, Month and Day
16	Su 1	6 ·86	22 ·55	5
17	Mo 2	7 ·77	23 ·49	6
18	Tu 3	8 ·68	24 ·42	7
19	We 4	9 ·58	25 ·35	8
20	Th 5	10 ·48	26 ·28	9
21	Fr 6	11 ·38	27 ·22	10
22	Sa 7	12 ·29	1 ·16	11
23	Su 8	13 ·21	2 ·11	12
24	Mo 9	14 ·15	3 ·07	13
25	Tu 10	P ·10	4 ·05	14
26	We 11	1 ·07	5 ·04	15
27	Th 12	2 ·06	6 ·05	16
28	Fr 13	3 ·07	7 ·08	17
29	Sa 14	4 ·11	8 ·13	18
—30	Su 15	5 ·16	9 ·21	19
1	Mo 16	6 ·23	10 ·31	20
2	Tu 17	7 ·31	11 ·41	21
3	We 18	8 ·40	12 ·51	22
4	Th 19	9 ·49	13 ·62	23
5	Fr 20	10 ·57	14 ·72	24
6	Sa 21	11 ·64	15 ·81	25
7	Su 22	12 ·68	16 ·88	26
8	Mo 23	13 ·72	17 ·92	27
9	Tu 24	14 ·73	18 ·95	28
10	We 25	—A ·72	19 ·96	29
11	Th 26	1 ·68	20 ·95	—30
12	Fr 27	2 ·64	21 ·92	1
13	Sa 28	3 ·57	22 ·88	2
14	Su 29	4 ·49	23 ·82	3
15	Mo 30	5 ·41	24 ·76	4
16	Tu 31	6 ·31	25 ·70	5

15. Svati. 16. Visak. 17. Anur. 18. Jyesh. 19. Mula. 20. P. Ash. 21. U. Ash. 22. Sravn. 23. Dani. 24. Satab. 25. P. Bhad. 26. U. Bhad. 27. Rev.

A. D. 1936.
Solar Eclipse. ●
Lunar Eclipse. ○

Mesha Sankranti (Commencement of Indian Sidereal Year).
(Surya Sid.) April 12·94.
(Arya Sid.) April 12·83.

Saka 1858. Kaliyuga 5037.
(S. Cycle) Dhatri.

SOLAR reckoning: Cyclic Sidereal Year, Month and Day; Week-Day English Month and Day. LUNAR reckoning: Tithi Ending Moment; Nakshatra Ending Moment; Muhammadan Year, Month and Day.

Jan.

Cyclic Sidereal Year, Month and Day	Week-Day English Month and Day	Tithi Ending Moment	Nakshatra Ending Moment	Muhammadan Year, Month and Day
Yuva Dhanus—Margali 17	We 1	Pausha Sukla 7 ·21	26 ·63	H. 1354 Shawwal 6
18	Th 2	8 ·11	27 ·56	7
19	Fr 3	9 ·02 / 10 ·94	1 ·50	8
20	Sa 4	11 ·86	2 ·44	9
21	Su 5	12 ·80	3 ·41	10
22	Mo 6	13 ·75	4 ·38	11
23	Tu 7	14 ·72	5 ·36	12
24	We ○ 8	P ·71	6 ·37	13
25	Th 9	1 ·73	7 ·40	14
26	Fr 10	2 ·76	8 ·44	15
27	Sa 11	3 ·81	9 ·52	16
28	Su 12	4 ·88	10 ·61	17
—29	Mo 13	5 ·96	11 ·70	18
Yuva Makara—Tai 1	Tu 14	Bahula	12 ·81	19
2	We 15	6 ·05	13 ·92	20
3	Th 16	7 ·14	... ...	21
4	Fr 17	8 ·22	14 ·02	22
5	Sa 18	9 ·29	15 ·11	23
6	Su 19	10 ·34	16 ·19	24
7	Mo 20	11 ·37	17 ·24	25
8	Tu 21	12 ·37	18 ·27	26
9	We 22	13 ·36	19 ·29	27
10	Th 23	14 ·32	20 ·28	28
11	Fr 24	—A ·28	21 ·26	—29
12	Sa 25	Sukla 1 ·21	22 ·21	1
13	Su 26	2 ·13	23 ·16	2
14	Mo 27	3 ·04 / 4 ·94	24 ·10	3
15	Tu 28	5 ·84	25 ·04 / 26 ·97	4
16	We 29	6 ·74	27 ·90	5
17	Th 30	7 ·65	1 ·83	6
18	Fr 31	8 ·56	2 ·77	7

Feb.

Cyclic Sidereal Year, Month and Day	Week-Day English Month and Day	Tithi Ending Moment	Nakshatra Ending Moment	Muhammadan Year, Month and Day
19	Sa 1	Magha 9 ·49	3 ·73	H. 1354 Zi-l-ka'da 8
20	Su 2	10 ·43	4 ·70	9
21	Mo 3	11 ·39	5 ·69	10
22	Tu 4	12 ·36	6 ·69	11
23	We 5	13 ·34	7 ·71	12
24	Th 6	14 ·36	8 ·76	13
25	Fr 7	P ·40	9 ·83	14
26	Sa 8	1 ·46	10 ·91	15
27	Su 9	2 ·53	... ...	16
28	Mo 10	3 ·61	11 ·00	17
29	Tu 11	4 ·69	12 ·11	18
—30	We 12	5 ·78	13 ·22	19
Yuva Kumbha—Masi 1	Th 13	Bahula 6 ·86	14 ·33	20
2	Fr 14	7 ·92	15 ·42	21
3	Sa 15	8 ·97	16 ·49	22
4	Su 16	... ...	17 ·55	23
5	Mo 17	9 ·00	18 ·60	24
6	Tu 18	10 ·01 / 11 ·99	19 ·62	25
7	We 19	12 ·95	20 ·61	26
8	Th 20	13 ·89	21 ·58	27
9	Fr 21	14 ·83	22 ·55	28
10	Sa 22	—A ·76	23 ·50	29
11	Su 23	Phalg. Suk. 1 ·67	24 ·44	—30
12	Mo 24	2 ·57	25 ·38	Zi-l-hijja 1
13	Tu 25	3 ·47	26 ·31	2
14	We 26	4 ·37	27 ·24	3
15	Th 27	5 ·27	1 ·17	4
16	Fr 28	6 ·18	2 ·12	5
17	Sa 29	7 ·11	3 ·07	6

March

Cyclic Sidereal Year, Month and Day	Week-Day English Month and Day	Tithi Ending Moment	Nakshatra Ending Moment	Muhammadan Year, Month and Day
18	Su 1	Phalguna Sukla 8 ·05	4 ·03	H. 1354 Zi-l-hijja 7
19	Mo 2	9 ·00 / 10 ·97	5 ·01	8
20	Tu 3	11 ·96	6 ·01	9
21	We 4	12 ·97	7 ·04	10
22	Th 5	... ...	8 ·08	11
23	Fr 6	13 ·01	9 ·13	12
24	Sa 7	14 ·07	10 ·21	13
25	Su 8	P ·14	11 ·30	14
26	Mo 9	1 ·22	12 ·41	15
27	Tu 10	2 ·31	13 ·52	16
28	We 11	3 ·40	14 ·63	17
29	Th 12	4 ·47	15 ·72	18
—30	Fr 13	5 ·53	16 ·80	19
Yuva Mina—Panguni 1	Sa 14	Bahula 6 ·57	17 ·87	20
2	Su 15	7 ·59	18 ·91	21
3	Mo 16	8 ·60	19 ·93	22
4	Tu 17	9 ·58	20 ·93	23
5	We 18	10 ·55	21 ·91	24
6	Th 19	11 ·49	22 ·88	25
7	Fr 20	12 ·43	23 ·84	26
8	Sa 21	13 ·35	24 ·78	27
9	Su 22	14 ·25	25 ·71	28
10	Mo 23	—A ·15	26 ·64	—29
11	Tu 24	Sukla 1 ·05 / 2 ·95	27 ·57	1
12	We 25	3 ·86	1 ·51	2
13	Th 26	4 ·77	2 ·45	3
14	Fr 27	5 ·69	3 ·40	4
15	Sa 28	6 ·62	4 ·36	5
16	Su 29	7 ·58	5 ·34	6
17	Mo 30	8 ·55	6 ·34	7
18	Tu 31	9 ·54	7 ·35	8

April

Cyclic Sidereal Year, Month and Day	Week-Day English Month and Day	Tithi Ending Moment	Nakshatra Ending Moment	Muhammadan Year, Month and Day
19	We 1	Chaitra 10 ·56	8 ·38	H. 1355 Muharram 9
20	Th 2	11 ·59	9 ·44	10
21	Fr 3	12 ·64	10 ·51	11
22	Sa 4	13 ·72	11 ·61	12
23	Su 5	14 ·80	12 ·71	13
24	Mo 6	P ·89	13 ·82	14
25	Tu 7	1 ·97	14 ·92	15
26	We 8	... ...	... ...	16
27	Th 9	2 ·04	15 ·02	17
28	Fr 10	3 ·09	16 ·11	18
29	Sa 11	4 ·14	17 ·18	19
—30	Su 12	5 ·16	18 ·23	20
Dhatri Mesha—Chittirai 1	Mo 13	Bahula 6 ·16	19 ·25	21
2	Tu 14	7 ·14	20 ·26	22
3	We 15	8 ·11	21 ·25	23
4	Th 16	9 ·05 / 10 ·98	22 ·22	24
5	Fr 17	11 ·90	23 ·18	25
6	Sa 18	12 ·81	24 ·12	26
7	Su 19	13 ·71	25 ·05 / 26 ·98	27
8	Mo 20	14 ·60	27 ·91	28
9	Tu 21	—A ·50	1 ·85	29
10	We 22	Vaisakha Sukla 1 ·40	2 ·79	—30
11	Th 23	2 ·31	3 ·73	H. 1355 Safar 1
12	Fr 24	3 ·23	4 ·69	2
13	Sa 25	4 ·17	5 ·67	3
14	Su 26	5 ·12	6 ·66	4
15	Mo 27	6 ·10	7 ·67	5
16	Tu 28	7 ·08	8 ·70	6
17	We 29	8 ·08	9 ·75	7
18	Th 30	9 ·12	10 ·82	8

May

Cyclic Sidereal Year, Month and Day	Week-Day English Month and Day	Tithi Ending Moment	Nakshatra Ending Moment	Muhammadan Year, Month and Day
19	Fr 1	Vaisakha Suk. 10 ·17	11 ·91	H. 1355 Safar 9
20	Sa 2	11 ·24	... ...	10
21	Su 3	12 ·32	12 ·01	11
22	Mo 4	13 ·41	13 ·12	12
23	Tu 5	14 ·48	14 ·22	13
24	We 6	P ·55	15 ·32	14
25	Th 7	1 ·62	16 ·41	15
26	Fr 8	2 ·67	17 ·49	16
27	Sa 9	3 ·69	18 ·54	17
28	Su 10	4 ·68	19 ·57	18
29	Mo 11	5 ·67	20 ·58	19
30	Tu 12	Bahula 6 ·63	21 ·58	20
—31	We 13	7 ·57	22 ·55	21
Dhatri Vrishabha—Vaikasi 1	Th 14	8 ·50	23 ·51	22
2	Fr 15	9 ·41	24 ·45	23
3	Sa 16	10 ·32	25 ·39	24
4	Su 17	11 ·22	26 ·33	25
5	Mo 18	12 ·12	27 ·26	26
6	Tu 19	13 ·02 / 14 ·92	1 ·19	27
7	We 20	—A ·82	2 ·13	28
8	Th 21	Sukla 1 ·74	3 ·07	—29
9	Fr 22	2 ·68	4 ·03	1
10	Sa 23	3 ·63	5 ·00 / 6 ·98	2
11	Su 24	4 ·60	7 ·99	3
12	Mo 25	5 ·58	... ...	4
13	Tu 26	6 ·60	8 ·01	5
14	We 27	7 ·63	9 ·06	6
15	Th 28	8 ·67	10 ·13	7
16	Fr 29	9 ·74	11 ·21	8
17	Sa 30	10 ·82	12 ·31	9
18	Su 31	11 ·90	13 ·42	10

June

Cyclic Sidereal Year, Month and Day	Week-Day English Month and Day	Tithi Ending Moment	Nakshatra Ending Moment	Muhammadan Year, Month and Day
19	Mo 1	Jyeshtha 12 ·98	14 ·53	H. 1355 Rabi-ul-awwal 11
20	Tu 2	... ...	15 ·63	12
21	We 3	13 ·06	16 ·72	13
22	Th 4	14 ·12	17 ·80	14
23	Fr 5	P ·15	18 ·85	15
24	Sa 6	1 ·17	19 ·89	16
25	Su 7	2 ·18	20 ·91	17
26	Mo 8	3 ·17	21 ·91	18
27	Tu 9	4 ·13	22 ·88	19
28	We 10	5 ·07	23 ·84	20
29	Th 11	Bahula 6 ·00 / 7 ·91	24 ·79	21
30	Fr 12	8 ·81	25 ·74	22
—31	Sa 13	9 ·71	26 ·67	23
Dhatri Mithuna—Ani 1	Su 14	10 ·61	27 ·60	24
2	Mo 15	11 ·51	1 ·53	25
3	Tu 16	12 ·41	2 ·46	26
4	We 17	13 ·32	3 ·41	27
5	Th 18	14 ·24	4 ·36	28
6	Fr ● 19	—A ·17	5 ·33	29
7	Sa 20	Ashadha Sukla 1 ·11	6 ·31	—30
8	Su 21	2 ·08	7 ·31	H. 1355 Rabi-ul-akhir 1
9	Mo 22	3 ·06	8 ·33	2
10	Tu 23	4 ·07	9 ·38	3
11	We 24	5 ·10	10 ·44	4
12	Th 25	6 ·15	11 ·52	5
13	Fr 26	7 ·21	12 ·61	6
14	Sa 27	8 ·29	13 ·71	7
15	Su 28	9 ·37	14 ·82	8
16	Mo 29	10 ·45	15 ·93	9
17	Tu 30	11 ·53	... ...	10

Naksh :—1. Asvn. 2. Bhar. 3. Krit. 4. Rohi. 5. Mrig. 6. Ardh. 7. Punar. 8. Push. 9. Aslesh. 10. Magh. 11. P. Phal. 12. U. Phal. 13. Hasta. 14. Chit.

A. D. 1936.
A.—Amavasya.
P.—Paurnami.

Kollam 1112, Commences { N. Malabar—Sept. / S. Malabar—Aug.

Hijra 1355, Commences, March 24.

Vikrama 1993.
Bengal San 1342.
(N. Cycle) Sarvadharin.

SOLAR reckoning: Cyclic Sidereal Year, Month and Day	Week-Day English Month and Day	LUNAR reckoning: Tithi Ending Moment	Nakshatra Ending Moment	Muhammadan Year, Month and Day
	July			
Dhatri *Mithuna—Adi.* 18	We 1	Ashadha *Suk.* 12 ·59	16 ·03	H. 1355 *Rabi-ul-akhir.* 11
19	Th 2	13 ·64	17 ·10	12
20	Fr 3	14 ·66	18 ·16	13
21	Sa ○ 4	P ·66	19 ·21	14
22	Su 5	*Bahula* 1 ·64	20 ·23	15
23	Mo 6	2 ·60	21 ·23	16
24	Tu 7	3 ·54	22 ·21	17
25	We 8	4 ·47	23 ·18	18
26	Th 9	5 ·39	24 ·14	19
27	Fr 10	6 ·29	25 ·08	20
28	Sa 11	7 ·19	26 ·01 27 ·94	21
29	Su 12	8 ·09 9 ·99	1 ·87	22
30	Mo 13	10 ·89	2 ·81	23
31	Tu 14	11 ·79	3 ·75	24
—32	We 15	12 ·71	4 ·70	25
Dhatri *Karkata—Adi.* 1	Th 16	13 ·64	5 ·66	26
2	Fr 17	14 ·59	6 ·63	27
3	Sa 18	—A ·56	7 ·63	28
4	Su 19	*Sukla* 1 ·55	8 ·65	—29
5	Mo 20	2 ·55	9 ·69	1
6	Tu 21	3 ·57	10 ·74	2
7	We 22	4 ·62	11 ·82	3
8	Th 23	5 ·68	12 ·91	4
9	Fr 24	6 ·76	... ...	5
10	Sa 25	7 ·84	13 ·02	6
11	Su 26	8 ·93	14 ·13	7
12	Mo 27	... ...	15 ·23	8
13	Tu 28	9 ·01	16 ·33	9
14	We 29	10 ·07	17 ·41	10
15	Th 30	11 ·12	18 ·48	11
16	Fr 31	12 ·14	19 ·53	12
	Aug.			
17	Sa 1	13 ·14	20 ·55	H. 1355 *Jumadal-awwal.* 13
18	Su 2	14 ·12	21 ·56	14
19	Mo 3	P ·09	22 ·54	15
20	Tu 4	Sravana~ 1 ·03 2 ·96	23 ·51	16
21	We 5	3 ·88	24 ·47	17
22	Th 6	4 ·79	25 ·42	18
23	Fr 7	5 ·69	26 ·35	19
24	Sa 8	6 ·59	27 ·28	20
25	Su 9	7 ·49	1 ·21	21
26	Mo 10	8 ·39	2 ·14	22
27	Tu 11	*Bahula* 9 ·30	3 ·08	23
28	We 12	10 ·22	4 ·03 5 ·99	24
29	Th 13	11 ·14	6 ·96	25
30	Fr 14	12 ·08	7 ·96	26
—31	Sa 15	13 ·05	8 ·97	27
Dhatri *Simha—Avani.* 1	Su 16	14 ·04	... ...	28
2	Mo 17	—A ·05	9 ·00	29
3	Tu 18	Adhika Bhadrapada *Sukla* 1 ·07	10 ·05	—30
4	We 19	2 ·11	11 ·12	H. 1355 *Jumadal-akhir.* 1
5	Th 20	3 ·18	12 ·22	2
6	Fr 21	4 ·26	13 ·32	3
7	Sa 22	5 ·34	14 ·42	4
8	Su 23	6 ·42	15 ·53	5
9	Mo 24	7 ·50	16 ·63	6
10	Tu 25	8 ·57	17 ·72	7
11	We 26	9 ·61	18 ·79	8
12	Th 27	10 ·63	19 ·84	9
13	Fr 28	11 ·64	20 ·87	10
14	Sa 29	12 ·62	21 ·88	11
15	Su 30	13 ·59	22 ·87	12
16	Mo 31	14 ·54	23 ·85	13

SOLAR reckoning: Cyclic Sidereal Year, Month and Day	Week-Day English Month and Day	LUNAR reckoning: Tithi Ending Moment	Nakshatra Ending Moment	Muhammadan Year, Month and Day
	Sep.			
Dhatri *Simha—Avani.* 17	Tu 1	Adhika~Bhadra. P ·47	24 ·80	H. 1355 *Jumadal-akhir.* 14
18	We 2	1 ·39	25 ·75	15
19	Th 3	2 ·30	26 ·69	16
20	Fr 4	3 ·20	27 ·63	17
21	Sa 5	4 ·10	1 ·56	18
22	Su 6	5 ·00 6 ·90	2 ·49	19
23	Mo 7	7 ·81	3 ·42	20
24	Tu 8	8 ·73	4 ·36	21
25	We 9	9 ·66	5 ·32	22
26	Th 10	10 ·60	6 ·30	23
27	Fr 11	*Bahula* 11 ·57	7 ·29	24
28	Sa 12	12 ·56	8 ·29	25
29	Su 13	13 ·58	9 ·31	26
30	Mo 14	14 ·60	10 ·36	27
—31	Tu 15	—A ·64	11 ·43	28
Dhatri *Kanya—Purattasi.* 1	We 16	1 ·70	12 ·52	—29
2	Th 17	2 ·77	13 ·62	*Rajab.* 1
3	Fr 18	3 ·85	14 ·72	2
4	Sa 19	4 ·94	15 ·83	3
5	Su 20	... ...	16 ·94	4
6	Mo 21	5 ·02	... ...	5
7	Tu 22	6 ·09	17 ·03	6
8	We 23	*Sukla* 7 ·14	18 ·10	7
9	Th 24	8 ·17	19 ·16	8
10	Fr 25	9 ·18	20 ·19	9
11	Sa 26	10 ·17	21 ·20	10
12	Su 27	11 ·14	22 ·20	11
13	Mo 28	12 ·08	23 ·18	12
14	Tu 29	13 ·01 14 ·93	24 ·14	13
15	We 30	P ·85	25 ·08	14
	Oct.			
16	Th 1	Nija Bhadrapada 1 ·75	26 ·02 27 ·96	H. 1355 15
17	Fr 2	2 ·65	1 ·89	16
18	Sa 3	3 ·55	2 ·82	17
19	Su 4	4 ·45	3 ·76	18
20	Mo 5	5 ·36	4 ·70	19
21	Tu 6	6 ·28	5 ·66	20
22	We 7	7 ·21	6 ·63	21
23	Th 8	8 ·16	7 ·61	22
24	Fr 9	9 ·14	8 ·61	23
25	Sa 10	10 ·13	9 ·63	24
26	Su 11	*Bahula* 11 ·14	10 ·68	25
27	Mo 12	12 ·16	11 ·74	26
28	Tu 13	13 ·20	12 ·82	27
29	We 14	14 ·26	13 ·92	28
30	Th 15	—A ·34	... ...	29
—31	Fr 16	1 ·43	14 ·02	—30
Dhatri *Tula—Aippasi.* 1	Sa 17	2 ·52	15 ·13	H. 1355 *Shaban.* 1
2	Su 18	3 ·60	16 ·24	2
3	Mo 19	4 ·67	17 ·33	3
4	Tu 20	5 ·72	18 ·41	4
5	We 21	6 ·75	19 ·47	5
6	Th 22	*Sukla* 7 ·76	20 ·51	6
7	Fr 23	8 ·75	21 ·53	7
8	Sa 24	9 ·72	22 ·53	8
9	Su 25	10 ·67	23 ·51	9
10	Mo 26	11 ·60	24 ·47	10
11	Tu 27	12 ·52	25 ·42	11
12	We 28	Asvina 13 ·43	26 ·36	12
13	Th 29	14 ·33	27 ·30	13
14	Fr 30	P ·23	1 ·23	14
15	Sa 31	1 ·13	2 ·16	15

SOLAR reckoning: Cyclic Sidereal Year, Month and Day	Week-Day English Month and Day	LUNAR reckoning: Tithi Ending Moment	Nakshatra Ending Moment	Muhammadan Year, Month and Day
	Nov.			
Dhatri *Tula—Aippasi.* 16	Su 1	Asvina~ 2 ·04 3 ·96	3 ·09	H. 1355 *Shaban.* 16
17	Mo 2	4 ·88	4 ·04 5 ·99	17
18	Tu 3	5 ·81	6 ·95	18
19	We 4	6 ·76	7 ·93	19
20	Th 5	7 ·73	8 ·93	20
21	Fr 6	8 ·71	9 ·95	21
22	Sa 7	*Bahula* 9 ·73	10 ·99	22
23	Su 8	10 ·76	... ...	23
24	Mo 9	11 ·81	11 ·05	24
25	Tu 10	12 ·88	12 ·12	25
26	We 11	13 ·95	13 ·22	26
27	Th 12	... ...	14 ·32	27
28	Fr 13	14 ·04	15 ·43	28
29	Sa 14	—A ·14	16 ·54	—29
—30	Su 15	1 ·22	17 ·63	*Ramzan.* 1
Dhatri *Vrischika—Kartigai.* 1	Mo 16	2 ·28	18 ·71	2
2	Tu 17	3 ·33	19 ·78	3
3	We 18	4 ·37	20 ·83	4
4	Th 19	5 ·38	21 ·85	5
5	Fr 20	6 ·36	22 ·85	6
6	Sa 21	*Sukla* 7 ·32	23 ·84	7
7	Su 22	8 ·28	24 ·81	8
8	Mo 23	9 ·22	25 ·77	9
9	Tu 24	10 ·14	26 ·71	10
10	We 25	Karttika~ 11 ·05 12 ·96	27 ·64	11
11	Th 26	13 ·86	1 ·57	12
12	Fr 27	14 ·76	2 ·50	13
13	Sa 28	P ·66	3 ·44	14
14	Su 29	1 ·57	4 ·38	15
15	Mo 30	2 ·50	5 ·33	16
	Dec.			
16	Tu 1	3 ·43	6 ·28	H. 1355 17
17	We 2	4 ·38	7 ·26	18
18	Th 3	5 ·35	8 ·25	19
19	Fr 4	6 ·34	9 ·27	20
20	Sa 5	*Bahula* 7 ·36	10 ·30	21
21	Su 6	8 ·39	11 ·36	22
22	Mo 7	9 ·44	12 ·43	23
23	Tu 8	10 ·51	13 ·52	24
24	We 9	11 ·59	14 ·63	25
25	Th 10	12 ·68	15 ·74	26
26	Fr 11	13 ·78	16 ·84	27
27	Sa 12	14 ·86	17 ·94	28
28	Su 13	—A ·93	... ...	29
—29	Mo 14	1 ·98	18 ·02	—30
Dhatri *Dhanus—Margali.* 1	Tu 15	... ...	19 ·09	H. 1355 *Shawwal.* 1
2	We 16	2 ·00	20 ·14	2
3	Th 17	3 ·01	21 ·17	3
4	Fr 18	*Sukla*~ 4 ·00 5 ·97	22 ·18	4
5	Sa 19	6 ·91	23 ·16	5
6	Su 20	7 ·84	24 ·14	6
7	Mo 21	8 ·76	25 ·10	7
8	Tu 22	9 ·67	26 ·04 27 ·98	8
9	We 23	Margasira 10 ·58	1 ·91	9
10	Th 24	11 ·49	2 ·84	10
11	Fr 25	12 ·39	3 ·78	11
12	Sa 26	13 ·29	4 ·72	12
13	Su 27	14 ·21	5 ·66	13
14	Mo 28	P ·13	6 ·61	14
15	Tu 29	*Bah.*~ 1 ·07	7 ·58	15
16	We 30	2 ·03	8 ·58	16
17	Th 31	3 ·00 4 ·99	9 ·59	17

15. Svati. 16. Visak. 17. Anur. 18. Jyesh. 19. Mula. 20. P. Ash. 21. U. Ash. 22. Sravn. 23. Dani. 24. Satab. 25. P. Bhad. 26. U. Bhad. 27. Rev,

A. D. 1937. **Mesha Sankranti** (Commencement of Indian Sidereal Year).
Solar Eclipse. ● (Surya Sid.) April 13·19. Saka 1859. Kaliyuga 5038.
Lunar Eclipse. ○ (Arya Sid.) April 13·08. (S. Cycle) Isvara.

Columns: SOLAR reckoning — Cyclic Sidereal Year, Month and Day; Week-Day English Month and Day. LUNAR reckoning — Tithi Ending Moment; Nakshatra Ending Moment; Muhammadan Year, Month and Day.

Jan. — Solar: Dhatri Dhanus—Margali (18–29); Dhatri Makara—Tai (1–19). Tithi: Marg., Bahula, Sukla, Pausha. Muhammadan: H. 1355 Shawwal; H. 1355 Zi-l-ka'da.

Cyclic Sidereal	Week-Day, Jan.	Tithi	Nakshatra	Muhammadan
18	Fr 1	... ...	10 ·62	18
19	Sa 2	5 ·00	11 ·66	19
20	Su 3	6 ·04	12 ·73	20
21	Mo 4	7 ·10	13 ·82	21
22	Tu 5	8 ·17	14 ·92	22
23	We 6	9 ·25	... ...	23
24	Th 7	10 ·34	15 ·08	24
25	Fr 8	11 ·43	16 ·14	25
26	Sa 9	12 ·51	17 ·24	26
27	Su 10	13 ·57	18 ·33	27
28	Mo 11	14 ·62	19 ·41	28
29	Tu 12	A ·65	20 ·46	29
1	We 13	1 ·66	21 ·49	1
2	Th 14	2 ·64	22 ·50	2
3	Fr 15	3 ·61	23 ·50	3
4	Sa 16	4 ·56	24 ·47	4
5	Su 17	5 ·49	25 ·43	5
6	Mo 18	6 ·41	26 ·38	6
7	Tu 19	7 ·32	27 ·32	7
8	We 20	8 ·22	1 ·26	8
9	Th 21	9 ·12	2 ·19	9
10	Fr 22	10 ·02 / 11 ·93	3 ·12	10
11	Sa 23	12 ·85	4 ·05 / 5 ·99	11
12	Su 24	13 ·78	6 ·95	12
13	Mo 25	14 ·72	7 ·92	13
14	Tu 26	P ·67	8 ·91	14
15	We 27	1 ·64	9 ·91	15
16	Th 28	2 ·63	10 ·93	16
17	Fr 29	3 ·65	11 ·97	17
18	Sa 30	4 ·69	... ...	18
19	Su 31	5 ·75	12 ·05	19

Feb. — Solar: Dhatri Kumbha—Masi. Tithi: Bahula, Sukla, Magha, Bah. Muhammadan: H. 1355 Zi-l-hijja.

Cyclic Sidereal	Week-Day, Feb.	Tithi	Nakshatra	Muhammadan
20	Mo 1	6 ·82	13 ·13	20
21	Tu 2	7 ·90	14 ·22	21
22	We 3	8 ·99	15 ·33	22
23	Th 4	... ...	16 ·44	23
24	Fr 5	9 ·08	17 ·55	24
25	Sa 6	10 ·15	18 ·64	25
26	Su 7	11 ·22	19 ·71	26
27	Mo 8	12 ·27	20 ·77	27
28	Tu 9	13 ·29	21 ·81	28
29	We 10	14 ·29	22 ·82	29
30	Th 11	A ·27	23 ·82	30
1	Fr 12	1 ·24	24 ·80	1
2	Sa 13	2 ·18	25 ·77	2
3	Su 14	3 ·11	26 ·71	3
4	Mo 15	4 ·03 / 5 ·94	27 ·65	4
5	Tu 16	6 ·85	1 ·59	5
6	We 17	7 ·75	2 ·53	6
7	Th 18	8 ·65	3 ·46	7
8	Fr 19	9 ·55	4 ·39	8
9	Sa 20	10 ·46	5 ·33	9
10	Su 21	11 ·38	6 ·29	10
11	Mo 22	12 ·33	7 ·25	11
12	Tu 23	13 ·29	8 ·23	12
13	We 24	14 ·27	9 ·23	13
14	Th 25	P ·26	10 ·25	14
15	Fr 26	1 ·27	11 ·29	15
16	Sa 27	2 ·31	12 ·35	16
17	Su 28	3 ·37	13 ·43	17

March — Solar: Dhatri Kumbha—Masi (18–30); Dhatri Mina—Panguni (1–18). Tithi: Magha, Bahula, Sukla, Phalguna. Muhammadan: H. 1355 Zi-l-hijja; H. 1356 Muharram.

Cyclic Sidereal	Week-Day, March	Tithi	Nakshatra	Muhammadan
18	Mo 1	4 ·44	14 ·52	18
19	Tu 2	5 ·53	15 ·63	19
20	We 3	6 ·62	16 ·74	20
21	Th 4	7 ·70	17 ·85	21
22	Fr 5	8 ·77	18 ·94	22
23	Sa 6	9 ·83	... ...	23
24	Su 7	10 ·88	19 ·02	24
25	Mo 8	11 ·90	20 ·08	25
26	Tu 9	12 ·90	21 ·12	26
27	We 10	13 ·89	22 ·15	27
28	Th 11	14 ·85	23 ·15	28
29	Fr 12	A ·79	24 ·13	29
30	Sa 13	1 ·72	25 ·10	30
1	Su 14	2 ·63	26 ·05	1
2	Mo 15	3 ·54	27 ·00 / 1 ·93	2
3	Tu 16	4 ·44	2 ·86	3
4	We 17	5 ·34	3 ·79	4
5	Th 18	6 ·24	4 ·73	5
6	Fr 19	7 ·15	5 ·67	6
7	Sa 20	8 ·06 / 9 ·98	6 ·62	7
8	Su 21	10 ·92	7 ·58	8
9	Mo 22	11 ·88	8 ·56	9
10	Tu 23	12 ·86	9 ·55	10
11	We 24	13 ·85	10 ·57	11
12	Th 25	14 ·87	11 ·61	12
13	Fr 26	P ·90	12 ·66	13
14	Sa 27	1 ·96	13 ·73	14
15	Su 28	... ...	14 ·82	15
16	Mo 29	2 ·03	15 ·92	16
17	Tu 30	3 ·11	... ...	17
18	We 31	4 ·20	16 ·03	18

April — Solar: Dhatri Mina—Panguni (19–30); Isvara Mesha—Chittirai (1–18). Tithi: Bahula, Sukla, Chaitra, Bah. Muhammadan: H. 1356 Muharram; H. 1356 Safar.

Cyclic Sidereal	Week-Day, April	Tithi	Nakshatra	Muhammadan
19	Th 1	5 ·28	17 ·14	19
20	Fr 2	6 ·35	18 ·24	20
21	Sa 3	7 ·41	19 ·33	21
22	Su 4	8 ·46	20 ·39	22
23	Mo 5	9 ·48	21 ·45	23
24	Tu 6	10 ·47	22 ·47	24
25	We 7	11 ·45	23 ·48	25
26	Th 8	12 ·41	24 ·46	26
27	Fr 9	13 ·36	25 ·43	27
28	Sa 10	14 ·29	26 ·39	28
29	Su 11	A ·20	27 ·34	29
30	Mo 12	1 ·10	1 ·27	30
1	Tu 13	2 ·00 / 3 ·90	2 ·20	1
2	We 14	4 ·80	3 ·13	2
3	Th 15	5 ·71	4 ·07	3
4	Fr 16	6 ·63	5 ·01 / 6 ·95	4
5	Sa 17	7 ·55	7 ·91	5
6	Su 18	8 ·48	8 ·88	6
7	Mo 19	9 ·44	9 ·88	7
8	Tu 20	10 ·41	10 ·89	8
9	We 21	11 ·39	11 ·92	9
10	Th 22	12 ·40	12 ·97	10
11	Fr 23	13 ·44	... ...	11
12	Sa 24	14 ·50	13 ·04	12
13	Su 25	P ·57	14 ·12	13
14	Mo 26	1 ·65	15 ·23	14
15	Tu 27	2 ·74	16 ·34	15
16	We 28	3 ·82	17 ·44	16
17	Th 29	4 ·89	18 ·54	17
18	Fr 30	5 ·94	19 ·68	18

May — Solar: Isvara Mesha—Chittirai (19–31); Isvara Vrishabha—Vaikasi (1–18). Tithi: Ch., Bahula, Sukla, Vaisakha. Muhammadan: H. 1356 Safar; H. 1356 Rabi-ul-awwal.

Cyclic Sidereal	Week-Day, May	Tithi	Nakshatra	Muhammadan
19	Sa 1	6 ·98	20 ·71	19
20	Su 2	... ...	21 ·76	20
21	Mo 3	7 ·00	22 ·79	21
22	Tu 4	8 ·01 / 9 ·99	23 ·80	22
23	We 5	10 ·94	24 ·79	23
24	Th 6	11 ·88	25 ·77	24
25	Fr 7	12 ·80	26 ·73	25
26	Sa 8	13 ·72	27 ·67	26
27	Su 9	14 ·63	1 ·61	27
28	Mo 10	A ·53	2 ·55	28
29	Tu 11	1 ·43	3 ·48	29
30	We 12	2 ·33	4 ·41	1
31	Th 13	3 ·23	5 ·35	2
1	Fr 14	4 ·14	6 ·29	3
2	Sa 15	5 ·05 / 6 ·99	7 ·24	4
3	Su 16	7 ·95	8 ·21	5
4	Mo 17	8 ·92	9 ·20	6
5	Tu 18	9 ·91	10 ·21	7
6	We 19	10 ·91	11 ·23	8
7	Th 20	11 ·95	12 ·28	9
8	Fr 21	... ...	13 ·35	10
9	Sa 22	12 ·01	14 ·43	11
10	Su 23	13 ·07	15 ·53	12
11	Mo 24	14 ·15	16 ·64	13
12	Tu 25	P ·23	17 ·74	14
13	We 26	1 ·32	18 ·84	15
14	Th 27	2 ·39	19 ·94	16
15	Fr 28	3 ·44	... ...	17
16	Sa 29	4 ·48	20 ·02	18
17	Su 30	5 ·50	21 ·07	19
18	Mo 31	6 ·50	22 ·10	20

June — Solar: Isvara Vrishabha—Vaikasi (19–31); Isvara Mithuna—Ani (1–17). Tithi: Bahula, Sukla, Jyeshtha, Bahula. Muhammadan: H. 1356 Rabi-ul-awwal; H. 1356 Rabi-ul-akhir.

Cyclic Sidereal	Week-Day, June	Tithi	Nakshatra	Muhammadan
19	Tu 1	7 ·48	23 ·12	21
20	We 2	8 ·45	24 ·13	22
21	Th 3	9 ·39	25 ·10	23
22	Fr 4	10 ·32	26 ·06	24
23	Sa 5	11 ·23	27 ·01 / 1 ·95	25
24	Su 6	12 ·13	2 ·89	26
25	Mo 7	13 ·03 / 14 ·93	3 ·82	27
26	Tu 8	A ·83	4 ·75	28
27	We 9	1 ·73	5 ·68	29
28	Th 10	2 ·64	6 ·62	30
29	Fr 11	3 ·55	7 ·57	1
30	Sa 12	4 ·48	8 ·55	2
31	Su 13	5 ·44	9 ·53	3
1	Mo 14	6 ·40	10 ·53	4
2	Tu 15	7 ·39	11 ·55	5
3	We 16	8 ·40	12 ·59	6
4	Th 17	9 ·44	13 ·66	7
5	Fr 18	10 ·49	14 ·74	8
6	Sa 19	11 ·55	15 ·83	9
7	Su 20	12 ·62	16 ·93	10
8	Mo 21	13 ·70	... ...	11
9	Tu 22	14 ·79	17 ·04	12
10	We 23	P ·86	18 ·15	13
11	Th 24	1 ·92	19 ·25	14
12	Fr 25	2 ·96	20 ·32	15
13	Sa 26	3 ·99	21 ·38	16
14	Su 27	4 ·98	22 ·42	17
15	Mo 28	5 ·96	23 ·45	18
16	Tu 29	6 ·93	24 ·45	19
17	We 30	7 ·87	25 ·43	20

Naksh :— 1. Asvn. 2. Bhar. 3. Krit. 4. Rohi. 5. Mrig. 6. Ardh. 7. Punar. 8. Push. 9. Aslesh. 10. Magh. 11. P. Phal. 12. U. Phal. 13. Hasta. 14. Chit.

A. D. 1937.
A.—Amavasya.
P.—Paurnami.

Kollam 1113, Commences { N. Malabar—Sept. / S. Malabar—Aug.

Hijra 1356, Commences, March 14.

Vikrama 1994.
Bengal San 1343.
(N. Cycle) Virodhin.

July

Solar month	Cyclic Sidereal Year, Month and Day	Week-Day	English Day	Lunar month / Paksha	Tithi Ending Moment	Nakshatra Ending Moment	Muhammadan month	Muhammadan Day
Isvara Mithuna—Ani	18	Th	1	Jyesh. Bahula	8 ·79	26 ·89	H. 1356 Rabi-ul-akhir.	21
	19	Fr	2		9 ·71	27 ·35		22
	20	Sa	3		10 ·62	1 ·29		23
	21	Su	4		11 ·51	2 ·23		24
	22	Mo	5		12 ·40	3 ·16		25
	23	Tu	6		13 ·29	4 ·09		26
	24	We	7		14 ·20	{ 5 ·02 / 6 ·96 }		27
	25	Th	8		—A ·11	7 ·92		28
	26	Fr	9		{ 1 ·03 / 2 ·96 }	8 ·88		—29
	27	Sa	10		3 ·91	9 ·85		1
	28	Su	11		4 ·89	10 ·85		2
	29	Mo	12		5 ·87	11 ·86		3
	30	Tu	13		6 ·87	12 ·91		4
	31	We	14		7 ·91	13 ·96		5
	—32	Th	15	Sukla	8 ·96	... ...		6
Isvara Karkata—Adi	1	Fr	16		... ...	14 ·04	H. 1356 Jumadal-awwal.	7
	2	Sa	17		9 ·02	15 ·13		8
	3	Su	18		10 ·09	16 ·23		9
	4	Mo	19		11 ·18	17 ·34		10
	5	Tu	20	Ashadha	12 ·26	18 ·45		11
	6	We	21		13 ·33	19 ·55		12
	7	Th	22		14 ·39	20 63		13
	8	Fr	23		P ·44	21 ·69		14
	9	Sa	24		1 ·46	22 ·74		15
	10	Su	25		2 ·46	23 ·77		16
	11	Mo	26		3 ·45	24 ·78		17
	12	Tu	27		4 ·41	25 ·76		18
	13	We	28		5 ·35	26 ·73		19
	14	Th	29	Bahula	6 ·28	27 ·68		20
	15	Fr	30		7 ·20	1 ·63		21
	16	Sa	31		8 ·10	2 ·57		22

Aug.

Solar month	Cyclic Sidereal Year, Month and Day	Week-Day	English Day	Lunar month / Paksha	Tithi Ending Moment	Nakshatra Ending Moment	Muhammadan month	Muhammadan Day
	17	Su	1		{ 9 ·00 / 10 ·90 }	3 ·50		23
	18	Mo	2		11 ·80	4 ·43		24
	19	Tu	3		12 ·70	5 ·36		25
	20	We	4		13 ·60	6 ·30		26
	21	Th	5		14 ·52	7 ·25		27
	22	Fr	6		—A ·45	8 ·21		28
	23	Sa	7		1 ·40	9 ·18		29
	24	Su	8		2 ·37	10 ·17		—30
	25	Mo	9		3 ·35	11 ·19		1
	26	Tu	10		4 ·36	12 ·22		2
	27	We	11		5 ·39	13 ·27		3
	28	Th	12		6 ·44	14 ·34		4
	29	Fr	13	Sukla	7 ·50	15 ·43		5
	30	Sa	14		8 ·58	16 ·54		6
	—31	Su	15		9 ·67	17 ·65		7
Isvara Simha—Avani	1	Mo	16		10 ·75	18 ·75	H. 1356 Jumadal-akhir.	8
	2	Tu	17		11 ·83	19 ·85		9
	3	We	18		12 ·88	20 ·94		10
	4	Th	19	Sravana	13 ·92	... ...		11
	5	Fr	20		14 ·96	21 ·00		12
	6	Sa	21		P ·96	22 ·06		13
	7	Su	22		1 ·95	23 ·09		14
	8	Mo	23		2 ·91	24 ·10		15
	9	Tu	24		3 ·86	25 ·09		16
	10	We	25		4 ·79	26 ·06		17
	11	Th	26		5 ·71	{ 27 ·02 / 1 ·97 }		18
	12	Fr	27	Bahula	6 ·61	2 ·90		19
	13	Sa	28		7 ·51	3 ·83		20
	14	Su	29		8 ·41	4 ·76		21
	15	Mo	30		9 ·31	5 ·70		22
	16	Tu	31		10 ·21	6 ·64		23

Sep.

Solar month	Cyclic Sidereal Year, Month and Day	Week-Day	English Day	Lunar month / Paksha	Tithi Ending Moment	Nakshatra Ending Moment	Muhammadan month	Muhammadan Day
Isvara Simha—Avani	17	We	1		11 ·12	7 ·58	Jumadal-akhir.	24
	18	Th	2		{ 12 ·04 / 13 ·97 }	8 ·54		25
	19	Fr	3		14 ·92	9 ·51		26
	20	Sa	4		—A ·88	10 ·50		27
	21	Su	5		1 ·86	11 ·51		28
	22	Mo	6		2 ·88	12 ·53		—29
	23	Tu	7		3 ·91	13 ·58		1
	24	We	8		4 ·96	14 ·65		2
	25	Th	9		... ...	15 ·73		3
	26	Fr	10		5 ·02	16 ·84		4
	27	Sa	11		6 ·10	17 ·94		5
	28	Su	12	Sukla	7 ·18	... ...		6
	29	Mo	13		8 ·27	18 ·05		7
	30	Tu	14		9 ·34	19 ·15		8
	31	We	15		10 ·41	20 ·24		9
	—32	Th	16		11 ·46	21 ·32		10
Isvara Kanya—Purattasi	1	Fr	17	Bhadrapada	12 ·48	22 ·38	H. 1356 Rajab.	11
	2	Sa	18		13 ·49	23 ·41		12
	3	Su	19		14 ·47	24 ·42		13
	4	Mo	20		P ·44	25 ·42		14
	5	Tu	21		1 ·39	26 ·40		15
	6	We	22		2 ·31	27 ·36		16
	7	Th	23		3 ·23	1 ·30		17
	8	Fr	24		4 ·14	2 ·24		18
	9	Sa	25	Bahula	{ 5 ·05 / 6 ·95 }	3 ·18		19
	10	Su	26		7 ·85	4 ·11		20
	11	Mo	27		8 ·75	{ 5 ·04 / 6 ·98 }		21
	12	Tu	28		9 ·66	7 ·92		22
	13	We	29		10 ·58	8 ·87		23
	14	Th	30		11 ·51	9 ·84		24

Oct.

Solar month	Cyclic Sidereal Year, Month and Day	Week-Day	English Day	Lunar month / Paksha	Tithi Ending Moment	Nakshatra Ending Moment	Muhammadan month	Muhammadan Day
	15	Fr	1		12 ·46	10 ·83		25
	16	Sa	2		13 ·43	11 ·88		26
	17	Su	3		14 ·42	12 ·85		27
	18	Mo	4		—A ·43	13 ·89		28
	19	Tu	5		1 ·46	14 ·95		29
	20	We	6		2 ·51	... ...		—30
	21	Th	7		3 ·57	15 ·04		1
	22	Fr	8		4 ·65	16 ·14		2
	23	Sa	9		5 ·74	17 ·24		3
	24	Su	10		6 ·83	18 ·35		4
	25	Mo	11		7 ·91	19 ·45		5
	26	Tu	12	Sukla	8 ·97	20 ·55		6
	27	We	13		... ...	21 ·63		7
	28	Th	14		9 ·02	22 ·69		8
	29	Fr	15		10 ·04	23 ·73		9
	—30	Sa	16		11 ·05	24 ·74	H. 1356 Shaban.	10
Isvara Tula—Aippasi	1	Su	17		12 ·04	25 ·74		11
	2	Mo	18	Asvina	{ 13 ·02 / 14 ·96 }	26 ·73		12
	3	Tu	19		P ·89	27 ·69		13
	4	We	20		1 ·81	1 ·64		14
	5	Th	21		2 ·72	2 ·58		15
	6	Fr	22		3 ·62	3 ·52		16
	7	Sa	23		4 ·52	4 ·45		17
	8	Su	24		5 ·42	5 ·38		18
	9	Mo	25		6 ·33	6 ·31		19
	10	Tu	26	Bahula	7 ·24	7 ·25		20
	11	We	27		8 ·16	8 ·20		21
	12	Th	28		9 ·09	9 ·17		22
	13	Fr	29		10 ·05	10 ·15		23
	14	Sa	30		11 ·02	11 ·15		24
	15	Su	31		12 ·01	12 ·16		25

Nov.

Solar month	Cyclic Sidereal Year, Month and Day	Week-Day	English Day	Lunar month / Paksha	Tithi Ending Moment	Nakshatra Ending Moment	Muhammadan month	Muhammadan Day
Isvara Tula—Aippasi	16	Mo	1	Bah.	13 ·01	13 ·20		26
	17	Tu	2		14 ·05	14 ·27		27
	18	We	3		—A ·11	15 ·34		28
	19	Th	4		1 ·18	16 ·44		—29
	20	Fr	5		2 ·26	17 ·54		1
	21	Sa	6		3 ·34	18 ·65		2
	22	Su	7		4 ·43	19 ·76		3
	23	Mo	8		5 ·51	20 ·86		4
	24	Tu	9		6 ·58	21 ·94		5
	25	We	10	Sukla	7 ·62	... ...		6
	26	Th	11		8 ·65	22 ·00		7
	27	Fr	12		9 ·66	23 ·04		8
	28	Sa	13		10 ·64	24 ·07		9
	29	Su	14		11 ·62	25 ·07		10
	—30	Mo	15		12 ·57	26 ·06		11
Isvara Vrischika—Kartigai	1	Tu	16	Kartika	13 ·50	{ 27 ·02 / 1 ·97 }	H. 1356 Ramzan.	12
	2	We	17		14 ·42	2 ·92		13
	3	Th ○	18		P ·33	3 ·86		14
	4	Fr	19		1 ·23	4 ·79		15
	5	Sa	20		2 ·13	5 ·72		16
	6	Su	21		{ 3 ·03 / 4 ·94 }	6 ·65		17
	7	Mo	22		5 ·86	7 ·59		18
	8	Tu	23		6 ·78	8 ·54		19
	9	We	24	Bahula	7 ·72	9 ·50		20
	10	Th	25		8 ·67	10 ·48		21
	11	Fr	26		9 ·64	11 ·47		22
	12	Sa	27		10 ·63	12 ·48		23
	13	Su	28		11 ·64	13 ·52		24
	14	Mo	29		12 ·68	14 ·58		25
	15	Tu	30		13 ·74	15 ·65		26

Dec.

Solar month	Cyclic Sidereal Year, Month and Day	Week-Day	English Day	Lunar month / Paksha	Tithi Ending Moment	Nakshatra Ending Moment	Muhammadan month	Muhammadan Day
	16	We	1		14 ·81	16 ·74		27
	17	Th	2		—A ·89	17 ·84		28
	18	Fr	3		1 ·98	18 ·95		29
	19	Sa	4		... ...	... ...		—30
	20	Su	5		2 ·07	19 ·06		1
	21	Mo	6		3 ·15	20 ·16		2
	22	Tu	7		4 ·22	21 ·24		3
	23	We	8		5 ·26	22 ·31		4
	24	Th	9		6 ·29	23 ·36		5
	25	Fr	10	Sukla	7 ·30	24 ·39		6
	26	Sa	11		8 ·29	25 ·40		7
	27	Su	12		9 ·25	26 ·38		8
	28	Mo	13		10 ·19	27 ·35		9
	—29	Tu	14		11 ·12	1 ·31		10
Isvara Dhanus—Margali	1	We	15	Margasira	{ 12 ·04 / 13 ·95 }	2 ·26	H. 1356 Shawwal.	11
	2	Th	16		14 ·86	3 ·20		12
	3	Fr	17		P ·76	4 ·13		13
	4	Sa	18		1 ·66	{ 5 ·06 / 6 ·99 }		14
	5	Su	19		2 ·56	7 ·93		15
	6	Mo	20		3 ·48	8 ·88		16
	7	Tu	21		4 ·41	9 ·83		17
	8	We	22		5 ·35	10 ·80		18
	9	Th	23		6 ·30	11 ·79		19
	10	Fr	24	Bahula	7 ·28	12 ·81		20
	11	Sa	25		8 ·27	13 ·84		21
	12	Su	26		9 ·29	14 ·88		22
	13	Mo	27		10 ·33	15 ·95		23
	14	Tu	28		11 ·38	... ...		24
	15	We	29		12 ·45	16 ·04		25
	16	Th	30		13 ·54	17 ·15		26
	17	Fr	31		14 ·64	18 ·26		27

A. D. 1938.
Solar Eclipse. ●
Lunar Eclipse. ○

Mesha Sankranti (Commencement of Indian Sidereal Year).
(Surya Sid.) April 13·45.
(Arya Sid.) April 13·34.

Saka 1860. **Kaliyuga 5039.**
(S. Cycle) Bahudhanya.

SOLAR reckoning: Cyclic Sidereal Year, Month and Day; Week-Day, English Month and Day. LUNAR reckoning: Tithi Ending Moment; Nakshatra Ending Moment; Muhammadan Year, Month and Day.

Jan.

Isvara *Dhanus—Margali.* / Isvara *Makara—Tai.* — *Sukla* / **Pausha** / *Bahula* — H. 1356 *Zil-ka'da.*

Cyclic Sidereal Year, Month and Day	Week-Day	English Day	Tithi	Tithi Ending Moment	Nakshatra	Nakshatra Ending Moment	Muhammadan Year, Month and Day
18	Sa	1	—A	·73	19	·36	28
19	Su	2	1	·80	20	·46	—29
20	Mo	3	2	·86	21	·55	1
21	Tu	4	3	·90	22	·62	2
22	We	5	4	·93	23	·68	3
23	Th	6	5	·94	24	·71	4
24	Fr	7	6	·93	25	·72	5
25	Sa	8	7	·90	26	·71	6
26	Su	9	8	·85	27	·68	7
27	Mo	10	9	·77	1	·65	8
28	Tu	11	10	·69	2	·60	9
29	We	12	11	·60	3	·54	10
—30	Th	13	12	·50	4	·47	11
1	Fr	14	13	·40	5	·40	12
2	Sa	15	14	·30	6	·33	13
3	Su	16	P	·21	7	·27	14
4	Mo	17	1	·13	8	·21	15
5	Tu	18	2	·06	9	·17	16
6	We	19	3 4	·00 ·95	10	·14	17
7	Th	20	5	·93	11	·13	18
8	Fr	21	6	·92	12	·13	19
9	Sa	22	7	·94	13	·15	20
10	Su	23	8	·97	14	·19	21
11	Mo	24	...	...	15	·26	22
12	Tu	25	9	·04	16	·34	23
13	We	26	10	·12	17	·44	24
14	Th	27	11	·20	18	·55	25
15	Fr	28	12	·29	19	·66	26
16	Sa	29	13	·38	20	·76	27
17	Su	30	14	·46	21	·85	28
18	Mo	31	—A	·52	22	·93	29

Feb.

Isvara *Kumbha—Masi.* — *Sukla* / **Magha** / *Bahula* — H. 1356 *Zil-hijja.*

Cyclic Sidereal Year, Month and Day	Week-Day	English Day	Tithi	Tithi Ending Moment	Nakshatra	Nakshatra Ending Moment	Muhammadan Year, Month and Day
19	Tu	1	1	·55	28	·99	—30
20	We	2	2	·57	...	...	1
21	Th	3	3	·58	24	·03	2
22	Fr	4	4	·57	25	·04	3
23	Sa	5	5	·53	26	·04	4
24	Su	6	6	·47	27 1	·02 ·99	5
25	Mo	7	7	·40	2	·93	6
26	Tu	8	8	·32	3	·87	7
27	We	9	9	·23	4	·81	8
28	Th	10	10	·13	5	·74	9
—29	Fr	11	11 12	·03 ·93	6	·67	10
1	Sa	12	13	·84	7	·61	11
2	Su	13	14	·75	8	·55	12
3	Mo	14	P	·68	9	·50	13
4	Tu	15	1	·63	10	·47	14
5	We	16	2	·59	11	·45	15
6	Th	17	3	·56	12	·45	16
7	Fr	18	4	·54	13	·47	17
8	Sa	19	5	·56	14	·50	18
9	Su	20	6	·60	15	·56	19
10	Mo	21	7	·66	16	·65	20
11	Tu	22	8	·74	17	·74	21
12	We	23	9	·83	18	·85	22
13	Th	24	10	·92	19	·96	23
14	Fr	25	...	...	...	...	24
15	Sa	26	11	·00	20	·06	25
16	Su	27	12	·07	21	·16	26
17	Mo	28	13	·13	22	·24	27

March

Isvara *Kumbha—Masi.* / Isvara *Mina—Panguni.* — *Sukla* / **Phalguna** / *Bahula* — H. 1357 *Muharram.*

Cyclic Sidereal Year, Month and Day	Week-Day	English Day	Tithi	Tithi Ending Moment	Nakshatra	Nakshatra Ending Moment	Muhammadan Year, Month and Day
18	Tu	1	14	·18	23	·30	28
19	We	2	—A	·20	24	·34	—29
20	Th	3	1	·20	25	·36	1
21	Fr	4	2	·18	26	·37	2
22	Sa	5	3	·14	27	·35	3
23	Su	6	4	·08	1	·32	4
24	Mo	7	5 6	·01 ·93	2	·27	5
25	Tu	8	7	·84	3	·21	6
26	We	9	8	·74	4	·15	7
27	Th	10	9	·64	5	·08	8
28	Fr	11	10	·54	6 7	·01 ·94	9
29	Sa	12	11	·44	8	·88	10
—30	Su	13	12	·35	9	·83	11
1	Mo	14	13	·28	10	·80	12
2	Tu	15	14	·22	11	·78	13
3	We	16	P	·18	12	·77	14
4	Th	17	1	·15	13	·78	15
5	Fr	18	2	·14	14	·82	16
6	Sa	19	3	·17	15	·88	17
7	Su	20	4	·21	16	·95	18
8	Mo	21	5	·26	...	...	19
9	Tu	22	6	·34	17	·04	20
10	We	23	7	·43	18	·14	21
11	Th	24	8	·52	19	·25	22
12	Fr	25	9	·60	20	·36	23
13	Sa	26	10	·67	21	·46	24
14	Su	27	11	·73	22	·55	25
15	Mo	28	12	·77	23	·61	26
16	Tu	29	13	·78	24	·66	27
17	We	30	14	·78	25	·69	28
18	Th	31	—A	·76	26	·70	29

April

Bahudhanya *Mesha—Chittirai.* — *Sukla* / **Chaitra** / *Bahula* — H. 1357 *Safar.*

Cyclic Sidereal Year, Month and Day	Week-Day	English Day	Tithi	Tithi Ending Moment	Nakshatra	Nakshatra Ending Moment	Muhammadan Year, Month and Day
19	Fr	1	1	·72	27	·68	—30
20	Sa	2	2	·66	1	·65	1
21	Su	3	3	·59	2	·60	2
22	Mo	4	4	·50	3	·55	3
23	Tu	5	5	·40	4	·49	4
24	We	6	6	·30	5	·42	5
25	Th	7	7	·20	6	·35	6
26	Fr	8	8	·10	7	·28	7
27	Sa	9	9 10	·00 ·92	8	·22	8
28	Su	10	11	·84	9	·17	9
29	Mo	11	12	·78	10	·13	10
—30	Tu	12	13	·74	11	·10	11
1	We	13	14	·71	12	·09	12
2	Th	14	P	·71	13	·10	13
3	Fr	15	1	·72	14	·14	14
4	Sa	16	2	·76	15	·19	15
5	Su	17	3	·82	16	·26	16
6	Mo	18	4	·90	17	·34	17
7	Tu	19	5	·98	18	·44	18
8	We	20	...	...	19	·55	19
9	Th	21	6	·06	20	·66	20
10	Fr	22	7	·14	21	·76	21
11	Sa	23	8	·21	22	·85	22
12	Su	24	9	·27	23	·92	23
13	Mo	25	10	·31	24	·98	24
14	Tu	26	11	·32	...	...	25
15	We	27	12	·32	25	·01	26
16	Th	28	13	·30	26	·02	27
17	Fr	29	14	·26	27 1	·01 ·98	28
18	Sa	30	—A	·19	2	·94	—29

May

Bahudhanya *Mesha—Chittirai.* / Bahudhanya *Vrishabha—Vaikasi.* — *Sukla* / **Vaisakha** / *Bahula* — H. 1357 *Rabi-ul-awwal.*

Cyclic Sidereal Year, Month and Day	Week-Day	English Day	Tithi	Tithi Ending Moment	Nakshatra	Nakshatra Ending Moment	Muhammadan Year, Month and Day
19	Su	1	1	·12	3	·89	1
20	Mo	2	2 3	·03 ·94	4	·83	2
21	Tu	3	4	·84	5	·76	3
22	We	4	5	·74	6	·69	4
23	Th	5	6	·64	7	·62	5
24	Fr	6	7	·54	8	·56	6
25	Sa	7	8	·45	9	·51	7
26	Su	8	9	·37	10	·46	8
27	Mo	9	10	·31	11	·43	9
28	Tu	10	11	·26	12	·41	10
29	We	11	12	·24	13	·42	11
30	Th	12	13	·23	14	·45	12
—31	Fr	13	14	·24	15	·50	13
1	Sa ○	14	P	·28	16	·56	14
2	Su	15	1	·33	17	·64	15
3	Mo	16	2	·40	18	·75	16
4	Tu	17	3	·49	19	·86	17
5	We	18	4	·57	20	·96	18
6	Th	19	5	·65	...	...	19
7	Fr	20	6	·72	21	·06	20
8	Sa	21	7	·78	22	·15	21
9	Su	22	8	·81	23	·23	22
10	Mo	23	9	·83	24	·29	23
11	Tu	24	10	·83	25	·33	24
12	We	25	11	·81	26	·34	25
13	Th	26	12	·77	27	·33	26
14	Fr	27	13	·70	1	·31	27
15	Sa	28	14	·62	2	·28	28
16	Su	29	—A	·53	3	·23	29
17	Mo	30	1	·43	4	·17	—30
18	Tu	31	2	·33	5	·10	1

June

Bahudhanya *Mithuna—Ani.* — *Sukla* / **Jyeshtha** / *Bahula* / *Suk.* — H. 1357 *Rabi-ul-akhir.*

Cyclic Sidereal Year, Month and Day	Week-Day	English Day	Tithi	Tithi Ending Moment	Nakshatra	Nakshatra Ending Moment	Muhammadan Year, Month and Day
19	We	1	3	·23	6 7	·03 ·96	2
20	Th	2	4	·13	8	·90	3
21	Fr	3	5 6	·04 ·95	9	·84	4
22	Sa	4	7	·87	10	·79	5
23	Su	5	8	·81	11	·76	6
24	Mo	6	9	·76	12	·75	7
25	Tu	7	10	·73	13	·75	8
26	We	8	11	·72	14	·77	9
27	Th	9	12	·74	15	·81	10
28	Fr	10	13	·77	16	·87	11
29	Sa	11	14	·82	17	·96	12
30	Su	12	P	·88	18	·05	13
31	Mo	13	1	·95	...	...	14
—32	Tu	14	...	...	19	·15	15
1	We	15	2	·04	20	·26	16
2	Th	16	3	·12	21	·36	17
3	Fr	17	4	·19	22	·46	18
4	Sa	18	5	·25	23	·55	19
5	Su	19	6	·30	24	·60	20
6	Mo	20	7	·32	25	·64	21
7	Tu	21	8	·31	26	·66	22
8	We	22	9	·29	27	·66	23
9	Th	23	10	·24	1	·65	24
10	Fr	24	11	·18	2	·61	25
11	Sa	25	12	·11	3	·56	26
12	Su	26	13 14	·02 ·92	4	·50	27
13	Mo	27	—A	·82	5	·44	28
14	Tu	28	1	·72	6	·38	—29
15	We	29	2	·62	7	·31	1
16	Th	30	3	·53	8	·24	2

Naksh :—1. Asvn. 2. Bhar. 3. Krit. 4. Rohi. 5. Mrig. 6. Ardh. 7. Punar. 8. Push. 9. Aslesh. 10. Magh. 11. P. Phal. 12. U. Phal. 13. Hasta. 14. Chit.

A. D. 1938.
A.—Amavasya.
P.—Paurnami.

Kollam 1114, Commences { **N. Malabar—Sept.** / **S. Malabar—Aug.**

Hijra 1357, Commences, **March 3.**

Vikrama 1995.
Bengal San 1344.
(N. Cycle) Vikrita.

SOLAR reckoning: Cyclic Sidereal Year, Month and Day; Week-Day English Month and Day. LUNAR reckoning: Tithi Ending Moment; Nakshatra Ending Moment; Muhammadan Year, Month and Day.

July — Solar: Bahudhanya *Mithuna—Ani*; Bahudhanya *Karkata—Adi*. Lunar: *Sukla*, **Ashadha**, *Bahula*. *H. 1357 Jumadal-awwal.*

Cyclic Sidereal Year, Month and Day	Week-Day	English Month and Day	Tithi	Tithi Ending Moment	Nakshatra	Nakshatra Ending Moment	Muhammadan Year, Month and Day
17	Fr	1	4	·44	9	·18	3
18	Sa	2	5	·36	10	·13	4
19	Su	3	6	·29	11	·10	5
20	Mo	4	7	·24	12	·07	6
21	Tu	5	8	·21	13	·07	7
22	We	6	9	·20	14	·08	8
23	Th	7	10	·21	15	·12	9
24	Fr	8	11	·24	16	·17	10
25	Sa	9	12	·29	17	·26	11
26	Su	10	13	·35	18	·35	12
27	Mo	11	14	·43	19	·45	13
28	Tu	12	P	·52	20	·56	14
29	We	13	1	·60	21	·66	15
30	Th	14	2	·67	22	·76	16
—31	Fr	15	3	·73	23	·85	17
1	Sa	16	4	·78	24	·92	18
2	Su	17	5	·79	25	·96	19
3	Mo	18	6	·79	26	·98	20
4	Tu	19	7	·77	27	·99	21
5	We	20	8	·72	1	·98	22
6	Th	21	9	·66	2	·95	23
7	Fr	22	10	·59	3	·90	24
8	Sa	23	11	·51	4	·84	25
9	Su	24	12	·42	5	·78	26
10	Mo	25	13	·32	6	·72	27
11	Tu	26	14	·22	7	·65	28
12	We	27	—A	·12	8	·58	29
13	Th	28	1 / 2	·02 / ·92	9	·52	—30
14	Fr	29	3	·84	10	·47	1
15	Sa	30	4	·77	11	·43	2
16	Su	31	5	·72	12	·40	3

Aug. — Solar: Bahudhanya *Simha—Avani*. Lunar: *Sukla*, **Sravana**, *Bahula*, **Bhad.** *Suk.* *H. 1357 Jumadal-akhir.* *Rajab.*

Cyclic Sidereal Year, Month and Day	Week-Day	English Month and Day	Tithi	Tithi Ending Moment	Nakshatra	Nakshatra Ending Moment	Muhammadan Year, Month and Day
17	Mo	1	6	·69	13	·39	4
18	Tu	2	7	·68	14	·40	5
19	We	3	8	·68	15	·43	6
20	Th	4	9	·71	16	·49	7
21	Fr	5	10	·76	17	·56	8
22	Sa	6	11	·83	18	·65	9
23	Su	7	12	·91	19	·75	10
24	Mo	8	13	·99	20	·86	11
25	Tu	9	...	...	21	·97	12
26	We	10	14	·08	...	...	13
27	Th	11	P	·15	22	·07	14
28	Fr	12	1	·21	23	·16	15
29	Sa	13	2	·25	24	·22	16
30	Su	14	3	·28	25	·27	17
31	Mo	15	4	·28	26	·31	18
—32	Tu	16	5	·26	27	·32	19
1	We	17	6	·22	1	·31	20
2	Th	18	7	·16	2	·28	21
3	Fr	19	8	·09	3	·23	22
4	Sa	20	9 / 10	·01 / ·92	4	·18	23
5	Su	21	11	·82	5	·12	24
6	Mo	22	12	·72	6 / 7	·05 / ·98	25
7	Tu	23	13	·62	8	·91	26
8	We	24	14	·52	9	·85	27
9	Th	25	—A	·43	10	·80	28
10	Fr	26	1	·35	11	·76	—29
11	Sa	27	2	·28	12	·73	1
12	Su	28	3	·23	13	·71	2
13	Mo	29	4	·19	14	·72	3
14	Tu	30	5	·18	15	·75	4
15	We	31	6	·19	16	·80	5

Sep. — Solar: Bahudhanya *Simha—Avani*; Bahudhanya *Kanya—Purattasi*. Lunar: *Sukla*, **Bhadrapada**, *Bahula*. *H. 1357 Rajab.*

Cyclic Sidereal Year, Month and Day	Week-Day	English Month and Day	Tithi	Tithi Ending Moment	Nakshatra	Nakshatra Ending Moment	Muhammadan Year, Month and Day
16	Th	1	7	·23	17	·87	6
17	Fr	2	8	·28	18	·95	7
18	Sa	3	9	·34	...	...	8
19	Su	4	10	·41	19	·05	9
20	Mo	5	11	·49	20	·16	10
21	Tu	6	12	·58	21	·27	11
22	We	7	13	·66	22	·37	12
23	Th	8	14	·72	23	·46	13
24	Fr	9	P	·77	24	·53	14
25	Sa	10	1	·81	25	·59	15
26	Su	11	2	·80	26	·63	16
27	Mo	12	3	·78	27	·64	17
28	Tu	13	4	·74	1	·63	18
29	We	14	5	·69	2	·61	19
30	Th	15	6	·62	3	·58	20
—31	Fr	16	7	·54	4	·52	21
1	Sa	17	8	·45	5	·46	22
2	Su	18	9	·35	6	·39	23
3	Mo	19	10	·25	7	·32	24
4	Tu	20	11	·15	8	·26	25
5	We	21	12 / 13	·05 / ·96	9	·20	26
6	Th	22	14	·88	10	·14	27
7	Fr	23	—A	·81	11	·09	28
8	Sa	24	1	·76	12	·06	29
9	Su	25	2	·74	13	·04	—30
10	Mo	26	3	·73	14	·05	1
11	Tu	27	4	·74	15	·07	2
12	We	28	5	·77	16	·11	3
13	Th	29	6	·82	17	·17	4
14	Fr	30	7	·88	18	·25	5

Oct. — Solar: Bahudhanya *Tula—Aippasi*. Lunar: *Sukla*, **Asvina**, *Bahula*, **Kartt.** *Sukla*. *H. 1357 Shaban.* *Ramzan.*

Cyclic Sidereal Year, Month and Day	Week-Day	English Month and Day	Tithi	Tithi Ending Moment	Nakshatra	Nakshatra Ending Moment	Muhammadan Year, Month and Day
15	Sa	1	8	·96	19	·35	6
16	Su	2	...	...	20	·46	7
17	Mo	3	9	·05	21	·57	8
18	Tu	4	10	·13	22	·67	9
19	We	5	11	·20	23	·76	10
20	Th	6	12	·27	24	·84	11
21	Fr	7	13	·32	25	·91	12
22	Sa	8	14	·35	26	·95	13
23	Su	9	P	·36	27	·96	14
24	Mo	10	1	·34	1	·96	15
25	Tu	11	2	·30	2	·94	16
26	We	12	3	·25	3	·91	17
27	Th	13	4	·18	4	·86	18
28	Fr	14	5	·10	5	·80	19
29	Sa	15	6 / 7	·01 / ·91	6	·73	20
—30	Su	16	8	·81	7	·66	21
1	Mo	17	9	·71	8	·59	22
2	Tu	18	10	·62	9	·53	23
3	We	19	11	·53	10	·47	24
4	Th	20	12	·46	11	·42	25
5	Fr	21	13	·40	12	·38	26
6	Sa	22	14	·35	13	·37	27
7	Su	23	—A	·32	14	·37	28
8	Mo	24	1	·31	15	·38	—29
9	Tu	25	2	·32	16	·42	1
10	We	26	3	·35	17	·48	2
11	Th	27	4	·40	18	·57	3
12	Fr	28	5	·48	19	·66	4
13	Sa	29	6	·56	20	·76	5
14	Su	30	7	·64	21	·87	6
15	Mo	31	8	·73	22	·97	7

Nov. — Solar: Bahudhanya *Tula—Aippasi*; Bahudhanya *Vrischika—Kartigai*. Lunar: *Sukla*, **Kartika**, *Bahula*, *Sukla*. *H. 1357 Ramzan.*

Cyclic Sidereal Year, Month and Day	Week-Day	English Month and Day	Tithi	Tithi Ending Moment	Nakshatra	Nakshatra Ending Moment	Muhammadan Year, Month and Day
16	Tu	1	9	·81	...	...	8
17	We	2	10	·87	23	·07	9
18	Th	3	11	·92	24	·16	10
19	Fr	4	12	·96	25	·22	11
20	Sa	5	13	·96	26	·26	12
21	Su	6	14	·94	27	·28	13
22	Mo ○	7	P	·90	1	·28	14
23	Tu	8	1	·85	2	·27	15
24	We	9	2	·79	3	·24	16
25	Th	10	3	·71	4	·19	17
26	Fr	11	4	·61	5	·14	18
27	Sa	12	5	·51	6	·08	19
28	Su	13	6	·41	7 / 8	·01 / ·94	20
29	Mo	14	7	·32	9	·87	21
—30	Tu	15	8	·23	10	·81	22
1	We	16	9	·14	11	·75	23
2	Th	17	10	·06	12	·72	24
3	Fr	18	11 / 12	·00 / ·95	13	·70	25
4	Sa	19	13	·93	14	·69	26
5	Su	20	14	·92	15	·70	27
6	Mo	21	—A	·94	16	·74	28
7	Tu	22	1	·97	17	·80	29
8	We	23	...	...	18	·87	—30
9	Th	24	2	·03	19	·96	1
10	Fr	25	3	·10	...	...	2
11	Sa	26	4	·18	20	·06	3
12	Su	27	5	·27	21	·16	4
13	Mo	28	6	·36	22	·27	5
14	Tu	29	7	·44	23	·37	6
15	We	30	8	·50	24	·46	7

Dec. — Solar: Bahudhanya *Dhanus—Margali*. Lunar: **Margasira**, *Bahula*, **Pausha** *Sukla*. *H. 1357 Shawwal.* *H. 1357 Zi-l-ka'da.*

Cyclic Sidereal Year, Month and Day	Week-Day	English Month and Day	Tithi	Tithi Ending Moment	Nakshatra	Nakshatra Ending Moment	Muhammadan Year, Month and Day
16	Th	1	9	·55	25	·53	8
17	Fr	2	10	·58	26	·58	9
18	Sa	3	11	·58	27	·60	10
19	Su	4	12	·56	1	·61	11
20	Mo	5	13	·52	2	·60	12
21	Tu	6	14	·47	3	·57	13
22	We	7	P	·41	4	·53	14
23	Th	8	1	·33	5	·47	15
24	Fr	9	2	·24	6	·41	16
25	Sa	10	3	·14	7	·35	17
26	Su	11	4 / 5	·04 / ·94	8	·28	18
27	Mo	12	6	·85	9	·21	19
28	Tu	13	7	·77	10	·15	20
29	We	14	8	·69	11	·10	21
—30	Th	15	9	·63	12	·05	22
1	Fr	16	10	·59	13	·02	23
2	Sa	17	11	·57	14	·01	24
3	Su	18	12	·57	15	·02	25
4	Mo	19	13	·58	16	·05	26
5	Tu	20	14	·62	17	·10	27
6	We	21	—A	·68	18	·17	28
7	Th	22	1	·75	19	·26	—29
8	Fr	23	2	·83	20	·36	1
9	Sa	24	3	·93	21	·46	2
10	Su	25	...	...	22	·57	3
11	Mo	26	4	·02	23	·68	4
12	Tu	27	5	·09	24	·77	5
13	We	28	6	·15	25	·84	6
14	Th	29	7	·20	26	·89	7
15	Fr	30	8	·22	27	·93	8
16	Sa	31	9	·23	1	·94	9

15. Svati. 16. Visak. 17. Anur. 18. Jyesh. 19. Mula. 20. P. Ash. 21. U. Ash. 22. Sravn. 23. Dani. 24. Satab. 25. P. Bhad. 26. U. Bhad. 27. Rev.

A. D. 1939. **Mesha Sankranti** (Commencement of Indian Sidereal Year).
Solar Eclipse. ● (Surya Sid.) April 13·71. Saka 1861. Kaliyuga 5040.
Lunar Eclipse. ○ (Arya Sid.) April 13·60. (S. Cycle) Pramathi.

Jan.

Solar: Cyclic Sidereal Year, Month and Day	Week-Day English Month and Day	Lunar: Tithi Ending Moment	Nakshatra Ending Moment	Muhammadan Year, Month and Day
Bahudhanya Dhanus—Margali 17	Su 1	Sukla 10 ·21	2 ·93	H. 1357 Zi'l-ka'da 10
18	Mo 2	11 ·17	3 ·90	11
19	Tu 3	12 ·11	4 ·86	12
20	We 4	13 ·04 / 14 ·96	5 ·82	13
21	Th 5	Pausha P ·87	6 ·76	14
22	Fr 6	Bahula 1 ·78	7 ·69	15
23	Sa 7	2 ·68	8 ·62	16
24	Su 8	3 ·59	9 ·55	17
25	Mo 9	4 ·50	10 ·49	18
26	Tu 10	5 ·41	11 ·43	19
27	We 11	6 ·34	12 ·39	20
28	Th 12	7 ·28	13 ·35	21
29	Fr 13	8 ·24	14 ·34	22
Bahudhanya Makara—Tai 1	Sa 14	9 ·21	15 ·34	23
2	Su 15	10 ·21	16 ·37	24
3	Mo 16	11 ·23	17 ·41	25
4	Tu 17	12 ·27	18 ·48	26
5	We 18	13 ·33	19 ·56	27
6	Th 19	14 ·41	20 ·66	28
7	Fr 20	A ·50	21 ·77	29
8	Sa 21	Sukla 1 ·59	22 ·88	30
9	Su 22	2 ·67	23 ·98	1
10	Mo 23	3 ·74	...	2
11	Tu 24	4 ·80	24 ·07	3
12	We 25	5 ·84	25 ·15	4
13	Th 26	6 ·87	26 ·21	5
14	Fr 27	7 ·87	27 ·25	6
15	Sa 28	8 ·85	1 ·26	7
16	Su 29	9 ·81	2 ·26	8
17	Mo 30	10 ·75	3 ·24	9
18	Tu 31	11 ·68	4 ·21	10

Feb.

Solar: Cyclic Sidereal Year, Month and Day	Week-Day English Month and Day	Lunar: Tithi Ending Moment	Nakshatra Ending Moment	Muhammadan Year, Month and Day
19	We 1	12 ·60	5 ·15	H. 1357 Zi'l-hijja 11
20	Th 2	13 ·51	6 ·09	12
21	Fr 3	Magha 14 ·41	7 ·02 / 8 ·95	13
22	Sa 4	P ·31	9 ·89	14
23	Su 5	Bahula 1 ·21	10 ·83	15
24	Mo 6	2 ·12	11 ·77	16
25	Tu 7	3 ·04 / 4 ·97	12 ·72	17
26	We 8	5 ·92	13 ·68	18
27	Th 9	6 ·87	14 ·66	19
28	Fr 10	7 ·84	15 ·67	20
29	Sa 11	8 ·85	16 ·69	21
Bahudhanya Kumbha—Masi 1	Su 12	9 ·87	17 ·73	22
2	Mo 13	10 ·91	18 ·78	23
3	Tu 14	11 ·97	19 ·86	24
4	We 15	...	20 ·96	25
5	Th 16	12 ·04	...	26
6	Fr 17	13 ·13	21 ·07	27
7	Sa 18	14 ·22	22 ·17	28
8	Su 19	A ·30	23 ·28	29
9	Mo 20	Phalg. Sukla 1 ·37	24 ·37	30
10	Tu 21	2 ·43	25 ·45	H. 1358 Muharram 1
11	We 22	3 ·47	26 ·52	2
12	Th 23	4 ·50	27 ·56	3
13	Fr 24	5 ·49	1 ·58	4
14	Sa 25	6 ·47	2 ·58	5
15	Su 26	7 ·42	3 ·57	6
16	Mo 27	8 ·36	4 ·54	7
17	Tu 28	9 ·29	5 ·49	8

March

Solar: Cyclic Sidereal Year, Month and Day	Week-Day English Month and Day	Lunar: Tithi Ending Moment	Nakshatra Ending Moment	Muhammadan Year, Month and Day
Bahudhanya Kumbha—Masi 18	We 1	Suk. 10 ·21	6 ·43	H. 1358 Muharram 9
19	Th 2	11 ·12	7 ·36	10
20	Fr 3	12 ·02 / 13 ·92	8 ·29	11
21	Sa 4	Phalguna 14 ·82	9 ·22	12
22	Su 5	P ·72	10 ·16	13
23	Mo 6	1 ·64	11 ·10	14
24	Tu 7	2 ·57	12 ·05	15
25	We 8	3 ·52	13 ·02	16
26	Th 9	4 ·48	14 ·00 / 15 ·99	17
27	Fr 10	Bahula 5 ·46	...	18
28	Sa 11	6 ·46	16 ·00	19
29	Su 12	7 ·48	17 ·04	20
30	Mo 13	8 ·51	18 ·09	21
Bahudhanya Mina—Panguni 1	Tu 14	9 ·56	19 ·17	22
2	We 15	10 ·64	20 ·26	23
3	Th 16	11 ·73	21 ·36	24
4	Fr 17	12 ·82	22 ·47	25
5	Sa 18	13 ·90	23 ·58	26
6	Su 19	14 ·97	24 ·68	27
7	Mo 20	...	25 ·77	28
8	Tu 21	A ·03	26 ·83	29
9	We 22	Sukla 1 ·07	27 ·88	30
10	Th 23	2 ·09	1 ·90	1
11	Fr 24	3 ·08	2 ·91	2
12	Sa 25	4 ·06	3 ·90	3
13	Su 26	5 ·02 / 6 ·96	4 ·87	4
14	Mo 27	7 ·88	5 ·82	5
15	Tu 28	8 ·79	6 ·76	6
16	We 29	9 ·70	7 ·70	7
17	Th 30	10 ·60	8 ·64	8
18	Fr 31	11 ·50	9 ·57	9

April

Solar: Cyclic Sidereal Year, Month and Day	Week-Day English Month and Day	Lunar: Tithi Ending Moment	Nakshatra Ending Moment	Muhammadan Year, Month and Day
19	Sa 1	12 ·40	10 ·50	H. 1358 Safar 10
20	Su 2	13 ·31	11 ·44	11
21	Mo 3	Chaitra 14 ·22	12 ·39	12
22	Tu 4	P ·15	13 ·35	13
23	We 5	1 ·09	14 ·32	14
24	Th 6	2 ·05	15 ·31	15
25	Fr 7	3 ·03	16 ·32	16
26	Sa 8	4 ·02	17 ·35	17
27	Su 9	5 ·04	18 ·41	18
28	Mo 10	Bahula 6 ·07	19 ·48	19
29	Tu 11	7 ·13	20 ·56	20
30	We 12	8 ·21	21 ·66	21
31	Th 13	9 ·29	22 ·77	22
Pramathi Mesha—Chittirai 1	Fr 14	10 ·38	23 ·88	23
2	Sa 15	11 ·46	24 ·98	24
3	Su 16	12 ·53	...	25
4	Mo 17	13 ·59	25 ·07	26
5	Tu 18	14 ·63	26 ·14	27
6	We 19	A ·64	27 ·19	28
7	Th 20	Sukla 1 ·63	1 ·22	29
8	Fr 21	2 ·60	2 ·24	H. 1358 Rabi-ul-awwal 1
9	Sa 22	3 ·55	3 ·23	2
10	Su 23	Vaisakha 4 ·49	4 ·20	3
11	Mo 24	5 ·42	5 ·16	4
12	Tu 25	6 ·34	6 ·10	5
13	We 26	7 ·25	7 ·04 / 8 ·98	6
14	Th 27	8 ·15	9 ·91	7
15	Fr 28	9 ·05 / 10 ·95	10 ·84	8
16	Sa 29	11 ·85	11 ·78	9
17	Su 30	12 ·76	12 ·73	10

May

Solar: Cyclic Sidereal Year, Month and Day	Week-Day English Month and Day	Lunar: Tithi Ending Moment	Nakshatra Ending Moment	Muhammadan Year, Month and Day
Pramathi Mesha—Chittirai 18	Mo 1	Suk. 13 ·68	13 ·68	H. 1358 Rabi-ul-awwal 11
19	Tu 2	14 ·62	14 ·65	12
20	We ○ 3	P ·58	15 ·63	13
21	Th 4	Vaisakha 1 ·56	16 ·64	14
22	Fr 5	2 ·55	17 ·67	15
23	Sa 6	3 ·57	18 ·72	16
24	Su 7	4 ·60	19 ·78	17
25	Mo 8	5 ·66	20 ·86	18
26	Tu 9	6 ·73	21 ·96	19
27	We 10	Bahula 7 ·81	...	20
28	Th 11	8 ·89	22 ·07	21
29	Fr 12	9 ·98	23 ·18	22
30	Sa 13	...	24 ·28	23
31	Su 14	10 ·05	25 ·37	24
Pramathi Vrishabha—Vaikasi 1	Mo 15	11 ·10	26 ·45	25
2	Tu 16	12 ·14	27 ·50	26
3	We 17	13 ·15	1 ·54	27
4	Th 18	14 ·15	2 ·56	28
5	Fr 19	A ·13	3 ·55	29
6	Sa 20	1 ·09	4 ·53	30
7	Su 21	2 ·02 / 3 ·94	5 ·49	1
8	Mo 22	4 ·85	6 ·45	2
9	Tu 23	5 ·75	7 ·39	3
10	We 24	6 ·65	8 ·32	4
11	Th 25	Sukla 7 ·55	9 ·25	5
12	Fr 26	8 ·45	10 ·18	6
13	Sa 27	9 ·35	11 ·12	7
14	Su 28	10 ·26	12 ·06	8
15	Mo 29	11 ·19	13 ·01 / 14 ·98	9
16	Tu 30	12 ·13	15 ·96	10
17	We 31	13 ·08	16 ·97	11

June

Solar: Cyclic Sidereal Year, Month and Day	Week-Day English Month and Day	Lunar: Tithi Ending Moment	Nakshatra Ending Moment	Muhammadan Year, Month and Day
18	Th 1	14 ·05	17 ·99	H. 1358 Rabi-ul-akhir 12
19	Fr 2	Jyeshtha P ·05	...	13
20	Sa 3	1 ·06	18 ·03	14
21	Su 4	2 ·09	19 ·09	15
22	Mo 5	3 ·15	20 ·17	16
23	Tu 6	4 ·22	21 ·26	17
24	We 7	5 ·30	22 ·37	18
25	Th 8	Bahula 6 ·39	23 ·48	19
26	Fr 9	7 ·47	24 ·58	20
27	Sa 10	8 ·53	25 ·68	21
28	Su 11	9 ·58	26 ·76	22
29	Mo 12	10 ·62	27 ·83	23
30	Tu 13	11 ·64	1 ·86	24
31	We 14	12 ·63	2 ·88	25
Pramathi Mithuna—Ani 1	Th 15	13 ·61	3 ·88	26
2	Fr 16	14 ·57	4 ·86	27
3	Sa 17	A ·51	5 ·83	28
4	Su 18	1 ·43	6 ·78	29
5	Mo 19	2 ·34	7 ·72	H. 1358 Jumadal-awwal 1
6	Tu 20	3 ·24	8 ·66	2
7	We 21	4 ·14	9 ·59	3
8	Th 22	5 ·04 / 6 ·94	10 ·52	4
9	Fr 23	Sukla 7 ·84	11 ·46	5
10	Sa 24	8 ·75	12 ·40	6
11	Su 25	9 ·67	13 ·35	7
12	Mo 26	Ashadha 10 ·61	14 ·31	8
13	Tu 27	11 ·56	15 ·29	9
14	We 28	12 ·53	16 ·29	10
15	Th 29	13 ·53	17 ·30	11
16	Fr 30	14 ·54	18 ·34	12

Nakah :—1. Asvn. 2. Bhar. 3. Krit. 4. Rohi. 5. Mrig. 6. Ardh. 7. Punar. 8. Push. 9 Aslesh. 10. Magh. 11. P. Phal. 12. U. Phal. 13. Hasta. 14. Chit.

A. D. 1939. A.—Amavasya. P.—Paurnami.	Kollam 1115, Commences { N. Malabar—Sept. S. Malabar—Aug.	Hijra 1358, Commences, Feb. 21.	Vikrama 1996. Bengal San 1345. (N. Cycle) Khara.

July — Solar: Pramathi *Mithuna—Ani* (17–32), Pramathi *Karkata—Adi* (1–15). Lunar: Ashadha, *Bahula*, *Sukla*, Sravana. Muhammadan: H. 1358 *Jumadal-awwal*, *Jumadal-akhir*.

Cyclic Sidereal Year, Month and Day	Week-Day English Month and Day	Tithi Ending Moment	Nakshatra Ending Moment	Muhammadan Year, Month and Day
17	Sa 1	P ·58	19 ·39	13
18	Su 2	1 ·63	20 ·47	14
19	Mo 3	2 ·70	21 ·57	15
20	Tu 4	3 ·78	22 ·67	16
21	We 5	4 ·86	23 ·78	17
22	Th 6	5 ·94	24 ·88	18
23	Fr 7	... ...	25 ·98	19
24	Sa 8	6 ·01	... ...	20
25	Su 9	7 ·07	26 ·07	21
26	Mo 10	8 ·10	27 ·14	22
27	Tu 11	9 ·12	1 ·18	23
28	We 12	10 ·11	2 ·20	24
29	Th 13	11 ·09	3 ·21	25
30	Fr 14	{12 ·04 13 ·98	4 ·20	26
31	Sa 15	14 ·91	5 ·17	27
—32	Su 16	—A ·82	6 ·12	28
1	Mo 17	1 ·72	7 ·06	29
2	Tu 18	2 ·62	8 ·00 9 ·93}	—30
3	We 19	3 ·52	10 ·86	1
4	Th 20	4 ·42	11 ·80	2
5	Fr 21	5 ·32	12 ·74	3
6	Sa 22	6 ·23	13 ·68	4
7	Su 23	7 ·15	14 ·64	5
8	Mo 24	8 ·09	15 ·62	6
9	Tu 25	9 ·05	16 ·61	7
10	We 26	10 ·03	17 ·62	8
11	Th 27	11 ·02	18 ·65	9
12	Fr 28	12 ·02	19 ·70	10
13	Sa 29	13 ·04	20 ·78	11
14	Su 30	14 ·09	21 ·87	12
15	Mo 31	P ·16	22 ·97	13

Aug. — Solar: Pramathi *Simha—Avani*. Lunar: Adhika, *Bahula*, *Sukla*, Nija Sravana. Muhammadan: H. 1358, H. 1358 *Rajab*.

Cyclic Sidereal Year, Month and Day	Week-Day English Month and Day	Tithi Ending Moment	Nakshatra Ending Moment	Muhammadan Year, Month and Day
16	Tu 1	1 ·24	... ...	14
17	We 2	2 ·33	23 ·08	15
18	Th 3	3 ·41	24 ·18	16
19	Fr 4	4 ·48	25 ·28	17
20	Sa 5	5 ·54	26 ·37	18
21	Su 6	6 ·58	27 ·44	19
22	Mo 7	7 ·61	1 ·49	20
23	Tu 8	8 ·60	2 ·52	21
24	We 9	9 ·58	3 ·54	22
25	Th 10	10 ·54	4 ·53	23
26	Fr 11	11 ·49	5 ·50	24
27	Sa 12	12 ·41	6 ·45	25
28	Su 13	13 ·32	7 ·40	26
29	Mo 14	14 ·22	8 ·34	27
30	Tu 15	—A ·12	9 ·27	28
—31	We 16	{1 ·02 2 ·92	10 ·20	—29
1	Th 17	3 ·82	11 ·13	1
2	Fr 18	4 ·73	12 ·07	2
3	Sa 19	5 ·65	13 ·02 14 ·98}	3
4	Su 20	6 ·59	15 ·95	4
5	Mo 21	7 ·54	16 ·93	5
6	Tu 22	8 ·51	17 ·94	6
7	We 23	9 ·50	18 ·97	7
8	Th 24	10 ·51	... ...	8
9	Fr 25	11 ·54	19 ·02	9
10	Sa 26	12 ·60	20 ·09	10
11	Su 27	13 ·67	21 ·17	11
12	Mo 28	14 ·74	22 ·27	12
13	Tu 29	P ·82	23 ·38	13
14	We 30	1 ·91	24 ·49	14
15	Th 31	2 ·99	25 ·59	15

Sep. — Solar: Pramathi *Simha—Avani* (16–31), Pramathi *Kanya—Purattasi* (1–14). Lunar: Nija Sravn., *Bahula*, *Sukla*, Bhadrapada. Muhammadan: H. 1358 *Rajab*, *Shaban*.

Cyclic Sidereal Year, Month and Day	Week-Day English Month and Day	Tithi Ending Moment	Nakshatra Ending Moment	Muhammadan Year, Month and Day
16	Fr 1	... ...	26 ·68	16
17	Sa 2	3 ·05	27 ·75	17
18	Su 3	4 ·09	1 ·81	18
19	Mo 4	5 ·12	2 ·84	19
20	Tu 5	6 ·11	3 ·86	20
21	We 6	7 ·09	4 ·85	21
22	Th 7	8 ·05	5 ·83	22
23	Fr 8	9 ·00 10 ·93	6 ·79	23
24	Sa 9	11 ·84	7 ·74	24
25	Su 10	12 ·74	8 ·68	25
26	Mo 11	13 ·64	9 ·61	26
27	Tu 12	14 ·54	10 ·54	27
28	We 13	—A ·44	11 ·47	28
29	Th 14	1 ·35	12 ·41	29
30	Fr 15	2 ·26	13 ·36	—30
—31	Sa 16	3 ·19	14 ·31	1
1	Su 17	4 ·12	15 ·27	2
2	Mo 18	5 ·07	16 ·26	3
3	Tu 19	6 ·04	17 ·26	4
4	We 20	7 ·03	18 ·29	5
5	Th 21	8 ·04	19 ·33	6
6	Fr 22	9 ·07	20 ·39	7
7	Sa 23	10 ·13	21 ·47	8
8	Su 24	11 ·20	22 ·57	9
9	Mo 25	12 ·28	23 ·68	10
10	Tu 26	13 ·36	24 ·79	11
11	We 27	14 ·44	25 ·89	12
12	Th 28	P ·52	26 ·98	13
13	Fr 29	1 ·59	... ...	14
14	Sa 30	2 ·63	27 ·06	15

Oct. — Solar: Pramathi *Tula—Aippasi*. Lunar: *Bahula*, *Sukla*, Asvina, *Bah.* Muhammadan: H. 1358, H. 1358 *Ramzan*.

Cyclic Sidereal Year, Month and Day	Week-Day English Month and Day	Tithi Ending Moment	Nakshatra Ending Moment	Muhammadan Year, Month and Day
15	Su 1	3 ·65	1 ·12	16
16	Mo 2	4 ·66	2 ·17	17
17	Tu 3	5 ·64	3 ·18	18
18	We 4	6 ·60	4 ·18	19
19	Th 5	7 ·54	5 ·16	20
20	Fr 6	8 ·47	6 ·12	21
21	Sa 7	9 ·39	7 ·08	22
22	Su 8	10 ·30	8 ·02 9 ·95}	23
·23	Mo 9	11 ·21	10 ·88	24
24	Tu 10	12 ·11	11 ·81	25
25	We 11	{13 ·01 14 ·91	12 ·75	26
26	Th 12	—A ·82	13 ·69	27
27	Fr 13	1 ·74	14 ·64	28
28	Sa 14	2 ·68	15 ·60	—29
29	Su 15	3 ·64	16 ·58	1
—30	Mo 16	4 ·61	17 ·59	2
1	Tu 17	5 ·60	18 ·60	3
2	We 18	6 ·61	19 ·64	4
3	Th 19	7 ·65	20 ·70	5
4	Fr 20	8 ·71	21 ·78	6
5	Sa 21	9 ·78	22 ·87	7
6	Su 22	10 ·86	23 ·98	8
7	Mo 23	11 ·94	... ...	9
8	Tu 24	... ...	24 ·09	10
9	We 25	12 ·03	25 ·19	11
10	Th 26	13 ·11	26 ·29	12
11	Fr 27	14 ·18	27 ·37	13
12	Sa ○ 28	P ·22	1 ·44	14
13	Su 29	1 ·25	2 ·48	15
14	Mo 30	2 ·25	3 ·50	16
15	Tu 31	3 ·23	4 ·50	17

Nov. — Solar: Pramathi *Tula—Aippasi* (16–30), Pramathi *Vrischika—Kartigai* (1–15). Lunar: Asv. *Bahula*, *Sukla*, Kartika. Muhammadan: H. 1358 *Ramzan*, H. 1358 *Shawwal*.

Cyclic Sidereal Year, Month and Day	Week-Day English Month and Day	Tithi Ending Moment	Nakshatra Ending Moment	Muhammadan Year, Month and Day
16	We 1	4 ·19	5 ·49	18
17	Th 2	5 ·14	6 ·46	19
18	Fr 3	{6 ·07 7 ·98	7 ·41	20
19	Sa 4	8 ·89	8 ·35	21
20	Su 5	9 ·79	9 ·29	22
21	Mo 6	10 ·69	10 ·23	23
22	Tu 7	11 ·60	11 ·16	24
23	We 8	12 ·51	12 ·09	25
24	Th 9	13 ·43	13 ·03 14 ·97}	26
25	Fr 10	14 ·35	15 ·93	27
26	Sa 11	—A ·28	16 ·92	28
27	Su 12	1 ·24	17 ·91	29
28	Mo 13	2 ·22	18 ·92	—30
29	Tu 14	3 ·21	19 ·95	1
—30	We 15	4 ·22	... ...	2
1	Th 16	5 ·26	20 ·01	3
2	Fr 17	6 ·32	21 ·08	4
3	Sa 18	7 ·40	22 ·18	5
4	Su 19	8 ·48	23 ·28	6
5	Mo 20	9 ·56	24 ·38	7
6	Tu 21	10 ·65	25 ·49	8
7	We 22	11 ·73	26 ·59	9
8	Th 23	12 ·80	27 ·68	10
9	Fr 24	13 ·84	1 ·75	11
10	Sa 25	14 ·87	2 ·80	12
11	Su 26	P ·87	3 ·82	13
12	Mo 27	1 ·85	4 ·83	14
13	Tu 28	2 ·81	5 ·82	15
14	We 29	3 ·76	6 ·79	16
15	Th 30	4 ·69	7 ·75	17

Dec. — Solar: Pramathi *Dhanus—Margali*. Lunar: *Bahula*, *Sukla*, Margasira, *Bah.* Muhammadan: H. 1358 *Zi-l-ka'da*.

Cyclic Sidereal Year, Month and Day	Week-Day English Month and Day	Tithi Ending Moment	Nakshatra Ending Moment	Muhammadan Year, Month and Day
16	Fr 1	5 ·61	8 ·69	18
17	Sa 2	6 ·52	9 ·63	19
18	Su 3	7 ·42	10 ·57	20
19	Mo 4	8 ·32	11 ·50	21
20	Tu 5	9 ·22	12 ·43	22
21	We 6	10 ·13	13 ·36	23
22	Th 7	{11 ·05 12 ·97	14 ·31	24
23	Fr 8	13 ·91	15 ·26	25
24	Sa 9	14 ·87	16 ·24	26
25	Su 10	—A ·85	17 ·23	27
26	Mo 11	1 ·85	18 ·24	28
27	Tu 12	2 ·87	19 ·27	—29
28	We 13	3 ·92	20 ·32	1
29	Th 14	4 ·98	21 ·39	2
—30	Fr 15	... ...	22 ·48	3
1	Sa 16	5 ·05	23 ·58	4
2	Su 17	6 ·13	24 ·68	5
3	Mo 18	7 ·22	25 ·79	6
4	Tu 19	8 ·30	26 ·90	7
5	We 20	9 ·38	27 ·99	8
6	Th 21	10 ·44	... ...	9
7	Fr 22	11 ·48	1 ·06	10
8	Sa 23	12 ·51	2 ·11	11
9	Su 24	13 ·51	3 ·14	12
10	Mo 25	14 ·50	4 ·16	13
11	Tu 26	P ·46	5 ·15	14
12	We 27	1 ·40	6 ·12	15
13	Th 28	2 ·33	7 ·08	16
14	Fr 29	3 ·25	8 ·03 9 ·97}	17
15	Sa 30	4 ·16	10 ·91	18
16	Su 31	{5 ·06 6 ·96	11 ·84	19

15. Svati. 16. Visak. 17. Anur. 18. Jyesh. 19. Mula. 20. P. Ash. 21. U. Ash. 22. Sravn. 23. Dani. 24. Satab. 25. P. Bhad. 26. U. Bhad. 27. Rev.

A. D. 1940. **Mesha Sankranti** (Commencement of Indian Sidereal Year).
Solar Eclipse. ● (Surya Sid.) April 12·97. Saka 1862. Kaliyuga 5041.
Lunar Eclipse. ○ (Arya Sid.) April 12·86. (S. Cycle) Vikrama.

Cyclic Sidereal Year, Month and Day.	Week-Day English Month and Day.	Tithi Ending Moment.	Nakshatra Ending Moment.	Muhammadan Year, Month and Day.
SOLAR reckoning.		LUNAR reckoning.		
	Jan.			
Pramathi *Dhanus—Margali.* 17	Mo 1	Marg. 7 ·86	12 ·77	H. 1358 *Zi-l-ka'da.* 20
18	Tu 2	8 ·77	13 ·70	21
19	We 3	9 ·69	14 ·64	22
20	Th 4	10 ·61	15 ·60	23
21	Fr 5	11 ·55	16 ·57	24
22	Sa 6	*Bahula* 12 ·52	17 ·56	25
23	Su 7	13 ·50	18 ·56	26
24	Mo 8	14 ·49	19 ·58	27
25	Tu 9	—A ·52	20 ·63	28
26	We 10	1 ·56	21 ·70	29
27	Th 11	2 ·62	22 ·78	—30
28	Fr 12	3 ·69	23 ·88	1
—29	Sa 13	4 ·77	24 ·99	2
1	Su 14	*Sukla* 5 ·86	... ...	3
2	Mo 15	6 ·95	25 ·10	4
3	Tu 16	... ...	26 ·20	5
4	We 17	7 ·03	27 ·29	6
5	Th 18	8 ·09	1 ·37	7
6	Fr 19	9 ·13	2 ·42	8
7	Sa 20	Pausha 10 ·16	3 ·46	9
8	Su 21	11 ·15	4 ·48	10
9	Mo 22	12 ·13	5 ·48	11
10	Tu 23	13 ·09	6 ·45	12
11	We 24	14 ·04 P ·97	7 ·41	13
Pramathi *Makara—Tai.* 12	Th 25	1 ·88	8 ·36	H. 1358 *Zi-l-hijja.* 14
13	Fr 26	2 ·79	9 ·31	15
14	Sa 27	3 ·69	10 ·24	16
15	Su 28	4 ·59	11 ·17	17
16	Mo 29	5 ·49	12 ·10	18
17	Tu 30	*Bahula* 6 ·40	13 ·04 14 ·99	19
18	We 31	7 ·32	15 ·94	20
	Feb.			
19	Th 1	8 ·25	16 ·90	21
20	Fr 2	9 ·19	17 ·88	22
21	Sa 3	10 ·16	18 ·88	23
22	Su 4	11 ·14	19 ·91	24
23	Mo 5	12 ·13	20 ·94	25
24	Tu 6	13 ·16	... ...	26
25	We 7	14 ·21	21 ·00	27
26	Th 8	—A ·27	22 ·08	28
27	Fr 9	1 ·34	23 ·18	—29
28	Sa 10	2 ·42	24 ·29	1
29	Su 11	3 ·51	25 ·40	2
—30	Mo 12	4 ·60	26 ·50	3
Pramathi *Kumbha—Masi.* 1	Tu 13	5 ·67	27 ·59	4
2	We 14	6 ·73	1 ·67	5
3	Th 15	*Sukla* 7 ·77	2 ·73	6
4	Fr 16	8 ·79	3 ·78	7
5	Sa 17	9 ·79	4 ·80	H. 1359 *Muharram.* 8
6	Su 18	10 ·77	5 ·80	9
7	Mo 19	11 ·72	6 ·78	10
8	Tu 20	12 ·66	7 ·75	11
9	We 21	Magha 13 ·59	8 ·71	12
10	Th 22	14 ·51	9 ·65	13
11	Fr 23	P ·41	10 ·58	14
12	Sa 24	1 ·31	11 ·51	15
13	Su 25	2 ·21	12 ·44	16
14	Mo 26	3 ·11	13 ·38	17
15	Tu 27	*Bah.* 4 ·02 5 ·94	14 ·32	18
16	We 28	6 ·87	15 ·27	19
17	Th 29	7 ·81	16 ·23	20

Cyclic Sidereal Year, Month and Day.	Week-Day English Month and Day.	Tithi Ending Moment.	Nakshatra Ending Moment.	Muhammadan Year, Month and Day.
SOLAR reckoning.		LUNAR reckoning.		
	March			
Pramathi *Kumbha—Masi.* 18	Fr 1	Magha 8 ·78	17 ·21	H. 1359 *Muharram.* 21
19	Sa 2	9 ·76	18 ·21	22
20	Su 3	10 ·75	19 ·22	23
21	Mo 4	11 ·77	20 ·26	24
22	Tu 5	12 ·81	21 ·31	25
23	We 6	*Bahula* 13 ·88	22 ·38	26
24	Th 7	14 ·96	23 ·48	27
25	Fr 8	... ...	24 ·58	28
26	Sa 9	—A ·05	25 ·69	29
27	Su 10	1 ·14	26 ·80	—30
28	Mo 11	2 ·22	27 ·89	1
29	Tu 12	3 ·28	1 ·98	2
30	We 13	4 ·33	... ...	3
—31	Th 14	5 ·37	2 ·05	4
Pramathi *Mina—Panguni.* 1	Fr 15	6 ·38	3 ·10	5
2	Sa 16	*Sukla* 7 ·38	4 ·12	6
3	Su 17	8 ·36	5 ·13	7
4	Mo 18	9 ·31	6 ·11	8
5	Tu 19	10 ·25	7 ·09	9
6	We 20	11 ·18	8 ·04 9 ·99	10
7	Th 21	12 ·09 13 ·99	10 ·92	11
8	Fr 22	Phalguna 14 ·89	11 ·85	12
9	Sa 23	P ·79	12 ·78	H. 1359 *Safar.* 13
10	Su 24	1 ·70	13 ·72	14
11	Mo 25	2 ·61	14 ·66	15
12	Tu 26	3 ·53	15 ·60	16
13	We 27	4 ·45	16 ·56	17
14	Th 28	5 ·39	17 ·54	18
15	Fr 29	6 ·36	18 ·53	19
16	Sa 30	7 ·34	19 ·54	20
17	Su 31	8 ·33	20 ·57	21
	April			
18	Mo 1	*Bahula* 9 ·35	21 ·62	22
19	Tu 2	10 ·40	22 ·69	23
20	We 3	11 ·46	23 ·79	24
21	Th 4	12 ·53	24 ·89	25
22	Fr 5	13 ·61	25 ·99	26
23	Sa 6	14 ·70	... ...	27
24	Su 7	—A ·78	26 ·10	28
25	Mo 8	1 ·85	27 ·20	—29
26	Tu 9	2 ·90	1 ·29	1
27	We 10	3 ·93	2 ·36	2
28	Th 11	4 ·94	3 ·41	3
—29	Fr 12	5 ·94	4 ·44	4
Vikrama *Mesha—Chittirai.* 1	Sa 13	6 ·92	5 ·45	5
2	Su 14	*Sukla* 7 ·87	6 ·45	6
3	Mo 15	8 ·81	7 ·42	7
4	Tu 16	9 ·74	8 ·38	H. 1359 *Rabi-ul-awwal.* 8
5	We 17	10 ·65	9 ·32	9
6	Th 18	11 ·55	10 ·26	10
7	Fr 19	12 ·45	11 ·20	11
8	Sa 20	Chaitra 13 ·35	12 ·13	12
9	Su 21	14 ·25	13 ·06 14 ·99	13
10	Mo ○ 22	P ·15	15 ·94	14
11	Tu 23	1 ·07 2 ·99	16 ·90	15
12	We 24	3 ·93	17 ·87	16
13	Th 25	4 ·89	18 ·86	17
14	Fr 26	5 ·87	19 ·86	18
15	Sa 27	6 ·87	20 ·88	19
16	Su 28	*Bahula* 7 ·88	21 ·93	20
17	Mo 29	8 ·92	... ...	21
18	Tu 30	9 ·98	22 ·00	22

Cyclic Sidereal Year, Month and Day.	Week-Day English Month and Day.	Tithi Ending Moment.	Nakshatra Ending Moment.	Muhammadan Year, Month and Day.
SOLAR reckoning.		LUNAR reckoning.		
	May			
Vikrama *Mesha—Chittirai.* 19	We 1	Ch.	23 ·09	*Rabi-ul-awwal.* 23
20	Th 2	10 ·06	24 ·18	24
21	Fr 3	11 ·15	25 ·29	25
22	Sa 4	*Bahula* 12 ·23	26 ·40	26
23	Su 5	13 ·30	27 ·51	27
24	Mo 6	14 ·37	1 ·60	28
25	Tu 7	—A ·43	2 ·67	29
26	We 8	1 ·47	3 ·72	—30
27	Th 9	2 ·48	4 ·76	1
28	Fr 10	3 ·47	5 ·78	2
29	Sa 11	4 ·45	6 ·77	3
30	Su 12	5 ·40	7 ·75	4
—31	Mo 13	6 ·33	8 ·71	5
Vikrama *Vrishabha—Vaikasi.* 1	Tu 14	*Sukla* 7 ·26	9 ·66	6
2	We 15	8 ·17	10 ·61	7
3	Th 16	9 ·07 10 ·97	11 ·54	8
4	Fr 17	11 ·87	12 ·47	9
5	Sa 18	Vaisakha 12 ·77	13 ·40	10
6	Su 19	13 ·67	14 ·33	11
7	Mo 20	14 ·58	15 ·27	12
8	Tu 21	P ·51	16 ·23	H. 1359 *Rabi-ul-akhir.* 13
9	We 22	1 ·45	17 ·20	14
10	Th 23	2 ·40	18 ·18	15
11	Fr 24	3 ·38	19 ·18	16
12	Sa 25	4 ·37	20 ·20	17
13	Su 26	5 ·39	21 ·25	18
14	Mo 27	6 ·44	22 ·31	19
15	Tu 28	*Bahula* 7 ·49	23 ·39	20
16	We 29	8 ·56	24 ·48	21
17	Th 30	9 ·64	25 ·59	22
18	Fr 31	10 ·72	26 ·70	23
	June			
19	Sa 1	11 ·80	27 ·81	24
20	Su 2	12 ·87	1 ·90	25
21	Mo 3	13 ·92	2 ·98	26
22	Tu 4	14 ·96	... ...	27
23	We 5	—A ·97	3 ·04	28
24	Th 6	1 ·96	4 ·08	—29
25	Fr 7	2 ·94	5 ·10	1
26	Sa 8	3 ·89	6 ·10	2
27	Su 9	4 ·83	7 ·08	3
28	Mo 10	5 ·76	8 ·04	4
29	Tu 11	6 ·66	9 ·00 10 ·94	5
30	We 12	*Sukla* 7 ·56	11 ·88	6
—31	Th 13	8 ·46	12 ·81	7
Vikrama *Mithuna—Ani.* 1	Fr 14	9 ·36	13 ·74	H. 1359 *Jumadal-awwal.* 8
2	Sa 15	10 ·26	14 ·68	9
3	Su 16	11 ·17	15 ·62	10
4	Mo 17	12 ·08	16 ·56	11
5	Tu 18	Jyeshtha 13 ·00 14 ·93	17 ·53	12
6	We 19	P ·88	18 ·50	13
7	Th 20	1 ·86	19 ·50	14
8	Fr 21	2 ·85	20 ·52	15
9	Sa 22	3 ·87	21 ·56	16
10	Su 23	4 ·90	22 ·62	17
11	Mo 24	5 ·96	23 ·69	18
12	Tu 25	... ...	24 ·78	19
13	We 26	6 ·03	25 ·89	20
14	Th 27	*Bahula* 7 ·11	... ...	21
15	Fr 28	8 ·19	26 ·00	22
16	Sa 29	9 ·27	27 ·10	23
17	Su 30	10 ·34	1 ·20	24

Naksh :—1. Asvn. 2. Bhar. 3. Krit. 4. Rohi. 5. Mrig. 6. Ardh. 7. Punar. 8. Push. 9. Aslesh. 10. Magh. 11. P. Phal. 12. U. Phal. 13. Hasta. 14. Chit.

A. D. 1940.
A.—Amavasya.
P.—Paurnami.

Kollam 1116, Commences { N. Malabar—Sept. / S. Malabar—Aug.

Hijra 1359, Commences, Feb. 10.

Vikrama 1997.
Bengal San 1346.
(N. Cycle) Nandana.

July

Solar: Vikrama Mithuna—Ani (18–32); Vikrama Karkata—Adi (1–16). Lunar: Jy. Bah., Sukla, Ashadha, Bahula. Muhammadan: J-awwal; H. 1359 Jumadal-akhir.

Cyclic Sidereal Year, Month and Day	Week-Day English Month and Day	Tithi Ending Moment	Nakshatra Ending Moment	Muhammadan Year, Month and Day
18	Mo 1	Jy. 11 ·39	2 ·29	25
19	Tu 2	12 ·43	3 ·36	26
20	We 3	13 ·45	4 ·40	27
21	Th 4	14 ·44	5 ·42	28
22	Fr 5	—A ·42	6 ·42	29
23	Sa 6	1 ·37	7 ·41	—30
24	Su 7	2 ·31	8 ·38	1
25	Mo 8	3 ·23	9 ·34	2
26	Tu 9	4 ·14	10 ·28	3
27	We 10	{ 5 ·04 / 6 ·94	11 ·21	4
28	Th 11	7 ·84	12 ·14	5
29	Fr 12	8 ·74	13 ·07	6
30	Sa 13	9 ·64	14 ·01 / 15 ·95 }	7
31	Su 14	10 ·55	16 ·90	8
—32	Mo 15	11 ·48	17 ·86	9
1	Tu 16	12 ·41	18 ·83	10
2	We 17	13 ·36	19 ·83	11
3	Th 18	14 ·34	20 ·84	12
4	Fr 19	P ·34	21 ·87	13
5	Sa 20	1 ·35	22 ·92	14
6	Su 21	2 ·38	23 ·99	15
7	Mo 22	3 ·43	... ...	16
8	Tu 23	4 ·50	24 ·09	17
9	We 24	5 ·58	25 ·19	18
10	Th 25	6 ·66	26 ·30	19
11	Fr 26	7 ·75	27 ·40	20
12	Sa 27	8 ·82	1 ·50	21
13	Su 28	9 ·87	2 ·60	22
14	Mo 29	10 ·91	3 ·67	23
15	Tu 30	11 ·93	4 ·71	24
16	We 31	12 ·92	5 ·74	25

Aug.

Solar: Vikrama Karkata—Adi (17–31); Vikrama Simha—Avani (1–16). Lunar: Sukla, Sravana, Bahula. Muhammadan: H. 1359 Rajab.

Cyclic Sidereal Year, Month and Day	Week-Day English Month and Day	Tithi Ending Moment	Nakshatra Ending Moment	Muhammadan Year, Month and Day
17	Th 1	13 ·90	6 ·75	26
18	Fr 2	14 ·86	7 ·74	27
19	Sa 3	—A ·80	8 ·72	28
20	Su 4	1 ·72	9 ·67	—29
21	Mo 5	2 ·63	10 ·62	1
22	Tu 6	3 ·53	11 ·55	2
23	We 7	4 ·43	12 ·48	3
24	Th 8	5 ·33	13 ·41	4
25	Fr 9	6 ·23	14 ·35	5
26	Sa 10	7 ·13	15 ·29	6
27	Su 11	{ 8 ·05 / 9 ·97	16 ·23	7
28	Mo 12	10 ·89	17 ·19	8
29	Tu 13	11 ·85	18 ·17	9
30	We 14	12 ·83	19 ·15	10
—31	Th 15	13 ·83	20 ·16	11
1	Fr 16	14 ·84	21 ·18	12
2	Sa 17	P ·87	22 ·23	13
3	Su 18	1 ·92	23 ·31	14
4	Mo 19	... ...	24 ·39	15
5	Tu 20	2 ·00	25 ·49	16
6	We 21	3 ·08	26 ·60	17
7	Th 22	4 ·16	27 ·70	18
8	Fr 23	5 ·24	1 ·80	19
9	Sa 24	6 ·31	2 ·90	20
10	Su 25	7 ·37	3 ·97	21
11	Mo 26	8 ·41	... ...	22
12	Tu 27	9 ·44	4 ·03	23
13	We 28	10 ·43	5 ·06	24
14	Th 29	11 ·40	6 ·07	25
15	Fr 30	12 ·36	7 ·07	26
16	Sa 31	13 ·30	8 ·05	27

Sep.

Solar: Vikrama Simha—Avani (17–31); Vikrama Kanya—Purattasi (1–15). Lunar: Sukla, Bhadrapada, Bahula. Muhammadan: Rajab; H. 1359 Shaban.

Cyclic Sidereal Year, Month and Day	Week-Day English Month and Day	Tithi Ending Moment	Nakshatra Ending Moment	Muhammadan Year, Month and Day
17	Su 1	14 ·23	9 ·01 / 10 ·95 }	28
18	Mo 2	—A ·14	11 ·89	29
19	Tu 3	{ 1 ·04 / 2 ·94	12 ·83	—30
20	We 4	3 ·84	13 ·76	1
21	Th 5	4 ·74	14 ·69	2
22	Fr 6	5 ·64	15 ·62	3
23	Sa 7	6 ·56	16 ·57	4
24	Su 8	7 ·49	17 ·53	5
25	Mo 9	8 ·43	18 ·49	6
26	Tu 10	9 ·38	19 ·48	7
27	We 11	10 ·36	20 ·48	8
28	Th 12	11 ·35	21 ·50	9
29	Fr 13	12 ·36	22 ·54	10
30	Sa 14	13 ·40	23 ·61	11
—31	Su 15	14 ·45	24 ·69	12
1	Mo 16	P ·52	25 ·79	13
2	Tu 17	1 ·60	26 ·89	14
3	We 18	2 ·68	... ...	15
4	Th 19	3 ·76	27 ·00	16
5	Fr 20	4 ·83	1 ·11	17
6	Sa 21	5 ·89	2 ·20	18
7	Su 22	6 ·94	3 ·28	19
8	Mo 23	7 ·96	4 ·34	20
9	Tu 24	8 ·96	5 ·38	21
10	We 25	9 ·94	6 ·40	22
11	Th 26	10 ·91	7 ·40	23
12	Fr 27	11 ·85	8 ·38	24
13	Sa 28	12 ·77	9 ·34	25
14	Su 29	13 ·68	10 ·29	26
15	Mo 30	14 ·59	11 ·24	27

Oct.

Solar: Vikrama Kanya—Purattasi (16–31); Vikrama Tula—Aippasi (1–15). Lunar: Sukla, Asvina, Bahula. Muhammadan: H. 1359 Ramzan.

Cyclic Sidereal Year, Month and Day	Week-Day English Month and Day	Tithi Ending Moment	Nakshatra Ending Moment	Muhammadan Year, Month and Day
16	Tu 1	—A ·50	12 ·17	28
17	We 2	1 ·40	13 ·10	—29
18	Th 3	2 ·30	14 ·03 / 15 ·96 }	1
19	Fr 4	3 ·20	16 ·91	2
20	Sa 5	4 ·11	17 ·86	3
21	Su 6	{ 5 ·03 / 6 ·97	18 ·82	4
22	Mo 7	7 ·93	19 ·80	5
23	Tu 8	8 ·92	20 ·80	6
24	We 9	9 ·92	21 ·81	7
25	Th 10	10 ·93	22 ·86	8
26	Fr 11	11 ·96	23 ·92	9
27	Sa 12	... ...	... ...	10
28	Su 13	12 ·01	24 ·00	11
29	Mo 14	13 ·08	25 ·09	12
30	Tu 15	14 ·16	26 ·19	13
—31	We 16	P ·25	27 ·30	14
1	Th 17	1 ·33	1 ·41	15
2	Fr 18	2 ·41	2 ·51	16
3	Sa 19	3 ·47	3 ·59	17
4	Su 20	4 ·52	4 ·65	18
5	Mo 21	5 ·55	5 ·70	19
6	Tu 22	6 ·54	6 ·72	20
7	We 23	7 ·52	7 ·72	21
8	Th 24	8 ·48	8 ·71	22
9	Fr 25	9 ·42	9 ·67	23
10	Sa 26	10 ·35	10 ·63	24
11	Su 27	11 ·27	11 ·57	25
12	Mo 28	12 ·18	12 ·51	26
13	Tu 29	{ 13 ·08 / 14 ·98	13 ·44	27
14	We 30	—A ·88	14 ·37	28
15	Th 31	1 ·79	15 ·30	29

Nov.

Solar: Vikrama Tula—Aippasi (16–30); Vikrama Vrischika—Kartigai (1–15). Lunar: Sukla, Kartika, Bahula. Muhammadan: H. 1359 Shawwal.

Cyclic Sidereal Year, Month and Day	Week-Day English Month and Day	Tithi Ending Moment	Nakshatra Ending Moment	Muhammadan Year, Month and Day
16	Fr 1	2 ·70	16 ·24	—30
17	Sa 2	3 ·63	17 ·19	1
18	Su 3	4 ·58	18 ·15	2
19	Mo 4	5 ·53	19 ·13	3
20	Tu 5	6 ·51	20 ·12	4
21	We 6	7 ·50	21 ·14	5
22	Th 7	8 ·52	22 ·17	6
23	Fr 8	9 ·56	23 ·23	7
24	Sa 9	10 ·62	24 ·30	8
25	Su 10	11 ·69	25 ·39	9
26	Mo 11	12 ·77	26 ·50	10
27	Tu 12	13 ·86	27 ·61	11
28	We 13	14 ·94	1 ·71	12
29	Th 14	... ...	2 ·81	13
—30	Fr 15	P ·02	3 ·90	14
1	Sa 16	1 ·08	4 ·97	15
2	Su 17	2 ·13	... ...	16
3	Mo 18	3 ·15	5 ·02	17
4	Tu 19	4 ·16	6 ·04	18
5	We 20	5 ·13	7 ·05	19
6	Th 21	6 ·09	8 ·03	20
7	Fr 22	{ 7 ·04 / 8 ·97	9 ·01 / 10 ·97 }	21
8	Sa 23	9 ·89	11 ·91	22
9	Su 24	10 ·80	12 ·85	23
10	Mo 25	11 ·70	13 ·78	24
11	Tu 26	12 ·60	14 ·71	25
12	We 27	13 ·50	15 ·65	26
13	Th 28	14 ·41	16 ·59	27
14	Fr 29	—A ·32	17 ·53	28
15	Sa 30	1 ·25	18 ·48	—29

Dec.

Solar: Vikrama Vrischika—Kartigai (16–29); Vikrama Dhanus—Margali (1–17). Lunar: Sukla, Margasira, Bahula, P. Suk. Muhammadan: H. 1359 Zi-l-ka'da.

Cyclic Sidereal Year, Month and Day	Week-Day English Month and Day	Tithi Ending Moment	Nakshatra Ending Moment	Muhammadan Year, Month and Day
16	Su 1	2 ·19	19 ·45	1
17	Mo 2	3 ·15	20 ·45	2
18	Tu 3	4 ·13	21 ·46	3
19	We 4	5 ·14	22 ·49	4
20	Th 5	6 ·16	23 ·54	5
21	Fr 6	7 ·20	24 ·60	6
22	Sa 7	8 ·26	25 ·70	7
23	Su 8	9 ·33	26 ·80	8
24	Mo 9	10 ·41	27 ·90	9
25	Tu 10	11 ·50	... ...	10
26	We 11	12 ·59	1 ·01	11
27	Th 12	13 ·67	2 ·11	12
28	Fr 13	14 ·73	3 ·20	13
—29	Sa 14	P ·77	4 ·28	14
1	Su 15	1 ·79	5 ·33	15
2	Mo 16	2 ·79	6 ·36	16
3	Tu 17	3 ·77	7 ·37	17
4	We 18	4 ·73	8 ·36	18
5	Th 19	5 ·67	9 ·34	19
6	Fr 20	6 ·60	10 ·30	20
7	Sa 21	7 ·52	11 ·25	21
8	Su 22	8 ·43	12 ·19	22
9	Mo 23	9 ·33	13 ·12	23
10	Tu 24	10 ·23	14 ·05 / 15 ·98 }	24
11	We 25	11 ·13	16 ·92	25
12	Th 26	{ 12 ·04 / 13 ·96	17 ·86	26
13	Fr 27	14 ·89	18 ·81	27
14	Sa 28	—A ·83	19 ·79	28
15	Su 29	1 ·80	20 ·78	29
16	Mo 30	2 ·78	21 ·78	—30
17	Tu 31	3 ·78	22 ·80	1

15. Svati. 16. Visak. 17. Anur. 18. Jyesh. 19. Mula. 20. P. Ash. 21. U. Ash. 22. Sravn. 23. Dani. 24. Satab. 25. P. Bhad. 26. U. Bhad. 27. Rev.

A. D. 1941. **Mesha Sankranti** (Commencement of Indian Sidereal Year).
Solar Eclipse. ● (Surya Sid.) April 13·23. Saka 1863. Kaliyuga 5042.
Lunar Eclipse. ○ (Arya Sid.) April 13·12. (S. Cycle) Vrisha.

Jan.

Solar: Vikrama *Dhanus—Margali* (to 30); Vikrama *Makara—Tai* (from 1). Lunar: Pausha Sukla; Bahula (from 6). Muhammadan: H. 1359 *Zi-l-hijja*.

Cyclic Sidereal Year, Month and Day	Week-Day	English Month and Day	Tithi	Ending Moment	Nakshatra	Ending Moment	Muhammadan Year, Month and Day
18	We	1	4	·80	23	·84	2
19	Th	2	5	·85	24	·91	3
20	Fr	3	6	·91	...	...	4
21	Sa	4	7	·98	25	·00	5
22	Su	5	...	...	26	·10	6
23	Mo	6	8	·07	27	·20	7
24	Tu	7	9	·16	1	·31	8
25	We	8	10	·24	2	·42	9
26	Th	9	11	·32	3	·51	10
27	Fr	10	12	·38	4	·59	11
28	Sa	11	13	·42	5	·64	12
29	Su	12	14	·44	6	·68	13
30	Mo	13	P	·44	7	·70	14
1	Tu	14	1	·41	8	·70	15
2	We	15	2	·37	9	·67	16
3	Th	16	3	·31	10	·63	17
4	Fr	17	4	·24	11	·58	18
5	Sa	18	5	·16	12	·52	19
6	Su	19	6 / 7	·07 / ·97	13	·46	20
7	Mo	20	8	·87	14	·39	21
8	Tu	21	9	·77	15	·32	22
9	We	22	10	·68	16	·26	23
10	Th	23	11	·60	17	·20	24
11	Fr	24	12	·53	18	·16	25
12	Sa	25	13	·48	19	·12	26
13	Su	26	14	·44	20	·10	27
14	Mo	27	A	·42	21	·10	28
15	Tu	28	1	·42	22	·12	29
16	We	29	2	·44	23	·16	1
17	Th	30	3	·49	24	·22	2
18	Fr	31	4	·56	25	·30	3

Feb.

Solar: Vikrama *Makara—Tai* (to 29); Vikrama *Kumbha—Masi* (from 1). Lunar: Sukla; Magha; Bahula; Suk. (from 27). Muhammadan: H. 1360 *Muharram*.

Cyclic Sidereal Year, Month and Day	Week-Day	English Month and Day	Tithi	Ending Moment	Nakshatra	Ending Moment	Muhammadan Year, Month and Day
19	Sa	1	5	·64	26	·40	4
20	Su	2	6	·72	27	·50	5
21	Mo	3	7	·81	1	·61	6
22	Tu	4	8	·89	2	·72	7
23	We	5	9	·96	3	·81	8
24	Th	6	...	...	4	·89	9
25	Fr	7	10	·02	5	·95	10
26	Sa	8	11	·06	6	·99	11
27	Su	9	12	·08	...	...	12
28	Mo	10	13	·07	7	·02	13
29	Tu	11	14	·05	8	·02	14
1	We	12	P / 1	·01 / ·95	9 / 10	·00 / ·97	15
2	Th	13	2	·87	11	·92	16
3	Fr	14	3	·78	12	·87	17
4	Sa	15	4	·69	13	·80	18
5	Su	16	5	·60	14	·73	19
6	Mo	17	6	·50	15	·66	20
7	Tu	18	7	·40	16	·59	21
8	We	19	8	·30	17	·54	22
9	Th	20	9	·22	18	·49	23
10	Fr	21	10	·15	19	·45	24
11	Sa	22	11	·10	20	·43	25
12	Su	23	12	·06	21	·42	26
13	Mo	24	13	·05	22	·44	27
14	Tu	25	14	·05	23	·48	28
15	We	26	A	·08	24	·53	29
16	Th	27	1	·12	25	·61	30
17	Fr	28	2	·18	26	·70	1

March

Solar: Vikrama *Kumbha—Masi* (to 30); Vikrama *Mina—Panguni* (from 1). Lunar: Sukla; Phalguna; Bahula. Muhammadan: H. 1360 *Safar*.

Cyclic Sidereal Year, Month and Day	Week-Day	English Month and Day	Tithi	Ending Moment	Nakshatra	Ending Moment	Muhammadan Year, Month and Day
18	Sa	1	3	·26	27	·80	2
19	Su	2	4	·35	1	·91	3
20	Mo	3	5	·44	...	...	4
21	Tu	4	6	·52	2	·02	5
22	We	5	7	·59	3	·12	6
23	Th	6	8	·64	4	·20	7
24	Fr	7	9	·68	5	·26	8
25	Sa	8	10	·69	6	·31	9
26	Su	9	11	·68	7	·34	10
27	Mo	10	12	·65	8	·35	11
28	Tu	11	13	·61	9	·33	12
29	We	12	14	·55	10	·30	13
30	Th ○	13	P	·47	11	·26	14
1	Fr	14	1	·39	12	·21	15
2	Sa	15	2	·29	13	·14	16
3	Su	16	3	·19	14	·07	17
4	Mo	17	4 / 5	·09 / ·99	15 / 16	·00 / ·94	18
5	Tu	18	6	·90	17	·88	19
6	We	19	7	·82	18	·82	20
7	Th	20	8	·75	19	·78	21
8	Fr	21	9	·69	20	·75	22
9	Sa	22	10	·65	21	·74	23
10	Su	23	11	·64	22	·76	24
11	Mo	24	12	·64	23	·79	25
12	Tu	25	13	·67	24	·84	26
13	We	26	14	·71	25	·91	27
14	Th	27	A	·77	...	...	28
15	Fr	28	1	·85	26	·00	29
16	Sa	29	2	·93	27	·10	1
17	Su	30	...	...	1	·21	2
18	Mo	31	8	·02	2	·32	3

April

Solar: Vrisha *Mesha—Chittirai*. Lunar: Sukla; Chaitra; Bahula; V. Suk. (from 27). Muhammadan: H. 1360 *Rabi-ul-awwal*.

Cyclic Sidereal Year, Month and Day	Week-Day	English Month and Day	Tithi	Ending Moment	Nakshatra	Ending Moment	Muhammadan Year, Month and Day
19	Tu	1	4	·10	3	·42	4
20	We	2	5	·17	4	·51	5
21	Th	3	6	·22	5	·58	6
22	Fr	4	7	·26	6	·63	7
23	Sa	5	8	·27	7	·66	8
24	Su	6	9	·26	8	·67	9
25	Mo	7	10	·23	9	·66	10
26	Tu	8	11	·18	10	·64	11
27	We	9	12	·12	11	·60	12
28	Th	10	13 / 14	·04 / ·95	12	·54	13
29	Fr	11	P	·85	13	·48	14
30	Sa	12	1	·75	14	·41	15
1	Su	13	2	·65	15	·34	16
2	Mo	14	3	·55	16	·28	17
3	Tu	15	4	·46	17	·22	18
4	We	16	5	·37	18	·16	19
5	Th	17	6	·30	19	·11	20
6	Fr	18	7	·24	20	·08	21
7	Sa	19	8	·21	21	·07	22
8	Su	20	9	·19	22	·08	23
9	Mo	21	10	·18	23	·10	24
10	Tu	22	11	·21	24	·15	25
11	We	23	12	·25	25	·22	26
12	Th	24	13	·31	26	·30	27
13	Fr	25	14	·39	27	·40	28
14	Sa	26	A	·48	1	·51	29
15	Su	27	1	·56	2	·62	30
16	Mo	28	2	·64	3	·72	1
17	Tu	29	3	·70	4	·82	2
18	We	30	4	·75	5	·89	3

May

Solar: Vrisha *Mesha—Chittirai* (to 31); Vrisha *Vrishabha—Vaikasi* (from 1). Lunar: Sukla; Vaisakha; Bahula. Muhammadan: H. 1360 *Rabi-ul-akhir*.

Cyclic Sidereal Year, Month and Day	Week-Day	English Month and Day	Tithi	Ending Moment	Nakshatra	Ending Moment	Muhammadan Year, Month and Day
19	Th	1	5	·79	6	·94	4
20	Fr	2	6	·80	7	·98	5
21	Sa	3	7	·79	8	·99	6
22	Su	4	8	·76	9	·99	7
23	Mo	5	9	·71	10	·97	8
24	Tu	6	10	·64	11	·93	9
25	We	7	11	·56	12	·88	10
26	Th	8	12	·48	13	·82	11
27	Fr	9	13	·38	14	·76	12
28	Sa	10	14	·28	15	·69	13
29	Su	11	P	·18	16	·62	14
30	Mo	12	1 / 2	·08 / ·98	17	·55	15
31	Tu	13	3	·89	18	·49	16
1	We	14	4	·81	19	·44	17
2	Th	15	5	·76	20	·42	18
3	Fr	16	6	·72	21	·40	19
4	Sa	17	7	·70	22	·40	20
5	Su	18	8	·70	23	·42	21
6	Mo	19	9	·73	24	·46	22
7	Tu	20	10	·77	25	·53	23
8	We	21	11	·82	26	·61	24
9	Th	22	12	·89	27	·70	25
10	Fr	23	13	·98	1	·81	26
11	Sa	24	...	...	2	·92	27
12	Su	25	14	·06	...	...	28
13	Mo	26	A	·14	3	·02	29
14	Tu	27	1	·21	4	·12	1
15	We	28	2	·26	5	·20	2
16	Th	29	3	·28	6	·26	3
17	Fr	30	4	·29	7	·29	4
18	Sa	31	5	·28	8	·31	5

June

Solar: Vrisha *Vrishabha—Vaikasi* (to 31); Vrisha *Mithuna—Ani* (from 1). Lunar: Sukla; Jyeshtha; Bahula; Ash. Suk. (from 25). Muhammadan: H. 1360 *Jumadi-ul-awwal*; *J.-akhir.* (from 1).

Cyclic Sidereal Year, Month and Day	Week-Day	English Month and Day	Tithi	Ending Moment	Nakshatra	Ending Moment	Muhammadan Year, Month and Day
19	Su	1	6	·25	9	·32	6
20	Mo	2	7	·21	10	·30	7
21	Tu	3	8	·15	11	·26	8
22	We	4	9 / 10	·07 / ·98	12	·21	9
23	Th	5	11	·88	13	·15	10
24	Fr	6	12	·78	14	·09	11
25	Sa	7	13	·68	15 / 16	·02 / ·95	12
26	Su	8	14	·58	17	·89	13
27	Mo	9	P	·48	18	·83	14
28	Tu	10	1	·40	19	·78	15
29	We	11	2	·32	20	·75	16
30	Th	12	3	·26	21	·72	17
31	Fr	13	4	·21	22	·72	18
1	Sa	14	5	·18	23	·73	19
2	Su	15	6	·18	24	·78	20
3	Mo	16	7	·20	25	·84	21
4	Tu	17	8	·24	26	·91	22
5	We	18	9	·29	...	...	23
6	Th	19	10	·36	27	·00	24
7	Fr	20	11	·45	1	·10	25
8	Sa	21	12	·53	2	·21	26
9	Su	22	13	·61	3	·32	27
10	Mo	23	14	·68	4	·42	28
11	Tu	24	A	·73	5	·50	29
12	We	25	1	·76	6	·57	30
13	Th	26	2	·78	7	·61	1
14	Fr	27	3	·76	8	·64	2
15	Sa	28	4	·73	9	·64	3
16	Su	29	5	·69	10	·63	4
17	Mo	30	6	·63	11	·59	5

Naksh :—1. Asvn. 2. Bhar. 3. Krit. 4. Rohi. 5. Mrig. 6. Ardh. 7. Punar. 8. Push. 9. Aslesh. 10. Magh. 11. P. Phal. 12. U. Phal. 13. Hasta. 14. Chit.

A. D. 1941.
A.—Amavasya.
P.—Paurnami.

Kollam 1117, Commences { N. Malabar—Sept. / S. Malabar—Aug.

Hijra 1360, Commences, Jan. 29.

Vikrama 1998.
Bengal San 1347.
(N. Cycle) Vijaya.

Column groups: SOLAR reckoning (Cyclic Sidereal Year, Month and Day; Week-Day English Month and Day) — LUNAR reckoning (Tithi Ending Moment; Nakshatra Ending Moment; Muhammadan Year, Month and Day).

July

Solar month	Sidereal day	Week-day	Date	Lunar month / Paksha	Tithi	Moment	Nakshatra	Moment	Muhammadan month	Day
Vrisha Mithuna—Ani.	18	Tu	1	Ashadha, Sukla	7	·55	12	·55	H. 1360 Jumada-l-akhir.	6
	19	We	2		8	·46	13	·50		7
	20	Th	3		9	·36	14	·43		8
	21	Fr	4		10	·26	15	·36		9
	22	Sa	5		11	·16	16	·29		10
	23	Su	6		12, 13	·06, ·96	17	·22		11
	24	Mo	7		14	·87	18	·17		12
	25	Tu	8		P	·79	19	·12		13
	26	We	9	Bahula	1	·78	20	·08		14
	27	Th	10		2	·69	21	·05		15
	28	Fr	11		3	·67	22	·04		16
	29	Sa	12		4	·66	23	·06		17
	30	Su	13		5	·68	24	·09		18
	31	Mo	14		6	·72	25	·14		19
	32	Tu	15		7	·77	26	·21		20
Vrisha Karkata—Adi.	1	We	16		8	·83	27	·30		21
	2	Th	17		9	·91	1	·40		22
	3	Fr	18		...	...	2	·51		23
	4	Sa	19		10	·00	3	·62		24
	5	Su	20		11	·08	4	·72		25
	6	Mo	21		12	·15	5	·81		26
	7	Tu	22		13	·21	6	·88		27
	8	We	23		14	·24	7	·93		28
	9	Th	24		A	·25	8	·96		29
	10	Fr	25		1	·24	9	·97		1
	11	Sa	26		2	·21	10	·96		2
	12	Su	27		3	·17	11	·93		3
	13	Mo	28		4	·12	12	·89		4
	14	Tu	29		5, 6	·04, ·95	13	·84		5
	15	We	30		7	·85	14	·77		6
	16	Th	31		8	·75	15	·70		7

Aug.

Solar month	Sidereal day	Week-day	Date	Lunar month / Paksha	Tithi	Moment	Nakshatra	Moment	Muhammadan month	Day
	17	Fr	1	Sravana, Sukla	9	·65	16	·63	H. 1360 Rajab.	8
	18	Sa	2		10	·55	17	·57		9
	19	Su	3		11	·45	18	·51		10
	20	Mo	4		12	·36	19	·45		11
	21	Tu	5		13	·28	20	·41		12
	22	We	6		14	·22	21	·38		13
	23	Th	7		P	·17	22	·37		14
	24	Fr	8	Bahula	1	·15	23	·38		15
	25	Sa	9		2	·14	24	·40		16
	26	Su	10		3	·16	25	·45		17
	27	Mo	11		4	·20	26	·52		18
	28	Tu	12		5	·26	27	·60		19
	29	We	13		6	·32	1	·71		20
	30	Th	14		7	·40	2	·82		21
	31	Fr	15		8	·49	3	·92		22
	32	Sa	16		9	·57	...	...		23
Vrisha Simha—Avani.	1	Su	17		10	·64	4	·02		24
	2	Mo	18		11	·69	5	·11		25
	3	Tu	19		12	·73	6	·19		26
	4	We	20		13	·75	7	·25		27
	5	Th	21		14	·74	8	·28		28
	6	Fr	22		A	·72	9	·29		29
	7	Sa	23	Bhadra., Sukla	1	·67	10	·29		30
	8	Su	24		2	·61	11	·27	H. 1360 Shaban.	1
	9	Mo	25		3	·54	12	·23		2
	10	Tu	26		4	·46	13	·17		3
	11	We	27		5	·36	14	·11		4
	12	Th	28		6	·26	15, 16	·04, ·97		5
	13	Fr	29		7	·16	17	·90		6
	14	Sa	30		8, 9	·06, ·96	18	·84		7
	15	Su	31		10	·87	19	·79		8

Sep.

Solar month	Sidereal day	Week-day	Date	Lunar month / Paksha	Tithi	Moment	Nakshatra	Moment	Muhammadan month	Day
Vrisha Simha—Avani.	16	Mo	1	Bhadrapada, Suk.	11	·80	20	·74	H. 1360 Shaban.	9
	17	Tu	2		12	·74	21	·71		10
	18	We	3		13	·69	22	·70		11
	19	Th	4		14	·66	23	·70		12
	20	Fr ○	5		P	·65	24	·72		13
	21	Sa	6	Bahula	1	·67	25	·76		14
	22	Su	7		2	·71	26	·82		15
	23	Mo	8		3	·77	27	·91		16
	24	Tu	9		4	·84	...	...		17
	25	We	10		5	·92	1	·01		18
	26	Th	11		...	...	2	·11		19
	27	Fr	12		6	·00	3	·22		20
	28	Sa	13		7	·08	4	·32		21
	29	Su	14		8	·16	5	·42		22
	30	Mo	15		9	·22	6	·50		23
	31	Tu	16		10	·26	7	·56		24
Vrisha Kanya—Purattasi.	1	We	17		11	·28	8	·60		25
	2	Th	18		12	·27	9	·62		26
	3	Fr	19		13	·24	10	·62		27
	4	Sa	20		14	·21	11	·60		28
	5	Su ●	21		A	·15	12	·56		29
	6	Mo	22	Sukla	1, 2	·07, ·99	13	·51		1
	7	Tu	23		3	·89	14	·45		2
	8	We	24		4	·79	15	·39		3
	9	Th	25		5	·69	16	·32		4
	10	Fr	26		6	·59	17	·25		5
	11	Sa	27		7	·50	18	·18		6
	12	Su	28		8	·41	19	·12		7
	13	Mo	29		9	·34	20	·07		8
	14	Tu	30		10	·28	21	·04		9

Oct.

Solar month	Sidereal day	Week-day	Date	Lunar month / Paksha	Tithi	Moment	Nakshatra	Moment	Muhammadan month	Day
	15	We	1	Asvina	11	·23	22	·02	H. 1360 Ramzan.	10
	16	Th	2		12	·21	23	·02		11
	17	Fr	3		13	·21	24	·03		12
	18	Sa	4		14	·22	25	·07		13
	19	Su	5		P	·26	26	·14		14
	20	Mo	6	Bahula	1	·31	27	·22		15
	21	Tu	7		2	·38	1	·31		16
	22	We	8		3	·47	2	·41		17
	23	Th	9		4	·56	3	·52		18
	24	Fr	10		5	·65	4	·63		19
	25	Sa	11		6	·73	5	·73		20
	26	Su	12		7	·79	6	·81		21
	27	Mo	13		8	·82	7	·87		22
	28	Tu	14		9	·84	8	·91		23
	29	We	15		10	·84	9	·93		24
	30	Th	16		11	·81	10	·94		25
Vrisha Tula—Aippasi.	1	Fr	17		12	·77	11	·92		26
	2	Sa	18		13	·72	12	·89		27
	3	Su	19		14	·65	13	·84		28
	4	Mo	20		A	·56	14	·79		29
	5	Tu	21	Kartt., Sukla	1	·47	15	·73		30
	6	We	22		2	·37	16	·66	H. 1360 Shawwal.	1
	7	Th	23		3	·27	17	·59		2
	8	Fr	24		4	·17	18	·52		3
	9	Sa	25		5	·08	19	·46		4
	10	Su	26		6, 7	·00, ·92	20	·41		5
	11	Mo	27		8	·86	21	·37		6
	12	Tu	28		9	·82	22	·35		7
	13	We	29		10	·80	23	·34		8
	14	Th	30		11	·80	24	·35		9
	15	Fr	31		12	·81	25	·39		10

Nov.

Solar month	Sidereal day	Week-day	Date	Lunar month / Paksha	Tithi	Moment	Nakshatra	Moment	Muhammadan month	Day
Vrisha Tula—Aippasi.	16	Sa	1	Kartika, Suk.	13	·86	26	·45	H. 1360 Shawwal.	11
	17	Su	2		14	·92	27	·52		12
	18	Mo	3		...	...	1	·61		13
	19	Tu	4		P	·00	2	·71		14
	20	We	5	Bahula	1	·08	3	·82		15
	21	Th	6		2	·17	4	·93		16
	22	Fr	7		3	·25	...	...		17
	23	Sa	8		4	·32	5	·03		18
	24	Su	9		5	·38	6	·11		19
	25	Mo	10		6	·42	7	·18		20
	26	Tu	11		7	·45	8	·23		21
	27	We	12		8	·44	9	·26		22
	28	Th	13		9	·41	10	·27		23
	29	Fr	14		10	·38	11	·25		24
	30	Sa	15		11	·33	12	·22		25
Vrisha Vrischika—Kartigai.	1	Su	16		12	·26	13	·18		26
	2	Mo	17		13	·17	14	·13		27
	3	Tu	18		14, A	·08, ·98	15	·07		28
	4	We	19	Sukla	1	·88	16, 17	·00, ·93		29
	5	Th	20		2	·78	18	·86		1
	6	Fr	21		3	·69	19	·80		2
	7	Sa	22		4	·61	20	·75		3
	8	Su	23		5	·54	21	·70		4
	9	Mo	24		6	·48	22	·67		5
	10	Tu	25		7	·45	23	·66		6
	11	We	26		8	·43	24	·68		7
	12	Th	27		9	·42	25	·71		8
	13	Fr	28		10	·44	26	·76		9
	14	Sa	29		11	·48	27	·82		10
	15	Su	30		12	·54	1	·91		11

Dec.

Solar month	Sidereal day	Week-day	Date	Lunar month / Paksha	Tithi	Moment	Nakshatra	Moment	Muhammadan month	Day
	16	Mo	1	Margasira	13	·62	...	...	H. 1360 Zi-l-ka'da.	12
	17	Tu	2		14	·70	2	·01		13
	18	We	3		P	·80	3	·12		14
	19	Th	4	Bahula	1	·88	4	·23		15
	20	Fr	5		2	·95	5	·33		16
	21	Sa	6		...	...	6	·42		17
	22	Su	7		3	·01	7	·49		18
	23	Mo	8		4	·06	8	·55		19
	24	Tu	9		5	·08	9	·58		20
	25	We	10		6	·07	10	·59		21
	26	Th	11		7	·05	11	·58		22
	27	Fr	12		8, 9	·01, ·95	12	·55		23
	28	Sa	13		10	·88	13	·52		24
	29	Su	14		11	·79	14	·47		25
Vrisha Dhanus—Margali.	1	Mo	15		12	·70	15	·40		26
	2	Tu	16		13	·61	16	·33		27
	3	We	17		14	·51	17	·26		28
	4	Th	18		A	·41	18	·20		29
	5	Fr	19	Pausha, Sukla	1	·32	19	·14		30
	6	Sa	20		2	·24	20	·08	H. 1360 Zi-l-hijja.	1
	7	Su	⊙21		3	·17	21	·03		2
	8	Mo	22		4	·12	22	·01		3
	9	Tu	23		5	·09	23	·00		4
	10	We	24		6	·07	24	·00		5
	11	Th	25		7	·06	25	·02		6
	12	Fr	26		8	·09	26	·06		7
	13	Sa	27		9	·14	27	·13		8
	14	Su	28		10	·20	1	·21		9
	15	Mo	29		11	·27	2	·31		10
	16	Tu	30		12	·35	3	·42		11
	17	We	31		13	·44	4	·53		12

15. Svati. 16. Visak. 17. Anur. 18. Jyesh. 19. Mula. 20. P. Ash. 21. U. Ash. 22. Sravn. 23. Dani. 24. Satab. 25. P. Bhad. 26. U. Bhad. 27. Rev.

A. D. 1942. | **Mesha Sankranti** (Commencement of Indian Sidereal Year).
Solar Eclipse. ● | (Surya Sid.) April 13·49. | Saka 1864. | Kaliyuga 5043.
Lunar Eclipse. ○ | (Arya Sid.) April 13·38. | (S. Cycle) Chitrabhanu.

Columns: SOLAR reckoning — Cyclic Sidereal Year, Month and Day; Week-Day English Month and Day. LUNAR reckoning — Tithi Ending Moment; Nakshatra Ending Moment; Muhammadan Year, Month and Day.

Jan.

Cyclic Sidereal Year, Month and Day	Week-Day English Month and Day	Tithi Ending Moment	Nakshatra Ending Moment	Muhammadan Year, Month and Day
Vrisha *Dhanus—Margali.* 18	Th 1	Pausha 14 ·58	5 ·63	*H. 1360 Zi-l-hijja.* 13
19	Fr 2	P ·61	6 ·72	14
20	Sa 3	1 ·67	7 ·80	15
21	Su 4	2 ·71	8 ·86	16
22	Mo 5	3 ·72	9 ·90	17
23	Tu 6	4 ·72	10 ·91	18
24	We 7	5 ·69	11 ·91	19
25	Th 8	*Bahula* 6 ·65	12 ·89	20
26	Fr 9	7 ·60	13 ·85	21
27	Sa 10	8 ·53	14 ·80	22
28	Su 11	9 ·44	15 ·74	23
29	Mo 12	10 ·35	16 ·68	24
—30	Tu 13	11 ·25	17 ·61	25
1	We 14	12 ·15	18 ·54	26
2	Th 15	13 ·05 14 ·97	19 ·48	27
3	Fr 16	—A ·89	20 ·42	28
4	Sa 17	1 ·82	21 ·37	29
5	Su 18	2 ·77	22 ·33	—30
6	Mo 19	3 ·73	23 ·32	1
7	Tu 20	4 ·71	24 ·32	2
8	We 21	5 ·71	25 ·34	3
9	Th 22	6 ·74	26 ·38	4
10	Fr 23	7 ·79	27 ·44	5
11	Sa 24	*Sukla* 8 ·86	1 ·52	6
Vrisha *Makara—Tai.* 12	Su 25	9 ·94	2 ·62	7
13	Mo 26	... ...	3 ·72	8
14	Tu 27	10 ·03	4 ·83	9
15	We 28	11 ·11	5 ·93	10
16	Th 29	12 ·19	... ...	11
17	Fr 30	13 ·26	6 ·03	12
18	Sa 31	14 ·32	7 ·11	13

Feb.

Cyclic Sidereal Year, Month and Day	Week-Day English Month and Day	Tithi Ending Moment	Nakshatra Ending Moment	Muhammadan Year, Month and Day
19	Su 1	Magha P ·35	8 ·17	*H. 1361 Muharram.* 14
20	Mo 2	1 ·36	9 ·21	15
21	Tu 3	2 ·36	10 ·23	16
22	We 4	3 ·34	11 ·24	17
23	Th 5	4 ·29	12 ·22	18
24	Fr 6	5 ·23	13 ·19	19
25	Sa 7	6 ·15	14 ·14	20
26	Su 8	*Bahula* 7 ·07 8 ·97	15 ·08	21
27	Mo 9	9 ·87	16 ·02 17 ·95	22
28	Tu 10	10 ·77	18 ·88	23
—29	We 11	11 ·68	19 ·81	24
1	Th 12	12 ·59	20 ·75	25
2	Fr 13	13 ·51	21 ·70	26
3	Sa 14	14 ·44	22 ·67	27
4	Su 15	—A ·39	23 ·64	28
5	Mo 16	1 ·36	24 ·64	29
6	Tu 17	2 ·34	25 ·65	—30
7	We 18	3 ·34	26 ·69	1
8	Th 19	*Sukla* 4 ·37	27 ·75	2
Vrisha *Kumbha—Masi.* 9	Fr 20	5 ·41	1 ·88	*H. 1361 Safar.* 3
10	Sa 21	6 ·48	2 ·92	4
11	Su 22	7 ·56	... ...	5
12	Mo 23	8 ·66	3 ·02	6
13	Tu 24	9 ·74	4 ·13	7
14	We 25	Phalguna 10 ·81	5 ·24	8
15	Th 26	11 ·88	6 ·34	9
16	Fr 27	12 ·93	7 ·42	10
17	Sa 28	13 ·97	8 ·48	11

March

Cyclic Sidereal Year, Month and Day	Week-Day English Month and Day	Tithi Ending Moment	Nakshatra Ending Moment	Muhammadan Year, Month and Day
18	Su 1	Phalguna 14 ·98	9 ·53	12
19	Mo ○ 2	P ·98	10 ·56	13
20	Tu 3	1 ·95	11 ·57	14
Vrisha *Kumbha—Masi.* 21	We 4	2 ·90	12 ·55	15
22	Th 5	3 ·84	13 ·52	16
23	Fr 6	4 ·77	14 ·47	17
24	Sa 7	5 ·63	15 ·41	18
25	Su 8	*Bahula* 6 ·58	16 ·35	*H. 1361 Safar.* 19
26	Mo 9	7 ·48	17 ·29	20
27	Tu 10	8 ·38	18 ·22	21
28	We 11	9 ·28	19 ·15	22
29	Th 12	10 ·19	20 ·09	23
—30	Fr 13	11 ·11	21 ·04	24
1	Sa 14	12 ·04 13 ·98	22 ·00 23 ·97	25
2	Su 15	14 ·95	24 ·96	26
3	Mo 16	--A ·93	25 ·97	27
4	Tu 17	1 ·93	... ...	28
5	We 18	2 ·97	26 ·01	—29
6	Th 19	... ...	27 ·06	1
7	Fr 20	3 ·02	1 ·13	2
8	Sa 21	4 ·08	2 ·22	3
9	Su 22	5 ·16	3 ·32	4
10	Mo 23	6 ·25	4 ·43	5
11	Tu 24	*Sukla* 7 ·33	5 ·54	6
Vrisha *Mina—Panguni.* 12	We 25	8 ·41	6 ·64	7
13	Th 26	9 ·48	7 ·72	8
14	Fr 27	10 ·53	8 ·79	9
15	Sa 28	11 ·56	9 ·84	10
16	Su 29	12 ·57	10 ·88	11
17	Mo 30	13 ·56	11 ·89	12
18	Tu 31	14 ·52	12 ·88	13

April

Cyclic Sidereal Year, Month and Day	Week-Day English Month and Day	Tithi Ending Moment	Nakshatra Ending Moment	Muhammadan Year, Month and Day
19	We 1	Chaitra P ·47	13 ·85	*H. 1361 Rabi-ul-awwal.* 14
20	Th 2	1 ·41	14 ·81	15
21	Fr 3	2 ·34	15 ·76	16
22	Sa 4	3 ·25	16 ·70	17
23	Su 5	4 ·15	17 ·63	18
24	Mo 6	*Bahula* 5 ·05 6 ·95	18 ·56	19
25	Tu 7	7 ·85	19 ·49	20
26	We 8	8 ·76	20 ·43	21
27	Th 9	9 ·67	21 ·37	22
28	Fr 10	10 ·60	22 ·33	23
29	Sa 11	11 ·55	23 ·30	24
—30	Su 12	12 ·51	24 ·28	25
1	Mo 13	13 ·49	25 ·30	26
2	Tu 14	14 ·49	26 ·33	27
3	We 15	—A ·52	27 ·37	28
4	Th 16	1 ·57	1 ·43	29
5	Fr 17	2 ·63	2 ·52	—30
6	Sa 18	3 ·71	3 ·62	1
7	Su 19	4 ·80	4 ·73	2
8	Mo 20	*Sukla* 5 ·88	5 ·84	3
9	Tu 21	6 ·95	6 ·94	4
Chitrabhanu *Mesha—Chittirai.* 10	We 22	... ...	... ...	5
11	Th 23	7 ·01	7 ·03	6
12	Fr 24	8 ·06	8 ·10	7
13	Sa 25	9 ·10	9 ·16	*H. 1361 Rabi-ul-akhir.* 8
14	Su 26	Vaisakha 10 ·11	10 ·20	9
15	Mo 27	11 ·10	11 ·21	10
16	Tu 28	12 ·07	12 ·20	11
17	We 29	13 ·02 14 ·95	13 ·18	12
18	Th 30	P ·87	14 ·15	13

May

Cyclic Sidereal Year, Month and Day	Week-Day English Month and Day	Tithi Ending Moment	Nakshatra Ending Moment	Muhammadan Year, Month and Day
19	Fr 1	Vaisakha 1 ·79	15 ·10	14
20	Sa 2	2 ·69	16 ·04 17 ·97	15
Chitrabhanu *Mesha—Chittirai.* 21	Su 3	3 ·59	18 ·90	*H. 1361 Rabi-ul-akhir.* 16
22	Mo 4	4 ·49	19 ·83	17
23	Tu 5	5 ·39	20 ·77	18
24	We 6	6 ·29	21 ·71	19
25	Th 7	*Bahula* 7 ·20	22 ·66	20
26	Fr 8	8 ·13	23 ·63	21
27	Sa 9	9 ·03	24 ·62	22
28	Su 10	10 ·04	25 ·62	23
29	Mo 11	11 ·02	26 ·64	24
30	Tu 12	12 ·02	27 ·68	25
—31	We 13	13 ·05	1 ·74	26
1	Th 14	14 ·09	2 ·82	27
2	Fr 15	—A ·14	3 ·92	28
3	Sa 16	1 ·21	... ...	—29
4	Su 17	2 ·30	4 ·03	1
5	Mo 18	3 ·39	5 ·13	2
6	Tu 19	*Sukla* 4 ·47	6 ·23	3
7	We 20	5 ·58	7 ·33	4
8	Th 21	6 ·58	8 ·42	5
9	Fr 22	7 ·60	9 ·48	6
10	Sa 23	8 ·61	10 ·51	7
11	Su 24	9 ·60	11 ·53	8
Chitrabhanu *Vrishabha—Vaikasi.* 12	Mo 25	Jyeshtha 10 ·58	12 ·53	*Jumadal-awwal.* 9
13	Tu 26	11 ·53	13 ·52	10
14	We 27	12 ·46	14 ·48	11
15	Th 28	13 ·38	15 ·43	12
16	Fr 29	14 ·29	16 ·37	13
17	Sa 30	P ·19	17 ·31	14
18	Su 31	1 ·09 2 ·99	18 ·24	15

June

Cyclic Sidereal Year, Month and Day	Week-Day English Month and Day	Tithi Ending Moment	Nakshatra Ending Moment	Muhammadan Year, Month and Day
19	Mo 1	Adhika 3 ·89	19 ·17	H. 1361 16
20	Tu 2	4 ·79	20 ·11	17
21	We 3	5 ·70	21 ·05 22 ·99	18
22	Th 4	6 ·63	23 ·96	19
23	Fr 5	7 ·57	24 ·94	20
24	Sa 6	*Bahula* 8 ·53	25 ·94	21
25	Su 7	9 ·51	26 ·95	22
26	Mo 8	10 ·50	27 ·99	23
27	Tu 9	11 ·53	... ...	24
28	We 10	12 ·57	1 ·05	25
29	Th 11	13 ·63	2 ·13	26
30	Fr 12	14 ·70	3 ·22	27
31	Sa 13	—A ·78	4 ·32	28
—32	Su 14	*Sukla* 1 ·86	5 ·43	29
1	Mo 15	2 ·94	6 ·54	—30
2	Tu 16	... ...	7 ·64	1
3	We 17	Jyeshtha 3 ·01	8 ·72	2
4	Th 18	4 ·06	9 ·79	3
5	Fr 19	5 ·09	10 ·83	4
6	Sa 20	6 ·10	11 ·85	5
Chitrabhanu *Mithuna—Ani.* 7	Su 21	7 ·09	12 ·86	*H. 1361 Jumadal-akhir.* 6
8	Mo 22	8 ·06	13 ·85	7
9	Tu 23	9 ·01 10 ·95	14 ·82	8
10	We 24	11 ·87	15 ·77	9
11	Th 25	Nija 12 ·78	16 ·71	10
12	Fr 26	13 ·68	17 ·65	11
13	Sa 27	14 ·58	18 ·58	12
14	Su 28	P ·48	19 ·51	13
15	Mo 29	*Bah.* 1 ·38	20 ·44	14
16	Tu 30	2 ·28	21 ·38	15

Naksh :—1. Asvn. 2. Bhar. 3. Krit. 4. Rohi. 5. Mrig. 6. Ardh. 7. Punar. 8. Push. 9. Aslesh. 10. Magh. 11. P. Phal. 12. U. Phal. 13. Hasta. 14. Chit.

A. D. 1942.
A.—Amavasya.
P.—Paurnami.

Kollam 1118, Commences { N. Malabar—Sept. / S. Malabar—Aug.

Hijra 1361, Commences, Jan. 19.

Vikrama 1999.
Bengal San 1348.
(N. Cycle) Manmatha.

SOLAR reckoning	Cyclic Sidereal Year, Month and Day	Week-Day English Month and Day	LUNAR reckoning	Tithi Ending Moment	Nakshatra Ending Moment		Muhammadan Year, Month and Day
		July					
Chitrabhanu *Mithuna—Ani.*	17	We 1	Nija—Jysh. *Bahula*	3 ·19	22 ·33	H. 1361 *Jumadal-akhir.*	16
	18	Th 2		4 ·12	23 ·30		17
	19	Fr 3		5 ·06	24 ·27		18
	20	Sa 4		6 ·01 7 ·99	25 ·26		19
	21	Su 5		8 ·98	26 ·27		20
	22	Mo 6		... ...	27 ·30		21
	23	Tu 7		9 ·00	1 ·36		22
	24	We 8		10 ·04	2 ·43		23
	25	Th 9		11 ·10	3 ·52		24
	26	Fr 10		12 ·17	4 ·62		25
	27	Sa 11		13 ·26	5 ·73		26
	28	Su 12		14 ·34	6 ·84		27
	29	Mo 13		—A ·42	7 ·94		28
	30	Tu 14	Ashadha *Sukla*	1 ·48	... ...		—29
	—31	We 15		2 ·53	8 ·03	H. 1361 *Rajab.*	1
Chitrabhanu *Karkata—Adi.*	1	Th 16		3 ·57	9 ·10		2
	2	Fr 17		4 ·58	10 ·14		3
	3	Sa 18		5 ·57	11 ·18		4
	4	Su 19		6 ·54	12 ·19		5
	5	Mo 20		7 ·49	13 ·18		6
	6	Tu 21		8 ·42	14 ·15		7
	7	We 22		9 ·34	15 ·11		8
	8	Th 23		10 ·26	16 ·06 17 ·99		9
	9	Fr 24		11 ·16	18 ·92		10
	10	Sa 25		12 ·06 13 ·96	19 ·85		11
	11	Su 26		14 ·86	20 ·78		12
	12	Mo 27		P ·76	21 ·72		13
	13	Tu 28		1 ·67	22 ·67		14
	14	We 29		2 ·59	23 ·63		15
	15	Th 30		3 ·53	24 ·60		16
	16	Fr 31		4 ·49	25 ·58		17
		Aug.					
	17	Sa 1	*Bahula*	5 ·47	26 ·59		18
	18	Su 2		6 ·47	27 ·63		19
	19	Mo 3		7 ·48	1 ·67		20
	20	Tu 4		8 ·52	2 ·74		21
	21	We 5		9 ·58	3 ·82		22
	22	Th 6		10 ·65	4 ·92		23
	23	Fr 7		11 ·73	... ...		24
	24	Sa 8		12 ·81	5 ·03		25
	25	Su 9		13 ·89	6 ·14		26
	26	Mo 10		14 ·96	7 ·24		27
	27	Tu 11		... ...	8 ·33		28
	28	We 12		—A ·02	9 ·40		29
	29	Th 13	Sravana *Sukla*	1 ·06	10 ·46		—30
	30	Fr 14		2 ·07	11 ·50	H. 1361 *Shaban.*	1
	31	Sa 15		3 ·06	12 ·51		2
	——32	Su 16		4 ·03 5 ·99	13 ·50		3
Chitrabhanu *Simha—Avani.*	1	Mo 17		6 ·93	14 ·48		4
	2	Tu 18		7 ·85	15 ·44		5
	3	We 19		8 ·76	16 ·39		6
	4	Th 20		9 ·66	17 ·33		7
	5	Fr 21		10 ·56	18 ·26		8
	6	Sa 22		11 ·46	19 ·19		9
	7	Su 23		12 ·36	20 ·12		10
	8	Mo 24		13 ·26	21 ·06		11
	9	Tu 25		14 ·18	22 ·01 23 ·96		12
	10	We○26		P ·11	24 ·92		13
	11	Th 27	*Bah.*	1 ·05	25 ·91		14
	12	Fr 28		2 ·00 3 ·97	26 ·92		15
	13	Sa 29		4 ·97	27 ·94		16
	14	Su 30		5 ·99	1 ·98		17
	15	Mo 31		... ...	... ...		18

SOLAR reckoning	Cyclic Sidereal Year, Month and Day	Week-Day English Month and Day	LUNAR reckoning	Tithi Ending Moment	Nakshatra Ending Moment		Muhammadan Year, Month and Day
		Sep.					
Chitrabhanu *Simha—Avani.*	16	Tu 1	Sravn. *Bahula*	6 ·03	2 ·04	H. 1361 *Shaban.*	19
	17	We 2		7 ·09	3 ·13		20
	18	Th 3		8 ·16	4 ·23		21
	19	Fr 4		9 ·24	5 ·34		22
	20	Sa 5		10 ·32	6 ·44		23
	21	Su 6		11 ·40	7 ·54		24
	22	Mo 7		12 ·47	8 ·63		25
	23	Tu 8		13 ·53	9 ·71		26
	24	We 9		14 ·57	10 ·78		27
	25	Th 10		—A ·60	11 ·82		28
	26	Fr 11	Bhadrapada *Sukla*	1 ·59	12 ·83		—29
	27	Sa 12		2 ·56	13 ·83	H. 1361 *Ramzan.*	1
	28	Su 13		3 ·51	14 ·81		2
	29	Mo 14		4 ·45	15 ·78		3
	30	Tu 15		5 ·38	16 ·73		4
	—31	We 16		6 ·29	17 ·67		5
Chitrabhanu *Kanya—Purattasi.*	1	Th 17		7 ·19	18 ·60		6
	2	Fr 18		8 ·09 9 ·99	19 ·53		7
	3	Sa 19		10 ·89	20 ·46		8
	4	Su 20		11 ·79	21 ·40		9
	5	Mo 21		12 ·71	22 ·34		10
	6	Tu 22		13 ·64	23 ·29		11
	7	We 23		14 ·58	24 ·25		12
	8	Th 24		P ·54	25 ·24		13
	9	Fr 25		1 ·52	26 ·24		14
	10	Sa 26		2 ·51	27 ·25		15
	11	Su 27		3 ·52	1 ·29		16
	12	Mo 28		4 ·57	2 ·35		17
	13	Tu 29		5 ·63	3 ·44		18
	14	We 30		6 ·70	4 ·53		19
		Oct.					
	15	Th 1	*Bahula*	7 ·78	5 ·63		20
	16	Fr 2		8 ·87	6 ·74		21
	17	Sa 3		9 ·95	7 ·84		22
	18	Su 4		... ...	8 ·94		23
	19	Mo 5		10 ·03	... ...		24
	20	Tu 6		11 ·09	9 ·03		25
	21	We 7		12 ·12	10 ·09		26
	22	Th 8		13 ·14	11 ·13		27
	23	Fr 9		14 ·14	12 ·15		28
	24	Sa 10		—A ·12	13 ·15		29
	25	Su 11	Asvina *Sukla*	1 ·08	14 ·14		—30
	26	Mo 12		2 ·02 3 ·94	15 ·11	H. 1361 *Shawwal.*	1
	27	Tu 13		4 ·85	16 ·06		2
	28	We 14		5 ·76	17 ·00 18 ·94		3
	29	Th 15		6 ·66	19 ·88		4
	—30	Fr 16		7 ·56	20 ·81		5
Chitrabhanu *Tula—Aippasi.*	1	Sa 17		8 ·46	21 ·74		6
	2	Su 18		9 ·37	22 ·68		7
	3	Mo 19		10 ·28	23 ·62		8
	4	Tu 20		11 ·21	24 ·59		9
	5	We 21		12 ·16	25 ·57		10
	6	Th 22		13 ·12	26 ·56		11
	7	Fr 23		14 ·10	27 ·57		12
	8	Sa 24		P ·10	1 ·60		13
	9	Su 25	*Bah.*	1 ·11	2 ·66		14
	10	Mo 26		2 ·15	3 ·74		15
	11	Tu 27		3 ·21	4 ·83		16
	12	We 28		4 ·28	5 ·93		17
	13	Th 29		5 ·37	... ...		18
	14	Fr 30		6 ·46	6 ·04		19
	15	Sa 31		7 ·55	7 ·15		20

SOLAR reckoning	Cyclic Sidereal Year, Month and Day	Week-Day English Month and Day	LUNAR reckoning	Tithi Ending Moment	Nakshatra Ending Moment		Muhammadan Year, Month and Day
		Nov.					
Chitrabhanu *Tula—Aippasi.*	16	Su 1	Asv. *Bahula*	8 ·63	8 ·25	H. 1361 *Shawwal.*	21
	17	Mo 2		9 ·68	9 ·33		22
	18	Tu 3		10 ·72	10 ·40		23
	19	We 4		11 ·75	11 ·45		24
	20	Th 5		12 ·74	12 ·47		25
	21	Fr 6		13 ·71	13 ·49		26
	22	Sa 7		14 ·67	14 ·47		27
	23	Su 8		—A ·61	15 ·44		28
	24	Mo 9	Karttika *Sukla*	1 ·54	16 ·40		—29
	25	Tu 10		2 ·46	17 ·34	H. 1361 *Zi-l-ka'da.*	1
	26	We 11		3 ·36	18 ·28		2
	27	Th 12		4 ·26	19 ·21		3
	28	Fr 13		5 ·16	20 ·14		4
	29	Sa 14		6 ·06 7 ·97	21 ·08		5
	—30	Su 15		8 ·89	22 ·02 23 ·96		6
Chitrabhanu *Vrischika—Kartigai.*	1	Mo 16		9 ·82	24 ·92		7
	2	Tu 17		10 ·76	25 ·89		8
	3	We 18		11 ·73	26 ·88		9
	4	Th 19		12 ·71	27 ·89		10
	5	Fr 20		13 ·71	1 ·93		11
	6	Sa 21		14 ·74	2 ·98		12
	7	Su 22		P ·78	... ...		13
	8	Mo 23		1 ·84	3 ·04		14
	9	Tu 24		2 ·91	4 ·13		15
	10	We 25		... ...	5 ·23		16
	11	Th 26		3 ·00	6 ·34		17
	12	Fr 27		4 ·09	7 ·45		18
	13	Sa 28		5 ·17	8 ·55		19
	14	Su 29		6 ·25	9 ·64		20
	15	Mo 30		7 ·31	10 ·71		21
		Dec.					
	16	Tu 1	*Bahula*	8 ·35	11 ·76		22
	17	We 2		9 ·37	12 ·80		23
	18	Th 3		10 ·36	13 ·81		24
	19	Fr 4		11 ·34	14 ·80		25
	20	Sa 5		12 ·29	15 ·77		26
	21	Su 6		13 ·23	16 ·73		27
	22	Mo 7		14 ·16	17 ·68		28
	23	Tu 8		A ·08 1 ·99	18 ·62		29
	24	We 9	Margasira *Sukla*	2 ·89	19 ·55		—30
	25	Th 10		3 ·79	20 ·48	H. 1361 *Zi-l-hijja.*	1
	26	Fr 11		4 ·69	21 ·42		2
	27	Sa 12		5 ·60	22 ·36		3
	28	Su 13		6 ·52	23 ·30		4
	29	Mo 14		7 ·45	24 ·25		5
	—30	Tu 15		8 ·39	25 ·22		6
Chitrabhanu *Dhanus—Margali.*	1	We 16		9 ·36	26 ·20		7
	2	Th 17		10 ·35	27 ·22		8
	3	Fr 18		11 ·36	1 ·24		9
	4	Sa 19		12 ·38	2 ·29		10
	5	Su 20		13 ·42	3 ·35		11
	6	Mo 21		14 ·48	4 ·43		12
	7	Tu 22		P ·56	5 ·53		13
	8	We 23	*Bahula*	1 ·65	6 ·64		14
	9	Th 24		2 ·75	7 ·75		15
	10	Fr 25		3 ·83	8 ·85		16
	11	Sa 26		4 ·90	9 ·94		17
	12	Su 27		5 ·96	... ...		18
	13	Mo 28		... ...	10 ·02		19
	14	Tu 29		6 ·00	11 ·08		20
	15	We 30		7 ·01	12 ·12		21
	16	Th 31		8 ·01 9 ·98	13 ·13		22

A. D. 1943.
Solar Eclipse. ●
Lunar Eclipse. ○

Mesha Sankranti (Commencement of Indian Sidereal Year).
(Surya Sid.) April 13·75.
(Arya Sid.) April 13·64.

Saka 1865. **Kaliyuga 5044.**
(S. Cycle) Subhanu.

Columns: SOLAR reckoning (Cyclic Sidereal Year, Month and Day; Week-Day English Month and Day) — LUNAR reckoning (Tithi Ending Moment; Nakshatra Ending Moment; Muhammadan Year, Month and Day).

Jan.

Solar: Chitrabhanu *Dhanus—Margali.* / Chitrabhanu *Makara—Tai.* — Lunar: *Bah.* **Marg.** / *Sukla* / **Pausha** / *Bahula* — Muhammadan: *Zil-hijja.* / H. 1362 *Muharram.*

Cyclic Sidereal	Week-Day	Day	Tithi	Nakshatra	Muhammadan
17	Fr	1	10 ·94	14 ·13	23
18	Sa	2	11 ·88	15 ·10	24
19	Su	3	12 ·81	16 ·07	25
20	Mo	4	13 ·73	17 ·02 } 18 ·96 }	26
21	Tu	5	14 ·63	19 ·89	27
22	We	6	—A ·53	20 ·82	28
23	Th	7	1 ·43	21 ·75	—29
24	Fr	8	2 ·34	22 ·69	1
25	Sa	9	3 ·25	23 ·63	2
26	Su	10	4 ·16	24 ·59	3
27	Mo	11	5 ·09	25 ·55	4
28	Tu	12	6 ·04	26 ·53	5
—29	We	13	7 ·01 8 ·99	27 ·54	6
1	Th	14	... ...	1 ·56	7
2	Fr	15	9 ·00	2 ·60	8
3	Sa	16	10 ·03	3 ·66	9
4	Su	17	11 ·08	4 ·74	10
5	Mo	18	12 ·14	5 ·84	11
6	Tu	19	13 ·22	6 ·94	12
7	We	20	14 ·31	... ...	13
8	Th	21	P ·40	7 ·05	14
9	Fr	22	1 ·48	8 ·15	15
10	Sa	23	2 ·55	9 ·24	16
11	Su	24	3 ·61	10 ·32	17
12	Mo	25	4 ·64	11 ·39	18
13	Tu	26	5 ·66	12 ·43	19
14	We	27	6 ·65	13 ·45	20
15	Th	28	7 ·62	14 ·45	21
16	Fr	29	8 ·57	15 ·44	22
17	Sa	30	9 ·51	16 ·41	23
18	Su	31	10 ·44	17 ·36	24

Feb.

Solar: Chitrabhanu *Kumbha—Masi.* — Lunar: *Sukla* / **Magha** / *Bahula* — Muhammadan: H. 1362 *Safar.*

Cyclic Sidereal	Week-Day	Day	Tithi	Nakshatra	Muhammadan
19	Mo	1	11 ·36	18 ·30	25
20	Tu	2	12 ·26	19 ·24	26
21	We	3	13 ·16	20 ·17	27
22	Th ●	4	{14 ·06 {A ·96	21 ·10	28
23	Fr	5	1 ·88	22 ·03 } 23 ·97 }	29
24	Sa	6	2 ·80	24 ·92	—30
25	Su	7	3 ·73	25 ·88	1
26	Mo	8	4 ·68	26 ·86	2
27	Tu	9	5 ·64	27 ·86	3
28	We	10	6 ·63	1 ·87	4
—29	Th	11	7 ·63	2 ·91	5
1	Fr	12	8 ·67	3 ·97	6
2	Sa	13	9 ·72	... ...	7
3	Su	14	10 ·78	4 ·05	8
4	Mo	15	11 ·86	5 ·14	9
5	Tu	16	12 ·95	6 ·24	10
6	We	17	... ...	7 ·34	11
7	Th	18	13 ·04	8 ·45	12
8	Fr	19	14 ·12	9 ·55	13
9	Sa ○	20	P ·18	10 ·64	14
10	Su	21	1 ·23	11 ·70	15
11	Mo	22	2 ·26	12 ·74	16
12	Tu	23	3 ·28	13 ·77	17
13	We	24	4 ·27	14 ·79	18
14	Th	25	5 ·24	15 ·77	19
15	Fr	26	6 ·19	16 ·74	20
16	Sa	27	7 ·13	17 ·69	21
17	Su	28	8 ·05 9 ·97	18 ·63	22

March

Solar: Chitrabhanu *Kumbha—Masi.* / Chitrabhanu *Mina—Panguni.* — Lunar: *Bah.* **Mag.** / *Sukla* / **Phalguna** / *Bahula* — Muhammadan: H. 1362 *Safar.* / H. 1362 *Rabi-ul-awwal.*

Cyclic Sidereal	Week-Day	Day	Tithi	Nakshatra	Muhammadan
18	Mo	1	10 ·87	19 ·57	23
19	Tu	2	11 ·77	20 ·51	24
20	We	3	12 ·67	21 ·44	25
21	Th	4	13 ·57	22 ·37 ○	26
22	Fr	5	14 ·48	23 ·31	27
23	Sa	6	—A ·40	24 ·25	28
24	Su	7	1 ·33	25 ·22	—29
25	Mo	8	2 ·28	26 ·19	1
26	Tu	9	3 ·25	27 ·18	2
27	We	10	4 ·24	1 ·19	3
28	Th	11	5 ·24	2 ·22	4
29	Fr	12	6 ·27	3 ·28	5
—30	Sa	13	7 ·32	4 ·35	6
1	Su	14	8 ·38	5 ·44	7
2	Mo	15	9 ·46	6 ·54	8
3	Tu	16	10 ·55	7 ·65	9
4	We	17	11 ·64	8 ·76	10
5	Th	18	12 ·72	9 ·86	11
6	Fr	19	13 ·79	10 ·94	12
7	Sa	20	14 ·84	... ...	13
8	Su	21	P ·87	11 ·01	14
9	Mo	22	1 ·88	12 ·06	15
10	Tu	23	2 ·86	13 ·10	16
11	We	24	3 ·83	14 ·11	17
12	Th	25	4 ·78	15 ·10	18
13	Fr	26	5 ·72	16 ·07	19
14	Sa	27	6 ·64	17 ·03 } 18 ·97 }	20
15	Su	28	7 ·55	19 ·91	21
16	Mo	29	8 ·45	20 ·85	22
17	Tu	30	9 ·35	21 ·78	23
18	We	31	10 ·25	22 ·71	24

April

Solar: Subhanu *Mesha—Chittirai.* — Lunar: *Sukla* / **Chaitra** / *Bahula* — Muhammadan: H. 1362 *Rabi-ul-akhir.*

Cyclic Sidereal	Week-Day	Day	Tithi	Nakshatra	Muhammadan
19	Th	1	11 ·15	23 ·65	25
20	Fr	2	{12 ·06 {13 ·98	24 ·60	26
21	Sa	3	14 ·91	25 ·55	27
22	Su	4	—A ·86	26 ·52	28
23	Mo	5	1 ·82	27 ·50	29
24	Tu	6	2 ·81	1 ·51	—30
25	We	7	3 ·81	2 ·54	1
26	Th	8	4 ·84	3 ·59	2
27	Fr	9	5 ·88	4 ·65	3
28	Sa	10	6 ·94	5 ·74	4
29	Su	11	... ...	6 ·84	5
30	Mo	12	7 ·03	7 ·95	6
—31	Tu	13	8 ·12	... ...	7
1	We	14	9 ·20	8 ·06	8
2	Th	15	10 ·28	9 ·16	9
3	Fr	16	11 ·34	10 ·25	10
4	Sa	17	12 ·39	11 ·32	11
5	Su	18	13 ·42	12 ·37	12
6	Mo	19	14 ·43	13 ·42	13
7	Tu	20	P ·42	14 ·43	14
8	We	21	1 ·38	15 ·42	15
9	Th	22	2 ·33	16 ·40	16
10	Fr	23	3 ·26	17 ·36	17
11	Sa	24	4 ·18	18 ·31	18
12	Su	25	5 ·09 6 ·99	19 ·25	19
13	Mo	26	7 ·89	20 ·19	20
14	Tu	27	8 ·79	21 ·12	21
15	We	28	9 ·69	22 ·05 } 23 ·99 }	22
16	Th	29	10 ·59	24 ·93	23
17	Fr	30	11 ·51	25 ·88	24

May

Solar: Subhanu *Mesha—Chittirai.* / Subhanu *Vrishabha—Vaikasi.* — Lunar: *Bah.* / *Sukla* / **Vaisakha** / *Bahula* — Muhammadan: *R.-akhir.* / H. 1362 *Jumadal-awwal.*

Cyclic Sidereal	Week-Day	Day	Tithi	Nakshatra	Muhammadan
18	Sa	1	12 ·44	26 ·85	25
19	Su	2	13 ·39	27 ·83	26
20	Mo	3	14 ·36	1 ·84	27
21	Tu	4	—A ·34	2 ·86	28
22	We	5	1 ·34	3 ·90	—29
23	Th	6	2 ·37	4 ·96	1
24	Fr	7	3 ·42	... ...	2
25	Sa	8	4 ·48	5 ·04	3
26	Su	9	5 ·55	6 ·14	4
27	Mo	10	6 ·63	7 ·25	5
28	Tu	11	7 ·72	8 ·35	6
29	We	12	8 ·80	9 ·45	7
30	Th	13	9 ·86	10 ·55	8
—31	Fr	14	10 ·91	11 ·63	9
1	Sa	15	11 ·93	12 ·69	10
2	Su	16	12 ·94	13 ·73	11
3	Mo	17	13 ·93	14 ·75	12
4	Tu	18	14 ·90	15 ·75	13
5	We	19	P ·85	16 ·73	14
6	Th	20	1 ·78	17 ·70	15
7	Fr	21	2 ·69	18 ·65	16
8	Sa	22	3 ·60	19 ·59	17
9	Su	23	4 ·50	20 ·52	18
10	Mo	24	5 ·40	21 ·45	19
11	Tu	25	6 ·30	22 ·39	20
12	We	26	7 ·20	23 ·33	21
13	Th	27	8 ·10	24 ·27	22
14	Fr	28	9 ·02 10 ·95	25 ·21	23
15	Sa	29	11 ·89	26 ·18	24
16	Su	30	12 ·85	27 ·16	25
17	Mo	31	13 ·83	1 ·16	26

June

Solar: Subhanu *Mithuna—Ani.* — Lunar: *Sukla* / **Jyeshtha** / *Bahula* — Muhammadan: H. 1362 *Jumadal-akhir.*

Cyclic Sidereal	Week-Day	Day	Tithi	Nakshatra	Muhammadan
18	Tu	1	14 ·84	2 ·17	27
19	We	2	—A ·86	3 ·21	28
20	Th	3	1 ·91	4 ·27	29
21	Fr	4	2 ·97	5 ·34	—30
22	Sa	5	... ...	6 ·44	1
23	Su	6	3 ·04	7 ·55	2
24	Mo	7	4 ·12	8 ·66	3
25	Tu	8	5 ·20	9 ·76	4
26	We	9	6 ·28	10 ·85	5
27	Th	10	7 ·34	11 ·94	6
28	Fr	11	8 ·39	... ...	7
29	Sa	12	9 ·42	12 ·01	8
30	Su	13	10 ·44	13 ·05	9
—31	Mo	14	11 ·42	14 ·07	10
1	Tu	15	12 ·39	15 ·07	11
2	We	16	13 ·34	16 ·06	12
3	Th	17	14 ·27	17 ·03 } 18 ·99 }	13
4	Fr	18	P ·19	19 ·93	14
5	Sa	19	1 ·10	20 ·87	15
6	Su	20	2 ·00 3 ·90	21 ·80	16
7	Mo	21	4 ·79	22 ·73	17
8	Tu	22	5 ·69	23 ·66	18
9	We	23	6 ·59	24 ·60	19
10	Th	24	7 ·51	25 ·55	20
11	Fr	25	8 ·44	26 ·52	21
12	Sa	26	9 ·38	27 ·49	22
13	Su	27	10 ·33	1 ·48	23
14	Mo	28	11 ·31	2 ·49	24
15	Tu	29	12 ·32	3 ·52	25
16	We	30	13 ·34	4 ·57	26

Naksh :—1. Asvn. 2. Bhar. 3. Krit. 4. Rohi. 5. Mrig. 6. Ardh. 7. Punar. 8. Push. 9. Aslesh. 10. Magh. 11. P. Phal. 12. U. Phal. 13. Hasta. 14. Chit.

A. D. 1943.
A.—Amavasya.
P.—Paurnami.

Kollam 1119, Commences { **N. Malabar—Sept.** / **S. Malabar—Aug.**

Hijra Commences, { **1362, Jan. 8.** / **1363, Dec. 28.**

Vikrama 2000.
Bengal San 1349.
(N. Cycle) Durmukha.

SOLAR reckoning: Cyclic Sidereal Year, Month and Day; Week-Day English Month and Day. LUNAR reckoning: Tithi Ending Moment; Nakshatra Ending Moment; Muhammadan Year, Month and Day.

July

Solar month	Cyclic Sidereal Day	Week-Day	English Day	Lunar month / Paksha	Tithi	Tithi Ending Moment	Nakshatra	Nakshatra Ending Moment	Muhammadan
Subhanu Mithuna—Ani.	17	Th	1		14	·38	5	·66	27
	18	Fr	2		—A	·44	6	·74	28
	19	Sa	3	Ashadha Sukla	1	·51	7	·84	—29
	20	Su	4		2	·59	8	·95	1 (H. 1362 Rajab.)
	21	Mo	5		3	·68	...	...	2
	22	Tu	6		4	·76	9	·06	3
	23	We	7		5	·82	10	·16	4
	24	Th	8		6	·87	11	·25	5
	25	Fr	9		7	·90	12	·32	6
	26	Sa	10		8	·91	13	·36	7
	27	Su	11		9	·90	14	·39	8
	28	Mo	12		10	·87	15	·41	9
	29	Tu	13		11	·82	16	·39	10
	30	We	14		12	·75	17	·36	11
	31	Th	15		13	·67	18	·32	12
	—32	Fr	16		14	·58	19	·27	13
Subhanu Karkata—Adi.	1	Sa	17		P	·48	20	·21	14
	2	Su	18	Bahula	1	·38	21	·14	15
	3	Mo	19		2	·28	22	·07	16
	4	Tu	20		3	·18	23 24	·00 ·94	17
	5	We	21		4 5	·08 ·99	25	·89	18
	6	Th	22		6	·92	26	·85	19
	7	Fr	23		7	·86	27	·82	20
	8	Sa	24		8	·82	1	·80	21
	9	Su	25		9	·80	2	·81	22
	10	Mo	26		10	·80	3	·84	23
	11	Tu	27		11	·82	4	·89	24
	12	We	28		12	·85	5	·96	25
	13	Th	29		13	·91	...	...	26
	14	Fr	30		14	·98	6	·04	27
	15	Sa	31		...	...	7	·14	28

Aug.

Solar month	Cyclic Sidereal Day	Week-Day	English Day	Lunar month / Paksha	Tithi	Tithi Ending Moment	Nakshatra	Nakshatra Ending Moment	Muhammadan
Subhanu Karkata—Adi.	16	Su ●	1		—A	·06	8	·25	29
	17	Mo	2	Sravana Sukla	1	·15	9	·36	—30
	18	Tu	3		2	·23	10	·46	1 (H. 1362 Shaban.)
	19	We	4		3	·30	11	·55	2
	20	Th	5		4	·35	12	·62	3
	21	Fr	6		5	·38	13	·63	4
	22	Sa	7		6	·40	14	·72	5
	23	Su	8		7	·38	15	·73	6
	24	Mo	9		8	·35	16	·72	7
	25	Tu	10		9	·30	17	·70	8
	26	We	11		10	·24	18	·66	9
	27	Th	12		11	·16	19	·60	10
	28	Fr	13		12 13	·07 ·97	20	·54	11
	29	Sa	14		14	·87	21	·48	12
	30	Su ○	15		P	·77	22	·41	13
	—31	Mo	16	Bahula	1	·67	23	·34	14
Subhanu Simha—Avani.	1	Tu	17		2	·57	24	·28	15
	2	We	18		3	·49	25	·22	16
	3	Th	19		4	·42	26	·17	17
	4	Fr	20		5	·36	27	·14	18
	5	Sa	21		6	·32	1	·13	19
	6	Su	22		7	·30	2	·13	20
	7	Mo	23		8	·29	3	·16	21
	8	Tu	24		9	·31	4	·20	22
	9	We	25		10	·35	5	·27	23
	10	Th	26		11	·41	6	·35	24
	11	Fr	27		12	·49	7	·44	25
	12	Sa	28		13	·57	8	·55	26
	13	Su	29		14	·65	9	·66	27
	14	Mo	30		—A	·73	10	·76	28
	15	Tu	31		1	·80	11	·85	—29

Sep.

Solar month	Cyclic Sidereal Day	Week-Day	English Day	Lunar month / Paksha	Tithi	Tithi Ending Moment	Nakshatra	Nakshatra Ending Moment	Muhammadan
Subhanu Simha—Avani.	16	We	1	Bhadrapada Sukla	2	·85	12	·98	1 (H. 1362 Ramzan.)
	17	Th	2		3	·89	...	...	2
	18	Fr	3		4	·91	13	·00	3
	19	Sa	4		5	·90	14	·04	4
	20	Su	5		6	·87	15	·05	5
	21	Mo	6		7	·82	16	·05	6
	22	Tu	7		8	·76	17 18	·03 ·99	7
	23	We	8		9	·68	19	·94	8
	24	Th	9		10	·59	20	·88	9
	25	Fr	10		11	·49	21	·82	10
	26	Sa	11		12	·39	22	·75	11
	27	Su	12		13	·29	23	·68	12
	28	Mo	13		14	·19	24	·62	13
	29	Tu	14		P	·10	25	·56	14
	30	We	15	Bahula	1 2	·02 ·95	26	·51	15
	—31	Th	16		3	·89	27	·47	16
Subhanu Kanya—Purattasi.	1	Fr	17		4	·84	1	·45	17
	2	Sa	18		5	·82	2	·46	18
	3	Su	19		6	·81	3	·48	19
	4	Mo	20		7	·84	4	·51	20
	5	Tu	21		8	·88	5	·57	21
	6	We	22		9	·94	6	·65	22
	7	Th	23		...	...	7	·75	23
	8	Fr	24		10	·01	8	·85	24
	9	Sa	25		11	·10	9	·93	25
	10	Su	26		12	·19	...	...	26
	11	Mo	27		13	·27	10	·06	27
	12	Tu	28		14	·34	11	·16	28
	13	We	29		—A	·39	12	·24	29
	14	Th	30		1	·43	13	·31	—30

Oct.

Solar month	Cyclic Sidereal Day	Week-Day	English Day	Lunar month / Paksha	Tithi	Tithi Ending Moment	Nakshatra	Nakshatra Ending Moment	Muhammadan
Subhanu Kanya—Purattasi.	15	Fr	1	Asvina Sukla	2	·45	14	·35	1 (H. 1362 Shawwal.)
	16	Sa	2		3	·44	15	·37	2
	17	Su	3		4	·41	16	·37	3
	18	Mo	4		5	·37	17	·35	4
	19	Tu	5		6	·30	18	·32	5
	20	We	6		7	·22	19	·28	6
	21	Th	7		8	·14	20	·22	7
	22	Fr	8		9 10	·05 ·95	21	·16	8
	23	Sa	9		11	·85	22	·10	9
	24	Su	10		12	·75	23 24	·03 ·96	10
	25	Mo	11		13	·66	25	·89	11
	26	Tu	12		14	·58	26	·84	12
	27	We	13		P	·51	27	·81	13
	28	Th	14	Bahula	1	·45	1	·79	14
	29	Fr	15		2	·41	2	·78	15
	30	Sa	16		3	·39	3	·79	16
	—31	Su	17		4	·40	4	·82	17
Subhanu Tula—Aippasi.	1	Mo	18		5	·42	5	·88	18
	2	Tu	19		6	·46	6	·96	19
	3	We	20		7	·51	...	...	20
	4	Th	21		8	·58	7	·05	21
	5	Fr	22		9	·67	8	·16	22
	6	Sa	23		10	·76	9	·26	23
	7	Su	24		11	·85	10	·36	24
	8	Mo	25		12	·92	11	·46	25
	9	Tu	26		13	·98	12	·55	26
	10	We	27		...	...	13	·62	27
	11	Th	28		14	·01	14	·67	28
	12	Fr	29		—A	·03	15	·69	—29
	13	Sa	30		1	·03	16	·70	1
	14	Su	31		2 3	·00 ·96	17	·69	2

Nov.

Solar month	Cyclic Sidereal Day	Week-Day	English Day	Lunar month / Paksha	Tithi	Tithi Ending Moment	Nakshatra	Nakshatra Ending Moment	Muhammadan
Subhanu Tula—Aippasi.	15	Mo	1	Karttika Sukla	4	·90	18	·66	3 (H. 1362 Zi-l-ka'da.)
	16	Tu	2		5	·82	19	·62	4
	17	We	3		6	·73	20	·56	5
	18	Th	4		7	·64	21	·50	6
	19	Fr	5		8	·54	22	·43	7
	20	Sa	6		9	·44	23	·36	8
	21	Su	7		10	·35	24	·29	9
	22	Mo	8		11	·26	25	·23	10
	23	Tu	9		12	·18	26	·18	11
	24	We	10		13	·11	27	·14	12
	25	Th	11		14	·05	1	·11	13
	26	Fr	12		P 1	·01 ·99	2	·10	14
	27	Sa	13	Bahula	...	...	3	·11	15
	28	Su	14		2	·01	4	·14	16
	—29	Mo	15		3	·03	5	·19	17
Subhanu Vrischika—Kartigai.	1	Tu	16		4	·07	6	·26	18
	2	We	17		5	·13	7	·35	19
	3	Th	18		6	·21	8	·45	20
	4	Fr	19		7	·30	9	·56	21
	5	Sa	20		8	·39	10	·66	22
	6	Su	21		9	·47	11	·77	23
	7	Mo	22		10	·54	12	·86	24
	8	Tu	23		11	·60	13	·93	25
	9	We	24		12	·64	14	·98	26
	10	Th	25		13	·66	...	...	27
	11	Fr	26		14	·65	15	·01	28
	12	Sa	27		—A	·62	16	·03	29
	13	Su	28	Margasira Sukla	1	·57	17 18	·02 ·99	—30
	14	Mo	29		2	·51	19	·95	1 (H. 1362 Zi-l-hijja.)
	15	Tu	30		3	·44	20	·90	2

Dec.

Solar month	Cyclic Sidereal Day	Week-Day	English Day	Lunar month / Paksha	Tithi	Tithi Ending Moment	Nakshatra	Nakshatra Ending Moment	Muhammadan
Subhanu Vrischika—Kartigai.	16	We	1	Margasira Sukla	4	·36	21	·84	3
	17	Th	2		5	·27	22	·77	4
	18	Fr	3		6	·17	23	·70	5
	19	Sa	4		7 8	·07 ·97	24	·63	6
	20	Su	5		9	·88	25	·57	7
	21	Mo	6		10	·80	26	·52	8
	22	Tu	7		11	·73	27	·47	9
	23	We	8		12	·68	1	·44	10
	24	Th	9		13	·65	2	·42	11
	25	Fr	10		14	·64	3	·43	12
	26	Sa	11		P	·64	4	·45	13
	27	Su	12	Bahula	1	·65	5	·50	14
	28	Mo	13		2	·71	6	·57	15
	29	Tu	14		3	·78	7	·65	16
	—30	We	15		4	·86	8	·75	17
Subhanu Dhanus—Margali.	1	Th	16		5	·95	9	·86	18
	2	Fr	17		...	...	10	·97	19
	3	Sa	18		6	·04	...	...	20
	4	Su	19		7	·12	11	·07	21
	5	Mo	20		8	·19	12	·16	22
	6	Tu	21		9	·24	13	·24	23
	7	We	22		10	·28	14	·29	24
	8	Th	23		11	·30	15	·33	25
	9	Fr	24		12	·29	16	·35	26
	10	Sa	25		13	·27	17	·35	27
	11	Su	26		14	·22	18	·32	28
	12	Mo	27		—A	·16	19	·23	—29
	13	Tu	28	P. Sukla	1 2	·08 ·99	20	·23	1 (H. 1363 Muharram.)
	14	We	29		3	·90	21	·17	2
	15	Th	30		4	·80	22	·11	3
	16	Fr	31		5	·70	23 24	·04 ·97	4

15. Svati. 16. Visak. 17. Anur. 18. Jyesh. 19. Mula. 20. P. Ash. 21. U. Ash. 22. Sravn. 23. Dani. 24. Satab. 25. P. Bhad. 26. U. Bhad. 27. Rev.

A. D. 1944. **Mesha Sankranti** (Commencement of Indian Sidereal Year).

Solar Eclipse. ● **(Surya Sid.) April 13·01.** **Saka 1866.** **Kaliyuga 5045.**

Lunar Eclipse. ○ **(Arya Sid.) April 12·90.** **(S. Cycle) Tarana.**

Columns: SOLAR reckoning (Cyclic Sidereal Year, Month and Day; Week-Day English Month and Day) — LUNAR reckoning (Tithi Ending Moment; Nakshatra Ending Moment; Muhammadan Year, Month and Day).

Jan.

Subhanu *Dhanus—Margali* (17–29); Subhanu *Makara—Tai* (1–18). Tithi: *Sukla*, Pausha, *Bahula*. H. 1363 *Muharram*.

Cyclic Sidereal Year, Month and Day	Week-Day	English Day	Tithi Ending Moment	Nakshatra Ending Moment	Muhammadan Year, Month and Day
17	Sa	1	6 ·61	25 ·91	5
18	Su	2	7 ·52	26 ·85	6
19	Mo	3	8 ·44	27 ·80	7
20	Tu	4	9 ·37	1 ·77	8
21	We	5	10 ·32	2 ·75	9
22	Th	6	11 ·29	3 ·75	10
23	Fr	7	12 ·28	4 ·78	11
24	Sa	8	13 ·28	5 ·82	12
25	Su	9	14 ·31	6 ·88	13
26	Mo	10	P ·36	7 ·95	14
27	Tu	11	1 ·43	... ...	15
28	We	12	2 ·51	8 ·05	16
—29	Th	13	3 ·59	9 ·16	17
1	Fr	14	4 ·68	10 ·27	18
2	Sa	15	5 ·76	11 ·37	19
3	Su	16	6 ·83	12 ·46	20
4	Mo	17	7 ·89	13 ·54	21
5	Tu	18	8 ·93	14 ·61	22
6	We	19	9 ·95	15 ·65	23
7	Th	20	10 ·93	16 ·67	24
8	Fr	21	11 ·90	17 ·67	25
9	Sa	22	12 ·85	18 ·65	26
10	Su	23	13 ·79	19 ·62	27
11	Mo	24	14 ·71	20 ·58	28
12	Tu	25	—A ·63	21 ·52	29
13	We	26	1 ·54	22 ·45	—30
14	Th	27	2 ·44	23 ·38	1
15	Fr	28	3 ·34	24 ·31	2
16	Sa	29	4 ·24	25 ·25	3
17	Su	30	5 ·16	26 ·19	4
18	Mo	31	6 ·08	27 ·14	5

Feb.

Subhanu *Kumbha—Masi*. Tithi: *Sukla*, Magha, *Bahula*, Pl. *Sukla*. H. 1363 *Safar*; *R.-awwal.*

Cyclic Sidereal Year, Month and Day	Week-Day	English Day	Tithi Ending Moment	Nakshatra Ending Moment	Muhammadan Year, Month and Day
19	Tu	1	7 ·02 / 8 ·97	1 ·10	6
20	We	2	9 ·94	2 ·07	7
21	Th	3	10 ·92	3 ·08	8
22	Fr	4	11 ·93	4 ·09	9
23	Sa	5	12 ·96	5 ·13	10
24	Su	6	... ...	6 ·18	11
25	Mo	7	13 ·01	7 ·26	12
26	Tu	8	14 ·08	8 ·36	13
27	We	9	P ·16	9 ·46	14
28	Th	10	1 ·25	10 ·57	15
29	Fr	11	2 ·33	11 ·67	16
—30	Sa	12	3 ·41	12 ·77	17
1	Su	13	4 ·48	13 ·85	18
2	Mo	14	5 ·53	14 ·92	19
3	Tu	15	6 ·56	15 ·97	20
4	We	16	7 ·53	16 ·99	21
5	Th	17	8 ·57	... ...	22
6	Fr	18	9 ·54	17 ·00 / 18 ·98	23
7	Sa	19	10 ·48	19 ·95	24
8	Su	20	11 ·41	20 ·91	25
9	Mo	21	12 ·33	21 ·85	26
10	Tu	22	13 ·25	22 ·79	27
11	We	23	14 ·16	23 ·72	28
12	Th	24	A ·06 / 1 ·96	24 ·65	—29
13	Fr	25	2 ·86	25 ·59	1
14	Sa	26	3 ·77	26 ·53	2
15	Su	27	4 ·69	27 ·47	3
16	Mo	28	5 ·63	1 ·43	4
17	Tu	29	6 ·58	2 ·41	5

March

Subhanu *Kumbha—Masi* (18–30); Subhanu *Mina—Panguni* (1–17). Tithi: *Sukla*, Phalguna, *Bahula*. H. 1363 *Rabi-ul-awwal.*

Cyclic Sidereal Year, Month and Day	Week-Day	English Day	Tithi Ending Moment	Nakshatra Ending Moment	Muhammadan Year, Month and Day
18	We	1	7 ·55	3 ·40	6
19	Th	2	8 ·53	4 ·41	7
20	Fr	3	9 ·54	5 ·44	8
21	Sa	4	10 ·57	6 ·49	9
22	Su	5	11 ·62	7 ·57	10
23	Mo	6	12 ·69	8 ·66	11
24	Tu	7	13 ·78	9 ·76	12
25	We	8	14 ·87	10 ·86	13
26	Th	9	P ·95	11 ·97	14
27	Fr	10	... ...	... ...	15
28	Sa	11	1 ·08	12 ·07	16
29	Su	12	2 ·09	13 ·16	17
30	Mo	13	3 ·14	14 ·23	18
—31	Tu	14	4 ·17	15 ·28	19
1	We	15	5 ·17	16 ·31	20
2	Th	16	6 ·15	17 ·32	21
3	Fr	17	7 ·12	18 ·32	22
4	Sa	18	8 ·07	19 ·29	23
5	Su	19	9 ·01 / 10 ·94	20 ·25	24
6	Mo	20	11 ·85	21 ·19	25
7	Tu	21	12 ·75	22 ·13	26
8	We	22	13 ·65	23 ·07	27
9	Th	23	14 ·55	24 ·00 / 25 ·93	28
10	Fr	24	—A ·45	26 ·87	29
11	Sa	25	1 ·36	27 ·81	—30
12	Su	26	2 ·28	1 ·77	1
13	Mo	27	3 ·22	2 ·74	2
14	Tu	28	4 ·17	3 ·72	3
15	We	29	5 ·13	4 ·73	4
16	Th	30	6 ·11	5 ·76	5
17	Fr	31	7 ·12	6 ·81	6

April

Tarana *Mesha—Chittirai*. Tithi: *Sukla*, Chaitra, *Bahula*, Vaisak. *Sukla*. H. 1363 *Rabi-ul-akhir*; *Jumadal-awwal.*

Cyclic Sidereal Year, Month and Day	Week-Day	English Day	Tithi Ending Moment	Nakshatra Ending Moment	Muhammadan Year, Month and Day
18	Sa	1	8 ·15	7 ·88	7
19	Su	2	9 ·20	8 ·96	8
20	Mo	3	10 ·27	... ...	9
21	Tu	4	11 ·35	9 ·06	10
22	We	5	12 ·44	10 ·16	11
23	Th	6	13 ·52	11 ·27	12
24	Fr	7	14 ·60	12 ·33	13
25	Sa	8	P ·66	13 ·47	14
26	Su	9	1 ·70	14 ·54	15
27	Mo	10	2 ·73	15 ·60	16
28	Tu	11	3 ·74	16 ·63	17
—29	We	12	4 ·72	17 ·65	18
1	Th	13	5 ·68	18 ·64	19
2	Fr	14	6 ·63	19 ·62	20
3	Sa	15	7 ·57	20 ·58	21
4	Su	16	8 ·49	21 ·53	22
5	Mo	17	9 ·40	22 ·47	23
6	Tu	18	10 ·30	23 ·41	24
7	We	19	11 ·20	24 ·34	25
8	Th	20	12 ·10	25 ·27	26
9	Fr	21	13 ·00 / 14 ·90	26 ·21	27
10	Sa	22	—A ·82	27 ·15	28
11	Su	23	1 ·73	1 ·10	—29
12	Mo	24	2 ·71	2 ·07	1
13	Tu	25	3 ·67	3 ·05	2
14	We	26	4 ·66	4 ·05	3
15	Th	27	5 ·67	5 ·07	4
16	Fr	28	6 ·69	6 ·12	5
17	Sa	29	7 ·73	7 ·18	6
18	Su	30	8 ·79	8 ·26	7

May

Tarana *Mesha—Chittirai* (19–31); Tarana *Vrishabha—Vaikasi* (1–18). Tithi: *Sukla*, Vaisakha, *Bahula*, *Sukla*. H. 1363 *Jumadal-awwal.*

Cyclic Sidereal Year, Month and Day	Week-Day	English Day	Tithi Ending Moment	Nakshatra Ending Moment	Muhammadan Year, Month and Day
19	Mo	1	9 ·87	9 ·35	8
20	Tu	2	10 ·96	10 ·46	9
21	We	3	... ...	11 ·57	10
22	Th	4	11 ·05	12 ·68	11
23	Fr	5	12 ·12	13 ·77	12
24	Sa	6	13 ·18	14 ·85	13
25	Su	7	14 ·22	15 ·91	14
26	Mo	8	P ·25	16 ·95	15
27	Tu	9	1 ·27	17 ·97	16
28	We	10	2 ·25	18 ·97	17
29	Th	11	3 ·22	19 ·95	18
30	Fr	12	4 ·16	20 ·92	19
—31	Sa	13	5 ·09	21 ·87	20
1	Su	14	6 ·01 / 7 ·91	22 ·81	21
2	Mo	15	8 ·81	23 ·74	22
3	Tu	16	9 ·71	24 ·67	23
4	We	17	10 ·61	25 ·60	24
5	Th	18	11 ·51	26 ·54	25
6	Fr	19	12 ·42	27 ·48	26
7	Sa	20	13 ·34	1 ·43	27
8	Su	21	14 ·27	2 ·39	28
9	Mo	22	—A ·22	3 ·37	29
10	Tu	23	1 ·18	4 ·37	—30
11	We	24	2 ·16	5 ·39	1
12	Th	25	3 ·17	6 ·43	2
13	Fr	26	4 ·19	7 ·49	3
14	Sa	27	5 ·24	8 ·56	4
15	Su	28	6 ·30	9 ·65	5
16	Mo	29	7 ·38	10 ·76	6
17	Tu	30	8 ·46	11 ·87	7
18	We	31	9 ·54	12 ·98	8

June

Tarana *Mithuna—Ani*. Tithi: Jyeshtha, *Bahula*, *Sukla*, Ashadha. H. 1363 *Jumadal-akhir*; *Rajab.*

Cyclic Sidereal Year, Month and Day	Week-Day	English Day	Tithi Ending Moment	Nakshatra Ending Moment	Muhammadan Year, Month and Day
19	Th	1	10 ·62	... ...	9
20	Fr	2	11 ·68	13 ·07	10
21	Sa	3	12 ·72	14 ·15	11
22	Su	4	13 ·75	15 ·22	12
23	Mo	5	14 ·76	16 ·27	13
24	Tu	6	P ·74	17 ·29	14
25	We	7	1 ·71	18 ·29	15
26	Th	8	2 ·66	19 ·28	16
27	Fr	9	3 ·59	20 ·25	17
28	Sa	10	4 ·51	21 ·21	18
29	Su	11	5 ·41	22 ·15	19
30	Mo	12	6 ·31	23 ·08	20
—31	Tu	13	7 ·21	24 ·01 / 25 ·94	21
1	We	14	8 ·11	26 ·88	22
2	Th	15	9 ·01 / 10 ·92	27 ·82	23
3	Fr	16	11 ·83	1 ·76	24
4	Sa	17	12 ·76	2 ·72	25
5	Su	18	13 ·70	3 ·70	26
6	Mo	19	14 ·66	4 ·70	27
7	Tu	20	—A ·64	5 ·71	28
8	We	21	1 ·65	6 ·74	—29
9	Th	22	2 ·67	7 ·79	1
10	Fr	23	3 ·71	8 ·87	2
11	Sa	24	4 ·77	9 ·96	3
12	Su	25	5 ·85	... ...	4
13	Mo	26	6 ·93	10 ·06	5
14	Tu	27	... ...	11 ·17	6
15	We	28	7 ·01	12 ·28	7
16	Th	29	8 ·09	13 ·38	8
17	Fr	30	9 ·16	14 ·47	9

Naksh :—1. Asvn. 2. Bhar. 3. Krit. 4. Rohi. 5. Mrig. 6. Ardh. 7. Punar. 8. Push. 9. Aslesh. 10. Magh. 11. P. Phal. 12. U. Phal. 13. Hasta. 14. Chit.

A. D. 1944. A.—Amavasya. P.—Paurnami.	Kollam 1120, Commences { N. Malabar—Sept. S. Malabar—Aug.	Hijra 1364, Commences, Dec. 17.	Vikrama 2001. Bengal San 1350. (N. Cycle) Hemalamba.

Columns: SOLAR reckoning — Cyclic Sidereal Year, Month and Day; Week-Day English Month and Day. LUNAR reckoning — Tithi Ending Moment; Nakshatra Ending Moment; Muhammadan Year, Month and Day.

July

Solar month	Cyclic Sidereal	Week-Day	July	Lunar month	Tithi	Nakshatra	Muhammadan
Tarana Mithuna—Ani	18	Sa	1	Sukla	10 ·21	15 ·54	10
	19	Su	2		11 ·23	16 ·58	11
	20	Mo	3		12 ·24	17 ·61	12
	21	Tu	4		13 ·23	18 ·62	13
	22	We	5		14 ·19	19 ·61	14
	23	Th	6		P ·13	20 ·58	15
	24	Fr	7	Ashadha	1 ·06 / 2 ·98	21 ·54	16 H. 1363 Rajab.
	25	Sa	8		3 ·89	22 ·48	17
	26	Su	9		4 ·79	23 ·42	18
	27	Mo	10		5 ·69	24 ·36	19
	28	Tu	11		6 ·59	25 ·29	20
	29	We	12		7 ·49	26 ·22	21
	30	Th	13		8 ·39	27 ·16	22
	31	Fr	14		9 ·31	1 ·10	23
	—32	Sa	15	Bahula	10 ·24	2 ·06	24
Tarana Karkata—Adi	1	Su	16		11 ·18	3 ·03	25
	2	Mo	17		12 ·14	4 ·02	26
	3	Tu	18		13 ·12	5 ·03	27
	4	We	19		14 ·13	6 ·06	28
	5	Th ●	20		—A ·15	7 ·10	29
	6	Fr	21	Sukla	1 ·19	8 ·18	—30
	7	Sa	22		2 ·25	9 ·27	1
	8	Su	23		3 ·32	10 ·37	2
	9	Mo	24		4 ·40	11 ·47	3
	10	Tu	25		5 ·48	12 ·58	4
	11	We	26		6 ·56	13 ·68	5
	12	Th	27		7 ·63	14 ·77	6
	13	Fr	28		8 ·68	15 ·85	7
	14	Sa	29		9 ·71	16 ·90	8
	15	Su	30		10 ·72	17 ·93	9
	16	Mo	31		11 ·70	18 ·94	10

Aug.

Solar month	Cyclic Sidereal	Week-Day	Aug.	Lunar month	Tithi	Nakshatra	Muhammadan
	17	Tu	1		12 ·67	19 ·94	11 H. 1363 Shaban.
	18	We	2		13 ·62	20 ·92	12
	19	Th	3		14 ·56	21 ·88	13
	20	Fr	4	Sravana	P ·48	22 ·82	14
	21	Sa	5		1 ·38	23 ·76	15
	22	Su	6		2 ·23	24 ·70	16
	23	Mo	7		3 ·18	25 ·63	17
	24	Tu	8		4 ·08 / 5 ·98	26 ·56	18
	25	We	9		6 ·89	27 ·49	19
	26	Th	10	Bahula	7 ·81	1 ·43	20
	27	Fr	11		8 ·73	2 ·39	21
	28	Sa	12		9 ·67	3 ·36	22
	29	Su	13		10 ·63	4 ·35	23
	30	Mo	14		11 ·61	5 ·35	24
	—31	Tu	15		12 ·62	6 ·37	25
Tarana Simha—Avani	1	We	16		13 ·64	7 ·42	26
	2	Th	17		14 ·68	8 ·49	27
	3	Fr	18		—A ·74	9 ·57	28
	4	Sa	19		1 ·81	10 ·66	—29
	5	Su	20		2 ·90	11 ·77	1
	6	Mo	21	Sukla	3 ·98	12 ·88	2
	7	Tu	22		... ...	13 ·99	3
	8	We	23	Bhadrapada	4 ·06	... ...	4 H. 1363 Ramzan.
	9	Th	24		5 ·12	14 ·08	5
	10	Fr	25		6 ·17	15 ·15	6
	11	Sa	26		7 ·20	16 ·21	7
	12	Su	27		8 ·23	17 ·25	8
	13	Mo	28		9 ·21	18 ·27	9
	14	Tu	29		10 ·18	19 ·27	10
	15	We	30		11 ·13	20 ·25	11
	16	Th	31		12 ·07 / 13 ·99	21 ·21	12

Sep.

Solar month	Cyclic Sidereal	Week-Day	Sep.	Lunar month	Tithi	Nakshatra	Muhammadan
Tarana Simha—Avani	17	Fr	1	Bhadrapada	14 ·90	22 ·16	13
	18	Sa	2		P ·80	23 ·10	14
	19	Su	3		1 ·70	24 ·04 / 25 ·97	15
	20	Mo	4		2 ·60	26 ·90	16
	21	Tu	5		3 ·50	27 ·84	17
	22	We	6		4 ·40	1 ·78	18
	23	Th	7		5 ·32	2 ·73	19
	24	Fr	8		6 ·25	3 ·69	20
	25	Sa	9	Bahula	7 ·19	4 ·67	21 H. 1363 Ramzan.
	26	Su	10		8 ·15	5 ·67	22
	27	Mo	11		9 ·13	6 ·70	23
	28	Tu	12		10 ·14	7 ·74	24
	29	We	13		11 ·16	8 ·79	25
	30	Th	14		12 ·21	9 ·87	26
	—31	Fr	15		13 ·27	10 ·96	27
Tarana Kanya—Purattasi	1	Sa	16		14 ·34	... ...	28
	2	Su	17		—A ·43	11 ·06	29
	3	Mo	18		1 ·51	12 ·17	—30
	4	Tu	19		2 ·58	13 ·28	1
	5	We	20		3 ·65	14 ·38	2
	6	Th	21		4 ·70	15 ·46	3
	7	Fr	22	Sukla	5 ·73	16 ·52	4
	8	Sa	23		6 ·75	17 ·57	5
	9	Su	24		7 ·74	18 ·59	6
	10	Mo	25		8 ·72	19 ·59	7
	11	Tu	26		9 ·67	20 ·57	8
	12	We	27	Asvina	10 ·60	21 ·54	9
	13	Th	28		11 ·52	22 ·50	10
	14	Fr	29		12 ·43	23 ·44	11
	15	Sa	30		13 ·34	24 ·38	12

Oct.

Solar month	Cyclic Sidereal	Week-Day	Oct.	Lunar month	Tithi	Nakshatra	Muhammadan
	16	Su	1		14 ·25	25 ·31	13 H. 1363 Shawwal.
	17	Mo	2		P ·15	26 ·24	14
	18	Tu	3		1 ·05 / 2 ·95	27 ·17	15
	19	We	4		3 ·87	1 ·11	16
	20	Th	5		4 ·80	2 ·06	17
	21	Fr	6		5 ·75	3 ·02	18
	22	Sa	7		6 ·71	4 ·00 / 5 ·99	19
	23	Su	8	Bahula	7 ·70	... ...	20
	24	Mo	9		8 ·70	6 ·01	21
	25	Tu	10		9 ·72	7 ·04	22
	26	We	11		10 ·76	8 ·10	23
	27	Th	12		11 ·82	9 ·17	24
	28	Fr	13		12 ·90	10 ·26	25
	29	Sa	14		... ...	11 ·37	26
	30	Su	15		13 ·00	12 ·48	27
	—31	Mo	16		14 ·08	13 ·58	28
Tarana Tula—Aippasi	1	Tu	17		—A ·15	14 ·68	—29
	2	We	18		1 ·22	15 ·76	1
	3	Th	19		2 ·28	16 ·83	2
	4	Fr	20		3 ·32	17 ·88	3
	5	Sa	21		4 ·34	18 ·91	4 H. 1363 Zi-l-ka'da.
	6	Su	22		5 ·32	19 ·92	5
	7	Mo	23		6 ·29	20 ·91	6
	8	Tu	24	Sukla	7 ·25	21 ·88	7
	9	We	25		8 ·19	22 ·84	8
	10	Th	26		9 ·11	23 ·78	9
	11	Fr	27		10 ·02 / 11 ·93	24 ·71	10
	12	Sa	28		12 ·83	25 ·64	11
	13	Su	29	Kartt.	13 ·73	26 ·57	12
	14	Mo	30		14 ·63	27 ·51	13
	15	Tu	31		P ·54	1 ·45	14

Nov.

Solar month	Cyclic Sidereal	Week-Day	Nov.	Lunar month	Tithi	Nakshatra	Muhammadan
Tarana Tula—Aippasi	16	We	1	Karttika	1 ·46	2 ·39	15
	17	Th	2		2 ·39	3 ·35	16
	18	Fr	3		3 ·33	4 ·32	17
	19	Sa	4		4 ·30	5 ·32	18
	20	Su	5		5 ·29	6 ·33	19
	21	Mo	6		6 ·29	7 ·36	20
	22	Tu	7		7 ·31	8 ·41	21
	23	We	8	Bahula	8 ·36	9 ·48	22 H. 1363 Zi-l-ka'da.
	24	Th	9		9 ·44	10 ·57	23
	25	Fr	10		10 ·52	11 ·67	24
	26	Sa	11		11 ·60	12 ·78	25
	27	Su	12		12 ·68	13 ·88	26
	28	Mo	13		13 ·76	14 ·98	27
	29	Tu	14		14 ·84	... ...	28
	—30	We	15		—A ·89	15 ·08	29
Tarana Vrischika—Kartigai	1	Th	16		1 ·93	16 ·15	—30
	2	Fr	17		2 ·04	17 ·20	1
	3	Sa	18		3 ·94	18 ·23	2
	4	Su	19		4 ·91	19 ·24	3
	5	Mo	20		5 ·86	20 ·24	4
	6	Tu	21	Sukla	6 ·80	21 ·21	5
	7	We	22		7 ·73	22 ·17	6
	8	Th	23		8 ·64	23 ·11	7
	9	Fr	24		9 ·55	24 ·05 / 25 ·99	8
	10	Sa	25	Margasira	10 ·45	26 ·92	9
	11	Su	26		11 ·35	27 ·85	10
	12	Mo	27		12 ·25	1 ·79	11 Zi-l-hijja
	13	Tu	28		13 ·16	2 ·73	12
	14	We	29		14 ·08	3 ·68	13
	15	Th	30		P ·01 / 1 ·96	4 ·65	14

Dec.

Solar month	Cyclic Sidereal	Week-Day	Dec.	Lunar month	Tithi	Nakshatra	Muhammadan
	16	Fr	1		2 ·93	5 ·64	15 H. 1363
	17	Sa	2		3 ·91	6 ·65	16
	18	Su	3		4 ·93	7 ·67	17
	19	Mo	4		5 ·96	8 ·72	18
	20	Tu	5		... ...	9 ·79	19
	21	We	6		6 ·00	10 ·87	20
	22	Th	7	Bahula	7 ·07	11 ·97	21
	23	Fr	8		8 ·14	... ...	22
	24	Sa	9		9 ·23	12 ·07	23
	25	Su	10		10 ·32	13 ·18	24
	26	Mo	11		11 ·41	14 ·28	25
	27	Tu	12		12 ·48	15 ·38	26
	28	We	13		13 ·53	16 ·46	27
	—29	Th	14		14 ·57	17 ·51	28
Tarana Dhanus—Margali	1	Fr	15		—A ·58	18 ·55	29
	2	Sa	16		1 ·57	19 ·57	—30
	3	Su	17		2 ·55	20 ·57	1
	4	Mo	18		3 ·50	21 ·54	2
	5	Tu	19		4 ·43	22 ·50	3
	6	We	20	Sukla	5 ·35	23 ·45	4 H. 1364 Muharram.
	7	Th	21		6 ·27	24 ·39	5
	8	Fr	22		7 ·17	25 ·33	6
	9	Sa	23		8 ·07 / 9 ·98	26 ·26	7
	10	Su	24		10 ·89	27 ·19	8
	11	Mo	25		11 ·80	1 ·12	9
	12	Tu	26	Pausha	12 ·72	2 ·06	10
	13	We	27		13 ·65	3 ·02 / 4 ·99	11
	14	Th	28		14 ·61	5 ·97	12
	15	Fr ○	29		P ·58	6 ·97	13
	16	Sa	30	Bah.	1 ·56	7 ·99	14
	17	Su	31		2 ·57	... ...	15

15. Svati. 16. Visak. 17. Anur. 18. Jyesh. 19. Mula. 20. P. Ash. 21. U. Ash. 22. Sravn. 23. Dani. 24. Satab. 25. P. Bhad. 26. U. Bhad. 27. Rev.

A. D. 1945. **Mesha Sankranti** (Commencement of Indian Sidereal Year).

Solar Eclipse. ● **(Surya Sid.) April 13·26.** **Saka 1867.** **Kaliyuga 5046.**

Lunar Eclipse. ○ **(Arya Sid.) April 13·15.** **(S. Cycle) Parthiva.**

SOLAR reckoning: Cyclic Sidereal Year, Month and Day; Week-Day English Month and Day. LUNAR reckoning: Tithi Ending Moment; Nakshatra Ending Moment; Muhammadan Year, Month and Day.

Jan.

Solar: Tarana Dhanus—Margali; Tarana Makara—Tai. Lunar: Pausha (Bahula, Sukla); Magha. Muhammadan: H. 1364 Muharram; H. 1364 Safar.

Cyclic Sidereal Year, Month and Day	Week-Day	English Day	Tithi	Tithi Ending Moment	Nakshatra	Nakshatra Ending Moment	Muhammadan Year, Month and Day
18	Mo	1	3	·60	8	·04	16
19	Tu	2	4	·65	9	·10	17
20	We	3	5	·72	10	·18	18
21	Th	4	6	·79	11	·27	19
22	Fr	5	7	·88	12	·37	20
23	Sa	6	8	·98	13	·48	21
24	Su	7	...	...	14	·59	22
25	Mo	8	9	·06	15	·69	23
26	Tu	9	10	·13	16	·76	24
27	We	10	11	·18	17	·82	25
28	Th	11	12	·21	18	·86	26
29	Fr	12	13	·22	19	·89	27
—30	Sa	13	14	·22	20	·89	28
1	Su	14	—A	·19	21	·87	29
2	Mo	15	1	·14	22	·84	—30
3	Tu	16	2	·07	23	·79	1
4	We	17	3 4	·00 ·91	24	·73	2
5	Th	18	5	·81	25	·67	3
6	Fr	19	6	·71	26	·60	4
7	Sa	20	7	·61	27	·53	5
8	Su	21	8	·52	1	·47	6
9	Mo	22	9	·44	2	·41	7
10	Tu	23	10	·37	3	·36	8
11	We	24	11	·30	4	·32	9
12	Th	25	12	·25	5	·29	10
13	Fr	26	13	·22	6	·29	11
14	Sa	27	14	·20	7	·31	12
15	Su	28	P	·21	8	·35	13
16	Mo	29	1	·24	9	·40	14
17	Tu	30	2	·30	10	·48	15
18	We	31	3	·37	11	·57	16

Feb.

Solar: Tarana Kumbha—Masi. Lunar: Magha (Bahula, Sukla); Phalguna. Muhammadan: H. 1364 Rabi-ul-awwal.

Cyclic Sidereal Year, Month and Day	Week-Day	English Day	Tithi	Tithi Ending Moment	Nakshatra	Nakshatra Ending Moment	Muhammadan Year, Month and Day
19	Th	1	4	·45	12	·68	17
20	Fr	2	5	·54	13	·79	18
21	Sa	3	6	·63	14	·89	19
22	Su	4	7	·71	15	·99	20
23	Mo	5	8	·77	...	...	21
24	Tu	6	9	·82	16	·07	22
25	We	7	10	·85	17	·13	23
26	Th	8	11	·87	18	·18	24
27	Fr	9	12	·85	19	·21	25
28	Sa	10	13	·82	20	·22	26
—29	Su	11	14	·77	21	·20	27
1	Mo	12	—A	·70	22	·17	28
2	Tu	13	1	·62	23	·13	—29
3	We	14	2	·53	24	·07	1
4	Th	15	3	.44	25 26	·01 ·94	2
5	Fr	16	4	·35	27	·87	3
6	Sa	17	5	·25	1	·80	4
7	Su	18	6	·15	2	·74	5
8	Mo	19	7 8	·05 ·97	3	·69	6
9	Tu	20	9	·91	4	·65	7
10	We	21	10	·87	5	·62	8
11	Th	22	11	·84	6	·61	9
12	Fr	23	12	·83	7	·63	10
13	Sa	24	13	·83	8	·63	11
14	Su	25	14	·87	9	·71	12
15	Mo	26	P	·92	10	·78	13
16	Tu	27	1	·99	11	·87	14
17	We	28	...	...	12	·97	15

March

Solar: Tarana Kumbha—Masi; Tarana Mina—Panguni. Lunar: Phalguna (Bahula); Adhika Chaitra (Sukla). Muhammadan: H. 1364 Rabi-ul-awwal; H. 1364 Rabi-ul-akhir.

Cyclic Sidereal Year, Month and Day	Week-Day	English Day	Tithi	Tithi Ending Moment	Nakshatra	Nakshatra Ending Moment	Muhammadan Year, Month and Day
18	Th	1	2	·08	...	...	16
19	Fr	2	3	·17	13	·08	17
20	Sa	3	4	·26	14	·19	18
21	Su	4	5	·33	15	·29	19
22	Mo	5	6	·39	16	·37	20
23	Tu	6	7	·44	17	·44	21
24	We	7	8	·47	18	·50	22
25	Th	8	9	·43	19	·53	23
26	Fr	9	10	·46	20	·54	24
27	Sa	10	11	·43	21	·53	25
28	Su	11	12	·38	22	·50	26
29	Mo	12	13	·31	23	·43	27
—30	Tu	13	14	·23	24	·41	28
1	We	14	—A	·11	25	·35	29
2	Th	15	1 2	·04 ·94	26	·29	—30
3	Fr	16	3	·84	27	·22	1
4	Sa	17	4	·74	1	·15	2
5	Su	18	5	·65	2	·08	3
6	Mo	19	6	·58	3 4	·02 ·98	4
7	Tu	20	7	·52	5	·95	5
8	We	21	8	·47	6	·94	6
9	Th	22	9	·43	7	·95	7
10	Fr	23	10	·42	8	·97	8
11	Sa	24	11	·43	...	...	9
12	Su	25	12	·47	9	·02	10
13	Mo	26	13	·52	10	·09	11
14	Tu	27	14	·59	11	·18	12
15	We	28	P	·67	12	·28	13
16	Th	29	1	·75	13	·38	14
17	Fr	30	2	·84	14	·49	15
18	Sa	31	3	.91	15	·59	16

April

Solar: Parthiva Mesha—Chittirai. Lunar: Adhika Chaitra (Bahula); Nija Chaitra (Sukla). Muhammadan: H. 1364 Jumadal-awwal.

Cyclic Sidereal Year, Month and Day	Week-Day	English Day	Tithi	Tithi Ending Moment	Nakshatra	Nakshatra Ending Moment	Muhammadan Year, Month and Day
19	Su	1	4	·97	16	·68	17
20	Mo	2	...	...	17	·76	18
21	Tu	3	5	·02	18	·82	19
22	We	4	6	·05	19	·85	20
23	Th	5	7	·05	20	·86	21
24	Fr	6	8 9	·08 ·99	21	·86	22
25	Sa	7	10	·94	22	·84	23
26	Su	8	11	·88	23	·80	24
27	Mo	9	12	·79	24	·75	25
28	Tu	10	13	·70	25	·68	26
29	We	11	14	·60	26	·61	27
—30	Th	12	—A	·50	27	·54	28
1	Fr	13	1	·40	1	·48	—29
2	Sa	14	2	·30	2	·42	1
3	Su	15	3	·21	3	·36	2
4	Mo	16	4	·13	4	·32	3
5	Tu	17	5	·06	5	·29	4
6	We	18	6 7	·02 ·99	6	·27	5
7	Th	19	8	·97	7	·27	6
8	Fr	20	9	·97	8	·29	7
9	Sa	21	...	...	9	·33	8
10	Su	22	10	·00	10	·40	9
11	Mo	23	11	·05	11	·48	10
12	Tu	24	12	·12	12	·58	11
13	We	25	13	·21	13	·68	12
14	Th	26	14	·30	14	·79	13
15	Fr	27	P	·38	15	·90	14
16	Sa	28	1	·44	16	·99	15
17	Su	29	2	·50	...	...	16
18	Mo	30	3	·55	17	·07	17

May

Solar: Parthiva Mesha—Chittirai; Parthiva Vrishabha—Vaikasi. Lunar: Nij. Chait. (Bahula); Vaisakha (Sukla). Muhammadan: H. 1364 Jumadal-awwal; H. 1364 Jumadal-akhir.

Cyclic Sidereal Year, Month and Day	Week-Day	English Day	Tithi	Tithi Ending Moment	Nakshatra	Nakshatra Ending Moment	Muhammadan Year, Month and Day
19	Tu	1	4	·53	18	·13	18
20	We	2	5	·58	19	·17	19
21	Th	3	6	·57	20	·19	20
22	Fr	4	7	·53	21	·19	21
23	Sa	5	8	·47	22	·17	22
24	Su	6	9	·40	23	·13	23
25	Mo	7	10	·32	24	·08	24
26	Tu	8	11	·23	25 26	·02 ·96	25
27	We	9	12	·13	27	·89	26
28	Th	10	13 14	·03 ·93	1	·82	27
29	Fr	11	—A	·83	2	·75	28
30	Sa	12	1	·73	3	·69	29
—31	Su	13	2	·65	4	·64	—30
1	Mo	14	3	·58	5	·61	1
2	Tu	15	4	·53	6	·59	2
3	We	16	5	·50	7	·59	3
4	Th	17	6	·48	8	·60	4
5	Fr	18	7	·49	9	·65	5
6	Sa	19	8	·52	10	·71	6
7	Su	20	9	·56	11	·78	7
8	Mo	21	10	·63	12	·88	8
9	Tu	22	11	·71	13	·98	9
10	We	23	12	·80	...	...	10
11	Th	24	13	·88	14	·09	11
12	Fr	25	14	·95	15	·20	12
13	Sa	26	...	...	16	·29	13
14	Su	27	P	·02	17	·37	14
15	Mo	28	1	·06	18	·44	15
16	Tu	29	2	·08	19	·48	16
17	We	30	3	·08	20	·51	17
18	Th	31	4	·07	21	·51	18

June

Solar: Parthiva Vrishabha—Vaikasi; Parthiva Mithuna—Ani. Lunar: Vaisakha (Bahula); Jyeshtha (Sukla, Bah.). Muhammadan: H. 1364 Rajab.

Cyclic Sidereal Year, Month and Day	Week-Day	English Day	Tithi	Tithi Ending Moment	Nakshatra	Nakshatra Ending Moment	Muhammadan Year, Month and Day
19	Fr	1	5 6	·08 ·98	22	·49	19
20	Sa	2	7	·91	23	·46	20
21	Su	3	8	·82	24	·42	21
22	Mo	4	9	·72	25	·36	22
23	Tu	5	10	·62	26	·30	23
24	We	6	11	·52	27	·23	24
25	Th	7	12	·42	1	·16	25
26	Fr	8	13	·32	2	·10	26
27	Sa	9	14	23	3 4	·04 ·99	27
28	Su	10	—A	·15	5	·95	28
29	Mo	11	1	·08	6	·92	—29
30	Tu	12	2 3	·03 ·99	7	·91	1
—31	We	13	4	·93	8	·93	2
1	Th	14	5	·97	9	·96	3
2	Fr	15	...	...	...	...	4
3	Sa	16	6	·00	10	·01	5
4	Su	17	7	·05	11	·09	6
5	Mo	18	8	·11	12	·18	7
6	Tu	19	9	·19	13	·28	8
7	We	20	10	·27	14	·39	9
8	Th	21	11	·34	15	·50	10
9	Fr	22	12	·42	16	·60	11
10	Sa	23	13	·49	17	·68	12
11	Su	24	14	·53	18	·75	13
12	Mo ○	25	P	·56	19	·80	14
13	Tu	26	1	·57	20	·83	15
14	We	27	2	·54	21	·84	16
15	Th	28	3	·51	22	·82	17
16	Fr	29	4	·46	23	·79	18
17	Sa	30	5	·39	24	·75	19

Naksh:—1. Asvn. 2. Bhar. 3. Krit. 4. Rohi. 5. Mrig. 6. Ardh. 7. Punar. 8. Push. 9. Aslesh. 10. Magh. 11. P. Phal. 12. U. Phal. 13. Hasta. 14. Chit.

A. D. 1945.			**Vikrama 2002.**
A.—Amavasya.	**Kollam 1121,** { **N. Malabar—Sept.**	**Hijra 1365,**	**Bengal San 1351.**
P.—Paurnami.	Commences { **S. Malabar—Aug.**	Commences, **Dec. 6.**	**(N. Cycle) Vilamba.**

Columns: SOLAR reckoning — Cyclic Sidereal Year, Month and Day; Week-Day, English Month and Day. LUNAR reckoning — Tithi Ending Moment; Nakshatra Ending Moment; Muhammadan Year, Month and Day.

July

Cyclic Sidereal Year, Month and Day	Week-Day	English Day	Tithi	Ending Moment	Nakshatra	Ending Moment	Muhammadan Year, Month and Day
(Parthiva Mithuna—Ani.) 18	Su	1	(Jyesh. Bahula) 6	·31	25	·70	(H. 1364 Rajab.) 20
19	Mo	2	7	·21	26	·64	21
20	Tu	3	8	·11	27	·57	22
21	We	4	9 10	·01 ·91	1	·50	23
22	Th	5	11	·81	2	·44	24
23	Fr	6	12	·71	3	·38	25
24	Sa	7	13	·62	4	·32	26
25	Su	8	14	·55	5	·28	27
26	Mo ●	9	—A	·50	6	·25	28
27	Tu	10	1	·46	7	·24	29
28	We	11	2	·45	8	·25	—30
29	Th	12	3	·45	9	·28	1
30	Fr	13	4	·48	10	·33	2
31	Sa	14	5	·52	11	·39	3
—32	Su	15	6	·58	12	·48	4
(Parthiva Karkata—Adi.) 1	Mo	16	(Ashadha Sukla) 7	·66	13	·58	5
2	Tu	17	8	·74	14	·69	6
3	We	18	9	·82	15	·80	7
4	Th	19	10	·89	16	·90	8
5	Fr	20	11	·96	17	·99	9
6	Sa	21	...	...	...	...	10
7	Su	22	12	·01	18	·06	11
8	Mo	23	13	·04	19	·12	12
9	Tu	24	14	·05	20	·15	13
10	We	25	P 1	·02 ·99	21	·16	(H. 1364 Shaban.) 14
11	Th	26	(Bahula) 2	·94	22	·15	15
12	Fr	27	3	·87	23	·13	16
13	Sa	28	4	·79	24	·09	17
14	Su	29	5	·70	25 26	·04 ·98	18
15	Mo	30	6	·60	27	·92	19
16	Tu	31	7	·49	1	·85	20

Aug.

Cyclic Sidereal Year, Month and Day	Week-Day	English Day	Tithi	Ending Moment	Nakshatra	Ending Moment	Muhammadan Year, Month and Day
17	We	1	8	·39	2	·78	21
18	Th	2	9	·29	3	·71	22
19	Fr	3	10	·20	4	·65	23
20	Sa	4	11	·11	5	·61	24
21	Su	5	12 13	·04 ·99	6	·58	25
22	Mo	6	14	·95	7	·57	26
23	Tu	7	—A	·98	8	·57	27
24	We	8	1	·93	9	·59	28
25	Th	9	2	·96	10	·63	—29
26	Fr	10	...	...	11	·70	(H. 1364 Ramzan.) 1
27	Sa	11	3	·00	12	·79	2
28	Su	12	4	·07	13	·89	3
29	Mo	13	5	·14	14	·99	4
30	Tu	14	6	·22	...	...	5
31	We	15	(Sravana Sukla) 7	·31	15	·09	6
—32	Th	16	8	·39	16	·20	7
(Parthiva Simha—Avani.) 1	Fr	17	9	·46	17	·30	8
2	Sa	18	10	·50	18	·37	9
3	Su	19	11	·53	19	·43	10
4	Mo	20	12	·54	20	·47	11
5	Tu	21	13	·52	21	·48	12
6	We	22	14	·49	22	·48	13
7	Th	23	P	·44	23	·46	14
8	Fr	24	(Bahula) 1	·37	24	·43	15
9	Sa	25	2	·29	25	·38	16
10	Su	26	3	·20	26	·32	17
11	Mo	27	4	·10	27	·26	18
12	Tu	28	5 6	·00 ·90	1	·19	19
13	We	29	7	·80	2	·12	20
14	Th	30	8	·71	3 4	·05 ·99	21
15	Fr	31	9	·63	5	·94	22

Sep.

Cyclic Sidereal Year, Month and Day	Week-Day	English Day	Tithi	Ending Moment	Nakshatra	Ending Moment	Muhammadan Year, Month and Day
(Parthiva Simha—Avani.) 16	Sa	1	(Sr. Bah.) 10	·56	6	·91	(Ramzan.) 23
17	Su	2	11	·51	7	·89	24
18	Mo	3	12	·47	8	·89	25
19	Tu	4	13	·45	9	·91	26
20	We	5	14	·44	10	·95	27
21	Th	6	—A	·47	...	...	28
22	Fr	7	1	·51	11	·01	29
23	Sa	8	2	·58	12	·09	—30
24	Su	9	3	·66	13	·18	(H. 1364 Shawwal.) 1
25	Mo	10	4	·74	14	·29	2
26	Tu	11	5	·82	15	·39	3
27	We	12	6	·90	16	·50	4
28	Th	13	7	·97	17	·60	5
29	Fr	14	(Sukla) ...	...	18	·68	6
30	Sa	15	8	·02	19	·74	7
—31	Su	16	9	·06	20	·78	8
(Parthiva Kanya—Purattasi.) 1	Mo	17	10	·07	21	·80	9
2	Tu	18	11	·06	22	·81	10
3	We	19	(Bhadrapada) 12 13	·02 ·97	23	·79	11
4	Th	20	14	·91	24	·76	12
5	Fr	21	P	·83	25	·71	13
6	Sa	22	(Bahula) 1	·74	26	·65	14
7	Su	23	2	·64	27	·59	15
8	Mo	24	3	·54	1	·52	16
9	Tu	25	4	·44	2	·45	17
10	We	26	5	·34	3	·39	18
11	Th	27	6	·25	4	·33	19
12	Fr	28	7	·17	5	·28	20
13	Sa	29	8	·10	6	·24	21
14	Su	30	9	·05	7	·22	22

Oct.

Cyclic Sidereal Year, Month and Day	Week-Day	English Day	Tithi	Ending Moment	Nakshatra	Ending Moment	Muhammadan Year, Month and Day
15	Mo	1	10 11	·01 ·99	8	·21	23
16	Tu	2	12	·99	9	·22	24
17	We	3	...	...	10	·26	25
18	Th	4	13	·02	11	·32	26
19	Fr	5	14	·06	12	·39	27
20	Sa	6	—A	·13	13	·48	28
21	Su	7	1	·21	14	·58	—29
22	Mo	8	2	·29	15	·69	(H. 1364 Zi-l-ka'da.) 1
23	Tu	9	3	·38	16	·80	2
24	We	10	4	·47	17	·90	3
25	Th	11	5	·54	18	·98	4
26	Fr	12	6	·59	...	...	5
27	Sa	13	(Asvina Sukla) 7	·62	19	·05	6
28	Su	14	8	·63	20	·10	7
29	Mo	15	9	·62	21	·13	8
—30	Tu	16	10	·59	22	·14	9
(Parthiva Tula—Aippasi.) 1	We	17	11	·55	23	·12	10
2	Th	18	12	·48	24	·09	11
3	Fr	19	13	·40	25	·05	12
4	Sa	20	14	·31	26 27	·00 ·93	13
5	Su	21	P	·21	1	·86	14
6	Mo	22	1	·11	2	·79	15
7	Tu	23	2 3	·01 ·92	3	·72	16
8	We	24	(Bahula) 4	·83	4	·66	17
9	Th	25	5	·75	5	·61	18
10	Fr	26	6	·68	6	·57	19
11	Sa	27	7	·63	7	·54	20
12	Su	28	8	·60	8	·53	21
13	Mo	29	9	·58	9	·55	22
14	Tu	30	10	·59	10	·58	23
15	We	31	11	·61	11	·63	24

Nov.

Cyclic Sidereal Year, Month and Day	Week-Day	English Day	Tithi	Ending Moment	Nakshatra	Ending Moment	Muhammadan Year, Month and Day
(Parthiva Tula—Aippasi.) 16	Th	1	(Bah.) 12	·66	12	·70	(Zi-l-ka'da.) 25
17	Fr	2	13	·73	13	·79	26
18	Sa	3	14	·81	14	·89	27
19	Su	4	—A	·90	...	...	28
20	Mo	5	1	·99	15	·00	29
21	Tu	6	...	...	16	·10	—30
22	We	7	2	·07	17	·20	(H. 1364 Zi-l-hijja.) 1
23	Th	8	3	·13	18	·29	2
24	Fr	9	4	·18	19	·36	3
25	Sa	10	5	·22	20	·42	4
26	Su	11	6	·24	21	·45	5
27	Mo	12	(Sukla) 7	·22	22	·46	6
28	Tu	13	8	·19	23	·45	7
29	We	14	9	·15	24	·48	8
—30	Th	15	10	·08	25	·39	9
(Parthiva Vrischika—Kartigai.) 1	Fr	16	(Karttika) 11 12	·00 ·91	26	·33	10
2	Sa	17	13	·82	27	·27	11
3	Su	18	14	·73	1	·20	12
4	Mo	19	P	·63	2	·13	13
5	Tu	20	1	·53	3	07	14
6	We	21	2	·44	4 5	·01 ·95	15
7	Th	22	3	·36	6	·90	16
8	Fr	23	4	·29	7	·87	17
9	Sa	24	5	·25	8	·86	18
10	Su	25	6	·22	9	·87	19
11	Mo	26	(Bahula) 7	·21	10	·89	20
12	Tu	27	8	·21	11	·91	21
13	We	28	9	·23	...	...	22
14	Th	29	10	·28	12	·00	23
15	Fr	30	11	·36	13	·09	24

Dec.

Cyclic Sidereal Year, Month and Day	Week-Day	English Day	Tithi	Ending Moment	Nakshatra	Ending Moment	Muhammadan Year, Month and Day
16	Sa	1	12	·44	14	·19	25
17	Su	2	13	·52	15	·30	26
18	Mo	3	14	·61	16	·40	27
19	Tu	4	—A	·70	17	·50	28
20	We	5	1	·77	18	·59	—29
21	Th	6	2	·82	19	·67	(H. 1365 Muharram.) 1
22	Fr	7	3	·86	20	·73	2
23	Sa	8	4	·87	21	·77	3
24	Su	9	(Sukla) 5	·85	22	·78	4
25	Mo	10	6	·82	23	·78	5
26	Tu	11	7	·78	24	·76	6
27	We	12	8	·71	25	·72	7
28	Th	13	9	·63	26	·67	8
—29	Fr	14	(Margasira) 10	·54	27	·61	9
(Parthiva Dhanus—Margali.) 1	Sa	15	11	·45	1	·55	10
2	Su	16	12	·35	2	·48	11
3	Mo	17	13	·26	3	·41	12
4	Tu	18	14	·17	4	·34	13
5	We ○	19	P 1	·08 ·99	5	·28	14
6	Th	20	2	·93	6	·24	15
7	Fr	21	3	·89	7	·21	16
8	Sa	22	4	·86	8	·19	17
9	Su	23	5	·85	9	·19	18
10	Mo	24	6	·86	10	·21	19
11	Tu	25	(Bahula) 7	·89	11	·25	20
12	We	26	8	·95	12	·31	21
13	Th	27	...	...	13	·40	22
14	Fr	28	9	·01	14	·49	23
15	Sa	29	10	·09	15	·59	24
16	Su	30	11	·18	16	70	25
17	Mo	31	12	·27	17	·80	26

15. Svati. 16. Visak. 17. Anur. 18. Jyesh. 19. Mula. 20. P. Ash. 21. U. Ash. 22. Sravn. 23. Dani. 24. Satab. 25. P. Bhad. 26. U. Bhad. 27. Rev.

A. D. 1946.
Solar Eclipse. ●
Lunar Eclipse. ○

Mesha Sankranti (Commencement of Indian Sidereal Year).
(Surya Sid.) April 13·52. = 31-12 Saka 1868. Kaliyuga 5047.
(Arya Sid.) April 13·41. = 24-36 (S. Cycle) Vyaya.

Cyclic Sidereal Year, Month and Day (SOLAR reckoning)	Week-Day English Month and Day (SOLAR reckoning)	Tithi Ending Moment (LUNAR reckoning)	Nakshatra Ending Moment (LUNAR reckoning)	Muhammadan Year, Month and Day (LUNAR reckoning)
	Jan.			
Parthiva, Dhanus—Margali. 18	Tu 1	Bah. 13 ·35	18 ·90	27
19	We 2	14 ·42	19 ·93	28
20	Th 3	—A ·47	... ...	29
21	Fr 4	Sukla 1 ·50	20 ·04	—30
22	Sa 5	2 ·51	21 ·08	1
23	Su 6	3 ·50	22 ·10	2
24	Mo 7	4 ·47	23 ·11	3
25	Tu 8	5 ·42	24 ·09	4
26	We 9	6 ·36	25 ·06	5
27	Th 10	7 ·28	26 ·01 27 ·95	6
28	Fr 11	8 ·19	1 ·89	7
29	Sa 12	9 ·10	2 ·82	8
—30	Su 13	10 ·00 11 ·90	3 ·75	9
1	Mo 14	12 ·80	4 ·69	H. 1365 Safar. 10
2	Tu 15	Pausha 13 ·72	5 ·63	11
3	We 16	14 ·64	6 ·58	12
4	Th 17	P ·58	7 ·54	13
5	Fr 18	Bahula 1 ·53	8 ·51	14
6	Sa 19	2 ·50	9 ·51	15
7	Su 20	3 ·49	10 ·52	16
8	Mo 21	4 ·50	11 ·56	17
9	Tu 22	5 ·53	12 ·62	18
10	We 23	6 ·60	13 ·70	19
Parthiva, Makara—Tai. 11	Th 24	7 ·67	14 ·79	20
12	Fr 25	8 ·74	15 ·89	21
13	Sa 26	9 ·83	... ...	22
14	Su 27	10 ·93	16 ·00	23
15	Mo 28	... ...	17 ·11	24
16	Tu 29	11 ·00	18 ·21	25
17	We 30	12 ·07	19 ·29	26
18	Th 31	13 ·12	20 ·35	27

Cyclic Sidereal Year, Month and Day	Week-Day English Month and Day	Tithi Ending Moment	Nakshatra Ending Moment	Muhammadan Year, Month and Day
	Feb.			
19	Fr 1	14 ·15	21 ·40	28
20	Sa 2	—A ·15	22 ·43	—29
21	Su 3	Sukla 1 ·14	23 ·44	1
22	Mo 4	2 ·11	24 ·42	2
23	Tu 5	3 ·05 4 ·98	25 ·39	3
24	We 6	5 ·90	26 ·35	4
25	Th 7	6 ·82	27 ·29	5
26	Fr 8	7 ·72	1 ·23	6
27	Sa 9	8 ·62	2 ·16	7
28	Su 10	9 ·52	3 ·09	8
—29	Mo 11	10 ·42	4 ·02 5 ·96	9
1	Tu 12	11 ·34	6 ·91	H. 1365 Rabi-ul-awwal. 10
2	We 13	12 ·26	7 ·87	11
3	Th 14	Magha 13 ·20	8 ·84	12
4	Fr 15	14 ·16	9 ·83	13
5	Sa 16	P ·14	10 ·84	14
6	Su 17	Bahula 1 ·12	11 ·88	15
7	Mo 18	2 ·14	12 ·93	16
8	Tu 19	3 ·17	... ...	17
9	We 20	4 ·22	13 ·00	18
Parthiva, Kumbha—Masi. 10	Th 21	5 ·29	14 ·09	19
11	Fr 22	6 ·37	15 ·19	20
12	Sa 23	7 ·47	16 ·30	21
13	Su 24	8 ·55	17 ·41	22
14	Mo 25	9 ·63	18 ·51	23
15	Tu 26	10 ·69	19 ·60	24
16	We 27	11 ·73	20 ·67	25
17	Th 28	12 ·76	21 ·72	26

Cyclic Sidereal Year, Month and Day	Week-Day English Month and Day	Tithi Ending Moment	Nakshatra Ending Moment	Muhammadan Year, Month and Day
	March			
Parthiva, Kumbha—Masi. 18	Fr 1	Bah. 13 ·77	22 ·75	27
19	Sa 2	14 ·75	23 ·76	28
20	Su 3	—A ·72	24 ·75	29
21	Mo 4	Sukla 1 ·67	25 ·72	—30
22	Tu 5	2 ·59	26 ·68	1
23	We 6	3 ·51	27 ·63	2
24	Th 7	4 ·43	1 ·57	3
25	Fr 8	5 ·34	2 ·50	4
26	Sa 9	6 ·24	3 ·43	5
27	Su 10	7 ·14	4 ·36	6
28	Mo 11	8 ·04 9 ·94	5 ·30	7
29	Tu 12	10 ·86	6 ·24	8
—30	We 13	11 ·80	7 ·20	9
1	Th 14	12 ·76	8 ·17	H. 1365 Rabi-ul-akhir. 10
2	Fr 15	Phalguna 13 ·73	9 ·15	11
3	Sa 16	14 ·71	10 ·17	12
4	Su 17	P ·73	11 ·20	13
5	Mo 18	1 ·77	12 ·25	14
6	Tu 19	2 ·83	13 ·31	15
7	We 20	3 ·90	14 ·39	16
8	Th 21	4 ·98	15 ·49	17
9	Fr 22	... ...	16 ·60	18
10	Sa 23	5 ·07	17 ·71	19
11	Su 24	Bahula 6 ·15	18 ·81	20
Parthiva, Mina—Panguni. 12	Mo 25	7 ·23	19 ·90	21
13	Tu 26	8 ·29	20 ·98	22
14	We 27	9 ·33	... ...	23
15	Th 28	10 ·36	21 ·04	24
16	Fr 29	11 ·35	22 ·07	25
17	Sa 30	12 ·34	23 ·08	26
18	Su 31	13 ·30	24 ·07	27

Cyclic Sidereal Year, Month and Day	Week-Day English Month and Day	Tithi Ending Moment	Nakshatra Ending Moment	Muhammadan Year, Month and Day
	April			
19	Mo 1	14 ·25	25 ·05	28
20	Tu 2	—A ·18	26 ·02 27 ·96	—29
21	We 3	Sukla 1 ·10	1 ·90	1
22	Th 4	2 ·00 3 ·90	2 ·83	2
23	Fr 5	4 ·80	3 ·76	3
24	Sa 6	5 ·70	4 ·70	4
25	Su 7	6 ·60	5 ·64	5
26	Mo 8	7 ·51	6 ·58	6
27	Tu 9	8 ·43	7 ·53	7
28	We 10	9 ·37	8 ·50	8
29	Th 11	10 ·32	9 ·49	9
—30	Fr 12	11 ·29	10 ·49	H. 1365 Jumadal-awwal. 10
1	Sa 13	12 ·27	11 ·51	11
2	Su 14	Chaitra 13 ·29	12 ·55	12
3	Mo 15	14 ·32	13 ·61	13
4	Tu 16	P ·38	14 ·70	14
5	We 17	1 ·45	15 ·80	15
6	Th 18	2 ·54	16 ·90	16
7	Fr 19	3 ·62	... ...	17
8	Sa 20	4 ·70	17 ·01	18
9	Su 21	5 ·76	18 ·11	19
Vyaya, Mesha—Chittirai. 10	Mo 22	6 ·82	19 ·20	20
11	Tu 23	Bahula 7 ·87	20 ·28	21
12	We 24	8 ·89	21 ·35	22
13	Th 25	9 ·90	22 ·39	23
14	Fr 26	10 ·88	23 ·40	24
15	Sa 27	11 ·85	24 ·40	25
16	Su 28	12 ·79	25 ·39	26
17	Mo 29	13 ·71	26 ·35	27
18	Tu 30	14 ·63	27 ·30	28

Cyclic Sidereal Year, Month and Day	Week-Day English Month and Day	Tithi Ending Moment	Nakshatra Ending Moment	Muhammadan Year, Month and Day
	May			
19	We 1	—A ·54	1 ·24	29
20	Th 2	Sukla 1 ·44	2 ·18	—30
21	Fr 3	2 ·34	3 ·11	1
Vyaya, Mesha—Chittirai. 22	Sa 4	3 ·24	4 ·04 5 ·97	2
23	Su 5	4 ·14	6 ·91	3
24	Mo 6	5 ·04 6 ·96	7 ·86	4
25	Tu 7	7 ·90	8 ·83	5
26	We 8	8 ·85	9 ·81	6
27	Th 9	9 ·81	10 ·81	7
28	Fr 10	10 ·80	11 ·82	8
29	Sa 11	11 ·81	12 ·86	9
30	Su 12	12 ·84	13 ·92	H. 1365 Jumadal-akhir. 10
—31	Mo 13	13 ·90	... ...	11
1	Tu 14	Vaisakha 14 ·96	14 ·00	12
2	We 15	... ...	15 ·10	13
3	Th 16	P ·04	16 ·20	14
4	Fr 17	1 ·12	17 ·30	15
5	Sa 18	2 ·21	18 ·41	16
6	Su 19	3 ·28	19 ·51	17
7	Mo 20	4 ·34	20 ·60	18
8	Tu 21	5 ·39	21 ·66	19
9	We 22	6 ·40	22 ·70	20
10	Th 23	Bahula 7 ·41	23 ·72	21
11	Fr 24	8 ·39	24 ·73	22
12	Sa 25	9 ·35	25 ·72	23
13	Su 26	10 ·29	26 ·69	24
Vyaya, Vrishabha—Vaikasi. 14	Mo 27	11 ·22	27 ·64	25
15	Tu 28	12 ·13	1 ·58	26
16	We 29	13 ·03 14 ·93	2 ·52	27
17	Th 30	—A ·83	3 ·45	28
18	Fr 31	1 ·73	4 ·38	—29

Cyclic Sidereal Year, Month and Day	Week-Day English Month and Day	Tithi Ending Moment	Nakshatra Ending Moment	Muhammadan Year, Month and Day
	June			
19	Sa 1	2 ·63	5 ·31	1
20	Su 2	3 ·55	6 ·25	2
21	Mo 3	4 ·47	7 ·20	3
22	Tu 4	5 ·40	8 ·16	4
23	We 5	6 ·34	9 ·14	5
24	Th 6	Sukla 7 ·31	10 ·18	6
25	Fr 7	8 ·30	11 ·14	7
26	Sa 8	9 ·30	12 ·17	8
27	Su 9	10 ·33	13 ·23	9
28	Mo 10	11 ·38	14 ·31	10
29	Tu 11	12 ·44	15 ·40	11
30	We 12	13 ·52	16 ·50	12
31	Th 13	Jyeshtha 14 ·60	17 ·61	H. 1365 Rajab. 13
—32	Fr ○ 14	P ·68	18 ·72	14
1	Sa 15	1 ·75	19 ·82	15
2	Su 16	2 ·82	20 ·90	16
3	Mo 17	3 ·87	21 ·97	17
4	Tu 18	4 ·89	... ...	18
5	We 19	5 ·89	22 ·01	19
6	Th 20	6 ·87	23 ·04	20
7	Fr 21	7 ·83	24 ·06	21
8	Sa 22	Bahula 8 ·78	25 ·04	22
Vyaya, Mithuna—Ani. 9	Su 23	9 ·71	26 ·01 27 ·97	23
10	Mo 24	10 ·62	1 ·92	24
11	Tu 25	11 ·52	2 ·86	25
12	We 26	12 ·42	3 ·79	26
13	Th 27	13 ·32	4 ·72	27
14	Fr 28	14 ·22	5 ·65	28
15	Sa 29	—A ·12	6 ·59	29
16	Su 30	1 ·03 2 ·95	7 ·53	—30

Naksh :—1. Asvn. 2. Bhar. 3. Krit. 4. Rohi. 5. Mrig. 6. Ardh. 7. Punar. 8. Push. 9. Aslesh. 10. Magh. 11. P. Phal. 12. U. Phal. 13. Hasta. 14. Chit.

A. D. 1946.
A.—Amavasya.
P.—Paurnami.

Kollam 1122, Commences { N. Malabar—Sept. / S. Malabar—Aug.

Hijra 1366, Commences, Nov. 25.

Vikrama 2003.
Bengal San 1352.
(N. Cycle) Vikarin.

July

Cyclic Sidereal Year, Month and Day (SOLAR reckoning)	Week-Day English Month and Day		Tithi Ending Moment (LUNAR reckoning)	Nakshatra Ending Moment	Muhammadan Year, Month and Day
Vyaya Mithuna—Ani 17	Mo	1	3 ·88	8 ·49	1
18	Tu	2	4 ·82	9 ·46	2
19	We	3	5 ·79	10 ·45	3
20	Th	4	6 ·77	11 ·46	4
21	Fr	5	Sukla 7 ·78	12 ·49	5
22	Sa	6	8 ·80	13 ·54	6
23	Su	7	9 ·85	14 ·61	7
24	Mo	8	10 ·92	15 ·70	8
25	Tu	9	11 ·99	16 ·80	9
26	We	10	... ...	17 ·91	10
27	Th	11	12 ·08	... ...	11
28	Fr	12	Ashadha 13 ·16	18 ·02	H. 1365 Shaban 12
29	Sa	13	14 ·23	19 ·12	13
30	Su	14	P ·29	20 ·21	14
31	Mo	15	1 ·34	21 ·28	15
Vyaya Karkata—Adi 1	Tu	16	2 ·37	22 ·34	16
2	We	17	3 ·36	23 ·37	17
3	Th	18	4 ·35	24 ·38	18
4	Fr	19	5 ·31	25 ·37	19
5	Sa	20	Bahula 6 ·26	26 ·35	20
6	Su	21	7 ·18	27 ·31	21
7	Mo	22	8 ·10	1 ·26	22
8	Tu	23	9 ·02 / 10 ·92	2 ·20	23
9	We	24	11 ·82	3 ·13	24
10	Th	25	12 ·72	4 ·06 / 5 ·99	25
11	Fr	26	13 ·62	6 ·93	26
12	Sa	27	14 ·52	7 ·87	27
13	Su	28	—A ·43	8 ·82	28
14	Mo	29	1 ·36	9 ·79	—29
15	Tu	30	2 ·30	10 ·78	1
16	We	31	3 ·27	11 ·79	2

Aug.

Cyclic Sidereal Year, Month and Day	Week-Day English Month and Day		Tithi Ending Moment	Nakshatra Ending Moment	Muhammadan Year, Month and Day
17	Th	1	4 ·25	12 ·81	3
18	Fr	2	5 ·27	13 ·85	4
19	Sa	3	6 ·29	14 ·92	5
20	Su	4	Sukla 7 ·32	... ...	6
21	Mo	5	8 ·39	15 ·00	7
22	Tu	6	9 ·47	16 ·10	8
23	We	7	10 ·56	17 ·21	9
24	Th	8	11 ·64	18 ·32	10
25	Fr	9	12 ·71	19 ·42	H. 1365 Ramzan 11
26	Sa	10	Sravana 13 ·77	20 ·51	12
27	Su	11	14 ·83	21 ·59	13
28	Mo	12	P ·86	22 ·65	14
29	Tu	13	1 ·86	23 ·69	15
30	We	14	2 ·84	24 ·70	16
31	Th	15	3 ·80	25 ·70	17
—32	Fr	16	4 ·76	26 ·68	18
Vyaya Simha—Avani 1	Sa	17	5 ·69	27 ·64	19
2	Su	18	6 ·60	1 ·59	20
3	Mo	19	Bahula 7 ·51	2 ·53	21
4	Tu	20	8 ·41	3 ·47	22
5	We	21	9 ·31	4 ·40	23
6	Th	22	10 ·21	5 ·33	24
7	Fr	23	11 ·11	6 ·27	25
8	Sa	24	12 ·01 / 13 ·93	7 ·21	26
9	Su	25	14 ·87	8 ·16	27
10	Mo	26	—A ·82	9 ·12	28
11	Tu	27	1 ·78	10 ·11	29
12	We	28	B. Sukla 2 ·75	11 ·11	—30
13	Th	29	3 ·77	12 ·13	1
14	Fr	30	4 ·79	13 ·16	2
15	Sa	31	5 ·84	14 ·22	3

Sep.

Cyclic Sidereal Year, Month and Day	Week-Day English Month and Day		Tithi Ending Moment	Nakshatra Ending Moment	Muhammadan Year, Month and Day
16	Su	1	6 ·90	15 ·31	4
17	Mo	2	7 ·98	16 ·41	5
18	Tu	3	... ...	17 ·51	6
19	We	4	Sukla 8 ·06	18 ·61	7
20	Th	5	9 ·15	19 ·72	8
21	Fr	6	10 ·23	20 ·82	9
Vyaya Simha—Avani 22	Sa	7	11 ·29	21 ·90	10
23	Su	8	12 ·34	22 ·96	11
24	Mo	9	13 ·36	... ...	12
25	Tu	10	Bhadrapada 14 ·38	23 ·00	13
26	We	11	P ·36	24 ·02	H. 1365 Shawwal 14
27	Th	12	1 ·33	25 ·02	15
28	Fr	13	2 ·28	26 ·01 / 27 ·98	16
29	Sa	14	3 ·21	1 ·93	17
30	Su	15	4 ·13	2 ·87	18
—31	Mo	16	5 ·04 / 6 ·95	3 ·81	19
1	Tu	17	Bahula 7 ·85	4 ·74	20
2	We	18	8 ·75	5 ·67	21
3	Th	19	9 ·65	6 ·60	22
4	Fr	20	10 ·55	7 ·54	23
5	Sa	21	11 ·47	8 ·49	24
6	Su	22	12 ·40	9 ·46	25
Vyaya Kanya—Purattasi 7	Mo	23	13 ·34	10 ·44	26
8	Tu	24	14 ·31	11 ·43	27
9	We	25	—A ·30	12 ·44	28
10	Th	26	1 ·32	13 ·48	—29
11	Fr	27	2 ·34	14 ·54	1
12	Sa	28	3 ·38	15 ·61	2
13	Su	29	4 ·44	16 ·70	3
14	Mo	30	5 ·52	17 ·80	4

Oct.

Cyclic Sidereal Year, Month and Day	Week-Day English Month and Day		Tithi Ending Moment	Nakshatra Ending Moment	Muhammadan Year, Month and Day
15	Tu	1	Sukla 6 ·60	18 ·91	5
16	We	2	7 ·69	... ...	6
17	Th	3	8 ·76	19 ·02	7
18	Fr	4	9 ·83	20 ·12	8
19	Sa	5	10 ·89	21 ·21	9
20	Su	6	11 ·92	22 ·27	10
21	Mo	7	12 ·93	23 ·31	11
22	Tu	8	Asvina 13 ·92	24 ·34	H. 1365 Zi-l-ka'da 12
23	We	9	14 ·90	25 ·36	13
24	Th	10	P ·85	26 ·34	14
25	Fr	11	1 ·78	27 ·31	15
26	Sa	12	2 ·69	1 ·27	16
27	Su	13	3 ·60	2 ·21	17
28	Mo	14	4 ·51	3 ·15	18
29	Tu	15	5 ·41	4 ·08	19
—30	We	16	6 ·31	5 ·01 / 6 ·94	20
1	Th	17	Bahula 7 ·21	7 ·88	21
2	Fr	18	8 ·12	8 ·88	22
3	Sa	19	9 ·04 / 10 ·97	9 ·79	23
4	Su	20	11 ·92	10 ·76	24
Vyaya Tula—Aippasi 5	Mo	21	12 ·89	11 ·75	25
6	Tu	22	13 ·88	12 ·76	26
7	We	23	14 ·90	13 ·80	27
8	Th	24	—A ·92	14 ·85	28
9	Fr	25	1 ·96	15 ·92	29
10	Sa	26	... ...	... ...	—30
11	Su	27	Kartt. Sukla 2 ·02	16 ·00	Zi-l-hijja 1
12	Mo	28	3 ·10	17 ·10	2
13	Tu	29	4 ·19	18 ·21	3
14	We	30	5 ·29	19 ·32	4
15	Th	31	6 ·37	20 ·42	5

Nov.

Cyclic Sidereal Year, Month and Day	Week-Day English Month and Day		Tithi Ending Moment	Nakshatra Ending Moment	Muhammadan Year, Month and Day
16	Fr	1	Sukla 7 ·44	21 ·51	6
17	Sa	2	8 ·48	22 ·58	7
18	Su	3	9 ·51	23 ·63	8
19	Mo	4	10 ·53	24 ·66	9
20	Tu	5	11 ·51	25 ·68	10
Vyaya Tula—Aippasi 21	We	6	12 ·48	26 ·67	11
22	Th	7	13 ·43	27 ·64	12
23	Fr	8	Karttika 14 ·37	1 ·60	13
24	Sa	9	P ·29	2 ·55	14
25	Su	10	1 ·21	3 ·49	H. 1365 Zi-l-hijja 15
26	Mo	11	2 ·11	4 ·42	16
27	Tu	12	3 ·01 / 4 ·91	5 ·35	17
28	We	13	5 ·81	6 ·29	18
29	Th	14	6 ·73	7 ·23	19
—30	Fr	15	Bahula 7 ·65	8 ·17	20
1	Sa	16	8 ·59	9 ·12	21
2	Su	17	9 ·54	10 ·09	22
3	Mo	18	10 ·51	11 ·07	23
4	Tu	19	11 ·49	12 ·08	24
5	We	20	12 ·50	13 ·11	25
6	Th	21	13 ·54	14 ·16	26
7	Fr	22	14 ·59	15 ·22	27
8	Sa	23	—A ·66	16 ·30	28
9	Su	24	1 ·74	17 ·40	—29
Vyaya Vrischika—Kartigai 10	Mo	25	2 ·83	18 ·51	1
11	Tu	26	3 ·91	19 ·62	2
12	We	27	4 ·99	20 ·72	3
13	Th	28	... ...	21 ·81	4
14	Fr	29	5 ·06	22 ·89	5
15	Sa	30	6 ·11	23 ·95	6

Dec.

Cyclic Sidereal Year, Month and Day	Week-Day English Month and Day		Tithi Ending Moment	Nakshatra Ending Moment	Muhammadan Year, Month and Day
16	Su	1	Sukla 7 ·15	24 ·99	7
17	Mo	2	8 ·15	... ...	8
18	Tu	3	9 ·14	25 ·00	9
19	We	4	10 ·10	26 ·00 / 27 ·98	10
20	Th	5	11 ·05 / 12 ·99	1 ·94	11
21	Fr	6	13 ·91	2 ·89	H. 1366 Muharram 12
22	Sa	7	Margasira 14 ·83	3 ·83	13
23	Su ○	8	P ·73	4 ·76	14
24	Mo	9	1 ·63	5 ·69	15
25	Tu	10	2 ·53	6 ·62	16
26	We	11	3 ·44	7 ·56	17
27	Th	12	4 ·35	8 ·50	18
28	Fr	13	5 ·28	9 ·45	19
29	Sa	14	6 ·22	10 ·42	20
—30	Su	15	Bahula 7 ·16	11 ·40	21
1	Mo	16	8 ·14	12 ·41	22
2	Tu	17	9 ·13	13 ·43	23
3	We	18	10 ·15	14 ·47	24
4	Th	19	11 ·18	15 ·53	25
5	Fr	20	12 ·23	16 ·61	26
Vyaya Dhanus—Margali 6	Sa	21	13 ·31	17 ·71	27
7	Su	22	14 ·39	18 ·81	28
8	Mo	23	—A ·48	19 ·92	29
9	Tu	24	1 ·57	... ...	—30
10	We	25	Sukla 2 ·65	20 ·02	H. 1366 Safar 1
11	Th	26	3 ·71	21 ·12	2
12	Fr	27	4 ·76	22 ·20	3
13	Sa	28	Pausha 5 ·79	23 ·26	4
14	Su	29	6 ·80	24 ·30	5
15	Mo	30	7 ·79	25 ·32	6
16	Tu	31	8 ·75	26 ·32	7

15. Svati. 16. Visak. 17. Anur. 18. Jyesh. 19. Mula. 20. P. Ash. 21. U. Ash. 22. Sravn. 23. Dani. 24. Satab. 25. P. Bhad. 26. U. Bhad. 27. Rev.

A. D. 1947. **Mesha Sankranti** (Commencement of Indian Sidereal Year).
Solar Eclipse. ● **(Surya Sid.) April 13·78.** **Saka 1869.** **Kaliyuga 5048.**
Lunar Eclipse. ○ **(Arya Sid.) April 13·67.** **(S. Cycle) Sarvajit.**

SOLAR reckoning: Cyclic Sidereal Year, Month and Day; Week-Day English Month and Day. LUNAR reckoning: Tithi Ending Moment; Nakshatra Ending Moment; Muhammadan Year, Month and Day.

Cyclic Sidereal Year, Month and Day	Week-Day English Month and Day	Tithi Ending Moment	Nakshatra Ending Moment	Muhammadan Year, Month and Day
	Jan.			
Vyaya Dhanus—Margali 17	We 1	Sukla 9 ·70	27 ·31	8
18	Th 2	10 ·64	1 ·28	9
19	Fr 3	11 ·56	2 ·23	10
20	Sa 4	12 ·47	3 ·17	11
21	Su 5	13 ·37	4 ·10	12
22	Mo 6	Pausha 14 ·27	5 ·03 / 6 ·96	13
23	Tu 7	P ·17	7 ·90	14
24	We 8	1 ·03	8 ·84	15
25	Th 9	2 ·00 / 3 ·93	9 ·79	H. 1366 Safar 16
26	Fr 10	4 ·86	10 ·75	17
27	Sa 11	5 ·82	11 ·73	18
28	Su 12	6 ·79	12 ·73	19
—29	Mo 13	Bahula 7 ·77	13 ·74	20
Vyaya Makara—Tai 1	Tu 14	8 ·79	14 ·78	21
2	We 15	9 ·83	15 ·84	22
3	Th 16	10 ·88	16 ·92	23
4	Fr 17	11 ·96	...	24
5	Sa 18	...	17 ·01	25
6	Su 19	12 ·04	18 ·11	26
7	Mo 20	13 ·13	19 ·22	27
8	Tu 21	14 ·22	20 ·33	28
9	We 22	—A ·30	21 ·43	—29
10	Th 23	Sukla 1 ·37	22 ·51	1
11	Fr 24	2 ·41	23 ·57	2
12	Sa 25	3 ·43	24 ·61	3
13	Su 26	4 ·45	25 ·64	4
14	Mo 27	5 ·43	26 ·66	5
15	Tu 28	6 ·39	27 ·64	6
16	We 29	7 ·34	1 ·61	7
17	Th 30	8 ·27	2 ·56	8
18	Fr 31	9 ·19	3 ·50	9
	Feb.			
19	Sa 1	10 ·10	4 ·44	H. 1366 Rabi-ul-awwal 10
20	Su 2	11 ·00 / 12 ·90	5 ·38	11
21	Mo 3	Magha 13 ·80	6 ·31	12
22	Tu 4	14 ·70	7 ·24	13
23	We 5	P ·62	8 ·17	14
24	Th 6	1 ·55	9 ·12	15
25	Fr 7	2 ·49	10 ·08	16
26	Sa 8	3 ·45	11 ·06	17
27	Su 9	4 ·42	12 ·05	18
28	Mo 10	5 ·41	13 ·06	19
29	Tu 11	6 ·42	14 ·09	20
—30	We 12	Bahula 7 ·47	15 ·15	21
Vyaya Kumbha—Masi 1	Th 13	8 ·53	16 ·22	22
2	Fr 14	9 ·59	17 ·31	23
3	Sa 15	10 ·67	18 ·41	24
4	Su 16	11 ·77	19 ·52	25
5	Mo 17	12 ·86	20 ·63	26
6	Tu 18	13 ·93	21 ·73	27
7	We 19	14 ·99	22 ·82	28
8	Th 20	...	23 ·88	29
9	Fr 21	—A ·04	24 ·93	—30
10	Sa 22	Sukla 1 ·06	25 ·96	Rabi-ul-akhir 1
11	Su 23	2 ·07	26 ·98	2
12	Mo 24	3 ·05	27 ·97	3
13	Tu 25	4 ·02 / 5 ·95	1 ·94	4
14	We 26	Phal. 6 ·88	2 ·90	5
15	Th 27	7 ·80	3 ·84	6
16	Fr 28	8 ·71	4 .78	7

Cyclic Sidereal Year, Month and Day	Week-Day English Month and Day	Tithi Ending Moment	Nakshatra Ending Moment	Muhammadan Year, Month and Day
	March			
17	Sa 1	Suk. 9 ·62	5 ·71	8
18	Su 2	10 ·52	6 ·64	9
19	Mo 3	11 ·42	7 ·57	10
20	Tu 4	12 ·32	8 ·51	11
21	We 5	13 ·24	9 ·46	12
Vyaya Kumbha—Masi 22	Th 6	Phalguna 14 ·16	10 ·42	13
23	Fr 7	P ·10	11 ·39	14
24	Sa 8	1 ·06	12 ·37	15
25	Su 9	2 ·03	13 ·38	16
26	Mo 10	3 ·02	14 ·41	H. 1366 Rabi-ul-akhir 17
27	Tu 11	4 ·03	15 ·46	18
28	We 12	5 ·08	16 ·53	19
—29	Th 13	6 ·13	17 ·61	20
1	Fr 14	Bahula 7 ·20	18 ·71	21
2	Sa 15	8 ·28	19 ·82	22
3	Su 16	9 ·37	20 ·93	23
4	Mo 17	10 ·46	...	24
5	Tu 18	11 ·53	21 ·03	25
6	We 19	12 ·60	22 ·12	26
7	Th 20	13 ·64	23 ·19	27
8	Fr 21	14 ·66	24 ·25	28
9	Sa 22	—A ·66	25 ·29	—29
10	Su 23	1 ·64	26 ·30	1
11	Mo 24	2 ·60	27 ·29	2
12	Tu 25	3 ·54	1 ·27	3
13	We 26	4 ·48	2 ·23	4
14	Th 27	5 ·40	3 ·18	5
Vyaya Mina—Panguni 15	Fr 28	6 ·30	4 ·12	6
16	Sa 29	Sukla 7 ·20	5 ·05 / 6 ·98	7
17	Su 30	8 ·10	7 ·92	8
18	Mo 31	9 ·00 / 10 ·90	8 ·86	9
	April			
19	Tu 1	11 ·82	9 ·80	H. 1366 Jumadal-awwal 10
20	We 2	12 ·74	10 ·75	11
21	Th 3	Chaitra 13 ·68	11 ·72	12
22	Fr 4	14 ·63	12 ·70	13
23	Sa 5	P ·60	13 ·71	14
24	Su 6	1 ·59	14 ·73	15
25	Mo 7	2 ·61	15 ·77	16
26	Tu 8	3 ·65	16 ·83	17
27	We 9	4 ·70	17 ·91	18
28	Th 10	5 ·77	...	19
29	Fr 11	6 ·84	18 ·01	20
30	Sa 12	7 ·93	19 ·12	21
—31	Su 13	Bahula ...	20 ·23	22
1	Mo 14	8 ·02	21 ·33	23
2	Tu 15	9 ·09	22 ·42	24
3	We 16	10 ·15	23 ·50	25
4	Th 17	11 ·19	24 ·57	26
5	Fr 18	12 ·21	25 ·61	27
6	Sa 19	13 ·21	26 ·62	28
7	Su 20	14 ·20	27 ·62	29
8	Mo 21	—A ·16	1 ·60	—30
9	Tu 22	1 ·09	2 ·57	Jumadal-akhir. 1
Sarvajit Mesha—Chittirai 10	We 23	Sukla 2 ·02 / 3 ·94	3 ·52	2
11	Th 24	4 ·85	4 ·46	3
12	Fr 25	5 ·75	5 ·39	4
13	Sa 26	6 ·65	6 ·32	5
14	Su 27	7 ·55	7 ·25	6
15	Mo 28	8 ·45	8 ·19	7
16	Tu 29	9 ·35	9 ·13	8
17	We 30	Vaisak. 10 ·26	10 ·08	9

Cyclic Sidereal Year, Month and Day	Week-Day English Month and Day	Tithi Ending Moment	Nakshatra Ending Moment	Muhammadan Year, Month and Day
	May			
18	Th 1	Suk. 11 ·21	11 ·04	10
19	Fr 2	12 ·17	12 ·02	11
20	Sa 3	13 ·14	13 ·02	12
21	Su 4	14 ·12	14 ·04	13
22	Mo 5	Vaisakha P ·13	15 ·08	14
Sarvajit Mesha—Chittirai 23	Tu 6	1 ·17	16 ·14	15
24	We 7	2 ·22	17 ·22	16
25	Th 8	3 ·29	18 ·32	17
26	Fr 9	4 ·37	19 ·42	18
27	Sa 10	5 ·45	20 ·53	19
28	Su 11	6 ·53	21 ·63	H. 1366 Jumadal-akhir. 20
29	Mo 12	Bahula 7 ·61	22 ·73	21
30	Tu 13	8 ·67	23 ·81	22
—31	We 14	9 ·71	24 ·88	23
1	Th 15	10 ·72	25 ·92	24
2	Fr 16	11 ·72	26 ·94	25
3	Sa 17	12 ·71	27 ·94	26
4	Su 18	13 ·67	1 ·93	27
5	Mo 19	14 ·61	2 ·90	28
6	Tu ● 20	—A ·54	3 ·85	—29
7	We 21	1 ·45	4 ·79	1
8	Th 22	2 ·35	5 ·73	2
9	Fr 23	3 ·25	6 ·67	3
10	Sa 24	4 ·15	7 ·60	4
11	Su 25	Sukla 5 ·05 / 6 ·95	8 ·53	5
Sarvajit Vrishabha—Vaikasi 12	Mo 26	7 ·86	9 ·47	6
13	Tu 27	8 ·78	10 ·42	7
14	We 28	9 ·72	11 ·38	8
15	Th 29	10 ·67	12 ·36	9
16	Fr 30	11 ·64	13 ·35	10
17	Sa 31	12 ·61	14 ·36	11
	June			
18	Su 1	13 ·63	15 ·39	H. 1366 Rajab. 12
19	Mo 2	14 ·66	16 ·45	13
20	Tu ○ 3	Jyeshtha P ·72	17 ·53	14
21	We 4	1 ·78	18 ·62	15
22	Th 5	2 ·86	19 ·72	16
23	Fr 6	3 ·95	20 ·82	17
24	Sa 7	...	21 ·93	18
25	Su 8	4 ·03	...	19
26	Mo 9	5 ·10	22 ·03	20
27	Tu 10	6 ·16	23 ·12	21
28	We 11	Bahula 7 ·20	24 ·19	22
29	Th 12	8 ·21	25 ·24	23
30	Fr 13	9 ·21	26 ·27	24
—31	Sa 14	10 ·20	27 ·28	25
1	Su 15	11 ·16	1 ·26	26
2	Mo 16	12 ·10	2 ·23	27
3	Tu 17	13 ·08 / 14 ·95	3 ·19	28
4	We 18	—A ·85	4 ·13	29
5	Th 19	1 ·75	5 ·07	—30
Sarvajit Mithuna—Ani 6	Fr 20	2 ·65	6 ·01 / 7 ·94	1
7	Sa 21	3 ·55	8 ·87	2
8	Su 22	Sukla 4 ·45	9 ·81	H. 1366 Shaban. 3
9	Mo 23	5 ·35	10 ·75	4
10	Tu 24	6 ·26	11 ·71	5
11	We 25	7 ·20	12 ·68	6
12	Th 26	8 ·15	13 ·67	7
13	Fr 27	9 ·11	14 ·68	8
14	Sa 28	10 ·09	15 ·71	9
15	Su 29	Ashadha 11 ·11	16 ·76	10
16	Mo 30	12 ·14	17 ·83	11

Naksh :—1. Asvn. 2. Bhar. 3. Krit. 4. Rohi. 5. Mrig. 6. Ardh. 7. Punar. 8. Push. 9. Aslesh. 10. Magh. 11. P. Phal. 12. U. Phal. 13. Hasta. 14. Chit.

A. D. 1947.
A.—Amavasya. **P.—Paurnami.**

Kollam 1123, Commences { **N. Malabar—Sept.** **S. Malabar—Aug.**

Hijra 1367, Commences, Nov. 15.

Vikrama 2004. **Bengal San 1353.** **(N. Cycle) Sarvari.**

SOLAR reckoning: Cyclic Sidereal Year, Month and Day; Week-Day English Month and Day. LUNAR reckoning: Tithi Ending Moment; Nakshatra Ending Moment; Muhammadan Year, Month and Day.

July

Solar: *Sarvajit Mithuna—Ani.* / *Sarvajit Karkata—Adi.* Lunar: *Ashadha Suk.* / *Bahula* / *Sukla* / *Sravana.* Muhammadan: *H. 1366 Shaban.* / *Ramzan.*

Cyclic Sidereal	Week-Day	Day	Tithi	Moment	Nakshatra	Moment	Muhammadan
17	Tu	1	13	·19	18	·92	12
18	We	2	14	·25	...	...	13
19	Th	3	P	·34	19	·02	14
20	Fr	4	1	·42	20	·12	15
21	Sa	5	2	·50	21	·23	16
22	Su	6	3	·57	22	·34	17
23	Mo	7	4	·58	23	·43	18
24	Tu	8	5	·67	24	·50	19
25	We	9	6	·69	25	·55	20
26	Th	10	7	·69	26	·59	21
27	Fr	11	8	·67	27	·60	22
28	Sa	12	9	·64	1	·60	23
29	Su	13	10	·58	2	·56	24
30	Mo	14	11	·50	3	·52	25
31	Tu	15	12	·42	4	·47	26
—32	We	16	13	·32	5	·42	27
1	Th	17	14	·22	6	·35	28
2	Fr	18	—A	·12	7	·28	—29
3	Sa	19	1 2	·02 ·92	8	·21	1
4	Su	20	3	·82	9	·14	2
5	Mo	21	4	·74	10	·09	3
6	Tu	22	5	·67	11	·05	4
7	We	23	6	·62	12	·01	5
8	Th	24	7	·59	13	·00	6
9	Fr	25	8	·58	14	·00	7
10	Sa	26	9	·59	15	·03	8
11	Su	27	10	·62	16	·07	9
12	Mo	28	11	·66	17	·14	10
13	Tu	29	12	·72	18	·22	11
14	We	30	13	·81	19	·32	12
15	Th	31	14	·89	20	·43	13

Aug.

Solar: *Sarvajit Simha—Avani.* Lunar: *Adhika* / *Bahula* / *Sukla* / *Nija Sravana.* Muhammadan: *H. 1366* / *H. 1366 Shawwal.*

Cyclic Sidereal	Week-Day	Day	Tithi	Moment	Nakshatra	Moment	Muhammadan
16	Fr	1	P	·97	21	·54	14
17	Sa	2	...	...	22	·64	15
18	Su	3	1	·04	23	·73	16
19	Mo	4	2	·11	24	·80	17
20	Tu	5	3	·15	25	·86	18
21	We	6	4	·17	26	·91	19
22	Th	7	5	·18	27	·92	20
23	Fr	8	6	·16	1	·92	21
24	Sa	9	7	·12	2	·89	22
25	Su	10	8	·07	3	·86	23
26	Mo	11	9 10	·00 ·92	4	·81	24
27	Tu	12	11	·82	5	·75	25
28	We	13	12	·72	6	·69	26
29	Th	14	13	·62	7	·62	27
30	Fr	15	14	·52	8	·55	28
—31	Sa	16	—A	·42	9	·49	29
1	Su	17	1	·34	10	·43	—30
2	Mo	18	2	·26	11	·38	1
3	Tu	19	3	·18	12	·34	2
4	We	20	4	·12	13	·32	3
5	Th	21	5	·09	14	·33	4
6	Fr	22	6	·08	15	·35	5
7	Sa	23	7	·08	16	·38	6
8	Su	24	8	·11	17	·44	7
9	Mo	25	9	·16	18	·52	8
10	Tu	26	10	·23	19	·62	9
11	We	27	11	·31	20	·73	10
12	Th	28	12	·39	21	·84	11
13	Fr	29	13	·47	22	·94	12
14	Sa	30	14	·54	...	...	13
15	Su	31	P	·61	23	·03	14

Sep.

Solar: *Sarvajit Simha—Avani.* / *Sarvajit Kanya—Purattasi.* Lunar: *Nija Sravana* / *Bahula* / *Sukla* / *Bhadrapada.* Muhammadan: *H. 1366 Shawwal.* / *Zi-l-ka'da.*

Cyclic Sidereal	Week-Day	Day	Tithi	Moment	Nakshatra	Moment	Muhammadan
16	Mo	1	1	·65	24	·11	15
17	Tu	2	2	·68	25	·18	16
18	We	3	3	·69	26	·22	17
19	Th	4	4	·67	27	·24	18
20	Fr	5	5	·64	1	·24	19
21	Sa	6	6	·58	2	·22	20
22	Su	7	7	·51	3	·20	21
23	Mo	8	8	·43	4	·15	22
24	Tu	9	9	·34	5	·09	23
25	We	10	10	·24	6 7	·02 ·95	24
26	Th	11	11	·14	8	·88	25
27	Fr	12	12 13	·04 ·94	9	·82	26
28	Sa	13	14	·85	10	·76	27
29	Su	14	—A	·77	11	·71	28
30	Mo	15	1	·71	12	·67	—29
—31	Tu	16	2	·65	13	·66	1
1	We	17	3	·62	14	·65	2
2	Th	18	4	·60	15	·66	3
3	Fr	19	5	·61	16	·70	4
4	Sa	20	6	·64	17	·75	5
5	Su	21	7	·69	18	·82	6
6	Mo	22	8	·75	19	·92	7
7	Tu	23	9	·83	...	...	8
8	We	24	10	·92	20	·02	9
9	Th	25	...	...	21	·13	10
10	Fr	26	11	·00	22	·24	11
11	Sa	27	12	·08	23	·33	12
12	Su	28	13	·15	24	·43	13
13	Mo	29	14	·19	25	·49	14
14	Tu	30	P	·22	26	·54	15

Oct.

Solar: *Sarvajit Tula—Aippasi.* Lunar: *Bahula* / *Sukla* / *Asvina* / *Bah.* Muhammadan: *H. 1366* / *H. 1366 Zi-l-hijja.*

Cyclic Sidereal	Week-Day	Day	Tithi	Moment	Nakshatra	Moment	Muhammadan
15	We	1	1	·23	27	·56	16
16	Th	2	2	·22	1	·57	17
17	Fr	3	3	·19	2	·56	18
18	Sa	4	4	·14	3	·53	19
19	Su	5	5 6	·06 ·98	4	·48	20
20	Mo	6	7	·89	5	·43	21
21	Tu	7	8	·80	6	·37	22
22	We	8	9	·71	7	·30	23
23	Th	9	10	·61	8	·23	24
24	Fr	10	11	·51	9	·16	25
25	Sa	11	12	·41	10	·10	26
26	Su	12	13	·33	11	·04	27
27	Mo	13	14	·27	12 13	·01 ·98	28
28	Tu	14	—A	·22	14	·97	29
29	We	15	1	·19	15	·98	—30
30	Th	16	2	·17	...	...	1
—31	Fr	17	3	·19	16	·01	2
1	Sa	18	4	·22	17	·06	3
2	Su	19	5	·27	18	·14	4
3	Mo	20	6	·33	19	·22	5
4	Tu	21	7	·41	20	·32	6
5	We	22	8	·50	21	·43	7
6	Th	23	9	·59	22	·54	8
7	Fr	24	10	·67	23	·64	9
8	Sa	25	11	·73	24	·73	10
9	Su	26	12	·78	25	·80	11
10	Mo	27	13	·80	26	·85	12
11	Tu	28	14	·81	27	·88	13
12	We	29	P	·81	1	·90	14
13	Th	30	1	·78	2	·89	15
14	Fr	31	2	·73	3	·86	16

Nov.

Solar: *Sarvajit Tula—Aippasi.* / *Sarvajit Vrischika—Kartigai.* Lunar: *Asv.* / *Bahula* / *Sukla* / *Karttika.* Muhammadan: *H. 1366 Zi-l-hijja.* / *Muharram.*

Cyclic Sidereal	Week-Day	Day	Tithi	Moment	Nakshatra	Moment	Muhammadan
15	Sa	1	3	·65	4	·82	17
16	Su	2	4	·58	5	·76	18
17	Mo	3	5	·49	6	·70	19
18	Tu	4	6	·39	7	·64	20
19	We	5	7	·29	8	·57	21
20	Th	6	8	·19	9	·50	22
21	Fr	7	9	·10	10	·43	23
22	Sa	8	10 11	·01 ·94	11	·38	24
23	Su	9	12	·87	12	·34	25
24	Mo	10	13	·82	13	·31	26
25	Tu	11	14	·79	14	·29	27
26	We	12	—A	·77	15	·30	28
27	Th	13	1	·80	16	·32	29
28	Fr	14	2	·83	17	·38	—30
—29	Sa	15	3	·88	18	·44	1
1	Su	16	4	·95	19	·52	2
2	Mo	17	...	...	20	·62	3
3	Tu	18	5	·03	21	·73	4
4	We	19	6	·12	22	·84	5
5	Th	20	7	·20	23	·94	6
6	Fr	21	8	·28	...	...	7
7	Sa	22	9	·35	24	·03	8
8	Su	23	10	·40	25	·11	9
9	Mo	24	11	·43	26	·16	10
10	Tu	25	12	·44	27	·20	11
11	We	26	13	·43	1	·22	12
12	Th	27	14	·39	2	·21	13
13	Fr	28	P	·34	3	·19	14
14	Sa	29	1	·28	4	·15	15
15	Su	30	2	·21	5	·10	16

Dec.

Solar: *Sarvajit Dhanus—Margali.* Lunar: *Bahula* / *Sukla* / *Margasira* / *Bahula.* Muhammadan: *H. 1367* / *H. 1367 Safar.*

Cyclic Sidereal	Week-Day	Day	Tithi	Moment	Nakshatra	Moment	Muhammadan
16	Mo	1	3	·12	6 7	·05 ·98	17
17	Tu	2	4 5	·02 ·92	8	·91	18
18	We	3	6	·82	9	·84	19
19	Th	4	7	·72	10	·78	20
20	Fr	5	8	·62	11	·72	21
21	Sa	6	9	·55	12	·67	22
22	Su	7	10	·49	13	·64	23
23	Mo	8	11	·45	14	·62	24
24	Tu	9	12	·42	15	·62	25
25	We	10	13	·41	16	·65	26
26	Th	11	14	·43	17	·69	27
27	Fr	12	—A	·46	18	·75	28
28	Sa	13	1	·52	19	·83	29
29	Su	14	2	·60	20	·92	—30
—30	Mo	15	3	·68	...	...	1
1	Tu	16	4	·77	21	·03	2
2	We	17	5	·86	22	·14	3
3	Th	18	6	·93	23	·24	4
4	Fr	19	7	·99	24	·34	5
5	Sa	20	...	...	25	·42	6
6	Su	21	8	·04	26	·48	7
7	Mo	22	9	·06	27	·52	8
8	Tu	23	10	·08	1	·54	9
9	We	24	11	·06	2	·54	10
10	Th	25	12 13	·04 ·98	3	·52	11
11	Fr	26	14	·91	4	·48	12
12	Sa	27	P	·83	5	·44	13
13	Su	28	1	·74	6	·38	14
14	Mo	29	2	·65	7	·32	15
15	Tu	30	3	·56	8	·25	16
16	We	31	4	·46	9	·18	17

15. Svati. 16. Visak. 17. Anur. 18. Jyesh. 19. Mula. 20. P. Ash. 21. U. Ash. 22. Sravn. 23. Dani. 24. Satab. 25. P. Bhad. 26. U. Bhad. 27. Rev.

A. D. 1948. **Mesha Sankranti** (Commencement of Indian Sidereal Year).
Solar Eclipse. ● **(Surya Sid.) April 13·04.** **Saka 1870.** **Kaliyuga 5049.**
Lunar Eclipse. ○ **(Arya Sid.) April 12·93.** **(S. Cycle) Sarvadhari.**

Solar month	Cyclic Sidereal Year, Month and Day	Week-Day	English Month and Day	Lunar month	Tithi Ending Moment	Nakshatra Ending Moment	Hijri month	Muhammadan Year, Month and Day
		Jan.						
Sarvajit Dhanus—Margali.	17	Th	1	Margasira Bahula	5 ·36	10 ·12	H. 1367 Safar.	18
	18	Fr	2		6 ·27	11 ·06		19
	19	Sa	3		7 ·20	12 ·01 / 13 ·97		20
	20	Su	4		8 ·13	14 ·94		21
	21	Mo	5		9 ·09	15 ·95		22
	22	Tu	6		10 ·07	16 ·96		23
	23	We	7		11 ·06	... ...		24
	24	Th	8		12 ·08	17 ·00		25
	25	Fr	9		13 ·12	18 ·05		26
	26	Sa	10		14 ·18	19 ·13		27
	27	Su	11		—A ·25	20 ·23		28
	28	Mo	12	Pausha Sukla	1 ·33	21 ·33		—29
	—29	Tu	13		2 ·42	22 ·44	H. 1367 Rabi-ul-awwal.	1
Sarvajit Makara—Tai.	1	We	14		3 ·50	23 ·54		2
	2	Th	15		4 ·58	24 ·64		3
	3	Fr	16		5 ·65	25 ·72		4
	4	Sa	17		6 ·69	26 ·80		5
	5	Su	18		7 ·72	27 ·84		6
	6	Mo	19		8 ·73	1 ·86		7
	7	Tu	20		9 ·71	2 ·86		8
	8	We	21		10 ·68	3 ·85		9
	9	Th	22		11 ·63	4 ·83		10
	10	Fr	23		12 ·56	5 ·78		11
	11	Sa	24		13 ·47	6 ·72		12
	12	Su	25		14 ·38	7 ·66		13
	13	Mo	26		P ·28	8 ·60		14
	14	Tu	27		1 ·18	9 ·53		15
	15	We	28		2 ·08 / 3 ·99	10 ·46		16
	16	Th	29		4 ·91	11 ·39		17
	17	Fr	30		5 ·84	12 ·34		18
	18	Sa	31		6 ·78	13 ·30		19
		Feb.						
	19	Su	1	Bahula	7 ·74	14 ·28		20
	20	Mo	2		8 ·72	15 ·27		21
	21	Tu	3		9 ·70	16 ·28		22
	22	We	4		10 ·72	17 ·31		23
	23	Th	5		11 ·76	18 ·36		24
	24	Fr	6		12 ·82	19 ·44		25
	25	Sa	7		13 ·90	20 ·53		26
	26	Su	8		14 ·98	21 ·63		27
	27	Mo	9		... ...	22 ·74		28
	28	Tu	10		—A ·06	23 ·84		29
	29	We	11	Magha Sukla	1 ·14	24 ·94		—30
	—30	Th	12		2 ·22	... ...	H. 1367 Rabi-ul-akhir.	1
Sarvajit Kumbha—Masi.	1	Fr	13		3 ·29	25 ·04		2
	2	Sa	14		4 ·38	26 ·10		3
	3	Su	15		5 ·35	27 ·15		4
	4	Mo	16		6 ·30	1 ·18		5
	5	Tu	17		7 ·35	2 ·19		6
	6	We	18		8 ·31	3 ·19		7
	7	Th	19		9 ·24	4 ·16		8
	8	Fr	20		10 ·17	5 ·11		9
	9	Sa	21		11 ·09	6 ·05 / 7 ·99		10
	10	Su	22		12 ·00 / 13 ·91	8 ·93		11
	11	Mo	23		14 ·81	9 ·86		12
	12	Tu	24		P ·71	10 ·79		13
	13	We	25	Bah.	1 ·61	11 ·73		14
	14	Th	26		2 ·52	12 ·67		15
	15	Fr	27		3 ·44	13 ·64		16
	16	Sa	28		4 ·39	14 ·61		17
	17	Su	29		5 ·35	15 ·59		18

Solar month	Cyclic Sidereal Year, Month and Day	Week-Day	English Month and Day	Lunar month	Tithi Ending Moment	Nakshatra Ending Moment	Hijri month	Muhammadan Year, Month and Day
		March						
Sarvajit Kumbha—Masi.	18	Mo	1	Magha Bahula	6 ·33	16 ·60	H. 1367 Rabi-ul-akhir.	19
	19	Tu	2		7 ·31	17 ·62		20
	20	We	3		8 ·33	18 ·67		21
	21	Th	4		9 ·37	19 ·75		22
	22	Fr	5		10 ·43	20 ·83		23
	23	Sa	6		11 ·51	21 ·93		24
	24	Su	7		12 ·59	... ...		25
	25	Mo	8		13 ·69	22 ·03		26
	26	Tu	9		14 ·77	23 ·14		27
	27	We	10		—A ·84	24 ·25		28
	28	Th	11	Phalguna Sukla	1 ·89	25 ·34		—29
	29	Fr	12		2 ·93	26 ·41	H. 1367 Jumadal-awwal.	1
	30	Sa	13		3 ·95	27 ·47		2
	—31	Su	14		4 ·95	1 ·50		3
Sarvajit Mina—Panguni.	1	Mo	15		5 ·94	2 ·52		4
	2	Tu	16		6 ·90	3 ·51		5
	3	We	17		7 ·84	4 ·49		6
	4	Th	18		8 ·77	5 ·45		7
	5	Fr	19		9 ·69	6 ·39		8
	6	Sa	20		10 ·59	7 ·33		9
	7	Su	21		11 ·49	8 ·27		10
	8	Mo	22		12 ·39	9 ·20		11
	9	Tu	23		13 ·29	10 ·13		12
	10	We	24		14 ·20	11 ·07		13
	11	Th	25		P ·11	12 ·02 / 13 ·97		14
	12	Fr	26		1 ·04 / 2 ·98	14 ·93		15
	13	Sa	27		3 ·94	15 ·92		16
	14	Su	28		4 ·91	16 ·92		17
	15	Mo	29		5 ·89	17 ·94		18
	16	Tu	30		6 ·92	18 ·99		19
	17	We	31		7 ·96	... ...		20
		April						
	18	Th	1	Bahula	... ...	19 ·05		21
	19	Fr	2		8 ·02	20 ·13		22
	20	Sa	3		9 ·09	21 ·23		23
	21	Su	4		10 ·17	22 ·33		24
	22	Mo	5		11 ·26	23 ·44		25
	23	Tu	6		12 ·34	24 ·55		26
	24	We	7		13 ·41	25 ·64		27
	25	Th	8		14 ·47	26 ·72		28
	26	Fr	9		—A ·51	27 ·78		29
	27	Sa	10	Chaitra Sukla	1 ·52	1 ·83		—30
	28	Su	11		2 ·52	2 ·84	H. 1367 Jumadal-akhir.	1
	—29	Mo	12		3 ·50	3 ·81		2
Sarvadhari Mesha—Chittirai.	1	Tu	13		4 ·46	4 ·82		3
	2	We	14		5 ·40	5 ·78		4
	3	Th	15		6 ·32	6 ·74		5
	4	Fr	16		7 ·24	7 ·68		6
	5	Sa	17		8 ·15	8 ·61		7
	6	Su	18		9 ·05 / 10 ·95	9 ·54		8
	7	Mo	19		11 ·85	10 ·47		9
	8	Tu	20		12 ·75	11 ·41		10
	9	We	21		13 ·66	12 ·35		11
	10	Th	22		14 ·58	13 ·30		12
	11	Fr ○	23		P ·52	14 ·26		13
	12	Sa	24	Bahula	1 ·48	15 ·24		14
	13	Su	25		2 ·45	16 ·24		15
	14	Mo	26		3 ·44	17 ·26		16
	15	Tu	27		4 ·45	18 ·30		17
	16	We	28		5 ·49	19 ·36		18
	17	Th	29		6 ·55	20 ·44		19
	18	Fr	30		7 ·62	21 ·53		20

Solar month	Cyclic Sidereal Year, Month and Day	Week-Day	English Month and Day	Lunar month	Tithi Ending Moment	Nakshatra Ending Moment	Hijri month	Muhammadan Year, Month and Day
		May						
Sarvadhari Mesha—Chittirai.	19	Sa	1	Chaitra Bah.	8 ·71	22 ·63	Jumadal-akhir.	21
	20	Su	2		9 ·79	23 ·74		22
	21	Mo	3		10 ·87	24 ·85		23
	22	Tu	4		11 ·94	25 ·95		24
	23	We	5		12 ·99	... ...		25
	24	Th	6		... ...	26 ·03		26
	25	Fr	7		13 ·04	27 ·10		27
	26	Sa	8		14 ·05	1 ·14		28
	27	Su ●	9		—A ·05	2 ·16		—29
	28	Mo	10	Vaisakha Sukla	1 ·03 / 2 ·99	3 ·16	H. 1367 Rajab.	1
	29	Tu	11		3 ·92	4 ·15		2
	30	We	12		4 ·81	5 ·12		3
	—31	Th	13		5 ·76	6 ·07		4
Sarvadhari Vrishabha—Vaikasi.	1	Fr	14		6 ·66	7 ·01 / 8 ·95		5
	2	Sa	15		7 ·56	9 ·88		6
	3	Su	16		8 ·46	10 ·81		7
	4	Mo	17		9 ·36	11 ·75		8
	5	Tu	18		10 ·26	12 ·69		9
	6	We	19		11 ·17	13 ·63		10
	7	Th	20		12 ·09	14 ·59		11
	8	Fr	21		13 ·03 / 14 ·99	15 ·57		12
	9	Sa	22		P ·96	16 ·57		13
	10	Su	23	Bahula	1 ·94	17 ·58		14
	11	Mo	24		2 ·93	18 ·61		15
	12	Tu	25		... ...	19 ·67		16
	13	We	26		3 00	20 ·74		17
	14	Th	27		4 ·05	21 ·84		18
	15	Fr	28		5 ·12	22 ·94		19
	16	Sa	29		6 ·21	... ...		20
	17	Su	30		7 ·29	23 ·04		21
	18	Mo	31		8 ·36	24 ·15		22
		June						
	19	Tu	1		9 ·48	25 ·25		23
	20	We	2		10 ·49	26 ·34		24
	21	Th	3		11 ·53	27 ·41		25
	22	Fr	4		12 ·54	1 ·46		26
	23	Sa	5		13 ·54	2 ·48		27
	24	Su	6		14 ·52	3 ·49		28
	25	Mo	7		—A ·49	4 ·47		29
	26	Tu	8	Jyeshtha Sukla	1 ·43	5 ·45		—30
	27	We	9		2 ·35	6 ·41	H. 1367 Shaban.	1
	28	Th	10		3 ·26	7 ·35		2
	29	Fr	11		4 ·16	8 ·29		3
	30	Sa	12		5 ·06 / 6 ·96	9 ·23		4
	—31	Su	13		7 ·86	10 ·16		5
Sarvadhari Mithuna—Ani.	1	Mo	14		8 ·76	11 ·09		6
	2	Tu	15		9 ·67	12 ·02 / 13 ·97		7
	3	We	16		10 ·59	14 ·92		8
	4	Th	17		11 ·53	15 ·90		9
	5	Fr	18		12 ·47	16 ·89		10
	6	Sa	19		13 ·44	17 ·90		11
	7	Su	20		14 ·48	18 ·93		12
	8	Mo	21		P ·44	19 ·93		13
	9	Tu	22	Bahula	1 ·47	... ...		14
	10	We	23		2 ·52	20 ·05		15
	11	Th	24		3 ·59	21 ·14		16
	12	Fr	25		4 ·67	22 ·24		17
	13	Sa	26		5 ·75	23 ·34		18
	14	Su	27		6 ·83	24 ·45		19
	15	Mo	28		7 ·90	25 ·55		20
	16	Tu	29		8 ·97	26 ·65		21
	17	We	30		... ...	27 ·72		22

Naksh :—1. Asvn. 2. Bhar. 3. Krit. 4. Rohi. 5. Mrig. 6. Ardh. 7. Punar. 8. Push. 9. Aslesh. 10. Magh. 11. P. Phal. 12. U. Phal. 13. Hasta. 14. Chit.

A. D. 1948.
A.—Amavasya.
P.—Paurnami.

Kollam 1124, Commences { **N. Malabar—Sept.** / **S. Malabar—Aug.**

Hijra 1368, Commences, **Nov. 3.**

Vikrama 2005.
Bengal San 1354.
(N. Cycle) Plava.

Cyclic Sidereal Year, Month and Day. (SOLAR reckoning)	Week-Day English Month and Day. (SOLAR reckoning)	Tithi Ending Moment. (LUNAR reckoning)	Nakshatra Ending Moment. (LUNAR reckoning)	Muhammadan Year, Month and Day. (LUNAR reckoning)
	July			
Sarvadhari *Mithuna—Ani.*		*Bahula*		H. 1367 *Shaban.*
18	Th 1	9 ·01	1 ·77	23
19	Fr 2	10 ·02	2 ·80	24
20	Sa 3	11 ·02	3 ·81	25
21	Su 4	12 ·00 13 ·96	4 ·81	26
22	Mo 5	14 ·90	5 ·78	27
23	Tu 6	—A ·83	6 ·74	28
24	We 7	1 ·74	7 ·69	—29
		Ashadha *Sukla*		
25	Th 8	2 ·64	8 ·63	1
26	Fr 9	3 ·54	9 ·57	2
27	Sa 10	4 ·44	10 ·50	3
28	Su 11	5 ·34	11 ·43	4
29	Mo 12	6 ·24	12 ·33	5
30	Tu 13	7 ·15	13 ·30	6
31	We 14	8 ·07	14 ·26	7
—32	Th 15	9 ·00 10 ·95	15 ·23	8
Sarvadhari *Karkata—Adi.*				H. 1367 *Ramzan.*
1	Fr 16	11 ·92	16 ·22	9
2	Sa 17	12 ·91	17 ·22	10
3	Su 18	13 ·92	18 ·24	11
4	Mo 19	14 ·95	19 ·29	12
5	Tu 20	P ·99	20 ·35	13
6	We 21	... ...	21 ·44	14
7	Th 22	1 ·06	22 ·53	15
8	Fr 23	2 ·14	23 ·64	16
9	Sa 24	3 ·22	24 ·75	17
10	Su 25	4 ·30	25 ·86	18
11	Mo 26	5 ·38	26 ·95	19
		Bahula		
12	Tu 27	6 ·44	... ...	20
13	We 28	7 ·48	27 ·02	21
14	Th 29	8 ·50	1 ·08	22
15	Fr 30	9 ·50	2 ·12	23
16	Sa 31	10 ·48	3 ·14	24
	Aug.			
17	Su 1	11 ·44	4 ·14	25
18	Mo 2	12 ·39	5 ·11	26
19	Tu 3	13 ·32	6 ·08	27
20	We 4	14 ·23	7 ·08 8 ·97	28
21	Th 5	—A ·14	9 ·90	29
		Sravana *Sukla*		H. 1367 *Shawwal.*
22	Fr 6	1 ·04 2 ·94	10 ·83	—30
23	Sa 7	3 ·84	11 ·76	1
24	Su 8	4 ·74	12 ·70	2
25	Mo 9	5 ·65	13 ·65	3
26	Tu 10	6 ·57	14 ·60	4
27	We 11	7 ·50	15 ·56	5
28	Th 12	8 ·44	16 ·54	6
29	Fr 13	9 ·41	17 ·54	7
30	Sa 14	10 ·40	18 ·56	8
—31	Su 15	11 ·41	19 ·60	9
Sarvadhari *Simha—Avani.*				
1	Mo 16	12 ·45	20 ·66	10
2	Tu 17	13 ·50	21 ·74	11
3	We 18	14 ·56	22 ·83	12
4	Th 19	P ·63	23 ·94	13
5	Fr 20	1 ·72	... ...	14
6	Sa 21	2 ·80	24 ·05	15
7	Su 22	3 ·88	25 ·16	16
8	Mo 23	4 ·94	26 ·25	17
		Bahula		
9	Tu 24	5 ·98	27 ·33	18
10	We 25	... ...	1 ·39	19
11	Th 26	6 ·01	2 ·44	20
12	Fr 27	7 ·00 8 ·99	3 ·46	21
13	Sa 28	9 ·95	4 ·46	22
14	Su 29	10 ·89	5 ·44	23
15	Mo 30	11 ·82	6 ·41	24
16	Tu 31	12 ·74	7 ·37	25

Cyclic Sidereal Year, Month and Day. (SOLAR reckoning)	Week-Day English Month and Day. (SOLAR reckoning)	Tithi Ending Moment. (LUNAR reckoning)	Nakshatra Ending Moment. (LUNAR reckoning)	Muhammadan Year, Month and Day. (LUNAR reckoning)
	Sep.			
Sarvadhari *Simha—Avani.*		*Bah.*		
17	We 1	13 ·65	8 ·31	26
18	Th 2	14 ·55	9 ·24	27
19	Fr 3	—A ·45	10 ·17	28
		Sukla		
20	Sa 4	1 ·35	11 ·10	—29
21	Su 5	2 ·25	12 ·04 13 ·98	1
22	Mo 6	3 ·16	14 ·93	2
23	Tu 7	4 ·08	15 ·89	3
24	We 8	5 ·01 6 ·96	16 ·87	4
25	Th 9	7 ·93	17 ·83	5
26	Fr 10	8 ·92	18 ·88	6
27	Sa 11	9 ·93	19 ·92	7
28	Su 12	10 ·97	20 ·97	8
29	Mo 13	... ...	... ...	9
30	Tu 14	11 ·02	21 ·04	10
—31	We 15	12 ·08	22 ·13	11
Sarvadhari *Kanya—Purattasi.*		**Bhadrapada**		H. 1367 *Zi-l-ka'da.*
1	Th 16	13 ·16	23 ·24	12
2	Fr 17	14 ·24	24 ·35	13
3	Sa 18	P ·32	25 ·46	14
4	Su 19	1 ·39	26 ·55	15
5	Mo 20	2 ·46	27 ·64	16
6	Tu 21	3 ·51	1 ·71	17
7	We 22	4 ·53	2 ·76	18
8	Th 23	5 ·54	3 ·78	19
		Bahula		
9	Fr 24	6 ·52	4 ·79	20
10	Sa 25	7 ·49	5 ·77	21
11	Su 26	8 ·43	6 ·74	22
12	Mo 27	9 ·36	7 ·70	23
13	Tu 28	10 ·28	8 ·65	24
14	We 29	11 ·19	9 ·58	25
15	Th 30	12 ·09 13 ·99	10 ·51	26
	Oct.			
16	Fr 1	14 ·89	11 ·44	27
17	Sa 2	—A ·79	12 ·38	28
18	Su 3	1 ·70	13 ·32	29
19	Mo 4	2 ·62	14 ·23	—30
		Sukla		H. 1367 *Zi-l-hijja.*
20	Tu 5	3 ·56	15 ·22	1
21	We 6	4 ·51	16 ·19	2
22	Th 7	5 ·49	17 ·19	3
23	Fr 8	6 ·49	18 ·20	4
24	Sa 9	7 ·50	19 ·23	5
25	Su 10	8 ·53	20 ·28	6
26	Mo 11	9 ·58	21 ·35	7
27	Tu 12	10 ·64	22 ·44	8
28	We 13	11 ·72	23 ·54	9
29	Th 14	12 ·80	24 ·65	10
30	Fr 15	13 ·89	25 ·76	11
—31	Sa 16	14 ·97	26 ·86	12
Sarvadhari *Tula—Aippasi.*		**Asvina**		
1	Su 17	... ...	27 ·95	13
2	Mo ○ 18	P ·04	... ...	14
3	Tu 19	1 ·08	1 ·02	15
4	We 20	2 ·11	2 ·07	16
5	Th 21	3 ·11	3 ·10	17
6	Fr 22	4 ·10	4 ·11	18
7	Sa 23	5 ·03	5 ·11	19
		Bahula		
8	Su 24	6 ·01 7 ·94	6 ·08	20
9	Mo 25	8 ·86	7 ·04 8 ·98	21
10	Tu 26	9 ·77	9 ·92	22
11	We 27	10 ·67	10 ·86	23
12	Th 28	11 ·57	11 ·79	24
13	Fr 29	12 ·48	12 ·72	25
14	Sa 30	13 ·39	13 ·66	26
15	Su 31	14 ·30	14 ·60	27

Cyclic Sidereal Year, Month and Day. (SOLAR reckoning)	Week-Day English Month and Day. (SOLAR reckoning)	Tithi Ending Moment. (LUNAR reckoning)	Nakshatra Ending Moment. (LUNAR reckoning)	Muhammadan Year, Month and Day. (LUNAR reckoning)
	Nov.			
Sarvadhari *Tula—Aippasi.*				
16	Mo ● 1	—A ·22	15 ·55	28
		Sukla		
17	Tu 2	1 ·16	16 ·53	—29
				H. 1368 *Muharram.*
18	We 3	2 ·11	17 ·51	1
19	Th 4	3 ·08	18 ·52	2
20	Fr 5	4 ·08	19 ·54	3
21	Sa 6	5 ·09	20 ·59	4
22	Su 7	6 ·12	21 ·66	5
23	Mo 8	7 ·17	22 ·75	6
24	Tu 9	8 ·25	23 ·85	7
25	We 10	9 ·33	24 ·95	8
26	Th 11	10 ·41	... ...	9
27	Fr 12	11 ·50	25 ·05	10
28	Sa 13	12 ·58	26 ·15	11
29	Su 14	13 ·65	27 ·25	12
—30	Mo 15	14 ·70	1 ·33	13
Sarvadhari *Vrischika—Kartigai.*		**Karttika**		
1	Tu 16	P ·73	2 ·38	14
2	We 17	1 ·72	3 ·42	15
3	Th 18	2 ·71	4 ·43	16
4	Fr 19	3 ·67	5 ·43	17
5	Sa 20	4 ·62	6 ·41	18
6	Su 21	5 ·56	7 ·37	19
7	Mo 22	6 ·48	8 ·32	20
		Bahula		
8	Tu 23	7 ·39	9 ·26	21
9	We 24	8 ·29	10 ·20	22
10	Th 25	9 ·19	11 ·13	23
11	Fr 26	10 ·10	12 ·06 13 ·99	24
12	Sa 27	11 ·01 12 ·92	14 ·93	25
13	Su 28	13 ·84	15 ·89	26
14	Mo 29	14 ·78	16 ·86	27
15	Tu 30	—A ·73	17 ·84	28
	Dec.			
		Sukla		
16	We 1	1 ·71	18 ·84	29
17	Th 2	2 ·70	19 ·86	—30
				H. 1368 *Safar.*
18	Fr 3	3 ·72	20 ·91	1
19	Sa 4	4 ·76	21 ·97	2
20	Su 5	5 ·81	... ...	3
21	Mo 6	6 ·88	22 ·05	4
22	Tu 7	7 ·96	23 ·14	5
23	We 8	... ...	24 ·24	6
24	Th 9	8 ·05	25 ·35	7
25	Fr 10	9 ·14	26 ·46	8
26	Sa 11	10 ·22	27 ·56	9
27	Su 12	11 ·29	1 ·64	10
28	Mo 13	12 ·34	2 ·70	11
—29	Tu 14	13 ·37	3 ·73	12
Sarvadhari *Dhanus—Margali.*		**Margasira**		
1	We 15	14 ·37	4 ·76	13
2	Th 16	P ·35	5 ·76	14
3	Fr 17	1 ·31	6 ·74	15
4	Sa 18	2 ·26	7 ·70	16
5	Su 19	3 ·19	8 ·65	17
6	Mo 20	4 ·11	9 ·60	18
		Bahula		
7	Tu 21	5 ·02 6 ·92	10 ·54	19
8	We 22	7 ·82	11 ·47	20
9	Th 23	8 ·73	12 ·40	21
10	Fr 24	9 ·64	13 ·34	22
11	Sa 25	10 ·55	14 ·28	23
12	Su 26	11 ·48	15 ·23	24
13	Mo 27	12 ·42	16 ·19	25
14	Tu 28	13 ·37	17 ·16	26
15	We 29	14 ·35	18 ·16	27
16	Th 30	—A ·35	19 ·17	28
17	Fr 31	1 ·37	20 ·21	—29

15. Svati. 16. Visak. 17. Anur. 18. Jyesh. 19. Mula. 20. P. Ash. 21. U. Ash. 22. Sravn. 23. Dani. 24. Satab. 25. P. Bhad. 26. U. Bhad. 27. Rev.

A. D. 1949. **Mesha Sankranti** (Commencement of Indian Sidereal Year).

Solar Eclipse. ● **(Surya Sid.) April 13·30.** **Saka 1871.** **Kaliyuga 5050.**

Lunar Eclipse. ○ **(Arya Sid.) April 13·19.** **(S. Cycle) Virodhi.**

SOLAR reckoning: Cyclic Sidereal Year, Month and Day; Week-Day English Month and Day. LUNAR reckoning: Tithi Ending Moment; Nakshatra Ending Moment; Muhammadan Year, Month and Day.

Jan. (Sarvadhari Dhanus—Margali; Sarvadhari Makara—Tai; Sukla; Pausha; Bahula; H. 1368 Rabi-ul-awwal)

Cyclic Sidereal Year, Month and Day	Week-Day English Month and Day	Tithi Ending Moment	Nakshatra Ending Moment	Muhammadan Year, Month and Day
18	Sa 1	2 ·40	21 ·27	1
19	Su 2	3 ·46	22 ·35	2
20	Mo 3	4 ·53	23 ·44	3
21	Tu 4	5 ·61	24 ·54	4
22	We 5	6 ·70	25 ·65	5
23	Th 6	7 ·79	26 ·76	6
24	Fr 7	8 ·87	27 ·86	7
25	Sa 8	9 ·93	1 ·94	8
26	Su 9	10 ·98	... ...	9
27	Mo 10	... ...	2 ·01	10
28	Tu 11	11 ·01	3 ·06	11
29	We 12	12 ·01	4 ·08	12
30	Th 13	13 ·00 / 14 ·96	5 ·08	13
1	Fr 14	P ·91	6 ·07	14
2	Sa 15	1 ·84	7 ·04	15
3	Su 16	2 ·76	8 ·00 / 9 ·94	16
4	Mo 17	3 ·66	10 ·87	17
5	Tu 18	4 ·56	11 ·80	18
6	We 19	5 ·46	12 ·73	19
7	Th 20	6 ·36	13 ·67	20
8	Fr 21	7 ·27	14 ·61	21
9	Sa 22	8 ·19	15 ·56	22
10	Su 23	9 ·12	16 ·52	23
11	Mo 24	10 ·06	17 ·49	24
12	Tu 25	11 ·02	18 ·48	25
13	We 26	12 ·00 / 13 ·99	19 ·50	26
14	Th 27	... ...	20 ·53	27
15	Fr 28	14 ·01	21 ·58	28
16	Sa 29	A ·05	22 ·65	29
17	Su 30	1 ·12	23 ·74	30
18	Mo 31	2 ·20	24 ·85	1

Feb. (Sarvadhari Kumbha—Masi; Sukla; Magha; Bahula; H. 1368 Rabi-ul-akhir)

Cyclic Sidereal Year, Month and Day	Week-Day English Month and Day	Tithi Ending Moment	Nakshatra Ending Moment	Muhammadan Year, Month and Day
19	Tu 1	3 ·28	25 ·96	2
20	We 2	4 ·36	... ...	3
21	Th 3	5 ·44	26 ·06	4
22	Fr 4	6 ·52	27 ·16	5
23	Sa 5	7 ·58	1 ·25	6
24	Su 6	8 ·62	2 ·32	7
25	Mo 7	9 ·65	3 ·37	8
26	Tu 8	10 ·65	4 ·40	9
27	We 9	11 ·63	5 ·41	10
28	Th 10	12 ·59	6 ·40	11
29	Fr 11	13 ·53	7 ·38	12
1	Sa 12	14 ·46	8 ·33	13
2	Su 13	P ·38	9 ·27	14
3	Mo 14	1 ·29	10 ·21	15
4	Tu 15	2 ·20	11 ·14	16
5	We 16	3 ·10	12 ·07	17
6	Th 17	4 ·00 / 5 ·90	13 ·01 / 14 ·95	18
7	Fr 18	6 ·81	15 ·89	19
8	Sa 19	7 ·73	16 ·85	20
9	Su 20	8 ·67	17 ·82	21
10	Mo 21	9 ·64	18 ·81	22
11	Tu 22	10 ·62	19 ·82	23
12	We 23	11 ·62	20 ·84	24
13	Th 24	12 ·64	21 ·89	25
14	Fr 25	13 ·67	22 ·96	26
15	Sa 26	14 ·73	... ...	27
16	Su 27	A ·81	23 ·05	28
17	Mo 28	1 ·90	24 ·15	29

March (Sarvadhari Kumbha—Masi; Sarvadhari Mina—Panguni; Sukla; Phalguna; Bahula; H. 1368 Jumadal-awwal)

Cyclic Sidereal Year, Month and Day	Week-Day English Month and Day	Tithi Ending Moment	Nakshatra Ending Moment	Muhammadan Year, Month and Day
18	Tu 1	2 ·99	25 ·26	1
19	We 2	... ...	26 ·36	2
20	Th 3	3 ·07	27 ·46	3
21	Fr 4	4 ·14	1 ·56	4
22	Sa 5	5 ·20	2 ·63	5
23	Su 6	6 ·25	3 ·69	6
24	Mo 7	7 ·26	4 ·72	7
25	Tu 8	8 ·26	5 ·73	8
26	We 9	9 ·24	6 ·73	9
27	Th 10	10 ·19	7 ·71	10
28	Fr 11	11 ·13	8 ·67	11
29	Sa 12	12 ·06 / 13 ·98	9 ·61	12
30	Su 13	14 ·89	10 ·55	13
1	Mo 14	P ·79	11 ·49	14
2	Tu 15	1 ·69	12 ·42	15
3	We 16	2 ·59	13 ·35	16
4	Th 17	3 ·49	14 ·29	17
5	Fr 18	4 ·40	15 ·23	18
6	Sa 19	5 ·33	16 ·18	19
7	Su 20	6 ·28	17 ·15	20
8	Mo 21	7 ·24	18 ·14	21
9	Tu 22	8 ·21	19 ·14	22
10	We 23	9 ·21	20 ·16	23
11	Th 24	10 ·23	21 ·20	24
12	Fr 25	11 ·27	22 ·27	25
13	Sa 26	12 ·33	23 ·35	26
14	Su 27	13 ·41	24 ·45	27
15	Mo 28	14 ·49	25 ·55	28
16	Tu 29	A ·58	26 ·66	29
17	We 30	1 ·66	27 ·77	30
18	Th 31	2 ·73	1 ·86	1

April (Virodhi Mesha—Chittirai; Sukla; Chaitra; Bahula; Suk.; H. 1368 Jumadal-akhir)

Cyclic Sidereal Year, Month and Day	Week-Day English Month and Day	Tithi Ending Moment	Nakshatra Ending Moment	Muhammadan Year, Month and Day
19	Fr 1	3 ·78	2 ·94	2
20	Sa 2	4 ·82	... ...	3
21	Su 3	5 ·84	3 ·00	4
22	Mo 4	6 ·83	4 ·04	5
23	Tu 5	7 ·81	5 ·05	6
24	We 6	8 ·76	6 ·06	7
25	Th 7	9 ·70	7 ·04	8
26	Fr 8	10 ·63	8 ·00 / 9 ·95	9
27	Sa 9	11 ·54	10 ·89	10
28	Su 10	12 ·45	11 ·83	11
29	Mo 11	13 ·35	12 ·76	12
30	Tu 12	14 ·25	13 ·69	13
1	We ○ 13	P ·15	14 ·62	14
2	Th 14	1 ·05 / 2 ·96	15 ·56	15
3	Fr 15	3 ·88	16 ·52	16
4	Sa 16	4 ·83	17 ·48	17
5	Su 17	5 ·79	18 ·46	18
6	Mo 18	6 ·77	19 ·46	19
7	Tu 19	7 ·76	20 ·47	20
8	We 20	8 ·78	21 ·52	21
9	Th 21	9 ·81	22 ·58	22
10	Fr 22	10 ·87	23 ·66	23
11	Sa 23	11 ·95	24 ·75	24
12	Su 24	... ...	25 ·85	25
13	Mo 25	12 ·03	26 ·96	26
14	Tu 26	13 ·12	... ...	27
15	We 27	14 ·20	27 ·07	28
16	Th 28	A ·27	1 ·17	29
17	Fr 29	1 ·32	2 ·25	1
18	Sa 30	2 ·35	3 ·31	2

May (Virodhi Mesha—Chittirai; Virodhi Vrishabha—Vaikasi; Sukla; Vaisakha; Bahula; H. 1368 Rajab)

Cyclic Sidereal Year, Month and Day	Week-Day English Month and Day	Tithi Ending Moment	Nakshatra Ending Moment	Muhammadan Year, Month and Day
19	Su 1	3 ·37	4 ·35	3
20	Mo 2	4 ·36	5 ·38	4
21	Tu 3	5 ·34	6 ·38	5
22	We 4	6 ·29	7 ·37	6
23	Th 5	7 ·23	8 ·33	7
24	Fr 6	8 ·15	9 ·28	8
25	Sa 7	9 ·07 / 10 ·98	10 ·23	9
26	Su 8	11 ·88	11 ·17	10
27	Mo 9	12 ·78	12 ·10	11
28	Tu 10	13 ·67	13 ·03 / 14 ·97	12
29	We 11	14 ·57	15 ·91	13
30	Th 12	P ·48	16 ·85	14
31	Fr 13	1 ·41	17 ·81	15
1	Sa 14	2 ·36	18 ·79	16
2	Su 15	3 ·31	19 ·78	17
3	Mo 16	4 ·28	20 ·80	18
4	Tu 17	5 ·27	21 ·83	19
5	We 18	6 ·29	22 ·89	20
6	Th 19	7 ·33	23 ·96	21
7	Fr 20	8 ·38	... ...	22
8	Sa 21	9 ·45	24 ·05	23
9	Su 22	10 ·53	25 ·15	24
10	Mo 23	11 ·62	26 ·26	25
11	Tu 24	12 ·70	27 ·37	26
12	We 25	13 ·77	1 ·47	27
13	Th 26	14 ·82	2 ·55	28
14	Fr 27	A ·85	3 ·62	29
15	Sa 28	1 ·87	4 ·68	30
16	Su 29	2 ·86	5 ·70	1
17	Mo 30	3 ·85	6 ·71	2
18	Tu 31	4 ·80	7 ·69	3

June (Virodhi Mithuna—Ani; Sukla; Jyeshtha; Bahula; Ash. Suk.; H. 1368 Shaban; Ramzan)

Cyclic Sidereal Year, Month and Day	Week-Day English Month and Day	Tithi Ending Moment	Nakshatra Ending Moment	Muhammadan Year, Month and Day
19	We 1	5 ·74	8 ·66	4
20	Th 2	6 ·66	9 ·63	5
21	Fr 3	7 ·57	10 ·57	6
22	Sa 4	8 ·47	11 ·51	7
23	Su 5	9 ·37	12 ·44	8
24	Mo 6	10 ·27	13 ·37	9
25	Tu 7	11 ·17	14 ·31	10
26	We 8	12 ·07 / 13 ·98	15 ·25	11
27	Th 9	14 ·91	16 ·19	12
28	Fr 10	P ·85	17 ·14	13
29	Sa 11	1 ·80	18 ·11	14
30	Su 12	2 ·77	19 ·10	15
31	Mo 13	3 ·75	20 ·12	16
32	Tu 14	4 ·77	21 ·15	17
1	We 15	5 ·80	22 ·20	18
2	Th 16	6 ·86	23 ·26	19
3	Fr 17	7 ·93	24 ·35	20
4	Sa 18	... ...	25 ·45	21
5	Su 19	8 ·01	26 ·56	22
6	Mo 20	9 ·09	27 ·67	23
7	Tu 21	10 ·17	1 ·77	24
8	We 22	11 ·24	2 ·86	25
9	Th 23	12 ·30	3 ·94	26
10	Fr 24	13 ·34	4 ·99	27
11	Sa 25	14 ·35	... ...	28
12	Su 26	A ·35	5 ·02	29
13	Mo 27	1 ·32	6 ·03	1
14	Tu 28	2 ·28	7 ·02	2
15	We 29	3 ·22	8 ·00 / 9 ·96	3
16	Th 30	4 ·14	10 ·91	4

Naksh:—1. Asvn. 2. Bhar. 3. Krit. 4. Rohi. 5. Mrig. 6. Ardh. 7. Punar. 8. Push. 9. Aslesh. 10. Magh. 11. P. Phal. 12. U. Phal. 13. Hasta. 14. Chit.

A. D. 1949. Kollam 1125, { N. Malabar—Sept. Hijra 1369, Vikrama 2006.
A.—Amavasya. Commences { S. Malabar—Aug. Commences, Oct. 24. Bengal San 1355.
P.—Paurnami. (N. Cycle) Subhakrit.

Columns: SOLAR reckoning (Cyclic Sidereal Year, Month and Day; Week-Day English Month and Day) — LUNAR reckoning (Tithi Ending Moment; Nakshatra Ending Moment; Muhammadan Year, Month and Day).

July — Solar: Virodhi *Mithuna—Ani.* (to 31), Virodhi *Karkata—Adi.* (from 1). Lunar: *Sukla* Ashadha, *Bahula*, *Sukla*. Muhammadan: H. 1368 *Ramzan.*

Cyclic Sidereal	Week-Day	Day	Tithi	Moment	Nakshatra	Moment	Muhammadan
17	Fr	1	5 / 6	·06 / ·96	11	·85	5
18	Sa	2	7	·86	12	·78	6
19	Su	3	8	·76	13	·71	7
20	Mo	4	9	·65	14	·64	8
21	Tu	5	10	·55	15	·58	9
22	We	6	11	·46	16	·52	10
23	Th	7	12	·38	17	·47	11
24	Fr	8	13	·32	18	·44	12
25	Sa	9	14	·28	19	·44	13
26	Su	10	P	·25	20	·44	14
27	Mo	11	1	·24	21	·46	15
28	Tu	12	2	·25	22	·50	16
29	We	13	3	·28	23	·57	17
30	Th	14	4	·33	24	·66	18
—31	Fr	15	5	·40	25	·76	19
1	Sa	16	6	·48	26	·86	20
2	Su	17	7	·56	27	·97	21
3	Mo	18	8	·64	...	...	22
4	Tu	19	9	·71	1	·07	23
5	We	20	10	·77	2	·17	24
6	Th	21	11	·81	3	·25	25
7	Fr	22	12	·83	4	·30	26
8	Sa	23	13	·83	5	·34	27
9	Su	24	14	·80	6	·35	28
10	Mo	25	—A	·76	7	·36	29
11	Tu	26	1	·70	8	·33	—30
12	We	27	2	·63	9	·29	1
13	Th	28	3	·54	10	·24	2
14	Fr	29	4	·45	11	·18	3
15	Sa	30	5	·35	12	·12	4
16	Su	31	6	·24	13 / 14	·05 / ·98	5

Aug. — Solar: Virodhi *Simha—Avani.* Lunar: Sravana, *Bahula*, Bhad. *Sukla*. Muhammadan: H. 1368 *Shawwal.*, H. 1368 *Zi-l-ka'da.*

Cyclic Sidereal	Week-Day	Day	Tithi	Moment	Nakshatra	Moment	Muhammadan
17	Mo	1	7	·14	15	·92	6
18	Tu	2	8 / 9	·04 / ·96	16	·86	7
19	We	3	10	·88	17	·81	8
20	Th	4	11	·81	18	·78	9
21	Fr	5	12	·76	19	·76	10
22	Sa	6	13	·73	20	·76	11
23	Su	7	14	·72	21	·78	12
24	Mo	8	P	·72	22	·81	13
25	Tu	9	1	·76	23	·88	14
26	We	10	2	·81	24	·96	15
27	Th	11	3	·88	...	...	16
28	Fr	12	4	·96	25	·06	17
29	Sa	13	...	...	26	·16	18
30	Su	14	5	·04	27	·26	19
31	Mo	15	6	·13	1	·37	20
—32	Tu	16	7	·20	2	·47	21
1	We	17	8	·26	3	·55	22
2	Th	18	9	·29	4	·61	23
3	Fr	19	10	·32	5	·65	24
4	Sa	20	11	·32	6	·68	25
5	Su	21	12	·30	7	·68	26
6	Mo	22	13	·26	8	·66	27
7	Tu	23	14	·20	9	·63	28
8	We	24	—A	·13	10	·58	—29
9	Th	25	1 / 2	·04 / ·95	11	·52	1
10	Fr	26	3	·85	12	·46	2
11	Sa	27	4	·75	13	·39	3
12	Su	28	5	·65	14	·32	4
13	Mo	29	6	·55	15	·25	5
14	Tu	30	7	·46	16	·19	6
15	We	31	8	·89	17	·15	7

Sep. — Solar: Virodhi *Simha—Avani.* (to 31), Virodhi *Kanya—Purattasi.* (from 1). Lunar: *Sukla* Bhadrapada, *Bahula*, *Sukla*. Muhammadan: H. 1368 *Zi-l-ka'da.*

Cyclic Sidereal	Week-Day	Day	Tithi	Moment	Nakshatra	Moment	Muhammadan
16	Th	1	9	·33	18	·11	8
17	Fr	2	10	·28	19	·09	9
18	Sa	3	11	·25	20	·03	10
19	Su	4	12	·24	21	·09	11
20	Mo	5	13	·24	22	·13	12
21	Tu	6	14	·27	23	·19	13
22	We	7	P	·32	24	·26	14
23	Th	8	1	·39	25	·35	15
24	Fr	9	2	·47	26	·46	16
25	Sa	10	3	·56	27	57	17
26	Su	11	4	·64	1	·68	18
27	Mo	12	5	·72	2	·77	19
28	Tu	13	6	·78	3	·85	20
29	We	14	7	·83	4	·92	21
30	Th	15	8	·86	5	·97	22
—31	Fr	16	9	·85	...	...	23
1	Sa	17	10	·84	6	·00	24
2	Su	18	11	·79	7 / 8	·01 / ·99	25
3	Mo	19	12	·73	9	·96	26
4	Tu	20	13	·66	10	·92	27
5	We	21	14	·57	11	·86	28
6	Th	22	—A	·48	12	·80	29
7	Fr	23	1	·39	13	·73	—30
8	Sa	24	2	·30	14	·66.	1
9	Su	25	3	·19	15	·60	2
10	Mo	26	4	·09	16	·54	3
11	Tu	27	5 / 6	·00 / ·98	17	·48	4
12	We	28	7	·87	18	·44	5
13	Th	29	8	·82	19	·41	6
14	Fr	30	9	·79	20	·40	7

Oct. — Solar: Virodhi *Tula—Aippasi.* Lunar: Asvina, *Bahula*, Karttika *Sukla*. Muhammadan: H. 1368 *Zi-l-hijja.*, H. 1369 *Muharram.*

Cyclic Sidereal	Week-Day	Day	Tithi	Moment	Nakshatra	Moment	Muhammadan
15	Sa	1	10	·78	21	·42	8
16	Su	2	11	·79	22	·45	9
17	Mo	3	12	·82	23	·50	10
18	Tu	4	13	·87	24	·57	11
19	We	5	14	·94	25	·66	12
20	Th	6	...	...	26	·76	13
21	Fr ○	7	P	·02	27	·87	14
22	Sa	8	1	·11	1	·98	15
23	Su	9	2	·20	...	...	16
24	Mo	10	3	·29	2	·08	17
25	Tu	11	4	·35	3	·16	18
26	We	12	5	·39	4	·23	19
27	Th	13	6	·42	5	·29	20
28	Fr	14	7	·41	6	·32	21
29	Sa	15	8	·40	7	·33	22
—30	Su	16	9	·36	8	·32	23
1	Mo	17	10	·31	9	·29	24
2	Tu	18	11	·23	10	·26	25
3	We	19	12	·14	11	·20	26
4	Th	20	13 / 14	·05 / ·96	12	·14	27
5	Fr	21	—A	·87	13	·07	28
6	Sa	22	1	·77	14 / 15	·00 / ·93	29
7	Su	23	2	·67	16	·87	—30
8	Mo	24	3	·58	17	·82	1
9	Tu	25	4	·51	18	·77	2
10	We	26	5	·45	19	·74	3
11	Th	27	6	·40	20	·73	4
12	Fr	28	7	·38	21	·74	5
13	Sa	29	8	·37	22	·76	6
14	Su	30	9	·38	23	·81	7
15	Mo	31	10	·41	24	·87	8

Nov. — Solar: Virodhi *Tula—Aippasi.* (to 30), Virodhi *Vrischika—Kartigai.* (from 1). Lunar: Karttika *Suk.*, *Bahula*, *Sukla*. Muhammadan: H. 1369 *Muharram.*

Cyclic Sidereal	Week-Day	Day	Tithi	Moment	Nakshatra	Moment	Muhammadan
16	Tu	1	11	·47	25	·96	9
17	We	2	12	·54	...	...	10
18	Th	3	13	·62	26	·06	11
19	Fr	4	14	·72	27	·17	12
20	Sa	5	P	·80	1	·28	13
21	Su	6	1	·88	2	·38	14
22	Mo	7	2	·94	3	·47	15
23	Tu	8	3	·99	4	·55	16
24	We	9	...	...	5	·60	17
25	Th	10	4	·02	6	·64	18
26	Fr	11	5	·01	7	·65	19
27	Sa	12	6 / 7	·00 / ·96	8	·64	20
28	Su	13	8	·91	9	·63	21
29	Mo	14	9	·84	10	·59	22
—30	Tu	15	10	·76	11	·54	23
1	We	16	11	·67	12	·48	24
2	Th	17	12	·57	13	·42	25
3	Fr	18	13	·47	14	·35	26
4	Sa	19	14	·37	15	·28	27
5	Su	20	—A	·28	16	·21	28
6	Mo	21	1	·20	17	·15	29
7	Tu	22	2	·13	18	·10	—30
8	We	23	3	·07	19	·07	1
9	Th	24	4 / 5	·02 / ·99	20	·06	2
10	Fr	25	6	·99	21	·06	3
11	Sa	26	...	...	22	·08	4
12	Su	27	7	·01	23	·12	5
13	Mo	28	8	·04	24	·18	6
14	Tu	29	9	·10	25	·27	7
15	We	30	10	·17	26	·36	8

Dec. — Solar: Virodhi *Dhanus—Margali.* Lunar: Margasira, *Bahula*, Pausha *Sukla*. Muhammadan: H. 1369 *Safar.*, H. 1369 *Rabi-ul-awwal.*

Cyclic Sidereal	Week-Day	Day	Tithi	Moment	Nakshatra	Moment	Muhammadan
16	Th	1	11	·26	27	·46	9
17	Fr	2	12	·35	1	·57	10
18	Sa	3	13	·43	2	·68	11
19	Su	4	14	·51	3	·78	12
20	Mo	5	P	·58	4	·86	13
21	Tu	6	1	·62	5	·92	14
22	We	7	2	·65	6	·95	15
23	Th	8	3	·65	7	·97	16
24	Fr	9	4	·63	8	·98	17
25	Sa	10	5	·59	9	·96	18
26	Su	11	6	·54	10	·92	19
27	Mo	12	7	·46	11	·87	20
28	Tu	13	8	·38	12	·81	21
—29	We	14	9	·29	13	·75	22
1	Th	15	10	·20	14	·69	23
2	Fr	16	11	·10	15	·62	24
3	Sa	17	12 / 13	·00 / ·91	16	·55	25
4	Su	18	14	·82	17	·49	26
5	Mo	19	—A	·75	18	·43	27
6	Tu	20	1	·70	19	·40	28
7	We	21	2	·66	20	·38	—29
8	Th	22	3	·63	21	·38	1
9	Fr	23	4	·64	22	·39	2
10	Sa	24	5	·66	23	·43	3
11	Su	25	6	·70	24	·49	4
12	Mo	26	7	·76	25	·57	5
13	Tu	27	8	·83	26	·66	6
14	We	28	9	·91	27	·76	7
15	Th	29	...	...	1	·87	8
16	Fr	30	10	·00	2	·98	9
17	Sa	31	11	·09	...	...	10

15. Svati. 16. Visak. 17. Anur. 18. Jyesh. 19. Mula. 20. P. Ash. 21. U. Ash. 22. Sravn. 23. Dani. 24. Şatab. 25 P. Bhad. 26. U. Bhad. 27. Rev.

A. D. 1950.
Solar Eclipse. ●
Lunar Eclipse. ○

Mesha Sankranti (Commencement of Indian Sidereal Year).
(Surya Sid.) April 13·56. **Saka 1872.** **Kaliyuga 5051.**
(Arya Sid.) April 13·43. **(S. Cycle) Vikrita.**

Jan. — Solar: Virodhi *Dhanus—Margali*; Virodhi *Makara—Tai*. Lunar: Pausha *Suk.*, *Bahula*, *Sukla*. Muhammadan: H. 1369 *Rabi-ul-awwal*.

SOLAR reckoning: Cyclic Sidereal Year, Month and Day	Week-Day English Month and Day		LUNAR reckoning: Tithi Ending Moment	Nakshatra Ending Moment	Muhammadan Year, Month and Day
18	Su	1	12 ·17	3 ·08	11
19	Mo	2	13 ·23	4 ·16	12
20	Tu	3	14 ·27	5 ·23	13
21	We	4	P ·29	6 ·27	14
22	Th	5	1 ·29	7 ·30	15
23	Fr	6	2 ·27	8 ·30	16
24	Sa	7	3 ·24	9 ·29	17
25	Su	8	4 ·18	10 ·26	18
26	Mo	9	5 ·11	11 ·21	19
27	Tu	10	6 ·03 / 7 ·94	12 ·15	20
28	We	11	8 ·84	13 ·09	21
29	Th	12	9 ·74	14 ·02 / 15 ·96	22
30	Fr	13	10 ·65	16 ·89	23
1	Sa	14	11 ·56	17 ·83	24
2	Su	15	12 ·47	18 ·78	25
3	Mo	16	13 ·40	19 ·74	26
4	Tu	17	14 ·34	20 ·71	27
5	We	18	A ·30	21 ·70	28
6	Th	19	1 ·28	22 ·71	29
7	Fr	20	2 ·28	23 ·75	30
8	Sa	21	3 ·29	24 ·80	1
9	Su	22	4 ·33	25 ·87	2
10	Mo	23	5 ·40	26 ·96	3
11	Tu	24	6 ·48	... ...	4
12	We	25	7 ·56	27 ·06	5
13	Th	26	8 ·65	1 ·17	6
14	Fr	27	9 ·74	2 ·28	7
15	Sa	28	10 ·81	3 ·38	8
16	Su	29	11 ·87	4 ·47	9
17	Mo	30	12 ·91	5 ·54	10
18	Tu	31	13 ·94	6 ·59	11

Feb. — Solar: Virodhi *Kumbha—Masi*. Lunar: Magha, *Bahula*, *Sukla*, Phalguna. Muhammadan: H. 1369 *Rabi-ul-akhir*; *Jumadal-awwal*.

Cyclic Sidereal Year, Month and Day	Week-Day English Month and Day		Tithi Ending Moment	Nakshatra Ending Moment	Muhammadan Year, Month and Day
19	We	1	14 ·93	7 ·62	12
20	Th	2	P ·91	8 ·63	13
21	Fr	3	1 ·87	9 ·62	14
22	Sa	4	2 ·81	10 ·59	15
23	Su	5	3 ·74	11 ·55	16
24	Mo	6	4 ·66	12 ·50	17
25	Tu	7	5 ·57	13 ·48	18
26	We	8	6 ·47	14 ·36	19
27	Th	9	7 ·37	15 ·29	20
28	Fr	10	8 ·27	16 ·23	21
29	Sa	11	9 ·18	17 ·17	22
1	Su	12	10 ·10	18 ·11	23
2	Mo	13	11 ·03 / 12 ·97	19 ·07	24
3	Tu	14	13 ·94	20 ·04	25
4	We	15	14 ·92	21 ·02	26
5	Th	16	A ·91	22 ·04	27
6	Fr	17	1 ·93	23 ·07	28
7	Sa	18	2 ·97	24 ·11	29
8	Su	19	... ...	25 ·18	1
9	Mo	20	3 ·08	26 ·26	2
10	Tu	21	4 ·10	27 ·37	3
11	We	22	5 ·19	1 ·48	4
12	Th	23	6 ·29	2 ·58	5
13	Fr	24	7 ·37	3 ·68	6
14	Sa	25	8 ·44	4 ·77	7
15	Su	26	9 ·50	5 ·85	8
16	Mo	27	10 ·58	6 ·91	9
17	Tu	28	11 ·55	7 ·94	10

March — Solar: Virodhi *Kumbha—Masi*; Virodhi *Mina—Panguni*. Lunar: Phalguna, *Bahula*, *Sukla*. Muhammadan: H. 1369 *Jumadal-awwal*.

Cyclic Sidereal Year, Month and Day	Week-Day English Month and Day		Tithi Ending Moment	Nakshatra Ending Moment	Muhammadan Year, Month and Day
18	We	1	12 ·55	8 ·95	11
19	Th	2	13 ·53	9 ·94	12
20	Fr	3	14 ·49	10 ·93	13
21	Sa	4	P ·48	11 ·89	14
22	Su	5	1 ·35	12 ·83	15
23	Mo	6	2 ·26	13 ·77	16
24	Tu	7	3 ·17	14 ·70	17
25	We	8	4 ·08 / 5 ·98	15 ·63	18
26	Th	9	6 ·88	16 ·57	19
27	Fr	10	7 ·79	17 ·51	20
28	Sa	11	8 ·70	18 ·45	21
29	Su	12	9 ·62	19 ·40	22
30	Mo	13	10 ·57	20 ·37	23
1	Tu	14	11 ·53	21 ·36	24
2	We	15	12 ·51	22 ·36	25
3	Th	16	13 ·50	23 ·38	26
4	Fr	17	14 ·53	24 ·42	27
5	Sa	18	A ·58	25 ·48	28
6	Su	19	1 ·64	26 ·57	29
7	Mo	20	2 ·72	27 ·67	30
8	Tu	21	3 ·80	1 ·77	1
9	We	22	4 ·89	2 ·88	2
10	Th	23	5 ·96	3 ·98	3
11	Fr	24	... ...	... ...	4
12	Sa	25	6 ·03	4 ·08	5
13	Su	26	7 ·09	5 ·16	6
14	Mo	27	8 ·13	6 ·22	7
15	Tu	28	9 ·14	7 ·26	8
16	We	29	10 ·13	8 ·27	9
17	Th	30	11 ·12	9 ·27	10
18	Fr	31	12 ·07	10 ·26	11

April — Solar: Vikrita *Mesha—Chittirai*. Lunar: Chaitra, *Bahula*, *Sukla*, Vaisakha. Muhammadan: H. 1369 *Jumadal-akhir*; H. 1369 *Rajab*.

Cyclic Sidereal Year, Month and Day	Week-Day English Month and Day		Tithi Ending Moment	Nakshatra Ending Moment	Muhammadan Year, Month and Day
19	Sa	1	13 ·01 / 14 ·93	11 ·22	12
20	Su ○	2	P ·85	12 ·17	13
21	Mo	3	1 ·75	13 ·11	14
22	Tu	4	2 ·65	14 ·05 / 15 ·98	15
23	We	5	3 ·55	16 ·91	16
24	Th	6	4 ·45	17 ·84	17
25	Fr	7	5 ·36	18 ·78	18
26	Sa	8	6 ·27	19 ·73	19
27	Su	9	7 ·19	20 ·70	20
28	Mo	10	8 ·13	21 ·68	21
29	Tu	11	9 ·10	22 ·68	22
30	We	12	10 ·07	23 ·69	23
1	Th	13	11 ·06	24 ·73	24
2	Fr	14	12 ·09	25 ·80	25
3	Sa	15	13 ·13	26 ·88	26
4	Su	16	14 ·19	27 ·97	27
5	Mo	17	A ·27	... ...	28
6	Tu	18	1 ·35	1 ·07	29
7	We	19	2 ·44	2 ·18	1
8	Th	20	3 ·52	3 ·29	2
9	Fr	21	4 ·58	4 ·39	3
10	Sa	22	5 ·63	5 ·47	4
11	Su	23	6 ·67	6 ·53	5
12	Mo	24	7 ·68	7 ·57	6
13	Tu	25	8 ·68	8 ·59	7
14	We	26	9 ·66	9 ·60	8
15	Th	27	10 ·61	10 ·59	9
16	Fr	28	11 ·55	11 ·55	10
17	Sa	29	12 ·47	12 ·50	11
18	Su	30	13 ·38	13 ·44	12

May — Solar: Vikrita *Mesha—Chittirai*; Vikrita *Vrishabha—Vaikasi*. Lunar: Vaisakha, *Bahula*, *Sukla*, Jyeshtha. Muhammadan: H. 1369 *Rajab*.

Cyclic Sidereal Year, Month and Day	Week-Day English Month and Day		Tithi Ending Moment	Nakshatra Ending Moment	Muhammadan Year, Month and Day
19	Mo	1	14 ·29	14 ·38	13
20	Tu	2	P ·19	15 ·32	14
21	We	3	1 ·09 / 2 ·99	16 ·25	15
22	Th	4	3 ·89	17 ·18	16
23	Fr	5	4 ·79	18 ·12	17
24	Sa	6	5 ·72	19 ·07	18
25	Su	7	6 ·66	20 ·03	19
26	Mo	8	7 ·63	21 ·01	20
27	Tu	9	8 ·60	22 ·00	21
28	We	10	9 ·59	23 ·02	22
29	Th	11	10 ·61	24 ·05	23
30	Fr	12	11 ·65	25 ·11	24
31	Sa	13	12 ·71	26 ·18	25
1	Su	14	13 ·78	27 ·27	26
2	Mo	15	14 ·86	1 ·37	27
3	Tu	16	A ·94	2 ·48	28
4	We	17	... ...	3 ·59	29
5	Th	18	1 ·03	4 ·69	30
6	Fr	19	2 ·10	5 ·77	1
7	Sa	20	3 ·15	6 ·84	2
8	Su	21	4 ·18	7 ·89	3
9	Mo	22	5 ·19	8 ·92	4
10	Tu	23	6 ·19	9 ·93	5
11	We	24	7 ·17	10 ·91	6
12	Th	25	8 ·13	11 ·88	7
13	Fr	26	9 ·06 / 10 ·98	12 ·84	8
14	Sa	27	11 ·89	13 ·79	9
15	Su	28	12 ·79	14 ·73	10
16	Mo	29	13 ·69	15 ·66	11
17	Tu	30	14 ·58	16 ·59	12
18	We	31	P ·48	17 ·52	13

June — Solar: Vikrita *Mithuna—Ani*. Lunar: *Bahula*, *Sukla*, Adh.—Ashadha. Muhammadan: H. 1369 *Shaban*; H. 1369 *Ramzan*.

Cyclic Sidereal Year, Month and Day	Week-Day English Month and Day		Tithi Ending Moment	Nakshatra Ending Moment	Muhammadan Year, Month and Day
19	Th	1	1 ·38	18 ·46	14
20	Fr	2	2 ·30	19 ·41	15
21	Sa	3	3 ·23	20 ·36	16
22	Su	4	4 ·16	21 ·33	17
23	Mo	5	5 ·12	22 ·32	18
24	Tu	6	6 ·10	23 ·34	19
25	We	7	7 ·09	24 ·37	20
26	Th	8	8 ·10	25 ·42	21
27	Fr	9	9 ·14	26 ·48	22
28	Sa	10	10 ·19	27 ·57	23
29	Su	11	11 ·26	1 ·67	24
30	Mo	12	12 ·34	2 ·78	25
31	Tu	13	13 ·42	3 ·89	26
32	We	14	14 ·50	4 ·99	27
1	Th	15	A ·57	... ...	28
2	Fr	16	1 ·63	5 ·08	29
3	Sa	17	2 ·67	6 ·15	1
4	Su	18	3 ·68	7 ·21	2
5	Mo	19	4 ·67	8 ·24	3
6	Tu	20	5 ·65	9 ·25	4
7	We	21	6 ·60	10 ·24	5
8	Th	22	7 ·54	11 ·21	6
9	Fr	23	8 ·47	12 ·18	7
10	Sa	24	9 ·38	13 ·13	8
11	Su	25	10 ·28	14 ·07	9
12	Mo	26	11 ·17	15 ·00 / 16 ·93	10
13	Tu	27	12 ·07 / 13 ·97	17 ·86	11
14	We	28	14 ·87	18 ·80	12
15	Th	29	P ·79	19 ·74	13
16	Fr	30	1 ·71	20 ·69	14

Naksh :—1. Asvn. 2. Bhar. 3. Krit. 4. Rohi. 5. Mrig. 6. Ardh. 7. Punar. 8. Push. 9. Aslesh. 10. Magh. 11. P. Phal. 12. U. Phal. 13. Hasta. 14. Chit.

A. D. 1950.
A.—Amavasya.
P.—Paurnami.

Kollam 1126, Commences { N. Malabar—Sept. / S. Malabar—Aug.

Hijra 1370, Commences, Oct. 13.

Vikrama 2007.
Bengal San 1356.
(N. Cycle) Sobhana.

SOLAR reckoning: Cyclic Sidereal Year, Month and Day; Week-Day English Month and Day. LUNAR reckoning: Tithi Ending Moment; Nakshatra Ending Moment; Muhammadan Year, Month and Day.

July — Cyclic: Vikrita Mithuna—Ani. / Vikrita Karkata—Adi. Tithi: Adhika Ashadha (Bahula, Sukla) / Nija Ashadha. Muhammadan: H. 1369 Ramzan. / H. 1369 Shawwal.

Cyclic Sidereal Year, Month and Day	Week-Day	English Day	Tithi	Tithi Ending Moment	Nakshatra	Nakshatra Ending Moment	Muhammadan Year, Month and Day
17	Sa	1	2	·64	21	·66	15
18	Su	2	3	·60	22	·65	16
19	Mo	3	4	·58	23	·66	17
20	Tu	4	5	·56	24	·68	18
21	We	5	6	·57	25	·72	19
22	Th	6	7	·61	26	·79	20
23	Fr	7	8	·67	27	·88	21
24	Sa	8	9	·74	1	·98	22
25	Su	9	10	·82	...	...	23
26	Mo	10	11	·90	2	·08	24
27	Tu	11	12	·98	3	·19	25
28	We	12	...	...	4	·29	26
29	Th	13	13	·05	5	·38	27
30	Fr	14	14	·11	6	·46	28
—31	Sa	15	—A	·14	7	·52	29
1	Su	16	1	·16	8	·56	—30
2	Mo	17	2	·15	9	·57	1
3	Tu	18	3	·13	10	·57	2
4	We	19	4	·08	11	·55	3
5	Th	20	5 / 6	·02 / ·95	12	·51	4
6	Fr	21	7	·87	13	·46	5
7	Sa	22	8	·77	14	·40	6
8	Su	23	9	·66	15	·33	7
9	Mo	24	10	·56	16	·26	8
10	Tu	25	11	·46	17	·20	9
11	We	26	12	·37	18	·14	10
12	Th	27	13	·28	19	·08	11
13	Fr	28	14	·19	20 / 21	·03 / ·99	12
14	Sa	29	P	·12	22	·98	13
15	Su	30	1	·07	23	·98	14
16	Mo	31	2	·05	...	...	15

Aug. — Cyclic: Vikrita Simha—Avani. Tithi: Bahula, Sukla, Sravana, Bah. Muhammadan: H. 1369 Zi-l-ka'da.

Cyclic Sidereal Year, Month and Day	Week-Day	English Day	Tithi	Tithi Ending Moment	Nakshatra	Nakshatra Ending Moment	Muhammadan Year, Month and Day
17	Tu	1	8	·04	24	·00	16
18	We	2	4	·06	25	·03	17
19	Th	3	5	·09	26	·09	18
20	Fr	4	6	·13	27	·18	19
21	Sa	5	7	·21	1	·28	20
22	Su	6	8	·29	2	·38	21
23	Mo	7	9	·38	3	·49	22
24	Tu	8	10	·46	4	·59	23
25	We	9	11	·53	5	·69	24
26	Th	10	12	·58	6	·77	25
27	Fr	11	13	·62	7	·83	26
28	Sa	12	14	·65	8	·87	27
29	Su	13	—A	·64	9	·89	28
30	Mo	14	1	·62	10	·90	—29
31	Tu	15	2	·58	11	·88	1
—32	We	16	3	·52	12	·85	2
1	Th	17	4	·45	13	·80	3
2	Fr	18	5	·36	14	·74	4
3	Sa	19	6	·26	15	·68	5
4	Su	20	7	·16	16	·61	6
5	Mo	21	8 / 9	·06 / ·96	17	·54	7
6	Tu	22	10	·86	18	·47	8
7	We	23	11	·78	19	·41	9
8	Th	24	12	·70	20	·36	10
9	Fr	25	13	·63	21	·33	11
10	Sa	26	14	·58	22	·31	12
11	Su	27	P	·56	23	·30	13
12	Mo	28	1	·54	24	·31	14
13	Tu	29	2	·55	25	·35	15
14	We	30	3	·59	26	·41	16
15	Th	31	4	·65	27	·49	17

Sep. — Cyclic: Vikrita Simha—Avani. / Vikrita Kanya—Purattasi. Tithi: Sravana (Bahula), Sukla, Bhadrapada. Muhammadan: H. 1369. Zi-l-ka'da. / H. 1369 Zi-l-hijja.

Cyclic Sidereal Year, Month and Day	Week-Day	English Day	Tithi	Tithi Ending Moment	Nakshatra	Nakshatra Ending Moment	Muhammadan Year, Month and Day
16	Fr	1	5	·72	1	·53	18
17	Sa	2	6	·80	2	·68	19
18	Su	3	7	·88	3	·79	20
19	Mo	4	8	·96	4	·90	21
20	Tu	5	...	...	...	...	22
21	We	6	9	·04	5	·00	23
22	Th	7	10	·10	6	·08	24
23	Fr	8	11	·14	7	·14	25
24	Sa	9	12	·16	8	·19	26
25	Su	10	13	·16	9	·22	27
26	Mo	11	14	·14	10	·23	28
27	Tu	12	—A	·10	11	·21	29
28	We	13	1 / 2	·04 / ·97	12	·18	—30
29	Th	14	3	·89	13	·13	1
30	Fr	15	4	·79	14	·08	2
—31	Sa	16	5	·69	15 / 16	·02 / ·95	3
1	Su	17	6	·59	17	·88	4
2	Mo	18	7	·49	18	·81	5
3	Tu	19	8	·39	19	·75	6
4	We	20	9	·30	20	·70	7
5	Th	21	10	·23	21	·66	8
6	Fr	22	11	·16	22	·63	9
7	Sa	23	12	·11	23	·62	10
8	Su	24	13	·09	24	·63	11
9	Mo	25	14	·09	25	·67	12
10	Tu ○	26	P	·10	26	·72	13
11	We	27	1	·13	27	·79	14
12	Th	28	2	·19	1	·88	15
13	Fr	29	3	·26	2	·98	16
14	Sa	30	4	·34	...	...	17

Oct. — Cyclic: Vikrita Tula—Aippasi. Tithi: Bahula, Sukla, Asvina, Bahula. Muhammadan: H. 1370 Muharram.

Cyclic Sidereal Year, Month and Day	Week-Day	English Day	Tithi	Tithi Ending Moment	Nakshatra	Nakshatra Ending Moment	Muhammadan Year, Month and Day
15	Su	1	5	·42	3	·09	18
16	Mo	2	6	·51	4	·20	19
17	Tu	3	7	·58	5	·30	20
18	We	4	8	·64	6	·38	21
19	Th	5	9	·69	7	·45	22
20	Fr	6	10	·71	8	·50	23
21	Sa	7	11	·71	9	·54	24
22	Su	8	12	·69	10	·55	25
23	Mo	9	13	·66	11	·54	26
24	Tu	10	14	·60	12	·51	27
25	We	11	—A	·53	13	·47	28
26	Th	12	1	·45	14	·42	—29
27	Fr	13	2	·35	15	·36	1
28	Sa	14	3	·25	16	·29	2
29	Su	15	4	·15	17	·22	3
—30	Mo	16	5 / 6	·05 / ·95	18	·15	4
1	Tu	17	7	·87	19	·09	5
2	We	18	8	·80	20 / 21	·04 / ·99	6
3	Th	19	9	·73	22	·96	7
4	Fr	20	10	·69	23	·94	8
5	Sa	21	11	·67	24	·96	9
6	Su	22	12	·67	25	·99	10
7	Mo	23	13	·68	...	...	11
8	Tu	24	14	·72	26	·03	12
9	We	25	P	·77	27	·09	13
10	Th	26	1	·84	1	·13	14
11	Fr	27	2	·92	2	·28	15
12	Sa	28	...	...	3	·39	16
13	Su	29	3	·01	4	·50	17
14	Mo	30	4	·11	5	·60	18
15	Tu	31	5	·18	6	·69	19

Nov. — Cyclic: Vikrita Tula—Aippasi. / Vikrita Vrischika—Kartigai. Tithi: Asvina (Bahula), Sukla, Kartika. Muhammadan: H. 1370 Muharram. / H. 1370 Safar.

Cyclic Sidereal Year, Month and Day	Week-Day	English Day	Tithi	Tithi Ending Moment	Nakshatra	Nakshatra Ending Moment	Muhammadan Year, Month and Day
16	We	1	6	·24	7	·76	20
17	Th	2	7	·28	8	·82	21
18	Fr	3	8	·30	9	·86	22
19	Sa	4	9	·31	10	·87	23
20	Su	5	10	·29	11	·86	24
21	Mo	6	11	·25	12	·84	25
22	Tu	7	12	·19	13	·81	26
23	We	8	13	·12	14	·76	27
24	Th	9	14 / A	·04 / ·95	15	·70	28
25	Fr	10	1	·85	16	·63	29
26	Sa	11	2	·75	17	·56	—30
27	Su	12	3	·65	18	·49	1
28	Mo	13	4	·56	19	·43	2
29	Tu	14	5	·48	20	·37	3
—30	We	15	6	·41	21	·32	4
1	Th	16	7	·34	22	·29	5
2	Fr	17	8	·29	23	·28	6
3	Sa	18	9	·28	24	·28	7
4	Su	19	10	·28	25	·30	8
5	Mo	20	11	·29	26	·34	9
6	Tu	21	12	·33	27	·40	10
7	We	22	13	·39	1	·48	11
8	Th	23	14	·47	2	·58	12
9	Fr	24	P	·55	3	·69	13
10	Sa	25	1	·64	4	·80	14
11	Su	26	2	·73	5	·90	15
12	Mo	27	3	·80	6	99	16
13	Tu	28	4	·86	...	...	17
14	We	29	5	·91	7	·08	18
15	Th	30	6	·94	8	·14	19

Dec. — Cyclic: Vikrita Dhanus—Margali. Tithi: Bahula, Sukla, Margasira, Bahula. Muhammadan: H. 1370 Rabi-ul-awwal.

Cyclic Sidereal Year, Month and Day	Week-Day	English Day	Tithi	Tithi Ending Moment	Nakshatra	Nakshatra Ending Moment	Muhammadan Year, Month and Day
16	Fr	1	7	·93	9	·17	20
17	Sa	2	8	·92	10	·19	21
18	Su	3	9	·87	11	·19	22
19	Mo	4	10	·81	12	·18	23
20	Tu	5	11	·74	13	·14	24
21	We	6	12	·66	14	·09	25
22	Th	7	13	·58	15 / 16	·03 / ·97	26
23	Fr	8	14	·48	17	·90	27
24	Sa	9	—A	·38	18	·83	28
25	Su	10	1	·28	19	·77	—29
26	Mo	11	2	·18	20	·71	1
27	Tu	12	3	·10	21	·65	2
28	We	13	4 / 5	·03 / ·98	22	·62	3
29	Th	14	6	·94	23	·60	4
—30	Fr	15	7	·92	24	·60	5
1	Sa	16	8	·92	25	·61	6
2	Su	17	9	·94	26	·65	7
3	Mo	18	10	·98	27	·71	8
4	Tu	19	...	...	1	·79	9
5	We	20	11	·04	2	·88	10
6	Th	21	12	·12	3	·98	11
7	Fr	22	13	·20	...	...	12
8	Sa	23	14	·29	4	·09	13
9	Su	24	P	·38	5	·20	14
10	Mo	25	1	·46	6	·30	15
11	Tu	26	2	·52	7	·38	16
12	We	27	3	·56	8	·45	17
13	Th	28	4	·58	9	·49	18
14	Fr	29	5	·57	10	·51	19
15	Sa	30	6	·56	11	·52	20
16	Su	31	7	·52	12	·51	21

15. Svati. 16. Visak. 17. Anur. 18. Jyesh. 19. Mula. 20. P. Ash. 21. U. Ash. 22. Sravn. 23. Dani. 24. Satab. 25. P. Bhad. 26. U. Bhad. 27. Rev.

A. D. 1951. **Mesha Sankranti** (Commencement of Indian Sidereal Year).
Solar Eclipse. ● **(Surya Sid.) April 13·82.** **Saka 1873.** **Kaliyuga 5052.**
Lunar Eclipse. ○ **(Arya Sid.) April 13·71.** **(S. Cycle) Khara.**

SOLAR reckoning: Cyclic Sidereal Year, Month and Day; Week-Day English Month and Day. LUNAR reckoning: Tithi Ending Moment; Nakshatra Ending Moment; Muhammadan Year, Month and Day.

Jan.

Cyclic Sidereal Year, Month and Day	Week-Day	English Day	Tithi	Tithi Ending Moment	Nakshatra	Nakshatra Ending Moment	Muhammadan Year, Month and Day
Vikrita Dhanus—Margali 17	Mo	1	Mar. Bah. 8	·46	13	·48	H. 1370 Rabi-ul-awwal 22
18	Tu	2	9	·38	14	·48	23
19	We	3	10	·30	15	·37	24
20	Th	4	11	·21	16	·31	25
21	Fr	5	12	·12	17	·24	26
22	Sa	6	13 14	·02 ·92	18	·17	27
23	Su	7	—A	·83	19	·10	28
24	Mo	8	1	·75	20 21	·04 ·99	29
25	Tu	9	2	·68	22	·96	—30
26	We	10	3	·62	23	·93	1
27	Th	11	4	·59	24	·92	2
28	Fr	12	5	·57	25	·93	3
—29	Sa	13	6	·56	26	·96	4
Vikrita Makara—Tai 1	Su	14	Pausha Sukla 7	·58	...	...	5
2	Mo	15	8	·62	27	·02	6
3	Tu	16	9	·69	1	·09	7
4	We	17	10	·77	2	·18	8
5	Th	18	11	·85	3	·28	9
6	Fr	19	12	·95	4	·39	10
7	Sa	20	...	...	5	·50	H. 1370 Rabi-ul-akhir 11
8	Su	21	13	·03	6	·60	12
9	Mo	22	14	·11	7	·69	13
10	Tu	23	P	·16	8	·76	14
11	We	24	1	·21	9	·80	15
12	Th	25	2	·22	10	·83	16
13	Fr	26	3	·21	11	·85	17
14	Sa	27	4	·20	12	·84	18
15	Su	28	5	·16	13	·81	19
16	Mo	29	6	·10	14	·76	20
17	Tu	30	7 8	·02 94	15	·71	21
18	We	31	9	·85	16	·65	22

Feb.

Cyclic Sidereal Year, Month and Day	Week-Day	English Day	Tithi	Tithi Ending Moment	Nakshatra	Nakshatra Ending Moment	Muhammadan Year, Month and Day
19	Th	1	Bahula 10	·75	17	·58	23
20	Fr	2	11	·65	18	·51	24
21	Sa	3	12	·55	19	·44	25
22	Su	4	13	46	20	·38	26
23	Mo	5	14	·38	21	·33	27
24	Tu	6	—A	·31	22	·29	28
25	We	7	1	·26	23	·26	—29
26	Th	8	2	·22	24	·24	1
27	Fr	9	3	·20	25	·25	2
28	Sa	10	4	·20	26	·28	3
29	Su	11	5	·23	27	·33	4
—30	Mo	12	6	·27	1	·40	5
Vikrita Kumbha—Masi 1	Tu	13	Magha Sukla 7	·33	2	·48	H. 1370 Jumadal-awwal 6
2	We	14	8	·40	3	·58	7
3	Th	15	9	·49	4	·69	8
4	Fr	16	10	·58	5	·80	9
5	Sa	17	11	·67	6	·90	10
6	Su	18	12	·74	7	·99	11
7	Mo	19	13	·80	...	...	12
8	Tu	20	14	·84	8	·06	13
9	We	21	P	·85	9	·12	14
10	Th	22	1	·83	10	·16	15
11	Fr	23	2	·82	11	·17	16
12	Sa	24	3	·78	12	·16	17
13	Su	25	4	·71	13	·14	18
14	Mo	26	5	·63	14	·10	19
15	Tu	27	Bahula 6	·55	15 16	·05 ·99	20
16	We	28	7	·46	17	·92	21

March

Cyclic Sidereal Year, Month and Day	Week-Day	English Day	Tithi	Tithi Ending Moment	Nakshatra	Nakshatra Ending Moment	Muhammadan Year, Month and Day
Vikrita Kumbha—Masi 17	Th	1	Mag. Bah. 8	·37	18	·85	Jumadal-awwal 22
18	Fr	2	9	·27	19	·78	23
19	Sa	3	10	·17	20	·72	24
20	Su	4	11 12	·07 ·98	21	·67	25
21	Mo	5	13	·91	22	·62	26
22	Tu	6	14	·86	23	·58	27
23	We	7	—A	·83	24	·57	28
24	Th	8	1	·81	25	·58	29
25	Fr	9	2	·81	26	·60	—30
26	Sa	10	3	·84	27	·64	1
27	Su	11	4	·88	1	·70	2
28	Mo	12	5	·94	2	·78	3
—29	Tu	13	...	...	3	·88	4
Vikrita Mina—Panguni 1	We	14	Phalguna Sukla 6	·01	4	·99	H. 1370 Jumadal-akhir 5
2	Th	15	7	·10	...	...	6
3	Fr	16	8	·19	5	·10	7
4	Sa	17	9	·27	6	·20	8
5	Su	18	10	·33	7	·29	9
6	Mo	19	11	·39	8	·37	10
7	Tu	20	12	·44	9	·44	11
8	We	21	13	·45	10	·48	12
9	Th	22	14	·44	11	·49	13
10	Fr	23	P	·41	12	·49	14
11	Sa	24	1	·37	13	·47	15
12	Su	25	2	·30	14	·44	16
13	Mo	26	3	·23	15	·39	17
14	Tu	27	4	·14	16	·33	18
15	We	28	Bahula 5 6	·04 ·94	17	·26	19
16	Th	29	7	·84	18	·19	20
17	Fr	30	8	·74	19	·12	21
18	Sa	31	9	·65	20	·06	22

April

Cyclic Sidereal Year, Month and Day	Week-Day	English Day	Tithi	Tithi Ending Moment	Nakshatra	Nakshatra Ending Moment	Muhammadan Year, Month and Day
19	Su	1	10	·57	21 22	·00 ·95	23
20	Mo	2	11	·50	23	·91	24
21	Tu	3	12	·44	24	·90	25
22	We	4	13	·40	25	·90	26
23	Th	5	14	·38	26	·91	27
24	Fr	6	—A	·38	27	·95	28
25	Sa	7	1	·41	...	...	—29
26	Su	8	2	·45	1	·01	1
27	Mo	9	3	·51	2	·10	2
28	Tu	10	4	·59	3	·19	3
29	We	11	5	·67	4	·29	4
30	Th	12	6	·75	5	·40	5
—31	Fr	13	Chaitra Sukla 7	·83	6	·50	H. 1370 Rajab 6
Khara Mesha—Chittirai 1	Sa	14	8	·89	7	·60	7
2	Su	15	9	·95	8	·69	8
3	Mo	16	10	·99	9	·75	9
4	Tu	17	...	...	10	·79	10
5	We	18	11 12	·00 ·99	11	·81	11
6	Th	19	13	·96	12	·81	12
7	Fr	20	14	·92	13	·80	13
8	Sa	21	P	·85	14	·77	14
9	Su	22	1	·77	15	·72	15
10	Mo	23	2	·68	16	·66	16
11	Tu	24	3	·59	17	·60	17
12	We	25	4	·49	18	·54	18
13	Th	26	5	·39	19	·47	19
14	Fr	27	Bahula 6	·29	20	·40	20
15	Sa	28	7	·19	21	·34	21
16	Su	29	8	·10	22	·28	22
17	Mo	30	9 10	·03 ·98	23	·25	23

May

Cyclic Sidereal Year, Month and Day	Week-Day	English Day	Tithi	Tithi Ending Moment	Nakshatra	Nakshatra Ending Moment	Muhammadan Year, Month and Day
Khara Mesha—Chittirai 18	Tu	1	Ch. Bah. 11	·94	24	·23	Rajab 24
19	We	2	12	·92	25	·22	25
20	Th	3	13	·91	26	·23	26
21	Fr	4	14	·93	27	·26	27
22	Sa	5	—A	·97	1	·32	28
23	Su	6	...	...	2	·40	29
24	Mo	7	1	·03	3	·49	—30
25	Tu	8	2	·11	4	·59	1
26	We	9	3	·19	5	·70	2
27	Th	10	4	·27	6	·81	3
28	Fr	11	5	·35	7	·91	4
29	Sa	12	6	·42	8	·99	5
30	Su	13	Vaisakha Sukla 7	·48	...	...	H. 1370 Shaban 6
—31	Mo	14	8	·51	9	·06	7
Khara Vrishabha—Vaikasi 1	Tu	15	9	·51	10	·11	8
2	We	16	10	·50	11	·13	9
3	Th	17	11	·48	12	·15	10
4	Fr	18	12	·44	13	·13	11
5	Sa	19	13	·37	14	·10	12
6	Su	20	14	·28	15	·06	13
7	Mo	21	P	·19	16 17	·00 ·94	14
8	Tu	22	1	·10	18	·88	15
9	We	23	2 3	·00 ·90	19	·81	16
10	Th	24	4	·80	20	·74	17
11	Fr	25	5	·70	21	·67	18
12	Sa	26	6	·61	22	·62	19
13	Su	27	Bahula 7	·54	23	·58	20
14	Mo	28	8	·48	24	·55	21
15	Tu	29	9	·43	25	·54	22
16	We	30	10	·42	26	·55	23
17	Th	31	11	·40	27	·58	24

June

Cyclic Sidereal Year, Month and Day	Week-Day	English Day	Tithi	Tithi Ending Moment	Nakshatra	Nakshatra Ending Moment	Muhammadan Year, Month and Day
18	Fr	1	12	·43	1	·64	25
19	Sa	2	13	·48	2	·71	26
20	Su	3	14	·54	3	·79	27
21	Mo	4	—A	·60	4	·89	28
22	Tu	5	1	·68	5	·99	—29
23	We	6	2	·77	...	...	1
24	Th	7	3	·85	6	·10	2
25	Fr	8	4	·91	7	·21	3
26	Sa	9	5	·96	8	·30	4
27	Su	10	Jyeshtha Sukla ...	...	9	·37	5
28	Mo	11	6	·00	10	42	6
29	Tu	12	7 8	·00 ·99	11	·46	7
30	We	13	9	·97	12	·47	8
—31	Th	14	10	·92	13	·46	H. 1370 Ramzan 9
Khara Mithuna—Ani 1	Fr	15	11	·86	14	·43	10
2	Sa	16	12	·78	15	·39	11
3	Su	17	13	·69	16	·34	12
4	Mo	18	14	·59	17	·28	13
5	Tu	19	P	·49	18	·21	14
6	We	20	1	·39	19	·14	15
7	Th	21	2	·29	20	·07	16
8	Fr	22	3	·19	21 22	·01 ·96	17
9	Sa	23	4	·10	23	·91	18
10	Su	24	Bahula 5 6	·02 ·96	24	·88	19
11	Mo	25	7	·92	25	·87	20
12	Tu	26	8	·89	26	·87	21
13	We	27	9	·88	27	·90	22
14	Th	28	10	·91	1	·95	23
15	Fr	29	11	·95	...	...	24
16	Sa	30	...	...	2	·01	25

Naksh:—1. Asvn. 2. Bhar. 3. Krit. 4. Rohi. 5. Mrig. 6. Ardh. 7. Punar. 8. Push. 9. Asesh. 10. Magh. 11. P. Phal. 12. U. Phal. 13. Hasta. 14. Chit.

A. D. 1951.
A.—Amavasya.
P.—Paurnami.

Kollam 1127, Commences { **N. Malabar—Sept.** / **S. Malabar—Aug.**

Hijra 1371, Commences, **Oct. 2.**

Vikrama 2008.
Bengal San 1357.
(N. Cycle) Krodhin.

SOLAR reckoning: Cyclic Sidereal Year, Month and Day; Week-Day, English Month and Day. LUNAR reckoning: Tithi Ending Moment; Nakshatra Ending Moment; Muhammadan Year, Month and Day.

July

Solar month	Cyclic Sidereal Day	Week-Day	Eng. Day	Paksha / Lunar month	Tithi	Nakshatra	Muh. month	Muh. Day
Khara *Mithuna—Ani.*	17	Su	1	*Bah.*	12 ·00	3 ·09	*Ramzan.*	26
	18	Mo	2		13 ·07	4 ·19		27
	19	Tu	3		14 ·15	5 ·30		28
	20	We	4		—A ·23	6 ·41		29
	21	Th	5		1 ·31	7 ·51		—30
	22	Fr	6		2 ·38	8 ·60		1
	23	Sa	7		3 ·43	9 ·68		2
	24	Su	8		4 ·47	10 ·74		3
	25	Mo	9		5 ·48	11 ·78		4
	26	Tu	10		6 ·47	12 ·79		5
	27	We	11	*Sukla*	7 ·44	13 ·79		6
	28	Th	12		8 ·40	14 ·76		7
	29	Fr	13		9 ·34	15 ·72		8
	30	Sa	14		10 ·26	16 ·68		9
	31	Su	15		11 ·17	17 ·62		10
	—32	Mo	16		{ 12 ·07 13 ·97	18 ·55		11
Khara *Karkata—Adi.*	1	Tu	17	Ashadha	14 ·87	19 ·48	H. 1370 *Shawwal.*	12
	2	We	18		P ·77	20 ·41		13
	3	Th	19		1 ·67	21 ·35		14
	4	Fr	20		2 ·58	22 ·30		15
	5	Sa	21		3 ·50	23 ·25		16
	6	Su	22		4 ·44	24 ·21		17
	7	Mo	23		5 ·40	25 ·19		18
	8	Tu	24	*Bahula*	6 ·37	26 ·20		19
	9	We	25		7 ·37	27 ·22		20
	10	Th	26		8 ·39	1 ·26		21
	11	Fr	27		9 ·42	2 ·31		22
	12	Sa	28		10 ·47	3 ·39		23
	13	Su	29		11 ·54	4 ·49		24
	14	Mo	30		12 ·62	5 ·60		25
	15	Tu	31		13 ·70	6 ·71		26

Aug.

Solar month	Cyclic Sidereal Day	Week-Day	Eng. Day	Paksha / Lunar month	Tithi	Nakshatra	Muh. month	Muh. Day
	16	We	1		14 ·78	7 ·81		27
	17	Th	2		—A ·85	8 ·90		28
	18	Fr	3		1 ·92	9 ·99		—29
	19	Sa	4		2 ·95	... ...		1
	20	Su	5		3 ·96	10 ·05		2
	21	Mo	6		4 ·96	11 ·09		3
	22	Tu	7		5 ·93	12 ·11		4
	23	We	8		6 ·89	13 ·11		5
	24	Th	9		7 ·83	14 ·09		6
	25	Fr	10	*Sukla*	8 ·76	15 ·07		7
	26	Sa	11		9 ·67	{ 16 ·02 17 ·96		8
	27	Su	12		10 ·57	18 ·89		9
	28	Mo	13	Sravana	11 ·47	19 ·82		10
	29	Tu	14		12 ·37	20 ·75		11
	30	We	15		13 ·27	21 ·69		12
	—31	Th	16		14 ·18	22 ·63	H. 1370 *Zi-l-ka'da.*	13
Khara *Simha—Avani.*	1	Fr	17		P [illegible]	23 ·58		14
	2	Sa	18		{ 1 ·01 2 ·94	24 ·54		15
	3	Su	19		3 ·89	25 ·52		16
	4	Mo	20		4 ·87	26 ·52		17
	5	Tu	21		5 ·87	27 ·53		18
	6	We	22		6 ·88	1 ·57		19
	7	Th	23		7 ·91	2 ·63		20
	8	Fr	24	*Bahula*	8 ·97	3 ·71		21
	9	Sa	25		... ...	4 ·80		22
	10	Su	26		9 ·05	5 ·90		23
	11	Mo	27		10 ·13	... ...		24
	12	Tu	28		11 ·21	6 ·00		25
	13	We	29		12 ·29	7 ·10		26
	14	Th	30		13 ·36	8 ·21		27
	15	Fr	31		14 ·42	9 ·30		28

Sep.

Solar month	Cyclic Sidereal Day	Week-Day	Eng. Day	Paksha / Lunar month	Tithi	Nakshatra	Muh. month	Muh. Day
Khara *Simha—Avani.*	16	Sa ●	1		—A ·45	10 ·36		29
	17	Su	2		1 ·48	11 ·41		—30
	18	Mo	3		2 ·47	12 ·43		1
	19	Tu	4		3 ·44	13 ·44		2
	20	We	5		4 ·40	14 ·43		3
	21	Th	6	*Sukla*	5 ·34	15 ·40		4
	22	Fr	7		6 ·27	16 ·35		5
	23	Sa	8		7 ·19	17 ·29		6
	24	Su	9		{ 8 ·09 9 ·99	18 ·23		7
	25	Mo	10		10 ·89	19 ·17		8
	26	Tu	11		11 ·79	20 ·10		9
	27	We	12		12 ·69	{ 21 ·03 22 ·97		10
	28	Th	13	Bhadrapada	13 ·61	23 ·91		11
	29	Fr	14		14 ·54	24 ·88		12
	30	Sa	15		P ·48	25 ·85		13
	—31	Su	16		1 ·43	26 ·84	H. 1370 *Zi-l-hijja.*	14
Khara *Kanya—Purattasi.*	1	Mo	17		2 ·40	27 ·85		15
	2	Tu	18		3 ·39	1 ·88		16
	3	We	19		4 ·40	2 ·94		17
	4	Th	20		5 ·44	... ...		18
	5	Fr	21		6 ·50	3 ·01		19
	6	Sa	22	*Bahula*	7 ·57	4 ·10		20
	7	Su	23		8 ·65	5 ·20		21
	8	Mo	24		9 ·74	6 ·30		22
	9	Tu	25		10 ·82	7 ·41		23
	10	We	26		11 ·90	8 ·52		24
	11	Th	27		12 ·96	9 ·60		25
	12	Fr	28		13 ·99	10 ·67		26
	13	Sa	29		... ...	11 ·72		27
	14	Su	30		14 ·01	12 ·75		28

Oct.

Solar month	Cyclic Sidereal Day	Week-Day	Eng. Day	Paksha / Lunar month	Tithi	Nakshatra	Muh. month	Muh. Day
	15	Mo	1		{ A ·01 1 ·99	13 ·77		—29
	16	Tu	2		2 ·95	14 ·76		1
	17	We	3		3 ·89	15 ·73		2
	18	Th	4		4 ·82	16 ·69		3
	19	Fr	5		5 ·74	17 ·64		4
	20	Sa	6		6 ·65	18 ·58		5
	21	Su	7	*Sukla*	7 ·55	19 ·51		6
	22	Mo	8		8 ·45	20 ·44		7
	23	Tu	9		9 ·35	21 ·37		8
	24	We	10		10 ·26	22 ·30		9
	25	Th	11		11 ·18	23 ·25		10
	26	Fr	12		12 ·10	24 ·21		11
	27	Sa	13		{ 13 ·04 14 ·99	25 ·18		12
	28	Su	14	Asvina	P ·97	26 ·16	H. 1371 *Muharram.*	13
	29	Mo	15		1 ·96	27 ·17		14
	30	Tu	16		2 ·98	1 ·19		15
	—31	We	17		... ...	2 ·25		16
Khara *Tula—Aippasi.*	1	Th	18		3 ·02	3 ·31		17
	2	Fr	19		4 ·07	4 ·40		18
	3	Sa	20		5 ·14	5 ·49		19
	4	Su	21		6 ·23	6 ·60		20
	5	Mo	22		7 ·32	7 ·71		21
	6	Tu	23	*Bahula*	8 ·41	8 ·82		22
	7	We	24		9 ·49	9 ·91		23
	8	Th	25		10 ·54	10 ·98		24
	9	Fr	26		11 ·58	... ...		25
	10	Sa	27		12 ·60	11 ·03		26
	11	Su	28		13 ·59	12 ·07		27
	12	Mo	29		14 ·58	13 ·09		28
	13	Tu	30		—A ·54	14 ·08		29
	14	We	31		1 ·48	15 ·06		—30

Nov.

Solar month	Cyclic Sidereal Day	Week-Day	Eng. Day	Paksha / Lunar month	Tithi	Nakshatra	Muh. month	Muh. Day
Khara *Tula—Aippasi.*	15	Th	1		2 ·41	{ 16 ·02 17 ·97		1
	16	Fr	2	*Sukla*	3 ·33	18 ·91		2
	17	Sa	3		4 ·24	19 ·85		3
	18	Su	4		5 ·14	20 ·78		4
	19	Mo	5		{ 6 ·04 7 ·94	21 ·71		5
	—20	Tu	6		8 ·85	22 ·65		6
	21	We	7		9 ·77	23 ·59		7
	22	Th	8		10 ·70	24 ·54		8
	23	Fr	9		11 ·64	25 ·51		9
	24	Sa	10		12 ·59	26 ·49		10
	25	Su	11	Karttika	13 ·57	27 ·49	H. 1371 *Safar.*	11
	26	Mo	12		14 ·56	1 ·52		12
	27	Tu	13		P ·59	2 ·56		13
	28	We	14		1 ·63	3 ·62		14
	29	Th	15		2 ·69	4 ·70		15
	—30	Fr	16		3 ·76	5 ·80		16
Khara *Vrischika—Kartigai.*	1	Sa	17		4 ·85	6 ·91		17
	2	Su	18		5 ·94	... ...		18
	3	Mo	19		... ...	7 ·02		19
	4	Tu	20		6 ·02	8 ·12		20
	5	We	21	*Bahula*	7 ·10	9 ·21		21
	6	Th	22		8 ·16	10 ·29		22
	7	Fr	23		9 ·21	11 ·36		23
	8	Sa	24		10 ·22	12 ·39		24
	9	Su	25		11 ·22	13 ·41		25
	10	Mo	26		12 ·19	14 ·41		26
	11	Tu	27		13 ·15	15 ·39		27
	12	We	28		14 ·10	16 ·36		28
	13	Th	29		{ A ·03 1 ·95	17 ·31		—29
	14	Fr	30		2 ·86	18 ·25		1

Dec.

Solar month	Cyclic Sidereal Day	Week-Day	Eng. Day	Paksha / Lunar month	Tithi	Nakshatra	Muh. month	Muh. Day
	15	Sa	1		3 ·76	19 ·18		2
	16	Su	2		4 ·66	20 ·11		3
	17	Mo	3		5 ·56	{ 21 ·05 22 ·99		4
	18	Tu	4		6 ·46	23 ·93		5
	19	We	5	*Sukla*	7 ·38	24 ·87		6
	20	Th	6		8 ·31	25 ·84		7
	21	Fr	7		9 ·26	26 ·81		8
	22	Sa	8		10 ·22	27 ·82		9
	23	Su	9		11 ·20	1 ·83		10
	24	Mo	10	Margasira	12 ·20	2 ·87		11
	25	Tu	11		13 ·23	3 ·93		12
	26	We	12		14 ·27	... ...		13
	27	Th	13		P ·33	4 ·00		14
	28	Fr	14		1 ·41	5 ·10		15
	—29	Sa	15		2 ·50	6 ·21	H. 1371 *Rabi-ul-awwal.*	16
Khara *Dhanus—Margali.*	1	Su	16		3 ·59	7 ·31		17
	2	Mo	17		4 ·68	8 ·42		18
	3	Tu	18		5 ·75	9 ·51		19
	4	We	19		6 ·80	10 ·60		20
	5	Th	20		7 ·84	11 ·67		21
	6	Fr	21	*Bahula*	8 ·86	12 ·71		22
	7	Sa	22		9 ·86	13 ·73		23
	8	Su	23		10 ·83	14 ·73		24
	9	Mo	24		11 ·80	15 ·72		25
	10	Tu	25		12 ·74	16 ·69		26
	11	We	26		13 ·67	17 ·65		27
	12	Th	27		14 ·59	18 ·59		28
	13	Fr	28		—A ·50	19 ·52		29
	14	Sa	29	P. Suk.	1 ·40	20 ·45		—30
	15	Su	30		2 ·30	21 ·38		1
	16	Mo	31		3 ·20	22 ·32		2

15. Svati. **16.** Visak. **17.** Anur. **18.** Jyesh. **19.** Mula. **20.** P. Ash. **21.** U. Ash. **22.** Sravn. **23.** Dani. **24.** Satab. **25.** P. Bhad. **26.** U. Bhad. **27.** Rev.

A. D. 1952. | **Mesha Sankranti** (Commencement of Indian Sidereal Year).
Solar Eclipse. ● | (Surya Sid.) April 13·08. | Saka 1874. | Kaliyuga 5053.
Lunar Eclipse. ○ | (Arya Sid.) April 12·07. | (S. Cycle) Nandana.

Jan.

SOLAR reckoning: Cyclic Sidereal Year, Month and Day	Week-Day English Month and Day	LUNAR reckoning: Tithi Ending Moment	Nakshatra Ending Moment	Muhammadan Year, Month and Day
17	Tu 1	4 ·11	23 ·26	3
18	We 2	5 ·03 6 ·96	24 ·21	4
19 *Khara Dhanus—Margali.*	Th 3	*Sukla* 7 ·90	25 ·17	5
20	Fr 4	8 ·86	26 ·15	6
21	Sa 5	9 ·85	27 ·14	7
22	Su 6	10 ·85	1 ·15	8
23	Mo 7	11 ·87	2 ·18	9
24	Tu 8	12 ·92	3 ·23	10
25	We 9	13 ·98	4 ·31	11
26	Th 10	... ...	5 ·40	12
27	Fr 11	**Pausha** 14 ·06	6 ·50	13
28	Sa 12	P ·15	7 ·61	14
—29	Su 13	1 ·24	8 ·72	15
1	Mo 14	2 ·32	9 ·82	16
2	Tu 15	3 ·39	10 ·91	17
3	We 16	4 ·45	11 ·98	18
4	Th 17	5 ·49	... ...	H. 1371 *Rabi-ul-akhir.* 19
5	Fr 18	6 ·50	12 ·02	20
6	Sa 19	*Bahula* 7 ·51	13 ·05	21
7	Su 20	8 ·48	14 ·06	22
8	Mo 21	9 ·44	15 ·06	23
9	Tu 22	10 ·38	16 ·03 17 ·98	24
10	We 23	11 ·31	18 ·93	25
11	Th 24	12 ·22	19 ·87	26
12	Fr 25	13 ·13	20 ·80	27
13	Sa 26	14 ·03 A ·93	21 ·73	28
14 *Khara Makara—Tai.*	Su 27	1 ·83	22 ·66	—29
15	Mo 28	2 ·74	23 ·60	1
16	Tu 29	3 ·66	24 ·54	2
17	We 30	4 ·60	25 ·51	3
18	Th 31	5 ·55	26 ·48	4

Feb.

SOLAR reckoning: Cyclic Sidereal Year, Month and Day	Week-Day English Month and Day	LUNAR reckoning: Tithi Ending Moment	Nakshatra Ending Moment	Muhammadan Year, Month and Day
19	Fr 1	6 ·50	27 ·46	5
20	Sa 2	7 ·48	1 ·47	6
21	Su 3	*Sukla* 8 ·49	2 ·50	7
22	Mo 4	9 ·52	3 ·55	8
23	Tu 5	10 ·57	4 ·62	9
24	We 6	11 ·63	5 ·70	10
25	Th 7	12 ·71	6 ·80	11
26	Fr 8	13 ·79	7 ·91	12
27	Sa 9	**Magha** 14 ·88	... ...	13
28	Su ○ 10	P ·96	8 ·02	14
29	Mo 11	... ...	9 ·12	15
—30	Tu 12	1 ·03	10 ·21	16
1	We 13	2 ·09	11 ·28	H. 1371 *Jumadal-awwal.* 17
2	Th 14	3 ·13	12 ·34	18
3	Fr 15	4 ·14	13 ·37	19
4	Sa 16	5 ·13	14 ·39	20
5	Su 17	*Bahula* 6 ·11	15 ·38	21
6	Mo 18	7 ·06	16 ·36	22
7	Tu 19	8 ·00 9 ·98	17 ·31	23
8 *Khara Kumbha—Masi.*	We 20	10 ·84	18 ·26	24
9	Th 21	11 ·75	19 ·21	25
10	Fr 22	12 ·65	20 ·14	26
11	Sa 23	13 ·55	21 ·07	27
12	Su 24	14 ·45	22 ·01 23 ·95	28
13	Mo ● 25	—A ·36	24 ·89	29
14	Tu 26	1 ·28	25 ·84	—30
15	We 27	**P.** *Suk.* 2 ·21	26 ·80	1
16	Th 28	3 ·16	27 ·79	2
17	Fr 29	4 ·12	1 ·79	3

March

SOLAR reckoning: Cyclic Sidereal Year, Month and Day	Week-Day English Month and Day	LUNAR reckoning: Tithi Ending Moment	Nakshatra Ending Moment	Muhammadan Year, Month and Day
18	Sa 1	5 ·11	2 ·82	4
19	Su 2	6 ·11	3 ·86	5
20	Mo 3	*Sukla* 7 ·14	4 ·92	6
21	Tu 4	8 ·19	... ...	7
22 *Khara Kumbha—Masi.*	We 5	9 ·24	5 ·01	8
23	Th 6	10 ·32	6 ·10	9
24	Fr 7	11 ·41	7 ·21	10
25	Sa 8	12 ·51	8 ·32	11
26	Su 9	13 ·59	9 ·42	12
27	Mo 10	14 ·66	10 ·52	13
28	Tu 11	**Phalguna** P ·70	11 ·59	14
29	We 12	1 ·73	12 ·65	15
30	Th 13	2 ·74	13 ·70	16
—31	Fr 14	3 ·78	14 ·71	H. 1371 *Jumadal-akhir.* 17
1	Sa 15	4 ·70	15 ·71	18
2	Su 16	5 ·66	16 69	19
3	Mo 17	6 ·60	17 ·65	20
4	Tu 18	*Bahula* 7 ·53	18 ·61	21
5	We 19	8 ·44	19 ·55	22
6	Th 20	9 ·34	20 ·48	23
7	Fr 21	10 ·24	21 ·41	24
8	Sa 22	11 ·14	22 ·34	25
9	Su 23	12 ·04 13 ·95	23 ·28	26
10	Mo 24	14 ·87	24 ·22	27
11	Tu 25	—A ·80	25 ·17	28
12	We 26	1 ·74	26 ·13	—29
13 *Khara Mina—Panguni.*	Th 27	2 ·70	27 ·11	1
14	Fr 28	3 ·69	1 ·11	2
15	Sa 29	4 ·69	2 ·13	3
16	Su 30	5 ·72	3 ·17	4
17	Mo 31	6 ·76	4 ·23	5

April

SOLAR reckoning: Cyclic Sidereal Year, Month and Day	Week-Day English Month and Day	LUNAR reckoning: Tithi Ending Moment	Nakshatra Ending Moment	Muhammadan Year, Month and Day
18	Tu 1	*Sukla* 7 ·82	5 ·31	6
19	We 2	8 ·90	6 ·40	7
20	Th 3	9 ·99	7 ·51	8
21	Fr 4	... ...	8 ·62	9
22	Sa 5	10 ·03	9 ·72	10
23	Su 6	11 ·15	10 ·82	11
24	Mo 7	12 ·22	11 ·90	12
25	Tu 8	13 ·27	12 ·97	13
26	We 9	**Chaitra** 14 ·31	... ...	H. 1371 *Rajab* 14
27	Th 10	P ·30	13 ·01	15
28	Fr 11	1 ·28	14 ·03	16
—29	Sa 12	2 ·26	15 ·03	17
1	Su 13	3 ·22	16 ·01 17 ·99	18
2	Mo 14	4 ·16	18 ·94	19
3	Tu 15	5 ·08 6 ·99	19 ·88	20
4	We 16	*Bahula* 7 ·90	20 ·82	21
5	Th 17	8 ·80	21 ·76	22
6	Fr 18	9 ·70	22 ·69	23
7	Sa 19	10 ·60	23 ·62	24
8 *Nandana Mesha—Chittirai.*	Su 20	11 ·50	24 ·56	25
9	Mo 21	12 ·41	25 ·50	26
10	Tu 22	13 ·33	26 ·46	27
11	We 23	14 ·28	27 ·44	28
12	Th 24	—A ·25	1 ·44	29
13	Fr 25	1 ·23	2 ·45	—30
14	Sa 26	2 ·23	3 ·48	1
15	Su 27	**Vaisak.** *Suk.* 3 ·26	4 ·54	*Shaban.* 2
16	Mo 28	4 ·30	5 ·61	3
17	Tu 29	5 ·36	6 ·71	4
18	We 30	6 ·43	7 ·81	5

May

SOLAR reckoning: Cyclic Sidereal Year, Month and Day	Week-Day English Month and Day	LUNAR reckoning: Tithi Ending Moment	Nakshatra Ending Moment	Muhammadan Year, Month and Day
19	Th 1	*Sukla* 7 ·52	8 ·92	6
20	Fr 2	8 ·61	... ...	7
21	Sa 3	9 ·68	9 ·02	8
22	Su 4	10 ·75	10 ·12	9
23	Mo 5	11 ·79	11 ·21	10
24 *Nandana Mesha—Chittirai.*	Tu 6	12 ·82	12 ·28	11
25	We 7	13 ·83	13 ·33	12
26	Th 8	14 ·83	14 ·35	13
27	Fr 9	**Vaisakha** P ·80	15 ·36	14
28	Sa 10	1 ·75	16 ·34	15
29	Su 11	2 ·68	17 ·32	16
30	Mo 12	3 ·60	18 ·28	17
—31	Tu 13	4 ·51	19 ·22	18
1	We 14	5 ·41	20 ·16	H. 1371 *Shaban.* 19
2	Th 15	6 ·31	21 ·09	20
3	Fr 16	*Bahula* 7 ·21	22 ·02 23 ·96	21
4	Sa 17	8 ·11	24 ·90	22
5	Su 18	9 ·01 10 ·92	25 ·84	23
6	Mo 19	11 ·85	26 ·79	24
7	Tu 20	12 ·80	27 ·77	25
8	We 21	13 ·76	1 ·76	26
9	Th 22	14 ·73	2 ·77	27
10	Fr 23	—A ·73	3 ·80	28
11	Sa 24	1 ·75	4 ·85	—29
12	Su 25	2 ·80	5 ·92	1
13 *Nandana Vrishabha—Vaikasi.*	Mo 26	3 ·86	... ...	2
14	Tu 27	4 ·93	6 ·01	3
15	We 28	... ...	7 ·11	4
16	Th 29	5 ·01	8 ·22	5
17	Fr 30	*Sukla* 6 ·09	9 ·33	6
18	Sa 31	7 ·17	10 ·43	7

June

SOLAR reckoning: Cyclic Sidereal Year, Month and Day	Week-Day English Month and Day	LUNAR reckoning: Tithi Ending Moment	Nakshatra Ending Moment	Muhammadan Year, Month and Day
19	Su 1	8 ·24	11 ·52	8
20	Mo 2	9 ·29	12 ·59	9
21	Tu 3	10 ·32	13 ·64	10
22	We 4	11 ·33	14 ·67	11
23	Th 5	12 ·32	15 ·68	12
24	Fr 6	13 ·29	16 ·68	13
25	Sa 7	**Jyeshtha** 14 ·25	17 ·65	H. 1371 *Ramzan.* 14
26	Su 8	P ·18	18 ·61	15
27	Mo 9	1 ·10	19 ·55	16
28	Tu 10	2 ·01 3 ·91	20 ·49	17
29	We 11	4 ·81	21 ·43	18
30	Th 12	5 ·71	22 ·36	19
—31	Fr 13	6 ·61	23 ·29	20
1	Sa 14	7 ·51	24 ·23	21
2	Su 15	*Bahula* 8 ·42	25 ·17	22
3	Mo 16	9 ·35	26 ·13	23
4	Tu 17	10 ·29	27 ·10	24
5	We 18	11 ·24	1 ·09	25
6	Th 19	12 ·22	2 ·09	26
7 *Nandana Mithuna—Ani.*	Fr 20	13 ·22	3 ·11	27
8	Sa 21	14 ·23	4 ·17	28
9	Su 22	—A ·27	5 ·23	29
10	Mo 23	1 ·33	6 ·31	—30
11	Tu 24	2 ·41	7 ·41	1
12	We 25	3 ·49	8 ·51	2
13	Th 26	**Ashadha** *Sukla* 4 ·57	9 ·62	*Shawwal.* 3
14	Fr 27	5 ·65	10 ·73	4
15	Sa 28	6 ·71	11 ·82	5
16	Su 29	7 ·77	12 ·90	6
17	Mo 30	8 ·80	13 ·95	7

Naksh :—1. Asvn. 2. Bhar. 3. Krit. 4. Rohi. 5. Mrig. 6. Ardh. 7. Punar. 8. Push. 9. Aslesh. 10. Magh. 11. P. Phal. 12. U. Phal. 13. Hasta. 14. Chit.

A. D. 1952.	Kollam 1128,	N. Malabar—Sept.	Hijra 1372,	Vikrama 2009.
A.—Amavasya.	Commences	S. Malabar—Aug.	Commences, Sep. 21.	Bengal San 1358.
P.—Paurnami.				(N. Cycle) Visvavasu.

Columns: SOLAR reckoning — Cyclic Sidereal Year, Month and Day; Week-Day English Month and Day. LUNAR reckoning — Tithi Ending Moment; Nakshatra Ending Moment; Muhammadan Year, Month and Day.

July

Solar month	Cyclic Sidereal Day	Week-Day	Day	Lunar month / Paksha	Tithi	Ending Moment	Nakshatra	Ending Moment	Muhammadan month	Muhammadan Day
	18	Tu	1	Sukla	9	·81	14	·99		8
	19	We	2		10	·80	...	...		9
	20	Th	3		11	·77	15	·01		10
	21	Fr	4		12	·72	16 / 17	·01 / ·98		11
Nandana Mithuna—Ani.	22	Sa	5	Ashadha	13	·66	18	·94		12
	23	Su	6		14	·58	19	·89		13
	24	Mo	7		P	·48	20	·83		14
	25	Tu	8		1	·38	21	·77	H. 1371 Shawwal.	15
	26	We	9		2	·28	22	·70		16
	27	Th	10		3	·18	23	·63		17
	28	Fr	11		4 / 5	·08 / ·98	24	·56		18
	29	Sa	12	Bahula	6	·90	25	·51		19
	30	Su	13		7	·83	26	·47		20
	31	Mo	14		8	·77	27	·43		21
	—32	Tu	15		9	·72	1	·41		22
	1	We	16		10	·70	2	·41		23
	2	Th	17		11	·69	3	·44		24
	3	Fr	18		12	·71	4	·48		25
	4	Sa	19		13	·75	5	·54		26
	5	Su	20		14	·81	6	·61		27
	6	Mo	21		—A	·88	7	·71		28
	7	Tu	22		1	·96	8	·82		—29
	8	We	23		...	...	9	·93		1
	9	Th	24		2	·04	...	...		2
Nandana Karkata—Adi.	10	Fr	25		3	·12	10	·03		3
	11	Sa	26		4	·19	11	·12		4
	12	Su	27		5	·23	12	·20		5
	13	Mo	28		6	·27	13	·26		6
	14	Tu	29	Sukla	7	·29	14	·31		7
	15	We	30		8	·27	15	·33		8
	16	Th	31		9	·25	16	·33		9

Aug.

Solar month	Cyclic Sidereal Day	Week-Day	Day	Lunar month / Paksha	Tithi	Ending Moment	Nakshatra	Ending Moment	Muhammadan month	Muhammadan Day
	17	Fr	1		10	·21	17	·31	H. 1371 Zi-l-ka'da.	10
	18	Sa	2		11	·15	18	·28		11
	19	Su	3	Sravana	12 / 13	·07 / ·98	19	·24		12
	20	Mo	4		14	·88	20	·18		13
	21	Tu ○	5		P	·78	21	·11		14
	22	We	6		1	·68	22 / 23	·04 / ·97		15
	23	Th	7		2	·58	24	·91		16
	24	Fr	8		3	·48	25	·85		17
	25	Sa	9		4	·39	26	·80		18
	26	Su	10		5	·32	27	·76		19
	27	Mo	11	Bahula	6	·26	1	·73		20
	28	Tu	12		7	·21	2	·73		21
	29	We	13		8	·19	3	·75		22
	30	Th	14		9	·18	4	·79		23
	—31	Fr	15		10	·20	5	·84		24
	1	Sa	16		11	·24	6	·92		25
	2	Su	17		12	·30	...	...		26
	3	Mo	18		13	·37	7	·01		27
	4	Tu	19		14	·45	8	·11		28
	5	We	20		—A	·54	9	·22		29
Nandana Simha—Avani.	6	Th	21		1	·62	10	·33		—30
	7	Fr	22	Sukla	2	·68	11	·43	H. 1371 Zi-l-hijja.	1
	8	Sa	23		3	·73	12	·51		2
	9	Su	24	Bhadrapada	4	·77	13	·58		3
	10	Mo	25		5	·79	14	·63		4
	11	Tu	26		6	·78	15	·65		5
	12	We	27		7	·76	16	·66		6
	13	Th	28		8	·72	17	·64		7
	14	Fr	29		9	·65	18	·62		8
	15	Sa	30		10	·57	19	·57		9
	16	Su	31		11	·49	20	·51		10

Sep.

Solar month	Cyclic Sidereal Day	Week-Day	Day	Lunar month / Paksha	Tithi	Ending Moment	Nakshatra	Ending Moment	Muhammadan month	Muhammadan Day
	17	Mo	1	Suk.	12	·39	21	·45		11
	18	Tu	2		13	·29	22	·39		12
	19	We	3		14	·19	23	·32		13
	20	Th	4		P	·09	24	·25		14
Nandana Simha—Avani.	21	Fr	5	Bhadrapada	1 / 2	·00 / ·91	25	·19		15
	22	Sa	6		3	·84	26	·13	H. 1371 Zi-l-hijja.	16
	23	Su	7		4	·78	27	·09		17
	24	Mo	8		5	·73	1	·06		18
	25	Tu	9		6	·71	2	·06		19
	26	We	10		7	·70	3	·07		20
	27	Th	11		8	·72	4	·10		21
	28	Fr	12		9	·76	5	·15		22
	29	Sa	13		10	·82	6	·22		23
	30	Su	14	Bahula	11	·89	7	·32		24
	—31	Mo	15		12	·97	8	·42		25
	1	Tu	16		...	...	9	·52		26
	2	We	17		13	·06	10	·63		27
	3	Th	18		14	·14	11	·73		28
	4	Fr	19		—A	·21	12	·82		29
	5	Sa	20		1	·26	13	·89		—30
	6	Su	21		2	·30	14	·94		1
	7	Mo	22		3	·31	15	·97		2
	8	Tu	23		4	·32	16	·98		3
	9	We	24		5	·30	17	·98		4
Nandana Kanya—Purattasi.	10	Th	25		6	·26	18	·95		5
	11	Fr	26	Sukla	7	·19	19	·91		6
	12	Sa	27		8	·11	20	·85		7
	13	Su	28		9 / 10	·03 / ·94	21	·79		8
	14	Mo	29		11	·84	22	·73		9
	15	Tu	30		12	·74	23	·66		10

Oct.

Solar month	Cyclic Sidereal Day	Week-Day	Day	Lunar month / Paksha	Tithi	Ending Moment	Nakshatra	Ending Moment	Muhammadan month	Muhammadan Day
	16	We	1	Asvina	13	·64	24	·59	H. 1372 Muharram.	11
	17	Th	2		14	·54	25	·53		12
	18	Fr	3		P	·46	26	·47		13
	19	Sa	4		1	·39	27	·42		14
	20	Su	5		2	·33	1	·40		15
	21	Mo	6		3	·28	2	·38		16
	22	Tu	7		4	·26	3	·39		17
	23	We	8		5	·26	4	·41		18
	24	Th	9		6	·28	5	·46		19
	25	Fr	10	Bahula	7	·32	6	·53		20
	26	Sa	11		8	·38	7	·62		21
	27	Su	12		9	·45	8	·72		22
	28	Mo	13		10	·53	9	·82		23
	29	Tu	14		11	·62	10	·93		24
	30	We	15		12	·71	...	...		25
	—31	Th	16		13	·78	11	·04		26
	1	Fr	17		14	·84	12	·13		27
	2	Sa	18		—A	·87	13	·20		28
	3	Su	19		1	·89	14	·25		29
	4	Mo	20		2	·89	15	·29		—30
	5	Tu	21		3	·87	16	·30		1
	6	We	22		4	·83	17	·30		2
Nandana Tula—Aippasi.	7	Th	23	Sukla	5	·77	18	·28	H. 1372 Safar.	3
	8	Fr	24		6	·70	19	·24		4
	9	Sa	25		7	·61	20	·19		5
	10	Su	26		8	·52	21	·13		6
	11	Mo	27	Karttika	9	·42	22	·07		7
	12	Tu	28		10	·32	23 / 24	·00 / ·93		8
	13	We	29		11	·22	25	·86		9
	14	Th	30		12	·13	26	·80		10
	15	Fr	31		13 / 14	·05 / ·98	27	·76		11

Nov.

Solar month	Cyclic Sidereal Day	Week-Day	Day	Lunar month / Paksha	Tithi	Ending Moment	Nakshatra	Ending Moment	Muhammadan month	Muhammadan Day
	16	Sa	1	Karttika	P	·91	1	·73		12
	17	Su	2		1	·87	2	·71		13
	18	Mo	3		2	·86	3	·71		14
	19	Tu	4		3	·86	4	·73		15
Nandana Tula—Aippasi.	20	We	5		4	·88	5	·78		16
	21	Th	6		5	·92	6	·84	H. 1372 Safar.	17
	22	Fr	7		6	·98	7	·92		18
	23	Sa	8		...	...	...	...		19
	24	Su	9	Bahula	7	·06	8	·01		20
	25	Mo	10		8	·15	9	·12		21
	26	Tu	11		9	·24	10	·23		22
	27	We	12		10	·32	11	·34		23
	28	Th	13		11	·39	12	·43		24
	29	Fr	14		12	·45	13	·51		25
	—30	Sa	15		13	·50	14	·57		26
	1	Su	16		14	·51	15	·60		27
	2	Mo	17		—A	·50	16	·63		28
	3	Tu	18		1	·48	17	·63		—29
	4	We	19		2	·44	18	·61		1
	5	Th	20		3	·38	19	·57		2
	6	Fr	21		4	·31	20	·52		3
	7	Sa	22		5	·23	21	·46		4
	8	Su	23		6	·14	22	·40		5
Nandana Vrischika—Kartigai.	9	Mo	24	Sukla	7 / 8	·04 / ·94	23	·83		6
	10	Tu	25		9	·84	24	·26		7
	11	We	26		10	·75	25	·20		8
	12	Th	27		11	·67	26	·14		9
	13	Fr	28		12	·59	27	·09		10
	14	Sa	29		13	·54	1	·06		11
	15	Su	30		14	·50	2	·03		12

Dec.

Solar month	Cyclic Sidereal Day	Week-Day	Day	Lunar month / Paksha	Tithi	Ending Moment	Nakshatra	Ending Moment	Muhammadan month	Muhammadan Day
	16	Mo	1	Margasira	P	·49	3	·03	H. 1372 Rabi-ul-awwal.	13
	17	Tu	2		1	·50	4	·05		14
	18	We	3		2	·52	5	·09		15
	19	Th	4		3	·56	6	·15		16
	20	Fr	5		4	·62	7	·22		17
	21	Sa	6		5	·70	8	·31		18
	22	Su	7		6	·78	9	·42		19
	23	Mo	8		7	·87	10	·53		20
	24	Tu	9	Bahula	8	·96	11	·64		21
	25	We	10		...	...	12	·73		22
	26	Th	11		9	·03	13	·81		23
	27	Fr	12		10	·09	14	·88		24
	28	Sa	13		11	·13	15	·93		25
	—29	Su	14		12	·15	16	·95		26
	1	Mo	15		13	·14	17	·95		27
	2	Tu	16		14	·12	18	·94		28
	3	We	17		—A	·07	19	·91		29
	4	Th	18		1 / 2	·01 / ·94	20	·87		—30
Nandana Dhanus—Margali.	5	Fr	19		3	·86	21	·81	H. 1372 Rabi-ul-akhir.	1
	6	Sa	20		4	·77	22	·74		2
	7	Su	21		5	·67	23	·67		3
	8	Mo	22		6	·57	24	·60		4
	9	Tu	23	Sukla	7	·47	25	·54		5
	10	We	24		8	·38	26	·48		6
	11	Th	25		9	·30	27	·43		7
	12	Fr	26		10	·23	1	·39		8
	13	Sa	27		11	·18	2	·36		9
	14	Su	28	Pausha	12	·15	3	·36		10
	15	Mo	29		13	·14	4	·37		11
	16	Tu	30		14	·14	5	·40		12
	17	We	31		P	·16	6	·45		13

15. Svati. 16. Visak. 17. Anur. 18. Jyesh. 19. Mula. 20. P. Ash. 21. U. Ash. 22. Sravn. 23. Dani. 24. Satab. 25. P. Bhad. 26. U. Bhad. 27. Rev.

A. D. 1953.
Solar Eclipse. ●
Lunar Eclipse. ○

Mesha Sankranti (Commencement of Indian Sidereal Year)
(Surya Sid.) April 13·33.
(Arya Sid.) April 13·22.

Saka 1875.
(S. Cycle) Vijaya.

Kaliyuga 5054.

Column groups: SOLAR reckoning (Cyclic Sidereal Year, Month and Day; Week-Day, English Month and Day) — LUNAR reckoning (Tithi Ending Moment; Nakshatra Ending Moment; Muhammadan Year, Month and Day).

Jan. (Solar: Nandana, Dhanus—Margali; then Nandana, Makara—Tai. Lunar: Pausha, Bahula; Sukla; Magha. Muhammadan: H 1372 Rabi-ul-akhir; Jumadal-awwal.)

Cyclic Sidereal Year, Month and Day	Week-Day	English Day	Tithi	Ending Moment	Nakshatra	Ending Moment	Muhammadan Year, Month and Day
18	Th	1	1	·20	7	·52	14
19	Fr	2	2	·26	8	·61	15
20	Sa	3	3	·34	9	·72	16
21	Su	4	4	·43	10	·83	17
22	Mo	5	5	·52	11	·94	18
23	Tu	6	6	·61	...	...	19
24	We	7	7	·69	12	·03	20
25	Th	8	8	·75	13	·12	21
26	Fr	9	9	·79	14	·20	22
27	Sa	10	10	·80	15	·24	23
28	Su	11	11	·79	16	·27	24
29	Mo	12	12	·77	17	·28	25
—30	Tu	13	13	·72	18	·27	26
1	We	14	14	·66	19	·25	27
2	Th	15	—A	·59	20	·20	28
3	Fr	16	1	·51	21	·14	—29
4	Sa	17	2	·41	22	·08	1
5	Su	18	3	·31	23 / 24	·01 / ·94	2
6	Mo	19	4	·21	25	·88	3
7	Tu	20	5	·11	26	·82	4
8	We	21	6 / 7	·02 / ·94	27	·76	5
9	Th	22	8	·88	1	·72	6
10	Fr	23	9	·82	2	·69	7
11	Sa	24	10	·79	3	·68	8
12	Su	25	11	·78	4	·69	9
13	Mo	26	12	·78	5	·72	10
14	Tu	27	13	·80	6	·76	11
15	We	28	14	·85	7	·88	12
16	Th ○	29	P	·92	8	·92	13
17	Fr	30	...	...	...	...	14
18	Sa	31	1	·00	9	·02	15

Feb. (Solar: Nandana, Kumbha—Masi. Lunar: Bahula; Sukla; Phalguna. Muhammadan: H. 1372; H. 1372 Jumadal-akhir.)

Cyclic Sidereal Year, Month and Day	Week-Day	English Day	Tithi	Ending Moment	Nakshatra	Ending Moment	Muhammadan Year, Month and Day
19	Su	1	2	·09	10	·13	16
20	Mo	2	3	·18	11	·23	17
21	Tu	3	4	·26	12	·33	18
22	We	4	5	·34	13	·43	19
23	Th	5	6	·39	14	·50	20
24	Fr	6	7	·43	15	·56	21
25	Sa	7	8	·45	16	·59	22
26	Su	8	9	·43	17	·60	23
27	Mo	9	10	·40	18	·60	24
28	Tu	10	11	·35	19	·58	25
—29	We	11	12	·28	20	·53	26
1	Th	12	13	·21	21	·48	27
2	Fr	13	14	·13	22	·42	28
3	Sa ●	14	A / 1	·03 / ·93	23	·36	29
4	Su	15	2	·83	24	·29	—30
5	Mo	16	3	·73	25	·22	1
6	Tu	17	4	·61	26	·15	2
7	We	18	5	·56	27	·09	3
8	Th	19	6	·49	1	·05	4
9	Fr	20	7	·44	2	·02	5
10	Sa	21	8	·41	3	·01	6
11	Su	22	9	·40	4	·01	7
12	Mo	23	10	·41	5	·03	8
13	Tu	24	11	·43	6	·07	9
14	We	25	12	·47	7	·15	10
15	Th	26	13	·54	8	·23	11
16	Fr	27	14	·62	9	·32	12
17	Sa	28	P	·72	10	·42	13

March (Solar: Nandana, Kumbha—Masi; then Nandana, Mina—Panguni. Lunar: Phalguna, Bahula; Sukla; Chaitra. Muhammadan: H. 1372 Jumadal-akhir; Rajab.)

Cyclic Sidereal Year, Month and Day	Week-Day	English Day	Tithi	Ending Moment	Nakshatra	Ending Moment	Muhammadan Year, Month and Day
18	Su	1	1	·80	11	·53	14
19	Mo	2	2	·88	12	·64	15
20	Tu	3	3	·95	13	·74	16
21	We	4	...	...	14	·81	17
22	Th	5	4	·00	15	·87	18
23	Fr	6	5	·04	16	·91	19
24	Sa	7	6	·05	17	·93	20
25	Su	8	7	·04	18	·93	21
26	Mo	9	8 / 9	01 / ·96	19	·91	22
27	Tu	10	10	·89	20	·87	23
28	We	11	11	·81	21	·82	24
29	Th	12	12	·73	22	·76	25
—30	Fr	13	13	·63	23	·70	26
1	Sa	14	14	·53	24	·63	27
2	Su	15	—A	·43	25	·56	28
3	Mo	16	1	·33	26	·49	—29
4	Tu	17	2	·24	27	·43	1
5	We	18	3	·16	1	·39	2
6	Th	19	4	·09	2	·35	3
7	Fr	20	5	·04	3	·33	4
8	Sa	21	6 / 7	·01 / ·99	4	·33	5
9	Su	22	...	...	5	·34	6
10	Mo	23	8	·00	6	·39	7
11	Tu	24	9	·03	7	·45	8
12	We	25	10	·07	8	·53	9
13	Th	26	11	13	9	·62	10
14	Fr	27	12	·21	10	·72	11
15	Sa	28	13	·30	11	·83	12
16	Su	29	14	·39	12	·94	13
17	Mo	30	P	·47	...	...	14
18	Tu	31	1	·53	13	·04	15

April (Solar: Vijaya, Mesha—Chittirai. Lunar: Bahula; Adhika Vaisakha, Sukla. Muhammadan: H. 1372; H. 1372 Shaban.)

Cyclic Sidereal Year, Month and Day	Week-Day	English Day	Tithi	Ending Moment	Nakshatra	Ending Moment	Muhammadan Year, Month and Day
19	We	1	2	·59	14	·12	16
20	Th	2	3	·62	15	·18	17
21	Fr	3	4	·63	16	·23	18
22	Sa	4	5	·61	17	·25	19
23	Su	5	6	·57	18	·25	20
24	Mo	6	7	·53	19	·23	21
25	Tu	7	8	·47	20	·20	22
26	We	8	9	·39	21	·15	23
27	Th	9	10	·30	22	·10	24
28	Fr	10	11	·20	23 / 24	·04 / ·97	25
29	Sa	11	12 / 13	·09 / ·99	25	·90	26
—30	Su	12	14	·89	26	·88	27
1	Mo	13	—A	·80	27	·77	28
2	Tu	14	1	·72	1	·72	29
3	We	15	2	·65	2	·68	—30
4	Th	16	3	·60	3	·66	1
5	Fr	17	4	·56	4	·65	2
6	Sa	18	5	·54	5	·67	3
7	Su	19	6	·55	6	·70	4
8	Mo	20	7	·58	7	·76	5
9	Tu	21	8	·62	8	·83	6
10	We	22	9	·68	9	·92	7
11	Th	23	10	·76	...	...	8
12	Fr	24	11	·85	10	·03	9
13	Sa	25	12	·93	11	·14	10
14	Su	26	...	...	12	·24	11
15	Mo	27	13	·00	13	·34	12
16	Tu	28	14	·07	14	·42	13
17	We	29	P	·13	15	·49	14
18	Th	30	1	·15	16	·55	15

May (Solar: Vijaya, Mesha—Chittirai; then Vijaya, Vrishabha—Vaikasi. Lunar: Adh. Vak., Bahula; Nija Vaisakha, Sukla. Muhammadan: H. 1372 Shaban; Ramzan.)

Cyclic Sidereal Year, Month and Day	Week-Day	English Day	Tithi	Ending Moment	Nakshatra	Ending Moment	Muhammadan Year, Month and Day
19	Fr	1	2	·16	17	·57	16
20	Sa	2	3	·15	18	·58	17
21	Su	3	4	·12	19	·56	18
22	Mo	4	5 / 6	·06 / ·99	20	·53	19
23	Tu	5	7	·91	21	·50	20
24	We	6	8	·82	22	·44	21
25	Th	7	9	·72	23	·37	22
26	Fr	8	10	·62	24	·30	23
27	Sa	9	11	·52	25	·23	24
28	Su	10	12	·42	26	·17	25
29	Mo	11	13	·32	27	·11	26
30	Tu	12	14	·24	1	·06	27
—31	We	13	—A	·17	2 / 3	·01 / ·98	28
1	Th	14	1	·12	4	·98	—29
2	Fr	15	2	·08	5	·99	1
3	Sa	16	3	·06	...	...	2
4	Su	17	4	·07	6	·02	3
5	Mo	18	5	·10	7	·07	4
6	Tu	19	6	·14	8	·14	5
7	We	20	7	·19	9	·22	6
8	Th	21	8	·27	10	·33	7
9	Fr	22	9	·35	11	·44	8
10	Sa	23	10	·43	12	·54	9
11	Su	24	11	·51	13	·64	10
12	Mo	25	12	·58	14	·73	11
13	Tu	26	13	·63	15	·81	12
14	We	27	14	·65	16	·86	13
15	Th	28	P	·66	17	·89	14
16	Fr	29	1	·64	18	·90	15
17	Sa	30	2	·62	19	·89	16
18	Su	31	3	·57	20	·87	17

June (Solar: Vijaya, Mithuna—Ani. Lunar: Bahula; Sukla; Jyeshtha; Bah. Muhammadan: H. 1372; H. 1372 Shawal.)

Cyclic Sidereal Year, Month and Day	Week-Day	English Day	Tithi	Ending Moment	Nakshatra	Ending Moment	Muhammadan Year, Month and Day
19	Mo	1	4	·50	21	·83	18
20	Tu	2	5	·41	22	·78	19
21	We	3	6	·32	23	·71	20
22	Th	4	7	·22	24	·64	21
23	Fr	5	8	·12	25	·57	22
24	Sa	6	9 / 10	·02 / ·92	26	·51	23
25	Su	7	11	·83	27	·45	24
26	Mo	8	12	·74	1	·39	25
27	Tu	9	13	·67	2	·34	26
28	We	10	14	·61	3	·32	27
29	Th	11	—A	·57	4	·30	28
30	Fr	12	1	·55	5	·31	29
31	Sa	13	2	·54	6	·33	—30
—32	Su	14	3	·57	7	·38	1
1	Mo	15	4	·61	8	·44	2
2	Tu	16	5	·67	9	·53	3
3	We	17	6	·75	10	·63	4
4	Th	18	7	·83	11	·73	5
5	Fr	19	8	·91	12	·84	6
6	Sa	20	9	·98	13	·94	7
7	Su	21	...	...	...	...	8
8	Mo	22	10	·05	14	·04	9
9	Tu	23	11	·10	15	·12	10
10	We	24	12	·14	16	·17	11
11	Th	25	13	·14	17	·21	12
12	Fr	26	14	·13	18	·22	13
13	Sa	27	P	·10	19	·23	14
14	Su	28	1 / 2	·05 / ·98	20	·20	15
15	Mo	29	3	·90	21	·16	16
16	Tu	30	4	·80	22	·11	17

Naksh :—1. Asvn. 2. Bhar. 3. Krit. 4. Rohi. 5. Mrig. 6. Ardh. 7. Punar. 8. Push. 9. Aslesh. 10. Magh. 11. P. Phal. 12. U. Phal. 13. Hasta. 14. Chit.

A. D. 1953.
A.—Amavasya.
P.—Paurnami.

Kollam 1129, Commences { **N. Malabar—Sept.** / **S. Malabar—Aug.**

Hijra 1373, Commences, **Sep. 10.**

Vikrama 2010.
Bengal San 1359.
(N. Cycle) Parabhava.

SOLAR reckoning: Cyclic Sidereal Year, Month and Day; Week-Day, English Month and Day. LUNAR reckoning: Tithi Ending Moment; Nakshatra Ending Moment; Muhammadan Year, Month and Day.

July

Solar (Cyclic Sidereal)	Day	Week-Day	July	Lunar month	Tithi	Ending Moment	Nakshatra	Ending Moment	Muhammadan	Day
Vijaya Mithuna—Ani	17	We	1	Jyeshtha	5	·70	23 24	·05 ·99	H. 1372 Shawwal	18
	18	Th	2		6	·60	25	·92		19
	19	Fr	3		7	·50	26	·85		20
	20	Sa	4		8	·40	27	·78		21
	21	Su	5		9	·31	1	·72		22
	22	Mo	6		10	·22	2	·67		23
	23	Tu	7	Bahula	11	·14	3	·65		24
	24	We	8		12	·08	4	·63		25
	25	Th	9		13	·04	5	·63		26
	26	Fr	10		14	·02	6	·65		27
	27	Sa	11		A	·02	7	·69		28
	28	Su	12	Ashadha Sukla	1	·05	8	·75		29
	29	Mo	13		2	·09	9	·88	H. 1372 Zi-l-ka'da	1
	30	Tu.	14		3	·14	10	·93		2
	31	We	15		4	·22	...	...		3
Vijaya Karkata—Adi	1	Th	16		5	·30	11	·03		4
	2	Fr	17		6	·38	12	·14		5
	3	Sa	18		7	·46	13	·25		6
	4	Su	19		8	·53	14	·34		7
	5	Mo	20		9	·58	15	·42		8
	6	Tu	21		10	61	16	·48		9
	7	We	22		11	·62	17	·52		10
	8	Th	23		12	·61	18	·55		11
	9	Fr	24		13	·57	19	·55		12
	10	Sa	25		14	·53	20	·53		13
	11	Su ○	26		P	·47	21	·50		14
	12	Mo	27	Bahula	1	·39	22	·45		15
	13	Tu	28		2	·29	23	·40		16
	14	We	29		3	·19	24	·33		17
	15	Th	30		4 5	·09 ·99	25	·26		18
	16	Fr	31		6	·89	26	·19		19

Aug.

Solar (Cyclic Sidereal)	Day	Week-Day	Aug.	Lunar month	Tithi	Ending Moment	Nakshatra	Ending Moment	Muhammadan	Day
Vijaya Karkata—Adi	17	Sa	1	Bahula	7	·79	27	·12	H. 1372 Zi-l-ka'da	20
	18	Su	2		8	·71	1	·06		21
	19	Mo	3		9	·63	2 3	·02 ·98		22
	20	Tu	4		10	·57	4	·95		23
	21	We	5		11	·53	5	·95		24
	22	Th	6		12	·51	6	·97		25
	23	Fr	7		13	·51	...	...		26
	24	Sa	8		14	·52	7	·01		27
	25	Su	9		A	·57	8	·06		28
	26	Mo	10	Sravana Sukla	1	·63	9	·14		29
	27	Tu	11		2	·70	10	·23		30
	28	We	12		3	·78	11	·33	H. 1372 Zi-l-hijja	1
	29	Th	13		4	·86	12	·44		2
	30	Fr	14		5	·94	13	·55		3
	31	Sa	15		...	...	14	·65		4
	32	Su	16		6	·01	15	·73		5
Vijaya Simha—Avani	1	Mo	17		7	·07	16	·79		6
	2	Tu	18		8	·10	17	·84		7
	3	We	19		9	·11	18	·87		8
	4	Th	20		10	·10	19	·88		9
	5	Fr	21		11	·07	20	·86		10
	6	Sa	22		12 13	·03 ·97	21	·83		11
	7	Su	23		14	·89	22	·78		12
	8	Mo	24		P	·80	23	·73		13
	9	Tu	25	Bahula	1	·70	24	·67		14
	10	We	26		2	·60	25	·60		15
	11	Th	27		3	·50	26	·53		16
	12	Fr	28		4	·40	27	·47		17
	13	Sa	29		5	·30	1	·41		18
	14	Su	30		6	·22	2	·35		19
	15	Mo	31		7	·15	3	·31		20

Sep.

Solar (Cyclic Sidereal)	Day	Week-Day	Sep.	Lunar month	Tithi	Ending Moment	Nakshatra	Ending Moment	Muhammadan	Day
Vijaya Simha—Avani	16	Tu	1	Sravn. Bah.	8	·09	4	·28	H. 1372 Zi-l-hijja	21
	17	We	2		9	·04	5	·27		22
	18	Th	3		10	·02	6	·29		23
	19	Fr	4		11	·03	7	·32		24
	20	Sa	5		12	·04	8	·37		25
	21	Su	6		13	·08	9	·44		26
	22	Mo	7		14	·13	10	·53		27
	23	Tu	8		A	·21	11	·63		28
	24	We	9	Bhadrapada Sukla	1	·29	12	·74		29
	25	Th	10		2	·38	13	·85	H. 1373 Muharram	1
	26	Fr	11		3	·46	14	·95		2
	27	Sa	12		4	·53	...	...		3
	28	Su	13		5	·59	15	·03		4
	29	Mo	14		6	·62	16	·11		5
	30	Tu	15		7	·65	17	·16		6
	31	We	16		8	·65	18	·19		7
Vijaya Kanya—Purattasi	1	Th	17		9	·62	19	·20		8
	2	Fr	18		10	·57	20	·19		9
	3	Sa	19		11	·50	21	·16		10
	4	Su	20		12	·42	22	·13		11
	5	Mo	21		13	·33	23	·07		12
	6	Tu	22		14	·23	24 25	·01 ·94		13
	7	We	23		P	·13	26	·87		14
	8	Th	24	Bahula	1 2	·03 ·93	27	·80		15
	9	Fr	25		3	·83	1	·74		16
	10	Sa	26		4	·74	2	·68		17
	11	Su	27		5	·68	3	·64		18
	12	Mo	28		6	·63	4	·61		19
	13	Tu	29		7	·59	5	·60		20
	14	We	30		8	·57	6	·61		21

Oct.

Solar (Cyclic Sidereal)	Day	Week-Day	Oct.	Lunar month	Tithi	Ending Moment	Nakshatra	Ending Moment	Muhammadan	Day
Vijaya Kanya—Purattasi	15	Th	1	Bahula	9	·56	7	·63	H. 1373 Muharram	22
	16	Fr	2		10	·58	8	·68		23
	17	Sa	3		11	·63	9	·75		24
	18	Su	4		12	·69	10	·84		25
	19	Mo	5		13	·76	11	·94		26
	20	Tu	6		14	·84	...	...		27
	21	We	7		A	·93	12	·04		28
	22	Th	8	Asvina Sukla	...	...	13	·15		29
	23	Fr	9		1	·02	14	·25		30
	24	Sa	10		2	·10	15	·34	H. 1373 Safar	1
	25	Su	11		3	·15	16	·42		2
	26	Mo	12		4	·18	17	·48		3
	27	Tu	13		5	·21	18	·51		4
	28	We	14		6	·19	19	·52		5
	29	Th	15		7	·17	20	·51		6
	30	Fr	16		8	·13	21	·50		7
Vijaya Tula—Aippasi	1	Sa	17		9 10	·07 ·99	22	·46		8
	2	Su	18		11	·90	23	·41		9
	3	Mo	19		12	·81	24	·35		10
	4	Tu	20		13	·71	25	·28		11
	5	We	21		14	·61	26	·21		12
	6	Th	22		P	·51	27	·14		13
	7	Fr	23	Bahula	1	·42	1	·08		14
	8	Sa	24		2	·34	2 3	·02 ·97		15
	9	Su	25		3	·27	4	·95		16
	10	Mo	26		4	·21	5	·93		17
	11	Tu	27		5	·17	6	·93		18
	12	We	28		6	·15	7	·95		19
	13	Th	29		7	·16	8	·99		20
	14	Fr	30		8	·18	...	...		21
	15	Sa	31		9	·23	9	·06		22

Nov.

Solar (Cyclic Sidereal)	Day	Week-Day	Nov.	Lunar month	Tithi	Ending Moment	Nakshatra	Ending Moment	Muhammadan	Day
Vijaya Tula—Aippasi	16	Su	1	Asv. Bah.	10	·29	10	·14	H. 1373 Safar	23
	17	Mo	2		11	·36	11	·23		24
	18	Tu	3		12	·44	12	·34		25
	19	We	4		13	·54	13	·45		26
	20	Th	5		14	·62	14	·55		27
	21	Fr	6		A	·69	15	·65		28
	22	Sa	7	Kartika Sukla	1	·74	16	·73		29
	23	Su	8		2	·78	17	·79	H. 1373 Rabi-ul-awwal	1
	24	Mo	9		3	·81	18	·82		2
	25	Tu	10		4	·79	19	·84		3
	26	We	11		5	·77	20	·85		4
	27	Th	12		6	·73	21	·83		5
	28	Fr	13		7	·67	22	·79		6
	29	Sa	14		8	·59	23	·74		7
	30	Su	15		9	·51	24	68		8
Vijaya Vrischika—Kartigai	1	Mo	16		10	·42	25	·62		9
	2	Tu	17		11	·32	26	·55		10
	3	We	18		·12	·22	27	·48		11
	4	Th	19		13	·12	1	·42		12
	5	Fr	20		14 P	·03 ·95	2	·36		13
	6	Sa	21	Bahula	1	·88	3	·31		14
	7	Su	22		2	·83	4	·28		15
	8	Mo	23		3	·79	5	·25		16
	9	Tu	24		4	·77	6	·25		17
	10	We	25		5	·78	7	·26		18
	11	Th	26		6	·81	8	·30		19
	12	Fr	27		7	·85	9	·37		20
	13	Sa	28		8	·91	10	·44		21
	14	Su	29		9	·99	11	·53		22
	15	Mo	30		...	...	12	·63		23

Dec.

Solar (Cyclic Sidereal)	Day	Week-Day	Dec.	Lunar month	Tithi	Ending Moment	Nakshatra	Ending Moment	Muhammadan	Day
Vijaya Vrischika—Kartigai	16	Tu	1	Kartika Bahula	10	·08	13	·74	H. 1373 Rabi-ul-awwal	24
	17	We	2		11	·16	14	·85		25
	18	Th	3		12	·24	15	·95		26
	19	Fr	4		13	·32	...	...		27
	20	Sa	5		14	·88	16	·03		28
	21	Su	6		A	·42	17	·10		29
	22	Mo	7	Margasira Sukla	1	·44	18	·14		30
	23	Tu	8		2	·43	19	·17	H. 1373 Rabi-ul-akhir	1
	24	We	9		3	·40	20	·17		2
	25	Th	10		4	·36	21	·16		3
	26	Fr	11		5	·30	22	·12		4
	27	Sa	12		6	·22	23	·08		5
	28	Su	13		7	·14	24 25	·03 ·96		6
	29	Mo	14		8 9	·05 ·95	26	·89		7
	30	Tu	15		10	·85	27	·82		8
Vijaya Dhanus—Margali	1	We	16		11	·75	1	·75		9
	2	Th	17		12	·66	2	·69		10
	3	Fr	18		13	·58	3	·64		11
	4	Sa	19		14	·51	4	·60		12
	5	Su	20		P	·46	5	·58		13
	6	Mo	21	Bahula	1	·43	6	·57		14
	7	Tu	22		2	·42	7	·58		15
	8	We	23		3	·42	8	·62		16
	9	Th	24		4	·45	9	·68		17
	10	Fr	25		5	·49	10	·75		18
	11	Sa	26		6	·56	11	·83		19
	12	Su	27		7	·64	12	·93		20
	13	Mo	28		8	·73	...	...		21
	14	Tu	29		9	·82	13	·04		22
	15	We	30		10	·90	14	·15		23
	16	Th	31		11	·97	15	·25		24

15. Svati. 16. Visak. 17. Anur. 18. Jyesh. 19. Mula. 20. P. Ash. 21. U. Ash. 22. Sravn. 23. Dani. 24. Satab. 25. P. Bhad. 26. U. Bhad. 27. Rev.

A. D. 1954.
Solar Eclipse. ●
Lunar Eclipse. ○

Mesha Sankranti (Commencement of Indian Sidereal Year).
(Surya Sid.) April 13·39.
(Arya Sid.) April 13·48.

Saka 1876.
(S. Cycle) Jaya.

Kaliyuga 5055.

SOLAR reckoning: Cyclic Sidereal Year, Month	Cyclic Sidereal Day	Week-Day	English Month and Day	LUNAR reckoning: Lunar month / paksha	Tithi	Tithi Ending Moment	Nakshatra	Nakshatra Ending Moment	Muhammadan Year, Month	Muhammadan Day
			Jan.							
Vijaya Dhanus—Margali.	17	Fr	1	Mr. Bah.	...	...	16	·34	R.-akhir.	25
	18	Sa	2		12	·03	17	·41		26
	19	Su	3		13	·06	18	·46		27
	20	Mo	4		14	·08	19	·49		28
	21	Tu	5		—A	·07	20	·50		—29
	22	We	6		1	·04	21	·48		1
	23	Th	7		2 3	·00 ·94	22	·45		2
	24	Fr	8		4	·86	23	·42		3
	25	Sa	9		5	·78	24	·36		4
	26	Su	10		6	·69	25	·30		5
	27	Mo	11	Sukla	7	·59	26	·23		6
	28	Tu	12		8	·49	27	·16		7
	—29	We	13		9	·39	1	·10		8
Vijaya Makara—Tai.	1	Th	14		10	·30	2 3	·04 ·98		9
	2	Fr	15		11	·22	4	·94	H. 1373 Jumadal-awwal.	10
	3	Sa	16		12	·15	5	·91		11
	4	Su	17	Pausha	13	·10	6	·89		12
	5	Mo	18		14	·07	7	·91		13
	6	Tu ○	19		P	·06	8	·94		14
	7	We	20		1	·07	9	·98		15
	8	Th	21		2	·10	...	...		16
	9	Fr	22		3	·15	10	·05		17
	10	Sa	23		4	22	11	·14		18
	11	Su	24		5	·30	12	·24		19
	12	Mo	25		6	·38	13	·35		20
	13	Tu	26	Bahula	7	·47	14	·46		21
	14	We	27		8	·55	15	·56		22
	15	Th	28		9	·62	16	·65		23
	16	Fr	29		10	·68	17	·73		24
	17	Sa	30		11	·71	18	·79		25
	18	Su	31		12	·73	19	·81		26
			Feb.							
Vijaya Kumbha—Masi.	19	Mo	1		13	·71	20	·82		27
	20	Tu	2		14	·68	21	·81		28
	21	We	3		—A	·64	22	·79		29
	22	Th	4		1	·57	23	·75		—30
	23	Fr	5		2	·49	24	·70	H. 1373 Jumadal-akhir.	1
	24	Sa	6		3	·41	25	·64		2
	25	Su	7		4	·32	26	·57		3
	26	Mo	8		5	·22	27	·50		4
	27	Tu	9		6	·12	1	·43		5
	28	We	10	Sukla	7 8	·02 ·92	2	·37		6
	—29	Th	11		9	·84	3	·31		7
	1	Fr	12		10	·78	4	·27		8
	2	Sa	13		11	·74	5	·24		9
	3	Su	14		12	·71	6	·23		10
	4	Mo	15	Magha	13	·70	7	·23		11
	5	Tu	16		14	·70	8	·25		12
	6	We	17		P	·73	9	·29		13
	7	Th	18		1	·78	10	·36		14
	8	Fr	19		2	·84	11	·45		15
	9	Sa	20		3	·92	12	·55		16
	10	Su	21		...	...	13	·65		17
	11	Mo	22		4	·01	14	·76		18
	12	Tu	23		5	·10	15	·86		19
	13	We	24	Bahula	6	·18	16	·96		20
	14	Th	25		7	·24	...	...		21
	15	Fr	26		8	·30	17	·08		22
	16	Sa	27		9	·33	18	·09		23
	17	Su	28		10	·34	19	·13		24

SOLAR reckoning: Cyclic Sidereal Year, Month	Cyclic Sidereal Day	Week-Day	English Month and Day	LUNAR reckoning: Lunar month / paksha	Tithi	Tithi Ending Moment	Nakshatra	Nakshatra Ending Moment	Muhammadan Year, Month	Muhammadan Day
			March							
Vijaya Kumbha—Masi.	18	Mo	1	Mg. Bah.	11	·33	20	·14	J.-akhir.	25
	19	Tu	2		12	·31	21	·14		26
	20	We	3		13	·25	22	·13		27
	21	Th	4		14	·18	23	·09		28
	22	Fr	5		—A	·10	24 25	·04 ·98		—29
	23	Sa	6		1 2	·02 ·92	26	·92		1
	24	Su	7		3	·82	27	·85		2
	25	Mo	8		4	·72	1	·78		3
	26	Tu	9		5	·63	2	·71		4
	27	We	10		6	·54	3	·65		5
	28	Th	11	Sukla	7	·45	4	·60		6
	29	Fr	12		8	·39	5	·57		7
	—30	Sa	13		9	·34	6	·55		8
Vijaya Mina—Panguni.	1	Su	14		10	·30	7	·55		9
	2	Mo	15		11	·29	8	·57		10
	3	Tu	16		12	·29	9	·61		11
	4	We	17	Phalguna	13	·33	10	·67	H. 1373 Rajab.	12
	5	Th	18		14	·38	11	·75		13
	6	Fr	19		P	·45	12	·84		14
	7	Sa	20		1	·53	13	·94		15
	8	Su	21		2	·61	...	...		16
	9	Mo	22		3	·70	14	·05		17
	10	Tu	23		4	·78	15	·16		18
	11	We	24		5	·84	16	·26		19
	12	Th	25		6	·89	17	·34		20
	13	Fr	26	Bahula	7	·93	18	·40		21
	14	Sa	27		8	·93	19	·44		22
	15	Su	28		9	·91	20	·46		23
	16	Mo	29		10	·88	21	·47		24
	17	Tu	30		11	·83	22	·45		25
	18	We	31		12	·77	23	·42		26
			April							
	19	Th	1		13	·69	24	·37		27
	20	Fr	2		14	·60	25	·31		28
	21	Sa	3		—A	·50	26	25		29
	22	Su	4		1	·40	27	·18		—30
	23	Mo	5		2	·30	1	·11		1
	24	Tu	6		3	·20	2 3	·05 ·99		2
	25	We	7		4	·11	4	·94		3
	26	Th	8		5 6	·02 ·95	5	·90		4
	27	Fr	9	Sukla	7	·90	6	·88		5
	28	Sa	10		8	·86	7	·87		6
	29	Su	11		9	·85	8	·88		7
	—30	Mo	12		10	·85	9	·92		8
Jaya Mesha—Chittirai.	1	Tu	13		11	·89	10	·98		9
	2	We	14		12	·94	...	...	H. 1373 Shaban.	10
	3	Th	15		...	...	11	·05		11
	4	Fr	16	Chaitra	13	·00	12	·14		12
	5	Sa	17		14	·08	13	·24		13
	6	Su	18		P	·17	14	·85		14
	7	Mo	19		1	·26	15	·46		15
	8	Tu	20		2	·34	16	·56		16
	9	We	21		3	·40	17	·64		17
	10	Th	22		4	·44	18	·71		18
	11	Fr	23		5	·47	19	·76		19
	12	Sa	24		6	·47	20	·79		20
	13	Su	25	Bahula	7	·46	21	·80		21
	14	Mo	26		8	·43	22	·78		22
	15	Tu	27		9	·37	23	·75		23
	16	We	28		10	·30	24	·71		24
	17	Th	29		11	·22	25	·66		25
	18	Fr	30		12	·13	26	·59		26

SOLAR reckoning: Cyclic Sidereal Year, Month	Cyclic Sidereal Day	Week-Day	English Month and Day	LUNAR reckoning: Lunar month / paksha	Tithi	Tithi Ending Moment	Nakshatra	Nakshatra Ending Moment	Muhammadan Year, Month	Muhammadan Day
			May							
Jaya Mesha—Chittirai.	19	Sa	1		13 14	·08 ·93	27	·52		27
	20	Su	2		—A	·83	1	·45		28
	21	Mo	3		1	·73	2	·39		—29
	22	Tu	4		2	·64	3	·33		1
	23	We	5		3	·55	4	·28		2
	24	Th	6		4	·48	5	·23		3
	25	Fr	7		5	·43	6	·20		4
	26	Sa	8		6	·40	7	·19		5
	27	Su	9	Sukla	7	·38	8	·20		6
	28	Mo	10		8	·38	9	·24		7
	29	Tu	11		9	·41	10	·29		8
	30	We	12		10	·46	11	·36		9
	—31	Th	13		11	·52	12	·44		10
Jaya Vrishabha—Vaikasi.	1	Fr	14		12	·60	13	·54		11
	2	Sa	15	Vaisakha	13	·68	14	·65		12
	3	Su	16		14	·76	15	·76		13
	4	Mo	17		P	·84	16	·86	H. 1373 Ramzan.	14
	5	Tu	18		1	·91	17	·95		15
	6	We	19		2	·96	...	...		16
	7	Th	20		3	·97	18	·02		17
	8	Fr	21		4	·98	19	·08		18
	9	Sa	22		5	·97	20	·11		19
	10	Su	23		6	·94	21	·12		20
	11	Mo	24	Bahula	7	·88	22	·11		21
	12	Tu	25		8	·80	23	·08		22
	13	We	26		9	·72	24	·05		23
	14	Th	27		10	·63	25 26	·00 ·93		24
	15	Fr	28		11	·53	27	·86		25
	16	Sa	29		12	·43	1	·79		26
	17	Su	30		13	·33	2	·73		27
	18	Mo	31		14	·28	3	·67		28
			June							
	19	Tu	1		—A	·14	4	·61		29
	20	We	2		1 2	·06 ·99	5	·56		—30
	21	Th	3		3	·93	6	·53		1
	22	Fr	4		4	·89	7	·51		2
	23	Sa	5		5	·87	8	·53		3
	24	Su	6		6	·88	9	·55		4
	25	Mo	7		7	·90	10	·60		5
	26	Tu	8	Sukla	8	·94	11	·66		6
	27	We	9		...	...	12	·74		7
	28	Th	10		9	·01	13	·84		8
	29	Fr	11		10	·08	14	·95		9
	30	Sa	12		11	·16	...	...		10
	31	Su	13		12	·24	15	·06		11
	—32	Mo	14	Jyeshtha	13	·31	16	·16	H. 1373 Shawwal.	12
Jaya Mithuna—Ani.	1	Tu	15		14	·38	17	·25		13
	2	We	16		P	·43	18	·33		14
	3	Th	17		1	·46	19	·39		15
	4	Fr	18		2	·47	20	·48		16
	5	Sa	19		3	·45	21	·44		17
	6	Su	20		4	·42	22	·44		18
	7	Mo	21		5	·36	23	·42		19
	8	Tu	22	Bahula	6	·29	24	·38		20
	9	We	23		7	·22	25	·33		21
	10	Th	24		8	·12	26	·27		22
	11	Fr	25		9 10	·02 ·92	27	·20		23
	12	Sa	26		11	·82	1	·13		24
	13	Su	27		12	·72	2	·06		25
	14	Mo	28		13	·62	3 4	·00 ·94		26
	15	Tu	29		14	·54	5	·89		27
	16	We ●	30		—A	·47	6	·86		28

Naksh :—1. Asvn. 2. Bhar. 3. Krit. 4. Rohi. 5. Mrig. 6. Ardh. 7. Punar. 8. Push. 9. Aslesh. 10. Magh. 11. P. Phal. 12. U. Phal. 13. Hasta. 14 Chit.

A. D. 1954.
A.—Amavasya.
P.—Paurnami.

Kollam 1130, Commences { N. Malabar—Sept. / S. Malabar—Aug.

Hijra 1374, Commences, Aug. 30.

Vikrama 2011.
Bengal San 1360.
(N. Cycle) Plavanga.

Columns: SOLAR reckoning — Cyclic Sidereal Year, Month and Day; Week-Day English Month and Day. LUNAR reckoning — Tithi Ending Moment; Nakshatra Ending Moment; Muhammadan Year, Month and Day.

July — Jaya Mithuna—Ani (17–30); Jaya Karkata—Adi (1–16); Sukla; Ashadha; Bahula; H. 1373 Zi-l-ka'da.

Cyclic Sidereal	Week-Day	Day	Tithi	Moment	Nakshatra	Moment	Muhammadan
17	Th	1	1	·41	7	·85	—29
18	Fr	2	2	·37	8	·85	1
19	Sa	3	3	·35	9	·87	2
20	Su	4	4	·35	10	·91	3
21	Mo	5	5	·37	11	·97	4
22	Tu	6	6	·42	...	...	5
23	We	7	7	·48	12	·05	6
24	Th	8	8	·56	13	·15	7
25	Fr	9	9	·64	14	·25	8
26	Sa	10	10	·72	15	·36	9
27	Su	11	11	·80	16	·46	10
28	Mo	12	12	·86	17	·56	11
29	Tu	13	13	·91	18	·64	12
30	We	14	14	·93	19	·70	13
—31	Th ○	15	P	·95	20	·74	14
1	Fr	16	1	·93	21	·76	15
2	Sa	17	2	·90	22	·76	16
3	Su	18	3	·84	23	·75	17
4	Mo	19	4	·77	24	·72	18
5	Tu	20	5	·70	25	·67	19
6	We	21	6	·61	26	·61	20
7	Th	22	7	·51	27	·55	21
8	Fr	23	8	·41	1	·48	22
9	Sa	24	9	·31	2	·41	23
10	Su	25	10	·21	3	·34	24
11	Mo	26	11	·11	4	·28	25
12	Tu	27	12 / 13	·03 / ·95	5	·23	26
13	We	28	14	·89	6	·20	27
14	Th	29	—A	·85	7	·17	28
15	Fr	30	1	·83	8	·17	29
16	Sa	31	2	·83	9	·18	—30

Aug. — Jaya Simha—Avani (1–15); Sukla; Sravana; Bahula; B. Suk.; H. 1373 Zi-l-hijja.

Cyclic Sidereal	Week-Day	Day	Tithi	Moment	Nakshatra	Moment	Muhammadan
17	Su	1	3	·85	10	·22	1
18	Mo	2	4	·90	11	·28	2
19	Tu	3	5	·95	12	·36	3
20	We	4	...	...	13	·45	4
21	Th	5	6	·03	14	·55	5
22	Fr	6	7	·11	15	·66	6
23	Sa	7	8	·20	16	·77	7
24	Su	8	9	·27	17	·87	8
25	Mo	9	10	·34	18	·95	9
26	Tu	10	11	·39	...	...	10
27	We	11	12	·42	19	·01	11
28	Th	12	13	·44	20	·06	12
29	Fr	13	14	·42	21	·08	13
30	Sa	14	P	·39	22	·10	14
31	Su	15	1	·34	23	·08	15
—32	Mo	16	2	·28	24	·05	16
1	Tu	17	3	·20	25 / 26	·00 / ·94	17
2	We	18	4	·11	27	·88	18
3	Th	19	5 / 6	·01 / 91	1	·82	19
4	Fr	20	7	·81	2	·75	20
5	Sa	21	8	·71	3	·68	21
6	Su	22	9	·61	4	·62	22
7	Mo	23	10	·52	5	·57	23
8	Tu	24	11	·45	6	·53	24
9	We	25	12	·39	7	·50	25
10	Th	26	13	·35	8	·49	26
11	Fr	27	14	·34	9	·50	27
12	Sa	28	—A	·34	10	·54	28
13	Su	29	1	·35	11	·59	—29
14	Mo	30	2	·39	12	·66	1
15	Tu	31	3	·46	13	·75	2

Sep. — Jaya Simha—Avani (16–31); Jaya Kanya—Purattasi (1–14); Sukla; Bhadrapada; Bahula; H. 1374 Muharram.

Cyclic Sidereal	Week-Day	Day	Tithi	Moment	Nakshatra	Moment	Muhammadan
16	We	1	4	·54	14	·85	3
17	Th	2	5	·63	15	·96	4
18	Fr	3	6	·71	...	...	5
19	Sa	4	7	·79	16	·07	6
20	Su	5	8	·86	17	·17	7
21	Mo	6	9	·90	18	·25	8
22	Tu	7	10	·93	19	·32	9
23	We	8	11	·95	20	·37	10
24	Th	9	12	·94	21	·41	11
25	Fr	10	13	·91	22	·42	12
26	Sa	11	14	·86	23	·41	13
27	Su	12	P	·80	24	·38	14
28	Mo	13	1	·72	25	·34	15
29	Tu	14	2	·63	26	·29	16
30	We	15	3	·53	27	·23	17
—31	Th	16	4	·43	1	·16	18
1	Fr	17	5	·33	2	·09	19
2	Sa	18	6	·23	3 / 4	·02 / ·96	20
3	Su	19	7	·14	5	·90	21
4	Mo	20	8 / 9	·06 / ·99	6	·86	22
5	Tu	21	10	·93	7	·83	23
6	We	22	11	·89	8	·81	24
7	Th	23	12	·87	9	·83	25
8	Fr	24	13	·86	10	·86	26
9	Sa	25	14	·89	11	·91	27
10	Su	26	—A	·94	12	·97	28
11	Mo	27	...	...	...	...	29
12	Tu	28	1	·00	13	05	—30
13	We	29	2	·08	14	·15	1
14	Th	30	3	·17	15	·26	2

Oct. — Jaya Tula—Aippasi (1–15); Sukla; Asvina; Bahula; Kart. Suk.; H. 1374 Safar; R. awwal.

Cyclic Sidereal	Week-Day	Day	Tithi	Moment	Nakshatra	Moment	Muhammadan
15	Fr	1	4	·25	16	·37	3
16	Sa	2	5	·33	17	·47	4
17	Su	3	6	·40	18	·56	5
18	Mo	4	7	·45	19	·63	6
19	Tu	5	8	·48	20	·69	7
20	We	6	9	·50	21	·73	8
21	Th	7	10	·49	22	·74	9
22	Fr	8	11	·46	23	·73	10
23	Sa	9	12	·42	24	·71	11
24	Su	10	13	·36	25	·68	12
25	Mo	11	14	·28	26	·63	13
26	Tu	12	P	·19	27	·56	14
27	We	13	1	·10	1	·49	15
28	Th	14	2 / 3	·00 / ·90	2	·42	16
29	Fr	15	4	·80	3	·36	17
—30	Sa	16	5	·71	4	·30	18
1	Su	17	6	·63	5	·24	19
2	Mo	18	7	·56	6	·19	20
3	Tu	19	8	·50	7	·16	21
4	We	20	9	·47	8	·14	22
5	Th	21	10	·45	9	·15	23
6	Fr	22	11	·46	10	·17	24
7	Sa	23	12	·48	11	·21	25
8	Su	24	13	·53	12	·27	26
9	Mo	25	14	·59	13	·35	27
10	Tu	26	—A	·66	14	·45	28
11	We	27	1	·75	15	·56	—29
12	Th	28	2	·84	16	·67	1
13	Fr	29	3	·93	17	·77	2
14	Sa	30	4	·99	18	·86	3
15	Su	31	...	...	19	·94	4

Nov. — Jaya Tula—Aippasi (16–30); Jaya Vrischika—Kartigai (1–15); Sukla; Kartika; Bahula; H. 1374 Rabi-ul-awwal.

Cyclic Sidereal	Week-Day	Day	Tithi	Moment	Nakshatra	Moment	Muhammadan
16	Mo	1	5	·04	...	...	5
17	Tu	2	6	·07	20	·01	6
18	We	3	7	·09	21	·05	7
19	Th	4	8	·08	22	·06	8
20	Fr	5	9	06	23	·03	9
21	Sa	6	10 / 11	·02 / ·95	24	05	10
22	Su	7	12	·87	25 / 26	·01 / ·96	11
23	Mo	8	13	·78	27	·90	12
24	Tu	9	14	·69	1	·84	13
25	We	10	P	·60	2	·77	14
26	Th	11	1	·50	3	·70	15
27	Fr	12	2	·40	4	·63	16
28	Sa	13	3	·31	5	·57	17
29	Su	14	4	·24	6	·52	18
—30	Mo	15	5	·17	7	·48	19
1	Tu	16	6	·11	8	·47	20
2	We	17	7	·07	9	·47	21
3	Th	18	8	·06	10	·48	22
4	Fr	19	9	·07	11	·52	23
5	Sa	20	10	·09	12	·58	24
6	Su	21	11	·13	13	·66	25
7	Mo	22	12	·20	14	·76	26
8	Tu	23	13	·29	15	·86	27
9	We	24	14	·37	16	·96	28
10	Th	25	—A	·45	...	...	29
11	Fr	26	1	·53	17	·07	—30
12	Sa	27	2	·61	18	·17	1
13	Su	28	3	·67	19	·25	2
14	Mo	29	4	·70	20	·32	3
15	Tu	30	5	·73	21	·36	4

Dec. — Jaya Dhanus—Margali (1–16); Sukla; Margasira; Bahula; Paush. Suk.; H. 1374 Rabi-ul-akhir; J.-awwal.

Cyclic Sidereal	Week-Day	Day	Tithi	Moment	Nakshatra	Moment	Muhammadan
16	We	1	6	·71	22	·38	5
17	Th	2	7	·68	23	·39	6
18	Fr	3	8	·63	24	·38	7
19	Sa	4	9	·57	25	·34	8
20	Su	5	10	·50	26	·30	9
21	Mo	6	11	·41	27	·24	10
22	Tu	7	12	·32	1	·18	11
23	We	8	13	·22	2	·11	12
24	Th	9	14	·12	3 / 4	·04 / ·97	13
25	Fr	10	P / 1	·02 / ·93	5	·91	14
26	Sa	11	2	·86	6	·86	15
27	Su	12	3	·79	7	·82	16
28	Mo	13	4	·75	8	·80	17
29	Tu	14	5	·71	9	·79	18
—30	We	15	6	·69	10	·80	19
1	Th	16	7	·71	11	·83	20
2	Fr	17	8	·74	12	·89	21
3	Sa	18	9	·79	13	·97	22
4	Su	19	10	·85	...	...	23
5	Mo	20	11	·93	14	·06	24
6	Tu	21	...	...	15	·16	25
7	We	22	12	·02	16	·27	26
8	Th	23	13	·11	17	·38	27
9	Fr	24	14	·19	18	·48	28
10	Sa	25	—A	·26	19	·56	—29
11	Su	26	1	·31	20	·63	1
12	Mo	27	2	·35	21	·68	2
13	Tu	28	3	·37	22	·71	3
14	We	29	4	·35	23	·72	4
15	Th	30	5	·33	24	·70	5
16	Fr	31	6	·28	25	·67	6

15. Svati. 16. Visak. 17. Anur. 18. Jyesh. 19. Mula. 20. P. Ash. 21. U. Ash. 22. Sravn. 23. Dani. 24. Satab. 25. P. Bhad. 26. U. Bhad. 27. Rev.

A. D. 1955.
Solar Eclipse. ●
Lunar Eclipse. ○

Mesha Sankranti (Commencement of Indian Sidereal Year).
(Surya Sid.) April 13·85.
(Arya Sid.) April 13·74.

Saka 1877.
(S. Cycle) Manmatha.

Kaliyuga 5056.

SOLAR reckoning: Cyclic Sidereal Year, Month and Day	Week-Day English Month and Day	LUNAR reckoning: Tithi Ending Moment	Nakshatra Ending Moment	Muhammadan Year, Month and Day
	Jan.			
Jaya, Dhanus—Margali. 17	Sa 1	Suk. 7 ·22	26 ·63	H. 1374 Jumadal-awwal. 7
18	Su 2	8 ·14	27 ·57	8
19	Mo 3	9 ·05 10 ·96	1 ·51	9
20	Tu 4	11 ·86	2 ·45	10
21	We 5	12 ·76	3 ·38	11
22	Th 6	Pausha 13 ·67	4 ·31	12
23	Fr 7	14 ·58	5 ·25	13
24	Sa 8	P ·50	6 ·20	14
25	Su 9	1 ·44	7 ·16	15
26	Mo 10	2 ·39	8 ·13	16
27	Tu 11	3 ·36	9 ·11	17
28	We 12	4 ·35	10 ·12	18
29	Th 13	5 ·35	11 ·16	19
Jaya, Makara—Tai. 1	Fr 14	6 ·38	12 ·20	20
2	Sa 15	Bahula 7 ·43	13 ·27	21
3	Su 16	8 ·51	14 ·36	22
4	Mo 17	9 ·59	15 ·46	23
5	Tu 18	10 ·68	16 ·57	24
6	We 19	11 ·77	17 ·68	25
7	Th 20	12 ·85	18 ·78	26
8	Fr 21	13 ·91	19 ·86	27
9	Sa 22	14 ·96	20 ·94	28
10	Su 23	... ...	21 ·99	29
11	Mo 24	A ·00	... ...	30
12	Tu 25	1 ·01 2 ·99	22 ·03	1
13	We 26	3 97	23 ·04	2
14	Th 27	4 ·92	24 ·03	3
15	Fr 28	5 ·85	25 ·01 26 ·97	4
16	Sa 29	Sukla 6 ·77	27 ·92	5
17	Su 30	7 ·69	1 ·86	6
18	Mo 31	8 ·60	2 ·79	7
	Feb.			
19	Tu 1	9 ·60	3 ·72	H. 1374 Jumadal-akhir. 8
20	We 2	10 ·40	4 ·65	9
21	Th 3	11 ·30	5 ·59	10
22	Fr 4	Magha 12 ·21	6 ·53	11
23	Sa 5	13 ·13	7 ·49	12
24	Su 6	14 ·07	8 ·46	13
25	Mo 7	P ·03	9 ·44	14
26	Tu 8	1 ·00 2 ·98	10 ·45	15
27	We 9	3 ·93	11 ·47	16
28	Th 10	... ...	12 ·51	17
29	Fr 11	4 ·01	13 ·58	18
30	Sa 12	5 ·07	14 ·66	19
Jaya, Kumbha—Masi. 1	Su 13	6 ·15	15 ·76	20
2	Mo 14	Bahula 7 ·23	16 ·87	21
3	Tu 15	8 ·31	17 ·98	22
4	We 16	9 ·40	... ...	23
5	Th 17	10 48	18 ·08	24
6	Fr 18	11 ·55	19 ·17	25
7	Sa 19	12 ·60	20 ·25	26
8	Su 20	13 ·62	21 ·31	27
9	Mo 21	14 ·63	22 ·35	28
10	Tu 22	A ·68	23 ·36	29
11	We 23	Phal. Sukla 1 ·60	24 ·36	H. 1374 Rajab. 1
12	Th 24	2 ·54	25 ·34	2
13	Fr 25	3 ·47	26 ·31	3
14	Sa 26	4 ·39	27 ·26	4
15	Su 27	5 ·30	1 ·20	5
16	Mo 28	6 ·21	2 ·13	6

SOLAR reckoning: Cyclic Sidereal Year, Month and Day	Week-Day English Month and Day	LUNAR reckoning: Tithi Ending Moment	Nakshatra Ending Moment	Muhammadan Year, Month and Day
	March			
Jaya, Kumbha—Masi. 17	Tu 1	7 ·12	3 ·06 4 ·99	H. 1374 Rajab. 7
18	We 2	Sukla 8 ·02 9 ·92	5 ·93	8
19	Th 3	10 ·82	6 ·87	9
20	Fr 4	11 ·74	7 ·82	10
21	Sa 5	Phalguna 12 ·67	8 ·78	11
22	Su 6	13 ·63	9 ·77	12
23	Mo 7	14 ·61	10 ·77	13
24	Tu 8	P ·59	11 ·79	14
25	We 9	1 ·60	12 ·82	15
26	Th 10	2 ·64	13 ·88	16
27	Fr 11	3 ·69	14 ·96	17
28	Sa 12	4 ·76	... ...	18
29	Su 13	5 ·81	15 ·06	19
Jaya, Mina—Panguni. 1	Mo 14	6 ·92	16 ·17	20
2	Tu 15	... ...	17 ·28	21
3	We 16	Bahula 7 ·00	18 ·38	22
4	Th 17	8 ·08	19 ·47	23
5	Fr 18	9 ·14	20 ·55	24
6	Sa 19	10 ·19	21 ·62	25
7	Su 20	11 ·23	22 ·66	26
8	Mo 21	12 ·23	23 ·68	27
9	Tu 22	13 ·22	24 ·68	28
10	We 23	14 ·18	25 ·67	29
11	Th 24	A ·13	26 ·64	30
12	Fr 25	1 ·07 2 ·99	27 ·59	1
13	Sa 26	3 ·89	1 ·53	2
14	Su 27	4 ·79	2 ·47	3
15	Mo 28	5 ·69	3 ·40	4
16	Tu 29	Sukla 6 ·59	4 ·33	5
17	We 30	7 ·50	5 ·26	6
18	Th 31	8 ·41	6 ·20	7
	April			
19	Fr 1	9 ·33	7 ·15	H. 1374 Shaban. 8
20	Sa 2	10 ·26	8 ·12	9
21	Su 3	11 ·21	9 ·10	10
22	Mo 4	12 ·18	10 ·09	11
23	Tu 5	Chaitra 13 ·16	11 ·10	12
24	We 6	14 ·17	12 ·13	13
25	Th 7	P ·21	13 ·19	14
26	Fr 8	1 ·26	14 ·27	15
27	Sa 9	2 ·32	15 ·36	16
28	Su 10	3 ·40	16 ·46	17
29	Mo 11	4 ·48	17 ·57	18
30	Tu 12	5 ·57	18 ·68	19
31	We 13	6 ·65	19 ·78	20
Manmatha, Mesha—Chittirai. 1	Th 14	Bahula 7 ·71	20 ·87	21
2	Fr 15	8 ·76	21 ·93	22
3	Sa 16	9 ·78	22 ·98	23
4	Su 17	10 ·79	... ...	24
5	Mo 18	11 ·77	23 ·00	25
6	Tu 19	12 ·73	24 ·02	26
7	We 20	13 ·68	25 ·00 26 ·97	27
8	Th 21	14 ·60	27 ·93	28
9	Fr 22	A ·52	1 ·87	29
10	Sa 23	Vak. Sukla 1 ·43	2 ·81	H. 1374 Ramzan. 1
11	Su 24	2 ·34	3 ·74	2
12	Mo 25	3 ·24	4 ·67	3
13	Tu 26	4 ·14	5 ·60	4
14	We 27	5 ·04 6 ·94	6 ·54	5
15	Th 28	7 ·86	7 ·48	6
16	Fr 29	8 ·79	8 ·45	7
17	Sa 30	9 ·75	9 ·42	8

SOLAR reckoning: Cyclic Sidereal Year, Month and Day	Week-Day English Month and Day	LUNAR reckoning: Tithi Ending Moment	Nakshatra Ending Moment	Muhammadan Year, Month and Day
	May			
Manmatha, Mesha—Chittirai. 18	Su 1	Sukla 10 ·71	10 ·41	H. 1374 Ramzan. 9
19	Mo 2	11 ·70	11 ·42	10
20	Tu 3	12 ·70	12 ·45	11
21	We 4	Vaisakha 13 ·74	13 ·51	12
22	Th 5	14 ·78	14 ·58	13
23	Fr 6	P ·84	15 ·66	14
24	Sa 7	1 ·92	16 ·76	15
25	Su 8	.. ...	17 ·87	16
26	Mo 9	2 ·01	18 ·98	17
27	Tu 10	3 ·09	... ...	18
28	We 11	4 ·16	19 ·08	19
29	Th 12	5 ·22	20 ·17	20
30	Fr 13	6 ·27	21 ·24	21
31	Sa 14	Bahula 7 ·29	22 ·29	22
Manmatha, Vrishabha—Vaikasi. 1	Su 15	8 ·30	23 ·33	23
2	Mo 16	9 ·28	24 ·34	24
3	Tu 17	10 ·25	25 ·33	25
4	We 18	11 ·20	26 ·30	26
5	Th 19	12 ·13	27 ·26	27
6	Fr 20	13 ·04 14 ·94	1 ·20	28
7	Sa 21	A ·84	2 ·14	29
8	Su 22	1 ·74	3 ·08	30
9	Mo 23	2 ·64	4 ·01 5 ·94	1
10	Tu 24	3 ·54	6 ·88	2
11	We 25	4 ·45	7 ·83	3
12	Th 26	5 ·37	8 ·78	4
13	Fr 27	6 ·30	9 ·75	5
14	Sa 28	Sukla 7 ·25	10 ·73	6
15	Su 29	8 ·21	11 ·74	7
16	Mo 30	9 ·20	12 ·77	8
17	Tu 31	10 ·20	13 ·82	9
	June			
18	We 1	11 ·23	14 ·88	H. 1374 Shawwal. 10
19	Th 2	12 ·28	15 ·96	11
20	Fr 3	Jyeshtha 13 ·34	... ...	12
21	Sa 4	14 ·41	16 ·06	13
22	Su 5	P ·50	17 ·17	14
23	Mo 6	1 ·59	18 ·28	15
24	Tu 7	2 ·66	19 ·38	16
25	We 8	3 ·71	20 ·47	17
26	Th 9	4 ·76	21 ·55	18
27	Fr 10	5 ·79	22 ·61	19
28	Sa 11	6 ·79	23 ·65	20
29	Su 12	Bahula 7 ·77	24 ·66	21
30	Mo 13	8 ·74	25 ·66	22
31	Tu 14	9 ·68	26 ·63	23
Manmatha, Mithuna—Ani. 1	We 15	10 ·61	27 ·59	24
2	Th 16	11 ·53	1 ·55	25
3	Fr 17	12 ·44	2 ·49	26
4	Sa 18	13 ·34	3 ·42	27
5	Su 19	14 ·24	4 ·35	28
6	Mo ● 20	A ·14	5 ·28	29
7	Tu 21	Sukla 1 ·04 2 ·94	6 ·22	H. 1374 Zil-ka'da. 1
8	We 22	3 ·86	7 ·16	2
9	Th 23	4 ·79	8 ·11	3
10	Fr 24	5 ·73	9 ·08	4
11	Sa 25	Ashadha 6 ·69	10 ·06	5
12	Su 26	7 ·67	11 ·07	6
13	Mo 27	8 ·68	12 ·09	7
14	Tu 28	9 ·71	13 ·13	8
15	We 29	10 ·75	14 ·19	9
16	Th 30	11 ·81	15 ·27	10

Naksh :—1. Asvn. 2. Bhar. 3. Krit. 4. Rohi. 5. Mrig. 6. Ardh. 7. Punar. 8. Push. 9. Aslesh. 10. Magh. 11. P. Phal. 12. U. Phal. 13. Hasta. 14. Chit.

A. D. 1955.
A.—Amavasya.
P.—Paurnami.

Kollam 1131, Commences { N. Malabar—Sept. S. Malabar—Aug.

Hijra 1375, Commences, Aug. 20.

Vikrama 2012.
Bengal San 1361.
(N. Cycle) Kilaka.

July — Solar: Manmatha, Mithuna—Ani (1–16); Manmatha, Karkata—Adi (17–31). Lunar: Ashadha, Sukla; Bahula; Sukla. Muhammadan: H. 1374 Zi-l-ka'da; Zi-l-hijja.

Cyclic Sidereal Year, Month and Day	Week-Day	English Month and Day	Tithi Ending Moment	Nakshatra Ending Moment	Muhammadan Year, Month and Day
17	Fr	1	12 ·90	16 ·37	11
18	Sa	2	13 ·98	17 ·47	12
19	Su	3	... ...	18 ·58	13
20	Mo	4	14 ·05	19 ·68	14
21	Tu	5	P ·12	20 ·78	15
22	We	6	1 ·19	21 ·85	16
23	Th	7	2 ·24	22 ·92	17
24	Fr	8	3 ·26	23 ·96	18
25	Sa	9	4 ·27	24 ·98	19
26	Su	10	5 ·25	25 ·98	20
27	Mo	11	6 ·21	26 ·96	21
28	Tu	12	7 ·16	27 ·93	22
29	We	13	8 ·10	1 ·89	23
30	Th	14	9 ·01 10 ·92	2 ·83	24
31	Fr	15	11 ·82	3 ·70	25
32	Sa	16	12 ·72	4 ·69	26
1	Su	17	13 ·61	5 ·62	27
2	Mo	18	14 ·51	6 ·56	28
3	Tu	19	A ·42	7 ·50	29
4	We	20	1 ·34	8 ·45	30
5	Th	21	2 ·26	9 ·41	1
6	Fr	22	3 ·21	10 ·39	2
7	Sa	23	4 ·18	11 ·39	3
8	Su	24	5 ·15	12 ·40	4
9	Mo	25	6 ·16	13 ·44	5
10	Tu	26	7 ·19	14 ·50	6
11	We	27	8 ·22	15 ·58	7
12	Th	28	9 ·28	16 ·67	8
13	Fr	29	10 ·36	17 ·77	9
14	Sa	30	11 ·44	18 ·88	10
15	Su	31	12 ·52	19 ·98	11

Aug. — Solar: Manmatha, Karkata—Adi (1–16); Manmatha, Simha—Avani (17–31). Lunar: Sravana, Sukla; Bahula; Adhika Bhadra. Sukla. Muhammadan: H. 1374 Zi-l-hijja; H. 1375 Muharram.

Cyclic Sidereal Year, Month and Day	Week-Day	English Month and Day	Tithi Ending Moment	Nakshatra Ending Moment	Muhammadan Year, Month and Day
16	Mo	1	13 ·60	... ...	12
17	Tu	2	14 ·66	20 ·08	13
18	We	3	P ·71	21 ·17	14
19	Th	4	1 ·74	22 ·23	15
20	Fr	5	2 ·75	23 ·28	16
21	Sa	6	3 ·74	24 ·30	17
22	Su	7	4 ·70	25 ·31	18
23	Mo	8	5 ·65	26 ·30	19
24	Tu	9	6 ·59	27 ·27	20
25	We	10	7 ·51	1 ·22	21
26	Th	11	8 ·42	2 ·16	22
27	Fr	12	9 ·32	3 ·10	23
28	Sa	13	10 ·22	4 ·04 5 ·97	24
29	Su	14	11 ·12	6 ·90	25
30	Mo	15	12 ·02 13 ·92	7 ·83	26
31	Tu	16	14 ·84	8 ·78	27
1	We	17	A ·76	9 ·75	28
2	Th	18	1 ·70	10 ·72	29
3	Fr	19	2 ·67	11 ·71	30
4	Sa	20	3 ·65	12 ·72	1
5	Su	21	4 ·66	13 ·75	2
6	Mo	22	5 ·68	14 ·80	3
7	Tu	23	6 ·72	15 ·88	4
8	We	24	7 ·78	16 ·97	5
9	Th	25	8 ·86	... ...	6
10	Fr	26	9 ·94	17 ·07	7
11	Sa	27	... ...	18 ·17	8
12	Su	28	10 ·03	19 ·28	9
13	Mo	29	11 ·10	20 ·39	10
14	Tu	30	12 ·17	21 ·48	11
15	We	31	13 ·22	22 ·54	12

Sep. — Solar: Manmatha, Simha—Avani (1–16); Manmatha, Kanya—Purattasi (17–30). Lunar: Adhika Bhadrapada, Bahula; Bhadrapada, Sukla. Muhammadan: H. 1375 Muharram.

Cyclic Sidereal Year, Month and Day	Week-Day	English Month and Day	Tithi Ending Moment	Nakshatra Ending Moment	Muhammadan Year, Month and Day
16	Th	1	14 ·25	23 ·59	13
17	Fr	2	P ·27	24 ·62	14
18	Sa	3	1 ·25	25 ·64	15
19	Su	4	2 ·22	26 ·63	16
20	Mo	5	3 ·18	27 ·60	17
21	Tu	6	4 ·11	1 ·55	18
22	We	7	5 ·02 6 ·93	2 ·50	19
23	Th	8	7 ·83	3 ·45	20
24	Fr	9	8 ·73	4 ·38	21
25	Sa	10	9 ·63	5 ·31	22
26	Su	11	10 ·53	6 ·24	23
27	Mo	12	11 ·44	7 ·17	24
28	Tu	13	12 ·36	8 ·11	25
29	We	14	13 ·29	9 ·08	26
30	Th	15	14 ·24	10 ·05	27
31	Fr	16	A ·20	11 ·03	28
1	Sa	17	1 ·18	12 ·04	29
2	Su	18	2 ·17	13 ·06	30
3	Mo	19	3 ·20	14 ·12	1
4	Tu	20	4 ·25	15 ·19	2
5	We	21	5 ·31	16 ·27	3
6	Th	22	6 ·39	17 ·37	4
7	Fr	23	7 ·47	18 ·48	5
8	Sa	24	8 ·56	19 ·59	6
9	Su	25	9 ·64	20 ·69	7
10	Mo	26	10 ·71	21 ·78	8
11	Tu	27	11 ·76	22 ·85	9
12	We	28	12 ·79	23 ·91	10
13	Th	29	13 ·81	24 ·95	11
14	Fr	30	14 ·79	25 ·96	12

Oct. — Solar: Manmatha, Kanya—Purattasi (1–17); Manmatha, Tula—Aippasi (18–31). Lunar: Nija, Bahula; Asvina, Sukla. Muhammadan: H. 1375 Safar; H. 1375 Rabi-ul-awwal.

Cyclic Sidereal Year, Month and Day	Week-Day	English Month and Day	Tithi Ending Moment	Nakshatra Ending Moment	Muhammadan Year, Month and Day
15	Sa	1	P ·77	26 ·95	13
16	Su	2	1 ·72	27 ·93	14
17	Mo	3	2 ·65	1 ·89	15
18	Tu	4	3 ·57	2 ·84	16
19	We	5	4 ·48	3 ·78	17
20	Th	6	5 ·39	4 ·71	18
21	Fr	7	6 ·29	5 ·64	19
22	Sa	8	7 ·19	6 ·57	20
23	Su	9	8 ·09	7 ·51	21
24	Mo	10	9 ·00 10 ·92	8 ·46	22
25	Tu	11	11 ·85	9 ·41	23
26	We	12	12 ·80	10 ·38	24
27	Th	13	13 ·76	11 ·36	25
28	Fr	14	14 ·75	12 ·36	26
29	Sa	15	A ·75	13 ·39	27
30	Su	16	1 ·78	14 ·43	28
31	Mo	17	2 ·82	15 ·49	29
1	Tu	18	3 ·88	16 ·57	1
2	We	19	4 ·96	17 ·67	2
3	Th	20	... ...	18 ·78	3
4	Fr	21	5 ·05	19 ·89	4
5	Sa	22	6 ·14	20 ·99	5
6	Su	23	7 ·22	... ...	6
7	Mo	24	8 ·30	21 ·08	7
8	Tu	25	9 ·34	22 ·16	8
9	We	26	10 ·37	23 ·23	9
10	Th	27	11 ·39	24 ·27	10
11	Fr	28	12 ·37	25 ·28	11
12	Sa	29	13 ·35	26 ·28	12
13	Su	30	14 ·31	27 ·26	13
14	Mo	31	P ·25	1 ·22	14

Nov. — Solar: Manmatha, Tula—Aippasi (1–16); Manmatha, Vrischika—Kartigai (17–30). Lunar: Asvina, Bahula; Karttika, Sukla. Muhammadan: H. 1375 Rabi-ul-awwal; Rabi-ul-akhir.

Cyclic Sidereal Year, Month and Day	Week-Day	English Month and Day	Tithi Ending Moment	Nakshatra Ending Moment	Muhammadan Year, Month and Day
15	Tu	1	1 ·16	2 ·18	15
16	We	2	2 ·07 3 ·98	3 ·12	16
17	Th	3	4 ·88	4 ·05 5 ·98	17
18	Fr	4	5 ·78	6 ·91	18
19	Sa	5	6 ·68	7 ·85	19
20	Su	6	7 ·59	8 ·79	20
21	Mo	7	8 ·51	9 ·74	21
22	Tu	8	9 ·45	10 ·70	22
23	We	9	10 ·40	11 ·68	23
24	Th	10	11 ·36	12 ·69	24
25	Fr	11	12 ·35	13 ·70	25
26	Sa	12	13 ·35	14 ·74	26
27	Su	13	14 ·38	15 ·80	27
28	Mo	14	A ·43	16 ·88	28
29	Tu	15	1 ·50	17 ·98	29
30	We	16	2 ·58	... ...	30
1	Th	17	3 ·66	18 ·08	1
2	Fr	18	4 ·76	19 ·18	2
3	Sa	19	5 ·84	20 ·29	3
4	Su	20	6 ·90	21 ·39	4
5	Mo	21	7 ·95	22 ·48	5
6	Tu	22	... ...	23 ·54	6
7	We	23	8 ·00	24 ·58	7
8	Th	24	9 ·01	25 ·60	8
9	Fr	25	10 ·00 11 ·97	26 ·60	9
10	Sa	26	12 ·92	27 ·59	10
11	Su	27	13 ·86	1 ·56	11
12	Mo	28	14 ·78	2 ·52	12
13	Tu	29	P ·70	3 ·46	13
14	We	30	1 ·60	4 ·39	14

Dec. — Solar: Manmatha, Vrischika—Kartigai (1–15); Manmatha, Dhanus—Margali (16–31). Lunar: Bahula; Margasira, Sukla. Muhammadan: H. 1375 Rabi-ul-akhir; H. 1375 Jumadal-awwal.

Cyclic Sidereal Year, Month and Day	Week-Day	English Month and Day	Tithi Ending Moment	Nakshatra Ending Moment	Muhammadan Year, Month and Day
15	Th	1	2 ·50	5 ·32	15
16	Fr	2	3 ·40	6 ·25	16
17	Sa	3	4 ·30	7 ·19	17
18	Su	4	5 ·21	8 ·13	18
19	Mo	5	6 ·13	9 ·08	19
20	Tu	6	7 ·07	10 ·04	20
21	We	7	8 ·03	11 ·02	21
22	Th	8	9 ·00 10 ·98	12 ·01	22
23	Fr	9	11 ·98	13 ·02	23
24	Sa	10	... ...	14 ·05	24
25	Su	11	12 ·02	15 ·11	25
26	Mo	12	13 ·07	16 ·19	26
27	Tu	13	14 ·15	17 ·28	27
28	We	14	A ·23	18 ·38	28
29	Th	15	1 ·32	19 ·48	29
1	Fr	16	2 ·41	20 ·59	1
2	Sa	17	3 ·49	21 ·69	2
3	Su	18	4 ·56	22 ·78	3
4	Mo	19	5 ·61	23 ·85	4
5	Tu	20	6 ·64	24 ·89	5
6	We	21	7 ·65	25 ·92	6
7	Th	22	8 ·64	26 ·93	7
8	Fr	23	9 ·61	27 ·92	8
9	Sa	24	10 ·57	1 ·89	9
10	Su	25	11 ·50	2 ·85	10
11	Mo	26	12 ·42	3 ·79	11
12	Tu	27	13 ·34	4 ·73	12
13	We	28	14 ·24	5 ·67	13
14	Th	29	P ·14	6 ·60	14
15	Fr	30	1 ·04 2 ·95	7 ·53	15
16	Sa	31	3 ·86	8 ·46	16

15. Svati. 16. Visak. 17. Anur. 18. Jyesh. 19. Mula. 20. P. Ash. 21. U. Ash. 22. Sravn. 23. Dani. 24. Satab. 25 P. Bhad. 26. U. Bhad. 27 Rev.

A. D. 1956. **Mesha Sankranti** (Commencement of Indian Sidereal Year).
Solar Eclipse. ● **(Surya Sid.) April 13·11.** **Saka 1878.** **Kaliyuga 5057.**
Lunar Eclipse. ○ **(Arya Sid.) April 13·00.** **(S. Cycle) Durmukha.**

SOLAR reckoning: Cyclic Sidereal Year, Month and Day	SOLAR reckoning: Week-Day	English Month and Day	LUNAR reckoning: Tithi Ending Moment	LUNAR reckoning: Nakshatra Ending Moment	Muhammadan Year, Month and Day
		Jan.			
Manmatha *Dhanus—Margali* 17	Su	1	Margasira *Bahula* 4 ·78	9 ·41	H. 1375 *Jumadal-awwal* 17
18	Mo	2	5 ·72	10 ·37	18
19	Tu	3	6 ·67	11 ·34	19
20	We	4	7 ·64	12 ·33	20
21	Th	5	8 ·63	13 ·34	21
22	Fr	6	9 ·64	14 ·37	22
23	Sa	7	10 ·67	15 ·42	23
24	Su	8	11 ·73	16 ·49	24
25	Mo	9	12 ·80	17 ·58	25
26	Tu	10	13 ·88	18 ·68	26
27	We	11	14 ·98	19 ·78	27
28	Th	12	... ...	20 ·89	28
29	Fr	13	A ·06	... ...	29
Manmatha *Makara—Tai* 1	Sa	14	Pausha *Sukla* 1 ·14	21 ·00	30
2	Su	15	2 ·20	22 ·09	H. 1375 *Jumadal-akhir* 1
3	Mo	16	3 ·26	23 ·10	2
4	Tu	17	4 ·29	24 ·21	3
5	We	18	5 ·29	25 ·24	4
6	Th	19	6 ·28	26 ·26	5
7	Fr	20	7 ·25	27 ·25	6
8	Sa	21	8 ·21	1 ·22	7
9	Su	22	9 ·14	2 ·18	8
10	Mo	23	10 ·06 11 ·97	3 ·13	9
11	Tu	24	12 ·87	4 ·08	10
12	We	25	13 ·77	5 ·01 6 ·94	11
13	Th	26	14 ·67	7 ·87	12
14	Fr	27	P ·58	8 ·80	13
15	Sa	28	1 ·49	9 ·74	14
16	Su	29	2 ·42	10 ·70	15
17	Mo	30	3 ·36	11 ·67	16
18	Tu	31	4 ·32	12 ·66	17
		Feb.			
19	We	1	*Bahula* 5 ·28	13 ·66	18
20	Th	2	6 ·26	14 ·68	19
21	Fr	3	7 ·28	15 ·73	20
22	Sa	4	8 ·32	16 ·80	21
23	Su	5	9 ·37	17 ·88	22
24	Mo	6	10 ·44	18 ·97	23
25	Tu	7	11 ·53	... ...	24
26	We	8	12 ·61	19 ·08	25
27	Th	9	13 ·69	20 ·19	26
28	Fr	10	14 ·77	21 ·30	27
29	Sa	11	A ·84	22 ·39	28
30	Su	12	Magha *Sukla* 1 ·90	23 ·46	29
Manmatha *Kumbha—Masi* 1	Mo	13	2 ·92	24 ·52	H. 1375 *Rajab* 1
2	Tu	14	3 ·93	25 ·57	2
3	We	15	4 ·92	26 ·58	3
4	Th	16	5 ·89	27 ·58	4
5	Fr	17	6 ·83	1 ·56	5
6	Sa	18	7 ·75	2 ·52	6
7	Su	19	8 ·67	3 ·47	7
8	Mo	20	9 ·58	4 ·41	8
9	Tu	21	10 ·49	5 ·35	9
10	We	22	11 ·40	6 ·28	10
11	Th	23	12 ·30	7 ·21	11
12	Fr	24	13 ·20	8 ·14	12
13	Sa	25	14 ·11	9 ·09	13
14	Su	26	P ·08 1 ·97	10 ·04	14
15	Mo	27	Magha *Bahula* 2 ·93	11 ·00 12 ·98	15
16	Tu	28	3 ·90	13 ·98	16
17	We	29	4 ·89	... ...	17

SOLAR reckoning: Cyclic Sidereal Year, Month and Day	SOLAR reckoning: Week-Day	English Month and Day	LUNAR reckoning: Tithi Ending Moment	LUNAR reckoning: Nakshatra Ending Moment	Muhammadan Year, Month and Day
		March			
Manmatha *Kumbha—Masi* 18	Th	1	Magha *Bahula* 5 ·90	14 ·01	H. 1375 *Rajab* 18
19	Fr	2	6 ·93	15 ·04	19
20	Sa	3	7 ·99	16 ·10	20
21	Su	4	... ...	17 ·18	21
22	Mo	5	8 ·06	18 ·27	22
23	Tu	6	9 ·14	19 ·38	23
24	We	7	10 ·23	20 ·49	24
25	Th	8	11 ·32	21 ·60	25
26	Fr	9	12 ·40	22 ·69	26
27	Sa	10	13 ·46	23 ·77	27
28	Su	11	14 ·50	24 ·84	28
29	Mo	12	A ·52	25 ·88	29
30	Tu	13	Phalguna *Sukla* 1 ·53	26 ·90	30
31	We	14	2 ·51	27 ·90	H. 1375 *Shaban* 1
Manmatha *Mina—Panguni* 1	Th	15	3 ·48	1 ·88	2
2	Fr	16	4 ·42	2 ·85	3
3	Sa	17	5 ·35	3 ·81	4
4	Su	18	6 ·27	4 ·75	5
5	Mo	19	7 ·18	5 ·68	6
6	Tu	20	8 ·08 9 ·98	6 ·61	7
7	We	21	10 ·88	7 ·54	8
8	Th	22	11 ·79	8 ·48	9
9	Fr	23	12 ·70	9 ·42	10
10	Sa	24	13 ·62	10 ·37	11
11	Su	25	14 ·55	11 ·33	12
12	Mo	26	P ·51	12 ·31	13
13	Tu	27	1 ·48	13 ·31	14
14	We	28	2 ·47	14 ·32	15
15	Th	29	3 ·49	15 ·36	16
16	Fr	30	4 ·52	16 ·41	17
17	Sa	31	5 ·57	17 ·48	18
		April			
18	Su	1	*Bahula* 6 ·64	18 ·58	19
19	Mo	2	7 ·72	19 ·68	20
20	Tu	3	8 ·80	20 ·79	21
21	We	4	9 ·89	21 ·90	22
22	Th	5	10 ·97	... ...	23
23	Fr	6	... ...	22 ·00	24
24	Sa	7	11 ·03	23 ·09	25
25	Su	8	12 ·07	24 ·15	26
26	Mo	9	13 ·10	25 ·20	27
27	Tu	10	14 ·09	26 ·22	28
28	We	11	A ·07	27 ·23	29
29	Th	12	Chaitra *Sukla* 1 ·04 2 ·98	1 ·21	H. 1375 *Ramzan* 1
Durmukha *Mesha—Chittirai* 1	Fr	13	3 ·91	2 ·18	2
2	Sa	14	4 ·83	3 ·14	3
3	Su	15	5 ·74	4 ·09	4
4	Mo	16	6 ·64	5 ·02 6 ·95	5
5	Tu	17	7 ·54	7 ·88	6
6	We	18	8 ·44	8 ·82	7
7	Th	19	9 ·34	9 ·76	8
8	Fr	20	10 ·25	10 ·70	9
9	Sa	21	11 ·16	11 ·66	10
10	Su	22	12 ·10	12 ·64	11
11	Mo	23	13 ·06	13 ·63	12
12	Tu	24	14 ·03	14 ·64	13
13	We	25	P ·01	15 ·67	14
14	Th	26	1 ·02	16 ·72	15
15	Fr	27	2 ·06	17 ·80	16
16	Sa	28	3 ·11	18 ·83	17
17	Su	29	*Bah.* 4 ·17	19 ·98	18
18	Mo	30	5 ·25	... ...	19

SOLAR reckoning: Cyclic Sidereal Year, Month and Day	SOLAR reckoning: Week-Day	English Month and Day	LUNAR reckoning: Tithi Ending Moment	LUNAR reckoning: Nakshatra Ending Moment	Muhammadan Year, Month and Day
		May			
Durmukha *Mesha—Chittirai* 19	Tu	1	Chaitra *Bahula* 6 ·34	20 ·09	H. 1375 *Ramzan* 20
20	We	2	7 ·42	21 ·19	21
21	Th	3	8 ·49	22 ·29	22
22	Fr	4	9 ·55	23 ·39	23
23	Sa	5	10 ·59	24 ·46	24
24	Su	6	11 ·62	25 ·51	25
25	Mo	7	12 ·62	26 ·54	26
26	Tu	8	13 ·61	27 ·55	27
27	We	9	14 ·57	1 ·55	28
28	Th	10	A ·51	2 ·52	29
29	Fr	11	Vaisakha *Sukla* 1 ·43	3 ·48	30
30	Sa	12	2 ·35	4 ·42	H. 1375 *Shawwal* 1
31	Su	13	3 ·26	5 ·36	2
Durmukha *Vrishabha—Vaikasi* 1	Mo	14	4 ·16	6 ·30	3
2	Tu	15	5 ·06 6 ·96	7 ·23	4
3	We	16	7 ·86	8 ·16	5
4	Th	17	8 ·76	9 ·10	6
5	Fr	18	9 ·68	10 ·04	7
6	Sa	19	10 ·62	11 ·00 12 ·97	8
7	Su	20	11 ·57	13 ·95	9
8	Mo	21	12 ·54	14 ·96	10
9	Tu	22	13 ·51	15 ·99	11
10	We	23	14 ·53	... ...	12
11	Th	24 ○	P ·56	16 ·04	13
12	Fr	25	1 ·61	17 ·10	14
13	Sa	26	2 ·68	18 ·18	15
14	Su	27	3 ·75	19 ·28	16
15	Mo	28	4 ·84	20 ·39	17
16	Tu	29	5 ·92	21 ·49	18
17	We	30	6 ·99	22 ·60	19
18	Th	31	... ...	23 ·69	20
		June			
19	Fr	1	*Bahula* 7 ·05	24 ·77	21
20	Sa	2	8 ·09	25 ·82	22
21	Su	3	9 ·12	26 ·86	23
22	Mo	4	10 ·12	27 ·88	24
23	Tu	5	11 ·10	1 ·88	25
24	We	6	12 ·07	2 ·85	26
25	Th	7	13 ·02 14 ·94	3 ·81	27
26	Fr	8	A ·86	4 ·76	28
27	Sa	9	Jyeshtha *Sukla* 1 ·76	5 ·71	29
28	Su	10	2 ·63	6 ·64	H. 1375 *Zi-l-ka'da* 1
29	Mo	11	3 ·56	7 ·57	2
30	Tu	12	4 ·46	8 ·50	3
31	We	13	5 ·33	9 ·43	4
Durmukha *Mithuna—Ani* 1	Th	14	6 ·26	10 ·38	5
2	Fr	15	7 ·18	11 ·33	6
3	Sa	16	8 ·11	12 ·30	7
4	Su	17	9 ·05	13 ·28	8
5	Mo	18	10 ·02	14 ·28	9
6	Tu	19	11 ·00	15 ·30	10
7	We	20	12 ·02	16 ·35	11
8	Th	21	13 ·04	17 ·41	12
9	Fr	22	14 ·09	18 ·49	13
10	Sa	23	P ·15	19 ·58	14
11	Su	24	1 ·23	20 ·68	15
12	Mo	25	2 ·31	21 ·79	16
13	Tu	26	3 ·39	22 ·90	17
14	We	27	4 ·43	... ...	18
15	Th	28	*Bahula* 5 ·52	23 ·00	19
16	Fr	29	6 ·57	24 ·07	20
17	Sa	30	7 ·30	25 ·13	21

Naksh :—1. Asvn. 2. Bhar. 3. Krit. 4. Rohi. 5. Mrig. 6. Ardh. 7. Punar. 8. Push. 9. Aslesh. 10. Magh. 11. P. Phal. 12. U. Phal. 13. Hasta. 14. Chit.

A. D. 1956.
A.—Amavasya.
P.—Paurnami.

Kollam 1132, Commences { N. Malabar—Sept. S. Malabar—Aug.

Hijra 1376, Commences, Aug. 8.

Vikrama 2013.
Bengal San 1362.
(N. Cycle) Saumya.

SOLAR reckoning: Cyclic Sidereal Year, Month and Day; Week-Day English Month and Day. LUNAR reckoning: Tithi Ending Moment; Nakshatra Ending Moment; Muhammadan Year, Month and Day.

July

Solar: Durmukha Mithuna—Ani; Durmukha Karkata—Adi. Lunar: Jyeshtha Bah.; Sukla, Ashadha; Bahula. Muhammadan: H. 1375 Zi-l-ka'da; H. 1375 Zi-l-hijja.

Cyclic Sidereal Year, Month and Day	Week-Day English Month and Day	Tithi Ending Moment	Nakshatra Ending Moment	Muhammadan Year, Month and Day
18	Su 1	8 ·60	26 ·18	22
19	Mo 2	9 ·58	27 ·20	23
20	Tu 3	10 ·54	1 ·20	24
21	We 4	11 ·49	2 ·18	25
22	Th 5	12 ·41	3 ·15	26
23	Fr 6	13 ·33	4 ·11	27
24	Sa 7	14 ·23	5 ·05 6 ·98	28
25	Su 8	—A ·13	7 ·91	29
26	Mo 9	1 ·03 2 ·93	8 ·84	30
27	Tu 10	3 ·83	9 ·77	1
28	We 11	4 ·73	10 ·72	2
29	Th 12	5 ·65	11 ·67	3
30	Fr 13	6 ·58	12 ·63	4
31	Sa 14	7 ·53	13 ·60	5
—32	Su 15	8 ·49	14 ·60	6
1	Mo 16	9 ·48	15 ·62	7
2	Tu 17	10 ·49	16 ·66	8
3	We 18	11 ·51	17 ·71	9
4	Th 19	12 ·55	18 ·79	10
5	Fr 20	13 ·61	19 ·88	11
6	Sa 21	14 ·69	20 ·99	12
7	Su 22	P ·77	... ...	13
8	Mo 23	1 ·86	21 ·10	14
9	Tu 24	2 ·93	22 ·20	15
10	We 25	3 ·99	23 ·30	16
11	Th 26	... ...	24 ·38	17
12	Fr 27	4 ·05	25 ·45	18
13	Sa 28	5 ·08	26 ·50	19
14	Su 29	6 ·08	27 ·52	20
15	Mo 30	7 ·06	1 ·53	21
16	Tu 31	8 ·03 9 ·97	2 ·51	22

Aug.

Solar: Durmukha Simha—Avani. Lunar: Sukla; Sravana; Bahula. Muhammadan: H. 1376 Muharram.

Cyclic Sidereal Year, Month and Day	Week-Day English Month and Day	Tithi Ending Moment	Nakshatra Ending Moment	Muhammadan Year, Month and Day
17	We 1	10 ·91	3 ·49	23
18	Th 2	11 ·83	4 ·44	24
19	Fr 3	12 ·73	5 ·38	25
20	Sa 4	13 ·63	6 ·32	26
21	Su 5	14 ·53	7 ·25	27
22	Mo 6	—A ·43	8 ·18	28
23	Tu 7	1 ·33	9 ·11	—29
24	We 8	2 ·23	10 ·05	1
25	Th 9	3 ·15	11 ·00 12 ·96	2
26	Fr 10	4 ·08	13 ·93	3
27	Sa 11	5 ·02 6 ·99	14 ·93	4
28	Su 12	7 ·97	15 ·94	5
29	Mo 13	8 ·98	16 ·97	6
30	Tu 14	... ...	... ...	7
—31	We 15	9 ·00	17 ·02	8
1	Th 16	10 ·05	18 ·09	9
2	Fr 17	11 ·11	19 ·19	10
3	Sa 18	12 ·19	20 ·29	11
4	Su 19	13 ·27	21 ·40	12
5	Mo 20	14 ·36	22 ·50	13
6	Tu 21	P ·43	23 ·60	14
7	We 22	1 ·50	24 ·69	15
8	Th 23	2 ·54	25 ·76	16
9	Fr 24	3 ·57	26 ·81	17
10	Sa 25	4 ·58	27 ·84	18
11	Su 26	5 ·56	1 ·85	19
12	Mo 27	6 ·53	2 ·84	20
13	Tu 28	7 ·48	3 ·82	21
14	We 29	8 ·41	4 ·77	22
15	Th 30	9 ·33	5 ·72	23
16	Fr 31	10 ·24	6 ·65	24

Sep.

Solar: Durmukha Simha—Avani; Durmukha Kanya—Purattasi. Lunar: Sukla; Bhadrapada; Bahula. Muhammadan: H. 1376 Muharram; H. 1376 Safar.

Cyclic Sidereal Year, Month and Day	Week-Day English Month and Day	Tithi Ending Moment	Nakshatra Ending Moment	Muhammadan Year, Month and Day
17	Sa 1	11 ·14	7 ·58	25
18	Su 2	12 ·04 13 ·94	8 ·51	26
19	Mo 3	14 ·84	9 ·45	27
20	Tu 4	—A ·74	10 ·39	28
21	We 5	1 ·66	11 ·33	29
22	Th 6	2 ·59	12 ·29	—30
23	Fr 7	3 ·53	13 ·27	1
24	Sa 8	4 ·50	14 ·25	2
25	Su 9	5 ·49	15 ·26	3
26	Mo 10	6 ·51	16 ·28	4
27	Tu 11	7 ·53	17 ·33	5
28	We 12	8 ·57	18 ·41	6
29	Th 13	9 ·63	19 ·49	7
30	Fr 14	10 ·71	20 ·59	8
—31	Sa 15	11 ·80	21 ·69	9
1	Su 16	12 ·88	22 ·80	10
2	Mo 17	13 ·96	23 ·91	11
3	Tu 18	... ...	... ...	12
4	We 19	14 ·02	24 ·00	13
5	Th 20	P ·07	25 ·07	14
6	Fr 21	1 ·10	26 ·13	15
7	Sa 22	2 ·11	27 ·16	16
8	Su 23	3 ·10	1 ·17	17
9	Mo 24	4 ·07	2 ·17	18
10	Tu 25	5 ·01 6 ·95	3 ·15	19
11	We 26	7 ·87	4 ·11	20
12	Th 27	8 ·78	5 ·05 6 ·99	21
13	Fr 28	9 ·69	7 ·93	22
14	Sa 29	10 ·59	8 ·86	23
15	Su 30	11 ·49	9 ·79	24

Oct.

Solar: Durmukha Tula—Aippasi. Lunar: Sukla; Asvina; Bahula. Muhammadan: H. 1376 Rabi-ul-awwal.

Cyclic Sidereal Year, Month and Day	Week-Day English Month and Day	Tithi Ending Moment	Nakshatra Ending Moment	Muhammadan Year, Month and Day
16	Mo 1	12 ·89	10 ·73	25
17	Tu 2	13 ·29	11 ·67	26
18	We 3	14 ·21	12 ·63	27
19	Th 4	—A ·15	13 ·60	28
20	Fr 5	1 ·09	14 ·58	—29
21	Sa 6	2 ·06	15 ·59	1
22	Su 7	3 ·04	16 ·60	2
23	Mo 8	4 ·06	17 ·65	3
24	Tu 9	5 ·09	18 ·71	4
25	We 10	6 ·13	19 ·79	5
26	Th 11	7 ·19	20 ·89	6
27	Fr 12	8 ·27	21 ·99	7
28	Sa 13	9 ·36	... ...	8
29	Su 14	10 ·44	22 ·10	9
30	Mo 15	11 ·52	23 ·21	10
—31	Tu 16	12 ·59	24 ·30	11
1	We 17	13 ·64	25 ·38	12
2	Th 18	14 ·67	26 ·44	13
3	Fr 19	P ·68	27 ·48	14
4	Sa 20	1 ·67	1 ·50	15
5	Su 21	2 ·64	2 ·50	16
6	Mo 22	3 ·60	3 ·48	17
7	Tu 23	4 ·53	4 ·44	18
8	We 24	5 ·45	5 ·39	19
9	Th 25	6 ·36	6 ·34	20
10	Fr 26	7 ·26	7 ·27	21
11	Sa 27	8 ·16	8 ·20	22
12	Su 28	9 ·06 10 ·97	9 ·13	23
13	Mo 29	11 ·89	10 ·06	24
14	Tu 30	12 ·81	11 ·01 12 ·96	25
15	We 31	13 ·74	13 ·92	26

Nov.

Solar: Durmukha Tula—Aippasi; Durmukha Vrischika—Karttigai. Lunar: Sukla; Karttika; Bahula. Muhammadan: H. 1376 Rabi-ul-akhir.

Cyclic Sidereal Year, Month and Day	Week-Day English Month and Day	Tithi Ending Moment	Nakshatra Ending Moment	Muhammadan Year, Month and Day
16	Th 1	14 ·68	14 ·90	27
17	Fr 2	—A ·65	15 ·90	28
18	Sa 3	1 ·64	16 ·92	29
19	Su 4	2 ·66	17 ·96	—30
20	Mo 5	3 ·68	... ...	1
21	Tu 6	4 ·73	18 ·02	2
22	We 7	5 ·79	19 ·09	3
23	Th 8	6 ·88	20 ·19	4
24	Fr 9	7 ·97	21 ·29	5
25	Sa 10	... ...	22 ·40	6
26	Su 11	8 ·05	23 ·51	7
27	Mo 12	9 ·13	24 ·61	8
28	Tu 13	10 ·20	25 ·68	9
29	We 14	11 ·26	26 ·75	10
—30	Th 15	12 ·29	27 ·80	11
1	Fr 16	13 ·30	1 ·82	12
2	Sa 17	14 ·28	2 ·82	13
3	Su 18	P ·25	3 ·80	14
4	Mo 19	1 ·21	4 ·77	15
5	Tu 20	2 ·15	5 ·73	16
6	We 21	3 ·07 4 ·98	6 ·68	17
7	Th 22	5 ·88	7 ·61	18
8	Fr 23	6 ·78	8 ·54	19
9	Sa 24	7 ·68	9 ·47	20
10	Su 25	8 ·59	10 ·41	21
11	Mo 26	9 ·50	11 ·35	22
12	Tu 27	10 ·42	12 ·29	23
13	We 28	11 ·35	13 ·25	24
14	Th 29	12 ·30	14 ·23	25
15	Fr 30	13 ·28	15 ·22	26

Dec.

Solar: Durmukha Dhanus—Margali. Lunar: Sukla; Margasira; Bahula. Muhammadan: H. 1376 Jumada-l-awwal.

Cyclic Sidereal Year, Month and Day	Week-Day English Month and Day	Tithi Ending Moment	Nakshatra Ending Moment	Muhammadan Year, Month and Day
16	Sa 1	14 ·26	16 ·24	27
17	Su 2	—A ·28	17 ·27	28
18	Mo 3	1 ·31	18 ·33	—29
19	Tu 4	2 ·36	19 ·40	1
20	We 5	3 ·43	20 ·49	2
21	Th 6	4 ·51	21 ·59	3
22	Fr 7	5 ·60	22 ·70	4
23	Sa 8	6 ·69	23 ·81	5
24	Su 9	7 ·76	24 ·91	6
25	Mo 10	8 ·83	25 ·99	7
26	Tu 11	9 ·89	... ...	8
27	We 12	10 ·92	26 ·07	9
28	Th 13	11 ·93	27 ·12	10
—29	Fr 14	12 ·92	1 ·14	11
1	Sa 15	13 ·89	2 ·15	12
2	Su 16	14 ·84	3 ·13	13
3	Mo 17	P ·77	4 ·11	14
4	Tu 18	1 ·69	5 ·07	15
5	We 19	2 ·60	6 ·01 7 ·95	16
6	Th 20	3 ·51	8 ·89	17
7	Fr 21	4 ·41	9 ·82	18
8	Sa 22	5 ·31	10 ·75	19
9	Su 23	6 ·21	11 ·68	20
10	Mo 24	7 ·13	12 ·63	21
11	Tu 25	8 ·06 9 ·99	13 ·58	22
12	We 26	10 ·95	14 ·55	23
13	Th 27	11 ·92	15 ·55	24
14	Fr 28	12 ·91	16 ·56	25
15	Sa 29	13 ·93	17 ·59	26
16	Su 30	14 ·96	18 ·63	27
17	Mo 31	... ...	19 ·70	28

15. Svati. 16. Visak. 17. Anur. 18. Jyesh. 19. Mula. 20. P. Ash. 21. U. Ash. 22. Sravn. 23. Dani. 24. Satab. 25. P. Bhad. 26. U. Bhad. 27. Rev.

A. D. 1957. — Mesha Sankranti (Commencement of Indian Sidereal Year).
Solar Eclipse. ● — (Surya Sid.) April 13·37. — Saka 1879. — Kaliyuga 5058.
Lunar Eclipse. ○ — (Arya Sid.) April 13·26. — (S. Cycle) Hemalamba.

Columns: SOLAR reckoning — Cyclic Sidereal Year, Month and Day; Week-Day, English Month and Day. LUNAR reckoning — Tithi Ending Moment; Nakshatra Ending Moment; Muhammadan Year, Month and Day.

Jan. (Solar: Durmukha, Dhanus—Margali; Durmukha, Makara—Tai. Lunar: Sukla, Pausha, Bahula. Muhammadan: H. 1376 Jumadal-akhir.)

Cyclic Sidereal	Week-Day	Day	Tithi	Moment	Nakshatra	Moment	Muhammadan
18	Tu	1	—A	·01	20	·80	29
19	We	2	1	·08	21	·90	—30
20	Th	3	2	·16	...	...	1
21	Fr	4	3	·25	22	·00	2
22	Sa	5	4	·34	23	·11	3
23	Su	6	5	·43	24	·21	4
24	Mo	7	6	·50	25	·31	5
25	Tu	8	7	·54	26	·38	6
26	We	9	8	·57	27	·43	7
27	Th	10	9	·58	1	·46	8
28	Fr	11	10	·56	2	·47	9
29	Sa	12	11	·53	3	·47	10
—30	Su	13	12	·48	4	·44	11
1	Mo	14	13	·42	5	·40	12
2	Tu	15	14	·34	6	·35	13
3	We	16	P	·25	7	·29	14
4	Th	17	1	·15	8	·23	15
5	Fr	18	2 3	·05 ·95	9	·16	16
6	Sa	19	4	·86	10	·09	17
7	Su	20	5	·78	11 12	·02 ·96	18
8	Mo	21	6	·70	13	·92	19
9	Tu	22	7	·64	14	·89	20
10	We	23	8	·59	15	·88	21
11	Th	24	9	·56	16	·88	22
12	Fr	25	10	·55	17	·90	23
13	Sa	26	11	·57	18	·95	24
14	Su	27	12	·62	...	...	25
15	Mo	28	13	·67	19	·02	26
16	Tu	29	14	·74	20	·10	27
17	We	30	—A	·82	21	·19	28
18	Th	31	1	·90	22	·30	—29

Feb. (Solar: Durmukha, Kumbha—Masi. Lunar: Sukla, Magha, Bahula. Muhammadan: H. 1376 Rajab.)

Cyclic Sidereal	Week-Day	Day	Tithi	Moment	Nakshatra	Moment	Muhammadan
19	Fr	1	2	·99	23	·41	1
20	Sa	2	...	...	24	·52	2
21	Su	3	3	·08	25	·61	3
22	Mo	4	4	·15	26	·68	4
23	Tu	5	5	·19	27	·74	5
24	We	6	6	·21	1	·78	6
25	Th	7	7	·22	2	·79	7
26	Fr	8	8	·21	3	·80	8
27	Sa	9	9	·17	4	·77	9
28	Su	10	10	·11	5	·74	10
—29	Mo	11	11 12	·04 ·96	6	·68	11
1	Tu	12	13	·88	7	·62	12
2	We	13	14	·78	8	·56	13
3	Th	14	P	·68	9	·49	14
4	Fr	15	1	·58	10	·42	15
5	Sa	16	2	·48	11	·36	16
6	Su	17	3	·40	12	·30	17
7	Mo	18	4	·32	13	·26	18
8	Tu	19	5	·26	14	·22	19
9	We	20	6	·21	15	·20	20
10	Th	21	7	·19	16	·20	21
11	Fr	22	8	·18	17	·22	22
12	Sa	23	9	·19	18	·26	23
13	Su	24	10	·23	19	·32	24
14	Mo	25	11	·28	20	·40	25
15	Tu	26	12	·36	21	·49	26
16	We	27	13	·45	22	·60	27
17	Th	28	14	·54	23	·71	28

March (Solar: Durmukha, Kumbha—Masi; Durmukha, Mina—Panguni. Lunar: Sukla, Phalguna, Bahula. Muhammadan: H. 1376 Shaban.)

Cyclic Sidereal	Week-Day	Day	Tithi	Moment	Nakshatra	Moment	Muhammadan
18	Fr	1	—A	·62	24	·82	29
19	Sa	2	1	·70	25	·91	30
20	Su	3	2	·76	26	·99	1
21	Mo	4	3	·80	...	...	2
22	Tu	5	4	·82	27	·05	3
23	We	6	5	·82	1	·09	4
24	Th	7	6	·81	2	·12	5
25	Fr	8	7	·78	3	·12	6
26	Sa	9	8	·72	4	·10	7
27	Su	10	9	·65	5	·07	8
28	Mo	11	10	·57	6 7	·02 ·97	9
29	Tu	12	11	·48	8	·90	10
—30	We	13	12	·38	9	·83	11
1	Th	14	13	·28	10	·76	12
2	Fr	15	14	·18	11	·69	13
3	Sa	16	P 1	·08 ·99	12	·64	14
4	Su	17	2	·92	13	·59	15
5	Mo	18	3	·86	14	·55	16
6	Tu	19	4	·82	15	·53	17
7	We	20	5	·79	16	·52	18
8	Th	21	6	·77	17	·54	19
9	Fr	22	7	·80	18	·58	20
10	Sa	23	8	·83	19	·63	21
11	Su	24	9	·88	20	·70	22
12	Mo	25	10	·95	21	·79	23
13	Tu	26	...	...	22	·89	24
14	We	27	11	·03	...	...	25
15	Th	28	12	·12	23	·00	26
16	Fr	29	13	·20	24	·11	27
17	Sa	30	14	·28	25	·21	28
18	Su	31	—A	·34	26	·30	29

April (Solar: Hemalamba, Mesha—Chittirai. Lunar: Sukla, Chaitra, Bahula. Muhammadan: H. 1376 Ramzan.)

Cyclic Sidereal	Week-Day	Day	Tithi	Moment	Nakshatra	Moment	Muhammadan
19	Mo	1	1	·39	27	·37	1
20	Tu	2	2	·41	1	·42	2
21	We	3	3	·40	2	·44	3
22	Th	4	4	·38	3	·45	4
23	Fr	5	5	·34	4	·43	5
24	Sa	6	6	·29	5	·40	6
25	Su	7	7	·22	6	·36	7
26	Mo	8	8	·14	7	·31	8
27	Tu	9	9 10	·04 ·94	8	·24	9
28	We	10	11	·84	9	·17	10
29	Th	11	12	·74	10	·10	11
—30	Fr	12	13	·64	11 12	·04 ·98	12
1	Sa	13	14	·55	13	·92	13
2	Su	14	P	·48	14	·88	14
3	Mo	15	1	·42	15	·85	15
4	Tu	16	2	·37	16	·85	16
5	We	17	3	·34	17	·86	17
6	Th	18	4	·32	18	·89	18
7	Fr	19	5	·34	19	·94	19
8	Sa	20	6	·38	...	...	20
9	Su	21	7	·43	20	·01	21
10	Mo	22	8	·49	21	·09	22
11	Tu	23	9	·57	22	·20	23
12	We	24	10	·66	23	·31	24
13	Th	25	11	·75	24	·41	25
14	Fr	26	12	·82	25	·51	26
15	Sa	27	13	·88	26	·60	27
16	Su	28	14	·93	27	·68	28
17	Mo	29	—A	·94	1	·73	29
18	Tu	30	1	·94	2	·76	30

May (Solar: Hemalamba, Mesha—Chittirai; Hemalamba, Vrishabha—Vaikasi. Lunar: Sukla, Vaisakha, Bahula. Muhammadan: H. 1376 Shawwal.)

Cyclic Sidereal	Week-Day	Day	Tithi	Moment	Nakshatra	Moment	Muhammadan
19	We	1	2	·92	3	·77	1
20	Th	2	3	·88	4	·76	2
21	Fr	3	4	·82	5	·74	3
22	Sa	4	5	·75	6	·70	4
23	Su	5	6	·66	7	·64	5
24	Mo	6	7	·57	8	·58	6
25	Tu	7	8	·47	9	·52	7
26	We	8	9	·37	10	·45	8
27	Th	9	10	·27	11	·38	9
28	Fr	10	11	·17	12	·31	10
29	Sa	11	12	·08	13	·26	11
30	Su	12	13 14	·00 ·94	14	·21	12
—31	Mo ○	13	P	·89	15	·18	13
1	Tu	14	1	·85	16	·17	14
2	We	15	2	·84	17	·18	15
3	Th	16	3	·85	18	·20	16
4	Fr	17	4	·89	19	·25	17
5	Sa	18	5	·94	20	·31	18
6	Su	19	...	...	21	·40	19
7	Mo	20	6	·00	22	·50	20
8	Tu	21	7	·08	23	·61	21
9	We	22	8	·17	24	·71	22
10	Th	23	9	·26	25	·81	23
11	Fr	24	10	·33	26	·91	24
12	Sa	25	11	·39	27	·99	25
13	Su	26	12	·43	...	...	26
14	Mo	27	13	·44	1	·04	27
15	Tu	28	14	·44	2	·08	28
16	We	29	—A	·42	3	·09	—29
17	Th	30	1	·38	4	·09	1
18	Fr	31	2	·33	5	·07	2

June (Solar: Hemalamba, Mithuna—Ani. Lunar: Sukla, Jyeshtha, Bahula, A. Suk. Muhammadan: H. 1376 Zil-ka'da.)

Cyclic Sidereal	Week-Day	Day	Tithi	Moment	Nakshatra	Moment	Muhammadan
19	Sa	1	3	·26	6 7	·03 ·98	3
20	Su	2	4	·16	8	·92	4
21	Mo	3	5 6	·03 ·96	9	·86	5
22	Tu	4	7	·86	10	·79	6
23	We	5	8	·76	11	·72	7
24	Th	6	9	·66	12	·65	8
25	Fr	7	10	·58	13	·59	9
26	Sa	8	11	·50	14	·54	10
27	Su	9	12	·43	15	·52	11
28	Mo	10	13	·38	16	·50	12
29	Tu	11	14	·34	17	·50	13
30	We	12	P	·33	18	·52	14
31	Th	13	1	·33	19	·56	15
—32	Fr	14	2	·37	20	·63	16
1	Sa	15	3	·42	21	·71	17
2	Su	16	4	·49	22	·80	18
3	Mo	17	5	·56	23	·90	19
4	Tu	18	6	·64	...	...	20
5	We	19	7	·73	24	·01	21
6	Th	20	8	·80	25	·12	22
7	Fr	21	9	·86	26	·22	23
8	Sa	22	10	·90	27	·30	24
9	Su	23	11	·93	1	·35	25
10	Mo	24	12	·92	2	·39	26
11	Tu	25	13	·90	3	·42	27
12	We	26	14	·87	4	·42	28
13	Th	27	A	·81	5	·40	29
14	Fr	28	1	·74	6	·36	—30
15	Sa	29	2	·65	7	·31	1
16	Su	30	3	·55	8	·25	2

Naksh:—1. Asvn. 2. Bhar. 3. Krit. 4. Rohi. 5. Mrig. 6. Ardh. 7. Punar. 8. Push. 9. Aslesh. 10. Magh. 11. P. Phal. 12. U. Phal. 13. Hasta. 14. Chit.

A. D. 1957.
A.—Amavasya.
P.—Paurnami.

Kollam 1133, Commences { N. Malabar—Sept. / S. Malabar—Aug.

Hijra 1377, Commences, July 29.

Vikrama 2014.
Bengal San 1363.
(N. Cycle) Sadharana.

SOLAR reckoning: Cyclic Sidereal Year, Month and Day; Week-Day English Month and Day. LUNAR reckoning: Tithi Ending Moment; Nakshatra Ending Moment; Muhammadan Year, Month and Day.

July

Hemalamba Mithuna—Ani. / Hemalamba Karkata—Adi. — Sukla, Ashadha, Bahula — H. 1376 Zi-l-hijja.

Cyclic Sidereal Year, Month and Day	Week-Day	English Day	Tithi	Tithi Ending Moment	Nakshatra	Nakshatra Ending Moment	Muhammadan Year, Month and Day
17	Mo	1	4	·45	9	·19	3
18	Tu	2	5	·35	10	·13	4
19	We	3	6	·25	11; 12	·06; ·99	5
20	Th	4	7	·15	13	·93	6
21	Fr	5	8; 9	·06; ·98	14	·89	7
22	Sa	6	10	·91	15	·85	8
23	Su	7	11	·85	16	·82	9
24	Mo	8	12	·82	17	·82	10
25	Tu	9	13	·80	18	·83	11
26	We	10	14	·81	19	·87	12
27	Th	11	P	·85	20	·93	13
28	Fr	12	1	·90	...	...	14
29	Sa	13	2	·96	21	·01	15
30	Su	14	...	...	22	·10	16
31	Mo	15	3	·04	23	·20	17
1	Tu	16	4	·12	24	·31	18
2	We	17	5	·20	25	·42	19
3	Th	18	6	·27	26	·52	20
4	Fr	19	7	·34	27	·60	21
5	Sa	20	8	·38	1	·67	22
6	Su	21	9	·40	2	·72	23
7	Mo	22	10	·40	3	·74	24
8	Tu	23	11	·38	4	·74	25
9	We	24	12	·34	5	·73	26
10	Th	25	13	·29	6	·70	27
11	Fr	26	14	·22	7	·65	28
12	Sa	27	A	·14	8	·60	29
13	Su	28	1; 2	·04; ·94	9	·54	30
14	Mo	29	3	·84	10	·47	1
15	Tu	30	4	·74	11	·40	2
16	We	31	5	·64	12	·33	3

Aug.

Hemalamba Simha—Avani. — Sukla, Sravana, Bahula, Sukla, B. — H. 1377 Muharram., Safar.

Cyclic Sidereal Year, Month and Day	Week-Day	English Day	Tithi	Tithi Ending Moment	Nakshatra	Nakshatra Ending Moment	Muhammadan Year, Month and Day
17	Th	1	6	·55	13	·27	4
18	Fr	2	7	·46	14	·22	5
19	Sa	3	8	·39	15	·18	6
20	Su	4	9	·34	16	·15	7
21	Mo	5	10	·31	17	·14	8
22	Tu	6	11	·29	18	·16	9
23	We	7	12	·31	19	·19	10
24	Th	8	13	·33	20	·24	11
25	Fr	9	14	·37	21	·31	12
26	Sa	10	P	·44	22	·40	13
27	Su	11	1	·52	23	·51	14
28	Mo	12	2	·61	24	·62	15
29	Tu	13	3	·69	25	·72	16
30	We	14	4	·76	26	·82	17
31	Th	15	5	·82	27	·91	18
32	Fr	16	6	·87	1	·98	19
1	Sa	17	7	·90	...	...	20
2	Su	18	8	·89	2	·03	21
3	Mo	19	9	·83	3	·06	22
4	Tu	20	10	·85	4	·07	23
5	We	21	11	·80	5	·06	24
6	Th	22	12	·73	6; 7	·03; ·99	25
7	Fr	23	13	·64	8	·94	26
8	Sa	24	14	·54	9	·87	27
9	Su	25	A	·44	10	·80	28
10	Mo	26	1	·34	11	·73	29
11	Tu	27	2	·24	12	·67	30
12	We	28	3	·14	13	·61	1
13	Th	29	4; 5	·05; ·97	14	·55	2
14	Fr	30	6	·90	15	·51	3
15	Sa	31	7	·85	16	·48	4

Sep.

Hemalamba Simha—Avani. / Hemalamba Kanya—Purattasi. — Sukla, Bhadrapada, Bahula — H. 1377 Safar.

Cyclic Sidereal Year, Month and Day	Week-Day	English Day	Tithi	Tithi Ending Moment	Nakshatra	Nakshatra Ending Moment	Muhammadan Year, Month and Day
16	Su	1	8	·82	17	·47	5
17	Mo	2	9	·80	18	·48	6
18	Tu	3	10	·82	19	·50	7
19	We	4	11	·84	20	·55	8
20	Th	5	12	·89	21	·62	9
21	Fr	6	13	·95	22	·71	10
22	Sa	7	...	...	23	·81	11
23	Su	8	14	·03	24	·91	12
24	Mo	9	P	·11	...	...	13
25	Tu	10	1	·19	25	·02	14
26	We	11	2	·27	26	·12	15
27	Th	12	3	·34	27	·21	16
28	Fr	13	4	·39	1	·29	17
29	Sa	14	5	·41	2	·35	18
30	Su	15	6	·43	3	·38	19
31	Mo	16	7	·41	4	·39	20
1	Tu	17	8	·38	5	·38	21
2	We	18	9	·32	6	·37	22
3	Th	19	10	·25	7	·33	23
4	Fr	20	11	·17	8	·27	24
5	Sa	21	12; 13	·08; ·98	9	·21	25
6	Su	22	14	·88	10	·15	26
7	Mo	23	A	·78	11	·08	27
8	Tu	24	1	·68	12; 13	·01; ·94	28
9	We	25	2	·59	14	·89	29
10	Th	26	3	·51	15	·84	1
11	Fr	27	4	·44	16	·82	2
12	Sa	28	5	·39	17	·80	3
13	Su	29	6	·36	18	·80	4
14	Mo	30	7	·35	19	·82	5

Oct.

Hemalamba Tula—Aippasi. — Sukla, Asvina, Bahula, Kartt. Suk. — H. 1377 Rabi-ul-awwal., Rabi-ul-akhir.

Cyclic Sidereal Year, Month and Day	Week-Day	English Day	Tithi	Tithi Ending Moment	Nakshatra	Nakshatra Ending Moment	Muhammadan Year, Month and Day
15	Tu	1	8	·37	20	·86	6
16	We	2	9	·39	21	·92	7
17	Th	3	10	·44	...	...	8
18	Fr	4	11	·50	22	·01	9
19	Sa	5	12	·58	23	·11	10
20	Su	6	13	·66	24	·21	11
21	Mo	7	14	·75	25	·32	12
22	Tu	8	P	·83	26	·42	13
23	We	9	1	·90	27	·52	14
24	Th	10	2	·95	1	·60	15
25	Fr	11	3	·97	2	·66	16
26	Sa	12	4	·99	3	·70	17
27	Su	13	5	·97	4	·71	18
28	Mo	14	6	·95	5	·72	19
29	Tu	15	7	·89	6	·70	20
30	We	16	8	·82	7	·66	21
1	Th	17	9	·74	8	·61	22
2	Fr	18	10	·65	9	·55	23
3	Sa	19	11	·55	10	·49	24
4	Su	20	12	·45	11	·42	25
5	Mo	21	13	·35	12	·35	26
6	Tu	22	14	·26	13	·28	27
7	We	23	A	·17	14	·22	28
8	Th	24	1	·09	15	·17	29
9	Fr	25	2; 3	·02; ·97	16	·14	30
10	Sa	26	4	·94	17	·12	1
11	Su	27	5	·93	18	·12	2
12	Mo	28	6	·94	19	·13	3
13	Tu	29	7	·98	20	·17	4
14	We	30	...	...	21	·24	5
15	Th	31	8	·03	22	·32	6

Nov.

Hemalamba Tula—Aippasi. / Hemalamba Vrischika—Kartigai. — Sukla, Karttika, Bahula, Sukla — H. 1377 Rabi-ul-akhir.

Cyclic Sidereal Year, Month and Day	Week-Day	English Day	Tithi	Tithi Ending Moment	Nakshatra	Nakshatra Ending Moment	Muhammadan Year, Month and Day
16	Fr	1	9	·09	23	·41	7
17	Sa	2	10	·17	24	·51	8
18	Su	3	11	·26	25	·62	9
19	Mo	4	12	·35	26	·73	10
20	Tu	5	13	·43	27	·83	11
21	We	6	14	·50	1	·91	12
22	Th	7	P	·55	2	·97	13
23	Fr	8	1	·58	...	...	14
24	Sa	9	2	·59	3	·01	15
25	Su	10	3	·57	4	·01	16
26	Mo	11	4	·54	5	·04	17
27	Tu	12	5	·49	6; 7	·03; ·99	18
28	We	13	6	·43	8	·94	19
29	Th	14	7	·35	9	·89	20
30	Fr	15	8	·26	10	·83	21
1	Sa	16	9	·16	11	·76	22
2	Su	17	10; 11	·06; ·96	12	·69	23
3	Mo	18	12	·87	13	·62	24
4	Tu	19	13	·78	14	·56	25
5	We	20	14	·70	15	·51	26
6	Th	21	A	·64	16	·47	27
7	Fr	22	1	·59	17	·45	28
8	Sa	23	2	·56	18	·44	29
9	Su	24	3	·55	19	·45	1
10	Mo	25	4	·57	20	·49	2
11	Tu	26	5	·60	21	·55	3
12	We	27	6	·65	22	·62	4
13	Th	28	7	·72	23	·71	5
14	Fr	29	8	·81	24	·81	6
15	Sa	30	9	·90	25	·92	7

Dec.

Hemalamba Dhanus—Margali. — Margasira, Bahula, Sukla, Pausha — H. 1377 Jumadal-awwal., Jumadal-akhir.

Cyclic Sidereal Year, Month and Day	Week-Day	English Day	Tithi	Tithi Ending Moment	Nakshatra	Nakshatra Ending Moment	Muhammadan Year, Month and Day
16	Su	1	10	·98	...	...	8
17	Mo	2	...	...	26	·03	9
18	Tu	3	11	·05	27	·13	10
19	We	4	12	·12	1	·21	11
20	Th	5	13	·18	2	·28	12
21	Fr	6	14	·21	3	·34	13
22	Sa	7	P	·22	4	·36	14
23	Su	8	1	·21	5	·37	15
24	Mo	9	2	·17	6	·35	16
25	Tu	10	3	·12	7	·32	17
26	We	11	4; 5	·05; ·97	8	·28	18
27	Th	12	6	·88	9	·23	19
28	Fr	13	7	·79	10	·17	20
29	Sa	14	8	·69	11	·10	21
30	Su	15	9	·59	12; 13	·03; ·96	22
1	Mo	16	10	·50	14	·90	23
2	Tu	17	11	·41	15	·85	24
3	We	18	12	·33	16	·80	25
4	Th	19	13	·27	17	·77	26
5	Fr	20	14	·23	18	·76	27
6	Sa	21	A	·21	19	·78	28
7	Su	22	1	·19	20	·81	29
8	Mo	23	2	·21	21	·85	30
9	Tu	24	3	·25	22	·92	1
10	We	25	4	·30	...	...	2
11	Th	26	5	·37	23	·01	3
12	Fr	27	6	·46	24	·11	4
13	Sa	28	7	·55	25	·22	5
14	Su	29	8	·63	26	·33	6
15	Mo	30	9	·71	27	·43	7
16	Tu	31	10	·78	1	·52	8

15. Svati. 16. Visak. 17. Anur. 18. Jyesh. 19. Mula. 20. P. Ash. 21. U. Ash. 22. Sravn. 23. Dani. 24. Satab. 25. P. Bhad. 26. U. Bhad. 27. Rev,

A. D. 1958.
Solar Eclipse. ●
Lunar Eclipse. ○

Mesha Sankranti (Commencement of Indian Sidereal Year).
(Surya Sid.) April 13·63.
(Arya Sid.) April 13·52.

Saka 1880. **Kaliyuga 5059.**
(S. Cycle) Vilamba.

Columns: SOLAR reckoning (Cyclic Sidereal Year, Month and Day; Week-Day English Month and Day) — LUNAR reckoning (Tithi Ending Moment; Nakshatra Ending Moment) — Muhammadan Year, Month and Day.

Jan.

Solar: Hemalamba Dhanus—Margali (17–29); Hemalamba Makara—Tai (1–18). Lunar: Pausha Suk., Bahula, Sukla. Muhammadan: H. 1377 Jumadal-akhir.

Cyclic Sidereal	Week-Day English	Tithi	Nakshatra	Muhammadan
17	We 1	11 ·82	2 ·60	9
18	Th 2	12 ·85	3 ·65	10
19	Fr 3	13 ·86	4 ·68	11
20	Sa 4	14 ·85	5 ·69	12
21	Su 5	P ·81	6 ·68	13
22	Mo 6	1 ·76	7 ·65	14
23	Tu 7	2 ·70	8 ·62	15
24	We 8	3 ·62	9 ·57	16
25	Th 9	4 ·53	10 ·51	17
26	Fr 10	5 ·43	11 ·44	18
27	Sa 11	6 ·33	12 ·37	19
28	Su 12	7 ·23	13 ·30	20
—29	Mo 13	8 ·14	14 ·24	21
1	Tu 14	9 ·05 / 10 ·98	15 ·18	22
2	We 15	11 ·92	16 ·14	23
3	Th 16	12 ·87	17 ·11	24
4	Fr 17	13 ·85	18 ·10	25
5	Sa 18	14 ·84	19 ·10	26
6	Su 19	—A ·86	20 ·12	27
7	Mo 20	1 ·90	21 ·16	28
8	Tu 21	2 ·96	22 ·23	—29
9	We 22	... ...	23 ·32	1
10	Th 23	3 ·08	24 ·42	2
11	Fr 24	4 ·11	25 ·52	3
12	Sa 25	5 ·20	26 ·63	4
13	Su 26	6 ·29	27 ·73	5
14	Mo 27	7 ·37	1 ·82	6
15	Tu 28	8 ·43	2 ·90	7
16	We 29	9 ·48	3 ·96	8
17	Th 30	10 ·50	... ...	9
18	Fr 31	11 ·51	4 ·00	10

Feb.

Solar: Hemalamba Kumbha—Masi. Lunar: Magha, Bahula, Sukla, Phalguna. Muhammadan: H. 1377 Rajab; H. 1377 Shaban.

Cyclic Sidereal	Week-Day English	Tithi	Nakshatra	Muhammadan
19	Sa 1	12 ·49	5 ·01	11
20	Su 2	13 ·45	6 ·01 / 7 ·99	12
21	Mo 3	14 ·89	8 ·96	13
22	Tu 4	P ·82	9 ·90	14
23	We 5	1 ·25	10 ·84	15
24	Th 6	2 ·16	11 ·78	16
25	Fr 7	3 ·03 / 4 ·96	12 ·71	17
26	Sa 8	5 ·86	13 ·64	18
27	Su 9	6 ·76	14 ·58	19
28	Mo 10	7 ·67	15 ·52	20
—29	Tu 11	8 ·60	16 ·47	21
1	We 12	9 ·55	17 ·44	22
2	Th 13	10 ·51	18 ·42	23
3	Fr 14	11 ·48	19 ·42	24
4	Sa 15	12 ·46	20 ·44	25
5	Su 16	13 ·49	21 ·47	26
6	Mo 17	14 ·53	22 ·54	27
7	Tu 18	—A ·59	23 ·62	28
8	We 19	1 ·63	24 ·71	29
9	Th 20	2 ·74	25 ·81	—30
10	Fr 21	3 ·83	26 ·92	1
11	Sa 22	4 ·92	... ...	2
12	Su 23	... ...	27 ·03	3
13	Mo 24	5 ·00	1 ·13	4
14	Tu 25	6 ·03	2 ·21	5
15	We 26	7 ·10	3 ·27	6
16	Th 27	8 ·11	4 ·31	7
17	Fr 28	9 ·12	5 ·33	8

March

Solar: Hemalamba Kumbha—Masi; Hemalamba Mina—Panguni. Lunar: Suk., Phalguna, Bahula, Sukla, Chaitra. Muhammadan: H. 1377 Shaban.

Cyclic Sidereal	Week-Day English	Tithi	Nakshatra	Muhammadan
18	Sa 1	10 ·11	6 ·34	9
19	Su 2	11 ·07	7 ·32	10
20	Mo 3	12 ·01 / 13 ·93	8 ·29	11
21	Tu 4	14 ·85	9 ·24	12
22	We 5	P 76	10 ·18	13
23	Th 6	1 ·67	11 ·12	14
24	Fr 7	2 ·57	12 ·05 / 13 ·98	15
25	Sa 8	3 ·47	14 ·91	16
26	Su 9	4 ·37	15 ·85	17
27	Mo 10	5 ·28	16 ·81	18
28	Tu 11	6 ·21	17 ·77	19
29	We 12	7 ·15	18 ·75	20
—30	Th 13	8 ·11	19 ·74	21
1	Fr 14	9 ·08	20 ·75	22
2	Sa 15	10 ·07	21 ·79	23
3	Su 16	11 ·08	22 ·85	24
4	Mo 17	12 ·13	23 ·92	25
5	Tu 18	13 ·19	... ...	26
6	We 19	14 ·27	24 ·01	27
7	Th 20	—A ·35	25 ·12	28
8	Fr 21	1 ·44	26 ·23	—29
9	Sa 22	2 ·52	27 ·34	1
10	Su 23	3 ·59	1 ·43	2
11	Mo 24	4 ·65	2 ·52	3
12	Tu 25	5 ·69	3 ·58	4
13	We 26	6 ·71	4 ·63	5
14	Th 27	7 ·71	5 ·66	6
15	Fr 28	8 ·69	6 ·67	7
16	Sa 29	9 ·65	7 ·65	8
17	Su 30	10 ·59	8 ·62	9
18	Mo 31	11 ·52	9 ·57	10

April

Solar: Vilamba Mesha—Chittirai. Lunar: Bahula, Vaisak. Sukla. Muhammadan: H. 1377 Ramzan; H. 1377 Shawwal.

Cyclic Sidereal	Week-Day English	Tithi	Nakshatra	Muhammadan
19	Tu 1	12 ·43	10 ·52	11
20	We 2	13 ·34	11 ·46	12
21	Th 3	14 ·24	12 ·39	13
22	Fr 4	P ·14	13 ·32	14
23	Sa 5	1 ·04 / 2 ·94	14 ·25	15
24	Su 6	3 ·86	15 ·19	16
25	Mo 7	4 ·78	16 ·14	17
26	Tu 8	5 ·72	17 ·10	18
27	We 9	6 ·67	18 ·07	19
28	Th 10	7 ·64	19 ·06	20
29	Fr 11	8 ·63	20 ·07	21
30	Sa 12	9 ·64	21 ·11	22
—31	Su 13	10 ·69	22 ·16	23
1	Mo 14	11 ·75	23 ·23	24
2	Tu 15	12 ·88	24 ·31	25
3	We 16	13 ·91	25 ·41	26
4	Th 17	14 ·9[illegible]	26 ·58	27
5	Fr 18	... ...	27 ·64	28
6	Sa ● 19	—A ·07	1 ·73	29
7	Su 20	1 ·14	2 ·82	—30
8	Mo 21	2 ·20	3 ·89	1
9	Tu 22	3 ·23	4 ·95	2
10	We 23	4 ·25	5 ·98	3
11	Th 24	5 ·25	6 ·99	4
12	Fr 25	6 ·24	7 ·98	5
13	Sa 26	7 ·20	8 ·95	6
14	Su 27	8 ·13	9 ·92	7
15	Mo 28	9 ·03 / 10 ·98	10 ·86	8
16	Tu 29	11 ·88	11 ·80	9
17	We 30	12 ·78	12 ·73	10

May

Solar: Vilamba Mesha—Chittirai; Vilamba Vrishabha—Vaikasi. Lunar: Vaisakha, Bahula, Sukla. Muhammadan: H. 1377 Shawwal.

Cyclic Sidereal	Week-Day English	Tithi	Nakshatra	Muhammadan
18	Th 1	13 ·68	13 ·66	11
19	Fr 2	14 ·38	14 ·59	12
20	Sa ○ 3	P ·48	15 ·53	13
21	Su 4	1 ·39	16 ·48	14
22	Mo 5	2 ·30	17 ·48	15
23	Tu 6	3 ·24	18 ·40	16
24	We 7	4 ·20	19 ·38	17
25	Th 8	5 ·18	20 ·40	18
26	Fr 9	6 ·16	21 ·42	19
27	Sa 10	7 ·17	22 ·47	20
28	Su 11	8 ·21	23 ·53	21
29	Mo 12	9 ·26	24 ·62	22
—30	Tu 13	10 ·34	25 ·72	23
1	We 14	11 ·42	26 ·83	24
2	Th 15	12 ·50	27 ·93	25
3	Fr 16	13 ·58	... ...	26
4	Sa 17	14 ·66	1 ·03	27
5	Su 18	—A ·72	2 ·12	28
6	Mo 19	1 ·76	3 ·20	—29
7	Tu 20	2 ·77	4 ·26	1
8	We 21	3 ·76	5 ·30	2
9	Th 22	4 ·75	6 ·31	3
10	Fr 23	5 ·72	7 ·30	4
11	Sa 24	6 ·65	8 ·28	5
12	Su 25	7 ·57	9 ·25	6
13	Mo 26	8 ·48	10 ·20	7
14	Tu 27	9 ·38	11 ·14	8
15	We 28	10 ·28	12 ·07	9
16	Th 29	11 ·18	13 ·00 / 14 ·93	10
17	Fr 30	12 ·08 / 13 ·98	15 ·87	11
18	Sa 31	14 ·89	16 ·81	12

June

Solar: Vilamba Mithuna—Ani. Lunar: Jyeshtha, Bahula, Ashadha Sukla. Muhammadan: H. 1377 Zi-l-kada; H. 1377 Zi-l-hijja.

Cyclic Sidereal	Week-Day English	Tithi	Nakshatra	Muhammadan
19	Su 1	P ·81	17 ·76	13
20	Mo 2	1 ·75	18 ·73	14
21	Tu 3	2 ·70	19 ·72	15
22	We 4	3 ·67	20 ·72	16
23	Th 5	4 ·65	21 ·74	17
24	Fr 6	5 ·67	22 ·78	18
25	Sa 7	6 ·70	23 ·84	19
26	Su 8	7 ·75	24 ·93	20
27	Mo 9	8 ·82	... ...	21
28	Tu 10	9 ·89	25 ·02	22
29	We 11	10 ·98	26 ·12	23
30	Th 12	... ...	27 ·23	24
31	Fr 13	11 ·06	1 ·34	25
—32	Sa 14	12 ·14	2 ·44	26
1	Su 15	13 ·19	3 ·52	27
2	Mo 16	14 ·23	4 ·58	28
3	Tu 17	—A ·25	5 ·61	29
4	We 18	1 ·26	6 ·63	—30
5	Th 19	2 ·23	7 ·63	1
6	Fr 20	3 ·19	8 ·62	2
7	Sa 21	4 ·14	9 ·58	3
8	Su 22	5 ·06 / 6 ·97	10 ·53	4
9	Mo 23	7 ·87	11 ·47	5
10	Tu 24	8 ·77	12 ·41	6
11	We 25	9 ·67	13 ·35	7
12	Th 26	10 ·57	14 ·28	8
13	Fr 27	11 ·47	15 ·21	9
14	Sa 28	12 ·38	16 ·15	10
15	Su 29	13 ·30	17 ·10	11
16	Mo 30	14 ·24	18 ·07	12

Naksh :—1. Asvn. 2. Bhar. 3. Krit. 4. Rohi. 5. Mrig. 6. Ardh. 7. Punar. 8. Push. 9. Aslesh. 10. Magh. 11. P. Phal. 12. U. Phal. 13. Hasta. 14. Chit.

A. D. 1958.
A.—Amavasya.
P.—Paurnami.

Kollam 1134, Commences { N. Malabar—Sept. / S. Malabar—Aug.

Hijra 1378, Commences, July 18.

Vikrama 2015.
Bengal San 1364.
(N. Cycle) Virodhakrit.

SOLAR reckoning: Cyclic Sidereal Year, Month and Day; Week-Day English Month and Day. LUNAR reckoning: Tithi Ending Moment; Nakshatra Ending Moment; Muhammadan Year, Month and Day.

July

Solar month	Cyclic Sidereal Day	Week-Day	English Day	Lunar month	Tithi	Ending Moment	Nakshatra	Ending Moment	Muhammadan month	Day
Vilamba Mithuna—Ani	17	Tu	1	Ashadha	P	·19	19	·04	H. 1377 Zi-l-hijja	13
	18	We	2	Bahula	1	·15	20	·04		14
	19	Th	3		2	·13	21	·05		15
	20	Fr	4		3	·14	22	·09		16
	21	Sa	5		4	·17	23	·15		17
	22	Su	6		5	·23	24	·23		18
	23	Mo	7		6	·30	25	·32		19
	24	Tu	8		7	·38	26	·42		20
	25	We	9		8	·46	27	·53		21
	26	Th	10		9	·54	1	·64		22
	27	Fr	11		10	·61	2	·74		23
	28	Sa	12		11	·67	3	·82		24
	29	Su	13		12	·72	4	·89		25
	30	Mo	14		13	·73	5	·93		26
	31	Tu	15		14	·73	6	·95		27
Vilamba Karkata—Adi	1	We	16		A	·71	7	·96		28
	2	Th	17	Sravana Sukla	1	·67	8	·95		29
	3	Fr	18		2	·61	9	·92	Muharram	1
	4	Sa	19		3	·54	10	·87		2
	5	Su	20		4	·46	11	·81		3
	6	Mo	21		5	·36	12	·75		4
	7	Tu	22		6	·26	13	·68		5
	8	We	23		7	·16	14	·61		6
	9	Th	24		8 9	·06 ·96	15	·55		7
	10	Fr	25		10	·86	16	·49		8
	11	Sa	26		11	·78	17	·44		9
	12	Su	27		12	·71	18	·40		10
	13	Mo	28		13	·67	19	·37		11
	14	Tu	29		14	·64	20	·36		12
	15	We	30		P	·61	21	·37		13
	16	Th	31		1	·62	22	·41		14

Aug.

Solar month	Cyclic Sidereal Day	Week-Day	English Day	Lunar month	Tithi	Ending Moment	Nakshatra	Ending Moment	Muhammadan month	Day
Vilamba Karkata—Adi	17	Fr	1	Adhika Sravana Bahula	2	·65	23	·46	H. 1378	15
	18	Sa	2		3	·71	24	·53		16
	19	Su	3		4	·77	25	·62		17
	20	Mo	4		5	·85	26	·72		18
	21	Tu	5		6	·93	27	·83		19
	22	We	6		...	...	1	·94		20
	23	Th	7		7	·02	...	...		21
	24	Fr	8		8	·09	2	·04		22
	25	Sa	9		9	·15	3	·13		23
	26	Su	10		10	·19	4	·19		24
	27	Mo	11		11	·21	5	·24		25
	28	Tu	12		12	·23	6	·28		26
	29	We	13		13	·20	7	·29		27
	30	Th	14		14	·16	8	·28		28
	31	Fr	15		A	·11	9	·25		29
	32	Sa	16	Nija Sravana Sukla	1 2	·04 ·95	10	·20		30
Vilamba Simha—Avani	1	Su	17		3	·85	11	·15	H. 1378 Safar	1
	2	Mo	18		4	·75	12	·09		2
	3	Tu	19		5	·65	13 14	·02 ·95		3
	4	We	20		6	·55	15	·89		4
	5	Th	21		7	·45	16	·83		5
	6	Fr	22		8	·36	17	·77		6
	7	Sa	23		9	·28	18	·73		7
	8	Su	24		10	·21	19	·70		8
	9	Mo	25		11	·16	20	·68		9
	10	Tu	26		12	·13	21	·69		10
	11	We	27		13	·12	22	·72		11
	12	Th	28		14	·13	23	·77		12
	13	Fr	29		P	·15	24	·84		13
	14	Sa	30		1	·20	25	·92		14
	15	Su	31		2	·27	...	...		15

Sep.

Solar month	Cyclic Sidereal Day	Week-Day	English Day	Lunar month	Tithi	Ending Moment	Nakshatra	Ending Moment	Muhammadan month	Day
Vilamba Simha—Avani	16	Mo	1	Nija Sravana Bahula	3	·85	26	·02	H. 1378 Safar	16
	17	Tu	2		4	·43	27	·13		17
	18	We	3		5	·52	1	·24		18
	19	Th	4		6	·60	2	·34		19
	20	Fr	5		7	·67	3	·43		20
	21	Sa	6		8	·71	4	·50		21
	22	Su	7		9	·72	5	·57		22
	23	Mo	8		10	·73	6	·60		23
	24	Tu	9		11	·71	7	·61		24
	25	We	10		12	·68	8	·60		25
	26	Th	11		13	·63	9	·58		26
	27	Fr	12		14	·56	10	·55		27
	28	Sa	13		A	·48	11	·49		28
	29	Su	14	Bhadrapada Sukla	1	·39	12	·43		29
	30	Mo	15		2	·29	13	·36	Rabi-ul-awwal	1
	31	Tu	16		3	·19	14	·29		2
Vilamba Kanya—Purattasi	1	We	17		4 5	·09 ·99	15	·23		3
	2	Th	18		6	·89	16	·17		4
	3	Fr	19		7	·81	17	·11		5
	4	Sa	20		8	·75	18	·06		6
	5	Su	21		9	·70	19	·02		7
	6	Mo	22		10	·67	20	·01		8
	7	Tu	23		11	·66	21	·02		9
	8	We	24		12	·67	22	·04		10
	9	Th	25		13	·69	23	·08		11
	10	Fr	26		14	·74	24	·14		12
	11	Sa	27		P	·81	25	·22		13
	12	Su	28		1	·89	26	·32		14
	13	Mo	29		2	·98	27	·48		15
	14	Tu	30		...	...	1	·54		16

Oct.

Solar month	Cyclic Sidereal Day	Week-Day	English Day	Lunar month	Tithi	Ending Moment	Nakshatra	Ending Moment	Muhammadan month	Day
	15	We	1	Bahula	3	·06	2	·64	H. 1378	17
	16	Th	2		4	·14	3	·73		18
	17	Fr	3		5	·21	4	·82		19
	18	Sa	4		6	·25	5	·88		20
	19	Su	5		7	·27	6	·92		21
	20	Mo	6		8	·28	7	·93		22
	21	Tu	7		9	·27	8	·93		23
	22	We	8		10	·24	9	·92		24
	23	Th	9		11	·19	10	·88		25
	24	Fr	10		12	·12	11	·83		26
	25	Sa	11		13 14	·03 ·94	12	·77		27
	26	Su	12		A	·85	13	·70		28
	27	Mo	13	Asvina Sukla	1	·75	14	·63		29
	28	Tu	14		2	·65	15	·56		30
	29	We	15		3	·55	16	·50	H. 1378 Rabi-ul-akhir	1
	30	Th	16		4	·46	17	·44		2
Vilamba Tula—Aippasi	1	Fr	17		5	·38	18	·39		3
	2	Sa	18		6	·32	19	·35		4
	3	Su	19		7	·27	20	·34		5
	4	Mo	20		8	·25	21	·34		6
	5	Tu	21		9	·24	22	·35		7
	6	We	22		10	·26	23	·39		8
	7	Th	23		11	·29	24	·45		9
	8	Fr	24		12	·33	25	·54		10
	9	Sa	25		13	·39	26	·63		11
	10	Su	26		14	·47	27	·73		12
	11	Mo	27		P	·56	1	·84		13
	12	Tu	28	Asvina Bah.	1	·65	2	·95		14
	13	We	29		2	·73	...	...		15
	14	Th	30		3	·80	3	·05		16
	15	Fr	31		4	·85	4	·13		17

Nov.

Solar month	Cyclic Sidereal Day	Week-Day	English Day	Lunar month	Tithi	Ending Moment	Nakshatra	Ending Moment	Muhammadan month	Day
Vilamba Tula—Aippasi	16	Sa	1	Asvina Bahula	5	·88	5	·19	H. 1378 Rabi-ul-akhir	18
	17	Su	2		6	·87	6	·23		19
	18	Mo	3		7	·86	7	·25		20
	19	Tu	4		8	·83	8	·25		21
	20	We	5		9	·78	9	·24		22
	21	Th	6		10	·71	10	·21		23
	22	Fr	7		11	·62	11	·16		24
	23	Sa	8		12	·53	12	·10		25
	24	Su	9		13	·44	13 14	·04 ·98		26
	25	Mo	10		14	·34	15	·91		27
	26	Tu	11		A	·25	16	·84		28
	27	We	12	Karttika Sukla	1	·16	17	·78		29
	28	Th	13		2	·08	18	·72	Jumadal-awwal	1
	29	Fr	14		3 4	·00 ·93	19	·69		2
	30	Sa	15		5	·87	20	·67		3
Vilamba Vrischika—Kartigai	1	Su	16		6	·85	21	·66		4
	2	Mo	17		7	·85	22	·67		5
	3	Tu	18		8	·86	23	·70		6
	4	We	19		9	·89	24	·77		7
	5	Th	20		10	·94	25	·84		8
	6	Fr	21		...	...	26	·93		9
	7	Sa	22		11	·02	...	...		10
	8	Su	23		12	·11	27	·03		11
	9	Mo	24		13	·20	1	·14		12
	10	Tu	25		14	·28	2	·25		13
	11	We	26		P	·36	3	·35		14
	12	Th	27		1	·42	4	·43		15
	13	Fr	28		2	·47	5	·50		16
	14	Sa	29		3	·49	6	·55		17
	15	Su	30		4	·51	7	·57		18

Dec.

Solar month	Cyclic Sidereal Day	Week-Day	English Day	Lunar month	Tithi	Ending Moment	Nakshatra	Ending Moment	Muhammadan month	Day
	16	Mo	1	Bahula	5	·49	8	·59	H. 1378	19
	17	Tu	2		6	·44	9	·57		20
	18	We	3		7	·39	10	·54		21
	19	Th	4		8	·33	11	·50		22
	20	Fr	5		9	·25	12	·44		23
	21	Sa	6		10	·16	13	·38		24
	22	Su	7		11 12	·07 ·98	14	·32		25
	23	Mo	8		13	·88	15	·25		26
	24	Tu	9		14	·78	16	·18		27
	25	We	10		A	·69	17	·11		28
	26	Th	11	Margasira Sukla	1	·62	18	·06		29
	27	Fr	12		2	·55	19 20	·02 ·99		30
	28	Sa	13		3	·52	21	·98	H. 1378 Jumadal-akhir	1
	29	Su	14		4	·49	22	·99		2
	30	Mo	15		5	·49	...	...		3
Vilamba Dhanus—Margali	1	Tu	16		6	·51	23	·03		4
	2	We	17		7	·54	24	·08		5
	3	Th	18		8	·60	25	·14		6
	4	Fr	19		9	·67	26	·23		7
	5	Sa	20		10	·75	27	·33		8
	6	Su	21		11	·84	1	·43		9
	7	Mo	22		12	·92	2	·54		10
	8	Tu	23		...	...	3	·65		11
	9	We	24		13	·00	4	·74		12
	10	Th	25		14	·07	5	·81		13
	11	Fr	26		P	·12	6	·86		14
	12	Sa	27	Margasira Bah.	1	·14	7	·90		15
	13	Su	28		2	·15	8	·91		16
	14	Mo	29		3	·13	9	·90		17
	15	Tu	30		4	·09	10	·87		18
	16	We	31		5 6	·04 ·97	11	·83		19

15. Svati. 16. Visak. 17. Anur. 18. Jyesh. 19. Mula. 20. P. Ash. 21. U. Ash. 22. Sravn. 23. Dani. 24. Satab. 25. P. Bhad. 26. U. Bhad. 27. Rev.

A. D. 1959. **Mesha Sankranti** (Commencement of Indian Sidereal Year).

Solar Eclipse. ● **(Surya Sid.) April 13·89.** **Saka 1881.** **Kaliyuga 5060.**

Lunar Eclipse. ○ **(Arya Sid.) April 13·78.** **(S. Cycle) Vikari.**

Columns: SOLAR reckoning — Cyclic Sidereal Year, Month and Day; Week-Day English Month and Day. LUNAR reckoning — Tithi Ending Moment; Nakshatra Ending Moment; Muhammadan Year, Month and Day.

Jan.

Solar month	Sidereal Day	Week-Day	Eng. Day	Lunar month	Tithi	Nakshatra	Muhammadan
Vilamba Dhanus—Margali	17	Th	1	Marg.	7 ·89	12 ·78	Jumadal-akhir. 20
	18	Fr	2		8 ·80	13 ·72	21
	19	Sa	3		9 ·71	14 ·66	22
	20	Su	4	Bahula	10 ·61	15 ·59	23
	21	Mo	5		11 ·51	16 ·52	24
	22	Tu	6		12 ·42	17 ·46	25
	23	We	7		13 ·34	18 ·40	26
	24	Th	8		14 ·26	19 ·35	27
	25	Fr	9		—A ·20	20 ·32	28
	26	Sa	10		1 ·16	21 ·31	—29
	27	Su	11		2 ·13	22 ·32	1
	28	Mo	12		3 ·13	23 ·34	2
	—29	Tu	13		4 ·15	24 ·38	3
	1	We	14		5 ·19	25 ·45	4
	2	Th	15	Sukla	6 ·24	26 ·53	5
	3	Fr	16		7 ·32	27 ·63	6
	4	Sa	17		8 ·41	1 ·74	7
	5	Su	18		9 ·49	2 ·86	8
	6	Mo	19		10 ·58	3 ·95	9
	7	Tu	20		11 ·66	... ...	10
	8	We	21		12 ·72	4 ·04	11
	9	Th	22	Pausha	13 ·76	5 ·12	12
	10	Fr	23		14 ·79	6 ·18	13
	11	Sa	24		P ·79	7 ·22	14
	12	Su	25		1 ·77	8 ·23	15
Vilamba Makara—Tai	13	Mo	26		2 ·74	9 ·23	16
	14	Tu	27		3 ·68	10 ·20	H. 1378 Rajab. 17
	15	We	28		4 ·61	11 ·17	18
	16	Th	29	Bahula	5 ·53	12 ·12	19
	17	Fr	30		6 ·44	13 ·06 / 14 ·99	20
	18	Sa	31		7 ·34	15 ·92	21

Feb.

Solar month	Sidereal Day	Week-Day	Eng. Day	Lunar month	Tithi	Nakshatra	Muhammadan
	19	Su	1		8 ·24	16 ·86	22
	20	Mo	2		9 ·14	17 ·80	23
	21	Tu	3		10 ·05 / 11 ·97	18 ·74	24
	22	We	4		12 ·90	19 ·69	25
	23	Th	5		13 ·84	20 ·65	26
	24	Fr	6		14 ·80	21 ·63	27
	25	Sa	7		—A ·77	22 ·64	28
	26	Su	8		1 ·77	23 ·66	29
	27	Mo	9		2 ·79	24 ·69	—30
	28	Tu	10		3 ·83	25 ·75	1
	29	We	11		4 ·89	26 ·83	2
	—30	Th	12		5 ·96	27 ·98	3
	1	Fr	13		... ...	... ...	4
	2	Sa	14		6 ·04	1 ·04	5
	3	Su	15	Sukla	7 ·13	2 ·15	6
	4	Mo	16		8 ·22	3 ·25	7
	5	Tu	17		9 ·30	4 ·34	H. 1378 Shaban. 8
Vilamba Kumbha—Masi	6	We	18		10 ·36	5 ·43	9
	7	Th	19		11 ·40	6 ·49	10
	8	Fr	20	Magha	12 ·42	7 ·53	11
	9	Sa	21		13 ·41	8 ·55	12
	10	Su	22		14 ·39	9 ·55	13
	11	Mo	23		P ·35	10 ·54	14
	12	Tu	24		1 ·29	11 ·51	15
	13	We	25	Bah.	2 ·22	12 ·46	16
	14	Th	26		3 ·14	13 ·40	17
	15	Fr	27		4 ·05 / 5 ·95	14 ·34	18
	16	Sa	28		6 ·85	15 ·27	19

March

Solar month	Sidereal Day	Week-Day	Eng. Day	Lunar month	Tithi	Nakshatra	Muhammadan
Vilamba Kumbha—Masi	17	Su	1	Magha	7 ·75	16 ·20	H. 1378 Shaban. 20
	18	Mo	2		8 ·66	17 ·13	21
	19	Tu	3		9 ·58	18 ·07	22
	20	We	4		10 ·50	19 ·02 / 20 ·98	23
	21	Th	5	Bahula	11 ·44	21 ·97	24
	22	Fr	6		12 ·40	22 ·96	25
	23	Sa	7		13 ·38	23 ·97	26
	24	Su	8		14 ·38	... ...	27
	25	Mo	9		—A ·41	24 ·01	28
	26	Tu	10		1 ·44	25 ·06	—29
	27	We	11		2 ·49	26 ·14	1
	28	Th	12		3 ·57	27 ·23	2
	—29	Fr	13		4 ·65	1 ·33	3
	1	Sa	14		5 ·74	2 ·44	4
	2	Su	15		6 ·82	3 ·55	5
	3	Mo	16	Sukla	7 ·89	4 ·65	6
	4	Tu	17		8 ·95	5 ·74	7
	5	We	18		9 ·99	6 ·80	8
	6	Th	19		... ...	7 ·85	9
	7	Fr	20		10 ·02	8 ·87	10
	8	Sa	21		11 ·01	9 ·89	11
	9	Su	22		12 ·00 / 13 ·95	10 ·87	12
	10	Mo	23		14 ·89	11 ·84	13
	11	Tu	24 ○		P ·82	12 ·79	14
Vilamba Mina—Panguni	12	We	25		1 ·74	13 ·74	H. 1378 Ramzan. 15
	13	Th	26	Phalguna	2 ·64	14 ·68	16
	14	Fr	27		3 ·54	15 ·61	17
	15	Sa	28		4 ·44	16 ·54	18
	16	Su	29		5 ·34	17 ·47	19
	17	Mo	30		6 ·25	18 ·41	20
	18	Tu	31		7 ·16	19 ·35	21

April

Solar month	Sidereal Day	Week-Day	Eng. Day	Lunar month	Tithi	Nakshatra	Muhammadan
	19	We	1		8 ·08	20 ·32	22
	20	Th	2		9 ·02 / 10 ·98	21 ·29	23
	21	Fr	3	Bahula	11 ·96	22 ·28	24
	22	Sa	4		12 ·95	23 ·29	25
	23	Su	5		13 ·97	24 ·32	26
	24	Mo	6		... ...	25 ·38	27
	25	Tu	7		14 ·01	26 ·45	28
	26	We	8		—A ·07	27 ·54	29
	27	Th	9		1 ·14	1 ·64	—30
	28	Fr	10		2 ·22	2 ·75	1
	29	Sa	11		3 ·30	3 ·86	2
	30	Su	12		4 ·38	4 ·96	3
	—31	Mo	13		5 ·45	... ...	4
	1	Tu	14		6 ·51	5 ·04	5
	2	We	15	Sukla	7 ·55	6 ·11	6
	3	Th	16		8 ·57	7 ·16	7
	4	Fr	17		9 ·57	8 ·20	H. 1378 Shawwal. 8
	5	Sa	18		10 ·55	9 ·21	9
	6	Su	19		11 ·50	10 ·20	10
Vikari Mesha—Chittirai	7	Mo	20	Chaitra	12 ·44	11 ·17	11
	8	Tu	21		13 ·37	12 ·13	12
	9	We	22		14 ·28	13 ·07	13
	10	Th	23		P ·18	14 ·01 / 15 ·95	14
	11	Fr	24		1 ·08 / 2 ·98	16 ·88	15
	12	Sa	25		3 ·88	17 ·81	16
	13	Su	26		4 ·79	18 ·75	17
	14	Mo	27		5 ·70	19 ·70	18
	15	Tu	28	Bahula	6 ·62	20 ·65	19
	16	We	29		7 ·56	21 ·62	20
	17	Th	30		8 ·52	22 ·60	21

May

Solar month	Sidereal Day	Week-Day	Eng. Day	Lunar month	Tithi	Nakshatra	Muhammadan
Vikari Mesha—Chittirai	18	Fr	1	Chait.	9 ·49	23 ·61	Shawwal. 22
	19	Sa	2		10 ·48	24 ·64	23
	20	Su	3		11 ·51	25 ·69	24
	21	Mo	4	Bah.	12 ·54	26 ·75	25
	22	Tu	5		13 ·59	27 ·84	26
	23	We	6		14 ·66	1 ·94	27
	24	Th	7		—A ·74	... ...	28
	25	Fr	8		1 ·82	2 ·05	—29
	26	Sa	9		2 ·91	3 ·16	1
	27	Su	10		3 ·98	4 ·26	2
	28	Mo	11		... ...	5 ·35	3
	29	Tu	12		4 ·03	6 ·42	4
	30	We	13		5 ·07	7 ·47	5
	—31	Th	14	Sukla	6 ·09	8 ·51	6
	1	Fr	15		7 ·09	9 ·53	7
	2	Sa	16		8 ·06	10 ·52	8
	3	Su	17		9 ·01 / 10 ·95	11 ·50	9
	4	Mo	18		11 ·88	12 ·46	10
	5	Tu	19		12 ·80	13 ·42	11
	6	We	20	Vaisakha	13 ·70	14 ·36	H. 1378 Zi-l-ka'da. 12
	7	Th	21		14 ·60	15 ·29	13
	8	Fr	22		P ·50	16 ·22	14
	9	Sa	23		1 ·40	17 ·15	15
	10	Su	24		2 ·30	18 ·09	16
Vikari Vrishabha—Vaikasi	11	Mo	25		3 ·21	19 ·03 / 20 ·99	17
	12	Tu	26		4 ·13	21 ·95	18
	13	We	27		5 ·07	22 ·93	19
	14	Th	28	Bahula	6 ·02 / 7 ·99	23 ·94	20
	15	Fr	29		8 ·99	24 ·96	21
	16	Sa	30		... ...	... ...	22
	17	Su	31		9 ·00	25 ·00	23

June

Solar month	Sidereal Day	Week-Day	Eng. Day	Lunar month	Tithi	Nakshatra	Muhammadan
	18	Mo	1		10 ·03	26 ·06	24
	19	Tu	2		11 ·09	27 ·14	25
	20	We	3		12 ·16	1 ·23	26
	21	Th	4		13 ·23	2 ·34	27
	22	Fr	5		14 ·32	3 ·45	28
	23	Sa	6		—A ·41	4 ·56	29
	24	Su	7		1 ·48	5 ·65	—30
	25	Mo	8		2 ·53	6 ·73	1
	26	Tu	9		3 ·56	7 ·80	2
	27	We	10		4 ·57	8 ·83	3
	28	Th	11		5 ·57	9 ·85	4
	29	Fr	12		6 ·55	10 ·85	5
	30	Sa	13	Sukla	7 ·50	11 ·83	6
	—31	Su	14		8 ·44	12 ·80	7
	1	Mo	15		9 ·37	13 ·75	8
	2	Tu	16		10 ·29	14 ·69	H. 1378 Zi-l-hijja. 9
	3	We	17		11 ·19	15 ·63	10
	4	Th	18		12 ·09 / 13 ·99	16 ·57	11
	5	Fr	19	Jyeshtha	14 ·89	17 ·50	12
Vikari Mithuna—Ani	6	Sa	20		P ·79	18 ·43	13
	7	Su	21		1 ·69	19 ·37	14
	8	Mo	22		2 ·61	20 ·31	15
	9	Tu	23		3 ·55	21 ·28	16
	10	We	24		4 ·50	22 ·26	17
	11	Th	25		5 ·47	23 ·26	18
	12	Fr	26		6 ·46	24 ·27	19
	13	Sa	27	Bahula	7 ·47	25 ·31	20
	14	Su	28		8 ·51	26 ·37	21
	15	Mo	29		9 ·56	27 ·44	22
	16	Tu	30		10 ·64	1 ·54	23

Nakah :—1. Asvn. 2. Bhar. 3. Krit. 4. Rohi. 5. Mrig. 6. Ardh. 7. Punar. 8. Push. 9. Aslesh. 10. Magh. 11. P. Phal. 12. U. Phal. 13. Hasta. 14. Chit.

A. D. 1959.
A.—Amavasya.
P.—Paurnami.

Kollam 1135, Commences { N. Malabar—Sept. / S. Malabar—Aug.

Hijra 1379, Commences, July 7.

Vikrama 2016.
Bengal San 1365.
(N. Cycle) Paridhavin.

SOLAR reckoning: Cyclic Sidereal Year, Month and Day; Week-Day, English Month and Day. LUNAR reckoning: Tithi Ending Moment; Nakshatra Ending Moment; Muhammadan Year, Month and Day.

July (Solar: Vikari Mithuna—Ani; from 32nd, Vikari Karkata—Adi. Lunar: Jy. Bah.; Sukla; Ashadha; Bahula. Muhammadan: Zi-l-hijja; H. 1379 Muharram.)

Cyclic Sidereal	Week-Day	English Day	Tithi	Tithi Moment	Nakshatra	Nakshatra Moment	Muhammadan
17	We	1	11	·70	2	·64	24
18	Th	2	12	·79	3	·75	25
19	Fr	3	13	·88	4	·85	26
20	Sa	4	14	·94	5	·95	27
21	Su	5	...	...	...	...	28
22	Mo	6	—A	·00	6	·04	—29
23	Tu	7	1	·04	7	·11	1
24	We	8	2	·06	8	·15	2
25	Th	9	3	·05	9	·17	3
26	Fr	10	4 5	·03 ·98	10	·18	4
27	Sa	11	6	·92	11	·17	5
28	Su	12	7	·85	12	·14	6
29	Mo	13	8	·76	13	·09	7
30	Tu	14	9	·66	14 15	·03 ·97	8
31	We	15	10	·56	16	·90	9
—32	Th	16	11	·46	17	·83	10
1	Fr	17	12	·36	18	·76	11
2	Sa	18	13	·26	19	·70	12
3	Su	19	14	·17	20	·65	13
4	Mo	20	P	·09	21	·61	14
5	Tu	21	1 2	·03 ·98	22	·59	15
6	We	22	3	·96	23	·58	16
7	Th	23	4	·94	24	·59	17
8	Fr	24	5	·95	25	·62	18
9	Sa	25	6	·98	26	·67	19
10	Su	26	...	...	27	·75	20
11	Mo	27	7	·03	1	·84	21
12	Tu	28	8	·10	2	·94	22
13	We	29	9	·18	...	...	23
14	Th	30	10	·27	3	·05	24
15	Fr	31	11	·35	4	·16	25

Aug. (Solar: Vikari Karkata—Adi; from 31st, Vikari Simha—Avani. Lunar: Sukla; Sravana; Bahula. Muhammadan: H. 1379 Safar.)

Cyclic Sidereal	Week-Day	English Day	Tithi	Tithi Moment	Nakshatra	Nakshatra Moment	Muhammadan
16	Sa	1	12	·42	5	·26	26
17	Su	2	13	·47	6	·35	27
18	Mo	3	14	·51	7	·42	28
19	Tu	4	—A	·54	8	·46	29
20	We	5	1	·53	9	·49	—30
21	Th	6	2	·51	10	·51	1
22	Fr	7	3	·47	11	·50	2
23	Sa	8	4	·42	12	·47	3
24	Su	9	5	·34	13	·42	4
25	Mo	10	6	·25	14	·37	5
26	Tu	11	7	·16	15	·31	6
27	We	12	8 9	·06 ·96	16	·24	7
28	Th	13	10	·86	17	·17	8
29	Fr	14	11	·76	18	·10	9
30	Sa	15	12	·67	19 20	·04 ·98	10
—31	Su	16	13	·59	21	·95	11
1	Mo	17	14	·52	22	·92	12
2	Tu	18	P	·47	23	·90	13
3	We	19	1	·45	24	·91	14
4	Th	20	2	·44	25	·93	15
5	Fr	21	3	·45	26	·99	16
6	Sa	22	4	·48	...	...	17
7	Su	23	5	·54	27	·06	18
8	Mo	24	6	·60	1	·14	19
9	Tu	25	7	·68	2	·24	20
10	We	26	8	·76	3	·35	21
11	Th	27	9	·85	4	·46	22
12	Fr	28	10	·93	5	·56	23
13	Sa	29	11	·98	6	·65	24
14	Su	30	...	...	7	·72	25
15	Mo	31	12	·02	8	·78	26

Sep. (Solar: Vikari Simha—Avani; from 31st, Vikari Kanya—Purattasi. Lunar: Bah.; Sukla; Bhadrapada; Bahula. Muhammadan: Safar; H. 1379 Rabi-ul-awwal.)

Cyclic Sidereal	Week-Day	English Day	Tithi	Tithi Moment	Nakshatra	Nakshatra Moment	Muhammadan
16	Tu	1	13	·05	9	·82	27
17	We	2	14	·04	10	·83	28
18	Th	3	A 1	·02 ·98	11	·82	—29
19	Fr	4	2	·93	12	·80	1
20	Sa	5	3	·86	13	·76	2
21	Su	6	4	·78	14	·70	3
22	Mo	7	5	·68	15	·64	4
23	Tu	8	6	·58	16	·58	5
24	We	9	7	·48	17	·51	6
25	Th	10	8	·38	18	·44	7
26	Fr	11	9	·28	19	·38	8
27	Sa	12	10	·19	20	·33	9
28	Su	13	11	·12	21	·28	10
29	Mo	14	12	·06	22	·24	11
30	Tu	15	13 14	·01 ·98	23	·23	12
—31	We ○	16	P	·97	24	·23	13
1	Th	17	1	·97	25	·26	14
2	Fr	18	...	...	26	·30	15
3	Sa	19	2	·00	27	·36	16
4	Su	20	3	·06	1	·44	17
5	Mo	21	4	·13	2	·54	18
6	Tu	22	5	·21	3	·65	19
7	We	23	6	·29	4	·76	20
8	Th	24	7	·37	5	·86	21
9	Fr	25	8	·45	6	·95	22
10	Sa	26	9	·51	...	...	23
11	Su	27	10	·56	7	·03	24
12	Mo	28	11	·58	8	·10	25
13	Tu	29	12	·59	9	·14	26
14	We	30	13	·57	10	·15	27

Oct. (Solar: Vikari Kanya—Purattasi; from 31st, Vikari Tula—Aippasi. Lunar: Sukla; Asvina; Bahula. Muhammadan: H. 1379 Rabi-ul-akhir.)

Cyclic Sidereal	Week-Day	English Day	Tithi	Tithi Moment	Nakshatra	Nakshatra Moment	Muhammadan
15	Th	1	14	·54	11	·15	28
16	Fr ●	2	—A	·48	12	·13	29
17	Sa	3	1	·40	13	·09	—30
18	Su	4	2	·32	14 15	·05 ·99	1
19	Mo	5	3	·23	16	·92	2
20	Tu	6	4	·14	17	·85	3
21	We	7	5 6	·04 ·94	18	·78	4
22	Th	8	7	·84	19	·72	5
23	Fr	9	8	·75	20	·66	6
24	Sa	10	9	·68	21	·61	7
25	Su	11	10	·62	22	·57	8
26	Mo	12	11	·57	23	·55	9
27	Tu	13	12	·55	24	·56	10
28	We	14	13	·54	25	·57	11
29	Th	15	14	·54	26	·61	12
30	Fr	16	P	·57	27	·67	13
—31	Sa	17	1	·63	1	·75	14
1	Su	18	2	·70	2	·84	15
2	Mo	19	3	·78	3	·95	16
3	Tu	20	4	·87	...	...	17
4	We	21	5	·96	4	·06	18
5	Th	22	...	...	5	·16	19
6	Fr	23	6	·04	6	·26	20
7	Sa	24	7	·10	7	·34	21
8	Su	25	8	·14	8	·41	22
9	Mo	26	9	·17	9	·45	23
10	Tu	27	10	·17	10	·47	24
11	We	28	11	·15	11	·47	25
12	Th	29	12	·12	12	·46	26
13	Fr	30	13	·07	13	·43	27
14	Sa	31	14 A	·00 ·92	14	·38	28

Nov. (Solar: Vikari Tula—Aippasi; from 30th, Vikari Vrischika—Kartigai. Lunar: Sukla; Karttika; Bahula. Muhammadan: H. 1379 Jumadal-awwal.)

Cyclic Sidereal	Week-Day	English Day	Tithi	Tithi Moment	Nakshatra	Nakshatra Moment	Muhammadan
15	Su	1	1	·82	15	·32	—29
16	Mo	2	2	·72	16	·26	1
17	Tu	3	3	·62	17	·20	2
18	We	4	4	·52	18	·13	3
19	Th	5	5	·43	19	·06	4
20	Fr	6	6	·35	20 21	·00 ·94	5
21	Sa	7	7	·27	22	·90	6
22	Su	8	8	·21	23	·89	7
23	Mo	9	9	·17	24	·88	8
24	Tu	10	10	·14	25	·89	9
25	We	11	11	·14	26	·92	10
26	Th	12	12	·15	27	·98	11
27	Fr	13	13	·18	...	...	12
28	Sa	14	14	·24	1	·05	13
29	Su	15	P	·32	2	·15	14
—30	Mo	16	1	·40	3	·25	15
1	Tu	17	2	·48	4	·35	16
2	We	18	3	·57	5	·46	17
3	Th	19	4	·65	6	·56	18
4	Fr	20	5	·71	7	·65	19
5	Sa	21	6	·76	8	·72	20
6	Su	22	7	·79	9	·77	21
7	Mo	23	8	·79	10	·79	22
8	Tu	24	9	·77	11	·80	23
9	We	25	10	·73	12	·79	24
10	Th	26	11	·68	13	·76	25
11	Fr	27	12	·62	14	·72	26
12	Sa	28	13	·53	15	·66	27
13	Su	29	14	·44	16	·60	28
14	Mo	30	—A	·35	17	·54	29

Dec. (Solar: Vikari Vrischika—Kartigai; from 29th, Vikari Dhanus—Margali. Lunar: Sukla; Margasira; Bahula. Muhammadan: H. 1379 Jumadal-akhir.)

Cyclic Sidereal	Week-Day	English Day	Tithi	Tithi Moment	Nakshatra	Nakshatra Moment	Muhammadan
15	Tu	1	1	·25	18	·47	—30
16	We	2	2	·15	19	·40	1
17	Th	3	3 4	·05 ·97	20	·33	2
18	Fr	4	5	·89	21	·28	3
19	Sa	5	6	·84	22	·23	4
20	Su	6	7	·80	23	·21	5
21	Mo	7	8	·78	24	·20	6
22	Tu	8	9	·77	25	·21	7
23	We	9	10	·78	26	·24	8
24	Th	10	11	·82	27	·29	9
25	Fr	11	12	·88	1	·36	10
26	Sa	12	13	·96	2	·45	11
27	Su	13	...	...	3	·55	12
28	Mo	14	14	·05	4	·65	13
—29	Tu	15	P	·14	5	·76	14
1	We	16	1	·22	6	·87	15
2	Th	17	2	·30	7	·96	16
3	Fr	18	3	·37	...	...	17
4	Sa	19	4	·41	8	·03	18
5	Su	20	5	·43	9	·08	19
6	Mo	21	6	·43	10	·11	20
7	Tu	22	7	·42	11	·13	21
8	We	23	8	·38	12	·12	22
9	Th	24	9	·33	13	·09	23
10	Fr	25	10	·25	14	·05	24
11	Sa	26	11	·16	15 16	·00 ·94	25
12	Su	27	12 13	·08 ·99	17	·88	26
13	Mo	28	14	·89	18	·81	27
14	Tu	29	—A	·79	19	·74	28
15	We	30	1	·70	20	·67	—29
16	Th	31	2	·61	21	·61	1

15. Svati. 16. Visak. 17. Anur. 18. Jyesh. 19. Mula. 20. P. Ash. 21. U. Ash. 22. Sravn. 23. Dani. 24. Satab. 25. P. Bhad. 26. U. Bhad. 27. Rev.

A. D. 1960.
Solar Eclipse. ●
Lunar Eclipse. ○

Mesha Sankranti (Commencement of Indian Sidereal Year).
(Surya Sid.) April 13·15.
(Arya Sid.) April 13·04.

Saka 1882. **Kaliyuga 5061.**
(S. Cycle) Sarvari.

Columns: SOLAR reckoning — Cyclic Sidereal Year, Month and Day; Week-Day English Month and Day. LUNAR reckoning — Tithi Ending Moment; Nakshatra Ending Moment; Muhammadan Year, Month and Day.

Jan. — Solar: Vikari *Dhanus—Margali* (to 29), Vikari *Makara—Tai* (from 1). Lunar: *Sukla*, Pausha, *Bahula*. Muhammadan: H. 1379 *Rajab*.

Cyclic Sidereal	Week-Day	Date	Tithi	Moment	Nakshatra	Moment	Muhammadan
17	Fr	1	3	·53	22	·57	2
18	Sa	2	4	·48	23	·54	3
19	Su	3	5	·44	24	·53	4
20	Mo	4	6	·42	25	·53	5
21	Tu	5	7	·41	26	·55	6
22	We	6	8	·44	27	·60	7
23	Th	7	9	·47	1	·67	8
24	Fr	8	10	·53	2	·75	9
25	Sa	9	11	·61	3	·85	10
26	Su	10	12	·69	4	·96	11
27	Mo	11	13	·78	...	...	12
28	Tu	12	14	·87	5	·07	13
—29	We	13	P	·95	6	·17	14
1	Th	14	...	...	7	·26	15
2	Fr	15	1	·01	8	·34	16
3	Sa	16	2	·05	9	·39	17
4	Su	17	3	·08	10	·43	18
5	Mo	18	4	·07	11	·45	19
6	Tu	19	5	·06	12	·45	20
7	We	20	6 / 7	·02 / ·97	13	·42	21
8	Th	21	8	·89	14	·38	22
9	Fr	22	9	·80	15	·33	23
10	Sa	23	10	·71	16	·28	24
11	Su	24	11	·61	17	·21	25
12	Mo	25	12	·51	18	·14	26
13	Tu	26	13	·42	19	·07	27
14	We	27	14	·33	20 / 21	·01 / ·96	28
15	Th	28	—A	·25	22	·91	29
16	Fr	29	1	·18	23	·87	—30
17	Sa	30	2	·13	24	·85	1
18	Su	31	3	·08	25	·85	2

Feb. — Solar: Vikari *Kumbha—Masi*. Lunar: *Sukla*, Magha, *Bahula*, *P. Suk.* Muhammadan: H. 1379 *Shaban*.

Cyclic Sidereal	Week-Day	Date	Tithi	Moment	Nakshatra	Moment	Muhammadan
19	Mo	1	4	·06	26	·88	3
20	Tu	2	5	·05	27	·91	4
21	We	3	6	·08	1	·97	5
22	Th	4	7	·12	...	...	6
23	Fr	5	8	·18	2	·05	7
24	Sa	6	9	·25	3	·15	8
25	Su	7	10	·34	4	·26	9
26	Mo	8	11	·43	5	·37	10
27	Tu	9	12	·51	6	·47	11
28	We	10	13	·59	7	·56	12
29	Th	11	14	·65	8	·64	13
—30	Fr	12	P	·69	9	·71	14
1	Sa	13	1	·71	10	·75	15
2	Su	14	2	·71	11	·77	16
3	Mo	15	3	·69	12	·77	17
4	Tu	16	4	·64	13	·75	18
5	We	17	5	·58	14	·72	19
6	Th	18	6	·51	15	·68	20
7	Fr	19	7	·43	16	·62	21
8	Sa	20	8	·34	17	·55	22
9	Su	21	9	·24	18	·48	23
10	Mo	22	10	·14	19	·41	24
11	Tu	23	11 / 12	·05 / ·95	20	·35	25
12	We	24	13	·86	21	·29	26
13	Th	25	14	·79	22	·24	27
14	Fr	26	—A	·73	23	·20	28
15	Sa	27	1	·70	24	·18	—29
16	Su	28	2	·68	25	·18	1
17	Mo	29	3	·68	26	·19	2

March — Solar: Vikari *Kumbha—Masi* (to 31), Vikari *Mina—Panguni* (from 1). Lunar: *Sukla*, Phalguna, *Bahula*. Muhammadan: H. 1379 *Ramzan*.

Cyclic Sidereal	Week-Day	Date	Tithi	Moment	Nakshatra	Moment	Muhammadan
18	Tu	1	4	·70	27	·23	3
19	We	2	5	·74	1	·28	4
20	Th	3	6	·80	2	·35	5
21	Fr	4	7	·88	3	·45	6
22	Sa	5	8	·97	4	·56	7
23	Su	6	...	...	5	·67	8
24	Mo	7	9	·05	6	·77	9
25	Tu	8	10	·13	7	·86	10
26	We	9	11	·20	8	·95	11
27	Th	10	12	·26	...	...	12
28	Fr	11	13	·30	9	·02	13
29	Sa	12	14	·31	10	·07	14
30	Su ○	13	P	·31	11	·09	15
—31	Mo	14	1	·29	12	·10	16
1	Tu	15	2	·24	13	·08	17
2	We	16	3	·18	14	·05	18
3	Th	17	4	·11	15 / 16	·01 / ·96	19
4	Fr	18	5 / 6	·02 / ·93	17	·89	20
5	Sa	19	7	·83	18	·82	21
6	Su	20	8	·73	19	·75	22
7	Mo	21	9	·63	20	·69	23
8	Tu	22	10	·54	21	·63	24
9	We	23	11	·46	22	·57	25
10	Th	24	12	·38	23	·53	26
11	Fr	25	13	·32	24	·51	27
12	Sa	26	14	·29	25	·50	28
13	Su	27	—A	·26	26	·51	29
14	Mo	28	1	·26	27	·54	—30
15	Tu	29	2	·28	1	·59	1
16	We	30	3	·32	2	·66	2
17	Th	31	4	·38	3	·75	3

April — Solar: Vikari *Mina—Panguni* (to 29), Sarvari *Mesha—Chittirai* (from 1). Lunar: *Sukla*, Chaitra, *Bahula*, *Vsk. Suk.* Muhammadan: H. 1379 *Shawwal*.

Cyclic Sidereal	Week-Day	Date	Tithi	Moment	Nakshatra	Moment	Muhammadan
18	Fr	1	5	·45	4	·85	4
19	Sa	2	6	·54	5	·96	5
20	Su	3	7	·62	...	...	6
21	Mo	4	8	·70	6	·07	7
22	Tu	5	9	·77	7	·17	8
23	We	6	10	·83	8	·26	9
24	Th	7	11	·87	9	·33	10
25	Fr	8	12	·89	10	·38	11
26	Sa	9	13	·87	11	·41	12
27	Su	10	14	·85	12	·42	13
28	Mo	11	P	·80	13	·42	14
—29	Tu	12	1	·74	14	·39	15
1	We	13	2	·67	15	·35	16
2	Th	14	3	·58	16	·29	17
3	Fr	15	4	·49	17	·23	18
4	Sa	16	5	·39	18	·17	19
5	Su	17	6	·29	19	·10	20
6	Mo	18	7	·19	20 / 21	·03 / ·96	21
7	Tu	19	8	·09	22	·91	22
8	We	20	9 / 10	·00 / ·92	23	·87	23
9	Th	21	11	·86	24	·84	24
10	Fr	22	12	·83	25	·82	25
11	Sa	23	13	·80	26	·83	26
12	Su	24	14	·80	27	·85	27
13	Mo	25	—A	·82	1	·90	28
14	Tu	26	1	·86	2	·97	—29
15	We	27	2	·92	...	...	1
16	Th	28	3	·98	3	·06	2
17	Fr	29	...	...	4	·15	3
18	Sa	30	4	·06	5	·26	4

May — Solar: Sarvari *Mesha—Chittirai* (to 31), Sarvari *Vrishabha—Vaikasi* (from 1). Lunar: *Sukla*, Vaisakha, *Bahula*. Muhammadan: H. 1379 *Zi-l-ka'da*.

Cyclic Sidereal	Week-Day	Date	Tithi	Moment	Nakshatra	Moment	Muhammadan
19	Su	1	5	·15	6	·37	5
20	Mo	2	6	·23	7	·48	6
21	Tu	3	7	·30	8	·57	7
22	We	4	8	·36	9	·64	8
23	Th	5	9	·39	10	·69	9
24	Fr	6	10	·41	11	·73	10
25	Sa	7	11	·40	12	·75	11
26	Su	8	12	·38	13	·74	12
27	Mo	9	13	·33	14	·72	13
28	Tu	10	14	·27	15	·68	14
29	We	11	P	·19	16	·63	15
30	Th	12	1	·10	17	·58	16
—31	Fr	13	2 / 3	·01 / ·91	18	·51	17
1	Sa	14	4	·81	19	·44	18
2	Su	15	5	·71	20	·37	19
3	Mo	16	6	·61	21	·30	20
4	Tu	17	7	·52	22	·24	21
5	We	18	8	·45	23	·20	22
6	Th	19	9	·39	24	·17	23
7	Fr	20	10	·34	25	·15	24
8	Sa	21	11	·32	26	·15	25
9	Su	22	12	·31	27	·17	26
10	Mo	23	13	·33	1	·22	27
11	Tu	24	14	·37	2	·28	28
12	We	25	—A	·42	3	·36	29
13	Th	26	1	·50	4	·45	—30
14	Fr	27	2	·58	5	·56	1
15	Sa	28	3	·66	6	·67	2
16	Su	29	4	·73	7	·78	3
17	Mo	30	5	·80	8	·87	4
18	Tu	31	6	·85	9	·95	5

June — Solar: Sarvari *Vrishabha—Vaikasi* (to 31), Sarvari *Mithuna—Ani* (from 1). Lunar: *Sukla*, Jyeshtha, *Bahula*, *Ash. Suk.* Muhammadan: H. 1379 *Zi-l-hijja*; H. 1380 *Muharram*.

Cyclic Sidereal	Week-Day	Date	Tithi	Moment	Nakshatra	Moment	Muhammadan
19	We	1	7	·88	...	...	6
20	Th	2	8	·91	10	·01	7
21	Fr	3	9	·90	11	·05	8
22	Sa	4	10	·88	12	·07	9
23	Su	5	11	·84	13	·07	10
24	Mo	6	12	·78	14	·05	11
25	Tu	7	13	·70	15 / 16	·01 / ·97	12
26	We	8	14	·61	17	·91	13
27	Th	9	P	·51	18	·85	14
28	Fr	10	1	·41	19	·78	15
29	Sa	11	2	·31	20	·71	16
30	Su	12	3	·21	21	·65	17
—31	Mo	13	4	·11	22	·59	18
1	Tu	14	5 / 6	·01 / ·93	23	·54	19
2	We	15	7	·87	24	·50	20
3	Th	16	8	·83	25	·47	21
4	Fr	17	9	·80	26	·47	22
5	Sa	18	10	·79	27	·49	23
6	Su	19	11	·81	1	·53	24
7	Mo	20	12	·84	2	·59	25
8	Tu	21	13	·90	3	·66	26
9	We	22	14	·97	4	·75	27
10	Th	23	...	...	5	·86	28
11	Fr	24	—A	·04	6	·97	29
12	Sa	25	1	·13	...	...	—30
13	Su	26	2	·21	7	·07	1
14	Mo	27	3	·27	8	·17	2
15	Tu	28	4	·33	9	·25	3
16	We	29	5	·37	10	·32	4
17	Th	30	6	·39	11	·37	5

Naksh:—1. Asvn. 2. Bhar. 3. Krit. 4. Rohi. 5. Mrig. 6. Ardh. 7. Punar. 8. Push. 9. Aslesh. 10. Magh. 11. P. Phal. 12. U. Phal. 13. Hasta. 14. Chit.

A. D. 1960. Kollam 1136, Commences { N. Malabar—Sept. S. Malabar—Aug. Hijra 1380, Commences, June 26. Vikrama 2017.
A.—Amavasya. Bengal San 1366.
P.—Paurnami. (N. Cycle) Pramadin.

July

SOLAR reckoning: Cyclic Sidereal Year, Month and Day	SOLAR reckoning: Week-Day English Month and Day	LUNAR reckoning: Tithi Ending Moment	LUNAR reckoning: Nakshatra Ending Moment	LUNAR reckoning: Muhammadan Year, Month and Day
Sarvari *Mithuna—Ani.* 18	Fr 1	Ashadha *Sukla* 7 ·39	12 ·39	H. 1380 *Muharram.* 6
19	Sa 2	8 ·37	13 ·39	7
20	Su 3	9 ·32	14 ·38	8
21	Mo 4	10 ·26	15 ·35	9
22	Tu 5	11 ·18	16 ·31	10
23	We 6	12 ·09 13 ·99	17 ·25	11
24	Th 7	14 ·89	18 ·18	12
25	Fr 8	P ·78	19 ·11	13
26	Sa 9	*Bahula* 1 ·68	20 ·04 21 ·98	14
27	Su 10	2 ·58	22 ·92	15
28	Mo 11	3 ·48	23 ·87	16
29	Tu 12	4 ·40	24 ·83	17
30	We 13	5 ·35	25 ·80	18
31	Th 14	6 ·31	26 ·80	19
—32	Fr 15	7 ·28	27 ·81	20
Sarvari *Karkata—Adi.* 1	Sa 16	8 ·27	1 ·84	21
2	Su 17	9 ·28	2 ·89	22
3	Mo 18	10 ·32	3 ·96	23
4	Tu 19	11 ·38	... ...	24
5	We 20	12 ·44	4 ·06	25
6	Th 21	13 ·52	5 ·16	26
7	Fr 22	14 ·60	6 ·27	27
8	Sa 23	—A ·68	7 ·37	28
9	Su 24	*Sukla* 1 ·75	8 ·47	29
10	Mo 25	2 ·81	9 ·57	—30
11	Tu 26	3 ·85	10 ·64	H. 1380 *Safar.* 1
12	We 27	4 ·87	11 ·68	2
13	Th 28	5 ·86	12 ·71	3
14	Fr 29	6 ·84	13 ·72	4
15	Sa 30	7 ·80	14 ·71	5
16	Su 31	8 ·73	15 ·69	6

Aug.

SOLAR reckoning: Cyclic Sidereal Year, Month and Day	SOLAR reckoning: Week-Day English Month and Day	LUNAR reckoning: Tithi Ending Moment	LUNAR reckoning: Nakshatra Ending Moment	LUNAR reckoning: Muhammadan Year, Month and Day
Sarvari *Simha—Avani.* 17	Mo 1	Sravana 9 ·66	16 ·65	7
18	Tu 2	10 ·58	17 ·59	8
19	We 3	11 ·48	18 ·52	9
20	Th 4	12 ·38	19 ·45	10
21	Fr 5	13 ·28	20 ·38	11
22	Sa 6	14 ·18	21 ·32	12
23	Su 7	P ·08 1 ·99	22 ·26	13
24	Mo 8	*Bahula* 2 ·91	23 ·20	14
25	Tu 9	3 ·84	24 ·16	15
26	We 10	4 ·80	25 ·14	16
27	Th 11	5 ·77	26 ·12	17
28	Fr 12	6 ·76	27 ·13	18
29	Sa 13	7 ·76	1 ·15	19
30	Su 14	8 ·80	2 ·20	20
—31	Mo 15	9 ·86	3 ·28	21
1	Tu 16	10 ·93	4 ·36	22
2	We 17	... ...	5 ·46	23
3	Th 18	11 ·01	6 ·57	24
4	Fr 19	12 ·09	7 ·67	25
5	Sa 20	13 ·18	8 ·77	26
6	Su 21	14 ·25	9 ·87	27
7	Mo 22	—A ·31	10 ·94	28
8	Tu 23	Bhadra. *Sukla* 1 ·84	... ...	—29
9	We 24	2 ·86	11 ·00	H.1380 *Rabi-ul-awwal.* 1
10	Th 25	3 ·36	12 ·03	2
11	Fr 26	4 ·34	13 ·04	3
12	Sa 27	5 ·30	14 ·04	4
13	Su 28	6 ·25	15 ·02 16 ·98	5
14	Mo 29	7 ·17	17 ·92	6
15	Tu 30	8 ·08 9 ·99	18 ·86	7
16	We 31	10 ·89	19 ·80	8

Sep.

SOLAR reckoning: Cyclic Sidereal Year, Month and Day	SOLAR reckoning: Week-Day English Month and Day	LUNAR reckoning: Tithi Ending Moment	LUNAR reckoning: Nakshatra Ending Moment	LUNAR reckoning: Muhammadan Year, Month and Day
Sarvari *Simha—Avani.* 17	Th 1	Bhadrapada *Suk.* 11 ·79	20 ·73	H. 1380 *Rabi-ul-awwal.* 9
18	Fr 2	12 ·69	21 ·66	10
19	Sa 3	13 ·59	22 ·59	11
20	Su 4	14 ·50	23 ·54	12
21	Mo ○ 5	P ·42	24 ·50	13
22	Tu 6	*Bahula* 1 ·36	25 ·46	14
23	We 7	2 ·31	26 ·45	15
24	Th 8	3 ·28	27 ·45	16
25	Fr 9	4 ·28	1 ·47	17
26	Sa 10	5 ·29	2 ·52	18
27	Su 11	6 ·33	3 ·58	19
28	Mo 12	7 ·38	4 ·66	20
29	Tu 13	8 ·45	5 ·76	21
30	We 14	9 ·54	6 ·86	22
—31	Th 15	10 ·62	7 ·97	23
Sarvari *Kanya—Purattasi.* 1	Fr 16	11 ·70	... ...	24
2	Sa 17	12 ·77	8 ·08	25
3	Su 18	13 ·83	9 ·17	26
4	Mo 19	14 ·87	10 ·25	27
5	Tu 20	—A ·89	11 ·31	28
6	We 21	*Sukla* 1 ·89	12 ·35	29
7	Th 22	2 ·88	13 ·37	—30
8	Fr 23	3 ·84	14 ·37	H. 1380 *Rabi-ul-akhir.* 1
9	Sa 24	4 ·77	15 ·35	2
10	Su 25	5 ·70	16 ·31	3
11	Mo 26	6 ·62	17 ·26	4
12	Tu 27	7 ·53	18 ·21	5
13	We 28	8 ·43	19 ·14	6
14	Th 29	9 ·33	20 ·07	7
15	Fr 30	10 ·28	21 ·00 22 ·94	8

Oct.

SOLAR reckoning: Cyclic Sidereal Year, Month and Day	SOLAR reckoning: Week-Day English Month and Day	LUNAR reckoning: Tithi Ending Moment	LUNAR reckoning: Nakshatra Ending Moment	LUNAR reckoning: Muhammadan Year, Month and Day
16	Sa 1	Asvina 11 ·13	23 ·88	9
17	Su 2	12 ·05 13 ·97	24 ·83	10
18	Mo 3	14 ·91	25 ·79	11
19	Tu 4	P ·86	26 ·77	12
20	We 5	*Bahula* 1 ·84	27 ·77	13
21	Th 6	2 ·83	1 ·79	14
22	Fr 7	3 ·84	2 ·83	15
23	Sa 8	4 ·88	3 ·89	16
24	Su 9	5 ·94	4 ·97	17
25	Mo 10	... ...	... ...	18
26	Tu 11	6 ·01	5 ·06	19
27	We 12	7 ·10	6 ·16	20
28	Th 13	8 ·18	7 ·27	21
29	Fr 14	9 ·26	8 ·38	22
30	Sa 15	10 ·34	9 ·48	23
—31	Su 16	11 ·40	10 ·56	24
Sarvari *Tula—Aippasi.* 1	Mo 17	12 ·44	11 ·62	25
2	Tu 18	13 ·47	12 ·67	26
3	We 19	14 ·46	13 ·69	27
4	Th 20	—A ·45	14 ·69	28
5	Fr 21	Karttika *Sukla* 1 ·41	15 ·68	—29
6	Sa 22	2 ·36	16 ·64	H. 1380 *Jumadal-awwal.* 1
7	Su 23	3 ·29	17 ·60	2
8	Mo 24	4 ·21	18 ·54	3
9	Tu 25	5 ·11	19 ·48	4
10	We 26	6 ·01 7 ·91	20 ·41	5
11	Th 27	8 ·81	21 ·34	6
12	Fr 28	9 ·72	22 ·28	7
13	Sa 29	10 ·64	23 ·22	8
14	Su 30	11 ·56	24 ·16	9
15	Mo 31	12 ·50	25 ·12	10

Nov.

SOLAR reckoning: Cyclic Sidereal Year, Month and Day	SOLAR reckoning: Week-Day English Month and Day	LUNAR reckoning: Tithi Ending Moment	LUNAR reckoning: Nakshatra Ending Moment	LUNAR reckoning: Muhammadan Year, Month and Day
Sarvari *Tula—Aippasi.* 16	Tu 1	Karttika 13 ·45	26 ·10	H. 1380 *Jumadal-awwal.* 11
17	We 2	14 ·43	27 ·09	12
18	Th 3	P ·43	1 ·11	13
19	Fr 4	*Bahula* 1 ·44	2 ·14	14
20	Sa 5	2 ·48	3 ·20	15
21	Su 6	3 ·54	4 ·27	16
22	Mo 7	4 ·61	5 ·36	17
23	Tu 8	5 ·70	6 ·47	18
24	We 9	6 ·79	7 ·58	19
25	Th 10	7 ·87	8 ·68	20
26	Fr 11	8 ·94	9 ·78	21
27	Sa 12	... ...	10 ·86	22
28	Su 13	9 ·00	11 ·94	23
29	Mo 14	10 ·05	12 ·99	24
—30	Tu 15	11 ·08	... ...	25
Sarvari *Vrischika—Kartigai.* 1	We 16	12 ·07	13 ·01	26
2	Th 17	13 ·06	14 ·02	27
3	Fr 18	14 ·02 A ·97	15 ·00 16 ·98	28
4	Sa 19	*Sukla* 1 ·90	17 ·94	29
5	Su 20	2 ·82	18 ·88	—30
6	Mo 21	3 ·73	19 ·82	1
7	Tu 22	4 ·63	20 ·75	2
8	We 23	5 ·53	21 ·68	3
9	Th 24	6 ·43	22 ·62	4
10	Fr 25	7 ·34	23 ·56	5
11	Sa 26	8 ·25	24 ·50	6
12	Su 27	9 ·18	25 ·45	7
13	Mo 28	10 ·11	26 ·42	8
14	Tu 29	11 ·07	27 ·42	9
15	We 30	12 ·06	1 ·43	10

Dec.

SOLAR reckoning: Cyclic Sidereal Year, Month and Day	SOLAR reckoning: Week-Day English Month and Day	LUNAR reckoning: Tithi Ending Moment	LUNAR reckoning: Nakshatra Ending Moment	LUNAR reckoning: Muhammadan Year, Month and Day
16	Th 1	Margasira 13 ·05	2 ·46	H. 1380 *Jumadal-akhir.* 11
17	Fr 2	14 ·07	3 ·51	12
18	Sa 3	P ·12	4 ·58	13
19	Su 4	*Bahula* 1 ·17	5 ·67	14
20	Mo 5	2 ·24	6 ·77	15
21	Tu 6	3 ·33	7 ·87	16
22	We 7	4 ·42	8 ·98	17
23	Th 8	5 ·50	... ...	18
24	Fr 9	6 ·58	9 ·08	19
25	Sa 10	7 ·64	10 ·18	20
26	Su 11	8 ·69	11 ·25	21
27	Mo 12	9 ·71	12 ·30	22
28	Tu 13	10 ·71	13 ·33	23
—29	We 14	11 ·70	14 ·34	24
Sarvari *Dhanus—Margali.* 1	Th 15	12 ·66	15 ·33	25
2	Fr 16	13 ·59	16 ·31	26
3	Sa 17	14 ·52	17 ·27	27
4	Su 18	—A ·44	18 ·22	28
5	Mo 19	Pausha *Sukla* 1 ·35	19 ·16	—29
6	Tu 20	2 ·23	20 ·09	H. 1380 *Rajab.* 1
7	We 21	3 ·16	21 ·02 22 ·95	2
8	Th 22	4 ·06 5 ·96	23 ·89	3
9	Fr 23	6 ·88	24 ·88	4
10	Sa 24	7 ·81	25 ·78	5
11	Su 25	8 ·76	26 ·76	6
12	Mo 26	9 ·72	27 ·75	7
13	Tu 27	10 ·70	1 ·75	8
14	We 28	11 ·70	2 ·77	9
15	Th 29	12 ·72	3 ·81	10
16	Fr 30	13 ·76	4 ·88	11
17	Sa 31	14 ·82	5 ·97	12

15. Svati. 16. Visak. 17. Anur. 18. Jyesh. 19. Mula. 20. P. Ash. 21. U. Ash. 22. Sravn. 23. Dani. 24. Satab. 25. P. Bhad. 26. U. Bhad. 27. Rev.

A. D. 1961. Solar Eclipse. ● Lunar Eclipse. ○

Mesha Sankranti (Commencement of Indian Sidereal Year). (Surya Sid.) April 13·40. (Arya Sid.) April 13·29.

Saka 1883. (S. Cycle) Plava. Kaliyuga 5062.

SOLAR reckoning: Cyclic Sidereal Year, Month and Day. LUNAR reckoning: Week-Day English Month and Day; Tithi Ending Moment; Nakshatra Ending Moment; Muhammadan Year, Month and Day.

Jan.

Cyclic Sidereal Year, Month and Day	Week-Day English Month and Day	Tithi Ending Moment	Nakshatra Ending Moment	Muhammadan Year, Month and Day
Sarvari *Dhanus—Margali.* 18	Su 1	Pausha P ·89	... ...	H. 1380 *Rajab.* 13
19	Mo 2	1 ·98	6 ·07	14
20	Tu 3	... ...	7 ·17	15
21	We 4	2 ·07	8 ·28	16
22	Th 5	3 ·16	9 ·39	17
23	Fr 6	4 ·24	10 ·48	18
24	Sa 7	5 ·30	11 ·56	19
25	Su 8	*Bahula* 6 ·34	12 ·61	20
26	Mo 9	7 ·36	13 ·65	21
27	Tu 10	8 ·36	14 ·67	22
28	We 11	9 ·34	15 ·67	23
29	Th 12	10 ·30	16 ·64	24
30	Fr 13	11 ·24	17 ·60	25
1	Sa 14	12 ·17	18 ·55	26
2	Su 15	13 ·09	19 ·50	27
3	Mo 16	14 ·00 / A ·90	20 ·43	28
4	Tu 17	1 ·80	21 ·36	29
5	We 18	2 ·70	22 ·29	30
6	Th 19	3 ·61	23 ·23	1
7	Fr 20	4 ·53	24 ·17	2
8	Sa 21	5 ·46	25 ·13	3
9	Su 22	6 ·40	26 ·09	4
10	Mo 23	*Sukla* 7 ·36	27 ·07	5
11	Tu 24	8 ·34	1 ·07	6
Sarvari *Makara—Tai.* 12	We 25	9 ·34	2 ·09	7
13	Th 26	10 ·36	3 ·13	8
14	Fr 27	11 ·41	4 ·19	9
15	Sa 28	Magha 12 ·47	5 ·27	*Shaban.* 10
16	Su 29	13 ·55	6 ·37	11
17	Mo 30	14 ·64	7 ·48	12
18	Tu 31	P ·73	8 ·59	13

Feb.

Cyclic Sidereal Year, Month and Day	Week-Day English Month and Day	Tithi Ending Moment	Nakshatra Ending Moment	Muhammadan Year, Month and Day
19	We 1	1 ·81	9 ·69	H. 1380 14
20	Th 2	2 ·88	10 ·78	15
21	Fr 3	3 ·94	11 ·86	16
22	Sa 4	4 ·98	12 ·92	17
23	Su 5	... ...	13 ·97	18
24	Mo 6	*Bahula* 5 ·00 / 6 ·99	14 ·99	19
25	Tu 7	7 ·97	15 ·99	20
26	We 8	8 ·93	16 ·97	21
27	Th 9	9 ·86	17 ·94	22
28	Fr 10	10 ·79	18 ·89	23
29	Sa 11	11 ·71	19 ·84	24
1	Su 12	12 ·62	20 ·77	25
2	Mo 13	13 ·53	21 ·70	26
3	Tu 14	14 ·43	22 ·63	27
4	We ● 15	A ·33	23 ·56	28
5	Th 16	1 ·23	24 ·51	29
6	Fr 17	2 ·15	25 ·46	1
7	Sa 18	3 ·08	26 ·42	2
Sarvari *Kumbha—Masi.* 8	Su 19	*Sukla* 4 ·02 / 5 ·98	27 ·40	H. 1380 *Ramzan.* 3
9	Mo 20	6 ·97	1 ·39	4
10	Tu 21	7 ·97	2 ·41	5
11	We 22	8 ·99	3 ·45	6
12	Th 23	... ...	4 ·50	7
13	Fr 24	Phalguna 9 ·04	5 ·58	8
14	Sa 25	10 ·10	6 ·67	9
15	Su 26	11 ·17	7 ·77	10
16	Mo 27	12 ·26	8 ·88	11
17	Tu 28	13 ·35	9 ·99	12

March

Cyclic Sidereal Year, Month and Day	Week-Day English Month and Day	Tithi Ending Moment	Nakshatra Ending Moment	Muhammadan Year, Month and Day
Sarvari *Kumbha—Masi.* 18	We 1	Phalguna 14 ·43	... ...	H. 1380 *Ramzan.* 13
19	Th ○ 2	P ·50	10 ·09	14
20	Fr 3	1 ·56	11 ·17	15
21	Sa 4	2 ·60	12 ·23	16
22	Su 5	3 ·61	13 ·28	17
23	Mo 6	4 ·60	14 ·31	18
24	Tu 7	5 ·58	15 ·32	19
25	We 8	6 ·54	16 ·30	20
26	Th 9	*Bahula* 7 ·48	17 ·27	21
27	Fr 10	8 ·40	18 ·23	22
28	Sa 11	9 ·31	19 ·18	23
29	Su 12	10 ·22	20 ·11	24
30	Mo 13	11 ·13	21 ·04 / 22 ·97	25
1	Tu 14	12 ·03 / 13 ·93	23 ·91	26
2	We 15	14 ·83	24 ·85	27
3	Th 16	A ·74	25 ·79	28
4	Fr 17	1 ·66	26 ·75	29
5	Sa 18	2 ·61	27 ·72	30
6	Su 19	3 ·58	1 ·72	1
7	Mo 20	4 ·57	2 ·73	2
8	Tu 21	5 ·56	3 ·76	3
9	We 22	6 ·59	4 ·81	4
10	Th 23	*Sukla* 7 ·63	5 ·88	5
11	Fr 24	8 ·69	6 ·98	6
Sarvari *Mina—Panguni.* 12	Sa 25	9 ·77	... ...	7
13	Su 26	10 ·85	7 ·08	8
14	Mo 27	11 ·94	8 ·18	9
15	Tu 28	... ...	9 ·29	*Shawwal.* 10
16	We 29	12 ·02	10 ·39	11
17	Th 30	13 ·09	11 ·47	12
18	Fr 31	14 ·14	12 ·54	13

April

Cyclic Sidereal Year, Month and Day	Week-Day English Month and Day	Tithi Ending Moment	Nakshatra Ending Moment	Muhammadan Year, Month and Day
19	Sa 1	Chaitra P ·18	13 ·60	H. 1380 14
20	Su 2	1 ·19	14 ·63	15
21	Mo 3	2 ·18	15 ·64	16
22	Tu 4	3 ·15	16 ·63	17
23	We 5	4 ·11	17 ·61	18
24	Th 6	*Bahula* 5 ·05 / 6 ·97	18 ·57	19
25	Fr 7	7 ·89	19 ·51	20
26	Sa 8	8 ·79	20 ·45	21
27	Su 9	9 ·69	21 ·39	22
28	Mo 10	10 ·59	22 ·32	23
29	Tu 11	11 ·49	23 ·25	24
30	We 12	12 ·39	24 ·19	25
1	Th 13	13 ·30	25 ·13	26
2	Fr 14	14 ·23	26 ·09	27
3	Sa 15	A ·17	27 ·06	28
4	Su 16	1 ·14	1 ·04	29
5	Mo 17	2 ·12	2 ·05	1
6	Tu 18	3 ·11	3 ·07	2
7	We 19	4 ·14	4 ·12	3
8	Th 20	5 ·18	5 ·19	4
9	Fr 21	6 ·23	6 ·28	5
Plava *Mesha—Chittirai.* 10	Sa 22	*Sukla* 7 ·30	7 ·38	H. 1380 *Zi-l-ka'da.* 6
11	Su 23	8 ·39	8 ·48	7
12	Mo 24	9 ·48	9 ·59	8
13	Tu 25	10 ·56	10 ·69	9
14	We 26	Vaisakha 11 ·63	11 ·79	10
15	Th 27	12 ·68	12 ·86	11
16	Fr 28	13 ·72	13 ·91	12
17	Sa 29	14 ·73	14 ·95	13
18	Su 30	P ·72	15 ·96	14

May

Cyclic Sidereal Year, Month and Day	Week-Day English Month and Day	Tithi Ending Moment	Nakshatra Ending Moment	Muhammadan Year, Month and Day
19	Mo 1	Vaisakha 1 ·69	16 ·96	H. 1380 *Zi-l-ka'da.* 15
20	Tu 2	2 ·64	17 ·94	16
21	We 3	3 ·58	18 ·90	17
Plava *Mesha—Chittirai.* 22	Th 4	4 ·50	19 ·85	18
23	Fr 5	5 ·41	20 ·79	19
24	Sa 6	6 ·31	21 ·73	20
25	Su 7	7 ·21	22 ·66	21
26	Mo 8	8 ·11	23 ·59	22
27	Tu 9	9 ·01 / 10 ·91	24 ·52	23
28	We 10	*Bahula* 11 ·82	25 ·46	24
29	Th 11	12 ·75	26 ·42	25
30	Fr 12	13 ·70	27 ·39	26
31	Sa 13	14 ·66	1 ·37	27
1	Su 14	A ·64	2 ·37	28
2	Mo 15	1 ·63	3 ·39	29
3	Tu 16	2 ·66	4 ·43	30
4	We 17	3 ·70	5 ·50	1
5	Th 18	4 ·76	6 ·58	2
6	Fr 19	*Sukla* 5 ·82	7 ·67	3
7	Sa 20	6 ·90	8 ·78	4
8	Su 21	7 ·99	9 ·89	5
9	Mo 22	... ...	... ...	6
Plava *Vrishabha—Vaikasi.* 10	Tu 23	Adhika Jyeshtha 8 ·07	10 ·00	7
11	We 24	9 ·14	11 ·09	8
12	Th 25	10 ·18	12 ·17	9
13	Fr 26	11 ·22	13 ·23	10
14	Sa 27	12 ·23	14 ·26	*Zi-l-hijja.* 11
15	Su 28	13 ·23	15 ·29	12
16	Mo 29	14 ·20	16 ·29	13
17	Tu 30	P ·16	17 ·27	14
18	We 31	1 ·09	18 ·23	15

June

Cyclic Sidereal Year, Month and Day	Week-Day English Month and Day	Tithi Ending Moment	Nakshatra Ending Moment	Muhammadan Year, Month and Day
19	Th 1	2 ·00 / 3 ·91	19 ·18	H. 1380 16
20	Fr 2	4 ·81	20 ·13	17
21	Sa 3	5 ·71	21 ·06 / 22 ·99	18
22	Su 4	6 ·61	23 ·92	19
23	Mo 5	*Bahula* 7 ·51	24 ·86	20
24	Tu 6	8 ·42	25 ·80	21
25	We 7	9 ·33	26 ·75	22
26	Th 8	10 ·25	27 ·72	23
27	Fr 9	11 ·19	1 ·69	24
28	Sa 10	12 ·15	2 ·69	25
29	Su 11	13 ·12	3 ·71	26
30	Mo 12	14 ·12	4 ·75	27
31	Tu 13	A ·14	5 ·81	28
32	We 14	1 ·17	6 ·88	29
1	Th 15	2 ·23	7 ·97	1
2	Fr 16	3 ·30	... ...	2
3	Sa 17	4 ·38	8 ·08	3
4	Su 18	5 ·46	9 ·19	4
5	Mo 19	6 ·54	10 ·30	5
6	Tu 20	*Sukla* 7 ·61	11 ·39	6
7	We 21	8 ·66	12 ·47	7
8	Th 22	9 ·70	13 ·54	8
Plava *Mithuna—Ani.* 9	Fr 23	10 ·72	14 ·59	H. 1381 *Muharram.* 9
10	Sa 24	11 ·70	15 ·61	10
11	Su 25	12 ·68	16 ·61	11
12	Mo 26	Nija Jyeshtha 13 ·64	17 ·60	12
13	Tu 27	14 ·57	18 ·57	13
14	We 28	P ·49	19 ·53	14
15	Th 29	1 ·40	20 ·47	15
16	Fr 30	2 ·30	21 ·40	16

Naksh:—1. Asvn. 2. Bhar. 3. Krit. 4. Rohi. 5. Mrig. 6. Ardh. 7. Punar. 8. Push. 9. Aslesh. 10. Magh. 11. P. Phal. 12. U. Phal. 13. Hasta. 14. Chit.

A. D. 1961.
A.—Amavasya.
P.—Paurnami.

Kollam 1137, Commences { **N. Malabar—Sept.** **S. Malabar—Aug.**

Hijra 1381, Commences, **June 15.**

Vikrama 2018.
Bengal San 1367.
(N. Cycle) Ananda.

SOLAR reckoning: Cyclic Sidereal Year, Month and Day; Week-Day English Month and Day. LUNAR reckoning: Tithi Ending Moment; Nakshatra Ending Moment; Muhammadan Year, Month and Day.

July

Marginal labels: Playa *Mithuna—Ani.*; Playa *Karkata—Adi.*; Nija—Jy. *Bahula*; *Sukla*; Ashadha; H. 1381 *Muharram.*; H. 1381 *Safar.*

Cyclic Sidereal Year, Month and Day	Week-Day English Month and Day	Tithi Ending Moment	Nakshatra Ending Moment	Muhammadan Year, Month and Day
17	Sa 1	3 ·20	22 ·33	17
18	Su 2	4 ·10	23 ·26	18
19	Mo 3	5 ·00 6 ·90	24 ·19	19
20	Tu 4	7 ·81	25 ·14	20
21	We 5	8 ·73	26 ·09	21
22	Th 6	9 ·67	27 ·05	22
23	Fr 7	10 ·62	1 ·02	23
24	Sa 8	11 ·60	2 ·01	24
25	Su 9	12 ·59	3 ·03	25
26	Mo 10	13 ·61	4 ·06	26
27	Tu 11	14 ·65	5 ·11	27
28	We 12	—A ·71	6 ·18	28
29	Th 13	1 ·78	7 ·27	29
30	Fr 14	2 ·86	8 ·38	—30
—31	Sa 15	3 ·94	9 ·49	1
1	Su 16	... ...	10 ·59	2
2	Mo 17	4 ·01	11 ·69	3
3	Tu 18	5 ·08	12 ·78	4
4	We 19	6 ·14	13 ·86	5
5	Th 20	7 ·18	14 ·90	6
6	Fr 21	8 ·20	15 ·93	7
7	Sa 22	9 ·18	16 ·94	8
8	Su 23	10 ·16	17 ·93	9
9	Mo 24	11 ·12	18 ·90	10
10	Tu 25	12 ·05 13 ·97	19 ·86	11
11	We 26	14 ·89	20 ·81	12
12	Th 27	P ·79	21 ·74	13
13	Fr 28	1 ·69	22 ·67	14
14	Sa 29	2 ·59	23 ·60	15
15	Su 30	3 ·49	24 ·54	16
16	Mo 31	4 ·39	25 ·48	17

Aug.

Marginal labels: Playa *Simha—Avani.*; *Bahula*; *Sukla*; Sravana; *Bahula*; H. 1381 *Rabi-ul-awwal.*

Cyclic Sidereal Year, Month and Day	Week-Day English Month and Day	Tithi Ending Moment	Nakshatra Ending Moment	Muhammadan Year, Month and Day
17	Tu 1	5 ·30	26 ·42	18
18	We 2	6 ·22	27 ·38	19
19	Th 3	7 ·16	1 ·35	20
20	Fr 4	8 ·11	2 ·34	21
21	Sa 5	9 ·09	3 ·35	22
22	Su 6	10 ·08	4 ·37	23
23	Mo 7	11 ·10	5 ·42	24
24	Tu 8	12 ·13	6 ·49	25
25	We 9	13 ·18	7 ·58	26
26	Th 10	14 ·26	8 ·68	27
27	Fr 11	—A ·34	9 ·79	28
28	Sa 12	1 ·43	10 ·89	—29
29	Su 13	2 ·50	11 ·99	1
30	Mo 14	3 ·57	... ...	2
31	Tu 15	4 ·68	12 ·08	3
—32	We 16	5 ·66	13 ·16	4
1	Th 17	6 ·69	14 ·22	5
2	Fr 18	7 ·67	15 ·25	6
3	Sa 19	8 ·65	16 ·26	7
4	Su 20	9 ·61	17 ·25	8
5	Mo 21	10 ·56	18 ·24	9
6	Tu 22	11 ·48	19 ·20	10
7	We 23	12 ·39	20 ·14	11
8	Th 24	13 ·29	21 ·08	12
9	Fr 25	14 ·19	22 ·02 23 ·95	13
10	Sa ⊙ 26	P ·09 1 ·99	24 ·88	14
11	Su 27	2 ·89	25 ·81	15
12	Mo 28	3 ·80	26 ·76	16
13	Tu 29	4 ·73	27 ·71	17
14	We 30	5 ·67	1 ·68	18
15	Th 31	6 ·62	2 ·67	19

Sep.

Marginal labels: Playa *Simha—Avani.*; Playa *Kanya—Purattasi.*; Sravana; *Bahula*; *Sukla*; Bhadrapada; H. 1381 *Rabi-ul-awwal.*; H. 1381 *Rabi-ul-akhir.*

Cyclic Sidereal Year, Month and Day	Week-Day English Month and Day	Tithi Ending Moment	Nakshatra Ending Moment	Muhammadan Year, Month and Day
16	Fr 1	7 ·60	3 ·67	20
17	Sa 2	8 ·59	4 ·69	21
18	Su 3	9 ·61	5 ·73	22
19	Mo 4	10 ·64	6 ·80	23
20	Tu 5	11 ·70	7 ·88	24
21	We 6	12 ·76	8 ·98	25
22	Th 7	13 ·84	... ...	26
23	Fr 8	14 ·93	9 ·08	27
24	Sa 9	... ...	10 ·19	28
25	Su 10	—A ·01	11 ·29	29
26	Mo 11	1 ·09	12 ·39	—30
27	Tu 12	2 ·15	13 ·47	1
28	We 13	3 ·20	14 ·53	2
29	Th 14	4 ·21	15 ·57	3
30	Fr 15	5 ·21	16 ·58	4
—31	Sa 16	6 ·18	17 ·59	5
1	Su 17	7 ·14	18 ·57	6
2	Mo 18	8 ·08	19 ·53	7
3	Tu 19	9 ·00 10 ·92	20 ·48	8
4	We 20	11 ·83	21 ·42	9
5	Th 21	12 ·73	22 ·36	10
6	Fr 22	13 ·63	23 ·29	11
7	Sa 23	14 ·53	24 ·22	12
8	Su 24	P ·43	25 ·15	13
9	Mo 25	1 ·34	26 ·09	14
10	Tu 26	2 ·27	27 ·05	15
11	We 27	3 ·21	1 ·01 2 ·99	16
12	Th 28	4 ·16	3 ·99	17
13	Fr 29	5 ·14	... ...	18
14	Sa 30	6 ·13	4 ·00	19

Oct.

Marginal labels: Playa *Tula—Aippasi.*; *Bahula*; *Sukla*; Asvina; *Bahula*; 1381 *Jumadal-awwal.*

Cyclic Sidereal Year, Month and Day	Week-Day English Month and Day	Tithi Ending Moment	Nakshatra Ending Moment	Muhammadan Year, Month and Day
15	Su 1	7 ·15	5 ·04	20
16	Mo 2	8 ·18	6 ·11	21
17	Tu 3	9 ·24	7 ·19	22
18	We 4	10 ·31	8 ·28	23
19	Th 5	11 ·40	9 ·38	24
20	Fr 6	12 ·48	10 ·49	25
21	Sa 7	13 ·56	11 ·60	26
22	Su 8	14 ·63	12 ·70	27
23	Mo 9	—A ·70	13 ·78	28
24	Tu 10	1 ·75	14 ·84	—29
25	We 11	2 ·77	15 ·88	1
26	Th 12	3 ·77	16 ·91	2
27	Fr 13	4 ·75	17 ·91	3
28	Sa 14	5 ·71	18 ·89	4
29	Su 15	6 ·65	19 ·86	5
—30	Mo 16	7 ·57	20 ·81	6
1	Tu 17	8 ·49	21 ·76	7
2	We 18	9 ·40	22 ·70	8
3	Th 19	10 ·30	23 ·63	9
4	Fr 20	11 ·20	24 ·56	10
5	Sa 21	12 ·11	25 ·49	11
6	Su 22	13 ·02 14 ·93	26 ·43	12
7	Mo 23	P ·85	27 ·38	13
8	Tu 24	1 ·79	1 ·34	14
9	We 25	2 ·74	2 ·32	15
10	Th 26	3 ·72	3 ·31	16
11	Fr 27	4 ·72	4 ·32	17
12	Sa 28	5 ·74	5 ·36	18
13	Su 29	6 ·78	6 ·42	19
14	Mo 30	7 ·84	7 ·49	20
15	Tu 31	8 ·91	8 ·58	21

Nov.

Marginal labels: Playa *Tula—Aippasi.*; Playa *Vrischika—Kartigai.*; Asvina; *Bah.*; *Sukla*; Kartika; *Bahula*; *Jumadal-awwal.*; H. 1381 *Jumadal-akhir.*

Cyclic Sidereal Year, Month and Day	Week-Day English Month and Day	Tithi Ending Moment	Nakshatra Ending Moment	Muhammadan Year, Month and Day
16	We 1	... ...	9 ·68	22
17	Th 2	9 ·00	10 ·79	23
18	Fr 3	10 ·09	11 ·90	24
19	Sa 4	11 ·18	... ...	25
20	Su 5	12 ·25	12 ·00	26
21	Mo 6	13 ·31	13 ·08	27
22	Tu 7	14 ·34	14 ·15	28
23	We 8	—A ·36	15 ·21	29
24	Th 9	1 ·37	16 ·23	—30
25	Fr 10	2 ·34	17 ·24	1
26	Sa 11	3 ·30	18 ·22	2
27	Su 12	4 ·25	19 ·19	3
28	Mo 13	5 ·18	20 ·16	4
29	Tu 14	6 ·10	21 ·10	5
—30	We 15	7 ·00 8 ·90	22 ·04 23 ·97	6
1	Th 16	9 ·80	24 ·90	7
2	Fr 17	10 ·71	25 ·83	8
3	Sa 18	11 ·62	26 ·77	9
4	Su 19	12 ·54	27 ·72	10
5	Mo 20	13 ·46	1 ·67	11
6	Tu 21	14 ·40	2 ·64	12
7	We 22	P ·36	3 ·63	13
8	Th 23	1 ·34	4 ·65	14
9	Fr 24	2 ·34	5 ·68	15
10	Sa 25	3 ·36	6 ·73	16
11	Su 26	4 ·40	7 ·79	17
12	Mo 27	5 ·46	8 ·88	18
13	Tu 28	6 ·54	9 ·98	19
14	We 29	7 ·62	... ...	20
15	Th 30	8 ·71	10 ·09	21

Dec.

Marginal labels: Playa *Dhanus—Margali.*; *Sukla*; Margasira; *Bahula*; H. 1381 *Rajab.*

Cyclic Sidereal Year, Month and Day	Week-Day English Month and Day	Tithi Ending Moment	Nakshatra Ending Moment	Muhammadan Year, Month and Day
16	Fr 1	9 ·80	11 ·20	22
17	Sa 2	10 ·87	12 ·30	23
18	Su 3	11 ·94	13 ·39	24
19	Mo 4	12 ·98	14 ·47	25
20	Tu 5	... ...	15 ·52	26
21	We 6	13 ·00 14 ·99	16 ·55	27
22	Th 7	—A ·97	17 ·56	28
23	Fr 8	1 ·93	18 ·55	—29
24	Sa 9	2 ·87	19 ·53	1
25	Su 10	3 ·80	20 ·49	2
26	Mo 11	4 ·72	21 ·44	3
27	Tu 12	5 ·63	22 ·37	4
28	We 13	6 ·53	23 ·30	5
29	Th 14	7 ·43	24 ·23	6
—30	Fr 15	8 ·34	25 ·17	7
1	Sa 16	9 ·25	26 ·11	8
2	Su 17	10 ·17	27 ·05	9
3	Mo 18	11 ·09	1 ·00 2 ·97	10
4	Tu 19	12 ·03 13 ·99	3 ·96	11
5	We 20	14 ·98	4 ·97	12
6	Th 21	P ·98	5 ·99	13
7	Fr 22	... ...	... ...	14
8	Sa 23	1 ·00	6 ·03	15
9	Su 24	2 ·05	7 ·10	16
10	Mo 25	3 ·11	8 ·19	17
11	Tu 26	4 ·19	9 ·29	18
12	We 27	5 ·28	10 ·39	19
13	Th 28	6 ·37	11 ·50	20
14	Fr 29	7 ·45	12 ·60	21
15	Sa 30	8 ·53	13 ·70	22
16	Su 31	9 ·59	14 ·78	23

15. Svati. 16. Visak. 17. Anur. 18. Jyesh. 19. Mula. 20. P. Ash. 21. U. Ash. 22. Sravn. 23. Dani. 24. Satab. 25 P. Bhad. 26. U. Bhad. 27. Rev.

A. D. 1962. **Mesha Sankranti** (Commencement of Indian Sidereal Year).

Solar Eclipse. ● **(Surya Sid.) April 13·66.** **Saka 1884.** **Kaliyuga 5063.**

Lunar Eclipse. ○ **(Arya Sid.) April 13·55.** **(S. Cycle) Subhakrit.**

Columns: SOLAR reckoning — Cyclic Sidereal Year, Month and Day; Week-Day English Month and Day. LUNAR reckoning — Tithi Ending Moment; Nakshatra Ending Moment; Muhammadan Year, Month and Day.

Jan. (Solar: Plava Dhanus—Margali; Plava Makara—Tai. Lunar: Mar. Bah.; Sukla; Pausha; Bahula; H. 1381 Rajab.; H. 1381 Shaban.)

Cyclic Sidereal	Week-Day	Tithi	Nakshatra	Muhammadan
17	Mo 1	Mar. 10 ·62	15 ·88	H. 1381 Rajab. 24
18	Tu 2	11 ·64	16 ·87	25
19	We 3	12 ·64	17 ·88	26
20	Th 4	Bah. 13 ·62	18 ·88	27
21	Fr 5	14 ·58	19 ·86	28
22	Sa 6	—A ·52	20 ·82	29
23	Su 7	1 ·45	21 ·77	—30
24	Mo 8	2 ·37	22 ·71	1
25	Tu 9	3 ·28	23 ·65	2
26	We 10	4 ·18	24 ·58	3
27	Th 11	{5 ·08 / 6 ·98	25 ·51	4
28	Fr 12	7 ·89	26 ·44	5
—29	Sa 13	8 ·81	27 ·39	6
1	Su 14	9 ·74	1 ·34	7
2	Mo 15	10 ·68	2 ·31	8
3	Tu 16	11 ·64	3 ·29	9
4	We 17	12 ·63	4 ·29	10
5	Th 18	13 ·63	5 ·31	11
6	Fr 19	14 ·66	6 ·35	12
7	Sa 20	P ·70	7 ·41	13
8	Su 21	1 ·77	8 ·49	14
9	Mo 22	2 ·85	9 ·59	15
10	Tu 23	3 ·93	10 ·69	16
11	We 24	... ...	11 ·80	17
12	Th 25	4 ·02	12 ·90	18
13	Fr 26	5 ·11	... ...	19
14	Sa 27	6 ·19	13 ·00	20
15	Su 28	7 ·24	14 ·08	21
16	Mo 29	8 ·27	15 ·14	22
17	Tu 30	9 ·28	16 ·18	23
18	We 31	10 ·28	17 ·20	24

Feb. (Solar: Plava Kumbha—Masi. Lunar: Sukla; Magha; Bahula; H. 1381 Ramzan.)

Cyclic Sidereal	Week-Day	Tithi	Nakshatra	Muhammadan
19	Th 1	11 ·26	18 ·21	25
20	Fr 2	12 ·21	19 ·19	26
21	Sa 3	13 ·15	20 ·16	27
22	Su 4	14 ·08	21 ·11	28
23	Mo ● 5	{A ·00 / 1 ·90	22 ·05 / 23 ·99}	—29
24	Tu 6	2 ·80	24 ·92	1
25	We 7	3 ·70	25 ·85	2
26	Th 8	4 ·60	26 ·78	3
27	Fr 9	5 ·51	27 ·72	4
28	Sa 10	6 ·43	1 ·68	5
—29	Su 11	7 ·37	2 ·64	6
1	Mo 12	8 ·32	3 ·61	7
2	Tu 13	9 ·28	4 ·61	8
3	We 14	10 ·26	5 ·62	9
4	Th 15	11 ·26	6 ·66	10
5	Fr 16	12 ·29	7 ·72	11
6	Sa 17	13 ·34	8 ·80	12
7	Su 18	14 ·40	9 ·89	13
8	Mo 19	P ·47	10 ·99	14
9	Tu 20	1 ·55	... ...	15
10	We 21	2 ·64	11 ·10	16
11	Th 22	3 ·73	12 ·21	17
12	Fr 23	4 ·81	13 ·31	18
13	Sa 24	5 ·86	14 ·39	19
14	Su 25	6 ·89	15 ·45	20
15	Mo 26	7 ·90	16 ·50	21
16	Tu 27	8 ·90	17 ·53	22
17	We 28	9 ·88	18 ·54	23

March (Solar: Plava Kumbha—Masi; Plava Mina—Panguni. Lunar: Mag. Bah.; Sukla; Phalguna; Bahula; Ramzan.; H. 1381 Shawwal.)

Cyclic Sidereal	Week-Day	Tithi	Nakshatra	Muhammadan
18	Th 1	Mag. 10 ·83	19 ·52	24
19	Fr 2	11 ·77	20 ·49	25
20	Sa 3	12 ·69	21 ·44	26
21	Su 4	Bah. 13 ·61	22 ·39	27
22	Mo 5	14 ·52	23 ·33	28
23	Tu 6	—A ·42	24 ·26	29
24	We 7	1 ·32	25 ·19	—30
25	Th 8	2 ·22	26 ·13	1
26	Fr 9	3 ·13	27 ·07	2
27	Sa 10	{4 ·04 / 5 ·97	1 ·01 / 2 ·97}	3
28	Su 11	6 ·91	3 ·94	4
29	Mo 12	7 ·88	4 ·93	5
—30	Tu 13	8 ·86	5 ·95	6
1	We 14	9 ·86	6 ·98	7
2	Th 15	10 ·89	... ...	8
3	Fr 16	11 ·93	7 ·03	9
4	Sa 17	12 ·99	8 ·10	10
	Su 18	... ...	9 ·19	11
	Mo 19	13 ·08	10 ·29	12
7	Tu 20	14 ·17	11 ·40	13
8	We 21	P ·25	12 ·51	14
9	Th 22	1 ·33	13 ·61	15
10	Fr 23	2 ·40	14 ·69	16
11	Sa 24	3 ·46	15 ·76	17
12	Su 25	4 ·49	16 ·82	18
13	Mo 26	5 ·49	17 ·85	19
14	Tu 27	6 ·48	18 ·86	20
15	We 28	7 ·45	19 ·85	21
16	Th 29	8 ·41	20 ·82	22
17	Fr 30	9 ·35	21 ·79	23
18	Sa 31	10 ·28	22 ·73	24

April (Solar: Subhakrit Mesha—Chittirai. Lunar: Sukla; Chaitra; Bahula; H. 1381 Zi-l-ka'da.)

Cyclic Sidereal	Week-Day	Tithi	Nakshatra	Muhammadan
19	Su 1	11 ·19	23 ·67	25
20	Mo 2	{12 ·09 / 13 ·99	24 ·60	26
21	Tu 3	14 ·89	25 ·53	27
22	We 4	—A ·79	26 ·47	28
23	Th 5	1 ·70	27 ·41	—29
24	Fr 6	2 ·62	1 ·35	1
25	Sa 7	3 ·55	2 ·30	2
26	Su 8	4 ·49	3 ·27	3
27	Mo 9	5 ·44	4 ·25	4
28	Tu 10	6 ·42	5 ·27	5
29	We 11	7 ·42	6 ·29	6
30	Th 12	8 ·45	7 ·34	7
—31	Fr 13	9 ·50	8 ·40	8
1	Sa 14	10 ·56	9 ·49	9
2	Su 15	11 ·64	10 ·59	10
3	Mo 16	12 ·72	11 ·70	11
4	Tu 17	13 ·80	12 ·81	12
5	We 18	14 ·88	13 ·91	13
6	Th 19	P ·95	... ...	14
7	Fr 20	... ...	14 ·00	15
8	Sa 21	1 ·01	15 ·08	16
9	Su 22	2 ·08	16 ·13	17
10	Mo 23	3 ·04	17 ·17	18
11	Tu 24	4 ·03	18 ·18	19
12	We 25	{5 ·00 / 6 ·95	19 ·17	20
13	Th 26	7 ·89	20 ·16	21
14	Fr 27	8 ·82	21 ·12	22
15	Sa 28	9 ·72	22 ·07	23
16	Su 29	10 ·62	23 ·01 / 24 ·94}	24
17	Mo 30	11 ·52	25 ·87	25

May (Solar: Subhakrit Mesha—Chittirai; Subhakrit Vrishabha—Vaikasi. Lunar: Bah.; Sukla; Vaisakha; Bahula; Zilka'da.; H. 1381 Zi-l-hijja.)

Cyclic Sidereal	Week-Day	Tithi	Nakshatra	Muhammadan
18	Tu 1	Bah. 12 ·42	26 ·80	Zilka'da. 26
19	We 2	13 ·32	27 ·74	27
20	Th 3	14 ·23	1 ·68	28
21	Fr 4	—A ·15	2 ·63	29
22	Sa 5	1 ·07	3 ·60	—30
23	Su 6	{2 ·02 / 3 ·98	4 ·59	1
24	Mo 7	4 ·96	5 ·59	2
25	Tu 8	5 ·95	6 ·61	3
26	We 9	6 ·97	7 ·65	4
27	Th 10	... ...	8 ·71	5
28	Fr 11	7 ·01	9 ·80	6
29	Sa 12	8 ·07	10 ·90	7
—30	Su 13	9 ·15	... ...	8
1	Mo 14	10 ·23	11 ·00	9
2	Tu 15	11 ·32	12 ·10	10
3	We 16	12 ·39	13 ·21	11
4	Th 17	13 ·46	14 ·31	12
5	Fr 18	14 ·51	15 ·39	13
6	Sa 19	P ·54	16 ·45	14
7	Su 20	1 ·55	17 ·48	15
8	Mo 21	2 ·54	18 ·50	16
9	Tu 22	3 ·52	19 ·51	17
10	We 23	4 ·47	20 ·49	18
11	Th 24	5 ·41	21 ·45	19
12	Fr 25	6 ·32	22 ·40	20
13	Sa 26	7 ·22	23 ·34	21
14	Su 27	8 ·12	24 ·28	22
15	Mo 28	9 ·02 / 10 ·92	25 ·21	23
16	Tu 29	11 ·82	26 ·14	24
17	We 30	12 ·73	27 ·08	25
18	Th 31	13 ·65	1 ·02 / 2 ·97}	26

June (Solar: Subhakrit Mithuna—Ani. Lunar: Sukla; Jyeshtha; Bahula; H. 1382 Muharram.)

Cyclic Sidereal	Week-Day	Tithi	Nakshatra	Muhammadan
19	Fr 1	14 ·58	3 ·94	27
20	Sa 2	—A ·52	4 ·91	28
21	Su 3	1 ·47	5 ·91	—29
22	Mo 4	2 ·45	6 ·92	1
23	Tu 5	3 ·44	7 ·96	2
24	We 6	4 ·47	... ...	3
25	Th 7	5 ·51	8 ·03	4
26	Fr 8	6 ·56	9 ·10	5
27	Sa 9	7 ·64	10 ·19	6
28	Su 10	8 ·72	11 ·30	7
29	Mo 11	9 ·80	12 ·41	8
30	Tu 12	10 ·88	13 ·52	9
31	We 13	11 ·95	14 ·61	10
—32	Th 14	12 ·99	15 ·69	11
1	Fr 15	... ...	16 ·76	12
2	Sa 16	13 ·03	17 ·80	13
3	Su 17	14 ·04	18 ·82	14
4	Mo 18	P ·03	19 ·83	15
5	Tu 19	1 ·00 / 2 ·95	20 ·82	16
6	We 20	3 ·89	21 ·78	17
7	Th 21	4 ·81	22 ·74	18
8	Fr 22	5 ·71	23 ·63	19
9	Sa 23	6 ·61	24 ·62	20
10	Su 24	7 ·51	25 ·55	21
11	Mo 25	8 ·41	26 ·48	22
12	Tu 26	9 ·31	27 ·41	23
13	We 27	10 ·21	1 ·35	24
14	Th 28	11 ·13	2 ·31	25
15	Fr 29	12 ·06	3 ·27	26
16	Sa 30	{13 ·00 / 14 ·95	4 ·24	27

Naksh :—1. Asvn. 2. Bhar. 3. Krit. 4. Rohi. 5. Mrig. 6. Ardh. 7. Punar. 8. Push. 9. Aslesh. 10. Magh. 11. P. Phal. 12. U. Phal. 13. Hasta. 14. Chit.

A. D. 1962.
A.—Amavasya.
P.—Paurnami.

Kollam 1138, Commences { N. Malabar—Sept. / S. Malabar—Aug.

Hijra 1382, Commences, June 4.

Vikrama 2019.
Bengal San 1368.
(N. Cycle) Rakshasa.

Cyclic Sidereal Year, Month and Day (SOLAR)	Week-Day	English Month and Day	Tithi Ending Moment (LUNAR)	Nakshatra Ending Moment	Muhammadan Year, Month and Day	Labels
		July				
17	Su	1	—A ·93	5 ·23	28	Subhakrit Mithuna—Ani
18	Mo	2	1 ·92	6 ·24	29	
19	Tu	3	2 ·94	7 ·28	—30	
20	We	4	3 ·98	8 ·33	1	
21	Th	5	... ...	9 ·41	2	
22	Fr	6	4 ·04	10 ·49	3	Sukla
23	Sa	7	5 ·11	11 ·59	4	
24	Su	8	6 ·20	12 ·70	5	
25	Mo	9	7 ·28	13 ·81	6	
26	Tu	10	8 ·35	14 ·91	7	
27	We	11	9 ·42	... ...	8	
28	Th	12	10 ·47	15 ·00	9	
29	Fr	13	11 ·50	16 ·07	10	
30	Sa	14	12 ·51	17 ·11	11	
—31	Su	15	13 ·51	18 ·15	12	Ashadha
1	Mo	16	14 ·48	19 ·16	13	Subhakrit Karkata—Adi
2	Tu	17	P ·43	20 ·14	14	
3	We	18	1 ·37	21 ·11	15	H. 1382 Safar
4	Th	19	2 ·29	22 ·07	16	
5	Fr	20	3 ·20	23 ·02 / 24 ·96	17	
6	Sa	21	4 ·10	25 ·89	18	
7	Su	22	5 ·00 / 6 ·90	26 ·82	19	Bahula
8	Mo	23	7 ·80	27 ·76	20	
9	Tu	24	8 ·70	1 ·70	21	
10	We	25	9 ·61	2 ·64	22	
11	Th	26	10 ·54	3 ·60	23	
12	Fr	27	11 ·48	4 ·57	24	
13	Sa	28	12 ·43	5 ·55	25	
14	Su	29	13 ·41	6 ·57	26	
15	Mo	30	14 ·41	7 ·60	27	
16	Tu ●	31	—A ·42	8 ·64	28	
		Aug.				
17	We	1	1 ·45	9 ·71	—29	
18	Th	2	2 ·52	10 ·79	1	
19	Fr	3	3 ·59	11 ·89	2	
20	Sa	4	4 ·67	... ...	3	
21	Su	5	5 ·75	12 ·00	4	
22	Mo	6	6 ·83	13 ·11	5	Sukla
23	Tu	7	7 ·90	14 ·21	6	
24	We	8	8 ·95	15 ·30	7	
25	Th	9	9 ·98	16 ·37	8	
26	Fr	10	... ...	17 ·43	9	
27	Sa	11	10 ·00	18 ·47	10	
28	Su	12	11 ·00 / 12 ·97	19 ·48	11	H. 1382 Rabi-ul-awwal
29	Mo	13	13 ·92	20 ·47	12	Sravana
30	Tu	14	14 ·87	21 ·45	13	
31	We	15	P ·79	22 ·41	14	
—32	Th	16	1 ·70	23 ·36	15	
1	Fr	17	2 ·60	24 ·30	16	Subhakrit Simha—Avani
2	Sa	18	3 ·50	25 ·23	17	
3	Su	19	4 ·40	26 ·16	18	
4	Mo	20	5 ·30	27 ·10	19	
5	Tu	21	6 ·20	1 ·04 / 2 ·98	20	Bahula
6	We	22	7 ·12 / 8 ·04	3 ·98	21	
7	Th	23	9 ·98	4 ·90	22	
8	Fr	24	10 ·93	5 ·89	23	
9	Sa	25	11 ·91	6 ·89	24	
10	Su	26	12 ·91	7 ·91	25	
11	Mo	27	13 ·92	8 ·95	26	
12	Tu	28	14 ·96	... ...	27	
13	We	29	... ...	9 ·01	28	
14	Th	30	—A ·02	10 ·10	29	
15	Fr	31	1 ·09	11 ·20	—30	

Cyclic Sidereal Year, Month and Day (SOLAR)	Week-Day	English Month and Day	Tithi Ending Moment (LUNAR)	Nakshatra Ending Moment	Muhammadan Year, Month and Day	Labels
		Sep.				
16	Sa	1	2 ·17	12 ·31	1	Subhakrit Simha—Avani
17	Su	2	3 ·26	13 ·41	2	
18	Mo	3	4 ·34	14 ·51	3	
19	Tu	4	5 ·41	15 ·61	4	Sukla
20	We	5	6 ·47	16 ·69	5	
21	Th	6	7 ·50	17 ·75	6	
22	Fr	7	8 ·52	18 ·79	7	
23	Sa	8	9 ·51	19 ·80	8	
24	Su	9	10 ·48	20 ·80	9	
25	Mo	10	11 ·44	21 ·79	10	Bhadrapada
26	Tu	11	12 ·38	22 ·75	11	H. 1382 Rabi-ul-akhir
27	We	12	13 ·31	23 ·70	12	
28	Th	13	14 ·22	24 ·64	13	
29	Fr	14	P ·13	25 ·58	14	
30	Sa	15	1 ·03 / 2 ·93	26 ·51	15	
—31	Su	16	3 ·83	27 ·44	16	
1	Mo	17	4 ·73	1 ·37	17	Subhakrit Kanya—Purattasi
2	Tu	18	5 ·64	2 ·31	18	
3	We	19	6 ·57	3 ·26	19	
4	Th	20	7 ·52	4 ·22	20	Bahula
5	Fr	21	8 ·47	5 ·21	21	
6	Sa	22	9 ·45	6 ·21	22	
7	Su	23	10 ·44	7 ·22	23	
8	Mo	24	11 ·45	8 ·26	24	
9	Tu	25	12 ·49	9 ·32	25	
10	We	26	13 ·55	10 ·41	26	
11	Th	27	14 ·63	11 ·50	27	
12	Fr	28	—A ·71	12 ·60	28	
13	Sa	29	1 ·80	13 ·71	—29	
14	Su	30	2 ·88	14 ·82	1	
		Oct.				
15	Mo	1	3 ·95	15 ·92	2	
16	Tu	2	... ...	... ...	3	
17	We	3	4 ·01	16 ·00	4	
18	Th	4	5 ·04	17 ·06	5	
19	Fr	5	6 ·06	18 ·10	6	Sukla
20	Sa	6	7 ·06	19 ·12	7	
21	Su	7	8 ·04	20 ·13	8	
22	Mo	8	9 ·00 / 10 ·94	21 ·11	9	H. 1382 Jumadal-awwal
23	Tu	9	11 ·87	22 ·08	10	
24	We	10	12 ·79	23 ·03 / 24 ·97	11	
25	Th	11	13 ·69	25 ·91	12	Asvina
26	Fr	12	14 ·59	26 ·85	13	
27	Sa	13	P ·49	27 ·78	14	
28	Su	14	1 ·39	1 ·71	15	
29	Mo	15	2 ·30	2 ·65	16	
—30	Tu	16	3 ·21	3 ·59	17	
1	We	17	4 ·14	4 ·56	18	
2	Th	18	5 ·08	5 ·54	19	
3	Fr	19	6 ·03	6 ·53	20	
4	Sa	20	7 ·02	7 ·54	21	Subhakrit Tula—Aippasi
5	Su	21	8 ·02	8 ·57	22	Bahula
6	Mo	22	9 ·04	9 ·64	23	
7	Tu	23	10 ·08	10 ·71	24	
8	We	24	11 ·14	11 ·80	25	
9	Th	25	12 ·21	12 ·90	26	
10	Fr	26	13 ·29	... ...	27	
11	Sa	27	14 ·38	13 ·01	28	
12	Su	28	—A ·46	14 ·12	29	
13	Mo	29	1 ·54	15 ·22	—30	K. Suk.
14	Tu	30	2 ·60	16 ·30	1	
15	We	31	3 ·64	17 ·37	2	

Cyclic Sidereal Year, Month and Day (SOLAR)	Week-Day	English Month and Day	Tithi Ending Moment (LUNAR)	Nakshatra Ending Moment	Muhammadan Year, Month and Day	Labels
		Nov.				
16	Th	1	4 ·66	18 ·42	3	Subhakrit Tula—Aippasi
17	Fr	2	5 ·65	19 ·45	4	
18	Sa	3	6 ·63	20 ·46	5	
19	Su	4	7 ·59	21 ·44	6	Sukla
20	Mo	5	8 ·54	22 ·41	7	
21	Tu	6	9 ·46	23 ·37	8	
22	We	7	10 ·38	24 ·32	9	
23	Th	8	11 ·29	25 ·26	10	
24	Fr	9	12 ·19	26 ·19	11	
25	Sa	10	13 ·09 / 14 ·99	27 ·12	12	H. 1382 Jumadal-akhir
26	Su	11	P ·90	1 ·05 / 2 ·99	13	Karttika
27	Mo	12	1 ·82	3 ·94	14	
28	Tu	13	2 ·75	4 ·89	15	
29	We	14	3 ·69	5 ·86	16	
—30	Th	15	4 ·65	6 ·85	17	
1	Fr	16	5 ·63	7 ·86	18	
2	Sa	17	6 ·63	8 ·90	19	
3	Su	18	7 ·65	9 ·95	20	Bahula
4	Mo	19	8 ·69	... ...	21	
5	Tu	20	9 ·76	10 ·01	22	
6	We	21	10 ·84	11 ·10	23	
7	Th	22	11 ·92	12 ·20	24	Subhakrit Vrischika—Kartigai
8	Fr	23	... ...	13 ·31	25	
9	Sa	24	12 ·01	14 ·42	26	
10	Su	25	13 ·09	15 ·52	27	
11	Mo	26	14 ·17	16 ·61	28	
12	Tu	27	—A ·23	17 ·68	—29	
13	We	28	1 ·27	18 ·73	1	
14	Th	29	2 ·28	19 ·77	2	
15	Fr	30	3 ·28	20 ·78	3	
		Dec.				
16	Sa	1	4 ·26	21 ·77	4	
17	Su	2	5 ·21	22 ·74	5	Sukla
18	Mo	3	6 ·15	23 ·70	6	
19	Tu	4	7 ·08	24 ·65	7	
20	We	5	8 ·01 / 9 ·92	25 ·59	8	
21	Th	6	10 ·82	26 ·52	9	
22	Fr	7	11 ·72	27 ·45	10	H. 1382 Rajab
23	Sa	8	12 ·62	1 ·39	11	
24	Su	9	13 ·52	2 ·33	12	Margasira
25	Mo	10	14 ·44	3 ·27	13	
26	Tu	11	P ·38	4 ·22	14	
27	We	12	1 ·33	5 ·19	15	
28	Th	13	2 ·29	6 ·17	16	
29	Fr	14	3 ·27	7 ·19	17	
—30	Sa	15	4 ·27	8 ·21	18	
1	Su	16	5 ·29	9 ·26	19	
2	Mo	17	6 ·34	10 ·32	20	
3	Tu	18	7 ·41	11 ·40	21	Bahula
4	We	19	8 ·48	12 ·50	22	
5	Th	20	9 ·57	13 ·61	23	Subhakrit Dhanus—Margali
6	Fr	21	10 ·66	14 ·72	24	
7	Sa	22	11 ·74	15 ·82	25	
8	Su	23	12 ·81	16 ·91	26	
9	Mo	24	13 ·87	17 ·99	27	
10	Tu	25	14 ·91	... ...	28	
11	We	26	—A ·92	18 ·05	29	
12	Th	27	1 ·93	19 ·09	—30	Pah. Sukla
13	Fr	28	2 ·90	20 ·10	1	Shaban
14	Sa	29	3 ·86	21 ·10	2	
15	Su	30	4 ·80	22 ·07	3	
16	Mo	31	5 ·72	23 ·04 / 24 ·99	4	

15. Svati. 16. Visak. 17. Anur. 18. Jyesh. 19. Mula. 20. P. Ash. 21. U. Ash. 22. Sravn. 23. Dani. 24. Satab. 25. P. Bhad. 26. U. Bhad. 27. Rev.

A. D. 1963. **Mesha Sankranti** (Commencement of Indian Sidereal Year).

Solar Eclipse. ● **(Surya Sid.) April 13·92.** **Saka 1885.** **Kaliyuga 5064.**

Lunar Eclipse. ○ **(Arya Sid.) April 13·81.** **(S. Cycle) Sobhana** (Sobhakrit).

Columns: SOLAR reckoning — Cyclic Sidereal Year, Month and Day; Week-Day, English Month and Day. LUNAR reckoning — Tithi Ending Moment; Nakshatra Ending Moment; Muhammadan Year, Month and Day.

Jan.

Solar: Subhakrit *Dhanus—Margali.* (to 29); Subhakrit *Makara—Tai.* (from 1). Lunar: Pausha — *Sukla*, *Bahula*. Muhammadan: H. 1382 *Shaban.*

Cyclic Sidereal Day	Week-Day	Day	Tithi	Ending Moment	Nakshatra	Ending Moment	Muhammadan Day
17	Tu	1	6	·64	25	·93	5
18	We	2	7	·55	26	·87	6
19	Th	3	8	·45	27	·80	7
20	Fr	4	9	·35	1	·73	8
21	Sa	5	10	·26	2	·66	9
22	Su	6	11	·17	3	·60	10
23	Mo	7	12	·09	4	·56	11
24	Tu	8	13 14	·02 ·96	5	·52	12
25	We ○	9	P	·93	6	·51	13
26	Th	10	1	·91	7	·51	14
27	Fr	11	2	·92	8	·53	15
28	Sa	12	3	·94	9	·57	16
29	Su	13	4	·99	10	·63	17
1	Mo	14	...	...	11	·71	18
2	Tu	15	5	·05	12	·81	19
3	We	16	6	·14	13	·91	20
4	Th	17	7	·23	...	...	21
5	Fr	18	8	·32	14	·02	22
6	Sa	19	9	·40	15	·12	23
7	Su	20	10	·47	16	·21	24
8	Mo	21	11	·52	17	·30	25
9	Tu	22	12	·56	18	·36	26
10	We	23	13	·57	19	·40	27
11	Th	24	14	·57	20	·42	28
12	Fr	25	A	·55	21	·42	29
13	Sa	26	1	·51	22	·41	1
14	Su	27	2	·44	23	·38	2
15	Mo	28	3	·36	24	·33	3
16	Tu	29	4	·27	25	·27	4
17	We	30	5	·18	26	·21	5
18	Th	31	6 7	·08 ·98	27	·14	6

Feb.

Solar: Subhakrit *Kumbha—Masi.* Lunar: Magha — *Sukla*, *Bahula*; *P. Sukla*. Muhammadan: H. 1382 *Ramzan.*; *Shawwal.*

Cyclic Sidereal Day	Week-Day	Day	Tithi	Ending Moment	Nakshatra	Ending Moment	Muhammadan Day
19	Fr	1	8	·89	1	·07	7
20	Sa	2	9	·80	2 3	·00 ·94	8
21	Su	3	10	·72	4	·89	9
22	Mo	4	11	·65	5	·86	10
23	Tu	5	12	·60	6	·83	11
24	We	6	13	·56	7	·83	12
25	Th	7	14	·55	8	·84	13
26	Fr	8	P	·56	9	·88	14
27	Sa	9	1	·58	10	·94	15
28	Su	10	2	·63	...	...	16
29	Mo	11	3	·70	11	·02	17
30	Tu	12	4	·78	12	·11	18
1	We	13	5	·86	13	·21	19
2	Th	14	6	·94	14	·31	20
3	Fr	15	...	...	15	·42	21
4	Sa	16	7	·03	16	·53	22
5	Su	17	8	·11	17	·61	23
6	Mo	18	9	·16	18	·67	24
7	Tu	19	10	·19	19	·72	25
8	We	20	11	·21	20	·74	26
9	Th	21	12	·19	21	·76	27
10	Fr	22	13	·17	22	·74	28
11	Sa	23	14	·12	23	·71	29
12	Su	24	A 1	·05 ·98	24	·66	30
13	Mo	25	2	·89	25	·60	1
14	Tu	26	3	·80	26	·54	2
15	We	27	4	·70	27	·48	3
16	Th	28	5	·60	1	·41	4

March

Solar: Subhakrit *Kumbha—Masi.* (to 29); Subhakrit *Mina—Panguni.* (from 1). Lunar: Phalguna — *Sukla*, *Bahula*. Muhammadan: H. 1382 *Shawwal.*

Cyclic Sidereal Day	Week-Day	Day	Tithi	Ending Moment	Nakshatra	Ending Moment	Muhammadan Day
17	Fr	1	6	·50	2	·34	5
18	Sa	2	7	·41	3	·28	6
19	Su	3	8	·33	4	·22	7
20	Mo	4	9	·26	5	·19	8
21	Tu	5	10	·21	6	·16	9
22	We	6	11	·18	7	·15	10
23	Th	7	12	·17	8	·16	11
24	Fr	8	13	·17	9	·19	12
25	Sa	9	14	·20	10	·25	13
26	Su	10	P	·24	11	·32	14
27	Mo	11	1	·30	12	·41	15
28	Tu	12	2	·38	13	·51	16
29	We	13	3	·47	14	·62	17
1	Th	14	4	·56	15	·73	18
2	Fr	15	5	·64	16	·83	19
3	Sa	16	6	·71	17	·91	20
4	Su	17	7	·76	18	·98	21
5	Mo	18	8	·79	...	...	22
6	Tu	19	9	·81	19	·03	23
7	We	20	10	·79	20	·07	24
8	Th	21	11	·76	21	·08	25
9	Fr	22	12	·71	22	·07	26
10	Sa	23	13	·65	23	·04	27
11	Su	24	14	·57	24 25	·00 ·95	28
12	Mo	25	A	·48	26	·89	29
13	Tu	26	1	·38	27	·82	1
14	We	27	2	·28	1	·75	2
15	Th	28	3	·18	2	·68	3
16	Fr	29	4	·09	3	·62	4
17	Sa	30	5 6	·00 ·91	4	·57	5
18	Su	31	7	·84	5	·52	6

April

Solar: Sobhana *Mesha—Chittirai.* Lunar: Chaitra — *Sukla*, *Bahula*; Vaisakha *Suk.* Muhammadan: H. 1382 *Zi-l-ka'da.*; *Zi-l-hijja.*

Cyclic Sidereal Day	Week-Day	Day	Tithi	Ending Moment	Nakshatra	Ending Moment	Muhammadan Day
19	Mo	1	8	·79	6	·49	7
20	Tu	2	9	·75	7	·47	8
21	We	3	10	·74	8	·48	9
22	Th	4	11	·74	9	·51	10
23	Fr	5	12	·77	10	·56	11
24	Sa	6	13	·81	11	·62	12
25	Su	7	14	·88	12	·71	13
26	Mo	8	P	·95	13	·81	14
27	Tu	9	...	...	14	·92	15
28	We	10	1	·03	...	...	16
29	Th	11	2	·12	15	·03	17
30	Fr	12	3	·20	16	·13	18
31	Sa	13	4	·27	17	·22	19
1	Su	14	5	·32	18	·29	20
2	Mo	15	6	·35	19	·34	21
3	Tu	16	7	·36	20	·38	22
4	We	17	8	·34	21	·40	23
5	Th	18	9	·31	22	·39	24
6	Fr	19	10	·26	23	·37	25
7	Sa	20	11	·20	24	·33	26
8	Su	21	12	·12	25	·28	27
9	Mo	22	13 14	·03 ·93	26	·22	28
10	Tu	23	A	·83	27	·16	29
11	We	24	1	·73	1	·09	30
12	Th	25	2	·63	2 3	·02 ·96	1
13	Fr	26	3	·53	4	·90	2
14	Sa	27	4	·45	5	·85	3
15	Su	28	5	·38	6	·82	4
16	Mo	29	6	·32	7	·80	5
17	Tu	30	7	·29	8	·81	6

May

Solar: Sobhana *Mesha—Chittirai.* (to 31); Sobhana *Vrishabha—Vaikasi.* (from 1). Lunar: Vaisakha — *Sukla*, *Bahula*; *Sukla*. Muhammadan: H. 1382 *Zi-l-hijja.*

Cyclic Sidereal Day	Week-Day	Day	Tithi	Ending Moment	Nakshatra	Ending Moment	Muhammadan Day
18	We	1	8	·27	9	·83	7
19	Th	2	9	·27	10	·87	8
20	Fr	3	10	·30	11	·93	9
21	Sa	4	11	·34	...	...	10
22	Su	5	12	·40	12	·01	11
23	Mo	6	13	·47	13	·11	12
24	Tu	7	14	·56	14	·22	13
25	We	8	P	·64	15	·33	14
26	Th	9	1	·72	16	·43	15
27	Fr	10	2	·79	17	·52	16
28	Sa	11	3	·84	18	·60	17
29	Su	12	4	·87	19	·67	18
30	Mo	13	5	·88	20	·70	19
31	Tu	14	6	·87	21	·72	20
1	We	15	7	·83	22	·72	21
2	Th	16	8	·78	23	·70	22
3	Fr	17	9	·71	24	·67	23
4	Sa	18	10	·63	25	·62	24
5	Su	19	11	·54	26	·56	25
6	Mo	20	12	·44	27	·50	26
7	Tu	21	13	·34	1	·43	27
8	We	22	14	·24	2	·36	28
9	Th	23	A	·14	3	·29	29
10	Fr	24	1 2	·04 ·96	4	·23	30
11	Sa	25	3	·89	5	·18	1
12	Su	26	4	·83	6	·15	2
13	Mo	27	5	·79	7	·13	3
14	Tu	28	6	·77	8	·13	4
15	We	29	7	·78	9	·14	5
16	Th	30	8	·79	10	·18	6
17	Fr	31	9	·83	11	·24	7

June

Solar: Sobhana *Mithuna—Ani.* Lunar: Jyeshtha — *Bahula*; Ashadha *Sukla*. Muhammadan: H. 1383 *Muharram.*; H. 1383 *Safar.*

Cyclic Sidereal Day	Week-Day	Day	Tithi	Ending Moment	Nakshatra	Ending Moment	Muhammadan Day
18	Sa	1	10	·89	12	·31	8
19	Su	2	11	·97	13	·41	9
20	Mo	3	...	...	14	·52	10
21	Tu	4	12	·05	15	·63	11
22	We	5	13	·14	16	·73	12
23	Th	6	14	·22	17	·82	13
24	Fr	7	P	·29	18	·91	14
25	Sa	8	1	·33	19	·98	15
26	Su	9	2	·36	...	...	16
27	Mo	10	3	·37	20	·02	17
28	Tu	11	4	·35	21	·04	18
29	We	12	5	·32	22	·04	19
30	Th	13	6	·28	23	·03	20
31	Fr	14	7	·21	24 25	·00 ·96	21
1	Sa	15	8	·13	26	·90	22
2	Su	16	9 10	·04 ·94	27	·84	23
3	Mo	17	11	·84	1	·77	24
4	Tu	18	12	·74	2	·70	25
5	We	19	13	·64	3	·63	26
6	Th	20	14	·54	4	·57	27
7	Fr	21	A	·45	5	·52	28
8	Sa	22	1	·38	6	·49	29
9	Su	23	2	·32	7	·46	30
10	Mo	24	3	·27	8	·45	1
11	Tu	25	4	·25	9	·46	2
12	We	26	5	·26	10	·49	3
13	Th	27	6	·28	11	·54	4
14	Fr	28	7	·32	12	·62	5
15	Sa	29	8	·37	13	·71	6
16	Su	30	9	·45	14	·81	7

Naksh:—1. Asvn. 2. Bhar. 3. Krit. 4. Rohi. 5. Mrig. 6. Ardh. 7. Punar. 8. Push. 9. Aslesh. 10. Magh. 11. P. Phal. 12. U. Phal. 13. Hasta. 14. Chit.

A. D. 1963. A.—Amavasya. P.—Paurnami.	Kollam 1139, Commences { N. Malabar—Sept. S. Malabar—Aug.	Hijra 1383, Commences, May 25.	Vikrama 2020. Bengal San 1369. (N. Cycle) Anala.

SOLAR reckoning: Cyclic Sidereal Year, Month and Day; Week-Day English Month and Day. LUNAR reckoning: Tithi Ending Moment; Nakshatra Ending Moment; Muhammadan Year, Month and Day.

July

Solar: Sobhana Mithuna—Ani (17–32); Sobhana Karkata—Adi (1–15). Lunar: Ashadha (Suk., Bahula, Sukla). Muhammadan: H. 1383 Safar.

Cyclic Sidereal	Week-Day	Day	Tithi	Moment	Nakshatra	Moment	Muhammadan
17	Mo	1	10	·52	15	·92	8
18	Tu	2	11	·61	...	...	9
19	We	3	12	·69	16	·03	10
20	Th	4	13	·75	17	·13	11
21	Fr	5	14	·81	18	·22	12
22	Sa ○	6	P	·84	19	·29	13
23	Su	7	1	·85	20	·33	14
24	Mo	8	2	·83	21	·36	15
25	Tu	9	3	·80	22	·38	16
26	We	10	4	·75	23	·36	17
27	Th	11	5	·68	24	·33	18
28	Fr	12	6	·61	25	·29	19
29	Sa	13	7	·52	26	·24	20
30	Su	14	8	·42	27	·18	21
31	Mo	15	9	·32	1	·11	22
—32	Tu	16	10	·22	2 / 3	·04 / ·97	23
1	We	17	11	·12	4	·91	24
2	Th	18	12 / 13	·02 / ·93	5	·85	25
3	Fr	19	14	·85	6	·82	26
4	Sa	20	—A	·79	7	·79	27
5	Su	21	1	·75	8	·77	28
6	Mo	22	2	·74	9	·78	—29
7	Tu	23	3	·73	10	·81	1
8	We	24	4	·75	11	·86	2
9	Th	25	5	·79	12	·93	3
10	Fr	26	6	·85	...	...	4
11	Sa	27	7	·92	13	·01	5
12	Su	28	...	...	14	·11	6
13	Mo	29	8	·00	15	·22	7
14	Tu	30	9	·09	16	·33	8
15	We	31	10	·16	17	·43	9

Aug.

Solar: Sobhana Karkata—Adi (16–31); Sobhana Simha—Avani (1–15). Lunar: Sravana (Bahula); Bhadrapada (Sukla). Muhammadan: H. 1383 Rabi-ul-awwal; H. 1383 Rabi-ul-akhir.

Cyclic Sidereal	Week-Day	Day	Tithi	Moment	Nakshatra	Moment	Muhammadan
16	Th	1	11	·22	18	·52	10
17	Fr	2	12	·28	19	·59	11
18	Sa	3	13	·32	20	·65	12
19	Su	4	14	·33	21	·69	13
20	Mo	5	P	·31	22	·70	14
21	Tu	6	1	·29	23	·69	15
22	We	7	2	·24	24	·67	16
23	Th	8	3	·18	25	·62	17
24	Fr	9	4	·10	26	·58	18
25	Sa	10	5 / 6	·01 / ·91	27	·52	19
26	Su	11	7	·81	1	·45	20
27	Mo	12	8	·71	2	·38	21
28	Tu	13	9	·61	3	·31	22
29	We	14	10	·52	4	·24	23
30	Th	15	11	·43	5	·19	24
—31	Fr	16	12	·35	6	·15	25
1	Sa	17	13	·29	7	·11	26
2	Su	18	14	·25	8	·10	27
3	Mo	19	—A	·23	9	·10	28
4	Tu	20	1	·23	10	·13	29
5	We	21	2	·25	11	·17	—30
6	Th	22	3	·29	12	·24	1
7	Fr	23	4	·34	13	·32	2
8	Sa	24	5	·41	14	·42	3
9	Su	25	6	·49	15	·53	4
10	Mo	26	7	·58	16	·63	5
11	Tu	27	8	·66	17	·73	6
12	We	28	9	·74	18	·82	7
13	Th	29	10	·78	19	·90	8
14	Fr	30	11	·82	20	·97	9
15	Sa	31	12	·84	...	...	10

Sep.

Solar: Sobhana Simha—Avani (16–31); Sobhana Kanya—Purattasi (1–14). Lunar: Bhadrapada (Bahula, Sukla). Muhammadan: H. 1383 Rabi-ul-akhir.

Cyclic Sidereal	Week-Day	Day	Tithi	Moment	Nakshatra	Moment	Muhammadan
16	Su	1	13	·82	21	·01	11
17	Mo	2	14	·80	22	·02	12
18	Tu	3	P	·76	23	·02	13
19	We	4	1	·70	24 / 25	·00 / ·96	14
20	Th	5	2	·62	26	·92	15
21	Fr	6	3	·52	27	·86	16
22	Sa	7	4	·42	1	·79	17
23	Su	8	5	·32	2	·72	18
24	Mo	9	6	·22	3	·65	19
25	Tu	10	7	·12	4	·59	20
26	We	11	8 / 9	·03 / ·95	5	·53	21
27	Th	12	10	·88	6	·48	22
28	Fr	13	11	·82	7	·44	23
29	Sa	14	12	·78	8	·42	24
30	Su	15	13	·76	9	·43	25
—31	Mo	16	14	·76	10	·44	26
1	Tu	17	—A	·77	11	·48	27
2	We	18	1	·81	12	·54	28
3	Th	19	2	·86	13	·62	—29
4	Fr	20	3	·94	14	·72	1
5	Sa	21	...	...	15	·82	2
6	Su	22	4	·03	16	·93	3
7	Mo	23	5	·11	...	...	4
8	Tu	24	6	·19	17	·03	5
9	We	25	7	·26	18	·13	6
10	Th	26	8	·32	19	·21	7
11	Fr	27	9	·36	20	·28	8
12	Sa	28	10	·38	21	·32	9
13	Su	29	11	·37	22	·34	10
14	Mo	30	12	·34	23	·34	11

Oct.

Solar: Sobhana Kanya—Purattasi (15–31); Sobhana Tula—Aippasi (1–14). Lunar: Adhika Asvina (Bahula); Nija Asvina (Sukla). Muhammadan: H. 1383 Jumadal-awwal; H. 1383 Jumadal-akhir.

Cyclic Sidereal	Week-Day	Day	Tithi	Moment	Nakshatra	Moment	Muhammadan
15	Tu	1	13	·30	24	·32	12
16	We	2	14	·24	25	·30	13
17	Th	3	P	·16	26	·25	14
18	Fr	4	1 / 2	·07 / ·98	27	·19	15
19	Sa	5	3	·88	1	·13	16
20	Su	6	4	·78	2	·07	17
21	Mo	7	5	·68	3 / 4	·00 / ·93	18
22	Tu	8	6	·59	5	·86	19
23	We	9	7	·51	6	·81	20
24	Th	10	8	·44	7	·77	21
25	Fr	11	9	·38	8	·76	22
26	Sa	12	10	·34	9	·75	23
27	Su	13	11	·32	10	·76	24
28	Mo	14	12	·33	11	·79	25
29	Tu	15	13	·34	12	·85	26
30	We	16	14	·38	13	·93	27
—31	Th	17	—A	·44	...	...	28
1	Fr	18	1	·51	14	·02	29
2	Sa	19	2	·60	15	·12	—30
3	Su	20	3	·69	16	·23	1
4	Mo	21	4	·78	17	·33	2
5	Tu	22	5	·85	18	·43	3
6	We	23	6	·90	19	·52	4
7	Th	24	7	·94	20	·59	5
8	Fr	25	8	·96	21	·64	6
9	Sa	26	9	·95	22	·66	7
10	Su	27	10	·92	23	·67	8
11	Mo	28	11	·89	24	·66	9
12	Tu	29	12	·83	25	·63	10
13	We	30	13	·76	26	·59	11
14	Th	31	14	·67	27	·53	12

Nov.

Solar: Sobhana Tula—Aippasi (15–30); Sobhana Vrischika—Kartigai (1–14). Lunar: Nija Asvina (Bahula); Kartika (Sukla). Muhammadan: H. 1383 Jumadal-akhir; Rajab.

Cyclic Sidereal	Week-Day	Day	Tithi	Moment	Nakshatra	Moment	Muhammadan
15	Fr	1	P	·57	1	·47	13
16	Sa	2	1	·47	2	·40	14
17	Su	3	2	·37	3	·33	15
18	Mo	4	3	·27	4	·26	16
19	Tu	5	4	·18	5	·20	17
20	We	6	5	·10	6	·15	18
21	Th	7	6 / 7	·03 / ·97	7	·11	19
22	Fr	8	8	·94	8	·08	20
23	Sa	9	9	·92	9	·07	21
24	Su	10	10	·93	10	·08	22
25	Mo	11	11	·95	11	·11	23
26	Tu	12	12	·99	12	·16	24
27	We	13	...	...	13	·23	25
28	Th	14	13	·06	14	·32	26
29	Fr	15	14	·14	15	·42	27
—30	Sa	16	—A	·22	16	·53	28
1	Su	17	1	·30	17	·64	—29
2	Mo	18	2	·39	18	·74	1
3	Tu	19	3	·46	19	·83	2
4	We	20	4	·52	20	·90	3
5	Th	21	5	·56	21	·95	4
6	Fr	22	6	·59	22	98	5
7	Sa	23	7	·57	...	...	6
8	Su	24	8	·54	23 / 24	·00 / ·99	7
9	Mo	25	9	·50	25	·96	8
10	Tu	26	10	·44	26	·92	9
11	We	27	11	·37	27	·87	10
12	Th	28	12	·28	1	·81	11
13	Fr	29	13	·19	2	·74	12
14	Sa	30	14 / P	·09 / ·99	3	·67	13

Dec.

Solar: Sobhana Vrischika—Kartigai (15–29); Sobhana Dhanus—Margali (1–16). Lunar: Kartika (Bahula); Margasira (Sukla). Muhammadan: H. 1383 Rajab; H. 1383 Shaban.

Cyclic Sidereal	Week-Day	Day	Tithi	Moment	Nakshatra	Moment	Muhammadan
15	Su	1	1	·89	4	·60	14
16	Mo	2	2	·80	5	·54	15
17	Tu	3	3	·72	6	·49	16
18	We	4	4	·65	7	·44	17
19	Th	5	5	·60	8	·41	18
20	Fr	6	6	·57	9	·39	19
21	Sa	7	7	·56	10	·40	20
22	Su	8	8	·56	11	·42	21
23	Mo	9	9	·58	12	·47	22
24	Tu	10	10	·63	13	·54	23
25	We	11	11	·70	14	·62	24
26	Th	12	12	·78	15	·72	25
27	Fr	13	13	·87	16	·83	26
28	Sa	14	14	·96	17	·94	27
—29	Su	15	...	...	...	...	28
1	Mo	16	—A	·04	18	·04	29
2	Tu	17	1	·11	19	·13	—30
3	We	18	2	·17	20	·21	1
4	Th	19	3	·20	21	·26	2
5	Fr	20	4	·22	22	·30	3
6	Sa	21	5	·21	23	·32	4
7	Su	22	6	·19	24	·32	5
8	Mo	23	7	·14	25	·29	6
9	Tu	24	8	·07	26	·25	7
10	We	25	9 / 10	·00 / ·92	27	·21	8
11	Th	26	11	·83	1	·15	9
12	Fr	27	12	·73	2	·08	10
13	Sa	28	13	·63	3 / 4	·01 / ·94	11
14	Su	29	14	·53	5	·87	12
15	Mo ○	30	P	·44	6	·82	13
16	Tu	31	1	·36	7	·77	14

15. Svati. 16. Visak. 17. Anur. 18. Jyesh. 19. Mula. 20. P. Ash. 21. U. Ash. 22. Sravn. 23. Dani. 24. Satab. 25. P. Bhad. 26. U. Bhad. 27. Rev.

A. D. 1964. | Mesha Sankranti (Commencement of Indian Sidereal Year).
Solar Eclipse. ● | (Surya Sid.) April 13·18. | Saka 1886. | Kaliyuga 5065.
Lunar Eclipse. ○ | (Arya Sid.) April 13·07. | (S. Cycle) Krodhi.

Jan.

SOLAR reckoning: Cyclic Sidereal Year, Month and Day	Week-Day English Month and Day	LUNAR reckoning: Tithi Ending Moment	Nakshatra Ending Moment	Muhammadan Year, Month and Day
Sobhana *Dhanus—Margali.* 17	We 1	**Margasira** 2 ·29	8 ·74	15
18	Th 2	3 ·24	9 ·72	16
19	Fr 3	4 ·21	10 ·72	17
20	Sa 4	5 ·20	11 ·75	18
21	Su 5	6 ·21	12 ·79	19
22	Mo 6	7 ·24	13 ·85	20
23	Tu 7	8 ·28	14 ·92	21
24	We 8	*Bahula* 9 ·34	... ...	H. 1383 *Shaban.* 22
25	Th 9	10 ·42	15 ·02	23
26	Fr 10	11 ·51	16 ·13	24
27	Sa 11	12 ·60	17 ·24	25
28	Su 12	13 ·69	18 ·34	26
—29	Mo 13	14 ·76	19 ·43	27
1	Tu 14	—A ·81	20 ·51	28
2	We 15	1 ·84	21 ·58	—29
3	Th 16	2 ·86	22 ·62	1
4	Fr 17	3 ·85	23 ·64	2
5	Sa 18	4 ·83	24 ·64	3
6	Su 19	5 ·79	25 ·62	4
7	Mo 20	6 ·73	26 ·60	5
8	Tu 21	*Sukla* 7 ·64	27 ·55	6
9	We 22	8 ·55	1 ·49	7
10	Th 23	9 ·46	2 ·42	8
11	Fr 24	10 ·36	3 ·35	9
12	Sa 25	11 ·26	4 ·28	10
13	Su 26	12 ·17	5 ·22	11
Sobhana *Makara—Tai.* 14	Mo 27	13 ·08	6 ·16	12
15	Tu 28	**Magha** 14 ·00 P ·94	7 ·11	*Ramzan.* 13
16	We 29	1 ·89	8 ·07	14
17	Th 30	2 ·85	9 ·04	15
18	Fr 31	3 ·84	10 ·05	16

Feb.

SOLAR reckoning: Cyclic Sidereal Year, Month and Day	Week-Day English Month and Day	LUNAR reckoning: Tithi Ending Moment	Nakshatra Ending Moment	Muhammadan Year, Month and Day
19	Sa 1	4 ·85	11 ·07	H. 1383 17
20	Su 2	5 ·89	12 ·10	18
21	Mo 3	6 ·94	13 ·15	19
22	Tu 4	... ...	14 ·23	20
23	We 5	*Bahula* 7 ·00	15 ·33	21
24	Th 6	8 ·07	16 ·43	22
25	Fr 7	9 ·16	17 ·53	23
26	Sa 8	10 ·25	18 ·64	24
27	Su 9	11 ·33	19 ·74	25
28	Mo 10	12 ·40	20 ·83	26
29	Tu 11	13 ·45	21 ·89	27
—30	We 12	14 ·49	22 ·94	28
1	Th 13	—A ·50	23 ·96	29
2	Fr 14	1 ·49	24 ·97	—30
3	Sa 15	2 ·46	25 ·95	1
4	Su 16	3 ·41	26 ·92	2
5	Mo 17	*Sukla* 4 ·34	27 ·88	3
Sobhana *Kumbha—Masi.* 6	Tu 18	5 ·26	1 ·82	4
7	We 19	6 ·18	2 ·76	H. 1383 *Shawwal.* 5
8	Th 20	7 ·09 8 ·99	3 ·70	6
9	Fr 21	9 ·89	4 ·63	7
10	Sa 22	10 ·79	5 ·56	8
11	Su 23	11 ·70	6 ·50	9
12	Mo 24	**Phalguna** 12 ·61	7 ·44	10
13	Tu 25	13 ·54	8 ·40	11
14	We 26	14 ·50	9 ·38	12
15	Th 27	P ·47	10 ·37	13
16	Fr 28	1 ·46	11 ·38	14
17	Sa 29	2 ·47	12 ·41	15

March

SOLAR reckoning: Cyclic Sidereal Year, Month and Day	Week-Day English Month and Day	LUNAR reckoning: Tithi Ending Moment	Nakshatra Ending Moment	Muhammadan Year, Month and Day
18	Su 1	**Phalguna** 3 ·50	13 ·46	16
19	Mo 2	4 ·54	14 ·54	17
20	Tu 3	5 ·61	15 ·63	18
Sobhana *Kumbha—Masi.* 21	We 4	6 ·69	16 ·73	H. 1383 *Shawwal.* 19
22	Th 5	7 ·78	17 ·83	20
23	Fr 6	8 ·87	18 ·94	21
24	Sa 7	9 ·95	... ...	22
25	Su 8	*Bahula*	19 ·04	23
26	Mo 9	10 ·01	20 ·13	24
27	Tu 10	11 ·06	21 ·20	25
28	We 11	12 ·09	22 ·25	26
29	Th 12	13 ·10	23 ·28	27
30	Fr 13	14 ·09	24 ·29	28
—31	Sa 14	—A ·06	25 ·29	—29
1	Su 15	1 ·01 2 ·94	26 ·26	1
2	Mo 16	3 ·86	27 ·22	2
3	Tu 17	4 ·77	1 ·16	3
4	We 18	5 ·68	2 ·10	4
5	Th 19	*Sukla* 6 ·58	3 ·04 4 ·97	5
6	Fr 20	7 ·48	5 ·90	6
7	Sa 21	8 ·38	6 ·83	7
8	Su 22	9 ·29	7 ·78	8
9	Mo 23	**Adhika Chaitra** 10 ·21	8 ·74	9
10	Tu 24	11 ·14	9 ·71	10
Sobhana *Mina—Panguni.* 11	We 25	12 ·09	10 ·69	11
12	Th 26	13 ·06	11 ·70	12
13	Fr 27	14 ·04	12 ·72	*Zi-l-ka'da.* 13
14	Sa 28	P ·05	13 ·78	14
15	Su 29	1 ·08	14 ·85	15
16	Mo 30	2 ·13	15 ·93	16
17	Tu 31	3 ·20	... ...	17

April

SOLAR reckoning: Cyclic Sidereal Year, Month and Day	Week-Day English Month and Day	LUNAR reckoning: Tithi Ending Moment	Nakshatra Ending Moment	Muhammadan Year, Month and Day
18	We 1	4 ·28	16 ·03	H. 1383 18
19	Th 2	5 ·36	17 ·13	19
20	Fr 3	6 ·44	18 ·24	20
21	Sa 4	*Bahula* 7 ·52	19 ·35	21
22	Su 5	8 ·58	20 ·44	22
23	Mo 6	9 ·64	21 ·51	23
24	Tu 7	10 ·67	22 ·57	24
25	We 8	11 ·67	23 ·60	25
26	Th 9	12 ·65	24 ·62	26
27	Fr 10	13 ·61	25 ·61	27
28	Sa 11	14 ·57	26 ·59	28
—29	Su 12	—A ·50	27 ·55	29
1	Mo 13	1 ·42	1 ·50	—30
2	Tu 14	2 ·33	2 ·44	1
3	We 15	3 ·23	3 ·38	2
4	Th 16	4 ·13	4 ·31	3
5	Fr 17	*Sukla* 5 ·03 6 ·93	5 ·24	4
6	Sa 18	7 ·84	6 ·18	H. 1383 *Zi-l-hijja.* 5
7	Su 19	8 ·76	7 ·12	6
8	Mo 20	9 ·69	8 ·07	7
Krodhi *Mesha—Chittirai.* 9	Tu 21	**Nija Chaitra** 10 ·64	9 ·04	8
10	We 22	11 ·60	10 ·02	9
11	Th 23	12 ·58	11 ·02	10
12	Fr 24	13 ·59	12 ·04	11
13	Sa 25	14 ·62	13 ·09	12
14	Su 26	P ·67	14 ·15	13
15	Mo 27	1 ·73	15 ·23	14
16	Tu 28	2 ·81	16 ·33	15
17	We 29	*Bah.* 3 ·89	17 ·44	16
18	Th 30	4 ·97	18 ·55	17

May

SOLAR reckoning: Cyclic Sidereal Year, Month and Day	Week-Day English Month and Day	LUNAR reckoning: Tithi Ending Moment	Nakshatra Ending Moment	Muhammadan Year, Month and Day
19	Fr 1	**N. Chait.**	19 ·65	18
20	Sa 2	5 ·05	20 ·74	19
Krodhi *Mesha—Chittirai.* 21	Su 3	6 ·11	21 ·82	H. 1383 *Zi-l-hijja.* 20
22	Mo 4	7 ·16	22 ·88	21
23	Tu 5	8 ·19	23 ·92	22
24	We 6	*Bahula* 9 ·20	24 ·94	23
25	Th 7	10 ·18	25 ·94	24
26	Fr 8	11 ·15	26 ·92	25
27	Sa 9	12 ·10	27 ·88	26
28	Su 10	13 ·03 14 ·94	1 ·84	27
29	Mo 11	—A ·85	2 ·78	28
30	Tu 12	1 ·75	3 ·71	—29
—31	We 13	2 ·65	4 ·64	1
1	Th 14	3 ·55	5 ·57	2
2	Fr 15	4 ·45	6 ·51	3
3	Sa 16	5 ·35	7 ·45	4
4	Su 17	6 ·27	8 ·40	5
5	Mo 18	*Sukla* 7 ·20	9 ·37	6
6	Tu 19	8 ·15	10 ·34	7
7	We 20	9 ·11	11 ·34	8
8	Th 21	10 ·10	12 ·36	9
9	Fr 22	11 ·10	13 ·40	10
Krodhi *Vrishabha—Vaikasi.* 10	Sa 23	**Vaisakha** 12 ·13	14 ·46	H. 1384 *Muharram.* 11
11	Su 24	13 ·17	15 ·53	12
12	Mo 25	14 ·23	16 ·62	13
13	Tu 26	P ·31	17 ·73	14
14	We 27	1 ·39	18 ·84	15
15	Th 28	2 ·48	19 ·95	16
16	Fr 29	3 ·56	... ...	17
17	Sa 30	4 ·62	20 ·04	18
18	Su 31	5 ·65	21 ·12	19

June

SOLAR reckoning: Cyclic Sidereal Year, Month and Day	Week-Day English Month and Day	LUNAR reckoning: Tithi Ending Moment	Nakshatra Ending Moment	Muhammadan Year, Month and Day
19	Mo 1	6 ·68	22 ·19	20
20	Tu 2	*Bahula* 7 ·70	23 ·24	21
21	We 3	8 ·68	24 ·26	22
22	Th 4	9 ·65	25 ·26	23
23	Fr 5	10 ·59	26 ·25	24
24	Sa 6	11 ·53	27 ·22	25
25	Su 7	12 ·45	1 ·18	26
26	Mo 8	13 ·35	2 ·12	27
27	Tu 9	14 ·25	3 ·05 4 ·98	28
28	We 10	—A ·15	5 ·91	29
29	Th 11	1 ·05 2 ·95	6 ·85	—30
30	Fr 12	3 ·86	7 ·79	1
—31	Sa 13	4 ·77	8 ·74	2
1	Su 14	5 ·70	9 ·69	3
2	Mo 15	6 ·64	10 ·67	4
3	Tu 16	*Sukla* 7 ·60	11 ·67	5
4	We 17	8 ·59	12 ·68	6
5	Th 18	9 ·59	13 ·71	H. 1384 *Safar.* 7
Krodhi *Mithuna—Ani.* 6	Fr 19	10 ·61	14 ·76	8
7	Sa 20	11 ·65	15 ·84	9
8	Su 21	12 ·71	16 ·93	10
9	Mo 22	**Jyeshtha** 13 ·78	... ...	11
10	Tu 23	14 ·86	17 ·03	12
11	We ○ 24	P ·95	18 ·14	13
12	Th 25	... ...	19 ·25	14
13	Fr 26	1 ·03	20 ·35	15
14	Sa 27	2 ·10	21 ·44	16
15	Su 28	3 ·14	22 ·51	17
16	Mo 29	*Bah.* 4 ·17	23 ·55	18
17	Tu 30	5 ·18	24 ·58	19

Naksh :—1. Asvn. 2. Bhar. 3. Krit. 4. Rohi. 5. Mrig. 6. Ardh. 7. Punar. 8. Push. 9. Aslesh. 10. Magh. 11. P. Phal. 12. U. Phal. 13. Hasta. 14. Chit.

N.B.—In this year the Lunar month **Pausha**

A. D. 1964.
A.—Amavasya.
P.—Paurnami.

Kollam 1140, Commences { N. Malabar—Sept. / S. Malabar—Aug.

Hijra 1384, Commences, May 13.

Vikrama 2021.
Bengal San 1370.
(N. Cycle) Pingala.

SOLAR reckoning: Cyclic Sidereal Year, Month and Day.	Week-Day English Month and Day.	LUNAR reckoning: Tithi Ending Moment.	Nakshatra Ending Moment.	Muhammadan Year, Month and Day.
	July			
18	We 1	Jy. 6 ·16	25 ·59	20
19	Th 2	7 ·13	26 ·58	21
20	Fr 3	8 ·07	27 ·55	22
21	Sa 4	9 ·00 / 10 ·92	1 ·51	H. 1384 Safar. 23
Krodhi Mithuna—Ani. 22	Su 5	Bahula 11 ·88	2 ·45	24
23	Mo 6	12 ·73	3 ·39	25
24	Tu 7	13 ·63	4 ·33	26
25	We 8	14 ·53	5 ·26	27
26	Th 9	—A ·43	6 ·19	28
27	Fr 10	1 ·33	7 ·13	—29
28	Sa 11	2 ·25	8 ·07	1
29	Su 12	3 ·18	9 ·03	2
30	Mo 13	4 ·12	10 ·01 / 11 ·99	3
31	Tu 14	5 ·08	... ...	4
—32	We 15	6 ·06	12 ·00	5
1	Th 16	Sukla 7 ·06	13 ·03	6
2	Fr 17	8 ·08	14 ·07	7
3	Sa 18	9 ·12	15 ·15	8
4	Su 19	10 ·18	16 ·24	9
5	Mo 20	11 ·25	17 ·34	10
6	Tu 21	12 ·34	18 ·44	11
7	We 22	Ashadha 13 ·42	19 ·55	12
8	Th 23	14 ·49	20 ·66	H. 1384 Rabi-ul-awwal. 13
9	Fr 24	P ·56	21 ·75	14
10	Sa 25	1 ·61	22 ·82	15
Krodhi Karkata—Adi. 11	Su 26	2 ·65	23 ·87	16
12	Mo 27	3 ·66	24 ·90	17
13	Tu 28	4 ·64	25 ·91	18
14	We 29	5 ·61	26 ·91	19
15	Th 30	6 ·56	27 ·89	20
16	Fr 31	7 ·49	1 ·84	21
	Aug.			
17	Sa 1	Bahula 8 ·41	2 ·79	22
18	Su 2	9 ·32	3 ·73	23
19	Mo 3	10 ·22	4 ·67	24
20	Tu 4	11 ·12	5 ·60	25
21	We 5	12 ·02 / 13 ·92	6 ·53	26
22	Th 6	14 ·83	7 ·46	27
23	Fr 7	—A ·74	8 ·40	28
24	Sa 8	1 ·66	9 ·36	29
25	Su 9	2 ·60	10 ·33	—30
26	Mo 10	3 ·57	11 ·32	1
27	Tu 11	4 ·55	12 ·32	2
28	We 12	5 ·55	13 ·34	3
29	Th 13	Sukla 6 ·57	14 ·39	4
30	Fr 14	7 ·61	15 ·46	5
—31	Sa 15	8 ·67	16 ·54	6
1	Su 16	9 ·75	17 ·63	7
2	Mo 17	10 ·83	18 ·74	H. 1384 Rabi-ul-akhir. 8
3	Tu 18	11 ·91	19 ·85	9
4	We 19	12 ·99	20 ·96	10
5	Th 20	... ...	... ...	11
Krodhi Simha—Avani. 6	Fr 21	Sravana 13 ·06	21 ·05	12
7	Sa 22	14 ·11	22 ·12	13
8	Su 23	P ·14	23 ·13	14
9	Mo 24	1 ·15	24 ·22	15
10	Tu 25	2 ·14	25 ·24	16
11	We 26	3 ·11	26 ·24	17
12	Th 27	4 ·07	27 ·22	18
13	Fr 28	Bahula 5 ·01 / 6 ·93	1 ·18	19
14	Sa 29	7 ·83	2 ·13	20
15	Su 30	8 ·73	3 ·08	21
16	Mo 31	9 ·63	4 ·01 / 5 ·94	22

SOLAR reckoning: Cyclic Sidereal Year, Month and Day.	Week-Day English Month and Day.	LUNAR reckoning: Tithi Ending Moment.	Nakshatra Ending Moment.	Muhammadan Year, Month and Day.
	Sep.			
17	Tu 1	Srv. 10 ·53	6 ·87	Rabi-ul-akhir. 23
18	We 2	11 ·48	7 ·81	24
19	Th 3	12 ·34	8 ·75	25
20	Fr 4	Bah. 13 ·26	9 ·70	26
21	Sa 5	14 ·19	10 ·66	27
Krodhi Simha—Avani. 22	Su 6	—A ·13	11 ·64	28
23	Mo 7	1 ·08	12 ·64	—29
24	Tu 8	2 ·06	13 ·67	1
25	We 9	3 ·07	14 ·71	2
26	Th 10	4 ·09	15 ·76	3
27	Fr 11	5 ·13	16 ·84	4
28	Sa 12	6 ·19	17 ·93	5
29	Su 13	Sukla 7 ·27	... ...	6
30	Mo 14	8 ·36	18 ·03	7
31	Tu 15	9 ·44	19 ·14	8
—32	We 16	10 ·52	20 ·25	9
1	Th 17	11 ·59	21 ·35	10
2	Fr 18	Bhadrapada 12 ·63	22 ·43	11
3	Sa 19	13 ·66	23 ·49	12
4	Su 20	14 ·69	24 ·54	13
5	Mo 21	P ·67	25 ·56	H. 1384 Jumadal-awwal. 14
6	Tu 22	1 ·64	26 ·56	15
7	We 23	2 ·60	27 ·54	16
Krodhi Kanya—Purattasi. 8	Th 24	3 ·53	1 ·51	17
9	Fr 25	4 ·46	2 ·47	18
10	Sa 26	Bahula 5 ·37	3 ·41	19
11	Su 27	6 ·28	4 ·34	20
12	Mo 28	7 ·18	5 ·27	21
13	Tu 29	8 ·08 / 9 ·98	6 ·20	22
14	We 30	10 ·88	7 ·14	23
	Oct.			
15	Th 1	11 ·80	8 ·08	24
16	Fr 2	12 ·72	9 ·03 / 10 ·99	25
17	Sa 3	13 ·66	11 ·97	26
18	Su 4	14 ·63	12 ·97	27
19	Mo 5	—A ·62	13 ·98	28
20	Tu 6	1 ·62	... ...	29
21	We 7	2 ·65	14 ·01	—30
22	Th 8	3 ·69	15 ·07	1
23	Fr 9	4 ·74	16 ·14	2
24	Sa 10	5 ·82	17 ·23	3
25	Su 11	6 ·92	18 ·34	4
26	Mo 12	Sukla	19 ·45	5
27	Tu 13	7 ·00	20 ·55	6
28	We 14	8 ·08	21 ·65	7
29	Th 15	9 ·15	22 ·73	8
—30	Fr 16	10 ·20	23 ·80	9
1	Sa 17	11 ·23	24 ·85	H. 1384 Jumadal-akhir. 10
2	Su 18	12 ·26	25 ·88	11
3	Mo 19	Asvina 13 ·24	26 ·89	12
4	Tu 20	14 ·22	27 ·87	13
5	We 21	P ·18	1 ·85	14
6	Th 22	1 ·12	2 ·81	15
7	Fr 23	2 ·04 / 3 ·95	3 ·75	16
Krodhi Tula—Aippasi. 8	Sa 24	4 ·85	4 ·68	17
9	Su 25	Bahula 5 ·75	5 ·61	18
10	Mo 26	6 ·65	6 ·54	19
11	Tu 27	7 ·55	7 ·48	20
12	We 28	8 ·47	8 ·42	21
13	Th 29	9 ·39	9 ·37	22
14	Fr 30	10 ·32	10 ·32	23
15	Sa 31	11 ·26	11 ·29	24

SOLAR reckoning: Cyclic Sidereal Year, Month and Day.	Week-Day English Month and Day.	LUNAR reckoning: Tithi Ending Moment.	Nakshatra Ending Moment.	Muhammadan Year, Month and Day.
	Nov.			
16	Su 1	Bah. 12 ·22	12 ·29	J.-akhir. 25
17	Mo 2	13 ·21	13 ·30	26
18	Tu 3	14 ·22	14 ·33	27
19	We 4	—A ·24	15 ·38	28
20	Th 5	1 ·28	16 ·45	—29
21	Fr 6	2 ·35	17 ·54	1
Krodhi Tula—Aippasi. 22	Sa 7	3 ·43	18 ·64	2
23	Su 8	4 ·52	19 ·75	3
24	Mo 9	5 ·61	20 ·85	4
25	Tu 10	Sukla 6 ·69	21 ·95	5
26	We 11	7 ·76	... ...	6
27	Th 12	8 ·81	22 ·05	7
28	Fr 13	9 ·85	23 ·12	8
29	Sa 14	10 ·86	24 ·17	9
—30	Su 15	11 ·85	25 ·20	10
1	Mo 16	12 ·83	26 ·21	11
2	Tu 17	Karttika 13 ·78	27 ·21	12
3	We 18	14 ·72	1 ·18	13
4	Th 19	P ·65	2 ·14	14
5	Fr 20	1 ·57	3 ·09	15
6	Sa 21	2 ·47	4 ·03 / 5 ·96	H. 1384 Rajab. 16
7	Su 22	3 ·37	6 ·89	17
Krodhi Vrischika—Kartigai. 8	Mo 23	4 ·27	7 ·82	18
9	Tu 24	5 ·17	8 ·76	19
10	We 25	6 ·09	9 ·70	20
11	Th 26	Bahula 7 ·01 / 8 ·94	10 ·65	21
12	Fr 27	9 ·88	11 ·63	22
13	Sa 28	10 ·85	12 ·61	23
14	Su 29	11 ·83	13 ·62	24
15	Mo 30	12 ·84	14 ·64	25
	Dec.			
16	Tu 1	13 ·87	15 ·69	26
17	We 2	14 ·92	16 ·76	27
18	Th ● 3	—A ·99	17 ·84	28
19	Fr 4	... ...	18 ·94	29
20	Sa 5	1 ·07	... ...	—30
21	Su 6	2 ·16	19 ·04	1
22	Mo 7	3 ·24	20 ·15	2
23	Tu 8	4 ·32	21 ·26	3
24	We 9	5 ·39	22 ·35	4
25	Th 10	6 ·45	23 ·43	5
26	Fr 11	Sukla 7 ·49	24 ·48	6
27	Sa 12	8 ·50	25 ·52	7
28	Su 13	9 ·49	26 ·54	8
—29	Mo 14	Margasira 10 ·46	27 ·54	9
1	Tu 15	11 ·41	1 ·51	10
2	We 16	12 ·35	2 ·47	H. 1384 Shaban. 11
3	Th 17	13 ·28	3 ·42	12
4	Fr 18	14 ·19	4 ·36	13
5	Sa ○ 19	P ·10	5 ·30	14
Krodhi Dhanus—Margali. 6	Su 20	1 ·00 / 2 ·90	6 ·23	15
7	Mo 21	3 ·81	7 ·16	16
8	Tu 22	4 ·72	8 ·09	17
9	We 23	5 ·64	9 ·08 / 10 ·99	18
10	Th 24	Bahula 6 ·58	11 ·96	19
11	Fr 25	7 ·53	12 ·94	20
12	Sa 26	8 ·50	13 ·94	21
13	Su 27	9 ·48	14 ·96	22
14	Mo 28	10 ·49	... ...	23
15	Tu 29	11 ·52	15 ·01	24
16	We 30	12 ·57	16 ·07	25
17	Th 31	13 ·64	17 ·15	26

15. Svati. 16. Visak. 17. Anur. 18. Jyesh. 19. Mula. 20. P. Ash. 21. U. Ash. 22. Sravn. 23. Dani. 24. Satab. 25. P. Bhad. 26. U. Bhad 27. Rev. ... is Kshaya, *i.e.*, suppressed.

A. D. 1965. **Mesha Sankranti** (Commencement of Indian Sidereal Year).
Solar Eclipse. ● **(Surya Sid.) April 13·44.** **Saka 1887.** **Kaliyuga 5066.**
Lunar Eclipse. ○ **(Arya Sid.) April 13·33.** **(S. Cycle) Visvavasu.**

SOLAR reckoning: Cyclic Sidereal Year, Month and Day; Week-Day English Month and Day. LUNAR reckoning: Tithi Ending Moment; Nakshatra Ending Moment; Muhammadan Year, Month and Day.

Jan.

Krodhi *Dhanus—Margali*; Krodhi *Makara—Tai*. *Sukla*, **Pausha**, *Bahula*. H. 1384 *Ramzan*.

Cyclic Sidereal Year, Month and Day	Week-Day English Month and Day		Tithi Ending Moment	Nakshatra Ending Moment	Muhammadan Year, Month and Day
18	Fr	1	14 ·72	18 ·24	27
19	Sa	2	—A ·81	19 ·34	28
20	Su	3	1 ·90	20 ·45	—29
21	Mo	4	2 ·98	21 ·56	1
22	Tu	5	... ...	22 ·66	2
23	We	6	3 ·05	23 ·73	3
24	Th	7	4 ·10	24 ·79	4
25	Fr	8	5 ·13	25 ·83	5
26	Sa	9	6 ·15	26 ·86	6
27	Su	10	7 ·14	27 ·86	7
28	Mo	11	8 ·11	1 ·84	8
29	Tu	12	9 ·06	2 ·81	9
—30	We	13	{10 ·00 11 ·93	3 ·76	10
1	Th	14	12 ·83	4 ·71	11
2	Fr	15	13 ·73	5 ·64	12
3	Sa	16	14 ·63	6 ·57	13
4	Su	17	P ·53	7 ·50	14
5	Mo	18	1 ·44	8 ·4[illegible]	15
6	Tu	19	2 ·36	9 ·38	16
7	We	20	3 ·29	10 ·33	17
8	Th	21	4 ·23	11 ·29	18
9	Fr	22	5 ·18	12 ·26	19
10	Sa	23	6 ·14	13 ·26	20
11	Su	24	7 ·12	14 ·28	21
12	Mo	25	8 ·13	15 ·32	22
13	Tu	26	9 ·16	16 ·37	23
14	We	27	10 ·22	17 ·45	24
15	Th	28	11 ·29	18 ·54	25
16	Fr	29	12 ·37	19 ·65	26
17	Sa	30	13 ·46	20 ·76	27
18	Su	31	14 ·54	21 ·86	28

Feb.

Krodhi *Kumbha—Masi*. *Sukla*, **Magha**, *Bahula*. H. 1384 *Shawwal*.

Cyclic Sidereal Year, Month and Day	Week-Day English Month and Day		Tithi Ending Moment	Nakshatra Ending Moment	Muhammadan Year, Month and Day
19	Mo	1	—A ·62	22 ·96	29
20	Tu	2	1 ·69	... ...	—30
21	We	3	2 ·75	23 ·04	1
22	Th	4	3 ·77	24 ·10	2
23	Fr	5	4 ·79	25 ·15	3
24	Sa	6	5 ·77	26 ·18	4
25	Su	7	6 ·74	27 ·19	5
26	Mo	8	7 ·69	1 ·17	6
27	Tu	9	8 ·62	2 ·14	7
28	We	10	9 ·55	3 ·10	8
—29	Th	11	10 ·46	4 ·04 5 ·98}	9
1	Fr	12	11 ·36	6 ·91	10
2	Sa	13	12 ·26	7 ·84	11
3	Su	14	13 ·16	8 ·77	12
4	Mo	15	{14 ·07 P ·98	9 ·71	13
5	Tu	16	1 ·91	10 ·66	14
6	We	17	2 ·85	11 ·62	15
7	Th	18	3 ·80	12 ·59	16
8	Fr	19	4 ·77	13 ·59	17
9	Sa	20	5 ·76	14 ·60	18
10	Su	21	6 ·76	15 ·63	19
11	Mo	22	7 ·79	16 ·68	20
12	Tu	23	8 ·84	17 ·75	21
13	We	24	9 ·91	18 ·84	22
14	Th	25	10 ·99	19 ·94	23
15	Fr	26	... ...	... ...	24
16	Sa	27	11 ·08	20 ·05	25
17	Su	28	12 ·17	21 ·16	26

March

Krodhi *Kumbha—Masi*; Krodhi *Mina—Panguni*. *Bah.*, *Sukla*, **Phalguna**, *Bahula*. H. 1384 *Zi-l-ka'da*.

Cyclic Sidereal Year, Month and Day	Week-Day English Month and Day		Tithi Ending Moment	Nakshatra Ending Moment	Muhammadan Year, Month and Day
18	Mo	1	13 ·25	22 ·26	27
19	Tu	2	14 ·31	23 ·34	28
20	We	3	—A ·36	24 ·42	—29
21	Th	4	1 ·39	25 ·47	1
22	Fr	5	2 ·40	26 ·50	2
23	Sa	6	3 ·38	27 ·51	3
24	Su	7	4 ·35	1 ·50	4
25	Mo	8	5 ·30	2 ·48	5
26	Tu	9	6 ·23	3 ·43	6
27	We	10	7 ·16	4 ·38	7
28	Th	11	{8 ·07 9 ·97	5 ·32	8
29	Fr	12	10 ·87	6 ·25	9
—30	Sa	13	11 ·77	7 ·18	10
1	Su	14	12 ·67	8 ·11	11
2	Mo	15	13 ·58	9 ·05 10 ·99}	12
3	Tu	16	14 ·50	11 ·95	13
4	We	17	P ·44	12 ·93	14
5	Th	18	1 ·39	13 ·91	15
6	Fr	19	2 ·36	14 ·92	16
7	Sa	20	3 ·35	15 ·94	17
8	Su	21	4 ·36	16 ·99	18
9	Mo	22	5 ·39	... ...	19
10	Tu	23	6 ·44	17 ·06	20
11	We	24	7 ·51	18 ·15	21
12	Th	25	8 ·59	19 ·25	22
13	Fr	26	9 ·67	20 ·35	23
14	Sa	27	10 ·76	21 ·46	24
15	Su	28	11 ·84	22 ·56	25
16	Mo	29	12 ·90	23 ·66	26
17	Tu	30	13 ·95	24 ·73	27
18	We	31	14 ·97	25 ·79	28

April

Visvavasu *Mesha—Chittirai*. *Sukla*, **Chaitra**, *Bahula*. H. 1384 *Zi-l-hijja*.

Cyclic Sidereal Year, Month and Day	Week-Day English Month and Day		Tithi Ending Moment	Nakshatra Ending Moment	Muhammadan Year, Month and Day
19	Th	1	—A ·98	26 ·82	29
20	Fr	2	1 ·96	27 ·83	—30
21	Sa	3	2 ·93	1 ·83	1
22	Su	4	3 ·88	2 ·81	2
23	Mo	5	4 ·81	3 ·77	3
24	Tu	6	5 ·73	4 ·72	4
25	We	7	6 ·63	5 ·66	5
26	Th	8	7 ·53	6 ·59	6
27	Fr	9	8 ·43	7 ·52	7
28	Sa	10	9 ·33	8 ·45	8
29	Su	11	10 ·23	9 ·39	9
—30	Mo	12	11 ·14	10 ·33	10
1	Tu	13	{12 ·06 13 ·99	11 ·28	11
2	We	14	14 ·94	12 ·26	12
3	Th	15	P ·91	13 ·24	13
4	Fr	16	1 ·90	14 ·24	14
5	Sa	17	2 ·91	15 ·26	15
6	Su	18	3 ·94	16 ·30	16
7	Mo	19	4 ·99	17 ·37	17
8	Tu	20	... ...	18 ·45	18
9	We	21	5 ·05	19 ·55	19
10	Th	22	6 ·13	20 ·65	20
11	Fr	23	7 ·21	21 ·76	21
12	Sa	24	8 ·30	22 ·87	22
13	Su	25	9 ·37	23 ·96	23
14	Mo	26	10 ·44	... ...	24
15	Tu	27	11 ·49	24 ·04	25
16	We	28	12 ·52	25 ·10	26
17	Th	29	13 ·52	26 ·14	27
18	Fr	30	14 ·50	27 ·16	28

May

Visvavasu *Mesha—Chittirai*; Visvavasu *Vrishabha—Vaikasi*. *Sukla*, **Vaisakha**, *Bahula*. H. 1385 *Muharram*.

Cyclic Sidereal Year, Month and Day	Week-Day English Month and Day		Tithi Ending Moment	Nakshatra Ending Moment	Muhammadan Year, Month and Day
19	Sa	1	—A ·47	1 ·16	—29
20	Su	2	1 ·41	2 ·14	1
21	Mo	3	2 ·34	3 ·10	2
22	Tu	4	3 ·26	4 ·05	3
23	We	5	4 ·17	5 ·00 6 ·93}	4
24	Th	6	{5 ·07 6 ·97	7 ·86	5
25	Fr	7	7 ·87	8 ·79	6
26	Sa	8	8 ·77	9 ·72	7
27	Su	9	9 ·67	10 ·66	8
28	Mo	10	10 ·58	11 ·62	9
29	Tu	11	11 ·51	12 ·58	10
30	We	12	12 ·47	13 ·56	11
—31	Th	13	13 ·44	14 ·56	12
1	Fr	14	14 ·42	15 ·58	13
2	Sa	15	P ·43	16 ·62	14
3	Su	16	1 ·46	17 ·68	15
4	Mo	17	2 ·51	18 ·75	16
5	Tu	18	3 ·57	19 ·85	17
6	We	19	4 ·64	20 ·95	18
7	Th	20	5 ·71	... ...	19
8	Fr	21	6 ·80	21 ·06	20
9	Sa	22	7 ·88	22 ·17	21
10	Su	23	8 ·95	23 ·26	22
11	Mo	24	... ...	24 ·34	23
12	Tu	25	9 ·00	25 ·41	24
13	We	26	10 ·01	26 ·46	25
14	Th	27	11 ·02	27 ·48	26
15	Fr	28	{12 ·01 13 ·97	1 ·48	27
16	Sa	29	14 ·91	2 ·47	28
17	Su	30	—A ·84	3 ·44	29
18	Mo	31	1 ·76	4 ·39	—30

June

Visvavasu *Mithuna—Ani*. *Sukla*, **Jyeshtha**, *Bahula*. H. 1385 *Safar*.

Cyclic Sidereal Year, Month and Day	Week-Day English Month and Day		Tithi Ending Moment	Nakshatra Ending Moment	Muhammadan Year, Month and Day
19	Tu	1	2 ·66	5 ·34	1
20	We	2	3 ·56	6 ·27	2
21	Th	3	4 ·46	7 ·20	3
22	Fr	4	5 ·36	8 ·13	4
23	Sa	5	6 ·26	9 ·07	5
24	Su	6	7 ·17	10 ·01 11 ·95}	6
25	Mo	7	8 ·09	12 ·91	7
26	Tu	8	{9 ·02 10 ·97	13 ·89	8
27	We	9	11 ·93	14 ·88	9
28	Th	10	12 ·90	15 ·90	10
29	Fr	11	13 ·91	16 ·93	11
30	Sa	12	14 ·94	17 ·98	12
31	Su ○	13	P ·98	... ...	13
—32	Mo	14	... ...	18 ·06	14
1	Tu	15	1 ·04	19 ·15	15
2	We	16	2 ·12	20 ·25	16
3	Th	17	3 ·20	21 ·36	17
4	Fr	18	4 ·28	22 ·47	18
5	Sa	19	5 ·36	23 ·57	19
6	Su	20	6 ·42	24 ·65	20
7	Mo	21	7 ·47	25 ·72	21
8	Tu	22	8 ·49	26 ·77	22
9	We	23	9 ·50	27 ·80	23
10	Th	24	10 ·48	1 ·81	24
11	Fr	25	11 ·45	2 ·79	25
12	Sa	26	12 ·39	3 ·76	26
13	Su	27	13 ·32	4 ·73	27
14	Mo	28	14 ·24	5 ·67	28
15	Tu	29	—A ·15	6 ·61	—29
16	We	30	{1 ·05 2 ·95	7 ·54	1

Naksh :—1. Asvn. 2. Bhar. 3. Krit. 4. Rohi. 5. Mrig. 6. Ardh. 7. Punar. 8. Push. 9. Aslesh. 10 Magh. 11. P. Phal. 12. U. Phal. 13. Hasta. 14. Chit

A. D. 1965.
A.—Amavasya.
P.—Paurnami.

Kollam 1141, Commences { **N. Malabar—Sept.** / **S. Malabar—Aug.**

Hijra 1385, Commences, **May 2.**

Vikrama 2022.
Bengal San 1371.
(N. Cycle) Kalayukta.

SOLAR reckoning: Cyclic Sidereal Year, Month and Day; Week-Day English Month and Day. LUNAR reckoning: Tithi Ending Moment; Nakshatra Ending Moment; Muhammadan Year, Month and Day.

July

Solar month	Cyclic Sidereal Day	Week-Day	English Day	Lunar month	Tithi Ending Moment	Nakshatra Ending Moment	Muhammadan Day	Muhammadan month
Visvavasu Mithuna—Ani.	17	Th	1	Ashadha, Sukla	3 ·85	8 ·47	2	H. 1385 Rabi-ul-awwal.
	18	Fr	2		4 ·75	9 ·41	3	
	19	Sa	3		5 ·65	10 ·35	4	
	20	Su	4		6 ·57	11 ·29	5	
	21	Mo	5		7 ·50	12 ·25	6	
	22	Tu	6		8 ·45	13 ·22	7	
	23	We	7		9 ·42	14 ·21	8	
	24	Th	8		10 ·40	15 ·22	9	
	25	Fr	9		11 ·39	16 ·25	10	
	26	Sa	10		12 ·41	17 ·29	11	
	27	Su	11		13 ·46	18 ·36	12	
	28	Mo	12		14 ·52	19 ·45	13	
	29	Tu	13		P ·60	20 ·55	14	
	30	We	14	Bahula	1 ·68	21 ·66	15	
	31	Th	15		2 ·77	22 ·77	16	
Visvavasu Karkata—Adi.	1	Fr	16		3 ·84	23 ·87	17	
	2	Sa	17		4 ·90	24 ·96	18	
	3	Su	18		5 ·95	... ...	19	
	4	Mo	19		6 ·97	25 ·04	20	
	5	Tu	20		7 ·99	26 ·09	21	
	6	We	21		8 ·97	27 ·12	22	
	7	Th	22		9 ·94	1 ·13	23	
	8	Fr	23		10 ·88	2 ·12	24	
	9	Sa	24		11 ·81	3 ·10	25	
	10	Su	25		12 ·73	4 ·06	26	
	11	Mo	26		13 ·64	5 ·01 / 6 ·95	27	
	12	Tu	27		14 ·54	7 ·89	28	
	13	We	28		A ·44	8 ·82	29	
	14	Th	29	Sukla	1 ·34	9 ·75	30	
	15	Fr	30		2 ·24	10 ·68	1	
	16	Sa	31		3 ·14	11 ·62	2	

Aug.

Solar month	Cyclic Sidereal Day	Week-Day	English Day	Lunar month	Tithi Ending Moment	Nakshatra Ending Moment	Muhammadan Day	Muhammadan month
	17	Su	1	Sravana, Sukla	4 ·06 / 5 ·98	12 ·58	3	H. 1385 Rabi-ul-akhir.
	18	Mo	2		6 ·93	13 ·55	4	
	19	Tu	3		7 ·89	14 ·54	5	
	20	We	4		8 ·87	15 ·54	6	
	21	Th	5		9 ·87	16 ·56	7	
	22	Fr	6		10 ·90	17 ·60	8	
	23	Sa	7		11 ·94	18 ·67	9	
	24	Su	8		... ...	19 ·76	10	
	25	Mo	9		12 ·00	20 ·86	11	
	26	Tu	10		13 ·07	21 ·96	12	
	27	We	11		14 ·16	... ...	13	
	28	Th	12		P ·25	22 ·06	14	
	29	Fr	13	Bahula	1 ·32	23 ·17	15	
	30	Sa	14		2 ·38	24 ·27	16	
	31	Su	15		3 ·43	25 ·34	17	
	32	Mo	16		4 ·47	26 ·40	18	
Visvavasu Simha—Avani.	1	Tu	17		5 ·48	27 ·44	19	
	2	We	18		6 ·46	1 ·45	20	
	3	Th	19		7 ·43	2 ·46	21	
	4	Fr	20		8 ·38	3 ·43	22	
	5	Sa	21		9 ·31	4 ·40	23	
	6	Su	22		10 ·23	5 ·35	24	
	7	Mo	23		11 ·14	6 ·29	25	
	8	Tu	24		12 ·04 / 13 ·94	7 ·23	26	
	9	We	25		14 ·84	8 ·16	27	
	10	Th	26		A ·74	9 ·09	28	
	11	Fr	27	Bhad. Suk.	1 ·65	10 ·02 / 11 ·96	29	
	12	Sa	28		2 ·56	12 ·92	1	J.-awwal.
	13	Su	29		3 ·49	13 ·89	2	
	14	Mo	30		4 ·44	14 ·87	3	
	15	Tu	31		5 ·40	15 ·86	4	

Sep.

Solar month	Cyclic Sidereal Day	Week-Day	English Day	Lunar month	Tithi Ending Moment	Nakshatra Ending Moment	Muhammadan Day	Muhammadan month
Visvavasu Simha—Avani.	16	We	1	Bhadrapada, Sukla	6 ·38	16 ·88	5	H. 1385 Jumadal-awwal.
	17	Th	2		7 ·38	17 ·92	6	
	18	Fr	3		8 ·41	18 ·98	7	
	19	Sa	4		9 ·45	... ...	8	
	20	Su	5		10 ·51	19 ·06	9	
	21	Mo	6		11 ·58	20 ·15	10	
	22	Tu	7		12 ·67	21 ·25	11	
	23	We	8		13 ·75	22 ·36	12	
	24	Th	9		14 ·83	23 ·47	13	
	25	Fr	10		P ·90	24 ·57	14	
	26	Sa	11	Bahula	1 ·95	25 ·65	15	
	27	Su	12		2 ·98	26 ·71	16	
	28	Mo	13		... ...	27 ·75	17	
	29	Tu	14		3 ·00 / 4 ·99	1 ·78	18	
	30	We	15		5 ·96	2 ·78	19	
	31	Th	16		6 ·91	3 ·76	20	
Visvavasu Kanya—Purattasi.	1	Fr	17		7 ·84	4 ·73	21	
	2	Sa	18		8 ·76	5 ·68	22	
	3	Su	19		9 ·67	6 ·63	23	
	4	Mo	20		10 ·58	7 ·56	24	
	5	Tu	21		11 ·48	8 ·49	25	
	6	We	22		12 ·38	9 ·42	26	
	7	Th	23		13 ·28	10 ·36	27	
	8	Fr	24		14 ·18	11 ·30	28	
	9	Sa	25		A ·10	12 ·25	29	
	10	Su	26		1 ·03 / 2 ·98	13 ·21	30	
	11	Mo	27		3 ·94	14 ·19	1	
	12	Tu	28		4 ·92	15 ·18	2	
	13	We	29		5 ·92	16 ·19	3	
	14	Th	30		6 ·95	17 ·23	4	

Oct.

Solar month	Cyclic Sidereal Day	Week-Day	English Day	Lunar month	Tithi Ending Moment	Nakshatra Ending Moment	Muhammadan Day	Muhammadan month
	15	Fr	1	Asvina, Sukla	7 ·99	18 ·29	5	H. 1385 Jumadal-akhir.
	16	Sa	2		... ...	19 ·36	6	
	17	Su	3		8 ·05	20 ·45	7	
	18	Mo	4		9 ·13	21 ·55	8	
	19	Tu	5		10 ·22	22 ·66	9	
	20	We	6		11 ·30	23 ·77	10	
	21	Th	7		12 ·38	24 ·87	11	
	22	Fr	8		13 ·45	25 ·96	12	
	23	Sa	9		14 ·51	... ...	13	
	24	Su	10		P ·55	26 ·03	14	
	25	Mo	11	Bahula	1 ·56	27 ·08	15	
	26	Tu	12		2 ·55	1 ·10	16	
	27	We	13		3 ·52	2 ·11	17	
	28	Th	14		4 ·48	3 ·09	18	
	29	Fr	15		5 ·41	4 ·06	19	
	30	Sa	16		6 ·33	5 ·02 / 6 ·97	20	
Visvavasu Tula—Aippasi.	1	Su	17		7 ·24	7 ·90	21	
	2	Mo	18		8 ·14	8 ·83	22	
	3	Tu	19		9 ·04 / 10 ·94	9 ·76	23	
	4	We	20		11 ·85	10 ·70	24	
	5	Th	21		12 ·76	11 ·64	25	
	6	Fr	22		13 ·68	12 ·58	26	
	7	Sa	23		14 ·61	13 ·54	27	
	8	Su	24		A ·56	14 ·51	28	
	9	Mo	25	Kart. Suk.	1 ·52	15 ·50	29	
	10	Tu	26		2 ·50	16 ·52	1	H. 1385 Rajab.
	11	We	27		3 ·51	17 ·55	2	
	12	Th	28		4 ·54	18 ·60	3	
	13	Fr	29		5 ·59	19 ·67	4	
	14	Sa	30		6 ·66	20 ·76	5	
	15	Su	31		7 ·74	21 ·86	6	

Nov.

Solar month	Cyclic Sidereal Day	Week-Day	English Day	Lunar month	Tithi Ending Moment	Nakshatra Ending Moment	Muhammadan Day	Muhammadan month
Visvavasu Tula—Aippasi.	16	Mo	1	Karttika, Sukla	8 ·82	22 ·97	7	H. 1385 Rajab.
	17	Tu	2		9 ·91	... ...	8	
	18	We	3		10 ·99	23 ·07	9	
	19	Th	4		... ...	24 ·17	10	
	20	Fr	5		11 ·06	25 ·26	11	
	21	Sa	6		12 ·11	26 ·34	12	
	22	Su	7		13 ·15	27 ·39	13	
	23	Mo	8		14 ·16	1 ·42	14	
	24	Tu	9		P ·15	2 ·43	15	
	25	We	10	Bahula	1 ·12	3 ·42	16	
	26	Th	11		2 ·08	4 ·39	17	
	27	Fr	12		3 ·01 / 4 ·93	5 ·36	18	
	28	Sa	13		5 ·84	6 ·30	19	
	29	Su	14		6 ·75	7 ·24	20	
	30	Mo	15		7 ·65	8 ·17	21	
Visvavasu Vrischika—Karthigai.	1	Tu	16		8 ·55	9 ·10	22	
	2	We	17		9 ·45	10 ·04 / 11 ·98	23	
	3	Th	18		10 ·37	12 ·92	24	
	4	Fr	19		11 ·29	13 ·87	25	
	5	Sa	20		12 ·22	14 ·84	26	
	6	Su	21		13 ·17	15 ·83	27	
	7	Mo	22		14 ·14	16 ·84	28	
	8	Tu	23		A ·13	17 ·86	29	
	9	We	24	Sukla	1 ·13	18 ·91	30	
	10	Th	25		2 ·15	19 ·97	1	
	11	Fr	26		3 ·20	... ...	2	
	12	Sa	27		4 ·27	20 ·06	3	
	13	Su	28		5 ·35	21 ·16	4	
	14	Mo	29		6 ·44	22 ·27	5	
	15	Tu	30		7 ·53	23 ·37	6	

Dec.

Solar month	Cyclic Sidereal Day	Week-Day	English Day	Lunar month	Tithi Ending Moment	Nakshatra Ending Moment	Muhammadan Day	Muhammadan month
	16	We	1	Margasira	8 ·61	24 ·47	7	H. 1385 Shaban.
	17	Th	2		9 ·68	25 ·57	8	
	18	Fr	3		10 ·74	26 ·65	9	
	19	Sa	4		11 ·78	27 ·70	10	
	20	Su	5		12 ·79	1 ·74	11	
	21	Mo	6		13 ·77	2 ·75	12	
	22	Tu	7		14 ·75	3 ·75	13	
	23	We	8		P ·70	4 ·73	14	
	24	Th	9	Bahula	1 ·63	5 ·69	15	
	25	Fr	10		2 ·55	6 ·64	16	
	26	Sa	11		3 ·47	7 ·58	17	
	27	Su	12		4 ·38	8 ·52	18	
	28	Mo	13		5 ·28	9 ·45	19	
	29	Tu	14		6 ·18	10 ·38	20	
	30	We	15		7 ·08	11 ·31	21	
Visvavasu Dhanus—Margali.	1	Th	16		8 ·00 / 9 ·92	12 ·25	22	
	2	Fr	17		10 ·86	13 ·21	23	
	3	Sa	18		11 ·81	14 ·18	24	
	4	Su	19		12 ·78	15 ·16	25	
	5	Mo	20		13 ·77	16 ·16	26	
	6	Tu	21		14 ·78	17 ·18	27	
	7	We	22		A ·81	18 ·22	28	
	8	Th	23	Pausha, Sukla	1 ·86	19 ·29	29	
	9	Fr	24		2 ·93	20 ·37	1	H. 1385 Ramzan.
	10	Sa	25		... ...	21 ·46	2	
	11	Su	26		3 ·01	22 ·56	3	
	12	Mo	27		4 ·10	23 ·67	4	
	13	Tu	28		5 ·19	24 ·78	5	
	14	We	29		6 ·27	25 ·88	6	
	15	Th	30		7 ·34	26 ·95	7	
	16	Fr	31		8 ·39	... ...	8	

15. Svati. 16. Visak. 17. Anur. 18. Jyesh. 19. Mula. 20. P. Ash. 21. U. Ash. 22. Sravn. 23. Dani. 24. Satab. 25. P. Bhad. 26. U. Bhad. 27. Rev.

A. D. 1966. **Mesha Sankranti** (Commencement of Indian Sidereal Year).

Solar Eclipse. ● **(Surya Sid.) April 13·70.** **Saka 1888.** **Kaliyuga 5067.**

Lunar Eclipse. ○ **(Arya Sid.) April 13·59.** **(S. Cycle) Parabhava.**

SOLAR reckoning: Cyclic Sidereal Year, Month and Day.	Week-Day English Month and Day.		LUNAR reckoning: Tithi Ending Moment.	Nakshatra Ending Moment.	Muhammadan Year, Month and Day.
	Jan.				
Visvavasu Dhanus—Margali. 17	Sa	1	Sukla 9 ·42	27 ·01	H. 1385 Ramzan. 9
18	Su	2	10 ·43	1 ·05	10
19	Mo	3	11 ·42	2 ·07	11
20	Tu	4	12 ·39	3 ·08	12
21	We	5	Pausha 13 ·34	4 ·06	13
22	Th	6	14 ·28	5 ·02 6 ·98	14
23	Fr	7	P ·20	7 ·92	15
24	Sa	8	1 ·12	8 ·86	16
25	Su	9	2 ·03 3 ·93	9 ·79	17
26	Mo	10	4 ·83	10 ·72	18
27	Tu	11	5 ·73	11 ·65	19
28	We	12	Bahula 6 ·64	12 ·59	20
—29	Th	13	7 ·56	13 ·55	21
1	Fr	14	8 ·50	14 ·51	22
2	Sa	15	9 ·45	15 ·48	23
3	Su	16	10 ·42	16 ·48	24
4	Mo	17	11 ·41	17 ·49	25
5	Tu	18	12 ·42	18 ·53	26
6	We	19	13 ·46	19 ·59	27
7	Th	20	14 ·51	20 ·67	28
8	Fr	21	—A ·58	21 ·76	29
9	Sa	22	1 ·66	22 ·86	—30
10	Su	23	2 ·76	23 ·97	1
11	Mo	24	3 ·84	... ...	2
Visvavasu Makara—Tai. 12	Tu	25	4 ·92	24 ·08	3
13	We	26	5 ·99	25 ·18	4
14	Th	27	... ...	26 ·26	5
15	Fr	28	6 ·04	27 ·32	6
16	Sa	29	7 ·07	1 ·37	7
17	Su	30	Sukla 8 ·08	2 ·40	8
18	Mo	31	9 ·07	3 ·41	9
	Feb.				
19	Tu	1	10 ·03 11 ·98	4 ·39	H. 1385 Shawwal. 10
20	We	2	12 ·91	5 ·36	11
21	Th	3	Magha 13 ·83	6 ·31	12
22	Fr	4	14 ·75	7 ·26	13
23	Sa	5	P ·65	8 ·20	14
24	Su	6	1 ·55	9 ·13	15
25	Mo	7	2 ·45	10 ·06 11 ·99	16
26	Tu	8	3 ·35	12 ·93	17
27	We	9	4 ·26	13 ·88	18
28	Th	10	5 ·18	14 ·84	19
—29	Fr	11	Bahula 6 ·18	15 ·81	20
1	Sa	12	7 ·09	16 ·80	21
2	Su	13	8 ·06	17 ·81	22
3	Mo	14	9 ·04	18 ·85	23
4	Tu	15	10 ·05	19 ·90	24
5	We	16	11 ·09	20 ·97	25
6	Th	17	12 ·15	... ...	26
7	Fr	18	13 ·22	21 ·06	27
8	Sa	19	14 ·30	22 ·16	28
9	Su	20	—A ·88	23 ·27	—29
Visvavasu Kumbha—Masi. 10	Mo	21	1 ·46	24 ·38	H. 1385 Zi-l-ka'da. 1
11	Tu	22	2 ·55	25 ·48	2
12	We	23	Sukla 3 ·62	26 ·57	3
13	Th	24	4 ·66	27 ·64	4
14	Fr	25	Phalg. 5 ·69	1 ·69	5
15	Sa	26	6 ·69	2 ·72	6
16	Su	27	7 ·68	3 ·73	7
17	Mo	28	8 ·65	4 ·72	8

SOLAR reckoning: Cyclic Sidereal Year, Month and Day.	Week-Day English Month and Day.		LUNAR reckoning: Tithi Ending Moment.	Nakshatra Ending Moment.	Muhammadan Year, Month and Day.
	March				
18	Tu	1	9 ·60	5 ·69	H. 1385 Zi-l-ka'da. 9
19	We	2	Sukla 10 ·53	6 ·65	10
20	Th	3	11 ·45	7 ·60	11
Visvavasu Kumbha—Masi. 21	Fr	4	12 ·36	8 ·54	12
22	Sa	5	13 ·26	9 ·47	13
23	Su	6	14 ·16	10 ·40	14
24	Mo	7	P ·06 1 ·97	11 ·33	15
25	Tu	8	2 ·88	12 ·27	16
26	We	9	3 ·80	13 ·21	17
27	Th	10	Phalguna 4 ·73	14 ·17	18
28	Fr	11	5 ·69	15 ·14	19
29	Sa	12	6 ·66	16 ·12	20
—30	Su	13	7 ·64	17 ·14	21
1	Mo	14	8 ·66	18 ·16	22
2	Tu	15	Bahula 9 ·69	19 ·21	23
3	We	16	10 ·74	20 ·28	24
4	Th	17	11 ·81	21 ·37	25
5	Fr	18	12 ·89	22 ·47	26
6	Sa	19	13 ·98	23 ·57	27
7	Su	20	... ...	24 ·68	28
8	Mo	21	14 ·07	25 ·78	29
9	Tu	22	—A ·15	26 ·87	—30
10	We	23	1 ·21	27 ·95	1
11	Th	24	2 ·26	... ...	2
12	Fr	25	3 ·29	1 ·01	3
13	Sa	26	4 ·29	2 ·04	4
Visvavasu Mina—Panguni. 14	Su	27	5 ·27	3 ·05	5
15	Mo	28	6 ·23	4 ·04	6
16	Tu	29	Sukla 7 ·18	5 ·03 6 ·99	7
17	We	30	8 ·11	7 ·93	8
18	Th	31	9 ·03 10 ·93	8 ·87	9
	April				
19	Fr	1	11 ·88	9 ·80	H. 1385 Zi-l-hijja. 10
20	Sa	2	12 ·73	10 ·73	11
21	Su	3	Chaitra 13 ·63	11 ·67	12
22	Mo	4	14 ·54	12 ·61	13
23	Tu	5	P ·45	13 ·55	14
24	We	6	1 ·37	14 ·50	15
25	Th	7	2 ·31	15 ·47	16
26	Fr	8	3 ·26	16 ·46	17
27	Sa	9	4 ·22	17 ·46	18
28	Su	10	5 ·20	18 ·48	19
29	Mo	11	6 ·21	19 ·52	20
30	Tu	12	Bahula 7 ·25	20 ·58	21
—31	We	13	8 ·30	21 ·67	22
1	Th	14	9 ·38	22 ·77	23
2	Fr	15	10 ·46	23 ·87	24
3	Sa	16	11 ·54	24 ·98	25
4	Su	17	12 ·63	... ...	26
5	Mo	18	13 ·71	25 ·08	27
6	Tu	19	14 ·77	26 ·18	28
7	We	20	--A ·81	27 ·26	29
8	Th	21	1 ·82	1 ·32	—30
9	Fr	22	2 ·83	2 ·36	H. 1386 Muharram. 1
Parabhava Mesha—Chittirai. 10	Sa	23	Sukla 3 ·81	3 ·37	2
11	Su	24	4 ·78	4 ·37	3
12	Mo	25	5 ·72	5 ·36	4
13	Tu	26	Vaisakha 6 ·64	6 ·32	5
14	We	27	7 ·57	7 ·27	6
15	Th	28	8 ·47	8 ·21	7
16	Fr	29	9 ·37	9 ·15	8
17	Sa	30	10 ·27	10 ·08	9

SOLAR reckoning: Cyclic Sidereal Year, Month and Day.	Week-Day English Month and Day.		LUNAR reckoning: Tithi Ending Moment.	Nakshatra Ending Moment.	Muhammadan Year, Month and Day.
	May				
18	Su	1	Suk. 11 ·17	11 ·01 12 ·94	10
19	Mo	2	12 ·07 13 ·98	13 ·88	11
20	Tu	3	14 ·90	14 ·83	12
Parabhava Mesha—Chittirai. 21	We ○	4	P ·83	15 ·80	13
22	Th	5	Vaisakha 1 ·73	16 ·78	14
23	Fr	6	2 ·75	17 ·78	15
24	Sa	7	3 ·74	18 ·79	H. 1386 Muharram. 16
25	Su	8	4 ·76	19 ·83	17
26	Mo	9	5 ·79	20 ·89	18
27	Tu	10	6 ·83	21 ·97	19
28	We	11	Bahula 7 ·89	... ...	20
29	Th	12	8 ·97	22 ·07	21
30	Fr	13	... ...	23 ·17	22
—31	Sa	14	9 ·05	24 ·27	23
1	Su	15	10 ·14	25 ·38	24
2	Mo	16	11 ·22	26 ·48	25
3	Tu	17	12 ·28	27 ·57	26
4	We	18	13 ·32	1 ·63	27
5	Th	19	14 ·34	2 ·67	28
6	Fr ●	20	—A ·35	3 ·69	29
7	Sa	21	1 ·33	4 ·70	—30
8	Su	22	2 ·29	5 ·69	1
9	Mo	23	3 ·23	6 ·65	2
10	Tu	24	4 ·16	7 ·61	3
Parabhava Vrishabha—Vaikasi. 11	We	25	5 ·07 6 ·98	8 ·55	4
12	Th	26	Sukla 7 ·88	9 ·49	5
13	Fr	27	8 ·78	10 ·42	6
14	Sa	28	9 ·68	11 ·35	7
15	Su	29	10 ·58	12 ·28	8
16	Mo	30	11 ·49	13 ·22	9
17	Tu	31	12 ·41	14 ·17	10
	June				
18	We	1	Jyeshtha 13 ·34	15 ·13	H. 1386 Safar. 11
19	Th	2	14 ·29	16 ·11	12
20	Fr	3	P ·25	17 ·10	13
21	Sa	4	1 ·23	18 ·11	14
22	Su	5	2 ·24	19 ·15	15
23	Mo	6	3 ·27	20 ·21	16
24	Tu	7	4 ·32	21 ·28	17
25	We	8	5 ·39	22 ·37	18
26	Th	9	6 ·46	23 ·47	19
27	Fr	10	Bahula 7 ·54	24 ·58	20
28	Sa	11	8 ·62	25 ·69	21
29	Su	12	9 ·69	26 ·79	22
30	Mo	13	10 ·75	27 ·87	23
—31	Tu	14	11 ·79	1 ·94	24
1	We	15	12 ·82	2 ·99	25
2	Th	16	13 ·83	... ...	26
3	Fr	17	14 ·81	3 ·02	27
4	Sa	18	—A ·77	4 ·03	28
5	Su	19	1 ·72	5 ·01 6 ·98	—29
6	Mo	20	2 ·65	7 ·94	H. 1386 Rabi-ul-awwal. 1
7	Tu	21	3 ·56	8 ·89	2
Parabhava Mithuna—Ani. 8	We	22	4 ·47	9 ·83	3
9	Th	23	5 ·37	10 ·76	4
10	Fr	24	Sukla 6 ·27	11 ·69	5
11	Sa	25	7 ·17	12 ·62	6
12	Su	26	8 ·07 9 ·97	13 ·56	7
13	Mo	27	Ashad. 10 ·89	14 ·51	8
14	Tu	28	11 ·82	15 ·46	9
15	We	29	12 ·77	16 ·43	10
16	Th	30	13 ·73	17 ·42	11

Naksh :—1. Asvn. 2. Bhar. 3. Krit. 4. Rohi. 5. Mrig. 6. Ardh. 7. Punar. 8. Push. 9. Aslesh. 10. Magh. 11. P. Phal. 12. U. Phal. 13. Hasta. 14. Chit.

A. D. 1966.
A.—Amavasya.
P.—Paurnami.

Kollam 1142, Commences { N. Malabar—Sept. / S. Malabar—Aug.

Hijra 1386, Commences, April 22.

Vikrama 2023.
Bengal San 1373.
(N. Cycle) Siddharthin.

July

Solar: Parabhava Mithuna—Ani; Parabhava Karkata—Adi. Lunar: Ashadha, Bahula; Sukla, Sravana. Muhammadan: H. 1386 Rabi-ul-awwal; Rabi-ul-akhir.

SOLAR reckoning: Cyclic Sidereal Year, Month and Day	Week-Day English Month and Day	LUNAR reckoning: Tithi Ending Moment	Nakshatra Ending Moment	Muhammadan Year, Month and Day
17	Fr 1	14 ·71	18 ·44	12
18	Sa 2	P ·72	19 ·47	13
19	Su 3	1 ·74	20 ·51	14
20	Mo 4	2 ·79	21 ·58	15
21	Tu 5	3 ·86	22 ·67	16
22	We 6	4 ·94	23 ·77	17
23	Th 7	... ...	24 ·88	18
24	Fr 8	5 ·02	25 ·99	19
25	Sa 9	6 ·10	... ...	20
26	Su 10	7 ·17	26 ·09	21
27	Mo 11	8 ·23	27 ·17	22
28	Tu 12	9 ·27	1 ·25	23
29	We 13	10 ·30	2 ·31	24
30	Th 14	11 ·31	3 ·34	25
31	Fr 15	12 ·29	4 ·35	26
—32	Sa 16	13 ·25	5 ·34	27
1	Su 17	14 ·20	6 ·31	28
2	Mo 18	—A ·13	7 ·28	29
3	Tu 19	1 ·05 2 ·96	8 ·23	—30
4	We 20	3 ·86	9 ·17	1
5	Th 21	4 ·76	10 ·10	2
6	Fr 22	5 ·66	11 ·03 12 ·96	3
7	Sa 23	6 ·56	13 ·90	4
8	Su 24	7 ·46	14 ·84	5
9	Mo 25	8 ·37	15 ·80	6
10	Tu 26	9 ·30	16 ·76	7
11	We 27	10 ·25	17 ·75	8
12	Th 28	11 ·21	18 ·76	9
13	Fr 29	12 ·19	19 ·78	10
14	Sa 30	13 ·21	20 ·82	11
15	Su 31	14 ·23	21 ·89	12

Aug.

Solar: Parabhava Simha—Avani. Lunar: Adhika, Bahula; Sukla, Nija Sravana. Muhammadan: H. 1386; H. 1386 Jumadal-awwal.

Cyclic Sidereal Year, Month and Day	Week-Day English Month and Day	Tithi Ending Moment	Nakshatra Ending Moment	Muhammadan Year, Month and Day
16	Mo 1	P ·27	22 ·97	13
17	Tu 2	1 ·33	... ...	14
18	We 3	2 ·40	23 ·07	15
19	Th 4	3 ·48	24 ·18	16
20	Fr 5	4 ·57	25 ·29	17
21	Sa 6	5 ·65	26 ·39	18
22	Su 7	6 ·71	27 ·48	19
23	Mo 8	7 ·75	1 ·56	20
24	Tu 9	8 ·78	2 ·62	21
25	We 10	9 ·79	3 ·66	22
26	Th 11	10 ·78	4 ·67	23
27	Fr 12	11 ·75	5 ·67	24
28	Sa 13	12 ·70	6 ·65	25
29	Su 14	13 ·63	7 ·62	26
30	Mo 15	14 ·55	8 ·56	27
—31	Tu 16	—A ·45	9 ·50	28
1	We 17	1 ·35	10 ·44	—29
2	Th 18	2 ·25	11 ·38	1
3	Fr 19	3 ·15	12 ·31	2
4	Sa 20	4 ·05 5 ·96	13 ·24	3
5	Su 21	6 ·88	14 ·18	4
6	Mo 22	7 ·80	15 ·13	5
7	Tu 23	8 ·74	16 ·09	6
8	We 24	9 ·71	17 ·08	7
9	Th 25	10 ·69	18 ·08	8
10	Fr 26	11 ·70	19 ·10	9
11	Sa 27	12 ·73	20 ·13	10
12	Su 28	13 ·77	21 ·19	11
13	Mo 29	14 ·83	22 ·27	12
14	Tu 30	P ·91	23 ·37	13
15	We 31	1 ·99	24 ·47	14

Sep.

Solar: Parabhava Simha—Avani; Parabhava Kanya—Purattasi. Lunar: Nija Sravana, Bahula; Sukla, Bhadrapada. Muhammadan: H. 1386 Jumadal-awwal; Jumadal-akhir.

Cyclic Sidereal Year, Month and Day	Week-Day English Month and Day	Tithi Ending Moment	Nakshatra Ending Moment	Muhammadan Year, Month and Day
16	Th 1	... ...	25 ·58	15
17	Fr 2	2 ·07	26 ·69	16
18	Sa 3	3 ·15	27 ·79	17
19	Su 4	4 ·22	1 ·87	18
20	Mo 5	5 ·27	2 ·93	19
21	Tu 6	6 ·29	3 ·97	20
22	We 7	7 ·31	4 ·99	21
23	Th 8	8 ·29	... ...	22
24	Fr 9	9 ·27	5 ·00 6 ·98	23
25	Sa 10	10 ·22	7 ·95	24
26	Su 11	11 ·15	8 ·90	25
27	Mo 12	12 ·07 13 ·98	9 ·85	26
28	Tu 13	14 ·88	10 ·78	27
29	We 14	—A ·78	11 ·71	28
30	Th 15	1 ·68	12 ·64	29
—31	Fr 16	2 ·58	13 ·57	—30
1	Sa 17	3 ·48	14 ·51	1
2	Su 18	4 ·40	15 ·46	2
3	Mo 19	5 ·33	16 ·43	3
4	Tu 20	6 ·27	17 ·41	4
5	We 21	7 ·24	18 ·40	5
6	Th 22	8 ·23	19 ·41	6
7	Fr 23	9 ·25	20 ·45	7
8	Sa 24	10 ·27	21 ·51	8
9	Su 25	11 ·31	22 ·58	9
10	Mo 26	12 ·37	23 ·67	10
11	Tu 27	13 ·45	24 ·77	11
12	We 28	14 ·53	25 ·88	12
13	Th 29	P ·62	26 ·99	13
14	Fr 30	1 ·70	... ...	14

Oct.

Solar: Parabhava Tula—Aippasi. Lunar: Bahula; Sukla, Asvina; Bah. Muhammadan: H. 1386; H. 1386 Rajab.

Cyclic Sidereal Year, Month and Day	Week-Day English Month and Day	Tithi Ending Moment	Nakshatra Ending Moment	Muhammadan Year, Month and Day
15	Sa 1	2 ·77	27 ·09	15
16	Su 2	3 ·82	1 ·18	16
17	Mo 3	4 ·84	2 ·24	17
18	Tu 4	5 ·86	3 ·29	18
19	We 5	6 ·84	4 ·31	19
20	Th 6	7 ·81	5 ·33	20
21	Fr 7	8 ·76	6 ·31	21
22	Sa 8	9 ·70	7 ·28	22
23	Su 9	10 ·63	8 ·23	23
24	Mo 10	11 ·54	9 ·18	24
25	Tu 11	12 ·44	10 ·12	25
26	We 12	13 ·34	11 ·05 12 ·98	26
27	Th 13	14 ·24	13 ·91	27
28	Fr 14	—A ·14	14 ·85	28
29	Sa 15	1 ·05 2 ·97	15 ·80	—29
—30	Su 16	3 ·90	16 ·76	1
1	Mo 17	4 ·85	17 ·78	2
2	Tu 18	5 ·81	18 ·72	3
3	We 19	6 ·80	19 ·73	4
4	Th 20	7 ·82	20 ·77	5
5	Fr 21	8 ·85	21 ·82	6
6	Sa 22	9 ·89	22 ·89	7
7	Su 23	10 ·96	23 ·97	8
8	Mo 24	... ...	... ...	9
9	Tu 25	11 ·03	24 ·07	10
10	We 26	12 ·11	25 ·18	11
11	Th 27	13 ·20	26 ·29	12
12	Fr 28	14 ·28	27 ·39	13
13	Sa ○ 29	P ·36	1 ·48	14
14	Su 30	1 ·41	2 ·55	15
15	Mo 31	2 ·44	3 ·60	16

Nov.

Solar: Parabhava Tula—Aippasi; Parabhava Vrischika—Kartigai. Lunar: Asvn. Bahula; Sukla, Karttika. Muhammadan: H. 1386 Rajab; Shaban.

Cyclic Sidereal Year, Month and Day	Week-Day English Month and Day	Tithi Ending Moment	Nakshatra Ending Moment	Muhammadan Year, Month and Day
16	Tu 1	3 ·45	4 ·64	17
17	We 2	4 ·43	5 ·65	18
18	Th 3	5 ·40	6 ·64	19
19	Fr 4	6 ·36	7 ·61	20
20	Sa 5	7 ·30	8 ·57	21
21	Su 6	8 ·22	9 ·52	22
22	Mo 7	9 ·13	10 ·46	23
23	Tu 8	10 ·04 11 ·94	11 ·89	24
24	We 9	12 ·84	12 ·32	25
25	Th 10	13 ·74	13 ·26	26
26	Fr 11	14 ·65	14 ·20	27
27	Sa 12	—A ·57	15 ·14	28
28	Su 13	1 ·51	16 ·09	29
29	Mo 14	2 ·46	17 ·06	—30
—30	Tu 15	3 ·43	18 ·04	1
1	We 16	4 ·41	19 ·06	2
2	Th 17	5 ·42	20 ·08	3
3	Fr 18	6 ·45	21 ·13	4
4	Sa 19	7 ·50	22 ·19	5
5	Su 20	8 ·57	23 ·27	6
6	Mo 21	9 ·65	24 ·37	7
7	Tu 22	10 ·75	25 ·48	8
8	We 23	11 ·83	26 ·59	9
9	Th 24	12 ·90	27 ·69	10
10	Fr 25	13 ·97	1 ·78	11
11	Sa 26	... ...	2 ·86	12
12	Su 27	14 ·03	3 ·92	13
13	Mo 28	P ·06	4 ·96	14
14	Tu 29	1 ·07	5 ·97	15
15	We 30	2 ·06	6 ·97	16

Dec.

Solar: Parabhava Dhanus—Margali. Lunar: Bahula; Sukla, Margasira; Bah. Muhammadan: H. 1386; H. 1386 Ramzan.

Cyclic Sidereal Year, Month and Day	Week-Day English Month and Day	Tithi Ending Moment	Nakshatra Ending Moment	Muhammadan Year, Month and Day
16	Th 1	3 ·03 4 ·98	7 ·94	17
17	Fr 2	5 ·91	8 ·91	18
18	Sa 3	6 ·84	9 ·86	19
19	Su 4	7 ·76	10 ·80	20
20	Mo 5	8 ·67	11 ·73	21
21	Tu 6	9 ·57	12 ·66	22
22	We 7	10 ·47	13 ·59	23
23	Th 8	11 ·37	14 ·53	24
24	Fr 9	12 ·27	15 ·47	25
25	Sa 10	13 ·19	16 ·42	26
26	Su 11	14 ·13	17 ·39	27
27	Mo 12	—A ·08	18 ·38	28
28	Tu 13	1 ·06	19 ·38	—29
29	We 14	2 ·05	20 ·40	1
—30	Th 15	3 ·07	21 ·44	2
1	Fr 16	4 ·10	22 ·50	3
2	Sa 17	5 ·15	23 ·58	4
3	Su 18	6 ·22	24 ·68	5
4	Mo 19	7 ·30	25 ·78	6
5	Tu 20	8 ·39	26 ·89	7
6	We 21	9 ·48	27 ·99	8
7	Th 22	10 ·56	... ...	9
8	Fr 23	11 ·63	1 ·09	10
9	Sa 24	12 ·68	2 ·17	11
10	Su 25	13 ·71	3 ·23	12
11	Mo 26	14 ·71	4 ·27	13
12	Tu 27	P ·70	5 ·29	14
13	We 28	1 ·67	6 ·29	15
14	Th 29	2 ·62	7 ·28	16
15	Fr 30	3 ·56	8 ·25	17
16	Sa 31	4 ·48	9 ·20	18

15. Svati. 16. Visak. 17. Anur. 18. Jyesh. 19. Mula. 20. P. Ash. 21. U. Ash. 22. Sravn. 23. Dani. 24. Satab. 25. P. Bhad. 26. U. Bhad. 27. Rev.

A. D. 1967. **Mesha Sankranti** (Commencement of Indian Sidereal Year).

Solar Eclipse. ● **(Surya Sid.) April 13·96.** **Saka 1889.** **Kaliyuga 5068.**

Lunar Eclipse. ○ **(Arya Sid.) April 13·85.** **(S. Cycle) Plavanga.**

SOLAR reckoning: Cyclic Sidereal Year, Month and Day; Week-Day, English Month and Day. LUNAR reckoning: Tithi Ending Moment; Nakshatra Ending Moment; Muhammadan Year, Month and Day.

Jan.

Solar month	Cyclic Sidereal Day	Week-Day	English Day	Lunar month / Paksha	Tithi	Tithi Ending Moment	Nakshatra	Nakshatra Ending Moment	Muhammadan month	Muhammadan Day
	17	Su	1	Marga.	5	·39	10	·14		19
	18	Mo	2		6	·30	11	·07		20
	19	Tu	3		7	·20	12 / 13	·00 / ·93		21
Parabhava Dhanus—Margali.	20	We	4		8	·10	14	·87		22
	21	Th	5		9 / 10	·01 / ·92	15	·81		23
	22	Fr	6	Bahula	11	·84	16	·76	H. 1386 Ramzan.	24
	23	Sa	7		12	·78	17	·72		25
	24	Su	8		13	·74	18	·71		26
	25	Mo	9		14	·71	19	·70		27
	26	Tu	10		—A	·69	20	·71		28
	27	We	11		1	·71	21	·75		29
	28	Th	12		2	·74	22	·81		—30
	—29	Fr	13		3	·80	23	·89		1
	1	Sa	14		4	·87	24	·98		2
	2	Su	15		5	·96	...	...		3
	3	Mo	16		...	...	25	·08		4
	4	Tu	17	Sukla	6	·05	26	·19		5
	5	We	18		7	·18	27	·30		6
	6	Th	19		8	·21	1	·40		7
	7	Fr	20		9	·28	2	·48		8
	8	Sa	21		10	·33	3	·54		9
	9	Su	22		11	·35	4	·59		10
	10	Mo	23		12	·36	5	·61		11
	11	Tu	24		13	·35	6	·63		12
	12	We	25	Pausha	14	·31	7	·61		13
	13	Th	26		P	·26	8	·58	H. 1386 Shawwal.	14
Parabhava Mekara—Tai.	14	Fr	27		1	·19	9	·53		15
	15	Sa	28		2	·11	10	·47		16
	16	Su	29		3 / 4	·02 / ·93	11	·41		17
	17	Mo	30		5	·83	12	·35		18
	18	Tu	31		6	·73	13	·28		19

Feb.

Solar month	Cyclic Sidereal Day	Week-Day	English Day	Lunar month / Paksha	Tithi	Tithi Ending Moment	Nakshatra	Nakshatra Ending Moment	Muhammadan month	Muhammadan Day
	19	We	1	Bahula	7	·64	14	·21		20
	20	Th	2		8	·55	15	·14		21
	21	Fr	3		9	·48	16	·09		22
	22	Sa	4		10	·42	17	·06		23
	23	Su	5		11	·37	18	·03		24
	24	Mo	6		12	·34	19	·02		25
	25	Tu	7		13	·34	20	·03		26
	26	We	8		14	·35	21	·06		27
	27	Th	9		—A	·38	22	·12		28
	28	Fr	10		1	·44	23	·19		—29
	29	Sa	11		2	·51	24	·28		1
	—30	Su	12		3	·60	25	·38		2
	1	Mo	13		4	·69	26	·49		3
	2	Tu	14		5	·77	27	·60		4
	3	We	15		6	·84	1	·70		5
	4	Th	16	Sukla	7	·91	2	·79		6
	5	Fr	17		8	·96	3	·85		7
Parabhava Kumbha—Masi.	6	Sa	18		9	·98	4	·90		8
	7	Su	19		10	·99	5	·93	H. 1386 Zi-l-ka'da.	9
	8	Mo	20		11	·97	6	·95		10
	9	Tu	21		12	·94	7	·94		11
	10	We	22		13	·88	8	·91		12
	11	Th	23	Magha	14	·81	9	·86		13
	12	Fr	24		P	·73	10	·81		14
	13	Sa	25		1	·64	11	·75		15
	14	Su	26		2	·55	12	·68		16
	15	Mo	27	Bah.	3	·45	13	·61		17
	16	Tu	28		4	·35	14	·54		18

March

Solar month	Cyclic Sidereal Day	Week-Day	English Day	Lunar month / Paksha	Tithi	Tithi Ending Moment	Nakshatra	Nakshatra Ending Moment	Muhammadan month	Muhammadan Day
	17	We	1	Mag.	5	·25	15	·48		19
	18	Th	2		6	·17	16	·43		20
	19	Fr	3		7	·09	17	·39		21
Parabhava Kumbha—Masi.	20	Sa	4		8 / 9	·02 / ·98	18	·36	H. 1386 Zi-l-ka'da.	22
	21	Su	5	Bahula	10	·95	19	·34		23
	22	Mo	6		11	·95	20	·35		24
	23	Tu	7		12	·96	21	·38		25
	24	We	8		...	...	22	·43		26
	25	Th	9		13	·00	23	·50		27
	26	Fr	10		14	·05	24	·58		28
	27	Sa	11		--A	·12	25	·68		29
	28	Su	12		1	·20	26	·79		—30
	29	Mo	13		2	·29	27	·90		1
	—30	Tu	14		3	·38	...	...		2
	1	We	15		4	·46	1	·00		3
	2	Th	16		5	·52	2	·09		4
	3	Fr	17		6	·56	3	·16		5
	4	Sa	18	Sukla	7	·58	4	·22		6
	5	Su	19		8	·59	5	26		7
	6	Mo	20		9	·57	6	·27		8
	7	Tu	21		10	·53	7	·26		9
	8	We	22		11	·47	8	·24		10
	9	Th	23	Phalguna	12	·40	9	·20		11
	10	Fr	24		13	·32	10	·15		12
	11	Sa	25		14	·23	11	·09		13
	12	Su	26		P	·13	12 / 13	·02 / ·95	H. 1386 Zi-l-hijja.	14
Parabhava Mina—Panguni.	13	Mo	27		1 / 2	·03 / ·93	14	·89		15
	14	Tu	28		3	·83	15	·83		16
	15	We	29		4	·75	16	·77		17
	16	Th	30		5	·67	17	·72		18
	17	Fr	31		6	·61	18	·69		19

April

Solar month	Cyclic Sidereal Day	Week-Day	English Day	Lunar month / Paksha	Tithi	Tithi Ending Moment	Nakshatra	Nakshatra Ending Moment	Muhammadan month	Muhammadan Day
	18	Sa	1	Bahula	7	·56	19	·67		20
	19	Su	2		8	·53	20	·68		21
	20	Mo	3		9	·52	21	·70		22
	21	Tu	4		10	·54	22	·74		23
	22	We	5		11	·58	23	·80		24
	23	Th	6		12	·63	24	·88		25
	24	Fr	7		13	·70	25	·98		26
	25	Sa	8		14	·78	...	...		27
	26	Su	9		—A	·86	26	·09		28
	27	Mo	10		1	·94	27	·20		—29
	28	Tu	11		...	...	1	·30		1
	29	We	12		2	·02	2	·39		2
	—30	Th	13		3	·08	3	·47		3
	1	Fr	14		4	·12	4	·54		4
	2	Sa	15		5	·14	5	·58		5
	3	Su	16	Sukla	6	·14	6	·59		6
	4	Mo	17		7	·13	7	·59		7
	5	Tu	18		8	·09	8	·57		8
Plavanga Mesha—Chittirai.	6	We	19		9 / 10	·03 / ·96	9	·54		9
	7	Th	20		11	·88	10	·49	H. 1387 Muharram.	10
	8	Fr	21		12	·78	11	·43		11
	9	Sa	22	Chaitra	13	·68	12	·36		12
	10	Su	23		14	·58	13	·29		13
	11	Mo	○ 24		P	·48	14	·22		14
	12	Tu	25		1	·38	15	·16		15
	13	We	26		2	·29	16	·10		16
	14	Th	27		3	·21	17	·05		17
	15	Fr	28	Bahula	4	·15	18	·01		18
	16	Sa	29		5	·10	19	·00		19
	17	Su	30		6	·07	20	·00		20

May

Solar month	Cyclic Sidereal Day	Week-Day	English Day	Lunar month / Paksha	Tithi	Tithi Ending Moment	Nakshatra	Nakshatra Ending Moment	Muhammadan month	Muhammadan Day
	18	Mo	1	Chait.	7	·05	21	·01		21
	19	Tu	2		8	·07	22	·05		22
	20	We	3		9	·11	23	·11		23
Plavanga Mesha—Chittirai.	21	Th	4		10	·16	24	·19		24
	22	Fr	5		11	·22	25	·29		25
	23	Sa	6	Bahula	12	·29	26	·39	H. 1387 Muharram.	26
	24	Su	7		13	·37	27	·50		27
	25	Mo	8		14	·46	1	·60		28
	26	Tu	9		—A	·54	2	·70		29
	27	We	10		1	·60	3	·79		—30
	28	Th	11		2	·64	4	·85		1
	29	Fr	12		3	·66	5	·89		2
	30	Sa	13		4	·66	6	·91		3
	—31	Su	14		5	·64	7	·91		4
	1	Mo	15		6	·60	8	·90		5
	2	Tu	16	Sukla	7	·54	9	·87		6
	3	We	17		8	·47	10	·82		7
	4	Th	18		9	·38	11	·76		8
	5	Fr	19		10	·29	12	·70		9
	6	Sa	20		11	·19	13	·64		10
	7	Su	21		12 / 13	·09 / ·99	14	·57		11
	8	Mo	22	Vaisakha	14	·89	15	·50		12
	9	Tu	23		P	·80	16	·44		13
	10	We	24		1	·72	17	·38		14
Plavanga Vrishabha—Vaikasi.	11	Th	25		2	·66	18	·34		15
	12	Fr	26		3	·61	19	·33	H. 1387 Safar.	16
	13	Sa	27		4	·58	20	·32		17
	14	Su	28		5	·55	21	·33		18
	15	Mo	29	Bahula	6	·57	22	·36		19
	16	Tu	30		7	·60	23	·42		20
	17	We	31		8	·65	24	·50		21

June

Solar month	Cyclic Sidereal Day	Week-Day	English Day	Lunar month / Paksha	Tithi	Tithi Ending Moment	Nakshatra	Nakshatra Ending Moment	Muhammadan month	Muhammadan Day
	18	Th	1		9	·72	25	·59		22
	19	Fr	2		10	·80	26	·69		23
	20	Sa	3		11	·88	27	·79		24
	21	Su	4		12	·96	1	·90		25
	22	Mo	5		...	...	...	...		26
	23	Tu	6		13	·03	2	·00		27
	24	We	7		14	·09	3	·09		28
	25	Th	8		—A	·13	4	·16		—29
	26	Fr	9		1	·15	5	·21		1
	27	Sa	10		2	·16	6	·23		2
	28	Su	11		3	·14	7	·25		3
	29	Mo	12		4	·10	8	·23		4
	30	Tu	13		5 / 6	·04 / ·97	9	·20		5
	—31	We	14	Sukla	7	·88	10	·16		6
	1	Th	15		8	·79	11	·10		7
	2	Fr	16		9	·69	12 / 13	·04 / ·98	H. 1387 Rabi-ul-awwal.	8
	3	Sa	17		10	·59	14	·91		9
	4	Su	18		11	·49	15	·84		10
	5	Mo	19		12	·39	16	·78		11
	6	Tu	20	Jyeshtha	13	·29	17	·72		12
	7	We	21		14	·21	18	·68		13
	8	Th	22		P	·14	19	·65		14
Plavanga Mithuna—Ani.	9	Fr	23		1	·09	20	·64		15
	10	Sa	24		2	·05	21	·65		16
	11	Su	25		3	·03	22	·68		17
	12	Mo	26		4	·05	23	·73		18
	13	Tu	27		5	·08	24	·80		19
	14	We	28	Bahula	6	·13	25	·89		20
	15	Th	29		7	·19	26	·99		21
	16	Fr	30		8	·27	...	...		22

Naksh :—1. Asvn. 2. Bhar. 3. Krit. 4. Rohi. 5. Mrig. 6. Ardh. 7. Punar. 8. Push. 9. Aslesh. 10. Magh. 11. P. Phal. 12. U. Phal. 13. Hasta. 14. Chit.

A. D. 1967. A.—Amavasya. P.—Paurnami.	Kollam 1143, Commences { N. Malabar—Sept. S. Malabar—Aug.	Hijra 1387, Commences, April 11.	Vikrama 2024. Bengal San 1373. (N. Cycle) Raudra.

Column headings (repeated in each of the three column groups): SOLAR reckoning: Cyclic Sidereal Year, Month and Day. — Week-Day English Month and Day. LUNAR reckoning: Tithi Ending Moment. — Nakshatra Ending Moment. — Muhammadan Year, Month and Day.

July

Cyclic Sidereal Year, Month and Day	Week-Day English Month and Day	Tithi Ending Moment	Nakshatra Ending Moment	Muhammadan Year, Month and Day
17	Sa 1	Jy. 9 ·34	27 ·10	Rabi-ul-awwal. 23
18	Su 2	10 ·43	1 ·21	24
19	Mo 3	Bahula 11 ·51	2 ·31	25
20	Tu 4	12 ·56	3 ·40	26
21	We 5	13 ·61	4 ·47	27
Playanga Mithuna—Ani. 22	Th 6	14 ·63	5 ·52	28
23	Fr 7	—A ·63	6 ·56	29
24	Sa 8	1 ·61	7 ·57	—30
25	Su 9	2 ·57	8 ·56	1
26	Mo 10	3 ·51	9 ·53	2
27	Tu 11	4 ·44	10 ·49	3
28	We 12	Sukla 5 ·36	11 ·44	4
29	Th 13	6 ·26	12 ·39	5
30	Fr 14	7 ·16	13 ·32	6
31	Sa 15	8 ·06 / 9 ·96	14 ·25	7
—32	Su 16	10 ·86	15 ·18	8
1	Mo 17	11 ·77	16 ·11	9
2	Tu 18	12 ·69	17 ·06	10
3	We 19	13 ·62	18 ·02 / 19 ·98	11
4	Th 20	Ashadha 14 ·56	20 ·97	12
5	Fr 21	P ·53	21 ·97	13
6	Sa 22	1 ·52	... ...	14
7	Su 23	2 ·53	22 ·00	15
8	Mo 24	3 ·56	23 ·04	16
9	Tu 25	4 ·60	24 ·11	H. 1387 Rabi-ul-akhir. 17
10	We 26	5 ·66	25 ·19	18
Playanga Karkata—Adi. 11	Th 27	6 ·73	26 ·29	19
12	Fr 28	Bahula 7 ·81	27 ·40	20
13	Sa 29	8 ·90	1 ·51	21
14	Su 30	9 ·98	2 ·61	22
15	Mo 31	... ...	3 ·70	23

Aug.

Cyclic Sidereal Year, Month and Day	Week-Day English Month and Day	Tithi Ending Moment	Nakshatra Ending Moment	Muhammadan Year, Month and Day
16	Tu 1	10 ·04	4 ·77	24
17	We 2	11 ·08	5 ·83	25
18	Th 3	12 ·11	6 ·87	26
19	Fr 4	13 ·12	7 ·89	27
20	Sa 5	14 ·09	8 ·89	28
21	Su 6	—A ·06	9 ·86	—29
22	Mo 7	1 ·02 / 2 ·94	10 ·83	1
23	Tu 8	3 ·85	11 ·78	2
24	We 9	4 ·76	12 ·72	3
25	Th 10	5 ·66	13 ·66	4
26	Fr 11	6 ·56	14 ·59	5
27	Sa 12	Sukla 7 ·46	15 ·52	6
28	Su 13	8 ·36	16 ·46	7
29	Mo 14	9 ·27	17 ·40	8
30	Tu 15	10 ·19	18 ·35	9
—31	We 16	11 ·12	19 ·31	10
1	Th 17	12 ·06	20 ·29	11
2	Fr 18	Sravana 13 ·02	21 ·30	12
3	Sa 19	14 ·01	22 ·32	H. 1387 Jumadal-awwal. 13
4	Su 20	P ·02	23 ·35	14
5	Mo 21	1 ·05	24 ·41	15
6	Tu 22	2 ·10	25 ·49	16
7	We 23	3 ·16	26 ·59	17
8	Th 24	4 ·23	27 ·70	18
Playanga Simha—Avani. 9	Fr 25	5 ·31	1 ·81	19
10	Sa 26	6 ·40	2 ·91	20
11	Su 27	Bahula 7 ·48	... ...	21
12	Mo 28	8 ·55	3 ·00	22
13	Tu 29	9 ·59	4 ·08	23
14	We 30	10 ·61	5 ·15	24
15	Th 31	11 ·62	6 ·19	25

Sep.

Cyclic Sidereal Year, Month and Day	Week-Day English Month and Day	Tithi Ending Moment	Nakshatra Ending Moment	Muhammadan Year, Month and Day
16	Fr 1	Bah. 12 ·61	7 ·21	J.-awwal. 26
17	Sa 2	13 ·57	8 ·21	27
18	Su 3	14 ·52	9 ·19	28
19	Mo 4	—A ·46	10 ·17	29
20	Tu 5	1 ·38	11 ·12	—30
Playanga Simha—Avani. 21	We 6	2 ·28	12 ·06 / 13 ·99	1
22	Th 7	3 ·18	14 ·92	2
23	Fr 8	4 ·08 / 5 ·98	15 ·85	3
24	Sa 9	6 ·88	16 ·79	4
25	Su 10	Sukla 7 ·79	17 ·73	5
26	Mo 11	8 ·71	18 ·68	6
27	Tu 12	9 ·65	19 ·64	7
28	We 13	10 ·59	20 ·63	8
29	Th 14	11 ·56	21 ·62	9
30	Fr 15	12 ·54	22 ·63	10
—31	Sa 16	13 56	23 ·67	11
1	Su 17	Bhadrapada 14 ·58	24 ·72	12
2	Mo 18	P ·62	25 ·79	13
3	Tu 19	1 ·63	26 ·89	14
4	We 20	2 ·76	27 ·99	15
5	Th 21	3 ·85	... ...	H. 1387 Jumadal-akhir. 16
6	Fr 22	4 ·93	1 ·10	17
7	Sa 23	... ...	2 ·21	18
8	Su 24	5 ·01	3 ·31	19
9	Mo 25	6 ·08	4 ·40	20
10	Tu 26	Bahula 7 ·12	5 ·46	21
Playanga Kanya—Purattasi. 11	We 27	8 ·15	6 ·51	22
12	Th 28	9 ·16	7 ·53	23
13	Fr 29	10 ·15	8 ·54	24
14	Sa 30	11 ·12	9 ·53	25

Oct.

Cyclic Sidereal Year, Month and Day	Week-Day English Month and Day	Tithi Ending Moment	Nakshatra Ending Moment	Muhammadan Year, Month and Day
15	Su 1	12 ·07	10 ·50	26
16	Mo 2	13 ·00 / 14 ·92	11 ·45	27
17	Tu 3	—A ·83	12 ·39	28
18	We 4	1 ·73	13 ·33	—29
19	Th 5	2 ·63	14 ·27	1
20	Fr 6	3 ·53	15 ·20	2
21	Sa 7	4 ·43	16 ·13	3
22	Su 8	5 ·34	17 ·07	4
23	Mo 9	6 ·26	18 ·01 / 19 ·98	5
24	Tu 10	Sukla 7 ·20	20 ·95	6
25	We 11	8 ·15	21 ·94	7
26	Th 12	9 ·12	22 ·95	8
27	Fr 13	10 ·10	23 ·98	9
28	Sa 14	11 ·12	... ...	10
29	Su 15	12 ·15	24 ·08	H. 1387 Rajab. 11
30	Mo 16	Asvina 13 ·20	25 ·11	12
—31	Tu 17	14 ·26	26 ·19	13
1	We ○ 18	P ·33	27 ·29	14
2	Th 19	1 ·41	1 ·40	15
3	Fr 20	2 ·50	2 ·51	16
4	Sa 21	3 ·59	3 ·61	17
5	Su 22	4 ·66	4 ·70	18
6	Mo 23	5 ·71	5 ·77	19
Playanga Tula—Aippasi. 7	Tu 24	6 ·73	6 ·82	20
8	We 25	Bahula 7 ·74	7 ·85	21
9	Th 26	8 ·72	8 ·87	22
10	Fr 27	9 ·69	9 ·86	23
11	Sa 28	10 ·65	10 ·83	24
12	Su 29	11 ·59	11 ·79	25
13	Mo 30	12 ·51	12 ·73	26
14	Tu 31	13 ·42	13 ·67	27

Nov.

Cyclic Sidereal Year, Month and Day	Week-Day English Month and Day	Tithi Ending Moment	Nakshatra Ending Moment	Muhammadan Year, Month and Day
15	We 1	14 ·32	14 ·61	28
16	Th 2	—A ·22	15 ·54	29
17	Fr 3	1 ·12	16 ·47	—30
18	Sa 4	2 ·03 / 3 ·94	17 ·40	1
19	Su 5	4 ·86	18 ·35	2
Playanga Tula—Aippasi. 20	Mo 6	5 ·79	19 ·31	3
21	Tu 7	6 ·74	20 ·28	4
22	We 8	Sukla 7 ·72	21 ·26	5
23	Th 9	8 ·70	22 ·27	6
24	Fr 10	9 ·72	23 ·30	7
25	Sa 11	10 ·75	24 ·35	8
26	Su 12	11 ·80	25 ·41	9
27	Mo 13	12 ·87	26 ·49	10
28	Tu 14	13 ·95	27 ·59	11
29	We 15	... ...	1 ·70	12
—30	Th 16	Karttika 14 ·04	2 ·81	13
1	Fr 17	P ·13	3 ·91	14
2	Sa 18	1 ·21	... ...	H. 1387 Shaban. 15
3	Su 19	2 ·27	4 ·00	16
4	Mo 20	3 ·32	5 ·08	17
5	Tu 21	4 ·85	6 ·13	18
6	We 22	5 ·87	7 ·17	19
7	Th 23	6 ·35	8 ·19	20
8	Fr 24	Bahula 7 ·31	9 ·18	21
9	Sa 25	8 ·26	10 ·16	22
Playanga Vrischika—Kartigai. 10	Su 26	9 ·20	11 ·12	23
11	Mo 27	10 ·13	12 ·08	24
12	Tu 28	11 ·04 / 12 ·94	13 ·02 / 14 ·95	25
13	We 29	13 ·84	15 ·88	26
14	Th 30	14 ·74	16 ·81	27

Dec.

Cyclic Sidereal Year, Month and Day	Week-Day English Month and Day	Tithi Ending Moment	Nakshatra Ending Moment	Muhammadan Year, Month and Day
15	Fr 1	—A ·64	17 ·74	28
16	Sa 2	1 ·55	18 ·69	—29
17	Su 3	2 ·47	19 ·64	1
18	Mo 4	3 ·41	20 ·61	2
19	Tu 5	4 ·37	21 ·59	3
20	We 6	5 ·34	22 ·59	4
21	Th 7	6 ·34	23 ·62	5
22	Fr 8	Sukla 7 ·35	24 ·66	6
23	Sa 9	8 ·38	25 ·72	7
24	Su 10	9 ·44	26 ·80	8
25	Mo 11	10 ·51	27 ·89	9
26	Tu 12	11 ·60	... ...	10
27	We 13	12 ·69	1 ·00	11
28	Th 14	Margasira 13 ·78	2 ·11	12
—29	Fr 15	14 ·85	3 ·21	13
1	Sa 16	P ·92	4 ·31	H. 1387 Ramzan. 14
2	Su 17	1 ·97	5 ·39	15
3	Mo 18	2 ·99	6 ·45	16
4	Tu 19	... ...	7 ·49	17
5	We 20	3 ·00 / 4 ·98	8 ·51	18
6	Th 21	5 ·95	9 ·51	19
Playanga Dhanus—Margali. 7	Fr 22	6 ·90	10 ·49	20
8	Sa 23	Bahula 7 ·83	11 ·45	21
9	Su 24	8 ·76	12 ·41	22
10	Mo 25	9 ·67	13 ·35	23
11	Tu 26	10 ·57	14 ·29	24
12	We 27	11 ·47	15 ·22	25
13	Th 28	12 ·38	16 ·15	26
14	Fr 29	13 ·29	17 ·09	27
15	Sa 30	14 ·20	18 ·03 / 19 ·98	28
16	Su 31	—A ·12	20 ·94	29

15. Svati. 16. Visak. 17. Anur. 18. Jyesh. 19. Mula. 20. P. Ash. 21. U. Ash. 22. Sravn. 23. Dani. 24. Satab. 25. P. Bhad. 26. U. Bhad. 27. Rev.

A. D. 1968.
Solar Eclipse. ●
Lunar Eclipse. ○

Mesha Sankranti (Commencement of Indian Sidereal Year).
(Surya Sid.) April 13·22.
(Arya Sid.) April 13·11.

Saka 1890. **Kaliyuga 5069.**
(S. Cycle) Kilaka.

SOLAR reckoning: Cyclic Sidereal Year, Month and Day; Week-Day English Month and Day. LUNAR reckoning: Tithi Ending Moment; Nakshatra Ending Moment; Muhammadan Year, Month and Day.

Jan.

Cyclic Sidereal Year, Month and Day	Week-Day	English Day	Tithi Ending Moment	Nakshatra Ending Moment	Muhammadan Year, Month and Day	Side labels
17	Mo	1	1 ·05	21 ·91	—30	
18	Tu	2	2 ·01 3 ·99	22 ·92	1	
19	We	3	4 ·98	23 ·93	2	Playanga Dhanus—Margali.
20	Th	4	5 ·99	24 ·97	3	
21	Fr	5	... ...	... ...	4	
22	Sa	6	6 ·03	25 ·02	5	Sukla
23	Su	7	7 ·09	26 ·10	6	
24	Mo	8	8 ·16	27 ·20	7	
25	Tu	9	9 ·24	1 ·30	8	
26	We	10	10 ·33	2 ·41	9	
27	Th	11	11 ·42	3 ·51	10	
28	Fr	12	12 ·50	4 ·61	11	H. 1387 Shawwal.
29	Sa	13	13 ·57	5 ·69	12	Pausha
—30	Su	14	14 ·61	6 ·76	13	
1	Mo	15	P ·64	7 ·81	14	
2	Tu	16	1 ·65	8 ·83	15	
3	We	17	2 ·63	9 ·83	16	
4	Th	18	3 ·60	10 ·82	17	
5	Fr	19	4 ·55	11 ·80	18	
6	Sa	20	5 ·48	12 ·75	19	
7	Su	21	6 ·40	13 ·69	20	Bahula
8	Mo	22	7 ·31	14 ·63	21	
9	Tu	23	8 ·21	15 ·57	22	
10	We	24	9 ·11	16 ·50	23	
11	Th	25	10 ·01 11 ·92	17 ·43	24	
12	Fr	26	12 ·83	18 ·36	25	Playanga Makara—Tai.
13	Sa	27	13 ·76	19 ·31	26	
14	Su	28	14 ·70	20 ·27	27	
15	Mo	29	—A ·66	21 ·25	28	
16	Tu	30	1 ·64	22 ·24	—29	
17	We	31	2 ·62	23 ·25	1	

Feb.

Cyclic Sidereal Year, Month and Day	Week-Day	English Day	Tithi Ending Moment	Nakshatra Ending Moment	Muhammadan Year, Month and Day	Side labels
18	Th	1	3 ·64	24 ·28	2	
19	Fr	2	4 ·68	25 ·33	3	
20	Sa	3	5 ·74	26 ·41	4	
21	Su	4	6 ·81	27 ·50	5	
22	Mo	5	7 ·89	1 ·60	6	Sukla
23	Tu	6	8 ·98	2 ·71	7	
24	We	7	... ...	3 ·81	8	
25	Th	8	9 ·07	4 ·91	9	
26	Fr	9	10 ·14	... ...	10	H. 1387 Zi-l-ka'da.
27	Sa	10	11 ·21	5 ·00	11	
28	Su	11	12 ·25	6 ·07	12	
—29	Mo	12	13 ·27	7 ·12	13	
1	Tu	13	14 ·28	8 ·15	14	Magha
2	We	14	P ·27	9 ·16	15	
3	Th	15	1 ·23	10 ·16	16	
4	Fr	16	2 ·17	11 ·13	17	
5	Sa	17	3 ·10	12 ·08	18	
6	Su	18	4 ·02 5 ·93	13 ·03 14 ·97	19	Playanga Kumbha—Masi.
7	Mo	19	6 ·83	15 ·90	20	
8	Tu	20	7 ·73	16 ·83	21	Bahula
9	We	21	8 ·63	17 ·76	22	
10	Th	22	9 ·54	18 ·70	23	
11	Fr	23	10 ·45	19 ·64	24	
12	Sa	24	11 ·37	20 ·61	25	
13	Su	25	12 ·31	21 ·58	26	
14	Mo	26	13 ·37	22 ·56	27	
15	Tu	27	14 ·25	23 ·57	28	
16	We	28	—A ·24	24 ·59	29	
17	Th	29	1 ·26	25 ·64	—30	

March

Cyclic Sidereal Year, Month and Day	Week-Day	English Day	Tithi Ending Moment	Nakshatra Ending Moment	Muhammadan Year, Month and Day	Side labels
18	Fr	1	2 ·30	26 ·72	1	
19	Sa	2	3 ·35	27 ·80	2	
20	Su	3	4 ·42	1 ·90	3	
21	Mo	4	5 ·51	... ...	4	
22	Tu	5	6 ·60	2 ·01	5	Playanga Kumbha—Masi.
23	We	6	7 ·69	3 ·12	6	Sukla
24	Th	7	8 ·77	4 ·22	7	
25	Fr	8	9 ·82	5 ·31	8	
26	Sa	9	10 ·86	6 ·38	9	
27	Su	10	11 ·88	7 ·44	10	
28	Mo	11	12 ·88	8 ·47	11	
29	Tu	12	13 ·87	9 ·49	12	
30	We	13	14 ·83	10 ·48	13	Phalguna
—31	Th	14	P ·77	11 ·46	14	
1	Fr	15	1 ·69	12 ·42	15	H. 1387 Zi-l-hijja.
2	Sa	16	2 ·61	13 ·36	16	
3	Su	17	3 ·52	14 ·30	17	
4	Mo	18	4 ·42	15 ·24	18	
5	Tu	19	5 ·32	16 ·17	19	
6	We	20	6 ·22	17 ·10	20	Bahula
7	Th	21	7 ·13	18 ·04 19 ·90	21	
8	Fr	22	8 ·05 9 ·97	20 ·94	22	
9	Sa	23	10 ·90	21 ·90	23	
10	Su	24	11 ·86	22 ·89	24	
11	Mo	25	12 ·84	23 ·89	25	Playanga Mina—Panguni.
12	Tu	26	13 ·82	24 ·92	26	
13	We	27	14 ·85	25 ·96	27	
14	Th	28	—A ·88	... ...	28	
15	Fr	29	1 ·94	26 ·02	29	
16	Sa	30	... ...	27 ·10	—30	
17	Su	31	2 ·01	1 ·20	1	

April

Cyclic Sidereal Year, Month and Day	Week-Day	English Day	Tithi Ending Moment	Nakshatra Ending Moment	Muhammadan Year, Month and Day	Side labels
18	Mo	1	3 ·10	2 ·31	2	
19	Tu	2	4 ·18	3 ·42	3	
20	We	3	5 ·26	4 ·52	4	
21	Th	4	6 ·33	5 ·61	5	
22	Fr	5	7 ·39	6 ·69	6	Sukla
23	Sa	6	8 ·44	7 ·75	7	
24	Su	7	9 ·46	8 ·79	8	
25	Mo	8	10 ·46	9 ·81	9	
26	Tu	9	11 ·44	10 ·81	10	H. 1388 Muharram.
27	We	10	12 ·39	11 ·79	11	Chaitra
28	Th	11	13 ·33	12 ·75	12	
—29	Fr	12	14 ·26	13 ·71	13	
1	Sa ○	13	P ·18	14 ·65	14	
2	Su	14	1 ·09 2 ·99	15 ·58	15	
3	Mo	15	3 ·89	16 ·51	16	
4	Tu	16	4 ·79	17 ·44	17	
5	We	17	5 ·69	18 ·38	18	
6	Th	18	6 ·60	19 ·32	19	Kilaka Mesha—Chittirai.
7	Fr	19	7 ·52	20 ·27	20	Bahula
8	Sa	20	8 ·45	21 ·23	21	
9	Su	21	9 ·41	22 ·21	22	
10	Mo	22	10 ·38	23 ·22	23	
11	Tu	23	11 ·37	24 ·24	24	
12	We	24	12 ·38	25 ·27	25	
13	Th	25	13 ·42	26 ·33	26	
14	Fr	26	14 ·48	27 ·41	27	
15	Sa	27	—A ·55	1 ·50	28	
16	Su	28	1 ·63	2 ·61	29	Y. Suk.
17	Mo	29	2 ·71	3 ·72	—30	
18	Tu	30	3 ·79	4 ·82	1	

May

Cyclic Sidereal Year, Month and Day	Week-Day	English Day	Tithi Ending Moment	Nakshatra Ending Moment	Muhammadan Year, Month and Day	Side labels
19	We	1	4 ·87	5 ·92	2	
20	Th	2	5 ·93	... ...	3	
21	Fr	3	6 ·97	6 ·00	4	Kilaka Mesha—Chittirai.
22	Sa	4	7 ·98	7 ·07	5	Sukla
23	Su	5	8 ·98	8 ·11	6	
24	Mo	6	9 ·96	9 ·13	7	
25	Tu	7	10 ·92	10 ·13	8	
26	We	8	11 ·86	11 ·12	9	
27	Th	9	12 ·79	12 ·09	10	
28	Fr	10	13 ·70	13 ·04 14 ·99	11	Vaisakha
29	Sa	11	14 ·60	15 ·92	12	H. 1388 Safar.
30	Su	12	P ·50	16 ·85	13	
—31	Mo	13	1 ·40	17 ·78	14	
1	Tu	14	2 ·30	18 ·72	15	
2	We	15	3 ·20	19 ·66	16	
3	Th	16	4 ·11	20 ·60	17	
4	Fr	17	5 ·03 6 ·97	21 ·56	18	
5	Sa	18	7 ·93	22 ·54	19	Bahula
6	Su	19	8 ·89	23 ·54	20	
7	Mo	20	9 ·88	24 ·55	21	
8	Tu	21	10 ·89	25 ·58	22	
9	We	22	11 ·93	26 ·64	23	
10	Th	23	12 ·98	27 ·71	24	
11	Fr	24	... ...	1 ·81	25	
12	Sa	25	13 ·05	2 ·91	26	Kilaka Vrishabha—Vaikasi.
13	Su	26	14 ·13	... ...	27	
14	Mo	27	—A ·21	3 ·01	28	
15	Tu	28	1 ·29	4 ·12	—29	
16	We	29	2 ·37	5 ·22	1	
17	Th	30	3 ·43	6 ·31	2	
18	Fr	31	4 ·46	7 ·38	3	

June

Cyclic Sidereal Year, Month and Day	Week-Day	English Day	Tithi Ending Moment	Nakshatra Ending Moment	Muhammadan Year, Month and Day	Side labels
19	Sa	1	5 ·48	8 ·43	4	
20	Su	2	6 ·48	9 ·45	5	
21	Mo	3	7 ·45	10 ·46	6	Sukla
22	Tu	4	8 ·42	11 ·45	7	
23	We	5	9 ·36	12 ·42	8	
24	Th	6	10 ·29	13 ·38	9	
25	Fr	7	11 ·20	14 ·32	10	H. 1388 Rabi-ul-awwal.
26	Sa	8	12 ·10	15 ·26	11	
27	Su	9	13 ·00 14 ·90	16 ·20	12	
28	Mo	10	P ·80	17 ·13	13	
29	Tu	11	1 ·70	18 ·06 19 ·99	14	Jyeshtha
30	We	12	2 ·61	20 ·94	15	
—31	Th	13	3 ·53	21 ·89	16	
1	Fr	14	4 ·46	22 ·87	17	
2	Sa	15	5 ·41	23 ·86	18	
3	Su	16	6 ·38	24 ·87	19	
4	Mo	17	7 ·37	25 ·90	20	Bahula
5	Tu	18	8 ·37	26 ·95	21	
6	We	19	9 ·41	... ...	22	
7	Th	20	10 ·46	27 ·02	23	
8	Fr	21	11 ·53	1 ·11	24	Kilaka Mithuna—Ani.
9	Sa	22	12 ·61	2 ·21	25	
10	Su	23	13 ·69	3 ·31	26	
11	Mo	24	14 ·77	4 ·42	27	
12	Tu	25	—A ·84	5 ·53	28	
13	We	26	1 ·90	6 ·62	29	Ash. Suk.
14	Th	27	2 ·93	7 ·69	—30	
15	Fr	28	3 ·96	8 ·74	1	
16	Sa	29	4 ·96	9 ·77	2	
17	Su	30	5 ·94	10 ·79	3	

Naksh :—1. Asvn. 2. Bhar. 3. Krit. 4. Rohi. 5. Mrig. 6. Ardh. 7. Punar. 8. Push. 9. Aslesh. 10. Magh. 11. P. Phal. 12. U. Phal. 13. Hasta. 14. Chit.

A. D. 1968. **Kollam 1144,** Commences { **N. Malabar—Sept.** / **S. Malabar—Aug.** **Hijra 1388,** Commences, **March 31.** **Vikrama 2025.**

A.—Amavasya. **Bengal San 1374.**

P.—Paurnami. **(N. Cycle) Durmati.**

July

Solar month	Cyclic Sidereal Year, Month and Day	Week-Day	English Month and Day	Lunar month	Tithi	Tithi Ending Moment	Nakshatra	Nakshatra Ending Moment	Muhammadan month	Muhammadan Day
Kilaka Mithuna—Ani.	18	Mo	1	Ashadha Sukla	6	·90	11	·78	H. 1388 Rabi-ul-akhir.	4
	19	Tu	2		7	·84	12	·75		5
	20	We	3		8	·77	13	·71		6
	21	Th	4		9	·68	14	·66		7
	22	Fr	5		10	·58	15	·60		8
	23	Sa	6		11	·48	16	·54		9
	24	Su	7		12	·38	17	·47		10
	25	Mo	8		13	·28	18	·40		11
	26	Tu	9		14	·18	19	·33		12
	27	We	10		P	·09	20	·27		13
	28	Th	11	Bahula	1 / 2	·01 / ·94	21	·23		14
	29	Fr	12		3	·89	22	·20		15
	30	Sa	13		4	·86	23	·19		16
	31	Su	14		5	·84	24	·19		17
	32	Mo	15		6	·85	25	·21		18
Kilaka Karkata—Adi.	1	Tu	16		7	·88	26	·26		19
	2	We	17		8	·93	27	·33		20
	3	Th	18		...	...	1	·41		21
	4	Fr	19		9	·00	2	·50		22
	5	Sa	20		10	·08	3	·61		23
	6	Su	21		11	·16	4	·72		24
	7	Mo	22		12	·24	5	·83		25
	8	Tu	23		13	·31	6	·92		26
	9	We	24		14	·37	7	·99		27
	10	Th	25		A	·41	...	...		28
	11	Fr	26	Sukla	1	·44	8	·05		29
	12	Sa	27		2	·44	9	·09		1
	13	Su	28		3	·42	10	·11		2
	14	Mo	29		4	·38	11	·11		3
	15	Tu	30		5	·32	12	·08		4
	16	We	31		6	·25	13 / 14	·04 / ·99		5

Aug.

Solar month	Cyclic Sidereal Year, Month and Day	Week-Day	English Month and Day	Lunar month	Tithi	Tithi Ending Moment	Nakshatra	Nakshatra Ending Moment	Muhammadan month	Muhammadan Day
	17	Th	1	Sravana	7	·17	15	·94	H. 1388 Jumadal-awwal.	6
	18	Fr	2		8 / 9	·07 / ·97	16	·87		7
	19	Sa	3		10	·87	17	·80		8
	20	Su	4		11	·77	18	·73		9
	21	Mo	5		12	·67	19	·67		10
	22	Tu	6		13	·58	20	·62		11
	23	We	7		14	·50	21	·57		12
	24	Th	8		P	·43	22	·53		13
	25	Fr	9	Bahula	1	·37	23	·51		14
	26	Sa	10		2	·34	24	·51		15
	27	Su	11		3	·32	25	·53		16
	28	Mo	12		4	·34	26	·57		17
	29	Tu	13		5	·37	27	·63		18
	30	We	14		6	·42	1	·71		19
	31	Th	15		7	·49	2	·80		20
	32	Fr	16		8	·57	3	·91		21
Kilaka Simha—Avani.	1	Sa	17		9	·66	...	...		22
	2	Su	18		10	·74	4	·02		23
	3	Mo	19		11	·81	5	·13		24
	4	Tu	20		12	·87	6	·22		25
	5	We	21		13	·91	7	·30		26
	6	Th	22		14	·93	8	·36		27
	7	Fr	23		A	·94	9	·41		28
	8	Sa	24	Bhadra. Sukla	1	·92	10	·43		29
	9	Su	25		2	·83	11	·43		30
	10	Mo	26		3	·83	12	·41	J.-akhir.	1
	11	Tu	27		4	·76	13	·38		2
	12	We	28		5	·68	14	·34		3
	13	Th	29		6	·59	15	·28		4
	14	Fr	30		7	·49	16	·21		5
	15	Sa	31		8	·39	17	·14		6

Sep.

Solar month	Cyclic Sidereal Year, Month and Day	Week-Day	English Month and Day	Lunar month	Tithi	Tithi Ending Moment	Nakshatra	Nakshatra Ending Moment	Muhammadan month	Muhammadan Day
Kilaka Simha—Avani.	16	Su	1	Bhadrapada Sukla	9	·29	18	·07	H. 1388 Jumadal-akhir.	7
	17	Mo	2		10	·19	19 / 20	·01 / ·95		8
	18	Tu	3		11	·10	21	·90		9
	19	We	4		12 / 13	·02 / ·95	22	·86		10
	20	Th	5		14	·89	23	·84		11
	21	Fr	6		P	·96	24	·84		12
	22	Sa	7	Bahula	1	·84	25	·85		13
	23	Su	8		2	·86	26	·89		14
	24	Mo	9		3	·89	27	·94		15
	25	Tu	10		4	·94	...	...		16
	26	We	11		...	...	1	·01		17
	27	Th	12		5	·00	2	·11		18
	28	Fr	13		6	·08	3	·22		19
	29	Sa	14		7	·17	4	·33		20
	30	Su	15		8	·26	5	·43		21
	31	Mo	16		9	·34	6	·52		22
Kilaka Kanya—Purattasi.	1	Tu	17		10	·40	7	·61		23
	2	We	18		11	·44	8	·68		24
	3	Th	19		12	·46	9	·73		25
	4	Fr	20		13	·47	10	·75		26
	5	Sa	21		14	·45	11	·76		27
	6	Su ●	22		A	·43	12	·74		28
	7	Mo	23	Sukla	1	·37	13	·72		29
	8	Tu	24		2	·30	14	·68		1
	9	We	25		3	·22	15	·62		2
	10	Th	26		4	·13	16	·55		3
	11	Fr	27		5 / 6	·03 / ·93	17	·48		4
	12	Sa	28		7	·83	18	·41		5
	13	Su	29		8	·73	19	·35		6
	14	Mo	30		9	·64	20	·29		7

Oct.

Solar month	Cyclic Sidereal Year, Month and Day	Week-Day	English Month and Day	Lunar month	Tithi	Tithi Ending Moment	Nakshatra	Nakshatra Ending Moment	Muhammadan month	Muhammadan Day
	15	Tu	1	Asvina	10	·56	21	·23	H. 1388 Rajab.	8
	16	We	2		11	·49	22	·19		9
	17	Th	3		12	·44	23	·17		10
	18	Fr	4		13	·41	24	·16		11
	19	Sa	5		14	·40	25	·17		12
	20	Su ○	6		P	·42	26	·20		13
	21	Mo	7	Bahula	1	·44	27	·25		14
	22	Tu	8		2	·49	1	·32		15
	23	We	9		3	·56	2	·41		16
	24	Th	10		4	·64	3	·51		17
	25	Fr	11		5	·73	4	·62		18
	26	Sa	12		6	·82	5	·73		19
	27	Su	13		7	·90	6	·83		20
	28	Mo	14		8	·97	7	·92		21
	29	Tu	15		...	...	8	·99		22
	30	We	16		9	·01	...	...		23
Kilaka Tula—Aippasi.	1	Th	17		10	·03	9	·04		24
	2	Fr	18		11	·04	10	·07		25
	3	Sa	19		12	·02	11	·08		26
	4	Su	20		13 / 14	·00 / ·95	12	·03		27
	5	Mo	21		A	·88	13	·05		28
	6	Tu	22	Karttika Sukla	1	·80	14 / 15	·00 / ·95		29
	7	We	23		2	·70	16	·89		30
	8	Th	24		3	·60	17	·83	H. 1388 Shaban.	1
	9	Fr	25		4	·50	18	·76		2
	10	Sa	26		5	·40	19	·69		3
	11	Su	27		6	·30	20	·62		4
	12	Mo	28		7	·22	21	·57		5
	13	Tu	29		8	·15	22	·53		6
	14	We	30		9	·08	23	·50		7
	15	Th	31		10	·03	24	·48		8

Nov.

Solar month	Cyclic Sidereal Year, Month and Day	Week-Day	English Month and Day	Lunar month	Tithi	Tithi Ending Moment	Nakshatra	Nakshatra Ending Moment	Muhammadan month	Muhammadan Day
Kilaka Tula—Aippasi.	16	Fr	1	Karttika Suk.	11 / 12	·00 / ·99	25	·49	H. 1388 Shaban.	9
	17	Sa	2		...	...	26	·51		10
	18	Su	3		13	·00	27	·56		11
	19	Mo	4		14	·04	1	·63		12
	20	Tu	5		P	·09	2	·72		13
	21	We	6	Bahula	1	·17	3	·82		14
	22	Th	7		2	·25	4	·92		15
	23	Fr	8		3	·33	...	...		16
	24	Sa	9		4	·42	5	·03		17
	25	Su	10		5	·50	6	·13		18
	26	Mo	11		6	·57	7	·22		19
	27	Tu	12		7	·61	8	·30		20
	28	We	13		8	·64	9	·35		21
	29	Th	14		9	·65	10	·39		22
	30	Fr	15		10	·64	11	·41		23
Kilaka Vrischika—Kartigai.	1	Sa	16		11	·60	12	·40		24
	2	Su	17		12	·55	13	·38		25
	3	Mo	18		13	·49	14	·34		26
	4	Tu	19		14	·41	15	·29		27
	5	We	20		A	·32	16	·24		28
	6	Th	21	Sukla	1	·22	17	·17		29
	7	Fr	22		2	·12	18	·10		1
	8	Sa	23		3 / 4	·02 / ·92	19 / 20	·03 / ·96		2
	9	Su	24		5	·84	21	·90		3
	10	Mo	25		6	·76	22	·86		4
	11	Tu	26		7	·70	23	·83		5
	12	We	27		8	·65	24	·81		6
	13	Th	28		9	·63	25	·81		7
	14	Fr	29		10	·63	26	·83		8
	15	Sa	30		11	·64	27	·88		9

Dec.

Solar month	Cyclic Sidereal Year, Month and Day	Week-Day	English Month and Day	Lunar month	Tithi	Tithi Ending Moment	Nakshatra	Nakshatra Ending Moment	Muhammadan month	Muhammadan Day
	16	Su	1	Margasira	12	·67	1	·94	H. 1388 Ramzan.	10
	17	Mo	2		13	·72	...	...		11
	18	Tu	3		14	·80	2	·02		12
	19	We	4		P	·89	3	·11		13
	20	Th	5	Bahula	1	·98	4	·22		14
	21	Fr	6		...	...	5	·33		15
	22	Sa	7		2	·06	6	·43		16
	23	Su	8		3	·14	7	·53		17
	24	Mo	9		4	·21	8	·61		18
	25	Tu	10		5	·25	9	·67		19
	26	We	11		6	·28	10	·71		20
	27	Th	12		7	·28	11	·73		21
	28	Fr	13		8	·27	12	·73		22
	29	Sa	14		9	·24	13	·71		23
Kilaka Dhanus—Margali.	1	Su	15		10	·18	14	·67		24
	2	Mo	16		11	·11	15	·62		25
	3	Tu	17		12 / 13	·03 / ·94	16	·57		26
	4	We	18		14	·84	17	·51		27
	5	Th	19		A	·74	18	·44		28
	6	Fr	20	Pausha Sukla	1	·64	19	·37		29
	7	Sa	21		2	·55	20	·31		30
	8	Su	22		3	·47	21	·25	H. 1388 Shawwal.	1
	9	Mo	23		4	·40	22	·20		2
	10	Tu	24		5	·34	23	·16		3
	11	We	25		6	·29	24	·13		4
	12	Th	26		7	·27	25	·13		5
	13	Fr	27		8	·27	26	·15		6
	14	Sa	28		9	·28	27	·19		7
	15	Su	29		10	·32	1	·24		8
	16	Mo	30		11	·38	2	·32		9
	17	Tu	31		12	·45	3	·41		10

15. Svati. 16. Visak. 17. Anur. 18. Jyesh. 19. Mula. 20. P. Ash. 21. U. Ash. 22. Sravn. 23. Dani. 24. Satab. 25. P. Bhad. 26. U. Bhad. 27. Rev.

A. D. 1969. **Mesha Sankranti** (Commencement of Indian Sidereal Year).

Solar Eclipse. ● **(Surya Sid.) April 13·47.** **Saka 1891.** **Kaliyuga 5070.**

Lunar Eclipse. ○ **(Arya Sid.) April 13·36.** **(S. Cycle) Saumya.**

SOLAR reckoning: Cyclic Sidereal Year, Month and Day; Week-Day, English Month and Day. LUNAR reckoning: Tithi Ending Moment; Nakshatra Ending Moment; Muhammadan Year, Month and Day.

Jan.

Solar: **Kilaka** *Dhanus—Margali* (18–30); **Kilaka** *Makara—Tai* (1–18). Lunar: **Pausha** *Bahula*, *Sukla*. Muhammadan: H. 1388 *Shawwal*.

Cyclic Sidereal Year, Month and Day	Week-Day	English Day	Tithi Ending Moment	Nakshatra Ending Moment	Muhammadan Year, Month and Day
18	We	1	13 ·53	4 ·52	11
19	Th	2	14 ·62	5 ·63	12
20	Fr	3	P ·71	6 ·73	13
21	Sa	4	1 ·79	7 ·83	14
22	Su	5	2 ·85	8 ·92	15
23	Mo	6	3 ·90	9 ·99	16
24	Tu	7	4 ·93	... ...	17
25	We	8	5 ·93	10 ·03	18
26	Th	9	6 ·92	11 ·05	19
27	Fr	10	7 ·88	12 ·05	20
28	Sa	11	8 ·82	13 ·04	21
29	Su	12	9 ·76	14 ·01 15 ·97	22
—30	Mo	13	10 ·68	16 ·91	23
1	Tu	14	11 ·59	17 ·84	24
2	We	15	12 ·49	18 ·77	25
3	Th	16	13 ·39	19 ·70	26
4	Fr	17	14 ·29	20 ·64	27
5	Sa	18	—A ·20	21 ·58	28
6	Su	19	1 ·12	22 ·53	—29
7	Mo	20	2 ·05 3 ·98	23 ·49	1
8	Tu	21	4 ·94	24 ·46	2
9	We	22	5 ·92	25 ·46	3
10	Th	23	6 ·91	26 47	4
11	Fr	24	7 ·93	27 ·50	5
12	Sa	25	8 ·98	1 ·55	6
13	Su	26	... ...	2 ·62	7
14	Mo	27	9 ·04	3 ·72	8
15	Tu	28	10 ·12	4 ·82	9
16	We	29	11 ·20	5 ·93	10
17	Th	30	12 ·28	... ...	11
18	Fr	31	13 ·36	6 ·03	12

Feb.

Solar: **Kilaka** *Makara—Tai* (19–29); **Kilaka** *Kumbha—Masi* (1–17). Lunar: **Magha** *Bahula*; *Sukla* **Phalguna**. Muhammadan: H. 1388 *Zi-l-ka'da*; H. 1388 *Zi-l-hijja*.

Cyclic Sidereal Year, Month and Day	Week-Day	English Day	Tithi Ending Moment	Nakshatra Ending Moment	Muhammadan Year, Month and Day
19	Sa	1	14 ·44	7 ·13	13
20	Su	2	P ·50	8 ·22	14
21	Mo	3	1 ·55	9 ·29	15
22	Tu	4	2 ·57	10 ·34	16
23	We	5	3 ·57	11 ·87	17
24	Th	6	4 ·55	12 ·38	18
25	Fr	7	5 ·51	13 ·37	19
26	Sa	8	6 ·45	14 ·35	20
27	Su	9	7 ·38	15 ·30	21
28	Mo	10	8 ·30	16 ·24	22
—29	Tu	11	9 ·21	17 ·18	23
1	We	12	10 ·12	18 ·12	24
2	Th	13	11 ·02 12 ·92	19 ·05 20 ·98	25
3	Fr	14	13 ·83	21 ·92	26
4	Sa	15	14 ·74	22 ·86	27
5	Su	16	—A ·67	23 ·82	28
6	Mo	17	1 ·61	24 ·80	29
7	Tu	18	2 ·57	25 ·78	—30
8	We	19	3 ·54	26 ·79	1
9	Th	20	4 ·54	27 ·81	2
10	Fr	21	5 ·56	1 ·86	3
11	Sa	22	6 ·60	2 ·94	4
12	Su	23	7 ·66	... ...	5
13	Mo	24	8 ·73	3 ·03	6
14	Tu	25	9 ·81	4 ·13	7
15	We	26	10 ·90	5 ·23	8
16	Th	27	11 ·99	6 ·33	9
17	Fr	28	... ...	7 ·43	10

March

Solar: **Kilaka** *Kumbha—Masi* (18–30); **Kilaka** *Mina—Panguni* (1–18). Lunar: *Suk.* **Phalguna** *Bahula*; *Sukla*. Muhammadan: H. 1388 *Zi-l-hijja*.

Cyclic Sidereal Year, Month and Day	Week-Day	English Day	Tithi Ending Moment	Nakshatra Ending Moment	Muhammadan Year, Month and Day
18	Sa	1	12 ·07	8 ·52	11
19	Su	2	13 ·13	9 ·60	12
20	Mo	3	14 ·17	10 ·66	13
21	Tu	4	P ·18	11 ·69	14
22	We	5	1 ·18	12 ·70	15
23	Th	6	2 ·15	13 ·70	16
24	Fr	7	3 ·11	14 ·68	17
25	Sa	8	4 ·06	15 ·64	18
26	Su	9	5 ·00 6 ·92	16 ·58	19
27	Mo	10	7 ·82	17 ·52	20
28	Tu	11	8 ·72	18 ·46	21
29	We	12	9 ·62	19 ·39	22
—30	Th	13	10 ·52	20 ·32	23
1	Fr	14	11 ·42	21 ·23	24
2	Sa	15	12 ·34	22 ·20	25
3	Su	16	13 ·23	23 ·16	26
4	Mo	17	14 ·20	24 ·13	27
5	Tu	● 18	—A ·16	25 ·11	28
6	We	19	1 ·14	26 ·11	—29
7	Th	20	2 ·14	27 ·13	1
8	Fr	21	3 ·16	1 ·17	2
9	Sa	22	4 ·20	2 ·24	3
10	Su	23	5 ·26	3 ·32	4
11	Mo	24	6 ·33	4 ·42	5
12	Tu	25	7 ·41	5 ·52	6
13	We	26	8 ·49	6 ·63	7
14	Th	27	9 ·57	7 ·74	8
15	Fr	28	10 ·64	8 ·83	9
16	Sa	29	11 ·71	9 ·91	10
17	Su	30	12 ·75	10 ·97	11
18	Mo	31	13 ·77	... ...	12

April

Solar: **Kilaka** *Mina—Panguni* (19–30); **Saumya** *Mesha—Chittirai* (1–18). Lunar: **Chaitra** *Bahula*; *Sukla* **Vaisakha**. Muhammadan: H. 1389 *Muharram*; H. 1389 *Safar*.

Cyclic Sidereal Year, Month and Day	Week-Day	English Day	Tithi Ending Moment	Nakshatra Ending Moment	Muhammadan Year, Month and Day
19	Tu	1	14 ·76	11 ·01	13
20	We	2	P ·74	12 ·03	14
21	Th	3	1 ·69	13 ·03	15
22	Fr	4	2 ·63	14 ·01 15 ·97	16
23	Sa	5	3 ·56	16 ·92	17
24	Su	6	4 ·48	17 ·87	18
25	Mo	7	5 ·39	18 ·80	19
26	Tu	8	6 ·29	19 ·73	20
27	We	9	7 ·18	20 ·66	21
28	Th	10	8 ·08 9 ·98	21 ·60	22
29	Fr	11	10 ·90	22 ·54	23
—30	Sa	12	11 ·82	23 ·49	24
1	Su	13	12 ·76	24 ·45	25
2	Mo	14	13 ·72	25 ·43	26
3	Tu	15	14 ·70	26 ·43	27
4	We	16	—A ·69	27 ·45	28
5	Th	17	1 ·71	1 ·49	29
6	Fr	18	2 ·75	2 ·55	—30
7	Sa	19	3 ·80	3 ·63	1
8	Su	20	4 ·86	4 ·72	2
9	Mo	21	5 ·94	5 ·82	3
10	Tu	22	... ...	6 ·93	4
11	We	23	6 ·04	... ...	5
12	Th	24	7 ·12	7 ·04	6
13	Fr	25	8 ·19	8 ·14	7
14	Sa	26	9 ·25	9 ·22	8
15	Su	27	10 ·29	10 ·28	9
16	Mo	28	11 ·31	11 ·33	10
17	Tu	29	12 ·30	12 ·35	11
18	We	30	13 ·28	13 ·35	12

May

Solar: **Saumya** *Mesha—Chittirai* (19–31); **Saumya** *Vrishabha—Vaikasi* (1–18). Lunar: *Suk.* **Vaisakha** *Bahula*; *Sukla* **Jyeshtha**. Muhammadan: H. 1389 *Safar*; *Rabi-ul-awwal*.

Cyclic Sidereal Year, Month and Day	Week-Day	English Day	Tithi Ending Moment	Nakshatra Ending Moment	Muhammadan Year, Month and Day
19	Th	1	14 ·23	14 ·33	13
20	Fr	2	P ·17	15 ·30	14
21	Sa	3	1 ·10	16 ·26	15
22	Su	4	2 ·02 3 ·92	17 ·20	16
23	Mo	5	4 ·82	18 ·14	17
24	Tu	6	5 ·72	19 ·07	18
25	We	7	6 ·62	20 ·00 21 ·94	19
26	Th	8	7 ·52	22 ·88	20
27	Fr	9	8 ·43	23 ·82	21
28	Sa	10	9 ·35	24 ·78	22
29	Su	11	10 ·29	25 ·76	23
30	Mo	12	11 ·24	26 ·75	24
—31	Tu	13	12 ·22	27 ·77	25
1	We	14	13 ·21	1 ·80	26
2	Th	15	14 ·22	2 ·86	27
3	Fr	16	—A ·26	3 ·93	28
4	Sa	17	1 ·31	... ...	—29
5	Su	18	2 ·38	4 ·02	1
6	Mo	19	3 ·46	5 ·13	2
7	Tu	20	4 ·54	6 ·23	3
8	We	21	5 ·32	7 ·34	4
9	Th	22	6 ·70	8 ·44	5
10	Fr	23	7 ·76	9 ·52	6
11	Sa	24	8 ·79	10 ·60	7
12	Su	25	9 ·81	11 ·65	8
13	Mo	26	10 ·80	12 ·67	9
14	Tu	27	11 ·78	13 ·68	10
15	We	28	12 ·74	14 ·66	11
16	Th	29	13 ·68	15 ·64	12
17	Fr	30	14 ·60	16 ·60	13
18	Sa	31	P ·51	17 ·54	14

June

Solar: **Saumya** *Vrishabha—Vaikasi* (19–32); **Saumya** *Mithuna—Ani* (1–16). Lunar: *Bahula*; *Sukla* **Adhika Ashadha**. Muhammadan: H. 1389; H. 1389 *Rabi-ul-akhir*.

Cyclic Sidereal Year, Month and Day	Week-Day	English Day	Tithi Ending Moment	Nakshatra Ending Moment	Muhammadan Year, Month and Day
19	Su	1	1 ·41	18 ·48	15
20	Mo	2	2 ·31	19 ·41	16
21	Tu	3	3 ·21	20 ·34	17
22	We	4	4 ·11	21 ·28	18
23	Th	5	5 ·01 6 ·93	22 ·22	19
24	Fr	6	7 ·85	23 ·16	20
25	Sa	7	8 ·78	24 ·11	21
26	Su	8	9 ·73	25 ·08	22
27	Mo	9	10 ·71	26 ·08	23
28	Tu	10	11 ·69	27 ·09	24
29	We	11	12 ·71	1 ·12	25
30	Th	12	13 ·74	2 ·17	26
31	Fr	13	14 ·80	3 ·24	27
—32	Sa	14	—A ·87	4 ·33	28
1	Su	15	1 ·94	5 ·43	29
2	Mo	16	... ...	6 ·53	—30
3	Tu	17	2 ·02	7 ·64	1
4	We	18	3 ·10	8 ·74	2
5	Th	19	4 ·17	9 ·84	3
6	Fr	20	5 ·23	10 ·91	4
7	Sa	21	6 ·27	11 ·96	5
8	Su	22	7 ·29	12 ·99	6
9	Mo	23	8 ·29	... ...	7
10	Tu	24	9 ·27	13 ·00 14 ·99	8
11	We	25	10 ·22	15 ·97	9
12	Th	26	11 ·16	16 ·93	10
13	Fr	27	12 ·09	17 ·87	11
14	Sa	28	13 ·00 14 ·90	18 ·80	12
15	Su	29	P ·80	19 ·75	13
16	Mo	30	1 ·70	20 ·68	14

Naksh:—1. Asvn. 2. Bhar. 3. Krit. 4. Rohi. 5. Mrig. 6. Ardh. 7. Punar. 8. Push. 9. Aslesh. 10. Magh. 11. P. Phal. 12. U. Phal. 13. Hasta. 14. Chit.

A. D. 1969.
A.—Amavasya.
P.—Paurnami.

Kollam 1145, { N. Malabar—Sept. / S. Malabar—Aug. } Commences

Hijra 1389, Commences, March 20.

Vikrama 2026.
Bengal San 1375.
(N. Cycle) Dundubhi.

July — Solar: Saumya, Mithuna—Ani.; Saumya, Karkata—Adi. Lunar: Adhika Ashadha (Bahula, Sukla); Nija—Ashadha. Muhammadan: H. 1389 Rabi-ul-akhir.; H. 1389 Jumadal-awwal.

SOLAR reckoning: Cyclic Sidereal Year, Month and Day	Week-Day English Month and Day		LUNAR reckoning: Tithi Ending Moment		Nakshatra Ending Moment		Muhammadan Year, Month and Day
17	Tu	1	2	·60	21	·61	15
18	We	2	3	·50	22	·55	16
19	Th	3	4	·41	23	·49	17
20	Fr	4	5	·33	24	·44	18
21	Sa	5	6	·26	25	·42	19
22	Su	6	7	·21	26	·41	20
23	Mo	7	8	·18	27	·41	21
24	Tu	8	9	·18	1	·43	22
25	We	9	10	·19	2	·47	23
26	Th	10	11	·22	3	·54	24
27	Fr	11	12	·27	4	·63	25
28	Sa	12	13	·34	5	·73	26
29	Su	13	14	·41	6	·83	27
30	Mo	14	—A	·49	7	·94	28
—31	Tu	15	1	·58	...	...	—29
1	We	16	2	·65	8	·04	1
2	Th	17	3	·70	9	·14	2
3	Fr	18	4	·74	10	·22	3
4	Sa	19	5	·77	11	·27	4
5	Su	20	6	·77	12	·30	5
6	Mo	21	7	·74	13	·32	6
7	Tu	22	8	·70	14	·33	7
8	We	23	9	·64	15	·30	8
9	Th	24	10	·57	16	·26	9
10	Fr	25	11	·49	17	·21	10
11	Sa	26	12	·39	18	·15	11
12	Su	27	13	·29	19	·09	12
13	Mo	28	14	·19	20; 21	·02; ·95	13
14	Tu	29	P; 1	·09; ·99	22	·89	14
15	We	30	2	·89	23	·83	15
16	Th	31	3	·81	24	·79	16

Aug. — Solar: Saumya, Simha—Avani. Lunar: Bahula; Sukla; Sravana; Bah. Muhammadan: H. 1389 Jumadal-akhir.

SOLAR reckoning: Cyclic Sidereal Year, Month and Day	Week-Day English Month and Day		LUNAR reckoning: Tithi Ending Moment		Nakshatra Ending Moment		Muhammadan Year, Month and Day
17	Fr	1	4	·74	25	·75	17
18	Sa	2	5	·70	26	·73	18
19	Su	3	6	·67	27	·73	19
20	Mo	4	7	·66	1	·75	20
21	Tu	5	8	·66	2	·79	21
22	We	6	9	·69	3	·85	22
23	Th	7	10	·74	4	·93	23
24	Fr	8	11	·81	...	...	24
25	Sa	9	12	·89	5	·03	25
26	Su	10	13	·98	6	·13	26
27	Mo	11	...	...	7	·23	27
28	Tu	12	14	·06	8	·34	28
29	We	13	—A	·13	9	·44	29
30	Th	14	1	·19	10	·52	—30
31	Fr	15	2	·23	11	·58	1
—32	Sa	16	3	·26	12	·62	2
1	Su	17	4	·26	13	·65	3
2	Mo	18	5	·23	14	·65	4
3	Tu	19	6	·19	15	·63	5
4	We	20	7	·14	16	·60	6
5	Th	21	8; 9	·07; ·99	17	·55	7
6	Fr	22	10	·89	18	·50	8
7	Sa	23	11	·79	19	·43	9
8	Su	24	12	·69	20	·36	10
9	Mo	25	13	·59	21	·29	11
10	Tu	26	14	·49	22	·22	12
11	We	27	P	·40	23	·17	13
12	Th	28	1	·32	24	·12	14
13	Fr	29	2	·25	25	·08	15
14	Sa	30	3	·20	26	·06	16
15	Su	31	4	·17	27	·05	17

Sep. — Solar: Saumya, Simha—Avani.; Saumya, Kanya—Purattasi. Lunar: Sravana (Bahula); Sukla; Bhadrapada. Muhammadan: H. 1389 Jumadal-akhir.; H. 1389 Rajab.

SOLAR reckoning: Cyclic Sidereal Year, Month and Day	Week-Day English Month and Day		LUNAR reckoning: Tithi Ending Moment		Nakshatra Ending Moment		Muhammadan Year, Month and Day
16	Mo	1	5	·17	1	·07	18
17	Tu	2	6	·18	2	·11	19
18	We	3	7	·21	3	·16	20
19	Th	4	8	·26	4	·23	21
20	Fr	5	9	·32	5	·32	22
21	Sa	6	10	·39	6	·43	23
22	Su	7	11	·48	7	·54	24
23	Mo	8	12	·57	8	·65	25
24	Tu	9	13	·65	9	·75	26
25	We	10	14	·71	10	·83	27
26	Th	11	—A	·75	11	·89	28
27	Fr	12	1	·78	12	·94	—29
28	Sa	13	2	·78	13	·97	1
29	Su	14	3	·76	14	·98	2
30	Mo	15	4	·72	15	·96	3
—31	Tu	16	5	·67	16	·93	4
1	We	17	6	·60	17	·89	5
2	Th	18	7	·51	18	·84	6
3	Fr	19	8	·42	19	·77	7
4	Sa	20	9	·32	20	·70	8
5	Su	21	10	·22	21	·63	9
6	Mo	22	11	·12	22	·57	10
7	Tu	23	12; 13	·02; ·93	23	·51	11
8	We	24	14	·86	24	·45	12
9	Th	25	P	·80	25	·41	13
10	Fr	26	1	·75	26	·38	14
11	Sa	27	2	·72	27	·37	15
12	Su	28	3	·71	1	·39	16
13	Mo	29	4	·72	2	·42	17
14	Tu	30	5	·75	3	·47	18

Oct. — Solar: Saumya, Tula—Aippasi. Lunar: Bahula; Sukla; Asvina; Bahula. Muhammadan: H. 1389 Shaban.

SOLAR reckoning: Cyclic Sidereal Year, Month and Day	Week-Day English Month and Day		LUNAR reckoning: Tithi Ending Moment		Nakshatra Ending Moment		Muhammadan Year, Month and Day
15	We	1	6	·80	4	·54	19
16	Th	2	7	·87	5	·63	20
17	Fr	3	8	·93	6	·73	21
18	Sa	4	...	...	7	·84	22
19	Su	5	9	·04	8	·95	23
20	Mo	6	10	·12	...	...	24
21	Tu	7	11	·20	9	·05	25
22	We	8	12	·26	10	·14	26
23	Th	9	13	·31	11	·21	27
24	Fr	10	14	·35	12	·26	28
25	Sa	11	—A	·34	13	·29	29
26	Su	12	1	·32	14	·30	—30
27	Mo	13	2	·28	15	·29	1
28	Tu	14	3	·23	16	·27	2
29	We	15	4	·16	17	·23	3
—30	Th	16	5; 6	·08; ·99	18	·17	4
1	Fr	17	7	·89	19	·11	5
2	Sa	18	8	·79	20; 21	·04; ·97	6
3	Su	19	9	·69	22	·91	7
4	Mo	20	10	·59	23	·85	8
5	Tu	21	11	·50	24	·79	9
6	We	22	12	·43	25	·74	10
7	Th	23	13	·37	26	·71	11
8	Fr	24	14	·32	27	·70	12
9	Sa	25	P	·30	1	·71	13
10	Su	26	1	·29	2	·73	14
11	Mo	27	2	·30	3	·77	15
12	Tu	28	3	·34	4	·84	16
13	We	29	4	·40	5	·93	17
14	Th	30	5	·47	...	...	18
15	Fr	31	6	·55	6	·03	19

Nov. — Solar: Saumya, Tula—Aippasi.; Saumya, Vrischika—Kartigai. Lunar: Asvina (Bahula); Sukla; Karttika. Muhammadan: H. 1389 Shaban.; H. 1389 Ramzan.

SOLAR reckoning: Cyclic Sidereal Year, Month and Day	Week-Day English Month and Day		LUNAR reckoning: Tithi Ending Moment		Nakshatra Ending Moment		Muhammadan Year, Month and Day
16	Sa	1	7	·63	7	·14	20
17	Su	2	8	·72	8	·25	21
18	Mo	3	9	·80	9	·35	22
19	Tu	4	10	·86	10	·45	23
20	We	5	11	·91	11	·52	24
21	Th	6	12	·94	12	·57	25
22	Fr	7	13	·94	13	·61	26
23	Sa	8	14	·92	14	·62	27
24	Su	9	—A	·88	15	·62	28
25	Mo	10	1	·83	16	·60	—29
26	Tu	11	2	·76	17	·56	1
27	We	12	3	·68	18	·51	2
28	Th	13	4	·59	19	·45	3
29	Fr	14	5	·50	20	·39	4
—30	Sa	15	6	·40	21	·32	5
1	Su	16	7	·30	22	·25	6
2	Mo	17	8	·20	23	·18	7
3	Tu	18	9	·12	24	·12	8
4	We	19	10; 11	·05; ·98	25	·07	9
5	Th	20	12	·94	26	·05	10
6	Fr	21	13	·92	27	·03	11
7	Sa	22	14	·91	1	·03	12
8	Su	23	P	·93	2	·05	13
9	Mo	24	1	·96	3	·09	14
10	Tu	25	...	...	4	·17	15
11	We	26	2	·02	5	·24	16
12	Th	27	3	·09	6	·33	17
13	Fr	28	4	·17	7	·44	18
14	Sa	29	5	·26	8	·55	19
15	Su	30	6	·35	9	·66	20

Dec. — Solar: Saumya, Dhanus—Margali. Lunar: Bahula; Sukla; Margasira; Bahula. Muhammadan: H. 1389 Shawwal.

SOLAR reckoning: Cyclic Sidereal Year, Month and Day	Week-Day English Month and Day		LUNAR reckoning: Tithi Ending Moment		Nakshatra Ending Moment		Muhammadan Year, Month and Day
16	Mo	1	7	·43	10	·75	21
17	Tu	2	8	·49	11	·83	22
18	We	3	9	·54	12	·89	23
19	Th	4	10	·57	13	·92	24
20	Fr	5	11	·57	14	·94	25
21	Sa	6	12	·55	15	·95	26
22	Su	7	13	·52	16	·93	27
23	Mo	8	14	·46	17	·89	28
24	Tu	9	—A	·39	18	·84	29
25	We	10	1	·31	19	·78	—30
26	Th	11	2	·22	20	·72	1
27	Fr	12	3	·13	21	·66	2
28	Sa	13	4; 5	·03; ·93	22	·59	3
29	Su	14	6	·83	23	·52	4
—30	Mo	15	7	·75	24	·46	5
1	Tu	16	8	·68	25	·41	6
2	We	17	9	·62	26	·38	7
3	Th	18	10	·58	27	·35	8
4	Fr	19	11	·55	1	·35	9
5	Sa	20	12	·56	2	·37	10
6	Su	21	13	·58	3	·41	11
7	Mo	22	14	·61	4	·47	12
8	Tu	23	P	·66	5	·54	13
9	We	24	1	·74	6	·63	14
10	Th	25	2	·83	7	·73	15
11	Fr	26	3	·92	8	·84	16
12	Sa	27	...	...	9	·95	17
13	Su	28	4	·01	...	...	18
14	Mo	29	5	·09	10	·05	19
15	Tu	30	6	·15	11	·13	20
16	We	31	7	·19	12	·20	21

15. Svati. 16. Visak. 17. Anur. 18. Jyesh. 19. Mula. 20. P. Ash. 21. U. Ash. 22. Sravn. 23. Dani. 24. Satab. 25. P. Bhad. 26. U. Bhad. 27. Rev.

A. D. 1970. **Mesha Sankranti** (Commencement of Indian Sidereal Year).
Solar Eclipse. ● **(Surya Sid.) April 13·73.** **Saka 1892.** **Kaliyuga 5071.**
Lunar Eclipse. ○ **(Arya Sid.) April 13·62.** **(S. Cycle) Sadharana.**

SOLAR reckoning: Cyclic Sidereal Year, Month and Day; Week-Day English Month and Day. LUNAR reckoning: Tithi Ending Moment; Nakshatra Ending Moment; Muhammadan Year, Month and Day.

Jan. (Solar: Saumya Dhanus—Margali to 29; Saumya Makara—Tai from 1. Lunar: Mr. Bah. to A; Pausha Sukla from 1, Bahula from P. Muhammadan: H. 1389 Shawwal to 29; H. 1389 Zi-l-ka'da from 1.)

Cyclic Sidereal Year, Month and Day	Week-Day English Month and Day	Tithi Ending Moment	Nakshatra Ending Moment	Muhammadan Year, Month and Day
17	Th 1	8 ·21	13 ·24	22
18	Fr 2	9 ·21	14 ·27	23
19	Sa 3	10 ·19	15 ·27	24
20	Su 4	11 ·16	16 ·26	25
21	Mo 5	12 ·10	17 ·23	26
22	Tu 6	13 ·08 14 ·95	18 ·18	27
23	We 7	—A ·87	19 ·13	28
24	Th 8	1 ·77	20 ·06 21 ·99	—29
25	Fr 9	2 ·67	22 ·92	1
26	Sa 10	3 ·57	23 ·85	2
27	Su 11	4 ·48	24 ·80	3
28	Mo 12	5 ·40	25 ·75	4
—29	Tu 13	6 ·33	26 ·71	5
1	We 14	7 ·27	27 ·68	6
2	Th 15	8 ·22	1 ·67	7
3	Fr 16	9 ·20	2 ·69	8
4	Sa 17	10 ·20	3 ·72	9
5	Su 18	11 ·22	4 ·77	10
6	Mo 19	12 ·26	5 ·84	11
7	Tu 20	13 ·32	6 ·93	12
8	We 21	14 ·40	... ...	13
9	Th 22	P ·48	7 ·03	14
10	Fr 23	1 ·57	8 ·14	15
11	Sa 24	2 ·66	9 ·25	16
12	Su 25	3 ·73	10 ·35	17
13	Mo 26	4 ·79	11 ·44	18
14	Tu 27	5 ·83	12 ·51	19
15	We 28	6 ·86	13 ·56	20
16	Th 29	7 ·85	14 ·59	21
17	Fr 30	8 ·84	15 ·60	22
18	Sa 31	9 ·80	16 ·59	23

Feb. (Solar: Saumya Kumbha—Masi from 1. Lunar: Magha Sukla from 1, Bahula from P. Muhammadan: H. 1389 Zi-l-hijja from 1.)

Cyclic Sidereal Year, Month and Day	Week-Day English Month and Day	Tithi Ending Moment	Nakshatra Ending Moment	Muhammadan Year, Month and Day
19	Su 1	10 ·74	17 ·56	24
20	Mo 2	11 ·66	18 ·52	25
21	Tu 3	12 ·58	19 ·47	26
22	We 4	13 ·49	20 ·40	27
23	Th 5	14 ·40	21 ·33	28
24	Fr 6	—A ·30	22 ·26	29
25	Sa 7	1 ·20	23 ·20	—30
26	Su 8	2 ·10	24 ·14	1
27	Mo 9	3 ·02 4 ·95	25 ·08	2
28	Tu 10	5 ·90	26 ·04	3
—29	We 11	6 ·86	27 ·01 1 ·99	4
1	Th 12	7 ·84	... ...	5
2	Fr 13	8 ·83	2 ·01	6
3	Sa 14	9 ·85	3 ·03	7
4	Su 15	10 ·90	4 ·08	8
5	Mo 16	11 ·96	5 ·15	9
6	Tu 17	... ...	6 ·24	10
7	We 18	12 ·03	7 ·34	11
8	Th 19	13 ·11	8 ·45	12
9	Fr 20	14 ·20	9 ·55	13
10	Sa ○ 21	P ·28	10 ·65	14
11	Su 22	1 ·36	11 ·74	15
12	Mo 23	2 ·42	12 ·82	16
13	Tu 24	3 ·46	13 ·88	17
14	We 25	4 ·48	14 ·91	18
15	Th 26	5 ·47	15 ·92	19
16	Fr 27	6 ·45	16 ·91	20
17	Sa 28	7 ·41	17 ·90	21

March (Solar: Saumya Kumbha—Masi to 30; Saumya Mina—Panguni from 1. Lunar: Mg. Bah. to A; Phalguna Sukla from 1, Bahula from P. Muhammadan: H. 1389 Zi-l-hijja to 29; H. 1390 Muharram from 1.)

Cyclic Sidereal Year, Month and Day	Week-Day English Month and Day	Tithi Ending Moment	Nakshatra Ending Moment	Muhammadan Year, Month and Day
18	Su 1	8 ·36	18 ·86	22
19	Mo 2	9 ·23	19 ·80	23
20	Tu 3	10 ·19	20 ·74	24
21	We 4	11 ·10	21 ·63	25
22	Th 5	12 ·01 13 ·91	22 ·61	26
23	Fr 6	14 ·81	23 ·54	27
24	Sa 7	—A ·72	24 ·47	28
25	Su 8	1 ·63	25 ·42	—29
26	Mo 9	2 ·55	26 ·37	1
27	Tu 10	3 ·50	27 ·34	2
28	We 11	4 ·46	1 ·34	3
29	Th 12	5 ·44	2 ·33	4
—30	Fr 13	6 ·43	3 ·35	5
1	Sa 14	7 ·46	4 ·39	6
2	Su 15	8 ·50	5 ·45	7
3	Mo 16	9 ·56	6 ·54	8
4	Tu 17	10 ·63	7 ·64	9
5	We 18	11 ·71	8 ·74	10
6	Th 19	12 ·81	9 ·85	11
7	Fr 20	13 ·89	10 ·95	12
8	Sa 21	14 ·96	... ...	13
9	Su 22	... ...	11 ·05	14
10	Mo 23	P ·02	12 ·13	15
11	Tu 24	1 ·06	13 ·19	16
12	We 25	2 ·07	14 ·23	17
13	Th 26	3 ·06	15 ·24	18
14	Fr 27	4 ·04 5 ·99	16 ·25	19
15	Sa 28	6 ·94	17 ·23	20
16	Su 29	7 ·87	18 ·19	21
17	Mo 30	8 ·78	19 ·14	22
18	Tu 31	9 ·68	20 ·08	23

April (Solar: Sadharana Mesha—Chittirai from 1. Lunar: Chaitra Sukla from 1, Bahula from P. Muhammadan: H. 1390 Safar from 1.)

Cyclic Sidereal Year, Month and Day	Week-Day English Month and Day	Tithi Ending Moment	Nakshatra Ending Moment	Muhammadan Year, Month and Day
19	We 1	10 ·58	21 ·02 22 ·95	24
20	Th 2	11 ·48	23 ·88	25
21	Fr 3	12 ·38	24 ·81	26
22	Sa 4	13 ·29	25 ·75	27
23	Su 5	14 ·20	26 ·70	28
24	Mo 6	—A ·13	27 ·67	29
25	Tu 7	1 ·07	1 ·65	—30
26	We 8	2 ·03	2 ·65	1
27	Th 9	3 ·00 4 ·99	3 ·66	2
28	Fr 10	... ...	4 ·70	3
29	Sa 11	5 ·02	5 ·77	4
30	Su 12	6 ·06	6 ·85	5
—31	Mo 13	7 ·12	7 ·94	6
1	Tu 14	8 ·19	... ...	7
2	We 15	9 ·28	8 ·04	8
3	Th 16	10 ·36	9 ·15	9
4	Fr 17	11 ·44	10 ·23	10
5	Sa 18	12 ·51	11 ·36	11
6	Su 19	13 ·57	12 ·44	12
7	Mo 20	14 ·61	13 ·50	13
8	Tu 21	P ·62	14 ·54	14
9	We 22	1 ·61	15 ·57	15
10	Th 23	2 ·59	16 ·57	16
11	Fr 24	3 ·54	17 ·56	17
12	Sa 25	4 ·48	18 ·52	18
13	Su 26	5 ·40	19 ·47	19
14	Mo 27	6 ·32	20 ·41	20
15	Tu 28	7 ·22	21 ·35	21
16	We 29	8 ·12	22 ·29	22
17	Th 30	9 ·02 10 ·92	23 ·22	23

May (Solar: Sadharana Mesha—Chittirai to 31; Sadharana Vrishabha—Vaikasi from 1. Lunar: Ch. Bah. to A; Vaisakha Sukla from 1, Bahula from P. Muhammadan: H. 1390 Safar to 29; H. 1390 Rabi-ul-awwal from 1.)

Cyclic Sidereal Year, Month and Day	Week-Day English Month and Day	Tithi Ending Moment	Nakshatra Ending Moment	Muhammadan Year, Month and Day
18	Fr 1	11 ·82	24 ·15	24
19	Sa 2	12 ·73	25 ·09	25
20	Su 3	13 ·35	26 ·04	26
21	Mo 4	14 ·59	27 ·00 1 ·93	27
22	Tu 5	—A ·55	2 ·97	28
23	We 6	1 ·53	3 ·98	—29
24	Th 7	2 ·53	... ...	1
25	Fr 8	3 ·55	4 ·02	2
26	Sa 9	4 ·58	5 ·08	3
27	Su 10	5 ·64	6 ·15	4
28	Mo 11	6 ·71	7 ·24	5
29	Tu 12	7 ·79	8 ·34	6
30	We 13	8 ·87	9 ·45	7
—31	Th 14	9 ·95	10 ·56	8
1	Fr 15	... ...	11 ·66	9
2	Sa 16	10 ·02	12 ·74	10
3	Su 17	11 ·08	13 ·81	11
4	Mo 18	12 ·12	14 ·86	12
5	Tu 19	13 ·13	15 ·89	13
6	We 20	14 ·13	16 ·90	14
7	Th 21	P ·10	17 ·88	15
8	Fr 22	1 ·05 2 ·99	18 ·85	16
9	Sa 23	3 ·92	19 ·81	17
10	Su 24	4 ·83	20 ·76	18
11	Mo 25	5 ·73	21 ·70	19
12	Tu 26	6 ·63	22 ·63	20
13	We 27	7 ·53	23 ·56	21
14	Th 28	8 ·43	24 ·49	22
15	Fr 29	9 ·33	25 ·43	23
16	Sa 30	10 ·24	26 ·38	24
17	Su 31	11 ·16	27 ·33	25

June (Solar: Sadharana Mithuna—Ani from 1. Lunar: Jyeshtha Sukla from 1, Bahula from P. Muhammadan: H. 1390 Rabi-ul-akhir from 1.)

Cyclic Sidereal Year, Month and Day	Week-Day English Month and Day	Tithi Ending Moment	Nakshatra Ending Moment	Muhammadan Year, Month and Day
18	Mo 1	12 ·10	1 ·30	26
19	Tu 2	13 ·06	2 ·29	27
20	We 3	14 ·03	3 ·31	28
21	Th 4	—A ·02	4 ·31	29
22	Fr 5	1 ·03	5 ·39	—30
23	Sa 6	2 ·07	6 ·45	1
24	Su 7	3 ·13	7 ·54	2
25	Mo 8	4 ·20	8 ·64	3
26	Tu 9	5 ·28	9 ·75	4
27	We 10	6 ·36	10 ·86	5
28	Th 11	7 ·43	11 ·96	6
29	Fr 12	8 ·50	... ...	7
30	Sa 13	9 ·56	12 ·05	8
—31	Su 14	10 ·60	13 ·12	9
1	Mo 15	11 ·62	14 ·18	10
2	Tu 16	12 ·61	15 ·21	11
3	We 17	13 ·59	16 ·22	12
4	Th 18	14 ·51	17 ·21	13
5	Fr 19	P ·48	18 ·18	14
6	Sa 20	1 ·41	19 ·15	15
7	Su 21	2 ·31	20 ·10	16
8	Mo 22	3 ·21	21 ·03 22 ·96	17
9	Tu 23	4 ·11	23 ·89	18
10	We 24	5 ·01 6 ·91	24 ·83	19
11	Th 25	7 ·81	25 ·77	20
12	Fr 26	8 ·72	26 ·71	21
13	Sa 27	9 ·64	27 ·66	22
14	Su 28	10 ·58	1 ·63	23
15	Mo 29	11 ·54	2 ·62	24
16	Tu 30	12 ·52	3 ·63	25

Nakśh :—1. Asvn. 2. Bhar. 3. Krit. 4. Rohi. 5. Mrig. 6. Ardh. 7. Punar. 8. Push. 9. Aslesh. 10. Magh. 11. P. Phal. 12. U. Phal. 13. Hasta. 14. Chit.

A. D. 1970.
A.—Amavasya.
P.—Paurnami.

Kollam 1146, Commences { **N. Malabar—Sept.** / **S. Malabar—Aug.**

Hijra 1390, Commences, **March 9.**

Vikrama 2027.
Bengal San 1376.
(N. Cycle) Rudhirodgarin.

SOLAR reckoning: Cyclic Sidereal Year, Month and Day; Week-Day English Month and Day. LUNAR reckoning: Tithi Ending Moment; Nakshatra Ending Moment; Muhammadan Year, Month and Day.

July

Solar month	Cyclic Sidereal Year, Month and Day	Week-Day	English Month and Day	Lunar label	Tithi Ending Moment	Nakshatra Ending Moment	Muhammadan Year, Month and Day
Sadharana Mithuna—Ani.	17	We	1	Bah.	13 ·50	4 ·65	R.-akhir. 26
	18	Th	2		14 ·51	5 ·69	27
	19	Fr	3		—A ·55	6 ·76	28
	20	Sa	4		1 ·00	7 ·85	—29
	21	Su	5		2 ·67	8 ·95	1
	22	Mo	6		3 ·75	... ...	2
	23	Tu	7		4 ·83	9 ·05	3
	24	We	8		5 ·91	10 ·16	4
	25	Th	9		6 ·98	11 ·26	5
	26	Fr	10		... ...	12 ·35	6
	27	Sa	11	Sukla	7 ·04	13 ·43	7
	28	Su	12		8 ·08	14 ·49	8
	29	Mo	13		9 ·10	15 53	9
	30	Tu	14		10 ·09	16 ·54	10
	31	We	15		11 ·07	17 ·54	11
	—32	Th	16		12 ·02 13 ·96	18 ·52	12
Sadharana Karkata—Adi.	1	Fr	17	Ashadha	14 ·88	19 ·48	H. 1390 Jumadal-awwal. 13
	2	Sa	18		P ·79	20 ·43	14
	3	Su	19		1 ·70	21 ·37	15
	4	Mo	20		2 ·60	22 ·31	16
	5	Tu	21		3 ·50	23 ·24	17
	6	We	22		4 ·40	24 ·17	18
	7	Th	23		5 ·30	25 ·11	19
	8	Fr	24		6 ·20	26 ·05	20
	9	Sa	25	Bahula	7 ·12	27 ·00 1 ·96	21
	10	Su	26		8 ·06	2 ·95	22
	11	Mo	27		9 ·02 10 ·99	3 ·95	23
	12	Tu	28		11 ·98	4 ·97	24
	13	We	29		... ...	... ...	25
	14	Th	30		12 ·00	5 ·00	26
	15	Fr	31		13 ·03	6 ·06	27

Aug.

Solar month	Cyclic Sidereal Year, Month and Day	Week-Day	English Month and Day	Lunar label	Tithi Ending Moment	Nakshatra Ending Moment	Muhammadan Year, Month and Day
	16	Sa	1		14 ·07	7 ·15	28
	17	Su	2		—A ·14	8 ·25	29
	18	Mo	3		1 ·22	9 ·35	—30
	19	Tu	4		2 ·31	10 ·46	1
	20	We	5		3 ·39	11 ·56	2
	21	Th	6		4 46	12 ·66	3
	22	Fr	7		5 ·52	13 ·74	4
	23	Sa	8	Sukla	6 ·56	14 ·80	5
	24	Su	9		7 ·58	15 ·84	6
	25	Mo	10		8 ·57	16 ·86	7
	26	Tu	11		9 ·56	17 ·87	8
	27	We	12		10 52	18 ·85	9
	28	Th	13	Sravana	11 ·46	19 ·82	10
	29	Fr	14		12 ·38	20 ·77	11
	30	Sa	15		13 ·30	21 ·71	12
	—31	Su	16		14 ·20	22 ·65	13
	1	Mo ○	17		P ·10	23 ·58	14
	2	Tu	18		1 ·00 2 ·90	24 ·51	H. 1390 Jumadal-akhir. 15
Sadharana Simha—Avani.	3	We	19		3 ·80	25 ·44	16
	4	Th	20		4 ·71	26 ·38	17
	5	Fr	21		5 ·63	27 ·33	18
	6	Sa	22		6 ·56	1 ·30	19
	7	Su	23	Bahula	7 ·51	2 ·28	20
	8	Mo	24		8 ·49	3 ·27	21
	9	Tu	25		9 ·48	4 ·28	22
	10	We	26		10 ·49	5 ·32	23
	11	Th	27		11 ·53	6 ·33	24
	12	Fr	28		12 ·58	7 ·46	25
	13	Sa	29		13 ·64	8 ·55	26
	14	Su	30		14 ·72	9 ·65	27
	15	Mo	31		—A ·81	10 ·76	28

Sep.

Solar month	Cyclic Sidereal Year, Month and Day	Week-Day	English Month and Day	Lunar label	Tithi Ending Moment	Nakshatra Ending Moment	Muhammadan Year, Month and Day
	16	Tu	1		1 ·89	11 ·87	—29
	17	We	2		2 ·97	12 ·97	1
	18	Th	3		... ...	... ...	2
	19	Fr	4		3 ·03	13 ·05	3
	20	Sa	5		4 ·07	14 ·11	4
Sadharana Simha—Avani.	21	Su	6	Sukla	5 ·10	15 ·16	5
	22	Mo	7		6 ·09	16 ·19	6
	23	Tu	8		7 ·07	17 ·20	7
	24	We	9		8 ·03 9 ·97	18 ·18	8
	25	Th	10		10 ·90	19 ·15	9
	26	Fr	11		11 ·82	20 ·10	10
	27	Sa	12	Bhadrapada	12 ·73	21 ·05 22 ·99	11
	28	Su	13		13 ·63	23 ·92	12
	29	Mo	14		14 ·53	24 ·85	13
	30	Tu	15		P ·43	25 ·78	14
	—31	We	16		1 ·33	26 ·72	H. 1390 Rajab. 15
	1	Th	17		2 ·24	27 ·67	16
	2	Fr	18		3 ·16	1 ·63	17
	3	Sa	19		4 ·09	2 ·60	18
	4	Su	20		5 ·05	3 ·59	19
	5	Mo	21		6 ·02	4 ·60	20
Sadharana Kanya—Purattasi.	6	Tu	22	Bahula	7 ·02	5 ·64	21
	7	We	23		8 ·03	6 ·69	22
	8	Th	24		9 ·06	7 ·76	23
	9	Fr	25		10 ·11	8 ·85	24
	10	Sa	26		11 ·18	9 ·95	25
	11	Su	27		12 ·26	... ...	26
	12	Mo	28		13 ·35	10 ·06	27
	13	Tu	29		14 ·44	11 ·17	28
	14	We	30		—A ·51	12 ·27	29

Oct.

Solar month	Cyclic Sidereal Year, Month and Day	Week-Day	English Month and Day	Lunar label	Tithi Ending Moment	Nakshatra Ending Moment	Muhammadan Year, Month and Day
	15	Th	1		1 ·57	13 ·35	—30
	16	Fr	2		2 ·61	14 ·42	1
	17	Sa	3		3 ·63	15 ·47	2
	18	Su	4		4 ·64	16 ·51	3
	19	Mo	5		5 ·62	17 ·52	4
	20	Tu	6		6 ·59	18 ·51	5
	21	We	7	Sukla	7 ·53	19 ·48	6
	22	Th	8		8 ·46	20 ·44	7
	23	Fr	9		9 ·38	21 ·39	8
	24	Sa	10		10 ·29	22 ·33	9
	25	Su	11		11 ·19	23 ·26	10
	26	Mo	12		12 ·09 13 ·99	24 ·19	11
	27	Tu	13	Asvina	14 ·89	25 ·12	H. 1390 Shaban. 12
	28	We	14		P ·81	26 ·06	13
	29	Th	15		1 ·73	27 ·01 1 ·96	14
	30	Fr	16		2 ·66	2 ·93	15
	—31	Sa	17		3 ·62	3 ·91	16
	1	Su	18		4 ·59	4 ·93	17
	2	Mo	19		5 ·59	5 ·96	18
	3	Tu	20		6 ·61	... ...	19
	4	We	21	Bahula	7 ·65	6 ·00	20
Sadharana Tula—Aippasi.	5	Th	22		8 ·70	7 ·06	21
	6	Fr	23		9 ·76	8 ·15	22
	7	Sa	24		10 ·84	9 ·25	23
	8	Su	25		11 ·93	10 ·36	24
	9	Mo	26		... ...	11 ·47	25
	10	Tu	27		12 ·02	12 ·57	26
	11	We	28		13 ·10	13 ·66	27
	12	Th	29		14 ·17	14 ·73	28
	13	Fr	30		—A ·21	15 ·79	—29
	14	Sa	31		1 ·24	16 ·83	1

Nov.

Solar month	Cyclic Sidereal Year, Month and Day	Week-Day	English Month and Day	Lunar label	Tithi Ending Moment	Nakshatra Ending Moment	Muhammadan Year, Month and Day
	15	Su	1		2 ·23	17 ·84	2
	16	Mo	2		3 ·21	18 ·88	3
	17	Tu	3		4 ·18	19 ·81	4
	18	We	4		5 ·13	20 ·78	5
Sadharana Tula—Aippasi.	19	Th	5		6 ·06 7 ·97	21 ·73	6
	20	Fr	6	Sukla	8 ·88	22 ·67	7
	21	Sa	7		9 ·78	23 ·60	8
	22	Su	8		10 ·68	24 ·53	9
	23	Mo	9		11 ·58	25 ·46	10
	24	Tu	10		12 ·49	26 ·40	11
	25	We	11	Karttika	13 ·41	27 ·34	12
	26	Th	12		14 ·33	1 ·29	13
	27	Fr	13		P ·27	2 ·26	14
	28	Sa	14		1 ·23	3 ·25	15
	—29	Su	15		2 ·20	4 ·25	H. 1390 Ramzan. 16
	1	Mo	16		3 ·20	5 ·27	17
	2	Tu	17		4 ·21	6 ·31	18
	3	We	18		5 ·25	7 ·37	19
	4	Th	19		6 ·31	8 ·45	20
	5	Fr	20	Bahula	7 ·39	9 ·55	21
	6	Sa	21		8 ·47	10 ·66	22
	7	Su	22		9 ·56	11 ·77	23
Sadharana Vrischika—Kartigai.	8	Mo	23		10 ·65	12 ·87	24
	9	Tu	24		11 ·72	13 ·96	25
	10	We	25		12 ·78	... ...	26
	11	Th	26		13 ·83	14 ·05	27
	12	Fr	27		14 ·86	15 ·11	28
	13	Sa	28		—A ·86	16 ·14	29
	14	Su	29		1 ·84	17 ·16	—30
	15	Mo	30		2 ·80	18 ·16	1

Dec.

Solar month	Cyclic Sidereal Year, Month and Day	Week-Day	English Month and Day	Lunar label	Tithi Ending Moment	Nakshatra Ending Moment	Muhammadan Year, Month and Day
	16	Tu	1		3 ·74	19 ·15	2
	17	We	2		4 ·68	20 ·11	3
	18	Th	3		5 ·60	21 ·06	4
	19	Fr	4		6 ·51	22 ·00 23 ·94	5
	20	Sa	5	Sukla	7 ·41	24 ·87	6
	21	Su	6		8 ·31	25 ·80	7
	22	Mo	7		9 ·21	26 ·74	8
	23	Tu	8		10 ·12	27 ·68	9
	24	We	9		11 ·03 12 ·96	1 ·62	10
	25	Th	10	Margasira	13 ·90	2 ·59	H. 1390 Shawwal. 11
	26	Fr	11		14 ·85	3 ·57	12
	27	Sa	12		P ·83	4 ·57	13
	28	Su	13		1 ·84	5 ·58	14
	29	Mo	14		2 ·86	6 ·62	15
	—30	Tu	15		3 ·90	7 ·68	16
	1	We	16		4 ·96	8 ·76	17
	2	Th	17		... ...	9 ·83	18
	3	Fr	18		5 ·04	10 ·95	19
	4	Sa	19		6 ·12	... ...	20
	5	Su	20	Bahula	7 ·21	11 ·06	21
Sadharana Dhanus—Margali.	6	Mo	21		8 ·30	12 ·17	22
	7	Tu	22		9 ·38	13 ·27	23
	8	We	23		10 ·44	14 ·35	24
	9	Th	24		11 ·48	15 ·42	25
	10	Fr	25		12 ·50	16 ·46	26
	11	Sa	26		13 ·49	17 ·48	27
	12	Su	27		14 ·48	18 ·49	28
	13	Mo	28		—A ·44	19 ·48	—29
	14	Tu	29	P. Suk.	1 ·39	20 ·44	1
	15	We	30		2 ·82	21 ·40	2
	16	Th	31		3 ·24	22 ·34	3

15. Svati. 16. Visak. 17. Anur. 18. Jyesh. 19. Mula. 20. P. Ash. 21. U. Ash. 22. Sravn. 23. Dani. 24. Satab. 25. P. Bhad. 26. U. Bhad. 27. Rev.

A. D. 1971.
Solar Eclipse. ●
Lunar Eclipse. ○

Mesha Sankranti (Commencement of Indian Sidereal Year).
(Surya Sid.) April 13·99.
(Arya Sid.) April 13·88.

Saka 1893. **Kaliyuga 5072.**
(S. Cycle) Virodhakrit.

Columns: SOLAR reckoning — Cyclic Sidereal Year, Month and Day; Week-Day, English Month and Day. LUNAR reckoning — Tithi Ending Moment; Nakshatra Ending Moment; Muhammadan Year, Month and Day.

Jan. — Sadharana Dhanus—Margali; Sadharana Makara—Tai. Sukla; Pausha; Bahula. H. 1390 Zi-l-ka'da.

Cyclic Sidereal Day	Week-Day	Jan.	Tithi	Nakshatra	Muhammadan
17	Fr	1	4 ·14	23 ·28	4
18	Sa	2	5 ·04 / 6 ·94	24 ·21	5
19	Su	3	7 ·84	25 ·14	6
20	Mo	4	8 ·76	26 ·07	7
21	Tu	5	9 ·68	27 ·01 / 1 ·96	8
22	We	6	10 ·61	2 ·93	9
23	Th	7	11 ·55	3 ·90	10
24	Fr	8	12 ·51	4 ·89	11
25	Sa	9	13 ·49	5 ·90	12
26	Su	10	14 ·48	6 ·93	13
27	Mo	11	P ·51	7 ·99	14
28	Tu	12	1 ·55	...	15
29	We	13	2 ·61	8 ·06	16
1	Th	14	3 ·68	9 ·15	17
2	Fr	15	4 ·77	10 ·25	18
3	Sa	16	5 ·87	11 ·36	19
4	Su	17	6 ·95	12 ·47	20
5	Mo	18	...	13 ·57	21
6	Tu	19	7 ·02	14 ·66	22
7	We	20	8 ·08	15 ·73	23
8	Th	21	9 ·13	16 ·78	24
9	Fr	22	10 ·14	17 ·81	25
10	Sa	23	11 ·15	18 ·82	26
11	Su	24	12 ·13	19 ·81	27
12	Mo	25	13 ·08	20 ·78	28
13	Tu	26	14 ·02 / A ·95	21 ·73	29
14	We	27	1 ·87	22 ·68	30
15	Th	28	2 ·78	23 ·62	1
16	Fr	29	3 ·68	24 ·55	2
17	Sa	30	4 ·58	25 ·48	3
18	Su	31	5 ·48	26 ·41	4

Feb. — Sadharana Kumbha—Masi. Sukla; Magha; Bahula; P. Suk. H. 1390 Zi-l-hijja.

Cyclic Sidereal Day	Week-Day	Feb.	Tithi	Nakshatra	Muhammadan
19	Mo	1	6 ·39	27 ·35	5
20	Tu	2	7 ·31	1 ·30	6
21	We	3	8 ·24	2 ·26	7
22	Th	4	9 ·18	3 ·23	8
23	Fr	5	10 ·14	4 ·21	9
24	Sa	6	11 ·12	5 ·22	10
25	Su	7	12 ·12	6 ·25	11
26	Mo	8	13 ·14	7 ·30	12
27	Tu	9	14 ·19	8 ·37	13
28	We ○	10	P ·25	9 ·45	14
29	Th	11	1 ·33	10 ·55	15
30	Fr	12	2 ·42	11 ·66	16
1	Sa	13	3 ·51	12 ·77	17
2	Su	14	4 ·59	13 ·87	18
3	Mo	15	5 ·66	14 ·96	19
4	Tu	16	6 ·72	...	20
5	We	17	7 ·76	15 ·04	21
6	Th	18	8 ·77	16 ·10	22
7	Fr	19	9 ·77	17 ·13	23
8	Sa	20	10 ·75	18 ·14	24
9	Su	21	11 ·70	19 ·13	25
10	Mo	22	12 ·64	20 ·11	26
11	Tu	23	13 ·57	21 ·07	27
12	We	24	14 ·49	22 ·02 / 23 ·96	28
13	Th	25	A ·39	24 ·89	29
14	Fr	26	1 ·29	25 ·82	30
15	Sa	27	2 ·19	26 ·75	1
16	Su	28	3 ·09	27 ·69	2

March — Sadharana Kumbha—Masi; Sadharana Mina—Panguni. Sukla; Phalguna; Bahula. H. 1391 Muharram.

Cyclic Sidereal Day	Week-Day	March	Tithi	Nakshatra	Muhammadan
17	Mo	1	4 ·00 / 5 ·92	1 ·64	3
18	Tu	2	6 ·85	2 ·59	4
19	We	3	7 ·79	3 ·55	5
20	Th	4	8 ·75	4 ·54	6
21	Fr	5	9 ·73	5 ·55	7
22	Sa	6	10 ·74	6 ·57	8
23	Su	7	11 ·76	7 ·61	9
24	Mo	8	12 ·81	8 ·67	10
25	Tu	9	13 ·87	9 ·75	11
26	We	10	14 ·94	10 ·85	12
27	Th	11	...	11 ·96	13
28	Fr	12	P ·03	...	14
29	Sa	13	1 ·12	12 ·07	15
30	Su	14	2 ·20	13 ·17	16
1	Mo	15	3 ·26	14 ·26	17
2	Tu	16	4 ·31	15 ·34	18
3	We	17	5 ·35	16 ·41	19
4	Th	18	6 ·36	17 ·45	20
5	Fr	19	7 ·36	18 ·46	21
6	Sa	20	8 ·34	19 ·46	22
7	Su	21	9 ·29	20 ·44	23
8	Mo	22	10 ·23	21 ·41	24
9	Tu	23	11 ·16	22 ·36	25
10	We	24	12 ·07 / 13 ·98	23 ·30	26
11	Th	25	14 ·88	24 ·23	27
12	Fr	26	A ·78	25 ·16	28
13	Sa	27	1 ·68	26 ·09	29
14	Su	28	2 ·58	27 ·03 / 1 ·97	30
15	Mo	29	3 ·50	2 ·92	1
16	Tu	30	4 ·43	3 ·88	2
17	We	31	5 ·37	4 ·87	3

April — Virodhakrit Mesha—Chittirai. Sukla; Chaitra; Bahula; V. Suk. H. 1391 Safar; R.-awwal.

Cyclic Sidereal Day	Week-Day	April	Tithi	Nakshatra	Muhammadan
18	Th	1	6 ·33	5 ·87	4
19	Fr	2	7 ·31	6 ·88	5
20	Sa	3	8 ·31	7 ·92	6
21	Su	4	9 ·33	8 ·98	7
22	Mo	5	10 ·38	...	8
23	Tu	6	11 ·44	9 ·06	9
24	We	7	12 ·52	10 ·16	10
25	Th	8	13 ·60	11 ·26	11
26	Fr	9	14 ·68	12 ·37	12
27	Sa	10	P ·76	13 ·47	13
28	Su	11	1 ·83	14 ·57	14
29	Mo	12	2 ·88	15 ·66	15
30	Tu	13	3 ·92	16 ·72	16
1	We	14	4 ·93	17 ·76	17
2	Th	15	5 ·92	18 ·78	18
3	Fr	16	6 ·90	19 ·78	19
4	Sa	17	7 ·85	20 ·77	20
5	Su	18	8 ·79	21 ·74	21
6	Mo	19	9 ·71	22 ·69	22
7	Tu	20	10 ·62	23 ·63	23
8	We	21	11 ·52	24 ·57	24
9	Th	22	12 ·42	25 ·51	25
10	Fr	23	13 ·32	26 ·44	26
11	Sa	24	14 ·22	27 ·37	27
12	Su	25	A ·12	1 ·31	28
13	Mo	26	1 ·04 / 2 ·97	2 ·25	29
14	Tu	27	3 ·91	3 ·22	1
15	We	28	4 ·87	4 ·20	2
16	Th	29	5 ·85	5 ·19	3
17	Fr	30	6 ·84	6 ·20	4

May — Virodhakrit Mesha—Chittirai; Virodhakrit Vrishabha—Vaikasi. Sukla; Vaisakha; Bahula. H. 1391 Rabi-ul-awwal.

Cyclic Sidereal Day	Week-Day	May	Tithi	Nakshatra	Muhammadan
18	Sa	1	7 ·86	7 ·23	5
19	Su	2	8 ·90	8 ·29	6
20	Mo	3	9 ·96	9 ·37	7
21	Tu	4	...	10 ·46	8
22	We	5	10 ·03	11 ·56	9
23	Th	6	11 ·11	12 ·67	10
24	Fr	7	12 ·20	13 ·78	11
25	Sa	8	13 ·28	14 ·88	12
26	Su	9	14 ·36	15 ·96	13
27	Mo	10	P ·41	...	14
28	Tu	11	1 ·44	16 ·03	15
29	We	12	2 ·45	17 ·08	16
30	Th	13	3 ·44	18 ·10	17
31	Fr	14	4 ·42	19 ·12	18
1	Sa	15	5 ·37	20 ·10	19
2	Su	16	6 ·30	21 ·07	20
3	Mo	17	7 ·22	22 ·03 / 23 ·98	21
4	Tu	18	8 ·13	24 ·92	22
5	We	19	9 ·04 / 10 ·94	25 ·85	23
6	Th	20	11 ·84	26 ·78	24
7	Fr	21	12 ·74	27 ·71	25
8	Sa	22	13 ·64	1 ·65	26
9	Su	23	14 ·55	2 ·60	27
10	Mo	24	A ·48	3 ·55	28
11	Tu	25	1 ·42	4 ·52	29
12	We	26	2 ·38	5 ·51	30
13	Th	27	3 ·36	6 ·52	1
14	Fr	28	4 ·34	7 ·55	2
15	Sa	29	5 ·36	8 ·61	3
16	Su	30	6 ·40	9 ·67	4
17	Mo	31	7 ·46	10 ·76	5

June — Virodhakrit Mithuna—Ani. Sukla; Jyeshtha; Bahula; Sukla; Ashadha. H. 1391 Rabi-ul-akhir; J.-awwal.

Cyclic Sidereal Day	Week-Day	June	Tithi	Nakshatra	Muhammadan
18	Tu	1	8 ·53	11 ·86	6
19	We	2	9 ·61	12 ·97	7
20	Th	3	10 ·70	...	8
21	Fr	4	11 ·78	13 ·08	9
22	Sa	5	12 ·85	14 ·18	10
23	Su	6	13 ·90	15 ·27	11
24	Mo	7	14 ·93	16 ·34	12
25	Tu	8	P ·94	17 ·39	13
26	We	9	1 ·93	18 ·43	14
27	Th	10	2 ·91	19 ·44	15
28	Fr	11	3 ·86	20 ·43	16
29	Sa	12	4 ·80	21 ·40	17
30	Su	13	5 ·72	22 ·36	18
31	Mo	14	6 ·63	23 ·31	19
1	Tu	15	7 ·53	24 ·25	20
2	We	16	8 ·43	25 ·18	21
3	Th	17	9 ·33	26 ·11	22
4	Fr	18	10 ·23	27 ·04 / 1 ·98	23
5	Sa	19	11 ·13	2 ·93	24
6	Su	20	12 ·04 / 13 ·96	3 ·88	25
7	Mo	21	14 ·90	4 ·85	26
8	Tu	22	A ·86	5 ·84	27
9	We	23	1 ·83	6 ·84	28
10	Th	24	2 ·82	7 ·87	29
11	Fr	25	3 ·85	8 ·92	1
12	Sa	26	4 ·88	9 ·98	2
13	Su	27	5 ·93	...	3
14	Mo	28	...	10 ·06	4
15	Tu	29	6 ·00	11 ·16	5
16	We	30	7 ·08	12 ·27	6

Naksh :—1. Asvn. 2. Bhar. 3. Krit. 4. Rohi. 5. Mrig. 6. Ardh. 7. Punar. 8. Push. 9. Aslesh. 10. Magh. 11. P. Phal. 12. U. Phal. 13. Hasta. 14. Chit.

A. D. 1971.
A.—Amavasya.
P.—Paurnami.

Kollam 1147, Commences { N. Malabar—Sept. S. Malabar—Aug.

Hijra 1391, Commences, Feb. 27.

Vikrama 2028.
Bengal San 1377.
(N. Cycle) Raktaksha.

SOLAR reckoning: Cyclic Sidereal Year, Month and Day. LUNAR reckoning: Tithi Ending Moment; Nakshatra Ending Moment; Muhammadan Year, Month and Day.

July

Cyclic Sidereal Year, Month and Day	Week-Day	English Month and Day	Tithi Ending Moment	Nakshatra Ending Moment	Muhammadan Year, Month and Day
17 (Virodhakrit, Mithuna—Ani.)	Th	1	(Ashadha, Sukla) 8 ·16	13 ·38	7 (H. 1391 Jumadal-awwal.)
18	Fr	2	9 ·24	14 ·48	8
19	Sa	3	10 ·32	15 ·57	9
20	Su	4	11 ·37	16 ·65	10
21	Mo	5	12 ·41	17 ·71	11
22	Tu	6	13 ·42	18 ·75	12
23	We	7	14 ·41	19 ·76	13
24	Th	8	P ·38	20 ·75	14
25	Fr	9	(Bahula) 1 ·35	21 ·73	15
26	Sa	10	2 ·27	22 ·69	16
27	Su	11	3 ·19	23 ·65	17
28	Mo	12	4 ·11	24 ·59	18
29	Tu	13	5 ·01, 6 ·91	25 ·52	19
30	We	14	7 ·81	26 ·45	20
31	Th	15	8 ·71	27 ·38	21
32	Fr	16	9 ·61	1 ·32	22
1 (Virodhakrit, Karkata—Adi.)	Sa	17	10 ·52	2 ·27	23
2	Su	18	11 ·44	3 ·22	24
3	Mo	19	12 ·38	4 ·18	25
4	Tu	20	13 ·34	5 ·16	26
5	We	21	14 ·31	6 ·17	27
6	Th	22	A ·31	7 ·19	28
7	Fr	23	(Sukla) 1 ·33	8 ·23	29
8	Sa	24	2 ·35	9 ·28	30
9	Su	25	3 ·41	10 ·36	1
10	Mo	26	4 ·48	11 ·46	2
11	Tu	27	5 ·56	12 ·57	3
12	We	28	6 ·64	13 ·68	4
13	Th	29	7 ·72	14 ·78	5
14	Fr	30	8 ·79	15 ·87	6
15	Sa	31	9 ·84	16 ·95	7

Aug.

Cyclic Sidereal Year, Month and Day	Week-Day	English Month and Day	Tithi Ending Moment	Nakshatra Ending Moment	Muhammadan Year, Month and Day
16	Su	1	(Sravana) 10 ·88	... ...	8 (H. 1391 Jumadal-akhir.)
17	Mo	2	11 ·90	17 ·02	9
18	Tu	3	12 ·90	18 ·06	10
19	We	4	13 ·87	19 ·08	11
20	Th	5	14 ·83	20 ·08	12
21	Fr ○	6	P ·77	21 ·06	13
22	Sa	7	(Bahula) 1 ·70	22 ·03, 23 ·99	14
23	Su	8	2 ·61	24 ·93	15
24	Mo	9	3 ·51	25 ·86	16
25	Tu	10	4 ·41	26 ·79	17
26	We	11	5 ·31	27 ·72	18
27	Th	12	6 ·21	1 ·66	19
28	Fr	13	7 ·11	2 ·60	20
29	Sa	14	8 ·02, 9 ·94	3 ·55	21
30	Su	15	10 ·87	4 ·51	22
31	Mo	16	11 ·83	5 ·49	23
1 (Virodhakrit, Simha—Avani.)	Tu	17	12 ·80	6 ·49	24
2	We	18	13 ·80	7 ·50	25
3	Th	19	14 ·81	8 ·54	26
4	Fr	20	A ·85	9 ·60	27
5	Sa	21	(Bhadrapada, Sukla) 1 ·91	10 ·68	28
6	Su	22	2 ·98	11 ·77	29
7	Mo	23	... ...	12 ·87	1 (H. 1391 Rajab.)
8	Tu	24	3 ·05	13 ·97	2
9	We	25	4 ·13	... ...	3
10	Th	26	5 ·22	14 ·08	4
11	Fr	27	6 ·29	15 ·13	5
12	Sa	28	7 ·35	16 ·27	6
13	Su	29	8 ·39	17 ·33	7
14	Mo	30	9 ·41	18 ·38	8
15	Tu	31	10 ·40	19 ·40	9

Sep.

Cyclic Sidereal Year, Month and Day	Week-Day	English Month and Day	Tithi Ending Moment	Nakshatra Ending Moment	Muhammadan Year, Month and Day
16	We	1	(Bhadrapada, Sukla) 11 ·38	20 ·41	10 (H. 1391 Rajab.)
17	Th	2	12 ·34	21 ·40	11
18	Fr	3	13 ·28	22 ·37	12
19	Sa	4	14 ·21	23 ·32	13
20	Su	5	P ·12	24 ·26	14
21 (Virodhakrit, Simha—Avani.)	Mo	6	(Bahula) 1 ·02, 2 ·92	25 ·20	15
22	Tu	7	3 ·82	26 ·14	16
23	We	8	4 ·72	27 ·07	17
24	Th	9	5 ·62	1 ·00, 2 ·94	18
25	Fr	10	6 ·54	3 ·89	19
26	Sa	11	7 ·47	4 ·85	20
27	Su	12	8 ·41	5 ·82	21
28	Mo	13	9 ·36	6 ·81	22
29	Tu	14	10 ·34	7 ·82	23
30	We	15	11 ·33	8 ·85	24
31	Th	16	12 ·34	9 ·91	25
1 (Virodhakrit, Kanya—Purattasi.)	Fr	17	13 ·38	10 ·98	26
2	Sa	18	14 ·43	... ...	27
3	Su	19	A ·50	11 ·07	28
4	Mo	20	(Sukla) 1 ·58	12 ·17	29
5	Tu	21	2 ·66	13 ·27	30
6	We	22	3 ·74	14 ·38	1
7	Th	23	4 ·31	15 ·48	2
8	Fr	24	5 ·88	16 ·57	3
9	Sa	25	6 ·92	17 ·64	4
10	Su	26	7 ·94	18 ·69	5
11	Mo	27	8 ·94	19 ·72	6
12	Tu	28	9 ·92	20 ·74	7
13	We	29	10 ·89	21 ·73	8
14	Th	30	11 ·83	22 ·70	9

Oct.

Cyclic Sidereal Year, Month and Day	Week-Day	English Month and Day	Tithi Ending Moment	Nakshatra Ending Moment	Muhammadan Year, Month and Day
15	Fr	1	(Asvina) 12 ·75	28 ·66	10 (H. 1391 Shaban.)
16	Sa	2	13 ·67	24 ·61	11
17	Su	3	14 ·58	25 ·55	12
18	Mo	4	P ·48	26 ·48	13
19	Tu	5	(Bahula) 1 ·38	27 ·41	14
20	We	6	2 ·28	1 ·34	15
21	Th	7	3 ·18	2 ·27	16
22	Fr	8	4 ·09	3 ·22	17
23	Sa	9	5 ·02, 6 ·96	4 ·18	18
24	Su	10	7 ·92	5 ·15	19
25	Mo	11	8 ·90	6 ·13	20
26	Tu	12	9 ·89	7 ·14	21
27	We	13	10 ·91	8 ·16	22
28	Th	14	11 ·94	9 ·22	23
29	Fr	15	... ...	10 ·29	24
30	Sa	16	12 ·00	11 ·37	25
31	Su	17	13 ·07	12 ·46	26
1 (Virodhakrit, Tula—Aippasi.)	Mo	18	14 ·15	13 ·57	27
2	Tu	19	A ·24	14 ·68	28
3	We	20	(Karttika, Sukla) 1 ·33	15 ·79	29
4	Th	21	2 ·41	16 ·88	1 (H. 1391 Ramzan.)
5	Fr	22	3 ·47	17 ·95	2
6	Sa	23	4 ·51	... ...	3
7	Su	24	5 ·53	18 ·00	4
8	Mo	25	6 ·52	19 ·04	5
9	Tu	26	7 ·50	20 ·06	6
10	We	27	8 ·46	21 ·05	7
11	Th	28	9 ·41	22 ·03, 23 ·99	8
12	Fr	29	10 ·34	24 ·95	9
13	Sa	30	11 ·26	25 ·89	10
14	Su	31	12 ·16	26 ·82	11

Nov.

Cyclic Sidereal Year, Month and Day	Week-Day	English Month and Day	Tithi Ending Moment	Nakshatra Ending Moment	Muhammadan Year, Month and Day
15	Mo	1	(Karttika) 13 ·06, 14 ·96	27 ·75	12 (H. 1391 Ramzan.)
16	Tu	2	P ·86	1 ·68	13
17	We	3	(Bahula) 1 ·77	2 ·62	14
18	Th	4	2 ·69	3 ·56	15
19 (Virodhakrit, Tula—Aippasi.)	Fr	5	3 ·62	4 ·51	16
20	Sa	6	4 ·56	5 ·48	17
21	Su	7	5 ·52	6 ·46	18
22	Mo	8	6 ·50	7 ·46	19
23	Tu	9	7 ·49	8 ·49	20
24	We	10	8 ·51	9 ·53	21
25	Th	11	9 ·55	10 ·59	22
26	Fr	12	10 ·61	11 ·67	23
27	Sa	13	11 ·69	12 ·76	24
28	Su	14	12 ·78	13 87	25
29	Mo	15	13 ·83	14 ·98	26
30	Tu	16	14 ·94	... ...	27
1 (Virodhakrit, Vrischika—Kartigai.)	We	17	... ...	15 ·09	28
2	Th	18	A ·01	16 ·18	29
3	Fr	19	(Sukla) 1 08	17 ·26	30
4	Sa	20	2 ·13	18 ·33	1
5	Su	21	3 ·14	19 ·36	2
6	Mo	22	4 ·14	20 ·38	3
7	Tu	23	5 ·12	21 ·38	4
8	We	24	6 ·08	22 ·36	5
9	Th	25	7 ·03, 8 ·96	23 ·33	6
10	Fr	26	9 ·88	24 ·28	7
11	Sa	27	10 ·79	25 ·22	8
12	Su	28	11 ·69	26 ·16	9
13	Mo	29	12 ·59	27 ·09	10
14	Tu	30	13 ·49	1 ·02, 2 ·96	11

Dec.

Cyclic Sidereal Year, Month and Day	Week-Day	English Month and Day	Tithi Ending Moment	Nakshatra Ending Moment	Muhammadan Year, Month and Day
15	We	1	(Margasira) 14 ·40	3 ·90	12 (H. 1391 Shawwal.)
16	Th	2	P ·31	4 ·84	13
17	Fr	3	(Bahula) 1 ·23	5 ·81	14
18	Sa	4	2 ·18	6 ·79	15
19	Su	5	3 ·14	7 ·79	16
20	Mo	6	4 ·12	8 ·80	17
21	Tu	7	5 ·13	9 ·84	18
22	We	8	6 ·15	10 ·90	19
23	Th	9	7 ·19	11 ·98	20
24	Fr	10	8 ·25	... ...	21
25	Sa	11	9 ·33	12 ·07	22
26	Su	12	10 ·42	13 ·18	23
27	Mo	13	11 ·51	14 ·29	24
28	Tu	14	12 ·59	15 ·39	25
29	We	15	13 ·66	16 ·48	26
1 (Virodhakrit, Dhanus—Margali.)	Th	16	14 ·72	17 ·57	27
2	Fr	17	A ·76	18 ·64	28
3	Sa	18	(Pausha, Sukla) 1 ·78	19 ·68	29
4	Su	19	2 ·78	20 ·70	1 (H. 1391 Zil-ka'da.)
5	Mo	20	3 ·76	21 ·70	2
6	Tu	21	4 ·72	22 ·69	3
7	We	22	5 ·66	23 ·66	4
8	Th	23	6 ·59	24 ·62	5
9	Fr	24	7 ·51	25 ·56	6
10	Sa	25	8 ·42	26 ·49	7
11	Su	26	9 ·32	27 ·42	8
12	Mo	27	10 ·22	1 ·35	9
13	Tu	28	11 ·12	2 ·29	10
14	We	29	12 ·03, 13 ·95	3 ·23	11
15	Th	30	14 ·88	4 ·18	12
16	Fr	31	P ·82	5 ·14	13

15. Svati. 16. Visak. 17. Anur. 18. Jyesh. 19. Mula. 20. P. Ash. 21. U. Ash. 22. Sravn. 23. Dani. 24. Satab. 25. P. Bhad. 26. U Bhad. 27. Rev.

A. D. 1972. **Mesha Sankranti** (Commencement of Indian Sidereal Year).
Solar Eclipse. ● **(Surya Sid.) April 13·25.** **Saka 1894.** **Kaliyuga 5073.**
Lunar Eclipse. ○ **(Arya Sid.) April 13·14.** **(S. Cycle) Paridhavi.**

SOLAR reckoning: Cyclic Sidereal Year, Month and Day; Week-Day English Month and Day. LUNAR reckoning: Tithi Ending Moment; Nakshatra Ending Moment; Muhammadan Year, Month and Day.

Jan.

Cyclic Sidereal Year, Month	Day	Week-Day	English Day	Lunar Month	Tithi	Ending Moment	Nakshatra	Ending Moment	Muhammadan Year, Month	Day
Virodhakrit *Dhanus—Margali.*	17	Sa	1	Pausha	1	·78	6	·12	H. 1391 *Zi-l-ka'da.*	14
	18	Su	2		2	·77	7	·11		15
	19	Mo	3		3	·77	8	·12		16
	20	Tu	4		4	·79	9	·15		17
	21	We	5		5	·84	10	·20		18
	22	Th	6		6	·90	11	·28		19
	23	Fr	7		7	·98	12	·37		20
	24	Sa	8	*Bahula*	...	...	13	·48		21
	25	Su	9		8	·07	14	·58		22
	26	Mo	10		9	·16	15	·69		23
	27	Tu	11		10	·24	16	·79		24
	28	We	12		11	·32	17	·88		25
	29	Th	13		12	·38	18	·95		26
	—30	Fr	14		13	·41	19	·99		27
	1	Sa	15		14	·43	...	...		28
	2	Su	16		—A	·43	20	·02		29
	3	Mo	17		1	·40	21	·03		—30
	4	Tu	18		2	·36	22	·02		1
	5	We	19		3	·31	23 24	·00 ·95		2
	6	Th	20		4	·24	25	·90		3
	7	Fr	21		5	·15	26	·84		4
	8	Sa	22		6 7	·05 ·95	27	·77		5
Virodhakrit *Makara—Tai.*	9	Su	23	Magha *Sukla*	8	·85	1	·70	*Zi-l-hijja.*	6
	10	Mo	24		9	·76	2	·63		7
	11	Tu	25		10	·67	3	·57		8
	12	We	26		11	·59	4	·51		9
	13	Th	27		12	·52	5	·48		10
	14	Fr	28		13	·46	6	·45		11
	15	Sa	29		14	·42	7	·43		12
	16	Su ○	30		P	·41	8	·44		13
	17	Mo	31		1	·41	9	·47		14

Feb.

Cyclic Sidereal Year, Month	Day	Week-Day	English Day	Lunar Month	Tithi	Ending Moment	Nakshatra	Ending Moment	Muhammadan Year, Month	Day
	18	Tu	1		2	·43	10	·52	H. 1391	15
	19	We	2		3	·48	11	·59		16
	20	Th	3		4	·55	12	·67		17
	21	Fr	4		5	·63	13	·77		18
	22	Sa	5		6	·71	14	·88		19
	23	Su	6	*Bahula*	7	·80	15	·99		20
	24	Mo	7		8	·89	...	...		21
	25	Tu	8		9	·96	16	·09		22
	26	We	9		...	...	17	·18		23
	27	Th	10		10	·01	18	·25		24
	28	Fr	11		11	·04	19	·31		25
	—29	Sa	12		12	·06	20	·34		26
	1	Su	13		13	·06	21	·36		27
	2	Mo	14		14 A	·04 ·99	22	·35		28
Virodhakrit *Kumbha—Masi.*	3	Tu	15	Phalguna *Sukla*	1	·93	23	·33	H. 1392 *Muharram.*	—29
	4	We	16		2	·86	24	·29		1
	5	Th	17		3	·78	25	·24		2
	6	Fr	18		4	·68	26	·18		3
	7	Sa	19		5	·58	27	·11		4
	8	Su	20		6	·48	1 2	·04 ·97		5
	9	Mo	21		7	·38	3	·91		6
	10	Tu	22		8	·29	4	·86		7
	11	We	23		9	·21	5	·81		8
	12	Th	24		10	·14	6	·77		9
	13	Fr	25		11	·09	7	·76		10
	14	Sa	26		12	·05	8	·76		11
	15	Su	27		13	·03	9	·79		12
	16	Mo	28		14	·03	10	·83		13
	17	Tu	29		P	·06	11	·89		14

March

Cyclic Sidereal Year, Month	Day	Week-Day	English Day	Lunar Month	Tithi	Ending Moment	Nakshatra	Ending Moment	Muhammadan Year, Month	Day
Virodhakrit *Kumbha—Masi.*	18	We	1	Phalguna	1	·11	12	·97	H. 1392 *Muharram.*	15
	19	Th	2		2	·17	...	...		16
	20	Fr	3		3	·25	13	·07		17
	21	Sa	4		4	·33	14	·18		18
	22	Su	5		5	·42	15	·29		19
	23	Mo	6		6	·51	16	·39		20
	24	Tu	7		7	·58	17	·49		21
	25	We	8	*Bahula*	8	·63	18	·56		22
	26	Th	9		9	·66	19	·62		23
	27	Fr	10		10	·67	20	·67		24
	28	Sa	11		11	·66	21	·68		25
	29	Su	12		12	·63	22	·68		26
	30	Mo	13		13	·59	23	·66		27
	—31	Tu	14		14	·58	24	·62		28
	1	We	15		—A	·46	25	·58		29
	2	Th	16		1	·37	26	·52		—30
	3	Fr	17		2	·27	27	·45		1
	4	Sa	18		3	·17	1	·38		2
	5	Su	19		4 5	·07 ·97	2	·31		3
	6	Mo	20		6	·88	3	·25		4
	7	Tu	21		7	·80	4	·19		5
	8	We	22		8	·73	5	·14		6
	9	Th	23		9	·67	6	·10		7
Virodhakrit *Mina—Panguni.*	10	Fr	24	Chaitra *Sukla*	10	·64	7	·08	*Safar.*	8
	11	Sa	25		11	·62	8	·08		9
	12	Su	26		12	·61	9	·10		10
	13	Mo	27		13	·64	10	·14		11
	14	Tu	28		14	·69	11	·20		12
	15	We	29		P	·75	12	·28		13
	16	Th	30		1	·83	13	·37		14
	17	Fr	31		2	·91	14	·48		15

April

Cyclic Sidereal Year, Month	Day	Week-Day	English Day	Lunar Month	Tithi	Ending Moment	Nakshatra	Ending Moment	Muhammadan Year, Month	Day
	18	Sa	1		...	...	15	·59	H. 1392	16
	19	Su	2		3	·00	16	·69		17
	20	Mo	3		4	·08	17	·79		18
	21	Tu	4		5	·15	18	·87		19
	22	We	5		6	·20	19	·94		20
	23	Th	6	*Bahula*	7	·23	20	·98		21
	24	Fr	7		8	·24	...	...		22
	25	Sa	8		9	·24	21	·00		23
	26	Su	9		10	·21	22 23	·00 ·98		24
	27	Mo	10		11	·15	24	·96		25
	28	Tu	11		12	·09	25	·91		26
	—29	We	12		13 14	·01 ·93	26	·85		27
Paridhavi *Mesha—Chittirai.*	1	Th	13	Adhika Vaisakha *Sukla*	—A	·83	27	·79	H. 1392 *Rabi-ul-awwal.*	28
	2	Fr	14		1	·73	1	·73		—29
	3	Sa	15		2	·63	2	·66		1
	4	Su	16		3	·53	3	·59		2
	5	Mo	17		4	·44	4	·53		3
	6	Tu	18		5	·35	5	·47		4
	7	We	19		6	·28	6	·43		5
	8	Th	20		7	·22	7	·41		6
	9	Fr	21		8	·18	8	·41		7
	10	Sa	22		9	·16	9	·42		8
	11	Su	23		10	·16	10	·45		9
	12	Mo	24		11	·19	11	·51		10
	13	Tu	25		12	·23	12	·58		11
	14	We	26		13	·29	13	·68		12
	15	Th	27		14	·36	14	·78		13
	16	Fr	28		P	·44	15	·89		14
	17	Sa	29		1	·53	16	·99		15
	18	Su	30		2	·61	...	...		16

May

Cyclic Sidereal Year, Month	Day	Week-Day	English Day	Lunar Month	Tithi	Ending Moment	Nakshatra	Ending Moment	Muhammadan Year, Month	Day
Paridhavi *Mesha—Chittirai.*	19	Mo	1	Adh. Vaisakha	3	·68	17	·09	H. 1392 *Rabi-ul-awwal.*	17
	20	Tu	2		4	·73	18	·18		18
	21	We	3		5	·76	19	·25		19
	22	Th	4		6	·77	20	·30		20
	23	Fr	5		7	·76	21	·32		21
	24	Sa	6		8	·73	22	·33		22
	25	Su	7		9	·68	23	·32		23
	26	Mo	8		10	·62	24	·29		24
	27	Tu	9		11	·54	25	·25		25
	28	We	10	*Bahula*	12	·45	26	·19		26
	29	Th	11		13	·35	27	·13		27
	30	Fr	12		14	·25	1 2	·06 ·99		28
	—31	Sa	13		—A	·15	3	·93		29
	1	Su	14		1 2	·05 ·95	4	·87		—30
	2	Mo	15		3	·87	5	·81		1
	3	Tu	16		4	·80	6	·76		2
	4	We	17		5	·74	7	·74		3
	5	Th	18		6	·69	8	·73		4
	6	Fr	19	*Sukla*	7	·67	9	·74		5
	7	Sa	20		8	·67	10	·77		6
	8	Su	21		9	·70	11	·82		7
	9	Mo	22		10	·74	12	·89		8
Paridhavi *Vrishabha—Vaikasi.*	10	Tu	23	Nija Vaisakha	11	·79	13	·98	*Rabi-ul-akhir.*	9
	11	We	24		12	·86	...	...		10
	12	Th	25		13	·94	14	·08		11
	13	Fr	26		...	...	15	·19		12
	14	Sa	27		14	·03	16	·30		13
	15	Su	28		P	·11	17	·40		14
	16	Mo	29		1	·18	18	·49		15
	17	Tu	30		2	·22	19	·53		16
	18	We	31		3	·25	20	·61		17

June

Cyclic Sidereal Year, Month	Day	Week-Day	English Day	Lunar Month	Tithi	Ending Moment	Nakshatra	Ending Moment	Muhammadan Year, Month	Day
	19	Th	1		4	·26	21	·64	H. 1392	18
	20	Fr	2		5	·26	22	·66		19
	21	Sa	3	*Bahula*	6	·23	23	·65		20
	22	Su	4		7	·18	24	·62		21
	23	Mo	5		8	·12	25	·58		22
	24	Tu	6		9 10	·04 ·95	26	·53		23
	25	We	7		11	·85	27	·47		24
	26	Th	8		12	·75	1	·40		25
	27	Fr	9		13	·65	2	·33		26
	28	Sa	10		14	·55	3	·26		27
	29	Su	11		—A	·46	4	·20		28
	30	Mo	12		1	·37	5	·14		—29
	—31	Tu	13		2	·29	6	·10		1
Paridhavi *Mithuna—Ani.*	1	We	14	Jyeshtha *Sukla*	3	·23	7	·07	H. 1392 *Jumadal-awwal.*	2
	2	Th	15		4	·18	8	·05		3
	3	Fr	16		5	·16	9	·06		4
	4	Sa	17		6	·15	10	·09		5
	5	Su	18		7	·17	11	·14		6
	6	Mo	19		8	·21	12	·20		7
	7	Tu	20		9	·26	13	·28		8
	8	We	21		10	·33	14	·38		9
	9	Th	22		11	·41	15	·49		10
	10	Fr	23		12	·49	16	·60		11
	11	Sa	24		13	·57	17	·70		12
	12	Su	25		14	·64	18	·79		13
	13	Mo	26		P	·70	19	·87		14
	14	Tu	27	*Bah.*	1	·73	20	·92		15
	15	We	28		2	·75	21	·96		16
	16	Th	29		3	·74	22	·98		17
	17	Fr	30		4	·71	23	·98		18

Naksh:—1. Asvn. 2. Bhar. 3. Krit. 4. Rohi. 5. Mrig. 6. Ardh. 7. Punar. 8. Push. 9. Aslesh. 10. Magh. 11. P. Phal. 12. U. Phal. 13. Hasta. 14. Chit.

A. D. 1972.				Vikrama 2029.
A.—Amavasya.	Kollam 1148, Commences	N. Malabar—Sept. S. Malabar—Aug.	Hijra 1392, Commences, Feb. 16.	Bengal San 1378.
P.—Paurnami.				(N. Cycle) Krodhana.

SOLAR reckoning (Cyclic Sidereal Year, Month and Day; Week-Day English Month and Day) — **LUNAR reckoning** (Tithi Ending Moment; Nakshatra Ending Moment; Muhammadan Year, Month and Day)

July

Cyclic Sidereal Year, Month and Day	Week-Day English Month and Day	Tithi Ending Moment	Nakshatra Ending Moment	Muhammadan Year, Month and Day
Paridhavi *Mithuna—Ani.* 18	Sa 1	Jyesh. *Bahula* 5 ·66	24 ·95	H. 1392 *Jumadal-awwal.* 19
19	Su 2	6 ·60	25 ·91	20
20	Mo 3	7 ·52	26 ·86	21
21	Tu 4	8 ·43	27 ·80	22
22	We 5	9 ·33	1 ·74	23
23	Th 6	10 ·23	2 ·67	24
24	Fr 7	11 ·13	3 ·60	25
25	Sa 8	12 ·02 13 ·92	4 ·53	26
26	Su 9	14 ·84	5 ·48	27
27	Mo 10	—A ·77	6 ·44	28
28	Tu 11	1 ·71	7 ·40	29
29	We 12	2 ·66	8 ·38	—30
30	Th 13	3 ·64	9 ·38	H. 1392 *Jumadal-akhir.* 1
31	Fr 14	4 ·63	10 ·41	2
—32	Sa 15	5 ·65	11 ·45	3
Paridhavi *Karkata—Adi.* 1	Su 16	Ashadha *Sukla* 6 ·69	12 ·51	4
2	Mo 17	7 ·74	13 ·58	5
3	Tu 18	8 ·81	14 ·68	6
4	We 19	9 ·89	15 ·79	7
5	Th 20	10 ·97	16 ·90	8
6	Fr 21	... ...	... ...	9
7	Sa 22	11 ·05	17 ·00	10
8	Su 23	12 ·12	18 ·09	11
9	Mo 24	13 ·18	19 ·17	12
10	Tu 25	14 ·21	20 ·23	13
11	We ○ 26	P ·23	21 ·28	14
12	Th 27	1 ·21	22 ·30	15
13	Fr 28	2 ·19	23 ·30	16
14	Sa 29	3 ·15	24 ·28	17
15	Su 30	4 ·09	25 ·25	18
16	Mo 31	5 ·01 6 ·92	26 ·21	19

Aug.

Cyclic Sidereal Year, Month and Day	Week-Day English Month and Day	Tithi Ending Moment	Nakshatra Ending Moment	Muhammadan Year, Month and Day
17	Tu 1	*Bahula* 7 ·82	27 ·15	20
18	We 2	8 ·72	1 ·08	21
19	Th 3	9 ·62	2 ·01 3 ·94	22
20	Fr 4	10 ·52	4 ·88	23
21	Sa 5	11 ·42	5 ·82	24
22	Su 6	12 ·34	6 ·77	25
23	Mo 7	13 ·26	7 ·73	26
24	Tu 8	14 ·19	8 ·70	27
25	We 9	—A ·15	9 ·71	28
26	Th 10	1 ·18	10 ·72	—29
27	Fr 11	2 ·12	11 ·76	H. 1392 *Rajab.* 1
28	Sa 12	3 ·13	12 ·81	2
29	Su 13	4 ·17	13 ·89	3
30	Mo 14	5 ·23	14 ·98	4
31	Tu 15	6 ·30	... ...	5
—32	We 16	Sravana *Sukla* 7 ·38	15 ·08	6
Paridhavi *Simha—Avani.* 1	Th 17	8 ·47	16 ·19	7
2	Fr 18	9 ·55	17 ·30	8
3	Sa 19	10 ·62	18 ·40	9
4	Su 20	11 ·67	19 ·48	10
5	Mo 21	12 ·71	20 ·55	11
6	Tu 22	13 ·72	21 ·60	12
7	We 23	14 ·71	22 ·62	13
8	Th 24	P ·69	23 ·63	14
9	Fr 25	1 ·65	24 ·61	15
10	Sa 26	2 ·60	25 ·59	16
11	Su 27	3 ·52	26 ·54	17
12	Mo 28	4 ·43	27 ·48	18
13	Tu 29	*Bahula* 5 ·33	1 ·42	19
14	We 30	6 ·23	2 ·35	20
15	Th 31	7 ·13	3 ·28	21

Sep.

Cyclic Sidereal Year, Month and Day	Week-Day English Month and Day	Tithi Ending Moment	Nakshatra Ending Moment	Muhammadan Year, Month and Day
Paridhavi *Simha—Avani.* 16	Fr 1	Srv. *Bah.* 8 ·03 9 ·93	4 ·22	H. 1392 *Rajab.* 22
17	Sa 2	10 ·65	5 ·16	23
18	Su 3	11 ·78	6 ·10	24
19	Mo 4	12 ·71	7 ·06	25
20	Tu 5	13 ·66	8 ·03	26
21	We 6	14 ·64	9 ·03	27
22	Th 7	—A ·64	10 ·04	28
23	Fr 8	1 ·65	11 ·07	29
24	Sa 9	2 ·69	12 ·12	—30
25	Su 10	3 ·75	13 ·19	H. 1392 *Shaban.* 1
26	Mo 11	4 ·82	14 ·29	2
27	Tu 12	5 ·90	15 ·39	3
28	We 13	6 ·99	16 ·49	4
29	Th 14	Bhadrapada *Sukla*	17 ·60	5
30	Fr 15	7 ·07	18 ·70	6
—31	Sa 16	8 ·14	19 ·79	7
Paridhavi *Kanya—Purattasi.* 1	Su 17	9 ·19	20 ·86	8
2	Mo 18	10 ·23	21 ·91	9
3	Tu 19	11 ·24	22 ·94	10
4	We 20	12 ·24	23 ·95	11
5	Th 21	13 ·22	24 ·95	12
6	Fr 22	14 ·19	25 ·92	13
7	Sa 23	P ·13	26 ·88	14
8	Su 24	1 ·05 2 ·96	27 ·82	15
9	Mo 25	*Bahula* 3 ·87	1 ·76	16
10	Tu 26	4 ·77	2 ·70	17
11	We 27	5 ·67	3 ·63	18
12	Th 28	6 ·57	4 ·56	19
13	Fr 29	7 ·47	5 ·49	20
14	Sa 30	8 ·39	6 ·44	21

Oct.

Cyclic Sidereal Year, Month and Day	Week-Day English Month and Day	Tithi Ending Moment	Nakshatra Ending Moment	Muhammadan Year, Month and Day
15	Su 1	9 ·32	7 ·40	22
16	Mo 2	10 ·26	8 ·37	23
17	Tu 3	11 ·21	9 ·35	24
18	We 4	12 ·19	10 ·36	25
19	Th 5	13 ·19	11 ·38	26
20	Fr 6	14 ·21	12 ·43	27
21	Sa 7	—A ·25	13 ·50	28
22	Su 8	1 ·31	14 ·59	—29
23	Mo 9	2 ·38	15 ·69	H. 1392 *Ramzan.* 1
24	Tu 10	3 ·46	16 ·79	2
25	We 11	4 ·55	17 ·90	3
26	Th 12	5 ·63	... ...	4
27	Fr 13	6 ·71	18 ·01	5
28	Sa 14	Asvina *Sukla* 7 ·77	19 ·10	6
29	Su 15	8 ·80	20 ·17	7
—30	Mo 16	9 ·82	21 ·22	8
Paridhavi *Tula—Aippasi.* 1	Tu 17	10 ·82	22 ·26	9
2	We 18	11 ·79	23 ·28	10
3	Th 19	12 ·76	24 ·27	11
4	Fr 20	13 ·71	25 ·25	12
5	Sa 21	14 ·63	26 ·21	13
6	Su 22	P ·54	27 ·16	14
7	Mo 23	1 ·45	1 ·10	15
8	Tu 24	2 ·35	2 ·04 3 ·97	16
9	We 25	3 ·25	4 ·90	17
10	Th 26	4 ·15	5 ·83	18
11	Fr 27	*Bahula* 5 ·06 6 ·98	6 ·77	19
12	Sa 28	7 ·91	7 ·73	20
13	Su 29	8 ·85	8 ·70	21
14	Mo 30	9 ·80	9 ·68	22
15	Tu 31	10 ·78	10 ·68	23

Nov.

Cyclic Sidereal Year, Month and Day	Week-Day English Month and Day	Tithi Ending Moment	Nakshatra Ending Moment	Muhammadan Year, Month and Day
Paridhavi *Tula—Aippasi.* 16	We 1	11 ·78	11 ·70	*Ramzan.* 24
17	Th 2	*Bah.* 12 ·80	12 ·75	25
18	Fr 3	13 ·85	13 ·81	26
19	Sa 4	14 ·91	14 ·89	27
20	Su 5	—A ·99	15 ·98	28
21	Mo 6	... ...	... ...	29
22	Tu 7	1 ·07	16 ·09	—30
23	We 8	2 ·16	17 ·20	H. 1392 *Shawwal.* 1
24	Th 9	3 ·24	18 ·31	2
25	Fr 10	4 ·31	19 ·40	3
26	Sa 11	5 ·37	20 ·48	4
27	Su 12	*Sukla* 6 ·41	21 ·54	5
28	Mo 13	7 ·44	22 ·58	6
29	Tu 14	8 ·43	23 ·60	7
—30	We 15	9 ·40	24 ·61	8
Paridhavi *Vrischika—Kartigai.* 1	Th 16	10 ·36	25 ·58	9
2	Fr 17	11 ·31	26 ·54	10
3	Sa 18	12 ·24	27 ·49	11
4	Su 19	13 ·16	1 ·44	12
5	Mo 20	Karttika 14 ·07 P ·97	2 ·37	13
6	Tu 21	1 ·87	3 ·30	14
7	We 22	2 ·77	4 ·23	15
8	Th 23	3 ·67	5 ·17	16
9	Fr 24	4 ·59	6 ·11	17
10	Sa 25	5 ·52	7 ·03	18
11	Su 26	6 ·47	8 ·03	19
12	Mo 27	*Bahula* 7 ·44	9 ·00	20
13	Tu 28	8 ·42	10 ·00	21
14	We 29	9 ·41	11 ·02	22
15	Th 30	10 ·43	12 ·03	23

Dec.

Cyclic Sidereal Year, Month and Day	Week-Day English Month and Day	Tithi Ending Moment	Nakshatra Ending Moment	Muhammadan Year, Month and Day
16	Fr 1	11 ·47	13 ·12	24
17	Sa 2	12 ·54	14 ·19	25
18	Su 3	13 ·62	15 ·28	26
19	Mo 4	14 ·71	16 ·39	27
20	Tu 5	—A ·80	17 ·50	28
21	We 6	1 ·88	18 ·61	—29
22	Th 7	2 ·95	19 ·70	H. 1392 *Zi-l-ka'da.* 1
23	Fr 8	... ...	20 ·78	2
24	Sa 9	3 ·01	21 ·85	3
25	Su 10	4 ·05	22 ·90	4
26	Mo 11	5 ·07	23 ·92	5
27	Tu 12	*Sukla* 6 ·06	24 ·92	6
28	We 13	7 ·04	25 ·91	7
—29	Th 14	8 ·00 9 ·94	26 ·88	8
Paridhavi *Dhanus—Margali.* 1	Fr 15	10 ·87	27 ·84	9
2	Sa 16	11 ·79	1 ·78	10
3	Su 17	12 ·70	2 ·71	11
4	Mo 18	Margasira 13 ·60	3 ·64	12
5	Tu 19	14 ·50	4 ·57	13
6	We 20	P ·40	5 ·51	14
7	Th 21	1 ·31	6 ·45	15
8	Fr 22	2 ·23	7 ·40	16
9	Sa 23	3 ·16	8 ·36	17
10	Su 24	4 ·11	9 ·33	18
11	Mo 25	5 ·07	10 ·33	19
12	Tu 26	6 ·06	11 ·34	20
13	We 27	*Bahula* 7 ·05	12 ·37	21
14	Th 28	8 ·08	13 ·42	22
15	Fr 29	9 ·13	14 ·50	23
16	Sa 30	10 ·19	15 ·59	24
17	Su 31	11 ·27	16 ·69	25

15. Svati. 16. Visak. 17. Anur. 18. Jyesh. 19. Mula. 20. P. Ash. 21. U. Ash. 22. Sravn. 23. Dani. 24. Satab. 25. P. Bhad. 26. U. Bhad. 27. Rev.

A. D. 1973. Mesha Sankranti (Commencement of Indian Sidereal Year).

Solar Eclipse. ● (Surya Sid.) April 13·51. Saka 1895. Kaliyuga 5074.

Lunar Eclipse. ○ (Arya Sid.) April 13·40. (S. Cycle) Pramadicha.

Jan.

SOLAR reckoning: Cyclic Sidereal Year, Month and Day	Week-Day	English Month and Day	LUNAR reckoning: Tithi	Tithi Ending Moment	Nakshatra	Nakshatra Ending Moment	Muhammadan Year, Month and Day
Paridhavi *Dhanus—Margali.* 18	Mo	1	*Bah.* 12	·35	17	·80	*Zi-l-kada.* 26
19	Tu	2	13	·44	18	·91	27
20	We	3	14	·53	...	...	28
21	Th	4	—A	·60	19	·00	29
22	Fr	5	1	·66	20	·03	—30
23	Sa	6	2	·70	21	·17	1
24	Su	7	3	·71	22	·21	2
25	Mo	8	4	·71	23	·24	3
26	Tu	9	5	·69	24	·25	4
27	We	10	6	·64	25	·23	5
28	Th	11	*Sukla* 7	·58	26	·21	6
29	Fr	12	8	·51	27	·17	7
—30	Sa	13	9	·43	1	·12	8
1	Su	14	10	·34	2 3	·05 ·98	9
2	Mo	15	11	·24	4	·91	10
3	Tu	16	12	·14	5	·85	11
4	We	17	13 14	·04 ·95	6	·79	12
5	Th	18	Pausha P	·87	7	·73	H. 1392 *Zi-l-hijja.* 13
6	Fr	19	1	·81	8	·69	14
7	Sa	20	2	·75	9	·67	15
8	Su	21	3	·71	10	·65	16
9	Mo	22	4	·70	11	·66	17
10	Tu	23	5	·70	12	·60	18
11	We	24	6	·73	13	·73	19
Paridhavi *Makara—Tai.* 12	Th	25	*Bahula* 7	·78	14	·80	20
13	Fr	26	8	·85	15	·89	21
14	Sa	27	9	·93	16	·99	22
15	Su	28	...	...	...	...	23
16	Mo	29	10	·02	17	·10	24
17	Tu	30	11	·10	18	·20	25
18	We	31	12	·18	19	·30	26

Feb.

Cyclic Sidereal Year, Month and Day	Week-Day	English Month and Day	Tithi	Tithi Ending Moment	Nakshatra	Nakshatra Ending Moment	Muhammadan Year, Month and Day
19	Th	1	13	·25	20	·40	27
20	Fr	2	14	·31	21	·47	28
21	Sa	3	—A	·34	22	·53	—29
22	Su	4	1	·35	23	·56	1
23	Mo	5	2	·35	24	·57	2
24	Tu	6	3	·33	25	·57	3
25	We	7	*Sukla* 4	·28	26	·55	4
26	Th	8	5	·22	27	·50	5
27	Fr	9	6	·14	1	·45	6
28	Sa	10	7 8	·06 ·97	2	·39	7
—29	Su	11	9	·87	3	·33	8
1	Mo	12	10	·77	4	·26	9
2	Tu	13	11	·67	5	·19	10
3	We	14	12	·57	6	·12	11
4	Th	15	13	·49	7	·06	12
5	Fr	16	Magha 14	·43	8 9	·02 ·99	H. 1393 *Muharram.* 13
Paridhavi *Kumbha—Masi.* 6	Sa	17	P	·38	10	·98	14
7	Su	18	1	·34	11	·98	15
8	Mo	19	2	·32	...	...	16
9	Tu	20	3	·32	12	·00	17
10	We	21	4	·35	13	·04	18
11	Th	22	5	·40	14	·11	19
12	Fr	23	6	·47	15	·20	20
13	Sa	24	*Bahula* 7	·55	16	·30	21
14	Su	25	8	·64	17	·40	22
15	Mo	26	9	·72	18	·50	23
16	Tu	27	10	·80	19	·61	24
17	We	28	11	·37	20	·71	25

March

Cyclic Sidereal Year, Month and Day	Week-Day	English Month and Day	Tithi	Tithi Ending Moment	Nakshatra	Nakshatra Ending Moment	Muhammadan Year, Month and Day
Paridhavi *Kumbha—Masi.* 18	Th	1	*Bah.* 12	·92	21	·73	*Muharam.* 26
19	Fr	2	13	·95	22	·84	27
20	Sa	3	14	·96	23	·88	28
21	Su	4	—A	·96	24	·90	29
22	Mo	5	1	·93	25	·90	—30
23	Tu	6	2	·89	26	·88	1
24	We	7	3	·83	27	·84	2
25	Th	8	4	·75	1	·79	3
26	Fr	9	5	·66	2	·74	4
27	Sa	10	6	·57	3	·67	5
28	Su	11	*Sukla* 7	·47	4	·60	6
29	Mo	12	8	·37	5	·53	7
—30	Tu	13	9	·27	6	·46	8
1	We	14	10	·17	7	·40	9
2	Th	15	11	·09	8	·36	10
3	Fr	16	12 13	·02 ·97	9	·82	11
4	Sa	17	Phalguna 14	·94	10	·80	12
5	Su	18	P	·92	11	·80	13
6	Mo	19	1	·92	12	·82	14
7	Tu	20	2	·95	13	·86	H. 1393 *Safar.* 15
8	We	21	...	...	14	·42	16
9	Th	22	3	·00	15	·50	17
10	Fr	23	4	·06	16	·59	18
11	Sa	24	5	·14	17	·69	19
Paridhavi *Mina—Panguni.* 12	Su	25	6	·23	18	·80	20
13	Mo	26	*Bahula* 7	·31	19	·91	21
14	Tu	27	8	·39	...	...	22
15	We	28	9	·46	20	·01	23
16	Th	29	10	·51	21	·09	24
17	Fr	30	11	·54	22	·15	25
18	Sa	31	12	·55	23	·20	26

April

Cyclic Sidereal Year, Month and Day	Week-Day	English Month and Day	Tithi	Tithi Ending Moment	Nakshatra	Nakshatra Ending Moment	Muhammadan Year, Month and Day
19	Su	1	13	·54	24	·22	27
20	Mo	2	14	·50	25	·22	28
21	Tu	3	—A	·45	26	·20	—29
22	We	4	1	·39	27	·17	1
23	Th	5	2	·32	1	·12	2
24	Fr	6	3	·23	2	·07	3
25	Sa	7	4	·13	3 4	·01 ·94	4
26	Su	8	5 6	·03 ·93	5	·87	5
27	Mo	9	*Sukla* 7	·83	6	·80	6
28	Tu	10	8	·73	7	·74	7
29	We	11	9	·65	8	·69	8
—30	Th	12	10	·58	9	·65	9
1	Fr	13	11	·53	10	·63	10
2	Sa	14	12	·49	11	·62	11
3	Su	15	13	·47	12	·64	12
4	Mo	16	Chaitra 14	·48	13	·67	13
5	Tu	17	P	·50	14	·73	14
6	We	18	1	·55	15	·80	15
7	Th	19	2	·61	16	·89	H. 1393 *Rabi-ul-awwal.* 16
8	Fr	20	3	·69	...	...	17
9	Sa	21	4	·77	17	·00	18
Pramadicha *Mesha—Chittirai.* 10	Su	22	5	·86	18	·11	19
11	Mo	23	6	·93	19	·21	20
12	Tu	24	...	...	20	·31	21
13	We	25	*Bahula* 7	·00	21	·39	22
14	Th	26	8	·05	22	·47	23
15	Fr	27	9	·09	23	·52	24
16	Sa	28	10	·10	24	·54	25
17	Su	29	11	·08	25	·55	26
18	Mo	30	12 13	·05 ·99	26	·53	27

May

Cyclic Sidereal Year, Month and Day	Week-Day	English Month and Day	Tithi	Tithi Ending Moment	Nakshatra	Nakshatra Ending Moment	Muhammadan Year, Month and Day
19	Tu	1	14	·92	27	·50	28
20	We	2	—A	·85	1	·46	29
21	Th	3	1	·76	2	·41	—30
Pramadicha *Mesha—Chittirai.* 22	Fr	4	2	·66	3	·34	1
23	Sa	5	3	·56	4	·27	2
24	Su	6	4	·46	5	·20	3
25	Mo	7	5	·36	6	·14	4
26	Tu	8	6	·27	7	·08	5
27	We	9	*Sukla* 7	·18	8 9	·03 ·98	6
28	Th	10	8	·10	10	·95	7
29	Fr	11	9	·05	11	·95	8
30	Sa	12	10	·01	12	·96	9
—31	Su	13	11	·00	13	·99	10
1	Mo	14	12	·00	...	...	11
2	Tu	15	Vaisakha 13	·02	14	·04	H. 1393 *Rabi-ul-akhir.* 12
3	We	16	14	·06	15	·11	13
4	Th	17	P	·12	16	·20	14
5	Fr	18	1	·20	17	·30	15
6	Sa	19	2	·28	18	·41	16
7	Su	20	3	·36	19	·51	17
8	Mo	21	4	·44	20	·61	18
9	Tu	22	5	·51	21	·70	19
10	We	23	6	·53	22	·78	20
11	Th	24	*Bahula* 7	·58	23	·83	21
Pramadicha *Vrishabha—Vaikasi.* 12	Fr	25	8	·60	24	·86	22
13	Sa	26	9	·58	25	·87	23
14	Su	27	10	·55	26	·86	24
15	Mo	28	11	·50	27	·84	25
16	Tu	29	12	·43	1	·80	26
17	We	30	13	·35	2	·75	27
18	Th	31	14	·26	3	·68	28

June

Cyclic Sidereal Year, Month and Day	Week-Day	English Month and Day	Tithi	Tithi Ending Moment	Nakshatra	Nakshatra Ending Moment	Muhammadan Year, Month and Day
19	Fr	1	—A	·16	4	·61	—29
20	Sa	2	1 2	·03 ·96	5	·54	1
21	Su	3	3	·86	6	·48	2
22	Mo	4	4	·76	7	·42	3
23	Tu	5	5	·63	8	·36	4
24	We	6	6	·61	9	·32	5
25	Th	7	*Sukla* 7	·55	10	·29	6
26	Fr	8	8	·51	11	·27	7
27	Sa	9	9	·49	12	·28	8
28	Su	10	10	·48	13	·30	9
29	Mo	11	11	·50	14	·35	10
30	Tu	12	12	·54	15	·42	11
31	We	13	13	·60	16	·50	12
—32	Th	14	Jyeshtha 14	·67	17	·60	13
1	Fr	15	P	·75	18	·70	14
2	Sa	16	1	·84	19	·81	15
3	Su	17	2	·92	20	·91	16
4	Mo	18	3	·99	...	...	H. 1393 *Jumadal-awwal.* 17
5	Tu	19	...	...	21	·01	18
6	We	20	4	·04	22	·09	19
7	Th	21	*Bahula* 5	·07	23	·14	20
Pramadicha *Mithuna—Ani.* 8	Fr	22	6	·08	24	·18	21
9	Sa	23	7	·07	25	·19	22
10	Su	24	8 9	·04 ·99	26	·20	23
11	Mo	25	10	·92	27	·17	24
12	Tu	26	11	·84	1	·13	25
13	We	27	12	·75	2	·08	26
14	Th	28	13	·65	3 4	·02 ·96	27
15	Fr	29	14	·55	5	·89	28
16	Sa ●	30	—A	·45	6	·82	29

Naksh:—1. Asvn. 2. Bhar. 3. Krit. 4. Rohi. 5. Mrig. 6. Ardh. 7. Punar. 8. Push. 9. Aslesh. 10. Magh. 11. P. Phal. 12. U. Phal. 13. Hasta. 14. Chit.

A. D. 1973.
A.—Amavasya.
P.—Paurnami.

Kollam 1149, Commences { N. Malabar—Sept. / S. Malabar—Aug.

Hijra 1393, Commences, Feb. 4.

Vikrama 2030.
Bengal San 1379.
(N. Cycle) Kshaya.

Pramadicha Mithuna—Ani; Pramadicha Karkata—Adi; Pramadicha Simha—Avani. Sukla; Ashadha; Bahula; Sukla; Sravana; Bahula; Suk. H. 1393 Jumadal-akhir; H. 1393 Rajab.

SOLAR reckoning: Cyclic Sidereal Year, Month and Day.	SOLAR reckoning: Week-Day English Month and Day.	LUNAR reckoning: Tithi Ending Moment.	LUNAR reckoning: Nakshatra Ending Moment.	LUNAR reckoning: Muhammadan Year, Month and Day.
	July			
17	Su 1	1 ·35	7 ·75	—30
18	Mo 2	2 ·25	8 ·69	1
19	Tu 3	3 ·16	9 ·65	2
20	We 4	4 ·08	10 ·62	3
21	Th 5	5 ·02 / 6 ·98	11 ·60	4
22	Fr 6	7 ·96	12 ·60	5
23	Sa 7	8 ·96	13 ·62	6
24	Su 8	9 ·98	14 ·66	7
25	Mo 9	... ...	15 ·73	8
26	Tu 10	10 ·02	16 ·81	9
27	We 11	11 ·08	17 ·90	10
28	Th 12	12 ·15	... ...	11
29	Fr 13	13 ·24	18 ·00	12
30	Sa 14	14 ·32	19 ·11	13
—31	Su 15	P ·40	20 ·22	14
1	Mo 16	1 ·47	21 ·31	15
2	Tu 17	2 ·52	22 ·39	16
3	We 18	3 ·55	23 ·45	17
4	Th 19	4 ·56	24 ·49	18
5	Fr 20	5 ·55	25 ·52	19
6	Sa 21	6 ·52	26 ·52	20
7	Su 22	7 ·47	27 ·50	21
8	Mo 23	8 ·40	1 ·47	22
9	Tu 24	9 ·32	2 ·42	23
10	We 25	10 ·24	3 ·37	24
11	Th 26	11 ·14	4 ·30	25
12	Fr 27	12 ·04 / 13 ·94	5 ·23	26
13	Sa 28	14 ·84	6 ·16	27
14	Su 29	—A ·74	7 ·09	28
15	Mo 30	1 ·65	8 ·04 / 9 ·99	—29
16	Tu 31	2 ·56	10 ·95	1
	Aug.			
17	We 1	3 ·50	11 ·92	2
18	Th 2	4 ·47	12 ·92	3
19	Fr 3	5 ·45	13 ·93	4
20	Sa 4	6 ·45	14 ·97	5
21	Su 5	7 ·46	... ...	6
22	Mo 6	8 ·50	15 ·03	7
23	Tu 7	9 ·55	16 ·11	8
24	We 8	10 ·62	17 ·20	9
25	Th 9	11 ·71	18 ·30	10
26	Fr 10	12 ·80	19 ·41	11
27	Sa 11	13 ·88	20 ·52	12
28	Su 12	14 ·95	21 ·62	13
29	Mo 13	... ...	22 ·70	14
30	Tu 14	P ·00	23 ·76	15
31	We 15	1 ·03	24 ·81	16
—32	Th 16	2 ·05	25 ·84	17
1	Fr 17	3 ·03	26 ·85	18
2	Sa 18	4 ·00 / 5 ·96	27 ·83	19
3	Su 19	6 ·90	1 ·80	20
4	Mo 20	7 ·83	2 ·76	21
5	Tu 21	8 ·74	3 ·70	22
6	We 22	9 ·64	4 ·64	23
7	Th 23	10 ·54	5 ·57	24
8	Fr 24	11 ·44	6 ·50	25
9	Sa 25	12 ·34	7 ·43	26
10	Su 26	13 ·24	8 ·37	27
11	Mo 27	14 ·16	9 ·32	28
12	Tu 28	—A ·08	10 ·28	29
13	We 29	1 ·02 / 2 ·97	11 ·25	—30
14	Th 30	3 ·95	12 ·24	1
15	Fr 31	4 ·96	13 ·26	2

Pramadicha Simha—Avani; Pramadicha Kanya—Purattasi; Pramadicha Tula—Aippasi. Sukla; Bhadrapada; Bahula; Sukla; Asvina; Bahula; K. Suk. H 1393 Shaban; H. 1393 Ramzan; Shawwal.

SOLAR reckoning: Cyclic Sidereal Year, Month and Day.	SOLAR reckoning: Week-Day English Month and Day.	LUNAR reckoning: Tithi Ending Moment.	LUNAR reckoning: Nakshatra Ending Moment.	LUNAR reckoning: Muhammadan Year, Month and Day.
	Sep.			
16	Sa 1	5 ·98	14 ·29	3
17	Su 2	... ...	15 ·34	4
18	Mo 3	6 ·02	16 ·41	5
19	Tu 4	7 ·07	17 ·50	6
20	We 5	8 ·14	18 ·60	7
21	Th 6	9 ·22	19 ·71	8
22	Fr 7	10 ·30	20 ·82	9
23	Sa 8	11 ·38	21 ·92	10
24	Su 9	12 ·46	... ...	11
25	Mo 10	13 ·52	22 ·01	12
26	Tu 11	14 ·56	23 ·08	13
27	We 12	P ·58	24 ·13	14
28	Th 13	1 ·56	25 ·16	15
29	Fr 14	2 ·54	26 ·17	16
30	Sa 15	3 ·49	27 ·16	17
—31	Su 16	4 ·43	1 ·14	18
1	Mo 17	5 ·36	2 ·10	19
2	Tu 18	6 ·27	3 ·04 / 4 ·98	20
3	We 19	7 ·17	5 ·91	21
4	Th 20	8 ·07 / 9 ·97	6 ·84	22
5	Fr 21	10 ·87	7 ·77	23
6	Sa 22	11 ·77	8 ·71	24
7	Su 23	12 ·69	9 ·65	25
8	Mo 24	13 ·61	10 ·61	26
9	Tu 25	14 ·56	11 ·58	27
10	We 26	—A ·52	12 ·57	28
11	Th 27	1 ·50	13 ·58	—29
12	Fr 28	2 ·49	14 ·60	1
13	Sa 29	3 ·51	15 ·65	2
14	Su 30	4 ·55	16 ·72	3
	Oct.			
15	Mo 1	5 ·61	17 ·81	4
16	Tu 2	6 ·69	18 ·91	5
17	We 3	7 ·77	... ...	6
18	Th 4	8 ·86	19 ·01	7
19	Fr 5	9 ·94	20 ·12	8
20	Sa 6	... ...	21 ·22	9
21	Su 7	10 ·01	22 ·32	10
22	Mo 8	11 ·07	23 ·39	11
23	Tu 9	12 ·11	24 ·45	12
24	We 10	13 ·14	25 ·48	13
25	Th 11	14 ·12	26 ·49	14
26	Fr 12	P ·10	27 ·48	15
27	Sa 13	1 ·06	1 ·47	16
28	Su 14	2 ·00 / 3 ·92	2 ·43	17
29	Mo 15	4 ·83	3 ·38	18
—30	Tu 16	5 ·74	4 ·32	19
1	We 17	6 ·64	5 ·25	20
2	Th 18	7 ·54	6 ·18	21
3	Fr 19	8 ·44	7 ·11	22
4	Sa 20	9 ·35	8 ·05 / 9 ·99	23
5	Su 21	10 ·27	10 ·94	24
6	Mo 22	11 ·20	11 ·92	25
7	Tu 23	12 ·14	12 ·90	26
8	We 24	13 ·10	13 ·90	27
9	Th 25	14 ·08	14 ·92	28
10	Fr 26	—A ·08	15 ·96	29
11	Sa 27	1 ·10	... ...	—30
12	Su 28	2 ·14	16 ·03	1
13	Mo 29	3 ·21	17 ·11	2
14	Tu 30	4 ·29	18 ·20	3
15	We 31	5 ·37	19 ·31	4

Pramadicha Tula—Aippasi; Pramadicha Vrischika—Kartigai; Pramadicha Dhanus—Margali. Sukla; Kartika; Bahula; Sukla; Margasira; Bahula; Suk.; Pausha. H. 1393 Shawwal; H. 1393 Zi-l-ka'da; Zi-l-hijja.

SOLAR reckoning: Cyclic Sidereal Year, Month and Day.	SOLAR reckoning: Week-Day English Month and Day.	LUNAR reckoning: Tithi Ending Moment.	LUNAR reckoning: Nakshatra Ending Moment.	LUNAR reckoning: Muhammadan Year, Month and Day.
	Nov.			
16	Th 1	6 ·45	20 ·42	5
17	Fr 2	7 ·53	21 ·52	6
18	Sa 3	8 ·61	22 ·62	7
19	Su 4	9 ·67	23 ·70	8
20	Mo 5	10 ·71	24 ·76	9
21	Tu 6	11 ·73	25 ·79	10
22	We 7	12 ·71	26 ·81	11
23	Th 8	13 ·69	27 ·82	12
24	Fr 9	14 ·65	1 ·80	13
25	Sa 10	P ·60	2 ·76	14
26	Su 11	1 ·52	3 ·71	15
27	Mo 12	2 ·43	4 ·65	16
28	Tu 13	3 ·34	5 ·59	17
29	We 14	4 ·24	6 ·52	18
—30	Th 15	5 ·14	7 ·45	19
1	Fr 16	6 ·04 / 7 ·96	8 ·39	20
2	Sa 17	8 ·88	9 ·33	21
3	Su 18	9 ·80	10 ·28	22
4	Mo 19	10 ·74	11 ·25	23
5	Tu 20	11 ·71	12 ·22	24
6	We 21	12 ·70	13 ·22	25
7	Th 22	13 ·70	14 ·24	26
8	Fr 23	14 ·72	15 ·28	27
9	Sa 24	—A ·76	16 ·34	28
10	Su 25	1 ·83	17 ·41	—29
11	Mo 26	2 ·91	18 ·50	1
12	Tu 27	... ...	19 ·61	2
13	We 28	3 ·00	20 ·72	3
14	Th 29	4 ·08	21 ·83	4
15	Fr 30	5 ·16	22 ·92	5
	Dec.			
16	Sa 1	6 ·24	... ...	6
17	Su 2	7 ·30	23 ·00	7
18	Mo 3	8 ·34	24 ·07	8
19	Tu 4	9 ·36	25 ·11	9
20	We 5	10 ·35	26 ·14	10
21	Th 6	11 ·32	27 ·14	11
22	Fr 7	12 ·28	1 ·12	12
23	Sa 8	13 ·22	2 ·09	13
24	Su 9	14 ·14	3 ·05	14
25	Mo ⊙ 10	P ·06 / 1 ·97	4 ·00 / 5 ·93	15
26	Tu 11	2 ·87	6 ·86	16
27	We 12	3 ·77	7 ·79	17
28	Th 13	4 ·67	8 ·73	18
29	Fr 14	5 ·58	9 ·67	19
—30	Sa 15	6 ·50	10 ·61	20
1	Su 16	7 ·44	11 ·57	21
2	Mo 17	8 ·38	12 ·55	22
3	Tu 18	9 ·35	13 ·54	23
4	We 19	10 ·33	14 ·55	24
5	Th 20	11 ·35	15 ·59	25
6	Fr 21	12 ·37	16 ·64	26
7	Sa 22	13 ·41	17 ·72	27
8	Su 23	14 ·48	18 ·80	28
9	Mo 24	—A ·56	19 ·90	29
10	Tu 25	1 ·65	... ...	—30
11	We 26	2 ·74	20 ·01	1
12	Th 27	3 ·82	21 ·12	2
13	Fr 28	4 ·89	22 ·22	3
14	Sa 29	5 ·95	23 ·31	4
15	Su 30	6 ·99	24 ·38	5
16	Mo 31	... ...	25 ·48	6

15. Svati. 16. Visak. 17. Anur. 18. Jyesh. 19. Mula. 20. P. Ash. 21. U. Ash. 22 Sravn. 23. Dani. 24. Satab. 25 P. Bhad. 26. U. Bhad. 27. Rev.

A. D. 1974. **Mesha Sankranti** (Commencement of Indian Sidereal Year).

Solar Eclipse. ● **(Surya Sid.) April 13·77.** **Saka 1896.** **Kaliyuga 5075.**

Lunar Eclipse. ○ **(Arya Sid.) April 13·66.** **(S. Cycle) Ananda.**

SOLAR reckoning: Cyclic Sidereal Year, Month and Day	Week-Day	English Month and Day	LUNAR reckoning: Tithi Ending Moment	Nakshatra Ending Moment	Muhammadan Year, Month and Day
		Jan.			
Pramadicha *Dhanus—Margali.*			**Pausha, *Sukla***		**H. 1393 *Zil-hijja.***
17	Tu	1	7 ·00 8 ·99	26 ·46	7
18	We	2	9 ·96	27 ·47	8
19	Th	3	10 ·92	1 ·45	9
20	Fr	4	11 ·86	2 ·42	10
21	Sa	5	12 ·79	3 ·38	11
22	Su	6	13 ·70	4 ·33	12
23	Mo	7	14 ·61	5 ·27	13
24	Tu	8	P ·52	6 ·20	14
25	We	9	1 ·42	7 ·13	15
26	Th	10	2 ·32	8 ·07	16
27	Fr	11	3 ·23	9 ·01 10 ·95	17
28	Sa	12	4 ·15	11 ·91	18
—29	Su	13	5 ·08	12 ·88	19
			Bahula		
1	Mo	14	6 ·03 7 ·99	13 ·86	20
2	Tu	15	8 ·98	14 ·88	21
3	We	16	9 ·99	15 ·91	22
4	Th	17	... ...	16 ·95	23
5	Fr	18	10 ·02	... ...	24
6	Sa	19	11 ·07	17 ·02	25
7	Su	20	12 ·14	18 ·11	26
8	Mo	21	13 ·22	19 ·21	27
9	Tu	22	14 ·30	20 ·32	28
10	We	23	—A ·40	21 ·43	29
11	Th	24	1 ·48	22 ·53	—30
Pramadicha *Makara—Tai.*					
12	Fr	25	2 ·55	23 ·62	1
13	Sa	26	3 ·61	24 ·70	2
14	Su	27	4 ·63	25 ·75	3
15	Mo	28	5 ·65	26 ·78	4
16	Tu	29	6 ·63	27 ·79	5
17	We	30	7 ·61	1 ·78	6
18	Th	31	8 ·56	2 ·76	7
		Feb.			
			Magha, *Sukla*		**H. 1394 *Muharram.***
19	Fr	1	9 ·49	3 ·72	8
20	Sa	2	10 ·42	4 ·67	9
21	Su	3	11 ·34	5 ·61	10
22	Mo	4	12 ·25	6 ·54	11
23	Tu	5	13 ·15	7 ·47	12
24	We	6	14 ·05 P ·95	8 ·40	13
25	Th	7	1 ·86	9 ·34	14
26	Fr	8	2 ·78	10 ·28	15
27	Sa	9	3 ·72	11 ·24	16
28	Su	10	4 ·67	12 ·21	17
29	Mo	11	5 ·63	13 ·20	18
—30	Tu	12	6 ·62	14 ·20	19
Pramadicha *Kumbha—Masi.*			***Bahula***		
1	We	13	7 ·62	15 ·22	20
2	Th	14	8 ·65	16 ·26	21
3	Fr	15	9 ·70	17 ·33	22
4	Sa	16	10 ·77	18 ·42	23
5	Su	17	11 ·85	19 ·52	24
6	Mo	18	12 ·93	20 ·62	25
7	Tu	19	... ...	21 ·73	26
8	We	20	13 ·02	22 ·83	27
9	Th	21	14 ·10	23 ·92	28
10	Fr	22	—A ·17	... ...	29
			Phalg. *Suk.*		
11	Sa	23	1 ·23	24 ·00	—30
					Safar.
12	Su	24	2 ·26	25 ·06	1
13	Mo	25	3 ·27	26 ·10	2
14	Tu	26	4 ·25	27 ·11	3
15	We	27	5 ·23	1 ·12	4
16	Th	28	6 ·18	2 ·10	5

SOLAR reckoning: Cyclic Sidereal Year, Month and Day	Week-Day	English Month and Day	LUNAR reckoning: Tithi Ending Moment	Nakshatra Ending Moment	Muhammadan Year, Month and Day
		March			
Pramadicha *Kumbha—Masi.*			**Phalguna, *Sukla***		**H. 1394 *Safar.***
17	Fr	1	7 ·12	3 ·06	6
18	Sa	2	8 ·04 9 ·95	4 ·01 5 ·95	7
19	Su	3	10 ·85	6 ·89	8
20	Mo	4	11 ·75	7 ·82	9
21	Tu	5	12 ·65	8 ·75	10
22	We	6	13 ·55	9 ·68	11
23	Th	7	14 ·47	10 ·62	12
24	Fr	8	P ·39	11 ·57	13
25	Sa	9	1 ·32	12 ·54	14
26	Su	10	2 ·27	13 ·52	15
27	Mo	11	3 ·23	14 ·52	16
28	Tu	12	4 ·22	15 ·54	17
—29	We	13	5 ·22	16 ·58	18
			Bahula		
1	Th	14	6 ·25	17 ·64	19
2	Fr	15	7 ·30	18 ·72	20
3	Sa	16	8 ·37	19 ·81	21
4	Su	17	9 ·45	20 ·91	22
5	Mo	18	10 ·54	... ...	23
6	Tu	19	11 ·63	21 ·02	24
7	We	20	12 ·71	22 ·13	25
8	Th	21	13 ·77	23 ·23	26
9	Fr	22	14 ·82	24 ·31	27
10	Sa	23	—A ·86	25 ·37	28
Pramadicha *Mina—Panguni.*					
11	Su	24	1 ·86	26 ·41	—29
					H. 1394 *Rabi-ul-awwal.*
12	Mo	25	2 ·84	27 ·43	1
13	Tu	26	3 ·81	1 ·44	2
14	We	27	4 ·76	2 ·42	3
15	Th	28	5 ·70	3 ·39	4
			Sukla		
16	Fr	29	6 ·62	4 ·34	5
17	Sa	30	7 ·53	5 ·28	6
18	Su	31	8 ·43	6 ·22	7
		April			
			Chaitra		
19	Mo	1	9 ·33	7 ·15	8
20	Tu	2	10 ·23	8 ·08	9
21	We	3	11 ·13	9 ·02 10 ·96	10
22	Th	4	12 ·04 13 ·96	11 ·91	11
23	Fr	5	14 ·89	12 ·87	12
24	Sa	6	P ·84	13 ·85	13
25	Su	7	1 ·81	14 ·84	14
26	Mo	8	2 ·78	15 ·85	15
27	Tu	9	3 ·78	16 ·89	16
28	We	10	4 ·81	17 ·95	17
29	Th	11	5 ·86	... ...	18
30	Fr	12	6 ·93	18 ·02	19
—31	Sa	13	... ...	19 ·11	20
Ananda *Mesha—Chittirai.*			***Bahula***		
1	Su	14	7 ·01	20 ·21	21
2	Mo	15	8 ·10	21 ·32	22
3	Tu	16	9 ·18	22 ·43	23
4	We	17	10 ·26	23 ·53	24
5	Th	18	11 ·32	24 ·61	25
6	Fr	19	12 ·37	25 ·68	26
7	Sa	20	13 ·41	26 ·73	27
8	Su	21	14 ·40	27 ·76	28
9	Mo	22	—A ·39	1 ·77	29
			Vsk. *Sukla*		
10	Tu	23	1 ·35	2 ·75	—30
					Rabi-ul-akhir.
11	We	24	2 ·30	3 ·72	1
12	Th	25	3 ·24	4 ·68	2
13	Fr	26	4 ·16	5 ·63	3
14	Sa	27	5 ·07 6 ·97	6 ·56	4
15	Su	28	7 ·87	7 ·49	5
16	Mo	29	8 ·77	8 ·42	6
17	Tu	30	9 ·67	9 ·36	7

SOLAR reckoning: Cyclic Sidereal Year, Month and Day	Week-Day	English Month and Day	LUNAR reckoning: Tithi Ending Moment	Nakshatra Ending Moment	Muhammadan Year, Month and Day
		May			
Ananda *Mesha—Chittirai.*			**Vaisakha, *Sukla***		**H. 1394 *Rabi-ul-akhir.***
18	We	1	10 ·57	10 ·30	8
19	Th	2	11 ·49	11 ·25	9
20	Fr	3	12 ·42	12 ·20	10
21	Sa	4	13 ·37	13 ·17	11
22	Su	5	14 ·33	14 ·16	12
23	Mo	6	P ·31	15 ·17	13
24	Tu	7	1 ·32	16 ·21	14
25	We	8	2 ·35	17 ·26	15
26	Th	9	3 ·39	18 ·33	16
27	Fr	10	4 ·45	19 ·41	17
28	Sa	11	5 ·52	20 ·51	18
29	Su	12	6 ·61	21 ·62	19
30	Mo	13	7 ·69	22 ·73	20
—31	Tu	14	8 ·77	23 ·83	21
			Bahula		
1	We	15	9 ·83	24 ·92	22
2	Th	16	10 ·88	25 ·99	23
3	Fr	17	11 ·91	... ...	24
4	Sa	18	12 ·92	26 ·05	25
5	Su	19	13 ·91	27 ·08	26
6	Mo	20	14 ·88	1 ·09	27
7	Tu	21	—A ·83	2 ·08	28
8	We	22	1 ·76	3 ·05	—29
					Jumad-al-awwal.
9	Th	23	2 ·67	4 ·02 5 ·97	1
Ananda *Vrishabha—Vaikasi.*			***Sukla***		
10	Fr	24	3 ·57	6 ·90	2
11	Sa	25	4 ·47	7 ·83	3
12	Su	26	5 ·37	8 ·76	4
13	Mo	27	6 ·27	9 ·70	5
14	Tu	28	7 ·17	10 ·64	6
15	We	29	8 ·07 9 ·99	11 ·58	7
16	Th	30	10 ·92	12 ·53	8
17	Fr	31	11 ·86	13 ·50	9
		June			
			Jyeshtha		**H. 1394 *Jumad-al-awwal.***
18	Sa	1	12 ·83	14 ·48	10
19	Su	2	13 ·81	15 ·50	11
20	Mo	3	14 ·81	16 ·53	12
21	Tu ○	4	P ·83	17 ·57	13
22	We	5	1 ·88	18 ·63	14
23	Th	6	2 ·95	19 ·71	15
24	Fr	7	... ...	20 ·81	16
25	Sa	8	3 ·02	21 ·92	17
26	Su	9	4 ·10	... ...	18
27	Mo	10	5 ·18	22 ·03	19
28	Tu	11	6 ·25	23 ·13	20
29	We	12	7 ·31	24 ·22	21
30	Th	13	8 ·36	25 ·30	22
—31	Fr	14	9 ·39	26 ·36	23
			Bahula		
1	Sa	15	10 ·41	27 ·40	24
2	Su	16	11 ·39	1 ·41	25
3	Mo	17	12 ·36	2 ·41	26
4	Tu	18	13 ·31	3 ·39	27
5	We	19	14 ·24	4 ·35	28
6	Th ●	20	—A ·16	5 ·30	29
Ananda *Mithuna—Ani.*			**Ashadha, *Sukla***		
7	Fr	21	1 ·06 2 ·96	6 ·24	—30
					H. 1394 *Jumad-al-akhir.*
8	Sa	22	3 ·86	7 ·17	1
9	Su	23	4 ·76	8 ·10	2
10	Mo	24	5 ·66	9 ·03 10 ·97	3
11	Tu	25	6 ·56	11 ·91	4
12	We	26	7 ·47	12 ·86	5
13	Th	27	8 ·40	13 ·88	6
14	Fr	28	9 ·35	14 ·82	7
15	Sa	29	10 ·31	15 ·82	8
16	Su	30	11 ·30	16 ·84	9

Naksh :— 1. Asvn. 2. Bhar. 3. Krit. 4. Rohi. 5. Mrig. 6. Ardh. 7. Punar. 8. Push. 9. Aslesh. 10. Magh. 11. P. Phal. 12. U. Phal. 13. Hasta. 14. Chit.-

A. D. 1974. | Kollam 1150, Commences { N. Malabar—Sept. S. Malabar—Aug. | Hijra 1394, Commences, Jan. 25. | Vikrama 2031.
A.—Amavasya. | | | Bengal San 1380.
P.—Paurnami. | | | (N. Cycle) Prabhava.

July — Solar: Ananda, Mithuna—Ani. (17–32); Ananda, Karkata—Adi. (1–15). Lunar: Ashadha Suk. (12–14), Ashadha (P–A, Bahula); Sukla. Muhammadan: H. 1394 Jumadal-akhir.

Cyclic Sidereal Year, Month and Day.	Week-Day English Month and Day.		Tithi Ending Moment.		Nakshatra Ending Moment.		Muhammadan Year, Month and Day.
17	Mo	1	12	·29	17	·88	10
18	Tu	2	13	·31	18	·94	11
19	We	3	14	·36	...	...	12
20	Th	4	P	·42	19	·02	13
21	Fr	5	1	·49	20	·12	14
22	Sa	6	2	·57	21	·22	15
23	Su	7	3	·65	22	·33	16
24	Mo	8	4	·73	23	·43	17
25	Tu	9	5	·79	24	·53	18
26	We	10	6	·84	25	·61	19
27	Th	11	7	·87	26	·67	20
28	Fr	12	8	·89	27	·71	21
29	Sa	13	9	·87	1	·73	22
30	Su	14	10	·84	2	·74	23
31	Mo	15	11	·79	3	·72	24
—32	Tu	16	12	·72	4	·69	25
1	We	17	13	·64	5	·64	26
2	Th	18	14	·55	6	·58	27
3	Fr	19	—A	·45	7	·52	28
4	Sa	20	1	·35	8	·45	—29
5	Su	21	2	·25	9	·38	1
6	Mo	22	3	·15	10	·31	2
7	Tu	23	4 5	·05 ·96	11	·25	3
8	We	24	6	·88	12	·20	4
9	Th	25	7	·83	13	·17	5
10	Fr	26	8	·79	14	·14	6
11	Sa	27	9	·77	15	·14	7
12	Su	28	10	·77	16	·15	8
13	Mo	29	11	·79	17	·19	9
14	Tu	30	12	·82	18	·25	10
15	We	31	13	·88	19	·33	11

Aug. — Solar: Ananda (16–31); Ananda, Simha—Avani. (1–15). Lunar: Sravana (14–4), Bahula; Adhika Bhadra. Sukla. Muhammadan: H. 1394 Rajab.; H. 1394 Shaban.

Cyclic Sidereal Year, Month and Day.	Week-Day English Month and Day.		Tithi Ending Moment.		Nakshatra Ending Moment.		Muhammadan Year, Month and Day.
16	Th	1	14	·96	20	·42	12
17	Fr	2	...	...	21	·52	13
18	Sa	3	P	·04	22	·63	14
19	Su	4	1	·13	23	·74	15
20	Mo	5	2	·20	24	·84	16
21	Tu	6	3	·27	25	·92	17
22	We	7	4	·32	26	·98	18
23	Th	8	5	·35	...	...	19
24	Fr	9	6	·37	27	·02	20
25	Sa	10	7	·35	1	·05	21
26	Su	11	8	·33	2	·07	22
27	Mo	12	9	·28	3	·05	23
28	Tu	13	10	·22	4 5	·02 ·97	24
29	We	14	11	·14	·6	·91	25
30	Th	15	12 13	·05 ·95	7	·85	26
—31	Fr	16	14	·85	8	·79	27
1	Sa	17	—A	75	9	·72	28
2	Su	18	1	·65	10	·65	29
3	Mo	19	2	·55	11	·59	—30
4	Tu	20	3	·46	12	·54	1
5	We	21	4	·39	13	·50	2
6	Th	22	5	·32	14	·47	3
7	Fr	23	6	·28	15	·46	4
8	Sa	24	7	·27	16	·47	5
9	Su	25	8	·27	17	·51	6
10	Mo	26	9	·29	18	·56	7
11	Tu	27	10	·33	19	·63	8
12	We	28	11	·39	20	·72	9
13	Th	29	12	·46	21	·82	10
14	Fr	30	13	·54	22	·93	11
15	Sa	31	14	·63	...	...	12

Sep. — Solar: Ananda, Simha—Avani. (16–31); Ananda, Kanya—Purattasi. (1–14). Lunar: Adhika Bhadrapada (P–12), Bahula; Bhadrapada Sukla. Muhammadan: H. 1394 Shaban.

Cyclic Sidereal Year, Month and Day.	Week-Day English Month and Day.		Tithi Ending Moment.		Nakshatra Ending Moment.		Muhammadan Year, Month and Day.
16	Su	1	P	·71	23	·04	13
17	Mo	2	1	·78	24	·14	14
18	Tu	3	2	·83	25	·22	15
19	We	4	3	·87	26	·29	16
20	Th	5	4	·89	27	·34	17
21	Fr	6	5	·87	1	·38	18
22	Sa	7	6	·84	2	·39	19
23	Su	8	7	·79	3	·38	20
24	Mo	9	8	·73	4	·35	21
25	Tu	10	9	·65	5	·31	22
26	We	11	10	·57	6	·26	23
27	Th	12	11	·48	7	·20	24
28	Fr	13	12	·38	8	·13	25
29	Sa	14	13	·28	9 10	·03 ·99	26
30	Su	15	14	·18	11	·93	27
—31	Mo	16	A 1	·08 ·99	12	·87	28
1	Tu	17	2	·92	13	·83	—29
2	We	18	3	·86	14	·80	1
3	Th	19	4	·82	15	·78	2
4	Fr	20	5	·80	16	·80	3
5	Sa	21	6	·80	17	·82	4
6	Su	22	7	·82	18	·87	5
7	Mo	23	8	·86	19	·94	6
8	Tu	24	9	·92	...	...	7
9	We	25	10	·99	20	·02	8
10	Th	26	..	...	21	·12	9
11	Fr	27	11	·08	22	·23	10
12	Sa	28	12	·17	23	·34	11
13	Su	29	13	·25	24	·44	12
14	Mo	30	14	·32	25	·53	13

Oct. — Solar: Ananda (15–31); Ananda, Tula—Aippasi. (1–14). Lunar: Nija (P–2), Bahula; Sukla; Asvina. Muhammadan: H. 1394 Ramzan.; H. 1394 Shawwal.

Cyclic Sidereal Year, Month and Day.	Week-Day English Month and Day.		Tithi Ending Moment.		Nakshatra Ending Moment.		Muhammadan Year, Month and Day.
15	Tu	1	P	·37	26	·60	14
16	We	2	1	·41	27	·66	15
17	Th	3	2	·43	1	·70	16
18	Fr	4	3	·42	2	·71	17
19	Sa	5	4	·39	3	·70	18
20	Su	6	5	·34	4	·68	19
21	Mo	7	6	·28	5	·65	20
22	Tu	8	7	·21	6	·60	21
23	We	9	8	·13	7	·53	22
24	Th	10	9 10	·03 ·93	8	·46	23
25	Fr	11	11	·83	9	·39	24
26	Sa	12	12	·73	10	·33	25
27	Su	13	13	·64	11	·27	26
28	Mo	14	14	·56	12	·21	27
29	Tu	15	—A	·49	13	·16	28
30	We	16	1	·43	14	·13	29
—31	Th	17	2	·39	15	·11	—30
1	Fr	18	3	·37	16	·12	1
2	Sa	19	4	·38	17	·14	2
3	Su	20	5	·40	18	·18	3
4	Mo	21	6	·45	19	·24	4
5	Tu	22	7	·51	20	·32	5
6	We	23	8	·59	21	·42	6
7	Th	24	9	·68	22	·53	7
8	Fr	25	10	·76	23	·64	8
9	Sa	26	11	·84	24	·74	9
10	Su	27	12	·91	25	·83	10
11	Mo	28	13	·97	26	·92	11
12	Tu	29	...	...	27	·98	12
13	We	30	14	·00	...	...	13
14	Th	31	P	·02	1	·02	14

Nov. — Solar: Ananda, Tula—Aippasi. (15–29); Ananda, Vrischika—Kartigai. (1–15). Lunar: Asvina, Bahula; Sukla; Karttika. Muhammadan: H. 1394 Shawwal.

Cyclic Sidereal Year, Month and Day.	Week-Day English Month and Day.		Tithi Ending Moment.		Nakshatra Ending Moment.		Muhammadan Year, Month and Day.
15	Fr	1	1 2	·01 ·98	2	·03	15
16	Sa	2	3	·94	3	·03	16
17	Su	3	4	·88	4 5	·02 ·98	17
18	Mo	4	5	·81	6	·93	18
19	Tu	5	6	·73	7	·87	19
20	We	6	7	·63	8	·81	20
21	Th	7	8	·53	9	·74	21
22	Fr	8	9	·43	10	·67	22
23	Sa	9	10	·33	11	·60	23
24	Su	10	11	·24	12	·54	24
25	Mo	11	12	·16	13	·49	25
26	Tu	12	13	·09	14	·45	26
27	We	13	14	·03	15	·44	27
28	Th	14	A 1	·00 ·98	16	·44	28
—29	Fr	15	2	·99	17	·45	—29
1	Sa	16	...	...	18	·49	1
2	Su	17	3	·01	19	·55	2
3	Mo	18	4	·06	20	·63	3
4	Tu	19	5	·13	21	·73	4
5	We	20	6	·21	22	·83	5
6	Th	21	7	·29	23	·93	6
7	Fr	22	8	·38	...	...	7
8	Sa	23	9	·46	24	·04	8
9	Su	24	10	·53	25	·14	9
10	Mo	25	11	·59	26	·22	10
11	Tu	26	12	·63	27	·29	11
12	We	27	13	·65	1	·33	12
13	Th	28	14	·63	2	·35	13
14	Fr ○	29	P	·61	3	·36	14
15	Sa	30	1	·56	4	·34	15

Dec. — Solar: Ananda (16–30); Ananda, Dhanus—Margali. (1–16). Lunar: Bahula; Sukla; Margasira. Muhammadan: H. 1394 Zi-l-ka'da.; H. 1394 Zi-l-hijja.

Cyclic Sidereal Year, Month and Day.	Week-Day English Month and Day.		Tithi Ending Moment.		Nakshatra Ending Moment.		Muhammadan Year, Month and Day.
16	Su	1	2	·49	5	·31	16
17	Mo	2	3	·42	6	·27	17
18	Tu	3	4	·34	7	·21	18
19	We	4	5	·25	8	·15	19
20	Th	5	6	·15	9	·08	20
21	Fr	6	7 8	·05 ·95	10 11	·01 ·94	21
22	Sa	7	9	·86	12	·88	22
23	Su	8	10	·78	13	·83	23
24	Mo	9	11	·72	14	·79	24
25	Tu	10	12	·67	15	·77	25
26	We	11	13	·63	16	·76	26
27	Th	12	14	·62	17	·77	27
28	Fr	13	—A	·63	18	·80	28
29	Sa	14	1	·65	19	·86	29
—30	Su	15	2	·70	20	·94	—30
1	Mo	16	3	·77	...	...	1
2	Tu	17	4	·85	21	·03	2
3	We	18	5	·94	22	·13	3
4	Th	19	...	...	23	·24	4
5	Fr	20	6	·03	24	·35	5
6	Sa	21	7	·11	25	·45	6
7	Su	22	8	·18	26	·53	7
8	Mo	23	9	·23	27	·60	8
9	Tu	24	10	·27	1	·65	9
10	We	25	11	·29	2	·68	10
11	Th	26	12	·27	3	·69	11
12	Fr	27	13	·25	4	·67	12
13	Sa	28	14	·20	5	·64	13
14	Su	29	P	·14	6	·60	14
15	Mo	30	1 2	·07 ·99	7	·54	15
16	Tu	31	3	·89	8	·48	16

15. Svati. 16. Visak. 17. Anur. 18. Jyesh. 19. Mula. 20. P. Ash. 21. U. Ash. 22. Sravn. 23. Dani. 24. Satab. 25. P. Bhad. 26. U. Bhad. 27. Rev.

A. D. 1975. **Mesha Sankranti** (Commencement of Indian Sidereal Year).

Solar Eclipse. ● **(Surya Sid.) April 14·03.** **Saka 1897.** **Kaliyuga 5076.**

Lunar Eclipse. ○ **(Arya Sid.) April 13·92.** **(S. Cycle) Rakshasa.**

SOLAR reckoning: Cyclic Sidereal Year, Month and Day; Week-Day, English Month and Day. LUNAR reckoning: Tithi Ending Moment; Nakshatra Ending Moment; Muhammadan Year, Month and Day.

Jan.

Solar year and month	Cyclic Sidereal Day	Week-Day	English Day	Lunar month	Tithi	Tithi Ending Moment	Nakshatra	Nakshatra Ending Moment	Muhammadan month	Muhammadan Day
Ananda Dhanus—Margali.	17	We	1	Margasira Bahula	4	·79	9	·42	H. 1394 *Zi-l-hijja.*	17
	18	Th	2		5	·69	10	·35		18
	19	Fr	3		6	·59	11	·28		19
	20	Sa	4		7	·50	12	·22		20
	21	Su	5		8	·42	13	·17		21
	22	Mo	6		9	·36	14	·13		22
	23	Tu	7		10	·31	15	·10		23
	24	We	8		11	·28	16	·08		24
	25	Th	9		12	·27	17	·09		25
	26	Fr	10		13	·27	18	·13		26
	27	Sa	11		14	·30	19	·18		27
	28	Su	12		A	·35	20	·24		28
	29	Mo	13	Pausha Sukla	1	·42	21	·32		29
Ananda Makara—Tai.	1	Tu	14		2	·50	22	·43	H. 1395 *Muharram.*	1
	2	We	15		3	·59	23	·54		2
	3	Th	16		4	·68	24	·65		3
	4	Fr	17		5	·77	25	·75		4
	5	Sa	18		6	·83	26	·83		5
	6	Su	19		7	·88	27	·90		6
	7	Mo	20		8	·92	1	·96		7
	8	Tu	21		9	·93	...	...		8
	9	We	22		10	·91	2	·00		9
	10	Th	23		11	·89	3	·01		10
	11	Fr	24		12	·84	4 5	·00 ·98		11
	12	Sa	25		13	·78	6	·94		12
	13	Su	26		14	·70	7	·89		13
	14	Mo	27		P	·62	8	·83		14
	15	Tu	28	Bahula	1	·52	9	·76		15
	16	We	29		2	·42	10	·69		16
	17	Th	30		3	·32	11	·62		17
	18	Fr	31		4	·23	12	·56		18

Feb.

Solar year and month	Cyclic Sidereal Day	Week-Day	English Day	Lunar month	Tithi	Tithi Ending Moment	Nakshatra	Nakshatra Ending Moment	Muhammadan month	Muhammadan Day
Ananda Makara—Tai.	19	Sa	1	Pausha Bahula	5	·14	13	·50	H. 1395 *Muharram.*	19
	20	Su	2		6	·06	14	·46		20
	21	Mo	3		7 8	·00 ·95	15	·43		21
	22	Tu	4		9	·92	16	·41		22
	23	We	5		10	·90	17	·42		23
	24	Th	6		11	·91	18	·44		24
	25	Fr	7		12	·95	19	·48		25
	26	Sa	8		...	...	20	·55		26
	27	Su	9		13	·00	21	·63		27
	28	Mo	10		14	·07	22	·73		28
	29	Tu	11		A	·15	23	·84		29
	30	We	12	Magha Sukla	1	·24	24	·95		30
Ananda Kumbha—Masi.	1	Th	13		2	·32	...	...	H. 1395 *Safar.*	1
	2	Fr	14		3	·40	25	·05		2
	3	Sa	15		4	·47	26	·14		3
	4	Su	16		5	·52	27	·21		4
	5	Mo	17		6	·55	1	·27		5
	6	Tu	18		7	·56	2	·32		6
	7	We	19		3	·55	3	·33		7
	8	Th	20		9	·52	4	·33		8
	9	Fr	21		10	·47	5	·31		9
	10	Sa	22		11	·40	6	·28		10
	11	Su	23		12	·32	7	·23		11
	12	Mo	24		13	·23	8	·17		12
	13	Tu	25		14	·14	9	·11		13
	14	We	26	Bah.	P 1	·04 ·94	10 11	·04 ·97		14
	15	Th	27		2	·84	12	·90		15
	16	Fr	28		3	·75	13	.84		16

March

Solar year and month	Cyclic Sidereal Day	Week-Day	English Day	Lunar month	Tithi	Tithi Ending Moment	Nakshatra	Nakshatra Ending Moment	Muhammadan month	Muhammadan Day
Ananda Kumbha—Masi.	17	Sa	1	Magha Bahula	4	·67	14	·79	H. 1395 *Safar.*	17
	18	Su	2		5	·61	15	·75		18
	19	Mo	3		6	·56	16	·74		19
	20	Tu	4		7	·53	17	·74		20
	21	We	5		8	·51	18	·76		21
	22	Th	6		9	·53	19	·79		22
	23	Fr	7		10	·56	20	·85		23
	24	Sa	8		11	·61	21	·93		24
	25	Su	9		12	·68	...	...		25
	26	Mo	10		13	·76	22	·03		26
	27	Tu	11		14	·85	23	·14		27
	28	We	12		A	·98	24	·25		28
	29	Th	13	Phalguna Sukla	...	...	25	·35		29
	30	Fr	14		1	·01	26	·44	H. 1395 *Rabi-ul-awwal.*	1
Ananda Mina—Panguni.	1	Sa	15		2	·07	27	·52		2
	2	Su	16		3	·12	1	·59		3
	3	Mo	17		4	·15	2	·63		4
	4	Tu	18		5	·15	3	·65		5
	5	We	19		6	·14	4	·65		6
	6	Th	20		7	·11	5	·64		7
	7	Fr	21		8 9	·06 ·99	6	·61		8
	8	Sa	22		10	·91	7	·56		9
	9	Su	23		11	·82	8	·50		10
	10	Mo	24		12	·72	9	·44		11
	11	Tu	25		13	·62	10	·37		12
	12	We	26		14	·52	11	·30		13
	13	Th	27		P	·43	12	·23		14
	14	Fr	28		1	·34	13	·17		15
	15	Sa	29		2	·26	14	·12		16
	16	Su	30		3	·20	15	·08		17
	17	Mo	31		4	·15	16	·07		18

April

Solar year and month	Cyclic Sidereal Day	Week-Day	English Day	Lunar month	Tithi	Tithi Ending Moment	Nakshatra	Nakshatra Ending Moment	Muhammadan month	Muhammadan Day
Ananda Mina—Panguni.	18	Tu	1	Phalguna Bahula	5	·11	17	·06	H. 1395 *Rabi-ul-awwal.*	19
	19	We	2		6	·09	18	·07		20
	20	Th	3		7	·10	19	·10		21
	21	Fr	4		8	·13	20	·16		22
	22	Sa	5		9	·19	21	·24		23
	23	Su	6		10	·26	22	·33		24
	24	Mo	7		11	·34	23	·43		25
	25	Tu	8		12	·42	24	·54		26
	26	We	9		13	·50	25	·65		27
	27	Th	10		14	·57	26	·75		28
	28	Fr	11		A	·63	27	·84		29
	29	Sa	12	Chaitra Sukla	1	·68	1	·90		30
	30	Su	13		2	·71	2	·95	H. 1395 *Rabi-ul-akhir.*	1
Rakshasa Mesha—Chittirai.	1	Mo	14		3	·72	3	·97		2
	2	Tu	15		4	·70	4	·99		3
	3	We	16		5	·66	5	·97		4
	4	Th	17		6	·61	6	·94		5
	5	Fr	18		7	·54	7	89		6
	6	Sa	19		8	·46	8	·84		7
	7	Su	20		9	·37	9	·78		8
	8	Mo	21		10	·27	10	·71		9
	9	Tu	22		11	·17	11	·64		10
	10	We	23		12 13	·07 ·97	12	·57		11
	11	Th	24		14	·88	13	·51		12
	12	Fr	25		P	·80	14	·46		13
	13	Sa	26	Bah.	1	·73	15	·42		14
	14	Su	27		2	·68	16	·39		15
	15	Mo	28		3	·64	17	·38		16
	16	Tu	29		4	·63	18	·39		17
	17	We	30		5	·63	19	·42		18

May

Solar year and month	Cyclic Sidereal Day	Week-Day	English Day	Lunar month	Tithi	Tithi Ending Moment	Nakshatra	Nakshatra Ending Moment	Muhammadan month	Muhammadan Day
Rakshasa Mesha—Chittirai.	18	Th	1	Chaitra Bahula	6	·66	20	·48	H. 1395 *Rabi-ul-akhir.*	19
	19	Fr	2		7	·72	21	·55		20
	20	Sa	3		8	·78	22	·63		21
	21	Su	4		9	·85	23	·73		22
	22	Mo	5		10	·93	24	·84		23
	23	Tu	6		...	...	25	·95		24
	24	We	7		11	·02	...	...		25
	25	Th	8		12	·10	26	·05		26
	26	Fr	9		13	·16	27	·14		27
	27	Sa	10		14	·21	1	·21		28
	28	Su	11		A	·23	2	·26		29
	29	Mo	12	Vaisakha Sukla	1	·24	3	·30	H. 1395 *Jumadal-awwal.*	1
	30	Tu	13		2	·22	4	·31		2
	31	We	14		3	·19	5	·30		3
Rakshasa Vrishabha—Vaikasi.	1	Th	15		4	·13	6	·27		4
	2	Fr	16		5 6	·06 ·98	7	·23		5
	3	Sa	17		7	·89	8	·18		6
	4	Su	18		8	·79	9	·12		7
	5	Mo	19		9	·69	10 11	05 ·98		8
	6	Tu	20		10	·59	12	·91		9
	7	We	21		11	·49	13	·85		10
	8	Th	22		12	·39	14	·79		11
	9	Fr	23		13	·31	15	·75		12
	10	Sa	24		14	·24	16	·72		13
	11	Su ○	25		P	·19	17	·70		14
	12	Mo	26		1	·15	18	·71		15
	13	Tu	27		2	·13	19	·74		16
	14	We	28		3	·13	20	·79		17
	15	Th	29		4	·16	21	·85		18
	16	Fr	30		5	·21	22	·93		19
	17	Sa	31		6	·27	...	...		20

June

Solar year and month	Cyclic Sidereal Day	Week-Day	English Day	Lunar month	Tithi	Tithi Ending Moment	Nakshatra	Nakshatra Ending Moment	Muhammadan month	Muhammadan Day
Rakshasa Vrishabha—Vaikasi.	18	Su	1	Vaisakha Bahula	7	·35	23	·03	H. 1395 *Jumadal-awwal.*	21
	19	Mo	2		8	·43	24	·14		22
	20	Tu	3		9	·51	25	·25		23
	21	We	4		10	·59	26	·35		24
	22	Th	5		11	·65	27	·44		25
	23	Fr	6		12	·70	1	·52		26
	24	Sa	7		13	·73	2	·58		27
	25	Su	8		14	·74	3	·62		28
	26	Mo	9		A	·72	4	·63		29
	27	Tu	10	Jyeshtha Sukla	1	·69	5	·63		30
	28	We	11		2	·63	6	·60	H. 1395 *Jumadal-akhir.*	1
	29	Th	12		3	·56	7	·56		2
	30	Fr	13		4	·48	8	·52		3
	31	Sa	14		5	·38	9	·46		4
Rakshasa Mithuna—Ani.	1	Su	15		6	·28	10	·39		5
	2	Mo	16		7	·18	11	·32		6
	3	Tu	17		8 9	·08 ·98	12	·25		7
	4	We	18		10	·88	13	·19		8
	5	Th	19		11	·80	14	·13		9
	6	Fr	20		12	·73	15	·08		10
	7	Sa	21		13	·67	16	·05		11
	8	Su	22		14	·63	17	·03		12
	9	Mo	23		P	·61	18	·04		13
	10	Tu	24	Bahula	1	·61	19	·06		14
	11	We	25		2	·64	20	·10		15
	12	Th	26		3	·69	21	·16		16
	13	Fr	27		4	·75	22	·24		17
	14	Sa	28		5	·82	23	·34		18
	15	Su	29		6	·90	24	·44		19
	16	Mo	30		7	·98	25	·55		20

Naksh:—1. Asvn. 2. Bhar. 3. Krit. 4. Rohi. 5. Mrig. 6. Ardh. 7. Punar. 8. Push. 9. Aslesh. 10. Magh. 11. P. Phal. 12. U. Phal. 13. Hasta. 14. Chit.

A. D. 1975.
A.—Amavasya.
P.—Paurnami.

Kollam 1151, Commences { N. Malabar—Sept. / S. Malabar—Aug.

Hijra 1395, Commences, Jan. 14.

Vikrama 2032.
Bengal San 1381.
(N. Cycle) Vibhava.

Columns: SOLAR reckoning — Cyclic Sidereal Year, Month and Day; Week-Day, English Month and Day. LUNAR reckoning — Tithi Ending Moment; Nakshatra Ending Moment; Muhammadan Year, Month and Day.

July

Rakshasa Mithuna—Ani; Rakshasa Karkata—Adi. Jyesh. Bahula; Sukla; Ashadha; Bahula. Jumadal-akhir; H. 1395 Rajab.

Cyclic Sidereal	Week-Day	Eng. Day	Tithi	Nakshatra	Muhammadan
17	Tu	1	... ...	26 ·65	21
18	We	2	8 ·06	27 ·74	22
19	Th	3	9 ·13	1 ·82	23
20	Fr	4	10 ·17	2 ·89	24
21	Sa	5	11 ·20	3 ·93	25
22	Su	6	12 ·21	4 ·95	26
23	Mo	7	13 ·19	5 ·95	27
24	Tu	8	14 ·16	6 ·93	28
25	We	9	—A ·10	7 ·90	—29
26	Th	10	1 ·08 / 2 ·95	8 ·86	1
27	Fr	11	3 ·86	9 ·80	2
28	Sa	12	4 ·76	10 ·73	3
29	Su	13	5 ·66	11 ·66	4
30	Mo	14	6 ·56	12 ·59	5
31	Tu	15	7 ·46	13 ·53	6
—32	We	16	8 ·36	14 ·47	7
1	Th	17	9 ·27	15 ·42	8
2	Fr	18	10 ·20	16 ·38	9
3	Sa	19	11 ·15	17 ·36	10
4	Su	20	12 ·12	18 ·36	11
5	Mo	21	13 ·09	19 ·37	12
6	Tu	22	14 ·10	20 ·41	13
7	We	23	P ·13	21 ·47	14
8	Th	24	1 ·16	22 ·55	15
9	Fr	25	2 ·22	23 ·64	16
10	Sa	26	3 ·29	24 ·74	17
11	Su	27	4 ·38	25 ·85	18
12	Mo	28	5 ·46	26 ·95	19
13	Tu	29	6 ·54	... ...	20
14	We	30	7 ·60	27 ·05	21
15	Th	31	8 ·64	1 ·14	22

Aug.

Rakshasa Simha—Avani. Sukla; Sravana; Bahula. H. 1395 Shaban.

Cyclic Sidereal	Week-Day	Eng. Day	Tithi	Nakshatra	Muhammadan
16	Fr	1	9 ·67	2 ·20	23
17	Sa	2	10 ·69	3 ·25	24
18	Su	3	11 ·68	4 ·27	25
19	Mo	4	12 ·64	5 ·28	26
20	Tu	5	13 ·59	6 ·27	27
21	We	6	14 ·53	7 ·24	28
22	Th	7	—A ·45	8 ·19	29
23	Fr	8	1 ·36	9 ·13	—30
24	Sa	9	2 ·26	10 ·07	1
25	Su	10	3 ·16	11 ·01 / 12 ·94	2
26	Mo	11	4 ·06 / 5 ·96	13 ·87	3
27	Tu	12	6 ·86	14 ·80	4
28	We	13	7 ·78	15 ·75	5
29	Th	14	8 ·70	16 ·72	6
30	Fr	15	9 ·64	17 ·69	7
—31	Sa	16	10 ·61	18 ·68	8
1	Su	17	11 ·58	19 ·69	9
2	Mo	18	12 ·59	20 ·72	10
3	Tu	19	13 ·61	21 ·77	11
4	We	20	14 ·66	22 ·85	12
5	Th	21	P ·72	23 ·94	13
6	Fr	22	1 ·78	... ...	14
7	Sa	23	2 ·86	24 ·04	15
8	Su	24	3 ·96	25 ·14	16
9	Mo	25	... ...	26 ·25	17
10	Tu	26	4 ·04	27 ·36	18
11	We	27	5 ·10	1 ·45	19
12	Th	28	6 ·15	2 ·51	20
13	Fr	29	7 ·18	3 ·56	21
14	Sa	30	8 ·20	4 ·59	22
15	Su	31	9 ·18	5 ·61	23

Sep.

Rakshasa Simha—Avani; Rakshasa Kanya—Purattasi. Bah.; Sukla; Bhadrapada; Bahula. Shaban; H. 1395 Ramzan.

Cyclic Sidereal	Week-Day	Eng. Day	Tithi	Nakshatra	Muhammadan
16	Mo	1	10 ·15	6 ·60	24
17	Tu	2	11 ·11	7 ·57	25
18	We	3	12 ·04 / 13 ·96	8 ·52	26
19	Th	4	14 ·87	9 ·47	27
20	Fr	5	—A ·77	10 ·42	28
21	Sa	6	1 ·67	11 ·35	—29
22	Su	7	2 ·57	12 ·28	1
23	Mo	8	3 ·47	13 ·21	2
24	Tu	9	4 ·38	14 ·14	3
25	We	10	5 ·30	15 ·09	4
26	Th	11	6 ·22	16 ·05	5
27	Fr	12	7 ·17	17 ·02	6
28	Sa	13	8 ·13	18 ·00	7
29	Su	14	9 ·12	19 ·01	8
30	Mo	15	10 ·12	20 ·03	9
—31	Tu	16	11 ·14	21 ·09	10
1	We	17	12 ·19	22 ·16	11
2	Th	18	13 ·24	23 ·24	12
3	Fr	19	14 ·31	24 ·34	13
4	Sa	20	P ·40	25 ·45	14
5	Su	21	1 ·49	26 ·56	15
6	Mo	22	2 ·56	27 ·66	16
7	Tu	23	3 ·63	1 ·75	17
8	We	24	4 ·68	2 ·82	18
9	Th	25	5 ·71	3 ·88	19
10	Fr	26	6 ·74	4 ·92	20
11	Sa	27	7 ·73	5 ·93	21
12	Su	28	8 ·71	6 ·92	22
13	Mo	29	9 ·65	7 ·90	23
14	Tu	30	10 ·58	8 ·86	24

Oct.

Rakshasa Tula—Aippasi. Sukla; Asvina; Bahula. H. 1395 Shawwal.

Cyclic Sidereal	Week-Day	Eng. Day	Tithi	Nakshatra	Muhammadan
15	We	1	11 ·50	9 ·81	25
16	Th	2	12 ·42	10 ·75	26
17	Fr	3	13 ·32	11 ·68	27
18	Sa	4	14 ·22	12 ·61	28
19	Su	5	—A ·12	13 ·54	29
20	Mo	6	1 ·02 / 2 ·93	14 ·48	—30
21	Tu	7	3 ·85	15 ·43	1
22	We	8	4 ·78	16 ·38	2
23	Th	9	5 ·73	17 ·35	3
24	Fr	10	6 ·69	18 ·33	4
25	Sa	11	7 ·68	19 ·33	5
26	Su	12	8 ·68	20 ·36	6
27	Mo	13	9 ·71	21 ·40	7
28	Tu	14	10 ·75	22 ·46	8
29	We	15	11 ·81	23 ·54	9
30	Th	16	12 ·88	24 ·64	10
—31	Fr	17	13 ·97	25 ·75	11
1	Sa	18	... ...	26 ·86	12
2	Su	19	14 ·06	27 ·96	13
3	Mo	20	P ·14	... ...	14
4	Tu	21	1 ·21	1 ·05	15
5	We	22	2 ·26	2 ·13	16
6	Th	23	3 ·29	3 ·20	17
7	Fr	24	4 ·32	4 ·24	18
8	Sa	25	5 ·30	5 ·25	19
9	Su	26	6 ·27	6 ·25	20
10	Mo	27	7 ·23	7 ·23	21
11	Tu	28	8 ·17	8 ·19	22
12	We	29	9 ·09	9 ·15	23
13	Th	30	10 ·01 / 11 ·91	10 ·09	24
14	Fr	31	12 ·81	11 ·02 / 12 ·95	25

Nov.

Rakshasa Tula—Aippasi; Rakshasa Vrischika—Kartigai. Bah.; Sukla; Kartika; Bahula. H. 1395 Zi-l-ka'da.

Cyclic Sidereal	Week-Day	Eng. Day	Tithi	Nakshatra	Muhammadan
15	Sa	1	13 ·71	13 ·88	26
16	Su	2	14 ·61	14 ·82	27
17	Mo	3	—A ·53	15 ·76	28
18	Tu	4	1 ·45	16 ·71	—29
19	We	5	2 ·38	17 ·67	1
20	Th	6	3 ·32	18 ·65	2
21	Fr	7	4 ·28	19 ·63	3
22	Sa	8	5 ·27	20 ·67	4
23	Su	9	6 ·28	21 ·71	5
24	Mo	10	7 ·31	22 ·77	6
25	Tu	11	8 ·35	23 ·85	7
26	We	12	9 ·42	24 ·95	8
27	Th	13	10 ·50	... ...	9
28	Fr	14	11 ·59	25 ·05	10
29	Sa	15	12 ·68	26 ·15	11
—30	Su	16	13 ·75	27 ·26	12
1	Mo	17	14 ·82	1 ·36	13
2	Tu ○	18	P ·88	2 ·45	14
3	We	19	1 ·92	3 ·51	15
4	Th	20	2 ·93	4 ·55	16
5	Fr	21	3 ·92	5 ·57	17
6	Sa	22	4 ·89	6 ·57	18
7	Su	23	5 ·85	7 ·56	19
8	Mo	24	6 ·79	8 ·53	20
9	Tu	25	7 ·71	9 ·49	21
10	We	26	8 ·63	10 ·43	22
11	Th	27	9 ·53	11 ·36	23
12	Fr	28	10 ·43	12 ·29	24
13	Sa	29	11 ·33	13 ·22	25
14	Su	30	12 ·24	14 ·16	26

Dec.

Rakshasa Dhanus—Margali. Sukla; Margasira; Bahula. H. 1395 Zi-l-hijja.

Cyclic Sidereal	Week-Day	Eng. Day	Tithi	Nakshatra	Muhammadan
15	Mo	1	13 ·15	15 ·10	27
16	Tu	2	14 ·06 / A ·99	16 ·05	28
17	We	3	1 ·95	17 ·01 / 18 ·99	29
18	Th	4	2 ·92	19 ·98	—30
19	Fr	5	3 ·90	20 ·99	1
20	Sa	6	4 ·92	... ...	2
21	Su	7	5 ·95	21 ·02	3
22	Mo	8	6 ·99	22 ·08	4
23	Tu	9	... ...	23 ·16	5
24	We	10	7 ·05	24 ·25	6
25	Th	11	8 ·14	25 ·35	7
26	Fr	12	9 ·24	26 ·45	8
27	Sa	13	10 ·33	27 ·56	9
28	Su	14	11 ·41	1 ·66	10
—29	Mo	15	12 ·47	2 ·75	11
1	Tu	16	13 ·52	3 ·82	12
2	We	17	14 ·56	4 ·86	13
3	Th	18	P ·57	5 ·89	14
4	Fr	19	1 ·56	6 ·90	15
5	Sa	20	2 ·53	7 ·89	16
6	Su	21	3 ·49	8 ·86	17
7	Mo	22	4 ·42	9 ·82	18
8	Tu	23	5 ·34	10 ·76	19
9	We	24	6 ·26	11 ·70	20
10	Th	25	7 ·17	12 ·64	21
11	Fr	26	8 ·07 / 9 ·97	13 ·57	22
12	Sa	27	10 ·88	14 ·50	23
13	Su	28	11 ·79	15 ·43	24
14	Mo	29	12 ·71	16 ·38	25
15	Tu	30	13 ·64	17 ·34	26
16	We	31	14 ·58	18 ·31	27

15. Svati. 16. Visak. 17. Anur. 18. Jyesh. 19. Mula. 20. P. Ash. 21. U. Ash. 22. Sravn. 23. Dani. 24. Satab. 25. P. Bhad. 26. U. Bhad. 27. Rev.

A. D. 1976.
Solar Eclipse. ●
Lunar Eclipse. ○

Mesha Sankranti (Commencement of Indian Sidereal Year).
(Surya Sid.) April 13·29. **Saka 1898.** **Kaliyuga 5077.**
(Arya Sid.) April 13·18. **(S. Cycle) Anala** (Nala).

Jan.

Rakshasa Dhanus—Margali; Sukla; Pausha; Bahula; H. 1396 Muharram; Rakshasa Makara—Tai.

SOLAR reckoning: Cyclic Sidereal Year, Month and Day	Week-Day English Month and Day	LUNAR reckoning: Tithi Ending Moment	Nakshatra Ending Moment	Muhammadan Year, Month and Day
17	Th 1	—A ·55	19 ·30	28
18	Fr 2	1 ·55	20 ·31	—29
19	Sa 3	2 ·56	21 ·34	1
20	Su 4	3 ·59	22 ·39	2
21	Mo 5	4 ·65	23 ·46	3
22	Tu 6	5 ·71	24 ·54	4
23	We 7	6 ·79	25 ·64	5
24	Th 8	7 ·89	26 ·75	6
25	Fr 9	8 ·97	27 ·86	7
26	Sa 10	... ...	1 ·96	8
27	Su 11	9 ·05	... ...	9
28	Mo 12	10 ·12	2 ·05	10
29	Tu 13	11 ·18	3 ·13	11
—30	We 14	12 ·21	4 ·18	12
1	Th 15	13 ·21	5 ·21	13
2	Fr 16	14 ·20	6 ·23	14
3	Sa 17	P ·17	7 ·22	15
4	Su 18	1 ·13	8 ·19	16
5	Mo 19	2 ·06 / 3 ·98	9 ·15	17
6	Tu 20	4 ·89	10 ·10	18
7	We 21	5 ·80	11 ·05 / 12 ·98	19
8	Th 22	6 ·70	13 ·91	20
9	Fr 23	7 ·60	14 ·84	21
10	Sa 24	8 ·50	15 ·77	22
11	Su 25	9 ·42	16 ·72	23
12	Mo 26	10 ·35	17 ·68	24
13	Tu 27	11 ·29	18 ·64	25
14	We 28	12 ·24	19 ·63	26
15	Th 29	13 ·20	20 ·63	27
16	Fr 30	14 ·19	21 ·65	28
17	Sa 31	—A ·20	22 ·70	29

Feb.

Sukla; Magha; Bahula; H. 1396 Safar; Rakshasa Kumbha—Masi.

SOLAR reckoning: Cyclic Sidereal Year, Month and Day	Week-Day English Month and Day	LUNAR reckoning: Tithi Ending Moment	Nakshatra Ending Moment	Muhammadan Year, Month and Day
18	Su 1	1 ·24	23 ·77	—30
19	Mo 2	2 ·29	24 ·85	1
20	Tu 3	3 ·36	25 ·94	2
21	We 4	4 ·44	... ...	3
22	Th 5	5 ·53	26 ·05	4
23	Fr 6	6 ·62	27 ·16	5
24	Sa 7	7 ·70	1 ·27	6
25	Su 8	8 ·77	2 ·36	7
26	Mo 9	9 ·82	3 ·43	8
27	Tu 10	10 ·84	4 ·49	9
28	We 11	11 ·85	5 ·54	10
—29	Th 12	12 ·84	6 ·55	11
1	Fr 13	13 ·81	7 ·55	12
2	Sa 14	14 ·75	8 ·52	13
3	Su 15	P ·68	9 ·49	14
4	Mo 16	1 ·61	10 ·44	15
5	Tu 17	2 ·53	11 ·38	16
6	We 18	3 ·43	12 ·32	17
7	Th 19	4 ·33	13 ·25	18
8	Fr 20	5 ·23	14 ·18	19
9	Sa 21	6 ·13	15 ·12	20
10	Su 22	7 ·04 / 8 ·96	16 ·06	21
11	Mo 23	9 ·89	17 ·01 / 18 ·97	22
12	Tu 24	10 ·85	19 ·95	23
13	We 25	11 ·82	20 ·95	24
14	Th 26	12 ·81	21 ·98	25
15	Fr 27	13 ·82	... ...	26
16	Sa 28	14 ·86	22 ·01	27
17	Su 29	—A ·91	23 ·07	28

March

Rakshasa Kumbha—Masi; Sukla; Phalguna; Bahula; H. 1396 Rabi-ul-awwal; Rakshasa Mina—Panguni.

SOLAR reckoning: Cyclic Sidereal Year, Month and Day	Week-Day English Month and Day	LUNAR reckoning: Tithi Ending Moment	Nakshatra Ending Moment	Muhammadan Year, Month and Day
18	Mo 1	1 ·98	24 ·15	—29
19	Tu 2	... ...	25 ·25	1
20	We 3	2 ·06	26 ·36	2
21	Th 4	3 ·15	27 ·47	3
22	Fr 5	4 ·24	1 ·57	4
23	Sa 6	5 ·32	2 ·66	5
24	Su 7	6 ·39	3 ·74	6
25	Mo 8	7 ·43	4 ·81	7
26	Tu 9	8 ·45	5 ·85	8
27	We 10	9 ·46	6 ·87	9
28	Th 11	10 ·44	7 ·87	10
29	Fr 12	11 ·40	8 ·85	11
30	Sa 13	12 ·35	9 ·83	12
—31	Su 14	13 ·29	10 ·78	13
1	Mo 15	14 ·21	11 ·72	14
2	Tu 16	P ·12	12 ·65	15
3	We 17	1 ·02 / 2 ·92	13 ·58	16
4	Th 18	3 ·82	14 ·51	17
5	Fr 19	4 ·72	15 ·45	18
6	Sa 20	5 ·63	16 ·39	19
7	Su 21	6 ·55	17 ·34	20
8	Mo 22	7 ·49	18 ·30	21
9	Tu 23	8 ·45	19 ·28	22
10	We 24	9 ·41	20 ·28	23
11	Th 25	10 ·40	21 ·29	24
12	Fr 26	11 ·40	22 ·33	25
13	Sa 27	12 ·44	23 ·38	26
14	Su 28	13 ·49	24 ·45	27
15	Mo 29	14 ·57	25 ·55	28
16	Tu 30	—A ·65	26 ·65	29
17	We 31	1 ·73	27 ·76	—30

April

Sukla; Chaitra; Bahula; H. 1396 Rabi-ul-akhir; Anala Mesha—Chittirai.

SOLAR reckoning: Cyclic Sidereal Year, Month and Day	Week-Day English Month and Day	LUNAR reckoning: Tithi Ending Moment	Nakshatra Ending Moment	Muhammadan Year, Month and Day
18	Th 1	2 ·82	1 ·87	1
19	Fr 2	3 ·90	2 ·97	2
20	Sa 3	4 ·96	... ...	3
21	Su 4	... ...	3 ·06	4
22	Mo 5	5 ·00	4 ·12	5
23	Tu 6	6 ·03	5 ·17	6
24	We 7	7 ·03	6 ·19	7
25	Th 8	8 ·01 / 9 ·97	7 ·20	8
26	Fr 9	10 ·92	8 ·19	9
27	Sa 10	11 ·85	9 ·16	10
28	Su 11	12 ·77	10 ·11	11
—29	Mo 12	13 ·68	11 ·06 / 12 ·99	12
1	Tu 13	14 ·58	13 ·92	13
2	We 14	P ·48	14 ·85	14
3	Th 15	1 ·38	15 ·79	15
4	Fr 16	2 ·28	16 ·73	16
5	Sa 17	3 ·19	17 ·67	17
6	Su 18	4 ·11	18 ·63	18
7	Mo 19	5 ·04 / 6 ·99	19 ·61	19
8	Tu 20	7 ·96	20 ·60	20
9	We 21	8 ·94	21 ·61	21
10	Th 22	9 ·94	22 ·64	22
11	Fr 23	10 ·98	23 ·69	23
12	Sa 24	... ...	24 ·76	24
13	Su 25	11 ·04	25 ·85	25
14	Mo 26	12 ·11	26 ·95	26
15	Tu 27	13 ·19	... ...	27
16	We 28	14 ·27	27 ·06	28
17	Th ● 29	—A ·35	1 ·17	—29
18	Fr 30	1 ·42	2 ·27	1

May

Anala Mesha—Chittirai; Sukla; Vaisakha; Bahula; H. 1396 Jumadal-awwal; Anala Vrishabha—Vaikasi.

SOLAR reckoning: Cyclic Sidereal Year, Month and Day	Week-Day English Month and Day	LUNAR reckoning: Tithi Ending Moment	Nakshatra Ending Moment	Muhammadan Year, Month and Day
19	Sa 1	2 ·48	3 ·36	2
20	Su 2	3 ·53	4 ·43	3
21	Mo 3	4 ·56	5 ·48	4
22	Tu 4	5 ·55	6 ·51	5
23	We 5	6 ·53	7 ·52	6
24	Th 6	7 ·50	8 ·52	7
25	Fr 7	8 ·45	9 ·49	8
26	Sa 8	9 ·38	10 ·45	9
27	Su 9	10 ·29	11 ·39	10
28	Mo 10	11 ·20	12 ·33	11
20	Tu 11	12 ·10	13 ·27	12
30	We 12	13 ·00 / 14 ·90	14 ·20	13
—31	Th ○ 13	P ·80	15 ·13	14
1	Fr 14	1 ·70	16 ·07	15
2	Sa 15	2 ·62	17 ·01 / 18 ·97	16
3	Su 16	3 ·56	19 ·94	17
4	Mo 17	4 ·51	20 ·92	18
5	Tu 18	5 ·47	21 ·93	19
6	We 19	6 ·45	22 ·95	20
7	Th 20	7 ·46	... ...	21
8	Fr 21	8 ·50	23 ·01	22
9	Sa 22	9 ·55	24 ·07	23
10	Su 23	10 ·61	25 ·15	24
11	Mo 24	11 ·68	26 ·25	25
12	Tu 25	12 ·76	27 ·36	26
13	We 26	13 ·85	1 ·47	27
14	Th 27	14 ·93	2 ·57	28
15	Fr 28	—A ·99	3 ·66	29
16	Sa 29	... ...	4 ·74	—30
17	Su 30	1 ·03	5 ·79	1
18	Mo 31	2 ·05	6 ·83	2

June

Sukla; Jyeshtha; Bahula; Suk.; H. 1396 Jumadal-akhir; Rajab.; Anala Mithuna—Ani.

SOLAR reckoning: Cyclic Sidereal Year, Month and Day	Week-Day English Month and Day	LUNAR reckoning: Tithi Ending Moment	Nakshatra Ending Moment	Muhammadan Year, Month and Day
19	Tu 1	3 ·05	7 ·85	3
20	We 2	4 ·04	8 ·85	4
21	Th 3	5 ·00 / 6 ·94	9 ·82	5
22	Fr 4	7 ·87	10 ·78	6
23	Sa 5	8 ·79	11 ·73	7
24	Su 6	9 ·69	12 ·68	8
25	Mo 7	10 ·59	13 ·61	9
26	Tu 8	11 ·49	14 ·54	10
27	We 9	12 ·39	15 ·47	11
28	Th 10	13 ·29	16 ·40	12
29	Fr 11	14 ·20	17 ·35	13
30	Sa 12	P ·12	18 ·30	14
31	Su 13	1 ·05	19 ·27	15
—32	Mo 14	2 ·00 / 3 ·96	20 ·25	16
1	Tu 15	4 ·94	21 ·25	17
2	We 16	5 ·94	22 ·28	18
3	Th 17	6 ·97	23 ·32	19
4	Fr 18	... ...	24 ·38	20
5	Sa 19	7 ·02	25 ·46	21
6	Su 20	8 ·08	26 ·55	22
7	Mo 21	9 ·16	27 ·65	23
8	Tu 22	10 ·24	1 ·76	24
9	We 23	11 ·32	2 ·87	25
10	Th 24	12 ·40	3 ·97	26
11	Fr 25	13 ·46	... ...	27
12	Sa 26	14 ·50	4 ·04	28
13	Su 27	—A ·58	5 ·10	—29
14	Mo 28	1 ·54	6 ·15	1
15	Tu 29	2 ·52	7 ·17	2
16	We 30	3 ·48	8 ·17	3

Naksh :—1. Asvn. 2. Bhar. 3. Krit. 4. Rohi. 5. Mrig. 6. Ardh. 7. Punar. 8. Push. 9. Aslesh. 10. Magh. 11. P. Phal. 12. U. Phal. 13. Hasta. 14. Chit.

A. D. 1976.	Kollam 1152, Commences	N. Malabar—Sept. / S. Malabar—Aug.	Hijra Commences,	1396, Jan. 3. / 1397, Dec. 23.	Vikrama 2033.
A.—Amavasya.					Bengal San 1383.
P.—Paurnami.					(N. Cycle) Sukla.

SOLAR reckoning: Cyclic Sidereal Year, Month and Day; Week-Day English Month and Day. LUNAR reckoning: Tithi Ending Moment; Nakshatra Ending Moment; Muhammadan Year, Month and Day.

Solar month	Cyclic Sidereal Day	Week-Day	English Day	Lunar month / Paksha	Tithi	Ending Moment	Nakshatra	Ending Moment	Muhammadan month	Muhammadan Day
		July								
	17	Th	1		4	·43	9	·15		4
	18	Fr	2		5	·36	10	·12		5
	19	Sa	3	Sukla	6	·27	11	·08		6
	20	Su	4		7	·17	12 / 13	·02 / ·95		7
Anala *Mithuna—Ani.*	21	Mo	5		8 / 9	·07 / ·97	14	·88		8
	22	Tu	6		10	·87	15	·81		9
	23	We	7		11	·77	16	·75		10
	24	Th	8		12	·67	17	·69		11
	25	Fr	9	Ashadha	13	·59	18	·64		12
	26	Sa	10		14	·52	19	·60		13
	27	Su	11		P	·47	20	·57	H. 1396 *Rajab.*	14
	28	Mo	12		1	·43	21	·57		15
	29	Tu	13		2	·42	22	·59		16
	30	We	14		3	·43	23	·63		17
	—31	Th	15		4	·45	24	·69		18
	1	Fr	16		5	·50	25	·76		19
	2	Sa	17		6	·56	26	·85		20
	3	Su	18	Bahula	7	·63	27	·96		21
	4	Mo	19		8	·71	...	...		22
	5	Tu	20		9	·79	1	·07		23
	6	We	21		10	·87	2	·17		24
	7	Th	22		11	·93	3	·27		25
	8	Fr	23		12	·98	4	·35		26
	9	Sa	24		...	...	5	·42		27
	10	Su	25		13	·01	6	·47		28
	11	Mo	26		14	·02	7	·49		29
Anala *Karkata—Adi.*	12	Tu	27		A / 1	·00 / ·96	8	·50		—30
	13	We	28		2	·91	9	·48		1
	14	Th	29		3	·85	10	·46		2
	15	Fr	30		4	·77	11	·41		3
	16	Sa	31		5	·67	12	·35		4
		Aug.								
	17	Su	1		6	·57	13	·29		5
	18	Mo	2		7	·47	14	·22		6
	19	Tu	3	Sukla	8	·37	15	·15		7
	20	We	4		9	·27	16	·09		8
	21	Th	5		10	·18	17 / 18	·03 / ·97		9
	22	Fr	6		11	·09	19	·93	H. 1396 *Shaban.*	10
	23	Sa	7		12 / 13	·02 / ·96	20	·90		11
	24	Su	8	Sravana	14	·92	21	·90		12
	25	Mo	9		P	·91	22	·91		13
	26	Tu	10		1	·92	23	·94		14
	27	We	11		2	·94	24	·99		15
	28	Th	12		3	·98	...	...		16
	29	Fr	13		...	...	25	·06		17
	30	Sa	14		4	·05	26	·16		18
	31	Su	15		5	·12	27	·26		19
	—32	Mo	16		6	·20	1	·37		20
	1	Tu	17	Bahula	7	·29	2	·47		21
	2	We	18		8	·36	3	·57		22
	3	Th	19		9	·42	4	·66		23
	4	Fr	20		10	·47	5	·73		24
	5	Sa	21		11	·51	6	·78		25
Anala *Simha—Avani.*	6	Su	22		12	·51	7	·81		26
	7	Mo	23		13	·49	8	·82		27
	8	Tu	24		14	·46	9	·82		28
	9	We	25		—A	·42	10	·79		—29
	10	Th	26		1	·35	11	·74	H. 1396 *Ramzan.*	1
	11	Fr	27	B.—Suk.	2	·27	12	·69		2
	12	Sa	28		3	·17	13	·62		3
	13	Su	29		4 / 5	·07 / ·97	14	·55		4
	14	Mo	30		6	·87	15	·48		5
	15	Tu	31		7	·77	16	·42		6

Solar month	Cyclic Sidereal Day	Week-Day	English Day	Lunar month / Paksha	Tithi	Ending Moment	Nakshatra	Ending Moment	Muhammadan month	Muhammadan Day
		Sep.								
	16	We	1	Sukla	8	·68	17	·36		7
	17	Th	2		9	·60	18	·30		8
	18	Fr	3		10	·53	19	·26		9
	19	Sa	4		11	·47	20	·24		10
	20	Su	5		12	·44	21	·22		11
Anala *Simha—Avani.*	21	Mo	6		13	·42	22	·23		12
	22	Tu	7		14	·44	23	·25		13
	23	We	8		P	·46	24	·30		14
	24	Th	9	Bhadrapada	1	·50	25	·38		15
	25	Fr	10		2	·56	26	·46		16
	26	Sa	11		3	·63	27	·56		17
	27	Su	12		4	·72	1	·66	H. 1396 *Ramzan.*	18
	28	Mo	13		5	·81	2	·77		19
	29	Tu	14		6	·88	3	·88		20
	30	We	15		7	·95	4	·97		21
	—31	Th	16		8	·99	...	...		22
	1	Fr	17	Bahula	...	...	5	·04		23
	2	Sa	18		9	·08	6	·10		24
	3	Su	19		10	·04	7	·13		25
	4	Mo	20		11	·03	8	·15		26
	5	Tu	21		12 / 13	·00 / ·95	9	·14		27
	6	We	22		14	·88	10	·12		28
	7	Th	23		—A	·80	11	·08		29
	8	Fr	24		1	·71	12 / 13	·02 / ·96		—30
Anala *Kanya—Purattasi.*	9	Sa	25		2	·62	14	·90		1
	10	Su	26		3	·52	15	·83		2
	11	Mo	27		4	·42	16	·76		3
	12	Tu	28		5	·32	17	·70		4
	13	We	29	Sukla	6	·22	18	·64		5
	14	Th	30		7	·14	19	·60		6
		Oct.								
	15	Fr	1		8	·07	20	·57		7
	16	Sa	2		9 / 10	·02 / ·99	21	·55		8
	17	Su	3		11	·97	22	·55		9
	18	Mo	4		12	·99	23	·57	H. 1396 *Shawwal.*	10
	19	Tu	5		...	...	24	·62		11
	20	We	6	Asvina	13	·01	25	·68		12
	21	Th	7		14	·05	26	·76		13
	22	Fr	8		P	·12	27	·86		14
	23	Sa	9		1	·20	1	·97		15
	24	Su	10		2	·29	...	...		16
	25	Mo	11		3	·37	2	·08		17
	26	Tu	12		4	·45	3	·18		18
	27	We	13		5	·52	4	·27		19
	28	Th	14		6	·57	5	·35		20
	29	Fr	15	Bahula	7	·60	6	·41		21
	—30	Sa	16		8	·61	7	·45		22
	1	Su	17		9	·60	8	·47		23
	2	Mo	18		10	·57	9	·47		24
	3	Tu	19		11	·53	10	·45		25
	4	We	20		12	·47	11	·41		26
	5	Th	21		13	·39	12	·36		27
	6	Fr	22		14	·29	13	·31		28
Anala *Tula—Aippasi.*	7	Sa ●	23		—A	·19	14	·24		—29
	8	Su	24		1 / 2	·09 / ·99	15	·17	H. 1396 *Zi-l-ka'da.*	1
	9	Mo	25	Suk.	3	·90	16	·10		2
	10	Tu	26		4	·81	17 / 18	·03 / ·98		3
	11	We	27	Karttika	5	·74	19	·93		4
	12	Th	28		6	·67	20	·89		5
	13	Fr	29		7	·61	21	·87		6
	14	Sa	30		8	·58	22	·87		7
	15	Su	31		9	·56	23	·89		8

Solar month	Cyclic Sidereal Day	Week-Day	English Day	Lunar month / Paksha	Tithi	Ending Moment	Nakshatra	Ending Moment	Muhammadan month	Muhammadan Day
		Nov.								
	16	Mo	1	Suk.	10	·57	24	·93		9
	17	Tu	2		11	·60	25	·99		10
	18	We	3		12	·65	...	...		11
	19	Th	4		13	·72	26	·07		12
Anala *Tula—Aippasi.*	20	Fr	5	Karttika	14	·80	27	·16		13
	21	Sa	6		P	·89	1	·27		14
	22	Su	7		1	·98	2	·33		15
	23	Mo	8		...	...	3	·48	H. 1396 *Zi-l-ka'da.*	16
	24	Tu	9		2	·06	4	·58		17
	25	We	10		3	·12	5	·65		18
	26	Th	11		4	·17	6	·72		19
	27	Fr	12		5	·21	7	·77		20
	28	Sa	13		6	23	8	·79		21
	29	Su	14	Bahula	7	·21	9	·79		22
	—30	Mo	15		8	·17	10	·78		23
	1	Tu	16		9	·13	11	·74		24
	2	We	17		10	·07	12	·70		25
	3	Th	18		11 / 12	·00 / ·91	13	·65		26
	4	Fr	19		13	·81	14	·58		27
	5	Sa	20		14	·71	15	·51		28
	6	Su	21		—A	·61	16	·44		29
	7	Mo	22		1	·52	17	·38		—30
	8	Tu	23		2	·43	18	·32		1
	9	We	24		3	·35	19	·26		2
Anala *Vrischika—Kartigai.*	10	Th	25		4	·28	20	·22		3
	11	Fr	26		5	·23	21	·20		4
	12	Sa	27		6	·20	22	·20		5
	13	Su	28		7	·19	23	·21		6
	14	Mo	29	Sukla	8	·21	24	·24		7
	15	Tu	30		9	·23	25	·30		8
		Dec.								
	16	We	1		10	·28	26	·37		9
	17	Th	2		11	·35	27	·46	H. 1396 *Zi-l-hijja.*	10
	18	Fr	3		12	·43	1	·56		11
	19	Sa	4	Margasira	13	·52	2	·67		12
	20	Su	5		14	·61	3	·78		13
	21	Mo	6		P	·69	4	88		14
	22	Tu	7		1	·76	5	·96		15
	23	We	8		2	·81	...	...		16
	24	Th	9		3	·84	6	·04		17
	25	Fr	10		4	·86	7	09		18
	26	Sa	11		5	·84	8	·11		19
	27	Su	12		6	·81	9	·12		20
	28	Mo	13		7	·76	10	·10		21
	—29	Tu	14	Bahula	8	·69	11	·08		22
	1	We	15		9	·62	12 / 13	·04 / ·98		23
	2	Th	16		10	·54	14	·92		24
	3	Fr	17		11	·44	15	·86		25
	4	Sa	18		12	·34	16	·79		26
	5	Su	19		13	·24	17	·72		27
	6	Mo	20		14	·14	18	·66		28
	7	Tu	21		A / 1	·05 / ·97	19	·60		29
Anala *Dhanus—Margali.*	8	We	22		2	·92	20	·55		—30
	9	Th	23		3	·87	21	·52	H. 1397 *Muharram.*	1
	10	Fr	24	Sukla	4	·84	22	·52		2
	11	Sa	25		5	·84	23	·53		3
	12	Su	26		6	·85	24	·56		4
	13	Mo	27		7	·88	25	·60		5
	14	Tu	28	Pausha	8	·94	26	·67		6
	15	We	29		...	...	27	·77		7
	16	Th	30		9	·01	1	·87		8
	17	Fr	31		10	·09	2	·97		9

15. Svati. 16. Visak. 17. Anur. 18. Jyesh. 19. Mula. 20. P. Ash. 21. U. Ash. 22. Sravn. 23. Dani. 24. Satab. 25. P. Bhad. 26. U. Bhad. 27. Rev.

A. D. 1977. | Mesha Sankranti (Commencement of Indian Sidereal Year). | Saka 1899. | Kaliyuga 5078.

Solar Eclipse. ● | (Surya Sid.) April 13·54. | (S. Cycle) Pingala.

Lunar Eclipse. ○ | (Arya Sid.) April 13·43.

SOLAR reckoning: Cyclic Sidereal Year, Month and Day; Week-Day English Month and Day. LUNAR reckoning: Tithi Ending Moment; Nakshatra Ending Moment; Muhammadan Year, Month and Day.

Jan. — Solar: Anala Dhanus—Margali; Anala Makara—Tai. Lunar: Pausha Suk.; Bahula; Sukla. Muhammadan: H. 1397 Muharram.

Cyclic Sidereal Year, Month and Day	Week-Day	English Day	Tithi	Tithi Ending Moment	Nakshatra	Nakshatra Ending Moment	Muhammadan Year, Month and Day
18	Sa	1	11	·17	...	...	10
19	Su	2	12	·26	3	·08	11
20	Mo	3	13	·34	4	·18	12
21	Tu	4	14	·41	5	·28	13
22	We	5	P	·46	6	·35	14
23	Th	6	1	·49	7	·40	15
24	Fr	7	2	·50	8	·48	16
25	Sa	8	3	·49	9	·44	17
26	Su	9	4	·46	10	·44	18
27	Mo	10	5	·41	11	·41	19
28	Tu	11	6	·35	12	·37	20
29	We	12	7	·27	13	·32	21
—30	Th	13	8	·18	14	·26	22
1	Fr	14	9 10	·08 ·98	15	·20	23
2	Sa	15	11	·89	16	·13	24
3	Su	16	12	·80	17 18	·06 ·99	25
4	Mo	17	13	·71	19	·93	26
5	Tu	18	14	·63	20	·89	27
6	We	19	—A	·57	21	·86	28
7	Th	20	1	·52	22	·85	29
8	Fr	21	2	·49	23	·85	—30
9	Sa	22	3	·48	24	·87	1
10	Su	23	4	·49	25	·92	2
11	Mo	24	5	·53	26	·99	3
12	Tu	25	6	·59	...	...	4
13	We	26	7	·66	27	·07	5
14	Th	27	8	·74	1	·16	6
15	Fr	28	9	·82	2	·27	7
16	Sa	29	10	·91	3	·38	8
17	Su	30	11	·99	4	·49	9
18	Mo	31	...	...	5	·58	10

Feb. — Solar: Anala Kumbha—Masi. Lunar: Magha; Bahula; Sukla; Phalguna. Muhammadan: H. 1397 Safar; Rabi-ul-awwal.

Cyclic Sidereal Year, Month and Day	Week-Day	English Day	Tithi	Tithi Ending Moment	Nakshatra	Nakshatra Ending Moment	Muhammadan Year, Month and Day
19	Tu	1	12	·06	6	·65	11
20	We	2	13	·11	7	·71	12
21	Th	3	14	·14	8	·75	13
22	Fr	4	P	·14	9	·77	14
23	Sa	5	1	·13	10	·77	15
24	Su	6	2	·09	11	·74	16
25	Mo	7	3 4	·03 ·97	12	·71	17
26	Tu	8	5	·89	13	·65	18
27	We	9	6	·80	14	·59	19
28	Th	10	7	·71	15	·53	20
—29	Fr	11	8	·61	16	·46	21
1	Sa	12	9	·51	17	·39	22
2	Su	13	10	·41	18	·33	23
3	Mo	14	11	·32	19	·27	24
4	Tu	15	12	·25	20	·23	25
5	We	16	13	·19	21	·19	26
6	Th	17	14	·14	22	·17	27
7	Fr	18	—A	·12	23	·17	28
8	Sa	19	1	·10	24	·19	—29
9	Su	20	2	·12	25	·23	1
10	Mo	21	3	·16	26	·29	2
11	Tu	22	4	·21	27	·37	3
12	We	23	5	·28	1	·46	4
13	Th	24	6	·36	2	·57	5
14	Fr	25	7	·46	3	·68	6
15	Sa	26	8	·54	4	·79	7
16	Su	27	9	·62	5	·88	8
17	Mo	28	10	·63	6	·96	9

March — Solar: Anala Kumbha—Masi; Anala Mina—Panguni. Lunar: Phalguna Suk.; Bahula; Sukla. Muhammadan: H. 1397 Rabi-ul-awwal.

Cyclic Sidereal Year, Month and Day	Week-Day	English Day	Tithi	Tithi Ending Moment	Nakshatra	Nakshatra Ending Moment	Muhammadan Year, Month and Day
18	Tu	1	11	·73	...	...	10
19	We	2	12	·75	7	·02	11
20	Th	3	13	·75	8	·07	12
21	Fr	4	14	·74	9	·09	13
22	Sa	5	P	·70	10	·09	14
23	Su	6	1	·65	11	·07	15
24	Mo	7	2	·58	12 13	·04 ·99	16
25	Tu	8	3	·50	14	·94	17
26	We	9	4	·41	15	·87	18
27	Th	10	5	·32	16	·80	19
28	Fr	11	6	·22	17	·73	20
29	Sa	12	7	·12	18	·66	21
—30	Su	13	8 9	·02 ·93	19	·61	22
1	Mo	14	10	·85	20	·56	23
2	Tu	15	11	·78	21	·52	24
3	We	16	12	·74	22	·50	25
4	Th	17	13	·72	23	·49	26
5	Fr	18	14	·71	24	·51	27
6	Sa	19	—A	·73	25	·55	28
7	Su	20	1	·76	26	·60	29
8	Mo	21	2	·81	27	·67	—30
9	Tu	22	3	·88	1	·76	1
10	We	23	4	·96	2	·87	2
11	Th	24	...	...	3	·98	3
12	Fr	25	5	·05	...	...	4
13	Sa	26	6	·13	4	·09	5
14	Su	27	7	·20	5	·18	6
15	Mo	28	8	·26	6	·26	7
16	Tu	29	9	·31	7	·33	8
17	We	30	10	·34	8	·39	9
18	Th	31	11	·33	9	·41	10

April — Solar: Pingala Mesha—Chittirai. Lunar: Chaitra; Bahula; Sukla; Vaisakha. Muhammadan: H. 1397 Rabi-ul-akhir; H. 1397 Jumadal-awwal.

Cyclic Sidereal Year, Month and Day	Week-Day	English Day	Tithi	Tithi Ending Moment	Nakshatra	Nakshatra Ending Moment	Muhammadan Year, Month and Day
19	Fr	1	12	·31	10	·42	11
20	Sa	2	13	·27	11	·40	12
21	Su	3	14	·22	12	·37	13
22	Mo ○	4	P	·15	13	·33	14
23	Tu	5	1 2	·07 ·98	14	·28	15
24	We	6	3	·88	15	·21	16
25	Th	7	4	·78	16	·14	17
26	Fr	8	5	·68	17	·07	18
27	Sa	9	6	·58	18 19	·01 ·95	19
28	Su	10	7	·40	20	·89	20
29	Mo	11	8	·41	21	·85	21
—30	Tu	12	9	·35	22	·82	22
1	We	13	10	·30	23	·82	23
2	Th	14	11	·27	24	·83	24
3	Fr	15	12	·25	25	·86	25
4	Sa	16	13	·27	26	·91	26
5	Su	17	14	·30	27	·98	27
6	Mo ●	18	—A	·36	...	...	28
7	Tu	19	1	·43	1	·07	—29
8	We	20	2	·51	2	·17	1
9	Th	21	3	·59	3	·28	2
10	Fr	22	4	·67	4	·38	3
11	Sa	23	5	·74	5	·48	4
12	Su	24	6	·80	6	·57	5
13	Mo	25	7	·85	7	·65	6
14	Tu	26	8	·87	8	·70	7
15	We	27	9	·88	9	·73	8
16	Th	28	10	·86	10	·74	9
17	Fr	29	11	·81	11	·78	10
18	Sa	30	12	·75	12	·71	11

May — Solar: Pingala Mesha—Chittirai; Pingala Vrishabha—Vaikasi. Lunar: Vaisakha; Bahula; Sukla. Muhammadan: H. 1397 Jumadal-awwal.

Cyclic Sidereal Year, Month and Day	Week-Day	English Day	Tithi	Tithi Ending Moment	Nakshatra	Nakshatra Ending Moment	Muhammadan Year, Month and Day
19	Su	1	13	·68	13	·67	12
20	Mo	2	14	·60	14	·61	13
21	Tu	3	P	·51	15	·55	14
22	We	4	1	·41	16	·49	15
23	Th	5	2	·31	17	·42	16
24	Fr	6	3	·21	18	·35	17
25	Sa	7	4	·11	19	·28	18
26	Su	8	5 6	·01 ·93	20	·23	19
27	Mo	9	7	·86	21	·19	20
28	Tu	10	8	·82	22	·16	21
29	We	11	9	·79	23	·14	22
30	Th	12	10	·78	24	·15	23
—31	Fr	13	11	·79	25	·17	24
1	Sa	14	12	·82	26	·22	25
2	Su	15	13	·87	27	·28	26
3	Mo	16	14	·94	1	·37	27
4	Tu	17	...	...	2	·47	28
5	We	18	—A	·02	3	·58	29
6	Th	19	1	·10	4	·68	—30
7	Fr	20	2	·18	5	·78	1
8	Sa	21	3	·26	6	·88	2
9	Su	22	4	·33	7	·96	3
10	Mo	23	5	·37	...	...	4
11	Tu	24	6	·38	8	·01	5
12	We	25	7	·38	9	·05	6
13	Th	26	8	·36	10	·06	7
14	Fr	27	9	·33	11	·06	8
15	Sa	28	10	·27	12	·04	9
16	Su	29	11	·19	13 14	·00 ·95	10
17	Mo	30	12	·10	15	·89	11
18	Tu	31	13 14	·01 ·91	16	·83	12

June — Solar: Pingala Mithuna—Ani. Lunar: Jyeshtha; Bahula; Sukla; Adhika Ashadha. Muhammadan: H. 1397 Jumadal-akhir; H. 1397 Rajab.

Cyclic Sidereal Year, Month and Day	Week-Day	English Day	Tithi	Tithi Ending Moment	Nakshatra	Nakshatra Ending Moment	Muhammadan Year, Month and Day
19	We	1	P	·81	17	·76	13
20	Th	2	1	·71	18	·69	14
21	Fr	3	2	·61	19	·62	15
22	Sa	4	3	·52	20	·56	16
23	Su	5	4	·44	21	·52	17
24	Mo	6	5	·38	22	·49	18
25	Tu	7	6	·32	23	·47	19
26	We	8	7	·28	24	·47	20
27	Th	9	8	·27	25	·49	21
28	Fr	10	9	·28	26	·53	22
29	Sa	11	10	·31	27	·60	23
30	Su	12	11	·35	1	·68	24
31	Mo	13	12	·42	2	·77	25
—32	Tu	14	13	·49	3	·87	26
1	We	15	14	·57	4	·93	27
2	Th	16	—A	·66	...	...	28
3	Fr	17	1	·74	5	·09	—29
4	Sa	18	2	·80	6	·19	1
5	Su	19	3	·84	7	·27	2
6	Mo	20	4	·87	8	·32	3
7	Tu	21	5	·86	9	·36	4
8	We	22	6	·84	10	·39	5
9	Th	23	7	·81	11	·39	6
10	Fr	24	8	·75	12	·37	7
11	Sa	25	9	·68	13	·33	8
12	Su	26	10	·59	14	·28	9
13	Mo	27	11	·50	15	·23	10
14	Tu	28	12	·40	16	·17	11
15	We	29	13	·30	17	·10	12
16	Th	30	14	·19	18 19	·03 ·96	13

Naksh :—1. Asvn. 2. Bhar. 3. Krit. 4. Rohi. 5. Mrig. 6. Ardh. 7. Punar. 8. Push. 9. Aslesh. 10. Magh. 11. P. Phal. 12. U. Phal. 13. Hasta. 14. Chit.

A. D. 1977. A.—Amavasya. P.—Paurnami.	Kollam 1153, Commences { N. Malabar—Sept. S. Malabar—Aug.	Hijra 1398, Commences, Dec. 12.	Vikrama 2034. Bengal San 1383. (N. Cycle) Pramoda.

SOLAR reckoning: Cyclic Sidereal Year, Month and Day; Week-Day English Month and Day. LUNAR reckoning: Tithi Ending Moment; Nakshatra Ending Moment; Muhammadan Year, Month and Day.

July

Cyclic Sidereal	Week-Day	Day	Tithi	Moment	Nakshatra	Moment	Muhammadan
17	Fr	1	P	·09	20	·90	14
18	Sa	2	1 / 2	·00 / ·92	21	·86	15
19	Su	3	3	·85	22	·82	16
20	Mo	4	4	·79	23	·79	17
21	Tu	5	5	·73	24	·79	18
22	We	6	6	·74	25	·80	19
23	Th	7	7	·76	26	·84	20
24	Fr	8	8	·79	27	·90	21
25	Sa	9	9	·83	1	·98	22
26	Su	10	10	·90	...	...	23
27	Mo	11	11	·98	2	·07	24
28	Tu	12	...	...	3	·17	25
29	We	13	12	·06	4	·23	26
30	Th	14	13	·14	5	·39	27
—31	Fr	15	14	·21	6	·49	28
1	Sa	16	—A	·27	7	·57	29
2	Su	17	1	·31	8	·64	—30
3	Mo	18	2	·34	9	·69	1
4	Tu	19	3	·34	10	·71	2
5	We	20	4	·33	11	·71	3
6	Th	21	5	·29	12	·70	4
7	Fr	22	6	·23	13	·67	5
8	Sa	23	7	·16	14	·62	6
9	Su	24	8 / 9	·07 / ·98	15	·57	7
10	Mo	25	10	·88	16	·51	8
11	Tu	26	11	·78	17	·44	9
12	We	27	12	·68	18	·37	10
13	Th	28	13	·58	19	·30	11
14	Fr	29	14	·49	20	·24	12
15	Sa	30	P	·40	21	·19	13
16	Su	31	1	·33	22	·15	14

Solar: Pingala *Mithuna—Ani.* (17–31); Pingala *Karkata—Adi.* (1–16). Lunar: Adh. Ashadha (*Bahula* from 12); *Sukla*; Ashadha. Muhammadan: H. 1397 *Rajab.*; *Shaban.*

Aug.

Cyclic Sidereal	Week-Day	Day	Tithi	Moment	Nakshatra	Moment	Muhammadan
17	Mo	1	2	·27	23	·12	15
18	Tu	2	3	·24	24	·11	16
19	We	3	4	·22	25	·13	17
20	Th	4	5	·24	26	·16	18
21	Fr	5	6	·27	27	·21	19
22	Sa	6	7	·31	1	·28	20
23	Su	7	8	·37	2	·37	21
24	Mo	8	9	·44	3	·48	22
25	Tu	9	10	·52	4	·59	23
26	We	10	11	·61	5	·69	24
27	Th	11	12	·70	6	·79	25
28	Fr	12	13	·76	7	·88	26
29	Sa	13	14	·80	8	·95	27
30	Su	14	—A	·83	...	...	28
31	Mo	15	1	·83	9	·00	—29
—32	Tu	16	2	·82	10	·03	1
1	We	17	3	·78	11	·04	2
2	Th	18	4	·73	12	·03	3
3	Fr	19	5	·66	13 / 14	·00 / ·96	4
4	Sa	20	6	·58	15	·91	5
5	Su	21	7	·48	16	·84	6
6	Mo	22	8	·38	17	·77	7
7	Tu	23	9	·28	18	·70	8
8	We	24	10	·18	19	·64	9
9	Th	25	11 / 12	·08 / ·99	20	·58	10
10	Fr	26	13	·92	21	·52	11
11	Sa	27	14	·85	22	·48	12
12	Su	28	P	·79	23	·45	13
13	Mo	29	1	·75	24	·44	14
14	Tu	30	2	·73	25	·45	15
15	We	31	3	·75	26	·47	16

Solar: Pingala *Simha—Avani.* (from 1). Lunar: Nija (Ashadha) *Bahula*; *Sukla*; Sravana. Muhammadan: H. 1397 (Shaban); H. 1397 *Ramzan.*

Sep.

Cyclic Sidereal	Week-Day	Day	Tithi	Moment	Nakshatra	Moment	Muhammadan
16	Th	1	4	·78	27	·52	17
17	Fr	2	5	·83	1	·59	18
18	Sa	3	6	·89	2	·68	19
19	Su	4	7	·96	3	·78	20
20	Mo	5	...	...	4	·88	21
21	Tu	6	8	·04	5	·99	22
22	We	7	9	·12	...	...	23
23	Th	8	10	·20	6	·09	24
24	Fr	9	11	·27	7	·18	25
25	Sa	10	12	·32	8	·26	26
26	Su	11	13	·34	9	·32	27
27	Mo	12	14	·35	10	·35	28
28	Tu	13	—A	·34	11	·36	29
29	We	14	1	·31	12	·35	—30
30	Th	15	2	·26	13	·34	1
—31	Fr	16	3	·19	14	·30	2
1	Sa	17	4	·10	15	·24	3
2	Su	18	5 / 6	·01 / ·92	16	·18	4
3	Mo	19	7	·82	17	·11	5
4	Tu	20	8	·72	18 / 19	·04 / ·98	6
5	We	21	9	·62	20	·92	7
6	Th	22	10	·53	21	·86	8
7	Fr	23	11	·45	22	·81	9
8	Sa	24	12	·38	23	·78	10
9	Su	25	13	·32	24	·77	11
10	Mo	26	14	·29	25	·77	12
11	Tu ○	27	P	·28	26	·79	13
12	We	28	1	·30	27	·83	14
13	Th	29	2	·32	1	·90	15
14	Fr	30	3	·36	2	·98	16

Solar: Pingala *Simha—Avani.* (16–31); Pingala *Kanya—Purattasi.* (1–14). Lunar: Sravana *Bahula*; *Sukla*; Bhadrapada. Muhammadan: H. 1397 *Ramzan.*; *Shawwal.*

Oct.

Cyclic Sidereal	Week-Day	Day	Tithi	Moment	Nakshatra	Moment	Muhammadan
15	Sa	1	4	·42	...	...	17
16	Su	2	5	·50	3	·08	18
17	Mo	3	6	·59	4	·18	19
18	Tu	4	7	·68	5	·29	20
19	We	5	8	·75	6	·39	21
20	Th	6	9	·82	7	·49	22
21	Fr	7	10	·87	8	·57	23
22	Sa	8	11	·90	9	·63	24
23	Su	9	12	·92	10	·67	25
24	Mo	10	13	·90	11	·68	26
25	Tu	11	14	·88	12	·69	27
26	We	12	—A	·82	13	·67	28
27	Th	13	1	·75	14	·63	—29
28	Fr	14	2	·67	15	·58	1
29	Sa	15	3	·58	16	·52	2
—30	Su	16	4	·48	17	·46	3
1	Mo	17	5	·38	18	·39	4
2	Tu	18	6	·28	19	·32	5
3	We	19	7	·18	20	·25	6
4	Th	20	8	·10	21	·19	7
5	Fr	21	9 / 10	·02 / ·96	22	·15	8
6	Sa	22	11	·90	23	·11	9
7	Su	23	12	87	24	·09	10
8	Mo	24	13	·86	25	·09	11
9	Tu	25	14	·88	26	·10	12
10	We	26	P	·90	27	·14	13
11	Th	27	1	·95	1	·21	14
12	Fr	28	...	...	2	·29	15
13	Sa	29	2	·02	3	·38	16
14	Su	30	3	·10	4	·48	17
15	Mo	31	4	·18	5	·59	18

Solar: Pingala *Tula—Aippasi.* (from 1). Lunar: (Bhadrapada) *Bahula*; *Sukla*; Asvina; *Bah.* Muhammadan: H. 1397 (Shawwal); H. 1397 *Zi-l-ka'da.*

Nov.

Cyclic Sidereal	Week-Day	Day	Tithi	Moment	Nakshatra	Moment	Muhammadan
16	Tu	1	5	·27	6	·70	19
17	We	2	6	·35	7	·80	20
18	Th	3	7	·42	8	·88	21
19	Fr	4	8	·47	9	·94	22
20	Sa	5	9	·50	10	·98	23
21	Su	6	10	·51	...	...	24
22	Mo	7	11	·49	11	·01	25
23	Tu	8	12	·46	12	·01	26
24	We	9	13	·42	13 / 14	·00 / ·96	27
25	Th	10	14	·36	15	·92	28
26	Fr	11	—A	·28	16	·87	29
27	Sa	12	1	·19	17	·80	—30
28	Su	13	2 / 3	·09 / ·99	18	·73	1
29	Mo	14	4	·89	19	66	2
—30	Tu	15	5	·80	20	·60	3
1	We	16	6	·71	21	·54	4
2	Th	17	7	·63	22	·48	5
3	Fr	18	8	·53	23	·44	6
4	Sa	19	9	·51	24	·42	7
5	Su	20	10	·49	25	·41	8
6	Mo	21	11	·48	26	·42	9
7	Tu	22	12	·49	27	·46	10
8	We	23	13	·52	1	·52	11
9	Th	24	14	·57	2	·59	12
10	Fr	25	P	·65	3	·68	13
11	Sa	26	1	·73	4	·78	14
12	Su	27	2	·82	5	·89	15
13	Mo	28	3	·90	...	...	16
14	Tu	29	4	·98	6	·00	17
15	We	30	...	...	7	·10	18

Solar: Pingala *Tula—Aippasi.* (16–30); Pingala *Vrischika—Kartigai.* (1–15). Lunar: Asvina *Bahula*; *Sukla*; Karttika. Muhammadan: H. 1397 *Zi-l-ka'da.*; H. 1397 *Zi-l-hijja.*

Dec.

Cyclic Sidereal	Week-Day	Day	Tithi	Moment	Nakshatra	Moment	Muhammadan
16	Th	1	5	·05	8	·18	19
17	Fr	2	6	·10	9	·25	20
18	Sa	3	7	·13	10	·31	21
19	Su	4	8	·14	11	·33	22
20	Mo	5	9	·13	12	·34	23
21	Tu	6	10	·09	13	·32	24
22	We	7	11 / 12	·04 / ·97	14	·29	25
23	Th	8	13	·89	15	·25	26
24	Fr	9	14	·81	16	·20	27
25	Sa	10	—A	·72	17	·14	28
26	Su	11	1	·62	18	·07	—29
27	Mo	12	2	·52	19 / 20	·00 / ·93	1
28	Tu	13	3	·42	21	·87	2
29	We	14	4	·33	22	·82	3
—30	Th	15	5	·25	23	·77	4
1	Fr	16	6	·19	24	·74	5
2	Sa	17	7	·15	25	·73	6
3	Su	18	8	·13	26	·75	7
4	Mo	19	9	·11	27	·78	8
5	Tu	20	10	·13	1	·82	9
6	We	21	11	·17	2	·89	10
7	Th	22	12	·22	3	·98	11
8	Fr	23	13	·29	...	...	12
9	Sa	24	14	·38	4	·08	13
10	Su	25	P	·47	5	·19	14
11	Mo	26	1	·56	6	·30	15
12	Tu	27	2	·64	7	·40	16
13	We	28	3	·70	8	·49	17
14	Th	29	4	·74	9	·57	18
15	Fr	30	5	·77	10	·62	19
16	Sa	31	6	·78	11	·65	20

Solar: Pingala *Dhanus—Margali.* (from 1). Lunar: (Karttika) *Bahula*; *Sukla*; Margasira; *Bahula*. Muhammadan: H. 1398 *Muharram.*

15. Svati. 16. Visak. 17, Anur. 18. Jyesh. 19. Mula. 20. P. Ash. 21. U. Ash. 22. Sravn. 23. Dani. 24. Satab. 25. P. Bhad. 26. U. Bhad. 27. Rev.

A. D. 1978.
Solar Eclipse. ●
Lunar Eclipse. ○

Mesha Sankranti (Commencement of Indian Sidereal Year).
(Surya Sid.) April 13·80.
(Arya Sid.) April 13·69.

Saka 1900. **Kaliyuga 5079.**
(S. Cycle) Kalayukta.

Columns: SOLAR reckoning — Cyclic Sidereal Year, Month and Day; Week-Day English Month and Day. LUNAR reckoning — Tithi Ending Moment; Nakshatra Ending Moment; Muhammadan Year, Month and Day.

Jan.

Cyclic Sidereal Year, Month	Day	Week-Day	Eng. Day	Lunar Month, Paksha	Tithi	Ending Moment	Nakshatra	Ending Moment	Muhammadan Year, Month	Day
Pingala Dhanus—Margali.	17	Su	1	Marga. Bahula	7	·77	12	·66	H. 1398 Muharram.	21
	18	Mo	2		8	·74	13	·65		22
	19	Tu	3		9	·69	14	·62		23
	20	We	4		10	·62	15	·59		24
	21	Th	5		11	·54	16	·54		25
	22	Fr	6		12	·45	17	·48		26
	23	Sa	7		13	·36	18	·41		27
	24	Su	8		14	·26	19	·34		28
	25	Mo	9		—A	·16	20	·27		29
	26	Tu	10	Pausha Sukla	1 2	·07 ·98	21	·21		—30
	27	We	11		3	·91	22	·15	H. 1398 Safar.	1
	28	Th	12		4	·84	23	·11		2
	—29	Fr	13		5	·79	24	·08		3
Pingala Makara—Tai.	1	Sa	14		6	·77	25	·07		4
	2	Su	15		7	·76	26	·07		5
	3	Mo	16		8	·78	27	·09		6
	4	Tu	17		9	·82	1	·13		7
	5	We	18		10	·88	2	·20		8
	6	Th	19		11	·95	3	·29		9
	7	Fr	20		...	...	4	·38		10
	8	Sa	21		12	·03	5	·49		11
	9	Su	22		13	·12	6	·60		12
	10	Mo	23		14	·21	7	·70		13
	11	Tu	24		P	·29	8	·79		14
	12	We	25	Bahula	1	·35	9	·87		15
	13	Th	26		2	·40	10	·93		16
	14	Fr	27		3	·42	11	·97		17
	15	Sa	28		4	·43	12	·98		18
	16	Su	29		5	·41	13	·98		19
	17	Mo	30		6	·38	14	·96		20
	18	Tu	31		7	·32	15	·93		21

Feb.

Cyclic Sidereal Year, Month	Day	Week-Day	Eng. Day	Lunar Month, Paksha	Tithi	Ending Moment	Nakshatra	Ending Moment	Muhammadan Year, Month	Day
	19	We	1		8	·25	16	·87		22
	20	Th	2		9	·17	17	·81		23
	21	Fr	3		10 11	·08 ·99	18	·75		24
	22	Sa	4		12	·89	19	·68		25
	23	Su	5		13	·79	20	·61		26
	24	Mo	6		14	·70	21	·55		27
	25	Tu	7		—A	·61	22	·49		28
	26	We	8	Magha Sukla	1	·53	23	·44		—29
	27	Th	9		2	·47	24	·41	H. 1398 Rabi-ul-awwal.	1
	28	Fr	10		3	·43	25	·39		2
	29	Sa	11		4	·40	26	·39		3
	—30	Su	12		5	·40	27	·41		4
Pingala Kumbha—Masi.	1	Mo	13		6	·41	1	·45		5
	2	Tu	14		7	·45	2	·51		6
	3	We	15		8	·51	3	·59		7
	4	Th	16		9	·58	4	·69		8
	5	Fr	17		10	·67	5	·79		9
	6	Sa	18		11	·76	6	·89		10
	7	Su	19		12	·84	...	...		11
	8	Mo	20		13	·91	7	·00		12
	9	Tu	21		14	·97	8	·10		13
	10	We	22		...	...	9	·18		14
	11	Th	23		P	·02	10	·24		15
	12	Fr	24	Bah.	1	·04	11	·28		16
	13	Sa	25		2	·05	12	·30		17
	14	Su	26		3 4	·08 ·99	13	·31		18
	15	Mo	27		5	·94	14	·29		19
	16	Tu	28		6	·87	15	·26		20

March

Cyclic Sidereal Year, Month	Day	Week-Day	Eng. Day	Lunar Month, Paksha	Tithi	Ending Moment	Nakshatra	Ending Moment	Muhammadan Year, Month	Day
Pingala Kumbha—Masi.	17	We	1	Magha Bahula	7	·79	16	·21	H. 1398 Rabi-ul-awwal.	21
	18	Th	2		8	·70	17	·15		22
	19	Fr	3		9	·60	18	·09		23
	20	Sa	4		10	·50	19 20	·02 ·95		24
	21	Su	5		11	·40	21	·88		25
	22	Mo	6		12	·30	22	·82		26
	23	Tu	7		13	·22	23	·78		27
	24	We	8		14	·14	24	·74		28
	25	Th	9		—A	·08	25	·72		29
	26	Fr	10	Phalguna Sukla	1	·04	26	·71		—30
	27	Sa	11		2	·01	27	·72	H. 1398 Rabi-ul-akhir.	1
	28	Su	12		3	·00	1	·76		2
	—29	Mo	13		4	·01	2	·82		3
Pingala Mina—Panguni.	1	Tu	14		5	·05	3	·89		4
	2	We	15		6	·11	4	·98		5
	3	Th	16		7	·18	...	...		6
	4	Fr	17		8	·26	5	·08		7
	5	Sa	18		9	·35	6	·19		8
	6	Su	19		10	·44	7	·30		9
	7	Mo	20		11	·52	8	·40		10
	8	Tu	21		12	·58	9	·49		11
	9	We	22		13	·62	10	·55		12
	10	Th	23		14	·64	11	·60		13
	11	Fr ○	24		P	·64	12	·63		14
	12	Sa	25	Bahula	1	·62	13	·64		15
	13	Su	26		2	·58	14	·62		16
	14	Mo	27		3	·52	15	·59		17
	15	Tu	28		4	·45	16	·55		18
	16	We	29		5	·37	17	·50		19
	17	Th	30		6	·27	18	·43		20
	18	Fr	31		7	·17	19	·36		21

April

Cyclic Sidereal Year, Month	Day	Week-Day	Eng. Day	Lunar Month, Paksha	Tithi	Ending Moment	Nakshatra	Ending Moment	Muhammadan Year, Month	Day
	19	Sa	1		8 9	·07 ·97	20	·29		22
	20	Su	2		10	·88	21	·22		23
	21	Mo	3		11	·79	22	·16		24
	22	Tu	4		12	·71	23	·11		25
	23	We	5		13	·65	24	·07		26
	24	Th	6		14	·61	25	·04		27
	25	Fr	7		—A	·58	26	·03		28
	26	Sa	8	Chaitra Sukla	1	·57	27	·04		—29
	27	Su	9		2	·57	1	·08	H. 1398 Jumadal-awwal.	1
	28	Mo	10		3	·61	2	·13		2
	29	Tu	11		4	·67	3	·20		3
	30	We	12		5	·75	4	·28		4
	—31	Th	13		6	·83	5	·38		5
Kalayukta Mesha—Chittirai.	1	Fr	14		7	·92	6	·49		6
	2	Sa	15		...	...	7	·60		7
	3	Su	16		8	·00	8	·70		8
	4	Mo	17		9	·07	9	·79		9
	5	Tu	18		10	·13	10	·86		10
	6	We	19		11	·17	11	·92		11
	7	Th	20		12	·19	12	·95		12
	8	Fr	21		13	·19	13	·96		13
	9	Sa	22		14	·17	14	·95		14
	10	Su	23		P	·12	15	·92		15
	11	Mo	24	Bahula	1 2	·06 ·99	16	·89		16
	12	Tu	25		3	·91	17	·83		17
	13	We	26		4	·82	18	·77		18
	14	Th	27		5	·72	19	·70		19
	15	Fr	28		6	·62	20	·63		20
	16	Sa	29		7	·52	21	·56		21
	17	Su	30		8	·42	22	·50		22

May

Cyclic Sidereal Year, Month	Day	Week-Day	Eng. Day	Lunar Month, Paksha	Tithi	Ending Moment	Nakshatra	Ending Moment	Muhammadan Year, Month	Day
Kalayukta Mesha—Chittirai.	18	Mo	1	Chait. Bah.	9	·32	23	·45	Jumadal-awwal.	23
	19	Tu	2		10	·24	24	·40		24
	20	We	3		11	·18	25	·37		25
	21	Th	4		12	·14	26	·35		26
	22	Fr	5		13	·11	27	·37		27
	23	Sa	6		14	·09	1	·39		28
	24	Su	7		—A	·11	2	·44		29
	25	Mo	8	Vaisakha Sukla	1	·15	3	·50		—30
	26	Tu	9		2	·20	4	·59	H. 1398 Jumadal-akhir.	1
	27	We	10		3	·26	5	·69		2
	28	Th	11		4	·34	6	·80		3
	29	Fr	12		5	·43	7	·90		4
	30	Sa	13		6	·51	...	...		5
	—31	Su	14		7	·59	8	·00		6
Kalayukta Vrishabha—Vaikasi.	1	Mo	15		8	·64	9	·09		7
	2	Tu	16		9	·68	10	·17		8
	3	We	17		10	·70	11	·23		9
	4	Th	18		11	·70	12	·27		10
	5	Fr	19		12	·68	13	·28		11
	6	Sa	20		13	·64	14	·27		12
	7	Su	21		14	·58	15	·25		13
	8	Mo	22		P	·51	16	·22		14
	9	Tu	23	Bahula	1	·42	17	·17		15
	10	We	24		2	·32	18	·11		16
	11	Th	25		3	·22	19 20	·04 ·97		17
	12	Fr	26		4	·12	21	·91		18
	13	Sa	27		5 6	·02 ·92	22	·85		19
	14	Su	28		7	·83	23	·79		20
	15	Mo	29		8	·75	24	·73		21
	16	Tu	30		9	·68	25	·70		22
	17	We	31		10	·64	26	·69		23

June

Cyclic Sidereal Year, Month	Day	Week-Day	Eng. Day	Lunar Month, Paksha	Tithi	Ending Moment	Nakshatra	Ending Moment	Muhammadan Year, Month	Day
	18	Th	1		11	·61	27	·69		24
	19	Fr	2		12	·59	1	·71		25
	20	Sa	3		13	·60	2	·75		26
	21	Su	4		14	·64	3	·81		27
	22	Mo	5		—A	·70	4	·89		28
	23	Tu	6	Jyeshtha Sukla	1	·76	5	·99		—29
	24	We	7		2	·83	...	...	H. 1398 Rajab.	1
	25	Th	8		3	·91	6	·09		2
	26	Fr	9		...	...	7	·20		3
	27	Sa	10		4	·00	8	·31		4
	28	Su	11		5	·08	9	·41		5
	29	Mo	12		6	·13	10	·49		6
	30	Tu	13		7	·17	11	·55		7
	—31	We	14		8	·19	12	·58		8
Kalayukta Mithuna—Ani.	1	Th	15		9	·18	13	·60		9
	2	Fr	16		10	·17	14	·60		10
	3	Sa	17		11	·13	15	·59		11
	4	Su	18		12 13	·07 ·99	16	·55		12
	5	Mo	19		14	·91	17	·50		13
	6	Tu	20		P	·82	18	·44		14
	7	We	21	Bahula	1	·72	19	·38		15
	8	Th	22		2	·61	20	·32		16
	9	Fr	23		3	·51	21	·25		17
	10	Sa	24		4	·41	22	·18		18
	11	Su	25		5	·32	23	·12		19
	12	Mo	26		6	·24	24	·07		20
	13	Tu	27		7	·17	25	·04		21
	14	We	28		8	·12	26	·01		22
	15	Th	29		9	·09	27	·01		23
	16	Fr	30		10	·07	1	·02		24

Naksh :—1. Asvn. 2. Bhar. 3. Krit. 4. Rohi. 5. Mrig. 6. Ardh. 7. Punar. 8. Push. 9. Aslesh. 10. Magh. 11. P. Phal. 12. U. Phal. 13. Hasta. 14. Chit.

A. D. 1978.
A.—Amavasya.
P.—Paurnami.

Kollam 1154, Commences { N. Malabar—Sept. / S. Malabar—Aug.

Hijra 1399, Commences, Dec. 2.

Vikrama 2035.
Bengal San 1384.
(N. Cycle) Prajapati.

SOLAR reckoning: Cyclic Sidereal Year, Month and Day.	SOLAR reckoning: Week-Day English Month and Day.	LUNAR reckoning: Tithi Ending Moment.	LUNAR reckoning: Nakshatra Ending Moment.	LUNAR reckoning: Muhammadan Year, Month and Day.
	July			
Kalayukta *Mithuna—Ani.* 17	Sa 1	*Jy. Bah.* 11 ·08	2 ·06	*Rajab.* 25
18	Su 2	12 ·11	3 ·11	26
19	Mo 3	13 ·17	4 ·20	27
20	Tu 4	14 ·23	5 ·29	28
21	We 5	—A ·31	6 ·39	29
22	Th 6	*Sukla* 1 ·39	7 ·50	—30
23	Fr 7	2 ·47	8 ·61	H. 1398 *Saban.* 1
24	Sa 8	3 ·54	9 ·71	2
25	Su 9	4 ·60	10 ·79	3
26	Mo 10	5 ·64	11 ·86	4
27	Tu 11	6 ·66	12 ·90	5
28	We 12	7 ·67	13 ·92	6
29	Th 13	8 ·65	14 ·93	7
30	Fr 14	9 ·61	15 ·92	8
31	Sa 15	10 ·55	16 ·89	9
—32	Su 16	**Ashadha** 11 ·47	17 ·84	10
Kalayukta *Karkata—Adi.* 1	Mo 17	12 ·39	18 ·78	11
2	Tu 18	13 ·30	19 ·72	12
3	We 19	14 ·20	20 ·65	13
4	Th 20	P ·10	21 ·58	14
5	Fr 21	{ 1 ·00 2 ·9)	22 ·52	15
6	Sa 22	*Bahula* 3 ·80	23 ·46	16
7	Su 23	4 ·72	24 ·41	17
8	Mo 24	5 ·65	25 ·37	18
9	Tu 25	6 ·60	26 ·34	19
10	We 26	7 ·57	27 ·33	20
11	Th 27	8 ·55	1 ·34	21
12	Fr 28	9 ·56	2 ·38	22
13	Sa 29	10 ·59	3 ·43	23
14	Su 30	11 ·63	4 ·50	24
15	Mo 31	12 ·70	5 ·59	25
	Aug.			
16	Tu 1	13 ·78	6 ·69	26
17	We 2	14 ·86	7 ·30	27
18	Th 3	—A ·94	8 ·91	28
19	Fr 4	... ...	... ...	—29
20	Sa 5	*Sukla* 1 ·02	9 ·01	H. 1398 *Ramzan.* 1
21	Su 6	2 ·08	10 ·10	2
22	Mo 7	3 ·12	11 ·16	3
23	Tu 8	4 ·14	12 ·21	4
24	We 9	5 ·15	13 ·25	5
25	Th 10	6 ·13	14 ·26	6
26	Fr 11	7 ·10	15 ·25	7
27	Sa 12	{ 8 ·05 9 ·98	16 ·22	8
28	Su 13	10 ·89	17 ·18	9
29	Mo 14	11 ·79	18 ·13	10
30	Tu 15	12 ·69	19 ·06 20 ·99 }	11
—31	We 16	**Sravana** 13 ·59	21 ·92	12
Kalayukta *Simha—Avani.* 1	Th 17	14 ·49	22 ·86	13
2	Fr 18	P ·39	23 ·80	14
3	Sa 19	*Bahula* 1 ·30	24 ·74	15
4	Su 20	2 ·22	25 ·70	16
5	Mo 21	3 ·16	26 ·67	17
6	Tu 22	4 ·10	27 ·65	18
7	We 23	5 ·06	1 ·66	19
8	Th 24	6 ·05	2 ·69	20
9	Fr 25	7 ·06	3 ·74	21
10	Sa 26	8 ·09	4 ·81	22
11	Su 27	9 ·14	5 ·89	23
12	Mo 28	10 ·21	6 ·99	24
13	Tu 29	11 ·28	... ...	25
14	We 30	12 ·35	7 ·10	26
15	Th 31	13 ·44	8 ·21	27

SOLAR reckoning: Cyclic Sidereal Year, Month and Day.	SOLAR reckoning: Week-Day English Month and Day.	LUNAR reckoning: Tithi Ending Moment.	LUNAR reckoning: Nakshatra Ending Moment.	LUNAR reckoning: Muhammadan Year, Month and Day.
	Sep.			
Kalayukta *Simha—Avani.* 16	Fr 1	14 ·52	9 ·31	28
17	Sa 2	—A ·59	10 ·40	29
18	Su 3	*Sukla* 1 ·63	11 ·48	—30
19	Mo 4	2 ·66	12 ·54	H. 1398 *Shawwal.* 1
20	Tu 5	3 ·67	13 ·57	2
21	We 6	4 ·65	14 ·58	3
22	Th 7	5 ·62	15 ·57	4
23	Fr 8	6 ·56	16 ·55	5
24	Sa 9	7 ·49	17 ·52	6
25	Su 10	8 ·41	18 ·46	7
26	Mo 11	9 ·32	19 ·40	8
27	Tu 12	10 ·22	20 ·33	9
28	We 13	11 ·12	21 ·26	10
29	Th 14	{ 12 ·02 13 ·92	22 ·20	11
30	Fr 15	**Bhadrapada** 14 ·83	23 ·14	12
—31	Sa ○ 16	P ·75	24 ·08	13
Kalayukta *Kanya—Purattasi.* 1	Su 17	1 ·68	25 ·03 26 ·99 }	14
2	Mo 18	*Bahula* 2 ·63	27 ·98	15
3	Tu 19	3 ·60	1 ·99	16
4	We 20	4 ·58	... ...	17
5	Th 21	5 ·60	2 ·01	18
6	Fr 22	6 ·62	3 ·05	19
7	Sa 23	7 ·67	4 ·11	20
8	Su 24	8 ·74	5 ·19	21
9	Mo 25	9 ·82	6 ·29	22
10	Tu 26	10 ·91	7 ·40	23
11	We 27	11 ·99	8 ·51	24
12	Th 28	... ...	9 ·61	25
13	Fr 29	12 ·06	10 ·70	26
14	Sa 30	13 ·13	11 ·78	27
	Oct.			
15	Su 1	14 ·17	12 ·85	28
16	Mo ● 2	—A ·20	13 ·89	—29
17	Tu 3	*Sukla* 1 ·21	14 ·90	H. 1398 *Zi-l-ka'da.* 1
18	We 4	2 ·20	15 ·90	2
19	Th 5	3 ·17	16 ·89	3
20	Fr 6	4 ·11	17 ·85	4
21	Sa 7	{ 5 ·04 6 ·96	18 ·80	5
22	Su 8	7 ·88	19 ·74	6
23	Mo 9	8 ·78	20 ·67	7
24	Tu 10	9 ·68	21 ·60	8
25	We 11	10 ·58	22 ·53	9
26	Th 12	11 ·48	23 ·47	10
27	Fr 13	12 ·39	24 ·41	11
28	Sa 14	13 ·31	25 ·36	12
29	Su 15	**Asvina** 14 ·25	26 ·32	13
30	Mo 16	P ·20	27 ·31	14
—31	Tu 17	1 ·17	1 ·31	15
Kalayukta *Tula—Aippasi.* 1	We 18	*Bahula* 2 ·15	2 ·32	16
2	Th 19	3 ·17	3 ·36	17
3	Fr 20	4 ·20	4 ·42	18
4	Sa 21	5 ·26	5 ·50	19
5	Su 22	6 ·32	6 ·60	20
6	Mo 23	7 ·40	7 ·70	21
7	Tu 24	8 ·49	8 ·81	22
8	We 25	9 ·58	9 ·92	23
9	Th 26	10 ·66	... ...	24
10	Fr 27	11 ·72	10 ·02	25
11	Sa 28	12 ·76	11 ·10	26
12	Su 29	13 ·79	12 ·16	27
13	Mo 30	14 ·80	13 ·20	28
14	Tu 31	—A ·79	14 ·22	29

SOLAR reckoning: Cyclic Sidereal Year, Month and Day.	SOLAR reckoning: Week-Day English Month and Day.	LUNAR reckoning: Tithi Ending Moment.	LUNAR reckoning: Nakshatra Ending Moment.	LUNAR reckoning: Muhammadan Year, Month and Day.
	Nov.			
Kalayukta *Tula—Aippasi.* 15	We 1	1 ·75	15 ·23	—30
16	Th 2	2 ·70	16 ·22	H. 1398 *Zi-l-hijja.* 1
17	Fr 3	3 ·63	17 ·18	2
18	Sa 4	4 ·56	18 ·13	3
19	Su 5	5 ·47	19 ·07	4
20	Mo 6	*Sukla* 6 ·37	20 ·01 21 ·95 }	5
21	Tu 7	7 ·27	22 ·88	6
22	We 8	8 ·17	23 ·81	7
23	Th 9	{ 9 ·08 10 ·99	24 ·75	8
24	Fr 10	11 ·91	25 ·69	9
25	Sa 11	12 ·85	26 ·66	10
26	Su 12	**Karttika** 13 ·81	27 ·64	11
27	Mo 13	14 ·78	1 ·63	12
28	Tu 14	P ·76	2 ·64	13
—29	We 15	1 ·78	3 ·67	14
Kalayukta *Vrischika—Karttigai.* 1	Th 16	2 ·81	4 ·73	15
2	Fr 17	3 ·87	5 ·81	16
3	Sa 18	4 ·94	6 ·90	17
4	Su 19	... ...	... ...	18
5	Mo 20	5 ·02	7 ·00	19
6	Tu 21	6 ·11	8 ·11	20
7	We 22	*Bahula* 7 ·20	9 ·22	21
8	Th 23	8 ·28	10 ·32	22
9	Fr 24	9 ·34	11 ·40	23
10	Sa 25	10 ·39	12 ·47	24
11	Su 26	11 ·42	13 ·52	25
12	Mo 27	12 ·43	14 ·55	26
13	Tu 28	13 ·41	15 ·56	27
14	We 29	14 ·38	16 ·54	28
15	Th 30	—A ·33	17 ·51	29
	Dec.			
16	Fr 1	1 ·26	18 ·47	—30
17	Sa 2	2 ·18	19 ·42	H. 1399 *Muharram.* 1
18	Su 3	3 ·09	20 ·36	2
19	Mo 4	{ 4 ·00 5 ·90	21 ·29	3
20	Tu 5	6 ·80	22 ·22	4
21	We 6	7 ·70	23 ·15	5
22	Th 7	*Sukla* 8 ·61	24 ·08	6
23	Fr 8	9 ·54	25 ·03 26 ·99 }	7
24	Sa 9	10 ·48	27 ·96	8
25	Su 10	11 ·44	1 ·95	9
26	Mo 11	**Margasira** 12 ·41	2 ·96	10
27	Tu 12	13 ·40	... ...	11
28	We 13	14 ·42	3 ·00	12
29	Th 14	P ·45	4 ·05	13
—30	Fr 15	1 ·51	5 ·11	14
Kalayukta *Dhanus—Margali.* 1	Sa 16	2 ·59	6 ·20	15
2	Su 17	3 ·68	7 ·30	16
3	Mo 18	4 ·77	8 ·41	17
4	Tu 19	5 ·85	9 ·52	18
5	We 20	6 ·92	10 ·62	19
6	Th 21	7 ·99	11 ·71	20
7	Fr 22	*Bahula*	12 ·78	21
8	Sa 23	8 ·04	13 ·83	22
9	Su 24	9 ·06	14 ·87	23
10	Mo 25	10 ·07	15 ·88	24
11	Tu 26	11 ·05	16 ·87	25
12	We 27	{ 12 ·02 13 ·97	17 ·84	26
13	Th 28	14 ·90	18 ·80	27
14	Fr 29	—A ·82	19 ·75	28
15	Sa 30	*Suk.* 1 ·73	20 ·69	29
16	Su 31	2 ·63	21 ·63	—30

15. Svati. 16. Visak. 17. Anur. 18. Jyesh. 19. Mula. 20. P. Ash. 21. U. Ash. 22. Sravn. 23. Dani. 24. Satab. 25. P. Bhad. 26. U. Bhad. 27. Rev.

A. D. 1979. **Mesha Sankranti** (Commencement of Indian Sidereal Year).

Solar Eclipse. ● **(Surya Sid.) April 14·06.** **Saka 1901.** **Kaliyuga 5080.**

Lunar Eclipse. ○ **(Arya Sid.) April 13·95.** **(S. Cycle) Siddharthi.**

SOLAR reckoning: Cyclic Sidereal Year, Month and Day; Week-Day, English Month and Day. LUNAR reckoning: Tithi Ending Moment; Nakshatra Ending Moment; Muhammadan Year, Month and Day.

Jan.

Solar: Kalayukta *Dhanus—Margali.*; Kalayukta *Makara—Tai.* Lunar: *Sukla*, **Pausha**, *Bahula*. Muhammadan: H. 1399 *Safar.*

Cyclic Sidereal	Week-Day	Day	Tithi	Moment	Nakshatra	Moment	Muhammadan
17	Mo	1	3	·53	22	·56	1
18	Tu	2	4	·48	23	·49	2
19	We	3	5	·34	24	·43	3
20	Th	4	6	·26	25	·37	4
21	Fr	5	7	·18	26	·32	5
22	Sa	6	8	·12	27	·29	6
23	Su	7	9	·08	1	·28	7
24	Mo	8	10	·05	2	·29	8
25	Tu	9	11	·05	3	·31	9
26	We	10	12	·06	4	·35	10
27	Th	11	13	·10	5	·42	11
28	Fr	12	14	·16	6	·50	12
—29	Sa	13	P	·24	7	·60	13
1	Su	14	1	·33	8	·71	14
2	Mo	15	2	·42	9	·82	15
3	Tu	16	3	·50	10	·92	16
4	We	17	4	·57	...	...	17
5	Th	18	5	·64	11	·01	18
6	Fr	19	6	·69	12	·09	19
7	Sa	20	7	·71	13	·15	20
8	Su	21	8	·71	14	·19	21
9	Mo	22	9	·69	15	·20	22
10	Tu	23	10	·66	16	·20	23
11	We	24	11	·61	17	·17	24
12	Th	25	12	·53	18	·14	25
13	Fr	26	13	·45	19	·09	26
14	Sa	27	14	·36	20 21	·03 ·96	27
15	Su	28	—A	·26	22	·89	28
16	Mo	29	1	·16	23	·88	—29
17	Tu	30	2 3	·06 ·97	24	·77	1
18	We	31	4	·89	25	·71	2

Feb.

Solar: Kalayukta *Kumbha—Masi.* Lunar: *Sukla*, **Magha**, *Bahula*, **P.** *Suk.* Muhammadan: H. 1399 *Rabi-ul-awwal.*

Cyclic Sidereal	Week-Day	Day	Tithi	Moment	Nakshatra	Moment	Muhammadan
19	Th	1	5	·82	26	·66	3
20	Fr	2	6	·77	27	·62	4
21	Sa	3	7	·72	1	·60	5
22	Su	4	8	·70	2	·61	6
23	Mo	5	9	·69	3	·63	7
24	Tu	6	10	·71	4	·66	8
25	We	7	11	·75	5	·72	9
26	Th	8	12	·81	6	·81	10
27	Fr	9	13	·88	7	·91	11
28	Sa	10	14	·97	...	...	12
29	Su	11	...	...	8	·01	13
—30	Mo	12	P	·06	9	·12	14
1	Tu	13	1	·14	10	·22	15
2	We	14	2	·21	11	·31	16
3	Th	15	3	·27	12	·40	17
4	Fr	16	4	·32	13	·46	18
5	Sa	17	5	·34	14	·50	19
6	Su	18	6	·34	15	·52	20
7	Mo	19	7	·33	16	·52	21
8	Tu	20	8	·29	17	·51	22
9	We	21	9	·22	18	·48	23
10	Th	22	10	·15	19	·43	24
11	Fr	23	11 12	·07 ·99	20	·37	25
12	Sa	24	13	·89	21	·31	26
13	Su	25	14	·79	22	·24	27
14	Mo	26	—A	·69	23	·17	28
15	Tu	27	1	·59	24	·10	29
16	We	28	2	·51	25 26	·04 ·99	—30

March

Solar: Kalayukta *Kumbha—Masi.*; Kalayukta *Mina—Panguni.* Lunar: *Sukla*, **Phalguna**, *Bahula*. Muhammadan: H. 1399 *Rabi-ul-akhir.*

Cyclic Sidereal	Week-Day	Day	Tithi	Moment	Nakshatra	Moment	Muhammadan
17	Th	1	3	·43	27	·96	1
18	Fr	2	4	·37	1	·94	2
19	Sa	3	5	·33	2	·93	3
20	Su	4	6	·31	3	·94	4
21	Mo	5	7	·30	4	·98	5
22	Tu	6	8	·32	...	...	6
23	We	7	9	·37	5	04	7
24	Th	8	10	·43	6	·11	8
25	Fr	9	11	·50	7	·20	9
26	Sa	10	12	·58	8	·30	10
27	Su	11	13	·67	9	·41	11
28	Mo	12	14	·75	10	·52	12
29	Tu ○	13	P	·82	11	·62	13
—30	We	14	1	·88	12	·71	14
1	Th	15	2	·92	13	·77	15
2	Fr	16	3	·94	14	·82	16
3	Sa	17	4	·93	15	·84	17
4	Su	18	5	·92	16	·86	18
5	Mo	19	6	·88	17	·84	19
6	Tu	20	7	·82	18	·81	20
7	We	21	8	·75	19	·76	21
8	Th	22	9	·67	20	·71	22
9	Fr	23	10	·57	21	·65	23
10	Sa	24	11	·47	22	·58	24
11	Su	25	12	·37	23	·51	25
12	Mo	26	13	·27	24	·44	26
13	Tu	27	14	·18	25	·38	27
14	We	28	—A	·09	26	·33	28
15	Th	29	1 2	·01 ·95	27	·29	—29
16	Fr	30	3	·91	1	·26	1
17	Sa	31	4	·89	2	·25	2

April

Solar: Siddharthi *Mesha—Chittirai.* Lunar: *Sukla*, **Chaitra**, *Bahula*, **V.** *Suk.* Muhammadan: H. 1399 *Jumadal-awwal.*

Cyclic Sidereal	Week-Day	Day	Tithi	Moment	Nakshatra	Moment	Muhammadan
18	Su	1	5	·88	3	·26	3
19	Mo	2	6	·91	4	·29	4
20	Tu	3	7	·95	5	·35	5
21	We	4	...	...	6	·42	6
22	Th	5	8	·09	7	·51	7
23	Fr	6	9	·07	8	·61	8
24	Sa	7	10	·16	9	·72	9
25	Su	8	11	·24	10	·83	10
26	Mo	9	12	·31	11	·93	11
27	Tu	10	13	·38	...	...	12
28	We	11	14	·44	12	·01	13
29	Th	12	P	·48	13	·08	14
—30	Fr	13	1	·50	14	·13	15
1	Sa	14	2	·50	15	·17	16
2	Su	15	3	·48	16	·18	17
3	Mo	16	4	·43	17	·17	18
4	Tu	17	5	·37	18	·14	19
5	We	18	6	·30	19	·10	20
6	Th	19	7	·22	20 21	·05 ·99	21
7	Fr	20	8	·12	22	·92	22
8	Sa	21	9 10	·02 ·92	23	·85	23
9	Su	22	11	·82	24	·78	24
10	Mo	23	12	·72	25	·71	25
11	Tu	24	13	·63	26	·66	26
12	We	25	14	·56	27	·62	27
13	Th	26	—A	·50	1	·59	28
14	Fr	27	1	·46	2	·57	29
15	Sa	28	2	·43	3	·58	—30
16	Su	29	3	·42	4	·61	1
17	Mo	30	4	·44	5	·66	2

May

Solar: Siddharthi *Mesha—Chittirai.*; Siddharthi *Vrishabha—Vaikasi.* Lunar: *Sukla*, **Vaisakha**, *Bahula*. Muhammadan: H. 1399 *Jumadal-akhir.*

Cyclic Sidereal	Week-Day	Day	Tithi	Moment	Nakshatra	Moment	Muhammadan
18	Tu	1	5	·47	6	·72	3
19	We	2	6	·52	7	·80	4
20	Th	3	7	·59	8	·90	5
21	Fr	4	8	·68	...	...	6
22	Sa	5	9	·76	9	·01	7
23	Su	6	10	·84	10	·12	8
24	Mo	7	11	·91	11	·23	9
25	Tu	8	12	·97	12	·32	10
26	We	9	...	...	13	·39	11
27	Th	10	13	·01	14	·45	12
28	Fr	11	14	·02	15	·49	13
29	Sa	12	P	·02	16	·50	14
30	Su	13	1 2	·00 ·96	17	·49	15
—31	Mo	14	3	·89	18	·47	16
1	Tu	15	4	·81	19	·44	17
2	We	16	5	·73	20	·39	18
3	Th	17	6	·64	21	·33	19
4	Fr	18	7	·54	22	·26	20
5	Sa	19	8	·44	23	·19	21
6	Su	20	9	·34	24	·12	22
7	Mo	21	10	·24	25	·06	23
8	Tu	22	11	·15	26 27	·00 ·95	24
9	We	23	12	·07	1	·92	25
10	Th	24	13 14	·00 ·96	2	·90	26
11	Fr	25	—A	·93	3	·91	27
12	Sa	26	1	·93	4	·93	28
13	Su	27	2	·94	5	·97	—29
14	Mo	28	3	·98	...	...	1
15	Tu	29	...	...	6	·03	2
16	We	30	4	·03	7	·11	3
17	Th	31	5	·09	8	·21	4

June

Solar: Siddharthi *Mithuna—Ani.* Lunar: *Sukla*, **Jyeshtha**, *Bahula*, **Ash.** *Sukla*. Muhammadan: H. 1399 *Rajab.*; *Shaban.*

Cyclic Sidereal	Week-Day	Day	Tithi	Moment	Nakshatra	Moment	Muhammadan
18	Fr	1	6	·17	9	·32	5
19	Sa	2	7	·25	10	·43	6
20	Su	3	8	·33	11	·53	7
21	Mo	4	9	·40	12	62	8
22	Tu	5	10	·46	13	·70	9
23	We	6	11	·50	14	·76	10
24	Th	7	12	·52	15	·80	11
25	Fr	8	13	·51	16	·82	12
26	Sa	9	14	·49	17	·82	13
27	Su	10	P	·45	18	·80	14
28	Mo	11	1	·39	19	·77	15
29	Tu	12	2	·32	20	·72	16
30	We	13	3	23	21	·66	17
—31	Th	14	4	·13	22	·60	18
1	Fr	15	5 6	·03 ·93	23	·53	19
2	Sa	16	7	·83	24	·46	20
3	Su	17	8	·73	25	·40	21
4	Mo	18	9	·64	26	·34	22
5	Tu	19	10	·56	27	·28	23
6	We	20	11	·49	1	·25	24
7	Th	21	12	·44	2	·23	25
8	Fr	22	13	·41	3	·23	26
9	Sa	23	14	·40	4	·24	27
10	Su	24	—A	·41	5	·28	28
11	Mo	25	1	·45	6	·34	29
12	Tu	26	2	·50	7	·42	—30
13	We	27	3	·56	8	·51	1
14	Th	28	4	·64	9	·61	2
15	Fr	29	5	·73	10	·72	3
16	Sa	30	6	·81	11	·82	4

Naksh :—1. Asvn. 2. Bhar. 3. Krit. 4. Rohi. 5. Mrig. 6. Ardh. 7. Punar. 8. Push. 9. Aslesh. 10. Magh. 11. P. Phal. 12. U. Phal. 13. Hasta. 14. Chit.

A. D. 1979.
A.—Amavasya.
P.—Paurnami.

Kollam 1155, Commences { **N. Malabar—Sept.** / **S. Malabar—Aug.**

Hijra 1400, Commences, **Nov. 21.**

Vikrama 2036.
Bengal San 1385.
(N. Cycle) Angiras.

Solar month	Cyclic Sidereal Year, Month and Day	Week-Day	English Month and Day	Lunar month / Paksha	Tithi	Tithi Ending Moment	Nakshatra	Nakshatra Ending Moment	Muhammadan Year and Month	Muhammadan Day
			July							
Siddharthi *Mithuna—Ani.*	17	Su	1	**Ashadha** Sukla	7	·87	12	·93	H. 1399 *Shaban.*	5
	18	Mo	2		8	·94	...	...		6
	19	Tu	3		9	·98	13	·01		7
	20	We	4		...	...	14	·08		8
	21	Th	5		10 / 11	·00 / ·99	15	·12		9
	22	Fr	6		12	·97	16	·14		10
	23	Sa	7		13	·92	17	·15		11
	24	Su	8		14	·87	18	·14		12
	25	Mo	9		P	·80	19	·11		13
	26	Tu	10	Bahula	1	·71	20	·06		14
	27	We	11		2	·61	21 / 22	·00 / ·93		15
	28	Th	12		3	·51	23	·86		16
	29	Fr	13		4	·41	24	·79		17
	30	Sa	14		5	·30	25	·73		18
	31	Su	15		6	·20	26	·67		19
	—32	Mo	16		7	·11	27	·62		20
Siddharthi *Karkata—Adi.*	1	Tu	17		8 / 9	·03 / ·97	1	·59		21
	2	We	18		10	·93	2	·56		22
	3	Th	19		11	·90	3	·55		23
	4	Fr	20		12	·83	4	·56		24
	5	Sa	21		13	·90	5	·59		25
	6	Su	22		14	·93	6	·65		26
	7	Mo	23		—A	·97	7	·72		27
	8	Tu	24	Sukla	...	...	8	·81		28
	9	We	25		1	·03	9	·91		—29
	10	Th	26		2	·11	...	...	*Ramzan.*	1
	11	Fr	27		3	·20	10	·02		2
	12	Sa	28		4	·28	11	·13		3
	13	Su	29		5	·85	12	·23		4
	14	Mo	30		6	·41	13	·32		5
	15	Tu	31		7	·45	14	·39		6
			Aug.							
	16	We	1	**Sravana**	8	·48	15	·43	H. 1399 *Ramzan.*	7
	17	Th	2		9	·47	16	·46		8
	18	Fr	3		10	·45	17	·48		9
	19	Sa	4		11	·41	18	·47		10
	20	Su	5		12	·36	19	·44		11
	21	Mo	6		13	·29	20	·39		12
	22	Tu	7		14	·20	21	·34		13
	23	We	8		P	·11	22	·28		14
	24	Th	9	Bahula	1 / 2	·01 / ·91	23	·21		15
	25	Fr	10		3	·81	24	·14		16
	26	Sa	11		4	·71	25	·07		17
	27	Su	12		5	·61	26 / 27	·01 / ·96		18
	28	Mo	13		6	·53	1	·92		19
	29	Tu	14		7	·47	2	·89		20
	30	We	15		8	·42	3	·87		21
	—31	Th	16		9	·39	4	·88		22
Siddharthi *Simha—Avani.*	1	Fr	17		10	·37	5	·91		23
	2	Sa	18		11	·38	6	·96		24
	3	Su	19		12	·41	...	...		25
	4	Mo	20		13	·47	7	·03		26
	5	Tu	21		14	·53	8	·11		27
	6	We	22		—A	·60	9	·21		28
	7	Th	23	**Bhadra.** Sukla	1	·68	10	·32		29
	8	Fr	24		2	·77	11	·43		—30
	9	Sa	25		3	·85	12	·53	*Shawwal.*	1
	10	Su	26		4	·91	13	·62		2
	11	Mo	27		5	·96	14	·69		3
	12	Tu	28		6	·98	15	·75		4
	13	We	29		7	·97	16	·79		5
	14	Th	30		8	·96	17	·80		6
	15	Fr	31		9	·92	18	·79		7

Solar month	Cyclic Sidereal Year, Month and Day	Week-Day	English Month and Day	Lunar month / Paksha	Tithi	Tithi Ending Moment	Nakshatra	Nakshatra Ending Moment	Muhammadan Year and Month	Muhammadan Day
			Sep.							
Siddharthi *Simha—Avani.*	16	Sa	1	**Bhadrapada** Suk.	10	·87	19	·77	H. 1399 *Shawwal.*	8
	17	Su	2		11	·80	20	·73		9
	18	Mo	3		12	·72	21	·68		10
	19	Tu	4		13	·62	22	·62		11
	20	We	5		14	·52	23	·55		12
	21	Th ○	6		P	·42	24	·48		13
	22	Fr	7	Bahula	1	·32	25	·41		14
	23	Sa	8		2	·22	26	·35		15
	24	Su	9		3	·13	27	·30		16
	25	Mo	10		4 / 5	·05 / ·99	1	·25		17
	26	Tu	11		6	·94	2	·21		18
	27	We	12		7	·91	3	·20		19
	28	Th	13		8	·90	4	·20		20
	29	Fr	14		9	·91	5	·23		21
	30	Sa	15		10	·95	6	·27		22
	—31	Su	16		...	...	7	·33		23
Siddharthi *Kanya—Purattasi.*	1	Mo	17		11	·00	8	·41		24
	2	Tu	18		12	·06	9	·51		25
	3	We	19		13	·13	10	·62		26
	4	Th	20		14	·21	11	·73		27
	5	Fr	21		—A	·30	12	·83		28
	6	Sa	22	Sukla	1	·38	13	·92		—29
	7	Su	23		2	·44	...	...	*Zi-l-ka'da.*	1
	8	Mo	24		3	·49	14	·00		2
	9	Tu	25		4	·51	15	·07		3
	10	We	26		5	·52	16	·11		4
	11	Th	27		6	·50	17	·12		5
	12	Fr	28		7	·47	18	·12		6
	13	Sa	29		8	·41	19	·10		7
	14	Su	30		9	·34	20	·07		8
			Oct.							
	15	Mo	1	**Asvina**	10	·26	21 / 22	·02 / ·96	H. 1399 *Zi-l-ka'da.*	9
	16	Tu	2		11	·17	23	·89		10
	17	We	3		12 / 13	·08 / ·98	24	·82		11
	18	Th	4		14	·88	25	·75		12
	19	Fr	5		P	·77	26	·69		13
	20	Sa	6	Bahula	1	·68	27	·68		14
	21	Su	7		2	·61	1	·58		15
	22	Mo	8		3	·55	2	·54		16
	23	Tu	9		4	·50	3	·52		17
	24	We	10		5	·47	4	·53		18
	25	Th	11		6	·47	5	·54		19
	26	Fr	12		7	·48	6	·58		20
	27	Sa	13		8	·51	7	·64		21
	28	Su	14		9	·56	8	·72		22
	29	Mo	15		10	·62	9	·82		23
	30	Tu	16		11	·70	10	·92		24
	—31	We	17		12	·79	...	...		25
Siddharthi *Tula—Aippasi.*	1	Th	18		13	·88	11	·03		26
	2	Fr	19		14	·96	12	·13		27
	3	Sa	20		...	...	13	·23		28
	4	Su	21		—A	·03	14	·32		29
	5	Mo	22	**Karttika** Sukla	1	·07	15	·38		—30
	6	Tu	23		2	·10	16	·42	H. 1399 *Zi-l-hijja.*	1
	7	We	24		3	·10	17	·44		2
	8	Th	25		4	·08	18	·44		3
	9	Fr	26		5 / 6	·04 / ·99	19	·48		4
	10	Sa	27		7	·92	20	·40		5
	11	Su	28		8	·85	21	·35		6
	12	Mo	29		9	·76	22	·29		7
	13	Tu	30		10	·66	23	·23		8
	14	We	31		11	·56	24	·17		9

Solar month	Cyclic Sidereal Year, Month and Day	Week-Day	English Month and Day	Lunar month / Paksha	Tithi	Tithi Ending Moment	Nakshatra	Nakshatra Ending Moment	Muhammadan Year and Month	Muhammadan Day
			Nov.							
Siddharthi *Tula—Aippasi.*	15	Th	1	**Kartika** Suk.	12	·46	25	·10	H. 1399 *Zi-l-hijja.*	10
	16	Fr	2		13	·36	26 / 27	·03 / ·97		11
	17	Sa	3		14	·27	1	·91		12
	18	Su	4		P	·20	2	·87		13
	19	Mo	5	Bahula	1	·14	3	·86		14
	20	Tu	6		2	·09	4	·85		15
	21	We	7		3	·06	5	·86		16
	22	Th	8		4	·06	6	·89		17
	23	Fr	9		5	·07	7	·95		18
	24	Sa	10		6	·11	...	...		19
	25	Su	11		7	·16	8	·03		20
	26	Mo	12		8	·23	9	·12		21
	27	Tu	13		9	·31	10	·22		22
	28	We	14		10	·41	11	·32		23
	29	Th	15		11	·50	12	·43		24
	—30	Fr	16		12	·57	13	·53		25
Siddharthi *Vrischika—Kartigai.*	1	Sa	17		13	·63	14	·62		26
	2	Su	18		14	·68	15	·69		27
	3	Mo	19		—A	·72	16	·74		28
	4	Tu	20	Sukla	1	·71	17	·76		—29
	5	We	21		2	·69	18	·77	H. 1400 *Muharram.*	1
	6	Th	22		3	·65	19	·76		2
	7	Fr	23		4	·60	20	·73		3
	8	Sa	24		5	·54	21	·69		4
	9	Su	25		6	·46	22	·68		5
	10	Mo	26		7	·38	23	·57		6
	11	Tu	27		8	·28	24	·51		7
	12	We	28		9	·18	25	·44		8
	13	Th	29		10 / 11	·08 / ·99	26	·37		9
	14	Fr	30		12	·90	27	·31		10
			Dec.							
	15	Sa	1	**Margasira**	13	·82	1	·25	H. 1400 *Muharram.*	11
	16	Su	2		14	·76	2	·21		12
	17	Mo	3		P	·72	3	·18		13
	18	Tu	4	Bahula	1	·70	4	·17		14
	19	We	5		2	·69	5	·18		15
	20	Th	6		3	·71	6	·21		16
	21	Fr	7		4	·75	7	·27		17
	22	Sa	8		5	·80	8	·34		18
	23	Su	9		6	·88	9	·42		19
	24	Mo	10		7	·97	10	·52		20
	25	Tu	11		...	...	11	·63		21
	26	We	12		8	·06	12	·74		22
	27	Th	13		9	·15	13	·84		23
	28	Fr	14		10	·23	14	·93		24
	—29	Sa	15		11	·28	...	...		25
Siddharthi *Dhanus—Margali.*	1	Su	16		12	·32	15	·00		26
	2	Mo	17		13	·36	16	·05		27
	3	Tu	18		14	·35	17	·08		28
	4	We	19		—A	·33	18	·10		29
	5	Th	20	**Pausha** Sukla	1	·29	19	·09		—30
	6	Fr	21		2	·24	20	·06	H. 1400 *Safar.*	1
	7	Sa	22		3	·17	21 / 22	·02 / ·97		2
	8	Su	23		4	·09	23	·91		3
	9	Mo	24		5 / 6	·01 / ·91	24	·85		4
	10	Tu	25		7	·81	25	·78		5
	11	We	26		8	·71	26	·71		6
	12	Th	27		9	·62	27	·65		7
	13	Fr	28		10	·53	1	·59		8
	14	Sa	29		11	·46	2	·54		9
	15	Su	30		12	·40	3	·51		10
	16	Mo	31		13	·36	4	·50		11

15. Svati. **16.** Visak. **17.** Anur. **18.** Jyesh. **19.** Mula. **20.** P. Ash. **21.** U. Ash. **22.** Sravn. **23.** Dani. **24.** Satab. **25.** P. Bhad. **26.** U. Bhad. **27.** Rev.

A. D. 1980.
Solar Eclipse. ●
Lunar Eclipse. ○

Mesha Sankranti (Commencement of Indian Sidereal Year).
(Surya Sid.) April 13·32.
(Arya Sid.) April 13·21.

Saka 1902.
(S. Cycle) Raudra.

Kaliyuga 5081.

SOLAR reckoning. Cyclic Sidereal Year, Month and Day.	Week-Day English Month and Day.		LUNAR reckoning. Tithi Ending Moment.		Nakshatra Ending Moment.		Muhammadan Year, Month and Day.
	Jan.						
Siddharthi *Dhanus—Margali.* 17	Tu	1	Pausha 14	·34	5	·50	H. 1400 *Safar.* 12
18	We	2	P	·33	6	·53	13
19	Th	3	1	·36	7	·57	14
20	Fr	4	2	·39	8	·64	15
21	Sa	5	3	·45	9	·72	16
22	Su	6	4	·53	10	·82	17
23	Mo	7	5	·61	11	·93	18
24	Tu	8	6	·70	...	...	19
25	We	9	*Bahula* 7	·79	12	·04	20
26	Th	10	8	·87	13	·14	21
27	Fr	11	9	·93	14	·23	22
28	Sa	12	10	·98	15	·31	23
29	Su	13	...	...	16	·36	24
—30	Mo	14	11 12	·00 ·99	17	·40	25
1	Tu	15	13	·98	18	·42	26
2	We	16	14	·94	19	·42	27
3	Th	17	—A	·89	20	·39	28
4	Fr	18	1	·81	21	·35	—29
5	Sa	19	2	·73	22	·31	1
6	Su	20	3	·64	23	·25	2
7	Mo	21	4	·54	24	·18	3
8	Tu	22	5	·44	25	·11	4
9	We	23	6	·34	26 27	·05 ·99	5
Siddharthi *Makara—Tai.* 10	Th	24	*Sukla* 7	·25	1	·93	*Rabi-ul-awwal.* 6
11	Fr	25	8	·17	2	·88	7
12	Sa	26	9	·11	3	·84	8
13	Su	27	10	·05	4	·82	9
14	Mo	28	11 12	·01 ·98	5	·83	10
15	Tu	29	13	·98	6	·85	11
16	We	30	...	...	7	·88	12
17	Th	31	14	·00	8	·94	13
	Feb.						
Siddharthi *Kumbha—Masi.* 18	Fr	1	Magha P	·04	...	...	H. 1400 14
19	Sa	2	1	·10	9	·02	15
20	Su	3	2	·18	10	·12	16
21	Mo	4	3	·27	11	·23	17
22	Tu	5	4	·35	12	·34	18
23	We	6	5	·43	13	·44	19
24	Th	7	6	·51	14	·53	20
25	Fr	8	*Bahula* 7	·57	15	·61	21
26	Sa	9	8	·62	16	·68	22
27	Su	10	9	·63	17	·72	23
28	Mo	11	10	·63	18	·74	24
—29	Tu	12	11	·62	19	·74	25
1	We	13	12	·57	20	·72	26
2	Th	14	13	·51	21	·70	27
3	Fr	15	14	·44	22	·65	28
4	Sa ●	16	—A	·36	23	·59	29
5	Su	17	1	·27	24	·52	—30
6	Mo	18	2	·17	25	·45	1
7	Tu	19	3 4	·07 ·97	26	·33	H. 1400 *Rabi-ul-akhir.* 2
8	We	20	*Sukla* 5	·87	27	·32	3
9	Th	21	6	·79	1	·26	4
10	Fr	22	7	·72	2	·21	5
11	Sa	23	8	·66	3	·17	6
12	Su	24	9	·63	4	·15	7
13	Mo	25	Phalguna 10	·60	5	·15	8
14	Tu	26	11	·60	6	·16	9
15	We	27	12	·63	7	·20	10
16	Th	28	13	·66	8	·25	11
17	Fr	29	14	·72	9	·32	12

SOLAR reckoning. Cyclic Sidereal Year, Month and Day.	Week-Day English Month and Day.		LUNAR reckoning. Tithi Ending Moment.		Nakshatra Ending Moment.		Muhammadan Year, Month and Day.
	March						
Siddharthi *Kumbha—Masi.* 18	Sa	1	Phalguna P	·80	10	·42	H. 1400 *Rabi-ul-akhir.* 13
19	Su	2	1	·89	11	·53	14
20	Mo	3	2	·98	12	·64	15
21	Tu	4	...	...	13	·74	16
22	We	5	3	·06	14	·83	17
23	Th	6	4	·13	15	·92	18
24	Fr	7	5	·19	16	·99	19
25	Sa	8	6	·23	...	...	20
26	Su	9	*Bahula* 7	·24	17	·04	21
27	Mo	10	8	·24	18	·06	22
28	Tu	11	9	·22	19	·07	23
29	We	12	10	·17	20	·05	24
30	Th	13	11	·11	21 22	·03 ·98	25
—31	Fr	14	12 13	·04 ·96	23	·92	26
1	Sa	15	14	·87	24	·86	27
2	Su	16	—A	·77	25	·80	28
3	Mo	17	1	·67	26	·73	—29
4	Tu	18	2	·57	27	·66	1
5	We	19	3	·47	1	·60	2
6	Th	20	4	·39	2	·54	3
7	Fr	21	5	·31	3	·50	4
8	Sa	22	6	·25	4	·48	5
9	Su	23	*Sukla* 7	·22	5	·47	6
Siddharthi *Mina—Panguni.* 10	Mo	24	8	·19	6	·48	*Jumadal-awwal.* 7
11	Tu	25	9	·19	7	·51	8
12	We	26	10	·21	8	·56	9
13	Th	27	11	·25	9	·64	10
14	Fr	28	Chaitra 12	·31	10	·73	11
15	Sa	29	13	·39	11	·82	12
16	Su	30	14	·47	12	·93	13
17	Mo	31	P	·55	...	...	14
	April						
18	Tu	1	1	·63	13	·04	H. 1400 15
19	We	2	2	·70	14	·14	16
20	Th	3	3	·76	15	·23	17
21	Fr	4	4	·80	16	·30	18
22	Sa	5	5	·82	17	·35	19
23	Su	6	*Bahula* 6	·81	18	·38	20
24	Mo	7	7	·78	19	·40	21
25	Tu	8	8	·73	20	·39	22
26	We	9	9	·67	21	·36	23
27	Th	10	10	·60	22	·32	24
28	Fr	11	11	·52	23	·26	25
—29	Sa	12	12	·42	24	·20	26
1	Su	13	13	·32	25	·14	27
2	Mo	14	14	·22	26	·07	28
3	Tu	15	—A	·12	27 1	·00 ·93	29
4	We	16	1 2	·02 ·94	2	·88	—30
Raudra *Mesha—Chittirai.* 5	Th	17	3	·87	3	·84	H. 1400 *Jumadal-akhir.* 1
6	Fr	18	4	·81	4	·81	2
7	Sa	19	5	·76	5	·79	3
8	Su	20	6	·74	6	·80	4
9	Mo	21	*Sukla* 7	·73	7	·82	5
10	Tu	22	8	·75	8	·88	6
11	We	23	9	·79	9	·95	7
12	Th	24	10	·84	...	...	8
13	Fr	25	11	·92	10	·03	9
14	Sa	26	Vaisakha ...	...	11	·12	10
15	Su	27	12	·01	12	·23	11
16	Mo	28	13	·09	13	·34	12
17	Tu	29	14	·16	14	·45	13
18	We	30	P	·23	15	·54	14

SOLAR reckoning. Cyclic Sidereal Year, Month and Day.	Week-Day English Month and Day.		LUNAR reckoning. Tithi Ending Moment.		Nakshatra Ending Moment.		Muhammadan Year, Month and Day.
	May						
Raudra *Mesha—Chittirai.* 19	Th	1	Vaisakha 1	·29	16	·61	H. 1400 *Jumadal-akhir.* 15
20	Fr	2	2	·33	17	·66	16
21	Sa	3	3	·35	18	·70	17
22	Su	4	4	·33	19	·72	18
23	Mo	5	5	·31	20	·71	19
24	Tu	6	6	·26	21	·69	20
25	We	7	7	·20	22	·65	21
26	Th	8	8	·18	23	·60	22
27	Fr	9	9 10	·04 ·95	24	·55	23
28	Sa	10	*Bahula* 11	·85	25	·48	24
29	Su	11	12	·75	26	·41	25
30	Mo	12	13	·65	27	·34	26
—31	Tu	13	14	·55	1	·28	27
1	We	14	—A	·46	2	·22	28
2	Th	15	1	·38	3	·17	—29
3	Fr	16	2	·33	4	·14	1
4	Sa	17	3	·29	5	·12	2
5	Su	18	*Sukla* 4	·26	6	·12	3
6	Mo	19	5	·24	7	·15	4
7	Tu	20	6	·26	8	·19	5
8	We	21	7	·30	9	·25	6
9	Th	22	8	·35	10	·33	7
Raudra *Vrishabha—Vaikasi.* 10	Fr	23	9	·42	11	·42	8
11	Sa	24	10	·50	12	·53	9
12	Su	25	11	·59	13	·64	10
13	Mo	26	12	·67	14	·75	11
14	Tu	27	13	·74	15	·84	12
15	We	28	Adhika Jyeshtha 14	·80	16	·92	13
16	Th	29	P	·83	17	·98	*Rajab.* 14
17	Fr	30	1	·84	...	...	15
.8	Sa	31	2	·83	18	·02	16
	June						
19	Su	1	3	·82	19	·04	H. 1400 17
20	Mo	2	4	·77	20	·04	18
21	Tu	3	5	·71	21 22	·02 ·98	19
22	We	4	*Bahula* 6	·63	23	·94	20
23	Th	5	7	·54	24	·88	21
24	Fr	6	8	·44	25	·82	22
25	Sa	7	9	·34	26	·75	23
26	Su	8	10	·24	27	·68	24
27	Mo	9	11	·14	1	·62	25
28	Tu	10	12 13	·04 ·95	2	·56	26
29	We	11	14	·88	3	·50	27
30	Th	12	—A	·81	4	·47	28
31	Fr	13	1	·76	5	·45	29
—32	Sa	14	2	·74	6	·45	—30
1	Su	15	3	·73	7	·46	1
2	Mo	16	4	·74	8	·50	2
3	Tu	17	5	·78	9	·56	3
4	We	18	*Sukla* 6	·84	10	·63	4
Raudra *Mithuna—Ani.* 5	Th	19	7	·90	11	·72	H. 1400 *Shaban.* 5
6	Fr	20	8	·98	12	·83	6
7	Sa	21	...	...	13	·94	7
8	Su	22	9	·06	...	...	8
9	Mo	23	10	·14	14	·04	9
10	Tu	24	11	·21	15	·14	10
11	We	25	12	·27	16	·23	11
12	Th	26	Nija Jyeshtha 13	·30	17	·30	12
13	Fr	27	14	·32	18	·34	13
14	Sa	28	P	·32	19	·36	14
15	Su	29	1	·30	20	·36	15
16	Mo	30	2	·25	21	·35	16

Naksh :—1. Asvn. 2. Bhar. 3. Krit. 4. Rohi. 5. Mrig. 6. Ardh. 7. Punar. 8. Push. 9. Aslesh. 10. Magh. 11. P. Phal. 12. U. Phal. 13. Hasta. 14. Chit.

A. D. 1980.	Kollam 1156, Commences { N. Malabar—Sept. / S. Malabar—Aug.	Hijra 1401, Commences, Nov. 9.	Vikrama 2037.
A.—Amavasya.			Bengal San 1386.
P.—Paurnami.			(N. Cycle) Srimukha.

SOLAR reckoning: Cyclic Sidereal Year, Month and Day; Week-Day English Month and Day. LUNAR reckoning: Tithi Ending Moment; Nakshatra Ending Moment; Muhammadan Year, Month and Day.

July

Solar: Raudra, Mithuna—Ani (to 31); Raudra, Karkata—Adi. Lunar: Jy. Nija—Jy. Bahula; Ashadha Sukla. Muhammadan: H. 1400 Shaban; H. 1400 Ramzan.

Cyclic Sidereal Year, Month and Day	Week-Day English Month and Day	Tithi Ending Moment	Nakshatra Ending Moment	Muhammadan Year, Month and Day
17	Tu 1	3 ·19	22 ·33	17
18	We 2	4 ·11	23 ·28	18
19	Th 3	5 ·02 6 ·92	24 ·22	19
20	Fr 4	7 ·82	25 ·15	20
21	Sa 5	8 ·72	26 ·08	21
22	Su 6	9 ·62	27 ·01 1 ·95	22
23	Mo 7	10 ·52	2 ·89	23
24	Tu 8	11 ·43	3 ·84	24
25	We 9	12 ·35	4 ·80	25
26	Th 10	13 ·29	5 ·78	26
27	Fr 11	14 ·25	6 ·77	27
28	Sa 12	A ·22	7 ·78	28
29	Su 13	1 ·21	8 ·81	29
30	Mo 14	2 ·22	9 ·86	1
31	Tu 15	3 ·25	10 ·93	2
1	We 16	4 ·31	... ...	3
2	Th 17	5 ·37	11 ·03	4
3	Fr 18	6 ·45	12 ·13	5
4	Sa 19	7 ·53	13 ·24	6
5	Su 20	8 ·61	14 ·34	7
6	Mo 21	9 ·63	15 ·44	8
7	Tu 22	10 ·74	16 ·54	9
8	We 23	11 ·78	17 ·61	10
9	Th 24	12 ·80	18 ·65	11
10	Fr 25	13 ·80	19 ·68	12
11	Sa 26	14 ·78	20 ·69	13
12	Su 27	P ·73	21 ·69	14
13	Mo 28	1 ·67	22 ·66	15
14	Tu 29	2 ·60	23 ·61	16
15	We 30	3 ·51	24 ·55	17
16	Th 31	4 ·42	25 ·49	18

Aug.

Solar: Raudra, Simha—Avani (from 1). Lunar: Bahula; Sukla; Sravana Bahula. Muhammadan: H. 1400 Shawwal.

Cyclic Sidereal Year, Month and Day	Week-Day English Month and Day	Tithi Ending Moment	Nakshatra Ending Moment	Muhammadan Year, Month and Day
17	Fr 1	5 ·82	26 ·43	19
18	Sa 2	6 ·22	27 ·36	20
19	Su 3	7 ·12	1 ·29	21
20	Mo 4	8 ·02 9 ·98	2 ·28	22
21	Tu 5	10 ·85	3 ·17	23
22	We 6	11 ·77	4 ·13	24
23	Th 7	12 ·73	5 ·11	25
24	Fr 8	13 ·70	6 ·09	26
25	Sa 9	14 ·69	7 ·10	27
26	Su 10	A ·70	8 ·12	28
27	Mo 11	1 ·78	9 ·17	29
28	Tu I2	2 ·78	10 ·24	30
29	We 13	3 ·85	11 ·33	1
30	Th 14	4 ·94	12 ·43	2
31	Fr 15	... ...	13 ·54	3
32	Sa 16	5 ·02	14 ·65	4
1	Su 17	6 ·10	15 ·75	5
2	Mo 18	7 ·17	16 ·84	6
3	Tu 19	8 ·28	17 ·91	7
4	We 20	9 ·27	18 ·97	8
5	Th 21	10 ·30	... ...	9
6	Fr 22	11 ·29	19 ·00	10
7	Sa 23	12 ·27	20 ·02	11
8	Su 24	13 ·23	21 ·01 22 ·99	12
9	Mo 25	14 ·18	23 ·95	13
10	Tu 26	P ·11	24 ·89	14
11	We 27	1 ·02 2 ·92	25 ·83	15
12	Th 28	3 ·82	26 ·77	16
13	Fr 29	4 ·72	27 ·70	17
14	Sa 30	5 ·62	1 ·63	18
15	Su 31	6 ·52	2 ·56	19

Sep.

Solar: Raudra, Simha—Avani (to 31); Raudra, Kanya—Purattasi. Lunar: Sravn. Bahula; Bhadrapada Sukla. Muhammadan: H. 1400 Shawwal; H. 1400 Zi-l-ka'da.

Cyclic Sidereal Year, Month and Day	Week-Day English Month and Day	Tithi Ending Moment	Nakshatra Ending Moment	Muhammadan Year, Month and Day
16	Mo 1	7 ·44	3 ·51	20
17	Tu 2	8 ·86	4 ·47	21
18	We 3	9 ·30	5 ·43	22
19	Th 4	10 ·24	6 ·42	23
20	Fr 5	11 ·21	7 ·42	24
21	Sa 6	12 ·21	8 ·44	25
22	Su 7	13 ·22	9 ·49	26
23	Mo 8	14 ·25	10 ·55	27
24	Tu 9	A ·31	11 ·63	28
25	We 10	1 ·37	12 ·73	29
26	Th 11	2 ·45	13 ·84	1
27	Fr 12	3 ·54	14 ·95	2
28	Sa 13	4 ·62	... ...	3
29	Su 14	5 ·70	15 ·05	4
30	Mo 15	6 ·77	16 ·14	5
31	Tu 16	7 ·80	17 ·22	6
1	We 17	8 ·82	18 ·28	7
2	Th 18	9 ·82	19 ·33	8
3	Fr 19	10 ·81	20 ·34	9
4	Sa 20	11 ·77	21 ·34	10
5	Su 21	12 ·71	22 ·32	11
6	Mo 22	13 ·64	23 ·28	12
7	Tu 23	14 ·56	24 ·23	13
8	We 24	P ·47	25 ·18	14
9	Th 25	1 ·37	26 ·11	15
10	Fr 26	2 ·27	27 ·04 1 ·97	16
11	Sa 27	3 ·17	2 ·91	17
12	Su 28	4 ·07 5 ·98	3 ·85	18
13	Mo 29	6 ·90	4 ·80	19
14	Tu 30	7 ·84	5 ·76	20

Oct.

Solar: Raudra, Tula—Aippasi (from 1). Lunar: Bahula; Sukla; Asvina; Bahula. Muhammadan: H. 1400 Zi-l-hijja.

Cyclic Sidereal Year, Month and Day	Week-Day English Month and Day	Tithi Ending Moment	Nakshatra Ending Moment	Muhammadan Year, Month and Day
15	We 1	8 ·79	6 ·74	21
16	Th 2	9 ·77	7 ·74	22
17	Fr 3	10 ·76	8 ·76	23
18	Sa 4	11 ·77	9 ·80	24
19	Su 5	12 ·81	10 ·86	25
20	Mo 6	13 ·86	11 ·94	26
21	Tu 7	14 ·93	... ...	27
22	We 8	... ...	12 ·03	28
23	Th 9	A ·01	13 ·14	29
24	Fr 10	1 ·10	14 ·25	30
25	Sa 11	2 ·19	15 ·35	1
26	Su 12	3 ·27	16 ·45	2
27	Mo 13	4 ·33	17 ·53	3
28	Tu 14	5 ·37	18 ·60	4
29	We 15	6 ·40	19 ·64	5
30	Th 16	7 ·39	20 ·66	6
1	Fr 17	8 ·38	21 ·66	7
2	Sa 18	9 ·34	22 ·65	8
3	Su 19	10 ·29	23 ·61	9
4	Mo 20	11 ·22	24 ·57	10
5	Tu 21	12 ·13	25 ·51	11
6	We 22	13 ·04 14 ·94	26 ·45	12
7	Th 23	P ·84	27 ·88	13
8	Fr 24	1 ·74	1 ·81	14
9	Sa 25	2 ·65	2 ·25	15
10	Su 26	3 ·57	3 ·19	16
11	Mo 27	4 ·50	4 ·13	17
12	Tu 28	5 ·43	5 ·09	18
13	We 29	6 ·38	6 ·07	19
14	Th 30	7 ·36	7 ·07	20
15	Fr 31	8 ·35	8 ·08	21

Nov.

Solar: Raudra, Tula—Aippasi (to 30); Raudra, Vrischika—Kartigai. Lunar: Asvn. Bah.; Kartika Sukla; Bahula. Muhammadan: Zi-l-hijja; H. 1401 Muharram.

Cyclic Sidereal Year, Month and Day	Week-Day English Month and Day	Tithi Ending Moment	Nakshatra Ending Moment	Muhammadan Year, Month and Day
16	Sa 1	9 ·37	9 ·11	22
17	Su 2	10 ·41	10 ·17	23
18	Mo 3	11 ·47	11 ·25	24
19	Tu 4	12 ·54	12 ·34	25
20	We 5	13 ·62	13 ·44	26
21	Th 6	14 ·71	14 ·55	27
22	Fr 7	A ·80	15 ·65	28
23	Sa 8	1 ·87	16 ·75	29
24	Su 9	2 ·93	17 ·83	1
25	Mo 10	3 ·97	18 ·90	2
26	Tu 11	... ...	19 ·96	3
27	We 12	4 ·00 5 ·99	20 ·98	4
28	Th 13	6 ·93	21 ·99	5
29	Fr 14	7 ·95	22 ·97	6
30	Sa 15	8 ·90	23 ·95	7
1	Su 16	9 ·83	24 ·91	8
2	Mo 17	10 ·75	25 ·85	9
3	Tu 18	11 ·66	26 ·79	10
4	We 19	12 ·56	27 ·73	11
5	Th 20	13 ·46	1 ·66	12
6	Fr 21	14 ·36	2 ·59	13
7	Sa 22	P ·27	3 ·52	14
8	Su 23	1 ·18	4 ·46	15
9	Mo 24	2 ·11	5 ·42	16
10	Tu 25	3 ·05	6 ·40	17
11	We 26	4 ·01 5 ·98	7 ·39	18
12	Th 27	6 ·97	8 ·40	19
13	Fr 28	... ...	9 ·43	20
14	Sa 29	7 ·00	10 ·48	21
15	Su 30	8 ·04	11 ·55	22

Dec.

Solar: Raudra, Dhanus—Margali (from 1). Lunar: Sukla; Margasira; Bahula. Muhammadan: H. 1401 Safar.

Cyclic Sidereal Year, Month and Day	Week-Day English Month and Day	Tithi Ending Moment	Nakshatra Ending Moment	Muhammadan Year, Month and Day
16	Mo 1	9 ·09	12 ·64	23
17	Tu 2	10 ·16	13 ·74	24
18	We 3	11 ·25	14 ·84	25
19	Th 4	12 ·34	15 ·95	26
20	Fr 5	13 ·43	... ...	27
21	Sa 6	14 ·51	16 ·05	28
22	Su 7	A ·57	17 ·14	29
23	Mo 8	1 ·61	18 ·22	30
24	Tu 9	2 ·63	19 ·27	1
25	We 10	3 ·64	20 ·30	2
26	Th 11	4 ·62	21 ·31	3
27	Fr 12	5 ·58	22 ·31	4
28	Sa 13	6 ·52	23 ·28	5
29	Su 14	7 ·45	24 ·24	6
30	Mo 15	8 ·37	25 ·19	7
1	Tu 16	9 ·28	26 ·13	8
2	We 17	10 ·19	27 ·06 1 ·99	9
3	Th 18	11 ·09 12 ·99	2 ·92	10
4	Fr 19	13 ·90	3 ·86	11
5	Sa 20	14 ·81	4 ·80	12
6	Su 21	P ·74	5 ·76	13
7	Mo 22	1 ·69	6 ·73	14
8	Tu 23	2 ·65	7 ·72	15
9	We 24	3 ·62	8 ·72	16
10	Th 25	4 ·68	9 ·74	17
11	Fr 26	5 ·65	10 ·79	18
12	Sa 27	6 ·69	11 ·86	19
13	Su 28	7 ·75	12 ·94	20
14	Mo 29	8 ·82	... ...	21
15	Tu 30	9 ·90	13 ·04	22
16	We 31	10 ·99	14 ·14	23

15. Svati. 16. Visak. 17. Anar. 18. Jyesh. 19. Mula. 20. P. Ash. 21. U. Ash. 22. Sravn. 23. Dani. 24. Satab. 25. P. Bhad. 26. U. Bhad. 27. Rev,

A. D. 1981.
Solar Eclipse. ●
Lunar Eclipse. ○

Mesha Sankranti (Commencement of Indian Sidereal Year).
(Surya Sid.) April 13·58.
(Arya Sid.) April 13·47.

Saka 1903.
(S. Cycle) Durmati.

Kaliyuga 5082.

SOLAR reckoning: Cyclic Sidereal Year, Month and Day; Week-Day English Month and Day. LUNAR reckoning: Tithi Ending Moment; Nakshatra Ending Moment; Muhammadan Year, Month and Day.

Jan. — Solar: Raudra *Dhanus—Margali* (17–29); Raudra *Makara—Tai* (1–18). Lunar: **Marg.** *Bah.* (… to A); *Sukla* (1–14); **Pausha** (P); *Bahula*. Muhammadan: *Safar.* (24–29); H. 1401 *Rabi-ul-awwal.* (1–25).

Cyclic Sidereal Year, Month and Day	Week-Day	English Day	Tithi	Ending Moment	Nakshatra	Ending Moment	Muhammadan Year, Month and Day
17	Th	1	…	…	15	·25	24
18	Fr	2	11	·08	16	·36	25
19	Sa	3	12	·16	17	·45	26
20	Su	4	13	·22	18	·53	27
21	Mo	5	14	·26	19	·58	28
22	Tu	6	—A	·28	20	·62	—29
23	We	7	1	·28	21	·64	1
24	Th	8	2	·27	22	·64	2
25	Fr	9	3	·23	23	·61	3
26	Sa	10	4	·18	24	·57	4
27	Su	11	5	·11	25	·52	5
28	Mo	12	6 7	·02 ·92	26	·47	6
—29	Tu	13	8	·82	27	·40	7
1	We	14	9	·72	1	·33	8
2	Th	15	10	·63	2	·26	9
3	Fr	16	11	·54	3	·20	10
4	Sa	17	12	·46	4	·14	11
5	Su	18	13	·39	5	·10	12
6	Mo	19	14	·33	6	·06	13
7	Tu	20	P	·29	7	·04	14
8	We	21	1	·26	8	·04	15
9	Th	22	2	·27	9	·06	16
10	Fr	23	3	·29	10	·10	17
11	Sa	24	4	·34	11	·16	18
12	Su	25	5	·40	12	·21	19
13	Mo	26	6	·48	13	·34	20
14	Tu	27	7	·56	14	·45	21
15	We	28	8	·64	15	·56	22
16	Th	29	9	·73	16	·66	23
17	Fr	30	10	·81	17	·75	24
18	Sa	31	11	·87	18	·83	25

Feb. — Solar: Raudra *Kumbha—Masi.* Lunar: *Sukla*; **Magha** (P); *Bahula*. Muhammadan: H. 1401 *Rabi-ul-akhir.*

Cyclic Sidereal Year, Month and Day	Week-Day	English Day	Tithi	Ending Moment	Nakshatra	Ending Moment	Muhammadan Year, Month and Day
19	Su	1	12	·90	19	·89	26
20	Mo	2	13	·98	20	·94	27
21	Tu	3	14	·92	21	·96	28
22	We	4	—A	·90	22	·96	29
23	Th	5	1	·85	23	·94	—30
24	Fr	6	2	·80	24	·91	1
25	Sa	7	3	·73	25	·87	2
26	Su	8	4	·64	26	·81	3
27	Mo	9	5	·55	27	·74	4
28	Tu	10	6	·45	1	·67	5
—29	We	11	7	·36	2	·60	6
1	Th	12	8	·26	3	·54	7
2	Fr	13	9	·16	4	·48	8
3	Sa	14	10	·08	5	·43	9
4	Su	15	11 12	·01 ·96	6	·39	10
5	Mo	16	13	·92	7	·37	11
6	Tu	17	14	·90	8	·36	12
7	We	18	P	·89	9	·38	13
8	Th	19	1	·91	10	·42	14
9	Fr	20	2	96	11	·47	15
10	Sa	21	…	…	12	·55	16
11	Su	22	3	·02	13	·64	17
12	Mo	23	4	·10	14	·74	18
13	Tu	24	5	·19	15	·85	19
14	We	25	6	·27	16	·96	20
15	Th	26	7	·35	…	…	21
16	Fr	27	8	·43	17	·06	22
17	Sa	28	9	·49	18	·14	23

March — Solar: Raudra *Kumbha—Masi.* (18–30); Raudra *Mina—Panguni.* (1–18). Lunar: **Mag.** *Bah.* (10 to A); *Sukla*; **Phalguna** (P); *Bahula*. Muhammadan: *R. akhir.* (24–29); H. 1401 *Jumadal-awwal.* (1–25).

Cyclic Sidereal Year, Month and Day	Week-Day	English Day	Tithi	Ending Moment	Nakshatra	Ending Moment	Muhammadan Year, Month and Day
18	Su	1	10	·53	19	·21	24
19	Mo	2	11	·54	20	·26	25
20	Tu	3	12	·53	21	·28	26
21	We	4	13	·52	22	·29	27
22	Th	5	14	·47	23	·27	28
23	Fr	6	—A	·41	24	·21	—29
24	Sa	7	1	·34	25	·20	1
25	Su	8	2	·25	26	·15	2
26	Mo	9	3	·16	27	·08	3
27	Tu	10	4 5	·06 ·96	1 2	·01 ·94	4
28	We	11	6	·86	3	·88	5
29	Th	12	7	·77	4	·82	6
—30	Fr	13	8	·68	5	·76	7
1	Sa	14	9	·60	6	·72	8
2	Su	15	10	·54	7	·69	9
3	Mo	16	11	·50	8	·69	10
4	Tu	17	12	·49	9	·70	11
5	We	18	13	·49	10	·73	12
6	Th	19	14	·52	11	·78	13
7	Fr	20	P	·55	12	·85	14
8	Sa	21	1	·62	13	·95	15
9	Su	22	2	·70	…	…	16
10	Mo	23	3	·78	14	·05	17
11	Tu	24	4	·87	15	·15	18
12	We	25	5	·95	16	·26	19
13	Th	26	…	…	17	·36	20
14	Fr	27	6	·02	18	·45	21
15	Sa	28	7	·07	19	·52	22
16	Su	29	8	·11	20	·57	23
17	Mo	30	9	·12	21	·60	24
18	Tu	31	10	·11	22	·61	25

April — Solar: Durmati *Mesha—Chittirai.* Lunar: *Sukla*; **Chaitra** (P); *Bahula*. Muhammadan: H. 1401 *Jumadal-akhir.*

Cyclic Sidereal Year, Month and Day	Week-Day	English Day	Tithi	Ending Moment	Nakshatra	Ending Moment	Muhammadan Year, Month and Day
19	We	1	11	·09	23	·60	26
20	Th	2	12 13	·04 ·98	24	·58	27
21	Fr	3	14	·91	25	·54	28
22	Sa	4	—A	·82	26	·48	29
23	Su	5	1	·72	27	·43	—30
24	Mo	6	2	·62	1	·36	1
25	Tu	7	3	·52	2	·29	2
26	We	8	4	·42	3	·22	3
27	Th	9	5	·33	4	·15	4
28	Fr	10	6	·24	5	·10	5
29	Sa	11	7	·17	6	·06	6
—30	Su	12	8	·11	7	·03	7
1	Mo	13	9	·07	8	·01	8
2	Tu	14	10	·05	9	·02	9
3	We	15	11	·04	10	·04	10
4	Th	16	12	·07	11	·09	11
5	Fr	17	13	·11	12	·16	12
6	Sa	18	14	·17	13	·25	13
7	Su	19	P	·25	14	·35	14
8	Mo	20	1	·34	15	·45	15
9	Tu	21	2	·41	16	·56	16
10	We	22	3	·48	17	·66	17
11	Th	23	4	·55	18	·76	18
12	Fr	24	5	·61	19	·83	19
13	Sa	25	6	·65	20	·88	20
14	Su	26	7	·66	21	·92	21
15	Mo	27	8	·66	22	·93	22
16	Tu	28	9	·63	23	·93	23
17	We	29	10	·57	24	·91	24
18	Th	30	11	·51	25	·87	25

May — Solar: Durmati *Mesha—Chittirai.* (19–31); Durmati *Vrishabha—Vaikasi.* (1–18). Lunar: *Bah.* (12 to A); *Sukla*; **Vaisakha** (P); *Bahula*. Muhammadan: H. 1401 *Rajab.*

Cyclic Sidereal Year, Month and Day	Week-Day	English Day	Tithi	Ending Moment	Nakshatra	Ending Moment	Muhammadan Year, Month and Day
19	Fr	1	12	·44	26	·82	26
20	Sa	2	13	·35	27	·76	27
21	Su	3	14	·25	1	·70	28
22	Mo	4	—A	·15	2	·63	—29
23	Tu	5	1 2	·05 ·95	3	·56	1
24	We	6	3	·85	4	·49	2
25	Th	7	4	·76	5	·43	3
26	Fr	8	5	·69	6	·39	4
27	Sa	9	6	·63	7	·36	5
28	Su	10	7	·59	8	·34	6
29	Mo	11	8	·57	9	·34	7
30	Tu	12	9	·57	10	·33	8
—31	We	13	10	·59	11	·41	9
1	Th	14	11	·62	12	·47	10
2	Fr	15	12	·68	13	·55	11
3	Sa	16	13	·75	14	·64	12
4	Su	17	14	·82	15	·75	13
5	Mo	18	P	·92	16	·86	14
6	Tu	19	…	…	17	·97	15
7	We	20	1	·00	…	…	16
8	Th	21	2	·07	18	·06	17
9	Fr	22	3	·13	19	·14	18
10	Sa	23	4	·17	20	·20	19
11	Su	24	5	·17	21	·23	20
12	Mo	25	6	·16	22	·26	21
13	Tu	26	7	·14	23	·26	22
14	We	27	8	·09	24	·24	23
15	Th	28	9 10	·02 ·94	25	·20	24
16	Fr	29	11	·85	26	·15	23
17	Sa	30	12	·75	27	·10	23
18	Su	31	13	·65	1 2	·03 ·96	27

June — Solar: Durmati *Mithuna—Ani.* Lunar: *Sukla*; **Jyeshtha** (P); *Bahula*. Muhammadan: H. 1401 *Shaban.*

Cyclic Sidereal Year, Month and Day	Week-Day	English Day	Tithi	Ending Moment	Nakshatra	Ending Moment	Muhammadan Year, Month and Day
19	Mo	1	14	·55	3	·89	28
20	Tu	2	—A	·45	4	·83	29
21	We	3	1	·35	5	·77	—30
22	Th	4	2	·27	6	·72	1
23	Fr	5	3	·20	7	·69	2
24	Sa	6	4	·13	8	·66	3
25	Su	7	5	·09	9	·66	4
26	Mo	8	6	·06	10	·68	5
27	Tu	9	7	·06	11	·72	6
28	We	10	8	·07	12	·78	7
29	Th	11	9	·11	13	·85	8
30	Fr	12	10	·16	14	·94	9
31	Sa	13	11	·23	…	…	10
—32	Su	14	12	·31	15	·05	11
1	Mo	15	13	·39	16	·16	12
2	Tu	16	14	·48	17	·27	13
3	We	17	P	·55	18	·36	14
4	Th	18	1	·60	19	·44	15
5	Fr	19	2	·64	20	·51	16
6	Sa	20	3	·66	21	·56	17
7	Su	21	4	·64	22	·58	18
8	Mo	22	5	·62	23	·58	19
9	Tu	23	6	·58	24	·57	20
10	We	24	7	·51	25	·54	21
11	Th	25	8	·43	26	·50	22
12	Fr	26	9	·34	27	·44	23
13	Sa	27	10	·24	1	·37	24
14	Su	28	11	·14	2	·30	25
15	Mo	29	12 13	·04 ·94	3	·28	26
16	Tu	30	14	·84	4	·17	27

Naksh:—1. Asvn. 2. Bhar. 3. Krit. 4. Rohi. 5. Mrig. 6. Ardh. 7. Punar. 8. Push. 9. Aslesh. 10. Magh. 11. P. Phal. 12. U. Phal. 13. Hasta. 14. Chit.

A. D. 1981.
A.—Amavasya.
P.—Paurnami.

Kollam 1157, Commences { **N. Malabar—Sept.** / **S. Malabar—Aug.**

Hijra 1402, Commences, **Oct. 30.**

Vikrama 2038.
Bengal San 1387.
(N. Cycle) Bhava.

SOLAR reckoning: Cyclic Sidereal Year, Month and Day; Week-Day, English Month and Day. LUNAR reckoning: Tithi Ending Moment; Nakshatra Ending Moment; Muhammadan Year, Month and Day.

July — Solar: Durmati Mithuna—Ani; Durmati Karkata—Adi. Lunar: Sukla; Ashadha; Bahula. Muhammadan: H. 1401 Ramzan.

Cyclic Sidereal Year, Month and Day	Week-Day	English Day	Tithi	Tithi Ending Moment	Nakshatra	Nakshatra Ending Moment	Muhammadan Year, Month and Day
17	We	1	—A	·75	5	·11	28
18	Th	2	1	·68	6	·06	—29
19	Fr	3	2	·61	7 8	·02 ·99	1
20	Sa	4	3	·57	9	·93	2
21	Su	5	4	·55	...	...	3
22	Mo	6	5	·53	10	·00	4
23	Tu	7	6	·54	11	·03	5
24	We	8	7	·58	12	·08	6
25	Th	9	8	·63	13	·15	7
26	Fr	10	9	·71	14	·24	8
27	Sa	11	10	·79	15	·35	9
28	Su	12	11	·88	16	·46	10
29	Mo	13	12	·95	17	·36	11
30	Tu	14	...	...	18	·66	12
—31	We	15	13	·02	19	·75	13
1	Th	16	14	·08	20	·83	14
2	Fr ○	17	P	·11	21	·87	15
3	Sa	18	1	·13	22	·90	16
4	Su	19	2	·12	23	·91	17
5	Mo	20	3	·10	24	·90	18
6	Tu	21	4 5	·05 ·98	25	·87	19
7	We	22	6	·91	26	·83	20
8	Th	23	7	·83	27	·78	21
9	Fr	24	8	·73	1	·71	22
10	Sa	25	9	·63	2	·64	23
11	Su	26	10	·53	3	·57	24
12	Mo	27	11	·43	4	·51	25
13	Tu	28	12	·33	5	·45	26
14	We	29	13	·23	6	·39	27
15	Th	30	14	·15	7	·35	28
16	Fr ●	31	—A	·09	8	·32	29

Aug. — Solar: Durmati Simha—Avani. Lunar: Sukla; Sravana; Bahula; Suk. Muhammadan: H. 1401 Shawwal.

Cyclic Sidereal Year, Month and Day	Week-Day	English Day	Tithi	Tithi Ending Moment	Nakshatra	Nakshatra Ending Moment	Muhammadan Year, Month and Day
17	Sa	1	1	·05	9	·31	—30
18	Su	2	2	·03	10	·32	1
19	Mo	3	3	·02	11	·34	2
20	Tu	4	4	·02	12	·39	3
21	We	5	5	·06	13	·46	4
22	Th	6	6	·11	14	·55	5
23	Fr	7	7	·18	15	·65	6
24	Sa	8	8	·26	16	·76	7
25	Su	9	9	·35	17	·86	8
26	Mo	10	10	·43	18	·96	9
27	Tu	11	11	·51	...	...	10
28	We	12	12	·56	19	·06	11
29	Th	13	13	·60	20	·13	12
30	Fr	14	14	·62	21	·19	13
31	Sa	15	P	·61	22	·22	14
—32	Su	16	1	·59	23	·23	15
1	Mo	17	2	·55	24	·22	16
2	Tu	18	3	·49	25	·21	17
3	We	19	4	·41	26	·17	18
4	Th	20	5	·33	27	·11	19
5	Fr	21	6	·23	1 2	·05 ·99	20
6	Sa	22	7	·13	3	·92	21
7	Su	23	8 9	·03 ·93	4	·85	22
8	Mo	24	10	·83	5	·78	23
9	Tu	25	11	·74	6	·73	24
10	We	26	12	·67	7	·68	25
11	Th	27	13	·61	8	·65	26
12	Fr	28	14	·55	9	·64	27
13	Sa	29	—A	·58	10	·64	28
14	Su	30	1	·52	11	·66	—29
15	Mo	31	2	·54	12	·70	1

Sep. — Solar: Durmati Simha—Avani; Durmati Kanya—Purattasi. Lunar: Sukla; Bhadrapada; Bahula. Muhammadan: H. 1401 Zi-l-ka'da.

Cyclic Sidereal Year, Month and Day	Week-Day	English Day	Tithi	Tithi Ending Moment	Nakshatra	Nakshatra Ending Moment	Muhammadan Year, Month and Day
16	Tu	1	3	·57	13	·77	2
17	We	2	4	·63	14	·85	3
18	Th	3	5	·70	15	·95	4
19	Fr	4	6	·78	...	...	5
20	Sa	5	7	·86	16	·05	6
21	Su	6	8	·94	17	·16	7
22	Mo	7	...	...	18	·27	8
23	Tu	8	9	·01	19	·37	9
24	We	9	10	·07	20	·44	10
25	Th	10	11	·12	21	·50	11
26	Fr	11	12	·14	22	·54	12
27	Sa	12	13	·14	23	·55	13
28	Su	13	14	·11	24	·56	14
29	Mo	14	P	·07	25	·54	15
30	Tu	15	1 2	·01 ·94	26	·50	16
—31	We	16	3	·86	27	·45	17
1	Th	17	4	·76	1	·39	18
2	Fr	18	5	·66	2	·33	19
3	Sa	19	6	·56	3	·26	20
4	Su	20	7	·46	4	·19	21
5	Mo	21	8	·36	5	·12	22
6	Tu	22	9	·27	6	·06	23
7	We	23	10	·20	7 8	·02 ·98	24
8	Th	24	11	·14	9	·96	25
9	Fr	25	12	·09	10	·96	26
10	Sa	26	13	·07	11	·98	27
11	Su	27	14	·07	...	...	28
12	Mo	28	—A	·08	12	·02	29
13	Tu	29	1	·11	13	·08	—30
14	We	30	2	·17	14	·16	1

Oct. — Solar: Durmati Tula—Aippasi. Lunar: Sukla; Asvina; Bahula; K. Suk. Muhammadan: H. 1401 Zi-l-hijja.

Cyclic Sidereal Year, Month and Day	Week-Day	English Day	Tithi	Tithi Ending Moment	Nakshatra	Nakshatra Ending Moment	Muhammadan Year, Month and Day
15	Th	1	3	·24	15	·25	2
16	Fr	2	4	·33	16	·35	3
17	Sa	3	5	·41	17	·46	4
18	Su	4	6	·49	18	·57	5
19	Mo	5	7	·56	19	·67	6
20	Tu	6	8	·62	20	·75	7
21	We	7	9	·67	21	·81	8
22	Th	8	10	·69	22	·85	9
23	Fr	9	11	·70	23	·88	10
24	Sa	10	12	·68	24	·88	11
25	Su	11	13	·64	25	·86	12
26	Mo	12	14	·58	26	·83	13
27	Tu	13	P	·50	27	·78	14
28	We	14	1	·42	1	·73	15
29	Th	15	2	·33	2	·67	16
—30	Fr	16	3	·23	3	·60	17
1	Sa	17	4	·13	4	·53	18
2	Su	18	5 6	·03 ·93	5	·47	19
3	Mo	19	7	·85	6	·41	20
4	Tu	20	8	·78	7	·35	21
5	We	21	9	·72	8	·31	22
6	Th	22	10	·67	9	·29	23
7	Fr	23	11	·65	10	·28	24
8	Sa	24	12	·65	11	·29	25
9	Su	25	13	·66	12	·33	26
10	Mo	26	14	·70	13	·39	27
11	Tu	27	—A	·76	14	·46	28
12	We	28	1	·84	15	·55	29
13	Th	29	2	·92	16	·65	—30
14	Fr	30	...	...	17	·76	1
15	Sa	31	3	·01	18	·87	2

Nov. — Solar: Durmati Tula—Aippasi; Durmati Vrischika—Kartigai. Lunar: Sukla; Karttika; Bahula. Muhammadan: H. 1402 Muharram.

Cyclic Sidereal Year, Month and Day	Week-Day	English Day	Tithi	Tithi Ending Moment	Nakshatra	Nakshatra Ending Moment	Muhammadan Year, Month and Day
16	Su	1	4	·09	19	·97	3
17	Mo	2	5	·16	...	...	4
18	Tu	3	6	·22	20	·05	5
19	We	4	7	·27	21	·12	6
20	Th	5	8	·30	22	·18	7
21	Fr	6	9	·29	23	·20	8
22	Sa	7	10	·26	24	·21	9
23	Su	8	11	·23	25	·19	10
24	Mo	9	12	·18	26	·16	11
25	Tu	10	13	·11	27	·13	12
26	We	11	14 P	·03 ·94	1	·07	13
27	Th	12	1	·84	2 3	·01 ·94	14
28	Fr	13	2	·74	4	·87	15
29	Sa	14	3	·64	5	·80	16
—30	Su	15	4	·54	6	·74	17
1	Mo	16	5	·46	7	·69	18
2	Tu	17	6	·39	8	·65	19
3	We	18	7	·33	9	·62	20
4	Th	19	8	·28	10	·60	21
5	Fr	20	9	·26	11	·62	22
6	Sa	21	10	·27	12	·65	23
7	Su	22	11	·29	13	·70	24
8	Mo	23	12	·32	14	·76	25
9	Tu	24	13	·38	15	·85	26
10	We	25	14	·46	16	·95	27
11	Th	26	—A	·55	...	...	28
12	Fr	27	1	·64	17	·06	29
13	Sa	28	2	·72	18	·17	—30
14	Su	29	3	·79	19	·27	1
15	Mo	30	4	·86	20	·36	2

Dec. — Solar: Durmati Dhanus—Margali. Lunar: Sukla; Margasira; Bahula; Pah. Suk. Muhammadan: H. 1402 Safar; R.-awwal.

Cyclic Sidereal Year, Month and Day	Week-Day	English Day	Tithi	Tithi Ending Moment	Nakshatra	Nakshatra Ending Moment	Muhammadan Year, Month and Day
16	Tu	1	5	·90	21	·44	3
17	We	2	6	·92	22	·49	4
18	Th	3	7	·91	23	·52	5
19	Fr	4	8	·90	24	·53	6
20	Sa	5	9	·86	25	·52	7
21	Su	6	10	·80	26	·50	8
22	Mo	7	11	·73	27	·46	9
23	Tu	8	12	·65	1	·41	10
24	We	9	13	·56	2	·34	11
25	Th	10	14	·46	3	·27	12
26	Fr	11	P	·36	4	·20	13
27	Sa	12	1	·26	5	·14	14
28	Su	13	2	·17	6	·08	15
29	Mo	14	3	·09	7 8	·02 ·97	16
—30	Tu	15	4 5	·02 ·96	9	·94	17
1	We	16	6	·92	10	·93	18
2	Th	17	7	·91	11	·91	19
3	Fr	18	8	·90	12	·96	20
4	Sa	19	9	·93	...	...	21
5	Su	20	10	·97	13	·00	22
6	Mo	21	...	...	14	·07	23
7	Tu	22	11	·03	15	·16	24
8	We	23	12	·11	16	·26	25
9	Th	24	13	·20	17	·36	26
10	Fr	25	14	·29	18	·47	27
11	Sa	26	—A	·37	19	·57	28
12	Su	27	1	·45	20	·67	—29
13	Mo	28	2	·51	21	·75	1
14	Tu	29	3	·54	22	·80	2
15	We	30	4	·57	23	·84	3
16	Th	31	5	·56	24	·85	4

A. D. 1982.
Solar Eclipse. ●
Lunar Eclipse. ○

Mesha Sankranti (Commencement of Indian Sidereal Year).
(Surya Sid.) April 13·84. **Saka 1904.** **Kaliyuga 5083.**
(Arya Sid.) April 13·73. **(S. Cycle) Dundubhi.**

Columns: SOLAR reckoning — Cyclic Sidereal Year, Month and Day; Week-Day, English Month and Day. LUNAR reckoning — Tithi Ending Moment; Nakshatra Ending Moment; Muhammadan Year, Month and Day.

Jan.

Solar: Durmati Dhanus—Margali (to 29); Durmati Makara—Tai (from 1). Lunar: Sukla, Pausha, Bahula. Muhammadan: H. 1402 Rabi-ul-awwal (to 30), then next month.

Solar	Week-Day	Day	Tithi	Moment	Nakshatra	Moment	Muhammadan
17	Fr	1	6	·54	25	·85	5
18	Sa	2	7	·50	26	·83	6
19	Su	3	8	·45	27	·79	7
20	Mo	4	9	·37	1	·74	8
21	Tu	5	10	·29	2	·68	9
22	We	6	11	·20	3	·62	10
23	Th	7	12	·10	4	·55	11
24	Fr	8	13 / 14	·00 / ·91	5	·48	12
25	Sa ○	9	P	·82	6	·41	13
26	Su	10	1	·74	7	·36	14
27	Mo	11	2	·67	8	·31	15
28	Tu	12	3	·61	9	·28	16
29	We	13	4	·56	10	·26	17
1	Th	14	5	·55	11	·26	18
2	Fr	15	6	·55	12	·28	19
3	Sa	16	7	·58	13	·32	20
4	Su	17	8	·62	14	·33	21
5	Mo	18	9	·69	15	·46	22
6	Tu	19	10	·76	16	·56	23
7	We	20	11	·85	17	·66	24
8	Th	21	12	·94	18	·77	25
9	Fr	22	...	...	19	·88	26
10	Sa	23	13	·03	20	·97	27
11	Su	24	14	·10	...	...	28
12	Mo	25	A	·15	21	·05	29
13	Tu	26	1	·19	22	·11	30
14	We	27	2	·21	23	·15	1
15	Th	28	3	·21	24	·17	2
16	Fr	29	4	·18	25	·18	3
17	Sa	30	5	·14	26	·16	4
18	Su	31	6	·08	27	·13	5

Feb.

Solar: Durmati Makara—Tai (to 30); Durmati Kumbha—Masi (from 1). Lunar: Sukla, Magha, Bahula, Phal. Suk. Muhammadan: H. 1402 Rabi-ul-akhir; J.-awwal.

Solar	Week-Day	Day	Tithi	Moment	Nakshatra	Moment	Muhammadan
19	Mo	1	7 / 8	·00 / ·92	1	·08	6
20	Tu	2	9	·83	2 / 3	·02 / ·96	7
21	We	3	10	·73	4	·89	8
22	Th	4	11	·63	5	·82	9
23	Fr	5	12	·53	6	·75	10
24	Sa	6	13	·44	7	·69	11
25	Su	7	14	·36	8	·65	12
26	Mo	8	P	·29	9	·61	13
27	Tu	9	1	·24	10	·58	14
28	We	10	2	·20	11	·58	15
29	Th	11	3	·18	12	·59	16
30	Fr	12	4	·18	13	·63	17
1	Sa	13	5	·21	14	·69	18
2	Su	14	6	·25	15	·77	19
3	Mo	15	7	·32	16	·86	20
4	Tu	16	8	·40	17	·96	21
5	We	17	9	·49	...	...	22
6	Th	18	10	·58	18	·07	23
7	Fr	19	11	·66	19	·18	24
8	Sa	20	12	·72	20	·28	25
9	Su	21	13	·78	21	·36	26
10	Mo	22	14	·82	22	·42	27
11	Tu	23	A	·82	23	·47	28
12	We	24	1	·83	24	·50	29
13	Th	25	2	·80	25	·51	1
14	Fr	26	3	·76	26	·49	2
15	Sa	27	4	·69	27	·46	3
16	Su	28	5	·62	1	·41	4

March

Solar: Durmati Kumbha—Masi (to 29); Durmati Mina—Panguni (from 1). Lunar: Sukla, Phalguna, Bahula. Muhammadan: H. 1402 Jumadal-awwal.

Solar	Week-Day	Day	Tithi	Moment	Nakshatra	Moment	Muhammadan
17	Mo	1	6	·54	2	·36	5
18	Tu	2	7	·44	3	·30	6
19	We	3	8	·34	4	·23	7
20	Th	4	9	·24	5	·16	8
21	Fr	5	10	·14	6	·09	9
22	Sa	6	11 / 12	·05 / ·97	7 / 8	·03 / ·98	10
23	Su	7	13	·90	9	·94	11
24	Mo	8	14	·84	10	·91	12
25	Tu	9	P	·81	11	·90	13
26	We	10	1	·79	12	·92	14
27	Th	11	2	·79	13	·95	15
28	Fr	12	3	·82	...	...	16
29	Sa	13	4	·86	14	·00	17
1	Su	14	5	·92	15	·07	18
2	Mo	15	...	...	16	·16	19
3	Tu	16	6	·00	17	·26	20
4	We	17	7	·09	18	·37	21
5	Th	18	8	·18	19	·48	22
6	Fr	19	9	·26	20	·58	23
7	Sa	20	10	·33	21	·66	24
8	Su	21	11	·39	22	·73	25
9	Mo	22	12	·42	23	·79	26
10	Tu	23	13	·42	24	·82	27
11	We	24	14	·41	25	·83	28
12	Th	25	A	·38	26	·82	29
13	Fr	26	1	·34	27	·79	30
14	Sa	27	2	·28	1	·76	1
15	Su	28	3	·21	2	·70	2
16	Mo	29	4	·12	3	·64	3
17	Tu	30	5 / 6	·02 / ·92	4	·57	4
18	We	31	7	·82	5	·50	5

April

Solar: Durmati Mina—Panguni (to 31); Dundubhi Mesha—Chittirai (from 1). Lunar: Sukla, Chaitra, Bahula, Sukla, Vaisak. Muhammadan: H. 1402 Jumadal-akhir; H. 1402 Rajab.

Solar	Week-Day	Day	Tithi	Moment	Nakshatra	Moment	Muhammadan
19	Th	1	8	·72	6	·44	6
20	Fr	2	9	·63	7	·38	7
21	Sa	3	10	·55	8	·32	8
22	Su	4	11	·48	9	·27	9
23	Mo	5	12	·42	10	·24	10
24	Tu	6	13	·38	11	·22	11
25	We	7	14	·36	12	·24	12
26	Th	8	P	·33	13	·26	13
27	Fr	9	1	·38	14	·31	14
28	Sa	10	2	·42	15	·37	15
29	Su	11	3	·48	16	·46	16
30	Mo	12	4	·56	17	·56	17
31	Tu	13	5	·65	18	·67	18
1	We	14	6	·73	19	·78	19
2	Th	15	7	·81	20	·88	20
3	Fr	16	8	·88	21	·97	21
4	Sa	17	9	·94	...	...	22
5	Su	18	10	·97	22	·05	23
6	Mo	19	11	·98	23	·10	24
7	Tu	20	12	·97	24	·14	25
8	We	21	13	·94	25	·15	26
9	Th	22	14	·88	26	·14	27
10	Fr	23	A	·82	27	·13	28
11	Sa	24	1	·75	1	·09	29
12	Su	25	2	·66	2 / 3	·04 / ·98	1
13	Mo	26	3	·57	4	·92	2
14	Tu	27	4	·47	5	·85	3
15	We	28	5	·37	6	·78	4
16	Th	29	6	·27	7	·71	5
17	Fr	30	7	·17	8	·65	6

May

Solar: Dundubhi Mesha—Chittirai (to 31); Dundubhi Vrishabha—Vaikasi (from 1). Lunar: Sukla, Vaisakha, Bahula, Sukla. Muhammadan: H. 1402 Rajab (to 30), then next month.

Solar	Week-Day	Day	Tithi	Moment	Nakshatra	Moment	Muhammadan
18	Sa	1	8	·08	9	·60	7
19	Su	2	9 / 10	·00 / ·95	10	·57	8
20	Mo	3	11	·91	11	·56	9
21	Tu	4	12	·85	12	·56	10
22	We	5	13	·88	13	·58	11
23	Th	6	14	·91	14	·62	12
24	Fr	7	P	·96	15	·68	13
25	Sa	8	...	...	16	·76	14
26	Su	9	1	·01	17	·86	15
27	Mo	10	2	·08	18	·97	16
28	Tu	11	3	·16	...	...	17
29	We	12	4	·25	19	·08	18
30	Th	13	5	·33	20	·18	19
31	Fr	14	6	·40	21	·28	20
1	Sa	15	7	·45	22	·36	21
2	Su	16	8	·48	23	·42	22
3	Mo	17	9	·50	24	·45	23
4	Tu	18	10	·48	25	·47	24
5	We	19	11	·45	26	·48	25
6	Th	20	12	·40	27	·46	26
7	Fr	21	13	·34	1	·42	27
8	Sa	22	14	·26	2	·37	28
9	Su	23	A	·17	3	·31	29
10	Mo	24	1 / 2	·07 / ·97	4	·25	30
11	Tu	25	3	·87	5	·18	1
12	We	26	4	·77	6	·11	2
13	Th	27	5	·67	7 / 8	·05 / ·99	3
14	Fr	28	6	·58	9	·94	4
15	Sa	29	7	·51	10	·91	5
16	Su	30	8	·46	11	·88	6
17	Mo	31	9	·41	12	·88	7

June

Solar: Dundubhi Vrishabha—Vaikasi (to 31); Dundubhi Mithuna—Ani (from 1). Lunar: Jyeshtha, Bahula, Sukla, Ashad. Muhammadan: H. 1402 Shaban (to 29); H. 1402 Ramzan.

Solar	Week-Day	Day	Tithi	Moment	Nakshatra	Moment	Muhammadan
18	Tu	1	10	·89	13	·89	8
19	We	2	11	·88	14	·93	9
20	Th	3	12	·41	...	...	10
21	Fr	4	13	·45	15	·00	11
22	Sa	5	14	·51	16	·07	12
23	Su	6	P	·58	17	·16	13
24	Mo	7	1	·66	18	·26	14
25	Tu	8	2	·74	19	·37	15
26	We	9	3	·82	20	·48	16
27	Th	10	4	·89	21	·58	17
28	Fr	11	5	·93	22	·66	18
29	Sa	12	6	·97	23	·73	19
30	Su	13	7	·98	24	·77	20
31	Mo	14	8	·96	25	·79	21
1	Tu	15	9	·94	26	·80	22
2	We	16	10	·90	27	·79	23
3	Th	17	11	·84	1	·75	24
4	Fr	18	12	·76	2	·71	25
5	Sa	19	13	·67	3	·65	26
6	Su	20	14	·57	4	·59	27
7	Mo	21	A	·46	5	·52	28
8	Tu	22	1	·36	6	·45	29
9	We	23	2	·26	7	·38	1
10	Th	24	3	·16	8	·32	2
11	Fr	25	4	·07	9	·28	3
12	Sa	26	5 / 6	·00 / ·93	10	·24	4
13	Su	27	7	·89	11	·21	5
14	Mo	28	8	·87	12	·20	6
15	Tu	29	9	·86	13	·21	7
16	We	30	10	·88	14	·25	8

Naksh :—1, Asvn, 2, Bhar, 3, Krit, 4, Rohi, 5, Mrig, 6, Ardh, 7, Punar, 8, Push, 9, Aslesh, 10, Magh, 11, P. Phal, 12, U. Phal, 13, Hasta, 14, Chit.

A. D. 1982.
A.—Amavasya.
P.—Paurnami.

Kollam 1158, Commences { **N. Malabar—Sept.** / **S. Malabar—Aug.**

Hijra 1403, Commences, Oct. 19.

Vikrama 2039.
Bengal San 1388.
(N. Cycle) Yuvan.

Column groups: SOLAR reckoning (Cyclic Sidereal Year, Month and Day; Week-Day English Month and Day) — LUNAR reckoning (Tithi Ending Moment; Nakshatra Ending Moment; Muhammadan Year, Month and Day).

July

Cyclic Sidereal Day	Week-Day	July	Tithi Ending Moment	Nakshatra Ending Moment	Muhammadan Day
17	Th	1	Suk. 11 ·92	15 ·30	9
18	Fr	2	12 ·98	16 ·37	10
19	Sa	3	... ...	17 ·46	11
20	Su	4	13 ·05	18 ·56	12
21	Mo	5	14 ·13	19 ·67	13
22	Tu ○	6	P ·21	20 ·78	14
23	We	7	1 ·29	21 ·88	15
24	Th	8	2 ·36	22 ·97	16
25	Fr	9	3 ·41	... ...	17
26	Sa	10	4 ·44	23 ·04	18
27	Su	11	5 ·45	24 ·09	19
28	Mo	12	6 ·45	25 ·12	20
29	Tu	13	7 ·42	26 ·13	21
30	We	14	8 ·37	27 ·12	22
31	Th	15	9 ·31	1 ·09	23
32	Fr	16	10 ·23	2 ·05	24
1	Sa	17	11 ·14	3 ·00 } 4 ·93	25
2	Su	18	{ 12 ·04 / 13 ·94	5 ·86	26
3	Mo	19	14 ·84	6 ·79	27
4	Tu	20	—A ·74	7 ·72	28
5	We	21	1 ·64	8 ·66	29
6	Th	22	2 ·55	9 ·61	—30
7	Fr	23	3 ·47	10 ·57	1
8	Sa	24	4 ·41	11 ·54	2
9	Su	25	5 ·37	12 ·52	3
10	Mo	26	6 ·35	13 ·54	4
11	Tu	27	7 ·34	14 ·57	5
12	We	28	8 ·36	15 ·61	6
13	Th	29	9 ·39	16 ·68	7
14	Fr	30	10 ·45	17 ·76	8
15	Sa	31	11 ·52	18 ·86	9

Solar: Dundubhi *Mithuna—Ani.* (to 32); Dundubhi *Karkata—Adi.* (from 1). Lunar: *Suk.*; Ashadha; *Bahula*; *Sukla*. Muhammadan: H. 1402 *Ramzan.*

Aug.

Cyclic Sidereal Day	Week-Day	Aug.	Tithi Ending Moment	Nakshatra Ending Moment	Muhammadan Day
16	Su	1	12 ·60	19 ·97	10
17	Mo	2	13 ·68	... ...	11
18	Tu	3	14 ·76	20 ·08	12
19	We	4	P ·83	21 ·18	13
20	Th	5	1 ·89	22 ·27	14
21	Fr	6	2 ·93	23 ·34	15
22	Sa	7	3 ·94	24 ·40	16
23	Su	8	4 ·93	25 ·44	17
24	Mo	9	5 ·90	26 ·45	18
25	Tu	10	6 ·86	27 ·44	19
26	We	11	7 ·81	1 ·42	20
27	Th	12	8 ·74	2 ·38	21
28	Fr	13	9 ·65	3 ·33	22
29	Sa	14	10 ·55	4 ·27	23
30	Su	15	11 ·45	5 ·20	24
—31	Mo	16	12 ·35	6 ·13	25
1	Tu	17	13 ·25	7 ·07	26
2	We	18	14 ·15	8 ·01 } 9 ·95	27
3	Th	19	{ A ·06 / 1 ·98	10 ·90	28
4	Fr	20	2 ·92	11 ·87	—29
5	Sa	21	3 ·87	12 ·86	1
6	Su	22	4 ·84	13 ·86	2
7	Mo	23	5 ·86	14 ·88	3
8	Tu	24	6 ·90	15 ·92	4
9	We	25	7 ·94	16 ·98	5
10	Th	26	8 ·98	... ...	6
11	Fr	27	... ...	17 ·07	7
12	Sa	28	9 ·03	18 ·17	8
13	Su	29	10 ·09	19 ·28	9
14	Mo	30	11 ·17	20 ·38	10
15	Tu	31	12 ·26	21 ·48	11

Solar: Dundubhi *Simha—Avani.* (from 1). Lunar: Sravana; *Bahula*; Bhadrapada *Sukla*. Muhammadan: H. 1402 *Shawwal.*; H. 1402 *Zi-l-ka'da.*

Sep.

Cyclic Sidereal Day	Week-Day	Sep.	Tithi Ending Moment	Nakshatra Ending Moment	Muhammadan Day
16	We	1	13 ·34	22 ·58	12
17	Th	2	14 ·40	23 ·66	13
18	Fr	3	P ·43	24 ·72	14
19	Sa	4	1 ·46	25 ·76	15
20	Su	5	2 ·45	26 ·77	16
21	Mo	6	3 ·42	27 ·77	17
22	Tu	7	4 ·38	1 ·76	18
23	We	8	5 ·32	2 ·72	19
24	Th	9	6 ·25	3 ·67	20
25	Fr	10	7 ·16	4 ·61	21
26	Sa	11	{ 8 ·06 / 9 ·96	5 ·55	22
27	Su	12	10 ·86	6 ·48	23
28	Mo	13	11 ·76	7 ·41	24
29	Tu	14	12 ·66	8 ·34	25
30	We	15	13 ·58	9 ·28	26
—31	Th	16	14 ·51	10 ·23	27
1	Fr	17	—A ·45	11 ·19	28
2	Sa	18	1 ·40	12 ·18	29
3	Su	19	2 ·38	13 ·18	—30
4	Mo	20	3 ·37	14 ·19	1
5	Tu	21	4 ·38	15 ·23	2
6	We	22	5 ·42	16 ·29	3
7	Th	23	6 ·47	17 ·37	4
8	Fr	24	7 ·55	18 ·47	5
9	Sa	25	8 ·63	19 ·57	6
10	Su	26	9 ·72	20 ·68	7
11	Mo	27	10 ·80	21 ·79	8
12	Tu	28	11 ·88	22 ·89	9
13	We	29	12 ·94	23 ·97	10
14	Th	30	13 ·97	... ...	11

Solar: Dundubhi *Simha—Avani.*; Dundubhi *Kanya—Purattasi.* (from 1). Lunar: Bhadrapada; *Bahula*; Asvina *Sukla*. Muhammadan: H. 1402 *Zi-l-ka'da.*

Oct.

Cyclic Sidereal Day	Week-Day	Oct.	Tithi Ending Moment	Nakshatra Ending Moment	Muhammadan Day
15	Fr	1	14 ·99	24 ·03	12
16	Sa	2	P ·99	25 ·07	13
17	Su	3	1 ·97	26 ·09	14
18	Mo	4	2 ·93	27 ·10	15
19	Tu	5	3 ·87	1 ·08	16
20	We	6	4 ·80	2 ·05	17
21	Th	7	5 ·71	3 ·00 } 4 ·94	18
22	Fr	8	6 ·62	5 ·88	19
23	Sa	9	7 ·52	6 ·82	20
24	Su	10	8 ·42	7 ·75	21
25	Mo	11	9 ·32	8 ·68	22
26	Tu	12	10 ·23	9 ·62	23
27	We	13	11 ·15	10 ·56	24
28	Th	14	12 ·08	11 ·53	25
29	Fr	15	{ 13 ·02 / 14 ·97	12 ·51	26
30	Sa	16	—A ·95	13 ·50	27
—31	Su	17	1 ·94	14 ·51	28
1	Mo	18	2 ·96	15 ·54	—29
2	Tu	19	... ...	16 ·60	1
3	We	20	3 ·00	17 ·68	2
4	Th	21	4 ·06	18 ·77	3
5	Fr	22	5 ·13	19 ·87	4
6	Sa	23	6 ·21	20 ·98	5
7	Su	24	7 ·31	... ...	6
8	Mo	25	8 ·39	21 ·09	7
9	Tu	26	9 ·46	22 ·19	8
10	We	27	10 ·52	23 ·27	9
11	Th	28	11 ·56	24 ·34	10
12	Fr	29	12 ·59	25 ·39	11
13	Sa	30	13 ·58	26 ·42	12
14	Su	31	14 ·56	27 ·43	13

Solar: Dundubhi *Tula—Aippasi.* (from 1). Lunar: Adhika; *Bahula*; Nija Asvina *Sukla*. Muhammadan: H. 1402 *Zi-l-hijja.*; H. 1403 *Muharram.*

Nov.

Cyclic Sidereal Day	Week-Day	Nov.	Tithi Ending Moment	Nakshatra Ending Moment	Muhammadan Day
15	Mo	1	P ·52	1 ·41	14
16	Tu	2	1 ·47	2 ·38	15
17	We	3	2 ·39	3 ·34	16
18	Th	4	3 ·31	4 ·29	17
19	Fr	5	4 ·21	5 ·23	18
20	Sa	6	5 ·11	6 ·16	19
21	Su	7	6 ·01 / 7 ·91	7 ·09	20
22	Mo	8	8 ·83	8 ·02 } 9 ·96	21
23	Tu	9	9 ·75	10 ·91	22
24	We	10	10 ·68	11 ·86	23
25	Th	11	11 ·61	12 ·83	24
26	Fr	12	12 ·57	13 ·82	25
27	Sa	13	13 ·56	14 ·83	26
28	Su	14	14 ·55	15 ·87	27
29	Mo	15	—A ·57	16 ·92	28
—30	Tu	16	1 ·61	17 ·99	29
1	We	17	2 ·68	... ...	—30
2	Th	18	3 ·76	18 ·07	1
3	Fr	19	4 ·85	19 ·17	2
4	Sa	20	5 ·93	20 ·28	3
5	Su	21	... ...	21 ·39	4
6	Mo	22	6 ·01	22 ·49	5
7	Tu	23	7 ·09	23 ·58	6
8	We	24	8 ·15	24 ·65	7
9	Th	25	9 ·19	25 ·71	8
10	Fr	26	10 ·21	26 ·74	9
11	Sa	27	11 ·21	27 ·75	10
12	Su	28	12 ·18	1 ·74	11
13	Mo	29	13 ·13	2 ·71	12
14	Tu	30	14 ·08	3 ·67	13

Solar: Dundubhi *Tula—Aippasi.*; Dundubhi *Vrischika—Kartigai.* (from 1). Lunar: Nija Asvn.; *Bahula*; *Sukla*; Karttika. Muhammadan: H. 1403 *Muharram.*

Dec.

Cyclic Sidereal Day	Week-Day	Dec.	Tithi Ending Moment	Nakshatra Ending Moment	Muhammadan Day
15	We	1	{ P ·01 / 1 ·93	4 ·62	14
16	Th	2	2 ·84	5 ·56	15
17	Fr	3	3 ·74	6 ·49	16
18	Sa	4	4 ·64	7 ·42	17
19	Su	5	5 ·54	8 ·36	18
20	Mo	6	6 ·45	9 ·30	19
21	Tu	7	7 ·37	10 ·24	20
22	We	8	8 ·30	11 ·19	21
23	Th	9	9 ·24	12 ·16	22
24	Fr	10	10 ·20	13 ·14	23
25	Sa	11	11 ·19	14 ·16	24
26	Su	12	12 ·19	15 ·18	25
27	Mo	13	13 ·21	16 ·23	26
28	Tu	14	14 ·26	17 ·29	27
—29	We ●	15	—A ·33	18 ·37	28
1	Th	16	1 ·41	19 ·47	—29
2	Fr	17	2 ·50	20 ·58	1
3	Sa	18	3 ·58	21 ·69	2
4	Su	19	4 ·66	22 ·79	3
5	Mo	20	5 ·73	23 ·88	4
6	Tu	21	6 ·79	24 ·96	5
7	We	22	7 ·83	... ...	6
8	Th	23	8 ·84	25 ·02	7
9	Fr	24	9 ·85	26 ·06	8
10	Sa	25	10 ·82	27 ·07	9
11	Su	26	11 ·78	1 ·07	10
12	Mo	27	12 ·72	2 ·04	11
13	Tu	28	13 ·65	3 ·01 } 4 ·96	12
14	We	29	14 ·57	5 ·90	13
15	Th ○	30	P ·48	6 ·83	14
16	Fr	31	1 ·38	7 ·76	15

Solar: Dundubhi *Dhanus—Margali.* (from 1). Lunar: *Bahula*; *Sukla*; Margasira. Muhammadan: H. 1403 *Safar.*; H. 1403 *Rabi-ul-awwal.*

15. Svati. 16. Visak. 17. Anur. 18. Jyesh. 19. Mula. 20. P. Ash. 21. U. Ash. 22. Sravn. 23. Dani. 24. Satab. 25. P. Bhad. 26. U. Bhad. 27. Rev.

A. D. 1983.
Solar Eclipse. ●
Lunar Eclipse. ○

Mesha Sankranti (Commencement of Indian Sidereal Year).
(Surya Sid.) April 14·10.
(Arya Sid.) April 13·99.

Saka 1905.
(S. Cycle) Rudhirodgari.

Kaliyuga 5084.

SOLAR reckoning: Cyclic Sidereal Year, Month and Day; Week-Day English Month and Day. LUNAR reckoning: Tithi Ending Moment; Nakshatra Ending Moment; Muhammadan Year, Month and Day.

Jan.

Cyclic Sidereal Day	Week-Day	English Day	Tithi Ending Moment	Nakshatra Ending Moment	Muhammadan Day
17	Sa	1	2 ·28	8 ·69	16
18	Su	2	3 ·18	9 ·63	17
19	Mo	3	4 ·09	10 ·57	18
20	Tu	4	5 ·01 6 ·94	11 ·53	19
21	We	5	7 ·89	12 ·49	20
22	Th	6	8 ·85	13 ·48	21
23	Fr	7	9 ·83	14 ·48	22
24	Sa	8	10 ·84	15 ·50	23
25	Su	9	11 ·86	16 ·54	24
26	Mo	10	12 ·91	17 ·60	25
27	Tu	11	13 ·98	18 ·68	26
28	We	12	... ...	19 ·78	27
—29	Th	13	14 ·05	20 ·88	28
1	Fr	14	—A ·14	21 ·99	29
2	Sa	15	1 ·23	... ...	—30
3	Su	16	2 ·31	22 ·09	1
4	Mo	17	3 ·38	23 ·18	2
5	Tu	18	4 ·44	24 ·26	3
6	We	19	5 ·48	25 ·33	4
7	Th	20	6 ·50	26 ·37	5
8	Fr	21	7 ·49	27 ·39	6
9	Sa	22	8 ·46	1 ·39	7
10	Su	23	9 ·42	2 ·38	8
11	Mo	24	10 ·36	3 ·35	9
12	Tu	25	11 ·28	4 ·30	10
13	We	26	12 ·20	5 ·24	11
14	Th	27	13 ·11	6 ·18	12
15	Fr	28	14 ·01 P ·91	7 ·11	13
16	Sa	29	1 ·81	8 ·04 9 ·97	14
17	Su	30	2 ·72	10 ·91	15
18	Mo	31	3 ·64	11 ·86	16

Dundubhi *Dhanus—Margali*; Dundubhi *Makara—Tai*. Marg. — *Bahula*; *Sukla*; Pausha. H. 1403 *Rabi-ul-awwal*; H. 1403 *Rabi-ul-akhir*.

Feb.

Cyclic Sidereal Day	Week-Day	English Day	Tithi Ending Moment	Nakshatra Ending Moment	Muhammadan Day
19	Tu	1	4 ·58	12 ·83	17
20	We	2	5 ·53	13 ·80	18
21	Th	3	6 ·49	14 ·80	19
22	Fr	4	7 ·47	15 ·81	20
23	Sa	5	8 ·47	16 ·85	21
24	Su	6	9 ·50	17 ·91	22
25	Mo	7	10 ·56	18 ·99	23
26	Tu	8	11 ·62	... ...	24
27	We	9	12 ·70	19 ·08	25
28	Th	10	13 ·78	20 ·18	26
29	Fr	11	14 ·87	21 ·28	27
—30	Sa	12	—A ·95	22 ·39	28
1	Su	13	... ...	23 ·50	—29
2	Mo	14	1 ·02	24 ·58	1
3	Tu	15	2 ·08	25 ·64	2
4	We	16	3 ·11	26 ·69	3
5	Th	17	4 ·13	27 ·71	4
6	Fr	18	5 ·12	1 ·73	5
7	Sa	19	6 ·09	2 ·71	6
8	Su	20	7 ·04 8 ·97	3 ·68	7
9	Mo	21	9 ·90	4 ·63	8
10	Tu	22	10 ·82	5 ·57	9
11	We	23	11 ·73	6 ·51	10
12	Th	24	12 ·63	7 ·45	11
13	Fr	25	13 ·53	8 ·38	12
14	Sa	26	14 ·43	9 ·31	13
15	Su	27	P ·34	10 ·25	14
16	Mo	28	1 ·26	11 ·19	15

Dundubhi *Kumbha—Masi*. *Bahula*; Adh. Phalguna — *Sukla*. H. 1403 *Jumadal-awwal*.

March

Cyclic Sidereal Day	Week-Day	English Day	Tithi Ending Moment	Nakshatra Ending Moment	Muhammadan Day
17	Tu	1	2 ·19	12 ·16	16
18	We	2	3 ·14	13 ·13	17
19	Th	3	4 ·10	14 ·12	18
20	Fr	4	5 ·09	15 ·13	19
21	Sa	5	6 ·09	16 ·16	20
22	Su	6	7 ·12	17 ·22	21
23	Mo	7	8 ·17	18 ·29	22
24	Tu	8	9 ·23	19 ·38	23
25	We	9	10 ·31	20 ·48	24
26	Th	10	11 ·40	21 ·59	25
27	Fr	11	12 ·49	22 ·70	26
28	Sa	12	13 ·57	23 ·80	27
29	Su	13	14 ·63	24 ·88	28
—30	Mo	14	—A ·68	25 ·95	29
1	Tu	15	1 ·71	... ...	—30
2	We	16	2 ·72	26 ·00	1
3	Th	17	3 ·71	27 ·04	2
4	Fr	18	4 ·68	1 ·05	3
5	Sa	19	5 ·64	2 ·04	4
6	Su	20	6 ·58	3 ·01 4 ·97	5
7	Mo	21	7 ·50	5 ·92	6
8	Tu	22	8 ·41	6 ·86	7
9	We	23	9 ·32	7 ·79	8
10	Th	24	10 ·22	8 ·72	9
11	Fr	25	11 ·12	9 ·65	10
12	Sa	26	12 ·02 13 ·93	10 ·59	11
13	Su	27	14 ·85	11 ·54	12
14	Mo	28	P ·78	12 ·49	13
15	Tu	29	1 ·72	13 ·46	14
16	We	30	2 ·68	14 ·44	15
17	Th	31	3 ·67	15 ·45	16

Dundubhi *Kumbha—Masi*; Dundubhi *Mina—Panguni*. Adh. Phalguna — *Bahula*; *Sukla*; Phalguna. H. 1403 *Jumadal-awwal*; H. 1403 *Jumadal-akhir*.

April

Cyclic Sidereal Day	Week-Day	English Day	Tithi Ending Moment	Nakshatra Ending Moment	Muhammadan Day
18	Fr	1	4 ·67	16 ·48	17
19	Sa	2	5 ·70	17 ·53	18
20	Su	3	6 ·74	18 ·60	19
21	Mo	4	7 ·81	19 ·68	20
22	Tu	5	8 ·89	20 ·78	21
23	We	6	9 ·97	21 ·89	22
24	Th	7	... ...	... ...	23
25	Fr	8	10 ·06	22 ·00	24
26	Sa	9	11 ·14	23 ·10	25
27	Su	10	12 ·20	24 ·19	26
28	Mo	11	13 ·25	25 ·26	27
29	Tu	12	14 ·28	26 ·32	28
—30	We	13	—A ·28	27 ·36	—29
1	Th	14	1 ·27	1 ·37	1
2	Fr	15	2 ·24	2 ·36	2
3	Sa	16	3 ·19	3 ·34	3
4	Su	17	4 ·13	4 ·30	4
5	Mo	18	5 ·05 6 ·97	5 ·25	5
6	Tu	19	7 ·87	6 ·19	6
7	We	20	8 ·77	7 ·13	7
8	Th	21	9 ·67	8 ·06 9 ·99	8
9	Fr	22	10 ·57	10 ·93	9
10	Sa	23	11 ·47	11 ·87	10
11	Su	24	12 ·39	12 ·82	11
12	Mo	25	13 ·32	13 ·79	12
13	Tu	26	14 ·23	14 ·77	13
14	We	27	P ·28	15 ·78	14
15	Th	28	1 ·21	16 ·80	15
16	Fr	29	2 ·20	17 ·84	16
17	Sa	30	3 ·23	18 ·90	17

Rudhirodgari *Mesha—Chittirai*. Nija — *Bahula*; *Sukla*; Chaitra; *Bah.* H. 1403 *Rajab*.

May

Cyclic Sidereal Day	Week-Day	English Day	Tithi Ending Moment	Nakshatra Ending Moment	Muhammadan Day
18	Su	1	4 ·27	19 ·98	18
19	Mo	2	5 ·34	... ...	19
20	Tu	3	6 ·42	20 ·08	20
21	We	4	7 ·50	21 ·19	21
22	Th	5	8 ·58	22 ·30	22
23	Fr	6	9 ·66	23 ·40	23
24	Sa	7	10 ·72	24 ·49	24
25	Su	8	11 ·77	25 ·58	25
26	Mo	9	12 ·80	26 ·64	26
27	Tu	10	13 ·81	27 ·67	27
28	We	11	14 ·80	1 ·69	28
29	Th	12	—A ·77	2 ·69	29
30	Fr	13	1 ·72	3 ·67	—30
—31	Sa	14	2 ·65	4 ·64	1
1	Su	15	3 ·57	5 ·59	2
2	Mo	16	4 ·48	6 ·53	3
3	Tu	17	5 ·38	7 ·46	4
4	We	18	6 ·28	8 ·39	5
5	Th	19	7 ·18	9 ·32	6
6	Fr	20	8 ·08 9 ·98	10 ·26	7
7	Sa	21	10 ·90	11 ·20	8
8	Su	22	11 ·83	12 ·15	9
9	Mo	23	12 ·77	13 ·12	10
10	Tu	24	13 ·73	14 ·10	11
11	We	25	14 ·71	15 ·10	12
12	Th	26	P ·71	16 ·11	13
13	Fr	27	1 ·73	17 ·15	14
14	Sa	28	2 ·78	18 ·21	15
15	Su	29	3 ·84	19 ·29	16
16	Mo	30	4 ·91	20 ·38	17
17	Tu	31	5 ·99	21 ·48	18

Rudhirodgari *Mesha—Chittirai*; Rudhirodgari *Vrishabha—Vaikasi*. Chaitra — *Bahula*; *Sukla*; Vaisakha. H. 1403 *Rajab*; H. 1403 *Shaban*.

June

Cyclic Sidereal Day	Week-Day	English Day	Tithi Ending Moment	Nakshatra Ending Moment	Muhammadan Day
18	We	1	... ...	22 ·59	19
19	Th	2	6 ·07	23 ·70	20
20	Fr	3	7 ·15	24 ·79	21
21	Sa	4	8 ·21	25 ·88	22
22	Su	5	9 ·26	26 ·95	23
23	Mo	6	10 ·30	27 ·99	24
24	Tu	7	11 ·30	... ...	25
25	We	8	12 ·29	1 ·01	26
26	Th	9	13 ·26	2 ·01	27
27	Fr	10	14 ·22	3 ·00 4 ·97	28
28	Sa ●	11	—A ·15	5 ·93	—29
29	Su	12	1 ·07 2 ·98	6 ·87	1
30	Mo	13	3 ·88	7 ·81	2
—31	Tu	14	4 ·78	8 ·74	3
1	We	15	5 ·68	9 ·67	4
2	Th	16	6 ·58	10 ·60	5
3	Fr	17	7 ·48	11 ·54	6
4	Sa	18	8 ·39	12 ·49	7
5	Su	19	9 ·32	13 ·46	8
6	Mo	20	10 ·26	14 ·43	9
7	Tu	21	11 ·21	15 ·42	10
8	We	22	12 ·19	16 ·43	11
9	Th	23	13 ·20	17 ·46	12
10	Fr	24	14 ·21	18 ·52	13
11	Sa ○	25	P ·25	19 ·60	14
12	Su	26	1 ·31	20 ·68	15
13	Mo	27	2 ·38	21 ·78	16
14	Tu	28	3 ·46	22 ·89	17
15	We	29	4 ·54	... ...	18
16	Th	30	5 ·63	23 ·00	19

Rudhirodgari *Vrishabha—Vaikasi*; Rudhirodgari *Mithuna—Ani*. *Bahula*; *Sukla*; Jyeshtha; *Bah.* H. 1403 *Ramzan*.

Naksh :—1. Asvn. 2. Bhar. 3. Krit. 4. Rohi. 5. Mrig. 6. Ardh. 7. Punar. 8. Push. 9. Aslesh. 10. Magh. 11. P. Phal. 12. U. Phal. 13. Hasta. 14. Chit.

N.B.—In this year, the Lunar month **Magha** is **Kshaya**, *i.e.*, suppressed.

A. D. 1983.
A.—Amavasya. **P.—Paurnami.**
Kollam 1159, Commences { **N. Malabar—Sept.** **S. Malabar—Aug.**
Hijra 1404, Commences, **Oct. 8.**
Vikrama 2040. **Bengal San 1389.** **(N. Cycle) Dhatri.**

SOLAR reckoning: Cyclic Sidereal Year, Month and Day; Week-Day English Month and Day. LUNAR reckoning: Tithi Ending Moment; Nakshatra Ending Moment; Muhammadan Year, Month and Day.

July — Solar: Rudhirodgari *Mithuna—Ani.* (to 32), Rudhirodgari *Karkata—Adi.* (from 1); Lunar: Jyeshtha Bahula, Ashadha Sukla; H. 1403 *Ramzan.* (to 30), H. 1403 *Shawwal.* (from 1)

Cyclic Sidereal	Week-Day	July	Tithi	Ending Moment	Nakshatra	Ending Moment	Muhammadan
17	Fr	1	6	·69	24	·10	20
18	Sa	2	7	·74	25	·19	21
19	Su	3	8	·78	26	·26	22
20	Mo	4	9	·78	27	·30	23
21	Tu	5	10	·77	1	·33	24
22	We	6	11	·74	2	·85	25
23	Th	7	12	·69	3	·33	26
24	Fr	8	13	·62	4	·30	27
25	Sa	9	14	·55	5	·26	28
26	Su	10	—A	·46	6	·21	29
27	Mo	11	1	·38	7	·15	—30
28	Tu	12	2	·26	8	·08	1
29	We	13	3	·16	9 10	·01 ·94	2
30	Th	14	4 5	·06 ·96	11	·88	3
31	Fr	15	6	·87	12	·83	4
—32	Sa	16	7	·79	13	·79	5
1	Su	17	8	·73	14	·76	6
2	Mo	18	9	·69	15	·74	7
3	Tu	19	10	·68	16	·75	8
4	We	20	11	·68	17	·78	9
5	Th	21	12	·69	18	·83	10
6	Fr	22	13	·73	19	·90	11
7	Sa	23	14	·78	20	·98	12
8	Su	24	P	·85	...	...	13
9	Mo	25	1	·93	21	·08	14
10	Tu	26	...	...	22	·19	15
11	We	27	2	·02	23	·30	16
12	Th	28	3	·10	24	·40	17
13	Fr	29	4	·17	25	·49	18
14	Sa	30	5	·22	26	·56	19
15	Su	31	6	·25	27	·62	20

Aug. — Solar: Rudhirodgari *Simha—Avani.* (from 1); Lunar: Bahula, Sukla, Sravana, Bahula; H. 1403 *Zi-l-ka'da.* (from 1)

Cyclic Sidereal	Week-Day	Aug.	Tithi	Ending Moment	Nakshatra	Ending Moment	Muhammadan
16	Mo	1	7	·27	1	·66	21
17	Tu	2	8	·25	2	·67	22
18	We	3	9	·22	3	·66	23
19	Th	4	10	·18	4	·64	24
20	Fr	5	11	·12	5	·60	25
21	Sa	6	12 13	·04 ·95	6	·55	26
22	Su	7	14	·85	7	·49	27
23	Mo	8	—A	·75	8	·42	28
24	Tu	9	1	·65	9	·35	—29
25	We	10	2	·55	10	·28	1
26	Th	11	3	·45	11	·21	2
27	Fr	12	4	·36	12	·16	3
28	Sa	13	5	·28	13	·12	4
29	Su	14	6	·22	14	·09	5
30	Mo	15	7	·18	15	·07	6
—31	Tu	16	8	·17	16	·07	7
1	We	17	9	·17	17	·10	8
2	Th	18	10	·18	18	·14	9
3	Fr	19	11	·21	19	·21	10
4	Sa	20	12	·27	20	·29	11
5	Su	21	13	·35	21	·39	12
6	Mo	22	14	·43	22	·50	13
7	Tu	23	P	·51	23	·60	14
8	We	24	1	·59	24	·70	15
9	Th	25	2	·66	25	·79	16
10	Fr	26	3	·72	26	·87	17
11	Sa	27	4	·76	27	·94	18
12	Su	28	5	·78	1	·98	19
13	Mo	29	6	·76	2	·99	20
14	Tu	30	7	·73	3	·99	21
15	We	31	8	·69	4	·97	22

Sep. — Solar: Rudhirodgari *Simha—Avani.* (to 31), Rudhirodgari *Kanya—Purattasi.* (from 1); Lunar: Sravn. Bah., Sukla, Bhadrapada, Bahula; H. 1403 *Zi-l-ka'da.* (to 30), H. 1403 *Zi-l-hijja.* (from 1)

Cyclic Sidereal	Week-Day	Sep.	Tithi	Ending Moment	Nakshatra	Ending Moment	Muhammadan
16	Th	1	9	·63	5	·94	23
17	Fr	2	10	·55	6	·89	24
18	Sa	3	11	·47	7	·83	25
19	Su	4	12	·37	8	·76	26
20	Mo	5	13	·26	9	·69	27
21	Tu	6	14	·16	10	·62	28
22	We	7	A 1	·06 ·97	11	·56	29
23	Th	8	2	·88	12	·50	—30
24	Fr	9	3	·81	13	·45	1
25	Sa	10	4	·75	14	·41	2
26	Su	11	5	·71	15	·39	3
27	Mo	12	6	·69	16	·40	4
28	Tu	13	7	·69	17	·41	5
29	We	14	8	·70	18	·45	6
30	Th	15	9	·74	19	·51	7
—31	Fr	16	10	·80	20	·59	8
1	Sa	17	11	·87	21	·69	9
2	Su	18	12	·95	22	·79	10
3	Mo	19	...	...	23	·90	11
4	Tu	20	13	·03	...	...	12
5	We	21	14	·11	24	·00	13
6	Th	22	P	·19	25	·10	14
7	Fr	23	1	·25	26	·19	15
8	Sa	24	2	·29	27	·25	16
9	Su	25	3	·31	1	·29	17
10	Mo	26	4	·30	2	·31	18
11	Tu	27	5	·28	3	·31	19
12	We	28	6	·24	4	·29	20
13	Th	29	7	·17	5	·26	21
14	Fr	30	8	·09	6	·22	22

Oct. — Solar: Rudhirodgari *Tula—Aippasi.* (from 1); Lunar: Sukla, Asvina, Bahula; H. 1404 *Muharram.* (from 1)

Cyclic Sidereal	Week-Day	Oct.	Tithi	Ending Moment	Nakshatra	Ending Moment	Muhammadan
15	Sa	1	9 10	·01 ·92	7	·16	23
16	Su	2	11	·82	8	·10	24
17	Mo	3	12	·72	9 10	·04 ·97	25
18	Tu	4	13	·62	11	·90	26
19	We	5	14	·52	12	·83	27
20	Th	6	—A	·43	13	·78	28
21	Fr	7	1	·36	14	·74	—29
22	Sa	8	2	·31	15	·73	1
23	Su	9	3	·27	16	·72	2
24	Mo	10	4	·25	17	·73	3
25	Tu	11	5	·26	18	·76	4
26	We	12	6	·27	19	·82	5
27	Th	13	7	·30	20	·90	6
28	Fr	14	8	·36	21	·99	7
29	Sa	15	9	·43	...	...	8
30	Su	16	10	·52	22	·09	9
—31	Mo	17	11	·61	23	·20	10
1	Tu	18	12	·69	24	·31	11
2	We	19	13	·77	25	·41	12
3	Th	20	14	·83	26	·49	13
4	Fr	21	P	·87	27	·56	14
5	Sa	22	1	·89	1	·61	15
6	Su	23	2	·88	2	·63	16
7	Mo	24	3	·85	3	·64	17
8	Tu	25	4	·81	4	·63	18
9	We	26	5	·75	5	·60	19
10	Th	27	6	·68	6	·56	20
11	Fr	28	7	·59	7	·50	21
12	Sa	29	8	·50	8	·44	22
13	Su	30	9	·40	9	·37	23
14	Mo	31	·10	·30	10	·30	24

Nov. — Solar: Rudhirodgari *Tula—Aippasi.* (to 30), Rudhirodgari *Vrischika—Kartigai.* (from 1); Lunar: Bah., Sukla, Karttika, Bahula; *Muharram.* (to 30), H. 1404 *Safar.* (from 1)

Cyclic Sidereal	Week-Day	Nov.	Tithi	Ending Moment	Nakshatra	Ending Moment	Muhammadan
15	Tu	1	11	·20	11	·23	25
16	We	2	12	·11	12	·17	26
17	Th	3	13 14	·03 ·96	13	·12	27
18	Fr	4	—A	·90	14	·08	28
19	Sa	5	1	·86	15	·05	29
20	Su	6	2	·84	16	·04	—30
21	Mo	7	3	·85	17	·05	1
22	Tu	8	4	·87	18	·08	2
23	We	9	5	·92	19	·14	3
24	Th	10	6	·98	20	·21	4
25	Fr	11	...	...	21	·29	5
26	Sa	12	7	·05	22	·39	6
27	Su	13	8	·13	23	·50	7
28	Mo	14	9	·23	24	·61	8
29	Tu	15	10	·31	25	·71	9
—30	We	16	11	·38	26	·80	10
1	Th	17	12	·44	27	·87	11
2	Fr	18	13	·49	1	·92	12
3	Sa	19	14	·51	2	·95	13
4	Su	20	P	·49	3	·97	14
5	Mo	21	1	·47	4	·96	15
6	Tu	22	2	·43	5	·93	16
7	We	23	3	·37	6	·89	17
8	Th	24	4	·30	7	·84	18
9	Fr	25	5	·22	8	·78	19
10	Sa	26	6	·13	9	·71	20
11	Su	27	7 8	·03 ·93	10	·64	21
12	Mo	28	9	·83	11	·57	22
13	Tu	29	10	·74	12	·51	23
14	We	30	11	·65	13	·46	24

Dec. — Solar: Rudhirodgari *Dhanus—Margali.* (from 1); Lunar: Sukla, Margasira, Bahula; H. 1404 *Rabi-ul-awwal.* (from 1)

Cyclic Sidereal	Week-Day	Dec.	Tithi	Ending Moment	Nakshatra	Ending Moment	Muhammadan
15	Th	1	12	·57	14	·41	25
16	Fr	2	13	·52	15	·38	26
17	Sa	3	14	·49	16	·36	27
18	Su ●	4	—A	·48	17	·37	28
19	Mo	5	1	·48	18	·40	—29
20	Tu	6	2	·51	19	·45	1
21	We	7	3	·56	20	·51	2
22	Th	8	4	·61	21	·59	3
23	Fr	9	5	·69	22	·69	4
24	Sa	10	6	·79	23	·80	5
25	Su	11	[illegible]	·87	24	·91	6
26	Mo	12	8	·95	...	...	7
27	Tu	13	...	...	25	·01	8
28	We	14	9	·03	26	·10	9
—29	Th	15	10	·09	27	·18	10
1	Fr	16	11	·13	1	·24	11
2	Sa	17	12	·15	2	·28	12
3	Su	18	13	·13	3	·29	13
4	Mo	19	14	·11	4	·29	14
5	Tu	20	P	·06	5	·26	15
6	We	21	1 2	·00 ·93	6	·22	16
7	Th	22	3	·84	7	·18	17
8	Fr	23	4	·75	8	·12	18
9	Sa	24	5	·66	9 10	·05 ·98	19
10	Su	25	6	·56	11	·91	20
11	Mo	26	7	·46	12	·85	21
12	Tu	27	8	·37	13	·79	22
13	We	28	9	·29	14	·74	23
14	Th	29	10	·22	15	·71	24
15	Fr	30	11	·17	16	·69	25
16	Sa	31	12	·13	17	·69	26

15. Svati. 16. Visak. 17. Anur. 18. Jyesh. 19. Mula. 20. P. Ash. 21. U. Ash. 22. Sravn. 23. Dani. 24. Satab. 25. P. Bhad. 26. U. Bhad. 27. Rev.

A. D. 1984. **Mesha Sankranti** (Commencement of Indian Sidereal Year).
Solar Eclipse. ● **(Surya Sid.) April 13·36.** **Saka 1906.** **Kaliyuga 5085.**
Lunar Eclipse. ○ **(Arya Sid.) April 13·25.** **(S. Cycle) Raktaksha.**

SOLAR reckoning: Cyclic Sidereal Year, Month and Day; Week-Day English Month and Day. LUNAR reckoning: Tithi Ending Moment; Nakshatra Ending Moment; Muhammadan Year, Month and Day.

Jan.

Solar month	Cyclic Sidereal Year, Month and Day	Week-Day	Day	Lunar	Tithi Ending Moment	Nakshatra Ending Moment	Muhammadan Year, Month and Day	Muhammadan month
Rudhirodgari *Dhanus—Margali.*	17	Su	1	*Bah.*	13 ·12	18 ·72	27	*R.-awwal.*
	18	Mo	2		14 ·12	19 ·76	28	
	19	Tu	3		—A ·15	20 ·82	29	
	20	We	4	*Sukla*	1 ·20	21 ·89	—30	
	21	Th	5		2 ·26	22 ·99	1	H. 1404 *Rabi-ul-akhir.*
	22	Fr	6		3 ·34	... ...	2	
	23	Sa	7		4 ·43	23 ·10	3	
	24	Su	8		5 ·52	24 ·21	4	
	25	Mo	9		6 ·60	25 ·31	5	
	26	Tu	10		7 ·68	26 ·40	6	
	27	We	11		8 ·74	27 ·48	7	
	28	Th	12		9 ·78	1 ·55	8	
	29	Fr	13		10 ·79	2 ·59	9	
	—30	Sa	14		11 ·77	3 ·61	10	
Rudhirodgari *Makara—Tai.*	1	Su	15	**Pausha**	12 ·75	4 ·61	11	
	2	Mo	16		13 ·71	5 ·59	12	
	3	Tu	17		14 ·65	6 ·57	13	
	4	We	18		P ·57	7 ·52	14	
	5	Th	19	*Bahula*	1 ·48	8 ·46	15	
	6	Fr	20		2 ·38	9 ·39	16	
	7	Sa	21		3 ·28	10 ·32	17	
	8	Su	22		4 ·18	11 ·25	18	
	9	Mo	23		5 ·09	12 ·19	19	
	10	Tu	24		6 ·01 7 ·93	13 ·13	20	
	11	We	25		8 ·87	14 ·08	21	
	12	Th	26		9 ·81	15 ·04	22	
	13	Fr	27		10 ·77	16 ·01	23	
	14	Sa	28		11 ·76	17 ·02	24	
	15	Su	29		12 ·77	18 ·04	25	
	16	Mo	30		13 ·80	19 ·07	26	
	17	Tu	31		14 ·85	20 ·12	27	

Feb.

Solar month	Cyclic Sidereal Year, Month and Day	Week-Day	Day	Lunar	Tithi Ending Moment	Nakshatra Ending Moment	Muhammadan Year, Month and Day	Muhammadan month
	18	We	1		—A ·92	21 ·20	28	
	19	Th	2	*Sukla*	... ...	22 ·30	—29	
	20	Fr	3		1 ·00	23 ·40	1	H. 1404 *Jumadal-awwal.*
	21	Sa	4		2 ·09	24 ·51	2	
	22	Su	5		3 ·17	25 ·61	3	
	23	Mo	6		4 ·25	26 ·71	4	
	24	Tu	7		5 ·32	27 ·80	5	
	25	We	8		6 ·38	1 ·86	6	
	26	Th	9		7 ·41	2 ·91	7	
	27	Fr	10		8 ·42	3 ·93	8	
	28	Sa	11		9 ·41	4 ·94	9	
	—29	Su	12		10 ·38	5 ·93	10	
Rudhirodgari *Kumbha—Masi.*	1	Mo	13	**Magha**	11 ·33	6 ·90	11	
	2	Tu	14		12 ·27	7 ·85	12	
	3	We	15		13 ·19	8 ·79	13	
	4	Th	16		14 ·11	9 ·73	14	
	5	Fr	17		P ·02 1 ·92	10 ·67	15	
	6	Sa	18	*Bahula*	2 ·81	11 ·60	16	
	7	Su	19		3 ·71	12 ·53	17	
	8	Mo	20		4 ·62	13 ·47	18	
	9	Tu	21		5 ·54	14 ·41	19	
	10	We	22		6 ·48	15 ·37	20	
	11	Th	23		7 ·43	16 ·35	21	
	12	Fr	24		8 ·40	17 ·34	22	
	13	Sa	25		9 ·38	18 ·35	23	
	14	Su	26		10 ·39	19 ·38	24	
	15	Mo	27		11 ·42	20 ·43	25	
	16	Tu	28		12 ·47	21 ·51	26	
	17	We	29		13 ·54	22 ·60	27	

March

Solar month	Cyclic Sidereal Year, Month and Day	Week-Day	Day	Lunar	Tithi Ending Moment	Nakshatra Ending Moment	Muhammadan Year, Month and Day	Muhammadan month
Rudhirodgari *Kumbha—Masi.*	18	Th	1		14 ·62	23 ·70	28	
	19	Fr	2		—A ·71	24 ·81	29	
	20	Sa	3	*Sukla*	1 ·79	25 ·91	—30	
	21	Su	4		2 ·87	... ...	1	H. 1404 *Jumadal-akhir.*
	22	Mo	5		3 ·93	26 ·01	2	
	23	Tu	6		4 ·98	27 ·10	3	
	24	We	7		... ...	1 ·17	4	
	25	Th	8		5 ·02	2 ·22	5	
	26	Fr	9		6 ·03	3 ·25	6	
	27	Sa	10		7 ·02 8 ·98	4 ·26	7	
	28	Su	11		9 ·93	5 ·26	8	
	29	Mo	12		10 ·87	6 ·23	9	
	30	Tu	13		11 ·80	7 ·19	10	
	—31	We	14		12 ·71	8 ·13	11	
Rudhirodgari *Mina—Panguni.*	1	Th	15	**Phalguna**	13 ·61	9 ·07	12	
	2	Fr	16		14 ·51	10 ·01 11 ·94	13	
	3	Sa	17		P ·41	12 ·87	14	
	4	Su	18	*Bahula*	1 ·31	13 ·80	15	
	5	Mo	19		2 ·22	14 ·74	16	
	6	Tu	20		3 ·14	15 ·71	17	
	7	We	21		4 ·07	16 ·68	18	
	8	Th	22		5 ·02 6 ·99	17 ·66	19	
	9	Fr	23		7 ·97	18 ·67	20	
	10	Sa	24		8 ·98	19 ·69	21	
	11	Su	25		... ...	20 ·75	22	
	12	Mo	26		9 ·01	21 ·82	23	
	13	Tu	27		10 ·06	22 ·90	24	
	14	We	28		11 ·12	... ...	25	
	15	Th	29		12 ·20	23 ·00	26	
	16	Fr	30		13 ·29	24 ·11	27	
	17	Sa	31		14 ·37	25 ·22	28	

April

Solar month	Cyclic Sidereal Year, Month and Day	Week-Day	Day	Lunar	Tithi Ending Moment	Nakshatra Ending Moment	Muhammadan Year, Month and Day	Muhammadan month
	18	Su	1		—A ·45	26 ·32	—29	
	19	Mo	2	*Sukla*	1 ·52	27 ·41	1	H. 1404 *Rajab.*
	20	Tu	3		2 ·57	1 ·48	2	
	21	We	4		3 ·60	2 ·54	3	
	22	Th	5		4 ·61	3 ·57	4	
	23	Fr	6		5 ·59	4 ·59	5	
	24	Sa	7		6 ·55	5 ·58	6	
	25	Su	8		7 ·50	6 ·56	7	
	26	Mo	9		8 ·43	7 ·52	8	
	27	Tu	10		9 ·36	8 ·47	9	
	28	We	11		10 ·27	9 ·41	10	
	—29	Th	12		11 ·17	10 ·35	11	
Raktaksha *Mesha—Chittirai.*	1	Fr	13	**Chaitra**	12 ·07 13 ·97	11 ·28	12	
	2	Sa	14		14 ·87	12 ·21	13	
	3	Su	15		P ·77	13 ·15	14	
	4	Mo	16	*Bahula*	1 ·69	14 ·09	15	
	5	Tu	17		2 ·62	15 ·04	16	
	6	We	18		3 ·57	16 ·01 17 ·99	17	
	7	Th	19		4 ·53	18 ·99	18	
	8	Fr	20		5 ·51	... ...	19	
	9	Sa	21		6 ·52	19 ·02	20	
	10	Su	22		7 ·55	20 ·06	21	
	11	Mo	23		8 ·60	21 ·12	22	
	12	Tu	24		9 ·67	22 ·20	23	
	13	We	25		10 ·76	23 ·30	24	
	14	Th	26		11 ·84	24 ·41	25	
	15	Fr	27		12 ·92	25 ·52	26	
	16	Sa	28		13 ·99	26 ·62	27	
	17	Su	29		... ...	27 ·71	28	
	18	Mo	30		14 ·05	1 ·79	29	

May

Solar month	Cyclic Sidereal Year, Month and Day	Week-Day	Day	Lunar	Tithi Ending Moment	Nakshatra Ending Moment	Muhammadan Year, Month and Day	Muhammadan month
Raktaksha *Mesha—Chittirai.*	19	Tu	1		—A ·10	2 ·85	—30	
	20	We	2	*Sukla*	1 ·13	3 ·89	1	H. 1404 *Shaban.*
	21	Th	3		2 ·14	4 ·91	2	
	22	Fr	4		3 ·12	5 ·91	3	
	23	Sa	5		4 ·09	6 ·89	4	
	24	Su	6		5 ·03 6 ·96	7 ·85	5	
	25	Mo	7		7 ·88	8 ·81	6	
	26	Tu	8		8 ·79	9 ·75	7	
	27	We	9		9 ·69	10 ·68	8	
	28	Th	10		10 ·59	11 ·61	9	
	29	Fr	11		11 ·49	12 ·54	10	
	30	Sa	12		12 ·39	13 ·48	11	
	—31	Su	13	**Vaisakha**	13 ·29	14 ·42	12	
Raktaksha *Vrishabha—Vaikasi.*	1	Mo	14		14 ·21	15 ·37	13	
	2	Tu	15		P ·14	16 ·34	14	
	3	We	16	*Bahula*	1 ·09	17 ·32	15	
	4	Th	17		2 ·06	18 ·32	16	
	5	Fr	18		3 ·04	19 ·33	17	
	6	Sa	19		4 ·03	20 ·37	18	
	7	Su	20		5 ·06	21 ·43	19	
	8	Mo	21		6 ·11	22 ·50	20	
	9	Tu	22		7 ·17	23 ·59	21	
	10	We	23		8 ·24	24 ·70	22	
	11	Th	24		9 ·32	25 ·81	23	
	12	Fr	25		10 ·41	26 ·92	24	
	13	Sa	26		11 ·49	... ...	25	
	14	Su	27		12 ·55	27 ·01	26	
	15	Mo	28		13 ·60	1 ·09	27	
	16	Tu	29		14 ·62	2 ·16	28	
	17	We	30		—A ·63	3 ·21	—29	
	18	Th	31		1 ·61	4 ·23	1	

June

Solar month	Cyclic Sidereal Year, Month and Day	Week-Day	Day	Lunar	Tithi Ending Moment	Nakshatra Ending Moment	Muhammadan Year, Month and Day	Muhammadan month
	19	Fr	1	*Sukla*	2 ·59	5 ·23	2	H. 1404 *Ramzan.*
	20	Sa	2		3 ·54	6 ·22	3	
	21	Su	3		4 ·47	7 ·19	4	
	22	Mo	4		5 ·38	8 ·15	5	
	23	Tu	5		6 ·29	9 ·09	6	
	24	We	6		7 ·19	10 ·02 11 ·95	7	
	25	Th	7		8 ·09 9 ·99	12 ·88	8	
	26	Fr	8		10 ·89	13 ·82	9	
	27	Sa	9		11 ·79	14 ·76	10	
	28	Su	10	**Jyeshtha**	12 ·71	15 ·71	11	
	29	Mo	11		13 ·64	16 ·66	12	
	30	Tu	12		14 ·57	17 ·64	13	
	31	We	13		P ·53	18 ·64	14	
	—32	Th	14	*Bahula*	1 ·52	19 ·65	15	
Raktaksha *Mithuna—Ani.*	1	Fr	15		2 ·52	20 ·68	16	
	2	Sa	16		3 ·54	21 ·73	17	
	3	Su	17		4 ·58	22 ·81	18	
	4	Mo	18		5 ·64	23 ·90	19	
	5	Tu	19		6 ·71	... ...	20	
	6	We	20		7 ·79	24 ·00	21	
	7	Th	21		8 ·88	25 ·11	22	
	8	Fr	22		9 ·95	26 ·22	23	
	9	Sa	23		... ...	27 ·32	24	
	10	Su	24		10 ·02	1 ·41	25	
	11	Mo	25		11 ·07	2 ·48	26	
	12	Tu	26		12 ·10	3 ·53	27	
	13	We	27		13 ·11	4 ·56	28	
	14	Th	28		14 ·10	5 ·56	29	
	15	Fr	29		—A ·07	6 ·55	—30	
	16	Sa	30		1 ·02 2 ·95	7 ·52	1	

Nakah:—1. Asvn. 2. Bhar. 3. Krit. 4. Rohi. 5. Mrig. 6. Ardh. 7. Punar. 8. Push. 9. Aslesh. 10. Magh. 11. P. Phal. 12. U. Phal. 13. Hasta. 14. Chit.

A. D. 1984.
A.—Amavasya.
P.—Paurnami.

Kollam 1160, Commences { N. Malabar—Sept. / S. Malabar—Aug.

Hijra 1405, Commences, Sep. 27.

Vikrama 2041.
Bengal San 1390.
(N. Cycle) Isvara.

SOLAR reckoning	Cyclic Sidereal Year, Month and Day	Week-Day	English Month and Day	LUNAR reckoning	Tithi	Ending Moment	Nakshatra	Ending Moment	Muhammadan Year, Month	Day
			July							
	17	Su	1		3	·87	8	·48		2
	18	Mo	2		4	·78	9	·42		3
	19	Tu	3		5	·68	10	·36		4
	20	We	4		6	·58	11	·30		5
	21	Th	5		7	·47	12	·23		6
Raktaksha *Mithuna—Asi.*	22	Fr	6	*Sukla*	8	·37	13	·16		7
	23	Sa	7		9	·27	14	·10		8
	24	Su	8		10	·19	15	·04		9
	25	Mo	9		11	·11	16 / 17	·00 / ·98		10
	26	Tu	10		12	·05	18	·96		11
	27	We	11		13	·02	19	·97	H. 1404 *Shawwal.*	12
	28	Th	12	Ashadha	14 / P	·00 / ·99	...	...		13
	29	Fr	13		...	...	20	·00		14
	30	Sa	14		1	·02	21	·05		15
	—31	Su	15		2	·06	22	·12		16
	1	Mo	16		3	·11	23	·21		17
	2	Tu	17		4	·18	24	·31		18
	3	We	18		5	·26	25	·41		19
	4	Th	19		6	·35	26	·52		20
	5	Fr	20	*Bahula*	7	·43	27	·62		21
	6	Sa	21		8	·50	1	·71		22
	7	Su	22		9	·55	2	·79		23
	8	Mo	23		10	·58	3	·84		24
	9	Tu	24		11	·59	4	·87		25
Raktaksha *Karkata—Adi.*	10	We	25		12	·58	5	·89		26
	11	Th	26		13	·55	6	·88		27
	12	Fr	27		14	·50	7	·86		28
	13	Sa	28		—A	·43	8	·82		—29
	14	Su	29		1	·35	9	·76		1
	15	Mo	30		2	·26	10	·70		2
	16	Tu	31		3	·16	11	·64		3
			Aug.							
	17	We	1	*Sukla*	4 / 5	·06 / ·96	12	·57		4
	18	Th	2		6	·86	13	·50		5
	19	Fr	3		7	·76	14	·43		6
	20	Sa	4		8	·67	15	·37		7
	21	Su	5		9	·60	16	·33		8
	22	Mo	6		10	·54	17	·30		9
	23	Tu	7		11	·50	18	·29		10
	24	We	8	Sravana	12	·48	19	·29	H. 1404 *Zi-l-ka'da.*	11
	25	Th	9		13	·49	20	·31		12
	26	Fr	10		14	·50	21	·36		13
	27	Sa	11		P	·54	22	·43		14
	28	Su	12		1	·60	23	·51		15
	29	Mo	13		2	·67	24	·60		16
	30	Tu	14		3	·75	25	·71		17
	31	We	15		4	·84	26	·82		18
	—32	Th	16		5	·92	27	·93		19
	1	Fr	17		6	·98	...	...		20
	2	Sa	18	*Bahula*	...	...	1	·02		21
	3	Su	19		7	·03	2	·09		22
	4	Mo	20		8	·07	3	·15		23
	5	Tu	21		9	·09	4	·19		24
Raktaksha *Simha—Avani.*	6	We	22		10	·07	5	·21		25
	7	Th	23		11	·04	6	·21		26
	8	Fr	24		12 / 13	·00 / ·94	7	·19		27
	9	Sa	25		14	·86	8	·15		28
	10	Su	26		—A	·77	9	·10		29
	11	Mo	27	Bhad. *Suk.*	1	·67	10 / 11	·04 / ·98		—30
	12	Tu	28		2	·57	12	·91	*Zi-l-hijja.*	1
	13	We	29		3	·47	13	·84		2
	14	Th	30		4	·37	14	·78		3
	15	Fr	31		5	·27	15	·72		4

SOLAR reckoning	Cyclic Sidereal Year, Month and Day	Week-Day	English Month and Day	LUNAR reckoning	Tithi	Ending Moment	Nakshatra	Ending Moment	Muhammadan Year, Month	Day
			Sep.							
	16	Sa	1	*Sukla*	6	·19	16	·67		5
	17	Su	2		7	·12	17	·63		6
	18	Mo	3		8	·07	18	·61		7
	19	Tu	4		9 / 10	·02 / ·99	19	·61		8
Raktaksha *Simha—Avani.*	20	We	5		...	...	20	·64		9
	21	Th	6	Bhadrapada	11	·00	21	·67		10
	22	Fr	7		12	·02	22	·73		11
	23	Sa	8		13	·06	23	·81		12
	24	Su	9		14	·12	24	·90	H. 1404 *Zi-l-hijja.*	13
	25	Mo	10		P	·19	...	...		14
	26	Tu	11		1	·27	25	·01		15
	27	We	12		2	·35	26	·12		16
	28	Th	13		3	·44	27	·22		17
	29	Fr	14		4	·51	1	·32		18
	30	Sa	15		5	·57	2	·40		19
	—31	Su	16		6	·60	3	·46		20
	1	Mo	17	*Bahula*	7	·62	4	·51		21
	2	Tu	18		8	·60	5	·53		22
	3	We	19		9	·58	6	·53		23
	4	Th	20		10	·54	7	·51		24
	5	Fr	21		11	·47	8	·48		25
	6	Sa	22		12	·39	9	·44		26
	7	Su	23		13	·31	10	·38		27
	8	Mo	24		14	·21	11	·32		28
Raktaksha *Kanya—Purattasi.*	9	Tu	25		—A	·11	12	·25		29
	10	We	26		1 / 2	·01 / ·91	13	·18		—30
	11	Th	27		3	·81	14	·11		1
	12	Fr	28		4	·73	15	·05		2
	13	Sa	29		5	·66	16 / 17	·00 / ·96		3
	14	Su	30		6	·61	18	·94		4
			Oct.							
	15	Mo	1	*Sukla*	7	·57	19	·94		5
	16	Tu	2		8	·55	20	·95		6
	17	We	3		9	·54	21	·98		7
	18	Th	4		10	·56	...	...		8
	19	Fr	5		11	·60	22	·04	H. 1405 *Muharram.*	9
	20	Sa	6		12	·66	23	·11		10
	21	Su	7	Asvina	13	·74	24	·20		11
	22	Mo	8		14	·83	25	·30		12
	23	Tu	9		P	·92	26	·41		13
	24	We	10		...	...	27	·52		14
	25	Th	11		1	·00	1	·62		15
	26	Fr	12		2	·07	2	·70		16
	27	Sa	13		3	·13	3	·77		17
	28	Su	14		4	·17	4	·82		18
	29	Mo	15	*Bahula*	5	·19	5	·85		19
	—30	Tu	16		6	·17	6	·86		20
	1	We	17		7	·15	7	·84		21
	2	Th	18		8	·10	8	·82		22
	3	Fr	19		9 / 10	·04 / ·97	9	·78		23
Raktaksha *Tula—Aippasi.*	4	Sa	20		11	·89	10	·72		24
	5	Su	21		12	·79	11	·65		25
	6	Mo	22		13	·69	12	·58		26
	7	Tu	23		14	·59	13	·51		27
	8	We	24		—A	·49	14	·45		28
	9	Th	25	Kartt. *Sukla*	1	·40	15	·39		29
	10	Fr	26		2	·32	16	·33		—30
	11	Sa	27		3	·25	17	·29	*Safar.*	1
	12	Su	28		4	·19	18	·27		2
	13	Mo	29		5	·15	19	·26		3
	14	Tu	30		6	·14	20	·27		4
	15	We	31		7	·14	21	·30		5

SOLAR reckoning	Cyclic Sidereal Year, Month and Day	Week-Day	English Month and Day	LUNAR reckoning	Tithi	Ending Moment	Nakshatra	Ending Moment	Muhammadan Year, Month	Day
			Nov.							
	16	Th	1	*Sukla*	8	·16	22	·35		6
	17	Fr	2		9	·20	23	·42		7
	18	Sa	3		10	·27	24	·51		8
	19	Su	4		11	·35	25	·61		9
Raktaksha *Tula—Aippasi.*	20	Mo	5		12	·43	26	·72		10
	21	Tu	6	Karttika	13	·52	27	·82		11
	22	We	7		14	·60	1	·92		12
	23	Th	8		P	·68	...	...		13
	24	Fr	9		1	·73	2	·03		14
	25	Sa	10		2	·77	3	·09	H. 1405 *Safar.*	15
	26	Su	11		3	·79	4	·14		16
	27	Mo	12		4	·78	5	·17		17
	28	Tu	13		5	·76	6	·13		18
	29	We	14		6	·71	7	·18		19
	—30	Th	15	*Bahula*	7	·65	8	·15		20
	1	Fr	16		8	·58	9	·11		21
	2	Sa	17		9	·50	10 / 11	·05 / ·99		22
	3	Su	18		10	·40	12	·93		23
	4	Mo	19		11	·30	13	·86		24
	5	Tu	20		12	·20	14	·79		25
	6	We	21		13	·11	15	·73		26
	7	Th	22		14 / A	·02 / ·93	16	·67		27
	8	Fr	23		1	·86	17	·63		28
Raktaksha *Vrischika—Kartigai.*	9	Sa	24		2	·81	18	·60		—29
	10	Su	25		3	·78	19	·58		1
	11	Mo	26		4	·76	20	·59		2
	12	Tu	27		5	·76	21	·61		3
	13	We	28	*Sukla*	6	·79	22	·66		4
	14	Th	29		7	·83	23	·73		5
	15	Fr	30		8	·90	24	·81		6
			Dec.							
	16	Sa	1		9	·98	25	·91		7
	17	Su	2		...	...	...	...		8
	18	Mo	3		10	·08	26	·02		9
	19	Tu	4		11	·16	27	·13	H. 1405 *Rabi-ul-awwal.*	10
	20	We	5	Margasira	12	·24	1	·23		11
	21	Th	6		13	·32	2	·32		12
	22	Fr	7		14	·37	3	·40		13
	23	Sa	8		P	·41	4	·45		14
	24	Su	9		1	·42	5	·49		15
	25	Mo	10		2	·42	6	·51		16
	26	Tu	11		3	·39	7	·51		17
	27	We	12		4	·34	8	·48		18
	28	Th	13		5	·28	9	·44		19
	29	Fr	14		6	·20	10	·39		20
	—30	Sa	15		7	·12	11	·33		21
	1	Su	16		8 / 9	·03 / ·93	12	·27		22
	2	Mo	17	*Bahula*	10	·83	13	·20		23
	3	Tu	18		11	·73	14	·13		24
	4	We	19		12	·65	15	·06		25
Raktaksha *Dhanus—Margali.*	5	Th	20		13	·57	16 / 17	·00 / ·96		26
	6	Fr	21		14	·50	18	·93		27
	7	Sa	22		—A	·45	19	·91		28
	8	Su	23		1	·42	20	·91		29
	9	Mo	24		2	·40	21	·93		—30
	10	Tu	25	Pausha *Sukla*	3	·42	22	·98	*Rabi-ul-akhir.*	1
	11	We	26		4	·45	...	...		2
	12	Th	27		5	·49	23	·04		3
	13	Fr	28		6	·56	24	·11		4
	14	Sa	29		7	·64	25	·21		5
	15	Su	30		8	·73	26	·32		6
	16	Mo	31		9	·81	27	·43		7

15. Svati. 16. Visak. 17. Anur. 18. Jyesh. 19. Mula. 20. P. Ash. 21. U. Ash. 22. Sravn. 23. Dani. 24. Satab. 25. P. Bhad. 26. U. Bhad. 27. Rev.

A. D. 1985. **Mesha Sankranti** (Commencement of Indian Sidereal Year).

Solar Eclipse. ● **(Surya Sid.) April 13·61.** **Saka 1907.** **Kaliyuga 5086.**

Lunar Eclipse. ○ **(Arya Sid.) April 13·50.** **(S. Cycle) Krodhana.**

SOLAR reckoning: Cyclic Sidereal Year, Month and Day. — LUNAR reckoning: Week-Day English Month and Day; Tithi Ending Moment; Nakshatra Ending Moment; Muhammadan Year, Month and Day.

Jan.

Solar month	Cyclic Sidereal Day	Week-Day	Jan.	Lunar month	Tithi Ending Moment	Nakshatra Ending Moment	Muhammadan Day	Muhammadan month
Raktaksha Dhanus—Margali.	17	Tu	1	Suk.	10 ·89	1 ·53	8	H. 1405 Rabi-ul-akhir.
	18	We	2		11 ·97	2 ·62	9	
	19	Th	3		... ...	3 ·70	10	
	20	Fr	4	Pausha	12 ·02	4 ·76	11	
	21	Sa	5		13 ·05	5 ·81	12	
	22	Su	6		14 ·07	6 ·83	13	
	23	Mo	7		P ·06	7 ·83	14	
	24	Tu	8		1 ·03 2 ·98	8 ·81	15	
	25	We	9		3 ·92	9 ·78	16	
	26	Th	10		4 ·85	10 ·73	17	
	27	Fr	11		5 ·77	11 ·67	18	
	28	Sa	12		6 ·67	12 ·61	19	
	29	Su	13	Bahula	7 ·57	13 ·54	20	
Raktaksha Makara—Tai.	1	Mo	14		8 ·47	14 ·47	21	
	2	Tu	15		9 ·38	15 ·41	22	
	3	We	16		10 ·29	16 ·35	23	
	4	Th	17		11 ·21	17 ·30	24	
	5	Fr	18		12 ·14	18 ·26	25	
	6	Sa	19		13 ·09	19 ·23	26	
	7	Su	20		14 ·06	20 ·23	27	
	8	Mo	21		A ·04	21 ·25	28	
	●9	Tu	22		1 ·03	22 ·29	29	
	10	We	23		2 ·09	23 ·35	1	
	11	Th	24		3 ·14	24 ·42	2	
	12	Fr	25		4 ·21	25 ·51	3	
	13	Sa	26		5 ·29	26 ·62	4	
	14	Su	27		6 ·38	27 ·73	5	
	15	Mo	28		7 ·47	1 ·83	6	
	16	Tu	29	Sukla	8 ·55	2 ·93	7	
	17	We	30		9 ·62	... ...	8	
	18	Th	31		10 ·67	3 ·01	9	

Feb.

Solar month	Cyclic Sidereal Day	Week-Day	Feb.	Lunar month	Tithi Ending Moment	Nakshatra Ending Moment	Muhammadan Day	Muhammadan month
	19	Fr	1		11 ·70	4 ·08	10	H. 1405 Jumadal-awwal.
	20	Sa	2		12 ·72	5 ·13	11	
	21	Su	3	Magha	13 ·70	6 ·15	12	
	22	Mo	4		14 ·66	7 ·16	13	
	23	Tu	5		P ·61	8 ·14	14	
	24	We	6		1 ·55	9 ·11	15	
	25	Th	7		2 ·48	10 ·07	16	
	26	Fr	8		3 ·39	11 ·01 12 ·95	17	
	27	Sa	9	Bahula	4 ·30	13 ·88	18	
	28	Su	10		5 ·20	14 ·81	19	
	29	Mo	11		6 ·10	15 ·74	20	
Raktaksha Kumbha—Masi.	1	Tu	12		7 ·00 8 ·91	16 ·68	21	
	2	We	13		9 ·83	17 ·63	22	
	3	Th	14		10 ·77	18 ·59	23	
	4	Fr	15		11 ·72	19 ·56	24	
	5	Sa	16		12 ·69	20 ·56	25	
	6	Su	17		13 ·68	21 ·57	26	
	7	Mo	18		14 ·68	22 ·60	27	
	8	Tu	19		A ·71	23 ·65	28	
	9	We	20		1 ·77	24 ·72	29	
	10	Th	21	Sukla	2 ·84	25 ·81	30	
	11	Fr	22		3 ·92	26 ·91	1	Jumadal-akhir.
	12	Sa	23		... ...	... ...	2	
	13	Su	24	Phalguna	4 ·01	27 ·02	3	
	14	Mo	25		5 ·09	1 ·13	4	
	15	Tu	26		6 ·17	2 ·23	5	
	16	We	27		7 ·24	3 ·32	6	
	17	Th	28		8 ·29	4 ·89	7	

March

Solar month	Cyclic Sidereal Day	Week-Day	March	Lunar month	Tithi Ending Moment	Nakshatra Ending Moment	Muhammadan Day	Muhammadan month
Raktaksha Kumbha—Masi.	18	Fr	1		9 ·32	5 ·44	8	H. 1405 Jumadal-akhir.
	19	Sa	2	Sukla	10 ·33	6 ·47	9	
	20	Su	3		11 ·31	7 ·48	10	
	21	Mo	4		12 ·28	8 ·47	11	
	22	Tu	5		13 ·22	9 ·45	12	
	23	We	6		14 ·16	10 ·41	13	
	24	Th	7		P ·09	11 ·35	14	
	25	Fr	8	Phalguna	1 ·00 2 ·90	12 ·29	15	
	26	Sa	9		3 ·80	13 ·23	16	
	27	Su	10		4 ·70	14 ·16	17	
	28	Mo	11		5 ·60	15 ·09	18	
	29	Tu	12		6 ·51	16 ·02 17 ·96	19	
	30	We	13		7 ·43	18 ·92	20	
Raktaksha Mina—Panguni.	1	Th	14	Bahula	8 ·86	19 ·90	21	
	2	Fr	15		9 ·31	20 ·88	22	
	3	Sa	16		10 ·28	21 ·89	23	
	4	Su	17		11 ·27	22 ·91	24	
	5	Mo	18		12 ·28	23 ·96	25	
	6	Tu	19		13 ·31	... ...	26	
	7	We	20		14 ·36	24 ·03	27	
	8	Th	21		A ·43	25 ·12	28	
	9	Fr	22		1 ·51	26 ·22	29	
	10	Sa	23		2 ·60	27 ·32	1	
	11	Su	24		3 ·69	1 ·43	2	
	12	Mo	25		4 ·77	2 ·53	3	
	13	Tu	26		5 ·83	3 ·62	4	
	14	We	27		6 ·87	4 ·70	5	
	15	Th	28		7 ·90	5 ·76	6	
	16	Fr	29	Sukla	8 ·91	6 ·79	7	
	17	Sa	30		9 ·89	7 ·80	8	
	18	Su	31		10 ·85	8 ·80	9	

April

Solar month	Cyclic Sidereal Day	Week-Day	April	Lunar month	Tithi Ending Moment	Nakshatra Ending Moment	Muhammadan Day	Muhammadan month
	19	Mo	1		11 ·80	9 ·78	10	H. 1405 Rajab.
	20	Tu	2		12 ·74	10 ·74	11	
	21	We	3	Chaitra	13 ·66	11 ·69	12	
	22	Th	4		14 ·56	12 ·63	13	
	23	Fr	5		P ·46	13 ·56	14	
	24	Sa	6		1 ·36	14 ·49	15	
	25	Su	7		2 ·26	15 ·42	16	
	26	Mo	8		3 ·16	16 ·36	17	
	27	Tu	9		4 ·07 5 ·99	17 ·30	18	
	28	We	10	Bahula	6 ·93	18 ·25	19	
	29	Th	11		7 ·88	19 ·23	20	
	30	Fr	12		8 ·84	20 ·21	21	
	31	Sa	13		9 ·83	21 ·21	22	
Krodhana Mesha—Chittirai.	1	Su	14		10 ·83	22 ·23	23	
	2	Mo	15		11 ·87	23 ·27	24	
	3	Tu	16		12 ·98	24 ·34	25	
	4	We	17		... ...	25 ·42	26	
	5	Th	18		13 ·00	26 ·52	27	
	6	Fr	19		14 ·08	27 ·63	28	
	7	Sa	20		A ·16	1 ·74	29	
	8	Su	21		1 ·24	2 ·84	30	
	9	Mo	22	Sukla	2 ·31	3 ·93	1	H. 1405 Shaban.
	10	Tu	23		3 ·37	... ...	2	
	11	We	24		4 ·42	4 ·01	3	
	12	Th	25		5 ·45	5 ·07	4	
	13	Fr	26	Vaisakha	6 ·45	6 ·11	5	
	14	Sa	27		7 ·44	7 ·13	6	
	15	Su	28		8 ·40	8 ·13	7	
	16	Mo	29		9 ·34	9 ·11	8	
	17	Tu	30		10 ·27	10 ·07	9	

May

Solar month	Cyclic Sidereal Day	Week-Day	May	Lunar month	Tithi Ending Moment	Nakshatra Ending Moment	Muhammadan Day	Muhammadan month
Krodhana Mesha—Chittirai.	18	We	1	Sukla	11 ·19	11 ·02 12 ·96	10	H. 1405 Shaban.
	19	Th	2		12 ·10	13 ·90	11	
	20	Fr	3		13 ·00 14 ·90	14 ·83	12	
	21	Sa ○	4	Vaisakha	P ·79	15 ·76	13	
	22	Su	5		1 ·69	16 ·69	14	
	23	Mo	6		2 ·60	17 ·63	15	
	24	Tu	7		3 ·52	18 ·59	16	
	25	We	8		4 ·46	19 ·55	17	
	26	Th	9		5 ·41	20 ·53	18	
	27	Fr	10		6 ·37	21 ·38	19	
	28	Sa	11	Bahula	7 ·35	22 ·55	20	
	29	Su	12		8 ·36	23 ·59	21	
	30	Mo	13		9 ·39	24 ·65	22	
Krodhana Vrishabha—Vaikasi.	1	Tu	14		10 ·44	25 ·73	23	
	2	We	15		11 ·50	26 ·82	24	
	3	Th	16		12 ·57	27 ·92	25	
	4	Fr	17		13 ·65	... ...	26	
	5	Sa	18		14 ·74	1 ·03	27	
	6	Su	19		A ·82	2 ·14	28	
	7	Mo	20		1 ·88	3 ·23	29	
	8	Tu	21		2 ·93	4 ·31	1	
	9	We	22		3 ·95	5 ·38	2	
	10	Th	23		4 ·96	6 ·43	3	
	11	Fr	24		5 ·94	7 ·45	4	
	12	Sa	25		6 ·91	8 ·45	5	
	13	Su	26	Sukla	7 ·86	9 ·43	6	
	14	Mo	27		8 ·79	10 ·40	7	
	15	Tu	28		9 ·70	11 ·36	8	
	16	We	29		10 ·60	12 ·31	9	
	17	Th	30		11 ·50	13 ·24	10	
	18	Fr	31		12 ·40	14 ·17	11	

June

Solar month	Cyclic Sidereal Day	Week-Day	June	Lunar month	Tithi Ending Moment	Nakshatra Ending Moment	Muhammadan Day	Muhammadan month
	19	Sa	1	Jyeshtha	13 ·30	15 ·10	12	H. 1405 Ramzan.
	20	Su	2		14 ·20	16 ·03 17 ·97	13	
	21	Mo	3		P ·11	18 ·92	14	
	22	Tu	4		1 ·08 2 ·96	19 ·88	15	
	23	We	5		3 ·91	20 ·86	16	
	24	Th	6		4 ·87	21 ·85	17	
	25	Fr	7		5 ·84	22 ·87	18	
	26	Sa	8		6 ·85	23 ·90	19	
	27	Su	9	Bahula	7 ·87	24 ·95	20	
	28	Mo	10		8 ·92	... ...	21	
	29	Tu	11		9 ·98	25 ·02	22	
	30	We	12		... ...	26 ·12	23	
	31	Th	13		10 ·05	27 ·23	24	
	32	Fr	14		11 ·13	1 ·34	25	
Krodhana Mithuna—Ani.	1	Sa	15		12 ·22	2 ·44	26	
	2	Su	16		13 ·30	3 ·54	27	
	3	Mo	17		14 ·36	4 ·62	28	
	4	Tu	18		A ·41	5 ·69	29	
	5	We	19		1 ·44	6 ·74	30	
	6	Th	20		2 ·45	7 ·77	1	H. 1405 Shawwal.
	7	Fr	21		3 ·42	8 ·78	2	
	8	Sa	22		4 ·39	9 ·76	3	
	9	Su	23	Sukla	5 ·34	10 ·73	4	
	10	Mo	24		6 ·27	11 ·70	5	
	11	Tu	25		7 ·19	12 ·64	6	
	12	We	26		8 ·09 9 ·99	13 ·58	7	
	13	Th	27	Ashad.	10 ·89	14 ·51	8	
	14	Fr	28		11 ·79	15 ·44	9	
	15	Sa	29		12 ·69	16 ·38	10	
	16	Su	30		13 ·59	17 ·32	11	

Naksh:—1. Asvn. 2. Bhar. 3. Krit. 4. Rohi. 5. Mrig. 6. Ardh. 7. Punar. 8. Push. 9. Aslesh. 10. Magh. 11. P. Phal. 12. U. Phal. 13. Hasta. 14. Chit.

A. D. 1985.
A.—Amavasya.
P.—Paurnami.

Kollam 1161, Commences { N. Malabar—Sept. / S. Malabar—Aug.

Hijra 1406, Commences, Sep. 16.

Vikrama 2042.
Bengal San 1391.
(N. Cycle) Bahudhanya.

July – August

SOLAR reckoning	Cyclic Sidereal Year, Month and Day	Week-Day	English Month and Day	LUNAR reckoning	Tithi Ending Moment	Nakshatra Ending Moment	Muhammadan Year, Month	Muhammadan Day
		July						
Krodhana Mithuna—Ani.	17	Mo	1	Ashadha	14 ·51	18 ·26	H. 1405 Shawwal.	12
	18	Tu	2		P ·44	19 ·22		13
	19	We	3		1 ·38	20 ·19		14
	20	Th	4		2 ·34	21 ·18		15
	21	Fr	5		3 ·32	22 ·19		16
	22	Sa	6		4 ·32	23 ·22		17
	23	Su	7		5 ·35	24 ·26		18
	24	Mo	8		6 ·40	25 ·33		19
	25	Tu	9	Bahula	7 ·46	26 ·42		20
	26	We	10		8 ·53	27 ·52		21
	27	Th	11		9 ·61	1 ·63		22
	28	Fr	12		10 ·70	2 ·74		23
	29	Sa	13		11 ·78	3 ·84		24
	30	Su	14		12 ·84	4 ·93		25
	—31	Mo	15		13 ·89	... ...		26
Krodhana Karkata—Adi.	1	Tu	16		14 ·91	5 ·01		27
	2	We	17		—A ·92	6 ·06		28
	3	Th	18	Sravana Sukla	1 ·90	7 ·09		—29
	4	Fr	19		2 ·87	8 ·10	Zi-l-ka'da.	1
	5	Sa	20		3 ·82	9 ·09		2
	6	Su	21		4 ·75	10 ·07		3
	7	Mo	22		5 ·67	11 ·03 } 12 ·98 }		4
	8	Tu	23		6 ·58	13 ·92		5
	9	We	24		7 ·48	14 ·86		6
	10	Th	25		8 ·38	15 ·79		7
	11	Fr	26		9 ·28	16 ·72		8
	12	Sa	27		10 ·18	17 ·65		9
	13	Su	28		11 ·08	18 ·59		10
	14	Mo	29		{ 12 ·00 { 13 ·92	19 ·55		11
	15	Tu	30		14 ·86	20 ·52		12
	16	We	31		P ·82	21 ·51		13
		Aug.						
	17	Th	1	Adhika	1 ·81	22 ·51	H. 1405	14
	18	Fr	2		2 ·81	23 ·53		15
	19	Sa	3		3 ·88	24 ·57		16
	20	Su	4		4 ·87	25 ·64		17
	21	Mo	5		5 ·93	26 ·72		18
	22	Tu	6		... ...	27 ·82		19
	23	We	7		6 ·01	1 ·93		20
	24	Th	8	Bahula	7 ·09	... ...		21
	25	Fr	9		8 ·17	2 ·04		22
	26	Sa	10		9 ·25	3 ·14		23
	27	Su	11		10 ·32	4 ·23		24
	28	Mo	12		11 ·37	5 ·31		25
	29	Tu	13		12 ·39	6 ·37		26
	30	We	14		13 ·41	7 ·41		27
	31	Th	15		14 ·39	8 ·42		28
	—32	Fr	16		—A ·37	9 ·42		29
Krodhana Simha—Avani.	1	Sa	17	Nija Sravana Sukla	1 ·32	10 ·40		—30
	2	Su	18		2 ·25	11 ·37	H. 1405 Zi-l-hijja.	1
	3	Mo	19		3 ·17	12 ·32		2
	4	Tu	20		{ 4 ·08 { 5 ·98	13 ·26		3
	5	We	21		6 ·88	14 ·20		4
	6	Th	22		7 ·77	15 ·13		5
	7	Fr	23		8 ·67	16 ·06 } 17 ·99 }		6
	8	Sa	24		9 ·58	18 ·93		7
	9	Su	25		10 ·50	19 ·88		8
	10	Mo	26		11 ·43	20 ·85		9
	11	Tu	27		12 ·37	21 ·83		10
	12	We	28		13 ·33	22 ·83		11
	13	Th	29		14 ·31	23 ·85		12
	14	Fr	30		P ·31	24 ·89		13
	15	Sa	31		1 ·33	25 ·95		14

September – October

SOLAR reckoning	Cyclic Sidereal Year, Month and Day	Week-Day	English Month and Day	LUNAR reckoning	Tithi Ending Moment	Nakshatra Ending Moment	Muhammadan Year, Month	Muhammadan Day
		Sep.						
Krodhana Simha—Avani.	16	Su	1	Nija Sravana	2 ·38	... ...	H. 1405 Zi-l-hijja.	15
	17	Mo	2		3 ·45	26 ·03		16
	18	Tu	3		4 ·52	27 ·12		17
	19	We	4		5 ·60	1 ·22		18
	20	Th	5		6 ·68	2 ·33		19
	21	Fr	6		7 ·76	3 ·44		20
	22	Sa	7		8 ·83	4 ·54		21
	23	Su	8		9 ·88	5 ·62		22
	24	Mo	9		10 ·91	6 ·68		23
	25	Tu	10	Bahula	11 ·93	7 ·72		24
	26	We	11		12 ·92	8 ·75		25
	27	Th	12		13 ·89	9 ·75		26
	28	Fr	13		14 ·84	10 ·78		27
	29	Sa	14		—A ·78	11 ·70		28
	30	Su	15		1 ·70	12 ·65		—29
	—31	Mo	16		2 ·61	13 ·60	Muharram.	1
Krodhana Kanya—Purattasi.	1	Tu	17	Bhadrapada Sukla	3 ·51	14 ·53		2
	2	We	18		4 ·41	15 ·46		3
	3	Th	19		5 ·31	16 ·39		4
	4	Fr	20		6 ·21	17 ·38		5
	5	Sa	21		7 ·11	18 ·27		6
	6	Su	22		{ 8 ·03 { 9 ·96	19 ·22		7
	7	Mo	23		10 ·91	20 ·18		8
	8	Tu	24		11 ·87	21 ·16		9
	9	We	25		12 ·85	22 ·15		10
	10	Th	26		13 ·84	23 ·16		11
	11	Fr	27		14 ·87	24 ·20		12
	12	Sa	28		P ·92	25 ·26		13
	13	Su	29		1 ·98	26 ·33		14
	14	Mo	30		... ...	27 ·42		15
		Oct.						
	15	Tu	1		2 ·06	1 ·52	H. 1406	16
	16	We	2		3 ·15	2 ·63		17
	17	Th	3		4 ·23	3 ·74		18
	18	Fr	4		5 ·31	4 ·84		19
	19	Sa	5	Bahula	6 ·38	5 ·92		20
	20	Su	6		7 ·43	6 ·99		21
	21	Mo	7		8 ·46	... ...		22
	22	Tu	8		9 ·48	7 ·04		23
	23	We	9		10 ·48	8 ·07		24
	24	Th	10		11 ·45	9 ·08		25
	25	Fr	11		12 ·41	10 ·06		26
	26	Sa	12		13 ·34	11 ·08 } 12 ·99 }		27
	27	Su	13		14 ·26	13 ·94		28
	28	Mo	14		—A ·17	14 ·87		29
	29	Tu	15		{ 1 ·07 { 2 ·97	15 ·80		—30
	—30	We	16	Asvina Sukla	3 ·87	16 ·73	H. 1406 Safar.	1
Krodhana Tula—Aippasi.	1	Th	17		4 ·77	17 ·66		2
	2	Fr	18		5 ·68	18 ·60		3
	3	Sa	19		6 ·60	19 ·55		4
	4	Su	20		7 ·54	20 ·51		5
	5	Mo	21		8 ·49	21 ·48		6
	6	Tu	22		9 ·45	22 ·47		7
	7	We	23		10 ·43	23 ·49		8
	8	Th	24		11 ·44	24 ·52		9
	9	Fr	25		12 ·46	25 ·57		10
	10	Sa	26		13 ·51	26 ·64		11
	11	Su	27		14 ·57	27 ·78		12
	12	Mo ○	28		P ·65	1 ·83		13
	13	Tu	29		1 ·73	2 ·94		14
	14	We	30	Bah.	2 ·83	... ...		15
	15	Th	31		3 ·91	3 ·04		16

November – December

SOLAR reckoning	Cyclic Sidereal Year, Month and Day	Week-Day	English Month and Day	LUNAR reckoning	Tithi Ending Moment	Nakshatra Ending Moment	Muhammadan Year, Month	Muhammadan Day
		Nov.						
Krodhana Tula—Aippasi.	16	Fr	1	Asvn. Bahula	4 ·97	4 ·14	H. 1406 Safar.	17
	17	Sa	2		... ...	5 ·23		18
	18	Su	3		5 ·02	6 ·31		19
	19	Mo	4		6 ·03	7 ·36		20
	20	Tu	5		7 ·08	8 ·39		21
	21	We	6		8 ·07	9 ·40		22
	22	Th	7		9 ·04	10 ·39		23
	23	Fr	8		{ 10 ·00 { 11 ·94	11 ·36		24
	24	Sa	9		12 ·86	12 ·32		25
	25	Su	10		13 ·77	13 ·27		26
	26	Mo	11		14 ·68	14 ·21		27
	27	Tu	12		—A ·58	15 ·14		28
	28	We	13	Kartika Sukla	1 ·48	16 ·07		—29
	29	Th	14		2 ·39	17 ·01 } 18 ·95 }	Rabi-ul-awwal.	1
	—30	Fr	15		3 ·30	19 ·89		2
Krodhana Vrischika—Kartigai.	1	Sa	16		4 ·22	20 ·84		3
	2	Su	17		5 ·15	21 ·81		4
	3	Mo	18		6 ·10	22 ·80		5
	4	Tu	19		7 ·06	23 ·81		6
	5	We	20		8 ·04	24 ·83		7
	6	Th	21		9 ·05	25 ·88		8
	7	Fr	22		10 ·08	26 ·95		9
	8	Sa	23		11 ·13	... ...		10
	9	Su	24		12 ·19	27 ·03		11
	10	Mo	25		13 ·27	1 ·13		12
	11	Tu	26		14 ·37	2 ·24		13
	12	We	27		P ·45	3 ·34		14
	13	Th	28		1 ·53	4 ·44		15
	14	Fr	29		2 ·60	5 ·54		16
	15	Sa	30		3 ·66	6 ·62		17
		Dec.						
	16	Su	1		4 ·69	7 ·67	H. 1406	18
	17	Mo	2		5 ·71	8 ·71		19
	18	Tu	3	Bahula	6 ·69	9 ·72		20
	19	We	4		7 ·67	10 ·72		21
	20	Th	5		8 ·62	11 ·70		22
	21	Fr	6		9 ·55	12 ·66		23
	22	Sa	7		10 ·48	13 ·61		24
	23	Su	8		11 ·40	14 ·55		25
	24	Mo	9		12 ·31	15 ·49		26
	25	Tu	10		13 ·21	16 ·42		27
	26	We	11		14 ·11	17 ·35		28
	27	Th	12		{ A ·01 { 1 ·92	18 ·28		29
	28	Fr	13	Margasira Sukla	2 ·85	19 ·22		—30
	29	Sa	14		3 ·78	20 ·18	H. 1406 Rabi-ul-akhir.	1
	—30	Su	15		4 ·78	21 ·15		2
Krodhana Dhanus—Margali.	1	Mo	16		5 ·70	22 ·13		3
	2	Tu	17		6 ·69	23 ·13		4
	3	We	18		7 ·69	24 ·15		5
	4	Th	19		8 ·72	25 ·19		6
	5	Fr.	20		9 ·77	26 ·26		7
	6	Sa	21		10 ·84	27 ·34		8
	7	Su	22		11 ·92	1 ·43		9
	8	Mo	23		... ...	2 ·53		10
	9	Tu	24		12 ·02	3 ·61		11
	10	We	25		13 ·11	4 ·74		12
	11	Th	26		14 ·19	5 ·84		13
	12	Fr	27		P ·26	6 ·92		14
	13	Sa	28		1 ·31	7 ·98		15
	14	Su	29		2 ·34	... ...		16
	15	Mo	30	Bah.	3 ·36	8 ·02		17
	16	Tu	31		4 ·34	9 ·04		18

15. Svati. 16. Visak. 17. Anur. 18. Jyesh. 19. Mula. 20. P. Ash. 21. U. Ash. 22. Sravn. 23. Dani. 24. Satab. 25. P. Bhad. 26. U. Bhad. 27. Rev.

A. D. 1986. **Mesha Sankranti** (Commencement of Indian Sidereal Year).

Solar Eclipse. ● **(Surya Sid.) April 13·87.** **Saka 1908.** **Kaliyuga 5087.**

Lunar Eclipse. ○ **(Arya Sid.) April 13·76.** **(S. Cycle) Kshaya** (Akshaya).

SOLAR reckoning: Cyclic Sidereal Year, Month and Day; Week-Day English Month and Day. LUNAR reckoning: Tithi Ending Moment; Nakshatra Ending Moment; Muhammadan Year, Month and Day.

Jan. (Solar: Krodhana *Dhanus—Margali.* / Krodhana *Makara—Tai.*; Lunar: Margasira *Bahula* / Pausha *Sukla*; Muhammadan: H. 1406 *Rabi-ul-akhir.* / H. 1406 *Jumadal-awwal.*)

Cyclic Sidereal Year, Month and Day	Week-Day English Month and Day	Tithi Ending Moment	Nakshatra Ending Moment	Muhammadan Year, Month and Day
17	We 1	5 ·31	10 ·05	19
18	Th 2	6 ·26	11 ·03 12 ·99	20
19	Fr 3	7 ·20	13 ·95	21
20	Sa 4	8 ·12	14 ·89	22
21	Su 5	9 ·04 10 ·95	15 ·83	23
22	Mo 6	11 ·85	16 ·76	24
23	Tu 7	12 ·75	17 ·69	25
24	We 8	13 ·66	18 ·62	26
25	Th 9	14 ·57	19 ·56	27
26	Fr 10	—A ·49	20 ·52	28
27	Sa 11	1 ·42	21 ·48	—29
28	Su 12	2 ·37	22 ·45	1
—29	Mo 13	3 ·34	23 ·45	2
1	Tu 14	4 ·33	24 ·46	3
2	We 15	5 ·33	25 ·50	4
3	Th 16	6 ·37	26 ·56	5
4	Fr 17	7 ·42	27 ·64	6
5	Sa 18	8 ·50	1 ·73	7
6	Su 19	9 ·59	2 ·83	8
7	Mo 20	10 ·68	3 ·94	9
8	Tu 21	11 ·76	... ...	10
9	We 22	12 ·84	4 ·05	11
10	Th 23	13 ·91	5 ·15	12
11	Fr 24	14 ·95	6 ·23	13
12	Sa 25	P ·98	7 ·29	14
13	Su 26	... ...	8 ·34	15
14	Mo 27	1 ·00 2 ·98	9 ·37	16
15	Tu 28	3 ·95	10 ·38	17
16	We 29	4 ·90	11 ·36	18
17	Th 30	5 ·84	12 ·33	19
18	Fr 31	6 ·76	13 ·28	20

Feb. (Solar: Krodhana *Kumbha—Masi.*; Lunar: *Bahula* / *Sukla* Magha / *Bah.*; Muhammadan: H. 1406 *Jumadal-akhir.*)

Cyclic Sidereal Year, Month and Day	Week-Day English Month and Day	Tithi Ending Moment	Nakshatra Ending Moment	Muhammadan Year, Month and Day
19	Sa 1	7 ·67	14 ·23	21
20	Su 2	8 ·58	15 ·17	22
21	Mo 3	9 ·48	16 ·10	23
22	Tu 4	10 ·38	17 ·03 18 ·96	24
23	We 5	11 ·28	19 ·90	25
24	Th 6	12 ·19	20 ·85	26
25	Fr 7	13 ·11	21 ·81	27
26	Sa 8	14 ·05	22 ·78	28
27	Su 9	A ·01 1 ·98	23 ·77	29
28	Mo 10	2 ·96	24 ·78	—30
29	Tu 11	3 ·97	25 ·82	1
—30	We 12	... ...	26 ·87	2
1	Th 13	4 ·01	27 ·94	3
2	Fr 14	5 ·06	... ...	4
3	Sa 15	6 ·13	1 ·03	5
4	Su 16	7 ·22	2 ·13	6
5	Mo 17	8 ·31	3 ·24	7
6	Tu 18	9 ·39	4 ·35	8
7	We 19	10 ·46	5 ·45	9
8	Th 20	11 ·53	6 ·53	10
9	Fr 21	12 ·58	7 ·60	11
10	Sa 22	13 ·62	8 ·66	12
11	Su 23	14 ·62	9 ·69	13
12	Mo 24	P ·61	10 ·70	14
13	Tu 25	1 ·57	11 ·69	15
14	We 26	2 ·52	12 ·66	16
15	Th 27	3 ·46	13 ·62	17
16	Fr 28	4 ·38	14 ·57	18

March (Solar: Krodhana *Kumbha—Masi.* / Krodhana *Mina—Panguni.*; Lunar: Mg. *Bahula* / *Sukla* Phalguna; Muhammadan: H. 1406 *Jumadal-akhir.* / H. 1406 *Rajab.*)

Cyclic Sidereal Year, Month and Day	Week-Day English Month and Day	Tithi Ending Moment	Nakshatra Ending Moment	Muhammadan Year, Month and Day
17	Sa 1	5 ·29	15 ·51	19
18	Su 2	6 ·19	16 ·44	20
19	Mo 3	7 ·09 8 ·99	17 ·37	21
20	Tu 4	9 ·90	18 ·30	22
21	We 5	10 ·81	19 ·24	23
22	Th 6	11 ·73	20 ·18	24
23	Fr 7	12 ·66	21 ·14	25
24	Sa 8	13 ·62	22 ·11	26
25	Su 9	14 ·59	23 ·09	27
26	Mo 10	—A ·57	24 ·11	28
27	Tu 11	1 ·58	25 ·14	—29
28	We 12	2 ·62	26 ·18	1
—29	Th 13	3 ·67	27 ·25	2
1	Fr 14	4 ·74	1 ·33	3
2	Sa 15	5 ·82	2 ·43	4
3	Su 16	6 ·91	3 ·54	5
4	Mo 17	7 ·99	4 ·65	6
5	Tu 18	... ...	5 ·75	7
6	We 19	8 ·07	6 ·84	8
7	Th 20	9 ·13	7 ·92	9
8	Fr 21	10 ·19	8 ·98	10
9	Sa 22	11 ·22	... ...	11
10	Su 23	12 ·21	9 ·01	12
11	Mo 24	13 ·20	10 ·02	13
12	Tu 25	14 ·16	11 ·01	14
13	We 26	P ·11	12 ·00 13 ·96	15
14	Th 27	1 ·04 2 ·96	14 ·90	16
15	Fr 28	3 ·87	15 ·84	17
16	Sa 29	4 ·77	16 ·77	18
17	Su 30	5 ·67	17 ·70	19
18	Mo 31	6 ·57	18 ·64	20

April (Solar: Kshaya *Mesha—Chittirai.*; Lunar: *Bahula* / *Sukla* Chaitra / *Bahula*; Muhammadan: H. 1406 *Shaban.*)

Cyclic Sidereal Year, Month and Day	Week-Day English Month and Day	Tithi Ending Moment	Nakshatra Ending Moment	Muhammadan Year, Month and Day
19	Tu 1	7 ·47	19 ·58	21
20	We 2	8 ·38	20 ·52	22
21	Th 3	9 ·30	21 ·47	23
22	Fr 4	10 ·24	22 ·44	24
23	Sa 5	11 ·19	23 ·43	25
24	Su 6	12 ·16	24 ·43	26
25	Mo 7	13 ·14	25 ·45	27
26	Tu 8	14 ·15	26 ·49	28
27	We 9	—A ·18	27 ·55	29
28	Th 10	1 ·23	1 ·64	—30
29	Fr 11	2 ·30	2 ·74	1
30	Sa 12	3 ·38	3 ·84	2
—31	Su 13	4 ·47	4 ·95	3
1	Mo 14	5 ·55	... ...	4
2	Tu 15	6 ·63	5 ·05	5
3	We 16	7 ·69	6 ·15	6
4	Th 17	8 ·74	7 ·23	7
5	Fr 18	9 ·76	8 ·29	8
6	Sa 19	10 ·77	9 ·33	9
7	Su 20	11 ·75	10 ·34	10
8	Mo 21	12 ·71	11 ·34	11
9	Tu 22	13 ·65	12 ·38	12
10	We 23	14 ·58	13 ·29	13
11	Th ○ 24	P ·50	14 ·24	14
12	Fr 25	1 ·41	15 ·18	15
13	Sa 26	2 ·31	16 ·12	16
14	Su 27	3 ·21	17 ·05 18 ·98	17
15	Mo 28	4 ·11	19 ·91	18
16	Tu 29	5 ·01 6 ·91	20 ·85	19
17	We 30	7 ·83	21 ·80	20

May (Solar: Kshaya *Mesha—Chittirai.* / Kshaya *Vrishabha—Vaikasi.*; Lunar: Chaitra *Bah.* / *Sukla* Yasakha; Muhammadan: H. 1406 *Shaban.* / H. 1406 *Ramzan.*)

Cyclic Sidereal Year, Month and Day	Week-Day English Month and Day	Tithi Ending Moment	Nakshatra Ending Moment	Muhammadan Year, Month and Day
18	Th 1	8 ·77	22 ·77	21
19	Fr 2	9 ·73	23 ·75	22
20	Sa 3	10 ·69	24 ·75	23
21	Su 4	11 ·67	25 ·76	24
22	Mo 5	12 ·67	26 ·80	25
23	Tu 6	13 ·71	27 ·87	26
24	We 7	14 ·76	1 ·95	27
25	Th 8	—A ·82	... ...	28
26	Fr 9	1 ·90	2 ·04	—29
27	Sa 10	2 ·98	3 ·14	1
28	Su 11	... ...	4 ·24	2
29	Mo 12	3 ·06	5 ·35	3
30	Tu 13	4 ·14	6 ·45	4
—31	We 14	5 ·21	7 ·54	5
1	Th 15	6 ·25	8 ·60	6
2	Fr 16	7 ·27	9 ·64	7
3	Sa 17	8 ·28	10 ·67	8
4	Su 18	9 ·26	11 ·67	9
5	Mo 19	10 ·23	12 ·65	10
6	Tu 20	11 ·17	13 ·62	11
7	We 21	12 ·10	14 ·58	12
8	Th 22	13 ·01 14 ·92	15 ·53	13
9	Fr 23	P ·82	16 ·46	14
10	Sa 24	1 ·72	17 ·39	15
11	Su 25	2 ·62	18 ·33	16
12	Mo 26	3 ·52	19 ·25	17
13	Tu 27	4 ·43	20 ·19	18
14	We 28	5 ·34	21 ·14	19
15	Th 29	6 ·27	22 ·10	20
16	Fr 30	7 ·22	23 ·08	21
17	Sa 31	8 ·18	24 ·07	22

June (Solar: Kshaya *Mithuna—Ani.*; Lunar: *Bahula* / *Sukla* Jyeshtha / *Bahula*; Muhammadan: H. 1406 *Shawwal.*)

Cyclic Sidereal Year, Month and Day	Week-Day English Month and Day	Tithi Ending Moment	Nakshatra Ending Moment	Muhammadan Year, Month and Day
18	Su 1	9 ·17	25 ·08	23
19	Mo 2	10 ·18	26 ·12	24
20	Tu 3	11 ·21	27 ·18	25
21	We 4	12 ·25	1 ·25	26
22	Th 5	13 ·32	2 ·34	27
23	Fr 6	14 ·40	3 ·44	28
24	Sa 7	—A ·48	4 ·55	29
25	Su 8	1 ·56	5 ·66	—30
26	Mo 9	2 ·64	6 ·76	1
27	Tu 10	3 ·70	7 ·84	2
28	We 11	4 ·74	8 ·91	3
29	Th 12	5 ·77	9 ·96	4
30	Fr 13	6 ·77	10 ·99	5
—31	Sa 14	7 ·74	... ...	6
1	Su 15	8 ·71	11 ·00 12 ·98	7
2	Mo 16	9 ·66	13 ·95	8
3	Tu 17	10 ·59	14 ·91	9
4	We 18	11 ·50	15 ·86	10
5	Th 19	12 ·41	16 ·80	11
6	Fr 20	13 ·31	17 ·73	12
7	Sa 21	14 ·20	18 ·66	13
8	Su 22	P ·10	19 ·59	14
9	Mo 23	1 ·00 2 ·91	20 ·53	15
10	Tu 24	3 ·83	21 ·48	16
11	We 25	4 ·76	22 ·43	17
12	Th 26	5 ·70	23 ·40	18
13	Fr 27	6 ·66	24 ·39	19
14	Sa 28	7 ·65	25 ·41	20
15	Su 29	8 ·65	26 ·44	21
16	Mo 30	9 ·68	27 ·48	22

Naksh :—1. Asvn. 2. Bhar. 3. Krit. 4. Rohi. 5. Mrig. 6. Ardh. 7. Punar. 8. Push. 9. Aslesh. 10. Magh. 11. P. Phal. 12. U. Phal. 13. Hasta. 14. Chit.

A. D. 1986.
A.—Amavasya.
P.—Paurnami.

Kollam 1162, Commences { N. Malabar—Sept. S. Malabar—Aug.

Hijra 1407, Commences, Sep. 6.

Vikrama 2043.
Bengal San 1392.
(N. Cycle) Pramathin.

SOLAR reckoning: Cyclic Sidereal Year, Month and Day; Week-Day English Month and Day. LUNAR reckoning: Tithi Ending Moment; Nakshatra Ending Moment; Muhammadan Year, Month and Day.

July

Solar: Kshaya Mithuna—Ani. (17–31); Kshaya Karkata—Adi. (1–15). Lunar: Jyesh. Bah.; Ashadha Sukla; Bahula. Muhammadan: Shawwal.; H. 1406 Zi-l-ka'da.

Cyclic Sidereal Year, Month and Day	Week-Day	English Day	Tithi	Ending Moment	Nakshatra	Ending Moment	Muhammadan Year, Month and Day
17	Tu	1	10	·73	1	·55	23
18	We	2	11	·80	2	·64	24
19	Th	3	12	·87	3	·74	25
20	Fr	4	13	·95	4	·85	26
21	Sa	5	...	...	5	·96	27
22	Su	6	14	·03	...	...	28
23	Mo	7	—A	·10	6	·06	—29
24	Tu	8	1	·16	7	·15	1
25	We	9	2	·21	8	·22	2
26	Th	10	3	·24	9	·28	3
27	Fr	11	4	·24	10	·31	4
28	Sa	12	5	·28	11	·32	5
29	Su	13	6	·19	12	·31	6
30	Mo	14	7	·13	13	·28	7
31	Tu	15	8 9	·06 ·98	14	·25	8
—32	We	16	10	·89	15	·20	9
1	Th	17	11	·79	16	·14	10
2	Fr	18	12	·69	17	·07	11
3	Sa	19	13	·59	18 19	·00 ·93	12
4	Su	20	14	·49	20	·87	13
5	Mo	21	P	·39	21	·81	14
6	Tu	22	1	·31	22	·77	15
7	We	23	2	·24	23	·74	16
8	Th	24	3	·18	24	·73	17
9	Fr	25	4	·15	25	·73	18
10	Sa	26	5	·13	26	·75	19
11	Su	27	6	·14	27	·79	20
12	Mo	28	7	·15	1	·86	21
13	Tu	29	8	·19	2	·95	22
14	We	30	9	·26	...	...	23
15	Th	31	10	·34	3	·05	24

Aug.

Solar: Kshaya Simha—Avani. (1–15). Lunar: Sukla; Sravana; Bahula. Muhammadan: H. 1403 Zi-l-hijja.

Cyclic Sidereal Year, Month and Day	Week-Day	English Day	Tithi	Ending Moment	Nakshatra	Ending Moment	Muhammadan Year, Month and Day
16	Fr	1	11	·42	4	·15	25
17	Sa	2	12	·50	5	·26	26
18	Su	3	13	·58	6	·36	27
19	Mo	4	14	·64	7	·45	28
20	Tu	5	—A	·69	8	·53	29
21	We	6	1	·73	9	·59	—30
22	Th	7	2	·73	10	·63	1
23	Fr	8	3	·71	11	·64	2
24	Sa	9	4	·67	12	·64	3
25	Su	10	5	·63	13	·62	4
26	Mo	11	6	·57	14	·59	5
27	Tu	12	7	·49	15	·53	6
28	We	13	8	·39	16	·47	7
29	Th	14	9	·29	17	·41	8
30	Fr	15	10	·19	18	·35	9
—31	Sa	16	11 12	·09 ·99	19	·28	10
1	Su	17	13	·89	20	·21	11
2	Mo	18	14	·81	21	·15	12
3	Tu	19	P	·74	22	·10	13
4	We	20	1	·69	23	·07	14
5	Th	21	2	·65	24	·05	15
6	Fr	22	3	·62	25	·05	16
7	Sa	23	4	·63	26	·07	17
8	Su	24	5	·65	27	·10	18
9	Mo	25	6	·70	1	·16	19
10	Tu	26	7	·77	2	·24	20
11	We	27	8	·84	3	·34	21
12	Th	28	9	·92	4	·45	22
13	Fr	29	...	...	5	·56	23
14	Sa	30	10	·00	6	·66	24
15	Su	31	11	·08	7	·76	25

Sep.

Solar: Kshaya Simha—Avani. (16–31); Kshaya Kanya—Purattasi. (1–14). Lunar: Bah.; Sukla; Bhadrapada; Bahula. Muhammadan: Zi-l-hijja.; H. 1407 Muharram.

Cyclic Sidereal Year, Month and Day	Week-Day	English Day	Tithi	Ending Moment	Nakshatra	Ending Moment	Muhammadan Year, Month and Day
16	Mo	1	12	·15	8	·84	26
17	Tu	2	13	·20	9	·90	27
18	We	3	14	·23	10	·94	28
19	Th	4	—A	·25	11	·96	29
20	Fr	5	1	·23	12	·97	—30
21	Sa	6	2	·20	13	·95	1
22	Su	7	3	·15	14	·92	2
23	Mo	8	4	·08	15	·87	3
24	Tu	9	5 6	·00 ·91	16	·81	4
25	We	10	7	·81	17	·75	5
26	Th	11	8	·71	18	·68	6
27	Fr	12	9	·61	19	·61	7
28	Sa	13	10	·51	20	·55	8
29	Su	14	11	·42	21	·49	9
30	Mo	15	12	·34	22	·44	10
—31	Tu	16	13	·27	23	·40	11
1	We	17	14	·21	24	·38	12
2	Th	18	P	·17	25	·37	13
3	Fr	19	1	·15	26	·38	14
4	Sa	20	2	·17	27	·42	15
5	Su	21	3	·19	1	·48	16
6	Mo	22	4	·24	2	·55	17
7	Tu	23	5	·30	3	·64	18
8	We	24	6	·37	4	·74	19
9	Th	25	7	·45	5	·85	20
10	Fr	26	8	·54	6	·96	21
11	Sa	27	9	·62	...	...	22
12	Su	28	10	·69	7	·06	23
13	Mo	29	11	·74	8	·14	24
14	Tu	30	12	·77	9	·21	25

Oct.

Solar: Kshaya Tula—Aippasi. (1–14). Lunar: Sukla; Asvina; Bahula. Muhammadan: H. 1407 Safar.

Cyclic Sidereal Year, Month and Day	Week-Day	English Day	Tithi	Ending Moment	Nakshatra	Ending Moment	Muhammadan Year, Month and Day
15	We	1	13	·79	10	·26	26
16	Th	2	14	·77	11	·29	27
17	Fr	3	—A	·75	12	·30	28
18	Sa	4	1	·70	13	·28	29
19	Su	5	2	·63	14	·25	—30
20	Mo	6	3	·55	15	·21	1
21	Tu	7	4	·46	16	·16	2
22	We	8	5	·37	17	·09	3
23	Th	9	6	·27	18 19	·02 ·95	4
24	Fr	10	7	·17	20	·88	5
25	Sa	11	8 9	·07 ·98	21	·82	6
26	Su	12	10	·90	22	·77	7
27	Mo	13	11	·83	23	·73	8
28	Tu	14	12	·78	24	·70	9
29	We	15	13	·74	25	·69	10
30	Th	16	14	·73	26	·70	11
—31	Fr ○	17	P	·74	27	·74	12
1	Sa	18	1	·76	1	·79	13
2	Su	19	2	·81	2	·86	14
3	Mo	20	3	·88	3	·94	15
4	Tu	21	4	·96	...	...	16
5	We	22	...	...	4	·04	17
6	Th	23	5	·04	5	·15	18
7	Fr	24	6	·13	6	·26	19
8	Sa	25	7	·21	7	·36	20
9	Su	26	8	·28	8	·45	21
10	Mo	27	9	·32	9	·52	22
11	Tu	28	10	·35	10	·58	23
12	We	29	11	·38	11	·61	24
13	Th	30	12	·36	12	·62	25
14	Fr	31	13	·33	13	·61	26

Nov.

Solar: Kshaya Tula—Aippasi. (15–30); Kshaya Vrischika—Kartigai. (1–14). Lunar: Sukla; Karttika; Bahula. Muhammadan: H. 1407 Rabi-ul-awwal.

Cyclic Sidereal Year, Month and Day	Week-Day	English Day	Tithi	Ending Moment	Nakshatra	Ending Moment	Muhammadan Year, Month and Day
15	Sa	1	14	·28	14	·58	27
16	Su	2	—A	·22	15	·55	28
17	Mo	3	1	·15	16	·49	—29
18	Tu	4	2 3	·06 ·96	17	·43	1
19	We	5	4	·86	18	·36	2
20	Th	6	5	·76	19	·29	3
21	Fr	7	6	·66	20	·23	4
22	Sa	8	7	·58	21	·17	5
23	Su	9	8	·50	22	·11	6
24	Mo	10	9	·43	23	·06	7
25	Tu	11	10	·37	24	·03	8
26	We	12	11	·34	25	·01	9
27	Th	13	12	·34	26	·03	10
28	Fr	14	13	·35	27	·06	11
29	Sa	15	14	·37	1	·10	12
—30	Su	16	P	·42	2	·16	13
1	Mo	17	1	·49	3	·24	14
2	Tu	18	2	·57	4	·34	15
3	We	19	3	·66	5	·45	16
4	Th	20	4	·75	6	·56	17
5	Fr	21	5	·83	7	·66	18
6	Sa	22	6	·90	8	·75	19
7	Su	23	7	·95	9	·83	20
8	Mo	24	8	·98	10	·89	21
9	Tu	25	9	·99	11	·93	22
10	We	26	10	·99	12	·94	23
11	Th	27	11	·95	13	·94	24
12	Fr	28	12	·90	14	·92	25
13	Sa	29	13	·84	15	·88	26
14	Su	30	14	·77	16	·83	27

Dec.

Solar: Kshaya Dhanus—Margali. (1–16). Lunar: Sukla; Margasira; Bahula. Muhammadan: H. 1407 Rabi-ul-akhir.

Cyclic Sidereal Year, Month and Day	Week-Day	English Day	Tithi	Ending Moment	Nakshatra	Ending Moment	Muhammadan Year, Month and Day
15	Mo	1	—A	·68	17	·77	28
16	Tu	2	1	·59	18	·70	29
17	We	3	2	·49	19	·63	—30
18	Th	4	3	·39	20	·56	1
19	Fr	5	4	·29	21	·50	2
20	Sa	6	5	·20	22	·44	3
21	Su	7	6	·12	23	·89	4
22	Mo	8	7	·06	24	·36	5
23	Tu	9	8 9	·01 ·98	25	·85	6
24	We	10	10	·97	26	·35	7
25	Th	11	11	·98	27	·37	8
26	Fr	12	...	...	1	·41	9
27	Sa	13	12	·01	2	·47	10
28	Su	14	13	·07	3	·55	11
—29	Mo	15	14	·14	4	·65	12
1	Tu	16	P	·22	5	·76	13
2	We	17	1	·32	6	·86	14
3	Th	18	2	·40	7	·96	15
4	Fr	19	3	·48	...	...	16
5	Sa	20	4	·54	8	·06	17
6	Su	21	5	·59	9	·14	18
7	Mo	22	6	·63	10	·20	19
8	Tu	23	7	·64	11	·24	20
9	We	24	8	·63	12	·26	21
10	Th	25	9	·59	13	·26	22
11	Fr	26	10	·54	14	·25	23
12	Sa	27	11	·48	15	·22	24
13	Su	28	12	·40	16	·17	25
14	Mo	29	13	·32	17	·11	26
15	Tu	30	14	·23	18 19	·05 ·98	27
16	We	31	—A	·13	20	·91	28

15. Svati. 16. Visak. 17. Anur. 18. Jyesh. 19. Mula. 20. P. Ash. 21. U. Ash. 22. Sravn. 23. Dani. 24. Sa...b. 25. P. Bhad. 26. U. Bhad. 27. Rev.

A. D. 1987. **Mesha Sankranti** (Commencement of Indian Sidereal Year).
Solar Eclipse. ● **(Surya Sid.) April 14·13.** **Saka 1909.** **Kaliyuga 5088.**
Lunar Eclipse. ⊙ **(Arya Sid.) April 14·02.** **(S. Cycle) Prabhava.**

SOLAR reckoning: Cyclic Sidereal Year, Month and Day; Week-Day English Month and Day. LUNAR reckoning: Tithi Ending Moment; Nakshatra Ending Moment; Muhammadan Year, Month and Day.

Jan. (Kshaya *Dhanus—Margali*; Kshaya *Makara—Tai*. Lunar: *Sukla*, **Pausha**, *Bahula*. H. 1407 *Jumadal-awwal*.)

Cyclic Sidereal Year, Month and Day	Week-Day	English Month and Day	Tithi Ending Moment	Nakshatra Ending Moment	Muhammadan Year, Month and Day
17	Th	1	1 ·03 2 ·93	21 ·84	—29
18	Fr	2	3 ·84	22 ·78	1
19	Sa	3	4 ·76	23 ·73	2
20	Su	4	5 ·70	24 ·70	3
21	Mo	5	6 ·66	25 ·67	4
22	Tu	6	7 ·63	26 ·67	5
23	We	7	8 ·61	27 ·68	6
24	Th	8	9 ·64	1 ·72	7
25	Fr	9	10 ·67	2 ·78	8
26	Sa	10	11 ·72	3 ·86	9
27	Su	11	12 ·79	4 ·95	10
28	Mo	12	13 ·87	... ...	11
—29	Tu	13	14 ·96	5 ·05	12
1	We	14	... ...	6 ·16	13
2	Th	15	P ·05	7 ·27	14
3	Fr	16	1 ·13	8 ·37	15
4	Sa	17	2 ·19	9 ·45	16
5	Su	18	3 ·24	10 ·51	17
6	Mo	19	4 ·28	11 ·55	18
7	Tu	20	5 ·28	12 ·58	19
8	We	21	6 ·27	13 ·59	20
9	Th	22	7 ·24	14 ·58	21
10	Fr	23	8 ·19	15 ·55	22
11	Sa	24	9 ·12	16 ·50	23
12	Su	25	10 ·04 11 ·95	17 ·44	24
13	Mo	26	12 ·86	18 ·38	25
14	Tu	27	13 ·76	19 ·32	26
15	We	28	14 ·66	20 ·25	27
16	Th	29	—A ·56	21 ·18	28
17	Fr	30	1 ·48	22 ·12	29
18	Sa	31	2 ·40	23 ·07	—30

Feb. (Kshaya *Kumbha—Masi*. Lunar: *Sukla*, **Magha**, *Bahula*. H. 1407 *Jumadal-akhir*.)

Cyclic Sidereal Year, Month and Day	Week-Day	English Month and Day	Tithi Ending Moment	Nakshatra Ending Moment	Muhammadan Year, Month and Day
19	Su	1	3 ·34	24 ·03	1
20	Mo	2	4 ·30	25 ·00 26 ·99	2
21	Tu	3	5 ·27	... ...	3
22	We	4	6 ·25	27 ·00	4
23	Th	5	7 ·27	1 ·03	5
24	Fr	6	8 ·31	2 ·09	6
25	Sa	7	9 ·37	3 ·16	7
26	Su	8	10 ·44	4 ·25	8
27	Mo	9	11 ·52	5 ·35	9
28	Tu	10	12 ·60	6 ·46	10
29	We	11	13 ·68	7 ·57	11
—30	Th	12	14 ·76	8 ·67	12
1	Fr	13	P ·83	9 ·75	13
2	Sa	14	1 ·88	10 ·82	14
3	Su	15	2 ·91	11 ·87	15
4	Mo	16	3 ·92	12 ·91	16
5	Tu	17	4 ·90	13 ·92	17
6	We	18	5 ·86	14 ·91	18
7	Th	19	6 ·80	15 ·88	19
8	Fr	20	7 ·73	16 ·84	20
9	Sa	21	8 ·66	17 ·78	21
10	Su	22	9 ·58	18 ·72	22
11	Mo	23	10 ·48	19 ·65	23
12	Tu	24	11 ·38	20 ·58	24
13	We	25	12 ·28	21 ·51	25
14	Th	26	13 ·18	22 ·45	26
15	Fr	27	14 ·09	23 ·40	27
16	Sa	28	A ·01 1 ·95	24 ·36	28

March (Kshaya *Kumbha—Masi*; Kshaya *Mina—Panguni*. Lunar: *Sukla*, **Phalguna**, *Bahula*. H. 1407 *Rajab*.)

Cyclic Sidereal Year, Month and Day	Week-Day	English Month and Day	Tithi Ending Moment	Nakshatra Ending Moment	Muhammadan Year, Month and Day
17	Su	1	2 ·91	25 ·33	—29
18	Mo	2	3 ·88	26 ·31	1
19	Tu	3	4 ·87	27 ·32	2
20	We	4	5 ·88	1 ·35	3
21	Th	5	6 ·91	2 ·40	4
22	Fr	6	7 ·97	3 ·47	5
23	Sa	7	... ...	4 ·55	6
24	Su	8	8 ·05	5 ·65	7
25	Mo	9	9 ·14	6 ·76	8
26	Tu	10	10 ·23	7 ·87	9
27	We	11	11 ·31	8 ·97	10
28	Th	12	12 ·38	... ...	11
29	Fr	13	13 ·44	9 ·06	12
—30	Sa	14	14 ·48	10 ·13	13
1	Su	15	P ·50	11 ·19	14
2	Mo	16	1 ·51	12 ·23	15
3	Tu	17	2 ·49	13 ·24	16
4	We	18	3 ·46	14 ·23	17
5	Th	19	4 ·41	15 ·21	18
6	Fr	20	5 ·34	16 ·18	19
7	Sa	21	6 ·26	17 ·12	20
8	Su	22	7 ·16	18 ·06 19 ·99	21
9	Mo	23	8 ·06 9 ·96	20 ·92	22
10	Tu	24	10 ·86	21 ·86	23
11	We	25	11 ·77	22 ·80	24
12	Th	26	12 ·68	23 ·74	25
13	Fr	27	13 ·60	24 ·69	26
14	Sa	28	14 ·54	25 ·66	27
15	Su ●	29	—A ·49	26 ·64	28
16	Mo	30	1 ·46	27 ·65	29
17	Tu	31	2 ·45	1 ·67	—30

April (Prabhava *Mesha—Chittirai*. Lunar: *Sukla*, **Chaitra**, *Bahula*, *Suk.* H. 1407 *Shaban*.)

Cyclic Sidereal Year, Month and Day	Week-Day	English Month and Day	Tithi Ending Moment	Nakshatra Ending Moment	Muhammadan Year, Month and Day
18	We	1	3 ·47	2 ·71	1
19	Th	2	4 ·50	3 ·77	2
20	Fr	3	5 ·55	4 ·85	3
21	Sa	4	6 ·62	5 ·95	4
22	Su	5	7 ·70	... ...	5
23	Mo	6	8 ·79	6 ·06	6
24	Tu	7	9 ·88	7 17	7
25	We	8	10 ·95	8 ·27	8
26	Th	9	... ...	9 ·37	9
27	Fr	10	11 ·00	10 ·45	10
28	Sa	11	12 ·04	11 ·51	11
29	Su	12	13 ·07	12 ·55	12
—30	Mo	13	14 ·07	13 ·56	13
1	Tu	14	P ·05	14 ·56	14
2	We	15	1 ·02 2 ·96	15 ·55	15
3	Th	16	3 ·89	16 ·52	16
4	Fr	17	4 ·81	17 ·47	17
5	Sa	18	5 ·72	18 ·40	18
6	Su	19	6 ·62	19 ·33	19
7	Mo	20	7 ·52	20 ·26	20
8	Tu	21	8 ·42	21 ·19	21
9	We	22	9 ·32	22 ·13	22
10	Th	23	10 ·22	23 ·07	23
11	Fr	24	11 ·14	24 ·02 25 ·98	24
12	Sa	25	12 ·08	26 ·97	25
13	Su	26	13 ·04	27 ·97	26
14	Mo	27	14 ·01 A ·99	1 ·98	27
15	Tu	28	... ...	... ...	28
16	We	29	1 ·00	2 ·02	—29
17	Th	30	2 ·03	3 ·08	1

May (Prabhava *Mesha—Chittirai*; Prabhava *Vrishabha—Vaikasi*. Lunar: *Sukla*, **Vaisakha**, *Bahula*. H. 1407 *Ramzan*.)

Cyclic Sidereal Year, Month and Day	Week-Day	English Month and Day	Tithi Ending Moment	Nakshatra Ending Moment	Muhammadan Year, Month and Day
18	Fr	1	3 ·08	4 ·16	2
19	Sa	2	4 ·15	5 ·26	3
20	Su	3	5 ·23	6 ·36	4
21	Mo	4	6 ·32	7 ·47	5
22	Tu	5	7 ·40	8 ·58	6
23	We	6	8 ·47	9 ·68	7
24	Th	7	9 ·53	10 ·76	8
25	Fr	8	10 ·58	11 ·82	9
26	Sa	9	11 ·60	12 ·86	10
27	Su	10	12 ·59	13 ·88	11
28	Mo	11	13 ·58	14 ·88	12
29	Tu	12	14 ·54	15 ·87	13
30	We	13	P ·48	16 ·84	14
—31	Th	14	1 ·41	17 ·79	15
1	Fr	15	2 ·32	18 ·73	16
2	Sa	16	3 ·23	19 ·67	17
3	Su	17	4 ·18	20 ·61	18
4	Mo	18	5 ·03 6 ·93	21 ·54	19
5	Tu	19	7 ·88	22 ·47	20
6	We	20	8 ·73	23 ·41	21
7	Th	21	9 ·65	24 ·35	22
8	Fr	22	10 ·59	25 ·32	23
9	Sa	23	11 ·54	26 ·30	24
10	Su	24	12 ·51	27 ·29	25
11	Mo	25	13 ·49	1 ·30	26
12	Tu	26	14 ·51	2 ·34	27
13	We	27	—A ·54	3 ·40	28
14	Th	28	1 ·58	4 ·47	29
15	Fr	29	2 ·65	5 ·56	—30
16	Sa	30	3 ·73	6 ·66	1
17	Su	31	4 ·81	7 ·77	2

June (Prabhava *Mithuna—Ani*. Lunar: *Sukla*, **Jyeshtha**, *Bahula*, **Ash.** *Suk.* H. 1407 *Shawwal*.)

Cyclic Sidereal Year, Month and Day	Week-Day	English Month and Day	Tithi Ending Moment	Nakshatra Ending Moment	Muhammadan Year, Month and Day
18	Mo	1	5 ·89	8 ·88	3
19	Tu	2	6 ·97	9 ·98	4
20	We	3	... ...	... ...	5
21	Th	4	7 ·03	10 ·06	6
22	Fr	5	8 ·07	11 ·13	7
23	Sa	6	9 ·09	12 ·18	8
24	Su	7	10 ·09	13 ·21	9
25	Mo	8	11 ·07	14 ·22	10
26	Tu	9	12 ·03 13 ·98	15 ·20	11
27	We	10	14 ·91	16 ·17	12
28	Th	11	P ·83	17 ·13	13
29	Fr	12	1 ·73	18 ·08	14
30	Sa	13	2 ·63	19 ·02 20 ·95	15
—31	Su	14	3 ·53	21 ·88	16
1	Mo	15	4 ·43	22 ·81	17
2	Tu	16	5 ·33	23 ·75	18
3	We	17	6 ·23	24 ·70	19
4	Th	18	7 ·15	25 ·65	20
5	Fr	19	8 ·08	26 ·62	21
6	Sa	20	9 ·02 10 ·99	27 ·61	22
7	Su	21	11 ·97	1 ·62	23
8	Mo	22	12 ·99	2 ·65	24
9	Tu	23	... ...	3 ·70	25
10	We	24	13 ·01	4 ·77	26
11	Th	25	14 ·06	5 ·86	27
12	Fr	26	—A ·12	6 ·96	28
13	Sa	27	1 ·20	... ...	—29
14	Su	28	2 ·28	7 ·07	1
15	Mo	29	3 ·36	8 ·18	2
16	Tu	30	4 ·44	9 ·28	3

Naksh:—1. Asvn. 2. Bhar. 3. Krit. 4. Rohi. 5. Mrig. 6. Ardh. 7. Punar. 8. Push. 9. Aslesh. 10. Magh. 11. P. Phal. 12. U. Phal. 13. Hasta. 14. Chit.

A. D. 1987.
A.—Amavasya.
P.—Paurnami.

Kollam 1163, Commences { **N. Malabar—Sept.** / **S. Malabar—Aug.**

Hijra 1408, Commences, **Aug. 26.**

Vikrama 2044.
Bengal San 1393.
(N. Cycle) Vikrama.

SOLAR reckoning: Cyclic Sidereal Year, Month and Day; Week-Day English Month and Day. LUNAR reckoning: Tithi Ending Moment; Nakshatra Ending Moment; Muhammadan Year, Month and Day.

July — Solar: Prabhava *Mithuna—Ani.* to 32, then Prabhava *Karkata—Adi.*; Lunar: Ashadha Sukla, Bahula, Sukla; Muhammadan: H. 1407 *Zi-l-ka'da.*

Cyclic Sidereal Year, Month and Day	Week-Day	English Month and Day	Tithi	Tithi Ending Moment	Nakshatra	Nakshatra Ending Moment	Muhammadan Year, Month and Day
17	We	1	5	·49	10	·37	4
18	Th	2	6	·55	11	·44	5
19	Fr	3	7	·57	12	·49	6
20	Sa	4	8	·57	13	·53	7
21	Su	5	9	·55	14	·54	8
22	Mo	6	10	·51	15	·53	9
23	Tu	7	11	·45	16	·50	10
24	We	8	12	·38	17	·46	11
25	Th	9	13	·30	18	·42	12
26	Fr	10	14	·21	19	·36	13
27	Sa	11	P	·11	20	·29	14
28	Su	12	1 2	·01 ·90	21	·22	15
29	Mo	13	3	·79	22	·15	16
30	Tu	14	4	·70	23	·09	17
31	We	15	5	·62	24 25	·03 ·99	18
—32	Th	16	6	·55	26	·96	19
1	Fr	17	7	·50	27	·94	20
2	Sa	18	8	·47	1	·95	21
3	Su	19	9	·46	2	·97	22
4	Mo	20	10	·46	...	...	23
5	Tu	21	11	·48	3	·01	24
6	We	22	12	·52	4	·08	25
7	Th	23	13	·58	5	·16	26
8	Fr	24	14	·66	6	·26	27
9	Sa	25	—A	·75	7	·37	28
10	Su	26	1	·84	8	·48	29
11	Mo	27	2	·92	9	·58	—30
12	Tu	28	3	·98	10	·67	1
13	We	29	...	...	11	·75	2
14	Th	30	4	·03	12	·81	3
15	Fr	31	5	·05	13	·85	4

Aug. — Solar: Prabhava *Karkata—Adi.* to 31, then Prabhava *Simha—Avani.*; Lunar: Sravana Sukla, Bahula, Bhadra. Suk.; Muhammadan: H. 1407 *Zi-l-hijja.*, then H. 1408 *Muharram.*

Cyclic Sidereal Year, Month and Day	Week-Day	English Month and Day	Tithi	Tithi Ending Moment	Nakshatra	Nakshatra Ending Moment	Muhammadan Year, Month and Day
16	Sa	1	6	·05	14	·86	5
17	Su	2	7	·03	15	·86	6
18	Mo	3	8 9	·00 ·94	16	·84	7
19	Tu	4	10	·87	17	·81	8
20	We	5	11	·79	18	·75	9
21	Th	6	12	·70	19	·69	10
22	Fr	7	13	·60	20	·63	11
23	Sa	8	14	·50	21	·56	12
24	Su	9	P	·40	22	·49	13
25	Mo	10	1	·30	23	·43	14
26	Tu	11	2	·21	24	·37	15
27	We	12	3	·13	25	·32	16
28	Th	13	4 5	·05 ·99	26	·28	17
29	Fr	14	6	·96	27	·26	18
30	Sa	15	7	·95	1	·27	19
—31	Su	16	8	·96	2	·29	20
1	Mo	17	9	·98	3	·32	21
2	Tu	18	...	...	4	·38	22
3	We	19	10	·02	5	·46	23
4	Th	20	11	·09	6	·56	24
5	Fr	21	12	·17	7	·67	25
6	Sa	22	13	·25	8	·78	26
7	Su	23	14	·33	9	·88	27
8	Mo	24	—A	·41	10	·97	28
9	Tu	25	1	·48	...	...	—29
10	We	26	2	·52	11	·05	1
11	Th	27	3	·55	12	·12	2
12	Fr	28	4	·56	13	·16	3
13	Sa	29	5	·53	14	·18	4
14	Su	30	6	·50	15	·18	5
15	Mo	31	7	·45	16	·17	6

Sep. — Solar: Prabhava *Simha—Avani.* to 31, then Prabhava *Kanya—Purattasi.*; Lunar: Sukla, Bhadrapada, Bahula, Sukla; Muhammadan: H. 1408 *Muharram.*

Cyclic Sidereal Year, Month and Day	Week-Day	English Month and Day	Tithi	Tithi Ending Moment	Nakshatra	Nakshatra Ending Moment	Muhammadan Year, Month and Day
16	Tu	1	8	·88	17	·14	7
17	We	2	9	·30	18	·09	8
18	Th	3	10	·21	19 20	·03 ·96	9
19	Fr	4	11	·11	21	·89	10
20	Sa	5	12 13	·01 ·91	22	·82	11
21	Su	6	14	·81	23	·76	12
22	Mo	7	P	·72	24	·70	13
23	Tu	8	1	·64	25	·65	14
24	We	9	2	·57	26	·61	15
25	Th	10	3	·51	27	·60	16
26	Fr	11	4	·48	1	·59	17
27	Sa	12	5	·47	2	·60	18
28	Su	13	6	·49	3	·64	19
29	Mo	14	7	·51	4	·69	20
30	Tu	15	8	·55	5	·77	21
—31	We	16	9	·61	6	·86	22
1	Th	17	10	·68	7	·96	23
2	Fr	18	11	·77	...	...	24
3	Sa	19	12	·85	8	·07	25
4	Su	20	13	·93	9	·18	26
5	Mo	21	...	...	10	·28	27
6	Tu	22	14	·00	11	·37	28
7	We	23	—A	·05	12	·43	29
8	Th	24	1	·08	13	·47	—30
9	Fr	25	2	·09	14	·50	1
10	Sa	26	3	·08	15	·52	2
11	Su	27	4 5	·04 ·99	16	·50	3
12	Mo	28	6	·93	17	·47	4
13	Tu	29	7	·85	18	·42	5
14	We	30	8	·76	19	·37	6

Oct. — Solar: Prabhava *Kanya—Purattasi.* to 31, then Prabhava *Tula—Aippasi.*; Lunar: Asvina Sukla, Bahula, Kartt. Sukla; Muhammadan: H. 1408 *Safar.*, then *Rabi-ul-awwal.*

Cyclic Sidereal Year, Month and Day	Week-Day	English Month and Day	Tithi	Tithi Ending Moment	Nakshatra	Nakshatra Ending Moment	Muhammadan Year, Month and Day
15	Th	1	9	·66	20	·31	7
16	Fr	2	10	·56	21	·24	8
17	Sa	3	11	·46	22	·17	9
18	Su	4	12	·36	23	·10	10
19	Mo	5	13	·27	24 25	·04 ·98	11
20	Tu	6	14	19	26	·95	12
21	We	7	P	·12	27	·92	13
22	Th	8	1	·07	1	·91	14
23	Fr	9	2	·05	2	·92	15
24	Sa	10	3	·03	3	·95	16
25	Su	11	4	·05	...	...	17
26	Mo	12	5	·07	4	·01	18
27	Tu	13	6	·11	5	·08	19
28	We	14	7	·17	6	·16	20
29	Th	15	8	·25	7	·26	21
30	Fr	16	9	·34	8	·37	22
—31	Sa	17	10	·43	9	·48	23
1	Su	18	11	·51	10	·53	24
2	Mo	19	12	·58	11	·67	25
3	Tu	20	13	·63	12	·74	26
4	We	21	14	·66	13	·79	27
5	Th	22	—A	·67	14	·82	28
6	Fr	23	1	·66	15	·84	—29
7	Sa	24	2	·63	16	·83	1
8	Su	25	3	·58	17	·80	2
9	Mo	26	4	·51	18	·76	3
10	Tu	27	5	·43	19	·71	4
11	We	28	6	·34	20	·65	5
12	Th	29	7	·25	21	·58	6
13	Fr	30	8	·15	22	·51	7
14	Sa	31	9 10	·05 ·95	23	·44	8

Nov. — Solar: Prabhava *Tula—Aippasi.* to 30, then Prabhava *Vrischika—Kartigai.*; Lunar: Karttika Suk., Bahula, Sukla; Muhammadan: H. 1408 *Rabi-ul-awwal.*

Cyclic Sidereal Year, Month and Day	Week-Day	English Month and Day	Tithi	Tithi Ending Moment	Nakshatra	Nakshatra Ending Moment	Muhammadan Year, Month and Day
15	Su	1	11	·86	24	·37	9
16	Mo	2	12	·79	25	·32	10
17	Tu	3	13	·73	26	·28	11
18	We	4	14	·67	27	·25	12
19	Th	5	P	·64	1	·23	13
20	Fr	6	1	·62	2	·24	14
21	Sa	7	2	·64	3	·27	15
22	Su	8	3	·67	4	·32	16
23	Mo	9	4	·72	5	·38	17
24	Tu	10	5	·79	6	·46	18
25	We	11	6	·87	7	·56	19
26	Th	12	7	·96	8	·67	20
27	Fr	13	...	...	9	·78	21
28	Sa	14	8	·05	10	·88	22
29	Su	15	9	·13	11	·97	23
—30	Mo	16	10	·19	...	...	24
1	Tu	17	11	·24	12	·03	25
2	We	18	12	·28	13	·11	26
3	Th	19	13	·29	14	·15	27
4	Fr	20	14	·27	15	·16	28
5	Sa	21	—A	·23	16	·15	29
6	Su	22	1	·19	17	·13	—30
7	Mo	23	2	·13	18	·09	1
8	Tu	24	3 4	·05 ·96	19 20	·05 ·99	2
9	We	25	5	·87	21	·92	3
10	Th	26	6	·77	22	·85	4
11	Fr	27	7	·67	23	·78	5
12	Sa	28	8	·57	24	·72	6
13	Su	29	9	·48	25	·66	7
14	Mo	30	10	·40	26	·61	8

Dec. — Solar: Prabhava *Vrischika—Kartigai.* to 29, then Prabhava *Dhanus—Margali.*; Lunar: Margasira, Bahula, Pausha Sukla; Muhammadan: H. 1408 *Rabi-ul-akhir.*, then H. 1408 *Jumadal-awwal.*

Cyclic Sidereal Year, Month and Day	Week-Day	English Month and Day	Tithi	Tithi Ending Moment	Nakshatra	Nakshatra Ending Moment	Muhammadan Year, Month and Day
15	Tu	1	11	·34	27	·58	9
16	We	2	12	·29	1	·56	10
17	Th	3	13	·26	2	·57	11
18	Fr	4	14	·25	3	·59	12
19	Sa	5	P	·27	4	·63	13
20	Su	6	1	·30	5	·69	14
21	Mo	7	2	·35	6	·77	15
22	Tu	8	3	·42	7	·86	16
23	We	9	4	·50	8	·97	17
24	Th	10	5	·59	...	...	18
25	Fr	11	6	·68	9	·08	19
26	Sa	12	7	·77	10	·18	20
27	Su	13	8	·84	11	·28	21
28	Mo	14	9	·89	12	·36	22
—29	Tu	15	10	·91	13	·42	23
1	We	16	11	·92	14	·46	24
2	Th	17	12	·91	15	·48	25
3	Fr	18	13	·88	16	·48	26
4	Sa	19	14	·82	17	·46	27
5	Su	20	—A	·75	18	·43	28
6	Mo	21	1	·68	19	·38	—29
7	Tu	22	2	·59	20	·32	1
8	We	23	3	·50	21	·26	2
9	Th	24	4	·40	22	·20	3
10	Fr	25	5	·30	23	·13	4
11	Sa	26	6	·20	24	·06	5
12	Su	27	7	·12	25 26	·00 ·05	6
13	Mo	28	8 9	·04 ·98	27	·91	7
14	Tu	29	10	·94	1	·89	8
15	We	30	11	·91	2	·89	9
16	Th	31	12	·90	3	·90	10

15. Svati. 16. Visak. 17. Anur. 18. Jyesh. 19. Mula. 20. P. Ash. 21. U. Ash. 22. Sravn. 23. Dani. 24. Satab. 25. P. Bhad. 26. U. Bhad. 27. Rev.

A. D. 1988.
Solar Eclipse. ●
Lunar Eclipse. ○

Mesha Sankranti (Commencement of Indian Sidereal Year).
(Surya Sid.) April 13·39. **Saka 1910.** **Kaliyuga 5089.**
(Arya Sid.) April 13·28. **(S. Cycle) Vibhava.**

Columns: SOLAR reckoning — Cyclic Sidereal Year, Month and Day; Week-Day English Month and Day. LUNAR reckoning — Tithi Ending Moment; Nakshatra Ending Moment; Muhammadan Year, Month and Day.

Jan.

Solar month	Cyclic Sidereal Day	Week-Day	English Day	Lunar month / Paksha	Tithi	Ending Moment	Nakshatra	Ending Moment	Muhammadan
Prabhava Dhanus—Margali.	17	Fr	1	Suk.	13	·92	4	·94	11 (H. 1408 Jumadal-awwal.)
	18	Sa	2		14	·96	5	·99	12
	19	Su	3	Pausha	...	...	...	...	13
	20	Mo	4		P	·01	6	·07	14
	21	Tu	5		1	·08	7	·17	15
	22	We	6		2	·16	8	·27	16
	23	Th	7		3	·25	9	·38	17
	24	Fr	8		4	·34	10	·48	18
	25	Sa	9		5	·42	11	·58	19
	26	Su	10		6	·49	12	·67	20
	27	Mo	11	Bahula	7	·53	13	·74	21
	28	Tu	12		8	·56	14	·78	22
	29	We	13		9	·57	15	·80	23
	—30	Th	14		10	·55	16	·81	24
Prabhava Makara—Tai.	1	Fr	15		11	·52	17	·80	25
	2	Sa	16		12	·47	18	·77	26
	3	Su	17		13	·40	19	·72	27
	4	Mo	18		14	·32	20	·66	28
	5	Tu	19		—A	·23	21	·60	29
	6	We	20		1	·18	22	·54	—30
	7	Th	21		2 / 3	·03 / ·93	23	·47	1
	8	Fr	22		4	·84	24	·40	2
	9	Sa	23		5	·76	25	·34	3
	10	Su	24		6	·69	26	·28	4
	11	Mo	25	Sukla	7	·63	27	·24	5
	12	Tu	26		8	·58	1	·22	6
	13	We	27		9	·55	2	·21	7
	14	Th	28		10	·54	3	·22	8
	15	Fr	29		11	·56	4	·25	9
	16	Sa	30		12	·60	5	·30	10
	17	Su	31		13	·66	6	·38	11

Feb.

Solar month	Cyclic Sidereal Day	Week-Day	English Day	Lunar month / Paksha	Tithi	Ending Moment	Nakshatra	Ending Moment	Muhammadan
	18	Mo	1	Magha	14	·73	7	·47	12 (H. 1408 Jumadal-akhir.)
	19	Tu	2		P	·81	8	·57	13
	20	We	3		1	·90	9	·68	14
	21	Th	4		2	·98	10	·79	15
	22	Fr	5		...	...	11	·89	16
	23	Sa	6		3	·06	12	·98	17
	24	Su	7		4	·13	...	...	18
	25	Mo	8		5	·18	13	·05	19
	26	Tu	9		6	·20	14	·10	20
	27	We	10	Bahula	7	·20	15	·12	21
	28	Th	11		8	·19	16	·14	22
	—29	Fr	12		9	·15	17	·13	23
Prabhava Kumbha—Masi.	1	Sa	13		10	·09	18	·10	24
	2	Su	14		11 / 12	·08 / ·95	19	·05	25
	3	Mo	15		13	·86	20 / 21	·00 / ·94	26
	4	Tu	16		14	·77	22	·87	27
	5	We	17		—A	·67	23	·80	28
	6	Th	18		1	·57	24	·73	—29
	7	Fr	19		2	·47	25	·67	1 (H. 1408 Rajab.)
	8	Sa	20		3	·38	26	·61	2
	9	Su	21		4	·30	27	·58	3
	10	Mo	22	Sukla	5	·24	1	·55	4
	11	Tu	23		6	·20	2	·53	5
	12	We	24		7	·18	3	·54	6
	13	Th	25	Phalguna	8	·16	4	·56	7
	14	Fr	26		9	·18	5	·62	8
	15	Sa	27		10	·22	6	·69	9
	16	Su	28		11	·28	7	·77	10
	17	Mo	29		12	·35	8	·87	11

March

Solar month	Cyclic Sidereal Day	Week-Day	English Day	Lunar month / Paksha	Tithi	Ending Moment	Nakshatra	Ending Moment	Muhammadan
Prabhava Kumbha—Masi.	18	Tu	1	Suk.	13	·44	9	·98	12
	19	We	2		14	·53	...	...	13
	20	Th	3	Phalguna	P	·61	10	·09	14
	21	Fr	4		1	·68	11	·19	15
	22	Sa	5		2	·74	12	·28	16
	23	Su	6		3	·79	13	·35	17
	24	Mo	7		4	·81	14	·41	18 (H. 1408 Rajab.)
	25	Tu	8		5	·81	15	·45	19
	26	We	9		6	·80	16	·46	20
	27	Th	10		7	·76	17	·45	21
	28	Fr	11	Bahula	8	·70	18	·43	22
	29	Sa	12		9	·63	19	·39	23
	30	Su	13		10	·55	20	·34	24
	—31	Mo	14		11	·46	21	·28	25
Prabhava Mina—Panguni.	1	Tu	15		12	·36	22	·21	26
	2	We	16		13	·26	23	·14	27
	3	Th	17		14	·16	24	·07	28
	4	Fr ●	18		A / 1	·06 / ·97	25 / 26	·01 / ·96	29
	5	Sa	19		2	·89	27	·91	—30
	6	Su	20		3	·83	1	·87	1
	7	Mo	21		4	·79	2	·86	2
	8	Tu	22		5	·77	3	·86	3
	9	We	23		6	·75	4	·89	4
	10	Th	24	Sukla	7	·78	5	·93	5
	11	Fr	25		8	·82	6	·99	6
	12	Sa	26		9	·87	...	...	7
	13	Su	27		10	·94	7	·07	8
	14	Mo	28		...	...	8	·17	9
	15	Tu	29		11	·02	9	·28	10
	16	We	30		12	·11	10	·39	11
	17	Th	31		13	·19	11	·49	12

April

Solar month	Cyclic Sidereal Day	Week-Day	English Day	Lunar month / Paksha	Tithi	Ending Moment	Nakshatra	Ending Moment	Muhammadan
	18	Fr	1	Chaitra	14	·27	12	·58	13 (H. 1408 Shaban.)
	19	Sa	2		P	·33	13	·66	14
	20	Su	3		1	·37	14	·72	15
	21	Mo	4		2	·39	15	·77	16
	22	Tu	5		3	·38	16	·78	17
	23	We	6		4	·36	17	·78	18
	24	Th	7		5	·32	18	·76	19
	25	Fr	8	Bahula	6	·26	19	·72	20
	26	Sa	9		7	·19	20	·68	21
	27	Su	10		8	·11	21	·62	22
	28	Mo	11		9 / 10	·02 / ·92	22	·55	23
	—29	Tu	12		11	·82	23	·48	24
Vibhava Mesha—Chittirai.	1	We	13		12	·72	24	·41	25
	2	Th	14		13	·62	25	·35	26
	3	Fr	15		14	·53	26	·29	27
	4	Sa	16		—A	·45	27	·24	28
	5	Su	17		1	·39	1	·20	—29
	6	Mo	18		2	·35	2	·18	1 (H. 1408 Ramzan.)
	7	Tu	19		3	·32	3	·19	2
	8	We	20		4	·29	4	·20	3
	9	Th	21	Sukla	5	·31	5	·24	4
	10	Fr	22		6	·35	6	·30	5
	11	Sa	23		7	·41	7	·38	6
	12	Su	24		8	·48	8	·48	7
	13	Mo	25	Vaisakha	9	·57	9	·58	8
	14	Tu	26		10	·65	10	·69	9
	15	We	27		11	·73	11	·79	10
	16	Th	28		12	·79	12	·89	11
	17	Fr	29		13	·85	13	·97	12
	18	Sa	30		14	·89	...	...	13

May

Solar month	Cyclic Sidereal Day	Week-Day	English Day	Lunar month / Paksha	Tithi	Ending Moment	Nakshatra	Ending Moment	Muhammadan
Vibhava Mesha—Chittirai.	19	Su	1	Vaisakha	P	·91	14	·04	14 (H. 1408 Ramzan.)
	20	Mo	2		1	·92	15	·08	15
	21	Tu	3		2	·90	16	·10	16
	22	We	4		3	·86	17	·10	17
	23	Th	5		4	·79	18	·09	18
	24	Fr	6		5	·72	19	·06	19
	25	Sa	7		6	·64	20 / 21	·01 / ·96	20
	26	Su	8	Bahula	7	·54	22	·89	21
	27	Mo	9		8	·44	23	·82	22
	28	Tu	10		9	·34	24	·75	23
	29	We	11		10	·24	25	·69	24
	30	Th	12		11	·14	26	·63	25
	—31	Fr	13		12 / 13	·04 / ·96	27	·57	26
Vibhava Vrishabha—Vaikasi.	1	Sa	14		14	·90	1	·53	27
	2	Su	15		—A	·86	2	·52	28
	3	Mo	16		1	·83	3	·51	29
	4	Tu	17		2	·82	4	·52	—30
	5	We	18		3	·82	5	·55	1
	6	Th	19		4	·86	6	·61	2
	7	Fr	20		5	·92	7	·69	3
	8	Sa	21		6	·98	8	·78	4
	9	Su	22	Sukla	...	...	9	·88	5
	10	Mo	23		7	·06	10	·98	6
	11	Tu	24		8	·15	...	...	7
	12	We	25		9	·23	11	·09	8
	13	Th	26		10	·30	12	·19	9
	14	Fr	27	Jyeshtha	11	·36	13	·28	10
	15	Sa	28		12	·39	14	·35	11
	16	Su	29		13	·41	15	·40	12
	17	Mo	30		14	·41	16	·42	13
	18	Tu	31		P	·39	17	·43	14

June

Solar month	Cyclic Sidereal Day	Week-Day	English Day	Lunar month / Paksha	Tithi	Ending Moment	Nakshatra	Ending Moment	Muhammadan
	19	We	1	Adhika	1	·36	18	·42	15 (H. 1408 Shawwal.)
	20	Th	2		2	·30	19	·39	16
	21	Fr	3		3	·22	20	·35	17
	22	Sa	4		4	·14	21	·29	18
	23	Su	5		5 / 6	·04 / ·94	22	·23	19
	24	Mo	6	Bahula	7	·84	23	·17	20
	25	Tu	7		8	·74	24	·10	21
	26	We	8		9	·64	25 / 26	·03 / ·96	22
	27	Th	9		10	·54	27	·91	23
	28	Fr	10		11	·46	1	·87	24
	29	Sa	11		12	·40	2	·84	25
	30	Su	12		13	·35	3	·83	26
	31	Mo	13		14	·31	4	·84	27
	—32	Tu	14		—A	·30	5	·87	28
Vibhava Mithuna—Ani.	1	We	15		1	·31	6	·92	—29
	2	Th	16		2	·34	7	·99	1 (H. 1408 Zil-ka'da.)
	3	Fr	17		3	·39	...	...	2
	4	Sa	18		4	·46	8	·08	3
	5	Su	19	Sukla	5	·54	9	·18	4
	6	Mo	20		6	·62	10	·28	5
	7	Tu	21		7	·70	11	·39	6
	8	We	22		8	·77	12	·50	7
	9	Th	23	Nija Jyeshtha	9	·83	13	·59	8
	10	Fr	24		10	·87	14	·66	9
	11	Sa	25		11	·90	15	·71	10
	12	Su	26		12	·89	16	·74	11
	13	Mo	27		13	·87	17	·76	12
	14	Tu	28		14	·84	18	·75	13
	15	We	29		P	·78	19	·72	14
	16	Th	30		1	·70	20	·68	15

Naksh :—1. Asvn. 2. Bhar. 3. Krit. 4. Rohi. 5. Mrig. 6. Ardh. 7. Punar. 8. Push. 9. Aslesh. 10. Magh. 11. P. Phal. 12. U. Phal. 13. Hasta. 14. Chit.

A. D. 1988. | Kollam 1164, { N. Malabar—Sept. / S. Malabar—Aug. } | Hijra 1409, Commences, Aug. 14. | **Vikrama 2045.**
A.—Amavasya. | | | **Bengal San 1394.**
P.—Paurnami. | | | **(N. Cycle) Vrisha.**

SOLAR reckoning: Cyclic Sidereal Year, Month and Day; Week-Day English Month and Day. LUNAR reckoning: Tithi Ending Moment; Nakshatra Ending Moment; Muhammadan Year, Month and Day.

July

Solar: Vibhava Mithuna—Ani (17–31); Vibhava Karkata—Adi (1–16). Lunar: Nija Jyesh. Bahula; Ashadha Sukla. Muhammadan: H. 1408 Zi-l-ka'da; H. 1408 Zi-l-hijja.

Cyclic Sidereal	Week-Day	Tithi	Nakshatra	Muhammadan
17	Fr 1	2 ·62	21 ·63	16
18	Sa 2	3 ·52	22 ·57	17
19	Su 3	4 ·42	23 ·51	18
20	Mo 4	5 ·32	24 ·44	19
21	Tu 5	6 ·22	25 ·37	20
22	We 6	7 ·12	26 ·30	21
23	Th 7	8 ·02; 9 ·94	27 ·24	22
24	Fr 8	10 ·87	1 ·20	23
25	Sa 9	11 ·83	2 ·17	24
26	Su 10	12 ·80	3 ·16	25
27	Mo 11	13 ·78	4 ·16	26
28	Tu 12	14 ·78	5 ·18	27
29	We 13	—A ·82	6 ·23	28
30	Th 14	1 ·87	7 ·30	29
—31	Fr 15	2 ·93	8 ·38	—30
1	Sa 16	... ...	9 ·48	1
2	Su 17	3 ·00	10 ·59	2
3	Mo 18	4 ·09	11 ·70	3
4	Tu 19	5 ·17	12 ·80	4
5	We 20	6 ·24	13 ·89	5
6	Th 21	7 ·30	14 ·96	6
7	Fr 22	8 ·35	... ...	7
8	Sa 23	9 ·37	15 ·02	8
9	Su 24	10 ·37	16 ·07	9
10	Mo 25	11 ·36	17 ·08	10
11	Tu 26	12 ·32	18 ·08	11
12	We 27	13 ·26	19 ·05	12
13	Th 28	14 ·19	20 ·02; 21 ·97	13
14	Fr 29	P ·11	22 ·91	14
15	Sa 30	1 ·01; 2 ·91	23 ·84	15
16	Su 31	3 ·81	24 ·77	16

Aug.

Solar: Vibhava Simha—Avani (from 1). Lunar: Bahula; Sukla; Sravana; Bah. Muhammadan: H. 1409 Muharram (from 14).

Cyclic Sidereal	Week-Day	Tithi	Nakshatra	Muhammadan
17	Mo 1	4 ·71	25 ·70	17
18	Tu 2	5 ·61	26 ·64	18
19	We 3	6 ·51	27 ·59	19
20	Th 4	7 ·43	1 ·54	20
21	Fr 5	8 ·36	2 ·50	21
22	Sa 6	9 ·31	3 ·48	22
23	Su 7	10 ·28	4 ·48	23
24	Mo 8	11 ·26	5 ·51	24
25	Tu 9	12 ·28	6 ·54	25
26	We 10	13 ·30	7 ·60	26
27	Th 11	14 ·34	8 ·68	27
28	Fr 12	—A ·41	9 ·77	28
29	Sa 13	1 ·49	10 ·88	—29
30	Su 14	2 ·58	11 ·99	1
31	Mo 15	3 ·66	... ...	2
—32	Tu 16	4 ·73	12 ·10	3
1	We 17	5 ·79	13 ·19	4
2	Th 18	6 ·84	14 ·27	5
3	Fr 19	7 ·87	15 ·33	6
4	Sa 20	8 ·87	16 ·38	7
5	Su 21	9 ·86	17 ·40	8
6	Mo 22	10 ·82	18 ·40	9
7	Tu 23	11 ·77	19 ·38	10
8	We 24	12 ·70	20 ·35	11
9	Th 25	13 ·62	21 ·31	12
10	Fr 26	14 ·52	22 ·25	13
11	Sa ○ 27	P ·42	23 ·18	14
12	Su 28	1 ·32	24 ·11	15
13	Mo 29	2 ·22	25 ·04; 26 ·98	16
14	Tu 30	3 ·12	27 ·92	17
15	We 31	4 ·03; 5 ·95	1 ·87	18

Sep.

Solar: Vibhava Simha—Avani (16–31); Vibhava Kanya—Purattasi (from 1). Lunar: Sravana Bahula; Sukla; Bhadrapada. Muhammadan: H. 1409 Muharram; H. 1409 Safar.

Cyclic Sidereal	Week-Day	Tithi	Nakshatra	Muhammadan
16	Th 1	6 ·88	2 ·83	19
17	Fr 2	7 ·83	3 ·81	20
18	Sa 3	8 ·80	4 ·81	21
19	Su 4	9 ·78	5 ·82	22
20	Mo 5	10 ·80	6 ·86	23
21	Tu 6	11 ·82	7 ·91	24
22	We 7	12 ·87	8 ·98	25
23	Th 8	13 ·93	... ...	26
24	Fr 9	... ...	9 ·08	27
25	Sa 10	14 ·01	10 ·19	28
26	Su ● 11	—A ·09	11 ·30	29
27	Mo 12	1 ·18	12 ·40	—30
28	Tu 13	2 ·26	13 ·49	1
29	We 14	3 ·32	14 ·58	2
30	Th 15	4 ·37	15 ·65	3
—31	Fr 16	5 ·39	16 ·70	4
1	Sa 17	6 ·40	17 ·72	5
2	Su 18	7 ·38	18 ·73	6
3	Mo 19	8 ·35	19 ·71	7
4	Tu 20	9 ·30	20 ·68	8
5	We 21	10 ·23	21 ·64	9
6	Th 22	11 ·15	22 ·59	10
7	Fr 23	12 ·06; 13 ·96	23 ·52	11
8	Sa 24	14 ·86	24 ·45	12
9	Su 25	P ·76	25 ·38	13
10	Mo 26	1 ·66	26 ·32	14
11	Tu 27	2 ·57	27 ·26	15
12	We 28	3 ·49	1 ·20	16
13	Th 29	4 ·42	2 ·16	17
14	Fr 30	5 ·37	3 ·14	18

Oct.

Solar: Vibhava Tula—Aippasi (from 1). Lunar: Bahula; Sukla; Asvina; Bahula. Muhammadan: H. 1409 Rabi-ul-awwal.

Cyclic Sidereal	Week-Day	Tithi	Nakshatra	Muhammadan
15	Sa 1	6 ·34	4 ·13	19
16	Su 2	7 ·33	5 ·14	20
17	Mo 3	8 ·35	6 ·17	21
18	Tu 4	9 ·37	7 ·22	22
19	We 5	10 ·42	8 ·29	23
20	Th 6	11 ·48	9 ·38	24
21	Fr 7	12 ·56	10 ·48	25
22	Sa 8	13 ·65	11 ·59	26
23	Su 9	14 ·74	12 ·70	27
24	Mo 10	—A ·82	13 ·80	28
25	Tu 11	1 ·88	14 ·89	—29
26	We 12	2 ·93	15 ·96	1
27	Th 13	3 ·95	... ...	2
28	Fr 14	4 ·97	16 ·01	3
29	Sa 15	5 ·95	17 ·04	4
—30	Su 16	6 ·92	18 ·05	5
1	Mo 17	7 ·87	19 ·05	6
2	Tu 18	8 ·80	20 ·02; 21 ·98	7
3	We 19	9 ·72	22 ·92	8
4	Th 20	10 ·63	23 ·86	9
5	Fr 21	11 ·54	24 ·80	10
6	Sa 22	12 ·44	25 ·73	11
7	Su 23	13 ·34	26 ·66	12
8	Mo 24	14 ·24	27 ·59	13
9	Tu 25	P ·15	1 ·54	14
10	We 26	1 ·07	2 ·50	15
11	Th 27	2 ·01; 3 ·96	3 ·47	16
12	Fr 28	4 ·93	4 ·45	17
13	Sa 29	5 ·92	5 ·46	18
14	Su 30	6 ·92	6 ·48	19
15	Mo 31	7 ·96	7 ·53	20

Nov.

Solar: Vibhava Tula—Aippasi (16–30); Vibhava Vrischika—Kartigai (from 1). Lunar: Asvina Bahula; Sukla; Karttika. Muhammadan: Rabi-ul-awwal; H. 1409 Rabi-ul-akhir.

Cyclic Sidereal	Week-Day	Tithi	Nakshatra	Muhammadan
16	Tu 1	... ...	8 ·60	21
17	We 2	8 ·02	9 ·69	22
18	Th 3	9 ·09	10 ·78	23
19	Fr 4	10 ·17	11 ·88	24
20	Sa 5	11 ·25	12 ·99	25
21	Su 6	12 ·34	... ...	26
22	Mo 7	13 ·42	13 ·10	27
23	Tu 8	14 ·49	14 ·19	28
24	We 9	—A ·54	15 ·27	29
25	Th 10	1 ·57	16 ·32	—30
26	Fr 11	2 ·57	17 ·36	1
27	Sa 12	3 ·55	18 ·38	2
28	Su 13	4 ·53	19 ·37	3
29	Mo 14	5 ·48	20 ·35	4
—30	Tu 15	6 ·41	21 ·31	5
1	We 16	7 ·33	22 ·26	6
2	Th 17	8 ·25	23 ·20	7
3	Fr 18	9 ·15	24 ·14	8
4	Sa 19	10 ·05; 11 ·95	25 ·07	9
5	Su 20	12 ·86	26 ·00; 27 ·93	10
6	Mo 21	13 ·77	1 ·87	11
7	Tu 22	14 ·69	2 ·83	12
8	We 23	P ·63	3 ·80	13
9	Th 24	1 ·58	4 ·78	14
10	Fr 25	2 ·55	5 ·78	15
11	Sa 26	3 ·54	6 ·80	16
12	Su 27	4 ·56	7 ·85	17
13	Mo 28	5 ·60	8 ·91	18
14	Tu 29	6 ·65	9 ·99	19
15	We 30	7 ·72	... ...	20

Dec.

Solar: Vibhava Dhanu—Margali (from 1). Lunar: Bahula; Sukla; Margasira; Bahula. Muhammadan: H. 1409 Jumadal-awwal.

Cyclic Sidereal	Week-Day	Tithi	Nakshatra	Muhammadan
16	Th 1	8 ·80	10 ·08	21
17	Fr 2	9 ·90	11 ·18	22
18	Sa 3	10 ·98	12 ·29	23
19	Su 4	... ...	13 ·40	24
20	Mo 5	11 ·06	14 ·50	25
21	Tu 6	12 ·13	15 ·58	26
22	We 7	13 ·17	16 ·64	27
23	Th 8	14 ·20	17 ·68	28
24	Fr 9	—A ·20	18 ·70	—29
25	Sa 10	1 ·20	19 ·70	1
26	Su 11	2 ·16	20 ·68	2
27	Mo 12	3 ·11	21 ·65	3
28	Tu 13	4 ·04; 5 ·96	22 ·60	4
29	We 14	6 ·87	23 ·54	5
—30	Th 15	7 ·77	24 ·48	6
1	Fr 16	8 ·67	25 ·41	7
2	Sa 17	9 ·57	26 ·34	8
3	Su 18	10 ·48	27 ·28	9
4	Mo 19	11 ·39	1 ·22	10
5	Tu 20	12 ·32	2 ·17	11
6	We 21	13 ·26	3 ·13	12
7	Th 22	14 ·22	4 ·10	13
8	Fr 23	P ·20	5 ·10	14
9	Sa 24	1 ·18	6 ·12	15
10	Su 25	2 ·20	7 ·16	16
11	Mo 26	3 ·24	8 ·22	17
12	Tu 27	4 ·29	9 ·29	18
13	We 28	5 ·37	10 ·38	19
14	Th 29	6 ·45	11 ·49	20
15	Fr 30	7 ·54	12 ·60	21
16	Sa 31	8 ·63	13 ·70	22

15. Svati. 16. Visak. 17. Anur. 18. Jyesh. 19. Mula. 20. P. Ash. 21. U. Ash. 22. Sravn. 23. Dani. 24. Satab. 25. P. Bhad. 26. U. Bhad. 27. Rev.

A. D. 1989. **Mesha Sankranti** (Commencement of Indian Sidereal Year).

Solar Eclipse. ● **(Surya Sid.) April 13·65.** **Saka 1911.** **Kaliyuga 5090.**

Lunar Eclipse. ○ **(Arya Sid.) April 13·54.** **(S. Cycle) Sukla.**

SOLAR reckoning: Cyclic Sidereal Year, Month and Day; Week-Day, English Month and Day. LUNAR reckoning: Tithi Ending Moment; Nakshatra Ending Moment; Muhammadan Year, Month and Day.

Jan.

Vibhava *Dhanus—Margali.* / Vibhava *Makara—Tai.* — Marg. *Bah.* / *Sukla* / Pausha *Bahula* — *Jumadal-awwal.* / H. 1409 *Jumadal-akhir.*

Cyclic Sidereal Year, Month and Day	Week-Day	English Month and Day	Tithi Ending Moment		Nakshatra Ending Moment		Muhammadan Year, Month and Day
17	Su	1	9	·71	14	·80	23
18	Mo	2	10	·77	15	·89	24
19	Tu	3	11	·81	16	·96	25
20	We	4	12	·83	...	...	26
21	Th	5	13	·85	17	·00	27
22	Fr	6	14	·84	18	·02	28
23	Sa	7	—A	·80	19	·02	29
24	Su	8	1	·75	20 21	·01 ·98	—30
25	Mo	9	2	·68	22	·94	1
26	Tu	10	3	·60	23	·88	2
27	We	11	4	·52	24	·81	3
28	Th	12	5	·42	25	·74	4
—29	Fr	13	6	·32	26	·67	5
1	Sa	14	7	·22	27	·61	6
2	Su	15	8	·13	1	·55	7
3	Mo	16	9 10	·04 ·97	2	·50	8
4	Tu	17	11	·91	3	·46	9
5	We	18	12	·87	4	·43	10
6	Th	19	13	·84	5	·43	11
7	Fr	20	14	·82	6	·44	12
8	Sa	21	P	·85	7	·47	13
9	Su	22	1	·89	8	·52	14
10	Mo	23	2	·95	9	·59	15
11	Tu	24	...	...	10	·68	16
12	We	25	3	·03	11	·79	17
13	Th	26	4	·11	12	·90	18
14	Fr	27	5	·20	...	...	19
15	Sa	28	6	·29	13	·00	20
16	Su	29	7	·37	14	·10	21
17	Mo	30	8	·43	15	19	22
18	Tu	31	9	·47	16	·26	23

Feb.

Vibhava *Kumbha—Masi.* — *Sukla* / Magha *Bahula* — H. 1409 *Rajab.*

Cyclic Sidereal Year, Month and Day	Week-Day	English Month and Day	Tithi Ending Moment		Nakshatra Ending Moment		Muhammadan Year, Month and Day
19	We	1	10	·49	17	·31	24
20	Th	2	11	·50	18	·34	25
21	Fr	3	12	·48	19	·35	26
22	Sa	4	13	·44	20	·34	27
23	Su	5	14	·38	21	·32	28
24	Mo	6	—A	·31	22	·28	—29
25	Tu	7	1	·23	23	·22	1
26	We	8	2	·14	24	·15	2
27	Th	9	3 4	·04 ·94	25	·08	3
28	Fr	10	5	·84	26 27	·01 ·95	4
—29	Sa	11	6	·75	1	·89	5
1	Su	12	7	·66	2	·83	6
2	Mo	13	8	·59	3	·79	7
3	Tu	14	9	·53	4	·77	8
4	We	15	10	·50	5	·75	9
5	Th	16	11	·47	6	·76	10
6	Fr	17	12	·45	7	·78	11
7	Sa	18	13	·47	8	·83	12
8	Su	19	14	·51	9	·90	13
9	Mo ○	20	P	·57	10	·99	14
10	Tu	21	1	·65	...	...	15
11	We	22	2	·74	11	·09	16
12	Th	23	3	·83	12	·20	17
13	Fr	24	4	·91	13	·30	18
14	Sa	25	5	·98	14	·40	19
15	Su	26	...	...	15	·49	20
16	Mo	27	6	·01	16	·57	21
17	Tu	28	7	·09	17	·63	22

March

Vibhava *Kumbha—Masi.* / Vibhava *Mina—Panguni.* — Mag. *Bah.* / *Sukla* / Phalguna *Bahula* — H. 1409 *Rajab.* / H. 1409 *Shaban.*

Cyclic Sidereal Year, Month and Day	Week-Day	English Month and Day	Tithi Ending Moment		Nakshatra Ending Moment		Muhammadan Year, Month and Day
18	We	1	8	·10	18	·66	23
19	Th	2	9	·11	19	·67	24
20	Fr	3	10	·09	20	·67	25
21	Sa	4	11 12	·05 ·99	21	·65	26
22	Su	5	13	·92	22	·61	27
23	Mo	6	14	·84	23	·55	28
24	Tu	7	—A	·75	24	·49	29
25	We	8	1	·65	25	·43	—30
26	Th	9	2	·55	26	·36	1
27	Fr	10	3	·45	27	·29	2
28	Sa	11	4	·35	1	·23	3
29	Su	12	5	·27	2	·17	4
—30	Mo	13	6	·19	3	·18	5
1	Tu	14	7	·13	4	·10	6
2	We	15	8	·09	5	·08	7
3	Th	16	9	·06	6	·03	8
4	Fr	17	10	·05	7	·10	9
5	Sa	18	11	·08	8	·14	10
6	Su	19	12	·12	9	·21	11
7	Mo	20	13	·18	10	·29	12
8	Tu	21	14	·25	11	·39	13
9	We	22	P	·33	12	·49	14
10	Th	23	1	·42	13	·60	15
11	Fr	24	2	·50	14	·71	16
12	Sa	25	3	·57	15	·80	17
13	Su	26	4	·64	16	·88	18
14	Mo	27	5	·68	17	·94	19
15	Tu	28	6	·69	18	·98	20
16	We	29	7	·69	...	...	21
17	Th	30	8	·67	19	·00	22
18	Fr	31	9	·63	20 21	·00 ·98	23

April

Sukla *Mesha—Chittirai.* — *Sukla* / Chaitra *Bahula* — H. 1409 *Ramzan.*

Cyclic Sidereal Year, Month and Day	Week-Day	English Month and Day	Tithi Ending Moment		Nakshatra Ending Moment		Muhammadan Year, Month and Day
19	Sa	1	10	·57	22	·94	24
20	Su	2	11	·50	23	·89	25
21	Mo	3	12	·41	24	·84	26
22	Tu	4	13	·32	25	·77	27
23	We	5	14	·22	26	·70	28
24	Th	6	—A	·12	27	·63	—29
25	Fr	7	1 2	·02 ·92	1	·56	1
26	Sa	8	3	·83	2	·51	2
27	Su	9	4	·75	3	·46	3
28	Mo	10	5	·69	4	·42	4
29	Tu	11	6	·65	5	·40	5
30	We	12	7	·62	6	·40	6
—31	Th	13	8	·62	7	·42	7
1	Fr	14	9	·63	8	·46	8
2	Sa	15	10	·68	9	·52	9
3	Su	16	11	·73	10	·60	10
4	Mo	17	12	·81	11	·69	11
5	Tu	18	13	·89	12	·79	12
6	We	19	14	·97	13	·90	13
7	Th	20	...	...	...	...	14
8	Fr	21	P	·05	14	·01	15
9	Sa	22	1	·12	15	·11	16
10	Su	23	2	·18	16	·19	17
11	Mo	24	3	·22	17	·25	18
12	Tu	25	4	·23	18	·30	19
13	We	26	5	·23	19	·32	20
14	Th	27	6	·22	20	·32	21
15	Fr	28	7	·18	21	·31	22
16	Sa	29	8	·11	22	·28	23
17	Su	30	9 10	·03 ·94	23	·23	24

May

Sukla *Mesha—Chittirai.* / Sukla *Vrishabha—Vaikasi.* — Chait. *Bah.* / *Sukla* / Vaisakha *Bahula* — *Ramzan.* / H. 1409 *Shawwal.*

Cyclic Sidereal Year, Month and Day	Week-Day	English Month and Day	Tithi Ending Moment		Nakshatra Ending Moment		Muhammadan Year, Month and Day
18	Mo	1	11	·85	24	·17	25
19	Tu	2	12	·75	25	·11	26
20	We	3	13	·65	26 27	·04 ·97	27
21	Th	4	14	·55	1	·90	28
22	Fr	5	—A	·15	2	·84	29
23	Sa	6	1	·36	3	·79	—30
24	Su	7	2	·28	4	·75	1
25	Mo	8	3	·22	5	·73	2
26	Tu	9	4	·18	6	·72	3
27	We	10	5	·15	7	·74	4
28	Th	11	6	·14	8	·77	5
29	Fr	12	7	·14	9	·83	6
—30	Sa	13	8	·19	10	·90	7
1	Su	14	9	·25	11	·99	8
2	Mo	15	10	·32	...	...	9
3	Tu	16	11	·40	12	·09	10
4	We	17	12	·48	13	·20	11
5	Th	18	13	·56	14	·31	12
6	Fr	19	14	·64	15	·41	13
7	Sa	20	P	·69	16	·50	14
8	Su	21	1	·72	17	·57	15
9	Mo	22	2	·75	18	·62	16
10	Tu	23	3	·74	19	·64	17
11	We	24	4	·72	20	·65	18
12	Th	25	5	·68	21	·63	19
13	Fr	26	6	·62	22	·61	20
14	Sa	27	7	·54	23	·57	21
15	Su	28	8	·45	24	·51	22
16	Mo	29	9	·35	25	·45	23
17	Tu	30	10	·25	26	·38	24
18	We	31	11	·15	27	·31	25

June

Sukla *Mithuna—Ani.* — *Sukla* / Jyeshtha *Bahula* — H. 1409 *Zi-l-ka'da.*

Cyclic Sidereal Year, Month and Day	Week-Day	English Month and Day	Tithi Ending Moment		Nakshatra Ending Moment		Muhammadan Year, Month and Day
19	Th	1	12 13	·05 ·95	1	·25	26
20	Fr	2	14	·86	2	·19	27
21	Sa	3	—A	·79	3	·13	28
22	Su	4	1	·72	4	·08	—29
23	Mo	5	2	·67	5	·05	1
24	Tu	6	3	·65	6	·05	2
25	We	7	4	·63	7	·06	3
26	Th	8	5	·65	8	·09	4
27	Fr	9	6	·68	9	·14	5
28	Sa	10	7	·73	10	·21	6
29	Su	11	8	·80	11	·30	7
30	Mo	12	9	·88	12	·40	8
31	Tu	13	10	·96	13	·50	9
—32	We	14	...	...	14	·61	10
1	Th	15	11	·04	15	·71	11
2	Fr	16	12	·11	16	·81	12
3	Sa	17	13	·17	17	·88	13
4	Su	18	14	·21	18	·93	14
5	Mo	19	P	·23	19	·96	15
6	Tu	20	1	·22	20	·97	16
7	We	21	2	·19	21	·96	17
8	Th	22	3	·15	22	·94	18
9	Fr	23	4	·10	23	·90	19
10	Sa	24	5 6	·03 ·94	24	·85	20
11	Su	25	7	·84	25	·79	21
12	Mo	26	8	·74	26	·72	22
13	Tu	27	9	·64	27	·65	23
14	We	28	10	·54	1	·58	24
15	Th	29	11	·44	2	·52	25
16	Fr	30	12	·35	3	·46	26

Naksh:—1. Asvn. 2. Bhar. 3. Krit. 4. Rohi. 5. Mrig. 6. Ardh. 7. Punar. 8. Push. 9. Aslesh. 10. Magh. 11. P. Phal. 12. U. Phal. 13. Hasta. 14. Chit.

A. D. 1989.
A.—Amavasya.
P.—Paurnami.

Kollam 1165, Commences { **N. Malabar—Sept.** / **S. Malabar—Aug.**

Hijra 1410, Commences, Aug. 4.

Vikrama 2046.
Bengal San 1395.
(N. Cycle) Chitrabhanu.

Solar reckoning: Cyclic Sidereal Year, Month and Day; Week-Day English Month and Day. Lunar reckoning: Tithi Ending Moment; Nakshatra Ending Moment; Muhammadan Year, Month and Day.

Cyclic Sidereal Year, Month and Day	Week-Day English Month and Day	Tithi Ending Moment	Nakshatra Ending Moment	Muhammadan Year, Month and Day
	July			
17	Sa 1	Bah. 13 ·27	4 ·41	Zilkada. 27
18	Su 2	14 ·21	5 ·39	28
19	Mo 3	—A ·16	6 ·38	29
20	Tu 4	1 ·12	7 ·38	—30
21	We 5	2 ·11	8 ·40	1
22	Th 6	3 ·13	9 ·44	2
23	Fr 7	4 ·16	10 ·51	3
24	Sa 8	5 ·21	11 ·60	4
25	Su 9	6 ·27	12 ·70	5
26	Mo 10	7 ·35	13 ·80	6
27	Tu 11	8 ·43	14 ·91	7
28	We 12	9 ·51	... ...	8
29	Th 13	10 ·58	15 ·02	9
30	Fr 14	11 ·64	16 ·11	10
—31	Sa 15	12 ·69	17 ·19	11
1	Su 16	13 ·71	18 ·24	12
2	Mo 17	14 ·70	19 ·28	13
3	Tu 18	P ·68	20 ·29	14
4	We 19	1 ·61	21 ·30	15
5	Th 20	2 ·58	22 ·27	16
6	Fr 21	3 ·50	23 ·23	17
7	Sa 22	4 ·42	24 ·18	18
8	Su 23	5 ·33	25 ·12	19
9	Mo 24	6 ·23	26 ·06 / 27 ·99	20
10	Tu 25	7 ·13	1 ·92	21
11	We 26	8 ·03 / 9 ·93	2 ·86	22
12	Th 27	10 ·83	3 ·80	23
13	Fr 28	11 ·75	4 ·76	24
14	Sa 29	12 ·68	5 ·72	25
15	Su 30	13 ·63	6 ·70	26
16	Mo 31	14 ·60	7 ·70	27

(Solar: Sukla Mithuna—Ani, to 31; Sukla Karkata—Adi, from 1. Lunar: Sukla, Ashadha, Bahula. Muhammadan: H. 1409 Zi-l-hijja, from 1.)

Cyclic Sidereal Year, Month and Day	Week-Day English Month and Day	Tithi Ending Moment	Nakshatra Ending Moment	Muhammadan Year, Month and Day
	Aug.			
17	Tu 1	—A ·60	8 ·72	28
18	We 2	1 ·61	9 ·76	29
19	Th 3	2 ·63	10 ·82	—30
20	Fr 4	3 ·68	11 ·90	1
21	Sa 5	4 ·74	... ...	2
22	Su 6	5 ·82	12 ·00	3
23	Mo 7	6 ·90	13 ·10	4
24	Tu 8	7 ·99	14 ·20	5
25	We 9	... ...	15 ·31	6
26	Th 10	8 ·07	16 ·41	7
27	Fr 11	9 ·13	17 ·49	8
28	Sa 12	10 ·17	18 ·55	9
29	Su 13	11 ·19	19 ·59	10
30	Mo 14	12 ·19	20 ·62	11
31	Tu 15	13 ·17	21 ·62	12
—32	We 16	14 ·13	22 ·60	13
1	Th ○ 17	P ·08	23 ·57	14
2	Fr 18	1 ·01 / 2 ·92	24 ·52	15
3	Sa 19	3 ·83	25 ·47	16
4	Su 20	4 ·73	26 ·40	17
5	Mo 21	5 ·63	27 ·33	18
6	Tu 22	6 ·53	1 ·26	19
7	We 23	7 ·43	2 ·19	20
8	Th 24	8 ·34	3 ·14	21
9	Fr 25	9 ·26	4 ·09	22
10	Sa 26	10 ·19	5 ·05	23
11	Su 27	11 ·14	6 ·03	24
12	Mo 28	12 ·11	7 ·02	25
13	Tu 29	13 ·10	8 ·04	26
14	We 30	14 ·10	9 ·08	27
15	Th 31	—A ·14	10 ·13	28

(Solar: Sukla Simha—Avani, from 1. Lunar: Sukla, Sravana, Bahula. Muhammadan: H. 1410 Muharram, from 1.)

Cyclic Sidereal Year, Month and Day	Week-Day English Month and Day	Tithi Ending Moment	Nakshatra Ending Moment	Muhammadan Year, Month and Day
	Sep.			
16	Fr 1	1 ·19	11 ·20	29
17	Sa 2	2 ·25	12 ·29	—30
18	Su 3	3 ·33	13 ·40	1
19	Mo 4	4 ·41	14 ·51	2
20	Tu 5	5 ·50	15 ·62	3
21	We 6	6 ·57	16 ·72	4
22	Th 7	7 ·63	17 ·80	5
23	Fr 8	8 ·68	18 ·86	6
24	Sa 9	9 ·72	19 ·91	7
25	Su 10	10 ·71	20 ·94	8
26	Mo 11	11 ·69	21 ·95	9
27	Tu 12	12 ·65	22 ·93	10
28	We 13	13 ·60	23 ·90	11
29	Th 14	14 ·53	24 ·86	12
30	Fr 15	P ·45	25 ·81	13
—31	Sa 16	1 ·36	26 ·74	14
1	Su 17	2 ·26	27 ·67	15
2	Mo 18	3 ·16	1 ·60	16
3	Tu 19	4 ·06 / 5 ·96	2 ·54	17
4	We 20	6 ·87	3 ·48	18
5	Th 21	7 ·79	4 ·42	19
6	Fr 22	8 ·73	5 ·38	20
7	Sa 23	9 ·68	6 ·35	21
8	Su 24	10 ·65	7 ·34	22
9	Mo 25	11 ·64	8 ·36	23
10	Tu 26	12 ·64	9 ·39	24
11	We 27	13 ·68	10 ·44	25
12	Th 28	14 ·73	11 ·51	26
13	Fr 29	—A ·79	12 ·60	27
14	Sa 30	1 ·87	13 ·70	28

(Solar: Sukla Simha—Avani, to 31; Sukla Kanya—Purattasi, from 1. Lunar: Sukla, Bhadrapada, Bahula. Muhammadan: H. 1410 Safar.)

Cyclic Sidereal Year, Month and Day	Week-Day English Month and Day	Tithi Ending Moment	Nakshatra Ending Moment	Muhammadan Year, Month and Day
	Oct.			
15	Su 1	2 ·96	14 ·81	—29
16	Mo 2	... ...	15 ·92	1
17	Tu 3	3 ·04	... ...	2
18	We 4	4 ·12	16 ·02	3
19	Th 5	5 ·19	17 ·11	4
20	Fr 6	6 ·23	18 ·18	5
21	Sa 7	7 ·26	19 ·23	6
22	Su 8	8 ·26	20 ·26	7
23	Mo 9	9 ·25	21 ·27	8
24	Tu 10	10 ·21	22 ·26	9
25	We 11	11 ·16	23 ·24	10
26	Th 12	12 ·09	24 ·20	11
27	Fr 13	13 ·01 / 14 ·92	25 ·14	12
28	Sa 14	P ·83	26 ·08	13
29	Su 15	1 ·73	27 ·01 / 1 ·94	14
—30	Mo 16	2 ·63	2 ·88	15
1	Tu 17	3 ·53	3 ·82	16
2	We 18	4 ·44	4 ·76	17
3	Th 19	5 ·36	5 ·71	18
4	Fr 20	6 ·31	6 ·68	19
5	Sa 21	7 ·26	7 ·67	20
6	Su 22	8 ·23	8 ·68	21
7	Mo 23	9 ·22	9 ·70	22
8	Tu 24	10 ·23	10 ·75	23
9	We 25	11 ·26	11 ·82	24
10	Th 26	12 ·31	12 ·90	25
11	Fr 27	13 ·38	... ...	26
12	Sa 28	14 ·46	13 ·00	27
13	Su 29	—A ·55	14 ·11	28
14	Mo 30	1 ·64	15 ·22	29
15	Tu 31	2 ·72	16 ·32	—30

(Solar: Sukla Tula—Aippasi, from 1. Lunar: Sukla, Asvina, Bahula, Suk. Muhammadan: H. 1410 Rabi-ul-awwal.)

Cyclic Sidereal Year, Month and Day	Week-Day English Month and Day	Tithi Ending Moment	Nakshatra Ending Moment	Muhammadan Year, Month and Day
	Nov.			
16	We 1	3 ·78	17 ·42	1
17	Th 2	4 ·83	18 ·49	2
18	Fr 3	5 ·86	19 ·54	3
19	Sa 4	6 ·86	20 ·58	4
20	Su 5	7 ·85	21 ·59	5
21	Mo 6	8 ·81	22 ·59	6
22	Tu 7	9 ·76	23 ·57	7
23	We 8	10 ·70	24 ·53	8
24	Th 9	11 ·62	25 ·48	9
25	Fr 10	12 ·53	26 ·42	10
26	Sa 11	13 ·43	27 ·36	11
27	Su 12	14 ·33	1 ·29	12
28	Mo 13	P ·23	2 ·22	13
29	Tu 14	1 ·14	3 ·15	14
—30	We 15	2 ·05 / 3 ·97	4 ·09	15
1	Th 16	4 ·91	5 ·04	16
2	Fr 17	5 ·87	6 ·02	17
3	Sa 18	6 ·84	7 ·00	18
4	Su 19	7 ·83	8 ·00	19
5	Mo 20	8 ·84	9 ·02	20
6	Tu 21	9 ·88	10 ·06	21
7	We 22	10 ·94	11 ·13	22
8	Th 23	... ...	12 ·21	23
9	Fr 24	11 ·01	13 ·30	24
10	Sa 25	12 ·09	14 ·41	25
11	Su 26	13 ·18	15 ·52	26
12	Mo 27	14 ·26	16 ·63	27
13	Tu 28	—A ·34	17 ·72	28
14	We 29	1 ·41	18 ·80	—29
15	Th 30	2 ·46	19 ·86	1

(Solar: Sukla Tula—Aippasi, to 30; Sukla Vrischika—Kartigai, from 1. Lunar: Sukla, Kartika, Bahula. Muhammadan: H. 1410 Rabi-ul-akhir.)

Cyclic Sidereal Year, Month and Day	Week-Day English Month and Day	Tithi Ending Moment	Nakshatra Ending Moment	Muhammadan Year, Month and Day
	Dec.			
16	Fr 1	3 ·49	20 ·89	2
17	Sa 2	4 ·49	21 ·91	3
18	Su 3	5 ·47	22 ·92	4
19	Mo 4	6 ·43	23 ·90	5
20	Tu 5	7 ·38	24 ·86	6
21	We 6	8 ·31	25 ·81	7
22	Th 7	9 ·24	26 ·76	8
23	Fr 8	10 ·15	27 ·70	9
24	Sa 9	11 ·05 / 12 ·95	1 ·63	10
25	Su 10	13 ·85	2 ·56	11
26	Mo 11	14 ·76	3 ·49	12
27	Tu 12	P ·67	4 ·43	13
28	We 13	1 ·60	5 ·38	14
29	Th 14	2 ·54	6 ·35	15
—30	Fr 15	3 ·50	7 ·32	16
1	Sa 16	4 ·48	8 ·32	17
2	Su 17	5 ·48	9 ·34	18
3	Mo 18	6 ·49	10 ·38	19
4	Tu 19	7 ·53	11 ·44	20
5	We 20	8 ·59	12 ·51	21
6	Th 21	9 ·66	13 ·60	22
7	Fr 22	10 ·74	14 ·70	23
8	Sa 23	11 ·84	15 ·81	24
9	Su 24	12 ·93	16 ·92	25
10	Mo 25	... ...	... ...	26
11	Tu 26	13 ·00	17 ·02	27
12	We 27	14 ·06	18 ·10	28
13	Th 28	—A ·11	19 ·17	29
14	Fr 29	1 ·13	20 ·21	—30
15	Sa 30	2 ·13	21 ·24	1
16	Su 31	3 ·12	22 ·24	2

(Solar: Sukla Dhanus—Margali, from 1. Lunar: Sukla, Margasira, Bahula, P. Suk. Muhammadan: H. 1410 Jumadal-awwal.)

15. Svati. 16. Visak. 17. Anur. 18. Jyesh. 19. Mula. 20. P. Ash. 21. U. Ash. 22. Sravn. 23. Dani. 24. Satab. 25. P.Bhad. 26. U. Bhad. 27. Rev.

A. D. 1990. **Mesha Sankranti** (Commencement of Indian Sidereal Year).
Solar Eclipse. ● **(Surya Sid.) April 13·91.** **Saka 1912.** **Kaliyuga 5091.**
Lunar Eclipse. ○ **(Arya Sid.) April 13·80.** **(S. Cycle) Pramodhuta.**

SOLAR reckoning: Cyclic Sidereal Year, Month and Day; Week-Day, English Month and Day. LUNAR reckoning: Tithi Ending Moment; Nakshatra Ending Moment; Muhammadan Year, Month and Day.

Jan.

Cyclic Sidereal Year, Month	Day	Week-Day	English Day	Lunar month	Tithi Ending Moment	Nakshatra Ending Moment	Muhammadan Year, Month	Day
Sukla Dhanus—Margali	17	Mo	1	Sukla Pausha	4 ·08	23 ·23	H. 1410 Jumadal-akhir	3
	18	Tu	2		5 ·02 6 ·95	24 ·20		4
	19	We	3		7 ·88	25 ·15		5
	20	Th	4		8 ·79	26 ·10		6
	21	Fr	5		9 ·69	27 ·03 1 ·96		7
	22	Sa	6		10 ·59	2 ·89		8
	23	Su	7		11 ·49	3 ·82		9
	24	Mo	8		12 ·40	4 ·77		10
	25	Tu	9		13 ·32	5 ·72		11
	26	We	10		14 ·24	6 ·63		12
	27	Th	11		P ·18	7 ·65		13
	28	Fr	12	Bahula	1 ·15	8 ·64		14
	—29	Sa	13		2 ·12	9 ·66		15
Sukla Makara—Tai	1	Su	14		3 ·12	10 ·69		16
	2	Mo	15		4 ·14	11 ·74		17
	3	Tu	16		5 ·18	12 ·81		18
	4	We	17		6 ·23	13 ·90		19
	5	Th	18		7 ·31	... ...		20
	6	Fr	19		8 ·40	14 ·00		21
	7	Sa	20		9 ·49	15 ·11		22
	8	Su	21		10 ·57	16 ·22		23
	9	Mo	22		11 ·65	17 ·32		24
	10	Tu	23		12 ·72	18 ·41		25
	11	We	24		13 ·76	19 ·48		26
	12	Th	25		14 ·78	20 ·53		27
	13	Fr	26		—A ·78	21 ·56		28
	14	Sa	27		1 ·76	22 ·57		—29
	15	Su	28		2 ·72	23 ·56		1
	16	Mo	29		3 ·66	24 ·53		2
	17	Tu	30		4 ·59	25 ·49		3
	18	We	31		5 ·51	26 ·44		4

Feb.

Cyclic Sidereal Year, Month	Day	Week-Day	English Day	Lunar month	Tithi Ending Moment	Nakshatra Ending Moment	Muhammadan Year, Month	Day
	19	Th	1	Sukla Magha	6 ·42	27 ·37	H. 1410 Rajab	5
	20	Fr	2		7 ·32	1 ·30		6
	21	Sa	3		8 ·22	2 ·23		7
	22	Su	4		9 ·12	3 ·17		8
	23	Mo	5		10 ·03 11 ·94	4 ·11		9
	24	Tu	6		12 ·87	5 ·05		10
	25	We	7		13 ·82	6 ·01 7 ·98		11
	26	Th	8		14 ·78	8 ·97		12
	27	Fr ○	9		P ·75	9 ·98		13
	28	Sa	10	Bahula	1 ·75	... ...		14
	29	Su	11		2 ·78	10 ·00		15
	—30	Mo	12		3 ·82	11 ·05		16
Sukla Kumbha—Masi	1	Tu	13		4 ·87	12 ·12		17
	2	We	14		5 ·95	13 ·21		18
	3	Th	15		... ...	14 ·31		19
	4	Fr	16		6 ·04	15 ·42		20
	5	Sa	17		7 ·13	16 ·52		21
	6	Su	18		8 ·21	17 ·62		22
	7	Mo	19		9 ·28	18 ·71		23
	8	Tu	20		10 ·34	19 ·79		24
	9	We	21		11 ·33	20 ·85		25
	10	Th	22		12 ·41	21 ·88		26
	11	Fr	23		13 ·40	22 ·89		27
	12	Sa	24		14 ·39	23 ·88		28
	13	Su	25		—A ·34	24 ·87		29
	14	Mo	26	P. Suk.	1 ·28	25 ·83		—30
	15	Tu	27		2 ·21	26 ·77		1
	16	We	28		3 ·13	27 ·71		2

March

Cyclic Sidereal Year, Month	Day	Week-Day	English Day	Lunar month	Tithi Ending Moment	Nakshatra Ending Moment	Muhammadan Year, Month	Day
Sukla Kumbha—Masi	17	Th	1	Sukla Phalguna	4 ·04 5 ·94	1 ·65	H. 1410 Shaban	3
	18	Fr	2		6 ·84	2 ·58		4
	19	Sa	3		7 ·74	3 ·51		5
	20	Su	4		8 ·64	4 ·44		6
	21	Mo	5		9 ·55	5 ·39		7
	22	Tu	6		10 ·48	6 ·34		8
	23	We	7		11 ·43	7 ·31		9
	24	Th	8		12 ·39	8 ·30		10
	25	Fr	9		13 ·37	9 ·30		11
	26	Sa	10		14 ·36	10 ·32		12
	27	Su	11		P ·39	11 ·36		13
	28	Mo	12	Bahula	1 ·42	12 ·42		14
	—29	Tu	13		2 ·48	13 ·51		15
Sukla Mina—Panguni	1	We	14		3 ·56	14 ·61		16
	2	Th	15		4 ·64	15 ·71		17
	3	Fr	16		5 ·73	16 ·82		18
	4	Sa	17		6 ·81	17 ·92		19
	5	Su	18		7 ·88	... ...		20
	6	Mo	19		8 ·94	18 ·02		21
	7	Tu	20		9 ·98	19 ·10		22
	8	We	21		... ...	20 ·16		23
	9	Th	22		10 ·00 11 ·99	21 ·20		24
	10	Fr	23		12 ·97	22 ·21		25
	11	Sa	24		13 ·92	23 ·22		26
	12	Su	25		14 ·86	24 ·20		27
	13	Mo	26		—A ·79	25 ·16		28
	14	Tu	27		1 ·71	26 ·11		—29
	15	We	28		2 ·62	27 ·05 1 ·99		1
	16	Th	29		3 ·52	2 ·92		2
	17	Fr	30		4 ·42	3 ·85		3
	18	Sa	31		5 ·32	4 ·78		4

April

Cyclic Sidereal Year, Month	Day	Week-Day	English Day	Lunar month	Tithi Ending Moment	Nakshatra Ending Moment	Muhammadan Year, Month	Day
	19	Su	1	Sukla Chaitra	6 ·22	5 ·72	H. 1410 Ramzan	5
	20	Mo	2		7 ·13	6 ·67		6
	21	Tu	3		8 ·06	7 ·64		7
	22	We	4		9 ·01 10 ·97	8 ·62		8
	23	Th	5		11 ·94	9 ·62		9
	24	Fr	6		12 ·93	10 ·63		10
	25	Sa	7		13 ·95	11 ·67		11
	26	Su	8		14 ·98	12 ·74		12
	27	Mo	9		... ...	13 ·82		13
	28	Tu	10		P ·01	14 ·91		14
	29	We	11	Bahula	1 ·12	... ...		15
	30	Th	12		2 ·21	15 ·01		16
	—31	Fr	13		3 ·29	16 ·12		17
Pramodhuta Mesha—Chittirai	1	Sa	14		4 ·37	17 ·23		18
	2	Su	15		5 ·44	18 ·33		19
	3	Mo	16		6 ·49	19 ·41		20
	4	Tu	17		7 ·53	20 ·47		21
	5	We	18		8 ·54	21 ·51		22
	6	Th	19		9 ·55	22 ·54		23
	7	Fr	20		10 ·52	23 ·54		24
	8	Sa	21		11 ·47	24 ·53		25
	9	Su	22		12 ·41	25 ·49		26
	10	Mo	23		13 ·33	26 ·44		27
	11	Tu	24		14 ·25	27 ·39		28
	12	We	25		—A ·16	1 ·33		29
	13	Th	26	Vsk. Suk.	1 ·06 2 ·96	2 ·26		—30
	14	Fr	27		3 ·86	3 ·19	Shawwal	1
	15	Sa	28		4 ·76	4 ·12		2
	16	Su	29		5 ·66	5 ·06		3
	17	Mo	30		6 ·59	6 ·01 7 ·97		4

May

Cyclic Sidereal Year, Month	Day	Week-Day	English Day	Lunar month	Tithi Ending Moment	Nakshatra Ending Moment	Muhammadan Year, Month	Day
Pramodhuta Mesha—Chittirai	18	Tu	1	Sukla Vaisakha	7 ·54	8 ·95	H. 1410 Shawwal	5
	19	We	2		8 ·50	9 ·94		6
	20	Th	3		9 ·47	10 ·95		7
	21	Fr	4		10 ·47	11 ·99		8
	22	Sa	5		11 ·48	... ...		9
	23	Su	6		12 ·52	12 ·05		10
	24	Mo	7		13 ·57	13 ·12		11
	25	Tu	8		14 ·64	14 ·21		12
	26	We	9		P ·72	15 ·31		13
	27	Th	10	Bahula	1 ·80	16 ·42		14
	28	Fr	11		2 ·89	17 ·53		15
	29	Sa	12		3 96	18 ·63		16
	30	Su	13		... ...	19 ·71		17
	—31	Mo	14		4 ·02	20 ·78		18
Pramodhuta Vrishabha—Vaikasi	1	Tu	15		5 ·06	21 ·83		19
	2	We	16		6 ·07	22 ·86		20
	3	Th	17		7 ·06	23 ·87		21
	4	Fr	18		8 ·04	24 ·85		22
	5	Sa	19		9 ·00 10 ·93	25 ·82		23
	6	Su	20		11 ·85	26 ·78		24
	7	Mo	21		12 ·76	27 ·73		25
	8	Tu	22		13 ·67	1 ·67		26
	9	We	23		14 ·57	2 ·60		27
	10	Th	24		—A ·46	3 ·53		28
	11	Fr	25		1 ·36	4 ·46		—29
	12	Sa	26		2 ·26	5 ·40		1
	13	Su	27		3 ·18	6 ·35		2
	14	Mo	28		4 ·11	7 ·30		3
	15	Tu	29		5 ·05	8 ·27		4
	16	We	30		6 ·00 7 ·96	9 ·26		5
	17	Th	31		8 ·96	10 ·28		6

June

Cyclic Sidereal Year, Month	Day	Week-Day	English Day	Lunar month	Tithi Ending Moment	Nakshatra Ending Moment	Muhammadan Year, Month	Day
	18	Fr	1	Sukla Jyeshtha	9 ·97	11 ·31	H. 1410 Zi-l-ka'da	7
	19	Sa	2		... ...	12 ·36		8
	20	Su	3		10 ·01	13 ·42		9
	21	Mo	4		11 ·06	14 ·51		10
	22	Tu	5		12 ·14	15 61		11
	23	We	6		13 ·22	16 ·72		12
	24	Th	7		14 ·30	17 ·83		13
	25	Fr	8		P ·38	18 ·93		14
	26	Sa	9	Bahula	1 ·44	... ...		15
	27	Su	10		2 ·49	19 ·02		16
	28	Mo	11		3 ·53	20 ·09		17
	29	Tu	12		4 ·56	21 ·15		18
	30	We	13		5 ·55	22 ·18		19
	—31	Th	14		6 ·52	23 ·19		20
Pramodhuta Mithuna—Ani	1	Fr	15		7 ·48	24 ·18		21
	2	Sa	16		8 ·42	25 ·15		22
	3	Su	17		9 ·35	26 ·12		23
	4	Mo	18		10 ·26	27 ·07		24
	5	Tu	19		11 ·16	1 ·00 2 ·93		25
	6	We	20		12 ·06 13 ·96	3 ·86		26
	7	Th	21		14 ·85	4 ·80		27
	8	Fr	22		—A ·75	5 ·74		28
	9	Sa	23	Ashadha Sukla	1 ·66	6 ·68		29
	10	Su	24		2 ·58	7 ·63		—30
	11	Mo	25		3 ·52	8 ·61	Zi-l-hijja	1
	12	Tu	26		4 ·47	9 ·60		2
	13	We	27		5 ·45	10 ·60		3
	14	Th	28		6 ·44	11 ·62		4
	15	Fr	29		7 ·45	12 ·66		5
	16	Sa	30		8 ·48	13 ·73		6

Naksh:—1. Asvn. 2. Bhar. 3. Krit. 4. Rohi. 5. Mrig. 6. Ardh. 7. Punar. 8. Push. 9. Aslesh. 10. Magh. 11. P. Phal. 12. U. Phal. 13. Hasta. 14. Chit.

A. D. 1990.
A.—Amavasya.
P.—Paurnami.

Kollam 1166, Commences { N. Malabar—Sept. / S. Malabar—Aug.

Hijra 1411, Commences, July. 24.

Vikrama 2047.
Bengal San 1396.
(N. Cycle) Subhanu.

SOLAR reckoning: Cyclic Sidereal Year, Month	Day	Week-Day	English Month and Day	LUNAR reckoning: Month	Tithi	Ending Moment	Nakshatra	Ending Moment	Muhammadan Year, Month	Day
			July							
Pramodhuta Mithuna—Ani.	17	Su	1	Ashadha Sukla	9	·53	14	·81	H. 1410 Zi-l-hijja.	7
	18	Mo	2		10	·60	15	·91		8
	19	Tu	3		11	·68	...	...		9
	20	We	4		12	·77	16	·02		10
	21	Th	5		13	·85	17	·13		11
	22	Fr	6		14	·92	18	·23		12
	23	Sa	7		P	·97	19	·32		13
	24	Su	8	Ashadha Bahula	...	...	20	·40		14
	25	Mo	9		1	·01	21	·46		15
	26	Tu	10		2	·04	22	·50		16
	27	We	11		3	·03	23	·51		17
	28	Th	12		4 5	·01 ·96	24	·51		18
	29	Fr	13		6	·90	25	·49		19
	30	Sa	14		7	·82	26	·45		20
	31	Su	15		8	·73	27	·40		21
	32	Mo	16		9	·64	1	·34		22
Pramodhuta Karkata—Adi.	1	Tu	17		10	·54	2	·28		23
	2	We	18		11	·44	3	·21		24
	3	Th	19		12	·34	4	·14		25
	4	Fr	20		13	·24	5	·08		26
	5	Sa	21		14	·14	6 7	·02 ·97		27
	6	Su ●	22		A	·06	8	·94		28
	7	Mo	23	Sravana Sukla	1 2	·00 ·95	9	·92		29
	8	Tu	24		3	·93	10	·92	H. 1411 Muharram.	1
	9	We	25		4	·92	11	·94		2
	10	Th	26		5	·94	12	·97		3
	11	Fr	27		6	·96	...	...		4
	12	Sa	28		...	...	13	·03		5
	13	Su	29		7	·01	14	·12		6
	14	Mo	30		8	·08	15	·22		7
	15	Tu	31		9	·15	16	·32		8
			Aug.							
	16	We	1		10	·24	17	·43		9
	17	Th	2		11	·32	18	·53		10
	18	Fr	3		12	·39	19	·63		11
	19	Sa	4		13	·45	20	·71		12
	20	Su	5		14	·49	21	·77		13
	21	Mo ○	6		P	·52	22	·81		14
	22	Tu	7	Sravana Bahula	1	·51	23	·83		15
	23	We	8		2	·49	24	·84		16
	24	Th	9		3	·45	25	·82		17
	25	Fr	10		4	·39	26	·79		18
	26	Sa	11		5	·32	27	·74		19
	27	Su	12		6	·24	1	·68		20
	28	Mo	13		7	·14	2	·62		21
	29	Tu	14		8 9	·04 ·94	3	·55		22
	30	We	15		10	·84	4	·48		23
	31	Th	16		11	·74	5	·41		24
Pramodhuta Simha—Avani.	1	Fr	17		12	·65	6	·35		25
	2	Sa	18		13	·57	7	·30		26
	3	Su	19		14	·51	8	·27		27
	4	Mo	20		A	·46	9	·25		28
	5	Tu	21	Bhadrapada Sukla	1	·43	10	·24		29
	6	We	22		2	·41	11	·25		30
	7	Th	23		3	·42	12	·29	H. 1411 Safar.	1
	8	Fr	24		4	·45	13	·35		2
	9	Sa	25		5	·51	14	·43		3
	10	Su	26		6	·58	15	·52		4
	11	Mo	27		7	·66	16	·62		5
	12	Tu	28		8	·74	17	·73		6
	13	We	29		9	·82	18	·84		7
	14	Th	30		10	·90	19	·94		8
	15	Fr	31		11	·96	...	...		9

SOLAR reckoning: Cyclic Sidereal Year, Month	Day	Week-Day	English Month and Day	LUNAR reckoning: Month	Tithi	Ending Moment	Nakshatra	Ending Moment	Muhammadan Year, Month	Day
			Sep.							
Pramodhuta Simha—Avani.	16	Sa	1	Bhadrapada Sukla	...	...	20	·02	H. 1411 Safar.	10
	17	Su	2		12	·00	21	·03		11
	18	Mo	3		13	·03	22	·13		12
	19	Tu	4		14	·03	23	·16		13
	20	We	5		P 1	·01 ·96	24	·17		14
	21	Th	6	Bhadrapada Bahula	2	·90	25	·15		15
	22	Fr	7		3	·83	26	·12		16
	23	Sa	8		4	·75	27	·07		17
	24	Su	9		5	·66	1 2	·02 ·96		18
	25	Mo	10		6	·56	3	·89		19
	26	Tu	11		7	·46	4	·82		20
	27	We	12		8	·36	5	·75		21
	28	Th	13		9	·26	6	·69		22
	29	Fr	14		10	·17	7	·64		23
	30	Sa	15		11	·09	8	·60		24
	31	Su	16		12 13	·03 ·99	9	·57		25
Pramodhuta Kanya—Purattasi.	1	Mo	17		14	·96	10	·56		26
	2	Tu	18		A	·95	11	·57		27
	3	We	19	Asvina Sukla	1	·95	12	·61		28
	4	Th	20		2	·98	13	·66		29
	5	Fr	21		...	...	14	·73	H. 1411 Rabi-ul-awwal.	1
	6	Sa	22		3	·04	15	·82		2
	7	Su	23		4	·11	16	·92		3
	8	Mo	24		5	·19	...	...		4
	9	Tu	25		6	·27	17	·03		5
	10	We	26		7	·36	18	·14		6
	11	Th	27		8	·44	19	·24		7
	12	Fr	28		9	·50	20	·32		8
	13	Sa	29		10	·54	21	·39		9
	14	Su	30		11	·56	22	·45		10
			Oct.							
	15	Mo	1		12	·57	23	·48		11
	16	Tu	2		13	·56	24	·49		12
	17	We	3		14	·53	25	·48		13
	18	Th	4		P	·46	26	·45		14
	19	Fr	5	Asvina Bahula	1	·39	27	·41		15
	20	Sa	6		2	·30	1	·36		16
	21	Su	7		3	·21	2	·30		17
	22	Mo	8		4	·12	3	·23		18
	23	Tu	9		5 6	·02 ·92	4	·16		19
	24	We	10		7	·83	5	·09		20
	25	Th	11		8	·74	6 7	·03 ·98		21
	26	Fr	12		9	·66	8	·93		22
	27	Sa	13		10	·59	9	·90		23
	28	Su	14		11	·55	10	·88		24
	29	Mo	15		12	·52	11	·90		25
	30	Tu	16		13	·52	12	·92		26
	31	We	17		14	·53	13	·97		27
Pramodhuta Tula—Aippasi.	1	Th	18		A	·56	...	...		28
	2	Fr	19	Karttika Sukla	1	·62	14	·04		29
	3	Sa	20		2	·70	15	·12		30
	4	Su	21		3	·78	16	·22	H. 1411 Rabi-ul-akhir.	1
	5	Mo	22		4	·86	17	·33		2
	6	Tu	23		5	·94	18	·44		3
	7	We	24		...	...	19	·54		4
	8	Th	25		6	·02	20	·63		5
	9	Fr	26		7	·09	21	·70		6
	10	Sa	27		8	·13	22	·76		7
	11	Su	28		9	·16	23	·80		8
	12	Mo	29		10	·16	24	·81		9
	13	Tu	30		11	·14	25	·80		10
	14	We	31		12	·10	26	·78		11

SOLAR reckoning: Cyclic Sidereal Year, Month	Day	Week-Day	English Month and Day	LUNAR reckoning: Month	Tithi	Ending Moment	Nakshatra	Ending Moment	Muhammadan Year, Month	Day
			Nov.							
Pramodhuta Tula—Aippasi.	15	Th	1	Karttika Sukla	13 14	·05 ·98	27	·75	H. 1411 Rabi-ul-akhir.	12
	16	Fr	2		P	·90	1	·70		13
	17	Sa	3	Karttika Bahula	1	·81	2	·61		14
	18	Su	4		2	·71	3	·57		15
	19	Mo	5		3	·61	4	·50		16
	20	Tu	6		4	·51	5	·43		17
	21	We	7		5	·42	6	·37		18
	22	Th	8		6	·34	7	·31		19
	23	Fr	9		7	·26	8	·26		20
	24	Sa	10		8	·19	9	·23		21
	25	Su	11		9	·15	10	·22		22
	26	Mo	12		10	·13	11	·22		23
	27	Tu	13		11	·12	12	·24		24
	28	We	14		12	·13	13	·28		25
	29	Th	15		13	·17	14	·34		26
	30	Fr	16		14	·23	15	·42		27
Pramodhuta Vrischika—Kartigai.	1	Sa	17		A	·31	16	·52		28
	2	Su	18	Margasira Sukla	1	·39	17	·63		29
	3	Mo	19		2	·48	18	·74	Jumadal-awwal.	1
	4	Tu	20		3	·56	19	·84		2
	5	We	21		4	·64	20	·93		3
	6	Th	22		5	·71	...	...		4
	7	Fr	23		6	·75	21	·02		5
	8	Sa	24		7	·78	22	·08		6
	9	Su	25		8	·77	23	·11		7
	10	Mo	26		9	·76	24	·13		8
	11	Tu	27		10	·72	25	·13		9
	12	We	28		11	·67	26	·11		10
	13	Th	29		12	·60	27	·08		11
	14	Fr	30		13	·52	1 2	·03 ·97		12
			Dec.							
	15	Sa	1		14	·43	3	·91	H. 1411	13
	16	Su	2		P	·33	4	·84		14
	17	Mo	3	Margasira Bahula	1	·23	5	·77		15
	18	Tu	4		2	·14	6	·71		16
	19	We	5		3 4	·05 ·96	7	·65		17
	20	Th	6		5	·88	8	·60		18
	21	Fr	7		6	·82	9	·57		19
	22	Sa	8		7	·78	10	·54		20
	23	Su	9		8	·76	11	·54		21
	24	Mo	10		9	·76	12	·55		22
	25	Tu	11		10	·78	13	·59		23
	26	We	12		11	·82	14	·65		24
	27	Th	13		12	·88	15	·73		25
	28	Fr	14		13	·96	16	·82		26
	29	Sa	15		...	...	17	·92		27
Pramodhuta Dhanus—Margali.	1	Su	16		14	·04	...	...		28
	2	Mo	17		A	·14	18	·03		29
	3	Tu	18	Pausha Sukla	1	·22	19	·14		30
	4	We	19		2	·29	20	·24	H. 1411 Jumadal-akhir.	1
	5	Th	20		3	·35	21	·32		2
	6	Fr	21		4	·39	22	·39		3
	7	Sa	22		5	·42	23	·43		4
	8	Su	23		6	·41	24	·45		5
	9	Mo	24		7	·40	25	·46		6
	10	Tu	25		8	·36	26	·44		7
	11	We	26		9	·31	27	·41		8
	12	Th	27		10	·24	1	·37		9
	13	Fr	28		11	·16	2	·31		10
	14	Sa	29		12 13	·07 ·97	3	·25		11
	15	Su	30		14	·87	4	·18		12
	16	Mo	31		P	·77	5	·11		13

15. Svati. 16. Visak. 17. Anur. 18. Jyesh. 19. Mula. 20. P. Ash. 21. U. Ash. 22. Sravn. 23. Dani. 24. Satab. 25. P. Bhad. 26. U. Bhad. 27. Rev.

A. D. 1991. **Mesha Sankranti** (Commencement of Indian Sidereal Year).

Solar Eclipse. ● **(Surya Sid.) April 14·17.** **Saka 1913.** **Kaliyuga 5092.**

Lunar Eclipse. ○ **(Arya Sid.) April 14·06.** **(S. Cycle) Prajapati.**

SOLAR reckoning: Cyclic Sidereal Year, Month and Day; Week-Day English Month and Day. LUNAR reckoning: Tithi Ending Moment; Nakshatra Ending Moment; Muhammadan Year, Month and Day.

Jan.

Solar month	Cyclic Sidereal	Week-Day	Jan.	Lunar month	Tithi Ending Moment	Nakshatra Ending Moment	Muhammadan	Muh. month
Pramodhuta Dhanus—Margali	17	Tu	1	Pausha	1 ·68	6 ·04 / 7 ·98	14	H. 1411 Jumadal-akhir
	18	We	2		2 ·60	8 ·94	15	
	19	Th	3		3 ·53	9 ·90	16	
	20	Fr	4		4 ·47	10 ·88	17	
	21	Sa	5		5 ·43	11 ·86	18	
	22	Su	6		6 ·41	12 ·87	19	
	23	Mo	7	Bahula	7 ·40	13 ·90	20	
	24	Tu	8		8 ·43	14 ·96	21	
	25	We	9		9 ·47	...	22	
	26	Th	10		10 ·53	15 ·03	23	
	27	Fr	11		11 ·60	16 ·12	24	
	28	Sa	12		12 ·69	17 ·22	25	
	—29	Su	13		13 ·78	18 ·33	26	
Pramodhuta Makara—Tai	1	Mo	14		14 ·86	19 ·44	27	
	2	Tu	15		—A ·93	20 ·54	28	
	3	We	16		...	21 ·63	—29	
	4	Th	17		1 ·00	22 ·70	1	Rajab
	5	Fr	18		2 ·04	23 ·75	2	
	6	Sa	19		3 ·06	24 ·78	3	
	7	Su	20		4 ·07	25 ·79	4	
	8	Mo	21		5 ·05	26 ·78	5	
	9	Tu	22	Sukla	6 ·01 / 7 ·95	27 ·75	6	
	10	We	23		8 ·88	1 ·71	7	
	11	Th	24		9 ·79	2 ·66	8	
	12	Fr	25		10 ·70	3 ·59	9	
	13	Sa	26		11 ·60	4 ·52	10	
	14	Su	27		12 ·50	5 ·45	11	
	15	Mo	28	Magha	13 ·40	6 ·38	12	
	16	Tu	29		14 ·31	7 ·32	13	
	17	We ○	30		P ·23	8 ·27	14	
	18	Th	31		1 ·16	9 ·23	15	

Feb.

Solar month	Cyclic Sidereal	Week-Day	Feb.	Lunar month	Tithi Ending Moment	Nakshatra Ending Moment	Muhammadan	Muh. month
	19	Fr	1		2 ·11	10 ·20	16	H. 1411
	20	Sa	2		3 ·07	11 ·18	17	
	21	Su	3		4 ·05	12 ·19	18	
	22	Mo	4		5 ·05	13 ·22	19	
	23	Tu	5	Bahula	6 ·07	14 ·27	20	
	24	We	6		7 ·11	15 ·34	21	
	25	Th	7		8 ·17	16 ·42	22	
	26	Fr	8		9 ·25	17 ·52	23	
	27	Sa	9		10 ·34	18 ·63	24	
	28	Su	10		11 ·43	19 ·74	25	
	29	Mo	11		12 ·51	20 ·84	26	
	—30	Tu	12		13 ·58	21 ·93	27	
Pramodhuta Kumbha—Masi	1	We	13		14 ·64	...	28	
	2	Th	14		—A ·68	22 ·00	29	
	3	Fr	15		1 ·69	23 ·06	—30	
	4	Sa	16		2 ·70	24 ·10	1	H. 1411 Shaban
	5	Su	17		3 ·68	25 ·11	2	
	6	Mo	18		4 ·63	26 ·10	3	
	7	Tu	19	Sukla	5 ·56	27 ·08	4	
	8	We	20		6 ·49	1 ·05 / 2 ·99	5	
	9	Th	21		7 ·41	3 ·93	6	
	10	Fr	22	Phal—guna	8 ·32	4 ·86	7	
	11	Sa	23		9 ·23	5 ·79	8	
	12	Su	24		10 ·13	6 ·72	9	
	13	Mo	25		11 ·03 / 12 ·93	7 ·66	10	
	14	Tu	26		13 ·85	8 ·61	11	
	15	We	27		14 ·78	9 ·56	12	
	16	Th	28		P ·72	10 ·52	13	

March

Solar month	Cyclic Sidereal	Week-Day	March	Lunar month	Tithi Ending Moment	Nakshatra Ending Moment	Muhammadan	Muh. month
Pramodhuta Kumbha—Masi	17	Fr	1	Phalguna	1 ·69	11 ·51	14	H. 1411 Shaban
	18	Sa	2		2 ·66	12 ·52	15	
	19	Su	3		3 ·66	13 ·54	16	
	20	Mo	4		4 ·68	14 ·58	17	
	21	Tu	5		5 ·73	15 ·64	18	
	22	We	6		6 ·79	16 ·72	19	
	23	Th	7		7 ·87	17 ·82	20	
	24	Fr	8	Bahula	8 ·96	18 ·93	21	
	25	Sa	9		...	...	22	
	26	Su	10		9 ·05	19 ·04	23	
	27	Mo	11		10 ·13	20 ·14	24	
	28	Tu	12		11 ·20	21 ·24	25	
	29	We	13		12 ·25	22 ·32	26	
	—30	Th	14		13 ·29	23 ·38	27	
Pramodhuta Mina—Panguni	1	Fr	15		14 ·30	24 ·42	28	
	2	Sa	16		—A ·29	25 ·48	—29	
	3	Su	17		1 ·27	26 ·43	1	Ramzan
	4	Mo	18		2 ·23	27 ·41	2	
	5	Tu	19		3 ·17	1 ·38	3	
	6	We	20		4 ·10	2 ·33	4	
	7	Th	21	Sukla	5 ·01 / 6 ·91	3 ·27	5	
	8	Fr	22		7 ·81	4 ·20	6	
	9	Sa	23		8 ·71	5 ·13	7	
	10	Su	24		9 ·61	6 ·06	8	
	11	Mo	25		10 ·52	7 ·00 / 8 ·94	9	
	12	Tu	26		11 ·44	9 ·89	10	
	13	We	27	Chaitra	12 ·36	10 ·85	11	
	14	Th	28		13 ·30	11 ·84	12	
	15	Fr	29		14 ·27	12 ·84	13	
	16	Sa	30		P ·24	13 ·85	14	
	17	Su	31		1 ·24	14 ·89	15	

April

Solar month	Cyclic Sidereal	Week-Day	April	Lunar month	Tithi Ending Moment	Nakshatra Ending Moment	Muhammadan	Muh. month
	18	Mo	1		2 ·26	15 ·95	16	H. 1411
	19	Tu	2		3 ·30	...	17	
	20	We	3		4 ·36	16 ·03	18	
	21	Th	4		5 ·44	17 ·13	19	
	22	Fr	5	Bahula	6 ·53	18 ·23	20	
	23	Sa	6		7 ·62	19 ·34	21	
	24	Su	7		8 ·70	20 ·45	22	
	25	Mo	8		9 ·76	21 ·55	23	
	26	Tu	9		10 ·81	22 ·63	24	
	27	We	10		11 ·85	23 ·69	25	
	28	Th	11		12 ·86	24 ·73	26	
	29	Fr	12		13 ·85	25 ·75	27	
	—30	Sa	13		14 ·83	26 ·75	28	
Prajapati Mesha—Chittirai	1	Su	14		—A ·78	27 ·74	29	
	2	Mo	15		1 ·71	1 ·71	—30	
	3	Tu	16		2 ·64	2 ·66	1	H. 1411 Shawwal
	4	We	17		3 ·56	3 ·60	2	
	5	Th	18		4 ·47	4 ·54	3	
	6	Fr	19	Sukla	5 ·37	5 ·48	4	
	7	Sa	20		6 ·27	6 ·41	5	
	8	Su	21		7 ·17	7 ·34	6	
	9	Mo	22		8 ·07 / 9 ·98	8 ·28	7	
	10	Tu	23	Adh. Vaisakha	10 ·90	9 ·22	8	
	11	We	24		11 ·84	10 ·19	9	
	12	Th	25		12 ·80	11 ·17	10	
	13	Fr	26		13 ·79	12 ·16	11	
	14	Sa	27		14 ·78	13 ·17	12	
	15	Su	28		P ·80	14 ·20	13	
	16	Mo	29		1 ·84	15 ·26	14	
	17	Tu	30		2 ·89	16 ·34	15	

May

Solar month	Cyclic Sidereal	Week-Day	May	Lunar month	Tithi Ending Moment	Nakshatra Ending Moment	Muhammadan	Muh. month
Prajapati Mesha—Chittirai	18	We	1	Adhika Vaisak.	3 ·97	17 ·43	16	H. 1411 Shawwal
	19	Th	2		...	18 ·53	17	
	20	Fr	3		4 ·06	19 ·64	18	
	21	Sa	4		5 ·14	20 ·75	19	
	22	Su	5		6 ·22	21 ·85	20	
	23	Mo	6		7 ·29	22 ·93	21	
	24	Tu	7		8 ·34	...	22	
	25	We	8		9 ·38	23 ·00	23	
	26	Th	9		10 ·39	24 ·05	24	
	27	Fr	10	Bahula	11 ·38	25 ·08	25	
	28	Sa	11		12 ·36	26 ·09	26	
	29	Su	12		13 ·31	27 ·07	27	
	30	Mo	13		14 ·25	1 ·04	28	
	—31	Tu	14		—A ·17	2 ·00 / 3 ·95	—29	
Prajapati Vrishabha—Vaikasi	1	We	15		1 ·08 / 2 ·98	4 ·89	1	Zi-l-ka'da
	2	Th	16		3 ·88	5 ·82	2	
	3	Fr	17		4 ·78	6 ·75	3	
	4	Sa	18		5 ·68	7 ·68	4	
	5	Su	19	Sukla	6 ·58	8 ·62	5	
	6	Mo	20		7 ·49	9 ·57	6	
	7	Tu	21		8 ·42	10 ·52	7	
	8	We	22		9 ·36	11 ·49	8	
	9	Th	23	Nija Vaisakha	10 ·31	12 ·48	9	
	10	Fr	24		11 ·29	13 ·49	10	
	11	Sa	25		12 ·28	14 ·52	11	
	12	Su	26		13 ·30	15 ·58	12	
	13	Mo	27		14 ·34	16 ·65	13	
	14	Tu	28		P ·40	17 ·73	14	
	15	We	29		1 ·47	18 ·83	15	
	16	Th	30		2 ·55	19 ·93	16	
	17	Fr	31		3 63	...	17	

June

Solar month	Cyclic Sidereal	Week-Day	June	Lunar month	Tithi Ending Moment	Nakshatra Ending Moment	Muhammadan	Muh. month
	18	Sa	1		4 ·71	20 ·04	18	H. 1411
	19	Su	2		5 ·79	21 ·15	19	
	20	Mo	3		6 ·84	22 ·24	20	
	21	Tu	4	Bahula	7 ·87	23 ·31	21	
	22	We	5		8 ·88	24 ·36	22	
	23	Th	6		9 ·87	25 ·40	23	
	24	Fr	7		10 ·85	26 ·41	24	
	25	Sa	8		11 ·80	27 ·40	25	
	26	Su	9		12 ·74	1 ·37	26	
	27	Mo	10		13 ·67	2 ·33	27	
	28	Tu	11		14 ·58	3 ·28	28	
	29	We	12		—A ·48	4 ·22	29	
	30	Th	13		1 ·38	5 ·15	—30	
	—31	Fr	14		2 ·27	6 ·08	1	H. 1411 Zi-l-hijja
Prajapati Mithuna—Ani	1	Sa	15		3 ·17	7 ·02 / 8 ·96	2	
	2	Su	16		4 ·07 / 5 ·98	9 ·90	3	
	3	Mo	17		6 ·90	10 ·85	4	
	4	Tu	18	Sukla	7 ·84	11 ·82	5	
	5	We	19		8 ·80	12 ·81	6	
	6	Th	20		9 ·77	13 ·81	7	
	7	Fr	21		10 ·76	14 ·84	8	
	8	Sa	22		11 ·78	15 ·89	9	
	9	Su	23	Jyeshtha	12 ·81	16 ·95	10	
	10	Mo	24		13 ·87	...	11	
	11	Tu	25		14 ·94	17 ·03	12	
	12	We	26		...	18 ·13	13	
	13	Th	27		P ·02	19 ·24	14	
	14	Fr	28		1 ·11	20 ·35	15	
	15	Sa	29	Bah.	2 ·19	21 ·45	16	
	16	Su	30		3 ·26	22 ·54	17	

Naksh:—1. Asvn. 2. Bhar. 3. Krit. 4. Rohi. 5. Mrig. 6. Ardh. 7. Punar. 8. Push. 9. Aslesh. 10. Magh. 11. P. Phal. 12. U. Phal. 13. Hasta. 14. Chit.

A. D. 1991.
A.—Amavasya.
P.—Paurnami.

Kollam 1167, Commences { **N. Malabar—Sept.** / **S. Malabar—Aug.**

Hijra 1412, Commences, **July. 13.**

Vikrama 2048.
Bengal San 1397.
(N. Cycle) Tarana.

SOLAR reckoning: Cyclic Sidereal Year, Month and Day; Week-Day English Month and Day. LUNAR reckoning: Tithi Ending Moment; Nakshatra Ending Moment; Muhammadan Year, Month and Day.

July

Side labels: Prajapati *Mithuna—Ani*; Jyesh. *Bahula*; H. 1411 *Zi-l-hijja*; *Sukla*; Ashadha; Prajapati *Karkata—Adi*; H. 1412 *Muharram*.

Cyclic Sidereal Year, Month and Day	Week-Day English Month and Day	Tithi Ending Moment	Nakshatra Ending Moment	Muhammadan Year, Month and Day
17	Mo 1	4 ·30	23 ·62	18
18	Tu 2	5 ·34	24 ·68	19
19	We 3	6 ·36	25 ·72	20
20	Th 4	7 ·35	26 ·73	21
21	Fr 5	8 ·33	27 ·73	22
22	Sa 6	9 ·29	1 ·70	23
23	Su 7	10 ·22	2 ·67	24
24	Mo 8	11 ·14	3 ·62	25
25	Tu 9	12 ·05 / 13 ·95	4 ·56	26
26	We 10	14 ·85	5 ·49	27
27	Th 11	—A ·75	6 ·42	28
28	Fr 12	1 ·65	7 ·35	—29
29	Sa 13	2 ·55	8 ·29	1
30	Su 14	3 ·46	9 ·24	2
31	Mo 15	4 ·38	10 ·19	3
—32	Tu 16	5 ·31	11 ·15	4
1	We 17	6 ·27	12 ·13	5
2	Th 18	7 ·25	13 ·14	6
3	Fr 19	8 ·25	14 ·16	7
4	Sa 20	9 ·26	15 ·20	8
5	Su 21	10 ·30	16 ·25	9
6	Mo 22	11 ·35	17 ·33	10
7	Tu 23	12 ·41	18 ·43	11
8	We 24	13 ·49	19 ·54	12
9	Th 25	14 ·58	20 ·65	13
10	Fr 26	P ·66	21 ·75	14
11	Sa 27	1 ·73	22 ·84	15
12	Su 28	2 ·78	23 ·92	16
13	Mo 29	3 ·82	24 ·99	17
14	Tu 30	4 ·84	... ...	18
15	We 31	5 ·83	25 ·03	19

Aug.

Side labels: *Bahula*; *Sukla*; Sravana; *Bahula*; Prajapati *Simha—Avani*; H. 1412 *Safar*.

Cyclic Sidereal Year, Month and Day	Week-Day English Month and Day	Tithi Ending Moment	Nakshatra Ending Moment	Muhammadan Year, Month and Day
16	Th 1	6 ·81	26 ·05	20
17	Fr 2	7 ·77	27 ·05	21
18	Sa 3	8 ·71	1 ·04	22
19	Su 4	9 ·63	2 ·01 / 3 ·96	23
20	Mo 5	10 ·54	4 ·90	24
21	Tu 6	11 ·45	5 ·83	25
22	We 7	12 ·35	6 ·76	26
23	Th 8	13 ·25	7 ·69	27
24	Fr 9	14 ·15	8 ·63	28
25	Sa 10	A ·05 / 1 ·96	9 ·57	29
26	Su 11	2 ·88	10 ·52	—30
27	Mo 12	3 ·81	11 ·48	1
28	Tu 13	4 ·76	12 ·46	2
29	We 14	5 ·74	13 ·46	3
30	Th 15	6 ·74	14 ·48	4
—31	Fr 16	7 ·75	15 ·51	5
1	Sa 17	8 ·78	16 ·56	6
2	Su 18	9 ·83	17 ·64	7
3	Mo 19	10 ·90	18 ·74	8
4	Tu 20	11 ·99	19 ·84	9
5	We 21	... ...	20 ·95	10
6	Th 22	12 ·07	... ...	11
7	Fr 23	13 ·15	21 ·06	12
8	Sa 24	14 ·22	22 ·16	13
9	Su 25	P ·28	23 ·24	14
10	Mo 26	1 ·32	24 ·30	15
11	Tu 27	2 ·35	25 ·34	16
12	We 28	3 ·34	26 ·37	17
13	Th 29	4 ·31	27 ·38	18
14	Fr 30	5 ·27	1 ·37	19
15	Sa 31	6 ·21	2 ·34	20

Sep.

Side labels: Sravn. *Bah.*; *Sukla*; Bhadrapada; *Bahula*; Prajapati *Simha—Avani*; Prajapati *Kanya—Purattasi*; H. 1412 *Safar*; H. 1412 *Rabi-ul-awwal*.

Cyclic Sidereal Year, Month and Day	Week-Day English Month and Day	Tithi Ending Moment	Nakshatra Ending Moment	Muhammadan Year, Month and Day
16	Su 1	7 ·14	3 ·29	21
17	Mo 2	8 ·05 / 9 ·96	4 ·23	22
18	Tu 3	10 ·86	5 ·17	23
19	We 4	11 ·76	6 ·11	24
20	Th 5	12 ·65	7 ·04 / 8 ·97	25
21	Fr 6	13 ·55	9 ·91	26
22	Sa 7	14 ·47	10 ·86	27
23	Su 8	—A ·40	11 ·82	28
24	Mo 9	1 ·34	12 ·79	—29
25	Tu 10	2 ·29	13 ·78	1
26	We 11	3 ·27	14 ·79	2
27	Th 12	4 ·26	15 ·82	3
28	Fr 13	5 ·26	16 ·88	4
29	Sa 14	6 ·30	17 ·95	5
30	Su 15	7 ·36	... ...	6
—31	Mo 16	8 ·43	18 ·04	7
1	Tu 17	9 ·51	19 ·14	8
2	We 18	10 ·59	20 ·25	9
3	Th 19	11 ·67	21 ·36	10
4	Fr 20	12 ·75	22 ·46	11
5	Sa 21	13 ·81	23 ·54	12
6	Su 22	14 ·85	24 ·61	13
7	Mo 23	P ·87	25 ·66	14
8	Tu 24	1 ·87	26 ·69	15
9	We 25	2 ·85	27 ·71	16
10	Th 26	3 ·82	1 ·70	17
11	Fr 27	4 ·78	2 ·67	18
12	Sa 28	5 ·68	3 ·63	19
13	Su 29	6 ·59	4 ·58	20
14	Mo 30	7 ·50	5 ·52	21

Oct.

Side labels: *Sukla*; Asvina; *Bahula*; Prajapati *Tula—Aippasi*; H. 1412 *Rabi-ul-akhir*.

Cyclic Sidereal Year, Month and Day	Week-Day English Month and Day	Tithi Ending Moment	Nakshatra Ending Moment	Muhammadan Year, Month and Day
15	Tu 1	8 ·41	6 ·45	22
16	We 2	9 ·31	7 ·38	23
17	Th 3	10 ·21	8 ·31	24
18	Fr 4	11 ·11	9 ·25	25
19	Sa 5	12 ·02 / 13 ·94	10 ·20	26
20	Su 6	14 ·88	11 ·15	27
21	Mo 7	—A ·84	12 ·12	28
22	Tu 8	1 ·83	13 ·10	29
23	We 9	2 ·82	14 ·11	—30
24	Th 10	3 ·83	15 ·14	1
25	Fr 11	4 ·87	16 ·19	2
26	Sa 12	5 ·93	17 ·25	3
27	Su 13	... ...	18 ·34	4
28	Mo 14	6 ·00	19 ·44	5
29	Tu 15	7 ·08	20 ·55	6
30	We 16	8 ·16	21 ·66	7
—31	Th 17	9 ·24	22 ·76	8
1	Fr 18	10 ·32	23 ·85	9
2	Sa 19	11 ·38	24 ·92	10
3	Su 20	12 ·43	25 ·97	11
4	Mo 21	13 ·46	... ...	12
5	Tu 22	14 ·45	26 ·01	13
6	We 23	P ·43	27 ·03	14
7	Th 24	1 ·39	1 ·02	15
8	Fr 25	2 ·33	2 ·00 / 3 ·96	16
9	Sa 26	3 ·26	4 ·91	17
10	Su 27	4 ·18	5 ·85	18
11	Mo 28	5 ·09 / 6 ·99	6 ·79	19
12	Tu 29	7 ·89	7 ·72	20
13	We 30	8 ·79	8 ·65	21
14	Th 31	9 ·70	9 ·59	22

Nov.

Side labels: Asv. *Bah.*; *Sukla*; Kartika; *Bahula*; Prajapati *Tula—Aippasi*; Prajapati *Vrischika—Kartigai*; *Rabi-ul-akhir*; H. 1412 *Jumada-l-awwal*.

Cyclic Sidereal Year, Month and Day	Week-Day English Month and Day	Tithi Ending Moment	Nakshatra Ending Moment	Muhammadan Year, Month and Day
15	Fr 1	10 ·61	10 ·53	23
16	Sa 2	11 ·54	11 ·48	24
17	Su 3	12 ·48	12 ·45	25
18	Mo 4	13 ·44	13 ·43	26
19	Tu 5	14 ·42	14 ·44	27
20	We 6	—A ·41	15 ·46	28
21	Th 7	1 ·43	16 ·50	—29
22	Fr 8	2 ·47	17 ·56	1
23	Sa 9	3 ·53	18 ·64	2
24	Su 10	4 ·60	19 ·74	3
25	Mo 11	5 ·68	20 ·85	4
26	Tu 12	6 ·77	21 ·96	5
27	We 13	7 ·86	... ...	6
28	Th 14	8 ·94	22 ·06	7
29	Fr 15	... ...	23 ·15	8
—30	Sa 16	9 ·00	24 ·23	9
1	Su 17	10 ·04	25 ·29	10
2	Mo 18	11 ·07	26 ·33	11
3	Tu 19	12 ·07	27 ·35	12
4	We 20	13 ·04	1 ·35	13
5	Th 21	14 ·00 / P ·95	2 ·33	14
6	Fr 22	1 ·88	3 ·30	15
7	Sa 23	2 ·80	4 ·25	16
8	Su 24	3 ·71	5 ·19	17
9	Mo 25	4 ·62	6 ·12	18
10	Tu 26	5 ·52	7 ·05 / 8 ·99	19
11	We 27	6 ·42	9 ·98	20
12	Th 28	7 ·32	10 ·87	21
13	Fr 29	8 ·23	11 ·81	22
14	Sa 30	9 ·16	12 ·78	23

Dec.

Side labels: *Sukla*; Margasira; *Bahula*; Prajapati *Dhanus—Margali*; H. 1412 *Jumada-l-akhir*.

Cyclic Sidereal Year, Month and Day	Week-Day English Month and Day	Tithi Ending Moment	Nakshatra Ending Moment	Muhammadan Year, Month and Day
15	Su 1	10 ·10	13 ·76	24
16	Mo 2	11 ·06	14 ·76	25
17	Tu 3	12 ·04	15 ·77	26
18	We 4	13 ·05	16 ·81	27
19	Th 5	14 ·07	17 ·87	28
20	Fr 6	—A ·11	18 ·94	29
21	Sa 7	1 ·17	... ...	—30
22	Su 8	2 ·24	19 ·04	1
23	Mo 9	3 ·32	20 ·15	2
24	Tu 10	4 ·41	21 ·26	3
25	We 11	5 ·50	22 ·36	4
26	Th 12	6 ·58	23 ·45	5
27	Fr 13	7 ·64	24 ·54	6
28	Sa 14	8 ·68	25 ·61	7
—29	Su 15	9 ·70	26 ·65	8
1	Mo 16	10 ·70	27 ·67	9
2	Tu 17	11 ·68	1 ·67	10
3	We 18	12 ·64	2 ·66	11
4	Th 19	13 ·58	3 ·63	12
5	Fr 20	14 ·51	4 ·59	13
6	Sa ○ 21	P ·43	5 ·53	14
7	Su 22	1 ·34	6 ·46	15
8	Mo 23	2 ·24	7 ·39	16
9	Tu 24	3 ·14	8 ·32	17
10	We 25	4 ·05 / 5 ·96	9 ·26	18
11	Th 26	6 ·88	10 ·20	19
12	Fr 27	7 ·80	11 ·15	20
13	Sa 28	8 ·74	12 ·11	21
14	Su 29	9 ·71	13 ·09	22
15	Mo 30	10 ·69	14 ·08	23
16	Tu 31	11 ·69	15 ·09	24

15. Svati. 16. Visak. 17. Anur. 18. Jyesh. 19. Mula. 20. P. Ash. 21. U. Ash. 22. Sravn. 23. Dani. 24. Satab. 25. P. Bhad. 26. U. Bhad. 27. Rev.

A. D. 1992. **Mesha Sankranti** (Commencement of Indian Sidereal Year).
Solar Eclipse. ● (Surya Sid.) April 13·43. **Saka 1914.** **Kaliyuga 5093.**
Lunar Eclipse. ○ (Arya Sid.) April 13·32. **(S. Cycle) Angirasa.**

SOLAR reckoning: Cyclic Sidereal Year, Month and Day; Week-Day English Month and Day. LUNAR reckoning: Tithi Ending Moment; Nakshatra Ending Moment; Muhammadan Year, Month and Day.

Jan.

Cyclic Sidereal Year, Month and Day	Week-Day English Month and Day	Tithi Ending Moment	Nakshatra Ending Moment	Muhammadan Year, Month and Day
Prajapati Dhanus—Margali. 17	We 1	Bah. 12 ·71	16 ·12	J.-akhir. 25
18	Th 2	13 ·76	17 ·17	26
19	Fr 3	14 ·82	18 ·25	27
20	Sa 4	—A ·90	19 ·34	28
21	Su 5	1 ·98	20 ·44	29
22	Mo 6	... ...	21 ·55	1
23	Tu 7	2 ·07	22 ·66	2
24	We 8	3 ·15	23 ·76	3
25	Th 9	4 ·23	24 ·85	4
26	Fr 10	5 ·29	25 ·92	5
27	Sa 11	6 ·33	26 ·96	6
28	Su 12	Sukla 7 ·36	27 ·99	7
29	Mo 13	8 ·35	... ...	8
—30	Tu 14	9 ·32	1 ·01	9
1	We 15	10 ·28	2 ·00 / 3 ·97	10
2	Th 16	11 ·23	4 ·92	11
3	Fr 17	12 ·16	5 ·87	12
4	Sa 18	Pausha 13 ·07 / 14 ·98	6 ·81	H. 1412 Rajab. 13
5	Su 19	P ·88	7 ·74	14
6	Mo 20	1 ·78	8 ·67	15
7	Tu 21	2 ·63	9 ·60	16
8	We 22	3 ·59	10 ·54	17
9	Th 23	4 ·51	11 ·49	18
10	Fr 24	5 ·44	12 ·45	19
Prajapati Makara—Tai. 11	Sa 25	Bahula 6 ·39	13 ·42	20
12	Su 26	7 ·36	14 ·40	21
13	Mo 27	8 ·34	15 ·41	22
14	Tu 28	9 ·33	16 ·44	23
15	We 29	10 ·35	17 ·49	24
16	Th ● 30	11 ·40	18 ·56	25
17	Fr 31	12 ·47	19 ·64	26

Feb.

Cyclic Sidereal Year, Month and Day	Week-Day English Month and Day	Tithi Ending Moment	Nakshatra Ending Moment	Muhammadan Year, Month and Day
18	Sa 1	13 ·55	20 ·74	27
19	Su 2	14 ·63	21 ·85	28
20	Mo 3	—A ·72	22 ·96	29
21	Tu 4	1 ·80	... ...	—30
22	We 5	2 ·87	23 ·06	1
23	Th 6	3 ·93	24 ·15	2
24	Fr 7	4 ·97	25 ·22	3
25	Sa 8	5 ·99	26 ·28	4
26	Su 9	6 ·98	27 ·31	5
27	Mo 10	Sukla 7 ·96	1 ·33	6
28	Tu 11	8 ·92	2 ·32	7
—29	We 12	9 ·86	3 ·29	8
1	Th 13	10 ·78	4 ·25	9
2	Fr 14	11 ·69	5 ·20	10
3	Sa 15	12 ·60	6 ·14	11
4	Su 16	13 ·51	7 ·08	12
5	Mo 17	Magha 14 ·41	8 ·01 / 9 ·94	H. 1412 Shaban. 13
Prajapati Kumbha—Masi. 6	Tu 18	P ·31	10 ·88	14
7	We 19	1 ·22	11 ·83	15
8	Th 20	2 ·13	12 ·78	16
9	Fr 21	3 ·06	13 ·74	17
10	Sa 22	4 ·02 / 5 ·98	14 ·73	18
11	Su 23	Bahula 6 ·96	15 ·73	19
12	Mo 24	7 ·95	16 ·76	20
13	Tu 25	8 ·98	17 ·80	21
14	We 26	... ...	18 ·86	22
15	Th 27	9 ·02	19 ·95	23
16	Fr 28	10 ·09	... ...	24
17	Sa 29	11 ·17	20 ·05	25

March

Cyclic Sidereal Year, Month and Day	Week-Day English Month and Day	Tithi Ending Moment	Nakshatra Ending Moment	Muhammadan Year, Month and Day
Prajapati Kumbha—Masi. 18	Su 1	Bah. 12 ·26	21 ·16	Shaban. 26
19	Mo 2	13 ·35	22 ·26	27
20	Tu 3	14 ·43	23 ·36	28
21	We 4	—A ·50	24 ·45	—29
22	Th 5	1 ·55	25 ·53	1
23	Fr 6	2 ·59	26 ·59	2
24	Sa 7	3 ·60	27 ·63	3
25	Su 8	4 ·59	1 ·65	4
26	Mo 9	5 ·56	2 ·65	5
27	Tu 10	6 ·52	3 ·63	6
28	We 11	Sukla 7 ·46	4 ·59	7
29	Th 12	8 ·39	5 ·55	8
30	Fr 13	9 ·30	6 ·49	9
—31	Sa 14	10 ·20	7 ·42	10
1	Su 15	11 ·10	8 ·35	11
2	Mo 16	12 ·00 / 13 ·90	9 ·28	12
3	Tu 17	Phalguna 14 ·81	10 ·22	H. 1412 Ramzan. 13
4	We 18	P ·73	11 ·16	14
5	Th 19	1 ·66	12 ·11	15
6	Fr 20	2 ·60	13 ·07	16
7	Sa 21	3 ·56	14 ·05	17
8	Su 22	4 ·55	15 ·06	18
9	Mo 23	5 ·55	16 ·07	19
10	Tu 24	6 ·58	17 ·11	20
Prajapati Mina—Panguni. 11	We 25	7 ·62	18 ·17	21
12	Th 26	Bahula 8 ·68	19 ·25	22
13	Fr 27	9 ·76	20 ·31	23
14	Sa 28	10 ·85	21 ·45	24
15	Su 29	11 ·93	22 ·56	25
16	Mo 30	... ...	23 ·66	26
17	Tu 31	12 ·01	24 ·76	27

April

Cyclic Sidereal Year, Month and Day	Week-Day English Month and Day	Tithi Ending Moment	Nakshatra Ending Moment	Muhammadan Year, Month and Day
18	We 1	13 ·08	25 ·84	28
19	Th 2	14 ·13	26 ·91	29
20	Fr 3	—A ·16	27 ·95	—30
21	Sa 4	1 ·17	1 ·97	1
22	Su 5	2 ·17	2 ·97	2
23	Mo 6	3 ·14	3 ·95	3
24	Tu 7	4 ·10	4 ·92	4
25	We 8	5 ·04 / 6 ·96	5 ·88	5
26	Th 9	Sukla 7 ·87	6 ·82	6
27	Fr 10	8 ·77	7 ·76	7
28	Sa 11	9 ·67	8 ·69	8
—29	Su 12	10 ·57	9 ·62	9
1	Mo 13	11 ·47	10 ·56	10
2	Tu 14	12 ·37	11 ·50	11
3	We 15	Chaitra 13 ·28	12 ·44	H. 1412 Shawwal. 12
4	Th 16	14 ·21	13 ·40	13
5	Fr 17	P ·15	14 ·39	14
6	Sa 18	1 ·12	15 ·38	15
Angirasa Mesha—Chittirai. 7	Su 19	2 ·10	16 ·39	16
8	Mo 20	3 ·09	17 ·42	17
9	Tu 21	4 ·12	18 ·48	18
10	We 22	5 ·16	19 ·55	19
11	Th 23	6 ·22	20 ·65	20
12	Fr 24	Bahula 7 ·30	21 ·75	21
13	Sa 25	8 ·39	22 ·86	22
14	Su 26	9 ·47	23 ·96	23
15	Mo 27	10 ·55	... ...	24
16	Tu 28	11 ·61	24 ·06	25
17	We 29	12 ·66	25 ·15	26
18	Th 30	13 ·70	26 ·22	27

May

Cyclic Sidereal Year, Month and Day	Week-Day English Month and Day	Tithi Ending Moment	Nakshatra Ending Moment	Muhammadan Year, Month and Day
Angirasa Mesha—Chittirai. 19	Fr 1	14 ·71	27 ·27	28
20	Sa 2	—A ·70	1 ·29	—29
21	Su 3	1 ·67	2 ·30	1
22	Mo 4	2 ·62	3 ·29	2
23	Tu 5	3 ·55	4 ·26	3
24	We 6	4 ·47	5 ·22	4
25	Th 7	5 ·39	6 ·16	5
26	Fr 8	6 ·29	7 ·10	6
27	Sa 9	Sukla 7 ·19	8 ·03 / 9 ·96	7
28	Su 10	8 ·09 / 9 ·99	10 ·90	8
29	Mo 11	10 ·89	11 ·84	9
30	Tu 12	11 ·81	12 ·78	10
—31	We 13	Vaisakha 12 ·73	13 ·73	11
1	Th 14	13 ·67	14 ·71	H. 1412 Zi-l-ka'da. 12
2	Fr 15	14 ·63	15 ·70	13
3	Sa 16	P ·61	16 ·71	14
4	Su 17	1 ·61	17 ·74	15
5	Mo 18	2 ·63	18 ·79	16
6	Tu 19	3 ·67	19 ·86	17
7	We 20	4 ·73	20 ·95	18
8	Th 21	5 ·80	... ...	19
9	Fr 22	6 ·88	21 ·05	20
Angirasa Vrishabha—Vaikasi. 10	Sa 23	7 ·97	22 ·16	21
11	Su 24	Bahula	23 ·27	22
12	Mo 25	8 ·05	24 ·37	23
13	Tu 26	9 ·12	25 ·46	24
14	We 27	10 ·17	26 ·53	25
15	Th 28	11 ·19	27 ·58	26
16	Fr 29	12 ·20	1 ·61	27
17	Sa 30	13 ·20	2 ·63	28
18	Su 31	14 ·17	3 ·62	29

June

Cyclic Sidereal Year, Month and Day	Week-Day English Month and Day	Tithi Ending Moment	Nakshatra Ending Moment	Muhammadan Year, Month and Day
19	Mo 1	—A ·12	4 ·59	—30
20	Tu 2	1 ·06 / 2 98	5 ·55	1
21	We 3	3 ·89	6 ·50	2
22	Th 4	4 ·79	7 ·44	3
23	Fr 5	5 ·69	8 ·37	4
24	Sa 6	Sukla 6 ·59	9 ·30	5
25	Su 7	7 ·49	10 ·28	6
26	Mo 8	8 ·39	11 ·17	7
27	Tu 9	9 ·30	12 ·11	8
28	We 10	10 ·22	13 ·07	9
29	Th 11	11 ·17	14 ·04	H. 1412 Zi-l-hijja. 10
30	Fr 12	12 ·12	15 ·02	11
31	Sa 13	Jyeshtha 13 ·00	16 ·03	12
—32	Su 14	14 ·09	17 ·05	13
1	Mo ○ 15	P ·11	18 ·11	14
2	Tu 16	1 ·15	19 ·17	15
3	We 17	2 ·21	20 ·25	16
4	Th 18	3 ·28	21 ·35	17
5	Fr 19	4 ·36	22 ·46	18
6	Sa 20	5 ·44	23 ·57	19
Angirasa Mithuna—Ani. 7	Su 21	6 ·52	24 ·67	20
8	Mo 22	Bahula 7 ·59	25 ·76	21
9	Tu 23	8 ·64	26 ·84	22
10	We 24	9 ·67	27 ·89	23
11	Th 25	10 ·69	1 ·98	24
12	Fr 26	11 ·67	2 ·95	25
13	Sa 27	12 ·64	3 ·95	26
14	Su 28	13 ·60	4 ·92	27
15	Mo 29	14 ·54	5 ·88	28
16	Tu 30	—A ·46	6 ·83	29

Nakah:—1. Asvn. 2. Bhar. 3. Krit. 4. Rohi. 5. Mrig. 6. Ardh. 7. Punar. 8. Push. 9. Aslesh. 10. Magh. 11. P. Phal. 12. U. Phal. 13. Hasta. 14. Chit.

A. D. 1992.
A.—Amavasya.
P.—Paurnami.

Kollam 1168, Commences { N. Malabar—Sept. / S. Malabar—Aug.

Hijra 1413, Commences, July. 2.

Vikrama 2049.
Bengal San 1398.
(N. Cycle) Parthiva.

Columns: SOLAR reckoning (Cyclic Sidereal Year, Month and Day; Week-Day English Month and Day) — LUNAR reckoning (Tithi Ending Moment; Nakshatra Ending Moment; Muhammadan Year, Month and Day).

July

Cyclic Sidereal Year, Month	Day	Week-Day	English Day	Lunar Month	Tithi	Ending Moment	Nakshatra	Ending Moment	Muhammadan Year, Month	Day
Angirasa Mithuna—Ani.	17	We	1	Ashadha Sukla	1	·37	7	·77		—30
	18	Th	2		2	·27	8	·71	H. 1413 Muharram.	1
	19	Fr	3		3	·17	9	·64		2
	20	Sa	4		4 / 5	·07 / ·97	10	·57		3
	21	Su	5		6	·87	11	·50		4
	22	Mo	6		7	·78	12	·45		5
	23	Tu	7		8	·70	13	·41		6
	24	We	8		9	·64	14	·37		7
	25	Th	9		10	·60	15	·35		8
	26	Fr	10		11	·58	16	·35		9
	27	Sa	11		12	·57	17	·38		10
	28	Su	12		13	·59	18	·42		11
	29	Mo	13		14	·63	19	·48		12
	30	Tu	14		P	·68	20	·55		13
	—31	We	15	Bahula	1	·74	21	·65		14
Angirasa Karkata—Adi.	1	Th	16		2	·82	22	·76		15
	2	Fr	17		3	·91	23	·87		16
	3	Sa	18		4	·99	24	·97		17
	4	Su	19		...	...	...	...		18
	5	Mo	20		5	·06	25	·06		19
	6	Tu	21		6	·12	26	·14		20
	7	We	22		7	·15	27	·20		21
	8	Th	23		8	·16	1	·25		22
	9	Fr	24		9	·15	2	·27		23
	10	Sa	25		10	·13	3	·27		24
	11	Su	26		11	·08	4	·25		25
	12	Mo	27		12 / 13	·02 / ·95	5	·22		26
	13	Tu	28		14	·86	6	·18		27
	14	We	29		—A	76	7	·12		28
	15	Th	30		1	·66	8 / 9	·05 / ·98		29
	16	Fr	31		2	·56	10	·91		—30

Aug.

Cyclic Sidereal Year, Month	Day	Week-Day	English Day	Lunar Month	Tithi	Ending Moment	Nakshatra	Ending Moment	Muhammadan Year, Month	Day
Angirasa Karkata—Adi.	17	Sa	1	Sravana Sukla	3	·46	11	·85	H. 1413 Safar.	1
	18	Su	2		4	·37	12	·79		2
	19	Mo	3		5	·28	13	·74		3
	20	Tu	4		6	·20	14	·70		4
	21	We	5		7	·13	15	·67		5
	22	Th	6		8	·08	16	·68		6
	23	Fr	7		9	·06	17	·70		7
	24	Sa	8		10	·05	18	·73		8
	25	Su	9		11	·07	19	·78		9
	26	Mo	10		12	·11	20	·86		10
	27	Tu	11		13	·16	21	·95		11
	28	We	12		14	·23	...	...		12
	29	Th	13		P	·31	22	·05		13
	30	Fr	14	Bahula	1	·40	23	·16		14
	31	Sa	15		2	·48	24	·27		15
	—32	Su	16		3	·55	25	·37		16
Angirasa Simha—Avani.	1	Mo	17		4	·60	26	·45		17
	2	Tu	18		5	·64	27	·52		18
	3	We	19		6	·66	1	·57		19
	4	Th	20		7	·65	2	·59		20
	5	Fr	21		8	·62	3	·60		21
	6	Sa	22		9	·58	4	·58		22
	7	Su	23		10	·53	5	·55		23
	8	Mo	24		11	·46	6	·51		24
	9	Tu	25		12	·37	7	·45		25
	10	We	26		13	·27	8	·39		26
	11	Th	27		14	·17	9	·33		27
	12	Fr	28	B. Suk.	A / 1	·06 / ·96	10	·26		28
	13	Sa	29		2	·87	11	·19		—29
	14	Su	30		3	·78	12	·13	H. 1413 Rabi-ul-awwal.	1
	15	Mo	31		4	·71	13	·07		2

Sep.

Cyclic Sidereal Year, Month	Day	Week-Day	English Day	Lunar Month	Tithi	Ending Moment	Nakshatra	Ending Moment	Muhammadan Year, Month	Day
Angirasa Simha—Avani.	16	Tu	1	Bhadrapada Sukla	5	·65	14	·03		3
	17	We	2		6	·61	15	·01		4
	18	Th	3		7	·58	16	·00		5
	19	Fr	4		8	·56	17	·01		6
	20	Sa	5		9	·58	18	·04		7
	21	Su	6		10	·62	19	·09		8
	22	Mo	7		11	·68	20	·16		9
	23	Tu	8		12	·75	21	·26		10
	24	We	9		13	·83	22	·36		11
	25	Th	10		14	·92	23	·46		12
	26	Fr	11		...	...	24	·57		13
	27	Sa	12		P	·00	25	·67		14
	28	Su	13	Bahula	1	·07	26	·76		15
	29	Mo	14		2	·13	27	·83		16
	30	Tu	15		3	·17	1	·88		17
	—31	We	16		4	·19	2	·91		18
Angirasa Kanya—Purattasi.	1	Th	17		5	·18	3	·92		19
	2	Fr	18		6	·16	4	·92		20
	3	Sa	19		7	·12	5	·89		21
	4	Su	20		8 / 9	·06 / ·98	6	·85		22
	5	Mo	21		10	·90	7	·79		23
	6	Tu	22		11	·81	8	·73		24
	7	We	23		12	·71	9	·67		25
	8	Th	24		13	·61	10	·60		26
	9	Fr	25		14	·51	11	·53		27
	10	Sa	26		—A	·41	12	·46		28
	11	Su	27	Asvina Sukla	1	·32	13	·41		29
	12	Mo	28		2	·25	14	·37		—30
	13	Tu	29		3	·19	15	·34	H. 1413 Rabi-ul-akhir.	1
	14	We	30		4	·14	16	·32		2

Oct.

Cyclic Sidereal Year, Month	Day	Week-Day	English Day	Lunar Month	Tithi	Ending Moment	Nakshatra	Ending Moment	Muhammadan Year, Month	Day
Angirasa Kanya—Purattasi.	15	Th	1	Asvina Sukla	5	·12	17	·33		3
	16	Fr	2		6	·12	18	·35		4
	17	Sa	3		7	·13	19	·40		5
	18	Su	4		8	·17	20	·47		6
	19	Mo	5		9	·22	21	·56		7
	20	Tu	6		10	·29	22	·66		8
	21	We	7		11	·38	23	·76		9
	22	Th	8		12	·47	24	·87		10
	23	Fr	9		13	·56	25	·98		11
	24	Sa	10		14	·64	...	...		12
	25	Su	11		P	·70	26	·07		13
	26	Mo	12	Bahula	1	·73	27	·14		14
	27	Tu	13		2	·75	1	·19		15
	28	We	14		3	·75	2	·23		16
	29	Th	15		4	·73	3	·25		17
	—30	Fr	16		5	·69	4	·24		18
Angirasa Tula—Aippasi.	1	Sa	17		6	·63	5	·22		19
	2	Su	18		7	·56	6	·18		20
	3	Mo	19		8	·47	7	·13		21
	4	Tu	20		9	·38	8	·07		22
	5	We	21		10	·28	9 / 10	·01 / ·94		23
	6	Th	22		11	·18	11	·87		24
	7	Fr	23		12 / 13	·08 / ·99	12	·80		25
	8	Sa	24		14	·91	13	·74		26
	9	Su	25		—A	·83	14	·70		27
	10	Mo	26	Kartt. Suk.	1	·77	15	·67		28
	11	Tu	27		2	·73	16	·65		—29
	12	We	28		3	·71	17	·65	J.-awwal.	1
	13	Th	29		4	·71	18	·67		2
	14	Fr	30		5	·72	19	·72		3
	15	Sa	31		6	·76	20	·78		4

Nov.

Cyclic Sidereal Year, Month	Day	Week-Day	English Day	Lunar Month	Tithi	Ending Moment	Nakshatra	Ending Moment	Muhammadan Year, Month	Day
Angirasa Tula—Aippasi.	16	Su	1	Karttika Sukla	7	·82	21	·86	H. 1413 Jumadal-awwal.	5
	17	Mo	2		8	·90	22	·95		6
	18	Tu	3		9	·99	...	...		7
	19	We	4		...	...	23	·06		8
	20	Th	5		10	·08	24	·17		9
	21	Fr	6		11	·16	25	·28		10
	22	Sa	7		12	·23	26	·37		11
	23	Su	8		13	·29	27	·45		12
	24	Mo	9		14	·33	1	·51		13
	25	Tu	10		P	·36	2	·55		14
	26	We	11	Bahula	1	·35	3	·57		15
	27	Th	12		2	·32	4	·57		16
	28	Fr	13		3	·29	5	·55		17
	29	Sa	14		4	·24	6	·51		18
	—30	Su	15		5	·17	7	·46		19
Angirasa Vrischika—Kartigai.	1	Mo	16		6 / 7	·08 / ·99	8	·40		20
	2	Tu	17		8	·89	9	·34		21
	3	We	18		9	·79	10	·27		22
	4	Th	19		10	·69	11	·20		23
	5	Fr	20		11	·60	12	·14		24
	6	Sa	21		12	·52	13	·08		25
	7	Su	22		13	·45	14	·03		26
	8	Mo	23		14	·39	15 / 16	·00 / ·98		27
	9	Tu	24		—A	·35	17	·97		28
	10	We	25	Margasira Sukla	1	·34	18	·99		29
	11	Th	26		2	·33	...	...		—30
	12	Fr	27		3	·35	19	·03	H. 1413 Jumadal-akhir.	1
	13	Sa	28		4	·40	20	·09		2
	14	Su	29		5	·46	21	·16		3
	15	Mo	30		6	·53	22	·25		4

Dec.

Cyclic Sidereal Year, Month	Day	Week-Day	English Day	Lunar Month	Tithi	Ending Moment	Nakshatra	Ending Moment	Muhammadan Year, Month	Day
Angirasa Vrischika—Kartigai.	16	Tu	1	Margasira Sukla	7	·61	23	·36		5
	17	We	2		8	·70	24	·47		6
	18	Th	3		9	·79	25	·58		7
	19	Fr	4		10	·87	26	·67		8
	20	Sa	5		11	·93	27	·75		9
	21	Su	6		12	·97	1	·82		10
	22	Mo	7		13	·99	2	·87		11
	23	Tu	8		14	·98	3	·89		12
	24	We ○	9		P	·96	4	·89		13
	25	Th	10	Bahula	1	·92	5	·88		14
	26	Fr	11		2	·86	6	·85		15
	27	Sa	12		3	·79	7	·81		16
	28	Su	13		4	·71	8	·75		17
	29	Mo	14		5	·62	9	·68		18
	—30	Tu	15		6	·52	10	·61		19
Angirasa Dhanus—Margali.	1	We	16		7	·42	11	·54		20
	2	Th	17		8	·32	12	·48		21
	3	Fr	18		9	·23	13	·42		22
	4	Sa	19		10	·15	14	·37		23
	5	Su	20		11	·08	15	·33		24
	6	Mo	21		12 / 13	·03 / ·99	16	·30		25
	7	Tu	22		14	·97	17	·30		26
	8	We ●	23		—A	·97	18	·31		27
	9	Th	24	Pausha Sukla	...	...	19	·34		28
	10	Fr	25		1	·00	20	·39		—29
	11	Sa	26		2	·05	21	·47	H.1413 Rajab.	1
	12	Su	27		3	·11	22	·56		2
	13	Mo	28		4	·18	23	·66		3
	14	Tu	29		5	·27	24	·77		4
	15	We	30		6	·36	25	·88		5
	16	Th	31		7	·44	26	·98		6

15. Svati. 16. Visak. 17. Anur. 18. Jyesh. 19. Mula. 20. P. Ash. 21. U. Ash. 22. Sravn. 23. Dani. 24. Satab. 25. P. Bhad. 26. U. Bhad. 27. Rev.

A. D. 1993. **Mesha Sankranti** (Commencement of Indian Sidereal Year).

Solar Eclipse. ● **(Surya Sid.) April 13·68.** **Saka 1915.** **Kaliyuga 5094.**

Lunar Eclipse. ○ **(Arya Sid.) April 13·57.** **(S. Cycle) Srimukha.**

Jan.

SOLAR reckoning: Cyclic Sidereal Year, Month	Day	Week-Day	English Day	LUNAR: Month	Tithi Ending Moment	Nakshatra Ending Moment	Muhammadan Year, Month	Day
Angirasa Dhanus—Margali.	17	Fr	1	Sukla	8 ·52	... ...		7
	18	Sa	2		9 ·58	27 ·06		8
	19	Su	3		10 ·62	1 ·13		9
	20	Mo	4		11 ·63	2 ·18		10
	21	Tu	5		12 ·63	3 ·21		11
	22	We	6	Pausha	13 ·61	4 ·22		12
	23	Th	7		14 ·57	5 ·20		13
	24	Fr	8		P ·52	6 ·18		14
	25	Sa	9		1 ·44	7 ·14		15
	26	Su	10		2 ·35	8 ·09		16
	27	Mo	11		3 ·26	9 ·02 10 ·95	H. 1413 Rajab.	17
	28	Tu	12		4 ·16	11 ·88		18
	—29	We	13	Bahula	5 ·06 6 ·96	12 ·82		19
	1	Th	14		7 ·88	13 ·76		20
	2	Fr	15		8 ·80	·14 ·70		21
	3	Sa	16		9 ·73	15 ·66		22
	4	Su	17		10 ·68	16 ·64		23
	5	Mo	18		11 ·64	17 ·62		24
	6	Tu	19		12 ·62	18 ·63		25
	7	We	20		13 ·62	19 ·66		26
	8	Th	21		14 ·65	20 ·70		27
	9	Fr	22		—A ·70	21 ·77		28
	10	Sa	23		1 ·77	22 ·86		29
	11	Su	24		2 ·85	23 ·96		—30
Angirasa Makara—Tai.	12	Mo	25		3 ·94	... ...		1
	13	Tu	26		... ...	24 ·07		2
	14	We	27		4 ·02	25 ·17		3
	15	Th	28		5 ·10	26 ·27		4
	16	Fr	29		6 ·17	27 ·37		5
	17	Sa	30	Sukla	7 ·23	1 ·44		6
	18	Su	31		8 ·26	2 ·50		7

Feb.

SOLAR reckoning: Cyclic Sidereal Year, Month	Day	Week-Day	English Day	LUNAR: Month	Tithi Ending Moment	Nakshatra Ending Moment	Muhammadan Year, Month	Day
	19	Mo	1		9 ·27	3 ·53		8
	20	Tu	2	Magha	10 ·28	4 ·54		9
	21	We	3		11 ·25	5 ·54	H. 1413 Shaban.	10
	22	Th	4		12 ·20	6 ·51		11
	23	Fr	5		13 ·14	7 ·47		12
	24	Sa	6		14 ·06 P ·93	8 ·42		13
	25	Su	7		1 ·89	9 ·36		14
	26	Mo	8		2 ·79	10 ·30		15
	27	Tu	9		3 ·69	11 ·23		16
	28	We	10		4 ·59	12 ·16		17
	—29	Th	11		5 ·50	13 ·09		18
Angirasa Kumbha—Masi.	1	Fr	12	Bahula	6 ·42	14 ·03 15 ·99		19
	2	Sa	13		7 ·35	16 ·96		20
	3	Su	14		8 ·30	17 ·95		21
	4	Mo	15		9 ·27	18 ·95		22
	5	Tu	16		10 ·25	19 ·97		23
	6	We	17		11 ·25	... ...		24
	7	Th	18		12 ·28	20 ·01		25
	8	Fr	19		13 ·32	21 ·08		26
	9	Sa	20		14 ·39	22 ·17		27
	10	Su	21		—A ·47	23 ·27		28
	11	Mo	22	Phalg. Sukla	1 ·57	24 ·37		—29
	12	Tu	23		2 ·65	25 ·48	Ramzan.	1
	13	We	24		3 ·72	26 ·58		2
	14	Th	25		4 ·79	27 ·67		3
	15	Fr	26		5 ·85	1 ·75		4
	16	Sa	27		6 ·89	2 ·81		5
	17	Su	28		7 ·90	3 ·85		6

March

SOLAR reckoning: Cyclic Sidereal Year, Month	Day	Week-Day	English Day	LUNAR: Month	Tithi Ending Moment	Nakshatra Ending Moment	Muhammadan Year, Month	Day
Angirasa Kumbha—Masi.	18	Mo	1	Sukla	8 ·89	4 ·87		7
	19	Tu	2		9 ·86	5 ·87		8
	20	We	3		10 ·81	6 ·85		9
	21	Th	4		11 ·75	7 ·81		10
	22	Fr	5		12 ·67	8 ·76		11
	23	Sa	6	Phalguna	13 ·59	9 ·71		12
	24	Su	7		14 ·50	10 ·64		13
	25	Mo	8		P ·40	11 ·57		14
	26	Tu	9		1 ·30	12 ·50	H. 1413 Ramzan.	15
	27	We	10		2 ·20	13 ·43		16
	28	Th	11		3 ·10	14 ·37		17
	29	Fr	12		4 ·02 5 ·95	15 ·32		18
	—30	Sa	13		6 ·89	16 ·29		19
	1	Su	14	Bahula	7 ·86	17 ·27		20
	2	Mo	15		8 ·84	18 ·27		21
	3	Tu	16		9 ·84	19 ·29		22
	4	We	17		10 ·88	20 ·33		23
	5	Th	18		11 ·93	21 ·39		24
	6	Fr	19		12 ·99	22 ·47		25
	7	Sa	20		... ...	23 ·56		26
	8	Su	21		13 ·07	24 ·66		27
	9	Mo	22		14 ·16	25 ·77		28
	10	Tu	23		—A ·25	26 ·88		29
	11	We	24		1 ·33	27 ·98		—30
Angirasa Mina—Panguni.	12	Th	25		2 ·39	... ...		1
	13	Fr	26		3 ·44	1 ·06		2
	14	Sa	27		4 ·47	2 ·12		3
	15	Su	28		5 ·48	3 ·17		4
	16	Mo	29		6 ·46	4 ·19		5
	17	Tu	30		7 ·43	5 ·19		6
	18	We	31		8 ·39	6 ·17		7

April

SOLAR reckoning: Cyclic Sidereal Year, Month	Day	Week-Day	English Day	LUNAR: Month	Tithi Ending Moment	Nakshatra Ending Moment	Muhammadan Year, Month	Day
	19	Th	1	Sukla	9 ·33	7 ·14		8
	20	Fr	2		10 ·25	8 ·10		9
	21	Sa	3		11 ·16	9 ·04 10 ·98	H. 1413 Shawwal.	10
	22	Su	4	Chaitra	12 ·06 13 ·96	11 ·91		11
	23	Mo	5		14 ·86	12 ·84		12
	24	Tu	6		P ·77	13 ·77		13
	25	We	7		1 ·68	14 ·71		14
	26	Th	8		2 ·59	15 ·66		15
	27	Fr	9		3 ·51	16 ·62		16
	28	Sa	10		4 ·46	17 ·60		17
	29	Su	11		5 ·42	18 ·59		18
	30	Mo	12		6 ·41	19 ·61		19
	—31	Tu	13	Bahula	7 ·40	20 ·64		20
Srimukha Mesha—Chittirai.	1	We	14		8 ·43	21 ·70		21
	2	Th	15		9 ·48	22 ·77		22
	3	Fr	16		10 ·54	23 ·86		23
	4	Sa	17		11 ·62	24 ·97		24
	5	Su	18		12 ·71	... ...		25
	6	Mo	19		13 ·80	25 ·08		26
	7	Tu	20		14 ·87	26 ·18		27
	8	We	21		—A ·93	27 ·28		28
	9	Th	22		1 ·98	1 ·37		—29
	10	Fr	23	Vaisak. Sukla	... ...	2 ·44	H. 1413 Zi-l-ka'da.	1
	11	Sa	24		2 ·01	3 ·49		2
	12	Su	25		3 ·02	4 ·51		3
	13	Mo	26		4 ·01 5 ·98	5 ·52		4
	14	Tu	27		6 ·93	6 ·50		5
	15	We	28		7 ·86	7 ·47		6
	16	Th	29		8 ·78	8 ·43		7
	17	Fr	30		9 ·69	9 ·38		8

May

SOLAR reckoning: Cyclic Sidereal Year, Month	Day	Week-Day	English Day	LUNAR: Month	Tithi Ending Moment	Nakshatra Ending Moment	Muhammadan Year, Month	Day
Srimukha Mesha—Chittirai.	18	Sa	1	Suk.	10 ·60	10 ·31		9
	19	Su	2	Vaisakha	11 ·50	11 ·24		10
	20	Mo	3		12 ·40	12 ·17		11
	21	Tu	4		13 ·30	13 ·11		12
	22	We	5		14 ·20	14 ·05		13
	23	Th	6		P ·12	15 ·00 16 ·95		14
	24	Fr	7		1 ·05	17 ·92	H. 1413 Zi-l-ka'da.	15
	25	Sa	8		2 ·00 3 ·96	18 ·92		16
	26	Su	9		4 ·93	19 ·93		17
	27	Mo	10		5 ·92	20 ·95		18
	28	Tu	11		6 ·95	... ...		19
	29	We	12	Bahula	... ...	21 ·01		20
	—30	Th	13		7 ·00	22 ·08		21
	1	Fr	14		8 ·06	23 ·17		22
	2	Sa	15		9 ·13	24 ·27		23
	3	Su	16		10 ·21	25 ·38		24
	4	Mo	17		11 ·30	26 ·48		25
	5	Tu	18		12 ·38	27 ·58		26
	6	We	19		13 ·45	1 ·67		27
	7	Th	20		14 ·49	2 ·75		28
	8	Fr ●	21		—A ·52	3 ·80		29
	9	Sa	22		1 ·53	4 ·83		—30
	10	Su	23		2 ·52	5 ·84		1
Srimukha Vrishabha—Vaikasi.	11	Mo	24		3 ·49	6 ·83		2
	12	Tu	25		4 ·44	7 ·81		3
	13	We	26		5 ·37	8 ·77		4
	14	Th	27	Sukla	6 ·29	9 ·72		5
	15	Fr	28		7 ·20	10 ·65		6
	16	Sa	29		8 ·10	11 ·58		7
	17	Su	30		9 ·00 10 ·89	12 ·51		8
	18	Mo	31		11 ·79	13 ·45		9

June

SOLAR reckoning: Cyclic Sidereal Year, Month	Day	Week-Day	English Day	LUNAR: Month	Tithi Ending Moment	Nakshatra Ending Moment	Muhammadan Year, Month	Day
	19	Tu	1	Jyeshtha	12 ·70	14 ·39	H. 1413 Zi-l-hijja.	10
	20	We	2		13 ·62	15 ·33		11
	21	Th	3		14 ·55	16 ·29		12
	22	Fr ○	4		P ·49	17 ·26		13
	23	Sa	5		1 ·44	18 ·24		14
	24	Su	6		2 ·42	19 ·25		15
	25	Mo	7		3 ·41	20 ·27		16
	26	Tu	8		4 ·44	21 ·32		17
	27	We	9		5 ·48	22 ·39		18
	28	Th	10		6 ·54	23 ·47		19
	29	Fr	11	Bahula	7 ·62	24 ·57		20
	30	Sa	12		8 ·71	25 ·67		21
	31	Su	13		9 ·79	26 ·78		22
	—32	Mo	14		10 ·86	27 ·88		23
Srimukha Mithuna—Ani.	1	Tu	15		11 ·92	1 ·98		24
	2	We	16		12 ·97	... ...		25
	3	Th	17		... ...	2 ·06		26
	4	Fr	18		13 ·01	3 ·11		27
	5	Sa	19		14 ·02	4 ·15		28
	6	Su	20		A ·01 1 ·98	5 ·16		—29
	7	Mo	21		2 ·93	6 ·17	H. 1414 Muharram.	1
	8	Tu	22		3 ·86	7 ·14		2
	9	We	23	Sukla	4 ·78	8 ·10		3
	10	Th	24		5 ·69	9 ·05 10 ·99		4
	11	Fr	25	Ashadha	6 ·59	11 ·93		5
	12	Sa	26		7 ·49	12 ·86		6
	13	Su	27		8 ·38	13 ·79		7
	14	Mo	28		9 ·28	14 ·72		8
	15	Tu	29		10 ·19	15 ·66		9
	16	We	30		11 ·10	16 ·62		10

Naksh:—1. Asvn. 2. Bhar. 3. Krit. 4. Rohi. 5. Mrig. 6. Ardh. 7. Punar. 8. Push. 9. Aslesh. 10. Magh. 11. P. Phal. 12. U. Phal. 13. Hasta. 14. Chit.

A. D. 1993.
A.—Amavasya.
P.—Paurnami.

Kollam 1169, Commences { **N. Malabar—Sept.** / **S. Malabar—Aug.**

Hijra 1414, Commences, **June. 21.**

Vikrama 2050.
Bengal San 1399.
(N. Cycle) Vyaya.

SOLAR reckoning: Cyclic Sidereal Year, Month and Day; Week-Day English Month and Day. LUNAR reckoning: Tithi Ending Moment; Nakshatra Ending Moment; Muhammadan Year, Month and Day.

July

Solar month	Cyclic Sidereal Year, Month and Day	Week-Day English Month and Day	Lunar month	Tithi Ending Moment	Nakshatra Ending Moment	Muhammadan month	Muhammadan Year, Month and Day
Srimukha Mithuna—Ani.	17	Th 1	Ashadha Bahula	12 ·03 / 13 ·97	17 ·59	H. 1414 Muharram.	11
	18	Fr 2		14 ·98	18 ·57		12
	19	Sa 3		P ·90	19 ·57		13
	20	Su 4		1 ·90	20 ·59		14
	21	Mo 5		2 ·92	21 ·63		15
	22	Tu 6		3 ·96	22 ·70		16
	23	We 7		... ...	23 ·78		17
	24	Th 8		4 ·02	24 ·87		18
	25	Fr 9		5 ·09	25 ·97		19
	26	Sa 10		6 ·17	... ...		20
	27	Su 11		7 ·26	26 ·08		21
	28	Mo 12		8 ·34	27 ·19		22
	29	Tu 13		9 ·40	1 ·23		23
	30	We 14		10 ·44	2 ·36		24
	31	Th 15		11 ·48	3 ·42		25
	—32	Fr 16		12 ·49	4 ·46		26
Srimukha Karkata—Adi.	1	Sa 17		13 ·48	5 ·49		27
	2	Su 18		14 ·45	6 ·49		28
	3	Mo 19		—A ·41	7 ·47		29
	4	Tu 20	Sukla	1 ·34	8 ·44		—30
	5	We 21		2 ·26	9 ·39	Safar.	1
	6	Th 22		3 ·18	10 ·34		2
	7	Fr 23		4 ·08 / 5 ·98	11 ·27		3
	8	Sa 24		6 ·68	12 ·20		4
	9	Su 25		7 ·78	13 ·13		5
	10	Mo 26		8 ·68	14 ·06		6
	11	Tu 27		9 ·59	15 ·01 / 16 ·96		7
	12	We 28		10 ·51	17 ·92		8
	13	Th 29		11 ·44	18 ·89		9
	14	Fr 30		12 ·40	19 ·89		10
	15	Sa 31		13 ·38	20 ·91		11

Aug.

Solar month	Cyclic Sidereal Year, Month and Day	Week-Day English Month and Day	Lunar month	Tithi Ending Moment	Nakshatra Ending Moment	Muhammadan month	Muhammadan Year, Month and Day
	16	Su 1	Sravana	14 ·38	21 ·95	H. 1414	12
	17	Mo 2		P ·40	... ...		13
	18	Tu 3	Bahula	1 ·43	22 ·01		14
	19	We 4		2 ·49	23 ·08		15
	20	Th 5		3 ·56	24 ·17		16
	21	Fr 6		4 ·61	25 ·27		17
	22	Sa 7		5 ·73	26 ·38		18
	23	Su 8		6 ·81	27 ·49		19
	24	Mo 9		7 ·87	1 ·59		20
	25	Tu 10		8 ·93	2 ·67		21
	26	We 11		9 ·97	3 ·73		22
	27	Th 12		10 ·99	4 ·78		23
	28	Fr 13		11 ·97	5 ·81		24
	29	Sa 14		12 ·94	6 ·82		25
	30	Su 15		13 ·90	7 ·83		26
	—31	Mo 16		14 ·84	8 ·77		27
Srimukha Simha—Avani.	1	Tu 17		—A ·76	9 ·73		28
	2	We 18	Adh. Bhad. Sukla	1 ·67	10 ·67		—29
	3	Th 19		2 ·58	11 ·61	H. 1414 Rabi-ul-awwal.	1
	4	Fr 20		3 ·48	12 ·54		2
	5	Sa 21		4 ·38	13 ·47		3
	6	Su 22		5 ·28	14 ·40		4
	7	Mo 23		6 ·18	15 ·34		5
	8	Tu 24		7 ·09	16 ·29		6
	9	We 25		8 ·01 / 9 ·95	17 ·25		7
	10	Th 26		10 ·91	18 ·22		8
	11	Fr 27		11 ·89	19 ·21		9
	12	Sa 28		12 ·89	20 ·23		10
	13	Su 29		13 ·90	21 ·26		11
	14	Mo 30		14 ·94	22 ·31		12
	15	Tu 31		... ...	23 ·38		13

Sep.

Solar month	Cyclic Sidereal Year, Month and Day	Week-Day English Month and Day	Lunar month	Tithi Ending Moment	Nakshatra Ending Moment	Muhammadan month	Muhammadan Year, Month and Day
Srimukha Simha—Avani.	16	We 1	Adhika Bhadrapada	P ·00	24 ·47	H. 1414 Rabi-ul-awwal.	14
	17	Th 2	Bahula	1 ·07	25 ·57		15
	18	Fr 3		2 ·15	26 ·68		16
	19	Sa 4		3 ·24	27 ·70		17
	20	Su 5		4 ·32	1 ·89		18
	21	Mo 6		5 ·39	2 ·98		19
	22	Tu 7		6 ·44	... ...		20
	23	We 8		7 ·48	3 ·05		21
	24	Th 9		8 ·51	4 ·10		22
	25	Fr 10		9 ·49	5 ·13		23
	26	Sa 11		10 ·47	6 ·14		24
	27	Su 12		11 ·43	7 ·13		25
	28	Mo 13		12 ·37	8 ·11		26
	29	Tu 14		13 ·29	9 ·07		27
	30	We 15		14 ·20	10 ·01 / 11 ·95		28
	—31	Th 16		—A ·11	12 ·88		29
Srimukha Kanya—Purattasi.	1	Fr 17	Bhadrapada Sukla	1 ·01 / 2 ·91	13 ·81		—30
	2	Sa 18		3 ·80	14 ·74	Rabi-ul-akhir.	1
	3	Su 19		4 ·70	15 ·68		2
	4	Mo 20		5 ·62	16 ·62		3
	5	Tu 21		6 ·55	17 ·58		4
	6	We 22		7 ·49	18 ·55		5
	7	Th 23		8 ·44	19 ·54		6
	8	Fr 24		9 ·43	20 ·55		7
	9	Sa 25		10 ·42	21 ·57		8
	10	Su 26		11 ·44	22 ·62		9
	11	Mo 27		12 ·48	23 ·69		10
	12	Tu 28		13 ·54	24 ·78		11
	13	We 29		14 ·61	25 ·88		12
	14	Th 30		P ·69	26 ·98		13

Oct.

Solar month	Cyclic Sidereal Year, Month and Day	Week-Day English Month and Day	Lunar month	Tithi Ending Moment	Nakshatra Ending Moment	Muhammadan month	Muhammadan Year, Month and Day
	15	Fr 1	Nija Bahula	1 ·78	... ...	H. 1414	14
	16	Sa 2		2 ·86	27 ·09		15
	17	Su 3		3 ·94	1 ·19		16
	18	Mo 4		... ...	2 ·29		17
	19	Tu 5		4 ·00	3 ·36		18
	20	We 6		5 ·04	4 ·42		19
	21	Th 7		6 ·06	5 ·45		20
	22	Fr 8		7 ·05	6 ·46		21
	23	Sa 9		8 ·03 / 9 ·99	7 ·45		22
	24	Su 10		10 ·93	8 ·43		23
	25	Mo 11		11 ·85	9 ·40		24
	26	Tu 12		12 ·76	10 ·35		25
	27	We 13		13 ·67	11 ·29		26
	28	Th 14		14 ·57	12 ·22		27
	29	Fr 15		—A ·47	13 ·15		28
	—30	Sa 16	Asvina Sukla	1 ·37	14 ·08		—29
Srimukha Tula—Aippasi.	1	Su 17		2 ·28	15 ·02 / 16 ·96	H 1414 Jumadal-awwal.	1
	2	Mo 18		3 ·19	17 ·92		2
	3	Tu 19		4 ·12	18 ·89		3
	4	We 20		5 ·06	19 ·87		4
	5	Th 21		6 ·02	20 ·87		5
	6	Fr 22		7 ·01	21 ·89		6
	7	Sa 23		8 ·01	22 ·93		7
	8	Su 24		9 ·02	... ...		8
	9	Mo 25		10 ·06	23 ·00		9
	10	Tu 26		11 ·12	24 ·08		10
	11	We 27		12 ·19	25 ·17		11
	12	Th 28		13 ·27	26 ·28		12
	13	Fr 29		14 ·37	27 ·39		13
	14	Sa 30		P ·46	1 ·50		14
	15	Su 31		1 ·54	2 ·59		15

Nov.

Solar month	Cyclic Sidereal Year, Month and Day	Week-Day English Month and Day	Lunar month	Tithi Ending Moment	Nakshatra Ending Moment	Muhammadan month	Muhammadan Year, Month and Day
Srimukha Tula—Aippasi.	16	Mo 1	Asvina Bahula	2 ·59	3 ·67	H. 1414 Jumadal-awwal.	16
	17	Tu 2		3 ·63	4 ·73		17
	18	We 3		4 ·65	5 ·76		18
	19	Th 4		5 ·65	6 ·78		19
	20	Fr 5		6 ·62	7 ·79		20
	21	Sa 6		7 ·58	8 ·77		21
	22	Su 7		8 ·52	9 ·73		22
	23	Mo 8		9 ·45	10 ·68		23
	24	Tu 9		10 ·37	11 ·62		24
	25	We 10		11 ·27	12 ·56		25
	26	Th 11		12 ·17	13 ·49		26
	27	Fr 12		13 ·07 / 14 ·97	14 ·42		27
	28	Sa 13		—A ·88	15 ·35		28
	29	Su 14	Karttika Sukla	1 ·80	16 ·29		29
	—30	Mo 15		2 ·73	17 ·25		—30
Srimukha Vrischika—Kartigai.	1	Tu 16		3 ·67	18 ·22	Jumadal-akhir.	1
	2	We 17		4 ·64	19 ·20		2
	3	Th 18		5 ·62	20 ·19		3
	4	Fr 19		6 ·62	21 ·21		4
	5	Sa 20		7 ·64	22 ·25		5
	6	Su 21		8 ·68	23 ·31		6
	7	Mo 22		9 ·74	24 ·38		7
	8	Tu 23		10 ·82	25 ·47		8
	9	We 24		11 ·91	26 ·58		9
	10	Th 25		... ...	27 ·69		10
	11	Fr 26		12 ·00	1 ·80		11
	12	Sa 27		13 ·09	2 ·89		12
	13	Su 28		14 ·16	3 ·97		13
	14	Mo ○ 29		P ·22	... ...		14
	15	Tu 30		1 ·26	4 ·04		15

Dec.

Solar month	Cyclic Sidereal Year, Month and Day	Week-Day English Month and Day	Lunar month	Tithi Ending Moment	Nakshatra Ending Moment	Muhammadan month	Muhammadan Year, Month and Day
	16	We 1	Bahula	2 ·28	5 ·08	H. 1414	16
	17	Th 2		3 ·27	6 ·11		17
	18	Fr 3		4 ·24	7 ·11		18
	19	Sa 4		5 ·20	8 ·09		19
	20	Su 5		6 ·14	9 ·06		20
	21	Mo 6		7 ·07 / 8 ·99	10 ·02 / 11 ·97		21
	22	Tu 7		9 ·90	12 ·90		22
	23	We 8		10 ·80	13 ·83		23
	24	Th 9		11 ·70	14 ·76		24
	25	Fr 10		12 ·60	15 ·69		25
	26	Sa 11		13 ·51	16 ·63		26
	27	Su 12		14 ·43	17 ·58		27
	28	Mo 13		—A ·36	18 ·54		28
	29	Tu 14	Margasira Sukla	1 ·30	19 ·52		—29
	—30	We 15		2 ·27	20 ·51		1
Srimukha Dhanus—Margali.	1	Th 16		3 ·25	21 ·52	H. 1414 Rajab.	2
	2	Fr 17		4 ·27	22 ·56		3
	3	Sa 18		5 ·29	23 ·62		4
	4	Su 19		6 ·33	24 ·69		5
	5	Mo 20		7 ·39	25 ·78		6
	6	Tu 21		8 ·47	26 ·88		7
	7	We 22		9 ·56	27 ·99		8
	8	Th 23		10 ·65	... ...		9
	9	Fr 24		11 ·73	1 ·10		10
	10	Sa 25		12 ·81	2 ·20		11
	11	Su 26		13 ·87	3 ·28		12
	12	Mo 27		14 ·91	4 ·35		13
	13	Tu 28		P ·92	5 ·40		14
	14	We 29	Bah.	1 ·91	6 ·48		15
	15	Th 30		2 ·89	7 ·44		16
	16	Fr 31		3 ·81	8 ·42		17

15. Svati. 16. Visak. 17. Anur. 18. Jyesh. 19. Mula. 20. P. Ash. 21. U. Ash. 22. Sravn. 23. Dani. 24. Satab. 25. P. Bhad. 26. U. Bhad. 27. Rev

A. D. 1994.
Solar Eclipse. ●
Lunar Eclipse. ○

Mesha Sankranti (Commencement of Indian Sidereal Year).
(Surya Sid.) April 13·94. (Arya Sid.) April 13·83.

Saka 1916. Kaliyuga 5095. (S. Cycle) Bhava.

SOLAR reckoning: Cyclic Sidereal Year, Month and Day; Week-Day English Month and Day. LUNAR reckoning: Tithi Ending Moment; Nakshatra Ending Moment; Muhammadan Year, Month and Day.

Jan.

Cyclic Sidereal Year, Month and Day	Week-Day	English Day	Tithi	Tithi Ending Moment	Nakshatra	Nakshatra Ending Moment	Muhammadan Year, Month and Day
17 (Srimukha, Dhanus—Margali)	Sa	1	4 (Margasira)	·78	9	·89	18 (H. 1414 Rajab)
18	Su	2	5	·71	10	·85	19
19	Mo	3	6	·63	11	·80	20
20	Tu	4	7	·54	12	·24	21
21	We	5	8	·44	13	·17	22
22	Th	6	9	·34	14	·10	23
23	Fr	7	10 (Bahula)	·24	15 / 16	·04 / ·98	24
24	Sa	8	11	·15	17	·92	25
25	Su	9	12	·07	18	·88	26
26	Mo	10	13 / 14	·00 / ·95	19	·85	27
27	Tu	11	A	·92	20	·83	28
28	We	12	1	·90	21	·85	29
29	Th	13	2	·91	22	·88	30
1 (Srimukha, Makara—Tai)	Fr	14	3	·93	23	·92	1 (H. 1414 Shaban)
2	Sa	15	4	·98	24	·99	2
3	Su	16	...	...	...	...	3
4	Mo	17	5 (Sukla)	·04	25	·08	4
5	Tu	18	6	·13	26	·18	5
6	We	19	7	·22	27	·29	6
7	Th	20	8	·31	1	·40	7
8	Fr	21	9	·39	2	·50	8
9	Sa	22	10	·46	3	·59	9
10	Su	23	11	·52	4	·67	10
11	Mo	24	12 (Pausha)	·55	5	·72	11
12	Tu	25	13	·57	6	·75	12
13	We	26	14	·56	7	·76	13
14	Th	27	P	·53	8	·75	14
15	Fr	28	1	·49	9	·73	15
16	Sa	29	2	·43	10	·69	16
17	Su	30	3	·35	11	·64	17
18	Mo	31	4	·26	12	·58	18

Feb.

Cyclic Sidereal Year, Month and Day	Week-Day	English Day	Tithi	Tithi Ending Moment	Nakshatra	Nakshatra Ending Moment	Muhammadan Year, Month and Day
19	Tu	1	5	·17	13	·51	19
20	We	2	6 / 7 (Bahula)	·07 / ·97	14	·44	20
21	Th	3	8	·87	15	·37	21
22	Fr	4	9	·78	16	·31	22
23	Sa	5	10	·70	17	·25	23
24	Su	6	11	·64	18	·21	24
25	Mo	7	12	·59	19	·18	25
26	Tu	8	13	·55	20	·17	26
27	We	9	14	·54	21	·17	27
28	Th	10	A	·55	22	·19	28
29	Fr	11	1	·58	23	·23	29
30	Sa	12	2	·63	24	·30	1 (H. 1414 Ramzan)
1 (Srimukha, Kumbha—Masi)	Su	13	3	·69	25	·39	2
2	Mo	14	4	·77	26	·48	3
3	Tu	15	5	·86	27	·58	4
4	We	16	6	·95	1	·69	5
5	Th	17	... (Sukla)	...	2	·80	6
6	Fr	18	7	·08	3	·90	7
7	Sa	19	8	·10	4	·97	8
8	Su	20	9	·15	...	...	9
9	Mo	21	10	·17	5	·03	10
10	Tu	22	11 (Magha)	·19	6	·07	11
11	We	23	12	·18	7	·08	12
12	Th	24	13	·15	8	·09	13
13	Fr	25	14	·10	9	·07	14
14	Sa	26	P / 1	·04 / ·96	10 / 11	·03 / ·98	15
15	Su	27	2 (Bah.)	·87	12	·92	16
16	Mo	28	3	·78	13	·86	17

March

Cyclic Sidereal Year, Month and Day	Week-Day	English Day	Tithi	Tithi Ending Moment	Nakshatra	Nakshatra Ending Moment	Muhammadan Year, Month and Day
17 (Srimukha, Kumbha—Masi)	Tu	1	4 (Magha)	·60	14	·79	18 (H. 1414 Ramzan)
18	We	2	5	·59	15	·72	19
19	Th	3	6	·49	16	·65	20
20	Fr	4	7	·40	17	·59	21
21	Sa	5	8	·31	18	·54	22
22	Su	6	9 (Bahula)	·24	19	·51	23
23	Mo	7	10	·19	20	·49	24
24	Tu	8	11	·16	21	·49	25
25	We	9	12	·15	22	·51	26
26	Th	10	13	·15	23	·55	27
27	Fr	11	14	·18	24	·61	28
28	Sa	12	A	·23	25	·69	29
29	Su	13	1	·29	26	·78	30
1 (Srimukha, Mina—Panguni)	Mo	14	2	·37	27	·88	1 (H. 1414 Shawwal)
2	Tu	15	3	·46	1	·99	2
3	We	16	4	·54	...	...	3
4	Th	17	5	·62	2	·10	4
5	Fr	18	6 (Sukla)	·69	3	·20	5
6	Sa	19	7	·75	4	·28	6
7	Su	20	8	·79	5	·34	7
8	Mo	21	9	·79	6	·38	8
9	Tu	22	10	·77	7	·40	9
10	We	23	11	·74	8	·41	10
11	Th	24	12 (Phalguna)	·69	9	·39	11
12	Fr	25	13	·63	10	·36	12
13	Sa	26	14	·55	11	·31	13
14	Su	27	P	·46	12	·26	14
15	Mo	28	1	·36	13	·20	15
16	Tu	29	2	·26	14	·13	16
17	We	30	3	·16	15 / 16	·06 / ·99	17
18	Th	31	4 / 5	·06 / ·97	17	·93	18

April

Cyclic Sidereal Year, Month and Day	Week-Day	English Day	Tithi	Tithi Ending Moment	Nakshatra	Nakshatra Ending Moment	Muhammadan Year, Month and Day
19	Fr	1	6 (Bahula)	·89	18	·88	19
20	Sa	2	7	·82	19	·84	20
21	Su	3	8	·77	20	·82	21
22	Mo	4	9	·74	21	·81	22
23	Tu	5	10	·72	22	·83	23
24	We	6	11	·72	23	·87	24
25	Th	7	12	·75	24	·92	25
26	Fr	8	13	·79	25	·99	26
27	Sa	9	14	·85	...	...	27
28	Su	10	A	·94	26	·08	28
29	Mo	11	...	...	27	·18	29
30	Tu	12	1	·03	1	·29	1 (H. 1414 Zi-l-ka'da)
31	We	13	2	·11	2	·40	2
1 (Bhava, Mesha—Chittirai)	Th	14	3	·18	3	·50	3
2	Fr	15	4 (Sukla)	·25	4	·58	4
3	Sa	16	5	·30	5	·65	5
4	Su	17	6	·33	6	·70	6
5	Mo	18	7	·34	7	·73	7
6	Tu	19	8 (Chaitra)	·33	8	·74	8
7	We	20	9	·29	9	·72	9
8	Th	21	10	·24	10	·69	10
9	Fr	22	11	·17	11	·65	11
10	Sa	23	12	·09	12	·60	12
11	Su	24	13 / 14	·00 / ·91	13	·53	13
12	Mo	25	P	·81	14	·46	14
13	Tu	26	1 (Bahula)	·71	15	·39	15
14	We	27	2	·61	16	·32	16
15	Th	28	3	·51	17	·26	17
16	Fr	29	4	·42	18	·21	18
17	Sa	30	5	·35	19	·17	19

May

Cyclic Sidereal Year, Month and Day	Week-Day	English Day	Tithi	Tithi Ending Moment	Nakshatra	Nakshatra Ending Moment	Muhammadan Year, Month and Day
18 (Bhava, Mesha—Chittirai)	Su	1	6 (Chaitra)	·30	20	·14	20 (H. 1414 Zi-l-ka'da)
19	Mo	2	7	·27	21	·13	21
20	Tu	3	8	·25	22	·15	22
21	We	4	9	·26	23	·18	23
22	Th	5	10	·28	24	·23	24
23	Fr	6	11	·32	25	·30	25
24	Sa	7	12 (Bahula)	·38	26	·38	26
25	Su	8	13	·46	27	·48	27
26	Mo	9	14	·55	1	·59	28
27	Tu	10	A	·63	2	·70	29
28	We	11	1	·71	3	·80	30
29	Th	12	2	·77	4	·89	1 (H. 1414 Zi-l-hijja)
30	Fr	13	3	·82	5	·96	2
31	Sa	14	4	·85	...	...	3
1 (Bhava, Vrishabha—Vaikasi)	Su	15	5	·85	6	·02	4
2	Mo	16	6 (Sukla)	·84	7	·05	5
3	Tu	17	7	·81	8	·06	6
4	We	18	8	·76	9	·05	7
5	Th	19	9	·69	10 / 11	·02 / ·99	8
6	Fr	20	10 (Vaisakha)	·61	12	·94	9
7	Sa	21	11	·51	13	·87	10
8	Su	22	12	·41	14	·80	11
9	Mo	23	13	·31	15	·73	12
10	Tu	24	14	·21	16	·67	13
11	We ○	25	P	·11	17	·61	14
12	Th	26	1 / 2	·01 / ·98	18	·55	15
13	Fr	27	3 (Bahula)	·86	19	·50	16
14	Sa	28	4	·80	20	·47	17
15	Su	29	5	·77	21	·46	18
16	Mo	30	6	·74	22	·47	19
17	Tu	31	7	·75	23	·49	20

June

Cyclic Sidereal Year, Month and Day	Week-Day	English Day	Tithi	Tithi Ending Moment	Nakshatra	Nakshatra Ending Moment	Muhammadan Year, Month and Day
18	We	1	8	·78	24	·54	21
19	Th	2	9	·83	25	·60	22
20	Fr	3	10	·89	26	·68	23
21	Sa	4	11	·96	27	·78	24
22	Su	5	...	...	1	·89	25
23	Mo	6	12	·04	...	...	26
24	Tu	7	13	·12	2	·00	27
25	We	8	14	·20	3	·10	28
26	Th	9	A	·26	4	·19	29
27	Fr	10	1	·31	5	·27	1 (H. 1415 Muharram)
28	Sa	11	2	·33	6	·33	2
29	Su	12	3	·35	7	·37	3
30	Mo	13	4	·33	8	·38	4
31	Tu	14	5	·30	9	·38	5
1 (Bhava, Mithuna—Ani)	We	15	6 (Sukla)	·25	10	·36	6
2	Th	16	7	·18	11	·32	7
3	Fr	17	8	·10	12	·27	8
4	Sa	18	9 / 10	·01 / ·91	13	·21	9
5	Su	19	11	·81	14	·15	10
6	Mo	20	12	·70	15	·08	11
7	Tu	21	13 (Jyeshtha)	·60	16 / 17	·01 / ·94	12
8	We	22	14	·51	18	·88	13
9	Th	23	P	·43	19	·83	14
10	Fr	24	1	·35	20	·80	15
11	Sa	25	2	·29	21	·79	16
12	Su	26	3	·25	22	·79	17
13	Mo	27	4 (Bahula)	·23	23	·81	18
14	Tu	28	5	·23	24	·85	19
15	We	29	6	·25	25	·91	20
16	Th	30	7	·30	...	...	21

Naksh :—1. Asvn. 2. Bhar. 3. Krit. 4. Rohi. 5. Mrig. 6. Ardh. 7. Punar. 8. Push. 9. Aslesh. 10. Magh. 11. P. Phal. 12. U. Phal. 13. Hasta. 14. Chit.

A. D. 1994.
A.—Amavasya.
P.—Paurnami.

Kollam 1170, Commences { **N. Malabar—Sept.** / **S. Malabar—Aug.**

Hijra 1415, Commences, **June 10.**

Vikrama 2051.
Bengal San 1400.
(N. Cycle) Sarvajit.

SOLAR reckoning: Solar month	Cyclic Sidereal Year, Month and Day.	Week-Day English Month and Day.		LUNAR reckoning: Lunar month	Tithi Ending Moment.	Nakshatra Ending Moment.	Muhammadan Year, Month and Day.
		July					
Bhava Mithuna—Ani.	17	Fr	1	Jyesh. Bah.	8 ·30	26 ·00	H. 1415 Muharram. 22
	18	Sa	2		9 ·43	27 ·00	23
	19	Su	3		10 ·51	1 ·19	24
	20	Mo	4		11 ·59	2 ·30	25
	21	Tu	5		12 ·67	3 ·40	26
	22	We	6		13 ·73	4 ·50	27
	23	Th	7		14 ·78	5 ·58	28
	24	Fr	8		—A ·81	6 ·64	29
	25	Sa	9	Ashadha Sukla	1 ·88	7 ·68	—30
	26	Su	10		2 ·81	8 ·70	H. 1415 Safar. 1
	27	Mo	11		3 ·78	9 ·71	2
	28	Tu	12		4 ·73	10 ·69	3
	29	We	13		5 ·66	11 ·66	4
	30	Th	14		6 ·58	12 ·61	5
	31	Fr	15		7 ·49	13 ·55	6
	—32	Sa	16		8 ·39	14 ·49	7
Bhava Karkata—Adi.	1	Su	17		9 ·29	15 ·42	8
	2	Mo	18		10 ·19	16 ·35	9
	3	Tu	19		11 ·09; 12 ·99	17 ·28	10
	4	We	20		13 ·90	18 ·22	11
	5	Th	21		14 ·82	19 ·17	12
	6	Fr	22		P ·76	20 ·14	13
	7	Sa	23	Bahula	1 ·72	21 ·12	14
	8	Su	24		2 ·71	22 ·11	15
	9	Mo	25		3 ·71	23 ·12	16
	10	Tu	26		4 ·74	24 ·16	17
	11	We	27		5 ·77	25 ·22	18
	12	Th	28		6 ·82	26 ·30	19
	13	Fr	29		7 ·89	27 ·39	20
	14	Sa	30		8 ·97	1 ·49	21
	15	Su	31		... ...	2 ·60	22
		Aug.					
	16	Mo	1		9 ·06	3 ·71	23
	17	Tu	2		10 ·14	4 ·81	24
	18	We	3		11 ·21	5 ·89	25
	19	Th	4		12 ·26	6 ·95	26
	20	Fr	5		13 ·30	... ...	27
	21	Sa	6		14 ·31	7 ·00	28
	22	Su	7		—A ·29	8 ·08	—29
	23	Mo	8	Sravana Sukla	1 ·26	9 ·04	H. 1415 Rabi-ul-awwal. 1
	24	Tu	9		2 ·21	10 ·02; 11 ·99	2
	25	We	10		3 ·15	12 ·94	3
	26	Th	11		4 ·07; 5 ·98	13 ·88	4
	27	Fr	12		6 ·88	14 ·82	5
	28	Sa	13		7 ·78	15 ·76	6
	29	Su	14		8 ·68	16 ·69	7
	30	Mo	15		9 ·58	17 ·62	8
	—31	Tu	16		10 ·49	18 ·56	9
Bhava Simha—Avani.	1	We	17		11 ·40	19 ·51	10
	2	Th	18		12 ·32	20 ·47	11
	3	Fr	19		13 ·26	21 ·44	12
	4	Sa	20		14 ·22	22 ·43	13
	5	Su	21		P ·21	23 ·45	14
	6	Mo	22	Bahula	1 ·20	24 ·48	15
	7	Tu	23		2 ·22	25 ·53	16
	8	We	24		3 ·26	26 ·60	17
	9	Th	25		4 ·32	27 ·69	18
	10	Fr	26		5 ·40	1 ·79	19
	11	Sa	27		6 ·48	2 ·90	20
	12	Su	28		7 ·56	... ...	21
	13	Mo	29		8 ·64	3 ·01	22
	14	Tu	30		9 ·71	4 ·11	23
	15	We	31		10 ·76	5 ·19	24

SOLAR reckoning: Solar month	Cyclic Sidereal Year, Month and Day.	Week-Day English Month and Day.		LUNAR reckoning: Lunar month	Tithi Ending Moment.	Nakshatra Ending Moment.	Muhammadan Year, Month and Day.
		Sep.					
Bhava Simha—Avani.	16	Th	1	Sr. Bah.	11 ·80	6 ·26	R.-awwal. 25
	17	Fr	2		12 ·82	7 ·31	26
	18	Sa	3		13 ·81	8 ·35	27
	19	Su	4		14 ·78	9 ·36	28
	20	Mo	5		—A ·74	10 ·35	29
	21	Tu	6	Bhadrapada Sukla	1 ·67	11 ·32	—30
	22	We	7		2 ·59	12 ·28	H. 1415 Rabi-ul-akhir. 1
	23	Th	8		3 ·50	13 ·23	2
	24	Fr	9		4 ·40	14 ·17	3
	25	Sa	10		5 ·30	15 ·10	4
	26	Su	11		6 ·20	16 ·03; 17 ·96	5
	27	Mo	12		7 ·10	18 ·90	6
	28	Tu	13		8 ·01; 9 ·98	19 ·84	7
	29	We	14		10 ·86	20 ·80	8
	30	Th	15		11 ·80	21 ·77	9
	—31	Fr	16		12 ·76	22 ·75	10
Bhava Kanya—Purattasi.	1	Sa	17		13 ·73	23 ·77	11
	2	Su	18		14 ·73	24 ·79	12
	3	Mo	19		P ·75	25 ·84	13
	4	Tu	20	Bahula	1 ·79	26 ·91	14
	5	We	21		2 ·85	... ...	15
	6	Th	22		3 ·92	27 ·00	16
	7	Fr	23		... ...	1 ·10	17
	8	Sa	24		4 ·00	2 ·20	18
	9	Su	25		5 ·09	3 ·31	19
	10	Mo	26		6 ·18	4 ·41	20
	11	Tu	27		7 ·25	5 ·50	21
	12	We	28		8 ·30	6 ·57	22
	13	Th	29		9 ·34	7 ·63	23
	14	Fr	30		10 ·36	8 ·67	24
		Oct.					
	15	Sa	1		11 ·35	9 ·68	25
	16	Su	2		12 ·33	10 ·67	26
	17	Mo	3		13 ·29	11 ·65	27
	18	Tu	4		14 ·22	12 ·62	28
	19	We	5		—A ·14	13 ·57	—29
	20	Th	6	Asvina Sukla	1 05; 2 ·96	14 ·50	H. 1415 Jumadal-awwal. 1
	21	Fr	7		3 ·85	15 ·48	2
	22	Sa	8		4 ·76	16 ·36	3
	23	Su	9		5 ·66	17 ·30	4
	24	Mo	10		6 ·57	18 ·24	5
	25	Tu	11		7 ·49	19 ·18	6
	26	We	12		8 ·42	20 ·13	7
	27	Th	13		9 ·36	21 ·10	8
	28	Fr	14		10 ·32	22 ·09	9
	29	Sa	15		11 ·30	23 ·09	10
	30	Su	16		12 ·31	24 ·11	11
	—31	Mo	17		13 ·33	25 ·15	12
Bhava Tula—Aippasi.	1	Tu	18		14 ·37	26 ·21	13
	2	We	19		P ·43	27 ·29	14
	3	Th	20	Bahula	1 ·50	1 ·30	15
	4	Fr	21		2 ·58	2 ·50	16
	5	Sa	22		3 ·67	3 ·61	17
	6	Su	23		4 ·76	4 ·71	18
	7	Mo	24		5 ·83	5 ·80	19
	8	Tu	25		6 ·89	6 ·88	20
	9	We	26		7 ·92	7 ·95	21
	10	Th	27		8 ·95	8 ·99	22
	11	Fr	28		9 ·93	... ...	23
	12	Sa	29		10 ·91	9 ·00	24
	13	Su	30		11 ·87	10 ·00; 11 ·99	25
	14	Mo	31		12 ·81	12 ·95	26

SOLAR reckoning: Solar month	Cyclic Sidereal Year, Month and Day.	Week-Day English Month and Day.		LUNAR reckoning: Lunar month	Tithi Ending Moment.	Nakshatra Ending Moment.	Muhammadan Year, Month and Day.
		Nov.					
Bhava Tula—Aippasi.	15	Tu	1	Bah.	13 ·73	13 ·90	27
	16	We	2		14 ·64	14 ·84	28
	17	Th	3		—A ·55	15 ·78	29
	18	Fr	4	Kartika Sukla	1 ·45	16 ·71	—30
	19	Sa	5		2 ·35	17 ·64	H. 1415 Jumadal-akhir. 1
	20	Su	6		3 ·25	18 ·57	2
	21	Mo	7		4 ·16	19 ·51	3
	22	Tu	8		5 ·08	20 ·46	4
	23	We	9		6 ·01; 7 ·96	21 ·43	5
	24	Th	10		8 ·92	22 ·41	6
	25	Fr	11		9 ·90	23 ·41	7
	26	Sa	12		10 ·91	24 ·42	8
	27	Su	13		11 ·93	25 ·46	9
	28	Mo	14		12 ·98	26 ·52	10
	29	Tu	15		... ...	27 ·60	11
	—30	We	16		13 ·04	1 ·70	12
Bhava Vrischika—Kartigai.	1	Th	17		14 ·12	2 ·80	13
	2	Fr	18		P ·21	3 ·90	14
	3	Sa	19	Bahula	1 ·30	... ...	15
	4	Su	20		2 ·38	4 ·01	16
	5	Mo	21		3 ·45	5 ·11	17
	6	Tu	22		4 ·51	6 ·19	18
	7	We	23		5 ·55	7 ·26	19
	8	Th	24		6 ·57	8 ·30	20
	9	Fr	25		7 ·56	9 ·32	21
	10	Sa	26		8 ·54	10 ·33	22
	11	Su	27		9 ·49	11 ·32	23
	12	Mo	28		10 ·42	12 ·29	24
	13	Tu	29		11 ·35	13 ·24	25
	14	We	30		12 ·27	14 ·18	26
		Dec.					
	15	Th	1		13 ·18	15 ·12	27
	16	Fr	2		14 ·08; A ·98	16 ·05; 17 ·98	28
	17	Sa	3	Margasira Sukla	1 ·88	18 ·91	—29
	18	Su	4		2 ·79	19 ·85	H. 1415 Rajab. 1
	19	Mo	5		3 ·71	20 ·80	2
	20	Tu	6		4 ·64	21 ·76	3
	21	We	7		5 ·59	22 ·74	4
	22	Th	8		6 ·55	23 ·73	5
	23	Fr	9		7 ·54	24 ·74	6
	24	Sa	10		8 ·55	25 ·77	7
	25	Su	11		9 ·58	26 ·83	8
	26	Mo	12		10 ·63	27 ·91	9
	27	Tu	13		11 ·69	... ...	10
	28	We	14		12 ·77	1 ·00	11
	—29	Th	15		13 ·86	2 ·10	12
Bhava Dhanus—Margali.	1	Fr	16		14 ·95	3 ·21	13
	2	Sa	17		... ...	4 ·32	14
	3	Su	18		P ·03	5 ·42	15
	4	Mo	19	Bahula	1 ·10	6 ·50	16
	5	Tu	20		2 ·15	7 ·57	17
	6	We	21		3 ·19	8 ·62	18
	7	Th	22		4 ·21	9 ·65	19
	8	Fr	23		5 ·20	10 ·66	20
	9	Sa	24		6 ·18	11 ·64	21
	10	Su	25		7 ·13	12 ·61	22
	11	Mo	26		8 ·07; 9 ·99	13 ·57	23
	12	Tu	27		10 ·90	14 ·52	24
	13	We	28		11 ·81	15 ·46	25
	14	Th	29		12 ·71	16 ·39	26
	15	Fr	30		13 ·61	17 ·32	27
	16	Sa	31		14 ·52	18 ·25	28

15. Svati. 16. Visak. 17. Anur. 18. Jyesh. 19. Mula. 20. P. Ash. 21. U. Ash. 22. Sravn. 23. Dani. 24. Satab. 25. P. Bhad. 26. U. Bhad. 27. Rev.

A. D. 1995.   **Mesha Sankranti** (Commencement of Indian Sidereal Year).
Solar Eclipse. ●   **(Surya Sid.) April 14·20.**   **Saka 1917.**   **Kaliyuga 5096.**
Lunar Eclipse. ○   **(Arya Sid.) April 14·09.**   **(S. Cycle) Yuva.**

Jan.

Solar: Bhava Dhanus—Margali (to 29); Bhava Makara—Tai (from 1). Lunar: Sukla; Pausha; Bahula. Muhammadan: H. 1415 Shaban.

SOLAR reckoning: Cyclic Sidereal Year, Month and Day	Week-Day English Month and Day	LUNAR reckoning: Tithi Ending Moment	Nakshatra Ending Moment	Muhammadan Year, Month and Day
17	Su 1	—A ·43	19 ·19	29
18	Mo 2	1 ·35	20 ·14	—30
19	Tu 3	2 ·28	21 ·10	1
20	We 4	3 ·23	22 ·07	2
21	Th 5	4 ·19	23 ·05	3
22	Fr 6	5 ·18	24 ·06	4
23	Sa 7	6 ·19	25 ·09	5
24	Su 8	7 ·22	26 ·14	6
25	Mo 9	8 ·27	27 ·21	7
26	Tu 10	9 ·34	1 ·30	8
27	We 11	10 ·42	2 ·40	9
28	Th 12	11 ·51	3 ·51	10
—29	Fr 13	12 ·60	4 ·62	11
1	Sa 14	13 ·68	5 ·72	12
2	Su 15	14 ·75	6 ·81	13
3	Mo 16	P ·80	7 ·88	14
4	Tu 17	1 ·84	8 ·94	15
5	We 18	2 ·85	9 ·97	16
6	Th 19	3 ·85	10 ·98	17
7	Fr 20	4 ·82	11 ·97	18
8	Sa 21	5 ·77	12 ·95	19
9	Su 22	6 ·70	13 ·91	20
10	Mo 23	7 ·62	14 ·86	21
11	Tu 24	8 ·54	15 ·80	22
12	We 25	9 ·45	16 ·73	23
13	Th 26	10 ·35	17 ·66	24
14	Fr 27	11 ·25	18 ·59	25
15	Sa 28	12 ·15	19 ·53	26
16	Su 29	13 ·06 / 14 ·98	20 ·47	27
17	Mo 30	—A ·92	21 ·42	28
18	Tu 31	1 ·87	22 ·39	—29

Feb.

Solar: Bhava Kumbha—Masi. Lunar: Sukla; Magha; Bahula. Muhammadan: H. 1415 Ramzan.

SOLAR reckoning: Cyclic Sidereal Year, Month and Day	Week-Day English Month and Day	LUNAR reckoning: Tithi Ending Moment	Nakshatra Ending Moment	Muhammadan Year, Month and Day
19	We 1	2 ·84	23 ·38	1
20	Th 2	3 ·83	24 ·39	2
21	Fr 3	4 ·83	25 ·41	3
22	Sa 4	5 ·87	26 ·45	4
23	Su 5	6 ·92	27 ·52	5
24	Mo 6	7 ·99	1 ·60	6
25	Tu 7	... ...	2 ·70	7
26	We 8	8 ·07	3 ·81	8
27	Th 9	9 ·16	4 ·92	9
28	Fr 10	10 ·24	... ...	10
29	Sa 11	11 ·32	5 ·02	11
—30	Su 12	12 ·39	6 ·11	12
1	Mo 13	13 ·44	7 ·19	13
2	Tu 14	14 ·47	8 ·25	14
3	We 15	P ·48	9 ·29	15
4	Th 16	1 ·48	10 ·30	16
5	Fr 17	2 ·45	11 ·30	17
6	Sa 18	3 ·39	12 ·28	18
7	Su 19	4 ·32	13 ·25	19
8	Mo 20	5 ·24	14 ·20	20
9	Tu 21	6 ·16	15 ·14	21
10	We 22	7 ·07 / 8 ·97	16 ·07	22
11	Th 23	9 ·87	17 ·00 / 18 ·98	23
12	Fr 24	10 ·77	19 ·87	24
13	Sa 25	11 ·68	20 ·81	25
14	Su 26	12 ·60	21 ·76	26
15	Mo 27	13 ·54	22 ·72	27
16	Tu 28	14 ·49	23 ·71	28

March

Solar: Bhava Kumbha—Masi (to 30); Bhava Mina—Panguni (from 1). Lunar: Sukla; Phalguna; Bahula. Muhammadan: H. 1415 Shawwal.

SOLAR reckoning: Cyclic Sidereal Year, Month and Day	Week-Day English Month and Day	LUNAR reckoning: Tithi Ending Moment	Nakshatra Ending Moment	Muhammadan Year, Month and Day
17	We 1	—A ·46	24 ·71	29
18	Th 2	1 ·44	25 ·73	—30
19	Fr 3	2 ·45	26 ·76	1
20	Sa 4	3 ·48	27 ·82	2
21	Su 5	4 ·53	1 ·90	3
22	Mo 6	5 ·60	... ...	4
23	Tu 7	6 ·69	2 ·00	5
24	We 8	7 ·78	3 ·11	6
25	Th 9	8 ·86	4 ·22	7
26	Fr 10	9 ·94	5 ·32	8
27	Sa 11	... ...	6 ·41	9
28	Su 12	10 ·00	7 ·49	10
29	Mo 13	11 ·05	8 ·56	11
—30	Tu 14	12 ·08	9 ·60	12
1	We 15	13 ·08	10 ·62	13
2	Th 16	14 ·07	11 ·62	14
3	Fr 17	P ·03 / 1 ·98	12 ·61	15
4	Sa 18	2 ·92	13 ·58	16
5	Su 19	3 ·85	14 ·53	17
6	Mo 20	4 ·76	15 ·47	18
7	Tu 21	5 ·66	16 ·41	19
8	We 22	6 ·56	17 ·34	20
9	Th 23	7 ·46	18 ·27	21
10	Fr 24	8 ·36	19 ·20	22
11	Sa 25	9 ·27	20 ·14	23
12	Su 26	10 ·19	21 ·09	24
13	Mo 27	11 ·13	22 ·06	25
14	Tu 28	12 ·08	23 ·04	26
15	We 29	13 ·04	24 ·03	27
16	Th 30	14 ·02	25 ·04	28
17	Fr 31	—A ·03	26 ·07	—29

April

Solar: Yuva Mesha—Chittirai. Lunar: Sukla; Chaitra; Bahula. Muhammadan: H. 1415 Zi-l-ka'da.

SOLAR reckoning: Cyclic Sidereal Year, Month and Day	Week-Day English Month and Day	LUNAR reckoning: Tithi Ending Moment	Nakshatra Ending Moment	Muhammadan Year, Month and Day
18	Sa 1	1 ·06	27 ·13	1
19	Su 2	2 ·11	1 ·21	2
20	Mo 3	3 ·18	2 ·30	3
21	Tu 4	4 ·26	3 ·40	4
22	We 5	5 ·35	4 ·51	5
23	Th 6	6 ·43	5 ·62	6
24	Fr 7	7 ·51	6 ·72	7
25	Sa 8	8 ·57	7 ·81	8
26	Su 9	9 ·61	8 ·87	9
27	Mo 10	10 ·64	9 ·92	10
28	Tu 11	11 ·65	10 ·94	11
29	We 12	12 ·63	11 ·96	12
—30	Th 13	13 ·60	12 ·94	13
1	Fr 14	14 ·54	13 ·91	14
2	Sa ○ 15	P ·47	14 ·87	15
3	Su 16	1 ·40	15 ·81	16
4	Mo 17	2 ·31	16 ·75	17
5	Tu 18	3 ·21	17 ·68	18
6	We 19	4 ·11	18 ·61	19
7	Th 20	5 ·01 / 6 ·91	19 ·54	20
8	Fr 21	7 ·81	20 ·48	21
9	Sa 22	8 ·73	21 ·43	22
10	Su 23	9 ·67	22 ·39	23
11	Mo 24	10 ·62	23 ·36	24
12	Tu 25	11 ·58	24 ·35	25
13	We 26	12 ·57	25 ·36	26
14	Th 27	13 ·57	26 ·39	27
15	Fr 28	14 ·59	27 ·45	28
16	Sa 29	—A ·64	1 ·52	29
17	Su 30	1 ·71	2 ·60	—30

May

Solar: Yuva Mesha—Chittirai (to 31); Yuva Vrishabha—Vaikasi (from 1). Lunar: Sukla; Vaisakha; Bahula. Muhammadan: H. 1415 Zi-l-hijja.

SOLAR reckoning: Cyclic Sidereal Year, Month and Day	Week-Day English Month and Day	LUNAR reckoning: Tithi Ending Moment	Nakshatra Ending Moment	Muhammadan Year, Month and Day
18	Mo 1	2 ·79	3 ·70	1
19	Tu 2	3 ·88	4 ·81	2
20	We 3	4 ·96	5 ·92	3
21	Th 4	... ...	... ...	4
22	Fr 5	5 ·04	6 ·02	5
23	Sa 6	6 ·10	7 ·11	6
24	Su 7	7 ·14	8 ·18	7
25	Mo 8	8 ·16	9 ·23	8
26	Tu 9	9 ·18	10 ·27	9
27	We 10	10 ·16	11 ·28	10
28	Th 11	11 ·13	12 ·27	11
29	Fr 12	12 ·07	13 ·24	12
30	Sa 13	13 ·00 / 14 ·92	14 ·20	13
—31	Su 14	P ·83	15 ·15	14
1	Mo 15	1 ·73	16 ·03	15
2	Tu 16	2 ·63	17 ·02 / 18 ·95	16
3	We 17	3 ·53	19 ·88	17
4	Th 18	4 ·43	20 ·82	18
5	Fr 19	5 ·34	21 ·77	19
6	Sa 20	6 ·25	22 ·72	20
7	Su 21	7 ·18	23 ·69	21
8	Mo 22	8 ·13	24 ·67	22
9	Tu 23	9 ·09	25 ·68	23
10	We 24	10 ·07	26 ·71	24
11	Th 25	11 ·07	27 ·76	25
12	Fr 26	12 ·10	1 ·82	26
13	Sa 27	13 ·15	2 ·90	27
14	Su 28	14 ·21	... ...	28
15	Mo 29	—A ·29	3 ·00	29
16	Tu 30	1 ·37	4 ·11	—30
17	We 31	2 ·45	5 ·22	1

June

Solar: Yuva Mithuna—Ani. Lunar: Sukla; Jyeshtha; Bahula; A. Suk. Muhammadan: H. 1416 Muharram.

SOLAR reckoning: Cyclic Sidereal Year, Month and Day	Week-Day English Month and Day	LUNAR reckoning: Tithi Ending Moment	Nakshatra Ending Moment	Muhammadan Year, Month and Day
18	Th 1	3 ·58	6 ·32	2
19	Fr 2	4 ·60	7 ·41	3
20	Sa 3	5 ·64	8 ·49	4
21	Su 4	6 ·66	9 ·55	5
22	Mo 5	7 ·67	10 ·59	6
23	Tu 6	8 ·66	11 ·60	7
24	We 7	9 ·63	12 ·60	8
25	Th 8	10 ·57	13 ·58	9
26	Fr 9	11 ·50	14 ·54	10
27	Sa 10	12 ·42	15 ·49	11
28	Su 11	13 ·32	16 ·43	12
29	Mo 12	14 ·22	17 ·36	13
30	Tu 13	P ·12	18 ·29	14
—31	We 14	1 ·02 / 2 ·92	19 ·22	15
1	Th 15	3 ·83	20 ·16	16
2	Fr 16	4 ·74	21 ·10	17
3	Sa 17	5 ·67	22 ·05	18
4	Su 18	6 ·62	23 ·02	19
5	Mo 19	7 ·58	24 ·00	20
6	Tu 20	8 ·55	25 ·01	21
7	We 21	9 ·55	26 ·03	22
8	Th 22	10 ·58	27 ·07	23
9	Fr 23	11 ·63	1 ·13	24
10	Sa 24	12 ·69	2 ·21	25
11	Su 25	13 ·76	3 ·31	26
12	Mo 26	14 ·84	4 ·41	27
13	Tu 27	—A ·92	5 ·52	28
14	We 28	... ...	6 ·62	29
15	Th 29	1 ·00	7 ·72	—30
16	Fr 30	2 ·07	8 ·80	1

Naksh:—1. Asvn. 2. Bhar. 3. Krit. 4. Rohi. 5. Mrig. 6. Ardh. 7. Punar. 8. Push. 9. Aslesh. 10. Magh. 11. P. Phal. 12. U. Phal. 13. Hasta. 14. Chit.

A. D. 1995.
A.—Amavasya.
P.—Paurnami.

Kollam 1171, Commences { **N. Malabar—Sept.** / **S. Malabar—Aug.**

Hijra 1416, Commences, **May 31.**

Vikrama 2052.
Bengal San 1401.
(N. Cycle) Sarvadharin

Columns: SOLAR reckoning — Cyclic Sidereal Year, Month and Day; Week-Day English Month and Day. LUNAR reckoning — Tithi Ending Moment; Nakshatra Ending Moment; Muhammadan Year, Month and Day.

Side labels: Solar: Yuva *Mithuna—Ani* (to 31); Yuva *Karkata—Adi* (from 32). Lunar: Ashadha (Sukla, then Bahula). Muhammadan: H. 1416 *Safar*.

Cyclic Sidereal	July		Tithi	Nakshatra	Muhammadan
17	Sa	1	3 ·11	9 ·86	2
18	Su	2	4 ·14	10 ·90	3
19	Mo	3	5 ·15	11 ·92	4
20	Tu	4	6 ·13	12 ·92	5
21	We	5	7 ·10	13 ·90	6
22	Th	6	8 ·05 / 9 ·98	14 ·87	7
23	Fr	7	10 ·89	15 ·83	8
24	Sa	8	11 ·80	16 ·77	9
25	Su	9	12 ·70	17 ·70	10
26	Mo	10	13 ·60	18 ·63	11
27	Tu	11	14 ·50	19 ·56	12
28	We	12	P ·40	20 ·50	13
29	Th	13	1 ·31	21 ·44	14
30	Fr	14	2 ·22	22 ·39	15
31	Sa	15	3 ·15	23 ·35	16
—32	Su	16	4 ·09	24 ·33	17
1	Mo	17	5 ·05	25 ·33	18
2	Tu	18	6 ·03	26 ·34	19
3	We	19	7 ·04	27 ·38	20
4	Th	20	8 ·06	1 ·44	21
5	Fr	21	9 ·10	2 ·52	22
6	Sa	22	10 ·16	3 ·61	23
7	Su	23	11 ·23	4 ·71	24
8	Mo	24	12 ·31	5 ·82	25
9	Tu	25	13 ·39	6 ·93	26
10	We	26	14 ·47	...	27
11	Th	27	—A ·54	7 ·03	28
12	Fr	28	1 ·59	8 ·11	—29
13	Sa	29	2 ·62	9 ·17	1
14	Su	30	3 ·62	10 ·21	2
15	Mo	31	4 ·61	11 ·24	3

Side labels: Solar: Yuva *Simha—Avani*. Lunar: Sravana (Sukla, then Bahula); B. Suk. Muhammadan: H. 1416 *Rabi-ul-awwal*; *R.-akhir*.

Cyclic Sidereal	Aug.		Tithi	Nakshatra	Muhammadan
16	Tu	1	5 ·58	12 ·25	4
17	We	2	6 ·53	13 ·24	5
18	Th	3	7 ·47	14 ·21	6
19	Fr	4	8 ·39	15 ·16	7
20	Sa	5	9 ·29	16 ·10	8
21	Su	6	10 ·19	17 ·04 / 18 ·98	9
22	Mo	7	11 ·09 / 12 ·99	19 ·91	10
23	Tu	8	13 ·89	20 ·84	11
24	We	9	14 ·80	21 ·77	12
25	Th	10	P ·72	22 ·72	13
26	Fr	11	1 ·65	23 ·69	14
27	Sa	12	2 ·58	24 ·66	15
28	Su	13	3 ·54	25 ·65	16
29	Mo	14	4 ·52	26 ·66	17
30	Tu	15	5 ·53	27 ·69	18
—31	We	16	6 ·55	1 ·75	19
1	Th	17	7 ·59	2 ·82	20
2	Fr	18	8 ·65	3 ·91	21
3	Sa	19	9 ·73	...	22
4	Su	20	10 ·81	4 ·01	23
5	Mo	21	11 ·89	5 ·11	24
6	Tu	22	12 ·97	6 ·22	25
7	We	23	...	7 ·33	26
8	Th	24	13 ·08	8 ·42	27
9	Fr	25	14 ·08	9 ·48	28
10	Sa	26	—A ·11	10 ·53	29
11	Su	27	1 ·13	11 ·56	—30
12	Mo	28	2 ·11	12 ·58	1
13	Tu	29	3 ·08	13 ·57	2
14	We	30	4 ·04 / 5 ·98	14 ·54	3
15	Th	31	6 ·90	15 ·49	4

Side labels: Solar: Yuva *Simha—Avani* (to 31); Yuva *Kanya—Purattasi* (from 32). Lunar: Sukla, Bhadrapada, Bahula, Sukla. Muhammadan: H. 1416 *Rabi-ul-akhir*.

Cyclic Sidereal	Sep.		Tithi	Nakshatra	Muhammadan
16	Fr	1	7 ·81	16 ·44	5
17	Sa	2	8 ·71	17 ·38	6
18	Su	3	9 ·61	18 ·32	7
19	Mo	4	10 ·51	19 ·25	8
20	Tu	5	11 ·41	20 ·18	9
21	We	6	12 ·31	21 ·11	10
22	Th	7	13 ·23	22 ·06	11
23	Fr	8	14 ·16	23 ·02 / 24 ·99	12
24	Sa	9	P ·11	25 ·97	13
25	Su	10	1 ·07	26 ·98	14
26	Mo	11	2 ·05	...	15
27	Tu	12	3 ·05	27 ·01	16
28	We	13	4 ·06	1 ·06	17
29	Th	14	5 ·11	2 ·13	18
30	Fr	15	6 ·17	3 ·21	19
31	Sa	16	7 ·25	4 ·31	20
—32	Su	17	8 ·34	5 ·42	21
1	Mo	18	9 ·42	6 ·53	22
2	Tu	19	10 ·49	7 ·63	23
3	We	20	11 ·56	8 ·72	24
4	Th	21	12 ·61	9 ·79	25
5	Fr	22	13 ·64	10 ·85	26
6	Sa	23	14 ·67	11 ·89	27
7	Su	24	—A ·65	12 ·90	28
8	Mo	25	1 ·62	13 ·89	—29
9	Tu	26	2 ·58	14 ·87	1
10	We	27	3 ·52	15 ·83	2
11	Th	28	4 ·44	16 ·78	3
12	Fr	29	5 ·35	17 ·72	4
13	Sa	30	6 ·26	18 ·65	5

Side labels: Solar: Yuva *Tula—Aippasi*. Lunar: Asvina (Sukla, then Bahula); Kartt. Suk. Muhammadan: H. 1416 *Jumadal-awwal*; *Jumadal-akhir*.

Cyclic Sidereal	Oct.		Tithi	Nakshatra	Muhammadan
14	Su	1	7 ·16	19 ·58	6
15	Mo	2	8 ·06 / 9 ·96	20 ·52	7
16	Tu	3	10 ·86	21 ·46	8
17	We	4	11 ·78	22 ·40	9
18	Th	5	12 ·71	23 ·35	10
19	Fr	6	13 ·66	24 ·32	11
20	Sa	7	14 ·62	25 ·30	12
21	Su	8	P ·61	26 ·30	13
22	Mo	9	1 ·61	27 ·33	14
23	Tu	10	2 ·63	1 ·37	15
24	We	11	3 ·68	2 ·43	16
25	Th	12	4 ·74	3 ·51	17
26	Fr	13	5 ·81	4 ·61	18
27	Sa	14	6 ·90	5 ·72	19
28	Su	15	7 ·98	6 ·83	20
29	Mo	16	...	7 ·93	21
—30	Tu	17	8 ·06	...	22
1	We	18	9 ·13	8 ·02	23
2	Th	19	10 ·19	9 ·10	24
3	Fr	20	11 ·23	10 ·17	25
4	Sa	21	12 ·25	11 ·21	26
5	Su	22	13 ·23	12 ·22	27
6	Mo	23	14 ·20	13 ·22	28
7	Tu	● 24	—A ·16	14 ·20	29
8	We	25	1 ·10	15 ·17	—30
9	Th	26	2 ·02 / 3 ·93	16 ·12	1
10	Fr	27	4 ·84	17 ·06 / 18 ·99	2
11	Sa	28	5 ·74	19 ·92	3
12	Su	29	6 ·64	20 ·85	4
13	Mo	30	7 ·54	21 ·79	5
14	Tu	31	8 ·45	22 ·73	6

Side labels: Solar: Yuva *Tula—Aippasi* (to 30); Yuva *Vrischika—Kartigai* (from 1). Lunar: Sukla, Kartika, Bahula, Sukla. Muhammadan: H. 1416 *Jumadal-akhir*.

Cyclic Sidereal	Nov.		Tithi	Nakshatra	Muhammadan
15	We	1	9 ·37	23 ·68	7
16	Th	2	10 ·31	24 ·64	8
17	Fr	3	11 ·25	25 ·62	9
18	Sa	4	12 ·21	26 ·63	10
19	Su	5	13 ·20	27 ·64	11
20	Mo	6	14 ·20	1 ·68	12
21	Tu	7	P ·22	2 ·74	13
22	We	8	1 ·27	3 ·82	14
23	Th	9	2 ·34	4 ·92	15
24	Fr	10	3 ·42	...	16
25	Sa	11	4 ·51	5 ·02	17
26	Su	12	5 ·59	6 ·12	18
27	Mo	13	6 ·67	7 ·23	19
28	Tu	14	7 ·74	8 ·33	20
29	We	15	8 ·80	9 ·42	21
—30	Th	16	9 ·84	10 ·48	22
1	Fr	17	10 ·85	11 ·52	23
2	Sa	18	11 ·85	12 ·54	24
3	Su	19	12 ·82	13 ·54	25
4	Mo	20	13 ·77	14 ·53	26
5	Tu	21	14 ·71	15 ·50	27
6	We	22	—A ·64	16 ·46	28
7	Th	23	1 ·55	17 ·40	—29
8	Fr	24	2 ·46	18 ·33	1
9	Sa	25	3 ·36	19 ·26	2
10	Su	26	4 ·26	20 ·19	3
11	Mo	27	5 ·16	21 ·13	4
12	Tu	28	6 ·07 / 7 ·99	22 ·07	5
13	We	29	8 ·92	23 ·02 / 24 ·98	6
14	Th	30	9 ·87	25 ·96	7

Side labels: Solar: Yuva *Dhanus—Margali*. Lunar: Margasira (Bahula); Pausha Sukla. Muhammadan: H. 1416 *Rajab*; H. 1416 *Shaban*.

Cyclic Sidereal	Dec.		Tithi	Nakshatra	Muhammadan
15	Fr	1	10 ·84	26 ·95	8
16	Sa	2	11 ·82	27 ·96	9
17	Su	3	12 ·84	1 ·99	10
18	Mo	4	13 ·87	...	11
19	Tu	5	14 ·91	2 ·05	12
20	We	6	P ·98	3 ·13	13
21	Th	7	...	4 ·22	14
22	Fr	8	1 ·06	5 ·32	15
23	Sa	9	2 ·14	6 ·43	16
24	Su	10	3 ·23	7 ·54	17
25	Mo	11	4 ·32	8 ·64	18
26	Tu	12	5 ·39	9 ·72	19
27	We	13	6 ·44	10 ·78	20
28	Th	14	7 ·48	11 ·83	21
—29	Fr	15	8 ·49	12 ·86	22
1	Sa	16	9 ·48	13 ·87	23
2	Su	17	10 ·46	14 ·86	24
3	Mo	18	11 ·41	15 ·83	25
4	Tu	19	12 ·34	16 ·79	26
5	We	20	13 ·26	17 ·73	27
6	Th	21	14 ·18	18 ·67	28
7	Fr	22	A ·09 / 1 ·99	19 ·61	29
8	Sa	23	2 ·89	20 ·54	—30
9	Su	24	3 ·80	21 ·47	1
10	Mo	25	4 ·71	22 ·40	2
11	Tu	26	5 ·63	23 ·35	3
12	We	27	6 ·56	24 ·31	4
13	Th	28	7 ·51	25 ·28	5
14	Fr	29	8 ·49	26 ·27	6
15	Sa	30	9 ·47	27 ·28	7
16	Su	31	10 ·48	1 ·31	8

15. Svati. 16. Visak. 17. Anur. 18. Jyesh. 19. Mula. 20. P. Ash. 21. U. Ash. 22. Sravn. 23. Dani. 24. Satab. 25. P. Bhad. 26. U. Bhad. 27. Rev.

A. D. 1996.
Solar Eclipse. ●
Lunar Eclipse. ○

Mesha Sankranti (Commencement of Indian Sidereal Year).
(Surya Sid.) April 13·46. **Saka 1918.** **Kaliyuga 5097.**
(Arya Sid.) April 13·35. **(S. Cycle) Dhatri.**

SOLAR reckoning: Cyclic Sidereal Year, Month and Day; Week-Day English Month and Day. LUNAR reckoning: Tithi Ending Moment; Nakshatra Ending Moment; Muhammadan Year, Month and Day.

Jan.

Solar: Yuva, Dhanus—Margali (17–30); Yuva, Makara—Tai (1–17). Lunar: Pausha, Suk. (11–P), Bahula (1–14, A), Sukla (1–11). Muhammadan: H. 1416 Shaban.

Cyclic Sidereal	Week-Day	Jan.	Tithi	Moment	Nakshatra	Moment	Muhammadan
17	Mo	1	11	·51	2	·36	9
18	Tu	2	12	·56	3	·43	10
19	We	3	13	·63	4	·52	11
20	Th	4	14	·71	5	·62	12
21	Fr	5	P	·80	6	·73	13
22	Sa	6	1	·89	7	·84	14
23	Su	7	2	·97	8	·94	15
24	Mo	8	...	...	...	...	16
25	Tu	9	3	·04	9	·08	17
26	We	10	4	·0J	10	·10	18
27	Th	11	5	·12	11	·15	19
28	Fr	12	6	·14	12	·18	20
29	Sa	13	7	·13	13	·20	21
—30	Su	14	8	·10	14	·19	22
1	Mo	15	9 10	·05 ·98	15	·16	23
2	Tu	16	11	·91	16	·12	24
3	We	17	12	·82	17	·07	25
4	Th	18	13	·72	18 19	·02 ·95	26
5	Fr	19	14	·62	20	·88	27
6	Sa	20	—A	·52	21	·81	28
7	Su	21	1	·48	22	·74	—29
8	Mo	22	2	·35	23	·69	1
9	Tu	23	3	·28	24	·65	2
10	We	24	4	·21	25	·62	3
11	Th	25	5	·16	26	·60	4
12	Fr	26	6	·13	27	·60	5
13	Sa	27	7	·11	1	·62	6
14	Su	28	8	·12	2	·67	7
15	Mo	29	9	·15	3	·74	8
16	Tu	30	10	·21	4	·82	9
17	We	31	11	·28	5	·91	10

Feb.

Solar: Yuva, Kumbha—Masi. Lunar: Magha (12–P), Bahula (1–14, A), Sukla, Phalguna. Muhammadan: H. 1416 Ramzan (11–30); H. 1416 Shawwal (1–9).

Cyclic Sidereal	Week-Day	Feb.	Tithi	Moment	Nakshatra	Moment	Muhammadan
18	Th	1	12	·36	...	...	11
19	Fr	2	13	·45	6	·02	12
20	Sa	3	14	·54	7	·13	13
21	Su	4	P	·62	8	·24	14
22	Mo	5	1	·68	9	·33	15
23	Tu	6	2	·73	10	·40	16
24	We	7	3	·76	11	·46	17
25	Th	8	4	·78	12	·50	18
26	Fr	9	5	·76	13	·52	19
27	Sa	10	6	·73	14	·52	20
28	Su	11	7	·68	15	·49	21
—29	Mo	12	8	·61	16	·46	22
1	Tu	13	9	·53	17	·41	23
2	We	14	10	·44	18	·35	24
3	Th	15	11	·35	19	·29	25
4	Fr	16	12	·26	20	·22	26
5	Sa	17	13	·16	21	·15	27
6	Su	18	14 A	·06 ·97	22	·09	28
7	Mo	19	1	·89	23 24	·03 ·98	29
8	Tu	20	2	·82	25	·94	—30
9	We	21	3	·78	26	·92	1
10	Th	22	4	·75	27	·92	2
11	Fr	23	5	·74	1	·95	3
12	Sa	24	6	·74	2	·98	4
13	Su	25	7	·78	...	...	5
14	Mo	26	8	·83	3	·04	6
15	Tu	27	9	·90	4	·12	7
16	We	28	10	·99	5	·22	8
17	Th	29	...	...	6	·33	9

March

Solar: Yuva, Kumbha—Masi (18–31); Yuva, Mina—Panguni (1–17). Lunar: Suk., Phalguna, Bahula, Sukla. Muhammadan: H. 1416 Shawwal.

Cyclic Sidereal	Week-Day	March	Tithi	Moment	Nakshatra	Moment	Muhammadan
18	Fr	1	11	·08	7	·44	10
19	Sa	2	12	·17	8	·54	11
20	Su	3	13	·24	9	·63	12
21	Mo	4	14	·30	10	·71	13
22	Tu	5	P	·35	11	·78	14
23	We	6	1	·38	12	·82	15
24	Th	7	2	·39	13	·84	16
25	Fr	8	3	·37	14	·84	17
26	Sa	9	4	·34	15	·82	18
27	Su	10	5	·28	16	·79	19
28	Mo	11	6	·21	17	·75	20
29	Tu	12	7	·13	18	·69	21
30	We	13	8 9	·04 ·95	19	·62	22
—31	Th	14	10	·85	20	·55	23
1	Fr	15	11	·75	21	·48	24
2	Sa	16	12	·65	22	·42	25
3	Su	17	13	·56	23	·36	26
4	Mo	18	14	·49	24	·31	27
5	Tu	19	—A	·43	25	·27	28
6	We	20	1	·38	26	·25	—29
7	Th	21	2	·34	27	·25	1
8	Fr	22	3	·33	1	·26	2
9	Sa	23	4	·33	2	·30	3
10	Su	24	5	·37	3	·35	4
11	Mo	25	6	·43	4	·42	5
12	Tu	26	7	·50	5	·52	6
13	We	27	8	·58	6	·62	7
14	Th	28	9	·66	7	·73	8
15	Fr	29	10	·75	8	·84	9
16	Sa	30	11	·82	9	·94	10
17	Su	31	12	·88	...	...	11

April

Solar: Dhatri, Mesha—Chittirai. Lunar: Chaitra, Bahula, Sukla, Vaisakha. Muhammadan: H. 1416 Zi-l-ka'da (12–30); H. 1416 Zi-l-hijja (1–11).

Cyclic Sidereal	Week-Day	April	Tithi	Moment	Nakshatra	Moment	Muhammadan
18	Mo	1	13	·93	10	·03	12
19	Tu	2	14	·96	11	·09	13
20	We ○	3	P	·96	12	·14	14
21	Th	4	1	·94	13	·16	15
22	Fr	5	2	·90	14	·17	16
23	Sa	6	3	·85	15	·16	17
24	Su	7	4	·79	16	·13	18
25	Mo	8	5	·71	17	·09	19
26	Tu	9	6	·61	18 19	·03 ·96	20
27	We	10	7	·51	20	·89	21
28	Th	11	8	·41	21	·82	22
—29	Fr	12	9	·31	22	·76	23
1	Sa	13	10	·21	23	·70	24
2	Su	14	11	·12	24	·64	25
3	Mo	15	12 13	·04 ·97	25	·60	26
4	Tu	16	14	·93	26	·58	27
5	We	17	—A	·90	27	·57	28
6	Th	18	1	·88	1	·58	29
7	Fr	19	2	·88	2	·61	—30
8	Sa	20	3	·91	3	·66	1
9	Su	21	4	·96	4	·73	2
10	Mo	22	...	...	5	·82	3
11	Tu	23	5	·03	6	·92	4
12	We	24	6	·12	...	...	5
13	Th	25	7	·21	7	·03	6
14	Fr	26	8	·29	8	·14	7
15	Sa	27	9	·36	9	·24	8
16	Su	28	10	·42	10	·33	9
17	Mo	29	11	·46	11	·40	10
18	Tu	30	12	·49	12	·45	11

May

Solar: Dhatri, Mesha—Chittirai (19–31); Dhatri, Vrishabha—Vaikasi (1–18). Lunar: Vaisakha, Bahula, Sukla, Jyeshtha. Muhammadan: H. 1416 Zi-l-hijja.

Cyclic Sidereal	Week-Day	May	Tithi	Moment	Nakshatra	Moment	Muhammadan
19	We	1	13	·49	13	·48	12
20	Th	2	14	·48	14	·49	13
21	Fr	3	P	·44	15	·49	14
22	Sa	4	1	·38	16	·46	15
23	Su	5	2	·31	17	·42	16
24	Mo	6	3	·23	18	·36	17
25	Tu	7	4	·14	19	·30	18
26	We	8	5 6	·04 ·94	20	·24	19
27	Th	9	7	·84	21	·17	20
28	Fr	10	8	·74	22	·10	21
29	Sa	11	9	·64	23 24	·04 ·98	22
30	Su	12	10	·56	25	·94	23
—31	Mo	13	11	·49	26	·91	24
1	Tu	14	12	·44	27	·89	25
2	We	15	13	·41	1	·90	26
3	Th	16	14	·39	2	·93	27
4	Fr	17	—A	·41	3	·98	28
5	Sa	18	1	·44	...	...	—29
6	Su	19	2	·48	4	·04	1
7	Mo	20	3	·54	5	·12	2
8	Tu	21	4	·62	6	·22	3
9	We	22	5	·71	7	·33	4
10	Th	23	6	·79	8	·44	5
11	Fr	24	7	·86	9	·54	6
12	Sa	25	8	·93	10	·63	7
13	Su	26	9	·97	11	·71	8
14	Mo	27	10	·99	12	·76	9
15	Tu	28	11	·99	13	·80	10
16	We	29	12	·98	14	·82	11
17	Th	30	13	·94	15	·82	12
18	Fr	31	14	·89	16	·79	13

June

Solar: Dhatri, Mithuna—Ani. Lunar: Bahula, Sukla, Adhika Ashadha. Muhammadan: H. 1417 Muharram (14–30); H. 1417 Safar (1–13).

Cyclic Sidereal	Week-Day	June	Tithi	Moment	Nakshatra	Moment	Muhammadan
19	Sa	1	P	·82	17	·75	14
20	Su	2	1	·73	18	·70	15
21	Mo	3	2	·63	19	·64	16
22	Tu	4	3	·53	20	·58	17
23	We	5	4	·43	21	·51	18
24	Th	6	5	·33	22	·44	19
25	Fr	7	6	·23	23	·37	20
26	Sa	8	7	·14	24	·32	21
27	Su	9	8 9	·06 ·99	25	·27	22
28	Mo	10	10	·94	26	·24	23
29	Tu	11	11	·90	27	·22	24
30	We	12	12	·87	1	·22	25
31	Th	13	13	·88	2	·25	26
—32	Fr	14	14	·91	3	·29	27
1	Sa	15	—A	·96	4	·35	28
2	Su	16	...	...	5	·43	29
3	Mo	17	1	·02	6	·52	—30
4	Tu	18	2	·10	7	·62	1
5	We	19	3	·18	8	·73	2
6	Th	20	4	·26	9	·84	3
7	Fr	21	5	·33	10	·94	4
8	Sa	22	6	·40	...	...	5
9	Su	23	7	·44	11	·01	6
10	Mo	24	8	·47	12	·07	7
11	Tu	25	9	·48	13	·12	8
12	We	26	10	·46	14	·14	9
13	Th	27	11	·42	15	·14	10
14	Fr	28	12	·36	16	·12	11
15	Sa	29	13	·20	17	·09	12
16	Su	30	14	·21	18 19	·05 ·99	13

Naksh :—1. Asvn. 2. Bhar. 3. Krit. 4. Rohi. 5. Mrig. 6. Ardh. 7. Punar. 8. Push. 9. Aslesh. 10. Magh. 11. P. Phal. 12. U. Phal. 13. Hasta. 14. Chit.

A. D. 1996.
A.—Amavasya.
P.—Paurnami.

Kollam 1172, Commences { N. Malabar—Sept. / S. Malabar—Aug.

Hijra 1417, Commences, May 19.

Vikrama 2053.
Bengal San 1403.
(N. Cycle) Virodhin.

July — Solar: Dhatri *Mithuna—Ani.*; Dhatri *Karkata—Adi.* Lunar: Adh. Ashadha, *Bahula*, *Sukla*, Ashadha *Bahula*. Muhammadan: H. 1417 *Safar*; *Rabi-ul-awwal*.

SOLAR reckoning: Cyclic Sidereal Year, Month and Day	Week-Day English Month and Day		LUNAR reckoning: Tithi Ending Moment	Nakshatra Ending Moment	Muhammadan Year, Month and Day
17	Mo	1	P ·12	20 ·92	14
18	Tu	2	{ 1 ·02, 2 ·92	21 ·65	15
19	We	3	3 ·82	22 ·78	16
20	Th	4	4 ·71	23 ·72	17
21	Fr	5	5 ·61	24 ·66	18
22	Sa	6	6 ·53	25 ·61	19
23	Su	7	7 ·46	26 ·57	20
24	Mo	8	8 ·41	27 ·55	21
25	Tu	9	9 ·37	1 ·54	22
26	We	10	10 ·36	2 ·56	23
27	Th	11	11 ·36	3 ·60	24
28	Fr	12	12 ·38	4 ·66	25
29	Sa	13	13 ·43	5 ·73	26
30	Su	14	14 ·49	6 ·82	27
—31	Mo	15	—A ·57	7 ·93	28
1	Tu	16	1 ·65	... ...	—29
2	We	17	2 ·73	8 ·04	1
3	Th	18	3 ·81	9 ·14	2
4	Fr	19	4 ·88	10 ·24	3
5	Sa	20	5 ·92	11 ·32	4
6	Su	21	6 ·95	12 ·39	5
7	Mo	22	7 ·96	13 ·44	6
8	Tu	23	8 ·94	14 ·46	7
9	We	24	9 ·90	15 ·47	8
10	Th	25	10 ·85	16 ·45	9
11	Fr	26	11 ·78	17 ·42	10
12	Sa	27	12 ·70	18 ·38	11
13	Su	28	13 ·61	19 ·32	12
14	Mo	29	14 ·51	20 ·26	13
15	Tu	30	P ·41	21 ·20	14
16	We	31	1 ·31	22 ·13	15

Aug. — Solar: Dhatri *Simha—Avani.* Lunar: Nija, *Bahula*, *Sukla*, Sravana, *Bah.* Muhammadan: H. 1417; H. 1417 *Rabi-ul-akhir.*

Cyclic Sidereal Year, Month and Day	Week-Day English Month and Day		Tithi Ending Moment	Nakshatra Ending Moment	Muhammadan Year, Month and Day
17	Th	1	2 ·21	{ 23 ·06, 24 ·99	16
18	Fr	2	3 ·11	25 ·94	17
19	Sa	3	{ 4 ·02, 5 ·95	26 ·90	18
20	Su	4	6 ·90	27 ·87	19
21	Mo	5	7 ·86	1 ·87	20
22	Tu	6	8 ·84	2 ·88	21
23	We	7	9 ·84	3 ·91	22
24	Th	8	10 ·87	4 ·96	23
25	Fr	9	11 ·92	... ...	24
26	Sa	10	12 ·98	5 ·03	25
27	Su	11	... ...	6 ·13	26
28	Mo	12	13 ·05	7 ·23	27
29	Tu	13	14 ·13	8 ·34	28
30	We	14	—A ·22	9 ·44	29
31	Th	15	1 ·30	10 ·54	—30
—32	Fr	16	2 ·37	11 ·63	1
1	Sa	17	3 ·41	12 ·70	2
2	Su	18	4 ·44	13 ·75	3
3	Mo	19	5 ·45	14 ·78	4
4	Tu	20	6 ·43	15 ·79	5
5	We	21	7 ·40	16 ·79	6
6	Th	22	8 ·35	17 ·76	7
7	Fr	23	9 ·28	18 ·72	8
8	Sa	24	10 ·20	19 ·66	9
9	Su	25	11 ·11	20 ·59	10
10	Mo	26	{ 12 ·01, 13 ·91	21 ·52	11
11	Tu	27	14 ·81	22 ·45	12
12	We	28	P ·71	23 ·39	13
13	Th	29	1 ·62	24 ·33	14
14	Fr	30	2 ·54	25 ·27	15
15	Sa	31	3 ·47	26 ·23	16

Sep. — Solar: Dhatri *Simha—Avani.*; Dhatri *Kanya—Purattasi.* Lunar: Sravana, *Bahula*, *Sukla*, Bhadrapada, *Bahula*. Muhammadan: H. 1417 *Rabi-ul-akhir.*; H. 1417 *Jumadal-awwal.*

Cyclic Sidereal Year, Month and Day	Week-Day English Month and Day		Tithi Ending Moment	Nakshatra Ending Moment	Muhammadan Year, Month and Day
16	Su	1	4 ·42	27 ·21	17
17	Mo	2	5 ·38	1 ·19	18
18	Tu	3	6 ·36	2 ·20	19
19	We	4	7 ·36	3 ·22	20
20	Th	5	8 ·38	4 ·27	21
21	Fr	6	9 ·42	5 ·34	22
22	Sa	7	10 ·48	6 ·43	23
23	Su	8	11 ·56	7 ·53	24
24	Mo	9	12 ·65	8 ·63	25
25	Tu	10	13 ·73	9 ·74	26
26	We	11	14 ·81	10 ·85	27
27	Th	12	—A ·88	11 ·94	28
28	Fr	13	1 ·93	... ...	—29
29	Sa	14	2 ·97	12 ·01	1
30	Su	15	3 ·98	13 ·07	2
—31	Mo	16	4 ·97	14 ·10	3
1	Tu	17	5 ·94	15 ·12	4
2	We	18	6 ·89	16 ·11	5
3	Th	19	7 ·82	17 ·09	6
4	Fr	20	8 ·74	{ 18 ·05, 19 ·99	7
5	Sa	21	9 ·65	20 ·93	8
6	Su	22	10 ·55	21 ·87	9
7	Mo	23	11 ·45	22 ·80	10
8	Tu	24	12 ·35	23 ·73	11
9	We	25	13 ·25	24 ·67	12
10	Th	26	14 ·16	25 ·61	13
11	Fr ○	27	P ·08	26 ·57	14
12	Sa	28	{ 1 ·01, 2 ·96	27 ·54	15
13	Su	29	3 ·92	1 ·52	16
14	Mo	30	4 ·90	2 ·52	17

Oct. — Solar: Dhatri *Tula—Aippasi.* Lunar: *Bahula*, *Sukla*, Asvina, *Bah.* Muhammadan: H. 1417 *Jumadal-akhir.*

Cyclic Sidereal Year, Month and Day	Week-Day English Month and Day		Tithi Ending Moment	Nakshatra Ending Moment	Muhammadan Year, Month and Day
15	Tu	1	5 ·90	3 ·54	18
16	We	2	6 ·93	4 ·58	19
17	Th	3	7 ·97	5 ·65	20
18	Fr	4	... ...	6 ·73	21
19	Sa	5	8 ·03	7 ·83	22
20	Su	6	9 ·11	8 ·94	23
21	Mo	7	10 ·20	... ...	24
22	Tu	8	11 ·29	9 ·05	25
23	We	9	12 ·38	10 ·15	26
24	Th	10	13 ·45	11 ·24	27
25	Fr	11	14 ·50	12 ·32	28
26	Sa	12	—A ·53	13 ·38	29
27	Su	13	1 ·54	14 ·42	—30
28	Mo	14	2 ·53	15 ·44	1
29	Tu	15	3 ·50	16 ·44	2
—30	We	16	4 ·46	17 ·42	3
1	Th	17	5 ·39	18 ·38	4
2	Fr	18	6 ·31	19 ·33	5
3	Sa	19	7 ·22	20 ·27	6
4	Su	20	8 ·13	21 ·21	7
5	Mo	21	{ 9 ·03, 10 ·93	22 ·14	8
6	Tu	22	11 ·83	23 ·07	9
7	We	23	12 ·74	{ 24 ·01, 25 ·95	10
8	Th	24	13 ·66	26 ·90	11
9	Fr	25	14 ·59	27 ·86	12
10	Sa	26	P ·54	1 ·84	13
11	Su	27	1 ·51	2 ·84	14
12	Mo	28	2 ·49	3 ·86	15
13	Tu	29	3 ·50	4 ·90	16
14	We	30	4 ·52	5 ·96	17
15	Th	31	5 ·57	... ...	18

Nov. — Solar: Dhatri *Tula—Aippasi.*; Dhatri *Vrischika—Kartigai.* Lunar: Asvina, *Bahula*, *Sukla*, Karttika. Muhammadan: H. 1417 *Jumadal-akhir.*; H. 1417 *Rajab.*

Cyclic Sidereal Year, Month and Day	Week-Day English Month and Day		Tithi Ending Moment	Nakshatra Ending Moment	Muhammadan Year, Month and Day
16	Fr	1	6 ·64	6 ·03	19
17	Sa	2	7 ·72	7 ·13	20
18	Su	3	8 ·81	8 ·24	21
19	Mo	4	9 ·89	9 ·35	22
20	Tu	5	10 ·97	10 ·45	23
21	We	6	... ...	11 ·55	24
22	Th	7	11 ·04	12 ·63	25
23	Fr	8	12 ·10	13 ·69	26
24	Sa	9	13 ·14	14 ·74	27
25	Su	10	14 ·15	15 ·76	28
26	Mo	11	—A ·13	16 ·76	29
27	Tu	12	1 ·09	17 ·74	1
28	We	13	{ 2 ·05, 3 ·99	18 ·71	2
29	Th	14	4 ·92	19 ·67	3
—30	Fr	15	5 ·83	20 ·62	4
1	Sa	16	6 ·74	21 ·55	5
2	Su	17	7 ·64	22 ·48	6
3	Mo	18	8 ·54	23 ·41	7
4	Tu	19	9 ·44	24 ·35	8
5	We	20	10 ·35	25 ·29	9
6	Th	21	11 ·27	26 ·23	10
7	Fr	22	12 ·20	27 ·19	11
8	Sa	23	13 ·16	1 ·17	12
9	Su	24	14 ·13	2 ·17	13
10	Mo	25	P ·12	3 ·18	14
11	Tu	26	1 ·12	4 ·21	15
12	We	27	2 ·14	5 ·27	16
13	Th	28	3 ·19	6 ·34	17
14	Fr	29	4 ·26	7 ·43	18
15	Sa	30	5 ·85	8 ·53	19

Dec. — Solar: Dhatri *Dhanus—Margali.* Lunar: *Bahula*, *Sukla*, Margasira, *Bahula*. Muhammadan: H. 1417 *Shaban.*

Cyclic Sidereal Year, Month and Day	Week-Day English Month and Day		Tithi Ending Moment	Nakshatra Ending Moment	Muhammadan Year, Month and Day
16	Su	1	6 ·43	9 ·64	20
17	Mo	2	7 ·52	10 ·75	21
18	Tu	3	8 ·60	11 ·85	22
19	We	4	9 ·67	12 ·94	23
20	Th	5	10 ·73	... ...	24
21	Fr	6	11 ·77	13 ·01	25
22	Sa	7	12 ·78	14 ·06	26
23	Su	8	13 ·76	15 ·08	27
24	Mo	9	14 ·73	16 ·09	28
25	Tu	10	—A ·69	17 ·07	29
26	We	11	1 ·62	18 ·05	—30
27	Th	12	2 ·54	{ 19 ·01, 20 ·95	1
28	Fr	13	3 ·45	21 ·89	2
29	Sa	14	4 ·36	22 ·83	3
—30	Su	15	5 ·27	23 ·76	4
1	Mo	16	6 ·17	24 ·69	5
2	Tu	17	{ 7 ·07, 8 ·98	25 ·62	6
3	We	18	9 ·90	26 ·56	7
4	Th	19	10 ·84	27 ·52	8
5	Fr	20	11 ·80	1 ·50	9
6	Sa	21	12 ·77	2 ·49	10
7	Su	22	13 ·76	3 ·50	11
8	Mo	23	14 ·77	4 ·53	12
9	Tu	24	P ·80	5 ·57	13
10	We	25	1 ·85	6 ·64	14
11	Th	26	2 ·92	7 ·74	15
12	Fr	27	... ...	8 ·84	16
13	Sa	28	3 ·00	9 ·94	17
14	Su	29	4 ·09	... ...	18
15	Mo	30	5 ·18	10 ·05	19
16	Tu	31	6 ·26	11 ·15	20

15. Svati. 16. Visak. 17. Anur. 18. Jyesh. 19. Mula. 20. P. Ash. 21. U. Ash. 22. Sravn. 23. Dani. 24. Satab. 25. P. Bhad. 26. U. Bhad. 27. Rev.

A. D. 1997. **Mesha Sankranti** (Commencement of Indian Sidereal Year).
Solar Eclipse. ● (Surya Sid.) April 13·72. Saka 1919. Kaliyuga 5098.
Lunar Eclipse. ○ (Arya Sid.) April 13·61. (S. Cycle) Isvara.

SOLAR reckoning: Cyclic Sidereal Year, Month and Day; Week-Day, English Month and Day. LUNAR reckoning: Tithi Ending Moment; Nakshatra Ending Moment; Muhammadan Year, Month and Day.

Jan.

Solar: Dhatri, Dhanus—Margali; Dhatri, Makara—Tai. Lunar: Marga, Bahula; Sukla; Pausha; Bahula. Muhammadan: H. 1417 Shaban; H. 1417 Ramzan.

Cyclic Sidereal Year, Month and Day	Week-Day	English Day	Tithi	Ending Moment	Nakshatra	Ending Moment	Muhammadan Year, Month and Day
17	We	1	7	·33	12	·25	21
18	Th	2	8	·38	13	·32	22
19	Fr	3	9	·42	14	·37	23
20	Sa	4	10	·42	15	·40	24
21	Su	5	11	·41	16	·41	25
22	Mo	6	12	·38	17	·41	26
23	Tu	7	13	·33	18	·38	27
24	We	8	14	·27	19	·34	28
25	Th	9	—A	·19	20	·29	—29
26	Fr	10	1	·10	21	·23	1
27	Sa	11	2 3	·01 ·91	22	·17	2
28	Su	12	4	·81	23	·10	3
—29	Mo	13	5	·72	24 25	·03 ·96	4
1	Tu	14	6	·68	26	·90	5
2	We	15	7	·55	27	·86	6
3	Th	16	8	·49	1	·83	7
4	Fr	17	9	·45	2	·82	8
5	Sa	18	10	·42	3	·82	9
6	Su	19	11	·40	4	·84	10
7	Mo	20	12	·41	5	·88	11
8	Tu	21	13	·44	6	·95	12
9	We	22	14	·50	...	...	13
10	Th	23	P	·58	7	·04	14
11	Fr	24	1	·66	8	·14	15
12	Sa	25	2	·75	9	·24	16
13	Su	26	3	·84	10	·35	17
14	Mo	27	4	·92	11	·46	18
15	Tu	28	5	·98	12	·55	19
16	We	29	...	...	13	·62	20
17	Th	30	6	·03	14	·68	21
18	Fr	31	7	·06	15	·72	22

Feb.

Solar: Dhatri, Kumbha—Masi. Lunar: Sukla; Magha; Bah. Muhammadan: H. 1417 Shawwal.

Cyclic Sidereal Year, Month and Day	Week-Day	English Day	Tithi	Ending Moment	Nakshatra	Ending Moment	Muhammadan Year, Month and Day
19	Sa	1	8	·06	16	·74	23
20	Su	2	9	·05	17	·74	24
21	Mo	3	10 11	·02 ·96	18	·71	25
22	Tu	4	12	·89	19	·67	26
23	We	5	13	·81	20	·62	27
24	Th	6	14	·73	21	·56	28
25	Fr	7	—A	·64	22	·50	29
26	Sa	8	1	·54	23	·48	—30
27	Su	9	2	·14	24	·36	1
28	Mo	10	3	·34	25	·30	2
—29	Tu	11	4	·25	26	·24	3
1	We	12	5	·17	27	·20	4
2	Th	13	6	·11	1	·16	5
3	Fr	14	7	·07	2	·14	6
4	Sa	15	8	·05	3	·14	7
5	Su	16	9	·03	4	·16	8
6	Mo	17	10	·05	5	·20	9
7	Tu	18	11	·08	6	·26	10
8	We	19	12	·13	7	·34	11
9	Th	20	13	·20	8	·48	12
10	Fr	21	14	·28	9	·54	13
11	Sa	22	P	·37	10	·65	14
12	Su	23	1	·46	11	·76	15
13	Mo	24	2	·54	12	·85	16
14	Tu	25	3	·60	13	·93	17
15	We	26	4	·64	14	·99	18
16	Th	27	5	·67	...	...	19
17	Fr	28	6	·68	15	·04	20

March

Solar: Dhatri, Kumbha—Masi; Dhatri, Mina—Panguni. Lunar: Magha, Bahula; Sukla; Phalguna; Bahula. Muhammadan: H. 1417 Shawwal; H. 1417 Zi-l-ka'da.

Cyclic Sidereal Year, Month and Day	Week-Day	English Day	Tithi	Ending Moment	Nakshatra	Ending Moment	Muhammadan Year, Month and Day
18	Sa	1	7	·67	16	·06	21
19	Su	2	8	·63	17	·06	22
20	Mo	3	9	·58	18	·04	23
21	Tu	4	10	·51	19 20	·01 ·96	24
22	We	5	11	·43	21	·90	25
23	Th	6	12	·34	22	·84	26
24	Fr	7	13	·25	23	·77	27
25	Sa	8	14	·15	24	·70	28
26	Su ●	9	A 1	·05 ·95	25	·64	—29
27	Mo	10	2	·86	26	·58	1
28	Tu	11	3	·78	27	·53	2
29	We	12	4	·71	1	·49	3
—30	Th	13	5	·66	2	·47	4
1	Fr	14	6	·64	3	·46	5
2	Sa	15	7	·62	4	·48	6
3	Su	16	8	·64	5	·52	7
4	Mo	17	9	·68	6	·57	8
5	Tu	18	10	·74	7	·64	9
6	We	19	11	·81	8	·73	10
7	Th	20	12	·89	9	·84	11
8	Fr	21	13	·98	10	·95	12
9	Sa	22	...	...	...	...	13
10	Su	23	14	·06	11	·06	14
11	Mo	24	P	·14	12	·15	15
12	Tu	25	1	·20	13	·23	16
13	We	26	2	·24	14	·30	17
14	Th	27	3	·27	15	·36	18
15	Fr	28	4	·27	16	·38	19
16	Sa	29	5	·25	17	·39	20
17	Su	30	6	·21	18	·37	21
18	Mo	31	7	·16	19	·35	22

April

Solar: Isvara, Mesha—Chittirai. Lunar: Sukla; Chaitra; Bahula. Muhammadan: H. 1417 Zi-l-hijja.

Cyclic Sidereal Year, Month and Day	Week-Day	English Day	Tithi	Ending Moment	Nakshatra	Ending Moment	Muhammadan Year, Month and Day
19	Tu	1	8	·09	20	·31	23
20	We	2	9 10	·01 ·91	21	·25	24
21	Th	3	11	·81	22	·18	25
22	Fr	4	12	·71	23	·11	26
23	Sa	5	13	·61	24 25	·04 ·98	27
24	Su	6	14	·51	26	·92	28
25	Mo	7	—A	·42	27	·86	29
26	Tu	8	1	·34	1	·82	—30
27	We	9	2	·28	2	·79	1
28	Th	10	3	·23	3	·79	2
29	Fr	11	4	·20	4	·80	3
30	Sa	12	5	·18	5	·83	4
—31	Su	13	6	·20	6	·88	5
1	Mo	14	7	·24	7	·95	6
2	Tu	15	8	·29	...	...	7
3	We	16	9	·36	8	·04	8
4	Th	17	10	·44	9	·14	9
5	Fr	18	11	·53	10	·25	10
6	Sa	19	12	·61	11	·35	11
7	Su	20	13	·67	12	·45	12
8	Mo	21	14	·73	13	·55	13
9	Tu	22	P	·78	14	·62	14
10	We	23	1	·80	15	·67	15
11	Th	24	2	·81	16	·70	16
12	Fr	25	3	·79	17	·71	17
13	Sa	26	4	·76	18	·71	18
14	Su	27	5	·70	19	·63	19
15	Mo	28	6	·62	20	·64	20
16	Tu	29	7	·54	21	·58	21
17	We	30	8	·45	22	·52	22

May

Solar: Isvara, Mesha—Chittirai; Isvara, Vrishabha—Vaikasi. Lunar: Bah.; Sukla; Vaisakha; Bahula. Muhammadan: H. 1417 Zi-l-hijja; H. 1418 Muharram.

Cyclic Sidereal Year, Month and Day	Week-Day	English Day	Tithi	Ending Moment	Nakshatra	Ending Moment	Muhammadan Year, Month and Day
18	Th	1	9	·35	23	·46	23
19	Fr	2	10	·25	24	·89	24
20	Sa	3	11	·15	25	·32	25
21	Su	4	12 13	·05 ·95	26	·25	26
22	Mo	5	14	·87	27	·20	27
23	Tu	6	—A	·81	1	·16	28
24	We	7	1	·76	2	·13	29
25	Th	8	2	·72	3	·11	—30
26	Fr	9	3	·71	4	·12	1
27	Sa	10	4	·72	5	·14	2
28	Su	11	5	·76	6	·19	3
29	Mo	12	6	·81	7	·26	4
30	Tu	13	7	·87	8	·34	5
—31	We	14	8	·95	9	·44	6
1	Th	15	...	...	10	·55	7
2	Fr	16	9	·03	11	·66	8
3	Sa	17	10	·12	12	·76	9
4	Su	18	11	·19	13	·85	10
5	Mo	19	12	·25	14	·93	11
6	Tu	20	13	·29	15	·98	12
7	We	21	14	·31	...	...	13
8	Th	22	P	·32	16	·02	14
9	Fr	23	1	·29	17	·03	15
10	Sa	24	2	·25	18	·02	16
11	Su	25	3	·20	19 20	·00 ·97	17
12	Mo	26	4	·13	21	·92	18
13	Tu	27	5 6	·05 ·95	22	·86	19
14	We	28	7	·85	23	·80	20
15	Th	29	8	·74	24	·73	21
16	Fr	30	9	·64	25	·66	22
17	Sa	31	10	·54	26	·59	23

June

Solar: Isvara, Mithuna—Ani. Lunar: Sukla; Jyeshtha; Bahula. Muhammadan: H. 1418 Safar.

Cyclic Sidereal Year, Month and Day	Week-Day	English Day	Tithi	Ending Moment	Nakshatra	Ending Moment	Muhammadan Year, Month and Day
18	Su	1	11	·45	27	·53	24
19	Mo	2	12	·38	1	·49	25
20	Tu	3	13	·31	2	·46	26
21	We	4	14	·25	3	·44	27
22	Th	5	—A	·22	4	·44	28
23	Fr	6	1	·21	5	·46	29
24	Sa	7	2	·21	6	·51	—30
25	Su	8	3	·24	7	·57	1
26	Mo	9	4	·29	8	·65	2
27	Tu	10	5	·35	9	·74	3
28	We	11	6	·43	10	·84	4
29	Th	12	7	·51	11	·95	5
30	Fr	13	8	·59	...	...	6
—31	Sa	14	9	·66	12	·06	7
1	Su	15	10	·73	13	·16	8
2	Mo	16	11	·78	14	·24	9
3	Tu	17	12	·80	15	·29	10
4	We	18	13	·80	16	·33	11
5	Th	19	14	·78	17	·36	12
6	Fr	20	P	·74	18	·36	13
7	Sa	21	1	·68	19	·34	14
8	Su	22	2	·61	20	·30	15
9	Mo	23	3	·53	21	·25	16
10	Tu	24	4	·44	22	·20	17
11	We	25	5	·34	23	·14	18
12	Th	26	6	·24	24	·07	19
13	Fr	27	7	·14	25 26	·00 ·94	20
14	Sa	28	8 9	·04 ·94	27	·88	21
15	Su	29	10	·85	1	·83	22
16	Mo	30	11	·78	2	·79	23

Naksh :—1. Asvn. 2. Bhar. 3. Krit. 4. Rohi. 5. Mrig. 6. Ardh. 7. Punar. 8. Push. 9. Aslesh. 10. Magh. 11. P. Phal. 12. U. Phal. 13. Hasta 14. Chit.

A. D. 1997.
A.—Amavasya.
P.—Paurnami.

Kollam 1173, Commences { N. Malabar—Sept. / S. Malabar—Aug.

Hijra 1418, Commences, **May 9.**

Vikrama 2054.
Bengal San 1403.
(N. Cycle) Vikrita.

Columns: SOLAR reckoning — Cyclic Sidereal Year, Month and Day; Week-Day English Month and Day. LUNAR reckoning — Tithi Ending Moment; Nakshatra Ending Moment; Muhammadan Year, Month and Day.

July

Solar: Isvara *Mithuna—Ani.* (to 32), Isvara *Karkata—Adi.* (from 1). Lunar: *Bah.*, Ashadha (*Sukla*, *Bahula*). Muhammadan: *Safar.*, H. 1418 *Rabi-ul-awwal.*

Cyclic Sidereal	Week-Day	Day	Tithi	Nakshatra	Muhammadan
17	Tu	1	12 ·73	3 ·76	24
18	We	2	13 ·70	4 ·76	25
19	Th	3	14 ·68	5 ·78	26
20	Fr	4	—A ·69	6 ·82	27
21	Sa	5	1 ·71	7 ·88	28
22	Su	6	2 ·76	8 ·95	—29
23	Mo	7	3 ·83	... ...	1
24	Tu	8	4 ·91	9 ·04	2
25	We	9	5 ·99	10 ·14	3
26	Th	10	... ...	11 ·25	4
27	Fr	11	6 ·07	12 ·36	5
28	Sa	12	7 ·14	13 ·46	6
29	Su	13	8 ·20	14 ·54	7
30	Mo	14	9 ·25	15 ·61	8
31	Tu	15	10 ·28	16 ·66	9
—32	We	16	11 ·27	17 ·68	10
1	Th	17	12 ·26	18 ·68	11
2	Fr	18	13 ·22	19 ·67	12
3	Sa	19	14 ·16	20 ·64	13
4	Su	20	P ·09	21 ·60	14
5	Mo	21	1 ·01 2 ·93	22 ·54	15
6	Tu	22	3 ·83	23 ·48	16
7	We	23	4 ·73	24 ·41	17
8	Th	24	5 ·63	25 ·34	18
9	Fr	25	6 ·53	26 ·27	19
10	Sa	26	7 ·43	27 ·21	20
11	Su	27	8 ·34	1 ·16	21
12	Mo	28	9 ·27	2 ·12	22
13	Tu	29	10 ·21	3 ·09	23
14	We	30	11 ·18	4 ·08	24
15	Th	31	12 ·16	5 ·10	25

Aug.

Solar: Isvara *Simha—Avani.* (from 1). Lunar: *Sukla*, Sravana (*Bahula*). Muhammadan: H. 1418 *Rabi-ul-akhir.*

Cyclic Sidereal	Week-Day	Day	Tithi	Nakshatra	Muhammadan
16	Fr	1	13 ·17	6 ·13	26
17	Sa	2	14 ·19	7 ·18	27
18	Su	3	—A ·24	8 ·25	28
19	Mo	4	1 ·30	9 ·34	29
20	Tu	5	2 ·38	10 ·45	—30
21	We	6	3 ·47	11 ·56	1
22	Th	7	4 ·55	12 ·66	2
23	Fr	8	5 ·62	13 ·76	3
24	Sa	9	6 ·68	14 ·85	4
25	Su	10	7 ·74	15 ·92	5
26	Mo	11	8 ·77	16 ·97	6
27	Tu	12	9 ·76	... ...	7
28	We	13	10 ·75	17 ·00	8
29	Th	14	11 ·72	18 ·01	9
30	Fr	15	12 ·67	19 ·00 20 ·98	10
—31	Sa	16	13 ·60	21 ·93	11
1	Su	17	14 ·52	22 ·88	12
2	Mo	18	P ·43	23 ·81	13
3	Tu	19	1 ·33	24 ·74	14
4	We	20	2 ·22	25 ·67	15
5	Th	21	3 ·12	26 ·61	16
6	Fr	22	4 ·02 5 ·93	27 ·55	17
7	Sa	23	6 ·85	1 ·49	18
8	Su	24	7 ·78	2 ·45	19
9	Mo	25	8 ·73	3 ·43	20
10	Tu	26	9 ·69	4 ·41	21
11	We	27	10 ·66	5 ·42	22
12	Th	28	11 ·68	6 ·44	23
13	Fr	29	12 ·70	7 ·49	24
14	Sa	30	13 ·75	8 ·56	25
15	Su	31	14 ·81	9 ·65	26

Sep.

Solar: Isvara *Simha—Avani.* (to 31), Isvara *Kanya—Purattasi.* (from 1). Lunar: *Sukla*, Bhadrapada (*Bahula*). Muhammadan: H. 1418 *Jumadal-awwal.*

Cyclic Sidereal	Week-Day	Day	Tithi	Nakshatra	Muhammadan
16	Mo	1	—A ·89	10 ·75	27
17	Tu	2	1 ·97	11 ·85	28
18	We	3	... ...	12 ·96	—29
19	Th	4	2 ·05	... ...	1
20	Fr	5	3 ·12	13 ·06	2
21	Sa	6	4 ·19	14 ·16	3
22	Su	7	5 ·24	15 ·24	4
23	Mo	8	6 ·27	16 ·29	5
24	Tu	9	7 ·29	17 ·32	6
25	We	10	8 ·27	18 ·33	7
26	Th	11	9 ·24	19 ·33	8
27	Fr	12	10 ·19	20 ·31	9
28	Sa	13	11 ·12	21 ·27	10
29	Su	14	12 ·04 13 ·95	22 ·21	11
30	Mo	15	14 ·86	23 ·15	12
—31	Tu ○	16	P ·76	24 ·09	13
1	We	17	1 ·66	25 ·02 26 ·95	14
2	Th	18	2 ·56	27 ·89	15
3	Fr	19	3 ·46	1 ·83	16
4	Sa	20	4 ·38	2 ·78	17
5	Su	21	5 ·31	3 ·75	18
6	Mo	22	6 ·25	4 ·74	19
7	Tu	23	7 ·22	5 ·74	20
8	We	24	8 ·21	6 ·76	21
9	Th	25	9 ·22	7 ·80	22
10	Fr	26	10 ·24	8 ·87	23
11	Sa	27	11 ·29	9 ·95	24
12	Su	28	12 ·35	... ...	25
13	Mo	29	13 ·43	10 ·05	26
14	Tu	30	14 ·51	11 ·15	27

Oct.

Solar: Isvara *Tula—Aippasi.* (from 1). Lunar: *Sukla*, Asvina (*Bahula*). Muhammadan: H. 1418 *Jumadal-akhir.*

Cyclic Sidereal	Week-Day	Day	Tithi	Nakshatra	Muhammadan
15	We	1	—A ·60	12 ·26	28
16	Th	2	1 ·68	13 ·37	29
17	Fr	3	2 ·75	14 ·46	—30
18	Sa	4	3 ·80	15 ·54	1
19	Su	5	4 ·82	16 ·60	2
20	Mo	6	5 ·84	17 ·64	3
21	Tu	7	6 ·83	18 ·66	4
22	We	8	7 ·81	19 ·66	5
23	Th	9	8 ·75	20 ·64	6
24	Fr	10	9 ·68	21 ·60	7
25	Sa	11	10 ·60	22 ·55	8
26	Su	12	11 ·51	23 ·49	9
27	Mo	13	12 ·42	24 ·43	10
28	Tu	14	13 ·32	25 ·36	11
29	We	15	14 ·22	26 ·29	12
—30	Th	16	P ·12	27 ·22	13
1	Fr	17	1 ·03 2 ·95	1 ·16	14
2	Sa	18	3 ·88	2 ·12	15
3	Su	19	4 ·83	3 ·08	16
4	Mo	20	5 ·80	4 ·06	17
5	Tu	21	6 ·79	5 ·06	18
6	We	22	7 ·80	6 ·08	19
7	Th	23	8 ·82	7 ·12	20
8	Fr	24	9 ·87	8 ·18	21
9	Sa	25	10 ·94	9 ·26	22
10	Su	26	... ...	10 ·35	23
11	Mo	27	11 ·02	11 ·45	24
12	Tu	28	12 ·10	12 ·56	25
13	We	29	13 ·20	13 ·67	26
14	Th	30	14 ·28	14 ·77	27
15	Fr	31	—A ·35	15 ·85	28

Nov.

Solar: Isvara *Tula—Aippasi.* (to 30), Isvara *Vrischika—Kartigai.* (from 1). Lunar: *Sukla*, Kartika (*Bahula*). Muhammadan: H. 1418 *Rajab.*

Cyclic Sidereal	Week-Day	Day	Tithi	Nakshatra	Muhammadan
16	Sa	1	1 ·39	16 ·91	—29
17	Su	2	2 ·42	17 ·95	1
18	Mo	3	3 ·44	18 ·98	2
19	Tu	4	4 ·42	19 ·98	3
20	We	5	5 ·39	20 ·97	4
21	Th	6	6 ·34	21 ·93	5
22	Fr	7	7 ·28	22 ·88	6
23	Sa	8	8 ·20	23 ·83	7
24	Su	9	9 ·12	24 ·77	8
25	Mo	10	10 ·02 11 ·92	25 ·70	9
26	Tu	11	12 ·82	26 ·63	10
27	We	12	13 ·72	27 ·56	11
28	Th	13	14 ·64	1 ·50	12
29	Fr	14	P ·56	2 ·45	13
—30	Sa	15	1 ·50	3 ·41	14
1	Su	16	2 ·45	4 ·39	15
2	Mo	17	3 ·42	5 ·38	16
3	Tu	18	4 ·40	6 ·40	17
4	We	19	5 ·41	7 ·43	18
5	Th	20	6 ·44	8 ·49	19
6	Fr	21	7 ·49	9 ·56	20
7	Sa	22	8 ·56	10 ·65	21
8	Su	23	9 ·64	11 ·75	22
9	Mo	24	10 ·74	12 ·86	23
10	Tu	25	11 ·82	13 ·97	24
11	We	26	12 ·90	... ...	25
12	Th	27	13 ·97	14 ·07	26
13	Fr	28	... ...	15 ·15	27
14	Sa	29	14 ·03	16 ·22	28
15	Su	30	—A ·06	17 ·27	29

Dec.

Solar: Isvara *Dhanus—Margali.* (from 1). Lunar: *Sukla*, Margasira (*Bahula*), *Suk.* Muhammadan: H. 1418 *Shaban.*

Cyclic Sidereal	Week-Day	Day	Tithi	Nakshatra	Muhammadan
16	Mo	1	1 ·06	18 ·30	—30
17	Tu	2	2 ·05	19 ·31	1
18	We	3	3 ·02 4 ·97	20 ·29	2
19	Th	4	5 ·90	21 ·26	3
20	Fr	5	6 ·82	22 ·22	4
21	Sa	6	7 ·74	23 ·17	5
22	Su	7	8 ·64	24 ·11	6
23	Mo	8	9 ·54	25 ·04 26 ·97	7
24	Tu	9	10 ·44	27 ·90	8
25	We	10	11 ·35	1 ·84	9
26	Th	11	12 ·26	2 ·79	10
27	Fr	12	13 ·18	3 ·74	11
28	Sa	13	14 ·12	4 ·71	12
29	Su	14	P ·07	5 ·71	13
—30	Mo	15	1 ·05	6 ·72	14
1	Tu	16	2 ·04	7 ·75	15
2	We	17	3 ·06	8 ·80	16
3	Th	18	4 ·09	9 ·86	17
4	Fr	19	5 ·14	10 ·95	18
5	Sa	20	6 ·21	... ...	19
6	Su	21	7 ·29	11 ·05	20
7	Mo	22	8 ·38	12 ·16	21
8	Tu	23	9 ·47	13 ·27	22
9	We	24	10 ·55	14 ·37	23
10	Th	25	11 ·62	15 ·46	24
11	Fr	26	12 ·68	16 ·54	25
12	Sa	27	13 ·70	17 ·59	26
13	Su	28	14 ·70	18 ·62	27
14	Mo	29	—A ·60	19 ·63	28
15	Tu	30	1 ·66	20 ·62	—29
16	We	31	2 ·61	21 ·60	1

15. Svati. 16. Visak. 17. Anur. 18. Jyesh. 19. Mula. 20. P. Ash. 21. U. Ash. 22. Sravn. 23. Dani. 24. Satab. 25. P.Bhad. 26. U. Bhad. 27. Rev.

A. D. 1998.
Solar Eclipse. ●
Lunar Eclipse. ○

Mesha Sankranti (Commencement of Indian Sidereal Year).
(Surya Sid.) April 13·98.
(Arya Sid.) April 13·87.

Saka 1920. Kaliyuga 5099.
(S. Cycle) Bahudhanya.

Columns: SOLAR reckoning — Cyclic Sidereal Year, Month and Day; Week-Day English Month and Day. LUNAR reckoning — Tithi Ending Moment; Nakshatra Ending Moment; Muhammadan Year, Month and Day.

Jan.

Isvara Dhanus—Margali (17–29); Isvara Makara—Tai (1–18). Sukla; Pausha; Bahula. H. 1418 Ramzan.

Cyclic Sidereal	Week-Day	Jan.	Tithi	Ending Moment	Nakshatra	Ending Moment	Muhammadan
17	Th	1	3	·54	22	·56	2
18	Fr	2	4	·47	23	·51	3
19	Sa	3	5	·38	24	·45	4
20	Su	4	6	·28	25	·39	5
21	Mo	5	7	·18	26	·32	6
22	Tu	6	8 9	·08 ·99	27	·25	7
23	We	7	10	·91	1	·18	8
24	Th	8	11	·83	2	·12	9
25	Fr	9	12	·77	3	·08	10
26	Sa	10	13	·73	4	·05	11
27	Su	11	14	·70	5	·04	12
28	Mo	12	P	·68	6	·04	13
29	Tu	13	1	·70	7	·06	14
1	We	14	2	·74	8	·10	15
2	Th	15	3	·79	9	·17	16
3	Fr	16	4	·87	10	·26	17
4	Sa	17	5	·96	11	·36	18
5	Su	18	...	...	12	·46	19
6	Mo	19	6	·04	13	·57	20
7	Tu	20	7	·12	14	·67	21
8	We	21	8	·20	15	·76	22
9	Th	22	9	·27	16	·84	23
10	Fr	23	10	·32	17	·90	24
11	Sa	24	11	·35	18	·94	25
12	Su	25	12	·36	19	·95	26
13	Mo	26	13	·34	20	·96	27
14	Tu	27	14	·30	21	·93	28
15	We	28	A	·25	22	·89	29
16	Th	29	1	·18	23	·84	30
17	Fr	30	2	·10	24	·78	1
18	Sa	31	3 4	·01 ·92	25	·72	2

Feb.

Isvara Kumbha—Masi. Sukla; Magha; Bahula; P. Suk. H. 1418 Shawwal.

Cyclic Sidereal	Week-Day	Feb.	Tithi	Ending Moment	Nakshatra	Ending Moment	Muhammadan
19	Su	1	5	·82	26	·65	3
20	Mo	2	6	·72	27	·58	4
21	Tu	3	7	·62	1	·52	5
22	We	4	8	·53	2	·46	6
23	Th	5	9	·46	3	·41	7
24	Fr	6	10	·40	4	·38	8
25	Sa	7	11	·36	5	·36	9
26	Su	8	12	·33	6	·36	10
27	Mo	9	13	·32	7	·38	11
28	Tu	10	14	·34	8	·42	12
29	We	11	P	·38	9	·48	13
30	Th	12	1	·43	10	·56	14
1	Fr	13	2	·50	11	·65	15
2	Sa	14	3	·58	12	·76	16
3	Su	15	4	·67	13	·87	17
4	Mo	16	5	·76	14	·98	18
5	Tu	17	6	·84	...	...	19
6	We	18	7	·90	15	·07	20
7	Th	19	8	·94	16	·15	21
8	Fr	20	9	·96	17	·21	22
9	Sa	21	10	·98	18	·25	23
10	Su	22	11	·06	19	·28	24
11	Mo	23	12	·98	20	·28	25
12	Tu	24	13	·87	21	·26	26
13	We	25	14	·80	22	·23	27
14	Th	26	A	·72	23	·18	28
15	Fr	27	1	·63	24	·12	29
16	Sa	28	2	·53	25 26	·06 ·99	1

March

Isvara Kumbha—Masi (17–30); Isvara Mina—Panguni (1–17). Sukla; Phalguna; Bahula. H. 1418 Zi-l-ka'da.

Cyclic Sidereal	Week-Day	March	Tithi	Ending Moment	Nakshatra	Ending Moment	Muhammadan
17	Su	1	3	·43	27	·92	2
18	Mo	2	4	·33	1	·85	3
19	Tu	3	5	·23	2	·79	4
20	We	4	6	·15	3	·74	5
21	Th	5	7	·07	4	·71	6
22	Fr	6	8 9	·01 ·97	5	·69	7
23	Sa	7	10	·94	6	·68	8
24	Su	8	11	·93	7	·70	9
25	Mo	9	12	·94	8	·74	10
26	Tu	10	13	·98	9	·79	11
27	We	11	...	...	10	·86	12
28	Th	12	14	·04	11	·95	13
29	Fr	13	P	·11	...	...	14
30	Sa	14	1	·19	12	·06	15
1	Su	15	2	·28	13	·17	16
2	Mo	16	3	·37	14	·28	17
3	Tu	17	4	·44	15	·37	18
4	We	18	5	·50	16	·45	19
5	Th	19	6	·55	17	·52	20
6	Fr	20	7	·58	18	·57	21
7	Sa	21	8	·57	19	·60	22
8	Su	22	9	·55	20	·62	23
9	Mo	23	10	·51	21	·59	24
10	Tu	24	11	·45	22	·56	25
11	We	25	12	·38	23	·52	26
12	Th	26	13	·30	24	·47	27
13	Fr	27	14	·21	25	·40	28
14	Sa	28	A	·11	26	·33	29
15	Su	29	1 2	·01 ·91	27	·26	30
16	Mo	30	3	·82	1	·19	1
17	Tu	31	4	·73	2	·13	2

April

Isvara Mina—Panguni (18–30); Bahudhanya Mesha—Chittirai (1–17). Sukla; Chaitra; Bahula; V. Suk. H. 1418 Zi-l-hijja.

Cyclic Sidereal	Week-Day	April	Tithi	Ending Moment	Nakshatra	Ending Moment	Muhammadan
18	We	1	5	·65	3	·08	3
19	Th	2	6	·59	4	·04	4
20	Fr	3	7	·54	5	·01	5
21	Sa	4	8	·51	6	·00	6
22	Su	5	9	·50	7	·02	7
23	Mo	6	10	·52	8	·05	8
24	Tu	7	11	·56	9	·10	9
25	We	8	12	·61	10	·17	10
26	Th	9	13	·68	11	·26	11
27	Fr	10	14	·76	12	·36	12
28	Sa	11	P	·85	13	·47	13
29	Su	12	1	·93	14	·58	14
30	Mo	13	...	...	15	·68	15
1	Tu	14	2	·00	16	·76	16
2	We	15	3	·06	17	·83	17
3	Th	16	4	·10	18	·89	18
4	Fr	17	5	·12	19	·92	19
5	Sa	18	6	·12	20	·93	20
6	Su	19	7	·10	21	·92	21
7	Mo	20	8 9	·06 ·99	22	·89	22
8	Tu	21	10	·92	23	·85	23
9	We	22	11	·84	24	·80	24
10	Th	23	12	·75	25	·74	25
11	Fr	24	13	·65	26	·67	26
12	Sa	25	14	·55	27	·60	27
13	Su	26	A	·45	1	·54	28
14	Mo	27	1	·35	2	·48	29
15	Tu	28	2	·26	3	·42	1
16	We	29	3	·18	4	·37	2
17	Th	30	4	·12	5	·34	3

May

Bahudhanya Mesha—Chittirai (18–31); Bahudhanya Vrishabha—Vaikasi (1–17). Sukla; Vaisakha; Bahula. H. 1419 Muharram.

Cyclic Sidereal	Week-Day	May	Tithi	Ending Moment	Nakshatra	Ending Moment	Muhammadan
18	Fr	1	5	·08	6	·33	4
19	Sa	2	6	·05	7	·34	5
20	Su	3	7	·03	8	·37	6
21	Mo	4	8	·04	9	·41	7
22	Tu	5	9	·08	10	·47	8
23	We	6	10	·13	11	·56	9
24	Th	7	11	·20	12	·66	10
25	Fr	8	12	·28	13	·77	11
26	Sa	9	13	·36	14	·87	12
27	Su	10	14	·44	15	·97	13
28	Mo	11	P	·52	...	...	14
29	Tu	12	1	·58	16	·06	15
30	We	13	2	·62	17	·14	16
31	Th	14	3	·63	18	·20	17
1	Fr	15	4	·63	19	·24	18
2	Sa	16	5	·62	20	·25	19
3	Su	17	6	·58	21	·24	20
4	Mo	18	7	·52	22	·22	21
5	Tu	19	8	·45	23	·19	22
6	We	20	9	·36	24	·14	23
7	Th	21	10	·26	25	·08	24
8	Fr	22	11	·16	26 27	·02 ·95	25
9	Sa	23	12 13	·06 ·96	1	·88	26
10	Su	24	14	·86	2	·81	27
11	Mo	25	A	·77	3	·75	28
12	Tu	26	1	·69	4	·71	29
13	We	27	2	·62	5	·68	30
14	Th	28	3	·57	6	·66	1
15	Fr	29	4	·54	7	·66	2
16	Sa	30	5	·52	8	·68	3
17	Su	31	6	·54	9	·72	4

June

Bahudhanya Vrishabha—Vaikasi (18–31); Bahudhanya Mithuna—Ani (1–16). Sukla; Jyeshtha; Bahula; Ashad. Suk. H. 1419 Safar; R.-awwal.

Cyclic Sidereal	Week-Day	June	Tithi	Ending Moment	Nakshatra	Ending Moment	Muhammadan
18	Mo	1	7	·57	10	·78	5
19	Tu	2	8	·62	11	·86	6
20	We	3	9	·69	12	·96	7
21	Th	4	10	·77	...	...	8
22	Fr	5	11	·86	13	·06	9
23	Sa	6	12	·94	14	·17	10
24	Su	7	...	...	15	·28	11
25	Mo	8	13	·01	16	·38	12
26	Tu	9	14	·06	17	·46	13
27	We	10	P	·10	18	·52	14
28	Th	11	1	·12	19	·55	15
29	Fr	12	2	·13	20	·57	16
30	Sa	13	3	·11	21	·58	17
31	Su	14	4	·07	22	·56	18
1	Mo	15	5 6	·01 ·94	23	·52	19
2	Tu	16	7	·86	24	·47	20
3	We	17	8	·76	25	·42	21
4	Th	18	9	·66	26	·36	22
5	Fr	19	10	·56	27	·29	23
6	Sa	20	11	·45	1	·22	24
7	Su	21	12	·35	2	·15	25
8	Mo	22	13	·26	3	·09	26
9	Tu	23	14	·18	4	·05	27
10	We	24	A	·11	5 6	·01 ·98	28
11	Th	25	1	·06	7	·98	29
12	Fr	26	2	·02	8	·99	1
13	Sa	27	3	·00	...	...	2
14	Su	28	4	·02	9	·03	3
15	Mo	29	5	·05	10	·00	4
16	Tu	30	6	·10	11	·17	5

Naksh :—1. Asvn. 2. Bhar. 3. Krit. 4. Rohi. 5. Mrig. 6. Ardh. 7. Punar. 8. Push. 9. Aslesh. 10. Magh. 11. P. Phal. 12. U. Phal. 13. Hasta. 14. Chit.

A. D. 1998. **A.—Amavasya.** **P.—Paurnami.**

Kollam 1174, Commences { **N. Malabar—Sept.** / **S. Malabar—Aug.**

Hijra 1419, Commences, April 28.

Vikrama 2055. Bengal San 1404. (N. Cycle) Khara.

July

Solar: Bahudhanya Mithuna—Ani. (17–32); Bahudhanya Karkata—Adi. (1–15). Lunar: Sukla; Ashadha; Bahula; Sukla. Muhammadan: H. 1419 Rabi-ul-awwal.

Cyclic Sidereal Year, Month and Day	Week-Day English Month and Day	Tithi Ending Moment	Nakshatra Ending Moment	Muhammadan Year, Month and Day
17	We 1	7 ·17	12 ·26	6
18	Th 2	8 ·25	13 ·36	7
19	Fr 3	9 ·33	14 ·47	8
20	Sa 4	10 ·41	15 ·58	9
21	Su 5	11 ·48	16 ·68	10
22	Mo 6	12 ·53	17 ·76	11
23	Tu 7	13 ·57	18 ·83	12
24	We 8	14 ·60	19 ·87	13
25	Th 9	P ·60	20 ·90	14
26	Fr 10	1 ·58	21 ·90	15
27	Sa 11	2 ·55	22 ·89	16
28	Su 12	3 ·49	23 ·86	17
29	Mo 13	4 ·42	24 ·82	18
30	Tu 14	5 ·33	25 ·76	19
31	We 15	6 ·23	26 ·69	20
—32	Th 16	7 ·13	27 ·62	21
1	Fr 17	8 ·03 / 9 ·93	1 ·55	22
2	Sa 18	10 ·83	2 ·49	23
3	Su 19	11 ·73	3 ·43	24
4	Mo 20	12 ·65	4 ·38	25
5	Tu 21	13 ·58	5 ·34	26
6	We 22	14 ·53	6 ·31	27
7	Th 23	—A ·50	7 ·30	28
8	Fr 24	1 ·49	8 ·31	29
9	Sa 25	2 ·50	9 ·35	—30
10	Su 26	3 ·52	10 ·40	1
11	Mo 27	4 ·57	11 ·47	2
12	Tu 28	5 ·63	12 ·56	3
13	We 29	6 ·71	13 ·66	4
14	Th 30	7 ·80	14 ·77	5
15	Fr 31	8 ·88	15 ·88	6

Aug.

Solar: Bahudhanya Simha—Avani. Lunar: Sravana; Bahula; Bhadrapada Sukla. Muhammadan: H. 1419 Rabi-ul-akhir; Jumadal-awwal.

Cyclic Sidereal Year, Month and Day	Week-Day English Month and Day	Tithi Ending Moment	Nakshatra Ending Moment	Muhammadan Year, Month and Day
16	Sa 1	9 ·95	16 ·98	7
17	Su 2	...	...	8
18	Mo 3	10 ·01	17 ·07	9
19	Tu 4	11 ·05	18 ·14	10
20	We 5	12 ·08	19 ·19	11
21	Th 6	13 ·09	20 ·22	12
22	Fr 7	14 ·06	21 ·23	13
23	Sa 8	P ·03 / 1 ·98	22 ·22	14
24	Su 9	2 ·91	23 ·19	15
25	Mo 10	3 ·83	24 ·15	16
26	Tu 11	4 ·73	25 ·10	17
27	We 12	5 ·63	26 ·03 / 27 ·96	18
28	Th 13	6 ·53	1 ·89	19
29	Fr 14	7 ·43	2 ·82	20
30	Sa 15	8 ·33	3 ·76	21
—31	Su 16	9 ·24	4 ·71	22
1	Mo 17	10 ·16	5 ·67	23
2	Tu 18	11 ·09	6 ·64	24
3	We 19	12 ·03	7 ·62	25
4	Th 20	13 ·00 / 14 ·99	8 ·63	26
5	Fr ● 21	—A ·90	9 ·66	27
6	Sa 22	...	10 ·71	28
7	Su 23	1 ·02	11 ·78	—29
8	Mo 24	2 ·07	12 ·87	1
9	Tu 25	3 ·14	13 ·97	2
10	We 26	4 ·22	...	3
11	Th 27	5 ·30	14 ·08	4
12	Fr 28	6 ·38	15 ·18	5
13	Sa 29	7 ·45	16 ·28	6
14	Su 30	8 ·51	17 ·37	7
15	Mo 31	9 ·56	18 ·45	8

Sep.

Solar: Bahudhanya Simha—Avani. (16–31); Bahudhanya Kanya—Purattasi. (1–14). Lunar: Bhadrapada Suk.; Bahula; Sukla. Muhammadan: H. 1419 Jumadal-awwal.

Cyclic Sidereal Year, Month and Day	Week-Day English Month and Day	Tithi Ending Moment	Nakshatra Ending Moment	Muhammadan Year, Month and Day
16	Tu 1	10 ·59	19 ·51	9
17	We 2	11 ·60	20 ·54	10
18	Th 3	12 ·59	21 ·55	11
19	Fr 4	13 ·55	22 ·54	12
20	Sa 5	14 ·49	23 ·52	13
21	Su 6	P ·42	24 ·49	14
22	Mo 7	1 ·34	25 ·43	15
23	Tu 8	2 ·25	26 ·37	16
24	We 9	3 ·15	27 ·30	17
25	Th 10	4 ·05 / 5 ·95	1 ·23	18
26	Fr 11	6 ·85	2 ·17	19
27	Sa 12	7 ·76	3 ·11	20
28	Su 13	8 ·68	4 ·05	21
29	Mo 14	9 ·62	5 ·00 / 6 ·97	22
30	Tu 15	10 ·57	7 ·96	23
—31	We 16	11 ·53	8 ·96	24
1	Th 17	12 ·51	9 ·98	25
2	Fr 18	13 ·53	...	26
3	Sa 19	14 ·56	10 ·02	27
4	Su 20	—A ·60	11 ·03	28
5	Mo 21	1 ·66	12 ·17	29
6	Tu 22	2 ·74	13 ·27	—30
7	We 23	3 ·83	14 ·37	1
8	Th 24	4 ·91	15 ·48	2
9	Fr 25	5 ·99	16 ·58	3
10	Sa 26	...	17 ·67	4
11	Su 27	6 ·06	18 ·75	5
12	Mo 28	7 ·10	19 ·82	6
13	Tu 29	8 ·13	20 ·86	7
14	We 30	9 ·14	21 ·87	8

Oct.

Solar: Bahudhanya Tula—Aippasi. Lunar: Asvina; Bahula; Karttika Sukla. Muhammadan: H. 1419 Jumadal-akhir; H. 1419 Rajab.

Cyclic Sidereal Year, Month and Day	Week-Day English Month and Day	Tithi Ending Moment	Nakshatra Ending Moment	Muhammadan Year, Month and Day
15	Th 1	10 ·13	22 ·87	9
16	Fr 2	11 ·10	23 ·86	10
17	Sa 3	12 ·04 / 13 ·97	24 ·82	11
18	Su 4	14 ·89	25 ·77	12
19	Mo 5	P ·80	26 ·71	13
20	Tu 6	1 ·71	27 ·65	14
21	We 7	2 ·61	1 ·58	15
22	Th 8	3 ·51	2 ·51	16
23	Fr 9	4 ·41	3 ·44	17
24	Sa 10	5 ·32	4 ·38	18
25	Su 11	6 ·24	5 ·33	19
26	Mo 12	7 ·18	6 ·30	20
27	Tu 13	8 ·13	7 ·28	21
28	We 14	9 ·10	8 ·28	22
29	Th 15	10 ·08	9 ·29	23
30	Fr 16	11 ·10	10 ·33	24
—31	Sa 17	12 ·13	11 ·40	25
1	Su 18	13 ·18	12 ·48	26
2	Mo 19	14 ·24	13 ·57	27
3	Tu 20	—A ·32	14 ·67	28
4	We 21	1 ·41	15 ·78	—29
5	Th 22	2 ·50	16 ·89	1
6	Fr 23	3 ·58	17 ·99	2
7	Sa 24	4 ·64	...	3
8	Su 25	5 ·69	18 ·07	4
9	Mo 26	6 ·71	19 ·13	5
10	Tu 27	7 ·72	20 ·17	6
11	We 28	8 ·72	21 ·19	7
12	Th 29	9 ·69	22 ·20	8
13	Fr 30	10 ·64	23 ·19	9
14	Sa 31	11 ·57	24 ·15	10

Nov.

Solar: Bahudhanya Tula—Aippasi. (15–30); Bahudhanya Vrischika—Karttigai. (1–14). Lunar: Suk.; Karttika; Bahula; Sukla. Muhammadan: H. 1419 Rajab.

Cyclic Sidereal Year, Month and Day	Week-Day English Month and Day	Tithi Ending Moment	Nakshatra Ending Moment	Muhammadan Year, Month and Day
15	Su 1	12 ·49	25 ·10	11
16	Mo 2	13 ·40	26 ·04 / 27 ·98	12
17	Tu 3	14 ·31	1 ·92	13
18	We 4	P ·21	2 ·85	14
19	Th 5	1 ·11	3 ·78	15
20	Fr 6	2 ·01 / 3 ·92	4 ·72	16
21	Sa 7	4 ·85	5 ·67	17
22	Su 8	5 ·78	6 ·63	18
23	Mo 9	6 ·73	7 ·61	19
24	Tu 10	7 ·70	8 ·60	20
25	We 11	8 ·68	9 ·61	21
26	Th 12	9 ·71	10 ·64	22
27	Fr 13	10 ·74	11 ·70	23
28	Sa 14	11 ·79	12 ·78	24
29	Su 15	12 ·86	13 ·87	25
—30	Mo 16	13 ·94	14 ·97	26
1	Tu 17	...	...	27
2	We 18	14 ·03	15 ·08	28
3	Th 19	—A ·11	16 ·19	29
4	Fr 20	1 ·19	17 ·29	—30
5	Sa 21	2 ·26	18 ·37	1
6	Su 22	3 ·31	19 ·44	2
7	Mo 23	4 ·34	20 ·49	3
8	Tu 24	5 ·35	21 ·52	4
9	We 25	6 ·34	22 ·53	5
10	Th 26	7 ·30	23 ·51	6
11	Fr 27	8 ·25	24 ·48	7
12	Sa 28	9 ·19	25 ·44	8
13	Su 29	10 ·12	26 ·39	9
14	Mo 30	11 ·03 / 12 ·93	27 ·33	10

Dec.

Solar: Bahudhanya Dhanus—Margali. Lunar: Margasira; Bahula; Pausha Sukla. Muhammadan: H. 1419 Shaban; H. 1419 Ramzan.

Cyclic Sidereal Year, Month and Day	Week-Day English Month and Day	Tithi Ending Moment	Nakshatra Ending Moment	Muhammadan Year, Month and Day
15	Tu 1	13 ·83	1 ·26	11
16	We 2	14 ·73	2 ·19	12
17	Th 3	P ·63	3 ·12	13
18	Fr 4	1 ·54	4 ·06	14
19	Sa 5	2 ·46	5 ·01 / 6 ·96	15
20	Su 6	3 ·40	7 ·93	16
21	Mo 7	4 ·36	8 ·92	17
22	Tu 8	5 ·33	9 ·93	18
23	We 9	6 ·33	10 ·97	19
24	Th 10	7 ·34	...	20
25	Fr 11	8 ·38	11 ·02	21
26	Sa 12	9 ·44	12 ·09	22
27	Su 13	10 ·51	13 ·17	23
28	Mo 14	11 ·59	14 ·27	24
—29	Tu 15	12 ·68	15 ·38	25
1	We 16	13 ·77	16 ·49	26
2	Th 17	14 ·85	17 ·59	27
3	Fr 18	—A ·91	18 ·68	28
4	Sa 19	1 ·95	19 ·75	—29
5	Su 20	2 ·98	20 ·81	1
6	Mo 21	3 ·99	21 ·84	2
7	Tu 22	4 ·97	22 ·85	3
8	We 23	5 ·94	23 ·84	4
9	Th 24	6 ·89	24 ·81	5
10	Fr 25	7 ·82	25 ·78	6
11	Sa 26	8 ·74	26 ·73	7
12	Su 27	9 ·65	27 ·67	8
13	Mo 28	10 ·56	1 ·60	9
14	Tu 29	11 ·47	2 ·53	10
15	We 30	12 ·37	3 ·46	11
16	Th 31	13 ·27	4 ·40	12

15. Svati. 16. Visak. 17. Anur. 18. Jyesh. 19. Mula. 20. P. Ash. 21. U. Ash. 22. Sravn. 23. Dani. 24. Satab. 25. P. Bhad. 26. U. Bhad. 27. Rev

A. D. 1999.
Solar Eclipse. ●
Lunar Eclipse. ○

Mesha Sankranti (Commencement of Indian Sidereal Year).
(Surya Sid.) April 14·24.
(Arya Sid.) April 14·13.

Saka 1921. **Kaliyuga 5100.**
(S. Cycle) Pramathi.

Columns: SOLAR reckoning — Cyclic Sidereal Year, Month and Day; Week-Day English Month and Day. LUNAR reckoning — Tithi Ending Moment; Nakshatra Ending Moment; Muhammadan Year, Month and Day.

Jan. — Solar: Bahudhanya *Dhanus—Margali.* (to 30); Bahudhanya *Makara—Tai.* Lunar: Suk. / Pausha — Bahula / Sukla / Magha. Muhammadan: H. 1419 *Ramzan.* (to 30); *Shawwal.*

Cyclic Sidereal Day	Week-Day	Jan.	Tithi	Ending Moment	Nakshatra	Ending Moment	Muhammadan Day
17	Fr	1	14	·18	5	·34	13
18	Sa	2	P	·10	6	·29	14
19	Su	3	1	·04	7	·26	15
20	Mo	4	2 3	·00 ·98	8	·25	16
21	Tu	5	4	·97	9	·26	17
22	We	6	5	·98	10	·28	18
23	Th	7	...	...	11	·32	19
24	Fr	8	6	·02	12	·39	20
25	Sa	9	7	·08	13	·48	21
26	Su	10	8	·16	14	·58	22
27	Mo	11	9	·24	15	·68	23
28	Tu	12	10	·33	16	·79	24
29	We	13	11	·41	17	·89	25
—30	Th	14	12	·49	18	·98	26
1	Fr	15	13	·56	...	...	27
2	Sa	16	14	·60	19	·06	28
3	Su	17	—A	·63	20	·12	29
4	Mo	18	1	·64	21	·16	—30
5	Tu	19	2	·62	22	·17	1
6	We	20	3	·59	23	·17	2
7	Th	21	4	·53	24	·15	3
8	Fr	22	5	·46	25	·11	4
9	Sa	23	6	·38	26	·06	5
10	Su	24	7	·29	27 1	·00 ·93	6
11	Mo	25	8	·20	2	·86	7
12	Tu	26	9	·10	3	·80	8
13	We	27	10 11	·00 ·90	4	·74	9
14	Th	28	12	·81	5	·68	10
15	Fr	29	13	·74	6	·63	11
16	Sa	30	14	·69	7	·59	12
17	Su	31	P	·65	8	·58	13

Feb. — Solar: Bahudhanya *Kumbha—Masi.* (from 1). Lunar: Bahula / Sukla / Phalguna. Muhammadan: H. 1419 (to 29); H. 1419 *Zi-l-ka'da.*

Cyclic Sidereal Day	Week-Day	Feb.	Tithi	Ending Moment	Nakshatra	Ending Moment	Muhammadan Day
18	Mo	1	1	·63	9	·58	14
19	Tu	2	2	·61	10	·60	15
20	We	3	3	·63	11	·63	16
21	Th	4	4	·67	12	·69	17
22	Fr	5	5	·73	13	·78	18
23	Sa	6	6	·80	14	·88	19
24	Su	7	7	·88	15	·98	20
25	Mo	8	8	·97	...	...	21
26	Tu	9	...	...	16	·08	22
27	We	10	9	·06	17	·19	23
28	Th	11	10	·14	18	·29	24
—29	Fr	12	11	·20	19	·37	25
1	Sa	13	12	·24	20	·43	26
2	Su	14	13	·26	21	·47	27
3	Mo	15	14	·26	22	·49	28
4	Tu	16	—A	·26	23	·49	—29
5	We	17	1	·22	24	·48	1
6	Th	18	2	·16	25	·45	2
7	Fr	19	3 4	·08 ·99	26	·40	3
8	Sa	20	5	·90	27	·34	4
9	Su	21	6	·81	1	·28	5
10	Mo	22	7	·72	2	·21	6
11	Tu	23	8	·62	3	·14	7
12	We	24	9	·52	4	·07	8
13	Th	25	10	·43	5 6	·01 ·96	9
14	Fr	26	11	·36	7	·93	10
15	Sa	27	12	·30	8	·91	11
16	Su	28	13	·26	9	·90	12

March — Solar: Bahudhanya *Kumbha—Masi.* (to 30); Bahudhanya *Mina—Panguni.* Lunar: Phalguna — Bahula / Sukla / Chaitra. Muhammadan: H. 1419 *Zi-l-ka'da.* (to 30); *Zi-l-hijja.*

Cyclic Sidereal Day	Week-Day	March	Tithi	Ending Moment	Nakshatra	Ending Moment	Muhammadan Day
17	Mo	1	14	·24	10	·91	13
18	Tu	2	P	·22	11	·95	14
19	We	3	1	·24	...	...	15
20	Th	4	2	·28	12	·01	16
21	Fr	5	3	·34	13	·08	17
22	Sa	6	4	·42	14	·17	18
23	Su	7	5	·51	15	·27	19
24	Mo	8	6	·60	16	·38	20
25	Tu	9	7	·68	17	·49	21
26	We	10	8	·75	18	·59	22
27	Th	11	9	·80	19	·68	23
28	Fr	12	10	·84	20	·74	24
29	Sa	13	11	·86	21	·78	25
—30	Su	14	12	·86	22	·81	26
1	Mo	15	13	·85	23	·83	27
2	Tu	16	14	·81	24	·81	28
3	We	17	—A	·75	25	·78	29
4	Th	18	1	·68	26	·73	—30
5	Fr	19	2	·60	27	·68	1
6	Sa	20	3	·50	1	·62	2
7	Su	21	4	·40	2	·55	3
8	Mo	22	5	·30	3	·48	4
9	Tu	23	6	·20	4	·41	5
10	We	24	7	·11	5	·35	6
11	Th	25	8 9	·02 ·94	6	·30	7
12	Fr	26	10	·88	7	·26	8
13	Sa	27	11	·84	8	·23	9
14	Su	28	12	·82	9	·22	10
15	Mo	29	13	·80	10	·23	11
16	Tu	30	14	·82	11	·27	12
17	We	31	P	·86	12	·32	13

April — Solar: Bahudhanya (to 30); Pramathi *Mesha—Chittirai.* Lunar: Bahula / Sukla / Vaisakha. Muhammadan: H. 1419 (to 29); H. 1420 *Muharram.*

Cyclic Sidereal Day	Week-Day	April	Tithi	Ending Moment	Nakshatra	Ending Moment	Muhammadan Day
18	Th	1	1	·92	13	·39	14
19	Fr	2	...	...	14	·48	15
20	Sa	3	2	·00	15	·58	16
21	Su	4	3	·08	16	·69	17
22	Mo	5	4	·17	17	·80	18
23	Tu	6	5	·25	18	·90	19
24	We	7	6	·32	19	·98	20
25	Th	8	7	·37	...	...	21
26	Fr	9	8	·41	20	·05	22
27	Sa	10	9	·42	21	·10	23
28	Su	11	10	·48	22	·14	24
29	Mo	12	11	·41	23	·15	25
—30	Tu	13	12	·37	24	·14	26
1	We	14	13	·31	25	·11	27
2	Th	15	14	·23	26	·07	28
3	Fr	16	—A	·15	27 1	·02 ·96	—29
4	Sa	17	1 2	·06 ·96	2	·89	1
5	Su	18	3	·86	3	·82	2
6	Mo	19	4	·76	4	·75	3
7	Tu	20	5	·66	5	·69	4
8	We	21	6	·57	6	·64	5
9	Th	22	7	·49	7	·59	6
10	Fr	23	8	·43	8	·56	7
11	Sa	24	9	·39	9	·54	8
12	Su	25	10	·36	10	·55	9
13	Mo	26	11	·35	11	·58	10
14	Tu	27	12	·36	12	·63	11
15	We	28	13	·39	13	·70	12
16	Th	29	14	·45	14	·78	13
17	Fr	30	P	·53	15	·87	14

May — Solar: Pramathi *Mesha—Chittirai.* (to 31); Pramathi *Vrishabha—Vaikasi.* Lunar: Vaisakha — Bahula / Sukla / Adhika Jyeshtha. Muhammadan: H. 1420 *Muharram.* (to 30); *Safar.*

Cyclic Sidereal Day	Week-Day	May	Tithi	Ending Moment	Nakshatra	Ending Moment	Muhammadan Day
18	Sa	1	1	·62	16	·98	15
19	Su	2	2	·70	...	...	16
20	Mo	3	3	·78	17	·09	17
21	Tu	4	4	·84	18	·20	18
22	We	5	5	·90	19	·29	19
23	Th	6	6	·94	20	·36	20
24	Fr	7	7	·95	21	·42	21
25	Sa	8	8	·96	22	·46	22
26	Su	9	9	·93	23	·47	23
27	Mo	10	10	·89	24	·46	24
28	Tu	11	11	·83	25	·44	25
29	We	12	12	·76	26	·41	26
30	Th	13	13	·67	27	·36	27
—31	Fr	14	14	·57	1	·30	28
1	Sa	15	—A	·47	2	·23	29
2	Su	16	1	·37	3	·16	—30
3	Mo	17	2	·27	4	·09	1
4	Tu	18	3	·17	5 6	·03 ·97	2
5	We	19	4	·08	7	·92	3
6	Th	20	5 6	·00 ·94	8	·89	4
7	Fr	21	7	·90	9	·87	5
8	Sa	22	8	·86	10	·88	6
9	Su	23	9	·85	11	·90	7
10	Mo	24	10	·86	12	·94	8
11	Tu	25	11	·90	...	...	9
12	We	26	12	·95	13	·00	10
13	Th	27	...	...	14	·08	11
14	Fr	28	13	·02	15	·18	12
15	Sa	29	14	·11	16	·29	13
16	Su	30	P	·19	17	·40	14
17	Mo	31	1	·27	18	·50	15

June — Solar: Pramathi (to 31); Pramathi *Mithuna—Ani.* Lunar: Bahula / Sukla / Nija Jyeshtha. Muhammadan: H. 1420 (to 29); H. 1420 *Rabi-ul-awwal.*

Cyclic Sidereal Day	Week-Day	June	Tithi	Ending Moment	Nakshatra	Ending Moment	Muhammadan Day
18	Tu	1	2	·34	19	·59	16
19	We	2	3	·40	20	·67	17
20	Th	3	4	·43	21	·73	18
21	Fr	4	5	·45	22	·77	19
22	Sa	5	6	·45	23	·79	20
23	Su	6	7	·43	24	·79	21
24	Mo	7	8	·39	25	·78	22
25	Tu	8	9	·33	26	·74	23
26	We	9	10	·26	27	·69	24
27	Th	10	11	·17	1	·63	25
28	Fr	11	12 13	·07 ·97	2	·57	26
29	Sa	12	14	·86	3	·51	27
30	Su	13	—A	·76	4	·44	28
—31	Mo	14	1	·66	5	·37	—29
1	Tu	15	2	·57	6	·31	1
2	We	16	3	·49	7	·25	2
3	Th	17	4	·43	8	·22	3
4	Fr	18	5	·38	9	·20	4
5	Sa	19	6	·34	10	·20	5
6	Su	20	7	·33	11	·21	6
7	Mo	21	8	·34	12	·25	7
8	Tu	22	9	·38	13	·31	8
9	We	23	10	·43	14	·39	9
10	Th	24	11	·50	15	·48	10
11	Fr	25	12	·58	16	·58	11
12	Sa	26	13	·66	17	·69	12
13	Su	27	14	·74	18	·80	13
14	Mo	28	P	·81	19	·90	14
15	Tu	29	1	·87	20	·98	15
16	We	30	2	·91	...	...	16

Naksh:—1. Asvn. 2. Bhar. 3. Krit. 4. Rohi. 5. Mrig. 6. Ardh. 7. Punar. 8. Push. 9. Aslesh. 10. Magh. 11. P. Phal. 12. U. Phal. 13. Hasta. 14. Chit.

A. D. 1999. A.—Amavasya. P.—Paurnami.	Kollam 1175, Commences { N. Malabar—Sept. S. Malabar—Aug.	Hijra 1420, Commences, April 17.	Vikrama 2056. Bengal San 1405. (N. Cycle) Nandana.

Columns: SOLAR reckoning (Cyclic Sidereal Year, Month and Day; Week-Day English Month and Day) — LUNAR reckoning (Tithi Ending Moment; Nakshatra Ending Moment; Muhammadan Year, Month and Day).

July

Cyclic Sidereal Year, Month and Day	Week-Day English Month and Day		Tithi Ending Moment	Nakshatra Ending Moment	Muhammadan Year, Month and Day	Labels
17	Th	1	3 ·93	21 ·05	17	Pramathi Mithuna—Ani; Nija Jyeshtha; H. 1420 Rabi-ul-awwal
18	Fr	2	4 ·93	22 ·09	18	
19	Sa	3	5 ·91	23 ·11	19	
20	Su	4	6 ·87	24 ·12	20	
21	Mo	5	7 ·81	25 ·11	21	
22	Tu	6	8 ·73	26 ·08	22	
23	We	7	9 ·64	27 ·03 / 1 ·97	23	
24	Th	8	10 ·55	2 ·91	24	
25	Fr	9	11 ·45	3 ·84	25	Bahula
26	Sa	10	12 ·35	4 ·77	26	
27	Su	11	13 ·25	5 ·70	27	
28	Mo	12	14 ·15	6 ·64	28	
29	Tu	13	A ·05 / 1 ·97	7 ·59	29	
30	We	14	2 ·91	8 ·56	—30	
31	Th	15	3 ·86	9 ·53	1	H. 1420 Rabi-ul-akhir
—32	Fr	16	4 ·83	10 ·52	2	
1	Sa	17	5 ·82	11 ·53	3	Pramathi Karkata—Adi
2	Su	18	6 ·83	12 ·56	4	Sukla
3	Mc	19	7 ·86	13 ·62	5	
4	Tu	20	8 ·90	14 ·69	6	
5	We	21	9 ·96	15 ·78	7	
6	Th	22	... ...	16 ·88	8	
7	Fr	23	10 ·04	17 ·99	9	
8	Sa	24	11 ·13	... ...	10	Ashadha
9	Su	25	12 ·21	18 ·10	11	
10	Mo	26	13 ·29	19 ·20	12	
11	Tu	27	14 ·35	20 ·29	13	
12	We○	28	P ·39	21 ·36	14	
13	Th	29	1 ·41	22 ·40	15	
14	Fr	30	2 ·41	23 ·43	16	
15	Sa	31	3 ·39	24 ·45	17	

Aug.

Cyclic Sidereal Year, Month and Day	Week-Day English Month and Day		Tithi Ending Moment	Nakshatra Ending Moment	Muhammadan Year, Month and Day	Labels
16	Su	1	4 ·35	25 ·44	18	Pramathi Karkata—Adi; Bahula; H. 1420 Rabi-ul-akhir
17	Mo	2	5 ·29	26 ·41	19	
18	Tu	3	6 ·22	27 ·36	20	
19	We	4	7 ·14	1 ·31	21	
20	Th	5	8 ·04 / 9 ·94	2 ·25	22	
21	Fr	6	10 ·84	3 ·18	23	
22	Sa	7	11 ·74	4 ·11	24	
23	Su	8	12 ·64	5 ·04 / 6 ·98	25	
24	Mo	9	13 ·55	7 ·93	26	
25	Tu	10	14 ·47	8 ·89	27	
26	We	11	—A ·40	9 ·86	28	
27	Th	12	1 ·35	10 ·84	—29	
28	Fr	13	2 ·32	11 ·85	1	H. 1420 Jumadal-awwal
29	Sa	14	3 ·31	12 ·88	2	
30	Su	15	4 ·32	13 ·93	3	
31	Mo	16	5 ·35	... ...	4	
—32	Tu	17	6 ·40	14 ·00	5	Sukla
1	We	18	7 ·46	15 ·08	6	Pramathi Simha—Avani
2	Th	19	8 ·54	16 ·18	7	
3	Fr	20	9 ·63	17 ·29	8	
4	Sa	21	10 ·71	18 ·40	9	
5	Su	22	11 ·78	19 ·50	10	Sravana
6	Mo	23	12 ·84	20 ·59	11	
7	Tu	24	13 ·89	21 ·66	12	
8	We	25	14 ·92	22 ·72	13	
9	Th	26	P ·92	23 ·76	14	
10	Fr	27	1 ·90	24 ·77	15	Bahula
11	Sa	28	2 ·86	25 ·76	16	
12	Su	29	3 ·80	26 ·74	17	
13	Mo	30	4 ·73	27 ·70	18	
14	Tu	31	5 ·65	1 ·65	19	

Sep.

Cyclic Sidereal Year, Month and Day	Week-Day English Month and Day		Tithi Ending Moment	Nakshatra Ending Moment	Muhammadan Year, Month and Day	Labels
15	We	1	6 ·56	2 59	20	Pramathi Simha—Avani; Sravana; H. 1420 Jumadal-awwal
16	Th	2	7 ·46	3 ·52	21	
17	Fr	3	8 ·36	4 ·45	22	
18	Sa	4	9 ·26	5 ·38	23	
19	Su	5	10 ·16	6 ·32	24	
20	Mo	6	11 ·07 / 12 ·99	7 ·27	25	Bah.
21	Tu	7	13 ·92	8 ·22	26	
22	We	8	14 ·87	9 ·19	27	
23	Th	9	—A ·84	10 ·17	28	
24	Fr	10	1 ·83	11 ·17	29	
25	Sa	11	2 ·84	12 ·20	—30	
26	Su	12	3 ·87	13 ·24	1	H. 1420 Jumadal-akhir
27	Mo	13	4 ·92	14 ·30	2	
28	Tu	14	5 ·99	15 ·38	3	
29	We	15	... ...	16 ·48	4	
30	Th	16	6 ·07	17 ·59	5	Sukla
—31	Fr	17	7 ·15	18 ·70	6	
1	Sa	18	8 ·23	19 ·80	7	Pramathi Kanya—Purattasi
2	Su	19	9 ·30	20 ·89	8	
3	Mo	20	10 ·36	21 ·97	9	
4	Tu	21	11 ·41	... ...	10	
5	We	22	12 ·44	22 ·04	11	Bhadrapada
6	Th	23	13 ·45	23 ·08	12	
7	Fr	24	14 ·43	24 ·09	13	
8	Sa	25	P ·40	25 ·09	14	
9	Su	26	1 ·34	26 ·07	15	
10	Mo	27	2 ·27	27 ·04 / 1 ·99	16	
11	Tu	28	3 ·19	2 ·93	17	
12	We	29	4 ·10	3 ·86	18	
13	Th	30	5 ·01 / 6 ·91	4 79	19	

Oct.

Cyclic Sidereal Year, Month and Day	Week-Day English Month and Day		Tithi Ending Moment	Nakshatra Ending Moment	Muhammadan Year, Month and Day	Labels
14	Fr	1	7 ·81	5 ·72	20	Pramathi Kanya—Purattasi; Bahula; H. 1420 Jumadal-akhir
15	Sa	2	8 ·71	6 ·66	21	
16	Su	3	9 ·62	7 ·60	22	
17	Mo	4	10 ·54	8 ·55	23	
18	Tu	5	11 ·47	9 ·51	24	
19	We	6	12 ·42	10 49	25	
20	Th	7	13 ·40	11 ·50	26	
21	Fr	8	14 ·40	12 ·51	27	
22	Sa	9	—A ·41	13 ·55	28	
23	Su	10	1 ·44	14 ·61	—29	
24	Mo	11	2 ·49	15 ·69	1	H. 1420 Rajab
25	Tu	12	3 ·55	16 ·79	2	
26	We	13	4 ·63	17 ·89	3	
27	Th	14	5 ·71	... ...	4	
28	Fr	15	6 ·80	18 ·00	5	Sukla
29	Sa	16	7 88	19 ·10	6	
—30	Su	17	8 ·95	20 ·20	7	
1	Mo	18	... ...	21 ·29	8	Pramathi Tula—Aippasi
2	Tu	19	9 ·00	22 ·35	9	
3	We	20	10 ·03	23 ·39	10	
4	Th	21	11 ·03	24 ·41	11	
5	Fr	22	12 ·01 / 13 ·97	25 ·42	12	Asvina
6	Sa	23	14 ·92	26 ·41	13	
7	Su	24	P ·86	27 ·37	14	
8	Mo	25	1 ·78	1 ·32	15	
9	Tu	26	2 ·69	2 ·26	16	
10	We	27	3 ·59	3 ·20	17	
11	Th	28	4 ·49	4 ·13	18	
12	Fr	29	5 ·39	5 ·06	19	Bahula
13	Sa	30	6 ·30	6 ·00 / 7 ·94	20	
14	Su	31	7 ·21	8 ·89	21	

Nov.

Cyclic Sidereal Year, Month and Day	Week-Day English Month and Day		Tithi Ending Moment	Nakshatra Ending Moment	Muhammadan Year, Month and Day	Labels
15	Mo	1	8 ·13	9 ·85	22	Pramathi Tula—Aippasi; Asv.; H. 1420 Rajab
16	Tu	2	9 ·07	10 ·83	23	
17	We	3	10 ·02 / 11 [illegible]	11 ·82	24	Bahula
18	Th	4	12 ·98	12 ·83	25	
19	Fr	5	13 ·99	13 ·86	26	
20	Sa	6	... ...	14 ·92	27	
21	Su	7	14 ·03	... ...	28	
22	Mo	8	—A ·09	15 ·00	29	
23	Tu	9	1 ·16	16 ·09	—30	
24	We	10	2 ·24	17 ·19	1	H. 1420 Shaban
25	Th	11	3 ·32	18 ·30	2	
26	Fr	12	4 ·41	19 ·41	3	
27	Sa	13	5 ·49	20 ·51	4	
28	Su	14	6 ·56	21 ·59	5	Sukla
29	Mo	15	7 ·60	22 ·66	6	
—30	Tu	16	8 ·63	23 ·71	7	
1	We	17	9 ·64	24 ·74	8	
2	Th	18	10 ·62	25 ·75	9	
3	Fr	19	11 ·58	26 ·73	10	
4	Sa	20	12 ·53	27 ·70	11	
5	Su	21	13 ·47	1 ·66	12	Karttika
6	Mo	22	14 ·39	2 ·60	13	Pramathi Vrischika—Kartigai
7	Tu	23	P ·30	3 ·54	14	
8	We	24	1 ·21	4 ·48	15	
9	Th	25	2 ·11	5 ·41	16	
10	Fr	26	3 ·01 / 4 ·92	6 ·34	17	
11	Sa	27	5 ·83	7 ·27	18	Bahula
12	Su	28	6 ·75	8 ·22	19	
13	Mo	29	7 ·69	9 ·18	20	
14	Tu	30	8 ·64	10 ·15	21	

Dec.

Cyclic Sidereal Year, Month and Day	Week-Day English Month and Day		Tithi Ending Moment	Nakshatra Ending Moment	Muhammadan Year, Month and Day	Labels
15	We	1	9 ·62	11 ·14	22	Pramathi Vrischika—Kartigai; H. 1420 Shaban
16	Th	2	10 ·62	12 ·15	23	
17	Fr	3	11 63	13 ·18	24	
18	Sa	4	12 ·67	14 ·23	25	
19	Su	5	13 ·72	15 ·30	26	
20	Mo	6	14 ·79	16 ·39	27	
21	Tu	7	—A ·87	17 ·49	28	
22	We	8	1 ·96	18 ·60	—29	
23	Th	9	... ...	19 ·71	1	H. 1420 Ramzan
24	Fr	10	2 ·06	20 ·81	2	
25	Sa	11	3 ·14	21 ·90	3	
26	Su	12	4 ·20	22 ·97	4	
27	Mo	13	5 ·25	... ...	5	
28	Tu	14	6 ·28	23 ·02	6	Sukla
—29	We	15	7 ·28	24 ·05	7	
1	Th	16	8 ·26	25 ·07	8	Pramathi Dhanus—Margali
2	Fr	17	9 ·22	26 ·06	9	
3	Sa	18	10 ·17	27 ·03 / 1 ·99	10	
4	Su	19	11 ·10	2 ·94	11	
5	Mo	20	12 ·02 / 13 ·93	3 ·88	12	Margasira
6	Tu	21	14 ·84	4 ·81	13	
7	We	22	P ·74	5 ·74	14	
8	Th	23	1 ·64	6 ·67	15	
9	Fr	24	2 ·55	7 ·61	16	
10	Sa	25	3 ·47	8 ·55	17	
11	Su	26	4 ·39	9 ·51	18	
12	Mo	27	5 ·33	10 ·48	19	
13	Tu	28	6 ·29	11 ·47	20	
14	We	29	7 ·27	12 ·47	21	Bahula
15	Th	30	8 ·26	13 ·50	22	
16	Fr	31	9 ·28	14 ·54	23	

15. Svati. 16. Visak. 17. Anur. 18. Jyesh. 19. Mula. 20. P. Ash. 21. U. Ash. 22. Sravn. 23. Dani. 24. Satab. 25. P. Bhad. 26. U. Bhad. 27. Rev.

APPENDIX I.

CORRECTIONS FOR SUNRISE FROM 8° TO 12° N. LATITUDE.

Day of Solar year.	Lat. 8° +·003 Long.			Lat. 9° +·010 Long.			Days of Solar months.	Lat. 10° +·007 Long.			Lat. 11° +·009 Long.			Lat. 12° +·002 Long.			English date.
	For Eqn. of time—fraction of a day.	For ☉'s Trop. Long. fraction of a day.	Total Correction—fraction of a day. Trivandram.	For Eqn. of time—fraction of a day.	For ☉'s Trop. Long. fraction of a day.	Total Correction—fraction of a day. Rameswaram.		For Eqn. of time—fraction of a day.	For ☉'s Trop. Long. fraction of a day.	Total Correction—fraction of a day. Madura.	For Eqn. of time—fraction of a day.	For ☉'s Trop. Long. fraction of a day.	Total Correction—fraction of a day. Tanjore.	For Eqn. of time—fraction of a day.	For ☉'s Trop. Long. fraction of a day.	Total Correction—fraction of a day. Maisur.	
							Tamil, Chittirai; *Malayalam*, Medam; *Bengal*, Vaisakha.										April.
1	−·005	+·000	+·006	−·005	+·000	+·013	1	−·005	+·000	+·010	−·005	+·000	+·013	−·005	+·000	+·007	13
2	...	+·001	...	...	+·001	...	2	...	+·001	...	...	+·001	+·014	...	+·001	...	14
3	...	...	...	...	...	...	3	...	...	+·011	...	...	...	...	...	+·008	15
4	...	...	+·007	...	+·002	+·014	4	...	+·002	...	...	+·002	...	...	+·002	...	16
5	...	+·002	...	...	...	...	5	...	...	...	...	...	+·015	...	...	...	17
6	...	...	+·008	...	...	+·015	6	...	...	+·012	...	...	...	...	+·003	+·009	18
7	...	...	...	...	+·003	...	7	...	+·003	...	...	+·003	+·016	...	...	...	19
8	...	+·003	...	...	...	...	8	...	...	+·013	...	...	...	...	...	+·010	20
9	...	...	+·009	...	...	+·016	9	...	+·004	...	...	+·004	+·017	...	+·004	...	21
10	...	+·004	...	...	+·004	...	10	...	...	+·014	...	...	...	...	...	+·011	22
11	...	...	...	...	...	...	11	...	...	...	...	+·005	...	...	+·005	...	23
12	...	...	...	...	...	+·017	12	...	+·005	...	...	...	...	...	...	...	24
13	...	+·005	+·010	...	+·005	...	13	...	...	...	...	...	+·018	...	+·006	...	25
14	...	...	...	...	...	...	14	...	+·006	...	...	+·006	...	...	...	+·012	26
15	...	...	...	...	+·006	...	15	...	...	...	...	...	...	...	+·007	...	27
16	...	+·006	...	...	...	...	16	...	...	+·015	...	+·007	...	...	...	...	28
17	...	...	...	...	...	...	17	...	+·007	...	...	...	+·019	...	...	...	29
18	...	...	...	...	+·007	+·018	18	...	...	...	...	...	...	−·004	+·008	+·013	30
19	...	+·007	+·011	...	...	...	19	...	...	...	−·004	+·008	...	...	...	...	1
20	...	...	...	...	...	...	20	−·004	+·008	...	...	...	...	...	+·009	...	2
21	...	...	...	−·004	+·008	...	21	...	...	+·016	...	+·009	...	...	...	...	3
22	−·004	+·008	...	...	...	...	22	...	+·009	...	...	...	+·020	...	+·010	...	4
23	...	...	...	...	+·009	+·019	23	...	...	...	...	+·010	...	...	...	+·014	5
24	...	+·009	...	...	...	...	24	...	...	...	...	...	...	...	...	...	6
25	...	...	+·012	...	...	...	25	...	+·010	...	...	...	...	...	+·011	...	7
26	...	...	...	...	+·010	...	26	...	...	+·017	...	+·011	+·021	...	...	...	8
27	...	+·010	...	...	...	...	27	...	+·011	...	...	...	...	...	+·012	+·015	9
28	...	...	...	...	...	...	28	...	...	...	...	+·012	...	...	...	...	10
29	...	...	...	...	+·011	+·020	29	...	...	...	...	...	...	...	+·013	...	11
30	...	+·011	...	...	...	...	30	...	+·012	...	...	...	...	...	...	...	12
31	...	...	+·013	...	...	...	31	...	...	+·018	...	+·013	+·022	...	...	...	13
							Tamil, Vaikasi; *Malayalam*, Edavam; *Bengal*, Jyeshtha.										May.
32	...	...	...	...	+·012	...	1	...	...	...	...	...	...	...	...	+·016	14
33	...	...	...	...	...	...	2	...	...	...	...	...	...	...	+·014	...	15
34	...	...	...	...	...	...	3	...	...	...	...	...	...	...	...	...	16
35	...	...	...	...	...	+·021	4	...	+·013	...	...	...	...	...	...	...	17
36	...	...	...	...	...	...	5	...	...	+·019	...	+·014	+·023	...	...	+·017	18
37	...	+·012	+·014	...	...	...	6	...	...	...	...	...	...	...	...	...	19
38	...	...	...	...	...	...	7	...	...	...	...	...	...	...	+·015	...	20
39	...	...	...	...	+·013	...	8	...	...	...	...	...	...	...	...	...	21
40	...	...	...	...	...	+·022	9	...	...	...	...	...	+·024	...	...	+·018	22
41	...	...	...	...	...	...	10	...	+·014	...	...	...	...	...	...	...	23
42	...	...	...	...	...	...	11	...	...	...	−·003	+·015	...	−·003	...	...	24
43	−·003	...	...	−·003	...	...	12	−·003	...	...	...	...	...	...	+·016	...	25
44	...	...	...	...	...	...	13	...	...	+·020	...	...	...	...	...	...	26
45	...	+·013	...	...	...	...	14	...	...	+·019	...	...	...	...	...	...	27
46	...	...	...	...	+·014	...	15	...	...	...	...	...	...	...	...	...	28
47	...	...	...	...	...	+·021	16	...	+·015	...	...	...	+·023	...	...	...	29
48	...	...	...	...	...	...	17	...	...	...	...	+·016	...	...	...	...	30
49	...	...	...	...	...	...	18	...	...	...	...	...	...	...	+·017	+·017	31
																	June.
50	...	...	...	...	...	...	19	...	...	...	...	...	...	...	...	...	1
51	...	...	...	...	...	...	20	...	...	...	...	...	...	...	...	...	2
52	...	...	...	...	...	...	21	...	...	...	...	...	...	...	...	...	3
53	...	...	...	...	+·015	...	22	...	+·016	...	...	+·017	...	...	...	...	4
54	...	+·014	+·013	...	...	...	23	...	...	...	...	...	...	−·002	+·018	...	5
55	−·002	...	...	−·002	...	...	24	−·002	...	...	−·002	...	...	...	...	...	6
56	...	...	...	...	...	...	25	...	...	...	...	...	...	...	...	...	7
57	...	...	...	...	...	...	26	...	...	...	...	...	...	...	...	...	8
58	...	...	...	...	...	...	27	...	...	...	...	...	...	...	...	...	9
59	...	...	...	...	...	...	28	...	...	...	...	+·018	...	...	+·019	...	10
60	...	...	...	...	+·016	...	29	...	+·017	+·018	...	...	...	...	...	...	11
61	...	...	...	...	...	...	30	...	...	...	...	...	...	...	...	...	12
62	...	...	...	...	+·015	+·020	31	...	...	...	...	...	+·022	...	...	...	13

APPENDIX I.

CORRECTIONS FOR SUNRISE FROM 8° TO 12° N. LATITUDE.

Day of Solar year.	Lat. 8° +·003 Long. For Eqn. of time—fraction of a day.	Lat. 8° For ⊙'s Trop. Long. fraction of a day.	Lat. 8° Total Correction—fraction of a day. **Trivandram.**	Lat. 9° +·010 Long. For Eqn. of time—fraction of a day.	Lat. 9° For ⊙'s Trop. Long. fraction of a day.	Lat. 9° Total Correction—fraction of a day. **Rameswaram.**	Days of Solar months.	Lat. 10° +·007 Long. For Eqn. of time—fraction of a day.	Lat. 10° For ⊙'s Trop. Long. fraction of a day.	Lat. 10° Total Correction—fraction of a day. **Madura.**	Lat. 11° +·009 Long. For Eqn. of time—fraction of a day.	Lat. 11° For ⊙'s Trop. Long. fraction of a day.	Lat. 11° Total Correction—fraction of a day. **Tanjore.**	Lat. 12° +·002 Long. For Eqn. of time—fraction of a day.	Lat. 12° For ⊙'s Trop. Long. fraction of a day.	Lat. 12° Total Correction—fraction of a day. **Maisur.**	English date.
63	−·002	+·014	+·013	−·002	+·015	+·020	1 (*Tamil*, Ani; *Malayalam*, Mithunam; *Bengal*, Ashadha.)	−·002	+·017	+·018	−·002	+·018	+·022	−·002	+·019	+·017	14 (June.)
64	...	...	...	...	...	...	2	...	+·016	...	...	...	...	...	...	...	15
65	...	...	...	...	...	...	3	...	...	...	...	+·017	...	...	+·018	...	16
66	...	...	...	...	...	...	4	...	...	...	...	...	...	...	...	...	17
67	−·001	...	...	−·001	...	...	5	−·001	...	...	−·001	...	...	−·001	...	...	18
68	...	+·013	...	...	...	...	6	...	...	...	...	...	...	...	...	...	19
69	...	...	...	...	+·014	...	7	...	...	...	...	...	...	...	...	+·016	20
70	...	...	...	...	...	...	8	...	...	...	...	...	...	...	...	...	21
71	...	...	+·012	...	...	...	9	...	+·015	...	...	...	...	...	...	...	22
72	...	...	...	...	...	...	10	...	...	...	...	+·016	...	...	...	...	23
73	...	...	...	...	...	...	11	...	...	...	...	...	...	...	+·017	...	24
74	...	...	...	...	...	...	12	...	...	...	...	...	...	...	...	...	25
75	...	+·012	...	...	...	+·019	13	...	...	+·017	...	...	...	...	...	...	26
76	−·000	...	...	−·000	+·013	...	14	−·000	...	...	−·000	...	+·021	−·000	...	...	27
77	...	...	...	...	...	...	15	...	...	...	...	...	...	...	...	+·015	28
78	...	...	+·011	...	...	...	16	...	+·014	...	...	...	...	...	...	...	29
79	...	...	...	...	...	...	17	...	...	...	...	+·015	...	...	...	...	30
80	...	...	...	...	...	...	18	...	...	...	...	...	...	...	+·016	...	1 (July.)
81	...	...	...	...	...	...	19	...	...	+·016	...	...	...	...	...	...	2
82	...	+·011	...	...	...	+·018	20	...	...	...	...	...	+·020	...	...	...	3
83	...	...	...	...	+·012	...	21	...	...	...	...	...	...	...	...	+·014	4
84	...	...	...	...	...	...	22	...	...	...	...	...	...	...	...	...	5
85	...	...	+·010	...	...	...	23	...	+·013	...	...	...	...	...	...	...	6
86	+·001	...	...	+·001	...	...	24	+·001	...	...	+·001	...	...	+·001	...	...	7
87	...	...	...	...	...	...	25	...	...	...	...	+·014	...	...	...	...	8
88	...	...	...	...	...	...	26	...	...	+·015	...	...	...	...	+·015	...	9
89	...	+·010	...	...	...	+·017	27	...	...	...	...	...	+·019	...	...	+·013	10
90	...	...	...	...	+·011	...	28	...	...	...	...	...	...	...	...	...	11
91	...	...	...	...	...	...	29	...	+·012	...	...	...	...	...	...	...	12
92	...	...	+·009	...	...	...	30	...	...	...	...	...	...	...	...	...	13
93	...	...	...	...	...	...	31	...	...	...	...	+·013	...	...	+·014	...	14
94	+·002	+·009	...	+·002	...	...	32	+·002	...	+·014	+·002	...	...	+·002	...	...	15
95	...	...	...	...	+·010	+·016	1 (*Tamil*, Adi; *Malayalam*, Karkatagam; *Bengal*, Sravana.)	...	+·011	...	...	...	+·018	...	...	...	16
96	...	...	...	...	...	...	2	...	...	...	...	+·012	...	...	...	+·012	17
97	...	...	...	...	...	...	3	...	...	...	...	...	...	...	+·013	...	18
98	...	+·008	+·008	...	+·009	...	4	...	...	...	...	...	...	...	...	...	19
99	...	...	...	...	...	...	5	...	+·010	...	...	...	...	...	...	...	20
100	...	...	...	...	...	...	6	...	...	...	...	+·011	...	...	...	...	21
101	...	+·007	...	...	...	...	7	...	...	+·013	...	...	...	...	+·012	...	22
102	...	...	...	...	+·008	+·015	8	...	...	...	...	...	+·017	...	...	+·011	23
103	+·003	...	...	+·003	...	...	9	+·003	+·009	...	+·003	...	...	+·003	...	...	24
104	...	...	...	...	...	...	10	...	...	...	...	+·010	...	...	+·011	...	25
105	...	+·006	...	...	...	...	11	...	...	...	...	...	...	...	...	...	26
106	...	...	...	...	+·007	...	12	...	...	...	...	...	...	...	...	...	27
107	...	...	...	...	...	...	13	...	+·008	...	...	...	...	...	...	...	28
108	...	...	...	...	...	...	14	...	...	...	...	+·009	...	...	+·010	...	29
109	...	+·005	...	...	...	...	15	...	...	...	...	...	...	...	...	...	30
110	...	...	...	...	+·006	...	16	...	+·007	...	...	...	...	...	...	...	31
111	...	...	...	...	...	...	17	...	...	...	...	+·008	...	...	...	...	1 (August.)
112	...	...	...	...	...	...	18	...	...	...	...	...	...	...	+·009	...	2
113	+·004	+·004	...	+·004	...	...	19	+·004	...	...	+·004	...	...	+·004	...	+·010	3
114	...	...	...	...	+·005	...	20	...	+·006	...	...	...	...	...	...	...	4
115	...	...	...	...	...	...	21	...	...	...	...	+·007	+·016	...	+·008	...	5
116	...	...	...	...	...	...	22	...	...	...	...	...	...	...	...	...	6
117	...	+·003	...	...	+·004	...	23	...	...	...	...	...	...	...	...	...	7
118	...	...	...	...	...	...	24	...	+·005	+·012	...	...	...	...	...	...	8
119	...	...	...	...	...	...	25	...	...	...	...	+·006	...	...	+·007	...	9
120	...	...	...	...	...	...	26	...	...	...	...	...	...	...	...	...	10
121	...	+·002	...	...	+·003	...	27	...	...	...	...	...	...	...	...	...	11
122	...	...	...	...	...	...	28	...	+·004	...	...	+·005	...	...	+·006	...	12
123	...	...	...	...	...	+·014	29	...	...	...	...	...	...	...	...	+·009	13
124	...	...	...	...	...	...	30	...	...	...	...	...	...	...	...	...	14
125	...	...	...	...	...	...	31	...	...	...	...	...	+·015	...	...	...	15

APPENDIX I.

CORRECTIONS FOR SUNRISE FROM 8° TO 12° N. LATITUDE.

Day of Solar year.	Lat. 8° +·003 Long.			Lat. 9° +·010 Long.			Days of Solar months.	Lat. 10° +·007 Long.			Lat. 11° +·009 Long.			Lat. 12° +·002 Long.			English date.
	For Eqn. of time—fraction of a day.	For ⊙'s Trop. Long. fraction of a day.	Total Correction—fraction of a day. **Trivandram.**	For Eqn. of time—fraction of a day.	For ⊙'s Trop. Long. fraction of a day.	Total Correction—fraction of a day. **Rameswaram.**		For Eqn. of time—fraction of a day.	For ⊙'s Trop. Long. fraction of a day.	Total Correction—fraction of a day. **Madura.**	For Eqn. of time—fraction of a day.	For ⊙'s Trop. Long. fraction of a day.	Total Correction—fraction of a day. **Tanjore.**	For Eqn. of time—fraction of a day.	For ⊙'s Trop. Long. fraction of a day.	Total Correction—fraction of a day. **Maisur.**	
126	+·004	+·002	+·008	+·004	+·003	+·014	*Tamil*, Avani; *Malayalam*, Chingam; *Bengal*, Bhadrapada. 1	+·004	+·004	+·012	+·005	+·005	+·015	+·005	+·006	+·000	**August. 16**
127	+·005	+·001	...	+·005	+·002	...	2	+·005	...	...	...	...	...	...	...	...	**17**
128	...	...	...	...	...	...	3	...	+·003	...	...	+·004	...	...	+·005	...	**18**
129	...	...	...	...	...	+·015	4	...	...	...	...	...	...	...	...	...	**19**
130	...	...	...	...	...	...	5	...	...	+·011	...	...	...	...	...	...	**20**
131	...	...	...	...	...	...	6	...	...	...	...	...	...	...	...	...	**21**
132	...	...	...	...	...	...	7	...	...	...	...	...	...	...	...	+·008	**22**
133	...	...	...	...	...	...	8	...	...	+·012	...	...	...	...	+·001	+·009	**23**
134	...	...	...	...	...	...	9	...	...	...	...	+·003	...	...	...	...	**24**
135	...	...	+·009	...	+·001	...	10	...	+·002	...	...	...	...	...	...	...	**25**
136	...	+·000	...	...	...	...	11	...	...	...	...	...	...	...	...	...	**26**
137	...	...	...	...	...	...	12	...	...	...	...	...	...	...	...	...	**27**
138	...	...	...	...	...	...	13	...	...	...	...	...	...	...	...	...	**28**
139	...	...	...	...	...	...	14	...	...	...	...	...	...	...	+·003	...	**29**
140	...	...	...	...	...	...	15	...	...	...	...	+·002	...	...	...	...	**30**
141	...	...	...	...	...	...	16	...	+·001	...	+·006	...	...	+·006	...	...	**31**
142	...	...	...	+·006	...	...	17	+·006	...	...	...	...	...	...	...	...	**September. 1**
143	+·006	...	...	...	+·000	...	18	...	...	...	...	...	...	...	...	...	**2**
144	...	...	...	...	...	...	19	...	...	...	...	...	...	...	+·002	...	**3**
145	...	...	...	...	...	...	20	...	...	...	...	...	...	...	...	...	**4**
146	...	...	...	...	...	+·016	21	...	...	...	...	+·001	...	...	...	...	**5**
147	...	...	...	...	...	...	22	...	...	...	...	...	...	...	...	...	**6**
148	...	...	...	...	...	...	23	...	+·000	...	...	...	...	...	...	...	**7**
149	...	...	...	...	...	...	24	...	...	...	...	...	...	...	...	...	**8**
150	...	...	...	...	...	...	25	...	...	...	...	...	...	...	+·001	...	**9**
151	...	...	...	...	...	...	26	...	...	...	...	...	...	...	...	...	**10**
152	...	...	...	...	...	...	27	...	...	...	...	+·000	...	...	...	...	**11**
153	...	...	...	...	...	...	28	...	...	...	...	...	...	...	...	...	**12**
154	...	...	...	...	...	...	29	...	...	...	...	...	...	...	...	...	**13**
155	...	...	...	...	...	...	30	...	...	...	...	...	...	...	...	...	**14**
156	...	...	...	...	...	...	31	...	...	...	...	...	...	...	...	...	**15**
157	...	...	...	...	...	...	*Tamil*, Purattasi; *Malayalam*, Kanni; *Bengal*, Asvina. 1	...	...	...	...	...	...	...	...	...	**16**
158	...	...	...	...	...	...	2	...	...	...	...	...	...	...	...	...	**17**
159	...	...	...	...	...	...	3	...	...	...	...	...	...	...	...	...	**18**
160	...	...	...	...	...	...	4	...	...	...	...	...	...	...	...	...	**19**
161	...	...	...	...	...	...	5	...	...	...	...	...	...	...	...	...	**20**
162	...	...	...	...	...	...	6	...	...	...	...	...	...	...	...	...	**21**
163	...	...	...	...	...	...	7	...	...	...	...	...	...	...	...	+·008	**22**
164	...	...	...	...	...	...	8	...	...	...	...	...	...	...	...	...	**23**
165	...	...	...	...	...	...	9	...	...	+·013	...	...	...	...	...	...	**24**
166	...	...	...	...	...	...	10	...	...	...	...	...	...	...	...	...	**25**
167	...	...	...	...	...	...	11	...	...	...	...	...	...	...	...	...	**26**
168	...	...	...	...	...	...	12	...	...	...	...	...	...	...	+·000	...	**27**
169	...	...	...	...	...	...	13	...	...	...	...	...	...	...	...	...	**28**
170	...	...	...	...	...	...	14	...	...	...	...	...	...	...	...	...	**29**
171	...	...	...	...	...	...	15	...	...	...	...	...	...	...	...	...	**30**
172	...	...	...	...	...	...	16	...	...	...	...	...	...	...	...	...	**October. 1**
173	...	...	...	...	...	...	17	...	...	...	...	...	...	...	...	...	**2**
174	...	...	...	...	...	...	18	...	...	...	...	...	...	...	...	...	**3**
175	...	...	...	...	...	...	19	...	...	...	...	...	...	...	...	...	**4**
176	...	...	...	...	...	...	20	...	...	...	...	...	...	...	...	...	**5**
177	...	...	...	...	...	...	21	...	...	...	...	...	...	...	...	...	**6**
178	...	...	...	...	...	...	22	...	...	...	...	...	...	...	...	...	**7**
179	...	...	...	...	...	...	23	...	...	...	...	...	...	...	...	...	**8**
180	...	...	...	...	...	...	24	...	...	+·012	...	...	...	...	...	...	**9**
181	...	...	...	...	...	...	25	...	...	...	...	...	...	...	...	...	**10**
182	...	...	...	...	...	...	26	...	...	...	...	...	...	...	...	...	**11**
183	...	...	...	...	...	...	27	...	...	...	...	...	...	...	...	...	**12**
184	...	...	...	...	...	...	28	...	...	...	...	...	...	...	...	...	**13**
185	...	...	...	...	...	...	29	...	...	...	...	...	...	...	...	...	**14**
186	...	...	...	...	...	...	30	...	...	...	...	...	...	...	...	...	**15**

APPENDIX I.

CORRECTIONS FOR SUNRISE FROM 8° TO 12° N. LATITUDE.

Day of Solar year.	Lat. 8° +·008 Long.			Lat. 9° +·010 Long.			Days of Solar months.	Lat. 10° +·007 Long.			Lat. 11° +·009 Long.			Lat. 12° +·002 Long.			English date.
	For Eqn. of time—fraction of a day.	For ⊙'s Trop. Long. fraction of a day.	Total Correction—fraction of a day. **Trivandram.**	For Eqn. of time—fraction of a day.	For ⊙'s Trop. Long. fraction of a day.	Total Correction—fraction of a day. **Rameswaram.**		For Eqn. of time—fraction of a day.	For ⊙'s Trop. Long. fraction of a day.	Total Correction—fraction of a day. **Madura.**	For Eqn. of time—fraction of a day.	For ⊙'s Trop. Long. fraction of a day.	Total Correction—fraction of a day. **Tanjore.**	For Eqn. of time—fraction of a day.	For ⊙'s Trop. Long. fraction of a day.	Total Correction—fraction of a day. **Maisur.**	
187	+·006	+·000	+·009	+·006	+·000	+·016	*Tamil*, Aippasi; *Malayalam*, Tulam; *Bengal*, Karttika. 1	+·006	+·000	+·012	+·006	+·000	+·015	+·006	+·000	+·008	October. 16
188	...	...	...	...	...	...	2	...	...	...	...	...	...	...	...	...	17
189	...	...	...	...	...	...	3	...	...	...	...	...	...	...	...	+·007	18
190	...	...	...	...	...	...	4	...	...	...	...	...	...	...	...	...	19
191	...	...	...	...	...	...	5	...	...	...	...	...	...	...	...	...	20
192	...	...	...	...	...	...	6	...	...	...	...	...	...	...	...	...	21
193	...	...	...	...	...	+·015	7	...	...	...	...	...	...	...	...	...	22
194	...	...	...	...	...	...	8	...	...	...	...	...	...	...	...	...	23
195	...	...	...	...	...	...	9	...	...	...	...	...	+·014	...	...	...	24
196	+·005	...	...	...	...	...	10	...	...	...	...	...	...	...	...	...	25
197	...	...	...	+·005	...	...	11	+·005	...	...	...	...	...	...	...	+·006	26
198	...	...	...	...	...	...	12	...	...	+·011	+·005	...	...	...	...	...	27
199	...	...	...	...	...	...	13	...	...	...	...	...	+·013	+·005	−·001	...	28
200	...	...	...	...	...	...	14	...	...	...	...	...	...	...	...	...	29
201	...	...	...	...	...	...	15	...	...	...	...	...	...	...	...	+·005	30
202	...	...	...	...	...	...	16	...	...	...	...	...	...	...	...	...	31
203	...	...	...	...	...	...	17	...	...	+·010	...	...	...	...	...	...	November. 1
204	...	...	...	...	...	+·014	18	...	...	...	...	...	+·012	...	...	...	2
205	...	...	...	...	...	...	19	...	...	...	...	...	...	...	...	+·004	3
206	...	...	+·008	...	...	...	20	...	...	...	...	...	...	...	...	...	4
207	...	...	...	...	...	...	21	...	...	...	...	...	...	...	...	...	5
208	...	...	...	...	...	...	22	...	...	+·009	...	...	+·011	...	...	...	6
209	...	...	...	...	...	+·013	23	...	...	...	...	...	...	...	...	+·003	7
210	...	...	...	...	...	...	24	...	...	...	...	...	...	...	...	...	8
211	..	...	...	...	...	...	25	...	..	...	...	...	...	...	...	...	9
212	...	...	+·007	...	...	...	26	...	...	...	...	...	...	...	...	...	10
213	...	...	...	...	...	...	27	...	...	...	...	...	+·010	...	...	...	11
214	...	...	...	...	...	...	28	...	...	+·008	...	−·001	...	...	...	+·002	12
215	...	...	...	...	...	+·012	29	...	...	...	...	...	...	...	...	...	13
216	...	...	...	...	...	...	30	...	...	...	...	...	...	...	−·002	...	14
217	...	...	...	...	...	...	*Tamil*, Kartigai; *Malayalam*, Vrischikam; *Bengal*, Margasira. 1	...	...	...	...	...	...	...	...	...	15
218	+·004	...	+·006	+·004	...	...	2	...	−·001	...	...	...	+·009	...	...	+·001	16
219	...	...	...	...	...	...	3	+·004	...	+·007	+·004	...	...	+·004	...	...	17
220	...	...	...	...	...	+·011	4	...	...	...	...	−·002	...	...	...	...	18
221	...	...	...	...	...	...	5	...	...	...	...	..	...	...	...	...	19
222	...	...	...	...	...	...	6	...	...	...	...	...	+·008	...	−·003	+·000	20
223	...	...	...	...	−·001	...	7	...	...	+·006	...	...	...	...	...	...	21
224	...	...	+·005	...	...	+·010	8	...	...	...	...	...	...	...	...	...	22
225	...	...	...	...	...	...	9	...	−·002	...	...	...	+·007	...	...	−·001	23
226	...	...	...	...	...	...	10	...	...	+·005	...	−·003	...	...	...	...	24
227	...	...	+·004	...	...	+·009	11	...	...	...	...	...	...	...	−·004	...	25
228	...	...	...	...	...	...	12	...	...	...	...	...	+·006	...	...	−·002	26
229	...	...	+·003	...	...	...	13	...	...	+·004	...	...	...	...	...	...	27
230	+·003	−·001	...	+·003	...	+·008	14	...	...	...	...	...	...	...	...	...	28
231	...	...	...	...	−·002	...	15	+·003	...	...	+·003	...	+·005	+·003	...	−·003	29
232	...	...	+·002	...	...	...	16	...	−·003	+·003	...	−·004	...	...	...	...	30
233	...	...	...	...	...	+·007	17	...	...	...	...	...	...	...	−·005	...	December. 1
234	...	...	...	...	...	...	18	...	...	+·002	...	...	+·004	...	...	−·004	2
235	...	...	+·001	...	...	...	19	...	...	...	...	...	...	...	...	...	3
236	...	...	...	...	...	+·006	20	...	...	...	...	...	+·003	...	...	−·005	4
237	...	...	...	...	...	...	21	...	...	+·001	...	...	...	...	...	...	5
238	...	...	+·000	...	...	+·005	22	...	−·004	...	...	−·005	...	...	−·006	...	6
239	...	−·002	...	...	−·003	...	23	...	...	...	...	...	+·002	...	...	−·006	7
240	+·002	...	...	...	...	...	24	...	...	+·000	...	...	...	...	...	...	8
241	...	...	−·001	+·002	...	+·004	25	+·002	...	...	+·002	...	...	...	...	...	9
242	...	...	...	...	...	...	26	...	...	...	...	...	+·001	+·002	...	−·007	10
243	...	...	...	...	...	...	27	...	...	−·001	...	...	...	...	...	...	11
244	...	...	−·002	...	...	+·003	28	...	−·005	...	...	−·006	...	...	−·007	−·008	12
245	...	−·003	...	...	−·004	...	29	...	...	...	...	...	+·000	...	...	...	13
246	...	...	−·003	...	...	...	30	...	...	−·002	...	...	...	...	...	...	14

APPENDIX I.

CORRECTIONS FOR SUNRISE FROM 8° TO 12° N. LATITUDE.

Day of Solar year.	Lat. 8° +·003 Long.			Lat. 9° +·010 Long.			Days of Solar months.	Lat. 10° +·007 Long.			Lat. 11° +·009 Long.			Lat. 12° +·002 Long.			English date.
	For Eqn. of time—fraction of a day.	For ☉'s Trop. Long. fraction of a day.	Total Correction—fraction of a day. **Trivandram.**	For Eqn. of time—fraction of a day.	For ☉'s Trop. Long. fraction of a day.	Total Correction—fraction of a day. **Rameswaram.**		For Eqn. of time—fraction of a day.	For ☉'s Trop. Long. fraction of a day.	Total Correction—fraction of a day. **Madura.**	For Eqn. of time—fraction of a day.	For ☉'s Trop. Long. fraction of a day.	Total Correction—fraction of a day. **Tanjore.**	For Eqn. of time—fraction of a day.	For ☉'s Trop. Long. fraction of a day.	Total Correction—fraction of a day. **Maisur.**	
247	+·002	−·003	−·003	+·002	−·004	+·002	*Tamil*, Margali; *Malayalam*, Dhanus; *Bengal*, Pausha. 1	+·002	−·005	−·002	+·002	−·007	−·001	+·002	−·008	−·009	**December.** **15**
248	...	...	...	...	...	...	2	...	−·006	−·003	...	...	...	...	...	...	**16**
249	...	−·004	−·004	...	−·005	+·001	3	...	...	...	...	...	...	...	...	−·010	**17**
250	+·001	...	...	+·001	...	...	4	+·001	...	...	+·001	...	−·002	+·001	...	...	**18**
251	...	...	...	...	...	...	5	...	...	−·004	..	−·008	...	...	−·009	...	**19**
252	...	...	−·005	...	−·006	+·000	6	...	−·007	...	...	...	−·003	...	...	−·011	**20**
253	...	−·005	...	...	...	...	7	...	...	−·005	...	...	...	...	...	...	**21**
254	...	...	−·006	...	...	...	8	...	...	...	...	...	...	...	−·010	−·012	**22**
255	...	...	...	...	...	−·001	9	...	...	...	...	−·009	−·004	...	...	...	**23**
256	...	...	...	...	−·007	...	10	...	−·008	...	...	...	...	...	...	...	**24**
257	...	−·006	...	...	...	...	11	...	..	−·006	...	...	...	...	...	...	**25**
258	...	...	−·007	...	...	...	12	...	...	...	...	...	...	...	−·011	−·013	**26**
259	+·000	...	...	+·000	...	−·002	13	+·000	−·009	...	+·000	−·010	−·005	+·000	...	...	**27**
260	...	...	...	...	−·008	...	14	...	...	...	...	...	...	...	...	...	**28**
261	...	−·007	...	...	...	...	15	...	...	−·007	...	...	...	...	...	...	**29**
262	...	...	−·008	...	...	...	16	...	...	...	...	−·011	...	...	−·012	−·014	**30**
263	...	...	...	...	...	−·003	17	...	−·010	...	...	...	−·006	...	...	...	**31**
264	...	...	...	...	−·009	...	18	...	...	−·008	...	...	...	...	...	...	**1**
265	...	−·008	...	...	...	...	19	...	...	...	...	...	...	...	−·013	...	**2**
266	...	...	−·009	...	...	...	20	...	...	...	...	−·012	...	...	...	...	**3**
267	...	...	...	...	...	−·004	21	...	−·011	...	...	...	−·007	...	...	−·015	**4**
268	−·001	−·009	...	−·001	−·010	...	22	−·001	...	−·009	−·001	...	...	−·001	...	...	**5**
269	...	...	...	...	...	...	23	...	...	...	...	...	...	...	−·014	...	**6**
270	...	...	−·010	...	...	−·005	24	...	...	...	...	−·013	...	...	...	...	**7**
271	...	...	...	...	−·011	...	25	...	−·012	...	...	...	−·008	...	...	−·016	**8**
272	...	−·010	...	...	...	...	26	...	...	−·010	...	...	...	...	...	...	**9**
273	...	...	−·011	...	...	...	27	...	...	...	...	−·014	...	...	−·015	...	**10**
274	...	...	...	...	...	−·006	28	...	...	...	...	...	...	...	...	...	**11**
275	...	...	...	...	...	...	29	...	−·013	...	...	...	−·009	...	...	−·017	**12**
276	...	...	...	...	−·012	...	*Tamil*, Tai; *Malayalam*, Magaram; *Bengal*, Magha. 1	...	...	...	...	...	...	...	...	...	**13**
277	...	−·011	...	...	...	...	2	...	...	−·011	...	...	...	...	...	...	**14**
278	−·002	...	−·012	−·002	...	...	3	−·002	...	...	−·002	...	...	−·002	−·016	...	**January.** **15**
279	...	...	...	...	...	−·007	4	...	...	...	...	−·015	...	...	...	...	**16**
280	...	...	...	...	...	...	5	...	...	...	...	...	−·010	...	...	−·018	**17**
281	...	...	...	...	...	...	6	...	−·014	−·012	...	...	...	...	...	...	**18**
282	...	...	−·013	...	...	...	7	...	..	...	...	...	...	...	...	...	**19**
283	...	...	...	...	−·013	−·008	8	...	...	...	...	...	...	...	...	...	**20**
284	...	−·012	...	...	...	...	9	...	...	...	...	...	−·011	...	...	−·019	**21**
285	...	...	...	...	...	...	10	...	...	...	...	...	−·010	...	...	−·018	**22**
286	...	...	...	...	...	...	11	...	...	...	...	...	...	...	−·017	...	**23**
287	...	...	...	...	...	...	12	...	...	...	...	−·016	...	...	...	...	**24**
288	...	...	...	...	...	...	13	...	−·015	...	...	...	...	...	...	...	**25**
289	...	...	...	...	...	...	14	...	...	...	...	...	...	...	...	...	**26**
290	−·003	...	...	−·003	−·014	−·007	15	−·003	...	...	−·003	...	...	...	...	...	**27**
291	...	−·013	...	...	...	...	16	...	...	...	...	...	...	−·003	...	...	**28**
292	...	...	...	...	...	...	17	...	...	...	...	...	...	...	...	...	**29**
293	...	...	...	...	...	...	18	...	...	...	...	...	...	...	−·018	...	**30**
294	...	...	...	...	...	...	19	...	...	...	...	−·017	...	...	...	−·017	**31**
295	...	...	...	...	...	...	20	...	−·016	−·011	...	...	−·009	...	...	...	**1**
296	...	...	...	...	...	...	21	...	...	...	...	...	...	...	...	...	**2**
297	...	...	...	...	−·015	...	22	...	...	...	...	..	...	...	...	...	**3**
298	...	−·014	...	...	...	...	23	...	...	...	...	...	...	...	...	...	**4**
299	...	...	...	...	...	...	24	...	...	...	...	...	...	...	...	...	**5**
300	...	...	−·012	...	...	...	25	...	...	...	...	...	...	...	...	...	**6**
301	−·004	...	...	...	...	...	26	...	...	...	...	−·018	...	...	−·010	...	**February.** **7**
302	...	...	...	−·004	..	...	27	−·004	−·017	...	−·004	...	...	−·004	...	...	**8**
303	...	...	...	...	...	...	28	...	...	...	...	...	...	...	...	−·016	**9**
304	...	...	...	...	−·016	...	29	...	...	...	...	...	...	...	...	...	**10**
305	...	...	...	...	...	...	30	...	...	...	...	...	−·008	...	...	...	**11**

APPENDIX I.

CORRECTIONS FOR SUNRISE FROM 8° TO 12° N. LATITUDE.

Day of Solar year.	Lat. 8° +·008 Long.			Lat. 9° +·010 Long.			Days of Solar months.	Lat. 10° +·007 Long.			Lat. 11° +·009 Long.			Lat. 12° +·002 Long.			English date.
	For Eqn. of time—fraction of a day.	For ⊙'s Trop. Long. fraction of a day.	Total Correction—fraction of a day. **Trivandram.**	For Eqn. of time—fraction of a day.	For ⊙'s Trop. Long. fraction of a day.	Total Correction—fraction of a day. **Rameswaram.**		For Eqn. of time—fraction of a day.	For ⊙'s Trop. Long. fraction of a day.	Total Correction—fraction of a day. **Madura.**	For Eqn. of time—fraction of a day.	For ⊙'s Trop. Long. fraction of a day.	Total Correction—fraction of a day. **Tanjore.**	For Eqn. of time—fraction of a day.	For ⊙'s Trop. Long. fraction of a day.	Total Correction—fraction of a day. **Maisur.**	
306	-·004	-·014	-·012	-·004	-·015	-·006	1 (*Tamil*, Masi; *Malayalam*, Kumbam; *Bengal*, Phalguna)	-·004	-·016	-·011	-·004	-·018	-·008	-·004	-·019	-·016	**February. 12**
307	...	...	...	...	...	...	2	...	...	-·010	...	-·017	...	...	-·018	...	**13**
308	...	...	...	...	...	...	3	...	...	...	...	...	...	...	...	...	**14**
309	...	...	...	...	...	...	4	...	...	...	...	...	...	...	...	...	**15**
310	...	...	...	...	...	...	5	...	...	...	...	...	...	...	...	-·015	**16**
311	...	...	...	...	...	...	6	...	...	...	...	...	...	...	...	...	**17**
312	...	-·013	...	...	...	...	7	...	...	...	...	...	...	...	-·017	...	**18**
313	...	...	...	...	-·014	...	8	...	-·015	...	...	-·016	-·007	...	...	...	**19**
314	...	...	-·011	...	...	...	9	...	...	...	...	...	...	...	...	...	**20**
315	...	...	...	...	...	...	10	...	...	-·009	...	...	...	...	...	...	**21**
316	...	...	...	...	...	-·005	11	...	...	...	...	...	...	...	...	-·014	**22**
317	...	...	...	...	...	...	12	...	...	...	...	...	-·006	...	-·016	...	**23**
318	...	...	-·010	...	...	...	13	...	...	-·008	...	-·015	...	...	...	-·013	**24**
319	...	...	...	...	...	-·004	14	...	-·014	...	...	...	...	...	...	...	**25**
320	...	...	...	...	-·013	...	15	...	...	...	...	...	-·005	...	...	...	**26**
321	...	-·012	-·009	...	...	...	16	...	...	-·007	...	...	...	...	...	-·012	**27**
322	...	...	...	...	...	-·003	17	...	...	...	...	...	-·004	...	...	...	**28**
323	-·005	...	...	...	...	...	18	...	...	...	...	...	...	...	-·015	...	**March. 1**
324	...	...	...	-·005	...	...	19	...	...	-·006	...	-·014	...	...	...	-·011	**2**
325	...	...	-·008	...	...	-·002	20	-·005	-·013	...	...	...	-·003	...	...	...	**3**
326	...	...	...	...	...	...	21	...	...	...	-·005	...	...	-·005	...	-·010	**4**
327	...	...	...	...	-·012	...	22	...	...	-·005	...	...	...	...	...	...	**5**
328	...	...	-·007	...	...	-·001	23	...	...	...	...	...	-·002	...	-·014	...	**6**
329	...	-·011	...	...	...	...	24	...	...	-·004	...	...	...	...	...	-·009	**7**
330	...	...	...	...	...	...	25	...	...	...	...	-·013	-·001	...	...	...	**8**
331	...	...	-·006	...	...	-·000	26	...	-·012	...	...	...	...	...	...	-·008	**9**
332	...	...	...	...	...	...	27	...	...	-·003	...	...	...	...	...	...	**10**
333	...	...	...	...	...	...	28	...	...	...	...	...	-·000	...	-·013	...	**11**
334	...	...	-·005	...	-·011	+·001	29	...	...	...	...	...	...	...	...	-·007	**12**
335	...	...	...	...	...	...	30	...	...	-·002	...	-·012	...	...	...	...	**13**
336	...	-·010	...	...	...	+·002	1 (*Tamil*, Panguni; *Malayalam*, Mînam; *Bengal*, Chaitra)	...	-·011	...	...	...	+·001	...	...	-·006	**14**
337	...	...	-·004	...	-·010	...	2	...	...	...	...	...	...	...	-·012	...	**15**
338	...	...	...	...	...	...	3	...	...	-·001	...	-·011	+·002	...	...	-·005	**16**
339	...	-·009	...	...	...	+·003	4	...	-·010	...	...	...	...	...	-·011	...	**17**
340	...	...	-·003	...	-·009	...	5	...	...	-·000	...	-·010	...	...	...	...	**18**
341	...	...	...	...	...	...	6	...	-·009	...	...	...	+·003	...	-·010	-·004	**19**
342	...	-·008	...	...	...	+·004	7	...	...	...	...	...	...	...	...	...	**20**
343	...	...	-·002	...	-·008	...	8	...	...	+·001	...	-·009	+·004	...	...	-·003	**21**
344	...	-·007	...	...	...	...	9	...	-·008	...	...	...	...	...	-·009	...	**22**
345	...	...	...	...	-·007	+·005	10	...	...	+·002	...	-·008	+·005	...	...	-·002	**23**
346	...	...	-·001	...	...	...	11	...	...	...	...	...	...	...	-·008	...	**24**
347	...	-·006	...	...	...	+·006	12	...	-·007	...	...	-·007	...	...	...	...	**25**
348	...	...	...	...	-·006	...	13	...	...	+·003	...	...	+·006	...	-·007	-·001	**26**
349	...	...	-·000	...	...	...	14	...	-·006	...	...	...	...	...	...	...	**27**
350	...	-·005	...	...	...	+·007	15	...	...	+·004	...	-·006	+·007	...	...	-·000	**28**
351	...	...	+·001	...	-·005	...	16	...	...	...	...	...	...	...	-·006	...	**29**
352	...	...	...	...	...	...	17	...	-·005	...	...	-·005	...	...	...	+·001	**30**
353	...	-·004	...	...	-·004	+·008	18	...	...	+·005	...	...	+·008	...	-·005	...	**31**
354	...	...	+·002	...	...	...	19	...	-·004	...	...	...	...	...	...	...	**April. 1**
355	...	...	...	...	...	...	20	...	...	...	...	-·004	+·009	...	-·004	+·002	**2**
356	...	-·003	...	...	-·003	+·009	21	...	...	+·006	...	...	...	...	...	...	**3**
357	...	...	+·003	...	...	...	22	...	-·003	...	...	-·003	...	...	-·003	+·003	**4**
358	...	-·002	...	...	...	+·010	23	...	...	+·007	...	...	+·010	...	...	...	**5**
359	...	...	...	...	-·002	...	24	...	-·002	...	...	-·002	...	...	...	+·004	**6**
360	...	...	+·004	...	...	...	25	...	...	...	...	...	+·011	...	-·002	...	**7**
361	...	-·001	...	...	-·001	+·011	26	...	...	+·008	...	...	...	...	...	...	**8**
362	...	...	...	...	...	...	27	...	-·001	...	...	-·001	...	...	-·001	+·005	**9**
363	...	...	+·005	...	...	...	28	...	...	+·009	...	...	+·012	...	...	...	**10**
364	...	-·000	...	...	-·000	+·012	29	...	-·000	...	...	-·000	...	...	-·000	+·006	**11**
365	...	...	...	...	...	...	30	...	...	...	...	...	+·013	...	...	...	**12**

APPENDIX I.

CORRECTIONS FOR SUNRISE FROM 13° TO 17° N. LATITUDE.

Day of Solar year.	Lat. 13° +·012 Long.			Lat. 14° +·012 Long.			Days of Solar months.	Lat. 15° +·002 Long.			Lat. 16° −·003 Long.			Lat. 17° +·008 Long.			English date.
	For Eqn. of time—fraction of a day.	For ☉'s Trop. Long. fraction of a day.	Total Correction—fraction of a day. **Madras.**	For Eqn. of time—fraction of a day.	For ☉'s Trop. Long. fraction of a day.	Total Correction—fraction of a day. **Nellore.**		For Eqn. of time—fraction of a day.	For ☉'s Trop. Long. fraction of a day.	Total Correction—fraction of a day. **Vijayanagar** (now Hampi, Bellary District).	For Eqn. of time—fraction of a day.	For ☉'s Trop. Long. fraction of a day.	Total Correction—fraction of a day. **Belgaum.**	For Eqn. of time—fraction of a day.	For ☉'s Trop. Long. fraction of a day.	Total Correction—fraction of a day. **Hyderabad.**	
– 1	− ·005	+·000	+·017	− ·005	+·000	+·017	1 (*Tamil,* Chittirai; *Malayalam,* Medam; *Bengal,* Vaisakha.)	− ·005	+·000	+·008	− ·005	+·001	+·002	− ·005	+·001	+·014	**April.** 13
2	...	+·001	...	...	+·001	...	2	...	+·001	...	...	...	+·003	...	...	+·015	14
3	...	...	+·018	...	...	+·018	3	...	...	+·009	...	+·002	+·004	...	+·002	...	15
4	...	+·002	...	...	+·002	...	4	...	+·002	...	...	...	...	...	...	+·016	16
5	..	...	+·019	...	...	+·019	5	...	...	+·010	...	+·003	+·005	...	+·003	...	17
6	...	+·003	...	...	+·003	...	6	...	+·003	...	...	...	...	...	...	+·017	18
7	...	...	+·020	...	...	+·020	7	...	...	+·011	...	+·004	+·006	...	+·004	...	19
8	...	+·004	...	...	+·004	...	8	...	+·004	...	...	...	...	...	...	+·018	20
9	...	...	+·021	...	...	+·021	9	...	...	+·012	...	+·005	+·007	...	+·005	...	21
–10	...	...	...	...	+·005	...	10	...	+·005	...	...	...	...	...	...	+·019	22
11	...	+·005	+·022	...	...	...	11	...	...	+·013	...	+·006	+·008	...	+·006	...	23
12	...	...	...	...	+·006	+·022	12	...	+·006	...	...	...	...	− ·004	...	+·020	24
13	...	+·006	...	...	...	...	13	...	...	...	...	+·007	...	...	+·007	...	25
14	...	...	...	...	+·007	...	14	...	+·007	...	− ·004	...	+·009	...	+·008	...	26
15	...	+·007	...	...	...	+·023	15	− ·004	...	+·014	...	+·008	...	...	...	+·021	27
16	...	...	+·023	− ·004	+·008	...	16	...	+·008	...	...	...	...	...	+·009	...	28
17	− ·004	+·008	...	...	...	...	17	...	...	...	...	+·009	...	...	...	...	29
18	...	...	...	...	+·009	...	18	...	+·009	...	...	...	+·010	...	+·010	+·022	30
19	...	+·009	...	...	...	+·024	19	...	...	+·015	...	+·010	...	...	...	...	1
–20	...	...	+·024	...	...	...	20	...	+·010	...	...	...	...	...	+·011	...	2
21	...	...	...	...	+·010	...	21	...	...	...	...	+·011	+·011	...	...	...	3
22	...	+·010	...	...	...	...	22	...	+·011	+·016	...	...	...	...	+·012	+·023	4
23	...	...	...	...	+·011	+·025	23	...	...	...	...	+·012	...	...	...	...	5
24	...	+·011	+·025	...	...	...	24	...	+·012	...	...	...	...	...	+·013	...	6
25	...	...	...	...	+·012	...	25	...	...	...	...	+·013	+·012	...	...	+·024	7
26	...	+·012	...	...	...	...	26	...	+·013	+·017	...	...	...	...	+·014	...	8
27	...	...	...	...	+·013	+·026	27	...	...	...	...	+·014	...	...	...	...	9
28	...	+·013	+·026	...	...	...	28	...	+·014	...	...	...	+·013	...	+·015	+·025	10
29	...	...	...	...	+·014	...	29	...	...	...	...	+·015	...	...	+·016	...	11
–30	...	+·014	...	...	...	...	30	...	+·015	+·018	...	...	...	...	...	...	12
31	...	...	...	...	...	+·027	31	...	...	...	...	+·016	...	...	...	...	13
32	...	...	+·027	...	+·015	...	1 (*Tamil,* Vaikasi; *Malayalam,* Edavam; *Bengal,* Jyeshtha.)	...	...	...	...	...	+·014	...	+·017	+·026	**May.** 14
33	...	...	...	...	...	...	2	...	+·016	...	...	...	...	...	...	...	15
34	...	...	...	...	...	...	3	...	...	+·019	...	...	...	...	...	...	16
35	...	+·015	...	...	...	+·028	4	...	...	...	...	+·017	+·015	...	...	...	17
36	...	...	+·028	...	+·016	...	5	...	...	...	...	...	...	...	+·018	+·027	18
37	...	...	...	...	...	...	6	...	+·017	+·020	...	...	...	...	...	...	19
38	...	...	...	...	...	...	7	...	...	...	...	+·018	+·016	...	...	+·028	20
39	...	...	...	.	...	+·029	8	...	...	...	...	...	...	...	+·019	...	21
–40	...	+·016	+·029	...	...	...	9	...	...	+·021	...	...	...	...	...	...	22
41	...	...	...	...	+·017	...	10	− ·003	+·018	...	− ·003	...	+·017	− ·003	...	+·029	23
42	− ·003	...	...	− ·003	...	...	11	...	...	...	...	+·019	...	...	...	...	24
43	...	...	...	...	...	...	12	...	...	...	...	...	+·016	...	+·020	...	25
44	...	+·017	...	...	...	...	13	...	...	...	...	...	...	...	...	...	26
45	...	...	...	...	+·018	...	14	...	+·019	...	...	...	...	...	...	...	27
46	...	...	...	...	...	...	15	...	...	...	...	+·020	...	...	...	...	28
47	...	...	...	...	...	...	16	...	...	...	...	...	...	...	+·021	...	29
48	...	...	...	...	...	...	17	...	...	...	...	...	...	...	...	...	30
49	...	+·018	...	...	+·019	...	18	...	+·020	...	...	...	...	...	...	...	31
–50	...	...	...	...	...	...	19	...	...	...	...	+·021	...	...	+·022	...	1
51	...	...	...	...	...	...	20	...	...	...	...	...	...	...	...	+·028	2
52	...	...	+·028	...	...	...	21	...	...	...	...	...	...	...	...	...	**June.** 3
53	...	...	...	...	...	...	22	...	...	+·020	...	...	...	− ·002	...	...	4
54	− ·002	+·019	...	− ·002	+·020	...	23	− ·002	+·021	...	− ·002	+·022	...	...	+·023	...	5
55	...	...	...	...	...	...	24	...	...	...	...	...	...	...	...	...	6
56	...	...	...	...	...	...	25	...	...	...	...	...	...	...	...	...	7
57	...	...	...	...	...	...	26	...	...	...	...	...	...	...	+·024	...	8
58	...	...	...	...	+·021	...	27	...	+·022	...	...	+·023	...	...	...	...	9
59	...	+·020	...	...	...	...	28	...	...	...	...	...	...	...	...	...	10
–60	...	...	...	...	...	...	29	...	...	...	...	...	...	...	...	...	11
61	...	...	...	...	...	...	30	...	...	...	...	...	...	...	+·025	...	12
62	...	...	...	...	...	+·028	31	...	...	...	...	...	...	...	...	...	13

APPENDIX I.

CORRECTIONS FOR SUNRISE FROM 13° TO 17° N. LATITUDE.

Day of Solar year.	Lat. 13° +·012 Long.			Lat. 14° +·012 Long.			Solar months	Days of Solar months.	Lat. 15° +·002 Long.			Lat. 16° −·003 Long.			Lat. 17° +·008 Long.			English month	English date.
	For Eqn. of time—fraction of a day.	For ⊙'s Trop. Long. fraction of a day.	Total Correction—fraction of a day. **Madras.**	For Eqn. of time—fraction of a day.	For ⊙'s Trop. Long. fraction of a day.	Total Correction—fraction of a day. **Nellore.**			For Eqn. of time—fraction of a day.	For ⊙'s Trop. Long. fraction of a day.	Total Correction—fraction of a day. **Vijayanagar** (now Hampi, Bellary District).	For Eqn. of time—fraction of a day.	For ⊙'s Trop. Long. fraction of a day.	Total Correction—fraction of a day. **Belgaum.**	For Eqn. of time—fraction of a day.	For ⊙'s Trop. Long. fraction of a day.	Total Correction—fraction of a day. **Hyderabad.**		
63	−·002	+·020	+·028	−·002	+·021	+·028	*Tamil*, Ani; *Malayalam*, Mithunam; *Bengal*, Ashadha.	1	−·002	+·022	+·020	−·002	+·023	+·016	−·002	+·024	+·028	June.	14
64	...	...	...	...	...	...		2	...	...	...	...	...	...	...	...	...		15
65	...	...	...	...	...	...		3	...	...	...	...	...	...	...	...	...		16
66	...	+·019	...	...	...	...		4	...	...	...	...	...	...	...	...	...		17
67	−·001	...	...	−·001	+·020	...		5	−·001	...	...	−·001	...	...	−·001	...	...		18
68	...	...	...	...	...	...		6	...	...	...	...	...	...	...	...	...		19
69	...	...	...	...	...	...		7	...	...	...	...	...	...	...	...	...		20
70	...	...	...	...	...	...		8	...	+·021	...	...	...	...	...	...	...		21
71	...	...	...	...	...	...		9	...	...	...	...	+·022	...	...	...	...		22
72	...	...	...	...	...	...		10	...	...	...	...	...	...	...	...	...		23
73	...	...	+·027	...	...	...		11	...	...	...	...	...	+·015	...	+·023	...		24
74	...	+·018	...	...	...	...		12	...	...	+·019	...	...	...	...	...	...		25
75	...	...	...	...	...	...		13	...	...	...	...	...	...	...	...	+·027		26
76	−·000	...	...	−·000	+·019	+·027		14	−·000	...	...	−·000	...	...	−·000	...	...		27
77	...	...	...	...	...	...		15	...	...	...	...	...	...	...	...	...		28
78	...	...	+·026	...	...	...		16	...	...	...	...	...	+·014	...	...	...		29
79	...	...	...	...	...	...		17	...	+·020	+·018	...	...	...	...	...	...		30
80	...	...	...	...	...	...		18	...	...	...	...	...	...	...	...	+·026	July.	1
81	...	...	...	...	...	+·026		19	...	...	...	...	+·021	...	...	...	...		2
82	...	+·017	...	...	...	...		20	...	...	...	...	...	...	...	...	...		3
83	...	...	...	...	...	...		21	...	...	...	...	...	...	...	+·022	...		4
84	...	...	+·025	...	...	...		22	...	...	...	...	...	+·013	...	...	...		5
85	...	...	...	...	+·018	...		23	...	...	+·017	...	...	...	...	...	+·025		6
86	+·001	...	...	+·001	...	...		24	+·001	...	...	+·001	...	...	+·001	...	...		7
87	...	...	...	...	...	+·025		25	...	...	...	...	...	...	...	...	...		8
88	...	...	...	...	...	...		26	...	+·019	...	...	...	...	...	...	...		9
89	...	...	...	...	...	...		27	...	...	...	...	...	+·012	...	...	...		10
90	...	+·016	+·024	...	...	...		28	...	...	+·016	...	+·020	...	...	...	+·024		11
91	...	...	...	...	...	...		29	...	...	...	...	...	...	...	...	...		12
92	...	...	...	...	+·017	...		30	...	...	...	...	...	...	...	+·021	...		13
93	...	...	...	...	...	+·024		31	...	+·018	...	...	...	...	...	...	...		14
94	+·002	+·015	...	+·002	...	...		32	+·002	...	...	+·002	+·019	+·011	+·002	...	...		15
95	...	...	...	...	...	...	*Tamil* Adi; *Malayalam*, Karkatagam; *Bengal*, Sravana.	1	...	...	...	...	...	...	...	+·020	+·023		16
96	...	...	+·023	...	+·016	...		2	...	...	+·015	...	...	...	...	...	...		17
97	...	...	...	...	...	...		3	...	+·017	...	...	...	...	...	...	...		18
98	...	+·014	...	...	...	...		4	...	...	...	...	+·018	...	...	...	...		19
99	...	...	...	...	+·015	+·023		5	...	...	...	...	...	...	...	+·019	...		20
100	...	...	...	...	...	...		6	...	+·016	...	...	...	+·010	...	...	+·022		21
101	...	...	...	...	...	...		7	...	...	...	...	+·017	...	...	...	...		22
102	...	+·013	+·022	...	+·014	...		8	...	...	+·014	...	...	...	...	+·018	...		23
103	+·003	...	...	+·003	...	...		9	+·003	...	...	+·003	...	...	+·003	...	...		24
104	...	...	...	...	...	...		10	...	+·015	...	...	+·016	...	...	...	...		25
105	...	+·012	...	...	...	+·022		11	...	...	...	...	...	...	...	+·017	...		26
106	...	...	...	...	+·013	...		12	...	...	...	...	...	+·009	...	...	+·021		27
107	...	...	...	...	...	...		13	...	+·014	...	...	...	...	...	...	...		28
108	...	...	...	...	...	...		14	...	...	...	...	+·015	...	...	+·016	...		29
109	...	+·011	...	...	+·012	...		15	...	...	+·013	...	...	...	...	...	...		30
110	...	...	...	...	...	...		16	...	+·013	...	...	...	...	...	...	...		31
111	...	...	...	...	...	...		17	...	...	...	...	+·014	...	...	...	...	August.	1
112	...	+·010	+·021	...	...	...		18	...	...	...	...	...	+·008	...	+·015	+·020		2
113	+·004	...	...	+·004	+·011	...		19	+·004	...	...	+·004	...	...	+·004	...	...		3
114	...	...	...	...	...	+·021		20	...	+·012	...	...	+·013	...	...	...	...		4
115	...	...	...	...	...	...		21	...	...	...	...	...	...	...	+·014	...		5
116	...	+·009	...	...	+·010	...		22	...	...	+·012	...	...	...	...	...	...		6
117	...	...	...	...	...	...		23	...	+·011	...	...	+·012	...	...	...	...		7
118	...	...	...	...	...	...		24	...	...	...	...	...	...	...	+·013	+·019		8
119	...	+·008	...	...	...	...		25	...	...	...	...	...	+·007	...	...	...		9
120	...	...	...	...	+·009	...		26	...	...	...	...	...	...	...	...	...		10
121	...	...	+·020	...	...	+·020		27	...	+·010	...	...	+·011	...	...	+·012	...		11
122	...	...	...	...	...	...		28	...	...	+·011	...	...	...	...	...	...		12
123	...	+·007	...	...	+·008	...		29	...	...	...	...	...	...	...	...	+·018		13
124	...	...	...	...	...	...		30	...	+·009	...	...	+·010	+·006	+·005	...	...		14
125	...	...	...	+·005	...	...		31	+·005	...	...	+·005	...	...	...	+·011	...		15

APPENDIX I.

CORRECTIONS FOR SUNRISE FROM 13° TO 17° N. LATITUDE.

Day of Solar year.	Lat. 13° +·012 Long.			Lat. 14° +·012 Long.			Days of Solar months.	Lat. 15° +·002 Long.			Lat. 16° −·003 Long.			Lat. 17° +·008 Long.			English date.
	For Eqn. of time—fraction of a day.	For ⊙'s Trop. Long. fraction of a day.	Total Correction—fraction of a day. **Madras.**	For Eqn. of time—fraction of a day.	For ⊙'s Trop. Long. fraction of a day.	Total Correction—fraction of a day. **Nellore.**		For Eqn. of time—fraction of a day.	For ⊙'s Trop. Long. fraction of a day.	Total Correction—fraction of a day. **Vijayanagar** (now Hampi, Bellary District).	For Eqn. of time—fraction of a day.	For ⊙'s Trop. Long. fraction of a day.	Total Correction—fraction of a day. **Belgaum.**	For Eqn. of time—fraction of a day.	For ⊙'s Trop. Long. fraction of a day.	Total Correction—fraction of a day. **Hyderabad.**	
126	+·005	+·007	+·020	+·005	+·008	+·020	1 (*Tamil*, Avani; *Malayalam*, Chingam; *Bengal*, Bhadrapada.)	+·005	+·009	+·011	+·005	+·010	+·006	+·005	+·011	+·018	**August.** 16
127	...	...	...	...	...	...	2	...	...	...	...	...	...	...	...	...	17
128	...	+·006	...	...	+·007	...	3	...	+·008	...	...	+·009	...	...	...	+·017	18
129	...	...	+·019	...	...	+·019	4	...	...	+·010	...	...	...	...	+·010	...	19
130	...	...	...	...	...	...	5	...	...	...	...	...	+·005	...	...	...	20
131	...	...	...	...	...	...	6	...	...	...	...	...	...	...	...	...	21
132	...	...	...	...	...	...	7	...	...	...	...	+·008	...	...	+·009	...	22
133	...	+·005	...	...	+·006	...	8	...	+·007	...	...	...	...	...	...	...	23
134	...	...	...	...	...	...	9	...	...	...	...	...	...	...	...	...	24
135	...	...	...	...	...	...	10	...	...	...	...	...	...	...	...	...	25
136	...	...	...	...	...	...	11	...	...	...	...	+·007	...	...	+·008	+·016	26
137	...	...	...	...	+·005	...	12	...	+·006	...	...	...	...	...	...	...	27
138	...	+·004	...	...	...	...	13	...	...	...	+·006	...	...	+·006	...	...	28
139	...	...	...	+·006	...	...	14	+·006	...	...	...	...	...	...	...	...	29
140	+·006	...	...	...	...	...	15	...	...	...	...	+·006	...	...	+·007	...	30
141	...	...	...	...	...	...	16	...	+·005	...	...	...	...	...	...	...	31
142	...	...	...	...	+·004	...	17	...	...	...	...	...	...	...	...	...	1
143	...	+·003	...	...	...	...	18	...	...	...	...	...	...	...	+·006	...	2
144	...	...	...	...	...	...	19	...	...	...	...	+·005	+·004	...	...	...	3
145	...	...	...	...	...	...	20	...	+·004	+·009	...	...	...	...	...	...	4
146	...	...	...	...	...	...	21	...	...	...	...	...	...	...	...	...	5
147	...	...	...	...	+·003	...	22	...	...	...	...	...	...	...	+·005	...	6
148	...	+·002	...	...	...	...	23	...	...	...	...	+·004	...	...	...	...	7
149	...	...	...	...	...	...	24	...	...	...	...	...	...	...	...	+·015	8
150	...	...	...	...	...	...	25	...	+·003	...	...	...	...	...	...	...	9
151	...	...	...	...	+·002	...	26	...	...	...	...	...	...	...	+·004	...	10
152	...	...	...	...	...	+·018	27	...	...	...	...	+·003	...	...	...	...	11
153	...	...	...	...	...	...	28	...	...	...	...	...	...	...	...	...	12
154	...	+·001	...	...	...	...	29	...	...	...	...	...	...	...	...	...	13
155	...	...	...	...	...	...	30	...	...	...	...	...	...	...	...	...	14
156	...	...	...	...	...	...	31	...	+·002	...	...	...	+·003	...	...	...	15
157	...	...	...	...	...	...	1 (*Tamil*, Purattasi; *Malayalam*, Kanni; *Bengal*, Asvina.)	...	...	...	...	...	...	...	+·003	+·014	16
158	...	...	...	...	...	...	2	...	...	+·008	...	...	...	...	...	...	17
159	...	...	...	...	...	...	3	...	...	...	...	...	...	...	...	...	18
160	...	...	...	...	...	...	4	...	...	...	...	...	...	...	...	...	19
161	...	...	...	...	...	...	5	...	...	...	...	+·002	...	...	...	...	20
162	...	...	...	...	+·001	...	6	...	...	...	...	...	...	...	...	...	21
163	...	...	+·018	...	...	...	7	...	...	...	...	...	...	...	...	...	22
164	...	...	...	...	...	...	8	...	...	...	...	...	...	...	+·002	...	23
165	...	...	...	...	...	...	9	...	...	...	...	...	...	...	...	...	24
166	...	...	...	...	...	...	10	...	...	...	...	...	+·002	...	...	+·013	25
167	...	...	...	...	...	...	11	...	+·001	...	...	...	...	...	...	...	26
168	...	...	...	...	...	+·017	12	...	...	...	...	...	...	...	...	...	27
169	...	...	...	...	...	...	13	...	...	...	...	...	...	...	...	...	28
170	...	...	...	...	...	...	14	...	...	...	...	+·001	...	...	...	...	29
171	...	...	...	...	...	...	15	...	...	+·007	...	...	...	...	...	...	30
172	...	...	...	...	...	...	16	...	...	...	...	...	...	...	+·001	...	**October.** 1
173	...	...	...	...	...	...	17	...	...	...	...	...	...	...	...	+·012	2
174	...	+·000	...	...	...	...	18	...	...	...	...	...	...	...	...	...	3
175	...	...	...	...	...	...	19	...	...	...	...	...	+·001	...	...	...	4
176	...	...	...	...	+·000	...	20	...	...	...	...	...	...	...	...	...	5
177	...	...	...	...	...	...	21	...	...	...	...	...	...	...	...	...	6
178	...	...	...	...	...	...	22	...	+·000	...	...	...	...	...	...	...	7
179	...	...	...	...	...	...	23	...	...	...	...	+·000	...	...	...	...	8
180	...	...	...	...	...	...	24	...	...	...	...	...	...	...	+·000	+·011	9
181	...	...	...	...	...	+·016	25	...	...	+·006	...	...	...	...	...	...	10
182	...	...	+·017	...	...	...	26	...	...	...	...	...	...	...	...	...	11
183	...	...	...	...	...	...	27	...	...	...	...	...	+·000	...	...	...	12
184	...	...	...	...	...	...	28	...	...	...	...	...	...	...	...	...	13
185	...	...	...	...	...	...	29	...	...	...	...	...	...	...	...	...	14
186	...	...	...	...	...	...	30	...	...	...	...	...	...	...	...	...	15

APPENDIX I.

CORRECTIONS FOR SUNRISE FROM 13° TO 17° N. LATITUDE.

Day of Solar year.	Lat. 13° +·012 Long. For Eqn. of time—fraction of a day.	Lat. 13° For ☉'s Trop. Long, fraction of a day.	Lat. 13° Total Correction—fraction of a day. **Madras.**	Lat. 14° +·012 Long. For Eqn. of time—fraction of a day.	Lat. 14° For ☉'s Trop. Long. fraction of a day.	Lat. 14° Total Correction—fraction of a day. **Nellore.**	Days of Solar months.	Lat. 15° +·002 Long. For Eqn. of time—fraction of a day.	Lat. 15° For ☉'s Trop. Long. fraction of a day.	Lat. 15° Total Correction—fraction of a day. **Vijayanagar** (now Hampi, Bellary District).	Lat. 16° −·003 Long. For Eqn. of time—fraction of a day.	Lat. 16° For ☉'s Trop. Long. fraction of a day.	Lat. 16° Total Correction—fraction of a day. **Belgaum.**	Lat. 17° +·008 Long. For Eqn. of time—fraction of a day.	Lat. 17° For ☉'s Trop. Long. fraction of a day.	Lat. 17° Total Correction—fraction of a day. **Hyderabad.**	English date.
187	+·006	+·000	+·017	+·006	+·000	+·016	1 (*Tamil*, Aippasi; *Malayalam*, Tulam; *Bengal*, Karttika.)	+·006	+·000	+·006	+·006	+·000	+·000	+·006	−·001	+·010	16 (**October.**)
188	...	...	...	...	...	...	2	...	...	...	...	−·001	...	...	...	...	17
189	...	...	...	...	...	...	3	...	−·001	+·005	...	...	...	...	...	...	18
190	...	...	...	...	−·001	...	4	...	...	...	...	...	−·001	...	...	...	19
191	...	...	...	...	...	+·015	5	...	...	...	...	...	...	...	...	...	20
192	...	...	...	...	...	...	6	...	...	...	...	...	...	...	...	...	21
193	...	−·001	...	...	...	...	7	...	...	...	...	...	...	...	...	+·009	22
194	...	...	+·016	...	...	...	8	...	...	...	...	...	...	...	...	...	23
195	...	...	...	...	...	...	9	...	...	+·004	...	...	−·002	...	−·002	...	24
196	...	...	...	...	...	+·014	10	...	...	...	...	...	...	...	...	+·008	25
197	...	...	...	...	...	...	11	...	...	...	...	−·002	...	...	...	...	26
198	...	...	+·015	...	...	...	12	...	...	...	...	...	...	...	...	...	27
199	...	...	...	...	...	...	13	...	−·002	+·003	...	...	−·003	...	...	...	28
200	+·005	...	...	...	...	+·013	14	...	...	...	...	...	...	...	...	+·007	29
201	...	...	...	+·005	...	...	15	+·005	...	...	...	...	...	...	...	...	30
202	...	...	+·014	...	...	...	16	...	...	+·002	+·005	...	−·004	...	−·003	...	31
203	...	...	...	...	...	...	17	...	...	...	...	...	...	+·005	...	+·006	1 (**November.**)
204	...	...	...	...	−·002	+·012	18	...	...	...	...	...	...	...	...	...	2
205	...	...	...	...	...	...	19	...	...	...	...	−·003	−·005	...	...	...	3
206	...	...	+·013	...	...	...	20	...	...	+·001	...	...	...	...	...	+·005	4
207	...	...	...	...	...	...	21	...	...	...	...	...	...	...	...	...	5
208	...	...	...	...	...	+·011	22	...	...	...	...	...	...	...	...	...	6
209	...	...	...	...	...	...	23	...	...	+·000	...	...	−·006	...	−·004	+·004	7
210	...	...	+·012	...	...	...	24	...	−·003	...	...	...	...	...	...	...	8
211	...	...	...	...	...	+·010	25	...	...	...	...	...	...	...	...	...	9
212	...	...	...	...	...	...	26	...	...	−·001	...	...	−·007	...	...	+·003	10
213	...	−·002	...	...	...	...	27	...	...	...	...	...	...	...	...	...	11
214	...	...	...	...	...	...	28	...	...	...	...	−·004	...	...	...	...	12
215	...	...	+·011	...	−·003	...	29	...	...	...	...	...	−·008	...	−·005	+·002	13
216	...	...	...	...	...	+·009	30	...	−·004	−·002	...	...	...	...	...	...	14
217	...	...	...	...	...	...	1 (*Tamil*, Kartigai; *Malayalam*, Vrischikam; *Bengal*, Margasira.)	...	...	...	...	...	...	...	...	...	15
218	...	−·003	+·010	...	...	...	2	...	...	...	...	−·005	−·009	...	...	+·001	16
219	+·004	...	...	...	−·004	+·008	3	...	...	−·003	...	...	...	...	−·006	...	17
220	...	...	...	+·004	...	...	4	+·004	−·005	...	+·004	...	...	...	...	...	18
221	...	...	...	...	...	...	5	...	...	...	...	...	−·010	+·004	...	+·000	19
222	...	...	+·009	...	...	+·007	6	...	...	...	...	−·006	...	...	...	...	20
223	...	−·004	...	...	...	...	7	...	...	−·004	...	...	...	...	−·007	...	21
224	...	...	...	...	−·005	...	8	...	...	...	...	...	−·011	...	...	−·001	22
225	...	...	+·008	...	...	+·006	9	...	−·006	−·005	...	...	...	...	...	...	23
226	...	...	...	...	...	...	10	...	...	...	...	−·007	...	...	−·008	−·002	24
227	...	...	+·007	...	...	...	11	...	...	...	...	...	−·012	...	...	...	25
228	...	−·005	...	...	...	+·005	12	...	...	−·006	...	...	...	...	...	...	26
229	...	...	...	...	−·006	...	13	...	−·007	...	...	...	−·013	...	...	−·003	27
230	...	...	+·006	...	...	+·004	14	...	...	...	...	−·008	...	...	−·009	...	28
231	+·003	...	...	+·003	...	...	15	+·003	...	−·007	+·003	...	...	...	...	−·004	29
232	...	...	...	...	...	...	16	...	...	...	...	...	−·014	+·003	...	...	30
233	...	−·006	+·005	...	−·007	+·003	17	...	−·008	−·008	...	...	...	...	...	...	1 (**December.**)
234	...	...	...	...	...	...	18	...	...	...	...	−·009	−·015	...	−·010	−·005	2
235	...	...	+·004	...	...	...	19	...	...	...	...	...	...	...	...	...	3
236	...	...	...	...	...	+·002	20	...	...	−·009	...	...	...	...	...	−·006	4
237	...	...	...	...	...	...	21	...	−·009	...	...	...	−·016	...	−·011	...	5
238	...	−·007	+·003	...	−·008	+·001	22	...	...	−·010	...	−·010	...	...	...	...	6
239	...	...	...	...	...	...	23	...	...	...	...	...	−·017	...	...	−·007	7
240	...	...	...	...	...	...	24	...	...	...	...	...	...	...	...	...	8
241	+·002	...	+·002	+·002	...	+·000	25	+·002	...	−·011	+·002	...	...	+·002	−·012	−·008	9
242	...	...	...	...	...	...	26	...	−·010	...	...	−·011	−·018	...	...	...	10
243	...	−·008	+·001	...	−·009	−·001	27	...	...	−·012	...	...	...	...	...	...	11
244	...	...	...	...	...	...	28	...	...	...	...	...	−·019	...	...	−·009	12
245	...	...	...	...	...	...	29	...	...	...	...	−·012	...	...	−·013	...	13
246	...	...	+·000	...	−·010	−·002	30	...	−·011	−·013	...	...	...	...	...	−·010	14

APPENDIX I.

CORRECTIONS FOR SUNRISE FROM 13° TO 17° N. LATITUDE.

Day of Solar year.	Lat. 13° +·012 Long. For Eqn. of time—fraction of a day.	For ☉'s Trop. Long fraction of a day.	Total Correction—fraction of a day. **Madras.**	Lat. 14° +·012 Long. For Eqn. of time—fraction of a day.	For ☉'s Trop. Long. fraction of a day.	Total Correction—fraction of a day. **Nellore.**	Days of Solar months.	Lat. 15° +·002 Long. For Eqn. of time—fraction of a day.	For ☉'s Trop. Long. fraction of a day.	Total Correction—fraction of a day. **Vijayanagar** (now Hampi, Bellary District).	Lat. 16° -·008 Long. For Eqn. of time—fraction of a day.	For ☉'s Trop. Long fraction of a day.	Total Correction—fraction of a day. **Belgaum.**	Lat. 17° +·008 Long. For Eqn. of time—fraction of a day.	For ☉'s Trop. Long. fraction of a day.	Total Correction—fraction of a day. **Hyderabad.**	English date.
247	+·002	-·009	+·000	+·002	-·010	-·002	1 *Tamil*, Margali; *Malayalam*, Dhanus; *Bengal*, Pausha.	+·002	-·011	-·013	+·002	-·012	-·020	+·002	-·013	-·010	**December. 15**
248	...	...	...	...	...	-·003	2	...	...	-·014	...	...	...	...	-·014	-·011	**16**
249	...	...	-·001	...	...	...	3	...	-·012	...	...	-·013	-·021	...	...	...	**17**
250	...	-·010	...	...	-·011	...	4	...	...	...	...	...	...	...	...	...	**18**
251	+·001	...	-·002	+·001	...	-·004	5	+·001	...	-·015	+·001	...	-·022	+·001	-·015	-·012	**19**
252	...	...	...	...	...	...	6	...	-·013	...	...	-·014	...	...	...	...	**20**
253	...	...	...	...	-·012	-·005	7	...	...	-·016	...	...	...	...	...	-·013	**21**
254	...	-·011	-·003	...	...	...	8	...	...	...	...	...	-·023	...	-·016	...	**22**
255	...	...	...	...	...	...	9	...	...	...	...	-·015	...	...	...	...	**23**
256	...	...	...	...	...	...	10	...	-·014	-·017	...	...	...	...	...	-·014	**24**
257	...	-·012	-·004	...	-·013	-·006	11	...	...	...	...	...	...	...	...	...	**25**
258	...	...	...	...	...	...	12	...	...	...	...	-·016	-·024	...	-·017	...	**26**
259	+·000	...	...	+·000	...	...	13	+·000	-·015	...	+·000	...	...	+·000	...	...	**27**
260	...	...	...	...	-·014	...	14	...	...	...	...	...	...	...	...	...	**28**
261	...	-·013	-·005	...	...	-·007	15	...	...	-·018	...	...	...	...	-·018	-·015	**29**
262	...	...	...	...	...	...	16	...	-·016	...	...	-·017	-·025	...	...	...	**30**
263	...	...	...	...	...	...	17	...	...	...	...	...	...	...	...	...	**31**
264	...	-·014	...	...	-·015	...	18	...	...	...	...	...	...	...	-·019	...	**1**
265	...	...	-·006	...	...	-·008	19	...	...	-·019	...	-·018	...	...	...	-·016	**2**
266	...	...	...	...	...	...	20	...	-·017	...	...	...	...	...	...	...	**3**
267	...	...	...	...	-·016	...	21	...	...	...	...	...	-·026	...	-·020	...	**4**
268	-·001	-·015	...	-·001	...	...	22	-·001	...	...	-·001	-·019	...	-·001	...	...	**5**
269	...	...	...	...	...	...	23	...	-·018	...	...	...	...	...	...	...	**6**
270	...	...	-·007	...	-·017	-·009	24	...	...	-·020	...	...	...	...	...	-·017	**7**
271	...	...	...	...	...	...	25	...	...	...	...	...	...	...	-·021	...	**8**
272	...	-·016	...	...	...	...	26	...	...	...	...	-·020	-·027	...	...	...	**9**
273	...	...	...	...	...	...	27	...	-·019	...	...	...	...	...	...	...	**10**
274	...	...	-·008	...	-·018	-·010	28	...	...	-·021	...	...	...	...	-·022	...	**11**
275	...	...	...	...	...	...	29	...	...	...	...	...	...	...	...	-·018	**12**
276	...	-·017	...	...	...	...	1 *Tamil*, Tai; *Malayalam*, Magaram; *Bengal*, Magha.	...	...	...	...	-·021	...	...	...	...	**January. 13**
277	...	...	...	...	...	...	2	...	...	...	...	...	-·028	...	...	...	**14**
278	-·002	...	...	-·002	...	...	3	...	-·020	...	-·002	...	...	...	...	...	**15**
279	...	...	-·009	...	...	-·011	4	-·002	...	...	...	...	...	-·002	...	...	**16**
280	...	...	...	...	...	...	5	...	...	-·022	...	...	...	...	...	...	**17**
281	...	...	...	...	-·019	...	6	...	...	...	...	...	...	...	...	-·019	**18**
282	...	...	...	...	...	...	7	...	...	...	...	...	-·029	...	...	...	**19**
283	...	...	...	...	...	...	8	...	...	...	...	...	...	...	-·023	...	**20**
284	...	-·018	-·010	...	...	-·012	9	...	...	...	...	...	...	...	...	...	**21**
285	...	...	...	...	...	-·011	10	...	...	...	...	...	...	...	...	...	**22**
286	...	...	-·009	...	...	...	11	...	...	...	...	-·022	...	...	...	...	**23**
287	...	...	...	...	...	...	12	...	-·021	...	...	...	-·028	...	...	...	**24**
288	...	...	...	...	...	...	13	...	...	...	...	...	...	...	...	-·018	**25**
289	...	...	...	...	...	...	14	...	...	...	...	...	...	...	...	...	**26**
290	...	...	...	-·003	-·020	...	15	...	...	-·021	...	...	...	...	...	...	**27**
291	-·003	...	...	...	...	...	16	...	...	...	-·003	...	...	-·003	...	...	**28**
292	...	-·019	...	...	...	-·010	17	-·003	...	...	...	...	...	...	...	...	**29**
293	...	...	...	...	...	...	18	...	...	...	...	...	-·027	...	-·024	-·017	**30**
294	...	...	-·008	...	...	...	19	...	...	...	...	...	...	...	...	...	**31**
295	...	...	...	...	...	...	20	...	...	...	...	-·023	...	...	...	...	**1**
296	...	...	...	...	...	...	21	...	-·022	-·020	...	...	...	...	...	...	**February. 2**
297	...	...	...	...	...	...	22	...	...	...	...	...	...	...	...	...	**3**
298	...	...	...	...	...	...	23	...	...	...	...	...	-·026	...	...	-·016	**4**
299	...	...	...	...	-·021	-·009	24	...	...	...	...	...	...	...	...	...	**5**
300	...	-·020	...	...	...	...	25	...	...	...	...	...	...	...	...	...	**6**
301	...	...	-·007	...	...	...	26	...	...	...	...	...	...	...	...	...	**7**
302	...	...	...	-·004	...	...	27	...	...	...	...	...	...	...	...	...	**8**
303	-·004	...	...	...	...	...	28	...	...	-·019	...	...	...	...	-·025	-·015	**9**
304	...	...	...	...	...	...	29	-·004	...	...	-·004	...	-·025	-·004	...	...	**10**
305	...	...	...	...	...	...	30	...	...	...	...	...	...	...	-·024	...	**11**

APPENDIX I.

CORRECTIONS FOR SUNRISE FROM 13° TO 17° N. LATITUDE.

Day of Solar year.	Lat. 13° +·012 Long			Lat. 14° +·012 Long.			Days of Solar months.	Lat. 15° +·002 Long.			Lat. 16° −·003 Long.			Lat. 17° +·008 Long.			English date.
	For Eqn. of time—fraction of a day.	For ☉'s Trop. Long. fraction of a day.	Total Correction—fraction of a day. **Madras.**	For Eqn. of time—fraction of a day.	For ☉'s Trop. Long. fraction of a day.	Total Correction—fraction of a day. **Nellore.**		For Eqn. of time—fraction of a day.	For ☉'s Trop. Long. fraction of a day.	Total Correction—fraction of a day. **Vijayanagar** (now Hampi, Bellary District).	For Eqn. of time—fraction of a day.	For ☉'s Trop. Long. fraction of a day.	Total Correction—fraction of a day. **Belgaum.**	For Eqn. of time—fraction of a day.	For ☉'s Trop. Long. fraction of a day.	Total Correction—fraction of a day. **Hyderabad.**	
							Tamil, Masi; *Malayalam*, Kumbham; *Bengal*, Phalguna.										
306	−·004	−·020	−·007	−·004	−·021	−·008	1	−·004	−·022	−·019	−·004	−·023	−·025	−·004	−·024	−·015	**February.** 12
307	...	−·019	...	...	...	...	2	...	...	...	...	...	...	...	...	−·014	13
308	...	...	−·006	...	−·020	...	3	...	−·021	−·018	...	−·022	−·024	...	...	...	14
309	...	...	...	...	...	...	4	...	...	...	...	...	...	...	−·023	...	15
310	...	...	...	...	...	...	5	...	...	...	...	...	...	...	...	...	16
311	...	...	...	...	...	−·007	6	...	...	...	...	...	...	...	...	...	17
312	...	−·018	...	...	−·019	...	7	...	−·020	...	...	−·021	...	...	−·022	−·013	18
313	...	...	...	...	...	...	8	...	...	−·017	...	...	−·023	...	...	...	19
314	...	...	−·005	...	...	...	9	...	...	...	...	...	...	...	...	...	20
315	...	...	...	...	...	...	10	...	...	...	...	...	...	...	...	...	21
316	...	...	...	...	...	−·006	11	...	...	...	...	−·020	−·022	...	−·021	−·012	22
317	...	−·017	−·004	...	−·018	...	12	...	−·019	−·016	...	...	...	...	...	...	23
318	...	...	...	...	...	−·005	13	...	...	...	...	...	−·021	...	...	−·011	24
319	...	...	...	...	...	...	14	...	...	−·015	...	...	...	...	...	...	25
320	...	...	−·003	...	...	−·004	15	...	...	...	...	−·019	−·020	...	−·020	−·010	26
321	...	...	...	...	−·017	...	16	...	−·018	−·014	...	...	...	...	...	...	27
322	...	−·016	−·002	...	...	...	17	...	...	...	...	...	−·019	...	...	−·009	28
323	...	...	...	...	...	−·003	18	...	...	−·013	...	...	...	...	−·019	...	**March.** 1
324	...	...	−·001	...	...	...	19	...	...	...	...	−·018	...	...	...	−·008	2
325	...	...	...	...	...	−·002	20	...	−·017	−·012	...	...	−·018	...	...	...	3
326	...	−·015	...	...	−·016	...	21	...	...	...	...	...	...	...	...	−·007	4
327	...	...	−·000	...	...	−·001	22	...	...	−·011	...	...	−·017	...	−·018	...	5
328	...	...	...	−·005	...	...	23	...	...	...	...	−·017	...	...	...	−·006	6
329	−·005	...	+·001	...	...	...	24	...	−·016	...	...	...	−·016	...	...	...	7
330	...	...	...	...	−·015	−·000	25	...	...	−·010	...	...	...	...	−·017	−·005	8
331	...	−·014	...	...	...	...	26	−·005	...	...	...	−·016	−·015	...	...	...	9
332	...	...	+·002	...	...	+·001	27	...	...	−·009	−·005	...	...	−·005	...	−·004	10
333	...	...	...	...	...	...	28	...	−·015	...	...	...	−·014	...	...	...	11
334	...	...	+·003	...	−·014	+·002	29	...	...	−·008	...	...	...	...	−·016	−·003	12
335	...	...	...	...	...	...	30	...	...	...	...	−·015	−·013	...	...	−·002	13
							Tamil, Panguni; *Malayalam*, Minam; *Bengal*, Chaitra.										
336	...	−·013	...	...	...	+·003	1	...	−·014	−·007	...	...	...	...	...	...	14
337	...	...	+·004	...	−·013	...	2	...	...	...	...	−·014	−·012	...	−·015	−·001	15
338	...	−·012	...	...	...	...	3	...	−·013	−·006	...	...	...	...	−·014	...	16
339	...	...	+·005	...	−·012	+·004	4	...	...	...	...	−·013	−·011	...	...	−·000	17
340	...	−·011	...	...	...	...	5	...	−·012	−·005	...	...	...	...	−·013	...	18
341	...	...	+·006	...	−·011	+·005	6	...	...	...	...	−·012	−·010	...	...	+·001	19
342	...	−·010	...	...	...	...	7	...	−·011	−·004	...	...	...	...	−·012	...	20
343	...	...	...	...	−·010	+·006	8	...	...	...	...	−·011	−·009	...	...	+·002	21
344	...	...	+·007	...	...	...	9	...	−·010	−·003	...	...	...	...	−·011	...	22
345	...	−·009	...	...	...	+·007	10	...	...	...	...	−·010	−·008	...	...	+·003	23
346	...	...	+·008	...	−·009	...	11	...	−·009	−·002	...	...	...	...	−·010	...	24
347	...	−·008	...	...	...	+·008	12	...	...	...	...	−·009	−·007	...	...	+·004	25
348	...	...	+·009	...	−·008	...	13	...	−·008	−·001	...	...	...	...	−·009	...	26
349	...	−·007	...	...	...	...	14	...	...	...	...	−·008	−·006	...	...	+·005	27
350	...	...	...	...	−·007	+·009	15	...	−·007	−·000	...	...	...	...	−·008	...	28
351	...	−·006	+·010	...	...	...	16	...	...	...	...	−·007	−·005	...	...	+·006	29
352	...	...	...	...	−·006	+·010	17	...	−·006	+·001	...	...	...	...	−·007	...	30
353	...	−·005	+·011	...	...	...	18	...	...	...	...	−·006	−·004	...	−·006	+·007	31
354	...	...	...	...	−·005	+·011	19	...	−·005	+·002	...	...	...	...	...	+·008	**April.** 1
355	...	...	+·012	...	...	...	20	...	...	...	...	−·005	−·003	...	−·005	...	2
356	...	−·004	...	...	−·004	+·012	21	...	−·004	+·003	...	...	...	...	...	+·009	3
357	...	...	+·013	...	...	...	22	...	...	...	...	−·004	−·002	...	−·004	...	4
358	...	−·003	...	...	−·003	+·013	23	...	...	+·004	...	...	...	...	...	+·010	5
359	...	...	+·014	...	...	...	24	...	−·003	...	...	−·003	−·001	...	−·003	...	6
360	...	−·002	...	...	−·002	+·014	25	...	...	+·005	...	...	...	...	...	+·011	7
361	...	...	+·015	...	...	...	26	...	−·002	...	...	−·002	−·000	...	−·002	...	8
362	...	−·001	...	...	−·001	+·015	27	...	...	+·006	...	...	...	...	...	+·012	9
363	...	...	...	...	...	...	28	...	−·001	...	...	−·001	+·001	...	−·001	...	10
364	...	−·000	+·016	...	−·000	+·016	29	...	−·000	...	...	...	...	...	...	+·013	11
365	...	...	...	...	...	...	30	...	...	+·007	...	−·000	+·002	...	−·000	...	12

APPENDIX II:—Geocentric (Indian) Longitudes of Sun and Major planets

(For the years 1840—1909,

Day of S. Yr.	0	10	20	30	40	50	60	70	80	90	100	110	120	130	140	150	160	170
⊙'s Mean L.	357·0	6·9	16·7	26·6	36·4	46·3	56·1	66·0	75·9	85·7	95·6	105·4	115·3	125·1	135·0	144·8	154·7	164·6
Actual do.	+2·1	+2·0	+1·9	+1·7	+1·4	+1·1	+0·8	+0·4	+0·0	−0·3	−0·7	−1·1	−1·4	−1·6	−1·9	−2·0	−2·1	−2·2
English date.	Ap 13	Ap 23	My 3	My 13	My 23	Je 2	Je 12	Je 22	Jl 2	Jl 12	Jl 22	Au 1	Au 11	Au 21	Au 31	S 10	S 20	S 30
Tamil month.	Chit	Chit	Chit	Chit	Vaik	Vaik	Vaik	Ani	Ani	Ani	Adi	Adi	Adi	Avani	Avani	Avani	Pura	Pura
Do. date.	1	11	21	31	10	20	30	9	19	29	7	17	27	6	16	26	5	15
1910 Mars ...	55·6	61·8	68·0	74·3	80·5	86·8	93·0	99·7	105·6	111·9	118·2	124·4	130·8	137·1	143·6	149·9	156·3	162·9
⊙'s L. Merc. ...	6·8	24·1	37·9	45·9	44·1	36·6	37·1	46·9	61·8	79·1	97·4	116·0	133·6	149·5	161·6	166·4	161·5	154·8
+·6 Jup. ...	161·8	163·7	162·5	161·6	161·1	161·0	161·1	161·3	162·3	163·4	164·6	166·1	167·9	169·7	171·6	173·7	175·7	177·9
Ven. ...	313·6	322·7	332·9	343·6	354·3	5·4	17·0	28·7	40·2	52·2	64·0	75·7	87·7	99·8	112·0	124·2	136·6	148·5
Sat. ...	2·3	3·6	4·9	6·3	7·5	8·6	9·9	10·9	11·8	12·7	13·1	13·6	13·9	13·7	13·6	13·5	12·9	12·2
1911 Mars ...	298·4	305·7	313·0	320·5	327·7	335·1	342·2	349·1	356·2	2·9	9·3	15·4	21·3	26·9	31·9	36·4	39·7	42·9
⊙'s L. Merc. ...	16·3	25·6	25·9	18·5	18·7	24·7	38·7	56·1	74·4	93·2	111·4	128·1	141·8	148·9	146·6	139·0	139·0	147·7
+·4 Jup. ...	198·8	197·6	197·0	194·9	193·8	192·8	191·9	191·4	191·4	191·4	191·7	192·6	193·5	194·9	196·3	198·0	199·7	201·7
Ven. ...	31·8	43·6	55·7	67·2	78·9	90·3	100·9	111.7	122·0	131·6	140·3	147·9	153·7	156·6	156·0	151·2	145·1	140·2
Sat. ...	14·3	15·7	17·1	18·5	19·8	21·1	22·4	23·7	25·2	26·5	26·9	27·2	27·6	27·7	27·9	28·0	27·5	27·1
Eng. Date.	Ap 12	Ap 22	My 2	My 12	My 22	Je 1	Je 11	Je 21	Jl 1	Jl 11	Jl 21	Jl 31	Au 10	Au 20	Au 30	S 9	S 19	S 29
1912 Mars ...	70·9	76·5	82·1	87·9	93·7	99·5	105·6	111·5	117·7	123·8	130·1	136·3	142·4	148·9	155·4	161·8	168·3	174·8
⊙'s L. Merc. ...	8·3	1·1	357·1	3·1	15·9	32·8	51·1	69·1	88·8	106·1	120·8	130·2	130·8	123·2	120·8	127·7	140·9	157·1
+·1 Jup. ...	232·4	231·0	230·6	229·9	228·6	227·3	225·9	224·8	223·7	222·9	222·2	222·0	222·0	222·4	223·3	224·4	225·4	226·8
Ven. ...	336·8	349·1	1·4	13·6	25·8	37·1	50·4	62·6	74·8	87·2	99·3	111·6	124·6	136·2	148·5	160·6	173·1	185·5
Sat. ...	26·9	28·2	29·5	30·8	32·1	33·4	34·8	36·1	37·3	38·5	39·4	40·2	41·2	41·6	42·1	42·5	42·4	42·3
1913 Mars ...	316·3	323·9	331·7	339·3	347·0	354·5	1·9	9·3	16·4	23·6	31·0	37·3	43·8	50·2	56·5	62·4	68·0	73·2
⊙'s L. Merc. ...	338·9	342·2	353·7	9·3	27·6	46·7	65·4	83·7	98·4	110·8	114·1	106·3	108·2	107·7	119·8	135·3	152·9	170·6
−·1 Jup. ...	264·0	264·6	264·8	264·7	264·4	263·6	262·6	261·4	260·1	258·8	257·5	256·3	255·5	254·7	254·4	254·4	254·6	255·3
Ven. ...	19·4	14·7	9·1	4·3	4·2	7·6	13·5	21·2	30·1	39·9	50·3	60·8	71·9	83·2	94·9	106·6	118·5	130·4
Sat. ...	39·5	40·7	41·9	43·1	44·5	45·9	47·3	48·6	49·9	51·3	52·3	53·4	54·4	55·2	55·9	56·4	56·7	56·9
Eng. Date.	Ap 13	Ap 23	My 3	My 13	My 23	Je 2	Je 12	Je 22	Jl 2	Jl 12	Jl 22	Au 1	Au 11	Au 21	Au 31	S 10	S 20	S 30
1914 Mars ...	88·7	93·0	97·9	103·0	108·4	114·1	119·4	125·1	131·0	137·0	143·0	149·1	155·5	161·7	168·3	174·8	181·4	188·0
⊙'s L. Merc. ...	333·3	318·4	6·3	25·3	44·2	62·5	78·6	90·8	95·4	90·2	84·4	88·4	100·0	115·5	132·9	150·8	168·5	184·9
+·6 Jup. ...	293·9	295·4	296·7	297·7	298·9	299·0	299·2	298·6	298·1	297·2	296·2	294·9	293·6	292·4	231·2	290·1	289·2	288·7
Ven. ...	14·7	27·1	39·5	51·6	63·7	75·7	87·6	99·5	111·1	123·1	134·7	146·3	157·6	168·9	179·7	190·1	199·8	209·1
Sat. ...	52·4	53·5	54·8	55·9	57·2	58·5	59·9	61·2	62·5	63·9	64·8	65·6	66·6	67·9	69·1	70·3	70·7	71·2
1915 Mars ...	333·7	341·6	349·3	356·8	4·6	12·1	19·4	26·8	34·0	41·1	48·0	54·8	61·6	68·1	74·5	80·8	86·8	92·7
⊙'s L. Merc. ...	344·3	1·9	20·8	39·2	56·1	69·9	76·5	73·1	66·1	68·3	78·5	93·3	111·8	129·0	147·0	164·1	179·1	189·2
+·4 Jup. ...	322·2	324·4	326·4	328·4	330·0	331·6	332·8	333·7	334·4	334·8	334·9	334·4	333·7	332·7	331·5	330·2	328·8	327·4
Ven. ...	320·7	332·5	344·6	356·8	8·5	20·8	32·9	44·9	57·0	69·1	81·3	93·4	105·7	118·0	130·4	142·6	155·0	167·4
Sat. ...	65·7	66·7	67·6	68·6	69·8	71·1	72·3	73·7	75·1	76·4	77·7	79·0	80·3	81·3	82·4	83·5	84·2	84·8
Eng. Date.	Ap 12	Ap 22	My 2	My 12	My 22	Je 1	Je 11	Je 21	Jl 1	Jl 11	Jl 21	Jl 31	Au 10	Au 20	Au 30	S 9	S 19	S 29
1916 Mars ...	110·8	113·2	116·4	120·1	124·4	129·2	134·0	139·3	145·3	151·0	156·7	162·6	168·7	175·1	181·6	188·2	194·7	201·6
⊙'s L. Merc. ...	357·6	14·9	33·4	47·8	56·6	55·8	48·3	47·6	56·5	71·1	88·3	106·4	124·8	142·5	158·4	170·5	175·8	171·1
+·1 Jup. ...	340·9	352·3	354·7	357·1	359·3	1·4	3·5	5·3	7·0	8·5	9·6	10·5	11·1	11·3	11·1	10·6	10·0	8·9
Ven. ...	34·4	54·8	64·3	73·0	80·0	85·5	88·4	86·7	82·9	75·3	70·7	71·1	74·5	80·3	88·3	97·1	107·2	117·6
Sat. ...	79·2	79·9	80·7	81·3	82·4	83·6	84·8	86·1	87·4	88·7	90·1	91·5	92·8	94·0	95·1	96·4	97·3	98·1
Eng. Date.	Ap 13	Ap 23	My 3	My 13	My 23	Je 2	Je 12	Je 22	Jl 2	Jl 12	Jl 22	Au 1	Au 11	Au 21	Au 31	S 10	S 20	S 30
1917 Mars ...	350·4	358·1	5·7	13·1	20·6	28·0	35·2	42·3	49.5	56·3	63·3	70·0	76·5	83·1	89·5	96·0	102·1	108·1
⊙'s L. Merc. ...	12·2	27·2	36·6	36·9	29·3	27·8	35·8	50·1	67·0	85·6	104·0	122·1	138·8	151·9	158·7	156·0	148·5	148·9
+·8 Jup. ...	17·7	20·1	22·5	24·9	27·3	29·7	32·0	34·4	36·5	38·6	40·5	42·2	43·8	45·0	46·1	46·8	47·2	47·3
Ven. ...	356·5	8·8	21·2	33·5	45·9	58·1	70·2	82·5	94·4	106·9	119·1	131·2	143·3	155·3	167·3	179·1	191·4	203·0
Sat. ...	92·9	93·4	93·9	94·5	95·4	96·3	97·4	98·6	99·8	101·1	102·4	103·7	105·1	106·3	107·6	108·9	110·0	111·0
1918 Mars ...	141·7	141·1	141·3	143·1	145·5	148·9	152·7	157·2	162·0	167·3	172·9	178·5	184·5	190·7	197·2	203·8	210·4	217·4
⊙'s L. Merc. ...	14·3	18·4	11·9	8·1	14·2	27·5	44·0	62·5	81·3	99·7	116·9	131·4	140·8	140·7	133·1	130·8	138·2	151·2
+·6 Jup. ...	45·3	47·5	49·6	51·8	53·7	56·4	58·7	61·0	63·4	65·7	68·0	70·2	72·2	73·9	75·8	77·5	78·9	80·0
Ven. ...	313·1	322·8	332·8	343·7	354·6	5·9	17·3	28·9	40·7	52·6	64·6	76·2	88·3	100·3	112·5	124·7	136·9	149·2
Sat. ...	106·6	106·9	107·2	107·6	108·3	109·1	109·8	110·9	112·1	113·2	114·5	116·8	117·0	118·3	119·6	121·0	122·2	123·3
1919 Mars ...	5·5	13·0	20·4	27·6	34·8	41·9	48·9	56·1	62·8	69·8	76·4	82·9	89·7	96·0	102·7	109·0	115·2	121·3
⊙'s L. Merc. ...	354·9	349·0	352·9	5·0	20·8	39·0	58·0	76·9	94·5	110·2	121·2	124·0	117·5	112·9	118·2	130·1	146·0	163·1
+·3 Jup. ...	73·9	75·2	76·9	78·6	80·5	82·5	84·6	86·8	89·1	91·4	93·6	95·9	98·3	100·5	102·6	104·7	106·7	108·4
Ven. ...	32·3	44·2	56·0	67·7	79·2	90·4	101·4	112·0	121·9	131·3	139·8	147·0	152·0	154·3	152·7	147·1	139·6	137·6
Sat. ...	119·5	120·6	120·5	120·6	121·0	121·6	122·1	122·8	123·6	124·3	125·4	126·5	127·7	129·0	130·3	131·5	132·8	134·1

Mesh.	Vrsh.	Mith.	Kat.	Sim.	Kan.	Tul.	Vrsch.	Dhan.	Mak.	Kum.	Min.	Asvn.	Bhar.	Krit.	Rohi.	Mrig.	Ardh.	Punar.	Push.	Asles.
30	60	90	120	150	180	210	240	270	300	330	360	13·3	26·7	40·0	53·3	66·7	80·0	93·3	106·7	120·0

at Ujjain mean Sunrise for every ten days from A.D. 1910 to A.D. 1919.

see *Indian Chronology*, Table XVIII).

180	190	200	210	220	230	240	250	260		270	280	290	300	310	320	330	340	350	360
174·4 −2·2 O 10 Pura 25	184·3 −2·1 O 20 Aipp 4	194·1 −1·9 O 30 Aipp 14	204·0 −1·7 N 9 Aipp 24	213·8 −1·5 N 19 Kart 4	223·7 −1·2 N 29 Kart 14	233·5 −0·9 D 9 Kart 24	243·4 −0·5 D 19 Marg 5	253·3 −0·1 D 29 Marg 15		263·1 +0·3 Ja 8 Marg 25	273·0 +0·6 Ja 18 Tai 5	282·8 +1·0 Ja 28 Tai 15	292·7 +1·3 F 7 Tai 25	302·5 +1·6 F 17 Masi 6	312·4 +1·8 F 27 Masi 16	322·2 +2·0 Mr 9 Masi 26	332·1 +2·1 Mr 19 Pang. 6	342·0 +2·2 Mr 29 Pang. 16	351·8 +2·2 Ap 8 Pang. 26
169·4	176·0	182·5	189·0	195·7	202·4	209·3	216·1	223·0	**11**	229·9	236·8	243·9	250·9	258·2	265·3	272·6	280·0	287·2	294·5
157·6	168·1	182·6	190·3	216·7	233·9	249·7	263·0	270·5		260·0	260·8	260·0	268·4	282·1	298·7	316·9	335·1	353·1	9·1
180·1	182·3	184·4	186·6	188·8	190·9	192·8	194·6	196·3		197·9	199·4	200·3	201·2	201·6	201·7	201·6	201·3	200·5	199·5
161·0	173·5	186·0	198·6	211·0	223·7	236·2	248·9	261·5		274·1	286·8	299·3	311·9	324·3	336·9	349·2	1·5	13·8	25·8
11·5	10·6	9·8	9·0	8·3	7·7	7·1	6·8	6·6		6·4	6·8	7·1	7·6	8·4	9·3	10·2	11·4	12·6	13·8
																Mr 8	Mr 18	Mr 28	Ap 7
44·8	45·7	44·9	42·7	40·1	37·0	34·5	32·8	32·0	**12**	32·7	34·4	37·0	40·3	44·0	48·1	52·1	57·6	62·9	68·1
161·7	178·3	195·8	213·8	229·5	243·6	252·9	254·2	246·8		243·0	248·8	261·3	277·1	294·5	312·7	330·3	347·2	0·6	7·8
208·8	205·8	207·9	210·2	212·4	214·6	216·8	219·0	221·1		223·2	225·0	226·7	228·3	229·8	230·9	231·8	232·4	232·7	232·7
139·9	142·4	149·4	157·1	166·2	176·2	186·5	197·7	209·2		220·7	232·2	244·8	257·0	269·1	281·5	293·5	305·8	318·2	330·7
26·7	25·9	25·1	24·4	23·6	22·9	22·1	21·6	21·1		20·7	20·8	20·9	20·9	21·6	22·2	23·0	24·0	25·2	26·2
O 9	O 19	O 29	N 8	N 18	N 28	D 8	D 18	D 28		Ja 7	Ja 17	Ja 27	F 6	F 16	F 26	Mr 8	Mr 18	Mr 28	Ap 7
181·4	188·2	195·0	201·8	208·6	216·1	223·1	230·2	237·4	**13**	244·5	251·9	259·3	266·8	274·3	281·9	289·5	297·1	304·9	312·6
174·4	192·0	208·6	224·0	235·2	239·1	233·6	227·3	230·2		240·8	255·7	272·9	290·8	308·4	325·1	339·5	348·3	348·0	340·4
228·6	230·4	232·4	234·5	236·7	238·9	241·1	243·3	245·7		247·9	250·1	252·3	254·3	256·3	258·2	259·9	261·5	262·8	263·6
197·8	210·1	222·4	234·7	247·0	259·4	271·4	283·5	295·4		307·2	319·4	329·8	340·5	350·6	0·2	8·4	14·9	19·6	20·6
42·1	41·2	40·2	39·2	38·6	38·1	37·6	36·9	36·3		35·5	35·3	35·2	34·9	35·4	35·8	36·2	37·0	37·9	38·9
78·1	82·5	86·3	89·4	91·7	92·7	92·9	91·4	88·8	**14**	85·5	81·7	78·5	76·0	74·9	75·3	76·9	79·3	82·5	86·1
188·0	204·2	216·9	223·5	221·1	213·2	212·8	221·3	234·8		251·4	269·1	286·7	308·6	318·5	328·9	331·2	324·4	320·5	326·2
256·2	257·6	259·2	260·8	262·5	264·5	266·6	268·0	271·0		273·3	275·6	278·0	280·3	282·7	284·9	287·1	289·2	291·2	293·2
142·4	154·7	166·9	179·4	191·7	204·1	216·8	229·2	241·7		254·4	267·1	279·6	292·4	305·3	318·2	329·9	342·5	355·0	7·2
57·0	56·6	56·1	55·7	55·9	54·1	53·3	52·5	51·8		51·0	50·6	50·1	49·7	49·7	49·8	49·8	50·5	51·2	51·9
O 10	O 20	O 30	N 9	N 19	N 29	D 9	D 19	D 29		Ja 8	Ja 18	Ja 28	F 7	F 17	F 27	Mr 9	Mr 19	Mr 29	Ap 8
194·9	201·7	208·6	215·6	222·8	230·1	237·4	244·7	252·1	**15**	259·7	267·3	275·1	282·7	290·4	298·3	306·2	314·1	321·9	329·8
198·5	207·1	206·2	198·6	196·5	203·6	216·4	232·2	249·7		267·1	284·0	299·2	310·3	313·8	307·5	301·7	306·7	318·6	334·6
288·5	288·8	289·3	290·1	291·3	292·6	294·2	295·9	298·2		300·3	302·4	304·8	307·1	309·4	311·8	314·3	316·7	319·1	321·4
217·1	223·8	227·5	228·7	224·6	218·5	213·6	212·6	215·4		220·9	228·3	237·2	247·1	257·6	268·5	279·6	291·1	302·8	314·7
71·5	71·3	71·2	71·0	70·3	69·5	68·9	68·1	67·4		66·5	65·9	65·2	·64·5	64·4	64·1	64·0	64·4	64·9	65·2
																Mr 8	Mr 18	Mr 28	Ap 7
98·4	103·8	108·9	113·4	117·9	121·8	124·9	127·1	128·4	**16**	128·6	127·5	125·3	122·0	118·0	114·2	111·4	109·7	109·2	110·1
191·7	185·1	180·3	184·8	196·4	211·7	228·6	245·9	262·9		278·6	291·2	296·8	292·8	294·4	296·2	306·5	321·2	338·1	348·3
326·3	325·6	324·9	324·4	324·3	324·7	325·3	326·3	327·6		329·2	329·8	332·7	334·8	337·0	339·2	341·6	344·0	346·4	348·8
179·9	192·4	205·0	217·5	229·9	242·5	255·5	267·7	280·1		292·6	304·9	317·2	329·3	341·5	353·5	5·1	17·0	28·1	39·2
85·4	85·5	85·7	85·8	85·3	84·9	84·4	83·6	82·8		82·0	81·1	80·3	79·4	79·1	78·7	78·4	78·5	73·5	78·6
O 9	O 19	O 29	N 8	N 18	N 28	D 8	D 18	D 28		Ja 7	Ja 17	Ja 27	F 6	F 16	F 26	Mr 8	Mr 18	Mr 28	Ap 7
208·5	215·6	222·6	229·9	237·1	244·6	252·0	259·6	267·2	**17**	275·0	282·9	290·6	298·6	306·4	314·1	322·1	330·0	338·0	345·6
164·5	166·7	176·6	191·1	207·5	224·9	242·0	258·2	271·7		279·5	278·4	270·8	267·3	277·2	290·9	307·4	323·3	342·1	0·5
7·8	6·4	5·0	3·8	2·6	1·7	1·0	0·9	0·9		1·4	2·1	3·2	4·4	6·1	7·9	9·7	11·9	14·1	16·4
128·6	139·9	151·5	163·2	175·3	187·3	199·5	211·7	224·0		236·5	249·2	261·5	274·2	287·0	299·0	311·6	324·1	336·6	349·0
98·9	99·3	99·7	100·1	99·8	99·6	99·4	98·7	98·0		97·4	96·6	96·9	95·0	94·3	93·7	93·0	92·9	92·7	92·5
O 10	O 20	O 30	N 9	N 19	N 29	D 9	D 19	D 29		Ja 8	Ja 18	Ja 28	F 7	F 17	F 27	Mr 9	Mr 19	Mr 29	Ap 8
114·1	119·9	125·6	131·0	136·1	141·2	145·8	149·9	153·6	**18**	156·4	158·8	159·9	160·2	158·6	155·8	152·6	148·4	145·2	142·4
157·8	171·9	188·3	205·6	222·9	239·4	253·3	262·5	263·0		255·6	252·3	258·5	271·3	287·4	305·1	323·2	341·1	357·9	11·3
47·0	46·4	45·5	44·3	43·1	36·7	40·3	39·2	38·1		37·3	36·9	36·7	37·0	37·6	38·5	39·6	40·9	42·5	44·3
215·0	226·7	237·8	249·2	260·1	270·5	280·2	289·2	296·8		302·2	304·8	303·7	298·4	292·1	289·1	290·3	294·1	300·8	308·7
111·9	112·6	113·2	113·8	113·9	113·9	114·0	113·9	113·1		112·5	111·7	110·9	110·2	109·4	108·6	107·8	107·4	106·9	106·6
224·4	231·4	238·6	246·0	253·5	260·9	268·7	276·3	283·9	**19**	291·8	299·6	307·5	315·0	323·2	331·0	338·8	346·6	354·2	1·4
167·3	184·7	202·1	218·7	233·7	244·6	248·1	242·0	236·4		239·7	250·8	265·9	283·2	301·3	319·0	334·8	350·2	358·9	358·6
80·9	81·1	81·8	81·6	81·2	80·3	79·0	78·1	76·8		75·6	74·3	73·2	72·2	71·6	71·3	71·3	71·5	72·3	73·3
161·5	174·0	186·4	198·7	211·5	224·1	236·7	249·4	262·0		274·7	287·3	299·6	312·4	325·0	327·8	349·7	2·0	14·3	26·2
124·4	125·1	125·9	126·7	127·1	127·3	127·7	127·7	127·8		127·9	126·3	125·6	124·9	124·0	123·2	122·4	122·4	120·5	119·6
																Mr 8	Mr 18	Mr 28	Ap 7
127·5	133·5	139·5	145·2	151·0	156·5	162·0	167·1	172·2	**20**	177·2	181·7	185·6	189·3	192·3	194·4	195·7	195·6	194·3	191·7
180·9	198·0	213·9	226·3	232·3	228·9	221·7	222·1	231·1		245·1	261·8	279·4	298·0	314·1	328·9	339·1	341·2	334·4	331·7
110·0	111·3	112·5	113·4	114·1	114·4	114·4	114·1	113·3		112·4	111·3	109·9	108·6	107·4	106·2	105·2	104·4	104·0	103·9
138·2	141·9	148·5	156·8	165·8	176·1	186·9	198·0	209·3		221·0	233·0	245·3	257·5	269·6	282·0	294·1	306·8	318·8	331·2
135·4	136·3	137·4	138·4	139·2	139·9	140·7	140·9	141·1		140·7	140·8	140·4	139·2	139·4	138·6	136·7	137·1	136·4	134·5

Mag.	P.Phal.	U.Phal.	Hasta.	Chit.	Svati.	Visak.	Anur.	Jyesh.	Mula.	P. Ash.	U.Ash.	Srav.	Dan.	Satab.	P. Bhad.	U. Bhad.	Revati.
133·3	146·7	160·0	173·3	186·7	200·0	213·3	226·7	240·0	253·3	266·7	280·0	293·3	306·7	320·0	333·3	346·7	360·0

APPENDIX II.—Geocentric (Indian) Longitudes of Sun and Major planets

(For the years 1840—1909,

Day of S. Yr.	0	10	20	30	40	50	60	70	80	90	100	110	120	130	140	150	160	170
☉'s Mean L.	357·0	6·9	16·7	26·6	36·4	46·3	56·1	66·0	75·9	85·7	95·6	105·4	115·3	125·1	135·0	144·8	154·7	164·6
Actual do.	+2·1	+2·0	+1·9	+1·7	+1·4	+1·1	+0·8	+0·4	+0·0	−0·3	−0·7	−1·1	−1·4	−1·6	−1·9	−2·0	−2·1	−2·2
English date.	Ap 12	Ap 22	My 2	My 12	My 22	Je 1	Je 11	Je 21	Jl 1	Jl 11	Jl 21	Jl 31	Au 10	Au 20	Au 30	S 9	S 19	S 29
Tamil month.	Chit	Chit	Chit	Chit	Vaik	Vaik	Vaik	Ani	Ani	Ani	Adi	Adi	Adi	Avani	Avani	Avani	Pura	Pura
Do. date.	1	11	21	31	10	20	30	9	19	29	7	17	27	6	16	26	5	15
1920 Mars ...	190·2	186·6	182·9	180·3	178·9	178·8	180·0	182·1	185·4	189·1	193·3	198·4	203·7	209·5	215·4	221·6	228·2	234·9
☉'s L. Merc. ...	332·8	342·8	357·9	15·4	34·3	53·3	71·7	88·1	100·9	106·5	102·0	95·6	98·4	109·1	124·3	141·4	160·2	176·8
+1 Jup. ...	103·8	104·2	104·9	105·9	107·1	108·5	110·3	112·1	114·0	116·2	118·3	120·4	122·6	124·9	127·0	129·2	131·5	133·5
Ven. ...	337·2	349·4	1·9	14·1	26·4	38·6	51·0	63·2	75·4	87·8	100·0	112·2	124·4	136·8	149·0	161·4	173·7	186·1
Sat. ...	134·2	133·9	133·6	133·4	133·7	134·1	134·4	135·2	136·0	136·7	137·9	139·0	140·1	141·3	142·5	143·8	145·0	146·2
Eng. Date.	Ap 13	Ap 23	My 3	My 13	My 23	Je 2	Je 12	Je 22	Jl 2	Jl 12	Jl 22	Au 1	Au 11	Au 21	Au 31	S 10	S 20	S 30
1921 Mars ...	20·7	27·9	35·0	42·1	49·0	55·9	62·7	69·4	76·3	82·8	89·4	95·9	102·4	108·9	115·3	121·6	127·9	134·0
☉'s L. Merc. ...	337·0	354·2	12·7	31·7	50·3	67·2	80·7	87·8	84·5	77·5	79·1	89·2	104·1	121·1	139·2	157·2	174·0	188·6
+·8 Jup. ...	135·8	135·2	134·9	135·0	135·2	136·0	136·9	138·0	139·4	141·1	142·8	144·7	146·8	148·9	151·0	153·2	155·4	157·5
Ven. ...	16·1	10·4	4·8	1·6	2·5	7·1	13·6	21·9	31·0	41·0	51·4	62·2	73·4	84·7	96·3	108·1	120·0	131·9
Sat. ...	148·0	147·5	147·0	146·6	146·6	146·7	146·7	147·3	147·9	148·5	149·5	150·5	151·5	152·7	153·9	155·0	156·3	157·6
1922 Mars ...	238·9	241·2	242·4	242·7	242·1	240·4	236·9	234·8	232·6	231·4	231·3	232·7	235·2	238·6	242·9	247·8	253·3	258·9
☉'s L. Merc. ...	349·7	8·5	27·0	44·3	59·0	67·8	67·2	59·7	58·9	67·7	81·9	99·0	116·9	135·2	152·6	168·4	180·3	185·4
+·6 Jup. ...	169·4	168·1	167·0	166·2	165·4	165·1	165·1	165·3	166·1	166·9	168·0	169·4	171·1	172·8	174·7	176·7	178·8	180·9
Ven. ...	15·3	27·6	39·9	51·9	64·1	76·0	88·1	100·0	111·8	123·5	135·0	146·5	157·7	168·9	179·6	189·9	199·7	208·8
Sat. ...	161·4	160·7	160·1	159·4	159·2	159·0	158·9	159·3	159·7	160·0	160·8	161·6	162·4	163·5	164·6	165·7	166·9	168·1
1923 Mars ...	35·1	41·8	48·6	55·3	62·0	68·7	75·3	81·8	88·2	94·9	101·4	107·6	114·2	120·5	126·8	133·2	139·6	146·0
☉'s L. Merc. ...	4·0	21·5	36·7	47·2	48·9	41·9	39·0	46·0	59·4	76·2	94·3	112·9	131·0	147·4	161·0	168·3	166·5	158·9
+·3 Jup. ...	203·5	202·3	201·1	199·7	198·5	197·3	196·3	195·7	195·3	195·3	195·5	196·2	197·0	198·1	199·6	201·2	202·9	204·9
Ven. ...	321·0	332·9	344·9	356·9	9·0	21·1	33·2	45·4	57·5	69·7	81·7	94·1	106·3	118·6	130·9	143·1	155·7	168·1
Sat. ...	174·5	173·8	173·0	172·2	171·8	171·4	171·0	171·2	171·4	171·5	172·1	172·7	173·3	174·3	175·3	176·3	177·5	178·7
Eng. Date.	Ap 12	Ap 22	My 2	My 12	My 22	Je 1	Je 11	Je 21	Jl 1	Jl 11	Jl 21	Jl 31	Au 10	Au 20	Au 30	S 9	S 19	S 29
1924 Mars ...	268·6	274·5	280·2	285·8	291·0	296·1	300·5	304·4	307·5	309·7	310·8	310·0	308·5	306·1	303·6	301·7	301·2	301·7
☉'s L. Merc. ...	14·6	26·2	30·0	24·2	19·5	24·5	36·9	53·3	71·4	90·1	108·6	125·7	140·6	150·1	151·2	144·0	140·8	147·0
+·0 Jup. ...	236·9	236·5	235·7	234·8	233·6	232·3	231·0	229·8	228·5	227·5	226·8	226·4	226·3	226·5	227·1	228·0	229·2	230·5
Ven. ...	44·3	54·7	64·1	72·5	79·6	84·2	85·7	83·6	77·6	71·3	68·3	68·9	73·2	79·8	88·0	97·3	107·3	118·0
Sat. ...	187·3	186·5	185·7	184·9	184·3	183·7	183·1	183·1	183·0	183·0	183·4	183·8	184·2	185·0	185·8	186·7	187·8	188·9
Eng. Date.	Ap 13	Ap 23	My 3	My 13	My 23	Je 2	Je 12	Je 22	Jl 2	Jl 12	Jl 22	Au 1	Au 11	Au 21	Au 31	S 10	S 20	S 30
1925 Mars ...	49·9	56·4	62·8	69·2	75·5	81·8	88·2	94·4	100·9	107·3	113·6	120·0	126·2	132·6	139·1	145·3	151·8	158·1
☉'s L. Merc. ...	11·1	6·1	0·3	4·2	15·8	31·9	50·0	68·8	87·6	105·4	120·7	131·8	134·4	127·9	123·4	128·4	140·5	156·2
+·8 Jup. ...	268·4	269·1	269·4	269·5	269·2	268·6	267·8	266·6	265·3	263·9	262·5	261·3	260·2	259·5	259·0	258·8	259·0	259·6
Ven. ...	357·1	9·5	21·8	34·1	46·5	58·6	70·8	83·1	95·2	107·4	119·4	131·7	143·6	155·8	167·6	179·7	191·7	203·4
Sat. ...	199·5	198·7	198·0	197·2	196·5	195·8	195·2	194·9	194·6	194·2	194·4	194·6	194·9	195·6	196·3	197·1	198·1	199·1
1926 Mars ...	290·8	297·9	305·0	312·2	319·3	326·2	333·1	339·7	346·2	352·5	358·3	3·8	9·1	13·3	17·2	20·0	21·5	21·8
☉'s L. Merc. ...	342·2	343·6	353·8	8·9	26·6	45·5	64·4	82·7	99·2	111·6	117·0	112·2	106·0	108·7	119·8	134·7	151·7	169·5
+·5 Jup. ...	297·9	299·6	301·1	302·2	303·1	303·7	303·9	303·8	303·3	302·6	301·5	300·3	299·0	297·5	296·2	295·1	294·2	293·5
Ven. ...	313·0	322·7	333·1	344·0	354·9	6·2	17·6	29·3	41·1	52·7	64·7	76·5	88·7	100·8	113·0	125·0	137·4	149·8
Sat. ...	211·7	211·0	210·3	209·6	208·8	208·0	207·3	206·8	206·3	205·9	205·9	205·9	205·9	206·4	206·9	207·5	208·4	209·3
1927 Mars ...	64·7	70·6	76·5	82·4	88·4	94·5	100·5	106·7	112·8	119·0	125·4	131·5	137·9	144·2	150·6	157·1	163·4	170·1
☉'s L. Merc. ...	332·2	346·3	3·5	22·1	41·2	59·5	76·6	90·4	98·2	95·8	88·5	89·3	98·6	113·0	130·0	147·8	165·6	182·5
+·3 Jup. ...	326·1	328·4	330·5	332·4	334·3	335·9	337·2	338·3	339·2	339·6	339·8	339·6	339·0	338·1	337·1	335·8	334·4	332·9
Ven. ...	32·7	44·5	56·4	68·0	79·4	90·5	101·4	111·9	121·9	131·1	139·5	146·2	150·7	152·1	149·2	143·3	137·9	135·1
Sat. ...	223·3	222·7	222·1	221·5	220·8	220·1	219·3	218·7	218·1	217·4	217·2	217·0	216·8	217·1	217·4	217·8	218·6	219·4
Eng. Date.	Ap 12	Ap 22	My 2	My 12	My 22	Je 1	Je 11	Je 21	Jl 1	Jl 11	Jl 21	Jl 31	Au 10	Au 20	Au 30	S 9	S 19	S 29
1928 Mars ...	309·2	317·0	324·5	332·2	339·7	347·2	354·5	1·8	9·2	16·1	22·9	29·7	36·0	42·2	48·2	53·7	58·9	63·6
☉'s L. Merc. ...	340·6	358·8	17·6	36·5	54·0	68·9	78·4	78·6	71·1	69·5	77·4	91·2	107·9	125·8	144·0	161·3	177·2	189·2
+·0 Jup. ...	353·8	356·2	358·6	1·0	3·3	5·5	7·5	9·6	11·3	12·8	14·2	15·2	15·9	16·4	16·3	16·0	15·3	14·4
Ven. ...	337·7	349·9	2·4	14·7	26·9	39·2	51·5	63·9	75·9	88·3	100·5	112·7	125·1	137·3	149·6	161·9	174·2	186·4
Sat. ...	234·9	234·4	233·9	233·4	232·7	232·0	231·2	230·4	229·6	228·9	228·5	228·1	227·8	228·0	228·2	228·3	228·9	229·5
Eng. Date.	Ap 13	Ap 23	My 3	My 13	My 23	Je 2	Je 12	Je 22	Jl 2	Jl 12	Jl 22	Au 1	Au 11	Au 21	Au 31	S 10	S 20	S 30
1929 Mars ...	81·4	86·4	91·6	97·1	102·5	108·2	114·1	119·9	125·9	131·9	138·0	144·3	150·6	156·9	163·3	169·7	176·3	182·9
☉'s L. Merc. ...	356·4	14·9	32·6	47·9	58·4	59·8	53·2	50·1	57·1	70·5	87·3	105·2	123·6	141·5	157·8	171·0	178·1	175·6
+·7 Jup. ...	21·5	23·8	26·2	28·6	31·0	33·4	35·8	38·1	40·3	42·4	44·4	46·2	47·9	49·4	50·5	51·4	51·9	52·1
Ven. ...	12·4	6·7	0·9	359·1	1·4	6·0	13·2	21·6	31·0	41·1	51·7	62·5	73·7	85·2	96·8	108·5	120·3	132·5
Sat. ...	246·1	245·8	245·5	245·1	244·4	243·7	242·9	242·1	241·3	240·6	240·1	239·6	239·1	239·0	238·9	238·9	239·4	239·9

Mesh.	Vrsh.	Mith	Kat.	Sim.	Kan.	Tul.	Vrsch.	Dhan.	Mak.	Kum.	Min.	Asvn.	Bhar.	Krit.	Rohi.	Mrig.	Ardh.	Punar.	Push	Asles.
30	60	90	120	150	180	210	240	270	300	330	360	13·3	26·7	40·0	53·3	66·7	80·0	93·3	106·7	120·0

at Ujjain mean Sunrise for every ten days from A.D. 1920 to A.D. 1929.

see *Indian Chronology*, Table XVIII).

180	190	200	210	220	230	240	250	260		270	280	290	300	310	320	330	340	350	360
174·4	184·3	194·1	204·0	213·8	223·7	233·5	243·4	253·3		263·1	273·0	282·8	292·7	302·5	312·4	322·2	332·1	342·0	351·8
−2·2	−2·1	−1·9	−1·7	−1·5	−1·2	−0·9	−0·5	−0·1		+0·3	+0·6	+1·0	+1·3	+1·6	+1·8	+2·0	+2·1	+2·2	+2·2
O 9	O 19	O 29	N 8	N 18	N 28	D 8	D 18	D 28		Ja 7	Ja 17	Ja 27	F 6	F 16	F 26	Mr 8	Mr 18	Mr 28	Ap 7
Pura	Aipp	Aipp	Aipp	Kart	Kart	Kart	Marg	Marg		Marg	Tai	Tai	Tai	Masi	Masi	Masi	Pang	Pang	Pang
25	4	14	24	4	14	24	5	15		25	5	15	25	6	16	26	6	16	26
241·8	248·9	256·1	263·4	270·8	278·4	285·9	293·4	301·1	**21**	308·7	316·5	324·2	331·7	339·3	346·9	354·3	1·8	9·0	16·4
193·2	207·0	215·9	215·7	208·8	205·4	212·0	224·5	240·5		257·7	275·2	292·4	307·9	319·5	324·2	318·9	313·0	316·6	328·0
135·5	137·6	139·4	140·9	142·3	143·6	144·5	145·1	145·5		145·5	145·1	144·5	143·6	142·5	141·2	140·0	138·6	137·3	136·3
198·4	210·7	223·0	235·2	247.4	259·5	271·8	283·7	295·6		307·4	318·7	329·8	340·4	350·6	359·7	7·6	14·0	17·7	18·0
147·5	148·6	149·7	150·9	151·6	152·3	153·1	153·3	153·6		153·8	153·5	153·2	152·9	152·2	151·5	150·7	149·9	149·1	148·3
O 10	O 20	O 30	N 9	N 19	N 29	D 9	D 19	D 29		Ja 8	Ja 18	Ja 28	F 7	F 17	F 27	Mr 9	Mr 19	Mr 29	Ap 8
140·3	146·6	152·7	158·7	164·8	170·9	176·8	182·5	188·6	**22**	194·2	200·0	205·4	210·7	216·0	220·9	225·8	230·1	233·9	237·5
198·9	200·9	194·2	189·5	194·3	206·1	221·3	238·2	255·6		272·8	288·4	300·9	306·7	302·9	296·0	297·7	307·0	322·9	340·3
159·7	161·9	164·0	165·9	167·9	169·7	171·2	172·7	173·8		174·7	175·4	175·7	175·7	175·3	174·7	173·8	172·6	171·5	170·1
144·1	156·4	168·6	181·0	193·3	205·8	218·3	230·9	243·4		256·1	268·7	281·5	294·1	306·6	319·3	331·6	344·2	356·6	9·1
158·8	159·9	161·0	162·2	163·1	164·0	164·9	165·3	165·7		166·2	166·1	166·0	165·9	165·5	165·1	164·2	163·4	162·6	161·7
265·0	271·5	278·1	285·0	292·1	299·0	306·3	313·4	320·6	**23**	327·9	335·0	342·4	349·5	356·7	3·6	10·7	17·8	24·6	31·5
180·4	173·8	176·1	186·3	200·8	217·4	234·6	251·8	267·9		281·2	280·2	287·9	280·3	279·3	287·3	301·1	317·9	336·1	354·6
183·1	185·3	187·5	189·6	191·8	193·9	195·9	197·9	199·6		201·2	202·7	203·9	204·8	205·4	205·9	205·9	205·5	205·0	201·0
216·3	222·3	225·7	225·2	221·2	215·1	210·8	210·3	214·0		220·0	228·0	237·2	247·1	257·8	268·6	280·0	291·4	303·3	315·0
169·4	170·6	171·8	173·0	174·0	175·0	176·0	176·6	177·2		177·9	178·0	178·2	178·3	177·9	177·4	177·0	176·3	175·6	174·9
																Mr 8	Mr 18	Mr 28	Ap 7
152·3	158·6	164·9	171·1	177·5	183·8	190·1	196·5	202·9	**24**	209·1	215·5	221·8	228·1	234·5	240·8	247·0	253·3	259·4	265·6
158·4	166·7	180·3	196·5	213·6	231·0	247·4	261·7	271·4		272·8	265·7	261·7	267·4	280·0	295·9	313·5	332·0	350·1	7·1
206·9	208·9	211·1	213·3	215·5	217·7	220·0	222·2	224·3		226·4	228·4	230·2	231·9	233·4	234·7	235·6	236·5	236·9	236·9
180·4	192·8	205·5	217·9	230·4	243·0	255·5	268·0	280·3		293·0	305·3	317·5	329·7	341·8	353·8	5·4	17·1	28·1	39·1
179·8	181·0	182·2	183·4	184·5	185·6	186·7	187·5	188·3		189·1	189·4	189·7	190·1	189·9	189·7	189·5	188·9	188·3	187·6
O 9	O 19	O 29	N 8	N 18	N 28	D 8	D 18	D 28		Ja 7	Ja 17	Ja 27	F 6	F 16	F 26	Mr 8	Mr 18	Mr 28	Ap 7
303·7	306·7	310·7	315·0	320·0	325·4	330·8	336·6	342·7	**25**	348·8	355·1	1·4	7·7	14·2	20·4	26·9	33·3	39·8	46·1
159·8	175·6	192·6	210·1	226·8	241·9	253·1	257·5	252·2		245·9	248·8	259·3	274·5	291·4	309·5	327·5	344·7	359·5	9·3
232·1	233·8	235·8	237·9	239·9	242·2	244·4	246·7	249·0		251·3	253·6	255·7	257·9	259·9	261·8	263·7	265·3	266·6	267·9
128·9	140·2	151·8	163·7	175·4	187·6	199·7	212·0	224·4		236·8	249·5	262·0	274·4	286·9	299·5	312·1	324·5	337·1	349·5
190·0	191·2	192·4	193·6	194·8	196·0	197·1	198·0	198·9		199·8	200·3	200·8	201·4	201·4	201·4	201·4	200·9	200·4	200·0
O 10	O 20	O 30	N 9	N 19	N 29	D 9	D 19	D 29		Ja 8	Ja 18	Ja 28	F 7	F 17	F 27	Mr 9	Mr 19	Mr 29	Ap 8
164·7	171·1	177·5	184·2	190·7	197·4	203·9	210·5	217·4	**26**	224·2	231·1	238·0	244·8	251·9	258·8	265·9	273·0	280·1	287·1
173·3	190·9	208·0	228·4	235·6	241·6	237·8	230·7	231·4		240·8	255·0	271·6	289·4	307·3	324·3	339·4	349·7	351·9	345·4
260·4	261·6	262·9	264·5	266·2	268·2	270·3	272·4	274·4		277·0	279·3	281·8	284·0	286·4	288·6	290·9	293·1	295·1	297·1
215·2	226·6	238·2	249·3	260·1	270·4	280·0	288·7	295·9		300·9	302·3	300·3	295·0	289·4	286·8	288·5	293·0	299·8	308·4
200·1	201·3	202·5	203·7	204·9	206·1	207·2	208·2	209·2		210·2	210·9	211·6	212·3	212·5	212·7	212·9	212·6	212·3	211·9
20·9	18·7	16·1	13·3	11·5	10·7	10·9	12·3	14·6	**27**	17·7	21·0	25·4	29·8	34·6	39·8	45·0	50·5	56·2	61·7
187·0	208·2	216·8	225·2	224·4	216·8	214·5	221·5	234·4		250·5	267·8	285·5	302·9	318·1	329·9	334·3	329·0	323·3	327·2
293·1	293·2	293·6	294·3	295·4	296·6	298·1	300·0	301·8		303·8	306·0	308·3	310·6	313·0	315·5	317·9	320·2	322·6	325·0
162·2	174·5	187·0	199·6	212·0	224·8	237·3	249·9	262·6		275·1	288·0	300·3	313·1	325·5	337·9	350·2	2·5	14·5	26·8
210·3	211·4	212·5	213·6	214·8	216·0	217·1	218·2	219·3		220·4	221·2	222·0	222·9	223·3	223·7	224·1	224·0	223·8	223·6
																Mr 8	Mr 18	Mr 28	Ap 7
176·7	183·2	189·9	196·7	203·4	210·4	217·2	224·3	231·4	**28**	238·5	245·7	253·0	260·3	267·7	275·3	282·7	290·2	297·8	305·5
197·2	207·6	210·1	203·6	198·5	202·9	214·5	229·5	246·6		264·0	281·4	297·3	310·1	316·5	313·3	306·3	308·1	317·2	331·9
331·7	330·6	329·7	329·3	329·0	329·2	329·8	330·6	331·7		333·1	334·8	336·6	338·5	340·8	343·0	345·3	347·7	350·1	352·3
136·3	141·2	148·1	156·5	166·1	176·4	187·0	198·3	209·8		221·5	233·4	245·7	257·6	270·0	282·1	294·5	306·8	319·3	331·5
220·2	221·3	222·4	223·4	224·5	225·6	226·8	227·9	229·0		230·2	231·1	232·0	233·0	233·6	234·2	234·7	234·7	234·8	234·8
O 9	O 19	O 29	N 8	N 18	N 28	D 8	D 18	D 28		Ja 7	Ja 17	Ja 27	F 6	F 16	F 26	Mr 8	Mr 18	Mr 28	Ap 7
67·9	71·3	74·1	75·7	76·5	75·7	73·7	70·7	67·1	**29**	68·5	61·3	60·0	60·1	61·3	63·4	66·6	70·1	74·3	78·6
194·5	190·2	182·8	184·9	194·7	209·0	225·6	243·0	260·1		276·5	290·2	298·6	297·9	290·3	288·6	296·3	310·1	326·8	345·0
13·2	11·9	10·5	9·1	7·9	6·9	6·3	5·6	5·6		5·9	6·5	7·4	8·6	10·1	11·7	13·6	15·7	17·8	20·0
198·9	211·0	223·3	235·5	247·9	260·1	272·1	284·1	295·9		307·7	318·8	329·9	340·3	350·3	359·5	6·9	12·8	15·8	14·7
230·1	231·1	232·1	233·1	234·3	235·5	236·6	237·8	239·0		240·1	241·1	242·1	243·1	243·8	244·5	245·3	245·6	245·9	246·1
O 10	O 20	O 30	N 9	N 19	N 29	D 9	D 19	D 29		Ja 8	Ja 18	Ja 28	F 7	F 17	F 27	Mr 9	Mr 19	Mr 29	Ap 8
189·7	196·5	203·3	210·4	217·4	224·6	231·8	239·0	246·4	**30**	253·9	261·3	268·8	276·5	284·3	292·0	299·9	307·6	315·4	323·3
168·0	167·8	176·4	190·3	206·9	223·7	240·9	257·4	271·6		281·0	282·1	274·8	271·4	277·4	290·3	306·4	324·3	342·7	0·9
52·0	51·5	50·7	49·6	48·4	47·1	45·7	44·4	43·3		42·4	41·7	41·4	41·5	41·8	42·6	43·6	44·0	46·5	48·1
144·6	156·7	169·1	181·5	193·8	206·3	218·9	231·4	244·2		256·8	269·5	282·0	294·6	307·3	319·8	332·3	344·7	357·2	9·6
240·3	241·2	242·1	243·0	244·1	245·2	246·3	247·5	248·7		249·8	250·9	252·0	253·1	254·0	254·9	255·7	256·1	256·5	257·0

Mag.	P.Phal.	U.Phal.	Hasta.	Chit.	Svati.	Visak.	Anur.	Jyesh.	Mula.	P. Ash.	U. Ash.	Srav.	Dan.	Satab.	P. Bhad.	U. Bhad.	Revati.
133·3	146·7	160·0	173·3	186·7	200·0	213·3	226·7	240·0	253·3	266·7	280·0	293·3	306·7	320·0	333·3	346·7	360·0

APPENDIX II:—Geocentric (Indian) Longitudes of Sun and Major planets

(For the years 1840—1909,

Day of S. Yr.	0	10	20	30	40	50	60	70	80	90	100	110	120	130	140	150	160	170
⊙'s Mean L.	357·0	6·9	16·7	26·6	36·4	46·3	56·1	66·0	75·9	85·7	95·6	105·4	115·3	125·1	135·0	144·8	154·7	164·6
Actual do.	+2·1	+2·0	+1·9	+1·7	+1·4	+1·1	+0·8	+0·4	+0·0	−0·3	−0·7	−1·1	−1·4	−1·6	−1·9	−2·0	−2·1	−2·2
English date.	Ap 13	Ap 23	My 3	My 13	My 23	Je 2	Je 12	Je 22	Jl 2	Jl 12	Jl 22	Au 1	Au 11	Au 21	Au 31	S 10	S 20	S 30
Tamil month.	Chit	Chit	Chit	Chit	Vaik	Vaik	Vaik	Ani	Ani	Ani	Adi	Adi	Adi	Avani	Avani	Avani	Pura	Pura
Do. date.	1	11	21	31	10	20	30	9	19	29	7	17	27	6	16	26	5	15
1930 Mars ...	327·2	335·0	342·7	350·4	358·0	5·6	13·0	20·8	27·6	34·8	41·7	48·5	55·1	61·7	68·2	74·2	80·3	86·0
⊙'s L. Merc. ...	9·7	25·6	37·3	41·1	35·3	30·5	35·7	48·1	64·4	82·4	101·1	119·4	136·4	150·8	160·2	160·7	153·3	150·4
+·5 Jup. ...	49·1	51·1	53·2	55·4	57·7	59·9	62·4	64·7	67·0	69·4	71·7	73·8	76·0	78·0	79·8	81·4	83·0	84·3
Ven. ...	15·8	28·1	40·4	52·4	64·6	76·6	88·6	100·4	112·2	123·8	135·3	146·8	158·0	169·0	179·8	190·0	199·5	208·3
Sat. ...	257·1	256·9	256·7	256·6	255·9	255·3	254·7	254·0	253·2	252·4	251·8	251·2	250·5	250·3	250·1	249·8	250·1	250·4
1931 Mars ...	101·2	104·5	108·5	112·8	117·5	122·7	127·9	133·6	139·3	145·0	151·1	157·1	163·4	169·7	176·1	182·7	189·3	196·2
⊙'s L. Merc. ...	16·8	22·1	17·7	11·5	14·5	25·7	41·5	59·4	78·1	96·6	114·5	130·0	141·2	144·6	138·4	133·3	137·8	149·4
+·2 Jup. ...	77·7	79·0	80·5	82·2	84·0	86·1	88·0	90·2	92·5	94·8	97·0	99·3	101·6	103·7	105·9	108·1	110·1	111·9
Ven. ...	321·5	333·4	345·4	357·4	9·5	21·6	33·8	45·9	58·1	70·2	82·3	94·6	106·8	119·1	131·4	143·7	156·2	168·7
Sat. ...	268·0	268·1	268·2	268·2	267·7	267·2	266·8	266·0	265·2	264·4	263·7	263·0	262·3	261·9	261·5	261·1	261·2	261·3
Eng. Date.	Ap 12	Ap 22	My 2	My 12	My 22	Je 1	Je 11	Je 21	Jl 1	Jl 11	Jl 21	Jl 31	Au 10	Au 20	Au 30	S 9	S 19	S 29
1932 Mars ...	343·4	351·2	358·7	6·5	13·9	21·3	28·7	35·9	43·1	50·1	57·0	63·7	70·3	76·9	83·5	89·7	95·0	101·8
⊙'s L. Merc. ...	0·6	353·3	353·9	3·5	18·3	35·9	54·7	73·6	92·0	108·5	121·2	127·1	123·2	116·5	118·4	128·8	143·4	160·3
−·0 Jup. ...	108·1	108·3	108·9	109·7	110·9	112·2	113·8	115·6	117·4	119·4	121·6	123·8	125·9	128·1	130·4	132·6	134·7	136·9
Ven. ...	44·5	54·6	63·9	72·0	78·5	82·5	83·4	79·7	73·8	68·4	66·1	67·6	72·4	79·4	87·8	97·2	107·4	118·1
Sat. ...	278·8	279·1	279·4	279·6	279·3	279·0	278·8	278·1	277·4	276·7	276·0	275·2	274·4	273·8	273·2	272·6	272·5	272·4
Eng. Date.	Ap 13	Ap 23	My 3	My 13	My 23	Je 2	Je 12	Je 22	Jl 2	Jl 12	Jl 22	Au 1	Au 11	Au 21	Au 31	S 10	S 20	S 30
1933 Mars ...	127·9	128·7	130·7	133·1	136·6	140·5	145·0	149·9	155·1	160·5	166·3	172·1	178·3	184·6	191·0	197·5	204·4	211·1
⊙'s L. Merc. ...	334·4	342·9	357·3	14·7	33·3	52·4	70·9	87·8	101·3	108·8	106·3	99·0	99·7	109·2	123·8	140·4	158·2	175·8
+·7 Jup. ...	140·4	139·6	139·2	138·9	139·3	139·8	140·6	141·7	143·0	144·4	146·2	148·1	150·0	152·1	154·2	156·4	158·6	160·8
Ven. ...	357·6	10·0	22·3	34·7	47·0	59·2	71·5	83·6	95·7	107·9	120·0	132·2	144·2	156·1	168·2	180·2	192·1	203·7
Sat. ...	289·8	290·2	290·6	291·1	291·0	290·9	290·8	290·2	289·6	289·1	288·3	287·5	286·8	286·1	285·4	284·7	284·4	284·1
1934 Mars ...	359·4	7·1	14·7	22·0	29·4	36·4	43·6	50·7	57·6	64·5	71·3	77·9	84·6	91·0	97·6	103·9	110·1	116·3
⊙'s L. Merc. ...	334·9	351·5	9·9	28·8	47·7	65·2	80·0	89·2	89·3	82·4	80·3	88·2	101·9	118·6	136·4	154·3	171·7	187·2
+·5 Jup. ...	174·1	172·8	171·5	170·7	169·9	169·3	169·2	169·4	169·8	170·6	171·7	173·0	174·4	176·2	178·0	179·9	182·1	184·1
Ven. ...	312·9	322·6	333·3	344·1	355·3	6·5	18·0	29·8	41·4	53·2	65·2	77·0	89·2	101·4	113·3	125·6	137·9	150·3
Sat. ...	300·6	301·2	301·8	302·5	302·6	302·7	302·9	302·5	302·1	301·8	301·1	300·4	299·6	298·8	298·0	297·3	296·8	296·3
1935 Mars ...	168·6	165·5	163·7	162·8	163·2	164·8	167·4	170·8	174·7	179·3	184·4	189·7	195·6	201·4	207·6	214·2	220·8	227·6
⊙'s L. Merc. ...	346·8	5·4	24·3	42·0	57·8	68·9	71·1	64·7	60·8	67·0	79·9	96·3	114·1	132·4	150·1	166·4	179·9	187·1
+·2 Jup. ...	208·2	207·1	205·8	204·5	203·1	202·0	201·0	200·1	199·6	199·4	199·5	200·0	200·8	201·9	203·1	204·7	206·3	208·2
Ven. ...	33·2	45·0	56·7	68·3	79·7	90·9	101·5	112·1	121·8	130·8	139·0	145·1	149·0	148·8	145·6	139·8	134·3	132·6
Sat. ...	311·5	312·3	313·1	314·0	314·4	314·8	315·1	314·9	314·7	314·6	314·0	313·4	312·8	312·0	311·2	310·3	309·6	308·9
Eng. Date.	Ap 12	Ap 22	My 2	My 12	My 22	Je 1	Je 11	Je 21	Jl 1	Jl 11	Jl 21	Jl 31	Au 10	Au 20	Au 30	S 9	S 19	S 29
1936 Mars ...	14·3	21·5	28·8	35·9	42·9	50·1	56·9	63·8	70·6	77·2	83·9	90·6	96·9	103·5	109·8	116·3	122·7	128·8
⊙'s L. Merc. ...	1·1	19·1	35·2	47·6	52·2	47·3	41·6	45·8	57·9	73·7	91·5	110·0	128·2	145·2	159·8	169·6	170·4	163·3
−·1 Jup. ...	241·3	241·2	240·5	269·7	238·7	237·4	236·0	234·6	233·4	232·3	231·4	230·9	230·7	230·7	231·3	231·9	232·9	234·2
Ven. ...	338·2	350·5	2·8	15·2	27·4	39·7	52·1	64·4	76·5	88·8	101·1	113·2	125·6	137·8	150·1	162·5	174·7	187·0
Sat. ...	322·5	323·5	324·5	325·5	326·1	326·7	327·3	327·4	327·5	327·5	327·0	326·5	326·1	325·3	324·5	328·8	323·0	322·2
Eng. Date.	Ap 13	Ap 23	My 3	My 13	My 23	Je 2	Je 12	Je 22	Jl 2	Jl 12	Jl 22	Au 1	Au 11	Au 21	Au 31	S 10	S 20	S 30
1937 Mars ...	222·3	222·0	220·2	217·8	214·9	211·7	209·7	208·3	208·9	210·2	212·8	216·3	220·4	225·3	230·4	236·2	242·3	248·6
⊙'s L. Merc. ...	14·5	27·3	33·0	28·8	22·5	25·5	36·9	52·7	70·4	89·1	107·6	125·2	140·6	151·4	154·3	148·0	143·0	147·6
+·7 Jup. ...	272·6	273·5	274·0	274·1	274·1	273·6	272·7	271·7	270·5	269·1	267·8	266·5	265·4	264·4	263·8	263·5	263·5	263·8
Ven. ...	9·0	2·6	357·9	356·8	359·9	5·1	12·7	21·5	30·9	41·3	51·8	63·0	74·0	85·6	97·1	108·9	120·8	132·9
Sat. ...	333·9	335·0	336·1	337·3	338·1	338·9	339·7	340·0	340·3	340·6	340·4	340·2	339·9	339·2	338·5	337·8	337·0	336·2
1938 Mars ...	29·4	36·5	43·2	50·0	56·9	63·7	70·4	77·0	83·4	90·1	96·6	103·1	109·5	115·9	122·3	128·6	134·9	141·4
⊙'s L. Merc. ...	13·6	11·4	4·5	4·9	14·6	29·7	47·2	66·0	84·9	103·0	119·1	131·8	137·4	133·0	126·5	128·0	139·0	153·6
+·4 Jup. ...	301·9	303·6	305·2	306·5	307·5	308·3	308·6	308·7	308·4	307·8	307·0	305·8	304·4	303·1	301·8	300·5	299·4	298·7
Ven. ...	16·3	28·7	40·9	53·1	65·1	77·1	88·9	100·9	112·6	124·3	135·7	147·1	158·4	169·3	179·9	189·9	199·4	207·6
Sat. ...	345·3	346·5	347·7	349·0	350·0	351·0	352·0	352·6	353·2	353·7	353·7	353·7	353·7	353·2	352·7	352·1	351·3	350·5
1939 Mars ...	258·4	263·3	268·0	272·2	275·9	278·9	280·7	281·8	282·0	280·6	277·9	275·6	273·0	272·1	272·3	274·1	276·8	280·6
⊙'s L. Merc. ...	346·6	344·8	352·8	6·8	24·0	42·5	61·6	80·0	97·1	111·0	119·0	117·2	109·6	109·6	118·4	132·6	140·1	166·8
+·2 Jup. ...	330·0	332·2	334·4	336·4	338·4	340·0	341·6	342·8	343·8	344·5	344·8	344·7	344·4	343·6	342·6	341·4	340·1	338·7
Ven. ...	321·9	333·7	345·8	357·9	10·1	22·1	34·3	46·4	58·6	70·7	82·8	95·2	107·5	119·7	131·9	144·4	156·7	169·2
Sat. ...	356·9	358·2	359·5	0·8	2·0	3·2	4·3	5·1	5·9	6·7	7·0	7·3	7·6	7·3	7·0	6·7	6·0	5·3

Mesh.	Vrsh.	Mith.	Kat.	Sim.	Kan.	Tul.	Vrsch.	Dhan.	Mak.	Kum.	Min.	Asvn.	Bhar	Krit.	Rohi.	Mrig.	Ardh.	Punar.	Push.	Asles.
30	60	90	120	150	180	210	240	270	300	330	360	13·3	26·7	40·0	53·3	66·7	80·0	93·3	106·7	120·0

at Ujjain mean Sunrise for every ten days from A.D. 1930 to A.D. 1939.

see *Indian Chronology,* **Table XVIII).**

180	190	200	210	220	230	240	250	260		270	280	290	300	310	320	330	340	350	360
174·4	184·3	194·1	204·0	213·8	223·7	233·5	243·4	253·3		263·1	273·0	282·8	292·7	302·5	312·4	322·2	332·1	342·0	351·8
−2·2	−2·1	−1·9	−1·7	−1·5	−1·2	−0·9	−0·5	−0·1		+0·3	+0·6	+1·0	+1·3	+1·6	+1·8	+2·0	+2·1	+2·2	+2·2
O 10	O 20	O 30	N 9	N 19	N 29	D 9	D 19	D 29		Ja 8	Ja 18	Ja 28	F 7	F 17	F 27	Mr 9	Mr 19	Mr 29	Ap 8
Pura	Aipp	Aipp	Aipp	Kart	Kart	Kart	Marg	Marg		Marg	Tai	Tai	Tai	Masi	Masi	Masi	Pang	Pang	Pang
25	4	14	24	4	14	24	5	15		25	5	15	25	6	16	26	6	16	26
91·4	96·4	101·1	105·5	108·9	111·8	114·1	115·1	115·3	**31**	113·9	111·4	107·9	103·9	100·5	97·7	96·4	96·4	97·7	99·8
157·2	169·8	185·7	202·7	220·0	236·7	251·6	262·8	266·6		260·9	254·8	258·4	269·4	284·7	301·9	320·1	338·3	355·6	10·4
85·2	86·0	86·3	86·3	86·0	85·4	84·4	83·2	82·0		80·6	79·3	78·1	77·0	76·2	75·8	75·6	75·8	76·3	77·2
215·5	220·8	223·4	222·1	217·1	211·1	207·7	208·5	212·7		219·4	227·5	237·1	247·0	257·9	268·9	280·3	291·8	303·6	315·4
250·7	251·4	252·1	252·9	253·9	254·9	256·0	257·2	258·4		259·6	260·8	262·0	263·1	264·0	264·9	265·9	266·5	267·1	267·8
																Mr 8	Mr 18	Mr 28	Ap 7
203·0	209·8	217·0	224·0	231·3	238·6	246·0	253·7	261·2	**32**	268·9	276·6	284·4	292·2	300·1	308·0	315·8	323·8	331·6	339·5
164·7	181·7	199·1	216·2	231·8	244·1	250·6	247·2	240·0		240·3	249·4	263·6	280·2	298·1	316·1	333·3	348·8	0·0	2·9
113·7	115·2	116·4	117·5	118·3	118·7	118·7	118·5	118·0		117·1	116·1	114·8	113·5	112·2	111·0	109·8	108·9	108·4	108·1
180·9	193·4	206·0	218·4	230·9	243·5	256·0	268·5	281·1		293·5	305·9	318·0	330·3	342·3	354·1	5·7	17·2	28·5	39·2
261·4	261·9	262·4	263·0	264·0	265·0	265·9	267·1	268·3		269·4	270·6	271·8	272·9	274·0	275·1	276·2	277·0	277·8	278·5
O 9	O 19	O 29	N 8	N 18	N 28	D 8	D 18	D 28		Ja 7	Ja 17	Ja 27	F 6	F 16	F 26	Mr 8	Mr 18	Mr 28	Ap 7
107·8	113·6	119·0	124·2	129·1	133·8	137·8	141·4	144·4	**33**	146·4	147·6	147·2	145·8	143·3	139·4	136·0	132·6	129·6	128·5
178·0	195·3	211·7	225·2	233·9	233·5	225·9	223·3	230·1		242·9	258·9	276·4	294·2	311·4	327·3	339·6	344·7	340·1	333·7
139·0	140·9	142·8	144·5	146·0	147·2	148·4	149·1	149·6		149·7	149·5	149·0	148·3	147·2	145·9	144·7	143·4	142·1	140·9
129·1	140·5	152·2	164·0	176·0	188·0	200·3	212·5	224·9		237·3	250·0	262·6	275·0	287·6	300·0	312·7	325·0	337·6	350·0
272·3	272·7	273·1	273·5	274·4	275·3	276·1	276·9	277·7		278·4	279·6	280·8	281·9	283·0	284·2	285·4	286·5	287·5	288·5
O 10	O 20	O 30	N 9	N 19	N 29	D 9	D 19	D 29		Ja 8	Ja 18	Ja 28	F 7	F 17	F 27	Mr 9	Mr 19	Mr 29	Ap 8
218·0	225·2	232·3	239·7	247·0	254·6	262·2	269·8	277·6	**34**	285·3	293·2	301·2	309·0	316·8	324·6	332·6	340·4	347·9	355·8
192·6	207·0	217·0	218·9	212·1	207·6	212·4	224·2	239·7		256·7	274·2	291·6	307·5	320·3	326·7	323·2	316·3	317·6	327·8
163·0	165·1	167·2	169·3	171·2	173·0	174·7	176·2	177·5		178·6	179·3	179·7	179·9	179·7	179·1	178·2	177·3	176·1	174·7
215·5	227·1	238·4	249·4	260·0	270·4	279·7	288·1	294·8		299·1	300·0	296·6	291·1	285·6	284·4	286·8	292·0	299·3	308·2
283·8	284·0	284·2	284·5	285·2	286·9	286·7	287·7	288·7		289·8	291·0	292·2	293·4	294·6	295·8	296·9	298·0	299·1	300·1
122·3	128·2	134·0	139·7	145·3	150·6	155·9	160·7	165·3	**35**	169·7	173·4	176·7	179·2	180·5	181·0	180·2	177·9	174·4	170·4
198·9	203·8	198·8	192·2	194·4	204·6	218·9	235·5	253·0		270·2	286·5	300·1	308·5	307·4	299·9	298·6	306·9	320·8	337·7
186·3	188·6	190·7	192·8	195·0	197·2	199·3	201·2	203·1		204·8	206·3	207·7	208·7	209·4	209·9	210·1	209·9	209·4	208·7
162·7	175·2	187·5	200·1	212·8	225·2	237·8	250·4	263·2		275·8	288·3	301·2	313·6	326·0	338·4	350·8	2·8	15·1	27·0
295·8	295·8	295·8	295·8	296·3	296·8	297·4	298·4	299·4		300·3	301·5	302·7	303·8	305·0	306·2	307·5	308·7	309·9	311·0
																Mr 8	Mr 18	Mr 28	Ap 7
234·6	241·6	249·0	256·2	263·7	271·1	278·8	286·6	294·2	**36**	302·0	309·8	317·5	325·1	332·9	340·7	348·1	355·6	3·3	10·5
185·2	177·5	176·9	185·1	198·5	214·7	231·9	249·2	265·7		280·2	290·2	291·9	284·8	280·8	286·5	299·1	315·4	333·1	351·8
210·2	212·3	214·4	216·6	218·9	221·1	223·2	225·6	227·7		229·8	231·7	233·8	235·5	237·1	238·5	239·6	240·4	241·1	241·3
134·9	140·1	147·6	156·2	166·0	176·3	187·3	198·7	210·1		221·9	233·9	246·0	258·1	270·3	282·6	295·0	307·4	319·6	332·1
308·3	308·1	307·9	307·7	308·0	308·3	308·7	309·5	310·3		311·2	312·3	313·4	314·5	315·7	316·9	318·2	319·4	320·6	321·9
O 9	O 19	O 29	N 8	N 18	N 28	D 8	D 18	D 28		Ja 7	Ja 17	Ja 27	F 6	F 16	F 26	Mr 8	Mr 18	Mr 28	Ap 7
135·0	141·0	147·2	153·1	159·1	164·9	170·7	176·4	181·9	**37**	187·5	192·8	197·7	202·7	207·1	211·2	215·0	218·2	220·5	222·0
150·8	166·1	178·4	194·0	210·9	228·3	245·1	260·1	271·6		276·0	270·7	264·5	267·5	278·2	293·5	310·7	329·0	347·5	4·8
235·8	237·4	239·3	241·4	243·4	245·6	247·8	250·2	252·4		254·6	257·0	259·2	261·4	263·6	265·5	267·4	269·1	270·6	271·9
199·2	211·6	223·8	236·1	248·2	260·4	272·4	284·4	296·3		307·8	319·2	330·1	340·5	350·0	359·0	6·2	11·3	13·4	12·0
321·5	321·1	320·7	320·2	320·3	320·4	320·5	321·1	321·7		322·4	323·5	324·6	325·6	326·8	328·0	329·2	330·5	331·8	333·0
O 10	O 20	O 30	N 9	N 19	N 29	D 9	D 19	D 29		Ja 8	Ja 18	Ja 28	F 7	F 17	F 27	Mr 9	Mr 19	Mr 29	Ap 8
255·2	262·0	269·0	276·1	283·3	290·8	298·1	305·6	313·0	**38**	320·4	327·9	335·3	342·7	350·1	357·2	4·6	11·7	18·8	25·9
159·5	174·7	191·7	209·1	226·1	241·5	253·9	259·6	255·8		248·8	249·8	259·4	273·7	290·7	308·5	326·8	344·1	359·5	10·5
264·6	265·5	266·7	268·4	270·0	271·9	274·0	276·1	278·2		280·6	282·9	285·2	287·6	290·0	292·3	294·6	296·9	298·9	300·9
145·0	157·2	169·7	182·0	194·5	206·9	219·4	231·9	244·6		257·3	270·0	282·6	295·1	307·9	320·3	332·9	345·2	357·7	10·1
335·4	334·8	334·2	333·6	333·5	333·4	333·2	333·7	334·2		334·7	335·5	336·3	337·1	338·3	339·5	340·7	342·0	343·3	344·6
147·5	153·9	160·0	166·3	172·5	178·8	185·0	191·0	197·1	**39**	203·4	209·5	215·6	221·7	227·6	233·5	239·3	244·9	250·5	255·8
170·5	188·1	205·3	221·4	234·8	243·0	242·3	234·7	232·6		239·7	252·9	269·1	286·7	304·5	322·0	337·8	350·0	355·2	350·4
298·2	298·0	298·2	298·8	299·6	300·9	302·2	303·8	305·7		307·7	309·8	312·0	314·4	316·8	319·1	321·6	324·0	326·4	328·7
214·6	219·4	220·7	218·7	212·9	207·5	204·9	206·6	211·6		218·5	227·3	237·0	247·2	258·0	269·1	280·6	292·1	303·9	315·9
349·8	349·0	348·2	347·4	347·0	346·6	346·3	346·5	346·7		347·0	347·7	348·4	349·1	350·2	351·3	352·4	353·7	355·0	356·3
																Mr 8	Mr 18	Mr 28	Ap 7
285·0	289·9	295·6	301·3	307·5	313·7	320·1	326·9	333·5	**40**	340·0	346·8	353·6	0·2	7·1	13·7	20·3	27·0	33·7	40·3
184·3	200·9	215·5	225·8	228·0	221·2	216·5	220·9	232·6		248·0	265·1	282·7	300·3	316·4	329·5	336·8	334·1	326·8	327·4
337·3	336·2	335·2	334·4	334·1	334·1	334·4	334·1	336·2		337·4	338·9	340·7	342·6	344·6	346·9	349·1	351·5	353·8	356·3
181·6	193·9	206·6	218·9	231·5	244·0	256·6	269·0	281·6		293·8	306·2	318·5	330·6	342·7	354·4	6·1	17·5	28·6	39·3
4·6	3·8	3·0	2·1	1·5	0·9	0·3	0·2	0·1		0·1	0·6	1·1	1·6	2·5	3·4	4·4	5·6	6·8	8·1

Mag.	P. Phal.	U. Phal.	Hasta.	Chit.	Svati.	Visak.	Anur.	Jyesh.	Mula.	P. Ash.	U. Ash.	Srav.	Dan.	Satab.	P. Bhad.	U. Bhad.	Revati.
133·3	146·7	160·0	173·3	186·6	200·0	213·3	226·7	240·0	253·3	266·7	280·0	293·3	306·7	320·0	333·3	346·7	360·0

APPENDIX II:—Geocentric (Indian) Longitudes of Sun and Major planets

(For the years 1840—1909.

Day of S. Yr.	0	10	20	30	40	50	60	70	80	90	100	110	120	130	140	150	160	170
☉'s Mean L.	357·0	6·9	16·7	26·6	36·4	46·3	56·1	66·0	75·9	85·7	95·6	105·4	115·3	125·1	135·0	144·8	154·7	164·6
Actual do.	+2·1	+2·0	+1·9	+1·7	+1·4	+1·1	+0·8	+0·4	+0·0	−0·3	−0·7	−1·1	−1·4	−1·6	−1·9	−2·0	−2·1	−2·2
English date.	Ap 12	Ap 22	My 2	My 12	My 22	Je 1	Je 11	Je 21	Jl 1	Jl 11	Jl 21	Jl 31	Au 10	Au 20	Au 30	S 9	S 19	S 29
Tamil month.	Chit	Chit	Chit	Chit	Vaik	Vaik	Vaik	Ani	Ani	Ani	Adi	Adi	Adi	Avani	Avani	Avani	Pura	Pura
Do. date.	1	11	21	31	10	20	30	9	19	29	7	17	27	6	16	26	5	15
1940 Mars ...	43·7	50·2	56·7	63·3	69·8	76·2	82·7	89·0	95·6	102·0	108·4	114·6	121·0	127·4	133·8	140·2	146·5	152·9
☉'s L. Merc. ...	331·5	344·4	0·8	19·3	38·0	56·9	74·6	89·7	99·4	100·4	93·2	90·5	97·9	111·0	127·4	145·0	162·9	180·2
−·1 Jup. ...	357·6	0·0	2·4	4·8	7·0	9·4	11·5	13·5	15·5	17·0	18·5	19·7	20·6	21·1	21·3	21·2	20·7	[illegible]
Ven. ...	44·6	54·6	63·6	71·4	77·4	80·7	80·8	76·6	69·0	65·2	63·8	66·3	71·5	78·9	87·7	97·3	107·6	118·2
Sat. ...	8·8	10·1	11·4	12·7	14·0	15·3	16·6	17·6	18·6	19·6	20·2	20·8	21·4	21·4	21·3	21·3	20·8	20·3
Eng. Date. ...	Ap 13	Ap 23	My 3	My 13	My 23	Je 2	Je 12	Je 22	Jl 2	Jl 12	Jl 22	Au 1	Au 11	Au 21	Au 31	S 10	S 20	S 30
1941 Mars ...	282·9	289·7	296·3	303·1	309·7	316·2	322·4	328·4	334·2	339·7	344·5	348·7	352·0	354·5	355·7	355·5	353·9	351·3
☉'s L. Merc. ...	330·8	357·9	16·6	35·4	53·2	68·9	79·7	82·1	75·5	71·8	77·9	90·8	107·1	124·8	142·8	160·6	176·8	189·7
+·6 Jup. ...	25·8	27·6	29·9	32·3	34·7	37·1	39·4	41·8	44·1	46·2	48·3	50·3	51·9	53·5	54·7	55·8	56·5	56·8
Ven. ...	358·1	10·6	22·8	35·2	47·5	59·7	72·1	84·2	96·3	108·5	120·5	132·7	144·7	156·5	168·7	180·6	192·4	204·3
Sat. ...	21·1	22·4	23·7	25·1	26·4	27·7	29·1	30·3	31·5	32·6	33·4	34·2	34·9	35·2	35·5	35·8	35·5	35·2
1942 Mars ...	58·8	64·9	71·0	77·1	83·2	89·4	95·7	101·9	108·0	114·4	120·7	127·0	133·3	139·6	146·0	152·4	158·9	165·3
☉'s L. Merc. ...	353·6	12·2	30·3	46·4	58·8	63·4	58·2	52·7	57·0	68·9	84·6	102·4	120·8	138·8	155·6	170·0	179·3	179·7
+·4 Jup. ...	53·0	54·9	56·9	59·1	61·3	63·5	65·9	68·2	70·6	72·9	75·2	77·4	79·5	81·6	83·6	85·3	86·9	88·3
Ven. ...	312·7	322·7	333·2	344·2	355·6	6·8	18·5	30·2	41·9	53·8	65·7	77·6	89·7	101·7	113·8	126·1	138·5	150·8
Sat. ...	33·5	34·8	36·1	37·5	38·8	40·1	41·5	42·8	44·1	45·3	46·4	47·5	48·7	49·1	49·5	50·0	50·0	49·9
1943 Mars ...	302·2	309·6	317·2	324·6	332·2	339·5	347·0	353·9	1·0	7·9	14·4	20·8	27·0	32·8	38·4	43·4	47·7	51·6
☉'s L. Merc. ...	7·3	21·0	37·3	44·1	40·6	33·8	35·9	46·6	62·0	79·7	98·1	116·5	134·2	149·4	160·8	164·0	158·1	152·6
+·1 Jup. ...	81·8	83·0	84·3	85·8	87·6	89·5	91·6	93·7	95·9	98·2	100·5	102·6	104·9	107·2	109·4	[illegible]	113·6	115·5
Ven. ...	33·5	45·4	57·2	68·7	80·0	91·0	101·6	112·0	121·8	130·5	138·2	143·8	147·2	146·5	142·6	[illegible]	131·2	130·4
Sat. ...	46·4	47·7	49·0	50·2	51·5	52·8	54·1	55·4	56·7	58·1	59·3	60·5	61·7	62·5	63·3	64·1	64·4	64·7
1944 Mars. ...	74·8	80·2	85·7	91·4	97·2	103·0	108·9	114·9	120·8	126·9	133·1	139·4	145·7	152·1	158·4	165·0	171·4	178·0
☉'s L. Merc. ...	16·7	24·4	22·2	14·9	15·8	25·8	40·9	58·4	77·1	95·8	113·7	129·9	142·2	147·2	141·6	136·1	138·6	149·2
+·9 Jup. ...	112·4	112·5	112·9	113·7	114·8	116·0	117·6	119·2	121·0	123·0	125·1	127·2	129·4	131·6	133·8	136·0	138·2	140·4
Ven. ...	339·9	352·2	4·6	17·1	29·4	41·6	53·8	66·0	78·4	90·6	102·8	115·2	127·3	139·6	151·8	164·2	176·4	188·9
Sat. ...	59·5	60·6	61·7	62·8	64·1	65·4	66·7	68·0	69·4	70·8	72·1	73·4	74·6	75·6	76·6	77·6	78·1	78·6
1915 Mars. ...	320·5	328·3	336·1	343·9	351·8	358·9	6·4	13·7	20·9	28·0	35·1	41·7	48·5	55·0	61·1	67·2	72·9	78·4
☉'s L. Merc. ...	4·5	357·3	355·8	3·3	17·9	35·1	53·7	72·7	91·1	108·1	121·7	129·3	127·3	119·7	119·9	128·8	142·9	159·6
+·6 Jup. ...	145·0	141·1	143·6	143·2	143·3	143·7	144·4	145·3	146·6	148·0	149·6	151·4	153·4	155·3	157·4	159·6	161·7	163·9
Ven. ...	5·1	358·8	355·0	354·3	358·4	4·5	12·4	21·5	31·0	41·2	52·1	63·0	74·4	85·9	97·7	109·5	121·4	133·3
Sat. ...	72·8	73·7	74·6	75·5	76·7	77·9	79·1	80·5	81·9	83·2	84·5	85·8	87·2	88·3	89·4	90·6	91·4	92·2
1916 Mars ...	92·0	97·0	101·5	106·3	111·6	116·7	122·4	127·9	133·7	139·8	145·6	151·9	158·2	164·4	170·8	177·4	184·2	190·8
☉'s L. Merc. ...	336·3	342·3	355·5	12·0	30·4	49·4	68·1	85·6	100·6	110·2	110·9	103·6	101·1	108·4	121·6	138·0	155·5	173·2
+·4 Jup. ...	178·8	177·5	176·2	175·2	174·4	173·7	173·3	173·4	173·7	174·4	175·3	176·5	177·9	179·5	181·4	183·3	185·2	187·4
Ven. ...	16·8	29·2	41·5	53·5	65·7	77·6	89·5	101·2	113·1	124·6	136·2	147·5	158·5	169·5	179·8	189·9	198·9	207·0
Sat. ...	86·3	87·0	87·7	88·3	89·4	90·5	91·6	92·9	94·2	95·4	96·7	98·0	99·4	100·7	102·0	103·2	104·2	105·2
1947 Mars ...	337·1	344·8	352·6	0·3	7·9	15·4	22·7	30·0	37·1	44·3	51·1	57·9	64·8	71·2	77·6	83·8	90·0	96·1
☉'s L. Merc. ...	333·4	349·0	7·0	25·3	44·9	63·0	78·7	90·1	93·2	86·8	82·4	87·6	100·0	116·0	133·5	151·6	169·2	185·2
+·1 Jup. ...	212·9	211·8	210·6	209·3	207·9	206·6	205·7	204·7	204·0	203·7	203·7	204·0	204·7	205·6	206·8	208·2	209·9	211·6
Ven. ...	322·2	334·2	346·3	358·4	10·4	22·7	34·9	47·0	59·1	71·2	83·5	95·6	107·9	120·2	132·5	144·9	157·3	169·7
Sat. ...	100·1	100·5	100·9	101·3	102·2	103·1	103·9	105·1	106·3	107·5	108·8	110·1	111·4	112·7	114·0	115·3	116·4	117·5
1948 Mars ...	116·6	118·5	121·2	121·6	123·6	133·2	138·1	143·4	148·8	154·4	160·2	166·1	172·5	178·6	185·2	191·7	198·5	205·4
☉'s L. Merc. ...	345·8	4·5	23·3	41·5	57·6	69·9	74·4	69·1	63·6	67·9	79·8	95·5	113·2	131·4	149·4	166·1	180·1	188·9
+·8 Jup ...	245·3	215·6	245·1	244·4	243·4	241·9	240·9	239·6	238·3	237·2	236·2	235·5	235·1	235·2	235·3	236·0	237·0	238·2
Ven. ...	45·5	55·3	64·0	71·3	76·5	79·1	77·3	72·4	66·0	61·9	61·8	65·4	71·4	79·4	88·4	98·2	108·7	119·6
Sat. ...	114·0	114·1	114·2	114·4	115·1	115·8	116·4	117·5	118·6	119·6	120·9	122·2	123·4	124·7	126·0	127·3	128·5	129·7
1940 Mars ...	353·5	1·1	8·3	16·2	23·6	30·9	38·2	45·2	52·3	59·2	66·1	72·8	79·4	86·0	92·3	98·7	104·9	111·1
☉'s L. Merc. ...	0·2	18·4	35·1	48·5	55·1	51·7	44·9	47·0	57·7	73·2	90·5	109·0	127·2	144·7	159·8	170·6	173·6	167·2
+·6 Jup. ...	276·7	277·6	278·4	278·8	278·8	278·5	277·9	276·9	275·7	274·5	273·1	271·8	270·6	269·5	268·7	268·3	268·2	268·3
Ven. ...	358·7	11·1	23·4	35·8	48·1	60·2	72·6	84·6	96·8	108·9	121·0	133·2	145·0	157·2	169·0	181·1	192·9	204·6
Sat. ...	127·9	127·7	127·5	127·4	127·8	128·2	128·7	129·6	130·5	131·3	132·5	133·7	134·9	136·2	137·5	138·7	139·9	141·2

Mesh.	Vrsh.	Mith.	Kat.	Sim.	Kan.	Tul.	Vrsch.	Dhan.	Mak.	Kum.	Min.	Asvn.	Bhar.	Krit.	Rohi.	Mrig.	Ardh.	Punar.	Push.	Asles.
30	60	90	120	150	180	210	240	270	300	330	360	13·3	26·7	40·0	53·3	66·7	80·0	93·3	106·7	120·0

at Ujjain mean Sunrise for every ten days from A.D. 1940 to A.D. 1949.

see *Indian Chronology*, **Table XVIII).**

180	190	200	210	220	230	240	250	260		270	280	290	300	310	320	330	340	350	360
174·4	184·3	194·1	204·0	213·8	223·7	233·5	243·4	253·3		263·1	273·0	282·8	292·7	302·5	312·4	322·2	332·1	342·0	351·8
−2·2	−2·1	−1·9	−1·7	−1·5	−1·2	−0·9	−0·5	−0·1		+0·3	+0·6	+1·0	+1·3	+1·6	+1·8	+2·0	+2·1	+2·2	+2·2
O 9	O 19	O 29	N 8	N 18	N 28	D 8	D 18	D 28		Ja 7	Ja 17	Ja 27	F 6	F 16	F 26	Mr 8	Mr 18	Mr 28	Ap 7
Pura	Aipp	Aipp	Aipp	Kart	Kart	Kart	Marg	Marg		Marg	Tai	Tai	Tai	Masi	Masi	Masi	Pang	Pang	Pang
25	4	14	24	4	14	24	5	15		25	5	15	25	6	16	26	6	16	26
159·3	165·7	172·3	178·6	185·0	191·6	198·2	204·7	211·3	**41**	217·8	224·5	231·3	238·0	244·6	251·3	258·1	265·0	272·0	278·8
195·8	207·6	212·8	208·3	201·4	203·2	218·0	227·3	243·9		261·4	278·7	295·3	309·1	318·1	317·8	310·5	308·6	316·2	330·0
18·9	17·6	16·2	14·8	13·5	12·4	11·4	10·9	10·5		10·7	11·1	11·9	12·9	14·3	15·9	17·6	19·5	21·7	23·9
128·4	140·8	152·5	164·4	176·3	188·6	200·8	213·1	225·4		237·9	250·5	263·1	275·5	288·1	300·6	313·2	325·6	338·1	350·6
19·7	18·9	18·1	17·2	16·5	15·8	15·0	14·6	14·2		13·9	14·1	14·3	14·6	15·4	16·2	16·9	18·0	19·1	20·8
O 10	O 20	O 30	N 9	N 19	N 29	D 9	D 19	D 29		Ja 8	Ja 18	Ja 28	F 7	F 17	F 27	Mr 9	Mr 19	Mr 29	Ap 8
348·8	346·3	345·4	345·6	347·2	349·5	352·5	356·3	0·4	**42**	5·1	10·1	15·3	20·8	26·4	31·9	37·9	44·0	49·8	55·7
196·6	194·1	186·4	186·2	194·7	208·4	224·6	241·8	259·4		275·9	290·3	300·0	301·3	294·3	290·8	296·7	300·7	326·1	344·0
56·9	56·7	56·0	55·1	53·8	52·5	51·1	49·9	48·6		47·5	46·8	46·3	46·1	46·5	47·0	47·8	49·0	50·4	52·1
215·8	227·3	238·5	249·6	260·1	270·1	279·2	287·2	293·3		297·1	297·0	292·6	286·8	282·5	281·9	285·3	291·1	298·9	307·9
34·8	34·1	33·4	32·6	31·8	31·0	30·1	29·5	28·9		28·4	28·4	28·3	28·3	28·8	29·3	29·9	30·9	31·9	32·9
171·7	178·4	185·1	191·7	198·4	205·2	212·0	218·8	225·9	**43**	232·8	239·8	247·0	254·1	261·4	268·6	276·2	283·6	290·9	298·6
172·4	169·2	175·8	188·2	203·9	220·8	238·3	255·1	270·2		281·3	285·2	279·6	273·8	277·3	288·5	303·9	321·3	339·8	358·3
89·4	90·2	90·8	90·9	90·7	90·2	89·5	88·4	87·1		85·8	84·5	83·2	82·1	81·1	80·5	80·2	80·3	80·6	81·3
163·3	175·5	188·1	200·6	213·1	225·8	238·4	250·9	263·6		276·4	288·8	301·6	314·1	326·6	338·9	351·1	3·3	15·6	27·6
49·9	49·3	48·7	48·2	47·4	46·6	45·7	45·0	44·3		43·5	43·2	42·9	42·5	42·8	43·1	43·3	44·1	44·9	45·7
																Mr 8	Mr 18	Mr 28	Ap 7
54·5	56·5	57·4	56·8	55·1	52·1	49·1	46·1	43·9	**44**	43·0	43·1	44·4	46·8	49·7	53·4	57·2	61·9	66·7	71·7
156·8	168·2	183·2	200·0	217·3	234·3	249·9	262·4	268·7		265·6	253·4	258·8	268·1	282·4	299·3	317·3	335·7	353·2	9·0
117·3	118·9	120·3	121·3	122·2	122·9	123·0	123·0	122·6		121·9	120·9	119·7	118·4	117·1	115·8	114·7	113·6	112·9	112·6
133·6	139·5	147·1	156·2	165·8	176·5	187·4	198·8	210·4		242·2	234·3	246·3	253·7	270·8	283·2	295·5	307·9	320·1	332·6
64·9	64·6	64·3	63·9	63·2	62·5	61·7	60·9	60·1		59·2	58·6	58·0	57·4	57·4	57·3	57·3	57·9	58·5	59·0
																Mr 9	Mr 19	Mr 29	Ap 8
184·6	191·3	198·2	205·1	212·2	219·2	226·1	233·4	240·7	**45**	248·1	255·3	262·7	270·3	277·9	285·7	293·3	301·1	309·0	316·7
168·9	180·7	198·0	215·2	231·3	244·6	252·4	251·1	243·3		241·8	249·6	263·0	279·2	297·0	315·1	332·6	348·6	1·0	5·8
142·4	144·5	146·4	148·1	149·6	151·0	152·2	153·0	153·7		153·9	153·8	153·5	152·8	151·3	150·5	149·3	147·9	146·6	145·6
200·9	213·3	225·5	237·7	250·1	262·2	274·2	286·0	297·8		309·1	320·5	331·1	341·4	350·8	359·3	5·8	10·0	11·1	7·7
79·1	79·1	79·0	79·0	78·4	77·8	77·3	76·4	75·5		74·7	74·0	73·3	72·5	72·2	71·9	71·6	71·9	72·2	72·5
83·5	88·1	92·3	95·8	98·7	100·7	101·5	101·0	99·5	**46**	96·6	92·5	88·9	85·9	83·4	82·9	83·4	85·1	87·8	91·0
177·0	194·3	210·9	225·3	235·0	236·7	229·7	225·4	230·5		242·6	258·1	275·4	293·2	310·6	327·0	340·2	347·2	344·4	337·8
166·2	168·3	170·4	172·5	174·5	176·4	178·1	179·8	181·1		182·2	183·1	183·7	183·9	183·9	183·6	182·9	181·8	180·8	179·5
145·5	157·7	170·2	182·6	194·9	207·4	219·9	232·5	245·1		257·9	270·3	283·1	295·6	308·4	320·9	333·4	345·8	358·2	10·7
92·9	93·1	93·3	93·6	93·3	93·0	92·6	91·8	91·0		90·3	89·5	88·7	87·8	87·3	86·8	86·2	86·2	86·1	86·1
197·5	204·4	211·4	218·6	225·8	232·9	240·3	247·7	255·3	**47**	262·8	270·4	278·2	286·0	293·8	301·7	309·5	317·4	325·4	333·2
190·3	205·6	217·2	221·7	216·8	210·1	212·5	222·7	237·3		253·8	271·6	289·0	305·6	319·6	328·3	327·9	320·3	318·9	326·8
189·5	191·7	193·9	196·1	198·3	200·4	202·6	204·6	206·5		208·3	209·9	211·2	212·4	213·3	214·0	214·2	214·3	213·9	213·3
213·5	217·5	218·4	214·7	208·9	203·7	202·5	205·1	210·6		218·0	227·0	236·7	247·3	258·1	269·4	281·0	292·6	304·3	316·2
106·1	106·6	107·1	107·5	107·5	107·4	107·4	106·8	106·2		105·5	104·7	103·9	103·0	102·3	101·6	100·9	100·6	100·3	100·0
																Mr 8	Mr 18	Mr 28	Ap 7
101·7	107·3	112·6	117·4	122·1	126·0	129·7	132·4	134·3	**48**	135·3	135·0	133·8	130·5	126·9	123·0	119·5	117·3	116·0	115·8
198·5	205·5	203·6	195·8	195·0	203·3	216·8	232·9	250·1		267·6	284·4	299·1	309·3	311·3	304·5	300·4	306·2	318·8	335·1
213·5	215·5	217·7	220·0	222·1	224·4	226·6	228·8	231·1		233·2	235·3	237·2	239·1	240·7	242·2	243·5	244·5	245·2	245·7
182·2	194·4	207·1	219·4	232·0	244·5	257·1	269·6	281·9		294·4	306·7	318·9	330·9	343·0	354·9	6·4	17·9	28·9	39·5
118·7	119·4	120·1	120·8	121·0	121·2	121·4	121·0	120·6		120·3	119·6	118·9	118·1	117·3	116·5	115·6	115·1	114·6	114·0
																Mr 9	Mr 19	Mr 29	Ap 8
212·3	219·1	226·3	233·6	241·1	248·5	256·0	263·7	271·2	**49**	279·1	286·9	294·7	302·7	310·6	318·4	326·2	334·1	342·0	349·7
188·7	181·3	178·7	185·4	198·1	213·8	230·9	248·2	265·1		280·2	291·2	294·8	289·1	283·4	287·4	298·9	314·6	332·1	350·8
239·6	241·3	243·1	245·0	247·1	249·3	251·5	253·8	256·1		258·4	260·6	263·0	265·2	267·3	269·4	271·4	273·1	274·7	276·1
130·9	142·4	154·2	166·1	178·0	190·3	202·3	214·9	227·2		239·8	252·3	264·9	277·3	289·8	302·6	314·9	327·6	340·0	352·3
130·8	131·7	132·6	133·5	134·0	134·5	134·9	134·8	134·7		134·5	133·8	133·1	132·5	131·7	130·9	130·1	129·4	128·7	128·1
117·1	122·8	128·7	134·1	139·5	144·6	149·4	154·0	157·9	**50**	161·4	164·4	166·4	167·5	167·1	165·3	162·7	159·0	155·1	151·3
162·1	166·4	178·1	193·2	209·9	227·2	244·4	259·9	272·3		278·1	274·6	267·5	268·5	278·3	292·7	309·8	328·0	346·5	4·2
268·8	269·7	270·9	272·2	273·9	275·6	277·6	279·7	282·0		284·1	286·4	288·9	291·2	293·5	296·0	298·3	300·5	302·7	304·7
216·1	227·6	238·9	249·5	260·1	269·8	278·3	286·3	292·0		294·6	293·4	288·8	282·9	279·5	280·0	283·8	290·4	298·4	307·8
142·5	143·5	144·5	145·5	146·2	146·9	147·5	147·6	147·7		147·8	147·4	147·0	146·6	145·8	145·0	144·3	143·5	142·7	141·9

Mag.	P. Phal.	U. Phal.	Hasta.	Chit.	Svati.	Visak.	Anur.	Jyesh.	Mula.	P. Ash.	U. Ash.	Srav.	Dan.	Satab.	P.Bhad.	U. Bhad.	Revati.
133·3	146·7	160·0	173·3	186·6	200·0	213·3	226·7	240·0	253·3	266·7	280·0	293·3	306·7	320·0	333·3	346·7	360·0

APPENDIX II:—Geocentric (Indian) Longitudes of Sun and Major planets

(For the years 1840—1909,

Day of S. Yr.		0	10	20	30	40	50	60	70	80	90	100	110	120	130	140	150	160	170
°'s Mean L.		357·0	6·9	16·7	26·6	36·4	46·3	56·1	66·0	75·9	85·7	95·6	105·4	115·3	125·1	135·0	144·8	154·7	164·6
Actual do.		+2·1	+2·0	+1·9	+1·7	+1·4	+1·1	+0·8	+0·4	+0·0	−0·3	−0·7	−1·1	−1·4	−1·6	−1·9	−2·0	−2·1	−2·2
English date.		Ap 13	Ap 23	My 3	My 13	My 23	Je 2	Je 12	Je 22	Jl 2	Jl 12	Jl 22	Au 1	Au 11	Au 21	Au 31	S 10	S 20	S 30
Tamil month.		Chit	Chit	Chit	Chit	Vaik	Vaik	Vaik	Ani	Ani	Ani	Ani	Adi	Adi	Avani	Avani	Avani	Pura	Pura
Do. date.		1	11	21	31	10	20	30	9	19	29	7	17	27	6	16	26	5	15
1950	Mars ...	150·2	148·8	148·6	149·2	151·4	153·9	157·5	161·7	166·1	171¯3	176·6	182·4	188·2	194·3	200·6	207·3	214·0	220·8
°'s L.	Merc. ...	12·4	26·8	35·0	33·9	26·6	26·4	35·7	50·3	67·7	86·1	104·8	122·6	138·9	151·4	157·0	153·2	146·0	147·8
+·3	Jup. ...	305·8	307·6	309·3	310·7	311·9	312·8	313·4	313·6	313·5	313·1	312·3	311·4	310·1	308·6	307·3	306·0	304·8	303·9
	Ven. ...	312·6	322·9	333·5	344·6	355·7	7·2	18·8	30·6	42·3	54·3	66·1	78·1	90·3	102·2	114·4	126·6	139·0	151·3
	Sat. ...	141·6	141·2	140·8	140·5	140·7	140·9	141·0	141·7	142·4	143·0	144·1	145·1	146·2	147·4	148·6	149·9	151·2	152·5
1951	Mars ...	8·5	15·9	23·3	30·4	37·7	44·7	51·6	58·7	65·6	72·3	79·0	85·5	92·3	98·7	105·1	111·4	117·6	123·9
°'s L.	Merc. ...	14·8	15·9	8·9	6·1	13·7	27·6	44·6	62·9	82·0	100·3	117·3	131·2	139·2	137·9	130·3	129·5	137·8	151·6
+·1	Jup. ...	333·8	336·0	338·3	340·4	342·4	344·2	345·7	347·2	348·3	349·1	349·8	349·8	349·7	349·1	348·3	347·0	345·8	344·5
	Ven. ...	34·0	45·9	57·6	69·0	80·4	91·3	102·0	111·9	121·7	130·0	137·3	142·5	144·0	143·5	138·3	132·2	128·1	128·6
	Sat. ...	155·2	154·6	151·0	153·4	153·3	153·3	153·2	153·7	151·2	154·6	155·5	156·4	157·3	158·4	159·5	160·6	161·9	163·2
1952	Mars ...	202·2	199·3	195·7	192·7	189·8	188·7	188·9	190·2	192·6	195·8	199·8	204·3	200·4	214·8	220·7	226·9	233·3	240·0
°'s L.	Merc. ...	351·0	347·1	353·3	6·4	23·2	41·5	60·6	79·3	96·7	111·3	120·6	121·1	113·7	111·7	118·8	132·0	148·3	165·6
+·8	Jup. ...	1·6	4·0	6·4	8·9	11·2	13·4	15·6	17·7	19·6	21·3	22·9	24·2	25·2	25·9	26·2	26·3	25·9	25·3
	Ven. ...	340·5	352·7	5·1	17·6	29·9	42·1	54·3	66·6	78·9	91·2	103·3	115·7	127·8	140·1	152·3	164·7	177·0	189·2
	Sat. ...	168·5	167·8	167·1	166·4	166·1	165·8	165·5	165·7	165·9	166·1	166·9	167·7	168·4	169·5	170·6	171·6	172·8	174·0
1953	Mars ...	23·8	30·8	37·8	44·8	51·6	58·6	65·4	72·0	78·7	85·3	92·0	98·3	104·8	111·3	117·6	124·1	130·4	136·6
°'s L.	Merc. ...	332·6	344·2	0·2	18·3	37·1	56·1	74·1	89·7	100·8	108·8	97·4	92·9	98·3	110·9	126·6	144·1	161·9	179·3
+·5	Jup. ...	29·1	31·3	33·6	36·1	38·4	40·8	43·2	45·5	47·7	50·0	52·1	54·1	55·8	57·6	58·9	60·1	61·0	61·5
	Ven. ...	1·0	355·1	352·1	353·2	357·4	3·8	12·0	21·2	31·2	41·5	52·3	63·3	74·9	86·3	98·0	109·9	121·7	133·9
	Sat. ...	181·4	180·6	179·8	179·1	178·6	178·1	177·6	177·6	177·6	177·6	178·1	178·6	179·2	180·1	181·0	181·9	183·1	184·3
1954	Mars ...	246·4	249·9	252·7	254·7	256·0	255·8	254·7	252·2	249·6	247·1	245·4	243·9	246·0	248·2	251·4	255·4	260·3	265·6
°'s L.	Merc. ...	337·5	355·0	13·8	32·7	51·0	67·5	79·9	85·5	80·7	74·7	77·9	89·3	104·5	122·0	140·0	158·1	174·7	188·7
+·3	Jup. ...	56·9	58·6	60·6	62·7	64·9	67·1	69·5	71·7	74·1	76·4	78·6	80·9	83·2	85·2	87·2	89·1	90·8	92·2
	Ven. ...	17·4	29·7	42·0	53·9	66·1	78·2	90·0	101·8	113·4	125·0	136·3	147·8	158·8	169·6	179·7	189·6	198·7	206·3
	Sat. ...	194·0	193·2	192·4	191·6	191·0	190·4	189·7	189·5	189·3	189·0	189·3	189·6	190·0	190·8	191·6	192·3	193·4	194·5
1955	Mars ...	38·0	44·6	51·4	58·0	64·8	71·3	77·8	84·3	90·8	97·4	103·8	110·1	116·5	122·8	129·4	135·6	141·9	148·3
°'s L.	Merc. ...	350·5	9·4	27·8	44·8	58·6	65·9	63·4	56·2	57·5	67·4	82·4	99·6	117·8	136·2	153·3	168·6	179·7	183·0
+·0	Jup ...	85·8	86·9	88·1	89·5	91·3	93·2	95·0	97·2	99·3	101·5	103·7	106·1	108·3	110·5	112·8	114·9	117·0	119·1
	Ven. ...	322·7	334·8	346·6	358·8	10·9	23·2	35·3	47·5	59·7	71·7	84·1	96·2	108·5	120·7	133·0	145·4	157·8	170·2
	Sat. ...	206·2	205·4	204·6	203·9	203·2	202·5	201·7	201·3	200·9	200·5	200·6	200·7	200·9	201·5	202·1	202·6	203·5	204·5
1956	Mars ...	274·3	280·5	286·8	292·9	298·6	304·3	309·5	314·4	318·7	322·4	325·3	326·0	327·3	325·8	323·4	321·0	318·6	317·5
°'s L.	Merc. ...	6·4	28·6	37·9	46·2	44·8	37·5	37·7	46·8	61·4	78·7	97·1	115·5	133·4	149·3	161·5	166·7	162·2	155·6
+·8	Jup. ...	116·8	116·8	117·1	117·7	118·6	119·7	121·0	122·8	124·5	126·4	128·5	130·5	132·7	134·8	137·1	139·3	141·5	143·7
	Ven. ...	45·6	55·1	63·7	70·4	75·4	76·8	74·6	68·7	62·5	59·2	60·2	64·3	71·0	79·2	88·3	98·4	109·0	119·9
	Sat. ...	218·0	217·3	216·6	215·9	215·1	214·3	213·6	213·0	212·4	211·9	211·8	211·7	211·7	212·1	212·5	213·0	213·9	214·8
1957	Mars ...	53·1	59·4	65·6	71·9	78·1	84·5	90·8	97·0	103·5	109·6	116·0	122·3	128·5	134·9	141·4	147·8	154·2	160·5
°'s L.	Merc. ...	15·9	25·8	26·7	19·8	17·2	25·0	38·8	55·8	74·1	92·8	111·0	127·8	141·7	149·2	147·5	139·9	139·5	147·8
+·5	Jup. ...	149·6	148·6	147·9	47·5	147·3	147·6	148·2	149·1	150·1	151·4	153·1	154·8	156·5	158·6	160·7	162·7	165·0	167·2
	Ven. ...	359·2	11·6	23·9	36·2	48·6	60·8	73·1	85·2	97·3	109·4	121·5	133·5	145·6	157·6	169·6	181·4	193·3	204·9
	Sat. ...	229·6	229·0	228·4	227·8	227·0	226·2	225·5	224·8	224·1	223·5	223·2	222·9	222·7	222·9	223·1	223·4	224·1	224·8
1958	Mars ...	294·8	302·2	309·5	316·8	323·9	331·1	338·2	345·0	351·9	358·3	4·6	10·5	16·1	21·4	25·8	29·8	32·9	34·7
°'s L.	Merc. ...	8·4	2·3	357·8	8·1	16·0	32·6	50·9	69·8	88·6	105·8	120·8	130·6	131·5	124·3	121·5	128·1	140·8	156·9
+·2	Jup. ...	183·5	182·2	180·9	179·8	178·8	178·1	177·6	177·4	177·6	178·2	179·1	180·1	181·5	183·0	184·7	186·4	188·5	190·6
	Ven. ...	312·5	323·0	333·6	344·9	356·0	7·7	19·2	30·9	42·7	54·6	66·6	78·6	90·6	102·7	114·9	127·2	139·5	151·9
	Sat. ...	241·0	240·6	240·2	239·7	239·0	238·3	237·5	236·8	236·1	235·3	234·8	234·3	233·9	233·9	234·0	234·0	234·6	235·2
1959	Mars ...	68·0	73·6	79·4	85·3	91·2	97·2	103·1	109·4	115·5	121·5	127·7	134·0	140·4	146·6	153·1	159·6	165·9	172·6
°'s L.	Merc. ...	339·2	342·3	353·8	·9·5	27·5	46·3	65·3	83·3	99·1	110·7	114·3	108·5	108·4	108·0	119·8	135·4	152·5	170·3
−·0	Jup. ...	217·5	216·6	215·4	214·1	212·8	211·6	210·3	209·2	208·6	208·0	207·9	208·1	208·6	209·3	210·5	211·8	213·4	215·0
	Ven. ...	34·6	46·2	57·9	69·3	80·7	91·4	101·9	112·0	121·4	129·6	136·6	141·4	142·4	140·5	134·4	128·7	125·6	126·7
	Sat. ...	251·9	251·7	251·5	251·2	250·6	250·0	249·3	248·6	247·9	247·1	246·4	245·7	245·1	245·0	244·9	244·8	245·2	245·6

Mesh.	Vrsh.	Mith.	Kat.	Sim.	Kan.	Tul.	Vrch.	Dhan.	Mak.	Kum.	Min.	Asvn.	Bhar.	Krit.	Rohi.	Mrig.	Ardh.	Punar.	Push.	Asles.
30	60	90	120	150	180	210	240	270	300	330	360	13·3	26·7	40·0	53·3	66·7	80·0	93·3	106·7	120·0

at Ujjain mean Sunrise for every ten days from A.D. 1950 to A.D. 1959.

see *Indian Chronology,* **Table XVIII).**

180	190	200	210	220	230	240	250	260		270	280	290	300	310	320	330	340	350	360
174·4	184·3	194·1	204·0	213·8	223·7	233·5	243·4	253·3		263·1	273·0	282·8	292·7	302·5	312·4	322·2	332·1	342·0	351·8
−2·2	−2·1	−1·9	−1·7	−1·5	−1·2	−0·9	−0·5	−0·1		+0·3	+0·6	+1·7	+1·3	+1·6	+1·8	+2·0	+2·1	+2·2	+2·2
O 10	O 20	O 30	N 9	N 19	N 29	D 9	D 19	D 29		Ja 8	Ja 18	Ja 28	F 7	F 17	F 27	Mr 9	Mr 19	Mr 29	Ap 8
Pura	Aipp	Aipp	Aipp	Kart	Kart	Kart	Marg	Marg		Marg	Tai	Tai	Tai	Masi	Masi	Masi	Pang	Pang	Pang
25	4	14	24	4	14	24	5	15		25	5	15	25	6	16	26	6	16	26
227·7	234·8	242·0	249·5	256·9	264·5	272·1	279·7	287·5	**51**	295·3	303·1	311·0	318·7	326·7	334·3	342·0	349·6	357·3	4·8
157·9	172·4	189·0	206·3	223·6	239·7	253·0	261·2	260·3		252·8	250·8	258·2	271·7	287·9	305·8	323·9	341·8	357·9	10·8
303·3	302·9	302·9	303·4	304·1	305·1	306·3	307·9	309·7		311·6	313·7	315·9	318·1	320·6	322·9	325·3	327·7	330·2	332·5
163·8	176·3	188·6	201·2	213·8	226·4	238·9	251·5	264·8		276·9	289·5	302·1	314·5	327·1	339·5	351·6	3·9	15·9	28·1
153·7	154·8	156·0	157·0	157·8	158·6	159·4	159·8	160·2		160·5	160·3	160·1	159·9	159·3	158·7	158·0	157·2	156·4	155·5
																Mr 8	Mr 18	Mr 28	Ap 7
130·0	136·2	142·1	148·0	153·8	159·5	165·0	170·4	175·7	**52**	180·9	185·6	190·2	194·3	197·9	200·8	203·2	204·3	204·7	203·5
167·8	185·4	202·7	219·3	233·8	243·8	245·8	239·1	234·4		230·1	251·0	266·6	283·8	301·7	319·6	336·1	349·6	357·5	355·5
343·1	341·8	340·7	339·8	339·3	339·1	339·2	339·8	340·6		341·7	343·2	344·8	346·6	348·6	350·7	352·9	355·3	357·7	0·0
132·3	138·6	146·8	156·1	166·0	176·6	187·6	199·1	210·8		222·5	234·6	246·8	259·0	271·3	283·7	296·1	308·2	320·7	333·1
164·4	165·6	166·8	167·9	168·9	169·9	170·9	171·4	171·9		172·5	172·5	172·6	172·6	172·1	171·6	171·1	170·4	169·7	168·9
																Mr 9	Mr 19	Mr 29	Ap 8
246·6	253·6	260·8	268·1	275·6	282·9	290·5	298·1	305·7	**53**	313·3	320·9	328·3	336·1	343·5	350·9	358·3	5·6	13·0	20·2
183·4	200·2	215·3	226·5	230·6	225·2	219·0	221·9	232·4		247·3	264·1	281·8	299·5	316·0	329·9	338·6	338·0	330·5	320·3
24·3	23·1	21·7	20·4	19·0	17·9	16·8	16·0	15·6		15·5	15·9	16·5	17·4	18·6	20·1	21·9	23·7	25·7	27·8
201·5	213·9	226·1	238·2	250·4	262·5	274·5	286·3	298·1		309·5	320·6	331·1	341·3	350·5	358·4	4·7	8·1	8·2	4·1
175·1	176·3	177·5	178·8	179·8	180·8	181·9	182·6	183·3		184·1	184·3	184·5	184·7	184·4	184·1	183·8	183·1	182·4	181·8
143·0	149·1	155·3	161·4	167·4	173·5	179·6	185·6	191·6	**54**	197·5	203·4	209·0	214·7	220·2	225·5	230·8	235·7	240·3	244·4
195·3	208·1	214·7	212·1	204·4	204·3	213·0	226·7	242·9		260·4	277·8	294·5	309·4	319·3	321·3	314·6	310·6	316·7	329·6
61·6	61·7	61·2	60·3	59·1	58·0	56·6	55·2	54·0		52·8	51·9	51·3	51·0	51·0	51·4	52·2	53·1	54·4	56·0
146·0	158·3	170·7	183·1	195·4	207·9	220·5	233·0	245·7		258·2	271·1	283·6	296·2	308·9	321·4	334·0	346·3	358·8	11·2
185·5	186·7	187·9	189·1	190·2	191·3	192·4	193·2	194·0		194·9	195·4	195·9	196·3	196·2	196·1	196·0	195·4	194·8	194·3
271·2	277·4	283·6	290·3	297·1	303·9	310·8	317·8	325·0	**55**	331·9	339·1	346·2	353·2	0·3	7·2	14·0	20·9	27·8	34·7
197·9	198·2	190·8	187·5	194·0	206·5	222·0	239·3	256·7		273·6	288·7	300·3	304·5	299·2	293·2	296·8	307·9	323·6	341·2
93·5	94·4	95·1	95·4	95·4	95·0	94·3	93·4	92·2		91·0	89·7	88·4	87·1	86·0	85·3	84·8	84·6	84·9	85·4
212·3	215·6	215·4	210·8	204·5	200·6	200·0	203·6	209·6		217·6	226·7	236·7	247·2	258·3	269·6	281·1	293·1	304·8	316·8
195·6	196·8	198·0	199·1	200·3	201·5	202·6	203·6	204·6		205·5	206·1	206·7	207·3	207·4	207·6	207·7	207·3	206·9	206·4
																Mr 8	Mr 18	Mr 28	Ap 7
154·6	161·1	167·5	173·7	180·2	186·5	192·9	199·3	205·7	**56**	212·2	218·7	225·2	231·7	238·1	244·6	251·0	257·5	264·0	270.3
177·0	171·6	175·4	186·6	201·4	218·3	235·6	252·7	268·3		281·0	287·7	284·6	277·2	277·7	287·2	301·5	318·8	337·0	355·5
120·3	122·4	123·9	125·2	126·2	126·8	127·3	127·4	127·1		126·6	125·7	124·6	123·3	122·0	120·6	119·3	118·4	117·6	116·9
182·7	195·0	207·6	220·1	232·5	245·1	257·4	270·1	282·5		294·9	307·3	319·4	331·5	343·5	355·3	6·7	18·0	29·0	39·6
205·5	206·7	207·9	209·0	210·2	211·4	212·5	213·6	214·7		215·7	216·4	217·1	217·9	218·2	218·5	218·9	218·7	218·5	218·3
																Mr 9	Mr 19	Mr 29	Ap 8
317·5	318·7	321·4	324·6	328·7	333·2	338·0	343·5	348·8	**57**	354·6	0·4	6·5	12·5	18·6	24·8	31·0	37·2	43·6	49·9
157·6	167·9	182·4	199·0	216·4	233·5	249·6	262·8	270·8		269·3	261·7	260·3	268·3	281·7	298·3	316·4	334·7	352·7	8·8
145·8	147·8	149·8	151·6	153·2	154·6	155·9	156·9	157·5		158·1	158·0	157·8	157·3	156·4	155·2	154·0	152·8	151·4	150·1
131·2	142·9	154·5	166·4	178·6	190·6	202·9	215·2	227·8		240·1	252·8	265·4	277·8	290·3	303·1	315·5	328·1	340·4	352·8
215·6	216·7	217·8	218·9	220·2	221·5	222·8	223·9	225·0		226·0	226·8	227·6	228·5	228·9	229·3	229·7	229·6	229·5	229·5
167·1	173·6	180·1	186·8	193·3	200·1	206·7	213·6	220·3	**58**	227·2	234·1	241·1	248·1	255·2	262·2	269·4	276·6	284·0	291·3
161·7	177·9	195·4	212·5	229·2	243·5	253·2	254·6	247·7		243·7	248·8	261·0	276·7	294·2	312·4	330·2	346·9	0·4	8·3
169·3	171·5	173·7	175·7	177·8	179·8	181·6	183·2	184·7		186·0	186·9	187·6	188·1	188·1	187·9	187·4	186·5	185·4	184·2
216·5	227·9	239·0	249·6	260·0	269·6	278·3	285·5	290·5		292·2	290·1	284·6	278·9	276·7	278·1	282·7	289·8	298·1	337·6
225·5	226·5	227·5	228·6	229·8	231·0	232·1	233·2	234·4		235·5	236·5	237·5	238·5	239·1	239·7	240·4	240·6	240·8	240·9
35·5	34·3	32·9	30·4	27·5	25·0	23·4	22·8	23·9	**59**	25·7	28·2	31·4	35·3	39·6	44·2	49·2	54·3	59·7	65·2
174·0	191·7	208·6	223·7	235·2	239·6	234·6	228·2	230·6		240·8	255·7	272·4	290·3	308·1	325·0	339·2	348·6	348·9	341·6
192·7	195·0	197·1	199·2	201·5	203·7	205·8	207·9	209·9		211·7	213·3	214·9	216·2	217·2	218·0	218·5	218·5	218·4	217·9
164·3	176·8	189·1	201·7	214·3	226·9	239·4	252·2	264·9		277·4	290·1	302·6	315·2	327·6	339·8	352·1	4·4	16·5	28·4
235·7	236·6	237·5	238·4	239·5	240·6	241·8	243·0	244·2		245·3	246·4	247·4	248·5	249·3	250·1	250·9	251·3	251·7	252·1
																Mr 8	Mr 18	Mr 28	Ap 7
179·2	185·9	192·5	199·3	206·3	213·1	220·1	227·1	234·3	**60**	241·5	248·8	256·1	263·6	271·0	278·5	286·2	293·8	301·5	309·2
187·9	203·6	216·7	223·7	221·4	213·5	213·1	221·3	235·0		251·1	268·6	286·4	303·3	318·4	328·9	331·7	325·2	320·7	326·2
217·0	218·9	221·1	223·3	225·4	227·6	230·0	232·2	234·3		236·5	238·7	240·7	242·6	244·5	246·0	247·3	248·5	249·4	250·0
131·3	137·9	146·4	155·8	165·9	176·7	187·9	199·4	211·1		222·8	235·1	247·2	259·5	271·7	284·2	296·4	308·7	321·2	333·6
246·0	246·8	247·6	248·3	249·4	250·5	251·6	252·8	254·0		255·1	256·2	257·3	258·4	259·4	260·3	261·3	261·8	262·3	262·9

Mag.	P. Phal.	U. Phal.	Hasta.	Chit.	Svati.	Visak.	Anur.	Jyesh.	Mula.	P. Ash.	U. Ash.	Srav.	Dan.	Satab.	P. Bhad.	U. Bhad.	Revati.
133·3	146·7	160·0	173·3	186·6	200·0	213·3	226·7	240·0	253;3	266·7	280·0	293·3	306·7	320·0	333·3	346·7	360·0

APPENDIX II:—Geocentric (Indian) Longitudes of Sun and Major planets

(For the years 1840—1909,

Day of S. Yr.	0	10	20	30	40	50	60	70	80	90	100	110	120	130	140	150	160	170
⊙'s Mean L.	357·0	6·9	16·7	26·6	36·4	46·3	56·1	66·0	75·9	85·7	95·6	105·4	115·3	125·1	135·0	144·8	154·7	164·6
Actual do.	+2·1	+2·0	+1·9	+1·7	+1·4	+1·1	+0·8	+0·4	+0·0	−0·3	−0·7	−1·1	−1·4	−1·6	−1·9	−2·0	−2·1	−2·2
English date.	Ap 13	Ap 23	My 3	My 13	My 23	Je 2	Je 12	Je 22	Jl 2	Jl 12	Jl 22	Au 1	Au 11	Au 21	Au 31	S 10	S 20	S 30
Tamil month.	Chit	Chit	Chit	Chit	Vaik	Vaik	Vaik	Ani	Ani	Ani	Adi	Adi	Adi	Avani	Avani	Avani	Pura	Pura
Do. date.	1	11	21	31	10	20	30	9	19	29	7	17	27	6	16	26	5	15
1960 Mars ...	313·7	321·3	329·2	336·8	344·3	352·0	359·3	6·7	13·9	21·0	27·7	34·6	41·1	47·3	53·5	59·2	64·6	69·6
⊙'s L. Merc. ...	333·2	348·5	6·0	24·0	43·9	62·2	78·5	91·0	96·1	91·3	85·4	83·7	99·9	115·2	132·6	150·5	168·2	184·6
+·7 Jup. ...	250·0	250·2	249·8	249·2	248·3	247·2	245·9	244·6	243·2	242·0	240·9	240·2	239·6	239·4	239·6	240·1	240·9	242·1
Ven. ...	340·5	353·5	5·6	18·0	30·4	42·6	54·9	67·3	79·4	91·7	103·9	116·2	128·4	140·6	152·9	165·2	177·5	189·7
Sat ...	263·1	263·0	262·9	262·8	262·3	261·8	261·2	260·4	259·6	258·9	258·2	257·5	256·8	256·5	256·2	255·8	256·0	256·2
1961 Mars ...	84·8	90·1	94·9	100·2	105·5	111·1	116·9	122·6	128·6	134·6	140·6	146·9	153·0	159·4	165·8	172·4	178·9	185·6
⊙'s L. Merc. ...	343·2	1·6	20·5	39·0	56·0	69·7	77·0	74·3	67·3	68·5	78·3	93·2	110·4	128·7	146·6	163·8	178·7	189·3
+·5 Jup. ...	280·8	281·9	282·8	283·4	283·5	283·3	282·8	282·1	281·0	279·7	278·5	277·1	275·8	274·7	273·8	273·1	272·8	272·9
Ven. ...	357·0	351·8	349·7	351·5	356·3	3·4	11·9	21·1	31·3	41·6	52·6	63·7	75·2	86·8	98·5	110·4	122·2	134·3
Sat. ...	273·8	274·0	274·2	274·4	274·0	273·6	273·3	272·5	271·7	271·0	270·3	269·6	268·8	268·3	267·8	267·2	267·2	267·2
1962 Mars ...	330·6	338·5	346·3	354·0	1·5	9·1	16·4	23·8	31·1	38·1	45·1	52·0	58·5	65·2	71·5	77·8	83·8	89·6
⊙'s L. Merc. ...	357·3	15·7	33·0	47·7	56·9	56·6	49·3	48·1	56·6	71·0	87·9	106·1	124·5	142·2	158·1	170·6	176·2	172·1
+·2 Jup. ...	309·6	311·6	313·4	314·9	316·3	317·2	318·1	318·4	318·6	318·3	317·7	316·7	315·7	314·4	313·0	311·5	310·3	309·2
Ven. ...	17·9	30·1	42·3	54·5	66·5	78·5	90·3	102·3	113·7	125·3	136·8	148·1	159·0	169·7	179·9	189·5	198·2	205·4
Sat. ...	284·7	285·0	285·3	285·7	285·5	285·3	285·2	284·6	284·0	283·4	282·6	281·8	281·1	280·4	279·7	279·1	278·9	278·7
1963 Mars ...	106·4	109·1	112·7	116·7	121·3	126·1	131·2	136·7	142·2	148·1	154·0	159·9	166·3	172·5	179·1	185·4	192·1	199·1
⊙'s L. Merc. ...	10·3	25·7	36·3	38·2	31·5	28·1	34·9	48·3	65·1	83·2	101·9	120·2	136·9	150·7	158·8	157·6	150·0	148·7
−·1 Jup. ...	337·5	339·8	342·1	344·3	346·4	348·3	350·0	351·5	352·8	353·8	354·5	354·7	354·9	354·5	353·7	352·8	351·6	350·2
Ven. ...	323·0	335·1	347·1	359·3	11·5	23·7	35·9	48·0	60·2	72·2	84·6	96·6	109·0	121·3	133·7	145·9	158·3	170·8
Sat. ...	295·5	296·1	296·7	297·2	297·3	297·4	297·4	296·9	296·4	296·0	295·2	294·4	293·6	292·9	292·2	291·5	291·1	290·7
1964 Mars ...	347·4	355·1	2·8	10·2	17·9	25·2	32·5	39·8	46·8	53·7	60·7	67·3	74·1	80·5	87·1	93·3	99·4	105·6
⊙'s L. Merc. ...	16·2	19·4	13·1	8·6	14·8	27·2	43·8	62·0	81·0	99·4	116·7	131·3	140·8	141·5	134·1	131·3	138·3	151·2
+·7 Jup. ...	5·4	7·8	10·2	12·5	14·9	17·3	19·5	21·6	23·6	25·5	27·1	28·6	29·7	30·5	31·1	31·2	31·0	30·5
Ven. ...	45·6	54·9	63·2	69·4	73·7	74·3	70·7	65·0	59·3	57·1	58·7	63·3	70·3	78·9	88·2	98·5	109·2	120·2
Sat. ...	306·5	307·2	307·9	308·7	309·0	309·3	309·5	309·2	308·9	308·6	308·0	307·4	306·7	305·9	305·1	304·2	303·7	303·2
1965 Mars ...	135·4	135·5	136·4	138·5	141·3	145·0	149·1	153·7	158·8	164·0	169·8	175·6	181·6	187·9	194·3	200·8	207·5	214·3
⊙'s L. Merc. ...	356·1	349·9	353·3	4·9	20·6	38·7	57·7	76·4	94·3	109·9	121·4	124·7	118·6	113·7	118·5	130·2	145·7	162·8
+·4 Jup. ...	32·7	35·0	37·3	39·6	42·1	44·4	46·8	49·2	51·5	53·7	55·8	57·9	59·8	61·5	63·1	64·3	65·3	66·1
Ven. ...	359·7	12·1	24·4	36·9	49·1	61·3	73·6	85·7	97·9	109·9	122·1	134·0	146·1	157·9	169·9	181·7	193·6	205·2
Sat. ...	317·5	318·4	319·3	320·3	320·8	321·3	321·8	321·7	321·6	321·6	321·1	320·6	320·0	319·2	318·4	317·6	316·9	316·2
1966 Mars ...	2·6	10·4	17·6	25·0	32·1	39·3	46·5	53·5	60·4	67·3	73·9	80·7	87·2	93·8	100·2	106·6	112·8	119·0
⊙'s L. Merc. ...	333·1	342·7	357·8	15·3	34·2	53·1	71·6	88·1	101·0	106·7	102·5	96·1	98·5	109·2	124·2	141·3	159·0	176·7
+·2 Jup. ...	60·8	62·4	64·3	66·4	68·5	70·6	73·0	75·2	77·6	79·9	82·2	84·5	86·6	88·9	90·9	92·8	94·6	96·0
Ven. ...	312·5	322·9	334·0	345·0	356·4	8·0	19·7	31·4	43·2	55·1	67·0	79·2	91·1	103·3	115·4	127·7	140·0	152·4
Sat. ...	328·6	329·7	330·8	331·8	332·5	333·2	333·9	334·1	334·3	334·5	334·2	333·9	333·5	332·8	333·1	331·3	330·5	329·7
1967 Mars ...	180·3	176·8	173·8	171·9	171·3	172·0	173·9	176·8	180·2	184·4	189·1	194·2	199·8	205·6	211·7	218·1	224·6	231·4
⊙'s L. Merc. ...	335·4	352·4	10·9	29·7	48·3	65·5	79·5	87·6	85·8	78·4	78·5	87·9	102·4	119·2	137·3	155·1	172·4	187·4
−·1 Jup. ...	90·0	90·8	92·0	93·3	94·9	96·8	98·6	100·6	102·7	105·0	107·1	109·4	111·7	113·9	116·1	118·3	120·4	122·4
Ven. ...	34·9	46·6	58·2	69·7	80·8	91·8	102·0	112·0	121·1	129·1	135·3	139·5	140·0	136·8	130·6	124·3	123·5	125·2
Sat. ...	339·8	341·0	342·2	343·4	344·3	345·2	346·2	346·7	347·2	347·6	347·5	347·4	347·3	346·7	346·1	345·5	344·7	343·9
1968 Mars ...	18·1	25·3	32·4	39·4	46·5	53·5	60·2	67·0	73·9	80·6	87·1	93·6	100·3	106·5	113·1	119·4	125·5	132·0
⊙'s L. Merc. ...	349·5	8·4	26·8	44·2	58·9	68·1	67·7	60·2	59·2	67·7	81·8	98·8	116·8	135·1	152·5	168·3	180·5	185·6
+·6 Jup. ...	121·2	121·0	121·1	121·6	122·3	123·5	124·7	126·2	127·9	129·7	131·7	133·7	135·9	138·1	140·3	142·6	144·8	146·9
Ven. ...	341·5	354·0	6·1	18·5	31·0	43·1	55·5	67·8	80·0	92·2	104·6	116·7	128·9	141·2	153·4	165·8	178·0	190·3
Sat. ...	351·6	352·9	354·2	355·4	356·5	357·6	358·6	359·3	0·0	0·7	0·9	1·1	1·2	0·8	0·4	0·0	359·2	358·4
1969 Mars ...	232·0	233·1	233·3	232·3	230·1	227·6	224·5	222·4	221·0	220·9	222·1	224·6	227·9	232·1	236·8	242·2	248·0	253·9
⊙'s L. Merc. ...	3·9	21·4	36·8	47·2	49·4	42·4	39·3	46·1	59·5	76·1	94·2	112·8	130·8	147·3	161·1	168·6	167·0	159·4
+·4 Jup. ...	154·2	153·2	152·3	151·7	151·6	151·6	152·0	152·7	153·7	155·0	156·4	158·1	159·9	161·9	163·9	166·0	168·1	170·2
Ven. ...	352·9	348·3	347·4	350·0	355·4	3·0	11·6	21·1	31·2	42·0	52·9	64·0	75·5	87·1	98·9	110·7	122·8	134·9
Sat. ...	3·4	4·7	6·0	7·3	8·5	9·7	10·9	11·8	12·7	13·7	14·1	14·5	15·0	14·9	14·8	14·6	14·0	13·4

Mesh.	Vrsh.	Mith.	Kat.	Sim.	Kan.	Tul.	Vrsch.	Dhan.	Mak.	Kum.	Min.	Asvn.	Bhar.	Kri.	Rohi.	Mrig.	Ardh.	Punar.	Push.	Asles.
30	60	90	120	150	180	210	240	270	300	330	360	13·3	26·7	40·0	53·3	66·7	80·0	93·3	106·7	120·0

at Ujjain mean Sunrise for every ten days from A.D. 1960 to A.D. 1969.

see *Indian Chronology*, Table XVIII).

180	190	200	210	220	230	240	250	260		270	280	290	300	310	320	330	340	350	360
174·4	184·3	194·1	204·0	213·8	223·7	233·5	243·4	253·3		263·1	273·0	282·8	292·7	302·5	312·4	322·2	332·1	342·0	351·8
− 2·2	− 2·1	− 1·9	− 1·7	− 1·5	− 1·2	− 0·9	− 0·5	− 0·1		+0·3	+0·6	+1·0	+1·3	+1·6	+1·8	+2·0	+2·1	+2·2	+2·2
O 10	O 20	O 30	N 9	N 19	N 29	D 9	D 19	D 29		Ja 8	Ja 18	Ja 28	F 7	F 17	F 27	Mr 9	Mr 19	Mr 29	Ap 8
Pura	Aipp	Aipp	Aipp	Kart	Kart	Kart	Marg	Marg		Marg	Tai	Tai	Tai	Masi	Masi	Masi	Pang	Pang	Pang
25	4	14	24	4	14	24	5	15		25	5	15	25	6	16	26	6	16	26
74·1	78·3	81·6	84·1	85·5	86·0	85·2	82·7	79·4	**61**	75·8	72·4	69·8	68·6	68·8	70·2	72·3	75·4	79·0	83·0
198·6	207·2	207·0	199·4	196·7	203·5	216·2	232·1	249·1		266·6	283·6	298·9	310·4	314·3	308·8	303·0	307·0	318·6	334·3
243·4	244·9	246·7	248·7	250·6	252·7	255·0	257·2	259·5		261·9	264·1	266·4	268·7	271·0	273·0	275·0	276·9	278·6	280·1
202·0	214·2	226·4	238·8	250·9	262·9	274·8	286·7	298·2		309·6	320·7	331·2	341·1	350·0	357·8	3·2	6·3	5·1	0·2
256·3	257·0	257·7	258·4	259·4	260·4	261·4	262·6	263·8		264·9	266·1	267·3	268·4	269·4	270·4	271·5	272·2	272·9	273·6
192·5	199·4	206·3	213·2	220·2	227·3	234·6	242·0	249·4	**62**	256·9	264·5	272·1	279·8	287·6	295·3	303·1	311·1	319·0	326·8
192·2	185·8	180·7	184·8	196·3	211·3	227·7	245·5	262·7		278·4	291·0	297·2	293·8	286·7	287·8	297·4	312·1	329·5	347·9
273·2	273·9	275·0	276·3	277·7	279·6	281·4	283·4	285·5		287·8	290·2	292·4	294·8	297·2	299·6	302·0	304·3	306·5	308·6
146·5	158·8	171·3	183·6	196·0	208·4	221·0	233·7	246·4		259·0	271·6	284·2	296·8	309·5	321·9	334·5	347·0	359·3	11·7
267·2	267·7	268·2	268·8	269·7	270·6	271·5	272·6	273·7		274·9	276·1	277·3	278·4	279·5	280·6	281·7	282·6	283·5	284·3
95·2	100·5	105·4	110·0	113·9	117·4	120·0	121·7	122·6	**63**	122·3	120·5	117·8	114·0	110·1	106·8	104·2	103·5	103·6	105·4
165·1	166·6	176·5	190·7	207·2	224·6	241·7	257·9	271·4		279·8	278·9	271·6	269·7	277·1	290·6	307·1	325·2	343·7	1·8
308·4	308·0	307·8	308·0	308·6	309·5	310·6	312·0	313·7		315·5	317·5	319·7	322·0	324·3	326·7	329·0	331·4	333·8	336·3
210·4	213·3	212·0	206·7	201·0	197·6	198·1	202·3	208·9		217·1	226·6	236·6	247·3	258·6	270·0	281·4	293·3	305·1	317·1
278·4	278·7	279·0	279·4	280·2	281·0	281·7	282·8	283·9		284·9	286·1	287·3	288·6	289·8	291·0	292·1	293·1	294·1	295·0
																Mr 8	Mr 18	Mr 28	Ap 7
205·8	212·9	219·9	227·0	234·4	241·8	249·2	256·8	264·4	**64**	272·2	279·7	287·7	295·6	303·4	311·3	319·1	327·2	335·0	342·7
156·8	170·3	186·3	203·6	221·0	237·4	251·9	262·0	264·1		257·2	252·8	257·6	269·7	285·3	302·8	321·2	339·1	356·1	10·2
348·8	347·5	346·3	345·2	344·6	344·1	344·1	344·5	345·2		346·1	347·4	348·9	350·6	352·5	354·7	356·8	359·1	1·4	3·8
183·2	195·7	208·1	220·6	233·0	245·6	258·2	270·6	283·1		295·4	307·6	319·7	331·8	343·8	355·6	7·1	18·3	29·2	39·5
290·2	290·3	290·4	290·4	291·1	291·8	292·4	293·4	294·4		295·3	296·5	297·7	298·8	300·0	301·2	302·5	303·6	304·7	305·9
																Mr 9	Mr 19	Mr 29	Ap 8
111·4	117·2	122·7	128·0	133·2	138·0	142·5	146·2	149·6	**65**	152·2	154·0	154·7	154·1	151·8	148·6	145·0	141·1	138·1	136·1
167·1	184·2	201·8	218·5	233·6	244·6	248·5	243·1	236·9		240·0	250·8	266·9	282·8	300·8	318·6	335·7	350·0	359·4	359·6
29·7	28·6	27·3	26·1	24·7	23·4	22·2	21·3	20·8		20·5	20·6	21·1	21·8	22·9	24·3	25·8	27·7	29·6	31·7
131·6	143·2	154·9	166·9	178·9	191·1	203·4	215·7	228·3		240·8	253·3	266·0	278·3	290·9	303·6	316·0	328·6	341·1	353·6
302·8	302·6	302·4	302·2	302·6	303·0	303·5	304·4	305·3		306·1	307·2	308·3	309·5	310·8	312·1	313·3	314·6	315·8	316·9
221·3	228·4	235·6	242·9	250·4	257·9	265·5	273·4	281·0	**66**	288·8	296·6	304·5	312·4	320·1	328·0	335·9	343·5	351·3	358·9
180·5	197·8	213·6	226·2	232·8	230·0	222·3	222·4	231·1		245·0	261·5	279·3	296·8	313·8	328·8	339·4	341·9	335·4	331·4
66·4	66·4	66·0	65·5	64·5	63·3	62·1	60·7	59·3		58·2	57·1	56·3	55·8	55·7	55·9	56·5	57·4	58·5	59·8
216·8	228·1	239·1	249·6	259·9	269·3	277·4	284·3	288·6		289·4	288·2	280·5	275·0	274·2	276·4	281·6	289·1	297·8	307·5
315·4	315·1	314·8	314·4	314·6	314·8	315·1	315·8	316·5		317·2	318·3	319·4	320·4	321·6	322·8	324·1	325·4	326·7	328·0
125·1	131·1	136·8	142·6	148·3	154·0	159·3	164·3	169·2	**67**	173·8	177·9	181·7	184·8	187·2	188·9	189·1	188·1	185·3	182·2
193·2	207·1	215·9	216·2	208·8	205·0	212·1	224·6	240·4		257·5	275·1	292·2	307·8	319·6	324·5	319·6	313·5	316·7	327·8
97·3	98·4	99·3	99·7	99·9	99·8	99·2	98·4	97·4		96·1	94·7	93·4	92·1	91·0	90·1	89·5	89·2	89·2	89·7
164·8	177·3	189·9	202·2	214·9	227·4	240·0	252·7	265·4		278·0	290·6	303·1	315·7	328·0	340·3	352·7	4·9	17·0	28·9
328·9	328·4	327·9	327·3	327·3	327·2	327·2	327·7	328·2		328·8	329·8	330·8	331·7	332·9	334·1	335·3	336·6	337·9	339·2
																Mr 8	Mr 18	Mr 28	Ap 7
238·4	245·5	252·6	259·9	267·3	275·0	282·5	290·1	297·9	**68**	305·5	313·3	321·0	328·7	336·2	344·0	351·5	359·0	6·3	13·7
198·3	201·5	195·5	189·8	193·7	204·7	219·5	236·4	253·8		271·1	286·9	299·9	306·7	304·2	296·9	297·2	306·6	321·2	338·6
124·3	126·1	127·6	128·9	130·1	130·9	131·5	131·8	131·5		131·1	130·3	129·4	128·1	126·9	125·6	124·3	123·1	122·2	121·4
130·2	137·4	146·1	155·8	166·0	177·1	188·2	199·8	211·5		223·5	235·4	247·7	259·8	272·2	284·6	296·9	309·4	321·7	334·2
343·0	342·3	341·6	340·9	340·6	340·3	340·1	340·4	340·7		341·0	341·8	342·6	343·4	344·5	345·6	346·8	348·1	349·4	350·7
																Mr 9	Mr 19	Mr 29	Ap 8
138·0	144·2	150·3	156·4	162·4	168·2	174·3	180·0	185·8	**69**	191·5	196·9	202·2	207·4	212·3	216·9	221·2	225·2	228·3	230·9
181·1	174·3	176·3	186·3	200·6	217·3	234·5	251·7	268·0		281·3	289·5	288·3	280·8	279·3	287·4	301·0	317·8	336·0	354·4
149·1	151·1	153·1	154·9	156·7	158·2	159·5	160·6	161·5		162·0	162·3	162·1	161·6	160·8	159·9	158·7	157·4	156·2	154·8
202·5	214·8	226·9	239·1	251·2	263·2	275·2	287·0	298·6		309·7	320·7	331·1	340·8	349·5	356·9	1·8	3·8	1·9	356·1
357·7	356·9	356·1	355·2	354·7	354·2	353·8	353·8	353·9		353·9	354·5	355·1	355·8	356·8	357·8	358·9	0·1	1·3	2·6
260·5	267·0	273·8	280·8	287·9	295·1	302·4	309·8	317·0	**70**	324·4	331·8	339·0	346·4	353·6	0·7	7·9	14·9	22·1	28·8
158·5	166·6	180·2	196·3	213·5	230·8	247·3	261·8	271·5		273·1	266·2	262·2	267·5	279·9	295·7	313·6	331·9	350·0	7·0
172·5	174·7	176·8	179·0	181·1	183·0	184·9	186·7	188·2		189·5	190·6	191·5	192·0	192·2	192·2	191·7	191·1	190·0	188·8
147·1	159·3	171·8	184·1	196·5	208·9	221·5	234·3	246·9		259·6	272·1	284·8	297·4	310·0	322·4	335·0	347·4	359·8	12·3
12·7	11·9	11·1	10·2	9·5	8·8	8·1	7·9	7·7		7·4	7·8	8·2	8·5	9·4	10·3	11·1	12·3	13·5	14·7

Mag.	P. Phal.	U. Phal.	Hasta.	Chit.	Svati.	Visak.	Anur.	Jyesh.	Mula.	P. Ash.	U. Ash.	Srav.	Dan.	Satab.	P.Bhad.	U. Bhad.	Revati.
133·3	146·7	160·0	173·3	186·6	200·0	213·3	226·7	240·0	253·3	266·7	280·0	293·3	306·7	320·0	333·3	346·7	360·0

APPENDIX II:—Geocentric (Indian) Longitudes of Sun and Major planets

(For the years 1840—1909,

Day of S. Yr.	0	10	20	30	40	50	60	70	80	90	100	110	120	130	140	150	160	170
☉'s Mean L.	357·0	6·9	16·7	26·6	36·4	46·3	56·1	66·0	75·9	85·7	95·6	105·4	115·3	125·1	135·0	144·8	154·7	164·6
Actual do.	+2·1	+2·0	+1·9	+1·7	+1·4	+1·1	+0·8	+0·4	+0·0	−0·3	−0·7	−1·1	−1·4	−1·6	−1·9	−2·0	−2·1	−2·2
English date.	Ap 13	Ap 23	My 3	My 13	My 23	Je 2	Je 12	Je 22	Jl 2	Jl 12	Jl 22	Au 1	Au 11	Au 21	Au 31	S 10	S 20	S 30
Tamil month.	Chit	Chit	Chit	Chit	Vaik	Vaik	Vaik	Ani	Ani	Ani	Adi	Adi	Adi	Avani	Avani	Avani	Pura	Pura
Do. date.	1	11	21	31	10	20	30	9	19	29	7	17	27	6	16	26	5	15
1970 Mars ...	32·2	39·3	46·1	52·9	59·5	66·3	73·0	79·5	86·0	92·5	99·0	105·5	111·9	118·5	124·8	131·1	137·4	143·7
☉'s L. Merc. ...	14·5	26·3	30·5	24·9	19·7	24·6	37·0	53·2	71·3	90·0	108·5	125·8	140·7	150·5	151·7	144·4	141·1	147·1
+·1 Jup. ...	188·3	186·9	185·5	184·5	183·3	182·4	181·8	181·7	181·6	182·1	182·8	183·7	184·9	186·4	188·1	189·9	191·8	193·9
Ven. ...	18·4	30·7	42·8	55·0	67·0	79·0	90·9	102·6	114·3	125·8	137·2	148·2	159·1	169·7	179·8	189·2	197·7	204·4
Sat. ...	15·4	16·7	18·0	19·4	20·7	22·0	23·3	24·4	25·5	26·6	27·3	28·0	28·7	28·9	29·1	29·2	28·8	28·4
1971 Mars ...	264·1	269·7	275·1	280·0	284·7	288·9	292·5	295·4	297·3	298·0	297·9	295·4	292·7	290·1	288·2	288·0	289·0	291·1
☉'s L. Merc. ...	11·4	7·6	1·0	3·4	14·5	30·1	48·2	66·9	86·0	103·7	119·3	131·1	134·0	129·5	123·7	127·7	130·0	154·3
−·1 Jup. ...	222·1	221·2	220·2	218·9	217·7	216·3	215·1	213·9	213·0	212·5	212·2	212·2	212·6	213·3	214·2	215·4	216·9	218·6
Ven. ...	323·6	335·6	347·7	359·8	12·0	24·2	36·4	48·6	60·5	72·8	85·1	97·2	109·5	121·8	134·2	146·5	158·8	171·3
Sat. ...	27·8	29·1	30·4	31·6	33·0	34·4	35·8	37·0	38·2	39·5	40·4	41·3	42·2	42·6	43·0	43·5	43·4	43·3
1972 Mars ...	47·4	53·7	60·3	66·7	73·1	79·5	85·8	92·4	98·6	105·0	111·4	117·6	124·0	130·5	136·8	143·1	149·6	156·1
☉'s L. Merc. ...	342·8	343·7	353·9	8·8	26·5	45·4	64·3	82·6	98·9	111·7	117·3	112·7	106·3	109·0	119·7	134·6	151·6	169·3
+·6 Jup. ...	254·5	254·7	254·6	254·1	253·3	252·3	251·1	249·7	248·3	247·1	245·9	245·0	244·4	244·0	244·0	244·4	245·1	246·0
Ven. ...	45·5	54·7	62·5	68·6	71·8	71·8	67·7	61·1	56·1	54·8	57·3	62·9	70·9	80·2	90·4	101·0	112·1	123·7
Sat. ...	40·4	41·7	43·0	44·3	45·6	46·9	48·3	49·6	50·9	52·2	53·3	54·4	55·5	56·2	56·9	57·6	57·7	57·8
1973 Mars ...	287·2	294·3	301·1	308·2	315·0	321·7	328·3	334·9	341·0	347·1	352·6	357·6	2·0	5·9	8·6	10·3	10·5	9·3
☉'s L. Merc. ...	332·2	346·2	3·4	22·0	40·9	59·6	76·7	90·6	98·5	96·3	80·0	89·4	98·7	113·1	130·0	147·7	165·5	182·6
+·4 Jup. ...	284·8	286·1	287·1	287·8	288·1	288·2	287·9	287·2	286·4	285·2	283·8	282·5	281·1	279·9	278·8	278·1	277·6	277·4
Ven. ...	0·2	12·6	25·0	37·4	49·7	61·8	74·2	86·2	98·4	110·4	122·6	134·6	146·6	158·5	170·4	182·3	193·9	205·6
Sat. ...	53·3	54·5	55·7	56·8	58·1	59·4	60·8	62·1	63·5	64·9	66·1	67·3	68·5	69·4	70·3	71·3	71·7	72·1
1974 Mars ...	61·8	68·0	73·8	79·9	86·0	92·0	98·2	104·4	110·6	116·9	122·9	129·3	135·6	142·0	148·4	154·7	161·3	167·8
☉'s L. Merc. ...	340·5	358·6	17·5	36·2	53·9	68·8	78·5	79·1	71·6	69·8	77·5	91·1	107·7	125·7	143·9	161·2	177·1	189·3
+·1 Jup. ...	318·6	315·6	317·4	319·0	320·5	321·7	322·6	323·2	323·5	323·3	322·9	322·2	321·1	319·8	318·6	317·2	315·9	314·7
Ven. ...	312·6	323·0	334·1	345·3	356·9	8·4	20·0	31·8	43·7	55·7	67·5	79·5	91·6	103·8	116·0	128·2	140·6	152·9
Sat. ...	66·5	67·5	68·5	69·5	70·8	72·1	73·3	74·7	76·0	77·3	78·6	79·9	81·2	82·3	83·4	84·5	85·2	85·9
Eng. Date.	Ap 14	Ap 24	My 4	My 14	My 24	Je 3	Je 13	Je 23	Jl 3	Jl 13	Jl 23	Au 2	Au 12	Au 22	S 1	S 11	S 21	O 1
1975 Mars ...	306·8	314·4	322·0	329·4	337·0	344·5	351·8	359·1	6·0	13·1	19·7	26·4	32·8	38·7	44·5	49·7	54·6	59·0
☉'s L. Merc. ...	356·2	15·0	32·6	48·0	58·4	60·4	53·6	50·4	57·2	70·6	87·2	105·1	128·5	141·4	157·7	171·1	178·4	176·1
+·8 Jup. ...	341·6	343·9	346·2	348·5	350·6	352·5	354·3	356·0	357·3	358·4	359·3	359·7	359·9	359·7	359·1	358·2	357·0	355·8
Ven. ...	36·6	48·3	59·7	71·1	82·2	92·8	103·2	112·9	121·7	129·0	134·9	138·0	137·4	132·5	126·2	121·8	121·2	124·4
Sat. ...	80·2	81·0	81·8	82·5	83·6	84·7	85·9	87·2	88·5	89·9	91·2	92·5	93·9	95·1	96·3	97·5	98·4	99·3
Eng. Date.	Ap 13	Ap 23	My 3	My 13	My 23	Je 2	Je 12	Je 22	Jl 2	Jl 12	Jl 22	Au 1	Au 11	Au 21	Au 31	S 10	S 20	S 30
1976 Mars ...	78·4	83·5	88·9	94·5	100·1	105·7	111·6	117·6	123·4	129·7	135·8	141·8	148·3	154·5	160·9	167·5	174·0	180·6
☉'s L. Merc. ...	9·8	25·7	37·4	41·6	35·9	30·9	35·8	48·2	64·3	82·3	100·9	119·3	136·3	150·9	160·4	161·2	153·7	150·7
+·6 Jup. ...	9·1	11·5	13·9	16·3	18·6	21·0	23·3	25·5	27·5	29·5	31·2	32·7	34·1	35·1	35·7	36·0	36·2	35·8
Ven. ...	342·1	354·5	6·9	19·2	31·5	43·6	56·0	68·2	80·4	92·8	104·9	117·2	129·4	141·7	153·9	166·3	178·5	190·8
Sat. ...	93·8	94·3	94·8	95·4	96·4	97·4	98·3	99·5	100·7	102·0	103·4	104·8	106·1	107·3	108·5	109·8	110·8	111·9
1977 Mars ...	324·2	332·0	339·8	317·3	354·9	2·4	10·0	17·4	24·6	31·6	38·5	45·4	52·2	58·7	64·9	71·1	77·0	82·6
☉'s L. Merc. ...	16·4	22·4	18·2	11·9	14·5	25·6	41·3	59·3	78·0	96·7	114·4	130·1	141·5	144·9	139·1	133·5	137·9	149·3
+·3 Jup. ...	36·6	38·7	41·0	43·3	45·7	48·1	50·5	52·8	55·1	57·4	59·6	61·6	68·7	65·5	67·0	68·5	69·6	70·4
Ven. ...	349·4	345·3	345·1	348·6	354·7	2·5	11·5	21·2	31·4	42·1	53·3	64·5	75·9	87·6	99·4	111·2	123·3	135·5
Sat. ...	107·6	107·8	108·0	108·3	109·1	109·9	110·6	111·7	112·8	114·0	115·3	116·6	117·8	119·1	120·4	121·3	122·9	124·0
1978 Mars ...	97·6	101·0	105·3	109·9	114·7	119·9	125·4	130·8	136·7	142·5	148·4	154·7	160·9	167·3	173·6	180·1	186·9	193·6
☉'s L. Merc. ...	1·1	353·8	354·0	3·4	18·4	36·0	54·8	73·5	91·9	108·4	121·4	127·4	123·7	116·8	118·7	128·7	143·3	160·2
+·1 Jup. ...	64·7	66·3	68·1	70·0	72·1	74·2	76·5	78·7	81·1	83·4	85·6	88·0	90·2	92·3	94·4	96·4	98·2	99·8
Ven. ...	19·0	31·2	43·4	55·5	67·6	79·4	91·2	103·0	114·6	126·2	137·5	148·6	159·2	169·8	179·7	188·8	197·0	203·3
Sat. ...	121·5	121·4	121·3	121·3	121·9	122·5	123·0	123·9	124·8	125·8	127·0	128·2	129·5	130·8	132·1	133·3	134·5	135·7
Eng. Date.	Ap 14	Ap 24	My 4	My 14	My 24	Je 3	Je 13	Je 23	Jl 3	Jl 13	Jl 23	Au 2	Au 12	Au 22	S 1	S 11	S 21	O 1
1979 Mars ...	341·3	349·2	356·7	4·4	11·9	19·2	26·5	33·8	41·1	48·1	54·8	61·7	68·3	75·0	81·4	87·6	93·9	99·9
☉'s L. Merc. ...	334·8	343·1	357·2	14·6	33·2	52·3	70·8	87·8	101·4	109·1	106·8	99·6	100·0	109·3	123·7	140·3	158·1	175·7
+·8 Jup. ...	94·3	95·0	95·9	97·2	98·8	100·4	102·3	104·4	106·4	108·5	110·8	113·0	115·2	117·4	119·7	121·9	123·9	126·1
Ven. ...	325·1	337·4	349·4	1·6	13·6	25·9	38·1	50·3	62·3	74·7	86·7	99·1	111·3	123·6	135·9	148·2	160·6	173·0
Sat. ...	135·3	135·0	134·7	134·5	134·8	135·1	135·4	136·2	137·0	137·7	138·8	139·9	141·1	142·3	143·5	144·8	146·1	147·4

Mesh.	Vrsh.	Mith.	Kat.	Sim.	Kan.	Tul.	Vrsch.	Dhan.	Mak.	Kum.	Min.	Asvn.	Bhar.	Krit.	Rohi.	Mrig.	Ardh.	Punar.	Push.	Asles.
30	60	90	120	150	180	210	240	270	300	330	360	13·3	26·7	40·0	53·3	66·7	80·0	93·3	106·7	120·0

at Ujjain mean Sunrise for every ten days from A.D. 1970 to A.D. 1979.

see *Indian Chronology*, **Table XVIII).**

180	190	200	210	220	230	240	250	260		270	280	290	300	310	320	330	340	350	360
174·4	184·3	194·1	204·0	213·8	223·7	233·5	243·4	253·3		263·1	273·0	282·8	292·7	302·5	312·4	322·2	332·1	342·0	351·8
−2·2	−2·1	−1·9	−1·7	−1·5	−1·2	−0·9	−0·5	−0·1		+0·3	+0·6	+1·7	+1·3	+1·6	+1·8	+2·0	+2·1	+2·2	+2·2
O 10	O 20	O 30	N 9	N 19	N 29	D 9	D 19	D 29		Ja 8	Ja 18	Ja 28	F 7	F 17	F 27	Mr 9	Mr 19	Mr 29	Ap 8
Pura 25	Aipp 4	Aipp 14	Aipp 24	Kart 4	Kart 14	Kart 24	Marg 5	Marg 15		Marg 25	Tai 5	Tai 15	Tai 25	Masi 6	Masi 16	Masi 26	Pang 6	Pang 16	Pang 26
150·1	156·4	162·5	169·0	175·1	181·5	187·7	194·0	200·2	**71**	206·4	212·7	219·0	225·1	231·3	237·5	243·7	249·5	255·5	261·3
159·7	175·5	192·5	210·0	226·7	241·8	253·4	257·8	252·7		246·2	248·9	259·4	274·4	291·5	309·4	327·6	344·6	359·5	9·4
196·0	198·1	200·4	202·6	204·7	207·0	209·1	211·2	213·1		215·1	216·9	218·5	219·9	221·0	221·9	222·5	222·8	222·9	222·3
209·3	210·9	208·3	202·6	197·3	194·6	196·1	201·2	208·1		216·7	226·6	236·7	247·5	258·6	270·3	281·7	293·6	305·4	317·6
27·9	27·1	26·3	25·6	24·8	24·0	23·1	22·6	22·1		21·6	21·7	21·8	21·9	22·6	23·3	23·9	25·0	26·1	27·1
																Mr 8	Mr 18	Mr 28	Ap 7
294·6	298·8	303·4	308·4	313·9	319·8	325·9	332·1	338·3	**72**	344·7	351·2	357·7	4·2	10·7	17·3	23·8	30·5	36·8	43·3
171·4	188·8	206·2	222·0	234·8	241·5	239·1	231·4	231·2		239·6	253·3	269·8	287·5	305·4	322·6	338·1	349·2	352·6	346·5
220·3	222·3	224·5	226·5	228·8	231·0	233·2	235·5	237·8		240·0	242·1	244·3	246·2	248·0	249·8	251·2	252·4	253·4	254·2
183·8	196·2	208·7	221·1	233·6	246·1	258·5	271·1	283·6		295·8	308·1	320·3	332·3	344·2	355·9	7·4	18·4	29·3	39·4
43·1	42·5	41·9	41·2	40·3	39·4	38·6	37·9	37·2		36·5	36·3	36·1	35·9	36·3	36·7	37·0	37·9	38·8	39·8
																Mr 9	Mr 19	Mr 29	Ap 8
162·5	169·0	175·4	181·7	188·5	195·0	201·6	208·1	214·8	**73**	221·5	228·2	235·1	241·9	248·7	255·7	262·6	269·6	276·5	283·7
186·9	203·3	216·9	225·3	224·9	217·3	214·8	221·6	234·3		250·4	267·6	285·4	302·8	318·2	330·0	334·6	329·5	323·6	327·3
247·2	248·7	250·3	252·1	254·2	256·3	258·4	260·8	263·0		265·3	267·6	270·0	272·2	274·4	276·6	278·7	280·6	282·6	284·1
135·3	147·0	158·8	170·7	182·6	194·5	206·3	218·1	230·0		241·7	253·8	266·3	279·1	291·6	304·0	316·5	329·2	341·6	354·1
57·9	57·5	57·1	56·6	55·8	55·0	54·2	53·4	52·6		51·8	51·4	51·0	50·5	50·6	50·7	50·8	51·5	52·2	52·9
7·1	4·6	1·9	0·5	359·9	0·7	2·1	4·7	7·9	**74**	11·6	15·9	20·5	25·6	30·8	36·0	41·6	47·3	53·1	58·9
197·3	207·7	210·3	204·0	198·8	203·0	214·4	229·6	246·5		263·9	281·3	297·1	310·0	316·8	313·8	306·8	307·4	317·3	332·1
277·7	278·3	279·1	280·3	281·8	283·3	285·1	287·2	289·3		291·5	293·9	296·1	298·4	300·9	303·2	305·6	307·9	310·2	312·4
216·9	228·2	239·2	249·7	259·7	268·8	276·8	282·8	286·5		286·5	282·5	276·1	272·1	271·5	274·9	280·8	288·6	297·6	307·4
72·5	72·4	72·2	72·1	71·4	70·7	70·1	69·2	68·3		67·5	66·8	66·1	65·4	65·2	65·0	64·9	65·3	65·7	66·2
174·3	180·9	187·7	194·4	201·1	207·9	214·7	221·6	228·7	**75**	235·9	243·1	250·1	257·5	264·9	272·1	279·7	287·1	294·7	302·2
194·8	190·6	183·6	185·0	194·8	209·0	225·5	242·9	260·0		276·4	290·1	298·9	298·4	290·8	288·8	296·4	310·0	326·7	345·1
313·7	313·0	312·9	312·8	313·1	313·9	314·9	316·2	317·7		319·5	321·4	323·6	325·8	328·0	330·3	332·8	335·2	337·6	340·0
165·4	177·8	190·4	202·7	215·4	227·9	240·7	252·9	265·9		278·5	291·1	303·7	316·2	328·5	340·8	353·2	5·3	17·3	29·3
86·6	86·7	86·8	86·8	86·4	86·0	85·5	84·7	83·9		83·1	82·3	81·5	80·7	80·3	79·9	79·4	79·5	79·6	79·7
O 11	O 21	O 31	N 10	N 20	N 30	D 10	D 20	D 30		Ja 9	Ja 19	Ja 29	F 8	F 18	F 28	Mr 9	Mr 19	Mr 29	Ap 8
62·7	65·6	67·4	68·3	67·7	65·7	63·0	59·6	56·4	**76**	53·9	52·5	52·8	53·9	56·2	58·9	62·6	66·6	71·1	76·0
168·8	167·1	176·5	190·2	206·2	223·6	240·7	257·3	271·6		281·1	282·6	275·3	271·7	277·5	290·2	306·3	324·2	342·8	0·8
351·5	353·1	351·8	350·7	349·8	349·3	349·2	349·3	349·9		350·7	351·8	353·2	355·0	356·8	358·7	0·9	3·2	5·4	7·8
130·1	138·0	147·0	156·7	167·2	178·2	189·6	201·1	213·1		225·0	237·3	249·2	261·7	274·0	286·4	298·6	311·1	323·5	335·9
100·2	100·5	100·8	101·2	101·0	100·8	100·7	100·0	99·3		98·6	97·7	96·8	96·0	95·4	94·8	94·1	93·9	93·8	93·7
O 10	O 20	O 30	N 9	N 19	N 29	D 9	D 19	D 29		Ja 8	Ja 18	Ja 28	F 7	F 17	F 27	Mr 9	Mr 19	Mr 29	Ap 8
187·3	194·1	201·0	207·8	214·8	222·0	229·1	236·4	243·6	**77**	251·1	258·4	266·1	273·7	281·3	289·0	296·9	304·7	312·4	320·2
157·3	169·7	185·6	202·7	220·1	236·6	251·7	262·8	266·8		261·4	255·3	258·5	269·5	284·6	301·8	320·0	338·1	355·5	10·4
35·1	34·2	33·0	31·6	30·3	29·0	27·7	26·7	26·0		25·5	25·4	25·8	26·3	27·2	28·5	30·0	31·6	33·4	35·5
203·1	215·3	227·5	239·6	251·8	263·7	275·5	287·3	298·9		310·1	320·8	331·1	340·5	349·1	355·6	0·3	1·3	358·2	352·4
112·9	113·5	114·1	114·8	114·9	115·0	115·0	114·5	114·0		113·5	112·7	111·9	111·2	110·4	109·6	108·8	108·4	108·0	107·6
87·9	92·8	97·4	101·1	104·6	107·2	108·9	109·5	108·7	**78**	106·4	103·5	99·7	95·9	92·8	91·0	90·4	91·2	93·1	95·7
164·6	181·6	199·1	216·1	231·7	244·3	250·7	247·7	240·2		240·6	249·5	263·5	280·1	297·8	316·0	333·2	348·7	0·0	3·2
71·0	71·1	71·0	70·5	69·8	68·6	67·3	66·1	64·7		63·4	62·3	61·3	60·7	60·4	60·5	60·9	61·6	62·6	63·9
147·6	159·9	172·1	184·7	197·0	209·5	222·0	234·8	247·4		260·1	272·7	285·3	298·1	310·5	323·2	335·5	348·1	0·3	12·8
125·2	126·0	126·8	127·7	128·0	128·3	128·7	128·5	128·3		128·0	127·3	126·6	125·9	125·2	124·5	123·7	123·1	122·5	121·9
200·5	207·4	214·2	221·5	228·6	235·9	243·4	250·8	258·3	**79**	266·0	273·8	281·5	289·2	297·2	304·9	312·9	320·9	328·6	336·6
177·8	195·2	211·6	225·3	234·0	234·0	226·6	223·5	230·2		242·8	258·8	276·3	294·0	311·5	327·2	339·7	345·0	340·6	335·0
101·3	102·5	103·4	104·0	104·3	104·3	104·0	103·3	102·3		101·1	99·8	98·5	97·1	96·1	95·0	94·1	93·8	93·6	93·9
207·4	208·1	204·7	198·9	198·7	192·3	194·7	200·1	207·6		216·5	226·3	236·7	247·6	259·1	270·4	282·1	293·9	305·8	317·9
137·0	138·0	139·0	140·0	140·6	141·2	141·7	141·7	141·7		141·7	141·2	140·7	140·2	139·4	138·6	137·8	137·1	136·4	135·6
O 11	O 21	O 31	N 10	N 20	N 30	D 10	D 20	D 30		Ja 9	Ja 19	Ja 29	F 8	F 18	F 28	Mr 9	Mr 19	Mr 29	Ap 8
105·7	111·3	116·5	121·6	126·4	130·8	134·6	137·8	140·3	**80**	141·8	142·7	141·2	139·1	135·9	131·9	128·5	125·2	123·0	122·7
192·5	207·1	217·3	219·3	212·6	207·9	212·5	224·3	239·6		256·6	274·1	291·5	307·4	320·4	327·0	323·7	316·8	317·9	327·9
128·0	129·7	131·4	132·8	134·0	134·9	135·6	135·9	135·9		135·7	135·0	134·0	132·9	131·6	130·3	128·9	127·7	126·6	125·8
185·5	198·0	210·4	222·9	235·4	248·0	260·3	272·8	285·1		297·6	309·7	321·8	333·8	345·7	357·5	8·7	19·8	30·4	40·6
148·6	149·7	150·8	151·9	152·6	153·3	154·1	154·3	154·5		154·8	154·5	154·2	153·9	153·2	152·5	151·7	151·0	150·2	149·4

Mag.	P. Phal.	U. Phal.	Hasta.	Chit.	Svati.	Visak.	Anur.	Jyesh.	Mula.	P. Ash.	U. Ash.	Srav.	Dan.	Satab.	P. Bhad.	U. Bhad.	Revati.
133·3	146·7	160·0	173·3	186·6	200·0	213·3	226·7	240·0	253·3	266·7	280·0	293·3	306·7	320·0	333·3	346·7	360·0

APPENDIX II:—Geocentric (Indian) Longitudes of Sun and Major planets

(For the years 1840—1909,

Day of S. Yr.		0	10	20	30	40	50	60	70	80	90	100	110	120	130	140	150	160	170
⊙'s Mean L.		357·0	6·9	16·7	26·6	36·4	46·3	56·1	66·0	75·9	85·7	95·6	105·4	115·3	125·1	135·0	144·8	154·7	164·6
Actual do.		+2·1	+2·0	+1·9	+1·7	+1·4	+1·1	+0·8	+0·4	+0·0	−0·3	−0·7	−1·1	−1·4	−1·6	−1·9	−2·0	−2·1	−2·2
English date.		Ap 13	Ap 23	My 3	My 13	My 23	Je 2	Je 12	Je 22	Jl 2	Jl 12	Jl 22	Au 1	Au 11	Au 21	Au 31	S 10	S 20	S 30
Tamil month.		Chit	Chit	Chit	Chit	Vaik	Vaik	Vaik	Ani	Ani	Ani	Adi	Adi	Adi	Avani	Avani	Avani	Pura	Pura
Do. date.		1	11	21	31	10	20	30	9	19	29	7	17	27	6	16	26	5	15
1980	Mars ...	122·8	124·0	126·2	129·2	132·9	137·0	141·8	146·7	152·1	157·7	163·5	169·3	175·5	181·7	188·3	194·8	201·5	208·4
⊙'s L.	Merc. ...	335·0	351·6	9·6	28·6	47·5	65·0	80·0	89·4	80·8	82·3	80·4	88·3	102·0	118·5	136·3	154·2	171·6	187·1
+·6	Jup. ...	125·6	125·3	125·3	125·6	126·3	127·1	128·4	129·8	131·4	133·1	135·1	137·1	139·2	141·4	143·5	145·7	148·0	150·2
	Ven. ...	45·4	54·2	61·6	67·3	70·0	68·5	63·9	57·5	53·1	52·7	56·0	62·0	69·8	78·8	88·3	98·8	109·6	120·7
	Sat. ...	149·0	148·5	148·0	147·5	147·5	147·6	147·6	148·2	148·8	149·3	150·3	151·2	152·2	153·4	154·6	155·8	157·1	158·4
1981	Mars ...	356·9	4·3	11·0	19·3	26·6	33·9	41·1	48·1	55·1	61·9	68·0	75·6	82·2	88·7	95·1	101·4	107·6	113·8
⊙'s L.	Merc. ...	346·7	5·3	24·2	42·1	57·9	69·0	71·6	65·2	61·3	67·1	80·0	96·2	114·0	132·3	150·1	165·5	179·8	187·4
+·3	Jup. ...	158·8	157·7	156·8	156·1	155·7	155·7	155·9	156·6	157·4	158·6	159·9	161·5	163·3	165·1	167·1	169·2	171·4	173·5
	Ven. ...	1·0	13·1	25·7	37·9	50·2	62·6	74·7	86·8	98·9	111·0	123·1	135·1	146·9	159·0	170·7	182·6	194·3	205·9
	Sat. ...	162·4	161·7	161·0	160·4	160·2	160·0	159·8	160·1	160·4	160·8	161·6	162·4	163·2	164·3	165·4	166·5	167·7	168·9
1982	Mars ...	160·2	157·5	156·2	156·6	157·4	159·7	162·7	166·5	170·7	175·4	180·7	186·2	191·9	198·2	204·3	210·7	217·5	224·3
⊙'s L.	Merc. ...	1·0	19·1	35·3	47·7	52·7	47·8	42·0	46·0	57·8	73·6	91·4	109·9	128·1	145·1	159·9	169·6	170·9	163·7
+·0	Jup. ...	192·9	191·6	190·4	189·0	187·8	186·9	186·2	185·8	185·8	186·0	186·6	187·5	188·6	189·9	191·4	193·2	195·1	197·1
	Ven. ...	312·7	323·2	334·4	345·7	357·2	8·7	20·5	32·3	44·1	56·0	68·1	80·0	92·2	104·3	116·5	128·7	141·1	153·4
	Sat. ...	175·4	174·7	174·0	173·2	172·8	172·4	172·0	172·1	172·2	172·2	172·8	173·4	174·1	175·0	176·0	177·0	178·2	179·4
Eng. Date.		Ap 14	Ap 24	My 4	My 14	My 24	Je 3	Je 13	Je 23	Jl 3	Jl 13	Jl 23	Au 2	Au 12	Au 22	S 1	S 11	S 21	O 1
1983	Mars ...	12·3	19·7	26·8	34·1	41·2	48·2	55·3	62·0	68·9	75·6	82·2	89·0	95·4	102·0	108·3	114·5	121·0	127·2
⊙'s L.	Merc. ...	14·4	27·4	33·8	29·3	23·0	25·7	36·8	52·4	70·3	89·0	107·5	125·1	140·5	151·5	154·6	148·5	148·2	147·9
+·8	Jup. ...	226·6	225·9	224·9	223·7	222·4	221·0	219·7	218·5	217·7	216·9	216·4	216·4	216·7	217·3	218·2	219·3	220·7	222·3
	Ven. ...	37·0	48·6	60·1	71·4	82·4	93·1	103·1	112·6	121·2	128·3	133·4	135·8	134·1	128·5	122·7	119·0	119·3	123·1
	Sat. ...	188·1	187·3	186·5	185·7	185·2	184·7	184·1	184·0	183·9	183·7	184·1	184·5	185·0	185·8	186·6	187·5	188·6	189·7
Eng. Date.		Ap 13	Ap 23	My 3	My 13	My 23	Je 2	Je 12	Je 22	Jl 2	Jl 12	Jl 22	Au 1	Au 11	Au 21	Au 31	S 10	S 20	S 30
1984	Mars ...	218·7	212·1	209·8	206·4	203·1	200·7	199·3	199·7	200·7	203·3	206·4	210·4	215·0	220·1	225·8	231·7	238·0	244·5
⊙'s L.	Merc. ...	13·7	11·8	4·6	5·0	14·5	29·6	47·2	65·9	84·7	102·9	119·1	131·9	137·7	133·5	126·8	128·7	139·1	153·5
+·5	Jup. ...	258·8	259·1	259·1	258·8	258·2	257·2	256·0	254·8	253·5	252·1	250·9	249·8	249·0	248·5	248·4	248·6	249·1	250·0
	Ven. ...	342·6	355·0	7·4	19·8	32·0	44·4	56·5	68·9	81·1	93·3	105·5	117·7	130·0	142·2	154·5	166·8	179·1	191·3
	Sat. ...	200·5	199·7	198·9	198·2	197·5	196·8	196·2	195·9	195·6	195·2	195·4	195·6	195·9	196·6	197·3	198·0	199·0	200·0
1985	Mars ...	26·9	33·8	40·7	47·7	54·4	61·2	68·0	74·7	81·2	87·8	94·5	100·9	107·3	113·8	120·2	126·6	132·8	139·2
⊙'s L.	Merc. ...	347·1	345·1	352·9	6·7	23·9	42·4	61·5	79·9	97·2	111·1	119·3	117·7	110·1	109·7	118·5	132·5	149·0	166·7
+·3	Jup. ...	288·8	290·2	291·3	292·3	292·8	292·0	292·8	292·3	291·6	290·5	289·2	287·8	286·4	285·2	284·1	283·1	282·6	282·2
	Ven. ...	315·7	342·4	343·5	347·5	353·9	2·2	11·3	21·1	31·5	42·4	53·6	64·9	76·4	88·0	99·7	111·8	123·8	135·9
	Sat. ...	212·6	211·9	211·2	210·4	209·6	208·8	208·1	207·7	207·3	206·8	206·8	206·7	206·7	207·2	207·7	208·2	209·1	210·0
1986	Mars ...	253·2	257·5	261·6	265·1	267·6	269·4	270·2	269·5	268·2	265·4	262·6	260·9	259·7	260·3	262·0	264·8	268·8	273·2
⊙'s L.	Merc. ...	331·7	314·4	0·9	19·1	38·1	57·0	74·5	89·6	99·7	100·0	93·5	90·8	97·7	111·1	127·3	144·9	162·8	180·1
−·0	Jup. ...	317·4	319·4	321·4	323·2	324·7	326·1	327·1	327·9	328·3	328·5	328·2	327·5	326·7	325·5	324·2	323·0	321·4	320·2
	Ven. ...	19·5	31·7	43·9	56·0	68·0	80·0	91·7	103·4	114·9	126·5	137·6	148·7	159·5	169·7	179·5	188·5	196·2	202·0
	Sat. ...	224·3	223·7	223·1	222·5	221·7	220·9	220·1	219·5	218·9	218·2	218·0	217·8	217·7	218·0	218·3	218·6	219·4	220·2
Eng. Date.		Ap 14	Ap 24	My 4	My 14	My 24	Je 3	Je 13	Je 23	Jl 3	Jl 13	Jl 23	Au 2	Au 12	Au 22	S 1	S 11	S 21	O 1
1987	Mars ...	41·6	48·2	54·8	61·4	68·0	74·5	81·0	87·5	93·9	100·3	106·7	113·1	119·6	126·0	132·3	138·7	145·1	151·4
⊙'s L.	Merc. ...	339·7	357·8	16·5	35·3	53·3	69·0	80·1	82·4	76·0	72·1	78·0	90·7	107·0	124·7	142·9	160·4	176·7	189·8
+·7	Jup. ...	345·3	347·7	350·0	352·3	354·4	356·6	358·5	0·2	1·7	2·9	3·9	4·7	4·9	4·9	4·5	3·8	2·8	1·4
	Ven. ...	325·6	337·7	349·9	2·1	14·1	26·4	38·7	50·8	62·9	75·2	87·3	99·6	111·8	124·1	136·4	148·9	161·1	173·6
	Sat. ...	235·7	235·5	235·3	234·2	233·4	232·6	231·9	231·2	230·5	229·7	229·3	228·9	228·6	228·8	229·0	229·1	229·7	230·3
Eng. Date.		Ap 13	Ap 23	My 3	My 13	My 23	Je 2	Je 12	Je 22	Jl 2	Jl 12	Jl 22	Au 1	Au 11	Au 21	Au 31	S 10	S 20	S 30
1988	Mars ...	278·9	285·7	292·0	298·5	304·9	311·0	316·9	322·6	327·9	332·6	336·9	340·1	342·3	343·2	342·8	340·8	338·1	335·8
⊙'s L.	Merc. ...	353·5	12·1	30·2	46·5	58·9	63·9	58·8	52·9	57·1	68·8	84·5	102·3	120·7	138·9	155·7	170·1	179·8	180·2
+·5	Jup. ...	12·8	15·2	17·6	20·1	22·5	24·8	27·1	29·4	31·5	33·4	35·2	36·9	38·3	39·5	40·4	40·8	41·1	41·0
	Ven. ...	45·2	53·9	61·0	65·8	67·8	66·1	60·1	53·8	50·4	51·0	55·0	61·2	69·3	78·5	88·4	99·0	109·9	121·0
	Sat. ...	246·9	246·6	246·3	245·9	245·3	244·7	244·0	243·2	242·4	241·7	241·1	240·5	240·0	239·9	239·8	239·8	240·2	240·6
1989	Mars ...	56·2	62·2	68·6	74·6	80·7	87·1	93·4	99·6	105·8	112·1	118·5	124·7	131·1	137·4	143·7	150·1	156·5	163·2
⊙'s L.	Merc. ...	7·3	23·9	37·4	44·2	41·1	34·3	36·2	46·7	61·8	79·6	98·2	116·4	134·1	149·5	160·9	164·5	158·6	153·1
+·2	Jup. ...	40·4	42·5	44·7	47·0	49·3	51·7	54·1	56·4	58·7	61·0	63·3	65·4	67·4	69·3	71·1	72·5	73·8	74·7
	Ven. ...	1·3	13·9	26·2	38·5	50·7	63·1	75·2	87·3	99·3	111·5	123·5	135·4	147·5	159·3	171·3	182·9	194·6	206·2
	Sat. ...	257·9	257·8	257·6	257·5	256·9	256·3	255·7	254·9	254·1	253·3	252·7	252·1	251·4	251·2	251·0	250·7	251·0	251·3

Mesh.	Vrsh.	Mith.	Kat.	Sim.	Kan.	Tul.	Vrch.	Dhan.	Mak.	Kum.	Min.
30	60	90	120	150	180	210	240	270	300	330	360

Asvn.	Bhar.	Krit.	Rohi.	Mrig.	Ardh.	Punar.	Push.	Asles.
13·3	26·7	40·0	53·3	66·7	80·0	93·3	106·7	120·0

at Ujjain mean Sunrise for every ten days from A.D. 1980 to A.D. 1989.

see *Indian Chronology,* Table XVIII).

	180	190	200	210	220	230	240	250	260	270	280	290	300	310	320	330	340	350	360
	174·4	184·3	194·1	204·0	213·8	223·7	233·5	243·4	253·3	263·1	273·0	282·8	292·7	302·5	312·4	322·2	332·1	342·0	351·8
	−2·2	−2·1	−1·9	−1·7	−1·5	−1·2	−0·9	−0·5	−0·1	+0·3	+0·6	+1·0	+1·3	+1·6	+1·8	+2·0	+2·1	+2·2	+2·2
	O 10	O 20	O 30	N 9	N 19	N 29	D 9	D 19	D 29	Ja 8	Ja 18	Ja 28	F 7	F 17	F 27	Mr 9	Mr 19	Mr 29	Ap 8
	Pura	Aipp	Aipp	Aipp	Kart	Kart	Kart	Marg	Marg	Marg	Tai	Tai	Tai	Masi	Masi	Masi	Pang	Pang	Pang
	25	4	14	24	4	14	24	5	15	25	5	15	25	6	16	26	6	16	26
81	215·2	222·4	229·4	236·8	244·2	251·6	259·3	266·9	274·5	282·4	290·1	298·2	306·0	313·8	321·7	329·6	337·5	345·1	352·8
	199·0	204·0	199·3	192·7	194·6	204·5	219·0	235·4	252·9	270·2	286·6	300·3	308·6	307·9	300·4	298·9	306·8	320·7	337·6
	152·2	154·3	156·4	158·3	160·1	161·8	163·2	164·3	165·3	165·9	166·3	166·3	166·0	165·3	164·4	163·5	162·1	160·8	159·5
	132·2	143·9	155·7	167·8	179·9	192·2	204·5	216·8	229·4	241·8	254·4	266·8	279·6	292·1	304·7	317·3	329·7	342·2	354·6
	159·6	160·7	161·8	163·0	163·9	164·8	165·7	166·1	166·5	167·0	166·9	166·9	166·8	166·2	165·6	165·1	164·3	163·5	162·7
82	119·8	125·7	131·4	137·1	142·6	147·9	152·9	157·8	162·1	166·2	169·5	172·1	174·1	174·8	174·6	172·5	169·4	165·6	161·8
	185·7	178·0	177·0	185·0	198·6	214·6	231·8	249·3	265·6	289·3	290·3	292·1	285·3	281·1	286·6	299·2	315·2	333·0	351·7
	175·7	177·9	180·1	182·2	184·3	186·4	188·3	190·0	191·7	193·1	194·3	195·3	195·9	196·3	196·5	196·1	195·5	194·5	193·5
	217·3	228·5	239·4	249·6	259·4	268·3	275·8	281·4	284·0	283·0	278·1	272·3	268·7	269·6	273·4	280·1	288·1	297·5	307·4
	170·2	171·4	172·6	173·8	174·8	175·8	176·8	177·4	178·0	178·7	178·9	179·1	179·2	178·8	178·4	178·1	177·3	176·5	175·8
83	231·4	238·5	245·7	253·0	260·4	268·0	275·7	283·3	291·0	298·8	306·7	314·4	322·3	329·9	337·6	345·4	352·9	0·4	7·8
	160·0	165·9	178·3	193·9	210·9	228·3	245·0	260·2	271·8	276·2	271·2	264·7	267·6	278·1	293·4	310·6	328·9	347·3	4·7
	199·2	201·4	203·6	205·8	208·0	210·2	212·4	214·6	216·6	218·5	220·3	222·0	223·6	224·9	225·8	225·6	226·9	227·1	226·9
	165·9	178·4	190·9	203·5	215·9	228·5	241·2	253·8	266·4	279·1	291·7	304·2	316·6	329·0	341·4	353·5	5·8	17·8	29·8
	180·5	181·7	182·9	184·2	185·3	186·4	187·5	188·3	189·1	189·9	190·2	190·5	190·9	190·7	190·5	190·4	189·8	189·2	188·6
	O 11	O 21	O 31	N 10	N 20	N 30	D 10	D 20	D 30	Ja 9	Ja 19	Ja 29	F 8	F 18	F 28	Mr 9	Mr 19	Mr 29	Ap 8
84	133·4	139·3	145·4	151·4	157·1	162·9	168·5	174·1	179·7	185·0	190·1	194·8	199·4	203·5	207·0	210·1	212·4	213·8	214·2
	159·3	174·6	191·6	209·0	226·0	241·6	253·8	259·9	256·5	249·3	250·1	259·4	273·6	290·6	308·4	326·7	341·0	359·6	10·9
	221·1	226·0	228·0	230·1	232·4	234·5	236·9	239·1	241·4	243·5	245·8	247·9	249·9	251·9	253·6	255·2	256·6	257·7	258·4
	129·4	137·5	147·0	156·8	167·4	178·5	190·0	201·6	213·4	225·3	237·6	249·7	262·2	274·6	[illegible]	299·2	311·6	324·0	336·4
	190·8	192·0	193·2	194·4	195·5	196·6	197·8	198·7	199·6	200·6	201·1	201·6	202·2	202·2	202·3	202·3	201·8	201·3	200·8
	O 10	O 20	O 30	N 9	N 19	N 29	D 9	D 19	D 29	Ja 8	Ja 18	Ja 28	F 7	F 17	F 27	Mr 9	Mr 19	Mr 29	Ap 8
85	251·2	258·1	265·2	272·4	279·7	287·1	294·5	302·0	309·6	317·1	324·5	332·2	339·6	346·9	354·4	1·5	9·0	16·0	23·1
	170·4	187·8	205·2	221·4	235·0	243·3	242·7	235·2	232·7	239·8	252·9	269·0	286·5	304·4	322·1	337·9	350·3	355·5	351·1
	251·1	252·4	254·1	255·8	257·8	259·8	262·0	264·3	266·5	268·9	271·1	273·4	275·8	278·1	280·3	282·4	284·4	286·3	288·0
	203·4	215·6	227·9	239·9	252·1	264·1	275·8	287·7	299·0	310·2	320·7	331·0	340·2	348·2	354·8	358·4	358·5	351·7	348·6
	201·0	202·2	203·4	204·5	205·7	206·9	208·0	209·0	210·0	211·0	211·7	212·4	213·2	213·4	213·6	213·8	213·5	213·2	212·9
86	145·3	151·6	157·8	163·9	170·2	176·3	182·4	188·5	194·5	200·8	206·6	212·5	218·4	224·2	229·9	235·5	240·8	246·0	250·9
	184·2	201·0	215·5	225·8	228·2	221·7	216·8	221·0	232·7	247·9	265·0	283·4	300·2	316·5	329·6	337·1	334·6	327·4	327·7
	282·3	282·7	283·5	284·4	285·8	287·3	289·1	290·9	293·0	295·2	297·4	299·9	302·2	304·5	306·9	309·3	311·7	313·9	316·3
	148·1	160·4	172·6	185·2	197·7	210·1	222·6	235·1	248·0	260·6	273·2	285·8	298·6	311·1	323·7	336·1	348·6	0·9	13·3
	210·9	212·0	213·1	214·3	215·5	216·7	217·8	218·9	220·0	221·1	222·0	222·9	223·7	224·1	224·5	224·8	225·0	225·2	224·5
87	278·3	283·9	289·9	296·2	302·6	309·3	315·8	322·5	329·4	336·2	343·2	350·1	357·0	3·8	10·7	17·4	24·2	30·8	37·6
	195·6	207·7	213·1	208·7	201·9	203·2	212·9	227·2	243·7	261·3	278·6	295·2	309·2	318·2	318·3	310·8	308·7	316·3	329·9
	319·2	318·3	317·8	317·6	318·0	318·4	319·3	320·6	322·0	323·6	325·5	327·5	329·6	331·8	334·2	336·5	338·9	341·4	343·8
	205·6	205·0	201·2	194·8	190·3	189·8	193·2	199·3	207·1	216·3	226·2	236·8	247·9	259·2	270·7	282·6	294·5	306·3	318·5
	220·9	222·0	223·0	224·0	225·2	226·4	227·5	228·6	229·7	230·9	231·0	232·9	233·8	234·4	235·0	235·6	235·7	235·8	235·8
	O 11	O 21	O 31	N 10	N 20	N 30	D 10	D 20	D 30	Ja 9	Ja 19	Ja 29	F 8	F 18	F 28	Mr 9	Mr 19	Mr 29	Ap 8
88	157·8	164·2	170·5	177·1	183·5	190·0	196·3	202·8	209·4	215·8	222·5	229·0	235·6	242·2	248·9	255·7	262·2	268·9	275·7
	196·7	194·6	186·9	186·5	194·8	208·3	224·5	241·7	259·3	275·8	290·4	300·1	301·8	291·8	291·1	296·8	309·6	325·9	343·9
	0·2	358·8	357·5	356·2	355·2	354·6	354·2	354·2	354·6	355·2	356·3	357·5	359·0	0·8	2·8	4·8	6·9	9·3	11·6
	186·0	198·6	210·9	223·4	235·9	248·5	260·8	273·3	285·7	297·9	310·3	322·3	334·2	346·0	357·8	9·0	19·9	30·5	40·5
	230·9	231·9	232·9	233·9	235·1	236·3	237·4	238·5	239·6	240·8	241·8	242·8	243·9	244·6	245·3	246·1	246·1	246·7	246·9
	O 10	O 20	O 30	N 9	N 19	N 29	D 9	D 19	D 29	Ja 8	Ja 18	Ja 28	F 7	F 17	F 27	Mr 9	Mr 19	Mr 29	Ap 8
89	333·7	333·3	333·7	335·4	338·2	341·7	345·7	350·1	355·0	0·1	5·6	11·2	16·8	22·8	28·6	34·7	40·7	46·8	53·0
	172·8	169·4	175·8	188·1	203·8	220·7	238·0	255·0	270·1	281·3	285·5	280·3	274·1	277·6	288·6	308·8	[illegible]	339·7	358·1
	40·4	39·6	38·5	37·3	35·8	34·4	33·2	32·1	31·1	30·6	30·3	30·4	30·8	31·7	32·7	34·0	35·6	37·4	39·2
	132·6	144·4	156·3	168·1	180·3	192·5	204·8	217·3	229·9	242·3	254·9	267·4	280·1	292·7	305·2	317·8	330·2	342·7	355·1
	241·0	241·9	242·8	243·7	244·8	245·9	247·0	248·2	249·4	250·5	251·6	252·7	253·8	254·7	255·6	256·4	256·9	257·3	257·8
90	169·5	176·1	182·8	189·4	196·1	202·8	209·4	216·3	223·2	230·1	237·2	244·1	251·4	258·5	265·7	273·1	280·4	287·7	295·0
	156·9	168·0	183·1	199·9	217·2	234·2	249·8	262·5	269·0	266·1	258·6	259·1	268·2	282·2	299·2	317·2	335·6	353·1	9·1
	75·5	75·8	75·9	75·5	74·8	73·9	72·8	71·4	70·2	68·7	67·4	66·3	65·7	65·3	65·1	65·4	65·9	66·7	67·9
	217·4	228·6	239·3	249·6	259·1	267·8	274·7	279·9	281·4	279·5	273·5	268·5	266·1	267·7	272·4	279·4	287·9	297·4	307·5
	251·5	252·2	252·9	253·7	254·7	255·7	256·7	257·9	259·1	260·3	261·5	262·7	263·8	264·7	265·7	266·7	267·3	267·9	268·6

Mag.	P. Phal.	U. Phal.	Hasta.	Chit.	Svati.	Visak.	Anur.	Jyesh.	Mula.	P. Ash.	U. Ash.	Srav.	Dan.	Satab.	P. Bhad.	U. Bhad.	Revati.
133·3	146·7	160·0	173·3	186·6	200·0	213·3	226·7	240·0	253·3	266·7	280·0	293·3	306·7	320·0	333·3	346·7	360·0

APPENDIX II :—Geocentric (Indian) Longitudes of Sun and Major planets

(For the years 1840—1909,

	Day of S. Yr.	0	10	20	30	40	50	60	70	80	90	100	110	120	130	140	150	160	170
	⊙'s Mean L.	357·0	6·9	16·7	26·6	36·4	46·3	56·1	66·0	75·9	85·7	95·6	105·4	115·3	125·1	135·0	144·8	151·7	154·6
	Actual do.	+2·1	+2·0	+1·9	+1·7	+1·4	+1·4	+0·8	+0·4	+0·0	−0·3	−0·7	−1·1	−1·4	−1·6	−1·9	−2·0	−2·1	−2·2
	English date.	Ap 13	Ap 23	My 3	My 13	My 23	Je 2	Je 12	Je 22	Jl 2	Jl 12	Jl 22	Au 1	Au 11	Au 21	Au 31	S 10	S 20	S 30
	Tamil month.	Chit	Chit	Chit	Chit	Vaik	Vaik	Vaik	Ani	Ani	Ani	Ani	Adi	Adi	Avani	Avani	Avani	Pura	Pura
	Do. date.	1	11	21	31	10	20	30	9	19	29	7	17	27	6	16	26	5	15
1900	Mars ...	298·8	306·3	313·6	321·2	328·5	335·6	343·0	350·0	357·0	3·7	10·0	16·5	2·23	28·1	33·2	37·6	41·6	44·9
⊙'s L.	Merc. ...	15·7	24·3	23·5	16·0	15·4	24·6	39·1	55·4	75·1	93·9	111·9	128·2	141·3	147·5	143·9	136·8	138·1	147·9
−0	Jup. ...	68·6	70·0	71·8	73·7	75·7	77·8	80·0	82·2	84·5	86·9	89·1	91·3	93·6	95·8	97·9	99·9	101·9	103·6
	Ven. ...	312·6	323·5	324·6	346·0	357·6	9·2	21·1	32·6	44·6	56·5	68·6	80·5	92·7	104·9	117·0	129·3	141·6	151·0
	Sat. ...	268·9	269·0	269·1	269·1	268·7	268·3	267·8	267·0	266·2	265·5	264·8	264·1	263·3	262·9	262·5	262·0	262·1	262·1
	Eng. Date.	Ap 14	Ap 24	My 4	My 14	My 24	Je 3	Je 13	Je 23	Jl 3	Jl 13	Jl 23	Au 2	Au 12	Au 22	S 1	S 11	S 21	O 1
1901	Mars ...	71·8	77·5	83·0	88·8	94·6	100·5	106·5	112·4	118·6	124·7	130·8	137·2	143·4	149·0	156·1	162·6	169·3	175·7
⊙'s L.	Merc. ...	5·3	357·7	355·9	3·9	17·8	35·0	53·6	72·6	91·1	108·0	121·8	129·6	127·7	120·2	120·2	128·7	142·8	159·5
+·7	Jup. ...	98·4	99·0	99·9	101·0	102·4	104·1	105·9	107·7	109·8	111·9	114·0	116·2	118·6	120·8	123·0	125·2	127·3	129·4
	Ven. ...	37·3	48·9	60·4	71·7	82·5	93·1	103·2	112·6	120·7	127·6	132·2	133·5	130·8	125·1	119·1	116·3	117·5	122·0
	Sat. ...	279·7	280·0	280·3	280·5	280·2	279·9	279·7	279·0	278·3	277·6	276·8	276·0	275·3	274·7	274·1	273·5	273·4	273·3
	Eng. Date.	Ap 13	Ap 23	My 3	My 13	My 23	Je 2	Je 12	Je 22	Jl 2	Jl 12	Jl 22	Au 1	Au 11	Au 21	Au 31	S 10	S 20	S 30
1992	Mars ...	317·5	325·1	332·9	340·4	348·2	355·6	3·2	10·4	17·7	24·8	31·8	38·7	45·1	51·6	57·8	63·7	69·4	74·6
⊙'s L.	Merc. ...	336·6	342·5	355·3	11·9	30·2	49·3	68·2	85·7	100·7	110·3	111·4	104·0	101·2	108·4	121·7	137·8	155·4	173·1
+·4	Jup. ...	130·0	129·6	129·5	129·6	130·1	130·9	132·0	133·3	134·9	136·6	138·4	140·5	142·5	144·6	146·7	149·0	151·2	153·3
	Ven. ...	343·1	355·4	7·9	20·3	32·5	44·9	57·1	69·4	81·7	93·8	106·1	118·2	130·5	142·7	155·0	167·1	179·6	191·9
	Sat. ...	290·6	291·0	291·4	291·9	291·8	291·7	291·7	291·2	290·7	290·2	289·4	288·6	287·7	287·0	286·3	285·7	285·4	285·1
1993	Mars ...	89·4	93·7	98·4	103·4	108·7	114·2	119·7	125·5	131·3	137·3	143·4	149·4	155·9	162·1	168·5	175·0	181·6	188·4
⊙'s L.	Merc. ...	333·3	348·9	6·9	25·7	44·8	62·8	78·6	90·2	93·5	87·5	82·7	87·9	100·1	115·9	133·4	151·4	169·1	185·3
+·2	Jup. ...	163·6	162·3	161·2	160·4	160·0	159·8	159·9	160·4	161·1	162·1	163·4	164·9	166·6	168·4	170·4	172·5	174·5	176·7
	Ven. ...	342·1	339·9	341·6	346·4	353·4	1·9	11·2	21·3	31·8	42·6	53·7	65·2	76·7	88·5	100·2	112·2	124·4	136·2
	Sat. ...	301·4	302·0	302·6	303·3	303·5	303·7	303.9	303·5	303·1	302·8	302·1	301·4	300·6	299·8	299·0	298·2	297·7	297·2
1994	Mars ...	334·2	341·9	349·7	357·3	4·9	12·3	19·9	27·0	34·4	41·4	48·4	55·1	61·9	68·5	74·9	81·1	87·3	93·0
⊙'s L.	Merc. ...	344·0	2·5	21·3	39·7	56·2	69·2	74·7	70·4	64·2	67·3	78·4	93·8	111·3	129·5	147·5	164·4	178·8	188·5
−·1	Jup. ...	197·7	196·4	195·0	193·7	192·5	191·3	190·6	190·1	189·9	190·1	190·4	191·2	192·2	193·5	194·9	196·6	198·6	200·5
	Ven. ...	20·0	32·3	44·4	56·4	68·5	80·3	92·2	103·9	115·5	126·8	138·0	149·0	159·5	169·8	179·4	188·0	195·5	200·8
	Sat. ...	312·2	313·1	314·0	314·8	315·2	315·6	316·1	315·9	315·7	315·6	315·0	314·4	313·8	313·0	312·2	311·4	310·7	310·0
	Eng. Date.	Ap 14	Ap 24	My 4	My 14	My 24	Je 3	Je 13	Je 23	Jl 3	Jl 13	Jl 23	Au 2	Au 12	Au 22	S 1	S 11	S 21	O 1
1995	Mars ...	112·0	114·2	117·3	121·2	125·5	130·2	135·0	140·4	145·9	151·7	157·6	163·5	169·7	176·1	182·4	189·2	195·8	202·5
⊙'s L.	Merc. ...	0·1	18·3	35·0	48·6	55·4	52·2	45·5	47·3	57·8	73·0	90·4	109·0	127·1	144·6	159·9	170·9	173·9	167·7
+·7	Jup. ...	231·2	230·5	229·7	228·6	227·3	225·9	224·6	223·4	222·2	221·5	220·9	220·7	220·9	221·3	222·0	223·0	224·4	225·9
	Ven. ...	326·2	338·2	350·3	2·4	14·7	26·9	39·2	51·3	63·4	75·7	87·8	100·2	112·5	124·7	137·1	149·3	161·6	174·3
	Sat. ...	323·4	324·4	325·4	326·5	327·1	327·7	328·3	328·4	328·5	328·5	328·1	327·7	327·2	326·4	325·6	324·8	324·0	323·2
	Eng. Date.	Ap 13	Ap 23	My 3	My 13	My 23	Je 2	Je 12	Je 22	Jl 2	Jl 12	Jl 22	Au 1	Au 11	Au 21	Au 31	S 10	S 20	S 30
1996	Mars ...	350·7	358·4	5·9	13·5	20.8	28·2	35·4	42·7	49·6	56·7	63·4	70·2	76·8	83·4	89·9	96·2	102·4	108·4
⊙'s L.	Merc. ...	12·5	26·7	35·3	34·4	26·9	26·6	35·8	50·2	67·6	86·2	104·6	122·7	139·0	151·5	157·3	153·5	146·5	147·9
+·4	Jup. ...	263·0	263·5	263·7	263·5	263·0	262·3	261·2	259·9	258·6	257·3	256·0	254·8	253·9	253·3	253·0	253·1	253·4	254·1
	Ven. ...	44·9	53·4	59·9	64·4	65·3	62·5	56·3	50·7	48·0	49·3	53·9	60·7	69·1	78·4	88·6	99·2	110·1	121·3
	Sat. ...	334·7	335·8	336·9	338·1	338·9	339·7	340·6	340·9	341·2	341·6	341·4	341·2	340·9	340·2	339·5	338·9	338·1	337·3
1997	Mars ...	143·6	142·6	142·7	144·3	146·7	149·8	153·4	157·8	162·6	167·9	173·4	179·1	185·1	191·4	197·8	204·2	210·8	217·8
⊙'s L.	Merc. ...	14·9	16·4	9·1	6·4	13·6	27·5	44·5	62·8	81·9	100·2	117·2	131·1	139·5	138·3	130·8	129·6	137·9	151·5
+·2	Jup. ...	292·8	294·4	295·6	296·5	297·4	297·7	297·7	297·5	296·8	295·8	294·7	293·3	291·9	290·6	289·4	288·3	287·6	287·2
	Ven. ...	2·0	14·4	26·7	39·0	51·3	63·4	75·7	87·8	99.9	111·8	124·0	135·9	148·0	159·8	171·6	183·5	195·1	206·4
	Sat. ...	346·1	347·3	348·5	349·6	350·9	351·9	352·9	353·5	354·1	354·7	354·7	354·8	354·8	354·4	354·0	353·3	352·5	351·7
1998	Mars ...	5·7	13·2	20·5	27·8	35·1	42·3	49·3	56·2	63·2	69·8	76·6	83·3	89·8	96·3	102·9	109·3	115·5	121·5
⊙'s L.	Merc. ...	352·3	347·2	352·5	4·9	21·3	39·6	58·6	77·3	94·9	110·2	120·3	122·0	115·0	111·5	117·7	130·5	146·6	163·7
−·1	Jup. ...	321·2	323·3	325.3	327·3	328·9	330·4	331·6	332·5	333·1	333·3	333·4	332·9	332·1	331·2	329·9	328·6	327·1	325·8
	Ven. ...	312·8	323·6	334·9	346·3	357·9	9·6	21·4	33·2	45·1	57·1	68·9	81·1	93·1	105·4	117·5	129·8	142·2	154·5
	Sat. ...	357·7	359·0	0·3	1·6	2·8	4·0	5·1	5·9	6·7	7·6	7·9	8·2	8·6	8·3	8·0	7·8	7·1	6·4
	Eng. Date.	Ap 14	Ap. 24	My 4	My 14	My 24	Je 3	Je 13	Je 23	Jl 3	Jl 13	Jl 23	Au 2	Au 12	Au 22	S 1	S 11	S 21	O 1
1999	Mars ...	192·2	189·0	185·8	182·7	181·1	180·8	181·7	183·8	186·8	190.6	194·8	199·7	205·1	210·9	216·8	223·1	229·6	236·1
⊙'s L.	Merc. ...	332·7	344·3	0·1	18·2	36·9	56·0	73·9	89·6	101·1	104·2	97·9	98·2	98·4	110·7	126·5	143·9	161·8	179·4
+·6	Jup. ...	349·1	351·5	353·8	356·2	358·4	0·5	2·6	4·4	6·0	7·4	8·5	9·8	9·7	10·0	9·7	9·2	8·4	7·2
	Ven. ...	37·8	49·3	60·9	71·9	82·8	93·2	108·1	112·3	120·3	126·5	130·6	131·0	127·5	121·2	115·7	113·8	116·0	121·0
	Sat. ...	9·8	11·1	12·4	13·7	15·0	16·3	17·6	18·6	19·6	20·6	21·2	21·8	22·4	22·3	22·3	22·3	21·8	21·3

Mesh.	Vrsh.	Mith.	Kat.	Sim.	Kan.	Tul.	Vrsch.	Dhan.	Mak	Kum.	Min.	Asvn.	Bhar	Krit.	Rohi.	Mrig.	Ardh.	Punar.	Push.	Asles.
30	60	90	120	150	180	210	240	270	300	330	360	13·3	26·7	40·0	53·3	66·7	80·0	93·3	106·7	120·0

at Ujjain mean Sunrise for every ten days from A.D. 1990 to A.D. 1999.

see *Indian Chronology*, Table XVIII).

180	190	200	210	220	230	240	250	260		270	280	290	300	310	320	330	340	350	360
174·4	181·3	194·1	204·0	213·8	223·7	233·5	243·4	253·3		263·1	273·0	282·8	292·7	302·5	312·4	322·2	332·1	342·0	351·8
−2·2	−2·1	−1·9	−1·7	−1·5	−1·2	−0·9	−0·5	−0·1		+0·3	+0·6	+1·0	+1·3	+1·6	+1·8	+2·0	+2·1	+2·2	+2·2
O 10	O 20	O 30	N 9	N 19	N 29	D 9	D 19	D 29		Ja 8	Ja 18	Ja 28	F 7	F 17	F 27	Mr 9	Mr 19	Mr 29	Ap 8
Pura	Aipp	Aipp	Aipp	Kart	Kart	Kart	Marg	Marg		Marg	Tai	Tai	Tai	Masi	Masi	Masi	Pang	Pang	Pang
25	4	14	24	4	14	24	5	15		25	5	15	25	6	16	26	6	16	26
46·9	47·8	47·5	46·3	43·5	40·3	37·4	35·5	34·5	**91**	34·7	36·2	38·3	41·3	44·9	49·0	53·5	58·3	63·4	68·6
162·3	178·8	196·2	213·6	229·7	243·3	252·1	252·0	244·4		241·8	248·6	261·4	277·5	295·0	313·2	330·9	347·1	0·1	6·1
105·1	106·5	107·4	108·2	108·7	108·8	108·6	108·0	107·2		106·1	104·8	103·5	102·2	100·9	99·8	98·9	98·3	98·0	98·2
166·4	178·9	191·4	204·0	216·5	229·0	241·8	254·3	267·0		279·6	292·2	304·7	317·1	329·5	341·9	354·1	6·3	18·4	30·1
262·2	262·8	263·4	263·9	264·8	265·7	266·7	267·9	269·1		270·2	271·4	272·6	273·7	274·8	275·9	277·0	277·8	278·6	279·5
O 11	O 21	O 31	N 10	N 20	N 30	D 10	D 20	D 30		Ja 9	Ja 19	Ja 29	F 8	F 18	F 28	Mr 9	Mr 19	Mr 29	Ap 8
182·3	189·0	195·7	202·8	209·6	216·6	223·6	230·7	237·9	**92**	245·3	252·6	260·1	267·5	275·1	282·6	290·4	298·0	305·7	313·5
176·9	194·2	210·8	225·2	235·3	237·0	230·2	225·7	230·6		242·5	258·0	275·3	293·0	310·5	326·8	340·1	347·5	344·9	337·6
131·5	133·3	134·9	136·4	137·8	138·8	139·5	140·1	140·2		140·0	139·6	138·7	137·6	136·4	135·1	133·7	132·4	131·4	130·4
128·[illegible]	137·2	146·7	156·9	167·5	178·6	190·1	202·0	213·7		225·9	238·1	250·3	262·5	275·1	287·4	299·7	312·2	324·5	337·0
273·2	273·6	274·0	274·4	275·3	276·2	277·0	278·1	279·2		280·3	281·5	282·7	283·9	285·1	286·3	287·4	288·3	289·2	290·1
O 10	O 20	O 30	N 9	N 19	N 29	D 9	D 19	D 29		Ja 8	Ja 18	Ja 28	F 7	F 17	F 27	Mr 9	Mr 19	Mr 29	Ap 8
79·4	83·8	87·8	91·1	93·2	94·5	94·8	93·5	91·1	**93**	87·8	83·8	80·7	77·9	76·7	76·8	78·4	80·6	83·6	87·5
190·2	205·5	217·3	222·0	217·2	210·6	212·5	222·6	237·2		253·7	271·5	288·9	305·5	319·6	328·4	328·3	320·8	319·1	326·9
155·5	157·6	159·7	161·7	163·6	165·1	166·6	168·0	169·1		169·8	170·3	170·5	170·3	169·9	169·0	167·9	166·8	165·5	164·1
208·9	216·2	228·3	240·5	252·4	264·4	276·1	287·8	299·2		310·3	320·7	330·7	339·8	347·5	353·5	356·3	355·2	350·8	344·5
284·7	284·9	285·1	285·3	286·0	283·7	287·4	288·4	289·4		290·5	291·7	292·9	294·1	295·3	296·5	297·7	298·8	299·9	300·9
195·1	202·0	209·0	216·0	223·2	230·3	237·5	244·9	252·4	**94**	260·1	267·7	275·3	283·2	290·8	298·8	306·5	314·3	322·2	330·2
198·4	205·8	203·8	196·1	195·3	203·4	216·7	232·7	250·0		267·7	284·3	299·2	309·4	311·8	305·2	300·7	306·2	318·9	334·9
178·9	181·3	183·3	185·5	187·5	189·6	191·6	193·5	195·1		196·8	198·0	199·1	199·9	200·4	200·5	200·4	200·0	199·2	198·2
148·7	160·9	173·2	185·5	198·2	210·6	223·3	235·9	248·5		261·2	273·7	286·6	299·1	311·6	324·2	336·7	349·1	1.6	13·8
296·7	296·7	296·7	296·7	297·2	297·7	298·3	299·2	300·1		301·0	302·2	303·4	304·5	305·7	306·9	308·2	309·4	310·6	311·8
98·7	104·3	109·3	114·1	118·3	122·3	125·8	128·1	129·3	**95**	129·7	128·8	126·5	123·7	119·9	115·8	112·8	110·8	110·3	111·0
189·6	182·6	178·6	184·5	196·5	212·2	229·1	246·4	263·3		278·7	290·6	295·1	290·1	283·9	286·7	297·4	312·8	330·3	348·8
202·5	204·7	206·8	209·0	211·2	213·5	215·6	217·8	219·9		222·0	223·8	225·7	227·2	228·6	229·6	230·6	231·1	231·4	231·4
203·3	202·0	196·8	191·0	187·4	188·0	191·9	198·6	206·6		216·2	226·2	236·9	248·1	259·5	271·1	282·9	294·8	306·8	318·8
309·3	309·1	308·9	308·6	308·9	309·2	309·6	310·4	311·2		311·9	313·0	314·1	315·3	316·5	317·7	319·0	320·2	321·4	322·7
O 11	O 21	O 31	N 10	N 20	N 30	D 10	D 20	D 30		Ja 9	Ja 19	Ja 29	F 8	F 18	F 28	Mr 9	Mr 19	Mr 29	Ap 8
209·6	216·5	223·7	230·9	238·1	245·7	253·1	260·7	268·3	**96**	276·1	284·0	291·7	299·6	307·6	315·4	323·3	331·2	339·0	346·9
162·4	166·7	178·0	193·1	210·0	227·3	244·3	259·8	272·2		278·4	275·1	267·9	268·8	278·2	292·8	309·9	327·9	346·4	4·1
227·6	229·5	231·5	233·5	235·8	238·0	240·2	242·4	244·8		246·9	249·2	251·4	253·5	255·5	257·4	258·9	260·4	261·6	262·6
183·5	199·1	211·5	223·9	233·5	248·8	261·4	273·8	286·2		298·4	310·6	322·7	334·7	346·4	357·9	9·2	20·0	30·5	40·4
322·5	322·1	321·7	321·2	321·3	321·4	321·5	322·1	322·7		323·4	324·4	325·5	326·5	327·7	328·9	330·2	331·5	332·8	334·1
O 10	O 20	O 30	N 9	N 19	N 29	D 9	D 19	D 29		Ja 8	Ja 18	Ja 28	F 7	F 17	F 27	Mr 9	Mr 19	Mr 29	Ap 8
114·4	120·3	125·8	131·5	136·6	141·6	146·3	150·5	154·3	**97**	157·4	160·0	161·3	161·6	160·6	158·2	154·6	150·7	147·1	144·5
158·0	172·2	188·9	203·1	223·5	239·6	253·1	261·5	260·8		253·2	251·1	258·3	271·6	287·8	305·7	323·8	341·7	357·8	10·9
255·1	255·4	257·8	259·5	261·5	263·5	265·5	267·8	270·0		272·3	274·7	277·0	279·3	281·6	284·0	286·1	288·2	290·2	292·0
132·9	144·7	156·6	168·6	180·8	193·1	205·3	217·9	230·4		242·9	255·5	268·1	280·4	293·2	305·8	318·3	330·8	343·2	355·7
335·4	335·8	335·2	334·6	334·4	334·2	334·1	334·5	334·9		335·4	336·3	337·2	338·0	339·2	340·4	341·6	342·9	344·2	345·4
224·8	231·8	239·1	246·3	253·9	261·4	269·0	276·6	284·5	**98**	292·3	300·1	308·0	315·8	323·5	331·3	339·1	346·8	354·4	1·9
157·7	183·5	202·5	219·2	233·6	243·9	246·3	239·6	234·7		239·2	251·1	266·5	283·7	301·6	319·5	335·9	349·7	357·6	356·0
287·0	287·2	287·6	283·7	289·9	291·3	293·0	294·3	296·8		299·0	301·2	303·5	305·8	308·2	310·6	312·9	315·4	317·8	320·0
217·7	228·3	239·2	249·5	258·8	266·9	273·7	277·9	279·0		275·5	270·1	264·5	263·6	266·0	271·5	278·7	287·6	297·2	307·5
350·9	350·1	349·3	[illegible]	348·1	347·7	347·4	347·6	347·8		347·9	348·6	349·3	350·0	351·1	352·2	353·2	354·5	355·8	357·0
127·8	133·7	139·6	145·5	151·2	157·0	162·3	167·8	172·9	**99**	177·5	182·3	186·4	190·2	193·4	195·6	197·2	197·4	196·6	194·2
181·6	193·5	213·9	225·9	231·0	223·5	219·7	221·3	231·2		245·5	262·3	279·8	297·6	314·3	328·8	338·3	339·1	331·8	329·2
324·6	323·6	323·1	322·7	322·6	323·1	323·8	324·8	326·2		327·7	329·4	331·3	333·5	335·7	337·9	340·4	342·7	345·2	347·6
167·0	179·4	192·0	204·5	217·0	229·5	242·3	254·9	267·5		280·2	292·7	305·1	317·6	330·1	342·2	354·6	6·6	18·7	30·7
5·7	4·9	4·1	3·2	2·6	2·0	1·4	1·3	1·2		1·1	1·6	2·1	2·5	3·4	4·3	5·1	6·4	7·7	8·9
O 11	O 21	O 31	N 10	N 20	N 30	D 10	D 20	D 30		Ja 9	Ja 19	Ja 29	F 8	F 18	F 28	Mr 9	Mr 19	Mr 29	Ap 8
248·2	250·3	257·4	264·8	272·2	279·7	287·3	294·9	302·5	**2000**	310·1	317·8	325·5	333·0	340·6	348·1	355·6	2·9	10·1	17·4
195·2	208·2	215·0	212·6	204·9	204·6	212·9	226·6	242·9		260·1	277·9	294·6	309·3	319·6	321·8	315·0	310·9	316·7	329·5
5·9	4·5	3·2	1·8	0·7	0·0	359·4	359·1	359·4		359·9	0·7	1·9	3·3	4·9	6·6	8·7	10·9	13·0	15·4
128·8	137·0	146·6	156·9	167·8	179·0	190·4	202·3	214·2		226·2	238·5	250·8	263·1	275·4	287·8	300·2	312·7	325·0	337·5
20·7	19·9	19·1	18·2	17·5	16·8	16·0	15·6	15·2		14·9	15·1	15·3	15·6	16·4	17·2	17·9	19·0	20·1	21·3

Mag.	P.Phal.	U.Phal.	Hasta.	Chit.	Svati.	Visak.	Anur.	Jyesh.	Mula.	P. Ash.	U. Ash.	Srav.	Dan.	Satab.	P. Bhad.	U.Bhad.	Revati.
133·3	146·7	160·0	173·3	186·7	200·0	213·3	226·7	240·0	253·3	266·7	280·0	293·3	306·7	320·0	333·3	346·7	360·0

Mean place of Rahu at Ujjain Sunrise on O day of each Solar Year, A.D. 1910—2000.

(For the years 1840—1909, see *Indian Chronology*, Table XVII-B.)

A.D.	Deg.	A.D.	Deg.	A.D	Deg.	A.D.	Deg.	A.D.	Deg.	A.D.	Deg.
1910	41·25	1925	110·96	1940	180·67	1955	250·38	1970	320·09	1985	29·79
1911	21·90	1926	91·61	1941	161·32	1956	231·03	1971	300·73	1986	10·44
1912	2·55	1927	72·26	1942	141·97	1957	211·67	1972	281·38	1987	351·09
1913	348·20	1928	52·91	1943	122·61	1958	192·32	1973	262·03	1988	331·73
1914	328·85	1929	33·55	1944	103·26	1959	172·97	1974	242·67	1989	312·38
1915	304·49	1930	14·20	1945	83·91	1960	153·61	1975	223·32	1990	293·03
1916	285·14	1931	354·85	1946	64·55	1961	134·26	1976	203·97	1991	273·68
1917	265·78	1932	335·49	1947	45·20	1962	114·91	1977	184·62	1992	254·32
1918	246·43	1933	316·14	1948	25·85	1963	95·56	1978	165·26	1993	234·97
1919	227·08	1934	296·79	1949	6·50	1964	76·20	1979	145·91	1994	215·62
1920	207·73	1935	277·44	1950	347·14	1965	56·85	1980	126·56	1995	196·26
1921	188·38	1936	258·08	1951	327·79	1966	37·50	1981	107·20	1996	176·91
1922	169·02	1937	238·73	1952	308·44	1967	18·14	1982	87·85	1997	157·56
1923	149·67	1938	219·38	1953	289·08	1968	358·79	1983	68·50	1998	138·21
1924	130·32	1939	200·02	1954	269·73	1969	339·44	1984	49·15	1999	118·85

Mean place of Rahu for every 10 days and for fractions of a day.

Day.	Deg.	Days.	Deg.	Days.	Deg.	Days.	Deg.	Days.	Deg.	Days.	Deg.
·1	— ·00	1	— ·05	10	— ·53	100	— 5·30	190	—10·07	280	—14·84
·2	·01	2	·11	20	1·06	110	5·83	200	10·60	290	15·36
·3	·02	3	·16	30	1·59	120	6·36	210	11·13	300	15·89
·4	·02	4	·21	40	2·12	130	6·89	220	11·66	310	16·42
·5	·03	5	·26	50	2·65	140	7·42	230	12·19	320	16·95
·6	·03	6	·32	60	3·18	150	7·95	240	12·72	330	17·48
·7	·04	7	·37	70	3·71	160	8·48	250	13·25	340	18·01
·8	·04	8	·42	80	4·24	170	9·01	260	13·78	350	18·54
·9	·05	9	·48	90	4·77	180	9·54	270	14·31	360	19·07

Latitudes and Longitudes of Chief places in the Madras Presidency and in the Native States of Mysore and Hyderabad.

(Longitudes are expressed by the time difference in fraction of a day as compared with Ujjain.)

No.	District.	Town.	Latitude in degrees.	Time difference in fraction of a day.
		Madras Presidency.		
1	Bellary ...	Adoni ...	15·7	+·004
		Bellary ...	15·2	+·003
2	Chingleput ...	Conjeeveram ...	12·8	+·011
3	Coimbatore ...	Coimbatore ...	11·0	+·003
4	Ganjam ...	Berhampore ...	19·3	+·025
5	Godavari ...	Cocanada ...	17·0	+·018
		Rajahmundry ...	17·0	+·017
6	Kistna ...	Bezwada ...	16·5	+·013
		Ellore ...	16·7	+·015
		Masulipatam ...	16·2	+·015
7	Guntur ...	Guntur ...	16·3	+·013
8	Kurnool ...	Kurnool ...	15·8	+·006
9	Madras ...	Madras ...	13·0	+·012
10	Madura ...	Madura ...	10·0	+·006
		Bodinayakkanur ...	10·0	+·004
		Dindigul ...	10·3	+·006
11	Malabar ...	Calicut ...	11·2	+·000
		Cannanore ...	11·8	-·001
		Palghat ...	10·8	+·002
		Tellicherry ...	11·7	-·001
12	Nellore ...	Nellore ...	14·5	+·012
13	North Arcot ...	Gudiyattam ...	13·0	+·009
		Vellore ...	12·9	+·009
14	Salem ...	Salem ...	11·7	+·007
15	South Arcot ...	Cuddalore ...	11·7	+·011
16	South Canara ..	Mangalore ...	12·8	-·003
17	Tanjore ...	Kumbakonam ...	11·0	+·010
		Negapatam ...	10·7	+·011
		Tanjore ...	10·7	+·009
		Mannargudi ...	10·7	+·010
		Mayavaram ...	11·1	+·011
18	Tinnevelly ...	Palamcottah ...	8·7	+·005
		Rajapalaiyam ...	9·5	+·003
		Srivilliputtur ...	9·5	+·005
		Tinnevelly ...	8·7	+·005
		Tiruchendur ...	8·5	+·006
		Tuticorin ...	8·8	+·007
		Madras Presidency—*(contd.)*		
19	Trichinopoly	Trichinopoly, Srirangam	10·8	+·008
20	Vizagapatam ...	Vizagapatam ...	17·7	+·021
21	Vizianagaram ...	Vizianagaram ...	18·2	+·021
		Madras Native States.		
22	Cochin ...	Ernakulam ...	10·0	+·001
		Mattancheri ...	10·0	+·001
23	Pudukkottai ...	Pudukkottai ...	10·3	+·008
24	Travancore ...	Alleppey ...	9·5	+·002
		Nagercoil ...	8·1	+·005
		Trivandrum ...	8·5	+·008
		Mysore State.		
25	Bangalore ...	Bangalore ...	13·0	+·005
26	Kolar ...	Kolar ...	13·1	+·007
27	Mysore ...	Mysore ...	12·3	+·002
		Hyderabad State.		
28	Gulbarga ...	Gulbarga ...	17·3	+·008
29	Hyderabad ...	Hyderabad ...	17·3	+·007
30	Raichur ...	Raichur ...	16·2	+·004
		Bombay Province.		
31	Belgaum ...	Belgaum ...	16·0	-·004
32	Bijapur ...	Bijapur ...	16·8	-·000
33	Dharwar ...	Hubli ...	15·3	-·002
		Dharwar ...	15·5	-·002
		Gadag ...	15·5	-·000
34	Surat ...	Surat ...	12·2	-·008
35	Kolhapur ...	Kolhapur ...	16·6	-·004

Equivalents of decimals of a day in (1) Ghatikas and Palas, (2) Hours and Minutes.

Decimals of a day.	Ghatikas.	Palas	Hours.	Minutes.	Decimals of a day.	Ghatikas.	Hours and Minutes.	Decimals of a day.	Ghatikas.	Hours and Minutes.
·000	0	0	0	0	·00	0	0, 0	·50	30	12, 0
·001	0	4	0	2	·01	0½	0,15	·51	30½	12,15
·002	0	7	0	3	·02	1	0,30	·52	31	12,30
·003	0	11	0	4	·03	2	0,45	·53	32	12,45
·004	0	14	0	6	·04	2½	1, 0	·54	32½	13, 0
·005	0	18	0	7	·05	3	1,15	·55	33	13,15
·006	0	22	0	9	·06	3½	1,30	·56	33½	13,30
·007	0	25	0	10	·07	4	1,45	·57	34	13,45
·008	0	29	0	11	·08	5	2, 0	·58	35	14 ,0
·009	0	32	0	13	·09	5½	2,10	·59	35½	14,10
·010	0	36	0	15	·10	6	2,30	·60	36	14,30
·011	0	40	0	16	·11	6½	2,40	·61	36½	14,40
·012	0	43	0	17	·12	7	2,50	·62	37	14,50
·013	0	47	0	19	·13	8	3,10	·63	38	15,10
·014	0	50	0	20	·14	8½	3,20	·64	38½	15,20
·015	0	54	0	22	·15	9	3,35	·65	39	15,35
·016	0	58	0	23	·16	9½	3,50	·66	39½	15,50
·017	1	1	0	25	·17	10	4, 5	·67	40	16, 5
·018	1	5	0	26	·18	11	4,20	·68	41	16,20
·019	1	8	0	27	·19	11½	4,30	·69	41½	16,30
·020	1	12	0	29	·20	12	4,45	·70	42	16,45
·021	1	16	0	30	·21	12½	5, 0	·71	42½	17, 0
·022	1	19	0	32	·22	13	5,20	·72	43	17,20
·023	1	23	0	33	·23	14	5,30	·73	44	17,30
·024	1	26	0	35	·24	14½	5,45	·74	44½	17,45
·025	1	30	0	36	·25	15	6, 0	·75	45	18, 0
·026	1	34	0	38	·26	15½	6,15	·76	45½	18,15
·027	1	37	0	39	·27	16	6,30	·77	46	18,30
·028	1	41	0	40	·28	17	6,45	·78	47	18,45
·029	1	44	0	42	·29	17½	7, 0	·79	47½	19, 0
·030	1	48	0	43	·30	18	7,10	·80	48	19,10
·031	1	52	0	45	·31	18½	7,30	·81	48½	19,30
·032	1	55	0	46	·32	19	7,40	·82	49	19,40
·033	1	59	0	48	·33	20	8, 0	·83	50	20, 0
·034	2	2	0	49	·34	20½	8,10	·84	50½	20,10
·035	2	6	0	50	·35	21	8,25	·85	51	20,25
·036	2	10	0	52	·36	21½	8,40	·86	51½	20,40
·037	2	13	0	53	·37	22	8,50	·87	52	20,50
·038	2	17	0	55	·38	23	9,10	·88	53	21,10
·039	2	20	0	56	·39	23½	9,20	·89	53½	21,20
·040	2	24	0	58	·40	24	9,35	·90	54	21,35
·041	2	28	0	59	·41	24½	9,50	·91	54½	21,50
·042	2	31	1	1	·42	25	10, 0	·92	55	22, 0
·043	2	35	1	2	·43	26	10,20	·93	56	22,20
·044	2	38	1	3	·44	26½	10,30	·94	56½	22,30
·045	2	42	1	5	·45	27	10,45	·95	57	22,45
·046	2	46	1	6	·46	27½	11, 0	·96	57½	23, 0
·047	2	49	1	8	·47	28	11,20	·97	58	23,20
·048	2	53	1	9	·48	29	11,30	·98	59	23,30
·049	2	56	1	10	·49	29½	11,45	·99	59½	23,45